WHAT DO
CHILDREN
READ
NEXT?

A Reader's Guide to
Fiction for Children

WHAT DO
CHILDREN
READ
NEXT?

A Reader's Guide to
Fiction for Children

VOLUME 2

PAM SPENCER
JANIS ANSELL

GALE

Detroit

New York

Toronto

London

Gale Research Staff

Coordinating Editor: Shelly Dickey
Contributing Editors: Beverly Baer, Victoria A. Coughlin, Nancy Franklin,
Paula Cutcher-Jackson, Kathleen Dallas, Lydia Fink, William Harmer,
Arlene M. Johnson, Debra M. Kirby, Prindle LaBarge,
Sharon McGilvray, Charles B. Montney, Dana Shonta, Kelly Sprague
Managing Editor: Ann V. Evory

Production Director: MaryBeth Trimper
External Production Assistant: Shanna P. Heilveil
Product Design Manager: Cynthia Baldwin
Senior Art Director/Cover Design: Mary Krzewinski

Manager Data Entry Services: Eleanor Allison
Data Entry Coordinator: Gwendolyn S. Tucker
Data Entry Associates: LySandra Davis, Maleka Imrana

Manager, Technical Support Services: Theresa Rocklin
Programmer/Analyst: Joshua E. Cohen

This book is printed on acid-free paper that meets the minimum requirements of American National Standard for Information Sciences—Permanence Paper for Printed Library Materials, ANSI Z39.48-1984.

ISBN 0-8103-6448-4

Printed in the United States of America

Reprint 10 9 8 7 6 5 4 3 2 1

Contents

Preface

What Do Children Read Next? is a readers advisory tool designed to match readers from Grades 1 through 8 with books that reflect their interests and concerns. It guides both reluctant and avid readers to new authors and titles or further reading. *What Do Children Read Next?* allows readers quick and easy access to specific information on both recent and classic juvenile titles. In addition, each entry provides alternate reading selections, giving children, parents, and librarians the answer to the frequently asked question "What do I read next?"

Highlights

● Compiled by Janis Ansell, educator and former school psychologist.

● Overview essay describes the history of children's literature and recent trends in the field.

● "Other books you might like," included in each entry, leads to the exploration of new authors or titles.

● Ten indexes help locate specific titles or offer suggestions for reading in favorite time periods or geographic locales, about special subjects or characters, or for a particular age level.

● All authors and titles listed in entries under "Other books by the author" and "Other books you might like" are indexed, allowing easy access to thousands of books recommended for further reading.

Details on over 1600 titles...

What Do Children Read Next? contains entries for over 1600 books aimed at young readers. About half of these titles were published in the past five years; the remaining fifty percent are older titles which have stood the test of time and still remain accessible and relevant to today's young readers. Titles have been selected on the basis of their currency, appeal to readers, and literary merit. The entries are listed alphabetically by author. Books by authors with more than one entry are then subarranged by title. The following information is provided where applicable:

☐ Author's name and real name if a pseudonym is used. Co-author, editor, and illustrator's names also given.

☐ Book title.

☐ Date and place of publication; name of publisher.

☐ Series name.

☐ Age Range: Indicates the grade levels for which the title is best suited.

☐ Subject(s): Up to three themes or topics covered in the story.

☐ Major character(s): Names of up to three featured characters and brief descriptions of them.

☐ Time Period(s): Tells when the story takes place.

☐ Locale(s): Tells where the story takes place.

☐ What the book is about: A brief plot summary.

☐ Where it's reviewed: Citations to reviews of the book, including the source of the review, date of the source, and page on which the review appears. Reviews are taken from general reviewing sources such as *Kirkus Reviews* and *Publishers Weekly*, as well as from sources which specialize in materials for younger readers, such as *School Library Journal* and *Horn Book*.

☐ Other books by the author: Titles and publication dates of other books the author has written, for those wanting to read more books by a particular writer.

☐ Other books you might like: Titles by other authors written on a similiar theme or in a similar style. A one sentence description of each of these titles whets the reader's appetite for additional titles.

Indexes Answer Reader's Questions...

The ten indexes in *What Do Children Read Next?* are the heart of the book.

Used separately or in conjunction, they create many pathways to the featured titles, answering general questions or locating specific titles. For example:

"What are the best books for children?"

The AWARDS INDEX lists awards and citations given by experts in the field of children's literature. These titles are especially noteworthy.

"Do you know of any books set during the Civil War?"

The TIME PERIOD INDEX is a chronological listing of the time settings in which the main entries take place.

"Are there any books set in Africa?"

The GEOGRAPHIC INDEX lists titles by their locale, helping readers pinpoint an area in which they may have a particular interest.

"I like stories with a mystery in them. What do you suggest?"

The SUBJECT INDEX lists books by what they are about. Topics include such things as fiction genres (e.g. Fantasy, Ghost Stories, Mystery and Detective Stories), life and relationships (e.g. Family Life, Friendship, School), and subjects of concern to today's children (e.g. Dinosaurs, Ethnic Identity, Sports).

"Do you have any books with kids whose name is the same as mine?"

The CHARACTER NAME INDEX lists the characters named in the entries, helping readers who remember some information about a book, but not an author or title.

"Do you have any books with cats in them?"

The CHARACTER DESCRIPTION INDEX identifies the major characters by occupation (e.g. Astronaut, Doctor) or persona (e.g. Cat, Toy, Twin).

"Which books are good for third graders?" The AGE LEVEL INDEX lists titles by grade levels for which they are best suited. The ability of individual readers may not necessarily reflect their actual age; the wide variety of age ranges allows the user to select titles for slower or more advanced readers.

"Which books have pictures by Bruce Degen?"

The ILLUSTRATOR INDEX is an alphabetical listing of the illustrators of the main entry titles.

"What has Marc Brown written recently?"

The AUTHOR INDEX contains the names of all authors featured in the entries and those listed under "Other books you might like."

"Are there any books like Peggy Parish's Amelia Bedelia?"

The TITLE INDEX includes all main entry titles and all titles recommended under "Other books by the author" and "Other books you might like" in one alphabetical listing. By searching for a specific title, the reader can find out what other books are similar to a title they like.

The indexes can also be used to narrow down or broaden choices. A reader interested in stories set in England during World War II would consult the SUBJECT and GEOGRAPHIC indexes to see which titles appear in both. Someone interested in detective stories set during the 1930s could compare titles in the TIME PERIOD and CHARACTER DESCRIPTION indexes. And with the AUTHOR and TITLE indexes, which include all books listed under "Other books by the author" and "Other books you might like," it is easy to compile an extensive list of titles for further reading, not only with the titles recommended in a main entry, but also by seeing other titles to which the main entry or its recommended titles are similar.

About the Author

As a school psychologist, teacher of young children, and board member, Janis Ansell wrote numerous psychological studies, lesson plans, student evaluations, and reports for meetings. But seldom did she have an opportunity to write book reviews until she began collaborating with Pam Spencer on *What Do Children Read Next?*

Ansell's writing for *What Do Children Read Next?* reflects her life-long interest in reading and her ability to adapt knowledge gained in one subject area to another. Her interest in reading isn't just personal; she aims to help children share her love of reading and develop their reading skills. Janis and her husband Charles, a self-employed architect, have brought up three enthusiastic readers—their children Jonathan (a student at The College of William and Mary), Carrie (a student at Randolph-Macon Woman's College), and Laurie (a 4th grader).

Professional expertise and affiliations and volunteer participation in libraries and classrooms augment her natural interest in books, especially those for children. Professionally affiliated with the Virginia Beach City Public Schools Task Force on the Hearing Impaired and the Randolph-Macon Woman's College Alumnae Association Executive Board, Ansell has been named an Honorary Life Member of the Virginia Congress of Parents and Teachers and Volunteer of the Year at Alanton Elementary School. She is a past board member of the Tidewater Association of Hearing Impaired Children and of the Alanton PTA.

Janis Ansell's psychological insight into young children, her love of books, and her practical experience as a professional, a parent, and a volunteer make her entries in *What Do Children Read Next?* exceptionally informative and useful.

Acknowledgements

The cooperative efforts of many people contributed to the completion of the second edition of *What Do Children Read Next?* I extend my appreciation to everyone involved, beginning with my sister, Pam Spencer, who planted the seed, nurtured the growth and supported the project in many ways, including the writing of 200 of the entries. My husband, Charles, and children, Jonathan, Carrie and Laurie, patiently allowed me to continue writing despite uncooked meals and overlooked housework. My father, Boyd "Gus" Gustafson

checked out books which could not be located closer to home from the Williamsburg (VA) Regional Library and, with the help of my mother, Jane Gustafson, delivered them to me. The staff at the Great Neck Branch of the Virginia Beach (VA) Public Library processed hundreds of reserve requests yet continued to greet me with a smile. Many publishers sent review copies of their 1994 - 1996 titles. As the completion date drew near, Peggy Howell wrote 135 entries of 1996 books. Editors, Deb Kirby and Shelly Dickey, were flexible and understanding as life events overshadowed publisher's deadlines. To my alma mater, Randolph-Macon Woman's College, I am indebted for the education which inspired me to accept opportunities and enabled me to succeed with challenges. I am grateful to each individual and institution for creating a "whole" which is indeed greater than "the sum of its parts".

Suggestions Are Welcome

The editors welcome any comments and suggestions for enhancing and improving *What Do Children Read Next?* Please address correspondence to:

Editor, *What Do Children Read Next?*, Gale Research, 835 Penobscot Bldg., Detroit, Michigan 48226-4094; or call toll-free 1-800-347-4253.

INTRODUCTION

For younger children, the question, "What do children read next?" can often be answered by considering what stories have been read to them during their earliest years. Children love to hear the same stories, especially at bedtime or during times of stress. Although parents may tire of nightly readings of *Goodnight, Moon* or the persistence of Sam-I-Am in *Green Eggs and Ham*, their offspring never do. As children begin to read independently, they choose the books with which they are most familiar, gaining confidence before reaching out to other titles. They may read to dolls, stuffed animals or younger siblings, first with their own made-up stories based on memory and interpretation of pictures and later actually following the words. As Kari discovered in Delores Johnson's book *Papa's Stories*, sometimes the made-up versions bring a special kind of pleasure that is as enjoyable as a literal reading of the text.

What are children in kindergarten through 5th grade reading now? The elementary-age child can choose from picture books to beginning chapter books to titles which overlap with some of those in *What Do Young Adults Read Next?* Topics of interest run the gamut from friendships, pets, and school to moving, death, and ghosts. This second volume of *What Do Children Read Next?* includes more than 1600 titles published primarily between 1993 and 1996 suitable for the wide-ranging interests of children who are five through ten years of age. Many of the titles designated for kindergarten or primary children will also be appropriate for storytime with preschoolers as they begin their journey into the wonderful world of reading. By using the indexes, teachers, parents and elementary librarians can use this book as a resource to identify thousands of other titles which their students or children will enjoy.

Children's Literature, 1993-1996

In 1993, the year that "Libraries Change Lives" was chosen as the theme of National Library Week, several authors and illustrators who have changed lives through their work were recognized. The Oregon Educational Media Association presented its Lifetime Achievement Award to Beverly Cleary, creator of unforgettable characters such as Ramona, Beezus, Henry and Ribsy for her "books loved by millions of children worldwide for over forty years." The Regina Medal of the Catholic Library Association was awarded to author/illustrator Chris Van Allsburg for his "continued distinguished contribution to children's literature" through books such as *The Widow's Broom*. Trina Schart Hyman, illustrator of many children's books, including the Caldecott Honor Books *Herschel and the Hanukkah Goblins* by Eric Kimmel and her own retelling of *Little Red Riding Hood* was recognized by the College of Information Studies with its Drexel Citation. At the 9th Annual Celebration of Black Writing, Eloise Greenfield author of many titles, including the ALA Notable book *Daydreamers* received a Lifetime Achievement Award. Mary Stolz, author of *Storm in the Night,* was presented the Kerlan Award for high achievement in the field of children's literature. The *Nashville Banner* Tennessee Writer Award went to Patricia and Frederick McKissack in recognition of their outstanding books for young readers. The Southern California Council on Literature for Children and Young People selected versatile author Eve Bunting as the recipient of its 1993 award in recognition of her "distinguished body of work." For "significant contribution to excellence in books for children," author/illustrator Jan Brett received the David McCord Children's Literature Citation. Changing lives on more than one continent, prolific author Margaret Mahy was given the Order of New Zealand for her international contribution to children's literature.

The first annual Marion Vannett Ridgway Award for a new author or illustrator was presented to Ian Schoenherr, illustrator of *Newf*. The biannual Ezra Jack Keats New Writer Award was claimed by Faith Ringgold for *Tar Beach*. Further encouragement to new writers and illustrators came from the Dr. Seuss Picture Book Award which included a cash prize and contract with Alfred A. Knopf Books for Young Readers; the recipient was first time author/illustrator Lisa Horstman. Other first time award-winning titles published in 1993 include Paul Brett Johnson's *The Cow Who Wouldn't Come Down*, recognized as both a *School Library Journal* Best Book and a *Booklinks* Good Book and *By the Light of the Halloween Moon* written by Caroline Stutson with illustrations by Kevin Hawkes, recipient of the 1993 Golden Kite Award for illustration. Fans of Laura Ingalls Wilder's *Little House* books can continue to read about the family's life with the publication of the first book in a new series, *Little House on Rocky Ridge* written by Roger Lea MacBride, adopted grandson of Rose Wilder Lane, daughter of Laura Ingalls Wilder.

Several first-time authors produced works which contributed to the growing body of multicultural literature available to children. In Sandra Belton's first picture book, *From Miss Ida's Front Porch* the children in the neighborhood receive a painless history lesson about two famous African Americans while listening to the stories told by their elders on a summer evening. A front porch is also featured in author/illustrator Jan Spivey Gilchrist's introspective book *Indigo and Moonlight Gold* as a young African American girl muses about her mother and her future. An element of magic is suggested in the first picture book for poet and storyteller Dakari Hru, *Joshua's Masai Mask*, as Joshua learns the full meaning of his uncle's gifts. A young girl's energetic urban lifestyle is portrayed in Karen Lotz's *Can't Sit Still* while Ronder Thomas Young's first novel *Learning by Heart* about a young girl's slowly developing awareness of racism is set in the South of the 1960s.

The typical preadolescent concerns about friends are compounded in Gayle Rogers Lockwood's first novel *Libbie Sims, Worry Wart* by Libbie's fears that her twice-divorced mother will remarry her first husband. Set in the 50s, first-time author Eileen Walsh Strauch captures the life of a rebellious 6th grader in *Hey You, Sister Rose*. The unexpected death of a sibling brings the carefree lifestyle of two sisters to an abrupt halt in the first novel by Carol Lynch Williams, *Kelly and Me*.

In February of 1993 the prestigious Caldecott and Newbery awards, for books published during the previous year, were announced at the mid-winter meeting of the American Library Association. The Newbery Medal

Committee selected *Missing May* by Cynthia Rylant for the 1993 Newbery Medal. The Caldecott Medal was awarded to *Mirette on the High Wire* written and illustrated by Emily Arnold McCully. Noted as Caldecott Honor Books were: *Seven Blind Mice* written and illustrated by Ed Young; Jon Scieszka's *The Stinky Cheese Man and Other Fairly Stupid Tales* illustrated by Lane Smith; and *Working Cotton* by Sherley Ann Williams with illustrations by Carole Byard. At the same time, the Coretta Scott King Committee presented the Coretta Scott King Author Award to Patricia McKissack for *The Dark Thirty: Southern Tales of the Supernatural*. The Coretta Scott King Illustrator Award went to Kathleen Atkins Wilson for her first book, *The Origin of Life on Earth: An African Creation Myth*. Three Illustrator Honor books were chosen: *Little Eight John* by Jan Wahl with illustrations by Wil Clay; Robert San Souci's *Sukey and the Mermaids*, illustrated by Brian Pinkney; and *Working Cotton*, cited above.

A new Picture Book category was created by the Jane Addams Children's Book Awards for books that "promote the cause of peace, social justice and world community"; the first award was presented to *Aunt Harriet's Underground Railroad in the Sky* by Faith Ringgold. The British Library Association awarded the Kate Greenaway Medal for illustration to Anthony Browne for *Zoo*. The National Jewish Book Award for Children's Literature, presented to books copyrighted during the preceding year, went to *Letters from Rifka* by Karen Hesse. In the picture book category, the National Jewish Book Award was won by *Elijah's Angel* by Michael J. Rosen with illustrations by Aminah Brenda Lynn Robinson. The 1993 *Weekly Reader* Book Club Award in the Picture Book category went to *Harry the Dirty Dog* by Gene Zion and in the Young Novel category the winner was Johanna Hurwitz's *Class Clown*. The picture book receiving the 1993 Christopher Award was *The Rainbow Fish* by Marcus Pfister while the same award for children's literature was claimed by Hesse's *Letters from Rifka*.

During the year that Peter Rabbit reached the 100th anniversary of his first raid on Farmer MacGregor's garden, several notable authors and illustrators died leaving us with the legacy of their work. Author/illustrator William Pene duBois passed way in February at the age of 76. Receiving the Newbery Medal in 1948 for *The Twenty-One Balloons*, duBois's other award-winning works include two books recognized as Caldecott Honor Books, *Lion* and *Bear Party*. Perhaps best known for her book *Molly's Pilgrim*, the movie version of which won an Academy Award in the short-subject category, author Barbara Kauder Cohen died in November at 60 years of age. Claire Bishop, author of two Newbery Honor Books, *Pancakes-Paris* and *All Alone*, passed away in March. Two-time winner of England's prestigious Carnegie Medal for Children's Literature, 53-year-old author Robert Westall died in April. Prior to her death in July at the age of 91, Ruth Krauss authored more than 30 books for children, including collaborations with illustrators Marc Simont and Maurice Sendak which were awarded Caldecott Honors. Fifty-three-year-old Anne Spencer Lindbergh, author of several books for children including *Three Lives to Live* died in December. Creator of one of the original interactive books, *Pat the Bunny* in print for more than 50 years, author/illustrator Margaret Van Doren Bevans passed away in July at the age of 75.

1994

Fortunately, well-stocked libraries enable children to enjoy the works of authors and illustrators even after their lives end. Children, parents and teachers in countries around the world can be thankful for the more than 200 children's books of author/illustrator Richard Scarry who passed away in April at the age of 74. Eighty-five-year-old Taro Yashima, illustrator of 3 Caldecott Honor Books—*Crow Boy*, *Umbrella* and *Seashore Story*, died in June. Fans of the *Hardy Boys* and *Nancy Drew* will need to accustom themselves to new illustrations following the death in November of 80-year-old illustrator Paul Frame. November also saw the demise of illustrator Janet Ahlberg who collaborated with her husband Allan Ahlberg to create the *Jolly Postman* series and other award-winning books, including *The Jolly Christmas Postman* and *Each Peach Pear Plum*, both winners of the Kate Greenaway Medal. Also on November 15th, Elizabeth George Speare, 85-year-old winner of Newbery Medals for *The Witch of Blackbird Pond* and *The Bronze Bow* as well as Newbery Honor recognition for her last novel *The Sign of the Beaver* passed away. Speare was the 1989 recipient of the Laura Ingalls Wilder Award for "distinguished and lasting contributions to children's literature."

While the writing careers of some ended, others were just beginning. Award-winning first-time authors included Jerdine Nolen whose depiction of a farmer's unique crop in *Harvey Potter's Balloon Farm*, with illustrations by Mark Buehner, was designated an ALA Notable Book in 1995 and won the 1996 Kentucky Bluegrass Award. Published in 1994, *Taxi, Taxi* by Cari Best received the 1995 Ezra Jack Keats New Writer's Award for Children's Books. *Casey Over There* by Staton Rabin with illustrations by Greg Shed claimed the 1995 Marion Vannett Ridgway Award for excellence in a first picture book. Zoe Hall's first book *It's Pumpkin Time!* was designated a *Booklist* Editors' Choice for 1994. A spider who dines on flowers rather than her nervous guests is featured in *Miss Spider's Tea Party* by David Kirk, winner of the International Reading Association's Children's Choice Award for 1995.

Other first-time authors used familiar themes for their works such as Katy Rydell's bedtime story, *Wind Says Good Night*. Friendship is the focus of Todd Starr Palmer's *Rhino and Mouse* as well as *Hamlet and the Enormous Chinese Dragon Kite* by Brian Lies and Laurie Jacob's *So Much in Common*. The way in which the imagination can help make family chores seem like fun is evident in first time author/illustrator Stephen Schlossberg's *Big Red Truck*. While retellings of Native American folkore continue to be popular, Leigh Casler produced an original story in the same spirit with *The Boy Who Dreamed of an Acorn*. A humorous portrayal of a dog's nightlife is seen in *The Night I Followed the Dog* by Nina Laden. The importance of quiet, shared time with a parent is conveyed by Troon Harrison's *The Long Weekend* in which a child selects a weekend at the beach with his mother for his birthday celebration. In Jane Mason's *River Day*, a child enjoys a relaxing day in a canoe with her Grandpa.

Created to "support writing of books for mid-graders," the first Annual Milkweed Prize for Children's Literature was presented to *A Bride for Anna's Papa* by Isabel Marvin. *Vejigante Masquerador* by Lulu Delacre received the Consortium of Latin American Studies Programs (CLASP) Children's Literature Award. The Mystery Writers of America selected Barbara Brooks Wallace's *The Twin in the Tavern* as the recipient of the Edgar Allan Poe Award for Best Juvenile Mystery published in the preceding year. The United Nations Children's Fund and the U.S. Board on Books for Young People chose Chris Raschka as the illustrator most deserving of the 1994 Ezra Jack Keats International Award for his work *Yo! Yes?* which "best exemplifies the cultural unity and diversity ideals of UNICEF." The ABBY Award of the American Booksellers Association was presented to *Stellaluna* by Janell Cannon. Susan Cooper's novel *The Boggart* claimed the WNBA/LA Judy Lopez Memorial Medal given by the Los Angeles Chapter of the Women's National Book Association, Inc. The Canada Council's Governor General's Literary Award for illustration was won by Murray Kimber, illustrator of *Josepha: A Prairie Boy's Story* written by Jim McGugan.

The American Folklore Society selected Julius Lester's retelling *John Henry*, with illustrations by Jerry Pinkney, for its 1994 Aesop Prize. Another retold tale, *Three Sacks of Truth: A Story from France* by Eric A. Kimmel with illustrations by Robert Rayevsky received the Bank Street College of Education's Children's Book Award. The 1994 National Jewish Book Award for Illustration was presented to Sheldon Oberman's *The Always Prayer Shawl* with illustrations by Ted Lewin. The Scott O'Dell Award for Historical Fiction went to *Bull Run* by Paul Fleischman. Missouri school children selected Phyllis Reynolds Naylor's *Shiloh* as the recipient of their state's Mark Twain Award as did South Dakota students who gave the book their Prairie Pasque Award. The popularity of the same book was recognized by Kansas school children with the William Allen White Children's Book Award and by children of the Pacific Northwest who proclaimed *Shiloh* winner of the Young Reader's Choice Award. The 1994 Irma S. and James H. Black Award for Excellence in Children's Literature given by

Bank Street College of Education was won by Patricia Polacco's moving story set during the Civil War, *Pink and Say*.

The Giver by Lois Lowry received the John Newbery Medal for 1994 with the Randolph Caldecott Medal going to Allen Say's *Grandfather's Journey*. The Caldecott Committee also designated five titles as Caldecott Honor Books: *In the Small, Small Pond* by Denise Fleming, *Owen* by Kevin Henkes, Elisa Bartone's *Peppe the Lamplighter* with illustrations by Ted Lewin, *Raven: A Trickster Tale from the Pacific Northwest* by Gerald McDermott, and *Yo! Yes?* by Christopher Raschka. *Grandfather's Journey* was also honored with the *Boston Globe-Horn Book* Picture Book Award and with a Silver Award from the Commonwealth Club of California. In the fiction category the *Boston Globe-Horn Book* Award went to *Scooter* by Vera B. Williams.

Myra Cohn Livingston was honored as the recipient of the 1994 Kerlan Award "in recognition of singular attainments in the creation of children's literature and in appreciation for generous donations of unique resources to the Kerlan Collection for the study of children's literature." The 1994 David McCord Children's Literature Citation was awarded to Joanna Cole, author of *The Magic School Bus* series and other works, for her "significant contribution to excellence in books for children."

1995

Awards determined by the popular vote of a state's school children continue to proliferate. Lowry's *The Giver* received both the Maine Student Book Award and Nebraska's Golden Sower Award for fiction. Children in Kentucky elected *The Cow Who Wouldn't Come Down* by Paul Brett Johnson to receive the 1995 Bluegrass Award. In Vermont, the Dorothy Canfield Fisher Award was given to *The Boggart* by Susan Cooper while the Oklahoma Library Association presented its Sequoyah Book Award to Peg Kehret's *Horror at the Haunted House*. *The Stinky Cheese Man and Other Fairly Stupid Tales* captured both the 1995 Texas Bluebonnet Award and the Buckeye Children's Book Award in the Picture Book category. The same biennial award from the children of Ohio in grades 3-5 was given to *Shiloh* by Phyllis Reynolds Naylor. Recognized by children in two states was Susan Meddaugh's book *Martha Speaks*. recipient of both the Nebraska Golden Sower Award for picture book and a California Young Reader Medal. Children in New Mexico selected *Terror at the Zoo* by Peg Kehret for the 1995 Land of Enchantment Children's Book Award as did students in the Pacific Northwest who gave it their Young Reader's Choice Award. Another of Kehret's works, *Horror at the Haunted House* was one of the winners named to receive the Young Hoosier Book Awards. Two other books receiving awards from the students in Indiana were *The Enchanted Wood* by Ruth Sanderson and *Whispers from the Dead* by Joan Lowry Nixon. The Virginia Young

Reader Awards for the 1994-1995 school year went to *Rough-Face Girl* by Rafe Martin in the primary division and *Ghost Cadet* by Elaine Alphin for elementary. In Missouri, *The Man Who Loved Clowns* by June Rae Wood was elected to receive the Mark Twain Award; students in Kansas chose the same book as recipient of the William Allen White Children's Book Award.

An author and an illustrator new to children's literature walked away with the Newbery and Caldecott Medals in February. Author of two adult novels, Sharon Creech turned to children's literature for the first time with *Walk Two Moons*, winner of the 1995 John Newbery Medal. Illustrator David Diaz received the Caldecott Medal for *Smoky Night*, his second book illustration, and one of many books authored by Eve Bunting. Three Caldecott Honor Books were also selected: Eric Rohman's *Time Flies; Swamp Angel*, illustrated by Paul O. Zelinksy and written by another first-time author Anne Isaacs; and Julius Lester's retelling of *John Henry* with illustrations by Jerry Pinkney. Outstanding achievement in African American literature was recognized by the Coretta Scott King Awards with the Author Award presented to Patricia C. McKissack and Frederick L. McKissack for their holiday story *Christmas in the Big House, Christmas in the Quarters*. James Ransome received the CSK Illustrator Award for *The Creation*.

Other first-time, award-winning authors include Kathi Appelt for her soothing, Cajun-inspired *Bayou Lullaby* which was selected a *School Library Journal* Best Book and *Home Lovely* by Lynne Rae Perkins which received a *Horn Book* Fanfare designation. A humorous look at illness, *Buz*, the first book also written by award-winning children's book illustrator Richard Egielski, was noted as one of the *New York Times* Best Illustrated Children's Books for 1995. An exuberant introduction to the orchestra, *Zin! Zin! Zin! A Violin* by first-time author Lloyd Moss with illustrations by Marjorie Priceman, received multiple awards. In Patricia Rae Wolff's ALA Notable Book *The Toll-Bridge Troll* illustrated by Kimberly Bulcken Root, a young boy creatively solves an unusual problem on his daily walk to school.

The Children's Literature Council of Pennsylvania selected Douglas Florian as the American poet or compiler to receive the 1995 Lee Bennett Hopkins Award for his work *Beast Feast*. The Children's and Young Adult Round Table of the Virginia Library Association presented their Jefferson Cup Award for distinguished historical fiction for young people to *Pink and Say* by Patricia Polacco. The Edgar Allan Poe Award for Best Juvenile Mystery during the preceding year went to *The Absolutely True Story . . . How I Visited Yellowstone Park with the Terrible Rupes: (No Names Have Been Changed to Protect the Guilty)* by Willo Davis Roberts. The American Booksellers selected *Rainbow Fish* by Marcus Pfister as the recipient of their 1995 ABBY Award to recognize a title frequently recommended to customers. The

Carolyn W. Field Award of the Pennsylvania Library Association which is presented annually to the most outstanding children's book written by a Pennsylvania author or illustrator during the preceding year was given to Marjorie Priceman's *How to Make an Apple Pie and See the World*.

Naomi Shihab Nye's story of a young American girl's visit to her Palestinian grandmother, *Sitti's Secrets* with illustrations by Nancy Carpenter, captured this year's Jane Addams Children's Book Award for its promotion of "peace, social justice and world community." The *Boston Globe-Horn Book* Award for Picture Book was conferred on Julius Lester's *John Henry* with illustrations by Jerry Pinkney. *Swamp Angel* by Anne Isaacs and Paul Zelinsky was noted an Honor Picture Book. The fiction title receiving the *Boston Globe-Horn Book* Award was *Some of the Kinder Planets* by Tim Wynne-Jones. Two Fiction Honor Books were chosen: *Jericho* by Janet Hickman and *Earthshine* by Theresa Nelson. The annual Christopher Awards for various age levels were presented to *I'll See You When the Moon Is Full* (ages 4-6) by Susi Gregg Fowler, illustrated by Jim Fowler and Bill Easterling's *Prize in the Snow* (ages 6-8) with illustrations by Mary Beth Owens. The annual Golden Kite Award for fiction was claimed by *The Watsons Go to Birmingham—1963* by Christopher Paul Curtis. For illustration, the Golden Kite Award went to Lauren Mills's *Fairy Wings* with illustrations by Lauren Mills and Dennis Nolan; an honor award in the same category was claimed by Agi Sogabe, illustrator of *The Loyal Cat* by Lensey Namioka. The Southern California Council on Literature for Children and Young People presented the following 1995 awards: Picture Book—*Smoky Night* by Eve Bunting and David Diaz; Folktale—*The Tale of Rabbit and Coyote* by Tony Johnston and Tomie dePaola; Fiction—*Earthshine* by Theresa Nelson.

Authors recognized during the year for their work include Tomie dePaola, recipient of the University of Southern Mississippi's Medallion for achievement in children's literature. For her books which have made a "substantial and lasting contribution to literature for children," Virginia Hamilton was presented the Laura Ingalls Wilder Award. For her "outstanding achievement in literature," Tove Jansson was awarded the Great Prize of the Swedish Academy. Todd Strasser claimed the Children's Literature Award given by the School Library Media Specialists of Southeastern New York to an author or illustrator who lives or works in that area. The 1995 Empire State Award for Excellence in Literature for Young People was given to New York author/illustrator Ed Young for his body of work. The very popular work of very talented writer and illustrator Eric Carle, well-known for his quartet of "Very" books was acknowledged by the 1995 David McCord Children's Literature Citation.

This year saw the lives of a number of authors come to an end, beginning with the deaths in January of Bernard

Wiseman, creator of the *Morris the Moose* books and Crosby Newall Bonsall whose beginning-reader mysteries were popular with children making the transition from picture books to chapter books. In February, Jack Sendak, author of *The Magic Tears* and collaborator with several illustrators including his brother Maurice, died. Jean Lee Latham winner of the 1955 Newbery Medal for *Carry On, Mr. Bowditch* passed away in June. The deaths of Thomas Aylesworth, author of more than 100 fiction and nonfiction titles, and Frances Temple, author/illustrator of *Tiger Soup: An Anansi Story from Jamaica* and several award-winning young adult novels were noted in July. In December, 99-year-old Ann Nolan Clark, 1963 recipient of the Regina Medal for lifetime achievement, passed away; she was also the winner of the 1953 Newbery Medal for *Secret of the Andes* which took the honor over E.B. White's *Charlotte's Web*.

1996

While the 2nd edition of *What Do Children Read Next?* does not include comprehensive coverage of 1996 titles, a sufficient sample can be found to reflect some of the trends in children's literature for the year. The awards presented in any year are often for titles published during previous years and certainly distinguished authors are worthy of note whether for an award or a report of their passing. Memorable characters are also deserving of attention—Happy 70th Birthday Winnie the Pooh!

Sadly, the year began with the death in January of 48-year-old Pam Conrad, author of both picture books and novels including *Stonewords* which received the Edgar Allan Poe Award for Best Juvenile Mystery. In March, Leo Politi, winner of the 1950 Caldecott Medal for *Song of the Swallows* and two Caldecott Honor awards, died at the age of 86. The creator of inimitable nanny *Mary Poppins*, 96-year-old Pamela L. Travers died in April. Renowned illustrator Garth Williams whose first assignment to illustrate E.B. White's *Stuart Little* was followed by the *Little House* Books, *Charlotte's Web* and *The Cricket in Times Square* passed away in May at 84 years of age. In June, death ended the writing career of 74-year-old Leon Garfield, author of historical novels and short stories for children. The author of more than 83 books of poetry, anthologies and critical works, Myra Cohn Livingston died in August at the age of seventy. Livingston's work was recogized in 1980 by the National Council for Teachers of English with their Award for Excellence in Poetry for Children. Creator of Harper & Row's first science "I Can Read Book," *Egg to Chick*, in print for over 50 years, 84-year-old Millicent Selsam passed away in October as did 102-year-old Roma Gans who began the HarperCollins "*Let's-Read-and-Find-Out* Science Series" after her retirement from Teachers College, Columbia University. *Curious George* is no doubt grieving the December passing of his co-creator Margaret E. Rey.

Two new awards were announced. The Pura Belpre Award was created to honor Latino authors and illustrators whose work "portrays and affirms the authentic cultural experience of Latino children." In the illustration category, the first Pura Belpre Award was presented to Susan Guevara for *Chato's Kitchen* written by Gary Soto. The Ohio State Children's Literature Conference has created the annual Jo Osborne Award for Humor in Children's Literature and named Patricia Polacco as its first recipient. A gifted storyteller, Polacco's works include *Chicken Sunday*, *My Rotten Red-Headed Older Brother*, and *Thunder Cake*.

Humor in children's literature was also acknowledged by the awarding of the 1996 Caldecott Medal to Peggy Rathmann for *Officer Buckle and Gloria*, a story of a police officer whose school safety programs are enlivened when he is assigned a new partner—a dog who enjoys the spotlight. Caldecott Honor Books for the year which marks the 150th birthday of Randolph Caldecott included: Stephen T. Johnson's *Alphabet City*; *Zin! Zin! Zin! A Violin* by Lloyd Moss with illustrations by Marjorie Priceman; Robert D. San Souci's *The Faithful Friend* illustrated by Brian Pinkney; and *Tops and Bottoms* by Janet Stevens. Karen Cushman, author of a 1995 Newbery Honor book, this year claimed the Newbery Medal for *The Midwife's Apprentice* set in Medieval England. The following titles were designated Newbery Honor Books: Jim Murphy's *The Great Fire; The Watsons Go to Birmingham—1963* by Christopher Paul Curtis; Carolyn Coman's *What Jamie Saw*; and *Yolonda's Genius* by Carol Fenner. Celebrating its 75th anniversary this year, the Newbery Medal honors "the most distinguished contribution to American literature for children" published during the preceding year.

Other awards announced at the Midwinter ALA Meeting were the Coretta Scott King Author Award presented to Virginia Hamilton for *Her Stories* and the Illustrator Award to Tom Feelings for *The Middle Passage: White Ships/Black Cargo*. CSK Illustrator Honor Books selected were *Her Stories* illustrated by Leo and Diane Dillon and *The Faithful Friend* illustrated by Brian Pinkney. The year's Andrew Carnegie Medal for Excellence in Children's Video was claimed by Paul R. Gagne for *Owen*, adapted from Kevin Henkes's picture book of the same title. One of this year's Batchelder Honor Awards for translated children's books went to *Star of Fear, Star of Hope* by Jo Hoestlandt which was translated from French by Mark Polizzotti.

The preceding year's new authors and illustrators were recognized with the 1996 Marion Vannett Ridgway Award for 1st picture book given to Marsha Diane Arnold for *Heart of a Tiger*. Honor recognitions were given to authors for the following books: *The Gift of a Traveler* by Wendy Matthews; *The Long Silk Strand* by Laura E. Williams; Karen Chinn's *Sam and the Lucky Money* and *Tsubu the Little Snail* by Carol Ann Williams. The African Studies Association's Annual Children's Book Award for Younger Children was presented to *It Takes a Village* by Jane Cowen-Fletcher. Virginia Hamilton's *Her Stories* with illustrations by Leo and Diane Dillon received the 1996 NAACP Image Award for Children's Books. The Virginia Library Association's annual Jefferson Cup Award went to *The Great Fire* by Jim Murphy and Mildred's Taylor's novel *The Well: David's Story* received the Jane Addams Children's Book Award. The *Boston Globe-Horn Book* Award for picture book was given to Amy Hest's *In the Rain with Baby Duck* illustrated by Jill Barton. The fiction title recognized for this year's *Boston Globe-Horn Book* Award was *Poppy* by Avi with illustrations by Brian Floca. The Carolyn W. Field Award for outstanding literature was presented by the Pennsylvania Library Association to *The Christmas Miracle of Jonathan Toomey* by Susan Wojciechowski with illustrations by P.J. Lynch. The title also received the 1996 Christopher Award for ages 6-9 for its "affirmation of the highest values of the human spirit" exemplified in the story and its "artistic and technical proficiency."

The Southern California Council on Literature for Children and Young People honored southern California author Alice Schertle for Distinguished Work in Two Genres (poetry and fiction) for her titles *Advice for a Frog* and *Down the Road*. For his "lifetime contribution to children's literature," Uri Orlev was presented the 1996 Hans Christian Andersen Award. Recognizing a New York author or illustrator, the Empire State Award of the New York Library Association was given to Nancy Willard for her body of work. Marion Dane Bauer and the late Paul Galdone were recipients of this year's Kerlan Award in "recognition of singular attainments in the creation of children's literature" and appreciation for their donations of original manuscripts and artwork to the University of Minnesota's Kerlan Collection of Children's Literature. The winner of this year's David McCord Children's Literature Citation was Patricia Polacco for her "significant contribution to excellence in books for children."

The children of America continue to read and cast their ballots for the books deemed worthy of receiving their state's children's book award. The New Jersey Library Association announced the following winners of the Garden State Children's Book Awards: *Henry and Mudge and the Wild Wind* by Cynthia Rylant with illustrations by Suci Stevenson for Easy-to-Read and Ellen Conford's *Nibble, Nibble, Jenny Archer* for Younger Fiction. Oklahoma school children elected *The Ghosts of Mercy Manor* by Betty Ren Wright to receive the Sequoyah Children's Book Award. In Connecticut, the Nutmeg Children's Book Award was claimed by Phyllis Reynolds Naylor for *The Grand Escape*. The same title received Nebraska's Golden Sower Award for grades 4-6. Younger students in Nebraska presented their state's award to *Soap, Soap, Don't Forget the Soap* by Tom Birdseye. The Colorado Book Award in the children's category went to *Tops and Bottoms* by Janet Stevens. Lois Lowry's novel *The Giver* continues to be popular with students, receiving the William Allen White Children's Book Award in Kansas and the Pacific Northwest Library Association's Young Readers' Choice Award, Senior Division. In the Youth Division, children from the Pacific Northwest selected *Boys Start the War* by Phyllis Reynolds Naylor as did students in South Carolina for their state's Children's Book Award. The South Carolina Association of School Librarians Junior Book Award went to Patricia MacLachlan's *Baby*. Vermont children chose *Time for Andrew: A Ghost Story* by Mary Downing Hahn to receive the Dorothy Canfield Fisher Award; the same title received a California Young Reader Medal from the intermediate grades. Primary grade students in California awarded *Stellaluna* by Jannell Cannon a Young Reader Medal. The Pennsylvania Young Readers' Choice Award for grades K-3 went to *The Three Little Wolves and the Big Bad Pig* by Eugene Trivizas and Helen Oxenbury while the 3rd-8th graders chose *The Sweetest Fig* by Chris Van Allsburg. In Kentucky the Bluegrass Award for grades 4-8 was presented to *The Christmas of the Reddle Moon* by J. Patrick Lewis and Gary Kelley.

1993-1996

As the cost of paper and printing has risen so has the cost of children's books. In 1993, the average price for preschool and primary books was $14.91 while books for 3rd to 6th graders averaged $14.40. By 1996 the average respective book prices were $15.28 and $15.34. Prices of 3rd to 6th grade books have climbed steadily while those for younger readers were as high as $16.03 in 1995 and have dropped slightly. It seems safe to say that prices will continue to climb as library acquisition budgets shrink.

While newly created series' entries allowed readers to meet friends such as Joyce Champion's *Emily and Alice* and a supportive family in Jonathan London's *Froggy* books, established characters continued to entertain. In the past few years, Marc Brown's lovable aardvark *Arthur* has survived chicken pox, a rained-out family vacation and a new puppy. James Howe's characters *Pinky and Rex* found their friendship was strong enough to handle the turmoil of a new baby adopted by Rex's family while Juanita Havill's *Jamaica and Brianna* coped with hurt feelings and peer acceptance.

Both the quality and quantity of beginning readers has increased. Cynthia Rylant's *Henry and Mudge* series continued to delight with tales of a boy and his dog while her new *Mr. Putter and Tabby* books presented a positive and light-hearted picture of the elderly. Laurie Krasny Brown introduced siblings Rex and Lilly in her new "Dino Easy Reader Series". Popular authors Suzy Kline, David Adler,

Patricia Reilly Giff and Betsy Duffey continued to write easy chapter books about school and friendships which enabled newly independent readers to make the transition from the controlled vocabulary of beginning readers to novels.

Life's tougher issues have also been tackled in recent children's fiction. Coping with the death of a pet is portrayed in Ellen Howard's *Murphy and Kate*, Michael J. Rosen's *Bonesy and Isabel* and *Maggie and Silky and Joe* by Amy Ehrlich. Parents and grandparents also died, leaving bewildered children facing tough issues in *Daddy's Climbing Tree* by C.S. Adler, Eve Bunting's *The In-Between Days*, Katherine Paterson's *Flip-Flop Girl* and *Granddad Bill's Song* by Jane Yolen. Moving is rarely popular with children, but Judith Viorst's *Alexander, Who's Not (Do You Hear Me? I Mean It!) Going to Move* may be the most adamantly opposed character seen recently. The theme was also addressed in Susan Patron's *Maybe Yes, Maybe No, Maybe Maybe* and *Scooter* by Vera Williams.

Society's growing awareness of and sensitivity to cultural diversity, is reflected in an expanding body of literature. The triumphs and troubles of immigrants from different countries and time periods were portrayed in titles such as Elisa Bartone's award-winning *Peppe the Lamplighter, My Name Is Maria Isabel* by Alma Flor Ada, *Sarah, Also Known as Hannah* by Lillian Hammer Ross and Sherry Garland's *The Lotus Seed*. African Americans were frequently seen as characters not only in historical fiction such as *Sweet Clara and the Freedom Quilt* by Deborah Hopkinson, *Uncle Jed's Barbershop* by Margaree Mitchell or Connie Porter's "Addy" series, but also in contemporary settings. The difficulty of life in the inner city and the successful coping strategies of impoverished children in such places were expressed in Alice Mead's *Junebug* and *The Secret Super Powers of Marco Polo* by Meredith Sue Willis. Works such as *Saturday at the New You* by Barbara E. Barber and Brian Pinkney's *Max Found Two Sticks* gave a glimpse of the joys of daily life.

Through children's literature, readers could travel around the world, visiting India with *Binya's Blue Umbrella* by Ruskin Bond, China in *First Apple* by Ching Yeung Russell or Japan in Rumer Godden's *Great-Grandfather's House*. Retold folktales continued to introduce children to other cultures from Native American legends such as Joseph Bruchac's *The Boy Who Lived with the Bears: And Other Iroquois Stories* to "pourquoi" tales from Africa by Verna Aardema which explained *How the Ostrich Got Its Long Neck*. As Flora, protagonist in Dick King-Smith's *The School Mouse*, learned, reading can be a life saver. It can also be an adventure as Cervantes experienced in *The Bookstore Mouse* by Peggy Christian. To get kids connected to a book, turn the page, find a story to fall into and you too may discover that reading can be the beginning of an unexpected journey!

WHAT DO CHILDREN

READ NEXT?

A Reader's Guide to
Fiction for Children

A

VERNA AARDEMA
MARCIA BROWN, Illustrator

How the Ostrich Got Its Long Neck

(New York: Scholastic Inc., 1995)

Subject(s): Folk Tales; Animals; Africa
Age range(s): Grades K-3
Major character(s): Ostrich, Ostrich; Crocodile, Crocodile; Fish Eagle, Bird (eagle)
Time period(s): Indeterminate Past
Locale(s): Africa

Summary: Long ago Ostrich had long legs, but a very short neck so he was unable to reach berries high in a bush or eat insects on the ground. Then, Crocodile asks for help with a toothache and kind Ostrich ignores Fish Eagle's warning, overcomes his timidity and peers into Crocodile's big mouth to find the tooth needing extraction. When Ostrich's head is deep in Crocodile's throat, Crocodile closes her mouth and a tug-of-war begins as Ostrich tries to free himself. Eventually, Ostrich is successful, but not before his neck has been stretched so much that now he can reach berries and bugs with ease. (32 pages)

Where it's reviewed:
Booklist, June 1995, page 1773
Children's Book Review Service, November 1995, page 25
Horn Book Guide, Spring 1996, page 88
Publishers Weekly, July 31, 1995, page 80
School Library Journal, November 1995, page 86

Other books by the same author:
Rabbit Makes a Monkey of Lion, 1989
Who's in Rabbit's House? A Masai Tale, 1977 (Lewis Carroll Shelf Award, 1978)
Why Mosquitoes Buzz in People's Ears: A West African Tale, 1975 (Caldecott Medal winner, 1976)

Other books you might like:
Michael Rosen, *How Giraffe Got Such a Long Neck. . .And Why Rhino Is So Grumpy: A Tale from East Africa*, 1993

The *pourquoi* tale explains that giraffe ate forgetful rhino's share of a magical neck-growing herb as well as his own to produce his extra long neck and rhino's grumpiness.
Mary-Joan Gerson, *Why the Sky Is Far Away: A Nigerian Folktale*, 1992
Award-winning illustrations enhance the original 1972 text explaining that the sky is no longer close to the earth because of people's wasteful habits.
Mwenye Hadithi, *Hungry Hyena*, 1994
After Hyena steals Fish Eagle's food, Fish Eagle devises a plan that teaches Hyena a lesson.
Barbara Knutson, *How the Guinea Fowl Got Her Spots: A Swahili Tale of Friendship*, 1990
When the Guinea Fowl does a favor for Cow she is given spots to help her hide from predators.

KAREN ACKERMAN
BARRY MOSER, Illustrator

Bingleman's Midway

(Honesdale, PA: Boyds Mills Press, Inc., 1995)

Subject(s): Carnivals; Fathers and Sons; Summer
Age range(s): Grades 1-4
Major character(s): Mr. McKinney, Farmer, Father; Drew McKinney, Brother (older); Nathaniel McKinney, Brother (younger)
Time period(s): Indeterminate Past
Locale(s): Ohio

Summary: When a flat tire stops a convoy of carnival trucks on the road near their farm, Nathaniel and Drew have their first glimpse of the Midway that will enliven their rural neighborhood. Drew is nonchalant, but Nathaniel begs to see the Midway. The next day, when chores are completed, Mr. McKinney takes his sons to see the attraction. The final act works its magic on Drew and that night he sneaks out of the house, intending to join Bingleman's Midway. (32 pages)

Where it's reviewed:
Booklist, October 15, 1995, page 409

Horn Book, March 1996, page 186
Kirkus Reviews, October 15, 1995, page 1486
New Advocate, Winter 1996, page 63
School Library Journal, December 1995, page 72

Other books by the same author:
By the Dawn's Early Light, 1994
Araminta's Paint Box, 1990
Song and Dance Man, 1988

Other books you might like:
Michael Garland, *Circus Girl*, 1993
   A day in the life of Alice and her family shows the excitement and the busyness of circus life.
David Merveille, *Thomas, the Circus Boy*, 1993
   Clumsy Thomas, lacking confidence in his ability to continue the family's acrobatic tradition, runs away from his circus home.
Ian Wallace, *Morgan the Magnificent*, 1987
   When the circus comes to town, Morgan discovers a place where her ability to do handstands in high places on the farm can finally be appreciated.

3

KAREN ACKERMAN
CATHERINE STOCK, Illustrator

By the Dawn's Early Light

(New York: Atheneum, 1994)

Subject(s): Single Parent Families; Working Mothers; Grandparents
Age range(s): Grades K-2
Major character(s): Mom, Single Mother, Worker; Nana, Grandmother, Babysitter; Rachel, Child, Student
Time period(s): 1990s (1994)
Locale(s): United States

Summary: Mom works the graveyard shift at a box factory while Nana cares for Rachel and her brother. Rachel knows exactly what Mom is doing at work while the family at home completes dinner, chores and homework. Sometimes, Rachel hears Mom arrive home at 4 in the morning and then she wakes her brother so they can snuggle with Mom "by the dawn's early light." (32 pages)

Where it's reviewed:
Booklist, April 1, 1994, page 1457
Bulletin of the Center for Children's Books, May 1994, page 280
Hungry Mind Review, Summer 1994, page 56
Kirkus Reviews, May 1, 1994, page 625
School Library Journal, June 1994, page 94

Other books by the same author:
Araminta's Paint Box, 1990
The Tin Heart, 1990
Song and Dance Man, 1988 (Caldecott Medal Winner, 1989)

Other books you might like:
Barbara E. Barber, *Saturday at the New You*, 1994
   Weekly, Shauna works with her mother in a beauty parlor, observing customers and helping with routine tasks.

Cari Best, *Red Light, Green Light, Mama and Me*, 1995
   When Grandma becomes ill and unable to babysit, Lizzie commutes to work with her mother, a children's librarian.
George Ella Lyon, *Mama Is a Miner*, 1994
   As a child goes through her day she reflects on her mother's job deep underground in a coal mine.

4

KAREN ACKERMAN
ELIZABETH SAYLES, Illustrator

The Night Crossing

(New York: Alfred A. Knopf, Inc., 1994)

Subject(s): World War II; Holocaust; Jews
Age range(s): Grades 3-4
Major character(s): Clara, Child, Sister (younger); Marta, Teenager, Sister
Time period(s): 1930s (1938)
Locale(s): Innsbruck, Austria

Summary: As the Nazi control in Austria strengthens and local Jews begin to vanish, Clara and Marta's parents decide to escape to Switzerland. The family valuables, with the exception of heirloom silver candlesticks, are sold. Travelling by night to avoid the Nazi patrols, the family reaches the Swiss border on foot. Clara's dolls hide the silver candlesticks and her wits trick the border guard into believing the family's story so they are able to safely enter Switzerland. An epilogue gives factual information about the family and the relatives left behind. (56 pages)

Where it's reviewed:
Booklist, March 15, 1994, page 1346
Children's Book Review Service, Spring 1994, page 139
Kirkus Reviews, April 1, 1994, page 477
Publishers Weekly, April 25, 1994, page 79
School Library Journal, July 1994, page 100

Other books by the same author:
The Leaves in October, 1991 (ALA Notable Book)

Other books you might like:
Claire Bishop, *Twenty and Ten*, 1952
   Ten Jewish children are hidden by twenty French school children during the Nazi occupation of their country.
Lois Lowry, *Number the Stars*, 1988
   An award-winning title describes the friendship of a young Dane and her Jewish friend during the German occupation of their country.
Uri Orlev, *Lydia, Queen of Palestine*, 1993
   Lydia's family and her world fall apart prior to her escape from Nazi-occupied Romania, alone, to Palestine where she resides in a kibbutz.

5

KAREN ACKERMAN
ELIZABETH SAYLES, Illustrator

The Sleeping Porch

(New York: Morrow Junior Books, 1995)

Subject(s): Moving, Household; Dwellings; Family Life

Age range(s): Grades K-3
Major character(s): Jonathan, Child
Time period(s): 1990s (1995)
Locale(s): United States

Summary: Excitedly, Jonathan and his family move from their cramped apartment into a large, older home. As the oldest of the five children, Jonathan has a room of his own, but such privilege does him no more good than the others when a summer thunderstorm reveals a very leaky roof on the house. When the storm subsides, the only dry place to sleep is on the ''sleeping'' porch. Cozily, the family settles down and begins a summertime tradition which they enjoy even after the roof is fixed. (40 pages)

Where it's reviewed:
Booklist, March 1, 1995, page 1246
Children's Book Review Service, April 1995, page 103
Horn Book Guide, Fall 1995, page 256
School Library Journal, May 1995, page 81

Other books by the same author:
In the Park with Dad, 1994
I Know a Place, 1992
This Old House, 1992

Other books you might like:
Marc Harshman, *The Storm*, 1995
    Alone on the farm, young Jonathan does not let his confinement to a wheelchair keep him from making preparations for a threatening tornado.
Amy Hest, *Ruby's Storm*, 1994
    Determined to keep her checkers date with Grampa, Ruby packs her picnic basket with supplies and sets off in a spring storm for a comforting evening.
Una Leavy, *Harry's Stormy Night*, 1994
    Coping with a loss of electric power during a storm, Harry and his family sing and tell stories by candlelight.
Anne F. Rockwell, *The Storm*, 1994
    In the comfort of her family's coastal home, a young girl reflects on the power of a major storm.

6

ALMA FLOR ADA
LESLIE TRYON, Illustrator

Dear Peter Rabbit
(New York: Atheneum, 1994)

Subject(s): Fairy Tale; Letters; Communication
Age range(s): Grades K-3
Major character(s): Peter Rabbit, Rabbit; Goldilocks McGregor, Child; Baby Bear, Bear
Time period(s): Indeterminate Past
Locale(s): Fictional City

Summary: Through the correspondence of various friends, who happen to be well-known fairy tale characters, plans are made for Peter Rabbit to attend the pigs' housewarming party (if his cold clears up in time) and for Goldilocks to have a return visit to Baby Bear's home to see his repaired chair. As the letters continue between the pairs of friends, it becomes obvious that all, except the infamous wolves, will be together at Goldilocks' birthday party. (40 pages)

Where it's reviewed:
Booklist, May 1, 1994, page 1606
Children's Book Review Service, May 1994, page 109
Kirkus Reviews, March 1, 1994, page 297
Publishers Weekly, February 21, 1994, page 253
School Library Journal, July 1994, page 73

Other books by the same author:
Mediopollito: Half Chicken, 1995
The Gold Coin, 1991
Friends—Amigos, 1989

Other books you might like:
Janet Ahlberg, *The Jolly Christmas Postman*, 1991
    Cards and letters from one nursery-rhyme character to another expand the story of the postman's rounds in a book co-authored by Allan Ahlberg.
Frank Asch, *Dear Brother*, 1992
    As two mice brothers read the letters of their ancestors they realize the importance of brothers and of letter writing.
Judith Caseley, *Dear Annie*, 1991
    In a work which also uses letter writing to tell the story, this one is correspondence between Annie and her grandfather.
Lisa Campbell Ernst, *Little Red Riding Hood: A Newfangled Prairie Tale*, 1995
    In a contemporary spoof of a classic fairy tale, Grandma surprises the wolf and the two reach a most unusual conclusion.
Eugene Trivizas, *The Three Little Wolves and the Big Bad Pig*, 1993
    A familiar tale takes a new turn in an award-winning title when the big bad pig tries to outmanuever the three little wolves and ends up surprising himself.

ALMA FLOR ADA
K. DYBLE THOMPSON, Illustrator

My Name Is Maria Isabel
(New York: Atheneum, 1993)

Subject(s): Moving, Household; Schools
Age range(s): Grades 3-4
Major character(s): Maria Isabel Salazar Lopez, 3rd Grader, Immigrant (Puerto Rican); Unnamed Character, Teacher
Time period(s): 1990s (1993)
Locale(s): United States

Summary: What's in a name? For Maria Isabel Salazar Lopez it is the cumulative heritage of the relatives for whom she is named and the country, Puerto Rico, from which she has come. Unfortunately, to the teacher at her new school, the name means simply a third Maria in the class and, for convenience, the teacher changes this Maria to Mary Lopez. Unable to adjust to that arbitrary renaming, Maria does not respond when the teacher calls on Mary Lopez and so her problems adjusting to the new school are compounded. A class assignment to write about one's greatest wish gives Maria an opportunity to claim her name as uniquely her own. Translated from Spanish by Ana M. Cerro. (64 pages)

Where it's reviewed:
Booklist, June 1, 1993, page 1828
Children's Book Review Service, June 1993, page 125
Five Owls, September 1993, page 14
Publisher's Weekly, April 19, 1993, page 62
School Library Journal, April 1993, page 117

Other books by the same author:
I Love Saturdays y Domingos, 1995
Dear Peter Rabbit, 1994
The Unicorn of the West: El Unicornio del Oeste, 1994
The Rooster Who Went to His Uncle's Wedding: A Latin American Folktale, 1992

Other books you might like:
Nicholasa Mohr, *Felita*, 1990
    When a Puerto Rican family moves to a non-Spanish speaking community, the language difference adds to the challenges they face in their new home.
Lillian Hammer Ross, *Sarah, Also Known as Hannah*, 1994
    When Sarah must emigrate to America in place of her older sister, Hannah, Sarah loses her home, her family, and her name.
Gary Soto, *The Skirt*, 1992
    To fourth-grader Miata, Mother's old skirt represents memories of childhood days in Mexico and serves as a link to the family's cultural heritage.

8

ADDIE ADAM
LISA THIESING, Illustrator

Hilda and the Mad Scientist
(New York: Dutton Children's Books, 1995)

Subject(s): Behavior; Conduct of Life; Humor
Age range(s): Grades 1-3
Major character(s): Hilda, Volunteer; Dr. Weinerstein, Scientist
Time period(s): Indeterminate Past
Locale(s): Fictional Country (Vampire Hill)

Summary: Helpful Hilda doesn't take "Go Away!" for an answer when she arrives at Dr. Weinerstein's castle with do-good intentions of keeping house, cooking and nursing his rheumatism. Unbeknowst to the frustrated mad scientist, Hilda has discarded his monster-making potions and replaced them with fresh grape juice and chocolate milk. Thus, when Dr. Weinerstein prepares the monster-making machine to create a monster which will s

Where it's reviewed:
Booklist, June 1995, page 1781
Horn Book Guide, Fall 1995, page 256
Library Talk, September 1995, page 26
Publishers Weekly, July 3, 1995, page 60
School Library Journal, August 1995, page 114

Other books you might like:
Pat Hutchins, *Three-Star Billy*, 1994
    A monster who doesn't want to be in school finds that his temper tantrum is rewarded by the teacher with three stars.

Rosemary Wells, *Fritz and the Mess Fairy*, 1991
    Messy Fritz meets his match when his science project goes awry creating Mess Fairy.
Anne Wilsdorf, *Philomene*, 1992
    Captured by a disagreeable witch, Philomene takes her by surprise when she befriends the witch's monster and the two of them create their own spell.

9

JOANN ADINOLFI, Author/Illustrator

The Egyptian Polar Bear
(Boston: Houghton Mifflin Company, 1994)

Subject(s): Animals/Bears; Kings, Queens, Rulers, etc.; Fantasy
Age range(s): Grades K-2
Major character(s): Nanook, Polar Bear; King Rahotep, 10-Year-Old, Royalty
Time period(s): Indeterminate Past
Locale(s): Egypt

Summary: Stranded on a iceberg floating south and gradually melting, Nanook ends up in the Mediterranean Sea from which he washes ashore, exhausted, in Egypt. He is found by sailors who are sure that he has been sent by the gods to be presented to King Rahotep. As a child, Rahotep finds the position of king to be lonely so he welcomes Nanook as a playmate, introducing him to the palace and Egypt. First book for the author/illustrator. (32 pages)

Where it's reviewed:
Booklist, November 1, 1994, page 504
Horn Book Guide, Spring 1995, page 24
Kirkus Reviews, August 15, 1994, page 1119
Publishers Weekly, September 5, 1994, page 109
School Library Journal, January 1995, page 81

Other books you might like:
Tomie De Paola, *Bill and Pete Go Down the Nile*, 1987
    A class trip to a Cairo museum provides unexpected excitement for Bill and his friend Pete.
Roy Gerrard, *Croco'nile*, 1994
    The rhyming text introduces Hamut and Nekatu whose adventures take the reader down the Nile for a tour of ancient Egypt.
Ann Turnbull, *The Queen Cat*, 1992
    When the Queen Cat of the temple dies, Mew-sheri must locate a successor.

10

C.S. ADLER

Courtyard Cat
(New York: Clarion Books, 1995)

Subject(s): Brothers and Sisters; City Life; Guilt
Age range(s): Grades 4-6
Major character(s): Lindsay, 11-Year-Old, Sister; Garth, 3-Year-Old, Brother; Sapphire, Cat
Time period(s): 1990s (1995)
Locale(s): Schenectady, New York

Summary: Following an accidental injury to Garth, Lindsay's family moves from a rural area of upstate New York to a small apartment near a hospital. While her parents find jobs to pay for Garth's surgery, Lindsay babysits. Because she blames herself for the accident, Lindsay has difficulty disciplining her strong-willed brother. New neighbors and a cat who frequents the courtyard of the apartment building help Lindsay adjust to the many changes in her life. (172 pages)

Where it's reviewed:
Booklist, August 1995, page 1945
Bulletin of the Center for Children's Books, September 1995, page 4
Horn Book Guide, Spring 1996, page 58
School Library Journal, September 1995, page 199

Other books by the same author:
Willie, the Frog Prince, 1994
One Sister Too Many, 1989
Good-Bye Pink Pig, 1986

Other books you might like:
Errol Broome, *Tangles*, 1994
    Sophie ''borrows'' a neighbor's money in order to purchase a kitten, but then is racked with guilt over her actions.
Janet Taylor Lisle, *Looking for Juliette*, 1994
    While Angela is away for a year, her cat disappears and Angela's friends suspect that the elderly caretaker of the house is responsible.
Lensey Namioka, *Yang the Third and Her Impossible Family*, 1995
    With her brother's help, Yingmei ''Mary'' Yang tries to hide a kitten from her family.
Phyllis Reynolds Naylor, *The Grand Escape*, 1993
    Housecats, Marco and Polo, escape to the wonderfully dangerous outside world, completing three missions for a cat group known as the Club of Mysteries.

11

C.S. ADLER

Daddy's Climbing Tree
(New York: Clarion Books, 1993)

Subject(s): Death; Fathers and Daughters; Grief
Age range(s): Grades 3-6
Major character(s): Jessica Turner, 11-Year-Old, Sister (older); Tycho Turner, 6-Year-Old, Brother (Jessica's); Judith Turner, Mother, Widow(er)
Time period(s): 1990s (1993)
Locale(s): Hammond, Indiana

Summary: Unable to accept her father's sudden accidental death soon after her family moves to a new community, Jessica convinces her brother to run away with her to search for him at their former home. Sure that she will find him high up in his special climbing tree, Jessica finds, not her daddy, but herself, an ability to accept his death and a determination to keep his memory alive within her. (136 pages)

Where it's reviewed:
Booklist, June 1, 1993, page 1828
Children's Book Review Service, June 1993, page 128

Horn Book, July 1993, page 455
Publishers Weekly, April 12, 1993, page 64
School Library Journal, May 1993, page 103

Other books by the same author:
That Horse Whiskey!, 1994
Mismatched Summer, 1991
Always and Forever Friends, 1990
Ghost Brother, 1990
If You Need Me, 1988

Other books you might like:
Katherine Paterson, *Flip-Flop Girl*, 1994
    Feeling very alone and confused, nine-year-old Vinnie is trying to cope with her father's death, her family's move, a new school, and a brother who hasn't talked since their dad died.
Jean Thesman, *Nothing Grows Here*, 1994
    Following the unexpected death of her father, Maryanne must learn to cope not only with her grief but also with the loss of her home and friends when her mother moves to an apartment.
Jane Breskin Zalben, *The Fortuneteller in 5B*, 1991
    Struggling to accept her father's death, Alexandra's life is also complicated by a neighbor who may be something more than she seems.

12

C.S. ADLER

Youn Hee and Me
(San Diego: Harcourt Brace & Co., 1995)

Subject(s): Adoption; Brothers and Sisters; Korean Americans
Age range(s): Grades 4-6
Major character(s): Caitlin Lacey, 11-Year-Old; Si Won ''Simon'' Lacey, Child; Youn Hee Lacey, 11-Year-Old
Time period(s): 1990s
Locale(s): New York

Summary: Caitlin is ecstatic when she discovers that her adopted Korean brother, Simon, has a sister who lives in an orphange in Korea. She thinks it will be great to have a sister her own age and convinces her mother to also adopt Youn Hee. But when Youn Hee arrives, it's obvious that she and Caitlin are opposites; Youn Hee is reserved and serious in direct contrast to Caitlin's exuberance. Though Youn Hee never liked living in a Korean orphanage, at least she knew how to be Korean; in America, she doesn't know exactly how to act. It takes time, understanding and many attempts at communication before Caitlin and Youn Hee work out a friendship. (183 pages)

Where it's reviewed:
Booklist, April 15, 1995, page 1497
Voice of Youth Advocates, August 1995, page 154
Publishers Weekly, May 1, 1995, page 59
Horn Book Guide, Fall 1995, page 293
Center for Children's Books. Bulletin, March 1995, page 226

Other books by the same author:
That Horse Whiskey!, 1994
Shell Lady's Daughter, 1983
In Our House Scott Is My Brother, 1980

Other books you might like:

Lauren Lee, *Stella: On the Edge of Popularity*, 1994
Stella must learn the difference between popularity and being true to her culture in this first novel.

Marie G. Lee, *If It Hadn't Been for Yoon Jun*, 1993
At first Alice is leery of Yoon Jun, a new student from Korea whom she considers weird, but through Yoon Jun she learns more about her culture.

Joyce McDonald, *Mail-Order Kid*, 1988
Flip adapts quickly when he and his newly adopted Korean brother have to share a bedroom.

Anna Myers, *Rosie's Tiger*, 1994
When her brother returns from Korea with his new Korean wife and their child, Rosie learns to accept her new relations.

13

DAVID A. ADLER
SUSANNA NATTI, Illustrator

Cam Jansen and the Chocolate Fudge Mystery

(New York: Viking, 1993)

Series: Cam Jansen Adventure
Subject(s): Mystery and Detective Stories
Age range(s): Grades 3-4
Major character(s): Jennifer ''Cam'' Jansen, Child, Detective; Eric Shelton, Child (Cam's friend)
Time period(s): 1990s (1993)
Locale(s): United States

Summary: As Cam and Eric walk through the neighborhood selling chocolate fudge bars and rice cakes to raise funds for the library, Cam observes a woman whose actions she considers peculiar. Using her curiosity and photographic memory, she determines the significance of some strange happenings at a home in the neighborhood, which leads to the apprehension of a bank robber. (49 pages)

Where it's reviewed:
Booklist, October 15, 1993, page 440
Horn Book Guide, Spring 1994, page 63
School Library Journal, September 1993, page 228

Other books by the same author:
Cam Jansen and the Mystery at the Haunted House, 1992
Cam Jansen and the Mystery of the Monster Movie, 1992
The Fourth Floor Twins and the Silver Ghost Express, 1987

Other books you might like:

Mary Blount Christian, *The Sebastian (Super Sleuth) Series*, 1982-
Although his owner considers himself the detective, the sheepdog Sebastian knows who really solves these mysteries.

Eth Clifford, *Help! I'm a Prisoner in the Library*, 1979
Unbeknownst to the librarian, Mary Rose and JoBeth run into the library to use the restroom and end up locked in for the night.

Marilyn Singer, *A Clue in Code*, 1985
Solving the mystery of the class's missing trip money is

the latest adventure for detective twins Sam and Dave Bean.

Donald J. Sobol, *The Encyclopedia Brown Series*, 1979-
Ten-year-old Leroy Brown operates his own detective agency and solves a variety of mysteries in his neighborhood.

Gertrude Chandler Warner, *The Mystery of the Hidden Painting*, 1992
The four children of the Boxcar Children Series are involved in another mysterious adventure.

14

DAVID A. ADLER
LLOYD BLOOM, Illustrator

One Yellow Daffodil: A Hanukkah Story

(San Diego: Harcourt Brace and Company, 1995)

Subject(s): Holidays, Jewish; Holocaust; Jews
Age range(s): Grades 1-4
Major character(s): Morris Kaplan, Businessman (florist), Survivor; Ilana Becker, Child, Sister; Jonathan Becker, Child, Brother
Time period(s): 1990s (1995)
Locale(s): United States

Summary: Daily, Ilana and Jonathan greet Mr. Kaplan as they walk to school and each Friday they stop on their way home to buy flowers for the Sabbath. When they unexpectedly come for flowers on a Tuesday, the siblings explain that they are buying flowers for the first night of Hanukkah. Their invitation to Mr. Kaplan to observe Hanukkah with their family revives his painful memories of a childhood in Poland, days in the concentration camp and lost family members, but celebrating the holiday also offers the promise of healing through friendship. (32 pages)

Where it's reviewed:
Booklist, November 1, 1995, page 476
Bulletin of the Center for Children's Books, December 1995, page 118
Five Owls, November 1995, page 36
Horn Book, March 1996, page 187
School Library Journal, October 1995, page 34

Other books by the same author:
Hilde and Eli: Children of the Holocaust, 1994
The Children's Book of Jewish Holidays, 1987
Hanukkah Game Book: Games, Riddles, Puzzles and More, 1978

Other books you might like:

Barbara Diamond Goldin, *Just Enough Is Plenty: A Hanukkah Tale*, 1988
Rivkeh worries that her poor family will be unable to celebrate Hanukkah, but when a stranger comes to the door, they generously share what they have.

Patricia Lakin, *Don't Forget*, 1994
As young Sarah gathers the supplies to surprise her mother with a birthday cake, she is assisted by Jewish shopkeepers in the neighborhood.

Myron Levoy, *The Hanukkah of Great-Uncle Otto*, 1984
Joshua learns a greater appreciation for the meaning of

Hanukkah as he helps his great-Uncle Otto make a menorah to replace the one lost during the Holocaust.

15

ALLAN AHLBERG
FRITZ WEGNER, Illustrator

The Giant Baby

(New York: Viking, 1995)

Subject(s): Family Life; Babies; Humor
Age range(s): Grades 3-5
Major character(s): Alice Hicks, Child; Unnamed Character, Child (giant's baby), Orphan; Horace, Cousin
Time period(s): Indeterminate Past
Locale(s): England

Summary: Alice's wish for a baby brother comes true in a most unusual way when she and her parents discover a giant baby on their doorstep. By the time the family can get the local welfare office to investigate the abandoned infant, Alice has rescued the baby from circus kidnappers and hidden him for safety. She enlists the help of mercenary Horace who charges other children to view the infant in order to raise money for supplies. Alice and her parents become attached to the giant baby and are forlorn when just as suddenly as he appeared, one night he is picked up by his mother giant and never seen again. (156 pages)

Where it's reviewed:
Children's Book Review Service, May 1995, apge 113
Junior Bookshelf, February 1995, page 14
Quill & Quire, February 1995, page 39
School Librarian, February 1995, page 20
School Library Journal, July 1995, page 76

Other books by the same author:
The Bear Nobody Wanted, 1993
Ten in a Bed, 1989
Woof!, 1986

Other books you might like:
Roald Dahl, *The BFG*, 1982
    After a Big Friendly Giant kidnaps Sophie from her orpanage, the duo devise a plan to save the world from some unfriendly giants.
Mordicai Gerstein, *The Giant*, 1995
    Clara, Reina and Amelia who frequently sit and watch the Giant on the other side of the ravine are unsure how to respond when he notices them.
Dick King-Smith, *Magnus Powermouse*, 19982
    A baby mouse's nonstop growth to a bigger-than-mouse size leads to capture by the rat catcher.

16

ALLAN AHLBERG
JANET AHLBERG, Illustrator

It Was a Dark and Stormy Night

(London: Viking, 1993)

Subject(s): Storytelling; Robbers and Outlaws; Adventure and Adventurers

Age range(s): Grades 2-4
Major character(s): Antonio Panetta, 8-Year-Old (brave), Kidnap Victim (storyteller); Chief, Outlaw, Leader
Time period(s): Indeterminate Past
Locale(s): Italy

Summary: Kidnapped by a band of brigands, Antonio is ordered by the bored leader to tell the group a story which he attempts to do while Chief and others in the band continually interrupt with editorial comments. Antonio soon notes that the brigands like a story with minimal violence, lots of food and successful outlaws. With his gift for gab, Antonio succeeds in turning the tale in such a way that the outlaws run away and Antonio gains his freedom. (32 pages)

Where it's reviewed:
Booklist, May 1, 1994, page 1606
Junior Bookshelf, April 1994, page 47
Publishers Weekly, February 28, 1994, page 88
School Librarian, February 1994, page 15
Wilson Library Bulletin, June 1994, page 129

Other books by the same author:
Burglar Bill, 1992
The Black Cat, 1990
Funnybones, 1981

Other books you might like:
Nancy Antle, *Sam's Wild West Show*, 1995
    A group of performing cowboys and cowgirls use their skills to trick a group of would-be bank robbers.
Barbara Ann Porte, *When Grandma Almost Fell Off the Mountain and Other Stories*, 1993
    Grandma doesn't consider herself a storyteller, but her visiting granddaughters are certainly entertained by her retelling a childhood trip.
James Thurber, *The Great Quillow*, 1994
    A newly illustrated version of the classic tale of a giant who is outwitted by a small, but clever toymaker.

17

JOAN AIKEN

Cold Shoulder Road

(New York: Delacorte Press, 1996, c1995)

Subject(s): Adventure and Adventurers; Extrasensory Perception; Religion
Age range(s): Grades 5-8
Major character(s): Is Twite, Cousin; Arun Twite, Cousin; Admiral Fishskin, Villain
Time period(s): Indeterminate Past
Locale(s): Folkstone, England

Summary: Is and Arun go to Folkstone to reunite Arun with his mother, but when they get there, she is gone and the house is locked up. In their search for her, the two young people find themselves involved in adventures, including smuggling with Admiral Fishskin and members of the Secret Sect. Fortunately the two can correspond with each other using ESP and are thus successful in doing away with the Merry Gentry and reuniting Arun and his mother. (283 pages)

Where it's reviewed:
Horn Book, March/April 1996, page 334

Bulletin of the Center for Children's Books, April 1996, page 255
Booklist, April 1, 1996, page 1352

Other books by the same author:
The Shoemaker's Boy, 1994
Is Underground, 1992
Return to Harken House, 1990

Other books you might like:
Lois Duncan, *A Gift of Magic*, 1971
Nancy learns how to handle her ESP.
Sheila Hayes, *Zoe's Gift*, 1994
Cory meets a girl with ESP and together they are able to solve a 100 year old mystery.
Peg Kehret, *Danger at the Fair*, 1995
Ellen receives a call for help from her brother when he is attacked in the fun house.
Kathryn Lasky, *Double Trouble Squared*, 1991
Liberty and Judy receive emanations from the former residence of Arthur Conan Doyle.
Betty Ren Wright, *A Ghost in the Window*, 1987
A man who died in a car wreck tries to communicate through Meg's dreams to prove he was innocent.

18

JOAN AIKEN
VICTOR G. AMBRUS, Illustrator

The Shoemaker's Boy

(New York: Simon & Schuster, 1994)

Subject(s): Fairy Tale; Illness; Good and Evil
Age range(s): Grades 2-4
Major character(s): Jem, Child (shoemaker's son); Unnamed Character, Father (shoemaker); Unnamed Character, Mother (ill)
Time period(s): Indeterminate Past
Locale(s): England (small village)

Summary: When Jem's mother falls ill, his father undertakes a pilgrimage to pray for her recovery, leaving Jem in charge of the shoemaking and the care of his unconscious mother. After some months, a tired Jem receives a series of strange visitors, the first two looking for three keys and the last one leaving a package in his care. During the night Jem hears the sounds of a struggle, but suspects that he is dreaming. In the morning, his mother awakens and speaks for the first time in months, apparently healed of her mysterious illness. Originally published in England in 1991. (31 pages)

Where it's reviewed:
Booklist, June 1, 1994, page 1815
Horn Book Guide, Fall 1994, page 298
Kirkus Reviews, June 15, 1994, page 839
Publishers Weekly, May 9, 1994, page 73
School Library Journal, June 1994, page 94

Other books by the same author:
The Erl King's Daughter, 1989

Other books you might like:
Philippa Gregory, *Florizella and the Wolves*, 1993
An original fairy tale about an unconventional princess who adopts four orphaned wolf cubs as pets.

George MacDonald, *The Light Princess and Other Tales*, 1961
The complete collection of MacDonald's fairy tales includes the story of the princess without gravity and the two youths in search of a keyhole for their golden key.
Margaret Mahy, *The Chewing-Gum Rescue*, 1992
The eleven short stories presented include elements of fairy tales and fantasy.

19

RICHARD E. ALBERT
SYLVIA LONG, Illustrator

Alejandro's Gift

(San Francisco: Chronicle Books, 1994)

Subject(s): Deserts; Loneliness; Animals
Age range(s): Grades 1-3
Major character(s): Alejandro, Aged Person, Gardener
Time period(s): 1990s (1994)
Locale(s): Southwest

Summary: Living alone in an isolated adobe home, Alejandro tends a garden to occupy his time. When he notices that his irrigation of the garden attracts a variety of wildlife, he digs a water hole to better serve the needs of the animals. In exchange for Alejandro's gift to the animals, their presence is a gift of companionship to him. A pictorial glossary gives factual information about the animals pictured in the book. First children's book for the author. (26 pages)

Where it's reviewed:
Booklist, April 15, 1994, page 1537
Children's Bookwatch, May 1994, page 4
Publishers Weekly, February 14, 1994, page 87
School Library Journal, July 1994, page 73

Awards the book has won:
Consortium of Latin American Studies Programs Commended Book, 1994

Other books you might like:
Byrd Baylor, *We Walk in Sandy Places*, 1976
For an observant person, animal tracks tell the story of what has walked in the desert.
Dale Fife, *The Empty Lot*, 1991
After Harry looks closely at his empty lot and sees the signs of life in it, he decides it cannot be described as empty at all.
Paul Brett Johnson, *Lost*, 1996
A lost dog meets many desert animals while searching for his owner. Co-author Celeste Lewis.

20

JEZ ALBOROUGH, Author/Illustrator

It's the Bear!

(Cambridge, MA: Candlewick Press, 1994)

Subject(s): Animals/Bears; Mothers and Sons; Stories in Rhyme
Age range(s): Grades K-2

Major character(s): Eddie, Child; Freddie, Bear, Toy; Mom, Mother
Time period(s): 1990s (1994)
Locale(s): Fictional Country
Summary: In the sequel to *Where's My Teddy?*, Eddie is remembering the events of his last walk in the woods as he tries to convince Mom not to plan a picnic there. Insisting that Freddie is the only bear in the forest, Mom cheerfully leaves Eddie alone while she goes back for the forgotten blueberry pie. In her absence, the bear arrives, clutching his own teddy, and devours all the food while terrified Eddie hides in the picnic basket. Mom returns just in time to unwittingly provide the bear with dessert. (32 pages)

Where it's reviewed:
Books for Keeps, November 1994, page 4
Horn Book Guide, Spring 1995, page 24
Instructor, May 1995, page 78
Publishers Weekly, November 21, 1994
School Library Journal, February 1995, page 72

Other books by the same author:
Cuddly Dudley, 1993
Where's My Teddy?, 1992
Beaky, 1990

Other books you might like:
Debi Gliori, *Mr. Bear's Picnic*, 1995
   The complaints of three young neighbors, uninvited guests at Mr. Bear's picnic, threaten to spoil this quiet activity.
Jimmy Kennedy, *The Teddy Bears' Picnic*, 1992
   A classic song telling of the day the teddy bears gather for a picnic is published in many versions by different illustrators.
John Prater, *Once Upon a Picnic*, 1996
   Mom and Dad don't seem to notice the storybook characters observed by their son as the family enjoys a quiet picnic near a stream.

■ **21**

ARLENE ALDA, Author/Illustrator

Pig, Horse, or Cow, Don't Wake Me Now
(New York: Doubleday Book for Young Readers, 1994)

Subject(s): Animals; Stories in Rhyme; Sleep
Age range(s): Grades K-1
Major character(s): Scott, Child
Time period(s): 1990s (1994)
Locale(s): United States

Summary: A peacock calling for his morning corn begins the cumulative process of awakening a variety of animals culminating with a cat intruding on Scott's sleep. Scott is dreaming and wants to linger under the covers a while longer, but his mother coaxes him out of bed and down to breakfast to begin another active day. (32 pages)

Where it's reviewed:
Booklist, October 15, 1994, page 434
Horn Book Guide, Spring 1995, page 24
Kirkus Reviews, November 15, 1994, page 1522
Publishers Weekly, October 10, 1994, page 69
School Library Journal, December 1994, page 71

Other books by the same author:
Sheep, Sheep, Sheep, Help Me Fall Asleep, 1992

Other books you might like:
Alyssa Satin Capucilli, *Inside a Barn in the Country*, 1995
   The mouse's squeak wakes the horse whose neigh awakens the next animal and so on until the farmer tells them all to go back to sleep until morning.
Sally Grindley, *Wake Up, Dad!*, 1988
   Unable to rouse her parents early one morning, a little girl decides to climb in their warm bed and keep them company.
Susan L. Roth, *Princess*, 1993
   Despite her mother's repeated attempts to wake her for school, a little girl tarries in bed imagining the freedom she would have if she were a princess.
Marisabina Russo, *Time to Wake Up!*, 1994
   Mama tickles the toes of reluctant riser Sam to encourage him to wake up and get out of bed.

■ **22**

LLOYD ALEXANDER

The Arkadians
(New York: Dutton, 1995)

Subject(s): Fantasy
Age range(s): Grades 6-7
Major character(s): Lucian, Accountant (bean counter); Fronto, Writer (poet changed into a jackass); Joy-in-the-Dance, Healer (prophetess)
Time period(s): Indeterminate Past
Locale(s): Fictional Country (Arkadia)

Summary: Orphaned at a young age, Lucian grows up in the king's palace and proves to be so capable that he's promoted to overseeing inventories. When he makes a mistake, Lucian leaves the palace before getting into bigger trouble. He escapes accompanied by a poet named Fronto who's been changed into a jackass; along the way they meet Joy-in-the-Dance who has given Lucian's king an unwelcome prophecy. As they search for the Lady of Wild Things, who they hope will solve their many problems, they become caught up in the disagreement between those who believe in the Lady of Wild Things and others who believe in the Olympian gods in this mythical adventure. (272 pages)

Where it's reviewed:
Publishers Weekly, June 12, 1995, page 62
Booklist, May 1, 1995, page 1561
School Library Journal, May 1995, page 104
Voice of Youth Advocates, December 1995, page 312
Horn Book Guide, Fall 1995, page 293

Awards the book has won:
ALA Notable Children's Book, 1996

Other books by the same author:
The Remarkable Journey of Prince Jen, 1991
The Drackenberg Adventure, 1988
Westmark, 1981

Other books you might like:

L. Frank Baum, *The Wonderful Wizard of Oz*, 1900
 The classic tale where Dorothy is caught in a tornado that drops her and her dog, Toto, in the magical land of Oz.

Alison Farthing, *Mystical Beast*, 1978
 In search of the ''Mystical Beast,'' Sara and Henry go to a distant land known as the ''other side.''

Zilpha Keatley Snyder, *Song of the Gargoyle*, 1991
 Hunting for his father, the court jester, Tymmon meets a gargoyle-like singing dog and enough knights to tarnish his image of them.

23

LLOYD ALEXANDER
DIANE GOODE, Illustrator

The House Gobbaleen

(New York: Dutton Children's Books, 1995)

Subject(s): Animals/Cats; Superstition; Humor
Age range(s): Grades 1-4
Major character(s): Gladsake, Cat (Tooley's pet); Tooley, Householder, Young Man; Hooks, Imposter, Bully
Time period(s): Indeterminate Past
Locale(s): Fictional Country

Summary: Considering himself the victim of bad luck, Tooley sets out food to attract the Friendly Folk in order to benefit from some of their luck. Convinced that a little man eating his offering one morning is the luck come at last, Tooley invites the fellow in despite Gladsake's warning to the contrary. Hooks turns out to be a bossy, rude, demanding guest who indeed brings Tooley lots of luck—all bad. Gladsake wisely concocts a plan which not only frees Tooley from the tyranny of Hooks, but also convinces him that he can bring about his own good fortune. (40 pages)

Where it's reviewed:

Booklist, July 1995, page 1882
Children's Book Review Service, November 1995, page 25
Horn Book, January 1996, page 58
Publishers Weekly, July 17, 1995, page 230
School Library Journal, September 1995, page 167

Awards the book has won:

School Library Journal Best Books, 1995

Other books by the same author:

The Fortune Tellers, 1992 (ALA Notable Book)

Other books you might like:

Jennifer Armstrong, *Chin Yu Min and the Ginger Cat*, 1993
 A ginger cat changes the fortunes of a haughty widow and teaches her the value of companionship over wealth.

Lily Toy Hong, *Two of Everything*, 1993
 When a poor farmer finds an old pot that turns out to be magic, he and his wife must learn to live with the consequences of their good fortune.

Steven Kroll, *Friday the 13th*, 1981
 Unlucky Harold hopes for a change of fortune.

24

MARTHA ALEXANDER, Author/Illustrator

You're a Genius, Blackboard Bear

(Cambridge, MA: Candlewick Press, 1995)

Subject(s): Animals/Bears; Imagination; Space Travel
Age range(s): Grades K-1
Major character(s): Anthony, Child (imaginative); Blackboard Bear, Bear (drawing)
Time period(s): 1990s (1995)
Locale(s): Earth

Summary: A bedtime story about the moon inspires Anthony to request a trip, but his father doesn't know how to build a spaceship. As Anthony sleeps, Blackboard Bear awakens and draws plans for a spaceship on the now-empty chalkboard. Together, he and Anthony assemble the spaceship, loading it so full with supplies that Anthony must stay behind while brave Blackboard Bear visits the moon to check it for monsters and brings back a souvenir star for Anthony. (32 pages)

Where it's reviewed:

Booklist, May 1, 1995, page 1578
Bulletin of the Center for Children's Books, June 1995, page 337
Horn Book, September 1995, page 625
Publishers Weekly, April 17, 1995, page 57
School Library Journal, June 1995, page 76

Other books by the same author:

We're in Big Trouble, Blackboard Bear, 1980
And My Mean Old Mother Will Be Sorry, Blackboard Bear, 1977
I Sure Am Glad to See You, Blackboard Bear, 1976

Other books you might like:

Frank Asch, *Mooncake*, 1978
 Believing the moon is made of cake, Bear builds a rocket to fly himself there in order to taste it.

Raymond Briggs, *The Bear*, 1994
 Only Tilly can see the huge, white bear that pays her a visit, creating more work than Tilly wants to do.

Crockett Johnson, *Harold and the Purple Crayon*, 1955
 Using his magic purple crayon, Harold draws himself into and out of adventure.

Else Holmelund Minarik, *Little Bear*, 1957
 The first entry in an easy reader series about Little Bear and his friends finds Little Bear planning a trip to the moon.

Hermann Moers, *Katie and the Big Brave Bear*, 1995
 While alone at home, fearful Katie is comforted by a large bear who emerges from the pages of her favorite story-book.

25

ALIKI, Author/Illustrator

Best Friends Together Again

(New York: Greenwillow Books, 1995)

Subject(s): Friendship; Moving, Household; Reunions
Age range(s): Grades K-2

Major character(s): Robert, Child, Friend; Peter, Child, Friend
Time period(s): 1990s (1995)
Locale(s): United States

Summary: The sequel to *We Are Best Friends* brings Robert and Peter together for a two-week visit. The best friends make room for Robert's new friend to join them in play before they all go to the park and meet other children who are also happy to see Peter again. The time passes too quickly, but Robert and Peter part knowing that they will see one another again. (32 pages)

Where it's reviewed:
Booklist, August 1995, page 1954
Horn Book, September 1995, page 584
Horn Book Guide, Spring 1996, page 18
School Library Journal, September 1995, page 167

Other books by the same author:
Jack and Jake, 1986
At Mary Bloom's, 1983
We Are Best Friends, 1982

Other books you might like:
Larry Dane Brimner, *Max and Felix*, 1993
   Frog friends experience the ups and downs of friendship in a beginning chapter book.
Kevin Henkes, *Chester's Way*, 1988
   Chester and Wilson do everything together in exactly the same way until Lilly moves in and shows them that friends can do things differently and remain friends.
Nette Hilton, *Andrew Jessup*, 1993
   Andrew Jessup remains a little girl's best "faraway friend" even after Madeline's family moves into his old house.
Pat Hutchins, *My Best Friend*, 1993
   A diversity of interests and abilities adds flavor to this friendship.

26

JONATHAN ALLEN, Author/Illustrator

Two by Two by Two

(New York: Dial Books for Young Readers, 1995)

Subject(s): Animals; Humor; Floods
Age range(s): Grades K-2
Major character(s): Noah, Historical Figure
Time period(s): Indeterminate Past
Locale(s): the Ark, At Sea

Summary: The Biblical story is reduced to a comic presentation of life aboard the Ark as it floats over the flooded world. Noah mediates disputes when the usually harmonious interactions between the animals need some direction and water skis with the help of a dolphin. Each animal is labelled for easy identification and contributions to the conversation are presented in comic-strip bubbles. (40 pages)

Where it's reviewed:
Booklist, July 1995, page 1882
Junior Bookshelf, April 1995, page 63
Publishers Weekly, May 22, 1995, page 59
School Librarian, May 1995, page 57
School Library Journal, June 1995, page 76

Other books by the same author:
Who's at the Door?, 1993
Mucky Moose, 1991
My Dog, 1989

Other books you might like:
Glen Rounds, *Washday on Noah's Ark: A Story of Noah's Ark According to Glen Rounds*, 1985
   When the sun finally shines after 40 days of rain, Mrs. Noah decides to wash clothes and improvises a clothesline in order to dry them.
Peter Spier, *Noah's Ark*, 1977
   In a Caldecott Medal winner, pictures tell the story of the pairs of animals who climbed aboard the Ark and survived the Flood.
Ann Turnbull, *Too Tired*, 1993
   The sloths are almost left behind because they are too tired to climb aboard Noah's Ark.

27

JUDY ALLEN
TUDOR HUMPHRIES, Illustrator

Eagle

(Cambridge, MA: Candlewick Press, 1994)

Subject(s): Animals/Birds; Wildlife Conservation; Fear
Age range(s): Grades 1-4
Major character(s): Miguel, Child, Student
Time period(s): 1990s (1994)
Locale(s): Philippines

Summary: On a two-day school trip to the jungle to study animals and their habitat, Miguel is frightened by the eagle hunting in the area. Then, when the eagle's quest to capture dinner also saves Miguel from a cobra snake, he loses his fear and begins to respect the powerful bird. A concluding fact sheet gives information about this endangered species and conservation efforts. (26 pages)

Where it's reviewed:
Booklist, September 1, 1994, page 47
Book World, December 4, 1994, page 17
Horn Book Guide, Spring 1995, page 24
Kirkus Reviews, September 15, 1994, page 1263
School Library Journal, October 1994, page 85

Other books by the same author:
Elephant, 1993
Whale, 1993
Tiger, 1992

Other books you might like:
Jacqueline Briggs Martin, *Washing the Willow Tree Loon*, 1995
   The rescue, treatment and rehabilitation of an oil-soaked loon is portrayed as a community effort following an oil spill.
Jane B. Mason, *River Day*, 1994
   A serene day on the river with her grandfather seems incomplete until Alex spots a bald eagle.
Sheryl McFarlane, *Eagle Dreams*, 1995
   Robin's dream that he can rehabilitate an injured eagle and see it fly again comes true through hard work and patience.

28

ELAINE MARIE ALPHIN
JOAN SANDIN, Illustrator

A Bear for Miguel

(New York: HarperCollins, 1996)

Series: I Can Read
Subject(s): Family Life; Toys
Age range(s): Grades 1-3
Major character(s): Maria, Child; Papa, Unemployed; Paco, Toy
Time period(s): 1990s
Locale(s): Felicidad, El Salvador

Summary: Maria and her father go to market to trade some of the last of their belongings for needed food, such as eggs and milk. As they drive the mule into town, they see soldiers on the street. They seem to be friendly and the market is busy. They are successful in trading chairs for food but then a couple inquires about Maria's toy, Paco. The young couple want the bear to give to their son, who was injured in the fighting. Maria hesitates, not wanting to give Paco up, until she thinks about the little boy lying in a bed with no toys. Maria and Papa return home with the food they need, but Maria knows she will always miss her toy. (60 pages)

Where it's reviewed:
Horn Book, May/June 1996, page 331
Booklist, August 1996, page 1910
Bulletin of the Center for Children's Books, February 1996, page 183

Other books by the same author:
Tournament of Time, 1994
The Ghost Cadet, 1991

Other books you might like:
Alma Flor Ada, *The Gold Coin*, 1991
    A thief follows a woman in order to steal the gold coin she has.
Alma Flor Ada, *My Name Is Maria Isabel*, 1993
    Maria's greatest wish is that she be called by her real name when she goes to school.
Ann Cameron, *The Most Beautiful Place in the World*, 1988
    Juan wants to go to school but is afraid to ask his grandmother for permission.
Nicholasa Mohr, *The Magic Shell*, 1995
    Jaime is not at all happy about moving to New York but is reconciled as he listens to the conch shell he brought with him.
Charlotte Pomerantz, *The Chalk Doll*, 1989
    Rose loves to hear about her mother's rag doll and how she was able to buy a present for three cents when she was a little girl.
Beatriz Zapater, *Fiesta!*, 1994
    Chucho and his family from Colombia plan a celebration in their new home.

29

LINDA JACOBS ALTMAN
ENRIQUE O. SANCHEZ, Illustrator

Amelia's Road

(New York: Lee & Low Books, 1993)

Subject(s): Migrant Labor; Mexican Americans
Age range(s): Grades K-3
Major character(s): Amelia Luisa Martinez, Child, Migrant Worker
Time period(s): 1990s (1993)
Locale(s): United States

Summary: The frequent moves, the remembering of family events by crops rather than dates, the interminable roads—all the things that Amelia hates about migrant life do not seem to bother others in her family. Amelia longs for permanence, for a classroom where the students and the teacher know her name, for a house with a yard, for a place to call home. During one apple harvest, Amelia's discovery of an old tree gives her such a place. (32 pages)

Where it's reviewed:
Booklist, September 15, 1993, page 155
Kirkus Reviews, August 15, 1993, page 1069
Publishers Weekly, August 9, 1993, page 476
Reading Teacher, April 1994, page 565
School Library Journal, December 1993, page 78

Other books you might like:
Arthur Dorros, *Radio Man = Don Radio: A Story in English and Spanish*, 1993
    As Diego and his family follow the crops, he searches for his friend David, succeeding with the help of the ever-present radio which he carries from cabbage fields to apple orchards.
Michele Benoit Slawson, *Apple Picking Time*, 1994
    Too young to pick as rapidly as her parents and grandparents, Anna sets her own goals in the apple orchard and meets them, proudly earning a half-moon punched into her very own ticket.
Jane Resh Thomas, *Lights on the River*, 1994
    While the adults in her family of migrant laborers pick the crops, Teresa serves as the babysitter, watching over the picking and the younger children from her shady spot.
Sherley Anne Williams, *Working Cotton*, 1992
    Shelan is proud of the work she and her family do laboring in the cotton fields.

30

SUZANNE ALTMAN
DIANE ALLISON, Illustrator

My Worst Days Diary

(New York: Bantam Books, 1995)

Series: Bank Street Ready-to-Read
Subject(s): Diaries; Self-Perception; School Life
Age range(s): Grades 2-3
Major character(s): Maureen ''Mo'' Murphy, Student
Time period(s): 1990s (1995)

Locale(s): United States

Summary: Every imaginable thing that can happen to embarrass a student happens to Mo, the new girl in class. Her teacher thinks she plans these horrid happenings, but, as Mo explains to her diary, she is simply a victim of bad luck . By the end of the school year, Mo has made two friends and put away her "worst days" diary for a brighter one labelled "greatest days." (48 pages)

Where it's reviewed:
Booklist, October 1, 1995, page 328
Horn Book Guide, Spring 1996, page 53
School Library Journal, January 1996, page 76

Other books you might like:
Marissa Moss, *Amelia's Notebook*, 1995
When her family moves, Amelia records her feelings about the changes in her life.
Jerry Spinelli, *Tooter Pepperday*, 1995
Tooter is so determined not to move with her family to Aunt Sally's farm that she handcuffs herself to the bathroom sink.
Vera B. Williams, *Stringbean's Trip to the Shining Sea*, 1988
Stringbean's postcards provide the record of a trip from the Midwest to the West Coast. Co-author Jennifer Williams

31

RUDOLFO ANAYA
EDWARD GONZALES, Illustrator

The Farolitos of Christmas
(New York: Hyperion Books for Children, 1995)

Subject(s): Christmas; Mexican Americans; Grandparents
Age range(s): Grades 1-4
Major character(s): Luz, Child (Mexican American), Friend (Reina's); Reina, Child, Indian; Abuelo, Grandfather
Time period(s): 1940s (1944)
Locale(s): San Juan, New Mexico

Summary: The night for lighting the traditional luminarias is quickly approaching and Abuelo is too ill to chop the necessary wood. Afraid that without the luminarias to light the way her family will not be included in the planned celebration, Luz tries to find her holiday spirit while helping Reina decorate her family's Christmas tree. Through all the preparations for the holiday, Luz is thinking of an alternative source of light using candles and, when she finally comes up with an idea, a new tradition of farolitos is begun. (32 pages)

Where it's reviewed:
Booklist, September 15, 1995, page 168
Horn Book, November 1995, page 727
Publishers Weekly, September 18, 1995, page 102
Quill & Quire, September 1995, page 76
School Library Journal, October 1995, page 34

Other books you might like:
Jean Ciavonne, *Carlos, Light the Farolito*, 1995
On the final night of Los Posadas, family and neighbors will gather at Carlos' home to complete the reenactment of the Christmas story.
Gary Soto, *Too Many Tamales*, 1993
Maria's attempts to help her mother prepare the traditional

Mexican-American Christmas Eve meal leads to a dilemma with a humorous solution.
Jane Resh Thomas, *Lights on the River*, 1994
While her family of migrant workers follows the crops, Teresa dreams of Abuela and the Christmas candles floating down the river near their Mexican village.

32

HANS CHRISTIAN ANDERSEN
P.J. LYNCH, Illustrator

The Snow Queen
(San Diego: Harcourt Brace and Company, 1994)

Subject(s): Fairy Tale; Winter; Voyages and Travels
Age range(s): Grades 3-6
Major character(s): Gerda, Heroine, Friend (Kay's); Kay, Kidnap Victim, Friend (Gerda's); Snow Queen, Sorceress
Time period(s): Indeterminate Past
Locale(s): Fictional Country

Summary: In Caroline Peachey's retelling of Andersen's tale, Kay vanishes on a snowy day when he ties his sled to that of the Snow Queen. Determined to find him when he does not return with the spring thaw, Gerda begins a quest which takes her to an enchanted garden, a princess's home, the abode of forest thieves, the hut of the Lapland woman and finally to the ice palace of the Snow Queen where the power of her love conquers the Snow Queen's spell and wins Kay's freedom. (48 pages)

Where it's reviewed:
Booklist, September 15, 1994, page 135
Kirkus Reviews, October 15, 1994, page 1403
Publishers Weekly, November 7, 1994, page 79
School Librarian, May 1994, page 53
School Library Journal, November 1994, page 102

Other books by the same author:
The Steadfast Tin Soldier, 1992
The Little Mermaid, 1988
The Little Match Girl: A Classic Tale, 1988

Other books you might like:
Virginia Haviland, *Favorite Fairy Tales Told in England*, 1994
The collection of English fairy tales was originally selected by Joseph Jacobs and published in 1892.
George MacDonald, *The Lost Princess: A Double Story*, 1992
The kidnapping of their spoiled daughter by a wise woman with magical powers begins a series of surprises for the princess's parents.
Margaret Mayo, *Magical Tales from Many Lands*, 1993
An international collection presents fairy tales and folklore from different countries.
Nancy Willard, *Beauty and the Beast*, 1992
A retelling set in New York City early in the 20th century retains the theme of the power of love to break a spell.

33

HANS CHRISTIAN ANDERSEN
ERIK BLEGVAD, Illustrator

Twelve Tales
(New York: Margaret K. McElderry Books, 1994)

Subject(s): Fairy Tale; Short Stories
Age range(s): Grades 3-6
Time period(s): Indeterminate Past
Locale(s): Europe

Summary: A native of Denmark, Erik Blegvad not only illustrates these twelve tales of his countryman, but also translates them from the original Danish. Thus, the collection contains familiar stories such as ''The Princess and the Pea'' as well as others such as ''The Sweethearts''which are less well known.

Where it's reviewed:
Booklist, October 1, 1994, page 328
Horn Book, November 1994, page 729
Kirkus Reviews, September 15, 1994, page 1263
Publishers Weekly, July 11, 1994, page 79
School Library Journal, October 1994, page 118

Other books by the same author:
The Fairy Tales of Hans Christian Andersen, 1995
The Snow Queen, 1994
The Little Mermaid, 1993

Other books you might like:
Cooper Edens, *Favorite Fairy Tales: A Classic Illustrated Edition*, 1991
    With co-author Harold Darling, Edens has collected 14 familiar tales.
Neil Philip, *American Fairy Tales: From Rip Van Winkle to the Rootabaga Stories*, 1996
    A collection of fairy tales includes the work of American authors from Washington Irving to Carl Sandburg.
Oscar Wilde, *The Happy Prince*, 1995
    An illustrated adaptation by Jane Ray of the 1888 tale tells of the little prince statue and the sparrow.

34

JOAN ANDERSON
GEORGE ANCONA, Illustrator

Sally's Submarine
(New York: Morrow Junior Books, 1995)

Series: You-Are-There Adventure
Subject(s): Submarines; Fathers and Daughters; Imagination
Age range(s): Grades K-3
Major character(s): Sally Sanford, Child
Time period(s): 1990s (1995)
Locale(s): United States

Summary: After helping her father load his boat with lobster traps, fishing poles and bait, Sally enters her cardboard submarine for a day of imaginative adventure. Today's trip hints of a touch of reality as Sally follows a seal, saves a lobster from a trap, and hides from a shark. (32 pages)

Where it's reviewed:
Booklist, March 15, 1995, page 1333
Horn Book Guide, Fall 1995, page 256
Library Talk, September 1995, page 32
School Library Journal, April 1995, page 97

Other books by the same author:
Richie's Rocket, 1993
Harry's Helicopter, 1990
Christmas on the Prairie, 1985

Other books you might like:
Eric Carle, *A House for Hermit Crab*, 1988
    When a hermit crab moves into a larger shell, he decorates the new residence with sea life he meets.
Milly Jane Limmer, *Where Will You Swim Tonight?*, 1991
    At bathtime a young girl imagines growing a tail and swimming with various sea creatures.
Joanne Ryder, *A House by the Sea*, 1994
    Imaginative children describe their fantasy life in a house by the sea and daily adventures with a variety of marine animals.

35

LAURENCE ANHOLT
CATHERINE ANHOLT, Illustrator

The New Puppy
(Racine, WI: Western Publishing Co., 1994)

Subject(s): Animals/Dogs; Pets; Responsibility
Age range(s): Grades K-1
Major character(s): Anna, Child; Tess, Dog
Time period(s): 1990s (1994)
Locale(s): England

Summary: Anna has every kind of dog imaginable, except a real dog. When she finally finds Tess, a wiggly, round puppy, Anna soon discovers that a puppy requires more attention than she expected. After Tess chews everything in sight, including Anna's favorite doggy slippers, Anna must consider the responsibility she has undertaken. First published in 1994 in Great Britain. (32 pages)

Where it's reviewed:
Booklist, August 1995, page 1954
Books for Keeps, November 1995, page 6
Bulletin of the Center for Children's Books, July 1995, page 376
Horn Book Guide, Fall 1995, page 256
School Library Journal, May 1995, page 81

Other books by the same author:
The Forgotten Forest, 1992
Camille and the Sunflowers, 1994

Other books you might like:
Norman Bridwell, *Clifford, the Small Red Puppy*, 1972
    Emily Elizabeth faces some out-of-the-ordinary puppy problems after choosing the runt of the litter as her pet.
Marc Brown, *Arthur's New Puppy*, 1993
    Arthur finds that caring for his new puppy presents challenges that he has not expected.
Cynthia Rylant, *Henry and Mudge*, 1987
    In this first book of a popular series, only-child Henry,

lonely for companionship, begs his parents to allow him to have a dog.

Rosemary Wells, *Lucy Comes to Stay*, 1994
Mary Elizabeth tolerates the puppy infractions of her new pet because she loves Lucy too much to scold her.

36

NANCY ANTLE
SIMMS TABACK, Illustrator

Sam's Wild West Show

(New York: Dial Books for Young Readers, 1995)

Series: Easy-to-Read Books
Subject(s): Robbers and Outlaws; American West
Age range(s): Grades 1-3
Major character(s): Sam, Cowboy, Entertainer
Time period(s): Indeterminate Past
Locale(s): United States

Summary: As Sam and the cowboys and cowgirls of his Wild West Show complete their performance in a small western town, a telegram arrives warning of outlaws heading into town. The marshall vamooses, the frightened citizens of the town hide behind locked doors, and the mayor pins a badge on Sam. Using the tricks of his trade, Sam and his troupe capture the would-be bank robbers before heading off to the next town and the next show. (40 pages)

Where it's reviewed:
Booklist, July 1995, page 1885
Bulletin of the Center for Children's Books, April 1995, page 264
Horn Book Guide, Fall 1995, page 288
Kirkus Reviews, May 15, 1995, page 706
School Library Journal, August 1995, page 114

Other books by the same author:
Beautiful Land: A Story of the Oklahoma Land Rush, 1994
Hard Times: A Story of the Great Depression, 1993
The Good Bad Cat, 1985

Other books you might like:
Barbara Brenner, *Wagon Wheels*, 1978
An entry in the I-Can-Read series relates the story of a widowed father and his three sons who seek free land in the West.
Betsy Byars, *The Golly Sisters Go West*, 1986
In six short stories, two intrepid sisters head West to try life on the frontier.
Eleanor Coerr, *Buffalo Bill and the Pony Express*, 1995
A beginning chapter book tells of Buffalo Bill who, while delivering mail for the Pony Express, escapes from wolves and outwits outlaws.

37

KATHI APPELT
NEIL WALDMAN, Illustrator

Bayou Lullaby

(New York: Morrow Junior Books, 1995)

Subject(s): Bedtime; Sleep; Stories in Rhyme

Age range(s): Grades K-1
Major character(s): Unnamed Character, Child
Time period(s): 1990s (1995)
Locale(s): United States

Summary: A parent soothes a little girl with a bedtime lullaby about the animals of the bayou who are also settling down for the night. Flickering fireflies provide the night light as the swishing cattails sigh softly. The author's first book includes a pronunciation guide and definitions for the Cajun words used in the text.

Where it's reviewed:
Booklist, March 15, 1995, page 1333
Children's Book Review Service, April 1995, page 97
Kirkus Reviews, March 15, 1995, page 378
Library Talk, May 1995, page 48
School Library Journal, April 1995, page 97

Awards the book has won:
School Library Journal Best Books, 1995

Other books you might like:
Molly Bang, *One Fall Day*, 1994
At bedtime as a young girl listens to her mom reviewing her day, she imagines her doll and toys recreating the events.
Margaret Wise Brown, *Goodnight Moon*, 1947
In the classic of bedtime stories, a small rabbit begins to settle for the night in the ''great green room'' saying goodnight to everything in sight, including the moon.
Mem Fox, *Time for Bed*, 1993
Mothers all over the world are putting their kittens, lambs, fawns and children to sleep.

38

JENNIFER ARMSTRONG
EMILY MARTINDALE, Illustrator

Black-Eyed Susan

(New York: Crown Publishers, Inc., 1995)

Subject(s): Frontier and Pioneer Life; Parent and Child; Depression
Age range(s): Grades 3-5
Major character(s): Susie, 10-Year-Old, Settler; Ma, Mother, Settler; Pa, Father, Farmer
Time period(s): 1870s
Locale(s): Medicine Fire, Midwest (Dakota Territory)

Summary: Susie rejoices in the vast beauty of the prairie when the sun rises and lights her world while she also worries about Ma who has become increasingly withdrawn, fearful and unhappy since the family settled in a sod house in this isolated territory. During a trip to town with Pa, Susie suggests items to purchase in order to cheer Ma, but discards her ideas and instead uses the sunrise that she loves and her own determination to bring happiness to Ma. (120 pages)

Where it's reviewed:
Bulletin of the Center for Children's Books, October 1995, page 45
Horn Book, March 1996, page 193
Kirkus Reviews, August 15, 1995, page 1184
Publishers Weekly, July 10, 1995, page 58

School Library Journal, October 1995, page 132

Awards the book has won:
Book Links Good Book, 1995

Other books by the same author:
Patrick Doyle Is Full of Blarney, 1996
The Puppy Project, 1990

Other books you might like:
Ann Nolan Clark, *All This Wild Land*, 1976
A Finnish family faces the difficulties of beginning a new life as they settle a Minnesota homestead in the late 1800s.
Brett Harvey, *My Prairie Year: Based on the Diary of Elenore Plaisted*, 1986
Nine-year-old Elenore records in her diary the activities of her family in Dakota Territory.
Laurie Lawlor, *Addie's Dakota Winter*, 1989
Stranded alone during a Dakota blizzard, 10-year-old settler Addie finds the courage to survive.
Patricia MacLachlan, *Skylark*, 1994
A severe drought tests Sarah's resolve to adapt to the prairie and remain with the family she joined as a mail-order bride.
Laura Ingalls Wilder, *On the Banks of Plum Creek*, 1961
When Laura and her family settle in Minnesota, they live in a dugout until a new home is built.

39

JENNIFER ARMSTRONG
MARY GRANDPRE, Illustrator

Chin Yu Min and the Ginger Cat

(New York: Crown Publishers, Inc., 1993)

Subject(s): Animals/Cats; Humor; Greed
Age range(s): Grades 2-4
Major character(s): Chin Yu Min, Widow(er); Ginger Cat, Cat, Fisherman
Time period(s): Indeterminate Past
Locale(s): Village near Kunming, China

Summary: When vain, wealthy Chin Yu Min is abruptly widowed she loses her source of income, but not her desire for a rich lifestyle. Scorning her neighbors offers of assistance, she rapidly spends her money and finds herself impoverished, but too proud to ask for help. While fishing, she spots a ginger cat with the ability to catch fish with his tail and invites him into her home. Again Chin Yu Min is prosperous, but not until she finds herself without Ginger Cat does she realize that his real value is as a companion. By giving away all her money in her search for the cat she finds the gift of generosity of spirit. (32 pages)

Where it's reviewed:
Booklist, February 15, 1993, page 1065
Children's Book Review Service, April 1993, page 97
Horn Book, May 1993, page 326
Publishers Weekly, March 15, 1993, page 86
School Library Journal, July 1993, page 84

Awards the book has won:
ALA Notable Book, 1994

Other books by the same author:
Little Salt Lick and the Sun King, 1994
That Terrible Baby, 1994
Hugh Can Do, 1992

Other books you might like:
Dayal Kaur Khalsa, *The Snow Cat*, 1992
Elsie's prayers are answered when she receives a large cat made of snow. Although the cat melts, it forms a cat-shaped pool where Elsie swims in the summer and skates in the winter.
Lily Toy Hong, *Two of Everything*, 1993
In this retelling of a Chinese folktale a poor couple find a magic pot which gives them with two of anything they put into it.
Margaret Mahy, *The Three-Legged Cat*, 1993
A humorous tale of wishes fulfilled involves a cat who is mistaken for a hat and realizes his dream of travel while the forgotten hat is mistaken for the desired docile cat.

40

JENNIFER ARMSTRONG

Patrick Doyle Is Full of Blarney

(New York: Random House, 1996)

Series: Stepping Stone
Subject(s): Irish Americans; Sports/Baseball
Age range(s): Grades 2-4
Major character(s): Patrick "Slugger" Doyle, Baseball Player, 9-Year-Old; Larry Doyle, Sports Figure (baseball player); Pug, Sports Figure (baseball player)
Time period(s): 1910s (1915)
Locale(s): New York, New York

Summary: In order to use the baseball field Patrick makes a bet with the Copperheads, led by Pug, that a Doyle will hit a ball over the fence. He plans to ask the professional baseball player, Larry Doyle, to come to the field and do it for him. He writes letters to Doyle and tries to see him but to no avail. And, since the letter had no return address, Doyle cannot get back in touch with Patrick. The day of the game Doyle does show up, but insists that Patrick hit the ball himself and lends him his bat. Patrick hits one out of the park and saves the day for the Irish. (69 pages)

Where it's reviewed:
School Library Journal, August 1996, page 115

Other books by the same author:
Black-Eyed Susan, 1995
Chin Yu Min and the Ginger Cat, 1993
Steal Away, 1992

Other books you might like:
Carla Heymsfeld, *Coaching Ms. Parker*, 1992
Mike and his friends try to get their teacher to play baseball before the annual teacher-student game.
Matt Christopher, *Return of the Home Run Kid*, 1992
Sylvester learns to be more aggressive on the field, but some of his friends don't like this.
Betsy Duffey, *Lucky in Left Field*, 1992
The team is not as good at fielding as George's dog.

Alison Cragin Herzig, *The Boonsville Bombers*, 1991
Emma loves baseball and is determined to play on her brother's team.

41

JENNIFER ARMSTRONG
SUSAN MEDDAUGH, Illustrator

That Terrible Baby
(New York: Tambourine Books, 1994)

Subject(s): Babies; Brothers and Sisters; Behavior
Age range(s): Grades K-3
Major character(s): Eleanor, Child, Sister; Mark, Child, Brother; Unnamed Character, Child (terrible baby)
Time period(s): 1990s (1994)
Locale(s): United States

Summary: Eleanor and Mark suffer through the disasters caused by a crawling baby who destroys their things, dumps over the garbage and floods the bathroom. Unfortunately, mother sees the terrible baby as a perfect angel who does no wrong and so she expects Eleanor and Mark to clean up the baby's messes. The older siblings imagine appropriate punishment for this crawling disaster maker, but when the baby crawls out the cat door and almost tumbles down the stairs they come to the rescue just in time, having decided that maybe the baby is not really so very awful. (32 pages)

Where it's reviewed:
Booklist, April 1, 1994, page 1457
Horn Book Guide, Fall 1994, page 262
Kirkus Reviews, April 15, 1994, page 551
Publishers Weekly, March 14, 1994, page 71
School Library Journal, June 1994, page 94

Awards the book has won:
International Reading Association Children's Choice, 1995

Other books by the same author:
Wan Hu Is in the Stars, 1995
Little Salt Lick and the Sun King, 1994
Hugh Can Do, 1992

Other books you might like:
Jane Cutler, *Darcy and Gran Don't Like Babies*, 1993
Although Darcy and Gran agree that they don't like babies, they both expect to like the new arrival at Darcy's house when the baby is a little older.
John Hassett, *We Got My Brother at the Zoo*, 1993
Mary Margaret has some unusual stories to tell about the origins of the new baby at her house. Co-author Ann Hassett.
Russell Hoban, *A Baby Sister for Frances*, 1964
Frances is not sure about the new addition to the family, but her patient, understanding parents help her adjust to the arrival of a baby sister.
Vera B. Williams, *More More More Said the Baby: 3 Love Stories*, 1990
In three brief stories, babies are played with lovingly by family members.

42

MARSHA ARNOLD
JAMICHAEL HENTERLY, Illustrator

Heart of a Tiger
(New York: Dial Books for Young Readers, 1995)

Subject(s): Animals/Cats; Animals/Tigers; Courage
Age range(s): Grades K-3
Major character(s): Number Four, Cat; Beautiful Bengal, Tiger
Time period(s): Indeterminate Past
Locale(s): India

Summary: In the author's first book, as Naming Day approaches, Number Four kitten searches for the name he knows rests in his heart. Although others in the litter think Smallest of All is an appropriate moniker, Number Four desires to be like the Beautiful Bengal and seeks a name to match. Number Four locates and follows Beautiful Bengal for days, learning to live wisely and move silently. When hunters come searching for Beautiful Bengal, Number Four warns him of the hunters' trick, saving Beautiful Bengal's life and earning the name Heart of a Tiger. (32 pages)

Where it's reviewed:
Children's Book Review Service, Winter 1996, page 61
Horn Book Guide, Spring 1996, page 19
Kirkus Reviews, October 15, 1995, page 1486
School Library Journal, January 1996, page 76

Awards the book has won:
Marion Vannett Ridgway Award, 1996

Other books you might like:
Antonia Barber, *Catkin*, 1994
A small, but brave cat agrees to enter the land of the little people to save a child stolen from her parents.
Libuse Palecek, *Brave as a Tiger*, 1995
The other tigers take timid Fang's stripes until he displays the courage expected of his breed.
Joan Phillips, *Tiger Is a Scaredy Cat*, 1986
In an award-winning beginning reader, a timid mouse shows the strength of a hero when he helps unite a lost baby mouse with its parents.

43

TEDD ARNOLD, Author/Illustrator

No More Water in the Tub!
(New York: Dial Books for Young Readers, 1995)

Subject(s): Humor; Brothers; Floods
Age range(s): Grades K-2
Major character(s): Walter, Child, Brother; William, Child, Brother
Time period(s): 1990s (1995)
Locale(s): United States

Summary: Walter's attempt to help William get the maximum amount of water into the tub during the "one-more-minute" allotted by Mom before the water is turned off, leads to an unexpected stream of events. Floating in his tub, William cascades out the door and down the apartment stairs, collecting neighbors at every floor. Or perhaps that is only Walter's story and what really happened is. . . (32 pages)

Where it's reviewed:
Booklist, December 15, 1995, page 707
Bulletin of the Center for Children's Books, September 1995, page 5
Horn Book, January 1996, page 59
Publishers Weekly, August 21, 1995, page 65
School Library Journal, October 1995, page 96

Other books by the same author:
Green Wilma, 1992
Mother Goose's Words of Wit and Wisdom: A Book of Months, 1990
No Jumping on the Bed!, 1987

Other books you might like:
Kyoko Matsuoka, *There's a Hippo in My Bath!*, 1989
   While bathing, a boy is joined by a turtle, penguins, a hippo and other animals.
David McPhail, *Andrew's Bath*, 1984
   The first time that Andrew is allowed to bathe himself, his efforts are undermined by an elephant drinking the shampoo and a hippo sitting on the soap.
Elvira Woodruff, *Tubtime*, 1990
   Enjoying a bubble bath, two sisters wonder if the chickens, frogs and alligator they see inside the bubbles are real or imaginary.

44

JIM ARNOSKY, Author/Illustrator

Little Champ
(New York: G. P. Putnam's Sons, 1995)

Subject(s): Dinosaurs; Brothers and Sisters; Grandparents
Age range(s): Grades 3-5
Major character(s): Bobby, Child, Brother (older); Gina, Child, Sister (younger); Charlie "Grandpa" Gennard, Grandfather, Store Owner
Time period(s): 1990s (1995)
Locale(s): Lake Champlain, Vermont

Summary: While helping their grandparents operate a lakeside general store and marina, Bobby and Gina happen to see the legendary creatures of Lake Champlain. Later in the summer, when Bobby and Gina run out of gas while fishing far from shore, Grandpa's rescue attempt runs aground. However, the unexpected movement of two powerful animals feeding nearby sets the boat free from the shoal and fulfills Grandpa's dream of one day seeing the underwater dinosaurs. (71 pages)

Where it's reviewed:
Booklist, September 15, 1995, page 158
Horn Book Guide, Spring 1996, page 53
School Library Journal, November 1995, page 96

Other books by the same author:
Long Spikes, 1992
Gray Boy, 1988
Secrets of a Wildlife Watcher, 1983

Other books you might like:
Debbie Dadey, *Monsters Don't Scuba Dive*, 1995
   The Bailey School Kids try to determine if the swimming teacher at Camp Lone Wolf is really a sea monster. Co-author Marcia Thornton Jones.
Jacques Duquennoy, *The Ghosts Trip to Loch Ness*, 1996
   Four ghosts travel to Scotland to see the legendary Loch Ness monster.
James Gurney, *Dinotopia: A Land Apart from Time*, 1992
   With his father, Will is somehow transported to a place where humans and dinosaurs coexist.

45

FRANCES ARRINGTON
AILEEN ARRINGTON, Illustrator

Stella's Bull
(Boston: Houghton Mifflin Company, 1994)

Subject(s): Animals/Bulls; Fear; Courage
Age range(s): Grades 1-3
Major character(s): Mary Wilson Montgomery, 4th Grader; Stella's Bull, Bull
Time period(s): 1930s
Locale(s): United States (rural area)

Summary: Although Mary Wilson has never seen Stella's bull, she's heard about it all her life and she knows that crazy bull is lurking in his pasture ready to attack anyone foolish enough to venture near. Mary Wilson's imagination has created such a monster that when her new spelling book accidently is thrown into the bull's pasture, she does without a book for 3 days before the daily humilation and taunts of classmates force her to face her fear in order to retrieve the book. (32 pages)

Where it's reviewed:
Booklist, September 15, 1994, page 141
Horn Book, November 1994, page 715
Kirkus Reviews, July 15, 1994, page 977
Publishers Weekly, June 27, 1994, page 77
School Library Journal, September 1994, page 180

Other books you might like:
Bill Martin Jr., *The Ghost-Eye Tree*, 1985
   As they walk down a dark road on a family errand, a brother and sister argue about who is afraid of the Ghost-Eye Tree. Co-author John Archambault.
Helena C. Pittman, *Once When I Was Scared*, 1988
   Grandfather tells a story from his youth when he was sent on a solitary journey one night through the dark and scary woods to fetch hot coals for the family's cabin.
Tres Seymour, *Hunting the White Cow*, 1993
   The difficulties the menfolks experience trying to capture a runaway cow do not deter a brave, young girl from attempting to locate and return the animal.

46

FRANK ASCH, Author/Illustrator

The Earth and I

(San Diego: Harcourt Brace & Company, 1994)

Series: A Gulliver Green Book
Subject(s): Conservation of Natural Resources; Nature
Age range(s): Grades K-1
Major character(s): Unnamed Character, Child
Time period(s): 1990s (1994)
Locale(s): Earth

Summary: A young boy's personal relationship with the earth demonstrates the principle of living in harmony with nature. The youth understands the impact of his actions on the earth and the benefits to be derived from caring for it as he would a good friend. (32 pages)

Where it's reviewed:
Booklist, January 15, 1995, page 934
Children's Book Review Service, November 1994, page 25
Horn Book Guide, Spring 1995, page 16
Kirkus Reviews, September 15, 1994, page 1264
Publishers Weekly, August 29, 1994, page 78

Other books by the same author:
Moon Bear, 1993
Bear Shadow, 1988
Skyfire, 1988

Other books you might like:
Nancy Carlson, *Northern Lullaby*, 1992
    A young Native American bids good night to Papa Star and Mama Moon, entreating all of nature to rest for the night.
Douglas Florian, *Nature Walk*, 1989
    Walking along a trail, a mother helps her two children notice the wildlife and plants they pass.
Mordicai Gerstein, *Daisy's Garden*, 1995
    Daisy's gardening philosophy reflects a willingness to work in harmony with all creatures.

47

FRANK ASCH
VLADIMIR VAGIN, Illustrator
VLADIMIR VAGIN, Illustrator

Insects from Outer Space

(New York: Scholastic Inc., 1995)

Subject(s): Animals/Insects; Aliens; Fantasy
Age range(s): Grades K-2
Major character(s): Unnamed Character, Insect; Hercules, Insect
Time period(s): Indeterminate
Locale(s): Fictional Country

Summary: The annual Bug Ball has an unexpected interruption when alien spaceships are observed landing on a nearby island. Realizing that the aliens have landed near his friend Hercules's home, a bug hurries to rescue his pal. The aliens turn out to be friendly bugs who join in the Bug Ball before returning to their own planet. (32 pages)

Where it's reviewed:
Booklist, February 1, 1995, page 1007
Horn Book Guide, Fall 1995, page 284
School Library Journal, April 1995, page 97

Other books by the same author:
Dear Brother, 1992
Here Comes the Cat!, 1991

Other books you might like:
David Kirk, *Miss Spider's Wedding*, 1995
    Match-making by some beetle friends adds suspense to Miss Spider's selection of a bridegroom, but love wins out.
Colin McNaughton, *Here Come the Aliens!*, 1995
    Rhyming descriptions of the aliens match the pictures of the creatures that are on an invasion path until stopped by an orbiting picture of a group of 4-year-olds.
Mark Teague, *Moog-Moog Space Barber*, 1990
    Elmo travels to outer space to ask the universe's greatest barber to repair the terrible haircut he received.
Daniel Manus Pinkwater, *Guys from Outer Space*, 1989
    When a boy travels to another planet with some guys from space, they discover talking rocks and other amazing things.

48

CAMILLA ASHFORTH, Author/Illustrator

Humphrey Thud

(Cambridge, MA: Candlewick Press, 1995)

Subject(s): Animals/Elephants; Animals/Rabbits; Toys
Age range(s): Grades K-1
Major character(s): Humphrey Thud, Elephant, Toy; Horatio, Rabbit, Toy; James, Bear, Toy
Time period(s): 1990s (1994)
Locale(s): Fictional Country

Summary: When Humphrey Thud tries to copy friend Horatio's disappearing trick, he discovers that no amount of magic can make an elephant disappear into a sock. James tries to help by offering a scarf to hide Humphrey, but it also is not large enough. Finally, the three decide to make only Humphrey's hat disappear and all are content. First published in Great Britain in 1994 (32 pages)

Where it's reviewed:
Booklist, March 15, 1995, page 1333
Books for Your Children, Summer 1995, page 19
Horn Book Guide, Fall 1995, page 246
Junior Bookshelf, April 1995, page 65
School Library Journal, July 1995, page 54

Other books by the same author:
Calamity, 1993
Monkey Tricks, 1993
Horatio's Bed, 1992

Other books you might like:
Jane Hissey, *Ruff*, 1994
    An abandoned toy dog joins a home filled with kindly animal toys who promptly give Ruff his first birthday party.

Shirley Isherwood, *Something for James*, 1995
    When a mysterious, rustling box arrives, the other toys help James learn what is inside.
Rodney Peppe, *The Magic Toy Box*, 1996
    Magically, a new friend appears in the magic toy box to be greeted by the other toys.

49

MARY JANE AUCH, Author/Illustrator

Hen Lake

(New York: Holiday House, 1995)

Subject(s): Animals/Chickens; Animals/Birds; Ballet
Age range(s): Grades K-3
Major character(s): Poulette, Hen, Dancer; Percival, Peacock
Time period(s): Indeterminate
Locale(s): United States (farmyard)

Summary: Poulette, star of *Peeping Beauty* returns with her desire to become a prima ballerina undiminished by anything, including boastful newcomer Percival. Challenging the braggart to a talent contest, Poulette choreographs a ballet and teaches the other hens the fine art of dance. During the performance, unexpected wind gusts assist the clumsy hens with some of their movements giving them enough self-confidence to believe they can dance, despite Percival's snide comments. (32 pages)

Where it's reviewed:
Booklist, August 1995, page 1954
Children's Book Review Service, December 1995, page 37
Horn Book Guide, Spring 1996, page 19
Publishers Weekly, September 11, 1995, page 85
School Library Journal, October 1995, page 96

Other books by the same author:
Eggs Mark the Spot, 1996
Monster Brother, 1994
Bird Dogs Can't Fly, 1993
The Easter Egg Farm, 1992

Other books you might like:
James Marshall, *Wings: A Tale of Two Chickens*, 1986
    Flighty Winnie's sense of adventure propels her into the fox's hot air balloon while sensible friend Harriet launches a rescue mission to keep both chickens out of the stew pot.
Ward Schumaker, *Dance!*, 1996
    A variety of animals gather for one purpose—to dance!
Hans Wilhelm, *The Royal Raven*, 1996
    Crawford's determination to be noticed leads him to a witch, a dramatic new look, and finally the realization that somethings are more important than outward appearances.

50

MARY JANE AUCH
CAT BOWMAN SMITH, Illustrator

The Latchkey Dog

(Boston: Little, Brown and Company , 1994)

Subject(s): Animals/Dogs; Latchkey Children; Single Parent Families

Age range(s): Grades 3-4
Major character(s): Amber, Dog (golden retriever); Sam, 8-Year-Old, Latch-Key Child; Jamie Diggs, 8-Year-Old, Friend
Time period(s): 1990s (1994)
Locale(s): United States

Summary: After Sam's parents' divorce, his mom goes to work and lonely Amber begins barking all day, disturbing the neighbors. Sam tries one idea after another to help Amber stop barking, but nothing seems to work. When his mom insists on giving his pet away, Sam and Jamie devise several schemes to try to keep her. Nothing works as they plan, but Sam's reluctant attendance at an after-school program turns out to be a blessing in disguise for Sam, Amber, and others. (120 pages)

Where it's reviewed:
Booklist, February 1, 1994, page 1005
Bulletin of the Center for Children's Books, April 1994, page 250
Kirkus Reviews, December 15, 1993, page 1586
Publishers Weekly, November 22, 1993, page 63
School Library Journal, January 1994, page 112

Other books by the same author:
Angel and Me and the Bayside Bombers, 1991
A Sudden Change of Family, 1990
Glass Slippers Give You Blisters, 1989

Other books you might like:
Beverly Cleary, *Strider*, 1991
    Leigh and his friend Barry share joint custody of an abandoned dog they find on the beach.
Karen Hesse, *Sable*, 1994
    Tate is excited to find a stray dog in the yard and works to keep her new pet despite parental objections and neighbor's complaints.
Eric Knight, *Lassie Come-Home*, 1940
    A classic story of the relationship between a boy and his loyal collie.
Jane Resh Thomas, *The Comeback Dog*, 1980
    After his own dog dies, Daniel finds a starving dog and nurses her back to health.

51

MARY JANE AUCH, Author/Illustrator

Monster Brother

(New York: Holiday House, 1994)

Subject(s): Monsters; Babies; Bedtime
Age range(s): Grades K-2
Major character(s): Rodney, Child (fearful), Brother (older); Sidney, Child (infant), Brother
Time period(s): 1990s (1994)
Locale(s): United States

Summary: Rodney and his parents try many imaginative approaches to prevent monsters from disturbing Rodney's sleep, but nothing works; the monsters come nightly. Although Rodney's monster fears are briefly overshadowed by concern about the new baby, Sidney turns out to be the ultimate monster-chaser. He shares Rodney's room and his cries are so loud that no monster dares come near. (32 pages)

Where it's reviewed:
Booklist, November 15, 1994, page 610
Bulletin of the Center for Children's Books, November 1994, page 79
Horn Book Guide, Spring 1995, page 25
Publishers Weekly, November 14, 1994, page 67
School Library Journal, November 1994, page 72

Other books by the same author:
Hen Lake, 1995
Bird Dogs Can't Fly, 1993
The Easter Egg Farm, 1992

Other books you might like:
Holly Keller, *Geraldine's Baby Brother*, 1994
An annoyed, awakened, yet ever resourceful Geraldine decides a heart-to-heart talk with the screaming baby will help the newcomer understand his place in the family.
Julia McClelland, *This Baby*, 1994
Andrew is not looking forward to the arrival of a sibling, but with support from his understanding parents he is able to welcome Jane when she is born.
Salvatore Murdocca, *Baby Wants the Moon*, 1995
Fear of displacement by the new baby are expressed in Sonny's dreams that his new sister is growing into a giant.
Susan Winter, *A Baby Just Like Me*, 1994
Martha and her friend Sam select toys and plan activities to include the new baby only to be very disappointed to discover that she does nothing but sleep and take up her mother's time.

52

MARY JANE AUCH, Author/Illustrator

Peeping Beauty

(New York: Holiday House, 1993)

Subject(s): Animals/Chickens; Animals/Foxes; Ballet
Age range(s): Grades K-2
Major character(s): Poulette, Chicken, Dancer (aspiring ballerina); Unnamed Character, Fox
Time period(s): 1990s (1993)
Locale(s): United States

Summary: The other hens may be content with bugs and gossip, but Poulette dreams of stardom as a ballerina. Her daily practices are observed by a wily fox who, in the guise of a talent scout, recruits Poulette for a new ballet. Despite the admonitions of the other hens and her own distrust of foxes, Poulette is won over by a stunning pink tutu and the opportunity to perform on a real stage. The true intentions of the fox become apparent during the grand finale of the performance. Not being one to give up a dream easily, Poulette manages to outfox the fox. (32 pages)

Where it's reviewed:
Booklist, March 1, 1993, page 1234
Emergency Librarian, September 1993, page 50
Kirkus Reviews, May 1, 1993, page 592
Publishers Weekly, April 12, 1993, page 62
School Library Journal, April 1993, page 90

Other books by the same author:
Bird Dogs Can't Fly, 1993
The Easter Egg Farm, 1992

Other books you might like:
Roger Duvoisin, *Petunia the Silly Goose Stories*, 1985
If ignorance is bliss, then the popular Petunia is in seventh heaven as shown in the tales of her many exploits gathered in this collection of stories.
James Marshall, *Wings: A Tale of Two Chickens*, 1986
Flighty Winnie's sense of adventure propels her into the fox's hot air balloon and her sensible friend Harriet into a rescue mission to keep both chickens out of the stew pot.
Ellen Stoll Walsh, *You Silly Goose*, 1992
Knowing that a fox has been reported in the neighborhood, Lulu panics and sounds the alarm when she spots George—who is really only a mouse.
Mary Wormell, *Hilda Hen's Happy Birthday*, 1995
Hilda Hen is so excited on her birthday that she assumes the horses' oats and the farmer's wife's tea and cookies are really intended as gifts for her.

53

GILLIAN AVERY
JULIE DOWNING, Illustrator

A Likely Lad

(New York: Simon & Schuster Books for Young Readers, 1994)

Subject(s): Family Life; Fathers and Sons; Historical
Age range(s): Grades 4-6
Major character(s): George Overs, 10-Year-Old, Brother (Willy's); William Cobbett "Willy" Overs, 11-Year-Old; Mr. Alfred Overs, Father, Businessman
Time period(s): 1890s (1895); 1900s (1901-1902)
Locale(s): Manchester, England (Ardwick)

Summary: Mr. Overs sees Willy as a lad who is likely to be successful; therefore, he aspires to place his son with an insurance company as an important step toward entrepreneurship and politics. Willy's ambitions lie in other areas and he's sufficiently proud and independent to seek his own fortune in life. In time, his father comes to accept Willy's aspirations for himself and the family is reconciled. Originally published in Great Britain in 1971, the book is reissued with illustrations. (299 pages)

Where it's reviewed:
Booklist, June 1, 1994, page 1815
Horn Book Guide, Fall 1994, page 305
Kirkus Reviews, June 15, 1994, page 840
Publishers Weekly, June 13, 1994, page 65
School Library Journal, July 1994, page 100

Other books by the same author:
Maria's Italian Spring, 1993
Maria Escapes, 1992

Other books you might like:
Natalie Babbitt, *Goody Hall*, 1986
The new tutor senses the mystery surrounding the ornate manor house at Goody Hall.
Karen Cushman, *Catherine, Called Birdy*, 1994
Birdy, daughter of an English country knight strives to

break away from the traditional expectations for women in medieval times.

Eileen Dunlop, *Finn's Island*, 1991

    Visiting a remote Scottish Island involves unexpected hardships and an opportunity for reconciliation between a boy and his father.

54

AVI (Pseudonym of Avi Wortis)

The Barn

(New York: Orchard Books, 1994)

Subject(s): Farm Life; Family Relations; Historical
Age range(s): Grades 3-6
Major character(s): Benjamin, 9-Year-Old; Nettie, 15-Year-Old; Harrison, 13-Year-Old
Time period(s): 1850s (1855)
Locale(s): Portland, Oregon (Oregon Territory); Yamhill County, Oregon (Willamette Valley of the Oregon Territory)

Summary: When his father suffers a "fit of palsy," Benjamin is summoned home from boarding school to care for his father while his older siblings, Harrison and Nettie, tend the farm. Benjamin becomes obsessed with the idea that if they build the barn their father has always wanted, then he will have a reason for wanting to live. The three undertake this physically demanding project, though only Benjamin is certain their father can improve. Everyday their father becomes weaker and weaker and finally, not even building a barn can save him. (106 pages)

Where it's reviewed:
School Library Journal, October 1994, page 118
Publishers Weekly, September 5, 1994, page 112
Horn Book, January 1995, page 57
Booklist, September 1, 1994, page 40
New York Times Book Review, January 1, 1995, page 15

Awards the book has won:
Booklist Editors' Choice/Books for Middle Readers, 1994

Other books by the same author:
Markham, 1996
City of Light, City of Dark: A Comic-Book Novel, 1993
Windcatcher, 1991
The Man Who Was Poe, 1989

Other books you might like:
Barbara Bonham, *Challenge of the Prairie*, 1965
    After Toby's father is killed, he must become the homesteader and deal with a plague of grasshoppers that destroy the crop.
Patricia MacLachlan, *Sarah, Plain and Tall*, 1985
    Sarah answers an ad and winds up as a wife to a farmer and mother to two children living on an isolated ranch.
Robert Newton Peck, *A Part of the Sky*, 1994
    After his father dies, 13-year-old Rob must assume responsibility for working the farm and caring for his mother and elderly aunt.

55

AVI (Pseudonym of Avi Wortis)
BRIAN FLOCA, Illustrator

City of Light, City of Dark: A Comic-Book Novel

(New York: Orchard Books, 1993)

Subject(s): Fantasy; Science Fiction; Good and Evil
Age range(s): Grades 4-7
Major character(s): Carlos Juarez, Student; Sarah Stubbs, Student; Asterel, Mother
Time period(s): Indeterminate
Locale(s): New York, New York

Summary: To save the city from the cold and darkness of the Kurbs, Asterel races against time to complete her mission as the designated searcher for the power. Carlos finds the special token in which the power resides, but does not realize its significance. Sarah, too, is on a quest for the token because she thinks it is connected to her father and a mysterious, evil man to whom he pays money. The search brings all three together and Sarah learns Asterel is the mother she has never known. With only moments to spare, they complete the requirements of the Kurbs and save the city for another year. (192 pages)

Where it's reviewed:
Booklist, September 15, 1993, page 142
Kirkus Reviews, October 1, 1993, page 1268
Library Talk, January 1994, page 41
Publishers Weekly, August 16, 1993, page 105
School Library Journal, September 1993, page 228

Other books by the same author:
Who Was That Masked Man, Anyway?, 1992
S.O.R. Losers, 1986
Who Stole the Wizard of Oz?, 1981

Other books you might like:
Robert Levy, *Clan of the Shape Changers*, 1994
    Using her inherited power to change into any animal shape, 16-year-old Susan fights against the greedy Ometerer who is trying to destroy her people.
Walter Dean Myers, *Shadow of the Red Moon*, 1995
    When Fens attack his New York City home, 15-year-old Jon and others are sent into the Wilderness to search for the ancient city.
Rosemary Sutcliff, *Chess-Dream in a Garden*, 1993
    When the white chess pieces living in a garden are attacked they must change into the animal shapes of their dreams in order to defeat the invaders.

56

AVI (Pseudonym of Avi Wortis)

The Fighting Ground

(New York: J.B. Lippincott, 1984)

Subject(s): Revolutionary War
Age range(s): Grades 4-7
Major character(s): Jonathan, 13-Year-Old
Time period(s): 1770s (April 3-April 4, 1778)

Locale(s): Trenton, New Jersey

Summary: Young Jonathan wants more than anything to take part in the Revolutionary War, but his father has forbidden him to do so. One day, while helping his father farm, they hear the tavern bell tolling and Jonathan's sent to find out the reason. Jonathan takes advantage of that opportunity and runs away to join up, though twenty-four hours later he returns home. In those twenty-four hours, however, he experiences enough of war to last a lifetime, including being imprisoned by Hessian soldiers. (157 pages)

Where it's reviewed:
School Library Journal, September 1984, page 124

Awards the book has won:
ALA Best Books for Young Adults, 1984

Other books by the same author:
The Barn, 1994
The True Confessions of Charlotte Doyle, 1990
The Man Who Was Poe, 1989
Something Upstairs: A Tale of Ghosts, 1988

Other books you might like:
Patricia Beatty, *Charley Skedaddle*, 1987
    Charley earns his nickname when he skedaddles from the horror of his first Civil War battle.
Howard Fast, *April Morning*, 1961
    Adam Cooper loses his excitement over the 1775 Battle of Lexington when his father is killed.
Carol Matas, *Code Name Kris*, 1990
    Jesper and his friend Stefan are captured by the Nazis for their resistance activities in the Danish Underground during World War II.

57

AVI (Pseudonym of Avi Wortis)
BRIAN FLOCA, Illustrator

Poppy
(New York: Orchard Books, 1995)

Subject(s): Animals/Mice; Animals/Owls; Survival
Age range(s): Grades 4-6
Major character(s): Poppy, Mouse, Heroine; Mr. Ocax, Owl, Ruler; Ragweed, Mouse, Boyfriend (Poppy's)
Time period(s): Indeterminate
Locale(s): Dimwood Forest, Fictional Country

Summary: Taunted by rebellious Ragweed, Poppy agrees to accompany him to Bannock's Hill without the required permission of Mr. Ocax, despotic ruler and self-proclaimed protector of the mice. The consequence for unapproved travel beyond the ruler's boundaries is to become Mr. Ocax's dinner and such is the fate of Ragweed. Barely escaping with her life, Poppy struggles home determined to avenge Ragweed's death and find independence from the cruel ruler for her brethren. (147 pages)

Where it's reviewed:
Booklist, October 15, 1995, page 402
Horn Book, January 1996, page 71
Kirkus Reviews, September 15, 1995, page 1346
Publishers Weekly, August 21, 1995, page 66

School Library Journal, December 1995, page 102

Awards the book has won:
Booklist Editors' Choice, 1995
School Library Journal Best Books, 1995

Other books by the same author:
The Barn, 1994 (ALA Notable Book)
Who Was That Masked Man, Anyway?, 1992 (ALA Notable Book)
The True Confessions of Charlotte Doyle, 1990

Other books you might like:
Dick King-Smith, *The School Mouse*, 1995
    In the old school Flora lives as the first school mouse, taking advantage of the daily lessons and eventually using her literacy to save her family.
Robert Lawson, *Rabbit Hill*, 1944
    The Newbery Medal winner describes the animal residents of Rabbit Hill pondering their fate as new occupants move into Big House.
Robert C. O'Brien, *Mrs. Frisby and the Rats of NIMH*, 1971
    Needing help, a widowed mouse bravely visits rats, retired from laboratory experiments which have made them wise and long-lived. Newbery Medal.

58

AVI (Pseudonym of Avi Wortis)
ALEXI NATCHEV, Illustrator

Tom, Babette, & Simon: Three Tales of Transformation
(New York: Macmillan Books for Young Readers, 1995)

Subject(s): Fairy Tale; Short Stories; Fantasy
Age range(s): Grades 4-6
Major character(s): Thomas Osborn ''Tom'' Pitz, 12-Year-Old; Babette, Royalty (princess); Simon, Young Man (greedy)
Time period(s): 1990s (1995); Indeterminate Past
Locale(s): Fictional Country

Summary: In each of three short stories a wish, whether directly spoken or implied, comes true and the wisher, too late, recognizes the error of blind desire. In a contemporary setting, bored Tom decides that the lazy life of a cat is more to his liking, but several weeks of such fare convince him he wants to be a boy again. The problem is the cat with whom he has changed places is happy as a boy and refuses to change back. Babette is a princess born to a queen who desired a ''flawless'' child. Her wish was realized when Babette was born invisible and must literally find the person she wants to become as she grows. When greedy, spoiled Simon learns that he is not the center of the universe, he finally finds true freedom. (100 pages)

Where it's reviewed:
Booklist, May 15, 1995, page 1643
Horn Book Guide, Fall 1995, page 294
Kirkus Reviews, June 1, 1995, page 776
Publishers Weekly, June 12, 1995, page 61
School Library Journal, June 1995, page 108

Other books by the same author:
Poppy, 1995
The Barn, 1994
Who Was That Masked Man, Anyway?, 1992

Other books you might like:
Joan Aiken, *Arabel and Mortimer*, 1981
   With her pet raven Mortimer as her companion, Arabel enjoys three unusual adventures.
Bruce Coville, *Bruce Coville's Book of Magic: Tales to Cast a Spell on You*, 1996
   Twelve fantasy tales by different authors weave a magical spell.
Annie M.G. Schmidt, *Minnie*, 1994
   A cat changed into a human must decide whether to continue her new life or return to her cat form.

59

JÍM AYLESWORTH
DAVID FRAMPTON, Illustrator

My Son John

(New York: Henry Holt and Company, Inc., 1994)

Subject(s): Farm Life
Age range(s): Grades K-2
Major character(s): Unnamed Character, Farmer
Time period(s): Indeterminate Past
Locale(s): Fictional Country

Summary: Read, read this book just for fun; hear what the kids do one by one. Mother Goose began this rhyme; it's grown and grown over time. From just one verse about son John; fourteen children go on and on. They do their chores and make Pa proud; you'll have fun if you read it aloud. (30 pages)

Where it's reviewed:
Bookist, April 1, 1994, page 1457
Children's Book Review Service, May 1994, page 109
Children's Bookwatch, May 1994, page 7
Publishers Weekly, March 7, 1994, page 69
School Library Journal, June 1994, page 94

Awards the book has won:
Notable Children's Books in the Language Arts, 1995

Other books by the same author:
The Cat & the Fiddle & More, 1992
Old Black Fly, 1992
The Completed Hickory Dickory Dock, 1990

Other books you might like:
Alan Benjamin, *Buck*, 1994
   An old dog is traded for a rooster and a hen which are in turn traded for other items until the poem returns Buck to his original owner.
Bill Martin Jr., *Brown Bear, Brown Bear, What Do You See?*, 1983
   The rhyme and repetition in this color concept book make it a favorite for reading to students who can participate in the response.
Bill Martin Jr., *Chicka Chicka Boom Boom*, 1989
   The letters of the alphabet have a rhythmic adventure in a read-aloud classic. Co-author John Archambault.

B

60

NATALIE BABBITT, Author/Illustrator

Bub: Or the Very Best Thing

(New York: HarperCollins Publishers, 1994)

Subject(s): Kings, Queens, Rulers, etc.; Parent and Child; Castles

Age range(s): Grades K-2

Major character(s): Prince, Child, Royalty; King, Father, Royalty; Queen, Mother, Royalty

Time period(s): Indeterminate Past

Locale(s): England (in a castle)

Summary: In their effort to be good parents, the King and Queen search for "the very best thing" for their only child. Everyone in the castle has a different idea, depending on their perspective, but no one asks Prince. Finally, the parents listen to Prince's answer, but do not understand that "bub" means love. (32 pages)

Where it's reviewed:
Booklist, February 15, 1994, page 1091
Children's Book Review Service, March 1994, page 85
Horn Book, May 1994, page 305
Publishers Weekly, January 3, 1994, page 80
School Library Journal, April 1994, page 96

Other books by the same author:
Nellie: A Cat on Her Own, 1989
The Something, 1987

Other books you might like:
Trish Cooke, *So Much*, 1994
    In this happy family there is no doubt that everyone loves the baby. . .so much!
Sam McBratney, *Guess How Much I Love You*, 1995
    Little Nutbrown Hare and his father share a tender bedtime moment expressing the extent of their love for one another.
Amy Schwartz, *A Teeny Tiny Baby*, 1994
    There's no misunderstanding who's in charge in this household, it's the teeny tiny baby with the doting parents and grandparents.

61

BARBARA BAKER
KATE DUKE, Illustrator

One Saturday Morning

(New York: Dutton Children's Books, 1994)

Series: Easy Reader

Subject(s): Animals/Bears; Family Life

Age range(s): Grades 1-3

Major character(s): Mama, Bear, Mother; Papa, Bear, Father

Time period(s): 1990s (1994)

Locale(s): Fictional Country

Summary: When Mama awakens before the family she looks forward to a quiet Saturday morning reading in bed. However, first Papa and then each of the other family members awaken, bringing her plans for quiet to an end. In the next five easy-to-read chapters, the family of bears enjoys a Saturday morning of activity and togetherness. (48 pages)

Where it's reviewed:
Booklist, January 1, 1995, page 827
Horn Book Guide, Spring 1995, page 63
Kirkus Reviews, October 15, 1994, page 140
School Library Journal, November 1994, page 72
Wilson Library Bulletin, December 1994, page 101

Awards the book has won:
School Library Journal Best Books, 1994

Other books by the same author:
Staying with Grandmother, 1994
Digby and Kate Again, 1989
Digby and Kate, 1988

Other books you might like:
Stan Berenstain, *The Berenstain Bears' New Baby*, 1974
    The Berenstain Bears' family grows in one of many stories about a well-known family of bears. Co-author Jan Berenstain.
Jill Murphy, *A Quiet Night In*, 1993
    Mrs. Large's plans to put the children to bed early and

spend a quiet night at home with Mr. Large on his birthday are not entirely successful.

Marjorie Dennis Murray, *Saturday with Little Rabbit*, 1993
Five brief chapters describe the activities of Little Rabbit and his friends Woodchuck and Raccoon.

62

SANNA ANDERSON BAKER
BILL FARNSWORTH, Illustrator

Grandpa Is a Flyer

(Morton Grove, IL: Albert Whitman & Company, 1995)

Subject(s): Grandparents; Airplanes; Storytelling
Age range(s): Grades 1-3
Major character(s): Anne, Child; Grandpa, Grandfather
Time period(s): 1920s; 1990s (1995)
Locale(s): Midwest

Summary: Visits to Grandpa are sure to include a ride in his plane. In response to his curious granddaughter's questions, Grandpa describes how he first became interested in flying when a barnstormer flew over his family's farm. Saving money from odd jobs enabled Grandpa and his older brother to pay a barnstormer for a plane ride that begins a life-long desire to earn a pilot's license. (32 pages)

Where it's reviewed:
Booklist, April 1, 1995, page 1422
Horn Book Guide, Fall 1995, page 257
School Library Journal, July 1995, page 54

Other books by the same author:
The Stormy Night, 1991
Who's a Friend of the Water Spurting Whale?, 1987

Other books you might like:
Robert Burleigh, *Flight: The Journey of Charles Lindbergh*, 1991
The life of Grandpa's hero and inspiration in presented in a picture book.
Douglas Florian, *Airplane Ride*, 1984
In his small plane, a pilot soars over the varied terrain of the United States.
Harriet Ziefert, *Tim and Jim Take Off*, 1990
A beginning reader describes the excitement of two boys during their first airplane ride.

63

HAEMI BALGASSI
CHRIS K. SOENTPIET, Illustrator

Peacebound Trains

(New York: Clarion Books, 1996)

Subject(s): Railroads and Railroading; Korean War; Grandparents
Age range(s): Grades 2-5
Major character(s): Harmuny, Grandmother; Harabujy, Grandfather; Sumi, Child (of single parent)
Time period(s): 1990s; 1950s (a story told of 1951)
Locale(s): East Blossom Hill; Seoul, Korea, South (train from Seoul to Pusan)

Summary: Sumi, disappointed that her mother is not home to celebrate her birthday, is also worried that she won't come home from the army on the train as promised. After Sumi has cried herself to sleep, her grandmother awakens her to tell her about how she and Sumi's mother escaped from Korea when the Chinese came over the border during the Korean War. Relating how her husband woke them in the night, how they found a train but had to ride on the roof, and how Sumi's grandfather decided to stay in Korea and fight for his country, she reassures Sumi that the two of them will soon meet the train bringing Sumi's mother home. (46 pages)

Where it's reviewed:
Booklist, September 15, 1996, page 238
School Library Journal, January 1997, page 75

Other books you might like:
Sook Nyul Choi, *Halmoni and the Picnic*, 1993
A little girl and her classmates help to make her grandmother comfortable when she arrives from Korea.
Sherry Garland, *The Lotus Seed*, 1993
A grandmother remembers her life in Vietnam and is saddened when a seed she brought with her is lost.
Amy Tan, *The Moon Lady*, 1992
Nai-Nai tells her grandchildren about an outing in China.

64

DUNCAN BALL
GEORGE ULRICH, Illustrator

Emily Eyefinger and the Lost Treasure

(New York: Simon & Schuster, 1994)

Series: Emily Eyefinger Books
Subject(s): Adventure and Adventurers; Humor; Mystery and Detective Stories
Age range(s): Grades 2-4
Major character(s): Emily Eyefinger, Child, Detective—Amateur
Time period(s): 1990s (1994)
Locale(s): United States; Cairo, Egypt

Summary: Emily flits from one mysterious adventure to another, solving mysteries with the assistance of a third eye on the end of her finger. When Emily wins a trip to Egypt, she and her parents fly to Cairo where Emily helps an archeologist find a lost treasure. (84 pages)

Where it's reviewed:
Booklist, February 15, 1995, page 1083
Horn Book Guide, Spring 1995, page 64
School Library Journal, January 1995, page 81

Other books by the same author:
Emily Eyefinger, Secret Agent, 1993
Emily Eyefinger, 1992

Other books you might like:
David A. Adler, *The Cam Jansen Series*, 1980-
Using her photographic memory Cam Jansen participates in the solving of a variety of mysteries.
Pat Hutchins, *The Mona Lisa Mystery*, 1981
A school trip to Paris becomes an adventure when the students find themselves involved in a mystery.

Donald J. Sobol, *Encyclopedia Brown, Boy Detective*, 1979
  The first book in the series introduces Encyclopedia Brown
  as he solves his first ten cases.

65

ROBIN BALLARD, Author/Illustrator

Good-Bye House

(New York: Greenwillow Books, 1994)

Subject(s): Dwellings; Moving, Household; Family Life
Age range(s): Grades K-1
Major character(s): Unnamed Character, Child; Mama,
  Mother; Papa, Father
Time period(s): 1990s (1994)
Locale(s): United States

Summary: With the family household goods packed and
loaded on a moving truck, a young girl walks through the
empty house recalling the special memories associated with
each room. Although she doesn't want to leave the only home
she's ever known, the discovery of a little girl just her age at
the new house helps her to understand that she will come to
like her new residence also. (24 pages)

Where it's reviewed:
Booklist, March 15, 1994, page 1369
Children's Book Review Service, Spring 1994, page 133
Horn Book, July 1994, page 439
Publishers Weekly, February 28, 1994, page 86
School Library Journal, June 1994, page 96

Other books by the same author:
Carnival!, 1995
Gracie, 1993
Granny and Me, 1992

Other books you might like:
Frank Asch, *Goodbye, House*, 1986
  Prior to the family's departure to a new home, Little Bear
  walks through the old house and yard saying goodbye to
  his favorite spots.
Barbara Shook Hazen, *Good-Bye, Hello*, 1995
  In brief rhyming phrases, a little girl says good-bye to her
  old home and neighborhood, repeating the routine with
  greetings upon arrival at her new home.
Ann Turner, *Stars for Sarah*, 1991
  Unable to sleep, Sarah wonders about life in her new home
  and is comforted by her mother's reassuring presence.

66

CATHERINE BANCROFT
HANNAH COALE GRUENBERG, Illustrator
HANNAH COALE GRUENBERG, Illustrator

Felix's Hat

(New York: Four Winds Press, 1993)

Subject(s): Animals/Frogs and Toads; Brothers and Sisters;
  Dreams and Nightmares
Age range(s): Grades K-2
Major character(s): Felix Frog, Frog
Time period(s): 1990s (1993)

Locale(s): United States

Summary: Felix constantly loses the special orange hat he is so
fond of. He always finds it again until the day he wears it on a
family outing to a pond. Alas, Felix is heartbroken and refuses
to have a bath or go to bed without his hat. Sensitive parents
and supportive siblings offer help which, in combination with
a dream, help Felix to accept his loss and find a solution to the
problem. (32 pages)

Where it's reviewed:
Booklist March 15, 1993, page 1354
Children's Book Review Service, April 1993, page 97
Five Owls, March 1993, page 88
Publishers Weekly, March 1, 1993, page 56
School Library Journal, July 1993, page 56

Other books by the same author:
That's Philomena!, 1995

Other books you might like:
Jez Alborough, *Where's My Teddy?*, 1992
  Oh no! After a walk in the forest, Eddie can't find his
  special teddy bear so he retraces his steps, surprised to find
  more than he lost.
Shirley Hughes, *David and Dog*, 1981
  With help from his older sister, David adjusts to the loss of
  his special toy dog, Dogger. This book won the 1978 Kate
  Greenaway Medal.
Deborah Turney Zagwyn, *The Pumpkin Blanket*, 1991
  Clee's blanket has always been very special. With support
  from a loving father she learns to get along without it.

67

CATHERINE BANCROFT
HANNAH COALE, Illustrator
HANNAH COALE, Illustrator

That's Philomena!

(New York: Simon & Schuster Books for Young Readers, 1995)

Subject(s): Animals/Frogs and Toads; Behavior; Brothers and
  Sisters
Age range(s): Grades K-2
Major character(s): Philomena, Frog, Sister (older); Felix,
  Frog, Brother (younger); Freda, Frog, Sister (younger)
Time period(s): 1990s (1995)
Locale(s): Fictional Country

Summary: Whenever Philomena wakes up on the wrong side
of the bed, her siblings call her Philomeany. One morning,
over her grumbling, she overhears the derogatory term and is
determined to restore her image as Philanicey or Philamazing.
Her plans to make brownies are interrupted repeatedly by
Freda's and Felix's pleas for help with the building of a
lemonade stand. Although the brownies finally make it into
the oven, while Philomena delivers lemonade to her siblings,
the brownies burn. Philomena now sees no choice but to
apologize. When she does, she is recognized for her many
contributions during the day to help her forgiving siblings. (30
pages)

Where it's reviewed:
Horn Book Guide, Fall 1995, page 257
Publishers Weekly, March 13, 1995, page 68

School Library Journal, May 1995, page 81

Other books by the same author:
Felix's Hat, 1993

Other books you might like:
Laurie Krasny Brown, *Rex and Lilly Family Time*, 1995
Rex and Lilly help plan Mom's birthday surprise, contend with an overeager robot helper and pick a family pet.
Russell Hoban, *Best Friends for Frances*, 1969
Being excluded from Albert's "no girls" baseball game gives Frances the idea that her little sister, Gloria, might be worthy of some attention.
Holly Keller, *Geraldine First*, 1996
Big sister Geraldine is annoyed by Willie's copy-cat ways, until she thinks of something he will not imitate.

68

LISA BANIM

Drums at Saratoga

(New York: Silver Moon Press, 1993)

Series: Stories of the States
Subject(s): Revolutionary War; American Colonies
Age range(s): Grades 4-6
Major character(s): Nathaniel Phillips, Orphan, Runaway; Ben Freeman, Servant (freed slave)
Time period(s): 1770s (1777)
Locale(s): Hudson River Valley, New York (Hudson River Valley)

Summary: Following British soldiers as they march against American forces seems far more exciting to young Nathaniel than continuing his apprenticeship to an abusive blacksmith. Impulsively he joins the throng of camp followers and, after days of tiresome marching, finds himself rescued from the danger of battle by Ben, servant to a British officer and informant to American forces. War no longer appears glamourous to Nathaniel as he experiences hunger and hardship and sees the death and destruction following a battle. (58 pages)

Where it's reviewed:
Children's Book Review Service, August 1993, page 164
Children's Bookwatch, July 1993, page 1
School Library Journal, October 1993, page 123
Small Press, Winter 1994, page 73

Other books by the same author:
A Spy in the King's Colony, 1994
A Thief on Morgan's Plantation, 1994
American Dreams, 1993

Other books you might like:
Avi, *The Fighting Ground*, 1984
Twenty-four hours on the frontlines give young Jonathan a new perspective of the Revolutionary War.
Nathaniel Benchley, *Sam the Minuteman*, 1969
Two of the early battles of the Revolutionary War are depicted through the eyes of young Minuteman Sam at first scared and finally angry with all he sees.
Nathaniel Benchley, *George the Drummer Boy*, 1977
The American Revolution is portrayed from the perspective of a young British drummer boy.

Alden R. Carter, *At the Forge of Liberty*, 1988
A factual review of causes, leaders and important events of the Revolutionary War. (nonfiction)

69

LISA BANIM
TATYANA YUDITSKAYA, Illustrator

A Spy in the King's Colony

(New York: Silver Moon Press, 1994)

Series: Mysteries in Time
Subject(s): American Colonies; Revolutionary War; Spies
Age range(s): Grades 3-5
Major character(s): Emily Parker, 11-Year-Old, Patriot; Mary Margaret "Maggie" Sullivan, 11-Year-Old, Friend; Robert Babcock, 18-Year-Old, Spy
Time period(s): 1770s (1775)
Locale(s): Boston, American Colonies

Summary: Chafing under the British occupation of her city, Emily is suspicious of anyone who may be loyal to the King. With her friend Maggie, she attempts to continue a routine life in the city all the while wondering about the movements of others, especially neighbor Robert whose family is definitely Loyalist. Robert, however, professes to be a Patriot, but still Emily wonders if she can trust him with an important message. (76 pages)

Where it's reviewed:
Horn Book Guide, Fall 1994, page 305
School Library Journal, July 1994, page 100

Other books by the same author:
A Thief on Morgan's Plantation, 1994
American Dreams, 1993
Drums at Saratoga, 1993

Other books you might like:
Drollene P. Brown, *Sybil Rides for Independence*, 1985
A non-fiction account of a 16-year-old's night ride through the countryside calling for support against the British army.
Judith Berry Griffith, *Phoebe the Spy*, 1977
In a story based on actual events in 1776, a 13-year-old black girl is sent to work for George Washington and gather information about possible traitors on his staff.
Byrna Stevens, *Deborah Sampson Goes to War*, 1984
A biography describes the war efforts of a patriot so dedicated to America's independence that she disguises herself as a man and joins the army.

70

JACQUELINE TURNER BANKS

Egg-Drop Blues

(Boston: Houghton Mifflin Co., 1995)

Subject(s): Twins; African Americans; Learning Disabilities
Age range(s): Grades 4-6
Major character(s): Jury Jenkins, Twin, 6th Grader; Judge Jenkins, Twin, Dyslexic
Time period(s): 1990s

Locale(s): Plank, Kentucky

Summary: This is the third book about the "posse," a group of friends who support one another and hang together. Led by twins Judge and Jury, Judge always tags after his more expert brother, until it's discovered that Judge has dyslexia. Once he learns the tricks of adapting to this disability, he finds he can compete with Jury. Right now the twins' biggest problem centers around the egg-drop competition to improve Judge's science grade. As Judge learns to adapt to his dyslexia, his self-esteem improves and he and his twin act more like equals. (120 pages)

Where it's reviewed:
Voice of Youth Advocates, June 1995, page 91
Booklist, April 15, 1995, page 1497
Horn Book, July 1995, page 483
Library Talk, September 1995, page 36
School Library Journal, August 1995, page 139

Other books by the same author:
The New One, 1994
Project Wheels, 1993

Other books you might like:
Cynthia Blair, *The Double Dip Disguise*, 1988
    In order to solve a mystery, a set of twins swap identities.
Lila Hopkins, *Talking Turkey*, 1989
    Croaker and his friend, Zeke, struggle with science fair projects during their seventh grade year.
Lee Kingman, *Head over Heels*, 1985
    A set of twins must adjust to a new lifestyle when one of the twins is severely injured in an automobile accident.

71

JACQUELINE TURNER BANKS

The New One
(Boston: Houghton Mifflin, 1994)

Subject(s): Twins; African Americans; Schools
Age range(s): Grades 6-7
Major character(s): Jury Jenkins, Twin, 6th Grader; Judge Jenkins, Twin, 6th Grader; Ayreal, 6th Grader
Time period(s): 1990s
Locale(s): Plank, Kentucky

Summary: Jury, his brother Judge and their friends, who call themselves "the posse," are part of a small number of minority students in a formerly all-white school. Jury confronts two problems as he begins 6th grade. First he doesn't like his mother's new boyfriend and plots to end their relationship. Second, he doesn't understand why Ayreal, a new student at his school, doesn't like any of his white friends. Life as a 6th grader becomes very complicated for Jury. (107 pages)

Where it's reviewed:
Voice of Youth Advocates, October 1994, page 204
Booklist, April 15, 1994, page 1533
Horn Book, July 1994, page 448
School Library Journal, June 1994, page 124
Children's Bookwatch, August 1994, page 4

Other books by the same author:
Egg-Drop Blues, 1995

Project Wheels, 1993

Other books you might like:
Walter Dean Myers, *Fast Sam, Cool Clyde and Stuff*, 1975
    Three young dudes in Harlem become the 116th Street Good People in a hilarious tale of city life and friendship.
Jacqueline Roy, *Soul Daddy*, 1992
    Hannah searches for her identity in a London world of differing values with her black, reggae music singer father and white working class mother.
Pieter Van Raven, *Pickle and Price*, 1990
    Pickle, an illiterate white teen, and Price, an ex-con, strike up an unlikely friendship in the 1950s South.

72

LYNNE REID BANKS
BARRY MOSER, Illustrator

The Magic Hare
(New York: Morrow Junior Books, 1993)

Subject(s): Animals/Rabbits; Magic; Short Stories
Age range(s): Grades 3-6
Major character(s): Unnamed Character, Hare (magic)
Time period(s): Indeterminate

Summary: Through 10 tales set in various times and places, the magic hare leaps, dances and conjures up magical relief to characters as diverse as rude queens and timid orphans. Confident, but somewhat naive, the hare is a bit of a trickster as he faces unexpected dilemmas with success. (49 pages)

Where it's reviewed:
Booklist, September 15, 1993, page 149
Books for Keeps, November 1993, page 12
Horn Book, November 1993, page 743
Publishers Weekly, July 5, 1993, page 69
School Library Journal, November 1993, page 104

Other books by the same author:
Broken Bridge, 1995
The Mystery of the Cupboard, 1993 (Indian in the Cupboard Series)
The Adventures of King Midas, 1992

Other books you might like:
Martin H. Greenberg, *A Newbery Zoo: A Dozen Animal Stories by Newbery Award-Winning Authors*, 1995
    Twelve animal stories from Newbery Award winning books are compiled by Greenberg and Charles G. Waugh.
Suzanne Crowder Han, *The Rabbit's Escape*, 1995
    In a retelling of a Korean folktale, wily rabbit tricks a turtle in order to keep his liver and his life.
Joel Chandler Harris, *Jump! The Adventures of Brer Rabbit*, 1986
    Five classic tales of trickster Brer Rabbit are adapted by Van Dyke Parks and Malcolm Jones.
James Howe, *Bunnicula: A Rabbit Tale of Mystery*, 1979
    Harold, the family dog, is convinced that Bunnicula is a vampire rabbit.

73

LYNNE REID BANKS
TOM NEWSOME, Illustrator

The Mystery of the Cupboard
(New York: Morrow, 1993)

Subject(s): Family Life; Magic; Toys
Age range(s): Grades 4-6
Major character(s): Omri, Child; Jessica Charlotte Driscoll, Actress, Aunt (Omri's great-great)
Time period(s): 1990s
Locale(s): London, England; England (countryside in Dorset)

Summary: After the *Indian in the Cupboard*, Omri vows to put away the magic cupboard. His family inherits an old farm house in the countryside and moves there. While their roof is being rethatched, Omri discovers a journal written by his relative Jessica Charlotte which explains the secret of the cupboard and the effect it has on their family. Omri knows he has to open the cupboard once again to right a wrong that affects his entire family. (246 pages)

Where it's reviewed:
School Library Journal, June 1993, page 102
Booklist, April 1, 1993, page 1430
Voice of Youth Advocates, October 1993, page 222
Horn Book, July 1993, page 483
New York Times Book Review, May 16, 1993, page 21

Other books by the same author:
The Return of the Indian, 1986
The Indian in the Cupboard, 1981

Other books you might like:
Mary Norton, *The Borrowers*, 1952
   People only several inches tall live under floorboards in homes and survive by ''borrowing'' from regular sized people.
Terry Pratchett, *Truckers*, 1990
   Masklin and his small group of gnomes move into the Arnold Bros. Store where they meet and join another group of gnomes.
Rosemary Wells, *Through the Hidden Door*, 1987
   Two boys explore a cave where they dig up an ancient town once inhabited by two-inch tall people.

74

SARA H. BANKS
BIRGITTA SAFLUND, Illustrator

Remember My Name
(Niwot, Colorado: Roberts Rinehart Publishers, 1993)

Subject(s): Indians of North America; Slavery; Indians of North America
Age range(s): Grades 3-6
Major character(s): Annie Rising Fawn Stuart, 11-Year-Old (half-Scottish, half-Cherokee), Orphan; William Blackfeather, Uncle (guardian), Indian (Cherokee); Rightous Cry, Slave
Time period(s): 19th century (1838)
Locale(s): New Echota, Georgia

Summary: Following the deaths of her parents, Annie is sent to live with her mother's brother, William Blackfeather, a respected, wealthy Cherokee. Annie faces many adjustments living on her uncle's plantation. She experiences slavery for the first time and attends a Cherokee school until it is closed by the government. With the Indian Removal Act of 1838, Annie's uncle must face the inevitable loss of the Cherokee land. He frees all his slaves and, with careful planning, arranges for Annie and Righteous Cry to escape to freedom before they, too, become victims of the ''Trail of Tears.'' (104 pages)

Where it's reviewed:
Booklist, September 1, 1993, page 59
Children's Bookwatch, October 1993, page 1
Library Talk, March 1994, page 35
Publishers Weekly, May 17, 1993, page 80
School Library Journal, June 1993, page 102

Other books by the same author:
Tomo-Chi Chi: Gentle Warrior, 1993

Other books you might like:
R. Conrad Stein, *The Trail of Tears*, 1993
   The story of the relocation of the Cherokee from their native lands to reservations set up by the government. (nonfiction)
Elisabeth Jane Stewart, *On the Long Trail Home*, 1994
   Separated from her family during the forced march to Oklahoma territory, 9-year-old Meli finds her brother and the two escape the Trail of Tears to return to their home in North Carolina.
Laura Ingalls Wilder, *Little House on the Prairie*, 1961
   Homesteading in Missouri Territory, the Ingalls family observes the Cherokee march by on the Trail of Tears.

75

ANTONIA BARBER
P.J. LYNCH, Illustrator

Catkin
(Cambridge, MA: Candlewick Press, 1994)

Subject(s): Fairy Tale; Animals/Cats; Adventure and Adventurers
Age range(s): Grades 1-3
Major character(s): Catkin, Cat; Carrie, Child; Wise Woman, Aged Person
Time period(s): Indeterminate Past
Locale(s): England

Summary: When Catkin fails to watch over sleeping Carrie, the little people take her to their underground kingdom, leaving a changling in her place. Feeling the burden of his failed vigilance, Catkin agrees to follow the Wise Woman's advice and try to retrieve the baby. Descending into the little people's kingdom, Catkin is befriended by the lord and lady who have Carrie and is given the task of solving three riddles to gain Carrie's freedom. In order to succeed Catkin must speak his own name, knowing that he will then be forever bound to the underground kingdom. Once again, the advice of the Wise Woman is sought for a solution which satisfies everyone. (48 pages)

Where it's reviewed:
Booklist, January 1, 1995, page 823
Kirkus Reviews, December 15, 1994, page 1558
Library Talk, September 1995, page 34
Publishers Weekly, November 21, 1994, page 76
School Library Journal, January 1995, page 101

Other books by the same author:
The Monkey and the Panda, 1995
The Enchanter's Daughter, 1994
The Mousehole Cat, 1990

Other books you might like:
Selma Lagerlof, *The Changeling*, 1992
    Despite the grief a farmer and his wife feel for their lost
    son, the wife cares for an ugly troll child left in his place
    and her kindness secures the return of her son.
Lauren Mills, *The Book of Little Folk: Faery Stories and
    Poems from around the World*, 1997
    The illustrated collection includes thirteen stories and six-
    teen poems drawn from the folklore of the elves, faeries,
    leprechauns and gnomes in many cultures.
Paul Robert Walker, *Little Folk: Stories from around the
    World*, 1997
    Stories and legends from Japan, Denmark, Ireland and
    Hawaii are retold in a collection of eight different tales
    about the wee folk.

76

ANTONIA BARBER
KARIN LITTLEWOOD, Illustrator

Gemma and the Baby Chick
(New York: Scholastic, Inc., 1993)

Subject(s): Animals/Chickens; Farm Life; Mothers and
    Daughters
Age range(s): Grades K-3
Major character(s): Gemma, Child; Unnamed Character,
    Mother
Time period(s): 1990s (1992)
Locale(s): England

Summary: Gemma learns a lesson when she warms a viable
unhatched egg until it yields a live chick. Her mother guides
her, explaining the actions of the hen and the need to return
the baby chick to its mother quickly. Gemma places "her"
chick under the mother hen and then walks proudly back to
the house with her mother. First published in England in 1992.
(32 pages)

Where it's reviewed:
Booklist, April 1, 1993, page 1441
Children's Book Review Service, May 1993, page 109
Kirkus Reviews, February 1, 1993, page 142
Publishers Weekly, January 18, 1993, page 468
School Library Journal, March 1993, page 170

Other books by the same author:
The Monkey and the Panda, 1995
Catkin, 1994
The Mousehole Cat, 1990

Other books you might like:
Carol Carrick, *Valentine*, 1995
    After Heather and Grandma bake Valentine cookies they
    check the newborn lambs and find one needing Heather's
    help.
Alice Provensen, *The Year at Maple Hill Farm*, 1978
    The seasons change and so do the activities on the farm.
    Co-author Martin Provensen.
Karen Wallace, *My Hen Is Dancing*, 1993
    A boy's observations of his hen's behavior are expanded
    with factual notes on selected pages of the story's text.

77

BARBARA E. BARBER
ANNA RICH, Illustrator

Saturday at the New You
(New York: Lee & Low Books Inc., 1994)

Subject(s): African Americans; Mothers and Daughters; Busi-
    ness Enterprises
Age range(s): Grades K-3
Major character(s): Shauna, 2nd Grader; Momma, Mother,
    Businesswoman
Time period(s): 1990s (1994)
Locale(s): United States (The New You Beauty Parlor)

Summary: Saturday is Shauna's favorite day of the week
because it's the day she works with her mother at The New
You. With her dolls for company, Shauna helps Momma open
the shop and prepare for the first customers. Throughout the
day she assists Momma and both share a contented tiredness
at the end of long, but satisfying work day. First picture book
by the author. (30 pages)

Where it's reviewed:
Booklist, December 1, 1994, page 684
Bulletin of the Center for Children's Books, December 1994,
    page 120
New York Times Book Review, February 26, 1995, page 21
Publishers Weekly, September 19, 1994, page 68
School Library Journal, January 1995, page 81

Other books you might like:
Mary Hoffman, *Amazing Grace*, 1991
    Grace realizes her dream of playing the lead role in the
    class play.
Karen Lynn Williams, *Tap-Tap*, 1994
    Sasifi helps her mother sell fruit in the local marketplace.
Vera B. Williams, *A Chair for My Mother*, 1982
    After a fire destroys the family's furniture, a young girl,
    her mother and grandmother save coins to buy a comfort-
    able chair for the girl's hard-working mother.

78

JOYCE ANNETTE BARNES

The Baby Grand, the Moon in July, & Me
(New York: Dial Books for Young Readers, 1994)

Subject(s): African Americans; Family Life; Poverty
Age range(s): Grades 4-6

Major character(s): Annie Armstrong, 10-Year-Old (determined), Sister; Matthew "Matty" Armstrong, Musician (aspiring), Brother (older)
Time period(s): 1960s (1969)
Locale(s): Ohio (154 Oakridge Avenue)
Summary: The author's first novel begins on the day that the Apollo 11 is launched toward the moon and Annie shares her dream of becoming an astronaut with her mother. The same day, unbeknownst to his parents, Matty purchases a baby grand piano on credit so that he can realize his own dream of being a jazz musician. His mother insists the piano be returned, but his father goes one step further and throws Matty out of the house along with the piano. Annie puts her creative energy to work to help her parents' accept Matty for the aspiring musician that he is and to accept his dreams as being legitimate ones for a poor boy to have. (134 pages)

Where it's reviewed:
Booklist, February 15, 1994, page 1078
Bulletin of the Center for Children's Books, January 1994, page 147
Kirkus Reviews, March 1, 1994, page 298
Publishers Weekly, February 7, 1994, page 88
School Library Journal, March 1994, page 220

Other books you might like:
Eloise Greenfield, *Koya DeLaney and the Good Girl Blues*, 1992
    Ever-cheerful Koya must learn to express other emotions, including anger, if she is to resolve some conflicts affecting her best friend which have Koya trapped in the middle.
Alice Mead, *Junebug*, 1995
    Living in the projects with the challenge of daily survival hasn't kept Junebug from having big dreams.
Mildred D. Taylor, *Roll of Thunder, Hear My Cry*, 1976
    Set in the South of the 1930's, the Newbery award-winning novel presents a black family trying to understand the prejudice and discrimination in their life.

79

DEBRA BARRACCA
SAL BARRACCA, Illustrator
ALAN AYERS, Illustrator

Maxi, the Star
(New York: Dial Books for Young Readers, 1993)

Subject(s): Animals/Dogs; Television
Age range(s): Grades 1-3
Major character(s): Jim, Taxi Driver (Maxi's owner); Maxi, Dog, Entertainer (TV star)
Time period(s): 1990s (1993)
Locale(s): New York, New York; Hollywood, California
Summary: Hollywood, here we come! Maxi's invitation to audition for a dog food commercial is the impetus for a cross-country trip in Jim's Checker cab. With the successful audition behind them, Jim and the new TV star, Maxi, return to New York and an exciting welcome from friends and neighbors. (32 pages)
Where it's reviewed:
Booklist, May 1, 1993, page 1601

Five Owls, May 1993, page 119
New York Times Book Review, May 30, 1993, page 19
Publishers Weekly, May 24, 1993, page 87
School Library Journal, October 1993, page 90

Other books by the same author:
A Taxi Dog Christmas, 1994
Maxi, the Hero, 1991
The Adventures of Taxi Dog, 1990

Other books you might like:
Maira Kalman, *Ooh-La-La (Max in Love)*, 1991
    The renowned poet dog, Max Stravinsky, is on tour in Paris when he is smitten by the charming Crepes Suzette.
James Marshall, *Fox Be Nimble*, 1990
    Fox's goal is to become a rock star, but Mom's plans send him babysitting and ultimately to some unexpected new heights.
Susan Meddaugh, *Martha Calling*, 1994
    Martha, the talking dog, has the winning answer to a radio contest. Unfortunately, the prize is a weekend for four at a resort with a "No Dogs Allowed" policy—until Martha arrives.

80

SHELLEY A. BARRE

Chive
(New York: Simon & Schuster, 1993)

Subject(s): Homeless; Sports/Skateboarding
Age range(s): Grades 5-6
Major character(s): Charles "Chive" Horton, Streetperson, 7th Grader; Terry Caldwell, 7th Grader
Time period(s): 1980s; 1990s
Locale(s): Buntsville; United States (Perkins County)
Summary: One day Terry's mother befriend's a raggedy-looking boy who helps her at the grocery store. Terry thinks his mother's being conned and is very resistant to her inviting Chive for dinner. The story of Chive's life eventually emerges and even Terry feels compassion for a young man whose family first loses their farm and now his mother and sister in a fire. Though all Chive's difficulties seem insurmountable, he and his father have also tried to help other homeless children in this first novel. (194 pages)

Where it's reviewed:
Publishers Weekly, October 25, 1993, page 64
Voice of Youth Advocates, February 1994, page 363
Horn Book Guide, Spring 1994, page 72
School Library Journal, November 1993, page 104
Publishers Weekly, October 25, 1993, page 64

Other books you might like:
Berlie Doherty, *Street Child*, 1994
    Based on a true story, orphaned Jim is saved by Dr. Barnardo who runs schools for destitute children in England.
Paula Fox, *Monkey Island*, 1991
    After Clay is abandoned in a hotel room by his parents, he takes to the streets where he is befriended by two homeless men.

Mark J. Harris, *Come the Morning*, 1989
   While searching for their father, Ben and his family become homeless and finally have to accept the fact that their father abandoned them.
Jonathan London, *Where's Home*, 1995
   Though homeless, Aaron and his father do their best to survive, eventually ending up in a shelter.
Jonathan Nasaw, *Shakedown Street*, 1993
   Homeless Caro meets many eccentric people who provide support and love to her and her mother, but she still wants her own house.

■ 81

MARY BRIGID BARRETT
SANDRA SPEIDEL, Illustrator

Sing to the Stars
(Boston: Little, Brown and Company, 1994)

Subject(s): Blind; Musicians; Friendship
Age range(s): Grades K-3
Major character(s): Ephram, Child, Musician (violinist); Mr. Washington, Musician (pianist), Blind; Grandma, Grandmother
Time period(s): 1990s (1995)
Locale(s): United States

Summary: Greeting Ephram as he walks home from a violin lesson, Mr. Washington compliments Ephram's ability and asks him to play at a neighborhood fundraiser the next night. Ephram is overwhelmed by the thought of performing on stage and discusses his concerns with Grandma over dinner. Surprised to learn that Mr. Washington was a professional pianist until an accident took his sight and his daughter's life, Ephram decides to invite Mr. Washington to perform with him. Mr.Washington is as reluctant as Ephram was initially to play before a crowd, but both musicians find their courage in time to make their music sing to the stars, as well as the audience. First children's book by the author. (32 pages)

Where it's reviewed:
Booklist, February 15, 1994, page 1092
Kirkus Reviews, May 1, 1994, page 626
New Advocate, Fall 1994, page 285
Publishers Weekly, April 18, 1994, page 61
School Library Journal, May 1994, page 84

Other books you might like:
Alice Faye Duncan, *Willie Jerome*, 1995
   On his trumpet, Willie Jerome plays "red hot bebop" from the apartment house roof.
Hoong Yee Lee Krakauer, *Rabbit Mooncakes*, 1994
   Hoong Wei worries about playing the piano in front of all her relatives.
Emily Arnold McCully, *Mirette on the High Wire*, 1992
   Instructing Mirette, who is determined to le the highwire, helps the Great Bellini overcome his own fear of performing again.
Brian Pinkney, *Max Found Two Sticks*, 1994
   With two twigs as drumsticks, Max uses every available surface as a drum, tapping out the rhythms of the city.

■ 82

SUSAN CAMPBELL BARTOLETTI
DAVID RAY, Illustrator

Silver at Night
(New York: Crown Publishers, Inc., 1994)

Subject(s): Emigration and Immigration; Italian Americans; Miners and Mining
Age range(s): Grades 1-3
Major character(s): Massimino, Immigrant, Miner; Perina, Girlfriend
Time period(s): Indeterminate Past
Locale(s): Italy; United States

Summary: Tired of laboring for the wealthy landlord, Massimino leaves his country and his beloved Perina in order to realize his dream of owning his own land. However, the new country has its own wealthy landlords and Massimino labors in the coal mines, saving his earnings, corresponding with Perina and waiting for the day when she joins him and they are indeed rich. First book for the author. (32 pages)

Where it's reviewed:
Booklist, November 1, 1994, page 505
Children's Book Review Service, February 1995, page 80
Kirkus Reviews, November 15, 1994, page 1523
Publishers Weekly, November 14, 1994, page 67
School Library Journal, November 1994, page 72

Other books you might like:
Elisa Bartone, *Peppe the Lamplighter*, 1993
   The Caldecott Honor book tells of hard-working Peppe who believes that each lamp he lights is a promise for a better future.
Riki Levinson, *Watch the Stars Come Out*, 1985
   After travelling alone to join their family in New York, Brother and Sister are happy to discover that from their top floor apartment they can see the stars at night.
Betsy Maestro, *Coming to America: The Story of Immigration*, 1996
   A factual account explains the immigrant experience from its beginnings to the present day.
Allen Say, *Grandfather's Journey*, 1993
   A grandson completes his grandfather's journey between homeland and adopted land, memory and desire.

■ 83

ELISA BARTONE
TED LEWIN, Illustrator

Peppe the Lamplighter
(New York: Lothrop, Lee & Shepard Books, 1993)

Subject(s): Fathers and Sons; Brothers and Sisters; Italian Americans
Age range(s): Grades 2-5
Major character(s): Peppe, Child (only son), Immigrant (substitute lamplighter)
Time period(s): 1900s
Locale(s): New York, New York (Mulberry Street, Little Italy)

Summary: With his mother dead and his father sick, young Peppe must find work to support his eight sisters. Delighted when the lamplighter offers him temporary work, Peppe hurries home with the good news only to be met with rejection by his father for accepting such an unimportant job. With support from his sisters, Peppe begins his work, only to face continuing disapproval from his father. Dejected, one night Peppe does not go to work, neighbors wonder what has become of him, and his little sister does not come home. Finally acknowledging the importance of Peppe's work, his father begs him to light the lamps so that his sister can find her way home. (32 pages)

Where it's reviewed:
Booklist, April 15, 1993, page 1522
Children's Book Review Service, May 1993, page 114
New Advocate, Winter 1994, page 68
Publishers Weekly, April 19, 1993, page 61
School Library Journal, July 1993, page 56

Awards the book has won:
ALA Notable Book, 1994
Caldecott Honor Book, 1994

Other books by the same author:
The Angel Who Forgot, 1992

Other books you might like:
Eve Bunting, *A Day's Work*, 1994
   The value of honesty is learned by a young boy when his efforts to help his immigrant grandfather backfire.
Eleanor Coerr, *Chang's Paper Pony*, 1988
   Working with his grandfather in a gold-mining camp, Chang dreams of owning a pony.
Brett Harvey, *Immigrant Girl, Becky of Eldridge Street*, 1987
   With her family, 10-year-old Becky lives in a New York tenement, adjusting to a new and different life.
Riki Levinson, *Watch the Stars Come Out*, 1985
   After travelling alone to join their family in New York, Brother and Sister are happy to discover that from their top floor apartment they can see the stars at night.

84

JENI BASSETT, Author/Illustrator

The Chick's Trick
(New York: Cobblehill Books, 1995)

Subject(s): Animals/Chickens; Conduct of Life; Mothers
Age range(s): Grades K-2
Major character(s): Mrs. Heckle, Chicken, Mother; Mrs. Peckle, Chicken, Mother
Time period(s): Indeterminate
Locale(s): Fictional Country

Summary: Overly competitive hens become so boastful when their chicks are born that the offspring devise a plan to fool Mrs. Heckle and Mrs. Peckle into realizing that both chicks are equally attractive and talented. The plan works so well that the chicks are able to solicit promises from their mothers to stop comparing the two. (32 pages)

Where it's reviewed:
Booklist, January 15, 1995, page 934
Children's Book Review Service, June 1995, page 121
Kirkus Reviews, February 15, 1995, page 220
Publishers Weekly, January 2, 1995, page 77
School Library Journal, March 1995, page 178

Other books by the same author:
Little Treasury of the Little People's Mother Goose, 1990

Other books you might like:
Lisa Campbell Ernst, *Zinnia and Dot*, 1992
   When a weasel comes searching for eggs, Zinnia and Dot decide it's time to stop bickering and unite to protect the eggs.
Julia Hoban, *Quick Chick*, 1989
   Eventually, Jenny Hen's youngest chick lives up to his Quick Chick nickname.
Megan Hallsey Lane, *Something to Crow About*, 1990
   Two seemingly identical chicks discover that, under their feathers, they have some basic differences.

85

MIRIAM BAT-AMI

Dear Elijah
(New York: Farrar, Straus & Giroux, 1995)

Subject(s): Jews; Holidays, Jewish; Fathers and Daughters
Age range(s): Grades 4-6
Major character(s): Rebecca Samuelson, 12-Year-Old; Elijah, Religious (Old Testament prophet)
Time period(s): 1990s
Locale(s): United States

Summary: Rebecca is distraught that, as Passover approaches, her father will not be in his customary role presiding over their family's celebration. Instead, he's hospitalized following a heart attack. To accept and understand this change in her life, Rebecca writes to Elijah, the Old Testament prophet who is suposed to visit Jewish homes during the Passover season. It's with Elijah that Rebecca is able to share her concerns about her father, thoughts about her religion, her heritage and the changes she experiences in her life as she approaches her teen years in a quiet, appealing work. (106 pages)

Where it's reviewed:
Booklist, April 1, 1995, page 1391
Publishers Weekly, January 16, 1995, page 455
School Library Journal, May 1995, page 104
Voice of Youth Advocates, August 1995, page 154
Horn Book Guide, Fall 1995, page 294

Other books by the same author:
When the Frost Is Gone, 1994

Other books you might like:
Susan Beth Pfeffer, *Turning Thirteen*, 1988
   Becky talks Dina into co-celebrating their Bat Mitzvah just so she can get Dina away from new student Amy.
Iris Rosofsky, *Miriam*, 1988
   Miriam gradually accepts that many of the Jewish rituals are not open to females, but only after she endures the shock of losing her brother Moshe.
Ferida Wolff, *Pink Slippers, Bat Mitzvah Blues*, 1989
   After Alyssa completes her Bat Mitzvah she considers continuing her lessons in Judaism.

86

ARTIE ANN BATES
JEFF CHAPMAN-CRANE, Illustrator

Ragsale

(Boston: Houghton Mifflin Company, 1995)

Subject(s): Shopping; Mothers and Daughters; Family Life
Age range(s): Grades 1-3
Major character(s): Jessann, Child, Sister; Eunice, Child, Sister
Time period(s): 1960s
Locale(s): Appalachians

Summary: The author's first book draws on childhood memories to describe a day of shopping at the ragsales. Everyone enjoys searching the barrels of used clothing and the tables filled with books and jewelry. For Eunice and Jessann the real excitement comes at the end of the day when they are allowed to open their surprise bundles. (32 pages)

Where it's reviewed:
Booklist, March 1, 1995, page 1246
Five Owls, May 1995, page 104
Horn Book, September 1995, page 585
Publishers Weekly, February 20, 1995, page 205
School Library Journal, April 1995, page 97

Other books you might like:
Dolly Parton, *Coat of Many Colors*, 1994
    Despite the teasing she hears at school, a young girl loves the coat her mother has carefully stitched for her out of rags.
Barbara Ann Porte, *When Aunt Lucy Rode a Mule and Other Stories*, 1994
    A visit with Aunt Lucy provides the opportunity for two sisters to hear some stories of Aunt Lucy's childhood visits to her grandparent's mountain home.
Cynthia Rylant, *When I Was Young in the Mountains*, 1982
    The shared experiences of two children evoke memories of a happy Appalachian childhood.

87

JOAN BAUER

Sticks

(New York: Delacorte, 1996)

Subject(s): Games; Mathematics; Grandparents
Age range(s): Grades 4-7
Major character(s): Mike "Mikey" Vernon, 10-Year-Old, Child (pool player); Arlen Pepper, 10-Year-Old; Poppy Vernon, Grandmother
Time period(s): 1990s
Locale(s): United States

Summary: Mikey is determined to win the pool championship in his family's pool hall, but is afraid he can't defeat the older pool player. He practices hard but things don't go right until an old friend of his dad's comes and starts giving him pointers. His best friend, Arlen, is a math whizz, and he too offers advice, using geometrical progression to explain the route of the ball. His grandmother, the owner of the pool hall, supports him as well and is proud when she is able to announce him the winner for the year. (182 pages)

Where it's reviewed:
Booklist, May 1, 1996, page 1505
School Library Journal, July 1996, page 120

Other books by the same author:
Thwonk, 1995

Other books you might like:
Sid Hite, *An Even Break*, 1995
    Frank wins a pool tournament and gets a summer job all in a very good year.
Alan Ritchie, *Erin McEwan, Your Days Are Numbered*, 1990
    Erin learns the importance and use of mathematics when she gets a job in a store.
Judith St. George, *What's Happening to My Junior Year?*, 1986
    Shooting pool and family problems are both important in the same year.
Alfred Slote, *The Trading Game*, 1990
    A baseball star comes to town and offers to coach the local team, but the trading of baseball cards gets in the way.

88

MARION DANE BAUER

A Question of Trust

(New York: Scholastic, 1994)

Subject(s): Mothers and Sons; Animals/Cats; Brothers
Age range(s): Grades 6-7
Major character(s): Bradley "Brad", 12-Year-Old; Charlie, Child, Brother (Brad's younger); Cat, Cat
Time period(s): 1990s
Locale(s): United States

Summary: Upset that their mother leaves them to "find herself," Brad refuses to visit her or allow his younger brother, Charlie, to answer her calls. Finding a stray cat has given birth in their storage shed, Brad empathizes with the two kittens, comparing their situation to that of he and his brother. When the brothers find one of the kittens dead, they mistakenly assume Cat has killed one of her offspring and in turn injure her. This act so horrifies them that they tell their father about the kittens, take Cat to the vet, and finally open dialogue about their changed family situation. (130 pages)

Where it's reviewed:
Booklist, January 15, 1994, page 924
Publishers Weekly, February 7, 1994, page 88
School Library Journal, March 1994, page 220
Voice of Youth Advocates, April 1994, page 22
New Advocate, Summer 1994, page 215

Other books by the same author:
Am I Blue? Coming Out from the Silence, 1993
A Taste of Smoke, 1993
Face to Face, 1991
On My Honor, 1987
Shelter from the Wind, 1979

Other books you might like:

Michael Behrens, *At the Edge*, 1988
  Lonely and vulnerable after his parents divorce, Dan learns to stop trying to please his father, going so far as to quit the swim team.

Natalie Honeycutt, *Ask Me Something Easy*, 1991
  After her parents divorce, Addie feels caught in the middle.

Jan Slepian, *Broccoli Tapes*, 1989
  Finding a stray cat trapped in rocks in a lava field brings Sara and her older brother Sam together as they adjust to their new Hawaiian home.

89

MARION DANE BAUER
ALLEN GARNS, Illustrator

When I Go Camping with Grandma

(Mahwah, NJ: BridgeWater Books, 1995)

Subject(s): Camps and Camping; Grandparents; Nature
Age range(s): Grades K-2
Major character(s): Grandma, Grandmother, Camper; Unnamed Character, Child, Camper
Time period(s): 1990s (1995)
Locale(s): United States

Summary: A young girl describes a camping trip with her grandmother. With Grandma's supportive companionship, she hikes deep into the woods and paddles across the lake to catch a fish. Both campers share an appreciation for the beauty and wonder of the natural environment. (32 pages)

Where it's reviewed:
Booklist, January 1, 1995, page 824
Children's BookWatch, May 1995, page 7
Kirkus Reviews, February 15, 1995, page 221
Publishers Weekly, April 17, 1995, page 58
School Library Journal, April 1995, page 97

Other books you might like:

Amy Hest, *Rosie's Fishing Trip*, 1994
  With Grampa for company, Rosie enjoys a quiet early morning fishing trip in the park.

Kathryn Lasky, *My Island Grandma*, 1993
  Abbey enjoys summer activities such as blueberry picking, swimming and hiking on an island with her grandma.

Elaine Moore, *Grandma's House*, 1985
  Summer is a memorable time of sharing for Kim and her grandmother.

90

NINA BAWDEN

Granny the Pag

(New York: Clarion, 1996)

Subject(s): Grandparents; Schools; Friendship
Age range(s): Grades 4-7
Major character(s): Catriona "Cat" Brooke, 11-Year-Old; Halina "Granny Pag" Luconirska, Doctor, Grandmother; Archibald "Willy" Green, 11-Year-Old, Bully

Time period(s): 1990s
Locale(s): London, England

Summary: Because her parents are actors and need to travel, Cat has been living with her grandmother ever since she was a very young girl. This, however, is a year of troubles, as she starts middle school and is taunted by the school bully, who even tries to burn her hair. Other adults are trying to take her away from her grandmother because they think Pag is not a fit caregiver, and her own parents think they would like to have her with them as a show child. Cat and Granny Pag (a name she's had since Cat spelled "pig" wrong) work together and with the help of an attorney, maintain their household, while Cat realizes the importance of family love and friendship. (184 pages)

Where it's reviewed:
School Library Journal, April 1996, page 132
Booklist, April 1, 1996, page 1362
Hornbook, September/October 1996, page 591

Awards the book has won:
Bulletin Blue Ribbon, 1996
School Library Journal Best Books, 1996

Other books by the same author:
Humbug, 1992
The Peppermint Pig, 1987
Carrie's War, 1973

Other books you might like:

Paula Fox, *Western Wind*, 1993
  Elizabeth resents being sent to her grandmother's house until she has gotten to know her better.

E.L. Konigsburg, *Jennifer, Hecate, Macbeth, William McKinley, and Me, Elizabeth*, 1967
  Elizabeth has to put up with the hazing of Jennifer when she moves to a new town.

Patricia MacLachlan, *Journey*, 1991
  Journey and her brother make themselves a new home on their grandparent's farm.

Brenda Seabrooke, *The Bridges of Summer*, 1992
  Jorah reluctantly joins her grandmother on an island off the coast of South Carolina.

Faythe Dyrud Thureen, *Jenna's Big Jump*, 1993
  Jenna is new in town and faces the class bully with the help of her mother and another newcomer.

91

DARLEEN BAILEY BEARD
LAURA KELLY, Illustrator

The Pumpkin Man from Piney Creek

(New York: Simon & Schuster Books for Young Readers, 1995)

Subject(s): Pumpkins; Farm Life; Fathers and Daughters
Age range(s): Grades 1-3
Major character(s): Hattie, Child; Pa, Father, Farmer; Pumpkin Man, Peddler
Time period(s): Indeterminate Past
Locale(s): United States

Summary: In the author's first book, Pa eagerly greets the arrival of the Pumpkin Man so he can sell the 100 pumpkins he's grown this year while Hattie secretly hides one for use as a jack-o-lantern later. However, Pa and the Pumpkin Man are counting as they load pumpkins and when they reach 99 and see an empty field, Hattie realizes that her deceit will not work and she relinquishes her hidden pumpkin. Before leaving, the Pumpkin Man discovers Hattie's wish and gives her the pumpkin from which he cut a sample slice, perfectly positioned to become a jack o' lantern's nose. (32pages)

Where it's reviewed:
Booklist, September 15, 1995, page 168
Children's Book Review Service, October 1995, page 13
Kirkus Reviews, October 1, 1995, page 1424
Publishers Weekly, September 18, 1995, page 90
School Library Journal, October 1995, page 96

Other books you might like:
Donald Hall, *Ox-Cart Man*, 1979
    A Caldecott Medal winner depicts the cycle of production of goods and their eventual sale or barter for one New England family in the 19th century.
Thomas Locker, *Family Farm*, 1988
    The hard work and financial uncertainty of farm life is depicted by a family that begins growing pumpkins and flowers to sell.
Scott Russell Sanders, *Here Comes the Mystery Man*, 1993
    The biannual visits from Merchant Meeks provide a pioneer family with access to his wares and the mysteries of the exotic places to which he travels.

92

MARGARET BECHARD

Really No Big Deal
(New York: Viking, 1994)

Subject(s): Friendship; Business Enterprises; Schools/Middle Schools
Age range(s): Grades 6-8
Major character(s): Jonah Truman, 7th Grader; Amanda "Moose" Matzinger, 7th Grader; Mallory Beckwith, 7th Grader
Time period(s): 1990s
Locale(s): Portland, Oregon

Summary: Jonah's a typical teenager—filled with worries! First he needs to earn money for his school's end-of-year beach trip, so he agrees to help his friend, Amanda, with her birthday party business by face-painting wiggly little kids. Then he worries if he'll ever outgrow being the shortest kid in his class. And then he thinks he has troubles because he can't get up the nerve to talk to Mallory on whom he has a crush. But his biggest anxiety arises when his mother tells him she's dating his school's principal! And that principal is Mallory's stepgrandfather! Life in 7th grade is too complicated for Jonah! (151 pages)

Where it's reviewed:
School Library Journal, May 1994, page 112
Publishers Weekly, May 2, 1994, page 309
Booklist, March 15, 1994, page 1347
Book Report, November 1994, page 41
Horn Book, July 1994, page 449

Other books by the same author:
Tory & Me and the Spirit of True Love, 1992
My Sister, My Science Report, 1990

Other books you might like:
Mary Jane Auch, *Mom Is Dating Weird Wayne*, 1988
    Jenna is horrified that her mother is dating the weird weatherman who always dresses in costumes on his television program.
Jeanne Betancourt, *Not Just Party Girls*, 1988
    Anne, Kate and Janet use their business of theme parties to also provide support for one another.
Betsy Byars, *Bingo Brown and the Language of Love*, 1989
    Bingo's venture into romance teaches him that speaking the ''language of love'' is like learning a foreign tongue.
Jan Greenberg, *Just the Two of Us*, 1988
    Holly convinces her mother to let her stay in New York to help Max with his business, Parties with Pizzazz, but soon misses her mother.

93

MARGARET BECHARD

Star Hatchling
(New York: Viking, 1995)

Subject(s): Science Fiction; Brothers and Sisters
Age range(s): Grades 4-6
Major character(s): Hanna, Space Explorer (lost), Teenager (Terran); Shem, Brother (Cheko's), Alien; Cheko, Sister (Shem's), Alien
Time period(s): Indeterminate Future
Locale(s): Planet—Imaginary

Summary: When Hanna accidently crash lands on an unknown planet she is found by adventurous Cheko and timid Shem. Together the bickering siblings hide the ''hatchling'' from the ''star'' which they assume the space ship to be and keep the secret of their discovery from their family. Hanna is intent on locating others from the spaceship with her transponder and leaving this strange planet. Before she returns to her own family, she rescues not only Cheko and Shem, but also her own rescuer after they are captured by ''Outsiders'' on the planet. (152 pages)

Where it's reviewed:
Booklist, September 15, 1995, page 158
Bulletin of the Center for Children's Books, January 1996, page 155
Children's Book Review Service, Winter 1996, page 68
Kirkus Reviews, August 1, 1995, page 1106
School Library Journal, August 1995, page 139

Other books by the same author:
Really No Big Deal, 1994
Tory & Me and the Spirit of True Love, 1992
My Sister, My Science Report, 1990

Other books you might like:
Bruce Coville, *The Search for Snout*, 1995
    Rod and his alien friends find themselves in danger as their search leads them into the area of the Mental Masters.
Debra Hess, *Spies, Incorporated*, 1994
    The fourth entry in Spies from Outer Space series finds

Cassie and alien friend Zeke solving the mystery of kidnapped pets.

Monica Hughes, *The Golden Aquarians*, 1995

When Walt Elliot accompanies his father to the planet Aqua he learns that his father's project threatens the native species.

Annette Curtis Klause, *Alien Secrets*, 1993

Puck's journey to her parents' workplace on a distant planet becomes one of danger when she befriends an alien seeking a mysterious object.

94

JOHN BELLAIRS
BRAD STRICKLAND, Co-Author

The Vengeance of the Witch-Finder
(New York: Dial, 1993)

Subject(s): Ghosts; Relatives
Age range(s): Grades 6-8
Major character(s): Lewis Barnavelt, 13-Year-Old; Jonathan Barnavelt, Magician, Uncle (Lewis'); Bertram "Bertie" Goodring, Blind
Time period(s): 1950s
Locale(s): London, England; Dinsdale, England (Sussex County)

Summary: Crotchety Uncle Jonathan takes his young nephew Lewis on a trip to England to visit the family's ancestral home. While staying at Barnavelt Manor, Lewis and Bertie, the blind son of the housekeeper, find a map which takes them to the center of an overgrown hedge maze. There they find a tomb from which they accidentally release an evil spirit, a witch finder from the 1600s who vows revenge on the Barnavelt family. When Uncle Jonathan disappears and Bertie's mother acts as if she's hypnotized, Lewis must save his friends in this posthumous work completed by Brad Strickland. (153 pages)

Where it's reviewed:
Book Report, January 1994, page 42
Booklist, October 15, 1993, page 440
Publishers Weekly, July 12, 1993, page 81
School Library Journal, September 1993, page 228
Voice of Youth Advocates, February 1994, page 377

Other books by the same author:
The Doom of the Haunted Opera, 1995
The Drum, the Doll and the Zombie, 1994
The Ghost in the Mirror, 1993

Other books you might like:
Gilbert B. Cross, *A Witch Across Time*, 1990
When Hannah visits her elderly aunt's New England home, she is used as a medium by a young girl hanged for witchcraft three hundred years before.

Catherine Dexter, *Mazemaker*, 1989
Stepping into the center of a painted maze in her schoolyard, Winnie is transported back one hundred years.

Robert Westall, *Urn Burial*, 1988
A shepherd finds a cat-like body inside a coffin hidden in a cairn of stones and puts his village in a battle between two alien groups.

95

SANDRA BELTON
FLOYD COOPER, Illustrator

From Miss Ida's Front Porch
(New York: Four Winds Press, 1993)

Subject(s): African Americans; Storytelling
Age range(s): Grades 2-5
Major character(s): Freda, Child; Miss Ida, Neighbor; Mr. Fisher "Pouissant", Storyteller
Time period(s): 1990s (1993)
Locale(s): United States (Church Street)

Summary: On a warm summer evening, neighbors gather on Miss Ida's front porch and the rememberings begin. The children sit quietly, spellbound by the tales of Duke Ellington and Marian Anderson. Through the stories, they learn of past discriminations against black people, develop an awareness of history and feel the strength and pride of their community. (40 pages)

Where it's reviewed:
Children's Book Review Service, November 1993, page 29
Horn Book, November 1993, page 743
Library Talk, March 1994, page 31
Publishers Weekly, July 26, 1993, page 73
School Library Journal, November 1993, page 76

Other books by the same author:
May'naise Sandwiches & Sunshine Tea, 1994

Other books you might like:
Verda Cross, *Great-Grandma Tells of Threshing Day*, 1992
Great-Grandma remembers the community effort to harvest the winter wheat.

Myra Cohn Livingston, *Keep on Singing: A Ballad of Marian Anderson*, 1994
The events of the life of Marian Anderson are described in this narrative poem. (nonfiction)

Mary Stolz, *Go Fish*, 1991
Thomas and Grandfather share a love of reading and storytelling in this warm family story.

96

SANDRA BELTON
GAIL GORDON CARTER, Illustrator

May'naise Sandwiches & Sunshine Tea
(New York: Four Winds Press, 1994)

Subject(s): Grandparents; African Americans; Storytelling
Age range(s): Grades K-3
Major character(s): Little Miss, Child (Big Mama's granddaughter); Big Mama, Grandmother, Storyteller
Time period(s): 1990s (1994); Indeterminate Past
Locale(s): United States

Summary: One of the things that Little Miss enjoys most when she visits Big Mama is thumbing through her scrapbook and listening to stories about relatives and events from the past. Her favorite story is one of a lesson of self-acceptance that Big Mama learned from a childhood picnic lunch of may'naise sandwiches and sunshine tea shared with a more affluent childhood friend. (32 pages)

Where it's reviewed:
Black Scholar, Fall 94, page 57
Children's Book Review Service, October 1994, page 13
Horn Book Guide, Spring 1995, page 25
School Library Journal, December 1994, page 71
Social Education, April 1995, page 224

Other books by the same author:
From Miss Ida's Front Porch, 1993

Other books you might like:
Elizabeth Fitzgerald Howard, *Aunt Flossie's Hats (and Crab Cakes Later)*, 1991
    Sarah and Susan remember Sunday afternoons at Aunt Flossie's house when they sip tea, eat cookies and try on her hats, each one prompting a story.
Margaree King Mitchell, *Uncle Jed's Barbershop*, 1993
    Sarah Jean fondly remembers her Uncle Jed who never lost sight of his dream to open his own barbershop.
Gloria Jean Pinkney, *The Sunday Outing*, 1994
    During weekly visits to the North Philadelphia Station to watch the trains, Ernestine and Great-Aunt Odessa share family stories and dreams for the future.

97

ROBERT BENDER, Author/Illustrator

A Most Unusual Lunch
(New York: Dial Books for Young Readers, 1994)

Subject(s): Food; Animals; Ecology
Age range(s): Grades K-2
Major character(s): Unnamed Character, Frog; Unnamed Character, Lion
Time period(s): Indeterminate
Locale(s): Fictional Country

Summary: Eating a beetle for lunch has surprising results for a frog who awakens the next day with antennae and six extra tiny legs. He has no time to worry because he is quickly eaten by a fish who is eaten by a snake who is eaten also. Each animal in turn sprouts characteristics of all the preceding animals. The last to partake of these unusual beasts is a lion who does not see his changed appearance as befitting the king of the jungle so he belches and the food chain begins to unravel. (32 pages)

Where it's reviewed:
Booklist, September 15, 1994, page 141
Children's Book Review Service, Winter 1995, page 61
Kirkus Reviews, August 15, 1994, page 1121
Publishers Weekly, September 26, 1994, page 69
School Library Journal, November 1994, page 72

Other books by the same author:
The Preposterous Rhinocerous, or, Alvin's Beastly Birthday, 1994
The Three Billy Goats Gruff, 1993
A Little Witch Magic, 1992

Other books you might like:
Eric Carle, *The Very Hungry Caterpillar*, 1969
    A caterpillar eats and eats and eats until he has an enormous stomachache.
Henrik Drescher, *The Boy Who Ate Around*, 1994
    When Mo decides to eat around his plate of food, he eats everything in the universe, except his dinner, before deciding to regurgitate all he has consumed and become a boy again.
David McPhail, *The Glerp*, 1972
    The Glerp goes for a walk, swallowing everything in its path until the elephant's tusks get stuck and cause all the swallowed animals to be coughed out.

98

AMANDA BENJAMIN, Author/Illustrator

Two's Company
(New York: Viking, 1995)

Subject(s): Mothers and Daughters; Remarriage; Change
Age range(s): Grades K-3
Major character(s): Maddy, Child; Unnamed Character, Single Mother; Simon, Fiance(e)
Time period(s): 1990s (1995)
Locale(s): Fictional Country

Summary: Maddy and her mother share an idyllic life until Simon arrives. Initially, Maddy sees Simon as a funny, enjoyable fellow, but when he begins taking up far too much of her mom's time, Maddy is resentful. When Maddy's mom tells her that she and Simon plan to marry, Maddy copes by planning a wedding of her own—to her stuffed lizard. As her supportive mother helps her prepare, Maddy comes to accept her mother's plans too. The author's first book. (30 pages)

Where it's reviewed:
Booklist, July 1995, page 1882
Children's Book Review Service, July 1995, page 145
Horn Book Guide, Fall 1995, page 258
Publishers Weekly, May 29, 1995, page 83
School Library Journal, July 1995, page 55

Other books you might like:
Joan E. Drescher, *My Mother's Getting Married*, 1986
    Katy is reluctant to face changes wrought by her mother's remarriage.
Anna Grossnickle Hines, *When We Married Gary*, 1996
    While she hasn't forgotten her absent father, Beth accepts her mother's new husband Gary as her Papa.
Candice F. Ransom, *We're Growing Together*, 1993
    Time and patience help a young girl and her stepfather learn to adjust to one another.
Danielle Steel, *Martha's New Daddy*, 1989
    Worried about her mother's upcoming marriage, 5-year-old Martha finds understanding and comfort in a chat with her father.

99

STAN BERENSTAIN, Author/Illustrator
JAN BERENSTAIN, Illustrator

The Berenstain Bears and the New Girl in Town

(New York: Random House, 1993)

Series: Big Chapter Book
Subject(s): Animals/Bears; Prejudice; Friendship
Age range(s): Grades 2-4
Major character(s): Brother Bear, Bear, Student; Sister Bear, Bear, Student; Bonnie Brown, Bear, Model (new girl in school)
Time period(s): 1990s (1993)
Locale(s): Bear Country, Fictional Country

Summary: A long-simmering feud between the Bear family and the Grizzly clan boils over and pulls even the children of the community into the dispute. Brother Bear is smitten with the new girl in town, Bonnie, the niece of a Grizzly who forbids her to have contact with a Bear. By carefully choosing the play *Romeo and Juliet* to perform, the students hope to teach the adults of Bear Country a lesson that will bring an end to the feud. (102 pages)

Where it's reviewed:
Horn Book Guide, Spring 1994, page 63
Publishers Weekly, June 7, 1993, page 71

Other books by the same author:
The Berenstain Bears and the Drug Free Zone, 1993
The Berenstain Bears and the Nerdy Nephew, 1993
The Berenstain Bears Gotta Dance!, 1993

Other books you might like:
Betsy Byars, *Hooray for the Golly Sisters!*, 1990
    Two pioneer sisters lead lives of humor and adventure.
Johanna Hurwitz, *Make Room for Elisa*, 1993
    In this beginning chapter book, five-year-old Elisa must adjust to new eyeglasses, starting school, and a new baby.
Elizabeth Levy, *The Something Queer Series*, 1971-
    Gwen, Jill, and basset hound Fletcher have one adventure after another while they solve mysterious occurrences.

100

BARBARA BERGER, Author/Illustrator

The Jewel Heart

(New York: Philomel Books, 1994)

Subject(s): Love; Music; Ballet
Age range(s): Grades K-2
Major character(s): Pavelle, Dancer (doll); Gemino, Musician (doll)
Time period(s): Indeterminate
Locale(s): Fictional Country

Summary: Gemino has no voice, a jewel for a heart, a talent for the violin and a love for Pavelle. He expresses this love through his playing as she dances. When Gemino does not appear one day, Pavelle learns from the shadows that he has fallen and a woodrat has stolen his jewel heart. Pavelle is saddened by the tattered, lifeless Gemino she finds on the path, but with help from the shadows she fashions new clothes and hair for him. With no jewel to replace his heart, Pavelle sews a seed into his chest, watering it with her tears. (32 pages)

Where it's reviewed:
Booklist, September 1, 1994, page 48
Horn Book Guide, Spring 1995, page 26
Kirkus Reviews, September 15, 1994, page 1265
Publishers Weekly, August 22, 1994, page 55
School Library Journal, October 1994, page 85

Other books by the same author:
The Donkey's Dream, 1986
Grandfather Twilight, 1986
When the Sun Rose, 1986

Other books you might like:
Hans Christian Andersen, *The Steadfast Tin Soldier*, 1979
    In one of many retellings of a classic tale, a one-legged tin soldier braves great dangers determined to find his way back to his beloved dancing paper doll.
Petra Mathers, *Victor and Christabel*, 1993
    Victor's love for Christabel frees her from the spell of her wicked cousin.
Domenico Vittorini, *The Thread of Life*, 1995
    A collection of 12 Italian folktales ranging from the romantic to the humorous is retold and newly illustrated.

101

FREDERICKA BERGER

The Green Bottle and the Silver Kite

(New York: Greenwillow, 1993)

Subject(s): Beaches; Brothers and Sisters
Age range(s): Grades 4-6
Major character(s): Phillip Grant, 10-Year-Old; Maggie Grant, 7-Year-Old
Time period(s): 1990s
Locale(s): Squan Beach, New Jersey

Summary: Summer at the beach hasn't been very much fun for Phil. The only kid his age wants to spend all his time fishing, so there's no one for Phil to hangout with. He loves to ride the waves, but has to share the raft with his younger sister, Maggie, who is no shrinking violet when it's her turn. One day he spies a silver kite, and knows he has to have one like it. Because it costs more money than he has, he tries several different ways to earn some cash, one of which leads to making a new friend. (131 pages)

Where it's reviewed:
Publishers Weekly, May 31, 1993, page 56
Horn Book, September 1993, page 595
Kirkus Reviews, June 1, 1993, page 716
Publishers Weekly, May 31, 1993, page 56

Other books by the same author:
Nuisance, 1983

Other books you might like:
Vicki Grove, *Junglerama*, 1989
    Creating a wildlife exhibit inside an abandoned carnival

trailer provides three boys with a place of escape one summer.

Carol J. Perry, *Going Overboard*, 1991

Tori's boring summer changes rapidly when her town decides to build the world's largest sandcastle.

William Sleator, *Interstellar Pig*, 1984

With fair skin that keeps him from enjoying the beach, Barney plays Interstellar Pig with three neighbors who happen to be aliens playing for control of Earth.

`102`

KATHRYN HOOK BERLAN
MAXIE CHAMBLISS, Illustrator

Andrew's Amazing Monsters
(New York: Atheneum, 1993)

Subject(s): Monsters; Imagination
Age range(s): Grades K-3
Major character(s): Andrew, Child (monster lover), Artist
Time period(s): 1990s (1993)
Locale(s): United States

Summary: Monsters, monsters everywhere! In an attempt to manage Andrew's love of monsters and his tendency to paint them on everything from sheets to shirts, his mother takes away his paints and his father gives him magic crayons that can only make monsters when used on the special paper provided by Andrew's parents. Andrew's room is soon decorated with monsters of all shapes, sizes, and colors. One night, when his bedtime wish is to have a real party with the monsters, Andrew learns just how much magic is in those crayons. (32 pages)

Where it's reviewed:
Booklist, March 1, 1993, page 1234
Children's Book Review Service, May 1993, page 109
Horn Book Guide, Fall 1993, page 250
Publishers Weekly, March 29, 1993, page 54
School Library Journal, October 1993, page 90

Other books you might like:
Johnny Alcorn, *Rembrandt's Beret*, 1991
On a trip to the Uffizi Gallery an artist observes all the paintings come to life.
Anthony Browne, *Bear Goes to Town*, 1989
Using his magic pencil, Bear is able to create all that he needs and come to the assistance of other animals too.
Crockett Johnson, *Harold and the Purple Crayon*, 1958
Harold has a magic purple crayon, a vivid imagination, and a talent for drawing himself into and out of trouble.
Maurice Sendak, *Where the Wild Things Are*, 1963
Max's imagination takes him to the land of the monstrous wild things and home again to his own room.
Mark Teague, *The Field Beyond the Outfield*, 1992
Monsters are all around says Ludlow Grebe, even on the baseball field.

`103`

RICHARD BERLETH
BEN OTERO, Illustrator

Mary Patten's Voyage
(Morton Grove, IL: Albert Whitman & Company, 1994)

Subject(s): Ships; Voyages and Travels; Sea Stories
Age range(s): Grades 3-5
Major character(s): Timothy Hare, Sailor; Captain Joshua Patten, Sailor, Spouse; Mary Patten, 18-Year-Old, Spouse
Time period(s): 1850s (1856)
Locale(s): At Sea (aboard *Neptune's Car*)

Summary: A clipper ship race from New York to San Francisco pits the *Neptune's Car* against two other ships. Captain Patten's reputation suggests that his clipper will win, but, when he takes ill with tuberculosis and his pregnant wife takes command, some of the superstitious sailors are troubled. Second mate Timothy Hare stands by Mary Patten as she charts course around the Horn and brings the ship and crew safely to San Francisco. (40 pages)

Where it's reviewed:
Booklist, January 1, 1995, page 820
Bulletin of the Center for Children's Books, December 1994, page 121
Horn Book Guide, Spring 1995, page 64
School Library Journal, December 1994, page 118

Other books by the same author:
Samuel's Choice, 1990

Other books you might like:
Loretta Krupinski, *Bluewater Journal: The Voyage of the Sea Tiger*, 1995
Benjamin Slocum records the daily events of the voyage on his father's clipper ship from Boston to the Sandwich Islands.
Thomas P. Lewis, *Clipper Ship*, 1978
When Jamie's father, captain of a clipper ship, falls ill his mother must take over and bring the ship safely to port.
Armstrong Sperry, *All Sail Set: A Romance of the ''Flying Cloud''*, 1935
The fictitious diary of a boy sailing on the maiden voyage of the clipper ship ''Flying Cloud'' was reissued in 1984.

`104`

CARI BEST
NIKI DALY, Illustrator

Red Light, Green Light, Mama and Me
(New York: Orchard Books, 1995)

Subject(s): Mothers and Daughters; Work; City Life
Age range(s): Grades K-2
Major character(s): Lizzie, Child; Mama, Mother, Librarian
Time period(s): 1990s (1995)
Locale(s): United States (Downtown Library)

Summary: Lizzie is excited to go to work with Mama. She rides the subway, watches her reflection in the window of a tall building, takes on the role of the Big Bad Wolf during storytime, and helps a coworker stamp papers. Quickly the day concludes and it is time to say good-bye to her library work-family and return home with Mama. (32 pages)

Where it's reviewed:
Booklist, September 1, 1995, page 82
Bulletin of the Center for Children's Books, September 1995, page 6
Children's Book Review Service, February 1996, page 73
Publishers Weekly, July 31, 1995, page 80
School Library Journal, October 1995, page 96

Other books by the same author:
Taxi! Taxi!, 1994

Other books you might like:
Barbara E. Barber, *Saturday at the New You*, 1994
    Weekly, Shauna works with her mother in a beauty parlor, observing the customers and helping with routine tasks.
Niki Daly, *Not So Fast, Songololo*, 1985
    A young boy shares a special day with his grandfather on a shopping trip to the city.
Karen Lynn Williams, *Tap-Tap*, 1994
    Old enough to assist her mother on market day, Sasifi is proud to be a skilled peddler of the family's oranges. She uses some of her earnings to pay for a ride home on the tap-tap.

105

CARI BEST
DALE GOTTLIEB, Illustrator

Taxi! Taxi!

(Boston: Little, Brown and Company, 1994)

Subject(s): Fathers and Daughters; City Life; Neighbors and Neighborhoods
Age range(s): Grades 1-2
Major character(s): Tina, Child of Divorced Parents; Papi, Single Father, Taxi Driver
Time period(s): 1990s (1994)
Locale(s): United States

Summary: Every Sunday Tina waits eagerly for Papi to drive up in his bright yellow taxi and take her away for the day. Some days Tina waits in vain, but today the taxi arrives and Tina and Papi travel past all the neighbors and into the country for a visit to Green Hill Farm. The brief time Tina and Papi have to share is over too quickly and they return to the city, offering rides to all the neighbors they pass along the way. The Spanish words and phrases sprinkled throughout the author's first book are easily understood from context. (32 pages)

Where it's reviewed:
Booklist, February 15, 1994, page 1092
Children's Book Review Service, Spring 1994, page 133
Horn Book, May 1994, page 306
Publisher's Weekly, March 7, 1994, page 69
School Library Journal, June 1994, page 96

Other books by the same author:
Red Light, Green Light, Mama and Me, 1995

Other books you might like:
Judith Caseley, *Priscilla Twice*, 1995
    Since her parents' divorce, Priscilla has two of everything when she would prefer one "all-together" family.
Kathryn O. Galbraith, *Holding onto Sunday*, 1995
    Sunday is the one day of the week that Jemma and Daddy can spend together and they enjoy every minute.
Linda Walvoord Girard, *At Daddy's on Saturday*, 1987
    When her parents divorce, Katie finds a way t o maintain a relationship with her father after he begins living in a different place.

106

JEANNE BETANCOURT

My Name Is Brain/Brian

(New York: Scholastic, 1993)

Subject(s): Learning Disabilities; School Life; Clubs
Age range(s): Grades 4-6
Major character(s): Brian Toomey, 6th Grader, Dyslexic; Dan Chester, 6th Grader, Friend; Isabel Morris, 6th Grader (unpopular)
Time period(s): 1990s (1993)
Locale(s): Sharon, Connecticut

Summary: The members of the Joker's Club concoct a plan to score points for jokes in class in hopes of making 6th grade more interesting. Little do they know that a new 6th grade teacher has been hired who finds no humor in their antics. Mr. Bigham does, however, detect Brian's previously undiagnosed learning disability and implements a plan of action to help him meet success at school. Learning to cope successfully with academic work is only one of the many challenges which Brian meets; he must deal with a changing understanding of the meaning of friendship too. (176 pages)

Where it's reviewed:
Booklist, April 1, 1993, page 1430
Kirkus Reviews, February 1, 1993, page 142
Language Arts, February 1994, page 139
Publishers Weekly, February 1, 1993, page 96
School Library Journal, April 1993, page 117

Other books by the same author:
Kate's Turn, 1992
Crazy Christmas, 1988
Puppy Love, 1986
The Rainbow Kid, 1983

Other books you might like:
Tom Birdseye, *Just Call Me Stupid*, 1993
    Fifth grader Patrick overcomes his reading disability and low self-esteem with support from his teacher, the love of his divorced mother, and the help of a new classmate.
Rose Blue, *Me and Einstein: Breaking through the Reading Barrier*, 1984
    Bobby wishes he could hide his inability to read, but it's a fact he can't conceal.
Barthe DeClements, *6th Grade Can Really Kill You*, 1985
    Helen is sure she will be in 6th grade forever, but a special reading teacher enables her to make progress.

Joyce Hansen, *Yellow Bird and Me*, 1986
  Doris befriends Yellow Bird, a dyslexic, and helps him
  with his school work.

107

CAROLINE BINCH, Author/Illustrator

Gregory Cool

(New York: Dial Books for Young Readers, 1994)

Subject(s): Relatives; Islands; Blacks
Age range(s): Grades 1-3
Major character(s): Gregory, Child (African American),
  Cousin; Lennox, Cousin (older than Gregory); Granny,
  Grandmother
Time period(s): 1990s (1994)
Locale(s): Trinidad and Tobago

Summary: On his first visit to his grandparents' home in
Tobago, all-American Gregory is initially overwhelmed by
the culture—Granny's strange food, the simple, small home,
the absence of a television set. The patience of his grandparents, the good-natured teasing from Lennox and the kindness
of the local people help Gregory to relax and look forward to
an enjoyable 4-week visit. Illustrator Binch makes her debut
as a writer with this tale. (32 pages)

Where it's reviewed:
Booklist, September 15, 1994, page 141
Bulletin of the Center for Children's Books, September 1994,
  page 5
Kirkus Reviews, August 15, 1994, page 1121
Publishers Weekly, August 1, 1994, page 78
School Library Journal, September 1994, page 180

Awards the book has won:
School Library Journal Best Books, 1994

Other books you might like:
Rachel Field, *If Once You Have Slept on an Island*, 1993
  A book of poetry describes the magical quality of an island
  experience.
Mary Hoffman, *Boundless Grace*, 1995
  Grace travels to Africa to visit the father she knows only
  from pictures and letters.
Rita Phillips Mitchell, *Hue Boy*, 1993
  On a Caribbean Island a young boy's family is eager for
  him to grow, but Hue Boy learns that size is a state of
  mind.

108

TOM BIRDSEYE

Just Call Me Stupid

(New York: Holiday House, 1993)

Subject(s): Friendship; Schools; Learning Disabilities
Age range(s): Grades 4-6
Major character(s): Patrick Lowe, 5th Grader (nonreader),
  Child of an Alcoholic; Paulette Lowe, Single Mother, Di-
  vorced Person (from Patrick's father); Celina Ortiz, 5th
  Grader (avid reader), Neighbor (new to neighborhood)
Time period(s): 1990s (1993)

Locale(s): Tucson, Arizona

Summary: Patrick remembers a time when books and the
anticipation of what might be discovered within them held
some interest for him. That was before his father shut him in
the closet, calling him stupid. Now, futile attempts to read
under the tutelage of an oppressive resource teacher only
remind him of his now-absent, alcoholic father. Patrick escapes from the pain of those memories into his fantasy life as
the White Knight, imagining the stories he cannot read for
himself. Through his mother's love and the help of Celina, a
new neighbor and classmate, the positive memories of the
hope of books return and Patrick begins to overcome some of
the emotional pain blocking his ability to read. (128 pages)

Where it's reviewed:
Booklist, January 15, 1994, page 930
Horn Book Guide, Spring 1994, page 73
Kirkus Reviews, November 1, 1993, page 1386
Publishers Weekly, October 25, 1993, page 62
School Library Journal, October 1993, page 123

Other books by the same author:
A Song of Stars, 1990
Tucker, 1990
I'm Going to Be Famous, 1986

Other books you might like:
Jeanne Betancourt, *My Name Is Brain/Brian*, 1993
  When 6th grader Brian's dyslexia is diagnosed and he
  obtains the necessary help for his reading problem, he
  comes to a new understanding of friendship and school.
Rose Blue, *Me and Einstein: Breaking through the Reading
  Barrier*, 1984
  Bobby wishes he could hide his inability to read, but it's a
  fact he can't conceal.
Barthe DeClements, *Sixth Grade Can Really Kill You*, 1985
  Helen is sure she will be in 6th grade forever, but a special
  reading teacher enables her to make progress.
Jamie Gilson, *Do Bananas Chew Gum?*, 1980
  An unlikely friendship between Alicia, the brightest stu-
  dent in the 6th grade class, and Sam, who has a learning
  disability, helps Sam to accept himself.
Joyce Hansen, *Yellow Bird and Me*, 1986
  Doris befriends Yellow Bird, a dyslexic, and helps him
  with his school work.

109

TOM BIRDSEYE
MEGAN LLOYD, Illustrator

A Regular Flood of Mishap

(New York: Holiday House, 1994)

Subject(s): Country Life; Family Life; Humor
Age range(s): Grades K-3
Major character(s): Ima Bean, 6-Year-Old
Time period(s): 1990s (1994)
Locale(s): Mossyrock Creek

Summary: In her efforts to be helpful, Ima Bean sets in motion
a series of events which trigger "a regular flood of mishap"
for her family. When she sees the calamity that has followed
her good intentions, Ima Bean packs her bags and heads down

the road. However, her family stops her and she learns that she is still loved despite her misdirected good intentions. (32 pages)

Where it's reviewed:
Booklist, March 15, 1994, page 1369
Horn Book Guide, Fall 1994, page 264
Kirkus Reviews, February 1, 1994, page 138
Publishers Weekly, December 20, 1993, page 71
School Library Journal, March 1994, page 190

Awards the book has won:
International Reading Association Children's Choice, 1995

Other books by the same author:
Soap! Soap! Don't Forget the Soap! An Appalachian Folktale, 1993
Waiting for Baby, 1991
Airmail to the Moon, 1988

Other books you might like:
David F. Birchman, *The Raggly, Scraggly, No-Soap, No-Scrub Girl*, 1995
An original folk tale tells of a family's reaction to a dirty, unexpected visitor who slips in and out of their life leaving behind a permanent bathtub ring.
Anne Isaacs, *Swamp Angel*, 1994
In tall tale fashion, the award-winning story tells of Angelica Longrider who can lasso a tornado and snore like a locomotive.
Arnold Lobel, *Owl at Home*, 1975
In a humorous beginning reader, Owl's attempts to be helpful do not meet with his expected success.
Tynia Thomassie, *Feliciana Feydra LeRoux: A Cajun Tall Tale*, 1995
Spoiled Feliciana disobeys Grampa Baby and secretly follows him when he goes "halligator huntin'," arriving just in time to use her doll to save Grampa Baby.

110

TOM BIRDSEYE

Tarantula Shoes
(New York: Holiday House, 1995)

Subject(s): Moving, Household; Brothers and Sisters; Twins
Age range(s): Grades 4-6
Major character(s): Ryan O'Keefe, 11-Year-Old; Fang, Tarantula; Gordon Schur, 6th Grader, Friend
Time period(s): 1990s (1995)
Locale(s): Macinburg, Kentucky

Summary: Ryan is not happy with the family's move from the Arizona desert to Kentucky. Among the reasons he's found to return to his former home is the news from Gordon that in this town, 6th graders go to junior high. This destroys all Ryan's plans of being the big guy in elementary school. Then, he learns that the coolest new shoes for basketball cost $124.99 and his parents, not feeling the least bit guilty about the move, refuse to buy them. Ryan decides to earn the money himself and when he runs out of work before he's raised enough money, he decides to sell tickets to see his pet, Fang, dine on crickets. Although he achieves his goal and acquires the

shoes, Ryan learns a much more important lesson from the experience. (131 pages)

Where it's reviewed:
Booklist, April 15, 1995, page 1497
Horn Book Guide, Fall 1995, page 294
Kirkus Reviews, April 15, 1995, page 552
Library Talk, September 1995, page 36
School Library Journal, May 1995, page 104

Other books you might like:
Susan Clymer, *There's a Tarantula in My Homework*, 1996
Micah's 3rd grade classroom acquires a tarantula as a class pet.
Peg Kehret, *The Richest Kids in Town*, 1994
Peter's money-making schemes provide a framework for a friendship with Wishbone Wyoming, but don't earn much cash.
Cynthia Stowe, *Not-So-Normal Norman*, 1995
When Anthony decides to earn extra money by pet-sitting for people, he doesn't expect his first client to be a tarantula.

111

BETTY G. BIRNEY
JOHN O'BRIEN, Illustrator

Tyrannosaurus Tex
(Boston: Houghton Mifflin Company, 1994)

Subject(s): Dinosaurs; American West; Folk Tales
Age range(s): Grades K-3
Major character(s): Tyrannosaurus Tex, Dinosaur (helpful); Pete, Cowboy, Assistant (to the cook); Cookie, Cook
Time period(s): Indeterminate Past
Locale(s): Texas

Summary: In an original tall tale, Cookie and Pete are manning the chuck wagon during a cattle drive when they are visited by Tyrannosaurus Tex. During the night, rustlers start a fire to scare the cattle. Tex comes to the rescue with his 10,000 gallon hat full of water which not only extinguishes the fire but also washes the rustlers all the way to El Paso. (32 pages)

Where it's reviewed:
Booklist, June 1, 1994, page 1835
Children's Book Review Service, April 1994, page 98
Horn Book, May 1994, page 306
Publishers Weekly, January 24, 1994, page 54
School Library Journal, May 1994, page 84

Other books by the same author:
Oh Brother! Someone's Afraid of the Dark!, 1994
Piglet Bakes Half a Haycorn Pie, 1992
Walt Disney's Winnie the Pooh and the Missing Pots, 1992

Other books you might like:
Ariane Dewey, *Pecos Bill*, 1983
The legend of a hero in the American West is retold in a tall tale.
Steven Kellogg, *Mike Fink: A Tall Tale*, 1992
Humorous illustrations compliment the tall tale of Mike Fink and his adventures after he runs away from home as a baby.

Robert D. San Souci, *Larger than Life: The Adventures of American Legendary Heroes*, 1991
A collection of tall tales includes such legendary figures as John Henry and Paul Bunyan.

112

CHARLES C. BLACK
JAMES STEVENSON, Illustrator

The Royal Nap

(New York: Viking, 1995)

Subject(s): Kings, Queens, Rulers, etc.; Sleep; Problem Solving
Age range(s): Grades K-3
Major character(s): King Gordo, Royalty; Gerald, Servant, Father (Phoebe's); Phoebe, Servant, Musician
Time period(s): Indeterminate Past
Locale(s): Fictional Country

Summary: Daily at one o'clock, a busy castle falls silent to allow King Gordo to have his royal nap. The slightest sound, even that of Gerald's hiccups, prevents King Gordo from sleeping. Although Gerald is banished to the "Cold and Snowy Land," other sounds continue to disturb the fatigued king. The sound of music turns out to be Phoebe plunking a sad tune on an old, one-string lute. Although Phoebe is able to lull King Gordo to sleep, she refuses to play again until her father returns. The tired king grants her wish. This is the author's first book. (32 pages)

Where it's reviewed:
Booklist, January 15, 1995, page 934
Bulletin of the Center for Children's Books, February 1995, page 192
Horn Book Guide, Fall 1995, page 258
Kirkus Reviews, February 15, 1995, page 221
School Library Journal, April 1995, page 97

Other books you might like:
Michael Grejniec, *Albert's Nap*, 1994
Hippo Albert's quiet, little nap is disturbed by a buzzing mosquito.
Mercer Mayer, *Hiccup*, 1976
While attempting to cure his friend's hiccups, Mr. Hippopotamus manages only to bother her with his outlandish ideas until he "catches" them himself.
M.L. Miller, *The Enormous Snore*, 1995
The problem of a snoring king is solved by Letty, a lost waif, who coincidentally finds her family about the same time the kingdom finds peace and quiet.

113

MALORIE BLACKMAN
LIS TOFT, Illustrator

Girl Wonder and the Terrific Twins

(New York: Dutton Children's Books, 1991)

Subject(s): Brothers and Sisters; Twins; Parent and Child
Age range(s): Grades 1-3

Major character(s): Maxine "Girl Wonder", Sister (African-American); Anthony, Brother, Twin; Edward, Brother, Twin
Time period(s): 1990s (1991)
Locale(s): England

Summary: It's not easy being a superhero. Maxine and her twin brothers intend to be helpful, but their childish interpretations of problems and the means to solve them backfire repeatedly, leaving them facing both a mess and an annoyed Mom. In and out of hot water, they seem to create their own adventures until a trip to the grocery store puts them in the right place at the right time to assist the police in capturing two thieves. Originally published in Great Britain. (70 pages)

Where it's reviewed:
Booklist, September 1, 1993, page 59
Books for Keeps, September 1993, page 7
Horn Book Guide, Fall 1993, page 284
Kirkus Reviews, February 15, 1993, page 222
School Library Journal, January 1994, page 82

Other books by the same author:
A New Dress for Maya, 1993

Other books you might like:
David A. Adler, *The Fourth Floor Twins and the Fish Snitch Mystery*, 1986
This entry in the Fourth Floor Twins Series involves Donna and Diane in a mystery involving missing newspapers.
Laura Lee Hope, *The Bobbsey Twins Series*, 1983-
There's never a dull moment in the Bobbsey household with two sets of twins lending a hand.
Joan M. Lexau, *Trouble Will Find You*, 1994
With the name Diz Aster, it's no wonder that Diz has a hard time staying out of trouble for one day in order to prove he can handle the reponsibility of a pet dog.
Susan Beth Pfeffer, *Sara Kate, Superkid*, 1994
Sara Kate's brother thinks it unfair that onlyfemales of the family inherit superpowers, usable on Tuesdays, Thursdays and occasional Saturdays, so he tries to capitalize on his sister's.

114

QUENTIN BLAKE, Author/Illustrator

Simpkin

(New York: Viking, 1994)

Subject(s): Behavior; Family Life; Stories in Rhyme
Age range(s): Grades K-1
Major character(s): Simpkin, Child
Time period(s): 1990s (1993)
Locale(s): England

Summary: The illustrations expand the brief story of mischievous Simpkin and the effects of his antics on his family, especially his older sister. Taking full advantage of Simpkin's unpredictable behavior, the text explores adjectives and opposites in a way which is simply funny. First published in the United Kingdom in 1993. (32 pages)

Where it's reviewed:
Booklist, February 15, 1994, page 1083

Horn Book, September 1994, page 572
Kirkus Reviews, February 1, 1994, page 139
Publishers Weekly, January 10, 1994, page 60
School Library Journal, June 1994, page 96

Other books by the same author:
Snuff, 1993
Cockatoos, 1992
All Join In, 1991

Other books you might like:
Jack Prelutsky, *My Parents Think I'm Sleeping*, 1985
    When the house is dark and quiet, a young boy thinks about what is happening at the midnight hour.
Maurice Sendak, *Pierre: A Cautionary Tale in Five Chapters and a Prologue*, 1962
    Pierre is an uncooperative lad who learns the importance of caring.
Dr. Seuss, *Marvin K. Mooney, Will You Please Go Now!*, 1972
    It doesn't matter how Marvin travels as long as he goes—now.

115

ROBERT J. BLAKE, Author/Illustrator

Dog
(New York: Philomel Books, 1994)

Subject(s): Old Age; Animals/Dogs
Age range(s): Grades K-2
Major character(s): Unnamed Character, Dog (stray); Peter, Aged Person (cemetery keeper)
Time period(s): Indeterminate Past
Locale(s): Ireland (seaside village)

Summary: Old Peter has no need for the companionship of a stray dog who comes calling or so he thinks until he remembers just how warm his toes were with the uninvited guest sleeping on them. Regretting that he has sent the stray out into a summer storm, he sets off in search of the animal. While Peter refuses to give the dog a name he does give him a home in exchange for his companionship to a lonely, stubborn old man. (32 pages)

Where it's reviewed:
Booklist, March 15, 1994, page 1369
Book World, May 8, 1994, page 18
Children's Book Review Service, May 1994, page 109
Children's Bookwatch, May 1994, page 4
School Library Journal, May 1994, page 84

Other books by the same author:
The Perfect Spot, 1992

Other books you might like:
Carol Carrick, *Lost in the Storm*, 1979
    Lost overnight in a storm, a frightened dog is relieved to be rescued by its owner.
Barbro Lindgren, *The Story of the Little Old Man*, 1992
    A friendship develops between a lonely old man and the dog who befriends him.
Charlotte Pomerantz, *The Outside Dog*, 1993
    Marisol's grandfather begrudgingly accepts the stray dog which has "adopted" his granddaughter into their home.

Tres Seymour, *Pole Dog*, 1993
    An abandoned dog sits forlornly near a telephone until rescued by a sympathetic family.

116

BENEDICT BLATHWAYT, Author/Illustrator

Stories from Firefly Island
(New York: Greenwillow Books, 1993)

Subject(s): Animals; Short Stories; Storytelling
Age range(s): Grades 2-4
Major character(s): Tortoise, Turtle, Storyteller
Time period(s): Indeterminate
Locale(s): Firefly Island, Fictional Country

Summary: Tortoise is very old, wise and respected by the other animals living on Firefly Island. To satisfy the animals, Tortoise tells ten stories of days gone by including those which explain why frogs croak at night and why the bear no longer lives with the other island animals. Originally published in Great Britain in 1992. (121 pages)

Where it's reviewed:
Booklist, January 15, 1994, page 935
Children's Book Review Service, January 1994, page 55
Horn Book Guide, Spring 1994, page 73
Publishers Weekly, November 1, 1993, page 79
School Library Journal, December 1993, page 80

Other books by the same author:
Little House by the Sea, 1994

Other books you might like:
Robin Moore, *The Cherry Tree Buck and Other Stories*, 1995
    Six humorous stories tell of a young boy's adventures with his grandfather and the wildlife in the mountains.
Paul Peabody, *Blackberry Hollow*, 1993
    Seven stories about the animal residents of Blackberry Hollow revolve around the inventions of Parnassus, a good-natured, but absent-minded bear.
William Steig, *Abel's Island*, 1976
    The Newbery Honor Book tells of a pampered mouse, marooned on an island, who must be resourceful and self-sufficient if he is to survive and find a way home.

117

LUCY JANE BLEDSOE
STERLING BROWN, Illustrator

The Big Bike Race
(New York: Holiday House, 1995)

Subject(s): Bicycles and Bicycling; Grandparents; African Americans
Age range(s): Grades 3-5
Major character(s): Ernest "Ernie" Peterson, 10-Year-Old; Sonny King, Neighbor (bicyclist); Grandma, Grandmother
Time period(s): 1990s (1995)
Locale(s): Washington, District of Columbia

Summary: Dreams of a racing bike are shattered when Ernie's practical Grandma gives him an affordable big yellow second-hand bike for his birthday. She has added baskets so that he can run errands for her and Ernie feels guilty that he is embarrassed by her gift. When Ernie accidently meets Sonny, he courageously asks for Sonny's help training for the Citywide Cup Race, hoping that he can win a racing bike. Although Ernie does not win the race, he learns a lot about competition and teaches Sonny a thing or two also in the author's first novel for children. (90 pages)

Where it's reviewed:
Booklist, October 1, 1995, page 313
Bulletin of the Center for Children's Books, December 1995, page 119
Children's Book Review Service, February 1996, page 80
Kirkus Reviews, October 15, 1995, page 1487
School Library Journal, November 1995, page 96

Other books you might like:
Matt Christopher, *Olympic Dream*, 1996
    Learning about the sport of cycling changes Doug Cannon's outlook on life and gives him the confidence to pursue his goals.
Franklin W. Dixon, *The Mystery of the Silver Star*, 1987
    A cyclist riding the famous Silver Star bicycle in a cross-country race must be rescued by Frank and Joe.
Cheryl Zach, *Benny and the Crazy Contest*, 1991
    The contest is crazy, but the prize is a new bike so Benny Holt decides to enter and win!

118

LENORE BLEGVAD
ERIK BLEGVAD, Illustrator

A Sound of Leaves
(New York, Margaret K. McElderry Books, 1996)

Subject(s): Beaches; Family Life; Friendship
Age range(s): Grades 3-5
Major character(s): Sylvie, 9-Year-Old; Clare, 10-Year-Old, Neighbor; Dell, 6-Year-Old, Sister
Time period(s): 1990s
Locale(s): United States (beach colony)

Summary: Sylvie and her family arrive for their first visit at the beach. Grandfather is quite pleased with getting away from the city, but the children are not so sure until Sylvie sees a tree right outside her window. They all go down to the beach but mother hurts her leg and is confined to the house for the rest of vacation. Sylvie, alone on the beach, meets Clare who invites her to her house to look at tree books, but Clare's friends arrive and want nothing to do with Sylvie. Sylvie returns home in tears after being called a ''slum child'', but when she sees Clare the next day decides that she can overlook name-calling and be friends. (58 pages)

Where it's reviewed:
Booklist, May 1, 1996, page 1505
Horn Book, September/October 1996, page 592
School Library Journal, May 1996, page 85

Other books by the same author:
Once Upon a Time and Grandma, 1993
Rainy Day Kate, 1987
Anna Banana and Me, 1985

Other books you might like:
Jacqueline Turner Banks, *The New One*, 1994
    Jury's brother does not want him to befriend a newcomer because he is an African-American.
Eileen Spinelli, *Lizzie Logan Wears Purple Sunglasses*, 1995
    Heather and Lizzie become friends even though they don't always like the same things.
Richard Wilbur, *A Game of Catch*, 1994
    Scho teases some boys because he feels shut out from their games.
Carol Beach York, *The Key to the Playhouse*, 1994
    Alice Ann and Megan lock their playhouse to keep out another child.

119

ODDS BODKIN
TED ROSE, Illustrator

The Banshee Train
(New York: Clarion Books, 1995)

Subject(s): Accidents; Trains; Ghosts
Age range(s): Grades 1-4
Major character(s): John Mercer, Engineer, Railroad Worker; Michael O'Reilly, Railroad Worker
Time period(s): 1920s (1929)
Locale(s): Colorado (Train Number 1)

Summary: John Mercer and Michael O'Reilly are manning a train approaching the Gore Canyon Trestle during the spring floods. Mercer intends to inspect the trestle, but the canyon is shrouded in fog. To complicate matters, the throttle is not acting properly and a train is bearing down on them. As they near the Gore Canyon Trestle, the throttle swings to off and they lose all pressure as the ghost train speeds by them with the banshee shrieking unintelligibly. Shaken, the men walk to the canyon's edge and see that the trestle has been washed out in the spring floods just as it had been twenty years earlier when a train unknowingly went into the abyss. First book for a master tale teller. (32 pages)

Where it's reviewed:
Booklist, June 1995, page 1782
Children's Book Review Service, Spring 1995, page 133
Horn Book Guide, Fall 1995, page 258
Publishers Weekly, April 24, 1995, page 71
School Library Journal, August 1995, page 115

Other books you might like:
Karen Ackerman, *The Banshee*, 1990
    The legendary, lonely banshee goes from house to house in the darkened village finding only love and warmth which leaves no room for her sad wail.
Washington Irving, *The Headless Horseman*, 1992
    The classic tale of the schoolmaster and the headless horseman is retold as a beginning chapter book by Natalie Standiford.
Alvin Schwartz, *Ghosts! Ghostly Tales from Folklore*, 1991
    A beginning reader includes ghost stories retold from folk tales and legends around the world.

120

MARIBETH BOELTS
MARTINE GOURBAULT, Illustrator

Grace and Joe

(Morton Grove, IL: Albert Whitman & Company, 1994)

Subject(s): Friendship; Neighbors and Neighborhoods; Loneliness
Age range(s): Grades K-3
Major character(s): Grace, Child; Joe, Postal Worker
Time period(s): 1990s
Locale(s): United States

Summary: Lonely Grace begins to tag along with Joe as he delivers the mail in her neighborhood. Daily, in every season of the year, they walk together until Grace begins kindergarten and is no longer available. Still, Grace finds a way to communicate with her friend—she writes him a letter! (32 pages)

Where it's reviewed:
Horn Book Guide, Spring 1995, page 26
School Library Journal, December 1994, page 71

Other books by the same author:
Summer's End, 1995
Dry Days, Wet Nights, 1994
Tornado, 1993

Other books you might like:
Melrose Cooper, *I Got Community*, 1995
  With a catchy rhythm, the text describes the important connections that make each person in a community significant.
Kevin Henkes, *Good-Bye, Curtis*, 1995
  After 42 years of delivering mail, Curtis spends his last work day in the familiar neighborhood and, when he reaches the last house on his route, is surprised by a retirement party.
Lynne Rae Perkins, *Home Lovely*, 1995
  Tiffany's beginning efforts at gardening are noticed and nurtured by Bob, the letter carrier on a rural route.

121

MARIBETH BOELTS
ELLEN KANDOIAN, Illustrator

Summer's End

(Boston: Houghton Mifflin Company, 1995)

Subject(s): Summer; Schools; Family Life
Age range(s): Grades K-2
Major character(s): Jill, 2nd Grader, Sister; Unnamed Character, 1st Grader, Sister (Jill's)
Time period(s): 1990s (1995)
Locale(s): United States

Summary: With mixed emotions, Jill faces the end of summer and the beginning of a new school year. While she does not want the carefree, active days of summer to end, she goes through the necessary school-year preparations—a haircut, shopping for school clothes and supplies, and cleaning her room. Observing her little sister's excitement about school

and recalling some past good times help Jill to go forth the first day with enthusiasm. (32 pages)

Where it's reviewed:
Booklist, April 1, 1995, page 1422
Bulletin of the Center for Children's Books, March 1995, page 228
Horn Book Guide, Fall 1995, page 258
School Library Journal, April 1995, page 98

Other books by the same author:
Dry Days, Wet Nights, 1994
Grace and Joe, 1994
Tornado, 1993

Other books you might like:
Janet Ahlberg, *Starting School*, 1988
  With customary humor the authors consider the conflicting emotions as a new school year begins. Co-author Allan Ahlberg.
Jonathan London, *Froggy Goes to School*, 1996
  Feeling nervous about the first day of school, Froggy not only survives sitting still but also enjoys the day.
Marisabina Russo, *I Don't Want to Go Back to School*, 1994
  After listening to his older sister's dire warnings about the upcoming school year, Ben is afraid for school to begin; when it does, he finds he has worried needlessly.

122

JANICE BOLAND
MEGAN HALSEY, Illustrator

Annabel Again

(New York: Dial Books for Young Readers, 1995)

Subject(s): Animals/Pigs; Self-Acceptance; Growing Up
Age range(s): Grades K-1
Major character(s): Annabel, Pig
Time period(s): 1990s (1995)
Locale(s): United States

Summary: The arrival of Spring gives Annabel the urge to find a residence more exciting than her mud puddle. She wanders away, telling each animal she meets of her search for a new home. Kindly, she is offered accommodations in a bird's nest, on a frog's lily pad and with a cat in a spooky, old barn. Annabel discovers, as she scurries back to her comforting mud puddle, there is no place like home. (32 pages)

Where it's reviewed:
Booklist, May 15, 1995, page 1650
Horn Book Guide, Fall 1995, page 259
School Library Journal, August 1995, page 115

Other books by the same author:
Annabel, 1993

Other books you might like:
Pat Hutchins, *Little Pink Pig*, 1994
  A mother pig asks the other animals for help locating her wandering child.
Abigail Pizer, *Penelope Pig*, 1988
  Tired of a muddy pig sty for a home, Penelope decides to move into the farmhouse.

Valerie Reddix, *Millie and the Mudhole*, 1992
    Other animals try without success to warn Millie her
    mudhole is too deep for her.
Martin Waddell, *The Pig in the Pond*, 1992
    An impulsive pig who can't swim creates an uproar on
    Farmer Neligan's farm when he jumps into the pond to
    cool off.

123

RUSKIN BOND
VERA ROSENBERRY, Illustrator

Binya's Blue Umbrella
(Honesdale, PA: Boyds Mills Press, 1995)

Subject(s): Possessions; Country Life; Jealousy
Age range(s): Grades 3-5
Major character(s): Binya, 10-Year-Old, Sister; Bijju, 12-
    Year-Old, Brother; Ram Bharosa, Aged Person, Store
    Owner (tea shop)
Time period(s): 1990s (1995)
Locale(s): Tibri, India (Himalayas)

Summary: When shy Binya appears in the village with the
beautiful blue umbrella traded to her by a wealthy woman
who desired Binya's leopard's claw necklace, she quickly
becomes the envy of all the villagers, especially Ram
Bharosa. The silk umbrella shelters Binya and Bijju from the
sun in summer and the rain during the monsoons. Though the
umbrella becomes faded and tattered, Ram Bharosa is so
desperate to own it that he tries to have it stolen. Kindly
Binya, seeing his torment, gives him the umbrella and in
exchange, Ram Bharosa has a bear's claw made into a pen-
dant for her. (68 pages)

Where it's reviewed:
Booklist, March 15, 1995, page 1327
Horn Book Guide, Fall 1995, page 294
Reading Teacher, October 1995, page 156
School Library Journal, March 1995, page 202

Awards the book has won:
Children's Literature Center Top Choice, 1995
Parenting Reading Magic Best Book, 1995

Other books by the same author:
Cherry Tree, 1991
The Hidden Pool, 1980
Tales Told at Twilight, 1970

Other books you might like:
Dave Jackson, *The Hidden Jewel*, 1992
    While traveling in India, John and his mother meet an Irish
    missionary and are drawn into her work.
Rudyard Kipling, *Rikki-Tikki-Tavi*, 1992
    Vigilantly protecting "his" family, a mongoose coura-
    geously battles and defeats two cobras who enter the home.
Robin McKinley, *Tales from the Jungle Book*, 1985
    An adaptation from Kipling's classic story tells of Mowgli,
    the child reared by wolves, and his many animal friends.

124

LOUISE BORDEN
ELIZABETH SAYLES, Illustrator

Albie the Lifeguard
(New York: Scholastic Inc., 1993)

Subject(s): Summer; Self-Confidence; Friendship
Age range(s): Grades K-2
Major character(s): Albie, Child (boy)
Time period(s): 1990s (1993)
Locale(s): United States

Summary: Reluctant to join his friends on the swim team early
in the summer because he cannot yet swim the length of the
pool, Albie contents himself "guarding" his backyard pool,
doing cannonballs into the town pool and watching his
friends' swim meets. Through his imaginative play as summer passes, Albie's confidence grows and he adds his own
name to the swim team list. (32 pages)

Where it's reviewed:
Booklist, February 15, 1993, page 1066
Children's Book Review Service, July 1993, page 145
Hornbook Guide, Fall 1993, page 250
Publishers Weekly, May 24, 1993, page 87
School Library Journal, June 1993, page 70

Other books by the same author:
Just in Time for Christmas, 1994
*Caps, Hats, Socks, and Mittens: A Book about the Four
    Seasons*, 1992
The Neighborhood Trucker, 1990

Other books you might like:
Marc Brown, *D.W. Flips*, 1987
    With a lot of practice and a little time, D. W. reaches her
    goal.
Mary Hoffman, *Amazing Grace*, 1991
    Grace refuses to be discouraged by others and pursues her
    acting dream.
Ann Herbert Scott, *Someday Rider*, 1989
    Determined to become a cowboy like his father, Kenny
    learns to ride a horse in time to join the roundup.

125

LOUISE BORDEN
TED LEWIN, Illustrator

Just in Time for Christmas
(New York, Scholastic Inc., 1994)

Subject(s): Christmas; Family Life; Animals/Dogs
Age range(s): Grades 1-3
Major character(s): Will Bryan, Child; Chandler, Friend;
    Luke, Dog
Time period(s): 1990s (1994)
Locale(s): Kentucky

Summary: As Christmas approaches, the Bryan relatives begin
arriving from homes in other states to the homestead where
Christmas has been celebrated for a hundred years. Although
Will worries about Luke who took off after a squirrel and
hasn't come home for five days, he becomes involved with his

cousins and other relatives in the making of the traditional cream candy. As the family stands on the porch pulling the sticky candy. Chandler walks up with Luke proving, once again, that Bryans always come home for Christmas. (32 pages)

Where it's reviewed:
Booklist, August 1994, page 2050
Horn Book Guide, Spring 1995, page 26
Library Talk, November 1994, page 30
New Advocate, Winter 1995, page 48
Publishers Weekly, September 19, 1994, page 30

Other books by the same author:
Albie the Lifeguard, 1993
Caps, Hats, Socks, and Mittens: A Book about the Four Seasons, 1992
The Neighborhood Trucker, 1990

Other books you might like:
Patricia Polacco, *The Trees of the Dancing Goats*, 1996
   A scarlet fever epidemic threatens to prevent any Christmas celebration until a healthy Jewish family provides a holiday treat for their Christian neighbors.
Candice F. Ransom, *One Christmas Dawn*, 1996
   During the winter of 1917, a young mountain girl's father left to find work in the city. On Christmas morning, she watches eagerly for his return.
Laura Ingalls Wilder, *Christmas in the Big Woods*, 1995
   Excerpted from *Little House in the Big Woods*, the story tells of the Wilder family gathering from afar to enjoy Christmas in their small Wisconsin cabin.
Susan Wojciechowski, *The Christmas Miracle of Jonathan Toomey*, 1995
   A bitter widower experiences the healing power of love as he carves a nativity set for a widow and her young son.

126

RUTH LERCHER BORNSTEIN, Author/Illustrator

Rabbit's Good News
(New York: Clarion Books, 1995)

Subject(s): Animals/Rabbits; Spring
Age range(s): Grades K-1
Major character(s): Rabbit, Rabbit
Time period(s): 1990s (1995)
Locale(s): United States

Summary: While her family sleeps in their burrow, early-rising Rabbit hops about in search of the faint sound she hears calling her. As the sun rises, Rabbit hops past a newly opened flower, a bee, and a worm. As she hops she also listens and finally knows what she's hearing, she quickly hops home to tell her family "Spring is here!" (32 pages)

Where it's reviewed:
Booklist, May 1, 1995, page 1579
Horn Book Guide, Fall 1995, page 259
Publishers Weekly, January 16, 1995, page 454
School Library Journal, April 1995, page 98

Other books by the same author:
A Beautiful Seashell, 1990
The Seedling Child, 1987

Little Gorilla, 1986

Other books you might like:
Craig Brown, *In the Spring*, 1994
   Illustrations support the brief text which describes the joy of spring on a farm.
Joyce Dunbar, *The Spring Rabbit*, 1994
   To compensate for being an only bunny, Smudge builds a leaf-and-twig brother in the fall and a snow sister in winter, but in spring his wish comes true with the birth of a real bunny.
Margaret Bloy Graham, *It's Spring!*, 1989
   Excitement about the arrival of spring prompts two cats to imagine how they could jump to express their happiness.

127

LADY BORTON
DEBORAH KOGAN RAY, Illustrator

Fat Chance!
(New York: Philomel Books, 1993)

Subject(s): Animals/Cats; Pets; Illness
Age range(s): Grades K-2
Major character(s): Marty Louise Whittsen, 1st Grader (lonely); Chancy, Cat (stray), Blind
Time period(s): Indeterminate Past
Locale(s): United States (farm)

Summary: Recovering from rheumatic fever, Marty is lonely when she is not allowed to return to school. Spotting a blind stray cat in the yard, Marty names him Chancy and feeds him all the while knowing that her mother's dislike of cats means that she has a "fat chance" of keeping him as a pet. By the time her mother notices the cat, Marty's patient care has tamed him leading her mother to accept the cat and use Marty's attachment to him to interest her in learning her letters. (32 pages)

Where it's reviewed:
Booklist, October 15, 1993, page 450
Children's Book Review Service, January 1994, page 49
Horn Book, September 1993, page 581
Reading Teacher, April 1994, page 563
School Library Journal, December 1993, page 80

Other books by the same author:
Junk Pile, 1995

Other books you might like:
Gloria Kamen, *Second-Hand Cat*, 1992
   When Louie moves he gives his cat to Nathan.
Inga Moore, *Six-Dinner Sid*, 1991
   Feline Sid is the pet to six different families until his secret is discovered.
Joan L. Nodset, *Come Here, Cat*, 1961
   A young girl's cat takes her on a merry chase to avoid being caught.

128

CANDY DAWSON BOYD

Chevrolet Saturdays

(New York: Macmillan, 1993)

Subject(s): Remarriage; Stepfathers; African Americans
Age range(s): Grades 5-7
Major character(s): Joey Davis, 5th Grader; Mr. Johnson, Stepfather
Time period(s): 1990s
Locale(s): Berkeley, California

Summary: Joey has a hard enough time accepting his parents' divorce, but finds it even more difficult to accept his mother's remarriage to Mr. Johnson. Joey's secret goal has always been to reunite his parents, but those plans have now been smashed. On top of that, Joey's fifth-grade teacher is difficult for him to get along with. A healing step occurs when Mr. Johnson goes to school to talk with the principal about Joey. As Joey learns to accept responsibility for his actions, he takes the first step to make his new family unit a cohesive one. (176 pages)

Where it's reviewed:
Booklist, May 15, 1995, page 1686
School Library Journal, May 1993, page 103
Publishers Weekly, May 24, 1993, page 88
Center for Children's Books. Bulletin, June 1993, page 309
Kirkus Reviews, June 1, 1993, page 716

Other books by the same author:
Fall Secrets, 1994
Seasons, 1994
Charles Pippin, 1987
Breadsticks and Blessing Places, 1985

Other books you might like:
Rosa Guy, *The Ups and Downs of Carl Davis III*, 1989
    Sent to live with his South Carolina grandmother, Carl encounters a prejudiced teacher for the first time which makes school miserable for him.
Lila Hopkins, *Talking Turkey*, 1989
    On Croaker's first day of 7th grade he ends up in the principal's office for gobbling like a turkey in class.
Michael Morpurgo, *Mr. Nobody's Eyes*, 1990
    When Harry decides that living with his stepfather is too much for him to bear, he runs away and takes his pet monkey with him.

129

CANDY DAWSON BOYD

Fall Secrets

(New York: Puffin, 1994)

Subject(s): African Americans; Acting; Self-Acceptance
Age range(s): Grades 6-7
Major character(s): Jessie Williams, Actress, Student—Junior High; Cassandra "Cass" Williams, Cheerleader, Student—High School (senior)
Time period(s): 1990s
Locale(s): Oakland, California

Summary: In Jessie's first year at a school for the performing arts, she worries about drama, grades and friends. Overriding these normal concerns is her feeling of inferiority compared to her older, lighter-skinned sister, Cass, who wants to be a doctor. The past few years have been hard for Jessie as she's had to endure the fires that swept through Berkeley and Oakland, her grandmother's Parkinson's disease and Cass's problems with her boyfriend. As Jessie quickly learns, this is all part of growing up. (216 pages)

Where it's reviewed:
Booklist, September 15, 1994, page 135
Publishers Weekly, August 8, 1994, page 440
School Library Journal, December 1994, page 104
Kliatt, January 1995, page 6

Other books by the same author:
Daddy, Daddy, Be There, 1995
Circle of Gold, 1994
Seasons, 1994
Forever Friends, 1992

Other books you might like:
Angela Johnson, *Toning the Sweep*, 1993
    Emily and her mother travel to the desert to help Emily's grandmother close up her home after she's diagnosed with cancer.
Rosa Guy, *The Music of Summer*, 1992
    Once-fun summer trips with light-skinned Cathy are now demoralizing for darker-skinned Sarah, as Cathy's friends treat her shabbily.
Brenda Seabrooke, *The Bridges of Summer*, 1992
    Sarah Jane is sent by her irresponsible mother to stay with her grandmother on her Gullah Island where she learns about being part of a family.
Rita Williams-Garcia, *Blue Tights*, 1988
    Joyce's attempts to succeed at classical ballet are defeated by her physical development; at last she finds her niche in an African dance troupe.

130

MARIE BRADBY
CHRIS K. SOENTPIET, Illustrator

More than Anything Else

(New York: Orchard Books, 1995)

Subject(s): African Americans; Historical; Determination
Age range(s): Grades K-3
Major character(s): Booker T. Washington, 9-Year-Old
Time period(s): Indeterminate Past
Locale(s): West Virginia

Summary: As Booker labors beside his father and brother packing salt into barrels he thinks only of his desire to learn to read. Booker yearns for the freedom that literacy will give him and vows to share his newly acquired skill with others. (32 pages)

Where it's reviewed:
Booklist, July 1995, page 1882
Children's Book Review Service, December 1995, page 43
Horn Book, September 1995, page 586
Kirkus Reviews, August 1, 1995, page 1107

School Library Journal, November 1995, page 64

Other books you might like:

Dolores Johnson, *Papa's Stories*, 1994
  Not until Kari learns to read does she discover that her illiterate father has been making up the stories he has "read" to her for years.
Tony Johnston, *Amber on the Mountain*, 1994
  Isolated in her family's mountain home, a new world opens to Amber when she is taught to read and write.
Nancy Smiler Levinson, *Clara and the Bookwagon*, 1988
  The arrival of a horse-drawn bookwagon at Clara's family farm provides her with the means to fulfill her dreams and expand her horizons through reading.
Andrea Davis Pinkney, *Dear Benjamin Banneker*, 1994
  Literacy played an important role in the life Benjamin Banneker, a free black man during the early years of America's development.

131

VIRGINIA BRADLEY

Wait and See

(New York: Cobblehill/Dutton, 1994)

Subject(s): Orphans; Friendship
Age range(s): Grades 4-6
Major character(s): Amy Ryker, 11-Year-Old, 6th Grader; Violetta Mills, 6th Grader; Judge Ryker, Judge, Grandfather (Amy's)
Time period(s): 1990s
Locale(s): Newton Grove

Summary: Orphaned since she was two, Amy's family consists of her grandfather, Judge Ryker, and Doff, their housekeeper. Doff returns to England to care for her own ailing mother and Amy knows she'll miss her terribly. When a new student, Violetta, arrives at school, Amy at first thinks she's just plain weird, but as she gets to know her, she looks forward to having Violetta as her friend. Unfortunately Violetta's mother decides to leave and moves to another town in her twelve-year quest to find the husband who abandoned her. Amy loses two friends, but immediately concocts a plan to get Violetta to return. (162 pages)

Where it's reviewed:
Publishers Weekly, July 4, 1994, page 65
Booklist, August 1994, page 2042
Voice of Youth Advocates, December 1994, page 270
Kirkus Reviews, July 15, 1994, page 978
Center for Children's Books. Bulletin, September 1994, page 6

Other books you might like:
Lois Lowry, *Rabble Starkey*, 1987
  Friends Rabble and Veronica share many adventures during their year as sixth graders.
Jan Slepian, *Getting on with It*, 1985
  After her parents divorce, Berry visits her grandmother, makes new friends, and sorts out her feelings about her changing life.

Phyllis Anderson Wood, *Then I'll Be Home Free*, 1986
  After losing her grandmother, Rosemary is thankful she has her friend, Arthur, to help her.

132

BERKELEY BREATHED, Author/Illustrator

Goodnight Opus

(Boston: Little, Brown and Company, 1993)

Subject(s): Imagination; Bedtime; Stories in Rhyme
Age range(s): Grades 1-3
Major character(s): Opus, Penguin; Grandma, Grandmother
Time period(s): Indeterminate Past
Locale(s): United States

Summary: On the night that Grandma begins reading Opus's favorite bedtime story for the 210th time, Opus impulsively interjects a few lines to the story. Grandma is not pleased with his antics, but she dozes off before completing the story so Opus carries on with his imaginative extension of the tale. (32 pages)

Where it's reviewed:
Booklist, January 1, 1994, page 832
Children's Bookwatch, January 1994, page 4
Horn Book Guide, Spring 1994, page 27
Publishers Weekly, September 27, 1993, page 62
School Library Journal, January 1994, page 82

Other books by the same author:
Red Ranger Came Calling, 1994
The Last Basselope: One Ferocious Story, 1992
A Wish for Wings That Work: An Opus Christmas Story, 1991

Other books you might like:
Arlene Alda, *Sheep, Sheep, Sheep, Help Me Fall Asleep*, 1992
  A child's attempt to hasten sleep by counting sheep is complicated by the arrival of many other animals before the sheep appear.
Margaret Wise Brown, *Goodnight Moon*, 1947
  In the original version of Opus's favorite bedtime story, the bunny says goodnight to all the objects in the great green room before bidding the moon goodnight.
Michael Foreman, *Dad! I Can't Sleep*, 1995
  Dad's going-to-sleep suggestions to Little Panda fail to produce the desired effect.

133

ROSEMARY BRECKLER
DEBORAH KOGAN RAY, Illustrator

Sweet Dried Apples: A Vietnamese Wartime Chldhood

(Boston: Houghton Mifflin, 1996)

Subject(s): Vietnam War; Grandparents
Age range(s): Grades K-2
Major character(s): Lieu Noi, Refugee; Ong Noi, Grandfather, Herbalist; Duc Noi, Brother (younger)
Time period(s): 1970s
Locale(s): Vietnam, South

Summary: Lieu awakens to find that her father has gone off to fight in the war and her grandfather has come to take care of them. Things are fine for a time and grandfather teaches them something about the herbs which he uses, but then, as the war comes closer, grandfather goes away. The children continue to pick the herbs and dry them as they were taught and when grandfather returns they are able to help heal the people hurt when the village is bombed. Life in Vietnam is over for the family, however, and they are able to find a boat which they hope will take them to freedom. (unpaged)

Where it's reviewed:
Booklist, September 1, 1996, page 124

Other books by the same author:
Hoang Breaks the Lucky Teapot, 1992

Other books you might like:
Sherry Garland, *The Lotus Seed*, 1993
    A grandmother brings a lotus seed with her from Vietnam to help her remember her life there.
Allen Say, *Grandfather's Journey*, 1993
    A Japanese American man remembers his grandfather and how the man was torn between his two homes.
Melanie Scheller, *My Grandfather's Hat*, 1992
    A young boy remembers his relationship with his grandfather and the hat he once had.

134

HERBIE BRENNAN

The Mystery Machine

(New York: Margaret K. McElderry Books, 1995)

Subject(s): Aliens; Science Fiction; Humor
Age range(s): Grades 4-6
Major character(s): Mrs. Pomfrey-Parkinson, Neighbor, Alien; Hubert Baker, Child, Friend (Slider's); Slider Coffrey, Friend (Hubert's)
Locale(s): Pugford, England

Summary: Hubert's new neighbor has such a reputation for being disagreeable that everyone in the village thinks she's a witch. However, when Hubert's plan to gain the experience needed to become a human cannonball with the circus launches him into the air and through the roof of Mrs. Pomfrey-Parkinson's shed, he finds himself face-to-face with a spaceship. After pressing a few buttons, Hubert has a surprising ride to an alien spaceship orbiting earth. When he returns to the shed, he is captured by Mrs. Pomfrey-Parkinson and threatened with death to prevent him from divulging the aliens' plan to take over Britain and then the world. Slider comes to his rescue and is also captured, but both boys escape and use the knowledge divulged by the aliens to bring the plot to an end. (91 pages)

Where it's reviewed:
Booklist, May 1, 1995, page 1571
Horn Book, September 1995, page 596
Horn Book Guide, Fall 1995, page 294
School Library Journal, July 1995, page 76

Other books by the same author:
Emily and the Werewolf, 1993

Other books you might like:
Janet Asimov, *The Norby Series*, 1983-1991
    With co-author Isaac Asimov, the series presents the adventures of Norby the robot and his human friend Jeff.
Annette Curtis Klause, *Alien Secrets*, 1993
    Puck, a human teenager, and her alien friend Hush must locate an important piece of alien art which Hush is transporting.
Pamela F. Service, *Stinker from Space*, 1988
    An alien takes the form of a skunk to disguise his presence on Earth.

135

JAN BRETT, Author/Illustrator

Armadillo Rodeo

(New York: G. P. Putnam's Sons, 1995)

Subject(s): Animals/Armadillos; Rodeos; American West
Age range(s): Grades K-3
Major character(s): Bo, Armadillo; Harmony Jean, Child, Rodeo Rider
Time period(s): 1990s (1995)
Locale(s): Curly H Ranch, Texas

Summary: Nearsighted Bo mistakes a pair of new red cowboy boots for a cute young armadillo and tries to get a closer look. On the feet of a young cowgirl heading for a rodeo, the boots are always one step ahead of Bo as he hurries through bucking horses and charging bulls to reach the bright red color. By the end of the day, when tired Harmony Jean kicks off her boots and Bo finally meets his "friend" face to face, he quickly realizes his error. (32 pages)

Where it's reviewed:
Booklist, September 15, 1995, page 174
Children's Book Review Service, November 1995, page 26
Horn Book, January 1996, page 59
Publishers Weekly, July 17, 1995, page 229
School Library Journal, October 1995, page 97

Other books by the same author:
The Trouble with Trolls, 1992
Annie and the Wild Animals, 1989
Fritz and the Beautiful Horses, 1981

Other books you might like:
Larry Dane Brimner, *Merry Christmas, Old Armadillo*, 1995
    Thinking his friends have forgotten him, Old Armadillo dozes in his easy chair while the friends arrive to decorate his yard.
Lynne Cherry, *The Armadillo from Amarillo*, 1994
    Curious Sasparillo tours his native state, sending postcards about his travels to his cousin Brillo.
Mary Elise Monsell, *Armadillo*, 1991
    Whenever it rains, Armadillo is cozy and warm inside his house.

136

PATIENCE BREWSTER, Author/Illustrator

Two Bushy Badgers

(Boston: Little, Brown and Company, 1995)

Subject(s): Animals/Badgers; Friendship; Stories in Rhyme
Age range(s): Grades K-2
Major character(s): Arthur, Badger, Friend; Ollie, Badger, Friend
Time period(s): 1990s (1995)
Locale(s): Fictional Country

Summary: Arthur and Ollie share a companionable life until the day they are both cranky and speak unkindly to one another. Harsh words stay suspended in the miserable silence now separating them. In time they recognize their friendship is more important than their anger and they resolve their differences. (32 pages)

Where it's reviewed:
Booklist, April 1, 1995, page 1422
Horn Book Guide, Fall 1995, page 259
Publishers Weekly, April 24, 1995, page 71
School Library Journal, June 1995, page 78

Other books by the same author:
Rabbit Inn, 1991

Other books you might like:
Russell Hoban, *Best Friends for Frances*, 1969
    When Albert excludes his friend Frances from his ''all boys'' game, Frances seeks out her younger sister and the two of them teach the boys a lesson.
Arnold Lobel, *Frog and Toad Are Friends*, 1970
    The award-winning celebration of friendship shows the give-and-take necessary to make it successful.
Nancy Jewell, *Two Silly Trolls*, 1992
    In a beginning reader, five brief stories showcase the challenges to a friendship of two trolls.

137

RAYMOND BRIGGS, Author/Illustrator

The Bear

(New York: Random House, 1994)

Subject(s): Animals/Bears; Imagination; Parent and Child
Age range(s): Grades K-3
Major character(s): Tilly, Child (imaginative); Bear, Bear
Time period(s): 1990s (1994)
Locale(s): England (Tilly's home)

Summary: When an enormous white bear climbs in the window of Tilly's room, he is promptly tucked into bed. The next morning, Tilly reports his arrival to her parents who nonchalantly ask all the appropriate questions to humor their daughter's imagination. Tilly becomes annoyed when she has to clean up after the non-housebroken bear, but still wants him to stay. The bear has his own plans and at bedtime slips out the window as quietly as he came. (36 pages)

Where it's reviewed:
Booklist, February 1, 1995, page 1008

Horn Book, March 1995, page 182
Kirkus Reviews, December 15, 1994, page 1558
Quill and Quire, September 1994, page 75
School Library Journal, February 1995, page 72

Other books by the same author:
Jim and the Beanstalk, 1989
Father Christmas, 1981
The Snowman, 1978

Other books you might like:
Jez Alborough, *It's the Bear!*, 1994
    Eddie and Mom are going back to the woods for a picnic and Eddie fears that he may meet the bear again.
Helen Cooper, *The Bear under the Stairs*, 1993
    William is so afraid of the bear he imagines living under the stairs that he throws food into the closet to feed it until his mother's nose leads to a closet cleaning.
Hermann Moers, *Katie and the Big Brave Bear*, 1995
    Katie's fear of being home alone is assuaged when a brave bear steps out of the pages of a favorite book and accompanies her on a search for her mother.
Nanette Newman, *There's a Bear in the Bath!*, 1994
    Liza's day is enlivened when she finds Jam, a friendly bear in her garden.
Joanne Ryder, *Bears out There*, 1995
    In his daydreams a young boy imagines the daily endeavors of a bear parallelling his own activities.

138

LARRY DANE BRIMNER
DOMINIC CATALANO, Illustrator

Merry Christmas, Old Armadillo

(Honesdale, PA: Boyds Mills Press, 1995)

Subject(s): Animals; Friendship; Christmas
Age range(s): Grades K-2
Major character(s): Old Armadillo, Armadillo
Time period(s): 1990s (1995)
Locale(s): Southwest

Summary: Christmas Eve finds Old Armadillo alone and lonely with no mail in the mailbox or friends stopping to visit. He settles into his easy chair for a nap near the fire while secretly his many animal friends arrive bringing gifts and decorations for his home. As Old Armadillo sleeps, preparations are completed and the friends awaken Old Armadillo and wish him a Merry Christmas. (32 pages)

Where it's reviewed:
Booklist, September 15, 1995, page 168
Children's Book Review Service, October 1995, page 14
Horn Book Guide, Spring 1996, page 21
Publishers Weekly, September 18, 1995, page 98
School Library Journal, October 1995, page 35

Other books by the same author:
Eliot Fry's Goodbye, 1994
Max and Felix, 1993
Country Bear's Surprise, 1991

Other books you might like:
Jan Brett, *Armadillo Rodeo*, 1995
> Nearsighted Bo mistakes a pair of red cowboy boots for a a cute armadillo and spends the day in pursuit of ''her.''
Lynne Cherry, *The Armadillo from Amarillo*, 1994
> Curious Sasparillo tours his native state, sending postcards about his travels to his cousin Brillo.
Jean Ciavonne, *Carlos, Light the Farolito*, 1995
> On the final night of Los Posadas, family and neighbors will gather at Carlos' home to complete the reenactment of the Christmas story.
Mary Elise Monsell, *Armadillo*, 1991
> Whenever it rains, Armadillo is cozy and warm inside his house.

139

PAT BRISSON
MARYANN COCCA-LEFFLER, Illustrator

Wanda's Roses
(Honesdale, PA: Boyds Mills Press, 1994)

Subject(s): Neighbors and Neighborhoods; City Life; Gardens and Gardening
Age range(s): Grades K-3
Major character(s): Wanda, Child, Gardener
Time period(s): 1990s (1994)
Locale(s): United States (corner of Fillmore and Hudson)

Summary: Noticing a bare, thorny bush in a litter-strewn vacant lot, Wanda is convinced that she has found a rose bush which simply needs a little more sun and air in order to bloom. Wanda's efforts to clean the debris from the lot attract the attention of her neighbors who are secretly skeptical of the potential for this bush to bloom. Wanda patiently tends the forlorn-looking bush and then invites everyone to a tea party in her ''Rose Garden.'' The guests arrive, each toting a rose bush, and Wanda's dream comes true. (32 pages)

Where it's reviewed:
Horn Book Guide, Fall 1994, page 265
Kirkus Reviews, May 15, 1994, page 696
Publishers Weekly, May 16, 1994, page 64
Reading Teacher, Fall 1995, page 422
School Library Journal, December 1994, page 71

Other books by the same author:
Kate on the Coast, 1992
Magic Carpet, 1991
Kate Heads West, 1990

Other books you might like:
Mary Louise Cuneo, *How to Grow a Picket Fence*, 1993
> The unobservant neighbors are oblivious to a child's efforts to grow a picket fence until the day it emerges fully grown in the vacant corner lot.
Satomi Ichikawa, *Nora's Roses*, 1993
> Observing passersby picking roses from her bush inspires an imaginary adventure for a bored, sick-in-bed child.
Alisandra Jezek, *Miloli's Orchids*, 1991
> Seeing orchids threatened by a volcano a young Hawaiian girl attempts to save them.

140

BILL BRITTAIN
JAMES WARHOLA, Illustrator

The Mystery of the Several Sevens
(New York: HarperCollinsPublishers, 1994)

Subject(s): Magic; Fantasy; Adventure and Adventurers
Age range(s): Grades 3-5
Major character(s): Mr. Merlin, Teacher (substitute), Wizard; Becky Rush, 5th Grader; Simon Toller, 5th Grader
Time period(s): 1990s (1994); Indeterminate
Locale(s): United States (Becky and Simon's classroom); Fictional Country (fairyland)

Summary: Once again Mr. Merlin substitutes in Becky and Simon's class, assuring them of an exciting day. Indeed, when the other fifth graders go outside for recess, Mr. Merlin transports Becky and Simon to a land populated by characters from fairy tales where they must solve the mystery of a stolen sack of diamonds. Using a witch's riddle and the morning math lesson on Roman numerals, Simon and Becky determine the name of the thief and return to the classroom just as the others are returning from recess. (79 pages)

Where it's reviewed:
Booklist, November 15, 1994, page 600
Horn Book Guide, Spring 1995, page 73
School Library Journal, December 1994, page 104

Other books by the same author:
Shape-Changer, 1994
The Wizards and the Monster, 1994
The Wish Giver, 1983 (Newbery Honor Book)

Other books you might like:
Eth Clifford, *Help! I'm a Prisoner in the Library*, 1979
> When two children are locked in the library, they must use their wits to find a way out.
Dick King-Smith, *Harry's Mad*, 1988
> After he is stolen, Mad, a talking parrot, is able to find his way home.
Lucinda Landon, *Meg Mackintosh and the Mystery in the Locked Library*, 1993
> Using clues that test their library skills Meg and her friend race the clock to find a missing book before the library opens.
Jon Scieszka, *Knights of the Kitchen Table*, 1991
> The TimeWarp Trio travels back in time to join Lancelot in his adventures.

141

ERROL BROOME
ANN JAMES, Illustrator

Tangles
(New York: Alfred A. Knopf, 1994)

Subject(s): Animals/Cats; Guilt; Honesty
Age range(s): Grades 3-4
Major character(s): Mrs. Cochran, Aged Person, Neighbor (kindly); Sophie, Child, Thief; Tangles, Cat
Time period(s): 1990s (1993)

Locale(s): Cattlesea, Australia

Summary: When Sophie spots kittens for sale, she is determined to own one as a replacement for her deceased cat, but her attempts to get enough money from her parents and brother are unsuccessful. Dejected, she finds a wallet belonging to her elderly neighbor on the ground from which she ''borrows'' five dollars to buy the kitten. Now consumed with guilt, she avoids Mrs. Cochran and antagonizes her family and friends with her irritable behavior. Eventually, Sophie realizes that she must face Mrs. Cochran, her fears, her guilt and, if necessary, the loss of her beloved Tangles. Orginally published in Australia in 1993. (108 pages)

Where it's reviewed:
Booklist, March 15, 1994, page 1347
Bulletin of the Center for Children's Books, February 1994, page 182
Kirkus Reviews, April 15, 1994, page 552
Publishers Weekly, February 28, 1994, page 88
School Library Journal, April 1994, page 124

Other books by the same author:
Dear Mr. Sprouts, 1993

Other books you might like:
C.S. Adler, *Courtyard Cat*, 1995
  Lindsay's friendship with a stray cat helps her to overcome the guilt which she feels for her younger brother's serious accident.
Johanna Hurwitz, *The Cold and Hot Winter*, 1988
  Three friends find that missing objects and suspicions about the identity of the thief put a strain on their relationship.
Colleen O'Shaughnessy McKenna, *Live from the Fifth Grade*, 1994
  Marsha agrees to join with class pest Roger and his friend to discover the identity of a thief who has taken school equipment.

142

JANE CLARK BROWN, Author/Illustrator

George Washington's Ghost
(Boston: Houghton Mifflin Company, 1994)

Subject(s): Theater; Family Life
Age range(s): Grades 3-5
Major character(s): Celinda Noodle, Child, Sister (youngest); Pliny Noodle, Child, Brother; Mrs. Noodle, Mother, Widow(er)
Time period(s): 19th century (1830-1840)
Locale(s): New England

Summary: After the death of her husband, a travelling puppeteer, Mrs. Noodle struggles to support her four children until the family realizes the puppet wagon can also be their source of income. Celinda, the shortest, is unable to operate the marionettes so she opens and closes the curtain and collects the money. As the performers practice and improve their act, Celinda's determination to turn Pliny into the curtain-puller and create her own act seems to get her into one scrape after another. (86 pages)

Where it's reviewed:
Bulletin of the Center for Children's Books, December 1994, page 122
Horn Book Guide, Spring 1995, page 73
Library Talk, May 1995, page 41
School Library Journal, November 1994, page 102

Other books you might like:
Carol Ryrie Brink, *Caddie Woodlawn*, 1935
  The Newbery Medal winner tells of the exploits of Caddie, a tomboy who preferred climbing trees with her brothers to traditional ''girl'' pursuits.
Marguerite De Angeli, *Thee, Hannah!*, 1940
  Strong-willed and imaginative, Hannah impulsively follows her ideas without considering if they are consistent with her Quaker faith.
Laura Ingalls Wilder, *Farmer Boy*, 1953
  Almanzo and his brother and sisters find time for simple pleasures when the farm chores are complete.

143

LAURIE KRASNY BROWN
MARC BROWN, Illustrator

Rex and Lilly Family Time
(Boston: Little, Brown and Company, 1995)

Series: Dino Easy Reader
Subject(s): Dinosaurs; Family Life; Brothers and Sisters
Age range(s): Grades K-2
Major character(s): Lilly, Dinosaur, Sister (older); Rex, Dinosaur, Brother (younger)
Time period(s): 1990s (1995)
Locale(s): Fictional Country

Summary: In the first of three stories, Lilly and Rex plan and implement a birthday surprise for their mother, refusing all offers from their parents to help until the party's over. Then, they gladly accept help with the clean-up. The second story describes how the family, overwhelmed with housework, acquires a robot who is a little too efficient and can't seem to recognize too much of a good thing. The last story tells of Rex and Lilly's search for the perfect pet. (32 pages)

Where it's reviewed:
Booklist, April 15, 1995, page 1509
Horn Book Guide, Fall 1995, page 288
Publishers Weekly, October 10, 1995, page 63
School Library Journal, August 1995, page 115

Other books by the same author:
Rex and Lilly Playtime, 1995
Dinosaurs Travel, 1991

Other books you might like:
Marc Brown, *Arthur's Family Vacation*, 1993
  When rain threatens to spoil their beach vacation, Arthur and his family work together to make the best of difficult circumstances.
Lillian Hoban, *Arthur's Honey Bear*, 1974
  Arthur plans to sell all his toys, but finds it hard to give up his special honey bear.

Russell Hoban, *A Bargain for Frances*, 1970
Frances's friend Thelma has eyes on her new china tea set and tries to trick Frances into parting with it.

Else Holmelund Minarik, *Little Bear*, 1957
The first I Can Read Book features the gentle family life of a bear and his loving mother and father.

144

M.K. BROWN, Author/Illustrator

Let's Go Camping with Mr. Sillypants
(New York: Crown Publishers, Inc., 1995)

Subject(s): Camps and Camping; Dreams and Nightmares; Humor
Age range(s): Grades K-2
Major character(s): Mr. Sillypants, Camper
Time period(s): 1990s (1995)
Locale(s): United States

Summary: Members of the Nature Club begin their camping weekend without Mr. Sillypants who oversleeps and misses the group's departure. Rather than miss the trip, when Mr. Sillypants awakens, he hurries into the forest trying to follow the footprints on the path. Soon he is distracted by birds and butterflies and finds that he is lost in the woods. After eating lunch he falls asleep and his dream gives him an idea for finding the rest of the group. (32 pages)

Where it's reviewed:
Booklist, September 15, 1995, page 174
Horn Book Guide, Fall 1995, page 259
New York Times Book Review, August 27, 1995, page 27
Publishers Weekly, June 19, 1995, page 59
School Library Journal, August 1995, page 115

Other books by the same author:
Let's Go Swimming with Mr. Sillypants, 1992
Sally's Room, 1992

Other books you might like:
Lillian Hoban, *Arthur's Camp-Out*, 1993
Arthur embarks on a solo camping trip in the woods near his home where he encounters unanticipated problems.
Robin Michal Koontz, *Chicago and the Cat: The Camping Trip*, 1994
On a camping trip with friend Cat, rabbit Chicago enjoys the hiking and rafting as well as the unexpected surprises.
Peggy Parish, *Amelia Bedelia Goes Camping*, 1985
Following directions literally, as always, Amelia Bedelia gives new meaning to camping terms such as ''pitch'' the tent.
Marilyn Sadler, *P.J. Funnybunny Camps Out*, 19993
On a ''boys only'' camping trip, P. J. and his friends are joined by some girls and they all discover that camping is hard work for everyone.

145

MARC BROWN, Author/Illustrator

Arthur Writes a Story
(Boston: Little, Brown, 1996)

Series: Arthur Adventure
Subject(s): Authorship; Family Life
Age range(s): Grades K-2
Major character(s): Arthur, Aardvark, Student; D.W., Aardvark, Sister; Mr. Ratburn, Rat, Teacher
Time period(s): 1990s
Locale(s): United States

Summary: Arthur's class is assigned to write a story and Arthur is having trouble deciding what to write about. At first he thinks he will write about how he got his dog but when he reads it to DW she thinks it is boring so he tries to find another subject. He decides on a science fiction fantasy story but keeps changing it as he talks to his friends. When he finally presents it to the class, it is not successful so he goes back to telling his original story which is much better received. (unpaged)

Where it's reviewed:
School Library Journal, September 1996, page 170
Booklist, September 15, 1996, page 245

Other books by the same author:
Arthur's TV Trouble, 1995
Arthur's First Sleepover, 1994
Arthur's Chicken Pox, 1994

Other books you might like:
Judy Delton, *The Goose Who Wrote a Book*, 1982
Goose changes the character in her book on the advice of friends, but the publisher advises her to return to her original idea.
Judith A. Enderle, *What's the Matter, Kelly Beans?*, 1996
Kelly loves to read and write but does not feel as talented as the rest of the family.
Maira Kalman, *Max Makes a Million*, 1990
Max, the dog, finally sells his book of poetry and is able to travel to Europe.
Marissa Moss, *Amelia's Notebook*, 1995
Amelia keeps a notebook of her feelings and ideas about moving, school, friends and other important things in her life.

146

MARC BROWN, Author/Illustrator

Arthur's Chicken Pox
(Boston: Little, Brown and Company, 1994)

Series: Arthur Adventure
Subject(s): Illness; Brothers and Sisters; Family Life
Age range(s): Grades K-3
Major character(s): Arthur, Aardvark, Brother (older); D.W., Aardvark, Sister (younger)
Time period(s): 1990s (1994)
Locale(s): United States

Summary: Arthur's family is planning a trip to the circus when Arthur becomes ill with the chicken pox. While he itches and worries about missing the circus, D.W. steams to see all the attention he receives, but kindly promises to bring him a balloon. As it turns out, by the morning of the circus trip, Arthur is healed, but D.W. is covered with spots. (32 pages)

Where it's reviewed:
Booklist, May 15, 1994, page 1683
Horn Book, May 1994, page 338
New York Times Book Review, May 22, 1994, page 34
Publishers Weekly, May 2, 1994, page 306
School Library Journal, June 1994, page 96

Awards the book has won:
International Reading Association Children's Choice, 1995

Other books by the same author:
Arthur Writes a Story, 1996
Arthur's TV Trouble, 1995
Arthur's First Sleepover, 1994
Arthur Meets the President, 1991

Other books you might like:
True Kelley, *I've Got Chicken Pox*, 1994
  The novelty of missing school and enjoying special foods is soon replaced by the agony of itching and fever for a young sufferer of chicken pox.
Grace Maccarone, *Itchy, Itchy Chickenpox*, 1992
  A rhyming, beginning reader expresses the humorous aspects of an itchy illness.
Gunilla Wolde, *Betsy and the Chicken Pox*, 1975
  When Betsy washes off the pretend spots she's painted on her face, she discovers real ones have appeared.
Harriet Ziefert, *When Daddy Had the Chicken Pox*, 1991
  Having Daddy sick with the chicken pox is no more fun than having them yourself.

147

MARC BROWN, Author/Illustrator

Arthur's Family Vacation

(Boston: Little Brown and Company, 1993)

Series: Arthur Adventure
Subject(s): Vacations; Family Life; Animals
Age range(s): Grades K-2
Major character(s): Arthur, Aardvark, Brother (older); D.W., Aardvark, Sister (middle child)
Time period(s): 1990s (1993)
Locale(s): United States (New England seashore)

Summary: A week-long family vacation is not appealing to Arthur who would prefer being at camp with his best friend to being cooped up in a motel room with D. W. while the rain pours down. Putting his camping experience to good use, Arthur initiates field trips, a favorite camp activity when it rains. By the final day of the vacation, the sun shines and the family has one day at the beach before returning home. (32 pages)

Where it's reviewed:
Booklist, May 15, 1993, page 1695
Horn Book, May 1993, page 311
Kirkus Reviews, May 15, 1993, page 656

Publishers Weekly, May 17, 1993, page 79
School Library Journal, May 1993, page 81

Other books by the same author:
Arthur Meets the President, 1991
Arthur's Pet Business, 1990
Arthur's Eyes, 1979

Other books you might like:
Stan Berenstain, *The Berenstain Bears and Too Much Vacation*, 1989
  The Bear family's vacation in the Great Grizzly Mountains turns out to be a succession of unfortunate mishaps. Co-author Jan Berenstain.
Franz Brandenberg, *A Fun Weekend*, 1991
  The plans for the weekend in the country do not proceed as expected, but the family has fun anyway.
David McPhail, *Emma's Vacation*, 1987
  Emma and her parents have differing opinions about what is a "good" vacation.

148

MARC BROWN, Author/Illustrator

Arthur's First Sleepover

(Boston: Little, Brown and Company, 1994)

Series: Arthur Adventure
Subject(s): Animals/Aardvarks; Sleep; Fear
Age range(s): Grades K-3
Major character(s): Arthur, Aardvark, Brother; D.W., Aardvark, Sister (younger); Buster, Rabbit, Friend (Arthur's)
Time period(s): 1990s (1994)
Locale(s): United States

Summary: All week, as Arthur prepares for his first sleepover in a backyard tent, D.W. and the kids at school talk about an alien spaceship sighting in their area. Fearful Buster suddenly is unable to come, but a phone call between the two moms straightens that out. Arthur and two friends settle into the tent, frightened first by strange footsteps from a pizza delivery man and later by a strange light that turns out to be D.W. Arthur and Buster have an idea that will settle the score with D.W. (32 pages)

Where it's reviewed:
Booklist, October 1, 1994, page 331
Horn Book, January 1995, page 75
Kirkus Reviews, November 15, 1994, page 1523
Publishers Weekly, October 24, 1994, page 61
School Library Journal, October 1994, page 86

Awards the book has won:
International Reading Association Children's Choice, 1995

Other books by the same author:
Arthur Writes a Story, 1996
Arthur's TV Trouble, 1995
Arthur and the True Francine, 1981

Other books you might like:
Carol Carrick, *Sleep Out*, 1973
  In his eagerness to try out his new camping gear, Christo-

pher does not wait until his father can accompany him and then regrets his decision. Co-author Donald Carrick.

Lillian Hoban, *Arthur's Camp-Out*, 1993
  Although Arthur has no friends to accompany him on a camp-out, he prefers to go alone rather than join his sister and her friends—at least until it gets dark.

Bernard Waber, *Ira Sleeps Over*, 1972
  Ira's excitement about sleeping over at a friends is dampened by concerns for his teddy bear who will be left behind.

149

MARC BROWN, Author/Illustrator

Arthur's New Puppy

(Boston: Little, Brown and Company, 1993)

Series: Arthur Adventure
Subject(s): Animals/Dogs; Pets; Animals/Aardvarks
Age range(s): Grades K-2
Major character(s): Pal, Dog; Arthur, Aardvark, Brother; D.W., Aardvark, Sister
Time period(s): 1990s (1993)
Locale(s): Fictional Country

Summary: Arthur's enthusiasm for a new puppy is soon dampened by myriad puppy misbehaviors such as crying at night and wetting on the carpet. When Arthur's parents state their intention to banish Pal to the garage, the key disappears so Pal stays in the house a little longer. D.W. has her own view of the puppy's future and it's not good. Arthur works diligently to train his pet and makes enough progress for Pal to be allowed to stay. (32 pages)

Where it's reviewed:
Booklist, December 1, 1993, page 696
Horn Book, January 1994, page 93
Kirkus Reviews, October 1, 1993, page 1270
Publishers Weekly, August 30, 1993, page 95
School Library Journal, February 1994, page 78

Other books by the same author:
Arthur's Pet Business, 1990
Arthur's Baby, 1987
Arthur's Tooth, 1985

Other books you might like:
Bunny Hoest, *Howard Huge Comes to Stay*, 1992
  When they find a stray St. Bernard, Jason and Jennifer try to hide it from their parents until they convince them to agree to a dog.
Mercer Mayer, *Just Me & My Puppy*, 1985
  Despite the inevitable misbehaviors of a young animal, a puppy is a wonderful pet.
Cynthia Rylant, *Henry and Mudge*, 1987
  In the first book of a popular series about a boy and his pet, Henry successfully lobbies his parents for a dog companion.
Rosemary Wells, *Lucy Comes to Stay*, 1994
  Mary Elizabeth endures typical puppy mischief such as chewed belongings as she learns to care for her new pet.

150

MARC BROWN, Author/Illustrator

D.W. Rides Again!

(Boston: Little, Brown and Company, 1993)

Series: D.W.
Subject(s): Bicycles and Bicycling; Brothers and Sisters
Age range(s): Grades K-2
Major character(s): D.W., Aardvark, Sister; Arthur, Aardvark, Brother; Father, Aardvark
Time period(s): 1990s (1993)
Locale(s): United States

Summary: Eager to use her new pink bicycle without the training wheels, D.W. accepts riding and safety lessons from patient and cautious older brother Arthur. After removing the training wheels, Father takes D.W. out for one final test of her ability to handle a two-wheeler. A mishap during the ride convinces D.W. that Father is the one who needs more practice and she offers him the training wheels. (28 pages)

Where it's reviewed:
Booklist, November 1, 1993, page 526
Horn Book, September 1993, page 582
Publishers Weekly, August 30, 1993, page 95
School Library Journal, December 1993, page 80

Other books by the same author:
D.W. the Picky Eater, 1995
Arthur's Chicken Pox, 1994
Arthur's First Sleepover, 1994
Arthur's New Puppy, 1993
D.W. Thinks Big, 1993

Other books you might like:
Stan Berenstain, *The Bike Lesson*, 1964
  A gift of a new bike comes with Dad's special lessons, but Small Bear learns to ride anyway. Jan Berenstain, co-author
Crescent Dragonwagon, *Annie Flies the Birthday Bike*, 1993
  With practice, Annie masters riding the two-wheeler she receives for her birthday.
Ashley Wolff, *Stella and Roy*, 1993
  Confident big sister Stella on her tricycle challenges her younger brother Roy on his coasting bike to a race.

151

MARC BROWN, Author/Illustrator

D.W. the Picky Eater

(Boston: Little, Brown and Company, 1995)

Subject(s): Animals/Aardvarks; Food; Behavior
Age range(s): Grades K-3
Major character(s): D.W., Aardvark, Sister (younger); Arthur, Aardvark, Brother; Grandma Thora, Aardvark, Grandmother
Time period(s): 1990s (1995)
Locale(s): United States

Summary: D.W. loudly expresses her food preferences, accidentally drops the snacks she doesn't like in the dirt and sneaks food to the dog while the family is eating. When D.W.

throws a temper tantrum in a restaurant because her salad contains a piece of spinach, she loses the privilege of going out to eat with her family. Staying home with a babysitter while the family dines out becomes boring, especially when she learns a special dinner is planned for Grandma Thora's birthday. Promising to be on her best behavior, D.W. is invited along and happily devours every bite of her Little Bo Peep Pot Pie. When she requests the recipe, she learns it is made with her most disliked vegetable. (24 pages)

Where it's reviewed:
Booklist, February 1, 1995, page 1008
Horn Book, July 1995, page 483
Horn Book Guide, Fall 1995, page 259
School Library Journal, March 1995, page 178

Other books by the same author:
D.W. Rides Again!, 1993
D.W. Thinks Big, 1993
D.W. Flips, 1987

Other books you might like:
Vivian French, *Oliver's Vegetables*, 1995
　Although Oliver says he only eats potatoes, Grandpa's idea has him sampling different vegetables from the garden.
Russell Hoban, *Bread and Jam for Frances*, 1965
　When Frances refuses to eat anything other than bread and jam, she is served a steady diet of it until she's ready to try something new.
Virginia Miller, *Eat Your Dinner!*, 1992
　George convinces Bartholomew the bear to finish all his dinner.

152

MARGARET WISE BROWN
ASHLEY WOLFF, Illustrator

Little Donkey Close Your Eyes
(New York: HarperCollins Publishers, 1995)

Subject(s): Sleep; Bedtime; Stories in Rhyme
Age range(s): Grades K-1
Major character(s): Little Donkey, Donkey; Unnamed Character, Child
Time period(s): 1990s (1995)
Locale(s): United States

Summary: The newly illustrated reissue of a poetic bedtime story features a succession of animals ending their daytime activities and settling down for a night of slumber. From the Little Donkey on the hill to the little child tucked in bed, each youngster is lovingly comforted by a mother's presence. (32 pages)

Where it's reviewed:
Horn Book, January 1996, page 60
School Library Journal, September 1995, page 167

Other books by the same author:
Goodnight Moon, 1947
A Child's Good Night Book, 1943
The Runaway Bunny, 1942

Other books you might like:
Michael Foreman, *Dad! I Can't Sleep*, 1995
　Little Panda tries to count animals to help him fall asleep, but the thirsty animals all want one last drink of water.
Mem Fox, *Time for Bed*, 1993
　Through appealing illustrations and comforting verse, the whole wide world is put to sleep.
Mirra Ginsburg, *Asleep, Asleep*, 1992
　The animals are quietly bid good night until only the sleepy child and the wind are awake.

153

MARGERY WHEELER BROWN
GEORGE FORD, Illustrator

Baby Jesus, Like My Brother
(East Orange, NJ: Just Us Books, 1995)

Subject(s): Christmas; Brothers and Sisters; African Americans
Age range(s): Grades K-2
Major character(s): Keisha, Child, Sister (older); Tony, Child, Brother
Time period(s): 1990s (1995)
Locale(s): United States

Summary: With the Boy's Club, Keisha and Tony ride the bus downtown on Christmas Eve to see the decorations. Tony pesters his sister with questions which she patiently answers as Tony develops an understanding of Jesus, a baby just like his newborn brother. (28 pages)

Where it's reviewed:
Publishers Weekly, September 18, 1995, page 96
School Library Journal, Ocotber 1995, page 35

Other books by the same author:
Afro-Bets: Book of Colors, 1991
Afro-Bets: Book of Shapes, 1991

Other books you might like:
Tomie De Paola, *The First Christmas*, 1984
　Simple text combines with three-dimensional scenes to tell the story of the nativity.
B.G. Hennessy, *The First Night*, 1993
　The Christmas story is retold with emphasis on the quiet time prior to the arrival of shepherds, angels and kings.
Nancy Jewell, *Christmas Lullaby*, 1994
　A story in rhyme describes the animals in attendance at the birth of Jesus.

154

RUTH BROWN, Author/Illustrator

Copycat
(New York: Dutton Children's Books, 1994)

Subject(s): Animals/Cats; Animals/Dogs; Pets
Age range(s): Grades K-2
Major character(s): Buddy, Cat
Time period(s): 1990s (1994)
Locale(s): England

Summary: Buddy is an imitator of the actions of the other family pets as well as the birds and squirrels in the yard. An attempt to mimic the dog chewing on a bone results in three broken teeth and a trip to the vet, but not a change in Buddy's copycat nature. (32 pages)

Where it's reviewed:
Booklist, October 1, 1994, page 331
Horn Book Guide, Spring 1995, page 27
Junior Bookshelf, August 1994, page 127
Publishers Weekly, August 22, 1994, page 54
School Library Journal, October 1994, page 86

Other books by the same author:
One Stormy Night, 1993
Ladybug, Ladybug, 1988
Our Cat Flossie, 1986

Other books you might like:
Patricia Casey, *My Cat Jack*, 1994
    A part of the *Read and Wonder Series*, the title illustrates the simple text describing the movements of a cat.
Isabelle Harper, *My Cats Nick and Nora*, 1995
    Cousins Emmie and Isabelle enjoy playing with each other and the family cats—once they locate their hiding place.
James Herriot, *Moses the Kitten*, 1984
    A stray black kitten is rescued and given the name Moses as ackowledgement of his adventures.

155

RUTH BROWN, Author/Illustrator

The Picnic
(New York: Dutton Children's Books, 1993)

Subject(s): Animals
Age range(s): Grades K-2
Major character(s): Rabbit, Rabbit
Time period(s): 1990s (1993)
Locale(s): England (a meadow)

Summary: An idyllic day in the country is spoiled for a group of animals when a family chooses their meadow for a picnic location. Just as the family's dog begins digging into the animals' underground home, a rain storm sends the humans scurrying for shelter, leaving the animals cheering both their departure and the forgotten food. Originally published in Great Britain (32 pages)

Where it's reviewed:
Booklist, February 15, 1993, page 1066
Horn Book, January 1993, page 103
Publishers Weekly, January 4, 1993, page 72
School Library Journal, March 1993, page 171

Other books by the same author:
Copycat, 1994
One Stormy Night, 1993
Ladybug, Ladybug, 1988
Our Cat Flossie, 1986
The Big Sneeze, 1985

Other books you might like:
Emily Arnold McCully, *Picnic*, 1984
    The Mouse family's picnic turns out to be more than they expected.
Patricia Polacco, *Picnic at Mudsock Meadow*, 1992
    An annual Halloween picnic gives William the opportunity to find the courage to explore a swamp.
Jane Yolen, *Picnic with Piggins*, 1988
    Even at a picnic, mysteries come up; fortunately Piggins, the trusty butler, is on hand to solve them.

156

ANTHONY BROWNE, Author/Illustrator

Zoo
(New York: Alfred A. Knopf, 1992)

Subject(s): Zoos; Animals
Age range(s): Grades K-3
Major character(s): Unnamed Character, Child, Brother (Harry's older); Harry, Child; Dad, Father
Time period(s): 1990s (1992)
Locale(s): England

Summary: Initially excited about a family trip to the zoo, Harry and his older brother find their enthusiasm waning as they endure a traffic jam, long lines, Dad's bad jokes, and their parent's plans for the day, which differ from the boys' approach to zoo exploration. The zoo animals seem real enough, but the surrealistic portrayal of the human observers presents a parallel wordless story. Published in Great Britain in 1992. (32 pages)

Where it's reviewed:
Booklist, December 15, 1992, page 730
Children's Book Review Service, April 1993, page 98
Junior Bookshelf, December 1992, page 232
Publishers Weekly, February 15, 1993, page 236
School Library Journal, March 1993, page 171

Awards the book has won:
Carnegie Medal, 1993
Kate Greenaway Medal, 1993

Other books by the same author:
The Big Baby, 1994
Through the Magic Mirror, 1992
Changes, 1991
Willy and Hugh, 1991

Other books you might like:
David Legge, *Bamboozled*, 1994
    Arriving for her weekly visit with her Grandfather, a young girl senses that something is a little out of the ordinary, but it takes a while before she notices just what it is.
Chris Van Allsburg, *Ben's Dream*, 1982
    While dreaming, Ben sees himself passing the great landmarks of the world.
David Wiesner, *Tuesday*, 1991
    This 1992 winner of the Caldecott Medal presents a wordless, surreal look at frogs and their habitat.

157

EILEEN BROWNE
DAVID PARKINS, Illustrator

Tick-Tock

(Cambridge, MA: Candlewick Press, 1994)

Subject(s): Animals/Squirrels; Problem Solving; Behavior
Age range(s): Grades K-1
Major character(s): Skip Squirrel, Squirrel; Brainy, Squirrel, Friend (Skip's)
Time period(s): 1990s (1993)
Locale(s): Fictional Country

Summary: Mom's away and Brainy comes to play! The combination of circumstances has Skip so excited that she forgets her mom's admonitions and begins jumping on the furniture. Brainy joins in and soon both squirrels are leaping through the air with such exuberance that they knock a prized cuckoo clock off the wall and break it. In a race against time they carry the heavy clock from one repair shop to another until they find one that specializes in clocks. Originally published in Great Britain in 1993. (32 pages)

Where it's reviewed:
Booklist, June 1, 1994, page 1835
Five Owls, May 1994, page 104
Kirkus Reviews, April 15, 1994, page 552
Publishers Weekly, February 28, 1994, page 86
School Library Journal, August 1994, page 126

Other books by the same author:
No Problem, 1993
Where's That Bus?, 1991

Other books you might like:
Dr. Seuss, *The Cat in the Hat*, 1957
 One rainy afternoon while Mom is away, an unexpected visitor creates havoc and a huge mess to clean up before being forced to leave.
Patty Thomas, *The One and Only, Super-Duper, Golly-Whopper, Jim-Dandy, Really-Handy Clock-Tock-Stopper*, 1990
 Bothered by the loud ticking of his clock, Porcupine asks Rabbit to stop the sound, with disappointingly noisy results.
Ann Tompert, *Sue Patch and the Crazy Clocks*, 1989
 A King seeks the services of Sue Patch to repair the palace clocks and set them all to the same time.

158

JOSEPH BRUCHAC
MURV JACOB, Illustrator

The Boy Who Lived with the Bears: And Other Iroquois Stories

(New York: HarperCollins Publishers, 1995)

Subject(s): Indians of North America; Animals; Folk Tales
Age range(s): Grades 1-4
Time period(s): Indeterminate Past
Locale(s): United States

Summary: The context for the retelling of six traditional Iroquois tales is established by an introductory summary of Iroquois history and storytelling tradition. The title story tells of an orphan boy cared for by a cruel uncle who resents his task and tricks the boy into a trap and certain death. The boy, however, is rescued by animals and adopted by bears. He happens to meet his remorseful uncle again while the uncle is bear-hunting, with the boy and his bear family as the targets. (62 pages)

Where it's reviewed:
Booklist, December 1, 1995, page 624
Horn Book, November 1995, page 740
Horn Book Guide, Spring 1996, page 88
School Library Journal, November 1995, page 88

Awards the book has won:
Booklist Editors' Choice, 1995
ALA Notable Book, 1996

Other books by the same author:
Gluskabe and the Four Wishes, 1995
The Earth under Sky Bear's Feet: Native American Poems of the Land, 1995
A Boy Called Slow, 1994

Other books you might like:
Gayle Ross, *How Rabbit Tricked Otter: And Other Cherokee Trickster Stories*, 1994
 Fifteen stories about Rabbit show him to be a trickster, getting the better of many animals and being responsible for some of their physical characteristics too.
Manitonquat, *The Children of the Morning Light: Wampanoag Tales*, 1994
 The oral traditions of the Wampanoag people presented by a first-time author include stories of creation and those that explain life and death.
Nancy Van Laan, *In a Circle Long Ago: A Treasury of Native Lore from North America*, 1995
 A collection of stories and poems includes source notes and descriptions of the tribes whose folklore is represented.

159

JOSEPH BRUCHAC

Children of the Longhouse

(New York: Dial, 1996)

Subject(s): Indians of North America; Brothers and Sisters; Twins
Age range(s): Grades 3-6
Major character(s): Otsi-stia, Indian, Twin; Ohkwa'ri, Indian, Twin; Grabber, Indian
Time period(s): 15th century
Locale(s): New York

Summary: Ohkwa'ri overhears Grabber and his friends planning an attack on a peaceful, neighboring tribe. When he reports this news to the elders, they punish Grabber. Determined to have revenge, Grabber attempts to carry it out during a game of lacrosse, but Ohkwa'ri runs away. Chasing him, Grabber falls down a cliff and is seriously injured. While Ohkwa'ri attempts to help him, his twin sister senses the danger and calls upon a medicine man from the other tribe to come to help. (146 pages)

Where it's reviewed:
School Library Journal, July 1996, page 82
Bulletin of the Center for Childrens Books, July/August 1996, page 364
Booklist, May 1, 1996, page 1506

Other books by the same author:
The First Strawberries: A Cherokee Story, 1992
Thirteen Moons on Turtle's Back, 1992
Keepers of the Earth, 1988

Other books you might like:
Brian Burks, *Runs with Horses*, 1995
　　Runs with Horses is eager to complete his training but the peace with the army ends his quest to become a warrior.
Michael Dorris, *Guests*, 1994
　　Moss and Trouble struggle with growing up in early Massachusetts.
Paul Pitts, *Racing the Sun*, 1988
　　A 12-year-old boy trying to learn about his roots must race the sun as part of his ritual.
Susan Sharpe, *Spirit Quest*, 1991
　　As part of their quest, two boys go on an overnight camping trip.

160

JOSEPH BRUCHAC
ANNA VOJTECH, Illustrator

The First Strawberries: A Cherokee Story
(New York: Dial Books for Young Readers, 1993)

Subject(s): Legends; Indians of North America; Conduct of Life
Age range(s): Grades K-3
Major character(s): Unnamed Character, Indian (Cherokee), Spouse; Unnamed Character, Indian (Cherokee), Spouse
Time period(s): Indeterminate Past
Locale(s): North America

Summary: In a retelling of a Cherokee story, the origin of different berries is explained as the sun's attempts to help a husband make amends to his wife who has walked away from her husband's angry words. Though the man regrets his outburst, he cannot reach his wife and, in pity for him, the sun puts a succession of berries in her path, all of which she ignores. Finally, strawberries appear and the woman stops to taste the sweet fruit and pick some for her husband. Her pause gives her husband time to reach her and apologize. (32 pages)

Where it's reviewed:
Booklist, July 1993, page 1969
Bulletin of the Center for Children's Books, September 1993, page 6
Kirkus Reviews, July 15, 1993, page 931
Publishers Weekly, June 28, 1993, page 76
School Library Journal, September 1993, page 222

Awards the book has won:
Book Links Good Book, 1993

Other books by the same author:
Gluskabe and the Four Wishes, 1995
A Boy Called Slow, 1994
Fox Song, 1993

Other books you might like:
Tomie De Paola, *The Legend of the Bluebonnet: An Old Tale of Texas*, 1983
　　The origin of the bluebonnet flower of Texas is explained in a retelling of a Comanche folktale.
Paul Goble, *Iktomi and the Berries: A Plains Indian Story*, 1989
　　In a humorous retelling of a Plains story, Iktomi attempts, unsuccessfully to gather buffalo berries.
Gerald McDermott, *Arrow to the Sun: A Pueblo Indian Tale*, 1974
　　The 1975 Caldecott Medal winner tells of the search a young Indian boy makes for his father, the Sun.

161

JOSEPH BRUCHAC
PAUL MORIN, Illustrator

Fox Song
(New York: Philomel Books, 1993)

Subject(s): Grandparents; Indians of North America; Death
Age range(s): Grades 2-4
Major character(s): Jamie, Child, Indian (Abenaki); Grama Bowman, Grandmother (Jamie's great-grandmother), Indian (Abenaki)
Time period(s): 1990s (1993)
Locale(s): Vermont (near the Winooski River)

Summary: In the six years that Grama lives with Jamie's family prior to her death, she develops a special relationship with her great granddaughter. After she dies, Jamie begins coping with Grama Bowman's death by staying in bed one morning and recalling their special times together. Finally she jumps from bed, runs out to a favorite tree, and greets the day with an Abenaki song taught her by Grama Bowman. When a fox appears while she is singing, she knows that all her Grama taught her is true. (32 pages)

Where it's reviewed:
Bulletin for the Center for Children's Books, October 1993, page 40
Horn Book, January 1994, page 60
Kirkus Reviews, July 15, 1993, page 931
Publishers Weekly, July 19, 1993, page 254
School Library Journal, February 1994, page 78

Other books by the same author:
Gluskabe and the Four Wishes, 1995
A Boy Called Slow, 1994
The First Strawberries: A Cherokee Story, 1993

Other books you might like:
Tomie De Paola, *Nana Upstairs & Nana Downstairs*, 1973
　　Loving memories of Tommy's grandmother and great-grandmother are shared as part of the reality of life and death.
Miska Miles, *Annie and the Old One*, 1972
　　Realizing that her beloved grandmother will soon die,

Annie tries to control the inevitable, but must learn to face and accept the cycle of life and death.

White Deer of Autumn, *The Great Change*, 1992
A Native American girl is helped to understand that her grandfather's death is part of the circle of life.

162

JOSEPH BRUCHAC
GAYLE ROSS, Illustrator
VIRGINIA A. STROUD, Illustrator

The Story of the Milky Way: A Cherokee Tale
(New York: Dial Books for Young Readers, 1995)

Subject(s): Indians of North America; Folk Tales; Legends
Age range(s): Grades K-3
Major character(s): Unnamed Character, Child, Indian (Cherokee); Unnamed Character, Dog, Spirit; Beloved Woman, Aged Person, Indian (Cherokee)
Time period(s): Indeterminate Past
Locale(s): United States

Summary: After an elderly couple discover cornmeal missing from their storage bin their concerned grandson hides nearby to catch the thief. The boy is surprised when a light in the shape of a dog appears and eats from the bins. The next day the grandson seeks the help of Beloved Woman, known for her wisdom. Her plan requires the cooperation of the entire community to frighten the spirit dog when he comes again to eat. As the dog runs away, leaping into the sky, each grain of cornmeal that spills from his mouth becomes a star forming the Milky Way. (32 pages)

Where it's reviewed:
Booklist, September 1, 1995, page 79
Horn Book, September 1995, page 611
Kirkus Reviews, August 15, 1995, page 1185
Publishers Weekly, October 2, 1995, page 74
School Library Journal, September 1995, page 190

Other books by the same author:
The Girl Who Married the Moon: Stories from Native North America, 1994

Other books you might like:
Jeanne M. Lee, *Legend of the Milky Way*, 1982
The stars of the Milky Way tell a Chinese legend of a celestial princess who came to earth to marry a mortal.
Gerald McDermott, *Raven: A Trickster Tale from the Pacific Northwest*, 1993
Saddened to see the world in darkness, Raven tricks the Sky Chief and steals the sun, hanging it in the dark sky to benefit everyone.
Gretchen Mayo, *Star Tales: North American Indian Stories about the Stars*, 1987
This collection of Indian legends focus on the stars, moon, and night sky.
Harriet Peck Taylor, *Coyote Places the Stars*, 1993
A Wasco Indian story explains that the constellations are due to Coyote's arrangement of the stars to make pictures in the sky so his friends could find their likenesses.

163

JENNIFER BRUTSCHY
EILEEN CHRISTELOW, Illustrator

Celeste and Crabapple Sam
(New York: Lodestar Books, 1994)

Subject(s): Friendship; Hermits; Grandparents
Age range(s): Grades K-2
Major character(s): Crabapple Sam, Recluse; Celeste, Child (outgoing); Arthur Hammond, Grandfather
Time period(s): 1990s (1994)
Locale(s): United States (seashore)

Summary: Crabapple Sam's quiet life is invaded by a little girl vacationing in a nearby beach cottage. For 20 years, Crabapple Sam has been angry with Celeste's grandfather, but Celeste ignores Sam's grumpiness, pets his dog, plays with his pig and invites herself along when he goes to gather mussels. Finally, Sam responds to her innocent friendliness and accepts an invitation to the fish fry at Grampa Hammond's cottage. (32 pages)

Where it's reviewed:
Booklist, December 15, 1993, page 762
Horn Book Guide, Fall 1994, page 266
Kirkus Reviews, December 15, 1993, page 1587
School Library Journal, March 1994, page 190

Other books by the same author:
The Winter Fox, 1993

Other books you might like:
Sharon Chmielarz, *Down at Angel's*, 1994
Other children in the town tease Angel, but two sisters find the lonely old woodworker to be a kind friend.
Laurie A. Jacobs, *So Much in Common*, 1994
Neighbors Philomena and Horace discover that, despite their obvious differences, they share a friendship.
Cynthia Rylant, *Mr. Putter and Tabby Pour the Tea*, 1994
In the first book of the Mr. Putter and Tabby series, the lonely, elderly gentleman decides to acquire a pet, one with creaking bones and thinning hair just like him.

164

BONNIE BRYANT
MARCY DUNN RAMSEY, Illustrator

Pony Crazy
(New York: Skylark, 1995)

Series: Pony Tails
Subject(s): Animals/Horses; Friendship; Clubs
Age range(s): Grades 3-5
Major character(s): May Grover, 8-Year-Old, Friend; Jasmine James, 8-Year-Old, Friend; Corey Takamura, 8-Year-Old
Time period(s): 1990s (1995)
Locale(s): Willow Creek, Virginia

Summary: When new neighbors move into the house next door, May is sure that the odd sounds and flickering lights coming from the property are the signs of mad scientists. She and Jasmine try to ignore their fears as they prepare for a pony competition and get to know the new team member, Corey.

When they share their thoughts about the neighbors with Corey, she runs away in tears. Later the girls learn that Corey's family now lives next door with a very logical explanation for the strange sounds and lights. (101 pages)

Where it's reviewed:
Booklist, July 1995, page 1877
School Library Journal, December 1995, page 102

Other books by the same author:
Corey's Pony Is Missing, 1995
Hay Fever, 1994
Ranch Hands, 1993

Other books you might like:
Jeanne Betancourt, *The Pony Pals Series*, 1995-
    A new series describes the adventures of a group of girls who enjoy riding and caring for their ponies.
Jessie Haas, *A Blue for Beware*, 1995
    Lily is worried the first time she and Blue compete in a horse show against Lily's best friend Mandy.
Elizabeth Henning Sutton, *The Pony Champions*, 1992
    Busy fourth grader Meg, involved with preparations for a dance recital and a pony competition, neglects her pony and Lady Jane becomes sick.

165

QUINT BUCHHOLZ, Author/Illustrator

Sleep Well, Little Bear
(New York: Farrar Straus Giroux, 1994)

Subject(s): Bedtime; Sleep; Toys
Age range(s): Grades K-2
Major character(s): Unnamed Character, Bear, Toy
Time period(s): 1990s (1993)
Locale(s): Germany

Summary: While a child sleeps, his wide-awake little bear climbs atop the bookcase to look out at the moon-covered land and review the play activities of the day. The bear thinks about where he's been and what he might do tomorrow until the child wakens and grabs the bear to cuddle in bed. Translated from the German by Peter F. Neumeyer. (30 pages)

Where it's reviewed:
Booklist, December 1, 1994, page 685
Children's Book Review Service, October 1994, page 13
Horn Book Guide, Spring 1995, page 27
Publishers Weekly, October 3, 1994, page 68
School Library Journal, December 1994, page 71

Other books you might like:
Margaret Wise Brown, *Goodnight Moon*, 1947
    In the classic of bedtime stories, a small rabbit begins to settle for the night in the "great green room" saying goodnight to everything in sight, including the moon.
Mem Fox, *Time for Bed*, 1993
    Mothers all over the world are putting their kittens, lambs, fawns and children to sleep.
Mirra Ginsburg, *Asleep, Asleep*, 1992
    The animals are quietly bid good night until only the sleepy child and the wind are awake.

Jan Ormerod, *Moonlight*, 1982
    Through illustrations alone a young girl's bedtime ritual is portrayed.
Shelley Moore Thomas, *Putting the World to Sleep*, 1995
    A mother rocks her baby to sleep as her daughter mimics her actions with her bear and the world outside the house turns to sleep as the indoor occupants do too.

166

CARALYN BUEHNER
MARK BUEHNER, Illustrator

Fanny's Dream
(New York: Dial, 1996)

Subject(s): Marriage; Family Life
Age range(s): Grades K-2
Major character(s): Fanny Agnes, Farmer; Heber Jensen, Farmer
Time period(s): Indeterminate Past
Locale(s): Europe (farm)

Summary: Fanny hears about a ball at the mayor's house so she dresses up and goes outside to wait for her fairy godmother who, she hopes, will take her to the ball to meet the prince. The fairy godmother does not come, but Heber comes with flowers and proceeds to court her. They marry and have children, survive a fire, and have a good life, working the land and helping each other in the house. Then comes another party at the mayor's and Fanny goes outside to look at the lights when who should arrive but her fairy godmother, apologizing that she is late. Fanny, however, decides to stay on the farm where she has found happiness. (unpaged)

Where it's reviewed:
Horn Book, July/August 1996, page 444
Bulletin of the Center for Children's Books, September 1996, page 7
Booklist, March 15, 1996, page 1261

Awards the book has won:
School Library Journal Best Books, 1996

Other books by the same author:
It's a Spoon, Not a Shovel, 1995
The Escape of Marvin the Ape, 1992
A Job for Wittilda, 1992

Other books you might like:
Judith Brown, *The Mask of the Dancing Princess*, 1989
    A Gypsy tribe reforms a spoiled princess.
Ellen Kindt McKenzie, *The King, the Princess, and the Tinker*, 1992
    A self-absorbed king pays no attention to his family while he looks in a mirror all day.
Margaret Mahy, *The Girl with the Green Ear: Stories about Magic in Nature*, 1992
    Wonderful adventures take place in a town called Trickle.
Gerda Marie Scheidl, *Loretta and the Little Fairy*, 1993
    Loretta tries to help the little fairy grow up to be a little girl again.
Nancy Willard, *Beauty and the Beast*, 1992
    Beauty meets her beast in the city of New York in a turn of the century setting.

167

CARALYN BUEHNER
MARK BUEHNER, Illustrator

A Job for Wittilda

(New York: Dial Books for Young Readers, 1993)

Subject(s): Witches and Witchcraft; Work; Animals/Cats
Age range(s): Grades K-2
Major character(s): Wittilda, Witch, Animal Lover (cat fancier)
Time period(s): 1990s (1993)
Locale(s): United States

Summary: Facing an empty cupboard and 47 hungry cats, Wittilda must find a job. First she tries Aunt Bort's Beauty Shop, but is fired after her first customer. She has more luck answering an ad for Dingaling Pizza where her use of her broom and her witch skills help her complete her pizza deliveries with amazing speed. (32 pages)

Where it's reviewed:
Booklist, July 1993, page 1973
Horn Book Guide, Spring 1994, page 28
Library Talk, November 1993, page 38
Publishers Weekly, June 28, 1993, page 76
School Library Journal, January 1994, page 87

Other books by the same author:
Fanny's Dream, 1995
The Escape of Marvin the Ape, 1992

Other books you might like:
Lorna Balian, *Humbug Witch*, 1987
    Despite her efforts, becoming a witch does not come easily to an apprentice.
Norman Bridwell, *The Witch Next Door*, 1986
    Having a witch for a neighbor makes life more interesting for a group of children.
Donna Guthrie, *The Witch Who Lives Down the Hall*, 1985
    A young boy's suspicions that his neighbor is a witch are confirmed when she takes him for a ride on her magic carpet.
James Stevenson, *Emma*, 1985
    Not your typical witch, Emma even needs flying lessons!
Jane Yolen, *Best Witches: Poems for Halloween*, 1989
    This collection of witch poems includes some surprising observations on the real activities of witches.

168

EMMA BULL
SUSAN GABER, Illustrator

The Princess and the Lord of Night

(San Diego: Harcourt Brace & Company, 1994)

Subject(s): Fairy Tale; Princes and Princesses
Age range(s): Grades 1-4
Major character(s): Unnamed Character, Royalty (princess), 13-Year-Old; Lord of Night, Sorcerer
Time period(s): Indeterminate Past
Locale(s): Fictional Country

Summary: The Lord of Night places a curse on a newborn princess, declaring that, if ever she does not receive what she wants, the kingdom will fall into ruin and her parents will die. Throughout her life all desires have been fulfilled by her loving parents, but on the morning of her 13th birthday, the princess awakens knowing that there is something she wants that she must get for herself. She sets off into the kingdom with her most-treasured belongings. As she travels she meets people in need and compassionately gives away her possessions, finally receiving in return a magic ring that enables her to confront the Lord of Night and receive what she truly wants2emdfreedom from the curse. (32 pages)

Where it's reviewed:
Booklist, June 1, 1994, page 1824
Children's Bookwatch, July 1994, page 4
Kirkus Reviews, March 1, 1994, page 300
Publishers Weekly, February 28, 1994, page 87
School Library Journal, May 1994, page 84

Awards the book has won:
International Reading Association Children's Choice, 1995

Other books you might like:
Hans Christian Andersen, *Twelve Tales*, 1994
    A dozen of Andersen's tales, including both the familiar and the less well known, selected, translated and illustrated by Erik Blegvad.
Ursula K. Le Guin, *A Ride on the Red Mare's Back*, 1992
    When her brother is stolen by trolls, a brave young girl is determined to rescue him, using only the everyday objects of her life in her quest.
Jane Yolen, *Tam Lin*, 1990
    In a retelling of a traditional Scottish tale, Jennet MacKenzie frees her home (and the handsome Tam Lin) from the spell of the fairies.

169

CLYDE ROBERT BULLA
JULIA NOONAN, Illustrator

A Place for Angels

(Mahwah, NJ: BridgeWater Books, 1995)

Subject(s): Fathers and Daughters; Artists and Art; Aunts and Uncles
Age range(s): Grades 3-5
Major character(s): Claudine, Orphan; Father, Father, Artist; Lona, Aunt
Time period(s): 1990s (1995)
Locale(s): United States

Summary: Claudine is the inspiration for the angels her widowed father creates and bequeaths to her on his death bed. Against Aunt Lona's wishes, Claudine insists that the angels move with Claudine to Aunt Lona's home. There they are stored in the stable while Aunt Lona secretly plans to send them to the dump. When Claudine learns of her aunt's plans, she finds a more suitable place for Father's angels and for herself. (79 pages)

Where it's reviewed:
Booklist, January 1996, page 832
Horn Book Guide, Spring 1996, page 53

Hungry Mind Review, Winter 1995, page 54
Kirkus Reviews, October 15, 1995, page 1488
School Library Journal, December 1995, page 102

Other books by the same author:
Charlie's House, 1993
The Cardboard Crown, 1984
A Lion to Guard Us, 1981

Other books you might like:
Frances Hodgson Burnett, *A Little Princess*, 1963
    Orphaned Sara Crewe is rescued from a British boarding
    school by a friend of her deceased father.
Jean Stratton Porter, *Pollyanna*, 1913
    A cheerful orphan is sent to live with a grumpy relative and
    spreads her special happiness to all who meet her.
Johanna Spyri, *Heidi*, 1945
    Orphan Heidi, sad to leave grandfather's home in the Alps,
    attends school and cares for an invalid girl in the city.

170

EVE BUNTING
IRVING TODDY, Illustrator

Cheyenne Again
(New York: Clarion Books, 1995)

Subject(s): Indian Reservations; Indians of North America;
    Schools/Boarding Schools
Age range(s): Grades 2-4
Major character(s): Young Bull, 10-Year-Old, Indian (Chey-
    enne)
Time period(s): 1880s
Locale(s): United States

Summary: Young Bull is forced to leave his family, the
reservation and the Cheyenne way of life to attend the ''White
Man's'' boarding school. There, he is forced to give up his
braids, his mocassins and his Cheyenne clothes in accordance
with the school's policy. After he attempts, unsuccessfully, to
run away, a sympathetic teacher cautions him not to let others
take his memories too. (32 pages)

Where it's reviewed:
Booklist, August 1995, page 1946
Bulletin of the Center for Children's Books, September 1995,
    page 8
Children's Book Review Service, December 1995, page 37
Language Arts, November 1995, page 543
School Library Journal, December 1995, page 72

Other books by the same author:
A Day's Work, 1994
Smoky Night, 1994
Fly Away Home, 1991

Other books you might like:
Anthony Hill, *The Burnt Stick*, 1995
    Five-year-old, mixed-race John is taken from his aborigi-
    nal mother and placed in a mission school to be taught
    ''white'' ways.
Arlene B. Hirschfelder, *Rising Voices: Writings of Young
    Native Americans*, 1992
    In the collection is an essay describing the life of a young

Chippewa girl who returns home a stranger after seven
years in a boarding school. Co-selector, Beverly R. Singer.
Scott O'Dell, *Sing Down the Moon*, 1970
    Although Bright Morning escapes from Spanish captors
    and returns to her tribe, she is forced to move with her
    people to a reservation.

171

EVE BUNTING
GREG SHED, Illustrator

Dandelions
(San Diego: Harcourt Brace & Company, 1995)

Subject(s): Frontier and Pioneer Life; Family Life; Surprises
Age range(s): Grades 2-4
Major character(s): Zoe Bolton, Child, Sister (older); Rebecca
    Bolton, Child, Sister (younger); Mama, Mother
Time period(s): Indeterminate Past
Locale(s): Nebraska

Summary: Leaving behind relatives and the family home in
Illinois, a family travels to a claim on the prairie. Zoe and
Rebecca wonder where the trees are and worry about lonely,
pregnant Mama who seems so far away and sad all the time.
Their father worries too as he digs the well, plants the crops
and builds a sod house to shelter his growing family. Returning from a trip to town for supplies, Zoe spots the bright
yellow of dandelions growing beside the trail. They dig some
as a symbol of their family's resilience and plant them on the
sod roof to cheer Mama. (48 pages)

Where it's reviewed:
Booklist, September 15, 1995, page 162
Bulletin of the Center for Children's Books, September 1995,
    page 8
Kirkus Reviews, August 15, 1995, page 1185
Quill & Quire, November 1995, page 47
School Library Journal, November 1995, page 65

Awards the book has won:
School Library Journal Best Books, 1995

Other books by the same author:
On Call Back Mountain, 1997
The Blue and the Gray, 1996
Sunflower House, 1996
Train to Somewhere, 1996

Other books you might like:
Jennifer Armstrong, *Black-Eyed Susan*, 1995
    While Susan shares her father's love of the prairie, Ma is
    overwhelmed by its vastness and saddened by its loneli-
    ness.
Brett Harvey, *My Prairie Year: Based on the Diary of Elenore
    Plaisted*, 1986
    Nine-year-old Elenore records in her diary the activities of
    her family in Dakota Territory.
Glen Rounds, *Sod Houses on the Great Plains*, 1995
    A non-fiction picture book describes the sod houses built
    by the early settlers on the treeless plains.

172

EVE BUNTING
RONALD HIMLER, Illustrator

A Day's Work

(New York: Clarion Books, 1994)

Subject(s): Mexican Americans; Work; Honesty
Age range(s): Grades 1-3
Major character(s): Francisco, Child (Mexican American); Abuelo, Grandfather, Immigrant (Mexican); Ben, Gardener, Employer
Time period(s): 1990s (1994)
Locale(s): California

Summary: After Francisco's father dies, Abuelo comes from Mexico to help the family. Francisco, acting as his interpreter, arranges day labor with a gardener despite Abuelo's protests that he is a carpenter. After a long hot day weeding a bank, dreaming all the while of the fine dinner to be purchased with the day's wages, Francisco must admit to Ben and Abuelo that he was not truthful in describing his grandfather's skill. Ben is understanding when Abuelo arranges to return early the next day to complete the job correctly and Francisco learns an important lesson. Spanish words sprinkled throughout the text are understandable from the context. (32 pages)

Where it's reviewed:
Booklist, November 1, 1994, page 505
Kirkus Reviews, September 15, 1994, page 1266
New Advocate, Winter 1995, page 49
Publishers Weekly, August 8, 1994, page 434
School Library Journal, January 1995, page 82

Awards the book has won:
Consortium of Latin American Studies Programs Commended Book, 1994

Other books by the same author:
Someday a Tree, 1993
Fly Away Home, 1991
The Wall, 1990

Other books you might like:
Susan Campbell Bartoletti, *Silver at Night*, 1994
  Massimino labors in the American coal mines saving for the day he will be joined by his beloved Perina.
Elisa Bartone, *Peppe the Lamplighter*, 1993
  After his mother's death, Peppe takes a job has a lamplighter to help support his father and sisters.
Muriel Stanek, *I Speak English for My Mom*, 1989
  A Mexican American child must be the interpreter whenever English is the spoken or written language.

173

EVE BUNTING
KATHRYN HEWITT, Illustrator

Flower Garden

(San Diego: Harcourt Brace & Company, 1994)

Subject(s): Gardens and Gardening; Parent and Child; Birthdays
Age range(s): Grades K-1
Major character(s): Unnamed Character, Child (African-American); Unnamed Character, Father (African-American); Mom, Mother (African-American)
Time period(s): 1990s (1994)
Locale(s): California (urban neighborhood)

Summary: With her father's help, a young girl purchases an assortment of colorful flowers which she carries home on the bus to the family's apartment. The girl and her father prepare a window-box garden which is presented to Mom as a birthday surprise. (32 pages)

Where it's reviewed:
Booklist, February 15, 1994, page 1076
Horn Book, May 1994, page 307
Kirkus Reviews, April 1, 1994, page 478
Publishers Weekly, April 4, 1994, page 79
School Library Journal, April 1994, page 96

Other books by the same author:
A Perfect Father's Day, 1991
Winter's Coming, 1990
The Big Red Barn, 1979

Other books you might like:
Lois Ehlert, *Planting a Rainbow*, 1988
  A mother and her child plant a family garden, carefully planning the placement of the flowers to create a rainbow of colors.
Diane Dawson Hearn, *Anna in the Garden*, 1994
  For her birhday, Anna receives a packet of seeds which her mother helps her plant in seed trays and transplant to the garden when the weather warms.
Julia Hoban, *Amy Loves the Sun*, 1988
  Amy takes advantage of a sunny day to go outside and pick flowers for her mother.
Helen Ketteman, *Not Yet, Yvette*, 1992
  With Dad's help Yvette plans a special surprise for Mom's birthday.
Arnold Lobel, *The Rose in My Garden*, 1984
  In the shade of the hollyhocks, a bee sleeps on the only rose in the garden.
Elaine Moore, *Grandma's Garden*, 1994
  Each Spring, Kim visits Grandma and helps to plant her vegetable garden.

174

EVE BUNTING
ALEXANDER PERTZOFF, Illustrator

The In-Between Days

(New York: HarperCollins Publishers, 1994)

Subject(s): Single Parent Families; Islands; Fathers and Sons
Age range(s): Grades 4-6
Major character(s): George ''Georgie'' Bowser, 11-Year-Old; David Bowser, Single Father, Businessman (bike shop owner); Caroline Best, Tourist, Divorced Person
Time period(s): 1990s (1994)
Locale(s): Dove Island, Michigan

Summary: In the five years since his mother's death, Georgie has settled into a comfortable routine with Dad, his younger brother and the solitude of their tiny island home. When

Caroline begins visiting the island, even in the winter after the tourist season ends, Georgie begins to resent her as a possible disruption. It is not until he plays a prank on Caroline which leaves the entire family without her during Christmas that Georgie begins to face the loneliness of his mother's death and the shame for the hurt he causes. (119 pages)

Where it's reviewed:
Booklist, October 1, 1994, page 325
Horn Book Guide, Spring 1995, page 73
Kirkus Reviews, September 15, 1994, page 1267
Library Talk, January 1995, page 21
School Library Journal, October 1994, page 118

Other books by the same author:
The Island of One, 1992
Sharing Susan, 1991
Karen Hepplewhite Is the World's Best Kisser, 1983

Other books you might like:
Mary Jane Auch, *Out of Step*, 1992
  When Jeremy's father remarries, Jeremy feels as if he no longer has a place in the family.
Lois Lowry, *The One Hundredth Thing about Caroline*, 1983
  Eleven-year-old Caroline and her older brother are suspicious of the man their mother is dating.
Patricia MacLachlan, *Sarah, Plain and Tall*, 1985
  Responding to the ad of a widowed father, adventurous, out-spoken Sarah adjusts to life on the prairie and waits for acceptance from Jacob and his motherless children.
Candice F. Ransom, *More than a Name*, 1995
  After her mother's remarriage, eight-year-old Cammie must adjust to a stepfather and a large family.

175

EVE BUNTING
DAVID WIESNER, Illustrator

Night of the Gargoyles

(New York: Clarion Books, 1994)

Subject(s): Fantasy; Monsters; Museums
Age range(s): Grades 1-3
Major character(s): Unnamed Character, Security Officer (night watchman)
Time period(s): Indeterminate
Locale(s): Fictional Country

Summary: As night falls, the carved stone gargoyles decorating a museum come to life. Resentful of the human hands which have carved them and placed them on buildings where pigeons roost, the gargoyles delight in frightening the night watchman who is unable to make the museum director believe that the gargoyles have a life of their own after dark. Before the break of day, all have returned to their positions on the building, to await the night's return.

Where it's reviewed:
Booklist, October 1, 1994, page 331
Horn Book Guide, Spring 1995, page 28
Kirkus Reviews, August 15, 1994, page 1122
Publishers Weekly, August 8, 1994, page 436
School Library Journal, October 1994, page 86

Awards the book has won:
School Library Journal Best Books, 1994

Other books by the same author:
Fly Away Home, 1991 (School Library Journal Best Book and ALA Notable Book)
The Wall, 1990 (School Library Journal Best Book and ALA Notable Book)
The Wednesday Surprise, 1989 (School Library Journal Best Book and ALA Notable Book)

Other books you might like:
Anthony Browne, *Through the Magic Mirror*, 1992
  When a young boy steps through a magic mirror he finds a world similar to his own, but with unique differences.
Chris Van Allsburg, *The Sweetest Fig*, 1993
  The surrealistic art work portrays the unusual experiences of a pompous dentist who eats a charmed fig.
David Wiesner, *Tuesday*, 1991
  In the wordless 1992 Caldecott Medal winner frogs atop lily pads soar through the air startling animals and humans alike.

176

EVE BUNTING
WENDELL MINOR, Illustrator

Red Fox Running

(New York, Clarion Books, 1993)

Subject(s): Animals/Foxes; Winter
Age range(s): Grades K-3
Major character(s): Unnamed Character, Fox, Hunter
Time period(s): 1990s (1993)
Locale(s): United States

Summary: Facing growing hunger pains, a red fox has a long day ahead, searching for food and avoiding predators who are equally hungry. Finally, as the moon begins to rise, the red fox is successful and hurries home to the warmth of a den, the companionship of a mate and cubs, a meal and sleep. (unpaged)

Where it's reviewed:
Booklist, November 15, 1993, page 632
Emergency Librarian, January 1994, page 47
Horn Book Guide, Spring 1994, page 28
Publishers Weekly, September 6, 1993, page 95
School Library Journal, December 1993, page 80

Other books by the same author:
Sunshine Home, 1994
Someday a Tree, 1993
Fly Away Home, 1991

Other books you might like:
Jim Arnosky, *Watching Foxes*, 1985
  Mom's away and the fox kits have a morning to play in their den.
Allison L. Blyler, *Finding Foxes*, 1991
  The life of the fox is described through a variety of short poems.
Hannah Giffard, *Red Fox on the Move*, 1992
  A bulldozer has destroyed their home so Red Fox and his family must find a new one.

177

EVE BUNTING
DAVID DIAZ, Illustrator

Smoky Night

(San Diego: Harcourt Brace & Company, 1994)

Subject(s): Neighbors and Neighborhoods; Interpersonal Relations; Fires
Age range(s): Grades 1-3
Major character(s): Daniel, Child; Gena, Single Mother; Jasmine, Cat
Time period(s): 1990s (1994)
Locale(s): Los Angeles, California

Summary: Observing rioting and looting in the streets below their apartment window, Daniel's mother tries to help him understand the anger which drives people to such behavior. During the night Daniel's apartment building burns and all the residents are evacuated to a nearby shelter. With no time to look for his beloved Jasmine, Daniel is worried about her fate until a firefighter arrives at the shelter with two cats found in the building—Jasmine and an unfriendly neighbor's cat. As the two cats share a bowl of milk, the need for the people residing in the neighborhood to get to know each other better becomes obvious. (32 pages)

Where it's reviewed:
Booklist, March 1, 1994, page 1267
Horn Book, May 1994, page 308
New Advocate, Winter 1995, page 57
Publishers Weekly, January 31, 1994, page 89
School Library Journal, May 1994, page 89

Awards the book has won:
Caldecott Medal, 1995
School Library Journal Best Books, 1994

Other books by the same author:
Night Tree, 1994
The Man Who Could Call Down Owls, 1984
The Big Red Barn, 1979

Other books you might like:
Patricia Polacco, *Chicken Sunday*, 1992
  Childhood memories inspire a story of different races and cultures working, playing and caring together.
Chris Raschka, *Yo! Yes?*, 1993
  An award-winning celebration of friendship shows two boys of different races becoming acquainted.
Michael J. Rosen, *Elijah's Angel: A Story for Chanukah and Christmas*, 1992
  A young Jewish boy and an elderly African American man ignore differences of race and religion and concentrate on the friendship they share.

178

EVE BUNTING
RONALD HIMLER, Illustrator

Someday a Tree

(New York: Clarion Books, 1993)

Subject(s): Trees; Pollution; Environmental Problems

Age range(s): Grades K-3
Major character(s): Alice, Child
Time period(s): 1990s (1993)
Locale(s): United States (Far Meadow)

Summary: Maybe the big old oak tree really has been growing since Columbus first came to America, just like Alice's dad says. Unfortunately, this favorite family relaxation spot, site of picnics, naps, and Alice's christening, is suffering the effects of illegally dumped chemicals. Using techniques ranging from removing the poisoned soil to offering the tree homemade chicken soup and knit scarves, the family and neighbors work in a futile attempt to save the tree. Feeling the pain of lost dreams, Alice spots her acorn collection and realizes that someday, with her help, there will be another tree. (32 pages)

Where it's reviewed:
Booklist, March 1, 1993, page 1234
Children's Bookwatch, May 1993, page 3
Kirkus Reviews, February 15, 1993, page 223
Publishers Weekly, March 15, 1993, page 86
School Library Journal, May 1993, page 81

Other books by the same author:
A Day's Work, 1994
Night Tree, 1994
Our Teacher's Having a Baby, 1992

Other books you might like:
Ruth Brown, *The World That Jack Built*, 1991
  Through the eyes of a black cat, the effects of pollution of the environment and the need to protect it are vividly portrayed.
Sheila MacGill Callahan, *And Still the Turtle Watched*, 1991
  Carved into a rock as a sentinel to watch over the Delaware peoples, the turtle observes many changes including the disappearance of his people and the pollution of the land and river.
Dr. Seuss, *The Lorax*, 1971
  The environmental changes that come with "progress" are recounted with sadness by the Lorax.
Chris Van Allsburg, *Just a Dream*, 1990
  A dreamlike vision of the future gives Walter a new perspective on the importance of recycling and respect for the environment.

179

EVE BUNTING

Spying on Miss Mueller

(New York: Clarion Books, 1995)

Subject(s): World War II; Schools/Boarding Schools; Historical
Age range(s): Grades 6-9
Major character(s): Jessie Drumm, Student (boarding school), 13-Year-Old; Daphne Muller, Teacher
Time period(s): 1940s
Locale(s): Belfast, Northern Ireland (Alveara School)

Summary: Jessica's life at boarding school changes once World War II begins. She and her friends once adored their language teacher Miss Muller, but now suspect that her half-

German heritage makes her a spy. Jessica and her classmates notice that Belfast is bombed the night after they see her climbing the bell tower and the maids report Miss Muller's picture of her father has a swastika on it. Jessica goes along with her friends when they accuse their once-favorite teacher of being a spy but, as Jessica sadly learns, their suspicions are wrong. (179 pages)

Where it's reviewed:
School Library Journal, May 1995, page 104
Booklist, March 15, 1995, page 1328
Voice of Youth Advocates, October 1995, page 216
Publishers Weekly, April 3, 1995, page 62

Awards the book has won:
Booklist Editors' Choice/Books for Youth, 1995

Other books by the same author:
For Always, 1993
Just Like Everyone Else, 1993
Such Nice Kids, 1990
A Sudden Silence, 1988
The Face at the Edge of the World, 1985

Other books you might like:
James Douglas Forman, *Ceremony of Innocence*, 1970
    Based on the true story of Hans and Sophie Scholl, this fictionalizes their anti-Nazi work and eventual execution during World War II.
Janet Taylor Lisle, *Sirens and Spies*, 1985
    Elsie eventually learns the story of her violin teacher's friendship with Germans during World War II.
Lois Lowry, *Number the Stars*, 1989
    Annemarie, a Danish youth, and her family join the Resistance Movement to save Jews during World War II.
Carol Matas, *Lisa's War*, 1989
    When Denmark is taken over by the Germans, Lisa and her brother, Stefan, both become active in the resistance movement.

180

EVE BUNTING
DIANE DE GROAT, Illustrator

Sunshine Home
(New York: Clarion Books, 1994)

Subject(s): Grandparents; Nursing Homes; Old Age
Age range(s): Grades 1-4
Major character(s): Timmie, Child; Gram, Grandmother
Time period(s): 1990s (1994)
Locale(s): New York

Summary: Timmie hasn't seen his grandmother for 5 weeks, since she broke her hip and had to move to a nursing home. On his first visit to the home with his parents he's nervous, but soon adjusts to seeing Gram in strange surroundings. Everyone tries to be cheerful, hiding the sadness they feel, until Timmie brings the family together for an honest sharing of feelings. (32 pages)

Where it's reviewed:
Booklist, March 15, 1994, page 1371
Children's Book Review Service, June 1994, page 121
Horn Book Guide, Fall 1994, page 266

Kirkus Reviews, February 15, 1994, page 223
School Library Journal, April 1994, page 96

Other books by the same author:
A Day's Work, 1994
Fly Away Home, 1991
The Wednesday Surprise, 1990

Other books you might like:
Mem Fox, *Wilfrid Gordon McDonald Partridge*, 1989
    When a young boy learns that his friend in a nursing home is losing her memory, he collects what he thinks she has lost to bring to her.
Lorraine Henriod, *Grandma's Wheelchair*, 1982
    Young Thomas enjoys helping his grandmother who is confined to a wheelchair.
Leslea Newman, *Remember That*, 1996
    The loving relationship between a child and her Bubbe endures the inevitability of aging and the eventual move of the grandmother to a nursing home.
Joel Strangis, *Grandfather's Rock*, 1993
    A family's difficult decision to place an infirm parent in a nursing home is given new perspective in a retelling of an Italian folktale.

181

EVE BUNTING
RONALD HIMLER, Illustrator

Train to Somewhere
(New York: Clarion Books, 1996)

Subject(s): Orphans
Age range(s): Grades 1-3
Major character(s): Marianne, Orphan; Nora, 5-Year-Old, Orphan; Miss Randolph, Child-Care Giver
Time period(s): 1870s (1878)
Locale(s): New York, New York; Iowa (train traveling west)

Summary: Marianne is traveling west with 13 other orphans to find a new home. She is also hoping to find her own mother who left her with promises to return. Marianne takes care of the younger children and hopes they can remain together, but Miss Randolph doubts this will happen. As the train stops at different towns along the way, each of the children is selected for adoption until only Marianne is left. When they arrive in Iowa, the Brooks', who were hoping for a little boy, are still thrilled to have a little girl, and Marianne realizes she has a new family. (32 pages)

Where it's reviewed:
School Library Journal, March 1966, page 166
Bulletin of the Center for Children's Books, March 1996, page 221

Awards the book has won:
Booklist Editors' Choice, 1996

Other books by the same author:
Dandelions, 1995
A Day's Work, 1994
Smoky Night, 1994
Fly Away Home, 1991
The Wall, 1990

Other books you might like:

Barbara Cohen, *Yussel's Prayer: A Yom Kippur Story*, 1981
An orphan boy wants to participate in Yom Kippur like others in his town.

Olga Cossi, *Orlanda and the Contest of Thiefs*, 1990
An ophan becomes involved in a contest to see who is the best pickpocket.

Emily Arnold McCully, *Little Kit or, the Industrious Flea Circus Girl*, 1995
A little orphan girl in Victorian England keeps herself alive by working with a flea circus.

Andrea Warren, *Orphan Train Rider: One Boy's True story*, 1996
Lee Nailling, an orphan train rider, tells his true story of events. (non-fiction)

182

JOHN BURNINGHAM, Author/Illustrator

Courtney
(New York: Crown Publishers, Inc., 1994)

Subject(s): Animals/Dogs; Family Life; Fantasy
Age range(s): Grades K-2
Major character(s): Courtney, Dog (old and unwanted)
Time period(s): 1990s (1994)
Locale(s): England

Summary: Pestered by the children, two uninterested parents finally agree to allow a dog, but only a proper dog with a pedigree, into the home. The children, however, are seeking a dog that no one else wants and return home with an old mongrel. Fortunately, Courtney's ability to cook, play the violin and entertain the baby make him a welcome addition to the family. (32 pages)

Where it's reviewed:
Booklist, September 15, 1994, page 141
Kirkus Reviews, July 15, 1994, page 979
Publishers Weekly, July 18, 1994, page 244
Quill & Quire, June 1994, page 51
School Library Journal, September 1994, page 180

Awards the book has won:
International Reading Association Children's Choice, 1995

Other books by the same author:
Aldo, 1992
Hey! Get Off Our Train, 1990
Come Away from the Water, Shirley, 1977

Other books you might like:

Debra Barracca, *Maxi, the Hero*, 1991
Maxi proves himself to be not just any dog when he apprehends a purse snatcher. Co-author Sal Barracca.

Norman Bridwell, *Clifford's Good Deeds*, 1985
Always desiring to be helpful, Clifford the big red dog finds that his efforts sometimes go awry.

Bernard Waber, *The House on East 88th Street*, 1962
In the first of the ''Lyle'' books, the Primms move into their new home and meet Lyle, the resident crocodile.

183

JOHN BURNINGHAM, Author/Illustrator

Harvey Slumfenburger's Christmas Present
(Cambridge, Massachusetts: Candlewick Press, 1993)

Subject(s): Santa Claus; Christmas; Transportation
Age range(s): Grades K-3
Major character(s): Santa Claus, Philanthropist, Mythical Creature
Time period(s): 1990s (1993)
Locale(s): Earth (heading for Roly Poly Mountain)

Summary: Just as Santa Claus is climbing into bed after a long night delivering presents, he notices a package for Harvey Slumfenberger at the bottom of his sack. Realizing that this is the only gift Harvey can expect to receive, Santa is determined to deliver it. Not wanting to awaken the tired reindeer, Santa sets off to seek other transportation to the top of Roly Poly Mountain and the Slumfenburger hut. Along the way, events force Santa to keep making new travel arrangements. Finally, the present is delivered and Santa begins an unusual trip home. (32 pages)

Where it's reviewed:
Booklist, October 15, 1993, page 450
Children's Book Review Service, Fall 1994, page 73
Five Owls, November 1993, page 43
Horn Book, March 1994, page 188
School Library Journal, October 1993, page 42

Other books by the same author:
Cannonball Simp, 1994
Hey! Get Off Our Train, 1990
Time to Get out of the Bath, Shirley, 1978

Other books you might like:

Raymond Briggs, *Father Christmas*, 1981
A pictorial view of Christmas Eve is seen from the perspective of ol' Saint Nick.

DuBose Heyward, *The Country Bunny and the Little Gold Shoes*, 1939
To prove her worth as one of the chosen Easter Bunnies, Cottontail is determined to see that her one last Easter egg is delivered.

Arthur Scholey, *Baboushka*, 1982
In this retelling of a traditional Russian Folk Tale, Baboushka is invited to accompany three kings who are following a star, but delays her departure until she has cleaned her home.

184

TIMOTHY BUSH, Author/Illustrator

James in the House of Aunt Prudence
(New York: Crown Publishers, Inc., 1993)

Subject(s): Aunts and Uncles; Imagination; Fantasy
Age range(s): Grades K-1
Major character(s): James, Child (imaginative); Prudence, Aunt
Time period(s): 1990s (1993)
Locale(s): United States

Summary: When James arrives for a visit at Aunt Prudence's Victorian mansion his hopes of receiving a tour are not realized in quite the way he expects. Great Aunt Prudence leaves James with tea and macaroons while she completes some work and James' tour begins with a ride on a bear's back. As his imagination runs wild so do the events in the house until Aunt Prudence enters the room and restores some semblance of order. First book by the author. (32 pages)

Where it's reviewed:
Booklist, November 1, 1993, page 526
Children's Book Review Service, Winter 1994, page 51
Horn Book Guide, Spring 1994, page 28
Publishers Weekly, September 6, 1993, page 94
School Library Journal, January 1994, page 87

Other books you might like:
Anthony Browne, *Changes*, 1991
    Waiting for his parents to return home, a young boy's anxieties contribute to his imagining many unusual and improbable changes.
David Legge, *Bamboozled*, 1994
    This week's visit to Grandpa's house leaves one little girl puzzled; things are not what they seem to be.
Maurice Sendak, *Where the Wild Things Are*, 1963
    Max's imagination sails away with him to the land of the wild things and then safely back to his home.

185

TIMOTHY BUSH, Author/Illustrator

Three at Sea
(New York: Crown Publishers, Inc., 1994)

Subject(s): Animals; Rivers; Adventure and Adventurers
Age range(s): Grades K-3
Major character(s): Alex, Child, Friend; Joel, Child, Friend; Zachariah Jr., Child, Friend
Time period(s): 1990s (1994)
Locale(s): United States

Summary: Absent-mindedly floating down a river in a large inner tube, Alex, Joel and Zachariah Jr. find themselves far out to sea and unable to get back to shore. They seek help from a passing sea turtle and dolphins, but neither endangered species is able to help them. Then a crocodile appears with plans to eat them until Zachariah remembers enough about crocodile physiology to devise a plan to save them all. After returning safely to their dock, the boys free the crocodile and go home. Zachariah Jr. begins writing letters to the president about caring for all animals. (32 pages)

Where it's reviewed:
Horn Book Guide, Spring 1995, page 28
Kirkus Reviews, July 15, 1994, page 979
Publishers Weekly, August 22, 1994, page 54
Reading Teacher, May 1995, page 708
School Library Journal, September 1994, page 180

Other books by the same author:
James in the House of Aunt Prudence, 1993

Other books you might like:
Gail Jorgensen, *Crocodile Beat*, 1989
    While lying partially submerged, listening to the nearby

animal sounds, Crocodile's plans for his next meal are compromised by Lion.
Michelle Koch, *World Water Watch*, 1993
    A picture-book, promoting conservation, explains the reasons why six animals, that depend on the sea for life, become endangered species.
Marcia Vaughan, *Snap!*, 1994
    Joey learns lots of great games playing with other animals, but when Crocodile plays "Snap!" Joey quickly invents "Tickle the Tonsils."

186

JEANNE BUSHEY
GERMAINE ARNAKTAUYOK, Illustrator

A Sled Dog for Moshi
(New York: Hyperion Books for Children, 1994)

Subject(s): Indians of North America; Animals/Dogs; Pets
Age range(s): Grades K-3
Major character(s): Moshi, Child, Indian (Inuit); Jessica, Child (newcomer); Nuna, Dog
Time period(s): 1990s (1994)
Locale(s): Iqaluit, Canada (Baffin Island)

Summary: Moshi's father is concerned and angry when his pregnant lead dog vanishes. Moshi, however, is more interested in playing with new friend Jessica and her pet terrier. When the girls walk to a nearby ridge on a spring day they become caught in a sudden snowstorm and are saved by Nuna who leads them to a shed where she has given birth. Jessica and Moshi rest with the puppies while Nuna goes for help. Moshi's father is proud of her Inuk survival skills and promises her one of the puppies. (40 pages)

Where it's reviewed:
Booklist, January 15, 1995, page 934
Horn Book Guide, Spring 1995, page 28
Publishers Weekly, October 24, 1994, page 61
Quill & Quire, August 1994, page 34
School Library Journal, January 1995, page 82

Other books you might like:
Mischa Damjan, *Atuk: A Story*, 1990
    When Atuk's puppy is killed by a wolf he learns that revenge is not always the answer to grief.
Jonathan London, *Red Wolf Country*, 1996
    She-Wolf and her mate roam the snowy countryside seeking a spot to safely deliver She-Wolf's cubs.
Nancy Luenn, *Nessa's Fish*, 1990
    During an ice-fishing trip, a young Inuit girl must defend herself and her ill grandmother from animal attacks.

187

JACK BUSHNELL
ROBERT ANDREW PARKER, Illustrator

Circus of the Wolves
(New York: Lothrop, Lee & Shepard Books, 1994)

Subject(s): Animals/Wolves; Circus
Age range(s): Grades 3-5

Major character(s): Kael, Wolf, Captive; Unnamed Character, Animal Trainer
Time period(s): 1990s (1994)
Locale(s): United States (near Lake Superior); Summerson-Appleby Circus

Summary: In the author's first book a timber wolf is captured and forced to join a circus. The animal trainer has many wolves which were born in captivity, but needs a wild wolf in order to teach the others to howl. Kael travels with the circus for a year until he returns to the area in which he was captured and escapes into the wild again. (32 pages)

Where it's reviewed:
Booklist, April 1, 1994, page 1458
Children's Book Review Service, June 1994, page 126
Kirkus Reviews, April 1, 1994, page 478
Publishers Weekly, April 25, 1994, page 77
School Library Journal, April 1994, page 124

Other books you might like:
Michael W. Fox, *The Wolf*, 1973
    Following five wolf cubs as they grow, the story shows their relationship to the family, pack, humans and the environment.
Jean Craighead George, *Julie of the Wolves*, 1974
    In a Newbery Award winning title, a pack of wolves comes to Julie's rescue during her trek across the Alaskan wilderness.
Jim Murphy, *The Call of the Wolves*, 1989
    In order to survive, a wounded wolf undertakes a treacherous journey.

188

MARIANNE BUSSER
RON SCHRODER, Illustrator
HANS DE BEER, Illustrator

On the Road with Poppa Whopper
(New York: North-South Books, 1995)

Series: Easy-to-Read
Subject(s): Work; Fathers and Daughters
Age range(s): Grades 2-4
Major character(s): Poppa Whopper, Father; Frannie Whopper, Child
Time period(s): 1990s (1995)
Locale(s): Europe

Summary: Poppa Whopper ignores official notices telling him his home is in the way of the new town hall, but he can't ignore the workman who's come to demolish the house. Packing their belongings in a used minicamper, Poppa Whopper and Frannie begin a life of independence and adventure. When they need money they work at a variety of jobs that come their way. Thanks to dumb luck rather than skill, they survive and prosper. Translated from the German by J. Alison James. (64 pages)

Where it's reviewed:
Booklist, July 1995, page 1878
Horn Book Guide, Fall 1995, page 290
School Library Journal, August 1995, page 115

Other books you might like:
Burny Bos, *More from the Molesons*, 1995
    A seemingly ordinary family of moles turns everyday activities into comical adventures.
Peggy Parish, *Come Back, Amelia Bedelia*, 1971
    Amelia has difficulty keeping a job because her literal interpretation of directions creates problems for her employers.
Mary Lyn Ray, *Alvah and Arvilla*, 1994
    Determined to see the Pacific Ocean, Arvilla has Alvah make a trailer greenhouse into which they load their livestock and their belongings for the trip.

189

NICK BUTTERWORTH, Author/Illustrator

The Secret Path
(Boston: Little, Brown and Company, 1995)

Subject(s): Gardens and Gardening; Animals; Surprises
Age range(s): Grades K-2
Major character(s): Percy, Gardener, Animal Lover
Time period(s): 1990s (1994)
Locale(s): England

Summary: The day Percy decides to trim the hedges in the maze, all his animal pals, except helper squirrel, hurry ahead to the center of the maze, planning a surprise. Percy's gardening chore takes so long the animals fall asleep while waiting and Percy tricks them instead. The biggest surprise comes when helper squirrel shows up with the string Percy had laid along the path to mark the way out. First published in Great Britain in 1994. (32 pages)

Where it's reviewed:
Booklist, April 15, 1995, page 1505
Books for Keeps, July 1995, page 7
Horn Book Guide, Fall 1995, page 260
School Librarian, February 1995, page 16
School Library Journal, June 1995, page 78

Other books by the same author:
The Rescue Party, 1993
One Blowy Night, 1992
One Snowy Night, 1990

Other books you might like:
David Martin, *Little Chicken Chicken*, 1996
    Little Chicken Chicken is an inventive thinker who is not fully appreciated by the other chickens until a thunderstorm blows the roof off the coop.
Gloria Rand, *Willie Takes a Hike*, 1996
    Willie prepares carefully for a hike in his new neighborhood so when he becomes lost, he is able to help rescuers find him.
Eve Rice, *Sam Who Never Forgets*, 1977
    All the animals look forward to seeing Sam the zookeeper and his wagon full of food.

190

NANCY BUTTS

Cheshire Moon

(Arden, NC: Front Street, 1996)

Subject(s): Death; Self-Acceptance; Deafness
Age range(s): Grades 4-7
Major character(s): Miranda Cooper, 12-Year-Old, Deaf; Boone Ligonier, 13-Year-Old, Artist; Mr. Leach, Store Owner, Storyteller
Time period(s): 1990s
Locale(s): Summerhaven, Maine

Summary: Against her will, Miranda is spending the summer with Aunt Kit on the island again. She doesn't want to go because she is haunted by memories of losing her best friend and cousin, Timothy. Upon arrival, she meets Boone, a new boy working in the store and helping her aunt. As they become friends and eventually overcome a communication problem, they realize that they are both having the same dreams. After hearing the story of a strange island, Boone and Miranda go there and find the spirit of Timothy, who tells Miranda that she can succeed on her own. She then has to help Boone get back to their island. Once home she determines to begin her life anew and face her handicap. (105 pages)

Where it's reviewed:
School Library Journal, November 1996, page 103

Other books you might like:
Jean F. Andrews, *The Secret in the Dorm Attic*, 1990
    While visiting a deaf friend, Donald discovers that there are strange things going on at the school and a nearby museum.
Claire H. Blatchford, *Nick's Mission*, 1995
    Nick, a deaf student, is upset about going to summer school but then he stumbles upon some smugglers and realizes he needs to know how to communicate.
John Neufeld, *Gaps in Stone Walls*, 1996
    Merry is a deaf child who lives on Martha's Vineyard in the 1800s, but when she is accused of murder she runs away.
Susan Richards Shreve, *The Gift of the Girl Who Couldn't Hear*, 1991
    Two friends help each other try out for the school play even though one of them is deaf.

191

BETSY BYARS

The Dark Stairs

(New York: Viking, 1994)

Subject(s): Mystery and Detective Stories
Age range(s): Grades 6-7
Major character(s): Herculeah Jones, Detective—Amateur, 13-Year-Old; Albert ''Meat'', Detective—Amateur, Neighbor (Herculeah's)
Time period(s): 1990s
Locale(s): United States

Summary: With a policeman father and a private investigator mother, Herculeah Jones has no choice but to be a female Sherlock Holmes. Right now she's interested in the disapppearance of Mr. Crewell several years ago. When she listens to her mother's tape of a client interview, she zeroes in on the mysterious mansion, Dead Oaks, as the probable location of the body. Enlisting her friend, Meat, to help protect her (though he falls asleep while standing guard at Dead Oaks) she solves the mystery of the missing body. But now somebody's after Herculeah. (130 pages)

Where it's reviewed:
Voice of Youth Advocates, February 1995, page 336
Publishers Weekly, July 18, 1994, page 246
Booklist, August 1994, page 2042
School Library Journal, September 1994, page 214
Kirkus Reviews, August 15, 1994, page 1122

Other books by the same author:
Growing Up Stories, 1995
McMummy, 1993
Coast to Coast, 1992
Wanted. . .Mud Blossom, 1991

Other books you might like:
Barbara Corcoran, *You're Allegro Dead*, 1981
    Two girls at summer camp discover a mystery when they find the abandoned loot from a bank robbery.
E.W. Hildick, *The Case of the Felon's Fiddle*, 1982
    Uncut diamonds and a note in a fiddle help McGurk solve this mystery.
Phyllis Reynolds Naylor, *The Bodies in the Bessledorf Hotel*, 1986
    When dead bodies start appearing at the Bessledorf Hotel, and then just as quickly disappearing, the manager's job is in trouble.

192

BETSY BYARS

Dead Letter

(New York: Viking, 1996)

Series: Herculeah Jones Mystery
Subject(s): Mystery and Detective Stories; Murder
Age range(s): Grades 4-7
Major character(s): Herculeah Jones, Detective—Amateur, Child of Divorced Parents; Albert ''Meat'', Sidekick, Detective—Amateur; Amanda Cole, Crime Victim (murdered), Equestrian
Time period(s): 1990s
Locale(s): North Carolina

Summary: Herculeah and Meat discover a letter hidden in the lining of a coat which leads them on another adventure. They try to discover what really happened to Amanda Cole, who died about the time the land she owned was being converted into a housing development. When some local businessmen discover Herculeah's interest in the case, she is followed by a strange black car and finds herself in danger from both men and dogs before the crime is solved. (147 pages)

Where it's reviewed:
Bulletin of the Center for Childrens Books, July/August 1996, page 365
School Library Journal, July 1996, page 84
Booklist, June 1, 1996, page 1715

Other books by the same author:
Tarot Says Beware, 1995
The Dark Stairs, 1994
The Summer of the Swans, 1970

Other books you might like:
Avi, *Who Stole the Wizard of Oz?*, 1990
   Books disappear from the book sale and young detectives are involved in finding them.
Eve Bunting, *Coffin on a Case*, 1992
   The son of a detective is enlisted to help find a missing woman.
E.W. Hildick, *The Case of the Desperate Drummer*, 1993
   MrGurk and his friends are involved in saving the drummer in a rock band. ,
James Howe, *Dew Drop Dead: A Sebastian Barth Mystery*, 1990
   Sebastian Barth finds a body but before he can investigate, it disappears.
Willo Davis Roberts, *What Could Go Wrong?*, 1989
   Children on a plane trip to visit relatives are involved in a mystery involving an older passenger.

193

BETSY BYARS
SUE TRUESDELL, Illustrator

The Golly Sisters Ride Again

(New York: HarperCollins Publishers, 1994)

Series: I Can Read
Subject(s): Sisters; Frontier and Pioneer Life; American West
Age range(s): Grades 1-3
Major character(s): May-May Golly, Entertainer, Sister; Rose Golly, Entertainer, Sister
Time period(s): Indeterminate Past
Locale(s): United States

Summary: The song and dance team of May-May and Rose returns in the third of their humorous adventures for beginning readers. Travelling by covered wagon, they perform in different towns and enjoy the sights as they journey to the next spot. (64 pages)

Where it's reviewed:
Booklist, April 1, 1994, page 1465
Bulletin of the Center for Children's Books, June 1994, page 314
Horn Book, July 1994, page 446
Parents Magazine, December 1994, page 24
School Library Journal, June 1994, page 96

Awards the book has won:
ALA Notable Book, 1995

Other books by the same author:
The Seven Treasure Hunts, 1992
Hooray for the Golly Sisters!, 1990
The Golly Sisters Go West, 1986

Other books you might like:
Kathryn O. Galbraith, *Roommates Again*, 1994
   Unexpectedly, sisters Beth and Mimi are roommates at camp when Mimi's friend Kelly is unable to go.
Lisa Westberg Peters, *The Hayloft*, 1995
   The three episodes in the beginning chapter book relate the summer activities of two sisters living on a farm.
Jean Van Leeuwen, *Two Girls in Sister Dresses*, 1994
   In five brief chapters, Molly and older sister Jennifer enjoy a day at the beach, a visit with a neighbor and the arrival of their baby brother.
Ferida Wolff, *Seven Loaves of Bread*, 1993
   When hard-working Milly falls ill, her less industrious sister Rose takes over the bread-baking chores with some humorous consequences.

194

BETSY BYARS
FRANK REMKIEWICZ, Illustrator

The Joy Boys

(New York: Delacorte, 1996)

Series: First Choice Chapter Book
Subject(s): Brothers; Farm Life; Animals/Dogs
Age range(s): Grades K-2
Major character(s): Harry Joy, Child, Brother; J.J. Joy, Child, Brother; Bono, Dog
Time period(s): 1990s
Locale(s): United States (farm)

Summary: The Joy brothers enjoy living on the farm and sharing adventures with their dog, like riding the cows and being chased by the bull. They also love playing in the mud, pillow fights, camping and looking for wild animals. (48 pages)

Where it's reviewed:
Bulletin of the Center for Children's Books, June 1996, page 328
School Library Journal, June 1996, page 93

Other books by the same author:
My Brother, Ant, 1996
The Golly Sisters Ride Again, 1994
McMummy, 1993

Other books you might like:
Ann Cameron, *Julian, Secret Agent*, 1987
   Two wonderful brothers share adventures with family and friends.
Stephen Krensky, *Lionel in the Spring*, 1990
   Lionel enjoys all kinds of things in the spring.
P.J. Petersen, *The Fireplug Is First Base*, 1990
   Joe's younger brother proves that he can play baseball.
Cynthia Rylant, *Henry and Mudge and the Best Dog of All*, 1995
   Henry and Mudge are such close friends that even though one is a dog they might be brothers.

195

BETSY BYARS

McMummy
(New York: Viking, 1993)

Subject(s): Supernatural; Single Parent Families
Age range(s): Grades 6-8
Major character(s): Robert "Mozie" Mozer, Babysitter; Howard "Batty" Batson, Babysitter; Valvoline Edwards, Beauty Pageant Contestant
Time period(s): 1990s
Locale(s): Downs City, South

Summary: Mozie thought he'd only have to set the timer to water the plants when he agreed to take care of Professor Orloff's greenhouse; never did he dream he'd find a pod that is as large as a human and shaped like a mummy. At first he's terrified of this pod, but gradually finds it calls to him. But what is it? And why does it call him? His best friend Batty, along with Valvoline, not only help him solve his dilemna about Professor Orloff's greenhouse but also accept his father's death. (150 pages)

Where it's reviewed:
Publishers Weekly, August 16, 1993, page 105
School Library Journal, September 1993, page 228
Center for Children's Books. Bulletin, October 1993, page 41
Horn Book Guide, Spring 1994, page 73
Library Talk, March 1994, page 50

Other books by the same author:
Growing Up Stories, 1995
The Dark Stairs, 1994
Bingo Brown and the Language of Love, 1989
House of Wings, 1972

Other books you might like:
Mel Gilden, *Outer Space and All That Junk*, 1989
    When Myron stays with eccentric Uncle Hugo, they spend the summer collecting junk, for Hugo's convinced that junk is just an alien in disguise.
Barbara Garland Polikoff, *Life's a Funny Proposition, Horatio*, 1992
    After Horatio's father dies, he has trouble accepting his grandfather's moving in with them, until O.P.'s dog dies which binds their hearts together.
William Sleator, *The Duplicate*, 1988
    David finds a gadget on the beach that duplicates himself; when there are three Davids, he knows things are out of control.
Robert Westall, *Urn Burial*, 1988
    A shepherd finds a cat-like body inside a coffin hidden in a cairn of stones, putting his village in a battle between two alien groups.

196

BETSY BYARS
MARC SIMONT, Illustrator

My Brother, Ant
(New York: Viking, 1996)

Series: Viking Easy to Read
Subject(s): Brothers; Family Life
Age range(s): Grades 1-3
Major character(s): Anthony "Ant", Child
Time period(s): 1990s
Locale(s): United States

Summary: Ant's big brother is so understanding and helpful in this easy reading book. He helps Ant get rid of the monster under his bed. He is upset but understanding when Ant draws a picture on his homework. He is willing to read to Ant and helps him write a letter to Santa. (32 pages)

Other books by the same author:
The Dark Stairs, 1994
The Golly Sisters Ride Again, 1993
McMummy, 1993

Other books you might like:
James Howe, *Pinky and Rex*, 1990
    Two very good friends enjoy all kinds of things together and support each other in this series.
Johanna Hurwitz, *Elisa in the Middle*, 1995
    Elisa is not the baby of the family anymore and so tries to help her big brother, including helping with his homework.
Jean Van Leeuwen, *Oliver & Amanda and the Big Snow*, 1995
    Oliver, the pig, helps his little sister face her fear of the snow until she is speeding down the hill on her sled.
Karen Lynn Williams, *First Grade King*, 1992
    Joey is worried about going to first grade.

197

BETSY BYARS
DORON BEN-AMI, Illustrator

Tornado
(New York: HarperCollins, 1996)

Subject(s): Animals/Dogs; Disasters; Weather
Age range(s): Grades 1-4
Major character(s): Pete, Animal Lover, Worker; Tornado, Dog
Time period(s): 1990s
Locale(s): United States

Summary: As the family waits out a tornado in the shelter, Pete tells them about his dog, Tornado, and how he first arrived, complete with his dog house, during another storm. The children have heard these stories before and ask for their favorites: the lying down place stolen by a cat, the card trick, the day the dog drank the turtle, and finally how Tornado returned after his original owner took him away. These stories keep the family entertained until the storm is over and father comes home. (49 pages)

Where it's reviewed:
School Library Journal, November 1996, page 78

Bulletin of the Center for Children's Books, November 1996, page 91

Booklist, September 15, 1996, page 238

Hornbook, November/December 1996, page 732

Other books by the same author:

Wanted. . .Mud Blossom, 1991

The Seven Treasure Hunts, 1991

The Summer of the Swans, 1970

Other books you might like:

Mary Jane Auch, *The Latchkey Dog*, 1994
Sam tries to arrange for a dog to live in his single parent family.

Helen Cresswell, *Posy Bates, Again!*, 1994
Posy tries different ways to keep the dog she found.

Karen Hesse, *Sable*, 1994
Tate's dog cannot be trained so she is given away until Tate is finally ready to care for her.

Phyllis Reynolds Naylor, *Shiloh*, 1991
When a beagle follows Marty home he finds that he must decide whether it is right to keep him.

Jane Resh Thomas, *The Comeback Dog*, 1981
Daniel tries to train a new dog following the death of his favorite setter.

C

198

B.B. CALHOUN
DANIEL MARK DUFFY, Illustrator

On the Right Track

(New York: W. H. Freeman and Company, 1994)

Series: Dinosaur Detective
Subject(s): Dinosaurs; Paleontology; Mystery and Detective Stories
Age range(s): Grades 3-5
Major character(s): Fenton Rumplemayer, 11-Year-Old, Detective—Amateur; Bill Rumplemeyer, Father, Scientist (paleontologist); Willy Whitefox, Child, Indian (Arapaho)
Time period(s): 1990s (1994)
Locale(s): New York, New York; Morgan, Wyoming (Sleeping Bear Mountain)

Summary: While Fenton's paleontologist mother studies in India, he and his father go to a dig site in Wyoming where dinosaur footprints which puzzle Fenton's dad and the other scientists are found. The tracks Fenton and Willy leave in the mud while riding their bikes to the dig site give Fenton an idea which provides an explanation to the mystery of the dinosaur tracks. (128 pages)

Where it's reviewed:
Booklist, May 15, 1994, page 1679
Horn Book Guide, Spring 1995, page 73
Publishers Weekly, April 11, 1994, page 65
School Library Journal, June 1994, page 126
Science Books and Films, November 1994, page 242

Other books by the same author:
Out of Place, 1994

Other books you might like:
Jean Craighead George, *The Fire Bug Connection: An Ecological Mystery*, 1993
When the fire bugs Maggie receives for her birthday grow so large they explode rather than metamorphose she enlists the aid of her friend Mitch to investigate.

Edward Packard, *Dinosaur Island*, 1993
In an entry in the Choose-Your-Own-Adventure series the reader determines the outcome.
Joel Matus, *Leroy and the Caveman*, 1993
In a cave, a 12-year-old boy finds a living specimen of a Neanderthal man.

199

MARY CALHOUN
ERICK INGRAHAM, Illustrator

Henry the Sailor Cat

(New York: Morrow Junior Books, 1994)

Subject(s): Animals/Cats; Sailing; Sea Stories
Age range(s): Grades K-2
Major character(s): Henry, Cat (pet Siamese); The Kid, Child; The Man, Father, Sailor
Time period(s): 1990s (1994)
Locale(s): At Sea

Summary: ''Hey, wait for me!'' says Henry to himself as he stows away on the family sailboat. The Man is giving The Kid sailing lessons and curious Henry wants to be a part of the action. The Man is annoyed to find him on board so Henry climbs the mast to stay out of the way. The trip is uneventful until The Man falls overboard just as a sudden storm approaches. Henry alerts The Kid and helps to guide him to The Man so the day ends successfully for The Man, The Kid and The Hero, Henry. (40 pages)

Where it's reviewed:
Booklist, May 1, 1994, page 1606
Horn Book, Sepember 1994, page 573
Kirkus Reviews, May 1, 1994, page 627
Publishers Weekly, April 4, 1994, page 80
School Library Journal, May 1994, page 89

Other books by the same author:
High-Wire Henry, 1991
Hot-Air Henry, 1981
Cross-Country Cat, 1979

Other books you might like:

Ruth Brown, *Copycat*, 1994
  Buddy the cat imitates the behavior of other animals until he tries to mimic the dog's habit of chewing on a bone and earns a trip to the vet.
Margaret Bloy Graham, *Benjy's Boat Trip*, 1977
  A ship's cat is not happy when a dog stows away on her ship hoping to find his vacationing family.
Curtis Parkinson, *Tom Foolery*, 1993
  Tom Foolery falls overboard from the family sailboat and is later retrieved from an island where he has sought refuge.
Amy Tan, *The Chinese Siamese Cat*, 1994
  Ming Miao tells her kittens of their ancestor's behavior thousands of years ago which resulted in the unique markings of their breed.

200

SHEILA MACGILL CALLAHAN
KRIS WALDHERR, Illustrator

The Seal Prince

(New York: Dial Books for Young Readers, 1995)

Subject(s): Fairy Tale; Folk Tales; Animals/Seals and Sea Lions
Age range(s): Grades 1-4
Major character(s): Grainne, Royalty; Deodatus, Seal, Royalty
Time period(s): Indeterminate Past
Locale(s): Skye, Scotland

Summary: On her eighth birthday, Princess Grainne rescues a young, injured seal trapped on the beach and returns him to the sea. Annually on her birthday, the seal returns and swims nearby as Grainne watches from the shore. On Grainne's 18th birthday, the seal takes human form as Deodatus and tries to entice Princess Grainne to join him in his kingdom. As an only child, Grainne refuses because of the duty she feels toward her parents and her people. Her love for Deodatus does not wain and she refuses all suitors until finally her father pledges to wed her to the man who brings the largest catch of fish by sunrise. Thus, Deodatus wins her hand, pledging to live on land until their eldest son is old enough to rule at which time he and Grainne will dwell in his land beneath the sea. (32 pages)

Where it's reviewed:
Booklist, February 1, 1996, page 935
Horn Book Guide, Spring 1996, page 92
School Library Journal, September 1995, page 195

Other books by the same author:
When Solomon Was King, 1995
The Children of Lir, 1993
And Still the Turtle Watched, 1991

Other books you might like:

Susan Cooper, *The Selkie Girl*, 1986
  Cooper retells the classic love story of a man and a seal-girl and the selkie's desire to return to her home in the sea.

Eric Jon Nones, *Caleb's Friend*, 1993
  Orphan Caleb and a mer-boy develop a mutually beneficial relationship.
Jill Paton Walsh, *Matthew and the Sea Singer*, 1993
  When the seal-queen steals Matthew, Birdy must strike a bargain to get him back.
Sylvia Peck, *Seal Child*, 1989
  During a winter visit to the Maine coast, Molly meets an unusual girl named Meara, a selkie.
Robert D. San Souci, *Nicholas Pipe*, 1997
  When Margaret, a fisherman's daughter, falls in love with the forbidden Nicholas Pipe, a merman, each forsakes family to remain together.

201

STEPHANIE CALMENSON
ELIVIA, Illustrator

Hotter than a Hot Dog!

(Boston: Little, Brown and Company, 1994)

Subject(s): Beaches; Summer; Grandparents
Age range(s): Grades K-2
Major character(s): Granny, Grandmother; Unnamed Character, Child
Time period(s): 1990s (1994)
Locale(s): United States

Summary: On a hot, hot day Granny and granddaughter decide to escape their steamy city stoop and seek relief at the beach. A day of sitting and swimming until the sun sets leaves them refreshed, tired and happy to return home to be greeted by a cool evening breeze.

Where it's reviewed:
Booklist, April 1, 1994, page 1458
Horn Book, May 1994, page 309
Language Arts, March 1995, page 222
Publishers Weekly, February 28, 1994, page 87
School Library Journal, May 1994, page 89

Awards the book has won:
International Reading Association Children's Choice, 1995

Other books by the same author:
Dinner at the Panda Palace, 1991
The Principal's New Clothes, 1989
Where's Rufus, 1988

Other books you might like:

Olof Landstrom, *Will Goes to the Beach*, 1995
  When Will and his mother bike to the beach for a picnic, even a little rain does not spoil Will's fun. Co-author Lena Landstrom; translation by Carla Wiberg.
Evan Levine, *Not the Piano, Mrs. Medley!*, 1991
  A trip to the beach with grandson Max is no simple matter for Mrs. Medley who wants to be prepared for anything and everything.
Marjory Wunsch, *Aunt Belle's Beach*, 1994
  Aunt Belle attracts attention at the beach with her flowered bathing cap, bright red suit and warm-up exercises.

202

STEPHANIE CALMENSON
MARY CHALMERS, Illustrator

Marigold and Grandma on the Town

(New York: HarperCollins, 1994)

Series: I Can Read
Subject(s): Animals/Rabbits; Grandparents; Shopping
Age range(s): Grades K-2
Major character(s): Marigold, Rabbit; Grandma, Grandmother
Time period(s): 1990s (1994)
Locale(s): United States

Summary: Four brief chapters describe Marigold and Grandma's day together as they shop for a new hat, eat in a restaurant, feed the ducks and enjoy each other. (64 pages)

Where it's reviewed:
Booklist, February 1, 1994, page 1012
Bulletin of the Center for Children's Books, March 1994, page 217
Horn Book, March 1994, page 194
Kirkus Reviews, January 1, 1994, page 64
School Library Journal, April 1994, page 101

Other books by the same author:
Hotter than a Hot Dog!, 1994
The Principal's New Clothes, 1991
One Little Monkey, 1982

Other books you might like:
Barbara Baker, *One Saturday Morning*, 1994
    Six members of the bear family are featured in an easy reader about their Saturday experiences.
Emily Arnold McCully, *Grandmas at Bat*, 1993
    Two competitive grandmothers with good intentions complicate things for Pip's baseball team in another entry in the ''I Can Read'' series.
Marjorie Dennis Murray, *Saturday with Little Rabbit*, 1993
    In an easy reader, Little Rabbit and his best friends enjoy a day of fishing, picking berries, climbing trees, and playing at the park.

203

JANELL CANNON, Author/Illustrator

Stellaluna

(New York: Harcourt Brace Jovanovich, Publishers, 1993)

Subject(s): Animals/Bats; Animals/Birds; Friendship
Age range(s): Grades K-3
Major character(s): Stellaluna, Bat (fruit bat)
Time period(s): 1990s (1993)
Locale(s): Earth (forest)

Summary: When an owl frightens her mother, baby Stellaluna tumbles away from her and lands in a birds' nest where she is befriended by three baby birds. The mother bird is not happy to find her offspring hanging upside down with Stellaluna, so the bat agrees to change her ways. When all the infants are old enough to fly, Stellaluna finds she cannot land on a branch as the birds do. Other fruit bats find her hanging the ''wrong''

way and instruct her in proper bat behavior. Mom finds her too and Stellaluna's life as a bat resumes. (48 pages)

Where it's reviewed:
Booklist, April 1, 1993, page 1436
Children's Book Review Service, Spring 1993, page 133
Kirkus Reviews, April 1, 1993, page 452
Publishers Weekly, April 26, 1993, page 78
School Library Journal, June 1993, page 70

Awards the book has won:
American Booksellers Book of the Year, 1994
Book Links Good Book, 1993

Other books by the same author:
Trupp: A Fuzzhead Tale, 1995

Other books you might like:
P.D. Eastman, *Are You My Mother?*, 1960
    A lost baby bird meets many different animals as it searches for its mother.
Kate Green, *A Number of Animals*, 1993
    Searching for his mother in a barnyard crowded with animals, a young chick is relieved to finally find her.
Keiko Kasza, *A Mother for Choco*, 1992
    Choco, a young, motherless bird, searches for someone who resembles him only to discover that looks can be deceiving.
Lynn Reiser, *The Surprise Family*, 1994
    Surprised when her newly hatched chicks decide to go swimming, Mother Chick realizes that she has ducklings for a family, but she accepts them as her own anyway.

204

KATHY CAPLE, Author/Illustrator

The Wimp

(Boston: Houghton Mifflin Company, 1994)

Subject(s): Bullies; Brothers and Sisters; Schools
Age range(s): Grades K-2
Major character(s): Arnold, Pig, Bullied Child; Rose, Pig, Sister (Arnold's); Clyde, Bully, Student
Time period(s): 1990s (1994)
Locale(s): United States

Summary: Rose is not sympathetic or particularly helpful when Arnold is bothered repeatedly by Clyde and his friend. When she steps forward to help him the bullies manage to leaves the siblings holding the evidence of their spray-painting just as the principal arrives. To avoid further contact with the duo, Rose and Arnold sneak to school early the next day and find the graffiti painters on the roof. Quick-witted Arnold seizes the opportunity and the ladder—just as the principal appears. (32 pages)

Where it's reviewed:
Booklist, June 1, 1994, page 1835
Horn Book Guide, Spring 1995, page 28
Kirkus Reviews, September 15, 1994, page 1267
Publishers Weekly, August 8, 1994, page 434
School Library Journal, September 1994, page 180

Awards the book has won:
International Reading Association Children's Choice, 1995

Other books by the same author:
Fox and Bear, 1992
The Coolest Place in Town, 1990
The Biggest Nose, 1985

Other books you might like:
Barbara Bottner, *Bootsie Barker Bites*, 1992
  Bootsie Barker terrorizes the daughter of her mother's friend whenever the two moms get together until the day Bootsie arrives to find her hostess has carefully prepared for the visit.
Anthony Browne, *Willy the Wimp*, 1985
  Chimp Willy is tired of being bullied so he sends away for a book to help him learn to deal with a gang of apes.
Keiko Kasza, *The Rat and the Tiger*, 1993
  Rat stands up for his rights when his friend Tiger uses his larger size to bully Rat.
James Marshall, *The Cut-Ups Cut Loose*, 1987
  Spud and Joe may have to change their ways; the new school principal does not tolerate their kind of behavior.

205

ALYSSA SATIN CAPUCILLI
CYNTHIA JABAR, Illustrator

Good Morning, Pond

(New York: Hyperion Books for Children, 1994)

Subject(s): Animals/Frogs and Toads; Animals; Stories in Rhyme
Age range(s): Grades K-1
Major character(s): Unnamed Character, Frog
Time period(s): 1990s (1994)
Locale(s): United States

Summary: By leaping into the pond, a little green frog signals the other pond animals to wake-up. One by one fish, snails, salamanders, grasshoppers and turtles begin moving about. When the dragonflies begin buzzing the signal for singing time, toads, ducks and geese respond with their individual calls. All the early morning pond activity is observed by three pajama-clad children who hurry to greet the day at the pond's edge. (32 pages)

Where it's reviewed:
Children's Book Review Service, February 1995, page 73
Horn Book Guide, Spring 1995, page 28
School Library Journal, November 1994, page 72

Other books by the same author:
Inside a Barn in the Country, 1995
Peekaboo Bunny, 1994

Other books you might like:
Ermanno Cristini, *In the Pond*, 1984
  A wordless picture book introduces the variety of life found in a pond. Co-author/illustrator Luigi Puricelli.
Kathryn Lasky, *Pond Year*, 1995
  Two best friends enjoy the pond near their home in every season of the year.
Nancy Tafuri, *Early Morning in the Barn*, 1983
  As the day begins, the sounds of waking animals are heard in the barn.

206

ALYSSA SATIN CAPUCILLI
TEDD ARNOLD, Illustrator

Inside a Barn in the Country: A Rebus Read-Along Story

(New York: Scholastic Inc., 1995)

Subject(s): Animals; Farm Life; Stories in Rhyme
Age range(s): Grades K-1
Major character(s): Unnamed Character, Mouse; Unnamed Character, Farmer
Time period(s): 1990s (1995)
Locale(s): United States

Summary: It starts with the squeak of a mouse, chased by a cat, waking a horse whose whinny wakes a cow and then one by one all the other barn animals. The commotion awakens the farmer who yells at the animals and tells them to go back to sleep until morning—and they do.

Where it's reviewed:
Booklist, January 15, 1995, page 935
Horn Book Guide, Fall 1995, page 260
Publishers Weekly, March 27, 1995, page 84
Reading Teacher, April 1996, page 571
School Library Journal, April 1995, page 98

Other books by the same author:
Good Morning, Pond, 1994
Peekaboo Bunny, 1994

Other books you might like:
Craig Brown, *My Barn*, 1991
  As the sun rises, Farmer Brown goes to the barn where he is greeted by the sounds of awakening animals.
Peter Harris, *Mouse Creeps*, 1997
  Innocently, a mouse crosses a room, initiating a chain of unexpected events that culminates with all the farm animals on the run.
David L. Harrison, *Wake Up, Sun!*, 1986
  A dog awakens unexpectedly during the night and thinks it's morning, but the sun is missing so he wakes all the other animals to help him search for it.
Colin West, *One Day in the Jungle*, 1995
  A butterfly's tiny sneeze is the first in a sequence of sneezes which concludes with an elephant whose very big sneeze blows away the jungle.
Sue Williams, *I Went Walking*, 1990
  A lively cumulative tale describes the animals a young child meets while walking.

207

PETER CAREY
ABIRA ALI, Illustrator

The Big Bazoohley

(New York: Henry Holt and Company, 1995)

Subject(s): Parent and Child; Contests; Money
Age range(s): Grades 3-5
Major character(s): Sam Kellow, 9-Year-Old; Earl Kellow, Father, Gambler; Vanessa Kellow, Mother, Artist

Time period(s): 1990s (1995)
Locale(s): Toronto, Ontario, Canada

Summary: Sam's life is one of endless travel as Earl Kellow seeks the ''Big Bazoohley'' or jackpot. However, it is Vanessa's artwork which brings the family to Toronto. With very little money, the family is so dependent on the sale that, when the rich buyer of the painting cannot be located, anxious Sam sleepwalks himself into adventure and a big bazoohley of his own making. First children's book for the author of adult novels. (133 pages)

Where it's reviewed:
Booklist, November 1, 1995, page 469
Bulletin of the Center for Children's Books, December 1995, page 121
Children's Book Review Service, November 1995, page 32
Publishers Weekly, September 18, 1995, page 134
School Library Journal, October 1995, page 132

Other books you might like:
Bill Brittain, *All the Money in the World*, 1979
     When Quentin's wish comes true he learns that riches do not make life trouble-free.
Paula Danziger, *Not for a Billion Gazillion Dollars*, 1992
     In the sequel to *Earth to Matthew*, Matthew learn s the value of money and starts his own business while trying to earn enough money for a computer program.
Stephen Manes, *Make Four Million Dollars by Next Thursday!*, 1991
     Jason follows the unconventional advice in a get-rich-quick book.
Thomas Rockwell, *How to Get Fabulously Rich*, 1990
     After winning the lottery, Billy finds the money creates problems with friends who want a share and will stoop to any means to get it.

208

VALERIE SCHO CAREY
DIRK ZIMMER, Illustrator

Tsugele's Broom

(New York: HarperCollins, 1993)

Subject(s): Parent and Child; Determination; Marriage
Age range(s): Grades K-3
Major character(s): Tsugele, Young Woman (independent), Housekeeper
Time period(s): Indeterminate Past
Locale(s): Potsk, Poland

Summary: Tsugele's parents imagine the future husband of their hard-working daughter as a lucky man indeed. Tsugele, however, has no interest in a husband. The suitors selected by the local matchmaker only confirm her intention to stick with her trusty broom, leave home, and seek employment in the next town. One night, Tsugele has an unusual dream in which she is attending her own wedding. Upon awakening, she searches in vain for her reliable broom, but finds instead a young man named Broom in the yard chopping wood. Accepting the miracle that was revealed to her in the dream, Tsugele concludes that this is the mate she's been waiting for—someone as reliable as her broom. (48 pages)

Where it's reviewed:
Booklist, March 1, 1993, page 1234
Children's Book Review Service, May 1993, page 110
Kirkus Reviews, February 15, 1993, page 223
Publishers Weekly, February 1, 1993, page 95
School Library Journal, June 1993, page 70

Awards the book has won:
ALA Notable Book, 1994

Other books by the same author:
Harriet & William & the Terrible Creature, 1990

Other books you might like:
Petra Mathers, *Victor and Christabel*, 1993
     Christabel, transformed into a painting by her evil cousin, is freed through the love of Victor.
Chris Van Allsburg, *The Widow's Broom*, 1992
     After the Widow Shaw assists a witch who has fallen into her garden, she discovers the broom left behind by the witch.
Jane Yolen, *Sleeping Ugly*, 1981
     In this twist on a classic fairy tale, beauty of spirit wins out over physical beauty and all live happily ever after.

209

ERIC CARLE, Author/Illustrator

My Apron

(New York: Philomel Books, 1994)

Subject(s): Aunts and Uncles; Construction; Work
Age range(s): Grades K-1
Major character(s): Adam, Uncle, Worker (plasterer); Elizabeth, Aunt, Seamstress; Unnamed Character, 8-Year-Old
Time period(s): Indeterminate Past
Locale(s): United States

Summary: When a young boy admires his uncle's work apron, Aunt Elizabeth sews another just for him and Uncle Adam allows him to help with the plastering work. The visit concludes with a sense of satisfaction for the young boy and his plans to visit again next year when he hopes to have a hat just like Uncle Adam's too. (20 pages)

Where it's reviewed:
Booklist, December 1, 1994, page 685
Kirkus Reviews, September 15, 1994, page 1268
Library Talk, January 1995, page 34
Publishers Weekly, August 1, 1994, page 79
School Library Journal, November 1994, page 73

Other books by the same author:
Walter the Baker, 1993
The Very Hungry Caterpillar, 1981
The Grouchy Ladybug, 1977

Other books you might like:
Candice Christiansen, *The Ice Horse*, 1993
     Jack is proud to be invited to help his uncle harvest the ice from the frozen Hudson River.
Patricia Edwards, *Chester and His Uncle Willoughby*, 1987
     Chester sits on the porch with his uncle, enjoying his company and swapping stories.

Emmy Payne, *Katy No-Pocket*, 1973

A mother kangaroo without a pocket has a real problem until a sympathetic carpenter gives her his work apron.

210

ERIC CARLE, Author/Illustrator

The Very Lonely Firefly

(New York: Philomel Books, 1995)

Subject(s): Animals/Insects; Loneliness
Age range(s): Grades K-1
Major character(s): Unnamed Character, Firefly (lonely)
Time period(s): 1990s (1995)
Locale(s): United States

Summary: Just as the sun sets, a firefly is born. In hopes of finding more fireflies, the lonely young firefly travels toward any light it sees, mistakenly flying toward a light, a candle, a lantern, car headlights, and a sky full of fireworks . When the bright lights of the fireworks subside, happily, the lonely firefly finds a group of flashing fireflies to join. (28 pages)

Where it's reviewed:
Booklist, May 15, 1995, page 1651
Horn Book, September 1995, page 625
Library Talk, September 1995, page 22
Publishers Weekly, June 5, 1995, page 63
School Library Journal, August 1995, page 115

Other books by the same author:
The Very Quiet Cricket, 1990
The Very Busy Spider, 1984
The Very Hungry Caterpillar, 1970

Other books you might like:
Julie Brinckloe, *Fireflies! Story and Pictures*, 1985
A jar of fireflies reminds a little boy of moonlight, but he realizes that the light will dim and he must release the insects.
Shulamith Levey Oppenheim, *Fireflies for Nathan*, 1994
While visiting his grandparents, Nathan catches fireflies just as his father did as a child.
Philemon Sturges, *Ten Flashing Fireflies*, 1995
Two children capture ten fireflies, then watch them fly away.

211

NANCY CARLSON, Author/Illustrator

Arnie and the Skateboard Gang

(New York: Viking , 1995)

Subject(s): Sports/Skateboarding; Courage; Peer Pressure
Age range(s): Grades K-3
Major character(s): Arnie, Cat; Tina, Squirrel; Fly, Dog
Time period(s): 1990s (1995)
Locale(s): Fictional Country

Summary: After receiving a skateboard for his birthday, Arnie is eager to become one of the "cool" kids. Tina takes him to the park where they meet Fly and other skaters more competent and daring. With practice Arnie and Tina are accepted into the "gang" and head over to Hairy Kerry Hill where Fly leads the way down, down, down. Returning with a bump on his head after wiping out, Fly badgers Arnie to go next. A confident Arnie goes—right back to the park with Tina and the other skaters. (32 pages)

Where it's reviewed:
Booklist, June 1995, page 1782
Horn Book Guide, Fall 1995, page 260
School Library Journal, August 1995, page 121

Other books by the same author:
Arnie and the New Kid, 1990
Arnie Goes to Camp, 1988
Arnie and the Stolen Markers, 1987
Harriet and the Roller Coaster, 1982

Other books you might like:
Kirsten Hall, *I'm Not Scared*, 1994
Two boys who think they fear nothing reconsider their courage as they listen to night sounds during an overnight camping trip.
Gail Herman, *Fievel's Big Showdown*, 1992
In a beginning reader, Fievel proves that he is not afraid by cleverly rescuing his sister and friends from a large cat.
Jane O'Connor, *Molly the Brave and Me*, 1990
While visiting admired friend Molly's rural home, Beth discovers courage within herself when the two are lost in a cornfield.

212

NANCY WHITE CARLSTROM
JAMES GRAHAM HALE, Illustrator

Barney Is Best

(New York: HarperCollins Publishers, 1994)

Subject(s): Toys; Hospitals; Hispanic Americans
Age range(s): Grades K-1
Major character(s): Unnamed Character, Child, Patient; Barney, Toy (elephant)
Time period(s): 1990s (1994)
Locale(s): United States

Summary: Feeling a little anxious the day before a scheduled tonsillectomy, a young boy tries to decide which stuffed animal to bring with him for comfort. Each member of the family has a different suggestion, but eventually they all agree that "Barney is best." (32 pages)

Where it's reviewed:
Booklist, November 1, 1994, page 505
Children's Book Review Service, November 1, 1994, page 505
Horn Book Guide, Spring 1995, page 28
Kirkus Reviews, October 15, 1994, page 1406
School Library Journal, October 1994, page 88

Other books by the same author:
What Would You Do If You Lived at the Zoo?, 1994
Who Gets the Sun out of Bed?, 1992
Wild, Wild Sunflower Child Anna, 1987

Other books you might like:

Martine Davison, *Rita Goes to the Hospital*, 1992
> When Rita goes to the hospital to have her tonsils removed, she finds the friendly staff to be comforting.

Deborah Hautzig, *A Visit to the Sesame Street Hospital*, 1985
> Prior to his tonsillectomy Grover visits the hospital in preparation for his surgery.

Elizabeth Winthrop, *Being Brave Is Best*, 1984
> Coping with a hospital stay for the removal of tonsils requires a brave outlook.

213

NANCY WHITE CARLSTROM
LISA DESIMINI, Illustrator

Fish and Flamingo

(Boston: Little, Brown and Company, 1993)

Subject(s): Friendship; Animals; Gifts
Age range(s): Grades K-3
Major character(s): Fish, Fish, Friend (to Flamingo); Flamingo, Bird, Friend (to Fish)
Time period(s): 1990s (1993)
Locale(s): Mexico

Summary: Where the sea meets the sand, Fish meets Flamingo and an unlikely friendship blossoms. Though each can never know the other's world, they share knowledge of their experiences. When it is time for Flamingo to join the other migrating birds, Fish receives, unbeknowst to Flamingo, a parting gift from the flock and also, with the other fish gathered to watch the flock depart, unknowingly gives one to Flamingo. (32 pages)

Where it's reviewed:
Booklist, March 15, 1993, page 1358
Children's Book Review Service, May 1993, page 110
Horn Book, May 1993, page 313
Publishers Weekly, April 12, 1993, page 62
School Library Journal, June 1993, page 70

Other books by the same author:
Happy Birthday, Jesse Bear!, 1994
Rise and Shine, 1993
I'm Not Moving, Mama!, 1990

Other books you might like:

Leo Lionni, *Swimmy*, 1987
> A small fish seeks the cooperation of others in a creative solution to an underwater problem.

Marcus Pfister, *Rainbow Fish*, 1992
> A unique, but lonely fish learns a lesson in sharing and friendship.

Jane Yolen, *Honkers*, 1993
> A lonely young girl and 3 abandoned geese share a summer of activity before the approach of winter forces them to part.

214

NANCY WHITE CARLSTROM
BRUCE DEGEN, Illustrator

Happy Birthday, Jesse Bear!

(New York: Macmillan Publishing Company, 1994)

Series: Jesse Bear
Subject(s): Animals/Bears; Birthdays; Stories in Rhyme
Age range(s): Grades K-2
Major character(s): Jesse Bear, Bear
Time period(s): 1990s (1994)
Locale(s): United States

Summary: The invitations have been sent, the preparations are complete, and Jesse waits impatiently for the party guests to arrive at his birthday party. The celebration is fun for everyone as the games are played, presents opened and cake eaten. When the party ends, the guests depart and Jesse's parents collapse, exhausted, while he plays with his new toys. (26 pages)

Where it's reviewed:
Horn Book Guide, Spring 1995, page 29
Publishers Weekly, October 3, 1994, page 67
School Library Journal, December 1994, page 72

Other books by the same author:
How Do You Say It Today, Jesse Bear?, 1992
It's About Time, 1990
Better Not Get Wet, Jesse Bear, 1988

Other books you might like:

Frank Asch, *Happy Birthday, Moon*, 1985
> A little bear is determined to present the moon with a gift for its birthday.

Lee Davis, *P.B. Bear's Birthday Party*, 1994
> Stuffed-animal friends gather to help P. B. Bear celebrate his birthday.

Helen Oxenbury, *It's My Birthday*, 1993
> When a young child decides to make a birthday cake, animal friends arrive with the ingredients, assist with the baking and then help to eat their handiwork.

215

CAROL CARRICK
PADDY BOUMA, Illustrator

Valentine

(New York: Clarion Books, 1995)

Subject(s): Animals/Sheep; Grandparents; Mothers and Daughters
Age range(s): Grades K-2
Major character(s): Mama, Mother, Office Worker; Heather, Child; Grandma, Grandmother
Time period(s): 1990s (1995)
Locale(s): United States

Summary: Heather doesn't understand why Mama must work on Valentine's Day. Grandma distracts and cheers her by baking cookies and checking on a pregnant sheep. Grandma and Heather find the sheep has delivered three lambs, but only two are strong enough to stand and nurse. Heather and

Grandma carry the sickly lamb to the house to warm and feed it. Caring for the lamb, whom she appropriately names Valentine, helps Heather forget her own sadness and pass the time until Mama returns. (29 pages)

Where it's reviewed:
Booklist, April 1, 1995, page 1422
Horn Book Guide, Fall 1995, page 260
Reading Teacher, December 1995, page 327
School Library Journal, May 1995, page 82
Smithsonian, November 1995, page 167

Other books by the same author:
The Very Little Sisters, 1993
In the Moonlight, Waiting, 1990
Left Behind, 1988

Other books you might like:
Antonia Barber, *Gemma and the Baby Chick*, 1993
    When Gemma's mother finds a rejected egg, Gemma helps to keep it warm until it hatches and then returns the baby chick to its sleeping mother.
Wende Devlin, *Cranberry Valentine*, 1986
    Maggie and her grandmother's sewing circle send secret valentines to Mr. Whiskers to cheer him.
Mick Inkpen, *If I Had a Sheep*, 1988
    With a sheep as a pet, a little girl imagines all the fun she would have.
Kim Lewis, *Emma's Lamb*, 1991
    While helping a lost lamb find his mother, Emma cares for and plays with him.

216

JOAN CARRIS

Stolen Bones

(Boston: Little, Brown and Co., 1993)

Subject(s): Grandparents; Mystery and Detective Stories; Archaeology
Age range(s): Grades 4-6
Major character(s): Alec Wright, 11-Year-Old; David A. ''Dr. D'' Dillon, Scientist (paleontologist), Grandfather (Alec's); Rina Grunder, 11-Year-Old
Time period(s): 1990s
Locale(s): Montana (The Badlands)

Summary: During what should be an exciting summer on a dinosaur dig, Alec feels he must prove himself to his distant, unfeeling grandfather, the paleontologist in charge of the dig. When Alec's mother says that his grandfather is upset because some dinosaur bones are missing, Alec and his friend Rina begin their own mystery investigation. In their search, they also come across clues to explain Dr. D's unease with his grandson. (160 pages)

Where it's reviewed:
Voice of Youth Advocates, June 1993, page 86
Booklist, May 1, 1993, page 1588
School Library Journal, April 1993, page 117
Center for Children's Books. Bulletin, June 1993, page 309
Kirkus Reviews, May 15, 1993, page 657

Other books by the same author:
Beware the Ravens, Aunt Morbelia, 1995

Rusty Timmons' First Million, 1985
Pets, Vets and Marty Howard, 1984

Other books you might like:
Lloyd Alexander, *The Illyrian Adventure*, 1986
    Holly Vesper begins the first of many adventures as she conducts archaeological research on an ancient legend.
Laurence R. Kittleman, *Canyons beyond the Sky*, 1985
    Evan has a chance to work on an archaeological dig with a father he scarcely knows but winds up traveling back in time.
Kathryn Lasky, *The Bone Wars*, 1988
    In the 1870s, teens Thad and Julian meet on a fossil dig in the Black Hills where their find astounds the paleontologists.
Cynthia Voigt, *The Vandemark Mummy*, 1991
    Someone steals a newly-donated mummy from Vandemark College's collection and Althea and Phineas help their father retrieve it.

217

MARY CASANOVA

Riot

(New York: Hyperion, 1996)

Subject(s): Fathers and Sons; Labor Conditions
Age range(s): Grades 4-7
Major character(s): Bryan Grant, 6th Grader; Chelsie Retting, 6th Grader; Stan Grant, Unemployed (union worker)
Time period(s): 1990s
Locale(s): United States

Summary: Bryan cannot decide what to do. His father is out of work and the company he worked for is hiring non-union workers. His dad and his friends are constantly speaking out against the ''rats'' who have come to take their jobs and their actions lead to a riot. Meanwhile Bryan has met a new girl in town and would like to know her better, but she is the daughter of one of the rats. Bryan's dad has always told him to stand up for what he thinks is right, but now he is confused. When the riot breaks out and his dad is arrested, Bryan faces a decision about doing the right thing because he has the whole thing on tape. (116 pages)

Where it's reviewed:
Booklist, November 1, 1996, page 497
School Library Journal, October 1996, page 120

Other books by the same author:
Moose Tracks, 1995

Other books you might like:
Bonnie Bader, *East Side Story*, 1993
    A young girl and her sister who are working in a sweatshop join a protest to try to improve the working conditions.
Barthe DeClements, *Breaking Out*, 1991
    Jerry is still trying to adjust to the fact that his father is in prison as he enters junior high school.
Judith Eichler Weber, *Forbidden Friendship*, 1993
    Molly befriends one of the Chinese workers brought in to replace the striking employees at her father's factory.

218

JUDITH CASELEY

Harry and Arney
(New York: Greenwillow Books, 1994)

Series: Kane Family Chronicles
Subject(s): Babies; Brothers and Sisters; Family Life
Age range(s): Grades 2-4
Major character(s): Harry Kane, 6-Year-Old, Brother; Lillian Kane, Mother; Arney Kane, Brother (baby)
Time period(s): 1990s (1994)
Locale(s): United States

Summary: Non-stop Harry is full of ideas and one of them lands him in the Emergency Room with a cut that needs stitching at the same time that his mother arrives to deliver her 4th baby. With two older sisters, Harry is relieved to have a brother and promptly names him Arney after the doctor who sews the cut in his leg. Harry's very patient family tolerates his never-ending ideas despite the problems they sometimes cause. (138 pages)

Where it's reviewed:
Booklist, September 1, 1994, page 39
Horn Book, January 1995, page 75
Horn Book Guide, Spring 1995, page 65
Kirkus Reviews, July 15, 1994, page 980
School Library Journal, September 1994, page 182

Other books by the same author:
Chloe in the Know, 1993
Starring Dorothy Kane, 1992
Hurricane Harry, 1991

Other books you might like:
Judy Blume, *Superfudge*, 1980
    A sequel to *Tales of a Fourth Grade Nothing* finds Peter continuing to endure the problems created by his energetic little brother.
Johanna Hurwitz, *Russell Sprouts*, 1987
    Six-year-old Russell is growing up fast and worrying about everything.
Philippa Pearce, *Here Comes Tod!*, 1994
    The episodic beginning chapter book features a lively 6-year-old and his loving family.

219

JUDITH CASELEY, Author/Illustrator

Mama, Coming and Going
(New York: Greenwillow Books, 1994)

Subject(s): Babies; Parent and Child; Memory
Age range(s): Grades K-2
Major character(s): Jenna, Child, Sister (Older); Mickey, Child (baby), Brother; Mama, Mother (forgetful)
Time period(s): 1990s (1994)
Locale(s): United States

Summary: After Mickey is born, Jenna notices that her mom is often forgetful. Some days nothing seems to go right and Mama says she doesn't know if she's "coming or going." Big sister Jenna helps to keep Mickey happy when he's acci-

dently locked in the car and finds Mama's lost sun hat. (32 pages)

Where it's reviewed:
Booklist, March 1, 1994, page 1268
Horn Book, May 1994, page 310
Horn Book Guide, Fall 1994, page 267
Kirkus Reviews, March 15, 1994, page 393
School Library Journal, May 1994, page 89

Other books by the same author:
Sophie and Sammy's Library Sleepover, 1993
Annie's Potty, 1990
Silly Baby, 1988

Other books you might like:
Jane Cutler, *Darcy and Gran Don't Like Babies*, 1993
    Big sister Darcy is relieved when Gran professes to share her lack of interest in the new baby and takes Darcy to the park.
Amy Schwartz, *A Teeny Tiny Baby*, 1994
    When the new baby arrives, this family has no big sister to help, but plenty of doting grandparents.
Carol Snyder, *One Up, One Down*, 1995
    With twins there is always one up when the other one is down keeping big sister Katie helping her parents.

220

JUDITH CASELEY, Author/Illustrator

Priscilla Twice
(New York: Greenwillow Books, 1995)

Subject(s): Divorce; Parent and Child; Family Problems
Age range(s): Grades K-2
Major character(s): Priscilla, Child of Divorced Parents; Mama, Mother; Papa, Father
Time period(s): 1990s (1995)
Locale(s): United States

Summary: Priscilla is aware of the friction between her parents, but not until she questions why they no longer speak to one another does she learn of their plan to divorce. Soon Papa moves into an apartment and Priscilla begins living one week with Mama and the other with Papa. While her parents assure Priscilla of their love and she adjusts to having two sets of toys, clothes and toothbrushes, she makes it clear that she would prefer an "all-together-family." (32 pages)

Where it's reviewed:
Booklist, August 1995, page 1954
Children's Book Review Service, September 1995, page 6
Horn Book, January 1996, page 61
Publishers Weekly, August 21, 1995, page 66
School Library Journal, September 1995, page 168

Other books by the same author:
Mr. Green Peas, 1995
Three Happy Birthdays, 1989
When Grandpa Came to Stay, 1986

Other books you might like:
C.B. Christiansen, *My Mother's House, My Father's House*, 1989

A child of divorced parents grows accustomed to the necessity of travelling between the two homes.

Linda Walvoord Girard, *At Daddy's on Saturday*, 1987
When her parents' divorce, Katie feels anger and concern, but finds a way to maintain a relationship with her father even after he begins living in a different place.

Joan Schuchman, *Two Places to Sleep*, 1979
David lives with his father and visits his mother on alternate weekends.

221

JUDITH CASELEY, Author/Illustrator

Sophie and Sammy's Library Sleepover

(New York: Greenwillow Books, 1993)

Subject(s): Brothers and Sisters; Libraries
Age range(s): Grades K-2
Major character(s): Sophie, Child (avid reader); Sammy, Child, Brother (Sophie's little)
Time period(s): 1990s (1993)
Locale(s): United States

Summary: Expressing their love for books in different ways— Sophie reads them, Sammy tears them—leads to some parental limits and privileges. Sophie enjoys her opportunity to go to the library for a night-time story time, but recognizes how much her brother would also appreciate the experience. Returning home, Sophie creates her own bedtime story time to share with him and teaches him how to treat books as friends, just as she does. (32 pages)

Where it's reviewed:
Booklist, February 15, 1993, page 1066
Children's Book Review Service, March 1993, page 90
Horn Book, July 1993, page 440
Reading Teacher, September 1993, page 49
School Library Journal, July 1993, page 57

Other books by the same author:
Mr. Green Peas, 1995
Mama, Coming and Going, 1994
Three Happy Birthdays, 1989

Other books you might like:
Julie Brillhart, *Story Hour—Starring Megan!*, 1992
When Mom's the librarian and the babysitter doesn't come, Megan and baby brother Nathan must go to work with Mom. One day Megan's love for books comes in handy at story time.

Angela Johnson, *Do Like Kyla*, 1990
Kyla's younger sister follows her all day, imitating every behavior.

Sarah Stewart, *The Library*, 1995
Elizabeth Brown is a most unusual child who likes to read and enjoys nothing else.

222

PATRICIA CASEY, Author/Illustrator

My Cat Jack

(Cambridge, MA: Candlewick Press, 1994)

Series: Read and Wonder
Subject(s): Animals/Cats; Behavior; Pets
Age range(s): Grades K-1
Major character(s): Jack, Cat
Time period(s): 1990s (1994)
Locale(s): United States

Summary: Jack, a yawning, stretching, playful cat, enjoys the company of his young human companion whose feet are sometimes seen in the illustrations. The illustrations mirror the descriptive text, making the tale of Jack accessible to beginning readers. (32 pages)

Where it's reviewed:
Horn Book, November 1994, page 750
Junior Bookshelf, October 1994, page 163
Kirkus Reviews, September 15, 1994, page 1268
New Advocate, Winter 1995, page 47
School Library Journal, January 1995, page 83

Awards the book has won:
American Booksellers Pick of the Lists, 1994

Other books by the same author:
Cluck, Cluck, 1988

Other books you might like:
Donald Hall, *I Am the Dog, I Am the Cat*, 1994
Poetically, a dog and a cat describe their separate interests.

Isabelle Harper, *My Cats Nick and Nora*, 1995
Two cousins wile away a Sunday afternoon playing dress-up with the patient cats.

Vivian Sathre, *Mouse Chase*, 1995
Brief rhyming sentences describe the actions of a mouse and the responses from a cat.

223

LEIGH CASLER
SHONTO BEGAY, Illustrator

The Boy Who Dreamed of an Acorn

(New York: Philomel Books, 1994)

Subject(s): Indians of North America; Dreams and Nightmares; Self-Acceptance
Age range(s): Grades 3-5
Major character(s): Unnamed Character, Indian (Chinook)
Time period(s): Indeterminate Past
Locale(s): Pacific Northwest

Summary: With two other boys from his village a young boy goes on a spirit quest seeking the dream that will explain each one's destiny. One boy dreams of a bear, another of an eagle and both are satisfied. The third boy dreams of an acorn and feels so confused about the message that he seeks the counsel of the village wise man. With time and maturity the boy understands the importance of his dream and finds his destiny for his people. The author's first book for children. (32 pages)

Where it's reviewed:
Booklist, September 1, 1994, page 49
New Advocate, Spring 1995, page 127
Publishers Weekly, September 19, 1994, page 70
Quill & Quire, October 1994, page 47
School Library Journal, December 1994, page 106

Other books you might like:
Caron Lee Cohen, *The Mud Pony: A Traditional Skidi Pawnee Tale*, 1988
  Mother Earth transforms a poor boy's pony into a real one, but the youth learns that a great leader must find his own strength.
Kathryn Lasky, *Cloud Eyes*, 1994
  Cloud Eyes fulfills his destiny by learning the dance of the bee and making peace with the bear thus enabling his people to once again harvest and enjoy honey.
Ann Herbert Scott, *Brave as a Mountain Lion*, 1996
  To conquer his fear during a spelling bee, Spider listens to his spirit and is brave as a mountain lion, clever as a coyote, and silent as a spider.

224

PETER CATALANOTTO, Author/Illustrator

The Painter

(New York: Orchard Books, 1995)

Subject(s): Artists and Art; Fathers and Daughters; Love
Age range(s): Grades K-2
Major character(s): Unnamed Character, Child; Daddy, Father, Artist; Mommy, Mother
Time period(s): 1990s (1995)
Locale(s): United States

Summary: Playfully cooking pancakes or joyfully dancing after dinner, Daddy makes the most of the time he has with his young daughter. Mommy looks on, commenting on their silliness, and also enjoys their time together when Daddy is not painting in his at-home studio. After a day of patiently waiting for a little more play time with Daddy, the daughter is rewarded with an after-dinner trip to the studio where she creates her own painting of a happy family. (32 pages)

Where it's reviewed:
Children's Book Review Service, December 1995, page 37
Five Owls, September 1995, page 10
Kirkus Reviews, August 15, 1995, page 1186
Publishers Weekly, August 21, 1995, page 64
School Library Journal, September 1995, page 168

Other books by the same author:
Christmas Always, 1991
Mr. Mumble, 1990
Dylan's Day Out, 1989

Other books you might like:
Allison Barrows, *The Artist's Model*, 1996
  After serving as a model for her artist-father, a young girl is able to watch the drawing proceed from first sketch through the process of becoming a printed illustration.
Thomas Locker, *Miranda's Smile*, 1994
  Miranda's artist father struggles to recreate her smile in a portrait until he realizes her unique smile is in her eyes.

Abigail Thomas, *Pearl Paints*, 1994
  A set of watercolors received for her birthday, inspires Pearl to start painting—everything!

225

DENYS CAZET, Author/Illustrator

Born in the Gravy

(New York: Orchard Books, 1993)

Subject(s): Mexican Americans; Schools; Fathers and Daughters
Age range(s): Grades K-1
Major character(s): Margarita, 5-Year-Old, Child (kindergartener); Papa, Father
Time period(s): 1990s (1993)
Locale(s): United States

Summary: At the conclusion of Margarita's first day of kindergarten, she and Papa head for the ice cream parlor to share her eventful day. Trying to understand the taunts of first graders about kindergarten babies born in the gravy, Margarita is relieved to learn from her father that she was actually born in Guadalajara. Text includes some Spanish. (32 pages)

Where it's reviewed:
Booklist, November 1, 1993, page 528
Horn Book Guide, Spring 1994, page 29
Kirkus Reviews, August 1, 1993, page 999
Publishers Weekly, July 29, 1993, page 69
School Library Journal, October 1993, page 92

Other books by the same author:
Nothing at All, 1994
Are There Any Questions?, 1992
Never Spit on Your Shoes, 1990

Other books you might like:
Miriam Cohen, *Will I Have a Friend?*, 1967
  First day of school jitters have Jim wondering if he will find a friend in his class.
Bernice Myers, *It Happens to Everyone*, 1990
  Michael learns that the first day of school presents challenges to teachers too.
Amy Schwartz, *Annabelle Swift, Kindergartner*, 1988
  Annabelle is not sure that school will be as much fun as she had anticipated.
Sylvia Root Tester, *We Laughed a Lot, My First Day of School*, 1979
  The first day of school is actually more fun than this Mexican-American boy had expected.
Rosemary Wells, *Timothy Goes to School*, 1981
  A friend assists Timothy when a bully almost spoils the first day of school.

226

DENYS CAZET, Author/Illustrator

Dancing

(New York: Orchard Books, 1995)

Subject(s): Babies; Fathers and Sons; Singing
Age range(s): Grades K-2

Major character(s): Alex, Child; Father, Father
Time period(s): 1990s (1995)
Locale(s): United States

Summary: Disgusted that he must contend with a screaming baby sibling, Alex storms out of the house to sit on the front steps. There, Father joins him and responds reassuringly to Alex's concerns with a song. Though the baby is ''paid for'' and can't be returned to the hospital as Alex hopes, Father assures him that his parents will love him always. A score by Craig Bond is included at the end of the book. (32 pages)

Where it's reviewed:
Booklist, September 15, 1995, page 175
Horn Book Guide, Spring 1996, page 12
Kirkus Reviews, July 15, 1995, page 1021
Publishers Weekly, September 11, 1995, page 84
School Library Journal, September 1995, page 168

Other books by the same author:
Nothing at All, 1994
Daydreams, 1990
Christmas Moon, 1984

Other books you might like:
Jane Cutler, *Darcy and Gran Don't Like Babies*, 1993
 Big sister Darcy is relieved when Gran professes to share her lack of interest in the new baby and spends time alone with Darcy.
Sam McBratney, *Guess How Much I Love You*, 1995
 Little Nutbrown Hare enjoys playing a game with his father in which each professes the magnitude of his love for the other.
Ingrid Mennen, *One Round Moon and a Star for Me*, 1994
 Papa reassures his son that the birth of a sibling will not mean the end of his parents' love for him.
Clara Vulliamy, *Ellen and Penguin and the New Baby*, 1996
 Ellen agrees with her stuffed Penguin's observation that having a new baby in the house is not such a good idea.

227

DENYS CAZET, Author/Illustrator

Nothing at All

(New York: Orchard Books, 1994)

Subject(s): Animals; Farm Life; Stories in Rhyme
Age range(s): Grades K-1
Major character(s): Scarecrow, Worker (farm)
Time period(s): Indeterminate
Locale(s): Fictional Country (farm)

Summary: One by one the farm animals awaken—bleating, mooing and neighing their greetings—but the scarecrow says nothing at all until. . .a mouse hides in his pants. At that moment the scarecrow comes to life to the relief of his farmyard friends. (32 pages)

Where it's reviewed:
Booklist, March 1, 1994, page 1268
Bulletin of the Center for Children's Books, July 1994, page 351
Children's Bookwatch, July 1994, page 3
Publishers Weekly, February 7, 1994, page 86
School Library Journal, May 1994, page 90

Other books by the same author:
Daydreams, 1990
Mother Night, 1989
A Fish in His Pocket, 1987

Other books you might like:
Denise Fleming, *Barnyard Banter*, 1994
 Award-winning illustrations enliven a goose's journey through the barnyard in pursuit of a butterfly.
Alison Lester, *My Farm*, 1994
 Based on recollections of the author's youth, one year in a child's life on a farm is described.
Jerdine Nolen, *Harvey Potter's Balloon Farm*, 1994
 An unusual crop is growing on Harvey Potter's farm and his friend is determined to learn the secret of his harvest.

228

MEL CEBULASH
DUANE KRYCH, Illustrator

Bat Boy

(Mankato, MN: Child's World, 1993)

Series: Sports
Subject(s): Sports/Baseball
Age range(s): Grades 6-9
Major character(s): Elliot Greeley, Student—Junior High, Baseball Player (catcher); Mike Piano, Student—Junior High, Baseball Player (bat boy)
Time period(s): 1990s
Locale(s): Union City

Summary: Mike is asked to show Elliot, a new student, around Kennedy Junior High School. Mike's height of 5'9'' is in sharp contrast to Elliot's 4'6'' prompting Mike to check reference books and ask his parents if Elliot's a midget. Mike doesn't want to hurt Elliot's feelings, but he is curious. However, a more serious concern about Elliot's feelings happens when he wants to join the local baseball team. Mike's not sure if his friends will accept Elliot on the team, but Elliot's enthusiasm and hard work more than compensate for his lack of inches. By the time he's in high school, he's the starting catcher for the school baseball team in this hi-lo book. (69 pages)

Where it's reviewed:
School Library Journal, January 1994, page 112
Horn Book Guide, Fall 1993, page 295

Other books by the same author:
Dirty Money: A Sully Gomez Mystery, 1993
Flipper's Boy, 1993
Muscle Bound, 1993

Other books you might like:
Matt Christopher, *Hit-Away Kid*, 1988
 Though Barry sometimes bends the rules, he receives a lesson in sports ethics from an opposing pitcher who wants to win at any cost.
Kenneth E. Ethridge, *Viola, Furgy, Bobbi, and Me*, 1989
 Old Mrs. Viola Spencer hires Stephen to do her yard work, but their mutual interest in baseball quickly leads to friendship.

Alfred Slote, *Hang Touch, Paul Mather*, 1973
Paul is the new kid in town who loves being a pitcher; he's also battling leukemia.

229

MEL CEBULASH
DUANE KRYCH, Illustrator

Flipper's Boy
(Mankato, MN: Child's World, 1993)

Series: Sports
Subject(s): Sports/Basketball; Fathers and Sons
Age range(s): Grades 6-9
Major character(s): Tommy Mandell, Basketball Player, Student—High School; Roger Mandell, Truck Driver, Father (Tommy's)
Time period(s): 1990s
Locale(s): Millersville

Summary: As one of the starters for his school's basketball team, Tommy has a nice jump shot and good moves up and down the court. But he's a little disturbed when townspeople call him Flipper, the nickname his father had twenty years ago when he played for the same high school team. Tommy hasn't seen his father since he was two years-old, when Roger abandoned his wife and child and moved west, and naturally doesn't want to be compared to him. As Tommy works on his hook shot, he begins to accept the fact that he is the son of ''Flipper'' but knows he'll develop his own basketball style in this hi-lo book. (69 pages)

Where it's reviewed:
School Library Journal, January 1994, page 112
Horn Book Guide, Fall 1993, page 295

Other books by the same author:
Bat Boy, 1993
Knockout Punch: A Sully Gomez Mystery, 1993
Rattler, 1992
Snooperman, 1992

Other books you might like:
Bruce Brooks, *The Moves Make the Man*, 1984
Black Jerome and white Bix become friends through their love of basketball in a story that is about more than just sports.
William Gault, *Showboat in the Back Court*, 1976
This book traces the careers of two basketball players who begin playing in high school situation and make it to the professionals.
Gary Soto, *Taking Sides*, 1991
After Lincoln moves from the barrio, he faces an uncomfortable when he has to play a game against his old team.

230

TIM CHADWICK
PIERS HARPER, Illustrator

Cabbage Moon
(New York: Orchard Books, 1994)

Subject(s): Animals/Rabbits; Food; Fantasy

Age range(s): Grades K-1
Major character(s): Albert, Rabbit
Time period(s): Indeterminate
Locale(s): Fictional Country; Moon—Imaginary

Summary: To his mother's dismay, curious Albert dislikes cabbage but ponders important questions about the color of the sky and how something made of rock and sand could change shape as the moon does. One night he is transported on a moonbeam to the moon where he discovers that the moon is actually a giant cabbage. Under the direction of a rather plump rabbit, Albert and others are instructed to eat the cabbage until it measures just the right size. Originally published in Great Britain in 1993. (32 pages)

Where it's reviewed:
Booklist, June 1, 1994, page 1835
Children's Book Review Service, April 1994, page 99
Horn Book Guide, Fall 1994, page 267
Publishers Weekly, December 6, 1993, page 72
School Library Journal, April 1994, page 101

Other books you might like:
Lois Ehlert, *Moon Rope: A Peruvian Folktale/Un Lazo a la Luna: Una Leyenda Peruana*, 1992
Translated by Amy Prince, the bilingual text explains why fox's face is seen in a full moon and mole's is seen only on a dark night.
Matthew Gollub, *The Moon Was at a Fiesta*, 1994
An original folktale explaining why the moon is sometimes visible in the morning sky.
Rodney Rigby, *The Night the Moon Fell Asleep*, 1993
Overtired from too many late nights, the moon falls asleep and crashes to the ground requiring a community effort to restore her to the night sky.
John Rowe, *Rabbit Moon*, 1992
With the moon hidden by a cloud, Albert thinks it has fallen and he ''repairs'' the problem by putting a fallen party decoration in the sky, just as the cloud moves away.

231

JOYCE CHAMPION
SUCIE STEVENSON, Illustrator

Emily and Alice
(New York: Gulliver Books, 1993)

Subject(s): Friendship; Neighbors and Neighborhoods
Age range(s): Grades K-1
Major character(s): Emily, Child, Friend (Alice's best); Alice, Child, Neighbor (Emily's new)
Time period(s): 1990s (1993)
Locale(s): United States (Emily and Alice's neighborhood)

Summary: Lonely Emily looks out the window and sees a family with a little girl moving in next door. From the moment Emily dashes out the door to meet Alice a friendship is formed which grows as these two get to know one another. (32 pages)

Where it's reviewed:
Booklist, September 15, 1993, page 156
Horn Book, November 1993, page 742
Horn Book Guide, Spring 1994, page 64

Publishers Weekly, September 9, 1993, page 96
School Library Journal, October 1993, page 92

Other books by the same author:
Emily and Alice Again, 1995

Other books you might like:
Russell Hoban, *Best Friends for Frances*, 1969
    Excluded from Albert's "boys only" baseball game, Frances plays with sister Gloria and Albert learns a lesson.
Dorothy Hoffman Levi, *A Very Special Friend*, 1989
    When Frannie learns that her new neighbor Laura is deaf, she discovers that the language of friendship is known to all.
James Howe, *Pinky and Rex*, 1990
    Pinky and Rex begin their friendship in the first book of the series.

232

JOYCE CHAMPION
SUCIE STEVENSON, Illustrator

Emily and Alice Again
(San Diego: Gulliver/Harcourt Brace & Company, 1995)

Subject(s): Friendship; Neighbors and Neighborhoods; Behavior
Age range(s): Grades 1-3
Major character(s): Emily, Child, Friend; Alice, Child, Friend; Nora, Child, Sister (Emily's)
Time period(s): 1990s (1995)
Locale(s): United States

Summary: In the first of three episodes, Emily is so taken by Alice's new pink, heart-shaped sunglasses she trades her sister for them. As Emily enjoys the sunglasses, alone, she hears Nora and Alice playing happily next door and decides she wants to trade back. Next, the best friends support one another in their selection of hats, enjoying the silliness of their purchases and ignoring the teasing of the neighborhood children. Finally, Alice accepts an invitation to sleep over at Emily's house and her anxiety about the first-time experience and the possibility of Snapigators under the bed keeps both girls wide-eyed. (32 pages)

Where it's reviewed:
Booklist, March 15, 1995, page 1333
Horn Book, May 1995, page 331
Kirkus Reviews, March 15, 1995, page 379
Language Arts, September 1995, page 372
School Library Journal, May 1995, page 82

Other books by the same author:
Emily and Alice, 1993

Other books you might like:
James Howe, *Pinky and Rex*, 1990
    A museum visit becomes complicated for good friends Pinky and Rex by the presence of Pinky's little sister Amanda.
Joanna Cole, *The Gator Girls*, 1995
    Best friends Allie and Amy have many plans for the time they have to spend together during summer vacation. Co-author Stephanie Calmenson.

Kevin Henkes, *Chester's Way*, 1988
    Chester and Wilson are content with their friendship and their way of doing things but when Lilly moves into the neighborhood they need to reconsider some ideas.
Nancy Jewell, *Two Silly Trolls*, 1992
    In a beginning reader, five brief stories showcase the challenges to a friendship of two trolls.
Arnold Lobel, *Frog and Toad Together*, 1972
    This Newbery Honor book is one of four titles describing the adventures and misadventures of loyal friends Frog and Toad.

233

VERONIKA MARTENOVA CHARLES, Author/Illustrator

The Crane Girl
(New York: Orchard Books, 1993)

Subject(s): Fairy Tale; Animals/Birds; Babies
Age range(s): Grades K-2
Major character(s): Yoshiko, Child, Sister (jealous); Katsumi, Brother (infant)
Time period(s): Indeterminate Past
Locale(s): Japan

Summary: Imagining a loss of parental love when her baby brother is born, a forlorn Yoshiko wanders off seeking kinship with fish, monkeys and finally cranes. In her sleep, Yoshiko is transformed into a baby crane and is raised with the flock. Flying over her family home, she hears her parents telling her brother of his lost sister. While trying to attract the parents' attention, she injures herself. When she realizes that the feelings which caused her to look elsewhere for love were incorrect, Yoshiko returns to human form in a happy ending to a classic tale. The first book both written and illustrated by the author was originally published in Canada in 1992. (32 pages)

Where it's reviewed:
Booklist, May 1, 1993, page 1601
Children's Book Review Service, July 1993, page 145
Publishers Weekly, March 29, 1993, page 54
Reading Teacher, October 1993, page 149
School Library Journal, July 1993, page 58

Other books you might like:
Mary Beth Owens, *Counting Cranes*, 1993
    The life of the endangered whooping crane gracefully unfolds in an artistic portrayal which concludes with factual information about the birds.
Florence Sakade, *Japanese Children's Favorite Stories*, 1958
    A collection of 20 folktales traditionally told to Japanese children.
Sumiko Yagawa, *The Crane Wife*, 1981
    In a retelling of a Japanese folktale, a farmer marries a beautiful stranger who is really a crane he has rescued and changed into human form.

234

JEROME CHARYN

Back to Bataan

(New York: Farrar Straus Giroux, 1993)

Subject(s): World War II; Gangs
Age range(s): Grades 5-7
Major character(s): Jack Dalton, 11-Year-Old, Runaway; Mauricette "Coco", 11-Year-Old, Girlfriend (Jack's former)
Time period(s): 1940s
Locale(s): New York, New York

Summary: Jack is tired of being a scholarship student at an expensive private school, saddened over his father's death at Bataan and upset that his girlfriend, Mauricette, throws him over for a rich kid. To retaliate against Mauricette's new boyfriend, Jack sets his mansion on fire. Scared about what he's done, Jack runs away to Central Park where he's taken in by a criminal gang who involve him in their nefarious activities. Jack finally redeems himself by helping the police stop the gang's illegal ways. (101 pages)

Where it's reviewed:
Voice of Youth Advocates, August 1993, page 148
School Library Journal, June 1993, page 126
Booklist, June 1, 1993, page 1830
New York Times Book Review, September 5, 1993, page 17
Children's Book Review Service, Spring 1993, page 141

Other books you might like:
Charles Dickens, *Oliver Twist*, 1837-1838
    Orphaned Oliver ends up in the clutches of The Artful Dodger and Fagin who train him to be a pickpocket.
Felice Holman, *Slake's Limbo*, 1974
    Living in the subway system of New York is lonely for young Aremis.
Jacqueline Woodson, *Maizon at Blue Hill*, 1992
    Maizon discovers how hard it is to be a minority scholarship student at a private school.

235

ANTON CHEKHOV
GENNADY SPIRIN, Illustrator

Kashtanka

(San Diego: Gulliver/Harcourt Brace & Company, 1995)

Subject(s): Animals/Dogs; Circus; Pets
Age range(s): Grades K-3
Major character(s): Kashtanka, Dog; Luka Alexandrych, Artisan
Time period(s): 19th century
Locale(s): Russia

Summary: Following Luka Alexandrych on an errand, Kashtanka loses sight of him on the snowy street and settles sadly into the shelter of a doorway. Attracted by her whimpering, a strange man opens the door and takes the forlorn dog into his home and, as it turns out, into his circus act. The first night that Kashtanka performs, cries are heard from the audi-

ence as Luka Alexandrych and his son recognize their lost pet and are happily reunited. (40 pages)

Where it's reviewed:
Christian Science Monitor, December 8, 1995, page 10
Horn Book Guide, Spring 1996, page 22
Kirkus Reviews, August 15, 1995, page 1186
Publishers Weekly, July 31, 1995, page 81
School Library Journal, December 1995, page 73

Awards the book has won:
Book Links Good Book, 1995
New York Times Best Illustrated Children's Books of the Year, 1995

Other books by the same author:
A Day in the Country, 1986

Other books you might like:
Paul Brett Johnson, *Lost*, 1996
    Lost in the Tonto National Forest, a beagle endures many hardships while searching for his family. Co-author Celeste Lewis.
Barbara Ann Porte, *Harry's Dog*, 1984
    Harry's excited to be given a dog, but his father's allergies to the pet pose a problem that seems insurmountable until Aunt Rose gets in the picture.
Lynn Reiser, *Any Kind of Dog*, 1992
    Mom offers Richard many kinds of pets, but all he really wants is a dog.

236

LYNNE CHERRY, Author/Illustrator

The Armadillo from Amarillo

(San Diego: Harcourt Brace & Company, 1994)

Subject(s): Animals/Armadillos; Stories in Rhyme; Transportation
Age range(s): Grades K-3
Major character(s): Sasparillo, Armadillo
Time period(s): 1990s (1994)
Locale(s): San Antonio, Texas; Amarillo, Texas

Summary: A curious armadillo travels across the state of Texas trying to discover where he is. Along the way he sends post cards to a cousin in the Philadelphia Zoo and hitches rides on an eagle and the space shuttle so he can better understand his location in relation to the rest of the world. (32 pages)

Where it's reviewed:
Booklist, March 1, 1994, page 1268
Children's Book Review Service, March 1994, page 91
Kirkus Reviews, March 1, 1994, page 300
Publishers Weekly, February 21, 1994, page 254
School Library Journal, April 1994, page 101

Other books by the same author:
The Dragon and the Unicorn, 1994
The Great Kapok Tree: A Tale of the Amazon Rain Forest, 1990
Who's Sick Today?, 1988

Other books you might like:

John Burningham, *Harvey Slumfenburger's Christmas Present*, 1993
    A weary Santa Claus uses a variety of alternative transportation methods to deliver an overlooked present.

Marjorie Priceman, *How to Make an Apple Pie and See the World*, 1994
    Finding the market closed, a young girl imagines travelling by various modes of transportation to different countries in order to locate the ingredients for an apple pie.

Mary Lyn Ray, *Alvah and Arvilla*, 1994
    To solve the problem of care for the animals while they travel, a farm couple takes the animals along on their cross-country trip.

237

LYNNE CHERRY, Author/Illustrator

The Dragon and the Unicorn
(San Diego: Harcourt Brace & Company, 1995)

Series: A Gulliver Green Book
Subject(s): Dragons; Unicorns; Conservation of Natural Resources
Age range(s): Grades 2-4
Major character(s): Valerio, Mythical Creature (dragon); Allegra, Unicorn; Arianna, Child, Royalty
Time period(s): Indeterminate Past
Locale(s): Ardet Forest, Fictional Country

Summary: For many years Valerio and Allegra live happily in the ancient forest. When humans arrive and cut down the trees to make a fortress, the two friends are hunted and hide deeper and deeper in the forest. Sensing Arianna is unafraid and interested in learning more about the forest, Allegra uses her knowledge to draw the child to her hiding place. For weeks Arianna remains with Valerio and Allegra learning to appreciate the forest while her father, the king, sends his knights to look for her. Finally, Arianna's father searches alone, finding both his daughter and the knowledge which convinces him to protect the forest. (40 pages)

Where it's reviewed:
Booklist, January 1996, page 842
Five Owls, March 1996, page 92
Horn Book Guide, Spring 1996, page 53
Publishers Weekly, October 30, 1995, page 61
School Library Journal, February 1996, page 82

Other books by the same author:
The Armadillo from Amarillo, 1994
A River Ran Wild, 1992
The Great Kapok Tree: A Tale of the Amazon Rain Forest, 1990

Other books you might like:

Alma Flor Ada, *The Unicorn of the West: El Unicornio del Oeste*, 1994
    A lonely unicorn who knows many forest creatures, begins to understand himself when he finally meets other unicorns.

Marianna Mayer, *The Unicorn and the Lake*, 1982
    When the waters become unusable to the creatures who

depend upon it, a unicorn uses its power to cleanse the lake of impurities.

Louise Moeri, *The Unicorn and the Plow*, 1982
    In a tale with a medieval setting, animals talk and the magic of a unicorn creates crops from fields of weeds.

Ruth Sanderson, *The Enchanted Wood*, 1991
    The youngest of the king's three sons fulfills a quest to free the land from a terrible drought by entering the Enchanted Wood and finding the Heart of the World.

238

EMMA CHICHESTER CLARK, Author/Illustrator

Across the Blue Mountains
(New York: Gulliver/Harcourt Brace, 1993)

Subject(s): Moving, Household; Pets
Age range(s): Grades K-2
Major character(s): Miss Bilberry, Wanderer, Eccentric
Time period(s): 1990s (1993)
Locale(s): Earth

Summary: Happy in her small, yellow home with her pets, Miss Bilberry is also curious to know what is on the other side of the blue mountains. One morning she packs up her household belongings, gathers her dog, cat and two birds, and sets off to find out for herself. Days of tiresome travel bring the weary companions to a small, yellow house into which they settle quite comfortably. Only the cat seems to realize what has really happened, but for the moment, Miss Bilberry is content. (32 pages)

Where it's reviewed:
Booklist, October 15, 1993, page 451
Horn Book, January 1994, page 60
Publishers Weekly, October 4, 1993, page 78
Reading Teacher, April 1994, page 564
School Library Journal, January 1994, page 87

Other books by the same author:
Lunch with Aunt Augusta, 1992
The Bouncing Dinosaur, 1990
Catch That Hat!, 1990

Other books you might like:

Burton Albert, *Where Does the Trail Lead?*, 1991
    A young boy follows a trail on Nantucket Island until it leads him back to his family.

Eve Merriam, *The Wise Woman and Her Secret*, 1991
    Of all the villagers who visit the old woman in the hills, only young Jenny seems to grasp the secret of her wisdom.

Jama Kim Rattigan, *Truman's Aunt Farm*, 1994
    Truman's Aunt Fran is one of a kind and so is the ant farm she sends him for his birthday.

239

SHARON CHMIELARZ
JILL KASTNER, Illustrator

Down at Angel's
(New York: Ticknor & Fields Books for Young Readers, 1994)

Subject(s): Neighbors and Neighborhoods; Sisters; Christmas

Age range(s): Grades K-3
Major character(s): Angel, Railroad Worker (Bulgarian immigrant), Artisan (woodworker); Unnamed Character, Child (narrator), Sister (older); Unnamed Character, Child, Sister
Time period(s): Indeterminate Past
Locale(s): United States (Midwest, near the Missouri River)

Summary: When Angel is not working at the railroad roundhouse, he's in the workshop in the cellar of his home. That's where two sisters in the neighborhood like to visit him to watch the sawdust fly, admire his handiwork and enjoy the chocolate bars which he passes out. On Christmas Eve they express their regret to their widowed mother that they have no money to buy a present for Angel and she leads them in packing a box of homemade goodies. Angel is touched by the gesture and gives them a much-admired inlaid table. (32 pages)

Where it's reviewed:
Booklist, August 1994, page 2050
Horn Book, November 1994, page 709
Horn Book Guide, Spring 1995, page 29
Kirkus Reviews, July 15, 1994, page 981
Publishers Weekly, June 27, 1994, page 76

Other books you might like:
Michael Bedard, *Emily*, 1992
    A reclusive neighbor, Emily Dickinson, is visited by a mother and child.
Bob Graham, *Rose Meets Mr. Wintergarten*, 1992
    In order to retrieve her ball, Rose must enter her grouchy neighbor's yard where she finds not only her ball, but also a new opinion of elderly Mr. Wintergarten.
Susan Wojciechowski, *The Christmas Miracle of Jonathan Toomey*, 1995
    A widow and her son ask a gruff woodcarver to carve the figures for their creche with unexpected results.

240

DEBORAH M. NEWTON CHOCOLATE
MELODYE ROSALES, Illustrator

On the Day I Was Born
(New York: Cartwheel Books/Scholastic Inc., 1995)

Subject(s): Babies; African Americans; Family Life
Age range(s): Grades K-1
Major character(s): "Pine", Child
Time period(s): 1990s (1995)
Locale(s): United States

Summary: Surrounded by family members, a young boy is welcomed and admired by all. He receives the nickname "Pine," a kente cloth and a kofia in the midst of a celebration of his birth. Most importantly, his father holds him up to the heavens saying, "Behold the only thing greater." A glossary defines the African Adkira symbols used to border the text. (32 pages)

Where it's reviewed:
Booklist, December 15, 1995, page 707
Horn Book Guide, Spring 1996, page 22
Publishers Weekly, October 23, 1995, page 68

School Library Journal, January 1996, page 77

Other books by the same author:
Imani in the Belly, 1994
Spider and the Sky God, 1992
Kwanzaa, 1990

Other books you might like:
Trish Cooke, *So Much*, 1994
    The relatives are gathering for a surprise party for a baby's father, but first they must hug, squeeze and kiss the baby because they love him "SO MUCH!"
Cathryn Falwell, *We Have a Baby*, 1993
    Whether one is caring for, holding, or simply watching a new baby, the excitement surrounding an infant's arrival is obvious.
Ingrid Mennen, *One Round Moon and a Star for Me*, 1994
    Feeling overwhelmed by the attention given to his newborn brother, a young African boy seeks reassurance from his father.

241

KAY CHORAO, Author/Illustrator

Annie and Cousin Precious
(New York: Dutton Children's Books, 1994)

Subject(s): Cousins; Behavior; Parent and Child
Age range(s): Grades K-1
Major character(s): Annie, Dog, Cousin (older); Precious, Dog, Cousin (younger)
Time period(s): 1990s (1994)
Locale(s): Fictional Country (Annie's house)

Summary: When Precious comes to visit, Annie tries to lock herself in her room, but her father insists that she be polite and play with her little cousin. As Annie predicts, a trip to the playhouse leads to a mess and the near destruction of Annie's dolls. Annie runs away, leaving Precious locked in the playhouse. When she begins to have second thoughts about her responsiblity, Annie finds Precious and then tries to establish some guidelines for a successful play experience. (32 pages)

Where it's reviewed:
Booklist, June 1, 1994, page 1836
Horn Book Guide, Fall 1994, page 268
Publishers Weekly, May 30, 1994, page 56
Reading Teacher, October 1995, page 137
School Library Journal, July 1994, page 74

Awards the book has won:
International Reading Association Children's Choice, 1995

Other books by the same author:
Carousel Round and Round, 1995
The Cherry Pie Baby, 1989
Cathedral Mouse, 1988

Other books you might like:
Barbara Bottner, *Bootsie Barker Bites*, 1992
    Bootsie Barker terrorizes the daughter of her mother's friend during visits until the day Bootsie arrives to find her hostess well prepared.

Kevin Henkes, *A Weekend with Wendell*, 1986
  Sophie Mouse thinks Wendell's visit will never end until they find they enjoy one another.
Cynthia Rylant, *Henry and Mudge and the Careful Cousin*, 1994
  Henry's cousin is unprepared for slobbery dog kisses and Henry's messy room, but she learns to be more comfortable during her visit.

242

EILEEN CHRISTELOW, Author/Illustrator

The Great Pig Escape

(New York: Clarion Books, 1994)

Subject(s): Animals/Pigs; Farm Life; Humor
Age range(s): Grades K-3
Major character(s): Bert, Farmer, Spouse; Ethel, Farmer, Spouse
Time period(s): 1990s (1994)
Locale(s): United States

Summary: Vegetable farmer Bert decides to raise pigs over the objections of his wife who would prefer to stick with turnips. Six little piglets rapidly grow into six marketable pigs who overhear Bert's plans to drive them to market the next day. The pigs have other ideas that quickly become obvious to Bert, Ethel and the townspeople who lose clothes from clotheslines, scarecrows and mannequins. (32 pages)

Where it's reviewed:
Booklist, September 15, 1994, page 143
Horn Book Guide, Spring 1995, page 29
Kirkus Reviews, July 15, 1994, page 981
Publishers Weekly, June 27, 1994, page 78
School Library Journal, November 1994, page 73

Other books by the same author:
The Five-Dog Night, 1993
Five Little Monkeys Sitting in a Tree, 1991
Olive and the Magic Hat, 1987

Other books you might like:
Amy Ehrlich, *Parents in the Pigpen, Pigs in the Tub*, 1993
  Accomodating farmers allow the animals to move into the house until the only room for the parents is in the pigpen.
Sid Fleischman, *Here Comes McBroom: Three More Tall Tales*, 1992
  There's no end to the surprises in store with Josh Mc-Broom and his very unusual farm.
Margaret Mahy, *The Boy Who Was Followed Home*, 1986
  Robert's parents do not share his love for hippopotamuses or his delight when one follows him home.
David McPhail, *Pigs Aplenty, Pigs Galore*, 1993
  A quiet evening becomes a noisy free-for-all when a man's home is invaded by pigs intent on enjoying pizza.
Trinka Hakes Noble, *The Day Jimmy's Boa Ate the Wash*, 1987
  What should be an educational field trip to a farm becomes a most unusual adventure for Jimmy's class when his pet boa gets loose.

243

MARY BLOUNT CHRISTIAN
LISA McCUE, Illustrator

Sebastian (Super Sleuth) and the Copycat Crime

(New York: Macmillan Publishing Company, 1993)

Series: Sebastian (Super Sleuth)
Subject(s): Mystery and Detective Stories; Animals/Dogs; Authors and Publishers
Age range(s): Grades 3-5
Major character(s): John Quincy Jones, Detective—Police; Sebastian, Dog, Detective
Time period(s): 1990s (1993)
Locale(s): United States

Summary: Despite the bungling of the official detective, John Quincy Jones, his pet, Sebastian, once again solves the mystery and apprehends the criminal. This time, Detective Jones is presiding over a mystery writer's conference when the hypothetical crime becomes a real one. (62 pages)

Where it's reviewed:
Booklist, January 1, 1994, page 827
Five Owls, March 1994, page 79
Horn Book Guide, Spring 1994, page 64
School Library Journal, March 1994, page 222

Other books by the same author:
Who'd Believe John Coulter?, 1993
Sebastian (Super Sleuth) and the Impossible Crime, 1992
The Pet Day Mystery, 1989
Penrod Again, 1987
Sebastian (Super Sleuth) and the Clumsy Cowboy, 1985

Other books you might like:
David A. Adler, *Cam Jansen and the Mystery at the Haunted House*, 1992
  Once again, Cam puts her legendary photographic memory to work to solve a mystery.
Sharon Cadwallader, *Cookie McCorkle and the Case of the Emerald Earrings*, 1991
  Moriarity may be a dog, but he's able to assist his 10-year old owner, Cookie, solve this mystery.
Donald J. Sobol, *Encyclopedia Brown, Boy Detective*, 1979
  In this first book of a series, Leroy Brown opens his detective agency and solves his first 10 crimes.
Gertrude Chandler Warner, *The Mystery of the Hidden Painting*, 1992
  In this Boxcar Children Mystery, the four children look for a lost necklace that once belonged to their grandmother.

244

MARY BLOUNT CHRISTIAN
LISA McCUE, Illustrator

Sebastian (Super Sleuth) and the Flying Elephant

(New York: Macmillan Publishing Company, 1994)

Series: Sebastian (Super Sleuth)

Subject(s): Animals/Dogs; Mystery and Detective Stories; Circus

Age range(s): Grades 3-4

Major character(s): Sebastian, Dog; John Quincy Jones, Detective—Police; Tahsha, Elephant

Time period(s): 1990s (1994)

Locale(s): United States

Summary: With his customary skill, Sebastian stays one clue ahead of his master when Detective Jones is assigned the case of the missing circus elephant. Donning a variety of disguises, Sebastian soon determines the guilty parties and enlists Tahsha's help in making their identities apparent to the circus owner and Jones. (57 pages)

Where it's reviewed:

Booklist, December 1, 1994, page 680

Horn Book Guide, Spring 1995, page 65

School Library Journal, December 1994, page 106

Other books by the same author:

Sebastian (Super Sleuth) and the Impossible Crime, 1992

Sebastian (Super Sleuth) and the Time Capsule Caper, 1989

Sebastian (Super Sleuth) and the Bone to Pick Mystery, 1983

Other books you might like:

David A. Adler, *Cam Jansen and the Mystery at the Monkey House*, 1985

In the 10th adventure of the series, Cam uses her photographic memory and her friend's help to determine why monkeys are disappearing from the zoo.

James Howe, *Dew Drop Dead: A Sebastian Barth Mystery*, 1990

Finding a body in the abandoned Dew Drop Inn, Sebastian plans to investigate, but the body vanishes.

Donald J. Sobol, *The Encyclopedia Brown Series*, 1979 -

Ten-year-old Leroy Brown operates his own detective agency and solves a variety of mysteries in his neighborhood.

245

PEGGY CHRISTIAN

GARY LIPPINCOTT, Illustrator

The Bookstore Mouse

(San Diego: Harcourt Brace & Company, 1995)

Subject(s): Animals/Mice; Dragons; Fantasy

Age range(s): Grades 4-6

Major character(s): Cervantes, Mouse; Milo, Cat; Sigfried, Religious (scribe)

Time period(s): 1990s (1995); Indeterminate Past

Locale(s): Ninth and Market; England

Summary: When a customer begins browsing through Cervantes's home, the reference section of a bookstore, Cervantes falls off the shelf and into an old book. Once there he begins reading and realizes the isolated words he's taught himself to read can be strung together to make a story which can become real. Cervantes finds himself in medieval England with Sigfried, a scribe who does not have a way with words, a giant who does, and a village needing rescue from a dragon. (134 pages)

Where it's reviewed:

Children's Book Review Service, January 1996, page 54

Horn Book Guide, Spring 1996, page 60

School Library Journal, November 1995, page 96

Other books you might like:

Norton Juster, *The Phantom Tollbooth*, 1961

The tollbooth Milo receives as a gift provides him with an opportunity to travel to a land where he learns to appreciate the importance of words and numbers.

Dick King-Smith, *The School Mouse*, 1995

Taking advantage of the daily lessons in the old school that is her home, Flora uses her literacy to save her family.

C.S. Lewis, *The Lion, the Witch, and the Wardrobe: A Story for Children*, 1950

The first of the seven volumes of the Narnia chronicles introduces three children to a magical land entered through their wardrobe.

246

DAVID CHRISTIANA, Author/Illustrator

A Tooth Fairy's Tale

(New York: Farrar Straus Giroux, 1994)

Subject(s): Fairy Tale; Giants; Greed

Age range(s): Grades K-2

Major character(s): Tooth Fairy, Mythical Creature; Sandman, Father; The Giant, Child, Human

Time period(s): Indeterminate

Locale(s): Fictional Country

Summary: Once upon a time, when all but one little Tooth Fairy has been turned to stone by the evil eye of The Giant, the lone fairy spots a beautiful blue stone in the possession of The Giant. The Sandman, who cleans The Giant's eyes nightly with tooth dust and a feather, notes that The Tooth Fairy's mother was wearing a gown just that color when she vanished. With her father's help, The Tooth Fairy devises a plan to retrieve the stone, freeing her mother. (32 pages)

Where it's reviewed:

Booklist, May 1, 1994, page 1606

Children's Book Review Service, May 1994, page 110

Horn Book Guide, Fall 1994, page 268

Publishers Weekly, March 7, 1994, page 70

School Library Journal, July 1994, page 74

Other books by the same author:

White Nineteens, 1992

Drawer in a Drawer, 1990

Other books you might like:

Peter Collington, *The Tooth Fairy*, 1995

With the author/illustrator's detailed pictures, words are not needed to explain the story of the tooth fairy and how she does her job.

Louise Gunther, *A Tooth for the Tooth Fairy*, 1978

Poor Rose! She's lost her tooth and fears the Tooth Fairy will not visit her now.

Marilyn Kaye, *The Real Tooth Fairy*, 1990

Elsie is sure she knows the identity of the "real" tooth fairy.

Ewa Lipniacka, *Tooth Fairy*, 1992
When young Luke first learns about the tooth fairy, he tries to acquire a tooth from various sources, including the family dog, to put under his pillow.

Verna Wilkins, *Dave & Tooth Fairy*, 1993
The familiar story of teeth and the tooth fairy is viewed from a new perspective.

247

C.B. CHRISTIANSEN
MELISSA SWEET, Illustrator

Sycamore Street

(New York: Atheneum, 1993)

Subject(s): Friendship; Seasons
Age range(s): Grades K-3
Major character(s): Angel, Child, Friend; Chloe, Child, Friend; Rupert Raguso, Child (new neighbor)
Time period(s): 1990s (1993)
Locale(s): United States

Summary: Any time is the right time to play with your best friend, especially when you both agree to avoid the obnoxious new kid on the block, Rupert. The loneliness that develops when one friend, in this case Angel, goes on vacation leads Chloe to seek a playmate in Rupert and to discover that he has something to offer in the way of friendship also. (42 pages)

Where it's reviewed:
Booklist, July 1993, page 1966
Horn Book Guide, Spring 1994, page 64
Library Talk, May 1994, page 43
Publishers Weekly, July 26, 1993, page 72
School Library Journal, November 1993, page 78

Other books by the same author:
Mara in the Morning, 1991
My Mother's House, My Father's House, 1989

Other books you might like:
Aliki, *We Are Best Friends*, 1982
Peter's moving away leaves Peter and his best friend, Robert, feeling sad and lonely. Both learn that they can make new friends while maintaining their own relationship.

Joyce Champion, *Emily and Alice Again*, 1995
Emily and Alice understand each other as only best friends can which is why even days that don't seem to be going well can turn out for the best.

Kevin Henkes, *Chester's Way*, 1988
Best friends, Chester and Wilson, have no use for the new kid, Lily, until she helps them out of a jam.

Rebecca C. Jones, *Matthew and Tilly*, 1991
Matthew and Tilly learn that their friendship is more important than some of their little disagreements.

Steven Kellogg, *Best Friends*, 1986
Kathy and Louise share the good times and the bad as friends do and learn how to remain friends despite typical childhood frustrations.

248

CANDICE CHRISTIANSEN
THOMAS LOCKER, Illustrator

The Ice Horse

(New York: Dial Books, 1993)

Subject(s): Historical; Animals/Horses; Winter
Age range(s): Grades 1-5
Major character(s): Jack, 12-Year-Old (uncle's helper); Joe, Uncle; Max, Horse
Time period(s): Indeterminate Past
Locale(s): Newtonhook, New York (Hudson River valley)

Summary: Before the days of refrigeration, when New York City is dependent on the ice cut from the Hudson River each winter, Jack learns the family business by assisting his Uncle Joe. Jack is proud of the reponsibility given him. Frightened when his uncle's horse, Max, plunges through the thinning ice, Jack is resourceful enough to participate in Max's successful rescue. (32 pages)

Where it's reviewed:
Booklist, November 15, 1993, page 622
Horn Book Guide, Spring 1994, page 29
Publishers Weekly, July 26, 1993, page 72
School Library Journal, October 1993, page 97
Social Education, April 1994, page 246

Other books by the same author:
The Mitten Tree, 1995
Calico and Tin Horns, 1992

Other books you might like:
Donald Hall, *Lucy's Christmas*, 1994
Lucy lives a simple life in rural New Hampshire early in this century.

Laura Ingalls Wilder, *Farmer Boy*, 1933
Almanzo's life on a farm in upstate New York, including the winter ritual of ice cutting, is depicted in this classic.

249

MATT CHRISTOPHER
KAREN MEYER, Illustrator

Double Play at Short

(Boston: Little, Brown and Co., 1995)

Subject(s): Sports/Baseball; Adoption; Twins
Age range(s): Grades 4-6
Major character(s): Danny Walker, Adoptee, Sports Figure (baseball player); Tammy Aiken, Adoptee, Sports Figure (baseball player)
Time period(s): 1990s
Locale(s): United States

Summary: Danny is sure he'll be the pick for shortstop on the all-star team, but he meets Tammy, the shortstop on the opposing team. Though Danny worries that Tammy will beat him out for the shortstop slot, he worries more that she looks so familiar to him and yet he doesn't know her. As he checks off their similarities, he notes they're both redheads, both bat left-handed and both field right-handed. When he realizes they're both adopted, he knows he must find out if they're related in a book where everyone's a winner. (151 pages)

Where it's reviewed:
Booklist, May 1, 1995, page 1572
School Library Journal, June 1995, page 108
Horn Book Guide, Fall 1995, page 295

Other books by the same author:
Hit-Away Kid, 1988
Shortstop from Tokyo, 1970
Baseball Flyhawk, 1963

Other books you might like:
Thomas J. Dygard, *Forward Pass*, 1989
    To have a winning football season, Coach Gardner convinces basketball star Jill Winston to try out for the high school team.
David Klass, *A Different Season*, 1987
    A female second baseman on the boys baseball team affects star pitcher Jim Roark's usually perfect throw.
Jerry Spinelli, *There's a Girl in My Hammerlock*, 1991
    When Maisie doesn't make cheerleading, her next plan to lure Eric away from Liz is to try out for his wrestling team—and she makes it!

250

MATT CHRISTOPHER
KARIN LIDBECK, Illustrator

Fighting Tackle

(Boston: Little, Brown and Co., 1995)

Subject(s): Sports/Football; Brothers; Down Syndrome
Age range(s): Grades 4-6
Major character(s): Terry McFee, Sports Figure (football player); Nicky McFee, Sports Figure (sprinter)
Time period(s): 1990s
Locale(s): United States

Summary: Once Terry had been the fastest defensive safety on the Clippers football team, but he's grown taller and larger and no longer has the needed speed. His coach wants to move him to nose tackle, but Terry wants both his speed and his old position back. To achieve this dream, he begins training as a sprinter but is humiliated to discover that his younger brother Nicky, a Down Syndrome child, is training as a sprinter for the Special Olympics and consistently beats him. Terry must resolve his conflicting feelings about his once-adored younger brother as well as accept his new position on his team. (147 pages)

Where it's reviewed:
Booklist, February 1, 1995, page 1004
School Library Journal, February 1995, page 96
Kirkus Reviews, February 15, 1995, page 223
Library Talk, May 1995, page 40

Other books by the same author:
Double Play at Short, 1995
Top Wing, 1994
The Winning Stroke, 1994

Other books you might like:
Thomas J. Dygard, *Halfback Tough*, 1986
    Joe is a star on the football team, but his rowdy past threatens to catch up with him.
Tommy Hallowell, *Last Chance Quarterback*, 1991
    Sam McCaskill receives a second chance to be the starting quarterback at the end of the season.
June Rae Wood, *The Man Who Loved Clowns*, 1992
    After her parents die, Delrita learns not to feel ashamed about her kind, loving Uncle Punky who has Down syndrome.

251

MATT CHRISTOPHER
ELLEN BEIER, Illustrator

Man Out at First

(Boston: Little Brown and Company, 1993)

Series: Peach Street Mudders
Subject(s): Sports/Baseball; Self-Confidence; Fear
Age range(s): Grades 2-4
Major character(s): Theodore "Turtleneck" Jones, 8-Year-Old, Baseball Player; Ebenezer Shaw, Aged Person (Turtleneck's neighbor), Blind; Coach Parker, Coach
Time period(s): 1990s (1993)
Locale(s): United States

Summary: After being hit in the chest and knocked out by a hard-thrown ball, Turtleneck loses his confidence and finds himself warming the bench. As he assists Mr. Shaw with the repairs of a broken porch step, he also receives some words of wisdom which he takes to heart. With Mr. Shaw in the stands he courageously returns to the ball field to ask Coach Parker for another chance. (60 pages)

Where it's reviewed:
Booklist, August 1993, page 2058
Horn Book Guide, Fall 1993, page 284
Reading Teacher, May 1994, page 651
School Library Journal, July 1993, page 58

Other books by the same author:
All-Star Fever, 1995
Zero's Slider, 1994
Centerfield Ballhawk, 1992

Other books you might like:
Betsy Duffey, *Lucky in Left Field*, 1992
    The new baseball coach doesn't allow dogs on the team so canine Lucky must find a way to regain his position in left field.
Patricia Reilly Giff, *Left-Handed Shortstop*, 1980
    Rather than disappoint his classmates with his poor playing ability, Walter makes a cast for his left arm in order to keep from playing on the class baseball team.
Constance Hiser, *Dog on Third Base*, 1991
    With help from his baseball-playing dog Tag, James helps to make Mean Mitchell a more cooperative member of the team.

252

MATT CHRISTOPHER

Olympic Dream

(New York: Little, Brown, 1996)

Subject(s): Bicycles and Bicycling; Weight Control
Age range(s): Grades 2-4
Major character(s): Doug Cannon, 12-Year-Old, Bicyclist; Red Roberts, Student—College, Bicyclist; Billy Torrant, Sports Figure (bicyclist)
Time period(s): 1990s
Locale(s): United States

Summary: Doug is disappointed when the video arcade burns down right at the beginning of summer. His sister is getting married and the family is caught up in the plans. Then Red, a friend of hers, comes to stay for the summer. He is a bicycle racing enthusiast and quickly gets Doug interested in the sport so much so that his father buys him a new bicycle. Doug has always been overweight but with bicycling and working on making trails, he begins to lose weight. He is not only able to participate in the bicycle races, but places as well. (171 pages)

Other books by the same author:
Fighting Tackle, 1995
The Winning Stroke, 1994
Man Out at First, 1993
Undercover Tailback, 1992

Other books you might like:
Helen Cavanaugh, *Panther Glade*, 1993
  Bill gains some self-confidence when he travels with his aunt on an archaeological dig.
Betsy Sachs, *Mountain Like Madness*, 1994
  Billy tries to earn money to buy a new bike.
Gary Soto, *Summer on Wheels*, 1995
  Hector and his friend take off on a six day bike trip.
Jean Van Leeuwen, *Benjy the Football Hero*, 1985
  Even though he is short and small, Benjy decides that he wants to be a football hero.
Bill Wallace, *Never Say Quit*, 1993
  Several misfits who cannot make the regular soccer team form one of their own.
Joan T. Zeier, *Stick Boy*, 1993
  A self-conscious boy comes to terms with himself when he attends a private school.

253

MATT CHRISTOPHER
KARIN LIDBECK, Illustrator

Pressure Play

(Boston: Little Brown and Company, 1993)

Subject(s): Sports/Baseball; Mystery and Detective Stories
Age range(s): Grades 4-6
Major character(s): Travis Bonelli, Baseball Player; Peter Hooper, Baseball Player
Time period(s): 1990s (1993)
Locale(s): Cloverdale

Summary: New to town, Travis' baseball skill leads to his acceptance by his peers, but also results in pressure to help the team win the championship. Travis is also interested in horror films, especially making his own from film clips, but only Peter seems to share that interest. The other team members are interested only in winning and when Travis' baseball performance slips, anonymous and threatening phone calls begin. (154 pages)

Where it's reviewed:
Booklist, August 1993, page 2058
Horn Book Guide, Fall 1993, page 295
School Library Journal, July 1993, page 84

Other books by the same author:
Double Play at Short, 1995
Challenge at Second Base, 1992
Catcher with a Glass Arm, 1985

Other books you might like:
David Halecroft, *Championship Summer*, 1991
  Rivalry between players effects performance on the field and threatens a team's chance to make the playoffs.
Dean Hughes, *All Together Now*, 1991
  Teamwork pays off for this baseball team on its way to the regional championship.
Johanna Hurwitz, *Baseball Fever*, 1981
  Ezra tries to help his European-born father appreciate his love for baseball.
Suzy Kline, *Herbie Jones and the Monster Ball*, 1988
  Best-known for his ability to strike out, Herbie sees a ruined summer ahead when his uncle agrees to coach the baseball team and expects Herbie to play.
Paul Robert Walker, *The Sluggers Club: A Sports Mystery*, 1993
  B. J. and his friend form the Slugger's Club to investigate the disappearance of equipment from their baseball team.

254

MATT CHRISTOPHER

The Winning Stroke

(Boston: Little, Brown and Co., 1994)

Subject(s): Sports/Swimming
Age range(s): Grades 6-7
Major character(s): Jerry Grayson, Baseball Player, Swimmer
Time period(s): 1990s
Locale(s): United States

Summary: Sliding into second base, Jerry feels a pain in his leg as the second baseman falls on him. Waking up later in the hospital, he's upset to realize he'll be in a cast for three months and then have therapy for several more months before he can return to his beloved sport of baseball. As he begins therapy, part of his routine is swimming, an activity he'd always considered great for the beach but never as a sport. As he watches his first meet and realizes the competitiveness, sportsmanship and feeling of being part of a team are just as strong as with baseball, it isn't long before Jerry's trying out for the swim team. (168 pages)

Where it's reviewed:
Voice of Youth Advocates, June 1994, page 81

Booklist, May 1, 1994, page 1601
School Library Journal, June 1994, page 81
Horn Book Guide, Fall 1994, page 299

Other books by the same author:
Double Play at Short, 1995
Fighting Tackle, 1995
Top Wing, 1994
Undercover Tailback, 1992

Other books you might like:
Chris Crutcher, *Stotan!*, 1986
　　You gotta be tough to endure the conditioning program imposed by the swim coach in this sports novel.
Deborah Davis, *My Brother Has AIDS*, 1994
　　Though a gifted swimmer, Lacy willingly shoves that aside when her brother comes home to die.
Tessa Duder, *In Lane Three, Alex Archer*, 1989
　　Alex must overcome great difficulties to be one of two girls chosen to represent New Zealand in the 1960 Rome Olympics.
Nancy J. Hopper, *Wake Me When the Band Starts Playing*, 1988
　　To try to slim down, Mike practices with the swim team.

255

MATT CHRISTOPHER
MOLLY DELANEY, Illustrator

Zero's Slider

(Boston: Little, Brown and Company, 1994)

Series: Springboard Books
Subject(s): Sports/Baseball; Aunts and Uncles; Self-Confidence
Age range(s): Grades 2-4
Major character(s): Zero Ford, Child, Baseball Player; Pete, Uncle, Unemployed
Time period(s): 1990s (1994)
Locale(s): United States

Summary: Frustrated with himself after a poorly pitched game, Zero accidentally slams his finger in the car door. Now his problems seem multiplied, but with Uncle Pete's help he begins to regain confidence in his pitching ability when he unintentionally throws a slider while practicing with a bandaged finger. Although he can't recreate the slider after his finger heals, Zero does regain his confidence and his pitching arm.

Where it's reviewed:
Booklist, June 1, 1994, page 1815
Horn Book Guide, Fall 1994, page 299
School Library Journal, October 1994, page 88

Other books by the same author:
Shadow over Second, 1996
The Lucky Baseball Bat, 1991
Hit-Away Kid, 1988

Other books you might like:
Fred Bowen, *T.J.'s Secret Pitch*, 1996
　　T.J. adopts an unorthodox pitching style in hopes that he can land a place on the neighborhood baseball team.

Betsy Duffey, *Lucky in Left Field*, 1992
　　When a losing baseball team acquires a new coach, Lucky the dog is kicked off the team.
Philip Hanft, *Never Fear, Flip the Dip Is Here*, 1991
　　When Buster, a former minor league baseball player, works with him, Flip gains both skills and self-confidence.

256

BEVERLY CLEARY
DAVID SMALL, Illustrator

Petey's Bedtime Story

(New York: Morrow Junior Books, 1993)

Subject(s): Bedtime; Parent and Child; Storytelling
Age range(s): Grades K-3
Major character(s): Petey, Child, Storyteller; Mommy, Mother; Daddy, Father
Time period(s): 1990s (1993)
Locale(s): United States

Summary: Petey is a little boy who loves bedtime—the bath, the stories, the nightly chases, everything except sleeping. The last item in the nightly ritual is Daddy's retelling of the story of Petey's birth. The night that Petey decides to do the storytelling for himself, the tale becomes so embellished and lengthy that by the time it concludes both his parents are asleep in Petey's room and Petey heads for a box of cookies and his parents' bed. (32 pages)

Where it's reviewed:
Booklist, September 1, 1993, page 67
Five Owls, January 1994, page 58
Horn Book Guide, Spring 1994, page 64
Publishers Weekly, July 12, 1993, page 80
School Library Journal, February 1994, page 78

Other books by the same author:
Janet's Thingamajigs, 1988
The Growing-Up Feet, 1987
Two Dog Biscuits, 1986

Other books you might like:
Eve Bunting, *No Nap*, 1989
　　Dad tries every trick he knows to entice Susie into sleeping at naptime, but when sleep finally comes, it's not as Dad plans it.
Russell Hoban, *Bedtime for Frances*, 1960
　　It's bedtime and Frances imagines one problem after another trying to delay the inevitable.
Angela Johnson, *Tell Me a Story, Mama*, 1989
　　Mama has responded so often to her daughter's plea for stories from Mama's childhood that there is no longer any distinction between storyteller and audience.
Marisabina Russo, *Waiting for Hannah*, 1989
　　Hannah wants to know what her mother did while awaiting Hannah's birth.

257

ANDREW CLEMENTS
BRIAN SELZNICK, Illustrator

Frindle

(New York: Simon & Schuster, 1996)

Subject(s): Language; Teacher-Student Relationships; Schools
Age range(s): Grades 3-5
Major character(s): Nicholas "Nick" Allen, 5th Grader; Mrs. Lorelei Granger, Teacher; Judy Morgan, Journalist
Time period(s): 1990s
Locale(s): Westfield, New Hampshire

Summary: Nick hates having to look up words in the dictionary for his language arts class so one day, after reading about how words are added to the English language, he decides to make up his own word for pen—frindle. The other students in the class quickly start using the word, much to their teacher's dismay. Nick gets into trouble but insists on his right to make up a word and eventually gets his side of the story reported. When school is over for the year, his teacher does admit that she did appreciate Nick's imagination. Ten years later the word appears in the dictionary. (105 pages)

Where it's reviewed:
School Library Journal, September 1996, page 201
Bulletin of the Center for Children's Books, October 1996, page 51
Booklist, September 1, 1996, page 124

Other books by the same author:
The Temple Cat, 1995
Billy and the Bad Teacher, 1992
Where Is Mr. Mole, 1989

Other books you might like:
Monalisa DeGross, *Donavan's Word Jar*, 1994
   Donavan loves words and keeps a jar-full which he eventually gives away.
Patricia Demuth, *In Trouble with Teacher*, 1995
   Montgomery writes wonderful stories and draws great pictures but he is concerned that his teacher only worries about spelling.
Louis Sachar, *Sideways Arithmetic from Wayside School*, 1989
   Amusing episodes occur in all the classrooms of the school which was built sideways and has one classroom per floor.
William Taylor, *Numbskulls*, 1995
   Chas has to deal with his neighbor who makes him do all kinds of funny things, but does develop him into a speller.

258

ETH CLIFFORD
BRIAN LIES, Illustrator

Flatfoot Fox and the Case of the Missing Whoooo

(Boston: Houghton Mifflin Company, 1993)

Subject(s): Mystery and Detective Stories; Animals; Humor
Age range(s): Grades 1-3
Major character(s): Flatfoot Fox, Fox, Detective (world's greatest detective); Secretary Bird, Bird, Assistant (to Flatfoot Fox); Mournful Owl, Owl (victim)
Time period(s): 1990s (1993)
Locale(s): Earth (a forest)

Summary: Ever eager to solve a mystery and maintain his self-proclaimed status as the greatest detective in the world, Flatfoot Fox accepts his third case over the protests of his trusted assistant, Secretary Bird. In his search for Mournful Owl's whoooo he is also accompanied by Silly Goose who reported the theft and Secretary Bird. In no time, Flatfoot has found Mournful Owl's whoooo and returned it to its proper place. (46 pages)

Where it's reviewed:
Booklist, December 15, 1993, page 753
Five Owls, March 1994, page 79
Horn Book Guide, Spring 1994, page 64
Library Talk, May 1994, page 42
School Library Journal, August 1993, page 140

Other books by the same author:
Flatfoot Fox and the Case of the Bashful Beaver, 1995
Flatfoot Fox and the Case of the Nosy Otter, 1992
The Dastardly Murder of Dirty Pete, 1981

Other books you might like:
David A. Adler, *Cam Jansen and the Mystery at the Monkey House*, 1985
   In her 10th adventure, Cam Jansen uses her photographic memory and the help of her friends to solve the mystery of disappearing monkeys.
Eve Bunting, *The Skate Patrol*, 1980
   Milton and James meet with success as they track down a thief.
Elizabeth Levy, *The Something Queer Series*, 1971-
   Gwen, Jill and basset hound Fletcher have one adventure after another while they solve mysterious occurrences.
Marjorie Weinman Sharmat, *Nate the Great Series*, 1989-
   With assistance from his dog Sludge, Nate the Great solves a succession of mysteries in this easy-to-read series.

259

ETH CLIFFORD

Harvey's Mystifying Raccoon Mix-Up

(Boston: Houghton Mifflin Company, 1994)

Subject(s): Mystery and Detective Stories; Cousins; Animals/Raccoons
Age range(s): Grades 3-5
Major character(s): Harvey Willson, 12-Year-Old, Cousin (Nora's); Nora Jean Adams, 11-Year-Old (imaginative), Cousin (Harvey's); Buttons, Raccoon
Time period(s): 1990s (1994)
Locale(s): United States (Harvey's house)

Summary: Whenever Nora visits, Harvey can be sure of excitement, but this time he gets more than he expected. A prowler's rifle shot breaks off a tree branch, causing it to crash through Harvey's window and bringing with it a raccoon clutching a counterfeiter's plate. The raccoon leads the family on a merry chase as they try to retrieve the plate to turn it over to the police. The counterfeiters break into the house to search Harvey's attic, briefly locking in the children, before both the raccoon and the crooks are caught. (112 pages)

Where it's reviewed:
Booklist, September 15, 1994, page 135
Horn Book Guide, Spring 1995, page 74
Kirkus Reviews, November 15, 1994, page 1524
Library Talk, September 1995, page 39
School Library Journal, October 1994, page 120

Other books by the same author:
Harvey's Wacky Parrot Adventure, 1991
Harvey's Marvelous Monkey Mystery, 1987
Harvey's Horrible Snake Disaster, 1984

Other books you might like:
Elizabeth Levy, *Gorgonzola Zombies in the Park*, 1993
Sam and Robert are accustomed to trouble when cousin Mabel visits, but this time some very unusual things begin to happen in the park after she arrives.
Margaret Mahy, *The Good Fortunes Gang*, 1993
When Pete Fortune's family moves to his father's hometown, Pete must prove himself worthy to be accepted by his cousins.
Willo Davis Roberts, *What Could Go Wrong?*, 1989
On what should have been an uncomplicated flight from Seattle to San Francisco, Gracie and her cousins find that a mix-up with some luggage creates problems and danger.

260

ETH CLIFFORD
GEORGE HUGHES, Illustrator

Never Hit a Ghost with a Baseball Bat

(Boston: Houghton Mifflin Company, 1993)

Series: Jo-Beth and Mary Rose Mystery
Subject(s): Museums; Mystery and Detective Stories; Homeless
Age range(s): Grades 3-5
Major character(s): Jo-Beth Onetree, 8-Year-Old; Mary Rose Onetree, 11-Year-Old
Time period(s): 1990s (1993)
Locale(s): Indiana

Summary: Jo-Beth and Mary Rose can't imagine anything more boring than accompanying their newspaper reporter father on assignment. However, after only a short time in the trolley car museum, strange events begin happening that not only keep them from being bored but also scare them plenty. Determined to learn who is behind the mysterious pranks, Mary Rose leads a terrified Jo-Beth from trolley to trolley until they find their father, the museum owner, and the culprits. (111 pages)

Where it's reviewed:
Booklist, April 15, 1994, page 1540
School Library Journal, June 1993, page 104

Other books by the same author:
Flatfoot Fox and the Case of the Bashful Beaver, 1995
Will Somebody Please Marry My Sister?, 1992
Help! I'm a Prisoner in the Library, 1979

Other books you might like:
Cynthia DeFelice, *The Light on Hogback Hill*, 1993
Hadley and Josh discover the real reason for the mysterious light that townsfolk think is from a witch on Hogback Hill.
Patricia Reilly Giff, *Tootsie Tanner, Why Don't You Talk?*, 1987
Detective Abby Jones and her friend Potsie investigate the mystery of some important stolen film.
James Howe, *Dew Drop Dead: A Sebastian Barth Mystery*, 1990
Finding a body in the abandoned Dew Drop Inn, Sebastian plans to investigate only to find that the body has vanished.
Donald J. Sobol, *The Encyclopedia Brown Series*, 1979-
Ten-year-old Leroy Brown operates his own detective agency and solves a variety of mysteries in his neighborhood.

261

SHIRLEY CLIMO
RUTH HELLER, Illustrator

The Korean Cinderella

(New York: HarperCollins Publishers, 1993)

Subject(s): Fairy Tale; Folk Tales; Stepfamilies
Age range(s): Grades K-3
Major character(s): Pear Blossom, Child (beautiful), Stepdaughter (mistreated); Omoni, Stepmother (cruel); Peony, Stepsister (unkind)
Time period(s): Indeterminate Past
Locale(s): Korea, South

Summary: After the death of her mother and remarriage of her elderly father, lovely Pear Blossom must endure cruel treatment from Omoni and Peony who force Pear Blossom to perform increasingly difficult tasks in order to avoid their wrath. Each time Pear Blossom is given a seemingly impossible chore, the *tokgabi* comes in the form of an animal to assist her. Kind Pear Blossom is rescued from this dreary life by the magistrate's offer of marriage. (48 pages)

Where it's reviewed:
Booklist, May 1, 1993, page 1598
Horn Book Guide, Fall 1993, page 324
Publishers Weekly, May 17, 1993, page 79
Reading Teacher, October 1993, page 156
School Library Journal, August 1993, page 156

Other books by the same author:
The Egyptian Cinderella, 1989
King of the Birds, 1988
Cobweb Christmas, 1982

Other books you might like:
Ellen Jackson, *Cinder Edna*, 1994
Here's Cinderella with a feminist twist. Cinder Edna doesn't wait for a fairy godmother; she takes charge of her life and gets the prince herself.
Charles Perrault, *Cinderella*, 1954
In a classic tale of love and inner beauty, Cinderella survives years of torment from her stepmother and stepsisters to win the Prince's hand in marriage.

Robert D. San Souci, *Sootface*, 1994

In a retelling of an Ojibwa Cinderella Story, Sootface, who is mistreated by her two older sisters, is chosen as the bride of a legendary hunter.

262

ELEANOR COERR
DON BOLOGNESE, Illustrator

Buffalo Bill and the Pony Express

(New York: HarperCollins Publishers, 1995)

Series: I Can Read
Subject(s): Historical; American West; Legends
Age range(s): Grades 2-4
Major character(s): Bill Cody, 15-Year-Old, Cowboy
Time period(s): 1860s (1860)
Locale(s): Red Buttes, West; Three Crossings, West

Summary: Responding to an help-wanted ad, Bill Cody begins an adventure-packed experience as a rider for the Pony Express. Although his letters to his mother suggest otherwise, Bill's life is now filled with danger—Indians, wolves and outlaws. Through it all, Bill delivers the mail on his 75-mile route. A concluding author's note gives factual information about this legendary American hero. (64 pages)

Where it's reviewed:
Booklist, April 15, 1995, page 1509
Five Owls, March 1995, page 83
Horn Book, July 1995, page 456
School Library Journal, May 1995, page 82

Other books by the same author:
Chang's Paper Pony, 1988
The Josefina Story Quilt, 1986
The Big Balloon Race, 1981

Other books you might like:
Clyde Robert Bulla, *Charlie's House*, 1993
Charlie leaves his impoverished home and travels to America where his dreams of designing his own house are eventually realized.
Joseph J. DiCerto, *The Pony Express: Hoofbeats in the Wilderness*, 1989
A factual overview of the long and hazardous Pony Express route.
Nancy Robison, *Buffalo Bill*, 1991
The life of Buffalo Bill is presented from his days on the frontier to his career in show business.
R. Conrad Stein, *The Story of the Pony Express*, 1981
A nonfiction book introduces the early days of postal delivery on the frontier.

263

ELEANOR COERR

Mieko and the Fifth Treasure

(New York: G.P. Putnam's Sons, 1993)

Subject(s): Artists and Art; School Life; Historical
Age range(s): Grades 3-5
Major character(s): Mieko, Child, Artist; Yoshi, Child, Friend

Time period(s): 1940s (1945, after bombing of Nagasaki)
Locale(s): Japan (countryside near Nagasaki)

Summary: Following Meiko's injury during the bombing of Nagasaki, she is sent to her grandparents' home for rest and healing. Depressed because her injured hand prevents her from painting and hurt by the teasing of students when she enters a new school, Mieko is sure that she has lost the most treasured quality of an artist, the inner beauty needed to guide the brush. With the loving support of her grandparents and the friendship of Yoshi, Mieko finds the courage to believe in herself and to overcome her physical loss. Calligraphy by Cecil H. Uyehara. (78 pages)

Where it's reviewed:
Booklist, April 1, 1993, page 1432
Children's Book Review Service, July 1993, page 153
Emergency Librarian, September 1993, page 49
Publishers Weekly, March 15, 1993, page 88
School Library Journal, July 1993, page 84

Other books by the same author:
Sadako, 1993
Sadako and the Thousand Paper Cranes, 1979

Other books you might like:
Pearl Buck, *The Big Wave*, 1973
A young Japanese boy shows his courage as he faces the loss of his family in a tidal wave.
Elizabeth Coatsworth, *The Cat Who Went to Heaven*, 1930
Winner of the 1930 Newbery Award, this book tells the miraculous story of a Japanese artist and his cat.
Rumer Godden, *Great Grandfather's House*, 1993
Resentful that she must stay in the countryside with her grandmother and great grandfather while her parents travel to England for 3 months, young Keiko is transformed by the experience.
Laurence Yep, *Hiroshima*, 1995
Sisters Sachi and Riko are forever effected by the atomic bomb dropped on Hiroshima.

264

NANCY COFFELT, Author/Illustrator

The Dog Who Cried Woof

(San Diego: Gulliver/Harcourt Brace & Company, 1995)

Subject(s): Animals/Dogs; Animals/Cats; Behavior
Age range(s): Grades K-2
Major character(s): Ernie, Dog; Unnamed Character, Cat
Time period(s): 1990s (1995)
Locale(s): United States

Summary: Ernie learns the hard way that non-stop barking does not attract the attention he needs from his family. By the time a cat moves into the neighborhood and begins stealing Ernie's food, his barking habits have put his family in ear muffs so no one hears his barks for help. As Ernie grows increasingly loud and frustrated with the cat, he loses his bark completely. His family is so pleased with the quiet that they praise him profusely. After a week, Ernie's bark returns and because he's learned to use it only when necessary, he finally attracts his family's attention and the cat problem is solved. (32 pages).

Where it's reviewed:

Booklist, April 1, 1995, page 1424
Emergency Librarian, September 1995, page 55
Horn Book, July 1995, page 447
Kirkus Reviews, April 1, 1995, page 465
School Library Journal, May 1995, page 82

Other books by the same author:

Tom's Fish, 1994
Dogs in Space, 1993
Good Night, Sigmund, 1992

Other books you might like:

Carol Barnett, *The Boy Who Cried Wolf*, 1990
  A bored shepherd boy learns too late his many false alarms undermine his credibility when he really needs the help.
Joanna Cole, *Give a Dog a Bone: Stories, Poems, Jokes, and Riddles about Dogs*, 1996
  The illustrated compilation concludes with factual information explaining why dogs bark at "nothing." Co-compiler Stephanie Calmenson.
David Milgrim, *Why Benny Barks*, 1994
  A puzzled child asks a series of rhyming questions in an attempt to understand why his dog barks.
Dav Pilkey, *Dog Breath: The Horrible Trouble with Hally Tosis*, 1994
  The Tosis family is ready to give away Hally until their pet's worst feature proves to be the undoing of two burglars.

265

NANCY COFFELT, Author/Illustrator

Tom's Fish

(San Diego: Gulliver Books, 1994)

Subject(s): Individuality; Pets
Age range(s): Grades K-1
Major character(s): Tom, 8-Year-Old; Jesse, Fish (pet); Flo, Fish (pet)
Time period(s): 1990s (1994)
Locale(s): United States (Tom's house)

Summary: Of all the presents he receives for his birthday, Tom's favorite is a goldfish with the unusual habit of swimming upside down. Although Tom tries all the suggestions offered by family and neighbors to change Jesse's behavior, including buying Flo to keep Jesse company, nothing works. Jesse is Jesse and it is Tom who will need to make some adjustments. (32 pages)

Where it's reviewed:

Booklist, March 15, 1994, page 1371
Children's Book Review Service, Spring 1994, page 134
Horn Book, September 1994, page 573
Publishers Weekly, April 18, 1994, page 61
School Library Journal, May 1994, page 90

Other books by the same author:

The Dog Who Cried Woof, 1994
Dogs in Space, 1993
Good Night, Sigmund, 1992

Other books you might like:

John Himmelman, *Ellen and the Goldfish*, 1990
  When a young girl befriends a goldfish she uses her talent for drawing to help the fish escape from the fisherman.
Robert Kraus, *Leo the Late Bloomer*, 1971
  His parents are concerned, but Leo's mother is sure that, given time, Leo will bloom . . . and she's right.
Helen Lester, *Three Cheers for Tacky*, 1994
  Despite his teammates efforts to mold him into a "perfect" cheerleader, Tacky remains true to himself.

266

BARBARA COHEN
JAN NAIMO JONES, Illustrator

Make a Wish, Molly

(New York: Doubleday Book for Young Readers, 1994)

Subject(s): Jews; Friendship; Birthdays
Age range(s): Grades 2-3
Major character(s): Molly Hyman, 3rd Grader, Immigrant (from Russia); Emma DeWitt, 3rd Grader, Friend (Molly's); Mama, Mother (Molly's), Immigrant (from Russia)
Time period(s): Indeterminate Past
Locale(s): Winter Hill, New Jersey

Summary: Molly's excitement over her invitation to Emma's birthday party, her first American party, is tempered by the realization that the party is during Passover. As Molly sits with a plate of cake and melting ice cream, she is reminded of Mama's admonition about the dietary laws of the religious holiday. Seeing her discomfort, another party guest taunts her until Molly leaves the party in tears. Mama settles the score a few weeks later when it is Molly's birthday and Emma, accompanied by the obnoxious party guest, unexpectedly arrives with a birthday gift. Mama's hospitality enriches her relationship with her daughter and helps Molly's friends appreciate her heritage. (38 pages)

Where it's reviewed:

Booklist, March 1, 1994, page 1269
Horn Book, May 1994, page 323
Publishers Weekly, December 13, 1993, page 69
Reading Teacher, September 1994, page 64
School Library Journal, April 1994, page 101

Other books by the same author:

Two Hundred Thirteen Valentines, 1991
The Carp in the Bathtub, 1987
Molly's Pilgrim, 1983

Other books you might like:

Amy Hest, *Party on Ice*, 1995
  At Casey's ninth birthday party, friend Kate falls while ice-skating and breaks her arm.
Janet Shaw, *Happy Birthday, Kirsten! A Springtime Story*, 1987
  The Larsen family takes time from farm chores to celebrate Kirsten's tenth birthday.
Jane Breskin Zalben, *Happy Passover, Rosie*, 1990
  Rosie celebrates her first Passover with her family.

267

RON COHEN, Author/Illustrator

My Dad's Baseball

(New York: Lothrop, Lee & Shepard Books, 1994)

Subject(s): Sports/Baseball; Fathers and Sons; Storytelling
Age range(s): Grades K-3
Major character(s): Max Cohen, 7-Year-Old; Ron Cohen, Father; Yogi Berra, Baseball Player
Time period(s): 1950s (1955); 1990s (1994)
Locale(s): New York, New York

Summary: Max's discovery of an autographed baseball in a long-forgotten box in his grandparents' attic prompts his dad to tell the story behind the ball. As a 7-year-old, Dad attended his first baseball game where he recovered a ball hit by Yogi Berra that the player autographed for him. Now that Dad has found the long-lost ball he presents it to his son. (32 pages)

Where it's reviewed:
Booklist, March 15, 1994, page 1371
Children's Book Review Service, March 1994, page 91
Horn Book Guide, Fall 1994, page 299
Publishers Weekly, February 7, 1994, page 87
School Library Journal, May 1994, page 90

Other books you might like:
Alexandra Day, *Frank and Ernest Play Ball*, 1990
    In order to manage a baseball team for one night, Frank and Ernest must learn baseball lingo.
William H. Hooks, *Mr. Baseball*, 1991
    A player on a Little League team must contend with the overly enthustiastic support of his younger brother.
David Spohn, *Home Field*, 1993
    Awakening early on a Saturday morning, Matt and his father enjoy a game of baseball on their own home field.

268

BABETTE COLE, Author/Illustrator

Winni Allfours

(Mahway, NJ: BridgeWater Books, 1994)

Subject(s): Animals/Horses; Parent and Child; Fantasy
Age range(s): Grades K-2
Major character(s): Winni Allfours, Child, Pony
Time period(s): 1990s (1993)
Locale(s): England; Kentucky

Summary: When Winni's vegetarian parents refuse to consider her desire to own a pony, she consumes so many vegetables that one day she begins to turn into a pony. While her parents aren't happy she's rolling on the organic vegetable garden in the yard, Winni is enjoying life without school. She joins a group of ponies in town and is taken to Kentucky to compete in a horse race. When her parents refuse to sell their daughter to a horse racer, she is kidnapped, but engineers her own escape by driving off in the kidnapper's truck. Promises of hamburgers and a pony of her own do not sway Winni Allfours who intends to remain a pony and never go to school again. First published in Great Britain in 1993. (32 pages)

Where it's reviewed:
Bulletin of the Center for Children's Books, May 1994, page 283
Junior Bookshelf, June 1994, page 93
Publishers Weekly, February 21, 1994, page 254
School Librarian, May 1994, page 53
School Library Journal, August 1994, page 127

Other books by the same author:
Dr. Dog, 1994
Supermoo!, 1993
Princess Smartypants, 1987

Other books you might like:
Peter Collington, *The Midnight Circus*, 1993
    A mechanical horse comes to life and takes a youngster on a midnight ride.
Liz Rosenberg, *The Carousel*, 1995
    The animals of a closed, and broken carousel become real and give two sisters rides.
Elizabeth Thiel, *The Polka Dot Horse*, 1993
    Fearing that he will be discarded, an old toy horse rolls away until he reaches a farm where he finds someone to care for him.

269

HENRY COLE, Author/Illustrator

Jack's Garden

(New York: Greenwillow Books, 1995)

Subject(s): Gardens and Gardening; Nature
Age range(s): Grades K-2
Major character(s): Jack, Child, Gardener
Time period(s): 1990s (1995)
Locale(s): United States

Summary: Jack stands in a fenced area of his back yard, shovel in hand, ready to prepare the soil to accept the seeds. The cumulative tale continues as the seeds sprout, then bud and finally blossom. As the garden grows, insects visit as well as birds and a garden snake. A concluding author's note gives factual information about planting a garden. (24 pages)

Where it's reviewed:
Booklist, April 1, 1995, page 1424
Bulletin of the Center for Children's Books, May 1995, page 301
Horn Book Guide, Fall 1995, page 261
Kirkus Reviews, April 15, 1995, page 555
School Library Journal, May 1995, page 82

Other books you might like:
Monica Hughes, *A Handful of Seeds*, 1993
    Heeding her deceased grandmother's advice, Concepcion plants a garden, saving enough seeds from her crop to begin again the next year.
Elaine Moore, *Grandma's Garden*, 1994
    Annually, Kim and Grandma plant a garden when the spring weather warms the soil.
Anne F. Rockwell, *How My Garden Grew*, 1982
    Simply, a young child explains how to plant and care for a garden.

Joanne Ryder, *My Father's Hands*, 1994

While digging in the garden, Father shows his patiently waiting daughter the treasures of nature that he finds.

270

JOANNA COLE
STEPHANIE CALMENSON, Illustrator
LYNN MUNSINGER, Illustrator

The Gator Girls

(New York: Morrow Junior Books, 1995)

Subject(s): Animals/Alligators; Friendship; Summer
Age range(s): Grades 2-3
Major character(s): Amy Gator, Child, Alligator; Allie Gator, Child, Alligator
Time period(s): 1990s (1995)
Locale(s): United States

Summary: When a last minute opening at Camp Wogga-Bog threatens to send Allie to camp without Amy, the best friends must compress a list of exciting summer plans into only a few days They hurry to complete their activities and bid one another a sad good-bye. The day before the camp bus comes, another space becomes available and the two friends no longer face a summer apart. (59 pages)

Where it's reviewed:
Booklist, April 15, 1995, page 1497
Horn Book Guide, Fall 1995, page 290
Library Talk, May 1995, page 41
School Library Journal, April 1995, page 100

Other books by the same author:
Yours 'til Banana Splits, 1995
Why Did the Chicken Cross the Road? And Other Riddles Old and New, 1994
The Laugh Book, 1986

Other books you might like:
Joyce Champion, *Emily and Alice Again*, 1995
Best friends return in this sequel to *Emily and Alice* and continue to enjoy a variety of activities.
James Howe, *Pinky and Rex Go to Camp*, 1992
Pinky doesn't share best friend Rex's enthusiasm for the summer camp experience ahead.
Arnold Lobel, *Frog and Toad Together*, 1972
The Newbery Honor book is one of four titles describing the adventures and misadventures of loyal friends Frog and Toad.

271

JOANNA COLE
MAXIE CHAMBLISS, Illustrator

How I Was Adopted: Samantha's Story

(New York: Morrow Junior Books, 1995)

Subject(s): Adoption; Parent and Child; Love
Age range(s): Grades K-2
Major character(s): Samantha "Sam", Adoptee
Time period(s): 1990s (1995)
Locale(s): United States

Summary: Cheerful Samantha tells the story of her adoption by loving parents. She relates her story to other adoptees encouraging them to consider their own story, which might be different, but is still valid. The book begins with a preface to families about adoption with tips for answering children's questions. (48 pages)

Where it's reviewed:
Booklist, August 1995, page 1955
Publishers Weekly, October 2, 1995, page 74
School Library Journal, September 1995, page 192

Other books by the same author:
The Magic School Bus on the Ocean Floor, 1994
Six Sick Sheep: One Hundred One Tongue Twisters, 1993
The Missing Tooth, 1988

Other books you might like:
Susi Gregg Fowler, *When Joel Comes Home*, 1993
A young girl eagerly plans her family's welcome of friends' newly adopted baby.
Betty Lifton, *Tell Me a Real Adoption Story*, 1994
A child requests a bedtime story "about me" to which the mother responds with a story about the child's adoption.
Jonathan London, *A Koala for Katie: An Adoption Story*, 1993
Katie "adopts" a toy koala from the zoo gift shop using the toy to work through feelings about her adoption.
Fred Rogers, *Let's Talk about It: Adoption*, 1995
A straightforward title examining the possible feelings adopted children may have.
Pat Mora, *Pablo's Tree*, 1994
A Mexican-American boy looks forward to his grandfather's annual decoration of the tree planted to commemorate his adoption.
Michael J. Rosen, *Bonesy and Isabel*, 1995
Befriending an old dog helps an adopted Salvadoran girl adjust to her new home in America but also brings grief when Bonesy dies.

272

JOANNA COLE, Editor
STEPHANIE CALMENSON, Co-Editor

Ready. . .Set. . .Read—and Laugh! A Funny Treasury for Beginning Readers

(New York: A Doubleday Book for Young Readers, 1995)

Subject(s): Short Stories; Humor; Poetry
Age range(s): Grades K-2
Time period(s): Indeterminate
Locale(s): Fictional Country

Summary: Humorous poems, stories, riddles, and songs are gathered from the works of well-known authors and illustrators for beginning readers. Entries are divided into sections in a table of contents. Indexes for title, author, and illustrator are included. (144 pages)

Where it's reviewed:
Booklist, October 1, 1995, page 329
Horn Book Guide, Spring 1996, page 134
Kirkus Reviews, July 15, 1995, page 1021
Publishers Weekly, September 11, 1995, page 87

School Library Journal, October 1995, page 125

Other books by the same author:
Six Sick Sheep: One Hundred One Tongue Twisters, 1993
Ready. . .Set. . .Read, 1990
The Laugh Book, 1986

Other books you might like:
Betsy Byars, *The Golly Sisters Go West*, 1986
Six stories trace the amusing travels of two comical sisters on the frontier.
James Marshall, *Rats on the Range and Other Stories*, 1993
This collection of humorous stories is a sequel to *Rats on the Roof*.
Barbara Ann Porte, *When Aunt Lucy Rode a Mule and Other Stories*, 1994
Two sisters are entertained by Aunt Lucy's stories of childhood visits to her grandparents' mountain home.
Robert Quackenbush, *Robert Quackenbush's Treasury of Humor*, 1990
Detective Mole and Sheriff Sally Gopher are featured characters in a collection of stories.

273

SHEILA COLE
BARBARA ROGOFF, Illustrator

The Hen That Crowed

(New York: Lothrop, Lee & Shepard Books, 1993)

Subject(s): Animals/Roosters; Fires
Age range(s): Grades K-3
Major character(s): Charlene, Rooster; Mr. Goodhart, Farmer (Charlene's kind owner)
Time period(s): 1990s (1993)
Locale(s): Bean Blossom, Earth

Summary: Knowing that it is against the law to own a rooster in the town of Bean Blossom, Mr. Goodhart is careful to request female chicks at the feed store. Unfortunately, looks can be deceiving and one of the babies, Charlene, grows up to sport a comb, beautiful colored feathers and a fine cock-a-doodle-doo. Mr. Goodhart feels obligated to put Charlene in the soup pot, but before he can, Charlene saves herself and the town by doing what comes naturally when she mistakes the light of a night-time fire for the rising sun and awakens the townsfolk who are able to successfully extinguish the flames. (32 pages)

Where it's reviewed:
Booklist, March 15, 1993, page 1358
Children's Book Review Service, April 1993, page 98
Horn Book, May 1993, page 313
Publishers Weekly, March 15, 1993, page 86
School Library Journal, August 1993, page 140

Other books by the same author:
When the Rain Stops, 1991
When the Tide Is Low, 1985

Other books you might like:
Sharon Phillips Denslow, *Hazel's Circle*, 1992
Young Hazel introduces her pet rooster, Ike, to the neighbors.

Bill Peet, *Cock-a-Doodle Dudley*, 1990
Cocky Dudley thinks that he controls the daily rising of the sun.
Colin Threadgall, *Proud Rooster and the Fox*, 1991
In his attempt to protect the hen house, rooster enters into a game of hide-and-seek with fox.

274

EVELYN COLEMAN
DANIEL MINTER, Illustrator

The Foot Warmer and the Crow

(New York: Macmillan Publishing Company, 1994)

Subject(s): Slavery; African Americans; Freedom
Age range(s): Grades 2-5
Major character(s): Hezekiah, Slave; Master Thompson, Plantation Owner, Bully; Unnamed Character, Crow
Time period(s): Indeterminate Past
Locale(s): United States

Summary: Hezekiah dreams of being as free as the birds with whom he communicates. One day a crow tells him a tale from cruel Master Thompson's childhood and suggests how Hezekiah can gain his freedom. Hezekiah follows the crow's advice, patiently gathering the information he needs, and confronts Master Thompson. He gains only the promise of one night's head start, but with the crow's help, Hezekiah gains his freedom. (32 pages)

Where it's reviewed:
Black Scholar, Fall 1994, page 58
Bulletin of the Center for Children's Books, December 1994, page 124
Children's Book Review Service, December 1994, page 42
Publishers Weekly, September 26, 1994, page 70
School Library Journal, November 1994, page 74

Other books by the same author:
White Socks Only, 1996
Cymbals, 1995

Other books you might like:
Virginia Hamilton, *The People Could Fly: American Black Folk Tales*, 1985
A collection of 24 folk tales includes a retelling of a slave's achieving freedom by stumping his master with a riddle.
William H. Hooks, *Freedom's Fruit*, 1996
Mama Marina, an enslaved conjure woman, gains freedom for her daughter and her beloved by using a powerful spell to trick the master.
Angela Shelf Medearis, *The Freedom Riddle*, 1995
With determination and ingenuity, a young slave wins freedom by besting his master in a riddle contest.

275

EVELYN COLEMAN
TYRONE GETER, Illustrator

White Socks Only

(New York: Whitman, 1996)

Subject(s): Race Relations; African Americans

Age range(s): Grades K-2
Major character(s): Grandma, Grandmother (as a child); Chicken Man, Aged Person
Time period(s): 1950s (a time of segregation)
Locale(s): Cole County, Mississippi

Summary: Grandma tells of a time when she was little and had been warned against walking into town. But it was a warm day and she started walking. Before she knew it, she was in town and very thirsty so she went to the water fountain. There she saw a sign which said "Whites Only". Well, she took off her black shoes and stood there in her white socks to get a drink of water. A town bully appeared and was whipping her when other black women from the town stopped by, took off their shoes and helped themselves to a drink of water. Chicken Man appeared and he, too, helped himself to a drink of water in his white socks. The people of the town made their point and the white man who had whipped them was never seen again. (32 pages)

Where it's reviewed:
School Library Journal, June 1996, page 99

Other books by the same author:
The Foot Warmer and the Crow, 1994

Other books you might like:
Eve Bunting, *The Blue and the Gray*, 1996
    Two boys moving to a new place look back over the history of that place, especially during the Civil War.
Robert Coles, *The Story of Ruby Bridges*, 1995
    A little girls helps integrate a New Orleans school in 1960 in this true story. (non-fiction)
Libba Moore Gray, *Dear Willie Rudd*, 1993
    A girl looks back at the fun times she had with her housekeeper and wishes she could apologize for the wrongs done in a segregated town.
Patricia Polacco, *Mrs. Katz and Tush*, 1992
    An African American and a Jewish widow become good friends when they find a kitten without a tail.
Faith Ringgold, *Tar Beach*, 1991
    A little girl remembers growing up in Harlem and some of the things her father was not allowed to do as she "flies" over the city.

276

CAROLYN COMAN

What Jamie Saw
(Arden, NC: Front Street Books, 1995)

Subject(s): Child Abuse; Family Problems
Age range(s): Grades 5-6
Major character(s): Jamie Beauville, Child; Nin Beauville, Child (baby); Patty Beauville, Mother
Time period(s): 1990s
Locale(s): Stark, New Hampshire

Summary: Something awakens Jamie and he opens his eyes in time to see his stepfather Van hurl his little sister Nin across the room. As he watches, Jamie's mother walks in from the hallway, raises her arms and catches Nin. With that incident, Patty moves her children to a little trailer on a hill where they can be safe from Jamie's stepfather. Terrified and lonely, they huddle in their trailer, supporting one another. Jamie's teacher steps forward to help them return to the normal world where they don't live in fear of Van in this slim but powerful book. (126 pages)

Where it's reviewed:
Booklist, December 15, 1995, page 703
School Library Journal, December 1995, page 128
Publishers Weekly, August 28, 1995, page 114
New York Times Book Review, February 11, 1996, page 24
Center for Children's Books. Bulletin, December 1995, page 123

Awards the book has won:
Newbery Honor Book, 1996
ALA Notable Children's Book, 1996

Other books by the same author:
Tell Me Everything, 1993

Other books you might like:
Tom Birdseye, *Tucker*, 1990
    After being separated for seven years because of his parents' divorce, a young boy and his sister are finally reunited.
Sarah Ellis, *A Family Project*, 1988
    A family is torn apart when their new baby dies of crib death.
Kathy Kennedy Tapp, *Smoke from the Chimney*, 1986
    It's very hard for Erin to put up with her alcoholic father.

277

ESTELLE CONDRA
LINDA CROCKETT-BLASSINGAME, Illustrator

See the Ocean
(Nashville, TN: Ideals Children's Books, 1994)

Subject(s): Vacations; Brothers and Sisters; Blind
Age range(s): Grades K-3
Major character(s): Nellie, Child, Blind; Gerald, Brother (older); Jamin, Brother (older)
Time period(s): 1990s
Locale(s): South Africa (sea coast)

Summary: The first book for both author and illustrator tells of the annual seashore vacations of Nellie and her family. At the beach, Nellie takes her first steps and is introduced to seaweed and fish. Each year as the car emerges from the Black Mountains, Gerald and Jamin compete to see who can spot the ocean first. One year, their contest is hampered by coastal fog and it is Nellie who wins for the first time as she describes the picture of the ocean that she clearly sees in her mind. (32 pages)

Where it's reviewed:
Booklist, October 15, 1994, page 434
Horn Book Guide, Spring 1995, page 30
Publishers Weekly, August 1, 1994, page 79
Reading Teacher, April 1995, page 606
School Library Journal, October 1994, page 88

Other books you might like:
Miriam Cohen, *See You Tomorrow, Charles*, 1983
    First graders accept their blind classmate.

Virginia L. Kroll, *Naomi Knows It's Springtime*, 1993
  Lacking sight, Naomi uses her other senses to tell her when Spring is here.
Patricia MacLachlan, *Through Grandpa's Eyes*, 1971
  By spending time with his blind grandfather, a young boy learns to see things differently.
Charlotte Zolotow, *The Seashore Book*, 1992
  With her descriptions, a mother creates for her son the seashore that he has never seen.

278

ELLEN CONFORD
DIANE PALMISCIANO, Illustrator

Get the Picture, Jenny Archer?

(Boston: Little, Brown and Company, 1994)

Series: Springboard Books
Subject(s): Photography; Imagination; Humor
Age range(s): Grades 2-4
Major character(s): Jenny Archer, Child (imaginative)
Time period(s): 1990s (1994)
Locale(s): United States

Summary: Receiving her grandparents' old camera is disappointing to Jenny until she decides to enter a photo contest. Using her family and neighbors as the subjects for candid shots, Jenny upsets some unsuspecting subjects whose reactions trigger Jenny's imagination and lead to problems for Jenny and the neighbors. (64 pages)

Where it's reviewed:
Booklist, December 1, 1994, page 680
Horn Book Guide, Spring 1995, page 65
Kirkus Reviews, December 15, 1994, page 1560
School Library Journal, December 1994, page 72
Wilson Library Bulletin, February 1995, page 93

Other books by the same author:
Can Do, Jenny Archer, 1993
What's Cooking, Jenny Archer?, 1989
A Case for Jenny Archer, 1988

Other books you might like:
David A. Adler, *The Cam Jansen Series*, 1980-
  Using her photographic memory Cam Jansen participates in the solving of a variety of mysteries.
Lucinda Landon, *The Meg Mackintosh Series*, 1986-
  In a series of solve-it-yourself mysteries, Meg Mackintosh is a winner any way you read the story.
Marjorie Weinman Sharmat, *Nate the Great Series*, 1972-
  Nate follows one clue after another in the style of Sherlock Holmes in this series for beginning readers.

279

ELLEN CONFORD

If This Is Love, I'll Take Spaghetti

(New York: Four Winds Press, 1983)

Subject(s): Short Stories; Romance
Age range(s): Grades 5-7
Time period(s): 1980s

Locale(s): United States

Summary: These nine stories represent the humorous side of falling in love and cover such situations as you and your best friend each dating the same guy, and not knowing it. Or dieting desperately to lose twenty pounds, only to have your date say "Gee, I liked you better the way you were before." And every girl's nightmare is to have a crush on a famous rock singer, only to discover he's a real loser. If you're having trouble with your love life, this is the book to read to get romance in perspective with what's important in life. (165 pages)

Other books by the same author:
I Love You, I Hate You, Get Lost, 1994
The Things I Did for Love, 1987
Strictly for Laughs, 1985
Dear Lovey Hart, I Am Desperate, 1975

Other books you might like:
Betsy Byars, *Bingo Brown and the Language of Love*, 1989
  Bingo's venture into romance teaches him that speaking the "language of love" is like learning a foreign tongue.
Lynn Hall, *Dagmar Schultz and the Angel Edna*, 1989
  Dagmar's attempts to find a boyfriend are continually bungled by a well-meaning spiritual guide, her Aunt Edna who "passed over" years ago.
Linda Lewis, *My Heart Belongs to That Boy*, 1989
  When Linda falls in love for the first time, she learns the importance of compromise in relationships.
Phyllis Reynolds Naylor, *Alice in Rapture, Sort Of*, 1989
  Although Alice's friends offer lots of advice on how to act, she decides to "be herself" in her first real romance.

280

PAM CONRAD
RICHARD EGIELSKI, Illustrator

Call Me Ahnighito

(New York: HarperCollins Publishers, 1995)

Subject(s): Historical; Loneliness; Transportation
Age range(s): Grades 1-3
Major character(s): Ahnighito, Celestial Body (meteorite)
Time period(s): 1890s; 1900s
Locale(s): Greenland; New York, New York

Summary: Ahnighito tells of years of loneliness half-buried in snow and ice as the Greenland natives visit to chip off chunks of its "star" stuff. After being discovered by the Peary expedition, the meteorite is, over a period of time, extracted from its landing spot and hauled to a ship for transport to New York where Ahnighito is eventually put on display in a museum. (32 pages)

Where it's reviewed:
Booklist, May 1, 1995, page 1579
Bulletin of the Center for Children's Books, July 1995, page 380
Horn Book, July 1995, page 448
Kirkus Reviews, May 15, 1995, page 708
School Library Journal, June 1995, page 78

Awards the book has won:
Book Links Good Book, 1995

School Library Journal Best Books, 1995

Other books by the same author:
Doll Face Has a Party!, 1994
The Lost Sailor, 1992
The Tub People, 1989

Other books you might like:
John Gustafson, *Planets, Moons and Meteors: The Young Stargazer's Guide to the Galaxy*, 1992
    A nonfiction book gives instructions for observing meteor showers and finding meteorites.
Patricia Polacco, *Meteor!*, 1987
    A meteor crashes into a family's front yard, adding unexpected excitement to a quiet, rural community.
Sidney Rosen, *Can You Catch a Falling Star?*, 1995
    A Question of Science Series entry describes meteors and meteorites in a text suitable for beginning readers.

281

PAM CONRAD
MARY SZILAGYI, Illustrator

Molly and the Strawberry Day
(New York: HarperCollins, 1994)

Subject(s): Food; Parent and Child
Age range(s): Grades K-2
Major character(s): Molly, Child
Time period(s): 1990s (1994)
Locale(s): United States

Summary: Molly's love for strawberries leads her to look forward to the annual strawberry picking with her parents. After an early start in the strawberry fields, Molly is ready to go home and enjoy the tasty fruit until it "comes out her ears" just as her dad predicts. (32 pages)

Where it's reviewed:
Booklist, June 1, 1994, page 1836
Children's Book Review Service, September 1994, page 1
Kirkus Reviews, June 15, 1994, page 842
Publishers Weekly, May 30, 1994, page 54
School Library Journal, July 1994, page 75

Other books by the same author:
Call Me Ahnighito, 1995 (School Library Journal Best Book)
Doll Face Has a Party!, 1994
The Tub People, 1989

Other books you might like:
Joseph Bruchac, *The First Strawberries: A Cherokee Story*, 1993
    The origin of strawberries is explained in a retelling of a Cherokee legend.
Antoon Krings, *Oliver's Strawberry Patch*, 1992
    Translated from the French, the tale describes Oliver's attempts to stop a thief from making off with his strawberries.
Lynn Reiser, *Tomorrow on Rocky Pond*, 1993
    On her family's annual visit to Rocky Pond, a tired youngster resists sleep to reminisce about the next day's activities.

282

PAM CONRAD
BRIAN SELZNICK, Illustrator

Our House: The Stories of Levittown
(New York: Scholastic Inc., 1995)

Subject(s): Neighbors and Neighborhoods; Short Stories; Housing
Age range(s): Grades 4-6
Time period(s): 20th century (1947-1995)
Locale(s): Levittown, New York (Long Island)

Summary: Beginning with the potato fields on which a new suburban community is built, each of six short stories tells a decade's-worth of history about one house in the development. The first occupant leaves his footprints in the concrete patio, has the first television set on the block and falls through the kitchen ceiling onto his mother's cake. Each decade is remembered with an event such as flash photography, Vietnam, pollution, or integration, which locates the story in its historical setting. (65 pages)

Where it's reviewed:
Booklist, January 1996, page 833
Bulletin of the Center for Children's Books, December 1995, page 123
Horn Book, November 1995, page 740
Kirkus Reviews, September 15, 1995, page 1347
Publishers Weekly, September 25, 1995, page 57

Other books by the same author:
Pedro's Journal: A Journey with Christopher Columbus, 1991
Prairie Visions: The Life and Times of Solomon Butcher, 1991
Staying Nine, 1988

Other books you might like:
Betsy Byars, *Growing Up Stories*, 1995
    A compilation of short stories and novel extracts from twenty-six authors focuses on the turning point in young people's lives as they mature.
Johanna Hurwitz, *Birthday Surprises: Ten Great Stories to Unwrap*, 1995
    Each of the ten original short stories is based on the receipt of a beautifully wrapped, empty box for one's birthday.
Patricia MacLachlan, *Journey*, 1991
    With help from his grandparents, Journey constructs a history for his life.

283

PAM CONRAD
ERIC BEDDOWS, Illustrator

The Rooster's Gift
(New York: HarperCollins, 1996)

Subject(s): Animals/Chickens
Age range(s): Grades K-2
Major character(s): Young Rooster, Chicken (rooster); Smallest Hen, Chicken (hen)
Time period(s): Indeterminate Past

Locale(s): United States (farm)

Summary: The farmer and his wife are hoping that one of their new chickens will have the gift and when the rooster starts crowing at the sunrise, they are sure that he does. Smallest Chicken is quite impressed and follows the rooster around even after the other chickens have become bored with the crowing. Rooster is sure that it is he who makes the sun come up, but one day he oversleeps and Smallest Chicken is the only one there to watch the sun rise. Rooster is upset until he hears that Smallest Chicken cannot crow. Realizing that his true gift is welcoming the sun, he knows he can be proud of this gift too. (32 pages)

Where it's reviewed:
School Library Journal, September 1996, page 177
Booklist, September 15, 1996, page 245
Hornbook, November/December 1996, page 712

Other books by the same author:
The Tub Grandfather, 1993
Pedro's Journal: A Journey with Christopher Columbus, 1991
Stonewords: A Ghost Story, 1990

Other books you might like:
Margaret Berrill, *Chanticleer*, 1986
   This is one of a number of retellings of the fable of the rooster who is tricked by a fox.
Mem Fox, *Feathers and Fools*, 1996
   The peacocks and the swans fight about which one of them is best.
Margaret Walden Froehlich, *The Kookoory*, 1995
   The rooster is so excited about the fair that he wakes his firends as well as the weasel.
Ragnhild Scamell, *Rooster Crows*, 1994
   Rooster bets Bluebird that he can make the sun come up at midnight.

284

TRISH COOKE
HELEN OXENBURY, Illustrator

So Much

(Cambridge, MA: Candlewick Press, 1994)

Subject(s): Babies; Relatives; Love
Age range(s): Grades K-1
Major character(s): Unnamed Character, Child; Mom, Mother; Daddy, Father
Time period(s): 1990s (1994)
Locale(s): England

Summary: One after another the relatives arrive and are unable to resist squeezing, hugging, kissing and wrestling with the baby. Each time the doorbell rings the group grows larger, until finally the person they've been waiting for —Daddy— arrives. All the relatives haven't gathered just because they want to see the baby ''SO MUCH,'' they're really here for Daddy's surprise birthday party. When everyone goes home, Mom tucks the tired baby into bed while he remembers the day's activities. (32 pages)

Where it's reviewed:
Booklist, March 1, 1995, page 1240

Five Owls, January 1995, page 59
Horn Book, November 1994, page 760
Publishers Weekly, November 14, 1994, page 66
School Library Journal, January 1995, page 83

Awards the book has won:
Booklist Editors' Choice, 1994

Other books by the same author:
Mr. Pam Pam and the Hullabazoo, 1994
When I Grow Bigger, 1994

Other books you might like:
Martin Baynton, *Why Do You Love Me?*, 1990
   A little boy tries to determine just which of his many behaviors (some not so lovable) are most appealing to his father.
Helen E. Buckley, *Grandfather and I*, 1961
   Newly illustrated in 1994, the story of the loving relationship between a grandfather and his young grandson is unchanged.
Pat Hutchins, *The Doorbell Rang*, 1986
   Each time the doorbell rings it heralds more friends arriving to enjoy Ma's freshly baked cookies.

285

TRISH COOKE
JOHN BENDALL-BRUNELLO, Illustrator

When I Grow Bigger

(Cambridge, MA: Candlewick Press, 1994)

Subject(s): Fathers and Sons; Growing Up; Babies
Age range(s): Grades K-2
Major character(s): Thomas, Child; Dad, Father; Leanne, Child, Sister (older)
Time period(s): 1990s (1994)
Locale(s): England

Summary: Leanne and two friends quibble about what they can or will do when they grow up while Thomas silently observes. Dad is working in the garden and intervenes whenever the discussion turns to arguing. When the children's plan to make Thomas grow bigger looks as if it will pull him apart, Dad scoops up Thomas and puts him on his shoulders where he is now as high as the sky. (32 pages)

Where it's reviewed:
Booklist, September 1, 1994, page 49
Horn Book Guide, Spring 1995, page 30
Kirkus Reviews, August 15, 1994, page 1124
Publishers Weekly, July 4, 1994, page 61
School Library Journal, September 1994, page 182

Other books by the same author:
Mr. Pam Pam and the Hullabazoo, 1994
So Much, 1994

Other books you might like:
Pat Hutchins, *Tidy Titch*, 1991
   When older siblings Mary and Peter clean out the toys they have outgrown, Titch has just the right spot for them in his room.
Holly Keller, *Maxine in the Middle*, 1989
   To Maxine the worst place to be is in the middle, neither

the oldest or the youngest, so she leaves and her siblings soon realize how much they miss her.

Martin Waddell, *Once There Were Giants*, 1989

A girl describes her growth from infancy when everyone around her is a giant to motherhood when she becomes one of the giants in her baby's life.

286

HELEN COOPER, Author/Illustrator

The Bear under the Stairs

(New York: Dial Books for Young Readers, 1993)

Subject(s): Fear; Imagination; Animals/Bears
Age range(s): Grades K-2
Major character(s): William, Child (imaginative); Mom, Mother
Time period(s): 1990s (1993)
Locale(s): England (William's house)

Summary: Both fearful and imaginative, William is especially afraid of bears and the space under the stairs at his house. When he sees a bear under the stairs, he begins feeding it daily in hopes of appeasing the bear before it decides to eat little boys. The food that William throws into the closet under the stairs naturally develops an odor and attracts Mom's attention. Together Mom and William clean up the mess and shop for a kindly, stuffed bear for William while the "real" bear moves to new quarters. (32 pages)

Where it's reviewed:
Booklist, June 1, 1993, page 1854
Children's Book Review Service, July 1993, page 146
Horn Book, May 1993, page 313
Publishers Weekly, June 14, 1993, page 68
School Library Journal, December 1993, page 81

Other books by the same author:
The House Cat, 1994
Ella and the Rabbit, 1990

Other books you might like:
Dick Gackenbach, *Harry and the Terrible Whatzit*, 1979
There's a 2-headed Whatzit in the cellar and Harry's mom is making him go down there!
Valiska Gregory, *Kate's Giants*, 1995
When Kate imagines scary things behind the attic door, her parents help her to find the courage to confront her fears.
Joanna Harrison, *Dear Bear*, 1994
At her mother's suggestion, Katie writes to the bear living under her stairs and asks it to go away.
Mercer Mayer, *There's a Nightmare in My Closet*, 1985
Sometimes inviting monsters out of the closet helps them seem less scary.
Maggie Smith, *There's a Witch under the Stairs*, 1991
In the basement, under the stairs, lives a witch and Frances saw it—honest!

287

ILENE COOPER

Trick or Trouble?

(New York: Viking, 1994)

Series: Holiday Five
Subject(s): Friendship; Schools; Holidays
Age range(s): Grades 6-7
Major character(s): Lia Greene, 7th Grader; Scott Tierney, 7th Grader
Time period(s): 1990s
Locale(s): Chicago, Illinois; Wisconsin (Camp Wildwood)

Summary: At Wildwood summer camp, Lia is voted best all-around camper, but when she returns to school, she's hardly acknowledged by the "in" group. Her only real friend is her nextdoor neighbor Scott, but he's gotten so cute over the summer all the girls in her class are after him. When Scott will only dance with Lia, the girls start malicious rumors about her "making-out" with Scott. Luckily friends of hers from camp, the Holiday Five, visit over Halloween and provide Lia the friendship and support she needs. (154 pages)

Where it's reviewed:
Book Report, March 1995, page 37
Publishers Weekly, July 4, 1994, page 64
School Library Journal, August 1994, page 154
Center for Children's Books. Bulletin, September 1994, page 10
Kirkus Reviews, August 15, 1994, page 1142

Other books by the same author:
Buddy Love: Now on Video, 1995
The Worst Noel, 1994
Lights, Camera, Attitude!, 1993
Choosing Sides, 1992

Other books you might like:
Virginia Bradley, *Wait and See*, 1994
Though Amy immediately dislikes new student Violetta, she comes to realize Violetta's not so weird after all.
Vicki Grove, *The Fastest Girl in the West*, 1990
Lori's best friend abandons her for the popular crowd; only weird Vern, a new girl at school, will have anything to do with her.
Phyllis Reynolds Naylor, *All but Alice*, 1992
Just piercing her ears seems to have made Alice popular, but she quickly realizes it's boring to be like everyone else.
Rachel Vail, *Wonder*, 1991
Jessica's tumultuous seventh grade year finds her seesawing between being a social pariah and having her own clique.

288

ILENE COOPER

The Worst Noel

(New York: Viking, 1994)

Series: Holiday Five
Subject(s): Stepfamilies; Friendship; Fathers and Daughters
Age range(s): Grades 6-7

Major character(s): Kathy Wallace, 12-Year-Old; Erin Moriarty, 12-Year-Old
Time period(s): 1990s
Locale(s): Lake Pointe, Illinois; Chicago, Illinois

Summary: Five friends who bond at Camp Wildwood call themselves the Holiday Five and try to get together with one another during holidays. As Christmas approaches, Kathy, the wealthiest of the group, doesn't feel very special since her parents divorce. To avoid spending the holidays with her father and new stepfamily, she concocts a plan to sneak out on Christmas Eve and visit Erin's large, but poor, family. (143 pages)

Where it's reviewed:
Booklist, August 1994, page 2050
Book Report, March 1995, page 37
Center for Children's Books. Bulletin, December 1994, page 124
Horn Book Guide, Spring 1995, page 74

Other books by the same author:
Buddy Love: Now on Video, 1995
Trick or Trouble?, 1994
Choosing Sides, 1992
Mean Streak, 1991
The Winning of Miss Lynn Ryan, 1987

Other books you might like:
C.G. Draper, *A Holiday Year*, 1988
    Ned and his family spend their holidays in a cottage on Cape Cod close to his grandparents.
Patricia Lee Gauch, *Night Talks*, 1983
    As they go camping together, three girls learn to overcome their differences.
Mary Downing Hahn, *Sara Summer*, 1979
    Sara and Emily become friends one summer.

289

MELROSE COOPER
DALE GOTTLIEB, Illustrator

I Got a Family

(New York: Henry Holt and Company, 1993)

Subject(s): Family Life; Relatives; Love
Age range(s): Grades K-2
Major character(s): Unnamed Character, Child
Time period(s): 1990s (1993)
Locale(s): United States

Summary: Reflecting on the individual members of her family, a young girl describes in rhyming verse the different ways in which each member of her extended family interacts with her and loves her so that she senses the security of a caring family. (32 pages)

Where it's reviewed:
Booklist, May 15, 1993, page 1691
Five Owls, May 1993, page 111
Instructor, October 1993, page 60
Publishers Weekly, May 24, 1993, page 85
School Library Journal, July 1993, page 58

Awards the book has won:
Booklist Editors' Choice, 1993

Other books by the same author:
I Got Community, 1995

Other books you might like:
Wade Hudson, *I Love My Family*, 1993
    Special memories of food and fun, with many generations gathered at an annual family reunion, are shared by a young boy.
Nina Pellegrini, *Families Are Different*, 1991
    In a family created through adoption, two Korean girls must also adjust to a new culture.
Patricia Polacco, *The Keeping Quilt*, 1988
    A special quilt connects the generations of a family.
Cynthia Rylant, *The Relatives Came*, 1985
    A visit from loving relatives brings humor.

290

SUSAN COOPER

The Boggart

(New York: Margaret K. McElderry Books, 1993)

Subject(s): Supernatural; Computers; Family Relations
Age range(s): Grades 4-7
Major character(s): The Boggart, Mythical Creature (Scottish), Spirit (shape-changing prankster); Emily Volnik, 12-Year-Old; Jessup Volnik, 10-Year-Old, Computer Expert
Time period(s): 1990s (1993)
Locale(s): Toronto, Ontario, Canada; Port Appin Argyll, Scotland (Castle Keep)

Summary: For centuries the mischievous Boggart has lived in the ancient Castle Keep, content to play pranks and work the Old Magic on members of the MacDevon clan. When the last MacDevon dies and wills the castle to an unsuspecting distant relative from Canada, the Boggart is inadvertently transported to Toronto. Wise in the ways of the Old Magic, the Boggart is fascinated by, but ignorant of, the ways of modern technology, such as electricity. Hence his mischief begins to be more than just baffling to the Volnik family, it becomes unintentionally dangerous. Emily and Jessup finally discover the basis for the strange occurrences that begin after their trip to Scotland and, with assistance from homesick Boggart and computer technology, devise a means of helping the Boggart return home. (196 pages)

Where it's reviewed:
Booklist, January 15, 1993, page 907
Five Owls, May 1993, page 117
Horn Book, May 1993, page 330
New Advocate, Summer 1993, page 229
School Library Journal, January 1993, page 96

Awards the book has won:
School Library Journal Best Books, 1993
ALA Notable Book, 1994

Other books by the same author:
Greenwitch, 1985
Silver on the Tree, 1980
The Grey King, 1975 (Newbery Award Winner, 1976)

Other books you might like:

Joan Carris, *Beware the Ravens, Aunt Morbelia*, 1995
 Visiting the old Fearing estate in London with his Aunt Morbelia and his friend Jeff becomes a journey through a part of family history that Todd Fearing had not expected.

William Mayne, *Hob and the Goblins*, 1994
 Unaware that their new home, Fairy Ring Cottage, is bewitched by unseen, evil forces, the Grimes family is protected by Hob, the family's "guardian" ghost.

Lila Sprague McGinnis, *The Ghost Upstairs*, 1982
 When he loses his home of 75 years, ghost Otis moves in with next-door neighbor Albert, creating havoc and humor as he experiences the many things that have been invented since his life ended.

Pamela F. Service, *Winter of Magic's Return*, 1985
 In this fantasy blending a post-holocaust future with Arthurian legend , three teens set off in search of King Arthur, seeking the restoration of his throne and the return of the age of magic.

291

ERIC COPELAND, Author/Illustrator

Milton, My Father's Dog

(Plattsburgh, NY: Tundra Books of Northern New York, 1994)

Subject(s): Animals/Dogs; Pets; Fathers and Sons
Age range(s): Grades 1-3
Major character(s): Milton, Dog; Fraser, Child
Time period(s): 1990s (1994)
Locale(s): Canada

Summary: When Fraser's parents go puppy shopping, they bring home not a puppy, but a one-year-old English sheep dog, a breed Fraser's father has always wanted. Fraser is not happy to have a rambunctious, enormous dog such as Milton. Although Milton's behavior never changes, Fraser does grow and, as he becomes more able to handle the large, lovable animal, he also becomes more accepting of his parents' choice in pets. (24 pages)

Where it's reviewed:
Books in Canada, March 1995, page 49
Children's Book News, Fall 1995, page 22
Horn Book Guide, Spring 1995, page 30
Quill & Quire, December 1994, page 32
School Library Journal, June 1995, page 78

Other books you might like:

Norman Bridwell, *Clifford, the Small Red Puppy*, 1972
 Emily Elizabeth chooses the runt of the litter for her pet and is pleased when Clifford begins growing.

Marc Brown, *Arthur's New Puppy*, 1993
 Arthur has problems because his new puppy is behaving just like a puppy and making a mess of the house.

Cynthia Rylant, *The Henry and Mudge Series*, 1987-
 The adventures of Henry and his lovable, slobbery dog Mudge entertain beginning readers.

292

NANCY COTE, Author/Illustrator

Palm Trees

(New York: Four Winds Press, 1993)

Subject(s): Friendship; Self-Reliance; African Americans
Age range(s): Grades K-2
Major character(s): Millie, Latch-Key Child; Renee, Child, Friend (Millie's best)
Time period(s): 1990s (1993)
Locale(s): United States

Summary: Cote's first book gives new meaning to the phrase "bad hair day." With Mom at work, Millie must manage alone with her head of unruly hair. Her pride in the pony tails she styles herself vanishes when Renee suggests that she has palm trees atop her head. Embarrassed, Millie decides to cut off her pony tails just as Renee appears with three "palm trees" adorning her head. Millie's hair and the friendship are saved! (32 pages)

Where it's reviewed:
Booklist, February 15, 1993, page 1067
Horn Book, September 1993, page 633
Kirkus Reviews, March 15, 1993, page 368
Publishers Weekly, March 29, 1993, page 54
School Library Journal, July 1993, page 58

Other books you might like:

Catherine Friend, *My Head Is Full of Colors*, 1994
 A young girl's many interests are expressed through unusual changes in her hair.

Linda Breiner Milstein, *Amanda's Perfect Hair*, 1993
 As far as Amanda is concerned, her beautiful, attention-getting locks are anything but perfect, until the day she takes scissors in hand and creates an image that pleases her.

Tricia Tusa, *Camilla's New Hairdo*, 1991
 Isolated in a tower, Camilla occupies her time fashioning her hair into animal shapes.

Camille Yarbrough, *Cornrows*, 1981
 The unique cornrow hairstyle is presented with some historical perspective and cultural background.

293

BRUCE COVILLE
KATHERINE COVILLE, Illustrator

Space Brat 4: Planet of the Dips

(New York: Pocket Books, 1995)

Series: Space Brat
Subject(s): Space Travel; Humor; Science Fiction
Age range(s): Grades 3-5
Major character(s): Captain Blork, Spaceship Captain; Skippy Hopbong III, Stowaway, Leader (Planet of the Dips); Moomie Peevik, Space Explorer
Time period(s): Indeterminate
Locale(s): Timboobia, Planet—Imaginary

Summary: Accidently, Captain Blork's space ship is pulled through a "Whoopee Warp" and crash lands on the Planet of the Dips, home of silliness with residents who wear propellor-topped beanies used for transportation. Skippy is chagrined to learn that the spaceship on which he stowed away trying to escape the Planet of Cranky People has carried him back to his disliked home planet. Getting off the dippy planet should be as easy as repairing the spaceship, but then the Dips decide that Blork's pet poodnoobie is the planet's long lost Lord of Silliness and Blork must come up with a plan to save him. (72 pages)

Where it's reviewed:
Booklist, November 1, 1995, page 473
Horn Book Guide, Spring 1996, page 53
School Library Journal, December 1995, page 79

Other books by the same author:
Space Brat 3: The Wrath of Squat, 1994
Aliens Ate My Homework, 1993
Space Brat, 1992

Other books you might like:
Janet Asimov, *The Norby Series*, 1983-1991
   With co-author Isaac Asimov, the series presents the adventures of Norby the robot and his human friend Jeff.
Gery Greer, *Jason and the Escape from Bat Planet*, 1993
   With alien neighbor Coop and a talking cat creature, Jason saves an absent-minded professor from the clutches of the Bat Planet leader. Co-author Bob Ruddick.
Pamela F. Service, *Stinker from Space*, 1988
   An alien takes the form of a skunk to disguise his presence on Earth.

294

JANE COWEN-FLETCHER, Author/Illustrator

Mama Zooms
(New York: Scholastic, Inc., 1993)

Subject(s): Physically Handicapped; Mothers and Sons; Imagination
Age range(s): Grades K-1
Major character(s): Unnamed Character, Child; Mama, Mother, Paraplegic
Time period(s): 1990s (1993)
Locale(s): United States

Summary: In this first picture book by the author, a young boy uses a little imagination, a willing Mom and her wheelchair to become a jockey on a race horse, an airplane pilot, and a captain of a ship. Of course, what the boy likes best is bedtime, when Mom is herself, caring, loving and capable. (32 pages)

Where it's reviewed:
Booklist, April 15, 1993, page 1523
Children's Book Review Service, May 1993, page 111
Five Owls, September 1993, page 4
Publishers Weekly, March 8, 1993, page 76
School Library Journal, May 1993, page 82

Other books you might like:
Joan Anderson, *Harry's Helicopter*, 1990
   With a little imagination, Harry's bright red, cardboard helicopter seems to fly.

Nicholas Heller, *The Front Hall Carpet*, 1990
   Without opening the front door, a little girl goes on magical adventures with the help of her imagination and the front hall carpet.
Alison Lester, *Isabella's Bed*, 1993
   Grandma's storytelling is so magical that her two grandchildren experience a fantastic trip on what appears to be, an ordinary bed.

295

JOY COWLEY
DAVID CHRISTIANA, Illustrator

The Mouse Bride
(New York: Scholastic Inc., 1995)

Subject(s): Animals/Mice; Marriage; Self-Perception
Age range(s): Grades K-2
Major character(s): Unnamed Character, Mouse
Time period(s): 1990s (1995)
Locale(s): United States

Summary: Dissatisfied with the fact she is small and weak, a little mouse sets out to marry someone stronger so at least her children will be strong. First she asks the sun to wed, but the sun refers her to the cloud who sends her to the wind who points her to a house that stands despite the force of the wind. The house, however, says a creature in the basement, gnawing at the house's timbers will some day topple the house. The mouse eagerly calls to the basement creature because he is the strongest of all. Who should appear up the basement stairs—a mouse! (32 pages)

Where it's reviewed:
Booklist, January 1, 1996, page 843
Children's Book Review Service, Winter 1996, page 61
Children's Bookwatch, February 1996, page 6
Horn Book Guide, Spring 1996, page 89
Kirkus Reviews, October 1, 1995, page 1425

Other books by the same author:
Gracias, the Thanksgiving Turkey, 1996
The Screaming Mean Machine, 1993
The Duck in the Gun, 1969

Other books you might like:
Linda Allen, *The Mouse Bride: A Tale from Finland*, 1992
   When three brothers seek brides, the youngest is able to find only a mouse. Fortunately, this is a folktale and the mouse is really a princess in disguise.
Judith Dupre, *The Mouse Bride: A Mayan Folk Tale*, 1993
   Proud parents search the rain forest to find the mightiest husband for their daughter to wed.
Eric A. Kimmel, *The Greatest of All: A Japanese Folktale*, 1991
   Chuko Mouse's father is displeased she is choosing to marry a humble field mouse.
Ekkehart Malotki, *The Mouse Couple: A Hopi Folktale*, 1988
   Another culture interprets the tale about mice planning their daughter's marriage to a strong husband.

296

HELEN CRAIG, Author/Illustrator

Charlie and Tyler at the Seashore

(Cambridge, MA: Candlewick Press, 1995)

Subject(s): Animals/Mice; Adventure and Adventurers; Beaches
Age range(s): Grades K-2
Major character(s): Tyler, Mouse, Cousin (Charlie's); Charlie, Mouse, Cousin (Tyler's)
Time period(s): 1990s (1995)
Locale(s): seacoast, England

Summary: Charlie, the country mouse, reluctantly accompanies his adventurous town-dwelling cousin on an excursion to the seashore. Initially, the day's events hold excitement for Tyler and terror for Charlie until a sea gull captures Tyler for her chick's next meal. Then, Charlie bravely rescues Tyler in time for both to return to the quiet of Charlie's country home. (32 pages)

Where it's reviewed:
Booklist, October 1, 1995, page 325
Books for Keeps, July 1995, page 24
Horn Book Guide, Spring 1996, page 23
School Library Journal, January 1996, page 77
Times Educational Supplement, July 7, 1995, page R2

Other books by the same author:
Susie and Alfred in a Busy Day in Town, 1994
I See the Moon and the Moon Sees Me, 1993
The Town Mouse and the Country Mouse, 1992

Other books you might like:
Arnold Lobel, *Frog and Toad Are Friends*, 1970
   While they don't always see eye-to-eye, Frog and Toad agree that they are the best of friends.
James Marshall, *George and Martha*, 1972
   The first book in a series about George and Martha uses several brief, humorous stories to describe the antics of two hippo buddies.
Ellen Schechter, *The Town Mouse and the Country Mouse*, 1995
   A retelling of Aesop's classic tale for beginning readers describes the different lifestyles of two mice.

297

JUNE CREBBIN
CLARA VULLIAMY, Illustrator

Danny's Duck

(Cambridge, MA: Candlewick Press, 1995)

Subject(s): Animals/Ducks; Schools; Nature
Age range(s): Grades K-2
Major character(s): Danny, Child, Student
Time period(s): 1990s (1995)
Locale(s): England

Summary: Danny spots a duck sitting on her nest near the school playground. His art work reflects the progress he observes from single duck to duck sitting on nine eggs and finally, sadly to an empty nest. His teacher has observed the progression and when Danny tearfully shows her the empty nest picture she leads him to a pond near the school to show him where his duck and her nine ducklings are swimming. (26 pages)

Where it's reviewed:
Booklist, June 1, 1995, page 1783
Horn Book Guide, Fall 1995, page 261
Junior Bookshelf, June 1995, page 93
Observer, April 9, 1995, page 19
School Library Journal, May 1995, page 83

Other books by the same author:
The Train Ride, 1995
Fly by Night, 1993

Other books you might like:
Eve Bunting, *Secret Place*, 1996
   A young boy discovers a nest of ducks near a polluted urban river.
Douglas Florian, *Nature Walk*, 1989
   Two children enjoy a trail hike through the woods learning more about nature.
Anna Grossnickle Hines, *What Joe Saw*, 1994
   As the preschoolers take a walk near their school only dawdling Joe is observant enough to see signs of nature along the way.
Kathryn Lasky, *Pond Year*, 1995
   Best friends enjoy the seasonal changes in the life of a pond near their home.
David Williams, *Walking to the Creek*, 1990
   Behind Grandma and Grandpa's farm is a path to the creek that is perfect for exploring the hidden treasures of nature.

298

JUNE CREBBIN
STEPHEN LAMBERT, Illustrator

Fly by Night

(Cambridge, Massachusetts: Candlewick Press, 1993)

Subject(s): Animals/Owls; Mothers and Sons
Age range(s): Grades K-2
Major character(s): Blink, Owl (young); Mother, Owl, Mother
Time period(s): 1990s (1993)
Locale(s): Earth (a forest)

Summary: In his eagerness to make his first flight, Blink pesters his sleeping mother throughout the day only to be told he must patiently keep waiting. As the day draws on, he finally dozes, only to be awakened by his mother. After soaring away on his first flight, Blink realizes the wisdom of waiting; he was meant to fly by night. (32 pages)

Where it's reviewed:
Booklist, March 15, 1993, page 1358
Children's Bookwatch, June 1993, page 5
Kirkus Reviews, June 1, 1993, page 719
Publishers Weekly, May 24, 1993, page 85
School Library Journal, April 1993, page 94

Other books by the same author:
Danny's Duck, 1995
The Train Ride, 1995

Other books you might like:

Lyn Littlefield Hoopes, *My Own Home*, 1991
   Lost and frightened, a young owl searches for his home.
Pat Hutchins, *Good-Night, Owl!*, 1972
   Trying to get a good day's sleep is not easy for an owl when an assortment of animals make use of his branch of the tree.
Martin Waddell, *Owl Babies*, 1992
   Waking to find themselves alone, these three owl babies really want mommy to come back!

299

HELEN CRESSWELL
KATE ALDOUS, Illustrator

Posy Bates, Again!

(New York: Macmillan Publishing Company, 1994)

Subject(s): Family Life; Animals/Dogs; Humor
Age range(s): Grades 2-4
Major character(s): Posy Bates, Child; Daff Bates, Mother; Buggins, Dog (stray)
Time period(s): 1990s (1991)
Locale(s): England

Summary: Posy has found a stray dog and is determined to convince Daff that the family needs Buggins as a watch dog. Her efforts to spare Buggins from the SPCA work better than some of her other plans to be helpful. Posy's heart is in the right place, but she has a way of turning a simple good deed into a disaster. First published in Great Britain in 1991. (112 pages)

Where it's reviewed:
Booklist, May 15, 1994, page 1679
Horn Book, July 1994, page 447
Horn Book Guide, Fall 1994, page 308
Kirkus Reviews, April 15, 1994, page 554
School Library Journal, June 1994, page 97

Other books by the same author:
Meet Posy Bates, 1992
The Secret World of Polly Flint, 1991
Time Out, 1990

Other books you might like:
Malorie Blackman, *Girl Wonder and the Terrific Twins*, 1993
   Maxine and her twin brothers only want to help their mother, but the children's plans seem to create more work not less.
Beverly Cleary, *Ramona Quimby, Age 8*, 1982
   One of several books about energetic Ramona and the ups and downs of life in the Quimby household; it is a Newbery Honor Book.
Susan Wojciechowski, *Don't Call Me Beanhead!*, 1994
   Beany is a worrier; her worries lead to plans and then the fun begins!

300

HELEN CRESSWELL

The Watchers: A Mystery at Alton Towers

(New York: Macmillan, 1994)

Subject(s): Space and Time; Magic; Amusement Parks
Age range(s): Grades 5-6
Major character(s): Katy, Runaway; Josh, Runaway
Time period(s): 1990s
Locale(s): England

Summary: Katy and Josh are sick of the temporary living arrangement that's been set up for them at Kirby House, a home for orphans, and unrealistically long to return to their own homes. When that doesn't seem possible, they run away to Alton Towers, an amusement park, where living on their own is an adventure at first. But after dark at Alton Towers, mysterious people roam the grounds and it becomes obvious that an alternate universe exists after sundown. Katy and Josh discover that there is a good King and an evil King and help destroy the evil one so that other homeless children can enjoy the alternate world while Katy and Josh realize they are better off at Kirby House. (206 pages)

Where it's reviewed:
Voice of Youth Advocates, April 1995, page 20
Horn Book, March 1995, page 192
Booklist, December 15, 1994, page 752
School Library Journal, February 1995, page 96
Kirkus Reviews, December 15, 1994, page 1561

Other books by the same author:
The Secret World of Polly Flint, 1991
Time Out, 1990
Moondial, 1987

Other books you might like:
Clive Barker, *The Thief of Always*, 1992
   At the strange Holiday House, Harvey decides he needs to leave when he sees one of the guests turn into a fish.
Ray Bradbury, *Something Wicked This Way Comes*, 1962
   When James and William discover the wonderful Pandemonium Shadow Show, they quickly wish they hadn't.
Richard Peck, *Secrets of the Shopping Mall*, 1979
   Barney and Theresa hide in a shopping mall to escape from a gang. Everything they need is there—food, shelter, clothing, plus other people who appear at night!

301

LINDA CREW
CHARLES ROBINSON, Illustrator

Nekomah Creek Christmas

(New York: Delacorte Press, 1994)

Subject(s): Christmas; Plays; Family Life
Age range(s): Grades 4-6
Major character(s): Robby Hummer, 10-Year-Old; Freddie Hummer, 3-Year-Old, Twin; Lucy Hummer, 3-Year-Old, Twin
Time period(s): 1990s (1994)
Locale(s): Nekomah Creek, Oregon

Summary: After seeing Freddie and Lucy perform in the Thanksgiving play, Robby succumbs to his mom's many hints and tries out for the school Christmas play. Secretly hoping not to get a part, he's disappointed to discover his name on the cast list and dismayed he has the role of chief elf. His parents expect him to follow through with his commitment but Robby dreads the embarrassment of appearing on stage in baggy green tights. Between the play, his parents' tax audit, and a Christmas visit from obnoxious cousins, Robby learns alot about the spirit of Christmas. (147 pages)

Where it's reviewed:
Booklist, August 1994, page 2050
Horn Book Guide, Spring 1995, page 75
Kirkus Reviews, December 15, 1994, page 1581
Library Talk, January 1995, page 30

Other books by the same author:
Someday I'll Laugh about This, 1992
Nekomah Creek, 1991 (ALA Notable Book, 1992)
Children of the River, 1989 (Golden Kite Award Honor Book, 1989)

Other books you might like:
Patricia Hermes, *Christmas Magic*, 1996
     As Christmas draws near, Katie finds herself with so many problems at school she wonders if Santa will visit her.
Beverly Lewis, *The Crazy Christmas Angel Mystery*, 1994
     With a mixture of kindness and curiosity, Eric and friends plan a Christmas visit to an elderly man who has recently moved in next door.
Ann M. Martin, *Mallory's Christmas Wish*, 1995
     All Mallory wants is an old-fashioned family Christmas, but it looks as if a disaster is in the making.
Connie Remlinger-Trounstine, *The Worst Christmas Ever*, 1994
     For the first Christmas after Grandma Mary's death, Callie's family change some traditions to make the holiday easier on Grandpa; Callie can't imagine anything worse.
Barbara Robinson, *The Best Christmas Pageant Ever*, 1972
     When the unruly Herdman children decide to participate in the traditional Christmas Pageant, the experience changes everyone.

302

DONALD CREWS, Author/Illustrator

Sail Away

(New York: Greenwillow Books, 1995)

Subject(s): Boats and Boating; Sailing; Weather
Age range(s): Grades K-3
Time period(s): 1990s (1995)
Locale(s): United States

Summary: A family of four sets off for a day of sailing in their small boat, enjoying the wind in the sails. Late in the day the perfect sailing weather abruptly becomes stormy and the family hurriedly shortens sail and motors for home as the storm clears and the sun sets. (32 pages)

Where it's reviewed:
Booklist, April 1, 1995, page 1424

Bulletin of the Center for Children's Books, April 1995, page 268
Horn Book, September 1995, page 587
Publishers Weekly, April 10, 1995, page 61
School Library Journal, May 1995, page 83

Awards the book has won:
Booklist Editors' Choice, 1995

Other books by the same author:
Bigmama's, 1991
Truck, 1980 (Caldecott Honor Book)
Freight Train, 1978 (Caldecott Honor Book)

Other books you might like:
Mary Calhoun, *Henry the Sailor Cat*, 1994
     As a stowaway on a family sailing trip, Henry proves himself useful when he leads the rescue of The Man who has fallen overboard.
Mary-Claire Helldorfer, *Sailing to the Sea*, 1991
     With his aunt at the helm, a young boy enjoys his first experience on a sailboat.
Thomas Locker, *Sailing with the Wind*, 1986
     On a sailing trip with her uncle, a young girl comes to appreciate the majesty of the ocean.

303

CAROLYN CRIMI
LINNEA ASPLIND RILEY, Illustrator

Outside, Inside

(New York: Simon & Schuster Books for Young Readers, 1995)

Subject(s): Weather; Nature
Age range(s): Grades K-1
Major character(s): Molly, Child
Time period(s): 1990s (1995)
Locale(s): United States

Summary: In the author's first book, Molly awakens inside a cozy house, while outside a storm begins. Inside, Molly eats breakfast, plays and bakes cookies while, outside, the rain pours and animals seek shelter. When the rain subsides and the sun peeks out, Molly opens the door to invite ''the outside in!'' (32 pages)

Where it's reviewed:
Booklist, June 1995, page 1784
Children's Book Review Service, Spring 1995, page 133
Horn Book, September 1995, page 587
Publishers Weekly, April 17, 1995, page 56
School Library Journal, May 1995, page 83

Other books you might like:
Molly Bang, *One Fall Day*, 1994
     As she listens to her mom reviewing her day, a young girl imagines her doll and toys recreating the events.
Ruth Brown, *The Picnic*, 1993
     The arrival of a picnicking family drives a group of animals from their meadow to underground shelter. Rain drives the family away allowing the animals to come out again.
Robert Kalan, *Rain*, 1978
     Illustrations by Donald Crews enhance the simple story of a rainy day.

Uri Shulevitz, *Rain Rain Rivers*, 1969

During a rain storm, a young girl sits in her attic bedroom, listening and imagining the effect of the rain on distant rivers, cities and even the sea.

304

MARTY CRISP

Buzzard Breath

(New York: Atheneum, 1995)

Subject(s): Animals/Dogs
Age range(s): Grades 4-6
Major character(s): Will Winkle, Animal Lover, 6th Grader; Mrs. Lydia Kingston, Aged Person; General/Buzzard Breath, Dog (German Shepard)
Time period(s): 1990s
Locale(s): Notchcliff

Summary: Will wants a purebred dog and constantly reads about them in the *American Kennel Club Complete Dog Book*. He saves his money from doing chores for Mrs. Kingston so he can buy one. Mrs. Kingston has a purebred dog, a German Shepard named General, nicknamed Buzzard Breath by one of Will's classmates. Though used as a guard dog, Buzzard Breath is just a softie and not at all the perfect purebred dog for him. When Mrs. Kingston replaces Buzzard Breath with a new dog called Assassin, Will knows he can't let the German Shepard go to the pound and so gives him a temporary home. Will cares more for this dog than he realizes and, when Buzz is accused of biting a child, sets out to prove his innocence in this author's first novel for young people. (140 pages)

Where it's reviewed:
Voice of Youth Advocates, June 1995, page 92
Publishers Weekly, July 3, 1995, page 61
New York Times Book Review, May 21, 1995, page 30
School Library Journal, June 1995, page 110
Children's Book Review Service, August 1995, page 163

Other books you might like:
Zachary Ball, *Bristle Face*, 1962
Jake, an orphan, and his dog Bristle Face are fast friends.
Barbara Corcoran, *Annie's Monster*, 1990
Annie's father agrees to let her have her longed-for Irish wolfhound, but that just signals the beginning of her problems.
Linda Oatman High, *Hound Heaven*, 1995
Though her grandfather doesn't want a dog in his house, orphaned Silver is determined to change his mind.
Phyllis Reynolds Naylor, *Shiloh*, 1991
Marty decides it's best to lie if it means saving the life of an abused beagle named Shiloh.

305

EMILY CROFFORD

A Place to Belong

(Minneapolis: Carolrhoda Books, 1994)

Series: Adventures in Time
Subject(s): Depression (Economic); Historical

Age range(s): Grades 6-8
Major character(s): Talmadge McLinn, 6th Grader, Handicapped (clubfoot), Brother (of Missy); Missy McLinn, Child, Sister
Time period(s): 1930s (1935)
Locale(s): Wild Hog Holler, Tennessee; Alabama (Limon Plantation)

Summary: Talmadge's family lost their Tennessee farm during the Depression and now settles in Alabama as tenant farmers. Talmadge dreads starting in a new school for his clubfoot usually makes him the butt of many jokes, but this time is different. His ability at schoolwork is appreciated and for the first time in his life he feels as though he's popular. His mother wants him to stop attending school after the sixth grade, but he convinces his father to let him continue. Schooling is short-lived, however, for Missy comes down with infantile paralysis and is sent to Memphis for special hospital care. When his mother joins Missy, Talmadge knows the family will relocate there soon and the battles about school will start again. (152 pages)

Where it's reviewed:
School Library Journal, June 1994, page 126
Booklist, May 15, 1994, page 1679
Kirkus Reviews, May 15, 1994, page 696
Horn Book Guide, Fall 1994, page 308
Childhood Education, Fall 1994, page 44

Other books by the same author:
Born in the Year of Courage, 1991
A Matter of Pride, 1981

Other books you might like:
Stephen Cole, *Growing Season*, 1966
Marie's life on an Iowa farm during the Depression is hard work.
Kathleen Karr, *The Cave*, 1994
With their South Dakota farm part of the Dust Bowl, Christine's brother's asthma worsens; finding a cave with running water helps them survive.
George Ella Lyon, *Borrowed Children*, 1988
Amanda is worn out from taking care of her sick mother; a trip to Memphis helps her recover during the Depression.

306

LYNN CULLEN

Meeting the Make-Out King

(New York: Clarion Books, 1994)

Subject(s): Schools; Popularity
Age range(s): Grades 6-7
Major character(s): Nora McKibben, 7th Grader; Mark DeAngelo, 7th Grader; Dawn, 7th Grader
Time period(s): 1990s
Locale(s): United States

Summary: As a new seventh grader, in addition to being the shortest girl in her class, Nora's determined not to be left out of the popular crowd. Hanging with Dawn and her friends makes Nora feel about seven feet tall, until Dawn decides Nora should get to know Mark, better known as the "make-out king." She's afraid she'll lose her new friends if she admits her inexperience, yet she's also terrified to flirt with Mark. Attending an unchaperoned party makes her realize the need to act as she knows is best. (131 pages)

Where it's reviewed:
School Library Journal, October 1994, page 120
Book Report, March 1995, page 35
Children's Book Review Service, December 1994, page 45
Horn Book Guide, Spring 1995, page 75

Other books by the same author:
The Three Lives of Harris Harper, 1996
The Backyard Ghost, 1993

Other books you might like:
Susan Haven, *Is it Them or Is it Me?*, 1990
    Molly finds her first year of high school without her best friend, Kathy, isn't so bad after all.
Phyllis Reynolds Naylor, *All but Alice*, 1992
    Just piercing her ears seems to have made Alice popular, but she quickly realizes it's boring to be like everyone else.
Susan Wojciechowski, *Promises to Keep*, 1991
    It takes awhile for Patty to realize that wealthy Penni is just using her to ensure that Penni's not-so-good writings are published in the school magazine.

307

PAT CUMMINGS, Author/Illustrator

Carousel
(New York: Bradbury Press, 1994)

Subject(s): Birthdays; Fathers and Daughters; Anger
Age range(s): Grades K-3
Major character(s): Alex, 5-Year-Old (African-American)
Time period(s): 1990s (1994)
Locale(s): United States

Summary: Angry that her father does not return from a business trip in time to celebrate her birthday, Alex lets her bad mood get the best of her behavior and finds herself sent to bed without any cake. There, Alex breaks the carousel her father has given her, falls asleep and dreams that all the animals have come to life and escaped from her room. After giving her a nighttime ride, the animals return to the carousel, Alex returns to bed and awakens in the morning to find her father waiting with belated birthday greetings. (32 pages)

Where it's reviewed:
Booklist, July 1994, page 1953
Children's Book Review Service, June 1994, page 121
Kirkus Reviews, April 1, 1994, page 478
Publishers Weekly, March 21, 1994, page 72
School Library Journal, August 1994, page 127

Other books by the same author:
Petey Moroni's Camp Runamok Diary, 1992
Clean Your Room, Harvey Moon!, 1991
Jimmy Lee Did It, 1985

Other books you might like:
Donald Crews, *Carousel*, 1982
    The joyful reality of a carousel ride is clearly presented.

Bill Martin Jr., *Up and Down on the Merry-Go-Round*, 1988
    With co-author John Archambault, the distinctive rhymes of Martin whirl the reader about on a carousel ride.
Liz Rosenberg, *The Carousel*, 1995
    Two sisters are taken on a fantastic ride by the magically alive horses of a closed carousel.

308

MARY LOUISE CUNEO
NADINE BERNARD WESTCOTT, Illustrator

How to Grow a Picket Fence
(New York: HarperCollins Publishers, 1993)

Subject(s): Imagination; Neighbors and Neighborhoods; Gardens and Gardening
Age range(s): Grades K-2
Major character(s): Unnamed Character, Child (imaginative)
Time period(s): 1990s (1993)
Locale(s): United States

Summary: First-time author Cuneo fancifully suggests that by finding an empty lot, some sticks, some big, brown, scarecrow gloves, and some white socks, and then following the directions for planting and watering with daisy pudding, one can produce a prize-winning picket fence. A little imagination is useful as is a supportive family to help find the ingredients. Voila! (32 pages)

Where it's reviewed:
Booklist, June 1, 1993, page 1854
Childrens Book Review Service, July 1993, page 146
Horn Book Guide, Fall 1993, page 255
Publishers Weekly, May 24, 1993, page 87
School Library Journal, September 1993, page 206

Other books by the same author:
What Can a Giant Do?, 1994

Other books you might like:
Walter Lyon Krudop, *Something Is Growing*, 1995
    Unnoticed, a young boy plants a seed in an urban neighborhood with results that get everyone's attention.
Greg Henry Quinn, *The Garden in Our Yard*, 1995
    Through the seasons of the year two children assist their parents with the family garden.
Elizabeth Spurr, *The Gumdrop Tree*, 1994
    Rather than eat a bag of gumdrops and then have none, a young girl decides to plant them in her garden.

309

JANE LOUISE CURRY

The Great Smith House Hustle
(New York: Margaret K. McElderry Books, 1993)

Subject(s): Brothers and Sisters; Grandparents; Mystery and Detective Stories
Age range(s): Grades 4-7
Major character(s): Belinda Rainbow "Boo" Smith, Student—Junior High (oldest of the Smith children); Francisco Moonlight "Cisco" Smith, 10-Year-Old, Brother;

Mrs. Matilda Tuttlebee, Aged Person, Neighbor (known as the ''wicked witch'')
Time period(s): 1990s (1993)
Locale(s): Pittsburgh, Pennsylvania

Summary: The many children in the Smith family are just settling in at Grandma's house after a long, hot, cross-country drive in the family van when a ''Sold'' sign appears in Grandma's front yard. Everyone gets involved in investigating this mistake and, in the process, discovers space that Mrs. Tuttlebee and her evil son are part of a scam to illegally take over people's property. Sequel to *The Big Smith Snatch*. (170 pages)

Where it's reviewed:
Booklist, May 1, 1993, page 1588
Horn Book Guide, Fall 1993, page 296
Kirkus Reviews, May 1, 1993, page 595
Library Talk, January 1994, page 39
School Library Journal, April 1993, page 163

Other books by the same author:
What the Dickens!, 1991
The Big Smith Snatch, 1989 (Prequel to *The Great Smith House Hustle*)
The Great Flood Mystery, 1985

Other books you might like:
Margaret Mahy, *Tangled Fortunes*, 1994
In this final book of The Cousins Quartet Series, siblings Jackson and Tracey begin to explore different interests, but as usual, all paths lead to mystery and adventure.
Phyllis Reynolds Naylor, *The Bodies in the Bessledorf Hotel*, 1986
If dead bodies don't stop appearing at the hotel, Bernie is afraid that his dad might lose his job as manager and, thus, his family's home.
Willo Davis Roberts, *What Could Go Wrong?*, 1989
An airplane flight to San Francisco should be uneventful, but three cousins find unexpected mystery and adventure.

310

JANE LOUISE CURRY

Moon Window
(New York: Margaret K. McElderry Books, 1996)

Subject(s): Haunted Houses; Mystery and Detective Stories; Ghosts
Age range(s): Grades 4-6
Major character(s): JoEllen Briggs, Stepdaughter; Granty Ellen Macallan, Cousin; Witch Ellen, Aged Person (200-year-old), Spirit
Time period(s): 1990s
Locale(s): New Hampshire (Winterbloom House)

Summary: JoEllen is furious about being sent to stay with a cousin while her mother is on her honeymoon. She is determined she will find a way to get her to return. Instead she finds herself intrigued by the old house, especially when she finds herself in another time whenever she steps out a window. She meets the original owner of the house and finds herself involved in trying to release Granty from a phobia about the house as it is destroyed. (170 pages)

Where it's reviewed:
School Library Journal, December 1996, page 120
Booklist, October 15, 1996, page 420
Bulletin of the Center for Children's Books, November 1996, page 94

Other books by the same author:
The Great Smith House Hustle, 1993
What the Dickens!, 1991
The Big Smith Snatch, 1989

Other books you might like:
Avi, *Something Upstairs: A Tale of Ghosts*, 1988
Kenny finds that the house is haunted by a slave who lived there in 1800.
Peg Kehret, *Horror at the Haunted House*, 1992
The festivities at the haunted house become too real for Ellen.
Marilyn Sachs, *Ghosts in the Family*, 1995
When her mother is killed in an accident, Gabriella stays with relatives and finds that her father's stories have not always been true.
Zilpha Keatley Snyder, *The Trespassers*, 1995
Neely and Grub enjoy playing in an abandoned house, even when the new owner seems strange, but then they discover the ghost of a former child.
Betty Ren Wright, *Out of the Dark*, 1995
Jessie is terrified to find a ghost in her dream, especially when she discovers something odd about her grandmother.

311

CHRISTOPHER PAUL CURTIS

The Watsons Go to Birmingham—1963
(New York: Delacorte, 1995)

Subject(s): African Americans; Family Life; Prejudice
Age range(s): Grades 4-6
Major character(s): Kenny Watson, 10-Year-Old; Byron ''By'' Watson, 13-Year-Old; Joetta Watson, Child
Time period(s): 1960s (1963)
Locale(s): Flint, Michigan; Birmingham, Alabama

Summary: The Watsons are a warm, loving family who move North in search of better jobs, but whose roots are firmly tied to the South. In addition to the parents, there's baby sister Joetta, narrator Kenny, and older brother Byron who recently has been getting into trouble. When by chemically straightens his hair, that's the straw that sends the Watsons to Birmingham where he can get a taste of his grandmother's discipline. The family heads south in their new Ultra-Glide automobile, well-stocked with food since stopping along the way could be foolhardy. The light-heartedness of the Watson family is altered forever when a church in Birmingham is blown up, four young children killed and there's the possibility that Joetta is one of the four. The innocence of childhood is lost for them, and for many others, in an act of cowardice in this first novel. (210 pages)

Where it's reviewed:
Voice of Youth Advocates, December 1995, page 298
School Library Journal, October 1995, page 152
Book Report, January 1996, page 42

Booklist, August 1995, page 1946
New York Times Book Review, November 12, 1995, page 23

Awards the book has won:
ALA Best Books for Young Adults, 1996
Coretta Scott King Honor Book, 1996

Other books you might like:
Ossie Davis, *Just Like Martin*, 1992
Ike and his father reconcile their opposite views of civil rights after a church bombing.
Yvette Moore, *Freedom Songs*, 1991
The death of her activist uncle makes Sheryl even more determined to put on a fundraising concert.
Walter Dean Myers, *The Glory Field*, 1994
The Lewis family is sustained and strengthened by a plot of land they call the glory field.
Mildred D. Taylor, *The Gold Cadillac*, 1987
A loving Ohio family is not prepared for the prejudice they experience when they are in Mississippi.

312

DOUG CUSHMAN, Author/Illustrator

Aunt Eater's Mystery Christmas
(New York: HarperCollins Publishers, 1995)

Series: I Can Read Books
Subject(s): Animals; Christmas; Mystery and Detective Stories
Age range(s): Grades 1-2
Major character(s): Aunt Eater, Aardvark
Time period(s): 1990s (1995)
Locale(s): Fictional Country

Summary: Aunt Eater's preparations for the Christmas holidays are sidetracked repeatedly by suspicious events which require curious Aunt Eater's attention. Each mysterious occurrence has a plausible explanation which Aunt Eater learns after she completes some judicious investigating. (64 pages)

Where it's reviewed:
Booklist, September 15, 1995, page 169
Children's Book Watch, December 1995, page 2
Horn Book Guide, Spring 1996, page 52
Parents' Choice, November 1995, page 7
School Library Journal, October 1995, page 36

Other books by the same author:
ABC Mystery, 1993
Aunt Eater's Mystery Vacation, 1992
Aunt Eater Loves a Mystery, 1987

Other books you might like:
Julia Hoban, *Buzby to the Rescue*, 1993
Buzby, the hotel cat, thinks he can solve the mystery of the missing jewels and catch the thieves.
Peggy Parish, *Come Back, Amelia Bedelia*, 1971
As usual, Amelia Bedelia interprets instructions literally causing her to lose a series of jobs.
Marjorie Weinman Sharmat, *Nate the Great and the Tardy Tortoise*, 1995
In one mystery in the series, Nate the Great tracks the culprit who has been eating the flower garden—a tortoise.

313

DOUG CUSHMAN, Author/Illustrator

The Mystery of King Karfu
(New York: HarperCollins, 1996)

Subject(s): Mystery and Detective Stories
Age range(s): Grades K-3
Major character(s): Seymour Sleuth, Detective, Wombat; Abbott Muggs, Photographer, Mouse; Professor Slagbottom, Anthropologist, Pig
Time period(s): 1990s
Locale(s): Cairo, Egypt

Summary: Seymour is called to Egypt to find the missing stone chicken which once belonged to King Karfu. The reader follows along as he looks for the item, interviews the suspects, examines clues, and puts the pieces together to expose a hieroglyphic code. (unpaged)

Where it's reviewed:
Booklist, January 1, 1997, page 866
School Library Journal, February 1997, page 74

Other books by the same author:
Mouse and Mole and the All Weather Train Ride, 1995
ABC Mystery, 1993
Aunt Eater's Mystery Vacation, 1992

Other books you might like:
Duncan Ball, *Emily Eyefinger and the Lost Treasure*, 1994
Emily has an extra eye on her finger and uses it to find a lost treasure in Egypt.
Robert Quackenbush, *Henry's World Tour*, 1992
Henry travels around the world to discover why he has a strange feather growing in his tail.
Mary Stolz, *Zekmet, the Stone Carver*, 1988
How the Sphinx may have been carved is told in text with hieroglyphic clues shown in the illustrations.
Jane Yolen, *Piggins*, 1987
Piggins discovers which of the guests has stolen the jewels.
Jill Paton Walsh, *Pepi and the Secret Names*, 1994
Pepi's father carves a tomb with the help of models his son finds for him and uses hieroglyphs to answer riddles.

314

KAREN CUSHMAN

The Ballad of Lucy Whipple
(New York: Clarion, 1996)

Subject(s): Frontier and Pioneer Life; Family Life; Miners and Mining
Age range(s): Grades 5-8
Major character(s): California Morning ''Lucy'' Whipple, Settler, Librarian; Arvella Whipple, Mother, Innkeeper; Jimmy Whiskers, Miner
Time period(s): 1840s; 1850s (1840-1850)
Locale(s): Lucky Diggins, California (gold mining town)

Summary: Lucy and her family have come to California to start over and run a boarding house. Lucy is homesick for New England and writes to her grandparents often, expressing her desire to return and live with them. Soon she is caught up in the life of the mining camp and is surprised to find that the miners are interested in reading as much as she is. Life is not easy for the family as there are fires, death, and evil people, but good wins out and Lucy finally has a chance to return East while her mother goes to the Pacific with her new husband. Lucy decides to stay, however, and become the official librarian, the role which she has been playing unofficially for some time. (195 pages)

Where it's reviewed:
School Library Journal, August 1996, page 142
Bulletin of the Center for Children's Books, September 1996, page 9
Booklist, August 1996, page 1904
Hornbook, September/October 1996, page 593

Awards the book has won:
School Library Journal Best Books, 1996
Booklist Editors' Choice, 1996

Other books by the same author:
The Midwife's Apprentice, 1995
Catherine, Called Birdy, 1994

Other books you might like:
Patricia Beatty, *Eight Mules from Monterey*, 1992
    Fayette and her mother find work in 1916 delivering books to the miners in California.
Laurie Lawlor, *Gold in the Hills*, 1995
    Hattie and her brother are left with a cousin but soon make friends with a hermit who teaches them survival.
Joan Lowery Nixon, *A Family Apart*, 1987
    Francis Mary sets out on her own in the first volume of the Orphan Train series.
Katherine Paterson, *Lyddie*, 1991
    A strong willed girl finds work in the New England mills.
Willo Davis Roberts, *Jo and the Bandit*, 1992
    Jo Whitman and her younger brother find adventure living in the West with their uncle.

315

JANE CUTLER
SUSANNAH RYAN, Illustrator

Darcy and Gran Don't Like Babies
(New York: Scholastic Inc., 1993)

Subject(s): Babies; Brothers and Sisters; Grandparents
Age range(s): Grades K-2
Major character(s): Darcy, Child; Gran, Grandmother; Baby, Brother
Time period(s): 1990s (1993)
Locale(s): United States

Summary: It's no secret. Darcy does not like babies, especially her new baby brother. Quick to express this opinion, Darcy still does not feel understood until Gran arrives for a visit and agrees with her. With Gran, she goes to the playground where they realize that babies are unable to enjoy the really important things that Darcy and Gran share such as the big swings and the tall slide. Darcy and Gran return home with a new appreciation for each other and an expectation that one day, each will feel differently about the baby. (32 pages)

Where it's reviewed:
Booklist, December 1, 1993, page 697
Horn Book, January 1994, page 62
Publishers Weekly, September 6, 1993, page 91
Reading Teacher, April 1994, page 565
School Library Journal, November 1993, page 78

Awards the book has won:
School Library Journal Best Books, 1993

Other books you might like:
Jennifer Armstrong, *That Terrible Baby*, 1994
    Mark and Eleanor have plans for the terrible baby at their house, but decide that perhaps the baby is not as bad as they first thought.
John Hassett, *We Got My Brother at the Zoo*, 1993
    Mary Margaret has some unusual stories to tell about the origins of the new baby at her house. Ann Hassett, co-author.
Russell Hoban, *A Baby Sister for Frances*, 1964
    Frances is not sure about the new addition to the family, but her patient, understanding parents help her adjust to the arrival of a baby sister.

316

JANE CUTLER

My Wartime Summers
(New York: Farrar, Straus & Giroux, 1994)

Subject(s): World War II; Historical; Relatives
Age range(s): Grades 4-6
Major character(s): Ellen, Child; Uncle Bob, Military Personnel, Uncle (Ellen's)
Time period(s): 1940s (1942-1945)
Locale(s): United States

Summary: World War II is just beginning, Uncle Bob is drafted, and Ellen just knows he'll be a hero and win the war for America. During the summer of 1942, she and her friends play war games and she faithfully writes Uncle Bob. Her father worries that Bob's so high-spirited he'll do something stupid and get killed. As the war progresses, Ellen gradually sheds her tomboyish ways, the letters from Uncle Bob become more somber as he withdraws and becomes depressed and Ellen's thoughts about war change. A Jewish refugee moves into her neighborhood, gold stars appear in the windows of homes where husbands or sons have been lost and Uncle Bob comes home so changed that Ellen and her family have a hard time dealing with him in this realistic treatment of the homefront. (153 pages)

Where it's reviewed:
Booklist, October 1, 1994, page 324
Publishers Weekly, August 15, 1994, page 96
Book Report, March 1995, page 35
School Library Journal, August 1994, page 102
Voice of Youth Advocates, April 1995, page 21

Other books by the same author:
Mr. Carey's Garden, 1996
Family Dinner, 1992
No Dogs Allowed, 1992

Other books you might like:

Avi, *Who Was That Masked Man, Anyway?*, 1992
  During the mid-1940s, Frankie pretends he's ''Chet Barker, Master Spy'' as he reenacts his life to match favorite radio serials.
Robert Cormier, *Other Bells for Us to Ring*, 1991
  Darcy becomes friends with Kathleen Mary as they wait for World War II to end and the bells to ring once more.
Connie Jordan Green, *The War at Home*, 1989
  Mattie adjusts to her new home when her father accepts a secret job in Oak Ridge, Tennessee during World War II.
Sollace Hotze, *Summer Endings*, 1991
  Though World War II ends, Christine worries for her family hasn't heard from her father since he was caught in Poland in 1939.

317

JANE CUTLER
TRACEY CAMPBELL PEARSON, Illustrator

No Dogs Allowed

(New York: Farrar Straus Giroux, 1992)

Subject(s): Family Life; Animals/Dogs; Brothers
Age range(s): Grades 2-4
Major character(s): Edward Fraser, 5-Year-Old (imaginative); Jason Fraser, 8-Year-Old (allergy sufferer)
Time period(s): 1990s (1992)
Locale(s): United States

Summary: While coping with his allergies, Jason's 5-year-old brother decides that, if he can't have a dog, he'll become one. The entire family must then contend with a barking Edward/Tuffles until swimming lessons lead Edward to change identities. These siblings endure new glasses, summer adventures, and a vacation that could prove to be surprising. (101 pages)

Where it's reviewed:
Booklist, October 15, 1992, page 423
Hornbook, January 1993, page 84
Kirkus Reviews, November 1, 1992, page 1374
Publishers Weekly, November 9, 1992, page 85
School Library Journal, December 1992, page 80

Other books by the same author:
Darcy and Gran Don't Like Babies, 1993
Family Dinner, 1992

Other books you might like:
Judy Blume, *Superfudge*, 1980
  In this sequel to *Tales of a Fourth Grade Nothing*, Peter continues to endure life with his irrepressible younger brother, Fudge.

Beverly Cleary, *Henry Huggins*, 1950
  Henry's knack for finding trouble where he least expects it may be what leads him to the mutt, Ribsy.
Johanna Hurwitz, *Aldo Peanut Butter*, 1990
  Aldo's two puppies, Peanut and Butter, add a new dimension to the fun that inevitably surrounds Aldo and his sisters.

318

JANE CUTLER
TRACEY CAMPBELL PEARSON, Illustrator

Rats!

(New York: Farrar, Straus, Giroux, 1996)

Subject(s): Brothers; Family Life; Animals/Rats
Age range(s): Grades 3-5
Major character(s): Jason Fraser, 4th Grader, Brother; Edward Fraser, 1st Grader, Brother; Andrew Kelley, 4th Grader, Classmate
Time period(s): 1990s
Locale(s): United States

Summary: This episodic book traces the different events that happen to the Fraser boys as they return to school in the Fall. The boys play and argue together as typical siblings and have amusing experiences. Edward enters his first haunted house and becomes really scared; Jason finds a girl friend; the boys are involved in raising rats and one of them turns out to be a surprise parent. (114 pages)

Where it's reviewed:
School Library Journal, August 1996, page 106

Other books by the same author:
My Wartime Summers, 1994
Family Dinner, 1993
No Dogs Allowed, 1992 (companion title to *Rats*)

Other books you might like:
Judy Blume, *Fudge-a-Mania*, 1990
  Two brothers share adventures and arguments.
Ann Cameron, *The Stories Huey Tells*, 1995
  A younger imaginative boy shares adventures with his brother and his loving family.
Pat Hutchins, *Rats!*, 1989
  Sam insists that he wants a rat for a pet and the result is a change in family routine as well as a surprise.
Phyllis Reynolds Naylor, *Being Danny's Dog*, 1995
  Two boys move to a new town and meet new friends.
P.J. Petersen, *The Amazing Magic Show*, 1994
  Hal finds a way of getting along with his older brother after he has a successful magic show.

D

319

NIKI DALY, Author/Illustrator

My Dad

(New York: Margaret K. McElderry Books, 1995)

Subject(s): Alcoholism; Fathers; Family Life
Age range(s): Grades 1-4
Major character(s): Dad, Father, Alcoholic; Gracie, Child, Sister (younger); Mr. Dickie, Teacher
Time period(s): 1990s (1995)
Locale(s): United States

Summary: Friday nights are a time of drinking and merriment for Dad and his buddies followed by family arguments as Gracie and her brother try to sleep. Although the children love Dad, they are embarrassed by his behavior and hide from him the fact that Mr. Dickie has asked them to perform in a school concert on Friday night. Before Dad comes home from work that day, Gracie, her brother, and mother hurry to the school. During the children's performance, they hear Dad shouting in the audience. Embarrassed, they leave the stage in tears and walk home with their mother. Mr. Dickie, a former alcoholic, drives Dad home and soon Dad begins attending AA meetings. (32 pages)

Where it's reviewed:
Booklist, May 1, 1995, page 1579
Bulletin of the Center for Children's Books, June 1995, page 341
Horn Book Guide, Fall 1995, page 262
Publishers Weekly, April 3, 1995, page 62
School Library Journal, June 1995, page 79

Other books by the same author:
Papa's Lucky Shadow, 1992
Mama, Papa and Baby Joe, 1991
Not So Fast, Songololo, 1986

Other books you might like:
Carol Carrick, *Banana Beer*, 1995
    Charlie wonders if there is anything he can do to keep his parents from arguing and his father from drinking so much.

Jane Resh Thomas, *Daddy Doesn't Have to Be a Giant Anymore*, 1996
    When a little girl's alcoholic father enters a treatment program, she begins to overcome her fear of him.
Judith Vigna, *I Wish Daddy Didn't Drink So Much*, 1988
    A little girl whose father is an alcoholic describes Christmas in her home.

320

PAULA DANZIGER
TONY ROSS, Illustrator

Amber Brown Is Not a Crayon

(New York: G.P. Putnam's Sons, 1994)

Subject(s): Friendship; Schools; Moving, Household
Age range(s): Grades 2-4
Major character(s): Amber Brown, 3rd Grader, Friend (Justin's); Justin Daniels, 3rd Grader, Friend
Time period(s): 1990s (1994)
Locale(s): New York

Summary: Amber Brown thought nothing could be worse than her parents' plan to divorce, but that was before she found out Justin's father has a new job in Alabama and her very best friend is moving. The tension of the impending move threatens to derail the friendship, but on Justin's last day of school, the two are able to begin communicating their sorrow over the separation. (80 pages)

Where it's reviewed:
Booklist, April 15, 1994, page 1533
Horn Book, July 1994, page 447
Kirkus Reviews, March 1, 1994, page 302
Publishers Weekly, February 21, 1994, page 254
School Library Journal, May 1994, page 90

Other books by the same author:
Amber Brown Goes Fourth, 1995
You Can't Eat Your Chicken Pox, Amber Brown, 1995
Everyone Else's Parents Said Yes, 1989

Other books you might like:

Marissa Moss, *Amelia's Notebook*, 1995
In a journal, 9-year-old Amelia records her thoughts about moving, the friend she's left behind, and her apprehensions about beginning a new school.

Jerry Spinelli, *Tooter Pepperday*, 1995
Tooter, determined not to move with her family to Aunt Sally's farm, handcuffs herself to the bathroom sink.

Vera B. Williams, *Scooter*, 1993
An out-going personality and an unfortunate accident on her scooter help Lanny make friends after her move to a New York apartment.

Jane O'Connor, *Corrie's Secret Pal*, 1993
Joining a Brownie Troop helps a lonely new student find friends.

321

PAULA DANZIGER
TONY ROSS, Illustrator

Amber Brown Wants Extra Credit

(New York: Putnam, 1996)

Subject(s): Divorce; Schools
Age range(s): Grades 2-5
Major character(s): Amber Brown, 9-Year-Old, Child of Divorced Parents; Sarah Thompson Brown, Mother, Divorced Person; Max Turner, Boyfriend
Time period(s): 1990s
Locale(s): United States

Summary: Amber is unhappy because her mother has found a boyfriend. She is determined not to meet him and, failing that, she is determined not to be nice. School is a hassle, too, as Amber forgets to hand in her homework and the teacher will not give her extra credit. When Amber does finally meet Max, he takes her out for ice cream and she admits that he really is a nice man. The bond is further strengthened when he and her mom help her make brownies for a school paper. Life will go on for Amber even as she finds that her father has a girl friend in France. (120 pages)

Where it's reviewed:
School Library Journal, August 1996, page 142
Booklist, June 1, 1996, page 1716

Other books by the same author:
Amber Brown Sees Read, 1997
Forever Amber Brown, 1996
Amber Brown Goes Fourth, 1995
Make Like a Tree and Leave, 1990

Other books you might like:

Judy Delton, *Angel's Mother's Boyfriend*, 1986
Angel and her brother are concerned when they hear that their mother has a boyfriend.

Anne Fine, *My War with Goggle-Eyes*, 1989
A little girl has problems with her new stepfather.

Patricia Reilly Giff, *Rat Teeth*, 1984
Radcliffe has problems adjusting to his parent's divorce and a new school.

322

PAULA DANZIGER
TONY ROSS, Illustrator

You Can't Eat Your Chicken Pox, Amber Brown

(New York: G.P. Putnam's Sons, 1995)

Subject(s): Divorce; Aunts and Uncles; Illness
Age range(s): Grades 2-4
Major character(s): Amber Brown, Child of Divorced Parents, 3rd Grader; Pam, Aunt; Phil Brown, Father
Time period(s): 1990s (1995)
Locale(s): New York; London, England

Summary: With half her class absent because of the chicken pox, Amber considers herself lucky to attend the end-of-the-year party. Even better, she's travelling with Aunt Pam to London for two weeks and then to Paris to visit her father. After arriving in London, Amber's luck runs out when she discovers what she thought were a few bug bites are actually chicken pox. Instead of going to Paris, Amber spends a week in bed in London and then has only a few days to visit with her father. Her hopes that she can convince her parents to reconcile don't work out, but Dad admits that he hopes to get a job assignment back in the States so he can see her more often. (101 pages)

Where it's reviewed:
Booklist, March 15, 1995, page 1330
Horn Book, May 1995, page 348
Library Talk, May 1995, page 40
Publishers Weekly, February 20, 1995, page 206
School Library Journal, June 1995, page 80

Other books by the same author:
Amber Brown Goes Fourth, 1995
Amber Brown Is Not a Crayon, 1994
Make Like a Tree and Leave, 1990

Other books you might like:

Beverly Lewis, *The Chicken Pox Panic*, 1993
Chicken pox forces Abby to change the plans she made to surprise her adopted Korean brother on his birthday.

Marilyn Kaye, *The Problem with Parents*, 1991
Secretly, Trina still hopes her divorced parents will reconcile.

P.J. Petersen, *I Want Answers and a Parachute*, 1993
Matt and his younger brother Jason visit their father for the first time since his remarriage, raising concerns for both of them.

323

MARGUERITE W. DAVOL

Papa Alonzo Leatherby: A Collection of Tall Tales from the Best Storyteller in Carroll County

(New York: Simon & Schuster Books for Young Readers, 1995)

Subject(s): Tall Tales; Storytelling; Humor
Age range(s): Grades 3-6

Major character(s): Papa Alonzo Leatherby, Father (of nine), Storyteller; Lulie Leatherby, Spouse
Time period(s): Indeterminate Past
Locale(s): Carroll County, Minnesota

Summary: For entertainment, Lulie and the nine Leatherby children listen to Papa Alonzo's stories. When a blizzard strikes and Papa's words freeze as he speaks, it takes Lulie's ingenuity to melt the words and bring the stories back to life. Cooped up, waiting for a thaw, Papa told so many stories that Lulie was able to save a year's worth by judicious canning of his frozen words. (70 pages)

Where it's reviewed:
Children's Book Review Service, December 1995, page 45
Horn Book Guide, Spring 1996, page 60
Kirkus Reviews, October 15, 1995, page 1489
School Library Journal, October 1995, page 133

Other books you might like:
Sid Fleischman, *Here Comes McBroom: Three More Tall Tales*, 1992
    The three previously published tales tell of Farmer Mc-Broom's zoo, his rain-making scheme to end a drought and a ghost who visits the family farm.
Robin Moore, *The Cherry Tree Buck and Other Stories*, 1995
    Six stories relate childhood adventures set in the Pennsylvania mountains involving animals, nature and a storytelling grandfather.
Mary Pope Osborne, *American Tall Tales*, 1991
    The collection includes traditional American folk heroes such as Pecos Bill and Sally Ann Thunder Ann Whirlwind Crockett.
Robert D. San Souci, *Larger than Life: The Adventures of American Legendary Heroes*, 1991
    Paul Bunyan, Sluefoot Sue, John Henry and Old Stormalong are the heroes featured in four short tales.
Alvin Schwartz, *Whoppers: Tall Tales and Other Lies*, 1975
    Selecting humorous tales of varying length, Schwartz has assembled a collection from many different authors.

324

ALEXANDRA DAY, Author/Illustrator

Frank and Ernest on the Road
(New York: Scholastic, Inc., 1994)

Series: Frank and Ernest
Subject(s): Animals; Transportation
Age range(s): Grades 2-3
Major character(s): Frank, Bear; Ernest, Elephant
Time period(s): 1990s (1994)
Locale(s): United States

Summary: Frank and Ernest receive a call to substitute for a long-distance truck driver. In order to do the job they must learn how to operate the truck and communicate on the CB radio. Readers learn the lingo too from the glossaries on the endpapers and the boxed inserts on each page. (48 pages)

Where it's reviewed:
Book Links, November 1994, page 52
Booklist, December 15, 1993, page 750
Five Owls, May 1994, page 106

Publishers Weekly, November 22, 1993, page 63
School Library Journal, February 1994, page 83

Other books by the same author:
Carl Makes a Scrapbook, 1994
Frank and Ernest Play Ball, 1990
Frank and Ernest, 1988

Other books you might like:
Hope Norman Coulter, *Uncle Chuck's Truck*, 1993
    While delivering food on the farm, Uncle Chuck's truck becomes mired in mud until the hungry cows come to the rescue.
Harriett Diller, *Grandaddy's Highway*, 1993
    As trucks drive along Route 30 past her home, Maggie imagines herself riding in one with her grandfather.
Keren Ludlow, *Benny the Breakdown Truck*, 1994
    Benny the tow truck helps other cars and trucks in this beginning reader co-authored by Willy Smax.

325

NANCY RAINES DAY
ANN GRIFALCONI, Illustrator

The Lion's Whiskers: An Ethiopian Folktale
(New York: Scholastic Inc., 1995)

Subject(s): Folk Tales; Stepmothers; Parent and Child
Age range(s): Grades K-3
Major character(s): Fanaye, Stepmother; Tesfa, Father, Trader; Abebe, Child (son), Stepson (to Fanaye)
Time period(s): Indeterminate Past
Locale(s): Ethiopia

Summary: When Fanaye marries the widowed Tesfa she considers his son a blessing. Abebe, however, still grieves for his mother and rejects Fanaye's overtures. Seeking guidance from a medicine man, Fanaye follows his instructions to pluck 3 whiskers from the chin of a lion. Months of patient planning are needed before Fanaye returns to the medicine man with her task completed. From the experience she learns to win Abebe's love in the same patient way she approached the lion. (32 pages)

Where it's reviewed:
Booklist, February 15, 1995, page 1085
Horn Book Guide, Fall 1995, page 329
Instructor, January 1996, page 75
Library Talk, September 1995, page 41
School Library Journal, April 1995, page 140

Other books you might like:
Jane Kurtz, *Pulling the Lion's Tail*, 1995
    When a young girl seeking the love of her stepmother follows her grandfather's advice to pluck a handful of hair from a lion's tail, she learns that some things take time.
Norman Leach, *My Wicked Stepmother*, 1993
    After a change of heart Tom gives his stepmother a hug. He realizes the power of love changes her from a witch to a fairy godmother.
Judith Vigna, *She's Not My Real Mother*, 1980
    Miles reconsiders his feelings toward his stepmother after she rescues him when he becomes lost.

326

HANS DE BEER, Author/Illustrator

Bernard Bear's Amazing Adventure
(New York: North-South Books, 1994)

Subject(s): Animals/Bears; Winter; Sleep
Age range(s): Grades K-3
Major character(s): Bernard Bear, Bear
Time period(s): 1990s (1994)
Locale(s): Europe

Summary: Bernard Bear prefers the family hibernation of his youth to the loneliness of the solo winter slumber of an older bear. When a sparrow suggests that an even better winter plan is to head south to a warm, sandy beach, Bernard tries to do just that. After days of walking a lost Bernard reaches an abandoned truck with three dormice for company and the warm coziness of his sunny dreams. Translated from the German by Marianne Martens. (26 pages)

Where it's reviewed:
Booklist, December 15, 1994, page 757
Children's Book Review Service, March 1995, page 86
Horn Book Guide, Spring 1995, page 31
Publishers Weekly, November 21, 1994, page 76
School Library Journal, July 1995, page 55

Other books by the same author:
Little Polar Bear Finds a Friend, 1990
Little Polar Bear, 1989
Ahoy There, Little Polar Bear, 1988

Other books you might like:
Jim Arnosky, *Every Autumn Comes the Bear*, 1993
    Annually a bear appears on the hillside behind the barn seeking his winter den.
Don Freeman, *Bearymore*, 1976
    Rather than plan his new circus act, Bearymore settles down for his winter's hibernation.
James Preller, *Wake Me in Spring*, 1994
    A mouse is sad he will not be able to play with his friend Bear again until Spring.

327

DIANE DE GROAT, Author/Illustrator

Annie Pitts, Swamp Monster
(New York, Simon & Schuster Books for Young Readers, 1994)

Subject(s): Movies; Actors and Actresses; Monsters
Age range(s): Grades 3-4
Major character(s): Annie Pitts, 3rd Grader, Actress (aspiring); Matthew McGill, 3rd Grader, Actor (amateur); Mark McGill, Student—High School, Brother (Matthew's)
Time period(s): 1990s (1994)
Locale(s): United States (Tibbetts Brook Park)

Summary: In the sequel to *Annie Pitts, Artichoke* star-struck Annie is excited to be acting in a video Mark is producing for a film class. Unfortunately, creepy Matthew is cast as the mummy, but Annie thinks her talented conversion of an artichoke costume into a swamp monster costume will be an important step on her road to stardom. The video shooting session doesn't go as well as Annie hopes, but it produces a video which is beyond her expectations. (71 pages)

Where it's reviewed:
Booklist, June 1, 1994, page 1815
Horn Book Guide, Fall 1994, page 308
Kirkus Reviews, June 15, 1994, page 843
School Library Journal, July 1994, page 102

Other books by the same author:
Annie Pitts, Artichoke, 1992

Other books you might like:
Beverly Cleary, *Emily's Runaway Imagination*, 1961
    Life on an Oregon farm is never boring for Emily as she follows her very active imagination into one mishap after another.
Patricia Reilly Giff, *Poopsie Pomerantz, Pick Up Your Feet*, 1989
    When Poopsie is chosen to play the pig in the class play, her self-esteem drops another notch.
Suzy Kline, *Song Lee and the Leech Man*, 1995
    Harry's plan to use a class field trip to the pond as an opportunity to get back at the class tattletale backfires.

328

TOMIE DE PAOLA, Author/Illustrator

Kit and Kat
(New York: Grosset & Dunlap, 1994)

Series: All Aboard Reading
Subject(s): Brothers and Sisters; Animals/Cats
Age range(s): Grades K-1
Major character(s): Kat, Cat, Sister; Kit, Cat, Brother
Time period(s): 1990s (1994)
Locale(s): Fictional Country

Summary: In three brief stories for beginning readers, older sister Kat helps Kit learn to ride a bike. Together they cope with a bully who is really not all bad and spend the night at Grandpa's house. (32 pages)

Where it's reviewed:
Booklist, January 1, 1995, page 827
Horn Book Guide, Fall 1995

Other books by the same author:
The Legend of the Indian Paintbrush, 1991
The Knight and the Dragon, 1980
Bill and Pete, 1978

Other books you might like:
Linda Breiner Milstein, *Miami-Nanny Stories*, 1994
    Three stories depict the special relationship between two children and their grandmother.
Janet Schulman, *Random House Book of Easy-to-Read Stories*, 1993
    A collection of fifteen stories from a variety of authors is accessible to the young beginning reader.
Rosemary Wells, *Max's Bedtime*, 1985
    Rejecting his sister's offer of substitute animals, Max must find his red rubber elephant in order to sleep.

329

TOMIE DE PAOLA, Author/Illustrator

Strega Nona Meets Her Match

(New York: G.P. Putnam's Sons, 1993)

Subject(s): Witches and Witchcraft
Age range(s): Grades K-3
Major character(s): Strega Nona, Witch; Strega Amelia, Witch (rival); Big Anthony, Assistant (bumbling)
Time period(s): Indeterminate Past
Locale(s): Calabria, Italy (a little town)

Summary: Strega Nona's quiet life is enlivened one day by an ostensibly neighborly visit from Strega Amelia. In fact, Strega Amelia must be looking over the potential competition, for within days, she has opened her own business dispensing advice to the lovelorn and home remedies for warts and hair loss with the aid of the latest scientific equipment, rather than the old-fashioned ways of Strega Nona. When the villagers flock to the new business, Strega Nona is forced to lay off her two assistants and Big Anthony is offered employment with Strega Amelia. Big Anthony's tendency to bumble into disaster proves to be the undoing of Strega Amelia's business. (32 pages)

Where it's reviewed:
Booklist, November 1, 1993, page 528
Horn Book, November 1993, page 730
Publishers Weekly, July 19, 1993, page 251
Quill & Quire, August 1993, page 40
School Library Journal, November 1993, page 78

Awards the book has won:
Book Links Good Book, 1993

Other books by the same author:
The Art Lesson, 1994
Merry Christmas Strega Nona, 1986
Strega Nona, 1975 (Caldecott Honor Book, 1976)

Other books you might like:
Patricia Coombs, *Dorrie and the Museum Case*, 1986
   An enchanter up to no good can not outwit lovable little witch Dorrie and her cousin Cosmo.
Paul Galdone, *The Magic Porridge Pot*, 1976
   Galdone's is one version of a familiar tale about a productive pot which will not stop until the correct words are spoken.
Robert D. San Souci, *The Talking Eggs: A Folktale from the American South*, 1989
   In this Caldecott Honor Book, a young girl's kindness is rewarded, while her greedy sister who seeks the same reward receives another.

330

CHRISTOPHER DE VINCK

Augusta & Trab

(New York: Four Winds Press, 1993)

Subject(s): Death; Animals/Cats; Fantasy
Age range(s): Grades 4-6
Major character(s): Augusta, 10-Year-Old; Trab, Cat (talking)

Time period(s): 1990s (1993)
Locale(s): England

Summary: A year after her mother's death, Augusta still feels a huge emptiness within her. Her father, a veterinarian, has little time for her so Augusta and her talking cat, Trab, spend their days wishing and imagining. One day their wishes come true in a fantastic adventure that helps Augusta learn to deal with the pain of her mother's death in this author's first book for children. (128 pages)

Where it's reviewed:
Booklist, October 15, 1993, page 442
Horn Book Guide, Spring 1994, page 75
Library Talk, May 1994, page 46
Publishers Weekly, November 1, 1993, page 80
School Library Journal, November 1993, page 106

Other books you might like:
L. Frank Baum, *The Emerald City of Oz*, 1910
   Dorothy returns to Oz with Aunt Em and Uncle Henry to give them a tour and an opportunity to meet the Wonderful Wizard.
Lewis Carroll, *Alice's Adventures in Wonderland*, 1865
   Alice's curiosity leads her on a fantastic adventure through a magical land.
Roald Dahl, *James and the Giant Peach*, 1961
   Finding a giant peach in his yard, James leaves his unhappy home to travel in the peach to some unusual places with an assortment of fantastic creatures.

331

BARTHE DECLEMENTS

The Pickle Song

(New York: Viking, 1993)

Subject(s): Friendship; Interpersonal Relations; Divorce
Age range(s): Grades 4-6
Major character(s): Paula Tomlin, 6th Grader, Child of Divorced Parents; Sukey Parsons, 6th Grader, Streetperson (homeless)
Time period(s): 1990s (1993)
Locale(s): Washington (near Seattle)

Summary: Curious about the new girl in class who seems to be living in a car parked near her home, Paula tries to befriend Sukey despite the girl's avoidance of questions. Paula's family also has problems: child support does not come regularly from Dad and her grandmother moves in when she loses her job. Cautiously, Paula and Sukey build a friendship which becomes strong enough for Paula and her family to provide support to Sukey and her mother. (151 pages)

Where it's reviewed:
Booklist, October 15, 1993, page 440
Horn Book Guide, Spring 1994, page 74
Kirkus Reviews, August 1, 1993, page 1000
Publishers Weekly, July 19, 1993, page 255
School Library Journal, August 1993, page 163

Other books by the same author:
Tough Loser, 1994
Breaking Out, 1993
Wake Me at Midnight, 1991

Other books you might like:

Sheila Greenwald, *My Fabulous New Life*, 1993
  When financial problems force Alison Fox's family to move from an elite suburb into an apartment in New York City, she comes face to face with the reality of homelessness and hunger.

Mark J. Harris, *Come the Morning*, 1989
  Homeless in Los Angeles, Ben Gibson, with his mother and siblings, searches for his father.

Alison Cragin Herzig, *Sam and the Moon Queen*, 1990
  Understanding the plight of the homeless occurs through Sam's attempts to help one homeless girl and her dog.

332

BARTHE DECLEMENTS

Tough Loser

(New York: Viking, 1994)

Subject(s): Brothers and Sisters; Anger; Sports/Hockey
Age range(s): Grades 3-5
Major character(s): Jenna Mason, 9-Year-Old, Sister (Mike's); Mike Mason, 13-Year-Old, Hockey Player (goalie)
Time period(s): 1990s (1994)
Locale(s): Washington

Summary: Mike is a good goalie, but a poor sport when his team loses a game and, unfortunately, they lose often. Jenna tries to defend him from their parents' anger when he takes his frustrations out on the maple tree and the family van, but when he shoves her after a losing game, their parents have had enough and take away his privilege of summer goalie camp until he learns to deal with his anger in an acceptable way. (118 pages)

Where it's reviewed:
Booklist, October 1, 1994, page 326
Horn Book Guide, Spring 1995, page 75
Library Talk, May 1995, page 40
Publishers Weekly, October 3, 1994, page 71
School Library Journal, October 94, page 120

Other books by the same author:
The Pickle Song, 1993
Five Finger Discount, 1989
The Fourth Grade Wizards, 1988

Other books you might like:

Matt Christopher, *The Hockey Machine*, 1986
  When Steve is abducted and forced to play hockey with a junior professional team, he soon realizes that surviving is as important as winning.

David Halecroft, *Power Play*, 1992
  Given the opportunity to play on the ninth grade team, seventh grader Derrick must choose between hockey and friends.

Nancy J. Hopper, *Ape Ears and Beaky*, 1984
  The experience of being kicked off one team and humiliated on another convinces Scott that he must learn to control his temper.

333

CARMEN AGRA DEEDY
MICHAEL P. WHITE, Illustrator

The Library Dragon

(Atlanta: Peachtree Publishers, Ltd., 1994)

Subject(s): Dragons; Libraries; Schools
Age range(s): Grades K-3
Major character(s): Miss Lotta Scales, Mythical Creature (dragon), Librarian; Molly Brickmeyer, Child (nearsighted), Student
Time period(s): 1990s (1994)
Locale(s): United States (Sunrise Elementary School)

Summary: When Miss Lotta Scales reads an ad seeking a "thick-skinned" librarian with a "burning" love for books and children she knows she has found the perfect job. Unfortunately, she sees her responsiblity to be guarding the books so that children do not touch or soil them. The principal and the faculty attempt to reason with her, but come away singed and smoky. Not until a very nearsighted student who has lost her glasses wanders into the library and begins reading a book does Miss Lotta Scales realize the value of books and their transforming power. (32 pages)

Where it's reviewed:
Children's Bookwatch, January 1995, page 6
Horn Book Guide, Spring 1995, page 31
Kirkus Reviews, November 15, 1994, page 1526
Publishers Weekly, November 14, 1994, page 68
School Library Journal, December 1994, page 73

Other books by the same author:
Treeman, 1993
Agatha's Feather Bed: Not Just Another Wild Goose Story, 1991

Other books you might like:

Crosby Bonsall, *Tell Me Some More*, 1961
  Andrew tells Tim about a special place where one can hold a lion or pat an elephant—the library.

Chris L. Demarest, *Clemen's Kingdom*, 1983
  Years of standing guard outside a library have so bored a stone lion that one day he strolls inside to determine if the facility is worth his continued vigilance.

John F. Green, *Alice and the Birthday Giant*, 1990
  Knowing that libraries are a source of information, Alice uses hers to learn how to get rid of the giant who has appeared in response to a birthday wish for something big.

Deborah Hautzig, *A Visit to the Sesame Street Library*, 1986
  Grover gives Big Bird a tour of the public library, describing the many services offerred.

334

CYNTHIA DEFELICE

The Apprenticeship of Lucas Whitaker

(New York: Farrar Straus Giroux, 1996)

Subject(s): Medicine; Orphans; Apprentices
Age range(s): Grades 4-7

Major character(s): Lucas Whitaker, Orphan, Apprentice; Uriah Beecher, Doctor; Sarah Stukeley, Teenager, Patient
Time period(s): 1850s
Locale(s): Southwick, Connecticut

Summary: Lucas is grief stricken over the death of his mother, especially when a neighbor tells him of a new and strange cure he could have used. Lucas leaves the farm and moves to the city where he becomes apprenticed to the local doctor, but consumption follows him there and he becomes involved in helping his new neighbors perform a superstitious rite; exhuming bodies in order to be rid of the person spreading the disease. Eventually he accepts that this rite does not work, especially when he returns home to find that his neighbor has died. (151 pages)

Where it's reviewed:
School Library Journal, August 1996, page 142
The Bulletin of Children's Literature, October 1996, page 54
Horn Book, January/February 1997, page 55

Awards the book has won:
School Library Journal Best Books, 1996

Other books by the same author:
Devil's Bridge, 1992
Weasel, 1990
The Strange Night Writing of Jessamine Colter, 1988

Other books you might like:
Sid Fleischman, *Saturnalia*, 1990
    A half-Indian boy finds himself involved in intrigue during the time of the epidemic in Philadelphia before the Revolution.
Stephen Krensky, *The Printer's Apprentice*, 1995
    A boy apprenticed to the printer in 1734 isn't sure what to make of the ideas of Peter Zenger.
Pilar M. Liorente, *The Apprentice*, 1993
    Being an apprentice during the Renaissance is not as wonderful as Arduino expected.

335

CYNTHIA DEFELICE

The Light on Hogback Hill

(New York: Macmillan Publishing Company, 1993)

Subject(s): Friendship; Mystery and Detective Stories; Physically Handicapped
Age range(s): Grades 3-6
Major character(s): Hadley Patterson, 11-Year-Old, Child of Divorced Parents; Josh Carter, 6th Grader (new boy in town)
Time period(s): 1990s (1993)
Locale(s): Possum Hollow (in the shadow of Hogback Hill)

Summary: Josh seeks friendship with Hadley, not realizing that they're both lonely: Hadley because of her mother's long work hours and Josh from being the new kid at school. The local folklore tells of the hag who lives on Hogback Hill which arouses the curiosity of Hadley and Josh. Together they climb the hill only to discover not only the identity of the hilltop resident, but also some insights into themselves. (139 pages)

Where it's reviewed:
Booklist, November 1, 1993, page 521
Hornbook, March 1994, page 198
Kirkus Reviews, November 1, 1993, page 1388
Publishers Weekly, October 25, 1993, page 62
School Library Journal, November 1993, page 106

Other books by the same author:
Lostman's River, 1994
Weasel, 1990
The Strange Night Writing of Jessamine Colter, 1988

Other books you might like:
Bill Brittain, *Who Knew There'd Be Ghosts?*, 1985
    Tommy and his friends are not expecting to find two ghosts in the deserted mansion they use for a playground, but they are able to use the ghosts to solve a mystery and save the ghosts' home.
Joan Lowery Nixon, *The House on Hackman's Hill*, 1986
    Curious about the old, supposedly haunted house, Jeff and Debbie become trapped inside by a blizzard.
Drew Stevenson, *One Ghost Too Many*, 1991
    When three friends decide to explore some unusual lights at the local haunted house, they find more than they were expecting.

336

CYNTHIA DEFELICE
MIKE SHENON, Illustrator

Mule Eggs

(New York: Orchard Books, 1994)

Subject(s): Animals; Farm Life; Humor
Age range(s): Grades K-3
Major character(s): Patrick, Farmer; Unnamed Character, Farmer
Time period(s): Indeterminate Past
Locale(s): United States

Summary: When Patrick arrives from the city determined to become a farmer, a neighbor sees an opportunity to take advantage of Patrick's ignorance and make some money by selling Patrick a "mule egg" (pumpkin) to hatch into a mule. Initially falling for the trick, Patrick soon realizes he's been duped and plans a response which earns back his money as well as some satisfaction. (32 pages)

Where it's reviewed:
Bulletin of the Center for Children's Books, October 1994, page 41
Horn Book, November 1994, page 717
Horn Book Guide, Spring 1995, page 31
Publishers Weekly, August 22, 1994, page 55
School Library Journal, September 1994, page 182

Other books by the same author:
Three Perfect Peaches: A French Folktale, 1995
When Grampa Kissed His Elbow, 1992
The Dancing Skeleton, 1989

Other books you might like:
Wilson Gage, *The Crow and Mrs. Gaddy*, 1984
    Because a farmer and a crow spend so much time tricking one another, the farmer has no time to tend the farm.

David McKee, *Elmer Again*, 1992
A patchwork elephant plays an amusing trick on his mono-chromatic, gray elephant friends.

Anne F. Rockwell, *The Gollywhopper Egg*, 1974
The beginning reader tells of the peddler Timothy Todd who sells a coconut which he claims has special attributes.

337

MONALISA DEGROSS
CHERYL HANNA, Illustrator

Donavan's Word Jar

(New York: HarperCollins, 1994)

Subject(s): Collectors and Collecting; Family Life; Problem Solving

Age range(s): Grades 2-4

Major character(s): Donavan Allen, 3rd Grader (African American), Collector

Time period(s): 1990s (1994)

Locale(s): United States

Summary: In the author's first children's book, all of Donavan's friends collect things, but Donavan is the only one who collects words. Fascinated by the sound and feel of unusual words as they are spoken, Donavan writes them on scraps of yellow paper and stores them in a jar. When the jar becomes full he asks the advice of his teacher and parents about what to do, but the solution he likes best is a ser-endipitous one. (80 pages)

Where it's reviewed:
Booklist, June 1, 1994, page 181
Children's Book Review Service, July 1994, page 152
New Advocate, Winter 1995, page 58
Publishers Weekly, June 13, 1994, page 65
School Library Journal, August 1994, page 128

Other books you might like:
Paula Fox, *Maurice's Room*, 1966
Maurice's collection of treasures is viewed by his parents as junk cluttering a messy room.

Jamie Gilson, *Harvey, the Beer Can King*, 1978
Harvey thinks that his fantastic collection of beer cans is his ticket to victory in the Super Kid Contest.

Ellen Leroe, *Ghost Dog*, 1993
Visiting his grandparents becomes an adventure for Artie when he encounters a ghost dog that only he can see.

338

LULU DELACRE, Author/Illustrator

Vejigante/Masquerader

(New York: Scholastic, 1993)

Subject(s): Holidays; Carnivals

Age range(s): Grades K-3

Major character(s): Ramon, Child (first-time vejigante)

Time period(s): 1990s (1993)

Locale(s): Ponce, Puerto Rico

Summary: Too small, too young, and too poor, Ramon has long admired the men and boys who dress as vejigantes and play pranks during the Carnival in the month of February. Secretly, he saves money for cloth, learns to sew, and makes his own costume. His masquerading career appears to end after only one parade when a goat tears his costume. Persistence, patience, and the help of a loving mother give Ramon the promise of more celebrations in the disguise of his long-sought role. Spanish text parallels the English. (40 pages)

Where it's reviewed:
Booklist, March 15, 1993, page 1359
Children's Book Review Service, April 1993, page 99
Kirkus Reviews, February 1, 1993, page 143
Publishers Weekly, January 11, 1993, page 63
School Library Journal, February 1993, page 71

Awards the book has won:
Consortium of Latin American Studies Programs Com-mended Book, 1994

Other books by the same author:
Arroz Con Leche: Popular Songs and Rhymes From Latin America, 1989
Nathan's Fishing Trip, 1988
Time for School Nathan, 1989

Other books you might like:
Bernice Chardiet, *Juan Bobo and the Pig: A Puerto Rican Folktale Retold*, 1973
Playing a trick on the family pig turns out in a way that Juan did not expect.

Phillis Gershator, *Rata-Pata-Scata-Fata: A Caribbean Story*, 1994
Daily chores interfere with Junjun's daydreaming so he tries wishing for things to go his way by invoking the magical West Indian nonsense words rata-pata-scata-fata.

Ann Grifalconi, *The Bravest Flute: A Story of Courage in the Mayan Tradition*, 1994
To bring honor to his family, an exhausted boy must lead the New Year's parade of renewal to the cathedral.

339

PATRICIA DEMUTH
TRUE KELLEY, Illustrator

In Trouble with Teacher

(New York: Dutton Children's Books, 1995)

Subject(s): Teacher-Student Relationships; Schools; Self-Per-ception

Age range(s): Grades 2-4

Major character(s): Mrs. Wix, Teacher; Montgomery Thorn-ton, 3rd Grader

Time period(s): 1990s (1995)

Locale(s): United States

Summary: Anxiously, Montgomery awaits the results of a spelling test for which he did not prepare. Third grade is harder than second, he is not a good speller and Mrs. Wix seems so strict that Montgomery fears the consequences of a failing paper. Although Montgomery's fear of failing the test is realized, his fear of Mrs. Wix vanishes when she offers encouragement and extra help before school while compli-menting Montgomery's writing and art skills. Maybe 3rd grade won't be so bad after all. (73 pages)

Where it's reviewed:
Booklist, April 1, 1995, page 1391
Bulletin of the Center for Children's Books, May 1995, page 304
Horn Book Guide, Fall 1995, page 290
School Library Journal, May 1995, page 84

Other books by the same author:
Max, the Bad-Talking Parrot, 1990

Other books you might like:
Beverly Cleary, *Henry Huggins*, 1950
  Third grader Henry Huggins, a neighbor of Beezus and Ramona Quimby, meets his mutt Ribsy in the first of the books about this adventurous pair.
Betsy Duffey, *How to Be Cool in the Third Grade*, 1993
  Robbie's plans to be a cool third grader are challenged by an over-protective mother and the class bully.
Suzy Kline, *Song Lee in Room 2B*, 1993
  Miss Mackle's classroom has a new student, a shy Korean immigrant who understands the language of friendship.

340

BARRY DENENBERG

When Will This Cruel War Be Over? The Civil War Diary of Emma Simpson

(New York: Scholastic, 1996)

Series: Dear America
Subject(s): Civil War; Diaries
Age range(s): Grades 4-8
Major character(s): Emma Simpson, Writer (diarist), Southern Belle; Talliaferro ''Tally'' Mills, Military Personnel (soldier), Boyfriend; Aunt Caroline, Companion, Southern Belle
Time period(s): 1860s (1864)
Locale(s): Virginia

Summary: Emma keeps a diary of life on the plantation during the final year of the war. She receives word that her brother has been killed, but the family hears little from her father. Her mother becomes ill and dies, and her Aunt Caroline and Cousin Rachel stay at the plantation to keep her company. Emma writes of both the big events of the war and the little things that keep life going. She shares letters from Tally which give a view of the life of the Southern soldier. When the war is over, she and Tally will marry but others in her tale do not have such a happy fate. (152 pages)

Other books by the same author:
American Hero: The True Story of Charles A. Lindbergh, 1996
Voice from Vietnam, 1995
Stealing Home: The True Story of Jackie Robinson, 1990

Other books you might like:
Patricia Beatty, *Turn Homeward, Hannalee*, 1984
  A girl from a mill-working town faces a different kind of life than the plantation girls.
James Forman, *Becca's Story*, 1992
  A courtship between a girl in Michigan and a Yankee soldier is carried on during the Civil War.

Gloria Houston, *Mountain Valor*, 1994
  Valor defends her home when her father and brother go off to fight in the Civil War.
Irene Hunt, *Across Five Aprils*, 1964
  A young boy expriences the war from the backwoods of southern Illinois when one brother fights for the Union and the other for the South.

341

SUE DENIM
DAV PILKEY, Illustrator

The Dumb Bunnies' Easter

(New York: The Blue Sky Press, 1995)

Subject(s): Humor; Animals/Rabbits; Holidays
Age range(s): Grades K-2
Major character(s): Momma Bunny, Rabbit, Mother; Poppa Bunny, Rabbit, Father; Baby Bunny, Rabbit
Time period(s): Indeterminate
Locale(s): Fictional Country

Summary: On the evening of December 24th, the Bunny family begins preparing for Easter by chopping down a neighbor's tree to decorate, nailing valentines to the walls and spray-painting fried eggs. The Easter goodies are delivered by a red minivan pulled by eight pilgrims who surely would have enjoyed seeing the roast turkey carved like a jack o' lantern. Momma Bunny, Poppa Bunny and Baby Bunny are thrilled with their holiday and hope the next one will be even worse. (32 pages)

Where it's reviewed:
Booklist, February 1, 1995, page 1009
Horn Book Guide, Fall 1995, page 262
School Library Journal, February 1995, page 72

Other books by the same author:
The Dumb Bunnies Go to the Zoo, 1997
Make Way for Dumb Bunnies, 1996
The Dumb Bunnies, 1994

Other books you might like:
Harry Allard, *The Stupids Have a Ball*, 1984
  The Stupid family plans a big celebration when the children bring home terrible report cards.
Edward Marshall, *Space Case*, 1980
  A creature from outer space visits Earth on Halloween night.
Francesca Simon, *The Topsy-Turvies*, 1995
  The goofy Topsy-Turvy family does everything backwards—they sleep, fully dressed, in the kitchen and awaken at midnight to change into pajamas and eat diinner on their bed.

342

SHARON PHILLIPS DENSLOW
G. BRIAN KARAS, Illustrator

On the Trail with Miss Pace

(New York: Simon & Schuster Books for Young Readers, 1995)

Subject(s): Teachers; Twins; Vacations

Age range(s): Grades K-2
Major character(s): Miss Pace, Teacher; Phil Trimble, Twin, Student; Bill Trimble, Twin, Student
Time period(s): 1990s (1995)
Locale(s): Miss Penelope Bartlett's Ranch, West

Summary: Miss Pace bids good-bye to her students, her classroom, and her teaching reponsibilities before beginning her vacation at a western ranch. Imagine her surprise to discover Bill and Phil are vacationing in the same spot. Patiently, she endures their interest in seeing the teacher out of school without allowing them to spoil her summer plans. (32 pages)

Where it's reviewed:
Booklist, June 1995, page 1784
Children's Book Review Service, July 1995, page 146
Kirkus Reviews, May 1, 1995, page 632
Publishers Weekly, May 22, 1995, page 59
School Library Journal, June 1995, page 80

Other books by the same author:
Radio Boy, 1995
Bus Riders, 1993
Hazel's Circle, 1992

Other books you might like:
Paula Kurzband Feder, *Where Does the Teacher Live?*, 1979
    Three children try to answer the title's question and determine the location of their teacher's residence.
Judy Finchler, *Miss Malarkey Doesn't Live in Room 10*, 1995
    Assuming his teacher lives in her classroom and eats in the cafeteria, a child is surprised when she moves into his apartment building.
Stephen Krensky, *My Teacher's Secret Life*, 1996
    A child is surprised to see her teacher at the grocery store, shopping in the mall, and even relaxing at the park.
Robin Pulver, *Miss Toggle's Beautiful Blue Shoe*, 1994
    While playing kickball with her class, Mrs. Toggle sends her blue shoe sailing when she kicks the ball.

343

SHARON PHILLIPS DENSLOW
NANCY COTE, Illustrator

Woollybear Good-bye

(New York: Four Winds Press, 1994)

Subject(s): Animals/Insects; Schools; Moving, Household
Age range(s): Grades 1-3
Major character(s): Joe Dean Castleberry, 8-Year-Old; Miss Rosemary, Teacher; Brenda Houser, 3rd Grader
Time period(s): 1990s (1994)
Locale(s): United States

Summary: Joe Dean's class is stunned when he announces his family's upcoming move to Michigan. Fortunately he will leave at the end of Woolleybear Week, an annual competition between the grades to collect woolleybear caterpillars. On the morning of the last day of the contest, the 3rd and 4th grades are tied. At recess Brenda spots a woolleybear in Miss Rosemary's redbud tree and risks her teacher's displeasure by climbing the tree to retrieve the winning entry. (32 pages)

Where it's reviewed:
Horn Book Guide, Spring 1995, page 31

Language Arts, Summer 1995, page 370
School Library Journal, December 1994, page 73

Other books by the same author:
Radio Boy, 1995
Bus Riders, 1993
Hazel's Circle, 1992

Other books you might like:
Betsy James, *Mary Ann*, 1994
    When her friend Mary Ann moves, Amy names a praying mantis that she finds after her and keeps it all winter as a pet.
Kathryn Lasky, *Pond Year*, 1995
    Best friends enjoy the plant, animal and insect life in and around a pond as it changes with the seasons.
Megan McDonald, *Insects Are My Life*, 1995
    Amanda's interest in insects is not appreciated by anyone until she meets a new classmate.

344

SALLY DERBY
LEONID GORE, Illustrator

Jacob and the Stranger

(New York: Ticknor & Fields, 1994)

Subject(s): Animals/Cats; Magic; Fantasy
Age range(s): Grades 1-4
Major character(s): Jacob, Young Man (kind and honest), Unemployed (lazy); Unnamed Character, Wizard (stranger)
Time period(s): Indeterminate Past
Locale(s): Slavda, Fictional Country

Summary: Jacob is content to be the person he is, one who works only when necessary, ''not too much and not too hard,'' and stops when he has money in his pockets. When a stranger offers to pay him a florin a day for caring for a plant, Jacob thinks he has come upon easy money. As it turns out, the plant is a most unusual one whose blossoms yield diminutive wild cats. Jacob doesn't mind the extra work, but he is reluctant to give up the pets when the stranger returns, demanding all that is his and refusing to pay the 20 florins. Jacob may be lazy, but he's no fool and the stranger finds himself matching wits with an honest, determined young man. (32 pages)

Where it's reviewed:
Booklist, September 1, 1994, page 40
Children's Book Review Service, September 1994, page 7
Horn Book, September 1994, page 583
Kirkus Reviews, June 15, 1994, page 843
School Library Journal, September 1994, page 182

Other books by the same author:
King Kenrick's Splinter, 1994
The Mouse Who Owned the Sun, 1993

Other books you might like:
Lloyd Alexander, *The Cat Who Wished to Be a Man*, 1973
    In love with the innkeeper, Lionel, the wizard's cat, wants to be changed into human form.
Dick King-Smith, *The Queen's Nose*, 1983
    A magic coin which can grant seven wishes is given to Harmony, a 10-year-old animal lover.

Patricia MacLachlan, *Tomorrow's Wizard*, 1982
Six short stories about a wizard with the power to grant wishes and bestow curses show insight into human nature.

345

SALLY DERBY
LEONID GORE, Illustrator

King Kenrick's Splinter

(New York: Walker and Company, 1994)

Subject(s): Kings, Queens, Rulers, etc.; Fear; Teasing
Age range(s): Grades K-3
Major character(s): King Kenrick, Royalty; Gloria, Cook, Niece; Archibald, Uncle (Gloria's)
Time period(s): Indeterminate Past
Locale(s): Fictional Country

Summary: On the day he is to lead the Hero's Day Parade, King Kenrick awakens to find a splinter in his big toe. Timidly, he hobbles to breakfast in his slippers where Gloria insists her Uncle Archibald be called for a splinter extraction. Uncle Archibald teases King Kenrick by pulling pliers and a saw out of his bag so that, by the time the actual extraction begins, any procedure seems preferable to amputation. Fearful King Kenrick is relieved of the splinter so quickly he doesn't know it's been removed. (32 pages)

Where it's reviewed:
Booklist, November 1, 1994, page 506
Children's Book Review Service, December 1994, page 37
Kirkus Reviews, November 15, 1994, page 1527
Publishers Weekly, October 31, 1994, page 61
School Library Journal, January 1995, page 84

Awards the book has won:
International Reading Association Children's Choice, 1995

Other books by the same author:
The Mouse Who Owned the Sun, 1993

Other books you might like:
Charles C. Black, *The Royal Nap*, 1995
The king finds it a problem making his kingdom quiet enough to allow him his daily nap.
Amy MacDonald, *Rachel Fister's Blister*, 1990
When no one else has a solution, the Queen offers advice to cure Rachel Fister's blister.
M.L. Miller, *The Enormous Snore*, 1995
The problem of a snoring king is solved by Letty, a lost waif, who coincidentally finds her family about the same time the kingdom finds peace and quiet.

346

DEBORAH DURLAND DESAIX, Author/Illustrator

Returning Nicholas

(New York: Farrar Strauss Giroux, 1995)

Subject(s): Animals/Horses; Fantasy; Carnivals
Age range(s): Grades K-3
Major character(s): Antonia, Child; Nicholas, Horse; Magda, Gypsy
Time period(s): Indeterminate Past
Locale(s): United States

Summary: Antonia hurries to the carousel of a small carnival set up in a field near her home. The horse she selects magically comes to life, so the next day Antonia hurries back and chooses the same horse. This time, she rides longer and meets a group of gypsies who are grateful to have Nicholas returned. Magda tells Antonia her grandfather carves horses to make a carousel. The next day Antonia learns she was carried to another time when, as the carnival leaves town, the grown Magda presents Antonia with a small carving showing her astride the horse. (32 pages)

Where it's reviewed:
Children's Book Review Service, January 1996, page 49
Children's Bookwatch, November 1995, page 8
Kirkus Reviews, October 15, 1995, page 1489
Publishers Weekly, October 30, 1995, page 61
School Library Journal, January 1996, page 77

Other books by the same author:
In the Back Seat, 1993

Other books you might like:
Pat Cummings, *Carousel*, 1994
The small music-box carousel which Alex receives for her birthday comes to life at bedtime and takes her for a nighttime ride.
Liz Rosenberg, *The Carousel*, 1995
Two sisters take a fantastic ride on magical horses of a closed carousel.
Brian Wildsmith, *Carousel*, 1988
Confined to bed, a sick child imagines riding on her favorite merry-go-round.

347

WENDE DEVLIN

The Trouble with Henriette!

(New York: Simon & Schuster Books for Young Readers, 1995)

Subject(s): Animals/Dogs; Grandparents; Farm Life
Age range(s): Grades K-2
Major character(s): Henriette, Dog; Jolie, Child; Grandfather, Grandfather, Farmer
Time period(s): Indeterminate Past
Locale(s): Paris, France

Summary: Grandfather is adamant that a farm dog must earn its keep and Henriette, having lost the ability to sniff out truffles, must go. A very unhappy Jolie tries to explain that Henriette has hay fever from sleeping in the barn and needs to be allowed to sleep in the house again. The threesome travel to Paris to trade Henriette for a more useful pet when she leaps from the car and dashes into the Hotel Eclair creating quite a scene as hotel employees, Grandfather, and Jolie chase after her. By the time she has located a bowl of truffles in the dining hall, demonstrating that her nose still works, she has left a trail of spilled souffles, tarts and cream pies. But now Henriette can go back to her happy days of truffle hunting on the farm. (32 pages)

Where it's reviewed:
Booklist, May 15, 1995, page 1651

Bulletin of the Center for Children's Books, June 1995, page 341

Horn Book Guide, Fall 1995, page 262

Publishers Weekly, May 29, 1995, page 84

School Library Journal, September 1995, page 168

Other books by the same author:

Maggie Has a Nightmare, 1994

Cranberry Autumn, 1993

Cranberry Summer, 1992

Other books you might like:

Joanna Cole, *Give a Dog a Bone: Stories, Poems, Jokes, and Riddles about Dogs*, 1996

The illustrated compilation concludes with factual information explaining why dogs bark at "nothing." Co-compiler Stephanie Calmenson.

Diana Hendry, *Dog Donovan*, 1995

The fearful Donovan family acquires a dog who is so timid that soon all the family members forget their own fears while caring for the dog.

Dav Pilkey, *Dog Breath: The Horrible Trouble with Hally Tosis*, 1994

The Tosis family is ready to give away Hally until their pet's worst feature proves to be the undoing of two burglars.

348

PETER DICKINSON
KEES DE KIEFTE, Illustrator

Chuck and Danielle

(New York: Delacorte, 1996)

Subject(s): Animals/Dogs; Fear
Age range(s): Grades 3-5
Major character(s): Danielle, Child (girl); Chuck, Dog
Time period(s): 1990s
Locale(s): England

Summary: Chuck, a whippet, is afraid of everything, from stuffed animals to loud noises, but Danielle is certain that she will save the world one day. In this episodic book, the dog and her mistress face a number of problems during which Chuck reacts as any frightened dog would, but with surprising results, such as the time that she actually catches the robber and the time that she wins the obedience trials. (115 pages)

Where it's reviewed:

School Library Journal, February 1996, page 100

Bulletin of the Center for Children's Books, February 1996, page 189

Booklist, March 1, 1996, page 1178

Hornbook, September/October 1996, page 593

Awards the book has won:

Bulletin Blue Ribbon, 1996

Booklist Editors' Choice, 1996

Other books by the same author:

Time and the Clockmice, Etcetera, 1994

Eva, 1988

Merlin Dreams, 1988

Other books you might like:

Meindert De Jong, *Along Came a Dog*, 1958

A friendship develops between a very timid dog and a hen.

James Howe, *Return to Howliday Inn*, 1994

This is one of a series of books about several dogs and cats and their strange fears.

Phyllis Reynolds Naylor, *The Grand Escape*, 1993

Two cats face fear and overcome bullies and dogs during their time of freedom from their owners.

Janice Lee Smith, *It's Not Easy Being George*, 1989

George is an underachieving dog with a very active owner in this episodic story.

Ann Turner, *One Brave Summer*, 1995

A little girl learns how to overcome her fears.

349

PETER DICKINSON
EMMA CHICHESTER-CLARK, Illustrator

Time and the Clockmice, Etcetera

(New York: Delacorte Press, 1993)

Subject(s): Animals/Mice; Fantasy; Animals, Treatment of
Age range(s): Grades 3-5
Major character(s): Tracy Dickory, Mouse (clock mouse); Unnamed Character, Repairman (clock), Aged Person
Time period(s): 1990s (1993)
Locale(s): Branton, England

Summary: The grandson of the builder of the Branton Town Hall Clock is called on to repair it when, after 100 years, it stops functioning. As he begins his work, he discovers that the clock is inhabited by Clock Mice, an unknown breed, who have kept the clock running all these years. During the lengthy repair work, he communicates with the mice telepathically, especially Tracy who, as this generation's clock expert, is interested in learning all she can from the repairman. (128 pages)

Where it's reviewed:

Booklist, August 1994, page 2042

Horn Book Guide, Fall 1994, page 307

Kirkus Reviews, June 1, 1994, page 773

Publishers Weekly, April 25, 1994, page 78

School Library Journal, June 1994, page 126

Other books by the same author:

Chuck and Danielle, 1996

A Box of Nothing, 1988

Emma Tupper's Diary, 1988

Other books you might like:

Avi, *Poppy*, 1995

The courage of one young mouse improves life for her large family.

Peggy Christian, *The Bookstore Mouse*, 1995

The routine of life for the bookstore mouse shifts from dining on the delicious words in cookbooks to unexpected adventure when he stumbles into a very old book.

Dick King-Smith, *The School Mouse*, 1995

In the old school Flora lives as the first school mouse, taking advantage of the daily lessons and eventually using her literacy to save her family.

350

TERRANCE DICKS
BLANCHE SIMS, Illustrator

Nurse Sally Ann

(New York: Simon & Schuster Books for Young Readers, 1994)

Subject(s): Dolls and Dollhouses; Illness; Toys
Age range(s): Grades 2-3
Major character(s): Sally Ann, Toy (doll); Jane, Child (selfish and rude), Asthmatic
Time period(s): 1980s (1988)
Locale(s): England (St. Mary's Hospital for Children)

Summary: When Jane has an asthma attack, she is rushed to the hospital with Sally Ann inadvertently accompanying her. Fortunately, Sally Ann has more manners than Jane and uses her social skills to try and improveJane's disposition so that she can make friends. Originally published in Great Britain in 1988. (60 pages)

Where it's reviewed:
Booklist, July 1994, page 1942
Horn Book Guide, Fall 1994, page 300
School Library Journal, August 1994, page 128

Other books by the same author:
Sally Ann and the Mystery Picnic, 1993
Sally Ann and the School Show, 1992
Sally Ann on Her Own, 1992

Other books you might like:
Michael Bond, *A Bear Called Paddington*, 1960
    A young bear is found at Paddington station by the Brown family and begins his humorous adventures.
Johnny Gruelle, *Raggedy Ann's Magical Wishes*, 1928
    One of several stories about a rag doll, Raggedy Ann, the series has long been a favorite of children.
Margery Williams, *The Velveteen Rabbit*, 1926
    A toy rabbit is so loved by a little boy that the rabbit, in time, becomes real.

351

HARRIETT DILLER
CHI CHUNG, Illustrator

The Waiting Day

(New York: Green Tiger Press, 1994)

Subject(s): Conduct of Life; Transportation; Rivers
Age range(s): Grades K-3
Major character(s): Unnamed Character, Aged Person (beggar); Unnamed Character, Worker (ferryman)
Time period(s): Indeterminate Past
Locale(s): China

Summary: As a ferryman readies for a day of transporting customers across the river he notices an elderly beggar sitting on the river bank. Assuming that the man is waiting for a free ride, the ferryman busies himself with the important people seeking his services, catering to their whims yet never satisfying their demands. As the day draws to a close the tired ferryman confronts the beggar and learns that the man has sat

in one spot all day patiently waiting to see the sunset and, as soon as he does, he goes home satisfied. (30 pages)

Where it's reviewed:
Booklist, November 15, 1994, page 610
Horn Book Guide, Spring 1995, page 32
School Library Journal, December 1994, page 73

Other books by the same author:
Grandaddy's Highway, 1993

Other books you might like:
Demi, *The Magic Boat*, 1990
    Tricked by wicked Ying, Chang enlists the help of his friend to help him win back his magic boat.
Rosalind C. Wang, *The Fourth Question*, 1991
    The story of Yee-Lee demonstrates that kindness is rewarded.
Jane Yolen, *The Emperor and the Kite*, 1967
    The oft-forgotten, smallest daughter of the emperor uses her kite to save her father from his tower prison.

352

DYANNE DISALVO-RYAN, Author/Illustrator

City Green

(New York: Morrow Junior Books, 1994)

Subject(s): Gardens and Gardening; City Life; Neighbors and Neighborhoods
Age range(s): Grades K-3
Major character(s): Marcy, Child, Activist; Miss Rosa, Aged Person, Neighbor; Old Man Hammer, Aged Person, Neighbor
Time period(s): 1990s (1994)
Locale(s): United States

Summary: After a building is torn down on Marcy's street, the empty lot accumulates garbage and litter. On the positive side, it is also full of dirt so Marcy and Miss Rosa decide they will plant a garden in the empty lot. They petition the neighbors and the city and soon even crabby Old Man Hammer is involved in the restoration of the neighborhood eyesore. (32 pages)

Where it's reviewed:
Booklist, November 15, 1994, page 611
Bulletin of the Center for Children's Books, September 1994, page 10
Kirkus Reviews, August 15, 1994, page 1125
Publishers Weekly, June 20, 1994, page 105
School Library Journal, September 1994, page 183

Other books by the same author:
Uncle Willie and the Soup Kitchen, 1991

Other books you might like:
Pat Brisson, *Wanda's Roses*, 1994
    When Wanda cleans up a littered vacant lot, the neighbors also take an interest and bring her rosebushes to plant.
Mary Louise Cuneo, *How to Grow a Picket Fence*, 1993
    An imaginative child demonstrates how to gather ingredients to grow a picket fence in an empty lot.
Arthur A. Levine, *Pearl Moscowitz's Last Stand*, 1993
    When elderly Pearl learns that the last tree on her street is

to be cut down, she becomes an environmental activist and, with support from her neighbors, saves the tree.

353

GARRY DISHER

The Bamboo Flute
(New York: Ticknor & Fields, 1993)

Subject(s): Music; Depression (Economic)
Age range(s): Grades 4-6
Major character(s): Paul, 12-Year-Old, 7th Grader; Eric the Red, Streetperson
Time period(s): 1930s (1932)
Locale(s): Tarlee, Australia

Summary: Over the last few years, Paul feels the music float out of his life. His father used to whistle and his mother used to play the piano, but now that his country's in the middle of a depression, there's no more music. Homeless men, called swagmen, roam the countryside and Paul's warned to stay away from them, warnings he ignores when he meets Eric the Red. Eric plays the flute and from him, Paul learns to carve and play a bamboo flute, bringing music back into his life. When he plays for his parents, his father finally shares with him some of his own carvings. (82 pages)

Where it's reviewed:
Publishers Weekly, June 28, 1993, page 79
School Library Journal, September 1993, page 229
Booklist, September 1, 1993, page 60
New York Times Book Review, April 24, 1994, page 24
Horn Book, January 1994, page 69

Other books by the same author:
Ratface, 1994

Other books you might like:
Jim Anderson, *Billarooby*, 1988
    Lindsay and his family eke out a living on dry, parched Australia land during the 1940s.
Sue Ellen Bridgers, *Home before Dark*, 1976
    When Stella and her migrant farm family return to her father's childhood Florida home, she never wants to leave its safety.
Rhea Beth Ross, *Hillbilly Choir*, 1991
    Laurie's singing ability provides her an opportunity to leave her small town during the Depression years.

354

BILL DODDS

My Sister Annie
(Honesdale, PA: Boyds Mill Press, 1993)

Subject(s): Mentally Handicapped; Down Syndrome
Age range(s): Grades 4-7
Major character(s): Charlie, 6th Grader; Annie, 13-Year-Old, Mentally Challenged Person (Down Syndrome)
Time period(s): 1990s
Locale(s): United States

Summary: The difficulty of having a handicapped sibling is felt by Charlie as he approaches middle school. While his problems of pitching a good game or taking a special girl to the dance or joining a club called the Bombers are similar to concerns all his peers have, overriding everything is Annie, his older sister who has Down Syndrome. Charlie is ashamed of Annie's loudness and the fact she always calls him Chuckie. It takes some understanding friends and coaches before Charlie can see how special his sister really is. (94 pages)

Where it's reviewed:
School Library Journal, February 1993, page 92
Booklist, February 15, 1993, page 1059
Children's Book Review Service, March 1993, page 92
Kirkus Reviews, December 15, 1992, page 1571
Horn Book Guide, Fall 1993, page 296

Other books by the same author:
The Hidden Fortune, 1991

Other books you might like:
Hazel Krantz, *For Love of Jeremy*, 1990
    Having a younger brother with Down Syndrome has upset Wendy's family.
Colby Rodowsky, *What about Me?*, 1989
    Dorrie resents the attention her younger brother receives just because he has Down Syndrome.
June Rae Wood, *The Man Who Loved Clowns*, 1992
    After her parents die, Delrita learns not to feel ashamed about her kind, loving Uncle Punky who has Down Syndrome.

355

BERLIE DOHERTY
CHRISTIAN BIRMINGHAM, Illustrator

The Magic Bicycle
(New York: Crown Publishers, Inc., 1995)

Subject(s): Bicycles and Bicycling; Dreams and Nightmares; Determination
Age range(s): Grades K-2
Major character(s): Unnamed Character, Child
Time period(s): 1990s (1995)
Locale(s): United States

Summary: Only in his dreams can a young boy successfully ride his shiny, new bicycle; his waking attempts all end in falls. Once he decides that success must be dependent on some kind of magic, the youngster is able to find the magic within himself and ride! (32 pages)

Where it's reviewed:
Booklist, October 15, 1995, page 410
Horn Book Guide, Spring 1996, page 25
Junior Bookshelf, October 1995, page 168
School Library Journal, December 1995, page 79

Other books by the same author:
Snowy, 1993

Other books you might like:
Marc Brown, *D.W. Rides Again!*, 1993
    With help from brother Arthur, D. W. learns to ride her new two-wheeler and proves to her father that she no longer needs training wheels.

Crescent Dragonwagon, *Annie Flies the Birthday Bike*, 1993
Persistent Annie succeeds in learning to ride her new bike so she can ''fly'' down the steep hill in front of her home with the other riders.

Donna Jakob, *My Bike*, 1994
First-time author Jakob portrays the determination and excitement of the new bike rider.

356

BERLIE DOHERTY
KEITH BOWEN, Illustrator

Snowy

(New York: Dial Books for Young Readers, 1993)

Subject(s): Animals/Horses; School Life; Pets
Age range(s): Grades K-2
Major character(s): Rachel, Child; Snowy, Horse; Miss Smith, Teacher
Time period(s): 1990s (1993)
Locale(s): England

Summary: To young Rachel, the best thing about living on a canal barge is Snowy, the big, white workhorse who pulls the barge. Rachel thinks of him as her pet and is upset when her mother does not allow Snowy to go to school for pet day. Fortunately, Rachel's parents and her understanding teacher devise a plan that enables Rachel to share her unique pet and home with the class. First published in Great Britain in 1992. (32 pages)

Where it's reviewed:
Booklist, December 15, 1992, page 745
Horn Book, January 1993, page 74
Kirkus Reviews, January 1, 1993, page 59
School Librarian, May 1993, page 54
School Library Journal, February 1993, page 72

Other books you might like:
Shari Halpern, *I Have a Pet!*, 1994
Eager children, unusual pets, and an understanding judge—this pet contest is a winner!
Marguerite Henry, *Five O'Clock Charlie*, 1962
Now retired from farm work, Charlie misses his more active life and especially his daily treats.
Scott Russell Sanders, *The Floating House*, 1995
In the early 1800s Jonathan and Mary live on a house floating down the Ohio River to a new life.

357

BERLIE DOHERTY
KIM LEWIS, Illustrator

Willa and Old Miss Annie

(Cambridge, MA: Candlewick Press, 1994)

Subject(s): Moving, Household; Friendship; Animals, Treatment of
Age range(s): Grades 2-4
Major character(s): Willa, Child; Miss Annie, Aged Person, Neighbor
Time period(s): 1990s (1994)

Locale(s): England

Summary: Poor lonely Willa moves far away from her best friend and at her new home a ''ghost'' in the neighbor's yard cries all night. When she meets the neighbor, old Miss Annie, Willa is initially frightened by her appearance, but she soons responds to Miss Annie's kindness and meets her ''ghost'' who turns out to be a lonely goat. Together, Willa and Miss Annie find friends for the lonely goat, save an abused pony, and meet an orphaned fox. (92 pages)

Where it's reviewed:
Booklist, July 1994, page 1947
Horn Book, September 1994, page 586
Kirkus Reviews, May 1, 1994, page 628
The New Advocate, Fall 1994, page 285
School Library Journal, July 1994, page 76

Awards the book has won:
Notable Children's Books in the Language Arts, 1995

Other books by the same author:
Street Child, 1994
Old Father Christmas, 1993

Other books you might like:
Maggie Harrison, *Lizzie's List*, 1993
Lizzie makes a list of individuals ''missing'' from her single-parent family, then finds a surrogate Grandmother to help her locate the other ''missing'' family members.
Karen Hesse, *Sable*, 1994
Tate wants desperately to keep the stray dog that wanders into the yard of her mountain home, but first she must demonstrate the ability to care for it responsibly.
Dick King-Smith, *The Stray*, 1996
A family with five children offers friendship and shelter to Henny Hickathrift who has run away from an old people's home.

358

JOHN DONAHUE

An Island Far from Home

(Minneapolis: Carolrhoda Books, 1994)

Subject(s): Civil War; Historical; Friendship
Age range(s): Grades 6-7
Major character(s): Joshua Loring, 12-Year-Old; Major Robert Pennington, Military Personnel; John Meadows, 14-Year-Old, Military Personnel (POW)
Time period(s): 1960s (1964)
Locale(s): Tilton, Massachusetts

Summary: Joshua's father is killed at the Battle of Fredericksburg and Joshua hopes the war won't end before he's old enough to enlist and avenge his father's death. His uncle, Major Pennington, is in charge of prisoners at the POW Camp at George's Island and asks Joshua to write to a lonely, frightened boy a few years older than him. Joshua wants nothing to do with this Union soldier, but for his uncle's sake he finally writes a letter to John. Their correspondence leads not only to a better understanding of one another but also a dangerous plan to meet at the prison camp. (179 pages)

Where it's reviewed:
Booklist, February 15, 1995, page 1083
School Library Journal, February 1995, page 98
Curriculum Review, January 1995, page 13

Other books you might like:
Patricia Polacco, *Pink and Say*, 1994
 Though one soldier is black and the other white and they fight on opposite sides in the Civil War, the lives of Pink and Say are forever linked.
Carolyn Reeder, *Shades of Gray*, 1989
 Orphaned Will Page has a hard time living with his Uncle Jed knowing that Jed didn't fight for either side in the Civil War that killed his father.
G. Clifton Wisler, *Red Cap*, 1991
 Young Union drummer, Ransom J. Powell, who lies about his age to join the army, is one of the few to survive the rigors of Andersonville Prison.

359

N.B. DORMAN

Petey and Miss Magic

(Hamden, Connecticut: Linnet Books, 1993)

Subject(s): Pets; Family Life; Schools
Age range(s): Grades 3-5
Major character(s): Petey, Child (poor and shy); Miss Magic, Worm (Petey's pet)
Time period(s): 1990s (1993)
Locale(s): United States

Summary: Although Petey longs for a pet, he knows he can never have one because his family is too poor, his sister has allergies, and the landlord evicts families with pets. A school assignment to write a paper about a pet creates a dilemma which Petey solves by finding an earthworm at the park. Miss Magic resides in a jar and, despite protests from other family members, is allowed to be Petey's pet. The effort which Petey puts into his class assignment and the uniqueness of his pet win Petey more attention than he ever imagined. (99 pages)

Where it's reviewed:
Horn Book Guide, Fall 1993, page 296
Kirkus Reviews, February 1, 1993, page 145
Publishers Weekly, April 5, 1993, page 79
School Library Journal, March 1993, page 196

Other books you might like:
Beverly Cleary, *Strider*, 1991
 Although the home he shares with his mother does not allow pets, Leigh makes room for an abandoned dog which he and friend Barry have found.
Pat Hutchins, *Rats!*, 1989
 Finally gaining consent from his parents to have a rat for a pet, Sam must now face the consequences when Nibbles arrives.
Elsie McCutcheon, *The Rat War*, 1986
 Life in postwar Britain is lonely for one shy boy until he befriends a rat and claims it as his pet.

360

MICHAEL DORRIS

Guests

(New York: Hyperion/Disney, 1994)

Subject(s): Coming of Age; Historical; Indians of North America
Age range(s): Grades 6-7
Major character(s): Moss, Indian; Trouble, Indian
Time period(s): Indeterminate Past
Locale(s): United States

Summary: Moss is out of sorts because his parents invite strangers who don't speak their language to be guests at their once-a-year harvest feast. Unable to convince his parents to uninvite these strangers, and not wanting to be part of the festivities, Moss runs away to the woods. There he meets Trouble, a young girl who feels even more out of touch with her family than Moss does. Gradually he understands himself better and, when he returns for the feast, realizes that the guests don't want to be at the feast either in this introspective coming of age story. (119 pages)

Where it's reviewed:
Horn Book, January 1995, page 58
Publishers Weekly, September 5, 1994, page 111
Kirkus Reviews, August 15, 1994, page 1125
Quill & Quire, September 1994, page 75
Tribune Books (Chicago), August 14, 1994, page 7

Other books by the same author:
Morning Girl, 1992
A Yellow Raft in Blue Water, 1987

Other books you might like:
J. Alison James, *Sing for a Gentle Rain*, 1990
 The songs of Spring Rain call James back in time to her Anasazi village where they overcome time and language barriers and fall in love.
Scott O'Dell, *Thunder Rolling in the Mountains*, 1992
 Sound of Running Feet, daughter of Chief Joseph, describes her people's defeat by the white man. Elizabeth Hall is the co-author.
John Ruemmler, *Smoke on the Water*, 1992
 Thomas and Eagle Owl meet for the third time when Eagle Owl rescues Thomas after the Powhatan Indians massacre the Jamestown colonists.

361

MICHAEL DORRIS

Sees Behind Trees

(New York: Hyperion, 1996)

Subject(s): Indians of North America; Blind; Physically Handicapped
Age range(s): Grades 4-8
Major character(s): Walnut "Sees Behind Trees", Indian, Blind; Gray Fire, Indian, Handicapped; Checha, Indian, Child
Time period(s): Indeterminate Past (before the time of Pocahontas)

Locale(s): Virginia (near the site of Jamestown)

Summary: Walnut tries to succeed with his bow and arrows but is so near-sighted that he cannot shoot well. His uncle suggests that he work on his other senses and he soon learns to hear and recognize people coming before they can be seen. He is asked by Gray Fire to accompany him in finding a site that he once visited and where his foot was injured. The two go off into the wilderness and come upon a family living alone in the woods. Staying with them for a brief time, Walnut, now called ''Sees Behind Trees'', finds the lake Gray Fire is looking for. It is there Gray Fire wishes to die so the boy must find his way home alone. On the way, he discovers the cabin has been destroyed and finds the child, Checha all alone. He takes the child with him as he finds his way home. (104 pages)

Where it's reviewed:

School Library Journal, October 1996, page 120
Booklist, September 15, 1996, page 239
Horn Book, September/October 1996, page 594
Bulletin of the Center for Children's Books, January 1997, page 168

Awards the book has won:

Booklist Editors' Choice, 1996
School Library Journal Best Books, 1996

Other books by the same author:

Guests, 1994
Morning Girl, 1992

Other books you might like:

Mary Louise Clifford, *When the Great Canoes Came*, 1993
    Life in Virginia when the settlers come through the eyes of the Indians.
John Ruemmler, *Smoke on the Water*, 1992
    A young English boy and the son of the Powhatan chief are caught up in the animosity of the peoples near Jameston in 1622.
Ruth Yaffe Radin, *Carver*, 1990
    Blind and fatherless since the age of two, Jon struggles to fit into his new school and learn the wood carving he loves.
Peter Roop, *Ahyoka and the Talking Leaves*, 1992
    Ahyoka follows her father in developing a language for the Cherokee.
Gloria Whelan, *Hannah*, 1991
    A blind girl living in Michigan in the late 19th century doesn't go to school until a teacher comes to live with and encourage her.

362

ARTHUR DORROS
ELISA KLEVEN, Illustrator

Isla

(New York: Dutton Children's Books, 1995)

Subject(s): Islands; Imagination; Hispanic Americans
Age range(s): Grades K-2
Major character(s): Abuela, Grandmother, Storyteller; Rosalba, Child
Time period(s): 1990s (1995)
Locale(s): New York, New York; Caribbean

Summary: In a sequel to *Abuela*, Rosalba is listening to one of her grandmother's stories. Abuela is such a gifted storyteller that Rosalba feels as if she's been transported with Abuela to her mother's childhood island home. She meets many relatives and enjoys a day of tropical island life. Using the stars as guides, Abuela and Rosalba fly home to New York when day is done. A concluding glossary provides definitions and a pronunciation guide for the Spanish words sprinkled throughout the test. (40 pages)

Where it's reviewed:

Booklist, November 1, 1995, page 476
Horn Book, March 1996, page 230
Kirkus Reviews, October 1, 1995, page 1426
Publishers Weekly, October 9, 1995, page 84
School Library Journal, September 1995, page 168

Other books by the same author:

Radio Man = Don Radio: A Story in English and Spanish, 1993
Abuela, 1991
Tonight Is Carnaval, 1991

Other books you might like:

Phillis Gershator, *Rata-Pata-Scata-Fata: A Caribbean Story*, 1994
    Junjun, a daydreamer, uses a magic phrase in order to get his chores completed with minimal effort.
Lynn Joseph, *Coconut Kind of Day: Island Poems*, 1990
    Poems describe the daily life of a young girl in the Caribbean.
Frane Lessac, *My Little Island*, 1984
    With a friend, a young boy visits the Caribbean island of his birth.
Faith Ringgold, *Tar Beach*, 1991
    In her dreams, Cassie Louise Lightfoot flies over New York and imagines the future.

363

ARTHUR DORROS, Author/Illustrator

Radio Man = Don Radio: A Story in English and Spanish

(New York: HarperCollins Publishers, 1993)

Subject(s): Migrant Labor; Mexican Americans; Family Life
Age range(s): Grades 1-4
Major character(s): Diego, Child (migrant); David, Child (migrant)
Time period(s): 1990s (1993)
Locale(s): United States

Summary: As Diego's family follows the crops, he is never without his radio which not only provides entertainment, but also serves as a compass to help him know the town his family is approaching. In each town Diego finds relatives or friends that he may not have seen in some time, but he does not find David until he uses a call-in radio program to get his message over the air. Each page carries the text in both English and Spanish, translated by Sandra Marulanda Dorros. (40 pages)

Where it's reviewed:

Booklist, January 15, 1994, page 924
Five Owls, January 1994, page 61

Horn Book Guide, Spring 1994, page 114
Library Talk, March 1994, page 33
Publishers Weekly, September 27, 1993, page 63

Awards the book has won:
Consortium of Latin American Studies Programs Commended Book, 1993

Other books by the same author:
Tonight Is Carnaval, 1991
Me and My Shadow, 1990
Rainforest Secrets, 1990

Other books you might like:
Linda Jacobs Altman, *Amelia's Road*, 1993
  The frequent moves of her migrant labor family make Amelia long for stability.
Jane Resh Thomas, *Lights on the River*, 1994
  While watching the work in the fields, Teresa thinks of her grandmother far away in the family village in Mexico.
Sherley Anne Williams, *Working Cotton*, 1992
  Shelan is proud of the work she and her family do laboring in the cotton fields.

364

CRESCENT DRAGONWAGON
EMILY ARNOLD MCCULLY, Illustrator

Annie Flies the Birthday Bike

(New York: Macmillan Publishing Company, 1993)

Subject(s): Bicycles and Bicycling; Birthdays
Age range(s): Grades K-2
Major character(s): Annie, Child
Time period(s): 1990s (1993)
Locale(s): United States

Summary: Eager to ''fly'' on a bike just like the older children who zoom down the hill in front of her home, Annie is thrilled to receive a new two-wheeler for her birthday. Soon she learns that mastering the bike requires patience and determination. One day, Annie experiences the pleasure of her bike as well as the pain of a fall as she, too, ''flies'' down the hill. (32 pages)

Where it's reviewed:
Booklist, March 1, 1993, page 1234
Children's Book Review Service, May 1993, page 112
Horn Book Guide, Fall 1993, page 256
Kirkus Reviews, March 15, 1993, page 370
School Library Journal, July 1993, page 59

Other books by the same author:
Home Place, 1990
I Hate My Sister Maggie, 1989
Always, Always, 1984

Other books you might like:
Stan Berenstain, *The Bike Lesson*, 1964
  A gift of a new bike comes with Dad's special lessons, but a little bear manages to ride a two-wheeler anyway. Jan Berenstain, co-author.
Marc Brown, *D.W. Rides Again!*, 1993
  With help from her brother Arthur, D.W. learns to ride her new two-wheeler and proves to her father that she no longer needs training wheels.
Donna Jakob, *My Bike*, 1994
  First-time author Jakob portrays the determination and excitement of the new bike rider.

365

HENRIK DRESCHER, Author/Illustrator

The Boy Who Ate Around

(New York: Hyperion Books for Children, 1994)

Subject(s): Monsters; Food; Fantasy
Age range(s): Grades 1-3
Major character(s): Mo, Child
Time period(s): 1990s (1994)
Locale(s): Earth

Summary: Seated at the dinner table facing a plate of string beans and cheese souffle which, to Mo, are really lizard guts and bullfrog heads, Mo decides that in order to avoid this plate of food he must eat around it. Mo changes into one monster after another, eating ever larger things as the monsters increase in size until only Mo, as an overstuffed monster tyrannosaurus rat, is left hanging from the moon, looking at the plate of string beans and souffle. (32 pages)

Where it's reviewed:
Booklist, November 1, 1994, page 506
Horn Book, September 1994, page 574
Library Talk, January 1995, page 36
Publishers Weekly, October 10, 1994, page 70
School Library Journal, October 1994, page 88

Other books by the same author:
Who's Furry Nose?, 1987
Simon's Book, 1983

Other books you might like:
Robert Bender, *A Most Unusual Lunch*, 1994
  As various animals eat their way up the food chain, each takes on characteristics of the animal just eaten, until the lion, offended by his new appearance, belches.
David McPhail, *The Glerp*, 1972
  As the glerp walks he eats everything in his path until the elephant's tusks become stuck and cause the glerp to cough.
J. Otto Seibold, *Mr. Lunch Takes a Plane Ride*, 1993
  The wacky illustrations compliment the silly story of a dog, riding in the baggage compartment of a plane, who explores the luggage and doesn't repack things as he found them.
Chung-Feng Sun, *On a White Pebble Hill*, 1994
  While seated at the dinner table a young girl takes an imaginary trip through the lake (noodle soup) and across the roasted chicken mountain.

366

MALKA DRUCKER
MICHAEL HALPERIN, Co-Author

Jacob's Rescue: A Holocaust Story
(New York: Bantam/Skylark, 1993)

Subject(s): Holocaust; World War II; Jews
Age range(s): Grades 5-7
Major character(s): Jacob ''Genyek'' Gutgeld, Child; Alex Roslan, Hero; David Gutgeld, Child
Time period(s): 1930s (1939); 1940s
Locale(s): Warsaw, Poland

Summary: During the Second World War, Jewish children, Jacob and his younger brother David, are hidden by Gentile Alex Roslan and his family. Sent to live in the Warsaw Ghetto, Jacob's parents fear daily that Jacob and his brother will be taken away. The two brothers must adapt to living in fear of discovery, hiding,in small spaces, even inside a couch, and at the end of the war, being sent away from the Roslans, whom they now consider as their parents. This fictionalized account of a true event reveals the risks people took during the war to help one another. (119 pages)

Where it's reviewed:
Booklist, February 15, 1993, page 1051
School Library Journal, May 1993, page 104
Voice of Youth Advocates, June 1993, page 88
Horn Book, September 1993, page 596
Pubishers Weekly, May 10, 1993, page 72

Other books by the same author:
The Family Treasury of Jewish Holidays, 1994
Frida Kahlo: Torment and Triumph in Her Life and Art, 1991

Other books you might like:
James Forman, *Survivor*, 1976
    Though David's family hides in an abandoned windmill, they are found and shipped to Auschwitz.
Anne Frank, *The Diary of Anne Frank*,
    Anne's diary covers the years she hides from the Nazis in an Amsterdam warehouse. (biography)
Lois Lowry, *Number the Stars*, 1989
    Annemarie, a Danish youth, and her family join the Resistance Movement to save Jews during World War II.
Ida Vos, *Anna Is Still Here*, 1993
    During World War II, Anna hides for three years in an attic and can't speak above a whisper when the war ends.

367

BETSY DUFFEY

Coaster
(New York: Viking, 1994)

Subject(s): Amusement Parks; Divorce; Single Parent Families
Age range(s): Grades 6-8
Major character(s): Hartwell ''Hart'' Patterson, 12-Year-Old; Frankie Cambardella, 12-Year-Old
Time period(s): 1990s
Locale(s): United States

Summary: Recently Hart's life has been filled with as many ups and downs as his favorite amusement park ride, a roller coaster. Since his parents' divorce two years ago, Hart and his dad see each other infrequently, and then usually just to try different roller coasters. His mother's dating a nerdy weatherman who took Hart to an amusement park, but got motion sickness at the thought of the roller coaster. Hart's so intrigued with roller coasters that he and his friend Frankie build one in the woods. As the time for his annual roller coaster ride with his father approaches, he and Frankie prepare to ride their own coaster, with disastrous results. (114 pages)

Where it's reviewed:
Booklist, August 1994, page 2042
Horn Book, January 1995, page 58
Kirkus Reviews, August 15, 1994, page 1125
School Library Journal, September 1994, page 214
Voice of Youth Advocates, April 1995, page 22

Awards the book has won:
ALA Recommended Books for the Reluctant Young Adult Reader, 1995

Other books by the same author:
Utterly Yours, Booker Jones, 1995
A Boy in the Doghouse, 1991
The Math Wiz, 1990

Other books you might like:
Marion Dane Bauer, *Face to Face*, 1991
    A white water rafting trip to reunite Michael with his father proves disastrous, but shows Michael the worth of his down-to-earth stepfather.
Richard Peck, *Unfinished Portrait of Jessica*, 1991
    At first angry with her mother because her father leaves them, Jessica calms down after a visit to her artist father in Mexico reveals his seamy side.
Barbara Wersba, *Run Softly, Go Fast*, 1970
    Nothing Davey does is right in his father's eyes, even when he tries to reconcile their love-hate relationship.

368

BETSY DUFFEY
ELLEN THOMPSON, Illustrator

Hey, New Kid!
(New York: Viking, 1996)

Subject(s): Schools; Moving, Household; Friendship
Age range(s): Grades 2-4
Major character(s): Cody Michaels, 3rd Grader; Ms. Harvey, Teacher; Holly, 3rd Grader
Time period(s): 1990s
Locale(s): United States

Summary: When Cody starts at a new school, he decides that his life has been too boring and starts making up all kinds of stories about his past, telling the others that he once lived in Alaska, owned an emu for a pet, and was a champion skater. The other kids are impressed but Cody finds it difficult to keep up with his lies. He discovers that all his information about emus is wrong and his lack of skating skills lands him in the girl's room at the rink. In the end he realizes that he doesn't have to be special to make friends. (89 pages)

Where it's reviewed:
Booklist, April 1, 1996, page 1362
School Library Journal, April 1996, page 132
Horn Book, July/August 1996, page 461

Other books by the same author:
Utterly Yours, Booker Jones, 1995
Coaster, 1994
The Gadget War, 1991

Other books you might like:
Jacqueline Turner Banks, *Egg-Drop Blues*, 1995
Twin boys work together on a science competition, although one is not sure this is really what he wants to do.
Johanna Hurwitz, *Ali Baba Bernstein, Lost and Found*, 1992
Ali Baba improves his lifestyle by becoming a detective and finding a dog.
Suzy Kline, *Horrible Harry and the Kickball Wedding*, 1992
Harry wants to plan the kick ball game but finds himself in a wedding with Song Lee.
Barbara Park, *The Kid in the Red Jacket*, 1987
Moving to a new town and making friends is hard to do, especially when the little girl next door wants to be your friend.

369

BETSY DUFFEY
JANET WILSON, Illustrator

How to Be Cool in the Third Grade

(New York: Viking, 1993)

Subject(s): Schools; Bullies; Self-Perception
Age range(s): Grades 2-4
Major character(s): Robert Hayes ''Robbie'' York, 3rd Grader; Clyde Elmer ''Bo'' Haney, 3rd Grader, Bully, Student (underachiever); Doug Daniels, 3rd Grader, Friend (Robbie's)
Time period(s): 1990s (1993)
Locale(s): United States (Danville School)

Summary: Entering third grade means a lot to Robert Hayes York. This is the year he wants to be cool, dump his nickname, Robbie, and wear jeans like the other kids. Implementing his plan is not easy with a mother who buys him a Pretty Pony ruler, Super Hero underwear and, worst of all, walks him to the school bus and takes pictures and kisses him in front of all the other kids! Although he's placed in a class with his good friend Doug, he's also in the same class as Bo, the meanest kid in school. When the teacher assigns Robbie to be Bo's ''Book Buddy,'' he's sure his life is over. In fact, the experience teaches him some understanding for Bo and helps him learn more about himself and how to achieve his goal of being cool in the third grade. (69 pages)

Where it's reviewed:
Booklist, September 1, 1993, page 72
Horn Book Guide, Spring 1994, page 75
Library Talk, January 1994, page 43
Reading Teacher, September 1994, page 70
School Library Journal, September 1993, page 206

Other books by the same author:
Lucky Christmas, 1994

The Wild Things, 1993
Puppy Love, 1992

Other books you might like:
Beverly Cleary, *Henry Huggins*, 1950
Third grader Henry Huggins, a neighbor of Beezus and Ramona Quimby, meets his mutt Ribsy in the first of the books about this adventurous pair.
Patricia Reilly Giff, *The Beast in Ms. Rooney's Room*, 1984
One of 12 titles in ''The Kids in the Polk Street School'' series, this one features Richard ''Beast'' Best.
Johanna Hurwitz, *The Up & Down Spring*, 1993
During vacation Rory and Derek travel to Bolivia's home for a visit that has some unexpected surprises.
Suzy Kline, *Song Lee in Room 2B*, 1993
The daily events in a 2nd grade classroom are enlivened with the arrival of a Korean immigrant who demonstrates that friendship can overcome language barriers.

370

BETSY DUFFEY
SUSANNA NATTI, Illustrator

Throw-Away Pets

(New York: Viking, 1993)

Series: Pet Patrol
Subject(s): Pets; Animals, Treatment of; Friendship
Age range(s): Grades 2-4
Major character(s): Evie, Student (Megan's friend); Megan, Student (Evie's friend)
Time period(s): 1990s (1993)
Locale(s): Douglasville

Summary: The deadline for a science project looms, but Evie and Megan have more urgent business—saving abandoned pets too old for adoption. The animal shelter attendant gives the girls 24 hours to find homes before the pets are destroyed. With teamwork and ingenuity, Evie and Megan manage to complete a blue-ribbon winning science project and save the animals. (80 pages)

Where it's reviewed:
Booklist, July 1993, page 1966
Horn Book Guide, Spring 1994, page 65
School Library Journal, September 1993, page 206

Other books by the same author:
Lucky on the Loose, 1993
Lucky in Left Field, 1992
A Boy in the Doghouse, 1991

Other books you might like:
Helen Cresswell, *Meet Posy Bates*, 1992
Posy tries to convince her mother that she should be allowed to have a pet.
N.B. Dorman, *Petey and Miss Magic*, 1993
Over his parents' objections, Petey finally finds an acceptable pet for an apartment.
Jerry Spinelli, *The Bathwater Gang Gets Down to Business*, 1992
The gang has an idea for a pet-washing business so Bertie dirties a few pets in an attempt to make the plan more successful.

371

BETSY DUFFEY

Utterly Yours, Booker Jones

(New York: Viking, 1995)

Subject(s): Authorship; Grandparents; Family Life
Age range(s): Grades 4-6
Major character(s): Booker Jones, Writer, 12-Year-Old; Pop, Grandfather (Booker's grandfather)
Time period(s): 1990s
Locale(s): Pickle Springs, Arkansas

Summary: Living under the dining room table is a little unusual, but then Booker's always been a little unusual. At the moment he's suffering from writer's block which began when he had to give up his bedroom to his grandfather, whose broken hip makes him a permanent resident of the Jones's family. Booker hopes that his first published work will be his science fiction adventure *Space Cows*, but work on that is at a standstill. For the moment, he must prepare a speech for a school rally about changing the school mascot from the Wolf Pack to the Fighting Pickles. He delivers a tongue-in-cheek speech, sees it written up in the local newspaper and shares his delight with Pop who, though unable to speak, shows great appreciation for his grandson's work in this warm novel. (116 pages)

Where it's reviewed:
School Library Journal, September 1995, page 199
Booklist, September 15, 1995, page 162
Horn Book, November 1995, page 740
Kirkus Reviews, July 15, 1995, page 1022
Center for Children's Books. Bulletin, October 1995, page 51

Other books by the same author:
Coaster, 1994
Lucky Christmas, 1994
A Boy in the Doghouse, 1991
The Gadget War, 1991

Other books you might like:
Betsy Byars, *The Two-Thousand-Pound Goldfish*, 1982
    Warren not only goes to horror movies, he also writes horror stories.
Anne Fine, *The Book of the Banshee*, 1991
    Siblings Will and Estelle were once friends, but then Estelle becomes a teenager!
Barbara Garland Polikoff, *Life's a Funny Proposition, Horatio*, 1992
    After Horatio's father dies, he has trouble accepting his grandfather's moving in with them, until O.P.'s dog dies, which binds their hearts together.

372

ALICE FAYE DUNCAN
TYRONE GETER, Illustrator

Willie Jerome

(New York: Macmillan Books for Young Readers, 1995)

Subject(s): Musicians; Brothers and Sisters; African Americans

Age range(s): Grades K-3
Major character(s): Willie Jerome, Child, Musician; Judy, Child, Sister; Mama, Single Mother
Time period(s): 1990s (1995)
Locale(s): Harlem, New York

Summary: Willie Jerome spends his summer days on the roof of his city apartment building blowing on a trumpet. His "red hot bebop" is appreciated only by Judy who takes the time to listen to the music behind the noise. The neighbors complain that he's too loud and even Mama is annoyed that he spends his time on the roof. Finally, Judy convinces Mama to relax after work by closing her eyes, resting her mind and hearing what Willie Jerome says with his horn. Thanks to Judy, Mama recognizes Willie Jerome's talent. (32 pages)

Where it's reviewed:
Booklist, June 1995, page 1784
Children's Book Review Service, Spring 1995, page 134
Kirkus Reviews, April 1, 1995, page 466
Publishers Weekly, April 17, 1995, page 59
School Library Journal, June 1995, page 80

Other books you might like:
Mary Brigid Barrett, *Sing to the Stars*, 1994
    A young violinist and a blind pianist perform at a neighborhood concert in the park.
Harriett Diller, *Big Band Sound*, 1996
    Determined to imitate the "big band sound" of a drummer on TV, Arlis gathers and "plays" discarded pots and cans which Mama at first thinks are just trash.
Brian Pinkney, *Max Found Two Sticks*, 1994
    With two twigs as drumsticks, Max uses every available surface as a drum, tapping out the rhythms of the city.
Alan Schroeder, *Satchmo's Blues*, 1996
    The fictionalized biography of Louis Armstrong's childhood in New Orleans portrays his single-minded desire to own and play a cornet.

373

EILEEN DUNLOP

Green Willow

(New York: Holiday House, 1993)

Subject(s): Ghosts; Mystery and Detective Stories
Age range(s): Grades 6-8
Major character(s): Catherine "Kit" Crawford, 11-Year-Old; Daniel Garth, 16-Year-Old; Kojima, Spirit
Time period(s): 1990s
Locale(s): Dundee, Scotland (Maddimoss House)

Summary: As the adopted daughter, Kit often feels unloved in comparison to her family's birth daughter; after Juliet's death, Kit feels even more distanced from her adoptive parents. Living in a rented house while their new home is being constructed, they provide shelter to Daniel, a young boy trying to find himself and whose last name matches the previous owners of Maddimoss House. The two explore the overgrown Japanese garden behind the house and immediately begin to restore it. A ghostly figure of a young Japanese man keeps appearing in the garden and the house's owner offers no clues to this mysterious apparition. (160 pages)

Where it's reviewed:
School Library Journal, January 1994, page 114
Booklist, December 1, 1993, page 684
Voice of Youth Advocates, April 1994, page 24
Horn Book Guide, Spring 1994, page 75
Locus, January 1994, page 51

Other books by the same author:
Websters' Leap, 1995
Finn's Search, 1994
Finn's Island, 1992
Clementina, 1987

Other books you might like:
Arlene Hale, *Nothing but a Stranger*, 1966
It's not until Holly writes an article about adoption for the newspaper that she discovers she, too, is adopted.
Eleanor Cameron, *Court of the Stone Children*, 1973
Nina is most unhappy about moving to San Francisco, until she meets a ghost in a museum.
Susan Beth Pfeffer, *Family of Strangers*, 1992
Conceived to take the place of a brother who died young, Abby has never felt loved or wanted.

374

EILEEN DUNLOP

Websters' Leap

(New York: Holiday House, 1995)

Subject(s): Space and Time; Brothers and Sisters; Historical
Age range(s): Grades 4-6
Major character(s): Jill Weaver, 11-Year-Old; Tad Weaver, Teenager
Time period(s): 1990s; 16th century (1562)
Locale(s): Gryffe, Scotland (Castle Gryffe)

Summary: Ever since her parents' divorce, Jill lives with her mother and her brother, Tad, lives with her father, except for the summers when the siblings switch parents. Jill's at Gryffe Castle in Scotland with her father, but finds she misses her brother and the relationship they used to have. One day she watches a video that her father and Tad have made about the castle and sees herself in 16th-century dress. Finding the file about the castle on her brother's computer, she manages to go back in time to the 1500s where she and her brother team up to save the lady of the castle. (168 pages)

Where it's reviewed:
School Library Journal, October 1995, page 133
Publishers Weekly, November 6, 1995, page 95
Booklist, October 1, 1995, page 313

Other books by the same author:
Green Willow, 1993
Finn's Search, 1994
Finn's Island, 1992
The House on the Hill, 1987

Other books you might like:
Marie D. Goodwin, *Where the Towers Pierce the Sky*, 1989
Young Lizzie Patterson time travels to France just as Jeanne D'Arc rises to fame.

Mary Downing Hahn, *The Doll in the Garden*, 1989
Finding an antique doll in an overgrown rose garden links Ashley with the present and the past.
Richard Peck, *Voices after Midnight*, 1989
Chad and his younger brother Luke are drawn back in time to the Great Blizzard of 1888 where they help save the former owners of their townhouse.

375

OLIVIER DUNREA, Author/Illustrator

The Painter Who Loved Chickens

(New York: Farrar Straus Giroux, 1995)

Subject(s): Artists and Art; Animals/Chickens
Age range(s): Grades K-3
Major character(s): Moel Eyris, Artist; Unnamed Character, Art Dealer
Time period(s): Indeterminate Past
Locale(s): Netherlands

Summary: A painter ekes out a living by painting what is popular while his heart's desire is to live in the country and paint chickens. In his spare time, Moel Eyris does paint what he loves so that, when a wealthy patron of the arts appears at his studio, he has something to show her that is out of the ordinary. The woman's purchase of all his chicken paintings enables Moel to move to a farm, raise chickens and paint only what he likes. (32 pages)

Where it's reviewed:
Booklist, March 1, 1995, page 1247
Horn Book, July 1995, page 448
Kirkus Reviews, March 15, 1995, page 381
Publishers Weekly, March 13, 1995, page 69
School Library Journal, June 1995, page 80

Other books by the same author:
The Broody Hen, 1992
Fergus and Bridey, 1992
Deep Down Underground, 1989

Other books you might like:
Paulette Bourgeois, *Too Many Chickens!*, 1991
When an elementary school classroom receives some chicken eggs, the results are surprising and funny!
Barbara Ann Porte, *Chickens! Chickens!*, 1995
After years of painting only chickens, an artist finds a market for his work when his wife calls his designs folk art and applies them to pillows.
Vera B. Williams, *Cherries and Cherry Pits*, 1986
Bidemmi is a young girl who loves art—creating it, making it and giving it to others.

376

ALAN DURANT
SUE HEAP, Illustrator

Mouse Party

(Cambridge, MA: Candlewick Press, 1995)

Subject(s): Animals; Dwellings; Stories in Rhyme
Age range(s): Grades K-1

Major character(s): Mouse, Mouse; Elephant, Elephant
Time period(s): Indeterminate
Locale(s): Fictional Country

Summary: When Mouse stumbles upon a large, empty house and decides to make it his own, he immediately sends invitations to all his friends to join him for a party. As each animal friend arrives toting an item that rhymes with the animal's name, the party grows increasingly lively. Just as the evening is in full swing, a loud knocking at the door is followed by the entry of angry Elephant, the actual home owner, returning from an extended vacation. Quickly, the animals welcome Elephant and invite him in for his welcome home party. (32 pages)

Where it's reviewed:
Booklist, September 1, 1995, page 84
Children's Book Review Service, September 1995, page 1
Kirkus Reviews, August 1, 1995, page 1108
Publishers Weekly, July 10, 1995, page 57
School Library Journal, September 1995, page 169

Other books by the same author:
Snake Supper, 1995

Other books you might like:
Henrietta, *A Mouse in the House*, 1991
    A photographic tour of a house shows a mouse eating her way through the birthday party preparations in each room.
Heather Maisner, *Find Mouse in the Yard*, 1994
    By lifting the flaps and following the clues, readers can locate a missing mouse.
Matt Novak, *Elmer Blunt's Open House*, 1992
    When Elmer Blunt hurries out one morning without closing the door, curious animals enter, explore, entertain and frighten aw ay a burglar.

377

ELISABETH DYJAK
JANET WILKINS, Illustrator

Bertha's Garden

(Boston: Houghton Mifflin Company, 1995)

Subject(s): Gardens and Gardening; Animals/Rabbits; Food
Age range(s): Grades K-1
Major character(s): Mr. Rabbit, Rabbit; Bertha, Wolf, Gardener
Time period(s): 1990s (1995)
Locale(s): Fictional Country

Summary: To supplement his bland diet of dandelions, Mr. Rabbit frolics through Bertha's garden sampling her vegetables and ignoring her innovative efforts to rid her garden of pests. Not until Mr. Rabbit accepts a luncheon invitation and learns, upon arrival, that he is the entree does he understand Bertha's intent. Yum, yum, dandelions! (32 pages)

Where it's reviewed:
Booklist, April 1, 1995, page 1427
Children's Book Review Service, May 1995, page 110
Five Owls, May 1995, page 102
Publishers Weekly, February 6, 1995, page 85
School Library Journal, August 1995, page 122

Other books you might like:
Philip Ross Norman, *The Carrot War*, 1992
    When the Hares steal the Rabbits' carrots, the Rabbits build a Trojan Carrot as part of their plan to seek revenge.
Beatrix Potter, *The Tale of Peter Rabbit*, 1902
    Against his mother's orders Peter visits Mr. McGregor's tempting vegetable garden and almost finds himself in the stew pot.
Janet Stevens, *Tops and Bottoms*, 1995
    Clever Hare outwits lazy Bear and grows enough vegetables to feed his family and open a vegetable stand.

E

378

BILL EASTERLING
MARY BETH OWENS, Illustrator

Prize in the Snow
(Boston: Little, Brown and Company, 1994)

Subject(s): Winter; Hunting; Animals/Rabbits
Age range(s): Grades K-3
Major character(s): Unnamed Character, Child, Hunter
Time period(s): 1990s (1994)
Locale(s): United States

Summary: Having watched his older brother and friends all week, a young boy is sure that he is capable of catching a bird or a rabbit. Armed with his brother's box trap and a carrot from the kitchen, the boy hikes into the woods near his home and sets the trap. Patiently, he waits, watching for a creature to take the bait. When a hungry rabbit hops to the carrot the boy pulls the string, trapping the rabbit inside the box. He fearfully approaches the box wondering what to do with the captured rabbit, but when he sees the starving creature he leaves the carrot for it to eat and decides to return with some bread crusts tomorrow. Then he hikes home to return the box trap. (32 pages)

Where it's reviewed:
Booklist, December 1, 1994, page 685
Children's Book Review Service, Winter 1995, page 62
Children's Bookwatch, January 1995, page 5
Publishers Weekly, October 31, 1994, page 60
School Library Journal, October 1994, page 88

Awards the book has won:
Christopher Award, 1995

Other books you might like:
Peggy Parish, *Good Hunting, Blue Sky*, 1989
Blue Sky's plan to use his new bow and arrow to bring home some food for his family doesn't work out quite as he expects.

Lynd Ward, *The Biggest Bear*, 1952
Johnny hunts for a bear to make a bearskin to hang on the family barn.
Brian Wildsmith, *Hunter and His Dog*, 1979
A trained bird dog finds he does not have the heart to retrieve the birds hunted by his master.

379

PAMELA DUNCAN EDWARDS
HENRY COLE, Illustrator

Four Famished Foxes and Fosdyke
(New York: HarperCollins Publishers, 1995)

Subject(s): Animals/Foxes; Food; Cooks and Cookery
Age range(s): Grades K-3
Major character(s): Fosdyke, Fox, Cook
Time period(s): 1990s (1995)
Locale(s): United States

Summary: When their mother flits off to Florida, five fox kits are left to fend for themselves. While four of the siblings attempt futile forays in the farm yard hoping to filch fowl, Fosdyke is busy preparing a feast of french fries, fruit flan, fish and figs. Finally, the four famished foxes give up their fowl plans and sample Fosdyke's fare. Fabulous! (32 pages)

Where it's reviewed:
Booklist, September 1, 1995, page 85
Children's Book Review Service, December 1995, page 38
Horn Book Guide, Spring 1996, page 25
Publishers Weekly, October 2, 1995, page 74
School Library Journal, December 1995, page 79

Other books by the same author:
Some Small Slug, 1996

Other books you might like:
Mary Jane Auch, *Peeping Beauty*, 1993
Starstruck Poulette belatedly discovers a fox masquerading as a talent scout is not interested in her dancing ability, but in her drumsticks.

Margrit Cruickshank, *Down by the Pond*, 1995
  Discovering a lurking fox, the farm animals noisily drive
  him into the nearby pond.
Judith Ross Enderle, *What Would Mama Do?*, 1995
  When Faraday Fox follows Little Lily Goose on her
  errands to town she considers how Mama would handle a
  fox looking for his next meal. Co-author Stephanie Gordon
  Tessler.
Vivian French, *Red Hen and Sly Fox*, 1995
  A clever hen outwits a fox who had hoped to enjoy her for
  dinner.

380

RICHARD EDWARDS
CAROLINE ANSTEY, Illustrator

Moles Can Dance

(Cambridge, MA: Candlewick Press, 1994)

Subject(s): Animals/Moles; Animals; Dancing
Age range(s): Grades K-2
Major character(s): Unnamed Character, Mole; Dodge, Child,
  Musician (drummer); Daisy, Child, Dancer
Time period(s): 1990s (1994)
Locale(s): England

Summary: A young mole wants to dance rather than dig
tunnels as he's told to do. The other moles offer no encouragement for such a goal so the young mole seeks advice from a
cow, a frog, a fox, and a woodpecker. Then, he hears a funny
noise and peeps through a hedge to see a child dancing to a
drum beat. Through observation and imitation the young mole
satisfies his desire and dances back to his home to inspire
other moles to join him. (26 pages)

Where it's reviewed:
Booklist, June 1, 1994, page 1837
Horn Book Guide, Spring 1995, page 33
Kirkus Reviews, August 15, 1994, page 1126
Learning, April 1995, page 22
School Library Journal, September 1994, page 183

Other books by the same author:
Moon Frog: Animal Poems for Young Children, 1993
Ten Tall Oak Trees, 1993
A Mouse in My Roof, 1990

Other books you might like:
Lois Ehlert, *Mole's Hill*, 1994
  A mole with a mind of her own ignores the demand of
  other animals to move her hill. Instead she beautifies it and
  tunnels a path through it.
Ward Schumaker, *Dance!*, 1996
  A rhyming celebration of movement and dance features
  animals bumping, stomping, and jumping to music.
Ellen Stoll Walsh, *Hop Jump*, 1993
  Daily hopping and jumping makes Betsy one bored frog.
  For variety, she imitates the leaves floating and becomes a
  dancing frog.
Jane Yolen, *Eeny, Meeny, Miney Mole*, 1992
  Meeny and Miney are content in the safety of their home,
  but Eeny wants to know what's ''Up Above'' and bravely
  ventures up to find out.

381

TIM EGAN, Author/Illustrator

Chestnut Cove

(Boston: Houghton Mifflin Company, 1995)

Subject(s): Greed; City Life; Animals/Hippos
Age range(s): Grades K-2
Major character(s): Eloise, Pig; King Milford, Royalty, Hippo
Time period(s): Indeterminate
Locale(s): Chestnut Cove, Fictional Country

Summary: Life is peaceful and friendly in Chestnut Cove until
King Milford offers his kingdom in exchange for the largest,
juiciest watermelon. Slowly, greed begins effecting the villagers' relationships as they put up fences and hide their
gardens from others. The rescue of Eloise brings the townspeople together again in a cooperative effort that reminds
them of the comfortable life they have abandoned. To celebrate, they eat all the watermelons, leaving nothing worthy of
King Milford's offer. (32 pages)

Where it's reviewed:
Booklist, March 15, 1995, page 1334
Horn Book, November 1995, page 732
Kirkus Reviews, March 15, 1995, page 382
Publishers Weekly, February 13, 1995, page 78
School Library Journal, March 1995, page 180

Other books by the same author:
Friday Night at Hodge's Cafe, 1994

Other books you might like:
Jean de Brunhoff, *Babar and Zephir*, 1937
  One of the classic stories about the elephant Babar in-
  cludes his adventures with his mischievous monkey friend.
John Vernon Lord, *The Giant Jam Sandwich*, 1973
  Citizens of Itching Down work together to rid their village
  of four million wasps.
James Marshall, *George and Martha Back in Town*, 1984
  A sense of humor helps two hippos survive the ups and
  downs of friendship.

382

TIM EGAN, Author/Illustrator

Friday Night at Hodge's Cafe

(Boston: Houghton Mifflin Company, 1994)

Subject(s): Animals/Tigers; Animals/Ducks; Restaurants
Age range(s): Grades K-3
Major character(s): Hodges, Elephant, Cook; Unnamed Char-
  acter, Duck (Hodge's Pet); Unnamed Character, Tiger,
  Bully
Time period(s): Indeterminate Past
Locale(s): Fictional Country (Hodges' Cafe)

Summary: Hodges' skill as a pastry chef makes his restaurant
a popular gathering spot where the regulars have learned to
ignore the antics of his ill-mannered duck. When three well-
dressed tigers march past the ''No Tigers'' sign on the door,
they intimidate everyone but the duck who responds to their
threatening remarks with caustic retorts and flying torts. The
melee ends with the largest tiger clutching the duck as quiet

Hodges smashes a chocolate souffle in the tiger's face. Having been forced to sample the real menu, the tigers decide to settle down and eat quietly, bringing the author's first book to an end. (32 pages)

Where it's reviewed:
Booklist, October 1, 1994, page 1334
Horn Book Guide, Spring 1995, page 33
Kirkus Reviews, July 15, 1994, page 982
Publishers Weekly, September 12, 1994, page 91
School Library Journal, September 1994, page 183

Other books by the same author:
Chestnut Cove, 1995

Other books you might like:
Laurent de Brunhoff, *Babar and the Wully-Wully*, 1975
    Babar must intercede to prevent the elephants and rhinos from waging war over the wully-wully which both groups want for a pet.
Keiko Kasza, *The Rat and the Tiger*, 1993
    Rat stands up for his rights when his friend Tiger uses his larger size to bully Rat.
Daniel Manus Pinkwater, *Ducks!*, 1984
    A boy frees a duck who purports to be an angel, unaware that his action will lead to bizare adventures.

383

RICHARD EGIELSKI, Author/Illustrator

Buz
(New York: HarperCollins, 1995)

Subject(s): Animals/Insects; Humor; Medicine
Age range(s): Grades K-2
Major character(s): Buz, Insect
Time period(s): 1990s (1995)
Locale(s): Fictional Country

Summary: In the first book both written and illustrated by this children's book illustrator, Buz is swallowed along with a young boy's spoonful of cereal. The boy goes to the doctor who peers into the child's eye at the trapped Buz peering back and observes that, indeed, the boy has "caught" a bug. The medication prescribed to drive the bug away looks very much like two cops who are in hot pursuit of Buz when he is freed by being washed out the boy's ear and into the bath tub. Feeling poorly, Buz goes the the doctor who notes that he has "caught" a germ and. . . (32 pages)

Where it's reviewed:
Booklist, August 1995, page 1955
Horn Book, January 1996, page 61
Kirkus Reviews, August 15, 1995, page 1187
Publishers Weekly, July 17, 1995, page 229
School Library Journal, September 1995, page 175

Other books you might like:
Joanna Cole, *The Magic School Bus: Inside the Human Body*, 1989
    Once again, Ms. Frizzle leads her class on a field trip aboard the Magic School Bus. While they don't meet Buz, the students do learn about the human body.

Pat McKissack, *Bugs!*, 1988
    In an easy reader, five different varieties of bugs are used to introduce the numbers one to five.
Chris Van Allsburg, *Two Bad Ants*, 1988
    After escaping from their colony, two bad ants decide they prefer the safety of the familiar to the danger of the unknown.

384

LOIS EHLERT, Author/Illustrator

Mole's Hill
(San Diego: Harcourt Brace and Company, 1994)

Subject(s): Animals/Moles; Animals/Foxes; Legends
Age range(s): Grades K-2
Major character(s): Mole, Mole; Fox, Fox
Time period(s): Indeterminate Past
Locale(s): Wisconsin

Summary: Based on a portion of a Seneca tale, the story evolves with Fox deciding that moles are simply too messy to remain in the neighborhood so he informs Mole that a new path, requiring the relocation of her hill, is to be built. Mole is happy in her home, so rather than submit to Fox's demands, she devises a plan to stay. Enlarging the molehill, she plants seeds and produces a beautiful mound of colorful flowers so appealing to Fox that he revises his plans and enlists Mole's help in building a tunnel through the hill instead. (32 pages)

Where it's reviewed:
Booklist, March 15, 1994, page 1366
Bulletin of the Center for Children's Books, April 1994, page 256
Horn Book, July 1994, page 462
Publishers Weekly, February 21, 1994, page 252
School Library Journal, May 1994, page 92

Other books by the same author:
Nuts to You!, 1993
Moon Rope: A Peruvian Folktale/Un Lazo a la Luna: Una Leyenda Peruana, 1992
Growing Vegetable Soup, 1990

Other books you might like:
Peter Firmin, *Basil Brush Builds a House*, 1973
    Basil, a helpful fox, tries to move his friend Harry (a mole) to an aboveground dwelling.
Jackie French Koller, *Mole and Shrew*, 1991
    Shrew tries to help displaced Mole find a new home.
Jane Yolen, *Eeny, Meeny, Miney Mole*, 1992
    One of three moles living underground finds the courage to explore the world "up above" for herself.
Harriet Ziefert, *A Clean House for Mole and Mouse*, 1988
    After spending the day cleaning house, mouse and mole decide to stay outside rather than dirty the house again.

385

LOIS EHLERT, Author/Illustrator

Nuts to You!

(New York: Harcourt Brace Jovanovich, Publishers, 1993)

Subject(s): Animals/Squirrels; Stories in Rhyme
Age range(s): Grades K-2
Major character(s): Unnamed Character, Squirrel
Time period(s): 1990s (1993)
Locale(s): Milwaukee, Wisconsin (an apartment building)

Summary: The antics of an intrepid squirrel are recounted by an unseen narrator. Not content with stealing bird seed and digging up bulbs from the window box, the squirrel enters an apartment through a torn window screen and must be enticed to leave with peanuts placed on the sidewalk and the cry ''Nuts to you!'' Factual information about squirrels is included at the end of the story. (32 pages)

Where it's reviewed:
Booklist, March 1, 1993, page 1226
Emergency Librarian, September 1993, page 49
Horn Book, May 1993, page 315
Publishers Weekly, February 15, 1993, page 237
School Library Journal, April 1993, page 96

Awards the book has won:
Book Links Good Book, 1993
ALA Recommended Books for the Reluctant Young Adult Reader, 1995

Other books by the same author:
Feathers for Lunch, 1993
Red Leaf, Yellow Leaf, 1991
Planting a Rainbow, 1988

Other books you might like:
Sue Alexander, *There's More. . .Much More*, 1987
    With guidance from a squirrel a little girl learns about the unique beauty of the forest.
Brent Ashabranner, *I'm in the Zoo, Too!*, 1989
    A squirrel who chooses to make his home at the zoo wonders why he is not fed by the zookeepers.
Marjorie Weinman Sharmat, *Attila the Angry*, 1985
    A squirrel with a bad attitude tries to change his ways.

386

AMY EHRLICH
ROBERT J. BLAKE, Illustrator

Maggie and Silky and Joe

(New York: Viking, 1994)

Subject(s): Animals/Dogs; Death (of a Pet); Farm Life
Age range(s): Grades K-3
Major character(s): Joe, Child; Maggie, Dog (Joe's pet); Silky, Dog (Joe's pet)
Time period(s): 1990s (1990 - 1994)
Locale(s): United States (farm)

Summary: Joe and Maggie are inseparable companions, sharing lazy, carefree summer days with each other and the stray puppy who arrives at the farm one day when Joe is seven and Maggie is eight. Time passes, the puppy, Silky, grows and one day during a thunder storm, a frightened Maggie vanishes. When her body is found, the entire family mourns her death. (32 pages)

Where it's reviewed:
Booklist, July 1994, page 1954
Horn Book Guide, Spring 1995, page 33
Publishers Weekly, July 25, 1994, page 55
School Library Journal, September 1994, page 184

Other books by the same author:
Leo, Zack and Emmie, 1992
Lucy's Winter Tale, 1992
Buck-Buck the Chicken, 1987

Other books you might like:
Michael J. Rosen, *Bonesy and Isabel*, 1995
    As a newly adopted child in a strange country, Isabel finds Bonesy's presence comforting and she grieves for the old dog when he dies.
David Updike, *The Sounds of Summer*, 1993
    When Sophocles is lost during a thunderstorm, Homer searches until he finds his pet who dies despite the efforts to save him.
Charlotte Zolotow, *The Old Dog*, 1995
    The revised and newly illustrated story relates the memories which flood a young boy's thoughts after finding his pet dog dead.

387

AMY EHRLICH
STEVEN KELLOGG, Illustrator

Parents in the Pigpen, Pigs in the Tub

(New York: Dial Books for Young Readers, 1993)

Subject(s): Animals; Farm Life; Humor
Age range(s): Grades K-2
Major character(s): Mary ''Ma'', Mother, Farmer; Calvin ''Pa'', Father, Farmer; Bossy, Cow
Time period(s): 1990s (1993)
Locale(s): United States (a farm)

Summary: Life on the farm is so much work for Ma and Pa that when Bossy the Cow decides to move into the house one day, Ma thinks one more mouth to feed is no problem. However, Bossy is a trend-setter and soon all the animals have moved from the barn to the house, taking over beds, hogging the bathroom, and expecting meals cooked to order. In order to get some sleep, Ma, Pa and the children move into the empty and mercifully quiet barn. Ma and Pa are comfortable in their pigpen, but soon find that with no animals to care for, farming becomes a little boring. The animals are ready to resume their former lives and invite the family into the house for a Thanksgiving dinner cooked by the pigs as a culminating celebration to a disastrous, though hilarious tale. (32 pages)

Where it's reviewed:
Booklist, January 15, 1994, page 870
Horn Book, January 1994, page 62
Publishers Weekly, August 16, 1993, page 102
Reading Teacher, April 1994, page 564
School Library Journal, October 1993, page 98

Awards the book has won:
Booklist Editors' Choice, 1993
Book Links Good Book, 1993

Other books by the same author:
Bunnies All Day Long, 1989
Buck-Buck the Chicken, 1987
Leo, Zack, and Emmie Together Again, 1987

Other books you might like:
Sid Fleischman, *Here Comes McBroom: Three More Tall Tales*, 1992
    There's no end to the surprises in store with Josh McBroom and his very unusual farm.
Margaret Mahy, *The Boy Who Was Followed Home*, 1986
    Robert's parents do not share his love for hippopotamuses or his delight when one follows him home.
Trinka Hakes Noble, *The Day Jimmy's Boa Ate the Wash*, 1987
    What should be an educational field trip to a farm becomes a most unusual adventure for Jimmy's class when his pet boa gets loose.

388

ROBERT ELMER

Into the Flames

(Minneapolis: Bethany House, 1995)

Series: Young Underground
Subject(s): World War II; Christian Life; Underground Resistance Movements
Age range(s): Grades 6-8
Major character(s): Elise Andersen, Twin, Resistance Fighter; Peter Andersen, Twin, Resistance Fighter; Morten Anderson, Prisoner (uncle of Elise and Peter)
Time period(s): 1940s
Locale(s): Denmark

Summary: Peter and Elise aid the Danish resistance movement against the Nazis who occupy their country during World War II. Though their Uncle Morten is imprisoned by the Nazis, they continue their resistance effort and help distribute the illegal newspaper ''Free Dane.'' They are caught and imprisoned in Gestapo Headquarters where they discover that their uncle has escaped during an allied bombing attack. They also make plans to escape and, with the help of a stray cat, manage to elude their captors. (192 pages)

Where it's reviewed:
School Library Journal, August 1995, page 140
Booklist, May 15, 1995, page 1645

Other books by the same author:
Beyond the River, 1994
Way through the Sea, 1994

Other books you might like:
Nathaniel Benchley, *Bright Candles*, 1974
    Young Jens helps the Danish Resistance smuggle Jews into Sweden.
Lois Lowry, *Number the Stars*, 1989
    Annemarie fears for her Jewish friend's life when the Germans occupy her Copenhagen neighborhood.

Carol Matas, *Lisa's War*, 1989
    Angry that Denmark gives up without a fight when the Germans invade, Lisa and her brother Stefan become active in the resistance movement.

389

MICHAEL EMBERLEY, Author/Illustrator

Welcome Back, Sun

(Boston: Little, Brown and Company, 1993)

Subject(s): Winter; Spring; Parent and Child
Age range(s): Grades 1-3
Major character(s): Unnamed Character, Child (Norwegian)
Time period(s): 1990s (1993)
Locale(s): Norway (a small village in the shadow of Mt. Gausta)

Summary: Living in a narrow valley in the Norwegian mountains means living without sunlight from September until March. When the excitement of the Winter holidays has ended, the absence of the sun begins to be oppressive to one little girl and eventually to her parents as well. Early one morning in March, following the path set by a child in a Norwegian legend, the family and many others in the village begin the long climb up Mt. Gausta in order to find the sun and bring it back to the village. Spring arrives with real joy in this village. Welcome back! (unpaged)

Where it's reviewed:
Booklist, October 15, 1993, page 452
Horn Book, March 1994, page 189
Kirkus Reviews, October 1, 1993, page 1272
Publishers Weekly, September 13, 1993, page 130
School Library Journal, January 1994, page 88

Other books by the same author:
More Dinosaurs! & Other Prehistoric Beasts, 1992
Ruby, 1990
Dinosaurs! A Drawing Book, 1985

Other books you might like:
Lynne Barasch, *A Winter Walk*, 1993
    Mother and daughter Sophie go walking one gray, dreary, winter day searching for the forgotten spots of color that still brighten the season.
Virginia L. Kroll, *The Seasons and Someone*, 1994
    The traditions and culture of Alaskan natives come to life through the eyes of a young girl describing seasonal changes.
Barbara Rogasky, *Winter Poems*, 1994
    This collection of poems celebrates winter and the promise of spring. Rogasky is editor.

390

REBECCA EMBERLEY, Author/Illustrator

Three Cool Kids

(Boston: Little, Brown and Company, 1995)

Subject(s): Fairy Tale; Folk Tales; Animals/Goats
Age range(s): Grades 4 and Up

Major character(s): Big Cool, Goat, Brother (older); Middle Cool, Goat, Sister; Little Cool, Goat, Brother
Time period(s): 1990s (1995)
Locale(s): United States

Summary: The take-off on the familiar fairy tale does not have a troll for an ogre. Big, Middle and Little Cool must contend with a rat who lives in the sewer under the street which they must cross to reach an empty lot with weeds and grass that look delicious. (32 pages)

Where it's reviewed:
Booklist, March 1, 1995, page 1243
Library Talk, September 1995, page 32
Publishers Weekly, April 24, 1995, page 70
Quill & Quire, April 1995, page 43
School Library Journal, March 1995, page 180

Other books by the same author:
City Sounds, 1989
Jungle Sounds, 1989

Other books you might like:
P.C. Asbjornsen, *The Three Billy Goats Gruff*, 1991
    A reissue of the classic Scandinavian tale of three clever goats outwitting the horrid troll is illustrated by Marcia Brown. Co-author J.E. Moe.
Ted Dewan, *3 Billy Goats Gruff*, 1994
    Sporting baseball caps, the smallest and middle-sized billy goats cross a bridge, convincing the resident troll to wait for the biggest goat to come.
Glen Rounds, *The Three Billy Goats Gruff*, 1993
    As in the original, the troll under the bridge meets his match when he tries to stop the biggest of the 3 billy goat brothers from crossing the bridge.
Janet Stevens, *The Three Billy Goats Gruff*, 1987
    An award-winning retelling brings the classic tale to life.

391

JUDITH ROSS ENDERLE
STEPHANIE GORDON TESSLER, Illustrator
JOHN O'BRIEN, Illustrator

Six Snowy Sheep

(Honesdale, PA: Boyds Mills Press, 1994)

Subject(s): Animals/Sheep; Winter
Age range(s): Grades K-2
Major character(s): Unnamed Character, Sheep
Time period(s): 1990s (1994)
Locale(s): Fictional Country

Summary: Six sheep receive a variety of snow-related items as Christmas gifts and hurry to put them to use. As the first five in turn try skis, skates, snowshoes, saucers, and a sled the result for each is a sheep in a snowbank. With five sheep in one snowbank, the sixth sheep goes into action with the last gift—a snow shovel enabling the freed sheep to join the rescuer for hot chocolate. (24 pages)

Where it's reviewed:
Horn Book Guide, Spring 1995, page 33
Reading Teacher, October 1995, page 139
School Library Journal, December 1994, page 74
Wilson Library Bulletin, December 1994, page 95

Awards the book has won:
International Reading Association Children's Choice, 1995

Other books by the same author:
A Pile of Pigs, 1993
Six Creepy Sheep, 1992
Six Sleepy Sheep, 1991

Other books you might like:
Holly Keller, *Ten Sleepy Sheep*, 1983
    Counting sheep does not help Lewis fall asleep because the sheep hold a noisy party in his bedroom.
Kevin Kiser, *Sherman the Sheep*, 1994
    An adventurous flock of sheep learn that home is the best place to be after all.
Nancy Shaw, *Sheep in a Jeep*, 1986
    In one of many books about a bunch of exuberant sheep, the group takes off in a jeep and, as usual, finds itself in a bit of a predicament.

392

JUDITH ROSS ENDERLE
STEPHANIE GORDON TESSLER, Illustrator
CHRIS L. DEMAREST, Illustrator

What Would Mama Do?

(Honesdale, PA: Boyds Mills Press, 1995)

Subject(s): Shopping; Humor; Animals
Age range(s): Grades K-3
Major character(s): Little Lily Goose, Goose; Mama Goose, Goose, Mother; Faraday Fox, Fox
Time period(s): Indeterminate
Locale(s): Fictional Country

Summary: With a long list of supplies for the winter, Little Lily Goose walks to town and soon notices that she is being followed by Faraday Fox. Wondering to herself how Mama Goose would handle the predicament, Little Lily solves the problem by giving the hungry Faraday her parcels to carry. Despite the burden and the snacks Little Lily gives him, Faraday soon tires of the game, puts down the groceries and makes a grab for Little Lily. He misses, slips, and slides down the hill on a firkin of butter until he is out of sight. (32 pages)

Where it's reviewed:
Booklist, October 1, 1995, page 325
Horn Book Guide, Spring 1996, page 26
Publishers Weekly, October 2, 1995, page 72

Other books by the same author:
Six Snowy Sheep, 1994
The Good-for-Something Dragon, 1993
Six Creepy Sheep, 1992

Other books you might like:
Mary Jane Auch, *Peeping Beauty*, 1993
    Starstruck Poulette belatedly discovers a fox masquerading as a talent scout is not interested in her dancing ability, but in her drumsticks.
Pamela Duncan Edwards, *Four Famished Foxes and Fosdyke*, 1995
    While Fosdyke cooks, four foxes find foraging in the farmyard futile and return home famished and ready for a feast.

Vivian French, *Red Hen and Sly Fox*, 1995
   A clever hen outwits a fox who had hoped to enjoy her for dinner.

393

DELIA EPHRON

The Girl Who Changed the World

(New York: Ticknor and Fields, 1993)

Subject(s): Brothers and Sisters; Revenge
Age range(s): Grades 3-5
Major character(s): Violet Dixie Sparks, 10-Year-Old (a "younger"); Simon Sparks, Brother (Violet's tormentor/ "older"); Melissa Lauren McFree, Child (a "younger"), Friend
Time period(s): 1990s (1993)
Locale(s): Mountain Terrace, California

Summary: That does it! Violet has put up with years of torment from her obnoxious older brother, but when he smashes a huge fly on her head during her piano recital she decides to organize all the younger siblings in town and declare war on the older siblings. With impressive organizational skill, "General" Violet Sparks gathers the "youngers" of the town to teach a lesson to all the "olders", their parents, and, surprisingly, themselves. (148 pages)

Where it's reviewed:
Booklist, November 15, 1993, page 623
Children's Book Review Service, November 1993, page 30
Library Talk, March 1994, page 47
Publishers Weekly, September 27, 1993, page 63
School Library Journal, November 1993, page 106

Other books you might like:
Ann M. Martin, *Eleven Kids, One Summer*, 1991
   Spending the summer in a rented beach house with a large family contributes to fun, mysteries and sibling conflicts.
Phyllis Reynolds Naylor, *The Boys Start the War*, 1993
   The boys start a neighborly battle giving new meaning to the term sibling rivalry and beginning a new series.
Stephen Roos, *Never Trust a Sister over Twelve*, 1993
   As these sisters grow up their relationship adjusts to accomodate their changing interests.

394

LISA CAMPBELL ERNST, Author/Illustrator

Little Red Riding Hood: A Newfangled Prairie Tale

(New York: Simon and Schuster, 1995)

Subject(s): Fairy Tale; Folk Tales; Animals/Wolves
Age range(s): Grades K-3
Major character(s): Little Red Riding Hood, Child; Grandma, Grandmother; Unnamed Character, Wolf
Time period(s): 1990s (1995)
Locale(s): Toad Road (prairie)

Summary: An updated version of the classic Brothers Grimm tale features a bike-riding, red sweatshirt-clad Little Red Riding Hood who pedals through the prairie fields to deliver homemade muffins to Grandma. The muffin's scent attracts a hungry wolf who plots to steal Grandma's secret recipe, but instead finds himself in the grip of Grandma's big, strong hands, staring into Grandma's big, glaring eyes. Little Red Riding Hood arrives just in time to save the wolf and all three share the muffins before beginning a bakery with the wolf as the baker and Little Red Riding Hood handling deliveries. (40 pages)

Where it's reviewed:
Booklist, July 1995, page 1881
Five Owls, September 1995, page 12
Horn Book, July 1996, page 80
Publishers Weekly, September 18, 1995, page 133
School Library Journal, September 1995, page 193

Other books by the same author:
The Luckiest Kid on the Planet, 1994
Ginger Jumps, 1990
When Bluebell Sang, 1989

Other books you might like:
Paul Galdone, *Little Red Riding Hood*, 1974
   In a traditional retelling of the Brothers Grimm tale, Little Red Riding Hood finds the wolf in Grandmother's bed, waiting for his next meal.
James Marshall, *Red Riding Hood*, 1987
   The story of an unsuspecting young girl meeting a hungry wolf in the forest is retold and illustrated by Marshall.
Vivian Vande Velde, *Tales from the Brothers Grimm and the Sisters Weird*, 1995
   Thirteen traditional fairy tales are humorously rewritten with some modifications.

395

LISA CAMPBELL ERNST, Author/Illustrator

The Luckiest Kid on the Planet

(New York: Bradbury Press, 1994)

Subject(s): Grandparents; Self-Perception
Age range(s): Grades K-3
Major character(s): Herbert "Lucky" Morgenstern, Child; Grandfather, Grandfather
Time period(s): 1990s (1994)
Locale(s): New Albany, Indiana

Summary: Lucky Morgenstern lives a happy, lucky life until the day a letter arrives addressed to Herbert Morgenstern. When Lucky learns that his "real" name is Herbert, his positive attitude changes. Believing he has been deceived by the nickname given to him at birth by his grandfather, Herbert's life becomes unlucky and dreary. When Herbert discovers Grandfather is sick in the hospital, he knows just how unlucky he is. The experience also gives him insight into how fortunate he is to have a grandfather and, as he heals himself, Grandfather recovers. (40 pages)

Where it's reviewed:
Booklist, September 1, 1994, page 49
Horn Book, November 1994, page 717
Horn Book Guide, Spring 1995, page 33
Publishers Weekly, August 15, 1994, page 94
School Library Journal, November 1994, page 74

Other books by the same author:
Zinnia and Dot, 1992
Ginger Jumps, 1990
When Bluebell Sang, 1989

Other books you might like:
Lloyd Alexander, *The House Gobbaleen*, 1995
  Tooley hopes to change his bad luck to good when he invites Hooks into his life.
Remy Charlip, *Fortunately*, 1964
  As he travels to Florida to attend a surprise party, Ned has lots of luck—some good, some bad.
Steven Kroll, *Friday the 13th*, 1981
  Unlucky Harold has a change of fortune.

396

LISA CAMPBELL ERNST, Author/Illustrator

Squirrel Park
(New York: Bradbury Press, 1993)

Subject(s): Animals/Squirrels; Fathers and Sons; Environmental Problems
Age range(s): Grades 1-3
Major character(s): Stuart Ivey, Child (nonconformist); Chuck, Squirrel, Friend (of Stuart); Mr. Ivey, Father, Architect (rigid, bossy and powerful)
Time period(s): 1990s (1993)
Locale(s): Springdale (at the last old oak tree in town)

Summary: An unlikely duo, Stuart and Chuck share a love of trees, especially the old oak tree standing in the center of town, which serves as Chuck's home. Over the years the other trees in town have been cut down to make way for the buildings designed by Stuart's father whose idea of development is to destroy the old and build anew. When Mr. Ivey gives Stuart the task of designing a town park around the old oak tree, it takes Chuck's ingenuity and Stuart's courage to convince Mr. Ivey of the merits of their plan. (40 pages)

Where it's reviewed:
Booklist, March 15, 1993, page 1358
Horn Book Guide, Fall 1993, page 285
Kirkus Reviews, March 15, 1993, page 370
Publishers Weekly, March 8, 1993, page 76
School Library Journal, June 1993, page 74

Other books by the same author:
Walter's Tail, 1992
When Bluebell Sang, 1989
Sam Johnson & the Blue Ribbon Quilt, 1983

Other books you might like:
Eve Bunting, *Someday a Tree*, 1993
  When poisons are carelessly dumped near a cherished oak tree, Alice's family and neighbors struggle to save it.
DyAnne DiSalvo-Ryan, *City Green*, 1994
  When a building is torn down leaving an ugly empty lot on Marcy's block, she takes charge and creates a garden in the space.
Lois Ehlert, *Nuts to You!*, 1993
  Squirrels and city-dwelling people coexist happily in this humorous book.

Constance Levy, *A Tree Place and Other Poems*, 1994
  This collection of poems celebrates ways to enjoy nature's beauty without controlling it.

397

ARNICA ESTERL
MAREK ZAWADZKI, Illustrator

Okino and the Whales
(San Diego: Harcourt Brace & Company, 1995)

Subject(s): Animals/Whales; Mothers and Sons; Fantasy
Age range(s): Grades K-3
Major character(s): Okino, Mother; Takumi, 5-Year-Old; Iwa, Deity
Time period(s): 1990s (1995); Indeterminate Past
Locale(s): Japan

Summary: For the first time Takumi is able to patiently sit with his mother and watch for the return of the whales. Excited to see the whales, Takumi eagerly listens to Okino tell a story of Iwa, the Great Mother of the Ocean, and the task she set before an earthly mother trying to reclaim her daughter from Iwa's palace beneath the sea. (32 pages)

Where it's reviewed:
Booklist, October 15, 1995, page 410
Children's Book Review Service, December 1995, page 43
Horn Book Guide, Spring 1996, page 26
Kirkus Reviews, October 15, 1995, page 1489
School Library Journal, January 1996, page 83

Other books by the same author:
The Fine Round Cake, 1991

Other books you might like:
Maggie Steincrohn Davis, *A Garden of Whales*, 1993
  Concerned that whales are diminishing in number, an imaginative young boy dreams of a way to save them.
Cynthia Rylant, *The Whales*, 1996
  The wonder of whales in the world's oceans and their profound impact on those who see them are sensitively portrayed.
Laurence Yep, *City of Dragons*, 1995
  With a caravan of kind giants, a young outcast journeys beneath the sea to the City of Dragons.

398

BETSY EVERITT, Author/Illustrator

TV Dinner
(San Diego: Harcourt Brace & Company, 1994)

Subject(s): Television; Food; Stories in Rhyme
Age range(s): Grades K-2
Major character(s): Daisy Lee, Child
Time period(s): 1990s (1994)
Locale(s): United States

Summary: Daisy Lee's distinctive food habits give new meaning to the term TV dinner. When Daisy Lee has a TV dinner she eats the television, piece by piece, program by program, saving the remote for last. For dessert, she'll have the house. (32 pages)

Where it's reviewed:
Booklist, October 1, 1994, page 332
Children's Book Review Service, Winter 1995, page 62
Kirkus Reviews, September 15, 1994, page 1269
Publishers Weekly, September 19, 1994, page 69
School Library Journal, December 1994, page 74

Other books by the same author:
Frida the Wondercat, 1990

Other books you might like:
Robert Bender, *A Most Unusual Lunch*, 1994
    As various animals eat their way up the food chain, each takes on characteristics of the animal just eaten, until the lion, offended by his new appearance, belches.
Henrik Drescher, *The Boy Who Ate Around*, 1994
    Dinner does not appeal to Mo so he decides to eat around it until he's consumed the world and is left with a plate of beans and cheese souffle.
Felice Haus, *Happy Birthday, Cookie Monster!*, 1986
    Cookie Monster has an appetite for cookies, cakes and anything else he can get in his mouth.
David McPhail, *The Glerp*, 1972
    As the glerp walks, he eats everything in his path until the elephant's tusks become stuck and cause the glerp to cough.

399

MARK EZRA
GAVIN ROWE, Illustrator

The Sleepy Dormouse
(New York: Crocodile Books, 1994)

Subject(s): Animals/Mice; Animals/Weasels; Spring

Age range(s): Grades K-2
Major character(s): Dormouse, Mouse (dormouse); Scraggly Sam, Weasel
Time period(s): 1990s (1994)
Locale(s): England (rural area)

Summary: The arrival of spring does not prompt a sleepy dormouse to leave his warm, cozy nest which is just where a hungry weasel finds him. Scraggly Sam captures Dormouse trapping him under a flower pot and dropping in water, nuts and seeds in order to fatten Dormouse sufficiently for a tasty Sunday dinner. The harvest mice observe what is happening, warn Dormouse and even suggest a plan which will set him free. (32 pages)

Where it's reviewed:
Booklist, January 1, 1995, page 825
Horn Book Guide, Fall 1994, page 271
Kirkus Reviews, May 15, 1994, page 697
Publishers Weekly, May 30, 1994, page 55
School Library Journal, August 1994, page 129

Other books you might like:
Arnold Lobel, *Mouse Soup*, 1977
    Mouse has a plan that he hopes will keep him out of Weasel's soup pot.
Susan Meddaugh, *Hog-Eye*, 1995
    A little pig with a mind of her own must put it to good use if she's to escape from the wolf who plans to have her for dinner.
Tony Ross, *Stone Soup*, 1987
    A hen cleverly avoids becoming a wolf's dinner by offering him a taste of her stone soup.

F

400

NANCY FARMER
SHELLEY JACKSON, Illustrator

Do You Know Me?

(New York: Orchard Books, 1993)

Subject(s): Africa; Aunts and Uncles; Family Life
Age range(s): Grades 3-5
Major character(s): Tapiwa, 9-Year-Old (shy and lonely); Uncle Zeka, Uncle (naive)
Time period(s): 1990s (1993)
Locale(s): Harare, Zimbabwe

Summary: In Uncle Zeka, first-time author Farmer has created a kindly personification of the trickster of traditional African folklore. Driven from his home in the bush country of Mozambique, Uncle Zeka seeks refuge at his brother's urban home. With irrepressible exuberance, Uncle Zeka attempts to continue the traditional life of the African countryside in the city by capturing and roasting termites and making caterpillar soup. Tapiwa sees parallels between her isolated position as a middle-class child in an elite girl's school and Uncle Zeka's country ways in an urban family. Tapiwa gains confidence in herself as she comes to know and appreciate her relative. A glossary of Shona and other African words is included. (105 pages)

Where it's reviewed:
Booklist, April 1, 1993, page 143
Horn Book, September 1993, page 597
Kirkus Reviews, May 1, 1993, page 596
Publishers Weekly, March 15, 1993, page 88
School Library Journal, April 1993, page 118

Other books by the same author:
The Ear, the Eye and the Arm, 1994 (Newbery Honor Book, 1994)

Other books you might like:
Hakim Adi, *African Migration*, 1994
    The historical look at the reasons for African migration and emigration shows the influence of African people on cultures throughout the world.
Tony Fairman, *Bury My Bones But Keep My Words: African Tales for Retelling*, 1993
    A collection of 17 tales includes traditional African stories.
Corlia Fourie, *Ganekwane and the Green Dragon: Four Stories from Africa*, 1994
    The four original tales feature female characters who use their wits and confidence to overcome unusual obstacles.
Colin Harris, *Taste of West Africa*, 1994
    A nonfiction look at the culture of both city and village life in West Africa includes recipes.

401

NANCY FARMER

The Warm Place

(New York: Orchard, 1995)

Subject(s): Fantasy; Animals/Giraffes; Zoos
Age range(s): Grades 4-6
Major character(s): Ruva, Giraffe; Nelson, Chameleon; Jabila, Runaway
Time period(s): 1990s
Locale(s): Africa; San Francisco, California

Summary: The evil Slopes steal Ruva from her home in Africa and transport her to the San Francisco zoo. She remembers her mother's advice to blend in with the shadows and the trees and hopes to use her camouflage to escape. With the help of Nelson, a chameleon who's also eager to leave, especially since the Gila monster has been talking about marriage, Ruva and Nelson stow away aboard a ship bound for Africa. The evil Slopes are encountered again, but this time Ruva teams with Jabila, a young boy they've kidnapped, and Nelson to outwith the Slopes and return to their home in ''the warm place'' in this heart-warming fantasy. (152 pages)

Where it's reviewed:
Publishers Weekly, March 20, 1995, page 62
Booklist, April 1, 1995, page 1391

School Library Journal, March 1995, page 204
Children's Book Review Service, June 1995, page 128
Christian Science Monitor, May 25, 1995, page B2

Other books by the same author:
A Girl Named Disasater, 1996
The Ear, the Eye and the Arm, 1994
Do You Know Me?, 1993

Other books you might like:
Roald Dahl, *James and the Giant Peach*, 1961
   James uses a magical peach to escape from his horrible life with his two mean aunts.
Brian Jacques, *Redwall*, 1986
   The evil rat Cluny destroys the peace of ancient Redwall Abbey as he and hordes of villians attempt to seize control.
Scott Russell Sanders, *The Engineer of Beasts*, 1988
   Mooch, conceived in a Petri dish, works at the "disney." a zoo populated by robots inside the skins of long-extinct animals.
Michael Slade, *The Horses of Central Park*, 1992
   Wendell releases the Central Park horses that pull the hansom cabs after they tell him they are drugged, ignored and work long hours.

402

PAULA KURZBAND FEDER
STACEY SHUETT, Illustrator

The Feather-Bed Journey

(Morton Grove, IL: Albert Whitman & Company, 1995)

Subject(s): Jews; Grandparents; Holocaust
Age range(s): Grades 1-4
Major character(s): Rachel, Child, Sister (older); Lewis, 7-Year-Old, Brother (Rachel's); Grandma, Grandmother, Survivor (Holocaust)
Time period(s): 1940s (1939-1945); 1990s (1995)
Locale(s): Poland; United States

Summary: When Rachel and Lewis accidently tear Grandma's special feather pillow, she shares the story of the pillow and its origins as a feather bed in her childhood home in Poland. Grandma tells the children of a happy childhood changed to one of fear, persecution by the Nazis, separation from her family and life in hiding. At the war's end, she is reunited with her mother and the two survivors emigrate to America where, on the final day of Hanukkah, a package arrives bearing the remants of the family's feather bed remade into a pillow. Now, Grandma will salvage the feathers she can and make an even smaller pillow to store the memories of her childhood. A concluding author's note gives factual information about the life of Polish Jews during the Holocaust. (32 pages)

Where it's reviewed:
Booklist, October 15, 1995, page 410
Bulletin of the Center for Children's Books, December 1995, page 125
Horn Book Guide, Spring 1996, page 54
School Library Journal, November 1995, page 71
Smithsonian, November 1995, page 172

Other books by the same author:
Did You Lose the Car Again?, 1991

Where Does the Teacher Live?, 1979

Other books you might like:
David A. Adler, *One Yellow Daffodil: A Hanukkah Story*, 1995
   Years after the war's end, the kindness of a neighborhood family helps Morris Kaplan heal some of the painful memories of his youth in a concentration camp.
Jo Hoestlandt, *Star of Fear, Star of Hope*, 1995
   Helen's childhood friendship with Lydia ends abruptly when Lydia and her family vanish during the Nazi occupation of France.
Jacqueline Jules, *The Grey Striped Shirt: How Grandma and Grandpa Survived the Holocaust*, 1995
   Frannie learns of her grandparent's experiences during the Holocaust through their responses to her searching questions.

403

JULES FEIFFER

The Man in the Ceiling

(New York: HarperCollins, 1993)

Subject(s): Cartoons and Comics
Age range(s): Grades 4-6
Major character(s): Jimmy Jibbett, 10-Year-Old, Artist (cartoonist); Charley Beemer, Sports Figure (baseball player); Uncle Lester, Writer (Broadway musicals), Uncle
Time period(s): 1990s
Locale(s): Upper Montclair, New Jersey

Summary: Jimmy's a failure; at least, that's what he thinks since he can't play ball. He can, however, draw, though his father thinks that's a waste of time. Jimmy feels like he's finally been accepted when Charley, the the-most-popular-guy in school, likes his drawings and teams up with Jimmy to produce a cartoon strip about the character "Bullethead." It's to his Uncle Lester that Jimmy really turns for support because Lester's the one who's written several failing broadway shows. The two of them want most to be recognized for their strengths, writing and cartooning, and operate under the belief that failure leads to success in this cartoonists first book for children. (185 pages)

Where it's reviewed:
Booklist, November 15, 1993, page 620
School Library Journal, February 1994, page 102
Five Owls, January 1994, page 66
Horn Book Guide, Spring 1994, page 75
New York Times Book Review, November 14, 1993, page 57

Awards the book has won:
Booklist Editors' Choice/Books for Middle Readers, 1993

Other books you might like:
Jessie Close, *The Warping of Al*, 1990
   Al and his father have a difference of opinion about his chosen career; Al wants to be a chef while his father wants him to be a metals trader.
Phyllis Reynolds Naylor, *The Year of the Gopher*, 1987
   George Richards is tired of being pressured by his parents to attend an Ivy League school, so after graduation he works as a "gopher."

Sally Warner, *Dog Years*, 1995
> Case, the new kid in school, creates a cartoon column for his school newspaper that reflects the way his life's gone recently and calls it "Dog Years."

404

CAROL FENNER

Yolanda's Genius

(New York: Margaret K. McElderry Books, 1995)

Subject(s): Brothers and Sisters; Gifted Children; Moving, Household
Age range(s): Grades 4-6
Major character(s): Yolanda Blue, 5th Grader (African-American); Andrew Blue, 6-Year-Old (African-American)
Time period(s): 1990s (1995)
Locale(s): Chicago, Illinois; Grand River, Michigan

Summary: Attempting tó shelter her family from the violence and drug culture of Chicago, Yolanda and Andrew's widowed mother moves them to a small town. Unfortunately, they cannot escape from all their problems. Yolanda's large size continues to draw teasing, taunting remarks from other students and Andrew still cannot read. In fact, he does not talk much either, preferring to communicate through the music he makes with a harmonica given to him by his deceased father. Also, the drug culture permeates even this small community, requiring Yolanda to use her street-smart toughness and her intelligence to protect Andrew and to convince everyone that he is the family genius. (208 pages)

Where it's reviewed:
Booklist, June 1995, page 1769
Children's Book Review Service, August 1995, page 164
Horn Book, September 1995, page 598
Publishers Weekly, June 19, 1995, page 61
School Library Journal, July 1995, page 76

Awards the book has won:
Book Links Good Book, 1995
ALA Notable Book, 1996

Other books by the same author:
Randall's Wall, 1991
A Summer of Horses, 1989
The Skates of Uncle Richard, 1978

Other books you might like:
Alice Mead, *Junebug*, 1995
> Living in the projects requires constant vigilance as Junebug protects himself and his younger sister, but still he is apprehensive about moving to a safer, unknown environment.
Katherine Paterson, *Flip-Flop Girl*, 1994
> A move to a small town following her father's death creates additional problems for Vinnie as she copes with grief and the responsibility she feels for her brother's mutism.
Meredith Sue Willis, *The Secret Super Powers of Marco*, 1994
> Marco's belief that he has super powers helps him to survive a friendship with a hyperactive bully and life in the inner city.

405

ALANE FERGUSON

Stardust

(New York: Bradbury Press, 1993)

Subject(s): Actors and Actresses; Identity; Schools
Age range(s): Grades 4-6
Major character(s): Haley "Samantha Love" Loring, 6th Grader (former actress); Andy Valdez, 6th Grader; Rosie, Toy (large stuffed gorilla)
Time period(s): 1990s (1993)
Locale(s): Hollywood, California; Garland (small town)

Summary: When eleven-year old Haley is written out of the script of a popular TV comedy, her family loses their only source of income. The parents decide to move to a small town in another state, forcing Haley to become a "regular" 6th grader at a small school. Upon arrival, she finds that everyone except Andy is excited to have "Samantha Love" in town so she hides her insecurities in her TV character, confiding only in Rosie, until she begins to find the real Haley Loring. (155 pages)

Where it's reviewed:
Booklist, May 15, 1993, page 1692
Horn Book Guide, Fall 1993, page 297
Kirkus Reviews, April 15, 1993, page 527
New Advocate, Spring 1994, page 152
School Library Journal, June 1993, page 105

Other books by the same author:
The Practical Joke War, 1991
Cricket and the Crackerbox Kid, 1990

Other books you might like:
Richard Peck, *Bel-Air Bambi and the Mall Rats*, 1993
> Moving from Los Angeles to the small town of Hickory Fork requires more than the usual after-a-move adjustments for Bambi and her sister Buffie.
Bill Wallace, *True Friends*, 1994
> Sixth grader Courtney learns a lot about dealing with her own perceived problems from a new girl in school.
Sharon Dennis Wyeth, *The World of Daughter McGuire*, 1994
> Living in a new neighborhood following her parent's separation, Daughter struggles to overcome personal and family problems.

406

JUDY FINCHLER
KEVIN O'MALLEY, Illustrator

Miss Malarkey Doesn't Live in Room 10

(New York: Walker and Company, 1995)

Subject(s): Teachers; Schools; Teacher-Student Relationships
Age range(s): Grades K-3
Major character(s): Unnamed Character, 1st Grader; Miss Malarkey, Teacher
Time period(s): 1990s (1995)
Locale(s): United States

Summary: A young boy's assumption that his teacher lives in the classroom, eats dinner in the cafeteria and sleeps in bunk beds in the Teacher's Room with the other staff is shattered when a moving van delivers Miss Malarkey and all her belongings to his apartment building. After she moves in, the child is suprised to discover that she dumps her own garbage, has parties when it's not a class member's birthday and goes barefoot with painted toe nails. First book by the author. (32 pages)

Where it's reviewed:
Booklist, November 15, 1995, page 563
Children's Book Review Service, October 1995, page 14
Kirkus Reviews, August 15, 1995, page 1188
Publishers Weekly, August 14, 1995, page 83
School Library Journal, December 1995, page 80

Other books you might like:
Eve Bunting, *Our Teacher's Having a Baby*, 1992
  A first grade class becomes so involved in their teacher's life that they write letters to her unborn baby, suggest names and plan the baby's room
Paula Kurzband Feder, *Where Does the Teacher Live?*, 1979
  Three children try to answer the title's question and determine the location of their teacher's residence.
Leatie Weiss, *My Teacher Sleeps in School*, 1984
  Because Mrs. Marsh is in the room when Mollie arrives in the morning and still there when the students depart, she assumes the teacher lives at school.

407

ANNE FINE

Step by Wicked Step

(New York: Little, Brown, 1996)

Subject(s): Divorce; Remarriage; Stepfamilies
Age range(s): Grades 4-6
Major character(s): Claudia, Child of Divorced Parents; Pixie, Child of Divorced Parents; Colin, Child of Divorced Parents
Time period(s): 1990s
Locale(s): England (Old Harwick Hall)

Summary: The children are going for an overnight trip to an old building but the cars become separated during a storm and the five children who have been placed together arrive early and go to a room in the tower. There they find an old diary written by a son of the owner, telling of his sorry family life. Once they read the story, each of the five tells their own sad story about their broken families and realize that it is because of this connection that their teacher placed them in the same car. (138 pages)

Where it's reviewed:
Horn Book, July/August 1996, page 463
Bulletin of the Center for Children's Books, May 1996, page 299
Booklist, May 15, 1996, page 1588

Awards the book has won:
School Library Journal Best Books, 1996

Other books by the same author:
Flour Babies, 1992

My War with Goggle-Eyes, 1989
Alias Madame Doubtfires, 1988

Other books you might like:
Terry Farish, *Why I'm Already Blue*, 1989
  Lucy must come to grips with the break-up of her parents' marriage while she's also facing problems at school.
Marilyn Sachs, *At the Sound of the Beep*, 1990
  Two children run away when they find they will be separated by their parents divorce.
Susan Richards Shreve, *The Formerly Great Alexander Family*, 1995
  Liam is unable to face the break-up of his perfect family until he takes time to talk with his father.
Zilpha Keatley Snyder, *The Gypsy Game*, 1997
  Toby fears a custody battle and so runs away to live with some homeless people until his friends bring him back.
Gina Willner-Pardo, *Jason and the Losers*, 1995
  Jason is sent to his aunt's house after his parents' divorce and finally realizes that being angry and resentful is not the way to be.

408

JOHN D. FITZGERALD
DIANE DE GROAT, Illustrator

The Great Brain Is Back

(New York: Dial Books for Young Readers, 1995)

Subject(s): Brothers; Frontier and Pioneer Life; Humor
Age range(s): Grades 4-6
Major character(s): Tom D. "The Great Brain" Fitzgerald, 13-Year-Old, Brother; J.D. Fitzgerald, 11-Year-Old, Brother
Time period(s): 1890s (1899)
Locale(s): Adenville, Utah

Summary: Now that he's reached the age when boys in town start working and courting, Tom rarely has time to pull one of his con games on J. D. or anyone else and life is pretty boring. Tom has not reformed, however, and in his spare moments, he is still able to swindle his brothers and friends, adding excitement to life in a small town. His "Great Brain" is also used to solve a bank robbery and capture the outlaw gang before he heads east with his older brother to school. (128 pages)

Where it's reviewed:
Booklist, January 1, 1995, page 822
Horn Book, May 1995, page 348
Horn Book Guide, Fall 1995, page 296
Library Talk, September 1995, page 37
School Library Journal, March 1995, page 204

Other books by the same author:
The Great Brain Does It Again, 1975
The Great Brain at the Academy, 1972
The Great Brain, 1967

Other books you might like:
David A. Adler, *Eaton Stanley and the Mind Control Experiment*, 1985
  For his science project, 6th grader Eaton plans to take control of his teacher's mind.

Tom Birdseye, *I'm Going to Be Famous*, 1986
  Arlo plans to set a new world record—for eating bananas.
Betsy Byars, *Bingo Brown and the Language of Love*, 1989
  Bingo's long distance calls to his girlfriend create a large
  debt that he must repay.
Peg Kehret, *The Richest Kids in Town*,
  Peter Dodge's get-rich-quick schemes backfire, jeopardiz-
  ing his friendship with Wishbone who is losing money.

409

SID FLEISCHMAN
PETER SIS, Illustrator

The 13th Floor: A Ghost Story

(New York: Greenwillow Books, 1995)

Subject(s): Time Travel; Pirates; Brothers and Sisters
Age range(s): Grades 4-6
Major character(s): Buddy Stebbins, 12-Year-Old, Orphan;
  Liz Stebbins, Sister (older), Lawyer; Abigail Parsons, 10-
  Year-Old
Time period(s): 1990s (1995); 17th century (1692)
Locale(s): San Diego, California; Massachusetts

Summary: Impoverished Buddy and Liz's struggle to meet
expenses after their parents' accidental deaths is complicated
when an ancestor communicates with them across time. Liz
answers the call hoping it's from a potential client and Buddy
goes in search of her, stepping off the elevator of an old
building on the 13th floor and into the past. From the deck of a
pirate ship to the witchcraft trial of young Abigail, Liz and
Buddy are challenged and assisted by the accouterments of
20th century life—from glow-in-the-dark shoe laces to present-day mannerisms. (131 pages)

Where it's reviewed:
Booklist, October 1, 1995, page 314
Horn Book, November 1995, page 741
Kirkus Reviews, October 1, 1995, page 1427
Publishers Weekly, October 9, 1995, page 86
School Library Journal, October 1995, page 133

Other books by the same author:
By the Great Horn Spoon, 1988
The Whipping Boy, 1986
The Ghost on Saturday Night, 1974

Other books you might like:
Pam Conrad, *Zoe Rising*, 1996
  In a sequel to *Stonewords*, Zoe travels back to the time of
  her mother's youth, intervening in past events in order to
  save the future.
Nancy Garden, *The Monster Hunters: Mystery of the Watch-
  ful Witches*, 1995
  In the fifth entry in a series, Darcy and friends must travel
  back in time to the Salem witch trials in order to save Aunt
  Eleanora from present-day accusations of witchcraft.
Jon Scieszka, *The Not-So-Jolly Roger*, 1991
  The Time Warp Trio travels back to the days of pirates,
  learning to see that time from a new perspective

410

VIRGINIA FLEMING
FLOYD COOPER, Illustrator

Be Good to Eddie Lee

(New York: Philomel Books, 1993)

Subject(s): Down Syndrome; Mentally Handicapped; Preju-
  dice
Age range(s): Grades K-2
Major character(s): Eddie Lee, Mentally Challenged Person
  (Down Syndrome), Child; Christy, Child, Neighbor (of
  Eddie Lee); JimBud, Child, Neighbor (prejudiced)
Time period(s): 1990s (1993)
Locale(s): South

Summary: Summer's here and Christy is not sure how to avoid
playing with her neighbor Eddie Lee. Her mama says to be
good to Eddie Lee because God made him different, but
Christy and neighbor JimBud still run off in search of frog
eggs without him. Undeterred, Eddie Lee finds them and
patiently shows Christy his own discoveries in the woods,
making it obvious that Eddie Lee has more insight into nature,
and possibly people, than either Christy or JimBud. (32
pages)

Where it's reviewed:
Booklist, January 15, 1994, page 936
Horn Book Guide, Spring 1994, page 65
Publishers Weekly, October 11, 1993, page 86
Reading Teacher, September 1994, page 65
School Library Journal, February 1994, page 84

Other books you might like:
Ada B. Litchfield, *Making Room for Uncle Joe*, 1984
  Adjustments, especially for three young children, are nec-
  essary when a handicapped uncle moves into their home.
Berniece Rabe, *Where's Chimpy?*, 1988
  Chimpy is lost and until her toy monkey is found it will be
  hard for one special little girl to sleep.
Maria Testa, *Thumbs Up, Rico!*, 1994
  Sometimes frustrated, always courageous, Rico copes with
  the challenges of friends, school and siblings.

411

RALPH FLETCHER

Fig Pudding

(New York: Clarion Books, 1995)

Subject(s): Family Life; Death; Christmas
Age range(s): Grades 6-7
Major character(s): Clifford Allyn "Cliff" Abernathy III, 12-
  Year-Old; Joshua Abernathy, Child (Cliff's youngest
  brother)
Time period(s): 1970s
Locale(s): United States

Summary: The Abernathy family is filled with love, lots and
lots of love, and it's a good thing for there are six children
who sop up all that extra care. Cliff, as the oldest, is the
narrator of a year in his family's life from one Christmas to
the next. The first Christmas is marked by baby Josh's stay in

the hospital when he tells everyone he wants a ''yidda yadda.'' No one can figure out what he's saying until he points to the ladder for a bunk bed in the hospital and exclaims a ''yidda yadda.'' Building that little ladder helps the Abernathy family keep their mind off Josh's illness in this warm family story filled with sad and funny happenings. (136 pages)

Where it's reviewed:
Publishers Weekly, April 24, 1995, page 72
Booklist, May 15, 1995, page 1645
School Library Journal, July 1995, page 78
Wilson Library Bulletin, May 1995, page 100
Horn Book Guide, Fall 1995, page 297

Other books by the same author:
I Am Wings: Poems about Love, 1994

Other books you might like:
Louise May Alcott, *Little Women*, 1868
   This classic tale describes life in the March household with four daughters, Jo, Amy, Beth and Meg.
Caroline B. Cooney, *Family Reunion*, 1989
   To Shelley's relief, the family reunion with her ''perfect'' relatives, the Preffyn's, shows they are anything but perfect.
Frank B. Gilbreth Jr., *Cheaper by the Dozen*, 1963
   This biography recounts the adventures of a family of twelve children whose efficiency expert father applies his beliefs to domestic life.

412

SUSAN FLETCHER

Sign of the Dove
(New York: Atheneum, 1996)

Subject(s): Dragons; Fantasy
Age range(s): Grades 4-8
Major character(s): Lyf, Child (girl); Kaeldra, Healer; Piro, Mythical Creature (dragon)
Time period(s): Indeterminate Past
Locale(s): Europe

Summary: Lyf looks after the doves in spite of warnings not to. One day her mother calls her home and she comes bringing one of the doves with her. Her mother hides her from the king's men but when the dove makes a noise, Lyf transports herself into the time of the bird. Since she is the one the men have been looking for, her family sends her off to stay with Kaeldra, who once healed her. There Lyf witnesses the birth of dragon hatchlings and cares for them until they are ready for freedom. Suffering the loss of the dragons, she sleeps until a bird comes to give her back her human life. (214 pages)

Where it's reviewed:
School Library Journal, May 1996, page 112
Horn Book, September/October 1996, page 595

Other books by the same author:
Flight of the Dragon Kyn, 1993
Dragon's Milk, 1989

Other books you might like:
Anne McCaffrey, *The Harper Hall Trilogy*, 1976
   The first in a series of books about a young harper who is also talented in raising dragons.
Patricia Wrede, *Dealing with Dragons*, 1990
   The princess who joins the dragons does not want to be rescued by the prince in this first in a series of dragon stories.
Laurence Yep, *Dragon War*, 1992
   The dragons work to restore their underwater home in this part of a series on dragons.
Jane Yolen, *Here There Be Dragons*, 1993
   This collection of dragon stories contains different kinds of stories by different authors.

413

VALERIE FLOURNOY
JERRY PINKNEY, Illustrator

Tanya's Reunion
(New York: Dial Books for Young Readers, 1995)

Subject(s): Grandparents; Farm Life; Reunions
Age range(s): Grades K-3
Major character(s): Tanya, Child; Grandma, Grandmother
Time period(s): 1990s (1995)
Locale(s): Virginia

Summary: In a sequel to *The Patchwork Quilt*, Tanya is allowed to accompany her grandmother to the family homestead to assist with preparations for an upcoming reunion. Her excitement quickly wanes when they arrive at the farm where city-bred and homesick Tanya sees dust and fly strips, while Grandma's view is colored with loving memories. Patiently, Grandma is able to share her memories with Tanya and help her to feel the love and the family history that make the old farm home so important. (40 pages)

Where it's reviewed:
Booklist, September 1, 1995, page 85
Bulletin of the Center for Children's Books, October 1995, page 53
Horn Book, September 1995, page 587
Publishers Weekly, September 18, 1995, page 131
School Library Journal, September 1995, page 175

Other books by the same author:
The Twins Strike Back, 1994
The Best Time of Day, 1992
The Patchwork Quilt, 1985

Other books you might like:
Juwanda G. Ford, *Kenya's Family Reunion*, 1996
   The annual family reunion has a special significance this year when the family gathers to celebrate the 50th anniversary of the farmhouse built by Kenya's grandfather.
Mary Hoffman, *Boundless Grace*, 1995
   In a sequel to *Amazing Grace*, Grace travels with Nana to visit the father she knows only from pictures and his new family in Gambia.
Elizabeth Fitzgerald Howard, *What's in Aunt Mary's Room*, 1996

Sarah and Susan discover that Aunt Mary's room is a treasure trove of family history.

414

VANESSA FLOURNOY
VALERIE FLOURNOY, Illustrator
JAMES E. RANSOME, Illustrator

Celie and the Harvest Fiddler
(New York: Tambourine Books, 1995)

Subject(s): Halloween; Magic; African Americans
Age range(s): Grades K-3
Major character(s): Celie, Child, Sister (Joshua's); Mr. Fiddler, Musician, Magician; Joshua, Child, Brother (Celie's)
Time period(s): 1870s
Locale(s): United States (rural South)

Summary: The harvest is complete and Celie hurries to put the finishing touches on her costume for the All Hallows' Eve festival. Determined to win first place, Celie races to town when she hears the sounds of the Fiddler, but stops, embarassed, when her homemade costume falls to a heap around her feet. The Fiddler follows her as she runs into the forest and gives her a mask that has the power to make wishes come true. (32 pages)

Where it's reviewed:
Booklist, September 15, 1995, page 170
Library Talk, September 1995, page 25
School Library Journal, November 1995, page 71

Other books you might like:
Dakari Hru, *Joshua's Masai Mask*, 1993
    A mask that Joshua receives from his uncle is imbued with unusual powers.
Pat McKissack, *Mirandy and Brother Wind*, 1988
    Mirandy hopes that, by catching Brother Wind for her partner, she will win first prize in the cake walk. Caldecott Medal and Coretta Scott King Illustrator Award.
Chris Van Allsburg, *The Widow's Broom*, 1992
    In an award-winning book, a witch's broom is discarded when it loses the ability to fly; fortunately it retains enough power to contribute to a widow's life.

415

MIELA FORD
SALLY NOLL, Illustrator

Sunflower
(New York: Greenwillow Books, 1995)

Subject(s): Gardens and Gardening
Age range(s): Grades K-1
Major character(s): Unnamed Character, Child, Gardener
Time period(s): 1990s (1995)
Locale(s): United States

Summary: Carefully, a young child plants a striped seed. Daily watering and watching produce a small plant which quickly grows to knee height, then nose height, and finally over-the-head height. The bright sunflower provides treats for butter-

flies, birds, and the child as well as seeds for next year's planting. (24 pages)

Where it's reviewed:
Booklist, February 15, 1995, page 1092
Children's Book Review Service, April 1995, page 99
Horn Book, May 1995, page 324
Kirkus Reviews, March 15, 1995, page 383
School Library Journal, May 1995, page 84

Other books by the same author:
Bear Play, 1995
Little Elephant, 1994

Other books you might like:
Eve Bunting, *Sunflower House*, 1996
    Sunflower seeds planted in a circle grow to make a fun summer house and produce seeds for next year.
Elizabeth King, *Backyard Sunflower*, 1993
    Color photographs compliment the description of a sunflower's life from seed to harvest by in a non-fiction book.
Jeanne Titherington, *Pumpkin, Pumpkin*, 1986
    Rhythmic text explains the life cycle of a pumpkin.

416

MICHAEL FOREMAN, Author/Illustrator

Dad! I Can't Sleep
(San Diego: Harcourt Brace & Company, 1995)

Subject(s): Sleep; Bedtime; Animals
Age range(s): Grades K-2
Major character(s): Little Panda, Bear, Child; Dad, Bear, Father
Time period(s): 1990s (1993)
Locale(s): England

Summary: Patiently, Dad responds to Little Panda's pleas for just one more drink to help him sleep. When the requests continue, however, Dad tells Little Panda to count sheep, cows and successively larger animals. Much to Dad's surprise, rather than putting Little Panda to sleep, the activity fills his room with thirsty animals all clamoring for one last drink. First published in England in 1993. (32 pages)

Where it's reviewed:
Booklist, March 1, 1995, page 1247
Horn Book Guide, Fall 1995, page 264
Junior Bookshelf, February 1995, page 9
School Librarian, February 1995, page 16
School Library Journal, July 1995, page 61

Other books by the same author:
Surprise! Surprise!, 1995
Grandfather's Pencil and the Room of Stories, 1994
Jack's Fantastic Voyage, 1992

Other books you might like:
Holly Berry, *Busy Lizzie*, 1994
    An active bedtime ritual helps Lizzie prepare for slumber.
Mordicai Gerstein, *Bedtime, Everybody!*, 1996
    Daisy has difficulty convincing her stuffed animals to settle down for the night.
Russell Hoban, *Bedtime for Frances*, 1960
    Anxious Frances imagines many obstacles to falling

asleep, but her patient parents offer firm reassurance and eventually she sleeps.

Kate McMullan, *Good Night, Stella*, 1994

An overly active imagination keeps Stella from falling asleep.

417

MICHAEL FOREMAN, Author/Illustrator

Surprise! Surprise!

(San Diego: Harcourt Brace & Company, 1995)

Subject(s): Fear; Birthdays; Gifts
Age range(s): Grades K-1
Major character(s): Little Panda, Panda; Mom, Mother, Panda
Time period(s): 1990s (1995)
Locale(s): Fictional Country

Summary: Although he's afraid of the dark, Little Panda bravely ventures into the unlit attic in order to hide Mom's birthday present. Reading the directions on the plant he's bought, he learns it needs sunlight. Little Panda can't provide that in the attic, but he can offer moonlight from his night light. Nightly, Little Panda sneaks his moonlight into the attic for the plant while he sleeps in the dark. By the time Mom's birthday arrives, Little Panda is no longer afraid of the dark and the plant has responded to his loving care. What a surprise! (32 pages)

Where it's reviewed:
Booklist, December 15, 1995, page 708
Horn Book Guide, Fall 1996, page 256
Junior Bookshelf, August 1995, page 128
School Library Journal, March 1996, page 173

Other books by the same author:
Dad! I Can't Sleep, 1994
Grandfather's Pencil and the Room of Stories, 1994
Cat and Canary, 1987

Other books you might like:
Eve Bunting, *Flower Garden*, 1994
    With her father's help a little girl shops for and secretly plants a window box garden as a birthday surprise for her mother.
Diane Goode, *Mama's Perfect Present*, 1996
    Two children search the shops of Paris to find just the right gift for Mama's birthday.
Martin Waddell, *Can't You Sleep, Little Bear?*, 1988
    Little Bear is frightened of the dark at bedtime so Big Bear comforts him and offers a nightlight.

418

MICHAEL FOREMAN, Author/Illustrator

War Game

(New York: Arcade Publishing Company, 1994)

Subject(s): World War I; War; Sports/Soccer
Age range(s): Grades 4-7
Major character(s): Will, Soccer Player, Military Personnel (soldier)
Time period(s): 1910s (1914)

Locale(s): England; France (front-line trenches)

Summary: Four young British soccer players respond to the excitement of recruiting posters and enlist in the army. The thrill of going off ''to see the world'' is soon replaced by the grim, horrid reality of war. Serving on the front-line in wet, cold vermin-infested trenches, the soldiers enjoy a brief respite on Christmas Eve to bury the dead and on Christmas Day when they have a soccer match with the Germans. Within a few days the fighting resumes. Intially published in Great Britain in 1993, the book is a tribute to the author's four uncles who died in World War I. (72 pages)

Where it's reviewed:
Books for Your Children, Summer 1994, page 12
Five Owls, September 1994, page 16
Horn Book Guide, Fall 1994, page 309
Kirkus Reviews, April 15, 1994, page 555
Publishers Weekly, April 25, 1994, page 78

Awards the book has won:
Britain's Smarties Book Prize, 1993

Other books by the same author:
One World, 1991
War Boy, 1990

Other books you might like:
Jean-Louis Besson, *October 45: Childhood Memories of the War*, 1995
    The author's memories of World War II, beginning when he was 7 years old, give a child's observations of shortages, air raids and German troops marching into town.
George Ella Lyon, *Cecil's Story*, 1991
    A boy considers the consequences for the family if his father leaves to fight in the Civil War.
Geraldine McCaughrean, *The Cherry Tree*, 1991
    With the village destroyed and their father killed by war, Taichi and Yumiko see hope for the future in the blossoms of a cherry tree.
Patricia Polacco, *Pink and Say*, 1994
    The senseless tragedy of war is eloquently portrayed through the brief friendship of two young Union soldiers.

419

TOBY FORWARD
LAURA CORNELL, Illustrator

Pie Magic

(New York: Tambourine Books, 1996)

Subject(s): Magic; Weight Control; Friendship
Age range(s): Grades 3-6
Major character(s): Bertie George, Student (overweight); Mr. Gupta, Businessman (shopowner), Magician; Norman, Bully
Time period(s): 1990s
Locale(s): England

Summary: Bertie is the fattest boy in school. Because he is self-conscious about his weight, he is lonely and has trouble making friends. He loves pie and one day when he visits the pie shop, he meets a mysterious customer who offers him a special formula to help him lose weight. But when Bertie wishes to be lighter and gets his wish, he doesn't lose weight, instead he is able to fly. While flying he notices all kinds of ways he can be helpful and friendly and as he becomes more friendly, his desire to eat becomes less. In the end he does lose weight and makes friends. (110 pages)

Where it's reviewed:
Horn Book, September/October 1996, page 595

Other books by the same author:
Ben's Christmas, 1996
Traveling Backward, 1992

Other books you might like:
Bill Brittain, *The Wish Giver*, 1983
 Three children make wishes and find that they need to be careful in wishing for exactly what they want.
Bruce Coville, *Jennifer Murdley's Toad*, 1992
 Jennifer gets a toad which can grant her wishes.
Willo Davis Roberts, *The Magic Book*, 1986
 Two friends discover that the spells they try on a bully do not always work the way they expect.
Elvira Woodruff, *The Summer I Shrank My Grandmother*, 1990
 A little girl uses a new potion on her grandmother and is shocked when she begins to become both younger and smaller.

▌420

TOBY FORWARD
LAURA CORNELL, Illustrator

Traveling Backward
(New York: Tambourine Books, 1994)

Subject(s): Grandparents; Death; Magic
Age range(s): Grades 4-5
Major character(s): Fanny Blake, Child; Grandpa, Aged Person (dying), Grandfather (Fanny's); Mrs. May, Aged Person, Neighbor (Fanny's)
Time period(s): 1990s (1992)
Locale(s): England

Summary: Fanny's fun-loving Grandpa lies dying while obnoxious relatives gather at his deathbed, waiting. Upset at the thought of losing him, Fanny seeks consolation from Mrs. May who seems to have the answer to aging. A sympathetic Mrs. May shares a potion with Fanny, giving specific instructions to return the leftovers when Grandpa is feeling better. After one glass, Grandpa feels so well he won't give up the elixir making Fanny question her wish to keep him around "forever" as Grandpa rapidly becomes younger and younger. Originally published in Great Britain in 1992. (123 pages)

Where it's reviewed:
Booklist, September 1, 1994, page 40
Horn Book Guide, Spring 1995, page 76
Kirkus Reviews, July 15, 1994, page 983
Publishers Weekly, July 11, 1994, page 79
School Library Journal, August 1994, page 154

Other books you might like:
Natalie Babbitt, *Tuck Everlasting*, 1975
 After drinking from a magic spring, the Tuck family must cope with the joy and the problems of eternal life.

Roald Dahl, *Charlie and the Chocolate Factory*, 1963
 Willy Wonka does not promise eternal life, but his inventions certainly make life more exciting for poor Charlie.
Betty MacDonald, *Mrs. Piggle-Wiggle*, 1947
 While Mrs. Piggle-Wiggle's magic potions may not promise eternity, they do put an end to the difficult behaviors of problem children.

▌421

SUSI GREGG FOWLER
JIM FOWLER, Illustrator

I'll See You When the Moon Is Full
(New York: Greenwillow Books, 1994)

Subject(s): Fathers and Sons; Love; Parent and Child
Age range(s): Grades K-1
Major character(s): Abe, Child; Daddy, Father
Time period(s): 1990s (1994)
Locale(s): United States

Summary: As Abe helps Daddy pack for a 2-week business trip, he relates just how much he misses his father during these trips. Daddy replies with his own examples of how much he misses Abe and offers Abe the reassurance of his return "when the moon is full." (24 pages)

Where it's reviewed:
Booklist, June 1, 1994, page 1837
Children's Book Review Service, Spring 1994, page 134
Five Owls, May 1995, page 110
Kirkus Reviews, February 15, 1994, page 224
School Library Journal, August 1994, page 130

Other books by the same author:
When Joel Comes Home, 1993
Fog, 1992
When Summer Ends, 1989

Other books you might like:
Pamela D. Greenwood, *I Found Mouse*, 1994
 To help Tessie pass the time during her mother's 3-week business trip, Dad suggests finding something to do. The kitten Tessie finds provides some focus for both of them.
Patricia Lakin, *Dad and Me in the Morning*, 1994
 A young boy and his father enjoy some special, private time together watching the sun rise.
Deborah Lee Rose, *Meredith's Mother Takes the Train*, 1991
 Meredith does not like going to day care while her mother goes to the office, but accepts the reassurance of her mother's return at the end of the work day.

▌422

MEM FOX
JANE DYER, Illustrator

Time for Bed
(New York: Gulliver Books, 1993)

Subject(s): Bedtime; Animals; Stories in Rhyme
Age range(s): Grades K-1
Major character(s): Unnamed Character, Mother; Unnamed Character, Child

Time period(s): 1990s (1993)
Locale(s): Earth

Summary: One by one, Mommy describes various animals being put to bed by their respective parents until, finally, she bids goodnight to her own child. The stage has been set in quiet lyrical verse and, of course, the child drifts peacefully off to sleep. (32 pages)

Where it's reviewed:
Children's Book Review Service, January 1994, page 51
Horn Book Guide, Spring 1994, page 33
Language Arts, April 1994, page 295
Publishers Weekly, August 9, 1993, page 475
School Library Journal, October 1993, page 98

Other books by the same author:
Sophie, 1994
Hattie and the Fox, 1988
Wilfrid Gordon McDonald Partridge, 1985

Other books you might like:
Margaret Wise Brown, *Little Donkey Close Your Eyes*, 1995
Animals throughout the world are bid good night in this gentle poem.
Michael Foreman, *Dad! I Can't Sleep*, 1995
Little Panda counts animals to help him fall asleep and they all want one last drink of water.
Mirra Ginsburg, *Asleep, Asleep*, 1992
The animals are quietly bid good night until only the sleepy child and the wind are awake.
Jan Ormerod, *Moonlight*, 1982
Through illustrations alone a young girl's bedtime ritual is portrayed.

423

MEM FOX
KATHRYN BROWN, Illustrator

Tough Boris

(San Diego: Harcourt Brace & Company, 1994)

Subject(s): Pirates; Pets; Grief
Age range(s): Grades K-2
Major character(s): Boris von der Borch, Pirate
Time period(s): Indeterminate Past
Locale(s): At Sea

Summary: In typical pirate fashion, Boris is tough, scruffy, mean and greedy. Yet, when his pet parrot dies, he cries and cries along with his crew. The illustrations expand the story and carry the subplot. (32 pages)

Where it's reviewed:
Booklist, March 1, 1994, page 1269
Children's Book Review Service, Spring 1994, page 135
Horn Book, May 1994, page 313
Kirkus Reviews, April 1994, page 479
School Library Journal, May 1994, page 92

Awards the book has won:
ALA Notable Book, 1995

Other books by the same author:
Sophie, 1994
Shoes from Grandpa, 1992

Koala Lou, 1989

Other books you might like:
Pat Hutchins, *One-Eyed Jake*, 1979
Trying to steal from just one more ship proves to be the comeuppance for greedy pirate One-Eyed Jake.
Leonard Kessler, *The Forgetful Pirate*, 1974
Accompanied by his crew and parrot, forgetful Ben attempts to locate the treasure which he has hidden somewhere.
Margaret Mahy, *The Horrendous Hullabaloo*, 1992
Peregrine the Pirate and his parrot are joined by his aunt who decides to sail the seven seas too.
Ingrid Schubert, *Wild Will*, 1994
Wild Will's stories of his life as a pirate inspire young Frank to suggest that he come out of retirement so the two of them can search for his buried treasure.
Kathy Tucker, *Do Pirates Take Baths?*, 1994
A story in rhyme provides details of the daily life of pirates.

424

KRISTINE L. FRANKLIN

Nerd No More

(New York: Candlewick Press, 1996)

Subject(s): Self-Acceptance; Schools; Mothers and Sons
Age range(s): Grades 4-6
Major character(s): Ludwig von Beethoven ''Wiggie'' Carter, 6th Grader; Callie Adams, 6th Grader; Marilyn M. Carter, Mother, Television Personality
Time period(s): 1990s
Locale(s): United States

Summary: Wiggie wants to be accepted by the ''in crowd'', but since he is the son of Mrs. Science, the TV scientist, and he is smart, he is considered a nerd. When Callie is promoted to 6th grade in the middle of the year they become friends but Wiggie still wants to do things with his old friend, Billy. Callie has started a science club and the boys want to be part of it. They go along on a field trip with the idea of causing trouble. It is trouble that finds them when a tree falls and Wiggie and Callie must work together to help rescue Eddie. (143 pages)

Where it's reviewed:
Bulletin of the Center for Children's Books, October 1996, page 57
School Library Journal, October 1996, page 122
Booklist, October 15, 1996, page 420
Horn Book, November/December 1996, page 735

Other books by the same author:
Eclipse, 1995

Other books you might like:
Margaret Bechard, *Really No Big Deal*, 1994
Jonah is involved in theme parties and helping his friend raise money, but then is embarrassed when his mom dates the principal.
Mame Farrell, *Marrying Malcolm Murgatroyd*, 1995
Hannah does not like the fact that the school geek likes her

and is really nice to her brother so she tries to do mean things to him.

Donna Jo Napoli, *On Guard*, 1997
Mikey wants to win a medal so he looks for a sport which he will be able to do.

David Skinner, *The Wrecker*, 1995
Michael is a new kid and doesn't like that the school ''geek'' seems to attach himself to him.

425

KRISTINE L. FRANKLIN
ROBERT ROTH, Illustrator

When the Monkeys Came Back

(New York: Atheneum, 1994)

Subject(s): Animals/Monkeys; Trees; Conservation of Natural Resources
Age range(s): Grades 1-3
Major character(s): Dona Marta, Mother
Time period(s): 1930s; 1990s (1994)
Locale(s): Costa Rica

Summary: As an adult, childhood memories of the forest filled with the sounds of monkeys inspire Dona Marta to restore the ravaged hillside near her home. She plants and tends the trees over the years as her eleven children are born, enlisting their help in her private restoration project. One night, an older, widowed Dona Marta hears again the sound of the monkeys who have returned to the forest that she has rebuilt. (32 pages)

Where it's reviewed:
Booklist, January 1, 1995, page 825
Children's Book Review Service, February 1995, page 75
Horn Book Guide, Spring 1995, page 34
Learning, March 1995, page 55
School Library Journal, December 1994, page 74

Awards the book has won:
Consortium of Latin American Studies Programs Commended Book, 1994

Other books by the same author:
The Blue-Eyed Goose, 1995
The Shepherd Boy, 1994
The Old, Old Man and the Very Little Boy, 1992

Other books you might like:
Virginia Lee Burton, *The Little House*, 1942
A city's growth swallows the little house until relatives of the original owner relocate the house to a country hillside. Caldecott Medal.

Lynne Cherry, *The Great Kapok Tree: A Tale of the Amazon Rain Forest*, 1990
A man changes his plans to cut down a kapok tree after his dreams are invaded by the animals who depend on the tree.

Arthur A. Levine, *Pearl Moscowitz's Last Stand*, 1993
Pearl's mother led the effort to have the trees planted on their urban street and Pearl is determined to keep the last one from being destroyed in the name of progress.

426

LISA ROWE FRAUSTINO

Grass and Sky

(New York: Orchard Books, 1994)

Subject(s): Grandparents; Summer
Age range(s): Grades 5-7
Major character(s): Timothea ''Timmi'' Lafler, 11-Year-Old, Baseball Player; Grampy Jim Lafler, Grandfather
Time period(s): 1990s
Locale(s): Scranton, Pennsylvania; Maine (summer camp on Fish Lake)

Summary: Timmi's not happy about missing the best two weeks of baseball season to go visit her grandfather, especially since he never answers any of her letters. At first it's difficult for Timmi to be nice to Grampy Lafler, remembering all those times she never heard from him, but gradually she responds to his attempts at friendship. And she does have fun visiting him as they go swimming and boating; Timmi even gets to play some baseball. Her parents eventually reveal they kept his letters from her as they didn't want her to know of Grampy's alcoholism. Though Grampy is obviously ill, Timmi and her father both make peace with him before his death in this first novel. (155 pages)

Where it's reviewed:
Publishers Weekly, February 28, 1994, page 88
Booklist, March 15, 1994, page 1347
Voice of Youth Advocates, June 1994, page 82
School Library Journal, April 1994, page 126
Kirkus Reviews, April 15, 1994, page 555

Other books by the same author:
Ash: A Novel, 1995

Other books you might like:
Sandra Markle, *The Fledglings*, 1992
Left an orphan, Kate realizes her grandfather doesn't know or want her; when he's shot by a poacher he welcomes her help with the eagles.

Norma Fox Mazer, *After the Rain*, 1987
Rachel takes daily walks with her grumpy grandfather and is surprised to find they like one another, which makes his death harder to bear.

Virginia Euwer Wolff, *The Mozart Season*, 1991
Allegra gives up her softball team to practice a Mozart Concert for a summer competition.

427

SIMON FRENCH

Change the Locks

(New York: Scholastic Inc., 1993)

Subject(s): Family Problems; Honesty; Fear
Age range(s): Grades 4-7
Major character(s): Steven Matovic, 11-Year-Old, Brother (older, of Dylan); Lisa Matovic, Single Mother (unemployed); Patrick Hetherington, 11-Year-Old, Friend (Steven's)
Time period(s): 1990s (1991)

Locale(s): Australia (Warrah Valley)

Summary: Bits and pieces of memories from the past flick in and out of Steven's conscious thoughts but he receives no help from his mum when he tries to make some sense of them. Recently deserted by her boyfriend who also stole her car, Lisa is too caught up with her own problems to lend support or comfort to Steven. As his friend Patrick shares memories of growing up in the community, Steven becomes more aware of his need to know more about his past and confronts his mum with his fears. Originally published in Australia in 1991. (103 pages)

Where it's reviewed:
Booklist, May 1, 1993, page 1588
Horn Book, May 1993, page 332
Language Arts, April 1994, page 300
School Library Journal, March 1993, page 218
Voice of Youth Advocates, June 1993, page 89

Other books you might like:
Paula Fox, *Monkey Island*, 1991
 Coping with the difficulties of homelessness in New York City presents challenges to daily life for 11-year-old Clay.
Patricia MacLachlan, *Journey*, 1991
 Journey tries to build a future to share with his sister Cat by reconstructing the past from old family photos.
June Rae Wood, *A Share of Freedom*, 1994
 Freedom struggles to keep her family together and learn about the past from her alcoholic mother.

428

VIVIAN FRENCH
RUSSELL AYTO, Illustrator

Lazy Jack
(Cambridge, MA: Candlewick Press, 1995)

Subject(s): Fairy Tale; Folk Tales; Humor
Age range(s): Grades K-3
Major character(s): Jack, Worker; Unnamed Character, Mother
Time period(s): Indeterminate Past
Locale(s): Fictional Country

Summary: In a retelling of the tradional tale about Jack, who prefers sleeping to any other activity, Jack's mother hires him out to various tradesman and farmers in the community. Although Jack manages to stay awake long enough to complete the day's work, he can't seem to arrive at home with the day's wages. As he goes from job to job, he remembers his mother's admonitions to keep from losing his earnings, but applies them inappropriately. While Jack doesn't become wealthy, he brings humor to his employers. (40 pages)

Where it's reviewed:
Booklist, September 1, 1995, page 73
Horn Book Guide, Spring 1996, page 90
Kirkus Reviews, July 1, 1995, page 945
Publishers Weekly, July 10, 1995, page 57
School Library Journal, October 1995, page 125

Awards the book has won:
Booklist Editors' Choice, 1995

Other books by the same author:
Spider Watching, 1995
Caterpillar, Caterpillar, 1993
Once Upon a Time, 1993

Other books you might like:
Anthea Bell, *Jack in Luck*, 1992
 A series of trades begins with Jack's wages going for a horse and then the horse for a cow until finally Jack decides he's better off with few possessions to encumber his journey home.
Tom Birdseye, *Soap! Soap! Don't Forget the Soap! An Appalachian Folktale*, 1993
 Plug Honeycutt tries to overcome his poor memory and remember the soap he is fetching from town for his mother.
Tony Ross, *Lazy Jack*, 1985
 In a more traditional retelling, the lazy boy who seems to do nothing right unwittingly makes a sad princess laugh and thus wins her hand in marriage.

429

VIVIAN FRENCH
ALISON BARTLETT, Illustrator

Oliver's Vegetables
(New York: Orchard Books, 1995)

Subject(s): Food; Grandparents; Gardens and Gardening
Age range(s): Grades K-1
Major character(s): Oliver, Child; Grandpa, Grandfather
Time period(s): 1990s (1995)
Locale(s): England

Summary: While spending a week at Grandpa's house, Oliver, who "only eats french fries," is told that he can eat french fries during his visit when he finds the potatoes in Grandpa's well-tended garden. The catch is that Oliver must eat any vegetable he selects while searching. By the time Oliver finds the potatoes on Saturday, his week is over and he has learned to eat and enjoy all of Grandpa's produce. (26 pages)

Where it's reviewed:
Booklist, September 15, 1995, page 175
Horn Book Guide, Spring 1996, page 27
Kirkus Reviews, July 15, 1995, page 1022
Publishers Weekly, October 9, 1995, page 84
School Library Journal, October 1, 1995, page 97

Other books by the same author:
A Song for Little Toad, 1995
Little Tiger Goes Shopping, 1993
One Ballerina Two, 1991

Other books you might like:
Judith Caseley, *Grandpa's Garden Lunch*, 1990
 Sarah's reward for helping Grandpa in his garden is a delicious lunch made from home-grown vegetables.
Douglas Florian, *Vegetable Garden*, 1990
 Rhyming text explains how a family plants a garden which yields a bountiful harvest.
Christopher King, *The Vegetables Go to Bed*, 1994
 A young child bids good night to each vegetable in the garden before falling asleep.

430

VIVIAN FRENCH
BARBARA FIRTH, Illustrator

A Song for Little Toad

(Cambridge, MA: Candlewick Press, 1995)

Subject(s): Animals; Bedtime; Parent and Child
Age range(s): Grades K-1
Major character(s): Old Mother Toad, Mother, Toad; Little Toad, Child, Toad
Time period(s): Indeterminate
Locale(s): Fictional Country

Summary: A sheep interrupts Old Mother Toad's lullaby to suggest that gentle baaing will be more effective. A mother duck disagrees and suggests quacking. Little Toad, however, knows that all he needs in order to fall asleep is the sweet croaking of his mother's voice. (32 pages)

Where it's reviewed:
Children's Bookwatch, October 1995, page 5
Horn Book, November 1995, page 768
Horn Book Guide, Spring 1996, page 27
Publishers Weekly, July 31, 1995, page 80
School Library Journal, September 1995, page 176

Other books by the same author:
Spider Watching, 1995
Little Tiger Goes Shopping, 1993
One Ballerina Two, 1991

Other books you might like:
Margaret Wise Brown, *Little Donkey Close Your Eyes*, 1995
  Animals throughout the world are bid good night in this gentle poem.
Michael Foreman, *Dad! I Can't Sleep*, 1995
  Little Panda counts animals to help him fall asleep and they all want one last drink of water.
Mem Fox, *Time for Bed*, 1993
  The gentle rhythm of various animal mothers bidding good night to their offspring concludes as a human mother soothes her tired child to sleep.
Mirra Ginsburg, *Asleep, Asleep*, 1992
  The animals are quietly bid good night until only the sleepy child and the wind are awake.

431

VIVIAN FRENCH
CHRIS FISHER, Illustrator

Under the Moon

(Cambridge, MA: Candlewick Press, 1994)

Subject(s): Fairy Tale; Short Stories
Age range(s): Grades 3-5
Time period(s): Indeterminate Past
Locale(s): Fictional Country

Summary: A collection of three fairy tales includes an original story of a fastidious woman whose reputation for cleanliness brings an invitation from the man in the moon to sweep the cobwebs from the sky. The second is a retelling of a folktale in which Old Mother Wolf tricks Little Ivan. The final origi-

nal story tells of the luck the apple child brings to Ben and then the entire village when he outsmarts the elder bogle. First published in Great Britain in 1993. (95 pages)

Where it's reviewed:
Booklist, March 15, 1994, page 1365
Horn Book Guide, Fall 1994, page 3376
Kirkus Reviews, April 1, 1994, page 479
Library Talk, September 1994, page 43
School Library Journal, June 1994, page 98

Other books by the same author:
A Christmas Carol, 1993 (abridged)
Little Tiger Goes Shopping, 1993
One Ballerina Two, 1991

Other books you might like:
Hans Christian Andersen, *Twelve Tales*, 1994
  Translated and illustrated by Erik Blegvad, the collection of twelve fairy tales includes both the familiar and the less well-known.
Philippa Gregory, *Florizella and the Wolves*, 1993
  An original fairy tale about an unconventional princess who defines her role in new ways.
Lauren Mills, *Tatterhood and the Hobgoblins*, 1993
  When her twin Isabella is enchanted, Tatterhood vows to find a way to break the hobgoblins' evil spell.
Neil Philip, *American Fairy Tales: From Rip Van Winkle to the Rootabaga Stories*, 1996
  Each of the tales includes background comments from the compiler.

432

MARGARET WALDEN FROEHLICH
MARLA FRAZEE, Illustrator

That Kookoory!

(San Diego: Harcourt Brace & Company, 1995)

Subject(s): Animals/Roosters; Fairs; Country Life
Age range(s): Grades K-3
Major character(s): Kookoory, Rooster; Weasel, Weasel
Time period(s): Indeterminate Past
Locale(s): Edgerton, Fictional Country

Summary: Kookoory is so excited about Fair Day that he doesn't notice Weasel following him in the hope of catching dinner, or breakfast or lunch. Blissfully ignorant of the lurking danger, Kookoory awakens friends and townfolk before he hurries off to the Fair. As Kookoory dines in a corn field while exhausted, famished Weasel naps, the awakened friends catch up with Kookoory, capture Weasel and put him in a cage at the Fair. There, Weasel finally dines—not on yummy rooster—but on cotton candy and popcorn fed to him by the fairgoers. (40 pages)

Where it's reviewed:
Booklist, April 15, 1995, page 1505
Children's Book Review Service, June 1995, page 122
Horn Book, July 1995, page 449
Publishers Weekly, April 3, 1995, page 62
School Library Journal, May 1995, page 84

Awards the book has won:
ALA Notable Book, 1996

Other books you might like:

Stephen Butler, *Henny Penny*, 1991
As a somewhat confused Henny Penny and her friends hurry to tell the king that the sky is falling they meet a hungry fox with his own plans.

Pat Hutchins, *Rosie's Walk*, 1968
Because she is oblivious to the presence of a fox intent on having her for dinner, Rosie is able to enjoy her walk.

Colin McNaughton, *Suddenly!*, 1994
As he walks home from school, Preston is happily unaware that a wolf is stalking him.

Mary Wormell, *Hilda Hen's Happy Birthday*, 1995
Confident that special surprises have been prepared in honor of her birthday, Hilda Hen enjoys all the treats she finds, not realizing that they were not intended for her.

433

DIANE MARCIAL FUCHS
KATHRYN BROWN, Illustrator

A Bear for All Seasons

(New York: Henry Holt and Company, 1995)

Subject(s): Animals; Seasons; Friendship
Age range(s): Grades K-2
Major character(s): Bear, Bear, Friend; Fox, Fox, Friend
Time period(s): Indeterminate
Locale(s): Fictional Country

Summary: As Bear is settling down for his long winter's nap, Fox arrives complaining about the cold and wishing for spring. For Fox, each season has drawbacks, but Bear quickly realizes that the most important thing about any time of year is the company of a good friend. (32 pages)

Where it's reviewed:
Booklist, October 1, 1995, page 326
Children's Book Review Service, October 1995, page 15
Horn Book Guide, Spring 1996, page 27
School Library Journal, December 1995, page 80

Other books you might like:

Arnold Lobel, *Frog and Toad All Year*, 1976
Through all seasons of the year, Frog and Toad maintain their friendship.

Anne F. Rockwell, *First Comes Spring*, 1985
Bear Child notices how clothing and activities change with the seasons.

Susan Pearson, *My Favorite Time of Year*, 1988
Any season is just right for Kelly and her family because they enjoy the changing activities and weather.

434

MONICA FURLONG

Robin's Country

(New York: Knopf, 1995)

Subject(s): Adventure and Adventurers; Orphans; Mutism
Age range(s): Grades 4-6
Major character(s): Robin Hood, Outlaw, Hero; Marian, Nurse; Richard ''Dummy'' Walter, Orphan (godson of King Richard)
Time period(s): Indeterminate Past
Locale(s): England (Sherwood Forest)

Summary: A mute orphan with a cruel master finally gathers his courage and runs away, only to find himself in the eerie Sherwood Forest where the legendary, and feared, Robin Hood lives. When Dummy accidentally stumbles into Robin Hood's camp, he is immediately taken under Marian's care and nursed back from starvation. Though Marian worries that Dummy might be a spy, Robin enjoys his pluckiness and teaches him archery. With the love and care shown to him, Dummy discovers who he is and recovers his voice. (139 pages)

Where it's reviewed:
School Library Journal, April 1995, page 132
Booklist, April 15, 1995, page 1497
Library Talk, September 1995, page 36
Horn Book Guide, Fall 1995, page 297
Center for Children's Books. Bulletin, June 1995, page 343

Other books by the same author:
Juniper, 1991
Wise Child, 1987

Other books you might like:

Julia Cunningham, *The Silent Voice*, 1981
A young mute lives in Paris where a mime performer helps him adjust.

Morris Gleitzman, *Blabber Mouth*, 1995
Born with ''bits missing'' from her throat, Rowena is mute but certainly a talker with her hands and inside her head.

Robin McKinley, *The Outlaws of Sherwood*, 1988
A realistic reworking of the story of Robin Hood with Robin as a more ordinary man.

G

435

LOUANN GAEDDERT

Hope

(New York: Atheneum/Simon & Schuster, 1995)

Subject(s): Shakers
Age range(s): Grades 5-6
Major character(s): Hope Douglas, 13-Year-Old; John Douglas, Child
Time period(s): 1850s
Locale(s): Pittsfield, Massachusetts

Summary: Hope and John's father is in California to try his luck at mining gold, their mother dies and their uncle hands them over to the Shaker community. The Shaker way of life is strange to Hope, with its separation of boys and girls so that she can't even talk to her brother, and she constantly rebels against it. John, however, thrives in their community with its abundant, well-prepared meals, the chance to learn woodworking and people to care for him during his asthma attacks. When the siblings finally hear from their father, it's not surprising that Hope chooses to join him while John remains with the Shakers. (165 pages)

Where it's reviewed:
Voice of Youth Advocates, December 1995, page 300
Publishers Weekly, November 13, 1995, page 62
School Library Journal, November 1995, page 98
Booklist, December 15, 1995, page 704
Horn Book Guide, Spring 1996, page 61

Other books by the same author:
Breaking Free, 1994
Ever After, 1990
Summer Like Turnips, 1989
Just Like Sisters, 1981

Other books you might like:
Kathryn Lasky, *Beyond the Divide*, 1983
    When Meribah's father is shunned by the Amish church, they endure the hardships of a trip west in 1850.

Robert Newton Peck, *A Day No Pigs Would Die*, 1972
    Living on a Vermont farm, a Shaker boy accepts the decisions that have to be made for the family to survive.
Virginia Sorensen, *Plain Girl*, 1955
    A young Amish girl realizes the conflict between her religion and that of the outside world.

436

KATHRYN O. GALBRAITH
MICHAEL HAYS, Illustrator

Holding onto Sunday

(New York: Margaret K. McElderry Books, 1995)

Subject(s): Fathers and Daughters; Dinosaurs; Museums
Age range(s): Grades 2-3
Major character(s): Jemma, Child; Daddy, Father; Grandma, Grandmother
Time period(s): 1990s (1995)
Locale(s): United States

Summary: Jemma eagerly awaits the beginning of her Sunday ritual. Grandma lets the early-rising child know when it's time to awaken her hard-working father so they can begin the day which is reserved for them. Daddy cooks breakfast for everyone before Jemma notices that it is beginning to rain. Though Jemma is disappointed to see rain on Sunday, Daddy grabs an umbrella and off they go to a natural history museum to spend their time together looking at dinosaurs. Grandma has dinner waiting when they come home and Jemma goes to sleep contentedly, knowing that Sunday will come again soon. (39 pages)

Where it's reviewed:
Booklist, May 15, 1995, page 1646
Horn Book Guide, Fall 1995, page 291
School Library Journal, September 1995, page 176

Other books by the same author:
Roommates Again, 1994
Roommates and Rachel, 1991
Roommates, 1990

Other books you might like:

Paula Danziger, *You Can't Eat Your Chicken Pox, Amber Brown*, 1995

Chicken pox delays a planned summer visit Amber Brown is making to her father.

Pamela D. Greenwood, *I Found Mouse*, 1994

With Mom away for a summer workshop and her brother camping, Tessie and her father are left to fend for themselves—a challenge for both.

James Howe, *Pinky and Rex and the Double-Dad Weekend*, 1995

When rain threatens to spoil the camping trip, Pinky and Rex's resourceful fathers set up the tent in a motel room and plan indoor fun.

437

KATHRYN O. GALBRAITH
MARK GRAHAM, Illustrator

Roommates Again

(New York: Margaret K. McElderry Books, 1994)

Subject(s): Sisters; Camps and Camping; Friendship
Age range(s): Grades 2-3
Major character(s): Mimi, Child, Sister (older); Beth, Child, Sister (younger); Kelly, Child, Friend (Mimi's)
Time period(s): 1990s (1994)
Locale(s): United States (Camp Sleep-Away)

Summary: Mimi and Kelly have plans for an exciting four days at camp. Beth's relief that she doesn't have to go is short-lived when Kelly comes down with the chicken pox and Beth is forced to go in her place. With the sisters assigned to be roommates again at camp, they learn more about each other and develop a deeper friendship. (44 pages)

Where it's reviewed:
Booklist, August 1994, page 2044
Horn Book Guide, Fall 1994, page 300
Library Talk, November 1994, page 40
School Library Journal, August 1994, page 130

Other books by the same author:
Holding onto Sunday, 1995
Roommates and Rachel, 1991
Roommates, 1990

Other books you might like:

Joanna Cole, *The Gator Girls*, 1995

A last-minute opening allows best friends Amy and Allie to be together at camp. Co-author Stephanie Calmenson.

James Howe, *Pinky and Rex Go to Camp*, 1992

Pinky does not share his friend Rex's enthusiasm for their upcoming trip to summer camp.

Lucinda Landon, *Meg Mackintosh and the Mystery at Camp Creepy*, 1990

First-time camper Meg puts her deductive skills to work in a solve-it-yourself mystery.

Ann M. Martin, *Mary Anne and Camp BSC*, 1995

Mary Anne's participation in the Baby-sitter's plans to operate a day camp is complicated by a sprained ankle.

438

DAVID GALE, Editor

Don't Give Up the Ghost: The Delacorte Book of Original Ghost Stories

(New York: Delacorte, 1993)

Subject(s): Short Stories; Ghosts
Age range(s): Grades 6-8
Time period(s): 20th century
Locale(s): United States

Summary: This collection of twelve original short stories by noted authors is divided into stories inhabited by ghosts from the past and ghosts "living" today. Barbara Ann Porte's "Grandmother's Ghost, the Gilded Bathroom and Other Home Improvements" features a grandmotherly ghost who doesn't like the renovations being done on her old home. In "The Last House on Crescent Road" by Mary Downing Hahn, young Adam with a little help from a caring ghost mysteriously becomes his baseball team's hero, instead of the strikeout king. And a young boy meets himself in the future in Theresa Nelson's "Andrew, Honestly." Each story includes the author's biographical sketch. (165 pages)

Where it's reviewed:
Booklist, August 1993, page 2062
Voice of Youth Advocates, December 1993, page 308
School Library Journal, September 1993, page 232
Horn Book Guide, Spring 1994, page 149
Locus, December 1993, page 50

Other books by the same author:
Funny You Should Ask, 1992

Other books you might like:

Gardner Dozois, *Isaac Asimov's Ghosts*, 1995

A collection of twelve ghost stories previously published in *Asimov's Science Fiction* magazine.

A.L. Furman, *Ghost Stories*, 1964

Eight ghost stories that are easy-to-read.

Jean Richardson, *Beware! Beware! Chilling Tales*, 1989

English authors contribute to this anthology of nine ghost stories.

439

KAY GALLWEY, Author/Illustrator

Dancing Daisy

(London: Gollancz Children's Paperbacks, 1994)

Subject(s): Ballet; Dancing; Friendship
Age range(s): Grades K-2
Major character(s): Daisy, Child, Dancer; Alice, Child, Dancer
Time period(s): 1990s (1993)
Locale(s): England

Summary: Exuberant Daisy sees her first ballet and is determined to be a ballerina. Nervously awaiting her first dance class, Daisy meets Alice in the dressing room and they enter class together. During class, their skill and friendship develop until they are chosen to perform as mice in a production of *Cinderella*. (32 pages)

Where it's reviewed:
Booklist, June 1995, page 1784
School Librarian, February 1994, page 16

Other books you might like:
Patricia Lee Gauch, *Tanya and Emily in a Dance for Two*, 1994
　　Unconventional Tanya and graceful Emily compliment each other's talents as they perform together during the winter dance recital.
Rachel Isadora, *Lili at Ballet*, 1993
　　Lili attends four dance classes each week in order to achieve her dream of becoming a ballerina.
Jane O'Connor, *Nina, Nina Ballerina*, 1993
　　Prior to her dance performance, Nina worries that her mom will not recognize her on stage.

440

TRICIA GARDELLA
MARGOT APPLE, Illustrator

Just Like My Dad

(New York: HarperCollins Publishers, 1993)

Subject(s): Ranch Life; Fathers and Sons
Age range(s): Grades K-3
Major character(s): Unnamed Character, Child; Unnamed Character, Father, Cowboy
Time period(s): 1990s (1993)
Locale(s): California

Summary: Each morning a young boy dresses in chaps, spurs and a cowboy hat to match his dad's attire and spends the day helping his father with ranch chores. At the end of the day a tired, but happy cowboy-in-training is tucked into bed by his father. The author's first book was inspired by her son's intent to become a fifth generation rancher. (32 pages)

Where it's reviewed:
Booklist, May 1, 1993, page 1602
Horn Book, July 1993, page 442
Language Arts, September 1993, page 417
Publishers Weekly, May 3, 1993, page 304
School Library Journal, September 1993, page 207

Other books you might like:
Laurie Lazzaro Knowlton, *Why Cowboys Sleep with Their Boots On*, 1994
　　The experiences of tired Slim Jim who loses his clothing nightly to a succession of thieving animals convince him to sleep fully dressed.
Ann Herbert Scott, *Cowboy Country*, 1993
　　An old cowhand gives an interested youngster an introduction to life as a cowboy.
Ann Herbert Scott, *One Good Horse*, 1990
　　A cowboy father and his son count all they see during a day of checking on the cattle on their ranch.

441

LEON GARFIELD
JOHN O'BRIEN, Illustrator

The Saracen Maid

(New York: Simon &Schuster Books for Young Readers, 1994)

Subject(s): Memory; Adventure and Adventurers; Humor
Age range(s): Grades 2-4
Major character(s): Gilbert Becket, Traveller (forgetful); Unnamed Character, Maiden (Saracen maid)
Time period(s): 12th century
Locale(s): London, England (Cheapside); Tyre, Ancient Civilization (northern coast)

Summary: As the son of a merchant, it is forgetful Gilbert's responsiblity to sail to the East and buy goods for his father's business. Feeling cheerful and confident, Gilbert sets off, enjoying a successful trip until his ship is attacked by Barbary pirates and everyone is sold into slavery. Alas, frightened Gilbert cannot remember his last name or address for the ransom note leaving him doomed to life in the dungeon until the Saracen maid befriends him, feeds him and frees him. First published in Great Britain in 1991. (26 pages)

Where it's reviewed:
Booklist, September 1, 1994, page 41
Children's Book Review Service, December 1994, page 42
Horn Book Guide, Spring 1995, page 66
Publishers Weekly, September 5, 1994, page 111
School Library Journal, October 1994, page 90

Other books by the same author:
King Nimrod's Tower, 1982
The Ghost Downstairs, 1972
Mr. Corbett's Ghost, 1968

Other books you might like:
Allan Ahlberg, *It Was a Dark and Stormy Night*, 1994
　　With tongue-in-cheek humor a young boy orchestrates his escape after being kidnapped by a band of brigands.
Philippa Gregory, *Florizella and the Wolves*, 1993
　　In a light-hearted look at another time, an independent princess has her own ideas as to how she should fulfill her role.
Margaret Mahy, *The Pirates' Mixed-Up Voyage*, 1993
　　To fulfill his dream of being a real pirate, Lionel sails away with the staff of his uncle's tea shoppe for a farcical journey of adventure, romance and mystery.

442

MICHAEL GARLAND, Author/Illustrator

Dinner at Magritte's

(New York: Dutton Children's Books, 1995)

Subject(s): Artists and Art; Country Life; Neighbors and Neighborhoods
Age range(s): Grades 3-5
Major character(s): Pierre, Child, Neighbor; Rene Magritte, Artist, Neighbor; Salvador Dali, Artist, Friend
Time period(s): Indeterminate Past
Locale(s): France

Summary: To escape the summer heat in Paris, Pierre and his family go to their country cottage for the weekend. Usually, Pierre is bored to be away from his friends because his parents are content to sit ''as still as stone'' and read or sew. Today, however, Pierre visits his neighbors and is invited to stay for a walk in the woods, a game of croquet and dinner. Rene Magritte and his wife are also joined by their fellow artist, Salvador Dali, for a day of completely surreal activity. A concluding author's note gives biographical information about the artists and their art. (32 pages)

Where it's reviewed:
Children's Book Review Service, July 1995, page 146
Horn Book, July 1995, page 450
Language Arts, November 1995, page 542
Publishers Weekly, May 22, 1995, page 59
School Library Journal, May 1995, page 106

Other books by the same author:
Circus Girl, 1993
My Cousin Katie, 1989

Other books you might like:
Anthony Browne, *The Tunnel*, 1990
 Following her more adventuresome brother into a tunnel, Rose finds herself in a dark, surreal woods and hurries to find Jack.
Chris Van Allsburg, *The Sweetest Fig*, 1993
 Annoyed to be paid for his services with two figs, Bibot learns to appreciate their magic, but never achieves his dreams.
David Wiesner, *June 29, 1999*, 1992
 Holly's science experiment has some unexpected results when enormous vegetables begin falling from the sky.

443

SHERRY GARLAND
TATSURO KIUCHI, Illustrator

The Lotus Seed

(San Diego: Harcourt Brace Jovanovich, Publishers, 1993)

Subject(s): Emigration and Immigration; Intergenerational Saga; Grandparents
Age range(s): Grades 2-5
Major character(s): Ba, Immigrant (from Vietnam), Grandmother; Unnamed Character, Child (grandson), Brother (to the story's narrator); Unnamed Character, Child (granddaughter)
Time period(s): 20th century (1945-1993)
Locale(s): Vietnam; United States

Summary: Ba remembers the day she saw her country's emperor cry when he abdicated his throne and she plucked a seed from a lotus pod in the Imperial garden. Through years of strife, hardship, marriage, escape from a fallen country and settling into a new country, Ba saved the seed as a link to her homeland and a symbol of good luck and long life. One day her grandson, having never seen an emperor or a lotus garden, plants the seed somewhere in the yard. Ba is distraught to lose this symbol of hope. The following spring, the lotus blooms, bringing joy to all and the opportunity to harvest the seeds for

all the grandchildren so they too may remember the story of their family's heritage. (32 pages)

Where it's reviewed:
Booklist, March 15, 1993, page 1320
Horn Book, May 1993, page 315
Publishers Weekly, April 5, 1993, page 78
Reading Teacher, October 1993, page 151
School Library Journal, July 1993, page 60

Awards the book has won:
ALA Notable Book, 1994
Book Links Good Book, 1993

Other books by the same author:
Summer Sands, 1995
I Never Knew Your Name, 1994
Shadow of the Dragon, 1993

Other books you might like:
Tricia Brown, *Lee Ann: The Story of a Vietnamese-American Girl*, 1991
 A non-fiction photographic essay depicts Lee Ann's love for her adopted home as well as her Vietnamese heritage.
Allen Say, *Grandfather's Journey*, 1993
 A grandson completes his grandfather's journey between homeland and adopted land, memory and desire.
Amy Tan, *The Moon Lady*, 1992
 Now living in the United States, a grandmother reminisces about her childhood in China.

444

SHERRY GARLAND
ROBERT J. LEE, Illustrator

Summer Sands

(San Diego: Harcourt Brace & Company, 1995)

Series: Gulliver Green Book
Subject(s): Beaches; Conservation of Natural Resources; Ecology
Age range(s): Grades K-3
Major character(s): Unnamed Character, Sister; Unnamed Character, Brother
Time period(s): 1990s (1995)
Locale(s): Texas

Summary: Two children who have enjoyed the sand dunes and beach near their grandfather's home are astonished to return after a storm and find the dunes and all signs of life washed away. In the winter, the brother and sister return to the beach with their Christmas trees and join other volunteers in placing the used trees along the beach to provide the framework for a new dune line. A concluding author's note gives factual information about the ecology of the barrier islands along the Gulf Coast. (32 pages)

Where it's reviewed:
Booklist, April 15, 1995, page 1505
Children's Book Review Service, Spring 1995, page 135
Horn Book Guide, Fall 1995, page 264
Reading Teacher, November 1995, page 253
School Library Journal, June 1995, page 80

Other books by the same author:
I Never Knew Your Name, 1994
The Lotus Seed, 1993
Why Ducks Sleep on One Leg, 1993

Other books you might like:
Douglas Florian, *A Beach Day*, 1990
　　A family enjoys a relaxing day at the beach looking for seashells.
Troon Harrison, *The Long Weekend*, 1994
　　For his fifth birthday, Michael chooses to spend three days playing at the beach with his mom.
Joanne Ryder, *A House by the Sea*, 1994
　　A child imagines life in a house by the sea, playing with seals, crabs and other marine life.

445

SUSAN GARRISON
MARJORIE PRICEMAN, Illustrator

How Emily Blair Got Her Fabulous Hair
(Mahwah, NJ: BridgeWater Books, 1995)

Subject(s): Self-Acceptance; Beauty; Friendship
Age range(s): Grades K-2
Major character(s): Emily Blair, 1st Grader, Friend; Pamela Paine, 1st Grader, Friend
Time period(s): 1990s (1995)
Locale(s): United States

Summary: As a five-year-old, Emily tries curling her very straight hair in her mom's rollers and gets strangely dented strands. In first grade she meets Pamela who, from Emily's perspective, is blessed with lots of curly hair. Emily indulges her creative impulses by styling Pamela's hair, but still she longs for curly hair of her own. Desperately she tries tying grapevine tendrils to her head, eating carrot curls, rubbing heads with a poodle and making a wig with glue and macaroni. The best solution arrives unexpectedly when she is unable to fulfill Pamela's request for a braid. Pamela takes on the role of stylist and quickly braids Emily's hair. Now Emily has the fabulous hair though Pamela still has the curls. (32 pages)

Where it's reviewed:
Booklist, January 1996, page 844
Horn Book Guide, Spring 1996, page 27
Kirkus Reviews, October 15, 1995, page 1490
Los Angeles Times Book Review, December 3, 1995, page 27
School Library Journal, January 1996, page 83

Other books you might like:
Nancy Cote, *Palm Trees*, 1993
　　A bad hair day threatens a friendship until two girls decide to make the most of it.
Linda Breiner Milstein, *Amanda's Perfect Hair*, 1993
　　As far as Amanda is concerned, her beautiful, attention-getting locks are anything but perfect until the day she takes scissors in hand and creates an image that pleases her.
Tricia Tusa, *Camilla's New Hairdo*, 1991
　　Isolated in a tower, Camilla occupies her time fashioning her hair into animal shapes.

John Sandford, *Nellie Lou's Hairdos*, 1993
　　Nellie Lou is eager to visit the hairdresser for a new hairdo.

446

PATRICIA LEE GAUCH
SATOMI ICHIKAWA, Illustrator

Tanya and Emily in a Dance for Two
(New York: Philomel Books, 1994)

Subject(s): Ballet; Dancing; Friendship
Age range(s): Grades K-3
Major character(s): Tanya, Child, Dancer; Emily, Child, Dancer
Time period(s): 1990s (1994)
Locale(s): United States

Summary: Spunky Tanya dances through life with far more enthusiasm than grace at the barre. When lonely, but talented Emily joins her class, Tanya is awed by the young ballerina. Then their paths cross at the park one afternoon and a friendship begins with the gifts of each enhancing the talents of the other. (32 pages)

Where it's reviewed:
Booklist, October 15, 1994, page 424
Horn Book, November 1994, page 718
Kirkus Reviews, September 15, 1994, page 1271
Publishers Weekly, July 4, 1994, page 62
School Library Journal, September 1994, page 184

Awards the book has won:
Booklist Editors' Choice, 1994

Other books by the same author:
Christina Katerina and the Box, 1993
Bravo, Tanya, 1992
Dance, Tanya, 1989 (ALA Notable Book)

Other books you might like:
Lucy Dickens, *Dancing Class*, 1992
　　A dance class gives children the chance to move like a bird.
Kay Gallwey, *Dancing Daisy*, 1995
　　Energetic Daisy and her graceful friend Alice are chosen for a special performance.
Rachel Isadora, *Lili at Ballet*, 1993
　　Four times a week Lili attends dance classes in order to realize her dream of becoming a ballerina.

447

RITA GOLDEN GELMAN
MARYANN KOVALSKI, Illustrator

I Went to the Zoo
(New York: Scholastic Inc., 1993)

Subject(s): Zoos; Animals
Age range(s): Grades K-2
Major character(s): Unnamed Character, Child, Animal Lover
Time period(s): 1990s (1993)
Locale(s): United States

Summary: When a young boy visits the zoo he notices the animals appear bored so he invites them all to follow him home. Once they're all in the apartment, and he hears the furniture breaking, and sees the mess, he realizes he's made a mistake and leads them back to the zoo. (32 pages)

Where it's reviewed:
Children's Book Review Service, November 1993, page 26
Horn Book Guide, Spring 1994, page 33
Library Talk, March 1994, page 29
Publishers Weekly, July 12, 1993, page 77
School Library Journal, November 1993, page 79

Other books by the same author:
Hello Cat You Need a Hat, 1993
Panda Grows Up, 1993
A Koala Grows Up, 1986

Other books you might like:
Nancy White Carlstrom, *What Would You Do If You Lived at the Zoo?*, 1994
  Many activities are possible if you live at the zoo and copy the animals' movements.
Mary Jean Hendrick, *If Anything Ever Goes Wrong at the Zoo*, 1993
  During a flood, the zookeepers recall Leslie's offer of her home, in the event anything goes wrong at the zoo, and bring the animals to her house.
Arnold Lobel, *A Zoo for Mister Muster*, 1962
  Mister Muster's zoo friends visit him at home for a change.
Peggy Rathmann, *Good Night, Gorilla*, 1994
  As a zoo keeper makes his final rounds, a little gorilla picks the keys out of his pocket and lets all the animals out of their cages to follow the unsuspecting man home.

448

JEAN CRAIGHEAD GEORGE

The Case of the Missing Cutthroats, an Ecological Mystery
(New York: HarperCollins, 1996, c1975)

Subject(s): Wildlife Conservation; Ecology; Mystery and Detective Stories
Age range(s): Grades 3-7
Major character(s): Spinner Shafter, Fisherman (Girl), 13-Year-Old; Cousin Allen "Alligator" Shafter, Fisherman, Teenager; Aunt Becky Shafter, Housewife
Time period(s): 1970s
Locale(s): Jackson Hole, Wyoming

Summary: Skinner and her dad are on a fishing vacation with his brother and family, including the boy cousins. Her dad is anxious to win the family fishing medal which he lost several years ago, so when Skinner catches a cutthroat trout the first day of fishing, he is quite pleased. But Skinner is not so sure since they are an endangered species. She and one of her cousin's take a side trip to locate some eggs for the trout when they meet another girl and her father who are looking for some of their own. When the family is trapped on a ledge, Skinner and Alligator come to the rescue but Alligator falls and breaks his leg when they are attacked by a grizzly. Skinner is able to get help and bring Alligator out from the

wild and the cousins are successful in replacing the trout eggs. (145 pages)

Where it's reviewed:
School Library Journal, June 1996, page 122

Other books by the same author:
There's an Owl in the Shower, 1995
The Fire Bug Connection: An Ecological Mystery, 1993
On the Far Side of the Mountain, 1990
Julie of the Wolves, 1972

Other books you might like:
Eve Bunting, *Blackbird Singing*, 1980
  Marcus's family farm is in danger from migrating blackbirds and he is involved in saving his family as well as solving the natural problem.
Nancy Bond, *The Voyage Begun*, 1981
  Children living in the not-too-distant future are involved in solving the problems brought by pollution of the river.
Virginia Hamilton, *Jacarundi*, 1995
  Animals feel threatened by the encroachment of humans but only Jrundi and Coati travel away to find a safer place.
Doris Buchanan Smith, *Remember the Red-Shouldered Hawk*, 1994
  John's grandmother is beginning to suffer from Altzheimer's disease and he tries to get her involved again by reminding her of birds they've learned about.

449

JEAN CRAIGHEAD GEORGE
LORETTA KRUPINSKI, Illustrator

Dear Rebecca, Winter Is Here
(New York: HarperCollins, 1993)

Subject(s): Winter; Seasons; Grandparents
Age range(s): Grades K-2
Major character(s): Unnamed Character, Grandmother
Time period(s): 1990s (1993)
Locale(s): United States (Grandmother's rural home)

Summary: In a letter to her granddaughter, a grandmother announces the arrival of winter and describes the seasonal events that have been leading up to this day. The letter tells about the changes in plants and weather as well as the adaptations of animals and humans that signal the approaching winter. An introductory note gives factual information about solstices and equinoxes. (32 pages)

Where it's reviewed:
Children's Book Review Service, October 1993, page 13
Horn Book Guide, Spring 1994, page 33
Library Talk, November 1993, page 36
Publishers Weekly, August 9, 1993, page 478
School Library Journal, December 1993, page 87

Other books by the same author:
First Thanksgiving, 1993
The Grizzly Bear with the Golden Ears, 1982
The Wounded Wolf, 1978

Other books you might like:

Nancy White Carlstrom, *Goodbye Geese*, 1991
　　Father and daughter exchange questions and answers which metaphorically describe the coming of winter.
Barbara Rogasky, *Winter Poems*, 1994
　　A collection of poems focuses simply and eloquently on the season of winter.
Ann Schweninger, *Wintertime*, 1990
　　Part of the Let's Look at the Seasons series, this book relates the wonder of winter.
Seymour Simon, *Winter Across America*, 1994
　　A factual photographic journey across America portrays the changes in nature during the winter season.

| 450 |

JEAN CRAIGHEAD GEORGE

The Fire Bug Connection: An Ecological Mystery

(New York: HarperCollins, 1993)

Subject(s): Animals/Insects; Mystery and Detective Stories; Ecology
Age range(s): Grades 6-7
Major character(s): Maggie Mercer, Scientist (entomologist), 12-Year-Old; Capek Has, Student—College (Czechoslovakian); Mitch Waterford, Computer Expert
Time period(s): 1990s
Locale(s): Orono, Maine; Maine (isolated spot in the mountains)

Summary: Like her scientist parents who study plants and soil, Maggie is also curious, but about insects. Every summer she and her parents head for the Biological Research Center in Maine, affectionately known to Maggie as Bug Camp. On her twelfth birthday, graduate student Capek gives her a collection of fire bugs which, when they molt, are supposed to be incredibly beautiful. When Maggie's bugs keep dying rather than transforming from their larvae state, she and young Mitch investigate to determine the cause of these deaths. (148 pages)

Where it's reviewed:
School Library Journal, June 1993, page 105
Booklist, May 15 1993, page 1693
Kirkus Reviews, June 1, 1993, page 721
Horn Book Guide, Fall 1993, page 298
Library Talk, January 1994, page 39

Other books by the same author:
Julie, 1994
The Missing 'Gator of Gumbo Limbo: An Ecological Mystery, 1992
Shark Beneath the Reef, 1989
Water Sky, 1987

Other books you might like:
Betty Ballantine, *The Secret Oceans*, 1994
　　While on a scientific expedition, a crew's deep-sea submersible is captured by Cetasapiens who explain to them how to stop destroying their world.

Alan Dean Foster, *The Deluge Drivers*, 1987
　　When the ecological balance on his planet is threatened, Ethan must stop those who will damage the environment.
David Klass, *California Blue*, 1994
　　John's discovery of an unknown species of butterfly means that many jobs at the lumber mill could be eliminated.

| 451 |

JEAN CRAIGHEAD GEORGE

Julie

(New York: HarperCollins, 1994)

Subject(s): Eskimos; Indians of North America; Animals/Wolves
Age range(s): Grades 6-8
Major character(s): Julie Edwards Miyax Kapugen, Indian (Eskimo); Kapu, Wolf; Kapugen, Indian (Eskimo), Father (Julie's)
Time period(s): 1990s
Locale(s): Kangik, Alaska

Summary: Just as Julie fought for survival in *Julie of the Wolves*, so must she fight again, though this time for the survival of others. As she returns to her village and reunites with her father, Kapugen, she finds he has added such modern conveniences as a telephone and a radio to his home and she worries about the survival of her Eskimo culture; hardest for her to accept is his new wife who is non-Eskimo. The wolves that saved her before are another worry, for the caribou tribes that normally provide food for the pack haven't come through this winter. When her father's herd of musk oxen is in danger from wolf attack, his solution is to kill the wolves, but Julie knows she can't allow that to happen. She makes contact with the dominant male, Kapu, and the rest of the wolf pack and forces them to move in the direction of the caribou herds before they are also eliminated from nature. (226 pages)

Where it's reviewed:
Booklist, October 15, 1994, page 424
Voice of Youth Advocates, December 1994, page 272
School Library Journal, October 1994, page 122
Publishers Weekly, August 22, 1994, page 56
Horn Book, November 1994, page 730

Awards the book has won:
Booklist Editors' Choice/Books for Middle Readers, 1994

Other books by the same author:
The Fire Bug Connection: An Ecological Mystery, 1993
The Missing 'Gator of Gumbo Limbo: An Ecological Mystery, 1992
Who Really Killed Cock Robin? An Ecological Mystery, 1991
On the Far Side of the Mountain, 1990
Julie of the Wolves, 1974

Other books you might like:
Melvin Burgess, *The Cry of the Wolf*, 1992
　　Ben blurts out the news that wolves, thought extinct in England, live near his family's farm; he instantly regrets his comment when a hunter shows interest.
Nancy J. Hopper, *The Interrupted Education of Huey B.*, 1991
　　Huey's attempt to help an old man save great blue herons

from a poacher means missing English class three days a week, jeopardizing his graduation.

Walt Morey, *Death Walk*, 1991

After the murder of his plane's pilot, Joel is stranded in the Alaskan wilderness until he's rescued by Mike and his two wolves.

Whitley Streiber, *Wolf of Shadows*, 1985

Following a nuclear war, a mother and her daughter attach themselves to a pack of wolves as they all attempt to find safety.

452

JEAN CRAIGHEAD GEORGE
CHRISTINE HERMAN MERRILL, Illustrator

There's an Owl in the Shower

(New York: HarperCollins Publishers, 1995)

Subject(s): Animals/Owls; Conservation of Natural Resources; Parent and Child
Age range(s): Grades 3-5
Major character(s): Borden Watson, Child; Leon Watson, Father, Lumberjack; Bardy, Owl
Time period(s): 1990s (1995)
Locale(s): Fresta, California

Summary: When a court order stops logging in the old growth forests and causes Leon Watson to lose his job as a cutter, Borden decides to solve the unemployment problem by killing spotted owls. Instead, Borden finds an immature, injured owl in the forest and, assuming it is a barred owl, takes it home to care for until it is able to be released into the wild. As the family becomes accustomed to Bardy, they begin to see another side to the conflict raging in their small logging community. (134 pages)

Where it's reviewed:
Booklist, September 1, 1995, page 77
Children's Book Review Service, September 1995, page 7
Horn Book Guide, Spring 1996, page 61
Kirkus Reviews, July 15, 1995, page 1023
School Library Journal, November 1995, page 98

Other books by the same author:
Animals Who Have Won Our Hearts, 1994
The Missing 'Gator of Gumbo Limbo: An Ecological Mystery, 1992
Julie of the Wolves, 1974

Other books you might like:
Twig C. George, *A Dolphin Named Bob*, 1995
A stranded bottle-nosed dolphin is taken to an aquarium for rehabilitation.
Kathryn Makris, *The Eco-Kids Series*, 1994-
Five Junior High students form a club to tackle environmental issues.
R.A. Montgomery, *The Owl Tree*, 1986
In a Choose-Your-Own Adventure series entry, your choice of talking owls determines the characteristics of your magical journey.

453

TWIG C. GEORGE
CHRISTINE HERMAN MERRILL, Illustrator

A Dolphin Named Bob

(New York: HarperCollins, 1996)

Subject(s): Animals/Dolphins
Age range(s): Grades 2-5
Major character(s): Bob, Dolphin; Aster, Dolphin; Mike, Animal Trainer
Time period(s): 1990s
Locale(s): Baltimore, Maryland

Summary: Aster performs in the dolphin show at the aquarium after being found on the shore and nursed to health. Her trainers are worried when she becomes pregnant and, when born, the baby dolphin, Bob, is quite thin but seems determined. Aster is soon able to perform in the show again and Bob becomes part of the show when he leaps over the wall into the performance tank and then is unable to leap back again. Finally, his trainers persuade him to leap high and return so that the other dolphins can perform. Meanwhile information about the dolphins is shared. (72 pages)

Where it's reviewed:
School Library Journal, May 1996, page 112

Other books you might like:
Kathryn Lasky, *Shadows in the Water: A Starbuck Family Adventure*, 1992
The family is involved in investigating toxic wastes which have an effect on dolphins.
Madeline L'Engle, *A Ring of Endless Light*, 1980
Vicki is able to face the death of her grandfather the summer she works with the dolphins.
Michael Morpurgo, *Why the Whales Came*, 1990
Two children help to save a beached whale with the help of the island's recluse.
Theodore Taylor, *The Hostage*, 1988
Jamie is surprised when his attempts to capture a whale are not understood.

454

ROY GERRARD, Author/Illustrator

Croco'nile

(New York: Farrar, Straus & Giroux, 1994)

Subject(s): Animals/Crocodiles; Brothers and Sisters; Stories in Rhyme
Age range(s): Grades 1-3
Major character(s): Hamut, Child, Brother; Nekatu, Child, Sister
Time period(s): Indeterminate Past
Locale(s): Egypt (Nile River)

Summary: Hamut and Nekatu raise a baby crocodile and enjoy daily swims with the creature. Impishly, during a swim, the two stow away on a boat and are a hundred miles downstream before they reveal themselves the next morning. The crew puts them ashore in a nearby town where they tour the pyramids and soon are found to have artistic talents which attract the attention not only of the Pharao h, but also of kidnappers eager to sell the talented children into slavery. Fortunately, their crocodile friend has been waiting. He rescues the children when the kidnappers' boat swamp s in the flooded Nile and returns them safely to their family. First published in Great Britain in 1994. (32 pages)

Where it's reviewed:
Booklist, October 15, 1994, page 435
Books for Keeps, May 1994, page 37
Children's Book Review Service, November 1994, page 26
Publishers Weekly, September 5, 1994, page 109
School Library Journal, November 1994, page 75

Other books by the same author:
A Pocketful of Posies, 1991
Mik's Mammoth, 1990
Rosie and the Rustlers, 1989

Other books you might like:
JoAnn Adinolfi, *The Egyptian Polar Bear*, 1994
    Stranded on an iceberg, a polar bear drifts to ancient Egypt where he becomes the pet of the lonely, 10-year-old king.
Tomie De Paola, *Bill and Pete Go Down the Nile*, 1987
    A class trip to a Cairo museum provides unexpected excitement for Bill and his friend Pete.
Jill Paton Walsh, *Pepi and the Secret Names*, 1995
    By befriending animals and learning their secret names, Pepi convinces them to pose for his father so he can make realistic paintings of them for Prince Dhutmose's tomb.

455

ROY GERRARD, Author/Illustrator

Wagons West

(New York: Farrar Straus Giroux, 1996)

Subject(s): Voyages and Travels; Frontier and Pioneer Life; Stories in Rhyme
Age range(s): Grades K-3
Major character(s): Buckskin Dan, Guide; Little Thunder, Indian; Cousin Jed, Teacher
Time period(s): 1850s
Locale(s): Independence, Illinois; Oregon (wagon train going West)

Summary: Buckskin Dan persuades his Illinois neighbors to travel West, so they join together to move. Along the way they face dangers, like buffalo and a lost Indian boy who is later returned to his chieftan father. The travelers defeat bandits with the help of the Indians and travel on across the Colombia River to their new land in Oregon and a successful farm. (unpaged)

Where it's reviewed:
Bulletin of the Center for Children's Books, February 1996, page 181
Booklist, March 15, 1996, page 1268

Other books by the same author:
Croco'nile, 1994
Mik's Mammoth, 1990
Sir Francis Drake, 1988

Other books you might like:
Brett Harvey, *Cassie's Journey: Going West in the 1860s*, 1988
    Cassie and her family travel by wagon from Illinois to California.
William H. Hooks, *Pioneer Cat*, 1988
    Kate smuggles a cat aboard their wagon as they travel on the Oregon Trail.
Sonia Levitin, *Nine for California*, 1996
    A family travels west on a stage coach to meet their father in California.
Gloria Whelan, *Next Spring an Oriole*, 1987
    Libby travels to Michigan from Virginia in a covered wagon.
Courtni C. Wright, *Wagon Train: A Family Goes West in 1865*, 1995
    Ginny and her family face all the trials as they join other former slaves to travel West.

456

DAVID GERSHATOR
PHILLIS GERSHATOR, Illustrator
EMMA SHAW-SMITH, Illustrator

Bread Is for Eating

(New York: Henry Holt and Company, 1995)

Subject(s): Bread; Multicultural; Mothers and Sons
Age range(s): Grades K-2
Major character(s): Mamita, Mother; Unnamed Character, Child
Time period(s): 1990s (1995)
Locale(s): Earth (rural area)

Summary: When a young boy does not finish eating his bread, his mother explains the importance of bread to peoples the world over as well as the process by which it is grown, harvested and processed. She intersperses her comments with a song about bread which is printed in Spanish and English, with music, at the conclusion of the book. (32 pages)

Where it's reviewed:
Booklist, June 1995, page 1784
Horn Book Guide, Fall 1995, page 265
School Library Journal, August 1995, page 122

Other books you might like:
Russell Hoban, *Bread and Jam for Frances*, 1965
    Picky-eater Frances soon grows tired of eating only bread and jam for breakfast, lunch and dinner.
John Vernon Lord, *The Giant Jam Sandwich*, 1987
    A wasp invasion leads a small town to an innovative solution to the problem using the talents of the local baker. Co-author Janet Burroway.
Gary Paulsen, *The Tortilla Factory*, 1995
    The nonfiction work traces the creation of a tortilla from planting to harvest and processing to consumption, thus giving strength to the farmer to begin the cycle again.
Dr. Seuss, *Green Eggs and Ham*, 1960
    Sam-I-Am will not take no for an answer when he offers an appetizing plate of green eggs and ham.

457

PHILLIS GERSHATOR
HOLLY MEADE, Illustrator

Rata-Pata-Scata-Fata: A Caribbean Story

(Boston: Little, Brown and Company, 1994)

Subject(s): Islands; Wishes; Work
Age range(s): Grades K-2
Major character(s): Junjun, Child; Mommy, Single Mother
Time period(s): 1990s (1994)
Locale(s): St. Thomas, Virgin Islands of the United States

Summary: Weary of chores that interrupt his daydreams, Junjun decides to resort to magic. Each time Mommy asks him to help her in some way, Junjun recites ''Rata-pata-scata-fata'' three times and closes his eyes. Coincidentally, but to Junjun's thinking magically, each time he opens his eyes, his wish has come true. By the end of the busy day, Junjun has convinced his mother to try the same technique to fill the rain barrel with water and that night he and Mommy hear the sounds ra-ta-pa-ta-sca-ta-fa-ta as the rain drops fall. (32 pages)

Where it's reviewed:
Booklist, April 15, 1994, page 1541
Horn Book, September 1994, page 574
Kirkus Reviews, May 1, 1994, page 629
Publishers Weekly, April 4, 1994, page 79
School Library Journal, June 1994, page 99

Awards the book has won:
Notable Children's Books in the Language Arts, 1995
Consortium of Latin American Studies Programs Commended Book, 1994

Other books by the same author:
Sweet, Sweet Fig Banana, 1996
The Iroko-Man: A Yoruba Folk Tale, 1994
Tukama Tootles the Flute, 1994
Honi and His Magic Circle

Other books you might like:
Nancy White Carlstrom, *Baby-O*, 1992
An island jitney carries three generations of a family and their goods to the local market to sell their wares.
Arthur Dorros, *Isla*, 1995
Abuela's vivid story carries Rosalba to the Caribbean island home of her relatives.
Lynn Joseph, *Coconut Kind of Day: Island Poems*, 1990
Poems describe the daily life of a young girl in the Caribbean.
Frane Lessac, *My Little Island*, 1984
With a friend, a young boy visits the Caribbean island of his birth.

458

MARY-JOAN GERSON
CARLA GOLEMBE, Illustrator

How Night Came from the Sea: A Story from Brazil

(Boston: Little, Brown and Company, 1994)

Subject(s): Fairy Tale; Folk Tales
Age range(s): Grades 2-5
Major character(s): Iemanja, Deity, Mother; Unnamed Character, Spouse
Time period(s): Indeterminate Past
Locale(s): Brazil

Summary: Long, long ago there was no night, only the bright light of day. Then, one of Iemanja's daughters left her home under the sea to marry a son of the earth people. Though she was happy with her husband, she longed for the comfort of darkness. To please her, the husband sent three men to Iemanja to ask for some night. Iemanja is happy to offer a bag of night spirits to soothe her daughter, but cautions the men not to open the bag until they have reached her daughter. Although the fearful men do not heed the instructions, the watchful daughter is nearby awaiting their return and she is able to quickly retrieve the night spirits. (32 pages)

Where it's reviewed:
Booklist, September 1, 1994, page 51
Kirkus Reviews, August 15, 1994, page 1128
Publishers Weekly, July 18, 1994, page 245
Quill & Quire, September 1995, page 75
School Library Journal, November 1994, page 75

Awards the book has won:
Consortium of Latin American Studies Programs Commended Book, 1994

Other books by the same author:
The People of Corn: A Mayan Story, 1995
Why the Sky Is Far Away: A Nigerian Folktale, 1992

Other books you might like:
George Crespo, *How the Sea Began: A Taino Myth*, 1993
A Puerto Rican folk tale explains the origins of the sea and the island.
Elphinstone Dayrell, *Why the Sun and the Moon Live in the Sky: An African Folktale*, 1968
This Caldecott Honor book tells of a time whensun and his wife moon lived on earth in a house too small to accommodate a visi t from friend water, so they were forced to move to the sky.
Audrey Wood, *The Rainbow Bridge*, 1995
When the Chumash people begin to overpopulate their island home, Hutash, their creator, makes a rainbow bridge to enable some to cross to the mainland.

459

MARY-JOAN GERSON
CARLA GOLEMBE, Illustrator

The People of Corn: A Mayan Story

(Boston: Little,Brown and Company, 1995)

Subject(s): Indians of Central America; Creation; Folk Tales
Age range(s): Grades K-3
Major character(s): Plumed Serpent, Deity; Heart of Sky, Deity; Grandmother of Light, Deity
Time period(s): 1990s (1995); Indeterminate Past
Locale(s): Guatemala

Summary: As the Mayas gather in a successful corn harvest, they pause to remember and give thanks for this source of life. Long ago when the world was empty, Plumed Serpent and Heart of Sky became lonely and decided to create life. Their first attempt produced animals, birds, and other creatures who could make many sounds, but could not communicate with the gods and offer thanks. Help from Grandmother of Light yielded people formed from wood who could talk but had no heart. As the earth recovers from a flood, Plumed Serpent and Heart of Sky realize corn is the basis of life; and from it they fashion the people who still tell this story at harvest time. (32 pages)

Where it's reviewed:
Booklist, January 1996, page 839
Horn Book, November 1995, page 751
Kirkus Reviews, October 15, 1995, page 1491
Quill & Quire, December 1995, page 40
School Library Journal, December 1995, page 96

Awards the book has won:
American Booksellers Pick of the Lists, 1995
Parent's Choice Award, 1995

Other books by the same author:
How Night Came from the Sea: A Story from Brazil, 1994
Why the Sky Is Far Away: A Nigerian Folktale, 1992

Other books you might like:
Deborah Nourse Lattimore, *Why There Is No Arguing in Heaven: A Mayan Myth*, 1989
    Hunab Ku, first creator god of the Maya challenges other gods to create a being to worship him; maize god succeeds.
Pat McKissack, *The Maya*, 1985
    A factual description of the culture, customs and history of the ancient Mayan civilization.
David Wisniewski, *Rain Player*, 1991
    Pik challenges the rain god to a game in hopes of winning rain for his thirsty people.

460

MORDICAI GERSTEIN
SUSAN YARD HARRIS, Co-Author

Daisy's Garden

(New York: Hyperion Books for Children, 1995)

Subject(s): Gardens and Gardening; Animals; Stories in Rhyme
Age range(s): Grades K-3
Major character(s): Daisy, Child, Gardener
Time period(s): 1990s (1995)
Locale(s): United States

Summary: Daisy is a gardener who cheerfully shares the work and the crop with bugs, birds and animals. Month by month, Daisy works in harmony with the wildlife—birds eat the bugs, moles dig the holes and raccoons help harvest the corn. (32 pages)

Where it's reviewed:
Booklist, July 1995, page 1882
Horn Book Guide, Fall 1995, page 265
School Library Journal, April 1995, page 101

Other books by the same author:
The Story of May, 1993
The Gigantic Baby, 1991
Anytime Mapleson and the Hungry Bears, 1990
Arnold of the Ducks, 1983

Other books you might like:
Lois Ehlert, *Planting a Rainbow*, 1988
    A mother and her child plant a family garden, carefully planning the placement of the flowers to create a rainbow of colors.
Diane Dawson Hearn, *Anna in the Garden*, 1994
    For her birthday, Anna receives a packet of seds which her mother helps her plant in seed trays and transplant to the garden when the weather warms.
Joanne Ryder, *My Father's Hands*, 1994
    While digging in the garden, Father shows his patiently waiting daughter the treasures of nature that he finds.

461

MORDICAI GERSTEIN, Author/Illustrator

The Giant

(New York: Hyperion Books for Children, 1995)

Subject(s): Giants; Fantasy; Friendship
Age range(s): Grades 2-4
Major character(s): Amelia, Child, Friend; Clara, Child, Friend; Reina, Child, Friend
Time period(s): Indeterminate Past
Locale(s): Fictional Country

Summary: Despite parental warnings to stay away from the giant's hill, Amelia, Clara, and Reina frequently sneak away town and stand atop the hill overlooking the giant's garden, calling and waving to him. The friends think their antics will cheer the giant, but he never seems to hear them. One day the girls laugh so much while watching the giant weed his garden that he finally hears them. Knowing they've been spotted, Reina admits to fear, while brazen Amelia decorates herself with flowers to attract the giant's attention. When the giant extends his hand in friendship the frightened trio throw flowers into it and race away. (34 pages)

Where it's reviewed:
Booklist, October 15, 1995, page 401
Horn Book Guide, Spring 1996, page 54
Kirkus Reviews, September 15, 1995, page 1350
School Library Journal, November 1995, page 71

Other books by the same author:
The Shadow of a Flying Bird: A Folktale from Kurdistan, 1994
The Mountains of Tibet, 1987
Arnold of the Ducks, 1983

Other books you might like:
Roald Dahl, *The BFG*, 1982
 The BFG (Big Friendly Giant) kidnaps Sophie because he needs her help to save the Queen and others from the wicked giants.
Walter De la Mare, *Molly Whuppie*, 1983
 The newly illustrated presentation of the Celtic story tells of a brave young girl who uses her wits to overcome a giant.
Mary Norton, *Are All the Giants Dead?*, 1997
 When young James travels to the land of Happily Ever After he learns a princess must be rescued from the last giant.

462

FAYE GIBBONS
ERICK INGRAHAM, Illustrator

Night in the Barn
(New York: Morrow Junior Books, 1995)

Subject(s): Fear; Cousins; Brothers
Age range(s): Grades 1-4
Major character(s): Mike, Child, Brother (younger); Willie, Child, Brother; Amos, Dog
Time period(s): 1990s (1995)
Locale(s): United States

Summary: On a dark, cold, windy fall night Willie challenges Mike and their visiting cousins to a night in the barn. No one's willing to admit any fear, so the four boys bid Amos good-bye, gather up snacks and sleeping bags and hurry to the barn. The sounds of the wind howling, mice scurrying, and owls hooting already have the boys on edge when a snuffling, snorting creature begins to mount the stairs to the loft. (32 pages)

Where it's reviewed:
Booklist, September 1, 1995, page 85
Horn Book, January 1996, page 63
Kirkus Reviews, July 1, 1995, page 945
School Library Journal, January 1996, page 83
Smithsonian, November 1995, page 173

Other books by the same author:
Mountain Wedding, 1996

Other books you might like:
Ray Bradbury, *Switch on the Night*, 1993
 A lonely little boy is helped by a new friend to overcome his fear of the dark.
Lillian Hoban, *Arthur's Camp-Out*, 1993
 Not to be outdone by his little sister and her friends, Arthur plans a solo camp-out in the woods near their home, but finds he does not feel as bold after dark.
Natalie Kinsey-Warnock, *On a Starry Night*, 1994
 On a hillside overlooking the family farm, a young girl

tries to ignore the dark shadows and scary night noises as she watches the stars with her mom.

463

DAVID GIFALDI

Toby Scudder, Ultimate Warrior
(New York: Clarion Books, 1993)

Subject(s): Behavior; Self-Perception; Schools
Age range(s): Grades 5-6
Major character(s): Tobias Michael ''Toby'' Scudder, 6th Grader; Mr. Fenning, Teacher
Time period(s): 1990s
Locale(s): Vancouver, British Columbia, Canada

Summary: Toby's cool! As a sixth-grader, and the biggest kid in his class, he thinks he's got it made this year. Toby has reasons to be a bully, for he's always defending himself against his older half-brother and half-sister. His father abandons the family and his mother's too busy with her boyfriends to pay him any attention, so he tries to get it in school by acting out. Between his new teacher Mr. Fenning, who has strict rules for class, and a new kid in his school, Toby's great year doesn't go as planned in this humorous look at a bully. (201 pages)

Where it's reviewed:
School Library Journal, October 1993, page 124
Booklist, October 15, 1993, page 442
Center for Children's Books. Bulletin, November 1993, page 81
Horn Book Guide, Spring 1994, page 76
Reading Teacher, September 1994, page 65

Other books by the same author:
Gregory, Maw and the Mean One, 1992
Yours Till Forever, 1989
One Thing for Sure, 1986

Other books you might like:
Susan Coryell, *Eaglebait*, 1989
 Wardy Spinks is labeled ''nerd'' when he starts high school, but a year of academic success thwarts his school's bullies.
Louis Sachar, *The Boy Who Lost His Face*, 1989
 Danny's brief foray in joining a group of bullies who harass an old woman ends quickly when he thinks she puts a curse on him.
Lee Wardlaw, *Seventh Grade Weirdo*, 1992
 With a mother who drives a pink van advertising her mail-order children's book business, Rob is immediately pegged as a weirdo by the school bully.

464

PATRICIA REILLY GIFF
SUSANNA NATTI, Illustrator

Good Luck, Ronald Morgan!
(New York: Viking, 1996)

Subject(s): Animals/Dogs; Friendship
Age range(s): Grades 1-3

Major character(s): Ronald Morgan, Child, Animal Lover; Lucky, Dog; Kelly, Neighbor, Animal Lover
Time period(s): 1990s
Locale(s): United States

Summary: Home alone during the summer, Ronald decides to train his dog, but nothing seems to work. A new neighbor, Kelly, has moved in with a cat. Naturally the dog and cat don't get along and all the things Ronald tries to have his dog do just don't work out. Lucky still jumps on people, chases the cat, digs in the yard, and rolls in the flowers. Then one day Lucky finds Kelly's favorite cap. This leads to a friendship that lasts until Ronald's friend returns from vacation with a large dog. (26 pages)

Where it's reviewed:
School Library Journal, September 1996, page 178

Other books by the same author:
Ronald Morgan Goes to Camp, 1995
Watch Out Ronald Morgan, 1985
Ronald Morgan Goes to Bat, 1988

Other books you might like:
Sara Swan Miller, *Three Stories You Can Read to Your Dog*, 1995
    A little girl tries to train her dog by reading him stories which should appeal to him, such as digging and napping.
Matt Christopher, *The Dog That Stole Home*, 1993
    A boy needs his dog to give him advice when he plays baseball, but he is gone.
Rose Impey, *Desperate for a Dog*, 1992
    Two sisters finally have a dog but they just can't decide on a name for it.
Steven Kroll, *Andrew Wants a Dog*, 1992
    A 7-year-old becomes a dog with a too-realistic costume at Halloween.
Louis Sachar, *Marvin Redpost: Alone in His Teacher's House*, 1994
    Marvin finds that there is a great deal of pressure in caring for a dog.

465

PATRICIA REILLY GIFF
BLANCHE SIMS, Illustrator

Look Out, Washington, D.C.!
(New York: Dell Books for Young Readers, 1995)

Series: Polk Street Special
Subject(s): School Life; Students; Behavior
Age range(s): Grades 2-4
Major character(s): Emily Arrow, Student; Derrick Grace, Student; Ms. Rooney, Teacher
Time period(s): 1990s (1995)
Locale(s): Washington, District of Columbia

Summary: An overnight class field trip is not proving to be all that Emily anticipated. She's forgotten to bring the required diary which Ms. Rooney plans to give to the President; she's stuck in an aisle seat on both the train and bus; and she has dorky Derrick for her partner. Finding a note from her mother eases her home sickness and, as she gets to know Derrick better, she realizes that he is a kind, knowledgeable person.

The book concludes with specific information about tourist attractions in the nation's capitol. (121 pages)

Where it's reviewed:
Booklist, June 1995, page 1770
Bulletin of the Center for Children's Books, July 1995, page 383
School Library Journal, October 1995, page 103

Other books by the same author:
Emily Arrow Promises to Do Better This Year, 1990
All about Stacy, 1988
The Beast in Ms. Rooney's Room, 1984

Other books you might like:
Paula Danziger, *Amber Brown Is Not a Crayon*, 1994
    Third grade is a confusing and sad time for Amber because her best friend is moving.
Suzy Kline, *Mary Marony and the Chocolate Surprise*, 1995
    Eager to be one of the five students to win a special pizza lunch with the teacher, Mary manipulates the outcome and is stuck with a guilty conscience.
Ann M. Martin, *Karen's School Surprise*, 1996
    Ms. Colman's class is selected to appear on a TV quiz show.

466

PATRICIA REILLY GIFF
MARYLIN HAFNER, Illustrator

Next Year I'll Be Special
(New York: Doubleday, 1993)

Subject(s): School Life; Imagination; Self-Confidence
Age range(s): Grades 1-2
Major character(s): Marilyn, 1st Grader
Time period(s): 1990s (1993)
Locale(s): United States

Summary: In this newly illustrated reissue of a 1980 title, Marylin's hopes and dreams remain unchanged. As a difficult year in the first grade classroom of mean Miss Minch draws to a close, Marylin looks forward to being in 2nd grade with a more understanding teacher. In her daydreams, Marylin becomes all the things she hopes to be. Good luck, Marylin—next year you'll be special. (32 pages)

Where it's reviewed:
Children's Book Review Service, October 1993, page 13
Horn Book, July 1993, page 442
Kirkus Reviews, September 1, 1993, page 1143
Publishers Weekly, July 5, 1993, page 72
School Library Journal, April 1994, page 102

Other books by the same author:
Wake Up, It's Mother's Day, 1991
Happy Birthday, Ronald Morgan!, 1986
The Almost Awful Play, 1985

Other books you might like:
Miriam Cohen, *See You in Second Grade!*, 1989
    First-grade friends plan to meet again in second grade.
Amy Schwartz, *Begin at the Beginning*, 1983
    The second grade is having an art show and Sara is not sure how to prepare for it.

Sue Stops, *Dulcie Dando, Soccer Star*, 1992

The boys don't like having a girl on the team until she helps to win the game.

467

PATRICIA REILLY GIFF
SUSANNA NATTI, Illustrator

Ronald Morgan Goes to Camp

(New York: Viking, 1995)

Subject(s): Camps and Camping; Friendship; Summer
Age range(s): Grades 1-3
Major character(s): Ronald Morgan, Child, Camper
Time period(s): 1990s (1995)
Locale(s): Camp Echo Lake

Summary: School is over and Ronald's friends are planning to go to camp. Reluctantly, Ronald agrees to go too although he's sure that, because he's not good at anything, he will win no medals. Throughout the week, Ronald participates in all the activities and seems to have just the right ideas to help his friends whenever a trouble spot appears. On the last day of camp the medals include one to Ronald for being a good friend. (26 pages)

Where it's reviewed:
Booklist, July 1995, page 1878
Horn Book Guide, Fall 1995, page 291
New Advocate, Winter 1996, page 65
School Library Journal, June 1995, page 80

Other books by the same author:
Good Luck, Ronald Morgan!, 1996
Ronald Morgan Goes to Bat, 1988
Happy Birthday, Ronald Morgan!, 1986
Today Was a Terrible Day, 1980

Other books you might like:
Eve Bunting, *I Don't Want to Go to Camp*, 1996
Lin has no intention of going to camp even when she's big enough, but after visiting her mother at a "Mom's only" camp she begins to reconsider.
Joanna Cole, *The Gator Girls*, 1995
Amy and Allie have such extensive summer plans that they fear a week at camp will interfer with their activities.
James Howe, *Pinky and Rex and the Double-Dad Weekend*, 1995
Good friends Pinky and Rex don't let a little rain spoil their plans for a weekend of camping with their fathers.

468

PATRICIA REILLY GIFF
BLANCHE SIMS, Illustrator

Shark in School

(New York: Delacorte Press, 1994)

Subject(s): Teacher-Student Relationships; Schools; Friendship
Age range(s): Grades 3-5
Major character(s): Matthew Jackson, 4th Grader, Learning Disabled Child; J.P. Peterson, 4th Grader, Outcast

Time period(s): 1990s (1994)
Locale(s): Deposit, Ohio

Summary: Matthew's apprehension about entering a new school gives way to despair when, the day before school opens, he finds under his bed the letter from the teacher assigning summer reading. A poor reader, Matthew has conveniently forgotten about the task and it seems too late to complete it. J.P. comes to his rescue by choosing simple library books and then reading with him. Not until his understanding teacher points out that Matthew always has his nose in a book, does Matthew realize that, thanks to J.P., he's learned to enjoy reading. By following the teacher's suggestion and helping Matthew, J.P. improves her social skills. (103 pages)

Where it's reviewed:
Booklist, July 1994, page 1947
Horn Book, September 1994, page 611
Horn Book Guide, Spring 1995, page 66
Kirkus Reviews, September 15, 1994, page 1271
School Library Journal, September 1994, page 184

Other books by the same author:
Matthew Jackson Meets the Wall, 1990
Fourth Grade Celebrity, 1979
The Girl Who Knew It All, 1979

Other books you might like:
Tom Birdseye, *Tarantula Shoes*, 1995
Unhappy about the family's move, Ryan thinks new shoes will help him be accepted so he uses his pet tarantula as a money-making attraction.
Betsy Duffey, *Hey, New Kid!*, 1996
To help overcome his fear of entering a new school, Cody Michaels creates a more exciting identity for himself and then must face the truth.
Walter Dean Myers, *Mop, Moondance and the Nagasaki Knights*, 1992
Adopted brothers reach out to help a homeless player on their baseball team.
Susan Richards Shreve, *Zoe and Columbo*, 1995
When Zoe and Columbo enter a new school, Columbo feels insecure and left out so he embellishes the true story of his life to keep people from knowing he's adopted.

469

JAN SPIVEY GILCHRIST, Author/Illustrator

Indigo and Moonlight Gold

(New York: Black Butterfly Children's Books, 1993)

Subject(s): Mothers and Daughters; Change; Imagination
Age range(s): Grades K-3
Major character(s): Autrie, Child (African American)
Time period(s): 1990s (1993)
Locale(s): United States

Summary: In the quiet of their home, after all the family members have gone to bed leaving only Autrie and her mama to share a special time together, Autrie likes to go the front porch of her home, secure in the knowledge that Mama is watching from the window. Autrie wishes she could hold this time forever with her beautiful, young mother providing a haven of comfort and strength as Autrie begins to explore in her mind the changes that will inevitably come with time. The first book both written and illustrated by this illustrator. (32 pages)

Where it's reviewed:
Booklist, March 1, 1994, page 1269
Children's Bookwatch, May 1994, page 3
Kirkus Reviews, September 1, 1993, page 1143
Publishers Weekly, November 8, 1993, page 77
School Library Journal, May 1994, page 94

Other books you might like:
Karen Ackerman, *By the Dawn's Early Light*, 1994
    A mom, who works the night shift, has her special time with her children each day as the sun is rising.
Mary Hoffman, *Amazing Grace*, 1991
    With the loving support of her family, Grace learns that one's dreams can come true.
Angela Shelf Medearis, *Our People*, 1994
    Father and daughter playfully share a history lesson and a hope for the future. (nonfiction)

470

JUDITH HEIDE GILLILAND
ELIZABETH SAYLES, Illustrator

Not in the House, Newton!

(New York: Clarion Books, 1995)

Subject(s): Artists and Art; Magic; Mothers and Sons
Age range(s): Grades K-1
Major character(s): Newton, Child, Artist; Unnamed Character, Mother
Time period(s): 1990s (1995)
Locale(s): United States

Summary: Newton's mother is so busy housecleaning and preparing for guests that she is pleased when Newton finds a red crayon and asks for drawing paper. Newton's sense that the crayon is magical is confirmed when he draws a crayon which bounces off the paper. Each object he draws subsequently becomes real and leads to his mother's admonition that the activity is not appropriate in the house. Finally, Newton tapes many sheets of paper together to draw an airplane which he assures his mother he will not fly in the house. Bye, Newton! (32 pages)

Where it's reviewed:
Booklist, December 15, 1995, page 708
Children's Book Review Service, January 1996, page 49
Horn Book Guide, Spring 1996, page 28
Kirkus Reviews, October 15, 1995, page 1491
School Library Journal, January 1996, page 83

Other books by the same author:
River, 1993

Other books you might like:
Martha Alexander, *You're a Genius, Blackboard Bear*, 1995
    With help from Blackboard Bear, Anthony builds a spaceship to the moon.
Anthony Browne, *Bear Goes to Town*, 1989
    Using his magic pencil, Bear is able to create all that he needs and come to the assistance of other animals too.

Crockett Johnson, *Harold and the Purple Crayon*, 1958
    Harold has a magic purple crayon, a vivid imagination, and a talent for drawing himself into and out of trouble.

471

RACHNA GILMORE
ALICE PRIESTLY, Illustrator

Lights for Gita

(Gardiner, ME: Tilbury House, Publishers, 1995)

Subject(s): Emigration and Immigration; Religion; Holidays
Age range(s): Grades K-3
Major character(s): Gita, Child, Immigrant; Amy, Child, Friend
Time period(s): 1990s (1994)
Locale(s): Canada

Summary: The difficulty of learning to live in a new country far from relatives is compounded when a freezing rain storm on Divali, the Hindu Festival of Lights, threatens to cancel the family celebration. Gita is disappointed when only Amy is able to reach her home to share in festivities and the weather cancels the fireworks that are an important part of the celebration. However, when the power goes out, Gita notices that the only light in the neighborhood comes from the *diyas*, the mustard oil lights used during the festival and finally she begins to appreciate the true meaning of the celebration. (24 pages)

Where it's reviewed:
Booklist, June 1995, page 1785
Emergency Librarian, March 1995, page 45
Five Owls, May 1995, page 106
Horn Book Guide, Fall 1995, page 265
Publishers Weekly, June 26, 1995, page 107

Other books by the same author:
Aunt Fred Is a Witch, 1991

Other books you might like:
Barbara Cohen, *Make a Wish, Molly*, 1994
    Molly's mother shows her friends how a Russian immigrant family celebrates a birthday.
Hoong Yee Lee Krakauer, *Rabbit Mooncakes*, 1994
    An immigrant Chinese family celebrates the Harvest Moon Festival.
Jama Kim Rattigan, *Dumpling Soup*, 1993
    The extended family gathers to celebrate the Hawaiian new year and, for the first time, Marisa is allowed to help make the dumplings.

472

JAMIE GILSON
DEE DEROSA, Illustrator

Soccer Circus

(New York: Lothrop, Lee & Shepard Books, 1993)

Series: Hobie Hanson
Subject(s): Hotels, Motels; Mystery and Detective Stories; Sports/Soccer
Age range(s): Grades 4-6

Major character(s): Hobie Hanson, 5th Grader, Soccer Player
Time period(s): 1990s (1993)
Locale(s): United States (Park District)

Summary: Hobie's hopes that his soccer team will bring home the trophy from this weekend's tournament contribute to his absentmindedly riding his bike through fresh cement and almost missing the trip to the game. Hobie promises to be on his best behavior during the weekend, not knowing that the presence of a murder mystery weekend and a clown wedding at the team's motel, in combination with his knack for being in the wrong place at the wrong time, portends potential disaster. While the team receives no trophy, Hobie does—one that will be hard to explain to his parents. (177 pages)

Where it's reviewed:
Booklist, April 1, 1993, page 1431
Horn Book Guide, Fall 1993, page 298
Kirkus Reviews, February 15, 1993, page 226
Publishers Weekly, March 8, 1993, page 79
School Library Journal, June 1993, page 106

Other books by the same author:
Sticks and Stones and Skeleton Bones, 1991
Hobie Hanson, Greatest Hero of the Mall, 1989
Hobie Hanson, You're Weird, 1987

Other books you might like:
Matt Christopher, *Top Wing*, 1994
 Dana faces problems both on and off the soccer field.
Joe Cottonwood, *The Adventures of Boone Barnaby*, 1990
 With friend and soccer teammate Danny, Boone experiences a variety of humorous adventures.
Karen Gardner, *The Case of the Basketball Joker and Other Mysteries*, 1991
 Four sports-related mysteries are solved by Jack B. Quick and his assistants.

473

JAMIE GILSON

Wagon Train 911

(New York: Lothrop, Lee & Shepard, 1996)

Subject(s): Schools; Pioneers; Voyages and Travels
Age range(s): Grades 4-6
Major character(s): Dinah Barnes, 5th Grader; Orin Philpot, 5th Grader; Mr. Marconi, Teacher
Time period(s): 1990s
Locale(s): Philadelphia, Pennsylvania (simulated travel across the United States)

Summary: Dinah's fifth grade class is studying the Westward movement and begins a simulation of the trip, selecting spouses, finding supplies, and making all the decisions involved in the trip. Dinah is not pleased about her partner, but as time goes by, she realizes that he is fun to be with and that they both enjoy doing funny things, like dying their hair green. Even though they do not make it over the mountains in their simulation, Dinah learns a great deal about history and herself. (191 pages)

Where it's reviewed:
School Library Journal, September 1996, page 201
Booklist, September 1, 1996, page 130

Bulletin of the Center for Children's Books, January 1997, page 170

Other books by the same author:
It Goes Eeeeeeeeeeeee, 1994
Soccer Circus, 1993
Sticks and Stones and Skeleton Bones, 1991
Hobie Hanson, Greatest Hero of the Mall, 1989

Other books you might like:
Laurie Lawlor, *Addie's Long Summer*, 1992
 Twelve-year-old Addie is looking forward to a visit from her cousin to their prairie home.
Jean Van Leeuwen, *Bound for Oregon*, 1994
 Mary Ellen Todd and her family travel from their home in Arkansas westward over the Oregon Trail in 1852.
Elvira Woodruff, *Dear Levi: Letters from the Overland Trail*, 1994
 Austin writes letters to his brother describing their trip from Pennsylvania to Oregon in 1851.
George Ella Lyon, *Here and There*, 1995
 A modern girl takes part in a reenactment that teaches her about the Civil War.

474

LINDA GLASER
SUSAN MCGINNIS, Illustrator

Tanya's Big Green Dream

(New York: Macmillan Publishing Company, 1994)

Subject(s): Environmental Problems; Trees; Schools
Age range(s): Grades 3-5
Major character(s): Tanya Cooper, 4th Grader
Time period(s): 1990s (1994)
Locale(s): Goshen City

Summary: Earth Day projects are due Monday and Tanya still needs a place to plant her project and the money to purchase it. Determined to achieve her goal, she collects donations and accepts help from classmates who have collected aluminum cans. On Monday at the tree-planting ceremony in the park the students recognize the importance of teamwork when they also help to dig the hole and plant the tree. (47 pages)

Where it's reviewed:
Booklist, May 15, 1994, page 1680
Children's Book Review Service, Spring 1994, page 140
Horn Book Guide, Fall 1994, page 300
Kirkus Reviews, April 15, 1994, page 556
School Library Journal, August 1994, page 154

Other books by the same author:
Keep Your Socks on, Albert!, 1992
Wonderful Worms, 1992

Other books you might like:
Eloise Greenfield, *Koya DeLaney and the Good Girl Blues*, 1992
 Cheerful Koya learns to accept her true feelings about unpleasant situations rather than use her smile to mask the truth.
Kathryn Makris, *The Eco-Kids Series*, 1994-
 In a new environmentally aware series, three friends res-

cue abandoned kittens, work to free performing dolphins and promote recycling efforts in their community.

Norma Fox Mazer, *Mrs. Fish, Ape, and Me, the Dump Queen*, 1980

Friendship with Mrs. Fish, the school custodian, helps a girl overcome the teasing she receives because her uncle manages the town dump.

Colleen O'Shaughnessy McKenna, *Live from the Fifth Grade*, 1994

A robbery at school encourages class trickster Roger to stop tormenting and start cooperating with Marsha in order to clear the school custodian from suspicion.

475

ANDREW GLASS, Author/Illustrator

Folks Call Me Appleseed John

(New York: A Doubleday Book for Young Readers, 1995)

Subject(s): Frontier and Pioneer Life; Folk Tales; Brothers
Age range(s): Grades 2-5
Major character(s): John ''Appleseed John'' Chapman, Frontiersman, Backwoodsman; Nathaniel Chapman, Brother (younger)
Time period(s): Indeterminate Past
Locale(s): French Creek, Pennsylvania

Summary: Appleseed John describes events in the wilderness when his half-brother Nathaniel, unaccustomed to such life, joins him to help tend apple seedlings. Nathaniel's inexperience causes John some concern for his well-being, especially when John must travel to Fort Pitt for supplies. Fortunately, friendly Indians find Nathaniel and offer him food, companionship, and survival tips until Appleseed John returns from his trip. A concluding author's note gives factual information on the life of this American legend. (42 pages)

Where it's reviewed:
Booklist, September 1, 1995, page 85
Kirkus Reviews, June 15, 1995, page 857
New York Times Book Review, September 24, 1995, page 29
Publishers Weekly, July 10, 1995, page 58
School Library Journal, August 1995, page 134

Other books by the same author:
Charles T. McBiddle, 1993

Other books you might like:
Carol Greene, *John Chapman: The Man Who Was Johnny Appleseed*, 1991
An easy-to-read biography tells the life of a simple apple grower who becomes an American folk hero.
Steven Kellogg, *Johnny Appleseed: A Tall Tale*, 1988
Humorous illustrations highlight this look at John Chapman, legendary traveller and sower of apple seeds.
Reeve Lindbergh, *Johnny Appleseed: A Poem*, 1990
A fanciful look at the activities of Johnny Appleseed.

476

ANDREW GLASS, Author/Illustrator

The Sweetwater Run: The Story of Buffalo Bill Cody and the Pony Express

(New York: Doubleday, 1996)

Subject(s): American West
Age range(s): Grades 1-3
Major character(s): William F. ''Buffalo Bill'' Cody, 13-Year-Old, Frontiersman; Mr. Slade, Businessman, Frontiersman
Time period(s): 1860s
Locale(s): Fort Laramie, Wyoming; Big Bend, Wyoming (Pony Express route)

Summary: Bill was attracted by the money offered for riders of the Pony Express but since he was too young, he was hired as a stable boy. When a rider arrived with news of President Lincoln's election but became too ill to continue, Bill took the news bag and jumped on a horse. He rode longer than most of the other riders and when he reached his final destination Mr. Slate, who at first had denied him a job, was glad to hire him for the future of the Pony Express. (upaged)

Where it's reviewed:
School Library Journal, October 1996, page 80
Bulletin of the Center for Children's Books, December 1996, page 135
Booklist, December 15, 1996, page 731

Other books by the same author:
Folks Call Me Appleseed John, 1995
Charles T. McBiddle, 1993
Chickpea and the Talking Cow, 1987

Other books you might like:
Eleanor Coerr, *Buffalo Bill and the Pony Express*, 1995
Buffalo Bill becomes a rider for the Pony Express.
Kristiana Gregory, *Jimmy Spoon and the Pony Express*, 1994
Jimmy searches once again for adventure on the Pony Express.
Steven Kroll, *Pony Express*, 1996
Includes a discussion of the 18-month history of the Pony Express. (non-fiction)

477

PETER GLASSMAN
TEDD ARNOLD, Illustrator

My Working Mom

(New York: Morrow Junior Books, 1994)

Subject(s): Working Mothers; Mothers and Daughters; Witches and Witchcraft
Age range(s): Grades K-3
Major character(s): Unnamed Character, Mother, Witch; Unnamed Character, Child
Time period(s): 1990s (1994)
Locale(s): Fictional Country

Summary: One glance at the illustrations confirms that the narrator's working mom has a most unusual job. When a witch brings work home, or plans a birthday party, excitement is guaranteed. (32 pages)

Where it's reviewed:
Children's Book Review Service, July 1994, page 147
Horn Book Guide, Fall 1994, page 272
Kirkus Reviews, March 15, 1994, page 395
Publishers Weekly, March 21, 1994, page 70
School Library Journal, August 1994, page 130

Other books by the same author:
The Wizard Next Door, 1993

Other books you might like:
Caralyn Buehner, *A Job for Wittilda*, 1993
    Wittilda is not a mother, but she does need to find a job in order to feed her many cats.
Norman Leach, *My Wicked Stepmother*, 1993
    With her black cat and broom in the corner, Tom is convinced his stepmother is a witch.
Liz Rosenberg, *Monster Mama*, 1993
    Patrick Edward has a loving, but unusual mother—she's a monster.

478

PETER GLASSMAN
STEVEN KELLOGG, Illustrator

The Wizard Next Door

(New York: Morrow Junior Books, 1993)

Subject(s): Imagination; Magic; Neighbors and Neighborhoods
Age range(s): Grades K-2
Major character(s): Unnamed Character, Child (imaginative); Mr. Myers, Wizard, Neighbor
Time period(s): 1990s (1993)
Locale(s): United States

Summary: When Mr. Myers moves into the neighborhood, the boy who lives next door begins to observe some very strange events. His parents think he is only imagining things for no one else sees the unusual events that happen next door or in the classroom when Mr. Myers substitutes for the teacher. Perhaps it is only the boy's imagination, or is it?

Where it's reviewed:
Children's Book Review Service, January 1994, page 51
Horn Book, November 1993, page 731
Kirkus Reviews, August 15, 1993, page 1074
Publishers Weekly, August 2, 1993, page 80
School Library Journal, November 1993, page 79

Other books by the same author:
My Working Mom, 1994

Other books you might like:
John Burningham, *Come Away from the Water, Shirley*, 1977
    Shirley has some very unusual adventures at the beach, but her parent's think she's only imagining.
Bill Martin Jr., *The Wizard*, 1994
    A wizard's clumsiness while conjuring leads to an unexpected result.

Ellen Stoll Walsh, *Pip's Magic*, 1994
    Pip searches for Old Abra, the wizard, in hopes that magic can help Pip overcome his fears.

479

MORRIS GLEITZMAN

Blabber Mouth

(San Diego: Harcourt Brace, 1995)

Subject(s): Fathers and Daughters; Mutism; Physically Handicapped
Age range(s): Grades 4-6
Major character(s): Rowena "Ro" Batts, Student, Handicapped (mute); Amanda Cosgrove, Student; Darryn Peck, Bully
Time period(s): 1990s
Locale(s): Australia

Summary: Born with "bits missing" from her throat, Rowena is mute but certainly a talker with her hands and inside her head. Moving to a new school, she is immediately picked on by the school bully, Darryn. Amanda befriends her, though at first it's just to fulfill a community service project. Eventually Amanda and Rowena band together to show Rowena's father what a source of embarrassment he can be when he wears his wild cowboy shirts and behaves strangely in front of her teacher. (137 pages)

Where it's reviewed:
School Library Journal, June 1995, page 110
Booklist, May 1, 1995, page 1561
Publishers Weekly, June 12, 1995, page 61
Voice of Youth Advocates, August 1995, page 159
Horn Book Guide, Fall 1995, page 297

Other books by the same author:
Sticky Beak, 1995
Misery Guts, 1993
Worry Warts, 1993

Other books you might like:
C.S. Adler, *Eddie's Blue-Winged Dragon*, 1988
    Tired of being picked on by the school bully, a young boy with cerebral palsy decides to fight back.
Julia Cunningham, *The Silent Voice*, 1981
    A young mute lives in Paris where a mime performer helps him adjust.
Virginia M. Scott, *Belonging*, 1986
    After Gustie has a bout of meningitis in her teens, she loses her hearing and must readjust her life.

480

MORRIS GLEITZMAN

Sticky Beak

(San Diego: Harcourt Brace, 1995)

Subject(s): Stepmothers; Fathers and Daughters; Mutism
Age range(s): Grades 4-6
Major character(s): Rowena "Ro" Batts, Student, Handicapped (mute); Ms. Dunning, Teacher, Stepmother
Time period(s): 1990s

Locale(s): Australia

Summary: In this sequel to *Blabber Mouth*, Rowena's fun-loving, country western singing father marries her teacher, Ms. Dunning. Pretty soon they're expecting a baby and Ro's worried that her parents will love this talkative baby more than they love her. Ro adopts an abused cockatoo and is finally able to express her concerns about her new siblings in this humorous family adventure. (140 pages)

Where it's reviewed:
School Library Journal, June 1995, page 110
Publishers Weekly, June 12, 1995, page 61
Voice of Youth Advocates, August 1995, page 159
Horn Book Guide, Fall 1995, page 297
Kliatt, November 1995, page 8

Other books by the same author:
Two Weeks with the Queen, 1992

Other books you might like:
Kate Dickerson, *Step Monsters*, 1989
     A young girl must adjust to life with a new stepfather and three stepbrothers.
Stella Pevsner, *A Smart Kid Like You*, 1979
     Imagine Vera's dismay when she realizes that her new stepmother is also her new math teacher.
Jacqueline Shannon, *Too Much T.J.*, 1987
     Razz's mother remarries and Razz finds herself very attracted to her new stepbrother. Unfortunately, he is oblivious to her interest.

481

DEBI GLIORI, Author/Illustrator

Mr. Bear's Picnic

(Racine, WI: Artists & Writers Guild Books, 1995)

Subject(s): Animals/Bears; Parent and Child; Problem Solving
Age range(s): Grades K-1
Major character(s): Mr. Bear, Bear, Father
Time period(s): 1990s (1995)
Locale(s): Fictional Country

Summary: Awakening on a beautiful morning, Mr. Bear declares it a perfect day for a picnic and sets off with his baby and a picnic basket. He hasn't gone far when he is joined by three opiniated young neighbors who complain about his choice of picnic site and criticize his fishing technique. When the picnic basket yields toys rather than sandwiches the neighbors become more vocal in their dissatisfaction. Calmly Mr. Bear climbs a honey tree and serves honey to all with enough left over for dinner. (32 pages)

Where it's reviewed:
Horn Book Guide, Fall 1995, page 265
Publishers Weekly, June 5, 1995, page 62
School Library Journal, August 1995, page 122

Other books by the same author:
Mr. Bear Babysits, 1994
When I'm Big, 1994
My Little Brother, 1992

Other books you might like:
Jez Alborough, *It's the Bear!*, 1994
     Eddie remembers what happened the last time he went into the woods with his teddy and now his mother plans to return for a picnic lunch.
John Prater, *Once Upon a Picnic*, 1996
     Mom and Dad don't seem to notice the storybook characters observed by their son as the family enjoys a quiet picnic near a stream.
Jimmy Kennedy, *The Teddy Bears' Picnic*, 1992
     A classic song telling of the day the teddy bears gather for a picnic is published in many versions by different illustrators.

482

DEBI GLIORI, Author/Illustrator

The Snowchild

(New York: Bradbury Press, 1994)

Subject(s): Loneliness; Shyness; Seasons
Age range(s): Grades K-2
Major character(s): Katie, Child (shy)
Time period(s): 1990s (1994)
Locale(s): England

Summary: As the seasons change, Katie's lonely, left-out routine remains the same. Her tentative attempts to play with neighborhood children are unsuccessful until the snowy day when she happily and single-handedly makes a snowman so small that she calls it a snowchild and hurries home to get the necessary adornments to complete it. When she returns, she finds a slightly larger snowman standing next to hers and a little girl with props to complete her design. Suddenly snowmen and lonely girls have friends on a happy winter afternoon. (24 pages)

Where it's reviewed:
Booklist, December 15, 1994, page 757
Children's Book Review Service, November 1994, page 26
School Librarian, November 1994, page 146
School Library Journal, December 1994, page 74
Times Educational Supplement, December 2, 1994, page 11

Other books by the same author:
Mr. Bear Babysits, 1994
When I'm Big, 1994
New Big House, 1992

Other books you might like:
Raymond Briggs, *The Snowman*, 1978
     In a wordless fantasy, a young boy's snowman comes to life and leads him on an incredible adventure.
Debra Hess, *Wilson Sat Alone*, 1994
     Shy Wilson sits alone overlooked by classmates who think he prefers solitude until a new student reaches out to him and the others see Wilson in a new light.
Ezra Jack Keats, *The Snowy Day*, 1962
     The Caldecott Medal Winner portrays a young child's enjoyment of the first snowfall.

483

RUMER GODDEN
VALERIE LITTLEWOOD, Illustrator

Great Grandfather's House

(New York: Greenwillow Books, 1993)

Subject(s): Behavior; Cousins; Grandparents
Age range(s): Grades 2-5
Major character(s): Keiko, 7-Year-Old (spoiled); Yoji, 6-Year-Old (small), Cousin; Great Grandfather, Grandfather
Time period(s): 1990s (1992)
Locale(s): Japan (a rural area)

Summary: Keiko is unhappy she is being sent to live temporarily at Great Grandfather's house where life follows the more traditional Japanese customs. Having cousin Yoji as a playmate is not appealing at first, but in time a willful and impulsive Keiko responds to Yoji's friendliness and Great Grandfather's patience. By the time her parents return for her, she is sad to leave. First published in Great Britain in 1992. (76 pages)

Where it's reviewed:
Booklist, May 15, 1993, page 1693
Children's Book Review Service, July 1993, page 150
Horn Book, September 1993, page 598
Publishers Weekly, May 24, 1993, page 88
School Library Journal, May 1993, page 105

Other books by the same author:
Listen to the Nightingale, 1994
Little Plum, 1987
Four Dolls, 1984

Other books you might like:
Eleanor Coerr, *Mieko and the Fifth Treasure*, 1993
    Sent to live with her grandparents after the bombing of Nagasaki, Mieko finds that not only her wounded hand, but also her heart is healed.
Petra Mathers, *Kisses from Rosa*, 1995
    Rosa lives with relatives far from home while her mother recuperates from an illness and finds that leaving them is as difficult as coming to them.
Yoshiko Uchida, *A Jar of Dreams*, 1981
    With the loving support of her extended family Rinko grows up in the 1930s, balancing the two cultures which are her heritage.

484

BARBARA DIAMOND GOLDIN
LOUISE AUGUST, Illustrator

Night Lights: A Sukkot Story

(San Diego: Harcourt Brace & Company, 1995)

Subject(s): Holidays, Jewish; Fear; Jews
Age range(s): Grades K-3
Major character(s): Daniel, Child, Brother (younger); Naomi, Child, Sister (older)
Time period(s): 1990s (1995)
Locale(s): United States

Summary: After enjoying a family dinner in the sukkah, Naomi and Daniel return to spend the night. Last year Grandpa was with them, but this year they're alone and Daniel is afraid without his night light. The night noises are a little frightening to Naomi too until she realizes they have the same night lights as their ancestors—the moon and stars shining through the branches used to roof the shelter. A concluding author's note relates the background of the holiday and the significance of the sukkah. (32 pages)

Where it's reviewed:
Booklist, September 1, 1995, page 59
Horn Book Guide, Spring 1996, page 28
School Library Journal, December 1995, page 80

Other books by the same author:
The Magician's Visit: A Passover Tale, 1993
Cakes and Miracles: A Purim Tale, 1991
Just Enough Is Plenty: A Hanukkah Tale, 1988

Other books you might like:
David A. Adler, *The House on the Roof: A Sukkot Story*, 1976
    Over his landlady's protests, an elderly man builds a sukkah on his apartment house roof in order to celebrate Sukkot with his grandchildren.
Malka Drucker, *The Family Treasury of Jewish Holidays*, 1994
    The traditions, songs, stories and recipes associated with nine holidays of the Jewish year are included in an award-winning collection.
Patricia Polacco, *Tikvah Means Hope*, 1994
    After a devastating fire only a backyard sukkah remains in which neighbors of all faiths gather to give thanks for their many blessings.
Shoshana Lepon, *Hillel Builds a House*, 1993
    A young boy who enjoys building realizes that Sukkot is the perfect holiday for him.

485

MATTHEW GOLLUB
LEOVIGILDO MARTINEZ, Illustrator

The Moon Was at a Fiesta

(New York: Tambourine Books, 1994)

Subject(s): Jealousy; Folk Tales; Mexicans
Age range(s): Grades 1-4
Major character(s): Unnamed Character, Celestial Body (moon); Unnamed Character, Celestial Body (sun)
Time period(s): Indeterminate Past
Locale(s): Oaxaca, Mexico

Summary: After years of peaceful coexistence with the moon watching over people's dreams and the sun overseeing the work day, the moon becomes jealous of the sun's daytime activities. Star gossip says that the day is filled with games and feasts and the moon struggles to stay awake to see for herself just what happens. Since the moon inevitably dozes in the daytime, she enlists the help of the night watchmen to plan a nighttime fiesta. By morning, however, she sees the difficulties caused by her plans and recognizes the importance of her role. (32 pages)

Where it's reviewed:
Booklist, May 1, 1994, page 1607
Bookwatch, May 8, 1994, page 21
Horn Book, May 1994, page 314
Publishers Weekly, March 28, 1994, page 97
School Library Journal, August 1994, page 131

Other books by the same author:
The Twenty-Five Mixtec Cats, 1993

Other books you might like:
Lois Ehlert, *Moon Rope: A Peruvian Folktale/Un Lazo a la Luna: Una Leyenda Peruana*, 1992
    Translated by Amy Prince, the bilingual text explains why fox's face is seen in a full moon and mole's is seen only on a dark night. *SPF
Rodney Rigby, *The Night the Moon Fell Asleep*, 1993
    When an overexhausted moon falls asleep and crashes to the ground the townspeople must convince her to return to the night sky.
Laura Simms, *Moon and Otter and Frog*, 1995
    In a retelling of a Modoc myth, lonely Moon visits earth where he is befriended by Otter who suggests he find a wife so he will not be lonely in the sky.
Susan Whitcher, *Moonfall*, 1993
    Sylvie finds the fallen moon in a neighbor's lilac bush and tries to restore its luster.

486

TARO GOMI, Author/Illustrator

The Crocodile and the Dentist

(Brookfield, CT: The Millbrook Press, 1994)

Subject(s): Animals/Crocodiles; Dentistry; Fear
Age range(s): Grades K-1
Major character(s): Unnamed Character, Crocodile; Unnamed Character, Dentist
Time period(s): 1980s (1984)
Locale(s): Japan

Summary: Translated from a Japanese title originally published in 1984, the story of a crocodile with a toothache shows that sometimes dentists are just as anxious about the patient being treated as the patient is about the dental procedure. (32 pages)

Where it's reviewed:
Booklist, January 1, 1995, page 825
Children's Book Review Service, December 1994, page 38
Curriculum Review, February 1995, page 12
Horn Book Guide, Spring 1995, page 36
School Library Journal, February 1995, page 73

Other books by the same author:
Who Hid It?, 1992
There's a Mouse in the House, 1991
Coco Can't Wait, 1985

Other books you might like:
Donald Charles, *Calico Cat's Sunny Smile*, 1990
    After a checkup by Dr. Dachsund, Calico Cat learns about proper dental hygiene and overcomes a fear of the dentist.

Harlow Rockwell, *My Dentist*, 1975
    A visit to the dentist is explained through simple text and clear illustrations.
William Steig, *Doctor De Soto*, 1982
    In pain from a toothache, a fox seeks help from Doctor De Soto, a mouse, creating an ethical dilemma for both.
Harriet Ziefert, *A Trip to the Dentist*, 1988
    Using a question-and-answer format the procedures and instruments used at a dentist's office are explained.

487

DIANE GOODE, Author/Illustrator

Diane Goode's Book of Scary Stories and Songs

(New York: Dutton Children's Books, 1994)

Subject(s): Folk Tales; Ghosts; Literature
Age range(s): Grades 1-4
Time period(s): Indeterminate Past
Locale(s): Fictional Country

Summary: The not-too-terrifying collection of scary stories also includes songs and poems, some familiar and some less so. With an emphasis on western folktales, entries also include folklore from Italian, Estonian, Native American and African American traditions. (64 pages)

Where it's reviewed:
Booklist, October 1, 1994, page 321
Horn Book, January 1995, page 75
New York Times Book Review, October 23, 1994, page 30
Publishers Weekly, July 4, 1994, page 60
School Library Journal, September 1994, page 207

Other books by the same author:
Diane Goode's Book of Silly Stories and Songs, 1992
Diane Goode's American Christmas, 1990

Other books you might like:
Marc Brown, *Scared Silly!*, 1994
    The collection of poems, riddles, jokes and stories designed to send a shiver down the reader's spine includes some nonthreatening illustrations.
Colin McNaughton, *Making Friends with Frankenstein: A Book of Monstrous Poems and Pictures*, 1994
    The horror of the subject is offset with humor in a collection of illustrated poems designed to appeal to lovers of the gross and grisly.
Jane Yolen, *The Haunted House: A Collection of Original Stories*, 1995
    Original stories describe the seven different families who, over the years, have lived in a house which is haunted. Co-editor Martin H. Greenberg.

488

CAROL GORMAN

Jennifer-the-Jerk Is Missing

(New York: Simon & Schuster, 1994)

Subject(s): Mystery and Detective Stories; Humor; Kidnapping

Age range(s): Grades 6-7
Major character(s): Amy Whipple, Babysitter, 13-Year-Old; Malcolm Wylie, Child; Jennifer "Jennifer-the-Jerk" Smith, Kidnap Victim, Classmate (Malcolm's)
Time period(s): 1990s
Locale(s): United States

Summary: There is no way that Amy wants to spend her weekend baby-sitting for obnoxious, storytelling Malcolm; however, since Malcolm's father is her dad's best client, she doesn't have much choice. As they walk to the park, Malcolm claims his classmate, Jennifer, is being kidnapped by some guy in a limousine. They report this information to the police, but are met with disbelief. Malcolm blackmails Amy to convince her to help him investigate. They track down Jennifer and her kidnappers, but are then locked in a closet in this comic mystery. (135 pages)

Where it's reviewed:
School Library Journal, June 1994, page 128
Publishers Weekly, June 6, 1994, page 66
Booklist, June 1, 1994, page 1816
Center for Children's Books. Bulletin, May 1994, page 287
Kirkus Reviews, June 15, 1994, page 845

Other books by the same author:
The Miraculous Makeover of Lizard Flanagan, 1994
The Taming of Roberta Parsley, 1994
Chelsey and the Green-Haired Kid, 1987

Other books you might like:
Alison Cragin Herzig, *Ten-Speed Babysitter*, 1987
   While Tony's babysitting for a three-year-old he must cope with a storm, robbers and a duck egg that hatches.
Willo Davis Roberts, *Baby-Sitting Is a Dangerous Job*, 1985
   Darcy babysits for three spoiled, rich kids; when they are kidnapped, Darcy outwits the kidnappers and their dog.
Gloria Whelan, *The Secret Keeper*, 1990
   Annie agrees to babysit young Matt at an exclusive resort, but gets in trouble when his estranged father kidnaps him.

489

CAROL GORMAN

The Miraculous Makeover of Lizard Flanagan

(New York: HarperCollins, 1994)

Subject(s): Schools; Friendship
Age range(s): Grades 4-6
Major character(s): Elizabeth "Lizard" Flanagan, Twin, 6th Grader; Sam Flanagan, Twin, 6th Grader
Time period(s): 1990s
Locale(s): United States

Summary: Middle school isn't easy for Lizard. She doesn't understand why her best friend wears a skirt on the first day of school, why her brother Sam is interested in girls or why she has to attend the "Welcome to Truman Middle School Sixth-Grade Dance." As Lizard continues through sixth grade, she adds makeup and hairstyles to her interests, while keeping her love for baseball and flag football. (185 pages)

Where it's reviewed:
School Library Journal, October 1994, page 122
Voice of Youth Advocates, April 1995, page 23
Booklist, October 15, 1994, page 426
Horn Book Guide, Spring 1995, page 76

Other books by the same author:
Jennifer-the-Jerk Is Missing, 1994
Million Dollar Winner, 1994
Graveyard Moon, 1993
The Great Director, 1993

Other books you might like:
Phyllis Reynolds Naylor, *All but Alice*, 1992
   Alice quickly tires of being popular, especially if it means she's supposed to be mean to her good friend Patrick.
Suzanne Weyn, *The Makeover Campaign*, 1990
   Rissa and Sara want Marsha to win the school presidential election, so they de-glamorize her to make her look more efficient.
Virginia Euwer Wolff, *The Mozart Season*, 1991
   Softball practice and violin lessons overlap in Allegra's life; each is important to her.

490

CHARLOTTE TOWNER GRAEBER
DYANNE DISALVO-RYAN, Illustrator

Olivia and the Real Live Pet

(New York: Macmillian Books for Young Readers, 1995)

Subject(s): Pets; Birthdays; Schools
Age range(s): Grades 2-3
Major character(s): Olivia Elizabeth Jones, 8-Year-Old; Kevin Spencer, 2nd Grader; Jess, Aunt
Time period(s): 1990s (1995)
Locale(s): United States

Summary: Olivia is counting the days until her 8th birthday when, finally, she will receive a real, live pet. Her thoughts about the pet Aunt Jess will give her are expressed in her creative writing at school, prompting Kevin to tease her by suggesting unpleasant possibilities. In fact, Aunt Jess gives her a parakeet and, at the party, Kevin wins the parakeet-naming contest using the name of his deceased pet as his entry. (120 pages)

Where it's reviewed:
Booklist, June 1995, page 1770
Bulletin of the Center for Children's Books, July 1995, page 384
Horn Book Guide, Fall 1995, page 297
School Library Journal, July 1995, page 61

Other books by the same author:
Fudge, 1987
Grey Cloud, 1984
In, Out and about Catfish Pond, 1984
Mustard, 1982

Other books you might like:
Helen Cresswell, *Meet Posy Bates*, 1990
   Posy Bates is willing to have either a dog or a cat, in fact, any pet will do.

N.B. Dorman, *Petey and Miss Magic*, 1993
> Restricted by poverty and the limitations of a small apartment, Petey has no pet to write about for a school assignment until he finds an earthworm.

Dick King-Smith, *Pretty Polly*, 1992
> When Abigail is not allowed to have an expensive parrot as a pet she teaches a barnyard hen to talk instead.

491

HARRIET GRAHAM

A Boy and His Bear

(New York: Margaret K. McElderry Books, 1996)

Subject(s): Animals/Bears; Friendship
Age range(s): Grades 4-7
Major character(s): Dickon, Apprentice; Master Nasche, Artisan; Nounou, Bear
Time period(s): 17th century
Locale(s): London, England; France

Summary: Dickon is working as a tanner's apprentice but he has always had a way with animals and likes to visit them. One day a new bear cub runs away to Dickon and the boy determines to save the cub. The people in the town accuse Dickon of witchcraft because of his abilities with the bear. With the help of a former servant and a girl he meets along the way, he joins a group of jugglers and travels with them to return the bear to France. There he is able to free it to return to the wild. The bear tells part of the story. (196 pages)

Where it's reviewed:
School Library Journal, November 1996, page 104
Booklist, October 15, 1996, page 426
Bulletin of the Center for Children's Books, February 1997, page 206

Awards the book has won:
School Library Journal Best Books, 1996

Other books you might like:
Betty Levin, *The Ice Bear*, 1986
> A girl, a bear cub and a baker's helper become pawns in a power struggle.
Pamela F. Service, *All's Faire*, 1993
> Kevin's parents were medieval buffs and appeared in medieval shows and Kevin, who did not like them, suddenly finds himself back in time.
Mary Stolz, *Bartholomew Fair*, 1990
> All types of people attend the fair during the time of Elizabeth I.
Theodore Taylor, *The Wierdo*, 1991
> Seventeen-year-old Chip fights to save a black bear.

492

LOIS G. GRAMBLING
H.B. LEWIS, Illustrator

Can I Have a Stegosaurus Mom? Can I? Please?

(Mahweh, NJ: BridgeWater Books, 1995)

Subject(s): Dinosaurs; Mothers and Sons; Pets

Age range(s): Grades K-2
Major character(s): Unnamed Character, Child
Time period(s): 1990s (1995)
Locale(s): United States

Summary: Repeatedly, a little boy begs his mother to allow him to have a stegosaurus. He lists the many reasons that such a pet would be of practical benefit to him. The most compelling reason for quickly getting his mom's permission is the huge egg that he has found which is hatching into... (32 pages)

Where it's reviewed:
Booklist, January 1, 1995, page 935
Children's Book Review Service, March 1995, page 86
Kirkus Reviews, February 15, 1995, page 224
Publishers Weekly, January 23, 1995, page 69
School Library Journal, June 1995, page 81

Awards the book has won:
Florida Reading Association Children's Book Award, 1996

Other books by the same author:
Mrs. Tittle's Turkey Farm, 1994
Elephant and Mouse Get Ready for Easter, 1991
A Hundred Million Reasons for Owning an Elephant, 1990

Other books you might like:
Lindsay Camp, *Dinosaurs at the Supermarket*, 1993
> After finding a strange bone in her backyard, a lonely girl imagines it came from a dinosaur and a herd of them is now following her.
Wolfram Hanel, *Lila's Little Dinosaur*, 1994
> While visiting a museum, Lila spots a little dinosaur who follows her home.
Lynn Sweat, *The Smallest Stegosaurus*, 1993
> Baby Stegosaurus wants to be helpful just like the bigger dinosaurs.

493

MICHELE GRANGER

Fifth Grade Fever

(New York: Dutton Children's Books, 1995)

Subject(s): Schools; Teachers; Students
Age range(s): Grades 4-5
Major character(s): Marty Gordon, 5th Grader, Friend; Nina Guardino, 5th Grader, Friend; Mr. Truesdale, Teacher
Time period(s): 1990s (1995)
Locale(s): United States

Summary: When Marty and Nina discover that they've been assigned to the new fifth grade teacher, gorgeous Mr. Truesdale, they plan to do whatever it takes to be the teacher's pet. Of course, they've never been a teacher's pet so they're not sure what it requires, but they think doing homework, improving their grades and not writing notes during class should be a good beginning. (133 pages)

Where it's reviewed:
Booklist, May 15, 1995, page 1646
Bulletin of the Center for Children's Books, June 1995, page 344
Horn Book Guide, Fall 1995, page 297

Library Talk, September 1995, page 36
School Library Journal, July 1995, page 78

Other books by the same author:
Eliza, the Hypnotizer: And Other Eliza & Francie Stories, 1993
The Summer House Cat, 1989

Other books you might like:
Barbara Shook Hazen, *Good-Bye, Hello*, 1994
  Sixth grade should be fun, but for Bobbie Jean, stuck in tough Sister Alice's class—what could be worse!
Colleen O'Shaughnessy Murphy, *The Truth about Sixth Grade*, 1991
  Instant popularity comes to Collette simply because her family knows a teacher considered by the other students to be extremely attractive.
Barbara Robinson, *The Best School Year Ever*, 1994
  In a sequel to *The Best Christmas Pageant Ever* the inimitable Herdmans are back for a school year of mayhem and disaster.
Eileen Walsh Strauch, *Hey You, Sister Rose*, 1993
  Outspoken Arlene struggles to meet strict Sister Rose's expectations of a 6th grader and learns about herself in the process.

494

JEANNE M. GRAVOIS
ALISON HILL, Illustrator

Quickly, Quigley

(New York: Tambourine Books, 1994)

Subject(s): Animals/Penguins; Family Life; Individuality
Age range(s): Grades K-1
Major character(s): Quigley, Penguin (slow)
Time period(s): Indeterminate
Locale(s): Fictional Country

Summary: Quigley tries, but can't seem to move quickly enough for anyone at home or at school. All day he hears pleas to speed up so the day he hurries out to play with some impatient friends he is happy to hear his younger brother say "slow down." The author's first book was originally published in Great Britain in 1993.

Where it's reviewed:
Booklist, April 15, 1994, page 1538
Children's Book Review Service, April 1994, page 99
Horn Book Guide, Fall 1994, page 273
Publishers Weekly, February 28, 1994, page 86
School Library Journal, June 1994, page 100

Other books you might like:
Robert Kraus, *Leo the Late Bloomer*, 1971
  Though slow to achieve parental expectations, at his own pace, Leo finally "blooms."
John Prater, *The Greatest Show on Earth*, 1995
  Harry's talented family performs with the circus, but Harry can't seem to do anything right.
Audrey Wood, *Oh My Baby Bear!*, 1990
  Although Baby Bear is now able to do many things for himself, he has not outgrown his need for a goodnight kiss.

495

LIBBA MOORE GRAY
ELIZABETH SAYLES, Illustrator

The Little Black Truck

(New York: Simon and Schuster Books for Young Readers, 1994)

Subject(s): Transportation; Seasons; Change
Age range(s): Grades K-1
Major character(s): Unnamed Character, Young Man
Time period(s): Indeterminate Past
Locale(s): United States (rural area)

Summary: Over the years a little black pickup truck lumbers over the roads, carrying pumpkins or Christmas trees or bushels of apples, depending on the season. Inevitably the day comes when the truck is simply too old to keep going and it is towed into the woods and abandoned. Years later it is found by a young man who, reminded of his grandfather's truck, works to restore it. (32 pages)

Where it's reviewed:
Booklist, June 1, 1994, page 1837
Children's Book Review Service, June 1994, page 122
Horn Book Guide, Fall 1994, page 273
Publishers Weekly, April 11, 1994, page 64
School Library Journal, August 1994, page 131

Other books by the same author:
Fenton's Leap, 1994
Dear Willie Rudd, 1993
Miss Tizzy, 1993

Other books you might like:
Virginia Lee Burton, *Mike Mulligan and His Steam Shovel*, 1939
  Mike Mulligan successfully demonstrates that his steam shovel Mary Anne is able to do work that the newer power shovels cannot.
Watty Piper, *The Little Engine That Could*, 1930
  The Little Engine proves that gumption is more important than size if there is a job to be done.
Peter Spier, *Tin Lizzie*, 1975
  The "life" of a Model T from its purchase in 1909 to its abandonment and final restoration is depicted.

496

LIBBA MOORE GRAY
RAUL COLON, Illustrator

My Mama Had a Dancing Heart

(New York: Orchard Books, 1995)

Subject(s): Dancing; Mothers and Daughters; Seasons
Age range(s): Grades K-3
Major character(s): Unnamed Character, Dancer; Mama, Mother
Time period(s): Indeterminate Past
Locale(s): United States

Summary: A ballerina reminisces about the seasons of her childhood, each greeted by an outdoor duet with her mother followed by a seasonal indoor activity. Mama and daughter share a love of movement as well as each other. The memories inspire the grown child when she performs as a dancer. (32 pages)

Where it's reviewed:
Booklist, September 15, 1995, page 160
Children's Book Review Service, February 1996, page 75
Kirkus Reviews, July 15, 1995, page 1023
Publishers Weekly, September 25, 1995, page 56
School Library Journal, September 1995, page 176

Awards the book has won:
Booklist Editors' Choice, 1995
ALA Notable Book, 1996

Other books by the same author:
Fenton's Leap, 1994
The Little Black Truck, 1994
Miss Tizzy, 1993

Other books you might like:
Patricia Lee Gauch, *Tanya and Emily in a Dance for Two*, 1994
Tanya's exuberance for movement makes her an unconventional, but inspirational ballet student.
Cynthia Jaber, *Shimmy Shake Earthquake: Don't Forget to Dance Poems*, 1992
A collection of poems includes works by Nash, Mahy and Prelutsky all celebrating the diverse rhythms and sounds of dance.
Linda Lowery, *Twist with a Burger, Jitter with a Bug*, 1995
The lively, rhyming text and bright illustrations encourage children to hop, jive, hula and boogie.
Jackie Jasina Schaefer, *Miranda's Day to Dance*, 1994
Each day of the week a different South American animal gives Miranda a piece of fruit to use in the headpiece she creates for her day to dance.

497

LULI GRAY

Falcon's Egg

(New York: Houghton Mifflin Company, 1995)

Subject(s): Dragons; Mothers and Daughters; Fantasy
Age range(s): Grades 4-6
Major character(s): Emily Falcon Davies, 11-Year-Old, Child of Divorced Parents; Ardene Taylor, Neighbor, Friend (Falcon's); Emily Meade, Aunt (Falcon's great-great aunt), Aged Person (eccentric)
Time period(s): 1990s (1995)
Locale(s): New York, New York

Summary: When Falcon finds a hot, glowing egg in Central Park she asks Ardene to hide the egg and great-great-aunt Emily to call an ornithologist friend to identify it. Soon enough, the egg hatches a dragon that quickly grows too large to be hidden. Reluctantly, Falcon recognizes the need to set the dragon free and sadly gathers family and friends for a ceremonial pre-dawn release. (133 pages)

Where it's reviewed:
Booklist, September 15, 1995, page 162
Children's Book Review Service, November 1995, page 32
Kirkus Reviews, July 1, 1995, page 945
Publishers Weekly, July 24, 1995, page 65

School Library Journal, September 1995, page 199

Awards the book has won:
ALA Notable Book, 1996
School Library Journal Best Books, 1995

Other books you might like:
Bruce Coville, *Jeremy Thatcher, Dragon Hatcher*, 1991
Jeremy buys a small, unusual ball which, in time, he learns is actually a dragon's egg.
Jackie French Koller, *A Dragon in the Family*, 1993
In a sequel to *The Dragonling*, Darek defends the orphaned dragon he has found from angry villagers and the Circle of Elders.
Betsy Sterman, *Backyard Dragon*, 1993
Owen, his grandfather and three friends help a dragon that shows up in their backyard to get back to medieval Wales.
Jane Yolen, *Here There Be Dragons*, 1993
A collection of poems and stories includes a variety of genres telling of good dragons as well as evil ones.

498

MARTIN H. GREENBERG, Editor
CHARLES G. WAUGH, Co-Editor

A Newbery Halloween: A Dozen Scary Stories by Newbery Award-Winning Authors

(New York: Delacorte Press, 1993)

Subject(s): Halloween; Short Stories
Age range(s): Grades 3 and Up
Time period(s): Indeterminate Past

Summary: Twelve tales selected from Newbery Award-winning books provide an opportunity for read-aloud stories and an introduction to acclaimed authors and their literature. The Halloween adventures range from the haunted to the hilarious, the supernatural to the simply spooky. (189 pages)

Where it's reviewed:
Booklist, September 1, 1993, page 61
Five Owls, September 1993, page 18
New Advocate, Winter 1994, page 61
Publishers Weekly, September 20, 1993, page 31
School Library Journal, October 1993, page 124

Other books by the same author:
A Newbery Zoo: A Dozen Animal Stories by Newbery Award-Winning Authors, 1995
A Newbery Christmas, 1991
The Newbery Award Reader, 1984

Other books you might like:
Carolyn Haywood, *Halloween Treats*, 1981
Trick or treat your way through 9 short stories with a Halloween theme.
Alice Low, *Spooky Stories for a Dark and Stormy Night*, 1994
From folklore and fiction, Low has collected stories to entertain those who like read to the company of goosebumps.
Betty Ren Wright, *The Ghost Witch*, 1993
Jenny persuades the ghost witch, residing in the home she and her mother have inherited, to find a new residence

499

MARTIN H. GREENBERG, Editor
CHARLES G. WAUGH, Co-Editor

A Newbery Zoo: A Dozen Animal Stories by Newbery Award-Winning Authors

(New York: Delacorte Press, 1995)

Subject(s): Animals; Short Stories
Age range(s): Grades 4-6
Time period(s): Indeterminate Past
Locale(s): Earth

Summary: A collection of animal stories and one poem from Newbery Award-winning authors offers an introduction to diverse genres. Realistic stories, fanatasy, fable and adventure are included. The work in which an author's selection was previously published is cited so readers eager for more will know where to turn. Brief biographies of each author are appended. (179 pages)

Where it's reviewed:
Booklist, January 15, 1995, page 929
Christian Science Monitor, May 25, 1995, page B2
Horn Book Guide, Fall 1995, page 374
Library Talk, January 1995, page 17
School Library Journal, April 1995, page 132

Other books by the same author:
A Newbery Halloween: A Dozen Scary Stories by Newbery Award-Winning Authors, 1993
A Newbery Christmas, 1991
The Newbery Award Reader, 1984

Other books you might like:
Dick King-Smith, *Dick King-Smith's Animal Friends*, 1996
    A collection of 31 stories tells the true tales of the many different animals in the author's life.
Rudyard Kipling, *Just So Stories*, 1912
    The classic book includes a dozen animal stories and has been reissued many times with different illustrations.
Carl Sandburg, *Rootabaga Stories: Part Two*, 1923
    A companion volume to *Rootabaga Stories*, the humorous collection of nonsense tales was reissued in 1989.
Elizabeth Segel, *Short Takes: A Short Story Collection for Young Readers*, 1986
    Nine stories from well-known authors focus on the thoughts of the child characters.

500

CONSTANCE C. GREENE
S.D. SCHINDLER, Illustrator

Odds on Oliver

(New York: Viking, 1993)

Subject(s): Hero; Humor; Small Town Life
Age range(s): Grades 2-4
Major character(s): Oliver, Child (would-be hero); Arthur, Child, Friend (Oliver's); Edna, Dog (Oliver's pet)
Time period(s): 1990s (1993)
Locale(s): United States (a small town)

Summary: Despite some early defeats, Oliver's dad still thinks that odds are he's a winner. As Oliver grows, he continually searches for the opportunity to be a hero, but most of his attempts end up with Oliver being the rescued rather than the rescuer. Undaunted, he keeps trying and, when he least expects it, finds success. (59 pages)

Where it's reviewed:
Booklist, January 15, 1993, page 908
Children's Book Review Service, April 1993, page 103
Kirkus Reviews, February 1, 1993, page 147
Publishers Weekly, March 8, 1993, page 79
School Library Journal, March 1993, page 198

Other books by the same author:
Isabelle the Itch, 1992
Starshine, 1987

Other books you might like:
Beverly Cleary, *Henry Huggins*, 1950
    The first of many stories about an unforgettable boy and his everyday adventures.
Betsy Duffey, *How to Be Cool in the Third Grade*, 1993
    Third grade begins with one mishap after another, but eventually Robbie comes to learn what it really means to be cool.
Johanna Hurwitz, *Aldo Peanut Butter*, 1990
    New puppies create many hilarious disasters for Aldo and his sisters.
Suzy Kline, *Herbie Jones*, 1985
    Herbie and his friend Raymond face the challenges of third grade with determination.

501

STEPHANIE GREENE
DEE DEROSA, Illustrator

Owen Foote, Second Grade Strongman

(New York: Clarion Books, 1996)

Subject(s): Self-Esteem; Schools
Age range(s): Grades 2-4
Major character(s): Owen Foote, 2nd Grader; Joseph Hobbes, 2nd Grader; Mrs. Jackson, Teacher
Time period(s): 1990s
Locale(s): United States

Summary: Owen is the smallest boy in second grade and his best friend, Joseph, is the heaviest. Knowing that his grandfather was a professional strongman, Owen writes to his grandmother to find out how he did it. While he waits for an answer, he gets into all kinds of trouble in school, even telling the teacher that her voice is too loud when she comments on Joseph's weight. He finds that standing up for his friends is something his grandfather also did. His grandfather was as proud of this as he was of his strength. (81 pages)

Where it's reviewed:
School Library Journal, April 1996, page 110
Booklist, April 15, 1996, page 1438
Bulletin of the Center for Children's Books, March 1996, page 227

Other books you might like:
Betsy Duffey, *The Math Wiz*, 1990
 Marty uses his math problem-solving skills to improve in gym class.
Jamie Gilson, *Itchy Richard*, 1991
 A rumor is spreading fast that someone in Richard's class has head lice.
Suzy Kline, *Herbie Jones*, 1985
 Herbie is determined to get out of the lowest reading group in third grade.
Louis Sachar, *Marvin Redpost: Why Pick on Me?*, 1993
 Marvin feels that he has problems with a student in 3rd grade and tries to find ways to overcome the false rumors he spreads.
Elizabeth Winthrop, *Luke's Bully*, 1990
 Luke is able to overcome the class bully with the help of his mother's ideas.

502

ELOISE GREENFIELD
JAN SPIVEY GILCHRIST, Illustrator

William and the Good Old Days
(New York: HarperCollins Publishers, 1993)

Subject(s): Grandparents; African Americans; Change
Age range(s): Grades K-3
Major character(s): William, Child; Grandma, Grandmother (former restaurant owner), Blind
Time period(s): 1990s (1993)
Locale(s): United States

Summary: In the good old days when Grandma was well, William enjoyed visiting her restaurant, talking with the customers, and eating Grandma's good food. Now Grandma is ill, she is unable to see, and she uses a wheelchair. William longs for those good old days to return, but recognizes that he needs to plan for the future and make some good new days with his beloved Grandma. (32 pages)

Where it's reviewed:
Booklist, February 15, 1994, page 1080
Horn Book Guide, Spring 1994, page 34
Publishers Weekly, August 2, 1993, page 79
School Library Journal, November 1993, page 79
Social Education, April 1994, page 249

Other books by the same author:
Night on Neighborhood Street, 1991
She Come Bringing Me That Little Baby Girl, 1990
Me & Neesie, 1975

Other books you might like:
Angela Johnson, *When I Am Old with You*, 1990
 Relaxing with Grandaddy, a young boy relates all the favorite activities they will do as they grow old together. A Coretta Scott King Honor Book.
Tony Johnston, *Grandpa's Song*, 1991
 The love of his granddaughter and memories of experiences shared with her, help one aging grandfather to cope with the changes he faces.

Jane Resh Thomas, *Saying Good-bye to Grandma*, 1988
 Suzie and her cousins remember their Grandma with love as the family gathers for the funeral.

503

SHEILA GREENWALD

My Fabulous New Life
(New York: Browndeer Press, 1993)

Subject(s): Moving, Household; Apartments; Friendship
Age range(s): Grades 4-6
Major character(s): Alison Fox, 11-Year-Old; K.J. Kendall, 6th Grader, Activist; Julie Fox, 7-Year-Old, Sister (Alison's)
Time period(s): 1990s (1993)
Locale(s): New York, New York

Summary: Alison Fox is hoping to find a fabulous new life in New York City. After months of unemployment, her father locates another job, moves the family into an apartment in New York City and leaves behind their former home, friends, swimming pool, and country club in an elite suburban neighborhood. Life is very different in a co-op in New York City. However, before she can become too engulfed in self-pity, Alison notices the homeless on the streets and, with socially aware but friendless K.J. Kendall, decides to tackle the problem. (172 pages)

Where it's reviewed:
Five Owls, November 1993, page 38
Horn Book Guide, Spring 1994, page 76
Publishers Weekly, September 23, 1993, page 72
School Library Journal, October 1993, page 124
Voice of Youth Advocates, June 1994, page 80

Other books by the same author:
Rosy Cole: She Walks in Beauty, 1994
Mariah Delany's Author-of-the-Month-Club, 1990
Will the Real Gertrude Hollings Please Stand Up?, 1985

Other books you might like:
Barthe DeClements, *The Pickle Song*, 1993
 Concerned about the new girl in her class, Paula attempts to befriend homeless Sukey and find a way to help her family.
Paula Fox, *Monkey Island*, 1991
 Finding himself abandoned by his parents in New York City, Clay runs away from the authorities and lives on the streets with other homeless people.
Alison Cragin Herzig, *Sam and the Moon Queen*, 1990
 Through the help she offers to one homeless girl and her dog, Sam gains some insight into the larger problem of homelessness in New York City.

504

SHEILA GREENWALD

Rosy Cole: She Walks in Beauty
(Boston: Little, Brown and Company, 1994)

Subject(s): Beauty; Peer Pressure; Models, Fashion
Age range(s): Grades 3-5

Major character(s): Rosy Cole, Student, Model; Christi Mc-Curry, Model, Student; Donald McCurry, 8th Grader, Brother
Time period(s): 1990s (1994)
Locale(s): New York, New York (Upper East Side of Manhattan)

Summary: Envious of the attention Christi receives from others for her good looks, Rosy decides she, too, will become one of the beautiful people. Her first attempts fail, but after touring the art museum with Donald, she finds inspiration in a portrait and a poem. While Rosy's new appearance gains attention and the modeling offer she seeks, the experience also teaches her that the time involved in the quest for superificial beauty is not worth the sacrifice of friends and fun. (83 pages)

Where it's reviewed:
Booklist, December 15, 1994, page 753
Bulletin of the Center for Children's Books, January 1995, page 165
Horn Book Guide, Spring 1995, page 76
Kirkus Reviews, December 15, 1994, page 1563
School Library Journal, January 1995, page 106

Other books by the same author:
Rosy Cole Discovers America!, 1992
Here's Hermione: A Rosy Cole Production, 1991
Valentine Rosy, 1986
Give Us a Great Big Smile, Rosy Cole, 1981

Other books you might like:
Candy Dawson Boyd, *Fall Secrets*, 1994
    Sixth grader Jessie enters a performing arts middle school to fulfill her dreams of being an actress, but insecurities plague her.
Kristine L. Franklin, *Nerd No More*, 1996
    When Wiggie Carter tries to be someone he isn't he creates problems for himself and others.
Margaret Mahy, *A Fortunate Name*, 1993
    Lolly decides to become more outgoing and claim her rightful place as a Fortunate cousin.

505

PAMELA D. GREENWOOD
JENNIFER PLECAS, Illustrator

I Found Mouse
(New York: Clarion Books, 1994)

Subject(s): Fathers and Daughters; Animals/Cats; Family Life
Age range(s): Grades 1-3
Major character(s): Tessie, Child; Mouse, Cat (stray); Dad, Father
Time period(s): 1990s (1994)
Locale(s): United States

Summary: Tessie is not happy! Her mom's on a 3-week trip, her brother is camping, her best friend is out of town and her Dad's work keeps him from having time for playing, cooking or remembering to buy milk for the cereal. After several days of boredom, Tessie takes Dad's advice and "finds something to do" when she finds a stray kitten. Caring for Mouse helps Dad and Tessie focus on caring for each other too and by the

time Mom comes home they're able to plan a homecoming celebration and share a final homecooked meal together. (47 pages)

Where it's reviewed:
Booklist, November 1, 1994, page 497
Horn Book Guide, Spring 1995, page 66
Kirkus Reviews, September 15, 1994, page 1272
School Library Journal, October 1994, page 90

Other books by the same author:
What about My Goldfish?, 1993

Other books you might like:
Lady Borton, *Fat Chance!*, 1993
    Lonely Marty befriends a stray, sick, blind cat, caring for it so well that her mother relents and allows her to keep it as a pet.
Gloria Kamen, *Second-Hand Cat*, 1992
    When Louie moves he gives his cat to Nathan.
Inga Moore, *Six-Dinner Sid*, 1991
    Feline Sid is the pet to six different families until his secret is discovered.
Joan L. Nodset, *Come Here, Cat*, 1961
    A young girl's cat takes her on a merry chase to avoid being caught.

506

PAMELA D. GREENWOOD
JENNIFER PLECAS, Illustrator

What about My Goldfish?
(New York, Clarion Books, 1993)

Subject(s): Moving, Household; Pets; Friendship
Age range(s): Grades K-2
Major character(s): Jamie, Child (pet owner); Freckles, Dog (Jamie's pet); Tim, Child (Jamie's new friend)
Time period(s): 1990s (1993)
Locale(s): United States

Summary: Facing the family's move to a new community, Jamie's anxieties are verbalized as concerns for his pets. His mother assures him that the dog and the goldfish will move with the family and gives his friends postcards with his new address. To facilitate his adjustment to a new school, Jamie invites classmates to a "Pond Party" asking each to bring a goldfish to join Jamie's in a fish pond at the new home. Both Jamie and the goldfish find new friends in the process. (40 pages)

Where it's reviewed:
Booklist, November 1, 1993, page 528
Kirkus Reviews, August 15, 1993, page 1074
Publishers Weekly, September 20, 1993, page 72
School Library Journal, January 1994, page 88
Wilson Library Bulletin, October 1993, page 120

Other books by the same author:
I Found Mouse, 1994

Other books you might like:
Robin Ballard, *Good-Bye House*, 1994
    Reluctantly, a young girl bids farewell to her house, room

by room. Meeting a friend upon arrival at her new home helps her to decide to like the new house too.

Nette Hilton, *Andrew Jessup*, 1993

Andrew Jessup has moved, leaving behind an empty house and a forlorn friend until the day that Madeleine Havenblower arrives.

Shirley Hughes, *Moving Molly*, 1988

Molly's loneliness following her family's move is lessened when she makes new friends.

507

GERY GREER, Editor
BOB RUDDICK, Illustrator
BLANCHE SIMS, Illustrator

Jason and the Escape from Bat Planet

(New York: HarperCollins Publishers, 1993)

Series: Intragalactic Troubleshooting Team
Subject(s): Science Fiction; Aliens; Rescue Work
Age range(s): Grades 2-5
Major character(s): Jason Harkness, Child (Coop's assistant); Cooper "Coop" Vor, Alien (Jason's neighbor), Leader (intergalactic troubleshooters); Lootna, Alien (talking cat-like creature)
Time period(s): Indeterminate
Locale(s): United States (Jason's neighborhood); Spaceship; Planet—Imaginary (Bluggax)

Summary: Once again Jason is summoned by his alien neighbor Coop to accompany him on a mission. Along with Lootna, the third team member, they are racing toward planet Bluggax, home of the Demon Bats, to rescue a friendly, but absentminded inventor imprisoned by the bat leader. (92 pages)

Where it's reviewed:
Booklist, March 1, 1994, page 1259
Horn Book Guide, Spring 1994, page 65
School Library Journal, December 1993, page 87

Other books by the same author:
Jason and the Lizard Pirates, 1992
Jason and the Aliens Down the Street, 1991
Let Me Off This Spaceship!, 1991

Other books you might like:
Bill Brittain, *Shape-Changer*, 1994

Frank meets a talking fire hydrant and joins this alien in disguise on his mission to save Earth.

Bruce Coville, *Aliens Ate My Homework*, 1993

When his school project is accidently destroyed by crash-landing aliens, Rod becomes involved in their search for an intergalactic fugitive.

Pamela F. Service, *Stinker's Return*, 1993

In this sequel to *Stinker from Space* the alien in the body of a skunk returns to earth in search of souvenirs.

508

KRISTIANA GREGORY

The Stowaway: A Tale of California Pirates

(New York: Scholastic, 1995)

Subject(s): Pirates; Adventure and Adventurers; Historical
Age range(s): Grades 5-6
Major character(s): Carlito, 11-Year-Old; Captain Hippolyte de Bouchard, Historical Figure, Pirate; Parvo, Pirate
Time period(s): 1810s (1818)
Locale(s): Monterey, California; At Sea (aboard *Argentina*)

Summary: When Carlito and his friends see the sails of the pirate ships on the horizon, they're excited at the thought of seeing real pirates. But when Captain de Bouchard and his pirates land and destroy their city, the boys become angry. After a pirate named Parvo kills Carlito's father, he plans revenge against all the pirates. Sabotaging one of the pirates' ships, Carlito is trapped aboard when it sets sail and is forced to become a cabin boy aboard a ship with a cruel captain. Carlito gets his chance at revenge, but realizes it won't bring back his father. (126 pages)

Where it's reviewed:
Voice of Youth Advocates, December 1995, page 308
School Library Journal, September 1995, page 200
Center for Children's Books. Bulletin, October 1995, page 55
Booklist, September 15, 1995, page 162

Other books by the same author:
Jimmy Spoon and the Pony Express, 1994
Earthquake at Dawn, 1992
The Legend of Jimmy Spoon, 1990

Other books you might like:
Avi, *The True Confessions of Charlotte Doyle*, 1990

A sea voyage under a tyrannical captain hones proper young lady, Charlotte, into a sailor who is able to fight for her life.

Leon Garfield, *Jack Holbrook*, 1965

Jack runs away from the cobbler he's apprenticed to, stows away on a ship captured by pirates and becomes the ship's cook.

Cynthia Voigt, *On Fortune's Wheel*, 1990

A couple of runaways are captured by pirates and sold into slavery.

509

KRISTIANA GREGORY

The Winter of Red Snow: The Revolutionary War Diary of Abigail Jane Stewart

(New York: Scholastic, 1996)

Series: Dear America
Subject(s): Revolutionary War; Diaries
Age range(s): Grades 4-7

Major character(s): Abigail Jane ''Abby'' Stewart, 11-Year-Old; John Edward Stewart, Child (baby); General George Washington, Historical Figure, Military Personnel
Time period(s): 1770s (1777-1778)
Locale(s): Valley Forge, Pennsylvania

Summary: It is the winter of Valley Forge and a new baby is born into the Stewart family. As the army under General Washington camps in Valley Forge, the Stewart family worries about the health of the new baby. They entertain Mrs. Washington and some of the other officers' wives, and the General comes to call at times. Abby writes about these visits in her diary and details the little day to day things that happen during that cold winter. (172 pages)

Where it's reviewed:
Bulletin of the Center for Children's Books, October 1996, page 55
School Library Journal, August 1996, page 144
Horn Book, September/October 1996, page 639

Other books by the same author:
Across the Wide and Lonesome Prairie, 1997
Jimmy Spoon and the Pony Express, 1994
Earthquake at Dawn, 1992
The Legend of Jimmy Spoon, 1990

Other books you might like:
Kathleen Duey, *Mary Alice Peale, Philadelphia 1777*, 1996
　　A girl goes against her father's wishes to help her brother, wounded in the Revolution.
Ruth Nulton Moore, *Distant Thunder*, 1991
　　Kate experiences the horrors of war when she sees the soldiers sent to Pennsylvania to recover from wounds.
Scott O'Dell, *Sarah Bishop*, 1980
　　A girl writes about her experiences during the Revolutionary War.
Seymour Reit, *Guns for General Washington*, 1990
　　Taking guns to Washington from Fort Ticonderoga is the basis of this novel of the Revolution.
Elvira Woodruff, *George Washington's Socks*, 1991
　　Children are transported back in time and join Washington as he crosses the Delaware.

510

PHILIPPA GREGORY
PATRICE AGGS, Illustrator

Florizella and the Wolves

(Cambridge, Massachusetts: Candlewick Press, 1993)

Subject(s): Fairy Tale; Princes and Princesses; Animals/Wolves
Age range(s): Grades 3-4
Major character(s): Florizella, Royalty (princess); Prince Bennett, Royalty (prince), Friend (from a neighboring kingdom); Samson, Wolf (Florizella's pet)
Time period(s): Indeterminate Past
Locale(s): Seven Kingdoms, Fictional Country

Summary: Headstrong Florizella is not the ordinary princess of her parents' dreams. Rather than making plans to settle down, marry a prince, and rule the kingdom, she spends her time riding her horse and playing with her friend, Prince Bennett. When Florizella befriends orphaned wolf cubs by raising them in her room, her parents have had enough of her unconventional ways and order her to release the cubs. After complying with her parents' demand, Florizella discovers that one cub returns to the palace so she quickly disguises him as a dog. When dog/wolf Samson saves Florizella from a panther, her parents realize that there is no hope for an ordinary life with Florizella and reluctantly agree to accept the wolf as a pet. First published in Great Britain in 1991. (80 pages)

Where it's reviewed:
Booklist, May 1, 1993, page 1588
Horn Book Guide, Fall 1993, page 285
Kirkus Reviews, March 15, 1993, page 371
School Library Journal, May 1993, page 105

Other books you might like:
Eva Ibbotson, *Which Witch?*, 1979
　　Arriman the Awful wants to marry a beautiful witch, hoping their baby will inherit his magic skills. However, not all witches are what they seem.
M.M. Kaye, *The Ordinary Princess*, 1989
　　Being the seventh daughter in the royal family should assure beauty but, alas, Amy is destined to be ordinary. Fortunately, that trait is appreciated by some.
Jane Yolen, *Sleeping Ugly*, 1981
　　In this twist on a classic fairy tale, beauty of spirit wins out over physical beauty and all live happily ever after.

511

VALISKA GREGORY
LYNN MUNSINGER, Illustrator

Babysitting for Benjamin

(Boston: Little, Brown and Company, 1993)

Subject(s): Babysitters; Animals/Rabbits; Animals/Mice
Age range(s): Grades K-2
Major character(s): Benjamin, Rabbit (active toddler); Ralph, Mouse, Babysitter (elderly); Frances, Mouse, Babysitter (elderly)
Time period(s): 1990s (1993)
Locale(s): United States (Frances & Ralph's immaculate home)

Summary: Seeking companionship, Frances and Ralph agree to care for little Benjamin, a young bunny who is much larger and considerably more active than his caretakers. Always looking at the positive side of Benjamin's visits to their home, Frances and Ralph finally learn how to cope with Benjamin, save their sanity, preserve their furniture and enjoy his visits. (32 pages)

Where it's reviewed:
Booklist, April 15, 1993, page 1523
Horn Book, September 1993, page 585
Kirkus Reviews, May 15, 1993, page 660
Publishers Weekly, May 17, 1993, page 78
School Library Journal, June 1993, page 76

Other books by the same author:
Through the Mickle Woods, 1992

Other books you might like:

Marc Brown, *Arthur Babysits*, 1992
> The terrible Tibble twins create chaos which babysitter Arthur tries to control.

Eileen Christelow, *Jerome and the Witchcraft Kids*, 1988
> Babysitting the Witchcraft kids on Halloween night is a greater challenge than alligator Jerome expected.

Dolores Johnson, *What Kind of Babysitter Is This?*, 1991
> Kevin's elderly babysitter surprises him by enjoying baseball also.

Rosemary Wells, *Max's Dragon Shirt*, 1991
> While on a shopping trip, Ruby loses younger brother Max in the store just long enough for Max to select a new shirt.

512

VALISKA GREGORY
VIRGINIA AUSTIN, Illustrator

Kate's Giants

(Cambridge, MA: Candlewick Press, 1995)

Subject(s): Fear; Imagination; Giants
Age range(s): Grades K-1
Major character(s): Kate, Child
Time period(s): 1990s (1995)
Locale(s): United States

Summary: Imaginative young Kate is trying to come to terms with a small door in the wall of her new bedroom. Her parents assure her it goes to the attic, but Kate thinks of monsters or giants lurking behind, waiting to come out as soon as she goes to bed. Taking her parents' advice to heart, Kate commands the apparitions to retreat behind the door and rethinks them back again as friendly companions. (32 pages)

Where it's reviewed:
Booklist, October 15, 1995, page 411
Children's Book Review Service, December 1995, page 38
Horn Book Guide, Spring 1996, page 28
Publishers Weekly, September 11, 1995, page 84
School Library Journal, December 1995, page 81

Other books by the same author:
Babysitting for Benjamin, 1993
Happy Burpday, Maggie McDougal!, 1992
Through the Mickle Woods, 1992

Other books you might like:

Joanna Harrison, *Dear Bear*, 1994
> At her mother's suggestion, Katie writes to the bear living under her stairs and asks it to go away.

Mercer Mayer, *There's a Nightmare in My Closet*, 1985
> Sometimes inviting monsters out of the closet helps them seem less scary.

Maggie Smith, *There's a Witch under the Stairs*, 1991
> Imaginative Frances is certain that a witch lives under the basement stairs.

513

MICHAEL GREJNIEC, Author/Illustrator

Who Is My Neighbor?

(New York: Alfred A. Knopf, 1994)

Subject(s): Neighbors and Neighborhoods; Fantasy; Magicians
Age range(s): Grades K-1
Major character(s): Phil, Child, Neighbor; Mr. Hart, Magician, Neighbor
Time period(s): 1990s (1994)
Locale(s): United States

Summary: Phil is a little leary of the upstairs neighbor whose face he never sees. When the power goes out and his mother asks him to go up to Mr. Hart's apartment and borrow some candles, Phil is understandably apprehensive. As Phil enters Mr. Hart's darkened apartment he is surprised to discover that the mysterious neighbor is a magician who loans him a twinkling star to light his way home. (33 pages)

Where it's reviewed:
Booklist, October 1, 1994, page 333
Horn Book Guide, Spring 1995, page 37
Kirkus Reviews, August 15, 1994, page 1129
Publishers Weekly, August 8, 1994, page 428
School Library Journal, November 1994, page 81

Other books by the same author:
Good Morning, Good Night, 1993
Look, 1993
What Do You Like?, 1992

Other books you might like:

Peter Glassman, *The Wizard Next Door*, 1993
> Strange things have been happening in the neighborhood since Mr. Myers moved in.

Bill Martin Jr., *The Wizard*, 1994
> A wizard's clumsiness while conjuring leads to an unexpected result.

Ellen Stoll Walsh, *Pip's Magic*, 1994
> Pip searches for Old Abra, the wizard, in hopes that magic can help Pip overcome his fears.

514

ARNOLD GRIESE
CHARLES RAGINS, Illustrator

Anna's Athabaskan Summer

(Honesdale, PA: Boyds Mills Press, 1995)

Subject(s): Indians of North America; Summer; Growing Up
Age range(s): Grades 2-5
Major character(s): Anna, Child, Indian (Athabaskan); Grandmother, Grandmother, Indian (Athabaskan); Mother, Mother, Indian (Athabaskan)
Time period(s): 1990s (1995)
Locale(s): Alaska

Summary: During the brief Alaskan summer, Anna, Grandmother, and Mother live at the family's fish camp beside a river. There they catch, clean, and dry salmon for the long winter ahead. While Anna picks berries with Grandmother or cleans fish with Mother she learns the ways of her people. (32 pages)

Where it's reviewed:
Appraisal: Science Books for Young People, Winter 1995, page 31
Booklist, June 1, 1995, page 1785
Horn Book Guide, Fall 1995, page 265
Reading Teacher, October 1995, page 156
School Library Journal, May 1995, page 84

Other books you might like:
Virginia L. Kroll, *The Seasons and Someone*, 1994
A young Inuit girl describes the seasonal changes in a life closely linked to time's natural cycle.
Nancy Luenn, *Nessa's Fish*, 1990
During an ice-fishing trip, a young Inuit girl must defend herself and her ill grandmother from animal attacks.
Michelle Renner, *The Girl Who Swam with the Fish: An Athabascan Legend*, 1995
Intrigued by the salmon her family catch to preserve for the winter, a young girl slips into the river and lives with the salmon for several years.

515

ANN GRIFALCONI, Author/Illustrator

The Bravest Flute: A Story of Courage in the Mayan Tradition
(Boston: Little, Brown and Company, 1994)

Subject(s): Indians of Central America; Holidays; Determination
Age range(s): Grades 1-4
Major character(s): Unnamed Character, Child, Musician
Time period(s): 1990s (1994)
Locale(s): Central America

Summary: An annual New Year's procession reenacts the Mayan welcome of the New Year. A poor farm boy, chosen to lead the parade, plays his bamboo flute while carrying a large drum on his back. The boy's first community service, if performed satisfactorily, could bring honor to his widowed mother and money to pay for food and seed. The way is long, the youth exhausted, but as he nears the final steps of the route, he is handed a silver flute by the widow of a master flutist and miraculously has the strength to continue. (32 pages)

Where it's reviewed:
Booklist, September 15, 1994, page 143
Children's Bookwatch, January 1995, page 5
Kirkus Reviews, September 15, 1994, page 1272
School Library Journal, September 15, 1994, page 143

Other books by the same author:
Osa's Pride, 1990 (International Reading Association Teachers' Choice, 1991)
Darkness and the Butterfly, 1987 (Booklist Editors' Choice, 1987)
The Village of Round and Square Houses, 1985 (Caldecott Honor Book, 1987)

Other books you might like:
Betty Baker, *No Help at All*, 1978
After saving a boy's life a Mayan rain god expects some help with his housework, but learns the boy is no help at all.
Jonathan London, *The Village Basket Weaver*, 1996
A young boy helps his grandfather finish a basket needed to carry on the village's traditional bread making.
David Wisniewski, *Rain Player*, 1991
Pik challenges the rain god to a game in hopes of winning some rain for his thirsty people.

516

ANN GRIFALCONI, Author/Illustrator

Kinda Blue
(Boston: Little, Brown and Company, 1993)

Subject(s): Relatives; Family Relations; Love
Age range(s): Grades K-2
Major character(s): Sissy, 6-Year-Old (sad and lonely); Uncle Dan, Farmer
Time period(s): 1990s (1993)
Locale(s): Georgia (a farm)

Summary: Feeling lonely for her deceased father, Sissy sits alone in the farm yard feeling as if other family members are too busy to notice her needs. Emerging from the corn field, Uncle Dan spots her and humors her into a ride on his shoulders to visit the "corn children" he is raising. Sissy's reluctance to give up her "kinda blue" mood is overcome by the sensitivity of Uncle Dan. He uses the allegorical tale of growing corn plants to give Sissy a lesson in family love. (32 pages)

Where it's reviewed:
Booklist, March 1, 1993, page 1235
Childen's Book Review Service, June 1993, page 122
Kirkus Reviews, March 15, 1993, page 371
Publishers Weekly, April 5, 1993, page 77
School Library Journal, May 1993, page 84

Other books by the same author:
Osa's Pride, 1990
Darkness and the Butterfly, 1987
The Village of Round and Square Houses, 1986 (Caldecott Honor Book)

Other books you might like:
Trish Cooke, *So Much*, 1994
Mom and baby are home alone when, one by one, relatives drop in to visit.
Russell Hoban, *Best Friends for Frances*, 1969
When best friend Albert excludes Frances from his "boys only" activities, she plays with sister Gloria.
SuAnn Kiser, *The Catspring Somersault Flying One-Handed Flip-Flop*, 1993
Feeling overlooked by her large and busy farm family, Willy decides to search for a more appreciative audience for her acrobatic tricks.

517

PENI R. GRIFFIN

The Brick House Burglars

(New York: Margaret K. McElderry, 1994)

Subject(s): Mystery and Detective Stories; Clubs; City Life
Age range(s): Grades 5-6
Major character(s): Mary Jane Wilson, Student—Junior High
Time period(s): 1990s
Locale(s): San Antonio, Texas

Summary: Living in cramped apartments with their families, four girls delight in their discovery of an abandoned brick house in their neighborhood and consider it their meeting house. With Mary Jane as the lookout, they slither and crawl into the house unseen by others; unfortunately someone else discovers their house and tries to burn it down. Not only do Mary Jane and the others want to save their meeting place, but they must also protect the mother cat and kittens they feed every day. The gang known as the ''Brick House Burglars'' adds detecting to their activities. (138 pages)

Where it's reviewed:
Voice of Youth Advocates, April 1994, page 26
School Library Journal, June 1994, page 128
Booklist, March 1, 1994, page 1259
Kirkus Reviews, February 1, 1994, page 143
Horn Book Guide, Fall 1994, page 310

Other books by the same author:
Vikki Vanishes, 1995
Switching Well, 1993
A Dig in Time, 1991

Other books you might like:
Felice Holman, *Secret City, U.S.A.*, 1990
    Benno and Moon restore an old house which becomes an oasis from the barrio for them and their homeless friends.
Walter Dean Myers, *The Young Landlords*, 1979
    Paul and his friends fix up a slum building to make some money.
Dorothy Whittaker, *Angels of the Swamp*, 1991
    Two orphans meet and set up camp in an abandoned house on Pelican Island in Florida.

518

HELEN V. GRIFFITH
NANCY BARNET, Illustrator

Dream Meadow

(New York: Greenwillow Books, 1994)

Subject(s): Old Age; Death; Animals/Dogs
Age range(s): Grades K-3
Major character(s): Jane, Aged Person; Frisky, Dog
Time period(s): 1990s (1994)
Locale(s): United States

Summary: An elderly woman spends her time in a rocking chair drifting in and out of a dream in which she is running in a meadow. At Jane's foot sits her old dog who shares her dream of running free. Each pulls the other out of their reverie until the day when Jane does not respond to Frisky's nuzzling and the dog is then free to return to the meadow as the two dreams become one. (24 pages)

Where it's reviewed:
Booklist, May 1, 1994, page 1608
Children's Book Review Service, July 1994, page 147
Kirkus Reviews, April 15, 1994, page 556
Publishers Weekly, March 28, 1994, page 97
School Library Journal, June 1994, page 100

Other books by the same author:
Grandaddy's Place, 1991
Georgia Music, 1990
Plunk's Dreams, 1990

Other books you might like:
Minna Jung, *William's Ninth Life*, 1993
    When William is asked to choose the next and final of his nine lives, the cat chooses to return to his elderly mistress.
Michael J. Rosen, *Bonesy and Isabel*, 1995
    An adopted girl grieves to lose a true companion in the elderly family dog who accepts Isabel's struggles to learn a new language as well as her lapses into Spanish.
Charlotte Zolotow, *The Old Dog*, 1995
    Memories fill a young boy's day after he finds his beloved dog dead one morning.

519

HELEN V. GRIFFITH
JAMES STEVENSON, Illustrator

Grandaddy and Janetta

(New York: Greenwillow Books, 1993)

Subject(s): Grandparents; Humor; Vacations
Age range(s): Grades 2-4
Major character(s): Janetta, Child; Grandaddy, Grandfather
Time period(s): 1990s (1993)
Locale(s): Baltimore, Maryland; Georgia (Grandaddy's farm)

Summary: In this third book about Janetta and Grandaddy, the two have not seen each other in a year. Janetta worries needlessly that Grandaddy may not recognize her when she arrives alone on her first train ride to visit him. Upon their reunion, the two set off for Grandaddy's farm so that Janetta can become reacquainted with the mule Star, the chickens, and the cat. The shared experiences of the two create a picture of relaxed comfort and lazy summer days. (32 pages)

Where it's reviewed:
Booklist, April 1, 1993, page 1431
Horn Book, May 1993, page 327
Kirkus Reviews, June 1, 1993, page 722
Publishers Weekly, May 3, 1993, page 308
School Library Journal, May 1993, page 85

Other books by the same author:
Grandaddy's Stars, 1995
Georgia Music, 1990
Grandaddy's Place, 1987

Other books you might like:
Simon James, *The Wild Woods*, 1993
    Grandad and Jess walk in the woods together, each sharing nature from his own perspective.

Walter Lyon Krudop, *Blue Claws*, 1993
> For a young boy, staying alone with Grandfather in his seaside cabin for the first time is an adventure.

Harvey Stevenson, *Grandpa's House*, 1994
> Woody and Grandpa renew their loving relationship during a family visit to Grandpa's house.

520

HELEN V. GRIFFITH
JAMES STEVENSON, Illustrator

Grandaddy's Stars
(New York: Greenwillow Books, 1995)

Subject(s): Grandparents; City Life; Humor
Age range(s): Grades 2-4
Major character(s): Janetta, Child; Grandaddy, Grandfather
Time period(s): 1990s (1995)
Locale(s): Baltimore, Maryland

Summary: With the return of summer comes another opportunity for Janetta and Grandaddy to spend some time together. This time Grandaddy leaves his mule and chickens to others' care and travels by train to Janetta's home. As usual, worrier Janetta frets unnecessarily because Grandaddy not only arrives safely but he also finds the activities that Janetta has planned to be just perfect. When Grandaddy tells Janetta that the sky outside her window has the same stars that he sees at home, Janetta finds a way to feel close to him even after their visit ends. (32 pages)

Where it's reviewed:
Booklist, April 15, 1995, page 1498
Horn Book, May 1995, page 332
Los Angeles Times Book Review, August 20, 1995, page 8
Publishers Weekly, May 15, 1995, page 72
School Library Journal, July 1995, page 62

Awards the book has won:
Booklist Editors' Choice, 1995
School Library Journal Best Books, 1995

Other books by the same author:
Grandaddy and Janetta, 1993
Georgia Music, 1990
Grandaddy's Place, 1987

Other books you might like:
Marc McCutcheon, *Grandfather's Christmas Camp*, 1995
> Searching for Grandfather's dog on Christmas Eve leads to a unique, shared experience for Lizzie and Grandfather.

Nicola Moon, *Lucy's Picture*, 1995
> In school, Lucy carefully considers the best way to create the perfect picture for her grandfather.

Silky Sullivan, *Grandpa Was a Cowboy*, 1996
> During a visit with his grandfather, a young, orphaned boy learns about his family's past.

521

JEREMY GRIMSDELL, Author/Illustrator

Kalinzu: A Story from Africa
(New York: Kingfisher Books, 1993)

Subject(s): Animals/Buffalo; Africa
Age range(s): Grades K-2
Major character(s): Kalinzu, Buffalo, Child (1-month-old); Amani, Buffalo, Mother
Time period(s): 1990s (1993)
Locale(s): Africa (grasslands)

Summary: Under attack by three hyenas, Kalinzu and Amani are separated in the buffalo stampede. Hurt, lost and frightened, Kalinzu learns to appreciate the bothersome ox-peckers on her back as they lead the calf back to the herd and the safety of her mother. This is the author's first book. (32 pages)

Where it's reviewed:
Children's Bookwatch, April 1994, page 6
Horn Book Guide, Spring 1994, page 35
Publishers Weekly, November 8, 1993, page 74
School Librarian, May 1994, page 54
School Library Journal, January 1994, page 88

Other books you might like:
Paul Geraghty, *The Hunter*, 1994
> In the African bush young Jamina is separated from her grandfather as she pretends to be on a hunt.

Dorian Haarhoff, *Desert December*, 1992
> An oryx helps a young African boy find his parents in Namibia.

Bijou Le Tord, *Elephant Moon*, 1993
> The way of life of elephants and other animals on the African plains is depicted.

522

PATRICIA GROSSMAN
ENRIQUE O. SANCHEZ, Illustrator

Saturday Market
(New York: Lothrop, Lee & Shepard Books, 1994)

Subject(s): Mexicans; City Life; Business Enterprises
Age range(s): Grades K-3
Major character(s): Pedro, Artisan (weaver); Ana, Cook (vendor)
Time period(s): 1990s (1994)
Locale(s): Oaxaca, Mexico

Summary: Pedro weaves stories of the Mayan people into his rugs and into his sales pitch to the market shoppers. Ana sets up her grill on the edge of the market and makes tortillas for hungry vendors and shoppers. Other vendors ply the product of the week's labor each Saturday on Market Day. (32 pages)

Where it's reviewed:
Booklist, September 1, 1994, page 51
Kirkus Reviews, July 15, 1994, page 984
Library Talk, November 1994, page 34
Publishers Weekly, June 27, 1994, page 77
School Library Journal, September 1994, page 184

Other books by the same author:
The Night Ones, 1991

Other books you might like:
Virginia Poulet, *Blue Bug Visits Mexico*, 1990
   Blue Bug enjoys the Mexican marketplace and fiesta
   where he dances with the jumping beans.
Leyla Torres, *Saturday Sancocho*, 1995
   Maria Lili and Mama Ana visit the market to barter their
   eggs for the ingredients to make the Saturday Sancocho.
Karen Lynn Williams, *Tap-Tap*, 1994
   Sasifi helps her mother sell fruit in the local marketplace.

523

GEORGIA GUBACK, Author/Illustrator

Luka's Quilt

(New York: Greenwillow Books, 1994)

Subject(s): Grandparents; Quilts
Age range(s): Grades K-2
Major character(s): Luka, Child; Tutu, Grandmother
Time period(s): 1990s (1994)
Locale(s): Hawaii

Summary: The special relationship between Luka and her
grandmother suffers a blow when Luka is unhappy with the
traditional two-color quilt which Tutu makes for her. Luka
believes that a flower quilt should be many colored and both
she and Tutu are hurt and sad. When Lei Day arrives, Tutu
suggests a truce so the two can enjoy the day together. At the
celebration Luka makes a multi-colored lei which inspires
Tutu to do a little more quilting to mend their relationship. (32
pages)

Where it's reviewed:
Booklist, June 1, 1994, page 1809
Horn Book, September 1994, page 577
New Advocate, Winter 1995, page 50
Publishers Weekly, May 2, 1994, page 307
School Library Journal, July 1994, page 76

Awards the book has won:
Booklist Editors' Choice, 1994

Other books by the same author:
The Carolers, 1992

Other books you might like:
Stephanie Feeney, *A Is for Aloha*, 1980
   A concept book introduces the uniqueness of Hawaii.
Jama Kim Rattigan, *Dumpling Soup*, 1993
   Marisa's Hawaiian heritage includes traditions from many
   cultures which are shared when the family gathers to-
   gether.
Joan Rothenberg, *Inside-Out Grandma*, 1995
   Rosie's grandmother relates the traditions surrounding the
   family's Hanukkah celebration.

524

LESLIE DAVIS GUCCIONE

Come Morning

(Minneapolis: Carolrhoda Books, 1995)

Subject(s): Underground Railroad; Slavery; African Ameri-
cans
Age range(s): Grades 4-6
Major character(s): Freedom Newcastle, 12-Year-Old;
Nehemiah Newcastle, Farmer (freed slave)
Time period(s): 1850s
Locale(s): Delaware (along the Brandywine River)

Summary: Freedom has tremendous respect for his father, for
the work he does on his farm and for the help he offers
runaway slaves along the Underground Railroad. Nehemiah is
a freed slave so he understands what people are willing to risk
for freedom. Free wants to help his father with the Underground Railroad activities, but is not prepared to take on the
job singlehanded as he must when his father is arrested by
slave patrollers in a story based on fact. (120 pages)

Where it's reviewed:
School Library Journal, November 1995, page 100
Center for Children's Books. Bulletin, January 1996, page
   159
Horn Book, November 1995, page 770

Other books by the same author:
Major Distractions, 1994
Nobody Listens to Me, 1991
Tell Me How the Wind Sounds, 1989

Other books you might like:
Jennifer Armstrong, *Steal Away*, 1992
   Yankee Susannah is displeased to be given her personal
   slave when she moves to Virginia; the two run away
   together to freedom.
Virginia Hamilton, *The House of Dies Drear*, 1968
   The Smalls family buys an old house and, when they find
   all its hidden passageways, discover their house used to be
   part of the Underground Railroad.
Lois Walfrid Johnson, *Escape into the Night*, 1995
   Libby joins her father aboard his riverboat, meets the cabin
   boy Caleb and together they assist runaway slaves on the
   Underground Railroad.

525

BRENDA Z. GUIBERSON
MEGAN LLOYD, Illustrator

Lobster Boat

(New York: Henry Holt and Company, 1993)

Subject(s): Animals/Lobsters; Sea Stories; Fishing
Age range(s): Grades K-2
Major character(s): Russ, Uncle (lobsterman); Tommy, Child,
Nephew
Time period(s): 1990s (1993)
Locale(s): Nellie Jean, At Sea (a lobster boat)

Summary: Early morning fog does not deter Tommy and his
Uncle Russ from the day's plans to tend their many lobster

pots. After loading the boat with fresh bait, the Nellie Jean moves through the foggy harbor and onto the area where the brightly painted buoys signal the location of Uncle Russ' pots. A sudden storm brings the lobstering day to an end, but not before the pair have hauled in, unloaded, and rebaited their many pots. (32 pages)

Where it's reviewed:
Booklist, April 15, 1993, page 1511
Kirkus Reviews, April 1, 1993, page 455
New Advocate, Summer 1994, page 208
Publishers Weekly, April 19, 1993, page 60
School Library Journal, July 1993, page 60

Other books by the same author:
Salmon Story, 1993
Spoonbill Swamp, 1992
Cactus Hotel, 1991

Other books you might like:
Jill Bailey, *Discovering Lobsters and Crabs*, 1987
    This title in the Discovering Nature series presents a factual look at two crustaceans.
Jerry Pallotta, *Going Lobstering*, 1990
    With her brother, a young girl spends an interesting day on a lobster boat.
Harriet Ziefert, *Bob and Shirley: A Tale of Two Lobsters*, 1991
    Destined for the dinner table, two old lobsters are saved.

526

DONNA GUTHRIE

Frankie Murphy's Kiss List
(New York: Simon & Schuster, 1993)

Subject(s): Schools
Age range(s): Grades 4-6
Major character(s): Frankie Murphy, 6th Grader; Travis Marshall, 6th Grader; Annie Davis, 6th Grader
Time period(s): 1990s
Locale(s): Harpersville, Indiana

Summary: As soon as Frankie Murphy moves to town, he brags about his expertise with girls. Travis finally gets tired of hearing Frankie tell about the five hundred girls he kissed back in Philadelphia, so he challenges Frankie to kiss all the girls in their class. Though there are only seven, Travis knows that one of them, Annie Davis, hates Frankie; surely she won't kiss him! Travis has no idea that someone can be so sneaky about collecting kisses. In the end, however, the girls claim revenge. (134 pages)

Where it's reviewed:
Voice of Youth Advocates, February 1994, page 367
Publishers Weekly, September 27, 1993, page 64
School Library Journal, September 1993, page 232
Horn Book Guide, Spring 1994, page 76

Kirkus Reviews, October 15, 1993, page 1330

Other books you might like:
Lynn Cullen, *Meeting the Make-Out King*, 1994
    Nora decides popularity is not worth it when her friends decide she has to get to know Mark, known as the "make-out king."
Phyllis Reynolds Naylor, *The Girls Get Even*, 1993
    The Malloy girls are determined to outwit the Hatford brothers in this sequel to *The Boys Start the War*.
Thomas Rockwell, *How to Eat Fried Worms*, 1973
    Billy wishes he'd never bet that he could eat 15 worms!

527

DAN GUTMAN

The Kid Who Ran for President
(New York: Scholastic Press, 1996)

Subject(s): Elections; Politics
Age range(s): Grades 4-6
Major character(s): Judson Moore, 12-Year-Old, Candidate; Lane Brainard, 12-Year-Old, Businessman (campaign manager); June Syers, Babysitter, Political Figure (candidate)
Time period(s): 2000s
Locale(s): Wisconsin

Summary: The elections of 1999 are over and the boys are discussing the results when they decide that Judd should run for president of the United States. Lane is his campaign manager and the boys plan their attack, including selecting Judd's former babysitter as a running mate as she will appeal to the older African-American community. Judd's parents, not taking him seriously, give him permission. Off he goes, getting enough signatures on the petition to run. The boys use modern day campaign methods, including television and modern communications and also get the support of children across America. When he wins, however, Judd realizes that a child should not be president and resigns. (155 pages)

Where it's reviewed:
Bulletin of the Center for Children's Books, November 1996, page 97
School Library Journal, November 1996, page 106
Booklist, November 1, 1996, page 498

Other books you might like:
Dean Hughes, *Re-Elect Nutty!*, 1995
    Nutty decides to run again although his past year as president was a disaster.
Claudia Mills, *Dinah for President*, 1992
    Dinah faces conflicting emotions as she runs for school president.
Judy K. Morris, *The Kid Who Ran for Principal*, 1989
    Bonnie is persuaded to become a candidate for interim principal of the school.

H

528

JESSIE HAAS
JOS. A. SMITH, Illustrator

Be Well, Beware

(New York: Greenwillow Books, 1996)

Subject(s): Animals/Horses
Age range(s): Grades 2-5
Major character(s): Lily Griffin, Animal Lover (horse owner); Beware, Horse; Dr. Brand, Veterinarian
Time period(s): 1990s
Locale(s): Massachusetts

Summary: Lily goes to greet her horse in the morning and is shocked to find that the horse is quite ill with colic. She calls the vet but what he tells her to do doesn't seem to work. She calls again and this time talks to Dr. Brand, who gives her several remedies to try with the horse, including constantly walking him. Lily spends days and nights walking Beware but the horse does not seem to be getting better until the doctor tries one last remedy. (66 pages)

Where it's reviewed:
School Library Journal, April 1996, page 132

Other books by the same author:
Beware the Mare, 1993
A Blue for Beware

Other books you might like:
C.S. Adler, *That Horse Whiskey!*, 1994
    Since her father won't buy a horse a little girl rides the one next door.
Marion Dane Bauer, *Touch the Moon*, 1987
    A little girl who wants a real horse and not a toy one, throws the toy away but then learns a lesson about responsibility.
Marguerite Henry, *Misty's Twilight*, 1992
    Dr. Price takes her children to Chincoteague to buy ponies.
Lisa Saunders, *Ride a Horse, Not an Elevator*, 1995
    City girl's grandparents insist that she learn how to ride a horse.

Nancy Springer, *Colt*, 1991
    A little boy who has spina bifida is helped when he takes riding lessons.

529

JESSIE HAAS
MARTHA HAAS, Illustrator

Beware the Mare

(New York: Greenwillow Books, 1993)

Subject(s): Animals/Horses; Grandparents
Age range(s): Grades 3-5
Major character(s): Beware, Horse; Lily, Child, Animal Lover (loves horses); Linwood Griffin, Grandfather (livestock dealer)
Time period(s): 1990s (1993)
Locale(s): Vermont (farm)

Summary: The day Gramp comes home with a mare, Lily hopes this one will become her horse to replace the pony she has outgrown. However, before Gramp will give her free rein with the new horse, he wants to know why the previous owners named her Beware. While Gramp researches the mystery of the name, he gives Lily the opportunity to demonstrate her horsemanship so that she can have the mare as a pet. (52 pages)

Where it's reviewed:
Booklist, July 1993, page 1966
Childhood Education, Winter 1993, page 105
Horn Book, May 1993, page 333
Library Talk, May 1994, page 42
School Library Journal, April 1993, page 118

Other books by the same author:
A Blue for Beware, 1995
Uncle Daney's Way, 1994
The Sixth Sense & Other Stories, 1988

213

Other books you might like:

C.S. Adler, *That Horse Whiskey!*, 1994
  Because her family cannot afford a horse for her, Lainey trains a neighbor's horse.

Jeanne Betancourt, *A Pony for Keeps*, 1995
  In this second book in the Pony Pals series, Anna must improve her grades if she wants to keep her pony.

Marguerite Henry, *Misty of Chincoteague*, 1990
  This classic horse story of the wild ponies of Virginia's barrier island has been reissued many times.

Sheila Kelly Welch, *A Horse for All Seasons*, 1995
  Twelve realistic horse tales use humor, mystery, adventure, and drama to describe events in relation to the four seasons.

530

JESSIE HAAS
JOS. A. SMITH, Illustrator

A Blue for Beware

(New York: Greenwillow Books, 1995)

Subject(s): Animals/Horses; Friendship
Age range(s): Grades 3-5
Major character(s): Lilian "Lily" Gifford, Child, Equestrian; Mandy, Child, Equestrian; Beware, Horse
Time period(s): 1990s (1995)
Locale(s): Vermont

Summary: Lily and best friend Mandy have graduated from the pony ring and are competing in their first junior horse show. In her eagerness to win a blue ribbon, Lily realizes that by competing against Mandy, one of them will go home the loser. The day includes many events with some more suitable to Lily and Beware's skills than to Mandy's so everyone wins many ribbons and has the satisfaction of accomplishment at the end of the day. (64 pages)

Where it's reviewed:
Booklist, May 15, 1995, page 1646
Bulletin of the Center for Children's Books, March 1995, page 236
Horn Book, May 1995, page 348
Library Talk, May 1995, page 42
School Library Journal, May 1995, page 106

Other books by the same author:
Beware the Mare, 1993

Other books you might like:
Jeanne Betancourt, *The Pony Pals Series*, 1994-
  The Pony Pals' love for ponies lead to adventures as well as problems which they work together to solve.

Jean Slaughter Doty, *The Crumb*, 1976
  A job helping at a stable involves a young girl and her pony in the horse show circuit.

Alison Hart, *The Craziest Horse Show Ever*, 1995
  Preparing for a horse show keeps four roommates at a boarding school busy.

531

JESSIE HAAS
YOSSI ABOLAFIA, Illustrator

Clean House

(New York: Greenwillow, 1996)

Subject(s): Cleanliness; Mothers and Daughters
Age range(s): Grades 2-4
Major character(s): Tess, Child; Milkshake, Cat; Kate, Child, Cousin
Time period(s): 1990s
Locale(s): United States

Summary: Aunt Kate and Cousin Kate call to tell Tess and her mother that they will be visiting. Mom, remembering how clean Aunt Kate's house is, begins a three day whirlwind of cleaning. Finally, all is spotless but when Kate arrives she complains to her mom about the lack of toys or books sitting around. This is quickly remedied and the visit is a great success. (56 pages)

Where it's reviewed:
Bulletin of the Center for Children's Books, March 1996, page 226
School Library Journal, May 1996, page 92
Booklist, April 15, 1996, page 1438

Other books by the same author:
Uncle Daney's Way, 1994
A Horse Like Barney, 1993
Keeping Barney, 1982

Other books you might like:
Ellen Conford, *Jenny Archer to the Rescue*, 1990
  Jenny is always getting involved in things at school and at home.

Sheila Greenwald, *Rosy Cole: She Walks in Beauty*, 1994
  Rosy is always trying to be as important as the rest of her family and friends and here she wants to be a model.

Jerry Spinelli, *Tooter Pepperday*, 1995
  Tooter does not want to move to the farm, in this first of a series about a feisty little girl.

Cathy Warrens, *Saturday Belongs to Sara*, 1994
  Sara and her mother save time on Saturday to do the things they like to do.

532

JESSIE HAAS

A Horse Like Barney

(New York: Greenwillow, 1993)

Subject(s): Animals/Horses
Age range(s): Grades 6-8
Major character(s): Missy, Student—College; Sarah, Horse Trainer; Barney, Horse (Morgan)
Time period(s): 1990s (1992)
Locale(s): United States

Summary: After spending a year looking after Barney for Missy, who's away at college, Sarah knows she'd like a horse just like him. Since her parents are busy, Missy offers to drive Sarah around until they find the perfect horse. The month of

August proves to be a busy one as Sarah searches for her horse while also conditioning a neighbor's horse for endurance competition and taking care of projects around her own house. Though Sarah is elated to have Missy take her horse hunting, she realizes that maybe her perfect horse isn't going to be that easy to find. (170 pages)

Where it's reviewed:
School Library Journal, October 1993, page 124
Horn Book, November 1993, page 744
Booklist, September 15, 1993, page 152
Kirkus Reviews, October 15, 1993, page 1330
Children's Bookwatch, December 1993, page 6

Other books by the same author:
Clean House, 1996
Uncle Daney's Way, 1994
Working Trot, 1983
Keeping Barney, 1982

Other books you might like:
Enid Bagnold, *National Velvet*, 1935
    A young girl named Velvet Brown wins a horse in a village lottery and later rides him in a major horse race.
Betty Cavanna, *Banner Year*, 1987
    When Cindy's horse, Banner, is injured, she works to raise money for the vet bills and ignores her special friend, Tad.
Lynn Hall, *Horse Trader*, 1981
    Karen buys a horse from Harley, an old friend, but finds he's lied about the horse.

533

JESSIE HAAS
JOS. A. SMITH, Illustrator

Mowing

(New York: Greenwillow Books, 1994)

Subject(s): Grandparents; Farm Life; Wildlife Conservation
Age range(s): Grades K-2
Major character(s): Nora, Child; Gramp, Grandfather, Farmer
Time period(s): Indeterminate Past
Locale(s): United States (hayfield)

Summary: Early one morning, Nora and Gramp head out to mow the hay field. Nora scouts the field for creatures that could be hurt by the mower's blades so that when their morning of mowing is complete islands of tall grass surround a killdeer's nest and a fawn. (32 pages)

Where it's reviewed:
Booklist, June 1, 1994, page 1838
Horn Book, May 1994, page 315
Kirkus Reviews, May 15, 1994, page 698
Reading Teacher, February 1995, page 422
School Library Journal, July 1994, page 76

Other books by the same author:
No Foal Yet, 1995
Busybody Brandy, 1994
Chipmunk!, 1993

Other books you might like:
David McPhail, *Farm Morning*, 1985
    A father and daughter enjoy their mornings on the farm as they feed the animals.
Patricia MacLachlan, *All the Places to Love*, 1994
    Eli has grown up to appreciate that ''all the places to love'' are on the family farm.
Linda Morris, *Morning Milking*, 1991
    A young girl wishes she could stop time and capture the moments when she helps her father milk the cows each morning.

534

JESSIE HAAS
JOS. A. SMITH, Illustrator

No Foal Yet

(New York: Greenwillow Books, 1995)

Subject(s): Animals/Horses; Birth; Farm Life
Age range(s): Grades 1-3
Major character(s): Nora, Child; Gramp, Grandfather, Farmer; Bonnie, Horse
Time period(s): 1990s (1995)
Locale(s): United States

Summary: When Bonnie is ready to foal, Nora and her grandparents take turns checking on her during the day and Gramps even gets up during the night to see if the foal has come. Days go by and everyone becomes tired of watching and waiting when, finally, Nora discovers Bonnie with her foal, successfully delivered with no one's help. (24 pages)

Where it's reviewed:
Booklist, June 1995, page 1785
Children's Bookwatch, August 1995, page 4
Horn Book, May 1995, page 349
Horn Book Guide, Fall 1995, page 265
School Library Journal, June 1995, page 81

Other books by the same author:
Busybody Brandy, 1994
Mowing, 1994

Other books you might like:
Carol Carrick, *Valentine*, 1995
    Heather helps Grandma care for a weak, newborn lamb.
Helen V. Griffith, *Grandaddy and Janetta*, 1993
    Janetta's visit to Grandaddy's farm livens up when the cat (who was thought to be male) surprises them both with kittens.
Jane Yolen, *Honkers*, 1993
    While staying with her grandparents a little girl watches daily for three abandoned goose eggs to hatch.

535

JESSIE HAAS

Uncle Daney's Way

(New York: Greenwillow, 1994)

Subject(s): Animals/Horses; Relatives; Country Life
Age range(s): Grades 6-7

Major character(s): Cole Tatro, 12-Year-Old; Daney, Uncle (Cole's great-uncle); Nip, Horse
Time period(s): 1990s
Locale(s): United States

Summary: Cole always envisioned loggers as huge, burly fellows, but his Uncle Daney isn't like that at all. Injured in a logging accident, Daney's now wheelchair-bound and comes to stay with Cole's family. Much to their dismay, he brings along his huge skidding horse, Nip, which will cost a fortune to feed. To offset that cost, Daney teaches Cole how to harness and drive Nip so that the horse can earn his keep. When they hear there'll be a cash prize in an upcoming Farm Horse Contest which would ensure Nip's survival, Cole and Daney step up the schooling. (117 pages)

Where it's reviewed:
School Library Journal, April 1994, page 126
Booklist, April 15, 1994, page 1533
Center for Children's Books. Bulletin, April 1994, page 259
Horn Book, July 1994, page 452
Kirkus Reviews, April 1, 1994, page 479

Other books by the same author:
A Horse Like Barney, 1993
Skipping School, 1992
Working Trot, 1983

Other books you might like:
Dona Schenker, *Throw a Hungry Loop*, 1990
 Tres Bomer lives up to his grandfather's expectations by performing all his ranch chores on muleback in order to buy a good horse.
Patti Sherlock, *Four of a Kind*, 1991
 Training Percheron horses isn't easy, but Andy's just as stubborn as his grandfather and convincing him to buy the team may be the hardest part.
Marya Smith, *Winter-Broken*, 1990
 Dawn's father is always abusive, but especially when he's been drinking; taking care of a horse helps her forget about him.

536

MWENYE HADITHI
ADRIENNE KENNAWAY, Illustrator

Hungry Hyena

(Boston: Little, Brown and Company, 1994)

Subject(s): Animals; Food; Folk Tales
Age range(s): Grades K-2
Major character(s): Fish Eagle, Eagle; Hungry Hyena, Hyena
Time period(s): Indeterminate Past
Locale(s): Africa

Summary: Swift Hungry Hyena tricks Fish Eagle out of the fish she has caught for her own meal. Frustrated, Fish Eagle, with help from other animals, devises a plan to teach Hungry Hyena not to steal. All the greedy hyenas fall for Fish Eagle's trap as they try to reach the sweetest meat in all the world. (30 pages)

Where it's reviewed:
Booklist, May 1, 1994, page 1608
Books for Keeps, July 1995, page 7

Horn Book Guide, Fall 1994, page 274
Kirkus Reviews, May 1, 1994, page 630
School Library Journal, May 1994, page 95

Other books by the same author:
Baby Baboon, 1993
Lazy Lion, 1990
Hot Hippo, 1986

Other books you might like:
Verna Aardema, *How the Ostrich Got Its Long Neck*, 1995
 When Ostrich ignores Fish Eagle's warning and offers to help Crocodile pull out a tooth, he comes away with his life, but with a very long neck.
Mary-Joan Gerson, *Why the Sky Is Far Away: A Nigerian Folktale*, 1992
 Award-winning illustrations enhance the original 1972 text explaining the sky is no longer close to the earth because of people's wasteful habits.
Barbara Knutson, *How the Guinea Fowl Got Her Spots: A Swahili Tale of Friendship*, 1990
 When the Guinea Fowl does a favor for Cow she is given spots to help her hide from predators.
Michael Rosen, *How Giraffe Got Such a Long Neck. . .And Why Rhino Is So Grumpy: A Tale from East Africa*, 1993
 The *pourquoi* tale explains that giraffe ate forgetful rhino's share of a magical neck-growing herb as well as his own to produce his extra long neck and rhino's grumpiness.

537

MARYLIN HAFNER, Author/Illustrator

Mommies Don't Get Sick

(Cambridge, MA: Candlewick Press, 1995)

Subject(s): Family Life; Illness; Parent and Child
Age range(s): Grades K-2
Major character(s): Abby, Child; Mommy, Mother; Daddy, Father
Time period(s): 1990s (1995)
Locale(s): United States

Summary: Saturday should be the best morning of the week because Mommy and Daddy don't work and the family gathers for a special breakfast. The Saturday that Abby's mother stays in bed sick changes the routine so much that even the family pets have some comments. While Daddy goes to the store, Abby tries to help care for her brother, clean up the kitchen mess and do the laundry. Nothing seems to go as Abby planned, but Daddy comes home to help and Mommy is well enough to join the family for lunch. (32 pages)

Where it's reviewed:
Booklist, September 1, 1995, page 86
Bulletin of the Center for Children's Books, November 1995, page 91
Children's Book Review Service, November 1995, page 27
Horn Book Guide, Spring 1996, page 28
School Library Journal, October 1995, page 103

Other books by the same author:
A Year with Molly and Emmett, 1997

Other books you might like:

Judith Caseley, *Mama, Coming and Going*, 1994
  Mama's not sick, just distracted by a new baby and happy for all the help provided by her daughter.

Ferne Sherkin-Langer, *When Mommy Is Sick*, 1995
  A nonfiction bibliotherapeutic offering tells about a young girl whose mother is hospitalized and how she and Dad cope at home without Mom.

Carol Snyder, *One Up, One Down*, 1995
  Twin brothers create extra work for big sister Katie as she tries to help her parents.

538

MARY DOWNING HAHN

Following My Own Footsteps
(New York: Clarion, 1996)

Subject(s): Family Problems; Parent and Child; Grandparents
Age range(s): Grades 5-8
Major character(s): Gordon "Gordy" Smith, 6th Grader; William Sullivan, Handicapped, Crime Victim (of polio); Donald "Donny" Smith, Military Personnel, Veteran (of World War II)
Time period(s): 1940s (1945)
Locale(s): North Carolina

Summary: Gordy and his family leave their College Hill home and go to North Carolina to live with grandmother and escape an abusive father. Gordy, a chip on his shoulder, fights his caring grandmother's attentions. Gradually she wears him down with her common sense and support of him when he gets into trouble. He makes friends with William next door, a polio victim confined to a wheelchair, and one day decides to make him walk the way Heidi made her friend walk. When this doesn't work he is unhappy, especially when William is subsequently taken away. In the midst of this, his father comes to visit but it is quickly clear that he has not changed his abusive ways. Gordy's mother, however, decides to leave with him and takes the younger children with her. Gordy, June, his younger sister, and Donny, who has returned from the war, decide to stay with their grandmother and try to start a new life. (186 pages)

Where it's reviewed:
Bulletin of the Center for Children's Books, October 1996, page 61
School Library Journal, November 1996, page 106
Booklist, September 15, 1996, page 240
Horn Book, September/October 1996, page 595

Other books by the same author:
Time for Andrew, 1994
Stepping on the Cracks, 1991 (Companion to *Following My Own Footsteps*)
The Spanish Kidnapping Disaster, 1991

Other books you might like:
Betsy Byars, *Cracker Jackson*, 1985
  A little boy tries to help his babysitter, wh o he thinks is being abused.

Carolyn Coman, *What Jamie Saw*, 1995
  Jamie and his mother leave his stepfather and begin to make a new life for themselves.

Julie Johnson, *Hero of Lesser Causes*, 1993
  Keely is devastated when her brother has polio and she tries to reawaken his interest in life.

Susan Richards Shreve, *Lucy Forever and Miss Rosetree, Shrinks*, 1987
  The girls help a mute child who they think is being abused.

539

MARY DOWNING HAHN

The Gentleman Outlaw and Me—Eli
(New York: Clarion Books, 1996)

Subject(s): Frontier and Pioneer Life; Robbers and Outlaws
Age range(s): Grades 5-7
Major character(s): Eliza "Elijah Bates" Yates, 12-Year-Old, Runaway; Calvin Thaddeus Featherbone, 18-Year-Old, Outlaw; Roscoe, Outlaw
Time period(s): 1880s (1887)
Locale(s): Tinville, Colorado (traveling to Tinville)

Summary: Eliza is tired of being the family scapegoat so she runs away to find her father. The first person she meets thinks it is easy to rob a girl, so she cuts off her hair and decides to go as a boy. Shortly thereafter, she witnesses the attempted robbery of Calvin and the two of them hook up together since they are both going to Tinville. Along the way she and Calvin make their money by begging and doing cardtricks, until they meet up again with Roscoe, who turns them in to the sheriff of Tinville. This sheriff turns out to be the man they are both looking for. (224 pages)

Where it's reviewed:
Bulletin of the Center for Children's Books, April 1996, page 265
Horn Book, September/October 1996, page 596

Other books by the same author:
The Doll in the Garden, 1989
Wait Till Helen Comes, 1986
The Time of the Witch, 1982

Other books you might like:
Avi, *Emily Upham's Revenge*, 1992
  7-year old Emily is sent to live with her uncle and becomes involved in his strange schemes.

Sid Fleischman, *By the Great Horn Spoon*, 1988
  Jack Fogg becomes involved in adventures during the California Gold Rush.

Leon Garfield, *Young Nick and Jubilee*, 1989
  A pickpocket and a student meet and set about a chain of events in London.

Willo Davis Roberts, *Jo and the Bandit*, 1992
  12-year-old Jo becomes involved with a young outlaw who tries to rob the stage.

540

SARAH JOSEPHA HALE
SALLEY MAVOR, Illustrator

Mary Had a Little Lamb

(New York: Orchard Books, 1995)

Subject(s): Poetry; Animals/Sheep; Schools
Age range(s): Grades K-1
Major character(s): Mary, Child, Student
Time period(s): Indeterminate Past
Locale(s): New England

Summary: The classic poem about the little girl whose lamb follows her to school is illustrated in fabric relief. Mary and her lamb cavort happily on each page until the teacher sends the lamb away for disrupting the classroom. A concluding note gives factual information about the origins of the poem. (32 pages)

Where it's reviewed:
Booklist, May 15, 1995, page 1649
Bulletin of the Center for Children's Books, May 1995, page 308
Christian Science Monitor, May 25, 1995, page B1
Horn Book, July 1995, page 472
School Library Journal, June 1995, page 81

Awards the book has won:
Boston Globe/Horn Book Fanfare, 1996

Other books you might like:
Carol Carrick, *Valentine*, 1995
　　While Mama works, Heather bakes cookies with Grandma and helps care for newborn lambs.
Tomie De Paola, *Mary Had a Little Lamb*, 1984
　　This illustrated retelling includes the music later written for the rhyme.
Bruce McMillan, *Mary Had a Little Lamb*, 1990
　　Using photographs the illustrator gives a contemporary look to the historical poem.

541

DONALD HALL
BARRY MOSER, Illustrator

The Farm Summer 1942

(New York: Dial Books, 1994)

Subject(s): Grandparents; Farm Life; World War II
Age range(s): Grades 1-3
Major character(s): Peter, 9-Year-Old
Time period(s): 1940s (1942)
Locale(s): San Francisco, California; Gale, New Hampshire

Summary: While his father serves on a destroyer in the Pacific and his mother works on a secret war project, Peter goes to his grandparents' farm for the summer. He learns to find eggs, milk cows and rake hay just as his father did as a boy. When summer ends, Peter is reluctant to leave the farm, his grandparents and cousins, but San Francisco, school and the hope of seeing his father call him back. (32 pages)

Where it's reviewed:
Booklist, June 1, 1994, page 1816
Horn Book, July 1994, page 441
Kirkus Reviews, May 15, 1994, page 698
Publishers Weekly, April 11, 1994, page 65
School Library Journal, June 1994, page 101

Other books by the same author:
I Am the Dog, I Am the Cat, 1994
Lucy's Christmas, 1994
Ox-Cart Man, 1979

Other books you might like:
George Shannon, *Climbing Kansas Mountains*, 1993
　　With his father, Sam shares an experience unique to their flat farm country.
Rosemary Wells, *Waiting for the Evening Star*, 1993
　　Life on a Vermont farm is appreciated in different ways by two brothers.
Jane Yolen, *Honkers*, 1993
　　Betsy spends the summer on her grandparents' farm watching the development of three abandoned Canadian geese.

542

DONALD HALL
BARRY MOSER, Illustrator

I Am the Dog, I Am the Cat

(New York: Dial Books, 1994)

Subject(s): Animals/Dogs; Animals/Cats; Behavior
Age range(s): Grades K-3
Major character(s): Dog, Dog; Cat, Cat
Time period(s): 1990s (1994)
Locale(s): United States

Summary: Two household pets explain their reason for being. Dog is interested in human contact and fearlessly defends his home from the UPS delivery man, yet admits to being frightened of thunder. Cat disdains Dog's concern about the opinions of others and confidently wanders around the house, avoiding babies ("Babies sit on you!"), working hard to catch mice, rubber bands or paper clips and, at its own discretion, seeking a comfortable lap. (32 pages)

Where it's reviewed:
Booklist, September 15, 1994, page 132
Horn Book, September 1994, page 577
Kirkus Reviews, August 15, 1994, page 1129
Publishers Weekly, July 18, 1994, page 243
School Library Journal, September 1994, page 185

Other books by the same author:
Lucy's Summer, 1995
The Farm Summer 1942, 1994
Ox-Cart Man, 1979

Other books you might like:
Alexandra Day, *Carl's Afternoon in the Park*, 1991
　　Carl, the family's pet rottweiler, "babysits" a puppy and a toddler while Mom visits with a friend.
Paul Fehlner, *Dog and Cat*, 1990
　　In an easy reader, an elderly dog and an overweight cat

have learned to coexist peacefully because such a life is all they are capable of physically.

Isabelle Harper, *Our New Puppy*, 1996

The arrival of Floyd, an 8-week-old puppy, is viewed with disdain by the family cat and accepted with patient tolerance by the older dog Rosie.

Gillian Rubenstein, *Dog In, Cat Out*, 1991

A busy dog and cat always seem to be in opposite places.

543

DONALD HALL
MICHAEL MCCURDY, Illustrator

Lucy's Christmas
(San Diego: Harcourt Brace & Company, 1994)

Subject(s): Christmas; Gifts; Family Life
Age range(s): Grades K-3
Major character(s): Lucy Wells, Child, Sister (older); Caroline Wells, 5-Year-Old, Sister (younger)
Time period(s): 1900s (1909)
Locale(s): South Danbury, New Hampshire

Summary: Lucy carefully plans and makes all the Christmas gifts she will give to family and friends. When she is finished with her own work, she helps Caroline to make gifts and paper chains for the Christmas Eve service at church. Even more exciting than the family's Christmas preparations is the arrival of a new kitchen range ordered from Sears. The range is such a modern wonder it attracts neighbors and relatives who stop by to see its features. (40 pages)

Where it's reviewed:
Booklist, August 1994, page 2051
Bulletin of the Center for Children's Books, October 1994, page 48
Horn Book, November 1994, page 711
Kirkus Reviews, October 15, 1994, page 1420
Publishers Weekly, September 19, 1994, page 31

Other books by the same author:
Old Home Day, 1996
Lucy's Summer, 1995
The Farm Summer 1942, 1994
Ox-Cart Man, 1979 (Caldecott Medal, 1980)

Other books you might like:
Tomie De Paola, *An Early American Christmas*, 1987
A German immigrant family finds themselves in a New England village where many people do not celebrate Christmas.
Mary Lyn Ray, *Pianna*, 1994
The simple life on a turn-of-the-century farm features a musically gifted child who travels over 100 miles by train for weekly piano lessons.
Laura Ingalls Wilder, *Farmer Boy*, 1953
The joys of a simple Christmas and the excitement of receiving handmade gifts is described in one chapter of this book about a young boy growing up on a farm.

544

DONALD HALL
BARRY MOSER, Illustrator

When Willard Met Babe Ruth
(New York: Harcourt Brace, 1996)

Subject(s): Sports/Baseball; Hero
Age range(s): Grades 5-7
Major character(s): Willard Babson, 12-Year-Old, Child (baseball fan); George Herman ''Babe'' Ruth, Historical Figure, Baseball Player; Ruth Babson, 10-Year-Old
Time period(s): 1910s (1917); 1930s (1935)
Locale(s): New Hampshire; Boston, Massachusetts (baseball stadium)

Summary: Willard and his dad are driving along the road when they come upon a car in the ditch. They get out to help and discover that they are helping Babe Ruth. As payment for the help, Babe gives Willard a baseball glove. Time goes by and Willard marries and has a daughter, Ruth, named after the baseball player. On her 10th birthday the family takes her to see Babe Ruth play. When he finally comes in to play, he notices the family and, remembering the story about his car, signs an autograph for Ruthie and proceeds to have a good day at bat. (42 pages)

Where it's reviewed:
Bulletin of the Center for Children's Books, June 1996, page 336
Booklist, March 15, 1996, page 1262
Horn Book, September/October 1996, page 589

Other books by the same author:
Old Home Day, 1996
The Farm Summer 1942, 1994
Oxcart Man, 1979

Other books you might like:
Ron Cohen, *My Dad's Baseball*, 1994
A father tells his son about his first baseball game and getting a ball signed by Yogi Berra.
Peter Golenbeck, *Teammates*, 1990
Pee Wee Reese and Jackie Robinson meet and play on the Dodgers team and when Pee Wee supports Jackie, they become firends.
Ken Mochizuki, *Baseball Saved Us*, 1993
A Japanese boy learns how to play baseball while in internment camp.
David Shannon, *How Georgie Radbourn Saved Baseball*, 1994
An outlaw business owner decrees that there will be no more baseball but Georgie discovers this old game and gets people involved in it again.

545

ELIZABETH HALL

Child of the Wolves
(Boston: Houghton Mifflin, 1996)

Subject(s): Animals/Dogs; Animals/Wolves
Age range(s): Grades 4-6

Major character(s): Granite, Dog; Snowdrift, Wolf; Ebony, Wolf
Time period(s): 1990s
Locale(s): Alaska

Summary: Granite is a happy puppy until the day a man buys him and takes him away from the life he has known. Since he does not like being held so tightly, he runs away into the wild where he meets up with a wolf pack. They accept him as one of their own and try to teach him to hunt. At first he doesn't do well and is ostracized by some of the pack, until the day, several years later, he saves the leader from an avalanche. (160 pages)

Where it's reviewed:
School Library Journal, April 1996, page 132
Booklist, April 1, 1996, page 1364

Other books you might like:
Melvin Burgess, *The Cry of the Wolf*, 1992
     Ben insists that the sounds he hears near the house are the sounds of wolves.
Jean Craighead George, *Julie of the Wolves*,
     Julie is able to live because she watches and is adopted by the wolf pack.
Elona Malterre, *The Last Wolf of Ireland*, 1990
     Devin and Katey hide wolf pups when they are threatened.
Bruce Weide, *There's a Wolf in the Classroom!*, 1995
     Bruce and co-author Patricia Tucker care for wolves and take them to school to show children how they act when cared for. (non-fiction)

546

ZOE HALL
SHARI HALPERN, Illustrator

It's Pumpkin Time!
(New York: Blue Sky Press, 1994)

Subject(s): Pumpkins; Halloween; Gardens and Gardening
Age range(s): Grades K-3
Major character(s): Unnamed Character, Child, Sister; Unnamed Character, Child, Brother
Time period(s): 1990s (1994)
Locale(s): United States

Summary: Excitedly a sister and brother prepare for their favorite holiday by planting a jack-o'-lantern patch. The children describe the stages of growth and development of the pumpkins until the biggest ones they've ever grown are ready for parental help with the picking and carving. The author's first book concludes with a factual note on the development of a pumpkin plant. (30 pages)

Where it's reviewed:
Booklist, August 1994, page 2053
Children's Book Review Service, October 1994, page 15
Library Talk, September 1994, page 16
Publishers Weekly, September 19, 1994, page 25
School Library Journal, November 1994, page 81

Awards the book has won:
Booklist Editors' Choice, 1994

Other books you might like:
Steven Kroll, *The Biggest Pumpkin Ever*, 1984
     Two mice, each intent on growing the biggest pumpkin, independently apply their secret gardening techniques to the same pumpkin with astounding results.
Erica Silverman, *Big Pumpkin*, 1992
     A witch learns to appreciate cooperative efforts when monsters assist her with a very large pumpkin.
Jeanne Titherington, *Pumpkin, Pumpkin*, 1986
     Carefully Jamie plants a seed, tends the plant, carves the pumpkin and saves some seeds to plant in the Spring.
Deborah Turney Zagwyn, *The Pumpkin Blanket*, 1990
     When frost threatens her pumpkin plant, a little girl uses her special blanket to protect it.

547

SHEILA HAMANAKA, Author/Illustrator

Bebop-a-Do-Walk!
(New York: Simon & Schuster Books for Young Readers, 1995)

Subject(s): Fathers and Daughters; Neighbors and Neighborhoods; Japanese Americans
Age range(s): Grades 1-3
Major character(s): Emi, Child (Japanese American), Friend (Martha's); Martha, Child (African American), Friend (Emi's); Daddy, Father (Emi's)
Time period(s): 1950s
Locale(s): New York, New York

Summary: Emi's father agrees to allow the girls to accompany him on his long and ususally solitary walk to Central Park. On the way, Emi and Martha briefly visit the Empire State Building, the Museum of Modern Art and Washington Square Park. In the park, while Daddy sketches, Emi and Martha float origami paper boats on the pond and share the lunch they brought. Too tired to walk home, the girls are treated to a bus ride complete with origami paper cranes for all the riders. (38 pages)

Where it's reviewed:
Booklist, September 1, 1995, page 86
Children's Book Review Service, September 1995, page 2
Five Owls, September 1995, page 13
Kirkus Reviews, August 1, 1995, page 1110
School Library Journal, October 1995, page 103

Other books by the same author:
Peace Crane, 1995
All the Colors of the Earth, 1994
Screen of Frogs: An Old Tale, 1993

Other books you might like:
Patricia Polacco, *My Ol' Man*, 1995
     Childhood memories of her father inspire the author's story of the traveling salesman who tells magical stories.
Eve Rice, *Swim!*, 1996
     Saturday mornings at the swimming pool with Dad lead to predicable activities.
Paul Showers, *The Listening Walk*, 1991
     A young girl and her father go for a quiet walk and try to identify the environmental sounds around them.

548

SHEILA HAMANAKA, Author/Illustrator

Peace Crane

(New York: Morrow Junior Books, 1995)

Subject(s): Peace; African Americans; Fantasy
Age range(s): Grades 2-3
Major character(s): Unnamed Character, Child
Time period(s): 1990s (1995)
Locale(s): United States

Summary: Drawing inspiration from the peace crane associated with the suffering following the bombing of Hiroshima, a young girl expresses her own desire for peace in the violent urban neighborhood in which she lives. In her dreams she flies with the Peace Crane and learns to recognize peace in the music of neighbors and efforts of others working for nonviolence. (40 peages)

Where it's reviewed:
Booklist, September 15, 1995, page 175
Children's Book Review Service, August 1995, page 157
Horn Book Guide, Spring 1996, page 29
Publishers Weekly, July 31, 1995, page 79
School Library Journal, September 1995, page 177

Other books by the same author:
All the Colors of the Earth, 1994
Screen of Frogs: An Old Tale, 1993

Other books you might like:
Eleanor Coerr, *Sadako*, 1993
   An illustrated abridgement of *Sadako and the Thousand Paper Cranes* tells the story of courageous Sadako, dying of leukemia, who folds paper cranes and hopes for healing.
Arthur Dorros, *Abuela*, 1991
   A little girl imagines that she and her grandmother are floating over New York City.
Junko Morimoto, *My Hiroshima*, 1990
   A young girl tells of her survival amid the destruction of her city during World War II.

549

VIRGINIA HAMILTON
JERRY PINKNEY, Illustrator

Drylongso

(New York: Harcourt Brace Jovanovich, 1992)

Subject(s): Drought; Farm Life; African Americans
Age range(s): Grades 3-6
Major character(s): Drylongso, Child (blown in with a dust storm); Lindy, Child (daughter of farmers); Mamalou, Mother
Time period(s): 1970s (1975)
Locale(s): United States (west of the Mississippi River)

Summary: As Lindy and her dad take refuge from a dust storm, they see, running before the wall of earth, a thin boy who stumbles into their home. The family's kindness is returned when Drylongso, using a divining rod, locates an underground spring and helps them prepare the land for a small garden. As abruptly as he came he departs, leaving behind the dowser and hope for a better, wetter future. (54 pages)

Where it's reviewed:
Booklist, July 1992, page 1938
Horn Book, September 1992, page 582
Language Arts, April 1993, page 308
Publishers Weekly, November 9, 1992, page 86
School Library Journal, January 1993, page 98

Other books by the same author:
Jaguarundi, 1995
Cousins, 1993
The People Could Fly: American Black Folk Tales, 1985

Other books you might like:
Emily Crofford, *A Matter of Pride*, 1991
   Raising cotton is hard work any time, but even more so during the Depression.
Shannon K. Jacobs, *Song of the Giraffe*, 1991
   Kisana tries to find the spring that can provide the water to save her tribe's crops.
Thomas Locker, *Family Farm*, 1988
   With ingenuity and commitment a family is able to save their home and livelihood.

550

VIRGINIA HAMILTON
LEO DILLON, Illustrator
DIANE DILLON, Illustrator

Her Stories: African American Folktales, Fairy Tales, and True Tales

(New York: The Blue Sky Press, 1995)

Subject(s): Folk Tales; Fairy Tale; African Americans
Age range(s): Grades 2-6
Time period(s): Indeterminate Past
Locale(s): United States

Summary: A collection of women's tales is retold without losing the qualities of the oral traditions on which they are based. The selections are grouped into animal tales, fairy tales, the supernatural, folk tales and legends and true recollections. In addition to background information at the beginning and end of the book, the author concludes each story with notes about that particular tale. (112 pages)

Where it's reviewed:
Booklist, November 1, 1995, page 470
Emergency Librarian, November 1995, page 45
Horn Book, January 1996, page 81
Publishers Weekly, November 6, 1995, page 68
School Library Journal, December 1995, page 21

Awards the book has won:
Coretta Scott King Author Award & Honor Book for Illustration, 1996
School Library Journal Best Books, 1995

Other books by the same author:
Many Thousand Gone: African Americans from Slavery to Freedom, 1992
The Dark Way: Stories from the Spirit World, 1990

The People Could Fly: American Black Folk Tales, 1985 (Coretta Scott King Book Award, 1986)

Other books you might like:

Julius Lester, *The Last Tales of Brer Rabbit*, 1994
The final adventures of Brer Rabbit, his friends, and enemies are gathered in an illustrated volume.

Pat McKissack, *The Dark Thirty: Southern Tales of the Supernatural*, 1992
An award-winning edition of ten original, suspenseful tales is inspired by the oral traditions of African American history.

Robert D. San Souci, *Cut from the Same Cloth: American Women of Myth, Legend and Tall Tale*, 1993
This illustrated collection of 20 stories, each with a female protagonist, is drawn from folktales, ballads and popular stories.

551

VIRGINIA HAMILTON
FLOYD COOPER, Illustrator

Jaguarundi
(New York: The Blue Sky Press, 1995)

Subject(s): Animals; Conservation of Natural Resources; Nature
Age range(s): Grades K-3
Major character(s): Rundi, Jaguarundi; Coati, Coatimundi
Time period(s): Indeterminate Past
Locale(s): Central America; South America

Summary: As their rain forest home is destroyed by settlers clearing trees to plant crops, the animals must adapt or flee. Rundi chooses to go north where he has heard there is still a forest canopy. At a farewell meeting of all the animals, only Coati chooses to travel with Rundi. When they reach the river to the north, Rundi and Coati find cities, little cover, and no forest canopy. They separate to find shelter until they feel ready to head north again to seek better habitat. A concluding pictorial glossary describes the many animals mentioned in the text. (40 pages)

Where it's reviewed:
Bulletin of the Center for Children's Books, February 1995, page 198
Library Talk, September 1995, page 34
Publishers Weekly, October 10, 1995, page 70
Reading Teacher, December 1995, page 325
School Library Journal, December 1994, page 75

Other books by the same author:
When Birds Could Talk & Bats Could Sing, 1996
Drylongso, 1992

Other books you might like:

Lynne Cherry, *The Great Kapok Tree: A Tale of the Amazon Rain Forest*, 1990
A man changes his plans to cut down a kapok tree after his dreams are invaded by the animals who depend on the tree.

Kristine L. Franklin, *When the Monkeys Came Back*, 1994
Dona Marta restores the ravaged hillside near her home so her children and grandchildren can appreciate the sound of a forest filled with monkeys.

Douglas Keister, *Fernando's Gift/El Regalo de Fernando*, 1995
Fernando learns the importance of respecting and restoring the rain forest.

Joanne Ryder, *Jaguar in the Rain Forest*, 1996
A young boy climbing a tree imagines himself to be a jaguar in a rain forest.

552

SUZANNE CROWDER HAN
YUMI HEO, Illustrator

The Rabbit's Escape
(New York: Henry Holt and Company, 1995)

Subject(s): Folk Tales; Animals/Rabbits; Animals/Turtles
Age range(s): Grades K-3
Major character(s): Dragon King, Royalty; Mr. Turtle, Turtle; Mr. Rabbit, Rabbit
Time period(s): Indeterminate Past
Locale(s): Korea, South

Summary: When the Dragon King falls ill, the prescribed treatment is the consumption of a rabbit's liver. Unfortunately, rabbits do not live in the Dragon King's underwater kingdom so his future looks bleak until a loyal turtle, being able to survive on land as well as under the water, volunteers to fetch a rabbit. Curious Mr. Rabbit eagerly travels with Mr. Turtle until he learns the real purpose of his visit. Being a clever fellow, Rabbit is able to trick the Dragon King and gain his freedom. Mr. Turtle's faithfulness is rewarded by a god who gives the turtle ginseng roots to cure the king's illness. An introductory author's note explains the character of rabbit in Korean folk tales and the Korean alphabet, Han-gul in which the bilingual text is written. (32 pages)

Where it's reviewed:
Booklist, May 15, 1995, page 1649
Bulletin of the Center for Children's Books, May 1995, page 308
Horn Book, September 1995, page 613
Publishers Weekly, April 3, 1995, page 62
School Library Journal, June 1995, page 101

Awards the book has won:
School Library Journal Best Books, 1995
ALA Notable Book, 1996

Other books by the same author:
The Rabbit's Judgment, 1994

Other books you might like:

Gayle Ross, *How Rabbit Tricked Otter: And Other Cherokee Trickster Stories*, 1994
Fifteen stories about Rabbit show him to be a trickster, getting the better of many animals and being responsible for some of their physical characteristics too.

Gerald McDermott, *Zomo the Rabbit: A Trickster Tale from West Africa*, 1992
Seeking wisdom in exchange, Zomo completes tasks for the Sky God which require courage and cunning.

Keizaburo Tejima, *Ho-Limlim: A Rabbit Tale from Japan*, 1990

As an aging rabbit takes a trip, he realizes that his eyes now play tricks on him and he should stay closer to home.

553

WOLFRAM HANEL
ALEX DE WOLF, Illustrator

Lila's Little Dinosaur

(New York: North-South Books, 1994)

Subject(s): Dinosaurs; Fathers and Daughters; Pets
Age range(s): Grades 2-3
Major character(s): Lila, 7-Year-Old; Unnamed Character, Father
Time period(s): 1990s (1994)
Locale(s): Europe

Summary: More than anything, Lila loves dinosaurs! Reluctantly, her father agrees to take her to the Museum of Natural History to see a special exhibit of mechanized dinosaurs. Before leaving, Lila crawls under one to examine the wiring used to create the realistic movement and is found by a small, rainbow-striped dinosaur who follows her home. Translated from the German by J. Alison James. (60 pages)

Where it's reviewed:
Booklist, January 1, 1995, page 820
Horn Book Guide, Spring 1995, page 66
Kirkus Reviews, November 15, 1994, page 1530
School Librarian, May 1995, page 63
School Library Journal, October 1994, page 90

Other books by the same author:
The Extraordinary Adventures of an Ordinary Hat, 1994
Mia the Beach Cat: A Story, 1994
The Old Man and the Bear, 1994

Other books you might like:
Lois G. Grambling, *Can I Have a Stegosaurus Mom? Can I? Please?*, 1995
  To convince mom to accept a stegosaurus as a family pet a child lists all the dinosaur's positive attributes.
Syd Hoff, *Danny and the Dinosaur*, 1958
  In a beginning reader, a dinosaur follows Danny out of the museum in order to continue playing with him.
William H. Hooks, *Mr. Dinosaur*, 1994
  Eli's brother offers a helping hand when Eli's fascination with dinosaurs begins to create problems.
James Mayhew, *Katie and the Dinosaurs*, 1992
  When Katie visits a natural history museum, she finds herself surrounded by real dinosaurs.

554

WOLFRAM HANEL
KRISTEN HOCKER, Illustrator

Mia the Beach Cat: A Story

(New York: North-South Books, 1994)

Subject(s): Animals/Cats; Beaches; Parent and Child
Age range(s): Grades 1-3
Major character(s): Maggie, Child; Mia, Cat; Felix, Toy (stuffed tiger)

Time period(s): 1990s (1994)
Locale(s): Ireland

Summary: While vacationing at the beach, Maggie quickly grows bored entertaining herself while her parents relax in beach chairs. One day a stray cat happens along and Maggie has a playmate livelier than Felix. Because Mia waits each morning for Maggie to arrive, Maggie is only momentarily saddened when Felix accidentally washes out to sea. When vacation comes to an end, Maggie uses the empty picnic basket to assure that Mia finds the way home. Translated from the German by J. Alison James. (45 pages)

Where it's reviewed:
Bulletin of the Center for Children's Books, January 1995, page 166
Horn Book Guide, Spring 1995, page 66
Kirkus Reviews, December 15, 1994, page 1563
School Librarian, February 1995, page 22
School Library Journal, December 1994, page 75

Other books by the same author:
The Extraordinary Adventures of an Ordinary Hat, 1994
Lila's Little Dinosaur, 1994
The Old Man and the Bear, 1994

Other books you might like:
Hans Fischer, *Pitschi*, 1996
  A kitten named Pitschi tries unsuccessfully to be many other animals before she learns the fun of simply being a kitten.
Cynthia Rylant, *Mr. Putter and Tabby Pour the Tea*, 1994
  Lonely Mr. Putter finds a lonely old cat at an animal shelter and makes a perfect pet for him.
Elisabeth Jane Stewart, *Bimmi Finds a Cat*, 1996
  Grieving for his deceased cat, an eight-year-old boy follows another cat to a new friend.

555

PETER HANSARD
FRANCESCA MARTIN, Illustrator

Jig, Fig, and Mrs. Pig

(Cambridge, MA: Candlewick Press, 1995)

Subject(s): Fairy Tale; Folk Tales; Animals/Pigs
Age range(s): Grades K-2
Major character(s): Jig, Pig, Servant; Fig, Pig, Bully; Mrs. Pig, Pig, Mother (Fig's)
Time period(s): Indeterminate Past
Locale(s): Fictional Country

Summary: Mrs. Pig and Fig are a disagreeable, nasty-tempered pair in contrast to the obedient Jig who completes her daily chores despite Fig's bullying and Mrs. Pig's unreasonable requests. One day Jig's kindness to an old pig is rewarded when the wizard in disguise grants her the gift of gold and diamonds which fall from her mouth as she speaks. When Mrs. Pig discovers what has happened, she sends Fig to town for milk. Given Fig's nature, his meeting with the wizard reaps the gift of toads and snakes pouring from his mouth. At the sight of her son, Mrs. Pig runs away with Fig clinging to her apron strings and Jig enjoys the peace and quiet of an empty house. (32 pages)

Where it's reviewed:
Booklist, June 1995, page 1785
Books for Keeps, May 1995, page 28
Children's Book Review Service, Spring 1995, page 135
Parents' Choice, Spring 1995, page 1
School Library Journal, June 1995, page 102

Other books by the same author:
A Field Full of Horses, 1994
Wag, Wag, Wag, 1994
I Like Monkeys Because, 1993

Other books you might like:
Ellen Jackson, *Cinder Edna*, 1994
Neighbors Cinderella and Cinder Edna have different philosophies of life yet each meets the prince of her dreams at the ball.
Barbara Karlins, *Cinderella*, 1989
James Marshall's illustrations add humor to a retelling of the classic story about the oppressed servant girl who meets the Prince and loses her glass slipper.
Janet Perlman, *Cinderella Penguin or, The Little Glass Flipper*, 1992
A spoof of the Cinderella story has penguins in the leading roles.

556

REGINA HANSON
HARVEY STEVENSON, Illustrator

The Tangerine Tree
(New York: Clarion Books, 1995)

Subject(s): Fathers and Daughters; Emigration and Immigration; Migrant Labor
Age range(s): Grades K-3
Major character(s): Ida, Child; Papa, Father; Mama, Mother
Time period(s): 1990s (1995)
Locale(s): Jamaica

Summary: In the author's first book, Ida, the youngest of three children, is saddened that Papa will travel to New York to work so that he can send money to Mama for Ida and her brothers. To keep him warm while he is in such a cold place, Ida squeezes the juice containing the Jamaican sun from the family's tangerines into a bottle and presents it to him as he departs. Papa's parting gift to Ida is a story book and the promise that he will return by the time Mama has taught her how to read the book. (32 pages)

Where it's reviewed:
Booklist, July 1995, page 1883
Children's Book Review Service, August 1995, page 158
Kirkus Reviews, July 1, 1995, page 946
Publishers Weekly, July 10, 1995, page 57
School Library Journal, September 1995, page 177

Other books you might like:
Rachel Isadora, *At the Crossroads*, 1991
South African children gather at the crossroads to welcome home their fathers when they return from working in the distant mines.
Mavis Jukes, *Like Jake and Me*, 1987
A simple little spider provides the avenue for communica-

tion and understanding between Alex and his stepfather Jake.
Hugh Lewin, *Jafta: The Homecoming*, 1994
A South African boy who has been separated from his father for a long time eagerly awaits his return.
Rita Phillips Mitchell, *Hue Boy*, 1993
The return of his father's ship makes small-for-his-age Hue Boy feel much taller.

557

BILL HARLEY
ANN MIYA, Illustrator

Nothing Happened
(Berkeley, CA: Tricycle Press, 1995)

Subject(s): Bedtime; Dwellings; Family Life
Age range(s): Grades K-2
Major character(s): Jack, Brother (younger); Will, Brother (older)
Time period(s): 1990s (1995)
Locale(s): United States

Summary: Convinced by Will's teasing that something exciting happens after he goes to sleep at night, Jack prepares to stay awake all night and find out for himself. His plan is carried out perfectly, he listens to the other family members retire for the night, he wanders the house looking for the secret party room and learns, just as his parents have told him, nothing happens. The first picture book for a storyteller and radio commentator. (32 pages)

Where it's reviewed:
Booklist, April 15, 1995, page 1506
Children's Book Review Service, Spring 1995, page 139
Children's Bookwatch, May 1995, page 7
Horn Book Guide, Fall 1995, page 266
School Library Journal, June 1995, page 81

Other books you might like:
Frank Asch, *Dear Brother*, 1992
When Joey and Marvin find a collection of family letters in the attic, they stay awake all night reading.
Frank B. Edwards, *Melody Mooner Stayed Up All Night!*, 1991
Melody discovers that staying awake after her family has gone to bed is not as much fun as she'd expected.
John Himmelman, *Lights Out!*, 1995
Something's happening in the cabin, or so the campers imagine and they are unable to fall sleep in the dark.
James Howe, *There's a Dragon in My Sleeping Bag*, 1994
Intimidated by his older brother's imaginary dragon, Alex conquers his fear by creating his own imaginary friend.

558

ISABELLE HARPER
BARRY MOSER, Illustrator

My Cats Nick and Nora
(New York: The Blue Sky Press, 1995)

Subject(s): Animals/Cats; Cousins; Behavior

Age range(s): Grades K-1
Major character(s): Emmie Martin, Cousin; Nick, Cat; Nora, Cat
Time period(s): 1990s (1995)
Locale(s): Massachusetts

Summary: Weekly visits from Emmie fill a Sunday afternoon with a successful search for Nick and Nora who then become the objects of play. First they are dressed in their finest for their birthday party and then taken for a stroll in a doll carriage. A neighbor cat who is not very nice gives chase and Nick and Nora leap out of their outfits and race away. By naptime, the girls and cats reunite for a much deserved rest. (32 pages)

Where it's reviewed:
Booklist, October 1, 1995, page 326
Horn Book Guide, Spring 1996, page 29
Parents Magazine, December 1995, page 230
Publishers Weekly, September 4, 1995, page 69
School Library Journal, October 1995, page 103

Other books by the same author:
Our New Puppy, 1996
My Dog Rosie, 1994

Other books you might like:
Aliki, *Tabby: A Story in Pictures*, 1995
    A kitten's first year is chronicled in a photo-essay of the kitten's bed, food and playmate—a loving little girl.
Patricia Casey, *My Cat Jack*, 1994
    A well-loved pet, Jack is a stretching, yawning, playful cat.
Donald Hall, *I Am the Dog, I Am the Cat*, 1994
    Poetically, a dog and a cat describe their separate interests.

559

ISABELLE HARPER
BARRY MOSER, Illustrator

My Dog Rosie

(New York: The Blue Sky Press, 1994)

Subject(s): Animals/Dogs; Pets; Behavior
Age range(s): Grades K-1
Major character(s): Rosie, Dog; Isabelle, 3-Year-Old; Grandpa, Grandfather, Artist
Time period(s): 1990s (1994)
Locale(s): Bear Run, Massachusetts

Summary: While Grandpa works in his studio, Isabelle is responsible for Rosie. She feeds him, bathes him and reads him a book. When they go outside to play catch, Rosie always brings back the ball. Soon Rosie is tired and ready for a nap; perhaps Isabelle is too. This is the first collaboration between illustrator Moser and his granddaughter. (32 pages)

Where it's reviewed:
Booklist, November 15, 1994, page 611
Bulletin of the Center for Children's Books, December 1994, page 129
Horn Book, November 1994, page 760
Publishers Weekly, September 5, 1994, page 108
School Library Journal, November 1994, page 81

Other books by the same author:
My Cats Nick and Nora, 1995

Other books you might like:
Alyssa Satin Capucilli, *Biscuit*, 1996
    In a beginning reader, a dog is unable to sleep until he's brought just one more thing.
Alexandra Day, *Carl Goes Shopping*, 1989
    While shopping, Baby crawls out of the buggy and onto Carl's back for a tour of the store, returning just in time to fool Mother who thinks dog and baby have waited patiently.
Rosemary Wells, *Lucy Comes to Stay*, 1994
    Mary Elizabeth endures typical puppy mischief such as chewed belongings as she learns to care for her new pet.

560

BEATRICE ORCUTT HARRELL
SUSAN L. ROTH, Illustrator

How Thunder and Lightning Came to Be: A Choctaw Legend

(New York: Dial Books for Young Readers, 1995)

Subject(s): Indians of North America; Legends; Folk Tales
Age range(s): Grades K-3
Major character(s): Heloha, Bird; Melatha, Bird; The Great Sun Father, Deity
Time period(s): Indeterminate Past
Locale(s): United States

Summary: When The Great Sun Father decides to warn his people of coming storms, he is too busy to think of an appropriate message. So he calls on Heloha and Melatha to devise one. The two birds are pleased to be selected, but Heloha's ideas are compromised by Melatha's clumsiness. Although the birds do not realize it, one of their inadvertent efforts is deemed worthy by The Great Sun Father; and, to this day, lightning and thunder forewarn of impending wind and rain. However, Melatha and Heloha are still trying to think of a good idea. The author's first book. (32 pages)

Where it's reviewed:
Booklist, August 1995, page 1952
Horn Book Guide, Fall 1995, page 330
Kirkus Reviews, May 15, 1995, page 710
Publishers Weekly, May 8, 1995, page 295
School Library Journal, August 1994, page 134

Other books you might like:
Paul Goble, *The Gift of the Sacred Dog*, 1982
    A retelling of the legend that explains how a young boy brings the gift of horses to his starving people.
Jonathan London, *Fire Race: A Karuk Coyote Tale about How Fire Came to the People*, 1992
    The wise Coyote who is suffering with his friends through a cold winter steals fire from the Yellow Jacket sisters. Co-author Lanny Pinola.
Lynn Reiser, *Night Thunder and the Queen of the Wild Horses*, 1995
    The fantasy explains thunder as the result of clamoring animals, each trying to outdo the bothersome noise made by the other.

Gayle Ross, *How Turtle's Back Was Cracked: A Traditional Cherokee Tale*, 1995
Boastful Turtle so provokes the wolves with his claims to be a hunter that they hurl him into the river intending to drown him, but he lands on a rock and cracks his shell.

561

MARIAN HARRIS
JIM HARRIS, Illustrator

Goose and the Mountain Lion

(Flagstaff, AZ: Northland Publishing Company, 1994)

Subject(s): Animals/Geese; Animals/Wild Cats; Animals/Rats
Age range(s): Grades K-3
Major character(s): Goose, Goose; Unnamed Character, Mountain Lion; Unnamed Character, Child (pack rat)
Time period(s): Indeterminate Past
Locale(s): Colorado

Summary: The morning Goose awakens to find one of her clutch of four eggs missing, the other barnyard animals agree to stand guard nightly to protect the remaining eggs from the mountain lion known to be prowling in the area. Because they are expecting to see a mountain lion, none of the guards notices the pack rat passing by each night with an egg in his wheelbarrow. When the last egg has vanished, the mountain lion, smelling goose, enters the barn and is attacked by a very angry Goose who considers him the kidnapper of her off-spring. The mountain lion flees the ''monster'' as the eggs hatch in pack rat's lair and all is well. (32 pages)

Where it's reviewed:
Booklist, July 1994, page 1954
Horn Book Guide, Fall 1994, page 274
Publishers Weekly, April 18, 1994, page 62
School Library Journal, August 1994, page 132

Other books you might like:
Frances Barnes-Murphy, *The Fables of Aesop*, 1994
A collection of the classic fables is faithful to the original retellings and humorously illustrated.
Mirra Ginsburg, *Merry-Go-Round: Four Stories*, 1992
Four of Ginsburg's animal fables are gathered together in one volume.
Sally Hobson, *Chicken Little*, 1994
In one of many retellings of the classic tale, Chicken Little and her feathered friends are still so concerned about the sky falling that they overlook the prowling fox.

562

MARK J. HARRIS

Solay

(New York: Bradbury Press, 1993)

Subject(s): Aliens; Self-Confidence; Bullies
Age range(s): Grades 3-5
Major character(s): Melissa ''Missy'' Ballard, 5th Grader (unhappy); Solay, Alien (from the planet Zironia)
Time period(s): 1990s (1993)

Locale(s): California (Crestwood Estates, a planned community)

Summary: Since her family moved from New York, life in California has been miserable for Melissa. She is not accepted by her classmates and her parents are too busy with new jobs to offer much support. Melissa's ho-hum existence undergoes an abrupt transformation when a space ship drops off Solay who is most disappointed to learn that she is not in her intended destination of New York. With completely opposite personalities, the two have much to learn from each other. (137 pages)

Where it's reviewed:
Booklist, April 15, 1993, page 1514
Children's Book Review Service, July 1993, page 153
Publishers Weekly, May 24, 1993, page 88
School Library Journal, May 1993, page 105
Science Fiction Chronicle, June 1993, page 33

Other books by the same author:
Come the Morning, 1989

Other books you might like:
Betsy Byars, *The Computer Nut*, 1984
Kate has met some interesting people via computer but BB-9 is the first alien.
Pamela F. Service, *Stinker from Space*, 1989
When an injured alien selects a skunk as a temporary host body, his rescuers are more than eager to help him return to his own planet.
Jeanne Willis, *The Long Blue Blazer*, 1987
The new kid at school is a puzzle to everyone. Why won't he remove that blazer?

563

JOANNA HARRISON, Author/Illustrator

Dear Bear

(Minneapolis: Carolrhoda Books, Inc., 1995)

Subject(s): Animals/Bears; Letters; Fear
Age range(s): Grades K-2
Major character(s): Katie, Child; Bear, Bear, Toy
Time period(s): 1990s (1994)
Locale(s): England

Summary: Having decided a terrifying bear lives under the stairs, Katie lives in fear of the imagined beast. Her mother suggests writing a letter to the bear and a correspondence begins which helps Katie develop courage to accept Bear's invitation to tea. With trepidation, Katie opens the door leading under the stairs and is greeted by a cheerful teddy bear sitting beside a tea service with a note asking permission to live upstairs with Katie. First published in England in 1994. (32 pages)

Where it's reviewed:
Booklist, January 1, 1995, page 825
Children's Book Review Service, March 1995, page 86
Publishers Weekly, November 21, 1994, page 76
School Librarian, November 1994, page 148
School Library Journal, February 1995, page 73

Other books you might like:

Helen Cooper, *The Bear under the Stairs*, 1993
Fearful William keeps the bear under the stairs well-fed so he won't eat William.

Dick Gackenbach, *Harry and the Terrible Whatzit*, 1979
There's a 2-headed Whatzit in the cellar and Harry's mom is making him go down there!

Valiska Gregory, *Kate's Giants*, 1995
When Kate imagines scary things behind the attic door, her parents help her find courage to confront her fears.

Maggie Smith, *There's a Witch under the Stairs*, 1991
Imaginative Frances is certain a witch lives under the basement stairs.

564

MAGGIE HARRISON
BETHAN MATTHEWS, Illustrator

Lizzie's List

(Cambridge, MA: Candlewick Press, 1993)

Subject(s): Family Life; Single Parent Families; Grandparents
Age range(s): Grades 3-5
Major character(s): Lizzie Giles, 9-Year-Old, Child of Divorced Parents (only child); Mrs. Giles, Single Mother, Mother (working); Mrs. Mildred Peabody, Grandmother ("adopted")
Time period(s): 1990s (1991)
Locale(s): England

Summary: Lizzie envies her friend who has a grandma with a cottage near the sea. All of Lizzie's grandparents are dead and her family consists simply of Lizzie and her mother. A determined youngster who knows how to plan and achieve a goal, Lizzie makes up a list of "missing" relatives and sets off in search of them. She begins by finding Mrs. Peabody whom she "adopts" as a grandmother, and then continues with her list to her mother's dismay. Lizzie does not find quite the family of her dreams, but she learns to accept the "family" that evolves from her efforts. Originally published in Great Britain in 1991. (105 pages)

Where it's reviewed:
Horn Book Guide, Spring 1994, page 76
Kirkus Reviews, August 1, 1993, page 1001
Reading Teacher, September 1994, page 71
School Librarian, February 1992, page 20
School Library Journal, November 1993, page 108

Other books by the same author:
Angels on Roller Skates, 1992

Other books you might like:

Beverly Cleary, *Ramona and Her Mother*, 1979
Lovable Ramona invites us into her family's life once again.

Sheila Greenwald, *Rosy Cole Discovers America!*, 1992
Rosy decides to make her class project a little more interesting by inventing ancestors that are more exciting than the those on her family tree.

Suzy Kline, *Mary Marony, Mummy Girl*, 1994
In the third book about Mary she continues to tackle problems and plan workable solutions.

565

TROON HARRISON
MICHAEL FOREMAN, Illustrator

The Long Weekend

(San Diego: Harcourt Brace & Company, 1994)

Subject(s): Mothers and Sons; Imagination; Beaches
Age range(s): Grades K-2
Major character(s): James, 5-Year-Old; Mommy, Mother
Time period(s): 1990s (1993)
Locale(s): England

Summary: To celebrate his fifth birthday, James prefers three days at the beach with his mother to a picnic with friends or a trip to the zoo. James knows how to make the most of his time on the beach, playing in the sand, building more elaborate structures each day and letting his imagination take him on fantastic adventures. The author's first book for children was originally published in England in 1993 (22 pages)

Where it's reviewed:
Booklist, July 1994, page 1954
Horn Book Guide, Fall 1994, page 274
Publishers Weekly, May 23, 1994, page 86
Quill and Quire, November 1993, page 37
School Library Journal, July 1994, page 77

Other books you might like:

Douglas Florian, *A Beach Day*, 1990
A simple descriptive tale of a family's day at the beach includes a list of seashells.

Sherry Garland, *Summer Sands*, 1995
Siblings enjoying a vacation at the seashore are surprised by the devastion of a late summer storm and work to rebuild the dunes.

Olof Landstrom, *Will Goes to the Beach*, 1995
In the latest of Will's adventures, he enjoys a holiday swimming at the beach.

Joanne Ryder, *A House by the Sea*, 1994
A child imagines life in a house by the sea, playing with seals, crabs and other marine life.

Peter Sis, *Beach Ball*, 1990
At the beach, Mary and her mother use their imaginations and the objects they find to see letters, numbers, colors and shapes in the marine environment.

566

MARC HARSHMAN
MARK MOHR, Illustrator

The Storm

(New York: Cobblehill Books, 1995)

Subject(s): Physically Handicapped; Self-Perception; Farm Life
Age range(s): Grades 2-4
Major character(s): Jonathan, Child, Accident Victim; Mom, Mother, Farmer; Dad, Father, Farmer
Time period(s): 1990s (1995)
Locale(s): Indiana

Summary: With a storm brewing and Mom and Dad away from home, Jonathan brings in the horses himself. Fortunately, since his accident, the barn doors and the horses' halters have been adjusted so Jonathan can handle them from his wheelchair. Although Jonathan is able to coax the frightened animals into their stall he must stay with them to keep them calm as the tornado hits. Frightened, but uninjured, Jonathan surveys the damage after the storm, thankful to be alive, and proud of what he's accomplished. (32 pages)

Where it's reviewed:
Booklist, May 1, 1995, page 1579
Children's Book Review Service, July 1995, page 151
Parents' Choice, September 1995, page 13
School Library Journal, July 1995, page 62
Smithsonian, November 1995, page 172

Other books by the same author:
Uncle James, 1993
Snow Company, 1990
A Little Excitement, 1989

Other books you might like:
Betsy Byars, *Tornado*, 1996
 During a tornado the family is sheltered in a storm cellar where their farmhand tells a childhood story of a dog blown into his life by a tornado.
Bonnie Dobkin, *Just a Little Different*, 1994
 Although his friend uses a wheelchair, a child finds that he shares much in common with him.
Anne F. Rockwell, *The Storm*, 1994
 A coastal storm knocks out power and produces quite a clean-up as it passes.

567

WENDY HARTMANN
NIKI DALY, Illustrator

All the Magic in the World

(New York: Dutton Children's Books, 1993)

Subject(s): Imagination; Magic
Age range(s): Grades K-2
Major character(s): Lena, Child (clumsy); Joseph, Collector (collects ''junk'')
Time period(s): 1990s (1993)
Locale(s): South Africa

Summary: Each Friday evening, rain or shine, hot or cold, Lena and other neighborhood children play happily in the dusty street, always ignoring Joseph because his habit of collecting ''junk'' and keeping it in a tin is considered odd. Being younger than the others, Lena also finds herself left out sometimes because she is perceived to be too clumsy. One night she befriends Joseph and is entranced with some of the simple, everyday items in his tin, watching as he transforms them into objects of wonder. Is the magic in the tin ask the children? Joseph knows where the magic is, do you? (32 pages)

Where it's reviewed:
Booklist, September 1, 1993, page 68
Children's Book Review Service, Winter 1994, page 62
Horn Book, November 1993, page 732

Publishers Weekly, July 19, 1993, page 254
School Library Journal, December 1993, page 88

Other books by the same author:
One Sun Rises: An African Wildlife Counting Book, 1994

Other books you might like:
Niki Daly, *Not So Fast, Songololo*, 1986
 Malusi and his grandmother travel to the city to buy sneakers.
Nigel Gray, *A Country Far Away*, 1989
 The similarities and differences of life in a Western country and in a rural African village are demonstrated through the activities of two boys.
Karen Lynn Williams, *Galimoto*, 1990
 Imaginative Kondi collects scraps in order to make his own toy car.

568

JAYNE HARVEY
ABBY CARTER, Illustrator

Great-Uncle Dracula and the Dirty Rat

(New York: Random House, 1993)

Series: Stepping Stone
Subject(s): Vampires; Brothers and Sisters; Pets
Age range(s): Grades 2-3
Major character(s): Emily Normal, Child (lives with Great-Uncle Dracula), Niece; Elliot Normal, Child (lives with Great-Uncle Dracula), Nephew; Finster, Rat (Elliot's pet)
Time period(s): 1990s (1993)
Locale(s): Transylvania (a town full of monsters)

Summary: Living in Great-Uncle Dracula's home with witches for friends, vampires for teachers and a principal named Frank N. Stein is not what the Normal children consider normal. In this sequel to *Great-Uncle Dracula*, Elliot's pet rat begins destroying Emily's school work and the two children's attempts to handle the problem themselves leads to even bigger problems. Ultimately the truth comes out and an understanding Great-Uncle Dracula sends Finster to obedience school. (62 pages)

Where it's reviewed:
Bulletin of the Center for Children's Books, December 1992, page 113
Horn Book Guide, Spring 1993, page 57
School Library Journal, February 1994, page 86

Other books by the same author:
Great-Uncle Dracula, 1992

Other books you might like:
Patricia Reilly Giff, *The Beast in Ms. Rooney's Room*, 1984
 One of many titles about the antics of students at Polk Street School.
James Howe, *Pinky and Rex and the Mean Old Witch*, 1991
 Pinky and Rex do not agree on the best approach to take with mean Mrs. Morgan.
Mary DeBall Kwitz, *Little Vampire and the Midnight Bear*, 1995
 Little vampire is more eager to learn to fly than to tackle Midnight Bear.

Ross Martin Madsen, *Perrywinkle and the Book of Magic Spells*, 1988
Perrywinkle finds that wizard training is hazardous if you're not careful.

569

LIBBY HATHORN
ELIVIA, Illustrator

Grandma's Shoes

(Boston: Little, Brown and Company, 1994)

Subject(s): Grandparents; Death; Fantasy
Age range(s): Grades K-3
Major character(s): Unnamed Character, Child; Grandma, Grandmother
Time period(s): 1990s (1994)
Locale(s): Fictional Country

Summary: Surrounded by adults following Grandma's funeral, a little girl repeatedly hears the comment, "Who could ever step into such a woman's shoes?" The granddaughter doesn't understand the remark, but when she finds the shoes under Grandma's chair she steps into them herself. Magically, she is transported into a land of fantasy and memory where she tries to find Grandma and comfort for her sorrow. (32 pages)

Where it's reviewed:
Children's Book Review Service, February 1995, page 75
Horn Book Guide, Spring 1995, page 39
Junior Bookshelf, August 1995, page 128
School Librarian, August 1995, page 108
School Library Journal, October 1994, page 91

Other books by the same author:
The Surprise Box, 1994
Looking for Felix, 1993
Freya's Fantastic Surprise, 1989

Other books you might like:
Aliki, *The Two of Them*, 1979
A young girl and her grandfather share a special relationship which she remembers after his death.
Tomie De Paola, *Nana Upstairs & Nana Downstairs*, 1973
With a loving family to console him, Tomie faces the death of his grandmother.
Karen Hesse, *Poppy's Chair*, 1993
After her grandfather dies, Leah is fearful that Gramm will also die. Gramm helps Leah cope with her fears and grieve for her grandfather.

570

JUANITA HAVILL
ANNE SIBLEY O'BRIEN, Illustrator

Jamaica and Brianna

(Boston: Houghton Mifflin Company, 1993)

Subject(s): Jealousy; Friendship; Peer Pressure
Age range(s): Grades K-3
Major character(s): Jamaica, Child (African American), Friend; Brianna, Child (Asian American), Friend

Time period(s): 1990s (1993)
Locale(s): United States

Summary: At the bus stop Brianna is quick to point out to Jamaica that she is wearing "boy" boots. Jamaica needs no reminding that the hated, hand-me-down boots are not fashionable. When, at last, the boots can no longer be worn, Jamaica selects a pair of fancy cowboy boots as their replacement. Now Brianna's hand-me-down boots look tarnished in comparison and the trading of insults continues until both girls face their feelings honestly and put their friendship back on a cooperative track. (32 pages)

Where it's reviewed:
Booklist, October 15, 1993, page 452
Horn Book, November 1993, page 732
Kirkus Reviews, September 1, 1993, page 1145
Publishers Weekly, July 26, 1993, page 71
School Library Journal, October 1993, page 100

Other books by the same author:
Jamaica's Blue Marker, 1995
Kentucky Troll, 1993
Jamaica's Find, 1986

Other books you might like:
Joyce Champion, *Emily and Alice Again*, 1995
Best friends Emily and Alice learn how to keep their friendship on a happy note.
Russell Hoban, *Best Friends for Frances*, 1969
Excluded from Albert's "boys only" baseball game, Frances plays with sister Gloria and Albert learns a lesson.
James Howe, *Pinky and Rex*, 1990
The first book about two close friends whose adventures continue in subsequent titles.

571

JUANITA HAVILL
ANNE SIBLEY O'BRIEN, Illustrator

Jamaica's Blue Marker

(Boston: Houghton Mifflin Company, 1995)

Subject(s): Schools; Moving, Household; Behavior
Age range(s): Grades K-2
Major character(s): Jamaica, Student; Russell, Student
Time period(s): 1990s (1995)
Locale(s): United States

Summary: Because Russell misbehaves in class and scribbles on her pictures, Jamaica is pleased that he is moving. However, when his last day arrives, Jamaica reconsiders and regrets not joining her classmates in making a good-bye card for Russell. Instead, she gives him her blue marker as a parting gift. (32 pages)

Where it's reviewed:
Booklist, July 1995, page 1881
Bulletin of the Center for Children's Books, October 1995, page 55
Horn Book Guide, Spring 1996, page 29
School Library Journal, January 1996, page 84

Other books by the same author:
Jamaica and Brianna, 1993

Jamaica Tag-Along, 1989
Jamaica's Find, 1986

Other books you might like:
Kevin Henkes, *Lilly's Purple Plastic Purse*, 1996
　Lilly's presentation of her weekend shopping treasures is not warmly received by her beloved teacher so she plots her revenge until the teacher's note changes her attitude.
Russell Hoban, *Best Friends for Frances*, 1994
　A newly illustrated edition of a 1969 title tells how Frances and little sister Gloria persevere when friends forsake them.
John Steptoe, *Stevie*, 1969
　When Robert's wish that pesky Stevie go away actually comes true, he begins to think of the fun times they shared and realizes that he misses the foster child.

572

JUANITA HAVILL
J.J. SMITH-MOORE, Illustrator

Jennifer, Too

(New York: Hyperion Books for Children, 1994)

Subject(s): Play; Brothers and Sisters
Age range(s): Grades 2-3
Major character(s): Jennifer, Child, Sister (younger); Matt, Child, Brother (older)
Time period(s): 1990s (1994)
Locale(s): United States

Summary: When Matt's friends come over to play they don't want Jennifer hanging around. She ignores their attempts to get rid of her and turns out to be a better spy than the boys are. In the second story, when she sneaks up the stairs to join the group in the attic in order to tell her own ghost story, she frightens away most of the audience. Last, Jennifer's ingenuity saves the day when the boys are not allowed to use trash can lids as shields for their game of knights. (56 pages)

Where it's reviewed:
Booklist, June 1, 1994, page 1820
Horn Book Guide, Fall 1994, page 300
Kirkus Reviews, June 1, 1994, page 775
School Library Journal, July 1994, page 78

Other books by the same author:
Saving Owen's Toad, 1994
Jamaica and Brianna, 1993
It Always Happens to Leona, 1989

Other books you might like:
Eth Clifford, *Family for Sale*, 1996
　When Mom goes away for two weeks she leaves behind five children with each having a turn to be in charge.
Elizabeth Levy, *Rude Rowdy Rumors: A Brian and Pea Brain Mystery*, 1994
　With unsolicited help from younger sister Penny (Pea Brain), Brian learns who is spreading rumors about him to others on the soccer team.
Lisa Westberg Peters, *The Hayloft*, 1995
　Sisters Caroline Rose and Ivy enjoy summer days at their farm home.

Suzanne Williams, *Edwin and Emily*, 1995
　Although younger sister Emily is often a pest, Edwin admits she's a nice pest.

573

JUANITA HAVILL

Saving Owen's Toad

(New York: Hyperion Books for Children, 1994)

Subject(s): Brothers; Animals/Frogs and Toads; Accidents
Age range(s): Grades 3-6
Major character(s): Owen, 9-Year-Old, Brother; Richard, 13-Year-Old, Brother; Buffy, Toad (Owen's)
Time period(s): 1990s (1994)
Locale(s): United States

Summary: When bossy Richard embarks on a money-making scheme selling ''pest-control'' toads to the neighbors, he underestimates Owen's knowledge of and love for animals. Fearing for the toads' lives, Owen frees them all, with the exception of Buffy, a three-legged toad he finds and claims as a pet. Richard extracts his revenge by stealing Buffy, prompting a desperate rescue attempt that results in Owen's injury and a trip to the emergency room. (124 pages)

Where it's reviewed:
Booklist, January 1, 1995, page 820
Bulletin of the Center for Children's Books, December 1994, page 130
Horn Book Guide, Spring 1995, page 77
Library Talk, May 1995, page 42
School Library Journal, March 1995, page 204

Other books by the same author:
Jennifer, Too, 1994

Other books you might like:
Ellen Leroe, *Leap Frog Friday*, 1992
　Using his new magic rocks, Oliver accidently changes his brother into a frog.
Phyllis Reynolds Naylor, *Being Danny's Dog*, 1995
　The relationship between T. R. and his older brother is so strong that T. R. thinks of himself as being Danny's loyal, protective dog.
P.J. Petersen, *The Amazing Magic Show*, 1994
　With knowledge gained from a magic show, Hal finds a way to deal with his obnoxious older brother.

574

NANCY HAYASHI, Author/Illustrator

Superbird to the Rescue

(New York: Dutton Children's Books, 1995)

Subject(s): Animals/Birds; Pets; Shoplifting
Age range(s): Grades 3-4
Major character(s): Jesse Beeman, Child, Friend; Walter Fujikawa, Child, Friend; Zenith, Bird (parrot)
Time period(s): 1990s (1995)
Locale(s): United States

Summary: When Jesse and Walter learn the shopping mall is having a problem with shoplifters they decide to become undercover detectives and catch the culprits. Jesse's plan to use Zenith backfires and he comes close to losing his pet in the parking lot. Just when the disappointed boys think they will have to go home unsuccessful, they spot a suspect and assist in her apprehension. (118 pages)

Where it's reviewed:
Bulletin of the Center for Children's Books, May 1995, page 309
Horn Book Guide, Fall 1995, page 298
School Library Journal, May 1995, page 106

Other books by the same author:
The Fantastic Stay-Home-from-School Day, 1992
Cosmic Cousin, 1990

Other books you might like:
Beverly Cleary, *Henry Huggins*, 1950
  This is the first of several stories about 3rd grader Henry, neighbor of the Beezus and Ramona, who adopts a dog, Ribsy.
Dick King-Smith, *Harry's Mad*, 1987
  Young Harry inherits an African gray parrot named Madison or ''Mad,'' who speaks both British and American.
Robert Newton Peck, *Soup*, 1974
  The first in a series of humorous stories tells of friends Soup and Rob who have unusual ideas which seem helpful, but don't work out.

575

SARAH HAYES
HELEN CRAIG, Illustrator

This Is the Bear and the Bad Little Girl
(Cambridge, MA: Candlewick Press, 1995)

Subject(s): Animals/Bears; Animals/Dogs; Stories in Rhyme
Age range(s): Grades K-1
Major character(s): Fred, Bear, Toy; Unnamed Character, Child; Unnamed Character, Child, Thief
Time period(s): 1990s (1995)
Locale(s): England

Summary: A boy and his beloved teddy bear await dessert in a tea room when the boy's jealous dog, angry to be stuck outside, trips a woman entering the tea room, making her fall into patrons waiting to pay. In the ensuing commotion, a little girl sitting at a nearby table grabs Fred and runs away with the dog in pursuit. The boy also enters the chase and, with his dog's help, retrieves Fred. (32 pages)

Where it's reviewed:
Booklist, November 15, 1995, page 564
Horn Book, November 1995, page 760
Horn Book Guide, Spring 1996, page 29
School Library Journal, December 1995, page 81

Other books by the same author:
This Is the Bear and the Scary Night, 1992
This Is the Bear and the Picnic Lunch, 1989
This Is the Bear, 1986

Other books you might like:
Jez Alborough, *Where's My Teddy?*, 1992
  When Eddie searches the dark woods for his lost teddy bear, he runs into a huge bear with the same problem.
Nancy White Carlstrom, *Barney Is Best*, 1994
  When a young child faces a brief hospital stay he chooses his well-loved, very worn, and bandaged Barney to be his comfort away from home.
Kim Lewis, *My Friend Harry*, 1995
  James and his stuffed animal Harry are inseparable until James starts school.

576

SHEILA HAYES

Zoe's Gift
(New York: Lodestar, 1994)

Subject(s): Mystery and Detective Stories; Extrasensory Perception; Friendship
Age range(s): Grades 4-6
Major character(s): Cory Gales, 11-Year-Old; Zoe Mitchell, 11-Year-Old, Psychic
Time period(s): 1990s (1994)
Locale(s): Olbourne, England (Rose Farm)

Summary: When Cory's parents decide to go to England to join an old acquaintance for an archeological dig they bring Cory along to visit with the friend's granddaughter while they are at the dig site. At first Cory considers Zoe to be snobbish, aloof and a little strange, but soon a friendship develops as Zoe confides that she is able to see things from the past. Zoe feels cursed by this gift, but Cory's enthusiasm for it helps Zoe to accept herself and solve a 100-year-old village mystery. (156 pages)

Where it's reviewed:
Booklist, September 1, 1994, page 41
Horn Book Guide, Spring 1995, page 77
Kirkus Reviews, July 15, 1994, page 985
Library Talk, March 1995, page 29
School Library Journal, August 1994, page 156

Other books by the same author:
No Autographs, Please, 1984
Speaking of Snapdragons, 1982
Me and My Mona Lisa Smile, 1981

Other books you might like:
Elaine Marie Alphin, *Tournament of Time*, 1994
  In England for a year, American Jess and her brothers solve murders from long ago with help from the victim's spirits who speak to her from the stained-glass windows.
E.L. Flood, *Ghost of a Chance*, 1994
  Molly and Josh solve the mystery of a ghost and a one-hundred-year-old murder.
Pamela F. Service, *Phantom Victory*, 1994
  With help from ancestral ghosts, two teenagers search for a necklace hidden many years ago.
Betty Ren Wright, *A Ghost in the House*, 1991
  The unusual occurrences that Sarah witnesses when she is home alone with her great aunt appear to be the work of a ghost seeking revenge.

577

BARBARA SHOOK HAZEN

Good-Bye, Hello

(New York: Greenwillow Books, 1994)

Subject(s): Teachers; Schools/Catholic Schools; Grandparents
Age range(s): Grades 4-6
Major character(s): Roberta Jean ''Bobbie Jean'' Callahan, 6th Grader (imaginative); Sister Alice, Teacher (strict), Religious (nun); Sarah ''Gramma'' Callahan, Grandmother, Aged Person
Time period(s): 1990s (1994)
Locale(s): Minnesota

Summary: In the picture-book author's first novel, Bobbie Jean must face the strictest teacher in school without the support of her best friend who moved away during the summer. On top of her school problems, Bobbie Jean notices that her lively, convertible-driving, fun-loving gramma just isn't herself. As Gramma's health fails, Bobbie Jean comes to accept her inevitable death just as she has learned to accept the challenge of 6th grade with her quick wit, imagination and flair for the dramatic. (155 pages)

Where it's reviewed:
Booklist, April 1, 1994, page 1444
Horn Book, July 1994, page 450
Kirkus Reviews, June 1, 1994, page 773
Publishers Weekly, May 2, 1994, page 310
School Library Journal, May 1994, page 112

Other books you might like:
Beverly Cleary, *Beezus and Ramona*, 1955
    Beezus struggles to understand how she can love a sister like Ramona who causes so many problems.
Lois Lowry, *Anastasia, Again!*, 1981
    In the sequel to *Anastasia Krupnik*, Anastasia faces a family move from the city to the suburbs with her characteristic wit and inventiveness.
Phyllis Reynolds Naylor, *The Agony of Alice*, 1985
    Motherless Alice is seeking a female role model and the only one available is her despised 6th grade teacher.
Eileen Walsh Strauch, *Hey You, Sister Rose*, 1993
    Knowing that she has stern Sister Rose this year, Arlene dreads beginning 6th grade.

578

BARBARA SHOOK HAZEN
TONI GOFFE, Illustrator

The Knight Who Was Afraid to Fight

(New York: Dial Books for Young Readers, 1994)

Subject(s): Knights and Knighthood; Fear; Humor
Age range(s): Grades K-3
Major character(s): Sir Fred, Knight; Lady Wendylyn, Noblewoman; Melvin the Miffed, Bully
Time period(s): Indeterminate Past
Locale(s): Fictional Country

Summary: Melvin the Miffed is jealous that Lady Wendylyn chooses cowardly Sir Fred as her beloved. Determined to show Sir Fred as the fearful knight that he is, Melvin challenges Sir Fred to a duel. Due to his honorable ways, Sir Fred triumphs over the foul play of Melvin the Miffed and rides off into the morning sunrise with his beloved Lady Wendylyn. (32 pages)

Where it's reviewed:
Booklist, May 15, 1994, page 1682
Horn Book Guide, Fall 1994, page 275
Publishers Weekly, May 9, 1994, page 72
School Library Journal, June 1994, page 101

Other books by the same author:
The Knight Who Was Afraid of the Dark, 1989
Very Shy, 1983
To Be Me, 1975

Other books you might like:
Tomie De Paola, *The Knight and the Dragon*, 1980
    A knight with little experience fighting dragons prepares to face an equally inexperienced dragon.
Joe Lasker, *A Tournament of Knights*, 1986
    As Justin prepares for his first tournament, a more experienced knight plans to defeat him.
Jane O'Connor, *Sir Small and the Dragonfly*, 1988
    Bravely, Sir Small mounts his trusty ant and pursues the dragonfly carrying away Lady Teena.

579

SHARON E. HEISEL

Wrapped in a Riddle

(Boston: Houghton Mifflin, 1993)

Subject(s): Mystery and Detective Stories
Age range(s): Grades 4-6
Major character(s): GrandAnn, Grandmother (Miranda's), Businesswoman (owner of Jumping Frog Inn); Miranda, 11-Year-Old
Time period(s): 1990s
Locale(s): Ashville, Oregon

Summary: In a story filled with riddles, allusions to Mark Twain and word play, Miranda stays at her grandmother's bed-andbreakfast while her parents are away on a biology field trip. Strange events occur and it's up to Miranda and her friends to solve them. First the housekeeper is hit on the head, then a strange key is found, and finally someone steals the love letters written by Mark Twain to Miranda's great-greatgrandmother in this mystery at the Jumping Frog Inn. (140 pages)

Where it's reviewed:
School Library Journal, February 1994, page 102
Booklist, October 1, 1993, page 344
Center for Children's Books. Bulletin, November 1993, page 84
Horn Book Guide, Spring 1994, page 77
Library Talk, September 1994, page 47

Other books by the same author:
A Little Magic, 1991

Other books you might like:

Lisa Eisenberg, *Mystery at Bluff Point Dunes*, 1988
　　Kate vacations at a classmate's home where jewelry, both hers and another guests, disappears; though police are called, Kate investigates.

Gordon Korman, *Our Man Weston*, 1986
　　The Weston twins work at a resort hotel where they're certain mystery is afoot.

Joan Lowery Nixon, *The Weekend Was Murder*, 1992
　　As part of a murder mystery enactment weekend at the hotel where she works, Liz is supposed to discover a body; unfortunately, it's real.

580

MARY-CLAIRE HELLDORFER
JULIE DOWNING, Illustrator

Cabbage Rose
(New York: Bradbury Press, 1993)

Subject(s): Fairy Tale; Artists and Art; Magic
Age range(s): Grades K-2
Major character(s): Cabbage Rose, Artist (independent); The Prince, Royalty (prince)
Time period(s): 16th century
Locale(s): Fictional City

Summary: When a magician visits the inn where a plain young girl works in service to her unkind brothers, he admires her paintings and gives her a new paintbrush as he departs. Cabbage, as her brothers call her to remind her of her insignificance, soon discovers that whatever she paints with the magician's brush becomes real. When her brothers take advantage of this magic for their own gain, Cabbage paints herself right out of the inn and heads for the king's city. She supports herself with her artwork, attracting the attention of The Prince who gives her the name Rose. Cabbage Rose learns that she does not need the magic paint brush to give this tale a happy ending. (32 pages)

Where it's reviewed:
Booklist, February 1, 1993, page 988
Children's Book Review Service, Spring 1993, page 135
Kirkus Reviews, March 1, 1993, page 299
Publishers Weekly, February 15, 1993, page 236
School Library Journal, November 1993, page 82

Other books by the same author:
Gather Up, Gather In: A Book of Seasons, 1994
The Mapmaker's Daughter, 1991
Daniel's Gift, 1987

Other books you might like:

Valerie Scho Carey, *Tsugele's Broom*, 1993
　　The ALA Notable Book tells of hard-working Tsugele's discovery that her trusty broom is also somewhat magical.

Demi, *Liang and the Magic Paintbrush*, 1980
　　A poor boy discovers that with a magic paintbrush all his pictures become real.

Ai-Ling Louie, *Yeh-Shen: A Cinderella Story from China*, 1982
　　In a retelling of a Chinese folktale a poor young girl over-

comes the wickedness of her stepmother and stepsister to marry the Prince.

581

KATHY HENDERSON
PATRICK BENSON, Illustrator

The Little Boat
(Cambridge, MA: Candlewick Press, 1995)

Subject(s): Beaches; Boats and Boating; Toys
Age range(s): Grades K-2
Major character(s): Unnamed Character, Child
Time period(s): 1990s (1995)
Locale(s): At Sea

Summary: A little boy constructs a boat out of styrofoam, sticks, and string which entertains him during a day at the beach. When he briefly turns away, the boat floats out beyond his reach and begins a journey past fishing boats, tugboats, and large ships. The sun sets and still the boat floats through night and storm and days of peril until it washes ashore near a little girl who plays with it all day long. (32 pages)

Where it's reviewed:
Booklist, September 1, 1995, page 86
Children's Book Review Service, Winter 1996, page 62
Children's Book Watch, October 1995, page 5
Publishers Weekly, August 7, 1995, page 460
School Library Journal, October 1995, page 104

Other books by the same author:
Bounce, Bounce, Bounce, 1994
Bumpety Bump, 1994
The Great Lakes, 1989

Other books you might like:

Molly Bang, *Yellow Ball*, 1991
　　A little boy momentarily forgets the yellow ball he's been playing with and it floats away, washing up on a distant shore.

Chris L. Demarest, *My Blue Boat*, 1995
　　In her bathtub a little girl imagines taking an ocean voyage with her toy boat.

Miriam Young, *If I Sailed a Boat*, 1971
　　In his imagination a young boy has adventures on each of fourteen different boats.

582

MARY JEAN HENDRICK
JANE DYER, Illustrator

If Anything Ever Goes Wrong at the Zoo
(New York: Harcourt Brace Jovanovich, 1993)

Subject(s): Zoos; Animals; Mothers and Daughters
Age range(s): Grades K-2
Major character(s): Leslie, Child, Animal Lover; Mom, Mother
Time period(s): 1990s (1993)
Locale(s): United States

Summary: In the author's first book, Leslie visits the zoo weekly with her mother, each time asking one of the keepers if she can take home an animal. When her invitation is refused, she describes a feature of her own house which would be suitable for the animal and departs by assuring the keeper that, if anything ever goes wrong at the zoo, the animals are welcome at her house. One rainy Saturday Leslie and her mom are unable to go to the zoo, but by bedtime, with the zoo flooding, the zoo begins arriving at Leslie's home, much to Mom's surprise. (32 pages)

Where it's reviewed:
Booklist, June 1, 1993, page 1857
Children's Book Review Service, July 1993, page 147
Five Owls, March 1993, page 81
Publishers Weekly, April 26, 1993, page 77
School Library Journal, July 1993, page 60

Other books you might like:
Nancy White Carlstrom, *What Would You Do If You Lived at the Zoo?*, 1994
   Many activities are possible if you live at the zoo and copy the animals' movements.
Rita Golden Gelman, *I Went to the Zoo*, 1993
   The animals at the zoo look so bored that one visitor invites them to come home with him.
Arnold Lobel, *A Zoo for Mister Muster*, 1962
   Mister Muster's zoo friends visit him at home for a change.
Eve Rice, *Sam Who Never Forgets*, 1977
   Elephant is fearful that zookeeper Sam has forgotten his daily food.
Pippa Unwin, *The Great Zoo Hunt!*, 1990
   Ten animals have escaped from the zoo and it's up to the reader to find them.

583

DIANA HENDRY
MARGARET CHAMBERLAIN, Illustrator

Dog Donovan
(Cambridge, MA: Candlewick Press, 1995)

Subject(s): Animals/Dogs; Fear; Pets
Age range(s): Grades K-2
Major character(s): Hero, Dog
Time period(s): 1990s (1995)
Locale(s): England

Summary: The seven members of the Donovan family decide the way to conquer their individual fears is to get a dog, so they proceed to the animal shelter and select Hero. As it turns out, their theory proves to be correct, though not in the way the family expected. While each of the Donovans is afraid of something, Hero is afraid of everything and the members of the family, in comforting the pet, forget their own fears and live more happily in their creaky, old house. (32 pages)

Where it's reviewed:
Booklist, March 1, 1995, page 1248
Children's Book Review Service, July 1995, page 147
Publishers Weekly, February 6, 1995, page 85
School Library Journal, April 1995, page 102
Wilson Library Bulletin, May 1995, page 99

Other books by the same author:
Why Father Christmas Was Late for Hartlepool, 1994

A Camel Called April, 1991
The Not-Anywhere House, 1991

Other books you might like:
Norman Bridwell, *Clifford, the Small Red Puppy*, 1972
   Emily Elizabeth faces some out-of-the-ordinary puppy problems after choosing the runt of the litter as her pet.
Wende Devlin, *The Trouble with Henriette!*, 1995
   Hay fever almost causes Jolie to lose her pet Henriette when the dog can no longer earn her keep by locating truffles.
Cynthia Rylant, *Henry and Mudge*, 1987
   In this first book of a popular series, only-child Henry, lonely for companionship, begs his parents to allow him to have a dog.

584

DIANA HENDRY
ADRIANO GON, Illustrator

Kid Kibble
(Cambridge, MA: Candlewick Press, 1994)

Subject(s): Tenant/Landlord Relations; Teachers; Behavior
Age range(s): Grades 3-5
Major character(s): Kid Kibble, Boarder, Teacher; Ned, Child, Brother (older); Jess, Child, Sister (younger)
Time period(s): 1990s (1992)
Locale(s): England

Summary: Kid Kibble is the eighth boarder Ned and Jess have had to contend with since their parents divorced and their mother began renting out the attic of their old home to help meet expenses. The first seven have been disasters of one kind or another so when Kid shows up with a trombone and a skeleton named Ernest everyone thinks history is ready to repeat itself. As a biology teacher, Kid has an assortment of pets which, in combination with some of his experiments, create unusual problems for the family. As the youngest in a large family, Kid tolerates Jess's practical jokes and eventually landlord and tenant find a way to share the space happily. Originally published in England in 1992. (80 pages)

Where it's reviewed:
Booklist, November 15, 1994, page 601
Horn Book Guide, Spring 1995, page 77
Kirkus Reviews, November 15, 1994, page 1531
Library Talk, May 1995, page 41
School Library Journal, November 1994, page 104

Other books by the same author:
The Carey Street Cat, 1991
The Rainbow Watchers, 1991
A Camel Called April, 1990

Other books you might like:
Mary Hoffman, *The Four-Legged Ghosts*, 1993
   After Alex and Carrie's first pet begins conjuring up the ghosts of previous household pets, they are fortunate the new tenant in the attic apartment is a magician.
Ellen Leroe, *Ghost Dog*, 1993
   The ghost of a dog in his grandpa's new home creates problems for Artie until he decides to use the dog to help solve a mystery.

Betty Ren Wright, *The Ghost of Popcorn Hill*, 1993
Martin and Peter solve their ghost problem by introducing the lonely ghost of a farmer to the ghost of a lonely sheep dog.

585

KEVIN HENKES, Author/Illustrator

Chrysanthemum
(New York: Greenwillow Books, 1991)

Subject(s): Schools; Teacher-Student Relationships; Self-Acceptance
Age range(s): Grades K-3
Major character(s): Chrysanthemum, Mouse, Student; Victoria, Mouse, Student; Mrs. Delphinium Twinkle, Teacher
Time period(s): 1990s (1991)
Locale(s): Fictional Country

Summary: When an absolutely perfect little mouse is born to adoring parents, they give her a name worthy of adorning their wonderful child—Chrysanthemum. As she grows, Chrysanthemum loves hearing her name and seeing it written, but when she enters school, her joy soon changes to despair as Victoria makes pointed comments about her being named after a flower. Daily, Chrysanthemum arrives home feeling humiliated about her name and daily her parents shower her with love and comfort. Fortunately, the class soon meets Mrs. Twinkle, the music teacher, who not only is also named after a flower but intends to name her baby Chrysanthemum if she has a girl. A chastised Victoria and her cronies instantly adopt long, flower names for themselves and Chrysanthemum goes home believing that her name is, indeed, absolutely perfect. (30 pages)

Where it's reviewed:
Booklist, March 15, 1992, page 1367
Horn Book, September 1991, page 583
Instructor, July 1992, page 14
Language Arts, November 1992, page 516
School Library Journal, December 1991, page 30

Awards the book has won:
Notable Children's Books in the Language Arts, 1991
ALA Notable Book, 1991

Other books by the same author:
Lilly's Purple Plastic Purse, 1996 (School Library Journal Best Books, 1996)
Chester's Way, 1988 (ALA Notable Book, 1988)
Sheila Rae, the Brave, 1987

Other books you might like:
Gibbs Davis, *The Other Emily*, 1984
On the first day of school, Emily is shocked to learn that there are other children with her name.
Diana Engel, *Josephina Hates Her Name*, 1989
Not until Grandma tells about the relative for whom Josephina is named does she begin to appreciate her name.
Belinda Rochelle, *When Jo Louis Won the Title*, 1994
Jo Louis is afraid to begin a new school because she is embarrassed by her name so her grandfather explains the story behind her name.

Bernard Waber, *But Names Will Never Hurt Me*, 1976
When Alison Wonderland learns how she came by her unusual name, she also begins to learn how to live with it.

586

KEVIN HENKES
MARISABINA RUSSO, Illustrator

Good-Bye, Curtis
(New York: Greenwillow Books, 1995)

Subject(s): Work; Neighbors and Neighborhoods; Surprises
Age range(s): Grades K-1
Major character(s): Curtis, Postal Worker
Time period(s): 1990s (1995)
Locale(s): United States

Summary: Today is the final day that Curtis will walk the route he has followed for 42 years, delivering mail to residents and businesses in the community. At each stop he receives a small gift as well as hugs from the customers he has served for so long. When Curtis reaches the last house on his route, his family and neighbors come out from their hiding places and surprise him with a retirement party. (24 pages)

Where it's reviewed:
Booklist, October 15, 1995, page 411
Hornbook, November 1995, page 733
Kirkus Reviews, July 15, 1995, page 1024
New York Times Book Review, January 14, 1996, page 23
School Library Journal, October 1995, page 104

Other books by the same author:
Lilly's Purple Plastic Purse, 1996
Owen, 1993 (Caldecott Honor Book)
Chrysanthemum, 1991

Other books you might like:
Maribeth Boelts, *Grace and Joe*, 1994
A lonely preschooler makes friends with the mail carrier and follows him about the neighborhood.
Melrose Cooper, *I Got Community*, 1995
With a catchy rhythm, the text describes the important connections that make each person in a community significant.
Elaine Know-Wagner, *My Grandpa Retired Today*, 1982
With mixed feelings, Margey helps Grandpa clean up his barber shop and close it for the last time as he prepares to retire.

587

KEVIN HENKES, Author/Illustrator

Lilly's Purple Plastic Purse
(New York: Greenwillow, 1996)

Subject(s): Schools; Teachers; Behavior
Age range(s): Grades K-2
Major character(s): Lilly, Mouse, 1st Grader; Mr. Slinger, Mouse, Teacher
Time period(s): 1990s
Locale(s): United States

Summary: Lilly loves school. Today she is excited about her new things and can't wait to share them with the class. When her teacher takes them away from her because she is too noisy, she is very upset and writes a nasty story about him. When she gets home she discovers that he has written her a nice note and realizes how bad she has been. She and her parents respond with a note of their own and make a snack to share with the class when she returns. (unpaged)

Where it's reviewed:
Horn Book, September/October 1996, page 577
School Library Journal, August 1996, page 122
Booklist, August 1996, page 1904
Bulletin of the Center for Children's Books, October 1996, page 62

Awards the book has won:
School Library Journal Best Books, 1996
ALA Notable Children's Book, 1997

Other books by the same author:
Owen, 1993
Chrysanthemum, 1992
Julius, the Baby of the World, 1990
Chester's Way, 1988

Other books you might like:
Maribeth Boelts, *Summer's End*, 1995
  Jill is not sure she really wants to return to school now that summer is over.
Sarah Garland, *Billy and Belle*, 1992
  Billy takes his sister to school but all kinds of troubles result.
Patricia Reilly Giff, *Today Was a Terrible Day*, 1980
  Ronald is having a very horrible day until the teacher writes him a very nice note.
Juanita Havill, *Jamaica's Blue Marker*, 1995
  When a student takes Jamaica's marker and uses it to write all over her papers, she forgives him when he moves away.
Amy Schwartz, *Annabelle Swift, Kindergartner*, 1988
  Annabelle is so upset in school because everything her sister told her is wrong, but then she is the only child who can count the money.

588

KEVIN HENKES, Author/Illustrator

Owen

(New York: Greenwillow Books, 1993)

Subject(s): Parent and Child; Possessions; Problem Solving
Age range(s): Grades K-2
Major character(s): Owen, Mouse; Mrs. Tweezers, Neighbor (busybody); Fuzzy, Toy (blanket)
Time period(s): 1990s (1993)
Locale(s): United States

Summary: Owen loves Fuzzy and takes the blanket with him wherever he goes. Soon Owen will begin school and Mrs. Tweezers has lots of unsolicited advice for Owen's parents to help them get rid of Fuzzy. When none of Mrs. Tweezer's ideas work, Owen's mother gets out her scissors and sewing machine and creates a supply of ''Fuzzy'' handkerchiefs for Owen to carry to school. (24 pages)

Where it's reviewed:
Booklist, August 1993, page 2060
Horn Book, November 1993, page 733
Publishers Weekly, September 20, 1993, page 71
Reading Teacher, September 1994, page 64
School Library Journal, November 1993, page 82

Awards the book has won:
Caldecott Honor Book, 1994
School Library Journal Best Books, 1993

Other books by the same author:
The Biggest Boy, 1995
Chrysanthemum, 1991
Julius, the Baby of the World, 1990

Other books you might like:
Shulamith Levey Oppenheim, *I Love You, Bunny Rabbit*, 1995
  Mama wants to replace Micah's beloved, well-worn bunny, but comes to understand the importance of Bunny Rabbit to her daughter.
Jean Van Leeuwen, *Emma Bean*, 1993
  Emma Bean, a stuffed rabbit, has been Molly's companion since birth, but will she go to kindergarten with her?
Deborah Turney Zagwyn, *The Pumpkin Blanket*, 1991
  Clee's blanket has always been very special, but with support from a loving father she learns to get along without it.

589

YUMI HEO, Author/Illustrator

Father's Rubber Shoes

(New York: Orchard Books, 1995)

Subject(s): Korean Americans; Friendship; Loneliness
Age range(s): Grades K-2
Major character(s): Yungsu, Child, Immigrant; Father, Father, Businessman; Alex, Child, Classmate
Time period(s): 1990s (1995)
Locale(s): United States

Summary: Lonely in America, Yungsu dreams of his friends in Korea and asks his mother if the family can return. Father gently explains about his desire to improve life for his family by coming to a new country. When Yungsu's mother makes his favorite Korean lunch, he carries some to Father at the store and on the way shares a little with Alex who seems to be open to friendship. (32 pages)

Where it's reviewed:
Booklist, September 15, 1995, page 175
Horn Book, November 1995, page 733
Kirkus Reviews, July 15, 1995, page 1025
Publishers Weekly, October 2, 1995, page 72
School Library Journal, November 1995, page 74

Other books by the same author:
One Afternoon, 1994

Other books you might like:
Sook Nyul Choi, *Halmoni and the Picnic*, 1993
  When lonely, homesick grandmother is able to help her

grandchild's 3rd grade class by sharing her Korean heritage, she begins to feel more comfortable in America.

Barbara M. Joosse, *The Morning Chair*, 1995

Quiet times with mom in the morning chair help Bram adjust to life in a strange, new country.

Min Paek, *Aekyung's Dream*, 1988

In a bilingual text, a young immigrant fostered by the words of an ancient Korean king adjusts to a new country.

590

CHARLOTTE HERMAN
HELEN COGANCHERRY, Illustrator

Millie Cooper and Friends

(New York: Viking, 1995)

Series: Millie Cooper
Subject(s): Friendship; Schools; Problem Solving
Age range(s): Grades 3-4
Major character(s): Millie Cooper, 4th Grader, Friend; Sandy Feinman, 4th Grader, Friend
Time period(s): 1940s (1947)
Locale(s): Chicago, Illinois

Summary: Millie's expectation of a perfect fourth grade year, free from last year's mean teacher, is short-lived. As the students file into the room on the first day of school, they learn that their third grade teacher has traded classrooms with the fourth grade teacher and now they all have her again. To make matters worse, a new student arrives and Sandy is selected to be her school companion for the week, leaving jealous Millie to figure out how to get along in a three-way friendship. (84 pages)

Where it's reviewed:
Booklist, September 15, 1995, page 163
Horn Book Guide, Spring 1996, page 62
School Library Journal, September 1995, page 200

Other books by the same author:
A Summer on Thirteenth Street, 1991
Millie Cooper, Take a Chance, 1989
Millie Cooper, 3B, 1985

Other books you might like:
Judy Delton, *Kitty from the Start*, 1987
In the 1940s, third grader Kitty adjusts to her family's move to a new neighborhood and her entry into a new school.

Kathleen Leverich, *Best Enemies Forever*, 1995
Priscilla's nemesis, Felicity, fails to undermine the respect Priscilla's classmates have for her ideas to provide service to others.

Maud Hart Lovelace, *Betsy-Tacy and Tib*, 1941
The Betsy-Tacy friendship finds the strength to expand and include Tib when she moves into town.

Colleen O'Shaughnessy McKenna, *Fourth Grade Is a Jinx*, 1989
It's hard for Collette to imagine what more could go wrong at school this year and then her mother is assigned to teach her class!

591

GAIL HERMAN
RON FRITZ, Illustrator

My Dog Talks

(New York: Cartwheel Books/Scholastic Inc., 1995)

Series: Hello Reader!
Subject(s): Animals/Dogs; Pets
Age range(s): Grades K-1
Major character(s): Sam, Dog
Time period(s): 1990s (1995)
Locale(s): United States

Summary: A little boy is happy to have a new dog, especially one that talks. The boy and the dog understand each other primarily because the boy interprets Sam's woofs to mean agreement with his thinking at the moment. When they finish playing in the neighborhood, they head home. (30 pages)

Where it's reviewed:
School Library Journal, September 1995, page 178

Other books by the same author:
What a Hungry Puppy!, 1993
The Puppy Who Went to School, 1992
Big Bird Visits Granny Bird, 1991

Other books you might like:
Marc Brown, *Arthur's New Puppy*, 1993
Arthur finds caring for his new puppy presents unexpected challenges.

Cynthia Rylant, *Henry and Mudge*, 1987
In this first book of a popular series, only-child Henry, lonely for companionship, begs his parents to allow him to have a dog.

Rosemary Wells, *Lucy Comes to Stay*, 1994
Mary Elizabeth tolerates the puppy infractions of her new pet because she loves Lucy too much to scold her.

592

PATRICIA HERMES

Nothing but Trouble, Trouble, Trouble

(New York: Scholastic, 1994)

Subject(s): Behavior; Growing Up
Age range(s): Grades 4-6
Major character(s): Alex Warner, 5th Grader; Meg Warner, Child (allergic to animals)
Time period(s): 1990s
Locale(s): United States

Summary: Though Alex means well, she is always in trouble. She wants to babysit, mainly to pay for having her ears pierced, but her parents won't let her until she shows some responsibility. When a school assignment requires her to watch a pet or a raw egg over a weekend, Alex chooses a pet. Unfortunately, she has no pets because of Meg's allergies, so instead "borrows" a pair of cats from a classmate. Whatever can go wrong, does go wrong, as Meg sneezes and her parents are furious with Alex. Yet through all the chaos, Alex starts to think of others first, which is a big step in growing up. (182 pages)

Where it's reviewed:
Publishers Weekly, January 24, 1994, page 56
School Library Journal, April 1994, page 126
Booklist, March 15, 1994, page 1365
Journal of Reading, September 1994, page 73
Kirkus Reviews, February 15, 1994, page 226

Other books by the same author:
On Winter's Wind, 1995
Take Care of My Girl, 1992
I Hate Being Gifted, 1990

Other books you might like:
Anne Fine, *The Book of the Banshee*, 1991
    When Estelle becomes a teenager, she turns life in the Flowers household upside-down.
Norma Howe, *The Game of Life*, 1989
    Cairo tackles several family problems in this humorous coming of age tale.
Alison Smith, *Help! There's a Cat Washing in Here*, 1981
    In charge of the house for two weeks while his mother works on a project, Henry has trouble with his siblings and a stray cat.

593

PATRICIA HERMES

On Winter's Wind

(Boston: Little, Brown and Co., 1995)

Subject(s): Family Life; Slavery; Conduct of Life
Age range(s): Grades 4-6
Major character(s): Genevieve "Gen", 11-Year-Old; Leila, Sister (Gen's younger); Israel, Fugitive (runaway slave)
Time period(s): 19th century (pre Civil War)
Locale(s): New Bedford, Massachusetts

Summary: Their father has been away at sea for three years, their mother is becoming stranger by the day, a harsh winter is upon them and Gen and her younger sister Leila have only themselves for comfort. With food running out, Gen secures a job at the general store but is caught in a moral dilemma about turning in a runaway slave for the $100 bounty. Israel is a runaway slave who is in hiding on the Underground Railroad with the storekeeper and, though Gen needs the money, she can't decide if she can take away another person's freedom. (163 pages)

Where it's reviewed:
Publishers Weekly, October 30, 1995, page 62
Booklist, October 1, 1995, page 313
Voice of Youth Advocates, October 1995, page 302
Horn Book, November 1995, page 742
Children's Book Review Service, September 1995, page 10

Other books by the same author:
I'm Going to Pulverize You, William, 1994
Nothing but Trouble, Trouble, Trouble, 1994
Someone to Count On, 1993
A Place for Jeremy, 1987

Other books you might like:
Jennifer Armstrong, *Steal Away*, 1992
    Yankee Susannah is displeased to be given her personal slave when she moves to Virginia; the two run away together to freedom.
Leslie Davis Guccione, *Come Morning*, 1995
    Freedom assumes more responsibility for helping with the Underground Railroad than he had intended when his father is arrested by slave patrollers.
Virginia Hamilton, *The House of Dies Drear*, 1968
    The Smalls family buys an old house and, when they find all its hidden passageways, discover their house used to be part of the Underground Railroad.
Lois Walfrid Johnson, *Escape into the Night*, 1995
    Libby joins her father aboard his riverboat, meets the cabin boy Caleb and together they assist runaway slaves on the Underground Railroad.

594

PATRICIA HERMES

Someone to Count On

(Boston: Little, Brown and Company, 1993)

Subject(s): Mothers and Daughters; Grandparents; Ranch Life
Age range(s): Grades 4-6
Major character(s): Samantha Marie "Sam" Leonard, 11-Year-Old; Elizabeth Leonard, Mother ("free spirit"), Widow(er) (estranged from her father); Sam Carter, Grandfather (Elizabeth's father), Rancher
Time period(s): 1990s (1993)
Locale(s): Carter, Colorado

Summary: Sam's father drowned a month before her birth and her unconventional mother is the only family she has ever known. Elizabeth has spent her life running away from conflict and leaving Sam to do the parenting. When Elizabeth decides to drive to Colorado to see her father from whom she has been estranged for many years, Sam hopes that at last she will have a stable home. The tension of the homecoming is compounded when Elizabeth meets her father's wife and Sam Carter meets a granddaughter he didn't know existed. The ranch becomes the home Sam has been seeking, but is it the place she will stay forever? (184 pages)

Where it's reviewed:
Booklist, October 15, 1993, page 443
Horn Book, January 1994, page 69
Publishers Weekly, November 8, 1993, page 78
School Library Journal, December 1993, page 112
Voice of Youth Advocates, December 1993, page 291

Other books by the same author:
Mama, Let's Dance, 1993
Heads, I Win, 1988
Kevin Corbett Eats Flies, 1986

Other books you might like:
Patricia MacLachlan, *Journey*, 1991
    Left at his grandparents' farm, Journey tries to build a future by reconstructing the past from old family photos which he finds.
Cynthia Stowe, *Dear Mom, in Ohio for a Year*, 1992
    Mom sends her sixth-grader to Vermont to live with relatives so she is free to attend college.

June Rae Wood, *A Share of Freedom*, 1994

Freedom struggles to keep her family together and learn about the past from her alcoholic mother.

595

KATHLEEN HERSHEY
JEANETTE WINTER, Illustrator

Cotton Mill Town

(New York: Dutton Children's Books, 1993)

Subject(s): Nature; Grandparents; Summer
Age range(s): Grades K-3
Major character(s): Unnamed Character, Child (vacationing at Grandmama's); Grandmama, Grandmother (widowed)
Time period(s): Indeterminate Past
Locale(s): United States (small town)

Summary: In the author's first book, the simple joys of lazy summer days in a small southern town are gently presented by a young girl. She tells of tadpoles from the pond, huckleberries growing near the creek, and wild honeysuckle blossoms in the woods. The days have a soothing rhythm— reading in the hammock of an afternoon, sitting on the porch in the evening, or simply watching the cotton flowers change colors as they mature. (32 pages)

Where it's reviewed:
Booklist, February 1, 1993, page 989
Children's Book Review Service, March 1993, page 86
Horn Book, January 1993, page 75
Publishers Weekly, January 18, 1993, page 468
School Library Journal, March 1993, page 179

Other books you might like:
Donald Hall, *Lucy's Summer*, 1995
    Lucy enjoys an unusual New England summer at the turn of the century.
Elaine Moore, *Grandma's House*, 1985
    Kim remembers summer activities shared with her grandmother.
Eve Rice, *At Grammy's House*, 1990
    A young boy and girl enjoy Sundays with their grandmother on her farm.

596

ALISON CRAGIN HERZIG
JANE LAWRENCE MALI, Co-Author

The Wimp of the World

(New York: Viking, 1994)

Subject(s): Brothers and Sisters; Hotels, Motels; Aunts and Uncles
Age range(s): Grades 3-5
Major character(s): Bridget Potter, 10-Year-Old, Sister (younger); Dawsie, Aunt
Time period(s): 1990s (1994)
Locale(s): Montana (Blue Moon Motel)

Summary: Poor Bridget! Her 14-year-old brothers (triplets) are so determined to keep her from being a wimp that they've instituted a fitness training program which does not include wearing a bridesmaid dress in Great Aunt Dawsie's wedding. Admittedly, the entire family is taken aback when 68-year-old Dawsie announces her intention to marry and move out of Cabin 13. Before she does, Aunt Dawsie and Bridget devise a plan to bring more customers to the motel that keeps the triplets so busy they forget about Bridget's training program. (74 pages)

Where it's reviewed:
Booklist, April 1, 1994, page 1448
Horn Book, September 1994, page 587
Kirkus Reviews, May 15, 1994, page 698
Library Talk, November 1994, page 43
School Library Journal, September 94, page 216

Other books by the same author:
Mystery on October Road, 1993
Sam and the Moon Queen, 1990
Ten-Speed Babysitter, 1988

Other books you might like:
Shirley Hughes, *Here Comes Charlie Moon*, 1980
    For Charlie, spending a summer at the beach with his aunt, the owner of a novelty shop, also means being with his disliked cousin.
Margaret Mahy, *The Good Fortunes Gang*, 1993
    The first book of the Cousins Quartet introduces the Fortune family to readers and Peter to his cousins who insist that he "prove" himself to be a true Fortune.
Phyllis Reynolds Naylor, *The Boys Start the War*, 1993
    Four brothers begin a "war" of practical jokes against three sisters who move into the neighborhood.

597

DEBRA HESS
CAROL NEWSOM, Illustrator

Alien Alert!

(New York: Hyperion Paperbacks for Children, 1993)

Series: Spy from Outer Space
Subject(s): Aliens; Science Fiction; Spies
Age range(s): Grades 3-4
Major character(s): Cassie Williams, 5th Grader, Spy (amateur); Zekephlon "Zeke", 10-Year-Old, Alien (from planet Triminica)
Time period(s): 1990s (1993)
Locale(s): Hillsdale

Summary: Although her friends have abandoned her for activities more befitting fifth graders, Cassie isn't ready to give up her interest in sleuthing. When she spots a spaceship landing on the outskirts of town she has a real spy mission to undertake. Meeting the occupants of the space ship, she befriends Zeke, a spy-in-training and the two of them share adventures while Zeke's parents attempt to locate the material needed to repair and fuel the spaceship for its return to Triminica. (121 pages)

Where it's reviewed:
Publishers Weekly, July 12, 1993, page 80
School Library Journal, September 1993, page 232

Other books by the same author:
Escape from Earth, 1994

Spies, Incorporated, 1994
Too Many Spies, 1993

Other books you might like:

Annette Curtis Klause, *Alien Secrets*, 1993
  Puck, a human teenager, and her alien friend Hush must locate an important piece of alien art which Hush is transporting.
Pamela F. Service, *Stinker from Space*, 1988
  An alien takes the form of a skunk to disguise his presence on Earth.
Janet Asimov, *The Norby Series*, 1983-1991
  With co-author Isaac Asimov, the series presents the adventures of Norby the robot and his human friend Jeff.

598

DEBRA HESS
DIANE GREENSEID, Illustrator

Wilson Sat Alone

(New York: Simon & Schuster Books for Young Readers, 1994)

Subject(s): Shyness; Interpersonal Relations; Schools
Age range(s): Grades K-3
Major character(s): Wilson, Student (shy); Sara, Student (outgoing)
Time period(s): 1990s (1994)
Locale(s): United States

Summary: Day after day Wilson sits alone, reads alone and eats alone because the other students think he prefers to be alone. Too shy to tell them otherwise, Wilson's solitary school life changes when a new student arrives. Sara is alone for only one day before she involves herself with the other children and reaches out to Wilson, bringing an end to his days of sitting alone. (32 pages)

Where it's reviewed:
Children's Book Review Service, January 1995, page 50
Horn Book Guide, Spring 1995, page 40
New York Times Book Review, November 13, 1994, page 52
School Library Journal, November 1994, page 82

Other books you might like:

Debi Gliori, *The Snowchild*, 1994
  One snowy day, lonely Katie builds a snowchild and finds a friend.
Marjorie Weinman Sharmat, *Say Hello, Vanessa*, 1979
  Shy mouse, Vanessa, finds it difficult to make friends.
Wendy Smith, *Say Hello, Tilly!*, 1991
  Meeting another bashful bear at Benny's birthday party helps Tilly overcome some of her own shyness.
Clara Vulliamy, *Ellen and Penguin*, 1993
  Shy Ellen and her special stuffed penguin meet a bashful girl with a toy monkey at the playground.

599

KAREN HESSE
ANDREW GLASS, Illustrator

Lavender

(New York: Henry Holt and Company, 1993)

Subject(s): Babies; Cousins; Aunts and Uncles
Age range(s): Grades 2-4
Major character(s): Codie, Child, Niece (Aunt Alix's favorite); Alixandra Moore, Aunt (pregnant); Lavender Moore, Child (newborn)
Time period(s): 1990s (1993)
Locale(s): United States

Summary: Codie and Aunt Alix share a special relationship. Thus, Codie's excitement about the impending birth of a cousin after Aunt Alix has suffered several miscarriages is tempered by fears that Aunt Alix will no longer have time for her. Lavender enters the world two weeks early, but not before Codie completes a baby quilt she has secretly made. (40 pages)

Where it's reviewed:
Booklist, October 1, 1993, page 344
Horn Book Guide, Spring 1994, page 66
Kirkus Reviews, October 1, 1993, page 1274
School Library Journal, December 1993, page 89

Other books by the same author:
Sable, 1994
Poppy's Chair, 1993

Other books you might like:

Eleanor Coerr, *The Josefina Story Quilt*, 1986
  Faith sews a quilt in remembrance of her pet hen.
Kathryn O. Galbraith, *Roommates*, 1990
  New babies bring changes at home which Mimi and Beth do not like.
James Howe, *Pinky and Rex and the New Baby*, 1993
  Fearing a lack of parental attention when the new baby arrives, Rex does not realize that she is neglecting her friend Pinky.

600

KAREN HESSE
NANCY CARPENTER, Illustrator

Lester's Dog

(New York: Crown Publishers, Inc., 1993)

Subject(s): Animals/Dogs; Fear; Courage
Age range(s): Grades K-3
Major character(s): Unnamed Character, Child (afraid of Lester's Dog); Corey, Deaf (neighborhood boy); Lester's Dog, Dog (mean)
Time period(s): 1940s (summer evening)
Locale(s): United States (Garrison Avenue in a small town)

Summary: One summer evening, Corey leads his neighbor down the street past the home of Lester's dog to show the boy the trapped kitten he found earlier. Corey insists on taking the kitten although neither boy can give the kitten a home. On the return trip, they do not safely pass Lester's house and the dog runs out to attack the boy and the kitten. In protecting the kitten, the boy finds the courage he lacked and a home for the kitten too. (40 pages)

Where it's reviewed:
Booklist, November 1, 1993, page 529
Horn Book, March 1994, page 190
Kirkus Reviews, October 1, 1993, page 1275
Publishers Weekly, August 30, 1993, page 95
School Library Journal, October 1993, page 100

Awards the book has won:
School Library Journal Best Books, 1993

Other books by the same author:
Poppy's Chair, 1993

Other books you might like:
Marc Harshman, *The Storm*, 1995
    When he faces a tornado alone, Jonathan finds the courage to save himself and the family's animals.
Bill Martin Jr., *The Ghost-Eye Tree*, 1985
    An errand requires children to walk past the dreaded ghost-eye tree. Co-author John Archambault.
Ian Wallace, *Morgan the Magnificent*, 1988
    In a dream come true, Morgan is on the high wire far above the crowd—and terrified.

601

KAREN HESSE
KAY LIFE, Illustrator

Poppy's Chair

(New York: Macmillan Publishing Company, 1993)

Subject(s): Death; Grandparents; Grief
Age range(s): Grades K-2
Major character(s): Leah, Child (grieving); Gramm, Grandmother, Widow(er); Poppy, Grandfather (deceased)
Time period(s): 1990s (1993)
Locale(s): United States

Summary: Since her beloved Poppy's death, Leah is uneasy during her first summer visit to her grandparent's home. Unwilling to look at his picture or sit in his chair, Leah is finally able to share her fears with her grandmother, who helps her to remember Poppy with joy, and accept the inevitable. (32 pages)

Where it's reviewed:
Booklist, March 15, 1993, page 1359
Children's Book Review Service, June 1993, page 122
Horn Book Guide, Fall 1993, page 261
Kirkus Reviews, February 15, 1993, page 227
School Library Journal, July 1993, page 61

Other books by the same author:
Lester's Dog, 1993

Other books you might like:
Aliki, *The Two of Them*, 1979
    A young girl and her grandfather share a special relationship which she remembers after his death.
Mem Fox, *Sophie*, 1994
    Because Grandpa has always been part of Sophie's life, his death leaves a sense of emptiness which, in time, is filled.

Mavis Jukes, *Blackberries in the Dark*, 1993
    Austin and his grandmother remember his recently deceased grandfather while continuing to cherish their own relationship. Reissue of a 1985 title.
Jane Yolen, *Grandad Bill's Song*, 1994
    Jon finds support from family members as he struggles to cope with his feelings, following the death of his grandfather.
Charlotte Zolotow, *My Grandson Lew*, 1974
    Six-year-old Lew shares his memories of his now-deceased grandfather.

602

KAREN HESSE
MARCIA SEWALL, Illustrator

Sable

(New York: Henry Holt and Company, 1994)

Subject(s): Animals/Dogs; Fathers and Daughters; Pets
Age range(s): Grades 3-5
Major character(s): Tate Marshall, 10-Year-Old; Sable, Dog (stray); Pap, Father, Artisan (furniture maker)
Time period(s): 1990s (1994)
Locale(s): Vermont

Summary: When a half-starved stray arrives on Tate's porch, her dreams of having a pet appear to have come true. Because her mother dislikes dogs, Tate must find a way to unobtrusively care for Sable. As the dog's strength returns, Sable begins to wander, prompting complaints from the neighbors and forcing Tate to give her away. However, the brief experience of a pet has taught Tate how to earn the privilege of having a pet in the future. (87 pages)

Where it's reviewed:
Booklist, June 1, 1994, page 1820
Horn Book, July 1994, page 452
Kirkus Reviews, April 15, 1994, page 557
Publishers Weekly, April 25, 1994, page 78
School Library Journal, May 1994, page 114

Awards the book has won:
School Library Journal Best Books, 1994

Other books by the same author:
Lavender, 1993
Letters from Rifka, 1992
Wish on a Unicorn, 1991

Other books you might like:
Mary Jane Auch, *The Latchkey Dog*, 1994
    Determined not to part with his dog Amber, Sam must come up with an acceptable plan to keep her in the family.
Hilary McKay, *Dog Friday*, 1995
    Nursing an injured, lost dog back to health helps Robin overcome the fear of dogs he has felt since being bitten by one.
Barbara Moe, *Dog Days for Dudley*, 1994
    Dudley is overjoyed when his parents finally agree to allow him to have a pet dog.

603

AMY HEST
LINDA DALAL SAWAYA, Illustrator

How to Get Famous in Brooklyn

(New York: Simon & Schuster Books for Young Readers, 1995)

Subject(s): Neighbors and Neighborhoods; City Life; Secrets
Age range(s): Grades 1-3
Major character(s): Janie, Child
Time period(s): 1990s (1995)
Locale(s): New York, New York (Brooklyn)

Summary: Observant Janie records the varied activities of her neighbors in a notebook. As part of her "spy" work, she writes about the many retail merchants on the street as well as the latest news about families. Janie carries the book at all times even in a rain storm when the wind tears the pages out of the notebook, scattering them about the street and giving Janie unexpected notoriety. (32 pages)

Where it's reviewed:
Booklist, August 1995, page 1955
Children's Book Review Service, September 1995, page 2
Kirkus Reviews, July 15, 1995, page 1025
Publishers Weekly, September 4, 1995, page 69
School Library Journal, September 1995, page 178

Other books by the same author:
Ruby's Storm, 1994
The Pajama Party, 1992
The Crack-of-Dawn Walkers, 1984

Other books you might like:
Duncan Ball, *Emily Eyefinger, Secret Agent*, 1993
    Emily uses her fingertip eye to catch a spy.
Louise Fitzhugh, *Harriet, the Spy*, 1964
    Secretly, Harriet records observations about her neighbors and classmates.
Dale Gottlieb, *My Stories, by Hildy Calpurnia Rose*, 1991
    In her diary, Brooklynite Hildy records the details of life in her apartment building.
Marjorie Weinman Sharmat, *The Sly Spy*, 1990
    Trying to learn an important secret, E. J. spies on Olivia.

604

AMY HEST
JILL BARTON, Illustrator

In the Rain with Baby Duck

(Cambridge, MA: Candlewick Press, 1995)

Subject(s): Weather; Animals/Ducks; Grandparents
Age range(s): Grades K-1
Major character(s): Baby Duck, Duck; Grampa, Duck, Grandfather
Time period(s): 1990s (1995)
Locale(s): Fictional Country

Summary: Baby Duck is unhappy that she has to walk in the rain to get to Grampa's house for Pancake Sunday. Her parents are not at all understanding of a duck who doesn't enjoy splashing in puddles and feeling the rain roll off her back. Grampa, however, remembers a daughter with much the same attitude and quickly retrieves boots and an umbrella from the attic so he and Baby Duck can have a post-pancake stroll through the rain. (26 pages)

Where it's reviewed:
Booklist, October 1, 1995, page 326
Children's Book Review Service, February 1996, page 75
Children's Bookwatch, December 1995, page 5
Horn Book, March 1996, page 188
Parents' Choice, November 1995, page 8

Awards the book has won:
Boston Globe/Horn Book Fanfare, 1996

Other books by the same author:
Rosie's Fishing Trip, 1994
Fancy Aunt Jess, 1990
The Purple Coat, 1986

Other books you might like:
Julia Hoban, *Amy Loves the Rain*, 1989
    When it is time to pick up Daddy, Amy enjoys driving through the rain with her mother.
Karla Kuskin, *James and the Rain*, 1995
    Wearing his yellow slicker, James goes outside to play rainy day games.
Christine Widman, *The Willow Umbrella*, 1993
    On a rainy day, two little girls are still able to find a way to play outside.
Taro Yashima, *Umbrella*, 1958
    After receiving red boots and an umbrella for her birthday, Momo eagerly awaits a rainy day. Conclusion disc WDCRN.396, Janis Ansell—100 entries

605

AMY HEST
AMY SCHWARTZ, Illustrator

Nana's Birthday Party

(New York: Morrow Junior Books, 1993)

Subject(s): Grandparents; Birthdays; Cousins
Age range(s): Grades K-3
Major character(s): Nana, Grandmother; Maggie, Child, Cousin; Brette, Child, Cousin
Time period(s): 1990s (1993)
Locale(s): New York, New York (Nana's apartment)

Summary: Annually, midway between Thanksgiving and Christmas, Nana has a birthday party for herself attended by all the family. Brette and Maggie have the privilege of arriving the night before to stay with Nana and help her prepare. Nana's policy of accepting only gifts made by the giver has Maggie and Brette in competition at first, but they soon see that by cooperating they can create the best birthday gift ever for Nana. (32 pages)

Where it's reviewed:
Booklist, August 1993, page 2060
Horn Book Guide, Spring 1994, page 37
Kirkus Reviews, July 15, 1993, page 934
Publishers Weekly, June 28, 1993, page 77
School Library Journal, October 1993, page 100

Awards the book has won:
Booklist Editors' Choice, 1993

Other books by the same author:
Rosie's Fishing Trip, 1994
Ruby's Storm, 1994
Best-Ever Good-Bye Party, 1989

Other books you might like:
Eileen Christelow, *Don't Wake Up Mama!*, 1992
While Mama sleeps, the five little monkeys prepare a surprise for her birthday.
Pat Mora, *A Birthday Basket for Tia*, 1992
Cecilia plans a special present for her great aunt's 90th birthday.
Jane Hissey, *Ruff*, 1994
A stuffed puppy who has never had a birthday party is feted with 7 of them by his stuffed animal friends.

606

AMY HEST
IRENE TRIVAS, Illustrator

Nannies for Hire

(New York: Morrow Junior Books, 1994)

Subject(s): Babies; Babysitters; Friendship
Age range(s): Grades 2-4
Major character(s): Casey, Child, Friend; Jenny Marks, Child, Friend; Kate, Child, Friend
Time period(s): 1990s (1994)
Locale(s): United States

Summary: When Jenny becomes a big sister with tired, frazzled parents, Kate, Jenny and Casey invent ''Nannies for Hire'' a child-care business intent on caring for the baby. Jenny's very worn-out mother turns the sleeping baby over to the ''Nannies'' and heads outside to the garden. An afternoon of diapers, splattered baby food and crying gives the threesome second thoughts about their latest scheme. (48 pages)

Where it's reviewed:
Booklist, March 1, 1994, page 1262
Horn Book, May 1994, page 339
Kirkus Reviews, February 15, 1994, page 226
School Library Journal, May 1994, page 95
Wilson Library Bulletin, December 1994, page 100

Other books by the same author:
The Pajama Party, 1992
Travel Tips from Harry: A Guide to Family Vacations in the Sun, 1989
Getting Rid of Krista, 1988

Other books you might like:
Judith Caseley, *Mama, Coming and Going*, 1994
After her brother Mickey is born Jenna notices that her mom is so busy she becomes forgetful and appreciates Jenna's help.
Jane Cutler, *Darcy and Gran Don't Like Babies*, 1993
Darcy and Gran take off for the park to get away from the baby. When he's older, they'll both like him better and invite him along.
James Howe, *Pinky and Rex and the New Baby*, 1993
Anxious that she will be displaced by the new baby, Rex becomes such a ''perfect'' big sister that she neglects her friend Pinky.
Janice Lee Smith, *The Baby Blues: An Adam Joshua Story*, 1994
The anxiety that Adam Joshua & his classmates feel about their teacher's upcoming maternity leave is heightened when they are assigned egg ''babies'' to parent.
Carol Snyder, *One Up, One Down*, 1995
Katie is kept busy helping her parents care for her twin brothers.

607

AMY HEST
SONJA LAMUT, Illustrator

The Private Notebook of Katie Roberts, Age 11

(Cambridge, MA: Candlewick Press, 1995)

Subject(s): Moving, Household; Remarriage; Diaries
Age range(s): Grades 3-5
Major character(s): Katie Roberts, 11-Year-Old
Time period(s): 1940s (1947-1948)
Locale(s): Langley, Texas

Summary: In the sequel to *Love You, Soldier*, Katie, who is still grieving her father's war-related death four years earlier, must now come to terms with a move from New York City to rural Texas and her mother's remarriage. Miserable lonely Katie pours her heart into a notebook and letters to a former neighbor as she struggles to make friends and find a place for herself in this new family. (75 pages)

Where it's reviewed:
Booklist, July 1995, page 1879
Horn Book, September 1995, page 599
Kirkus Reviews, May 15, 1995, page 710
Publishers Weekly, June 5, 1995, page 64
School Library Journal, September 1995, page 200

Awards the book has won:
Book Links Good Book, 1995

Other books by the same author:
Love You, Soldier, 1991
Where in the World is the Perfect Family, 1991
Getting Rid of Krista, 1988

Other books you might like:
Paula Danziger, *Forever Amber Brown*, 1996
More changes are possible for Amber Brown whose best friend moved away, whose father lives in France, and whose mother is considering remarriage.
Karen Hirsch, *Ellen Anders on Her Own*, 1994
Eleven-year-old Ellen gains insight into her relationships with friends by reading the childhood diary of her deceased mother.
Candice F. Ransom, *More than a Name*, 1995
After her mother's remarriage, Cammie must adjust to a stepfather and a large extended family.

608

AMY HEST
PAUL HOWARD, Illustrator

Rosie's Fishing Trip

(Cambridge, MA: Candlewick Press, 1994)

Subject(s): Fishing; Grandparents
Age range(s): Grades K-2
Major character(s): Rosie, Child; Grampa, Grandfather; Mama, Mother
Time period(s): Indeterminate Past
Locale(s): United States (Periwinkle Pond)

Summary: Rising at dawn to meet Grampa for their fishing trip, Rosie pedals swiftly through the dark streets racing the sun to the corner rendezvous. The two share a snack and set to fishing. Their catch for the day is a fish too little to keep, Rosie's drawings, and one of Grampa's famous poems. Fortunately, Mama has lunch waiting when they return home. (32 pages)

Where it's reviewed:
Booklist, October 15, 1994, page 435
Kirkus Reviews, December 15, 1994, page 1564
Language Arts, September 1995, page 371
Reading Teacher, September 1995, page 54
School Library Journal, February 1995, page 74

Other books by the same author:
Ruby's Storm, 1994
The Purple Coat, 1992
The Crack-of-Dawn Walkers, 1984

Other books you might like:
Diana Engel, *Fishing*, 1993
　　After Loretta moves to a new town she realizes how much she misses her grandfather and the time they shared fishing.
Tony Johnston, *Fishing Sunday*, 1996
　　A young boy learns to appreciate some of Grandfather's ways of doing things while on a fishing trip with him.
Jane B. Mason, *River Day*, 1994
　　Alex and her grandfather spend a peaceful day canoeing on the river.
N.L. Sharp, *Today I'm Going Fishing With My Dad*, 1993
　　Although he secretly dislikes the sport of fishing, a young boy goes on fishing trips because he values the time with his father.
Catherine Stock, *Armien's Fishing Trip*, 1990
　　When Armien stows away on his uncle's fishing boat, he becomes a hero before the day ends.

609

AMY HEST
NANCY COTE, Illustrator

Ruby's Storm

(New York: Four Winds Press, 1994)

Subject(s): Weather; Grandparents; City Life
Age range(s): Grades K-2
Major character(s): Ruby, Child; Grampa, Grandfather

Time period(s): 1990s (1994)
Locale(s): New York, New York

Summary: The threat of a storm will not keep Ruby from her visit with Grampa. She packs her basket with goodies, dons her new yellow poncho and bids her mother good-bye. On the windy streets she watches the grocer chase blowing fruit and the newspaper vendor struggle to protect his papers. The rain tickles her nose, but Ruby keeps on hurrying to reach Grampa's cozy apartment for a cup of hot chocolate and a game of checkers. (32 pages)

Where it's reviewed:
Booklist, March 1, 1994, page 1270
Horn Book Guide, Fall 1994, page 275
Kirkus Reviews, March 15, 1994, page 396
Publishers Weekly, December 6, 1993, page 72
School Library Journal, April 1994, page 106

Other books by the same author:
Rosie's Fishing Trip, 1994
The Go-Between, 1992
The Mommy Exchange, 1988

Other books you might like:
Marc Harshman, *The Storm*, 1995
　　Alone on the farm, young Jonathan does not let his confinement to a wheelchair keep him from making preparations for a threatening tornado.
Una Leavy, *Harry's Stormy Night*, 1994
　　Coping with a loss of electric power during a storm, Harry and his family sing and tell stories by candlelight.
Anne F. Rockwell, *The Storm*, 1994
　　In the comfort of her family's coastal home, a young girl reflects on the power of a major storm.

610

AMY HEST
HARVEY STEVENSON, Illustrator

Weekend Girl

(New York: Morrow Junior Books, 1993)

Subject(s): Grandparents; Photography; City Life
Age range(s): Grades 1-3
Major character(s): Sophie, Child (younger than 9 years old); Grampa, Grandfather, Photographer; Gram, Grandmother, Teacher (ballet)
Time period(s): 1990s (1993)
Locale(s): New York, New York

Summary: It's a tradition. Every year Sophie's parents go on a no-kids trip and every year Sophie stays with her grandparents who always plan a special activity to surprise her. While it's fun to help Grampa in his darkroom and to walk the dog with Gram, Sophie still misses her parents and grows impatient waiting to learn what has been planned as this year's special event. (32 pages)

Where it's reviewed:
Booklist, May 1, 1993, page 1603
Bulletin of the Center for Children's Books, April 1993, page 251
Horn Book Guide, Fall 1993, page 286
School Library Journal, August 1993, page 145

Other books by the same author:
Rosie's Fishing Trip, 1994
Nana's Birthday Party, 1993
Fancy Aunt Jess, 1990

Other books you might like:
Kate Aver, *Joey's Way*, 1992
   When the seasons change, Joey and her siblings share outdoor activities with their grandparents.
Stephanie Calmenson, *Marigold and Grandma on the Town*, 1994
   Young rabbit Marigold and her grandmother enjoy a day together in this cheerful beginning reader.
Helen V. Griffith, *Grandaddy and Janetta*, 1993
   In the third book about this pair, Janetta travels alone by train to visit her Grandaddy in Georgia.

611

JANET HICKMAN

Jericho
(New York: Greenwillow, 1994)

Subject(s): Grandparents; Family Life; Small Town Life
Age range(s): Grades 6-8
Major character(s): Angela, 7th Grader; Arminda "GrandMin" Dutton, Grandmother (Angela's great-grandmother)
Time period(s): 1990s
Locale(s): Gatesville (originally called Jericho)

Summary: The youngest and oldest members of four generations of women tell their stories the summer Angela and her family extend their vacation to care for GrandMin, the greatgrandmother of the family. Angela is upset to be stuck in a small town with no shopping mall, confined with her brother and caring for GrandMin who doesn't even remember who she is. Interspersed with Angela's accounts of self-pity are flashbacks to Min's younger days when she had to care for her widowed father in this intergenerational tale representative of the cyclical pattern of families. (135 pages).

Where it's reviewed:
Publishers Weekly, August 8, 1994, page 436
School Library Journal, September 1994, page 216
Booklist, September 1, 1994, page 41
Kirkus Reviews, August 15, 1994, page 1139
New Advocate, Fall 1994, page 295

Other books by the same author:
Thunder-Pup, 1981
Zoar Blue, 1978
Stones, 1976

Other books you might like:
Betsy Byars, *Coast to Coast*, 1992
   Birch and her ailing grandfather steal away on a crosscountry flying trip in his Piper J-3 Cub.
K.M. Peyton, *Darkling*, 1990
   When Jenny's successful race horse has a chance to compete in America she elects to stay home and care for her cancer-stricken grandfather.
Jean Thesman, *The Rain Catchers*, 1991
   Raised by her grandmother, Grayling's mother finally asks

her to move to San Francisco; one visit convinces Grayling to remain with her grandmother.

612

LINDA OATMAN HIGH

Hound Heaven
(New York: Holiday House, 1995)

Subject(s): Animals/Dogs; Grandparents; Mountain Life
Age range(s): Grades 6-7
Major character(s): Silver Iris Nickles, 12-Year-Old, Animal Lover (of dogs), Orphan; Walter "Papaw" Bills, Grandfather
Time period(s): 1990s
Locale(s): Muckwater Mountain, West Virginia

Summary: Silver has lived with Papaw ever since her parents and younger sister were killed in an automobile accident. Though she loves her grandfather, Silver wants a dog to love more than anything else to make up for being orphaned. She even has pictures of 52 dogs stuck on the ceiling over her bed in a collage her Papaw refers to as "Hound Heaven." Though Papaw doesn't want a dog in his house, Silver is determined to win him over and even works in a kennel to earn money to buy a dog. (194 pages)

Where it's reviewed:
School Library Journal, November 1995, page 100
Voice of Youth Advocates, February 1996, page 372
Children's Book Review Service, November 1995, page 33
Center for Children's Books. Bulletin, December 1995, page 129
Kirkus Reviews, October 15, 1995, page 1493

Other books by the same author:
Maizie, 1995

Other books you might like:
Barbara Corcoran, *Annie's Monster*, 1990
   Annie's father agrees to let her have her longed-for Irish wolfhound, but this just signals the beginning of her problems.
Marty Crisp, *Buzzard Breath*, 1995
   Though Will thinks the German shepherd, nicknamed Buzzard Breath, is not the dog he always dreamed of owning, he can't let himstay in the pound.
Lynn Hall, *Windsong*, 1992
   Marty saves a greyhound who's the runt of the litter, but then has to find a home for Windsong when her brother's allergies prevent her from keeping him.
Kevin Henkes, *Protecting Marie*, 1995
   Tied in with Fanny's desire for a dog is her concern that if her father really cared for her, he'd let her have one; "Dinner's" arrival unites the entire family.

613

LINDA OATMAN HIGH

Maizie
(New York: Holiday House, 1995)

Subject(s): Mothers and Daughters; Sisters; Mountain Life

Age range(s): Grades 6-8
Major character(s): Maizie Musser, 12-Year-Old; Grace Musser, Child
Time period(s): 1990s
Locale(s): Pennsylvania (Welsh Mountain)

Summary: For four years Maizie supports her family, both emotionally and financially. Before her sister, Grace, is even a year old, Maizie's mother leaves and abandons the girls to their alcoholic father who has difficulty earning enough to support the family. Maizie receives support from her Wish Books, including her Mama Wish Book and her Horse Wish Book. No matter the obstacle, she operates around it. Working in a nursing home to earn money for the electric bill and a horse, she writes her mother letters and tries to understand why a mother would leave her children. Maizie stops writing when she throws away the Wish Books, understanding that she'll always be fine and able to make it on her own. (180 pages)

Where it's reviewed:
Voice of Youth Advocates, October 1995, page 220
Booklist, April 15, 1995, page 1500
Horn Book, May 1995, page 332
School Library Journal, April 1995, page 132
Library Talk, September 1995, page 35

Other books by the same author:
Hound Heaven, 1995

Other books you might like:
A.E. Cannon, *Amazing Gracie*, 1991
Gracie pulls her stepfamily together with her cooking and cleaning, but even she's unsure if she can save her mother from another suicide attempt.
Vera Cleaver, *Where the Lilies Bloom*, 1969
When Mary Call's father dies, she must bury her father in secret so that the welfare authorities don't find out she's in charge of her family.
Barbara Hall, *Dixie Storms*, 1990
Fourteen-year-old Dutch is the binding force for her motherless Virginia farm family.
Jean Thesman, *When the Road Ends*, 1992
Three foster children and a brain-damaged accident victim make a home and a family in a cabin located "when the road ends."
Cynthia Voigt, *Dicey's Song*, 1981
After being abandoned by their mother, Dicey and her younger siblings make the long journey on foot to their eccentric grandmother's home.

614

E.W. HILDICK

The Case of the Absent Author

(New York: Macmillan/Simon & Schuster, 1995)

Series: McGurk Mystery
Subject(s): Mystery and Detective Stories
Age range(s): Grades 4-6
Major character(s): Bill Legrand, Writer (crime); Jack P. McGurk, Detective—Amateur, 12-Year-Old
Time period(s): 1990s

Locale(s): West Milford

Summary: When crime writer Bill Legrand is missing, along with his stash of already-written manuscripts, his literary agent hires the McGurk gang to handle the investigation. Jack McGurk leads the team of investigators, which includes specialists in the areas of science, tree climbing, smells and voice throwing. They filter through clues based on Edgar Allan Poe stories to find the missing author. (151 pages)

Where it's reviewed:
Voice of Youth Advocates, August 1995, page 159
Booklist, August 1995, page 1946
School Library Journal, July 1995, page 78
Horn Book Guide, Spring 1996, page 298
Kirkus Reviews, June 15, 1995, page 857

Other books by the same author:
The Case of the Fantastic Footprints, 1994 (A McGurk Mystery)
The Case of the Nervous Newsboy, 1991 (A McGurk Mystery)
The Case of the Wandering Weathervanes, 1988 (A McGurk Mystery)

Other books you might like:
Willo Davis Roberts, *Baby-Sitting Is a Dangerous Job*, 1985
While Darcy's baby-sitting for three spoiled kids, all four are kidnapped; luckily Darcy is able to outwit their captors.
Pieter Van Raven, *The Great Man's Secret*, 1989
Told to interview reclusive author Paul Bernard for his first school newspaper assignment, Jerry is overwhelmed when the "great man" meets him.
Marcia Wood, *The Search for Jim McGwynn*, 1989
Jamie uses the summer to track down P.J. Ross, a writer who's rumored to live in his hometown.

615

E.W. HILDICK

The Case of the Desperate Drummer

(New York: Macmillan Publishing Company, 1993)

Series: McGurk Mystery
Subject(s): Mystery and Detective Stories
Age range(s): Grades 3-5
Major character(s): Jack P. McGurk, Detective—Amateur, Leader (of the McGurk Organization); Mari Yoshimura, Detective—Amateur (officer in McGurk Organization); Yoshito Nakanishi, Cousin (Mari's), Entertainer (drummer in a rock band)
Time period(s): 1990s (1993)
Locale(s): New York

Summary: The McGurk Organization is in training to provide witness protection services when they receive a real plea for help from Yosihito Nakanishi who has escaped from 2 men trying to kill him. Not knowing why his life is in danger, he goes into hiding as McGurk and his officers seek to solve the mystery in time for Yoshito to perform at a benefit concert in their community. (157 pages)

Where it's reviewed:
Booklist, April 1, 1993, page 1431
Five Owls, March 1994, page 80

Horn Book Guide, Fall 1993, page 298
School Library Journal, April 1993, page 120

Other books by the same author:
The Case of the Fantastic Footprints, 1994 (McGurk Mystery)
The Case of the Weeping Witch, 1992 (McGurk Mystery)
The Ghost Squad and the Halloween Conspiracy, 1986

Other books you might like:
Seymour Simon, *Einstein Anderson, Science Sleuth*, 1986
A 12-year-old undertakes the solving of the first of many mysteries.
Donald J. Sobol, *Encyclopedia Brown, Boy Detective*, 1979
Confident and affordable, Encyclopedia Brown opens a detective agency, charging 25 cents per case.
Gertrude Chandler Warner, *The Boxcar Children Mystery Series*, 1953-
Four children are involved in a variety of mysteries in this timeless series.

616

E.W. HILDICK

The Case of the Fantastic Footprints

(New York: Macmillan Publishing Company, 1994)

Series: McGurk Mystery
Subject(s): Mystery and Detective Stories; Animals/Cats
Age range(s): Grades 3-6
Major character(s): Jack P. McGurk, 12-Year-Old, Detective—Amateur; Sandra Ennis, 12-Year-Old, Crime Victim
Time period(s): 1990s (1994)
Locale(s): New York

Summary: A complex case begins with the simple act of a cat walking in wet cement. McGurk and his organization members absolve the cat and are subsequently called in to solve additional incidents of deliberately vandalized wet concrete, blacktop and cars. No friend of McGurk, Sandra accuses him of the crimes, but ultimately saved by his detective work, he proves that the real culprit is trying to pin the blame on Sandra. (155 pages)

Where it's reviewed:
Booklist, April 1, 1994, page 1448
Horn Book Guide, Fall 1994, page 311
Library Talk, November 1994, page 49
School Library Journal, September 1994, page 216

Other books by the same author:
The Case of the Absent Author, 1995
The Case of the Weeping Witch, 1992
The Case of the Nervous Newsboy, 1991

Other books you might like:
Franklin W. Dixon, *Footprints under the Window*, 1965
The amateur detectives take on their 8th case in the popular Hardy Boys Mystery series.
Peg Kehret, *Cat Burglar on the Prowl*, 1995
In the first Frightmares Series entry, Kayo and Rosie enter their pets in a cat show hoping to win the cash prize; instead they lose both the contest and Kayo's cat.

Gary Paulsen, *Scam Artists*, 1993
Part of the Culpepper Adventure Series, Dunc and Amos, amateur sleuths, try to save an elderly woman from becoming a scam artist's next victim.

617

E.W. HILDICK

The Case of the Wiggling Wig

(New York: Simon & Schuster, 1996)

Series: McGurk Mystery
Subject(s): Mystery and Detective Stories
Age range(s): Grades 4-6
Major character(s): Jack P. McGurk, Detective—Amateur; Joey Rockaway, Detective—Amateur; Mari Yoshimina, Detective—Amateur
Time period(s): 1990s
Locale(s): United States

Summary: McGurk's friends arrive at his house to find that he has broken his leg and will have to stay in his room for awhile. When the friends return they come with presents, such as puppets and books, but McGurk is more interested in spying on the next-door-neighbors. He has noticed that the woman next door is actually a man wearing a wig and asks his organization to look into their activities. The detectives follow the neighbors to the store and around town until it becomes apparent that the neighbors are planning a robbery. (154 pages)

Where it's reviewed:
Booklist, May 15, 1996, page 1588
School Library Journal, May 1996, page 113

Other books by the same author:
The Case of the Absent Author, 1995
The Case of the Fantastic Footprints, 1994
The Case of the Desperate Drummer, 1993
The Case of the Purloined Parrot, 1990

Other books you might like:
Shannon Gillegan, *The Clue in the Clock Tower*, 1991
Four students solve vandalism in a clock tower.
E.M. Goldman, *Getting Lincoln's Goat*, 1995
Elliot finds that becoming a detective is harder than it looks on television.
James Howe, *Dew Drop Dead: A Sebastian Barth Mystery*, 1990
A boy finds a dead body which later disappears.
Suzy Kline, *Orp and the FBI*, 1995
As soon as Orp creates the Famous Bathtub Investigators they are involved in amusing mysteries.
Joan Lowery Nixon, *The Haunted House on Honeycutt Street*, 1991
Four friends join to publish a newspaper and solve mysteries.

618

ANTHONY HILL
MARK SOFILAS, Illustrator

The Burnt Stick

(Boston: Houghton Mifflin Company, 1995)

Subject(s): Mothers and Sons; Australian Aborigines; Schools/Boarding Schools
Age range(s): Grades 4-6
Major character(s): John Jagamarra, 5-Year-Old, Kidnap Victim; Liyan, Mother
Time period(s): Indeterminate Past
Locale(s): Dryborough Station, Australia; Pearl Bay Mission, Australia (Pearl Bay Mission for Aboriginal Children)

Summary: When Liyan learns the Big Man from Welfare is coming to take her half-breed son to be taught the White Man's ways in accord with the White Man's law, she is grief-stricken. To hide John, she covers his skin with charcoal from a burnt stick so his lighter brown skin will be as dark as the others in her tribe. Her trick fools the authorities twice, but when they return without forewarning Liyan has no time to protect John. He is taken to the mission school to be raised by the Fathers, forced to wear white man's clothes and learn white man's customs. As an adult, John returns to his now abandoned homeplace with his own son to search for his family. First published in Australia in 1994. (53 pages)

Where it's reviewed:
Booklist, July 1995, page 1878
Children's Book Review Service, August 1995, page 164
Horn Book, November 1995, page 743
Publishers Weekly, July 10, 1995, page 58
School Library Journal, October 1995, page 133

Other books you might like:
Eve Bunting, *Cheyenne Again*, 1995
    Forced from his reservation, a young Cheyenne boy attends a boarding school where he learns white man's ways, but struggles to remain Cheyenne on the inside.
Mildred D. Taylor, *The Friendship*, 1987
    In the 1930s, four children witness a confrontation between an elderly black man and a storekeeper when the black man refuses to address the storekeeper as "Mister."
Maria Testa, *Nine Candles*, 1996
    On his 7th birthday, Raymond visits his mother in prison and wishes time could fly until his 9th birthday when his mama promises to be home.

619

NETTE HILTON
CATHY WILCOX, Illustrator

Andrew Jessup

(New York: Ticknor & Fields, 1993)

Subject(s): Friendship; Moving, Household
Age range(s): Grades K-2
Major character(s): Unnamed Character, Child, Friend (Andrew's best); Madeleine Havenblower, Child, Neighbor (new)

Time period(s): 1990s (1992)
Locale(s): Australia

Summary: Andrew Jessup moves away and leaves a saddened best friend watching over the empty house next door, remembering her fun times with Andrew. Nothing is the same until Madeleine Havenblower moves in taking Andrew's place as best friend while Andrew becomes the best "faraway" friend. Originally published in Australia in 1992. (32 pages)

Where it's reviewed:
Booklist, December 15, 1993, page 764
Horn Book Guide, Spring 1994, page 37
Magpies, May 1993, page 26
Publishers Weekly, July 12, 1993, page 78
School Library Journal, October 1993, page 101

Other books by the same author:
The Long Red Scarf, 1990

Other books you might like:
Aliki, *Best Friends Together Again*, 1995
    Robert faces Peter's visit with mixed emotions—eager to see his friend, yet wondering if Peter's move has changed their relationship.
Larry Dane Brimner, *Max and Felix*, 1993
    Frog friends experience the ups and downs of friendship in begining chapter book.
Kevin Henkes, *Chester's Way*, 1988
    Chester and Wilson do everything together in exactly the same way until Lilly moves in and shows them that friends can do things differently.
Pat Hutchins, *My Best Friend*, 1993
    A diversity of interests and abilities adds flavor to this friendship.

620

JOHN HIMMELMAN, Author/Illustrator

Lights Out!

(Mahwah, NJ: BridgeWater Books, 1995)

Subject(s): Camps and Camping; Bedtime; Fear
Age range(s): Grades K-2
Major character(s): Jim, Counselor
Time period(s): 1990s (1995)
Locale(s): Camp Badger

Summary: Six Badger Scouts are unable to sleep because they imagine lions outside the window, eyeballs on the ceiling, and enormous mosquitoes drinking all their body fluids. Frustrated counselor Jim finally gives them each a flashlight to ease their fears and they promptly march off to the the mess hall for a drink and then visit the outhouse. Finally, the scouts settle down and counselor Jim tries to get some sleep only to have the scouts' imagined fears filling his room. (32 pages)

Where it's reviewed:
Booklist, April 1, 1995, page 1427
Horn Book Guide, Fall 1995, page 267
Kirkus Reviews, February 15, 1995, page 225
Publishers Weekly, May 1, 1995, page 58
School Library Journal, August 1995, page 124

Other books by the same author:
Wanted: Perfect Parents, 1993
The Super Camper Caper, 1991
Amanda and the Witch Switch, 1987

Other books you might like:
Stan Berenstain, *The Berenstain Bears Go to Camp*, 1982
    Although the cubs enjoy day camp, they are not eager to
    attend the final event—a sleep-out atop Skull Rock. Co-
    author Jan Bernenstain.
Marc Brown, *Arthur Goes to Camp*, 1982
    Already apprehensive about attending Camp
    Meadowcroak, the strange events Arthur experiences after
    his arrival are enough to convince him to run away.
Nancy Carlson, *Arnie Goes to Camp*, 1988
    Arnie learns that camp is not as bad as he feared it would
    be before he arrived.
James Marshall, *The Cut-Ups at Camp Custer*, 1989
    Spud and Joe try to catch the prankster responsible for
    getting them in trouble at camp.

621

ANNA GROSSNICKLE HINES, Author/Illustrator

Big Help!
(New York: Clarion Books, 1995)

Subject(s): Brothers and Sisters; Play; Problem Solving
Age range(s): Grades K-1
Major character(s): Sam, Child, Brother (older); Lucy, Child
    (toddler), Sister (younger); Daddy, Father
Time period(s): 1990s (1995)
Locale(s): United States

Summary: Trying to be helpful, instead, Lucy accidently collapses the tunnel Sam builds in the sandbox and tumbles his
block tower. Daddy tries to distract Lucy, but she has no
interest in doing her own thing, she only wants to help Sam.
Finally, Sam pulls her in the wagon until she falls asleep and
then Sam is able to sit contentedly coloring a picture with no
help at all. (32 pages)

Where it's reviewed:
Booklist, March 1, 1995, page 1248
Horn Book Guide, Fall 1995, page 250
School Library Journal, April 1995, page 102

Other books by the same author:
Even If I Spill My Milk?, 1994
Remember the Butterflies, 1991
Big Like Me, 1989

Other books you might like:
Judith Caseley, *Mama, Coming and Going*, 1994
    Jenna helps her busy and distracted mother after the birth
    of her baby brother.
Russell Hoban, *A Baby Sister for Frances*, 1964
    Patiently, Frances's parents help her adjust to the arrival of
    her sister.
Carol Snyder, *One Up, One Down*, 1995
    Katie has twice as many ''helpers'' with whom to contend
    when her twin brothers are born.

622

ANNA GROSSNICKLE HINES, Author/Illustrator

What Joe Saw
(New York: Greenwillow Books, 1994)

Subject(s): Individuality; Schools/Preschool; Nature
Age range(s): Grades K-2
Major character(s): Joe, Child, Student
Time period(s): 1990s (1994)
Locale(s): United States

Summary: When Joe's classmates line up for a walk to the
duck pond, Joe is last in line. Ignoring everyone's taunts of
slowpoke, Joe takes the time to observe what speedier students miss—a blue bird, a trail of ants, a turtle. As the class
heads back to school, one student stops to tie his shoe and
finally appreciates what Joe has been seeing all along. (32
pages)

Where it's reviewed:
Booklist, September 15, 1994, page 144
Children's Book Review Service, October 1994, page 16
Horn Book, November 1994, page 760
Kirkus Reviews, August 15, 1994, page 1130
School Library Journal, September 1994, page 186

Other books by the same author:
Grandma's Walk, 1993
It's Just Me, Emily, 1987
Come to the Meadow, 1984

Other books you might like:
Nancy White Carlstrom, *Wild, Wild Sunflower Child Anna*,
    1987
    Anna enjoys her day outside under the sun and sky, sur-
    rounded by grass, flowers, frogs and beetles.
Douglas Florian, *Nature Walk*, 1989
    Two children enjoy a trail hike through the woods learning
    more about nature.
Kathryn Lasky, *Pond Year*, 1995
    Best friends enjoy the seasonal changes in the life of a
    pond near their home.
David Williams, *Walking to the Creek*, 1990
    Behind Grandma and Grandpa's farm is a path to the creek
    that is perfect for exploring the hidden treasures of nature.
Ashley Wolff, *Stella and Roy*, 1993
    Stella's interest in nature distracts her from her intention to
    win the race around the lake.

623

S.E. HINTON
JACQUELINE ROGERS, Illustrator

The Puppy Sister
(New York: Delacorte Press, 1995)

Subject(s): Animals/Dogs; Pets; Fantasy
Age range(s): Grades 2-4
Major character(s): Nick Davidson, Child, Brother; Aleasha,
    Dog, Sister; Miss Kitty, Cat
Time period(s): 1990s (1995)
Locale(s): United States

Summary: From the moment of her arrival, puppy Aleasha is treated as a member of the family, the sister and playmate Nick wants. Aleasha assumes she will grow up to be like the human members of her family and is horrified to learn she's destined to be a dog. Taking matters into her own paws, Aleasha uses all her willpower to transform from an Australian shepherd pup into a human being. During the year she changes, the family hides her, telling neighbors they've given away the puppy and are trying to adopt a little girl. (122 pages)

Where it's reviewed:
Children's Book Review Service, November 1995, page 30
Horn Book Guide, Spring 1996, page 62
Kirkus Reviews, August 1, 1995, page 1111
Publishers Weekly, July 17, 1995, page 230
School Library Journal, October 1995, page 104

Other books by the same author:
Big David, Little David, 1995

Other books you might like:
Dick King-Smith, *Babe: The Gallant Pig*, 1985
  Babe is an extraordinary pig whose friendship with a sheep dog assures his place on the farm and keeps him off the dinner table.
Annie M.G. Schmidt, *Minnie*, 1994
  Minnie, a ginger cat, is accidentally changed into human form and must choose whether to continue life as a young woman or return to cat form.
E.B. White, *Stuart Little*, 1945
  A classic fantasy tells of the Little Family whose second born son appears to be a mouse.

624

HILARY HORDER HIPPELY
JO ELLEN MCALLISTER STAMMEN, Illustrator

The Crimson Ribbon
(New York: G. P. Putnam's Sons, 1994)

Subject(s): Aunts and Uncles; Imagination; Fantasy
Age range(s): Grades 1-3
Major character(s): Nell, Child (imaginative)
Time period(s): 1990s (1994)
Locale(s): United States

Summary: As an antidote to boredom on a cold November day, Nell's mother invites her up to the attic where Nell finds a box of hair ribbons, childhood gifts to her mother from her aunts. Nell sits in the window seat as the snow begins to fall, imagining herself as the little girl who visits the two elderly aunts and has her hair combed and tied with a ribbon. The author's first picture book. (32 pages)

Where it's reviewed:
Booklist, December 1, 1994, page 686
Children's Book Review Service, February 1995, page 75
Horn Book Guide, Spring 1995, page 40
Publishers Weekly, October 3, 1994, page 68
School Library Journal, September 1994, page 186

Other books you might like:
Barbara Berger, *When the Sun Rose*, 1986
  A young girl pretends to be playing happily with another child who brings a pet lion along for the day.
Robyn Harbert Eversole, *The Magic House*, 1992
  April tries to share her unique perspective of their home in which the stairs become a waterfall and the living room a desert, but her sister is preoccupied.
Anna Grossnickle Hines, *Gramma's Walk*, 1993
  Donnie and wheelchair-bound Gramma imagine a walk on the beach, feeling the warm sand and smelling the salty air.
Susan Tews, *Nettie's Gift*, 1993
  Playing in the woods near her grandmother's childhood home, Sarah imagines herself playing with a little girl named Nettie.

625

KAREN HIRSCH

Ellen Anders on Her Own
(New York: Macmillan, 1994)

Subject(s): Diaries; Friendship; Death
Age range(s): Grades 4-6
Major character(s): Ellen Anders, 6th Grader; Abby Wickers, 6th Grader
Time period(s): 1990s
Locale(s): Wisconsin

Summary: Since her mother's death, Ellen has relied on the support of her best friend Abby, especially as they enter 6th grade when she could use her mother's advice. But then Abby drifts away from Ellen and hangs out with a group they used to refer to as the ''Dandy Dames'' due to their flirty ways. At the same time, Ellen finds and reads her mother's diary from when she was 12-years-old and discovers that her mother was a 1960's version of a ''Dandy Dame.'' Suddenly that term doesn't sound too bad! (110 pages)

Where it's reviewed:
Voice of Youth Advocates, February 1995, page 339
School Library Journal, June 1994, page 128
Booklist, May 1, 1994, page 1601
Kirkus Reviews, May 1, 1994, page 630

Other books you might like:
Cynthia D. Grant, *Phoenix Rising: Or How to Survive Your Life*, 1989
  Finding her sister Helen's diary after her death from cancer, provides Jessie with the insight she needs to accept the loss of her sister.
Kit Pearson, *A Handful of Time*, 1988
  Patricia is able to travel back in time to observe her mother as a young girl, which helps her accept her parents' divorce.
Marc Talbert, *Dead Birds Singing*, 1985
  A drunk driver robs Matt of his mom and sister, but luckily his friend Jamie helps him overcome his grief.

626

JULIA HOBAN
JOHN HIMMELMAN, Illustrator

Buzby to the Rescue

(New York: HarperCollins Publishers, 1993)

Series: I Can Read
Subject(s): Animals/Cats; Animals/Chickens; Hotels, Motels
Age range(s): Grades K-2
Major character(s): Serena Lovejoy, Chicken (glamorous), Actress (movie star); Buzby, Cat, Hotel Worker
Time period(s): 1990s (1993)
Locale(s): United States

Summary: In this sequel to *Buzby*, the hotel manager assigns Buzby the task of attending to Serena Lovejoy during her stay at the hotel. The absent-minded Serena's refusal to leave her jewelry case in the hotel safe and the arrival of two suspicious-looking guests lead Buzby to assume the worst when Serena is unable to locate some of her jewelry. All's well that ends well and so it does in this silly mystery. (64 pages)

Where it's reviewed:
Booklist, September 15, 1993, page 163
Horn Book Guide, Spring 1994, page 62
School Library Journal, February 1994, page 87

Other books by the same author:
Buzby, 1990
Amy Loves the Rain, 1989
Quick Chick, 1989

Other books you might like:
Eth Clifford, *Flatfoot Fox and the Case of the Missing Whoooo*, 1993
   In the third title of the series detective Flatfoot Fox locates Owl's missing whoooo.
Richard Scarry, *Richard Scarry's Great Steamboat Mystery*, 1975
   A wedding party on a steamboat is enlivened by two detectives hot on the trail of jewel thieves.
Marjorie Weinman Sharmat, *Nate the Great Series*, 1972-
   Nate follows one clue after another in the style of Sherlock Holmes in this mystery series for beginning readers.

627

LILLIAN HOBAN, Author/Illustrator

Arthur's Camp-Out

(New York: HarperCollins, 1993)

Series: Arthur Adventure
Subject(s): Camps and Camping; Animals/Chimpanzees; Brothers and Sisters
Age range(s): Grades K-2
Major character(s): Arthur, Chimpanzee, Brother; Violet, Chimpanzee, Sister
Time period(s): 1990s (1993)
Locale(s): United States

Summary: Arthur's plans to entertain himself during vacation by going on a field trip to collect scientific specimens change when his sister and helper, Violet, is invited on a camp-out

with her friends. Offended by Arthur's offer to accompany them for their own protection, the girls refuse to include Arthur in the plans and he is left to fend for himself. Alone, Arthur meets with one misfortune after another. Finding himself wet, lonely, and hungry after dark, he follows the scent of roasting hot dogs, joins the girls and learns that they do know a few things about science and camping after all. (64 pages)

Where it's reviewed:
Booklist, March 1, 1993, page 1239
Horn Book, September 1993, page 633
Kirkus Reviews, April 15, 1993, page 530
School Library Journal, April 1993, page 96

Other books by the same author:
Joe and Betsy the Dinosaur, 1995
Turtle Spring, 1992
Arthur's Halloween Costume, 1984
Arthur's Funny Money, 1981

Other books you might like:
James Howe, *Pinky and Rex Go to Camp*, 1992
   Preparing for camp puts some unexpected strains on the friendship between Pinky and Rex.
Peggy Parish, *Amelia Bedelia Goes Camping*, 1985
   As usual, when she tries something new, Amelia Bedelia has her own way of doing things but she eventually learns the right way to pitch a tent.
Howie Schneider, *Amos Camps Out: A Couch Adventure in the Woods*, 1992
   Even on a camping trip Amos does not leave behind his old, but very special couch.

628

MARGARET HODGES
KIMBERLY BULCKEN ROOT, Illustrator

Gulliver in Lilliput

(New York: Holiday House, 1995)

Subject(s): Fantasy; Shipwrecks; Adventure and Adventurers
Age range(s): Grades 3-6
Major character(s): Lemuel Gulliver, Captive
Time period(s): 17th century; 1700s (1699-1702)
Locale(s): Lilliput, Fictional Country; Blefuscu, Fictional Country

Summary: When his ship breaks apart in a storm, Gulliver, the only survivor, washes ashore and awakens to find himself held captive by hundreds of tiny people. The emperor eventually recognizes that the very large captive means no harm and allows him to live freely. In time, Gulliver resolves a dispute between Blefuscu and Lilliput, finds an overturned boat in the sea, restores it and sails away. Based on Part I of *Gulliver's Travels* by Jonathan Swift, the story of Gulliver's capture by the Lilliputians includes illustrations which demonstrate the size disparity between Gulliver and his tiny captors. (32 pages)

Where it's reviewed:
Booklist, April 15, 1995, page 1500
Five Owls, May 1995, page 107
Horn Book, July 1995, page 450
Kirkus Reviews, March 15, 1995, page 384

School Library Journal, June 1995, page 114

Awards the book has won:
School Library Journal Best Books, 1995

Other books by the same author:
Saint Patrick and the Peddler, 1993
The Golden Deer, 1992
The Kitchen Knight, 1990

Other books you might like:
Hans Christian Andersen, *Thumbelina*, 1990
The retelling by Deborah Hautzig of the tale of tiny Thumbelina includes adventures which would be routine for Gulliver, until a happy ending lands her with others her own size.
William Steig, *Abel's Island*, 1976
A castaway on an isolated island, Abel, a pampered mouse accustomed to comfort, struggles to survive and find a way home.
Jonathan Swift, *Gulliver's Adventures in Lilliput*, 1993
The retelling, by Ann Keay Beneduce, of Swift's 1726 novel includes the tale of Gulliver in the land of Lilliput.

629

JO HOESTLANDT
JOHANNA KANG, Illustrator

Star of Fear, Star of Hope
(New York: Walker and Company, 1995)

Subject(s): Holocaust; Friendship; World War II
Age range(s): Grades 2-4
Major character(s): Helen, 9-Year-Old; Lydia, Child (Jewish), Friend (Helen's)
Time period(s): 1940s (1942)
Locale(s): France

Summary: After the Germans invade northern France, Lydia and her family must begin wearing yellow stars on their clothes. Then on the eve of Helen's birthday, when Lydia is spending the night, word comes that Jewish citizens are being arrested. Lydia insists on going home to warn her family and Helen sees her for the last time, never learning what has happened to Lydia or her family. Translated from the French by Mark Polizzotti, the book was originally published in France in 1993. (32 pages)

Where it's reviewed:
Booklist, May 1, 1995, page 1573
Christian Science Monitor, September 28, 1995, page B1
Horn Book, September 1995, page 588
Publishers Weekly, June 5, 1995, page 63
School Library Journal, August 1995, page 124

Awards the book has won:
Bologna Book Fair Graphics Prize, 1994

Other books by the same author:
Back to School with Mom, 1990

Other books you might like:
Karen Ackerman, *The Night Crossing*, 1994
In 1938, fearing persecution, Clara and her family leave their Austrian home and flee to the safety of Switzerland.

David A. Adler, *Hilde and Eli: Children of the Holocaust*, 1994
The lives of two children, victims of the Holocaust, are described through the recollections of surviving siblings.
Inge Auerbacher, *I Am a Star: Child of the Holocaust*, 1986
The autobiography describes childhood years in Germany, many of which were spent in a concentration camp, and includes original poetry.

630

SYD HOFF, Author/Illustrator

Arturo's Baton
(New York: Clarion Books, 1995)

Subject(s): Concerts; Musicians; Orchestra
Age range(s): Grades K-3
Major character(s): Arturo, Conductor
Time period(s): 1990s (1995)
Locale(s): United States

Summary: Arturo, a renowned conductor, believes that his success rests with his baton. When the baton cannot be located prior to a performance, Arturo wants to cancel the concert and the upcoming world tour. When he is finally convinced to try using only his hands to conduct, he learns that the gift for calling forth music from the orchestra is within him. (32 pages)

Where it's reviewed:
Booklist, September 1, 1995, page 87
Horn Book Guide, Spring 1996, page 31
School Library Journal, September 1995, page 179

Other books by the same author:
Captain Cat, 1993
Mrs. Brice's Mice, 1988
Little Chief, 1961

Other books you might like:
Scott Gustafson, *Scott Gustafson's Animal Orchestra*, 1988
Members of the orchestra are introduced in a counting book which begins with one conductor.
Leah Komaiko, *I Like the Music*, 1987
A grandmother escorts her music-loving granddaughter to an outdoor symphony concert.
Karla Kuskin, *The Philharmonic Gets Dressed*, 1982
The action begins behind stage as the 105 members of the Philharmonic prepare for a performance.
Lloyd Moss, *Zin! Zin! Zin! a Violin*, 1995
The playful rhymes and zany illustrations introduce the instruments of the orchestra.

631

SYD HOFF, Author/Illustrator

Bernard on His Own
(New York: Clarion, 1993)

Subject(s): Animals/Bears; Growing Up; Parent and Child
Age range(s): Grades K-2
Major character(s): Bernard, Bear (cub)
Time period(s): 1990s (1993)

Locale(s): United States

Summary: Frustrated that he can't successfully climb a tree, retrieve honey or catch a fish, without being rescued by his parents, Bernard is reassured that one day he will be able to do things on his own. (32 pages)

Where it's reviewed:
Booklist, March 15, 1993, page 1359
Horn Book Guide, Fall 1993, page 261
Publishers Weekly, February 2, 1993, page 86
School Library Journal, May 1993, page 86

Other books by the same author:
Captain Cat, 1993
Mrs. Brice's Mice, 1988
Danny and the Dinosaur, 1958

Other books you might like:
Robert Kraus, *Leo the Late Bloomer*, 1971
    Father is impatient for Leo to learn to do things, but Mother knows that Leo will bloom in his own time.
Arnold Lobel, *Owl at Home*, 1975
    Owl likes to be helpful; unfortunately his attempts are not always successful.
Jean Van Leeuwen, *Amanda Pig on Her Own*, 1991
    Now that brother is in school all day, Amanda must learn to do things for herself.

632

SYD HOFF, Author/Illustrator

Duncan the Dancing Duck
(New York: Clarion Books, 1994)

Subject(s): Animals/Ducks; Dancing
Age range(s): Grades K-2
Major character(s): Duncan, Duck, Dancer
Time period(s): 1990s (1994)
Locale(s): United States

Summary: His siblings are swimming in line just as mother expects, but Duncan is dancing in the pond, past the farm animals and into the farm house where the farmer and his wife are so impressed that they take Duncan to town. After his success on stage, Duncan goes on television and eventually performs on Broadway, winning the Golden Duck Award. Fame is exhausting and Duncan is happy to see his mother and his pond again. (32 pages)

Where it's reviewed:
Horn Book Guide, Fall 1994, page 276
Publishers Weekly, April 4, 1994, page 78
Reading Teacher, October 1995, page 137
School Library Journal, July 1994, page 78

Awards the book has won:
International Reading Association Children's Choice, 1995

Other books by the same author:
Bernard on His Own, 1993
Albert the Albatross, 1961
Oliver, 1960

Other books you might like:
Mary Jane Auch, *Hen Lake*, 1995
    Poulette, the determined hen ballerina, challenges a conceited barnyard peacock to a talent contest.
Richard Edwards, *Moles Can Dance*, 1994
    Despite admonitions to the contrary, a young mole decides to dance, not dig. By observing two children dancing, he teaches himself and then his fellow moles.
Elise Primavera, *The Three Dots*, 1993
    Three dot-covered animals share the bond of being misfits when they meet in New York City, forming a friendship and a musical group until jealousy separates them.
Erica Silverman, *Don't Fidget a Feather*, 1994
    Friendship triumphs as the competiveness between Duck and Gander almost leads to both becoming a Fox's dinner before one sacrifices victory to save the other.
Ellen Stoll Walsh, *Hop Jump*, 1993
    Bored with hopping and jumping like all the other frogs, Betsy dances instead, starting a trend in frog movement.

633

SYD HOFF, Author/Illustrator

Happy Birthday, Danny and the Dinosaur!
(New York: HarperCollins Publishers, 1995)

Series: I Can Read
Subject(s): Dinosaurs; Birthdays; Humor
Age range(s): Grades K-2
Major character(s): Danny, 6-Year-Old; Unnamed Character, Dinosaur
Time period(s): Indeterminate Past
Locale(s): United States

Summary: Danny hurries to the museum to invite his dinosaur friend to his 6th birthday party. The dinosaur is eager to accompany Danny and enjoy party games and refreshements. (32 pages)

Where it's reviewed:
Booklist, October 1, 1995, page 329
Bulletin of the Center for Children's Books, October 1995, page 56
Horn Book Guide, Spring 1996, page 52
School Library Journal, September 1995, page 179

Other books by the same author:
Chester, 1961
Sammy the Seal, 1959
Danny and the Dinosaur, 1958

Other books you might like:
Wolfram Hanel, *Lila's Little Dinosaur*, 1994
    Only Lila can see the rainbow-striped baby dinosaur that follows her home from the Natural History Museum.
Lillian Hoban, *Joe and Betsy the Dinosaur*, 1995
    Betsy's large size creates some problems, as the dinosaur tries to play in the snow with her human buddy Joe.
William H. Hooks, *Mr. Dinosaur*, 1994
    Eli is so intrigued by dinosaurs that his single-minded interest begins to create problems for him.

634

MARY HOFFMAN
CAROLINE BINCH, Illustrator

Boundless Grace

(New York: Dial Books for Young Readers, 1995)

Subject(s): Stepfamilies; African Americans; Africa
Age range(s): Grades K-3
Major character(s): Grace, Child of Divorced Parents; Nana, Grandmother; Papa, Father
Time period(s): 1990s (1995)
Locale(s): Gambia

Summary: In the sequel to *Amazing Grace*, Grace dreams of having a storybook perfect family. When her father sends money for Grace and Nana to fly to The Gambia for a visit, Grace uses her knowledge of stepfamilies in storybooks to prepare her for meeting Papa's new wife and children. Although Grace tries to make all the people fit as they do in a fairy tale, she finally accepts Nana's observation that stories, like families, are what you make them. Grace decides to write her own story about a family just like hers—living ''happily ever after, though not all in the same place.'' (32 pages)

Where it's reviewed:
Booklist, April 15, 1995, page 1506
Horn Book, July 1995, page 450
Language Arts, September 1995, page 371
Publishers Weekly, May 8, 1995, page 294
School Library Journal, May 1995, page 85

Other books by the same author:
Babies' Hotel, 1993
Leon's Lucky Lunch-Break, 1993
Amazing Grace, 1991

Other books you might like:
Cari Best, *Getting Used to Harry*, 1996
    Cynthia's mother remarries and now Cynthia must get used to having Harry around all the time.
Nancy Raines Day, *The Lion's Whiskers: An Ethiopian Folktale*, 1995
    In an African folktale, a stepmother seeks advice on how to gain her stepson's acceptance.
Sharon Dennis Wyeth, *Ginger Brown: Too Many Houses*, 1996
    After 6-year-old Ginger's parents divorce, she lives first with one set of grandparents and then the other.
Judith Vigna, *She's Not My Real Mother*, 1980
    Miles reconsiders his feelings toward his stepmother after she rescues him.

635

MARY HOFFMAN
LAURA L. SEELEY, Illustrator

The Four-Legged Ghosts

(New York: Dial Books for Young Readers, 1993)

Subject(s): Ghosts; Magic; Pets
Age range(s): Grades 3-5

Major character(s): Alex Brodie, 11-Year-Old, Brother; Carrie Brodie, Sister (younger), Asthmatic; Cedric Whitgift Blanco 57th, Mouse (magical)
Time period(s): 1990s (1992)
Locale(s): England

Summary: Carrie is as excited as Alex when her doctor allows the family to have a small mouse for a pet. However, the children soon learn that no ordinary pet has entered their lives, but the seventeenth son of the seventeenth son which means a magical mouse. Taking pity on the children when he hears they would like more pets, Cedric proudly conjures up the ghosts of all the animals who have ever lived in the house. Unfortunately, he is unable to stop the spell and the ghostly menagerie begins to create problems for the children who are the only ones who can see the animals. Originally published in Great Britain in 1992 as *The Ghost Menagerie*. (96 pages)

Where it's reviewed:
Booklist, September 1, 1993, page 60
Children's Book Review Service, Winter 1994, page 68
Horn Book Guide, Spring 1994, page 66
Publishers Weekly, July 12, 1993, page 80
School Library Journal, August 1993, page 164

Awards the book has won:
Book Links Good Book, 1993

Other books by the same author:
Henry's Baby, 1993
Dracula's Daughter, 1989

Other books you might like:
Susan Cooper, *The Boggart*, 1993
    Emily and Jessup must find a way to deal with a shape-changing, mischievous spirit before they get into any more trouble due to his tricks.
Ellen Leroe, *Ghost Dog*, 1993
    The ghost of a dog in his grandpa's new home creates problems for Artie until he decides to use the dog to help solve a mystery.
Betty Ren Wright, *The Ghost of Popcorn Hill*, 1993
    Martin and Peter solve their ghost problem by introducing the lonely ghost of a farmer to the ghost of a lonely sheep dog.

636

MARY HOFFMAN
SUSAN WINTER, Illustrator

Henry's Baby

(New York: Dorling Kindersley, 1993)

Subject(s): Popularity; Babies; Brothers
Age range(s): Grades K-3
Major character(s): Henry Moon, Child, Brother (older); George Moon, Brother (baby)
Time period(s): 1990s (1993)
Locale(s): United States

Summary: They're hip, they're cool, they're the ''in'' group at his new school and Henry wants to belong. When ''they'' ask to hold their weekly meeting at his house, Henry is thrilled that his mother consents and agrees to take baby brother George to a neighbor's home during the meeting. Unfortunately a problem next door leaves Henry unexpectedly baby-sitting George and fearing his tentative acceptance will become ridicule. Rather, Henry's baby is the hit of the meeting and the group asks to return. Yes! (32 pages)

Where it's reviewed:
Booklist, November 15, 1993, page 631
Five Owls, May 1994, page 106
New Advocate, Summer 1994, page 206
Publishers Weekly, August 23, 1993, page 71
School Library Journal, November 1993, page 82

Other books by the same author:
Amazing Grace, 1991
My Grandma Has Black Hair, 1988
Nancy No-Size, 1987

Other books you might like:
Betsy Duffey, *How to Be Cool in the Third Grade*, 1993
    Robbie's plans to become ''cool'' require ingenuity and courage to ensure their success.
Johanna Hurwitz, *Make Room for Elisa*, 1993
    Russell and his younger sister Elisa prepare for the arrival of a baby brother and a move to a bigger apartment.
Russell Hoban, *Best Friends for Frances*, 1969
    Frances and her younger sister Gloria learn some important lessons about friendship and family.

637

ISABELLE HOLLAND

The Promised Land

(New York: Scholastic, 1996)

Subject(s): Orphans; Prejudice; Frontier and Pioneer Life
Age range(s): Grades 4-6
Major character(s): Maggie Lavin, Orphan, 15-Year-Old; Annie Lavine, Orphan, 10-Year-Old; Aunt Priscilla Russell, Foster Parent
Time period(s): 1800s
Locale(s): Kansas

Summary: Maggie and Annie have been living in Kansas with the Russells for several years now and are quite happy there. Only one problem mars their home; the girls are Catholic and the Russells are Protestant. This problem comes to a head when their mother's brother appears wanting to take them and raise them in a Catholic home. He stays in the town for some time, getting to know the girls better and scrutinizing their new life. On a picnic, Annie almost drowns and Maggie's friend, Tom, rescues her. It is then that Annie recognizes that her life is now bonded to the Russels and Kansas. Uncle Michael, who has gotten to know the Russells better, agrees and returns home, promising to write. (155 pages)

Where it's reviewed:
Bulletin of the Center for Children's Books, April 1996, page 264
School Library Journal, April 1996, page 144
Booklist, April 15, 1996, page 1438

Other books by the same author:
Behind the Lines, 1994
The Journey Home, 1990 (prequel to *The Promised Land*)
The Island, 1984

Other books you might like:
Joan Lowery Nixon, *A Place to Belong*, 1989
    Danny plots to have his foster father send for and marry his mother and come live on the Missouri farm.
Jean Van Leeuwen, *Going West*, 1992
    A family moves from the East and settles in Kansas in the 1800s.
Charlene Joy Talbot, *An Orphan for Nebraska*, 1979
    A young Irish boy makes his own way to Nebraska and works for a newspaper.
Annette R. Fry, *The Orphan Trains*, 1994
    Charles Brace despaired at the plight of the orphans in New York and so developed the orphan train idea. (nonfiction)

638

NATALIE HONEYCUTT

Lydia Jane and the Baby-Sitter Exchange

(New York: Bradbury Press, 1993)

Subject(s): Babysitters; Family Life; Humor
Age range(s): Grades 3-4
Major character(s): Lydia Jane Bly, 8-Year-Old (independent), Sister (older); Gabrielle Bly, 4-Year-Old, Sister (younger); Mrs. Humphrey, Child-Care Giver (strict)
Time period(s): 1990s (1993)
Locale(s): Westmont, California

Summary: Mrs. Humphrey has one word for all of Lydia Jane's creative ideas, ''No!'' So, Lydia Jane puts her inquisitive, curious mind to work on a new babysitting plan that will meet her parents' approval. Although the children's retired science-professor grandmother does not agree to move in and take over the baby-sitting duties, she does help Lydia Jane and Gabrielle devise a solution that is acceptable to all. (117 pages)

Where it's reviewed:
Booklist, March 1, 1994, page 1261
Horn Book Guide. Spring 1994, page 77
Kirkus Reviews, September 1, 1993, page 1146
Publishers Weekly, September 23, 1993, page 72
School Library Journal, November 1993, page 108

Other books by the same author:
Juliet Fisher and the Foolproof Plan, 1992
The Best-Laid Plans of Jonah Twist, 1988
The All New Jonah Twist, 1986

Other books you might like:
Beverly Cleary, *Ramona Quimby, Age 8*, 1982
    One of several books about energetic Ramona and the ups and downs of life in a household with (hopefully) working parents; it is a Newbery Honor Book.
P.L. Travers, *Mary Poppins: Revised Edition*, 1962
    Mary Poppins' unique approach to child-care is an eye-opening experience for the Banks family of Cherry Tree Lane.
Susan Wojciechowski, *Don't Call Me Beanhead!*, 1994
    Beany is a worrier; her worries lead to plans and then the fun begins!

639

NATALIE HONEYCUTT
ANNIE CANNON, Illustrator

Whistle Home

(New York: Orchard Books, 1993)

Subject(s): Fear; Aunts and Uncles; Babysitters
Age range(s): Grades K-2
Major character(s): Unnamed Character, Child (young); Dooley, Dog; Aunt Whistle, Babysitter (skilled whistler)
Time period(s): 1990s (1993)
Locale(s): United States (rural area)

Summary: When Mom goes to town and Dooley runs off after a rabbit, reassurance of everyone's return comes in the form of Aunt Whistle's famous whistle. While that whistle brings Dooley back, Mama comes home on her own, bringing hugs and surprises for everyone. This is YA author Honeycutt's first picture book. (32 pages)

Where it's reviewed:
Booklist, December 1, 1993, page 698
Horn Book, January 1994, Page 64
Publishers Weekly, August 9, 1993, page 476
Reading Teacher, March 1994, page 494
School Library Journal, November 1993, page 84

Other books you might like:
Ezra Jack Keats, *Whistle for Willie*, 1964
   Peter experiences satisfaction when his attempts to whistle are finally successful.
Kathryn Lasky, *I Have an Aunt on Marlborough Street*, 1992
   A young girl shares a special relationship with her aunt during visits to her home in Boston.
Christine Widman, *The Lemon Drop Jar*, 1992
   The warmth of an autumn day is reflected in the glow of memories shared during a visit with Great-aunt Emma.

640

LILY TOY HONG, Author/Illustrator

The Empress and the Silkworm

(Morton Grove, IL: Albert Whitman & Company, 1995)

Subject(s): Silk; Legends; Animals/Worms
Age range(s): Grades K-3
Major character(s): Si Ling-Chi, Royalty (Empress)
Time period(s): Indeterminate Past
Locale(s): China

Summary: When a silkworm cocoon drops from a mulberry tree into the Empress Si Ling-Chi's tea cup, she studies the effects of the warm tea on the cocoon and enlists the help of her servants to unravel the thread. As a result of her curiosity and belief in a subsequent dream, the silkworm culture of China begins, initially to produce a robe for Si Ling-Chi's husband, the Emperor, and ultimately as a valuable export product. A concluding page gives factual information about silkworms. (32 pages)

Where it's reviewed:
Booklist, September 15, 1995, page 175
Horn Book Guide, Spring 1996, page 31

Publishers Weekly, September 4, 1995, page 69
School Library Journal, November 1995, page 90

Other books by the same author:
Two of Everything, 1993
How the Ox Star Fell from Heaven, 1991

Other books you might like:
Jeanne M. Lee, *The Song of Mu Lan*, 1995
   The Chinese folk poem tells the tale of a young girl who, in disguise, takes her father's place in battle.
Doreen Rappaport, *The Long-Haired Girl: A Chinese Legend*, 1995
   Courageous Ah-mei risks her life to save her village during a drought.
Amy Tan, *The Chinese Siamese Cat*, 1994
   An original folk tale explaining the facial markings of a Siamese cat's kittens is told from the perspective of a cat.

641

LILY TOY HONG, Author/Illustrator

Two of Everything

(Morton Grove, IL: Albert Whitman & Co., 1993)

Subject(s): Folk Tales; Magic; Poverty
Age range(s): Grades K-3
Major character(s): Mrs. Haktak, Spouse (poor), Aged Person (Chinese); Mr. Haktak, Spouse (poor), Aged Person (Chinese)
Time period(s): Indeterminate Past
Locale(s): China

Summary: While digging in his small garden Mr. Haktak finds a brass pot which magically duplicates anything that is put into it. Mr. & Mrs. Haktak happily take advantage of this discovery. The magic loses some of its charm when first one and then the other Haktak fall into the pot, but the now-duplicated Haktaks find a way to adjust to having two of everything - even each other. (32 pages)

Where it's reviewed:
Booklist, March 15, 1993, page 1320
Horn Book, July 1993, page 469
Kirkus Reviews, February 15, 1993, page 227
Publishers Weekly, March 8, 1993, page 78
School Library Journal, June 1993, page 101

Awards the book has won:
Booklist Editors' Choice, 1993

Other books by the same author:
How the Ox Star Fell from Heaven, 1991

Other books you might like:
Tomie De Paola, *Strega Nona*, 1975
   Oh no! Strega Nona has left Big Anthony alone with her magic pot and he's cooking pasta in it.
Paul Galdone, *The Magic Porridge Pot*, 1976
   This magic pot cooks porridge and more porridge and more porridge because the words which tell it to stop are forgotten.
Virginia Haviland, *The Talking Pot: A Danish Folktale*, 1990
   In a retelling of a classic folktale a pot which a poor man

acquires in exchange for his cow turns out to be a better bargain than anticipated.

642

WILLIAM H. HOOKS
ANGELA TROTTA THOMAS, Illustrator

The Mighty Santa Fe
(New York: Macmillan Publishing Company, 1993)

Subject(s): Christmas; Trains; Grandparents
Age range(s): Grades K-3
Major character(s): William, Child (train lover); Granny Blue, Grandmother (William's great grandmother)
Time period(s): 1990s (1993)
Locale(s): United States

Summary: William is a reluctant participant in the family trip to Granny Blue's home for Christmas because he could not bring his train set. Arriving in a blizzard, pouting William must also endure a power failure which heightens his fear of eccentric Granny Blue. Long after the families are asleep, William lies awake and Granny Blue leads him to the attic for a fantastic train trip. (32 pages)

Where it's reviewed:
Booklist, November 15, 1993, page 632
Children's Book Review Service, February 1994, page 74
Horn Book Guide, Spring 1994, page 66
Publishers Weekly, November 1993, page 79
School Library Journal, October 1993, page 44

Other books by the same author:
Mr. Dinosaur, 1994
Peach Boy, 1992
The Three Little Pigs and the Fox, 1989

Other books you might like:
Angela McAllister, *Jessie's Journey*, 1992
    Jessie imagines a train ride to visit her grandfather.
David McPhail, *The Train*, 1977
    As he drifts off to sleep, a young boy is taken on a fantastic train ride.
Chris Van Allsburg, *The Polar Express*, 1985
    The Caldecott Medal winner describes memories of a train ride to the North Pole on Christmas Eve.

643

PATRICIA HOOPER
SUSAN L. ROTH, Illustrator

How the Sky's Housekeeper Wore Her Scarves
(Boston: Little, Brown and Company, 1995)

Subject(s): Work; Weather; Problem Solving
Age range(s): Grades K-2
Major character(s): Unnamed Character, Aged Person, Housekeeper
Time period(s): Indeterminate Past
Locale(s): Earth

Summary: The sky's housekeeper is a methodical old woman who uses a different colored scarf for each day's chore. The old woman performs her work daily for many years until the rain asks to see the beautiful scarves also. Now the kindly old woman is afraid of losing her way in the darkness of the rain so she asks the sun to shine while the rain is out, but sun refuses. Cowering under a table while the rain taps on her window, the old woman forgets her chores for an entire week and then has to do them all on one rainy day. To keep herself from becoming lost in the gloom, she ties each scarf to the fence post and thereby creates the first rainbow. (32 pages)

Where it's reviewed:
Booklist, March 15, 1995, page 1334
Horn Book Guide, Fall 1995, page 267
Kirkus Reviews, April 15, 1995, page 558
Publishers Weekly, May 8, 1995, page 295
School Library Journal, June 1995, page 87

Other books by the same author:
A Bundle of Beasts, 1987

Other books you might like:
Frank Asch, *Skyfire*, 1984
    When Bear sees his first rainbow he thinks the sky is on fire and he should extinguish the blaze.
Don Freeman, *A Rainbow of My Own*, 1966
    A young boy imagines what it would be like to play with a personal rainbow.
Ruth Robbins, *How the First Rainbow Was Made: An American Indian Tale*, 1980
    The Indians on Mt. Shasta ask Coyote to give them a signal when the rain will stop so they can gather seeds.
Sara Yamaka, *The Gift of Driscoll Lipscomb*, 1995
    Annually, Molly receives a brush and a different color of paint from an artist friend until eventually she has all the colors of the rainbow.

644

DEBORAH HOPKINSON
JAMES E. RANSOME, Illustrator

Sweet Clara and the Freedom Quilt
(New York: Alfred A. Knopf, 1993)

Subject(s): Slavery; Quilts; Freedom
Age range(s): Grades K-3
Major character(s): Sweet Clara, Child (African American), Slave (separated from her mother); Young Jack, Child (African American), Slave (friend of Sweet Clara's); Aunt Rachel, Slave (African American), Seamstress
Time period(s): 19th century
Locale(s): Home Plantation

Summary: Separated from her mother, and sold to another slave owner, Sweet Clara finds herself working in the cotton fields and dreaming of escape and a reunion with her mother. When she is taught to sew and joins Aunt Rachel in the Big House as a seamstress, she also has access to all the visitors that come into the kitchen. The information that she overhears she pieces together into a quilt which serves as a map to show the way to the Ohio River and the beginning of the Underground Railroad. (32 pages)

Where it's reviewed:
Booklist, April 15, 1993, page 1514
Five Owls, March 1993, page 89
Horn Book, May 1993, page 328
Publishers Weekly, February 8, 1993, page 87
School Library Journal, June 1993, page 76

Awards the book has won:
International Reading Association Children's Books, 1994

Other books you might like:
Virginia Hamilton, *The People Could Fly: American Black Folk Tales*, 1985
    A collection of African-American folktales relate stories of slavery and people's escape from bondage.
Connie Porter, *Meet Addy: An American Girl*, 1993
    Addy and her mother escape to freedom from a North Carolina plantation.
Courtni C. Wright, *Journey to Freedom: A Story of the Underground Railroad*, 1994
    Eight-year-old Joshua tells of Harriet Tubman leading his family and other escaped slaves to safety on the Underground Railroad.

645

NANCY J. HOPPER

I Was a Fifth-Grade Zebra

(New York: Dial Books for Young Readers, 1993)

Subject(s): Schools; Interpersonal Relations; Peer Pressure
Age range(s): Grades 4-5
Major character(s): Chelsea Zeller, 5th Grader (not interested in boys), Child of Divorced Parents; Rachel, 5th Grader, Friend (Chelsea's)
Time period(s): 1990s (1993)
Locale(s): United States

Summary: When Rachel's birthday party invitation requires that each guest bring a boy, Chelsea, who is far more interested in pet tarantulas than boys, faces one dilemma after another. Teased by her classmates and desperate to show that she is like the others, Chelsea accepts a blind date arranged by her sister. When the "date" arrives with a frog in each pocket, the party is enlivened with frog races and smashed cake. Embarrassed, Chelsea makes an early exit, but learns to accept the value of her own interests. (136 pages)

Where it's reviewed:
Booklist, July 1993, page 1966
Horn Book Guide, Fall 1993, page 299
Library Talk, January 1994, page 42
Publishers Weekly, June 14, 1993, page 71
School Library Journal, September 1993, page 232

Other books by the same author:
The Queen of Put-Down, 1993
Hang on, Harvey!, 1984
The Seven and One-Half Sins of Stacey Kendall, 1983

Other books you might like:
Judy Blume, *Otherwise Known as Sheila the Great*, 1972
    As Sheila begins to understand herself she finds that maybe she is great after all.

Ellen Conford, *Dreams of Victory*, 1973
    In her dreams, Vicki is no longer a shy, unpopular person.
Colleen O'Shaughnessy McKenna, *Fifth Grade: Here Comes Trouble*, 1991
    An invitation to her first boy-girl party makes Collette uneasy.

646

NANCY J. HOPPER

What Happened in Mr. Fisher's Room

(New York: Dial, 1995)

Subject(s): School Life; Teacher-Student Relationships; Behavior
Age range(s): Grades 6-8
Major character(s): Mr. Fisher, Teacher (science); Vincent "Vinnie" Charles, 8th Grader; Melanie "Lanie" Strata, 8th Grader
Time period(s): 1990s
Locale(s): United States

Summary: Lanie is stuck with absolutely the worst science teacher in her school, Mr. Fisher. He can't make his students behave, he can't teach and worst of all, he accuses her of cheating. She dislikes Mr. Fisher so much, she plots revenge and thinks of killing his fish or his violets. Thinking of revenge is one thing, doing it is another and Lanie doesn't dislike anyone enough to actually carry out this kind of mischief. But someone in her class does, and Lanie is confused about her responsibility in these incidents. It's all part of Lanie's eighth grade year as the wretched Vinnie has a crush on her, problems of loyalty and responsibility arise, her mother returns to work and a best friend moves; Lanie's growing up and she finds it's not an easy process. (137 pages)

Where it's reviewed:
School Library Journal, August 1995, page 140
Booklist, September 1, 1995, page 78
Voice of Youth Advocates, February 1996, page 372
Kirkus Reviews, July 15, 1995, page 1025
Center for Children's Books. Bulletin, October 1995, page 57

Other books by the same author:
The Interrupted Education of Huey B., 1991
The Queen of Put-Down, 1991
The Truth or Dare Trap, 1988
Hang on, Harvey!, 1984

Other books you might like:
Jim Arter, *Gruel and Unusual Punishment*, 1991
    Arnold spends a lot of time in Mr. Applin's detention room, but he's angelic compared to the new student, Edward Straight.
Lois Duncan, *Killing Mr. Griffin*, 1978
    Kidnapping Mr. Griffin begins as a prank; his students never meant to kill him.
Chuck Hanners, *Frankie, Stoney and the Last Chance Boys*, 1990
    Frankie's assigned to Mr. Hansen's Opportunity Class for his "last chance" before being kicked out of school; he wrongly thinks Mr. Hansen is a bespectacled wimp.

647

POLLY HORVATH

The Happy Yellow Car

(New York: Farrar, Straus & Giroux, 1994)

Subject(s): Family Life; Depression (Economic); Humor
Age range(s): Grades 6-7
Major character(s): Betty Grunt, 12-Year-Old; Althea Finnerty Grunt, Mother (Betty's)
Time period(s): 1930s
Locale(s): Missouri

Summary: It's the middle of the Depression and Betty isn't sure where she's going to find the dollar for the flowers she needs after her classmates elect her Pork-Fry Queen. Without the dollar, the title will go to the teacher's pet. Betty's mother has even greater financial worries when she discovers her husband has spent her secret college fund for Betty on a bright yellow car, and he doesn't even know how to drive! This crazy but lovable family encounters even more adventures when Betty rounds up everyone to try to find the treasure rumored to be hidden on her deceased grandmother's farm. (151 pages)

Where it's reviewed:
Booklist, August 1994, page 2044
School Library Journal, September 1994, page 216
Publishers Weekly, July 25, 1994, page 56
Voice of Youth Advocates, December 1994, page 274
Kirkus Reviews, September 15, 1994, page 1274

Other books by the same author:
No More Cornflakes, 1993
An Occasional Cow, 1989

Other books you might like:
Betsy Byars, *The Not-Just-Anybody Family*, 1986
   Maggie and Vern have an amazing family—their mother's off with the rodeo, their brother's in the hospital and their grandfather's in the pokey.
Helen Cresswell, *The Bagthorpes Series*, 1978-
   The Bagthorpe family encounters one adventure after another, whether they're at home or on vacation.
Harvey Watson, *Bob War and Poke*, 1991
   Bob War and his older brother, Poke, get mixedup with a pair of criminals when they dislodge a beautiful Maxwell roadster from a muddy ditch.

648

ERIC L. HOUCK JR.
DOMINIC CATALANO, Illustrator

Rabbit Surprise

(New York: Crown Publishers, Inc., 1993)

Subject(s): Magic; Animals/Foxes; Animals/Rabbits
Age range(s): Grades K-1
Major character(s): Richard Fox, Fox, Brother; Johnny Fox, Fox, Brother
Time period(s): 1990s (1993)
Locale(s): United States

Summary: First-time author Houck presents Richard Fox with a package from his grandmother containing a magician's black hat and four rabbits. The rabbits, however, multiply faster than Richard can find cooking pans for them so he calls on brother Johnny for help. With the house hopping with little rabbits, a very large rabbit emerges from the hat ready to perform magic tricks. Richard outsmarts the big rabbit but not without eliminating breakfast too. Oh well, Johnny invites Richard to his house to dine on the contents of the basket which he received from Grandmother. (32 pages)

Where it's reviewed:
Horn Book Guide, Fall 1993, page 261
Publishers Weekly, March 1, 1993, page 56
School Library Journal, June 1993, page 76

Other books you might like:
Doug Cushman, *Possum Stew*, 1990
   Bear and Gator are tired of being tricked by Possum so they invite him to dinner, yum.
Jama Kim Rattigan, *Truman's Aunt Farm*, 1994
   Truman's birthday gift from his beloved Aunt Fran delivers far more than the ants he was expecting.
Elvira Woodruff, *Show and Tell*, 1991
   Finding a magical bubble jar enlivens Andy's contributions to show-and-tell time at school.

649

ELIZABETH FITZGERALD HOWARD
GAIL GORDON CARTER, Illustrator

Mac and Marie and the Train Toss Surprise

(New York: Four Winds Press, 1993)

Subject(s): Trains; Brothers and Sisters; African Americans
Age range(s): Grades K-1
Major character(s): Mac, 9-Year-Old, Brother (older); Marie, Sister; Clem, Uncle, Railroad Worker
Time period(s): 1900s
Locale(s): Maryland

Summary: In the deepening twilight of a summer evening, Mac and Marie wait beside the train tracks near their home for the Seaboard Florida Limited to pass. Uncle Clem has written that he will be tossing a package to the children and they are eager to receive the surprise. The author has used a family experience as the basis for the story. (32 pages)

Where it's reviewed:
Booklist, February 15, 1993, page 1067
Horn Book May 1993, page 317
Kirkus Reviews, March 1, 1993, page 300
Publishers Weekly, March 15, 1993, page 85
School Library Journal, June 1993, page 76

Other books by the same author:
Papa Tells Chita a Story, 1995
Chita's Christmas Tree, 1989 (ALA Notable Book)
The Train to Lulu's, 1988

Other books you might like:
Jeff Hagen, *Hiawatha Passing*, 1995
   A young boy, spending the night at his grandparent's farm,

watches a train pass by on a snowy night, wondering about the people aboard.

Paul Fleischman, *Time Train*, 1991

A class trip becomes a time travel fantasy when the train takes the students to their destination, but in prehistoric time.

Kim Lewis, *The Last Train*, 1994

After hearing Dad's stories of steam trains from his boyhood days, Sara and James imagine they see one rushing down the no-longer existent track.

Liz Rosenberg, *Adelaide and the Night Train*, 1989

One night Adelaide boards the train that passes her house, or perhaps she's only dreaming.

650

ELIZABETH FITZGERALD HOWARD
FLOYD COOPER, Illustrator

Papa Tells Chita a Story
(New York: Simon & Schuster Books for Young Readers, 1995)

Subject(s): Spanish-American War; Fathers and Daughters; African Americans
Age range(s): Grades K-2
Major character(s): Chita McCard, Child; Papa, Father, Storyteller
Time period(s): Indeterminate Past
Locale(s): Baltimore, Maryland; Cuba

Summary: After Chita finishes drying the supper dishes, Papa takes time from his busy day as a doctor to tell her a story about the days when he was a soldier. Chita loves the story of her brave Papa and knows just when the snake or the alligator will appear. When the story concludes with Papa safely completing his mission, Chita hurries off to bed. (28 pages)

Where it's reviewed:
Booklist, April 1, 1995, page 1427
Horn Book, September 1995, page 626
Horn Book Guide, Fall 1995, page 267
New York Times Book Review, June 18, 1995, page 25
School Library Journal, June 1995, page 87

Other books by the same author:
What's in Aunt Mary's Room, 1996
Aunt Flossie's Hats (and Crab Cakes Later), 1991
Chita's Christmas Tree, 1989
The Train to Lulu's, 1988

Other books you might like:
Sandra Belton, *From Miss Ida's Front Porch*, 1993
Neighbors gather on Miss Ida's porch and the rememberings begin, entrancing children with stories of famous African Americans.

Dolores Johnson, *Papa's Stories*, 1994
No one can read stories in the extra-special way of Kari's father.

Mary Stolz, *Go Fish*, 1991
Thomas and Grandfather share a love of reading and storytelling in this warm family story.

651

ELLEN HOWARD

A Different Kind of Courage
(New York: Simon & Schuster, 1996)

Subject(s): World War II; Refugees; Courage
Age range(s): Grades 4-8
Major character(s): Bertrand "Berti" Cole, Refugee; Zina Sarach, Refugee; Martha Sharp, Hero (rescuer)
Time period(s): 1940s
Locale(s): Paris, France (enroute to Lisbon, Portugal)

Summary: Bertie and his sister are running away from their home and connect with a group of young people being led to safety. As Bertie tells his story, Zina's family is also running away from Russia. The two groups join up, and with the help of Martha Sharp, are able to get on a train which will deliver them to Lisbon and from there they will continue to safety. The trip is not without its dangers, as when Bertie's sister refuses to cross into another country because a favorite adult is not with her and Bertie has a fistfight with a German boy who is acting like a bully. All 27 children do make it to safety. Based on a true story.(170 pages)

Other books by the same author:
The Cellar, 1991
Sister, 1990
Edith Herself, 1987
Circle of Giving, 1984

Other books you might like:
Lois Lowry, *Number the Stars*, 1989
A Danish girl helps her friend escape from the Nazis.

Judith Kerr, *When Hitler Stole Pink Rabbit*, 1987
A German-Jewish family escapes from the Nazis before the start of World War II.

David Kherdian, *The Road from Home: The Story of an Armenian Girl*, 1970
Memoir of a girl who escaped the slaughter of the Armenians. (non-fiction)

Joan B. Manley, *She Flew No Flags*, 1995
Janet and her family are able to escape on board a ship from India in 1944.

Michael Morpurgo, *Waiting for Anya*, 1990
A man leads a group of children to freedom from the Germans but refuses to leave for safety until Anya comes.

Uri Orlev, *Lydia, Queen of Palestine*, 1993
Lydia deals with her parent's divorce as well as the dangers of escaping from Romania to Israel before World War II.

652

ELLEN HOWARD
RONALD HIMLER, Illustrator

The Log Cabin Quilt
(New York: Holiday House, 1996)

Subject(s): Quilts; Family Life
Age range(s): Grades 1-3

Major character(s): Elvirey, Child (of a single parent), Settler; Granny, Grandmother, Seamstress (quilter); Pap, Settler, Widow(er)
Time period(s): 1800s
Locale(s): Michigan

Summary: When Elviry's mother dies, she and her family move to Michigan. Though Granny insists on bringing quilting pieces with her, the family is not interested in anything that reminds them of their mother. Then the winter sets and one evening, while Pap is away, the cabin gets so cold the chinks in the walls freeze and fall out. Remembering her mother's quilting scraps, Elviry and her brother push them into the holes in the walls. When Pap returns he is surprised and warmed by the sight of the quilting scraps and it is only then that the family can talk about memories of their mother. (32 pages)

Where it's reviewed:
School Library Journal, October 1996, page 122
Bulletin of the Center for Children's Books, October 1996, page 64
Booklist, December 1996, page 731

Other books by the same author:
The Big Seed, 1993
The Cellar, 1990
Sister, 1990

Other books you might like:
Eve Bunting, *Dandelions*, 1995
    Life on the prairie is so hard that even the sight of dandelions makes one more cheerful.
Tony Johnston, *The Quilt Story*, 1985
    A pioneer mother makes a quilt for her daughter and later this same daughter shares it with her daughter.
Patricia Polacco, *The Keeping Quilt*, 1988
    A quilt serves as a reminder of several generations of a Jewish family.
Ann Turner, *Sewing Quilts*, 1994
    Memories of a family are sewn into the quilts which a pioneer girl and her mother make.

653

ELLEN HOWARD
MARK GRAHAM, Illustrator

Murphy and Kate

(New York: Simon and Schuster Books for Young Readers, 1995)

Subject(s): Animals/Dogs; Pets; Death (of a Pet)
Age range(s): Grades 1-4
Major character(s): Kate, 14-Year-Old; Murphy, Dog
Time period(s): 1990s (1995)
Locale(s): United States

Summary: Kate is saddened by the death of her 14-year-old pet and best friend. She fills the void in her life with poignant memories of her activities with Murphy—teaching him to walk, playing with him on the swing, pushing him in her baby buggy and sharing her bed with him. By remembering, she knows the pain of her loss will lessen. (32 pages)

Where it's reviewed:
Booklist, May 1, 1995, page 1580

Horn Book Guide, Fall 1995, page 268
Instructor, September 1995, page 107
School Library Journal, June 1995, page 87

Other books by the same author:
The Cellar, 1992
The Chickenhouse House, 1991

Other books you might like:
Amy Ehrlich, *Maggie and Silky and Joe*, 1994
    Joe and his family are saddened by the death of faithful friend and pet Maggie.
Michael J. Rosen, *Bonesy and Isabel*, 1995
    As a newly adopted child in a strange country, Isabel finds Bonesy's presence comforting and she grieves for the old dog when he dies.
David Updike, *The Sounds of Summer*, 1993
    Homer mourns the death of his dog Sophocles, consoled by the sounds of summer which spark memories of his pet.
Charlotte Zolotow, *The Old Dog*, 1995
    The revised and newly illustrated story relates the memories which flood a young boy's thoughts after finding his pet dog dead.

654

JAMES HOWE
MELISSA SWEET, Illustrator

Pinky and Rex and the Bully

(New York: Atheneum Books for Young Readers, 1996)

Series: Ready to Read
Subject(s): Identity; Bullies; Friendship
Age range(s): Grades 1-3
Major character(s): Pinky, 2nd Grader, Child (boy); Rex, 2nd Grader, Child (girl); Kevin, Bully
Time period(s): 1990s
Locale(s): United States

Summary: Pinky loves the color pink and is good friends with a girl, two matters that Kevin makes fun of him about. Pinky does not know how to handle this so he goes to talk with his neighbor, Mrs. Morgan, where he also gets lemonade and cookies. Pinky thinks that maybe he should give up his name and even gives his stuffed animals to his little sister, but Mrs. Morgan tells him about giving up the art she loved as a child and her regret over it. Pinky then decides that he should stick with what he likes no matter what, and buys Mrs. Morgan some paints so that she can return to her earlier love. (40 pages)

Other books by the same author:
Pinky and Rex and the Double-Dad Weekend, 1995
Pinky and Rex Go to Camp, 1992
Scared Silly: A Halloween Treat, 1989
Bunnicula: A Rabbit Tale of Mystery, 1979

Other books you might like:
Kathy Caple, *The Wimp*, 1994
    Arnold the pig and his sister give two classmates a taste of their own medicine.
Amy Ehrlich, *Leo, Zack, and Emmie Together Again*, 1987
    The three friends enjoy second grade.

Karen Lynn Williams, *First Grade King*, 1992
   Making friends, learning to read and dealing with the class bully all make for a busy first grade.

655

JAMES HOWE
MELISSA SWEET, Illustrator

Pinky and Rex and the Double-Dad Weekend

(New York: Atheneum Books for Young Readers, 1995)

Series: Pinky and Rex
Subject(s): Fathers; Camps and Camping; Friendship
Age range(s): Grades 2-3
Major character(s): Rex, Child, Friend; Pinky, Child, Friend
Time period(s): 1990s (1995)
Locale(s): United States

Summary: The camping trip Pinky and Rex have been planning with their fathers finally happens. Unfortunately, a rain storm necessitates some modifications in their plans. The new tent is set up in a motel room and their hiking is through an underground cavern. They are able to find a variety of indoor activities to visit on the way home so the weekend turns out to be a pleasurable shared experience despite the uncooperative weather. (40 pages)

Where it's reviewed:
Booklist, April 15, 1995, page 1500
Horn Book Guide, Fall 1995, page 291
School Library Journal, August 1995, page 124

Other books by the same author:
Pinky and Rex Go to Camp, 1992
Pinky and Rex and the Spelling Bee, 1991
Pinky and Rex, 1990

Other books you might like:
Stan Berenstain, *The Berenstain Bears and Too Much Vacation*, 1989
   The Bear family's vacation in the Great Grizzly Mountains turns out to be a succession of unfortunate mishaps. Co-author Jan Berenstain.
Franz Brandenberg, *A Fun Weekend*, 1991
   The plans for a weekend in the country do not proceed as expected, but the family has fun anyway.
Marc Brown, *Arthur's Family Vacation*, 1993
   A week-long family vacation at the beach is spent in the motel room until Arthur's ingenuity finds activities which can be enjoyed despite the rain.

656

JAMES HOWE
MELISSA SWEET, Illustrator

Pinky and Rex and the New Baby

(New York: Atheneum, 1993)

Series: Pinky and Rex
Subject(s): Babies; Adoption; Friendship
Age range(s): Grades 2-4

Major character(s): Rex, Child, Sister; Pinky, Child, Friend; Matthew, Brother, Adoptee
Time period(s): 1990s (1993)
Locale(s): United States

Summary: Content as the only child, Rex feels threatened by the arrival of an adopted baby brother. To assure that her parents do not overlook her, she decides to become the perfect big sister and dotes over Matthew so much that she neglects her friend and playmate, Pinky. Fortunately, their friendship withstands the excitement of a new baby and life soon returns to normal. (40 pages)

Where it's reviewed:
Booklist, March 1, 1993, page 1230
Horn Book Guide, Fall 1993, page 287
Kirkus Reviews, March 15, 1993, page 372
School Library Journal, June 1993, page 76

Other books by the same author:
Pinky and Rex and the Double-Dad Weekend, 1995
Rabbit-Cadabra!, 1993
There's a Monster under My Bed, 1990

Other books you might like:
Kevin Henkes, *Julius, the Baby of the World*, 1990
   Lilly does not share her parents' high opinion of baby brother Julius until cousin Garland speaks up in a disparaging way.
Russell Hoban, *A Baby Sister for Frances*, 1976
   Frances is not sure how she will fit into the family now that baby Gloria is here.
Phoebe Koehler, *The Day We Met You*, 1990
   A family remembers with joy and celebration their adopted child's homecoming.
Patricia Lakin, *Don't Touch My Room*, 1988
   Slowly Aaron's unhappy feelings about his new brother change to more positive ones.

657

JAMES HOWE
ALAN DANIEL, Illustrator

Rabbit-Cadabra!

(New York: Morrow Junior Books, 1993)

Subject(s): Magicians; Animals; Vampires
Age range(s): Grades K-3
Major character(s): Bunnicula, Rabbit (pet), Magician (vampire); The Amazing Karlovsky, Magician; Harold, Dog (pet)
Time period(s): 1990s (1993)
Locale(s): Centerville

Summary: The Monroe family pets are alarmed to learn that a magic show being held at the local elementary school features Bunnicula, the family rabbit with the strange ability to turn carrots white. Convinced that they must save the audience from danger, Harold leads the pets to the school in order to stop The Amazing Karlovsky before the rabbit is out of the hat. What ensues is an unexpected disaster, hilarious to the audience, embarrassing to Harold and the Monroe family, but fun for all. (48 pages)

Where it's reviewed:
Booklist, April 15, 1993, page 1523
Horn Book Guide, Fall 1993, page 261
Library Talk, May 1994, page 43
Publishers Weekly, April 5, 1993, page 77
School Library Journal, April 1993, page 96

Other books by the same author:
Bunnicula Escapes! A Pop-up Adventure, 1994
Creepy Crawly Birthday, 1991
The Day the Teacher Went Bananas, 1984

Other books you might like:
Joanna Cole, *Mixed-Up Magic*, 1987
    Maggie and an overly confident elf find that a sense of humor helps their friendship develop.
Susan Meddaugh, *Martha Speaks*, 1992
    In an award-winning book, Martha is an ordinary family pet until a meal of alphabet soup enables her to talk and talk and talk!
Chris Van Allsburg, *The Garden of Abdul Gasazi*, 1979
    When Alan follows a wandering dog into the garden of a retired magician, he is in for a surprise.

658

DAKARI HRU
ANNA RICH, Illustrator

Joshua's Masai Mask

(New York: Lee & Low Books Inc., 1993)

Subject(s): African Americans; Magic; Self-Acceptance
Age range(s): Grades K-3
Major character(s): Joshua, Child (African American); Zambezi, Art Dealer (African American), Uncle
Time period(s): 1990s (1993)
Locale(s): United States

Summary: Joshua likes the kalimba given him by his Uncle Zambezi, but not his family's advice that he play it in the school talent show. His fears are confirmed at rehearsal when the other students laugh at his instrument. Seeking solace in his uncle's art gallery, Joshua also comes away with three gifts and an important piece of advice. With this support from his uncle, Joshua is able to appreciate his own gifts. This is the first picture book for both author and illustrator. (32 pages)

Where it's reviewed:
Booklist, April 1, 1993, page 1438
Essence, February 1994, page 118
MultiCultural Review, December 1993, page 88
Publishers Weekly, May 10, 1993, page 71
School Library Journal, March 1994, page 198

Other books you might like:
Virginia L. Kroll, *Masai and I*, 1992
    Inspired by a school lesson, a young girl contrasts her life in America with the life of the Masai in East Africa.
Angela Shelf Medearis, *Our People*, 1994
    Daddy's stories about the historical contributions of Africans, inspire a young girl to imagine the ways she might have participated and how she will in the future.

Belinda Rochelle, *When Jo Louis Won the Title*, 1994
    Grandfather reassures Jo Louis when she expresses a fear of being teased at her new school because of her name.

659

DEAN HUGHES

One-Man Team

(New York: Random, 1994)

Subject(s): Sports/Basketball; Interpersonal Relations; Schools
Age range(s): Grades 6-7
Major character(s): Aaron Reeves, Basketball Player, 8th Grader
Time period(s): 1990s
Locale(s): Greenwood, Oregon

Summary: The Greenwood Timber Wolves are winning their basketball season for the first time in many years, thanks to tall Aaron Reeves. Aaron is an outstanding player but, because his dad works in construction and the family moves so much, he's never learned to play as part of a team. The Timber Wolves resent his hotdogging and his coach calls him a ball hog. When Aaron realizes that his family is going to stay in the Greenwood area for a while, he finally gets a chance to become part of a team. (118 pages)

Where it's reviewed:
Booklist, January 15, 1995, page 928

Other books by the same author:
Re-Elect Nutty!, 1995
End of the Race, 1993
Nutty's Ghost, 1993
Family Pose, 1989

Other books you might like:
Russell Davis, *Some Town You Brought Me To*, 1969
    Without any status in his new school, Bud feels he has no choice but to quit the basketball team, even though the incident isn't his fault.
Gary Soto, *Taking Sides*, 1991
    After Lincoln moves from the barrio, he faces an uncomfortable game when he has to play against his old team.
Theodore Weesner, *Winning the City*, 1990
    Dale learns to fight back when he's replaced on his school's basketball tournament team by the sponsor's son.

660

DEAN HUGHES

Re-Elect Nutty!

(New York: Atheneum, 1995)

Subject(s): Politics; Schools
Age range(s): Grades 4-6
Major character(s): Frederick "Nutty" Nutsell, 6th Grader
Time period(s): 1990s
Locale(s): Warrensburg, Missouri

Summary: When Nutty decides to run again for student council president, he decides the only way to win is to tell the truth. Unfortunately, the truth is that he did a terrible job as president his first year, but promises to improve if he's re-elected. His attempt at honesty is admirable, but someone is posting flyers discrediting him. His attempts to discover the identity of the mysterious mud-slinger result in a series of mishaps in this sequel to *Nutty for President*.

Where it's reviewed:
Booklist, May 1, 1995, page 1573
Voice of Youth Advocates, August 1995, page 159
School Library Journal, June 1995, page 111
Horn Book Guide, Fall 1995, page 299

Other books by the same author:
One-Man Team, 1994
End of the Race, 1993
Nutty's Ghost, 1993

Other books you might like:
Jonah Kalb, *Kids' Candidate*, 1975
    Running for school board, Barnaby advocates no homework and better food in the school cafeterias.
Stephen Mooser, *It's a Weird, Weird School*, 1989
    When Carrie is elected school board president at their city's Youth Day activities, she immediately appoints her friend Jamie as school principal.
Suzanne Weyn, *The Makeover Campaign*, 1990
    Rissa and Sara want Marsha to win the school presidential election, so they de-glamorize her to make her look more efficient.

661

DEAN HUGHES

Team Picture

(New York: Atheneum, 1996)

Subject(s): Foster Homes; Sports/Baseball
Age range(s): Grades 5-8
Major character(s): David, 13-Year-Old (plays pony league baseball), Foster Child; Paul, Foster Parent; Melissa, Student—College, Friend (acts as mother)
Time period(s): 1990s
Locale(s): United States

Summary: David is concerned because Paul seems to be having difficulty again with his drinking. He also cannot seem to make friends with the other players on his baseball team because he thinks he is better than they are and even tells them so. Melissa has returned and is going to school. David would really like her to marry Paul and become his foster mother but, though she supports them as much as she can, she has other plans. Both David and Paul reach a turning point at about the same time when Paul realizes that he must stop his drinking and David sees that being friends with his teammates is as important as treating them as his inferiors. (155 pages)

Where it's reviewed:
Booklist, November 15, 1996, page 584
School Library Journal, November 1996, page 107

Other books by the same author:
Nutty's Ghost, 1993
Back Up Goalie, 1992
Family Pose, 1989 (prequel to *Team Picture*)

Other books you might like:
Betsy Byars, *The Pinballs*, 1977
    Three misfits in a foster home band together to solve their problems.
Judy K. Morris, *Nightwalkers*, 1996
    A young boy helps an elephant find its family at the same time he is finding his own foster father.
Gail Radley, *The Golden Days*, 1991
    Cory decides to run away because he is sure that his new foster family does not really want him.
Jean Thesman, *When the Road Ends*, 1992
    Three foster children are abandoned by their caretaker and must survive alone with an older woman who is trying to survive an accident.

662

DEAN HUGHES

The Trophy

(New York: Alfred A. Knopf, 1994)

Subject(s): Sports/Basketball; Fathers and Sons; Alcoholism
Age range(s): Grades 4-6
Major character(s): Danny Williams, 10-Year-Old, Child of an Alcoholic; Alan Call, Basketball Player, Friend (Danny's); Evan Williams, Father, Alcoholic
Time period(s): 1990s (1994)
Locale(s): Ogden, Utah

Summary: Danny pressures himself to improve his basketball game in order to please his father, thinking that somehow his success on the courts will make his father stop drinking. As Danny begins to understand how his father's drinking is affecting the family, he seeks help from Alan's father, a Mormon bishop. (135 pages)

Where it's reviewed:
Booklist, February 15, 1995, page 1083
Horn Book Guide, Spring 1995, page 78
Kirkus Reviews, December 15, 1994, page 1565
Library Talk, March 1995, page 53
School Library Journal, December 1994, page 109

Other books by the same author:
One-Man Team, 1994
Quick Moves, 1993
Nutty Can't Miss, 1987

Other books you might like:
Matt Christopher, *Red-Hot Hightops*, 1987
    Wearing the red sneakers which she's found, Kelly is able to overcome her fear of playing in front of a crowd.
Ilene Cooper, *Choosing Sides*, 1990
    When he loses interest in playing for the school team and wants to drop out, Jonathan worries that his father will consider him a quitter.
Barthe DeClements, *No Place for Me*, 1987
    With her mom in treatment for alcoholism, Copper is sent from one relative to another to live, learning that she must stand up for herself.
David Halecroft, *Benched!*, 1992
    Woody and Bannister are so focussed on making the school basketball team that they neglect their schoolwork.

June Rae Wood, *A Share of Freedom*, 1994
     Freedom struggles to keep her family together while her mother is treated for her alcoholism.

663

IRENE HUNT

Up a Road Slowly

(Chicago: Follett Publishing Co., 1966)

Subject(s): Family Life; Historical
Age range(s): Grades 5-7
Major character(s): Julie Trelling, Sister (younger sister to Chris); Christopher ''Chris'' Trelling, Brother (older brother to Julie); Aunt Cordelia Bishop, Teacher, Spinster
Time period(s): Indeterminate Past
Locale(s): United States

Summary: When Julie is seven, her mother dies and she and her older brother Christopher are sent to live with their maiden aunt. After the first year, Christopher is sent to boarding school. Aunt Cordelia is both her guardian and her school teacher and Julie spends the next ten years living on the farm with her. During that time, Julie matures from a somewhat spoiled young girl into a caring individual who leaves Aunt Cordelia's filled with a strong sense of who she is. (192 pages)

Awards the book has won:
Newbery Medal, 1967

Other books by the same author:
Everlasting Hills, 1985
William, 1977
Across Five Aprils, 1964

Other books you might like:
Iris Rosofsky, *My Aunt Ruth*, 1991
     Patty loves her Aunt Ruth and suffers with her as she first loses her legs to diabetes and then her husband through divorce.
Ferrol Sams, *Runs with the Horsemen*, 1984
     Family life on a cotton farm during the Depression is humorously narrated by Porter T. Osbourne, who believes he is ''raised right.''
Rona S. Zable, *Landing on Marvin Gardens*, 1989
     Forced to live with Aunt Rose, Katie is embarrassed by this well-meaning but bossy woman.

664

MOLLIE HUNTER
DONNA DIAMOND, Illustrator

Day of the Unicorn

(New York: HarperCollins Publishers, 1994)

Series: Knight of the Golden Plain Story
Subject(s): Knights and Knighthood; Unicorns; Magic
Age range(s): Grades 2-4
Major character(s): Sir Dauntless, Knight; Lady Dorabella, Noblewoman, Heroine; Sir Maladroit, Knight, Uncle (Dorabella's)
Time period(s): Indeterminate Past
Locale(s): Crag Castle, Fictional Country

Summary: Summoned by Lady Dorabella, Sir Dauntless hastens to his one true love and learns that she and her parents are distressed by her uncle's intention to use magic to cure his toothache. Since everything Sir Maladroit does seems to create a bigger problem than the one he thinks he is solving, Sir Dauntless attempts, unsuccessfully, to dissuade him from his plan. When Sir Maladroit recites the magic words, his pain is transferred to a tapestry unicorn who comes alive in torment and races away. In pursuit of the unicorn, Sir Dauntless is forced to summon Lady Dorabella as only a maiden can perform the act of bravery needed to confront the animal. (59 pages)

Where it's reviewed:
Booklist, September 1, 1994, page 41
Horn Book Guide, Fall 1994, page 301
Kirkus Reviews, June 15, 1994, page 846
Library Talk, November 1994, page 49
School Library Journal, November 1994, page 104

Other books by the same author:
The Mermaid Summer, 1988
The Three-Day Enchantment, 1985
The Knight of the Golden Plain, 1983

Other books you might like:
Michael Morpurgo, *Arthur, High King of Britain*, 1994
     Upon awakening from a long subterranean sleep, Arthur Pendragon shares exciting stories of his past with the boy who discovers him.
Mary Pope Osborne, *The Knight at Dawn*, 1993
     Using a magic tree house, eight-year-old Jack and his younger sister travel back in time to the Middle Ages.
Jon Scieszka, *Knights of the Kitchen Table*, 1991
     The Time Warp Trio rely on their magic book for round-trip transportation to a land of dragons, wizards and the Knights of the Round Table.

665

BELINDA HURMENCE

Dixie in the Big Pasture

(New York: Clarion, 1994)

Subject(s): Frontier and Pioneer Life; Indians of North America
Age range(s): Grades 6-8
Major character(s): Dixie Watson, 12-Year-Old, 7th Grader; John Three Sixteen, Indian (Kiowa, from Bible verse)
Time period(s): 1900s (1907-1908)
Locale(s): Chattanooga, Tennessee; Fairview Township, Oklahoma

Summary: This book is based on the author's aunt's childhood experiences when Dixie moves to the Oklahoma territory, referred to as the Big Pasture by the resident Kiowa Indians, from city life in Tennessee. After her dog disappears, Dixie's parents buy her a pony from the neighboring Kiowa family, but the oldest son, John Three Sixteen, feels she's been sold his horse and resents Dixie. Gradually Dixie and John become friends, though her mother always disapproves of their friendship. This nine-month slice reveals the struggle of life on the frontier, complete with grass fires, displacement of the Native Americans and hard, lonely work. (169 pages)

Where it's reviewed:
Book Report, November 1994, page 44
School Library Journal, May 1994, page 114
Booklist, April 15, 1994, page 1526
Kirkus Reviews, April 15, 1994, page 558
Horn Book Guide, Fall 1994, page 311

Other books by the same author:
Nightwalker, 1988
Tancy, 1984
A Girl Called Boy, 1982
Tough Tiffany, 1980

Other books you might like:
Kristiana Gregory, *The Legend of Jimmy Spoon*, 1990
   Two Shoshone boys offer Jimmy a horse to come visit their camp; when he accepts, he doesn't realize his stay will be permanent.
Laurie Lawlor, *Addie's Long Summer*, 1992
   Addie's unhappy that her cousins will be spending the summer with her family in their Dakota sod house, until she learns the reason for their visit.
Bill Wallace, *Buffalo Gal*, 1992
   Dragged to Texas by her mother, a member of the American Bison Society, debutante Amanda is not ready for the rigors of Western life.

666

JOHANNA HURWITZ
GAIL OWENS, Illustrator

Down and Up Fall

(New York: Morrow, 1996)

Subject(s): Friendship; Schools; Jealousy
Age range(s): Grades 3-6
Major character(s): Bolivia Raab, 6th Grader; Rory Dunn, 6th Grader; Derek Curry, 6th Grader
Time period(s): 1990s
Locale(s): Woodside, New Jersey

Summary: Bolivia's parents are off on an archaeological dig so she is spending the school year with her aunt and uncle and her good friends. The three of them begin middle school where Bolivia quickly makes new friends with DeeDee and Aldo Sossi. Derek and Rory are not at all pleased with this and jealously refuse to have anything to do with Bolivia and her new friends. It is only when the children form a nature club with a leaking rainforest, that things begin to work out again and they are all able to spend some of the holidays together. Bolivia keeps her parents informed of her activities with letters and post cards. (165 pages)

Where it's reviewed:
Bulletin of the Center for Children's Books, September 1996, page 16
School Library Journal, September 1996, page 202
Booklist, October 1, 1996, page 424

Other books by the same author:
School Spirit, 1994
The Up & Down Spring, 1993

Ali Baba Bernstein, Lost and Found, 1992
Aldo Peanut Butter, 1990

Other books you might like:
Mary Anderson, *Who Says Nobody's Perfect?*, 1987
   Ingvild arrives in New York as an exchange student but her hostess becomes jealous of her popularity at school.
Betsy Haynes, *Taffy Sinclair, Queen of the Soaps*, 1985
   Taffy wins a part on a soap opera and Jana's jealousy becomes so overpowering that she mixes some fantasy with real life.
Sheila Hayes, *You've Been Away All Summer*, 1986
   Fran returns after being away all summer only to find that Sarah has a new friend.
Constance Hiser, *Sixth-Grade Star*, 1992
   Jill is jealous of the attention her mother pays to her younger sister.
Lynn Hall, *Dagmar Schultz and the Green-Eyed Monster*, 1991
   Dagmar's family helps her when she becomes consumed with jealousy.

667

JOHANNA HURWITZ
MARK GRAHAM, Illustrator

A Llama in the Family

(New York: Morrow Junior Books, 1994)

Subject(s): Animals/Llamas; Family Life; Business Enterprises
Age range(s): Grades 3-4
Major character(s): Adam Fine, 10-Year-Old, Brother (April's); April Fine, 3-Year-Old, Sister (younger); Ethan Allen, Llama
Time period(s): 1990s (1994)
Locale(s): Vermont (rural area)

Summary: When Adam learns there's a surprise for him, he's expecting the mountain bike he's been wanting for a long time. Instead, he is truly surprised when April leads him to a llama which his mother has purchased in order to begin a tourist atraction offering llama treks thorugh the Vermont mountains with his mother as guide and preparer of the picnic lunch. The business begins slowly, but soon is doing so well that Adam thinks another llama may be more important than a bicycle. (98 pages)

Where it's reviewed:
Booklist, September 1, 1994, page 41
Bulletin of the Center for Children's Books, September 1994, page 15
Horn Book Guide, Spring 1995, page 78
Publishers Weekly, August 1, 1994, page 80
School Library Journal, September 1994, page 218

Other books by the same author:
Roz and Ozzie, 1992
The Cold and Hot Winter, 1988
Aldo Applesauce, 1979

Other books you might like:
Ann Nolan Clark, *Secret of the Andes*, 1952
   The Newbery Medal winner tells of a young Inca boy who

ponders his future while tending a llama herd high in the Peruvian mountains.

Susan Clymer, *Llama Pajamas*, 1996
Sarah and her parents go on a camping vacation in Colorado using llamas as pack animals.

Laura Ingalls Wilder, *Farmer Boy*, 1933
Growing up on a farm in upstate New York, Almanzo tells of a loving family life with siblings, parents, and lots of hard work.

668

JOHANNA HURWITZ
LILLIAN HOBAN, Illustrator

Make Room for Elisa
(New York: Morrow Junior Books, 1993)

Subject(s): Brothers and Sisters; Family Life; Apartments
Age range(s): Grades 1-3
Major character(s): Elisa Michaels, 5-Year-Old, Sister; Russell Michaels, 9-Year-Old, Brother
Time period(s): 1990s (1993)
Locale(s): New York

Summary: The year that Elisa turns five is one of surprises. Not only is she looking forward to beginning kindergarten wearing her new glasses, but her parents announce that the family is moving to another apartment in their building in order to have more room for the new baby soon to join the family. Russell is excited to have a room of his own, but Elisa needs some time to become comfortable sleeping alone. By the time Marshall is born, the family is well-settled in their new home. (82 pages)

Where it's reviewed:
Booklist, August 1993, page 2062
Horn Book, January 1994, page 94
Library Talk, January 1994, page 43
Reading Teacher, September 1994, page 71
School Library Journal, November 1993, page 84

Other books by the same author:
Russell and Elisa, 1989
Russell Rides Again, 1985
Rip-Roaring Russell, 1983

Other books you might like:
Beverly Cleary, *Ramona the Brave*, 1975
Ramona faces the privileges and perils of growing up as she enters first grade and adjusts to having a room of her own.

Maud Hart Lovelace, *Betsy and Tacy*, 1940
In the first book of a series, Betsy and Tacy, neighbors and best friends, share adventures at school and at home.

Colleen O'Shaughnessy McKenna, *Too Many Murphys*, 1988
Tired of her three pestering, younger siblings, Collette wishes to be an only child and then fears that her wish might come true.

Bonnie Pryor, *Jumping Jenny*, 1992
An energetic five-year-old experiences many of the same anxieties as others her age.

669

JOHANNA HURWITZ
JERRY PINKNEY, Illustrator

New Shoes for Silvia
(New York: Morrow Junior Books, 1993)

Subject(s): Gifts; Aunts and Uncles; Growing Up
Age range(s): Grades K-2
Major character(s): Silvia, Child
Time period(s): 1990s (1993)
Locale(s): South America

Summary: From an aunt in America, Silvia's family receives a package. For Silvia the most wonderful item in the gift box is her new pair of red shoes. While she waits to grow into them, the shoes become beds for her dolls, train cars and the repository for treasured shells and pebbles. Finally the day comes when the shoes fit perfectly and Silvia wears them on a walk to town where she hopes to find another package—containing blue shoes. (32 pages)

Where it's reviewed:
Booklist, October 15, 1993, page 452
Horn Book, November 1993, page 734
Kirkus Reviews, August 15, 1993, page 1074
Publishers Weekly, August 9, 1993, page 478
School Library Journal, October 1993, page 101

Other books by the same author:
Make Room for Elisa, 1993
New Neighbors for Nora, 1991
Busybody Nora, 1982

Other books you might like:
Marilee Robin Burton, *My Best Shoes*, 1994
A rhyming celebration of shoes is complemented by illustrations of joyous children and their activities.

Denise Lewis Patrick, *Red Dancing Shoes*, 1993
Grandma's gift of red shoes sets her grandaughter's feet to dancing around the neighborhood.

Amanda Vesey, *Hector's New Sneakers*, 1993
The sneakers Hector receives for his birthday teach him to adjust his expectations and accept something that is a little different.

670

JOHANNA HURWITZ
EILEEN MCKEATING, Illustrator

Ozzie on His Own
(New York: Morrow Junior Books, 1995)

Subject(s): Fathers and Sons; Family Life; Death
Age range(s): Grades 3-4
Major character(s): Ozzie Sims, 8-Year-Old; Ryan Richards, 2nd Grader; Candy Henderson, 9-Year-Old
Time period(s): 1990s (1995)
Locale(s): United States

Summary: A long, lonely, boring summer looms ahead for Ozzie without his vacationing best friend until he converts an old chicken coop in a neighbor's backyard into a clubhouse and makes three friends to share it with him. When his father has a heart attack the support of Ryan and Candy help him cope with his fears of his parents' possible deaths. (115 pages)

Where it's reviewed:
Book World, May 7, 1995, page 16
Booklist, March 1, 1995, page 1242
Horn Book, July 1995, page 484
Library Talk, May 1995, page 42
School Library Journal, June 1995, page 111

Other books by the same author:
Roz and Ozzie, 1992
Russell and Elisa, 1989
Aldo Ice Cream, 1981

Other books you might like:
Ann Cameron, *Julian's Glorious Summer*, 1987
    Rather than admit his fear, Julian makes excuses when his friend asks him to try riding her new bicycle, thus prompting his father to teach him a lesson in honesty.
Colby Rodowsky, *Jenny and the Grand Old Great-Aunts*, 1992
    Visiting her great aunts seems boring to Jenny until she discovers the attic in their old home.
Sally Wittman, *Stepbrother Sabotage*, 1990
    The discovery that they share the same problem finally unites warring stepbrothers and provides the basis for a friendship.

671

JOHANNA HURWITZ
KAREN DUGAN, Illustrator

School Spirit
(New York: Morrow Junior Books, 1994)

Subject(s): School Spirit; Student Protests; Problem Solving
Age range(s): Grades 3-5
Major character(s): Julio Sanchez, 5th Grader, Activist; Mr. Flores, Teacher; Cricket Kaufman, 5th Grader
Time period(s): 1990s (1994)
Locale(s): United States

Summary: When Julio, the class president, learns the school board is planning to close Edison-Armstrong Elementary School he enlists the help of his vice president Cricket to rally other students in an effort to keep the building open. With guidance from Mr. Flores and careful planning, a well-orchestrated protest convinces the School Board to change its plans and Edison-Armstrong does not close. (144 pages)

Where it's reviewed:
Booklist, May 1, 1994, page 1601
Horn Book, July 1994, page 478
Instructor, September 1994, page 104
Kirkus Reviews, May 1, 1994, page 631
School Library Journal, May 1994, page 114

Other books by the same author:
Class President, 1990
The Cold and Hot Winter, 1988
DeDe Takes Charge!, 1984

Other books you might like:
Frank Asch, *Hands Around Lincoln School*, 1994
    Sixth grader Lindsay's techniques for heightening awareness of Save the Earth Club jeopardize her friendship with Amy.
Dean Hughes, *Re-Elect Nutty!*, 1995
    Nutty runs for his second term as student council president.
Rebecca C. Jones, *Germy in Charge*, 1993
    When Germy is elected the sixth grade representative to the School Board he finds the job more complicated and wields less power than he expected.
Gary Soto, *Off and Running*, 1996
    Friends Rudy and Alex, the class clowns of fifth grade, are in a tough election race against Miata and her friend Ana.

672

JOHANNA HURWITZ
GAIL OWENS, Illustrator

The Up & Down Spring
(New York: Morrow Junior Books, 1993)

Subject(s): Friendship; Fear; Vacations
Age range(s): Grades 2-4
Major character(s): Bolivia Raab, 11-Year-Old, Friend; Rory Dunn, 11-Year-Old (from New Jersey), Friend; Derek Curry, 10-Year-Old (almost 11), Friend
Time period(s): 1990s (1993)
Locale(s): Ithaca, New York

Summary: In this third adventure, Rory and Derek travel by bus from New Jersey to Bolivia's home during vacation. Determined to make this reunion visit absolutely perfect, Bolivia plans a rigid, hectic schedule and then must deal with unexpected events that effect her plans. All three friends learn more about themselves and their friendship as they face fears and new experiences. (105 pages)

Where it's reviewed:
Booklist, February 15, 1993, page 1060
Horn Book Guide, Fall 1993, page 299
Kirkus Reviews, May 15, 1993, page 662
Publishers Weekly, May 31, 1993, page 55
School Library Journal, July 1993, page 61

Other books by the same author:
School Spirit, 1994
The Cold and Hot Winter, 1988
The Hot and Cold Summer, 1984

Other books you might like:
Pat Brisson, *Your Best Friend, Kate*, 1989
    Kate's family is travelling and Kate is sending friend Lucy letters and post cards about the trip.
Jamie Gilson, *Sticks and Stones and Skeleton Bones*, 1991
    Hobie and Nick find that fifth grade challenges, but does not end, their friendship.
Colby Rodowsky, *Dog Days*, 1990
    Rosie Rigg's summer vacation looks pretty hopeless until a famous dog and his owner move in next door.

673

PAT HUTCHINS, Author/Illustrator

Little Pink Pig

(New York: Greenwillow Books, 1994)

Subject(s): Animals/Pigs; Animals; Bedtime
Age range(s): Grades K-1
Major character(s): Little Pink Pig, Pig
Time period(s): 1990s (1994)
Locale(s): United States (farmyard)

Summary: Little Pink Pig's mother is wandering the farmyard in one direction looking for her offspring and asking each of the animals she meets to help her search. Meanwhile, behind the growing group of searchers and oblivious to the commotion he's causing is curious Little Pink Pig, tipping over apple barrels, falling into a cart of hay, or creating another problem that blocks the sound of his voice calling ''Wait for me!'' (32 pages)

Where it's reviewed:
Booklist, April 1, 1994, page 1460
Horn Book, May 1994, page 315
Kirkus Reviews, May 1, 1994, page 631
Publishers Weekly, March 21, 1994, page 70
School Library Journal, May 1994, page 96

Awards the book has won:
International Reading Association Children's Choice, 1995

Other books by the same author:
Three-Star Billy, 1994
Good-Night, Owl!, 1972
Rosie's Walk, 1968

Other books you might like:
Denise Fleming, *Barnyard Banter*, 1994
 The rhythmic banter of barnyard animals is heard as all search for goose who, of course, announces her presence at the book's conclusion.
Arthur Geisert, *Oink, Oink*, 1993
 Through the repetition of one word the story of eight piglets who wander away from their sleeping mother is told.
Colin McNaughton, *Suddenly!*, 1994
 Cheerful, but absent-minded Preston the pig follows a circuitous route home from school, unaware that a wolf is on his trail.
Susan Meddaugh, *Hog-Eye*, 1995
 A literate pig uses her reading ability to outwit a wolf intent on making her into his next meal.
Mary Wormell, *Hilda Hen's Happy Birthday*, 1995
 Hilda wanders the farmyard finding what she assumes, incorrectly, to be birthday treats left for her enjoyment.

674

JOANNE HYPPOLITE
COLIN BOOTMAN, Illustrator

Seth and Samona

(New York: Delacorte Press, 1995)

Subject(s): Friendship; Family Life; Multicultural
Age range(s): Grades 4-5
Major character(s): Seth Michelin, 5th Grader (Haitian-American), Friend (Samona's); Samona Gemini, 5th Grader (African-American), Friend (Seth's)
Time period(s): 1990s (1995)
Locale(s): Boston, Massachusetts

Summary: In the author's first novel, quiet Seth finds himself drawn into a friendship with exuberant, off-beat Samona. Because Samona is quiet when near his family, they encourage the friendship not realizing that Samona's odd-ball schemes all seem to end with Seth getting into trouble. Initially wary of Samona's company, as the two children grow and change, Seth comes to realize just how much he values the friendship with this unusual girl. (121 pages)

Where it's reviewed:
Booklist, May 1, 1995, page 1573
Children's Book Review Service, June 1995, page 130
Library Talk, May 1995, page 44
Publishers Weekly, June 19, 1995, page 60
School Library Journal, May 1995, page 108

Awards the book has won:
Marguerite de Angeli Prize, 1995

Other books you might like:
Carol Gorman, *The Miraculous Makeover of Lizard Flanagan*, 1994
 Tomboy Lizard enters middle school observing the changes in her friends and wondering about her own transition from kid to girl.
Peg Kehret, *The Richest Kids in Town*, 1994
 Peter's money-making schemes all seem to lead to more problems, but friend Wyoming never gives up on him or their friendship.
Angela Shelf Medearis, *The Adventures of Sugar and Junior*, 1995
 When a new girl moves into Junior's apartment building, he is relieved to have a friend his age.
Eileen Spinelli, *Lizzie Logan Wears Purple Sunglasses*, 1995
 On moving-in day, off-beat Lizzie Logan greets Heather and her family with a store-bought pie and an offer of friendship.

I

SATOMI ICHIKAWA, Author/Illustrator

Nora's Surprise
(New York: Philomel Books, 1994)

Subject(s): Animals/Sheep; Behavior
Age range(s): Grades K-1
Major character(s): Nora, Child; Benjy, Sheep
Time period(s): 1990s (1992)
Locale(s): Fictional Country

Summary: Nora is disappointed to arrive at an eagerly anticipated tea party to find the host geese's house less than she
expected and Benjy, a fat and hungry party guest who downs
not only the food but also the flower centerpiece provided by
Nora. Initially annoyed with Benjy, Nora follows when he is
called home and discovers that Benjy is no longer fat or fluffy;
now, she feels more forgiving. Translated from the original
1992 publication in Japanese. (32 pages)

Where it's reviewed:
Booklist, March 15, 1994, page 1373
Five Owls, September 1994, page 12
Horn Book Guide, Fall 1994, page 276
School Library Journal, May 1994, page 96

Other books by the same author:
Fickle Barbara, 1993
Nora's Roses, 1993
Nora's Duck, 1991

Other books you might like:
Elsa Beskow, *Pelle's New Suit*, 1929
    Pelle observes the progress of his new suit from the fleece
    being shorn to the final tailoring.
Mick Inkpen, *If I Had a Sheep*, 1988
    In her imagination, a young girl plans all that she would do
    with a sheep for a pet.
Kim Lewis, *Emma's Lamb*, 1991
    Emma comforts a lost lamb and helps to locate the mother.

Ragnhild Scamell, *Three Bags Full*, 1993
    Kindly Millie gives away so much of her fleece that her
    owner must knit a sweater to warm her through the winter.
Barbara Brooks Wallace, *Argyle*, 1987
    Perhaps it's something the sheep ate; the multi-colored
    fleece which he grows creates great changes on the farm.

MIKO IMAI, Author/Illustrator

Lilly's Secret
(Cambridge, MA: Candlewick Press, 1994)

Subject(s): Animals/Cats; Friendship; Self-Acceptance
Age range(s): Grades K-1
Major character(s): Lilly, Cat, Friend; Joey, Cat, Friend
    (Lilly's); Coco, Cat, Neighbor
Time period(s): 1990s (1994)
Locale(s): Fictional Country

Summary: When Coco stops by to share tea and biscuits with
Lilly, she comments on Lilly's "weird" paws, so an
embarassed Lilly tries to find a way to cover them. When Joey
comes by later for a walk, Lilly refuses to hold his paw and
runs away when she sees Coco. Joey—with a crooked tail—
finds Lilly and expresses an appreciation for her unique paws.
(32 pages)

Where it's reviewed:
Booklist, December 15, 1994, page 758
Five Owls, January 1995, page 59
Horn Book Guide, Spring 1995, page 41
Kirkus Reviews, December 15, 1994, page 1565
Publishers Weekly, November 28, 1994, page 60

Other books by the same author:
Sebastian's Trumpet, 1995
Little Lumpty, 1994

Other books you might like:
Linda Jennings, *Tom's Tail*, 1995
    Tom considers his tail to be too curly, but his attempts to

straighten it create problems so he decides to accept it the way it is.

Holly Keller, *Horace*, 1991

Horace, sensitive to the difference in his spotted appearance and his parents' stripes, learns that belonging to a family is based on feeling, not appearance.

Eve Titus, *The Kitten Who Couldn't Purr*, 1991

Trying to find someone to teach him how to purr thank you, Jonathan meets animals who make other sounds and a puppy who tells him many ways to say thank you.

677

HADLEY IRWIN

Jim-Dandy

(New York: Margaret K. McElderry Books, 1994)

Subject(s): Frontier and Pioneer Life; Animals/Horses; Indians of North America

Age range(s): Grades 6-8

Major character(s): Caleb, 13-Year-Old; Dancy, Horse; Colonel George Armstrong Custer, Historical Figure, Military Personnel

Time period(s): 1870s

Locale(s): Kansas (homestead between Fort Hays and Fort Larned); Kansas (Fort Hays)

Summary: For young Caleb, life on the frontier goes beyond harshness; he loses his mother and is left with his taciturn stepfather who thinks only of work. When a foal is born and Caleb is asked to raise Dandy, his spirits soar at the thought of finally having a companion. Over the summer Caleb secretly trains the foal for riding, much against his stepfather's wishes. That fall his stepfather, faced with mounting debts, sells Dandy to General Custer. Caleb runs away to continue caring for "his" horse, but becomes disillusioned when involved in the bloody battles against the Indians whom he regards as his friends. The story is based on a real horse named Dandy who was one of Custer's favorite mounts. (135 pages)

Where it's reviewed:
Publishers Weekly, March 21, 1994, page 73
Booklist, April 15, 1994, page 1534
School Library Journal, May 1994, page 116
Horn Book, July 1994, page 452
New Advocate, March 21, 1994, page 116

Other books by the same author:
The Original Freddie Ackerman, 1992
Can't Hear You Listening, 1990
I Be Somebody, 1984

Other books you might like:
Avi, *The Barn*, 1994

After they lose their father, three motherless children struggle to survive on their Oregon farm in the 1850s.

Kristiana Gregory, *The Legend of Jimmy Spoon*, 1990

Two Shoshone boys offer Jimmy a horse to come visit their camp; when he accepts, he doesn't realize his stay will be permanent.

Marya Smith, *Winter-Broken*, 1990

When Mr. Everley lets Dawn take care of his horse, it's the

first time an adult has ever been nice to her; the horse helps her forget her home life.

678

ANNE ISAACS
PAUL O. ZELINSKY, Illustrator

Swamp Angel

(New York: Dutton Children's Books, 1994)

Subject(s): Folk Tales; Frontier and Pioneer Life; Animals/Bears

Age range(s): Grades K-3

Major character(s): Angelica "Swamp Angel" Longrider, Frontierswoman

Time period(s): 19th century (1815-1835)

Locale(s): Tennessee

Summary: An original tall tale by a first-time author describes young Angelica who was "scarcely taller than her mother" at birth and two years old before she completed her first log cabin. At the age of 12 she earned the nickname Swamp Angel by rescuing a wagon train stuck in Dejection Swamp. Her greatest claim to fame comes from her 5-day struggle to vanquish an enormous bear known as Thundering Tarnation. (40 pages)

Where it's reviewed:
Booklist, October 15, 1994, page 424
Horn Book, March 1995, page 184
Library Talk, January 1995, page 36
Publishers Weekly, October 3, 1994, page 69
School Library Journal, December 1994, page 76

Awards the book has won:
Caldecott Honor Book, 1995
School Library Journal Best Books, 1994

Other books you might like:
David F. Birchman, *The Raggly, Scraggly, No-Soap, No-Scrub Girl*, 1995

A hungry, dirty child whirls into a family's home at dinner time, downing most of the food, and leaving behind dust, grease and a permanent bathtub ring.

Steven Kellogg, *Paul Bunyan, A Tall Tale*, 1984

Paul Bunyan, a lumberjack of extraordinary size and strength, leads a life of unusual adventures.

Steven Kellogg, *Sally Ann Thunder Ann Whirlwind Crockett: A Tall Tale*, 1995

In a retelling of a tall tale, Sally Ann departs for the frontier on her eighth birthday where she continues her larger than life exploits and marries Davy Crockett.

Julius Lester, *John Henry*, 1994

The Caldecott Honor Book retells the tradtional tale of John Henry, a legendary steel-driving man.

679

RACHEL ISADORA, Author/Illustrator

Lili at Ballet

(New York: G. P. Putnam's Sons, 1993)

Subject(s): Ballet; Dancing

Age range(s): Grades K-3
Major character(s): Lili, Child, Dancer (student of ballet)
Time period(s): 1990s (1993)
Locale(s): New York, New York

Summary: Four afternoons a week Lili attends ballet classes hoping to achieve her dream of becoming a ballerina. Lili's story concludes as her dream begins to be realized when she is chosen to dance the role of the Flower Fairy. The illustrations and captions give factual information about ballet. (32 pages)

Where it's reviewed:
Booklist, February 1, 1993, page 982
Horn Book, May 1993, page 318
Language Arts, January 1994, page 58
Reading Teacher, May 1994, page 649
School Library Journal, March 1993, page 179

Other books by the same author:
Firebird, 1994
Swan Lake, 1991
My Ballet Class, 1980

Other books you might like:
Lucy Dickens, *Dancing Class*, 1992
    A dance class gives children the chance to move like a bird.
Patricia Lee Gauch, *Dance, Tanya*, 1989
    Toddler Tanya imitates her older sister's performance.
Jane O'Connor, *Nina, Nina Ballerina*, 1993
    Prior to her dance performance, Nina worries that her mom will not recognize her on stage.

680

RACHEL ISADORA, Author/Illustrator

Lili on Stage

(New York: G. P, Putnam's Sons, 1995)

Subject(s): Ballet; Dancing

Age range(s): Grades K-3
Major character(s): Lili, Child, Dancer
Time period(s): 1990s (1995)
Locale(s): United States

Summary: As Lili waits nervously for the curtain to go up, she thinks over the months of practice and the last minute instructions from the ballet mistress. Tonight she will perform in the party scene of *The Nutcracker* for the first time, but already she knows the role she wants in next year's performance. (32 pages)

Where it's reviewed:
Booklist, November 15, 1995, page 564
Dance, December 1995, page 57
Horn Book, January 1996, page 98
Kirkus Reviews, October 1, 1995, page 1429
School Library Journal, December 1995, page 81

Other books by the same author:
Lili on Stage, 1993
Swan Lake, 1991
My Ballet Class, 1980

Other books you might like:
Eve Bunting, *The Day Before Christmas*, 1992
    Allie attends a Christmas Eve performance of *The Nutcracker* with her grandfather.
Lucy Dickens, *Dancing Class*, 1992
    Five young aspiring dancers have the opportunity to perform as birds during class.
Jane O'Connor, *Nina, Nina Ballerina*, 1993
    Nina worries that she will be lost in the flock of butterflies on stage, but an unfortunate accident helps her to stand out in the crowd.

J

681

ELLEN JACKSON
KEVIN O'MALLEY, Illustrator

Cinder Edna

(New York: Lothrop, Lee & Shepard Books, 1994)

Subject(s): Fairy Tale; Humor; Resourcefulness
Age range(s): Grades K-3
Major character(s): Cinderella, Stepdaughter; Cinder Edna, Stepdaughter; Rupert, Royalty (Prince)
Time period(s): 1960s
Locale(s): United States (suburbia)

Summary: Next-door neighbors, Cinderella and Cinder Edna both have wicked stepmothers and stepsisters who expect them to do all the work, but there the similarity between the two stops. Cinderella is vain and helpless, depending on a fairy godmother to get her to the ball. Cinder Edna is practical and resourceful, riding the bus to the ball in a dress she's purchased on layaway. Fortunately, the king has two sons, a vain, self-absorbed one for Cinderella and dorky Rupert, a recycler and caretaker of orphaned kittens. The story concludes with a double wedding and at least one couple who surely will live ''happily ever after.'' (32 pages)

Where it's reviewed:
Booklist, March 15, 1994, page 1373
Children's Book Review Service, May 1994, page 114
Kirkus Reviews, April 1, 1994, page 480
Publishers Weekly, February 14, 1994, page 88
School Library Journal, April 1994, page 107

Other books by the same author:
The Winter Solstice, 1994
The Tree of Life: The Wonders of Evolution, 1993
Ants Can't Dance, 1991

Other books you might like:
Marcia Brown, *Cinderella, or, The Little Glass Slipper*, 1954
One of the many illustrated retellings of Charles Perrault's classic tale of the lonely girl with the wicked stepmother is a Caldecott Medal Winner.

Valerie Scho Carey, *Tsugele's Broom*, 1993
An award-winning story of an industrious, resourceful young woman and her hard-working broom/groom.
Janet Perlman, *Cinderella Penguin or, The Little Glass Flipper*, 1992
In a spoof of the Cinderella story, penguins play the leading roles.

682

LAURIE A. JACOBS
VALERI GORBACHEV, Illustrator

So Much in Common

(Honesdale, PA: Boyds Mills Press, 1994)

Subject(s): Friendship; Animals/Hippos; Animals/Goats
Age range(s): Grades K-3
Major character(s): Philomena Midge, Hippo, Collector; Horace Abercrombie, Goat (neat)
Time period(s): 1990s (1994)
Locale(s): Fictional Country

Summary: With the exception of their shared backyard fence, Philomena and Horace really have nothing in common. One lives in the clutter of her collections and loves to cook while the other lives with stark essentials and eats take-out food. However, Horace loves Philomena's cooking and Philomena laughs at Horace's jokes. In her first book the author shows that just a little bit in common is just about enough to build a friendship. (28 pages)

Where it's reviewed:
Children's Book Review Service, September 1994, page 2
Kirkus Reviews, July 15, 1994, page 986
Publishers Weekly, June 13, 1994, page 63
School Library Journal, December 1994, page 76
Smithsonian, November 1994, page 37

Other books you might like:
Anthony Browne, *Willy and Hugh*, 1991
A difference in size does not stop a friendship from developing between Willy the chimp and Hugh the gorilla.

Arnold Lobel, *Frog and Toad Are Friends*, 1970
In five brief tales frog and toad agree on little other than the value of their friendship.

James Marshall, *George and Martha*, 1972
One of many humorous stories introduces two hippos and the adventures they enjoy together.

Sheila White Samton, *Tilly and the Rhinoceros*, 1993
Kindly Tilly wins over a grumpy rhinoceros with her unconditional caring.

683

DONNA JAKOB
NELLE DAVIS, Illustrator

My Bike

(New York: Hyperion Books for Children, 1994)

Subject(s): Bicycles and Bicycling; Family Life
Age range(s): Grades K-1
Major character(s): Unnamed Character, Child
Time period(s): 1990s (1994)
Locale(s): United States

Summary: A young boy recounts the frustration he felt yesterday as he tried to learn to ride a bike and the joy and satisfaction he feels today as he successfully soars along on his two-wheeler. The illustrations show the supportive parents assisting and the younger sister watching with some trepidation as her brother tries to ride solo. (32 pages)

Where it's reviewed:
Booklist, August 1994, page 2054
Children's Book Review Service, May 1994, page 111
Horn Book Guide, Fall 1994, page 276
Publishers Weekly, March 28, 1994, page 96
School Library Journal, August 1994, page 132

Other books you might like:
Stan Berenstain, *The Bike Lesson*, 1964
A gift of a new bike comes with Dad's special lessons, but little bear manages to ride a two-wheeler anyway. Co-author Jan Berenstain

Marc Brown, *D.W. Rides Again!*, 1993
With help from brother Arthur, D. W. learns to ride her new two-wheeler and proves to her father that she no longer needs training wheels.

Crescent Dragonwagon, *Annie Flies the Birthday Bike*, 1993
Annie's excitement with her birthday gift turns to frustration and finally elation as she masters the art of riding a two-wheeled bicycle.

684

TEDDY JAM
IAN WALLACE, Illustrator

The Year of Fire

(New York: Margaret K. McElderry Books, 1993)

Subject(s): Fires; Grandparents; Storytelling
Age range(s): Grades K-3
Major character(s): Howard, Grandfather, Storyteller; Unnamed Character, Child (granddaughter); John, Uncle

Time period(s): 1910s (1919); 1990s (1992)
Locale(s): Canada

Summary: While helping her grandfather tend the fire under the maple sap, a young girl asks if he has ever seen a fire any bigger than the one under the boiling pan. Indeed, Grandfather has and tells of a forest fire in the area when he was only a child. The fire singed John's eyebrows right off his face and, despite rain and snow, continued to burn underground all winter so that in the spring 10,000 trees toppled when the snow melted. The story, originally published in Canada in 1992, becomes part of Grandfather's legacy to his granddaughter. (40 pages)

Where it's reviewed:
Books in Canada, December 1992, page 32
Booklist, March 15, 1993, page 1360
Childrens Book Review Service, April, 1993, page 103
Publishers Weekly, February 1, 1993, page 95
School Library Journal, May 1993, page 86

Other books by the same author:
Dr. Kiss Says Yes, 1992

Other books you might like:
Sandra Belton, *From Miss Ida's Front Porch*, 1993
On warm, summer evenings the children gather to hear the older folks share stories of days gone by.

Helen Ketteman, *The Year of No More Corn*, 1993
Beanie's Old Grampa shares a tall tale about the year 1928 when there was no corn to harvest.

Patricia Polacco, *My Ol' Man*, 1995
A magic rock and a gift for storytelling help an unemployed father find work.

685

BETSY JAMES
ANNA VOJTECH, Illustrator

Blow Away Soon

(New York: G. P. Putnam's Sons, 1995)

Subject(s): Deserts; Grandparents; Possessions
Age range(s): Grades K-2
Major character(s): Sophie, Child; Nana, Grandmother
Time period(s): 1990s (1995)
Locale(s): Southwest

Summary: Sophie doesn't like the wind that blows away her hat and rolls her wagon into the street. Comforting her, Nana compares the wind to an old lady and teaches Sophie how to make a ''blow-away-soon'' so that Sophie is able to freely let go with the wind. (32 pages)

Where it's reviewed:
Booklist, June 1995, page 1786
Bulletin of the Center for Children's Books, September 1995, page 18
Horn Book Guide, Fall 1995, page 268
School Library Journal, August 1995, page 124

Other books by the same author:
The Mud Family, 1994
He Wakes Me, 1991
The Dream Stair, 1990

Other books you might like:

Marie Hall Ets, *Gilberto and the Wind*, 1963
> Through his play, a young boy learns to understand and appreciate the wind.

Pat Hutchins, *The Wind Blew*, 1974
> A rhyming story describes the cumulative effect of a wind which blows away many objects.

Joan L. Nodset, *Who Took the Farmer's Hat?*, 1963
> A farmer searches for his lost hat which was actually carried away by the wind.

686

BETSY JAMES, Author/Illustrator

Mary Ann

(New York: Dutton Children's Books, 1994)

Subject(s): Animals/Insects; Friendship; Moving, Household
Age range(s): Grades K-2
Major character(s): Amy, Child, Friend (Mary Ann's); Mary Ann, Child, Neighbor (moving)
Time period(s): 1990s (1994)
Locale(s): United States

Summary: After Mary Ann's family moves, lonely Amy names a praying mantis which she finds after her friend. She keeps the insect in her terrarium and spends the summer feeding and playing with it. After the praying mantis builds an egg case, the insect dies, leaving Amy without a friend once again. Amy carefully watches the egg case for signs of life which come when she least expects it. A concluding page gives factual information about praying mantises. (32 pages)

Where it's reviewed:
Booklist, January 1, 1994, page 832
Children's Book Review Service, March 1994, page 87
Horn Book Guide, Fall 1994, page 276
Kirkus Reviews, December 15, 1993, page 1591
School Library Journal, February 1994, page 87

Awards the book has won:
School Library Journal Best Books, 1994

Other books by the same author:
Blow Away Soon, 1995
The Mud Family, 1994
The Dream Stair, 1990

Other books you might like:

Jerry Booth, *Big Bugs*, 1994
> A factual look at many bugs, including praying mantises, describes habitats, characteristics and insect pets.

Kathryn Lasky, *Pond Year*, 1995
> Best friends enjoy the plant, animal and insect life in and around a pond as it changes with the seasons.

Megan McDonald, *Insects Are My Life*, 1995
> Amanda's interest in insects is not appreciated by anyone until she meets a new classmate.

687

BETSY JAMES
PAUL MORIN, Illustrator

The Mud Family

(New York: G. P. Putman's Sons, 1994)

Subject(s): Indians of North America; Drought; Family Relations
Age range(s): Grades K-3
Major character(s): Sosi, Child, Indian (Anasazi)
Time period(s): Indeterminate Past
Locale(s): Utah

Summary: When the lack of rain brings short tempers as well as dried corn plants, Sosi seeks refuge beside a small mud pond where she fashions a mud family for herself. In her play, her mud family responds the way Sosi would like her real family to treat her. Because she is considered too young to participate in the rain dance, Sosi stages her own dance with her mud family and, just as the family is prepared to move, the rains come, washing away the mud family, but bringing Sosi's real family together again. (32 pages)

Where it's reviewed:
Booklist, October 15, 1994, page 435
Children's Book Review Service, January 1995, page 51
Library Talk, November 1994, page 34
Publishers Weekly, October 31, 1994, page 61
School Library Journal, January 1995, page 87

Other books by the same author:
Blow Away Soon, 1995
He Wakes Me, 1991
The Dream Stair, 1990

Other books you might like:

Byrd Baylor, *And It Is Still That Way: Legends Told by Arizona Indian Children*, 1987
> The compilation of folktales and legends records the oral tradition of the American Southwest.

Caron Lee Cohen, *The Mud Pony: A Traditional Skidi Pawnee Tale*, 1988
> Legend tells of a poor Indian youth whose mud pony becomes real for a time, inspiring his selection as a leader of his people.

Ann Turner, *Dust for Dinner*, 1995
> Drought forces a family to sell their Oklahoma farm and move.

688

MARY JAMES

Shoebag Returns

(New York: Scholastic Press, 1996)

Subject(s): Animals/Cockroaches; Schools; Fantasy
Age range(s): Grades 4-6
Major character(s): Stuart "Shoebag" Bagg, Cockroach, Student; Stanley Sweetsong, 10-Year-Old, Student; Josephine Jiminez, Student
Time period(s): 1990s
Locale(s): Pennsylvania (Bucks County)

Summary: Shoebag is enjoying life as a cockroach again when he realizes he needs to return to his human form in order to help two students at Miss Rattray's school. Stanley has been sent to the school even though he will be the only boy there, and Josephine is not accepted by the other girls, mainly because of her desire to play-act. The children are not invited to join the Betters Club so they form their own secret club, the Butters, and then perform a prank on career day. Shoebag almost meets his end when he is picked up by Josephine, but he is rescued by Stanley and proceeds home to Tennessee. (144 pages)

Where it's reviewed:
Bulletin of the Center for Children's Books, February 1997, page 210
Booklist, February 1, 1997, page 941
School Library Journal, February 1997, page 103

Other books by the same author:
The Shuteyes, 1993
Shoebag, 1990 (prequel to *Shoebag Returns*)

Other books you might like:
Marion Dane Bauer, *Ghost Eye*, 1992
  A Cornish rex show cat sees ghosts and leads the household on various adventures.
Anna Coates, *Dog Magic*, 1991
  A dog who speaks English takes some children on a trip to find some missing puppies.
Janet W. Coleman, *Fast Eddie*, 1983
  Eddie is a raccoon who faces danger when he starts playing tricks on humans.
Bruce Coville, *Jennifer Murdley's Toad*, 1992
  Jennifer is surprised to learn that the toad she bought for a pet is a magical animal.
Annabel Johnson, *I Am Leaper*, 1990
  A talking kangaroo mouse feels that she must warn the world that a monster is destroying the desert.

689

MARY JAMES (Pseudonym of M.E. Kerr)

The Shuteyes

(New York: Scholastic Inc., 1993)

Subject(s): Fantasy; Prejudice; Sleep
Age range(s): Grades 4-6
Major character(s): Chester Dumbello, 11-Year-Old; Lornge, Bird (parrot); Molly Dumbello, Mother (Chester's), Psychic
Time period(s): 1990s (1993)
Locale(s): Lucy, Mississippi; Alert, Planet—Imaginary

Summary: Chester's life in a small town with Molly who interprets dreams while beating on a drum, becomes even stranger when a one-eyed parrot who never sleeps flies into their home. As Chester becomes increasingly frustrated with life, he absentmindedly says "Get me out of here!" and Lornge does. Chester is transported (actually he flies, thanks to Lornge) to the planet Alert where sleep is forbidden and "shuteyes" are considered criminals. Quickly, Chester learns to appreciate the life he no longer has and wonders how he can return to it. (167 pages)

Where it's reviewed:
Children's Book Review Service, April 1993, page 106
Kirkus Reviews, January 1, 1993, page 62
Library Talk, May 1993, page 52
Publishers Weekly, January 11, 1993, page 64
School Library Journal, April 1993, page 120

Other books by the same author:
Shoebag Returns, 1996
Frankenlouse, 1994
Shoebag, 1990

Other books you might like:
Avi, *Tom, Babette, & Simon: Three Tales of Transformation*, 1995
  Three short stories describe the unusual and unexpected results of three different children's wishes.
L. Frank Baum, *The Wizard of Oz*, 1996
  A reillustrated version of the 1900 classic about Dorothy and her dog Toto who, after being hurled into a strange land by a toado, find a way to return to Kansas.
Madeline L'Engle, *A Wrinkle in Time*, 1962
  The first in a four-book series about the Murry family finds the children searching for their father, a missing scientist.

690

CAROLINE JANOVER

The Worst Speller in Jr. High

(Minneapolis: Free Spirit Publishing, 1994)

Subject(s): Learning Disabilities; Cancer; School Life
Age range(s): Grades 6-7
Major character(s): Katie Kelso, 7th Grader, Dyslexic; Spud Larson, 7th Grader; Brian Straus, 7th Grader
Time period(s): 1990s
Locale(s): North Kent, Massachusetts

Summary: Classified as a nerd since elementary school, Katie's determined to be a P.K., or "Popular Kid," in junior high and doesn't want dyslexia to hamper her goal. One of her first decisions is whether to date Spud, who repeated first grade with her, or Brian, who's wealthy but lonely. And what should she do about the literary magazine that her teacher urges her to join? Katie knows she's the "worst speller in Jr. High" but she doesn't want everyone else to know! Katie charges ahead, assumes control of her dyslexia, helps her mother battle breast cancer and makes the right decision about dating in this book written by a dyslexic author. (200 pages)

Where it's reviewed:
Publishers Weekly, November 21, 1994, page 78
School Library Journal, February 1995, page 98
Booklist, February 1, 1995, page 1005
Kliatt, March 1995, page 8
Voice of Youth Advocates, June 1995, page 95

Other books by the same author:
Josh: A Boy with Dyslexia, 1988

Other books you might like:
C.S. Adler, *Kiss the Clown*, 1986
  Joel covers up his problem of dyslexia by always playing the role of the class clown.

Lynn Hall, *Just One Friend*, 1985
   Learning-disabled Dory is unintentionally responsible for an automobile accident that kills a friend.
Virginia Euwer Wolff, *Probably Still Nick Swansen*, 1988
   Prom night turns into a disaster for Nick, a special student who's never been mainstreamed.

691

GAIL JARROW

Beyond the Magic Sphere

(San Diego: Harcourt Brace, 1994)

Subject(s): Country Life; Fantasy Games; Friendship
Age range(s): Grades 6-7
Major character(s): Strawberry "S.B." Field, 11-Year-Old; Finis Hatcher, 13-Year-Old; Cally, Teenager
Time period(s): 1990s
Locale(s): New York (small town)

Summary: The only thing S.B. has from her deceased mother is her name, which she hates so much she prefers to be called by her initials. This summer, S.B. is living with a cousin while her father travels in Europe. She resents this change to her usually satisfying, highly-structured, and spoiled life. Her cousin takes in a ward named Finis who drives S.B. crazy with morbid facts; luckily she meets Cally with whom she feels great affinity. Cally leads S.B. through a mirrored lawn ornament into a fantasy world where Cally escapes her abusive family life. S.B. slowly realizes why she's been sent to stay with her cousin as she learns to get along with others, becomes involved in a neighborhood squabble about trees and finally accepts her mother's abandonment and eventual death. (198 pages)

Where it's reviewed:
Voice of Youth Advocates, December 1994, page 223
School Library Journal, November 1994, page 104
Horn Book Guide, Spring 1995, page 78

Other books by the same author:
The Two-Ton Secret, 1989
If Phyllis Were Here, 1987

Other books you might like:
Richard E. Allen, *Ozzy on the Outside*, 1989
   When Ozzy's mother is killed in a freak accident, he is so shattered that he runs away from his family.
Eric Houghton, *Gates of Glass*, 1987
   A young girl's mirror draws her into a subterranean world made of glass.
Marya Smith, *Across the Creek*, 1989
   After Rye's mother dies, he's sent to live in the country with his grandmother.

692

LINDA JENNINGS
TIM WARNES, Illustrator

Tom's Tail

(Boston: Little, Brown and Company, 1995)

Subject(s): Animals/Pigs; Self-Acceptance; Problem Solving

Age range(s): Grades K-2
Major character(s): Tom, Pig
Time period(s): 1990s (1995)
Locale(s): England

Summary: Tom is a lovely, young pig with just one complaint—his tail is too curly. With assistance from the other farm animals he tries to stretch his tail, but inevitably it recurls itself. The cow suggests stretching it and placing it in the mud until the mud dries on it. The technique works beautifully! Tom now has a tail that is as straight—and stiff—as a pencil but every time he turns around he pokes someone and his irritated siblings throw him out of the pig sty. Fortunately, he's stuck outside in a rain shower, the mud washes off, and his curly tail returns to normal. (32 pages)

Where it's reviewed:
Booklist, March 15, 1995, page 1334
Children's Book Review Service, June 1995, page 123
Magpies, May 1995, page 26
Publishers Weekly, May 1, 1995, page 58
School Library Journal, June 1995, page 88

Other books by the same author:
Easy Peasy!, 1997
The Best Christmas Present of All, 1996
The Dog Who Found Christmas, 1993

Other books you might like:
Eric Carle, *The Mixed-Up Chameleon*, 1984
   Dissatisfied with his appearance, a chameleon tries on characteristics of other animals but ultimately decides he just wants to be himself.
James Howe, *I Wish I Were a Butterfly*, 1987
   While cricket feels ugly and wishes he could fly, a butterfly hears the music he makes and wishes he could be a cricket.
Holly Keller, *Horace*, 1991
   Horace, sensitive to the difference in his spotted appearance and his parents' stripes, learns that belonging to a family is based on feeling and not appearance.
Theo. LeSeig, *I Wish that I Had Duck Feet*, 1965
   The silliness of a boy's desire for unique features is cleverly illustrated.

693

PATRICK JENNINGS

Faith and the Electric Dogs

(New York: Scholastic, 1996)

Subject(s): Animals/Dogs; Runaways
Age range(s): Grades 3-6
Major character(s): Faith, 10-Year-Old; Edison, Dog; Beverly Sinclair Glum, Castaway
Time period(s): 1990s
Locale(s): San Cristobal de las Casas, Mexico

Summary: Faith does not like Mexico as she can't speak the language and the students in her school make fun of her. One day she rescues an electric dog and the two start adventures together. Faith makes a very rudimentary rocket and the two take off to return to San Francisco but they crash-land on an island and spend some time there, where they learn more about themselves and get ready to try again to accept life in Mexico. (148 pages)

Where it's reviewed:
Booklist, December 1, 1996, page 653
School Library Journal, December 1996, page 122

Awards the book has won:
Booklist Editors' Choice, 1996

Other books you might like:
Anne Fine, *The Chicken Gave It to Me*, 1993
   Andrew claims he has a book written by a chicken about adventures in outer space.
S.E. Hinton, *The Puppy Sister*, 1995
   A boy really wanted a sister but he got a dog instead. As time goes on, however, she turns into the sister he wanted.
Kevin McColley, *The Walls of Pedro Garcia*, 1993
   Pedro tries to prove his strengh by a confrontaton with a grounds keeper in a house in Mexico.
Emily Rodda, *The Best-Kept Secret*, 1990
   Two friends are whisked into the future on a carousel.
Eduard Uspenskii, *Uncle Fedya, His Dog, and His Cat*, 1993
   A boy is unhappy that his mom won't let him keep the cat he found so he runs away and sets up housekeeping with some unconventional creatures.

694

PAUL JENNINGS

Unbearable! More Bizarre Stories
(New York: Viking, 1995)

Subject(s): Supernatural; Short Stories; Humor
Age range(s): Grades 4-6
Time period(s): 1990s (1990)
Locale(s): Australia

Summary: Eight short stories exude references to kids' gross behavior—licking "dirty" fly swatters in order to offend the dinner guest, having smelly feet capable of putting others to sleep, and searching goat poo for a swallowed opal. Parents and teachers lack understanding of the children's rationale for such behavior, but kids understand the logic behind using any means to save a sea turtle or a dying kangaroo. First published in Australia in 1990. (116 pages)

Where it's reviewed:
Booklist, June 1995, page 1771
Bulletin of the Center for Children's Books, July 1995, page 386
Horn Book Guide, Fall 1995, page 299
School Library Journal, July 1995, page 78

Other books by the same author:
Unmentionable!, 1993
Uncanny!, 1991
Unreal!, 1991

Other books you might like:
Bruce Coville, *Oddly Enough: Stories by Bruce Coville*, 1994
   An odd assortment of characters such as unicorns, vampires, angels and werewolves appear in nine short horror tales.

Diana Wynne Jones, *Stopping for a Spell*, 1993
   Three fantasies explore the impact of unexpected magic on everyday events.
Patrick F. McManus, *Never Cry Arp: And Other Great Adventures*, 1996
   Thirteen short stories give humorous insight into outdoor adventures.
Jane Yolen, *The Haunted House: A Collection of Original Stories*, 1995
   With co-editor Martin Greenberg, Yolen presents seven stories explaining the unusual events experienced by families renting an old house with a past waiting to be told.

695

ANITA JERAM, Author/Illustrator

Daisy Dare
(Cambridge, MA: Candlewick Press, 1995)

Subject(s): Animals/Mice; Behavior; Courage
Age range(s): Grades K-1
Major character(s): Daisy Dare, Mouse
Time period(s): 1990s (1995)
Locale(s): Fictional Country

Summary: If her friends dare her, fearless Daisy Dare will walk on a wall, eat a worm or stick out her tongue at an elderly neighbor. However, when they dare her to take the bell off the cat, she has second thoughts—but not for long. The cat is asleep as Daisy approaches, the bell comes off easily, but not quietly, waking the cat who pursues Daisy and her friends all the way to the safety of home. (18 pages)

Where it's reviewed:
Booklist, November 15, 1995, page 564
Horn Book Guide, Spring 1996, page 32
Kirkus Reviews, August 15, 1995, page 1189
Publishers Weekly, September 18, 1995, page 131
School Library Journal, December 1995, page 82

Other books by the same author:
Contrary Mary, 1995
The Most Obedient Dog in the World, 1994
It Was Jake, 1991

Other books you might like:
Bill Martin Jr., *A Beautiful Feast for a Big King Cat*, 1994
   The third time a mouse taunts a large cat he finds the path to safety blocked by the frustrated animal intent on lunch. Co-author Bill Martin, Jr.
Anna Currey, *Tickling Tigers*, 1996
   Boastful Hannibal is in a quandry when the other mice call his bluff and want to watch him tickle a tiger as he claims he can.
Robert Kraus, *Big Squeak, Little Squeak*, 1996
   Bored with a life of cheese curls and cartoons two mice venture into a cheese shop for a free treat and find more adventure than they ever imagined.

696

ANGELA JOHNSON
DAV PILKEY, Illustrator

Julius

(New York: Orchard Books, 1993)

Subject(s): Animals/Pigs; Friendship; Love
Age range(s): Grades K-2
Major character(s): Maya, Child (African American); Julius, Pig (Alaskan)
Time period(s): 1990s (1993)
Locale(s): Alabama

Summary: When Maya's Granddaddy brings her a special gift from Alaska to teach her fun and sharing, no one expects a pig, but that's what comes. Julius and Maya learn a lot from each other and eventually overcome Maya's parents reluctance to have a pig for a pet. (30 pages)

Where it's reviewed:
Booklist, March 1, 1993, page 1236
Children's Book Review Service, April 1993, page 100
Horn Book, March 1993, page 196
Publishers Weekly, January 18, 1993, page 468
School Library Journal, March 1993, page 179

Awards the book has won:
School Library Journal Best Books, 1993
ALA Notable Book, 1994

Other books by the same author:
The Girl Who Wore Snakes, 1993
Do Like Kyla, 1990
When I Am Old with You, 1990 (Coretta Scott King Honor Book)

Other books you might like:
Laurie Krasny Brown, *Rex and Lilly Family Time*, 1995
    The family tries to decide which pet is the best for Rex and Lilly.
Amy Ehrlich, *Parents in the Pigpen, Pigs in the Tub*, 1993
    The farm animals move into the house and the family heads for the barn in a humorous reversal of roles.
Carol Purdy, *Mrs. Merriwether's Musical Cat*, 1994
    An unusual cat changes Mrs. Merriwether's outlook on life.

697

DOLORES JOHNSON, Author/Illustrator

Papa's Stories

(New York: Macmillan Publishing Company, 1994)

Subject(s): African Americans; Fathers and Daughters; Literacy
Age range(s): Grades K-3
Major character(s): Kari, Child; Papa, Father (illiterate)
Time period(s): 1990s (1994)
Locale(s): United States

Summary: Kari enjoys the time she spends with Papa as he reads to her and never suspects that Papa's creative storytelling results from his inability to read. When she is in kindergarten, an older neighbor child reads to her from a favorite book and, of course, it is different from Papa's telling. Shaken, Kari talks to her mother and then confronts Papa who explains why he has misled her. Although Papa demonstrates his beginning reading skill by reading their favorite book correctly, Kari asks him to ''read'' it again the old way. (32 pages)

Where it's reviewed:
Booklist, February 15, 1994, page 1092
Bulletin of the Center for Children's Books, July 1994, page 361
Children's Book Review Service, April 1994, page 100
Kirkus Reviews, February 15, 1994, page 227
School Library Journal, September 1994, page 186

Other books by the same author:
Seminole Diary: Rembrances of a Slave, 1994
Now Let Me Fly: The Story of a Slave Family, 1993
The Best Bug to Be, 1992

Other books you might like:
Eve Bunting, *The Wednesday Surprise*, 1989
    Every Wednesday when Grandma babysits, she and Anna work on Papa's birthday surprise.
Tony Johnston, *Amber on the Mountain*, 1994
    With no school on the isolated mountain where she lives, Amber is unable to read until Anna comes into her life, determined to teach her.
Carol Purdy, *Least of All*, 1987
    A young girl in a large farm family teaches herself to read during a long winter's confinement.
Dr. Seuss, *I Can Read with My Eyes Shut*, 1978
    The Cat in the Hat instructs Young Cat in the joys of reading

698

DOLORES JOHNSON, Author/Illustrator

Your Dad Was Just Like You

(New York: Macmillan Publishing Company, 1993)

Subject(s): Fathers and Sons; Grandparents; Growing Up
Age range(s): Grades 1-3
Major character(s): Peter, Child (unhappy); Grandpa, Grandfather (understanding); Dad, Father (critical)
Time period(s): 1990s (1993)
Locale(s): United States

Summary: Frustrated because his father never seems satisfied with him, Peter decides to move in with his grandfather. In a conversation with his grandfather, Peter gains insight into his relationship with his own father and decides on a plan to help the two of them get along better. (32 pages)

Where it's reviewed:
Booklist, March 1, 1993, page 1236
Five Owls, September 1993, page 11
Instructor, October 1993, page 61
New Advocate, Fall 1993, page 293
School Library Journal, August 1993, page 146

Other books by the same author:
Papa's Stories, 1994
The Best Bug to Be, 1992

What Will Mommy Do When I'm at School?, 1990

Other books you might like:

Virginia L. Kroll, *Africa Brothers and Sisters*, 1993
 With his Dad, Jesse researches his heritage to learn more about the connection between African people and his life in America.

David Spohn, *Home Field*, 1993
 A father and son enjoy each other's company in the warmth of an early summer morning.

Sharon Dennis Wyeth, *Always My Dad*, 1995
 On a warm summer evening while staying with grandparents, a brother and sister enjoy a special, infrequent visit from their Dad.

699

DOUG JOHNSON
ABBY CARTER, Illustrator

Never Ride Your Elephant to School

(New York: Henry Holt and Company, Inc., 1995)

Subject(s): Animals/Elephants; Schools; Humor
Age range(s): Grades K-2
Major character(s): Unnamed Character, Student
Time period(s): 1990s (1995)
Locale(s): United States

Summary: When you ride your elephant to school, one normal elephantine behavior follows another with predictably calamitous results until utter mayhem ensues. So, take the author's advice and leave your elephant at home. (32 pages)

Where it's reviewed:
Booklist, September 15, 1995, page 175
Horn Book Guide, Spring 1996, page 32
Kirkus Reviews, August 15, 1995, page 1189
Publishers Weekly, August 21, 1995, page 65
School Library Journal, December 1995, page 82

Other books by the same author:
Never Babysit the Hippopotamuses!, 1993

Other books you might like:

Sarah Josepha Hale, *Mary Had a Little Lamb*, 1995
 Even an animal as small and gentle as a lamb can create problems in the classroom. One of many retellings is illustrated by Mavor.

Laura Numeroff, *If You Give a Moose a Muffin*, 1991
 Think carefully before giving a moose a muffin because that offer can lead to some unexpected happenings.

Laura Numeroff, *If You Give a Mouse a Cookie*, 1985
 When you give a mouse a cookie, the mouse will request milk and a napkin and one thing will lead to another until you may have a problem.

700

LOIS WALFRID JOHNSON

Escape into the Night

(Minneapolis: Bethany House, 1995)

Series: Riverboat Adventures

Subject(s): Slavery; African Americans; Underground Railroad
Age range(s): Grades 6-8
Major character(s): Libby Norstad, 12-Year-Old; Caleb Whitney, Worker (cabin boy); Captain Norstad, Shipowner
Time period(s): 1850s (1857)
Locale(s): Mississippi River

Summary: After her mother dies, Libby lived with her wealthy aunt in Chicago. Now she's joined her father, Captain Norstad of the riverboat *Christina*, named after her mother, that travels the Mississippi River. Her quiet, sedate life changes rapidly once she meets the cabin boy Caleb, who assists runaway slaves on the Underground Railroad. Together the two help Jordan, a fugitive who is being pursued by bloodhounds. (176 pages)

Where it's reviewed:
School Library Journal, October 1995, page 134
Booklist, November 15, 1995, page 559

Other books by the same author:
Disaster at Windy Hill, 1994
Mystery of the Missing Map, 1994
Mysterious Hideaway, 1992
Trouble at Wild River, 1991

Other books you might like:

Jennifer Armstrong, *Steal Away*, 1992
 Yankee Susannah is displeased to be given a personal slave when she moves to Virginia; the two run away together to freedom.

James Lincoln Collier, *Jump Ship to Freedom*, 1981
 A young slave, Daniel, tries to save enough money to buy freedom for himself and his mother.

Barbara Smucker, *Runaway to Freedom: A Story of the Underground Railroad*, 1979
 The Underground Railroad is the hope for two young slave girls fleeing their masters for freedom.

701

PAUL BRETT JOHNSON, Author/Illustrator

The Cow Who Wouldn't Come Down

(New York: Orchard Books, 1993)

Subject(s): Animals/Cows; Problem Solving; Behavior
Age range(s): Grades K-3
Major character(s): Miss Rosemary, Aged Person (problem solver); Gertrude, Cow (strong-willed)
Time period(s): 1990s (1993)
Locale(s): United States

Summary: In the author's first book, Miss Rosemary understands that Gertrude has a mind of her own and she tolerates most ideas, but when Gertrude has a mind to fly, Miss Rosemary has had enough. Not knowing how to milk a flying cow, Miss Rosemary instead tries a number of ideas to convince Gertrude to return to earth. Finally, Miss Rosemary is successful and Gertrude stops flying, but not thinking for herself. (30 pages)

Where it's reviewed:
Booklist, February 1, 1993, page 989
Children's Book Review Service, July 1993, page 147

Horn Book, May 1993, page 319
Publishers Weekly, March 29, 1993, page 53
School Library Journal, May 1993, page 86

Awards the book has won:
School Library Journal Best Books, 1993
Book Links Good Book, 1993

Other books by the same author:
Frank Fister's Hidden Talent: Story and Pictures, 1994

Other books you might like:
Chris Babcock, *No Moon, No Milk!*, 1993
   Martha refuses to give her owner any milk until she fulfills her dream to be a ''cowsmonaut'' and walk on the moon.
Jennifer A. Ericsson, *No Milk*, 1993
   A city boy learns through trial and error how to get milk from a cow.
Phyllis Krasilovsky, *The Cow Who Fell in the Canal*, 1985
   Hendrika, a discontented Dutch cow, finds life much more exciting when she falls onto a raft and floats down the canal.
Tres Seymour, *Hunting the White Cow*, 1993
   The independent, crafty white cow is able to evade all attempts to capture her and bring her home.
Toby Speed, *Two Cool Cows*, 1995
   Maude and Millie, two cool cows in borrowed boots and sunglasses jump to the moon to frolic with their bovine buddies.

702

TONY JOHNSTON
ROBERT DUNCAN, Illustrator

Amber on the Mountain
(New York: Dial Books for Young Readers, 1994)

Subject(s): Literacy; Friendship; Mountain Life
Age range(s): Grades K-3
Major character(s): Amber, Child (illiterate); Anna, Child (reader)
Time period(s): Indeterminate Past
Locale(s): United States (Amber's home on a mountain)

Summary: The opportunity to learn to read does not exist for Amber in her home with her grandmother high on an inaccessible mountain. When a crew comes through to build a road, the daughter of one of the workers teaches Amber how to read. Amber and Anna become friends, learning from one another. In time the road is finished and Anna moves away, but the friendship continues through correspondence as soon as Amber teaches herself to write. (32 pages)

Where it's reviewed:
Booklist, September 1, 1994, page 52
Children's Book Review Service, September 1994, page 2
Kirkus Reviews, June 15, 1994, page 847
Publishers Weekly, May 16, 1994, page 63
School Library Journal, August 1994, page 132

Awards the book has won:
Notable Children's Books in the Language Arts, 1995

Other books by the same author:
Alice Nizzy Nazzy, the Witch of Santa Fe, 1995

The Last Snow of Winter, 1993
Yonder, 1988

Other books you might like:
Miriam Cohen, *When Will I Read?*, 1977
   Eager to learn to read, an impatient first grader learns that there is more to reading than books.
Florence Parry Heide, *The Day of Ahmed's Secret*, 1990
   The award-winning story tells the joy of achieving a small step toward literacy for a poor Egyptian lad. Co-author Judith Heide Gilliland.
Dolores Johnson, *Papa's Stories*, 1994
   Kari is shaken to learn that Papa's inability to read creates the interesting stories which change with every telling.
Carol Purdy, *Least of All*, 1987
   A young girl in a large family teaches herself to read during a long, confining winter on her Vermont farm.

703

TONY JOHNSTON
S.D. SCHINDLER, Illustrator

The Ghost of Nicholas Greebe
(New York: Dial, 1996)

Subject(s): Ghosts; Humor
Age range(s): Grades K-3
Major character(s): Nicholas Greebe, Spirit
Time period(s): 1750s; 1850s (1750-1850)
Locale(s): Massachusetts (trip around the world)

Summary: A year after Nicholas' death, his dog digs up one of his leg bones. Thus begins the story of the travels of the bone over land and sea. For 100 years the bone tours the world and every anniversary Nicholas comes back to haunt his house asking for his missing part. One day a distant relative returns with the bone which a new dog reburies in the old grave to end the ghost's quest. (unpaged)

Where it's reviewed:
Bulletin of the Center for Children's Books, October 1996, page 65
Hornbook, November/December 1996, page 725

Awards the book has won:
School Library Journal Best Books, 1996

Other books by the same author:
The Wagon, 1996
Amber on the Mountain, 1994
The Cowboy and the Black-Eyed Pea, 1992

Other books you might like:
Laura Cecil, *Boo! Stories to Make You Jump*, 1990
   This is a collection of short stories about strange events.
Washington Irving, *Rip Van Winkle*, 1905
   Rip falls asleep for 100 years and awakens to find the world around him completely changed.
Maria Leach, *The Thing at the Foot of the Bed*, 1987
   This collection of spine-tingling ghost stories makes for shivery reading.
Judy Sierra, *Wiley and the Hairy Man*, 1995
   The scary monster in the marsh tries to capture a boy but is fooled by a number of tricks.

Robert D. San Souci, *The Faithful Friend*, 1995
> A young man realizes that he can save his friend only with his own sacrifice.

Jan Wahl, *Tailypo*, 1991
> A ghost returns to claim the tail which a man has eaten for dinner.

704

TONY JOHNSTON
MARK TEAGUE, Illustrator

The Iguana Brothers: A Tale of Two Lizards

(New York: The Blue Sky Press, 1995)

Subject(s): Brothers; Animals/Reptiles; Humor
Age range(s): Grades K-3
Major character(s): Dom, Iguana, Brother; Tom, Iguana, Brother
Time period(s): 1990s (1995)
Locale(s): Mexico

Summary: Tom, the thoughtful brother, decides bugs are gross and will no longer eat them. Dom continues to munch the delicacies while worrying about Tom, who eventually eats flowers and convinces Dom to do the same. Then Tom realizes he and Dom, must be dinosaurs so the two of them practice roaring until they are frightened by a little lizard. Finally, Tom searches unsuccessfully for a friend for Dom who decides that, if a brother can be a friend, then he's already got one. The Spanish words sprinkled throughout the text are understandable from context. (32 pages)

Where it's reviewed:
Booklist, January 15, 1995, page 924
Emergency Librarian, September 1995, page 56
Horn Book Guide, Fall 1995, page 268
Publishers Weekly, February 20, 1995, page 205
School Library Journal, April 1995, page 103

Awards the book has won:
National Parenting Publications Award, Picture Story Book, 1995

Other books by the same author:
The Magic Maguey, 1996
The Tale of Rabbit and Coyote, 1994
The Cowboy and the Black-Eyed Pea, 1992

Other books you might like:
Kelli C. Foster, *Whiptail of Blackshale Trail*, 1993
> In an easy reader an iguana tells two friends about spooky creature lurking about.

Nancy Jewell, *Two Silly Trolls*, 1992
> The silly experiences of troll brothers Nip and Tuck include getting lost on the way to their own picnic and building a house with no roof.

Bonnie Pryor, *The Porcupine Mouse*, 1988
> Mouse brothers Louie and Dan have difficulty agreeing on the perfect house until they meet a cat with an idea neither of them like.

705

TONY JOHNSTON
HARVEY STEVENSON, Illustrator

Little Rabbit Goes to Sleep

(New York: HarperCollins Publishers, 1994)

Subject(s): Fear; Bedtime; Grandparents
Age range(s): Grades K-2
Major character(s): Little Rabbit, Rabbit; Grandpa, Grandfather
Time period(s): 1990s (1994)
Locale(s): Fictional Country

Summary: Little Rabbit's fear of the dark and night noises keeps him awake long after bedtime. The comforting sound of Grandpa's porch rocker attracts him. He joins his grandfather, sharing his fears and is comforted sufficiently to return to bed . (32 pages)

Where it's reviewed:
Booklist, March 1, 1994, page 1270
Children's Book Review Service, March 1994, page 87
Kirkus Reviews, December 15, 1993, page 1591
Publishers Weekly, November 15, 1993, page 77
School Library Journal, April 1994, page 107

Other books by the same author:
Amber on the Mountain, 1994
Yonder, 1988
Whale Song, 1987

Other books you might like:
Michael Foreman, *Dad! I Can't Sleep*, 1994
> When Little Panda tries Dad's suggestion to count animals as an aid to falling asleep, the result surprises both of them.

Russell Hoban, *Bedtime for Frances*, 1960
> Each time Frances presents a problem keeping her from sleep, her parents have a matter-of-fact, but soothing reply.

Martin Waddell, *Can't You Sleep, Little Bear?*, 1988
> Little Bear is comforted by Big Bear when a fear of the dark interfers with his ability to fall asleep.

706

TONY JOHNSTON
TOMIE DE PAOLA, Illustrator

The Tale of Rabbit and Coyote

(New York: G.P. Putnam's Sons, 1994)

Subject(s): Folk Tales; Legends; Animals
Age range(s): Grades K-3
Major character(s): Rabbit, Rabbit; Coyote, Coyote
Time period(s): Indeterminate Past
Locale(s): Mexico

Summary: Rabbit gets himself into trouble and almost into hot water, until a surprisingly gullible Coyote comes along. Taking advantage of Coyote, Rabbit escapes from one predicament after another with Coyote in hot pursuit, determined to eat the troublesome trickster. Finally, Rabbit climbs a ladder to the moon and hides. Frustrated because he cannot find the ladder to follow Rabbit, Coyote howls at the moon to this day because he is still very angry with Rabbit. (32 pages)

Where it's reviewed:
Booklist, May 15, 1994, page 1678
Kirkus Reviews, May 15, 1994, page 700
New Advocate, Fall 1994, page 282
Publishers Weekly, April 18, 1994, page 60
School Library Journal, June 1994, page 121

Awards the book has won:
Consortium of Latin American Studies Programs, Commended Book, 1994

Other books by the same author:
The Magic Maguey, 1996
The Iguana Brothers: A Tale of Two Lizards, 1995
Old Lady and the Birds, 1994
The Cowboy and the Black-Eyed Pea, 1992

Other books you might like:
Verna Aardema, *Borreguita and the Coyote: A Tale from Ayutla, Mexico*, 1991
   In an award-winning tale, a lamb cleverly finds a way to keep herself from becoming a coyote's next meal.
Joel Chandler Harris, *Jump on Over! The Adventures of Brer Rabbit and His Family*, 1989
   A collection with illustrations by Barry Moser includes five tales of the wily rabbit and his family.
Linda Hayward, *Hello, House!*, 1988
   Cunning Brer Rabbit uses his wits to get the best of Brer Wolf.

■707■

TONY JOHNSTON
DOUGLAS FLORIAN, Illustrator

Very Scary

(San Diego: Harcourt Brace & Company, 1995)

Subject(s): Pumpkins; Halloween; Witches and Witchcraft
Age range(s): Grades K-2
Major character(s): Unnamed Character, Plant
Time period(s): 1990s (1995)
Locale(s): United States

Summary: On Halloween night the biggest pumpkin in a field absorbs the moonlight. Its glowing appearance attracts an owl, a cat, crickets and a witch intending to bake it into a pie. Before the witch can carry the pumpkin away, a group of costumed trick-or-treaters arrive and carve the big pumpkin into a jack o' lantern. When they put in the candle, the jack o' lantern proudly says "Boo!" and scares everyone away. (32 pages)

Where it's reviewed:
Booklist, September 15, 1995, page 170
Horn Book Guide, Spring 1996, page 32
Library Talk, September 1995, page 25
Publishers Weekly, September 18, 1995, page 89
School Library Journal, November 1995, page 74

Other books by the same author:
The Ghost of Nicholas Greebe, 1996
The Magic Maguey, 1996
Little Wild Parrot, 1995

Other books you might like:
Steven Kroll, *The Biggest Pumpkin Ever*, 1984
   Unbeknownst to each other, two mice have selected the same pumpkin for their secret work to grow an enormous one.
Dav Pilkey, *The Hallo-Wiener*, 1995
   Oscar's bravery on Halloween night wins him some respect despite the embarassing costume his mother has made him.
Anita Riggio, *Beware the Brindlebeast*, 1994
   On All Hallow's Eve Birdie carries home a pot of gold which is really the shape-changing brindlebeast who proves to be more hungry than scary.
Bethany Roberts, *Halloween Mice!*, 1995
   A group of cavorting mice cleverly take advantage of their flashlight to scare away a menacing cat.

■708■

TONY JOHNSTON
JAMES E. RANSOME, Illustrator

The Wagon

(New York, Morrow, 1996)

Age range(s): Grades K-3
Major character(s): Papa, Slave; Abraham Lincoln, Historical Figure (President)
Time period(s): 1860s
Locale(s): North Carolina

Summary: Born into slavery in North Carolina, a young boy tells the story of his life which centers around the wagon he and his father build for the master. When the Civil War begins, the boy is anxious to join the soldiers fighting for freedom but when he is refused, attacks the wagon wheels and is beaten. Freedom finally comes when he is twelve, but on the way North the family learns that President Lincoln has been killed. Inspired by the story of his life and work and upset that he is dead, the family stops in Washington to say goodbye. (unpaged)

Where it's reviewed:
Booklist, January 1, 1997, page 869

Other books by the same author:
The Iguana Brothers: A Tale of Two Lizards, 1995
Amber on the Mountain, 1994
Yonder, 1988

Other books you might like:
William H. Hooks, *Freedom's Fruit*, 1996
   Mama Marina casts a spell on her master's grapes so that her daughter can win her freedom and go away with the man she loves.
Dolores Johnson, *Now Let Me Fly: The Story of a Slave Family*, 1993
   Minna is captured in Africa, then lives the life of a slave on a Southern plantation in the 1800s.
Ann Turner, *Nettie's Trip South*, 1987
   A girl from the North views a slave sale in Richmond and is so upset she becomes ill.

Connie Porter, *Meet Addy: An American Girl*, 1993
Nine year old Addie escapes to freedom from her home in Virginia.
Alan Schroeder, *Minty: A Story of Young Harriet Tubman*, 1996
Harriet Tubman is beaten and mistreated before she first runs away to freedom.

709

DIANA WYNNE JONES
JOS. A. SMITH, Illustrator

Stopping for a Spell
(New York: Greenwillow Books, 1993)

Subject(s): Short Stories; Humor; Magic
Age range(s): Grades 3-5
Time period(s): 1990s (1993)
Locale(s): England

Summary: Three fantasies, which give younger readers an introduction to the humor of YA author Jones, explore the impact of magic where it is least expected. In the first story, an old arm chair ready to be discarded by the family is transformed into ''Chair Person''; in ''Four Grannies'' a chopstick begins behaving like a magic wand; and in the last story the household furnishings turn on an unpleasant houseguest. (160 pages)

Where it's reviewed:
Children's Book Review Service, July 1993, page 154
Horn Book Guide, Fall 1993, page 299
Kirkus Reviews, May 15, 1993, page 663
Publishers Weekly, May 24, 1993, page 88
School Library Journal, July 1993, page 85

Other books by the same author:
Fantasy Stories: A Spellbinding Collection, 1994

Other books you might like:
Daniel Cohen, *Great Ghosts*, 1990
A haunted house is the setting for each of nine ghost stories flavored with British humor and suspense.
David Gale, *Don't Give Up the Ghost: The Delacorte Book of Original Ghost Stories*, 1993
A collection of stories by well-known authors, focuses on contacts of humans with the supernatural.
Michael Stearns, *A Wizard's Dozen: Stories of the Fantastic*, 1993
Tales of dragons, giants, and wizards are among the thirteen fantasies presented in this collection.

710

REBECCA C. JONES
SHELLEY JACKSON, Illustrator

Great Aunt Martha
(New York: Dutton Children's Books, 1995)

Subject(s): Aunts and Uncles; Old Age; Family Relations
Age range(s): Grades K-3
Major character(s): Martha, Aunt (great aunt), Aged Person; Unnamed Character, Child, Niece; Skipper, Dog

Time period(s): 1990s (1995)
Locale(s): United States

Summary: Even before Great-Aunt Martha arrives, she has ruined her niece's fun. The house is cleaned from top to bottom, the grocery shopping includes fish and prune juice rather than pizza or pretzels and Skipper is banished to the garage lest he bark. Great-Aunt Martha seems to politely tolerate the bland diet, the quiet conversation and the suggested rest. However, the morning after Great-Aunt Martha arrives, her niece finds her tap dancing in her bedroom and eager to liven the place up with music and pizza. (32 pages)

Where it's reviewed:
Children's Book Review Service, August 1995, page 158
Horn Book, September 1995, page 589
Instructor, January 1996, page 77
Publishers Weekly, June 26, 1995, page 106
School Library Journal, July 1995, page 64

Other books by the same author:
Down at the Bottom of the Deep Dark Sea, 1991
Matthew and Tilly, 1991
I Am Not Afraid, 1987

Other books you might like:
Leah Komaiko, *Aunt Elaine Does the Dance from Spain*, 1992
Katy has an energetic aunt who dances in a show and invites Katy to join in the fun.
Jill Paton Walsh, *When Grandma Came*, 1992
Nothing Grandma has seen in her travels around the world compares to the wonder of granddaughter Madeleine.
Cynthia Rylant, *The Relatives Came*, 1985
When the relatives travel from Virginia in an old station wagon for a family visit, their stay is filled with hugs and laughter.

711

BARBARA M. JOOSSE
SUE TRUESDELL, Illustrator

The Losers Fight Back
(New York: Clarion Books, 1994)

Series: Wild Willie Mystery
Subject(s): Friendship; Sports/Soccer; Mystery and Detective Stories
Age range(s): Grades 3-5
Major character(s): Willie, Soccer Player; Lucy, Soccer Player; Chuckie Herman, Bully
Time period(s): 1990s (1994)
Locale(s): United States

Summary: In order to change the fortunes of their losing soccer team, Willie and Lucy plan to recruit one big player. Unfortunately, the only big kid available is Chuckie and both players prefer to avoid him. However, the thought of winning a game is overpowering, so they approach Chuckie and end up having to bribe him to join the team. The future doesn't look bright until Lucy and Willie think of a way to deal with Chuckie and to have a winning team. (98 pages)

Where it's reviewed:
Booklist, September 15, 1994, page 135

Horn Book Guide, Spring 1995, page 67
Kirkus Reviews, October 15, 1994, page 1408
School Library Journal, November 1994, page 82

Other books by the same author:
Wild Willie and King Kyle Detectives, 1993
Anna and the Cat Lady, 1992
Anna, the One and Only, 1990

Other books you might like:
Matt Christopher, *The Comeback Challenge*, 1996
   Team captain Vince resents the loss of attention and glory when Mark joins the team and proves himself to be a skilled player.
Jamie Gilson, *Soccer Circus*, 1993
   Even when Hobie Hanson tries to stay out of trouble his helpful antics create humorous near disasters.
Elizabeth Levy, *Rude Rowdy Rumors: A Brian and Pea Brain Mystery*, 1994
   With help from sister Penny, Brian tries to determine which of his soccer teammates is starting rumors about him.
Donna Jo Napoli, *Soccer Shock*, 1991
   Adam plots how to use his discovery that his freckles are able to see and talk to assure a spot on the school soccer team.

712

BARBARA M. JOOSSE
MARCIA SEWALL, Illustrator

The Morning Chair
(New York: Clarion Books, 1995)

Subject(s): Emigration and Immigration; Mothers and Sons; City Life
Age range(s): Grades K-3
Major character(s): Bram, Child, Immigrant; Mama, Mother, Immigrant; Papa, Father, Immigrant
Time period(s): 1950s (1950)
Locale(s): Netherlands; New York, New York

Summary: Bram is content living in their small seaside village, but Papa is looking for work in America so the family packs up all their belongings and boards an ocean liner. Mama, Papa and Bram reach the new apartment before the furniture does; so for a while they sleep on the floor and Bram tries to accustom himself to the noisy city and the strange food. When their belongings finally arrive, Bram is happy to sleep in a bed which smells of Holland and sit with Mama in the morning chair sipping tea. (32 pages)

Where it's reviewed:
Booklist, June 1995, page 1786
Five Owls, May 1995, page 101
Horn Book, May 1995, page 325
Kirkus Reviews, April 15, 1995, page 559
School Library Journal, June 1995, page 88

Other books by the same author:
Nobody's Cat, 1992
Mama, Do You Love Me?, 1991
Dinah's Mad, Bad Wishes, 1989

Other books you might like:
Sherry Garland, *The Lotus Seed*, 1993
   Fleeing her defeated country, Ba carries a lotus seed from the emperor's garden. Years later it is planted, yielding seeds and memories to share with her grandchildren.
Riki Levinson, *Watch the Stars Come Out*, 1985
   Grandma relates the story of her voyage to America as a child.
Marissa Moss, *In America*, 1994
   Grandpa explains to his grandson Walter why he chose to leave his homeland and family as a child and come to America.
Mary Watson, *The Butterfly Seeds*, 1995
   Jake is sad to leave Grandpa when his family emigrates to America. Grandpa's parting gift helps him remember the home he's left behind.

713

BARBARA M. JOOSSE
JENNIFER PLECAS, Illustrator

Snow Day!
(New York: Clarion Books, 1995)

Subject(s): Winter; Weather; Family Life
Age range(s): Grades K-2
Major character(s): Robby, Child; Zippy, Dog
Time period(s): 1990s (1995)
Locale(s): United States

Summary: While Robby and Zippy are sleeping, snow falls to such a depth that when they awaken they realize it's a snow day. Robby's family prefers to sleep in when school is cancelled, but Robby and Zippy quickly hurry outside to be the first to play in the new-fallen snow. One by one, other family members join in the activity which culminates in a snowball fight until snow again begins to fall and everyone heads inside to enjoy cocoa in front of the fire. (32 pages)

Where it's reviewed:
Horn Book Guide, Spring 1996, page 33
Kirkus Reviews, July 1, 1995, page 947
New York Times Book Review, November 12, 1995, page 42
School Library Journal, September 1995, page 179

Other books by the same author:
The Morning Chair, 1995
Mama, Do You Love Me?, 1991
Dinah's Mad, Bad Wishes, 1989

Other books you might like:
Maryann Cocca-Leffler, *Ice-Cold Birthday*, 1992
   Although snow interferes with a young girl's brthday party, it also provides the venue for some special fun.
Stephen Krensky, *Lionel in the Winter*, 1994
   In four brief, easy-to-read stories, Lionel makes the most of the winter weather which others in his family dislike.
Jean Van Leeuwen, *Oliver & Amanda and the Big Snow*, 1995
   Oliver and his younger sister enjoy sledding, tossing snow balls and making a snow pig.

714

LYNN JOSEPH
ANN GRIFALCONI, Illustrator

Jasmine's Parlour Day

(New York: Lothrop, Lee & Shepard Books, 1994)

Subject(s): Mothers and Daughters; Beaches; Business Enterprises

Age range(s): Grades K-2

Major character(s): Jasmine, Child; Mama, Mother

Time period(s): Indeterminate Past

Locale(s): Maracas Bay, Trinidad and Tobago

Summary: To Mama's cries of ''Parlour day!'' Jasmine leaps from bed and prepares to carry the sugar cakes and fresh fish to market. While Mama sets up the stall or ''parlour,'' Jasmine visits with friends at the many other shops. As customers arrive, she hurries back to help Mama amid the shouts of different vendors. (32 pages)

Where it's reviewed:
Booklist, February 15, 1994, page 1092
Horn Book, May 1994, page 316
Kirkus Reviews, May 15, 1994, page 700
Publishers Weekly, May 16, 1994, page 64
School Library Journal, September 1994, page 186

Other books by the same author:
An Island Christmas, 1992
Coconut Kind of Day: Island Poems, 1990

Other books you might like:
Caroline Binch, *Gregory Cool*, 1994
    When Gregory visits his grandparents in their Tobago home for the first time, he learns to appreciate the simplicity of island life.
Patricia Grossman, *Saturday Market*, 1994
    A Mexican marketplace is busy on Saturday with vendors selling everything from hand-woven rugs to parrots to sandals.
Alan Schroeder, *Carolina Shout!*, 1995
    The songs, calls and cries of many different workers add to the melody of life in Charleston.
Karen Lynn Williams, *Tap-Tap*, 1994
    Weekly, Sasifi works with her mother at the Haitian street market where they sell their crop of oranges.

715

WILLIAM JOYCE, Author/Illustrator

Santa Calls

(New York: HarperCollins Publishers, 1993)

Subject(s): Brothers and Sisters; Christmas; Santa Claus

Age range(s): Grades 1-3

Major character(s): Art Atchinson Aimesworth, Brother (older), Inventor; Spaulding Littlefeets, Indian (Comanche), Friend; Esther Aimesworth, Sister (younger)

Time period(s): 1900s (1908)

Locale(s): Abilene, Texas; North Pole, Earth

Summary: When adventurous Art Aimesworth finds a large box monogrammed SC in his yard he carries it into his laboratory. With Spaulding's help he assembles a flying machine and takes off for the North Pole, reluctantly agreeing to let Esther come along. The North Pole visit becomes more than the excitement of seeing Santa's workshop. It brings danger from dark elves and their leader and Art's use of a new invention to rescue Esther. Before morning Santa returns them to their bed to awaken and find just the gifts they want. (40 pages)

Where it's reviewed:
Booklist, August 1993, page 2060
Five Owls, November 1993, page 43
Horn Book, November 1993, page 725
Publishers Weekly, September 20, 1993, page 33
School Library Journal, October 1993, page 44

Other books by the same author:
Bently and Egg, 1992 (ALA Notable Book, 1993)

Other books you might like:
Berkeley Breathed, *Red Ranger Came Calling*, 1994
    The autobiographical Christmas tale of the author's father matches a cynical boy, a retired Santa, and a wish fulfilled in a unique way.
Elizabeth Fitzgerald Howard, *Chita's Christmas Tree*, 1989
    A turn-of-the-century Christmas in Baltimore is based on the recollections of the adult Chita.
David McPhail, *Santa's Book of Names*, 1993
    When Edward returns the book of names that Santa left at his house, Edward is invited to be Santa's helper for the night.
Chris Van Allsburg, *The Polar Express*, 1985
    The Caldecott Medal winner relates the memory of a Christmas Eve train ride to the North Pole.

716

MINNA JUNG
VERA ROSENBERRY, Illustrator

William's Ninth Life

(New York: Orchard Books, 1993)

Subject(s): Animals/Cats; Old Age; Love

Age range(s): Grades 1-3

Major character(s): William, Cat (old); Elizabeth, Aged Person; Unnamed Character, Cat (gray-green), Spirit

Time period(s): 1990s (1993)

Locale(s): England (a cottage by the sea)

Summary: William and Elizabeth are perfect companions - both old, thin and ugly. When a strange cat appears to William in a dream and presents him with a variety of exotic choices for his ninth life, William insists that he wants to remain with Elizabeth. This is the author's first book. (32 pages)

Where it's reviewed:
Booklist, September 1, 1993, page 68
Horn Book Guide, Spring 1994, page 66
Publishers Weekly, August 9, 1993, page 476
School Library Journal, January 1994, page 92

Other books you might like:
Helen V. Griffith, *Dream Meadow*, 1994
    An elderly woman and her aged dog spend their days

dreaming of youth as life slowly slips away from each of them.

Connie Heckert, *Dribbles*, 1993
Friendship, aging and grief are presented from the perspective of three cats who must say good-bye to their peer, elderly Dribbles.

Natalie Kinsey-Warnock, *Wilderness Cat*, 1992
Serena's pet, Moses, does not let time, distance, or harsh weather conditions keep him from finding her when the family moves.

Cynthia Rylant, *Mr. Putter and Tabby Bake the Cake*, 1994
Elderly Mr. Putter and his pet cat must learn how to bake a cake before they can give one as a present to a neighbor.

Ruth Wallace-Brodeur, *Goodbye, Mitch*, 1995
Michael's mom tries to prepare him for the inevitable death of his old cat.

K

717

ESTHER KALMAN
LAURA FERNANDEZ, Illustrator
RICK JACOBSON, Illustrator

Tchaikovsky Discovers America
(New York: Orchard Books, 1995)

Subject(s): Diaries; Russian Americans; Historical
Age range(s): Grades 3-5
Major character(s): Eugenia "Jenny" Petroff, 11-Year-Old; Peter Ilich Tchaikovsky, Composer, Conductor
Time period(s): 1890s (1891)
Locale(s): New York, New York; Niagara Falls, New York

Summary: The American-born child of Russian immigrants, Jenny is treated to a performance of guest conductor Tchaikovsky in the new Carnegie Music Hall. A week later, while travelling by train to Niagara Falls, she spots Mr. Tchaikovsky sitting alone and introduces herself. Through serendipitous contacts with him during his American tour, as described in her diary, Jenny learns to appreciate the humanity of this revered composer. First published in Canada in 1994. (32 pages)

Where it's reviewed:
Booklist, March 15, 1995, page 1331
Five Owls, May 1995, page 107
Horn Book, March 1995, page 190
Kirkus Reviews, March 15, 1995, page 385
School Library Journal, April 1995, page 132

Other books you might like:
Kathleen Krull, *Lives of the Musicians: Good Times, Bad Times (and What the Neighbors Thought)*, 1993
  A collection of biographies of famous musicians includes references and an index.
Floyd C. Moore, *I Gave Thomas Edison My Sandwich*, 1995
  An elderly gentleman recalls the day years ago when the celebrity train came to town and he shared his souse sandwich with Thomas Edison.
Barbara Nichol, *Beethoven Lives Upstairs*, 1994
  In letters to his uncle, Peter describes the difficulties of

having a tempermental artist renting an upstairs room in his home.

718

NURIT KARLAN, Author/Illustrator

The Fat Cat Sat on the Mat
(New York: HarperCollins, 1996)

Series: I Can Read
Subject(s): Animals/Cats; Animals/Rats; Stories in Rhyme
Age range(s): Grades K-2
Major character(s): Cat, Cat; Rat, Rat; Wilma, Witch
Time period(s): Indeterminate Past
Locale(s): United States

Summary: Wilma has gone off for the day and while she is gone the cat decides to lie on the mat which belongs to the rat. This starts a number of wild attempts by the rat to get back his mat, none of which work until finally the rat and other animals lie on top of the cat. When Wilma returns, the cat decides he is hungry and gets up to eat some fish. As he gets up, the other animals fall off, leaving the mat happily empty. (32 pages)

Where it's reviewed:
Bulletin of the Center for Children's Books, October 1996, page 65

Other books by the same author:
The Dream Factory, 1988
The Tooth Witch, 1988

Other books you might like:
Bill Apablasa, *Rhymin' Simon and the Mystery of the Fat Cat*, 1991
  Al and Annie try to find their missing cat, Wendell.
Nola Buck, *Sid & Sam*, 1996
  Sam finds a way to make his bird friend stop singing alliterative text.
Paul Fehlner, *Dog and Cat*, 1991
  The animals decide they are too old to chase each other anymore.

719

MARK KARLINS
ELAINE GREENSTEIN, Illustrator

Mendel's Ladder

(New York: Simon & Schuster Books for Young Readers, 1995)

Subject(s): Drought; Weather; Problem Solving
Age range(s): Grades K-3
Major character(s): Mendel Moscowitz, 7-Year-Old; Maxwell Butterbarrel, Mythical Creature (rainmaker)
Time period(s): 1990s (1995)
Locale(s): New York, New York

Summary: After 61 days without rainfall, Mendel uses scraps to build a ladder to the clouds so that he can find a rainmaker. In the clouds the family meets Maxwell, enjoying a newspaper with no intention of returning to work because he and the other rainmakers are not appreciated. When Mendel's father gives Maxwell some candies as a token of gratitude, the rainmaker relents and uses Mendel and his family to help create a thunderstorm. (32 pages)

Where it's reviewed:
Children's Book Review Service, July 1995, page 147
Horn Book Guide, Fall 1995, page 291
Kirkus Reviews, April 15, 1995, page 559
School Library Journal, September 1995, page 180
Smithsonian, November 1995, page 169

Other books by the same author:
Salmon Moon, 1993

Other books you might like:
Judi Barrett, *Cloudy with a Chance of Meatballs*, 1978
    Grandpa tells a story of a town named Chew and Swallow in which the expression "raining cats and dogs" takes on new meaning.
Pat Cummings, *C.L.O.U.D.S.*, 1986
    Assigned to paint the skies over New York City, reluctant Chuku the angel grows to enjoy the work.
Debi Gliori, *Willie Bear and the Wish Fish*, 1995
    Tired of hearing the Bears complain about the weather, the weather makers send them a wish fish who instantly creates any weather condition the Bears mention.
Michael Lustig, *Willy Whyner, Cloud Designer*, 1994
    Willy invents a cloud-making machine which he uses to make floating advertisements. Co-author Esther Lustig

720

KATHLEEN KARR

The Cave

(New York: Farrar, Straus & Giroux, 1994)

Subject(s): Depression (Economic); Caves; Farm Life
Age range(s): Grades 6-7
Major character(s): Christine, 12-Year-Old; Michael, Child, Asthmatic
Time period(s): 1930s
Locale(s): South Dakota

Summary: With their South Dakota farm part of the Dust Bowl, Christine feels as beaten down as her parents do as they struggle to eke out a living. Escaping from her family, Christine often walks in the foothills around the farm and one day discovers the entrance to a vast, unexplored cave. She tells Michael about it and when he's inside the cave his asthma improves because of the lakes and waterfalls running through it. The cave becomes their retreat from the dust and drought of the farm. The family fortune also improves when Christine and Michael return with amethyst geodes which their father sells for food and supplies. But when her father demands to know where they found the geodes, Christine doesn't want to tell him for fear their magical cave will be ruined; nature resolves her dilemma. (165 pages)

Where it's reviewed:
Booklist, September 15, 1994, page 136
Book Report, January 1995, page 47
Voice of Youth Advocates, December 1994, page 275
Publishers Weekly, September 12, 1994, page 92
School Library Journal, September 1994, page 218

Other books by the same author:
Gideon and the Mummy Professor, 1993
Oh, Those Harper Girls! Or Young and Dangerous, 1992
It Ain't Always Easy, 1990

Other books you might like:
Lonnie Coleman, *Orphan Jim*, 1975
    During the Depression, Trudy and her brother avoid being sent to an Orphanage.
Emily Crofford, *A Place to Belong*, 1994
    After losing the family farm during the Depression, Talmadge's family moves to Alabama until his sister Missy becomes ill and they all have to move again.
Libby Gleeson, *Eleanor, Elizabeth*, 1990
    Reading her grandmother's diary provides Eleanor with knowledge about a cave which saves her life during a brush fire.
Zilpha Keatley Snyder, *Cat Running*, 1994
    The reality of poverty in the Depression hits home to Cat when she and her rival, Zane, combine their running ability to seek help from the doctor for Zane's sick sister.

721

KEIKO KASZA, Author/Illustrator

Grandpa Toad's Last Secret

(New York: G.P. Putnam's Sons, 1995)

Subject(s): Grandparents; Animals/Frogs and Toads; Conduct of Life
Age range(s): Grades K-1
Major character(s): Grandpa Toad, Toad, Grandfather; Little Toad, Toad
Time period(s): Indeterminate
Locale(s): Fictional Country

Summary: From his grandfather, Little Toad learns the secrets of survival in a world of hungry enemies. The first of Grandpa Toad's secrets is to be brave and the second is to be smart. Before Grandpa Toad can deliver his third and final secret, a huge monster scoops up Grandpa and puts him in a sandwich. A frightened Little Toad peeks out of his hiding place, the first two secrets and bravely puts his smart plan into action, thus rescuing Grandpa Toad. Psst! The third secret is—always have a dependable friend with you. (30 pages)

Where it's reviewed:
Children's Bookwatch, July 1995, page 7
Learning, April 1995, page 71
Library Talk, September 1995, page 28
Publishers Weekly, April 10, 1995, page 62
School Library Journal, May 1995, page 86

Other books by the same author:
A Mother for Choco, 1992
When the Elephant Walks, 1990
The Pigs' Picnic, 1988

Other books you might like:
Russell E. Erickson, *Warton and the Contest*, 1986
  Quick, creative problem-solving is needed when Grandpa and Warton Toad are taken hostage by crows.
Dick Gackenbach, *Crackle Gluck and the Sleeping Toad*, 1979
  Crackle begins to doubt the virtue of a pampered toad who has been considered good luck for her generations of her farm family.
Arnold Lobel, *Days with Frog and Toad*, 1979
  The adventures of Frog and Toad continue as the two friends enjoy shared activities.

722

KEIKO KASZA, Author/Illustrator

The Rat and the Tiger
(New York: G. P. Putnam's Sons, 1993)

Subject(s): Bullies; Anger; Friendship
Age range(s): Grades K-2
Major character(s): Rat, Rat (small), Friend (courageous); Tiger, Tiger (large), Bully (Rat's friend)
Time period(s): 1990s (1993)
Locale(s): Fictional Country

Summary: Mismatched in size, playmates Rat and Tiger learn that speaking up for oneself and sharing cooperatively are necessary elements of a successful friendship. Now if they can only share the lesson they've learned the hard way with the new kid on the block. (32 pages)

Where it's reviewed:
Booklist, January 15, 1993, page 920
Horn Book, May 1993, page 319
Kirkus Reviews, February 1, 1993, page 149
Publishers Weekly, March 15, 1993, page 86
School Library Journal, April 1993, page 98

Other books by the same author:
Grandpa Toad's Last Secret, 1995
When the Elephant Walks, 1990
The Wolf's Chicken Stew, 1987 (ALA Notable Book for Children)

Other books you might like:
Barbara Brenner, *Mr. Tall and Mr. Small*, 1994
  Mouse and Giraffe are arguing and almost endanger themselves, but the experience helps them to see each other's value.

Anthony Browne, *Willy and Hugh*, 1991
  Despite the difference in their size, Willy and Hugh enjoy spending time together.
Diane Marcial Fuchs, *A Bear for All Seasons*, 1995
  Bear and Fox disagree about many things but not about the value of their friendship.
Sheila White Samton, *Tilly and the Rhinoceros*, 1993
  Kind Tilly teaches Rhinocerous a lesson in friendship and cooperation.

723

JEFF KAUFMANN, Author/Illustrator

Milk Rock
(New York: Henry Holt and Company, Inc., 1994)

Subject(s): Farm Life; Magic; Humor
Age range(s): Grades K-3
Major character(s): Farmer Foster, Farmer
Time period(s): 1990s (1994)
Locale(s): United States (farm)

Summary: Down-on-his-luck Farmer Foster awakens from a nap to find a large rock with a message painted on it. Following the rock's instructions, Farmer Foster cares for the rock and the rock magically produces milk. About the time Farmer Foster thinks he is sitting pretty the rock just as abruptly stops delivering. Refusing to abandon the rock, Farmer Foster finds his faith in the rock rewarded with .

Where it's reviewed:
Booklist, November 1, 1994, page 507
Children's Book Review Service, October 1994, page 16
Horn Book Guide, Spring 1995, page 42
Publishers Weekly, September 19, 1994, page 70
School Library Journal, December 1994, page 76

Other books you might like:
Ariane Dewey, *Feobold Feoboldson*, 1984
  Troubles never stop for a Nebraska farmer who creatively contends with cyclones, blizzards, fog and grasshoppers.
Sid Fleischman, *McBroom's Wonderful One-Acre Farm: Three Tall Tales*, 1992
  A collection of humorous tall tales about Farmer Mc-Broom and his family originally published in 1967.
Helen Ketteman, *Luck with Potatoes*, 1995
  Hard-luck farmer Clemmon Hardigree has a change of fortune when his potato crop yields enormous vegetables, each one containing a cow.

724

PEG KEHRET

Don't Go Near Mrs. Tallie
(New York: Minstrel/Pocket Books, 1995)

Series: Frightmares
Subject(s): Animals/Cats; Mystery and Detective Stories; Clubs
Age range(s): Grades 5-6
Major character(s): Rosie Saunders, 12-Year-Old; Kayo Benton, 12-Year-Old; Mrs. Hilda Tallie, Aged Person

Time period(s): 1990s
Locale(s): United States

Summary: Rosie and her best friend Kayo are members of the Care Club, which stands for We Care for Animals. They know Mrs. Tallie is sick so they volunteer to find a home for her cat Muffin. All of a sudden they receive an anonymous phone call warning them to stay away from Mrs. Tallie, which makes them all the more determined to be at her home. There they find a poisonous plant in her yard which they're convinced is making her sick. Now they just have to worry about who the anonymous phone caller is. (131 pages)

Where it's reviewed:
School Library Journal, December 1995, page 104
Booklist, October 1, 1995, page 314
Voice of Youth Advocates, February 1996, page 373
Horn Book Guide, Spring 1996, page 64

Other books by the same author:
Danger at the Fair, 1995
Night of Fear, 1994
Cages, 1991

Other books you might like:
Robbie Branscum, *Cameo Rose*, 1989
    When a despicable neighbor is killed, Cameo helps her sheriff grandfather locate the murderer.
Norma Johnston, *Return to Morocco*, 1988
    Tori accompanies her grandmother to Morocco, not realizing that the trip is a cover for Nannie to prove a French politician is a double agent.
Mary C. Ryan, *The Voice from the Mendelsohn's Maple*, 1990
    Thanks to Penny, who hears Miss Cooper calling from the branches of her neighbor's maple tree, Beacon Manor retirement home improves.

725

PEG KEHRET

Earthquake Terror

(New York: Cobblehill Books, 1996)

Subject(s): Earthquakes; Survival; Physically Handicapped
Age range(s): Grades 4-6
Major character(s): Jonathan Palmer, 12-Year-Old; Abby Palmer, Handicapped, 6-Year-Old; Moose, Dog
Time period(s): 1990s
Locale(s): Magpie Campground, California

Summary: Jonathan and his family have just arrived in the campground when mother has an accident and father drives her back to the mainland, leaving Jonathan, Abby and Moose alone. A major earthquake damages the camper and the camp site and actually changes the formation of the island. Fearing that the land will soon be flooded, Jonathan knows they must get to the mainland, but the bridge is down and, as the water rises, Jonathan must cope with his handicapped sister. (132 pages)

Where it's reviewed:
School Library Journal, February 1996, page 700
Booklist, January 1, 1996, page 834

Other books by the same author:
The Richest Kids in Town, 1994
Horror at the Haunted House, 1992
Terror at the Zoo, 1991

Other books you might like:
Matt Christopher, *Earthquake*, 1975
    Jeff faces all kinds of ordeals, including an earthquake, after he runs away from camp in the Adirondacks.
Joe Cottonwood, *Quake: A Novel*, 1995
    Francie tells of her family's adventures when they were caught in an earthquake in California.
Seymour Simon, *Earthquakes*, 1991
    The phenomenon of earthquakes, describing how and why they occur, is examined. (non-fiction)
Susan Hart Lindquist, *Walking the Rim*, 1992
    Rudy is separated from his family when an earthquake strikes while they are on a summer camping trip.
Gloria Skurzynski, *Caught in the Moving Mountains*, 1984
    Two brothers on a camping trip must use all their skills to survive after they are caught in an earthquake.

726

PEG KEHRET

The Richest Kids in Town

(New York: Cobblehill Books, 1994)

Subject(s): Moving, Household; Money; Friendship
Age range(s): Grades 3-5
Major character(s): Peter Dodge III, 4th Grader; Winston ''Wishbone'' Wyoming III, 4th Grader
Time period(s): 1990s (1994)
Locale(s): United States

Summary: The pain of moving and leaving behind a best friend is lessened for Peter when he meets Wishbone, a classmate with a terrific sense of humor and a willingness to be a partner in Peter's schemes to make money. The two have as many troubles as ideas, however. Though their business enterprises are not financially successful, they do provide the framework for a growing friendship between the two boys. (115 pages)

Where it's reviewed:
Booklist, September 1, 1994, page 41
Horn Book, November 1994, page 732
Kirkus Reviews, August 15, 1994, page 1131
Library Talk, May 1995, page 41
School Library Journal, September 1994, page 218

Other books by the same author:
Horror at the Haunted House, 1992
Wally Amos Presents Chip and Cookie: The First Adventure, 1991
Deadly Stranger, 1988

Other books you might like:
Nancy Lamb, *The Great Mosquito, Bull and Coffin Caper*, 1992
    To assure his unforgettable friendship with Jimmy remains so after Zander's move, the two friends dare each other to share three memorable moments.

Barbara Park, *The Kid in the Red Jacket*, 1988
> Ten-year-old Howard's move to another state necessitates an adjustment to a new school and a different neighborhood.

Phyllis Reynolds Naylor, *Being Danny's Dog*, 1995
> After the family's move, T. R. compares his relationship to his brother to that of a loyal, protective dog as both try to make friends and cope with many changes.

727

GARRISON KEILLOR
STEVE JOHNSON, Illustrator
LOU FANCHER, Illustrator

Cat, You Better Come Home

(New York: Viking, 1995)

Subject(s): Animals/Cats; Pets; Stories in Rhyme
Age range(s): Grades 2-4
Major character(s): Puff, Cat; Jack, Child
Time period(s): 1990s
Locale(s): United States; Europe

Summary: When her complaints about food selection are ignored, Puff leaves home over Jack's pleas for her to return. She turns up again in a TV commercial for cat food with a new name and permed fur. The celebrity cat tours Europe, overeats, hangs out with rich friends and loses her fame almost as fast as she first found it. Puff eventually returns home, tired, dishevelled, overweight and forgiven by a relieved Jack. (40 pages)

Where it's reviewed:
Children's Book Review Service, June 1995, page 124
Children's Bookwatch, July 1995, page 7
Library Talk, September 1995, page 31
Publishers Weekly, May 8, 1995, page 294
School Library Journal, July 1995, page 78

Other books by the same author:
The Old Man Who Loved Cheese, 1996

Other books you might like:
Francoise Richard, *On Cat Mountain*, 1994
> Sho's pet cat is forced out of the house by Sho's cruel mistress, but when Sho's search for her is successful Secret remembers and rewards her kindness.

Gary Soto, *Chato's Kitchen*, 1995
> The coolest cat in East L.A., Chato invites his new neighbors to a welcoming dinner party.

Gina Wilson, *Prowlpuss*, 1995
> A rough, tough, one-eyed, one-eared alley cat returns home after a night of carousing to become a pampered pussy.

728

DOUGLAS KEISTER, Author/Illustrator

Fernando's Gift/El Regalo de Fernando

(San Francisco: Sierra Club Books for Children, 1995)

Subject(s): Conservation of Natural Resources; Friendship; Gifts
Age range(s): Grades K-3
Major character(s): Fernando Vanegas, Child; Carmina, 8-Year-Old
Time period(s): 1990s (1995)
Locale(s): Costa Rica

Summary: Deep in the Costa Rican rain forest Fernando and Carmina discover that someone has chopped down her favorite climbing tree. The discovery helps Fernando choose the perfect birthday gift for CarminaWemda new cristobal tree. With the help of Fernando's father, the children find a safe, secret spot in the forest to plant the tree in hopes that it will survive and be a part of the reforestation effort. The Spanish translation for the bilingual text was provided by Mario Reposo and Margaret E. Hines. (32 pages)

Where it's reviewed:
Booklist, June 1, 1995, page 1786
Bulletin of the Center for Children's Books, May 1995, page 312
Horn Book Guide, Fall 1995, page 339
Language Arts, November 1995, page 539
School Library Journal, July 1995, page 64

Other books you might like:
Lynne Cherry, *The Great Kapok Tree: A Tale of the Amazon Rain Forest*, 1990
> A man changes his plans to cut down a kapok tree after his dreams are invaded by the animals who depend on the tree.

Helen Cowcher, *Rain Forest*, 1988
> Photographs portray the beauty of the rain forest habitat and the threats from man and machine.

Kristine L. Franklin, *When the Monkeys Came Back*, 1994
> Dona Marta restores the ravaged hillside near her home so her children and grandchildren can appreciate the sound of a forest filled with monkeys.

Gail Gibbons, *Nature's Green Umbrella: Tropical Rain Forests*, 1994
> A factual exploration of the significance of rain forests explains the need to preserve them.

Virginia Hamilton, *Jaguarundi*, 1995
> As their habitat is destroyed Rundi Jaguarundi and his friend Coati travel north in hopes of finding better shelter.

729

DEBRA KELLER
SHANNON MCNEILL, Illustrator

The Trouble with Mister

(San Francisco: Chronicle Books, 1995)

Subject(s): Animals/Dogs; Imagination; Pets
Age range(s): Grades K-3
Major character(s): Alex, Child, Animal Lover; Mister, Dog
Time period(s): 1990s (1995)
Locale(s): United States

Summary: When his family ignores his constant pleas for a dog, Alex contents himself by painting the dog of his dreams with long purple hair, one blue eye, one green eye, and bright yellow socks to keep his feet warm. Happily, Alex carries the folded picture with him and sleeps with it under his pillow. When Mister comes to life, Alex is briefly elated, but then the dog vanishes. After weeks of searching, Mister returns, folded into an envelope and that's just where Alex keeps him. First book for both author and illustrator. (32 pages)

Where it's reviewed:
Booklist, January 1996, page 846
Children's Book Review Service, January 1996, page 50
Kirkus Reviews, October 1, 1995, page 1431
Publishers Weekly, October 16, 1995, page 60
School Library Journal, February 1996, page 86

Other books you might like:
Judith Heide Gilliland, *Not in the House, Newton!*, 1995
    With his magical red crayon Newton makes an airplane and flies right out the window.
Syd Hoff, *The Horse in Harry's Room*, 1970
    A level one I-Can-Read book describes the special relationship between Harry and his imaginary pet horse.
Crockett Johnson, *Harold and the Purple Crayon*, 1958
    Harold has a magic purple crayon, a vivid imagination, and a talent for drawing himself into and out of trouble.
Daniel Lehan, *Wipe Your Feet!*, 1993
    The animals in a painting come to life and leave footprints all over the house.
Elizabeth MacDonald, *John's Picture*, 1991
    John draws a picture which comes to life and begins creating more pictures.

730

HOLLY KELLER, Author/Illustrator

Geraldine's Baby Brother

(New York: Greenwillow Books, 1994)

Subject(s): Babies; Brothers and Sisters; Family Life
Age range(s): Grades K-2
Major character(s): Geraldine, Pig, Sister (older); Willie, Pig, Brother (younger)
Time period(s): 1990s (1994)
Locale(s): Fictional Country

Summary: The baby brother that Geraldine wished for has arrived and he is not what Geraldine planned. He is noisy and commands the attention of a houseful of adults who forget Geraldine's lunch and bath. Ever resourceful, Geraldine ignores her parents in retaliation, puts herself to bed and refuses her favorite dinner. When Geraldine awakens and hears Willie rustling she marches into the nursery and establishes some big sister rules such as, "No more crying." Then she settles into the rocker and reads a story to Willie until they both fall back to sleep. (32 pages)

Where it's reviewed:
Booklist, August 1994, page 2054
Horn Book, November 1994, page 720
Kirkus Reviews, August 15, 1994, page 1131
Publishers Weekly, June 27, 1994, page 77
School Library Journal, August 1994, page 133

Other books by the same author:
Geraldine's Big Snow, 1988
Geraldine's Blanket, 1984
Cromwell's Glasses, 1982

Other books you might like:
Jennifer Armstrong, *That Terrible Baby*, 1994
    Mark and Eleanor have plans for the terrible baby at their house, but decide that perhaps the baby is not as bad as they first thought.
Jane Cutler, *Darcy and Gran Don't Like Babies*, 1993
    Although Darcy and Gran agree that they don't like babies, they both expect to like the new arrival at Darcy's house when the baby is a little older.
Kevin Henkes, *Julius, the Baby of the World*, 1990
    Although Lilly is jealous of the attention shown to her baby brother, she comes to his defense after a cousin makes an insulting remark about him.
Russell Hoban, *A Baby Sister for Frances*, 1964
    Frances is not sure about the new addition to the family, but her patient, understanding parents help her adjust to the arrival of a baby sister.

731

HOLLY KELLER

Grandfather's Dream

(New York: Greenwillow Books, 1994)

Subject(s): Conservation of Natural Resources; Animals/Birds; Grandparents
Age range(s): Grades K-3
Major character(s): Nam, Child; Grandfather, Grandfather; Papa, Father
Time period(s): 1990s (1994)
Locale(s): Tam Nong, Vietnam (Mekong Delta)

Summary: Grandfather remembers the days before the war when a defensive effort drained the wetlands and the Sarus crane lost its habitat. Now, his dream is to see the wetlands restored and the cranes return. Others, including Papa's generation, think the land should be used for growing rice, but Nam believes in Grandfather's dream and rejoices with him the day they spot the cranes flying over the wetlands again. (32 pages)

Where it's reviewed:
Booklist, March 15, 1994, page 1373
Horn Book Guide, May 1994, page 316
New Advocate, Winter 1995, page 49
Publishers Weekly, March 7, 1994, page 70
School Library Journal, June 1994, page 107

Other books by the same author:
Island Baby, 1992
Horace, 1991
Maxine in the Middle, 1989
Cromwell's Glasses, 1982

Other books you might like:
Lynne Cherry, *The Great Kapok Tree: A Tale of the Amazon Rain Forest*, 1990
    A man changes his plans to cut down a kapok tree after his dreams are invaded by the animals who depend on the tree.
Kristine L. Franklin, *When the Monkeys Came Back*, 1994
    Dona Marta restores the ravaged hillside near her home so her children and grandchildren can appreciate the sound of a forest filled with monkeys.

Douglas Keister, *Fernando's Gift/El Regalo de Fernando*, 1995

Fernando learns the importance of respecting and restoring the rain forest.

732

HOLLY KELLER, Author/Illustrator

Harry and Tuck

(New York: Greenwillow Books, 1993)

Subject(s): Twins; Individuality; Schools
Age range(s): Grades K-1
Major character(s): Harrison "Harry", 5-Year-Old, Twin; Tucker "Tuck", 5-Year-Old, Twin
Time period(s): 1990s (1990-1993)
Locale(s): United States

Summary: Twins Harrison and Tucker are inseparable and totally identical until the first day of kindergarten when they are placed in different classrooms. As they meet again at the end of their first day apart they discover that each has had an enjoyable day and has received a nickname from his teacher. The next morning Harry and Tuck dress in different outfits for their return to school. (24 pages)

Where it's reviewed:
Booklist, July 1993, page 1974
Horn Book, July 1993, page 444
Kirkus Reviews, April 15, 1993, page 531
Publishers Weekly, April 26, 1993, page 77
School Library Journal, July 1993, page 61

Other books by the same author:
Geraldine's Baby Brother, 1994
Horace, 1991
Ten Sleepy Sheep, 1983

Other books you might like:
Beverly Cleary, *The Growing-Up Feet*, 1987
  Twins Jimmy and Janet have red boots which seem to grow right along with their feet.
Mary Serfozo, *Benjamin Bigfoot*, 1993
  Benjamin has reservations about beginning kindergarten which vanish after a visit to the teacher.
Carol Snyder, *One Up, One Down*, 1995
  When twin brothers are born, Katie becomes a busy, big sister.

733

TRUE KELLEY, Author/Illustrator

I've Got Chicken Pox

(New York: Dutton Children's Books, 1994)

Subject(s): Illness; Mothers and Daughters; Brothers and Sisters
Age range(s): Grades K-3
Major character(s): Anna, Friend (Jess's); Jess, Friend (Anna's); Mark, Brother (Jess's)
Time period(s): 1990s (1994)
Locale(s): United States

Summary: The day Anna returns to school after a bout with the chicken pox, Jess develops a headache. By morning she's found several red pox marks and gleefully stays home from school. While Mark begs to be breathed on (Jess only charges a dime), the initial euphoria Jess feels about no school, lots of ice cream and unlimited ginger ale begins to wane as the illness progresses and the misery of fever and itching increase. Each page has factual information about chicken pox across the bottom. (32 pages)

Where it's reviewed:
Booklist, May 15, 1994, page 1683
Horn Book Guide, Fall 1994, page 277
New York Times Book Review, May 22, 1994, page 34
Publishers Weekly, May 2, 1994, page 306
School Library Journal, June 1994, page 107

Other books by the same author:
Day-Care Teddy Bear, 1990
Let's Eat, 1989
The Mouse's Terrible Christmas, 1978

Other books you might like:
Marc Brown, *Arthur's Chicken Pox*, 1994
  Arthur fears chicken pox may keep him from the circus, but he heals in time. However, his sister D.W., previously envious of the attention Arthur received, develops spots on circus morning.
Grace Maccarone, *Itchy, Itchy Chickenpox*, 1992
  A rhyming beginning reader expresses the humorous aspects of an itchy illness.
Gunilla Wolde, *Betsy and the Chicken Pox*, 1975
  When Betsy washes off the pretend spots she's painted on her face, she discovers real ones have appeared.
Harriet Ziefert, *When Daddy Had the Chicken Pox*, 1991
  Having Daddy sick with the chicken pox is no more fun than having them yourself.

734

STEVEN KELLOGG, Author/Illustrator

Sally Ann Thunder Ann Whirlwind Crockett: A Tall Tale

(New York: Morrow Junior Books, 1995)

Subject(s): Folk Tales; Legends; Humor
Age range(s): Grades 1-3
Major character(s): Sally Ann Thunder Crockett, Frontierswoman; Davy Crockett, Frontiersman
Time period(s): Indeterminate Past
Locale(s): Kentucky

Summary: From the moment of her birth Sally Ann Thunder Ann Whirlwind is destined to be a legend. On her eighth birthday she leaves home to begin life on the frontier, eventually she rescues and marries Davy Crockett and settles into a home overlooking the Mississippi River. When a hoard of alligators begin playing King of the Mountain on her roof, she beats them at their own game. (48 pages)

Where it's reviewed:
Booklist, August 1995, page 1952
Bulletin of the Center for Children's Books, September 1995, page 18

Kirkus Reviews, August 1, 1995, page 1112
Publishers Weekly, September 25, 1995, page 55
School Library Journal, October 1995, page 127

Other books by the same author:
Mike Fink: A Tall Tale, 1992
Johnny Appleseed: A Tall Tale, 1988
Paul Bunyan, A Tall Tale, 1984

Other books you might like:
David F. Birchman, *The Raggly, Scraggly, No-Soap, No-Scrub Girl*, 1995
A hungry, dirty child whirls into a family's home at dinner time, downing most of the food, and leaving behind dust, grease, and a permanent bathtub ring.
Caron Lee Cohen, *Sally Ann Thunder Ann Whirlwind Crockett: A Tall Tale*, 1985
The tale of the legendary figure who fears nothing is retold by a different author and illustrator.
Anne Isaacs, *Swamp Angel*, 1994
The award-winning original tall tale introduces Angelica Longrider who saves settlers in Tennessee before moving to Montana and continuing her heroic exploits.
Mercer Mayer, *Liza Lou and the Yeller Belly Swamp*, 1976
Liza Lou outwits all the witches, haunts and spooks in the Yeller Belly Swamp.

735

TRISH KENNEDY, Editor
TIMOTHY SCHODORF, Co-Editor

Baseball Card Crazy
(New York: Charles Scribner's Sons, 1993)

Subject(s): Collectors and Collecting; Grandparents; Sports/Baseball
Age range(s): Grades 3-5
Major character(s): Oliver O'Malley, 5th Grader, Collector (baseball cards); Grandad, Grandfather, Farmer; Samantha O'Malley, 7-Year-Old, Sister
Time period(s): 1990s (1993)
Locale(s): United States

Summary: A three-week trip to the farm where his father lived as a boy gives Oliver the opportunity to find his father's old baseball card collection. Futile searches of closets, the attic, basement, and his dad's old clubhouse yield some interesting relics of the past, but no obvious baseball cards. Finally, the night before he and Samantha are to return home, Oliver finds what he has been seeking in a most unexpected place. This is the first book by the authors who are mother and son. (72 pages)

Where it's reviewed:
Booklist, March 15, 1993, page 1319
Children's Book Review Service, March 1993, page 94
Horn Book Guide, Fall 1993, page 300
Publishers Weekly, February 8, 1993, page 87
School Library Journal, May 1993, page 106

Other books you might like:
Casey Childress, *A Beginner's Guide to Baseball Card Collecting: A Step-by-Step Guide for the Young Collector*, 1990

A nonfiction guide to collecting and storing baseball cards. Co-author Linda McKenzie.
Jamie Gilson, *Harvey, the Beer Can King*, 1978
Harvey thinks that his fantastic collection of beer cans is his ticket to victory in the Super Kid Contest.
Ellen Leroe, *Ghost Dog*, 1993
Visiting his grandparents becomes an adventure for Artie when he encounters a ghost dog that only he can see.

736

WILLIAM KENNEDY
BRENDAN KENNEDY, Illustrator
S.D. SCHINDLER, Illustrator

Charlie Malarkey and the Singing Moose
(New York: Viking, 1994)

Subject(s): Animals/Moose; Circus; Singing
Age range(s): Grades 1-4
Major character(s): Charlie Malarkey, Child, Friend; Barnaby, Moose (sad), Singer; Ralph T. Bungaroo, Kidnapper
Time period(s): 1990s (1994)
Locale(s): North Albany, New York

Summary: When Charlie visits the circus he notices that the singing moose appears sad. Investigating further, Charlie learns that Barnaby has been kidnapped by Ralph T. Bungaroo and forced to perform, using a magic tie to make him sing. This knowledge gives Charlie an idea to free Barnaby and put an end to Ralph T. Bungaroo's evil deeds. (32 pages)

Where it's reviewed:
Booklist, June 1, 1994, page 1839
Horn Book Guide, Fall 1994, page 301
Kirkus Reviews, June 15, 1994, page 847
Publishers Weekly, June 6, 1994, page 64
School Library Journal, July 1994, page 78

Other books by the same author:
Charlie Malarkey and the Belly Button Machine, 1990

Other books you might like:
Jim Latimer, *Moose and Friends*, 1993
The adventures of Moose continue in this tale of Moose and his animal friends.
Laura Numeroff, *If You Give a Moose a Muffin*, 1991
There's no telling what can happen if you give a moose that first muffin; he may just ask for something more.
Daniel Manus Pinkwater, *Blue Moose*, 1975
A restaurant owner hires a talking blue moose to serve as the head waiter for the winter.
John Stadler, *The Ballad of Wilbur and the Moose*, 1989
A humorous story of the Wild West features a cowboy, a large blue moose and pig rustlers.
Bernard Wiseman, *Morris and Boris at the Circus*, 1988
Morris and Boris are looking forward to seeing the circus and are surprised when they become participants.

737

WENDY KESSELMAN
RONALD HIMLER, Illustrator

Sand in My Shoes

(New York: Hyperion Books for Children, 1995)

Subject(s): Beaches; Summer; Stories in Rhyme
Age range(s): Grades K-3
Major character(s): Unnamed Character, Child
Time period(s): 1990s (1995)
Locale(s): United States

Summary: On the last day of summer vacation a young girl takes a nostalgic walk along the beach experiencing one last time the joys of her summer days. As the family begins the journey home, she bids good-bye to all the animals that are part of her beach environment as well as fog and storms. Returning to school in the city she sits in class wondering why she is inside and not at the beach. (32 pages)

Where it's reviewed:
Booklist, June 1995, page 1786
Horn Book Guide, Fall 1995, page 269
Kirkus Reviews, May 15, 1995, page 712
School Library Journal, July 1995, page 64

Other books by the same author:
There's a Train Going by My Window, 1982
Emma, 1980
Time for Jody, 1975

Other books you might like:
Douglas Florian, *A Beach Day*, 1990
    A family enjoys a relaxing day at the beach looking for sea shells.
Sherry Garland, *Summer Sands*, 1995
    After a storm two children are surprised to see the devastation of the dunes on which they have romped all summer.
Troon Harrison, *The Long Weekend*, 1994
    For his fifth birthday Michael chooses to spend three days playing at the beach with his mom.
Joanne Ryder, *A House by the Sea*, 1994
    A young boy imagines a rollicking life with a variety of marine animals.

738

CRISTINA KESSLER
IAN SCHOENHERR, Illustrator

One Night: A Story from the Desert

(New York: Philomel Books, 1995)

Subject(s): Deserts; Africa; Animals/Goats
Age range(s): Grades 1-3
Major character(s): Muhamad, 8-Year-Old (Tuareg), Shepherd (goat herder)
Time period(s): Indeterminate Past
Locale(s): Niger

Summary: For the Tuareg the grandmother is a boy's first teacher and so Muhamad learns of the beauty and danger of the desert and how to live in harmony with it. When the grandmother's lessons are complete, the father begins the instructions that will make a boy a man. Muhamad is given responsibilty for grazing the family's goats each day. Returning to the family's settlement one evening he notices one pregnant goat unable to continue the journey and so he spends the night alone on the desert, protecting his herd. In the morning, carrying the newborn goat, and leading the herd, he returns home to a man's welcome. (32 pages)

Where it's reviewed:
Booklist, July 1995, page 1882
Children's Book Review Service, June 1995, page 124
Library Talk, May 1995, page 50
Publishers Weekly, May 1, 1995, page 58
School Library Journal, June 1995, page 89

Awards the book has won:
Book Links Good Book, 1995

Other books you might like:
Robin Bernard, *Juma and the Honey-Guide: An African Story*, 1996
    A father teaches his son how to follow the honey-guide bird to find honey and to always share some honey with the bird as a token of thanks.
Ann Grifalconi, *Darkness and the Butterfly*, 1987
    Fearless by day, little Osa becomes afraid as darkness falls and she imagines the terrifying things that might be hidden by the night.
Tololwa M. Mollel, *Big Boy*, 1995
    Little Oli looks forward to the day when he is big enough to take on more responsibility.

739

HELEN KETTEMAN
JAMES WARHOLA, Illustrator

The Christmas Blizzard

(New York: Scholastic Inc., 1995)

Subject(s): Weather; Christmas; Folk Tales
Age range(s): Grades K-3
Major character(s): Maynard Jenkins, Aged Person, Storyteller; Sissy McNab, Child; Miz Pendersnarf, Aged Person
Time period(s): 1990s (1995); 1920s (1922)
Locale(s): Lizzard, Indiana

Summary: When Sissy McNab excitedly tells Mr. Jenkins about the prediction for snow, Maynard Jenkins relates a memory of the blizzard of '22. The crazy winter began with cold, dry weather in Indiana, but the North Pole was so warm the elves had no interest in making toys. Santa moved his workshop to Maynard's hometown, but the lack of snow still hampered toy production. With one of Miz Pendersnarf's spells to help, a wind whips moisture-laden clouds over town, Unfortunately, the clouds freeze and fall from the sky in clumps. It takes some ingenuity to get the clouds back into the sky and warm enough to snow a Christmas blizzard for Santa. (32 pages)

Where it's reviewed:
Booklist, September 15, 1995, page 170
Children's Book Review Service, January 1996, page 50
Horn Book Guide, Spring 1996, page 33
School Library Journal, October 1995, page 38

Other books by the same author:
Luck with Potatoes, 1995
The Year of No More Corn, 1993
Not Yet, Yvette, 1992

Other books you might like:
Daniil Kharms, *The Story of a Boy Named Will, Who Went Sledding down the Hill*, 1993
    When Will sleds down the hill he gathers speed and passengers before he reaches the bottom.
Mary Pope Osborne, *American Tall Tales*, 1991
    This award-winning collection features legendary figures such as Paul Bunyan and Johnny Appleseed.
Judith Benet Richardson, *Old Winter*, 1996
    As Old Winter prepares for his trip south he's angered by the complaints of the townsfolk about the cold, dreary weather and decides to stay put for 2 more months.

740

HELEN KETTEMAN
BRIAN FLOCA, Illustrator

Luck with Potatoes
(New York: Orchard Books, 1995)

Subject(s): Animals/Cows; Farm Life; Tall Tales
Age range(s): Grades 1-4
Major character(s): Clemmon Hardigree, Farmer
Time period(s): 1990s (1995)
Locale(s): Tennessee

Summary: A life of hard luck and failed crops prepares Clemmon Hardigree for disaster when his mountain cows gain so much weight that they collapse their pasture and vanish into newly created Cow Hollow. Undeterred, Clemmon next invests in seed potatoes to plant in Cow Hollow. Trying to ignore the mooing from the ghost cows, Clemmon tends the crop which grows to gigantic proportions. At harvest time Clemmon discovers that each potato holds a cow and so begins his luck with potatoes. (32 pages)

Where it's reviewed:
Booklist, October 1, 1995, page 326
Horn Book, January 1996, page 64
Horn Book Guide, Spring 1996, page 33
School Library Journal, October 1995, page 105

Other books by the same author:
The Christmas Blizzard, 1995
The Year of No More Corn, 1993
Not Yet, Yvette, 1992

Other books you might like:
Ariane Dewey, *Feobold Feoboldson*, 1984
    Troubles never stop for a Nebraska farmer who creatively contends with cyclones, blizzards, fog and grasshoppers.
Sid Fleischman, *McBroom's Wonderful One-Acre Farm: Three Tall Tales*, 1992
    A collection of humorous tall tales about Farmer McBroom and his family originally published in 1967.
Tres Seymour, *Hunting the White Cow*, 1993
    An ordinary white cow becomes legendary when she escapes and eludes capture.

741

HELEN KETTEMAN
ROBERT ANDREW PARKER, Illustrator

The Year of No More Corn
(New York: Orchard Books, 1993)

Subject(s): Folk Tales; Storytelling; Farm Life
Age range(s): Grades K-3
Major character(s): Old Grampa, Grandfather, Storyteller; Beanie, Child (bored)
Time period(s): 1990s (1993); 1920s (1928)
Locale(s): Indiana (family farm)

Summary: Beanie and Old Grampa are, respectively, too young and too old to help with the planting of the corn crop. Beanie seeks Old Grampa's company and is entertained with a tall tale of the year 1928 when one disaster after another wipes out the corn crop until Grampa's skill at whittling saves the day. (32 pages)

Where it's reviewed:
Booklist, September 15, 1993, page 158
Horn Book Guide, Spring 1994, page 40
Kirkus Reviews, August 1, 1993, page 1003
Publishers Weekly, July 26 1993, page 70
School Library Journal, September 1993, page 209

Other books by the same author:
One Baby Boy, 1994
Aunt Hilarity's Bustle, 1992
Not Yet, Yvette, 1992

Other books you might like:
Sid Fleischman, *McBroom's Wonderful One-Acre Farm: Three Tall Tales*, 1992
    A collection of humorous tall tales about Farmer McBroom and his family originally published in 1967.
Jacqueline Briggs Martin, *Good Times on Grandfather Mountain*, 1992
    Optimistic Old Washburn faces challenges by whittling himself right out of hardship.
Tres Seymour, *Hunting the White Cow*, 1993
    A wayward cow becomes a legend in a mountain community as attempts to capture her fail.

742

ERIC A. KIMMEL
TRINA SCHART HYMAN, Illustrator

The Adventures of Hershel of Ostropol
(New York: Holiday House, 1995)

Subject(s): Folk Tales; Legends; Jews
Age range(s): Grades 3-5
Major character(s): Hershel, Wanderer
Time period(s): 19th century
Locale(s): Ostropol, Ukraine

Summary: Ten stories relate the misfortunes of a wandering beggar who approaches barriers on the road of life with wit, determination, and inventiveness. He outwits a bandit in the forest and finds a miraculous way to keep his family from starving. When his life ends, he banters with the angel at heaven's gates before being invited to enter. (64 pages)

Where it's reviewed:
Booklist, October 15, 1995, page 405
Horn Book, January 1996, page 83
Instructor, November 1995, page 59
Kirkus Reviews, October 1, 1995, page 1431
School Library Journal, November 1995, page 112

Other books by the same author:
The Spotted Pony: A Collection of Hanukkah Stories, 1992
Bearhead: A Russian Folktale, 1991
Hershel and the Hanukkah Goblins, 1989 (Caldecott Honor Book)

Other books you might like:
Adele Geras, *My Grandmother's Stories: A Collection of Jewish Folk Tales*, 1990
This award-winning collection of stories told by a grandmother to her granddaughter includes customs and recipes.
Steve Sanfield, *The Feather Merchants and Other Tales of the Fools of Chelm*, 1991
Thirteen tales drawn from Jewish folklore offer humor and heritage.
Isaac Bashevis Singer, *Stories for Children*, 1984
Yiddish tradition inspires this collection of tales.

743

ERIC A. KIMMEL
ROBERT RAYEVSKY, Illustrator

Bernal & Florinda: A Spanish Tale

(New York: Holiday House, 1994)

Subject(s): Love; Animals/Insects; Problem Solving
Age range(s): Grades 1-4
Major character(s): Bernal, Gentleman; Florinda Garcilaso, Gentlewoman; Don Garcilaso, Father (Florinda's), Government Official (mayor)
Time period(s): Indeterminate Past
Locale(s): Seville, Spain

Summary: Greedy Don Garcilaso cares nothing for his daughter's love for poor Bernal and forbids their marriage. Bernal is determined to make his fortune from the grasshopper-infested field he owns and succeeds by trading his sack of grasshoppers for a goose. Each time Bernal trades one item he receives something in exchange which he is also able to swap until finally he has traded his way into a trick on Don Garcilaso and marriage to Florinda. (32 pages)

Where it's reviewed:
Booklist, September 15, 1994, page 144
Bulletin of the Center for Children's Books, September 1994, page 15
Horn Book Guide, Spring 1995, page 43
Publishers Weekly, July 4, 1994, page 62
School Library Journal, November 1994, page 83

Other books by the same author:
Three Sacks of Truth: A Story from France, 1993
I Took My Frog to the Library, 1990
Anansi and the Moss-Covered Rock, 1988

Other books you might like:
Sharon Creeden, *Fair Is Fair: World Folktales of Justice*, 1994
A collection of folktales relating to the theme of justice includes bibliographic references for each entry.
Cynthia DeFelice, *Three Perfect Peaches: A French Folktale*, 1995
When a king breaks his promise to marry his daughter to anyone bringing three perfect peaches, the kindly lad who fulfills the quest must use his wits to achieve his goal.
Andrej Dugin, *Dragon Feathers*, 1993
An artistic retelling of a German folktale tells of a woodcutter's son who must pluck three feathers from a dragon in order to win his true love. Co-author Olga Dugina.
Petra Mathers, *Victor and Christabel*, 1993
Victor's loving devotion to a sleeping woman in a painting breaks the spell and returns Christabel to life.

744

ERIC A. KIMMEL
ROBERT RAYEVSKY, Illustrator

Three Sacks of Truth: A Story from France

(New York: Holiday House, 1993)

Subject(s): Fairy Tale; Dishonesty; Kings, Queens, Rulers, etc.
Age range(s): Grades K-3
Major character(s): Petit Jean, Peddler (honest); Unnamed Character, Royalty (dishonest); Unnamed Character, Royalty (princess)
Time period(s): Indeterminate Past
Locale(s): France

Summary: In this adaptation of a French folk tale, a humble, but clever peasant outwits a greedy, unscrupulous king. To satisfy his craving for peaches, a king promises his daughter in marriage to anyone who can bring him the perfect peach. Many suitors appear, each bearing a peach, but no peach fulfills the king's requirements. Petite Jean's honesty, aided by a little magic from an old woman, triumphs over the peach-eating king's trickery and the princess becomes his bride. (32 pages)

Where it's reviewed:
Booklist, April 15, 1993, page 1519
Children's Bookwatch, May 1993, page 2
Horn Book Guide, Fall 1993, page 327
Publishers Weekly, April 19, 1993, page 60
School Library Journal, July 1993, page 80

Awards the book has won:
Irma and James H. Black Award, 1993

Other books by the same author:
Baba Yaga: A Russian Folktale, 1991
I Took My Frog to the Library, 1990
Hershel and the Hanukkah Goblins, 1989

Other books you might like:
Cynthia DeFelice, *Three Perfect Peaches: A French Folktale*, 1995

Another retelling of the French folktale humorously depicts the kind country lad who outwits the king and marries the princess. Co-author Mary DeMarsh.

Andrej Dugin, *Dragon Feathers*, 1993

To win his true love, a young man plucks 3 feathers from a dragon. Co-author Olga Dugina.

Arthur Ransome, *The Fool of the World and the Flying Ship*, 1968

A Caldecott Medal winning folktale in which a peasant reveals himself to be no fool as his attention to good advice enables him to marry the princess.

Anne F. Rockwell, *Puss in Boots and Other Stories*, 1988

Twelve well-known tales are retold and illustrated.

745

DIANA KIMPTON
ANNA KIERNAN, Illustrator

The Bear Santa Claus Forgot

(New York: Scholastic Inc., 1995)

Subject(s): Christmas; Animals/Bears; Santa Claus
Age range(s): Grades K-2
Major character(s): Unnamed Character, Bear, Toy; Maddie, Child
Time period(s): 1990s (1994)
Locale(s): England

Summary: The little bear, planned as Maddie's stocking gift, falls out of the sack, out of the sleigh and onto the roof of Maddie's house. Falling down the chimney makes the bear very dirty, but he is determined to position himself before morning so Maddie will find him when she awakens. Her stocking is too high to reach so the damp, soiled teddy bear wraps himself in some leftover paper and waits patiently to be discovered by a very appreciative little girl. First published in Great Britain in 1994. (32 pages)

Where it's reviewed:
Booklist, September 15, 1995, page 170
Horn Book Guide, Spring 1996, page 14
School Library Journal, October 1995, page 38

Other books you might like:
John Burningham, *Harvey Slumfenburger's Christmas Present*, 1993

Wearily, Santa returns home to discover that he's forgotten to deliver one child's present and so he sets off using a variety of transportation alternatives to reach his goal.

Don Freeman, *Corduroy*, 1968

A lonely department-store bear who tries to make himself more appealing to customers by finding his missing button eventually is purchased and given a home.

Jacqueline McQuade, *Christmas with Teddy Bear*, 1996

In preparation for Christmas, Teddy Bear writes a letter to Santa, decorates the tree, sings carols and tries to stay awake and watch for Santa's arrival.

746

CHRISTOPHER KING
MARY GRANDPRE, Illustrator

The Vegetables Go to Bed

(New York: Crown Publishers, Inc., 1994)

Subject(s): Bedtime; Stories in Rhyme
Age range(s): Grades K-2
Major character(s): Unnamed Character, Child
Time period(s): 1990s (1994)
Locale(s): United States

Summary: A young boy quietly reminds everyone that the vegetables are settling down for the night. As he continues the narration, the illustrations show the child going through his own bedtime routine until both boy and garden are asleep. (24 pages)

Where it's reviewed:
Children's Book Review Service, July 1994, page 148
Horn Book Guide, Fall 1994, page 277
Library Talk, May 1995, page 48
Publishers Weekly, April 11, 1994, page 63
School Library Journal, July 1994, page 79

Other books you might like:
Margaret Wise Brown, *Goodnight Moon*, 1947

A young rabbit bids good night to the items in his room and, finally, the moon before sleeping.

Mem Fox, *Time for Bed*, 1993

A mother reading to her child, puts the animals of the world to bed for the night as she gently encourages her own child's slumber.

Mirra Ginsburg, *Asleep, Asleep*, 1992

The animals are quietly bid good night until only the sleepy child and the wind are awake.

747

DICK KING-SMITH
LESLIE W. BOWMAN, Illustrator

The Cuckoo Child

(New York: Hyperion Books for Children, 1993)

Subject(s): Animals/Ostriches; Animals/Geese; Farm Life
Age range(s): Grades 2-5
Major character(s): Jack Daw, 8-Year-Old (bird lover); Oliver, Ostrich; Lydia, Goose (Jack's pet)
Time period(s): 1990s (1991)
Locale(s): England

Summary: On a class field trip to Wildlife Park, Jack sees an ostrich for the first time and is so determined to add one to his collection of pet birds that he steals an egg and places it beneath Lydia, who thinks she is sitting atop a clutch of her own eggs. When the "cuckoo child" hatches, the unusual gosling creates some humorous experiences for Jack and the geese "parents". First published in Great Britain in 1991. (127 pages)

Where it's reviewed:
Book List, April 15, 1993, page 1514
Children's Book Review Service, May 1993, page 114

Language Arts, April 1994, page 299
Publishers Weekly, March 8, 1993, page 79
School Library Journal, April 1993, page 121

Awards the book has won:
Book Links Good Book, 1993
School Library Journal Best Books, 1993

Other books by the same author:
Lady Daisy, 1993
Pretty Polly, 1992
Babe: The Gallant Pig, 1984 (Boston Globe-Horn Book Honor Book)

Other books you might like:
Robert Lawson, *The Fabulous Flight*, 1984
   A boy shrinks in size for an exciting trip on his pet seagull.
Frank O'Rourke, *Burton and Stanley*, 1993
   When a storm transports two African storks to the Midwest, they communicate in Morse code to find a way home.
E.B. White, *The Trumpet of the Swan*, 1970
   Louis, a voiceless trumpeter swan, is observed and assisted by Sam during the swans' annual migratory stop near Sam's ranch home.

748

DICK KING-SMITH
ROGER ROTH, Illustrator

The Invisible Dog
(New York: Crown Publishers, Inc., 1993)

Subject(s): Animals/Dogs; Pets; Family Life
Age range(s): Grades 1-3
Major character(s): Janie, 7-Year-Old (imaginative); Mrs. Garrow, Widow(er); Henry, Dog (imaginary, Great Dane)
Time period(s): 1990s (1993)
Locale(s): England

Summary: Eager to have another dog to replace the pet who died when she was two, Janie uses the old collar she finds to invent an invisible dog named Henry. Her pet saves the family a lot of money since he eats invisible food paid for with invisible money. Befriended by a neighborhood widow, who also likes the invisible Henry, Janie finds an unusual set of coincidences concludes with her ownership of a real pet having all the characteristics of her imagined one. (73 pages)

Where it's reviewed:
Booklist, March 1, 1993, page 1230
Horn Book, May 1993, page 329
Kirkus Reviews, May 15, 1993, page 663
Publishers Weekly, May 31, 1993, page 55
School Library Journal, May 1993, page 87

Other books by the same author:
Sophie in the Saddle, 1994
Paddy's Pot of Gold, 1992
Martin's Mice, 1988 (ALA Notable Book)

Other books you might like:
Lygia Bojunga-Nunes, *The Companions*, 1989
   A translation by Ellen Watson, this is the fantasy of three animals' friendship.

Helen Cresswell, *Meet Posy Bates*, 1992
   Posy's mom says no, no, no to her requests for a pet.
Cynthia Rylant, *Henry and Mudge: The First Book of Their Adventures*, 1987
   The first of many stories about this duo explains how Henry and the large dog Mudge become buddies.

749

DICK KING-SMITH
BRIAN FLOCA, Illustrator

Jenius, the Amazing Guinea Pig
(New York: Hyperion Books, 1996)

Subject(s): Animals/Guinea Pigs; Schools
Age range(s): Grades 2-4
Major character(s): Judy, 8-Year-Old, Animal Lover; Jenius, Guinea Pig; Molly, Guinea Pig, Mother (of Jenius)
Time period(s): 1990s
Locale(s): England

Summary: Judy is excited when her guinea pigs have a new baby and it seems so smart. Even more exciting, she discovers that she can talk to Jenius and he can learn tricks. Since her parents are too busy to pay attention to Judy and her guinea pig who does tricks, she records everything in her diary. When Judy takes Jenius to school to show him off, he is so frightened by a cat that he cannot perform. (52 pages)

Where it's reviewed:
School Library Journal, November 1996, page 87
Booklist, October 1, 1996, page 352

Other books by the same author:
The School Mouse, 1995
I Love Guinea Pigs, 1995 (non-fiction)
The Invisible Dog, 1993

750

DICK KING-SMITH
MARK TEAGUE, Illustrator

Mr. Potter's Pet
(New York: Hyperion, 1996)

Subject(s): Pets; Animals/Birds; Friendship
Age range(s): Grades 2-4
Major character(s): Peter Potter, Aged Person (50-year-old), Young Man (bachelor); Margaret "Peggy" Flower, Aged Person (50-year-old), Housekeeper; Everest, Bird, Matchmaker
Time period(s): 1990s
Locale(s): England

Summary: After his parents' funeral, Mr. Potter buys a very talkative mynah bird. The bird at first flies away but returns home quickly when he discovers cats outside. He then begins to rule the household and the two decide that they need a housekeeper. The first two applicants do not suit Everest so he chases them away, but the third is just right. Imagine the surprise when Mr. Potter finds that the new housekeeper is his long lost girl friend and she fits right in, especially when she buys her own bird. (63 pages)

Where it's reviewed:
Booklist, April 1, 1996, page 1366
Horn Book, March 1996, page 231
School Library Journal, April 1996, page 112

Other books by the same author:
The School Mouse, 1995
Sophie's Lucky, 1995
Harriet's Hare, 1995
Pretty Polly, 1992

Other books you might like:
Joan Aiken, *Arabel and Mortimer*, 1981
  Arabel and her raven share some adventures.
Roald Dahl, *Esio Trot*, 1990
  Mr. Hopper is taken with Mrs. Silver but she is too concerned with her pet turtle.
Frank O'Rourke, *Burton and Stanley*, 1993
  Two talking birds are swept along by a tornado to a small town in the Middle West.
Eudora Welty, *The Shoe'Bird*, 1993
  Arturo, the parrot, works in a shoe store and tries to fit all her bird friends with shoes.

751

DICK KING-SMITH
CYNTHIA FISHER, Illustrator

The School Mouse

(New York: Hyperion Books for Children, 1995)

Subject(s): Animals/Mice; Literacy; Schools
Age range(s): Grades 2-4
Major character(s): Flora, Mouse, Student; Hyacinth, Mouse, Mother; Ragged Robin, Mouse, Father
Time period(s): 1990s (1995)
Locale(s): England

Summary: Of Hyacinth's first litter of ten, only Flora takes an interest in education in the kindergarten classroom in which she is born. She is able to read the warning label on a package of mouse poison left by an exterminator but her warnings go unheeded by her siblings and the other school mice. Practical Hyacinth listens and convinces Ragged Robin to delay eating the pellets until a survey is taken of the other mice. When the fatal outcome is learned, Hyacinth, Ragged Robin, and their new litter move out of the school leaving Flora to continue her studies. As her knowledge grows, Flora learns how to live safely in the school house and her surviving family members return. (124 pages)

Where it's reviewed:
Booklist, October 15, 1995, page 404
Bulletin of the Center for Children's Books, January 1996, page 164
Kirkus Reviews, October 15, 1995, page 1494
Publishers Weekly, September 11, 1995, page 86
School Library Journal, December 1995, page 82

Awards the book has won:
School Library Journal Best Books, 1995

Other books by the same author:
Mr. Potter's Pet, 1996
Sophie's Lucky, 1995

Ace: The Very Important Pig, 1990

Other books you might like:
Avi, *Poppy*, 1995
  The courage of one young mouse improves life for her large family.
Peggy Christian, *The Bookstore Mouse*, 1995
  The routine of life for the bookstore mouse shifts from dining on the delicious words in cookbooks to unexpected adventure when he stumbles into a very old book.
Peter Dickinson, *Time and the Clockmice, Etcetera*, 1993
  When a repairman is called in to fix an old town hall clock he finds it inhabited by a breed of mice who have kept the clock running for years.

752

DICK KING-SMITH
DAVID PARKINS, Illustrator

Sophie in the Saddle

(Cambridge, MA: Candlewick Press, 1994)

Subject(s): Pets; Animals; Vacations
Age range(s): Grades 1-4
Major character(s): Sophie, 6-Year-Old; Puddles, Dog (puppy); Bumblebee, Pony
Time period(s): 1990s (1993)
Locale(s): England

Summary: In the fourth book of her adventures Sophie is more determined than ever to achieve her goal of being a lady farmer. She takes charge of the house-breaking of Puddles and continues the care of her growing collection of pets. When her parents plan a vacation to the seashore with accomodations at a nearby farm, Sophie has the opportunity to learn to ride on Bumblebee, a gentle pony. First published in Great Britain in 1993. (92 pages)

Where it's reviewed:
Booklist, April 1, 1994, page 1448
Bulletin of the Center for Children's Books, March 1994, page 224
Horn Book Guide, Fall 1994, page 301
Library Talk, September 1994, page 44
School Library Journal, April 1994, page 107

Other books by the same author:
Sophie Hits Six, 1993
Sophie's Tom, 1992
Sophie's Snail, 1991

Other books you might like:
Beverly Cleary, *Ramona the Brave*, 1975
  Ramona faces the privileges and perils of growing up as she enters first grade and adjusts to having a room of her own.
Johanna Hurwitz, *Make Room for Elisa*, 1993
  Six chapters tell the story of likeable Elisa and her adventures.
Laura Ingalls Wilder, *Little House in the Big Woods*, 1953
  In the first book of a classic series, lovable, determined Laura and her family are introduced.

753

DICK KING-SMITH
DAVID PARKINS, Illustrator

Sophie Is Seven
(Cambridge, MA: Candlewick Press, 1995)

Subject(s): Farm Life; Determination; Schools
Age range(s): Grades 2-4
Major character(s): Sophie, 7-Year-Old, Student; Andrew, Student, Friend
Time period(s): 1990s (1995)
Locale(s): England

Summary: Sophie, approaching her seventh birthday and the promise of riding lessons, continues following her career goal of becoming a lady farmer. All her plans are made with farming in mind. Her teacher, hoping to develop some academic interests, plans a unit on farming with humorous results. The only student Sophie deems worthy of friendship is Andrew, son of a farmer. Money-making ideas to add to her farm-fund coffers are never-ending. Direct, determined and endearing Sophie seems destined to achieve her goal. First published in England in 1994. (123 pages)

Where it's reviewed:
Booklist, July 1995, page 1880
Book World, May 7, 1995, page 16
Junior Bookshelf, April 1995, page 71
Magpies, March 1995, page 25
School Library Journal, July 1995, page 65

Other books by the same author:
Sophie's Lucky, 1996
Sophie Hits Six, 1993
Sophie's Tom, 1992

Other books you might like:
Beverly Cleary, *Ramona the Brave*, 1975
    Ramona faces the privileges and perils of growing up as she enters first grade and adjusts to having a room of her own.
Berlie Doherty, *Willa and Old Miss Annie*, 1994
    When Willa develops a friendship with an elderly neighbor, she and Miss Annie help a lonely goat, rescue an abused pony, and care for an orphaned fox.
Maggie Harrison, *Lizzie's List*, 1993
    Lizzie makes a list of individuals "missing" from her single-parent family, then finds a surrogate Grandmother to help her locate the other "missing" family members.
Karen Hesse, *Sable*, 1994
    Tate wants desperately to keep the stray dog that wanders into the yard of her mountain home, but first she must demonstrate the ability to care for it responsibly.
Johanna Hurwitz, *Make Room for Elisa*, 1993
    Six chapters tell the story of likeable Elisa and her adventures.

754

DICK KING-SMITH
DAVID PARKINS, Illustrator

Sophie's Lucky
(Cambridge, MA: Candlewick Press, 1996, c1995)

Subject(s): Animals/Horses; Aunts and Uncles
Age range(s): Grades 2-4
Major character(s): Sophie, 7-Year-Old; Great-Great Aunt Al, Aged Person (85-Year-Old); Lucky, Horse
Time period(s): 1990s
Locale(s): England; Scotland (farm)

Summary: Sophie is saving her money so that she can have a farm of her own. Her rabbit and cat are very important to her but she really wants a horse. Her great-aunt invites her to visit Scotland and, while there, she goes daily to the nearby farm and rides Lucky. She returns home for school and is saddened by the death of this favorite aunt. On her 8th birthday, however, she is surprised by a gift from this aunt—Lucky. (110 pages)

Other books by the same author:
Sophie in the Saddle, 1993
Sophie's Tom, 1991
Sophie's Snail, 1989

Other books you might like:
Crescent Dragonwagon, *Margaret Ziegler Is Horse-Crazy*, 1988
    Maggie is only 8-years-old, but she is as horse crazy as the older girls.
Jessie Haas, *A Blue for Beware*, 1995
    Lily wins a ribbon at the horse show but her friendship with another horse owner may lead to rivalry.
Cam Parker, *A Horse in New York*, 1989
    Tiffin persuades her parents to board the horse that she rode over the summer.
Krista Ruepp, *Midnight Rider*, 1995
    A little girl rides a horse at night and, although she realizes it was wrong, she does become friends with the owner of the horse.
Jo Ann Simon, *Star*, 1989
    Riding lessons help Toni gain self esteem.

755

DICK KING-SMITH
WAYNE PARMENTER, Illustrator

The Stray
(New York: Crown, 1996)

Subject(s): Old Age; Runaways; Family Life
Age range(s): Grades 2-4
Major character(s): Henrietta "Henny" Hickathrift, Aged Person (75-year-old), Runaway; Angela Good, 13-Year-Old; Rosie Good, 7-Year-Old
Time period(s): 1990s
Locale(s): Saltmouth, England

Summary: Henny is so bored in the old age home that she runs away to the beach where she quickly runs out of money. The

Good children are on the beach and, seeing a note she has written in the sand, decide to take her home just as they would a stray dog. There she quickly adjusts to the family and is asked to stay if she will help with some of the chores and care for the children. Even though the father is at first opposed, they all soon settle into a routine and the children and parents insist on giving her presents and treating her like the grandmother they don't have around. She takes in Sweep, a stray dog, which adds another mouth to the family but when she wins a portion of the lottery their future seems secure. (139 pages)

Where it's reviewed:
School Library Journal, November 1996, page 87
Bulletin of the Center for Children's Books, November 1996, page 102
Booklist, September 15, 1996

Other books by the same author:
The School Mouse, 1995
Sophie Is Seven, 1994
Harry's Mad, 1984
Babe: The Gallant Pig, 1983

Other books you might like:
Barbara Dagan, *Loop the Loop*, 1994
    A young girl and an older woman form a firm friendship.
Berlie Doherty, *Willa and Old Miss Annie*, 1994
    Old Miss Annie introduces Willa to a goat, a pony and a fox.
Kristi Hall, *Just Like a Real Family*, 1983
    A family adopts grandparents from a retirement home.

756

DICK KING-SMITH
MARIE CORNER, Illustrator

The Swoose
(New York: Hyperion Books for Children, 1994)

Subject(s): Animals; Fantasy; Pets
Age range(s): Grades 2-4
Major character(s): Fitzherbert, Swan; Victoria, Royalty (queen)
Time period(s): Indeterminate Past
Locale(s): Windsor Castle, England

Summary: Fitzherbert is teased by the other goslings because of his strange appearance. When his mother shares with him the secret that his father is actually a swan and not the farm's old gray gander, Fitzherbert decides to search for his father. Lost, he finds himself on the Thames near Windsor Castle and decides to visit the queen. Captured by the royal ornithologist, Fitzherbert amuses dour Queen Victoria and is made her pet. First published in England in 1993. (46 pages)

Where it's reviewed:
Booklist, January 15, 1995, page 929
Bulletin of the Center for Children's Books, December 1994, page 133
Horn Book Guide, Spring 1995, page 67
School Library Journal, January 1995, page 108
Times Educational Supplement, May 5, 1995, page 16

Other books by the same author:
The Queen's Nose, 1994
Babe: The Gallant Pig, 1993
The Cuckoo Child, 1993

Other books you might like:
Ted Allan, *Willie the Squowse*, 1991
    Willie who is part mouse and part squirrel makes his home in the wall adjoining the houses of two families with very different life styles.
Dick Gackenbach, *Beauty, Brave and Beautiful*, 1990
    An ugly, but endearing mutt is the star of this story.
Efner Tudor Holmes, *Amy's Goose*, 1977
    Although Amy grows attached to a wild goose she cares for until it is healthy again, she accepts that the goose must return to the wild.
Ursula K. Le Guin, *Wonderful Alexander and the Catwings*, 1994
    Alexander's exploration beyond his home boundaries leads to unexpected adventures and his introduction to cats with wings.

757

DICK KING-SMITH
MARK TEAGUE, Illustrator

Three Terrible Trins
(New York: Crown Publishers, Inc., 1994)

Subject(s): Animals/Cats; Animals/Mice; Fantasy
Age range(s): Grades 3-5
Major character(s): Thomas Gray, Mouse, Brother (''trin'' or triplet); Richard Gray, Mouse, Brother (''trin'' or triplet); Henry Gray, Mouse, Brother (''trin'' or triplet)
Time period(s): 1990s (1994)
Locale(s): England (Orchard Farm)

Summary: After the untimely death of her third husband, a widowed mouse devotes herself to her triplet sons, training them to avenge their father's death by tormenting the two house cats. To fulfill their mission of ridding the house of cats, Thomas, Richard and Henry join forces with a ''cellar'' mouse, one of the lowliest caste and far beneath their lofty position as ''attic'' mice. However, the alliance is success not only in its battle with the cats and the disagreeable farmer but also in bridging the class distinction between the four clans of mice in the farmhouse. (105 pages)

Where it's reviewed:
Booklist, November 15, 1994, page 594
Horn Book, November 1994, page 733
Kirkus Reviews, October 15, 1994, page 1409
Publishers Weekly, October 17, 1994, page 81
School Library Journal, November 1994, page 105

Awards the book has won:
Booklist Editors' Choice, 1994
International Reading Association Children's Choice, 1995

Other books by the same author:
Babe: The Gallant Pig, 1993
The Mouse Butcher, 1992
Martin's Mice, 1988

Other books you might like:

Jane Leslie Conly, *Racso & the Rats of NIMH*, 1988
    In a sequel to *Mrs. Frisby & the Rats of NIMH* Timothy joins forces with Racso, a young rat, to save a secret community of literate rats.

Beverly Cleary, *The Mouse and the Motorcycle*, 1965
    Ralph Mouse's friendship with a young boy gives him an opportunity to experience the joy of motorcycle riding.

Roald Dahl, *Twits*, 1981
    The dirty tricks of two elderly people come to an end when they are outwitted by monkeys. SPF

E.B. White, *Stuart Little*, 1945
    A dapper young mouse sets off on a trip to find his beloved sparrow.

758

NATALIE KINSEY-WARNOCK, Editor
HELEN KINSEY, Illustrator
TED RAND, Illustrator

The Bear That Heard Crying

(New York: Cobblehill Books, 1993)

Subject(s): Survival; Animals/Bears; Historical
Age range(s): Grades 1-3
Major character(s): Sarah Whitcher, 3-Year-Old (lost in the woods), Settler; Unnamed Character, Bear (Sarah's protector)
Time period(s): 1780s (1783)
Locale(s): Warren, New Hampshire (Pine Hill Woods)

Summary: On a pleasant Sunday afternoon, Sarah, left at home with her older siblings, instead tries to follow her parents to her uncle's home for a visit. Before she's travelled far she becomes lost and, when she begins to cry, the sound attracts a bear who offers her comfort and protection during the four days that she is lost in the woods. Sarah feels no fear because she thinks she has been befriended by a large dog. (32 pages)

Where it's reviewed:
Booklist, August 1993, page 2070
Horn Book Guide, Spring 1994, page 41
Kirkus Reviews, August 1, 1993, page 1003
Publishers Weekly, September 6, 1993, page 95
School Library Journal, September 1993, page 209

Other books by the same author:
When Spring Comes, 1993
Wilderness Cat, 1992
Wild Horses of Sweetbriar, 1990

Other books you might like:
Efner Tudor Holmes, *Deer in the Hollow*, 1993
    A boy who befriends woodland animals is in turn protected by them.
Rudyard Kipling, *Rikki-Tikki-Tavi*, 1992
    A mongoose protects a family in India from cobra snakes.
Ann McGovern, *If You Lived in Colonial Times*, 1985
    A factual look at daily life during the early days of colonial settlement.

759

NATALIE KINSEY-WARNOCK
DAVID MCPHAIL, Illustrator

On a Starry Night

(New York: Orchard Books, 1994)

Subject(s): Nature; Mothers and Daughters; Fear
Age range(s): Grades K-2
Major character(s): Unnamed Character, Child; Mama, Mother; Papa, Father, Farmer
Time period(s): 1990s (1994)
Locale(s): Vermont

Summary: Confident in Mama, a young girl tries to ignore the dark shadows and scary night noises that surround her as she and Mama spread their blankets on a hillside and watch the stars. Papa joins the duo when he finishes the nightly milking and, as he swings his daughter in the air, she imagines herself soaring through the constellations and feels her fear of the dark abating. (32 pages)

Where it's reviewed:
Booklist, February 1, 1994, page 1010
Children's Bookwatch, May 1994, page 4
Horn Book, July 1994, page 441
Publishers Weekly, February 21, 1994, page 252
School Library Journal, May 1994, page 96

Other books by the same author:
When Spring Comes, 1993
Wilderness Cat, 1992
Wild Horses of Sweetbriar, 1990

Other books you might like:
Robert J. Blake, *The Perfect Spot*, 1992
    A father and son find the perfect spot in the woods for the boy to catch insects and the father to paint.
Joanne Ryder, *Step Into the Night*, 1988
    One night a child stands outside a well-lit house and imagines the lives of the night creatures.
Martin Waddell, *The Big, Big Sea*, 1994
    By the light of a full moon a mother and daughter stroll along the beach making memories.
Jane Yolen, *Owl Moon*, 1987
    The Caldecott Medal winner eloquently portrays the wonder of a snowy, moonlit night, the companionship of father and child, and the magic of sighting an owl.

760

DAVID KIRK, Author/Illustrator

Miss Spider's Tea Party

(New York: Scholastic Inc., 1994)

Subject(s): Animals/Insects; Loneliness; Stories in Rhyme
Age range(s): Grades K-3
Major character(s): Miss Spider, Spider
Time period(s): Indeterminate
Locale(s): Fictional Country

Summary: The author's first book tells a tale of lonely Miss Spider who cannot understand why passing bugs will not accept her invitation to tea and cake. A rain-drenched moth, too wet to fly away, tries to make the best of a dreadful situation and learns Miss Spider has no intention of eating any bugs; she just wants company while she sips tea and dines on the floral centerpiece. (32 pages)

Where it's reviewed:
Booklist, January 15, 1994, page 937
Kirkus Reviews, May 1, 1994, page 632
Parents Magazine, December 1994, page 22
Publishers Weekly, March 14, 1994, page 70
School Library Journal, June 1994, page 107

Awards the book has won:
International Reading Association Children's Choice, 1995

Other books by the same author:
Miss Spider's Wedding, 1995

Other books you might like:
Eric Carle, *The Very Busy Spider*, 1984
A spider persists in spinning a web despite distractions from the farm animals.
Vivian French, *Spider Watching*, 1995
Cousins with an interest in arachnids help Helen overcome her fear of spiders in this Read and Wonder series entry which parallels facts with a story.
Amy MacDonald, *The Spider Who Created the World*, 1996
When sun, moon and cloud refuse to make room for Spider's egg case, she solves the problem by creating the world and sets the egg down on it.

761

PATRICIA KIRKPATRICK
JOEY KIRKPATRICK, Illustrator

Plowie: A Story from the Prairie

(San Diego: Harcourt Brace & Company, 1994)

Subject(s): Dolls and Dollhouses; Grandparents; Farm Life
Age range(s): Grades K-3
Major character(s): Unnamed Character, Child; Plowie, Toy
Time period(s): Indeterminate Past
Locale(s): Iowa

Summary: While following behind her father as he plows, a little girl finds a small porcelain doll in newly turned earth. Naming the doll Plowie, the little girl plays with her, wonders about her origin and, years later, passes her along to a grandchild who also reveres her and passes on Plowie's story to succeeding generations. A concluding author's note gives the family background to the story. First children's book for the sister author/illustrators. (32 pages)

Where it's reviewed:
Booklist, October 15, 1994, page 436
Children's Book Review Service, Winter 1995, page 64
Kirkus Reviews, September 15, 1994, page 1274
Publishers Weekly, September 29, 1994, page 70
School Library Journal, November 1994, page 83

Other books you might like:
Virginia Lee Burton, *The Little House*, 1942
The passage of time and family connectedness over generations is chronicled in the experiences of a house. Caldecott Medal Winner.

Barbara Cooney, *Miss Rumphius*, 1982
Great-aunt Alice's life is a fulfillment of her childhood resolve to travel, live by the sea and leave the world a more beautiful place.
Anne Shelby, *Homeplace*, 1995
While rocking a grandchild, a grandmother traces the history of the family from the building of the family homestead by the great-great-great-great granpa to the present.

762

KEVIN KISER
ROWAN BARNES-MURPHY, Illustrator

Sherman the Sheep

(New York: Macmillan Publishing Company, 1994)

Subject(s): Animals/Sheep; Humor
Age range(s): Grades K-1
Major character(s): Sherman, Sheep, Leader; Wayne, Sheep, Cousin (Sherman's)
Time period(s): 1990s (1994)
Locale(s): United States

Summary: At the flock's request, Wayne asks Sherman to lead the discontented sheep to "the best field in the whole valley" and he does. As Sherman leads, the sheep follow, complaining and grumbling, but always "rescued" from the discomfort of the moment by Sherman's "reading" of the signs ahead. Of course, Sherman can't read, but he pretends to and no one is the wiser. At last the tired sheep return to their original ranch, Sherman's destination all along, viewing it with greater appreciation now that they have seen the alternatives. (32 pages)

Where it's reviewed:
Booklist, July 1994, page 1955
Children's Book Review Service, July 1994, page 148
Horn Book Guide, Fall 1994, page 277
Publishers Weekly, April 11, 1994, page 65
School Library Journal, May 1994, page 96

Other books by the same author:
The Birthday Thing, 1989 (Co-author SuAnn Kiser)

Other books you might like:
Emma Chichester Clark, *Across the Blue Mountains*, 1993
When Miss Bilberry leaves her comfortable home to move to the other side of the mountain, she and her pets have an arduous and circular journey back to. . . home.
Roger Duvoisin, *Petunia*, 1950
An overly confident goose, Petunia carries a book under her wing assuming that she now has the gift of knowledge.
Nancy Shaw, *Sheep Take a Hike*, 1994
In their usually chaotic way, the sheep get lost on their hike and follow the trail of wool they have left behind in order to get out of the woods.
Monica Wellington, *The Sheep Follow*, 1992
All day a flock of sheep follows any animal that walks by until the shepherd arrives to find them too tired to follow him home.

763

SUANN KISER
PETER CATALANOTTO, Illustrator

The Catspring Somersault Flying One-Handed Flip-Flop

(New York: Orchard Books, 1993)

Subject(s): Family Life; Runaways; Farm Life
Age range(s): Grades K-2
Major character(s): Wilma Letitia ''Willy'' Carper, Child (tomboy)
Time period(s): Indeterminate Past
Locale(s): United States (family farm)

Summary: Inspired by stories of her mother's large family, the first-time author presents Willy, one of twelve children. Eager to show her family the astounding trick she has learned, Willy races from one part of the farm to another, seeking an appreciative audience. When the family is too busy with chores to watch her trick, Willy runs away to town expecting to find someone with some spare time to view her performance. Still unsuccessful, she returns home just in time for dinner and the opportunity to show her gathered family her Catspring Somersault Flying One-handed Flip-flop. (32 pages)

Where it's reviewed:
Booklist, December 1, 1993, page 698
Horn Book, September 1993, page 586
Language Arts, April 1994, page 297
Publishers Weekly, July 26, 1993, page 70
School Library Journal, October 1993, page 101

Awards the book has won:
Book Links Good Book, 1993

Other books you might like:
Marc Brown, *D.W. Flips*, 1987
   When D. W. begins a gymnastics class, she is determined to learn how to do a flip.
Patricia Lee Gauch, *Tanya and Emily in a Dance for Two*, 1994
   Tanya's free-spirited, unconventional dance technique inspires creativity in Emily, a proper ballerina.
Denise Lewis Patrick, *Red Dancing Shoes*, 1993
   Excited because she has new shoes, a young girl dances all over town to show everyone.

764

SUANN KISER
BETSY DAY, Illustrator

Hazel Saves the Day

(New York: Dial Books for Young Readers)

Series: Easy-to-Read Books
Subject(s): Animals; Friendship; Moving, Household
Age range(s): Grades K-3
Major character(s): Hazel Hen, Chicken
Time period(s): 1990s (1994)
Locale(s): Fictional Country

Summary: As Hazel Hen unpacks in her new home she realizes that the next day is Friday the 13th. Determined to share the day with good food and friends, she prepares for a good luck party, distributing invitations to those she meets as she walks about her new community. When the doorbell rings later that night she realizes that she has forgotten one detail in her preparations. (48 pages)

Where it's reviewed:
Booklist, April 1, 1994, page 1466
Horn Book Guide, Fall 1994, page 296
Library Talk, November 1994, page 39
School Library Journal, July 1994, page 79

Other books by the same author:
The Hog Call to End All!, 1994
The Catspring Somersault Flying One-Handed Flip-Flop, 1993

Other books you might like:
Shirley Albert, *Doll Party*, 1994
   When young mouse Becky receives a new doll she invites her friends over for a party to celebrate.
Syd Hoff, *Happy Birthday, Danny and the Dinosaur!*, 1995
   Six-year-old Danny invites his friend the dinosaur to his birthday party.
Doris Orgel, *The Spaghetti Party*, 1995
   Annie invites her friends to come over on the spur of the moment, just as they are, for a spaghetti party.

765

SUANN KISER
JOHN STEVEN GURNEY, Illustrator

The Hog Call to End All!

(New York: Orchard Books, 1994)

Subject(s): Animals/Pigs; Fairs; Contests
Age range(s): Grades K-2
Major character(s): Minerva, Child; Tillie, Hog
Time period(s): Indeterminate Past
Locale(s): United States (County fairgrounds)

Summary: Minerva is certain that Tillie will win a long-desired blue ribbon at the County Fair. Her family arrives early and Tillie is placed in the animal barn to await the hog contest while Minerva enjoys the fair. Impulsively, Minerva enters a hog-calling contest which inadvertently wins her the blue-ribbon when Tillie, in response to her call, comes racing all the way from the barn on the other side of the fairgrounds. (32 pages)

Where it's reviewed:
Horn Book Guide, Spring 1995, page 43
Publishers Weekly, September 19, 1994
School Library Journal, November 1994, page 83

Other books by the same author:
Hazel Saves the Day, 1994
The Catspring Somersault Flying One-Handed Flip-Flop, 1993

Other books you might like:

Tom Birdseye, *A Regular Flood of Mishap*, 1994
Six-year-old Ima Bean only intends to help her grandpa, but her attempts seem to be one mishap after another.

Tres Seymour, *Hunting the White Cow*, 1993
A young girl thinks she can catch a wayward cow who has eluded the men folk.

Tasha Tudor, *The County Fair*, 1940
The events of a typical county fair of long ago are beautifully illustrated and simply related.

766

SHEILA SOLOMON KLASS

A Shooting Star: A Novel about Annie Oakley

(New York: Holiday House, 1996)

Subject(s): American West; Entertainment; Sex Roles
Age range(s): Grades 4-7
Major character(s): Phoebe Anne "Annie Oakley" Moses, Historical Figure; Sarah Eddington, Teacher, Seamstress; Emmeline Sue Smathers, Orphan
Time period(s): 1860s (1860-1870)
Locale(s): Ohio

Summary: Annie is born into a large Quaker family and, although her mother is a nurse, there is not enough money for all the family needs so Annie shoots rabbits for dinner. She is sent away to the poorhouse where she learns to sew and goes to school for a brief time. Then she is sent to a farmer and his wife to help care for their baby. When she runs away from there, she is replaced by her enemy from school, Emmeline Sue, who lasts all of two days. Annie returns home and becomes so skillful as a shooter that she enters contests and joins the Wild West Show where she meets her old nemesis, Emmeline Sue, again. (173 pages)

Where it's reviewed:
Booklist, December 1996, page 726

Other books by the same author:
Cool Ada, 1991
Credit Card Carol, 1987
Nobody Knows Me in Miami, 1981

Other books you might like:

David Kherdian, *Bridger: The Story of a Mountain Man*, 1987
This story covers two years in the life of the famous mountain man.

Laurie Lawlor, *Addie's Long Summer*, 1992
Addie is disappointed that her cousin does not like to do the same things she does in the growing West.

Scott O'Dell, *Streams to the River, River to the Sea: A Novel of Sagagawea*, 1986
Sacagawea travels West with Lewis and Clark in this fictionalized account.

Maryann N. Weidt, *Wild Bill Hickock*, 1992
A story of the highlights of the life of Wild Bill.

767

ELISA KLEVEN, Author/Illustrator

The Paper Princess

(New York: Dutton Children's Books, 1994)

Subject(s): Princes and Princesses; Fantasy; Adventure and Adventurers
Age range(s): Grades K-3
Major character(s): Unnamed Character, Child, Artist
Time period(s): 1990s (1994)
Locale(s): United States

Summary: After a little girl draws a picture of a princess, she cuts it out to play with it while she decides on a hair style. Alas, a gust of wind carries the bald princess away on a series of adventures which give her hair, but also leave her crumpled and eager to find the little girl again. (32 pages)

Where it's reviewed:
Booklist, July 1994, page 1955
Horn Book Guide, Fall 1994, page 278
Kirkus Reviews, June 1, 1994, page 776
Publishers Weekly, April 11, 1994, page 64
School Library Journal, June 1994, page 107

Other books by the same author:
The Lion and the Little Red Bird, 1992
Ernst, 1989

Other books you might like:

Hans Christian Andersen, *The Steadfast Tin Soldier*, 1979
In one of many retellings of a classic tale, a one-legged tin soldier braves great dangers determined to find his way back to his beloved dancing paper doll.

Judith Heide Gilliland, *Not in the House, Newton!*, 1995
When Newton sees that his new red crayon creates drawings that become real, he quickly throws his paper airplane out the window.

Crockett Johnson, *Harold and the Purple Crayon*, 1955
Using his magic purple crayon, Harold draws himself into and out of adventure.

Arcadio Lobato, *Paper Bird*, 1994
An artist's unfinished picture of a bird floats out the window and begins a quest to learn to fly.

768

SUZY KLINE
CARL CASSLER, Illustrator

Herbie Jones and the Birthday Showdown

(New York: G.P. Putnam's Sons, 1993)

Series: Herbie Jones
Subject(s): Birthdays; Schools; Friendship
Age range(s): Grades 2-4
Major character(s): Herbie Jones, 3rd Grader; Ray Martin, 3rd Grader; John Greenwood, 3rd Grader (stubborn)
Time period(s): 1990s (1993)
Locale(s): Connecticut

Summary: What a problem! Herbie's classmates Ray and John share the same birthday, and this year, for the first time, Ray has decided that he will not change his party to a different date. John refuses to compromise so Ray and Herbie plan a party to rival John's. It still looks as if Ray will not win the best party contest when an accident a few days before the parties changes everyone's outlook. (94 pages)

Where it's reviewed:
Booklist, November 15, 1993, page 623
Horn Book Guide, Spring 1994, page 78
School Library Journal, November 1993, page 85

Other books by the same author:
Mary Marony, Mummy Girl, 1994
Herbie Jones and the Dark Attic, 1992
Horrible Harry in Room 2B, 1988

Other books you might like:
David A. Adler, *My Dog and the Birthday Mystery*, 1987
   The real mystery here is how to get Jenny to her surprise birthday party.
Valiska Gregory, *Happy Burpday, Maggie McDougal!*, 1992
   Maggie must think creatively when she has no money to buy her best friend a birthday gift.
Robert Newton Peck, *Little Soup's Birthday*, 1991
   Rob and Soup make plans to celebrate his 9th birthday.

769

SUZY KLINE
FRANK REMKIEWICZ, Illustrator

Horrible Harry and the Dungeon
(New York: Viking, 1996)

Subject(s): Schools; Teachers; Animals/Insects
Age range(s): Grades 2-3
Major character(s): Harry, 2nd Grader; Mr. Skooghammer, Teacher; Song Lee, 2nd Grader
Time period(s): 1990s
Locale(s): United States

Summary: The second grade is involved in a butterfly project and Harry and his friends have been told not to touch them when they hatch. At the same time, a new teacher has arrived at school and is placed in charge of the in-house detention room. He does not look like a teacher, wearing shorts and a beard. Harry is afraid and yet curious, so on the day that Song Lee touches one of the butterflies, Harry says that he did it. Sent to detention, he finds that Mr. Skooghammer is not as scarry as he looks and has the students doing all kinds of interesting things. Even when Song Lee admits that it was she who touched the butterfly, Harry wants to stay in the Dungeon.

Other books by the same author:
Orp and the FBI, 1995
Mary Marony and the Chocolate Surprise, 1995
Song Lee and the Leech Man, 1994
Herbie Jones and the Birthday Showdown, 1993

Other books you might like:
Betsy Duffey, *Hey, New Kid!*, 1996
   A new boy in school tries to be something he isn't with some amusing results.
Johanna Hurwitz, *Class Clown*, 1987
   What happens when Hobie tries to be a good student for a change?

P.J. Petersen, *The Sub*, 1993
   Two boys switch places to try and fool the sub, but she is smarter than they are.
Karen Lynn Williams, *Baseball and Butterflies*, 1990
   Daniel finds his butterfly project threatened by his little brother and his freinds' love for baseball.

770

SUZY KLINE
BLANCHE SIMS, Illustrator

Mary Marony Hides Out
(New York: G.P. Putnam's Sons, 1993)

Subject(s): Self-Acceptance; Problem Solving; Schools
Age range(s): Grades 2-3
Major character(s): Mary Marony, 2nd Grader (stutterer); Kitty Allen, 3rd Grader; Jan Berry, Writer (Mary's favorite author)
Time period(s): 1990s (1993)
Locale(s): United States (Elm School)

Summary: When Jan Berry visits Mary's school, Mary brings the author's newest book to school in hopes of getting it autographed. Unfortunately, when the author calls on Mary at the school-wide assembly, Mary's stuttering keeps her from being able to say her name. Embarrassed, Mary hides until two friends find her and coax her to try again. Mary learns a lesson in bravery and succeeds in getting her book autographed. (80 pages)

Where it's reviewed:
Booklist, September 1, 1993, page 61
Horn Book Guide, Spring 1994, page 67
Reading Teacher, Spring 1994, page 65
School Library Journal, November 1993, page 85

Other books by the same author:
Song Lee and the Hamster Hunt, 1994
Mary Marony and the Snake, 1992
Horrible Harry in Room 2B, 1988

Other books you might like:
Beverly Cleary, *Muggie Maggie*, 1990
   Third grade presents many challenges to Maggie, including cursive writing.
Patricia Reilly Giff, *The Secret at the Polk Street School*, 1987
   One title in a series about the many adventures of students at Polk Street School.
Johanna Hurwitz, *The Adventures of Ali Baba Bernstein*, 1985
   Changing his boring name is only one of many adventures for 8-year-old David.

771

SUZY KLINE

Orp and the FBI
(New York: G.P. Putnam's Sons, 1995)

Series: Orp
Subject(s): Brothers and Sisters; Friendship; Mystery and Detective Stories
Age range(s): Grades 3-6

Major character(s): Orville Rudemeyer ''Orp'' Pygenski, 12-Year-Old, Detective—Amateur; Chloe Pygenski, 5th Grader, Detective—Amateur; Derrick Jones, Friend (Orp's), Detective—Amateur
Time period(s): 1990s (1995)
Locale(s): Hartford, Connecticut

Summary: Orp and Derrick form a detective agency called the Famous Bathtub Investigators in recognition of the room they use for their office. When they reject the help that Chloe offers, she begins her own agency and is sometimes allowed to consult with Derrick and Orp or participate in stake-outs. The mystery that they finally solve turns out to be a case of simple misunderstanding, but before the solution is reached, the detectives have some scares, as well as some humorous moments. (94 pages)

Where it's reviewed:
Booklist, April 15, 1995, page 1500
Horn Book Guide, Fall 1995, page 300
Library Talk, September 1995, page 38
School Library Journal, May 1995, page 108

Other books by the same author:
Who's Orp's Girlfriend?, 1993
Orp and the Chop Suey Burgers, 1990
Orp, 1989

Other books you might like:
Franklin W. Dixon, *Footprints under the Window*, 1965
    The amateur detectives take on their 8th case in the popular Hardy Boys Mystery series.
Peg Kehret, *Cat Burglar on the Prowl*, 1995
    In the first Frightmares Series entry, Kayo and Rosie enter their pets in a cat show hoping to win the cash prize; instead they lose both the contest and Kayo's cat.
Margaret Mahy, *A Fortune Branches Out*, 1994
    Events surrounding Tessa's practice efforts to prepare for a future in corporate finance, while being successful in terms of fund-raising, cause her to reconsider her goals.

772

SUZY KLINE
FRANK REMKIEWICZ, Illustrator

Song Lee and the Leech Man
(New York: Viking, 1995)

Subject(s): Schools; Teacher-Student Relationships; Korean Americans
Age range(s): Grades 1-3
Major character(s): Song Lee, 2nd Grader; Harry, 2nd Grader; Sidney, 2nd Grader
Time period(s): 1990s (1995)
Locale(s): Connecticut

Summary: Sidney, the tattletale, hopes to keep Harry from earning the last sticker he needs to earn the privilege of going on the class field trip. Kind Song Lee successfully intervenes whenever she can so Harry earns his sticker. At the pond Harry's plan for revenge on Sidney goes awry when he falls into the pond and becomes covered with leeches. Fortunately Sidney's lunch contains the salt needed to get rid of the leeches and the animosity between the two boys. (53 pages)

Where it's reviewed:
Booklist, October 1, 1995, page 316
Horn Book Guide, Spring 1996, page 55
School Library Journal, December 1995, page 83

Other books by the same author:
Song Lee and the Hamster Hunt, 1994
Mary Marony and the Snake, 1992
Horrible Harry and the Ant Invasion, 1989

Other books you might like:
Beverly Cleary, *Ramona the Brave*, 1975
    In one of several titles about Ramona, she is adjusting to first grade and a room of her own.
Paula Danziger, *Amber Brown Is Not a Crayon*, 1994
    Third grader Amber is unhappy to learn that her best friend is moving.
Patricia Reilly Giff, *The Secret at the Polk Street School*, 1987
    One title in a series about the many adventures of students at Polk Street School.

773

SUZY KLINE
FRANK REMKIEWICZ, Illustrator

Song Lee in Room 2B
(New York: Viking, 1993)

Subject(s): School Life; Korean Americans; Shyness
Age range(s): Grades 1-3
Major character(s): Miss Mackle, Teacher (2nd grade); Doug, 2nd Grader; Song Lee, 2nd Grader (shy), Immigrant (Korean American)
Time period(s): 1990s (1993)
Locale(s): Connecticut (Room 2B, South School)

Summary: Song Lee's kindness toward her classmates shows that friendship knows no language barriers. She provides the inspiration needed to help Doug overcome his writer's block and finds a clever way to overcome her shyness when a homework assignment requires public speaking. During a fire drill everyone in class learns the importance of following directions. (56 pages)

Where it's reviewed:
Booklist, April 15, 1993, page 1514
Horn Book Guide, Spring 1994, page 67
Instructor, Spring 1994, page 104
School Library Journal, September 1993, page 209

Other books by the same author:
Who's Orp's Girlfriend?, 1993
Horrible Harry and the Kickball Wedding, 1992
Herbie Jones and the Class Gift, 1987

Other books you might like:
Alma Flor Ada, *My Name Is Maria Isabel*, 1993
    A Puerto Rican immigrant adjusts to a new school and a class which already has 2 girls named Maria.
Patricia Reilly Giff, *Fish Face*, 1984
    One of many titles about the antics of students at Polk Street School.
Maud Hart Lovelace, *Betsy-Tacy and Tib*, 1941
    Best friends Betsy and Tacy invite Tib to join them for more fun.

774

SUZY KLINE

Who's Orp's Girlfriend?

(New York: Putnam, 1993)

Subject(s): Friendship; Plays; Schools
Age range(s): Grades 5-6
Major character(s): Orville Rudemeyer "Orp" Pygenski, 7th
   Grader; Ellen Fairchild, 7th Grader; Jennifer "Jenny Lee"
   Washburn, Basketball Player
Time period(s): 1990s
Locale(s): Connecticut

Summary: Orp's back! And his misadventures continue. This
time he has two girlfriends, but since one is his pen pal he
doesn't have to worry that Jenny Lee and Ellen will ever meet.
Or does he? Orp has a date to go to the movies with Ellen, but
receives a call from Jenny Lee saying she'll be coming to visit
that weekend and attend the rehearsal for his school play.
Now he's got a date with two girls for the same night! Turning
to his father for advice, he gets his dad in hot water with his
mom while his bachelor uncle offers dancing lessons, but that
still leaves Orp in a pickle with Jenny and Ellen in this
humorous tale of romance. (94 pages)

Where it's reviewed:
School Library Journal, July 1993, page 86
Booklist, August 1993, page 2062
Horn Book Guide, Fall 1993, page 300

Other books by the same author:
Orp Goes to the Hoop, 1991
Orp and the Chop Suey Burgers, 1990
Orp, 1989

Other books you might like:
Betsy Byars, *Bingo Brown and the Language of Love*, 1989
   Bingo's venture into romance teaches him that speaking
   the "language of love" is like learning a foreign language.
Mary E. Ryan, *Me, My Sister, and I*, 1992
   Mattie is so busy helping her mother run for city council
   that she accidentally invites two boys to the Sadie Hawkins
   Dance.
Rachel Vail, *Do-Over*, 1992
   While Whit's adjusting to his parents' impending divorce,
   he's also interested in dating three different girls.

775

LEAH KOMAIKO
ABBY CARTER, Illustrator

Annie Bananie Moves to Barry Avenue

(New York: Delacorte, 1996)

Subject(s): Friendship; Clubs; Animals/Dogs
Age range(s): Grades 2-4
Major character(s): Annie, Child; Libby Johnson, Child; Gert,
   Grandmother
Time period(s): 1990s
Locale(s): United States

Summary: Annie Bananie moves to Barry Avenue, where
nothing ever seems to happen, and quickly makes friends with
Libby, the girl across the street. The girls decide to form a
club with other girls in the neighborhood. Libby would like to
be president, but the others will only let her if her grandmother, who hates dogs, kisses the new dog on the block. The
girls, with grandmother's help, work out their problems and
stay friends. (85 pages)

Other books by the same author:
Aunt Elaine Does the Dance from Spain, 1992
Earl's Too Cool for Me, 1988
Annie Bananie, 1987

Other books you might like:
Paula Danziger, *Amber Brown Is Not a Crayon*, 1994
   Amber realizes that friendship can withstand someone
   moving away.
Lisa Eisenberg, *Happy Birthday, Lexis*, 1991
   Lexis is disappointed when her birthday party is the same
   day as that of another student.
Patricia Reilly Giff, *Matthew Jackson Meets the Wall*, 1990
   Matthew moves to Ohio, where he finds that making
   friends is not easy.
Amy Hest, *Nannies for Hire*, 1994
   Three girls who are good friends, try their hand at earning
   money as nannies, only to find that it is not as easy as it
   looks.
Susan Beth Pfeffer, *Sara Kate, Superkid*, 1994
   Sara Kate is jealous that her brother is allowed to do things
   that she isn't.
Jerry Spinelli, *The Bathwater Gang*, 1990
   Bertie wants to form a girls only club but the boys cause
   trouble until grandmother intervenes.

776

LEAH KOMAIKO
JEFFREY GREENE, Illustrator

Just My Dad & Me

(New York: HarperCollins, 1995)

Subject(s): Fathers and Daughters; Fantasy; Stories in Rhyme
Age range(s): Grades K-3
Major character(s): Unnamed Character, Child; Dad, Father
Time period(s): Indeterminate Past
Locale(s): United States

Summary: A young girl hopes to spend a day in the water with
just Dad, but plans change when car loads of relatives arrive
to share in the water play. To find some solitude, the girl
imagines herself underwater with only the fish for company.
Of course, she realizes a solitary life is incomplete; she needs
her family. (32 pages)

Where it's reviewed:
Children's Book Review Service, July 1995, page 148
Horn Book Guide, Fall 1995, page 270
Publishers Weekly, May 29, 1995, page 83
School Library Journal, July 1995, page 65

Other books by the same author:
Fritzi Fox Flew in from Florida, 1995
Great-Aunt Ida and Her Great Dane, Doc, 1994
Aunt Elaine Does the Dance from Spain, 1992

Other books you might like:

Joan Anderson, *Sally's Submarine*, 1995
    When Sally enters her cardboard submarine for a day of pretend play, she finds herself on an underwater journey.

Milly Jane Limmer, *Where Will You Swim Tonight?*, 1991
    At bathtime a young girl imagines growing a tail and swimming with various sea creatures.

Joanne Ryder, *A House by the Sea*, 1994
    Imaginative children describe their fantasy life in a house by the sea and daily adventures with a variety of marine animals.

777

E.L. KONIGSBURG

The View from Saturday
(New York: Atheneum, 1996)

Subject(s): Friendship; Contests; Schools
Age range(s): Grades 4-6
Major character(s): Noah Gershom, 6th Grader, Child of Divorced Parents; Julian Singh, 6th Grader, Immigrant; Mrs. Eva Marie Olinski, Teacher, Handicapped
Time period(s): 1990s
Locale(s): New York (Ephiphany School); Florida

Summary: Four children are joined together by Mrs. Olinski to form a team, ''The Souls,'' to compete in the academic bowl. We meet them as we hear the questions they are given in the finals, and discover their relationship to each other. Two of them have grandparents who have married, one has learned to understand her father after helping him save some turtles, one is a new boy in town facing teasing and prejudice and one cannot let him face this alone. As the four stories proceed and merge for the contest the teacher begins to understand why these four were selected, how they support each other and earn the respect of the other students. (163 pages)

Where it's reviewed:
School Library Journal, September 1996, page 204
Bulletin of the Center for Children's Books, November 1996, page 103
Booklist, October 15, 1996, page 424

Awards the book has won:
Newbery Medal, 1997
School Library Journal Best Books, 1996

Other books by the same author:
T-Backs, T-Shirts, Coat and Suit, 1993
From the Mixed-Up Files of Mrs. Basil E. Frankweiler, 1967
Jennifer, Hecate, Macbeth, William McKinley, and Me, Elizabeth, 1967

Other books you might like:
Avi, *Romeo and Juliet, Together (and Alive) Again*, 1987
    Students work together to put on a play and to attempt to assist a budding romance.

Anne Fine, *Step by Wicked Step*, 1996
    Five children are joined on a camping trip and share their separate stories.

Vaunda Micheaux Nelson, *Mayfield Crossing*, 1993
    Children who move to a new school face prejudice but work together and give each other support while playing baseball.

Ellen Raskin, *The Westing Game*, 1979
    A number of people are trying to prove that they should gain from a will.

Andrea Wyman, *Faith, Hope and Chicken Feathers*, 1994
    Three students in 6th grade give each other support in a new school situation.

778

ROBIN MICHAL KOONTZ, Author/Illustrator

Chicago and the Cat
(New York: Cobblehill, 1993)

Series: Little Chapter Books
Subject(s): Animals/Rabbits; Animals/Cats; Friendship
Age range(s): Grades 1-3
Major character(s): Chicago, Rabbit; Unnamed Character, Cat (uninvited)
Time period(s): 1990s (1993)
Locale(s): United States (Chicago's house)

Summary: One blustry, snowy evening Chicago heads outside to get a load of firewood when a cat skiis into his house. Quickly making herself at home, the cat turns out to be a capable cook and a lively friend. At first Chicago doesn't know quite what to make of this assertive, uninvited guest, but eventually the pair settle into a peaceful co-existence and a unique friendship. (32 pages)

Where it's reviewed:
Booklist, February 15, 1993, page 1060
Horn Book Guide, Fall 1993, page 287
Kirkus Reviews, January 1, 1994, page 69
Publishers Weekly, January 1, 1993, page 73
School Library Journal, March 1993, page 180

Other books by the same author:
Chicago and the Cat: The Camping Trip, 1994
Chicago and the Cat: The Halloween Party, 1994
I See Something You Don't See: A Riddle-Me Picture Book, 1992

Other books you might like:
Barbara Baker, *Digby and Kate*, 1988
    Despite their differences, a dog and a cat manage to maintain a friendship.

Ida Luttrell, *Tillie and Mert*, 1985
    A skunk and a mouse enjoy a rewarding, though unusual, friendship.

Dr. Seuss, *The Cat in the Hat*, 1956
    An uninvited cat livens up a rainy afternoon for a young brother and sister.

779

ROBIN MICHAL KOONTZ, Author/Illustrator

Chicago and the Cat: The Halloween Party
(New York: Cobblehill Books, 1994)

Series: Little Chapter Books
Subject(s): Halloween; Animals/Rabbits; Animals/Cats

Age range(s): Grades 1-2
Major character(s): Chicago, Rabbit; Unnamed Character, Cat
Time period(s): 1990s (1994)
Locale(s): United States

Summary: On Halloween night nothing seems to go the way Chicago and the cat planned. Wearing their horse costume, they try to trick-or-treat as they walk to the party and then they arrive too late for the costume contest. As far as cat is concerned the worst news is that all the food has been eaten. Ever cheerful, Chicago simply invites everyone to come home with them and the evening's merriment continues. (32 pages)

Where it's reviewed:
Booklist, September 15, 1994, page 147
Horn Book Guide, Spring 1995, page 63
Publishers Weekly, September 19, 1994, page 26
School Library Journal, September 1994, page 187

Other books by the same author:
Chicago and the Cat: The Camping Trip, 1994
Chicago and the Cat, 1993

Other books you might like:
Sylvia Cassedy, *The Best Cat Suit of All*, 1991
    A cold keeps Mike from trick-or-treating in his favorite cat costume, but he is cheered by the final trick-or-treater who's wearing the best cat suit of all.
Dav Pilkey, *Dragon's Halloween*, 1993
    The fifth entry in a beginning reader series has Dragon busy making a jack o' lantern, going to a costume party, and walking in a dark, scary forest.
Bernard Wiseman, *Halloween with Morris and Boris*, 1974
    The humorous antics of two good friends continue as they enjoy Halloween together.

780

BRUCE KOSCIELNIAK, Author/Illustrator

Geoffrey Groundhog Predicts the Weather
(Boston: Houghton Mifflin Company, 1995)

Subject(s): Holidays; Animals; Weather
Age range(s): Grades K-2
Major character(s): Geoffrey Groundhog, Groundhog
Time period(s): 1990s (1995)
Locale(s): Fictional Country (Mooseflats County)

Summary: The first time Geoffrey tries his hand at predicting the weather based on his mom's saying about his shadow, he is so successful that the townspeople are depending on Geoffrey's observation the next year. In fact, expectations are so high that the media are surrounding the entrance to Geoffrey's hole and when he appears he sees only the popping flashbulbs of reporters' cameras. The town is in an uproar without a valid weather plan so Geoffrey turns to the expert—his mother—to ask if she saw her shadow on February 2nd. (32 pages)

Where it's reviewed:
Booklist, October 15, 1995, page 411
Bulletin of the Center for Children's Books, November 1995, page 95
Children's Book Review Service, September 1995, page 3
Publishers Weekly, August 21, 1995, page 65

School Library Journal, October 1995, page 105

Other books by the same author:
Bear and Bunny Grow Tomatoes, 1993

Other books you might like:
Lorna Balian, *A Garden for Groundhog*, 1985
    While Mr. O'Leary finds the groundhog's weather predictions helpful, he still wants to keep the rodent from eating his garden.
Marvin Glass, *What Happened Today Freddy Groundhog?*, 1989
    As February 2nd approaches, Freddy Groundhog finds himself busily preparing for the big day.
Crockett Johnson, *Will Spring Be Early? Or Will Spring Be Late?*, 1959
    An aritificial flower fools an overeager grounhog into thinking Spring has arrived.
Steven Kroll, *It's Groundhog Day!*, 1987
    Ski resort owner Roland Raccoon wants to extend his season by assuring another 6 weeks of winter so he tries to manipulate Godfrey Groundhog's findings.

781

DEBORAH KOVACS
WILLIAM SHATTUCK, Illustrator

Moonlight on the River
(New York: Viking, 1993)

Subject(s): Rivers; Fishing; Brothers
Age range(s): Grades K-3
Major character(s): Ben, Child, Brother (younger); Will, Child, Brother (older); Joshua Slocum, Spirit, Sailor
Time period(s): 1990s (1993)
Locale(s): Slocum River, Massachusetts

Summary: Two brothers slip quietly out of the house on a moonlit night when the bluefish are biting. At first they sail over placid waters, but unexpectedly a squall changes their calm trip into one filled with danger. In the first light of dawn, Will and Ben realize that the mysterious sailor who guided them to shelter during the storm must have been the spirit of Joshua Slocum, namesake of the river. (32 pages)

Where it's reviewed:
Booklist, May 1, 1993, page 1604
Horn Book Guide, Fall 1993, page 287
Language Arts, April 1994, page 298
Publishers Weekly, May 31, 1993, page 53
School Library Journal, August 1993, page 146

Other books by the same author:
All about Whales, 1994
The Tooth Fairy Book, 1992
A Day under Water, 1987

Other books you might like:
Eric Jon Nones, *Caleb's Friend*, 1993
    During a storm, Caleb's ship is guided to safety by a sea creature.
Allen Say, *A River Dream*, 1988
    Mark dreams that he is on a river trout fishing with his uncle.

Chris Van Allsburg, *The Wreck of the Zephyr*, 1983
Pride comes before the fall in a fantasy of a young boy who aspires to be a great sailor.

782

HANNA KRAAN
ANNEMARIE VAN HAERINGEN, Illustrator

Tales of the Wicked Witch

(Arden, NC: Front Street, 1995)

Subject(s): Witches and Witchcraft; Animals; Anger
Age range(s): Grades 3-5
Major character(s): Unnamed Character, Witch
Time period(s): Indeterminate Past
Locale(s): Fictional Country

Summary: The resident witch of a forest is prone to fits of rage when things don't go her way. When angry she's in the habit of turning everything in sight into something else. Fortunately, when her anger subsides she undoes her spells so things return to normal. The animals of the forest hide from her rages, prepare celebrations for her on Witch's Day and boldly steal her book of magic to prevent her from annoying them further. Originally published in the Netherlands in 1990 and translated from the Dutch by Elisabeth Koolschijn. (107 pages)

Where it's reviewed:
Booklist, January 1996, page 834
Children's Book Review Service, January 1996, page 55
Kirkus Reviews, December 15, 1995, page 1772
Publishers Weekly, December 11, 1995, page 71
School Library Journal, January 1996, page 88

Other books you might like:
Alice Low, *Spooky Stories for a Dark and Stormy Night*, 1994
Folktales, adaptations of classics and contemporary stories by a variety of popular authors make up an illustrated collection.
Inna Rayevsky, *The Talking Tree: An Old Italian Tale*, 1990
A king who desires to add a talking tree to his collection learns that the tree is actually a princess imprisoned by a witch's spell.
Elizabeth Winthrop, *Vasilissa the Beautiful: A Russian Folktale*, 1991
To protect her from the cruel stepmother and her stepsisters, as well as the witch Baba Yaga, the beautiful heroine has a magical doll.

783

HOONG YEE LEE KRAKAUER, Author/Illustrator

Rabbit Mooncakes

(Boston: Little, Brown and Company, 1994)

Subject(s): Music; Fear; Asian Americans
Age range(s): Grades K-3
Major character(s): Hoong Yee, Child, Sister (older); Hoong Wei, Child, Sister (younger)
Time period(s): Indeterminate Past
Locale(s): Queens, New York

Summary: It is the day of the Harvest Moon Festival and Hoong Yee and Hoong Wei must help mother and grandmother prepare for tonight's festivities. During all the busyness, Hoong Wei worries about the evening piano recital she and her sister will perform for all the relatives. Hoong Wei knows that Hoong Yee will play perfectly, but worries she will make many mistakes and all the visitors will laugh. The author's first book concludes with the piano recital which, though not flawless, is appreciated by the family and rewarded with the first two rabbit mooncakes. (32 pages)

Where it's reviewed:
Booklist, April 1, 1994, page 1460
Kirkus Reviews, May 15, 1994, page 701
Library Talk, November 1994, page 24
Publishers Weekly, May 16, 1994, page 63
School Library Journal, July 1994, page 79

Other books you might like:
Riki Levinson, *I Go With My Family to Grandma's*, 1986
A large family travels to Grandma's home in New York.
Jama Kim Rattigan, *Dumpling Soup*, 1993
The extended family gathers to celebrate the Hawaiian new year and, for the first time, Marisa is allowed to help make the dumplings.
Cynthia Rylant, *The Relatives Came*, 1985
A Caldecott Honor Book celebrates childhood memories of the joyful confusion of a houseful of relatives.

784

FARA LYNN KRASNOPOLSKY
GENNADY SCHIKARIOFF, Illustrator
TATAYNA MAMONOVA, Illustrator

I Remember

(New York: Clarion Books, 1995)

Subject(s): Family Life; Jews; Historical
Age range(s): Grades 4-6
Major character(s): Hannah, Child
Time period(s): 1910s
Locale(s): Pochep, Russia (Bryansk Province)

Summary: This fictionalized account of the author's life, well-known as a ballerina during her adult years, takes place as she is nearing her teen years. Living in a small Russian town, Hannah, as she is called in the story, learns early the importance of giving up some things to obtain others, such as a new dress for piano lessons. She describes her Hebrew lessons, necessary when she's prevented from attending school because of the Jewish quota. The author remembers a time when many Russians went hungry because of shortages of food and money following the war and Jews began to emigrate to escape persecution. (165 pages)

Where it's reviewed:
School Library Journal, July 1995, page 79
Booklist, June 1, 1995, page 1771
Library Talk, September 1995, page 36
Children's Book Review Service, June 1995, page 130
Horn Book Guide, Fall 1995, page 300

Other books you might like:

Marie Bloch, *Displaced Person*, 1978
  Stefan and his father roam around Eastern Europe to escape from both the Russians and the Germans.
Esther Hautzig, *The Endless Steppe*, 1968
  Esther shares a description of what she and her family endured when they were shipped from Poland to Siberia during World War II.
Johanna Reiss, *The Upstairs Room*, 1972
  The story of a Jewish family who, though separated and living in different farmhouse attics, managed to survive the war.

785

ROBERT KRAUS, Author/Illustrator

Fables Aesop Never Wrote: But Robert Kraus Did

(New York, Viking, 1994)

Subject(s): Fables; Short Stories; Humor
Age range(s): Grades 3-5
Time period(s): Indeterminate Past
Locale(s): Fictional Country

Summary: Fifteen original fables are written as spoofs of Aesop's original ones. At the conclusion of each brief story, the moral is clearly stated lest the reader be so bemused by the unique turn of events that the lesson is lost in the laughter. (32 pages)

Where it's reviewed:
Booklist, January 1, 1995, page 820
Children's Book Review Service, January 1995, page 54
Horn Book Guide, Spring 1995, page 43
Publishers Weekly, November 7, 1994, page 79
School Library Journal, February 1995, page 74

Other books by the same author:
The Adventures of Wise Old Owl, 1992
Another Mouse to Feed, 1987
Three Friends, 1975

Other books you might like:
Jon Scieszka, *The Stinky Cheese Man: And Other Fairly Stupid Tales*, 1992
  The Caldecott Honor book features nontraditional (truly bizarre) retellings of well-known fairy tales.
Vivian Vande Velde, *Tales from the Brothers Grimm and the Sisters Weird*, 1995
  Thirteen classic stories are rewritten with a new twist in a collection of ''fractured'' fairy tales.
Jane Yolen, *Sleeping Ugly*, 1981
  A classic fairy tale is modified to reward a poor, kind but ugly maiden. Conventionally, they all live happily ever after.

786

ROBERT KRAUS, Author/Illustrator

Strudwick: A Sheep in Wolf's Clothing

(New York: Viking, 1995)

Subject(s): Animals/Sheep; Animals/Wolves; Humor
Age range(s): Grades K-3
Major character(s): Strudwick, Sheep; Mr. Wolf, Wolf; Grandpa, Grandfather
Time period(s): Indeterminate Past
Locale(s): Sheep Dip Road, Fictional Country

Summary: Taking his father's advice to heart, Strudwick outfits himself in a wolf costume to outsmart the wolf who has been known to disguise himself as a sheep. Unfortunately, Strudwick's costume doesn't fool anyone he meets so he decides to visit near-sighted Grandpa. On the way he meets the disguised wolf who races ahead of Strudwick, changes costumes and knocks on Grandpa's door. No fool, the elderly sheep has a costume of his own to don that defeats the wolf and allows Grandpa and Strudwick to safely enjoy the basket of goodies. (32 pages)

Where it's reviewed:
Booklist, April 1, 1995, page 1428
Library Talk, September 1995, page 32
Publishers Weekly, April 10, 1995, page 62
School Library Journal, April 1995, page 104
Wilson Library Bulletin, May 1995, page 98

Other books by the same author:
Fables Aesop Never Wrote: But Robert Kraus Did, 1994
The Adventures of Wise Old Owl, 1992
Another Mouse to Feed, 1987

Other books you might like:
Lisa Campbell Ernst, *Little Red Riding Hood: A Newfangled Prairie Tale*, 1995
  Grandma proves to be more than the wolf bargained for in this updated retelling of a fairy tale.
Jon Scieszka, *The Stinky Cheese Man: And Other Fairly Stupid Tales*, 1992
  Classic fairy tales take on a new look in these humorous retellings.
Vivian Vande Velde, *Tales from the Brothers Grimm and the Sisters Weird*, 1995
  Thirteen traditional fairy tales are humorously rewritten with some modifications.

787

STEPHEN KRENSKY
JOHN FULWEILER, Illustrator

The Iron Dragon Never Sleeps

(New York: Delacorte Press, 1994)

Subject(s): Frontier and Pioneer Life; Chinese Americans; Strikes and Lockouts
Age range(s): Grades 3-5
Major character(s): Winnie Tucker, 10-Year-Old; Lee Cheng, Child, Construction Worker
Time period(s): 1860s (1867)

Locale(s): Cisco, California

Summary: Winnie and her mother spend the summer of 1867 in the small town of Cisco so they can be with her father, a mining engineer, working on the construction of the transcontinental railroad. During the few months she's in Cisco, Winnie experiences more than her first train ride. She meets Lee Cheng and develops a view of the Chinese laborers different from the prejudiced reactions of the construction supervisors and townspeople. An afterword gives the factual basis for the story. (90 pages)

Where it's reviewed:
Booklist, June 1, 1994, page 1820
Horn Book Guide, Fall 1994, page 301
Kirkus Reviews, June 1, 1994, page 776
Publishers Weekly, May 2, 1994, page 309
School Library Journal, June 1994, page 132

Other books by the same author:
Fraidy Cats, 1993
Witching Hour, 1990
Who Really Discovered America?, 1987

Other books you might like:
Eleanor Coerr, *Chang's Paper Pony*, 1988
   In San Francisco at the time of the Gold Rush, a son of Chinese immigrants wants a pony which he knows his parents cannot afford.
Leonard Everett Fisher, *Tracks across America: The Story of the American Railroad 1825-1900*, 1992
   A nonfiction account of the challenges to building a transcontinental railroad in America.
Barbara Diamond Goldin, *Red Means Good Fortune: A Story of San Francisco Chinatown*, 1994
   In an entry in the Once Upon America Series, 12-year-old Jun Mun works in his father's laundry.
Thomas L. Tedrow, *Land of Promise*, 1992
   Attempts by Chinese immigrants to settle in a Missouri pioneer community lead to problems with racism and cultural clashes.

788

STEPHEN KRENSKY
SUSANNA NATTI, Illustrator

Lionel in the Winter

(New York: Dial Books for Young Readers, 1994)

Series: Easy-to-Read Books
Subject(s): Winter; Family Life; Weather
Age range(s): Grades 1-3
Major character(s): Lionel, Brother; Louise, Sister
Time period(s): 1990s (1994)
Locale(s): United States

Summary: On a cold, wintry night that threatens snow, Lionel thinks of all the wonderful advantages of winter while Louise shivers and gets an extra sweater and their parents check supplies to be sure the family is prepared. The snow inspires imaginative play and the creation of four snow people. (48 pages)

Where it's reviewed:
Booklist, April 1, 1994, page 1466

Bulletin of the Center for Children's Books, February 1994, page 190
Emergency Librarian, May 1994, page 44
Horn Book, March 1994, page 195
School Library Journal, March 1994, page 202

Other books by the same author:
Lionel and Louise, 1992
Lionel in the Fall, 1987
Lionel at Large, 1986

Other books you might like:
Nancy White Carlstrom, *The Snow Speaks*, 1992
   Two children enjoy the sights and sounds of the season's first snow.
Maryann Cocca-Leffler, *Ice-Cold Birthday*, 1992
   Although snow interferes with a young girl's brthday party, it also provides the venue for some special fun.
Barbara M. Joosse, *Snow Day!*, 1995
   When snow forces the cancellation of school, Robby and his family have a day to play outside.
Jean Van Leeuwen, *Oliver & Amanda and the Big Snow*, 1995
   Siblings Oliver and Amanda enjoy the day romping in the snow with their parents.

789

STEVEN KROLL
BETSY LEWIN, Illustrator

I'm George Washington and You're Not!

(New York: Hyperion Books for Children, 1994)

Subject(s): Actors and Actresses; Fear; Schools
Age range(s): Grades 2-4
Major character(s): Eric Mills, Student (timid), Friend (Danny's); Danny Fontina, Student, Friend (Eric's); Marty Boomer, Bully, Classmate
Time period(s): 1990s (1994)
Locale(s): United States

Summary: Afraid of performing on stage, Eric declines the opportunity to star in the class play in order to be a tree beside his friend Danny. The teacher then assigns the starring role to Marty, the only student without a part. Marty's behavior almost gets him thrown out of the play at rehearsal, and during the show he literally throws himself off the stage and into the audience forcing Eric to step out from behind his tree costume and complete the show. (57 pages)

Where it's reviewed:
Booklist, April 1, 1994, page 1448
Horn Book Guide, Fall 1994, page 301
School Library Journal, April 1994, page 108
Wilson Library Bulletin, December 1994, page 100

Other books by the same author:
Pitching Trouble, 1994 (The Hit and Run Gang, No. 5)
Andrew Wants a Dog, 1993
New Kid in Town, 1992 (The Hit and Run Gang, No. 1)

Other books you might like:
Stan Berenstain, *The Berenstain Bears and the Red-Handed Thief*, 1993
   A new teacher at Bear Country School hopes that the class

bully understands the lesson about democracy. Co-author Jan Berenstain.

Larry Dane Brimner, *Cory Coleman, Grade 2*, 1990
   Cory's seventh birthday party is spoiled by the class bully who turns out to be not so tough after all.

Patricia Reilly Giff, *The Secret at the Polk Street School*, 1987
   One title in a series about the many adventures of students at Polk Street School.

Suzy Kline, *Horrible Harry in Room 2B*, 1988
   In the first book about Harry, a classmate learns that being friends with Harry is often difficult, but usually fun.

790

STEVEN KROLL
ROBERTA WILSON, Illustrator

Patrick's Tree House
(New York: Macmillan Publishing Company, 1994)

Subject(s): Grandparents; Behavior; Summer
Age range(s): Grades 2-4
Major character(s): Patrick, 9-Year-Old; Grandad, Grandfather; Sarah, Friend
Time period(s): 1990s (1994)
Locale(s): Maine

Summary: Patrick's annual summer vacation with his grandparents begins with a surprise from Grandad—a tree house built just for him. Unfortunately, the first time he tries to play in it with Sarah, he finds it has been taken over by the twins who live across the street. Not wanting to worry Grandad or create problems with the neighbors, Patrick and Sarah try to solve the problem themselves. (64 pages)

Where it's reviewed:
Booklist, May 1, 1994, page 1602
Children's Book Review Service, Spring 1994, page 140
Five Owls, November 1994, page 30
Library Talk, September 1994, page 44
School Library Journal, August 1994, page 139

Other books by the same author:
Andrew Wants a Dog, 1992
The Streak, 1992 (The Hit and Run Gang, No. 4)
Mary McLean and the St. Patrick's Day Parade, 1990

Other books you might like:
Rumer Godden, *Great Grandfather's House*, 1993
   Three months at her great grandfather's home transforms spoiled Keiko into a compassionate child.
Margaret Mahy, *The Good Fortunes Gang*, 1993
   Although his last name is Fortune, Pete finds he must prove himself to be a "real" Fortune in order to be accepted into his cousins' Good Fortunes Gang.
Carol Beach York, *The Key to the Playhouse*, 1994
   While visiting Grandmother, two cousins enjoy playing in the playhouse, but lock out a neighborhood child.

791

STEVEN KROLL
JENI BASSETT, Illustrator

The Pigrates Clean Up
(New York: Henry Holt and Company, 1993)

Subject(s): Animals/Pigs; Pirates; Stories in Rhyme
Age range(s): Grades K-2
Major character(s): Captain Dan, Pig, Pirate; Kate, Pig, Bride
Time period(s): Indeterminate Past
Locale(s): At Sea

Summary: Eager to make their pirate vessel ship-shape, Captain Dan and his crew of pigrates (pig pirates) work on their personal cleanliness as well as that of their ship. The motivation is the upcoming wedding of Captain Dan and Kate. As the ship reaches port all is spotless and the nuptials proceed. (32 pages)

Where it's reviewed:
Booklist, July 1993, page 1974
Children's Book Watch, June 1993, page 5
Horn Book Guide, Fall 1993, page 264
Publishers Weekly, April 26, 1993, page 78
School Library Journal, May 1993, page 87

Other books by the same author:
Queen of the May, 1993
Branigan's Cat and the Halloween Ghost, 1990
It's Groundhog Day!, 1987

Other books you might like:
Helme Heine, *The Pigs' Wedding*, 1979
   Aptly named pigs Curlytail and Porker celebrate their wedding with many friends.
David McPhail, *Pigs Ahoy!*, 1995
   Expecting a quiet vacation cruise, a man finds his cabin full of pigs who enliven the trip for everyone.
Laura Robb, *Snuffles and Snouts*, 1995
   A collection of poems humorously illustrated by Stephen Kellogg all focus on the subject of pigs.

792

VIRGINIA L. KROLL
JILL KASTNER, Illustrator

Naomi Knows It's Springtime
(Honesdale, PA: Boyd's Mill Press, Inc., 1993)

Subject(s): Spring; Blind; Seasons
Age range(s): Grades K-1
Major character(s): Naomi, Child (happy), Blind
Time period(s): 1990s (1993)
Locale(s): United States

Summary: Naomi uses the taste of seasonal foods, the changing sound of the wind, and the touch of warm air on her cheeks to let her know that spring is here. She does not share her neighbor's concern that she cannot see the blue of the sky because she has a rainbow in her mind. (31 pages)

Where it's reviewed:
Five Owls, February 1995, page 54

Horn Book Guide, Fall 1993, page 264
Kirkus Reviews, May 15, 1993, page 664
Reading Teacher, March 1994, page 492
School Library Journal, September 1993, page 210

Other books by the same author:
Hats Off to Hair!, 1995
Masai and I, 1992
My Sister, Then and Now, 1992

Other books you might like:
Miriam Cohen, *See You Tomorrow, Charles*, 1983
    First graders accept their blind classmate.
Estelle Condra, *See the Ocean*, 1994
    A family's annual trips to the beach are enjoyed by a blind girl.
Patricia MacLachlan, *Through Grandpa's Eyes*, 1971
    By sharing time with his blind grandfather, a young boy learns to see things differently.
Patricia McMahon, *Listen for the Bus: David's Story*, 1995
    A factual account of a young blind boy's first day at school.

793

VIRGINIA L. KROLL
NANCY L. CLOUSE, Illustrator

Pink Paper Swans

(Grand Rapids, MI: William B. Eerdmans Publishing Company, 1994)

Subject(s): Japanese Americans; City Life; Artists and Art
Age range(s): Grades 1-3
Major character(s): Janetta Jackson, 8-Year-Old; Mrs. Tsujimoto, Aged Person (arthritic), Artist (origami)
Time period(s): 1990s (1994)
Locale(s): United States

Summary: Janetta is entranced by the paper animals which seem to fly from the fingers of her neighbor Mrs. Tsujimoto. She watches her work all summer before gathering the courage to speak to her. Janetta's reward is a pink paper swan which she cherishes. When Mrs. Tsujimoto stops coming outside to fold her origami, Janetta seeks her out and discovers that arthritis keeps her from venturing out or folding origami. Determined to help, Janetta offers to be Mrs. Tsujimoto's fingers. (32 pages)

Where it's reviewed:
Booklist, July 1994, page 1955
Kirkus Reviews, June 15, 1994, page 847
Library Talk, November 1994, page 24
Publishers Weekly, June 13, 1994, page 63
School Library Journal, August 1994, page 139

Other books by the same author:
New Friends, True Friends, Stuck-Like-Glue Friends, 1994
Sweet Magnolia, 1994
My Sister, Then and Now, 1992

Other books you might like:
Sharon Chmielarz, *Down at Angel's*, 1994
    Two sisters befriend a reclusive neighbor, receiving far more in return than they expect.

DyAnne DiSalvo-Ryan, *City Green*, 1994
    A young girl and an elderly neighbor transform an empty lot into a community garden.
Libba Moore Gray, *Miss Tizzy*, 1993
    When loving neighbor Miss Tizzy becomes ill the children have an opportunity to return the love she has shown them.

794

VIRGINIA L. KROLL
TATSURO KIUCHI, Illustrator

The Seasons and Someone

(San Diego: Harcourt Brace & Company, 1994)

Subject(s): Eskimos; Indians of North America; Seasons
Age range(s): Grades K-3
Major character(s): Someone, Child, Indian (Inuit)
Time period(s): 1990s (1994)
Locale(s): Alaska

Summary: Someone ponders the changes with each season, reflecting on the actitivity of each family member at different times of the year. Following the signs in the sky, on the earth and in the movements and appearance of animals, Someone thinks only of once again eating ripe berries. She carefully watches the bushes for the first signs of growth, chases away the birds and plants new seeds saved from last year's berries. An author's note gives background information for the story. (32 pages)

Where it's reviewed:
Booklist, December 1, 1994, page 686
Children's Book Review Service, February 1995, page 76
Five Owls, January 1995, page 54
Horn Book Guide, Spring 1995, page 43
School Library Journal, January 1995, page 88

Other books by the same author:
Fireflies, Peaches and Lullabies, 1995
Sweet Magnolia, 1994
Masai and I, 1992

Other books you might like:
Douglas Florian, *A Year in the Country*, 1989
    Scenes from a farmyard show the seasonal changes in both monthly activities and signs in nature.
Leo Lionni, *A Busy Year*, 1992
    Two mice learn from a tree about the seasonal changes of a plant's annual cycle.
Gerda Muller, *Circle of Seasons*, 1995
    The seasons are reflected in the outdoor play of children and the ever-changing sky and landscape about them.

795

WALTER LYON KRUDOP, Author/Illustrator

Blue Claws

(New York: Atheneum, 1993)

Subject(s): Grandparents; Summer; Fishing
Age range(s): Grades K-3
Major character(s): Unnamed Character, Child; Grandpa, Grandfather

Time period(s): 1990s (1993)
Locale(s): Long Island, New York

Summary: In the author's first children's book, a young boy accompanies his grandfather for a day of crabbing. Grandpa is no more knowledgeable about communicating with a child than his grandson is about catching crabs, but during the day both become more skilled. (36 pages)

Where it's reviewed:
Booklist, July 1993, page 1975
Horn Book, July 1993, page 445
New Advocate, Summer 1994, page 207
Publishers Weekly, March 22, 1993, page 79
School Library Journal, May 1993, page 88

Other books you might like:
Brenda Z. Guiberson, *Lobster Boat*, 1993
　　Tommy and his uncle spend a day on a lobster boat, checking pots, replacing bait and hurrying home before a storm.
Amy Hest, *Rosie's Fishing Trip*, 1994
　　When Rosie and Grandpa spend the morning fishing, Rosie learns that catching fish is not the most important reason for going fishing.
Jane B. Mason, *River Day*, 1994
　　Alex has a privilege not enjoyed by her younger brother — a quiet day on the river with her grandfather.
Elaine Moore, *Deep River*, 1994
　　When Grandpa takes Jess on her first fly-fishing trip, she worries needlessly that her brother's predictions of snagged logs or scared fish will happen.

796

WALTER LYON KRUDOP, Author/Illustrator

Something Is Growing
(New York: Atheneum Books for Young Readers, 1995)

Subject(s): Gardens and Gardening; City Life
Age range(s): Grades K-2
Major character(s): Peter, Child, Gardener; Professor Thornbine, Explorer
Time period(s): 1990s (1995)
Locale(s): New York, New York

Summary: Peter finds a seed and plants it in a small patch of dirt exposed by a broken bit of sidewalk. He carefully tends the plant, talking to it daily. No one notices Peter, but a neighborhood busybody notices the large plant and calls Professor Thornbine to investigate. Professor Thornbine identifies a very rare plant which not only grows rapidly, but also begins spreading when the curious busybody touches it and releases millions of spores. Soon, greenery covers every flat surface in the city. In true explorer style, Professor Woodbine searches for the source of the rapidly growing jungle. Eventually, he finds Peter and thanks him for his fine plant care. (32 pages)

Where it's reviewed:
Booklist, June 1995, page 124
Children's Book Review Service, June 1995, page 124
Horn Book Guide, Fall 1995, page 270
School Library Journal, June 1995, page 89

Other books by the same author:
Blue Claws, 1993

Other books you might like:
Margaret Mahy, *The Pumpkin Man and the Crafty Creeper*, 1990
　　Mr. Parkin, caretaker of quiet pumpkins, has his life changed by a plant with an attitude.
Nancy J. Peteraf, *A Plant Called Spot*, 1994
　　Teddy's mom buys him a plant pet so he can practice caring for the animal kind.
Elise Primavera, *Plantpet*, 1994
　　Bertie is given a plant which grows to have a life of its own.

797

LORETTA KRUPINSKI, Author/Illustrator

Bluewater Journal: The Voyage of the Sea Tiger
(New York: HarperCollins Publishers, 1995)

Subject(s): Ships; Diaries; Voyages and Travels
Age range(s): Grades 2-5
Major character(s): Benjamin Slocum, 12-Year-Old, Brother; Isabel Slocum, Sister (younger); Papa, Father, Sea Captain
Time period(s): 1860s (1860)
Locale(s): At Sea (aboard the *Sea Tiger*); Honolulu, Hawaii

Summary: Racing from Boston to Honolulu against another ship, Benjamin records in his journal the events of life at sea. He and Isabel must continue with their studies, but Benjamin also likes to spend time on deck learning all he can about the sea. One day he hopes to be a sea captain like Papa. After the *Sea Tiger* wins the race, Papa receives a new telescope and all the crew are given an extra dollar. An afterword gives factual information about clipper ships and a glossary defines nautical terms. (32 pages)

Where it's reviewed:
Bulletin of the Center for Children's Books, June 1995, page 351
Children's Book Review Service, July 1995, page 152
Kirkus Reviews, May 1, 1995, page 635
Publishers Weekly, June 5, 1995, page 63
School Library Journal, July 1995, page 65

Other books by the same author:
Lost in the Fog, 1990

Other books you might like:
Richard Berleth, *Mary Patten's Voyage*, 1994
　　With her husband bed-ridden with tuberculosis and the first mate in the brig, Mary Patten takes the helm and safely brings the *Neptune Car* to port.
Thomas P. Lewis, *Clipper Ship*, 1978
　　When Jamie's father, captain of a clipper ship, falls ill his mother must take over and bring the ship safely to port.
Armstrong Sperry, *All Sail Set: A Romance of the "Flying Cloud"*, 1935
　　The fictitious diary of a boy sailing on the maiden voyage of the clipper ship "Flying Cloud" was reissued in 1984.

798

KATHLEEN V. KUDLINSKI
RONALD HIMLER, Illustrator

Earthquake! A Story of Old San Francisco
(New York: Viking, 1993)

Series: Once Upon America
Subject(s): Earthquakes; Fires; Animals/Horses
Age range(s): Grades 3-5
Major character(s): Phillip MacMillan, 12-Year-Old (livery stable helper); Chester MacMillan, 4-Year-Old, Brother; Papa, Businessman (livery stable owner)
Time period(s): 1900s (1906)
Locale(s): San Francisco, California (Van Ness Avenue)

Summary: On the morning of April 18, 1906, Phillip awakens to the strange sights and sounds of barking dogs, whinnying horses, and scurrying mice. As he begins the chores in the family's livery stable, the reason for the animal's unusual behavior becomes apparent as the city is struck by a violent earthquake. Horses are injured, but Phillip's family is alive. Papa drives Chester and Mama out of the city to a relative's home and leaves Phillip alone to care for the horses and guard against looters. Factual information about the earthquake is included in an afterword. (56 pages)

Where it's reviewed:
Booklist, July 1993, page 1965
Bulletin of the Center for Children's Books, May 1993, page 286
Horn Book Guide, Fall 1993, page 287
Kirkus Reviews, June 15, 1993, page 786
School Library Journal, August 1993, page 164

Other books by the same author:
Facing West: A Story of the Oregon Trail, 1994
Hero over Here, 1990
Helen Keller: A Light for the Blind, 1989

Other books you might like:
Joe Cottonwood, *Quake: A Novel*, 1995
    In her parent's absence, Franny must cope with the aftereffects of the 1989 California earthquake.
Kristiana Gregory, *Earthquake at Dawn*, 1992
    A fictionalized account of the 1906 San Francisco earthquake as it is witnessed by two young women, one a photographer.
Susan Lowell, *I Am Lavina Cumming*, 1993
    Mountain-bred Lavina feels out of place in San Francisco until the 1906 earthquake forces her to use her camping and survival skills.

799

KARLA KUSKIN, Author/Illustrator

City Dog
(New York: Clarion Books, 1994)

Subject(s): Animals/Dogs; Nature; Stories in Rhyme
Age range(s): Grades K-2
Major character(s): Unnamed Character, Dog
Time period(s): 1990s (1994)

Locale(s): United States

Summary: Accustomed to the definition of space provided by a city street with corners and buildings, a city dog is amazed to find herself in an environment with no boundaries. Racing over the countryside, the city dog is free to bark, run and explore rabbit holes, crows and waves on the beach. Even the setting sun does not slow the dog's activities—she continues to frolic by the light of the moon. (32 pages)

Where it's reviewed:
Booklist, March 1, 1994, page 1270
Bulletin of the Center for Children's Books, May 1994, page 292
Kirkus Reviews, March 1, 1994, page 307
Publishers Weekly, March 28, 1994, page 96
School Library Journal, March 1994, page 202

Other books by the same author:
James and the Rain, 1995
City Noise, 1994
Which Horse Is William?, 1992

Other books you might like:
Janet McLean, *Dog Tales*, 1995
    A rhyming text describes the varied activities in the daily lives of five dogs.
Susan Meddaugh, *Martha Calling*, 1994
    Martha makes the most of the vacation she wins in a radio call-in contest despite the resort's "No Dogs Allowed" policy.
Danny Shanahan, *Buckledown the Workhound*, 1993
    Buckledown, an overworked executive, discovers that he enjoys the life of a dog at the Shirttail Wagon Farm.

800

KARLA KUSKIN
REG CARTWRIGHT, Illustrator

James and the Rain
(New York: Simon & Schuster Books for Young Readers, 1995)

Subject(s): Animals; Weather; Stories in Rhyme
Age range(s): Grades K-2
Major character(s): James, Child
Time period(s): Indeterminate Past
Locale(s): United States

Summary: This newly illustrated reissue of a 1957 title features a young boy bedecked in a yellow raincoat strolling outside under a large black umbrella. Not willing to let the weather interfere with his play, James wanders from one animal to another asking for advice on games to play in the rain. As the day draws to a close James and all the animals gather in front of the fireplace to enjoy a warm nap. (32 pages)

Where it's reviewed:
Booklist, June 1, 1995, page 1787
Horn Book Guide, Spring 1996, page 34
New York Times Book Review, August 13, 1995, page 23
Publishers Weekly, May 29, 1995, page 86
School Library Journal, July 1995, page 66

Other books by the same author:
City Noise, 1994

The Philharmonic Gets Dressed, 1982
Roar and More, 1977

Other books you might like:
Amy Hest, *In the Rain with Baby Duck*, 1995
   Mr. and Mrs. Duck do not understand a Baby Duck who
   dislikes rain, but Grampa Duck does and he knows just
   how to improve the rainy day.
Jack Prelutsky, *Rainy Rainy Saturday*, 1980
   Fourteen poems celebrate the fun to be had on a rainy day,
   even if you're stuck inside.
Christine Widman, *The Willow Umbrella*, 1993
   On a rainy day, two little girls find a way to play outside.
Taro Yashima, *Umbrella*, 1958
   After receiving red boots and an umbrella for her birthday,
   Momo eagerly awaits a rainy day.

801

MARY DEBALL KWITZ
S.D. SCHINDLER, Illustrator

Little Vampire and the Midnight Bear

(New York: Dial Books for Young Readers, 1995)

Series: Easy-to-Read
Subject(s): Vampires; Animals/Bears; Family Relations
Age range(s): Grades 1-3
Major character(s): Little Vampire, Vampire, Brother; Baby
   Vampira, Vampire, Sister; Midnight Bear, Bear
Time period(s): 1990s (1995)

Locale(s): Fictional Country

Summary: Little Vampire is unable to use any of his birthday
gifts until he learns to fly. The night after his birthday party,
Little Vampire's parents fly away to a meeting leaving Little
Vampire with Baby Vampira and Grandpa. After Grandpa
flies home, Little Vampire forgets to lock the shutters and
ferocious Midnight Bear comes in to eat Baby Vampira. In
Little Vampire's hurried attempt to save Baby Vampira, he
forgets that he cannot fly, grabs her and flies out the window
away from Midnight Bear's grasping claws. (48 pages)

Where it's reviewed:
Booklist, October 1, 1995, page 329
Horn Book Guide, Spring 1996, page 52
School Library Journal, September 1995, page 180

Other books by the same author:
Gumshoe Goose: Private Eye, 1988

Other books you might like:
Jayne Harvey, *Great-Uncle Dracula*, 1992
   An easy-reader features Emily Normal's adjustment to a
   new school populated with witches, ghosts and were-
   wolves.
Deborah Hautzig, *Happy Birthday, Little Witch*, 1985
   In a beginning chapter book, Little Witch needs more than
   magic to find the three friends she wants invited to her
   party.
Ross Martin Madsen, *Perrywinkle and the Book of Magic
   Spells*, 1988
   Perrywinkle finds that wizard training is hazardous if one
   is not careful.

L

802

DOROTHEA LACHNER
THE, TJONG-KHING, Illustrator

Andrew's Angry Words

(New York: North-South Books, 1995)

Subject(s): Anger; Behavior; Fantasy
Age range(s): Grades K-2
Major character(s): Andrew, Child, Brother (younger); Marion, Sister
Time period(s): 1990s (1995)
Locale(s): Europe

Summary: When Marion trips over Andrew and his toys while racing for the phone, angry words spill out of Andrew's mouth and are passed from Marion to her friend on the other end of the phone. Andrew races after the words, but they stay just ahead of him and out of reach. Finally, the words reach a woman who lets them fall to the ground, unheard, where she bundles them into a sack and throws them into the ocean. When Andrew reaches her, she gives him a bundle of happy words in exchange and he distributes these on his way home. (24 pages)

Where it's reviewed:
Booklist, April 15, 1995, page 1506
Books for Keeps, May 1995, page 29
Children's Book Review Service, August 1995, page 159
Horn Book Guide, Fall 1995, page 270
School Library Journal, June 1995, page 90

Other books you might like:
Betsy Everitt, *Mean Soup*, 1992
    After a bad day, Horace helps his mother make Mean Soup and he begins to feel better.
Barbara M. Joosse, *Dinah's Mad, Bad Wishes*, 1989
    After fighting with her mom, Dinah is so angry she thinks of some really bad wishes.
Mercer Mayer, *I Was So Mad*, 1983
    A child tries different techniques to dissipate angry feelings.

Maurice Sendak, *Where the Wild Things Are*, 1963
    When Max's temper gets out of hand, he is sent to his room, but he journeys to the Land of the Wild Things until he feels calmer and then he comes home again.

803

DOROTHEA LACHNER
MAJA DUSIKOVA, Illustrator

The Gift from Saint Nicholas

(New York: North-South Books, 1995)

Subject(s): Holidays; Weather; Wishes
Age range(s): Grades K-3
Major character(s): Misha, Child; Anna, Child; Saint Nicholas, Aged Person
Time period(s): Indeterminate Past
Locale(s): Europe

Summary: For a week snow falls on a small village until it is impossible for the villagers to leave their homes. Because it is Saint Nicholas Eve, Anna and Misha send a wish to Saint Nicholas that he will blow away the snow so the people of the village can be together again. Saint Nicholas responds to the wish, although not in the way Anna and Misha expect. Translated from the German by J. Alison James. (26 pages)

Where it's reviewed:
Booklist, November 1, 1995, page 476
Children's Book Review Service, January 1996, page 51
Horn Book Guide, Spring 1996, page 34
Publishers Weekly, September 18, 1995, page 102
School Library Journal, October 1995, page 38

Other books by the same author:
Andrew's Angry Words, 1995

Other books you might like:
John Burningham, *Harvey Slumfenburger's Christmas Present*, 1993
    Wearily, Santa Claus resumes his journey to deliver one last, almost forgotten, present.

Carole Kismaric, *A Gift from Saint Nicholas*, 1988
Saint Nicholas is out of presents when he arrives at Cecile's house, but she helps him solve his dilemma.
Gerda Marie Scheidl, *Can We Help You, Saint Nicholas?*, 1992
The forest animals hurry to assist Saint Nicholas when they realize he has overslept on Christmas Eve.

804

JULIE LACOME, Author/Illustrator

I'm a Jolly Farmer

(Cambridge, MA: Candlewick Press, 1994)

Subject(s): Play; Imagination; Stories in Rhyme
Age range(s): Grades K-1
Major character(s): Unnamed Character, Child; Fred, Dog
Time period(s): 1990s (1994)
Locale(s): England

Summary: Using a chair and Fred as props, a young girl pretends that she is driving a cart or riding an elephant. When her imagination takes her from an underwater race with a dolphin to a confrontation with a wolf disguised as granny she decides she'd rather stay home with Fred. (25 pages)

Where it's reviewed:
Booklist, June 1, 1994, page 1840
Horn Book Guide, Fall 1994, page 257
Junior Bookshelf, October 1994, page 164
Kirkus Reviews, March 15 1994, page 397
School Library Journal, August 1994, page 139

Other books by the same author:
Garden Fingerwiggles, 1995
Walking through the Jungle, 1993

Other books you might like:
Joan Anderson, *Harry's Helicopter*, 1990
With a little imagination Harry's bright red, cardboard helicopter seems to fly.
Jane Cowen-Fletcher, *Mama Zooms*, 1993
With his mom and her wheelchair as inspiration, a young boy imagines himself in many roles.
Chris L. Demarest, *My Blue Boat*, 1995
Sitting in the bathtub with her blue boat a young girl "sails away" on a make-believe adventure.
Heidi Goennel, *I Pretend*, 1995
The routine events of a little girl's day are imagined to be exciting and fanciful escapades.
Nicholas Heller, *The Front Hall Carpet*, 1990
Without opening the front door, this little girl goes on magical adventures with the help of her imagination and the front hall carpet.

805

NINA LADEN, Author/Illustrator

The Night I Followed the Dog

(San Francisco: Chronicle Books, 1994)

Subject(s): Animals/Dogs; Imagination; Pets
Age range(s): Grades 1-4

Major character(s): Unnamed Character, Child; Unnamed Character, Dog
Time period(s): 1990s (1994)
Locale(s): United States

Summary: The morning a young boy observes his dog, dressed in a tuxedo, exiting a limousine, he becomes suspicious about his pet's after-dark activities. That night he follows his dog and discovers his pet owns a private club where dogs come to relax, and get treats without having to lie down or roll over. The author's first book gives new meaning to the phrase "in the doghouse."(32 pages)

Where it's reviewed:
Children's Book Review Service, September 1994, page 8
Kirkus Reviews, August 15, 1994, page 1131
Parents' Choice, April 1994, page 5
Publishers Weekly, July 11, 1994, page 78
School Library Journal, February 1994, page 74

Other books you might like:
Susan Meddaugh, *Martha Calling*, 1994
Martha makes the most of the vacation she wins in a radio call-in contest, despite the resort's "No Dogs Allowed" policy.
Danny Shanahan, *Buckledown the Workhound*, 1993
Buckledown is dog-tired from his work as president of a large company so he schedules a well-deserved vacation where he's able to lead a dog's life.
Alan Snow, *How Dogs Really Work!*, 1993
Answers to questions you may have not even considered are in a humorous, illustrated manual for pet owners.

806

PATRICIA LAKIN
ROBERT G. STEELE, Illustrator

Dad and Me in the Morning

(Morton Grove, IL: Albert Whitman & Company, 1994)

Subject(s): Fathers and Sons; Deafness; Beaches
Age range(s): Grades K-2
Major character(s): Jacob, Child, Deaf; Dad, Father
Time period(s): 1990s (1994)
Locale(s): United States (northeastern seacoast)

Summary: Awakened by his flashing alarm clock, Jacob hurries to dress, put on his hearing aids and tiptoe into his parent's room to wake his father. Quietly leaving the house, he and Dad walk to the beach and watch the sunrise. (28 pages)

Where it's reviewed:
Booklist, April 1, 1994, page 1460
Children's Book Review Service, May 1994, page 112
Five Owls, May 1995, page 110
Kirkus Reviews, March 15, 1994, page 397
School Library Journal, June 1994, page 108

Other books by the same author:
Don't Forget, 1994
Up a Tree, 1994
The Palace of Stars, 1993

Other books you might like:
Uri Shulevitz, *Dawn*, 1974
    The coming of dawn is simply yet eloquently described in poetic text and illustrations.
Mary Stolz, *Say Something*, 1993
    On a fishing trip, a father answers his young son's questions about the world around them.
Martin Waddell, *The Big, Big Sea*, 1994
    On a bright moonlit night a young girl and her mother walk by the sea, splashing in the water and counting stones on the seashore.
Rosemary Wells, *Night Sounds, Morning Colors*, 1994
    A young boy describes the sensations he experiences living in a rural area and sharing quiet moments with family.

807

PATRICIA LAKIN
TED RAND, Illustrator

Don't Forget

(New York: Tambourine Books, 1994)

Subject(s): Jews; Surprises; Neighbors and Neighborhoods
Age range(s): Grades K-3
Major character(s): Sarah, 8-Year-Old; Mrs. Singer, Store Owner (Holocaust survivor)
Time period(s): 1940s (post WWII)
Locale(s): United States (ethnic urban neighborhood)

Summary: Shopping for the ingredients to make her first cake, a surprise for her mother's birthday, Sarah is offered a secret for success from each of the merchants she visits in her multi-ethnic neighborhood. With each piece of cake-baking advice comes the admonition, "Don't forget." Reluctant to visit the Singers' shop because of the blue numbers on the shopkeepers' arms, Sarah goes there last for the final ingredients. Sensing Sarah's discomfort, Mrs. Singer kindly states that it is important not to forget bad things lest they happen again. Mrs. Singer not only offers a tip for successful cake baking, but allows Sarah to borrow a pan and use her oven so Sarah can prepare the surprise for her mother. (32 pages)

Where it's reviewed:
Booklist, May 15, 1994, page 1683
Kirkus Reviews, June 1, 1994, page 776
Library Talk, May 1994, page 15
Publishers Weekly, May 16, 1994, page 64
School Library Journal, June 1994, page 108

Other books by the same author:
Dad and Me in the Morning, 1994
The Palace of Stars, 1993

Other books you might like:
David A. Adler, *The Number on My Grandfather's Arm*, 1987
    A Holocaust survivor helps his grandchild understand the past in hopes of shaping a better future.
Eve Bunting, *Flower Garden*, 1994
    With her father's help a young girl shops for the ingredients to make a windowbox garden for her mother's birthday.

Melissa Madenski, *In My Mother's Garden*, 1995
    Rosie enlists the help of a neighbor to plant a flower garden as a birthday surprise for her mother.

808

PATRICIA LAKIN
KIMBERLY BULCKEN ROOT, Illustrator

The Palace of Stars

(New York: Tambourine Books, 1993)

Subject(s): Aunts and Uncles; Surprises; Theater
Age range(s): Grades 1-3
Major character(s): Max, Uncle, Aged Person; Amanda, Child, Niece
Time period(s): Indeterminate Past
Locale(s): Mattapan, Massachusetts

Summary: Saturday outings with Great-uncle Max include trolley car rides to the zoo, shopping, and ice cream—all Uncle Max's treat to Amanda. An appreciative Amanda saves her money for weeks so that one Saturday she is able to surprise her uncle with a trip to the theater—Amanda's palace of stars. (32 pages)

Where it's reviewed:
Booklist, November 1, 1993, page 530
Children's Book Review Service, Winter 1994, page 63
Horn Book Guide, Spring 1994, page 41
Publishers Weekly, September 13, 1993, page 132
School Library Journal, February 1994, page 88

Other books by the same author:
Dad and Me in the Morning, 1994
Don't Forget, 1994
Jet Black Pickup Truck, 1990

Other books you might like:
Karen Ackerman, *Just Like Max*, 1990
    Aaron helps his elderly and ill Great-Uncle Max complete a tailoring assignment.
Erica Magnus, *My Secret Place*, 1994
    A young boy and his teddy bear have a special place that can become anything imaginable.
Pat Mora, *A Birthday Basket for Tia*, 1992
    Cecelia plans a very special surprise for beloved Great-aunt Tia.
Mary Lyn Ray, *A Rumbly Tumbly Glittery Gritty Place*, 1993
    In a young girl's imagination, a gravel pit is transformed into a mountain, a beach and many other wonderful places.

809

PRISCILLA LAMONT, Author/Illustrator

Out to Lunch

(New York: Kingfisher, 1995)

Subject(s): Conduct of Life; Animals/Dogs; Change
Age range(s): Grades K-2
Major character(s): Mrs. Burdle, Dog, Friend; Mr. Howgego, Dog, Friend
Time period(s): Indeterminate Past
Locale(s): Fictional Country

Summary: Mrs. Burdle and Mr. Howgego, good friends, differ in one way—one is very punctual and one is always late. To prove that she can change her habits, Mrs. Burdle invites her friend to lunch precisely at noon. Using an alarm clock and an organized list, Mrs. Burdle begins preparing at seven on the morning of the luncheon. Unfortunately, Mr. Howgego, through a series of misadventures, does not arrive until four in the afternoon, with a new appreciation for his friend's motto—"better late than never." (26 pages)

Where it's reviewed:
Horn Book Guide, Fall 1995, page 271
Publishers Weekly, April 17, 1995, page 58
School Library Journal, August 1995, page 125

Other books you might like:
Donald Crews, *Shortcut*, 1992
Children using a railroad track as a shortcut find it's a dangerous route when a train approaches.
David Macaulay, *Shortcut*, 1995
As Albert and his horse, June, make their weekly trip to market, their simple acts create havoc for those who come after them.
Mark Teague, *The Secret Shortcut*, 1996
To keep from being tardy again, Wendell and Floyd try a secret shortcut to school which proves to be unexpectedly adventurous, but does help them arrive on time.

810

KATHRYN LANCE

Going to See Grassy Ella

(New York, Lothrop, Lee & Shepard Books, 1993)

Subject(s): Cancer; Sisters; Crime and Criminals
Age range(s): Grades 4-6
Major character(s): Peggy Jean "Peej" West, 12-Year-Old, Cancer Patient; Annie West, Teenager, Sister; Graciella "Grassy Ella" Bujold, Healer, Psychic
Time period(s): 1990s (1993)
Locale(s): Columbus, Ohio; New York, New York

Summary: Determined to take command of her cancer treatment, Peej decides to take advantage of her parents' 3-day trip to a convention to travel to New York and locate a faith healer. Enlisting Annie's reluctant help in the deception, the two use Peej's savings to fly to New York where their careful plans begin falling apart. While chasing a thief who has stolen their backpacks, they meet the run-away daughter of a mobster who offers to help them, but inadvertently leads them into the clutches of kidnappers. Eventually, everyone ends up at Grassy Ella's, including the police who haul off the bad guys enabling Peej to finally meet with healer. From Annie's perspective, the real miracle worker is Peej. (134 pages)

Where it's reviewed:
Booklist, June 1, 1993, page 1831
Five Owls, May 1993, page 116
Horn Book, May 1993, page 333
Publishers Weekly, May 24, 1993, page 88
School Library Journal, April 1993, page 121

Other books you might like:
E.L. Konigsburg, *From the Mixed-Up Files of Mrs. Basil E. Frankweiler*, 1967
The 1968 Newbery Award winning story features the humorous adventures of Claudia and her younger brother, hiding for a week in the Metropolitan Museum of Art.
Cynthia Voigt, *Homecoming*, 1981
Dicey takes charge of her younger siblings when they are abandoned by their emotionally disturbed mother and by wits, luck and determination finds a home with other relatives.
June Rae Wood, *A Share of Freedom*, 1994
When her alcoholic mother is forced into treatment, Freedom runs away with her younger brother to save them being separated and placed in foster care.

811

LUCINDA LANDON, Author/Illustrator

Meg Mackintosh and the Mystery in the Locked Library

(Boston: Little, Brown and Company, 1993)

Series: Solve-It-Yourself Mysteries
Subject(s): Libraries; Mystery and Detective Stories; Brothers and Sisters
Age range(s): Grades 2-4
Major character(s): Meg Mackintosh, Detective—Amateur, Sister (Peter's); Peter Mackintosh, Detective—Amateur, Brother (Meg's); Alice, Cousin, Librarian
Time period(s): 1990s (1993)
Locale(s): United States (Hudson Public Library)

Summary: Following mysterious, rhyming clues left by cousin Alice, Meg and Peter use their powers of deduction (and their library skills) to locate a valuable item which Alice has hidden in the closed library. When they arrive at the hiding place, the book is missing, but Meg solves the mystery and confronts the thief, recovering the valuable package before it leaves the library. (44 pages)

Where it's reviewed:
Booklist, February 1, 1993, page 984
Five Owls, March 1994, page 79
Horn Book Guide, Fall 1993, page 288
Language Arts, September 1993, page 422
School Library Journal, March 1993, page 180

Other books by the same author:
Meg Mackintosh and the Mystery at the Medieval Castle, 1993
Meg Mackintosh and the Case of the Curious Whale Watch, 1987
Meg Mackintosh and the Case of the Missing Babe Ruth Baseball, 1986

Other books you might like:
David A. Adler, *The Cam Jansen Series*, 1980-
Using her photographic memory Cam Jansen participates in the solving of a variety of mysteries.
Mary Blount Christian, *Sebastian (Super Sleuth) and the Stars-in-His-Eyes Mystery*, 1987
On this case Sebastian, the sheepdog detective, goes to

Hollywood to solve a mystery of a problem-plagued movie production.

Eth Clifford, *Help! I'm a Prisoner in the Library*, 1979
When two children are locked in the library, they must use their wits to find a way out.

Elizabeth Levy, *The Something Queer Series*, 1971 -
Gwen, Jill and basset hound Fletcher have one adventure after another while they solve mysterious occurrences.

Marjorie Weinman Sharmat, *Nate the Great Series*, 1972-
Nate follows one clue after another copying the style of Sherlock Holmes in this series for beginning readers.

812

KIRBY LARSON
NANCY POYDAR, Illustrator

Second-Grade Pig Pals

(New York: Holiday House, 1994)

Subject(s): Friendship; Schools; Animals/Pigs
Age range(s): Grades 2-3
Major character(s): Quinn Kelley, 2nd Grader; Manuela, 2nd Grader
Time period(s): 1990s (1994)
Locale(s): Washington

Summary: In her eagerness to make friends with the new student in class, Quinn unintentionally offends Manuela by suggesting her beautiful name in the pig-naming contest. To make matters worse, Quinn is the only student who has not brought in a contribution to the classroom "Pig Patch" display. In one last attempt to establish a friendship, Quinn comes up with an idea which includes Manuela and ensures fun for everyone. (87 pages)

Where it's reviewed:
Booklist, November 1, 1994, page 497
Bulletin of the Center for Children's Books, December 1994, page 134
Children's Book Review Service, February 1995, page 81
Horn Book Guide, Spring 1995, page 79
School Library Journal, November 1994, page 84

Other books by the same author:
Cody and Quinn, Sitting in a Tree, 1996

Other books you might like:
Betsy Duffey, *Hey, New Kid!*, 1996
Dreading his entry into a new school, newly moved third grader Jeremy "reinvents" himself in the hope of impressing his new classmates.

Bonnie B. Graves, *The Best Worst Day*, 1996
Hoping that the new girl in class will choose her as a friend, Lucy tries to impress Maya.

Arnold Lobel, *The Book of Pigericks*, 1983
Pigs are the theme in this book of limericks.

Angela Shelf Medearis, *The Adventures of Sugar and Junior*, 1995
When a new girl moves into Junior's apartment building, he is relieved to have a friend his age.

813

KATHRYN LASKY
BARRY MOSER, Illustrator

Cloud Eyes

(San Diego: Harcourt Brace & Company, 1994)

Subject(s): Animals/Bears; Animals/Bees; Indians of North America
Age range(s): Grades 1-4
Major character(s): Cloud Eyes, Indian, Daydreamer
Time period(s): Indeterminate Past
Locale(s): United States

Summary: Cloud Eyes is a dreamer, a visionary whose gift is to read the sky and understand the stories in clouds. So it is possible for Cloud Eyes to solve the problem of destruction by bears of the honey trees which makes the bees angry and deprives his people of the sweet honey. In a dream, Cloud Eyes receives instructions he follows carefully, subduing the bears and establishing a peaceful relationship between his people, the bears and the honey bees. (32 pages)

Where it's reviewed:
Children's Book Review Index, December 1994, page 43
Kirkus Reviews, November 15, 1994, page 1533
The New Advocate, Spring 1995, page 125
Publishers Weekly, November 7, 1994, page 78
School Library Journal, October 1994, page 124

Other books by the same author:
Days of the Dead, 1994
The Librarian Who Measured the Earth, 1994
Surtsey: The Newest Place on Earth, 1992

Other books you might like:
Joseph Bruchac, *The Boy Who Lived with the Bears: And Other Iroquois Stories*, 1995
An award-winning collection of six traditional Iroquois tales written for younger children includes historical and cultural background for the tales.

Caron Lee Cohen, *The Mud Pony: A Traditional Skidi Pawnee Tale*, 1988
Mother Earth transforms a poor boy's pony into a real one, but the youth learns that to be a great leader he must find his own strength.

Manitonquat, *The Children of the Morning Light: Wampanoag Tales*, 1994
A collection of stories presents the oral traditions of Wampanoag people in print for the first time.

814

KATHRYN LASKY
JANET STEVENS, Illustrator

The Gates of the Wind

(San Diego: Harcourt Brace and Company, 1995)

Subject(s): Mountain Life; Moving, Household; Change
Age range(s): Grades K-3
Major character(s): Gamma Lee, Aged Person; Louise, Mule
Time period(s): Indeterminate Past
Locale(s): Gates of the Wind, Fictional Country

Summary: The other villagers consider their home to be the best in the world, but Gamma Lee feels trapped and ready to relocate to the legendary Gates of the Wind atop the nearby mountains. To that end, Gamma Lee loads her worldly possessions onto Louise and the two set off up the mountain. Upon arrival, Gamma Lee soon learns she will have to adapt her manner of living to survive in a windy location. She does so willingly and revels in the newness and wonder of her home. (32 pages)

Where it's reviewed:
Horn Book, March 1996, page 189
Horn Book Guide, Spring 1996, page 35
Publishers Weekly, July 31, 1995, page 81
School Library Journal, October 1995, page 105

Other books by the same author:
The Solo, 1994
The Tantrum, 1993
Fourth of July Bear, 1991

Other books you might like:
Mary Calhoun, *Jack and the Whoopee Wind*, 1987
   With friends in Whoopee, Wyoming, Jack tries to tame a wind that is capable of blowing the feathers off a chicken.
Emma Chichester Clark, *Across the Blue Mountains*, 1992
   Curiosity leads Miss Bilberry to pack her belongings and travel to the other side of the blue mountains where she finds a home just to her liking.
Pat Hutchins, *The Wind Blew*, 1974
   A rhyming story describes the cumulative effect of a wind which blows away many objects.
Betsy James, *Blow Away Soon*, 1995
   Nana understands the wind and helps young Sophie appreciate rather than fear it.
Carol P. Saul, *Someplace Else*, 1995
   After a lifetime in the white house, Mrs. Tillby is ready to live someplace else, but has a hard time deciding just where.

815

KATHRYN LASKY

A Journey to the New World: The Diary of Remember Patience Whipple

(New York, Scholastic, 1996)

Series: Dear America
Subject(s): Pilgrims and Pilgrimages; Ships; Voyages and Travels
Age range(s): Grades 4-7
Major character(s): Remember Patience ''Mem'' Whipple, Settler, 12-Year-Old; Humility ''Hummy'' Sawyer, Settler, 12-Year-Old; William Brewster, Historical Figure, Sea Captain
Time period(s): 17th century
Locale(s): Plymouth, Massachusetts; At Sea (aboard the *Mayflower*, from England to America)

Summary: Mem leaves with her family on the Mayflower to find religous freedom in America. Early on she meets Hummy and the two of them become fast friends. Mem decides to keep a diary, but instead of writing ''Dear Diary'' she makes up an imaginary friend called Imp to whom she tells the general history of the trip as well as the little details about the voyage. Arriving in Plymouth she continues to write about the group's trials and tribulations; the burning of the shed, the illnesses, the running away of John Billington, and the work of Captain Brewster. (172 pages)

Where it's reviewed:
Bulletin of the Center for Children's Books, October 1996, page 55
School Library Journal, August 1996, page 144
Voice of Youth Advocates, October 1996, page 210

Other books by the same author:
A Voice in the Wind, 1993
The Night Journey, 1991
The Bone Wars, 1988
Double Trouble Squared, 1986

Other books you might like:
Patricia Clapp, *Constance: A Story of Early Plymouth*, 1968
   A story of the first year in Plymouth.
Rachel Field, *Calico Bush*, 1931
   A French girl who is loaned to a family in Maine, describes a year in her life as an early settler.
Cheryl Harness, *Three Young Pilgrims*, 1992
   Three children describe how life might have been coming over on the Mayflower.
Jean Van Leeuwen, *Across the Wide Dark Sea: The Mayflower Journey*, 1995
   A boy describes the nine week journey and the first winter in Plymouth.
Kate Waters, *On the Mayflower: Voyage of the Ship's Apprentice and a Passenger Girl*, 1996
   A 12-year-old apprentice and a young passenger tell about their trip to the new world in a story illustrated by photographs.
G. Clifton Wisler, *This New Land*, 1987
   A ten-year-old boy describes his trip to America on the Mayflower and the first year in Plymouth.

816

KATHRYN LASKY
AMY SCHWARTZ, Illustrator

My Island Grandma

(New York: Morrow Junior Books, 1993)

Subject(s): Islands; Grandparents; Summer
Age range(s): Grades K-2
Major character(s): Grandma, Grandmother; Abbey, Child; Shadow, Dog (Grandma's pet)
Time period(s): 1990s (1993)
Locale(s): Maine

Summary: Originally published in 1979 this book is reissued with new illustrations. Abbey and Grandma share a special relationship during their time together each summer. They sail the island waters, pick blueberries, and look at stars on a clear night. When summer ends, they close up the cabins, pack their memories and head to the mainland. (32 pages)

Where it's reviewed:
Booklist, March 15, 1993, page 1361

Horn Book Guide, Fall 1993, page 264
Publishers Weekly, March 8, 1993, page 80
Reading Teacher, March 1994, page 493
School Library Journal, May 1993, page 88

Other books by the same author:
The Solo, 1994
The Tantrum, 1993
I Have an Aunt on Marlborough Street, 1992

Other books you might like:
Lena Anderson, *Stina's Visit*, 1991
  In a sequel to *Stina* a young girl returns to her grandfather's island for another memorable summer visit.
Marion Dane Bauer, *When I Go Camping with Grandma*, 1995
  A granddaughter's description of her camping trip with grandma reflects the beauty of nature and of a special relationship.
Helen V. Griffith, *Georgia Music*, 1986
  A young girl and her grandfather enjoy a summer of music at his cabin in Georgia.
Elaine Moore, *Grandma's House*, 1985
  Summer is a memorable time of sharing for Kim and her grandmother.

817

KATHRYN LASKY
MIKE BOSTOCK, Illustrator

Pond Year

(Cambridge, MA: Candlewick Press, 1995)

Subject(s): Nature; Play; Friendship
Age range(s): Grades K-3
Major character(s): Carole, 6-Year-Old, Friend; Unnamed Character, 6-Year-Old, Friend
Time period(s): Indeterminate Past
Locale(s): United States

Summary: Throughout the year, the pond is the favorite place for Carole and her best friend to play. Always together, the friends enjoy the special pleasures of each season—wading, watching tadpoles hatch, playing with salamanders, catching crawdaddies or even skating when ice covers the pond. (32 pages)

Where it's reviewed:
Booklist, May 15, 1995, page 1652
Book World, September 3, 1995, page 11
Publishers Weekly, May 29, 1995, page 84
School Library Journal, September 1995, page 181
Times Educational Supplement, August 18, 1995, page 18

Other books by the same author:
Lunch Bunnies, 1993
I Have an Aunt on Marlborough Street, 1992
Sea Swan, 1988

Other books you might like:
Jim Arnosky, *I See Animals Hiding*, 1995
  A simply written, beautifully illustrated, nonfiction look at animals' use of camouflage to protect themselves.
William T. George, *Fishing at Long Pond*, 1991
  A fishing trip to Long Pond includes observation of the

plants and animals that Katie and her grandfather see along the way.
Lynn Reiser, *Tomorrow on Rocky Pond*, 1993
  Annually, a family returns to Rocky Pond for vacation where they enjoy observing everything from bugs to loons.
David Williams, *Walking to the Creek*, 1990
  A walk to a nearby creek is an opportunity to explore and appreciate nature.

818

KATHRYN LASKY

True North

(New York: Blue Sky Press, 1996)

Subject(s): Runaways; Slavery; Underground Railroad
Age range(s): Grades 4-8
Major character(s): Lucy Bradford, 14-Year-Old; Africa, Slave; Levi "Pap" Bradford, Grandfather, Worker (abolitionist)
Time period(s): 1850s (1858)
Locale(s): Boston, Massachusetts; Virginia (Great Dismal Swamp and route North)

Summary: As Lucy and Africa's lives become entwined, they both write in their diaries about their individual adventures. Lucy is troubled about her grandfather breaking the law, but, as she learns more about the slave laws, she understands his position. It is when she is called upon to help Africa reach the next station, and then Canada, that she truly understands the meaning of what she is doing. (266 pages)

Where it's reviewed:
Bulletin of the Center for Children's Books, November 1996, page 104

Other books by the same author:
The Bone Wars, 1988
Double Trouble Squared, 1986
The Night Journey, 1986

Other books you might like:
Jennifer Armstrong, *Steal Away*, 1992
  A girl helps her slave escape to Canada and later arranges that their grandchildren meet.
Anita Riggio, *Secret Signs: Along the Underground Railroad*, 1997
  A deaf boy and his mother work on the Underground Railroad.
Courtni C. Wright, *Jumping the Broom*, 1994
  A slave describes some of the customs of slavery.
Pat McKissack, *A Picture of Freedom: The Diary of Clotee, a Slave Girl*, 1997
  Clotee writes about life on the plantation in the 1850s.

819

KATHRYN LASKY

A Voice in the Wind

(New York: Harcourt Brace and Company, 1993)

Series: Starbuck Family Adventure

Subject(s): Extrasensory Perception; Brothers and Sisters; Mystery and Detective Stories
Age range(s): Grades 4-6
Major character(s): Liberty Starbuck, 12-Year-Old (telepathic), Twin (July's); Charlotte ''Charly'' Starbuck, 5-Year-Old (telepathic), Twin (Molly's); Zanny Duggan, Child-Care Giver (children's favorite)
Time period(s): 1990s (1993)
Locale(s): Washington, District of Columbia (Dakota Street); New Mexico (Anasazi ruins)

Summary: Once again the Starbuck twins accompany their father on an EPA project with Zanny the Nanny in tow. The Southwest curriculum, which Zanny devises to educate them about the heritage of the area they are visiting, is enlivened when the telepathic twins are contacted by the spirit of a young Anasazi potter seeking to be reunited with the fragments of her last pot. (256 pages)

Where it's reviewed:
Horn Book Guide, Spring 1994, page 78
Kirkus Reviews, December 15, 1993, page 1592
Library Talk, March 1994, page 49
School Library Journal, December 1993, page 114
Voice of Youth Advocates, April 1994, page 27

Other books by the same author:
Shadows in the Water: A Starbuck Family Adventure, 1992 (2nd Starbuck Family Adventure)
Double Trouble Squared, 1991 (1st Starbuck Family Adventure)
Sugaring Time, 1983

Other books you might like:
Laura Lee Hope, *The Bobbsey Twins: Campfire Mystery*, 1982
   One of many titles about a family with two sets of twins who seem to find a mystery to solve wherever they go.
Annette Curtis Klause, *Alien Secrets*, 1993
   Puck's journey to join her parents working on another planet becomes more of an adventure than she anticipated.
Barbara Steiner, *Ghost Cave*, 1990
   Two boys find the grave of an Indian boy in a cave, but become lost in the process.

820

JURGEN LASSIG
ULI WAAS, Illustrator

Spiny

(New York: North-South Books, 1995)

Series: Easy-to-Read
Subject(s): Dinosaurs; Parent and Child; Problem Solving
Age range(s): Grades 1-3
Major character(s): Spiny, Dinosaur
Time period(s): Indeterminate Past
Locale(s): Earth

Summary: A newly hatched dinosaur wanders from its nest in search of its parents only to become hopelessly lost. The frantic parent dinosaurs enlist the help of other, friendly creatures to search for Spiny before tyrannosaurus rex finds the youngster. Although Spiny runs into the feared tyr-

annosaurus, he survives, is rescued, and hurries home to his many newly hatched siblings. Translated from the German by J. Alison James. (58 pages)

Where it's reviewed:
Booklist, May 1, 1995, page 1575
Horn Book Guide, Fall 1995, page 292
School Library Journal, June 1995, page 90

Other books by the same author:
Where's Molly?, 1993

Other books you might like:
Lorinda Bryan Cauley, *The Trouble with Tyrannosaurus Rex*, 1988
   Duckbill and Ankylosaurus are friends with a plan to prevent Tyrannosaurus Rex from dining on their neighbors.
Wolfram Hanel, *Lila's Little Dinosaur*, 1994
   After visiting a museum Lila notices that a rainbow-colored dinosaur has followed her home.
Hudson Talbott, *Your Pet Dinosaur: An Owner's Manual*, 1992
   This humorous guide explains the care, feeding and discipline of a pet dinosaur.

821

JIM LATIMER
BETSY FRANCO-FEENEY, Illustrator

James Bear and the Goose Gathering

(New York: Charles Scribner's Sons, 1994)

Subject(s): Animals/Bears; Animals/Geese; Storytelling
Age range(s): Grades K-3
Major character(s): James Bear, Bear, Storyteller; Skunk, Skunk, Friend
Time period(s): Indeterminate Past
Locale(s): Fictional Country

Summary: To compensate for a boring vegetarian diet, James Bear entertains himself with caterpillar rugby, cricket choirs, and gentle practical jokes on the geese. Doubting Skunk makes James Bear promise not to tell the geese any more stories, but one last tale which shows even Skunk the power of belief as the geese become what James Bear foretold. (32 pages)

Where it's reviewed:
Booklist, March 1, 1994, page 1270
Horn Book Guide, Fall 1994, page 279
Kirkus Reviews, February 1, 1994, page 146
School Library Journal, April 1994, page 108

Other books by the same author:
James Bear's Pie, 1992
Fox Under First Base, 1991
When Moose Was Young, 1990

Other books you might like:
Ida Luttrell, *The Bear Next Door*, 1991
   Vic Bear becomes friends with neighbor Arlo Gopher.
Margaret Mayo, *Tortoise's Flying Lesson*, 1994
   A collection of animal stories includes one about a father bear and his naughty bear cubs.

Janet Stevens, *Tops and Bottoms*, 1995
> Bear is the brunt of the joke in this story about how clever gardener Hare shares his crop.

822

DEBORAH NOURSE LATTIMORE, Author/Illustrator

Frida Maria: A Story of the Old Southwest

(San Diego: Browndeer Press, 1994)

Subject(s): Sex Roles; Behavior; Mothers and Daughters
Age range(s): Grades 1-3
Major character(s): Frida Maria, Child; Mama, Mother; Tio Narizo, Uncle
Time period(s): Indeterminate Past
Locale(s): California

Summary: In contrast to Mama's image of a proper senorita, Frida Maria sews her fiesta gown into a pair of pants suitable for horseback riding and, during a cooking lesson, accurately flings her well-formed dough at a rat scurrying through the kitchen. Even Frida Maria's dancing is too fast to be acceptable to Mama who wants proper behavior from her youngest. At the Fiesta, Frida Maria watches forlornly rather than do something unacceptable. Then she hears Tio Narizo place a wager on his horse to win a race. Impulsively, Frida Maria leaps on the horse and unexpectedly wins. A concluding author's note explains the historical background to the story and a glossary defines the Spanish words used in the text. (32 pages)

Where it's reviewed:
Horn Book Guide, Fall 1994, page 279
Los Angeles Times Book Review, October 16, 1994, page 16
Publishers Weekly, April 4, 1994, page 80
School Library Journal, May 1994, page 97

Other books by the same author:
Punga: The Goddess of Ugly, 1993
The Winged Cat: A Tale of Ancient Egypt, 1992
The Dragon's Robe, 1990

Other books you might like:
Alma Flor Ada, *My Name Is Maria Isabel*, 1993
> When Maria moves to a new school, she is the third Maria in the class and must be assertive in order maintain her individuality.
Philippa Gregory, *Florizella and the Wolves*, 1993
> An original fairy tale about an unconventional princess who defines her role in new ways.
Karen Papagapitos, *Socorro, Daughter of the Desert*, 1993
> With her mother working the fields while her father is sick, 8-year-old Socorro helps care for her family and entertains her brothers with stories.

823

DENIZE LAUTURE
REYNOLD RUFFINS, Illustrator

Running the Road to ABC

(New York: Simon & Schuster, 1996)

Subject(s): Schools; Blacks

Age range(s): Grades K-2
Major character(s): Dyesal, Child (boy), Student; Milsen, Child (boy), Student; Loud, Child (girl), Student
Time period(s): 1990s
Locale(s): Haiti

Summary: Dyesel and his friends go to school six days a week, running down the road in the early morning. As they run they watch the sun rise and pass the sights and sounds of early morning in Haiti, illustrated in bright colors. They rush to go to school so they can learn reading and writing and add to their song of joy in learning. (unpaged)

Where it's reviewed:
School Library Journal, June 1996, page 102
Horn Book, May/June, page 327

Awards the book has won:
Coretta Scott King Honor Book, 1997

Other books by the same author:
Father and Son, 1992

Other books you might like:
Susan Saunders, *Tyrone Goes to School*, 1992
> When Tyrone goes to school he learns things and finds out things about himself.
Catherine Stock, *Where Are You Going, Manyoni?*, 1993
> A little girl sees all kinds of wildlife on her way to school in Kenya.
Nancy Van Laan, *Mama Rocks, Papa Sings*, 1995
> A Haitian family welcomes other members by singing and dancing.
Karen Lynn Williams, *Tap-Tap*, 1994
> A little Haitian girl and her grandmother get to ride on the bus, the tap tap, after they have a successful day at market.

824

LAURIE LAWLOR

Gold in the Hills

(New York: Walker, 1995)

Subject(s): Frontier and Pioneer Life; Miners and Mining
Age range(s): Grades 5-6
Major character(s): Harriet Elizabeth "Hattie" Proctor, 10-Year-Old; Alexander Phimester "Pheme" Proctor, 12-Year-Old (stutterer); Old Judge, Recluse
Time period(s): 19th century
Locale(s): Colorado

Summary: After their mother dies, Hattie and her shy, older brother leave Illinois to live with their aunt while their father searches for gold in Colorado. The two are considered a burden by their aunt and plucky Hattie finds herself sticking up for her brother Pheme, who retreats into silence to buffer the insults of his cousins. Hattie and Pheme befriend the reclusive hermit, Old Judge, who prevents their being turned over to a crooked prospector who wants them as cheap labor while they wait for their father to return. (146 pages)

Where it's reviewed:
Voice of Youth Advocates, October 1995, page 220
Publishers Weekly, May 29, 1995, page 86
Booklist, June 1, 1995, page 1771

Library Talk, September 1995, page 37
School Library Journal, August 1995, page 142

Other books by the same author:
The Worm Club, 1994
Addie's Long Summer, 1992
Addie's Dakota Winter, 1989
Addie Across the Prairie, 1986

Other books you might like:
Patricia Beatty, *The Nickle-Plated Beauty*, 1964
 The seven Kimball children embark on money-making schemes to raise the twenty-seven dollars needed to pay for their nickle-plated stove.
Laura Leonard, *Finding Papa*, 1991
 The three motherless Edwards children travel to California to find their father only to discover he's prospecting for gold in Nevada.
Gary Paulsen, *Mr. Tucket*, 1994
 Francis' troubles are just beginning as he tries out his new rifle, lags behind the wagon train to shoot and is kidnapped by Pawnee Indians.

825

JULIE LAWSON
PAUL MORIN, Illustrator

The Dragon's Pearl

(New York: Clarion, 1993)

Subject(s): Fairy Tale; Dragons; Pearls
Age range(s): Grades 1-4
Major character(s): Xiao Sheng, Child (cheerful), Worker (poor); Mama, Mother (poor)
Time period(s): Indeterminate Past
Locale(s): Szechuan, China (River Min)

Summary: When drought parches the land and dries the grasses which Xiao Sheng and his mother depend on for income, he must walk farther and farther each day searching for fuel. Finding a patch of lush green grass, he returns daily to harvest more as it magically grows during the night. Xiao Sheng learns the secret of this renewal when he digs up a magic pearl buried in the grass. To prevent two evil men from stealing the pearl, Xiao Sheng swallows it and is transformed into a benevolent river dragon. A final note gives factual information about the Chinese folklore which serves as the background for this tale. First published in Canada. (32 pages)

Where it's reviewed:
Booklist, April 15, 1993, page 1513
Emergency Librarian, September 1993, page 49
New Advocate, Summer 1993, page 215
Publishers Weekly, March 22, 1993, page 79
School Library Journal, July 1993, page 62

Other books by the same author:
Kate's Castle, 1994

Other books you might like:
Michael Hague, *The Book of Dragons*, 1995
 Seventeen short selections for dragon lovers include fantasy and folktales from different countries.

Walter Dean Myers, *The Dragon Takes a Wife*, 1972
 A lonely dragon seeks help from Mabel Mae, a most unusual fairy, with his quest for a wife.
Susan Miho Nunes, *The Last Dragon*, 1995
 In Chinatown a young boy finds an old ten-person dragon in a shop and encourages others to help him restore it to a useful life.
Laurence Yep, *City of Dragons*, 1995
 A young boy, shunned in his village because of his appearance, runs away to the city of dragons where he comes to understand the meaning of beauty.

826

URSULA K. LE GUIN
S.D. SCHINDLER, Illustrator

Wonderful Alexander and the Catwings

(New York: Orchard Books, 1994)

Series: Catwings
Subject(s): Animals/Cats; Fantasy; Fear
Age range(s): Grades 2-4
Major character(s): Alexander Furby, Kitten, Adventurer; Jane Catwing, Cat
Time period(s): 1990s (1994)
Locale(s): United States (Overhill Farm)

Summary: Wonderful Alexander, largest and bossiest of the Furby kittens, sets off to explore while his family sleeps. Alexander finds more than he bargains for and ends up spending the night at the top of a tall pine where he has sought refuge from two hounds. Afraid to come down, he is rescued the next morning by Jane who takes him to her home at Overhill Farm where he is accepted by the Catwing family. (48 pages)

Where it's reviewed:
Booklist, September 15, 1994, page 136
Horn Book Guide, Spring 1995, page 68
Kirkus Reviews, August 15, 1994, page 1132
School Library Journal, September 1994, page 188

Other books by the same author:
Fish Soup, 1992
Catwings Return, 1989
Catwings, 1988

Other books you might like:
Christopher de Vinck, *Augusta & Trab*, 1993
 Augusta and her talking cat Trab unlock a door in the peach tree and enter a magical land of fantastic adventures.
Dick King-Smith, *Sophie's Tom*, 1991
 Five-year-old Sophie finds a stray cat comforting as she adjusts to school, making friends and achieving her dream to be a farmer.
Phyllis Reynolds Naylor, *The Grand Escape*, 1993
 House cats Marco and Polo escape to an outside world of wonder, adventure and danger.
Dyan Sheldon, *Harry and Chicken*, 1992
 When Chicken adopts a stray cat, she discovers that Harry is actually an alien from another planet.

827

BIJOU LE TORD, Author/Illustrator

Elephant Moon

(New York: Doubleday Book for Young Readers, 1993)

Subject(s): Animals/Elephants; Africa; Environmental Problems

Age range(s): Grades K-3

Major character(s): Unnamed Character, Elephant

Time period(s): 1990s (1993)

Locale(s): Africa

Summary: The life of elephants on the African plains is gently described in both words and pictures. The simple story conveys an image of grace to the elephants' daily routine. A one-page introduction gives factual information about elephants and the international organizations working to save them from extinction. (32 pages)

Where it's reviewed:

Booklist, September 15, 1993, page 158

Children's Book Review Service, August 1993, page 160

Horn Book Guide, Fall 1993, page 265

Publishers Weekly, June 14, 1993, page 70

School Library Journal, August 1993, page

Other books by the same author:

The River and the Rain: The Lord's Prayer, 1994

Rabbit Seeds, 1993

Little Shepherd: The Twenty-Third Psalm, 1991

Other books you might like:

Verna Aardema, *Bringing the Rain to Kapiti Plain: A Nandi Tale*, 1981

In rhyme, the author retells an African folktale explaining how Ki-pat brought the rain to the dry Kapiti Plain and its wildlife.

Miela Ford, *Little Elephant*, 1994

A baby elephant describes a day of play under the watchful eye of his mother.

Richard Sobol, *One More Elephant: The Fight to Save Wildlife in Uganda*, 1995

A factual account of the efforts to protect elephant herds in Uganda's Queen Elizabeth National Park.

828

NORMAN LEACH

JANE BROWNE, Illustrator

My Wicked Stepmother

(New York: Macmillan Publishing Company, 1993)

Subject(s): Stepmothers; Love; Family Relations

Age range(s): Grades K-3

Major character(s): Tom, 7-Year-Old, Stepson; Dad, Father (remarried); Annie, Stepmother

Time period(s): 1990s (1992)

Locale(s): England

Summary: Feeling threatened by his father's marriage to Annie, Tom is determined to avoid a relationship with the woman he fears is a witch. One evening he speaks his inner thoughts about Annie for the first time and sees the hurt he

causes. This emotional airing enables the family to begin building a positive relationship. Tom now believes that he is a wizard because, with one kiss, he has transformed the wicked stepmother into a fairy godmother. This first book by the now-deceased author was first published in England in 1992. (26 pages)

Where it's reviewed:

Booklist, February 15, 1993, page 1067

Children's Book Review Service, Spring 1993, page 135

Instructor, October 1993, page 61

New Advocate, Fall 1993, page 293

School Library Journal, March 1993, page 180

Other books you might like:

Nancy Raines Day, *The Lion's Whiskers: An Ethiopian Folktale*, 1995

The advice of a wise man helps a stepmother understand the need for patience in building a relationship with her stepson.

Peter Glassman, *My Working Mom*, 1994

Hilarious illustrations communicate the unique advantage of having a mom who really is a witch.

Gina Willner-Pardo, *What I'll Remember When I Am a Grownup*, 1994

Knowing that a surprise awaits him during his weekend visit with his father and stepmother, Daniel fears the worst.

829

UNA LEAVY

PETER UTTON, Illustrator

Harry's Stormy Night

(New York: Margaret K.McElderry Books, 1995)

Subject(s): Weather; Fear; Family Life

Age range(s): Grades K-2

Major character(s): Harry, Child, Brother (older); Baby Tom, Child, Brother

Time period(s): 1990s (1994)

Locale(s): England

Summary: When the north wind blows fiercely a power line breaks down, and Harry and his family gather in the shelter of their rural home, warmed by the wood stove and comforted by apple tarts and story telling. At bedtime, Harry's fear of the dark begins to get the best of him when he hears the sound of Baby Tom crying. Bravely, he goes to Baby Tom's room and, by soothing him, also calms his own fears. The author's first book was originally published in London in 1994. (32 pages)

Where it's reviewed:

Booklist, April 1, 1995, page 1428

Children's Book Review Service, June 1995, page 124

Horn Book Guide, Fall 1995, page 271

School Library Journal, May 1995, page 86

Smithsonian, November 1995, page 172

Other books you might like:

Karen Ackerman, *The Sleeping Porch*, 1995

When a thunderstorm reveals leaks in the roof of their new home, a family gathers together to sleep in the only dry place—the porch.

Amy Hest, *Ruby's Storm*, 1994
Determined to keep her checkers date with Grampa, Ruby packs her picnic basket with supplies and sets off in a spring storm for a comforting evening.

Anne F. Rockwell, *The Storm*, 1994
In the comfort of her family's coastal home, a young girl reflects on the power of a major storm.

Cynthia Rylant, *Henry and Mudge and the Wild Wind*, 1993
Both Henry and his dog Mudge are afraid of thunderstorms, but Henry's father helps ease their fear with a game.

830

HUY VOUN LEE, Author/Illustrator

In the Snow

(New York: Henry Holt and Company, 1995)

Subject(s): Winter; Mothers and Sons; Chinese Americans
Age range(s): Grades 1-3
Major character(s): Xiao Ming, Child; Unnamed Character, Mother
Time period(s): 1990s (1995)
Locale(s): United States

Summary: The ground is covered with fresh white snow providing Xiao Ming's mother with the perfect canvas for a lesson in Chinese characters. As the two walk over the snowy ground, Xiao Ming watches his mother form characters in the snow with her stick and guesses their meaning. A glossary on the endpapers defines the characters and gives their approximate pronunciations in Mandarin Chinese. (32 pages)

Where it's reviewed:
Booklist, October 15, 1995, page 412
Children's Book Review Service, October 1995, page 18
Kirkus Reviews, September 1, 1995, page 1282
Publishers Weekly, September 4, 1995, page 69
School Library Journal, December 1995, page 84

Other books by the same author:
At the Beach, 1994

Other books you might like:
Cheryl Chapman, *Snow on Snow on Snow*, 1994
While sledding, a young boy loses and then finds his dog.

Lois Ehlert, *Snowballs*, 1995
The celebration of snow is enlivened with collage illustrations and expanded with factual information.

Ezra Jack Keats, *The Snowy Day*, 1962
The Caldecott Medal winner expresses a young boy's joy with the first snowfall.

831

DAVID LEGGE

Bamboozled

(New York: Scholastic, Inc., 1995)

Subject(s): Grandparents; Family Life; Fantasy
Age range(s): Grades K-3
Major character(s): Unnamed Character, Child; Grandpa, Grandfather
Time period(s): 1990s (1995)
Locale(s): Fictional Country

Summary: During her weekly visit with Grandpa, a young girl is certain something is different from previous visits. While Grandpa and granddaughter visit, drink tea (served in flower pots), and play cards (with a deck that includes only the eight of hearts) in a home which can only be described as bizarre, the girl still cannot determine what is odd. Even as she helps with the housework (by mowing his ''carpet'') she is troubled that she can't quite figure out what it is. As the girl bids Grandpa good-bye, she realizes what has been bothering her—Grandpa's socks don't match! The author's first children's book was originally published in Australia in 1994. (32 pages)

Where it's reviewed:
Booklist, January 15, 1995, page 936
Children's Book Review Service, May 1995, page 110
Library Talk, September 1995, page 32
Publishers Weekly, February 6, 1995, page 84
School Library Journal, March 1995, page 182

Other books you might like:
Anthony Browne, *Changes*, 1991
Waiting for his parents to return, a young boy imagines what his father might have meant by the comment, ''Things are going to change around here.''

Michael Garland, *Dinner at Magritte's*, 1995
Pierre's home is so quiet it's boring so he visits his artist neighbors where things are not exactly as they seem to the eye.

Harvey Stevenson, *Grandpa's House*, 1994
Grandpa has many surprises waiting for grandson Woody when he arrives for a weekend visit.

832

DANIEL LEHAN, Author/Illustrator

Wipe Your Feet!

(New York: Dutton Children's Books, 1993)

Subject(s): Animals; Artists and Art; Fantasy
Age range(s): Grades K-1
Major character(s): Nancy, Householder (painting owner)
Time period(s): 1990s
Locale(s): England

Summary: After Nancy purchases a painting of wild animals at a yard sale she begins to notice strange footprints on her bath mat which she discovers are coming from the painting's animals. Nancy establishes some ground rules to keep the footprints confined to the bath mat and now she has a new painting every day thanks to the animals' inability to remember the spot to which they are to return. Originally published in Great Britain in 1992. (32 pages)

Where it's reviewed:
Booklist, March 1, 1993, page 1236
Horn Book, January 1993, page 75
Kirkus Reviews, February 1, 1993, page 149
Publishers Weekly, January 4, 1993, page 73
School Library Journal, April 1993, page 100

Other books by the same author:
Crocodile Snaps—Kangaroo Jumps, 1993
This Is Not a Book about Dodos, 1992

Other books you might like:
Anthony Browne, *Gorilla*, 1985
  A little girl's fascination with gorillas leads to a visit from one who is interested in taking her on an adventure.
Elizabeth MacDonald, *John's Picture*, 1991
  John draws a picture which comes to life and begins creating more pictures.
William Steig, *Gorky Rises*, 1980
  In a book with award-winning illustrations, a frog named Gorky concocts a potion which enables him to fly.
Tim Wynne-Jones, *Zoom Away*, 1985
  In a surrealistic fantasy, feline Zoom embarks on another adventure with his human friend Maria.

833

PASCAL LEMAITRE, Author/Illustrator

Emily the Giraffe
(New York: Hyperion Books for Children, 1993)

Subject(s): Animals/Giraffes; Play; Change
Age range(s): Grades K-1
Major character(s): Emily, Giraffe (friendly)
Time period(s): 1990s (1993)
Locale(s): Africa

Summary: Happy to play with her friends in the African bush, Emily is also content to accept an offer of a boat trip to an unspecified northern destination. There she tries her hand at a variety of jobs including chimney sweep and circus performer. When she saves a child's life, the queen offers to grant her any wish and Emily cheerily choses to return to her friends in Africa. First published in Belgium in 1991. (32 pages)

Where it's reviewed:
Booklist, May 15, 1993, page 1696
Children's Book Review Service, July 1993, page 148
Junior Bookshelf, December 1992, page 235
Publishers Weekly, April 19, 1993, page 58
School Library Journal, August 1993, page 147

Other books you might like:
Judi Barrett, *Animals Should Definitely Not Wear Clothing*, 1970
  Silliness abounds as the many possibilities for animals in attire are discussed and appropriately illustrated.
Jean de Brunhoff, *The Story of Babar*, 1937
  Now a classic, the story of Babar, a most unusual, orphaned elephant, begins.
H. A. Rey, *Curious George*, 1941
  Curiosity leads a little monkey into captivity and a life of adventure with the man with the yellow hat.

834

ANNE LEMIEUX
DIANE DE GROAT, Illustrator

Fruit Flies, Fish & Fortune Cookies
(New York: Tambourine Books, 1994)

Subject(s): Superstition; Friendship; Moving, Household
Age range(s): Grades 4-6
Major character(s): Mary Ellen Bobowick, 6th Grader, Friend (Justine's); Justine Kelly, 11-Year-Old, Friend (Mary Ellen's); Ben, 6th Grader
Time period(s): 1990s (1994)
Locale(s): United States

Summary: As a future scientist, Mary Ellen doesn't believe in superstitions, but the events of her life seem determined to prove the fortune cookie right and her scientific methodology wrong. After reading the foreboding fortune, Mary Ellen breaks a mirror, her best friend Justine learns that her family is moving to Paris, and she spills pizza on her blouse in the cafeteria. What else can go wrong? Plenty, but meeting Ben, a new student, helps life look a little brighter. (187 pages)

Where it's reviewed:
Booklist, November 1, 1994, page 497
Children's Book Review Service, Winter 1995, page 71
Kirkus Reviews, November 15, 1994, page 1534
Library Talk, November 1994, page 43
School Library Journal, October 1994, page 124

Other books by the same author:
Do Angels Sing the Blues?

Other books you might like:
C.S. Adler, *Always and Forever Friends*, 1990
  Meg moves away leaving 11-year-old Wendy struggling to make new friends.
Sheila Greenwald, *Give Us a Great Big Smile, Rosy Cole*, 1981
  Uncle Ralph decides to make 10-year-old Rosy and her violin the subjects of his next book.
Gary Paulsen, *Dunc and the Scam Artists*, 1993
  An entry in the Culpepper Adventure Series finds clumsy Amos being talked into various schemes by amateur sleuth Dunc as the duo try to capture a scam artist.

835

MARGO LEMIEUX
ROBERT ANDREW PARKER, Illustrator

Full Worm Moon
(New York: Tambourine Books, 1994)

Subject(s): Indians of North America; Legends; Animals/Worms
Age range(s): Grades 1-3
Major character(s): Atuk, Brother, Indian (Algonquin); Monamie, Mother, Indian (Algonquin); Mequin, Sister, Indian (Algonquin)
Time period(s): Indeterminate Past
Locale(s): New England

Summary: Long before the Pilgrims arrived to settle America, an Algonquin family celebrates the return of spring. Through the winter, Atuk and Mequin ask to be told the story of the Full Worm Moon until Monamie is tired of retelling it. When their father enters the wigwam one evening and announces that the night of the Full Worm Moon is upon them, the family gathers elk robes and goes out into the open fields to await the return of the worms which signal the warming of the earth as spring returns. This is the first book written by the children's book illustrator. (32 pages)

Where it's reviewed:
Booklist, May 15, 1994, page 1683
Children's Book Review Service, June 1994, page 124
Kirkus Reviews, April 1, 1994, page 481
Publishers Weekly, April 25, 1994, page 77
School Library Journal, August 1994, page 139

Other books you might like:
Virginia L. Kroll, *The Seasons and Someone*, 1994
    A young Inuit girl marks the changes of the seasons by watching the sky, the animals, the plants and especially her cherished berry bushes.
Charles Larry, *Peboan and Seegwun*, 1993
    The Ojibway legend describes the change of seasons from winter to spring as the culmination of a dialog between Old Man Winter and the younger Spirit of Spring.
Nancy Van Laan, *In a Circle Long Ago: A Treasury of Native Lore from North America*, 1995
    This is a collection of stories and poems including source notes and descriptions of the tribes whose folklore is represented.

836

ELLEN LEROE
BILL BASSO, Illustrator

Ghost Dog

(New York: Hyperion Books for Children, 1993)

Subject(s): Mystery and Detective Stories; Animals/Dogs; Ghosts
Age range(s): Grades 2-4
Major character(s): Aristotle "Artie" Jensen, 9-Year-Old (imaginative); Grandpa Noonie, Grandfather; Ghost Dog, Dog, Spirit (ghost)
Time period(s): 1990s (1993)
Locale(s): Pennsylvania (small town near Philadelphia)

Summary: When Artie and his family arrive at Grandpa Noonie's new home for a visit, Artie is quick to discover that the place is haunted. Unfortunately, only Artie can see Ghost Dog and only Artie is blamed for the trouble that the spirit causes. When an important baseball card disappears, Artie uses Ghost Dog to help him solve the mystery and recover the valuable card. (63 pages)

Where it's reviewed:
Booklist, April 1, 1993, page 1431
Horn Book Guide, Fall 1993, page 300
Reading Teacher, September 1994, page 71
School Library Journal, June 1993, page 78

Other books by the same author:
Leap Frog Friday, 1992

Other books you might like:
Daniel Greenberg, *The Great Baseball Card Hunt*, 1992
    A Southside Sluggers Baseball Mystery involves a winless team's search for three valuable baseball cards.
Dian Curtis Regan, *The Mystery of the Haunted Castle*, 1995
    In the 8th entry of the Ghost Twins Series Robbie and Beka discover their dog has wandered into the picture of a book Beka is reading and they must retrieve him.
Betty Ren Wright, *The Ghost of Popcorn Hill*, 1993
    To rid themselves of a lonely ghost's nightly visits, Martin and Peter match him up with a ghost dog that's been visiting them too.

837

HELEN LESTER
LYNN MUNSINGER, Illustrator

Listen, Buddy

(Boston: Houghton Mifflin Company, 1995)

Subject(s): Animals/Rabbits; Parent and Child; Communication
Age range(s): Grades K-2
Major character(s): Buddy, Rabbit, Daydreamer; Scruffy Varmint, Monster
Time period(s): 1990s (1995)
Locale(s): Fictional Country

Summary: Inattentive Buddy's habit of tuning into his own activities rather than parental requests leads to some humorous misunderstandings. On his first venture far from home, Buddy forgets his parents' directions and turns the wrong way, finding himself face to face with hungry Scruffy Varmint. Buddy soon learns that Scruffy Varmint is not as patient as his parents are when the little rabbit doesn't listen to directions. (32 pages)

Where it's reviewed:
Booklist, October 15, 1995, page 412
Horn Book Guide, Spring 1996, page 36
Five Owls, January 1996, page 57
Publishers Weekly, July 24, 1995, page 64
School Library Journal, November 1995, page 76

Other books by the same author:
The Revenge of the Magic Chicken, 1990
Tacky the Penguin, 1988
It Wasn't My Fault, 1985

Other books you might like:
Tom Birdseye, *Soap! Soap! Don't Forget the Soap! An Appalachian Folktale*, 1993
    Plug Honeycutt tries to overcome his poor memory and remember the soap he is fetching from town for his mother.
Vivian French, *Lazy Jack*, 1995
    Inattentive, absent-minded Jack never seems to accurately remember his mother's instructions.
Susan Meddaugh, *Hog-Eye*, 1995
    When an absent-minded piglet misses her bus stop and

takes a shortcut through the woods to reach school, she finds herself in a battle of wits with a hungry wolf.

838

HELEN LESTER
LYNN MUNSINGER, Illustrator

Three Cheers for Tacky

(Boston: Houghton Mifflin Company, 1994)

Subject(s): Animals/Birds; Individuality; Contests
Age range(s): Grades K-2
Major character(s): Tacky, Penguin
Time period(s): Indeterminate
Locale(s): Antarctica

Summary: When Tacky's team decides to enter the Penguin Cheering Contest, the other team members are concerned that Tacky will ruin their chances of winning. However, with practice, Tacky masters the routine. Unfortunately, on the day of the performance, after the preceding groups have bored the judges into slumber, Tacky seems to forget the steps and the resulting laughter from the audience awakens the judges who are so entertained that they declare Tacky's team the contest winners. (32 pages)

Where it's reviewed:
Booklist, February 15, 1994, page 1092
Horn Book, September 1994, page 578
New Advocate, Fall 1994, page 284
Publishers Weekly, December 20, 1993, page 71
School Library Journal, May 1994, page 98

Awards the book has won:
International Reading Association Children's Choice, 1995

Other books by the same author:
The Revenge of the Magic Chicken, 1990
Tacky the Penguin, 1988
The Wizard, the Fairy and the Magic Chicken, 1983

Other books you might like:
Nancy Coffelt, *Tom's Fish*, 1994
    Tom has a most unusual pet goldfish—Jesse swims upside down and seems happy that way!
Janet Perlman, *Cinderella Penguin or, The Little Glass Flipper*, 1993
    A familiar tale is humorously recast with penguins as the leading characters.
Ellen Stoll Walsh, *Hop Jump*, 1993
    A blue frog decides she is tired of hopping and learns to dance, setting a new trend for other frogs also.

839

JULIUS LESTER
JERRY PINKNEY, Illustrator

John Henry

(New York: Dial Books, 1994)

Subject(s): Legends; Folk Tales; African Americans
Age range(s): Grades 1-3
Major character(s): John Henry, Hero
Time period(s): Indeterminate Past

Locale(s): West Virginia

Summary: In a retelling of the folk tale, John Henry grows through the porch roof on the day of his birth. The next day he is felling trees and stacking firewood. When he decides to make his way in the world, his father gives him the two sledge hammers passed down from his grandfather. With them John Henry is able to demolish a boulder impenetrable to dynamite at a road-building site and seek work on the railroad. Although John Henry wins his legendary contest with a steam drill, his great heart gives out from the effort and he dies. (40 pages)

Where it's reviewed:
Booklist, June 1, 1994, page 1809
Horn Book, November 1994, page 739
Kirkus Reviews, October 15, 1994, page 1410
Publishers Weekly, September 5, 1994, page 108
School Library Journal, November 1994, page 98

Awards the book has won:
ALA Notable Book, 1995
Caldecott Honor Book, 1995

Other books by the same author:
The Last Tales of Uncle Remus, 1994
More Tales of Uncle Remus: Further Adventures of Brer Rabbit, His Friends, Enemies, and Others, 1988
The Tales of Uncle Remus, 1987

Other books you might like:
Ezra Jack Keats, *John Henry, an American Legend*, 1965
    The legend of John Henry is retold in a fictionalized version that has stood the test of time.
Steven Kellogg, *Paul Bunyan, A Tall Tale*, 1984
    Paul Bunyan, a lumberjack of extraordinary size and strength, leads a life of unusual adventures.
Terry Small, *The Legend of John Henry*, 1994
    While adhering to the legend of a larger than life man, the author uses verse to tell the story.

840

KATHLEEN LEVERICH
WALTER LORRAINE, Illustrator

Best Enemies Forever

(New York: Greenwillow Books, 1995)

Series: Best Enemies
Subject(s): Schools; Clubs; Behavior
Age range(s): Grades 2-4
Major character(s): Priscilla Robin, 4th Grader, Sister (Eve's); Felicity Doll, 4th Grader, Dancer; Eve Robin, Sister, Student—High School
Time period(s): 1990s (1995)
Locale(s): United States

Summary: Felicity, the star, is jealous of the attention given to ordinary little Priscilla, especially when Priscilla tries to emulate Eve's service club by starting a volunteer organization for fourth graders. The service efforts of Ordinary Little People are recognized by the community and the attendant publicity brings out the worst in obnoxious Felicity. Finally, when she takes over the club Priscilla founded, the club members all resign and join Priscilla's new club. (136 pages)

Where it's reviewed:
Booklist, August 1995, page 1946
Horn Book, January 1996, page 71
Kirkus Reviews, August 1, 1995, page 1113
Publishers Weekly, September 18, 1995, page 135
School Library Journal, October 1995, page 105

Other books by the same author:
Hilary and the Troublemakers, 1992
Best Enemies Again, 1991
Best Enemies, 1989

Other books you might like:
Patricia Reilly Giff, *Fourth Grade Celebrity*, 1979
   Cassandra Eleanor Valentine realizes her dream of becoming a celebrity at school, but not in quite the way she expected.
Sheila Greenwald, *Rosy Cole's Great American Guilt Club*, 1985
   To achieve her goal of being attired in the trendy finery to which she feels entitled, Rosy forms a club to allow her rich friends to donate their used clothing for her benefit.
Charlotte Herman, *Millie Cooper and Friends*, 1995
   Millie's expectations for a terrific year in fourth grade are complicated by a difficult teacher and a new student.

841

KATHLEEN LEVERICH
DAN ANDREASEN, Illustrator

Brigid the Bad

(New York: Random House, 1995)

Series: First Stepping Stone Book
Subject(s): Behavior; Magic; Fairies
Age range(s): Grades 2-4
Major character(s): Brigid Thrush, Child; Maribel Jump, Mythical Creature
Time period(s): 1990s (1995)
Locale(s): United States

Summary: Impatient Brigid thinks that all her plans would work out perfectly if others would simply listen to her and do what she says. To achieve that goal, Brigid turns to her fairy godmother, Maribel, for assistance. The first wish Maribel grants makes others unhappily compliant with Brigid's demands. Then, Brigid asks to modify the wish and her friends and family become cheerful zombies when she orders them around. When she complains again to Maribel, the lesson she learns is that getting along with others depends on hard work, not magic. (72 pages)

Where it's reviewed:
Booklist, December 15, 1995, page 705
School Library Journal, March 1996, page 177

Other books by the same author:
Best Enemies Forever, 1995
Brigid Bewitched, 1994
Best Enemies, 1989

Other books you might like:
Ellen Conford, *Jenny Archer to the Rescue*, 1992
   In order to make her plan to be a hero successful, Jenny must find someone to save.

Magdalen Nabb, *Josie Smith and Eileen*, 1992
   Josie and Eileen learn that a successful friendship requires some practice.
Bonnie Pryor, *Vinegar Pancakes and Vanishing Cream*, 1987
   Trying to get some recognition is a challenge for Martin who is stuck between a cute younger brother and older, super-siblings.

842

BETTY LEVIN

Away to Me, Moss

(New York: Greenwillow, 1994)

Subject(s): Animals/Dogs; Physically Handicapped; Family Problems
Age range(s): Grades 5-6
Major character(s): Zanna Wald, 10-Year-Old; Rob Catherwood, Animal Trainer (of sheep dogs); Moss, Dog (Border collie)
Time period(s): 1990s
Locale(s): United States (Ragged Mountain)

Summary: Zanna doesn't understand why her father works so far away from home, her mother cares for a stroke victim, and the Border collie, Moss, is tied up behind the barn. As Zanna befriends Moss, she realizes that her mother's stroke victim, Mr. Catherwood, is Moss's owner and trainer. Convinced she can help Moss, Zanna helps Mr. Catherwood continue training Moss to have him work the sheep once again in this warm, touching story. (161 pages)

Where it's reviewed:
School Library Journal, October 1994, page 124
Booklist, October 1, 1994, page 327
Five Owls, January 1995, page 63
New York Times Book Review, March 12, 1995, page 20
Library Talk, November 1994, page 41

Other books by the same author:
Fire in the Wind, 1995
Brother Moose, 1990
The Trouble with Gramary, 1988

Other books you might like:
Jessie Haas, *Uncle Daney's Way*, 1994
   Though Uncle Daney's now wheelchair-bound, he teaches his nephew Cole how to train and work with his skidding horse, Nip.
Lynn Hall, *The Soul of the Silver Dog*, 1992
   Though Cory's Bedlington terrier has glaucoma, she spends hours training him for competition in the obstacle course event.
Patti Sherlock, *Some Fine Dog*, 1992
   Though poor, Terry's mother agrees to let him keep the stray Border collie he finds.

843

BETTY LEVIN

Fire in the Wind

(New York: Greenwillow, 1995)

Subject(s): Fires; Cousins; Brothers and Sisters
Age range(s): Grades 4-6
Major character(s): Meg Yeadon, 12-Year-Old, Cousin (Orin's); Orin Gray, 13-Year-Old, Mentally Challenged Person
Time period(s): 1940s (1947)
Locale(s): Prescott Falls, Maine

Summary: A dry summer envelops Maine and the drought has everyone concerned about the chance of an outbreak of fires. Meg is always told by her grandmother that she's like a "fire in the wind" since she often makes matters worse by her reaction to each situation. Meg, however, does a good job of protecting her younger brother and her older, "backward" cousin Orin. When fire does break out, it's Orin who becomes the leader and Meg who listens to his advice in a reversal of roles. (137 pages)

Where it's reviewed:
School Library Journal, October 1995, page 136
Children's Book Review Service, January 1996, page 59
Center for Children's Books. Bulletin, January 1996, page 165
Kirkus Reviews, October 15, 1995, page 1495
Horn Book, March 1996, page 196

Other books by the same author:
Away to Me, Moss, 1994
Brother Moose, 1990
Binding Spell, 1984

Other books you might like:
Caroline B. Cooney, *Flash Fire*, 1995
    When a flash fire overtakes their canyon home, Danny breaks her leg and her younger brother Hall must try to save her.
Ivan Southall, *Ash Road*, 1965
    A group of youngsters are trapped by a terrible fire.
Maureen Crane Wartski, *The Lake Is on Fire*, 1981
    When their cabin catches on fire, only a blind boy and his dog are at home.

844

BETTY LEVIN
JOS. A. SMITH, Illustrator

Starshine and Sunglow

(New York: Greenwillow Books, 1994)

Subject(s): Farm Life; Problem Solving; Neighbors and Neighborhoods
Age range(s): Grades 3-5
Major character(s): Ben Addario, Child, Friend; Foster Baring, Child, Friend; Kate, Child, Friend
Time period(s): 1990s (1994)
Locale(s): United States (Flint Farm Road)

Summary: When 3 friends learn that their favorite local sweet corn will not be grown this year, they rally all the neighbors to show the farmers that, by working together, the neighborhood can conquer the crows, blackbirds and raccoons which dine on the corn before it can be picked for market. While their idea is self-serving—Ben, Kate and Foster love eating that corn—it convinces the owners of Flint Farm to plant one more time so the children can try out the scarecrows they have made. The scarecrows, which take on a life of their own, are only the first of the innovative ideas of a corn-loving neighborhood. (91 pages)

Where it's reviewed:
Booklist, May 1, 1994, page 1598
Horn Book, September 1994, page 587
Kirkus Reviews, May 15, 1994, page 702
Library Talk, September 1994, page 44
School Library Journal, June 1994, page 132

Other books by the same author:
Away to Me, Moss, 1994
The Trouble with Gramary, 1988

Other books you might like:
Carol Ryrie Brink, *Caddie Woodlawn*, 1935
    A Newbery Award winner details the adventures and resourcefulness of Caddie and her brothers.
Eleanor Estes, *The Moffats*, 1941
    The first of four titles about the Moffats introduces a lively family with four children and their friends, and neighbors in a small Connecticut town.
Susan Beth Pfeffer, *Kid Power*, 1992
    With her mother unexpectedly out of work, a young girl takes the initiative and forms an employment agency to locate jobs for herself and her friends.

845

ARTHUR A. LEVINE
SUSAN GUEVARA, Illustrator

The Boardwalk Princess

(New York: Tambourine Books, 1993)

Subject(s): Folk Tales; Witches and Witchcraft; Brothers and Sisters
Age range(s): Grades K-3
Major character(s): Sadie, Orphan (Myron's sister), Seamstress (talented); Myron, Orphan (Sadie's brother), Tailor (talented); Unnamed Character, Witch (evil)
Time period(s): Indeterminate Past
Locale(s): New York, New York (Brooklyn)

Summary: The Grimm fairy tale *Brother and Sister* is transported to Brooklyn where Myron and Sadie are adopted by an evil witch who forces them to work in her garment shop as she becomes rich from their talents. When Myron and Sadie run away, they are followed by the witch who transforms Myron into a mouse. Sadie protects Myron from further harm and, when the witch reappears on the eve of Sadie's wedding to a well-dressed real estate tycoon, Myron outwits her so all can live happily ever after. (32 pages)

Where it's reviewed:
Booklist, April 15, 1993, page 1519

Horn Book Guide, Fall 1993, page 265
Kirkus Reviews, April 15, 1993, page 533
Publishers Weekly, May 3, 1993, page 308
School Library Journal, June 1993, page 98

Other books by the same author:
Bono and Nonno, 1995
The Boy Who Drew Cats: A Japanese Folktale, 1994
All the Lights in the Night, 1991

Other books you might like:
Jacob Grimm, *Rumpelstiltskin*, 1990
  In Alison Sage's retelling of the traditional tale, the future queen is assisted by a strange little man with magical powers, but then, as queen, must outwit him to save her child.
Peggy Thomson, *The Tinderbox*, 1991
  To gain control of a magical tinderbox, a soldier must match wits with a witch.
Jane Yolen, *Sleeping Ugly*, 1981
  In a clever retelling of a classic fairy tale, inner beauty triumphs and the deserving live happily ever after.

846

ARTHUR A. LEVINE
ROBERT ROTH, Illustrator

Pearl Moscowitz's Last Stand

(New York: Tambourine Books, 1993)

Subject(s): Trees; Neighbors and Neighborhoods; Courage
Age range(s): Grades K-3
Major character(s): Pearl Moscowitz, Aged Person (caring neighbor), Activist
Time period(s): 1990s (1993)
Locale(s): Elmont, New York (Gingko Street)

Summary: Urban renewal and Pearl Moscowitz come face to face and Pearl wins. As a life-long resident of her city neighborhood, Pearl and the gingko trees are the stabilizing presence on an urban street. When the last tree and neighborhood gathering spot is slated for removal in the name of development, Pearl is determined that the time for change is over. (32 pages)

Where it's reviewed:
Booklist, November 1, 1993, page 530
Children's Book Review Service, December 1993, page 43
Horn Book, November 1993, page 735
Publishers Weekly, August 9, 1993, page 478
School Library Journal, December 1993, page 90

Other books by the same author:
The Boardwalk Princess, 1993
Sheep Dreams, 1993
All the Lights in the Night, 1991

Other books you might like:
Eve Bunting, *Someday a Tree*, 1993
  When poisons are carelessly dumped near a cherished oak Alice's family and neighbors struggle to·save the tree.
DyAnne DiSalvo-Ryan, *City Green*, 1994
  When a building is torn down leaving an ugly empty lot on Marcy's block, she takes charge and creates a garden in the space.

Lisa Campbell Ernst, *Squirrel Park*, 1993
  Stuart Ivey and a friendly squirrel make sure that development plans spare the last big oak tree in town.
Alexandra Wallner, *Since 1920*, 1992
  A story of urbanization, decline and revitilization of a neighborhood centers on one family's home and the changes it endures over the generations.

847

ARTHUR A. LEVINE
JUDY LANFREDI, Illustrator

Sheep Dreams

(New York: Dial Books for Young Readers, 1993)

Subject(s): Animals/Sheep; Shyness; Plays
Age range(s): Grades K-1
Major character(s): Liza Shetland, Sheep (shy), Actress (aspiring); Cashmere LaFondue, Sheep (classmate of Liza's), Actress (starring role in class play)
Time period(s): 1990s (1993)
Locale(s): Fictional City

Summary: In the privacy of her living room Liza becomes the star of her dreams, but at the school auditions she is unable to say a word. On the night of the play Liza prepares for her nonspeaking role when Cashmere is overcome with stage fright and unable to perform. Liza finds herself on stage as the curtain goes up and steps into the lead role without "baaating" an eye or skipping a bleat. (32 pages)

Where it's reviewed:
Horn Book, May 1993, page 320
Horn Book Guide, Fall 1993, page 265
Publishers Weekly, January 18, 1993, page 468
School Library Journal, May 1993, page 88

Other books by the same author:
Bono and Nonno, 1995
The Boardwalk Princess, 1993
All the Lights in the Night, 1991

Other books you might like:
Wendy Cheyette Lewison, *Shy Vi*, 1993
  Too shy to speak up for herself, shy Vi finds her voice and her confidence on stage.
Emily Arnold McCully, *Speak Up, Blanche!*, 1991
  Timid Blanche finds a way to participate in the Farm Theater as a set designer.
Rosemary Wells, *Shy Charles*, 1988
  When his babysitter falls and needs assistance, Charles overcomes his shyness to call for help.

848

CAROLINE LEVINE
BETSY LEWIN, Illustrator

The Detective Stars and the Case of the Super Soccer Team

(New York: Cobblehill Books, 1994)

Subject(s): Mystery and Detective Stories; Sports/Soccer
Age range(s): Grades 2-3

Major character(s): Veronica, Child, Detective—Amateur; Ernest, Child, Detective—Amateur
Time period(s): 1990s (1994)
Locale(s): United States

Summary: The Detective Stars Agency is called into action by the coach of the Eagles soccer team when the Foxes, a team with a losing season, are suddenly challenging the Eagles for the championship. No one can understand the sudden good fortune of a losing team until Veronica and Ernest use their detective skills to solve the case. (45 pages)

Where it's reviewed:
Booklist, January 15, 1994, page 931
Horn Book Guide, Fall 1994, page 302
School Library Journal, May 1994, page 98

Other books by the same author:
Riddles to Tell Your Cat, 1992
Silly School Riddles and Other Classroom Crack-Ups, 1984
The Silly Kid Joke Book, 1983

Other books you might like:
Mary Jane Auch, *Angel and Me and the Bayside Bombers*, 1989
    Brian has the desire to play soccer, but not the skill and stoops to bribery to gain a place on a team.
Steven Otfinoski, *The Stolen Signs: A Southside Sluggers Baseball Mystery*, 1992
    The Southside Sluggers must learn who is stealing their team's pitching signals.
Donald J. Sobol, *Encyclopedia Brown and the Case of the Disgusting Sneakers*, 1990
    In a series entry Leroy Brown, boy detective, uses his wits and his detective agency to solve yet another mystery.

849

EVAN LEVINE
BETSY LEWIN, Illustrator

What's Black and White and Came to Visit?

(New York: Orchard Books, 1994)

Subject(s): Animals/Skunks; Problem Solving; Humor
Age range(s): Grades K-3
Major character(s): Lily, Child
Time period(s): 1990s (1994)
Locale(s): United States

Summary: Lily discovers a skunk stuck in the rain gutter and calls for help which begins an influx of community helpers intent on solving the problem of how to remove a stuck skunk. While the fire department, the police, the mayor, and the town yodeler consider what to do, the skunk, bothered by all the noise, quietly walks away. (32 pages)

Where it's reviewed:
Booklist, October 15, 1994, page 436
Horn Book Guide, Spring 1995, page 68
Publishers Weekly, August 8, 1994, page 428
School Library Journal, September 1994, page 188

Other books by the same author:
Not the Piano, Mrs. Medley!, 1991

Other books you might like:
Ida Luttrell, *Tillie and Mert*, 1985
    Best friends Tillie the skunk and Mert the mouse frolic through three tales.
Mona R. Reeves, *The Spooky Eerie Night Noise*, 1989
    Oh dear, that strange noise outside the window is skunks!
Rosemary Wells, *Fritz and the Mess Fairy*, 1991
    Fritz the skunk is such a slob that he receives a visit from the Mess Fairy.

850

MARILYN LEVINSON

No Boys Allowed

(Mahwah, NJ: BridgeWater Books, 1993)

Subject(s): Divorce; Family Life; Relatives
Age range(s): Grades 5-6
Major character(s): Cassie Landauer, 11-Year-Old, 6th Grader; Uncle Harry Landauer, Uncle (Cassie's great-uncle); Corinne Landauer, 15-Year-Old
Time period(s): 1990s
Locale(s): New York (near Glen Haven)

Summary: When their father abandons his family to move to another state with a younger woman, only Cassie eradicates all men from her life. Her sister, Corinne, is interested in a boy at school and her normally disorganized mother goes to work for the first time. Cassie sticks by her new motto of "no boys allowed." Her life is disrupted when her Great-Uncle Harry comes to stay, sleeps in her bed and houses his cat in her bedroom. As Uncle Harry talks to her about her father, Cassie comes to realize that her life is sterile and devoid of some special people when she excludes all males. (124 pages)

Where it's reviewed:
Publishers Weekly, November 1, 1993
Booklist, October 1, 1993, page 344
Horn Book Guide, Spring 1994, page 78
School Library Journal, November 1993, page 109
Library Talk, March 1994, page 47

Other books you might like:
Judy Blume, *It's Not the End of the World*, 1972
    Karen tries to reunite her parents, not realizing that they can never again be a regular family.
Natalie Honeycutt, *Ask Me Something Easy*, 1991
    Addie feels left out after her parents divorce, especially when her mother takes her anger out on Addie.
Robert Lehrman, *Separations*, 1990
    When Kim's parents separate, her whole life changes. She must adjust to a move to Manhattan, a new tennis coach and adjustment to her father's young girlfriend.

851

NANCY SMILER LEVINSON
BETH PECK, Illustrator

Sweet Notes, Sour Notes

(New York: Lodestar Books, 1993)

Subject(s): Musicians; Jews; Self-Discipline

Age range(s): Grades 3-5
Major character(s): David Raskin, 4th Grader; Zayde, Grandfather; Madame Markov, Teacher (violin)
Time period(s): 1920s
Locale(s): United States

Summary: After hearing a violin concert by a famous artist, David dreams of becoming a gifted violinist. Only Zayde shares his dreams and encourages David's parents to rent a violin and arrange for lessons. Much to David's chagrin the violin does not sing beautifully on his first attempts to play and he learns that practice and perseverance are necessary if his dream is to come true. (64 pages)

Where it's reviewed:
Booklist, April 15, 1993, page 1515
Horn Book Guide, Spring 1994, page 78
Kirkus Reviews, July 1, 1993, page 862
Publishers Weekly, June 14, 1993, page 71
School Library Journal, August 1993, page 164

Other books by the same author:
Turn of the Century: Our Nation One Hundred Years Ago, 1994
Christopher Columbus: Voyager to the Unknown, 1990
Clara and the Bookwagon, 1988

Other books you might like:
Riki Levinson, *Boys Here—Girls There*, 1993
    During the Depression, Jennie faces many changes — beginning school, her father's loss of his job and a new baby in the family.
Lensey Namioka, *Yang the Youngest and His Terrible Ear*, 1992
    Newly-arrived from China, Yang the Youngest is expected to give a violin recital in order to attract new students for his father.
Sydney Taylor, *All-of-a-Kind Family*, 1951
    The first of several adventures about five sisters growing up in early 20th century New York.

852

RIKI LEVINSON
JULIE DOWNING, Illustrator

Soon, Annala

(New York: Orchard Books, 1993)

Subject(s): Jews; Emigration and Immigration; Reunions
Age range(s): Grades K-3
Major character(s): Anna Sarah "Annala", Child, Immigrant; Papa, Father, Immigrant; Mama, Mother, Immigrant
Time period(s): 1910s (1911)
Locale(s): New York, New York

Summary: The sequel to *Watch the Stars Come Out* describes Anna and her family a year after their arrival in America as they wait for the day when Anna's two younger brothers will join them. Each time Anna asks what day they will arrive she hears the reply, "Soon, Annala." One day, soon becomes now, the family is joyfully reunited and Anna can share America with her little brothers. (32 pages)

Where it's reviewed:
Booklist, November 1, 1993, page 530

Horn Book, November 1993, page 735
Publishers Weekly, July 5, 1993, page 70
Reading Teacher, March 1994, page 495
School Library Journal, October 1993, page 102

Other books by the same author:
Country Dawn to Dusk, 1992
Our Home Is the Sea, 1988
Watch the Stars Come Out, 1985 (ALA Notable Book)

Other books you might like:
Elisa Bartone, *Peppe the Lamplighter*, 1993
    A young boy works to support his family and win his father's approval in an award-winning account of the immigrant experience.
Brett Harvey, *Immigrant Girl, Becky of Eldridge Street*, 1987
    Becky and her family flee Russia, seeking religious freedom and safety in New York City.
Joan Sandin, *The Long Way to a New Land*, 1981
    A family of Swedish emigrants travels to New York and a new home in the 1860s.

853

SONIA LEVITIN
VINCENT NASTE, Illustrator

Adam's War

(New York: Dial, 1994)

Subject(s): Clubs; Violence
Age range(s): Grades 5-6
Major character(s): Adam, Child, Leader (Angels club); Hector, Child (member of the Angels); Brendan, Child (member of the Angels)
Time period(s): 1990s
Locale(s): United States

Summary: Adam locates an abandoned shack to use as a clubhouse and is thrilled because he thinks this will invigorate his club members who aren't doing anything. Grabbing a marker, he writes the club name "Angels" on the wooden side to claim the shack and rushes off to tell Hector and Brendan about his find. But when the boys return, the Terrestrials have claimed the shack and suddenly feelings erupt. When a vet's dog is accidentally killed because of the rivalry between the Angels and the Terrestrials, Adam knows events have gotten out of hand. And it's up to Adam, as club leader, to set a better example for his members. (87 pages)

Where it's reviewed:
Publishers Weekly, June 13, 1994, page 65
School Library Journal, June 1994, page 132
Booklist, July 1994, page 1949
Horn Book Guide, Fall 1994, page 312
Kirkus Reviews, June 15, 1994, page 848

Other books by the same author:
Annie's Promise, 1993
The Golem and the Dragon Girl, 1993
The Mark of Conte, 1976
Jason and the Money Tree, 1974

Other books you might like:
Marion Dane Bauer, *On My Honor*, 1986
    Good friends Jore and Tony swim in a river off limits to

them; when Tony drowns, Jore is terrified to tell either set of parents.

Dick Cate, *Flames*, 1989

Billy and his neighborhood gang confront a mysterious stranger in Doggy Wood and wonder if he's the one who's been setting fires in their community.

Walter Dean Myers, *Scorpions*, 1988

Jamal takes over as leader of his brother's gang, but makes a big mistake when he thinks he can handle the gun someone gives him.

| 854 |

SONIA LEVITIN
CAT BOWMAN SMITH, Illustrator

Nine for California

(New York: Orchard Books, 1996)

Subject(s): Frontier and Pioneer Life; American West
Age range(s): Grades K-3
Major character(s): Amanda, Child, Traveller; Miss Camilla, Teacher, Traveller; Mama, Mother, Traveller
Time period(s): 1850s (1850-1880)
Locale(s): Missouri; California (on the trail west)

Summary: Amanda, her mother, four brothers and sisters travel by stagecoach to meet their father in California. Joining a teacher, a banker and a cowboy, they face all kinds of perils together, including being stuck in the mud, buffalos, Indians, and robbers. Mama keeps everyone supplied with beans, prunes and bread from her sack. The children keep the travelers amused with songs and lists of memorized items. At first the older travelers are not too pleased, but by the time they reach California, they're all friends. (unpaged)

Where it's reviewed:
School Library Journal, September 1996, page 184
Bulletin of the Center for Children's Books, December 1996, page 141

Awards the book has won:
School Library Journal Best Books, 1996

Other books by the same author:
The Golem and the Dragon Girl, 1993
The Man Who Kept His Heart in a Bucket, 1993
Roanoke, 1973

Other books you might like:
Celia Barker Lottridge, *The Wind Wagon*, 1995
A Kansas blacksmith builds a prairie schooner which sails to Denver, powered by the wind.
Scott Russell Sanders, *The Floating House*, 1995
The McClures sail their flatboard from Pittsburgh down the Ohio River to settle in Indiana in 1815.
David Williams, *Grandma Essie's Covered Wagon*, 1993
Grandma Essie describes how her family left Missouri looking for a better life in Kansas and Oklahoma.

| 855 |

SIDNEY LEVITT, Author/Illustrator

The Mighty Movers

(New York: Hyperion Books for Children, 1994)

Subject(s): Ghosts; Animals/Bears; Moving, Household
Age range(s): Grades K-3
Major character(s): Fred, Bear, Businessman; Ted, Bear, Businessman; Hamilton, Spirit (ghost)
Time period(s): Indeterminate Past
Locale(s): Fictional Country

Summary: Fred and Ted claim to be able to move anything, but when a customer calls wanting them to move a ghost, Ted is reluctant to take on such a scary job. Fred, however, appreciates the challenge and together they try unsuccessfully to capture Hamilton. When Ted inadvertently becomes entangled in a sheet and scares Hamilton right out of the house, the Mighty Movers' claims about moving anything appear to be true. The first book both written and illustrated by the children's book illustrator. (48 pages)

Where it's reviewed:
Booklist, April 1, 1994, page 1466
Children's Book Review Service, July 1994, page 148
Horn Book Guide, Fall 1994, page 297
Publishers Weekly, April 25, 1994, page 78
School Library Journal, August 1994, page 139

Other books you might like:
Laura Jean Allen, *Rollo and Tweedy and the Ghost at Dougal Castle*, 1992
In an I-Can-Read mystery, Lord Dougal hires Detective Tweedy and his assistant Rollo when he suspects a ghost is haunting his castle.
Dayle Ann Dodds, *Ghosts and Pete*, 1995
In a beginning reader, Pete goes trick-or-treating with his new friend Ghost who can't remember the correct Halloween greeting.
Nicole Rubel, *The Ghost Family Meets Its Match*, 1992
For 100 years a family of ghosts has successfully frightened away all potential tenants of the haunted house, but the latest residents have some tricks of their own.

| 856 |

MYRON LEVOY

Alan and Naomi

(New York: Harper & Row, 1977)

Subject(s): Friendship; Mental Illness; Historical
Age range(s): Grades 6-8
Major character(s): Alan Silverman, 7th Grader; Naomi Kirshenbaum, 7th Grader
Time period(s): 1940s
Locale(s): New York, New York

Summary: The last thing Alan wants to do is give up playing stickball with his own friends to pay attention to some crazy girl who lives upstairs. But his mother is persistent and he's so stunned by the horrible experiences the girl endured during the war years in France, that he finally agrees to visit Naomi.

With the help of his dummy, Charlie McCarthy, who talks to Naomi's doll Yvette, Alan gradually gets her to come out of her shell until the two of them share their homework and their thoughts as they become friends. But the horror of what Naomi's seen goes very deep and anything can cause a setback, as Alan sadly discovers. (192 pages)

Other books by the same author:
A Shadow Like a Leopard, 1994
Kelly n' Me, 1992
Pictures of Adam, 1986
The Hanukkah of Great-Uncle Otto, 1984

Other books you might like:
Rachel Anderson, *Paper Faces*, 1993
    Sent to the English countryside during World War II, Dot dreads returning home because of all the changes.
Peter Carter, *The Hunted*, 1994
    While retreating home after Italy surrendered during World War II, Corporal Salvani finds himself responsible for a young Jewish boy.
Anne Frank, *The Diary of Anne Frank*,
    Anne's diary covers the years she hides from the Nazis in an Amsterdam warehouse. (biography)
Lois Lowry, *Number the Stars*, 1989
    Annemarie, a Danish youth, and her family join the Resistance Movement to save Jews during World War II.
Ida Vos, *Anna Is Still Here*, 1993
    Though World War II has ended and she no longer needs to be concealed from the Nazis, the effect of living alone for three years in an attic is still with Anna.

857

ELIZABETH LEVY

Cheater, Cheater

(New York: Scholastic, 1993)

Subject(s): Friendship; Schools; Cheating
Age range(s): Grades 6-8
Major character(s): Lucy Lovello, 7th Grader; Joey Rich, 7th Grader
Time period(s): 1990s
Locale(s): Indianapolis, Indiana

Summary: At a friend's bowling birthday party, Lucy makes a big mistake when she lies about her score so that she and her partner, Joey Rich, will be the winners. A boy at the party knows what's happened and suddenly everyone at school calls her ''Cheater.'' Lucy knows she's been dishonest and tries to shed the label, but even when she studies for a test and brings up her grade honestly, no one believes her, including the teacher. Lucy learns the hard way that some mistakes are harder to correct than others. (164 pages)

Where it's reviewed:
Booklist, October 1, 1993, page 330
School Library Journal, October 1993, page 126
Publishers Weekly, August 9, 1993, page 479
Voice of Youth Advocates, December 1993, page 294
Horn Book Guide, Spring 1994, page 79

Other books by the same author:
The Drowned, 1995

Team Trouble, 1992
Tough at the Top, 1991
Cold as Ice, 1988

Other books you might like:
David Klass, *Wrestling with Honor*, 1989
    Eagle Scout, Ron, can't believe that his mandatory drug test has come back positive and that no one believes his view that the test could be wrong.
P.J. Petersen, *Liars*, 1992
    Sam is surprised to discover that his arms tingle when someone is lying; even more surprising is how many people lie, including his own father!
Laura A. Sonenmark, *The Lie*, 1992
    Norrie's lie comes back to haunt her and ruins her summer plans with heartthrob Mark.

858

ELIZABETH LEVY
GEORGE ULRICH, Illustrator

Gorgonzola Zombies in the Park

(New York: HarperCollins, 1993)

Series: Sam and Robert Bamford
Subject(s): Cousins; Monsters; Teasing
Age range(s): Grades 2-4
Major character(s): Sam Bamford, Child (Mabel's cousin), Brother (older); Robert Bamford, 7-Year-Old (Mabel's cousin), Brother (younger); Mabel, 8-Year-Old (annoying), Cousin (visiting)
Time period(s): 1990s (1993)
Locale(s): New York, New York (Central Park)

Summary: Remembering an unpleasant visit from Mabel three years earlier, Sam and Robert are not eager to have her return. When she steps off the plane with an attitude and a suitcase full of her favorite snack, smelly Gorgonzola cheese, they are determined to make her stay in New York as unpleasant as possible. Their stories about zombies in Central Park that use Gorgonzola breath to turn living things into statues begin as teasing but soon take on a air of reality when the Park's statues are vandalized with Gorgonzola cheese. (82 pages)

Where it's reviewed:
Booklist, December 1, 1993, page 691
Horn Book Guide, Spring 1994, page 79
Reading Teacher, Spring 1994, page 71
School Library Journal, December 1993, page 91

Other books by the same author:
The Case of the Tattletale Heart, 1992
Dracula Is a Pain in the Neck, 1983
Frankenstein Moved in on the Fourth Floor, 1979

Other books you might like:
David A. Adler, *The Fourth Floor Twins and the Skyscraper Parade*, 1988
    When a museum exhibit disappears, Donna and Diane investigate once again.
Mary Blount Christian, *The Sebastian (Super Sleuth) Series*, 1982-
    The real crime solver in this series is a sheepdog who solves the cases for his detective owner.

Marilyn Singer, *A Clue in Code*, 1985
The class trip money is gone and detective twins Sam and Dave must recover it.

859

ELIZABETH LEVY
GEORGE ULRICH, Illustrator

A Mammoth Mix-Up
(New York: HarperCollins Publishers, 1995)

Series: Brian and Pea Brain Mystery
Subject(s): Brothers and Sisters; Mystery and Detective Stories; Museums
Age range(s): Grades 3-5
Major character(s): Penny ''Pea Brain'' Casanova, Child (kindergartener), Sister; Brian Casanova, Brother (older)
Time period(s): 1990s (1995)
Locale(s): United States

Summary: When Penny begins disappearing into a sink hole that appears in the backyard, Brian leaps in to save her and together they find a piece of a mammoth's tusk under all the mud. Now Brian has an entry for the science-fair at the local museum although Pea Brain insists on sharing their common find. Unfortunately, the tusk disappears prior to the judging of the entry starting the sibling sleuths off on another mystery hunt. (87 pages)

Where it's reviewed:
Booklist, September 15, 1995, page 164
Horn Book Guide, Spring 1996, page 55
School Library Journal, December 1995, page 104

Other books by the same author:
Rude Rowdy Rumors: A Brian and Pea Brain Mystery, 1994
School Spirit Sabotage, 1994
Dracula Is a Pain in the Neck, 1984

Other books you might like:
David A. Adler, *Cam Jansen and the Mystery at the Monkey House*, 1985
In her 10th adventure, Cam Jansen uses her photographic memory and the help of her friends to solve the mystery of disappearing monkeys.
Elizabeth Levy, *The Something Queer Series*, 1971 -
Gwen, Jill and basset hound Fletcher have one adventure after another while they solve mysterious occurrences.
Lucinda Landon, *The Meg Mackintosh Series*, 1986-
In a series of solve-it-yourself mysteries, Meg Mackintosh is a winner any way you read the story.
Marjorie Weinman Sharmat, *Nate the Great Series*, 1972-
Nate follows one clue after another in the style of Sherlock Holmes in this series for beginning readers.

860

ELIZABETH LEVY
GEORGE ULRICH, Illustrator

School Spirit Sabotage
(New York: HarperCollins Publishers, 1994)

Series: Brian and Pea Brain Mystery

Subject(s): Mystery and Detective Stories; Schools; Brothers and Sisters
Age range(s): Grades 2-4
Major character(s): Penny ''Pea Brain'' Casanova, Child (Kindergartner), Sister; Brian Casanova, 2nd Grader, Brother
Time period(s): 1990s (1994)
Locale(s): United States (Pine Beach School)

Summary: Someone is trying to sabotage School Spirit Week. At first, Brian and Pea Brain each suspect the other. To protect his sibling, Brian decides to find the real culprit and Pea Brain wants to lend a hand. (87 pages)

Where it's reviewed:
Booklist, June 1, 1994, page 1822
Horn Book Guide, Fall 1994, page 312
Library Talk, November 1994, page 49
Publishers Weekly, May 23, 1994, page 89
School Library Journal, July 1994, page 102

Other books by the same author:
Rude Rowdy Rumors: A Brian and Pea Brain Mystery, 1994
The Schoolyard Mystery, 1994
The Case of the Mind-Reading Mommies, 1990

Other books you might like:
David A. Adler, *The Fourth Floor Twins and the Disappearing Parrot*, 1986
When the parrot used in the school talent show for a magic trick really vanishes, the Fourth Floor Twins go into action.
Laura Lee Hope, *The Bobbsey Twins and the Mystery at School*, 1962
In this one of many titles in the series about the two sets of twins in the Bobbsey family the mysterious events that need solving have happened at school.
Ann M. Martin, *Mary Anne and the Library Mystery*, 1994
One episode in the Babysitter's Club series finds Mary Anne with a problem at the library that needs attention.

861

ELIZABETH LEVY
MORDICAI GERSTEIN, Illustrator

Something Queer in Outer Space
(New York: Hyperion Books for Children, 1993)

Series: Something Queer Books
Subject(s): Mystery and Detective Stories; Animals/Dogs; Space Travel
Age range(s): Grades K-3
Major character(s): Gwen, Child, Detective—Amateur, Friend (Jill's best); Jill, Child; Fletcher, Dog (Jill's pet)
Time period(s): 1990s (1993)
Locale(s): Houston, Texas (Houston Space Center)

Summary: When Fletcher is selected for a NASA space mission, Gwen and Jill accompany him to Houston for training prior to the flight. Strange things happen on the ground and in space, requiring some sleuthing from Gwen, ever suspicious of an unexplained occurrence. (48 pages)

Where it's reviewed:
Booklist, October 15, 1993, page 443

Horn Book Guide, Spring 1994, page 67
School Library Journal, February 1994, page 88

Other books by the same author:
Something Queer in the Cafeteria, 1994
Keep Ms. Sugarman in the Fourth Grade, 1992
Something Queer at the Library, 1989

Other books you might like:
David A. Adler, *The Cam Jansen Series*, 1980-
   Using her photographic memory Cam Jansen participates in the solving of a variety of mysteries.
Lucinda Landon, *The Meg Mackintosh Series*, 1986-
   In a series of solve-it-yourself mysteries, Meg Mackintosh is a winner any way you read the story.
Marjorie Weinman Sharmat, *Nate the Great Series*, 1972-
   Nate follows one clue after another in the style of Sherlock Holmes in this series for beginning readers.

862

ELIZABETH LEVY
BILL BASSO, Illustrator

Wolfman Sam

(New York: HarperCollins, 1996)

Subject(s): Radio Broadcasting; Werewolves
Age range(s): Grades 2-5
Major character(s): Sam Bamford, 5th Grader; Echo Elmo, Radio Personality; Robert Bamford, Brother
Time period(s): 1990s
Locale(s): New York, New York

Summary: When Sam starts growing hair under his arms, he realizes he is growing up, but his brother thinks this is gross. Then Sam is selected to be the school disc jockey for the Halloween dance and assumes the name Wolfman. It isn't long before his brother starts playing tricks on him, like leaving hair in his bed, which reveal that he is turning into a werewolf. Sam finds out who is playing tricks on him but does go through with a cure just the same and is then a success at the party. (72 page)

Where it's reviewed:
Booklist, November 15, 1966, page 588

Other books by the same author:
Something Queer at the Birthday Party, 1992
The Case of the Mind-Reading Mommies, 1990
Something Queer at the Ball Park, 1984

Other books you might like:
Margery Cuyler, *Invisible in the Third Grade*, 1995
   Alex loves to chew gum and hopes that this will get him the attention of his big brother during the Halloween season.
Jamie Gilson, *It Goes Eeeeeeeeeeeee*, 1994
   Children combine to work on a science experiment that involves a bat, even though some of the children are afraid of them.
Michele Granger, *Fifth Grade Fever*, 1995
   Marty and Nina try to beat out Beverly as teacher's pet for the year in 5th grade.
Nancy J. Hopper, *What Happened in Mr. Fisher's Room*, 1995

All things are going wrong in Mr. Fisher's room and Lanie is trying to find out who is causing all the trouble.
Gordon Korman, *Radio Fifth Grade*, 1989
   Benjy thinks that he can develop his announcing skills with the aid of a local radio station.

863

BETSY LEWIN, Author/Illustrator

Booby Hatch

(New York: Clarion Books, 1995)

Subject(s): Animals/Birds; Islands; Animals
Age range(s): Grades K-2
Major character(s): Pepe, Bird (blue-footed booby)
Time period(s): 1990s (1995)
Locale(s): Galapagos Islands, Pacific Islands

Summary: On a rocky island a solitary white egg hatches. Pepe is fed and protected by his parents until he learns to fly and fend for himself. By year's end, Pepe is a mature blue-footed booby who finds a mate. The book closes with a solitary white egg sitting in a rocky island nest. (32 pages)

Where it's reviewed:
Appraisal: Science Books for Young People, Autumn 1995, page 31
Booklist, March 1, 1995, page 1248
Horn Book Guide, Fall 1995, page 271
Reading Teacher, October 1995, page 150
School Library Journal, May 1995, page 86

Awards the book has won:
School Library Journal Best Books, 1995

Other books by the same author:
Chubbo's Pool, 1996
Cat Count, 1981

Other books you might like:
Darice Bailer, *Puffin's Homecoming: The Story of an Atlantic Puffin*, 1993
   A factually based story in the Smithsonian Wild Heritage Collection tells of a puffin who returns to his island home to raise a chick.
Holly Keller, *Island Baby*, 1992
   At an island hospital for birds, Simon assists Pops as he treats an injured baby bird so it can be returned to the wild.
Nicholas Millhouse, *Blue-Footed Booby: Bird of the Galapagos*, 1986
   A non-fiction account describes the life cycle of the blue-footed booby of the Galapagos Islands.

864

HUGH LEWIN
LISA KOPPER, Illustrator

Jafta: The Homecoming

(New York: Alfred A. Knopf, 1994)

Series: Umbrella Book
Subject(s): Fathers and Sons; Africa; Work
Age range(s): Grades K-2
Major character(s): Jafta, Child

Time period(s): 1990s (1992)
Locale(s): South Africa

Summary: Jafta's father has been away for a long time working in a big city. As Jafta awaits his return, he reflects on all the events that his father has missed—a big storm, a wedding, and a freedom rally. There is so much that Jafta wants to share with his father and, now that he's returning, Jafta will. First published in Great Britain in 1992. (24 pages)

Where it's reviewed:
Booklist, December 1, 1993, page 700
Bulletin of the Center for Children's Books, March 1994, page 225
Kirkus Reviews, January 1, 1994, page 71
Publishers Weekly, November 29, 1993, page 64
School Library Journal, March 1994, page 203

Other books by the same author:
Jafta's Mother, 1988
Jafta: The Town, 1984
Jafta and the Wedding, 1983
Jafta's Father, 1983

Other books you might like:
Regina Hanson, *The Tangerine Tree*, 1995
    The loneliness of families separated by work in distant places is apparent in Ida's simple parting gift to her Papa.
Rachel Isadora, *At the Crossroads*, 1991
    South African children gather at the crossroads to welcome home their fathers when they return from working in the distant mines.
Rita Phillips Mitchell, *Hue Boy*, 1993
    The return of his father's ship makes small-for-his-age Hue Boy feel much taller.

865

TED LEWIN, Author/Illustrator

Amazon Boy
(New York: Macmillan Publishing Company, 1993)

Subject(s): Fathers and Sons; Rivers; Environmental Problems
Age range(s): Grades K-3
Major character(s): Paulo, Child; Unnamed Character, Father
Time period(s): 1990s (1993)
Locale(s): Brazil (deep in the Amazon jungle); Levino Filho, Brazil (on the Amazon River); Belem, Brazil (port city)

Summary: In honor of Paulo's birthday, his father treats him to his first trip out of the jungle on a steamship to the harbor in Belem. Knowing that over-fishing and disregard for the environment may someday mean the loss of the fish on display at the harbor market, Paulo's father shows him the bounty of nature and teaches him a regard for the environment. (32 pages)

Where it's reviewed:
Booklist, April 15, 1993, page 1523
Horn Book, May 1993, page 320
Kirkus Reviews, May 1, 1993, page 599
Publishers Weekly, April 26, 1993, page 78
School Library Journal, June 1993, page 78

Other books by the same author:
The Reindeer People, 1994
Tiger Trek, 1990

Other books you might like:
Timothy Bush, *Three at Sea*, 1994
    Three boys tubing on a river are carried out to sea where they meet a succession of endangered animals.
Glenn Alan Cheney, *The Amazon*, 1984
    In a non-fiction book, the Amazon River and its impact on the land, people, and economy of the area through which it flows, is described.
Lynne Cherry, *The Great Kapok Tree: A Tale of the Amazon Rain Forest*, 1990
    The many animals living in a kapok tree try to convince a man not to chop down their home.
Douglas Keister, *Fernando's Gift/El Regalo de Fernando*, 1995
    The bilingual text describes the efforts of one family in Costa Rica to preserve the rain forest.

866

J. PATRICK LEWIS
MARCY DUNN RAMSEY, Illustrator

One Dog Day
(New York: Atheneum, 1993)

Subject(s): Animals/Dogs; Contests; Country Life
Age range(s): Grades 3-5
Major character(s): Jilly Hawkes, 12-Year-Old (contest participant); Poetry, Dog (collie); Fairborn Farley "Twef" Garland, Child (son)
Time period(s): 1990s (1993)
Locale(s): Effingham, Illinois

Summary: The Third Annual Coon Dog Race and Corn Feed Contest is ready to begin when an unexpected entry appears. With nothing better to do Jilly Hawkes enters her collie, Poetry, in the contest. She knows Poetry has no interest in raccoons, but the dog likes to swim and the contest seems like fun. Jilly makes a new friend when Twef takes an interest in standing up for her against the teasing she and Poetry receive. Soon, coon dog enthusiasts are eating their own words along with the roasted corn being served. (52 pages)

Where it's reviewed:
Booklist, April 15, 1993, page 1515
Horn Book Guide, Fall 1993, page 301
Kirkus Reviews, May 1, 1993, page 600
Library Talk, January 1994, page 45
School Library Journal, June 1993, page 107

Other books by the same author:
The Christmas of the Reddle Moon, 1994
A Hippopotamusn't: And Other Animal Poems, 1994
July Is a Mad Mosquito, 1994

Other books you might like:
Helen Cresswell, *Posy Bates, Again!*, 1994
    Posey's determination to keep the stray dog she has befriended leads to one hilarious episode after another.

Dick King-Smith, *Babe: The Gallant Pig*, 1993
  The sheep dog in this story is really a pig — one with a unique and effective herding technique.
Betty Levin, *Away to Me, Moss*, 1994
  Zanna assists an elderly dog owner by preparing his Border collie for sheepdog trials.

867

KIM LEWIS, Author/Illustrator

First Snow

(Cambridge, MA: Candlewick Press, 1993)

Subject(s): Animals/Sheep; Parent and Child; Weather
Age range(s): Grades K-1
Major character(s): Teddy, Toy (Sara's special bear); Sara, Child; Mommy, Mother
Time period(s): 1990s (1993)
Locale(s): England (sheep farm in northern England)

Summary: One cold, winter morning, Mommy, Sara, and Teddy hurry up the hill to feed the sheep before the first snow begins. Before they finish, snow is falling and Sara, in her enjoyment of the first snow, does not notice that she has dropped Teddy. As Sara and Mommy return home, one of the faithful sheep dogs appears through the swirling snow, gently carrying Teddy. (32 pages)

Where it's reviewed:
Booklist, September 15, 1993, page 158
Horn Book Guide, Spring 1994, page 42
Junior Bookshelf, December 1993, page 227
School Library Journal, November 1993, page 86

Other books by the same author:
The Last Train, 1994
Floss, 1992
Emma's Lamb, 1991

Other books you might like:
Jez Alborough, *Where's My Teddy?*, 1992
  After a walk in the woods, a little boy realizes that he's lost his special teddy bear.
Ezra Jack Keats, *The Snowy Day*, 1962
  Keats' book is a classic portrayal of a young boy's enjoyment of a snowfall.
Scott Russell Sanders, *Warm as Wool*, 1992
  Concerned about keeping her pioneer family warm in the cold winter months, Betsy Ward saves coins to purchase sheep so that she can make woolen clothing for all.

868

KIM LEWIS, Author/Illustrator

My Friend Harry

(Cambridge, MA: Candlewick Press, 1995)

Subject(s): Toys; Animals/Elephants; Play .
Age range(s): Grades K-1
Major character(s): James, Child; Harry, Toy, Elephant
Time period(s): 1990s (1995)
Locale(s): England

Summary: Harry is a constant, silent companion to James, playing with him by day, listening to the stories he reads each night. As the years pass, and Harry endures baths to clean him from his daytime activities, he begins to grow limp and faded. One day James begins school and Harry stays home alone all day. The next day James bring him along, "just this once," until Harry can grow accustomed to being alone all day. (32 pages)

Where it's reviewed:
Booklist, October 15, 1995, page 412
Children's Book Review Service, October 1995, page 15
Horn Book Guide, Spring 1996, page 14
School Library Journal, September 1995, page 181
Times Educational Supplement, December 8, 1995, page 12

Other books by the same author:
One Summer Day, 1996
The Last Train, 1994
Emma's Lamb, 1991

Other books you might like:
Kevin Henkes, *Jessica*, 1989
  A shy preschooler insists her friend Jessica is not imaginary and, in time, her assertions turn out to be true.
Jean Van Leeuwen, *Emma Bean*, 1993
  Emma Bean, a stuffed rabbit, is a constant presence in Molly's life and helps her through the first days of kindergarten.
Selina Young, *Ned*, 1993
  Emily and Ned, her green cloth donkey, are inseparable until Ned is lost, and then found again, on the first day of school.

869

WENDY CHEYETTE LEWISON
STEPHEN JOHN SMITH, Illustrator

Shy Vi

(New York: Simon & Schuster Books for Young Readers, 1993)

Subject(s): Shyness; Animals/Mice; Parent and Child
Age range(s): Grades K-2
Major character(s): Violet, Mouse (shy)
Time period(s): 1990s (1993)
Locale(s): United States

Summary: The shy member of a loud, exuberant family, Violet is content speaking in her quiet voice, but her parents are eager for her to SPEAK UP! Violet is too shy to decline her parents' efforts and so she dutifully attends self-confidence lessons, voice lessons, and acting lessons. The acting lessons culminate in a play. Violet is unchanged, but her experiences lead to some acceptance of her from the other family members. (32 pages)

Where it's reviewed:
Booklist, May 1, 1993, page 1604
Children's Book Review Service, May 1, 1993, page 1604
Kirkus Reviews, April 15, 1993, page 533
Publishers Weekly, April 19, 1993, page 59
School Library Journal, July 1993, page 67

Other books by the same author:
Hello, Snow!, 1994

Buzz Said the Bee, 1992
Going to Sleep on the Farm, 1992

Other books you might like:

Arthur A. Levine, *Sheep Dreams*, 1993

Liza dreams of stardom but shyness leads her to settle for a nonspeaking part in the school play until a last minute crisis puts her in the spotlight.

Emily Arnold McCully, *Speak Up, Blanche!*, 1991

Shy Blanche finds a way to participate in the Farm Theater as a set designer.

Rosemary Wells, *Shy Charles*, 1988

When his babysitter falls and needs assistance, Charles overcomes his shyness to call for help.

870

JOAN M. LEXAU
MICHAEL CHESWORTH, Illustrator

Trouble Will Find You

(Boston: Houghton Mifflin Company, 1994)

Subject(s): Animals/Dogs; Burglary; Pets
Age range(s): Grades 3-4
Major character(s): Desmond "Diz" Aster, Child; Pepper Rooney, Child
Time period(s): 1990s (1994)
Locale(s): United States (Spring Street)

Summary: With a nickname like Diz Aster and a horoscope reading "Trouble will find you if you let it." the day promises to be full of problems. Poor Diz, his parents have promised that if he stays out of trouble for just one day he can have a dog. Diz really wants a pet, but when he spots a puppy being threatened with harm, he must make a decision between his own needs and the puppy's safety. His conscience wins out and although he does have a day full of troubles as he unintentionally interrupts the same burglars twice, his good deeds demonstrate his ability to be responsible and earn him the privilege of a pet. (68 pages)

Where it's reviewed:

Booklist, April 1, 1994, page 1448
Five Owls, September 1994, page 16
Horn Book Guide, Fall 1994, page 302
Kirkus Reviews, March 1, 1994, page 307
School Library Journal, April 1994, page 128

Other books by the same author:

The Dog Food Caper, 1985
Rooftop Mystery, 1968
Striped Ice Cream, 1968 (Charlie Mae Simon Award)

Other books you might like:

Richard Boughton, *Rent-a-Puppy, Inc.*, 1992

When the family beagle has a litter of six puppies, Nikki devises a plan to keep them all by renting them to other families on an hourly basis.

Betsy Duffey, *Puppy Love*, 1992

In an entry in the Pet Patrol series, Evie and Megan seek a good home for the runt of a litter of pups.

Bill Wallace, *Watchdog and the Coyotes*, 1995

The misconceptions of Sweetie, a Great Dane desiring a stable home, are revealed from the dog's perspective.

871

JANICE LIDDELL
LINDA NICKENS, Illustrator

Imani and the Flying Africans

(Trenton, NJ: Africa World Press, Inc., 1994)

Subject(s): African Americans; Slavery; Dreams and Nightmares
Age range(s): Grades 2-4
Major character(s): Imani, Child; Mama, Mother
Time period(s): Indeterminate Past
Locale(s): Savannah, Georgia

Summary: To relieve Imani's boredom on a long trip to Savannah to visit grandparents, Mama tells him a story from her childhood about slaves who could fly back to Africa to regain their freedom. After hearing the story, Imani dreams that he is kidnapped and escapes by flying away from the kidnapper to find his family. (32 pages)

Where it's reviewed:

Horn Book Guide, Spring 1995, page 68
Publishers Weekly, October 3, 1994, page 70
School Library Journal, November 1994, page 84

Other books you might like:

Virginia Hamilton, *The People Could Fly: American Black Folk Tales*, 1985

A collection of African folk tales includes one relating the ability of slaves to take flight away from oppressive conditions.

Angela Shelf Medearis, *The Freedom Riddle*, 1995

In this retelling of a folk tale, a slave uses his wits to win his freedom.

Courtni C. Wright, *Journey to Freedom: A Story of the Underground Railroad*, 1994

Not all slaves "flew" to freedom, some travelled more slowly in groups led by Harriet Tubman on the Underground Railroad.

872

BRIAN LIES, Author/Illustrator

Hamlet and the Enormous Chinese Dragon Kite

(Boston: Houghton Mifflin Company, 1994)

Subject(s): Adventure and Adventurers; Animals; Friendship
Age range(s): Grades K-3
Major character(s): Hamlet, Pig; Quince, Porcupine
Time period(s): Indeterminate
Locale(s): Fictional Country

Summary: In the author/illustrator's first book, adventurous Hamlet, undeterred by the concerns of timid friend Quince, buys an enormous dragon kite. When the wind carries the kite away with Hamlet clinging to the end of the string, he begins to wish he'd listened to Quince's advice. A helpful eagle thinks Hamlet is being kidnapped and enlists other eagles to attack the kite, bringing Hamlet's adventure to an unexpected ending. (26 pages)

Where it's reviewed:
Booklist, October 15, 1994, page 437
Horn Book Guide, Spring 1995, page 44
Kirkus Reviews, August 15, 1994, page 1133
Publishers Weekly, June 20, 1994, page 105
School Library Journal, August 1994, page 140

Other books you might like:
Arcadio Lobato, *Paper Bird*, 1994
    An artist's rendering of a paper bird achieves its dream of flying when the drawing is made into a kite.
Maryann McDonald, *Rabbit's Birthday Kite*, 1991
    Without waiting for Hedgehog's instructions, Rabbit hurries to fly his birthday kite, realizing too late that he does need some assistance.
Valerie Reddix, *Dragon-Kite of the Autumn Moon*, 1991
    When his grandfather becomes ill, Tad-Tin flies his dragon kite to symbolically carry away all troubles.
Margaret Rey, *Curious George Flies a Kite*, 1958
    Once again the curiosity of a little monkey leads to a problem requiring his rescue.

873

BECKY THOMAN LINDBERG
NANCY POYDAR, Illustrator

Thomas Tuttle, Just in Time

(Morton Grove, IL: Albert Whitman & Company, 1994)

Subject(s): Schools; Behavior
Age range(s): Grades 3-4
Major character(s): Thomas Tuttle, 3rd Grader, Friend; Arthur Wilmot, 3rd Grader, Friend
Time period(s): 1990s (1994)
Locale(s): Baltimore, Maryland

Summary: Disorganized Thomas has a hard time remembering to complete school assignments, especially projects, and his forgetfulness is reflected in poor grades. Thomas is determined to improve, so he tries to plan a successful costume for Maryland Day. Each time he becomes discouraged and tries to give up, Arthur tries to put him back on track and by the time the day is over, Thomas is recognized as the "most improved" student. (111 pages)

Where it's reviewed:
Booklist, November 15, 1994, page 602
Horn Book Guide, Spring 1995, page 68
School Library Journal, October 1994, page124

Other books by the same author:
Chelsea Martin Turns Green, 1993
Speak Up, Chelsea Martin!, 1991

Other books you might like:
Beverly Cleary, *Henry Huggins*, 1950
    Third grader Henry Huggins, a neighbor of Beezus and Ramona Quimby, meets his mutt Ribsy in the first of the books about this adventurous pair.
Betsy Duffey, *How to Be Cool in the Third Grade*, 1993
    Robbie views third grade as an opportunity to mature and change.

Patricia Reilly Giff, *The Beast in Ms. Rooney's Room*, 1984
    One of twelve titles in "The Kids in the Polk Street School" series, this features Richard "Beast" Best.

874

REEVE LINDBERGH
KIMBERLY BULCKEN ROOT, Illustrator

If I'd Known Then What I Know Now

(New York: Viking, 1994)

Subject(s): Dwellings; Fathers; Stories in Rhyme
Age range(s): Grades K-3
Major character(s): Dad, Father, Handyman
Time period(s): Indeterminate Past
Locale(s): United States

Summary: Dad's efforts to construct a house and complete the plumbing and wiring, while well-intentioned, are bumbling and inept. The roof leaks, the refrigerator's hot and the oven cold, the cows must climb a ladder to reach the barn stalls, but family members love and accept Dad just the way he is. (32 pages)

Where it's reviewed:
Bulletin of the Center for Children's Books, June 1994, page 326
Horn Book Guide, Fall 1994, page 280
Publishers Weekly, May 9, 1994, page 71
School Library Journal, July 1994, page 79

Other books by the same author:
Grandfather's Lovesong, 1993
There's a Cow in the Road?, 1993
The Day the Goose Got Loose, 1990

Other books you might like:
Steven Kellogg, *Pinkerton, Behave!*, 1979
    Despite his unconventional and sometimes frustrating behavior, Pinkerton is accepted and loved by his family.
Susan Patron, *Dark Cloud, Strong Breeze*, 1994
    When her bumbling daddy locks his keys in the car, a cheerful little girl describes the sequence of events which lead to the car keys' recovery before a rain storm begins.
Harriet Ziefert, *When Daddy Had the Chicken Pox*, 1991
    A family celebrates when poor Daddy finally recovers from the chicken pox.

875

LEO LIONNI, Author/Illustrator

An Extraordinary Egg

(New York: Alfred A. Knopf, 1994)

Subject(s): Animals/Frogs and Toads; Animals/Alligators; Friendship
Age range(s): Grades K-3
Major character(s): Jessica, Frog, Wanderer; Marilyn, Frog, Friend (Jessica's); August, Frog
Time period(s): Indeterminate
Locale(s): Pebble Island, Fictional Country

Summary: Daily, Jessica finds objects of wonder which are usually of no interest to either Marilyn or August. However, the day Jessica comes home with a very large pebble which Marilyn knowingly declares to be a chicken egg, everyone is curious to observe its hatching. The frogs are impressed by how well the "chicken" can swim, especially when it saves Jessica from drowning. When the "chicken" is spotted by a bird, she learns that her mother is looking for her "sweet little alligator." (33 pages)

Where it's reviewed:
Booklist, June 1, 1994, page 1841
Horn Book, July 1994, page 479
Kirkus Reviews, April 15, 1994, page 559
Publishers Weekly, March 7, 1994, page 68
School Library Journal, June 1994, page 109

Awards the book has won:
School Library Journal Best Books, 1994

Other books by the same author:
A Color of His Own, 1993
Fish Is Fish, 1974
Alexander & the Wind-Up Mouse, 1969

Other books you might like:
William Joyce, *Bently and Egg*, 1992
  When a shy, singing frog takes on responsiblity for a special egg the ensuing events change the frog's life.
Lynn Reiser, *The Surprise Family*, 1994
  Much to the surprise of a mother hen, the "chicks" she's hatched from a clutch of abandoned eggs enjoy swimming—like ducks.
Dr. Seuss, *Horton Hatches the Egg*, 1940
  More interested in a vacation than in mothering, a lazy bird leaves elephant Horton to sit on her egg through all kinds of weather and adversity.

876

JANET TAYLOR LISLE

Angela's Aliens

(New York: Orchard Books, 1996)

Series: Investigators of the Unknown
Subject(s): Identity; Aliens; Friendship
Age range(s): Grades 3-5
Major character(s): Angela Harrall, Traveller, Child of Divorced Parents; Georgina Rusk, Detective, Companion; Poco Lambert, Detective, Companion
Time period(s): 1990s
Locale(s): United States

Summary: Angela has returned from Mexico but appears strange to her old friends. Remembering some odd goings on at the reservoir, they cannot decide whether an alien has arrived and taken Angela's place or whether she is just trying to attract her mother's attention. Out of concern for her, Angela's family comes home and all seems to be well. . . (120 pages)

Where it's reviewed:
Booklist, September 1, 1996, page 498
School Library Journal, November 1996, page 108

Other books by the same author:
Looking for Juliette, 1995

A Message from the Match Girl, 1995
Afternoon of the Elves, 1989

Other books you might like:
Beatrice Gormley, *Six Guys to White Cat*, 1991
  Alison has to share her best friend and at the same time finds out that her cat is an alien spy.
Dick King-Smith, *Harriet's Hare*, 1995
  An alien takes the shape of a hare and is able to help Harriet find a new mother.
Daniel Manus Pinkwater, *Fat Men from Space*, 1977
  William hears messages from space through his tooth and then sees the aliens as they come looking for junk food.
Pamela F. Service, *Stinker from Space*, 1988
  An alien takes the shape of a skunk and makes friends with two human children.
Dyan Sheldon, *My Brother Is a Visitor from Another Planet*, 1993
  Adam's brother claims he is an alien and has fun bullying Adam.

877

JANET TAYLOR LISLE

Forest

(New York: Orchard Books, 1993)

Subject(s): Fantasy; Animals/Squirrels
Age range(s): Grades 6-7
Major character(s): Amber Padgett, 12-Year-Old; Woodbine, Squirrel; Barker, Squirrel
Time period(s): 1990s
Locale(s): Fictional Country (Forest)

Summary: Forest is divided into two levels, the Upper Forest and the Lower Forest and the inhabitants don't talk to those living on a different level. Amber climbs a tree and unknowingly trespasses in the home of the squirrels of the Upper Forest. The squirrels dislike having their space invaded by humans from the Lower Forest and are quick to declare war. Amber's father feels threatened by the squirrels and begins shooting them; the squirrels in turn, led by the evil Barker, retaliate even more fiercely. Caught in the middle are Amber and her younger brother, whose sympathies lie with the squirrels and Woodbine, a squirrel who wants to make friends, in this thought-provoking satire. (150 pages)

Where it's reviewed:
School Library Journal, November 1993, page 109
Publishers Weekly, August 30, 1993, page 97
Booklist, October 15, 1993, page 443
Horn Book, March 1994, page 199
New York Times Book Review, November 14, 1993, page 47

Other books by the same author:
The Gold Dust Letters, 1994
The Lampfish of Twill, 1991
Afternoon of the Elves, 1989
Sirens and Spies, 1985

Other books you might like:
Nina Bawden, *Henry*, 1988
  The antics of Henry the squirrel keep everyone living on

the Jones' British farm from thinking about the terror and destruction of World War II.

Jane Leslie Conly, *R-T, Margaret and the Rats of NIMH*, 1986

Rat Rasco and his friends must save Thorn Valley from discovery after two children accidentally stumble across it.

Peni R. Griffin, *Hobkin*, 1992

Runaways Kay and Liza Franklin move into a deserted house which comes complete with a Hobkin, a friendly spirit which helps with household chores.

Brian Jacques, *Redwall*, 1987

Martin, a mouse, must organize the inhabitants of Redwall Abbey to defend themselves against the evil Cluny and his vicious army of rats.

878

JANET TAYLOR LISLE

The Gold Dust Letters

(New York: Orchard Books, 1994)

Series: Investigators of the Unknown
Subject(s): Fathers and Daughters; Divorce; Friendship
Age range(s): Grades 3-5
Major character(s): Angela Harrall, 9-Year-Old, Friend; Georgina Rusk, Friend; Poco Lambert, Friend
Time period(s): 1990s (1994)
Locale(s): United States

Summary: When Angela receives a reply from her fairy godmother, she eagerly shares the information in the gold-dust sprinkled letter with Georgina and Poco. Skeptic Georgina thinks an investigation is needed so the threesome declare themselves the Investigators of the Unknown and make plans for a sleepover planning session at Angela's house. The correspondence continues for several weeks until the fairy invites the girls to a fairy banquet. As Georgina expects, there is an explanation for the magic, well, almost all the magic; they never do learn how the gold dust spills from the letters. (116 pages)

Where it's reviewed:
Booklist, February 1, 1994, page 1007
Children's Book Review Service, Spring 1994, page 142
Kirkus Reviews, March 15, 1994, page 399
Publishers Weekly, January 10, 1994, page 62
School Library Journal, April 1994, page 128

Other books by the same author:
Forest, 1993
Afternoon of the Elves, 1989 (Newbery Honor Book, 1990)
The Dancing Cats of Applesap, 1985

Other books you might like:
Joanna Cole, *Mixed-Up Magic*, 1987
A girl's friendship with an elf leads to some humorous adventures.

Gerda Marie Scheidl, *Loretta and the Little Fairy*, 1993
Loretta tries to help a little fairy with the task of "growing up" although she isn't quite sure what that means to a fairy.

Ann Turner, *Elfsong*, 1995
A routine summer visit to Grandpa's becomes Maddy's introduction to the usually unseen world of elves.

Jean Ure, *The Children Next Door*, 1996
In a time travel fantasy, shy Laura uncovers a mystery when she tries to meet the children next door.

879

JANET TAYLOR LISLE

Looking for Juliette

(New York: Orchard Books, 1994)

Series: Investigators of the Unknown
Subject(s): Supernatural; Animals/Cats; Old Age
Age range(s): Grades 3-5
Major character(s): Juliette, Cat; Georgina Rusk, Child, Friend; Poco Lambert, Child, Friend
Time period(s): 1990s (1994)
Locale(s): United States

Summary: The three investigators lose a member when one of the founders moves to Mexico for a year. Poco agrees to care for Juliette, but when the cat vanishes after being struck by a car, the investigators must find her. They enlist the help of a student with a Ouija board and initially suspect the housesitter of being a witch and turning Juliette into a furry hat. After a month Juliette returns on her own and the mystery is solved. (120 pages)

Where it's reviewed:
Booklist, September 15, 1994, page 136
Bulletin of the Center for Children's Books, December 1994, page 136
Kirkus Reviews, November 15, 1994, page 1535
Publishers Weekly, October 24, 1994, page 62
School Library Journal, August 1994, page 158

Other books by the same author:
The Gold Dust Letters, 1994
The Lampfish of Twill, 1991
Afternoon of the Elves, 1989 (Newbery Honor Book, 1990)

Other books you might like:
Luli Gray, *Falcon's Egg*, 1995
Falcon finds an unusual egg in the park which hatches into a dragon.

Ursula K. Le Guin, *Catwings*, 1988
The first of three books about winged, talking cats seeking a safe home.

Jane Yolen, *The Faery Flag: Stories and Poems of Fantasy and the Supernatural*, 1989
This collection includes poetry as well as writings based on the folklore of fairy tradition.

880

JANET TAYLOR LISLE

A Message from the Match Girl

(New York: Orchard Books, 1995)

Series: Investigators of the Unknown
Subject(s): Supernatural; Friendship; Identity

Age range(s): Grades 4-6
Major character(s): Walter Kew, 9-Year-Old, Orphan; Georgina Rusk, Friend (Walter's); Poco Lambert, Friend
Time period(s): 1990s (1995)
Locale(s): United States (Andersen Park)

Summary: Walter, an orphan longing for a personal history, believes he is being spoken to by the ghost of his mother who sends messages and leaves tokens from his infancy at the park statue of the Little Match Girl. Practical Georgina tries to determine a logical explanation for these strange events while Poco (who communicates with robins) simply enjoys the wonder of it all. Both friends are concerned for Walter and support him as he learns a little more about his past from his ''grandmother'' who has raised him since infancy. (121 pages)

Where it's reviewed:
Booklist, October 1, 1995, page 316
Bulletin of the Center for Children's Books, November 1995, page 98
Kirkus Reviews, October 1, 1995, page 1432
Publishers Weekly, September 25, 1995, page 57
School Library Journal, October 1995, page 136

Awards the book has won:
School Library Journal Best Books, 1995

Other books by the same author:
Looking for Juliette, 1994
Afternoon of the Elves, 1989
The Great Dimpole Oak, 1987

Other books you might like:
Bill Brittain, *Who Knew There'd Be Ghosts?*, 1985
    Tommy discovers two ghosts who help him solve a mystery.
Stella Pevsner, *Would My Fortune Cookie Lie?*, 1995
    Learning that her father has a son he didn't know about creates more concerns for Alexis about her arguing parents.
Jean Ure, *The Children Next Door*, 1995
    Settling into an old house in London, Laura notices ghost children playing next door and learns they are linked to the memories of an elderly woman living in the house.

881

JEAN LITTLE
KIM LAFAVE, Illustrator

Bats about Baseball
(New York: Viking, 1995)

Subject(s): Grandparents; Sports/Baseball; Humor
Age range(s): Grades K-3
Major character(s): Ryder, Child; Nana, Grandmother, Fanatic
Time period(s): 1990s (1994)
Locale(s): United States

Summary: Ryder's Nana is so intent on watching a baseball game on TV that she pays Ryder little attention. However, each remark he makes about a potential career is followed by a comment on the game in baseball lingo related to the career choice. Even a power outage does not stop Nana's obsession,

as she simply pulls a battery-operated radio from her bag and never misses a play. (32 pages)

Where it's reviewed:
Booklist, June 1995, page 1787
Books in Canada, September 1995, page 50
Horn Book Guide, Fall 1995, page 271
Kirkus Reviews, May 15, 1995, page 713
School Library Journal, August 1995, page 125

Other books by the same author:
Revenge of the Small Small, 1993

Other books you might like:
Leonard Kessler, *Here Comes the Strikeout!*, 1965
    The story of hard-working Bobby's efforts to learn to hit a baseball was reissued with new illustrations in 1992.
Emily Arnold McCully, *Grandmas at Bat*, 1993
    Thinking they're being helpful, Pip's grandmothers volunteer to coach her baseball team.
Peggy Parish, *Play Ball, Amelia Bedelia*, 1972
    In her usual, literal way, Amelia decides to learn how to play baseball which leads to a humorous game as she misunderstands the meaning of baseball terms.

882

JEAN LITTLE
JANET WILSON, Illustrator

Revenge of the Small Small
(New York: Viking, 1992)

Subject(s): Brothers and Sisters; Revenge; Family Relations
Age range(s): Grades K-2
Major character(s): Patsy Small, Child (youngest in the family)
Time period(s): 1990s (1992)
Locale(s): Canada (Patsy's home)

Summary: Being the youngest child in the Small family is not easy for Patsy. Although she helps to care for her siblings during their illness with chicken pox, they do not return her kindness when she is ill. While Patsy is convalescing, Dad brings home a large box of art supplies to entertain her. Envious, her siblings continue to disparage her work until the day they discover that she has ''buried'' them in the cemetary of her paper village. (32 pages)

Where it's reviewed:
Booklist, February 1, 1993, page 984
Childhood Education, May 1993, page 305
Kirkus Reviews, February 1, 1993, page 150
Publishers Weekly, March 8, 1993, page 76
Quill & Quire, October 1992, page 31

Other books by the same author:
Jess Was the Brave One, 1992

Other books you might like:
Catherine Bancroft, *That's Philomena!*, 1995
    When Philomena learns that her younger siblings call her Philomeany, she is determined to change their impression of her. Hannah Coale, co-author.

Patricia Polacco, *My Rotten Redheaded Older Brother*, 1994
Patricia's only wish is to beat her older brother at something - anything!

Judith Viorst, *I'll Fix Anthony*, 1969
Look out Anthony! Your little brother is making plans to get even with you.

883

AMY LITTLESUGAR
BARBARA GARRISON, Illustrator

Josiah True and the Art Maker

(New York: Simon & Schuster Books for Young Readers, 1995)

Subject(s): Artists and Art; Historical
Age range(s): Grades 1-3
Major character(s): Patience Cage, Artist; Josiah True, Child; Thomas True, Father
Time period(s): 1810s (1817)
Locale(s): Connecticut

Summary: On a trip to town, Josiah and Thomas True contract with Patience Cage for a family portrait. When Patience, the "art maker," arrives at Josiah's farm, he helps her unload supplies and watches her paint. Through her art, Patience makes wishes come true; thus she paints Josiah's mother in a red dress, his father in a new waistcoat and Josiah with a dog, just they requested. When the artist departs she gives Josiah a paint brush because the interest he's shown suggests that he will learn to use it—and he does. (32 pages)

Where it's reviewed:
Booklist, July 1995, page 1884
Children's Book Review Service, July 1995, page 148
Horn Book Guide, Fall 1995, page 271
School Library Journal, July 1995, page 66
Smithsonian, November 1995, page 173

Other books by the same author:
The Spinner's Daughter, 1994

Other books you might like:
Jane Johnson, *The Princess and the Painter*, 1994
The artist Diego Velasquez watches Princess Margarita, her parents, and court view the completed painting *Las Meninas* for the first time.
Wendy Kesselman, *Emma*, 1980
When Emma receives a set of paints for her 72nd birthday, she tries her hand at painting for the first time.
Thomas Locker, *The Young Artist*, 1989
A commission to paint the King's courtiers, who all want an improved appearance, creates a struggle for a young artist who seeks honesty in his portraits.
Sara Yamaka, *The Gift of Driscoll Lipscomb*, 1995
Annual gifts from an artist-neighbor teach Molly to see the colors in the world around her.

884

PENELOPE LIVELY
ADRIANO GON, Illustrator

Good Night, Sleep Tight

(Cambridge, MA: Candlewick Press, 1995)

Subject(s): Play; Bedtime; Toys
Age range(s): Grades K-1
Major character(s): Unnamed Character, Child; Mary Ann, Toy
Time period(s): 1990s (1994)
Locale(s): England

Summary: After playing all day with her stuffed animals and doll Mary Ann, a little girl gets herself and all her special friends ready for bed. The animals and doll are not quite willing to settle down to sleep and propose to take the little girl on an adventure. One by one she is taken by each of the animals to their real habitat where they do many of the things that children are discouraged by adults from doing. Last, Mary Ann takes the little girl dancing and then they all tuck themselves back into bed and go to sleep. First published in Great Britain in 1994. (26 pages)

Where it's reviewed:
Booklist, June 1, 1995, page 1787
Junior Bookshelf, April 1995, page 68
Publishers Weekly, April 10, 1995, page 61
School Librarian, May 1995, page 59
School Library Journal, June 1995, page 91

Other books by the same author:
The Cat, the Crow, and the Banyan Tree, 1994

Other books you might like:
Michael Foreman, *Dad! I Can't Sleep*, 1995
Dad's going-to-sleep suggestions to Little Panda fail to produce the desired effect.
Mordicai Gerstein, *Bedtime, Everybody!*, 1996
Daisy's stuffed animals do not cooperate with her efforts to get them settled for bed.
Kate McMullan, *Good Night, Stella*, 1994
It's bedtime, but Stella is wide awake so she plays with her toys, reads a scary story to her bears for which they need some comfort and, somehow, she's asleep.
Claire Masurel, *Good Night!*, 1994
A young girl walks about the house gathering her stuffed animals from their varied daytime activities and gets them ready for bed.

885

ARCADIO LOBATO
EMILIO URBERUAGA, Illustrator

Paper Bird

(Minneapolis: Carolrhoda Books, Inc., 1994)

Subject(s): Animals/Birds; Artists and Art; Animals/Cats
Age range(s): Grades K-3
Major character(s): Unnamed Character, Bird (paper); Unnamed Character, Cat
Time period(s): Indeterminate Past

Locale(s): Fictional Country

Summary: For his daughter's birthday, an artist is determined to make a drawing of a bird so beautiful that it will fly. The paper bird tries to make the artist's wish come true by seeking help from the cat who becomes annoyed and throws the drawing out the window, thus beginning a series of unsuccessful flying lessons. Not until the cat returns the drawing to the artist's studio so that the artist can complete his gift does the bird become able to fly. Translated from the German of the original publication in Switzerland in 1993. (32 pages)

Where it's reviewed:
Five Owls, November 1994, page 33
Horn Book Guide, Spring 1995, page 44
Kirkus Reviews, December 15, 1994, page 1568
Publishers Weekly, November 21, 1994, page 76
School Library Journal, February 1995, page 75

Other books by the same author:
The Greatest Treasure, 1991
Just One Wish, 1991

Other books you might like:
Hans Christian Andersen, *The Steadfast Tin Soldier*, 1979
    In one of many retellings of a classic tale, a one-legged tin soldier braves great dangers determined to find his way back to his beloved dancing paper doll.
Judith Heide Gilliland, *Not in the House, Newton!*, 1995
    When Newton sees that his new red crayon creates drawings that become real, he quickly hops on his paper airplane and flies out the window.
Crockett Johnson, *Harold and the Purple Crayon*, 1955
    Using his magic purple crayon, Harold draws himself into and out of adventure.
Elisa Kleven, *The Paper Princess*, 1994
    A child's drawing of a princess sails away on the wind through a series of adventures before finding its way back to the girl again.

886

THOMAS LOCKER, Author/Illustrator

Miranda's Smile
(New York: Dial Books)

Subject(s): Artists and Art; Fathers and Daughters
Age range(s): Grades K-2
Major character(s): Miranda, Child; Daddy, Father, Artist
Time period(s): 1990s (1994)
Locale(s): United States

Summary: Miranda regularly delivers homemade chocolate chip cookies to her father in his studio. Attracted by her smile, he decides to capture it in a portrait. The sittings are complicated when one of Miranda's front teeth falls out. When Daddy realizes that Miranda's smile is in her eyes he is able to complete the portrait. (32 pages)

Where it's reviewed:
Booklist, September 1, 1994, page 52
Children's Book Review Service, Spring 1995, page 51
Horn Book Guide, Spring 1995, page 44
Publishers Weekly, July 11, 1994, page 77
School Library Journal, September 1994, page 189

Other books by the same author:
Anna and the Bagpiper, 1994
The Boy Who Held Back the Sea, 1991
The Young Artist, 1989

Other books you might like:
Johnny Alcorn, *Rembrandt's Beret*, 1991
    While visiting the Uffizi Gallery, a painter observes the paintings come to life.
Peter Catalanotto, *The Painter*, 1995
    The loving relationship between daughter and artist-father includes time in the studio for the girl to express her creativity.
Diane Stanley, *The Gentleman and the Kitchen Maid*, 1994
    Nightly, the portraits in an art museum converse about the feelings of a gentleman in one portrait for a kitchen maid in another.

887

GAYLE ROGERS LOCKWOOD

Libbie Sims, Worry Wart
(New York, Viking, 1993)

Subject(s): Divorce; Friendship; Remarriage
Age range(s): Grades 4-6
Major character(s): Libbie Sims, 11-Year-Old, Child of Divorced Parents; Maggie Sims, 16-Year-Old, Sister (Libbie's); Gretchen Van Dyke, 6th Grader, Friend (of Libbie)
Time period(s): 1990s (1993)
Locale(s): Salem, Oregon

Summary: When Libbie's mother's first husband shows up unannounced at the front door, the night before she begins sixth grade, Libbie's fear that her mother may remarry is added to the worries she's already carrying about friends, boys, school and growing up. As sixth grade continues, both Libbie and her mother come to new insights about relationships and Libbie learns to worry less. First novel. (122 pages)

Where it's reviewed:
Booklist, October 1, 1993, page 345
Book Report, January 1994, page 48
Horn Book Guide, Spring 1994, page 79
Publishers Weekly, November 1, 1993, page 80
School Library Journal, October 1993, page 126

Other books you might like:
Barthe DeClements, *The Pickle Song*, 1993
    Paula worries about the new girl at school and her single mother's financial problems
Phyllis Reynolds Naylor, *The Agony of Alice*, 1985
    Alice survives the frustrations of sixth grade with humor and self-discovery.
Bonnie Pryor, *Horses in the Garage*, 1992
    Making friends with Jasmine helps Samantha adjust to the many changes in her life.

888

JONATHAN LONDON
FRANK REMKIEWICZ, Illustrator

Froggy Learns to Swim
(New York: Viking, 1995)

Subject(s): Animals/Frogs and Toads; Fear; Mothers and Sons
Age range(s): Grades K-1
Major character(s): Froggy, Frog; Mommy, Frog, Mother
Time period(s): 1990s (1994)
Locale(s): Fictional Country

Summary: Froggy refuses to join his parents in the pond, saying that he prefers to swing. When his overzealous swinging wraps the swing around the crossbar and flings Froggy into the pond, Mommy is waiting to begin swimming lessons. Once Froggy has his flippers, mask, snorkel and lessons, he enjoys the water so much he refuses to get out. (32 pages)

Where it's reviewed:
Horn Book, Fall 1995, page 272
Reading Teacher, May 1996, page 649
School Library Journal, January 1996, page 90

Other books by the same author:
Froggy Goes to School, 1996
Let's Go, Froggy!, 1994
Froggy Gets Dressed, 1992

Other books you might like:
Susan Akass, *Swim, Number Nine Duckling*, 1995
    Eight ducklings follow their mother into the water, but Number Nine duckling is afraid of the water. Reassurance from mother helps him learn what ducks like best.
Louise Borden, *Albie the Lifeguard*, 1993
    Albie guards his backyard "pool" until he gains the confidence to join his friends on the swim team.
Marc Brown, *D.W. All Wet*, 1988
    When her family goes to the beach, D.W. is determined to stay dry, but Arthur helps her find a way to have fun in the water.
Rosemary Wells, *Edward in Deep Water*, 1995
    Edward discovers that he is not ready for birthday pool parties with big bears.
Martha Weston, *Tuck in the Pool*, 1995
    A reluctant participant in the swimming class, Tuck's need to rescue his lucky spider from the pool bottom helps him to gain confidence.

889

JONATHAN LONDON
WOODLEIGH HUBBARD, Illustrator

Hip Cat
(San Francisco: Chronicle Books, 1993)

Subject(s): Animals/Cats; Musicians; Stories in Rhyme
Age range(s): Grades K-3
Major character(s): Oobie-do John the Sax Man, Cat (from the "sticks"), Musician (jazz saxophonist)
Time period(s): 1990s (1993)
Locale(s): San Francisco, California

Summary: One day Oobie-do John, the Sax Man, leaves his riverside home and hops the night train to San Francisco where he feels free to play the jazz that he loves. It takes time for this hip cat to make a living doing what he loves, but eventually his hard work is rewarded with gigs that pay the bills. (48 pages)

Where it's reviewed:
Children's Book Review Service, February 1994, page 75
Children's Bookwatch, October 1993, page 4
Horn Book, March 1994, page 225
Publishers Weekly, August 16, 1993, page 102
School Library Journal, January 1994, page 93

Other books by the same author:
Like Butter on Pancakes, 1995
Into This Night We Are Rising, 1993
The Owl Who Became the Moon, 1993

Other books you might like:
Alice Faye Duncan, *Willie Jerome*, 1995
    Only Willie's sister appreciates the bebop music he plays on his trumpet.
Rachel Isadora, *Ben's Trumpet*, 1979
    Ben dreams of becoming a jazz musician.
Robert Kraus, *Musical Max*, 1992
    When hippo Max stops playing his music, the neighbors are surprised that they miss it.

890

JONATHAN LONDON
JON VAN ZYLE, Illustrator

Honey Paw and Lightfoot
(San Francisco: Chronicle Books, 1995)

Subject(s): Animals/Bears; Nature; Wildlife Conservation
Age range(s): Grades K-3
Major character(s): Honeypaw, Bear (brown bear), Mother; Lightfoot, Bear (cub)
Time period(s): 1990s (1995)
Locale(s): Alaska (wilderness)

Summary: The fictionalized account of the life cycle of a brown or grizzly bear realistically portrays one year in the life of Honeybear and Lightfoot. Honeybear patiently teaches her young cub how to forage for food, plays with him on slippery snowbanks and protects him from danger. (32 pages)

Where it's reviewed:
Booklist, March 15, 1995, page 1335
Children's Bookwatch, May 1995, page 1
Horn Book, September 1995, page 590
Horn Book Guide, Fall 1995, page 272
Publishers Weekly, May 1, 1995, page 58

Other books by the same author:
Condor's Egg, 1994
The Eyes of Gray Wolf, 1993
Gray Fox, 1993

Other books you might like:
Jim Arnosky, *Every Autumn Comes the Bear*, 1993
    Annually, a bear appears in the woods near a farm seeking a den in which to hibernate.

Dieter Betz, *The Bear Family*, 1992
> A nonfiction title set in the Alaskan wilderness uses photographs to support the story of a grizzly bear and her two cubs.

Natalie Kinsey-Warnock, *The Bear That Heard Crying*, 1993
> When young Sarah becomes lost in the woods, she is befriended by a bear until found several days later by a search party. Co-author Helen Kinsey.

891

JONATHAN LONDON
CYNTHIA JABAR, Illustrator

A Koala for Katie: An Adoption Story

(Morton Grove, IL: Albert Whitman & Company, 1993)

Subject(s): Adoption; Parent and Child
Age range(s): Grades K-1
Major character(s): Katie, Child, Adoptee
Time period(s): 1990s (1993)
Locale(s): United States

Summary: Following a trip to the zoo with her sensitive and loving parents, Katie asks to have a toy koala similar to the real one she has seen clinging to a mother koala. Katie pretends to adopt the koala, using the experience to reassure herself of the security and love of her own adoptive parents. The story is preceded by a factual note to adoptive parents. (32 pages)

Where it's reviewed:
Booklist, November 15, 1993, page 632
Children's Book Review Service, January 1994, page 51
Horn Book Guide, Spring 1994, page 43
Publishers Weekly, August 16, 1993, page 101
School Library Journal, October 1993, page 104

Other books by the same author:
Condor's Egg, 1994
Into This Night We Are Rising, 1993
Froggy Gets Dressed, 1992

Other books you might like:
Suzanne Bloom, *A Family for Jamie: An Adoption Story*, 1991
> A couple prepares for the arrival of their adopted child.

Susi Gregg Fowler, *When Joel Comes Home*, 1993
> A little girl plans how best to greet her family's friends and the baby they have adopted.

Pat Mora, *Pablo's Tree*, 1994
> The tree planted in honor of his adoption is decorated each year for Pablo's birthday.

892

JONATHAN LONDON
FRANK REMKIEWICZ, Illustrator

Let's Go, Froggy!

(New York: Viking, 1994)

Subject(s): Animals/Frogs and Toads; Fathers and Sons; Possessions
Age range(s): Grades K-2

Major character(s): Froggy, Frog; Daddy, Father, Frog
Time period(s): Indeterminate
Locale(s): Fictional Country

Summary: Froggy wakens to a beautiful, sunny day and is eager to go out to play. Daddy suggests a bike ride and picnic, so Froggy hurries to get ready. Before he can go he must locate several items that he considers essential, such as his bike helmet, a ball and a butterfly net. Each item requires so much searching that by the time the two are ready to leave, Froggy is hungry and they eat their picnic lunch on the patio before peddling off into the sunset for their bike ride. (32 pages)

Where it's reviewed:
Horn Book Guide, Fall 1994, page 280
Publishers Weekly, March 7, 1994, page 68
Reading Teacher, October 1995, page 135
School Library Journal, May 1994, page 99

Awards the book has won:
International Reading Association Children's Choice, 1995

Other books by the same author:
Froggy Goes to School, 1996
Froggy Learns to Swim, 1995
Froggy Gets Dressed, 1992

Other books you might like:
Peggy Perry Anderson, *To the Tub*, 1996
> While Joe, a young frog, understands it's bathime, his father has quite a challenge actually getting him ready and into the tub.

Catherine Bancroft, *Felix's Hat*, 1993
> When Felix loses his favorite hat, his family works together to find an acceptable substitute because Felix refuses to do anything without it.

Beatrix Potter, *The Tale of Mr. Jeremy Fisher*, 1987
> A reissue of the original edition of a classic story tells of a frog fishing from his lily pad boat, who finds himself caught by a fish rather than the other way round.

893

JONATHAN LONDON
G. BRIAN KARAS, Illustrator

Like Butter on Pancakes

(New York: Viking, 1995)

Subject(s): Farm Life; Family Life; Parent and Child
Age range(s): Grades K-1
Major character(s): Unnamed Character, Child; Mama, Mother; Papa, Father, Farmer
Time period(s): 1990s (1995)
Locale(s): United States

Summary: As the sun rises, light creeps into a young boy's room, a rooster crows and bacon sizzles in the pan. When Mama calls her son to breakfast, he finally awakens and joins his parents. Papa goes out to the fields to work while the boy plays with the barnyard animals until the sun begins to set and he is called in to dinner. The sun soon sleeps as does the boy while Mama sings and Papa hums. (32 pages)

Where it's reviewed:
Booklist, April 1, 1995, page 1428
Kirkus Reviews, February 15, 1995, page 228
Library Talk, September 1995, page 28
Publishers Weekly, January 23, 1995, page 69
School Library Journal, February 1995, page 75

Awards the book has won:
School Library Journal Best Books, 1995

Other books by the same author:
Let's Go, Froggy!, 1994
Into This Night We Are Rising, 1993
The Owl Who Became the Moon, 1993

Other books you might like:
Reeve Lindbergh, *What Is the Sun?*, 1994
A grandmother's rhyming answers to her grandson's many questions about nature comfort him at bedtime.
Elizabeth Lee O'Donnell, *Sing Me a Window*, 1993
The favorite activities of a family's day are poetically presented.
Maryann N. Weidt, *Daddy Played Music for the Cows*, 1995
A young girl reminisces about her life growing up on a dairy farm.

894

JONATHAN LONDON
SYLVIA LONG, Illustrator

Liplap's Wish
(San Francisco: Chronicle Books, 1994)

Subject(s): Animals/Rabbits; Grandparents; Death
Age range(s): Grades K-2
Major character(s): Liplap, Rabbit
Time period(s): 1990s (1994)
Locale(s): Fictional Country

Summary: Still grieving for his recently deceased grandmother, Liplap is not able to fully enjoy the first snowfall. Half-heartedly he makes a snowbunny, but reminders of his grandma fill him with sadness as he works. When his mother shares with him a consoling story about deceased rabbits becoming stars, he is able to realize that, in spirit, his grandmother will always be with him. (32 pages)

Where it's reviewed:
Booklist, January 15, 1995, page 937
Five Owls, September 1994, page 10
Horn Book Guide, Spring 1995, page 45
Publishers Weekly, October 3, 1994, page 68
School Library Journal, November 1994, page 84

Other books by the same author:
Into This Night We Are Rising, 1993
The Owl Who Became the Moon, 1993
Froggy Gets Dressed, 1992

Other books you might like:
Aliki, *The Two of Them*, 1979
A young girl and her grandfather share a special relationship which she remembers after his death.

Mem Fox, *Sophie*, 1994
Because Grandpa has always been part of Sophie's life, his death leaves a sense of emptiness which, in time, is filled.
Karen Hesse, *Poppy's Chair*, 1993
Leah's grandmother helps her to understand her grandfather's death and to appreciate the reminders of him in her life.
Mavis Jukes, *Blackberries in the Dark*, 1993
Austin and his grandmother remember his recently deceased grandfather while continuing to cherish their own relationship. Reissue of a 1985 title.
Jane Yolen, *Grandad Bill's Song*, 1994
Jon finds support from family members as he struggles to cope with his feelings following the death of his grandfather.
Charlotte Zolotow, *My Grandson Lew*, 1974
Six-year-old Lew shares his memories of his now-deceased grandfather.

895

JONATHAN LONDON
GILLES PELLETIER, Illustrator

The Sugaring-Off Party
(New York: Dutton Children's Books, 1995)

Subject(s): Grandparents; Food; Storytelling
Age range(s): Grades K-3
Major character(s): Paul, Child; Grand-mere, Grandmother, Storyteller; Tante Loulou, Aunt (grand-mere's)
Time period(s): 1990s (1995); Indeterminate Past
Locale(s): Mont-Saint-Hilaire, Canada

Summary: On the eve of Paul's first sugaring-off party, he asks Grand-mere to tell the story of her first such party. Grand-mere relates the events of the day 60 years earlier when, with her family, she travelled to Tante Loulou's for a day of playing with cousins, eating with family, dancing with everyone and, of course, sampling the results of the day's work. A glossary defines the French terms sprinkled throughout the text. (32 pages)

Where it's reviewed:
Booklist, January 1, 1995, page 825
Kirkus Reviews, February 15, 1995, page 228
Publishers Weekly, November 21, 1994, page 75
Quill & Quire, March 1995, page 78
School Library Journal, January 1995, page 89

Other books by the same author:
Fireflies, Fireflies, Light My Way, 1996
Froggy Learns to Swim, 1995
Voices of the Wild, 1993

Other books you might like:
Diane L. Burns, *Sugaring Season: Making Maple Syrup*, 1990
A nonfiction work uses photographs and diagrams to explain the process of making maple syrup.
Eve Rice, *At Grammy's House*, 1990
Sunday lunches at Grammy's farm are a special time for siblings to learn about and enjoy their immigrant grandmother's French heritage.

Laura Ingalls Wilder, *Dance at Grandpa's*, 1994
     Adapted from the Little House series, the story tells of the day Laura's family helped to gather and boil the maple syrup prior to a celebratory dance to Granpa's.

896

CELIA BARKER LOTTRIDGE
DANIEL CLIFFORD, Illustrator

The Wind Wagon

(Parsippany, NJ: Silver Burdett Press, 1995)

Subject(s): Frontier and Pioneer Life; Historical; Inventions
Age range(s): Grades 2-4
Major character(s): Sam Peppard, Blacksmith, Inventor; Joe Willard, Friend (Sam's)
Time period(s): 1850s (1859); 1860s (1860)
Locale(s): Oskaloosa (Kansas Territory); Denver, Colorado

Summary: From the moment Sam arrives in Oskaloosa to open his blacksmith shop, he is intrigued by the wind which blows incessantly across the prairie. To satisfy his curiosity, he builds a windwagon and, with Joe and two other young men in town, sets off for Denver, passing the ox-drawn prairie schooners and racing Indian ponies along the way. A tornado brings the trip to an abrupt halt in sight of the Rockies but still 80 miles east of Denver. A concluding author's note gives background information. (56 pages)

Where it's reviewed:
Quill & Quire, June 1995, page 58
School Library Journal, August 1995, page 125

Other books by the same author:
Ten Small Tales, 1994
The Name of the Tree: A Bantu Folktale, 1990

Other books you might like:
Barbara Brenner, *Wagon Wheels*, 1978
     A family travels by wagon to Kansas seeking free land under the provisions of the Homestead Act.
Brett Harvey, *Cassie's Journey: Going West in the 1860s*, 1988
     Cassie tells of her family's difficult journey by covered wagon from Illinois to California.
Edna Shapiro, *Windwagon Smith*, 1966
     An American tall tale relates the adventures of a group of pioneers who travel west with a sailor at the helm of an unusual wagon.
Jean Van Leeuwen, *Going West*, 1992
     In a prairie schooner, a family emigrates from the East across the plains to Kansas.

897

KAREN E. LOTZ
COLLEEN BROWNING, Illustrator

Can't Sit Still

(New York: Dutton Children's Books, 1993)

Subject(s): Seasons; City Life; African Americans
Age range(s): Grades K-2

Major character(s): Unnamed Character, Child (African-American); Momma, Mother (African-American)
Time period(s): 1990s (1993)
Locale(s): United States (urban neighborhood)

Summary: With boundless enthusiasm a young girl skips, hops and slides through the four seasons in her urban neighborhood. Her mother's steady presence weaves in and out of the girl's activities which express such joy for living that she simply can't sit still. (48 pages)

Where it's reviewed:
Booklist, June 1, 1993, page 1858
Kirkus Reviews, June 15, 1993, page 787
Library Talk, January 1994, page 48
Publishers Weekly, June 7, 1993, page 69
School Library Journal, September 1993, page 210

Other books by the same author:
Snowsong Whistling, 1993

Other books you might like:
Kathryn Lasky, *I Have an Aunt on Marlborough Street*, 1992
     Phoebe and her Aunt Phoebe enjoy the seasonal changes in the city.
Thylias Moss, *I Want to Be*, 1993
     A lively, imaginative, confident young girl expresses her dreams for her future.
Chris K. Soentpiet, *Around Town*, 1994
     A mother and daughter enjoy a fun-filled summer tour of New York City.

898

D. ANNE LOVE
RONALD HIMLER, Illustrator

Bess's Log Cabin Quilt

(New York: Holiday House, 1995)

Subject(s): Frontier and Pioneer Life; Quilts; Historical
Age range(s): Grades 4-6
Major character(s): Bess Morgan, 10-Year-Old, Artisan (quilter); Nathan Trask, Collector (money lender)
Time period(s): 19th century
Locale(s): Oregon (near Salem)

Summary: Bess and her mother await her father's return as he accompanies a wagon train heading west to the Oregon Territory where their family settled last year. Her dad's more than a month late and Bess and her mother are quilting to pass the time until he comes back. Bess hates to quilt, but finds that quilting may be the only way to pay Mr. Trask the $100 he claims her father borrowed before leaving to join the wagon train. Bess works and works on the Log Cabin quilt and eventually wins second place in the quilting contest at the fair just as her father returns home to hear the good news in this first novel. (123 pages)

Where it's reviewed:
Voice of Youth Advocates, October 1995, page 220
Center for Children's Books. Bulletin, June 1995, page 352
Horn Book Guide, Fall 1995, page 300
Kirkus Reviews, April 1, 1995, page 472
Booklist, February 15, 1995, page 1085

Other books you might like:
Patricia Beatty, *Bonanza Girl*, 1993
When Mrs. Scott can't find a job as a teacher around the gold camps to support herself and her two children, she opens a restaurant.
Kathryn Lasky, *Beyond the Divide*, 1983
When Meribah's father is shunned by his Amish church, they endure the hardships of a trip west in 1850.
Willo Davis Roberts, *Jo and the Bandit*, 1992
As a victim of a stagecoach robbery on her way to live with her uncle, Judge Macklin, Jo is used as bait to catch the bandits.
Theodore Taylor, *Walking Up a Rainbow*, 1986
To settle her deceased parent's debts, Susan drives a herd of sheep to California.

899

D. ANNE LOVE
RONALD HIMLER, Illustrator

Dakota Spring

(New York: Holiday House, 1995)

Subject(s): Grandparents; Frontier and Pioneer Life; Behavior
Age range(s): Grades 3-5
Major character(s): Jess, 9-Year-Old, Brother; Caroline, 13-Year-Old, Sister; Mrs. Abigail Ravenell, Grandmother
Time period(s): 19th century (post Civil War)
Locale(s): Dakota Territory

Summary: Caroline looks at the dirt road leading to the farmstead and is reminded of the sorrow of the past year—first the news of mother's death and then father, returning injured from a fall while helping a neighbor build a barn. In desperation, Jess and Caroline's father writes to his deceased wife's mother in Charleston to request her assistance while he recovers. Mrs. Ravenell is strict and demanding of "proper" behavior, but the children and the prairie beauty soften her resolve and melt her unspoken sorrow over the loss of her daughter. (90 pages)

Where it's reviewed:
Booklist, November 15, 1995, page 559
Horn Book Guide, Spring 1996, page 65
School Library Journal, November 1995, page 103

Other books by the same author:
My Lone Star Summer, 1996
Bess's Log Cabin Quilt, 1995

Other books you might like:
Jennifer Armstrong, *Black-Eyed Susan*, 1995
Susan uses the awe-inspiring prairie sunrise to draw her depressed mother out of the dugout home and into life.
Pam Conrad, *Prairie Songs*, 1985
As a lifelong resident, Louisa understands the lonely beauty of the Nebraska prairie and tries to help a new neighbor as she struggles unsuccessfully to adapt.
Laurie Lawlor, *Addie Across the Prairie*, 1986
As the oldest child of a family homesteading in a sod house on the Dakota prairie, Addie dutifully helps her mother as she tries to accept the isolation of their new life.

Patricia MacLachlan, *Sarah, Plain and Tall*, 1985
A Newbery Award winning book tells of Sarah, a mail-order bride from Maine and her adjustment to life on the prairie farm of Jacob, Caleb and Anna

900

ALICE LOW, Editor
GAHAN WILSON, Illustrator

Spooky Stories for a Dark and Stormy Night

(New York: Hyperion Books for Children, 1994)

Subject(s): Folk Tales; Horror; Ghosts
Age range(s): Grades 3-6
Time period(s): Indeterminate Past

Summary: Nineteen short stories grouped into five categories include classics such as *The Legend of Sleepy Hollow*, familiar folktales such as *Taily-po*, and tales by contemporary authors Yep, Coville and Lively. The collection also includes stories from different countries and time periods as well as some with a humorous ending. (128 pages)

Where it's reviewed:
Booklist, October 1, 1994, page 321
Bulletin of the Center for Children's Books, January 1995, page 171
Kirkus Reviews, November 15, 1994, page 1535
Publishers Weekly, September 19, 1994, page 26
School Library Journal, November 1994, page 105

Other books by the same author:
The Family Read-Aloud Holiday Treasury, 1991
The Family Read-Aloud Christmas Treasury, 1989
The Macmillan Book of Greek Gods and Heroes, 1985

Other books you might like:
Marc Brown, *Scared Silly!*, 1994
A collection of poems, riddles, jokes, and stories including works by Yolen, Nash and Prelutsky Brown tickle the funny bone without being too frightening.
Bruce Coville, *Bruce Coville's Book of Ghosts: Tales to Haunt You*, 1994
A compilation of 13 entries from different authors range from frightening to funny.
Diana Wynne Jones, *Stopping for a Spell*, 1993
Three short stories in which seemingly ordinary objects or people react in extraordinary ways.

901

SUSAN LOWELL
JIM HARRIS, Illustrator

The Tortoise and the Jackrabbit

(Flagstaff, AZ: Northland Publishing, 1994)

Subject(s): Animals/Turtles; Animals/Rabbits; Deserts
Age range(s): Grades K-3
Major character(s): Tortoise, Turtle; Jackrabbit, Hare
Time period(s): Indeterminate Past
Locale(s): United States (southwest)

Summary: The classic fable of the tortoise and the hare is retold with a southwestern flair. On a fine Spring morning, elderly Tortoise challenges feisty Jackrabbit to a race so that he can prove that he is indeed the fastest runner in the desert. The animals gather round and Jackrabbit is off with a long, low leap while Tortoise scritch scratches her way along. By the time Jackrabbit wakes up from his nap, he's too far behind to beat Tortoise to the finish line. (32 pages)

Where it's reviewed:
Booklist, January 15, 1995, page 937
Horn Book Guide, Spring 1995, page 108
Publishers Weekly, November 7, 1994, page 77
School Library Journal, February 1995, page 76

Other books by the same author:
The Three Little Javelinas, 1992

Other books you might like:
Gerald McDermott, *Coyote: A Trickster Tale from the American Southwest*, 1994
    Coyote is aided by the crows until his boastful attitude becomes so obnoxious that the crows abandon him at an inopportune moment.
Janet Stevens, *The Tortoise and the Hare: An Aesop Fable*, 1984
    A retelling of the classic Aesop story has sprightly illustrations depicting the two protagonists in the contest which comes to a surprise ending for the hare.
David Vozar, *M.C. Turtle and the Hip Hop Hare: A Nursery Rap*, 1995
    The traditional tale takes on a modern rhythm, but the race comes to the same conclusion.

902

LOIS LOWRY
DIANE DEGROAT, Illustrator

See You Around, Sam!

(Boston: Houghton Mifflin, 1996)

Subject(s): Runaways; Neighbors and Neighborhoods; Humor
Age range(s): Grades 1-5
Major character(s): Sam Krupnik, Child (preschooler), Runaway; Anastasia Krupnik, 7th Grader, Sister; Gertrude Stein, Neighbor
Time period(s): 1990s
Locale(s): Cambridge, Massachusetts

Summary: Sam is quite excited about his fangs when he comes home from school but his mother is less than pleased with him wearing them all the time. Sam decides that he will run away to Alaska and packs the things he thinks he will need, but when he reaches the street he decides he needs some additional supplies and begins dropping in on his neighbors for cookies, naps, to play with a baby, and for help in locating Alaska on the globe. By the end of the day he is tired and willing to return home with Anastasia, after which the family celebrates with dinner and presents for all, including new fangs for Sam. (113 pages)

Where it's reviewed:
School Library Journal, October 1996, page 102

Bulletin of the Center for Children's Books, November 1996, page 105
Horn Book, September/October 1996, page 597

Awards the book has won:
School Library Journal Best Books, 1996

Other books by the same author:
Anastasia's Chosen Career, 1995
Attaboy Sam!, 1992
Number the Stars, 1989
All about Sam, 1988

Other books you might like:
Betsy Byars, *The Seven Treasure Hunts*, 1991
    Jackson and Goat try to outsmart each other during their treasure hunts.
Constance C. Greene, *Odds on Oliver*, 1993
    Oliver tries all kinds of ways to be a hero in his neighborhood.
Stephanie Greene, *Owen Foote, Second Grade Strongman*, 1996
    Owen finds that although he was small, his grandfather was a strongman.
Johanna Hurwitz, *Russell Sprouts*, 1987
    Russell worries about his family and living in an apartment.
Janice Lee Smith, *The Baby Blues: An Adam Joshua Story*, 1994
    Adam Joshua faces problems with his friends and his siblings.

903

BARBARA M. LUCAS
CATHERINE STOCK, Illustrator

Snowed In

(New York: Bradbury Press, 1993)

Subject(s): Winter; Frontier and Pioneer Life; Schools
Age range(s): Grades K-3
Major character(s): Grace, Child, Sister (older); Luke, Child, Brother (younger); Father, Settler, Farmer
Time period(s): 1910s (1915)
Locale(s): Wyoming

Summary: As winter approaches, the supplies that Father, Grace and Luke gather from town include paper, pencils and library books. When the snows confine the family to the ranch, their parents use the supplies to continue the children's education at home. With the spring thaw, Grace and Luke return to school in town, well-prepared to continue their schooling. (32 pages)

Where it's reviewed:
Booklist, November 15, 1993, page 633
Horn Book, September 1993, page 587
Kirkus Reviews, November 15, 1993, page 1464
New Advocate, Spring 1994, page 145
School Library Journal, January 1994, page 94

Other books you might like:
Judith Alter, *Growing Up in the Old West*, 1989
    A nonfiction look at the life of a child on the American frontier during the second half of the nineteenth century.

Brett Harvey, *My Prairie Year: Based on the Diary of Elenore Plaisted*, 1986

The life of Dakota homesteaders is portrayed through a biographical account of a year in the life of a child on the prairie.

Ann Turner, *Dakota Dugout*, 1985

Children learn about early life on the prairie from their grandmother's memories.

904

HARRIETT LUGER

Bye, Bye, Bai Kai

(New York: Browndeer Press, 1996)

Subject(s): Family Problems; Homeless; Friendship
Age range(s): Grades 4-6
Major character(s): Suzie Cooke, 11-Year-Old; Dawn Carter, Classmate; Lila Cooke, 13-Year-Old
Time period(s): 1990s
Locale(s): United States

Summary: Suzie's father has lost his job and the family is trying to save money but Suzie wants $20 to buy a costume for Halloween. When she is unable to get the money and join her friend Meredith, Meredith finds someone else to be the other half of Barney. To prove that her family is as good as others, Suzie gives her extra clothes away to the homeless, only to discover that her family is now among the homeless. They have been evicted and are moving to a motel. While there she meets Dawn, another homeless child, and it is through Dawn's family that Mr. Cooke is able to find a new job and Suzie realizes what a friend really is. (150 pages)

Other books you might like:

Barbara Corcoran, *Stay Tuned*, 1991
Stevie befriends two homeless youngsters in New York City.

Jean Sparks Ducey, *The Bittersweet Time*, 1995
Jane keeps a diary of events and her feelings about them after her father loses his job.

Vicki Grove, *The Fastest Friend in the West*, 1990
A girl becomes friends with a girl whose family lives in a car.

Mark J. Harris, *Come the Morning*, 1989
Ben and his family end up on the streets of Los Angeles, looking for their father.

905

JANET LUNN

The Root Cellar

(New York: Charles Scribner's Sons, 1981)

Subject(s): Space and Time; Orphans; Farm Life
Age range(s): Grades 5-7
Major character(s): Nan Henry, Aunt; Rose Larkin, Orphan, Time Traveller
Time period(s): 1860s; 1980s
Locale(s): Canada (Hawthorn Bay)

Summary: Orphaned at the age of three, Rose lives with her grandmother. Actually, Rose lives in hotels because her grandmother's work requires her to travel and Rose accompanies her. Taught by her grandmother, Rose spends no time with other children and divides her day among homework in the morning, museums in the afternoon and lessons with her grandmother in the evenings. After Grandmother dies, Rose is sent to live with her aunt Nan who has four boys. Rose is used to being alone and those four boys are terrifying to her, so she sneaks away to the root cellar when she needs her privacy. It's there that she time-travels back one hundred years and helps save Will when he heads off to fight in America's Civil War. (229 pages)

Other books by the same author:
Shadow in Hawthorn Bay, 1987
Double Spell, 1986
Twin Spell, 1968

Other books you might like:
Elaine Marie Alphin, *The Ghost Cadet*, 1991
Benjy helps a ghost find a pocket watch he lost during the Battle of New Market in the Civil War.

George Ella Lyon, *Here and Then*, 1994
Abby feels a connection with Eliza, a Civil War nurse, so she collects medicine and blankets and travels back in time to deliver the supplies.

Brenda Seabrooke, *The Haunting of Holroyd Hill*, 1995
In a new home, Melinda sees two different ghosts and realizes they're tied in with next-door neighbor Dan's grandfather and the Civil War.

Karen Weinberg, *Window of Time*, 1991
Climbing through a window in a basement he's cleaning, Ben Leeds discovers he's landed in the middle of preparations for the Battle of Gettysburg.

906

MICHAEL LUSTIG
ESTHER LUSTIG, Illustrator
MICHAEL LUSTIG, Illustrator

Willy Whyner, Cloud Designer

(New York: Four Winds Press, 1994)

Subject(s): Inventions; Fantasy; Humor
Age range(s): Grades 1-3
Major character(s): Willy Whyner, 3rd Grader, Inventor; Wilber Whyner, Father; Wanda Whyner, Mother
Time period(s): 1990s (1994)
Locale(s): Buzzard Creek, Idaho

Summary: Willy's humorless parents don't share his curiousity about clouds and are not understanding of his experiments which short out all the electricity in town. Willy perseveres and in time becomes the creator of unusually shaped clouds and, in an astute business move, the inventor of cloud advertisements. This is the first book for the co-authors. (34 pages)

Where it's reviewed:
Children's Book Review Service, Spring 1994, page 137
Horn Book Guide, Fall 1994, page 281
Library Talk, September 1994, page 30

New York Times Book Review, September 25, 1994, page 32
School Library Journal, July 1994, page 79

Other books you might like:
Judi Barrett, *Cloudy with a Chance of Meatballs*, 1978
　Grandpa tells a story of a town named Chew and Swallow
　in which the expression "raining cats and dogs" takes on
　new meaning.
Pat Cummings, *C.L.O.U.D.S.*, 1986
　Assigned to paint the skies over New York City, reluctant
　Chuku the angel grows to enjoy the work.
Peter Spier, *Dreams*, 1986
　Watching cloud formations, two children allow their imag-
　inations to guide their interpretations.
Ronald Wegen, *Sky Dragon*, 1982
　Using the clouds for inspiration, three children build dif-
　ferent animal shapes in the snow.

907

IDA LUTTRELL
BETSY LEWIN, Illustrator

Mattie's Little Possum Pet
(New York: Atheneum, 1993)

Subject(s): Pets; Animals; Humor
Age range(s): Grades K-2
Major character(s): Mattie, Farmer (kind-hearted); Unnamed
　Character, Possum (wily)
Time period(s): 1990s (1993)
Locale(s): United States

Summary: When kind-hearted Mattie finds a poorly-looking
possum she takes him home to nurse him back to health. It is
obvious to her dog and cat that this possum is a malingerer
and a trouble maker. Eventually Mattie comes to understand
the truth of her pets' suspicions and sends the wily varmit
packing. (40 pages)

Where it's reviewed:
Booklist, August 1993, page 2071
Horn Book Guide, Spring 1994, page 43
Publishers Weekly, July 19, 1993, page 253
School Library Journal, September 1993, page 210

Other books by the same author:
The Star Counters, 1994
Milo's Toothache, 1992
The Bear Next Door, 1991

Other books you might like:
Mary Blount Christian, *Penrod's Pants*, 1986
　Penrod, an adventurous porcupine, makes mischief again
　with his friend Griswold Bear.
Doug Cushman, *Possum Stew*, 1990
　Bear and Gator grow tired of Possum's tricks and invite
　him to a delicious dinner of, they hope, possum stew.
Thacher Hurd, *Pea Patch Jig*, 1988
　Nothing, even being picked with the lettuce and almost
　going into the salad, seems to diminish Baby Mouse's
　attraction to Farmer Clem's garden.

908

GEORGE ELLA LYON
PETER CATALANOTTO, Illustrator

Dreamplace
(New York: Orchard Books, 1993)

Subject(s): Indians of North America; Historical
Age range(s): Grades K-2
Major character(s): Unnamed Character, Child, Tourist
Time period(s): 1990s (1993)
Locale(s): Mesa Verde, Colorado

Summary: On a visit to the ruins of a cliff dwelling, a young
girl imagines the daily life of the Pueblo people when they
lived. The illustrations follow the girl's daydreaming, inter-
mingling images of the present tourist attraction with the
possible reality of the past. (32 pages)

Where it's reviewed:
Booklist, March 15, 1993, page 1321
Children's Book Review Service, March 1993, page 87
Horn Book, March 1993, page 199
Publishers Weekly, January 25, 1993, page 86
School Library Journal, March 1993, page 182

Awards the book has won:
Carolyn W. Field Award, 1994

Other books by the same author:
Together, 1994
Who Came Down That Road?, 1992
Come a Tide, 1990

Other books you might like:
Ann Nolan Clark, *In My Mother's House*, 1941
　A Caldecott Medal winner, the poetic narrative of the book
　evokes the harmony of the communal life of one group of
　Indian people.
Ruth Radlauer, *Mesa Verde National Park*, 1984
　The nonfiction book describes the cliff dwellings of the
　park.
Dyan Sheldon, *Under the Moon*, 1994
　The discovery of an arrowhead sparks a young girl's imag-
　inings of life long ago.

909

GEORGE ELLA LYON
JACQUELINE ROGERS, Illustrator

Five Live Bongos
(New York: Scholastic Inc., 1994)

Subject(s): Music; Brothers and Sisters; Stories in Rhyme
Age range(s): Grades K-2
Major character(s): Daddy, Father, Artist
Time period(s): 1990s (1994)
Locale(s): United States

Summary: Five lively, noisy, music-making children disturb
the solitude Daddy needs for his work. When they begin
parading around the house with pots, pans, skillets and trays,
Daddy sends them to the garage to build a drum set. The

imaginative bunch turns the idea and their creation into the Found Sound Band. (32 pages)

Where it's reviewed:
Booklist, October 15, 1994, page 437
Children's Book Review Service, February 1995, page 76
Horn Book Guide, Spring 1995, page 45
Reading Teacher, April 1995, page 605
School Library Journal, October 1994, page 93

Other books by the same author:
Cecil's Story, 1991
Come a Tide, 1990
Together, 1989

Other books you might like:
Jonathan London, *Hip Cat*, 1993
   Here's a cool cat celebrating the joys of jazz, man!
Linda Lowery, *Twist with a Burger, Jitter with a Bug*, 1995
   The lively read-aloud tale encourages movement to the syncopated rhythm of the text.
Lloyd Moss, *Zin! Zin! Zin! a Violin*, 1995
   With more formality than the Found Sound Band, but no less exuberance, the musicians of an orchestra begin playing.
Peter Spier, *Crash! Bang! Boom!*, 1990
   Environmental and manmade sounds are illustrated and described in a simple text.
Mildred Pitts Walter, *Ty's One-Man Band*, 1980
   Ty meets a man who uses a washboard, comb, spoons and pail to fill the air with music.

910

GEORGE ELLA LYON
PETER CATALANOTTO, Illustrator

Mama Is a Miner

(New York: Orchard Books, 1994)

Subject(s): Working Mothers; Miners and Mining; Family Life

Age range(s): Grades K-3
Major character(s): Unnamed Character, Child; Mama, Mother, Miner
Time period(s): 1990s (1994)
Locale(s): Black Mountain

Summary: A child sits at the kitchen table drawing as Mama prepares dinner. The young girl's thoughts are of her mother at work deep in the heart of Black Mountain. The illustrations alternate between mining scenes and home scenes as the proud daughter expresses her knowledge about the difficult job Mama has and her fears for Mama's safety. (32 pages)

Where it's reviewed:
Booklist, June 1, 1994, page 1810
Bulletin of the Center for Children's Books, September 1994, page 18
Kirkus Reviews, August 15, 1994, page 1133
Publishers Weekly, July 11, 1994, page 78
School Library Journal, September 1994, page 189

Other books by the same author:
Dreamplace, 1993
Who Came Down That Road?, 1992
Come a Tide, 1990

Other books you might like:
Barbara E. Barber, *Saturday at the New You*, 1994
   Shauna is proud and happy to be able to help her mom with her work as the proprietor of a beauty salon.
Barbara Shook Hazen, *Mommy's Office*, 1992
   Emily learns about her mother's more conventional job by accompanying her to the office.
Vera B. Williams, *A Chair for My Mother*, 1982
   In a Caldecott Honor book, Rosa heads the family's coin-saving effort in order to buy a comfortable chair for her hard-working mother.

M

911

DAVID MACAULAY, Author/Illustrator

Shortcut

(Boston: Houghton Mifflin Comany, 1995)

Subject(s): Country Life; Behavior; Humor
Age range(s): Grades 2-4
Major character(s): Albert, Farmer; June, Horse
Time period(s): Indeterminate Past
Locale(s): Fictional Country

Summary: Weekly, Albert and June trek to market to peddle their wagonload of melons. En route, their simple actions, such as untying a rope which blocks the road or hanging a jacket on a signpost, set off a chain of events which impact the lives of others in ways that Albert and June do not even suspect. Blissfully unaware of the chaos they have caused, they return home content, the melons sold as planned. Alert, thoughtful readers can follow the clues in the illustrations which supplement the nonlinear text. (64 pages)

Where it's reviewed:
Booklist, October 15, 1995, page 412
Five Owls, September 1995, page 14
Horn Book, January 1996, page 65
Publishers Weekly, July 17, 1995, page 228
School Library Journal, September 1995, page 182

Awards the book has won:
ALA Notable Book, 1996
Boston Globe/Horn Book Fanfare, 1996

Other books by the same author:
Black and White, 1990 (Caldecott Medal, 1991)
Why the Chicken Crossed the Road, 1987
Cathedral, 1973 (Caldecott Honor Book, 1974)

Other books you might like:
Lorna Balian, *Humbug Potion: An A-B-Cipher*, 1984
   In order to decode the secret recipe for beauty, a homely witch must decipher an alphabet-based code.
Susan Meddaugh, *Hog-Eye*, 1995
   The shortcut through the woods used by a young pig who is late for school brings her face-to-face with a wolf and his dinner plans.
James Stevenson, *Quick: Turn the Page!*, 1990
   Each of the problems posed in the book has a humorous solution which is obvious when the page is turned to the next scene.

912

ROGER LEA MACBRIDE
DAVID GILLEECE, Illustrator

In the Land of the Big Red Apple

(New York: HarperCollins Publishers, 1995)

Series: Rocky Ridge Years
Subject(s): Frontier and Pioneer Life; Farm Life; Family Life
Age range(s): Grades 4-6
Major character(s): Rose Wilder, 9-Year-Old; Swiney Baird, Orphan, 8-Year-Old
Time period(s): 1890s (1895-1896)
Locale(s): Mansfield, Missouri (Rocky Ridge Farm)

Summary: A year ago, Rose and her parents began life on their new farm. The first crops are harvested, Rose has friends, and Swiney's older brother works as a farm hand. It will be some time before the apple orchard begins producing, but until it does, life goes on with farm chores, birthday celebrations, school and Christmas. (338 pages)

Where it's reviewed:
Booklist, May 15, 1995, page 1646
Horn Book Guide, Fall 1995, page 301
School Library Journal, September 1995, page 202

Other books by the same author:
Little Farm in the Ozarks, 1994
Little House on Rocky Ridge, 1993

Other books you might like:
Thomas L. Tedrow, *Good Neighbors*, 1992
   During the harsh winter of 1905, the Wilder family and their neighbors work together to assure everyone's survival.

Kate Douglas Wiggins, *Rebecca of Sunnybrook Farm*, 1925
Many editions exist of this story of a curious, young girl growing up in Maine in the nineteenth century.

Laura Ingalls Wilder, *Farmer Boy*, 1953
The illustrated version of the previously published novel tells of Almanzo Wilder's boyhood on a farm in upstate New York.

913

ROGER LEA MACBRIDE
DAVID GILLEECE, Illustrator

Little House on Rocky Ridge

(New York: HarperCollins Publishers, 1993)

Series: Little House: The Rocky Ridge Years
Subject(s): Frontier and Pioneer Life; Moving, Household; Family Life
Age range(s): Grades 3-5
Major character(s): Rose Wilder, 7-Year-Old; Laura Ingalls "Bess" Wilder, Mother; Almanzo "Manly" Wilder, Father
Time period(s): 1890s (1894)
Locale(s): DeSmet, South Dakota; Mansfield, Missouri (Rocky Ridge Farm)

Summary: Drought and crop failures drive the Wilder family from the only home that young Rose has ever known. Leaving behind Grandparents and Aunts, she embarks on a journey by wagon with her parents and another family to find a better future in Missouri. In this first book of a series continuing the story begun in the Little House books, MacBride, the adopted grandson of Rose Wilder Lane, recreates the warmth and strength of a loving family as well as the hardships and simple pleasures of frontier life. (349 pages)

Where it's reviewed:
Booklist, June 1, 1993, page 1832
Children's Book Review Service, September 1993, page 11
Kirkus Reviews, July 1, 1993, page 863
Publishers Weekly, June 14, 1993, page 71
School Library Journal, September 1993, page 234

Other books by the same author:
In the Land of the Big Red Apple, 1995 (3rd in the series)
Little Farm in the Ozarks, 1994 (2nd in the series)

Other books you might like:
Jennifer Armstrong, *Black-Eyed Susan*, 1995
Sharing her father's love for the prairie, Susan is able to help her mother appreciate it also, despite the hardships of homesteading.
Rebecca S. Curtis, *Charlotte Avery on Isle Royale*, 1995
Daily life on the Midwest frontier is depicted as Charlotte moves with her family from Chicago to Isle Royale in Lake Superior.
Laura Ingalls Wilder, *Little House in the Big Woods*, 1961
This book originally published in 1932 begins the Little House series introducing Laura, sister Mary, Ma, Pa, and the life journey of this pioneer family.
Jeanette Winter, *Klara's New World*, 1992
A long journey lies ahead when Klara's family decides to leave Sweden and start a new life in America.

914

MARYANN MACDONALD
ABBY CARTER, Illustrator

The Pink Party

(New York: Hyperion Books for Children, 1994)

Subject(s): Friendship; Jealousy; Possessions
Age range(s): Grades 1-3
Major character(s): Lisa, Child, Friend (Amy's); Amy, Child, Friend (Lisa's)
Time period(s): 1990s (1994)
Locale(s): United States

Summary: Best friends Lisa and Amy can't get enough of the color pink. Each time Lisa gets something new, Amy gets something bigger and pinker. Together they plan a pink party with pink fairy costumes. Lisa is pleased with hers until she sees Amy and then she quietly leaves the party. The experience helps the girls appreciate that their friendship is more important than all the pink things they have. (40 pages)

Where it's reviewed:
Booklist, October 15, 1994, page 427
Horn Book Guide, Spring 1995, page 63
School Library Journal, January 1995, page 89

Other books by the same author:
Rosie and the Poor Rabbits, 1994
Secondhand Star, 1994
Ben at the Beach, 1991

Other books you might like:
Joyce Champion, *Emily and Alice Again*, 1995
Best friends Emily and Alice learn how to keep their friendship on a happy note.
Juanita Havill, *Jamaica and Brianna*, 1993
Envy over a friend's new boots leads to harsh words, hurt feelings and, with time, reconciliation between two best friends.
Russell Hoban, *Best Friends for Frances*, 1969
Excluded from Albert's "boys only" baseball game, Frances plays with sister Gloria teaching Albert an important lesson.
James Howe, *Pinky and Rex*, 1990
The first book about two close friends whose adventures continue in subsequent titles.

915

YVONNE MACGRORY
TERRY MYLER, Illustrator

The Secret of the Ruby Ring

(Minneapolis: Milkweed, 1994)

Subject(s): Space and Time; Time Travel; Historical
Age range(s): Grades 4-6
Major character(s): Lucy McLaughlin, 10-Year-Old; Martha "Granny" McLaughlin, Grandmother; Robert Tyrconnell, Child
Time period(s): 1990s (1991); 1880s (1885)
Locale(s): Glenoran, Ireland; Langley Castle, Ireland

Summary: On the eve of Lucy's eleventh birthday Granny McLaughlin gives her a star ruby ring and the story which has passed with it through the generations in the family. Lucy soon discovers that the ring has the magic power to grant two wishes. Her first wish sends her back in time to Langley Castle where she finds herself in service at Langley Castle and unable to find the ring to wish herself home to the comforts of the modern day. Lucy must confide in Robert and hope that, with his help, she can locate the ring or else she is trapped forever. Originally published in Ireland in 1991. (189 pages)

Where it's reviewed:
Booklist, March 1, 1994, page 1262
Bulletin of the Center for Children's Books, May 1994, page 294
Library Talk, March 1995, page 30
School Library Journal, March 1994, page 222

Other books you might like:
Edward Eager, *Knight's Castle*, 1956
    Four children magically travel to an earlier time when Ivanhoe and Robin Hood were alive.
Peni R. Griffin, *A Dig in Time*, 1991
    While digging in their grandmother's yard, two children find artifacts which carry them back in time to experience important moments in the family history.
Mollie Hunter, *The Three-Day Enchantment*, 1985
    A day-dream becomes reality when a boy is tranformed into Sir Dauntless, a brave knight.
Jon Scieszka, *Knights of the Kitchen Table*, 1991
    Joe's birthday present is a book which holds the power to transport him and two friends to other times and places.

916

PATRICIA MACLACHLAN
MIKE WIMMER, Illustrator

All the Places to Love
(New York: HarperCollins Publishers, 1994)

Subject(s): Farm Life; Country Life; Family Life
Age range(s): Grades K-3
Major character(s): Eli, Child, Brother (older); Sylvie, Child, Sister (Eli's)
Time period(s): 1980s; 1990s
Locale(s): United States (rural area)

Summary: Three generations live on a family farm which holds "all the places to love" that anyone could ever want. Eli grows up with an appreciation for family and land that he vows to share with his little sister Sylvie. (32 pages)

Where it's reviewed:
Booklist, June 1, 1994, page 1810
Children's Book Review Service, June 1994, page 126
Kirkus Reviews, June 15, 1994, page 848
Publishers Weekly, March 21, 1994, page 70
School Library Journal, June 1994, page 110

Awards the book has won:
International Reading Association Teachers' Choice, 1995
Notable Children's Books in the Language Arts, 1995

Other books by the same author:
Three Names, 1991

Mama One, Mama Two, 1982
Through Grandpa's Eyes, 1971

Other books you might like:
Jane B. Mason, *River Day*, 1994
    With her grandfather, Alex spends a quiet day in a canoe enjoying the beauty of the river.
George Shannon, *Climbing Kansas Mountains*, 1993
    In an award-winning work, father and son share time enjoying each other and the countryside near their farm home.
Rosemary Wells, *Waiting for the Evening Star*, 1993
    Young Berty appreciates the simple pleasures of life in rural Vermont while his older brother is eager to see beyond the distant mountains.

917

PATRICIA MACLACHLAN

Skylark
(New York: HarperCollins Publishers, 1994)

Subject(s): Stepmothers; Drought; Frontier and Pioneer Life
Age range(s): Grades 3-5
Major character(s): Sarah Witting, Stepmother; Anna Witting, Stepdaughter, Sister (older); Caleb Witting, Stepson, Brother (younger)
Time period(s): Indeterminate Past
Locale(s): Kansas; Maine

Summary: In the sequel to *Sarah, Plain and Tall*, Caleb's vision of living "happily ever after" comes face to face with the reality of prairie life during a drought. Wells go dry, forcing neighbors to move; crops die; the barn burns; the wind blows the dust, but no rain comes. Finally, Sarah, Anna and Caleb board a train for Maine to spend the summer with Sarah's aunts. Sarah's husband and the children's father stays behind to rebuild the barn and wait for the rain that will signal the reuniting of the family and their return to their prairie home. (87 pages)

Where it's reviewed:
Booklist, January 1, 1994, page 827
Horn Book, July 1994, page 453
Publishers Weekly, November 29, 1993, page 65
Reading Teacher, September 1994, page 71
School Library Journal, March 1994, page 222

Other books by the same author:
Sarah, Plain and Tall, 1985 (Newbery Medal)
Seven Kisses in a Row, 1983
Cassie Binegar, 1982

Other books you might like:
Carol Ryrie Brink, *Caddie Woodlawn*, 1935
    The Newbery Medal winner describes an adventurous young girl and her loving family on the frontier in Wisconsin.
Ann Turner, *Grasshopper Summer*, 1989
    A grasshopper plague combines with harsh living conditions to threaten the survival of Sam and his family in the Dakota territory.
Laura Ingalls Wilder, *On the Banks of Plum Creek*, 1937
    A Newbery Honor book in the Little House series de-

scribes the impact of a plague of grasshoppers on the Wilder family's farm life.

918

PATRICIA MACLACHLAN
BARRY MOSER, Illustrator

What You Know First

(New York: HarperCollins, 1995)

Subject(s): Farm Life; Country Life; Moving, Household
Age range(s): Grades 1-3
Major character(s): Unnamed Character, Child; Mama, Mother; Papa, Father, Farmer
Time period(s): Indeterminate Past
Locale(s): Midwest (prairie)

Summary: As a family prepares to move from their farm home, a young girl relates the many reasons she will not move and suggests alternatives to leaving the prairie. Mama and Papa are also sad when the farm is sold, but encourage their daughter to stay with the family. Finally, the girl gathers reminders of her prairie life so that she can help her baby brother understand what he knew first. (32 pages)

Where it's reviewed:
Children's Book Review Service, September 1995, page 7
Horn Book, January 1996, page 66
Kirkus Reviews, August 15, 1995, page 1190
Publishers Weekly, July 31, 1995, page 79
School Library Journal, November 1995, page 78

Other books by the same author:
All the Places to Love, 1994
Three Names, 1991
Through Grandpa's Eyes, 1971

Other books you might like:
Marc Harshman, *Moving Days*, 1994
    As his family prepares to move, a boy shares memories of his country home and his concerns about living in the city.
Candice F. Ransom, *When the Whippoorwill Calls*, 1995
    When the Shenandoah National Park is created, Polly and her family are forced off their mountain farmland and relocated to a house in the Flatlands.
Ann Turner, *Dust for Dinner*, 1995
    Drought and depression force Jake and Maggy's parents to sell their Oklahoma farm and move to California.
Judith Viorst, *Alexander, Who's Not (Do You Hear Me? I Mean It!) Going to Move*, 1995
    Alexander plans many ways to avoid the family's move to a new home and job 1000 miles away from his friends.
Jane Yolen, *Letting Swift River Go*, 1992
    A government decision forces Sally Jane, her family and friends to leave their village before it is flooded by the waters of a reservoir.

919

MELISSA MADENSKI
SANDRA SPEIDEL, Illustrator

In My Mother's Garden

(Boston: Little, Brown and Company, 1995)

Subject(s): Gardens and Gardening; Birthdays; Mothers and Daughters
Age range(s): Grades K-2
Major character(s): Rosie, Child; Mom, Single Mother, Gardener; Joe, Aged Person, Neighbor
Time period(s): 1990s (1995)
Locale(s): United States

Summary: With Joe's help, Rosie plans and implements a special birthday surprise for her mother. While Mom thinks Joe is helping Rosie learn to ride a two-wheeler, they are actually shopping at the nursery and secretly planting purple pansies in a remote corner of the garden. (32 pages)

Where it's reviewed:
Booklist, April 15, 1995, page 1506
Children's Book Review Service, Spring 1995, page 136
Horn Book Guide, Fall 1995, page 274
School Library Journal, April 1995, page 104

Other books by the same author:
Some of the Pieces, 1991

Other books you might like:
Eve Bunting, *Flower Garden*, 1994
    With her father's help, a young girl purchases the supplies necessary to plant a window box flower garden as a birthday surprise for her mother.
Lois Ehlert, *Planting a Rainbow*, 1988
    A mother and her child plant a family garden, carefully planning the placement of the flowers to create a rainbow of colors.
Diane Dawson Hearn, *Anna in the Garden*, 1994
    For her birhday, Anna receives a packet of seeds which her mother helps her plant in seed trays and transplant to the garden when the weather warms.

920

GREGORY MAGUIRE
DIRK ZIMMER, Illustrator

Seven Spiders Spinning

(New York: Clarion Books, 1994)

Subject(s): Schools; Humor; Fantasy
Age range(s): Grades 3-6
Major character(s): Pearl Hotchkiss, Student; Miss Germaine Earth, Teacher
Time period(s): 1990s (1994)
Locale(s): Hamlet, Vermont

Summary: Seven prehistoric Siberian snow spiders, frozen for centuries in a glacier, are discovered and tranported to Harvard for study. Alas, in route, they fall out of their refrigerated crate, the ice melts and the seven poisonous spiders are lost in a small Vermont town. Pearl captures one to use for Show and Tell, which, unexpectedly, becomes the last of the spiders to survive. By studying its behavior the students deduce the antidote to save the beloved, spider-bitten Miss Earth. (132 pages)

Where it's reviewed:
Booklinks, November 1994, page 34
Booklist, September 15, 1994, page 136
Children's Book Review Service, September 1994, page 12
Publishers Weekly, August 1, 1994, page 80
School Library Journal, October 1994, page 126

Other books by the same author:
Missing Sisters, 1994

Other books you might like:
Shirley Climo, *Someone Saw a Spider: Spider Facts and Folktales*, 1985
　　Spider lovers can read spider folklore, spider poems, spider stories and spider facts all in one volume.
Roald Dahl, *George's Marvelous Medicine*, 1982
　　George thinks he's found relief when he concocts a potion to transform his crabby grandmother.
Dick King-Smith, *The Fox Busters*, 1988
　　The chickens on a farm take the offensive to protect themselves from foxes.

921

MARGARET MAHY
MARGARET CHAMBERLAIN, Illustrator

A Busy Day for a Good Grandmother
(New York: Margaret K. McElderry Books, 1993)

Subject(s): Grandparents; Transportation; Humor
Age range(s): Grades K-2
Major character(s): Mrs. Oberon, Grandmother; Scrimshaw Oberon, Father (Mrs. Oberon's son); Sweeney Oberon, Child (infant)
Time period(s): 1990s (1993)
Locale(s): Hambone Hills, Fictional Country

Summary: In a frantic attempt to soothe his teething son, Scrimshaw phones his mother to request a delivery of cock-a-hoop honey cake. Cheerfully, Mrs. Oberon, a grandmother with traits to be envied by Indiana Jones, packs her backpack and sets off via trail bike, raft, airplane and skate board overcoming difficult terrain and dangerous animals with her quick wits. It's unlikely that Mrs. Oberon intends to rescue Scrimshaw again for she teaches him how to bake cock-a-hoop honey cake before she returns to her own home in Hambone Hills. Next time little Sweeney cries, Scrimshaw's on his own. (32 pages)

Where it's reviewed:
Booklist, October 15, 1993, page 453
Horn Book Guide, Spring 1994, page 44
Junior Bookshelf, February 1994, page 18
Publishers Weekly, July 12, 1993, page 79
School Library Journal, September 1993, page 215

Other books by the same author:
The Rattlebang Picnic, 1994
The Dragon of an Ordinary Family, 1992
The Boy Who Was Followed Home, 1983

Other books you might like:
Nancy Carlson, *A Visit to Grandma's*, 1991
　　Tina and her parents are surprised to learn how Grandma has changed since she moved into a Florida condominium!
Kathryn Lasky, *The Gates of the Wind*, 1995
　　Desiring to experience a more adventurous life, Gamma Lee moves out of her snug valley home to a windy mountaintop.
Patricia Polacco, *Babushka Baba Yaga*, 1993
　　Baba Yaga realizes her heart's desire when she becomes the adopted grandmother of a young boy in the village.
Margaret Wild, *Our Granny*, 1994
　　In an award-winning look at the diversity of grandmothers and their activities, two children remember their own granny who lives with them.

922

MARGARET MAHY
MARIAN YOUNG, Illustrator

The Good Fortunes Gang
(New York: Delacorte Press, 1993)

Series: Cousins Quartet
Subject(s): Moving, Household; Cousins; Family Relations
Age range(s): Grades 3-5
Major character(s): Pete Fortune, 10-Year-Old, Cousin (outsider); Tracey Fortune, 11-Year-Old, Cousin (leader)
Time period(s): 1990s (1993)
Locale(s): Fairfield, New Zealand

Summary: Abandoning a nomadic life in Australia, Pete Fortune and his family return to his father's hometown and move into his father's childhood home. One cousin, Tracey, does not welcome Pete into the Good Fortunes Gang which she leads and puts him to a test to prove that he is a "real" Fortune. The experience tests Tracey as well as Pete and ultimately links them and others in the Fortune family. (100 pages)

Where it's reviewed:
Booklist, September 1, 1993, page 61
Books for Your Children, Autumn 1993, page 21
Horn Book, July 1993, page 458
Publishers Weekly, June 7, 1993, page 71
School Library Journal, June 1993, page 108

Other books by the same author:
A Fortune Branches Out, 1994
The Greatest Show off Earth, 1994
The Pirates' Mixed-Up Voyage, 1993

Other books you might like:
Elizabeth Levy, *Gorgonzola Zombies in the Park*, 1993
　　The Bamford brothers must learn to work with obnoxious cousin Mabel to stop the vandalism in Central Park.
Susan Lowell, *I Am Lavina Cumming*, 1993
　　Moving to a different state, to live with her aunt and bratty cousin, leaves Lavina homesick but learning to appreciate new opportunites.
Phyllis Reynolds Naylor, *The Boys Start the War*, 1993
　　The boys start a neighborly battle giving new meaning to the term sibling rivalry and beginning a new series.

923

MARGARET MAHY
WENDY SMITH, Illustrator

The Greatest Show off Earth

(New York: Viking, 1994)

Subject(s): Circus; Science Fiction; Humor
Age range(s): Grades 4-6
Major character(s): Delphinium, 10-Year-Old (calculator); Jason Jones, Child (walking library); Mangold, Pilot
Time period(s): Indeterminate
Locale(s): Space Station Vulnik, Outer Space

Summary: Living on a space station where fun is forbidden makes it difficult to enjoy a birthday celebration. Perhaps it's that irritant which leads Delphinium to show off her calculator skills to Jason who then responds in a bit of one-up-manship by pushing a forbidden button. In no time Delphinium and Jason are racing through space toward a far-off circus. Delphinium's attempts to delete the program and return to Vulnik instead awaken Mangold, a pilot who has never actually flown anything. Together the trio take off for an adventure which returns fun to the universe. (186 pages)

Where it's reviewed:
Horn Book, November 1994, page 734
Junior Bookshelf, June 1994, page 96
Library Talk, March 1995, page 30
Publishers Weekly, September 12, 1994, page 92
School Library Journal, September 1994, page 105

Other books by the same author:
Aliens in the Family, 1991
The Blood-and-Thunder Adventure on Hurricane Peak, 1989
The Haunting, 1982

Other books you might like:
Roald Dahl, Charlie and the Great Glass Elevator, 1972
    In the sequel to Charlie and the Chocolate Factory Charlie and his family enter a glass elevator for a trip into space.
Gery Greer, Jason and the Aliens Down the Street, 1991
    Jason discovers his neighbors are aliens who invite him along on their travels to distant planets. Co-author Robert Ruddick.
Daniel Manus Pinkwater, Fat Men from Space, 1977
    William learns Earth is being invaded by fat men intent on stealing all the world's junk food.

924

MARGARET MAHY
MARGARET CHAMBERLAIN, Illustrator

The Pirates' Mixed-Up Voyage

(New York: Dial Books for Young Readers, 1993)

Subject(s): Pirates; Humor; Adventure and Adventurers
Age range(s): Grades 4-6
Major character(s): Captain Lionel Wafer, Pirate (former tea-shop employee), Adventurer (nonreader); Toothpick, Bird (parrot); Mrs. Hatchett, Teacher
Time period(s): Indeterminate

Locale(s): Hookywalker, Fictional City (homeport); The Sinful Sausage, At Sea (heading for the Thousand Islands)

Summary: Tired of his life as the operator of his retired uncle's tea shop, Lionel Wafer determines to live up to the legend of his name sake and become a pirate. Fortunately, Ye Olde Pyratte Tea Shoppe is located in a ship so Lionel simply cuts the moorings, renames the shop The Sinful Sausage and sets sail with the employees who also aspire to a life of piracy. Complicated by their inability to read, the trip to the Thousand Islands to kidnap a wealthy inventor is more comical than dastardly. (180 pages)

Where it's reviewed:
Booklist, January 15, 1993, page 908
Horn Book, May 1993, page 334
Kirkus Reviews, April 1, 1993, page 461
Publishers Weekly, February 15, 1993, page 239
School Library Journal, April 1993, page 124

Other books by the same author:
The Greatest Show off Earth, 1994
The Chewing-Gum Rescue, 1991
The Blood-and-Thunder Adventure on Hurricane Peak, 1989

Other books you might like:
Roald Dahl, James and the Giant Peach, 1961
    A flying peach and unusual insect travel companions are some of the surprises James receives from a bag of magic.
Betty MacDonald, Hello, Mrs. Piggle Wiggle, 1957
    Laughs and lessons are in store as Mrs.Piggle Wiggle delivers her unique remedies to problem children.
Ellen Raskin, The Mysterious Disappearance of Leon (I Mean Noel), 1989
    Using word puzzle clues, child bride Caroline Fish searches for her husband Leon (I mean Noel).

925

MARGARET MAHY
STEVEN KELLOGG, Illustrator

The Rattlebang Picnic

(New York: Dial Books for Young Readers, 1994)

Subject(s): Automobiles; Family Life; Humor
Age range(s): Grades K-3
Major character(s): Jack McTavish, Spouse, Father; Marion McGillicuddy Tavish, Spouse, Mother; Granny McTavish, Grandmother
Time period(s): Indeterminate
Locale(s): Fictional Country

Summary: As newlyweds, Jack and Marion McTavish decide not to spend their money on an expensive car, but to purchase an ''old rattlebang'' car so they can afford to have seven children. Adoring grandchildren, Granny McTavish heartily endorses the idea. Together, they enjoy picnics to the beach and the river with Granny providing pizza and pies which are so inedible they even break the shark's teeth when the kids dump them into the water. Granny's poor cooking saves the day when a wheel falls off the rattlebang just as the family is escaping from an erupting volcano. With no spare tire, Granny's pizza is put to good use as the family flees just ahead of the lava. (32 pages)

Where it's reviewed:
Booklist, June 1, 1994, page 1810
Horn Book, September 1994, page 579
Publishers Weekly, July 4, 1994, page 62
School Library Journal, October 1994, page 93
Wilson Library Bulletin, February 1995, page 94

Awards the book has won:
Booklist Editors' Choice, 1994
School Library Journal Best Books, 1994

Other books by the same author:
A Busy Day for a Good Grandmother, 1993
Seven Chinese Brothers, 1990
The Boy Who Was Followed Home, 1983

Other books you might like:
Alan Benjamin, *A Change of Plans*, 1982
    The Brown family must unexpectedly modify their plans for a picnic and boat ride due to the number of people they have invited.
Mercer Mayer, *Appelard and Liverwurst*, 1978
    With help from an unusual rhinoceros, farmer Appelard manages to bring in a successful harvest.
Trinka Hakes Noble, *Jimmy's Boa Bounces Back*, 1984
    Jimmy's pet boa constrictor is loose again and this time he's at a garden party creating the usual chaos whenever he's around.
Patricia Polacco, *Picnic at Mudsock Meadow*, 1992
    Although he tries again and again, William cannot seem to impress Hester at the Halloween picnic.

926

MARGARET MAHY
MARIAN YOUNG, Illustrator

Tangled Fortunes
(New York: Delacorte Press, 1994)

Series: Cousins Quartet
Subject(s): Brothers and Sisters; Cousins; Growing Up
Age range(s): Grades 4-6
Major character(s): Tracey Fortune, Sister (older); Jackson Fortune, Brother (younger); Tessa Fortune, Cousin
Time period(s): 1990s (1994)
Locale(s): Fairfield, New Zealand

Summary: The Fortune families find their lives becoming increasingly complicated. Inseparable Tracey and Jackson are developing different interests and trying to be more independent of one another. One cousin is planning a wedding—tomboy Tracey wants to be a bridesmaid and Jackson wants his newly formed band to play at the reception. When Tessa, sister of the bride, alerts all the cousins to a mysterious motorcycle rider in the neighborhood, everyone's plans begin to change. (105 pages)

Where it's reviewed:
Booklist, October 1, 1994, page 328
Horn Book Guide, Spring 1995, page 80
Junior Bookshelf, June 1994, page 96
Kirkus Reviews, December 15, 1994, page 1570
School Library Journal, November 1994, page 106

Other books by the same author:
A Fortune Branches Out, 1994
A Fortunate Name, 1993
The Good Fortunes Gang, 1993

Other books you might like:
C.S. Adler, *A Tribe for Lexi*, 1991
    Vacationing at a cousin's farm in upstate New York, Lexi finds that only cousin Jeb offers friendship.
Eth Clifford, *Harvey's Wacky Parrot Adventure*, 1990
    Begrudgingly, Harvey accepts the help of disliked cousin Nora in a search for hidden treasure.
Michael Morpurgo, *The Ghost of Grania O'Malley*, 1996
    With help from her American cousin and a pirate's ghost, Jessie saves her Irish island home from developers.
Phyllis Reynolds Naylor, *Beetles, Lightly Toasted*, 1987
    Determined to beat his cousin in the fifth grade essay contest, Andy tries unusual recipe ideas on his unsuspecting family.

927

MARGARET MAHY
ROBERT STARMOSE, Illustrator

Tingleberries, Tuckertubs and Telephones
(New York: Viking, 1996)

Subject(s): Pirates; Mystery and Detective Stories; Humor
Age range(s): Grades 3-5
Major character(s): Saracen Hobday, Orphan, Gardener; Grudge Gallows, Pirate, Thief; Granny, Detective—Private
Time period(s): Indeterminate Past
Locale(s): Australia (Island off the coast)

Summary: Saracen's grandmother, a retired detective, leaves him alone when she sets off to find an old pirate who's escaped. She sends him a new plant she has discovered on her travels which he grows with a great deal of success. Saracen also spends a lot of time on the phone as he has fallen in love with the operator's voice. Later, he discovers that this operator is also a boat captain and the girl who saves him when the pirate arrives on the island to steal some gold. (96 pages)

Where it's reviewed:
Horn Book, May/June 1996, page 336
School Library Journal, February 1996, page 102

Other books by the same author:
Clancy's Cabin, 1995
The Christmas Tree Tangle, 1994
A Fortune Branches Out, 1994
The Chewing-Gum Rescue, 1991

Other books you might like:
Bill Brittain, *My Buddy, the King*, 1989
    When Tim saves the king from choking on a hot dog, the two become friends and are able to outwit a plot to kill the king.
Anna Fienberg, *Wiggy and Boa*, 1990
    Boa must find help to escape the pirates she's inadvertently freed.

Sid Fleischman, *The Ghost in the Noonday Sun*, 1989
12-year-old Oliver tries to escape from pirates who have taken him to an island.
Jon Scieszka, *The Not-So-Jolly Roger*, 1991
The time warp trio is transported to a pirate ship and tries to find ways to escape.

928

JOAN B. MANLEY

She Flew No Flags

(Boston: Houghton Mifflin, 1995)

Subject(s): World War II; Ships; Voyages and Travels
Age range(s): Grades 5-6
Major character(s): Janet Baylor, 10-Year-Old
Time period(s): 1940s (1944)
Locale(s): At Sea (troopship)

Summary: Janet has spent most of her life living in India but World War II forces her family back to America. Their trip home aboard a disguised naval vessel is fraught with tension and boredom, tension from never knowing if they'll be attacked to the boredom faced by any young kids cooped up for six weeks. Janet, who must wear her lifebelt at all times, occupies her time figuring out the secrets of the other passengers, including the Chinese boy who is really a girl fleeing from an abusive father, in this semi-autobiographical first novel. (269 pages)

Where it's reviewed:
Booklist, March 15, 1995, page 1323
School Library Journal, April 1995, page 134
Publishers Weekly, May 1, 1995, page 59
Voice of Youth Advocates, June 1995, page 96
New York Times Book Review, June 11, 1995, page 43

Other books you might like:
Michael Morpurgo, *King of the Cloud Forests*, 1988
When the Japanese invade China, Ashley and his father's aide flee across the Himalayas trying to reach England.
Kit Pearson, *Looking at the Moon*, 1992
Norah and her brother are living in Canada after being evacuated from England during World War II.
Richard Peck, *Those Summer Girls I Never Met*, 1988
Drew and his sister spend the summer aboard a cruise ship with their grandmother, a famous singer from years ago.

929

FRAN MANUSHKIN
NED BITTINGER, Illustrator

The Matzah That Papa Brought Home

(New York: Scholastic Inc., 1995)

Subject(s): Holidays, Jewish; Spring; Jews
Age range(s): Grades K-2
Major character(s): Papa, Father; Mama, Mother
Time period(s): Indeterminate Past
Locale(s): United States

Summary: Papa arrives home with the matzah Mama uses to make for the feast the large, happy family gathers to share at the Passover Seder. The cumulative tale explains Passover traditions with terms defined in a concluding historical note. (32 pages)

Where it's reviewed:
Booklist, January 15, 1995, page 937
Children's Book Review Service, March 1995, page 87
New York Times Book Review, April 9, 1995, page 25
Publishers Weekly, December 12, 1994, page 61
School Library Journal, February 1995, page 76

Awards the book has won:
ALA Notable Book, 1996

Other books by the same author:
Peeping and Sleeping, 1994
Latkes and Applesauce: A Hanukkah Story, 1990
Baby, Come Out!, 1984

Other books you might like:
Malka Drucker, *The Family Treasury of Jewish Holidays*, 1994
With stories, games, songs and recipes, ten Jewish holidays and their traditions are explained. (nonfiction)
Shulamith Levey Oppenheim, *Appleblossom*, 1991
Naphtali hopes that his careful Seder plans will convince his father of the importance of a family pet such as a talking cat.
Roni Schotter, *Passover Magic*, 1995
Molly and Ben eagerly welcome the relatives arriving for the special Passover dinner.
Lauren Wohl, *Matzoh Mouse*, 1991
While preparing for Passover, Sarah is unable to resist the temptation to sample the chocolate matzos.
Jane Breskin Zalben, *Happy Passover, Rosie*, 1990
A young bear celbrates her first passover with her family.
Harriet Ziefert, *What Is Passover?*, 1994
Jake and his family prepare a special family seder.

930

FRAN MANUSHKIN
JENNIFER PLECAS, Illustrator

Peeping and Sleeping

(New York: Clarion Books, 1994)

Subject(s): Animals/Frogs and Toads; Fathers and Sons; Spring
Age range(s): Grades K-2
Major character(s): Barry, Child; Daddy, Father
Time period(s): 1990 (1994)
Locale(s): United States

Summary: Disturbed by the constant sound of peeping as he tries to go to sleep one Spring night, Barry's curiosity is satisfied by a walk with his father toward the direction of the sound. The flashlight reveals many tiny frogs known as Spring Peepers emerging from the mud around the pond. At the sight of the frogs, Barry forgets his fear of the dark and the strange sounds and decides to hop and peep his way home and into bed. (32 pages)

Where it's reviewed:
Booklist, June 1, 1994, page 1841

Bulletin of the Center for Children's Books, July 1994, page 367

Horn Book, May 1994, page 317

Publishers Weekly, April 25, 1994, page 77

School Library Journal, June 1994, page 110

Other books by the same author:

Let's Go Riding in Our Strollers, 1993

Buster Loves Buttons!, 1985

Baby, Come Out!, 1984

Other books you might like:

Patricia Lakin, *Dad and Me in the Morning*, 1994

Jacob and his dad share an early morning walk to the beach to watch the sunrise.

Cynthia Rylant, *A Night in the Country*, 1986

Text and illustrations provide an understanding of the sounds of the night, removing fear of the unknown.

Jane Yolen, *Owl Moon*, 1987

Father and child take a moonlit winter walk in hopes of seeing a great owl.

931

FRAN MANUSHKIN

JACQUELINE CHWAST, Illustrator

Starlight and Candles: The Joys of the Sabbath

(New York: Simon & Schuster Books for Young Readers, 1995)

Subject(s): Jews; Religion; Family Life

Age range(s): Grades K-2

Major character(s): Jake Jacobson, Child, Brother; Rosy Jacobson, Child, Sister

Time period(s): 1990s (1995)

Locale(s): United States

Summary: On the eve of the Sabbath, Jake and Rosy help their father with the weekly baking of the challah. After school the next day they help their mother prepare for the family dinner with grandparents and guests. Saturday morning the family attends synagogue and then has lunch together. At sunset Shabbat ends, but Rosy and Jake know it will continue to be celebrated forever and ever. A glossary defines the Yiddish words used in the text. (32 pages)

Where it's reviewed:

Booklist, September 1, 1995, page 59

Horn Book Guide, Spring 1996, page 38

Kirkus Reviews, July 15, 1995, page 1028

Publishers Weekly, September 11, 1995, page 38

School Library Journal, December 1995, page 87

Other books by the same author:

The Matzah That Papa Brought Home, 1994

Latkes and Applesauce: A Hanukkah Story, 1990

Buster Loves Buttons!, 1985

Other books you might like:

David A. Adler, *One Yellow Daffodil: A Hanukkah Story*, 1995

The kindness of a neighborhood family helps lonely Morris Kaplan celebrate his faith.

Patricia Polacco, *Tikvah Means Hope*, 1994

Following a fire during Sukkot, a Jewish family finds symbols of hope in the ashes.

Joan Rothenberg, *Inside-Out Grandma*, 1995

As a reminder to purchase the oil needed for making potato latkes, Rosie's grandma wears her clothes inside out.

932

JAN MARINO

The Mona Lisa of Salem Street

(Boston: Little, Brown and Co., 1995)

Subject(s): Brothers and Sisters; Orphans; Grandparents

Age range(s): Grades 6-7

Major character(s): Nettie DeAngelus, 12-Year-Old; John Peter DeAngelus, Child; Frank ''Pa'' DeAngelus, Grandfather

Time period(s): 1990s

Locale(s): Boston, Massachusetts

Summary: Shuffled from relative to relative after their parents die, but always winding up back with their crabby grandmother, Nettie and John Peter are finally sent to Boston to stay with their paternal grandfather. Afraid to become attached and dismayed that Pa's not rich like they'd been told, Nettie tries to keep her distance. John Peter, however, likes Pa immediately, even losing his stutter after a few weeks. It takes a while, but Nettie finally believes Pa when he tells her they'll always be together as a family. (155 pages)

Where it's reviewed:

Publishers Weekly, April 17, 1995, page 61

Booklist, March 1, 1995, page 1242

Voice of Youth Advocates, August 1995, page 161

School Library Journal, April 1995, page 134

Horn Book, July 1995, page 459

Other books by the same author:

Like Some Kind of Hero, 1992

The Day That Elvis Came to Town, 1991

Eighty-Eight Steps to September, 1989

Other books you might like:

Kristi D. Holl, *No Strings Attached*, 1988

June and her mother, Anne, live with old, cranky Mr. Cooper in a housing arrangement beneficial for all of them.

John Peel, *Uptime, Downtime*, 1992

When Karyn and Mike think their uncle doesn't want to adopt them, they wish themselves away from his home and discover they can time travel wherever they like.

Jean Thesman, *The Rain Catchers*, 1991

Raised by her grandmother, Grayling is asked by her mother to move to San Francisco; one visit convinces Grayling to remain with her grandmother.

933

MICHELLE MARKEL
DIANE PATERSON, Illustrator

Gracias, Rosa

(Morton Grove, IL: Albert Whitman & Company, 1995)

Subject(s): Babysitters; Friendship; Mothers and Daughters
Age range(s): Grades K-3
Major character(s): Kate, Child; Rosa Arqueta, Child-Care Giver (Guatemalan); Juana, 6-Year-Old (Rosa's daughter)
Time period(s): 1990s (1995)
Locale(s): Los Angeles, California

Summary: As the new babysitter, Rosa depends on her kind nature to conquer Kate's sadness and prepare the way for a loving relationship to grow between the two. Being separated from her daughter is difficult for Rosa and when she is financially able to return to Guatemala she does, bringing Kate's favorite doll as a gift for Juana. The Spanish words used in the text are understandable from context and also defined in a one-page glossary at the end of the book. (32 pages)

Where it's reviewed:
Booklist, June 1995, page 1787
Children's Book Review Service, July 1995, page 148
Horn Book Guide, Fall 1995, page 274
School Library Journal, May 1995, page 87

Other books you might like:
Susan Hellard, *Eleanor and the Babysitter*, 1991
    Resisting a change in child-care, Eleanor is happy to learn the new babysitter is friendly.
Angela Johnson, *Shoes Like Miss Alice's*, 1995
    Energetic Miss Alice is the liveliest babysitter a child has ever had!
Dolores Johnson, *What Kind of Babysitter Is This?*, 1991
    Kevin wants no babysitter at all until he meets one who loves baseball.
Jean Richardson, *Thomas's Sitter*, 1991
    When he meets Dan and learns more about the fun activities he plans, Thomas begins to have some interest in the new baby-sitting arrangements his mother is making.

934

MARION M. MARKHAM
KAREN A. JEROME, Illustrator

The St. Patrick's Day Shamrock Mystery

(Boston: Houghton Mifflin Company, 1995)

Series: Dixon Twins
Subject(s): Twins; Mystery and Detective Stories; Holidays
Age range(s): Grades 2-4
Major character(s): Kate Dixon, Twin; Mickey Dixon, Twin
Time period(s): 1990s (1994)
Locale(s): Springvale

Summary: The discovery of a shamrock painted in poster paint on a neighbor's front door and a missing kitten lead Kate and Mickey on the trail of another mystery. Using their heads and carefully noting their clues the twins locate the kitten and find a new friend at the same time. (48 pages)

Where it's reviewed:
Booklist, September 15, 1995, page 164
Horn Book Guide, Spring 1996, page 56
School Library Journal, December 1995, page 87

Other books by the same author:
The Valentine's Day Mystery, 1992
The April Fool's Day Mystery, 1991
The Birthday Party Mystery, 1989

Other books you might like:
David A. Adler, *The Fourth Floor Twins and the Skyscraper Parade*, 1988
    When Donna and Diane discover an exhibit is missing from the museum, they uncover the clues needed to find it.
Ellen Conford, *Nibble, Nibble, Jenny Archer*, 1993
    The seventh story about a likable character tells of Jenny's dreams of fame after she is filmed during a taste test for a commercial for—gerbil food!
Laura Lee Hope, *The Bobbsey Twins of Lakeport*, 1989
    The revised and abridged edition updates a classic mystery series about the two sets of Bobbsey twins who seem to find adventure wherever they go.

935

PATRICIA MALONEY MARKUN
ROBERT CASILLA, Illustrator

The Little Painter of Sabana Grande

(New York: Bradbury Press, 1993)

Subject(s): Artists and Art; Problem Solving; Country Life
Age range(s): Grades 1-3
Major character(s): Fernando Espino, Child, Artist; Senora Arias, Teacher
Time period(s): 1990s (1993)
Locale(s): Sabana Grande, Panama

Summary: During school vacation Fernando uses information from Senora Arias to make brightly colored paints. After all the work of gathering the natural materials and mixing the colors, Fernando realizes he cannot paint because he has no paper. When no one in the entire village has a scrap of paper, the frustrated artist asks permission to paint the white adobe walls of his home. His parents say no, but relent when they see his disappointment. As Fernando's picture begins to take shape on his home, the neighbors pull up chairs to watch him work and Senora Arias comes from a nearby town to see the famous painter of Sabana Grande. (30 pages)

Where it's reviewed:
Booklist, March 1, 1993, page 1234
Kirkus Reviews, March 15, 1993, page 375
New Advocate, Fall 1993, page 292
Publishers Weekly, February 15, 1993, page 237
School Library Journal, July 1993, page 68

Awards the book has won:
Book Links Good Book, 1993
Consortium of Latin American Studies Programs Commended Book, 1993

Other books you might like:

Karen Ackerman, *Araminta's Paint Box*, 1990
> During her journey by covered wagon from Boston to California, Araminta loses her treasured paint box which eventually finds its way to her in California.

Abigail Thomas, *Pearl Paints*, 1994
> After receiving a set of paints for her birthday, Pearl puts all her creative energy into making a mural for her bedroom wall.

Sara Yamaka, *The Gift of Driscoll Lipscomb*, 1995
> Annually, Molly receives a brush and a different color of paint from an artist friend until eventually she has all the colors of the rainbow.

936

JAMES MARSHALL, Author/Illustrator

Fox on Stage

(New York: Dial Books for Young Readers, 1993)

Series: Easy-to-Read Books
Subject(s): Animals/Foxes; Magicians; Plays
Age range(s): Grades K-3
Major character(s): Fox, Fox
Time period(s): 1990s (1993)
Locale(s): United States

Summary: In each of the three short stories Fox's plans, as usual, go a little awry, but still keep him in the middle of the action. First he tries to cheer his bored, hospitalized Grannie by making home videos; next his muttering comments during a magic show land him on stage; and, last, he directs and stars in a ''spooky'' play which turns out to be more of a comedy. (48 pages)

Where it's reviewed:
Booklist, July 1993, page 1980
Horn Book, March 1993, page 227
Kirkus Reviews, March 15, 1993, page 376
Language Arts, January 1994, page 55
School Library Journal, April 1993, page 100

Other books by the same author:
Fox Be Nimble, 1994
Fox Outfoxed, 1992
George and Martha Round and Round, 1988

Other books you might like:

Laurie Krasny Brown, *Rex and Lilly Playtime*, 1995
> The action never stops when these dinosaur siblings are playing.

Tomie De Paola, *Kit and Kat*, 1994
> Three stories about two kittens visiting grandparents, riding bikes and coping with a bully.

Julia Hoban, *Buzby to the Rescue*, 1993
> Buzby, the hotel cat, solves the mystery of a movie star's missing jewels.

937

JAMES MARSHALL

Rats on the Range and Other Stories

(New York: Dial Books for Young Readers, 1993)

Subject(s): Animals; Short Stories; Humor
Age range(s): Grades 2-4
Time period(s): 1990s (1993)
Locale(s): United States

Summary: In the sequel to *Rats on the Roof* eight animal stories tickle the readers' funny bones with adventures ranging from a family of rats vacationing at a dude ranch owned by, of all critters, rat terriers to a mouse keeping house for a tomcat whose diet she tries to change before she becomes a menu item. Pig is also featured learning proper table manners to impress his date and terrorizing the town as a newly licensed driver.

Where it's reviewed:
Booklist, June 1, 1993, page 1832
Horn Book, May 1993, page 329
Kirkus Reviews, June 15, 1993, page 788
Publishers Weekly, June 7, 1993, page 70
School Library Journal, November 1993, page 86

Other books by the same author:
Rats on the Roof: And Other Stories, 1991 (ALA Notable Book and SLJ Best Book)
Wings: A Tale of Two Chickens, 1986
George and Martha Encore, 1977

Other books you might like:

Kenneth Grahame, *The Wind in the Willows*, 1908
> The classic tale of 4 animal friends living along the banks of a river in England has been revised, reillustrated and retold many times.

Paul Peabody, *Blackberry Hollow*, 1993
> In an animal fantasy, kindly Parnassus expects his latest invention to put an end to Tom McPaddy's homesickness.

Tor Seidler, *A Rat's Tale*, 1986
> Facing extermination, the rats beneath New York City accept help from a member of the community whom they had previously viewed with disdain.

938

BILL MARTIN JR.
BRUCE DEGEN, Illustrator

A Beautiful Feast for a Big King Cat

(New York: HarperCollins Publishers, 1994)

Subject(s): Animals/Mice; Animals/Cats; Stories in Rhyme
Age range(s): Grades K-3
Major character(s): Unnamed Character, Mouse (young); Unnamed Character, Cat (big)
Time period(s): Indeterminate
Locale(s): Fictional Country

Summary: A cocky little mouse taunts a rather large cat and then runs to the safety of his mother who is twice able to distract the cat and achieve her offspring's safety. The third time the mouse tries his teasing ploy he finds that the cat is one step ahead of him. Racing down a shortcut, the cat reaches mouse's home first and lies in wait for a well-deserved meal. This time the mouse must do some quick thinking to save his own skin. (32 pages)

Where it's reviewed:
Booklist, July 1994, page 1952
Horn Book Guide, Fall 1994, page 262
Library Talk, January 1995, page 35
Publishers Weekly, May 30, 1994, page 55
School Library Journal, July 1994, page 73

Awards the book has won:
International Reading Association Children's Choice, 1995

Other books by the same author:
Listen to the Rain, 1988
Barn Dance!, 1988

Other books you might like:
Alyssa Satin Capucilli, *Inside a Barn in the Country*, 1995
    One by one the animals in a barn wake one another with their individual sounds.
Margrit Cruickshank, *Down by the Pond*, 1995
    Noisy farm animals chase away a fox.
Garry Disher, *Switch Cat*, 1995
    Next-door neighbor cats solve the problem of incompatibility with their owners by switching homes.
David Vozar, *M.C. Turtle and the Hip Hop Hare: A Nursery Rap*, 1995
    While the rhythm of the tale has a modern beat, the hare's challenge to turtle is the same.
Wong Herbert Yee, *Eek! There's a Mouse in the House*, 1992
    When a mouse is discovered in the house, larger and larger animals are sent to dispatch it.

939

BILL MARTIN JR.
BARRY ROOT, Illustrator

Old Devil Wind

(San Diego: Harcourt Brace & Company, 1993)

Subject(s): Halloween; Ghosts; Haunted Houses
Age range(s): Grades K-2
Major character(s): Ghost, Spirit; Witch, Witch
Time period(s): Indeterminate
Locale(s): United States

Summary: Originally copyrighted in 1971 this Halloween story is reissued with new illustrations which compliment and expand the cumulative tale. The ghost gets the night's activities started by floating out of the wall and wailing. Then one by one a broom, a stool, and many other objects join the cacophony as a witch arrives to fly around the house. The wind joins in last and brings an end to all the noise until next Halloween. (32 pages)

Where it's reviewed:
Booklist, October 1, 1993, page 353
Emergency Librarian, January 1994, page 47
Horn Book, January 1994, page 65
Publishers Weekly, September 20, 1993, page 29
School Library Journal, November 1993, page 86

Other books by the same author:
Fire! Fire! Said Mrs. McGuire, 1995
The Wizard, 1994
Polar Bear, Polar Bear, What Do You Hear?, 1991

Other books you might like:
Sylvia Andrews, *Rattlebone Rock*, 1995
    In the graveyard, tombstones, skeletons and ghosts begin a rhythmic Halloween beat which attracts the attention of the townspeople.
Marc Brown, *Scared Silly!*, 1994
    A collection of poems, riddles, jokes and stories provides a not too frightening introduction to scary, but nonthreatening, literature.
Ruth Brown, *A Dark, Dark Tale*, 1981
    A black cat surprises the only occupant of a dark abandoned house.
Kenn Compton, *Granny Greenteeth and the Noise in the Night*, 1993
    Granny asks her unusual and somewhat spooky housemates to investigate a noise under her bed. Co-author Joanne Compton.
Linda Williams, *The Little Old Lady Who Was Not Afraid of Anything*, 1986
    On a night-time walk through the woods an old woman is followed by many scary objects which attempt to frighten her.

940

BILL MARTIN JR.
ALEX SCHAEFER, Illustrator

The Wizard

(San Diego: Harcourt Brace & Company, 1994)

Subject(s): Wizards; Magic; Stories in Rhyme
Age range(s): Grades K-2
Major character(s): Unnamed Character, Wizard
Time period(s): Indeterminate
Locale(s): Fictional Country

Summary: As the cauldron boils, a lively wizard is cheered on by his assistants, entertained by their antics, and rated as to the success of his growl. While sliding on bars of soap, the wizard slips, flips, loops the loop and finally disappears into the bubbling cauldron. (32 pages)

Where it's reviewed:
Booklist, October 15, 1994, page 437
Children's Book Review Service, October 1994, page 17
Kirkus Reviews, August 15, 1994, 1135
Publishers Weekly, July 18, 1994, page 244
School Library Journal, February 1995, page 77

Other books by the same author:
Fire! Fire! Said Mrs. McGuire, 1995
Old Devil Wind, 1993
Polar Bear, Polar Bear, What Do You Hear?, 1991

Other books you might like:
Peter Glassman, *The Wizard Next Door*, 1993
    His parents say he's imagining things, but a young boy is certain that the family's new neighbor, Mr. Myers, is a wizard.

Helen Lester, *The Wizard, the Fairy and the Magic Chicken*, 1983

Three magicians trying to outdo one another create a problem that they must work together to solve.

Janice Lee Smith, *Wizard and Wart*, 1994

As Wizard begins his new business, he finds the confusion resulting from his response to requests is so tiring that he needs a vacation.

Ellen Stoll Walsh, *Pip's Magic*, 1994

Pip searches for Old Abra, the wizard, in hopes that magic can help Pip overcome his fears.

941

JACQUELINE BRIGGS MARTIN
PETRA MATHERS, Illustrator

Grandmother Bryant's Pocket

(Boston: Houghton Mifflin, 1996)

Subject(s): Fear; Dreams and Nightmares; Grandparents
Age range(s): Grades K-3
Major character(s): Sarah Bryant, 8-Year-Old; Grandmother Bryant, Healer; Beck Chadwick, Neighbor, Thief
Time period(s): 1780s (1787)
Locale(s): New Hampshire

Summary: Sarah has had nightmares ever since her dog was killed in a barn fire. Grandmother Bryant invites her to come and stay with them for a time to help her get over her fears, but Sarah still doesn't sleep well and is afraid of all kinds of things, including the geese. Grandmother gives her a little pocket which says ''fear not'' and which holds herbs, scissors and buttons. Beck finds it one day and sells items from it. When Beck is hurt, Sarah must go past the geese to get the scissors from the pocket. This helps her overcome her fears and she is able to return home again. (48 pages)

Where it's reviewed:
Booklist, May 15, 1996, page 1592
School Library Journal, June 1996, page 105
Horn Book, July/August 1996, page 460

Awards the book has won:
School Library Journal Best Books, 1996
ALA Notable Children's Book, 1997

Other books by the same author:
Good Times on Grandfather Mountain, 1992
Bizzy Bones and the Lost Quilt, 1988
Bizzy Bones and Uncle Ezra, 1984

Other books you might like:
Ann Cameron, *Julian's Glorious Summer*, 1987
Julian does not want to admit that he is afraid of riding his bike.
Jenny Koralek, *The Boy and the Cloth of Dreams*, 1994
A boy gets over his fears by cutting up a cloth he feels contains dreams.
Melissa Milich, *Can't Scare Me!*, 1995
Children help an older man get over his fears of ghosts by telling him stories.
Patricia Polacco, *Thunder Cake*, 1990
A little girl gets over her fear of thunderstorms by collecting the ingredients for a cake.

Ann Tompert, *The Tzar's Bird*, 1990
The tzar learns that fear of the unknown is the worst fear of all.

942

JACQUELINE BRIGGS MARTIN
NANCY CARPENTER, Illustrator

Washing the Willow Tree Loon

(New York: Simon & Schuster Books for Young Readers, 1995)

Subject(s): Animals/Birds; Wildlife Rescue; Pollution
Age range(s): Grades 2-4
Major character(s): Unnamed Character, Bird (loon)
Time period(s): 1990s (1995)
Locale(s): Turtle Bay

Summary: When a barge hits a bridge, spilling oil into Turtle Bay, many water birds are covered with the oil and must be rescued and treated. The loon who swims near the willow tree tries to hide from the rescuers, but finally is caught, treated, and released into the wild at the end of her rehabilitation. In a concluding note, the author gives information about bird rehabilitation. (32 pages)

Where it's reviewed:
Booklist, December 15, 1995, page 709
Horn Book, September 1995, page 591
Horn Book Guide, Spring 1996, page 38
Kirkus Reviews, October 15, 1995, page 1496
School Library Journal, October 1995, page 108

Other books by the same author:
The Finest Horse in Town, 1992
Good Times on Grandfather Mountain, 1992
Bizzy Bones and the Lost Quilt, 1988

Other books you might like:
Ron Hirschi, *Loon Lake*, 1991
Photographs and text introduce loons, their unique behaviors and their habitat.
Sheryl McFarlane, *Eagle Dreams*, 1995
Following the vet's treatment plan, Robin is able to care for an injured eagle and see it return to the wild when it is healed.
Gloria Rand, *Prince William*, 1992
Denny follows the recovery of a baby seal injured during an oil spill.

943

RAFE MARTIN
DAVID SHANNON, Illustrator

The Boy Who Lived with the Seals

(New York: G. P. Putnam's Sons, 1993)

Subject(s): Indians of North America; Animals/Seals and Sea Lions; Legends
Age range(s): Grades K-3
Major character(s): Unnamed Character, Child, Indian; Unnamed Character, Father, Indian; Unnamed Character, Mother, Indian
Time period(s): Indeterminate Past

Locale(s): Pacific Northwest

Summary: A Chinook legend tells of a young Indian boy who vanishes one day near the great river. When a search is unsuccessful in locating him, the tribe continues on its migratory route while the parents lag behind, seeking their son. One day the boy is spotted sunning with the seals and is captured and reintroduced to the languages and customs of his people. He learns to carve, but still longs for the river. Pulled by the call of the seals, he finally leaps into the water to return to his underwater life. (32 pages)

Where it's reviewed:
Booklist, March 15, 1993, page 1321
Horn Book, July 1993, page 472
Kirkus Reviews, May 1, 1993, page 601
Publishers Weekly, April 5, 1993, page 77
School Library Journal, April 1993, page 112

Awards the book has won:
Booklist Editors' Choice, 1993

Other books by the same author:
The Rough-Face Girl, 1992
A Storyteller's Story, 1992
Will's Mammoth, 1989

Other books you might like:
Nancy Lyon, *Totem Poles and Tribes*, 1977
    A nonfiction book explains the history of totem poles and the tribes that used these carvings.
Gerald McDermott, *Raven: A Trickster Tale from the Pacific Northwest*, 1993
    A Caldecott Medal Honor book explains how shape-changing Raven steals the sun from the Sky Chief in order to bring light to all people.
Michelle Renner, *The Girl Who Swam with the Fish: An Athabascan Legend*, 1995
    Intrigued by the salmon her family catch to preserve for the winter, a young girl slips into the river and lives with the salmon for several years.
Margaret Shaw-MacKinnon, *Tiktala*, 1996
    When Tiktala, a young Inuit, is changed into a seal she learns their ways and the harm they experience from humans.
David Wisniewski, *The Wave of the Sea-Wolf*, 1994
    This original story set in the Pacific Northwest is based on a Tlingit legend.

944

JEAN MARZOLLO
BLANCHE SIMS, Illustrator

Slam Dunk Saturday

(New York: Random House, 1994)

Series: Stepping Stone
Subject(s): Sports/Basketball; Schools; Contests
Age range(s): Grades 2-4
Major character(s): Billy Castello, 9-Year-Old, Child of Divorced Parents; Chad Smith, Bully; Ace, Student—High School, Basketball Player
Time period(s): 1990s (1994)
Locale(s): Spring Town

Summary: To raise money for a new playground, a shoot-out contest is held for the elementary school kids. Although everyone acknowledges the important number is the pledges each child has from donors, each entrant really wants to make the most baskets in order to beat obnoxious Chad. Ace gives Billy and his friends encouragement and skill instruction to help them achieve their goals. (79 pages)

Where it's reviewed:
Booklist, January 1, 1995, page 821
Wilson Library Bulletin, April 1995, page 113

Other books by the same author:
Red Ribbon Rosie, 1988
Cannonball Chris, 1987
Soccer Sam, 1987

Other books you might like:
Elizabeth Burton, *Cinderfella and the Slam Dunk Contest*, 1994
    Cinderfella is able to go to the Slam Dunk Contest after his fairy godfather Michael Jordan helps him reconsider and make amends for his mistreatment of his stepbrothers.
Dean Marney, *Dirty Socks Don't Win Games*, 1992
    Brent and his friends enter a basketball tournament against a girl's team so well-organized that it has a coach and a sponsor.
Robert Newton Peck, *Soup's Hoop*, 1990
    In order to help the town's basketball team, Soup and Rob try to enlist the services of a basketball star for one important game.

945

JEAN MARZOLLO
JACQUELINE ROGERS, Illustrator

Snow Angel

(New York: Scholastic Inc., 1995)

Subject(s): Winter; Angels; Fantasy
Age range(s): Grades K-3
Major character(s): Jamie, Child, Student; Unnamed Character, Angel; Mama, Mother
Time period(s): 1990s (1995)
Locale(s): United States

Summary: As a blizzard rapidly dumps snow on a community, the school closes early and Mama picks up her children and the neighbors. Not until Mama arrives home does she realize that she does not have Jamie in the car. While Mama hurries back to the school, Jamie is flying overhead with her snow angel who has kept her company while she's waiting. (32 pages)

Where it's reviewed:
Children's Book Review Service, January 1996, page 51
Horn Book Guide, Spring 1996, page 38
School Library Journal, December 1995, page 88

Other books by the same author:
Valentine Cats, 1996
Pretend You're a Cat, 1990
Close Your Eyes, 1978

Other books you might like:

Nancy White Carlstrom, *The Snow Speaks*, 1992
> Two children enjoy the sights and sounds of the season's first snow.

Cheryl Chapman, *Snow on Snow on Snow*, 1994
> While sledding, a young boy loses and then finds his dog.

Lois Ehlert, *Snowballs*, 1995
> A brightly decorated snow family, complete with pets, meets its inevitable end when the sun comes out.

946

JEAN MARZOLLO
LAURA REGAN, Illustrator

Sun Song

(New York: HarperCollins Publishers, 1995)

Subject(s): Nature; Stories in Rhyme; Bedtime
Age range(s): Grades K-2
Major character(s): Sun, Celestial Body (sun)
Time period(s): 1990s (1995)
Locale(s): United States

Summary: From sunrise to sunset and back to sunrise again, the gentle rhyming text follows the sun as it awakens the world and all the creatures in it. The natural cycle of plants and animals in response to the sun is portrayed as the earth's rotation brings day and night. (32 pages)

Where it's reviewed:
Booklist, June 1, 1995, page 1788
Children's Bookwatch, July 1995, page 7
Horn Book Guide, Fall 1995, page 274
Publishers Weekly, May 22, 1995, page 59
School Library Journal, July 1995, page 66

Other books by the same author:
Ten Cats Have Hats, 1994
The Teddy Bear Book, 1989
Close Your Eyes, 1978

Other books you might like:

Teryl Euvremer, *Sun's Up*, 1987
> Awakening each morning, the sun spends an active day moving across the sky before returning to sleep as night falls.

Mordicai Gerstein, *The Sun's Day*, 1989
> A day in the life of the sun is described as the sun rises, moves across the sky and sets again.

Mirra Ginsburg, *The Sun's Asleep Behind the Hill*, 1982
> The adaption describes the end of a long, tiring day as the sun, the leaves, the animals and a child fall asleep.

Christopher King, *The Vegetables Go to Bed*, 1994
> As part of his bedtime routine, a young boy bids good night to the vegetables in the garden.

Eileen Spinelli, *If You Want to Find Golden*, 1993
> Sunlight on the city creates many different colors.

947

JANE B. MASON
HENRI SORENSEN, Illustrator

River Day

(New York: Macmillan Publishing Company, 1994)

Subject(s): Canoeing; Grandparents; Rivers
Age range(s): Grades K-3
Major character(s): Alex, Child; Grampa, Grandfather
Time period(s): 1990s (1994)
Locale(s): Wisconsin

Summary: The author's first book is set on a special day when Grampa is taking only Alex and not her pesky little brother out on the river in his canoe. Alex is sure that today she will see a bald eagle. Although Grampa and Alex eat a picnic lunch within sight of the eagle's nest, their hopes are not realized and they reluctantly begin their homeward trip. As the canoe carries them home a large bird swoops down to the water, rising again with a trout clutched in its talons. The river day is now complete for Alex. (32 pages)

Where it's reviewed:
Booklist, June 1, 1994, page 1842
Children's Book Review Service, May 1994, page 112
Horn Book Guide, Fall 1994, page 283
Publishers Weekly, January 24, 1994, page 55
School Library Journal, May 1994, page 100

Other books you might like:

William T. George, *Fishing at Long Pond*, 1991
> A fishing trip to Long Pond includes observation of the plants and animals that Katie and her grandfather see along the way.

Walter Lyon Krudop, *Blue Claws*, 1993
> A young child spends the day crabbing with his Grandfather.

Elaine Moore, *Deep River*, 1994
> When Grandpa takes Jess on her first fly-fishing trip, she worries needlessly that her brother's predictions of snagged logs or scared fish will happen.

Lynn Reiser, *Tomorrow on Rocky Pond*, 1993
> As she settles into her vacation cabin, a young girl's thoughts turn to the family's activities the next day on Rocky Pond.

948

SUSAN ROWAN MASTERS
BEATA SZPURA, Illustrator

Libby Bloom

(New York: Henry Holt and Company, 1995)

Subject(s): Self-Confidence; Schools; Bands
Age range(s): Grades 3-4
Major character(s): Libby Bloom, 4th Grader, Musician (beginning tuba player); Noel Bloom, Sister (older), Student—Junior High
Time period(s): 1990s (1995)
Locale(s): United States

Summary: ''Perfect'' Noel is quick to point out Libby's short-comings as if Libby is not well aware of her inability to sing and her embarassing clumsiness. When the chorus teacher recommends Libby's transfer from chorus to band, the involuntary switch turns out to be an opportunity for Libby to find herself and some hidden talent. (86 pages)

Where it's reviewed:
Booklist, July 1995, page 1880
Bulletin of the Center for Children's Books, July 1995, page 390
Horn Book Guide, Fall 1995, page 292
School Library Journal, September 1995, page 202

Other books by the same author:
Summer Song, 1995

Other books you might like:
C.S. Adler, *The Lump in the Middle*, 1989
Feeling lost and overlooked between her ''perfect'' older sister and cute younger sister, Kelsey begins to find acceptance and confidence after making a new friend.
Sheila Greenwald, *Here's Hermione: A Rosy Cole Production*, 1991
Despite the fact that she plays a cello, Hermione is determined to become a rock star with her friend Rosy as the manager.
Ann M. Martin, *Karen's Tuba*, 1993
Another adventure with Karen and friends is presented in the 37th entry in the Baby Sitter's Little Sister series.
Phyllis Shalant, *Beware of Kissing Lizard Lips*, 1995
Small sixth grader Zach is teased by his classmates until he learns a little Tae Kwon Do and develops some self-confidence.

949

PETRA MATHERS, Author/Illustrator

Kisses from Rosa
(New York: Alfred A Knopf, Inc., 1995)

Subject(s): Farm Life; Mothers and Daughters; Illness
Age range(s): Grades 1-3
Major character(s): Rosa, Child, Cousin; Mookie, Aunt; Birgit, Child, Cousin (three years older than Rosa)
Time period(s): 1940s (1949)
Locale(s): Black Forest, Germany

Summary: While her mother is being treated for tuberculosis, Rosa is sent to a farm in the Black Forest to live with Aunt Mookie and her daughter Birgit. Gradually, Rosa becomes accustomed to the farm and her temporary family. Rosa and her mother exchange letters and look forward to the day they can be together again. (42 pages)

Where it's reviewed:
Booklist, November 1, 1995, page 476
Horn Book, November 1995, page 729
Los Angeles Times Book Review, August 20, 1995, page 8
Publishers Weekly, July 10, 1995, page 56
School Library Journal, November 1995, page 79

Other books by the same author:
Victor and Christabel, 1993
Sophie & Lou, 1991

Maria Theresa, 1985

Other books you might like:
Rumer Godden, *Great Grandfather's House*, 1993
Three months in the traditional country home of Great Grandfather while her parents travel, lead to surprising changes in a spoiled child.
Susan Hill, *The Glass Angels*, 1992
Illness and an accident threaten to interfer with Tilly's plans to enjoy Christmas with her mother.
Jane Yolen, *Honkers*, 1992
Raising three abandoned geese at her grandparents' farm helps a young girl cope with the separation from home during her mother's difficult pregnancy.

950

PETRA MATHERS, Author/Illustrator

Victor and Christabel
(New York: Alfred A. Knopf, Inc., 1993)

Subject(s): Museums; Magic; Love
Age range(s): Grades K-3
Major character(s): Victor, Crocodile, Guard; Christabel, Crocodile (entrapped in a painting); Anatole Fidibus, Crocodile (Christabel's cousin), Magician
Time period(s): 1990s (1993)
Locale(s): United States

Summary: Obnoxious, over-bearing, and usually incompetent Anatole transforms his cousin Christabel and her room into a painting and dumps the framed print at an obscure art museum. Christabel is hung in a remote gallery where the museum guard, Victor, feels strangely attracted to her. His devotion is expressed with flowers, a night light, and conversation. Finally, thanks to the steam from his cup of tea, the spell is broken and Christabel returns to life. (40 pages)

Where it's reviewed:
Booklist, July 1993, page 1975
Bulletin for the Center for Children's Books, October 1993, page 51
Kirkus Reviews, July 15, 1993, page 937
Publishers Weekly, July 19, 1993, page 252
School Library Journal, December 1993, page 91

Other books by the same author:
Sophie & Lou, 1991
Maria Theresa, 1985

Other books you might like:
Barbara Berger, *The Jewel Heart*, 1994
In this fantasy, injured Gemino is healed by the transforming power of Pavelle's love.
James Marshall, *George and Martha*, 1972
In this first book about two lovable hippos, George and Martha share humorous adventures.
Max Velthuijs, *Crocodile's Masterpiece*, 1992
The painting which Crocodile gives to Elephant is actually a blank canvas, allowing Elephant to imagine any masterpiece he desires.
Bernard Waber, *Lovable Lyle*, 1977
The adventures of Lyle the crocodile and his life with the Primm family continue.

951

MARY MATTHEWS
E.B. LEWIS, Illustrator

Magid Fasts for Ramadan

(New York: Clarion, 1996)

Subject(s): Holidays; Religion
Age range(s): Grades 2-5
Major character(s): Magid, 8-Year-Old; Aisha, Sister; Giddu, Grandmother
Time period(s): 1990s
Locale(s): Cairo, Egypt

Summary: Majid wakes up on the first day of Ramadan and thinks he is old enough to fast, though it is not necessary for children to do so. Majid plans to anyway, especiallly since his sister is fasting. His mother does agree to let him skip breakfast. She does not know that he fed his lunch to ducks or that he has not eaten dinner, so she lets him sleep through the evening meal. After several days Majid becomes ill because he is not following the usual rules for fasting. His family explains why it is not necessry for him to fast. (48 pages)

Where it's reviewed:
Bulletin of the Center for Children's Books, February 1996, page 196
School Library Journal, July 1996, page 69
Booklist March 1, 1996, page 1184

Other books you might like:
Ann Paxton El-Moslilmany, *Zaki's Ramadan Fast*, 1994
Zaki learns that he can fast part of the day.
Suhaib Hamid Ghazi, *Ramadan*, 1996
A family describes the meaning and importance of this holiday to the Islamic religion. (non-fiction)
Dianne MacMillan, *Ramadan and Id al-Fitr*, 1994
The author details the meaning and importance of Ramadan. (non-fiction)

952

WENDY MATTHEWS
ROBERT VAN NUTT, Illustrator

The Gift of a Traveler

(Mahwah, NJ: BridgeWater Books, 1995)

Subject(s): Christmas; Grandparents; Storytelling
Age range(s): Grades 1-3
Major character(s): Christine, 7-Year-Old; Anica, Grandmother (Christine's great-grandmother); Unnamed Character, Traveller, Gypsy
Time period(s): 1990s (1995); 1910s (1910)
Locale(s): United States; Romania

Summary: As Christine helps her aged great-grandmother decorate the tree on Christmas Eve she is shown an unusual ornament and told the story of the ornament's origin many years earlier when, as a 7-year-old, Anica became lost in the woods on Christmas Eve. Anica was found by a man describing himself as a traveler and his pet wolf. In return for Anica's kind invitation into her home for dinner, the traveler leaves the ornament which she finds in her hand when she awakens

Christmas morning. The author's first picture book concludes as great-grandmother passes on the ornament to Christine. (32 pages)

Where it's reviewed:
Booklist, September 15, 1995, page 171
Horn Book Guide, Spring 1996, page 56
Kirkus Reviews, October 15, 1995, page 1497
Publishers Weekly, September 18, 1995, page 102
School Library Journal, Ocober 1995, page 39

Other books you might like:
J. Patrick Lewis, *The Christmas of the Reddle Moon*, 1994
When Liddy and Will become lost in a snowstorm on Christmas Eve they are rescued by Wee Mary Fever who summons St. Nicholas to carry them safely home.
Patricia Polacco, *The Trees of the Dancing Goats*, 1996
Recollections of a childhood story tell of a family's Christmas gift to sick members of a community.
Laura Ingalls Wilder, *Christmas in the Big Woods*, 1995
An adaptation from *Little House in the Big Woods* describes the simple Christmas celebration of a loving pioneer family.
Susan Wojciechowski, *The Christmas Miracle of Jonathan Toomey*, 1995
A commission to carve the figures for a nativity set transforms embittered woodcarver Jonathan Toomey.

953

WILLIAM MAXWELL
JAMES STEVENSON, Illustrator

Mrs. Donald's Dog Bun and His Home Away From Home

(New York: Alfred A. Knopf, 1995)

Subject(s): Animals/Dogs; Dwellings; Humor
Age range(s): Grades 1-3
Major character(s): Bun, Dog
Time period(s): 1990s (1995)
Locale(s): United States

Summary: Bun, after years of sleeping on an old piece of carpet, is pleased to find an unused playhouse in the back yard of his owner's new home. In no time, Bun cleans, paints and repairs the roof to make a home for himself. Just as quickly all the neighborhood dogs arrive to visit and soon Bun has no place to sit, but on the playhouse's front porch. Tired of being crowded out of his new place, Bun locks the door, posts a for rent sign and enters his owner's home in search of his old piece of carpet. (30 pages)

Where it's reviewed:
Booklist, September 1, 1995, page 88
Kirkus Reviews, August 1, 1995, page 1114
Publishers Weekly, July 24, 1995, page 64
School Library Journal, October 1995, page 108
Smithsonian, November 1995, page 171

Other books you might like:
Diana Hendry, *Dog Donovan*, 1995
Giving new meaning to the term ''watch dog,'' a newly acquired and fearful pet helps family members learn to overlook their own fears in order to protect the dog.

Jackie French Koller, *Mole and Shrew*, 1991
Shrew tries to locate another house for Mole after Mole's many relatives arrive and take over his home.
Dav Pilkey, *Dog Breath: The Horrible Trouble with Hally Tosis*, 1994
The Tosis family is ready to get rid of their dog Hally because of her horrible breath until she uses it to overpower would-be burglars.

954

WILLIAM MAYNE
NORMAN MESSENGER, Illustrator

Hob and the Goblins
(New York: Dorling Kindersley, 1994)

Subject(s): Ghosts; Fantasy; Good and Evil
Age range(s): Grades 4-6
Major character(s): Hob, Spirit; Tom Grimes, Child; Meg Grimes, Child
Time period(s): 1990s (1993)
Locale(s): England (Fairy Ring Cottage)

Summary: A house spirit whose job it is to keep a household happy and running smoothly is no match for the evil of witches and goblins. Yet Hob must take on the challenge when his family moves into Fairy Ring Cottage, well-known to Hob from the activities of 100 years ago. Visible to Meg and Tom, Hob is accepted by them without question and appreciated for his protection. (140 pages)

Where it's reviewed:
Booklist, November 1, 1994, page 497
Horn Book, March 1995, page 193
Kirkus Reviews, July 15, 1994, page 990
Publishers Weekly, August 29, 1994, page 79
School Library Journal, November 1994, page 85

Awards the book has won:
ALA Notable Book, 1995
School Library Journal Best Books, 1994

Other books by the same author:
Low Tide, 1993
All the King's Men, 1988
The Green Book of Hob Stories, 1984

Other books you might like:
L. Frank Baum, *The Wizard of Oz*, 1900
Dorothy finds herself in Oz assisted by a timid lion, befuddled scarecrow, heartless tin man, and ruby slippers in her quest to locate the Wizard and her home in Kansas.
Susan Cooper, *The Boggart*, 1993
When the Volnik family inherits a boggart along with a Scottish castle, Emily and Jessup must find a way to send the unhappy, mischievous spirit home.
J.R.R. Tolkien, *The Hobbit*, 1938
In the first book of a fantasy trilogy, the Hobbit finds himself on a journey with dwarves, elves, goblins and trolls.

955

MARGARET MAYO
EMILY BOLAM, Illustrator

Tortoise's Flying Lesson
(San Diego: Harcourt Brace & Company, 1995)

Subject(s): Animals; Folk Tales; Short Stories
Age range(s): Grades 2-4
Time period(s): Indeterminate Past
Locale(s): Earth

Summary: A collection of retold and adapted folk tales tells of animals supporting, tricking, and learning from one another. A brief introductory note explains the source or country of origin for each story. The book was first published in Great Britain in 1994. (76 pages)

Where it's reviewed:
Booklist, May 1, 1995, page 1577
Center for Children's Books Bulletin, June 1995, page 353
Horn Book Guide, Fall 1995, page 332
Publishers Weekly, May 1, 1995, page 58
School Library Journal, May 1995, page 101

Other books by the same author:
Magical Tales from Many Lands, 1993

Other books you might like:
Naomi Adler, *The Dial Book of Animal Tales from Around the World*, 1996
Tales from nine different countries feature animals such as frogs, rabbits, monkeys, spiders and pelicans.
Dick King-Smith, *Dick King-Smith's Animal Friends*, 1996
A collection of 31 stories tells the true tales of the many different animals in the author's life.
Rudyard Kipling, *Just So Stories*, 1912
The classic book includes a dozen animal stories and has been reissued many times with different illustrations.

956

ANNE MAZER

The Accidental Witch
(New York: Hyperion Books for Children, 1995)

Subject(s): Witches and Witchcraft; Magic; Fantasy
Age range(s): Grades 3-5
Major character(s): Phoebe, 5th Grader
Time period(s): 1990s (1995)
Locale(s): United States

Summary: Clumsy Bee dreams of being a witch for many years and, true to character, she becomes one by accidentally falling out of a tree and into a circle of witches. Though she absorbs the power of the spells, Bee lacks training and her accident-prone nature leads to chaos. Finally, the local witches decide Bee will be less trouble if they take the time to train her even though she did not join the group by the proper application process. (123 pages)

Where it's reviewed:
Booklist, November 1, 1995, page 473
Horn Book Guide, Spring 1996, page 65

School Library Journal, January 1996, page 108

Other books by the same author:
Going Where I'm Coming From, 1994 (Booklist Editor's Choice)
The Oxboy, 1993 (ALA Notable Book)
Moose Street, 1992

Other books you might like:
Ruth Chew, *The Witch and the Ring*, 1992
    The magic ring found by two siblings leads to unexpected adventure.
Catherine Dexter, *A Is for Apple, W Is for Witch*, 1996
    Barnaby's constant teasing vexes Apple, daughter of a witch, so much that, despite her lack of training, she decides to try a tiny spell on him.
Jill Murphy, *The Worst Witch*, 1987
    As a first-year student, Mildred brings chaos to Miss Cackle's Academy for Witches.

957

ANGELA MCALLISTER
ANGELA BARRETT, Illustrator

The Ice Palace

(New York: G. P. Putnam's Sons, 1994)

Subject(s): Illness; Dreams and Nightmares; Fathers and Daughters
Age range(s): Grades 1-3
Major character(s): Anna, Child; Unnamed Character, Father
Time period(s): Indeterminate Past
Locale(s): Fictional Country

Summary: Confined to bed with a fever, Anna can see from her window the palace on the hill where her father works. Each night before her father returns to the palace kitchens to work on a secret project, he tells Anna a story as she drifts off to sleep. The story is incorporated into her fevered dreaming of icy lands, snowy mountains and frozen lakes. The day the fever breaks is also the day Anna's father can reveal the secret project. (32 pages)

Where it's reviewed:
Booklist, October 15, 1994, page 437
Children's Book Review Service, February 1995, page 77
Junior Bookshelf, October 1994, page 165
Publishers Weekly, October 24, 1994, page 61
School Library Journal, October 1994, page 125

Other books by the same author:
The Babies of Cockle Bay, 1994
One Breeze-Scented, Sun-Sparkling Morning, 1993
The Snow Angel, 1993

Other books you might like:
Patricia Hermes, *When Snow Lay Soft on the Mountains*, 1996
    Throughout her father's lengthy illness, Hallie wishes for the day when he will again be strong enough for moonlit walks on the mountain.
Allen Say, *The Lost Lake*, 1989
    While on a camping trip in the mountains, a young boy and his father develop a closer relationship.

Amy Zerner, *The Dream Quilt*, 1994
    After touching the squares of a magic quilt, Alex has dreams of adventure.

958

ANGELA MCALLISTER
CLAIRE FLETCHER, Illustrator

The Wind Garden

(New York: Lothrop, Lee & Shepard Books, 1995)

Subject(s): Gardens and Gardening; Grandparents; Problem Solving
Age range(s): Grades K-2
Major character(s): Ellie, Child; Grandpa, Grandfather
Time period(s): 1990s (1994)
Locale(s): England

Summary: Daily, Ellie visits her Grandpa whose legs will no longer carry him up and down the stairs of his "high house." Because Grandpa misses walking in the park, Ellie tries to grow a garden in pots on the building's roof. All her plants are killed or blown away by the incessant wind. One night Ellie, too, is blown away to the wind garden where she sees all the things the wind has carried away. The experience gives her an idea for a roof-top garden that will please Grandpa and survive the wind. First published in Great Britain in 1994. (22 pages)

Where it's reviewed:
Booklist, March 15, 1995, page 1335
Horn Book Guide, Fall 1995, page 272
Junior Bookshelf, October 1994, page 165
School Librarian, November 1994, page 146
School Library Journal, April 1995, page 104

Other books by the same author:
The Ice Palace, 1994
One Breeze-Scented, Sun-Sparkling Morning, 1993
Paradise Park, 1992

Other books you might like:
Tomie De Paola, *Now One Foot, Now the Other*, 1981
    Following his grandfather's stroke, Bobby helps him to regain his ability to speak and walk.
Arthur Dorros, *Abuela*, 1991
    A bus ride becomes a soaring experience as a young girl and her grandmother float over New York City.
John Himmelman, *Amanda and the Magic Garden*, 1987
    Grown from magic seed, Amanda's vegetables have an unusual effect on the animals who eat them.
Faith Ringgold, *Tar Beach*, 1991
    From the rooftop of her New York apartment, Cassie soars over the city, gaining a new perspective of her surroundings.

959

SAM MCBRATNEY
LISA THIESING, Illustrator

The Ghastly Gerty Swindle: With the Ghosts of Hungryhouse Lane

(New York: Henry Holt and Company, 1994)

Subject(s): Ghosts; Mystery and Detective Stories; Crime and Criminals
Age range(s): Grades 3-5
Major character(s): Amy Steadings, Aged Person (kind); Gertrude Elizabeth "Gerty" Moag, Thief, Mother (Alexander's); Alexander the Grate, Thief
Time period(s): 1990s (1994)
Locale(s): Tunwold, England

Summary: In the sequel to *The Ghosts of Hungryhouse Lane* Amy's advertisement for a live-in companion to assist with the cleaning of her old home attracts Gerty, a swindler who writes her own references and has her eyes on the antiques. At the first opportunity, Gerty and Alexander load a van with the household valuables, unwittingly carting off two resident ghosts from the attic. Fortunately, Amy has three visitors who have the energy to track down the thieves, reclaim the furniture and return the ghosts to their proper home. (119 pages)

Where it's reviewed:
Booklist, November 1, 1994, page 500
Horn Book Guide, Spring 1995, page 79
Library Talk, Spring 1995, page 38
School Library Journal, December 1994, page 110

Other books by the same author:
The Ghosts of Hungryhouse Lane, 1989

Other books you might like:
Susan Cooper, *The Boggart*, 1993
    When a family inherits a Scottish castle and its contents they also become owners of the Boggart, a shape-changing, ageless mischief-maker.
Mary Hoffman, *The Four-Legged Ghosts*, 1993
    Alex receives a pet mouse with the power to call up the ghosts of all the animals who have lived in Alex's old home.
Betty Ren Wright, *A Ghost in the House*, 1991
    While alone with her Great Aunt Margaret, Sarah observes strange happenings which suggest that her aunt is a victim of a ghost seeking revenge.

960

SAM MCBRATNEY
ANITA JERAM, Illustrator

Guess How Much I Love You

(Cambridge, MA: Candlewick Press, 1995)

Subject(s): Animals/Rabbits; Fathers and Sons; Bedtime
Age range(s): Grades K-1
Major character(s): Little Nutbrown Hare, Rabbit; Big Nutbrown Hare, Rabbit, Father
Time period(s): Indeterminate
Locale(s): Fictional Country

Summary: Little Nutbrown Hare declares his love for his father in increasingly expansive terms. Each expression he makes is countered by Big Nutbrown Hare who, being larger, appears to express more love when he can say "I love you this much." while stretching his arms out wide. Little Nutbrown Hare tries bigger and grander ideas until he drifts off to sleep saying, "I love you right up to the moon." First published in Great Britain in 1994. (32 pages)

Where it's reviewed:
Booklist, March 15, 1995, page 1328
Five Owls, March 1995, page 82
Horn Book, July 1995, page 452
Junior Bookshelf, February 1995, page 11
School Library Journal, May 1995, page 86

Awards the book has won:
Booklist Editors' Choice, 1995
Book Links Good Book, 1995

Other books by the same author:
The Dark at the Top of the Stairs, 1996

Other books you might like:
Michael Foreman, *Dad! I Can't Sleep*, 1995
    Little Panda counts animals to help him fall asleep and they all want one last drink of water.
Mem Fox, *Time for Bed*, 1993
    Through appealing illustrations and comforting verse, the whole wide world is put to sleep.
Mirra Ginsburg, *Asleep, Asleep*, 1992
    The animals are quietly bid good night until only the sleepy child and the wind are awake.

961

HELEN MCCANN
ELLEN EAGLE, Illustrator

What's French for HELP, George?

(New York: Simon & Schuster, 1993)

Subject(s): Travel; Humor; Friendship
Age range(s): Grades 6-7
Major character(s): George Aitken, 13-Year-Old
Time period(s): 1990s
Locale(s): United States; France

Summary: When George's school announces that there's one free ticket for the school trip to France, George is determined to be the one using it. He certainly can't afford the trip, but knows his friends won't have any fun if he isn't with them. The only stumbling block George has is that the computer teacher has written a software program that will select a student at random to receive the ticket. George hacks into the program, rewrites it and accompanies his friends to France where incredible adventures await both the students and the French. (200 pages)

Where it's reviewed:
Booklist, October 15, 1993, page 443
Horn Book Guide, Fall 1993, page 301

Other books by the same author:
What Do We Do Now, George?, 1993

Other books you might like:

Johanna Hurwitz, *Class Clown*, 1987

> Though Lucas has a good sense of humor, he has yet to learn how to best use it.

Gordon Korman, *A Semester in the Life of a Garbage Bag*, 1987

> Raymond is trying to win a trip to a Greek Island but his friend Sean is about to spoil his plans.

Louis Sachar, *Dogs Don't Tell Jokes*, 1991

> Goon thinks he tells great jokes though his family and classmates disagree; by the time of the school talent show, he's improved considerably.

962

EMILY ARNOLD MCCULLY, Author/Illustrator

The Amazing Felix

(New York: G. P. Putnam's Sons, 1993)

Subject(s): Magic; Musicians; Castles
Age range(s): Grades K-3
Major character(s): Felix, Child, Brother; Fanny, Child, Sister; Papa, Father, Musician (famous pianist)
Time period(s): 1920s
Locale(s): Magnifique, At Sea; England (in a castle)

Summary: With their mother, Felix and Fanny are travelling by luxury liner to join their father at the conclusion of his world tour. While Fanny follows Papa's instructions to practice a Bach fugue, Felix is bored practicing scales and instead spends his time at sea learning to palm a coin. Reunited at the castle where Papa is giving a recital, Fanny follows other children to the castle tower where all become trapped leaving dawdling Felix to come to the rescue. (32 pages)

Where it's reviewed:

Booklist, October 1, 1993, page 342
Children's Book Review Service, November 1993, page 27
Horn Book Guide, Spring 1994, page 44
Publishers Weekly, August 16, 1993, page 102
School Library Journal, October 1993, page 104

Other books by the same author:

Crossing the New Bridge, 1994
Mirette on the High Wire, 1992 (Caldecott Medal)
Zaza's Big Break, 1989

Other books you might like:

Elisa Bartone, *Peppe the Lamplighter*, 1993

> Disappointed that his only son has chosen to work as a lamplighter, Peppe's father learns to accept him and to appreciate the value of his job.

David Merveille, *The Circus Boy*, 1993

> Clumsy Thomas is not good at tricks like his father, a star performer, but he does foresee a future with the circus as a veterinarian.

Eileen Spinelli, *Boy, Can He Dance!*, 1993

> Tony's father expects him to become a chef and join the family business, but Tony's real talent is dancing.

963

EMILY ARNOLD MCCULLY, Author/Illustrator

The Ballot Box Battle

(New York: Knopf, 1996)

Subject(s): Historical; Women's Rights
Age range(s): Grades 2-4
Major character(s): Elizabeth Cady Stanton, Suffragette, Historical Figure; Cordelia, Child (girl); Howard, Child (boy)
Time period(s): 1880s
Locale(s): Tenafly, New Jersey

Summary: Cleaning Mrs. Stanton's stable provides Cordelia with the opportunity to hear how Mrs. Stanton became involved in women's rights. On election day Mrs. Stanton takes Cordelia with her when she tries to vote and is turned away. She convinces Cordelia that one day she will be able to vote. Cordelia's friends, led by Howard, make fun of her, but she leaps onto the back of Jule, the old horse, and they fly over a fence as Cordelia envisions her future to be as good as this ride. (unpaged)

Where it's reviewed:

Bulletin of the Center for Children's Books, September 1996, page 22
School Library Journal, August 1996, page 114
Booklist, April 15, 1996, page 1439

Other books by the same author:

The Pirate Queen, 1995
Mirette on the High Wire, 1992
The Evil Spell, 1990

Other books you might like:

Joan W. Blos, *The Heroine of the Titanic*, 1991

> Molly Brown is both a heroine of the Titanic and a leading woman in the West.

Rhoda Blumberg, *Bloomers!*, 1993

> Women try to become liberated by wearing trousers called bloomers.

Kathryn Lasky, *She's Wearing a Dead Bird on Her Head*, 1995

> Harriet Hemenway and other founders of the Audubon Society work to keep people from killing and wearing birds.

Zibby Oneal, *A Long Way to Go*, 1990

> Lila's grandmother is jailed for fighting for women's rights.

964

EMILY ARNOLD MCCULLY, Author/Illustrator

The Bobbin Girl

(New York: Dial, 1996)

Subject(s): Strikes and Lockouts
Age range(s): Grades 1-3
Major character(s): Rebecca Putney, 10-Year-Old, Worker; Ruth, Worker; Judith, Worker
Time period(s): 1830s
Locale(s): Lowell, Massachusetts

Summary: Rebecca is happy when she goes to work in the mill because she is now able to earn money to help her mother, who runs a local boarding house for the mill girls. She is worried about Ruth who has developed the ''mill cough'' and is injured in a mill accident. She admires Judith who is willing to stand up to the owners of the mill for the rights of the girls. The girls plan a walk-out to object to their treatment and reduced pay, but when the mill owners simply send away for more girls, the walk-out fails and things go back to the way they were, at least for a time. (unpaged)

Where it's reviewed:
School Library Journal, April 1996, page 114
Booklist, April 15, 1996, page 1439
Bulletin of the Center for Children's Books, March 1996, page 235

Other books by the same author:
Little Kit or, the Industrious Flea Circus Girl, 1995
The Pirate Queen, 1995
Crossing the New Bridge, 1994
Mirette on the High Wire, 1992

Other books you might like:
Susan M. Adler, *Meet Samantha*, 1986
    This is the story of an orphan who lived in the early part of the century when the rights of women were just being introduced.
Barbara Diamond Goldin, *Fire! The Beginning of the Labor Movement*, 1992
    A girl describes the Triangle Shirtwaist Factory fire which began the labor movement.
Carla Stevens, *Lily and Miss Liberty*, 1992
    Lily, who has come from France, wants to raise money for the Statue of Liberty.

965

EMILY ARNOLD MCCULLY, Author/Illustrator

Crossing the New Bridge

(New York: G. P. Putnam's Sons, 1994)

Subject(s): City Life; Construction; Problem Solving
Age range(s): Grades K-3
Major character(s): Mayor, Government Official; Unnamed Character, Aged Person
Time period(s): Indeterminate Past
Locale(s): Europe

Summary: When the ''Old Bridge'' collapses into the river, the mayor hurriedly directs the Jubilatti family to build a new one lest the townspeople suffer. A local crone reminds the mayor that, according to tradition, the first person across the new bridge must be the happiest person in town or the town will be forever cursed. The mayor searches the town for the happiest person as the bridge nears completion. In the end the problem is solved for the mayor in a most satisfying way. (32 pages)

Where it's reviewed:
Booklist, November 1, 1994, page 507
Bulletin of the Center for Children's Books, September 1994, page 18
Horn Book Guide, Spring 1995, page 45

Publishers Weekly, September 5, 1994, page 109
School Library Journal, September 1994, page 190

Other books by the same author:
Mirette on the High Wire, 1992 (Caldecott Medal)
Speak Up, Blanche!, 1991
Zaza's Big Break, 1989

Other books you might like:
Anita Lobel, *Sven's Bridge*, 1992
    When a king blows up his drawbridge, Sven the watchman is out of work.
Robert Yagelski, *The Day the Lifting Bridge Stuck*, 1992
    The activity of Old Joe's lifting bridge comes to a halt when the busy bridge becomes stuck.

966

EMILY ARNOLD MCCULLY, Author/Illustrator

Grandmas at Bat

(New York: HarperCollins Publishers)

Series: I Can Read
Subject(s): Grandparents; Sports/Baseball; Humor
Age range(s): Grades 1-3
Major character(s): Pip, Child, Baseball Player; Grandma Nan, Grandmother, Coach (substitute); Grandma Sal, Grandmother, Coach (substitute)
Time period(s): 1990s (1993)
Locale(s): United States

Summary: Pip's baseball team has a problem—a sick coach and no chance to play in Saturday's game. When Pip's two grandmothers offer to coach, the team has an even bigger problem—how to keep the feuding grandmothers on the sidelines. On the day of the game, Grandma Nan comes as a cheerleader, Grandma Sal as a clown and together they cheer the team to a come-from-behind victory. (64 pages)

Where it's reviewed:
Booklist, March 1, 1993, page 1240
Horn Book, July 1993, page 452
Horn Book Guide, Fall 1993, page 281
Kirkus Reviews, March 15, 1993, page 374
School Library Journal, June 1993, page 83

Other books by the same author:
Crossing the New Bridge, 1994
The Grandma Mix-Up, 1988
School, 1987

Other books you might like:
Kathryn Cristaldi, *Baseball Ballerina*, 1992
    When her mother forces her to attend ballet classes, a young girl worries about her baseball teammate's reactions.
Jean Little, *Bats about Baseball*, 1995
    Ryder's grandmother is so interested in baseball that attempts at conversation with her are met with responses in baseball lingo. Co-author Claire Mackay.
Peggy Parish, *Play Ball, Amelia Bedelia*, 1972
    In her usual, literal way Amelia decides to learn how to play baseball leading to a humorous game as she misundertands the meaning of baseball terms.

967

EMILY ARNOLD MCCULLY, Author/Illustrator

Little Kit or, the Industrious Flea Circus Girl

(New York: Dial Books for Young Readers, 1995)

Subject(s): Orphans; Poverty; Animals, Treatment of
Age range(s): Grades K-3
Major character(s): Little Kit, Orphan, Abuse Victim; Professor Malefetta, Con Artist; Nell Derry, Child, Friend
Time period(s): 19th century
Locale(s): London, England; Nettlegreen, England

Summary: Little Kit is eager to believe the too-good-to-be-true offer to assist Professor Malefetta and escape her impoverished life in the alley. Soon, Little Kit learns the truth of cruel man's pitch—the "artists" in the novelty act are fleas, the promised bed is a board and a blanket, the meals are crusts and gruel, and the offerred pence is never seen. Truth be told, Little Kit is not all she promised either for Professor Malefetta thinks he's hired a boy. When the traveling flea circus visits the Nettlegreen Fair, Little Kit is left to manage the tent almost all the time and is befriended by Nell Derry who brings her food every day. Kit's actions run afoul of both Professor Malefetta and a vengeful pickpocket, so kind Little Kit runs away (with the fleas) rather than face another beating. As luck would have it she's taken in by Nell's family and never goes hungry again. (32 pages)

Where it's reviewed:
Booklist, January 1, 1995, page 821
Bookwatch, May 7, 1995, page 17
Kirkus Reviews, February 15, 1995, page 228
Publishers Weekly, December 12, 1994, page 62
School Library Journal, October 1995, page 108

Other books by the same author:
The Bobbin Girl, 1996
Mirette on the High Wire, 1992 (Caldecott Medal winner)
The Christmas Gift, 1988

Other books you might like:
Eve Bunting, *Train to Somewhere*, 1996
    In a story based on the Orphan Trains of the 1850s to the 1920s, Marianne travels west with 14 other children hoping to find her mother or, at least, a kind home.
Mary Hastings, *Oliver!*, 1968
    An adaptation of a screenplay based on Dickens' classic novel tells the story of orphan Oliver who is saved from a life of crime by the kind Mr. Brownlow.
Margaret Hillert, *Pinocchio*, 1982
    Retold as a beginning reader, the well-known story of a wooden marionette with a lie-detector nose describes the trials and adventures that lead to his becoming a real boy.

968

EMILY ARNOLD MCCULLY, Author/Illustrator

My Real Family

(New York: Browndeer Press, 1994)

Subject(s): Adoption; Parent and Child; Runaways

Age range(s): Grades K-3
Major character(s): Blanche, Sheep, Adoptee; Sarah, Bear, Runaway; Bruno, Bear, Father
Time period(s): 1990s (1994)
Locale(s): United States

Summary: At the conclusion of the Bear Family Theater's greatest hit production, young Sarah faces one disappointment after another. Not only does her work with props and costumes go unnoticed, but Bruno, her father, announces the adoption of Blanche and her mother gives Sarah's room to the new family member. Deciding that such a lack of concern must mean that these are not her real parents, Sarah runs away to search for her real family. When night falls and she finds herself lost in the woods, Sarah begins to doubt her ideas. Looking for a way home, she finds a campfire surrounded by the family she has left, including Blanche, who all welcome her back to her real family. (32 pages)

Where it's reviewed:
Booklist, April 1, 1994, page 1461
Horn Book, July 1994, page 479
Kirkus Reviews, June 1, 1994, page 777
Publishers Weekly, March 28, 1994, page 96
School Library Journal, June 1994, page 110

Awards the book has won:
School Library Journal Best Books, 1994

Other books by the same author:
Crossing the New Bridge, 1994
Grandmas at Bat, 1993
Mirette on the High Wire, 1992 (Caldecott Medal Winner, 1993)
Speak Up, Blanche!, 1991
The Evil Spell, 1990

Other books you might like:
Beverly Cleary, *Runaway Ralph*, 1981
    Ralph, the mouse, uses a motorcycle as he runs off to seek adventure.
SuAnn Kiser, *The Catspring Somersault Flying One-Handed Flip-Flop*, 1993
    Willy's large family has no time to watch her latest gymnastic trick so she runs away, sure that no one will notice her absence.
Joan Robins, *Addie Runs Away*, 1989
    Once again Addie seeks her own solution, this time by running away.

969

MARC MCCUTCHEON
KATE KIESLER, Illustrator

Grandfather's Christmas Camp

(New York: Clarion Books, 1995)

Subject(s): Christmas; Animals/Dogs; Grandparents
Age range(s): Grades K-3
Major character(s): Mr. Biggins, Dog; Grandfather, Grandfather, Mountain Man; Lizzie, Child
Time period(s): 1990s (1995)
Locale(s): United States (snow-covered mountain)

Summary: When Grandfather's three-legged dog chases a doe up the mountain on Christmas Eve, Lizzie begs to be allowed to help Grandfather fetch him home. With snow falling, the two trudge off on snowshoes, but stop for a campfire dinner and a hastily constructed igloo for their night's rest. In the morning Mr. Biggins has appeared and the threesome rides home on a sled which has magically appeared as a Christmas gift to them all. (32 pages)

Where it's reviewed:
Booklist, September 15, 1995, page 171
Children's Book Review Service, September 1995, page 3
Five Owls, November 1995, page 44
Horn Book Guide, Spring 1996, page 37
School Library Journal, October 1995, page 39

Other books you might like:
J. Patrick Lewis, *The Christmas of the Reddle Moon*, 1994
When Liddy and Will become lost in a snowstorm on Christmas Eve they are rescued by Wee Mary Fever who summons St. Nicholas to carry them safely home.
Laura Ingalls Wilder, *Christmas in the Big Woods*, 1995
An adaptation from *Little House in the Big Woods* describes the simple Christmas celebration of a loving pioneer family.
Susan Wojciechowski, *The Christmas Miracle of Jonathan Toomey*, 1995
A commission to carve the figures for a nativity set transforms embittered woodcarver Jonathan Toomey.

970

GERALD MCDERMOTT, Author/Illustrator

Coyote: A Trickster Tale from the American Southwest

(San Diego: Harcourt Brace & Company, 1994)

Subject(s): Animals/Coyotes; Indians of North America; Legends
Age range(s): Grades K-3
Major character(s): Coyote, Coyote
Time period(s): Indeterminate Past
Locale(s): Southwest

Summary: Coyote has grandiose plans, but a penchant for getting into trouble. So it happens that when blue Coyote seeks to dance and fly just like the crows, he gets his opportunity and also his comeuppance when he refuses to change his rude boastful behavior. Thus, Coyote's attempt to fly flops and because of it his blue fur is the color of dust with a burnt, blackened tail tip. (32 pages)

Where it's reviewed:
Booklist, August 1994, page 2041
Five Owls, September 1994, page 13
Kirkus Reviews, October 15, 1994, page 1411
Publishers Weekly, September 19, 1994, page 70
School Library Journal, November 1994, page 99

Other books by the same author:
Raven: A Trickster Tale from the Pacific Northwest, 1993
Zomo the Rabbit: A Trickster Tale from West Africa, 1992
Arrow to the Sun: A Pueblo Indian Tale, 1974

Other books you might like:
Tom Pohrt, *Coyote Goes Walking*, 1995
Four legends present coyote as a mythical creator, a trickster, and a victim of his own cockiness.
Janet Stevens, *Coyote Steals the Blanket: A Ute Tale*, 1993
Coyote refuses to accept advice from anyone and suffers the consequences.
Harriet Peck Taylor, *Coyote and the Laughing Butterflies*, 1995
When butterflies play a trick on coyote they laugh so hard at their own cleverness that, to this day, they cannot fly straight.

971

GERALD MCDERMOTT, Author/Illustrator

Raven: A Trickster Tale from the Pacific Northwest

(San Diego: Harcourt Brace Jovanovich, Publishers, 1993)

Subject(s): Indians of North America; Legends; Animals/Birds
Age range(s): Grades K-3
Major character(s): Raven, Bird
Time period(s): Indeterminate Past
Locale(s): United States (Pacific Northwest)

Summary: Saddened that the world is in darkness, Raven searches for a way to brighten the earth. When he finds light emanating from a chief's home, he devises a plan to learn the source of the light and to steal it for the benefit of all. (32 pages)

Where it's reviewed:
Booklist, March 1, 1993, page 1227
Horn Book, July 1993, page 470
Publishers Weekly, March 22, 1993, page 79
Reading Teacher, November 1993, page 248
School Library Journal, May 1993, page 100

Awards the book has won:
ALA Notable Book, 1994
Caldecott Honor Book, 1994

Other books by the same author:
Coyote: A Trickster Tale from the American Southwest, 1995
Anansi the Spider: A Tale from the Ashanti, 1987
Arrow to the Sun: A Pueblo Indian Tale, 1974

Other books you might like:
Margaret Hodges, *The Fire Bringer: A Paiute Indian Legend*, 1972
A young Indian boy brings fire to his tribe with help from Coyote.
Gretchen Mayo, *Star Tales: North American Indian Stories about the Stars*, 1987
These Indian legends focus on the stars, moon and night sky.
Gail Robinson, *Raven, the Trickster: Legends of the North American Indians*, 1982
Nine retellings of Raven tales reveal a trickster who is also willing to help those in danger.

972

JOYCE MCDONALD

Comford Creek

(New York: Delacorte Press, 1996)

Subject(s): Fathers and Daughters; Moving, Household; Family Life

Age range(s): Grades 4-7

Major character(s): Quinnella "Quinn" Ellerbee, 11-Year-Old; Pa-Daddy Ellerbee, Unemployed; Ed Earl Murdoch, 11-Year-Old, Artisan (lamp-maker)

Time period(s): 1990s

Locale(s): Comfort Creek, Florida

Summary: When Quinn's father is laid off from the mines, the family moves, taking their house with them. Quinn is already depressed because her mother has left to sing with a group and has not yet been heard from. Now, with the move, Quinn will not get a chance to be on the school newspaper. The family has trouble settling in and battles financial problems at first but then Quinn meets Ed Earl and, with his help, is able to make and sell some lamps made from cypress logs. While Pa-Daddy looks for work, the others settle in with their great-grandmother. Pa-Daddy plans to manage the orange groves and Quinn hopes that she will be able to go to school. They hear from their mother and begin to settle into their new life. (194 pages)

Where it's reviewed:
School Library Journal, November 1996, page 108

Other books by the same author:
Mail-Order Kid, 1988

Other books you might like:
Sheila Greenwald, *My Fabulous New Life*, 1993
Sheila is not happy moving to New York, especially as she sees so much homelessness around her.
Jessie Haas, *Skipping School*, 1992
Phillip has trouble coping with his father's illness as well as the family move to the suburbs.
Phyllis Reynolds Naylor, *Being Danny's Dog*, 1996
Danny does not like the move he must make after the divorce.

973

MEGAN MCDONALD

TED LEWIN, Illustrator

The Great Pumpkin Switch

(New York: Orchard Books, 1992)

Subject(s): Grandparents; Brothers and Sisters; Pumpkins

Age range(s): Grades K-3

Major character(s): Otto, Child, Friend; Grampa, Brother (Rosie's); Rosie, Child, Sister (younger)

Time period(s): 1990s (1992); Indeterminate Past

Locale(s): United States

Summary: With his grandchildren gathered at his feet, Grandpa begins a story from his childhood about Rosie's prize pumpkin. After a storm, as young Grandpa and his friend Otto are removing a fallen tree with the help of a forbidden saw, Grandpa accidently cuts the vine to Rosie's pumpkin and it bounces down the 34 steps in front of the house and smashes to pieces. The boys hide the evidence by feeding it to the neighbor's pig and then hurry off to find the vegetable vendor in order to replace Rosie's pumpkin before she discovers her loss. (32 pages)

Where it's reviewed:
Booklist, September 15, 1992, page 146
Horn Book Guide, Spring 1993, page 38
Kirkus Reviews, July 1, 1992, page 851
Library Talk, September 1992, page 26
School Library Journal, August 1992, page 143

Awards the book has won:
Carolyn W. Field Award, 1993

Other books by the same author:
Insects Are My Life, 1995
The Potato Man, 1991
Is This a House for a Hermit Crab?, 1990 (International Reading Association's Children's Book Award)

Other books you might like:
Steven Kroll, *The Biggest Pumpkin Ever*, 1984
Unaware of the other's plans, two mice work to build an enormous pumpkin.
Elaine Moore, *Grandma's Smile*, 1995
The expression on Kim's jack-o-lantern is inspired by her Grandma's smile.
Laura Ingalls Wilder, *Farmer Boy*, 1933
One chapter of this classic book about growing up on a farm in upstate New York relates Almanzo's efforts to grow a prized pumpkin for the fair.

974

MEGAN MCDONALD

PAUL BRETT JOHNSON, Illustrator

Insects Are My Life

(New York: Orchard Books, 1995)

Subject(s): Animals/Insects; Schools; Family Life

Age range(s): Grades K-3

Major character(s): Amanda Frankenstein, Animal Lover (insects), Child; Victor, Classmate, Bully; Maggie, Classmate, Animal Lover (reptiles)

Time period(s): 1990s (1995)

Locale(s): United States

Summary: Ignoring taunts from her brother, teasing by Victor, and a lack of understanding from her mother, Amanda single-mindedly pursues her interest in insects. She does everything she can to protect them, recites poetry about bugs and opens the windows at night to let the bugs into the house. In an effort to keep Amanda and Victor apart, the teacher moves Amanda next to Maggie and instantly Amanda spots a soulmate, a friend with a similar devotion, not to bugs but to reptiles. (32 pages)

Where it's reviewed:
Booklist, March 1, 1995, page 1249
Horn Book, March 1995, page 185
Kirkus Reviews, March 15, 1995, page 387
Publishers Weekly, January 16, 1995, page 454

School Library Journal, March 1995, page 183

Other books by the same author:
The Great Pumpkin Switch, 1992
The Potato Man, 1991
Is This a House for a Hermit Crab?, 1990

Other books you might like:
Sharon Phillips Denslow, *Woollybear Good-bye*, 1994
    Just prior to Joe Dean's move he helps lead his class to victory in the annual woolleybear contest.
Vivian French, *Spider Watching*, 1995
    Cousins with an interest in arachnids help Helen overcome her fear of spiders in this Read and Wonder series entry which parallels facts with a story.
Betsy James, *Mary Ann*, 1994
    Amy is saddened by the death of a pet praying mantis and surprised when the egg case yields a houseful of baby insects.
Kathryn Lasky, *Pond Year*, 1995
    Best friends enjoy the plant, animal and insect life in and around a pond as it changes with the seasons.
Arnold Lobel, *Grasshopper on the Road*, 1978
    An award-winning entry in the I-Can-Read Series features Grasshopper whose travel disrupts the routine of some inflexible insects.

975

IAN MCEWAN
ANTHONY BROWNE, Illustrator

The Daydreamer
(New York: HarperCollins Publishers, 1994)

Subject(s): Imagination; Family Life; Fantasy
Age range(s): Grades 3-6
Major character(s): Peter Fortune, 10-Year-Old, Daydreamer; Kate Fortune, 7-Year-Old, Sister
Time period(s): 1990s (1994)
Locale(s): England

Summary: Superficially, Peter seems a quiet lad, but in his daydreams he has some fantastic adventures. Unfortunately, while daydreaming, he has gotten off a bus leaving Kate behind or failed to pay attention in class causing problems with his schoolwork. Well-known for his books for adult readers, the author in his first book for children portrays Peter's life in such a way that it is not only Peter who sometimes wonders what is reality and what is imagination. (192 pages)

Where it's reviewed:
Booklist, September 1, 1994, page 43
Children's Book Review Service, November 1994, page 34
Kirkus Reviews, August 15, 1994, page 1133
Publishers Weekly, July 11, 1994, page 79
School Library Journal, October 1994, page 126

Awards the book has won:
Notable Children's Books in the Language Arts, 1995
School Library Journal Best Books, 1994

Other books you might like:
Avi, *Who Was That Masked Man, Anyway?*, 1992
    In an award-winning story, Frankie finds himself with

problems because of the time he spends listening to his favorite radio program.
Edward Eager, *Half-Magic*, 1954
    Finding a coin which is only half magic, the children who use it must learn to phrase their wishes carefully.
Bjarne B. Reuter, *Buster, "The Sheikh of Hope Street"*, 1991
    Usually Buster's imagination leads to trouble, but on the night of the opening performance of the school play it enables him to step into the leading role.

976

SHERYL MCFARLANE
RON LIGHTBURN, Illustrator

Eagle Dreams
(New York: Philomel Books, 1995)

Subject(s): Animals/Birds; Wildlife Rescue; Fathers and Sons
Age range(s): Grades 2-4
Major character(s): Robin, Child, Animal Lover; Unnamed Character, Father, Farmer
Time period(s): 1990s (1994)
Locale(s): Canada

Summary: Robin is a dreamer, unlike his practical father, and when the boy finds an injured eagle, he envisions the day when the bird will fly again. Over his father's protests, the vet is called to treat the eagle. Robin carefully follows the vet's instructions during the bird's lengthy rehabilitation. In time, the eagle is able to return to its mate in the wild and Robin's father develops a new appreciation for his son's ideas. The book was originally published in 1994 in Canada. (32 pages)

Where it's reviewed:
Bookist, May 1, 1995, page 1580
Children's Bookwatch, July 1995, page 7
Horn Book Guide, Fall 1995, page 273
Quill & Quire, September 1994, page 69
School Library Journal, June 1995, page 91

Other books by the same author:
Waiting for the Whales, 1993

Other books you might like:
Byrd Baylor, *Hawk, I'm Your Brother*, 1976
    When a young boy frees a captured hawk, he finally begins to realize his own dream of flying. Caldecott Honor Book, 1977.
Jacqueline Briggs Martin, *Washing the Willow Tree Loon*, 1995
    The rescue, treatment and rehabilitation of an oil-soaked loon is portrayed as a community effort following an oil spill.
Jane B. Mason, *River Day*, 1994
    A serene day on the river with her grandfather seems incomplete until Alex spots a bald eagle.

977

SHERYL MCFARLANE
RON LIGHTBURN, Illustrator

Waiting for the Whales
(New York: Philomel Books, 1993)

Subject(s): Animals/Whales; Grandparents; Death
Age range(s): Grades K-3
Major character(s): Unnamed Character, Aged Person (lonely), Grandfather; Unnamed Character, Child (granddaughter); Unnamed Character, Mother
Time period(s): 1980s; 1990s
Locale(s): British Columbia, Canada

Summary: Living alone in his home overlooking the sea, an elderly man's life has a certain regularity touched with loneliness. When his daughter returns with a child, the old man shares the routines of his life with her, and she learns how to plant the garden, dig for clams, and look for the whales to return each summer. In time her grandfather dies and her mother comforts the child by telling her that grandfather's spirit is with the whales. A first children's book for both author and illustrator originally published in 1991 in Canada. (32 pages)

Where it's reviewed:
Booklist, May 15, 1993, page 1696
Canadian Literature, August 1992, page 164
Children's Book Review Service, June 1993, page 127
Publishers Weekly, March 15, 1993, page 86
School Library Journal, June 1993, page 83

Awards the book has won:
Canadian National Book Award, 1992
Amelia Frances Howard-Gibbons Award, 1992

Other books you might like:
Joseph Bruchac, *Fox Song*, 1993
    Jamie misses seeing Grama Bowman daily, but draws comfort from an Abenaki song which attracts a fox, symbolic of Grama's spirit.
Arnica Esterl, *Okino and the Whales*, 1995
    Awaiting the return of the whales, Takumi sits quietly with his mother listening to her tales of family and the sea.
Dyan Sheldon, *The Whales' Song*, 1990
    Learning from her grandmother about the whales' song, Lilly dreams of hearing it herself.

978

ELOISE JARVIS MCGRAW

The Moorchild
(New York: Margaret K. McElderry Books, 1996)

Subject(s): Fantasy; Fairies; Identity
Age range(s): Grades 4-8
Major character(s): Saaski, Child (changeling); Tam, Orphan, Farmer; Bess, Grandmother, Healer
Time period(s): Indeterminate Past
Locale(s): Europe

Summary: Saaski is born of the folk but is unable to change herself quickly and hide from the humans. She is also the child of a human, so she is placed in a house in lieu of a human child, a changeling. Grandmother, sensing that Saaski is different, advises the mother to put her out but the mother is unable to do this and raises Saaski as her own. The village people know that she is different and blame Saaski for all the bad things that happen. When they determine to get rid of her, Saaski decides to go get the original child, then leave the village on her own terms. This accomplished, she and Tam leave together to find their own place. (241 pages)

Where it's reviewed:
School Library Journal, April 1996, page 136
Bulletin of the Center for Children's Books, June 1996, page 345
Booklist, March 1, 1996, page 1176
Horn Book, September/October 1996, page 598

Awards the book has won:
Newbery Honor Book, 1997
School Library Journal Best Books, 1996

Other books by the same author:
The Tangled Web, 1993
The Money Room, 1991
The Seventeenth Swap, 1986

Other books you might like:
Melvin Burgess, *Burning Issy*, 1995
    Issy discovers she is tied to a pre-Christian culture and goes back for help when she and her aunt are accused of witchcraft.
Grace Chetwin, *Gom on Windy Mountain*, 1986
    Gom knows the language of the animals and thus is one with nature.
Lee Kisling, *The Fool's War*, 1992
    Clemmy is left in charge of the farm when his father dies. Not satisfied to be a farmer, he is involved in saving the land with miracles and magic.
Janet Taylor Lisle, *Forest*, 1993
    The squirrels and the humans interact and fight until Amber and Woodbine combine to save the day.
Ann Turner, *Alfsong*, 1995
    Maddy is visiting grandpa when she spies a cat with a rider and a tiny elf who fears that his family of elves will face danger from the owl.

979

JIM MCGUGAN
MURRAY KIMBER, Illustrator

Josepha: A Prairie Boy's Story
(San Francisco: Chronicle Books, 1994)

Subject(s): Friendship; Frontier and Pioneer Life; Schools
Age range(s): Grades 2-5
Major character(s): Josepha, Teenager, Immigrant; Unnamed Character, Child, Classmate
Time period(s): 1900s
Locale(s): United States (prairie)

Summary: Although Josepha is much older than the story's narrator, the two are classmates in the "primary row" because of Josepha's poor English skills. Frustrated by the unfamiliar language, Josepha ignores his teacher's attempts to convince him to stay and leaves school as soon as he is old enough. Miserable to think of being without his good friend, the young boy offers an appropriate parting gift which will convey the message that words cannot. (32 pages)

Where it's reviewed:
Booklist, October 1, 1994, page 328
Horn Book Guide, Spring 1995, page 45
Publishers Weekly, October 24, 1994, page 62
Quill & Quire, July 1994, page 60
School Library Journal, November 1994, page 84

Other books you might like:
Dorothy Hinshaw Patent, *West by Covered Wagon: Retracing the Pioneer Trails*, 1995
  A nonfiction work describing travel during the mid-1800s in comparison with present-day reenactments of wagon-trains.
Jean Van Leeuwen, *Going West*, 1992
  Seven-year-old Hannah tells the story of her family's journey by covered wagon to the prairie where they build a cabin and try to begin a new life.
David Williams, *Grandma Essie's Covered Wagon*, 1993
  A rich oral history told by the author's grandmother shares the experience of crossing prairies in a covered wagon and attending a one-room schoolhouse.

980

HILARY MCKAY

Dog Friday
(New York: Margaret McElderry Books, 1995)

Subject(s): Animals/Dogs; Friendship; Humor
Age range(s): Grades 4-6
Major character(s): Robin Brogan, 10-Year-Old; Friday, Dog (stray); Mrs. Brogan, Mother, Widow(er)
Time period(s): 1990s (1994)
Locale(s): England (coast of Yorkshire)

Summary: With help from a family with four irrepressible children and an old dog who move in next door to Robin and his mother's bed-and-breakfast, Robin overcomes his fear of dogs and eventually finds and adopts Friday. The ingenuous efforts of the neighbor children to be helpful lead to hilarious events which unexpectedly improve business for Mrs. Brogan. First published in Great Britain in 1994. (133 pages)

Where it's reviewed:
Booklist, November 15, 1995, page 560
Horn Book, January 1996, page 74
Junior Bookshelf, April 1995, page 72
School Librarian, May 1995, page 64
School Library Journal, October 1995, page 136

Awards the book has won:
Booklist Editors' Choice, 1995
School Library Journal Best Books, 1995

Other books by the same author:
The Exiles at Home, 1994 (Smarties Prize Winner)
The Exiles, 1992 (Notable Children's Books in the Language Arts)

Other books you might like:
Betsy Byars, *Wanted. . .Mud Blossom*, 1991
  The unique adventures of the Blossom family continue with the dog, Mud, being accused of responsibility for the disappearance of the class hamster.
Eleanor Estes, *The Moffats*, 1941
  The first of several books about a Connecticut family introduces the four lively children and their equally adventurous friends.
Barbara Robinson, *The Best School Year Ever*, 1994
  The incorrigible Herdmann's return, unchanged, and every class in school not only feels their presence, but also learns something about looking within to find the real person.

981

HILARY MCKAY

The Exiles at Home
(New York: McElderry, 1994)

Subject(s): Sisters; Charity; Humor
Age range(s): Grades 4-6
Major character(s): Ruth Conroy, 13-Year-Old; Joseck, Student
Time period(s): 1990s
Locale(s): England; Africa

Summary: In a burst of Christmas generosity, Ruth pledges ten pounds a month to support the schooling for Joseck, a young boy in Africa. When she discovers that her mother disapproves of this program, she has to secretly beg, borrow, earn or steal the money for her year commitment. By the end of that year, with the help of her three sisters, their grandmother, and even their vicar, everyone has contributed to the cause. Even better, an unexpected inheritance leaves money in trust for Joseck and pays for a trip to Africa for the sisters. (200 pages)

Where it's reviewed:
School Library Journal, March 1995, page 99
Booklist, January 15, 1995, page 925
Center for Children's Books. Bulletin, January 1995, page 172
Voice of Youth Advocates, April 1995, page 24
Horn Book Guide, Spring 1995, page 80

Other books by the same author:
The Exiles, 1992

Other books you might like:
Judie Angell, *Leave the Cooking to Me*, 1990
  Shirley helps a friend's mother with her dinner party and ends up forming Vanessa's Catering.
Kathleen Karr, *Oh, Those Harper Girls! Or Young and Dangerous*, 1992
  Lily and her five sisters try to earn money to help their father save his ranch; unfortunately, all their schemes are illegal.
Tricia Springstubb, *Eunice Gottlieb and the Unwhitewashed Truth about Life*, 1987
  Eunice and Joy set up their own cake-making business to earn some extra money.

982

THOMAS MCKEAN
CHRIS L. DEMAREST, Illustrator

Hooray for Grandma Jo!
(New York: Crown Publishers, Inc., 1994)

Subject(s): Animals/Lions; Grandparents; Humor
Age range(s): Grades K-3
Major character(s): Grandma Jo, Grandmother (nearsighted)
Time period(s): 1990s (1994)
Locale(s): United States

Summary: Grandma Jo is looking forward to a visit from her grandson when she loses her glasses and is unable to read the letter cancelling his trip and the newspaper report of an escaped lion. Unsuspecting, she travels to the train station and grabs the nearest "person" in a coat with a fluffy collar, assuming that it is her grandson. Rather, Grandma Jo has the lion, a potentially dangerous situation that proves helpful later in the evening when a burglar breaks into her home. (32 pages)

Where it's reviewed:
Booklist, August 1994, page 2054
Children's Book Review Service, Spring 1994, page 138
Kirkus Reviews, May 15, 1994, page 703
Publishers Weekly, May 2, 1994, page 307
School Library Journal, May 1994, page 100

Other books you might like:
Babette Cole, *The Trouble with Gran*, 1987
    A grandmother who is literally "out of this world" adds to the excitement of a field trip for school children and senior citizens.
Alison Dexter, *Grandma*, 1993
    Grandma's energetic activity at the beach is exhausting to her granddaughter.
Margaret Wild, *Our Granny*, 1994
    An award-winning look at the many different grannies in the world.

983

COLLEEN O'SHAUGHNESSY MCKENNA

Good Grief. . .Third Grade
(New York: Scholastic, Inc., 1993)

Subject(s): Schools/Catholic Schools; Humor; Behavior
Age range(s): Grades 3-4
Major character(s): Marsha Cessano, 3rd Grader; Roger Friday, 3rd Grader (class troublemaker); Collette Murphy, 3rd Grader (Marsha's friend)
Time period(s): 1990s (1993)
Locale(s): United States

Summary: This is the year that Marsha is determined to change her behavior. She promises herself and her parents that she will have a neat desk and a trouble-free year. Unfortunately, on the first day of school Marsha discovers that troublesome Roger Friday has not moved during the summer and the student teacher has assigned Marsha and Roger to be

classroom buddies! How will Marsha ever survive the year trouble-free now? (151 pages)

Where it's reviewed:
Booklist, September 1, 1993, page 61
Horn Book Guide, Spring 1994, page 80
Kirkus Reviews, July 15, 1993, page 937
School Library Journal, January 1994, page 116

Other books by the same author:
Roger Friday: Live from the Fifth Grade, 1994
Camp Murphy, 1993
Merry Christmas, Miss McConnell, 1991

Other books you might like:
Betsy Duffey, *How to Be Cool in the Third Grade*, 1993
    Robbie's determination to be cool faces the challenge of being assigned as a reading buddy to the class bully.
Charlotte Herman, *Millie Cooper, 3B*, 1985
    Third grade is a time of coping and self-discovery for Millie.
Natalie Honeycutt, *The All New Jonah Twist*, 1986
    This is the year that Jonah Twist is determined to become an attentive and responsible student.

984

COLLEEN O'SHAUGHNESSY MCKENNA

Live from the Fifth Grade
(New York: Scholastic Inc., 1994)

Subject(s): Stealing; Schools; Humor
Age range(s): Grades 3-5
Major character(s): Roger Friday, 5th Grader; Marsha Cessano, 5th Grader; Patrick Frank, 5th Grader, Friend (Roger's)
Time period(s): 1990s (1994)
Locale(s): United States (Sacred Heart Elementary)

Summary: Roger and Marsha have been best enemies since kindergarten. The problem, as Roger sees it, is that he's a natural comedian and Marsha has no sense of humor. Patrick, on the other hand, thinks Roger is so cool that he purposely gets in trouble so he can go to detention with Roger. When the school custodian is accused of stealing school equipment, friends and enemies join together to find the real thief. (148 pages)

Where it's reviewed:
Booklist, November 15, 1994, page 602
Horn Book Guide, Spring 1995, page 80
Library Talk, November 1994, page 43
School Library Journal, October 1994, page 126

Other books by the same author:
Mother Murphy, 1993
Fifth Grade: Here Comes Trouble, 1991
Too Many Murphys, 1988

Other books you might like:
Johanna Hurwitz, *Class Clown*, 1987
    Class clown Lucas learns more appropriate ways of using humor in the classroom.
Gordon Korman, *This Can't Be Happening at MacDonald Hall!*, 1972

Two friends with a love for practical jokes keep life interesting at their boarding school.

Eileen Walsh Strauch, *Hey You, Sister Rose*, 1993

During the course of a trying school year, Arlene and Sister Rose learn to respect one another for being the independent, unconventional individuals they are.

985

ELLEN KINDT MCKENZIE

Under the Bridge

(New York: Holt, 1994)

Subject(s): Brothers and Sisters; Parent and Child
Age range(s): Grades 4-6
Major character(s): Richard "Ritchie" Willis, 5th Grader; Rosemary "Rosie" Willis, Child; Thad Grailowsky, Musician, Neighbor
Time period(s): 1940s
Locale(s): Illinois

Summary: One morning Ritchie awakens and finds his mother's not at home and his father won't tell him anything except that his mother's sick and in the hospital. Luckily Ritchie's teacher talks to him about his mother's nervous breakdown, but neither he nor his sister Rosie receive any support from their taciturn father. Thad, a neighbor, explains what could have happened and begins writing messages for the children from the troll in *The Three Billy Goats Gruff* just as if the troll were living under his bridge. Creating this fantasy for Ritchie and Rosie helps them draw comfort through the dismal months until their mother returns home. (140 pages)

Where it's reviewed:
Publishers Weekly, November 7, 1994, page 79
Booklist, December 1, 1994, page 681
School Library Journal, March 1995, page 206
Horn Book Guide, Spring 1995, page 80
Voice of Youth Advocates, June 1995, page 96

Other books by the same author:
A Bowl of Mischief, 1992
Taash and the Jesters, 1992
Kashka, 1987

Other books you might like:
Harry Mazer, *Someone's Mother Is Missing*, 1990
After Lisa's father dies, and the family realizes he's left them almost penniless, her mother can't cope and simply disappears.
Joan Phipson, *Bianca*, 1988
Teen, Hubert Hamilton, and his sister reunite vulnerable, young Bianca with her mother, who happens to be a patient of their father's.
William Taylor, *Paradise Lane*, 1987
Neighbor Michael Geraghty's friendship helps Rosie Perkins when she's left alone with her father after her mother is hospitalized for alcoholism.

986

PAT MCKISSACK
DENA SCHUTZER, Illustrator

A Million Fish. . .More or Less

(New York: Alfred A. Knopf, 1992)

Subject(s): Fishing; Tall Tales
Age range(s): Grades K-3
Major character(s): Hugh Thomas, Child, Fisherman; Papa-Daddy, Fisherman, Storyteller; Elder Abbajon, Fisherman, Storyteller
Time period(s): 1990s (1992)
Locale(s): Bayou Clapateaux, Louisiana

Summary: The solitude of Hugh Thomas' early morning fishing venture is broken by Papa-Daddy and Elder Abbajon rowing by and swapping tales of the strange happenings on the Bayou Clapateaux. After the tale-tellers row on, Hugh Thomas' experience on the Bayou gives him a chance to share a tall tale of his own. (40 pages)

Where it's reviewed:
Horn Book Guide, Fall 1992, page 239
Booklist, January 1, 1992, page 834
Publishers' Weekly, January 27, 1992, page 97
School Library Journal, March 1992, page 217

Awards the book has won:
Notable Children's Books in the Language Arts, 1993

Other books by the same author:
Nettie Jo's Friends, 1989
Mirandy and Brother Wind, 1988
Tall Phil and Small Bill, 1987
Flossie and the Fox, 1986
It's the Truth, Christopher, 1984

Other books you might like:
Steven Kellogg, *Mike Fink: A Tall Tale*, 1992
Unusual skill, strength, and intelligence mark the legendary Mike Fink from an early age as one who will achieve fame in unexpected ways.
Eric A. Kimmel, *Anansi Goes Fishing*, 1992
Once again the trickster Anansi sets out to get the best of others.
Charles Temple, *Shanty Boat*, 1994
Uncle Sheb's life on an old boat on the Mississippi becomes a legend following his death and burial in the boat in the river.
Tynia Thomassie, *Feliciana Feydra LeRoux: A Cajun Tall Tale*, 1995
Grampa Baby will do anything his favorite grandchild asks, except take her alligator hunting so Feliciana Feydra LeRoux comes up with a plan of her own.

987

BRUCE MCMILLAN, Author/Illustrator

Grandfather's Trolley

(Cambridge, MA: Candlewick Press, 1995)

Subject(s): Transportation; Grandparents; Historical
Age range(s): Grades K-2

Major character(s): Unnamed Character, Child; Grandfather, Grandfather, Driver (trolley motorman)
Time period(s): 1900s
Locale(s): New England

Summary: On a breezy summer day a little girl patiently waits for the trolley to arrive. As he has many times before, Grandfather saves her a seat in the back and she rides all the way to end of line with him. She disembarks to play until Grandfather calls his "number one helper" to assist with the return trip. (32 pages)

Where it's reviewed:
Booklist, October 15, 1995, page 412
Center for Children's Books Bulletin, December 1995, page 133
Children's Book Review Service, January 1996, page 51
Children's Bookwatch, December 1995, page 5
School Library Journal, December 1995, page 86

Other books by the same author:
Going on a Whale Watch, 1992
Eating Fractions, 1991
Counting Wildflowers, 1986

Other books you might like:
Jessie Haas, *Mowing*, 1994
    Nora and Grandpa have a special way of mowing so they do not disturb the wildlife living in the field.
Riki Levinson, *Grandpa's Hotel*, 1995
    A large family gathers at Grandpa's hotel to enjoy good food, fun activities and family togetherness.
Helen V. Griffith, *Grandaddy's Place*, 1991
    Janetta's first impression of Grandaddy's place is enough to send her home on the train, but she stays and learns to understand his chickens, cat and mule, too.

`988`

KATE MCMULLAN
EMMA CHECHESTER-CLARK, Illustrator

Good Night, Stella

(Cambridge, MA: Candlewick Press, 1994)

Subject(s): Bedtime; Imagination; Sleep
Age range(s): Grades K-1
Major character(s): Stella, Child; Dad, Father
Time period(s): 1990s (1994)
Locale(s): United States

Summary: Stella's mom is out for the evening, Dad is babysitting, and Stella's imagination is working overtime. She pesters Dad with so many questions that finally he tries a bit of reverse psychology and asks Stella to wait up for her mother to return so that he can go to bed. Happily, Stella plays with her dolls and stuffed bears offerring them the reassurance and comfort she needs herself. As she inadvertently soothes her own fears, she simply falls asleep. (26 pages)

Where it's reviewed:
Booklist, November 15, 1994, page 612
Children's Book Review Service, March 1995, page 88
Horn Book, November 1994, page 722
Publishers Weekly, November 28, 1994, page 60
School Library Journal, March 1995, page 184

Other books by the same author:
Nutcracker Noel, 1993
The Noisy Giants' Tea Party, 1992

Other books you might like:
Frank B. Edwards, *Melody Mooner Stayed Up All Night!*, 1991
    Melody discovers that staying awake after her family has gone to bed is not as much fun as she'd expected.
Russell Hoban, *Bedtime for Frances*, 1960
    Frances imagines so many scary things in her room that she is unable to sleep.
Penelope Lively, *Good Night, Sleep Tight*, 1994
    All day a little girl cares for her stuffed animals. At bedtime, rather than settling down to sleep, the animals come alive and take the little girl on an adventure.

`989`

KATE MCMULLAN
JIM MCMULLAN, Illustrator

Nutcracker Noel

(New York: HarperCollins, 1993)

Subject(s): Ballet; Dancing; Dreams and Nightmares
Age range(s): Grades K-3
Major character(s): Noel, Child, Dancer; Mia, Child, Dancer; Miss Olga, Teacher (ballet)
Time period(s): 1990s (1993)
Locale(s): United States

Summary: Learning that her dance class will perform *The Nutcracker*, Noel is sure that her dreams of being a ballet dancer have come true. Much to her disappointment, Noel is cast as a tree while obnoxious Mia is a gingerbread cookie. Noel follows Miss Olga's advice to dream of being a tree so that she can really understand her part. At the dress rehearsal, it is Mia who is disappointed when she sees her costume, and Noel, who is an elegant tree. (32 pages)

Where it's reviewed:
Booklist, October 15, 1993, page 454
Five Owls, November 1993, page 43
Horn Book Guide, Spring 1994, page 44
Publishers Weekly, September 20, 1993, page 37
School Library Journal, March 1994, page 204

Other books by the same author:
Good Night, Stella, 1994

Other books you might like:
Melissa Hayden, *The Nutcracker Ballet*, 1992
    The story of the classic ballet is retold in another illustrated version.
Kathryn Lasky, *The Solo*, 1994
    Thinking her friends have excluded her from a dance routine, Grace prepares to perform solo.
Jane O'Connor, *Nina, Nina Ballerina*, 1993
    Prior to her dance performance, Nina worries that her mom will not recognize her on stage.

990

COLIN MCNAUGHTON, Author/Illustrator

Captain Abdul's Pirate School

(Cambridge, MA: Candlewick Press, 1994)

Subject(s): Pirates; Schools; Humor
Age range(s): Grades K-3
Major character(s): Maisie Pickles, Child, Student; Captain Abdul, Pirate
Time period(s): Indeterminate Past
Locale(s): England; West Indies

Summary: Maisie is annoyed when her parents enroll her in Captain Abdul's Pirate School. With other somewhat reluctant students, she attends classes where cheating and bad manners are rewarded. On the evening before Parent's Day, Maisie overhears Captain Abdul plotting with the crew to kidnap the students and hold them for ransom. Outraged, Maisie organizes the other students in a mutiny which leaves Captain Abdul and crew trussed on the quay while the students sail to the West Indies for a more carefree, enjoyable life. (40 pages)

Where it's reviewed:
Booklist, October 15, 1994, page 438
Kirkus Reviews, August 15, 1994, page 1134
Language Arts, February 1995, page 141
Library Talk, January 1995, page 36
School Library Journal, January 1995, page 90

Awards the book has won:
International Reading Association Children's Choices, 1995

Other books by the same author:
Making Friends with Frankenstein: A Book of Monstrous Poems and Pictures, 1994
Who's That Banging on the Ceiling?, 1994
Jolly Roger and the Pirates of Captain Abdul, 1988

Other books you might like:
Allan Ahlberg, *It Was a Dark and Stormy Night*, 1994
    Kidnapped by a band of outlaws, Antonio skillfully crafts a tale which enables him to sneak away.
Pat Hutchins, *One-Eyed Jake*, 1994
    Bravely, the cook, the bo'sun, and the cabin boy escape from evil Jake to lead the peaceful life of their dreams.
Emily Arnold McCully, *The Pirate Queen*, 1995
    The account of the life and adventures of a 16th century pirate, Grania O'Malley, is based on both legend and history.

991

COLIN MCNAUGHTON, Author/Illustrator

Suddenly!

(San Diego: Harcourt Brace & Company, 1995)

Subject(s): Animals/Pigs; Animals/Wolves; Surprises
Age range(s): Grades K-1
Major character(s): Preston, Pig; Unnamed Character, Wolf
Time period(s): Indeterminate
Locale(s): Fictional Country

Summary: Preston cheerfully walks home from school when he suddenly remembers that he was to do some shopping for his mother on the way home. As he abruptly changes direction, a lurking wolf crashes to the sidewalk. The seen-but-not-heard wolf continues to stalk him, but Preston's absentmindedness causes the wolf to have one accident after another. Finally, Preston arrives home with the groceries and the lingering sense that someone has been following him. First published in Great Britain in 1994. (32 pages)

Where it's reviewed:
Booklist, May 15, 1995, page 1652
Guardian Weekly, December 18, 1994, page 28
Junior Bookshelf, December 1994, page 204
Horn Book Guide, Fall 1995, page 273
School Library Journal, June 1995, page 92

Awards the book has won:
Notable Children's Books in the Language Arts, 1995

Other books by the same author:
Boo!, 1996
Here Come the Aliens!, 1995
Captain Abdul's Pirate School, 1994
Walk Rabbit Walk, 1992

Other books you might like:
Stephen Butler, *Henny Penny*, 1991
    As a somewhat confused Henny Penny and her friends hurry to tell the king that the sky is falling they meet a hungry fox with his own plans.
Margaret Walden Froehlich, *That Kookoory!*, 1995
    Rooster Kookoory is so excited about attending today's fair that he doesn't realize he's being followed by a hungry weasel.
Pat Hutchins, *Rosie's Walk*, 1968
    Because she is oblivious to the presence of a fox intent on having her for dinner, Rosie is able to enjoy her walk.

992

FAITH MCNULTY
TED RAND, Illustrator

A Snake in the House

(New York: Scholastic Inc., 1994)

Subject(s): Animals/Reptiles; Nature
Age range(s): Grades K-3
Major character(s): Unnamed Character, Child; Unnamed Character, Snake
Time period(s): 1990s (1994)
Locale(s): United States

Summary: On a spring day a young boy captures a grass snake in a glass jar and hurries home to find a cage in which to keep it. While the boy and his mother search the attic for a cage, the snake escapes from the jar and begins searching for a route back to the pond. For days the snake eludes the boy, the cat, the vacuum cleaner and other household dangers with nothing to eat but an occasional spider, until he hides in a basket which, unexpectedly, becomes the way home. (32 pages)

Where it's reviewed:
Booklist, May 1, 1994, page 1609

Bulletin of the Center for Children's Books, February 1994, page 194

Five Owls, September 1994, page 21

Publishers Weekly, December 6, 1993, page 72

School Library Journal, March 1994, page 204

Awards the book has won:

International Reading Association Children's Book Award 1995

Other books by the same author:

Dancing with Manatees, 1994

With Love from Koko, 1990

The Lady and the Spider, 1986

Other books you might like:

Keith Baker, *Hide and Snake*, 1991

Alert readers will spot the snake hiding on each page of this book.

Libba Moore Gray, *Small Green Snake*, 1994

A sassy, flashy garter snake does not heed his mother's warning and wanders into unexpected danger.

Jill Kastner, *Snake Hunt*, 1993

Inspired by Grandad's storytelling, a young girl follows Grandad into the woods on a snake hunt.

993

DAVID MCPHAIL, Author/Illustrator

Moony B. Finch, the Fastest Draw in the West

(Racine, WI: Artists and Writers, 1994)

Subject(s): Magic; Trains; Fantasy

Age range(s): Grades K-2

Major character(s): Moony B. Finch, Child, Artist; Wild Willie, Outlaw

Time period(s): 1990s (1994)

Locale(s): Ossipee

Summary: Moony B. Finch is so good at drawing that he need only touch his pictures and they come to life. Then, when he is ready to get rid of his animated art work, he begins erasing. His talent works to his advantage when he draws a train, climbs aboard and finds himself looking down the barrel of Wild Willie's gun. With nothing of value to give the outlaw, Moony defends himself with his pencil, eraser, and quick wits. (32 pages)

Where it's reviewed:

Christian Science Monitor, September 16, 1994, page 10

Horn Book Guide, Fall 1994, page 282

School Library Journal, July 1994, page 85

Smithsonian, November 1994, page 34

Other books by the same author:

First Flight, 1991

Snow Lion, 1987

The Train, 1977

Other books you might like:

Judith Heide Gilliland, *Not in the House, Newton!*, 1995

When Newton sees that his new red crayon creates drawings that become real, he quickly hops on his paper airplane and flies out the window.

Crockett Johnson, *Harold and the Purple Crayon*, 1955

Using his magic purple crayon, Harold draws himself into and out of adventure.

Elizabeth MacDonald, *John's Picture*, 1991

The picture John draws comes to life and begins to draw other people and objects.

Chris Van Allsburg, *Bad Day at Riverbend*, 1995

Residents of the town of Riverbend are alarmed when a "greasy slime" begins to cover some of the people, buildings and livestock.

994

DAVID MCPHAIL, Author/Illustrator

Pigs Ahoy!

(New York: Dutton Children's Books, 1995)

Subject(s): Cruise Ships; Animals/Pigs; Stories in Rhyme

Age range(s): Grades K-3

Major character(s): Unnamed Character, Human, Vacationer; Captain Krutch, Sea Captain; Fred, Pig

Time period(s): 1990s (1995)

Locale(s): At Sea

Summary: A solo vacationer enters his assigned cabin on a cruise ship and finds Fred in his bunk with a host of other pajama-clad pigs sharing the space. The pigs' behavior aboard ship attracts Captain Krutch's attention when their antics create such chaos that he has them all expelled from the ship and loaded into a life boat. The remainder of the cruise is a little too quiet, but when the vacationer returns home he finds a life boat in the hall and piggy welcome. (32 pages)

Where it's reviewed:

Booklist, October 1, 1995, page 308

Children's Bookwatch, November 1995, page 7

Kirkus Reviews, September 15, 1995, page 1354

Publishers Weekly, October 2, 1995, page 72

School Library Journal, December 1995, page 86

Other books by the same author:

Pigs Aplenty, Pigs Galore, 1993

Pig Pig Rides Again, 1992

Pig Pig Goes to Camp, 1983

Other books you might like:

Amy Ehrlich, *Parents in the Pigpen, Pigs in the Tub*, 1993

The farm animals move into the house and the family heads for the barn in a humorous reversal of roles.

Colin McNaughton, *Boo!*, 1996

Preston soon learns that no one appreciates his role as the "Masked Avenger" who tiptoes about town scaring people with loud shouts of "Boo!"

Mark Teague, *Pigsty*, 1994

Wendell's room becomes so cluttered that pigs move in and then the mess really begins!

995

DAVID MCPHAIL, Author/Illustrator

Pigs Aplenty, Pigs Galore
(New York: Dutton Children's Books, 1993)

Subject(s): Animals/Pigs; Stories in Rhyme; Humor
Age range(s): Grades K-1
Major character(s): Unnamed Character, Human
Time period(s): 1990s (1993)
Locale(s): United States

Summary: One evening while quietly reading, an unsuspecting man finds himself host to a bevy of uninvited pigs. As more and more pigs arrive leaving him with an enormous pizza bill and a messy house, the man loses his temper and the pigs agree to clean up before they all settle down for a well-deserved night's rest. (32 pages)

Where it's reviewed:
Booklist, April 1, 1993, page 1433
Childhood Education, Winter 1993, page 106
New Advocate, Spring 1994, page 138
Publishers Weekly, May 19, 1993, page 77
School Library Journal, July 1993, page 68

Awards the book has won:
Booklist Editors' Choice, 1993
ALA Notable Book, 1994

Other books by the same author:
Pig Pig Gets a Job, 1990
The Train, 1977
The Bear's Toothache, 1972

Other books you might like:
Amy Ehrlich, *Parents in the Pigpen, Pigs in the Tub*, 1993
    The farm animals move into the house and the family heads for the barn in a humorous reversal of roles.
Cynthia Rylant, *The Relatives Came*, 1985
    A visit from a boisterous, fun-loving group of relatives is recalled in an award-winning, humorous book.
Dr. Seuss, *The Cat in the Hat*, 1956
    An uninvited cat livens up a rainy afternoon for a young brother and sister.

996

DAVID MCPHAIL, Author/Illustrator

Yesterday I Lost a Sneaker (and Found the Great Goob Sick)
(Parsippany, NJ: Silver Press, 1995)

Subject(s): Monsters; Imagination; Food
Age range(s): Grades K-2
Major character(s): Unnamed Character, Child; Great Goob, Monster
Time period(s): Indeterminate Past
Locale(s): United States

Summary: In a reissue of a 1973 title, a young boy hears a moaning sound coming from the neighbor's yard. Climbing over the fence into the forbidden yard, the boy finds the Great Goob very sick and needing carrots from the neighbor's garden to help him feel better. The carrots aren't enough so he also tries peaches and finally grapes. By then the neighbor's dog is chasing the two and, as the boy climbs the fence, the dog yanks off the sneaker. At least, that's the story he tells his mother just before he goes to his room with a stomach ache. (32 pages)

Where it's reviewed:
Horn Book Guide, Fall 1995, page 273
School Library Journal, May 1995, page 87

Other books by the same author:
Ed & Me, 1990
Andrew's Bath, 1984
The Train, 1977

Other books you might like:
Katie Evans, *Hunky Dory Ate It*, 1992
    An insatiable appetite creates problems for puppy Hunky Dory.
Denise Fleming, *Lunch*, 1992
    The tempting goodies on a banquet table attract a mouse who samples everything in sight.
Beatrix Potter, *The Tale of Peter Rabbit*, 1902
    Against his mother's orders Peter visits Mr. McGregor's tempting vegetable garden and comes home with quite a stomach ache.

997

ALICE MEAD

Crossing the Starlight Bridge
(New York: Bradbury Press, 1994)

Subject(s): Indians of North America; Fathers and Daughters; Moving, Household
Age range(s): Grades 3-5
Major character(s): Rayanne Sunipass, 9-Year-Old, Indian (Penobscot); Gram, Grandmother, Storyteller; Mom, Single Mother
Time period(s): 1990s (1994)
Locale(s): Two Rivers Island, Maine; Springbrook, Maine

Summary: Rayanne's ninth birthday is shattered by her father's announcement that he is leaving the family and the island home of the Penobscot to travel west. Several months later, financial hardship forces Rayanne and her mother to also leave the island and move into Gram's apartment on the mainland. In the author's first novel, Gram's good humor and stories of Penobscot tradition help Rayanne face her loss and gain the self-confidence to find herself. (122 pages)

Where it's reviewed:
Booklist, June 1, 1994, page 1811
Children's Book Review Service, July 1994, page 155
Horn Book, September 1994, page 589
Publishers Weekly, April 18, 1994, page 64
School Library Journal, June 1994, page 132

Other books you might like:
Susan Patron, *Maybe Yes, Maybe No, Maybe Maybe*, 1993
    In an award-winning title, middle child PK begrudgingly adjusts to a move to a new apartment with her mother and two sisters.

Bonnie Pryor, *Horses in the Garage*, 1992
> Samantha's adjustment to a stepfather, new home and school is facilitated when she makes a friend who helps her learn to ride a horse.

Ruth Wallace-Brodeur, *The Godmother Tree*, 1992
> After her family's latest move, ten-year-old Laura slowly connects to her surroundings by finding a secret place for herself.

998

ALICE MEAD

Junebug

(New York: Farrar Straus Giroux, 1995)

Subject(s): Single Parent Families; Brothers and Sisters; City Life
Age range(s): Grades 4-6
Major character(s): Reeve ''Junebug'' McClain Jr., 4th Grader, Brother; Tasha McClain, 5-Year-Old, Sister; Mama, Single Mother
Time period(s): 1990s (1995)
Locale(s): New Haven, Connecticut (Auburn Street projects)

Summary: Junebug hopes to skip his tenth birthday this year because any boy in the projects celebrating a tenth birthday becomes a target for rival gangs and drug dealers. Sometimes feeling trapped in a dead-end life, Junebug dreams of sailing his own boat. When Mama is offered a job that includes housing in another part of town, Junebug and Tasha move away from the projects and Junebug is able to make his dream come true. (102 pages)

Where it's reviewed:
Booklist, September 15, 1995, page 164
Children's Book Review Service, September 1995, page 11
Horn Book, March 1996, page 198
Kirkus Reviews, September 1, 1995, page 1284
School Library Journal, November 1995, page 104

Awards the book has won:
Book Links Good Book, 1995

Other books by the same author:
Crossing the Starlight Bridge, 1994

Other books you might like:
Carol Fenner, *Yolanda's Genius*, 1995
> After moving from the inner city to a small community Yolanda must continue to protect her younger brother from drug dealers.

Linda Oatman High, *Maizie*, 1995
> After her mother deserts the family, twelve-year-old Maizie ably cares for her younger sister and her alcoholic father while working to realize her own dreams.

Meredith Sue Willis, *The Secret Super Powers of Marco*, 1994
> Marco's belief that he has super powers helps him to survive a friendship with a hyperactive bully and the dangers of life in the inner city.

999

ALICE MEAD

Walking the Edge

(Morton Grove, IL: Albert Whitman, 1995)

Subject(s): Divorce; Fathers and Sons; Animals/Clams
Age range(s): Grades 5-6
Major character(s): Scott Easton, 13-Year-Old
Time period(s): 1990s
Locale(s): Prescott Harbor, Maine

Summary: Tired of his alcoholic father's abuse, Scott often walks along the cliff edge and leans into the wind, trying to forget the poverty that has followed his parents' divorce. When he has a chance to take part in a 4-H project of raising clams to restock the bay of his coastal village, Scott loves the project and becomes keenly interested in the cycles of bay life. He also tries to help his family by spying on his father's illegal drug-selling activities; luckily Scott doesn't have to go to court to testify against him after the Coast Guard apprehends his father. (190 pages)

Where it's reviewed:
School Library Journal, December 1995, page 106
Horn Book Guide, Spring 1996, page 66

Other books by the same author:
Junebug, 1995
Crossing the Starlight Bridge, 1994

Other books you might like:
Mildred Ames, *Who Will Speak for the Lamb?*, 1989
> Julie is caught in a dilemma when her new friends are animal rights activists and her father is a research scientist.

Jean Craighead George, *The Missing 'Gator of Gumbo Limbo: An Ecological Mystery*, 1992
> A twelve-foot alligator keeps a waterhole in the Everglades pristine pure by eating the polluting algae but nearby condo residents complain.

Welwyn Wilton Katz, *Whalesinger*, 1991
> While on a conservation project on the California coast, Marty is attracted to a mother whale and her sickly calf.

1000

SUSAN MEDDAUGH, Author/Illustrator

Hog-Eye

(Boston: Houghton Mifflin Company, 1995)

Subject(s): Animals/Pigs; Animals/Wolves; Storytelling
Age range(s): Grades K-3
Major character(s): Unnamed Character, Pig (imaginative), Storyteller; Unnamed Character, Wolf
Time period(s): 1990s (1995)
Locale(s): Piggiboro

Summary: In order to explain her absence from school, a little pig tells her family how she takes the wrong school bus and then, realizing she's late for school, gets off and hurries down a short-cut through the woods. Predictably, she is captured by a wolf intent on including her in his dinner plans. When the wolf pulls out a recipe book, the pig discovers that he cannot read, giving the clever pig the opportunity to devise a plan of escape. (32 pages)

Where it's reviewed:
Book Links, January 1996, page 9
Booklist, September 1, 1995, page 88
Horn Book, January 1996, page 67
Publishers Weekly, July 24, 1995, page 63
School Library Journal, October 1995, page 108

Awards the book has won:
Book Links Good Book, 1995
School Library Journal Best Books, 1995

Other books by the same author:
Martha Calling, 1994 (School Library Journal Best Books, 1994; Booklist Editors' Choice, 1994)
Martha Speaks, 1992 (ALA Notable Book, 1993; Notable Children's Books in the Language Arts, 1993)
The Witches' Supermarket, 1991

Other books you might like:
Arnold Lobel, *Mouse Soup*, 1977
    Mouse has a plan that he hopes will keep him out of Weasel's soup pot.
Colin McNaughton, *Suddenly!*, 1995
    A little pig's absentminded walk home from school frustrates the wolf who is stalking him.
Mary Rayner, *Garth Pig and the Ice Cream Lady*, 1978
    When Garth discovers that the ice cream vendor is not what she appears to be, only quick thinking keeps him from becoming the wolf''s next meal.
Tony Ross, *Stone Soup*, 1987
    A hen cleverly avoids becoming a wolf's dinner by offering him a taste of her stone soup.
Gary Soto, *Chato's Kitchen*, 1995
    Cool cat Chato thinks he's in for a delicious meal when he invites his new neighbors to dinner, but the family of mice brings a friend who ruins Chato's appetite.

1001

SUSAN MEDDAUGH, Author/Illustrator

Martha Calling

(Boston: Houghton Mifflin Company, 1994)

Subject(s): Animals/Dogs; Vacations
Age range(s): Grades K-3
Major character(s): Martha, Dog (talking family pet); Helen, Child
Time period(s): 1990s (1994)
Locale(s): United States

Summary: Martha's family is thrilled when the talking dog enters a radio contest and wins a weekend for four at the Come-On-Inn. To circumvent the No-Dogs-Allowed policy, Martha is disguised as Grandma in a wheelchair. Martha's difficulty staying in disguise creates a commotion, but also changes policy. (32 pages)

Where it's reviewed:
Center for Children's Books, Bulletin, September 1994, page 19
Horn Book, November 1994, page 723
Publishers Weekly, August 15, 1994, page 95

School Library Journal, November 1994, page 85

Awards the book has won:
School Library Journal Best Books, 1994

Other books by the same author:
Martha Speaks, 1992
The Witches' Supermarket, 1991
Tree of Birds, 1990
Beast, 1985

Other books you might like:
Lisa Campbell Ernst, *When Bluebell Sang*, 1989
    The fame and fortune of a talented, singing cow turn to hardship and homesickness in the hands of a greedy talent agent.
James Howe, *Hot Fudge*, 1990
    The Monroe family's pets try to solve the mystery of the missing fudge.
Robert Kraus, *Phil the Ventriloquist*, 1989
    Being a ventriloquist never brings Phil much acclaim in his family until the day a burglar breaks into the house.
Emily Arnold McCully, *Speak Up, Blanche!*, 1991
    Shy Blanche finds the right spot with the Farm Theater when she goes behind the scenes and uses her talents as a set designer.
Andrew Sharmat, *Smedge*, 1989
    This family thinks they have one lazy dog for a pet when actually Smedge holds a very important job as adviser to the president.

1002

SUSAN MEDDAUGH, Author/Illustrator

Martha Speaks

(Boston: Houghton Mifflin Company, 1992)

Subject(s): Animals/Dogs; Pets; Family Life
Age range(s): Grades K-3
Major character(s): Martha, Dog
Time period(s): 1990s (1992)
Locale(s): United States

Summary: Until the day she eats a bowl of alphabet soup Martha is just an ordinary family pet. When the letters in the soup go to her brain and not her stomach, Martha begins talking and talking and talking. The novelty of a speaking dog quickly wears off with the family because Martha has not learned the social appropriateness of her comments. In frustration, the family collectively yells "Shut up!" and Martha does, until an emergency gives her the incentive to speak up again. (32 pages)

Where it's reviewed:
Booklist, September 1, 1992, page 54
Five Owls, November 1992, page 33
Horn Book, January 1993, page 76
Publishers Weekly, August 3, 1992, page 71
School Library Journal, November 1992, page 73

Awards the book has won:
ALA Notable Book, 1993
Notable Children's Books in the Language Arts, 1993

Other books by the same author:
The Witches' Supermarket, 1991
Tree of Birds, 1990
Beast, 1985

Other books you might like:
John Burningham, *Courtney*, 1994
  Adopted mongrel Courtney does not have much to say, but the dog is quite a chef!
Thacher Hurd, *Art Dog*, 1996
  Art Dog captures the thieves who have stolen the Mona Woofa from the Dogopolis Museum.
Dav Pilkey, *Dog Breath: The Horrible Trouble with Hally Tosis*, 1994
  Hally Tosis, the dog with the worst breath in the world, finds that her one flaw also brings her fame and security.

| 1003 |

ANGELA SHELF MEDEARIS
NANCY POYDAR, Illustrator

The Adventures of Sugar and Junior
(New York: Holiday House, 1995)

Subject(s): Friendship; Neighbors and Neighborhoods
Age range(s): Grades 2-3
Major character(s): Junior Ramirez, Child (Hispanic-American), Friend; Sugar Johnson, Child (African-American), Friend
Time period(s): 1990s (1995)
Locale(s): United States

Summary: When Sugar moves into the apartment building, Junior is happy to finally have a playmate his age nearby. The two quickly become friends enjoying basketball, baking cookies, movies and ice cream cones together. (32 pages)

Where it's reviewed:
Booklist, October 15, 1995, page 404
Children's Book Review Service, October 1995, page 15
Horn Book Guide, Spring 1996, page 39
School Library Journal, December 1995, page 88

Other books by the same author:
Poppa's New Pants, 1995
Annie's Gifts, 1993
Picking Peas for a Penny, 1990

Other books you might like:
Joyce Champion, *Emily and Alice*, 1993
  In several brief chapters, Emily and Alice become acquainted and learn the joys and challenges of friendship
Juanita Havill, *Jamaica and Brianna*, 1993
  Hand-me-downs and new boots create hurt feelings and problems for friends who soon realize that friendship is most important.
James Howe, *Pinky and Rex*, 1990
  Pinky and Rex begin their friendship in the first book of the series.
Joanna Cole, *The Gator Girls*, 1995
  Best friends Amy and Allie have big plans for summer fun. Co-author Stephanie Calmenson.

| 1004 |

ANGELA SHELF MEDEARIS
JOHN WARD, Illustrator

The Freedom Riddle
(New York: Lodestar Books, 1995)

Subject(s): Folk Tales; African Americans; Slavery
Age range(s): Grades 2-5
Major character(s): Jim, Slave, Foreman; Master Brown, Plantation Owner
Time period(s): 1850s (1850-1851)
Locale(s): Virginia

Summary: In an effort to gain his freedom, Jim wagers Master Brown that, if he stumps him with a riddle, Master Brown will free him. For one year, Jim thinks, plans, and memorizes the clues to the riddle as he fashions it. On Christmas morning, a year after making the wager, Jim is ready. Jim's plan works and, true to his word, Master Brown frees him. An author's note explains the origin of the story. (32 pages)

Where it's reviewed:
Booklist, November 15, 1995, page 556
Horn Book Guide, Spring 1996, page 93
Kirkus Reviews, October 1, 1995, page 1434
School Library Journal, October 1995, page 39

Other books by the same author:
The Singing Man: A West African Folktale, 1994
Annie's Gifts, 1993
Picking Peas for a Penny, 1990

Other books you might like:
Virginia Hamilton, *The People Could Fly: American Black Folk Tales*, 1985
  A collection of 24 folk tales includes a retelling of a slave's achieving freedom by stumping his master with a riddle.
William H. Hooks, *Freedom's Fruit*, 1996
  Mama Marina, an enslaved conjure woman, gains freedom for her daughter and her beloved by using a powerful spell to trick the master.
Deborah Hopkinson, *Sweet Clara and the Freedom Quilt*, 1993
  Using her skills as a seamstress and the information she overhears in the Big House, Clara embroiders a quilt which is a roadmap to freedom for escaping slaves.
Courtni C. Wright, *Journey to Freedom: A Story of the Underground Railroad*, 1994
  Harriet Tubman leads a family of escaping slaves to Canada and freedom.

| 1005 |

ANGELA SHELF MEDEARIS
JOHN WARD, Illustrator

Poppa's New Pants
(New York: Holiday House, 1995)

Subject(s): Family Life; Clothes; Ghosts
Age range(s): Grades K-3
Major character(s): George, Child; Poppa, Grandfather; Grandma Tiny, Grandmother

Time period(s): Indeterminate Past
Locale(s): United States

Summary: While Grandma Tiny prepares for a visit from her mother and sister, George and Poppa go to the general store where Poppa finds a pair of plaid pants for himself. Unfortunately, the pants are much too long and none of the women have the energy to shorten them before church in the morning. During the night, a displaced George cowers on the kitchen floor as one "ghost" after another comes into the moonlit kitchen, making snipping and rocking sounds. In the morning, the mystery of the ghostly visits is solved when Poppa tries on his new pants. (32 pages)

Where it's reviewed:
Booklist, June 1995, page 1788
Five Owls, May 1995, page 105
Horn Book Guide, Fall 1995, page 274
New Advocate, Winter 1996, page 64
School Library Journal, June 1995, page 92

Other books by the same author:
Annie's Gifts, 1995
Our People, 1994
Dancing with the Indians, 1991

Other books you might like:
Sandra Belton, *May'naise Sandwiches & Sunshine Tea*, 1994
    During visits to Big Mama's home, Little Miss enjoys hearing stories about relatives and life when Big Mama was a child.
Margaree King Mitchell, *Uncle Jed's Barbershop*, 1993
    Sarah Jean fondly remembers her Uncle Jed who never lost sight of his dream to open his own barbershop.
Gloria Jean Pinkney, *The Sunday Outing*, 1994
    During weekly visits to the North Philadelphia Station to watch the trains, Ernestine and Great-Aunt Odessa share family stories and dreams for the future.

1006

ANGELA SHELF MEDEARIS
STEFANO VITALE, Illustrator

Too Much Talk

(Cambridge, MA: Candlewick Press, 1995)

Subject(s): Folk Tales; Africa; Fear
Age range(s): Grades K-3
Major character(s): Unnamed Character, Farmer; Unnamed Character, Chieftain
Time period(s): Indeterminate Past
Locale(s): Africa

Summary: As a farmer digs up a yam, the yam complains because the farmer did not water or weed the plant, and is not deserving of the harvest. Alarmed by a talking yam, the farmer runs away, meeting in quick succession a fisherman, a weaver, and a swimmer who agree a yam cannot talk, but are then contradicted by their own product's comments. Seeking advice, they run to the chief who dismisses both the tale and the tale-tellers. However, when the chief's own chair disputes the contention that yam's cannot talk, the chief has heard enough and quickly departs. (32 pages)

Where it's reviewed:
Booklist, January 1, 1996, page 840
Horn Book, November 1995, page 752
Kirkus Reviews, October 1, 1995, page 1434
Publishers Weekly, October 23, 1995, page 67
School Library Journal, December 1995, page 98

Other books by the same author:
Poppa's New Pants, 1995
The Singing Man: A West African Folktale, 1994
Dancing with the Indians, 1991

Other books you might like:
Verna Aardema, *Why Mosquitoes Buzz in People's Ears: A West African Tale*, 1975
    The illustrated retelling of a folk tale about the consequences of a mosquito's lie won the Caldecott Medal.
Mary-Joan Gerson, *Why the Sky Is Far Away: A Nigerian Folktale*, 1992
    Misused by the peasants, the sky responds by moving farther away.
Julius Lester, *How Many Spots Does a Leopard Have?*, 1989
    A retelling of twelve folk tales includes ten of African origin.

1007

LAURA KRAUSS MELMED
ED YOUNG, Illustrator

The First Song Ever Sung

(New York: Lothrop, Lee and Shepard Books, 1993)

Subject(s): Music; Singing; Bedtime
Age range(s): Grades K-1
Major character(s): Unnamed Character, Child (curious)
Time period(s): 1990s (1993)
Locale(s): Japan

Summary: A little boy asks each family member, the dog and even the birds of the air, "What was the first song ever sung?" Each responds from his or her own experience and, of course, each response is different. He asks his mother last and her response closes the book with love as she sings the little boy to sleep. (32 pages)

Where it's reviewed:
Booklist, September 1, 1993, page 69
Children's Book Review Service, June 1993, page 123
Horn Book Guide, Spring 1994, page 45
Language Arts, January 1994, page 54
School Library Journal, June 1993, page 84

Other books by the same author:
Prince Nautilus, 1994
I Love You as Much. . ., 1993
The Rainbabies, 1992

Other books you might like:
Margaret Wise Brown, *Little Donkey Close Your Eyes*, 1995
    Animals throughout the world are bid good night in this gentle poem.
Mem Fox, *Time for Bed*, 1993
    One by one mothers put their babies to bed until all are asleep.

Elizabeth Lee O'Donnell, *Sing Me a Window*, 1993
  A young girl requests a bedtime song that details the day's activities with her father.

1008

LAURA KRAUSS MELMED
HENRI SORENSEN, Illustrator

Prince Nautilus

(New York: Lothrop, Lee & Shepard Books, 1994)

Subject(s): Fairy Tale; Sisters; Princes and Princesses
Age range(s): Grades 1-4
Major character(s): Fiona, Sister (kind); Columbine, Sister (selfish); Prince Nautilus, Royalty (prince), Prisoner
Time period(s): Indeterminate Past
Locale(s): Fictional Country (seacoast)

Summary: Kindly Fiona selflessly cares for her beautiful but selfish sister and widowed father. When her daily work is completed, Fiona walks the beach, one day finding a shell that speaks. Imprisoned within the shell is Prince Nautilus, the victim of a sorcerer. Fiona shares her discovery with Columbine and, together, the sisters follow the Prince's instructions in hopes of freeing him from the evil spell. Fiona's kindness to animals that cross the sisters' path is repaid when they encounter difficulty along the way. When the sisters succeed in breaking the sorcerer's spell, the Prince asks for Fiona's hand in marriage and Columbine, true to character, sneaks away with a stolen bag of gold. (32 pages)

Where it's reviewed:
Booklist, November 15, 1994, page 613
Children's Bookwatch, January 1995, page 6
Horn Book Guide, Spring 1995, page 47
Publishers Weekly, July 4, 1994, page 63
School Library Journal, October 1994, page 94

Other books by the same author:
The First Song Ever Sung, 1993
I Love You as Much..., 1993
The Rainbabies, 1992

Other books you might like:
Hans Christian Andersen, *Twelve Tales*, 1994
  The collection of Andersen's classic fairy tales is selected, translated and illustrated by Erik Blegvad.
Fiona Moodie, *The Boy and the Giants*, 1993
  A kind-hearted fisherboy rescues his beloved Kate from giants.
Charles Perrault, *Cinderella*, 1985
  A retelling by Amy Ehrlich of the classic story of a gentle girl who, though mistreated by her stepsisters, wins the Prince's heart.
Jane Yolen, *The Girl in the Golden Bower*, 1994
  With help from her animal friends, Aurea is able to outwit a sorceress determined to steal her magic comb.

1009

INGRID MENNEN
NIKI DALY, Illustrator

One Round Moon and a Star for Me

(New York: Orchard Books, 1994)

Subject(s): Babies; Birth; Fathers and Sons
Age range(s): Grades K-2
Major character(s): Unnamed Character, Child; Papa, Father
Time period(s): 1990s (1994)
Locale(s): Lesotho, South Africa (rural countryside)

Summary: A young boy celebrates the birth of his younger brother by placing the traditional stalks of grass above the door to announce the birth. Relatives come to assist and to admire the infant as the young child begins to wonder about his own place in the family. Hearing Papa say, "I am the baby's father," he asks if Papa is also his father. Papa reassures him and at nightfall shows him the round moon and a falling star in the sky just for his first-born son. (32 pages)

Where it's reviewed:
Booklist, February 15, 1994, page 1093
Kirkus Reviews, March 15, 1994, page 400
Library Talk, May 1994, page 14
Publishers Weekly, January 3, 1994, page 80
School Library Journal, September 1994, page 190

Other books by the same author:
Somewhere in Africa, 1992 (Co-author Niki Daly)

Other books you might like:
Denys Cazet, *Dancing*, 1995
  Dad joins disgruntled Alex and sings a song about the moon sharing the sky with the stars to assure Alex that the family has love enough for both children.
Deborah M. Newton Chocolate, *On the Day I Was Born*, 1995
  All the relatives gather to celebrate the birth of a baby as the father holds him up to the moon and others present gifts of kente cloth or a kofia.
Trish Cooke, *So Much*, 1994
  The relatives are gathering for a surprise party for a baby's father, but first they must hug, squeeze and kiss the baby because they love him "SO MUCH!"

1010

MELISSA MILICH
TYRONE GETER, Illustrator

Can't Scare Me!

(New York: Doubleday Book for Young Readers, 1995)

Subject(s): Ghosts; Fear; Storytelling
Age range(s): Grades 1-3
Major character(s): Mr. Munroe, Neighbor (fearful); Mr. Hayman, Father, Storyteller; Eugenia Hayman, Child
Time period(s): Indeterminate Past
Locale(s): United States

Summary: Nightly, while Eugenia and her sister play on the porch, they listen to stories their father tells to Mr. Munroe. The rhythm of the porch rockers varies with the drama of the story but, inevitably, the ghost stories strike such fear in Mr.

Munroe that he is unable to walk home alone. Although brave Eugenia enjoys walking Mr. Munroe home and skipping alone back to her own house, Mr. Hayman decides to spin a special tale designed to cure Mr. Munroe of his fear of ghosts. (32 pages)

Where it's reviewed:
Booklist, January 1, 1995, page 826
Children's Book Review Service, April 1995, page 104
Kirkus Reviews, February 15, 1995, page 229
Publishers Weekly, December 19, 1994, page 54
School Library Journal, April 1995, page 113

Other books you might like:
Sandra Belton, *From Miss Ida's Front Porch*, 1993
 Miss Ida's front porch is the gathering spot for neighborhood "rememberings" that entrance the children, but scare no one.
Marjorie Weinman Sharmat, *Two Ghosts on a Bench*, 1982
 When two ghosts become bored with haunting their bench, they relax by telling stories about previous happenings at the bench.
Eleanora E. Tate, *Front Porch Stories at the One-Room School*, 1992
 Listening to Margie's father tell stories about their small Missouri town entertains Margie and her younger cousin.

1011

JUDI MILLER

My Crazy Cousin Courtney
(New York: Pocket/Minstrel, 1993)

Subject(s): Cousins; Friendship; Divorce
Age range(s): Grades 6-7
Major character(s): Cathy Bushwick, 7th Grader; Courtney Alicia Green, 7th Grader, Cousin
Time period(s): 1990s
Locale(s): New York, New York

Summary: Though Cathy and Courtney are cousins, they have not seen one another since they were five years old and could not be any more different. When Cathy goes to the airport to pick up Courtney for her summer visit, she sees a young girl wearing a bright pink T-shirt that says "Kiss Me Quick." Cathy suddenly finds her orderly life is turned upside-down as the girls are locked in Tiffany's after hours, Courtney leaps into a pool at the aquarium and they become involved with the police after witnessing what they think is a murder. Suddenly the summer ends too quickly and Cathy realizes she and Courtney are more alike than she thought. (134 pages)

Where it's reviewed:
Booklist, March 1, 1993, page 1230
Publishers Weekly, February 8, 1993, page 87
Children's Bookwatch, April 1994, page 4

Other books by the same author:
My Crazy Cousin Courtney Comes Back, 1994
Cry in the Night, 1990
Ghost a La Mode, 1989

Other books you might like:
Caroline B. Cooney, *Family Reunion*, 1989
 A summer trip to visit her "perfect" cousins proves to

Shelley that life in a small town, like life in her cousins' family, is less than perfect.
Linda Crew, *Someday I'll Laugh about This*, 1990
 Shelby's long-awaited summer trip to the family cottage turns into a disaster when she realizes her cousin, Kirsten, has a boyfriend.
Willo Davis Roberts, *What Could Go Wrong?*, 1989
 Gracie knows that a flight to anywhere can go awry with her cousin Charlie along; sure enough, they are chased around the airport by criminals.

1012

M.L. MILLER
KEVIN HAWKES, Illustrator

The Enormous Snore
(New York: G.P. Putnam's Sons, 1995)

Subject(s): Sleep; Kings, Queens, Rulers, etc.; Problem Solving
Age range(s): Grades K-3
Major character(s): Letty, Child
Time period(s): Indeterminate Past
Locale(s): Fictional Country

Summary: While travelling during a storm, poor Letty is separated from her family. As Letty searches for her parents, she discovers the source of a loud sound emanating from the castle and is instrumental in bringing peaceful slumber to the kingdom. Inadvertently, her efforts also reunite her with her family. (32 pages)

Where it's reviewed:
Booklist, December 1, 1995, page 641
Horn Book Guide, Fall 1996, page 268
Kirkus Reviews, August 15, 1995, page 1191
Publishers Weekly, August 28, 1995, page 113
School Library Journal, January 1996, page 90

Other books by the same author:
Those Bottles!, 1994
Dizzy from Fools, 1991

Other books you might like:
Charles C. Black, *The Royal Nap*, 1995
 King Gordo's daily nap requires absolute silence throughout the kingdom!
Angela McAllister, *The King Who Sneezed*, 1988
 King Parsimonious is too mean and stingy to care about his subjects' comfort, so his efforts to learn why the castle is so cold seem puzzling.
Mwalimu, *Awful Aardvark*, 1989
 Because aardvark snores so loudly all night long, the other animals are unable to sleep.

1013

MARY JANE MILLER

Fast Forward
(New York: Viking, 1993)

Subject(s): Friendship; Conduct of Life; Schools/Junior High School

Age range(s): Grades 4-7
Major character(s): Kayla Ann Redmond, 11-Year-Old, Friend (Margy's); Margy McKenna, 11-Year-Old, Friend (moving away)
Time period(s): 1990s (1993)
Locale(s): Elmpark, Illinois; Chicago, Illinois

Summary: A summer of pre-junior high jitters becomes one of life's major setbacks when Kayla's best friend moves to Chicago. Nothing is the same and Kayla wants to fast forward to a time when she and Margy can be together again with nothing changed. When their weekend visit arrives, Kayla finds that Margy has a new friend and the girls must find a way to have a long-distance friendship. Kayla's mixed-up feelings are reflected in poor grades and a desperate attempt to avoid failing science by cheating on a project. Eventually, both girls begin to find themselves, sort out their confusing emotions, and learn some independence. (216 pages)

Where it's reviewed:
Booklist, July 1993, page 1967
Horn Book Guide, Spring 1994, page 80
Library Talk, March 1994, page 47
Publishers Weekly, July 5, 1993, page 74
School Library Journal, August 1993, page 164

Other books by the same author:
Going the Distance, 1994
Upside Down, 1992
Me and My Name, 1990

Other books you might like:
C.S. Adler, *Always and Forever Friends*, 1990
When her best friend Meg moves away Wendy struggles to make new friends.
Johanna Hurwitz, *Tough-Luck Karen*, 1982
Her siblings adjust to the family's move, but Karen finds her grades slipping.
Phyllis Reynolds Naylor, *Josie's Troubles*, 1992
Josie learns that a friendship can be strong enough to include others.

`1014`

MARY JANE MILLER

Going the Distance

(New York: Viking, 1994)

Subject(s): Moving, Household; Sports/Swimming; Artists and Art
Age range(s): Grades 5-6
Major character(s): Loren Monroe, 6th Grader; Cornelia "Nelia" Monroe, Grandmother, Writer (mysteries)
Time period(s): 1990s
Locale(s): Los Olas, Florida; Chicago, Illinois

Summary: Loren's had it! Everytime she settles into a new home and a new school, a few months later her parents pack up and move again. Now they're going to Europe for a few months to see one of her mother's paintings, *Loren in the Garden*, exhibited beside her grandfather's works, and Loren doesn't want to go along. She doesn't have to, but she doesn't get to stay in Florida either. Instead, she moves to Chicago and lives with her grandmother Nelia. There she goes out for

the swim team, has controversy about her long hair and tries to make her parents understand that she's growing up. (151 pages)

Where it's reviewed:
Book Report, March 1995, page 39
Publishers Weekly, September 19, 1994, page 71
Children's Book Review Service, January 1995, page 58
Center for Children's Books. Bulletin, December 1994, page 140
Horn Book Guide, Spring 1995, page 81

Other books by the same author:
Fast Forward, 1993
Upside Down, 1992
Me and My Name, 1990

Other books you might like:
Brock Cole, *Celine*, 1989
Sixteen-year-old Celina adjusts to life with a stepmother while her father lectures in Europe.
Libby Gleeson, *Eleanor, Elizabeth*, 1990
Eleanor resents moving to her mother's childhood home and dreads her first day of school.
Sheri Cooper Sinykin, *Next Thing to Strangers*, 1991
Two prickly teenagers meet when they're each visiting grandparents at a retirement trailer park.

`1015`

SARA SWAN MILLER
TRUE KELLEY, Illustrator

Three Stories You Can Read to Your Dog

(Boston: Houghton Mifflin Company, 1995)

Subject(s): Animals/Dogs; Pets; Humor
Age range(s): Grades 1-3
Major character(s): Unnamed Character, Dog
Time period(s): 1990s (1995)
Locale(s): United States

Summary: Three short stories tell of a typical dog's adventures such as digging holes in the yard to find a bone or barking when a "burglar" knocks at the door. Each escapade so exhausts the dog that he curls up and sleeps until the next story begins. (42 pages)

Where it's reviewed:
Booklist, April 15, 1995, page 1500
Christian Science Monitor, March 30, 1995, page B3
Language Arts, September 1995, page 369
Publishers Weekly, February 20, 1995, page 206
School Library Journal, April 1995, page 113

Other books you might like:
Joanna Cole, *Give a Dog a Bone: Stories, Poems, Jokes, and Riddles about Dogs*, 1996
With co-compiler Stephanie Calmenson, Cole has gathered stories, jokes, poems, and some true facts to entertain dog lovers.
David Milgrim, *Why Benny Barks*, 1994
A child offers a variety of reasons to explain why his dog Benny barks.

Cynthia Rylant, *The Henry and Mudge Series*, 1987-
The adventures of Henry and his lovable, slobbery dog Mudge continue to entertain beginning readers.

Maggie Smith, *Argo, You Lucky Dog*, 1994
While his owners are out-of-town, Argo uses the proceeds from a winning lottery ticket to make some doggone fine improvements to their home.

Alan Snow, *How Dogs Really Work!*, 1993
A humorous "instruction" manual explains all about dogs and their owners.

1016

CLAUDIA MILLS

Dinah in Love

(New York: Macmillan, 1993)

Subject(s): Schools; Interpersonal Relations; Dating (Social Customs)
Age range(s): Grades 6-7
Major character(s): Dinah Seabrooke, 12-Year-Old; Nick Tribble, 12-Year-Old
Time period(s): 1990s
Locale(s): Riverdale

Summary: Attention-seeking Dinah is at it again; this time she's chair of the publicity committee for the Sadie Hawkins sock hop. Though she's great at selecting mismatched socks to wear, she's not great at selecting a boy to invite. Her friends suggest she invite her debate opponent Nick, but she knows she doesn't want to invite the boy who threw a pink exercise bra over her head when she was a living mannequin. Gradually Nick's antics reveal his desire to have Dinah notice him and in a surprising turn of events, Dinah realizes that maybe Nick's not so bad after all. (143 pages)

Where it's reviewed:
School Library Journal, December 1993, page 114
Voice of Youth Advocates, April 1994, page 29
Horn Book, March 1994, page 225
Booklist, November 15, 1993, page 626
Library Talk, March 1994, page 46

Other books by the same author:
Dinah Forever, 1995
Dynamite Dinah, 1990
Boardwalk with Hotel, 1986
The One and Only Cynthia Jane Thornton, 1986
What about Annie?, 1985

Other books you might like:
Betsy Byars, *Bingo Brown, Gypsy Lover*, 1990
Bingo has to adjust to a new baby and the difficult task of buying his long-distance girlfriend a Christmas present.

Lynn Hall, *Dagmar Schultz and the Green-Eyed Monster*, 1991
Dagmar succumbs to the "green-eyed monster" of jealousy when blonde Ashley moves to town and steals Dagmar's boyfriend from her.

Phyllis Reynolds Naylor, *All but Alice*, 1992
Alice gives up popularity when she realizes it means giving up her good friend Patrick.

1017

CLAUDIA MILLS

The Secret Life of Bethany Barrett

(New York: Macmillan Publishing Company, 1994)

Subject(s): Mothers and Daughters; Brothers and Sisters; Schools
Age range(s): Grades 4-6
Major character(s): Bethany Barrett, 6th Grader; Jane Owen, 6th Grader, Friend (Bethany's); Brandon Barrett, 3-Year-Old (shy), Brother
Time period(s): 1990s (1994)
Locale(s): Pinevale, Colorado

Summary: Middle-child Bethany seems to have inherited her mother's tendency to worry. To spare her mother more anxiety Bethany hides from her the fact that her best friend is really quiet Jane, someone her mother considers a bad influence for a slight incident at a birthday party years ago. Out of concern for Brandon's delayed speech development and her mother's worries, Bethany decides to enlist Jane's help in her quest to become a "genius" and solve her own and her family's problems. (163 pages)

Where it's reviewed:
Booklist, January 1, 1995, page 821
Bulletin of the Center for Children's Books, January 1995, page 173
Horn Book Guide, Spring 1995, page 81
School Library Journal, February 1995, page 99

Other books by the same author:
Dinah for President, 1992
Hannah on Her Way, 1991
After Fifth Grade, 1989

Other books you might like:
C.S. Adler, *Always and Forever Friends*, 1988
When Meg moves away, Wendy discovers that finding another special friend is not easy.

Gayle Rogers Lockwood, *Libbie Sims, Worry Wart*, 1993
In an attempt to eliminate one of the many worries in her life, Libbie and her friends collaborate on a plan which gets attention.

Phyllis Reynolds Naylor, *The Agony of Alice*, 1985
Motherless Alice worries about an appropriate female role model, finding one and some needed insight in an unexpected person.

Katherine Paterson, *Flip-Flop Girl*, 1994
After her father's death, Vinnie's family moves, her younger brother stops talking, and her mother is so busy working that Vinnie must find her own solutions to problems.

Susan Beth Pfeffer, *What Do You Do When Your Mouth Won't Open?*, 1981
The excitement of winning a school essay contest is short-lived for Reesa when she learns she must present the essay to a large audience.

`1018`

LAUREN MILLS
DENNIS NOLAN, Illustrator
LAUREN MILLS, Illustrator

Fairy Wings

(Boston: Little, Brown and Company, 1995)

Subject(s): Fairy Tale; Fairies; Prejudice
Age range(s): Grades 1-4
Major character(s): Fia, Mythical Creature (fairy), Heroine; Kip, Mythical Creature (fairy), Royalty; Troll, Mythical Creature (fairy)
Time period(s): Indeterminate Past
Locale(s): Fictional Country

Summary: Ostracized by her own sisters because she is a wingless fairy, Fia contents herself with woodland animal friends and constructing alternative forms of transportation. Kip invites her to the May Dance and sends a special chair for her, but Fia leaves in disgrace when his parents, the King and Queen, notice she has no wings. Her lack of wings and kindness to others proves to be an advantage when the wicked Troll kidnaps all the fairies from the dance and Fia uses her resources to rescue them. (32 pages)

Where it's reviewed:
Booklist, November 1, 1995, page 478
Children's Book Watch, November 1995, page 8
Kirkus Reviews, October 15, 1995, page 1498
Publishers Weekly, November 6, 1995, page 94
School Library Journal, January 1996, page 90

Awards the book has won:
Golden Kite Award, Illustration, 1996

Other books by the same author:
Tatterhood and the Hobgoblins, 1993
The Rag Coat, 1991

Other books you might like:
Hans Christian Andersen, *Thumbelina*, 1990
   In this retelling by Deborah Hautzig the kindly Thumbelina is transported, by a swallow whom she saved, from freezing to a warm garden where she reigns as queen.
Emma Bull, *The Princess and the Lord of Night*, 1994
   On her thirteenth birthday a princess born under a curse takes the initiative to free herself forever.
Susan L. Roth, *Brave Martha and the Dragon*, 1996
   Martha is not frightened of the dragon threatening a small French village. She simply captures him, throws him in the dungeon, and brings peace to the town.

`1019`

LINDA BREINER MILSTEIN
SUSAN MEDDAUGH, Illustrator

Amanda's Perfect Hair

(New York: Tambourine Books, 1993)

Subject(s): Individuality; Independence; Self-Acceptance
Age range(s): Grades K-2
Major character(s): Amanda, Child
Time period(s): 1990s (1993)

Locale(s): United States

Summary: Amanda is the only person who thinks her head of curly, blond hair is less than perfect. Tired of her friends playing with her hair or comparing it to waterfalls or pythons, Amanda decides to remedy the situation by giving herself a haircut. Now, she hopes people will notice her and not her hair. (32 pages)

Where it's reviewed:
Booklist, November 1, 1993, page 531
Horn Book, September 1993, page 589
Horn Book Guide, Spring 1994, page 45
Publishers Weekly, August 2, 1993, page 79
School Library Journal, January 1994, page 95

Other books by the same author:
Coconut Mon, 1995
Miami-Nanny Stories, 1994
Grandma's Jewelry Box, 1992

Other books you might like:
Nancy Cote, *Palm Trees*, 1993
   A bad hair day threatens a friendship until two girls decide to make the most of it.
Catherine Friend, *My Head Is Full of Colors*, 1994
   This young girl's many interests are expressed through unusual changes in her hair.
Susan Garrison, *How Emily Blair Got Her Fabulous Hair*, 1995
   Emily enjoys styling friend Pamela's curly locks while desperately seeking a remedy for her own straight hair.

`1020`

JOHN A. MINAHAN
ROBERT QUACKENBUSH, Illustrator

Abigail's Drum

(New York: Pippin Press, 1995)

Subject(s): War of 1812; Lighthouses; Historical
Age range(s): Grades 3-5
Major character(s): Rebecca Bates, 11-Year-Old, Heroine; Abigail Bates, 8-Year-Old, Heroine; Simeon Bates, Father, Lighthouse Keeper
Time period(s): 1810s (1812)
Locale(s): Scituate, Massachusetts

Summary: While Rebecca dutifully completes her chores and helps her father tend the lighthouse, she also takes time to practice her fife as Abigail plays a colonial rhythm on her drum. The girls' musical efforts pay off the night a boatload of British soldiers lands at Cedar Point and takes Simeon Bates hostage. Rebecca runs away from her would-be captors and finds Abigail. The two of them play a military march on their fife and drum which scares the British into believing the army is returning. A historical note to the author's first book indicates that his story is based on a true incident. (64 pages)

Where it's reviewed:
Booklist, February 16, 1996, page 1022
Bulletin of the Center for Children's Books, February 1996, page 197
Horn Book Guide, Fall 1996, page 295
School Library Journal, February 1996, page 102

Other books you might like:

Patricia Lee Gauch, *This Time, Tempe Wick?*, 1974
During the Revolutionary War, the determination of Temperance Wick saves her family's horse from a soldier intent on stealing it.

Doreen Rappaport, *The Boston Coffee Party*, 1988
Based on an actual incident during the Revolutionary War, a group of women forces a greedy merchant to relinquish the coffee he's been hiding.

Gloria Whelan, *Once on This Island*, 1995
With her older siblings, 12-year-old Mary works to maintain the family farm on Mackinac Island while their father fights against the British during the War of 1812.

1021

BARBARA MITCHELL
JOHN SANDFORD, Illustrator

Down Buttermilk Lane

(New York: Lothrop, Lee & Shepard Books, 1993)

Subject(s): Amish; Family Life; Farm Life
Age range(s): Grades K-3
Major character(s): Mam, Mother (Old Order Amish); Dat, Father (Old Order Amish), Farmer
Time period(s): 1990s (1993)
Locale(s): Lancaster, Pennsylvania

Summary: A style of life that could be from an earlier century is presented through the day's activities of Mam, Dat and children travelling, by horse and buggy of course, to town for supplies and dinner at the grandparents' home. Set on a sunny autumn day, the serene pictures and simple text communicate as much understanding of the Old Order Amish as the words of the text. (32 pages)

Where it's reviewed:
Booklist, October 1, 1993, page 353
Children's Book Review Service, Winter 1994, page 68
Horn Book, November 1993, page 736
Quill & Quire, February 1994, page 40
School Library Journal, November 1993, page 87

Other books by the same author:
Hush, Puppies, 1983

Other books you might like:
Thomas Locker, *Family Farm*, 1988
The hard work and financial uncertainty of farm life is depicted by a family which begins growing pumpkins and flowers to sell.

Patricia Polacco, *Just Plain Fancy*, 1990
When Naomi finds an unusual egg which hatches into a peacock she is concerned that the bird may violate her simple Amish lifestyle.

Alice Provenson, *Town & Country*, 1984
A nonfiction story comparing life in a town with life on a farm near a village. Co-author Martin Provenson.

Mary Lyn Ray, *Shaker Boy*, 1994
Caleb learns to appreciate the order and simplicity of the Shaker community in which he lives.

1022

MARGAREE KING MITCHELL
JAMES E. RANSOME, Illustrator

Uncle Jed's Barbershop

(New York: Simon & Schuster Books for Young Readers, 1993)

Subject(s): Aunts and Uncles; African Americans; Segregation
Age range(s): Grades K-3
Major character(s): Jedediah "Jed" Johnson, Uncle, Worker (barber); Sarah Jean, Niece
Time period(s): 20th century
Locale(s): United States (rural South)

Summary: In the still-segregated South, Sarah Jean's Uncle Jed is the only black barber in the county. By horseback, he travels to all the farms and homes plying his trade, but saving and dreaming for the day when he will have his own barbershop. Over the years his savings are depleted by Sarah Jane's operation and the failure of banks during the Depression. Uncle Jed perseveres and when he is 79 years old he finally realizes his dream. This is the first children's book by the author. (32 pages)

Where it's reviewed:
Booklist, March 15, 1994, page 135
Horn Book, November 1993, page 737
Library Talk, March 1994, page 31
Publishers Weekly, August 2, 1993, page 78
School Library Journal, October 1993, page 105

Awards the book has won:
ALA Notable Book, 1993
Coretta Scott King Honor Book, 1993

Other books you might like:
Gwendolyn Battle-Lavert, *The Barber's Cutting Edge*, 1994
Rashaad visits Mr. Bigalow, the proprietor of a barber shop that is also a local gathering spot.

Libba Moore Gray, *Dear Willie Rudd*, 1993
In a letter to a now-deceased housekeeper, an elderly woman reminisces about the family's treatment of her in the Southern society of 50 years ago.

Mary Hoffman, *Amazing Grace*, 1991
With support from her family and belief in herself, Grace learns that she can realize her dreams.

1023

RITA PHILLIPS MITCHELL
CAROLINE BINCH, Illustrator

Hue Boy

(New York: Dial Books for Young Readers, 1993)

Subject(s): Growing Up; Islands; Family Life
Age range(s): Grades K-3
Major character(s): Hue Boy, Child (very small for his age)
Time period(s): 1990s (1993)
Locale(s): Belize (Caribbean coastal community)

Summary: As the smallest child in his class, Hue Boy is subject to teasing from his classmates, the concern of his family and the remedies offered by the village healer. Nothing works to make Hue Boy grow any taller. Then his daddy's ship returns and Hue Boy is so happy to see his father that he feels taller. First book by the author. (32 pages)

Where it's reviewed:
Booklist, May 1, 1993, page 1605
Horn Book Guide, Fall 1993, page 269
Reading Teacher, April 1994, page 562
Publisher's Weekly, May 24, 2993, page 85
School Library Journal, December 1993, page 91

Other books you might like:
Steven Kellogg, *Much Bigger than Martin*, 1976
    Henry tries to compensate for his brother's larger size.
Ruth Krauss, *The Growing Story*, 1947
    A young boy surprises himself when he realizes how much he has grown.
Tololwa M. Mollel, *Big Boy*, 1995
    Tired of being the youngest and smallest, Oli imagines himself bigger and magically he is!

1024

KEN MOCHIZUKI
DOM LEE, Illustrator

Heroes

(New York: Lee & Low Books, Inc. 1995)

Subject(s): Japanese Americans; Racism; Problem Solving
Age range(s): Grades 2-4
Major character(s): Donnie Okada, Bullied Child; Dad, Father, Veteran; Yosh, Uncle, Veteran
Time period(s): 1960s
Locale(s): United States

Summary: Although Donnie tries to encourage football games, the other kids only want to play "war" with Donnie as the "bad guy" because, to them, he looks like the enemy. Donnie protests that his Dad and Uncle Yosh fought as Americans, but no one believes him. When the extent of the bullying finally becomes apparent to Donnie's father and uncle they show up after school in uniform to settle the question of just who the heroes are. (32 pages)

Where it's reviewed:
Booklist, March 15, 1995, page 1335
Children's Bookwatch, May 1995, page 7
Horn Book, May 1995, page 327
Kirkus Reviews, March 15, 1995, page 389
School Library Journal, July 1995, page 79

Other books by the same author:
Baseball Saved Us, 1993

Other books you might like:
Kathleen V. Kudlinski, *Pearl Harbor Is Burning! A Story of World War II*, 1991
    New to the island of Hawaii, Frank meets Kenji and learns about friendship and patriotism.
Jean Thesman, *Molly Donnelly*, 1993
    When World War II begins, Molly faces many changes including the disappearance of her neighbor Emily Tamanaka and her family.
Yoshiko Uchida, *A Jar of Dreams*, 1981
    The prejudicial attitudes of others in the community make

life in 1930s California difficult for Rinko and her Japanese-American family.

1025

JEANNE MODESITT
ROBIN SPOWART, Illustrator

Lunch with Milly

(New York: BridgeWater Books, 1995)

Subject(s): Animals; Fantasy; Imagination
Age range(s): Grades K-2
Major character(s): Unnamed Character, Child; Milly, Friend
Time period(s): 1990s (1995)
Locale(s): United States

Summary: Having invited her grown-up friend to lunch, a young hostess is disconcerted when she realizes she has neglected to make dessert. Milly, however, calmly takes her by the hand and the two fly away to gather the ingredients from a fox, a frog, and a turtle in exchange for the child's singing, dancing and acting. With the ingredients in hand, the two friends fly home to enjoy a delightful dessert. (32 pages)

Where it's reviewed:
Horn Book Guide, Fall 1995, page 275
Kirkus Reviews, February 15, 1995, page 229
Publishers Weekly, January 2, 1995, page 76
School Library Journal, March 1995, page 184

Other books by the same author:
Momma, If You Had a Wish, 1993
Sometimes I Feel Like a Mouse, 1992
Vegetable Soup, 1988

Other books you might like:
Arthur Dorros, *Abuela*, 1991
    Riding a city bus with her grandmother, a young girl imagines instead flying with her over New York City.
Faith Ringgold, *Tar Beach*, 1991
    In an award-winning book, Cassie Lightfoot soars over the rooftops of Harlem, viewing familiar sites from a new perspective.
Jeanne Titherington, *Sophy and Auntie Pearl*, 1995
    Great-Aunt Pearl appreciates Sophy's new-found flying ability because she, too, can fly enabling the pair to travel together above the neighborhood.

1026

BARBARA MOE
SYLVIE WICKSTROM, Illustrator

Dog Days for Dudley

(New York: Bradbury Press, 1994)

Subject(s): Animals/Dogs; Fathers and Sons; Pets
Age range(s): Grades 2-3
Major character(s): Dudley Wolf, 7-Year-Old; Jason Jackson, 2nd Grader, Friend (Dudley's); Mutt, Dog (puppy)
Time period(s): 1990s (1994)
Locale(s): United States

Summary: In the author's first novel, Dudley envies his new friend Jason whose family has three dogs, two cats, a bird and a guinea pig. Dudley only wants one puppy to sit in his lap and keep him company. Unfortunately, Dudley's father is interested in his work to raise money for the zoo animals and not in family pets. A visit from Jason and Mutt and some good news about a zoo fund-raising project contribute to Dudley's father's reconsideration of his opposition to a puppy. (64 pages)

Where it's reviewed:
Booklist, October 1, 1994, page 329
Horn Book Guide, Spring 1995, page 69
School Library Journal, October 1994, page 94

Other books you might like:
Richard Boughton, *Rent-a-Puppy, Inc.*, 1992
    Rather than part with even one of the litter of six puppies, Nikki devises to plan to rent them out for an hour a day.
Betsy Duffey, *Puppy Love*, 1992
    In an adventure in the Pet Patrol Series, Evie and Megan find it difficult to locate a good home for the runt of a litter of pups.
Eve Feldman, *Dog Crazy*, 1992
    Sara Fine wants a dog and will try anything to get one!
Rose Impey, *Desperate for a Dog*, 1991
    Two sisters try some ingenious ideas to convince Dad the family should get a dog. Co-author Jolyne Knox.

1027

NICHOLASA MOHR
RUDY GUTIERREZ, Illustrator

The Magic Shell

(New York: Scholastic Inc., 1995)

Subject(s): Emigration and Immigration; Moving, Household; Loneliness
Age range(s): Grades 3-5
Major character(s): Jaime Ramos, 3rd Grader, Immigrant; Ernesto, Uncle (great uncle); Pedro Ramos, Father, Engineer
Time period(s): 1990s (1995)
Locale(s): Montana Verde, Dominican Republic; New York, New York

Summary: When an American company hires Pedro Ramos, he willingly moves his family to New York to take advantage of the new job opportunity. Jaime, however, is sad and angry to leave behind the only home he's ever known. The cold winter weather that greets the family does nothing to change his feelings about the move. Miserable because he's stuck inside without friends in a country with a language he does not speak, Jaime turns to his parting gift from Tio Ernesto—a large conch shell. As Tio Ernesto foretold, when Jaime holds it to his ear, his memories of friends and homeland come back to him as if they are real. Also as promised, the magic seems to stop working as Jaime becomes adjusted to his new life, because the power is really within Jaime. (90 pages)

Where it's reviewed:
Booklist, August 1995, page 1947
Bulletin of the Center for Children's Books, December 1995, page 134
Children's Book Review Service, September 1995, page 8
Kirkus Reviews, August 1, 1995, page 1114

School Library Journal, October 1995, page 138

Other books by the same author:
All for the Better: A Story of El Barrio, 1992
Going Home, 1986
Felita, 1979

Other books you might like:
Alma Flor Ada, *My Name Is Maria Isabel*, 1993
    When Maria's family moves to a "better" neighborhood, Maria misses her many friends.
Barbara Kerley, *Songs of Papa's Island*, 1995
    A mother tells her daughter about the tropical island on which the parents lived before the child's birth.
Gary Soto, *Taking Sides*, 1991
    When Lincoln Mendoza's family moves from the barrio to the suburbs, unhappy Lincoln feels torn by his loyalty to his former team and his desire to play basketball at his new school.

1028

TOLOLWA M. MOLLEL
E.B. LEWIS, Illustrator

Big Boy

(New York: Clarion Books, 1995)

Subject(s): Family Life; Africa; Magic
Age range(s): Grades K-3
Major character(s): Oli, Child, Brother (younger); Mbachu, Brother (older); Tunukia-zawadi, Bird (magical)
Time period(s): 1990s (1995)
Locale(s): Tanzania

Summary: Oli wants to be bigger and go bird hunting with Mbachu, not stay home with his mother and have a nap. So, after he's tucked in, he slips out of bed and out the door. He meets Tunukia-zawadi who grants his wish to be as "big as a mountain and as strong as the wind." Instantly he is so big that he strides over trees, elephants and villages until he jumps into the ocean and causes a tidal wave. Tired, he sits down and thinks another wish just as Tunukia-zawadi flies past. When Oli awakens he's under a tree in his mother's arms, back to his normal size again, and ready to ride home on his mother's back. A concluding glossary defines the Kiswahili words used in the story (28 pages)

Where it's reviewed:
Booklist, March 1, 1995, page 1248
Horn Book, July 1995, page 453
Library Talk, September 1995, page 41
Quill & Quire, August 1995, page 33
School Library Journal, June 1995, page 93

Other books by the same author:
The King and the Tortoise, 1993
Rhinos for Lunch and Elephants for Supper!, 1992
The Orphan Boy, 1991

Other books you might like:
Trish Cooke, *When I Grow Bigger*, 1994
    After watching Thomas endure teasing from his older sister and her friends, Dad helps him become bigger than everyone by lifting Thomas onto his shoulders.

Heidi Goennel, *While I Am Little*, 1993

A little boy revels in the pleasures that are uniquely his because he's young enough and small enough to do them.

Mercer Mayer, *When I Get Bigger*, 1983

A youngster imagines all the things that he'll be able to do as a big kid.

Rita Phillips Mitchell, *Hue Boy*, 1993

Everyone in the village tries unsuccessfully to help little Hue Boy grow. When Hue Boy sees his dad's ship return his size no longer matters because now Hue Boy feels tall.

Martin Waddell, *Once There Were Giants*, 1989

A girl describes her growth from infancy when everyone around her is a giant to motherhood when she becomes one of the giants in her baby's life.

1029

LUCIA MONFRIED

BETSY JAMES, Illustrator

No More Animals!

(New York: Dutton Children's Books, 1995)

Series: Speedsters
Subject(s): Animals; Pets; Mothers and Sons
Age range(s): Grades 2-4
Major character(s): Charlie, Animal Lover; Mom, Mother; Billy, Friend (Charlie's)
Time period(s): 1990s (1995)
Locale(s): United States

Summary: When Billy gives Charlie a skink he unwittingly creates a quandry for Charlie because Mom has said ''No more animals!'' While Charlie is trying to figure out a way to convince Mom to let him keep the skink, he absentmindly allows all his other animals to escape from his room. Frantically, he scrambles to safely locate and capture them all before Mom discovers what has happened. (64 pages)

Where it's reviewed:
Booklist, November 15, 1995, page 560
Horn Book Guide, Spring 1996, page 56
School Library Journal, November 1995, page 79

Other books you might like:
Marc Brown, *Arthur's Pet Business*, 1990

To show that he is able to handle the responsiblity of his pet, Arthur opens a pet-care business which is far more popular than he anticipated.

Vivian Sathre, *J.B. Wigglebottom and the Parade of Pets*, 1993

Petless J. B. has an ingenious idea for an entry in the annual Parade of Pets.

Karen Waggoner, *Partners*, 1995

Jamie's plans to raise mice as pets are complicated by his sister's cat and his brothers plan to sell the animals as snake food.

1030

FIONA MOODIE, Author/Illustrator

The Boy and the Giants

(New York: Farrar Straus Giroux, 1993)

Subject(s): Folk Tales; Giants; Kidnapping
Age range(s): Grades K-3
Major character(s): Thomas, Hero (kind), Fisherman; Kate, Kidnap Victim, Artisan (weaver); Unnamed Character, Kidnapper (giant)
Time period(s): Indeterminate Past
Locale(s): Scotland (island)

Summary: Thomas and his beloved Kate live happily on their island until the giant kidnaps Kate and makes plans to eat her as soon as she weaves a coat of nettles for him. The animals that Thomas has saved over the years assist him in rescuing Kate from the clutches of the giant and his greedy wife. (32 pages)

Where it's reviewed:
Booklist, June 1, 1993, page 1848
Horn Book Guide, Fall 1993, page 328
Kirkus Reviews, June 15, 1993, page 788
Publishers Weekly, June 21, 1993, page 103
School Library Journal, August 1993, page 148

Other books by the same author:
The Sugar Prince, 1987

Other books you might like:
Kevin Hawkes, *His Royal Buckliness*, 1992

When giants kidnap Lord Buckley to their frozen lands, he grows irritable from the cold and sends a message to his loyal followers who bring Spring.

Steven Kellogg, *Jack and the Beanstalk*, 1991

In one of many retellings of the 1889 English tale, Jack outsmarts the giant and his wife in order to save himself and provide for his mother.

Audrey Wood, *Rude Giants*, 1993

Persuasive Beatrix convinces two rude giants to clean up their act and become good neighbors.

1031

NICOLA MOON

ALEX AYLIFFE, Illustrator

Lucy's Picture

(New York: Dial Books for Young Readers, 1995)

Subject(s): Grandparents; Blind; Schools/Preschool
Age range(s): Grades K-2
Major character(s): Lucy, Child, Student; Grandpa, Grandfather, Blind
Time period(s): 1990s (1994)
Locale(s): England

Summary: While her classmates paint colorful pictures, Lucy asks permission to create a collage for her visiting grandfather. Carefully she selects green velvet for hills, shiny blue paper for a lake, twigs for trees and a lock of her own hair for the dog's fur. When she proudly presents her picture to Grandpa after school, the reader becomes aware that Lucy has been sensitive to his blindness as she created a textured work of art. Originally published in England in 1994. (32 pages)

Where it's reviewed:
Booklist, January 15, 1995, page 938
Children's Book Review Service, May 1995, page 111
Kirkus Reviews, February 15, 1995, page 230
Language Arts, September 1995, page 370
School Library Journal, March 1995, page 184

Other books by the same author:
At the Beginning of a Pig, 1994

Other books you might like:
Estelle Condra, *See the Ocean*, 1994
Nellie is the first to sense the ocean as the fog along the coast prevents the sighted members of her family from seeing it.
Patricia MacLachlan, *Through Grandpa's Eyes*, 1980
John learns to appreciate the world from the perspective of his blind grandfather.
Susan Pearson, *Happy Birthday, Grampie*, 1987
Martha makes a very special birthday card for her blind, elderly grandfather.

1032

ELAINE MOORE
HENRI SORENSEN, Illustrator

Deep River

(New York: Simon & Schuster Books for Young Readers, 1994)

Subject(s): Fishing; Grandparents; Rivers
Age range(s): Grades K-2
Major character(s): Jess, Child; Grandpa, Grandfather
Time period(s): 1990s (1994)
Locale(s): United States

Summary: The privilege of going on an early morning fly-fishing trip with Grandpa has finally come to Jess. Her father and brother are experienced fisherman and her brother's words of advice echo like warnings inside Jess's head. Though Jess is anxious, Grandpa is calm and reassuring as the two enjoy the day together. (33 pages)

Where it's reviewed:
Horn Book Guide, Fall 1994, page 284
Publishers Weekly, May 9, 1994, page 72
School Library Journal, August 1994, page 141
Southern Living, October 1994, page 96

Other books by the same author:
Grandma's Garden, 1994
Grandma's Promise, 1988
Grandma's House, 1985

Other books you might like:
William T. George, *Fishing at Long Pond*, 1991
A fishing trip to Long Pond includes observation of the plants and animals that Katie and her grandfather see along the way.
Nina Kidd, *June Mountain Secret*, 1991
With her father, Jen fishes for rainbow trout in a mountain stream.

Walter Lyon Krudop, *Blue Claws*, 1993
A young child spends the day crabbing with his grandfather.
Jane B. Mason, *River Day*, 1994
Alex and Grandpa enjoy the day together in a canoe on the river.
Sally Ward, *Punky Goes Fishing*, 1991
Punky and Grandpa have a fun-filled day of fishing.

1033

ELAINE MOORE
DAN ANDREASEN, Illustrator

Grandma's Garden

(New York: Lothrop, Lee & Shepard Books, 1994)

Subject(s): Gardens and Gardening; Grandparents; Family Relations
Age range(s): Grades K-2
Major character(s): Grandmother, Gardener; Kim, Child (grandaughter)
Time period(s): 1990s (spring of 1994)
Locale(s): United States (rural setting)

Summary: Once again, Kim is visiting Grandma. Now it is spring and Kim is helping Grandma prepare her garden. Despite a frightening thunder storm which washes away the carefully planted seeds and a late frost which threatens the plum trees, Grandma and Kim patiently complete their preparations. Kim is reluctant to leave the garden and her loving grandmother but knows that the carrots which she has planted will be ripe when she returns in the summer. (unpaged)

Where it's reviewed:
Booklist, June 1, 1994, page 1842
Kirkus Reviews, May 1, 1994, page 634
School Library Journal, May 1994, page 100

Other books by the same author:
Deep River, 1994
Grandma's Promise, 1988
Grandma's House, 1985

Other books you might like:
Marion Dane Bauer, *When I Go Camping with Grandma*, 1995
A loving relationship between a child and her grandmother is shared on a camping trip.
Lenore Blegvad, *Once Upon a Time and Grandma*, 1993
Grandma shares memories with her grandchildren in the house where she lived as a child.
Patricia Polacco, *Thunder Cake*, 1990
An understanding grandmother helps her grandaughter conquer her fear of thunderstorms.

1034

ELAINE MOORE
DAN ANDREASEN, Illustrator

Grandma's Smile

(New York: Lothrop, Lee & Shepard Books, 1995)

Subject(s): Grandparents; Pumpkins; Fall

Age range(s): Grades K-2
Major character(s): Kim, Child; Grandma, Grandmother
Time period(s): 1990s (1995)
Locale(s): United States (rural area)

Summary: The pumpkin seeds that Kim planted in *Grandma's Garden* have produced an enormous pumpkin to take to the local fall festival. While waiting for the jack-o-lantern contest to begin, Kim and Grandma enjoy the other attractions of the festival on a beautiful fall day. (32 pages)

Where it's reviewed:
Booklist, September 1, 1995, page 88
Horn Book Guide, Spring 1996, page 39
Library Talk, September 1995, page 26
Publishers Weekly, September 18, 1995, page 90
School Library Journal, October 1995, page 110

Other books by the same author:
Good Morning, City, 1995
Grandma's Promise, 1988
Grandma's House, 1985

Other books you might like:
Zoe Hall, *It's Pumpkin Time!*, 1994
   In preparation for their favorite holiday a brother and sister plant pumpkins seeds and tend their garden until the pumpkins are ready for carving.
Anne F. Rockwell, *Apples & Pumpkins*, 1989
   A family picks apples and pumpkins from a nearby farm to use on Halloween night.
Tasha Tudor, *Pumpkin Moonshine*, 1966
   Visiting her grandparents' farm, a little girl selects the perfect pumpkin which leads her on a merry chase back to the house.

1035

ROBIN MOORE
KEES DE KIEFTE, Illustrator

The Cherry Tree Buck and Other Stories
(New York: Alfred A. Knopf, 1995)

Subject(s): Grandparents; Animals; Humor
Age range(s): Grades 3-5
Major character(s): Robin Moore, Child; Grandpa, Grandfather
Time period(s): 1950s; 1960s
Locale(s): Pennsylvania

Summary: As a boy, Robin and his grandfather enjoyed the woods of Pennsylvania, sharing experiences that, in the retelling, take on the appearance of tall tales. Grandpa's advice to a storyteller is to ''start with the facts and go on from there.'' The facts in this case have grown to six stories that include a rattlesnake who knows Morse Code, a bear stuffed as a trophy and an eagle who thinks he's a chicken. (112 pages)

Where it's reviewed:
Booklist, April 15, 1995, page 1500
Horn Book Guide, Fall 1995, page 301
School Library Journal, June 1995, page 112

Other books by the same author:
Grandpa's True Tales from the Woods, 1995

The Bread Sister of Sinking Creek, 1992
Maggie Among the Seneca, 1990

Other books you might like:
Benedict Blathwayt, *Stories from Firefly Island*, 1993
   Tortoise tells ten stories which explain the origins of some present-day animal behaviors.
Lesly O'Mara, *Classic Animal Stories*, 1991
   From those of Aesop to Joel Chandler Harris, animal folktales are collected into an illustrated volume.
Alvin Schwartz, *Whoppers: Tall Tales and Other Lies*, 1975
   Selecting humorous tales of varying length, Schwartz has assembled a collection from many different authors.

1036

PAT MORA
CECILY LANG, Illustrator

A Birthday Basket for Tia
(New York: Macmillan Publishing Company, 1992)

Subject(s): Birthdays; Aunts and Uncles; Gifts
Age range(s): Grades K-2
Major character(s): Cecilia, Child, Niece; Chica, Cat; Tia, Aunt
Time period(s): 1990s (1992)
Locale(s): United States

Summary: Cecilia has an idea for just the right birthday gift for her beloved great aunt. With Chica's help she selects items from the house which remind her of the many special ''together'' activities that she and Tia share. The basket, decorated with flowers, is opened at the family birthday gathering with Tia recognizing the significance of Cecilia's carefully chosen present. (32 pages)

Where it's reviewed:
Booklist, September 15, 1992, page 156
Children's Book Review Service, Winter 1993, page 65
Horn Book, January 1993, page 76
Kirkus Reviews, September 1, 1992, page 1132
School Library Journal, January 1993, page 82

Awards the book has won:
Southwest Book Award, 1993

Other books by the same author:
The Desert Is My Mother, 1994
Listen to the Desert, 1994
Pablo's Tree, 1994

Other books you might like:
Eve Bunting, *Flower Garden*, 1994
   With her father's help, a young girl prepares a birthday surprise for her mother.
Eileen Christelow, *Don't Wake Up Mama!*, 1992
   While mom is sleeping, five little monkeys ''quietly'' bake a birthday cake in order to surprise her.
Amy Hest, *Nana's Birthday Party*, 1993
   It's an annual tradition for Nana's two granddaughters to create a homemade birthday gift.
George Shannon, *Heart to Heart*, 1995
   When Squirrel forgets to buy a valentine card for Mole, he creates a special tribute to their friendship instead.

1037

PAT MORA
CECILY LANG, Illustrator

Pablo's Tree

(New York: Macmillan Publishing Company, 1994)

Subject(s): Birthdays; Grandparents; Adoption
Age range(s): Grades K-3
Major character(s): Pablo, 5-Year-Old (Mexican-American), Adoptee; Lito, Grandfather (Mexican-American); Mama, Mother (Mexican-American)
Time period(s): 1990s (1994)
Locale(s): Texas

Summary: Annually Lito decorates a tree for Pablo's birthday in remembrance of the day the grandfather first met Pablo. Mama drives Pablo to Lito's home with an overnight bag filled with birthday toys and the day after the birthday is spent with Lito, sitting under the tree and retelling the story of Pablo's adoption, the tree, and the decorations which change each year. (32 pages)

Where it's reviewed:
Booklist, November 1, 1994, page 507
Bulletin of the Center for Children's Books, September 1994, page 20
Horn Book Guide, November 1994, page 723
Kirkus Reviews, September 15, 1994, page 1276
School Library Journal, July 1995, page 27

Awards the book has won:
Consortium of Latin American Studies Programs Commended Book, 1994

Other books by the same author:
Agua, Agua, Agua, 1994
Listen to the Desert, 1994
A Birthday Basket for Tia, 1992

Other books you might like:
Joanna Cole, *How I Was Adopted: Samantha's Story*, 1995
Samatha tells one of her favorite stories—the explanation of her adoption.
Susi Gregg Fowler, *When Joel Comes Home*, 1993
A young girl eagerly plans her family's welcome of friends' newly adopted baby.
Betty Lifton, *Tell Me a Real Adoption Story*, 1994
A child requests a bedtime story "about me" to which the mother responds with a story about the child's adoption.
Jonathan London, *A Koala for Katie: An Adoption Story*, 1993
Katie "adopts" a toy koala from the zoo gift shop using the toy to work through feelings about her adoption.
Fred Rogers, *Let's Talk about It: Adoption*, 1995
A straightforward title examining the possible feelings adopted children may have.

1038

MICHAEL MORPURGO
MICHAEL FOREMAN, Illustrator

Arthur, High King of Britain

(San Diego: Harcourt Brace & Company, 1995)

Subject(s): Arthurian Legend; Knights and Knighthood; Storytelling
Age range(s): Grades 3-6
Major character(s): Unnamed Character, 12-Year-Old; Arthur Pendragon, Royalty (High King of Britain), Aged Person (legendary figure)
Time period(s): Indeterminate Past
Locale(s): England

Summary: When a boy attempts to cross to the Eastern Isles between tides, he becomes lost in the fog and is rescued, near death, by an elderly man and his dog. The man claims to be Arthur, High King of Britain, trapped in another place and another time, awaiting the designated moment for his return. To entertain the recuperating child, Arthur relates 9 stories of the Knights of the Round Table before sending the boy home to his unsuspecting family. (144 pages)

Where it's reviewed:
Booklist, August 1995, page 1947
Books for Your Children, Spring 1995, page 17
Horn Book Guide, Fall 1995, page 301
School Library Journal, July 1995, page 89
Times Educational Supplement, November 4, 1994, page 16

Other books by the same author:
The Sandman and the Turtles, 1994
Twist of Gold, 1993
King of the Cloud Forests, 1988

Other books you might like:
Robin Lister, *The Legend of King Arthur*, 1990
The story of Arthur's life from his birth at Tintagel to his death is told by Merlin.
Robert D. San Souci, *Young Merlin*, 1990
One of many retellings of the Arthurian legends focusses on Merlin's youth and the vision of his future with King Arthur.
Marcia Williams, *King Arthur and the Knights of the Round Table*, 1996
The adventures of King Arthur and his nights are simply retold with detailed illustrations.
Jane Yolen, *Merlin and the Dragons*, 1995
In response to sleepless young Arthur's doubts, Merlin tells the tale of young Emrys, his troubled dreams and the battle they foretold.

1039

MICHAEL MORPURGO

The Ghost of Grania O'Malley

(New York: Viking, 1996)

Subject(s): Ghosts; Pirates; Physically Handicapped
Age range(s): Grades 4-7

Major character(s): Grania O'Malley, Pirate, Spirit; Jessie, 10-Year-Old, Handicapped; Jack, Cousin
Time period(s): 1990s
Locale(s): Clare Island, Ireland

Summary: Jessie loves the mountain on the island and is determined to climb it, even with cerebral palsy. The day she manages it she hears the voice of a woman commending her, but sees nothing. That evening she meets her cousin Jack, visiting from America, and the two of them climb the mountain together. This time Grania appears to them and enlists them in helping her save the mountain from destruction by gold diggers. The three of them working together, merging the old ideas from the 1500s with the new, are finally successful in saving the island and Jessie finds the strength to overcome her handicap and make friends with others on the island. (184 pages)

Where it's reviewed:
Booklist, June 1, 1996, page 1720
School Library Journal, July 1996, page 85

Other books by the same author:
The War of Jenkins' Ear, 1995
The Wreck of the Zanzibar, 1995
Waiting for Anya, 1990
King of the Cloud Forests, 1988

Other books you might like:
Marion Dane Bauer, *A Taste of Smoke*, 1993
    A boy who died in a fire years before appears to campers until they are able to absolve him of blame.
Pam Conrad, *Stonewords: A Ghost Story*, 1990
    A girl is visited by a new friend for a time before she realizes that she is a ghost.
Lynn Cullen, *The Backyard Ghost*, 1993
    A family finds that a ghost from the Civil War is living in their back yard.

1040

MICHAEL MORPURGO
FRANCOIS PLACE, Illustrator

The Wreck of the Zanzibar
(New York: Viking, 1995)

Subject(s): Shipwrecks; Islands; Diaries
Age range(s): Grades 4-6
Major character(s): Laura Perryman, 14-Year-Old
Time period(s): 1900s; 1990s
Locale(s): England (Bryher Island in the Scilly Isles)

Summary: The island of Bryher off the British Coast is constantly wracked by storms which makes a harsh life for Laura and her family. Ships often founder along their coastline and the islanders row out in small boats to rescue the crew and salvage the cargo. That cargo is often all that enables them to survive a winter. Laura's dream is to row one of the salvage boats, although that's considered men's work. Laura finally gets her chance to help when the *Zanzibar* begins to sink off their island and she tells her story in a beautifully illustrated diary that she leaves to her great-nephew after her death. (69 pages)

Where it's reviewed:
Publishers Weekly, October 30, 1995, page 62
Kirkus Reviews, October 15, 1995, page 1498
Booklist, November 15, 1995, page 740
Center for Children's Books. Bulletin, December 1995, page 135
Horn Book, March 1996, page 198

Other books by the same author:
The War of Jenkins' Ear, 1995
Twist of Gold, 1993
Waiting for Anya, 1991
Mr. Nobody's Eyes, 1990

Other books you might like:
Libby Gleeson, *Eleanor, Elizabeth*, 1990
    Finding a diary kept by her grandmother helps Eleanor adjust to being the new kid in school.
Katherine Kirkpatrick, *Keeping the Good Light*, 1995
    Eliza's world living on Stepping Stones lighthouse is an isolated one, but that changes when a ship's captain finds a note she places in a bottle.
Jill Paton Walsh, *Grace*, 1992
    One night Grace and her lighthouse keeper father row from their island to save the survivors of the wrecked ship *Forfarshine*.

1041

JUDY K. MORRIS

Nightwalkers
(New York: HarperCollins, 1996)

Subject(s): Animals/Elephants; Foster Homes; African Americans
Age range(s): Grades 3-6
Major character(s): James, Foster Child, 4th Grader; Daisy, Elephant; Big Jim, Foster Parent
Time period(s): 1990s
Locale(s): Washington, District of Columbia

Summary: James is in yet another foster home and misses his last foster father. Now he lives in an apartment near the zoo and one day, while on a class trip, he feels that a new elephant is trying to commmunicate with him and watches as the elephant works on releasing the lock on the gate. That evening the elephant escapes from the zoo and comes to take James on a trip through the city. She appears to be looking for something and during the next few days James realizes that she is looking for another elephant, just as he is looking for a happy foster home. It is only when James and Big Jim are able to unite the two elephants again that James also gets his wish to return to live with Big Jim. (133 pages)

Where it's reviewed:
Booklist, November 15, 1996, page 665
School Library Journal, December 1996, page 123

Other books by the same author:
The Kid Who Ran for Principal, 1989
The Crazies and Sam, 1983

Other books you might like:
Carol Carrick, *The Elephant in the Dark*, 1988
   Will helps the village storekeeper feed the elephants for the winter.
Gillian Cross, *The Great American Elephant Chase*, 1993
   Two children try to get an elephant to Nebraska.
Barbara Smucker, *Incredible Jumbo*, 1991
   An African elephant joins the circus in America.
Thomas Tryon, *The Adventures of Opal and Cupid*, 1992
   An elephant and a little girl have an adventure with the circus.

1042

LLOYD MOSS
MARJORIE PRICEMAN, Illustrator

Zin! Zin! Zin! a Violin

(New York: Simon & Schuster Books for Young Readers, 1995)

Subject(s): Orchestra; Music; Stories in Rhyme
Age range(s): Grades 1-4
Major character(s): Unnamed Character, Musician
Time period(s): 1990s (1995)
Locale(s): United States

Summary: Beginning with solo trombone, various instruments are introduced until a full orchestra performs onstage. In addition to describing the sounds of each instrument, terms such as quartet, septet and nonet are explained as the number of performers on stage grows in the author's first book. (28 pages)

Where it's reviewed:
Booklist, May 15, 1995, page 1650
Children's Book Review Service, April 1995, page 105
Kirkus Reviews, March 15, 1995, page 390
Publishers Weekly, February 20, 1995, page 204
School Library Journal, May 1995, page 87

Awards the book has won:
School Library Journal Best Books, 1995
Caldecott Honor Book, 1996

Other books you might like:
Rachel Isadora, *Ben's Trumpet*, 1991
   In a Caldecott Honor Book, Ben hears the jazz musicians at the Zig Zag Club play and joins them on his imaginary trumpet.
Michele Lemieux, *Peter and the Wolf*, 1996
   One of many illustrated retellings, the story was originally created by Prokofiev as a child's introduction to the orchestra.
Bill Martin Jr., *The Maestro Plays*, 1994
   Creatively, the maestro plays, while rhymingly the author describes his distinctively unique performance.

1043

MARISSA MOSS, Author/Illustrator

Amelia Writes Again

(Berkeley, CA: Tricycle Press, 1996)

Subject(s): Family Life; Diaries; Schools

Age range(s): Grades 1-3
Major character(s): Amelia, 10-Year-Old, Writer
Time period(s): 1990s
Locale(s): California

Summary: Amelia receives another notebook and proceeds to keep a journal about her daily life including the serious fire at school which ruined some of the classrooms. She also writes about the ups and downs of friendship with students in school and those to whom she writes letters. She talks about her school subjects and about how she does not like math so she gives personalities to numbers. The drawings and comments she makes help to show what kind of a little girl she is. (unpaged)

Where it's reviewed:
Booklist, November 1, 1996, page 501
School Library Journal, October 1996, page 122

Other books by the same author:
Amelia's Notebook, 1995 (prequel to *Amelia Writes Again*)
In America, 1994
But Not Kate, 1992
After-School Monster, 1991

Other books you might like:
Suzanne Altman, *My Worst Days Diary*, 1995
   A little girl writes about the embarrassing things that happen to her during her first year in a new school.
Pat Brisson, *Kate Heads West*, 1990
   Kate is traveling West to live and travel and writes letters and post cards back to her friends.
Marc Brown, *Arthur Writes a Story*, 1996
   Arthur, the aardvark, tries different stories until he finds one both he and his teacher liks.
Sheila Greenwald, *Write on Rosy*, 1988
   Rosy tries her best to be good in the family by talking up writing.

1044

MARISSA MOSS, Author/Illustrator

Amelia's Notebook

(Berkeley, CA: Tricycle Press, 1995)

Subject(s): Moving, Household; Sisters; Friendship
Age range(s): Grades 3-4
Major character(s): Leah, Friend (Amelia's); Amelia, 9-Year-Old, Writer; Cleo, Sister (Amelia's)
Time period(s): 1990s (1995)
Locale(s): California

Summary: In her special notebook, Amelia pours out her thoughts and feelings about moving, her older, revolting sister, the best friend she's left behind, the new friend she's seeking and her new school. Amelia's journal entries are adorned with colorful drawings and captions which expand on her thoughts and infuriate Cleo who, according to Amelia, has no business reading a private notebook anyway. (32 pages)

Where it's reviewed:
Booklist, April 1, 1995, page 1391
Horn Book Guide, Fall 1995, page 276
Kirkus Reviews, March 15, 1995, page 390
Publishers Weekly, March 20, 1995, page 61

School Library Journal, July 1995, page 79

Other books by the same author:
In America, 1994
Regina's Big Mistake, 1990
Who Was It?, 1989

Other books you might like:
Paula Danziger, *Amber Brown Is Not a Crayon*, 1994
 Amber's long-time best friend Justin is moving and Amber's feeling miserable.
Jerry Spinelli, *Tooter Pepperday*, 1995
 Tooter is so determined not to move with her family to Aunt Sally's farm that she handcuffs herself to the bathroom sink.
Vera B. Williams, *Scooter*, 1993
 An out-going personality and an unfortunate accident on her scooter help Lanny make friends after her move to a New York apartment.

1045

MARISSA MOSS, Author/Illustrator

In America
(New York: Dutton Children's Books, 1994)

Subject(s): Grandparents; Emigration and Immigration; Jews
Age range(s): Grades K-3
Major character(s): Walter, Child; Grandpa, Grandfather
Time period(s): 1990s (1994); Indeterminate Past
Locale(s): California; Pikeli, Lithuania

Summary: While walking to the post office, Grandpa tells Walter the story of his decision to come to America as a 10-year-old seeking freedom to worship his faith without persecution. The illustrations alternate between scenes of the walk on an urban American street and scenes in Pikeli as Grandpa reminisces about his life as a child. Walter reflects on the story wondering if he could be as courageous as his grandfather. (32 pages)

Where it's reviewed:
Booklist, May 15, 1994, page 1683
Horn Book Guide, Fall 1994, page 284
Library Talk, September 1994, page 11
Publishers Weekly, May 16, 1994, page 63
School Library Journal, June 1994, page 112

Other books by the same author:
But Not Kate, 1992
After-School Monster, 1991
Regina's Big Mistake, 1990

Other books you might like:
Judith Caseley, *Apple Pie and Onions*, 1987
 Although Rebecca enjoys hearing stories of her grandma's early life in America, she is embarassed when Grandma speaks publicly with old friends about life in Russia.
Riki Levinson, *Watch the Stars Come Out*, 1985
 Grandma relates the story of her voyage to America as a child.
Patricia Polacco, *The Keeping Quilt*, 1988
 A homemade quilt represents the love linking four generations of an immigrant Jewish family.

Mary Watson, *The Butterfly Seeds*, 1995
 When Jake's family emigrates to America, his beloved grandfather gives him a box of "butterfly" seeds which, when planted in America, provide a reminder of Grandpa.

1046

THYLIAS MOSS
JERRY PINKNEY, Illustrator

I Want to Be
(New York: Dial Books for Young Readers, 1993)

Subject(s): Growing Up; Imagination
Age range(s): Grades 1-3
Major character(s): Unnamed Character, Child (African American)
Time period(s): 1990s (1993)
Locale(s): United States

Summary: A young girl gives serious consideration to the questions from others as to what she wants to be. Her response is not a list of careers, but a list of qualities of being, joyfully expressed in poetic imagery. That's all she wants to be. (32 pages)

Where it's reviewed:
Booklist, October 1, 1993, page 353
Essence, February 1994, page 120
Library Talk, March 1994, page 31
Publishers Weekly, July 5, 1993, page 71
School Library Journal, September 1993, page 216

Other books you might like:
Mary Hoffman, *Amazing Grace*, 1991
 Grace is an imaginative girl who learns that she can become anything if she works for it.
Tololwa M. Mollel, *Big Boy*, 1995
 A magical bird grants a young boy's wish to be bigger and stronger.
Sarah Perry, *If. . .*, 1995
 A fanciful book explores a range of seemingly implausible ideas.

1047

MASSIMO MOSTACCHI
MONICA MICELI, Illustrator

The Beast and the Boy
(New York: North-South Books, 1995)

Subject(s): Friendship; Loneliness; Parent and Child
Age range(s): Grades K-2
Major character(s): Marco, Child, Friend; Unnamed Character, Monster (beast), Friend
Time period(s): Indeterminate Past
Locale(s): Fictional Country

Summary: Two lost, lonely souls unexpectedly meet in the forest when Marco runs away from home seeking a friend. A misunderstood beast becomes that friend and together they save Marco's searching parents from wolves and then return to Marco's home to live. The village children soon see in Marco and the beast what they see in each other—a friend who accepts them as they are. English adaptation by Andrew Clements. (29 pages)

Where it's reviewed:
Booklist, August 1995, page 1956
Children's Book Review Service, August 1995, page 149
Horn Book Guide, Fall 1995, page 276
Kirkus Reviews, May 1, 1995, page 637
School Library Journal, August 1995, page 127

Other books you might like:
Jan Brett, *Beauty and the Beast*, 1989
In a simplified retelling of the fairy tale, the love of a beautiful maiden releases a handsome prince from the spell which made him an ugly beast.
Patricia Polacco, *Babushka Baba Yaga*, 1993
Misunderstood and feared, Baba Yaga proves herself to be as loving a babushka as the others in the village.
Maurice Sendak, *Pierre: A Cautionary Tale in Five Chapters and a Prologue*, 1962
Pierre's response to every question, including those from the lion threatening to eat him, is "I don't care," but before the tale is through, Pierre changes his tune.

1048

JO ANN MUCHMORE

Johnny Rides Again
(New York: Holiday House, 1995)

Subject(s): Death; Animals/Dogs; Family Life
Age range(s): Grades 4-6
Major character(s): Rose Marlin, 10-Year-Old, Sister; Johnny, Dog; Luke Marlin, 14-Year-Old, Brother
Time period(s): 1990s (1995)
Locale(s): Temple, Texas

Summary: In the author's first novel, Rose feels she's the only one in the family who remembers their recently deceased mother and dog. The deaths of two loved ones so close together seems to be most difficult for Rose, the middle of three children. She resents the puppy they acquire and name Johnny after the first dog. When her father begins dating, Rose is the only one upset, angry, and suspicious about the woman he's seeing. Slowly, Rose comes to terms with her losses and begins to accept the changes in her family. (106 pages)

Where it's reviewed:
Children's Book Review Service, May 1995, page 119
Horn Book Guide, Fall 1995, page 301
Library Talk, September 1995, page 36
Publishers Weekly, April 17, 1995, page 60
School Library Journal, April 1995, page 134

Other books you might like:
C.S. Adler, *Daddy's Climbing Tree*, 1993
Jessica is unable to accept her beloved father's accidental death.
Dawna Lisa Buchanan, *The Falcon's Wing*, 1992
After her mother's death, Bryn and her father stay temporarily with her mother's older sister and Bryn forms a bond with her cousin Winnie, a Down's child.

Susan McLean, *Pennies for the Piper*, 1981
Alone, 10-year-old Bicks handles the arrangements for her mother's funeral, spending her bus money on flowers so she walks to her aunt's house in another state.

1049

GERDA MULLER, Author/Illustrator

Around the Oak
(New York: Dutton Children's Books, 1994)

Subject(s): Trees; Nature; Seasons
Age range(s): Grades 1-4
Major character(s): Nick, Child, Cousin; Ben, Brother (Caroline's), Cousin (Nick's); Caroline, Sister (Ben's), Cousin (Nick's)
Time period(s): 1990s (1991)
Locale(s): Germany (forest)

Summary: When Ben and Caroline visit their uncle, a forest ranger, they enjoy planning outdoor adventures with Nick. The activities vary with the season, but all their adventures provide opportunities for learning more about the forest, the life within it and how to protect it for the future. Intertwined with the story is factual information. Translated from the German, the book was originally published in Germany in 1991. (39 pages)

Where it's reviewed:
Booklist, June 1, 1994, page 1842
Bulletin of the Center for Children's Books, June 1994, page 329
Horn Book Guide, Fall 1994, page 302
Publishers Weekly, June 6, 1994, page 65
School Library Journal, July 1994, page 85

Other books by the same author:
The Garden in the City, 1992

Other books you might like:
Jim Arnosky, *Crinkleroot's Guide to Knowing the Trees*, 1991
A nonfiction introduction to trees describes how to identify trees and how animals use trees.
Eve Bunting, *Someday a Tree*, 1993
The community rallies to save a family's oak tree when it is poisoned by illegally dumped pollutants.
Lark Carrier, *A Tree's Tale*, 1996
A 400-year-old oak relates the story of the people observed during a lifetime as a guidepost to the forest.
Anne F. Rockwell, *Up a Tall Tree*, 1981
While exploring the forest, a woodcutter's son makes discoveries which profoundly effect his life.
Janice May Udry, *A Tree Is Nice*, 1956
The Caldecott Medal winner celebrates the many simple pleasures that a tree offers.

1050

ELSPETH CAMPBELL MURPHY
JOE NORDSTROM, Illustrator

The Mystery of the Dancing Angels
(Minneapolis, MN: Bethany House Publishers, 1995)

Series: Three Cousins Detective Club
Subject(s): Mystery and Detective Stories; Cousins; Christian Life
Age range(s): Grades 2-4
Major character(s): Sarah-Jane Cooper, 10-Year-Old, Cousin; Timothy Dawson, Child, Cousin; Titus McKay, Child, Cousin
Time period(s): 1990s (1995)
Locale(s): United States

Summary: Sarah-Jane, Timothy, and Titus are looking forward to spending a week with their grandparents when their plans are interrupted by the arrival of an annoying 4-year-old third cousin. As they unsuccessfully try to keep track of the younger cousin while the two grandmothers tour an historical home, a mystery develops for the Three Cousins Detective Club to solve. In the process of finding their young cousin, the threesome also solves a 100-year-old mystery in the house. (63 pages)

Where it's reviewed:
Booklist, October 1, 1995, page 316
School Library Journal, September 1995, page 183

Other books by the same author:
The Mystery of the Hobo's Message, 1995
The Mystery of the White Elephant, 1994
Pug McConnell, 1986

Other books you might like:
David A. Adler, *Cam Jansen and the Mystery at the Haunted House*, 1992
  Once again Cam uses her photographic memory to solve a case.
Ellen Conford, *A Case for Jenny Archer*, 1988
  Unwittingly, aspiring detective Jenny prevents a burglary.
Elizabeth Levy, *Something Queer on Vacation*, 1980
  The efforts of Gwen and Jill to win the sandcastle contest are repeatedly foiled.

1051

JILL MURPHY, Author/Illustrator

The Last Noo-Noo
(Cambridge, MA: Candlewick Press, 1995)

Subject(s): Growing Up; Mothers and Sons; Grandparents
Age range(s): Grades K-1
Major character(s): Marlon, Monster
Time period(s): 1990s (1995)
Locale(s): Fictional Country

Summary: Marlon's granny thinks he's too old for a pacifier. Marlon's mom defends his need for a ''noo-noo'' at bedtime, but finally gives in and throws away all the pacifiers she can find. Anticipating just such a move, Marlon hides noo-noos all over the house and taps his hidden supply whenever he's in need. Eventually, his mom's efforts and the teasing of neighborhood bullies convince him to give up pacifiers. Just in case he changes his mind, Marlon plants one in the backyard so he can reap its harvest in time of need. (32 pages)

Where it's reviewed:
Booklist, November 1, 1995, page 478
Children's Book Review Service, February 1996, page 77
Parents Magazine, December 1995, page 230
Publishers Weekly, October 9, 1995, page 85
School Library Journal, January 1996, page 91

Other books by the same author:
Five Minutes Peace, 1986
What Next, Baby Bear!, 1984
Peace at Last, 1980

Other books you might like:
Kevin Henkes, *Owen*, 1993
  Mrs. Tweezers offers unsolicited advice to Owen and his parents for getting rid of his special fuzzy blanket before school opens.
Holly Keller, *Geraldine's Blanket*, 1984
  Although Mama and Papa say it's time for Geraldine's old blanket to go, she finds a way to keep it nearby.
Shulamith Levey Oppenheim, *I Love You, Bunny Rabbit*, 1995
  Mama wants to replace Micah's beloved, well-worn bunny, but comes to understand the importance of Bunny Rabbit to her daughter.

1052

JILL MURPHY, Author/Illustrator

A Quiet Night In
(Cambridge, MA: Candlewick Press, 1994)

Subject(s): Animals/Elephants; Bedtime; Parenthood
Age range(s): Grades K-2
Major character(s): Mrs. Large, Elephant, Mother; Mr. Large, Elephant, Father
Time period(s): 1990s (1994)
Locale(s): Fictional Country

Summary: In preparation for Mr. Large's quiet birthday dinner at home, Mrs. Large has the four children bathed and ready for bed before sundown. Mr. Large arrives home very tired from his day's work, but agrees to read the bedtime story. Before he reaches the end of the book he falls asleep, so Mrs. Large finishes the book and dozes off too. The children cover their parents with a blanket, quietly take the birthday dinner upstairs to their rooms and put themselves to bed. (32 pages)

Where it's reviewed:
Booklist, May 1, 1994, page 1609
Children's Bookwatch, May 1994, page 4
Magpies, July 1994, page 26
Publishers Weekly, February 7, 1994, page 86
School Library Journal, May 1994, page 100

Other books by the same author:
A Piece of Cake, 1997
All in One Piece, 1987
Peace at Last, 1980

Other books you might like:

Russell Hoban, *Bedtime for Frances*, 1960
Frances is a master at avoiding sleep, but her patient parents have a response for every problem.

Ewa Lipniacka, *Asleep at Last*, 1992
Mommy wonders why it's taking Daddy so long to put Jamie and Luke to bed.

Elizabeth Winthrop, *Asleep in a Heap*, 1993
While waiting for Julia to finish her bubble bath, Daddy falls asleep on the bathroom floor. He's joined by Mama, sister Molly, the dog, four cats and finally Julia.

Audrey Wood, *The Napping House*, 1984
Though everyone begins napping in their own spot, they all end up asleep on top of Granny until a wide-awake flea bites a mouse beginning a wake-up alarm.

1053

JILL MURPHY, Author/Illustrator

The Worst Witch at Sea
(Cambridge, MA: Candlewick Press, 1995)

Subject(s): Witches and Witchcraft; Schools; Animals/Cats
Age range(s): Grades 3-5
Major character(s): Mildred Hubble, Student, Witch; Tabby, Cat
Time period(s): 1990s (1995)
Locale(s): England

Summary: With Mildred's reputation as the worst witch at Miss Cackle's Academy for Witches, no one is surprised when she can't fly proficiently or has problems with her spells. Everyone thinks she should be pleased to have a new, proper black cat, but Mildred is sad to be forced to give Tabby to the kitchen as a mouser. Knowing Tabby is just as afraid of mice as of flying, Mildred rescues her and hides her pet during a class trip to a wizard's castle near the sea. When, the boat Tabby is hidden on accidently floats out to sea, Mildred rescues her and finds a long-lost buried treasure at the same time, proving to everyone she can do some things right. First published in England in 1993. (222 pages)

Where it's reviewed:
Horn Book Guide, Spring 1996, page 66
School Library Journal, October 1995, page 138

Other books by the same author:
A Bad Spell for the Worst Witch, 1991
The Worst Witch Strikes Again, 1982
The Worst Witch, 1982

Other books you might like:

Catherine Dexter, *A Is for Apple, W Is for Witch*, 1996
Barnaby's constant teasing vexes Apple, daughter of a witch, so much that, despite her lack of training, she decides to try a tiny spell on him.

Eleanor Estes, *The Witch Family*, 1960
The imaginative story of two young girls and three witches (Old, Little and Weeny) blends fantasy and reality.

Anne Mazer, *The Accidental Witch*, 1995
When clumsy Bee tumbles into a circle of witches, absorbing some of their power, but none of their experience, her enthusiastic, uneducated use of spells creates chaos.

1054

JIM MURPHY
JEFFREY GREENE, Illustrator

Backyard Bear
(New York: Scholastic, Inc., 1993)

Subject(s): Animals/Bears; Survival; Fear
Age range(s): Grades K-2
Major character(s): Unnamed Character, Bear (young)
Time period(s): 1990s (1993)
Locale(s): United States (a suburban neighborhood)

Summary: A hungry, young bear attracted by the scent of food from garbage cans wanders into a suburban neighborhood one night in search of food. The noise awakens a family who call the police. Cornered, the bear escapes, eludes would-be captors and safely returns to the forest—hungry, but wiser. (32 pages)

Where it's reviewed:
Booklist, January 15, 1993, page 923
Language Arts, Summer 1993, page 421
New Advocates, Summer 1993, page 219
Publishers Weekly, January 25, 1993, page 87
School Library Journal, April 1993, page 101

Other books by the same author:
Dinosaur for a Day, 1992
The Call of the Wolves, 1989
The Last Dinosaur, 1988

Other books you might like:

Shelly Gill, *Alaska's Three Bears*, 1990
Three types of bears from Alaska are described in an original folktale.

Syd Hoff, *Grizzwold*, 1963
When his home is destroyed, Grizzwold the bear finds a new one.

Ian Stirling, *Bears*, 1992
An award-winning volume of the Sierra Club Wildlife Library describes 8 species of bear, their habitats, behavior, and the impact of humans on their future. (nonfiction)

1055

ANNA MYERS

Rosie's Tiger
(New York: Walker, 1994)

Subject(s): Korean Americans; Historical; Brothers and Sisters
Age range(s): Grades 6-7
Major character(s): Rosie Taylor, 6th Grader; Ronny Taylor, Military Personnel; Cassandra Carter, 6th Grader
Time period(s): 1950s
Locale(s): Guthrie, Oklahoma

Summary: Rosie worries about her brother, Ronny, being stationed in Korea and is elated when she hears he's returning home. However, this event is spoiled by the news that he's accompanied by his new Korean wife and their child. Rosie's so jealous that she turns to her friend Cassandra, who she thinks has magical powers, and asks her to work a spell to return her brother's wife and son to Korea. Rosie quickly learns to be careful what you wish for in this endearing story. (128 pages)

Where it's reviewed:
Publishers Weekly, August 22, 1994, page 56
Booklist, September 15, 1994, page 136
School Library Journal, November 1994, page 106
Horn Book, March 1995, page 194
Kirkus Reviews, September 15, 1994, page 1277

Other books by the same author:
Red-Dirt Jessie, 1992

Other books you might like:
Julie Reece Deaver, *First Wedding, Once Removed*, 1990
    When Gib marries, his younger sister Pokie has a hard time accepting their changed relationship.
Anne Fine, *My War with Goggle-Eyes*, 1989
    Kitty brings out all her artillery in an attempt to get rid of this Gerald Faulkner her mother is dating.
Theresa Nelson, *And One for All*, 1989
    Geraldine's world changes forever when her brother enlists in the Marines and heads for Vietnam.

1056

ANNA MYERS

Spotting the Leopard
(New York: Walker, 1996)

Subject(s): Brothers and Sisters; Animals/Leopards; Family Life
Age range(s): Grades 4-8
Major character(s): Jessie Harper, Teenager; H.J. Harper, Brother, Child; Lucky, Leopard
Time period(s): 1940s
Locale(s): Oklahoma City, Oklahoma

Summary: Jessie dreams of going to college and becoming a vet. She is good with animals and helps save the family dog, Ring, when he is bitten by a snake. Unfortunately, there is no money in the family for her to go to school. H.J. longs to help his sister and when he hears that a leopard has escaped from the zoo he formulates a plan. When he finds the animal in the woods and is able to catch it in a pen, he thinks he can get money for it as well as save it from the hunters who are after it. On the day of the hunt, however, he is unable to move the pen away into the woods. Lucky gets out and is shot and killed. H.J. is afraid that he has spoiled everything until he meets the zoo keeper who is willing to help him and his sister because of their interest in and love for the animals. (146 pages)

Where it's reviewed:
Bulletin of the Center for Children's Books, February 1997, page 216
Horn Book, January/February 1997, page 63

Other books by the same author:
Graveyard Girl, 1995
Rosie's Tiger, 1994
Red-Dirt Jessie, 1992 (prequel to *Spotting the Leopard*)

Other books you might like:
Betsy Byars, *The Midnight Fox*, 1968
    A boy persuades his uncle to save the fox he has been watching in the woods.
Deborah Davis, *The Secret of the Seal*, 1989
    A young Eskimo must save the life of a seal pup he befriended.
Peter Parnell, *Marsh Cat*, 1991
    A large black cat learns to trust humans but then decides that the wild life is best for him.
Peter Parnell, *Water Pup*, 1993
    A wild dog becomes attached to a vixen and her pups and becomes part of the family.

1057

WALTER DEAN MYERS
ASHLEY BRYAN, Illustrator

The Story of the Three Kingdoms
(New York: Harper Collins Publishers, 1995)

Subject(s): Animals; Human Behavior; Storytelling
Age range(s): Grades 2-5
Major character(s): Elephant, Elephant, Ruler (of earth); Shark, Shark, Ruler (of sea); Hawk, Hawk, Ruler (of air)
Time period(s): Indeterminate Past
Locale(s): Fictional Country

Summary: The three kingdoms are each ruled by an animal who depends on strength or fear to dominate its domain. When People come they hang their heads and remain on the mountaintops for fear of being crushed by Elephant. With time and experience, they learn that their stories contain wisdom which gives them strength to share the kingdoms with Elephant, Shark and Hawk. (32 pages)

Where it's reviewed:
Booklist, June 1995, page 1788
Children's Book Review Service, July 1995, page 152
Five Owls, May 1995, page 104
Publishers Weekly, May 8, 1995, page 296
School Library Journal, July 1995, page 67

Other books by the same author:
The Dragon Takes a Wife, 1994
Brown Angels: An Album of Pictures and Verse, 1993 (ALA Notable Book)
Young Martin's Promise, 1992

Other books you might like:
Benedict Blathwayt, *Stories from Firefly Island*, 1993
    Wise, old Tortoise tells the animal inhabitants of Firefly Island stories of their ancestors and events of the past which explain certain present-day customs.
Marguerite W. Davol, *How Snake Got His Hiss*, 1996
    Originally round and self-absorbed, snake rolls along with no concern for others, inadvertently causing spots on the hyena, the mane on the lion and his own slender shape.
Gerald McDermott, *Raven: A Trickster Tale from the Pacific Northwest*, 1993
    Saddened that the world is in darkness, shape-changing Raven steals the source of light from the Sky Chief to share with all the world.

N

1058

MAGDALEN NABB
JULEK HELLER, Illustrator

The Enchanted Horse
(New York: Orchard Books, 1993)

Subject(s): Animals/Horses; Magic; Farm Life
Age range(s): Grades 3-6
Major character(s): Irina, Child (lonely); Bella, Horse, Toy (enchanted); Unnamed Character, Aged Person, Blind
Time period(s): Indeterminate Past
Locale(s): England

Summary: Lonely and friendless, with busy parents who have little time for her, Irina is allowed to choose one Christmas gift from an old man's toy shop. The battered, old, toy horse she selects is banished to the barn where Irina cares for it so lovingly that at night it becomes real. Bella's return to life brings joy to Irina during their nightly rides across the snowy countryside. When Bella joins a herd of wild horses, Irina experiences the pain of loving and losing, but she begins to understand the wisdom of the blind man's statement that no living creature can be owned by anyone. (90 pages)

Where it's reviewed:
Booklist, November 15, 1993, page 623
Horn Book, November 1993, page 744
Junior Bookshelf, February 1993, page 23
School Librarian, May 1993, page 63
School Library Journal, October 1993, page 126

Other books by the same author:
Josie Smith and Eileen, 1992
Josie Smith at School, 1991
Josie Smith at the Seashore, 1990

Other books you might like:
Walter Farley, *The Black Stallion*, 1941
  The champion black stallion is featured in a series of 19 books for horse lovers.

Jessie Haas, *Beware the Mare*, 1993
  Gram and Gramps don't share Lily's excitement about the new mare that Lily hopes will be hers.
Anna Sewell, *Black Beauty*, 1877
  The classic story of a beautiful black horse has been reissued and reillustrated many times.

1059

LENSEY NAMIOKA
AKI SOGABE, Illustrator

The Loyal Cat
(San Diego: Browndeer Press, 1995)

Subject(s): Fairy Tale; Animals/Cats; Magic
Age range(s): Grades 1-4
Major character(s): Tetsuzan, Religious; Huku, Cat
Time period(s): Indeterminate Past
Locale(s): Hukuzo-ji, Japan

Summary: A poor, kindly priest rescues a kitten and offers it a home at his temple. Huku grows up to possess secret, magical powers which prove useful when Tetsuzan's temple becomes so poor he is forced to beg food for the cat because even the mice have left. A funeral for the nearby lord gives Huku an opportunity to put his magical powers to use in such a way that it appears Tetsuzan's prayers have solved the problem. Although the humble priest asks for only three gold pieces as a reward, the money is sufficient to repair the temple and buy food, so all are happy again. (40 pages)

Where it's reviewed:
Booklist, September 15, 1995, page 175
Horn Book, January 1996, page 68
Kirkus Reviews, August 15, 1995, page 1192
Publishers Weekly, September 4, 1995, page 69
School Library Journal, October 1995, page 110

Other books you might like:
Eric Quayle, *The Shining Princess and Other Japanese Legends*, 1989
  A collection of Japanese folktales includes a retelling of the story upon which *Lily and the Wooden Bowl* is based.

Francoise Richard, *On Cat Mountain*, 1994
 Sho's pet cat is forced out of the house by Sho's cruel mistress, but when Sho's search for her is successful Secret remembers and rewards her kindness.
Carol Ann Williams, *Tsubu the Little Snail*, 1995
 The love of a poor couple who faithfully care for the snail child sent by the water god in answer to their prayers is rewarded when the spell is broken and Tsubu becomes a young man.

1060

LENSEY NAMIOKA

Yang the Third and Her Impossible Family
(Boston: Little, Brown and Co., 1995)

Subject(s): Chinese Americans; Family Life; Animals/Cats
Age range(s): Grades 4-6
Major character(s): Mary´Yingmei Yang, Musician (cellist)
Time period(s): 1990s
Locale(s): Seattle, Washington

Summary: Mary's family has recently arrived from China. Mary is trying hard to become Americanized and make friends with the popular kids at school while retaining her Chinese culture. Her parents continually embarrass her as her father mispronounces words and her mother compliments someone on being fat. When Mary adopts a kitten from a popular girl at school, knowing that she's not allowed to have pets, she and her brother hide the kitten noises withoff-key violin playing. This sequel to *Yang the Youngest and His Terrible Ear* continues the humorous cross-cultural adventures of the Yang family. (143 pages)

Where it's reviewed:
Voice of Youth Advocates, June 1995, page 97
Booklist, April 15, 1995, page 1500
Horn Book, May 1995, page 350
School Library Journal, August 1995, page 144
Center for Children's Books. Bulletin, May 1995, page 318

Other books by the same author:
April and the Dragon Lady, 1994
Yang the Youngest and His Terrible Ear, 1994
The Coming of the Bear, 1992

Other books you might like:
Vicki Grove, *The Crystal Garden*, 1995
 Moving to a new town, Eliza meets only one other girl in her class; older schoolmates just take advantage of her newness to their school.
Bette Bao Lord, *In the Year of the Boar and Jackie Robinson*, 1984
 The love of baseball helps Shirley Wong adjust to life in America.
Laurence Yep, *The Star Fisher*, 1991
 Joan, a Chinese-American, feels like the starfisher who is caught between heaven and earth, only she is trying to bridge two cultures.

1061

DONNA JO NAPOLI
JUDITH BYRON SCHACHNER, Illustrator

Jimmy, the Pickpocket of the Palace
(New York: Dutton Children's Books, 1995)

Subject(s): Animals/Frogs and Toads; Fantasy; Magic
Age range(s): Grades 4-6
Major character(s): Jimmy, Frog, Child; Pin, Frog (Jimmy's father), Royalty (Prince); Sally, Royalty (Princess)
Time period(s): Indeterminate Past
Locale(s): Fictional Country

Summary: In the sequel to *The Prince of the Pond* Jimmy braves a trip to the palace to steal the hag's ring and save the pond from her curse. Unfortunately, Jimmy carries with him a curse from the hag which needs only the kiss of a princess to bring it to completion. As luck would have it, impetuous, but sensitive Sally finds Jimmy and fulfills the curse changing Jimmy into a boy with a lisp. Eventually, Jimmy realizes that this man called Pin from whom he is trying to get the hag's magic ring is actually his daddy. The kiss of a princess released Pin from a previous spell which had changed him from a Prince to a frog. Jimmy succeeds in his mission though not in the way he expects. (166 pages)

Where it's reviewed:
Booklist, March 15, 1995, page 1331
Bulletin of the Center for Children's Books, June 1995, page 355
Horn Book Guide, Fall 1995, page 301
Publishers Weekly, June 12, 1995, page 61
School Library Journal, June 1995, page 112

Other books by the same author:
When the Water Closes over My Head, 1994
The Prince of the Pond, 1992
Soccer Shock, 1991

Other books you might like:
S.E. Hinton, *The Puppy Sister*, 1995
 A young boy is surprised when his new puppy changes into the shape of a girl who claims to be his loving sister.
Mary James, *Shoebag*, 1990
 Life changes dramatically, but temporarily for Shoebag, a young cockroach who becomes a boy.
Annie M.G. Schmidt, *Minnie*, 1994
 Unexpectedly transformed into a human, Minnie must choose between staying in her new form or returning to life as a cat.

1062

KEIKO NARAHASHI, Author/Illustrator

Is That Josie?
(New York: Margaret K. McElderry Books, 1994)

Subject(s): Mothers and Daughters; Imagination; Asian Americans
Age range(s): Grades K-1
Major character(s): Josie, Child
Time period(s): 1990s (1994)

Locale(s): United States

Summary: Alternating questions from her mother with Josie's replies show Josie's activity and her imaginative response as she interprets what she is doing as an animal's actions. The day's playfulness concludes as "Mommy's big girl," is tucked into bed. (32 pages)

Where it's reviewed:
Booklist, November 1, 1994, page 508
Five Owls, January 1995, page 58
Horn Book, January 1995, page 50
Publishers Weekly, August 22, 1994, page 55
School Library Journal, November 1994, page 86

Other books by the same author:
I Have a Friend, 1987

Other books you might like:
Kady MacDonald Denton, *Would They Love a Lion?*, 1995
Hoping to divert attention from the new baby, Anna pretends to be a series of different animals.
Jean Marzollo, *Pretend You're a Cat*, 1990
Rhyming verse encourages children to imitate various animals' sounds and actions.
Janice May Udry, *Is Susan Here?*, 1993
Susan "vanishes" right after breakfast, reappearing happily at bedtime after a day visiting her parents while wearing various disguises.

1063

PHYLLIS REYNOLDS NAYLOR

The Bomb in the Bessledorf Bus Depot

(New York: Atheneum, 1996)

Subject(s): Mystery and Detective Stories; Brothers and Sisters
Age range(s): Grades 4-6
Major character(s): Bernie Magruder, 11-Year-Old, Detective; Officer Hiram Ignatius Feeney, Police Officer; Dolores Magruder, Sister, Crime Suspect
Time period(s): 1990s
Locale(s): United States

Summary: Bernie is awakened when the bus depot next to the hotel is bombed and quickly finds himself caught up in solving the crime. At first, he suspects his sister because her ex-boyfriend is either going or coming whenever the bombs go off. Concerned with solving the mystery and saving his family at the same time, he finally solves the case when he notices another man who has also been at all the sites. (136 pages)

Other books by the same author:
Ice, 1995
Boys Against Girls, 1994
The Face in the Bessledorf Funeral Parlor, 1993
Shiloh, 1991
Bernie and the Bessledorf Ghost, 1990

Other books you might like:
Gary Crews, *Angel's Gate*, 1995
A reclusive miner is murdered and the children of the local

doctor, especially the older daughter, are involved in solving the crime.
Jane Louise Curry, *The Great Smith House Hustle*, 1993
The Smith children uncover a plot to swindle their grandmother out of her house.
Shannon Gillighan, *There's a Body in the Brontosaurus Room!*, 1992
The Millerton Detective Gang is hot on the trail of the thief at a camp-in at the museum.
E.W. Hildick, *The Case of the Fantastic Footprints*, 1994
McGurk's crew sets out to find out who made the prints in the concrete and why they are being blamed.
Willo Davis Roberts, *The Absolutely True Story. . .How I Visited Yellowstone Park with the Terrible Rupes*, 1994
A boy and his sister join neighbors on a trip to Yellowstone, but they are quickly disenchanted and worried about the car following them.

1064

PHYLLIS REYNOLDS NAYLOR

The Boys Start the War

(New York: Delacorte, 1993)

Subject(s): Humor; Brothers; Sisters
Age range(s): Grades 4-6
Major character(s): Edith Ann "Eddie" Malloy, 11-Year-Old; Caroline Malloy, 8-Year-Old; Beth Malloy, 10-Year-Old
Time period(s): 1990s
Locale(s): Buckman, West Virginia

Summary: When several families move away from their town, the four Hatford boys are left waiting for new neighbors to arrive. Never do the four of them think that the new arrivals could be girls! Yet that's exactly who moves in, Eddie, Beth and Caroline who give tit-for-tat with everything the boys cook up. When the Hatford boys strew dead animals on the Malloy side of the creek to show the pollution around their town, the girls don't even blink. The pranks and jokes continue, but nothing the Hatford boys do can make the Malloy family want to move in this battle of the Hatford Hooligans versus the Malloy Musketeers. (133 pages)

Where it's reviewed:
Voice of Youth Advocates, June 1993, page 92
Booklist, February 15, 1993, page 1060
School Library Journal, March 1993, page 200
Library Talk, May 1993, page 46
Publishers Weekly, April 26, 1993, page 79

Other books by the same author:
Being Danny's Dog, 1995
The Girls Get Even, 1993
A String of Chances, 1982

Other books you might like:
Joan Carris, *When the Boys Ran the House*, 1982
Four siblings take care of themselves and the house when their mother is hospitalized and their father is away on a trip.
Stanley Kiesel, *The War between the Pitiful Teachers and the Splendid Kids*, 1980

Mr. Forclosure declares war on the students and they do the same to him in a humorous account of school life.

Mary C. Ryan, *Who Says I Can't?*, 1988
When a boy comes on a little too strong in the romance department, Tessa decides to exact revenge.

1065

PHYLLIS REYNOLDS NAYLOR

The Face in the Bessledorf Funeral Parlor
(New York: Atheneum, 1993)

Subject(s): Mystery and Detective Stories; Family Life
Age range(s): Grades 4-7
Major character(s): Bernie Magruder, 11-Year-Old; Weasel, Child; Georgene Riley, Child
Time period(s): 1990s (1993)
Locale(s): Middleburg, Indiana

Summary: Strange things are happening in the quiet town of Middleburg. Before the furor over the addition of a drive-in window to the local funeral parlor subsides, the Higgins Roofing Company experiences the theft of its retirement fund and the disappearance of its Vice President. In this fourth book about the Bessledorf Hotel, Bernie and friends Weasel and Georgene put their detective skills to work trying to solve the mystery. (144 pages)

Where it's reviewed:
Booklist, October 15, 1993, page 443
Five Owls, March 1994, page 80
Horn Book Guide, Spring 1994, page 80
School Library Journal, October 1993, page 126

Other books by the same author:
Boys Against Girls, 1994
The Fear Place, 1994
Bernie and the Bessledorf Ghost, 1992
Josie's Troubles, 1992
Shiloh, 1991

Other books you might like:
Jean F. Andrews, *The Secret in the Dorm Attic*, 1990
Visiting his friend, Matt, at a residential school, Donald discovers some stolen jewels and both boys become victims of a kidnapping.
Patricia Elmore, *Susannah and the Purple Mongoose Mystery*, 1992
The mongoose in this story is a delivery boys's trail bike; the mystery is the connection between the boy, the bike, and some suspicious fires.
Carol Farley, *The Case of the Vanishing Villian*, 1986
Trapped on a ferry with an escaped convict, two sisters solve the mystery of his disappearance.
Patricia Reilly Giff, *Have You Seen Hyacinth Macaw?*, 1981
Abby Jones has good intentions, but her lack of skill as a detective leads her to suspect her own brother as a thief.
James Howe, *Dew Drop Dead: A Sebastian Barth Mystery*, 1990
Despite the fact a dead body discovered at an abandoned inn disappears, Sebastian and friends solve the mystery.

1066

PHYLLIS REYNOLDS NAYLOR

The Fear Place
(New York: Atheneum, 1994)

Subject(s): Brothers; Camps and Camping; Survival
Age range(s): Grades 6-8
Major character(s): Doug Grillo, 12-Year-Old; Gordon Grillo, 14-Year-Old; Charlie, Cougar
Time period(s): 1990s
Locale(s): Colorado (North Fork Trailhead in the Rocky Mountains)

Summary: Two years after balking at crossing a narrow rock ledge, Doug and his older brother, Gordon, are on another camping trip. This time the two boys are left alone after their parents get called away for an unexpected family funeral. Their intense sibling rivalry causes Gordon to head up higher into the mountains. When he doesn't return after a few days, and a cougar has been making regular visits to Doug's campsite, Doug hikes to find him. With the cougar, nicknamed Charlie, acting partly as a prod and partly as a companion, Doug manages to hike over the narrow rock ledge that is his "fear place" as he searches for his brother. Finding Gordon with a broken leg forces both brothers to work together as Doug carries him down the mountain in this tale of survival. (118 pages)

Where it's reviewed:
Publishers Weekly, October 17, 1994, page 82
School Library Journal, December 1994, page 111
Booklist, December 15, 1994, page 753
Voice of Youth Advocates, April 1995, page 24
Center for Children's Books. Bulletin, January 1995, page 174

Other books by the same author:
Being Danny's Dog, 1995
Ice, 1995
The Grand Escape, 1993

Other books you might like:
Eric Campbell, *The Place of Lions*, 1991
After a plane crash on the Serengeti, Chris trudges off to find help, trailed by an old lion who becomes his protector.
Gary Paulsen, *Hatchet*, 1987
Enroute to visit his father, Brian's plane crashes in the Canadian Northwoods; as the sole survivor, he relies on his hatchet to live.
Ivy Ruckman, *No Way Out*, 1988
A group of campers are hiking through Utah's Zion Narrows when a flash flood traps them in a canyon.

1067

PHYLLIS REYNOLDS NAYLOR

The Girls Get Even
(New York: Delacorte, 1993)

Subject(s): Brothers and Sisters; Revenge; Halloween
Age range(s): Grades 4-6

Major character(s): Caroline Malloy, 4th Grader; Wally Hatford, 4th Grader
Time period(s): 1990s
Locale(s): Buckman, West Virginia

Summary: In this sequel to *The Boys Start the War*, Caroline and her sisters are determined to outwit the Hatford brothers. They attempt to sabotage the boys' camping trip, but somehow everything backfires and the girls are left defeated, as well as sopping wet. But with Halloween approaching and Caroline selected as the Goblin Queen for the school play, she knows there are possibilities for tricks with Wally playing her footman. The Malloy girls are certain they'll outdo the Hatford boys in the Halloween costume contest, but once again no one wins. (129 pages)

Where it's reviewed:
Voice of Youth Advocates, April 1994, page 29

Other books by the same author:
The Boys Start the War, 1993
Beetles, Lightly Toasted, 1987
The Bodies in the Bessledorf Hotel, 1986

Other books you might like:
Donna Guthrie, *Frankie Murphy's Kiss List*, 1993
    When Frankie tries to kiss the girls in his class, they claim revenge.
Lois Lowry, *Anastasia, Again!*, 1981
    Added to Anastasia's list of troubles are boys, including her young brother.
Robert Newton Peck, *Trig or Treat*, 1982
    Trig comes costumed as a sultry Delilah for the church Halloween costume party.

1068

PHYLLIS REYNOLDS NAYLOR

Shiloh Season
(New York: Atheneum, 1996)

Subject(s): Animals/Dogs
Age range(s): Grades 3-6
Major character(s): Marty Preston, Teenager; Judd Travers, Young Man; Shiloh, Dog
Time period(s): 1990s
Locale(s): West Virginia

Summary: Judd, Shiloh's former owner, has been drinking, hunting and driving heedlessly around the county. Marty is fearful that he will try to reclaim and mistreat or kill Shiloh, so he keeps him tied up at home. One evening Shiloh awakens him and they go out on the road to find that Judd has wrecked his truck and is badly hurt. When Judd returns from the hospital the Prestons take him food. It is then, when Marty sees Judd gently touch Shiloh, that he reallizes how hurt Judd has been and how long it takes to heal.

Where it's reviewed:
School Library Journal, November 1996, page 110
Bulletin of the Center for Children's Books, December 1996, page 145
Horn Book, November/December 1996, page 737
Booklist, November 15, 1996, page 584

Other books by the same author:
Being Danny's Dog, 1995
Josie's Troubles, 1992
Shiloh, 1991 (prequel to *Shiloh Season*)

Other books you might like:
Jim Arnosky, *Gray Boy*, 1988
    Gray Boy goes back to the wild despite his attachment to the young boy who raised him.
Alane Ferguson, *Cricket and the Crackerbox Kid*, 1990
    Two children who have just become friends learn that they each think they own the same dog and go to court to decide who is right.
Rose Impey, *Desperate for a Dog*, 1988
    Two sisters are desperate to get a dog but their father does not agree until they take care of a neighbor's dog for several weeks.
Jo Ann Muchmore, *Johnny Rides Again*, 1995
    Its bad enough that Rose's dog has died and she is mad at her mother, but things get worse when her father quickly replaces the dog and begins dating.
Erika Tamar, *The Junkyard Dog*, 1995
    Katie and her new stepfather work together to save a dog which is mistreated by a junkyard owner.

1069

SHIRLEY NEITZEL
NANCY WINSLOW PARKER, Illustrator

The Bag I'm Taking to Grandma's
(New York: Greenwillow Books, 1995)

Subject(s): Toys; Stories in Rhyme
Age range(s): Grades K-1
Major character(s): Unnamed Character, Child
Time period(s): 1990s (1995)
Locale(s): United States

Summary: Carefully packing his bag for a trip to Grandma's house, a young boy puts in all the items that he considers essential. His mother has her own ideas and dumps out his bag with instructions as to just what he should pack. Her son has the last word. (32 pages)

Where it's reviewed:
Booklist, June 1995, page 1788
Horn Book, May 1995, page 327
Horn Book Guide, Fall 1995, page 277
School Library Journal, April 1995, page 114
Tribune Books, April 9, 1995, page 7

Other books by the same author:
The Dress I'll Wear to the Party, 1992
The Jacket I Wear in the Snow, 1989

Other books you might like:
David A. Adler, *Bunny Rabbit Rebus*, 1983
    After Little Rabbit devours the family food, Mother Rabbit trades with friends for more.
Lee Davis, *P.B. Bear's Birthday Party*, 1994
    Using rebuses to assist the beginning reader, the story describes a teddy bear's birthday celebration.

Sigrud Heuck, *Who Stole the Apples*, 1986
  A rebus adventure shows how a horse and a bear try to discover what has happened to some vanished apples.

1070

VAUNDA MICHEAUX NELSON
LEONARD JENKINS, Illustrator

Mayfield Crossing

(New York: G. P. Putnam's Sons, 1993)

Subject(s): School Life; Prejudice; Sports/Baseball
Age range(s): Grades 4-6
Major character(s): Meg Turner, 4th Grader (Mo's best friend); Billie Turner, 6th Grader, Brother (older); Mo, 4th Grader (Meg's best friend)
Time period(s): 1960s (1960)
Locale(s): Mayfield Crossing

Summary: When the elementary school in Mayfield Crossing is closed, the children on the east side of town are sent to Parkview Elementary where all of them, black and white, are rejected by the Parkview students. Meg, Billy and the other "colored" children experience prejudice for the first time because, as their parents forewarned them, everyplace is not like Mayfield Crossing. Eventually the Mayfield kids use their skill at baseball to gain acceptance. (88pages)

Where it's reviewed:
Booklist, April 1, 1993, page 1433
Children's Book Review Service, March 1993, page 95
Horn Book, September 1993, page 601
Kirkus Reviews, December 15, 1992, page 1575
School Library Journal, January 1993, page 101

Other books by the same author:
Always Gramma, 1988

Other books you might like:
Deborah M. Newton Chocolate, *NEATE to the Rescue!*, 1992
  When her mother's position on a local council is threatened by a racist, a teenager and her friends take action.
Mildred D. Taylor, *The Gold Cadillac*, 1987
  When an African-American family from Ohio visits relatives in the South they face the racism that is a part of life in the South in the 1950s.
Ronder Thomas Young, *Learning by Heart*, 1993
  In the 1960s Rachel becomes aware of racial prejudices and their impact on friendships in her small southern town.

1071

LESLEA NEWMAN
CATHERINE STOCK, Illustrator

Too Far Away to Touch

(New York: Clarion Books, 1995)

Subject(s): AIDS (Disease); Aunts and Uncles; Death
Age range(s): Grades 1-3
Major character(s): Zoe, Child, Niece; Leonard, Uncle
Time period(s): 1990s (1995)
Locale(s): New York, New York

Summary: Zoe looks forward to visits from Uncle Leonard, but lately he's been tired and sick so they are not able to go out as often. During a trip to the planetarium Uncle Leonard explains to Zoe that stars are too far away to touch, but close enough to see, just as he will be if he should die. (32 pages)

Where it's reviewed:
Advocate, April 18, 1995, page 66
Booklist, March 15, 1995, page 1336
Horn Book, May 1995, page 328
New York Times Book Review, August 27, 1995, page 27
School Library Journal, September 1995, page 183

Other books by the same author:
Saturday Is Payday, 1993
Belinda's Bouquet, 1991
Heather Has Two Mommies, 1991

Other books you might like:
MaryKate Jordan, *Losing Uncle Tim*, 1989
  Though he grieves for the loss of his beloved Uncle Tim, Daniel finds comfort in the legacy of joy and courage left by his favorite relative.
Patricia Quinlan, *Tiger Flowers*, 1994
  After his uncle's death, Joel consoles himself and his little sister with memories of their shared activities.
Jane Yolen, *Grandad Bill's Song*, 1994
  With support from family and friends, a young boy begins to accept his feelings following his grandfather's death.

1072

NANETTE NEWMAN
MICHAEL FOREMAN, Illustrator

There's a Bear in the Bath!

(San Diego: Harcourt Brace & Company, 1994)

Subject(s): Animals/Bears; Imagination; Behavior
Age range(s): Grades K-3
Major character(s): Liza, Child; Jam, Bear
Time period(s): 1990s (1993)
Locale(s): England

Summary: When Liza notices a bear in her yard, she makes the mistake of inviting the creature in for a visit. Jam is a pompous, boastful and very large guest who drinks coffee, knocks over lamps while dancing and wanders off when he's satisfied his curiosity. Liza is left to write a homework assignment about her day's activities which, of course, no one believes. First published in Great Britain in 1993. (32 pages)

Where it's reviewed:
Booklist, March 15, 1994, page 1374
Children's Bookwatch, July 1994, page 4
Kirkus Reviews, March 1, 1994, page 308
Publishers Weekly, February 14, 1994, page 88
School Library Journal, July 1994, page 85

Other books by the same author:
Spider the Horrible Cat, 1993
That Dog!, 1992
Sharing, 1990

Other books you might like:

Jez Alborough, *It's the Bear!*, 1994

Eddie and Mom are going back to the woods for a picnic and Eddie fears that he may meet the bear again.

Raymond Briggs, *The Bear*, 1994

Tilly's parents consider her remarks about a large white bear sleeping in her bed to be signs of her imagination at work.

Helen Cooper, *The Bear under the Stairs*, 1993

William is so afraid of the bear he imagines living under the stairs that he throws food into the closet to feed it until his mother's nose leads to a closet cleaning.

Hermann Moers, *Katie and the Big Brave Bear*, 1995

Katie's fear of being home alone is assuaged when a brave bear steps out of the pages of a favorite book and accompanies her on a search for her mother.

Dr. Seuss, *The Cat in the Hat*, 1957

On a rainy afternoon, a mischievous cat visits two children, leaving behind an enormous mess.

1073

BARBARA NICHOL
SCOTT CAMERON, Illustrator

Beethoven Lives Upstairs

(New York: Orchard Books, 1994)

Subject(s): Aunts and Uncles; Letters; Historical
Age range(s): Grades 3-5
Major character(s): Christoph, 10-Year-Old; Karl, Uncle, Student (of music); Ludwig van Beethoven, Composer, Deaf
Time period(s): 1820s (1822-1827)
Locale(s): Vienna, Austria

Summary: After his father's death, Christoph's family rents the vacant upstairs study to Beethoven whose strange, noisy ways are of such concern to Christoph that he writes to Uncle Karl describing the intolerable situation and pleading for intervention. In reply, Uncle Karl's letters offer insight into Beethoven's life and, in time, help Christoph to understand and grow more tolerant of the composer's eccentricities. The author's first children's book. (48 pages)

Where it's reviewed:

Booklist, January 1, 1994, page 821
Children's Book Review Service, May 1994, page 115
Horn Book, July 1994, page 455
Publishers Weekly, December 13, 1993, page 69
School Library Journal, April 1994, page 130

Awards the book has won:
Booklist Editors' Choice, 1994

Other books you might like:

Beverly Cleary, *Dear Mr. Henshaw*, 1983

In a Newbery Award winning book Leigh Botts writes letters about the problems in his life to an admired author.

Kathleen Krull, *Lives of the Musicians: Good Times, Bad Times (and What the Neighbors Thought)*, 1993

A collection of biographies of famous musicians includes references and an index.

Elvira Woodruff, *Dear Napoleon, I Know You're Dead, But. . .*, 1992

When his beloved grandfather is ill, Marty writes descriptive letters about him to Napoleon Bonaparte

---

1074

LAURA F. NIELSEN
CHRISTINE M. SCHNEIDER, Illustrator

Jeremy's Muffler

(New York: Atheneum Books for Young Readers, 1995)

Subject(s): Clothes; Gifts; Aunts and Uncles
Age range(s): Grades K-2
Major character(s): Jeremy, Child, Student; Alice Appleflinger, Aunt
Time period(s): 1990s (1995)
Locale(s): United States

Summary: For his birthday, Jeremy's forgetful Aunt Alice has created a hand-knit muffler from three miles of green, purple and orange yarn. Expected to wear it, Jeremy has so many problems with his very long muffler that he tries losing it. Unfortunately, the distinctive muffler is always returned. Finally, Jeremy is able to put the voluminous scarf to good use when he uses it to rescue an ice skater who has fallen through thin ice. Now he's a hero and the muffler has a place of honor in the town museum. First book for the author and illustrator. (32 pages)

Where it's reviewed:

Booklist, December 15, 1995, page 709
Children's Book Review Service, January 1996, page 51
Horn Book Guide, Spring 1996, page 39
Kirkus Reviews, October 15, 1995, page 1498
School Library Journal, December 1995, page 89

Other books you might like:

Nette Hilton, *The Long Red Scarf*, 1987

When Grandfather can find no relative willing to make a scarf for him, he learns to knit.

Trinka Hakes Noble, *Jimmy's Boa and the Big Splash Birthday Bash*, 1989

Anytime Jimmy's boa comes along for an activity, the outcome is unpredictable and Jimmy's birthday party is no exception.

Jama Kim Rattigan, *Truman's Aunt Farm*, 1994

A birthday gift from Aunt Fran becomes something more than Truman expects.

1075

JOAN LOWERY NIXON

Keeping Secrets

(New York: Delacorte, 1995)

Series: Orphan Train
Subject(s): Civil War; Spies
Age range(s): Grades 5-6
Major character(s): Peggy Kelly, 11-Year-Old; Violet Hennessey, Spy
Time period(s): 1860s (1863)
Locale(s): St. Joseph, Missouri

Summary: When Violet arrives at the Kelly home, Peggy thinks there's more to her story than Violet being just a refugee from the Confederate army. It turns out that Violet is a spy for the Union army and must get information to them about the siege at Chattanooga. Peggy agrees to pose as her daughter to help Violet get past Union patrols and Confederate bushwhackers. (163 pages)

Where it's reviewed:
Voice of Youth Advocates, April 1995, page 25
School Library Journal, March 1995, page 206
Booklist, March 1, 1995, page 1243
Library Talk, September 1995, page 37
Horn Book Guide, Fall 1995, page 302

Other books by the same author:
Spirit Seeker, 1995
A Dangerous Promise, 1994
Land of Promise, 1993
The Name of the Game Was Murder, 1993

Other books you might like:
Patricia Clapp, *The Tamarack Tree*, 1986
  Rosemary begins the Civil War as a spoiled Southern lady; her stand against slavery helps her grow up.
Paul Fleischman, *Bull Run*, 1993
  Sixteen characters offer their accounts of the Civil War from its beginning to the first battle of Bull Run in a unique snapshot of the Civil War.
Lou Kassem, *Listen for Rachel*, 1986
  Though the Civil War divides her family, it also brings romance to Rachel.
Ann Rinaldi, *In My Father's House*, 1993
  In a bizarre coincidence, the Civil War begins and ends on McLean land with Grant and Lee surrendering in their parlor.

1076

JOAN LOWERY NIXON

Search for the Shadowman
(New York: Delacorte, 1996)

Subject(s): Family Life; Ancestry; Mystery and Detective Stories
Age range(s): Grades 5-8
Major character(s): Andy Thomas, 12-Year-Old, Researcher; Cole Joseph ''Coley Joe'' Bonner, Settler; J.J. Gasper, Friend, Student
Time period(s): 1990s
Locale(s): Hermosa, Texas

Summary: Assigned to research his family's genealogy, Andy discovers an ancestor about whom no one wants to talk; he supposedly stole money years before. Refusing to believe the allegation's true, he delves more deeply into his family history in libraries, on the Internet and in personal interviews. The more he learns, the more he believes ''Coley Joe'' was falsely accused. Warnings not to pursue his study convince him even more. His persistence finally pays off when he discovers that Coley Joe was murdered by a friend who was, later, a founder of their town. Deciding that publicly sharing his knowledge would only hurt his friend, Andy decides to share it with the great-aunt who's always refused to recognize Coley Joe's existence and ends the family's denial. (149 pages)

Where it's reviewed:
School Library Journal, November 1996, page 110
Booklist, October 1, 1996, page 352
Bulletin of the Center for Children's Books, January 1997, page 182
Horn Book, January/February 1996, page 65

Other books by the same author:
Keeping Secrets, 1995
A Deadly Promise, 1992
The Other Side of Dark, 1986

Other books you might like:
Joan Carris, *Beware the Ravens, Aunt Morbelia*, 1995
  As Todd tries to decipher old symbols found in a journal, he discovers that he is being followed.
Aileen Kilgore Henderson, *The Summer of the Bonepile Monster*, 1995
  While Hollis is investigating an area filled with fossils, he solves a family mystery.
Brenda Seabrooke, *The Haunting of Holroyd Hill*, 1995
  Ghostly visitors lead Melinda and Kevin to discover a family secret from Civil War times.

1077

JOAN LOWERY NIXON
DICK GACKENBACH, Illustrator

When I Am Eight
(New York: Dial Books for Young Readers, 1994)

Subject(s): Growing Up; Brothers; Imagination
Age range(s): Grades K-3
Major character(s): Herbie, Child, Brother (younger); Unnamed Character, 8-Year-Old, Brother
Time period(s): 1990s (1994)
Locale(s): United States

Summary: Whenever Herbie wants to do something with his brother, he is told that he is too little. So, Herbie fantasizes about the day when he will be eight, just like his brother, and he can have the best of everything for himself. (32 pages)

Where it's reviewed:
Booklist, January 15, 1994, page 938
Horn Book Guide, Fall 1994, page 285
Kirkus Reviews, February 1, 1994, page 147
Publishers Weekly, November 6, 1993, page 73
School Library Journal, March 1994, page 206

Other books by the same author:
Will You Give Me a Dream?, 1994
Beats Me, Claude, 1986
The Valentine Mystery, 1979

Other books you might like:
Steven Kellogg, *Much Bigger than Martin*, 1976
  Henry considers how to overcome his older brother's larger size.

Jean Little, *Revenge of the Small Small*, 1993
   Tired of her older siblings teasing, Patsy used a box of art supplies to plot her revenge.
Judith Viorst, *I'll Fix Anthony*, 1969
   Look out Anthony because your little brother has a plan to get back at you!

1078

JERDINE NOLEN
MARK BUEHNER, Illustrator

Harvey Potter's Balloon Farm
(New York: Lothrop, Lee & Shepard Books, 1994)

Subject(s): Balloons; Farm Life; Fantasy
Age range(s): Grades K-3
Major character(s): Harvey Potter, Farmer; Unnamed Character, Child
Time period(s): 1920s (1929)
Locale(s): United States

Summary: A young girl is fascinated by a neighboring farmer with a most unusual crop. Harvey Potter grows balloons in all shapes, sizes and colors. Curious to know more about the process, the girl befriends Harvey and then hides in a nearby sycamore tree to watch him plant his crop by the light of a full moon. Her childhood endeavors pay off when she grows up to become a balloon farmer herself. First book by the author. (32 pages)

Where it's reviewed:
Booklist, April 15, 1994, page 1541
Horn Book, July 1994, page 442
Kirkus Reviews, March 15, 1994, page 401
Publishers Weekly, April 11, 1994, page 65
School Library Journal, May 1994, page 102

Awards the book has won:
ALA Notable Book, 1995
Kentucky Bluegrass Award, 1996

Other books you might like:
Sid Fleischman, *McBroom's Almanac*, 1984
   McBrooms's unique almanac contains amazing and true farm tips, but no instructions for growing balloons.
Jeff Kaufmann, *Milk Rock*, 1994
   Farmer Foster has a rock which produces milk in abundance.
Helen Ketteman, *Luck with Potatoes*, 1995
   Hard-luck farmer Clemmon Hardigree grows a potato crop that comes complete with cows.

1079

SALLY NOLL, Author/Illustrator

Lucky Morning
(New York: Greenwillow Books, 1994)

Subject(s): Grandparents; Vacations; Fishing
Age range(s): Grades K-1
Major character(s): Nora, Child; Granddaddy, Grandfather, Fisherman
Time period(s): 1990s (1994)
Locale(s): Montana

Summary: For the first time, Nora joins her grandparents during their vacation in Montana. As she and Granddaddy walk toward the river for a morning of fishing, Nora wonders if they will see any wild animals. Her wish comes true on this lucky morning as they return to the vacation cabin, pausing along the way to admire the wildlife. (32 pages)

Where it's reviewed:
Horn Book Guide, Fall 1994, page 285
Publishers Weekly, March 21, 1994, page 71
School Library Journal, May 1994, page 102

Other books by the same author:
I Have a Loose Tooth, 1992
That Bothered Kate, 1991
Jiggle, Wiggle, Prance, 1987

Other books you might like:
William T. George, *Fishing at Long Pond*, 1991
   A fishing trip to Long Pond includes observation of the plants and animals that Katie and her grandfather see along the way.
Nina Kidd, *June Mountain Secret*, 1991
   With her father, Jen fishes for rainbow trout in a mountain stream.
Jane B. Mason, *River Day*, 1994
   Alex and Grandpa enjoy the day together in a canoe on the river.
Elaine Moore, *Deep River*, 1994
   Jess feels privileged and a little anxious to be invited to accompany Grandpa on her first fishing trip.
Sally Ward, *Punky Goes Fishing*, 1991
   Punky and Grandpa have a fun-filled day of fishing.

1080

ERIC JON NONES, Author/Illustrator

Angela's Wings
(New York: Farrar Straus Giroux, 1995)

Subject(s): Fantasy; Self-Acceptance; Individuality
Age range(s): Grades K-3
Major character(s): Angela, Child
Time period(s): 1990s (1995)
Locale(s): United States

Summary: Angela's attempts to hide wings that sprouted overnight on her back do not work. Her family notices as soon as she appears for breakfast. Although her brother thinks the wings are cool, Angela's feelings are hurt by the teasing of other children. Then kind remarks about making the most of one's special features help Angela accept the wings and enjoy the advantages of flight. (32 pages)

Where it's reviewed:
Booklist, September 15, 1995, page 176
Children's Book Review Service, October 1995, page 15
Children's Bookwatch, November 1995, page 8
Kirkus Reviews, August 1, 1995, page 1115
School Library Journal, October 1995, page 110

Other books by the same author:
Caleb's Friend, 1993

The Canary Prince, 1991
Wendell, 1989

Other books you might like:
Tedd Arnold, *Green Wilma*, 1993
  Despite awakening with a green, frog-like appearance, Wilma goes to school where she discovers she also has a taste for flies.
Mercer Mayer, *Purple Pickle Juice*, 1996
  With help from a magical aunt, Thistle begins to accept herself just the way she is.
Dr. Seuss, *Did I Ever Tell You How Lucky You Are?*, 1973
  No matter what troubles you think you might have, you're fortunate not to have the ones listed in this book.
David Small, *Imogene's Antlers*, 1985
  The morning Imogene wakes up to find antlers growing out of her head she begins to attract a lot of attention.

1081

ERIC JON NONES, Author/Illustrator

Caleb's Friend

(New York: Farrar, Straus & Giroux, 1993)

Subject(s): Sea Stories; Mermaids; Friendship
Age range(s): Grades 2-4
Major character(s): Caleb, Orphan (lonely), Fisherman; Unnamed Character, Mythical Creature (boy/fish), Friend
Time period(s): Indeterminate Past
Locale(s): United States (rocky coastal community)

Summary: When work on the fishing boat is finished for the day, lonely Caleb plays the harmonica left to him by his deceased father. The sound attracts a sea creature who retrieves the harmonica when Caleb drops it overboard. The two lonely beings communicate their appreciation for one another by sharing gifts from their own worlds. When the boy from the sea is trapped in a fishing net, Caleb saves him, and in turn, his ship is saved during a storm by guidance from the sea creature. (32 pages)

Where it's reviewed:
Children's Book Review Service, July 1993, page 151
Horn Book Guide, Fall 1993, page 270
Kirkus Reviews, June 15, 1993, page 789
Publishers Weekly, June 7, 1993, page 70
School Library Journal, September 1993, page 216

Other books by the same author:
Angela's Wings, 1995
The Canary Prince, 1991
Wendell, 1989

Other books you might like:
Susan Cooper, *The Selkie Girl*, 1986
  Cooper retells the classic love story of a man and a seal-girl and the selkie's desire to return to her home in the sea.
Jill Paton Walsh, *Matthew and the Sea Singer*, 1993
  Matthew's beautiful voice attracts the seal-queen who steals him for her own pleasure.
Robert D. San Souci, *Sukey and the Mermaid*, 1992
  In a mermaid tale based on African tradition, Mama Jo befriends unhappy Sukey.

1082

MATT NOVAK, Author/Illustrator

Gertie and Gumbo

(New York: Orchard Books, 1995)

Subject(s): Animals/Alligators; Fathers and Daughters; Loneliness
Age range(s): Grades K-3
Major character(s): Gertie Goomba, Child; Salvatore Goomba, Father, Animal Trainer; Gumbo, Alligator
Time period(s): 1990s (1995)
Locale(s): United States

Summary: Lonely Gertie has no playmates near her home at the Goomba Palace where her father performs with his five wrestling alligators. Salvatore will not allow his daughter to wrestle the alligators, so she plays the piano and dances to while away the time. When a baby alligator is born, Gertie cares for Gumbo and shares her musical talents with him to the horror of her father and the other alligators. However, when Salvatore injures his foot and is not allowed to wrestle for three weeks, it is Gertie and Gumbo who go on with the show. (32 pages)

Where it's reviewed:
Booklist, September 1, 1995, page 89
Horn Book Guide, Spring 1996, page 40
Publishers Weekly, August 7, 1995, page 460
School Library Journal, October 1995, page 110

Other books by the same author:
Mouse TV, 1994
The Last Christmas Present, 1993
Elmer Blunt's Open House, 1992

Other books you might like:
Shirley Mozelle, *Zack's Alligator*, 1989
  After soaking his new alligator key chain in water, Zack finds himself face-to-face with a large alligator ready for fun.
James Stevenson, *Monty*, 1979
  When Monty leaves his river home for a vacation, he takes away the "bridge" used by smaller animals on their way to school.
Kazuko G. Stone, *Goodnight Twinklegator*, 1990
  When Alligay uses the stars for connect-the-dots, an imaginary friend named Twinklegator appears to play.
Tynia Thomassie, *Feliciana Feydra LeRoux: A Cajun Tall Tale*, 1995
  An original tall tale describes how Feliciana defies her grandfather and sneaks out to join in the menfolk's alligator hunt.

1083

MATT NOVAK, Author/Illustrator

Mouse TV

(New York: Orchard Books, 1994)

Subject(s): Television; Family Life; Animals/Mice
Age range(s): Grades K-2

Major character(s): Papa Mouse, Mouse, Father; Mama
  Mouse, Mouse, Mother
Time period(s): 1990s (1994)
Locale(s): United States

Summary: The nightly arguments in the mouse household
regarding which TV channel to watch cease the night that the
television breaks and the family finds that their divergent
interests which create conflict in channel selection now make
for an enjoyable evening together. (32 pages)

Where it's reviewed:
Booklist, September 1, 1994, page 53
Kirkus Reviews, August 15, 1994, page 1136
Publishers Weekly, July 4, 1994, page 60
School Library Journal, October 1994, page 95

Awards the book has won:
School Library Journal Best Books, 1994

Other books by the same author:
The Last Christmas Present, 1993
Elmer Blunt's Open House, 1992
While the Shepherd Slept, 1991

Other books you might like:
David McPhail, *Fix-It*, 1984
  A broken TV is upsetting to Emma Bear who's only
  solution is to "Fix It!"
Dan West, *The Day the TV Blew Up*, 1988
  When Ralph's TV watching stops due to an exploding
  television, his friend suggests that he visit the library.
Harriet Ziefert, *When the TV Broke*, 1993
  A broken TV calls for some creative thinking.

1084

MATT NOVAK, Author/Illustrator

Newt
(New York: HarperCollins, 1996)

Series: I Can Read
Subject(s): Animals/Salamanders; Friendship
Age range(s): Grades K-2
Major character(s): Newt, Salamander; Mouse, Mouse
Time period(s): 1990s
Locale(s): United States

Summary: Newt really likes the flower he sees, but when he
digs it up to take home, he needs a vase for it. Mouse has a
vase, but is sad because the flower he found is gone. Newt
puts the flower in the vase but it doesn't look right, so he
replants it, hoping they can both enjoy it. When he awakens
next day, a bug has taken up residence on his porch. This bug
is not talented, pretty or strong, but it is a friend, like the moon
who joins Newt in lighting the dark corners of his room to
scare away monsters. (48 pages)

Where it's reviewed:
School Library Journal, July 1996, page 70

Awards the book has won:
International Reading Association Children's Choice, 1997

Other books by the same author:
Gertie and Gumbo, 1995
Mouse TV, 1994

Elmer Blunt's Open House, 1993

Other books you might like:
Barbara Baker, *Digby and Kate*, 1988
  The dog and cat weather all kinds of differences but keep
  their friendship intact.
Mary Blockman, *Yoo Hoo, Moon!*, 1992
  Bear can't sleep because he can't see the moon.
Ida Luttrell, *The Bear Next Door*, 1991
  A gopher tries to make friends with the grouchy bear who
  lives next door.

1085

SUSAN MIHO NUNES
CHRIS K. SOENTPIET, Illustrator

The Last Dragon
(New York: Clarion Books, 1995)

Subject(s): Chinese Americans; Dragons; Aunts and Uncles
Age range(s): Grades 1-4
Major character(s): Peter Chang, Child; Great Aunt, Aunt
Time period(s): 1990s (1995)
Locale(s): Chinatown

Summary: Peter is unhappy to be spending his summer in
Great Aunt's tiny apartment over a noodle factory, but he tries
to make the best of it. Returning from errands one day, he
spies an old, bedraggled dragon in a shop window and convinces Great Aunt to allow him to bring it home. Through his
restoration of the dragon he discovers the Chinese-American
community, enlists the help of different shopkeepers in his
project and learns about dragon culture and lore. A concluding author's note gives factual information about dragons
and their place in Chinese folklore. (32 pages)

Where it's reviewed:
Booklist, May 1, 1995, page 1580
Children's Bookwatch, July 1995, page 7
Horn Book Guide, Fall 1995, page 277
Language Arts, January 1996, page 58
School Library Journal, May 1995, page 93

Awards the book has won:
Notable Children's Trade Books in the Field of Social Studies, 1996

Other books by the same author:
To Find the Way, 1992
Tiddalick the Frog, 1989
Coyote Dreams, 1988

Other books you might like:
Karen Chinn, *Sam and the Lucky Money*, 1995
  For the Chinese New Year, Sam receives the traditional
  lucky money and now wonders how to spend it.
Margaret Leaf, *Eyes of the Dragon*, 1987
  An artist paints a dragon on the village wall, adding eyes at
  the insistance of the mayor. Everyone is surprised by the
  results.
Catherine Stock, *Emma's Dragon Hunt*, 1984
  When Emma's grandfather emigrates from China, she be-
  gins to learn from him of the power of dragons.

1086

NAOMI SHIHAB NYE
YU CHA PAK, Illustrator

Benito's Dream Bottle

(New York: Simon & Schuster Books for Young Readers, 1995)

Subject(s): Dreams and Nightmares; Grandparents; Problem Solving
Age range(s): Grades K-3
Major character(s): Benito, Child
Time period(s): 1990s (1995)
Locale(s): United States

Summary: Although he seeks the opinions of others, Benito has his own theory about the source of dreams. Dreams come from a bottle inside each person, which must be refilled in order to continue to supply dreams to the individual. So, when Benito learns his grandmother no longer dreams, he realizes her dream bottle must be empty and he helps her refill it. (32 pages)

Where it's reviewed:
Booklist, May 1, 1995, page 1580
Children's Book Review Service, Spring 1995, page 137
Horn Book Guide, Fall 1995, page 277
Publishers Weekly, April 24, 1995, page 71
School Library Journal, June 1994, page 94

Other books by the same author:
Sitti's Secrets, 1994

Other books you might like:
Mem Fox, *Wilfrid Gordon McDonald Partridge*, 1984
    A young boy collects items which he thinks might be instrumental in restoring an elderly friend's memory.
Laura McGee Kvasnosky, *What Shall I Dream?*, 1996
    Though many well-intentioned people try to help by offering dream suggestions, Prince Alexander realizes he must select his own dreams.
Joan Lowery Nixon, *Will You Give Me a Dream?*, 1994
    In response to Matthew's request, Mother begins a dream for him to finish as he sleeps.

1087

NAOMI SHIHAB NYE
NANCY CARPENTER, Illustrator

Sitti's Secrets

(New York: Four Winds Press, 1994)

Subject(s): Grandparents; Family Relations; Love
Age range(s): Grades K-3
Major character(s): Mona, Child (Palestinian-American); Sitti, Grandmother (Palestinian-Arab)
Time period(s): 1990s (1994)
Locale(s): West Bank, Israel

Summary: Traveling to the other side of the world to visit her grandmother, Mona finds that love quickly transcends the language barriers. Sitti shares with Mona the secrets of her simple life: making lemonade from the tree in her yard, seeing the lentil fields nearby, buying milk from a neighbor's cow, baking flatbread in a stone oven. Beyond time and space, culture and governments, this family remains connected. (32 pages)

Where it's reviewed:
Booklist, March 15, 1994, page 1374
Children's Book Review Service, Spring 1994, page 138
Five Owls, September 1994, page 14
Horn Book, May 1994, page 317
School Library Journal, June 1994, page 112

Awards the book has won:
School Library Journal Best Books, 1994

Other books by the same author:
Benito's Dream Bottle, 1995

Other books you might like:
Sharon Hart Addy, *A Visit with Great-Grandma*, 1989
    Barbara's Great-Grandma speaks little English, but still the two communicate with pictures and stories, sharing with their hearts Great-Grandma's life in Czechoslovakia long ago.
Patricia Polacco, *Thunder Cake*, 1990
    One little girl's fear of thunder is conquered with help from her Russian grandmother and the baking of a special thunder cake.
Marisabina Russo, *A Visit to Oma*, 1991
    During their weekly visits, Great-grandmother Oma entertains Celeste with stories told in a language which Celeste cannot understand so she happily concocts her own dialogue.

O

1088

GRAHAM OAKLEY, Author/Illustrator

The Foxbury Force

(New York: Atheneum, 1994)

Subject(s): Crime and Criminals; Burglary; Humor
Age range(s): Grades K-3
Major character(s): Inspector Flannel, Police Officer, Fox; Foreman Burglar, Criminal, Fox
Time period(s): Indeterminate Past
Locale(s): Foxbury, England

Summary: To keep the skills of the Foxbury Constabulary honed in their crime-free town, Inspector Flannel arranges for a monthly "burglary" by the town burglars. On the day the plan calls for the jewelry store to be robbed, Foreman Burglar decides to stop acting and escape with the gems. Foreman Burglar's schemes turn out to be no match for Inspector Flannel's dumb luck, enabling the constables to solve a real crime in spite of themselves. (32 pages)

Where it's reviewed:
Books for Your Children, Summer 1994, page 6
Horn Book Guide, Spring 1995, page 49
Junior Bookshelf, June 1994, page 97
Publishers Weekly, October 24, 1994, page 61
School Library Journal, November 1994, page 87

Other books by the same author:
The Church Mice and the Ring, 1992
Church Mice at Christmas, 1980
The Church Mice Spread Their Wings, 1976

Other books you might like:
Eth Clifford, *Flatfoot Fox and the Case of the Bashful Beaver*, 1995
  Detective Flatfoot Fox gives his assistant, Secretary Bird, an opportunity to solve a case.
James Marshall, *Fox Outfoxed*, 1992
  In an easy-to-read beginning chapter book, Fox competes in a race and trick-or-treats with friends.

Ursel Scheffler, *The Return of Rinaldo, the Sly Fox*, 1993
  Tricky Rinaldo eludes Detective Bruno, but ends up being outfoxed by a clever cat.

1089

SHELDON OBERMAN
TED LEWIN, Illustrator

The Always Prayer Shawl

(Honesdale, PA: Boyds Mills Press, 1994)

Subject(s): Jews; Religion; Emigration and Immigration
Age range(s): Grades 2-4
Major character(s): Adam, Immigrant; Adam, Grandfather
Time period(s): 20th century (1915-1994)
Locale(s): Russia; United States

Summary: When the Russian Revolution threatens, Adam and his family emigrate to the United States. Believing that he is too old for such change, Adam's grandfather stays in the village giving his grandson, as a parting gift, the prayer shawl which his grandfather had passed on to him. Adam treasures the prayer shawl as a constant in a life of changes, repairing it as time and use begin to fray it and then passes it on to his own grandson. (32 pages).

Where it's reviewed:
Booklist, December 15, 1993, page 750
Children's Book Review Service, March 1994, page 93
New Advocate, Winter 1995, page 51
Publishers Weekly, November 29, 1993, page 65
School Library Journal, March 1994, page 206

Awards the book has won:
Booklist Editors' Choice, 1994
National Jewish Book Award, 1994

Other books by the same author:
The White Stone of Casa Loma, 1994
Lion in the Lake, 1988

Other books you might like:
Patricia Polacco, *The Keeping Quilt*, 1988
  The lives, love and faith of four generations of an immi-

437

grant Jewish family are symbolically bound in a home-made quilt.

Maida Silverman, *The Glass Menorah and Other Stories for Jewish Holidays*, 1992
Eight stories tell of a family's celebration of various Jewish holidays.

Mary Watson, *The Butterfly Seeds*, 1995
When Jake's family emigrates to America, his grandfather's parting gift becomes a special reminder of the relative left behind.

1090

JANE O'CONNOR
DYANNE DISALVO-RYAN, Illustrator

Nina, Nina Ballerina
(New York: Grosset & Dunlap, 1993)

Series: All Aboard Reading
Subject(s): Ballet; Accidénts
Age range(s): Grades K-2
Major character(s): Nina, Child, Dancer
Time period(s): 1990s (1993)
Locale(s): United States

Summary: Nina goes to dance class weekly in order to achieve her goal of becoming a ballerina. Because she is one of a flock of butterflies in the recital, she worries that her mother will not know her from the other butterflies on stage. An unfortunate accident the night before the recital does not keep Nina from performing, but it does make her stand out in the crowd. (32 pages)

Where it's reviewed:
Booklist, July 1993, page 1980
Horn Book Guide, Fall 1993, page 282
School Library Journal, August 1993, page 148

Other books by the same author:
Lauren and the New Baby, 1994
Corrie's Secret Pal, 1993
Molly the Brave and Me, 1990

Other books you might like:
Lucy Dickens, *Dancing Class*, 1992
Five young aspiring dancers have the opportunity to perform as birds during class.
Rachel Isadora, *Lili on Stage*, 1995
A sequel to *Lili at Ballet* finds young Lili performing in *The Nutcracker* for the first time.
Kathryn Lasky, *The Solo*, 1994
When bossy Grace is excluded from her dance group before a performance, she prepares to go on stage solo.

1091

ELIZABETH LEE O'DONNELL
JACQUELINE ROGERS, Illustrator

Patrick's Day
(New York: Morrow Junior Books, 1994)

Subject(s): Identity; Holidays; Conduct of Life
Age range(s): Grades K-3

Major character(s): Patrick Quinn Murphy, Child
Time period(s): 1990s (1994)
Locale(s): Ireland

Summary: Patrick has grown up believing that the town's annual St. Patrick's Day parade is held in his honor. While he thought of himself as special, he treated everyone well, as a special person should. When he discovers that the parade is really for Saint Patrick, Patrick is so devasted that he runs away and adopts "ordinary" behavior. Unhappy with the quarreling that comes with being ordinary, Patrick tries to strike a compromise with himself and begrudgingly attends the parade. (32 pages)

Where it's reviewed:
Booklist, April 1, 1994, page 1461
Horn Book Guide, Fall 1994, page 285
New Advocate, Fall 1994, page 287
School Library Journal, May 1994, page 102

Other books by the same author:
Sing Me a Window, 1993
I Can't Get My Turtle to Move, 1989
Maggie Doesn't Want to Move, 1987

Other books you might like:
Eve Bunting, *Saint Patrick's Day in the Morning*, 1983
Being too small to parade with his family, Jamie plans his own early-morning celebration of St. Patrick's Day.
Steven Kroll, *Mary McLean and the St. Patrick's Day Parade*, 1991
On St. Patrick's Day a leprechaun visits a young Irish girl.
Alice Schertle, *Jeremy Bean's St. Patrick's Day*, 1987
Forgetting to wear something green on St. Patrick's Day humiliates shy Jeremy.

1092

JEAN DAVIES OKIMOTO
DOUG KEITH, Illustrator

A Place for Grace
(Seattle: Sasquatch Books, 1993)

Subject(s): Animals/Dogs; Deafness; Schools
Age range(s): Grades K-3
Major character(s): Charlie, Deaf; Grace, Dog; Mrs. Lombardi, Teacher (guide dog trainer)
Time period(s): 1990s (1993)
Locale(s): San Francisco, California

Summary: Grace is too small to realize her dream of being a guide dog for the blind, but Charlie thinks she would make a perfect companion for him. Although she does not share Charlie's enthusiasm, Mrs. Lombardi agrees to include Grace in the lessons. Only with some creative accomodations on Charlie's part is Grace able to receive her certification as a hearing ear dog. (32 pages)

Where it's reviewed:
Horn Book Guide, Fall 1993, page 270
Publishers Weekly, April 19, 1993, page 61
School Library Journal, August 1993, page 149

Other books by the same author:
Blumpoe the Grumpoe Meets Arnold the Cat, 1990

Other books you might like:

Deborah Abbott, *One TV Blasting and a Pig Outdoors*, 1994
With co-author Henry Kisor, Abbott describes a son's view of daily life with a deaf father including the accomodations used to facilitate communication.

Catherine Arthur, *My Sister's Silent World*, 1979
A girl tells about living with her younger sister who is deaf.

Ada B. Litchfield, *Words in Our Hands*, 1980
Life with deaf parents is described by their nine-year-old son.

1093

JAMIE OLIVIERO
SHARON HITCHCOCK, Illustrator

The Day Sun Was Stolen

(New York: Hyperion Books for Children, 1995)

Subject(s): Indians of North America; Folk Tales; Legends
Age range(s): Grades K-2
Major character(s): Raven, Bird (raven); Bear, Bear; Ts'ina dabju, Child, Indian
Time period(s): Indeterminate Past
Locale(s): Pacific Northwest

Summary: A *pourquoi* tale explains why some animals grow thicker coats in the winter while Bear hibernates in a cave. Originally, Raven created Bear by rolling clay many times in moss, which made Bear's coat so much thicker than those of the other animals that he became too warm. To cool himself, Bear caught the sun and put it in a cave. Now, Bear was happy, but the other animals and people were very cold so Ts'ina dabju thought of a plan to change Bear's mind. Tricking Bear into taking him into the cave with him, Ts'ina dabju takes off his fish disguise while Bear sleeps and shaves some of Bear's fur so his coat is less thick. When Bear awakens he feels so cool he quickly finds warm sun and throws it back into the sky. (32 pages)

Where it's reviewed:
Booklist, November 1, 1995, page 474
Horn Book Guide, Spring 1996, page 93
Kirkus Reviews, August 1, 1995, page 1115
School Library Journal, December 1995, page 100

Other books by the same author:
Som See and the Magic Elephant, 1995
The Fish Skin, 1993

Other books you might like:

Ann Dixon, *How Raven Brought Light to People*, 1992
Raven is the conveyer of light in this tale from the Tlingit Indians of Alaska.

Margaret Hodges, *The Fire Bringer: A Paiute Indian Legend*, 1972
A young Indian boy brings fire to his tribe with help from Coyote.

Gerald McDermott, *Raven: A Trickster Tale from the Pacific Northwest*, 1993
Saddened to see the world in darkness, Raven tricks the Sky Chief and steals the sun, hanging it in the dark sky to benefit everyone.

1094

JAMIE OLIVIERO
JO' ANNE KELLY, Illustrator

Som See and the Magic Elephant

(New York: Hyperion Books for Children, 1995)

Subject(s): Aunts and Uncles; Death; Animals/Elephants
Age range(s): Grades 1-3
Major character(s): Som See, Child, Niece; Pa Nang, Aunt (great aunt); Chang, Elephant
Time period(s): Indeterminate Past
Locale(s): Thailand

Summary: Pa Nang tells Som See a childhood story of the king's magnificent white elephant said to bring good luck to anyone who touches its trunk. Wishing to find Chang so her weak, aging great aunt can once again touch the magical trunk, Som See walks into the rain forest. Soon lost, a magic fish tells her how to find Chang. When Som See explains her need to Chang he carries her home, allowing Pa Nang to touch him. During the night, as Som See sleeps, Pa Nang begins her "great journey" and Som See knows it is a peaceful one. (32 pages)

Where it's reviewed:
Booklist, May 1, 1995, page 1580
Children's Book Review Service, June 1995, page 125
Horn Book Guide, Fall 1995, page 277
School Library Journal, May 1995, page 93

Other books by the same author:
The Day Sun Was Stolen, 1995
The Fish Skin, 1993

Other books you might like:

Helen V. Griffith, *Dream Meadow*, 1994
An elderly woman and her dog enjoy dreams of running in a meadow; one day, together, they run up to the sky.

Pegi Deitz Shea, *The Whispering Cloth: A Refugee's Story*, 1995
With Grandmother's guidance, Mai learns to stitch the story of her life experiences, including her parents' murder and her escape with Grandmother to a refugee camp.

Marion Davies Toth, *Tales from Thailand: Folklore, Culture and History*, 1971
The eighteen folktales are retold with additional factual information about Thailand and its people.

Laura E. Williams, *The Long Silk Strand*, 1995
Before her death, Grandmother tells her granddaughter stories of her life, tying a silk thread to a lengthening strand for each story, until her life is wound into a silk ball.

1095

SHULAMITH LEVEY OPPENHEIM
JOHN WARD, Illustrator

Fireflies for Nathan

(New York: Tambourine Books, 1994)

Subject(s): Grandparents; Summer
Age range(s): Grades K-1

Major character(s): Nathan, 6-Year-Old (African American); Nana, Grandmother; Poppy, Grandfather
Time period(s): 1990s (1994)
Locale(s): United States

Summary: While visiting Nana and Poppy, Nathan asks about his father's favorite childhood activities. Nana not only remembers that Nathan's father liked to catch fireflies, but she still has the jar he used ready and waiting for Nathan to try his hand at firefly catching too. (32 pages)

Where it's reviewed:
Children's Book Review Service, September 1994, page 3
Kirkus Reviews, August 15, 1994, page 1136
Publishers Weekly, June 27, 1994, page 78
School Library Journal, October 1994, page 96
Tribune Books, October 16, 1994, page 7

Other books by the same author:
The Lily Cupboard, 1992
Appleblossom, 1991
Waiting for Noah, 1990

Other books you might like:
Julie Brinckloe, *Fireflies! Story and Pictures*, 1985
    Proud to catch a full jar of fireflies, a young boy also realizes that he must set them free before they die.
Eric Carle, *The Very Lonely Firefly*, 1995
    Through the night, one very lonely firefly searches for others.
Jonathan London, *Fireflies, Fireflies, Light My Way*, 1996
    A child asks the fireflies to light the way so he can find otters, turtles, beavers and other animals.

1096

SHULAMITH LEVEY OPPENHEIM
MICHAEL HAYS, Illustrator

The Hundredth Name

(Honesdale, PA: Boyds Mills Press, 1995)

Subject(s): Animals/Camels; Muslims; Friendship
Age range(s): Grades K-3
Major character(s): Salah, 7-Year-Old, Animal Lover; Qadiim, Camel; Father, Father
Time period(s): Indeterminate Past
Locale(s): Egypt

Summary: Saddened to see Qadiim, his favorite of all animals, appearing to be sad, Salah lies awake considering how to cheer him. Remembering Father's words about the 100 names of Allah—only 99 of which are known to man—Salah decides that if Qadiim could only know the 100th name he would be a proud and happy camel. So, taking Father's prayer rug, Salah creeps quietly out of the sleeping house and prays to Allah. In the morning when he sees a proud, happy Qadiim, Salah knows that his prayer has been answered. (32 pages)

Where it's reviewed:
Booklist, September 15, 1995, page 176
Horn Book, January 1996, page 68
Kirkus Reviews, September 1, 1995, page 1285
Publishers Weekly, September 18, 1995, page 132
School Library Journal, January 1996, page 92

Other books by the same author:
Fireflies for Nathan, 1994
The Lily Cupboard, 1992
Waiting for Noah, 1992

Other books you might like:
Sue Alexander, *Nadia the Willful*, 1983
    After her oldest brother is lost on the desert, Nadia's father forbids the family to speak his name, but Nadia teaches her father that remembering is a part of grieving.
Berniece Freschet, *The Happy Dromedary*, 1977
    This story explains the reason for camels' long necks and their habit of holding their heads high.
Florence Parry Heide, *The Day of Ahmed's Secret*, 1990
    As Ahmed delivers bottled gas from his donkey cart he holds within him the secret he will share later with his family. Co-author Judith Heide Gilliland.

1097

SHULAMITH LEVEY OPPENHEIM
CYD MOORE, Illustrator

I Love You, Bunny Rabbit

(Honesdale, PA: Boyds Mills Press, Inc., 1995)

Subject(s): Toys; Mothers and Sons; Love
Age range(s): Grades K-1
Major character(s): Micah, Child; Bunny Rabbit, Toy; Mama, Mother
Time period(s): 1990s (1995)
Locale(s): United States

Summary: Micah's well-worn Bunny Rabbit is soiled with applesauce, chocolate milk and puddle mud. When a bath fails to remove all the stains, Mama decides it's time to shop for a new rabbit. To Micah, Bunny Rabbit is no more replaceable than he is and, eventually Mama comes to understand that too. (32 pages)

Where it's reviewed:
Booklist, January 1, 1995, page 826
Horn Book Guide, Fall 1995, page 253
Kirkus Reviews, February 15, 1995, page 230
Publishers Weekly, December 12, 1994, page 61
School Library Journal, February 1995, page 78

Awards the book has won:
Book Links Good Book, 1995

Other books by the same author:
Fireflies for Nathan, 1994
The Lily Cupboard, 1992
Waiting for Noah, 1990

Other books you might like:
Jean Van Leeuwen, *Emma Bean*, 1993
    Emma Bean, a stuffed rabbit, has been Molly's companion since birth, but will she go to kindergarten with her?
Margery Williams, *The Velveteen Rabbit*, 1926
    A toy rabbit is so loved by a little boy that the rabbit, in time, becomes real.
Deborah Turney Zagwyn, *The Pumpkin Blanket*, 1991
    Clee's blanket has always been very special. With support from a loving father she learns to get along without it.

1098

HIAWYN ORAM
SUSAN VARLEY, Illustrator

Badger's Bring Something Party
(New York: Lothrop, Lee & Shepard Books, 1995)

Subject(s): Animals; Individuality; Friendship
Age range(s): Grades K-2
Major character(s): Badger, Badger; Mole, Mole
Time period(s): Indeterminate Past
Locale(s): Fictional Country

Summary: Mole attempts to decline Badger's invitation to his
"Bring Something Party" because he is too busy building a
new home to make something to bring. However, Badger
encourages him to come and just "bring himself" so he does.
Other party guests are not as understanding as the host and an
embarassed Mole retreats to a corner. When Badger reminds
Mole that his instructions to "bring himself" referred to
Mole's "interesting" self and not his feel-sorry-for-himself
self, Mole quickly finds his interesting self and becomes the
life of the party. (32 pages)

Where it's reviewed:
Booklist, April 15, 1995, page 1507
Horn Book, May 1995, page 329
Junior Bookshelf, February 1995, page 11
School Librarian, February 1995, page 18
School Library Journal, July 1995, page 67

Other books by the same author:
Reckless Ruby, 1992
Angry Arthur, 1989
In the Attic, 1985

Other books you might like:
Eileen Browne, *No Problem*, 1993
    All Mouse's friends offer suggestions for the assembly of a
    construction kit which Mouse receives unexpectedly in the
    mail.
Mary Blount Christian, *Penrod's Party*, 1990
    A beginning reader includes four tales of good friends
    Penrod Porcupine and Griswold Bear.
Pat Hutchins, *Titch and Daisy*, 1996
    Unable to find friend Daisy at a party, Titch moves from
    one hiding place to another until he finds Daisy doing the
    same thing.
Jackie French Koller, *Mole and Shrew*, 1991
    When relatives crowd Mole out of his house, his friend
    Shrew tries to help him find another home.

1099

HIAWYN ORAM
TONY ROSS, Illustrator

The Second Princess
(Racine, WI: Western Publishing Company, Inc., 1994)

Subject(s): Sisters; Princes and Princesses; Problem Solving
Age range(s): Grades K-2

Major character(s): Second Princess, Royalty (princess);
    Queen, Mother, Royalty (queen); King, Father, Royalty
    (king)
Time period(s): Indeterminate Past
Locale(s): England

Summary: Second Princess is so determined to take over her
sister's position as First Princess that she enlists the cook's
help. While stealing the required payment of the Queen's
jewels, Second Princess is discovered in her mother's room
with her hand in the jewelry box and sent to explain herself to
the King. When the King and Queen discover the reason for
her behavior, they split the privilege of being First Princess
between the two daughters on alternate days of the week with
the entire family being first on Sundays. (32 pages)

Where it's reviewed:
Booklist, October 15, 1994, page 438
Books for Keeps, May 1994, page 36
Junior Bookshelf, February 1995, page 12
School Library Journal, January 1995, page 90
Wilson Library Bulletin, February 1995, page 94

Other books by the same author:
Reckless Ruby, 1992
A Boy Wants a Dinosaur, 1991
Angry Arthur, 1989

Other books you might like:
Sandy Asher, *Princess Bee and the Royal Good-Night Story*,
    1990
    Although other family members tell Princess Bee bedtime
    stories, none compare to those of her absent mother.
Judy Blume, *The Pain and the Great One*, 1974
    A brother and sister each resents the other for being the
    best-loved in the family.
Carol Diggory Shields, *I Am Really a Princess*, 1993
    A young girl's parents provide a reality check to her
    imagined perfect, privileged life as a princess.

1100

URI ORLEV

Lydia, Queen of Palestine
(Boston: Houghton Mifflin Company, 1993)

Subject(s): Jews; World War II; Divorce
Age range(s): Grades 4-7
Major character(s): Lydia Hoffman, 10-Year-Old (Romanian
    Jew), Child of Divorced Parents
Time period(s): 1940s
Locale(s): Bucharest, Romania; Palestine (a kibbutz)

Summary: A self-described terror, Lydia survives her parent's
divorce, the war-forced changes in her life and her escape,
alone, from Romania to the communal life of a kibbutz in
Palestine by retreating into a fantasy world in which she can
do whatever she pleases. Using her dolls as her cast of
characters, she becomes the Queen of Palestine married to
Prince Michael, son of the former king and queen of Romania.
In time, she seeks out her remarried father in Palestine, her
mother emigrates to the kibbutz with a new husband, and
Lydia begins to accept herself and the life events she cannot

control. Originally published in Israel in 1991 and translated from the Hebrew by Hillel Halkin. (170 pages)

Where it's reviewed:
Booklist, October 1, 1993, page 339
Horn Book, March 1994, page 200
Library Talk, May 1994, page 45
Publishers Weekly, October 25, 1993, page 64
School Library Journal, October 1993, page 126

Awards the book has won:
Booklist Editors' Choice, 1993

Other books by the same author:
The Man from the Other Side, 1991
The Island on Bird Street, 1984

Other books you might like:
Judith Kerr, *When Hitler Stole Pink Rabbit*, 1987
The adventures of a Jewish family escaping from Nazi Germany are presented through the eyes of the 9-year-old daughter.
Lois Lowry, *Number the Stars*, 1989
Sheltering her Jewish friend Ellen from the Nazis, 10-year-old Annemarie learns about herself and the meaning of courage.
Doris Orgel, *Devil in Vienna*, 1978
Changes in pre-World War II Austria put a strain on the relationship of two best friends, one a Jew, the other the daughter of a Nazi.

1101

FRANK O'ROURKE
JONATHAN ALLEN, Illustrator

Burton and Stanley
(Boston: David R. Godine, 1993)

Subject(s): Animals/Birds; Communication; Humor
Age range(s): Grades 4-6
Major character(s): Burton, Stork (lost); Stanley, Stork (lost); Franklin Kraft, Agent (railway depot agent)
Time period(s): 1930s (1935)
Locale(s): Cherrygrove, Nebraska

Summary: Two marabou storks caught in a storm are transported from Africa to Nebraska and have the good fortune of landing on the roof of a train depot where they are able to communicate in Morse Code with the depot agent. Being a bird lover, Mr. Kraft is sympathetic to their plight and manages to arrange their transportation back to Africa. This is the author's first book for children. (64 pages)

Where it's reviewed:
Booklist, May 15, 1993, page 1693
Five Owls, March 1993, page 91
Horn Book Guide, Fall 1993, page 302
Publishers Weekly, February 1, 1993, page 96
School Library Journal, May 1993, page 108

Other books you might like:
L. Frank Baum, *The Wonderful Wizard of Oz*, 1900
When a storm transports Dorothy from Kansas to Oz, she seeks help from the Wizard to find her way home.

Dick King-Smith, *Harry's Mad*, 1987
Harry receives a talking African parrot, Madison or Mad for short, from an American relative.
E.B. White, *Stuart Little*, 1945
A classic fantasy relates the story of Stuart Little who leaves the comfort of home to follow a beautiful wren, Margalo.

1102

MARY POPE OSBORNE
VICTORIA CHESS, Illustrator

Spider Kane and the Mystery at Jumbo Nightcrawler's
(New York: Alfred A. Knopf, 1993)

Subject(s): Mystery and Detective Stories; Animals/Insects; Humor
Age range(s): Grades 2-4
Major character(s): Spider Kane, Detective—Amateur (spider), Musician (jazz clarinetist); Leon Leafwing, Butterfly (assistant to Spider Kane); Saratoga D'Bee, Singer (bee), Imposter (villain)
Time period(s): 1990s
Locale(s): Fictional Country

Summary: The sequel to *Spider Kane and the Mystery under the May-Apple* finds the intrepid Spider Kane in the seamy underworld of Jumbo Nightcrawler's Supper Club where the good guys are being kidnapped. Spider Kane sees a connection to the theft of gold belonging to the United Ant Charities. With his trusty lieutenants in the Order of the MOTH, Spider weaves a cunning and rather sticky web which ensnares the culprits and solves the case.

Where it's reviewed:
Booklist, March 15, 1993, page 1319
Bulletin for the Center of Children's Books, June 1993, page 326
Hornbook Guide, Fall 1993, page 303
Kirkus Reviews, May 15, 1993, page 667
School Library Journal, April 1993, page 102

Other books by the same author:
Pirates Past Noon, 1994 (The Magic Tree House Series #4)
Mummies in the Morning, 1993
Spider Kane and the Mystery under the May-Apple, 1992

Other books you might like:
David A. Adler, *The Cam Jansen Series*, 1980-
Using her photographic memory, Cam Jansen participates in the solving of a variety of mysteries.
Mary Blount Christian, *Sebastian (Super Sleuth) and the Stars-in-His-Eyes Mystery*, 1987
On this case, Sebastian, the sheepdog detective, goes to Hollywood to solve a mystery of a problem-plagued movie production.
Lucinda Landon, *The Meg Mackintosh Series*, 1986-
In a series of solve-it-yourself mysteries, Meg Mackintosh is a winner any way you read the story.
Mary Elise Monsell, *The Mysterious Cases of Mr. Pin*, 1989
Mr. Pin, a penguin from the South Pole, travels to Chicago to become a detective.

Marjorie Weinman Sharmat, *Nate the Great Series*, 1972-
Nate follows one clue after another copying the style of
Sherlock Holmes in this series for beginning readers.

1103

HELEN OXENBURY, Author/Illustrator

It's My Birthday
(Cambridge, MA: Candlewick Press, 1994)

Subject(s): Birthdays; Food; Animals
Age range(s): Grades K-1
Major character(s): Unnamed Character, Child
Time period(s): 1990s (1993)
Locale(s): Fictional Country

Summary: A young child plans to make a birthday cake and
asks different animals to supply the ingredients. The chicken
gives eggs, the bear borrows flour, the cat raids the refrigerator for butter and milk, the dog buys some sugar and the
monkey climbs the tree for the cherries to go on top. When the
cake is ready, the animals sit down with the child to enjoy the
fruits of their labors. First published in Great Britain in 1993.
(24 pages)

Where it's reviewed:
Booklist, July 1994, page 1956
Horn Book, March 1995, page 186
Kirkus Reviews, July 15, 1994, page 992
Publishers Weekly, June 20, 1994, page 104
School Library Journal, November 1994, page 87

Other books by the same author:
The Birthday Party, 1993
Tom and Pippo's Day, 1989
Tom and Pippo Make a Mess, 1988

Other books you might like:
Frank Asch, *Happy Birthday, Moon*, 1985
A little bear is determined to present the moon with a gift
for its birthday.
Nancy White Carlstrom, *Happy Birthday, Jesse Bear!*, 1994
From the first preparations, through the party fun, to the
last good night kiss, Jesse Bear excitedly describes his
fourth birthday.

Lee Davis, *P.B. Bear's Birthday Party*, 1994
Stuffed-animal friends gather to help P. B. Bear celebrate
his birthday.

1104

HELEN OXENBURY, Author/Illustrator

Tom and Pippo and the Bicycle
(Cambridge, MA: Candlewick Press, 1994)

Subject(s): Bicycles and Bicycling; Toys; Problem Solving
Age range(s): Grades K-1
Major character(s): Tom, Child; Pippo, Toy, Monkey; Ste-
phanie, Child, Neighbor
Time period(s): 1990s (1993)
Locale(s): England

Summary: Poor Pippo! He likes to ride on the back of Tom's
bicycle, but each time the bike goes over a bump in the yard,
Pippo falls off. Fortunately, Stephanie rides by with her teddy
bear buckled safely into the kiddie seat of her bike. She has
the perfect solution to the problem. First published in Great
Britain in 1993. (24 pages)

Where it's reviewed:
Horn Book, January 1995, page 51
Horn Book Guide, Spring 1995, page 21
School Library Journal, January 1995, page 91

Other books by the same author:
Tom and Pippo on the Beach, 1993
Tom and Pippo Make a Friend, 1989
Tom and Pippo Read a Story, 1988

Other books you might like:
Antoon Krings, *Oliver's Bicycle*, 1992
On a rainy day, Oliver learns that bicycles were not in-
tended for riding in the house.
Dorothy Stott, *Little Duck's Bicycle Ride*, 1991
When Little Duck goes for a bicycle ride he encounters
many problems
Ashley Wolff, *Stella and Roy*, 1993
Patiently, Roy scoots his 4-wheeler bike along the path
determined to beat his overly confident sister Stella astride
her threewheeler.

P

1105

MARGIE PALATINI
HOWARD FINE, Illustrator

Piggie Pie!
(New York: Clarion Books, 1995)

Subject(s): Witches and Witchcraft; Animals; Humor
Age range(s): Grades K-3
Major character(s): Gritch, Witch
Time period(s): Indeterminate
Locale(s): Fictional Country

Summary: In her quest to find the eight piggies needed for a piggie pie recipe, overly confident and hungry Gritch the Witch flies over Old MacDonald's farm sky-writing ''Surrender Piggies!'' prior to arriving to claim ''her'' piggies. Forewarned by the message the pigs don disguises that completely fool a very frustrated (and perhaps nearsighted) Gritch. As she ponders what to eat, a battered, bandaged wolf hiding in the bushes advises her to forget about pigs; he's been chasing three pigs for days with no success. Together the hungry duo saunter off to Gritch's home, each in anticipation of a delicious lunch. (32 pages)

Where it's reviewed:
Booklist, September 1, 1995, page 74
Horn Book, March 1996, page 189
Horn Book Guide, Spring 1996, page 41
Kirkus Reviews, August 15, 1995, page 1192
School Library Journal, November 1995, page 80

Awards the book has won:
Booklist Editors' Choice, 1995
ALA Notable Book, 1996

Other books you might like:
Colin McNaughton, *Suddenly!*, 1995
  A little pig's absentminded walk home from school frustrates the wolf who is stalking him.
Susan Meddaugh, *Hog-Eye*, 1995
  According to the story she tells her family, only quick wits

and reading ability keep a little pig from becoming a wolf's dinner.
Gary Soto, *Chato's Kitchen*, 1995
  Cool cat Chato thinks he's in for a delicious meal when he invites his new neighbors to dinner, but the family of mice brings a friend who ruins Chato's appetite.

1106

TODD STARR PALMER
JUDY LANFREDI, Illustrator

Rhino and Mouse
(New York: Dial Books for Young Readers, 1994)

Series: Dial Easy-to-Read
Subject(s): Animals/Mice; Animals/Rhinoceroses; Friendship
Age range(s): Grades 1-2
Major character(s): Mouse, Mouse, Friend; Rhino, Rhinoceros, Friend
Time period(s): 1990s (1994)
Locale(s): Fictional Country

Summary: The author's first book describes an unusual friendship between Mouse and Rhino which supports the observation that opposites attract. While Mouse and Rhino each have good intentions, their efforts do not always come across in a positive, helpful way. Despite arguments, apologies and forgiveness abound and the two very different animals remain friends. (40 pages)

Where it's reviewed:
Booklist, January 1, 1995, page 828
Horn Book Guide, Spring 1995, page 63
School Library Journal, February 1995, page 79
Wilson Library Bulletin, April 1995, page 113

Other books you might like:
Robin Michal Koontz, *Chicago and the Cat: The Halloween Party*, 1994
  A humorous tale for beginning readers describes two friends' attempts to agree on a costume which requires their cooperation.

Arnold Lobel, *Frog and Toad Are Friends*, 1970

While they don't always see eye-to-eye, Frog and Toad agree that they are the best of friends.

James Marshall, *George and Martha*, 1972

The first book in a series about George and Martha uses several brief, humorous stories to describe the antics of two hippo buddies.

1107

BETTY PARASKEVAS
MICHAEL PARASKEVAS, Illustrator

Monster Beach

(San Diego: Harcourt Brace & Company, 1995)

Subject(s): Monsters; Beaches; Stories in Rhyme
Age range(s): Grades K-2
Major character(s): Unnamed Character, Child, Vacationer; Grandfather, Grandfather, Vacationer
Time period(s): 1990s (1995)
Locale(s): United States

Summary: Arriving at Grandfather's fishing shack, a young boy thinks he sees a large monster in the moonlit water. The next morning the threatening form briefly appears again. When ill-behaved triplets swim too far out just as a storm roils the waters, the monster rescues the children before collapsing on the beach. A tire patch and a bicycle pump breathe new life into the limp shell of the ''monster.'' (32 pages)

Where it's reviewed:
Booklist, June 1995, page 1788
Horn Book Guide, Fall 1995, page 279
School Library Journal, June 1995, page 94
Smithsonian, November 1995, page 172

Other books by the same author:
Junior Kroll and Company, 1994
Shamlanders, 1993
On the Edge of the Sea, 1992

Other books you might like:
Steven Kellogg, *Ralph's Secret Weapon*, 1983
Ralph's musical talents are so poor, eccentric Aunt Georgina suggests he use his bassoon to charm a sea serpent.
Yasuko Kimura, *Fergus and the Sea Monster*, 1976
Fergus is being followed by an unusual blue monster which seems to be growing larger and larger.
Bill Peet, *Cyrus the Unsinkable Sea Serpent*, 1975
Finally, shy but friendly Cyrus has an opportunity to help others by rescuing boaters during a storm and stopping some pirates.

1108

PEGGY PARISH
LYNN SWEAT, Illustrator

Good Driving, Amelia Bedelia

(New York: Greenwillow Books, 1995)

Series: Amelia Bedelia
Subject(s): Automobiles; Humor; Birthdays

Age range(s): Grades 1-2
Major character(s): Amelia Bedelia, Housekeeper; Mr. Rogers, Employer
Time period(s): 1990s (1995)
Locale(s): United States

Summary: Continuing the series begun by the late Peggy Parish, her nephew presents Amelia Bedelia with the day off in honor of her birthday. When she decides to go for a drive to visit her cousin, Mr. Rogers agrees to loan her his car after he accompanies her on a practice ride in the country. As usual, Amelia Bedelia takes all Mr. Rogers' directions literally resulting in a long, harrowing day for Mr. Rogers before he and Amelia Bedelia are able to return home for the birthday celebration. (40 pages)

Where it's reviewed:
Booklist, April 15, 1995, page 1509
Bulletin of the Center for Children's Books, March 1995, page 245
Horn Book Guide, Fall 1995, page 279
Publishers Weekly, April 10, 1995, page 63
School Library Journal, April 1995, page 114

Other books by the same author:
Good Work, Amelia Bedelia, 1976
Come Back, Amelia Bedelia, 1971
Amelia Bedelia and the Surprise Shower, 1966

Other books you might like:
Lucy Bate, *How Georgina Drove the Car Very Carefully from Boston to New York*, 1989
Georgina pretends to drive her family to Grandma's house in New York City.
George Mendoza, *Traffic Jam*, 1990
A family's drive comes to a halt due to traffic congestion.
Susan Schade, *Toad on the Road*, 1992
Toad takes his animal friends for an adventurous drive.

1109

BARBARA PARK
DENISE BRUNKUS, Illustrator

Junie B. Jones and Some Sneaky Peeky Spying

(New York: Random House, 1994)

Series: First Stepping Stone Book
Subject(s): Schools; Teachers; Humor
Age range(s): Grades 1-3
Major character(s): Junie B. Jones, 6-Year-Old, Child (kindergartener); Mrs., Teacher
Time period(s): 1990s (1994)
Locale(s): United States

Summary: Impetuous Junie B. is the sort of kindergartener who could make a teacher look for other work. Shocked to see Mrs. at the grocery store kissing a strange man and ''stealing'' grapes, Junie B. holds onto her secret until the middle of Grandparents' Day when her suspicions come blurting out, causing embarrassment for Mrs. but a good laugh for the grandparents. (66 pages)

Where it's reviewed:
Booklist, November 15, 1994, page 602
Horn Book Guide, Spring 1995, page 69
Instructor, September 1994, page 103
School Library Journal, October 1994, page 96

Other books by the same author:
Junie B. Jones and the Yucky Blucky Fruitcake, 1995
Junie B. Jones and Her Big Fat Mouth, 1993
Junie B. Jones and the Stupid Smelly Bus, 1992

Other books you might like:
Beverly Cleary, *Ramona the Pest*, 1968
    Spirited Ramona enters kindergarten with a curiousity that
    leads to humorous adventures.
Louise Fitzhugh, *Harriet, the Spy*, 1964
    Sneaking about her Manhattan neighborhood, Harriet rec-
    ords all she sees, good or bad, about anybody and every-
    body.
Johanna Hurwitz, *Russell Sprouts*, 1987
    Six-year-old Russell worries about everything.

1110

BARBARA PARK

Mick Harte Was Here

(New York: Knopf/Apple Soup Books, 1995)

Subject(s): Brothers and Sisters; Death
Age range(s): Grades 6-9
Major character(s): Phoebe Harte, 13-Year-Old; Mick Harte,
    12-Year-Old
Time period(s): 1990s
Locale(s): United States

Summary: As Phoebe announces at the beginning of this book,
''I don't want to make you cry. I just want to tell you about
Mick.that he's not here anymore.'' And Phoebe, who is older
than Mick by ten months, tells wonderful stories about impish
Mick. Mick who always stashed away the prizes from the
cereal boxes, who put a ceramic eye in a defrosted chicken,
who called his mother a ''Wascally Wabbit'' in an Elmer
Fudd impersonation and who would be alive if he had worn a
bicycle helmet. (89 pages)

Where it's reviewed:
Booklist, March 1, 1995, page 1242
Book Report, September 1995, page 40
Publishers Weekly, February 27, 1995, page 104
Library Talk, September 1995, page 35
School Library Journal, May 1995, page 109

Awards the book has won:
School Library Journal Best Books, 1995

Other books by the same author:
My Mother Got Married (And Other Disasters), 1989
Beanpole, 1988
Don't Make Me Smile, 1983
Skinnybones, 1982

Other books you might like:
Eve Bunting, *A Sudden Silence*, 1988
    Jesse turns his grief into action as he searches for the hit-
    and-run driver who killed his deaf brother.

Ralph Fletcher, *Fig Pudding*, 1995
    Cliff recounts the year when his gentle, younger brother,
    Brad, is killed while riding his bicycle.
Susan Beth Pfeffer, *The Year without Michael*, 1987
    Michael leaves home to play softball and never returns.
    Was he kidnapped? Did he run away? No one ever knows.

1111

CURTIS PARKINSON
CATHY BOBAK, Illustrator

Tom Foolery

(New York: Bradbury Press, 1993)

Subject(s): Animals/Cats; Islands; Boats and Boating
Age range(s): Grades K-3
Major character(s): Tom Foolery, Cat (family pet); Captain
    Andy, Father (pet owner); Megan, Child (pet owner)
Time period(s): 1990s (1993)
Locale(s): At Sea

Summary: First-time author Parkinson dumps a curious Tom
Foolery into the ocean as his owners sleep aboard their boat.
Fortunately, there is an island nearby and an exhausted Tom
struggles ashore. Captain Andy and Megan search one way
for Tom while he wanders another, but eventually all are
reunited. (32 pages)

Where it's reviewed:
Horn Book Guide, Fall 1993, page 271
Publishers Weekly, February 22, 1993, page 95
Quill and Quire, June 1993, page 36
School Library Journal, May 1993, page 90

Other books you might like:
Mary Calhoun, *Henry the Sailor Cat*, 1994
    Stowaway Henry proves to be a capable sailor who knows
    just what to do when Man falls overboard.
Margaret Bloy Graham, *Benjy's Boat Trip*, 1977
    A ship's cat is unhappy when a dog stows away on her ship
    hoping to find his vacationing family.
Tim Wynne-Jones, *Zoom at Sea*, 1993
    Zoom is a cat who likes water so much that he goes on a
    fantastic ocean adventure.

1112

KATHERINE PATERSON

Flip-Flop Girl

(New York: Lodestar Books, 1994)

Subject(s): Brothers and Sisters; Grief; Death
Age range(s): Grades 3-7
Major character(s): Vinnie Matthews, 4th Grader, Sister; Ma-
    son Matthews, 5-Year-Old, Brother (mute); Lupe Maho-
    ney, 4th Grader, Classmate
Time period(s): 1990s (1994)
Locale(s): Brownsville, Virginia

Summary: Grieving over her father's recent death and angered
by the family's move from Washington, D.C. to her Grandmother's home in Virginia, 9-year old Vinnie struggles to deal
with her confusing feelings, her silent brother, the lack of

acceptance by classmates, and the possiblity of friendship with Lupe, the class outcast. (128 pages)

Where it's reviewed:
Booklist, December 15, 1993, page 755
Horn Book, March/April 1994, page 200
Kirkus Reviews, December 15, 1993, page 1596
Publishers Weekly, November 22, 1993, page 64
School Library Journal, May 1994, page 117

Awards the book has won:
School Library Journal Best Books, 1994

Other books by the same author:
The King's Equal, 1992
Lyddie, 1991
Come Sing, Jimmy Jo, 1985
The Great Gilly Hopkins, 1978
Bridge to Terabithia, 1977

Other books you might like:
C.S. Adler, *Daddy's Climbing Tree*, 1993
    Unable to accept her father's death, Jessica convinces her younger brother to run away with her to their former home, sure that Daddy is there.
Jean Thesman, *Nothing Grows Here*, 1994
    Following the unexpected death of her father, Maryanne must learn to cope not only with her grief but also with the loss of her home and friends when her mother moves to an apartment.
Jane Breskin Zalben, *The Fortuneteller in 5B*, 1991
    Struggling to accept her father's death, Alexandra's life is complicated by a neighbor who may be something more than she seems.

1113

KATHERINE PATERSON

Jip: His Story

(New York: Lodestar Books, 1996)

Subject(s): Identity; Slavery; African Americans
Age range(s): Grades 5-9
Major character(s): Jip, Foundling, Fugitive (slave); Put, Mentally Ill Person; Lyddie Worthen, Teacher
Time period(s): 1850s (1855)
Locale(s): Vermont

Summary: Jip was dropped off a wagon in Vermont when he was three and has lived in the local poor house since then, helping to run the place for the owners. This year new people have come to join Jip, a woman and her daughter as well as a madman. A stranger has also come to town and seems to have a special interest in Jip. Since Jip does not know his background, he cannot answer the stranger's questions and wonders about this interest. Jips luck changes as he begins school with Lucy. There he meets Lyddie, the teacher, who with the help of her friend and the sacrifice of Put, are able to send Jip to Canada and safety from his former owner and the slave catcher. (181 pages)

Where it's reviewed:
School Library Journal, October 1996, page 124
Booklist, September 1, 1996, page 127

Bulletin of the Center for Children's Books, December 1996, page 147
Hornbook, November/December 1996, page 739

Awards the book has won:
School Library Journal Best Books, 1996
ALA Notable Children's Book, 1997

Other books by the same author:
Lyddie, 1991
Jacob Have I Loved, 1980
Bridge to Terabithia, 1977

Other books you might like:
Jennifer Armstrong, *Steal Away*, 1992
    Susannah and the slave she has been given plan to run away to Canada.
Joan W. Blos, *A Gathering of Days*, 1979
    A young girl's diary gives a view of life in New England in the 1850's.
Virginia Hamilton, *Plain City*, 1993
    A young girl learns more about her own past as she learns about her missing father.
Belinda Hurmence, *A Girl Called Boy*, 1982
    A young girl is tired of hearing about slavery until one day she goes to the mailbox and finds herself back in time.
Michael J. Rosen, *A School for Pompey Walker*, 1993
    A former slave tells of his and his master's adventures to raise money for a school.

1114

JILL PATON WALSH
ALAN MARKS, Illustrator

Matthew and the Sea Singer

(New York: Farrar Straus Giroux, 1993)

Subject(s): Orphans; Folk Tales; Singing
Age range(s): Grades 1-4
Major character(s): Birdy, Child (self-confident and kind); Matthew, Orphan (sold to Birdy), Singer (untrained); Pagan, Mythical Creature (seal-child)
Time period(s): Indeterminate Past
Locale(s): Zennor, England (seacoast near Zennor)

Summary: To save a pitiful boy too starved to be of use to anyone, Birdy pays her birthday shilling to the Orphan Master and takes Matthew home. The next morning the family hears Matthew singing beautifully to himself and seeks lessons from the pastor in Zennor. The pastor's voice lessons develop Matthew's natural ability so well that the seal-queen steals him for her own pleasure. Birdy negotiates with the seal-queen for his release by accepting one of the seal-queen's pups for musical training. Originally published in Great Britain in 1992. (46 pages)

Where it's reviewed:
Booklist, April 15, 1993, page 1518
Horn Book Guide, Fall 1993, page 292
Kirkus Reviews, April 15, 1993, page 535
New Advocate, Fall 1993, page 291
School Library Journal, May 1993, page 90

Awards the book has won:
ALA Notable Book, 1994

Other books by the same author:
Pepi and the Secret Names, 1995

Other books you might like:
Susan Cooper, *The Selkie Girl*, 1986
    Cooper retells the classic love story of a man and a seal-girl and the selkie's desire to return to her home in the sea.
Eric Jon Nones, *Caleb's Friend*, 1993
    Orphan Caleb and a mer-boy develop a mutually beneficial relationship.
Robert D. San Souci, *Sukey and the Mermaid*, 1992
    In a mermaid tale based on African tradition, Mama Jo befriends unhappy Sukey.

1115

JILL PATON WALSH
FIONA FRENCH, Illustrator

Pepi and the Secret Names
(New York: Lothrop, Lee & Shepard Books, 1995)

Subject(s): Animals; Artists and Art; Secrets
Age range(s): Grades 3-5
Major character(s): Pepi, Child; Father, Artist; Prince Dhutmose, Royalty
Time period(s): Indeterminate Past
Locale(s): Egypt

Summary: When Pepi's father is commissioned to paint the decorations on the tomb of Prince Dhutmose, he lacks live models of the animals to be included. Wanting Father's work to be of the highest quality, Pepi persuades the desert animals to model by threatening to reveal their secret names. Each animal is so impressed with the quality of Father's work that each returns when the tomb is completed to observe Prince Dhutmose's appreciation. The secret names are expressed in hieroglyphics with an appendix to assist the reader in deciphering and in creating original picture writing. (32 pages)

Where it's reviewed:
Booklist, April 15, 1995, page 1501
Children's Book Review Service, May 1995, page 115
Junior Bookshelf, December 1994, page 200
Publishers Weekly, March 13, 1995, page 69
School Library Journal, April 1995, page 119

Other books by the same author:
Matthew and the Sea Singer, 1993
Birdie and the Ghosties, 1989
Children of the Fox, 1978

Other books you might like:
JoAnn Adinolfi, *The Egyptian Polar Bear*, 1994
    Stranded on an ice berg, a polar bear drifts to ancient Egypt where he becomes the pet of the lonely 10-year-old king.
Roy Gerrard, *Croco'nile*, 1994
    A key helps readers decipher the ten hidden heiroglyphic messages in a rhyming adventure about Hamut and his sister Nekatu.
Deborah Nourse Lattimore, *The Winged Cat: A Tale of Ancient Egypt*, 1992
    Solving the mystery surrounding the death of a sacred cat requires finding the correct spells in the Book of the Dead to open the 12 gates of the Netherworld.

1116

DENISE LEWIS PATRICK
JAMES E. RANSOME, Illustrator

Red Dancing Shoes
(New York: Tambourine Books, 1993)

Subject(s): Dancing; Gifts; Grandparents
Age range(s): Grades K-2
Major character(s): Unnamed Character, Child; Big Sister, Teenager; Grandmama, Grandmother
Time period(s): 1990s (1993)
Locale(s): United States

Summary: When Grandmama returns from a trip with gifts for all the family, the best gift of all is a pair of red dancing shoes for the youngest grandaughter. In the company of Big Sister she dances around the neighborhood showing off the shoes until she trips and the shoes become scuffed and muddy. A little attention and shoe polish restore the shine to the shoes and the smile to the little girl's face. (32 pages)

Where it's reviewed:
Booklist, March 1, 1993, page 1237
Five Owls, January 1993, page 59
Horn Book, September 1993, page 635
Publishers Weekly, December 7, 1993, page 63
School Library Journal, March 1993, page 183

Other books by the same author:
The Car Washing Street, 1993
Disney's Peek-a-Boo Bambi, 1992

Other books you might like:
Niki Daly, *Not So Fast, Songololo*, 1986
    A slow-moving boy finds a new speed when he laces up a pair of red sneakers.
Johanna Hurwitz, *New Shoes for Silvia*, 1993
    Silvia finds many uses for her new red shoes while she waits to grow into them.
Linda Lowery, *Twist with a Burger, Jitter with a Bug*, 1995
    Get out your dancing shoes and get ready to boogie to the rhythm of this lively celebration of dance.

1117

SUSAN PATRON
MIKE SHENON, Illustrator

Bobbin Dustdobbin
(New York: Orchard Books, 1993)

Subject(s): Fantasy; Cleanliness; Fear
Age range(s): Grades K-2
Major character(s): Bobbin Dustbobbin, Child (afraid of brooms), Mythical Creature (small); PapaHob Dustbobbin, Father, Friend; Billy Que, Aged Person (homeowner)
Time period(s): Indeterminate Past
Locale(s): Fictional Country (Billy Que's home)

Summary: Shy Bobbin, terrified of the broom, lives in the dust under Billy Que's bed. Fortunately for Bobbin, Billy Que is not inclined to use the broom, but some friends have other plans. While PapaHob plays checkers with Billy Que and is invited to share in his birthday cake, the five bad boys of the neighborhood decide to clean Billy Que's house as a birthday surprise. A frightened, but resourceful Bobbin must take action before the broom is put to use. (32 pages)

Where it's reviewed:
Horn Book, March 1994, page 225
Kirkus Reviews, September 1, 1993, page 1149
Publishers Weekly, September 6, 1993, page 95
School Library Journal, October 1993, page 107

Other books by the same author:
Dark Cloud, Strong Breeze, 1994
Five Bad Boys, Billy Que, and the Dustbobbin, 1992
Burgoo Stew, 1991

Other books you might like:
Pam Conrad, *The Tub Grandfather*, 1993
    In a sequel to *The Tub People* long lost Tub Grandfather is found sleeping in the dust under the radiator.
Valiska Gregory, *Kate's Giants*, 1995
    Fearful of the dark and the giants that she imagines come out of the attic door at night, Kate realizes that her imagination can also work to her advantage.
John Sabraw, *I Wouldn't Be Scared*, 1989
    A fearful young boy envisions the many ways he will seek and destroy the imaginary monsters which might confront him.

1118

SUSAN PATRON
DOROTHY DONAHUE, Illustrator

Maybe Yes, Maybe No, Maybe Maybe

(New York: Orchard Books, 1993)

Subject(s): Moving, Household; Sisters; Mothers and Daughters
Age range(s): Grades 2-4
Major character(s): PK, 8-Year-Old (imaginative), Sister, middle child; Megan, Child (gifted), Sister (oldest); Rebecca "Rabbit", Child (stubborn), Sister (youngest)
Time period(s): 1990s (1993)
Locale(s): Los Angeles, California

Summary: Stuck in the middle, that's how PK sees herself—wedged between the hormonal, almost-a-teenager Megan and the stubborn, nervous -about-kindergarten Rabbit. When her single-parent family moves to a new, larger apartment, PK hates the changes, especially the loss of a magical built-in clothes hamper from which she "finds" the stories to entertain Rabbit. PK shares her inner thoughts and feelings with her bicycle, the most sympathetic listener in her life, and learns to let go, move on, and find the magic within herself. (96 pages)

Where it's reviewed:
Booklist, March 15, 1993, page 1322
Five Owls, May 1993, page 115
Horn Book, July 1993, page 459
Publishers Weekly, April 5, 1993, page 78
School Library Journal, March 1993, page 184

Awards the book has won:
School Library Journal Best Books, 1993
ALA Notable Book, 1994

Other books you might like:
Beverly Cleary, *Ramona Quimby, Age 8*, 1981
    An entry in the classic series about the Quimby family in which adventuresome Ramona continues to keep her family guessing as she enters third grade.
Lois Lowry, *Anastasia Krupnik*, 1979
    The first book in a humorous series about the Krupnik family introduces 4th grader Anastasia and her younger brother Sam.
Vera B. Williams, *Scooter*, 1993
    When Lanny, her scooter and her mother move to a new apartment, Lanny's out-going personality help her to make new friends.

1119

GARY PAULSEN

Brian's Winter

(New York: Delacorte Press, 1996)

Subject(s): Survival; Winter
Age range(s): Grades 5-9
Major character(s): Brian Robeson, 13-Year-Old, Survivor; David Smallhorn, Indian, Trapper
Time period(s): 1990s
Locale(s): Alaska

Summary: No plane has come to pick up Brian and he faces the fact that he must survive the winter alone with only his ax. The first danger he faces is a local bear, but that incident makes him more aware that he must know what is going on around him at all times. He is able to survive by fishing, then finds a fire rock to make fires for warmth. He follows wolves and eats the meat they leave. Finally he makes a bow from an exploded tree and learns to kill his own meat. Near the end of winter he follows some tracks and finds David, a Cree trapper, with whom he lives until the rescue plane lands for him. (133 pages)

Where it's reviewed:
School Library Journal, February 1996, page 102
Bulletin of the Center for Children's Books, February 1996, page 199

Other books by the same author:
Dogteam, 1993
The River, 1991 (companion book to *Hatchet*)
Hatchet, 1987 (prequel to *Brian's Winter*)

Other books you might like:
Kirkpatrick Hill, *Toughboy and Sister*, 1990
    Two children are able to survive in the Alaskan wilderness.
William Mayne, *Low Tide*, 1993
    Three children are swept inland during a tidal wave.
Harry Mazer, *Snow Bound*, 1987
    Two young people spend 11 days surviving in a wintry world.
Phyllis Reynolds Naylor, *The Fear Place*, 1994
    Doug must face the trail through the Rockies alone when it is up to him to save his brother.

1120

GARY PAULSEN
RUTH WRIGHT PAULSEN, Illustrator

Dogteam
(New York: Delacorte Press, 1993)

Subject(s): Animals/Dogs; Winter
Age range(s): Grades K-3
Major character(s): Unnamed Character, Animal Lover (dog sled operator)
Time period(s): 1990s (1993)
Locale(s): Alaska

Summary: A solitary nighttime dogsled run is a time of excitement for the dogteam as well as the sled driver. The run is enhanced by the beauty and wonder of moonlight on snow and the appearance of wolves who pace the dogs briefly and then vanish. (32 pages)

Where it's reviewed:
Booklist, November 15, 1993, page 633
Children's Book Review Service, February 1994, page 79
Horn Book, November 1993, page 738
Publishers Weekly, August 30, 1993, page 94
School Library Journal, October 1993, page 120

Other books by the same author:
The Tortilla Factory, 1995

Other books you might like:
Jonathan London, *The Eyes of Gray Wolf*, 1993
    Hunting alone on a moonlit winter night, Gray Wolf infringes on another pack's territory.
Leo Yerxa, *Last Leaf First Snowflake to Fall*, 1994
    Stunning collage illustrations depict the night of a parent-child camping trip when the seasons change, the last leaf falls and the snow begins.
Jane Yolen, *Owl Moon*, 1987
    The Caldecott Medal winner eloquently portrays the wonder of a snowy, moonlit night, the companionship of father and child and the magic of sighting an owl.

1121

GARY PAULSEN

Harris and Me: A Summer Remembered
(San Diego: Harcourt Brace and Co., 1994)

Subject(s): Farm Life; Cousins; Humor
Age range(s): Grades 6-12
Major character(s): Unnamed Character, Cousin (narrator); Harris Larson, 9-Year-Old, Cousin; Glennis Larson, Cousin, 14-Year-Old
Time period(s): 1950s
Locale(s): Minnesota

Summary: Shipped off to the farm of distant relatives, the narrator once again spends a summer away from his alcoholic parents. Arriving at the Larson's farm, the narrator meets Harris, with whom he feels an immediate bond, and his older sister, Glennis, who constantly hits Harris to curtail his swearing. The two boys spend the summer working, with the narrator doing many of Harris's chores, and out-daring one another. Together the boys wrestle pigs slick with muck, dodge the hired man's testy cat Buzzer, attach a washing machine motor to an old bicycle and pee on an electric fence, with catapultive results. Though summer has to end, as do all good summers, "Harris and me" have a wonderful, memory-filled time. (157 pages)

Where it's reviewed:
Booklist, December 1, 1993, page 685
Book Report, March 1994, page 36
Voice of Youth Advocates, February 1994, page 371
School Library Journal, January 1994, page 132
Publishers Weekly, October 18, 1993, page 73

Awards the book has won:
ALA Best Books for Young Adults, 1994
Booklist Editors' Choice/Books for Youth, 1993

Other books by the same author:
Call Me Francis Tucket, 1994
Mr. Tucket, 1994
The Cookcamp, 1991

Other books you might like:
Lynn Hall, *Murder in a Pig's Eye*, 1990
    Bodie searches all over Henry Silver's farm, including the manure pile, to find the murdered body of Henry's wife in this hilarious tale.
Kathleen Karr, *Oh, Those Harper Girls! Or Young and Dangerous*, 1992
    Lily and her five sisters try to earn money to help their father save his ranch; unfortunately, all their schemes are illegal.
Harvey Watson, *Bob War and Poke*, 1991
    Bob War and his older brother Poke get mixed up with a pair of criminals when they dislodge a beautiful Maxwell roadster from a muddy ditch.

1122

TOM PAXTON
MICHAEL DOOLING, Illustrator

The Story of Santa Claus
(New York: Morrow Junior Books, 1995)

Subject(s): Santa Claus; Christmas; Toys
Age range(s): Grades K-3
Major character(s): Claus, Artisan (woodcarver); Eva, Spouse (Claus')
Time period(s): Indeterminate Past
Locale(s): Old Forest, Fictional Country (North Country); North Pole, Earth

Summary: As word of his wooden toy figures spreads through the Old Forest, Claus finds that he cannot keep up with the chldren's demand for his carvings. Eva enlists the help of the neighboring elves who initially have more energy than talent. Soon. they outgrow the cottage in the woods and Claus moves workshop, wife and elves to the North Pole. Here he has the space to work, but the distance from the children requires that he use some local reindeer to help him with his Christmas Eve deliveries—or so the story goes. (40 pages)

Where it's reviewed:
Booklist, September 15, 1995, page 172

Children's Book Review Service, October 1995, page 19
Horn Book Guide, Spring 1996, page 41
Quill & Quire, September 1995, page 76
School Library Journal, October 1995, page 40

Other books by the same author:
Engelbert Moves the House, 1995
Engelbert the Elephant, 1990
Jennnifer's Rabbit, 1988

Other books you might like:
Sheila Black, *Santa's Christmas Storybook*, 1995
  A collection of illustrated stories tell about the preparations of elves and Saint Nick for the one night that keeps them busy all year.
Henrietta Strickland, *The Christmas Bear*, 1993
  When he is unable to sleep a young bear wanders into Santa's workshop just in time to offer some much-needed help.
Viveca Larn Sundvall, *Santa's Winter Vacation*, 1994
  On a family vacation, three brothers meet an elderly, bearded man and his wife who may be—guess who?

1123

PAUL PEABODY, Author/Illustrator

Blackberry Hollow
(New York: Philomel Books, 1993)

Subject(s): Animals/Bears; Animals/Frogs and Toads; Inventions
Age range(s): Grades 2-5
Major character(s): Tom McPaddy, Frog (Scottish); Parnassus, Bear (storekeeper), Inventor; Esq. Jeremy Field Mouse, Mouse
Time period(s): Indeterminate
Locale(s): Blackberry Hollow, Fictional Country

Summary: The residents of Blackberry Hollow are eager to find some relief from Tom McPaddy's bagpipe playing. To ease Tom's homesickness, kindly Parnassus invents his grandest contraption yet, to help poor Tom return to Scotland. Unfortunately, while demonstrating his invention, Parnassus became a little more involved than he planned. This is the author's first novel. (147 pages)

Where it's reviewed:
Booklist, January 1, 1994, page 833
Children's Book Review Service, Winter 1994, page 71
Horn Book Guide, Spring 1994, page 81
Publishers Weekly, August 2, 1993, page 82
School Library Journal, January 1994, page 97

Awards the book has won:
Book Links Good Book, 1993

Other books you might like:
Benedict Blathwayt, *Stories from Firefly Island*, 1993
  Tortoise is the resident storyteller for the animals living on Firefly Island.
Kenneth Grahame, *The Wind in the Willows*, 1908
  Mole, Ratty, Badger and Mr. Toad are involved in many adventures in this classic story set in the English countryside.

A.A. Milne, *Winnie the Pooh*, 1926
  Christopher Robin and Winnie the Pooh share good times and bad with their friends in the Hundred Acre Wood.

1124

PHILIPPA PEARCE
ADRIANO GON, Illustrator

Here Comes Tod!
(Cambridge, MA: Candlewick Press, 1994)

Subject(s): Family Life; Play; Parent and Child
Age range(s): Grades 1-2
Major character(s): Tod, Child
Time period(s): 1990s (1992)
Locale(s): England

Summary: Six adventures showcase the everyday activities of curious, imaginative, sometimes outspoken Tod. With supportive, loving parents he's given space to find his own way through the learning opportunities that present themselves whether he's finding a surprise present for his mom or learning to share with a playmate. First published in Great Britain in 1992. (95 pages)

Where it's reviewed:
Booklist, March 1, 1994, page 1262
Books for Keeps, January 1994, page 6
Bulletin of the Center for Children's Books, March 1994, page 229
Kirkus Reviews, February 1, 1994, page 148
School Library Journal, April 1994, page 110

Other books by the same author:
Emily's Own Elephant, 1988
Who's Afraid? and Other Strange Stories, 1986
Tom's Midnight Garden, 1958

Other books you might like:
Judith Caseley, *Harry and Arney*, 1994
  Harry's curious enthusiasm sometimes leads to unexpected problems.
Ann Cameron, *More Stories Julian Tells*, 1986
  In the award-winning sequel to *The Stories Julian Tells* typical childhood activities such as sending a message in a bottle are described from Julian's perspective.
Jane Cutler, *Rats!*, 1996
  Everyday activities for Jason and his younger brother Edward include shopping for school clothes, acquiring pet rats and receiving not birthday gifts from Aunt Bea.
Lois Lowry, *Attaboy Sam!*, 1992
  Sam does a better job helping Anastasia write a poem for Mom's birthday than he does with his own gift—homemade perfume.

1125

GAYLE PEARSON

The Fog Doggies and Me
(New York: Atheneum, 1993)

Subject(s): Friendship; Sisters; Family Life
Age range(s): Grades 6-8

Major character(s): Starr, 7th Grader; Ivy, 7th Grader; Stephen Salazar, 9th Grader
Time period(s): 1990s
Locale(s): San Francisco, California
Summary: Starr's father refers to their San Francisco fog as being composed of "fog doggies," and that's just how Starr views her life right now. She looks forward to spring break, to be with her best friend Ivy and have a special family dinner for Ivy's thirteenth birthday. But all of a sudden Ivy's interested in a 9th grade boy which propels her into the world of diets and dating. At the same time that Ivy's tiring of Starr, Starr is tiring of the adoration of her younger sister. It takes a while, but Starr finally understands that people vary and maturity occurs at different rates, which makes it easier for her to accept the changes in her life. (119 pages)
Where it's reviewed:
Booklist, January 15, 1994, page 919
School Library Journal, January 1994, page 116
Book Report, March 1994, page 37
Voice of Youth Advocates, February 1994, page 371
Horn Book, March 1994, page 201
Other books by the same author:
One Potato, Tu: Seven Stories, 1992
Fish Friday, 1986
Other books you might like:
Francine Pascal, *Love and Betrayal and Hold the Mayo!*, 1985
    Good friends Victoria and Steffi are at camp together for the summer when boy problems emerge.
Marilyn Sachs, *Thirteen Going on Seven*, 1993
    It's hard for Deezy to accept being different from her popular, twin sister Dee; after their grandmother dies, Deezy and her grandfather become close.
Rachel Vail, *Wonder*, 1991
    Jessica's tumultuous 7th grade year finds her seesawing between being a social pariah and having her own clique.

1126

RICHARD PECK

Lost in Cyberspace

(New York: Dial, 1995)

Subject(s): Time Travel; Brothers and Sisters; Schools
Age range(s): Grades 6-8
Major character(s): Josh Lewis, 6th Grader, Time Traveller; Aaron Zimmer, 6th Grader, Time Traveller; Heather Lewis, 12-Year-Old
Time period(s): 1990s
Locale(s): New York, New York
Summary: Josh's life isn't exactly great these days since his parents' divorce. His mother hires these au pairs who are terrible, he finds being a prep school student is chaotic and his older sister Heather is twelve going on twenty. Added to that, Josh's friend Aaron, a computer geek, manages to transport himself and Josh through cyberspace back to 1923. Luckily they only remain a little while and when they return, so does a housemaid from that time period to try and organize Josh's life in a crazy, madcap adventure. (151 pages)

Where it's reviewed:
Book Report, September 4, 1995, page 70
School Library Journal, September 1995, page 202
Booklist, October 15, 1995, page 402
Emergency Librarian, November 1995, page 45
Children's Book Review Service, January 1996, page 60
Other books by the same author:
Bel-Air Bambi and the Mall Rats, 1993
Voices after Midnight, 1989
Remembering the Good Times, 1985
The Ghost Belonged to Me, 1975
Other books you might like:
Grace Chetwin, *Friends in Time*, 1992
    Emma is thrilled when time traveller Abigail appears from 1846. To keep her new friend, she hides the magic doll that would allow Abigail to return home.
Caroline B. Cooney, *Both Sides of Time*, 1995
    Falling back in time, Annie meets and falls in love with Strat, heir to the family fortune. In time, she witnesses a murder and becomes one of the supsects.
Peni R. Griffin, *Switching Well*, 1993
    When a fairy hears their wishes, she sends Ada forward in time and Amber back. Each quickly realizes she's traded one set of problems for another.
Anne Lindbergh, *Nick of Time*, 1994
    When Jericho and Allison time travel to 2094, Allison decides to remain there though Jericho returns home.

1127

ROBERT NEWTON PECK
CHARLES ROBINSON, Illustrator

Soup Ahoy

(New York: Alfred A. Knopf)

Series: Soup
Subject(s): Boats and Boating; Contests; Humor
Age range(s): Grades 3-6
Major character(s): Luther Wesley "Soup" Vinson, Child, Friend (Rob's); Robert Newton "Rob" Peck, Child, Friend (Soup's); Sinker O. Sailor, Radio Personality
Time period(s): Indeterminate Past
Locale(s): Learning, Vermont
Summary: When a contest is announced on Rob and Soup's favorite radio show, they make plans to enter. With their usual enthusiasm Rob and Soup complete the contest requirements and win a visit to their hometown from Sinker O. Sailor himself. The hilarious preparations for this celebrity's visit to their town are topped only by the escapades of the planned entertainment for the illustrious guest. (118 pages)
Where it's reviewed:
Booklist, February 15, 1994, page 1082
Book World, May 8, 1994, page 20
Bulletin of the Center for Children's Books, March 1994, page 229
Kirkus Reviews, April 15, 1994, page 562
School Library Journal, March 1994, page 223
Other books by the same author:
Soup 1776, 1995

Soup in the Saddle, 1983
Soup and Me, 1975

Other books you might like:

Tom Birdseye, *I'm Going to Be Famous*, 1986
Arlo has plans to set a new banana-eating record and gain fame in the *Guinness Book of World Records*.
Gordon Korman, *Radio Fifth Grade*, 1989
By using a local radio station's Saturday afternoon program, Benjy hopes to improve his skill as an announcer.
Stephen Manes, *Make Four Million Dollars by Next Thursday!*, 1991
With plans to become a millionaire, Jason thinks he's a found the book to show how to do it.

1128

MALKA PENN

The Hanukkah Ghosts

(New York: Holiday House, 1995)

Subject(s): Time Travel; Holidays, Jewish; Aunts and Uncles
Age range(s): Grades 4-5
Major character(s): Susan, Child, Niece; Hanni, Spirit, Refugee; Elizabeth, Aunt (Susan's great-aunt)
Time period(s): 1990s (1995); 1940s (1940-1945)
Locale(s): Wimsley Hall, England

Summary: Susan travels from Connecticut to England for a week-long visit with the great-aunt who raised her father during World War II. Each day near dusk, Susan meets people and experiences events that could only have happened 50 years earlier. Meeting Hanni, Susan begins to understand her deceased mother's Jewish faith and participates in the lighting of the Menorah with Aunt Elizabeth and again with Hanni. (76 pages)

Where it's reviewed:
Booklist, September 15, 1995, page 172
Children's Book Watch, December 1995, page 4
Horn Book Guide, Spring 1996, page 67
School Library Journal, October 1995, page 40

Other books by the same author:
The Miracle of the Potato Latkes: A Hanukkah Story, 1994

Other books you might like:
Elaine Marie Alphin, *Tournament of Time*, 1994
In England for a year, American Jess and her brothers solve murders from long ago with help from the victim's spirits who speak to her from the stained-glass windows.
E.L. Flood, *Ghost of a Chance*, 1994
Molly and Josh solve the mystery of a ghost and a one-hundred-year-old murder.
Sheila Hayes, *Zoe's Gift*, 1994
While visiting a small English village Cory meets Zoe and comes to understand her gift for seeing the past.

1129

MALKA PENN
GIORA CARMI, Illustrator

The Miracle of the Potato Latkes: A Hanukkah Story

(New York: Holiday House, 1994)

Subject(s): Jews; Holidays, Jewish; Food
Age range(s): Grades K-3
Major character(s): Tante Golda, Cook
Time period(s): Indeterminate Past
Locale(s): Russia

Summary: The year of a drought Tante Golda doesn't find enough potatoes in the village to make latkes for her traditional Hanukkah party. Tante Golda has the only potato in town and, trusting in a miracle from God, the kind woman uses her potato to make latkes for a starving beggar who appears at her door on the first night of Hanukkah. For the remainder of the week, each morning she awakens to find one more potato at the base of her mennorah until the 8th day of Hanukkah when she has eight, enough to have her Hanukkah party. First picture book for the author. (32 pages)

Where it's reviewed:
Booklist, August 1994, page 2052
Children's Book Review Service, September 1994, page 4
Kirkus Reviews, September 15, 1994, page 1286
Library Talk, November 1994, page 29
Publishers Weekly, September 19, 1994, page 27

Other books you might like:
David A. Adler, *Malke's Secret Recipe: A Chanukah Story from Chelm*, 1989
Malke's recipe for latkes is one of many for each family in Chelm claims to have a secret recipe for the potato pancakes.
Barbara Diamond Goldin, *Just Enough Is Plenty: A Hanukkah Tale*, 1988
A poor family is willing to include a stranger at their holiday table because Mama can cook enough to be plenty for all.
Eric A. Kimmel, *The Chanukkah Guest*, 1990
Bubba Brayna prepares latkes for the rabbi's visit, but serves them to a bear whom she mistakes for the bearded rabbi.

1130

MARY E. PENSON

You're an Orphan, Mollie Brown

(Fort Worth, TX: Texas Christian University, 1993)

Subject(s): Frontier and Pioneer Life; Historical
Age range(s): Grades 4-6
Major character(s): Mollie Brown, Twin; Caleb Brown, Twin
Time period(s): 1870s
Locale(s): Texas

Summary: After their mother dies, Mollie and her brother Caleb are farmed out to relatives while their father travels to find work. Though the relatives are kind to the siblings,

Mollie misses her father and longs for the day he returns home, builds them a house and finds a new mother for them in this work filled with details of the period. (121 pages)

Where it's reviewed:
Publishers Weekly, April 15, 1993, page 79
Voice of Youth Advocates, August 1993, page 156

Other books you might like:
LouAnn Gaeddert, *Hope*, 1995
 Hope's father is in California mining gold and her mother dies. She hates being in the Shaker community and waits for her father to return so she can leave with him.
Laura Leonard, *Finding Papa*, 1991
 The three Edwards children travel to California to join their adventuring father, only to find out he's prospecting for gold in Nevada.
Patricia MacLachlan, *Sarah, Plain and Tall*, 1986
 Caleb and Anna are entranced by the mail-order bride from Maine who travels west to be a new mother for them.

1131
LYNNE RAE PERKINS, Author/Illustrator

Home Lovely
(New York: Greenwillow Books, 1995)

Subject(s): Gardens and Gardening; Mothers and Daughters; Loneliness
Age range(s): Grades 1-3
Major character(s): Tiffany, Latch-Key Child, Gardener; Janelle, Single Mother; Bob, Postal Worker
Time period(s): 1990s (1995)
Locale(s): United States (rural area)

Summary: After Tiffany and Janelle move into an isolated trailer, Tiffany spends the summer days home alone while her mother works. She quickly tires of dolls and TV so, when she spots some seedlings growing near the garbage can, she asks permission to transplant them. Tiffany's visions of trees and flowers growing around the porch and along the driveway are shattered when Bob compliments her on her fine-looking tomato, melon and potato plants. Noticing her disappointment, in a few days, kindly Bob delivers some flowering plants along with the mail, setting the stage for a satisfying conclusion to the author's first book. (32 pages)

Where it's reviewed:
Booklist, January 1, 1996, page 829
Bulletin of the Center for Children's Books, September 1995, page 24
Children's Book Review Service, Winter 1996, page 64
Horn Book, November 1995, page 736
Publishers Weekly, October 9, 1995, page 86

Awards the book has won:
Boston Globe/Horn Book Fanfare, 1996

Other books you might like:
Mordicai Gerstein, *Daisy's Garden*, 1995
 When Daisy plants a garden she includes everyone from the mice who help sow the seeds to the raccoons who help harvest the corn. Coauthor/illustrator Susan Yard Harris.
Helen V. Griffith, *Grandaddy's Place*, 1987
 As Janetta becomes accustomed to the animals on

Grandaddy's farm, she grows to like them and the different pace of life in the country.
Elaine Moore, *Grandma's Garden*, 1993
 Together, Grandma and Kim plant their garden, make a scarecrow and repair the damage of an early thunderstorm.

1132
JANET PERLMAN, Author/Illustrator

The Emperor Penguin's New Clothes
(New York: Viking, 1995)

Subject(s): Animals/Penguins; Fairy Tale; Kings, Queens, Rulers, etc.
Age range(s): Grades K-3
Major character(s): Emperor Penguin, Penguin, Royalty
Time period(s): Indeterminate Past
Locale(s): Fictional Country

Summary: Andersen's classic tale is retold with penguins as the characters. A vain ruler hires two tailors who promise a wonderful cloth which is invisible to those who are dishonest or simpleminded. The weavers are swindlers who work at empty looms deceiving the most trusted officials, none of whom want to admit being unable to see the cloth or they'll suffer the consequences. Not until Emperor Penguin parades through the town in his new suit of clothes and a very young penguin notes loudly that the Emperor wears nothing does everyone else acknowledge the truth. (32 pages)

Where it's reviewed:
Canadian Book Review Annual, 1994, page 462
Children's Bookwatch, February 1995, page 5
Horn Book Guide, Fall 1995, page 279
Publishers Weekly, April 24, 1995, page 70
School Library Journal, August 1995, page 127

Other books by the same author:
Cinderella Penguin or, The Little Glass Flipper, 1993

Other books you might like:
Hans Christian Andersen, *The Emperor's New Clothes*, 1985
 One of many retellings, this one by Janet Stevens portrays the emperor as a pig and the weavers as sly foxes.
Anthea Bell, *The Emperor's New Clothes*, 1986
 This retelling is more traditional in text and illustration but with the same outcome for the emperor.
Riki Levinson, *The Emperor's New Clothes*, 1991
 In Levinson's version of the frequently retold tale the emperor is a lion and the other characters are all animals.
Hans Wilhelm, *The Royal Raven*, 1996
 Crawford is determined to be noticed, but when he finally succeeds he discovers that some things in life are more important than appearance.

1133
JULIE ANNE PETERS
CYNTHIA FISHER, Illustrator

B.J.'s Billion-Dollar Bet
(Boston: Little, Brown and Company, 1994)

Series: Springboard Books

Subject(s): Lottery; Friendship; Gambling
Age range(s): Grades 2-3
Major character(s): B.J. Byner, 4th Grader, Gambler; Mavis Mae Clarry, 5th Grader; John Elway, Guinea Pig
Time period(s): 1990s (1994)
Locale(s): United States

Summary: When Mavis Mae moves in down the street, B.J. covets many of her things. Since Mavis Mae is not allowed to trade her things for B.J.'s, he enters into wagers with her. Unfortunately, his luck is not good and he loses everything he bets including his mother's winning lottery ticket. His efforts to get the ticket back only cause him to lose more things, including John Elway, before he finally admits to his family that he is responsible for the missing ticket. (64 pages)

Where it's reviewed:
Horn Book, September 1994, page 583
Horn Book Guide, Fall 1994, page 303
Kirkus Reviews, June 1, 1994, page 779

Other books by the same author:
The Stinky Sneakers Contest, 1992

Other books you might like:
Crosby Bonsall, *The Case of the Hungry Stranger*, 1963
    The Private Eyes Club solves the mystery of a disappearing blueberry pie in an I Can Read Book reissued in 1992.
Ann Cameron, *The Stories Julian Tells*, 1981
    Six episodes of happy family interaction are told from the perspective of Julian in the first award-winning book about his family.
Joanna Cole, *Bully Trouble*, 1989
    Arlo and Robby have a plan that they hope will protect future lunch treats from a hungry bully.

1134

JULIE ANNE PETERS

How Do You Spell Geek?
(New York: Little Brown, 1996)

Subject(s): Friendship; Divorce; Contests
Age range(s): Grades 4-7
Major character(s): Ann Keller, 8th Grader; Kimberly Tyne, 8th Grader; Lurlene Brueggenmeyer, 8th Grader
Time period(s): 1990s
Locale(s): Denver, Colorado

Summary: Ann and Kimberly have been preparing for their last spelling bee for years and then Lurlene comes to school and Ann is asked to sponsor her. At first Ann is turned off by Lurlene's actions and clothes, but as time passes she realizes that Lurlene can be a real friend and is also a good speller. As the girls prepare for and compete in the state spelling finals, Ann begins to realize what friendship means. (139 pages)

Where it's reviewed:
Bulletin of the Center for Children's Books, October 1996, page 72
School Library Journal, October 1996, page 124
Booklist, September 15, 1996, page 242

Other books by the same author:
B.J.'s Billion-Dollar Bet, 1994

The Sneaky Sneakers Contest, 1992

Other books you might like:
Ilene Cooper, *Queen of the Sixth Grade*, 1988
    Robin learns what it means to be an outsider when she and her best friend fight and her friend joins another group of girls.
Nancy J. Hopper, *The Queen of Put-Down*, 1991
    Cassie has to decide between loyalty to an old friend and her wish to get to know a new girl better.
Suzy Kline, *Orp and the Chop Suey Burgers*, 1990
    Orp enters a cooking contest where he thinks he can win a free trip to Disneyland.
E.L. Konigsburg, *The View from Saturday*, 1996
    Four students who are involved in an academic contest become good friends and bring pride to their school.

1135

LISA WESTBERG PETERS
K.D. PLUM, Illustrator

The Hayloft
(New York: Dial Books for Young Readers, 1995)

Series: Easy-to-Read Books
Subject(s): Sisters; Play; Farm Life
Age range(s): Grades 1-2
Major character(s): Caroline Rose, Child, Sister (older); Ivy, Child, Sister (younger); Hebby, Cat
Time period(s): 1990s (1995)
Locale(s): United States

Summary: Summer on the farm is a time for fun. To fulfill Ivy's desire for a dog, she and Caroline Rose pretend Hebby the cat is a dog. Predictably, Hebby does not approve of the idea and runs away. Next the sisters try various means to cool themselves on a hot day. Finally, they plan a sleepover in the hayloft with Hebby who, fortunately, likes to chase bats. (48 pages)

Where it's reviewed:
Booklist, January 1, 1995, page 828
Bulletin of the Center for Children's Books, February 1995, page 212
Horn Book Guide, Fall 1995, page 289
Kirkus Reviews, February 15, 1995, page 231
School Library Journal, February 1995, page 79

Other books by the same author:
The Room, 1994
Tania's Trolls, 1992
The Sun, the Wind and the Rain, 1990

Other books you might like:
Juanita Havill, *Jennifer, Too*, 1994
    Although Matt prefers to play with his own friends, at times he admits his younger sister Jennifer has some good ideas.
Siv Widerberg, *The Big Sister*, 1989
    A young girl admires her older sister although she knows that, being younger, she will never be the biggest, tallest or strongest.

Laura Ingalls Wilder, *On the Banks of Plum Creek*, 1937
Laura and her sisters enjoy the simple pleasures of life on a farm at the turn of the century.

1136

LISA WESTBERG PETERS
BRAD SNEED, Illustrator

When the Fly Flew In...

(New York: Dial Books for Young Readers, 1994)

Subject(s): Cleanliness; Pets; Animals/Insects
Age range(s): Grades K-2
Major character(s): Unnamed Character, Insect (fly)
Time period(s): 1990s (1994)
Locale(s): United States

Summary: Sleeping pets prevent a child from cleaning his room as his mother asks. A pesky fly has no qualms about entering the room and as it buzzes around, it disturbs the various animals whose tail swishes, leaps and zig-zaggy attempts to catch the fly instead restore some order to the clutter in the room. The fly, however . . . flew out. (32 pages)

Where it's reviewed:
Booklist, July 1994, page 1944
Horn Book Guide, Spring 1995, page 50
Kirkus Reviews, September 15, 1994, page 1278
Publishers Weekly, August 15, 1994, page 95
School Library Journal, September 1994, page 192

Awards the book has won:
International Reading Association Children's Choices, 1995

Other books by the same author:
Purple Delicious Blackberry Jam, 1992
Water's Way, 1991
The Sun, the Wind and the Rain, 1988

Other books you might like:
Verna Aardema, *Why Mosquitoes Buzz in People's Ears: A West African Tale*, 1975
    The folktale which explains, from a mosquito's perspective, why the pesky insects buzz in people's ears won the Caldecott Medal.
Byron Barton, *Buzz Buzz Buzz*, 1973
    When a bee stings a bull, a chain of events begins that affects everyone on the farm.
Teri Sloat, *The Thing That Bothered Farmer Brown*, 1995
    An annoying mosquito keeps tired Farmer Brown from enjoying his night's sleep.

1137

P.J. PETERSEN
BETSY JAMES, Illustrator

I Hate Company

(New York: Dutton Children's Books, 1994)

Subject(s): Behavior; Apartments; Single Parent Families
Age range(s): Grades 3-5
Major character(s): Dan Barton, Child of Divorced Parents; Jimmy, 3-Year-Old; Carol Barton, Single Mother
Time period(s): 1990s (1994)

Locale(s): United States

Summary: Dan and his mom live contentedly in a two-bedroom apartment until Carol's friend moves in with her young son while she searches for a job and an apartment. Jimmy is an active child living under difficult circumstances and Dan is expected to politely accept the intrusion into his life, the loss of his bedroom and the destruction of his toys by the younger child. The situation is difficult for all the participants, but each attempts to survive with good humor and patience. (96 pages)

Where it's reviewed:
Booklist, November 11, 1994, page 500
Horn Book Guide, Spring 1995, page 69
Instructor, Spring 1995, page 106
Library Talk, May 1995, page 40
School Library Journal, October 1994, page 126

Other books by the same author:
The Amazing Magic Show, 1994
The Sub, 1993
The Fireplug Is First Base, 1990

Other books you might like:
Barbara Baker, *Oh, Emma*, 1991
    Emma would like to have her own room instead of living in a crowded housing project.
Judy Blume, *Superfudge*, 1980
    Poor Peter Hatcher, life with his uniquely difficult little brother Fudge is not improving in this sequel to *Tales of a Fourth Grade Nothing*.
Eve Bunting, *The In-Between Days*, 1994
    Eleven-year-old George fears the changes his widowed father's girlfriend may cause in his life.

1138

P.J. PETERSEN
ANNA DIVITO, Illustrator

I Want Answers and a Parachute

(New York: Simon & Schuster Books for Young Readers, 1993)

Subject(s): Brothers; Fathers and Sons; Divorce
Age range(s): Grades 3-5
Major character(s): Jason, 1st Grader (fearful), Brother (younger); Matt, Brother (older), Child of Divorced Parents; Dad, Father (remarried)
Time period(s): 1990s (1993)
Locale(s): Tucson, Arizona; San Francisco, California

Summary: Jason is on his first plane ride with Matt to meet their dad's new wife and her daughter. Jason is fearful and loudly demands a parachute, just in case. Matt tries to keep him from becoming too much of an embarrassment, while also serving as the understanding and protective big brother, during a weekend filled with activity and new experiences. (112 pages)

Where it's reviewed:
Booklist, October 1, 1993, page 345
Children's Bookwatch, April 1994, page 4
Horn Book Guide, Spring 1994, page 81
Library Talk, January 1994, page 54
School Library Journal, December 1993, page 114

Other books by the same author:
The Amazing Magic Show, 1994
I Hate Camping, 1991
The Fireplug Is First Base, 1990

Other books you might like:
Judy Blume, *Superfudge*, 1980
> Peter's life is filled with the unexpected as the family tries to stay one step ahead of little brother Fudge.
Diana Hendry, *Kid Kibble*, 1992
> Making ends meet, by renting out the attic room, has meant a succession of boring boarders until Kid Kibble arrives.
Patricia Hermes, *Nothing but Trouble, Trouble, Trouble*, 1994
> Alex's attempts to prove that she is growing into a responsible person seem to end in nothing but trouble.

1139

P.J. PETERSEN
MEREDITH JOHNSON, Illustrator

The Sub

(New York: Dutton Children's Books, 1993)

Subject(s): Schools; Teachers; Friendship
Age range(s): Grades 3-4
Major character(s): Mrs. Walters, Teacher (substitute); James Parker, Child, Friend; Ray Nelson, Child, Friend
Time period(s): 1990s (1993)
Locale(s): United States

Summary: James and Ray are disappointed to find a substitute teacher in the classroom, but decide to make the day more interesting by switching places. Unfortunately, Mrs. Walters returns a second and a third day, making it increasingly difficult to keep up the ruse. The boys find that their plan tests their friendship because of the unexpected and unpleasant consequences. (86 pages)

Where it's reviewed:
Booklist, June 1, 1993, page 1836
Horn Book Guide, Fall 1993, page 289
Instructor, Spring 1994, page 104
Library Talk, November 1993, page 17
School Library Journal, July 1993, page 86

Other books by the same author:
The Amazing Magic Show, 1994
I Hate Company, 1994
I Want Answers and a Parachute, 1993

Other books you might like:
Patricia Reilly Giff, *Fourth Grade Celebrity*, 1979
> Casey's desire to be a celebrity is realized, but not in the way she intended.
Jamie Gilson, *13 Ways to Sink a Sub*, 1982
> A fourth grade class decides to hold a contest to see who can be the first to make the substitute cry.
Elizabeth Levy, *Keep Ms. Sugarman in the Fourth Grade*, 1992
> Troublesome Jackie is progressing well in 4th grade until her teacher is promoted to principal in the middle of the year.

1140

PALLE PETERSEN
JENS ROSING, Illustrator

Inunguak: The Little Greenlander

(New York: Lothreop, Lee & Shepard Books, 1993)

Subject(s): Eskimos; Storytelling; Grandparents
Age range(s): Grades 3-5
Major character(s): Inunguak, Child (Inuit); Grandfather, Aged Person (Inuit), Storyteller
Time period(s): Indeterminate Past
Locale(s): Greenland

Summary: Unlike the other boys in the village, Inunguak is not interested in or skilled at hunting or fishing. He prefers to sit by Grandfather and listen to the stories of his people. When the villagers scorn him and ignore the words of their ancestors, tragedy befalls the village and many die. Inunguak uses one of the stories he has learned to save the village. The book is a translation of a work originally published in Denmark in 1987. (32 pages)

Where it's reviewed:
Bulletin of the Center for Children's Books, December 1993, page 130
Horn Book Guide, Spring 1994, page 68
Kirkus Reviews, August 15, 1993, page 1077
Social Education, April 1994, page 244
School Library Journal, March 1994, page 223

Other books you might like:
Bryan Alexander, *An Eskimo Family*, 1985
> A nonfiction work describes the life of a boy and his family living in a Greenland village which is the most northern in the world.
Jan Andrews, *Very Last First Time*, 1985
> Realizing that there is a first time for everything, a young Eskimo girl walks alone under the ice after the tide recedes to gather mussels.
Deborah Davis, *The Secret of the Seal*, 1989
> A challenging moral dilemma faces Kyo as he struggles to choose between his friendship with a seal or loyalty to his family.
Jean Rogers, *Goodbye, My Island*, 1983
> The last winter of her people's residence on King Island, Alaska is described by an Eskimo girl.

1141

JEANNE WHITEHOUSE PETERSON
SANDRA SPEIDEL, Illustrator

My Mama Sings

(New York: HarperCollins Publishers, 1994)

Subject(s): Mothers and Sons; Singing; African Americans
Age range(s): Grades K-2
Major character(s): Unnamed Character, Child; Mama, Single Mother
Time period(s): 1990s (1994)
Locale(s): United States

Summary: Mama has a song for every occasion, adding constancy to a young boy's life experiences, until the day the car won't start and the bus is late. Then, Mama loses her job and stops singing. With hope that she will soon sing again, the boy makes up a song of his own and feels comforted as he drifts off to sleep, hearing Mama sing his new song. (32 pages)

Where it's reviewed:
Booklist, June 1, 1994, page 1843
Christian Science Monitor, September 16, 1994, page 10
Kirkus Reviews, June 1, 1994, page 779
Publishers Weekly, April 8, 1994, page 61
School Library Journal, August 1994, page 142

Other books by the same author:
I Have a Sister, My Sister Is Deaf, 1977
Sometimes I Dream Horses, 1987

Other books you might like:
Sandra Belton, *From Miss Ida's Front Porch*, 1993
　　On a warm summer evening Miss Ida's front porch is the gathering spot as the older neighbors share their memories with the neighborhood children.
Alice Faye Duncan, *Willie Jerome*, 1995
　　Until Mama takes the time to listen carefully, she thinks Willie Jerome can only make "noise" on his trumpet.
Jan Spivey Gilchrist, *Indigo and Moonlight Gold*, 1993
　　Autrie and her mother share a strong, supportive relationship that allows room for the growth and change that is inevitable.

1142

SUSAN BETH PFEFFER

Nobody's Daughter

(New York: Delacorte, 1995)

Subject(s): Orphans; Historical
Age range(s): Grades 4-6
Major character(s): Emily Lathrop Hasbrouck, Orphan, 11-Year-Old; Gracie Dodge, Orphan; Alice Webber, Librarian
Time period(s): 1910s
Locale(s): Oakbridge

Summary: When Emily's great-aunt dies, she's sent to the Mary Austen Home for Orphaned Girls where she finally becomes friends with several girls, including Gracie. Sent to the local public school, the three friends are continually tormented by the daughters of the wealthy mill owners. Luckily, Emily becomes friends with Alice Webber, the librarian, who drives a newfangled car and maintains her independence. When the town girls are responsible for the death of Gracie, Emily realizes that it's important to show her courage and let the town know what really happened. (153 pages)

Where it's reviewed:
School Library Journal, March 1995, page 206
Book Report, September 1995, page 41
Booklist, January 1, 1995, page 822
Publishers Weekly, January 2, 1995, page 77
Voice of Youth Advocates, April 1995, page 25

Other books by the same author:
Twice Taken, 1994
Make Believe, 1993
The Ring of Truth, 1993

Other books you might like:
Virginia Bradley, *Wait and See*, 1994
　　Though orphaned Amy immediately dislikes new student Violetta, she comes to realize Violetta's not so weird after all.
Marita Conlon-McKenna, *Wildflower Girl*, 1992
　　Orphan Peggy immigrates from Ireland to Boston where she finds a place to stay for young girls and works for a wealthy family.
Katherine Paterson, *Lyddie*, 1991
　　Lyddie hates being an inn servant. She leaves to work in a factory but her interest in unions causes her to be fired for "moral turpitude."

1143

SUSAN BETH PFEFFER
TONY DELUNA, Illustrator

Sara Kate Saves the World

(New York: Henry Holt and Company, 1995)

Subject(s): Supernatural; Schools; Bullies
Age range(s): Grades 2-4
Major character(s): Sara Kate, 3rd Grader; Ashley, 3rd Grader; Dicky Logan, 3rd Grader, Bully
Time period(s): 1990s (1995)
Locale(s): United States

Summary: In the sequel to *Sara Kate, Superkid*, Sara Kate is frustrated that her super powers, when they come on Tuesdays, Thursdays and sometimes Saturdays, are unpredictable and do not give her the ability to rescue people or even deal with a bully like Dicky Logan. On her "off" days, she enjoys school and her new friend Ashley much more because she's not worrying about the power that may unexpectedly arrive. Finally, she briefly receives the power of x-ray vision and subdues Dicky by threatening to reveal his teddy bear underwear to everyone. (58 pages)

Where it's reviewed:
Booklist, September 1, 1995, page 78
Bulletin of the Center for Children's Books, September 1995, page 24
Horn Book Guide, Spring 1996, page 57
School Library Journal, November 1995, page 80

Other books by the same author:
Sara Kate, Superkid, 1994
Twin Troubles, 1992
Twin Surprises, 1991

Other books you might like:
Malorie Blackman, *Girl Wonder and the Terrific Twins*, 1993
　　Most of Superhero Maxine and her twin brothers' good intentions backfire until they are finally in the right place at the right time to help police capture two thieves.
Betsy Duffey, *How to Be Cool in the Third Grade*, 1993
　　Robbie's determination to be "cool" in 3rd grade is chal-

lenged by the class bully who tells everyone about his Super Hero underwear.

Meredith Sue Willis, *The Secret Super Powers of Marco*, 1994

Marco's belief that he has super powers helps him to survive a friendship with a hyperactive bully and life in the inner city.

1144

MARCUS PFISTER, Author/Illustrator

Dazzle the Dinosaur
(New York: North-South Books, 1994)

Subject(s): Dinosaurs; Friendship; Individuality
Age range(s): Grades K-2
Major character(s): Dazzle, Dinosaur; Maia, Dinosaur
Time period(s): Indeterminate Past
Locale(s): Earth

Summary: Confined to a limited area of small valley and guarded carefully by adults, Dazzle and Maia decide to find their ancestral cave and drive away the dragonsaurus that has overtaken it and forced all the maiasaurus out. Other dinosaurs assist the youngsters with their quest and warn them that, because the dragonsaurus hates light, he sleeps by day and hunts at night. This knowledge enables Dazzle to save the brazen Maia when she hurries into the cave and awakens the vicious creature. Reflected light from Dazzle's glittering spines send the dragonsaurus running. Translated from the German by J. Alison James. (32 pages)

Where it's reviewed:
Booklist, February 1, 1995 page 101
Children's Book Review Service, December 1994, page 39
Horn Book Guide, Spring 1995, page 50
Publishers Weekly, October 3, 1994, page 69
School Library Journal, January 1995, page 91

Other books by the same author:
Chris and Croc, 1994
The Christmas Star, 1993
Rainbow Fish, 1992

Other books you might like:
Lorinda Bryan Cauley, *The Trouble with Tyrannosaurus Rex*, 1988
    Duckbill and Ankylosaurus plan to prevent Tyrannosaurus Rex from dining on their neighbors.
Wolfram Hanel, *Lila's Little Dinosaur*, 1994
    After visiting a museum Lila notices a rainbow-colored dinosaur has followed her home.
Jurgen Lassig, *Spiny*, 1995
    Newly Hatched Spiny wanders away from his nestand is almost eaten by Tyrannosaurus before being rescued by his babysitter.

1145

MARCUS PFISTER, Author/Illustrator

Rainbow Fish to the Rescue!
(New York: North-South Books, 1995)

Subject(s): Friendship; Courage; Peer Pressure
Age range(s): Grades K-2
Major character(s): Rainbow Fish, Fish
Time period(s): Indeterminate
Locale(s): Undersea Environment/Habitat

Summary: In a sequel to *Rainbow Fish*, the little fish with the sparkling scales watches a plain, striped fish suffer the exclusion of the group that Rainbow Fish so well remembers. When a shark threatens, Rainbow Fish finds the courage to exhort his friends to accompany him on a rescue mission to save the striped fish. Translated from the German by J. Alison James. (32 pages)

Where it's reviewed:
Booklist, September 15, 1995, page 176
Horn Book Guide, Spring 1996, page 41
Kirkus Reviews, July 15, 1995, page 1029
Publishers Weekly, July 17, 1995, page 229
School Library Journal, September 1995, page 184

Other books by the same author:
Dazzle the Dinosaur, 1994
Rainbow Fish, 1992
Penguin Pete, 1987

Other books you might like:
Eric Carle, *The Very Lonely Firefly*, 1995
    Through the night sky flies a lonely firefly searching for friends.
James Stevenson, *Mr. Hacker*, 1990
    After moving to the country, Mr. Hacker is lonely until a stray cat and dog befriend him.
Andrew Clements, *Big Al*, 1988
    Ignored by the other fish because of his ugly appearance, Big Al is finally appreciated when his scary looks save them all from a fisherman's net.
Leo Lionni, *Swimmy*, 1963
    One lonely, little, black fish in a school of red fish devises a plan to protect them all from their enemies.
James Stevenson, *Mr. Hacker*, 1990
    After moving to the country, Mr. Hacker is lonely until a stray cat and dog befriend him.

1146

PAT PFLIEGER
RUTH GAMPER, Illustrator

The Fog's Net
(Boston: Houghton Mifflin Company, 1994)

Subject(s): Brothers and Sisters; Folk Tales; Weather
Age range(s): Grades 1-3
Major character(s): Devora, Artisan (weaver), Heroine; Jarem, Brother (Devora's)
Time period(s): Indeterminate Past
Locale(s): Fictional Country (village by the sea)

Summary: Each time the fog creeps in from the sea the villagers say it is hungry and has come to satisfy its appetite by casting its net and capturing the village residents. Already, Devora's parents have vanished and the fog threatens to take Jarem if Devora does not weave a new net for its use. Although Devora complies, the fog does not keep its promise and Jarem vanishes with a determined Devora in pursuit, rowing toward the sound of a bell which she has wisely woven into the net. The heroine triumphs in this first picture book by the author. (32 pages)

Where it's reviewed:
Booklist, September 15, 1994, page 144
Children's Book Review Service, Winter 1995, page 71
Horn Book Guide, Spring 1995, page 50
Publishers Weekly, August 8, 1994, page 434
School Library Journal, January 1995, page 92

Other books you might like:
Mary-Claire Helldorfer, *Cabbage Rose*, 1993
    With the help of a magic paint brush Cabbage escapes from her greedy brothers and begins a new life for herself.
Steven Kroll, *Queen of the May*, 1993
    Sylvie's goodness triumphs over the wickedness in her life as she is crowned Queen of the May.
Lauren Mills, *Tatterhood and the Hobgoblins*, 1993
    In a retelling of a Norwegian folktale, unconventional Tatterhood breaks the evil spell cast on her beautiful twin.

1147

ANN PHILLIPS

A Haunted Year

(New York: Macmillan, 1994)

Subject(s): Ghosts; Cousins; Historical
Age range(s): Grades 4-6
Major character(s): Florence Gage, 11-Year-Old, Cousin; Georges Valery, Cousin (deceased)
Time period(s): 1910s
Locale(s): England (Paragon House)

Summary: With her mother dead and her father cataloging an art collection in Italy, lonely Florence stays with two maiden aunts. Spotting an old photograph of a deceased cousin, half-French George, she is able to invoke his spirit and call him to join her. At first George eases her loneliness and comes only when she calls him, but gradually he appears all the time and she can't get rid of him. When she's told that George was thought to have caused the drowning of several girls when he was alive, she wants more than ever to send him back. It takes the help of friends and her new stepbrother to return George to his grave. (175 pages)

Where it's reviewed:
Publishers Weekly, February 14, 1994, page 89
School Library Journal, April 1994, page 130
Book Report, September 1994, page 43
Booklist, March 15, 1994, page 1365
Center for Children's Books. Bulletin, March 1994, page 230

Other books by the same author:
The Peace Child, 1988
The Multiplying Glass, 1987

Other books you might like:
Lois Duncan, *Stranger with My Face*, 1981
    Laurie's astral twin Lia attempts to enter her body so that she can become Laurie and assume her place in the family.
Mary Downing Hahn, *The Doll in the Garden*, 1989
    Finding an antique doll in an overgrown rose garden links Ashley with the present and the past.
Hadley Irwin, *The Original Freddie Ackerman*, 1992
    With more step-relatives than he knows or wants, Trevor decides to spend the summer in Maine with his unknown great-aunts.

1148

DAV PILKEY, Author/Illustrator

Dog Breath: The Horrible Trouble with Hally Tosis

(New York: The Blue Sky Press, 1994)

Subject(s): Animals/Dogs; Humor; Pets
Age range(s): Grades K-2
Major character(s): Hally Tosis, Dog
Time period(s): 1990s (1994)
Locale(s): United States

Summary: The Tosis family love their pet Hally, but her bad breath is forcing them to give her away to a good home. Although the children plan many exciting activities in hopes of taking her breath away, Hally's problem persists. When two burglars break into the house and are overcome by Hally Tosis's welcoming kiss, the family begins to see some advantages to having such a unique pet. (32 pages)

Where it's reviewed:
Booklist, September 15, 1994, page 144
Horn Book Guide, Spring 1995, page 50
Observer, July 23, 1995, page 12
Publishers Weekly, September 12, 1994, page 90
School Library Journal, January 1995, page 92

Other books by the same author:
God Bless the Gargoyles, 1996
The Paperboy, 1996 (Caldecott Honor Book, 1997)
Dogzilla, 1993
Kat Kong, 1993

Other books you might like:
Susan Meddaugh, *Martha Calling*, 1994
    Martha makes the most of the vacation she wins in a radio call-in contest despite the resort's "No Dogs Allowed" policy.
Peggy Rathmann, *Officer Buckle and Gloria*, 1995
    Police dog Gloria enlivens Officer Buckle's safety presentations.
Danny Shanahan, *Buckledown the Workhound*, 1993
    Hard-working Buckledown is dog-tired and ready for a vacation at the Shirttail Wagon Farm.
Alan Snow, *How Dogs Really Work!*, 1993
    A winner of the New York Times Best Illustrated Children's Book Award is a humorous instruction manual for dog owners.

1149

DAV PILKEY, Author/Illustrator

Dogzilla

(San Diego: Harcourt Brace & Company, 1993)

Subject(s): Animals/Mice; Animals/Dogs; Monsters
Age range(s): Grades 1-3
Major character(s): Dogzilla, Dog, Monster; Big Cheese, Mouse, Leader; Scarlett O'Hairy, Mouse, Professor
Time period(s): 1990s (1993)
Locale(s): Mousopolis, Fictional Country

Summary: When the scent of the First Annual Mousopolis Barbeque Cook-Off wafts into a long dormant volcano, the fumes awaken large and hungry Dogzilla. At first the mice are powerless against this larger creature, but with careful planning they unleash the ultimate anti-dog weapon—a bath. Confident that they will never again be bothered by Dogzilla, the mice stage their Second Annual Barbeque Cook-Off with unexpected results. (32 pages)

Where it's reviewed:
Booklist, September 1, 1993, page 69
Children's Book Review Service, October 1993, page 17
Horn Book Guide, Spring 1994, page 49
Publishers Weekly, August 16, 1993, page 101
School Library Journal, December 1993, page 92

Other books by the same author:
Dog Breath: The Horrible Trouble with Hally Tosis, 1994
Kat Kong, 1993
Dragon Gets By, 1991

Other books you might like:
Jon Scieszka, *The Frog Prince, Continued*, 1991
An award-winning, satirical and rather different view of the fate of the frog who is transformed into a prince by the kiss of a princess.
Eugene Trivizas, *The Three Little Wolves and the Big Bad Pig*, 1993
A familiar tale takes a new turn when the big, bad pig tries to outmanuever the 3 little wolves and ends up surprising himself.
William Wegman, *Cinderella*, 1993
The classic fairy tale has been recast with dogs playing all the roles, but Cinderella still loses her glass slipper.

1150

DAV PILKEY, Author/Illustrator

Dragon's Halloween

(New York: Orchard Books, 1993)

Series: Dragon Tales
Subject(s): Dragons; Halloween; Humor
Age range(s): Grades K-2
Major character(s): Dragon, Mythical Creature (dragon)
Time period(s): Indeterminate
Locale(s): Fictional Country

Summary: In the first of three episodes, Dragon creatively uses six small pumpkins to make one large and scary jack o'lantern. Then his costume for the Halloween party acci-dently becomes more frightening than he expects and in the last episode the growling of his hungry stomach terrifies him as he walks home alone through the dark woods. (46 pages)

Where it's reviewed:
Booklist, September 15, 1993, page 163
Five Owls, September 1993, page 18
Horn Book Guide, Spring 1994, page 62
Publishers Weekly, September 20, 1993, page 30
School Library Journal, October 1993, page 107

Other books by the same author:
Dragon's Fat Cat, 1992
Dragon Gets By, 1991
Dragon's Merry Christmas, 1991

Other books you might like:
Sue Alexander, *Who Goes out on Halloween?*, 1990
The beginning reader answers the title's question with descriptions of monsters, pirates, small witches and ghosts.
Patricia Reilly Giff, *Beast and the Halloween Horror*, 1990
Beast does not expect an author to accept his invitation to the school's Halloween parade; now that he has, Beast faces a Halloween horror of his own making.
Robin Michal Koontz, *Chicago and the Cat: The Halloween Party*, 1994
Chicago the rabbit and Cat find that, despite their careful planning, the Halloween party has some unexpected surprises.
Bernard Wiseman, *Halloween with Morris and Boris*, 1975
Good friends Morris and Boris share a Halloween night of fun and fear with typical silly humor.

1151

DAV PILKEY, Author/Illustrator

The Hallo-Wiener

(New York: Scholastic, Inc., 1995)

Subject(s): Animals/Dogs; Halloween; Humor
Age range(s): Grades K-3
Major character(s): Oscar, Dog (dachshund)
Time period(s): 1990s (1995)
Locale(s): United States

Summary: Teased by the other dogs, Oscar endures not only their mean name-calling, but also his well-meaning mother's affectionate nicknames such as "my little sausage link." Rather than hurt his mother's feelings, Oscar resignedly dons the Halloween costume she makes and trots off as a giant hot dog. Encumbered by the costume, Oscar cannot keep up with the other dogs, but at least he is in time to save the bullies from a frightening Halloween monster and finally win some respect. (32 pages)

Where it's reviewed:
Booklist, September 15, 1995, page 172
Bookwatch, September 3, 1995, page 11
Horn Book Guide, Spring 1996, page 41
Library Talk, September 1995, page 25
School Library Journal, October 1995, page 113

Awards the book has won:
School Library Journal Best Books, 1995

Other books by the same author:
The Moonglow Roll-a-Rama, 1995
Dogzilla, 1993
Dragon's Halloween, 1993

Other books you might like:
Helen Craig, *Night of the Paper Bag Monsters*, 1994
On Halloween night two youngsters are frightened when each meets an unrecognizable monster until each notices their friend in disguise.
Robin Michal Koontz, *Chicago and the Cat: The Halloween Party*, 1994
Creating a costume for the two of them to share leads to unexpected surprises for rabbit Chicago and his feline friend.
Jane Yolen, *Beneath the Ghost Moon*, 1994
One small mouse inspires the others to scare away the creepy-crawlies and reclaim their home.

1152

BRIAN PINKNEY, Author/Illustrator

JoJo's Flying Side Kick

(New York: Simon & Schuster Books for Young Readers, 1995)

Subject(s): Martial Arts; Courage; African Americans
Age range(s): Grades K-3
Major character(s): JoJo, Child, Student (Tae Kwon Do); P.J., Friend; Grandaddy, Grandfather
Time period(s): 1990s (1995)
Locale(s): United States

Summary: After class, JoJo's martial arts instructor tells her she is to be tested at the next class for her yellow belt promotion by breaking a board with a flying side kick. Nervously, JoJo spends a sleepless night considering the different advice of Granddaddy, P.J., and her mother. In class, JoJo uses all the advice to her advantage, shattering both the board and a hidden fear. (32 pages)

Where it's reviewed:
Booklist, October 15, 1995, page 412
Bulletin of the Center for Children's Books, December 1995, page 136
Horn Book, September 1995, page 591
Publishers Weekly, September 11, 1995, page 85
School Library Journal, September 1995, page 184

Other books by the same author:
Max Found Two Sticks, 1994

Other books you might like:
Andrew Glass, *Charles T. McBiddle*, 1993
Charles T. McBiddle bolsters his confidence in order to master the art of bike riding.
Mary Hoffman, *Amazing Grace*, 1991
Grace learns she can succeed at anything if she has the courage and determination to persevere.
Ann Herbert Scott, *Brave as a Mountain Lion*, 1996
When Spider is selected for a Spelling Bee he must conquer his fear of standing on stage in front of a crowded audience.

1153

BRIAN PINKNEY, Author/Illustrator

Max Found Two Sticks

(New York: Simon & Schuster Books for Young Readers, 1994)

Subject(s): Musicians; African Americans; Communication
Age range(s): Grades K-3
Major character(s): Max, Child, Musician (drummer)
Time period(s): 1990s (1994)
Locale(s): United States

Summary: One day when Max isn't interested in conversation, he picks up two twigs and responds to questions by drumming a rhythm on a succession of objects that cross his path. Max imitates the sound of pigeons flying, rain on the windows, nearby church bells and the train on which his father works. Without missing a beat, he grabs a pair of real drum sticks tossed to him by a drummer in a passing marching band to conclude the story. (32 pages)

Where it's reviewed:
Booklist, April 1, 1994, page 1441
Bulletin of the Center for Children's Books, July 1994, page 370
Horn Book, May 1994, page 319
Publishers Weekly, February 21, 1994, page 253
School Library Journal, July 1994, page 86

Other books by the same author:
JoJo's Flying Side Kick, 1995

Other books you might like:
Alice Faye Duncan, *Willie Jerome*, 1995
Until Mama takes the time to listen carefully, she thinks Willie Jerome can only make "noise" on his trumpet.
Linda Lowery, *Twist with a Burger, Jitter with a Bug*, 1995
The lively read-aloud tale encourages movement to the syncopated rhythm of the text.
George Ella Lyon, *Five Live Bongos*, 1994
Five lively children create the "Found Sound Band" with everyday household items and discards.

1154

GLORIA JEAN PINKNEY
JERRY PINKNEY, Illustrator

The Sunday Outing

(New York: Dial Books for Young Readers, 1994)

Subject(s): Trains; African Americans; Family Life
Age range(s): Grades 1-3
Major character(s): Ernestine, 8-Year-Old; Odessa Powell, Aunt (great-aunt)
Time period(s): Indeterminate Past
Locale(s): Philadelphia, Pennsylvania

Summary: Every Sunday afternoon Ernestine and Aunt Odessa visit the train station to watch the trains arrive and depart. Ernestine's dream is to travel to the family home in Lumberton, North Carolina to meet relatives and see a farm. The family works together, each sacrificing a little, to find the money for a ticket so that Ernestine can make the trip. (32 pages)

Where it's reviewed:
Booklist, May 1, 1994, page 1609
Horn Book, September 1994, page 581
New Advocate, Winter 1995, page 50
Publishers Weekly, May 23, 1994, page 88
School Library Journal, July 1994, page 86

Other books by the same author:
Back Home, 1992 (ALA Notable Book)

Other books you might like:
Sandra Belton, *May'naise Sandwiches & Sunshine Tea*, 1994
Looking through a photo album with her granddaughter prompts Big Mama to share memories of a special childhood picnic.
Valerie Flournoy, *Tanya's Reunion*, 1995
While helping Grandma prepare for a family reunion, Tanya visits and learns about the Virginia farm where Grandma lived as a child.
Elizabeth Fitzgerald Howard, *Mac and Marie and the Train Toss Surprise*, 1993
Excitedly, Mac and Marie wait beside the tracks for the surprise their uncle has promised to throw to them from the passing train.

1155

DANIEL MANUS PINKWATER, Author/Illustrator

Mush, a Dog from Space

(New York: Atheneum Books for Young Readers, 1995)

Subject(s): Animals/Dogs; Moving, Household; Humor
Age range(s): Grades 2-4
Major character(s): Kelly Mangiaro, Child; Mush, Dog, Alien
Time period(s): 1990s (1995)
Locale(s): United States

Summary: While walking in the woods behind her new home Kelly meets a talking, educated, fastidious "mushamute" from the Planet Growf-Woof-Woof and invites the creature home to stay. Although Kelly's parents are opposed to the idea of a pet, Mush's gourmet cooking ability helps them to accept her as Kelly's pet and companion. (40 pages)

Where it's reviewed:
Booklist, October 1, 1995, page 317
Horn Book, November 1995, page 761
School Library Journal, November 1995, page 80

Other books by the same author:
Ned Feldman, Space Pirate, 1994
Jolly Roger: A Dog of Hoboken, 1985
The Hoboken Chicken Emergency, 1984

Other books you might like:
Dick King-Smith, *Harriet's Hare*, 1995
When Harriet befriends a talking hare who is actually a shape-changing alien, her quiet life on the farm is changed.
Dyan Sheldon, *Harry and Chicken*, 1992
Chicken adopts a stray cat who turns out to be an alien from the planet Arcana.
Catherine Siracusa, *The Banana Split from Outer Space*, 1995
After Stanley meets Zelmo, an alien who has crash-landed on earth, his ice cream business improves.

1156

DANIEL MANUS PINKWATER, Author/Illustrator

Ned Feldman, Space Pirate

(New York: Macmillan Publishing Company, 1994)

Subject(s): Aliens; Science Fiction; Humor
Age range(s): Grades 3-5
Major character(s): Ned Feldman, 9-Year-Old; Captain Lumpy "Bugbeard" Lugo, Pirate, Alien
Time period(s): 1990s (1994)
Locale(s): United States (Ned's apartment); Outer Space

Summary: While Ned is home alone for a few hours, he discovers Captain Lugo a. k. a. Bugbeard the Pirate under the kitchen sink. Bugbeard commands a space ship resembling Ned's kitchen sink cabinet and cheerfully takes Ned off on a trip through outer space, returning to Ned's kitchen just as his parents come home. (48 pages)

Where it's reviewed:
Booklist, November 1, 1994, page 500
Bulletin of the Center for Children's Books, October 1994, page 62
Horn Book Guide, Spring 1995, page 69
Instructor, March 1995, page 72
School Library Journal, December 1994, page 112

Other books by the same author:
Spaceburger, 1993
The Muffin Fiend, 1986
Jolly Roger: A Dog of Hoboken, 1984

Other books you might like:
Herbie Brennan, *The Mystery Machine*, 1995
Hubert discovers that his next-door-neighbor is not the witch everyone suspects, but an alien with plans to take-over Earth.
Gery Greer, *Jason and the Escape from Bat Planet*, 1993
In a series entry Jason and his alien friend, Coop, rescue an absent-minded professor imprisoned in outer space. Co-author Bod Ruddick.
Pamela F. Service, *Stinker's Return*, 1993
Alien Tsynq Yr returns the space shuttle he "borrowed" in order to escape from Earth in *Stinker from Space*.

1157

FELIX PITRE
CHRISTY HALE, Illustrator

Pace and the Witch: A Puerto Rican Folktale

(New York: Lodestar Books, 1995)

Subject(s): Folk Tales; Witches and Witchcraft
Age range(s): Grades K-3
Major character(s): Paco, Child; Casi Lampu'a Lentemue, Witch
Time period(s): Indeterminate Past
Locale(s): Puerto Rico

Summary: As Paco walks to the grocery store in town, he fails to heed his mother's admonition not to stop along the way.

Tired and hot, he sits beside the road and accepts an elderly woman's offer of a cool drink. Too late, he realizes that he has been tricked by a witch and is now under her spell. In order to free himself, Paco must guess the witch's name. After failing twice, Paco weeps beside a stream, when a crab happens along who gladly tells him the witch's name. Paco is freed, but the witch's anger now makes the crab scurry away from people and hide under rocks for fear that the witch is coming to get him for revealing her secret. An author's note gives the background information and a glossary defines the Spanish words used. (32 pages)

Where it's reviewed:
Booklist, May 15, 1995, page 1650
Bulletin of the Center for Children's Books, May 1995, page 320
Horn Book Guide, Fall 1995, page 333
Publishers Weekly, May 29, 1995, page 84
School Library Journal, August 1995, page 137

Other books by the same author:
Juan Bobo and the Pig: A Puerto Rican Folktale, 1993

Other books you might like:
Carmen Bernier-Grand, *Juan Bobo: Four Folktales from Puerto Rico*, 1994
    Juan Bobo means well but his literal interpretations of his mother's instructions lead to one humorous misunderstanding after another.
Janet Palazzo-Craig, *Bobo's Magic Wishes: A Story from Puerto Rico*, 1996
    A magical horse offers a man seven wishes which he uses in a comical way and inadvertently cheers a sad princess.
Paul O. Zelinsky, *Rumpelstiltskin*, 1986
    The miller's daughter strikes a bargain with a strange little man who helps her spin straw into gold, but then she must guess his name or sacrifice her first-born child.

1158

ETHEL POCHOCKI
BARRY MOSER, Illustrator

The Mushroom Man
(New York: Green Tiger Press, 1993)

Subject(s): Animals/Moles; Loneliness; Friendship
Age range(s): Grades 1-4
Major character(s): Unnamed Character, Worker (lonely); Beatrice, Cat (pet); Unnamed Character, Mole (lonely)
Time period(s): 1990s (1993)
Locale(s): United States

Summary: Long hours in the dark working his mushroom farm leave an elderly man feeling lonely for companionship. Isolated by the townspeople who mock him as the mushroom man, he decides to acquire a pet. At first he invites Beatrice to live with him, but she soon decides she needs more freedom and wanders away. When he meets a mole who is also lonely, the two find that they are perfectly suited for friendship. (32 pages)

Where it's reviewed:
Booklist, September 15, 1993, page 159
Horn Book Guide, Spring 1994, page 69

Library Talk, November 1993, page 35
Publishers Weekly, September 6, 1993, page 91
School Library Journal, January 1994, page 97

Other books by the same author:
Attic Mice, 1993
Wildflower Tea, 1993
Rosebud and Red Flannel, 1991

Other books you might like:
Nancy White Carlstrom, *Blow Me a Kiss, Miss Lilly*, 1990
    Young Sara and elderly Miss Lilly enjoy a special friendship.
Mem Fox, *Wilfrid Gordon McDonald Partridge*, 1989
    When he learns that his elderly friend is losing her memory, a young boy collects some things for her she may have lost.
Minna Jung, *William's Ninth Life*, 1993
    As a cat about to enter his ninth life William has many choices, but he prefers to stay with elderly Elizabeth.
Cynthia Rylant, *An Angel for Solomon Singer*, 1992
    Lonely Solomon Singer wanders the city until he finds a friendly waiter who smiles at him.

1159

PATRICIA POLACCO, Author/Illustrator

Babushka Baba Yaga
(New York: Philomel Books, 1993)

Subject(s): Legends; Grandparents; Russians
Age range(s): Grades K-3
Major character(s): Baba Yaga, Witch, Child-Care Giver; Victor, Child
Time period(s): Indeterminate Past
Locale(s): Russia (small village)

Summary: From her vantage point in the woods, lonely Baba Yaga enviously watches the village babushkas with their grandchildren each day. Finally, dressing herself in stolen clothes with a scarf to hide her pointed ears, she enters the village and offers to care for Victor while his mother works. Baba Yaga and Victor share a loving relationship until the other babushkas begin to tell tales of the horrible Baba Yaga in the woods. Fearing that her true identity will be discovered, she runs away, leaving a saddened Victor. Ultimately, she reveals herself and her true nature when she rescues Victor from wolves and is accepted by the village as Babushka Baba Yaga. (32 pages)

Where it's reviewed:
Booklist, August 1993, page 2071
Horn Book Guide, Spring 1994, page 49
Kirkus Reviews, August 1, 1993, page 1007
Publishers Weekly, July 12, 1993, page 78
School Library Journal, October 1993, page 108

Other books by the same author:
Tikvah Means Hope, 1994
The Bee Tree, 1993
The Keeping Quilt, 1988

Other books you might like:
Glenn Halak, *A Grandmother's Story*, 1992
    With no explanation to the neighbors who suspect she's a

bit daft, an old woman rows out to sea until she saves her grandson from drowning.

Eric A. Kimmel, *Baba Yaga: A Russian Folktale*, 1991
    In a retelling of the traditional tale, Marina's stepmother sends her into the forest to the wicked witch.

Myra Cohn Livingston, *Poems for Grandmothers*, 1990
    The compiled works of many poets celebrate grandmothers in different times, places and walks of life.

1160

PATRICIA POLACCO, Author/Illustrator

The Bee Tree
(New York: Philomel Books, 1993)

Subject(s): Animals/Bees; Grandparents; Neighbors and Neighborhoods
Age range(s): Grades K-3
Major character(s): Mary Ellen, Child; Grampa, Grandfather
Time period(s): Indeterminate Past
Locale(s): Michigan (rural area)

Summary: When Mary Ellen comments to her grandfather that she is ready for a reading break he suggests finding a bee tree. Grampa and Mary Ellen find a bee returning to its hive and follow it, collecting assorted neighbors, passers-by and animals along the way. The adventure becomes a tea party for all with the newly harvested honey and a lesson for Mary Ellen about the value of books and reading. (32 pages)

Where it's reviewed:
Booklist, March 1, 1993, page 1237
Horn Book, May 1993, page 322
New Advocate, Fall 1993, page 292
Publishers Weekly, March 1, 1993, page 57
School Library Journal, June 1993, page 86

Other books by the same author:
Tikvah Means Hope, 1994
Picnic at Mudsock Meadow, 1992
Thunder Cake, 1990

Other books you might like:
Berthe Amoss, *The Cajun Gingerbread Boy*, 1994
    Flavored with Cajun wit and words, a classic tale is retold with the well-known chase of a cocky Gingerbread Boy who ends up, not at a tea party, but as lunch for a hungry crocodile.
Helen V. Griffith, *Grandaddy's Place*, 1987
    A sequel to *Georgia Music* continues developing the relationship between Janetta and her Grandaddy.
Dr. Seuss, *I Can Read with My Eyes Shut*, 1978
    The joys of reading are exuberantly explained by the notorious Cat in the Hat.

1161

PATRICIA POLACCO, Author/Illustrator

My Rotten Redheaded Older Brother
(New York: Simon & Schuster, 1994)

Subject(s): Brothers and Sisters; Grandparents; Family Life
Age range(s): Grades K-3

Major character(s): Richie Barber, Brother (older); Bubbie, Grandmother; Patricia Barber, Sister
Time period(s): 1950s
Locale(s): Union City, Michigan

Summary: Try as she might, Patricia cannot beat her rotten, teasing, older brother at anything and he never lets her forget it! One night she learns from Bubbie how to make a wish on a falling star. Patricia's wish that she do something, anything, better than her brother comes true, but not in a way she expects. (unpaged)

Where it's reviewed:
Booklist, September 15, 1994, page 144
Kirkus Reviews, September 15, 1994, page 1279
Publishers Weekly, July 4, 1994, page 61
School Library Journal, October 1994, p. 96

Awards the book has won:
School Library Journal Best Books, 1994

Other books by the same author:
Tikvah Means Hope, 1994
Babushka Baba Yaga, 1993
The Bee Tree, 1993
Chicken Sunday, 1992
Some Birthday!, 1991

Other books you might like:
Judy Blume, *The Pain and the Great One*, 1984
    Here's a look at sibling rivalry from the perspective of one little brother who is a real pain and a big sister who thinks she's great. Both are sure that Mom and Dad like the other one best.
Marc Brown, *Arthur's Chicken Pox*, 1994
    D. W. is so jealous of the attention that chicken pox brings to her brother, Arthur, that she plans a little attention-getting behavior for herself and ends up with more than she expected.
Molly Delaney, *My Sister*, 1989
    Being the little sister may mean hand-me-downs and teasing, but life with a big sister has its advantages too.
Susan Beth Pfeffer, *The Riddle Streak*, 1993
    When Amy discovers that she has a talent for riddles that even big brother Peter can't solve, she can finally beat him at something.

1162

PATRICIA POLACCO, Author/Illustrator

Pink and Say
(New York: Philomel Books, 1994)

Subject(s): Civil War; Friendship; Death
Age range(s): Grades 3-6
Major character(s): Sheldon "Say" Curtis, 15-Year-Old, Military Personnel; Pinkus "Pink" Aylee, Military Personnel, Slave; Moe Moe Bay Aylee, Mother, Slave
Time period(s): 1860s
Locale(s): Georgia

Summary: Wounded and alone, Say is found by Pink who lost his unit. Valiantly, Pink carries Say to the slave quarters of the burned out plantation where he once lived. Moe Moe Bay nurses Say back to health and soothes his fear of returning to battle. After marauders kill Moe Moe Bay, Pink and Say set out to find Pink's unit, but are captured and taken to Andersonville prison where Pink is hanged. Say survives to return home and tell the story to his children and grandchildren. (48 pages)

Where it's reviewed:
Booklist, September 1, 1994, page 54
Horn Book, November 1994, page 724
Kirkus Reviews, September 15, 1994, page 1279
Publishers Weekly, August 15, 1994, page 95
School Library Journal, October 1994, page 126

Awards the book has won:
Jefferson Cup Award, 1994
School Library Journal Best Books, 1994

Other books by the same author:
My Ol' Man, 1995
Chicken Sunday, 1992
Uncle Vova's Tree, 1989

Other books you might like:
Karen Ackerman, *The Tin Heart*, 1990
    Mahaley and Flora are determined to maintain their friendship despite their fathers' differing positions on the Civil War.
Eve Bunting, *The Blue and the Gray*, 1996
    As a young boy and his friend watch the construction of their new homes, the boy's father tells them about the Civil War battle that was fought in the nearby fields.
George Ella Lyon, *Cecil's Story*, 1991
    During the Civil War, a worried, young child is left with a neighbor while his mother goes to find and bring home his wounded father.
Ann Turner, *Nettie's Trip South*, 1987
    When 10-year-old Nettie travels from her northern home to Virginia, she sees her first slave auction and begins to understand the awful realities of slavery.
Jeanette Winter, *Follow the Drinking Gourd*, 1988
    A song about the Big Dipper, taught to slaves, gives them the necessary information to escape and find a safe route to the North.

1163

PATRICIA POLACCO, Author/Illustrator

Tikvah Means Hope

(New York: Doubleday Book for Young Readers, 1994)

Subject(s): Fires; Holidays, Jewish; Animals/Cats
Age range(s): Grades K-3
Major character(s): Tikvah, Cat; Justine, Child, Friend; Duane, Child, Friend
Time period(s): 1990s (1991)
Locale(s): Oakland, California

Summary: The morning after Justine and Duane sleep overnight in the Sukkah, they help their elderly Jewish neighbors build, they accompany the neighbor as he shops for the ingredients to prepare a feast for Sukkoth. While the trio shops, homes in the hills are engulfed in fire and a firefighter will not let them return to their neighborhood. Fortunately, they find their families safe and, after two days in a shelter, are

allowed to return to their unrecognizable neighborhood. Only chimneys and, miraculously, the Sukkah still stand. While the neighborhood residents gather in a feast of thanksgiving in the Sukkah, Tikvah crawls out of the backyard barbecue where she sought shelter from the fire, giving them all hope. A concluding author's note gives factual information about the fire. (48 pages)

Where it's reviewed:
Horn Book Guide, Spring 1995, page 51
New Advocate, Winter 1995, page 51
Parents Magazine, December 1994, page 22
Publishers Weekly, September 12, 1994, page 90
School Library Journal, December 1994, page 80

Other books by the same author:
Chicken Sunday, 1992 (Golden Kite Award for Illustration, 1992)
Mrs. Katz and Tush, 1992 (Jane Addams Honor Picture Book, 1993)
Thunder Cake, 1990

Other books you might like:
David A. Adler, *The House on the Roof: A Sukkot Story*, 1976
    Over his landlady's protests, an elderly man builds a sukkah on his apartment house roof in order to celebrate Sukkot with his grandchildren.
Malka Drucker, *The Family Treasury of Jewish Holidays*, 1994
    The traditions, songs, stories and recipes associated with nine holidays of the Jewish year are included in an award-winning collection.
Barbara Diamond Goldin, *Night Lights: A Sukkot Story*, 1995
    Daniel and Naomi reflect on the history behind the sukkah and the celebration of Sukkot as they sleep under the stars.

1164

CHARLOTTE POMERANTZ
NANCY WINSLOW PARKER, Illustrator

Here Comes Henny

(New York: Greenwillow Books, 1994)

Subject(s): Animals/Chickens; Food; Stories in Rhyme
Age range(s): Grades K-1
Major character(s): Henny, Chicken, Mother
Time period(s): 1990s (1994)
Locale(s): Fictional Country

Summary: Henny packs a picnic snicky-snacky for her picky little chickies who demand a snacky-snicky instead. Frustrated, Henny devours the entire picnic herself and falls asleep leaving her hungry and somewhat remorseful chicks to pack their own snacky-snicky. (24 pages)

Where it's reviewed:
Booklist, October 15, 1994, page 438
Kirkus Reviews, July 15, 1994, page 993
Publishers Weekly, June 20 1994, page 104
School Library Journal, September 1994, page 192
Wilson Library Bulletin, January 1995, page 119

Other books by the same author:
Where's the Bear?, 1991
One Duck, Another Duck, 1984

The Piggy in the Puddle, 1974

Other books you might like:

Elinor J. Pinczes, *One Hundred Hungry Ants*, 1993
Hungry ants marching toward a picnic attempt different realignments in order to move more quickly, all to no avail.

Nancy Shaw, *Sheep Take a Hike*, 1994
In the fifth rhyming tale about a flock of silly sheep, the group discovers that, while they appear to be lost, they are able to find the way home.

Mary Wormell, *Hilda Hen's Happy Birthday*, 1995
Hilda Hen is not at all picky; she snacks on everything in her path, assuming it to be part of her birthday celebration.

1165

CHARLOTTE POMERANTZ
JENNIFER PLECAS, Illustrator

The Outside Dog

(New York: HarperCollins Publishers, 1993)

Series: I Can Read
Subject(s): Animals/Dogs; Grandparents
Age range(s): Grades K-3
Major character(s): Marisol, Child (granddaughter); Grandfather, Grandfather (Marisol's)
Time period(s): 1990s (1993)
Locale(s): Puerto Rico

Summary: Despite Marisol's longing for a dog, Grandfather wants nothing to do with the flea-bitten, hungry strays that frequent the hillside near their home. When one of the stray dogs "adopts" Marisol, Grandfather begrudgingly concedes that the outside dog now owns them and Marisol's wish comes true. (64 pages)

Where it's reviewed:

Booklist, September 5, 1993, page 151
Five Owls, September 1993, page 10
Horn Book, January 1994, page 68
Reading Teacher, September 1994, page 71
School Library Journal, November 1993, page 88

Awards the book has won:

Booklist Editors' Choice, 1993
ALA Notable Book, 1994

Other books by the same author:

Here Comes Henny, 1994
Halfway to Your House, 1993
The Chalk Doll, 1989
Timothy Tall Feather, 1986
Whiff, Sniff, Nibble, and Chew, 1984

Other books you might like:

Steven Kroll, *Andrew Wants a Dog*, 1992
Andrew is desperate! He really wants a dog and he has one more idea that may convince his parents to agree to a pet.

Cynthia Rylant, *Henry and Mudge: The First Book of Their Adventures*, 1987
Henry's parents finally accept his desire for a dog and agree to have a pet in the family.

Marjorie Weinman Sharmat, *I'm the Best!*, 1991
Following a succession of owners and name changes,

canine Dudley hopes that his current home and name will be permanent for he truly loves his new owner, Robert.

1166

BARBARA ANN PORTE
YOSSI ABOLAFIA, Illustrator

Harry's Birthday

(New York: Greenwillow Books, 1994)

Series: Harry Books
Subject(s): Birthdays; Gifts; Wishes
Age range(s): Grades 2-3
Major character(s): Harry, 8-Year-Old
Time period(s): 1990s (1994)
Locale(s): United States

Summary: In preparation for his birthday Harry plans a party with a cowboy theme and tells everyone one he sees that he's hoping to receive a cowboy hat. When Harry opens his gifts he discovers that his wish has come true—in many colors. (47 pages)

Where it's reviewed:

Booklist, April 1, 1994, page 1466
Bulletin of the Center for Children's Books, May 1994, page 298
Horn Book, September 1994, page 584
Kirkus Reviews, May 15, 1994, page 704
School Library Journal, May 1994, page 103

Other books by the same author:

Harry Gets an Uncle, 1991
Harry's Mom, 1985
Harry's Dog, 1983

Other books you might like:

Syd Hoff, *Happy Birthday, Danny and the Dinosaur!*, 1995
A beginning reader features 6-year-old Danny 's birthday party to which he invites his pal dinosaur.

Suzy Kline, *Herbie Jones and the Birthday Showdown*, 1993
Herbie tries to help his friend Ray come up with a great, but inexpensive, idea for a birthday party.

Cynthia Rylant, *Henry and Mudge and the Best Day of All*, 1995
Both Henry and his pet dog Mudge enjoy Henry's birthday party so much they declare May 1st to be the best day ever.

1167

BARBARA ANN PORTE
YOSSI ABOLAFIA, Illustrator

A Turkey Drive and Other Tales

(New York: Greenwillow Books, 1993)

Subject(s): Storytelling; Family Life; Humor
Age range(s): Grades 2-4
Major character(s): Abigail, Child, Sister; Sam, Child, Brother
Time period(s): 1990s (1993)
Locale(s): United States

Summary: The story-telling family introduced in *The Take-Along Dog* and followed in *Taxicab Tales* is back again with more humorous tall tales. Sam and Abigail find their parent's stories amusing although not always quite believable. (63 pages)

Where it's reviewed:
Booklist, April 15, 1993, page 1516
Horn Book, May 1993, page 348
Kirkus Reviews, April 1, 1993, page 463
Publishers Weekly, April 19, 1993, page 62
School Library Journal, May 1993, page 90

Other books by the same author:
Harry's Birthday, 1994
Ruthann and Her Pig, 1989
Harry's Mom, 1985

Other books you might like:
Sid Fleischman, *McBroom Tells the Truth*, 1981
　　The unusual adventures of a New England farmer continue in another tall tale.
Margaret Mahy, *The Good Fortunes Gang*, 1993
　　The Fortune cousins are part of a large, story-telling, silly-song-singing family.
Barbara Park, *Junie B. Jones and the Stupid Smelly Bus*, 1992
　　Junie's retelling of her first day of school is one of humor and vivid imagination.

1168

BARBARA ANN PORTE
MAXIE CHAMBLISS, Illustrator

When Aunt Lucy Rode a Mule and Other Stories
(New York: Orchard Books, 1994)

Subject(s): Aunts and Uncles; Sisters; Mountain Life
Age range(s): Grades 1-3
Major character(s): Lucy, Aunt; Zelda, Niece, Sister; Stella, Niece, Sister
Time period(s): 1990s (1994); Indeterminate Past
Locale(s): United States

Summary: During a visit with Aunt Lucy, Zelda and Stella listen to stories about Aunt Lucy's childhood visits to the mountain home of her grandparents. The sisters only know of the tales about the escapades of relatives from stories, photos or visits with elderly people who give Zelda and Stella a new perspective on family history. (30 pages)

Where it's reviewed:
Booklist, September 1, 1994, page 54
Horn Book Guide, Spring 1995, page 69
Kirkus Reviews, August 15, 1994, page 1138
Publishers Weekly, August 1, 1994, page 79
School Library Journal, November 1994, page 88

Other books by the same author:
A Turkey Drive and Other Tales, 1993
When Grandma Almost Fell Off the Mountain and Other Stories, 1993
Taxicab Tales, 1992

Other books you might like:
Donald Crews, *Bigmama's*, 1991
　　Memories of summer visits to Bigmama's and Bigpa's

farm home include recollections of 3-day train rides, cool well water, the chicken coop and a big comfortable house.
Patricia MacLachlan, *Three Names*, 1991
　　A great-grandfather tells of his childhood on the prairie with his dog, Three Names.
Cynthia Rylant, *When I Was Young in the Mountains*, 1982
　　Set in Appalachia, the book celebrates the needed support of family to endure the hardship of life in the simple beauty of the mountain world.

1169

CONNIE PORTER
MELODYE ROSALES, Illustrator

Meet Addy: An American Girl
(Middleton, WI: Pleasant Company, 1993)

Series: American Girls Collection
Subject(s): Slavery; African Americans; Freedom
Age range(s): Grades 2-5
Major character(s): Addy Walker, 9-Year-Old, Slave; Ruth Walker, Mother, Slave
Time period(s): 1860s (1864)
Locale(s): North Carolina (Stevens Plantation)

Summary: Addy overhears her parents talking about running away to freedom in the North. Her momma wants to wait for the war to end, but when the master sells her father and brother, Ruth realizes that she and Addy must fulfill the parents' plan. Leaving the baby in the care of older slaves, they escape to a safe house, determined to reach Philadelphia and freedom. Factual information about slavery is included at the end of the book. (69 pages)

Where it's reviewed:
Booklist, August 1993, page 2063
Bulletin of the Center for Children's Books, October 1993, page 55
Kirkus Reviews, September 1, 1993, page 1150
Publishers Weekly, July 5, 1993, page 73
School Library Journal, January 1994, page 116

Other books by the same author:
Addy Saves the Day, 1994
Changes for Addy, 1994
Addy Learns a Lesson: A School Story, 1993

Other books you might like:
Patricia Beatty, *Who Comes with Cannons?*, 1992
　　The Underground Railroad is presented from the perspective of a young Quaker girl whose family assists escaping slaves.
Deborah Hopkinson, *Sweet Clara and the Freedom Quilt*, 1993
　　Clara uses information from overheard conversations to fashion a quilt/map showing her planned escape route to freedom.
Courtni C. Wright, *Journey to Freedom: A Story of the Underground Railroad*, 1994
　　Historically accurate, the author presents one family's journey to freedom with Harriet Tubman as their guide.

1170

MINDY AVRA PORTNOY
KATHERINE JANUS KAHN, Illustrator

Matzah Ball: A Passover Story

(Rockville, MD: Kar-Ben Copies, Inc., 1994)

Subject(s): Jews; Holidays, Jewish; Sports/Baseball
Age range(s): Grades K-3
Major character(s): Aaron, Child
Time period(s): 1990s (1994)
Locale(s): Baltimore, Maryland

Summary: The excitement Aaron feels about an invitation to a baseball game lessens when his mother reminds him that it is Passover and he will not be able to eat from the concession stands. Embarassed to be carrying his own lunch, Aaron is also soon hungry as his friends enjoy the kosher items that he is unwilling to eat. When they go the concessions for more food, Aaron remains in his seat where he is visited by a stranger who shares matzah, a few words of wisdom, and memories of a youth packing a lunch to the ball game during Passover. As luck (or miracles) would have it, Aaron is fortunate to catch a ball hit into the stands before his friends return. (32 pages)

Where it's reviewed:
Horn Book Guide, Fall 1994, page 287
Library Talk, March 1995, page 21
Publishers Weekly, March 28, 1994, page 97
School Library Journal, August 1994, page 143

Other books by the same author:
Mommy Never Went to Hebrew School, 1989

Other books you might like:
Barbara Cohen, *Make a Wish, Molly*, 1994
 In an earlier era, Molly attends a party during Passover and watches others eat a beautiful birthday cake while enduring the taunts of some party guests.
Harriet K. Feder, *Not Yet, Elijah!*, 1989
 Impatiently, Elijah waits to be invited into the Passover Seder.
Lauren Wohl, *Matzoh Mouse*, 1991
 Sarah finds some of the Passover offerings so tempting that she has difficulty waiting for the Seder.
Jane Breskin Zalben, *Happy Passover, Rosie*, 1990
 In the company of her family, young bear Rosie celebrates her first Passover.

1171

ROXANNE DYER POWELL
WILL HILLENBRAND, Illustrator

Cat, Mouse, and Moon

(Boston: Houghton Mifflin Company, 1994)

Subject(s): Animals/Cats; Animals/Mice
Age range(s): Grades K-3
Major character(s): Cat, Cat, Hunter; Mouse, Mouse; Moon, Celestial Body (moon)
Time period(s): 1990s (1994)
Locale(s): United States

Summary: The author's first book explains the behavior of an ordinary house cat at night when Moon is full and Cat is hungrily searching for a meal. Mouse is unaware that Cat is so close until Moon shakes the clouds away, illuminating the night and revealing Cat's presence just in time for Mouse to seek refuge in his burrow. Disappointed, Cat hurries home as the sun rises for a meal and a nap as the crafty night-Cat becomes the docile day-Cat, dreaming of future adventures. (32 pages)

Where it's reviewed:
Booklist, January 1, 1995, page 826
Five Owls, November 1994, page 33
Horn Book Guide, Spring 1995, page 51
Publishers Weekly, September 26, 1994, page 70
School Library Journal, November 1994, page 88

Other books you might like:
Frank Asch, *Moongame*, 1984
 While playing hide-and-seek with his friend Bear, Moon hides behind a cloud.
Patricia Casey, *My Cat Jack*, 1994
 Jack is a stretching, yawning, scratching cat and a child's beloved pet.
Kit Wright, *Tigerella*, 1993
 A polite, quiet child by day, Ella becomes a fierce tiger at night, enjoying adventures with the stars.
Jane Yolen, *Beneath the Ghost Moon*, 1994
 After their costumes are destroyed by the wicked crawlies, the mice band together to save their home and their spoiled celebration beneath the Ghost Moon.

1172

CHRIS POWLING, Editor
PETER BAILEY, Illustrator

Faces in the Dark: A Book of Scary Stories

(New York: Kingfisher, 1994)

Subject(s): Ghosts; Supernatural; Short Stories
Age range(s): Grades 3-6
Time period(s): Indeterminate Past
Locale(s): Earth

Summary: Ten stories set in various countries and different time periods offer a mixture of scariness and subtle humor. All but two tales in the collection are original and all are intended to be read aloud. An introductory note by the editor suggests reading them out of the hearing of younger siblings, but none of these entries are really terrifying. (80 pages)

Where it's reviewed:
Booklist, January 1, 1995, page 820
Horn Book Guide, Spring 1995, page 143
Library Talk, January 1995, page 30
School Library Journal, December 1994, page 112

Other books by the same author:
Hiccup Harry, 1988

Other books you might like:
Marc Brown, *Scared Silly!*, 1994
 A collection of poems, riddles, jokes and stories including

works by Yolen, Nash and Prelutsky tickle the funny bone wit hout being too frightening.

Bruce Coville, *Bruce Coville's Book of Ghosts: Tales to Haunt You*, 1994
A compilation of 13 entries ranging from frightening to funny.

Alice Low, *Spooky Stories for a Dark and Stormy Night*, 1994
Folktales, adaptations of classics, and contemporary stories by a variety of popular authors make up an illustrated collection.

1173

NANCY POYDAR, Author/Illustrator

Busy Bea

(New York: Margaret K. McElderry Books, 1994)

Subject(s): Grandparents; Behavior; Memory
Age range(s): Grades K-2
Major character(s): Bea, Child (African American), Student; Grandma, Grandmother
Time period(s): 1990s (1994)
Locale(s): United States

Summary: Energetic Bea is so busy getting onto the next activity that she doesn't notice what she has left behind. Bea leaves for school with a lunch box, or a raincoat, or a jacket, but comes home empty-handed. However, Grandma is not at all worried about Bea's memory because Bea is the one on whom Grandma depends to find her lost glasses or knitting needles. The day Bea loses a sweater Grandma has just knit for her is the day she learns about the lost and found at school where she finds far more than the sweater. This is the first book both written and illustrated by the author. (32 pages)

Where it's reviewed:
Booklist, November 1, 1994, page 508
Children's Book Review Service, February 1995, page 78
Horn Book Guide, Spring 1995, page 51
School Library Journal, December 1994, page 80

Other books you might like:
Juanita Havill, *Jamaica's Find*, 1986
When Jamaica finds a stuffed dog in the park, she decides to give it a new home.

Anna Grossnickle Hines, *Moompa, Toby and Bomp*, 1993
Toby enjoys a visit to the park with Grandpa Moompa until Toby's doll Bomp is lost.

Barbara Ann Porte, *Harry in Trouble*, 1989
After losing his library card three times, Harry is comforted to know that even his father sometimes misplaces things.

1174

JOHN PRATER, Author/Illustrator

The Greatest Show on Earth

(Cambridge, MA: Candlewick Press, 1995)

Subject(s): Circus; Self-Acceptance; Individuality
Age range(s): Grades K-2
Major character(s): Harry, Child; Wellington, Dog

Time period(s): Indeterminate
Locale(s): Fictional Country

Summary: Harry is the klutz in a family of circus performers. While Harry's parents perform on the trapeze, his sister juggles and his grandfather rides a unicycle, Harry's attempts to emulate his relatives flop. Even Wellington has a balancing act. So Harry's job is to care for him, get him ready for the show and hold his leash when he performs. The night Wellington chases a mouse during a performance, with Harry still clinging to the leash, Harry finds his true circus calling—he's a clown! (32 pages)

Where it's reviewed:
Booklist, October 15, 1995, page 412
Books for Keeps, May 1995, page 29
Junior Bookshelf, April 1995, page 65
Publishers Weekly, July 24, 1995, page 63
School Library Journal, October 1995, page 113

Other books by the same author:
Once Upon a Picnic, 1996
Tim and the Blanket Thief, 1993
"No!" Said Joe, 1992
The Gift, 1986

Other books you might like:
Michael Bond, *Paddington at the Circus*, 1992
With Paddington's knack for turning a simple outing into an adventure, the Brown family's trip to the circus leads to Paddington becoming part of the show.

Lisa Campbell Ernst, *Ginger Jumps*, 1990
A performing circus dog finds the courage to do a new trick when she meets the girl of her dreams.

David Merveille, *Thomas, the Circus Boy*, 1993
Lacking his father's and grandfather's talentsThomas believes he has no future in the circus and runs away, only to discover hs talent is to care for the animals.

1175

MARJORIE PRICEMAN

How to Make an Apple Pie and See the World

(New York: Alfred A. Knopf, 1994)

Subject(s): Food; Voyages and Travels; Imagination
Age range(s): Grades 1-3
Major character(s): Unnamed Character, Child, Baker
Time period(s): Indeterminate Past
Locale(s): Earth

Summary: As a young baker prepares to make an apple pie, she imagines how she will proceed if she finds the market closed and thus begins a culinary geography lesson as the cook travels the globe selecting the finest ingredients for making her apple pie. A concluding recipe enables readers to make their own pie, travel optional. (40 pages)

Where it's reviewed:
Booklinks, November 1994, page 55
Booklist, April 15, 1994, page 1532
Horn Book, September 1994, page 581
Publishers Weekly, April 11, 1994, page 64

School Library Journal, June 1994, page 112

Awards the book has won:
Booklist Editors' Choice, 1994
ALA Notable Book, 1995

Other books by the same author:
Friend or Frog, 1989

Other books you might like:
Tony Blundell, *Beware of Boys*, 1992
Captured by a wolf, a small boy suggests suitable recipes for the wolf to use when cooking him.
Stella Blackstone, *Grandma Went to Market: A Round-the-World Counting Rhyme*, 1996
Beginning with one flying carpet, Grandma tours the word purchasing items from many locales.
Jo Ellen Boggart, *Gifts*, 1995
Around-the-world travels bring a grandmother home with gifts for her granddaughter.
Jeanne Modesitt, *Lunch with Milly*, 1995
To provide the forgotten dessert, Milly takes her young luncheon guest on a fanciful journey to collect the ingredients.

1176

ELISE PRIMAVERA, Author/Illustrator

Plantpet
(New York: G. P. Putnam's Sons, 1994)

Subject(s): Pets; Gardens and Gardening; Loneliness
Age range(s): Grades K-2
Major character(s): Bertie, Collector (of junk); Plantpet, Plant
Time period(s): 1990s (1994)
Locale(s): Fictional Country

Summary: Bertie's discovery of a caged plant in his junkyard, begins a tale of companionship and caring. As Bertie follows the care directions on the cage, the plant grows and changes until it walks out of the cage and begins digging holes and planting a garden. When Plantpet refuses to stop digging bigger and bigger holes, Bertie banishes it to an out-of-the-way corner. Forgotten, Plantpet begins shrinking until a lonely Bertie digs the last hole, plants Plantpet in it and watches the effect of light, love and caring. (32 pages)

Where it's reviewed:
Bulletin of the Center for Children's Books, September 1994, page 24
Children's Book Review Service, December 1994, page 39
Library Talk, January 1995, page 35
Publishers Weekly, August 8, 1994, page 434
School Library Journal, November 1994, page 88

Other books by the same author:
The Three Dots, 1993
Ralph's Frozen Tale, 1991

Other books you might like:
Margaret Mahy, *The Pumpkin Man and the Crafty Creeper*, 1990
Mr. Parkin, caretaker of quiet pumpkins, has his life changed by a plant with an attitude.

Nancy J. Peteraf, *A Plant Called Spot*, 1994
Teddy's mom buys him a plant pet so he can practice caring for the animal kind.
Shel Silverstein, *The Giving Tree*, 1964
For years, a tree shares all that it has with a little boy as he grows into a man, asking only to be loved in return.

1177

LAURENCE PRINGLE
KATE SALLEY PALMER, Illustrator

Octopus Hug
(Honesdale, PA: Boyds Mills Press, 1993)

Subject(s): Family Life; Fathers; Bedtime
Age range(s): Grades K-2
Major character(s): Dad, Father (African-American), Babysitter; Jesse, Child (African-American); Becky, Child (African-American)
Time period(s): 1990s (1993)
Locale(s): United States

Summary: When Mom goes out for the evening, leaving Jesse and Becky in Dad's care, the children are unhappy until Dad cheers them with an octopus hug. Then, he introduces one active, imaginative game after another until the children are worn out and ready to sleep. (32 pages)

Where it's reviewed:
Horn Book Guide, Spring 1994, page 49
Instructor, October 1993, page 60
Publishers Weekly, October 4, 1993, page 79
Reading Teacher, May 1994, page 654
School Library Journal, January 1994, page 97

Other books by the same author:
Jesse Builds a Road, 1989

Other books you might like:
Trish Cooke, *So Much*, 1994
All the relatives want to hug and squeeze and play with the baby SO MUCH!
Melrose Cooper, *I Got a Family*, 1993
A young girl relates the varied ways in which each member of her family expresses love for her.
Elizabeth Fitzgerald Howard, *Papa Tells Chita a Story*, 1995
Papa entertains Chita with stories of such grand adventures that Chita feels transported to another world.

1178

BONNIE PRYOR
MARK GRAHAM, Illustrator

The Dream Jar
(New York: Morrow, 1996)

Subject(s): Emigration and Immigration; Family Life; Russian Americans
Age range(s): Grades K-3
Major character(s): Valentina, Immigrant; Michael, Immigrant; Papa, Store Owner, Immigrant
Time period(s): 1890s
Locale(s): New York, New York

Summary: Valentina remembers when Papa used to sing all the time. Now he is worried and working hard to raise money to buy a store. Mam and Michael work too and Valentina wants to help, but no one will hire a little girl. One day a neighbor brings over a letter to be read and learns that Valentina can read. She hires the little girl to teach her family English and when other people in the neighborhood find out about this, they, too, join her class. The money adds up in the jar until the family is finally able to buy a small corner store and Papa sings again. (unpaged)

Where it's reviewed:
Booklist, March 1, 1996, page 1189
School Library Journal, March 1996, page 181
Horn Book, July/August 1996, page 454

Other books by the same author:
Poison Ivy and Eyebrow Wigs, 1993
Lottie's Dream, 1992
The Plum Tree War, 1989
Seth of the Lion People, 1988

Other books you might like:
Elisa Bartone, *American Too*, 1996
   A little girl wants to show that she is American so she dresses like the Statue of Liberty for her Italian festival in New York.
Elisa Bartone, *Peppe the Lamplighter*, 1993
   Peppe goes out one night to light the lamps and help his sister find her way home in turn of the century New York.
Eve Bunting, *How Many Days to America? A Thanksgiving Story*, 1988
   A family heads for the United States from their home in the Caribbean.

1179

BONNIE PRYOR
MELISSA SWEET, Illustrator

Marvelous Marvin and the Pioneer Ghost

(New York: Morrow Junior Books, 1995)

Subject(s): Mystery and Detective Stories; Ghosts; Brothers and Sisters
Age range(s): Grades 3-5
Major character(s): Marvin Fremont, 4th Grader, Twin; Sarah Fremont, 4th Grader, Twin; Ernie Farrow, 4th Grader, Bully (reformed)
Time period(s): 1990s (1995)
Locale(s): Liberty Corners

Summary: Returning to the creek where Marvin thinks he's seen a ghost, Marvin, Sarah and Ernie discover that someone has been illegally dumping chemicals there. An elderly, kindly factory owner is suspected and the three young detectives set out to prove the suspicions wrong and find the true culprit. (145 pages)

Where it's reviewed:
Booklist, May 1, 1995, page 1575
Horn Book Guide, Fall 1995, page 302
School Library Journal, July 1995, page 80

Other books by the same author:
Marvelous Marvin and the Wolfman Mystery, 1994

The Twenty-Four Hour Lipstick Mystery, 1989
Vinegar Pancakes and Vanishing Cream, 1987

Other books you might like:
Ellen Leroe, *Racetrack Robbery*, 1996
   Once again, invisible Ghost Dog helps Artie solve a mystery.
Sara St. Antoine, *The Green Musketeers and the Fabulous Frogs*, 1994
   Samantha and her fifth grade class fight City Hall and a group of developers to save the habitat of endangered tree frogs.
Betty Ren Wright, *The Ghost Comes Calling*, 1994
   On vacation in a haunted lakeside cabin, Chad tries to clear the name of the cabin's resident ghost.

1180

BONNIE PRYOR
GAIL OWENS, Illustrator

Poison Ivy and Eyebrow Wigs

(New York: Morrow Junior Books, 1993)

Subject(s): Identity; Family Life; Schools
Age range(s): Grades 3-5
Major character(s): Martin Elwood Snodgrass, 4th Grader; Jamie Jamison, 4th Grader, Friend (Martin's); Willie Smith, 4th Grader
Time period(s): 1990s (1993)
Locale(s): New Albany (Pleasant Street Elementary)

Summary: Being one of four children in an overachieving family leaves Martin feeling as if he is unworthy of recognition. His older siblings tease him about his bushy eyebrows; he hates sports, but likes animals; and he's sensitive enough to care about Willie, the class misfit. These traits make it difficult for Martin to successfully achieve the goal he and Jamie have established for the year—to join the "in-crowd" of 4th grade boys. In time, Martin sees that the popular group may not be the place for him. Fourth grade is complicated! (162 pages)

Where it's reviewed:
Booklist, April 15, 1993, page 1516
Horn Book Guide, Fall 1993, page 303
School Library Journal, June 1993, page 109

Other books by the same author:
Horses in the Garage, 1992
Vinegar Pancakes and Vanishing Cream, 1987
Rats, Spiders and Love, 1986

Other books you might like:
Judy Blume, *Tales of a Fourth Grade Nothing*, 1976
   Nine-year-old Peter's life is complicated by a stereotypically terrible two-year-old brother.
Betsy Byars, *Beans on the Roof*, 1988
   George feels like the only member of the family who is unable to write poetry.
Beverly Cleary, *Henry Huggins*, 1950
   A neighbor of Beezus and Ramona, Henry begins to find his own identity when he is "adopted" by a dog, Ribsy.

Johanna Hurwitz, *Aldo Ice Cream*, 1981
Nine-year-old Aldo discovers the intangible rewards of volunteering for a community service project.

1181

CAROL PURDY
PETRA MATHERS, Illustrator

Mrs. Merriwether's Musical Cat
(New York: G.P. Putnam's Sons, 1994)

Subject(s): Music; Animals/Cats
Age range(s): Grades K-3
Major character(s): Mrs. Merriwether, Teacher (of piano); Mr. Crump, Neighbor; Beethoven, Cat
Time period(s): 1990s (1994)
Locale(s): United States (an ordinary town)

Summary: Mrs. Merriwether, an ordinary piano teacher, with ordinary, untalented students and an ordinary, complaining neighbor finds an extraordinary stray cat with a rhythmic tail and an unusual effect on her students. Beethoven's transforming impact on Mrs. Merriwether, her students and the neighborhood is short-lived when the cat vanishes suddenly.

Fortunately, the misnamed Beethoven returns with her three kittens and the beat goes on. (32 pages)

Where it's reviewed:
Horn Book, March 1995, page 188
Publishers Weekly, August 1, 1994, page 78
School Library Journal, October 1994, page 97

Awards the book has won:
School Library Journal Best Books, 1994

Other books by the same author:
Least of All, 1993
Iva Dunnit and the Big Wind, 1985

Other books you might like:
Leslie Baker, *The Antique Store Cat*, 1992
Wandering away from her third-floor apartment, Alice cannot find her way home and takes up temporary residence in an antique store.
Mary Calhoun, *High-Wire Henry*, 1991
In this latest book about Henry, the high-jinks are indeed high. Feeling displaced by the family's new puppy, Henry decides to regain their attention by tightrope walking.
Judy Hindley, *Mrs. Mary Malarky's Seven Cats*, 1990
Each of these seven cats has its own special history which Mrs. Malarky has woven into bedtime stories for the children in her care.

Q

1182

MARY QUATTLEBAUM
ROBIN OZ, Illustrator

Jazz, Pizzaz, and the Silver Threads
(New York: Delacrote Press, 1996)

Subject(s): Animals; Self-Reliance; Magicians
Age range(s): Grades 2-5
Major character(s): Calvin Hastings, 9-Year-Old; Jenny Teitletot, 9-Year-Old, Magician; Pizzazz, Hamster
Time period(s): 1990s
Locale(s): United States

Summary: Calvin goes next door with Jenny every day after school to stay with Ms. Eva. Calvin really wants a pet but his parents do not believe him responsible enough. Meanwhile, Jenny is practicing her magic act and decides that she needs an animal to spice up the act, so she buys a hamster. Calvin is not too interested in the hamster until the day he gets sick and Calvin takes him to the vet. Meanwhile, Ms. Eva teaches dancing to older women and being present at her class one day, Calvin gets turned on to the jazz and decides to arrange a show for the neighborhood. His success at this and Jenny's purchase of a guinea pig give Calvin a chance at a pet of his own. (120 pages)

Where it's reviewed:
School Library Journal, March 1996, page 198

Other books by the same author:
The Magic Squad and the Dog of Great Potential, 1997 (sequel to *Jazz, Pizzazz and the Silver Threads*)
Jackson Jones and the Puddle of Thorns, 1994

Other books you might like:
Eve Feldman, *Dog Crazy*, 1992
Sara is just desperate to have a dog for a pet.
Charlotte Towner Graeber, *Fudge*, 1987
Chad Garcia has to prove to his parents that he is responsible enough to take care of a pet.
Johanna Hurwitz, *Ozzie on His Own*, 1995
Ozzie is concerned about the health of his father but upset when the nurse tells him his pet mouse might bring germs into the hospital.
Donna Jo Napoli, *The Bravest Thing*, 1995
Laurel has had a wide range of pets but something always goes wrong. This time she has a rabbit and really wants it to have babies.
Judith Bernie Strommen, *Champ Hobarth*, 1993
Marty is pressured by his father to succeed and does so when he works at an animal shelter.

1183

PATRICIA QUINLAN
JANET WILSON, Illustrator

Tiger Flowers
(New York: Dial Books for Young Readers, 1994)

Subject(s): AIDS (Disease); Death; Grief
Age range(s): Grades K-2
Major character(s): Joel, Child, Nephew; Tara, 3-Year-Old, Sister; Michael, Uncle
Time period(s): 1990s (1994)
Locale(s): United States

Summary: After Michael dies, Joel tries to explain to Tara that he will not return, realizing that a 3-year-old doesn't understand the finality of death. Joel depends on his memories of activities shared with Michael and the comforting reassurance of his mother to cope with his grief. (32 pages)

Where it's reviewed:
Booklist, June 1, 1994, page 1843
Bulletin of the Center for Children's Books, July 1994, page 371
Publishers Weekly, April 18, 1994, page 62
Quill & Quire, April 1994, page 87
School Library Journal, July 1994, page 87

Other books by the same author:
Brush Them Bright, 1992
Emma's Sea Journey, 1991
Anna's Red Sled, 1989

Other books you might like:

MaryKate Jordan, *Losing Uncle Tim*, 1989
    Though he grieves for the loss of his beloved Uncle Tim, Daniel finds comfort in the legacy of joy and courage left by his favorite relative.

Leslea Newman, *Too Far Away to Touch*, 1995
    Uncle Leonard takes Zoe to a planetarium to help her understand that, if he dies, he will be just like the stars—too far away to touch, but close enough to see.

Jane Yolen, *Grandad Bill's Song*, 1994
    With support from family and friends, a young boy begins to accept his feelings following his grandfather's death.

R

1184

STATON RABIN
GREG SHED, Illustrator

Casey over There

(San Diego: Harcourt Brace & Company, 1994)

Subject(s): World War I; Brothers; Letters
Age range(s): Grades 1-3
Major character(s): Aubrey Wheeler, 7-Year-Old, Brother;
Casey Wheeler, Military Personnel, Brother
Time period(s): 1910s (1917-1918)
Locale(s): Brooklyn, New York; France

Summary: Responding to a recruiting poster featuring Uncle Sam, Casey enlists and is sent ''over there'' to fight. Aubrey and Casey correspond, but the letters take two months to arrive. When three months go by and Aubrey has not received any mail from Casey, he writes to Uncle Sam and asks if Uncle Sam is ''done with him'' yet. The reply Aubrey receives is from President Wilson who regretfully informs Aubrey that Uncle Sam is not yet ''done'' with his brother. It is another year before, to everyone's joy, a thin Casey comes limping home. (32 pages)

Where it's reviewed:
Booklist, March 15, 1994, page 1374
Children's Book Review Service, Spring 1994, page 138
Horn Book Guide, Fall 1994, page 287
Publishers Weekly, March 14, 1994, page 72
School Library Journal, May 1994, page 103

Awards the book has won:
Notable Children's Trade Book in the Field of Social Studies, 1994
International Reading Association Award, 1994

Other books you might like:
Michael Foreman, *War Game*, 1994
A memorial to the author's four uncles who fought in World War I presents the paradox of war—alluring and terrifying, at times boring, grim and ultimately deadly.

Kathleen V. Kudlinski, *Hero over Here*, 1990
With his father and brother fighting in World War I and his mother and sister stricken by an influenza epidemic, Theodore becomes a home front hero.
James Stevenson, *Don't You Know There's a War On?*, 1992
A nonfiction picture book presents the author's childhood recollections of life during World War II when his brother joins the Navy and gas and food are rationed.
Rosemary Wells, *Waiting for the Evening Star*, 1993
While Berty is content on the family's Vermont farm, his older brother Luke enlists in the war effort to fulfill a lifelong dream to see what lies beyond the mountains.

1185

GAIL RADLEY

Odd Man Out

(New York: Macmillan/Simon & Schuster, 1995)

Subject(s): Twins; Mentally Handicapped; Friendship
Age range(s): Grades 4-6
Major character(s): Oakley Duster, Mentally Challenged Person; Kit Harper, Twin; Jordy Harper, Twin
Time period(s): 1990s
Locale(s): Clary, Missouri

Summary: Kit and Jordy move one county over after the death of their father and readjust to that change as well as to their mother's new job and new friends. One of the new friends they make is Oakley, a mentally handicapped young man who appeared in their town about a year before they did. Not much is known about Oakley, but that doesn't bother Kit and Jordy. What does bother Jordy is when he sees a gang of teens intimidate Oakley and realizes Kit has a crush on one of the boys in the gang; Jordy knows he must do something about the situation. (131 pages)

Where it's reviewed:
Voice of Youth Advocates, August 1995, page 164
Booklist, August 1995, page 1947
Kirkus Reviews, June 1, 1995, page 785

Center for Children's Books. Bulletin, September 1995, page 26

Other books by the same author:
Oakley Duster Day, 1995
The Golden Days, 1991

Other books you might like:
Victor Kelleher, *Baily's Bones*, 1989
   Two brothers fight to keep their retarded brother's spirit from being possessed by spirits of long-dead Australian aborigines.
Morton Rhue, *The Wave*, 1981
   A high school experiments with social interactions, but the plan backfires when some of the students form a clique.
June Rae Wood, *The Man Who Loved Clowns*, 1992
   After her parents die, Delrita learns not to feel ashamed about her kind, loving Uncle Punky who has Down syndrome.

1186

ELSA OKON RAEL
MARJORIE PRICEMAN, Illustrator

What Zeesie Saw on Delancey Street
(New York: Simon & Schuster, 1996)

Subject(s): Emigration and Immigration; Jews
Age range(s): Grades 1-3
Major character(s): Zeesie, 7-Year-Old; Max Mendelson, Friend
Time period(s): 1930s
Locale(s): New York, New York

Summary: Zeesie is excited to attend her first "package party," where items are auctioned off to raise the money needed to bring more friends from Europe. The party is also the site of the "money room" where the men of the families leave money for those who need it, and alternately, go to help themselves to whatever they need. Zeesie is disappointed because this is a male-only event. She sneaks into the room only to see her favorite family friend take money. Zeesie knows she shouldn't have witnessed this and leaves her own $1.00 birthday present as a gift for others. (unpaged)

Where it's reviewed:
School Library Journal, December 1996, page 130
Booklist, September 1, 1996, page 144
Bulletin of the Center for Children's Books, December 1996, page 149

Awards the book has won:
ALA Notable Children's Book, 1997

Other books by the same author:
Maruska's Egg, 1993

Other books you might like:
Roslyn Bresnick-Perry, *Leaving for America*, 1992
   Zisl is preparing to leave for America from Russia but she is sad knowing she leaves relatives behind who were killed in the Holocaust.
Barbara M. Joosse, *The Morning Chair*, 1995
   Bram is excited about coming to America and what he will

eat here, but when he gets here he does not like the things he thought he would.
Jeanette Winter, *Klara's New World*, 1992
   Klara and her family leave Sweden for the long journey to America.
Maxinne R. Leighton, *An Ellis Island Christmas*, 1992
   A young Polish girl arrives at Ellis Island at Christmas.

1187

GLORIA RAND
TED RAND, Illustrator

The Cabin Key
(San Diego: Harcourt Brace & Company, 1994)

Subject(s): Nature; Family Life; Winter
Age range(s): Grades 1-3
Major character(s): Mom, Mother; Dad, Father; Unnamed Character, Child
Time period(s): 1990s (1994)
Locale(s): Washington

Summary: Arriving at her family's cabin on a winter day, a young girl goes about her chores, helping Dad bring in wood or drawing water from the creek for Mom. As she works, she remembers the stories that have become a part of the cabin's legacy. Despite the lack of indoor plumbing or heat, the young girl enjoys the cabin that has been a part of her family for generations. (32 pages)

Where it's reviewed:
Booklist, November 1, 1994, page 509
Five Owls, November 1994, page 28
Library Talk, November 1994, page 32
Publishers Weekly, July 25, 1994, page 54
School Library Journal, November 1994, page 89

Other books by the same author:
Prince William, 1992
Salty Sails North, 1992
Salty Dog, 1991

Other books you might like:
Patricia MacLachlan, *All the Places to Love*, 1994
   Growing up in a close, loving family, Eli comes to understand that all the places to love are right here on the family farm.
Lynn Reiser, *Tomorrow on Rocky Pond*, 1993
   Annually, a family returns to their vacation cabin at Rocky Pond eager to enjoy the same activities they remember from previous trips.
Jane Yolen, *Owl Moon*, 1987
   A Caldecott Medal winner describes a father's d daughter's snowy, nighttime, moonlit quest through the hushed woods in hopes of spotting an owl.

1188

CANDICE F. RANSOM
SHELLY O. HAAS, Illustrator

Jimmy Crack Corn

(Minneapolis: Carolrhoda Books Inc., 1994)

Subject(s): Depression (Economic); Fathers and Sons; Historical
Age range(s): Grades 3-5
Major character(s): Jimmy Watkins, 9-Year-Old; Mr. Watkins, Father, Unemployed
Time period(s): 1930s (1932)
Locale(s): Virginia; Washington, District of Columbia

Summary: Like many others in the country, Mr Watkins loses his job during the Great Depression and the family falls on hard times. When he joins the march to Washington to claim the bonus money promised to the veterans of World War I, Jimmy accompanies him. For weeks they camp with the many other veterans living in makeshift huts near the capitol until Congress rejects the veterans' pleas and sends the army to roust them from their camp. Jimmy and his father are fortunate for they have a home to which to return. (72 pages)

Where it's reviewed:
Booklist, July 1994, page 1948
Bulletin of the Center for Children's Books, June 1994, page 331
Horn Book Guide, Fall 1994, page 315
Kirkus Reviews, May 15, 1994, page 705
School Library Journal, June 1994, page 134

Other books by the same author:
Why Are Boys So Weird?, 1994
Listening to Crickets: A Story about Rachel Carson, 1993
Who Needs Third Grade?, 1992

Other books you might like:
Robert Burch, *Tyler, Wilkin and Skee*, 1990
    One year in the life of a farm family during the Great Depression is seen through the eyes of three brothers.
Eth Clifford, *The Man Who Sang in the Dark*, 1987
    During the Depression a widow with two children is befriended by other residents of a Philadelphia boarding house.
Anna Myers, *Red-Dirt Jessie*, 1992
    A young girl living in the Oklahoma dust bowl tries to help her father recover from a nervous breakdown and tame a wild dog.
Carolyn Reeder, *Grandpa's Mountain*, 1991
    During eleven-year-old Carrie's annual summer visit to the Blue Ridge home of relatives she observes her grandfather fighting the government takeover of his land.

1189

CANDICE F. RANSOM

More than a Name

(New York: Macmillan Books for Young Readers, 1995)

Subject(s): Remarriage; Stepfamilies; Identity
Age range(s): Grades 3-5

Major character(s): Cammie Bradley, 8-Year-Old; William Bixby, 9-Year-Old, Cousin
Time period(s): 1990s (1995)
Locale(s): United States (Bennett Elementary School)

Summary: When Cammie's mother remarries, Cammie is stuck with a different last name and an obnoxious cousin. William's persistent teasing adds to Cammie's worries about how to tell her mother and stepfather of her desire to be adopted and have the same name as the rest of the family. Although Cammie's afraid to stand up to her cousin and risk upsetting her acceptance into her new family, she learns that she must take action to get what she wants. (115 pages)

Where it's reviewed:
Booklist, July 1995, page 1880
Children's Book Review Service, August 1995, page 167
Horn Book Guide, Spring 1996, page 67
Publishers Weekly, July 3, 1995, page 61
School Library Journal, July 1995, page 80

Other books by the same author:
Why Are Boys So Weird?, 1994
Shooting Star Summer, 1992
Who Needs Third Grade?, 1992

Other books you might like:
Kevin Henkes, *Two under Par*, 1987
    Ten-year-old Wedge resents his mother's remarriage to a disliked miniature golf course owner.
Amy Hest, *The Private Notebook of Katie Roberts, Age 11*, 1995
    Katie keeps a record of her thoughts and feelings when her widowed mother remarries, moving them from New York to Texas.
Joan Lowery Nixon, *A Place to Belong*, 1989
    The entry in the Orphan Train Quartet series tells of Danny and his younger sister, their trip to a foster father in Missouri and Danny's matchmaking efforts.

1190

CANDICE F. RANSOM
KIMBERLY BULCKEN ROOT, Illustrator

When the Whippoorwill Calls

(New York: Tambourine Books, 1995)

Subject(s): Mountain Life; Moving, Household; Historical
Age range(s): Grades 2-4
Major character(s): Polly, 7-Year-Old; Pap, Father, Farmer; Mama, Mother
Time period(s): 1920s
Locale(s): Blue Ridge Mountains, Virginia

Summary: When the government creates the Shenandoah National Park, Polly and her family are forced to move when their tenant farm is sold to the government. Now, the family has a home with electricity and running water, but Pap does not sing as cheerfully as he once did and Mama has no wild huckleberries to make jam. A springtime hike up the mountain to the old homestead helps Polly and Pap put their forced move into perspective and find some good in the change. (32 pages)

Where it's reviewed:
Booklist, September 15, 1995, page 176
Children's Book Review Service, December 1995, page 40
Five Owls, January 1996, page 58
Horn Book, March 1996, page 190
School Library Journal, November 1995, page 80

Other books by the same author:
Jimmy Crack Corn, 1993

Other books you might like:
Alice Provenson, *Shaker Lane*, 1987
A town's plan to build a reservoir forces residents of Shaker Lane to move from their homes. Co-author, Martin Provenson.
Cynthia Rylant, *When I Was Young in the Mountains*, 1982
The shared experiences of two children evoke memories of a happy Appalachian childhood.
Jane Yolen, *Letting Swift River Go*, 1992
When a dam is built across the Swift River, the waters quickly cover Sally Jane's home, village and the simple, country life that she knows.

1191

RASCAL
LOUIS JOOS, Illustrator

Oregon's Journey
(Mahwah, NJ: BridgeWater Books, 1994)

Subject(s): Circus; Animals/Bears; Voyages and Travels
Age range(s): Grades K-2
Major character(s): Oregon, Bear; Duke, Sidekick (clown)
Time period(s): 1990s (1994)
Locale(s): Pittsburgh, Pennsylvania; Oregon

Summary: In response to Oregon's plea, Duke agrees to help him find his way back to the "big forest" in his home state. The dwarf and the bear run away from the circus hitching a ride in a 10-wheeler, stowing away on a freight train and walking until they reach Oregon. Fulfilling his promise to Oregon is also a voyage of self-discovery for Duke. (40 pages)

Where it's reviewed:
Booklist, April 15, 1994, page 1532
Children's Book Review Service, May 1994, page 115
Five Owls, September 1994, page 2
Publishers Weekly, March 28, 1994, page 96
School Library Journal, August 1994, page 144

Other books by the same author:
Orson, 1994

Other books you might like:
Joan W. Blos, *Nellie Bly's Monkey: His Remarkable Story in His Own Words*, 1996
Monkey McGinty travels with his new owner from Singapore to New York.
Michael Bond, *Paddington at the Circus*, 1992
When Paddington Bear accompanies the Brown family to the circus he inadvertently becomes part of the trapeze act.
William Corderoy, *Leaves*, 1994
Curious, a little bear is determined to stay awake all winter in order to learn how the leaves reappear in Spring.

1192

RASCAL
MARIO RAMOS, Illustrator

Orson
(New York: Lothrop, Lee & Shepard Books, 1994)

Subject(s): Animals/Bears; Friendship; Love
Age range(s): Grades K-3
Major character(s): Orson, Bear
Time period(s): 1990s (1994)
Locale(s): Fictional Country (forest)

Summary: Being a very large bear, Orson has few friends or playmates because the other forest creatures are afraid of him. Thus, when Orson awakens from winter's hibernation to find a toy bear sitting under the tree outside his cave, Orson considers himself to have a friend and companion. Through spring and summer the two enjoy each other, but, as winter approaches and the teddy bear has still not become real, Orson reluctantly places it back under the tree. (32 pages)

Where it's reviewed:
Booklist, January 1, 1995, page 827
Horn Book Guide, Spring 1995, page 52
School Library Journal, February 1995, page 80

Other books by the same author:
Oregon's Journey, 1994

Other books you might like:
Jez Alborough, *Where's My Teddy?*, 1992
As Eddie searches the dark woods for his lost teddy bear he encounters a large bear with a similar problem.
Michael Ratnett, *Jenny's Bear*, 1991
Although Jenny loves her many stuffed bears, most of all, she wants to meet a real bear.
Margery Williams, *The Velveteen Rabbit*, 1926
The classic story of the power of love to make even a stuffed bunny real has been reissued in many different illustrated editions.

1193

CHRIS RASCHKA, Author/Illustrator

Can't Sleep
(New York: Orchard Books, 1995)

Subject(s): Animals/Dogs; Bedtime; Sleep
Age range(s): Grades K-1
Major character(s): Unnamed Character, Dog
Time period(s): 1990s (1995)
Locale(s): Fictional Country

Summary: A young dog lies awake listening anxiously to his family's bedtime preparations. When the lights go out, the silence tells him the others are sleeping as he remains fearfully awake. Comforted by the knowledge that the moon is staying awake to watch over him, eventually the youngster also sleeps, awakening in the morning to watch over the moon so she can sleep. (32 pages)

Where it's reviewed:
Booklist, September 15, 1995, page 176

Horn Book, March 1996, page 191
Kirkus Reviews, July 15, 1995, page 1030
Publishers Weekly, August 17, 1995,page 228
School Library Journal, September 1995, page 184

Other books by the same author:
Yo! Yes?, 1993 (Caldecott Honor Book)
Charlie Parker Played Be Bop, 1992

Other books you might like:
Margaret Wise Brown, *Goodnight Moon*, 1947
   Gently a little rabbit bids goodnight to all the objects in his great, green room and, finally, the moon.
Beverly Cleary, *Petey's Bedtime Story*, 1993
   Petey likes the familiar bedtime routine although he never quite falls asleep as expected.
Mem Fox, *Time for Bed*, 1993
   In gently rhyming text, animals bid their little ones good night.

1194

CHRIS RASCHKA, Author/Illustrator

Yo! Yes?

(New York: Orchard Books, 1993)

Subject(s): Friendship; Race Relations; African Americans
Age range(s): Grades K-2
Major character(s): Unnamed Character, Child (African American); Unnamed Character, Child (Caucasian)
Time period(s): 1990s (1993)
Locale(s): New York, New York

Summary: Two boys, one timid and one outgoing, meet on a city street and begin a monosyllabic dialogue which gradually draws the boys closer together. The illustrations portray the tentativeness of the beginning overtures and the eventual excitement as the two recognize the potential for friendship. (32 pages)

Where it's reviewed:
Book List, March 15, 1993, page 1361
Five Owls, May 1993, page 112
Horn Book, May 1993, page 323
Publishers Weekly, February 15, 1993, page 236
School Library Journal, May 1993, page 90

Awards the book has won:
Caldecott Honor Book, 1994
Ezra Jack Keats Book Illustration Award, 1994

Other books by the same author:
Elizabeth Imagined an Iceberg, 1994
Charlie Parker Played Be Bop, 1992

Other books you might like:
Juanita Havill, *Jamaica and Brianna*, 1993
   Two young girls learn that their friendship is more important than clothes or new boots.
Laurie A. Jacobs, *So Much in Common*, 1994
   Philomena the hippo and Horace the goat are very different animals who have one important thing in common—their friendship.

William Steig, *Amos and Boris*, 1971
   A classic tale of the improbable friendship between a whale and a mouse is told with humor and compassion.

1195

PEGGY RATHMANN, Author/Illustrator

Good Night, Gorilla

(New York: G. P. Putnam's Sons, 1994)

Subject(s): Animals; Zoos; Bedtime
Age range(s): Grades K-1
Major character(s): Gorilla, Gorilla; Unnamed Character, Zoo Keeper
Time period(s): 1990s (1994)
Locale(s): United States

Summary: Beginning with Gorilla, the zoo keeper makes his rounds, bidding good night to each animal. Behind him, Gorilla, who has stolen the zoo keeper's keys, unlocks each cage as the zoo keeper passes. A parade of animals follows the zoo keeper home and settles down in his bedroom. When his wife hears seven voices responding to her "Good Night" she marches everyone back to the zoo where almost everyone stays for the night. (40 pages)

Where it's reviewed:
Booklist, July 1994, page 1956
Horn Book, July 1994, page 443
Parents, December 1994, page 22
Publishers Weekly, March 14, 1994, page 71
School Library Journal, July 1994, page 87

Awards the book has won:
ALA Notable Book, 1995
Boston Globe/Horn Book Fanfare, 1995

Other books by the same author:
Officer Buckle and Gloria, 1995
Ruby the Copycat, 1991

Other books you might like:
Rita Golden Gelman, *I Went to the Zoo*, 1993
   Assuming that the zoo animals are bored, a young visitor invites them home to his apartment and quickly realizes that they belong at the zoo.
Mary Jean Hendrick, *If Anything Ever Goes Wrong at the Zoo*, 1993
   When the zoo floods, the keepers take Leslie up on her offer to shelter the animals, much to her mother's surprise.
Eve Rice, *Sam Who Never Forgets*, 1977
   Elephant is fearful that zookeeper Sam has forgotten his daily food.

1196

PEGGY RATHMANN, Author/Illustrator

Officer Buckle and Gloria

(New York: G. P. Putnam's Sons, 1995)

Subject(s): Animals/Dogs; Schools; Humor
Age range(s): Grades K-3
Major character(s): Officer Buckle, Police Officer; Gloria, Dog

Time period(s): 1990s (1995)
Locale(s): Napville

Summary: Officer Buckle is a diligent, but dull policeman, giving safety assemblies to student audiences who quickly fall asleep. When the department acquires a police dog, Gloria accompanies Officer Buckle and the students' attentiveness improves along with the town's safety record. While viewing a tape of the program Officer Buckle discovers that Gloria, rather than sitting at attention during his lectures, has been humorously acting out his tips. Humiliated, Officer Buckle turns the programs over to Gloria who is also no good as a solo act. Finally, the duo writes the best safety tip of all and returns to a team approach to safety instruction. (32 pages)

Where it's reviewed:
Booklist, November 1, 1995, page 471
Children's Book Review Service, September 1995, page 3
Horn Book, November 1995, page 736
Publishers Weekly, July 17, 1995, page 229
School Library Journal, September 1995, page 185

Awards the book has won:
Caldecott Medal, 1996
School Library Journal Best Books, 1995

Other books by the same author:
Goodnight Gorilla, 1994
Ruby the Copycat, 1991

Other books you might like:
Margaret Bloy Graham, *Benjy and His Friend Fifi*, 1988
    Well-intentioned mutt Benjy accompanies his nervous poodle friend Fifi to her first dog show intending only to offer moral support.
Doug Johnson, *Never Ride Your Elephant to School*, 1995
    Here's an important safety tip that Officer Buckle overlooked—never ride your elephant to school!
Constance McGeorge, *Boomer Goes to School*, 1996
    Boomer, a golden retriever, accompanies his owner to school for show-and-tell.

1197

JAMA KIM RATTIGAN
LILLIAN HSU-FLANDERS, Illustrator

Dumpling Soup

(Boston: Little, Brown and Company, 1993)

Subject(s): Family Life; Cooks and Cookery; Asian Americans
Age range(s): Grades K-3
Major character(s): Marisa, 7-Year-Old; Grandma, Grandmother (Korean)
Time period(s): 1990s (1993)
Locale(s): Oahu, Hawaii

Summary: Marisa is excited and a little nervous now that she is old enough to assist the cooks in making dumplings for the New Year's Eve celebration. Her concerns about her odd-looking dumplings are forgetten as she enjoys playing with the many cousins who have gathered at Grandma's house to share a time for family togetherness and lots of good food, including Marisa's dumplings. A glossary defines words of 4 different languages used in the text. (32 pages)

Where it's reviewed:
Booklist, September 15, 1993, page 160
Horn Book, November 1993, page 727
Publishers Weekly, October 25, 1993, page 60
Quill and Quire, October 1993, page 44
School Library Journal, December 1993, page 93

Awards the book has won:
New Voices, New World Multicultural Fiction Contest, 1990

Other books by the same author:
Truman's Aunt Farm, 1994

Other books you might like:
Sook Nyul Choi, *Halmoni and the Picnic*, 1993
    Yunmi's grandmother, a newly arrived immigrant from Korea, gains acceptace from Yunmi's classmates when she provides traditional Korean food for a class picnic.
Georgia Guback, *Luka's Quilt*, 1994
    When Luka's grandmother decides to make Luka a traditional Hawaiian quilt, her efforts strain the friendship between the two, but also teach a lesson in compromise and understanding.
Riki Levinson, *I Go With My Family to Grandma's*, 1986
    A large family travels to Grandma's home in New York.
Cynthia Rylant, *The Relatives Came*, 1985
    A Caldecott Honor Book celebrates childhood memories of the joyful confusion of a houseful of relatives.

1198

JAMA KIM RATTIGAN
G. BRIAN KARAS, Illustrator

Truman's Aunt Farm

(Boston: Houghton Mifflin, 1994)

Subject(s): Aunts and Uncles; Birthdays
Age range(s): Grades K-2
Major character(s): Truman, Nephew; Fran, Aunt, Eccentric
Time period(s): 1990s (1994)
Locale(s): United States

Summary: Truman never knows what to expect when Aunt Fran sends a package so he is excited to receive an ant farm for his birthday. Sending in the card that should result in a delivery of ants for the farm, Truman is surprised when, instead, he finds aunts at his door. Truman makes the most of this abundance of aunts, sharing his bounty with other children and eventually enjoying a visit with his favorite Aunt Fran. (unpaged)

Where it's reviewed:
Booklist, February 15, 1994, page 1093
Children's Book Review Service, Spring 1994, page 138
Publishers Weekly, January 10, 1994, page 62
School Library Journal, June 1994, page 112

Awards the book has won:
School Library Journal Best Books, 1994

Other books by the same author:
Dumpling Soup, 1993

Other books you might like:
Kathryn Lasky, *I Have an Aunt on Marlborough Street*, 1992
Phoebe enjoys a special relationship with her Aunt Phoebe.
Peggy Parish, *Amelia Bedelia Helps Out*, 1979
Amelia doesn't confuse words intentionally, but her misunderstandings lead to some humorous events.
Pat Thomson, *Beware of the Aunts!*, 1992
There's no end to the surprises when these nine aunts choose Christmas gifts.

1199

MARY LYN RAY
BARRY ROOT, Illustrator

Alvah and Arvilla

(San Diego: Harcourt Brace & Company, 1994)

Subject(s): Farm Life; Animals; Voyages and Travels
Age range(s): Grades K-3
Major character(s): Arvilla, Spouse, Housewife; Alvah, Spouse, Farmer
Time period(s): Indeterminate Past
Locale(s): New England

Summary: For the past thirty-one years Arvilla has longed to see the Pacific Ocean, but the demands of a farm prevent travel. Finally, Arvilla decides that if the animals are keeping them from travelling, she and Alvah will simply take the animals along on the trip. So, Alvah builds a greenhouse on wheels into which they load all the cows, sheep, cats, dogs and chickens and head west across unnamed territories until they reach the Pacific. When they have seen all that they came to see, they load up the wagon and head east. (32 pages)

Where it's reviewed:
Horn Book, November 1994, page 725
Kirkus Reviews, September 15, 1994, page 1279
Publishers Weekly, September 5, 1994, page 109
Quill & Quire, December 1994, page 35
School Library Journal, January 1995, page 92

Other books by the same author:
Pianna, 1994
A Rumbly Tumbly Glittery Gritty Place, 1993
Pumpkins: A Story for a Field, 1992

Other books you might like:
Bonnie Pryor, *Lottie's Dream*, 1992
When she's growing up in Kentucky, Lottie dreams of the day when she will see the ocean.
Penny Carter, *A New House for the Morrisons*, 1993
After a day of fruitless searching for a new house, the Morrisons return to the one they like best—their own home.
Emma Chichester Clark, *Across the Blue Mountains*, 1992
Curiosity leads Miss Bilberry to pack her belongings and travel to the other side of the blue mountains where she finds a home just to her liking.
Carol P. Saul, *Someplace Else*, 1995
Until her purchase of a travel trailer enables Mrs. Tilby to live any place else, she finds that just living somewhere

other than the white house in which she's always lived is not satisfying.

1200

MARY LYN RAY
BOBBIE HENBA, Illustrator

Pianna

(San Diego: Harcourt Brace & Company, 1994)

Subject(s): Musicians; Talent; Trains
Age range(s): Grades 1-3
Major character(s): Anna, Aged Person, Musician
Time period(s): 1910s; 1990s (1994)
Locale(s): South Danbury, New Hampshire

Summary: When her parents discover that 7-year-old Anna has a talent for music, they arrange for her to have weekly piano lessons in Boston, a 107-mile train ride. Now, as an eighty-year-old widow, Anna continues to live in her childhood home and play her beloved piano. Through her memories, we learn how she develops the talent which provides her with pleasure all her life. (32 pages)

Where it's reviewed:
Booklist, March 15, 1994, page 1375
Children's Book Review Service, March 1994, page 89
Kirkus Reviews, March 1, 1994, page 309
Publishers Weekly, March 7, 1994, page 69
School Library Journal, May 1994, page 103

Other books by the same author:
Alvah and Arvilla, 1994
Shaker Boy, 1994
Pumpkins: A Story for a Field, 1992

Other books you might like:
Virginia Lee Burton, *The Little House*, 1942
The passage of time and connectedness of family over the generations is chronicled in the experiences of a house. Caldecott Medal Winner.
Donald Hall, *Old Home Day*, 1996
The cycle of growth, decline and renewal of a New England town is described through the history of its settlers.
Alice Schertle, *Maisie*, 1994
The story of 90-year-old Maisie's life is also a record of the changes in America during her lifetime and the celebration of family ties.
Anne Shelby, *Homeplace*, 1995
While rocking a grandchild, a grandmother traces the history of the family from the building of the family homestead by the great-great-great-great granpa to the present.

1201

MARY LYN RAY
JEANETTE WINTER, Illustrator

Shaker Boy

(San Diego: Harcourt Brace & Company, 1994)

Subject(s): Shakers; Religious Communes; Behavior
Age range(s): Grades 1-3

Major character(s): Caleb Whitcher, 6-Year-Old
Time period(s): Indeterminate Past
Locale(s): Canterbury, New Hampshire

Summary: After his father is killed in the Civil War, young Caleb's mother is forced to find work in the mills and sends Caleb to live in the Shaker community. Caleb adapts to the orderly way of life, especially enjoying the rule about "Shakering" his plate which requires him to eat all the food he is given. Like everyone in the community, Caleb is assigned jobs with the type of work changing as he grows older. Frequently, Caleb hears the angels singing and records the songs he is given. At nineteen, he is made deacon of the apple orchard where he picks both apples and songs until his death as an old man. (48 pages)

Where it's reviewed:
Booklist, November 15, 1994, page 6
Horn Book, January 1995, page 52
Kirkus Reviews, October 15, 1994, page 1415
Publishers Weekly, October 17, 1994, page 80
School Library Journal, November 1994, page 89

Awards the book has won:
Notable Children's Trade Book in the Field of Social Studies, 1994

Other books by the same author:
Alvah and Arvilla, 1994
Pianna, 1994
A Rumbly Tumbly Glittery Gritty Place, 1993
Angel Baskets: A Little Story about the Shakers, 1987

Other books you might like:
Raymond Bial, *Shaker Home*, 1994
    A nonfiction photo-essay describes the daily life of residents in a Shaker village.
Jane Boulton, *Only Opal: The Diary of a Young Girl*, 1994
    The sad life story of orphaned Opal Whiteley is based on the diary written while she lived with an adoptive family in Oregon.
LouAnn Gaeddert, *Hope*, 1995
    Orphaned siblings adjust to a new way of life in the Shaker community in which they have been placed.

1202

MARY RAYNER, Author/Illustrator

Garth Pig Steals the Show
(New York: Dutton Children's Books, 1993)

Subject(s): Animals/Pigs; Family Life; Musicians
Age range(s): Grades K-3
Major character(s): Garth Pig, Pig, Musician (piccolo player); Unnamed Character, Musician (sousaphonist), Wolf; William Pig, Pig (Garth's brother), Musician (trumpet)
Time period(s): 1990s (1993)
Locale(s): England

Summary: With all ten piglets learning to play an instrument, the Pig parents decide to form a band. Their advertisement for a tuba player is answered by a rather furry, suspicious-looking character who lurks behind her large instrument while licking her chops. When Garth disappears during the concert and William notices the sousaphonist sneaking off-stage, he takes

the baton from his father and orchestrates a sousaphone solo which is appreciated by everyone but the soloist. The pig family triumphs again! (32 pages)

Where it's reviewed:
Booklist, April 1, 1993, page 1441
Horn Book, May 1993, page 324
Kirkus Reviews, May 15, 1993, page 668
Publishers Weekly, May 31, 1993, page 53
School Library Journal, May 1993, page 90

Awards the book has won:
Book Links Good Book, 1993

Other books by the same author:
Mrs. Pig Gets Cross and Other Stories, 1987
Garth Pig and the Ice Cream Lady, 1978
Mr. and Mrs. Pig's Evening Out, 1976

Other books you might like:
Mary Jane Auch, *Peeping Beauty*, 1993
    When a fox takes advantage of Poulette's love for the stage, she almost makes her first and last performance.
Tony Blundell, *Beware of Boys*, 1992
    Captured by a wolf, a resourceful, little boy uses his quick wits to save himself.
Michael Emberley, *Ruby*, 1990
    In an urban tale, Ruby, a mouse in a red cloak, encounters not one but two strangers on her way to Granny's with a delivery of pies.
Colin McNaughton, *Suddenly!*, 1994
    Oblivious to the danger lurking in wait for him, Preston walks calmly and absent-mindedly home from school, creating havoc for the skulking wolf.
Susan Meddaugh, *Hog-Eye*, 1995
    A piglet describes to her family how she escaped the clutches of the hungry wolf after being captured on her way to school.

1203

DIAN CURTIS REGAN
LAURA CORNELL, Illustrator

Monster of the Month Club
(New York: Henry Holt and Company, 1994)

Subject(s): Monsters; Fantasy
Age range(s): Grades 4-6
Major character(s): Rilla Harmony Earth, Child; Sparrow Harmony Earth, Mother
Time period(s): 1990s (1994)
Locale(s): United States

Summary: Rilla's peaceful life in the Harmony House Bed and Breakfast run by Sparrow and her sister becomes much livelier when a package arrives holding the first monster from her gift subscription to the "Monster of the Month Club." Expecting a year's worth of stuffed animals, Rilla is surprised to receive a live creature which she cleverly hides and feeds in her attic room. When the second monster arrives in February, Rilla's ingenuity and allowance are severely strained by the care and feeding of two monsters. In March, the guest responsible for the subscription arrives along with the third package, explaining the mystery and helping Rilla solve her dilemma. (143 pages)

Where it's reviewed:
Booklist, January 1, 1995, page 822
Bulletin of the Center for Children's Books, January 1995, page 175
Children's Book Review Service, December 1994, page 47
Horn Book Guide, Spring 1995, page 82
School Library Journal, March 1995, page 206

Other books by the same author:
Monsters in the Attic, 1995 (sequel to *Monster of the Month Club*)
The Mystery of the Disappearing Dogs, 1995 (Ghost Twins Series)
The Mystery at Kickingbird Lane, 1994 (Ghost Twins Series)
My Zombie Valentine, 1993

Other books you might like:
Vivien Alcock, *The Monster Garden*, 1988
    Trying her hand at her father's profession of genetic engineering, Frankie creates a rapidly growing baby monster.
Bruce Coville, *Bruce Coville's Book of Monsters: Tales to Give You the Creeps*, 1993
    A collection of short stories focusses on the theme of monsters.
Diane De Groat, *Annie Pitts, Swamp Monster*, 1993
    Eager to become a star, Annie willingly agrees to be a swamp monster for a student video only to learn that "acting" is hard work.

`1204`

LYNN REISER, Author/Illustrator

Night Thunder and the Queen of the Wild Horses
(New York: Greenwillow Books, 1995)

Subject(s): Sleep; Bedtime; Animals
Age range(s): Grades K-2
Major character(s): Unnamed Character, Child
Time period(s): 1990s (1995)
Locale(s): United States

Summary: On a stormy night a young girl is awakened by crashing, banging and booming. The noises also awaken and bring to life the girl's painting of the Queen of the Wild Horses and together they fly into the night to find the source of the noise. Each group of large, clamoring animals that they locate refuses to be quiet because the noise of the others is keeping them awake. Finally the little girl and her animated painting find the source of the trouble so that everyone can have a quiet night's rest. (32 pages)

Where it's reviewed:
Booklist, October 15, 1995, page 413
Five Owls, January 1996, page 57
Horn Book Guide, Spring 1996, page 43
Publishers Weekly, September 25, 1995, page 56
School Library Journal, December 1995, page 90

Other books by the same author:
Any Kind of Dog, 1992

Christmas Counting, 1992
Bedtime Cat, 1991

Other books you might like:
Kathryn Hook Berlan, *Andrew's Amazing Monsters*, 1993
    Andrew is awakened to find that his artwork has come to life and prepared a surprise party for him.
Pat Cummings, *Carousel*, 1994
    The animals on Alex's birthday carousel come to life and take her for a nighttime flight.
Kit Wright, *Tigerella*, 1994
    A polite, quiet child by day, Ella becomes a fierce tiger at night, enjoying adventures with the stars.

`1205`

LYNN REISER, Author/Illustrator

The Surprise Family
(New York: Greenwillow Books, 1994)

Subject(s): Animals/Chickens; Animals/Ducks; Family Relations
Age range(s): Grades K-3
Major character(s): The Boy, Child (chick's "mother"); The Hen, Mother, Chicken
Time period(s): 1990s (1994)
Locale(s): United States (rural setting)

Summary: A baby chick hatches and accepts a boy as her mother. Despite his devoted attention, as the chick matures into a little hen, she begins to long for her own family and builds a nest into which the boy puts a clutch of abandoned eggs. The little hen raises the hatchlings as her own and is alarmed when they ignore her motherly warnings and swim away in the pond. Only after they return does the little hen realize that her beloved babies are really ducks. (32 pages)

Where it's reviewed:
Booklist, June 1, 1994, page 1844
Kirkus Reviews, June 1, 1994, page 780
School Library Journal, July 1994, page 87

Awards the book has won:
ALA Notable Book, 1995

Other books by the same author:
Two Mice in Three Fables, 1995
Tomorrow on Rocky Pond, 1993
Any Kind of Dog, 1992
Christmas Counting, 1992
Dog and Cat, 1991

Other books you might like:
Janell Cannon, *Stellaluna*, 1993
    Separated from her mother, Stellaluna the fruit bat, falls into a bird's nest where she is treated like one of the family.
P.D. Eastman, *Are You My Mother?*, 1986
    After falling from the nest, a baby bird tries to find its mother.
Keiko Kasza, *A Mother for Choco*, 1992
    While searching for its mother, a young bird is adopted by a bear.

1206

LYNN REISER, Author/Illustrator

Tomorrow on Rocky Pond

(New York: Greenwillow Books, 1993)

Subject(s): Fishing; Vacations; Family Life
Age range(s): Grades K-2
Major character(s): Unnamed Character, Child, Sister (older);
    Unnamed Character, Child, Brother (younger)
Time period(s): 1990s (1993)
Locale(s): Connecticut (Rocky Pond)

Summary: Today a young girl and her brother are tired from their trip to the family vacation cabin in the woods, but tomorrow is a fishing trip to Rocky Pond. As she tries to drift off to sleep, the girl recalls previous fishing trips and details exactly what tomorrow will bring. (32 pages)

Where it's reviewed:
Booklist, August 1993, page 2071
Horn Book, September 1993, page 589
Language Arts, April 1994, page 296
Publishers Weekly, May 31, 1993, page 53
School Library Journal, September 1993, page 218

Other books by the same author:
The Surprise Family, 1994
Any Kind of Dog, 1992
Christmas Counting, 1992

Other books you might like:
Jim Arnosky, *I See Animals Hiding*, 1995
    A simply written, beautifully illustrated, nonfiction look at animals' use of camouflage to protect themselves.
William T. George, *Fishing at Long Pond*, 1991
    A fishing trip to Long Pond includes observation of the plants and animals that Katie and her grandfather see along the way.
Kathryn Lasky, *Pond Year*, 1995
    Two friends enjoy the seasonal changes observed in the pond near their homes.
Gloria Rand, *The Cabin Key*, 1994
    Returning to the family cabin in the woods brings back happy memories for a young girl.

1207

LYNN REISER, Author/Illustrator

Two Mice in Three Fables

(New York: Greenwillow Books, 1995)

Subject(s): Fables; Animals
Age range(s): Grades K-2
Major character(s): Unnamed Character, Mouse (indoor); Unnamed Character, Mouse (outdoor)
Time period(s): 1990s (1995)
Locale(s): United States

Summary: The indoor mouse meets the outdoor mouse for three adventures. In the first, the outdoor mouse finds the options which the indoor mouse has for activity to be too tame for his tastes. In the next two fables the two mice wander about the yard, successfully evading the efforts of an owl, a raccoon and a snake to capture and eat them. The moral of each fable is clearly explained at the story's conclusion. (30 pages)

Where it's reviewed:
Booklist, March 1, 1995, page 1249
Children's Book Review Service, June 1995, page 125
Kirkus Reviews, March 15, 1995, page 392
Library Talk, September 1995, page 29
School Library Journal, April 1995, page 114

Other books by the same author:
Margaret and Margarita, 1993
Any Kind of Dog, 1992
Bedtime Cat, 1991

Other books you might like:
Janet Stevens, *The Town Mouse and the Country Mouse: An Aesop Fable*, 1987
    One of many retellings of the classic tale of two mice attempting to adapt to differing life styles.
Mark Ezra, *The Sleepy Dormouse*, 1994
    Kindly harvest mice save a sleepy dormouse from becoming a weasel's dinner.
Arnold Lobel, *Mouse Soup*, 1977
    Mouse has a plan that he hopes will keep him out of Weasel's soup pot.

1208

FRANK REMKIEWICZ, Author/Illustrator

The Bone Stranger

(New York: Lothrop, Lee & Shepard Books, 1994)

Subject(s): Animals/Dogs; American West; Humor
Age range(s): Grades 2-3
Major character(s): Boney, Dog, Store Owner; Wolfgang, Wolf, Companion
Time period(s): Indeterminate Past
Locale(s): United States (dusty little town)

Summary: When the stagecoach carrying the strongbox filled with the bedtime treats for the orphans is robbed, Boney knows he must do something to help the poor, young widow who runs the orphanage. With Wolfgang's assistance, Boney rides after the bandits, armed with hard salami and jump ropes, and nabs the scoundrels. (32 pages)

Where it's reviewed:
Bulletin of the Center for Children's Books, June 1994, page 332
Horn Book, May 1994, page 319
Publishers Weekly, May 23, 1994, page 87
School Library Journal, July 1994, page 88
Tribune Books, June 12, 1994, page 9

Other books by the same author:
There's Only One Harris, 1993
Greedy Anna, 1992
The Last Time I Saw Harris, 1991

Other books you might like:
Roy Gerrard, *Rosie and the Rustlers*, 1989
    A story in rhyme describes how Rosie catches the rustlers who have stolen her cattle.

Eric A. Kimmel, *Four Dollars and Fifty Cents*, 1990
When a ne'er-do-well cowboy tries to avoid paying a debt by faking his own death he almost finds himself buried alive.

Chris Van Allsburg, *Bad Day at Riverbend*, 1995
Sheriff Hardy investigates the colorful slime which mysteriously coats the town and its residents.

1209

FRANCOISE RICHARD
ANNE BUGUET, Illustrator

On Cat Mountain

(New York: G.P. Putnam's Sons, 1994)

Subject(s): Folk Tales; Animals/Cats; Conduct of Life
Age range(s): Grades 2-4
Major character(s): Sho, Servant, Animal Lover; Secret, Cat
Time period(s): Indeterminate Past
Locale(s): Japan

Summary: Sho kindly tries to hide her pet, appropriately named Secret, from her cruel, cat-hating mistress, but the animal is spotted and Sho loses her only friend. When a travelling fortune-teller comes to town, Sho ignores her mistress's instruction and seeks his advice for finding Secret. Overheard by the mistress, Sho is forced to make a dangerous trip to Cat Mountain from which no one has ever returned. On Cat Mountain, Sho finds Secret who saves her not only from the mountain, but also from a life of misery with the cruel mistress. The mistress, however, does not fare as well when she attempts to repeat Sho's successful journey. Originally published in France in 1993, the English language adaptation is by Arthur A. Levine. (40 pages)

Where it's reviewed:
Booklist, May 1, 1994, page 1599
Children's Book Review Service, June 1994, page 127
Horn Book, May 1994, page 328
Publishers Weekly, April 4, 1994, page 80
School Library Journal, June 1994, page 141

Awards the book has won:
Booklist Editors' Choice, 1994

Other books you might like:
Eric Quayle, *The Shining Princess and Other Japanese Legends*, 1989
A collection of Japanese folktales includes a retelling of the story upon which *Lily and the Wooden Bowl* is based.

Alan Schroeder, *Lily and the Wooden Bowl*, 1994
By faithfully fulfilling a promise made to her dying grandmother, Lily is protected from the evil Matsu and rewarded with true love and riches.

Carol Ann Williams, *Tsubu the Little Snail*, 1995
The love of a poor couple who faithfully care for the snail child sent by the water god in answer to their prayers is rewarded when the spell is broken and Tsubu becomes a young man.

1210

JUDITH BENET RICHARDSON

First Came the Owl

(New York: Henry Holt, 1996)

Subject(s): Self-Confidence; Asian Americans; Depression
Age range(s): Grades 4-7
Major character(s): Nita Orson, 10-Year-Old, Student; Anne Stillwater, Student; Captain Pudge, Sailor (coastguardsman), Artisan (woodworker)
Time period(s): 1990s
Locale(s): Maushope's Landing, Massachusetts

Summary: Nita and her family live on the coast guard base where Nita's father is an officer. Since a visit to her family in Thailand, Nita's mother has been depressed and is hospitalized when Nita's father goes to sea. Nita stays with her friend, Anne, where she finds herself doing new things, like trying out for a play. Gaining more confidence as she becomes more involved in school-life, Nita recalls what her mother once told her about Thailand and is disturbed that they don't talk about her homeland anymore. She determines to explore her heritage with her mother and decides to show her mom the snowy owl which has taken up residence on the base and which serves as the analogy for the story. (153 pages)

Other books by the same author:
Old Winter, 1996
Come to My Party, 1993
David's Landing, 1984

Other books you might like:
Sherry Garland, *Song of the Buffalo*, 1992
A Vietnamese girl wants to go to America and find her American father.

Bette Bao Lord, *In the Year of the Boar and Jackie Robinson*, 1984
A Chinese child comes to America and wants to blend in with the other students.

Lensey Namioka, *Yang the Third and Her Impossible Family*, 1995
Mary Yang tries to make new friends and still maintain her Chinese heritage.

Jayne Pettit, *My Name Is San Ho*, 1992
A Vietnamese boy comes to America after the war to be with his mother.

Laurence Yep, *Thief of Hearts*, 1995
A young girl is asked to show a new Chinese girl around and when she has to follow her to China Town, begins to understand her own culture better.

1211

ENID RICHEMONT
JAN ORMEROD, Illustrator

The Magic Skateboard

(Cambridge, MA: Candlewick Press, 1993)

Subject(s): Magic; Sports/Skateboarding; Fantasy
Age range(s): Grades 3-5

Major character(s): Danny, Child; Unnamed Character, Aged Person, Spirit
Time period(s): 1990s (1991)
Locale(s): England

Summary: With only five more days until Christmas, Danny is enjoying his skateboard and anticipating his school vacation. A very tall, elderly woman stops him on the street, borrows his skateboard, and demonstrates some most unusual manuvers. Returning the board, she gives Danny a gift of 30 minutes of ''her'' time on the skateboard in which he can go wherever he pleases simply by wishing himself there. Although he's a little late getting home, the series of fantastic adventures he has along the way makes the possible consequences bearable. First published in Great Britain in 1991. (80 pages)

Where it's reviewed:
Books for Keeps, September 1992, page 10
Horn Book Guide, Fall 1993, page 303
Kirkus Reviews, March 15, 1993, page 378
New Advocate, Fall 1993, page 301
School Library Journal, May 1993, page 108

Other books by the same author:
The Glass Bird, 1993
The Time Tree, 1990

Other books you might like:
Roald Dahl, *The Wonderful Story of Henry Sugar and Six More*, 1977
Seven brief, humorous tales of fantasy in typical Dahl style.
Constance Hiser, *No Bean Sprouts, Please!*, 1989
James receives a lunch box from Uncle Wesley which seems to have the magical ability to transform his boring lunches into something more appealing .
Hazel Hutchins, *Anastasia Morningstar*, 1992
Sarah and Ben notice that the next-door neighbor seems to have some magical ability.

1212

RODNEY RIGBY, Author/Illustrator

The Night the Moon Fell Asleep
(New York: Hyperion Books for Children, 1993)

Subject(s): Fantasy; Sleep; Problem Solving
Age range(s): Grades K-2
Major character(s): Moon, Celestial Body
Time period(s): Indeterminate
Locale(s): England

Summary: The night the moon falls asleep and crashes to the ground the townspeople come running to wake her and encourage her to return to her proper place in the night sky. Moon feels neglected and must be cajoled by everyone before she decides that, if she will be appreciated, then she will resume her position. Originally published in Great Britain in 1992. (32 pages)

Where it's reviewed:
Booklist, April 15, 1993, page 1524
Horn Book Guide, Fall 1993, page 272
Publishers Weekly, March 8, 1993, page 77

School Library Journal, August 1993, page 150

Other books by the same author:
Hello, This Is Your Penguin Speaking, 1992
There's a Building on Sixth Avenue, 1992

Other books you might like:
Lois Ehlert, *Moon Rope: A Peruvian Folktale/Un Lazo a la Luna: Una Leyenda Peruana*, 1992
Translated by Amy Prince, the bilingual text explains why fox's face is seen in a full moon and mole's is seen only on a dark night. *SPF
Mary-Claire Helldorfer, *Moon Trouble*, 1994
When the moon lands in the river, the local folk know to call Paul Bunyan to solve the problem.
Laura Simms, *Moon and Otter and Frog*, 1995
In a retelling of a Modoc myth, lonely Moon visits earth where he is befriended by Otter who suggests he find a wife so he will not be lonely in the sky.
Susan Whitcher, *Moonfall*, 1993
Sylvie finds the fallen moon in a neighbor's lilac bush and tries to restore its luster.

1213

ANITA RIGGIO, Author/Illustrator

Beware the Brindlebeast
(Honesdale, PA: Boyds Mills Press, 1994)

Subject(s): Folk Tales; Halloween; Monsters
Age range(s): Grades 1-3
Major character(s): Birdie, Aged Person; Brindlebeast, Monster (shape-changer)
Time period(s): Indeterminate Past
Locale(s): England

Summary: As the author retells the traditional British tale, Birdie is walking home in the gathering dusk of All Hallow's Eve when she spots a pot filled with gold coins in her path. As she drags it home, Birdie notices the pot change into a barrel of apples and then a large pumpkin. Cheerfully, Birdie sees each item as being useful and carves the pumpkin into a jack-o'lantern which transforms into the large, monstrous Brindlebeast. When Birdie shows no fear, the Brindlebeast reveals itself to be a little man who enjoys Birdie's company. (32 pages)

Where it's reviewed:
Booklist, September 15, 1994, page 141
Children's Book Review Service, October 1994, page 18
Horn Book Guide, Spring 1995, page 109
New Advocate, Winter 1995, page 47
Publishers Weekly, September 19, 1994, page 25

Other books by the same author:
A Moon in My Teacup, 1993

Other books you might like:
Ida DeLage, *The Old Witch and Her Magic Basket*, 1978
Using her magic basket of tricks, a witch entertains a little girl who is sick and unable to enjoy Halloween.
Tony Johnston, *The Soup Bone*, 1990
While looking for a soup bone, an elderly woman finds a hungry skeleton.

Phyllis Root, *Aunt Nancy and Old Man Trouble*, 1996
Aunt Nancy turns her troubles into triumphs, confounding Old Man Trouble and sending him on his way to bother someone less clever.

1214

ANN RINALDI

Keep Smiling Through

(San Diego, CA: Harcourt Brace, 1996)

Subject(s): World War II; Courage
Age range(s): Grades 4-7
Major character(s): Kay Hennings, 10-Year-Old, Stepdaughter; Mrs. Leudloff, Farmer (Egg lady); Amazing Grace Hennings, Stepmother
Time period(s): 1940s
Locale(s): United States

Summary: Kay and her family have trouble with their new stepmother, who likes to lie around and let the children take care of the house. Life is also hard in World War II America and money is not available for things like new shoes. One day, while Kay's grandfather and another man are talking in support of Germany, a group of young men attack them thinking them Nazis supporters. Kay goes to the rescue of her grandfather. Questioned later, she admits that she heard them saying things that might be considered spying. Though her stepmother is quite angry, the police let her know that she has done the right thing. (188 pages)

Where it's reviewed:
School Library Journal, July 1996, page 124
Booklist, July 1996, page 1824

Other books by the same author:
The Secret of Sarah Revere, 1995
Finishing Becca, 1994
The Fifth of March, 1993

Other books you might like:
Avi, *Who Was That Masked Man, Anyway?*, 1992
Two boys, caught up in listening to the mystery stories on the radio, decide that a neighbor is really a German spy.
Mary Downing Hahn, *Stepping on the Cracks*, 1991
Girls keep an eye on a deserted cabin in the woods where they suspect all kinds of things until they find that a boy is hiding a deserter.
Charlotte Herman, *A Summer on Thirteenth Street*, 1991
A Chicago neighborhood is affected by World War II as relatives join the army and others are suspected of being German spies.
Katherine Marko, *Hang out the Flag*, 1992
While waiting for her father to come home from the war a sixth grade girl wants to do something exciting like catch a German spy.
Harry Paige, *The Summer War*, 1983
A boy discovers that there was hatred of German Americans during World War II, just as there was of the Japanese.

1215

FAITH RINGGOLD, Author/Illustrator

Tar Beach

(New York: Crown Publishers, Inc., 1991)

Subject(s): African Americans; Imagination
Age range(s): Grades K-3
Major character(s): Cassie Louise Lightfoot, 8-Year-Old, Daydreamer; Be Be Lightfoot, Brother; Daddy, Father, Construction Worker
Time period(s): 1930s (1939)
Locale(s): New York, New York (Harlem)

Summary: Cassie Louise Lightfoot knows how to rise above the poverty and discrimination faced by her family. Under a starry sky, she lies on her mattress on the tar beach of her apartment rooftop and, in her dreams, flies over the city, imagining the future. (32 pages)

Where it's reviewed:
Booklist, January 15, 1992, page 875
Horn Book, May 1992, page 322
Publishers Weekly, November 1, 1991, page 22
Reading Teacher, February 1992, page 453
School Library Journal, December 1991, page 31

Awards the book has won:
Caldecott Honor Book, 1992
Coretta Scott King Award Illustration, 1992

Other books by the same author:
Aunt Harriet's Underground Railroad in the Sky, 1993
Dinner at Aunt Connie's House, 1993

Other books you might like:
Diane Worfolk Allison, *This Is the Key to the Kingdom*, 1992
In her imagination, a young child travels through a fantasy land filled with beauty and love. Although her own neighborhood is less splendid, it is still filled with love.
Michael Chesworth, *Rainy Day Dream*, 1992
One stormy day, the wind carries a young boy and his umbrella over the countryside.
Arthur Dorros, *Abuela*, 1991
In this ALA Notable Book, art and language bl end to illustrate a young girl's fantasy of flying with her grandmother over New York City.
Eloise Greenfield, *Daydreamers*, 1981
Calling all daydreamers! Here's a book that really appreciates you.
Liz Rosenberg, *Adelaide and the Night Train*, 1989
Drifting off to sleep one night, a young girl boards the train that travels past her house, or perhaps she is only dreaming.

1216

BETHANY ROBERTS
DOUG CUSHMAN, Illustrator

Halloween Mice!

(New York: Clarion Books, 1995)

Subject(s): Animals/Mice; Animals/Cats; Halloween
Age range(s): Grades K-1

Major character(s): Unnamed Character, Mouse; Unnamed Character, Cat
Time period(s): 1990s (1995)
Locale(s): United States
Summary: Four mice dressed for Halloween skitter, scamper, scurry and swirl to a party of their own making in the pumpkin patch. When they hear the swish, swish of a cat lurking nearby they use their wits, a lantern and costume parts to create the illusion of a monster which scares the cat away. Though the mice are able to return safely home, the littlest one is not quite through with Halloween pranks. (32 pages)

Where it's reviewed:
Booklist, September 15, 1995, page 172
Horn Book Guide, Spring 1996, page 43
Library Talk, September 1995, page 25
Publishers Weekly, September 18, 1995, page 89
School Library Journal, September 1995, page 185

Other books by the same author:
Cat Parade!, 1995
Waiting-for-Christmas Stories, 1994
The Two O'Clock Secret, 1993

Other books you might like:
True Kelley, *The Mouse's Terrible Halloween*, 1980
    Halloween is here, bringing more troublesome adventures for the Mouse family.
Steven Kroll, *The Biggest Pumpkin Ever*, 1984
    Unbeknownst to each other, two mice have selected the same pumpkin for their secret work to grow an enormous one.
Tasha Tudor, *Pumpkin Moonshine*, 1938
    Seeking the very best pumpkin in her grandparents' patch, a little girl selects one which rolls down the hill and arrives home ahead of her.
Jane Yolen, *Beneath the Ghost Moon*, 1994
    When the creepy crawlies destroy their costumes, the mice are ready to give up until cajoled by one small mouse to stand up for their rights and to forgive the misdeeds.

1217

WILLO DAVIS ROBERTS

The Absolutely True Story. . .How I Visited Yellowstone Park with the Terrible Rupes
(New York: Atheneum, 1994)

Subject(s): Mystery and Detective Stories; Brothers and Sisters; Vacations
Age range(s): Grades 4-6
Major character(s): Lewis Q. Dodge, Twin, Vacationer; Alison Dodge, Twin, Vacationer
Time period(s): 1990s
Locale(s): Marysville, Washington; Yellowstone National Park, Wyoming

Summary: Lewis is overwhelmed at their good fortune when he and his sister Alison are invited on a trip to Yellowstone Park with their new neighbors the Rupes. He envisions what fun it'll be traveling in a rented motor home, eating junk food and not having any rules, though he quickly figures out his sister is stuck with baby-sitting the younger Rupe children.

Junk food rapidly becomes unappetizing, a lack of rules unsettling and $100 bills hidden in the motor home discomfiting. When all five children are kidnapped, Lewis and Alison use every tactic imaginable to escape in this humorous mystery. (154 pages)

Where it's reviewed:
Booklist, January 15, 1995, page 929
School Library Journal, March 1995, page 200
Horn Book Guide, Spring 1995, page 82
Kirkus Reviews, December 15, 1994, page 1576
Library Talk, September 1995, page 39

Awards the book has won:
Edgar Allen Poe Award/Juvenile, 1995

Other books by the same author:
What Are We Going to Do About David?, 1993
To Grandmother's House We Go, 1990
What Could Go Wrong?, 1989
Pet Sitting Peril, 1983

Other books you might like:
Lois Lowry, *Taking Care of Terrific*, 1983
    Fourteen-year-old Enid encounters all sorts of adventures in a baby-sitting job.
P.J. Petersen, *How Can You Hijack a Cave?*, 1988
    While working as tour guides at a cave, the daughter of the owner is kidnapped and Lori and Curt try to save their coworker.
Bruce Stone, *Half Nelson, Full Nelson*, 1985
    In an attempt to reunite his parents, Nelson Gato kidnaps his younger sister.

1218

HARRIETTE GILLEM ROBINET

Washington City Is Burning
(New York: Atheneum, 1996)

Subject(s): War of 1812; Slavery
Age range(s): Grades 4-6
Major character(s): Virginia, Slave, Teenager; Dolley Madison, Historical Figure (first lady); Tobias, Slave
Time period(s): 1810s (1814)
Locale(s): Washington, District of Columbia

Summary: Virginia comes to the White House from the Virginia plantation and is soon caught up in working for Miss Dolley. Because of her past, she is also soon driving a wagon to help slaves escape the city to freedom. Everyone is kind to her except Rosetta Bell, who mistreats her and lies about her to Miss Dolley in order to get her in trouble. When the War of 1812 breaks out in the city, many slaves run to freedom. While Virginia does help them get new clothes from the White House, she decides that she will stay on there because it is where she feels wanted, and she is sure she will eventually be freed. (149 pages)

Where it's reviewed:
Booklist, November 1, 1996, page 501

Other books by the same author:
Mississippi Chariot, 1995
If You Please, Mr. Lincoln, 1995

Children of the Fire, 1991

Other books you might like:

Gloria Whelan, *Once on This Island*, 1995
 A young girl sees her life changed as the British take over the island during the War of 1812.

Sandra Forester, *Sound the Jubilee*, 1995
 A young girl writes about how her family was able to find life after slavery on an island.

Barbara Diamond Goldin, *Red Means Good Fortune: A Story of San Francisco Chinatown*, 1994
 A Chinese boy in San Francisco discovers that a slave girl is living next door.

Pat McKissack, *A Picture of Freedom: The Diary of Clotee, a Slave Girl*, 1997
 A slave girl keeps a diary about her life on a Virginia plantation before the Civil War.

1219

NANCY K. ROBINSON

Countess Veronica

(New York: Scholastic, 1994)

Series: Veronica
Subject(s): Games; Humor
Age range(s): Grades 4-6
Major character(s): Veronica Schmidt, 5th Grader; Carlton Count, Chess Player
Time period(s): 1990s
Locale(s): United States

Summary: Veronica's at it again! The only child of divorced parents, she is forever plotting new ways for each parent to find a mate. When her favorite librarian moves near her father, she ensures they meet one another. Hearing that her jet-set mother's newest boyfriend, Count Carleton, is coming to dinner, she tells everyone that she'll soon become a Countess. Because Count Carleton is coming to town to take part in a chess tournament, Veronica implies that she's also an expert at chess. Luckily her friends come to her aid when her exaggerations backfire in this light-hearted story. (146 pages)

Where it's reviewed:
Voice of Youth Advocates, April 1994, page 30
School Library Journal, April 1994, page 130
Booklist, February 1, 1994, page 1007
Library Talk, May 1994, page 95

Other books by the same author:
Veronica Meets Her Match, 1990
Veronica Knows Best, 1987
Veronica the Show-Off, 1984

Other books you might like:
Ellen Conford, *A Royal Pain*, 1986
 Abby discovers she's been brought up by the wrong parents and she's really a princess from Saxony Coburn.
Frances Lantz, *Dear Celeste, My Life Is a Mess*, 1992
 Amanda and Leigh decide their favorite newspaper columnist doesn't fit her image, so they embark on ''Operation Celeste'' to remake her.
Ivy Ruckman, *Who Invited the Undertaker?*, 1989
 Dale knows his mother misses her deceased husband, so he

puts an ad in the personal section of their newspaper to find her a man.

1220

BELINDA ROCHELLE
LARRY JOHNSON, Illustrator

When Jo Louis Won the Title

(Boston: Houghton Mifflin Company, 1994)

Subject(s): African Americans; Grandparents; Storytelling
Age range(s): Grades K-2
Major character(s): Jo Louis, Child, Student; John Henry, Grandfather
Time period(s): 1990s (1994); Indeterminate Past
Locale(s): United States; New York, New York (Harlem)

Summary: When John Henry finds his granddaughter sitting glumly on the steps of her home awaiting his return, he tries to learn what is troubling her. Although Jo Louis expresses a variety of concerns about the first day of school, she doesn't admit that her real fear is of people's reactions to her name. However, her sensitive grandfather relates the story of his journey, as a young man, from the South, his arrival in Harlem and how the events of that particular night determined her father's name and in turn hers. (32 pages)

Where it's reviewed:
Booklist, July 1994, page 1956
Children's Book Review Service, December 1994, page 40
New Advocate, Winter 1995, page 49
Publishers Weekly, July 25, 1994, page 54
School Library Journal, September 1994, page 192

Other books by the same author:
Witnesses to Freedom: Young People Who Fought for Civil Rights, 1993

Other books you might like:
Sandra Belton, *May'naise Sandwiches & Sunshine Tea*, 1994
 Big Mama shares with her granddaughter the story of a childhood friendship .
Jacob Lawrence, *The Great Migration*, 1993
 Through paintings, a nonfiction work depicts the lives of African-Americans who left the rural South seeking opportunity in the industrial North.
Margaree King Mitchell, *Uncle Jed's Barbershop*, 1993
 In an awarding-winning story, Sarah Jean recalls the determination of her Uncle Jed to save enough money to open his own barbershop.

1221

ANNE F. ROCKWELL, Author/Illustrator

No! No! No!

(New York: Macmillan Books for Young Readers, 1995)

Subject(s): Behavior; Family Life; Bedtime
Age range(s): Grades K-1
Major character(s): Unnamed Character, Child
Time period(s): 1990s (1995)
Locale(s): United States

Summary: From the moment he awakens, a little boy knows it's not going to be one of his good days. At breakfast he has the wrong cereal and spills his orange juice which he didn't want to drink anyway. It's raining, he has to wear a yucky shirt to school and someone makes fun of his new shoes. By the time he's listening to a great bedtime story he realizes that tomorrow will begin a better day. (24 pages)

Where it's reviewed:
Booklist, May 1, 1995, page 1580
Horn Book Guide, Fall 1995, page 254
New York Times Book Review, August 27, 1995, page 27
School Library Journal, July 1995, page 68

Other books by the same author:
When Hugo Went to School, 1991
At the Beach, 1987
When We Grow Up, 1981

Other books you might like:
Anita Jeram, *Contrary Mary*, 1995
    Mary is having an uncooperative day. She puts her shoes on the wrong feet, refuses to walk under the umbrella and reads books upside down.
Miranda Hapgood, *Martha's Mad Day*, 1977
    Martha wakes up in a bad mood which stays with her all the long mad day.
Judith Viorst, *Alexander and the Terrible, Horrible, No Good Very Bad Day*, 1972
    Alexander is having a day when everything that can possibly go wrong does.

1222

ANNE F. ROCKWELL
ROBERT SAUBER, Illustrator

The Storm

(New York: Hyperion Books for Children, 1994)

Subject(s): Weather; Fall; Family Life
Age range(s): Grades K-3
Major character(s): Unnamed Character, Child
Time period(s): 1990s (1994)
Locale(s): New England

Summary: A young girl and her family hurry to prepare for an approaching storm in their coastal community. As the storm rages during the night, the family loses power, but is otherwise safe. When the girl awakens her father has already left for his city job to help with the clean-up and she and her mother go for a walk on the beach to see the changes wrought by the force of nature. (32 pages)

Where it's reviewed:
Children's Book Review Service, December 1994, page 40
Horn Book Guide, Spring 1995, page 53
Learning, May 1995, page 71
School Library Journal, November 1994, page 90

Other books by the same author:
The Way to Captain Yankee's, 1994
Our Yard Is Full of Birds, 1992
First Comes Spring, 1985

Other books you might like:
Lena Anderson, *Stina*, 1989
    Visiting her grandfather's home by the sea, Stina is frightened by a storm until grandfather joins her to share the experience.
Una Leavy, *Harry's Stormy Night*, 1994
    Coping with a loss of electric power during a storm, Harry and his family sing and tell stories by candlelight.
Cynthia Rylant, *Henry and Mudge and the Wild Wind*, 1993
    During a thunderstorm, Henry's father suggests a game as a distraction from the power failure while frightened Mudge tries to hide.

1223

KRISTINA RODANAS, Author/Illustrator

Dance of the Sacred Circle: A Native American Tale

(Boston: Little, Brown and Company, 1994)

Subject(s): Legends; Indians of North America; Animals/ Horses
Age range(s): Grades 2-4
Major character(s): Great Chief, Deity; Unnamed Character, Orphan, Indian
Time period(s): Indeterminate Past
Locale(s): United States

Summary: Long ago the people who roam the prairies in search of buffalo have only dogs as beasts of burden. Hunting the buffalo on foot becomes more and more difficult and the people begin to go hungry. After listening as the tribal elders pass the sacred pipe and discuss the problem, an orphan boy decides to walk to the highest mountain and find the Great Chief in the Sky to ask his help. After many days the boy's quest ends and the Great Chief fashions an animal of mud and calls a council of all the animals and trees of the forest to contribute something to its the creation. When the sacred circle concludes, a horse is presented to the boy to ride back to his people. (32 pages)

Where it's reviewed:
Booklist, October 1, 1994, page 331
Children's Bookwatch, January 1995, page 5
Kirkus Reviews, October 15, 1994, page 1415
Quill & Quire, March 1995, page 79
School Library Journal, January 1995, page 105

Awards the book has won:
International Reading Association Teachers' Choice, 1995

Other books by the same author:
Dragonfly's Tale, 1992 (Southwest Book Award)
The Story of Wali Dad, 1988

Other books you might like:
Joseph Bruchac, *Native American Animal Stories*, 1992
    The collection of animal tales is drawn from the folklore of North American tribes.
Caron Lee Cohen, *The Mud Pony: A Traditional Skidi Pawnee Tale*, 1988
    An Indian boy is too poor to own a pony; when a mud pony magically becomes real, his people see it as a sign of leadership ability.

Paul Goble, *The Gift of the Sacred Dog*, 1982
The Plains Indians are saved from starvation when the sacred dog—a horse—is given to them for buffalo hunting.

1224

EMILY RODDA
NOELA YOUNG, Illustrator

The Timekeeper
(New York: Greenwillow Books, 1993)

Subject(s): Time Travel; Brothers and Sisters; Fantasy
Age range(s): Grades 4-6
Major character(s): Patrick Minter, Child; Danny Minter, 4-Year-Old, Brother (younger); Claire Minter, Sister (older)
Time period(s): 1990s (1992)
Locale(s): Australia; Fictional Country (other side of the Barrier)

Summary: In this sequel to *Finders Keepers*, originally published in Australia in 1992, Patrick must travel to the world on the other side of the invisible Barrier to get help with the computer used for communication with the other side. Patrick finds himself in a race against time to rescue his brother and sister who have followed him and to fix a broken timepiece before both worlds come to an end. (160 pages)

Where it's reviewed:
Booklist, December 1, 1993, page 691
Horn Book Guide, Spring 1994, page 81
Kirkus Reviews, October 1, 1993, page 1278
Library Talk, January 1994, page 40
School Library Journal, October 1993, page 128

Other books by the same author:
The Best-Kept Secret, 1991
Finders Keepers, 1991
The Pigs Are Flying!, 1988

Other books you might like:
Peni R. Griffin, *Switching Well*, 1993
    Two girls standing in front of a well in different centuries receive their wish for escape when they change eras.
Jon Scieszka, *2095*, 1995
    The latest entry in the Time Warp Trio Series finds Joe, Fred, and Sam travelling into the future where they meet their great-grandchildren.
Jan Slepian, *Back to Before*, 1993
    Cousins Hilary and Linny find a magical ring which enables them to go back in time.

1225

SUSANNA RODELL
KIM GAMBLE, Illustrator

Dear Fred
(New York: Ticknor & Fields Books for Young Readers, 1995)

Subject(s): Brothers and Sisters; Divorce; Letters
Age range(s): Grades K-2

Major character(s): Grace, Child of Divorced Parents, Sister (Fred's half-sister); Fred, Child of Divorced Parents, Brother (Grace's half-brother)
Time period(s): 1990s (1995)
Locale(s): New York, New York; Australia

Summary: It's been almost a year since Grace left Fred in Australia and moved with her mother and her mother's new husband to America. Grace writes nostagically to Fred of the fun times she remembers sharing with him in a home which had a backyard for playing. The letter closes with Grace's expression of love for Fred, her hope that he remembers her, and wistful anticipation of a future visit. This is the author's first picture book. (32 pages)

Where it's reviewed:
Booklist, August 1995, page 1956
Children's Book Review Service, June 1995, page 125
Horn Book Guide, Fall 1995, page 280
New York Times Book Review, August 13, 1995, page 23
School Library Journal, April 1995, page 116

Other books you might like:
Pat Brisson, *Kate on the Coast*, 1992
    In letters to her best friend, Kate describes her family's move to the Pacific Northwest.
Judith Caseley, *Priscilla Twice*, 1995
    When her parents' separate, Priscilla must adjust to life in two different households.
Nette Hilton, *Andrew Jessup*, 1993
    Andrew Jessup moves away leaving a lonely and sad "best" friend behind watching his house for a new family.

1226

STEPHEN ROOS
DIANE DE GROAT, Illustrator

Never Trust a Sister over Twelve
(New York: Delacorte Press, 1993)

Subject(s): Sisters; Family Life; School Life
Age range(s): Grades 4-6
Major character(s): Suki Johnson, 9-Year-Old (impulsive), Sister; Ginger Johnson, 12-Year-Old, Sister; Lyman Johnson, 5-Year-Old, Brother
Time period(s): 1990s (1993)
Locale(s): New Eden

Summary: When Suki decides to take scissors in hand and cut her hair to match her adored older sister's new style, her family is horrified and Lyman offers her his helmet to wear. At her new school, however, Suki fabricates an adventurous story to explain her almost-bald head and attracts the attention of a group called the Hijinxers. They convince her that any sister who has had her 12th birthday can no longer be a friend to a younger sister and events prove them right. With her new group, Suki plans revenge. Look out Ginger, you're going to be hijinxed! (145 pages)

Where it's reviewed:
Booklist, November 1, 1993, page 524
Horn Book Guide, Spring 1994, page 81
Kirkus Reviews, October 1, 1993, page 1279
Publishers Weekly, October 18, 1993, page 73

School Library Journal, September 1993, page 234

Other books by the same author:
Cottontail Caper: The Pet Lover's Club, 1994
Love Me, Love My Werewolf, 1993
And the Winner Is..., 1989

Other books you might like:
Betsy Byars, *Wanted...Mud Blossom*, 1991
In one of several stories about an unusual family, Junior accuses the family dog of causing the disappearance of a hamster & demands Mud's "trial" for the crime.
Beverly Cleary, *Beezus and Ramona*, 1955
Two sisters who try to get along find that it's not always easy.
Lois Lowry, *Anastasia Krupnik*, 1979
The first book in a humorous series about 4th grader Anastasia and her family.

1227

PHYLLIS ROOT
SANDRA SPEIDEL, Illustrator

Coyote and the Magic Words

(New York: Lothrop, Lee and Shepard Books, 1993)

Subject(s): Animals/Coyotes; Creation; Folk Tales
Age range(s): Grades 2-4
Major character(s): Maker-of-all-things, Deity; Coyote, Coyote (trickster)
Time period(s): Indeterminate Past
Locale(s): United States (American Southwest)

Summary: The harmony of the world created by the Maker-of-all-things is disturbed by bored Coyote, who uses the magic in the words to create dissension among the people. The Maker-of-all-things is not pleased when she sees the mischief Coyote is making and she takes away the magic, proclaiming that it can only return when a story is told. To this day Coyote tells stories trying to bring back the magic. (32 pages)

Where it's reviewed:
Booklist, November 15, 1993, page 633
Children's Book Review Service, Winter 1994, page 65
Horn Book Guide, Spring 1994, page 51
Reading Teacher, May 1994, page 653
School Library Journal, January 1994, page 97

Other books by the same author:
Sam, Who Was Swallowed by a Shark, 1994
The Old Red Rocking Chair, 1992
Moon Tiger, 1985

Other books you might like:
Gerald McDermott, *Coyote: A Trickster Tale from the American Southwest*, 1994
In a retelling of a Native American folk tale, Coyote begs the crows to teach him to sing, dance and fly.
Tom Pohrt, *Coyote Goes Walking*, 1995
The four tales of the mischievous coyote are rooted in Native American storytelling tradition.
Harriet Peck Taylor, *Coyote Places the Stars*, 1993
A curious coyote seeks to learn the secrets of the heavens and rearranges the stars into the shapes of animal friends.

1228

DEBORAH LEE ROSE
GREG SHED, Illustrator

The Rose Horse

(San Diego: Harcourt Brace and Company, 1995)

Subject(s): Jews; Babies; Historical
Age range(s): Grades 2-5
Major character(s): Lily, Child, Sister (older); Totte, Father, Artisan (wood-carver); Momme, Mother
Time period(s): 1900s (1909)
Locale(s): New York, New York (Coney Island)

Summary: When Lily's sister is born prematurely Momme and the baby are sent to a special clinic operated as an attraction at Coney Island. To keep the family as close as possible, Lily and Totte move in with Totte's cousin who carves carousel horses. Totte, an accomplished carver himself, helps in the woodshop while Lily helps her aunt sell tickets for the carousel ride. Yiddish words and Jewish holidays used in the story are defined in a concluding glossary. (60 pages)

Where it's reviewed:
Booklist, September 1, 1995, page 58
Bulletin of the Center for Children's Books, November 1995, page 104
Children's Book Review Service, November 1995, page 30
Horn Book Guide, Spring 1996, page 68
School Library Journal, January 1996, page 94

Other books by the same author:
Meredith's Mother Takes the Train, 1991
The People Who Hugged the Trees, 1990

Other books you might like:
Barbara Cohen, *Make a Wish, Molly*, 1994
Recently emigrated with her family from Russia, Molly finds American birthday traditions conflict with her family's observance of Passover.
Riki Levinson, *Dinnie Abbie Sister-r-r*, 1987
Growing up in Brooklyn, Jennie helps care for one of her brothers during a serious illness.
Bonnie Pryor, *The Dream Jar*, 1996
After reaching America each member of a Russian family works to contribute to the family's dream.

1229

MICHAEL J. ROSEN
JAMES E. RANSOME, Illustrator

Bonesy and Isabel

(San Diego: Harcourt Brace & Company, 1995)

Subject(s): Adoption; Animals/Dogs; Death (of a Pet)
Age range(s): Grades 1-4
Major character(s): Bonesy, Dog; Isabel, Adoptee
Time period(s): 1990s (1995)
Locale(s): Sunbury Road

Summary: In a family with many pets, elderly Bonesy is the only one of nine dogs, all formerly strays, to be allowed inside the house. Bonesy's special place is under the dining room table where he receives scraps of food and listens to Isabel practice her English. Although Isabel cannot understand many of the English words she hears, she and Bonesy communicate with no difficulty. The night Isabel finds Bonesy under the table, dead, her adoptive parents join her in a moment of shared grieving. (32 pages)

Where it's reviewed:
Booklist, April 15, 1995, page 1507
Children's Book Review Service, May 1995, page 114
Emergency Librarian, September 1995, page 55
Publishers Weekly, April 24, 1995, page 71
School Library Journal, June 1995, page 94

Other books by the same author:
All Eyes on the Pond, 1994
Moving, 1993
Elijah's Angel: A Story for Chanukah and Christmas, 1992
Little Rabbit Foo Foo, 1990

Other books you might like:
Amy Ehrlich, *Maggie and Silky and Joe*, 1994
   Joe and his family are saddened by the death of faithful friend and pet Maggie.
Ellen Howard, *Murphy and Kate*, 1995
   Kate and Murphy grow up together, but Murphy, the older dog, dies after 14 years, leaving a still young Kate to mourn his passing.
Maureen Wittbold, *Mending Peter's Heart*, 1995
   Grieving over the death of his pet, Peter is comforted by Mr. MacIntyre, a widowed neighbor, who helps Peter understand how to remember a lost loved one with joy.

◼1230◼

MICHAEL J. ROSEN
AMINAH BRENDA LYNN ROBINSON, Illustrator

A School for Pompey Walker
(San Diego: Harcourt Brace & Company, 1995)

Subject(s): Slavery; Schools; Underground Railroad
Age range(s): Grades 3-5
Major character(s): Pompey Bibb Walker, Slave, Friend; Jeremiah Walker, Friend
Time period(s): Indeterminate Past; 1920s (1923)
Locale(s): South; Madisonville, Ohio

Summary: Addressing students at a school bearing his name, 88-year-old Pompey Walker tells the story of his courageous life as a slave and his use of slavery to achieve his goal of educating black children. Born a slave, Pompey Bibb, as a young teen, is rescued from slavery when Jeremiah Walker, a Northerner, buys him. They become lifelong friends and partners in a strange business venture of raising money by selling Pompey on the trading block and then stealing him from the new owner. Splitting the money from each transaction, these two friends save enough to achieve Pompey's goal of building a school. A concluding author's note gives background for the story. (48 pages)

Where it's reviewed:
Booklist, October 15, 1995, page 405
Bulletin of the Center for Children's Books, January 1996, page 170
Children's Book Review Service, September 1995, page 12

Kirkus Reviews, August 15, 1995, page 1193
School Library Journal, November 1995, page 81

Other books by the same author:
The Greatest Table: A Banquet to Fight Against Hunger, 1994
Elijah's Angel: A Story for Chanukah and Christmas, 1992
The Kid's Book of Fishing, 1991

Other books you might like:
Marie Bradby, *More than Anything Else*, 1995
   This fictionalized account describes Booker T. Washington as a child learning to read his name.
Dolores Johnson, *Now Let Me Fly: The Story of a Slave Family*, 1993
   In 1815 Minna is captured in Africa and sold into slavery on an American plantation.
Connie Porter, *Addy Learns a Lesson: A School Story*, 1993
   With her mother, Addy escapes to freedom in Philadelphia where she begins attending school for the first time.
Courtni C. Wright, *Journey to Freedom: A Story of the Underground Railroad*, 1994
   Historically accurate, the author presents one family's journey to freedom with Harriet Tubman as their guide.

◼1231◼

LIZ ROSENBERG
JIM LAMARCHE, Illustrator

The Carousel
(San Diego: Harcourt Brace & Company, 1995)

Subject(s): Sisters; Animals/Horses; Fantasy
Age range(s): Grades K-3
Major character(s): Unnamed Character, Sister; Unnamed Character, Sister
Time period(s): 1990s (1995)
Locale(s): United States

Summary: Two sisters, who should hurry home to cook dinner for their father, take a shortcut through the park past the closed carousel and discover the horses have come to life. The youngest sister mounts her favorite gray mare while the older girl clambers aboard a zebra as they all race through the park and over the treetops of the town. Realizing the horses become wild because they are broken, the younger sister gets a toolbox to fix the carousel and the older sister plays a lullaby on her flute. Soon the carousel is back to normal and they continue their walk home, arriving in time to greet their father. (32 pages)

Where it's reviewed:
Booklist, November 15, 1995, page 565
Emergency Librarian, January 1996, page 56
Five Owls, January 1996, page 59
Publishers Weekly, September 25, 1995, page 56
School Library Journal, January 1996, page 94

Other books by the same author:
Grandmother and the Runaway Shadow, 1996
Moonbathing, 1996
Monster Mama, 1993
The Scrap Doll, 1991

Other books you might like:
Pat Cummings, *Carousel*, 1994
   The small music-box carousel Alex receives for her birthday comes to life at bedtime and takes her for a nighttime ride.
Bill Martin Jr., *Up and Down on the Merry-Go-Round*, 1988
   With co-author John Archambault, the distinctive rhymes of Martin whirl the reader about on a carousel ride.
David McPhail, *The Train*, 1977
   After his father puts him to bed, Matthew boards his toy train and takes a fantastic trip.
Chris Van Allsburg, *The Polar Express*, 1985
   The Caldecott Medal winner relates the memory of a magical Christmas Eve train ride to the North Pole.

1232

LIZ ROSENBERG
STEPHEN GAMMELL, Illustrator

Monster Mama

(New York: Philomel Books, 1993)

Subject(s): Mothers and Sons; Bullies; Monsters
Age range(s): Grades K-1
Major character(s): Patrick Edward, Child (son); Monster Mama, Mother, Monster
Time period(s): 1990s (1993)
Locale(s): United States

Summary: Three bullies make the mistake of picking on Patrick Edward, only son of a monster. Unafraid, Patrick Edward is outmatched by the bullies until their teasing mentions his mother, provoking him to respond. What a surprise the bullies are in for when Monster Mama hears the commotion and comes to Patrick Edward's rescue. (32 pages)

Where it's reviewed:
Booklist, January 15, 1993, page 899
Horn Book, March 1993, page 200
Kirkus Reviews, February 1, 1993, page 153
Publishers Weekly, January 25, 1993, page 87
School Library Journal, June 1993, page 87

Awards the book has won:
Booklist Editors' Choice, 1993

Other books by the same author:
The Carousel, 1995
Grandmother and the Runaway Shadow, 1994
The Scrap Doll, 1991
Adelaide and the Night Train, 1989

Other books you might like:
Babette Cole, *The Trouble with Mom*, 1984
   When your mom is a witch, life can be full of interesting surprises.
Pat Hutchins, *Silly Billy!*, 1992
   Even in a monster family, big sisters must learn to get along with bothersome little brothers.
Maurice Sendak, *Where the Wild Things Are*, 1988
   When Max's overly exuberant playing results in a trip to his room without dinner, he imagines himself traveling to the land of the wild things.

Scott Taylor, *Dinosaur James*, 1990
   James' obsession with dinosaurs becomes an asset when the schoolyard bully singles out James for attention.
Elizabeth Winthrop, *Maggie and the Monster*, 1987
   Maggie learns to deal with the nightly visits of a little monster.
Audrey Wood, *Weird Parents*, 1990
   This young boy wishes that his weird parents were more typical of other parents he knows, or does he?

1233

LILLIAN HAMMER ROSS
HELEN COGANCHERRY, Illustrator

Sarah, Also Known as Hannah

(Morton Grove, IL: Albert Whitman & Company, 1994)

Subject(s): Emigration and Immigration; Jews; Fear
Age range(s): Grades 3-5
Major character(s): Hannah Kamornick, 16-Year-Old, Sister; Sarah Kamornick, 12-Year-Old, Sister; Benjamin, Uncle
Time period(s): 1910s (1910)
Locale(s): Lisec, Austria-Hungary; New York, New York

Summary: After Sarah's father dies, her mother writes to Sarah's Uncle Benjamin in America, asking him to take her two daughters. Uncle Benjamin, able to pay for the passage of only one of the girls, asks for Hannah because she is old enough to work. After Hannah secures her passport and tickets, Sarah's mother sends Sarah in her place. Saddened and frightened, Sarah departs by train and boat for America, taking on Hannah's identity until Uncle Benjamin greets her and she can be Sarah again. (63 pages)

Where it's reviewed:
Booklist, April 1, 1994, page 1451
Bulletin of the Center for Children's Books, March 1994, page 232
Kirkus Reviews, April 1, 1994, page 484
Publishers Weekly, April 25, 1994, page 79
School Library Journal, May 1994, page 118

Other books by the same author:
Buba Leah and Her Paper Children, 1991

Other books you might like:
Alma Flor Ada, *My Name Is Maria Isabel*, 1993
   In her new school, Puerto Rican Maria Isabel expresses the importance of her name when writing a school assignment about her greatest wish.
Jamie Gilson, *Hello, My Name Is Scrambled Eggs*, 1985
   The Americanization of a Vietnamese refugee becomes the reponsibility of Harvey Trumble whose family shelters Tuan's family until they are settled.
Jeanette Winter, *Klara's New World*, 1992
   When drought forces Klara's family from their Swedish home, they endure the long journey to America in hopes of an improved life.

1234

JOYCE ROSSI, Author/Illustrator

The Gullywasher

(Flagstaff, AZ: Northland Publishing, 1995)

Subject(s): Grandparents; Storytelling; Weather
Age range(s): Grades 1-3
Major character(s): Leticia, Child; Abuelito, Grandfather, Cowboy
Time period(s): 1990s (1995)
Locale(s): United States (Southwest)

Summary: While waiting for a gullywasher of a storm to subside, Abuelito entertains his granddaughter with tales of his life as a young vaquero or cowboy. As he tells of a gullywasher from years ago, he also explains to Leticia how this storm and its aftermath caused him to have white hair, a potbelly and a stooped back. In the author's first book, a beginning author's note gives historical background and a concluding glossary defines the Spanish words which sprinkle the text. (32 pages)

Where it's reviewed:
Booklist, December 15, 1995, page 705
Horn Book Guide, Spring 1996, page 43
Publishers Weekly, October 16, 1995, page 61
School Library Journal, January 1996, page 95

Other books you might like:
Jo Harper, *Jalapeno Hal*, 1993
    Jalapeno Hal assists the residents of a small Texas town solve a drought problem and bring on the rain.
Steven Kellogg, *Pecos Bill: A Tall Tale*, 1986
    The origin of some unique features of the American West are explained in a retelling of a frequently told tall tale about a legendary folk hero.
Helen Ketteman, *The Year of No More Corn*, 1993
    Old Grampa tells Beanie how he saved the 1928 corn crop by planting whittled corn kernels which grew into corn trees.
Susan Lowell, *The Three Little Javelinas*, 1992
    The tale of the Three Little Pigs is retold with a Southwestern twist.

1235

SUSAN L. ROTH, Author/Illustrator

Princess

(New York: Hyperion Books for Children, 1993)

Subject(s): Mothers and Daughters; Imagination
Age range(s): Grades K-1
Major character(s): Princess, Child (imaginative); Mother, Mother
Time period(s): 1990s
Locale(s): United States

Summary: Ignoring her mother's repeated calls to wake up for school, Princess imagines all the things she will do as a real princess. One of the things that she will surely *not* do is go to school. Unfortunately for Princess, Mother has different ideas. (32 pages)

Where it's reviewed:
Children's Book Review Service, January 1994, page 53
Horn Book Guide, Spring 1994, page 51
Publishers Weekly, October 25, 1993, page 60
School Library Journal, January 1994, page 97

Other books by the same author:
Thump, Creak, Bump!, 1995
Another Christmas, 1992
Gypsy Bird Song, 1991
The Story of Light, 1990
We'll Ride Elephants through Brooklyn, 1989

Other books you might like:
Marisabina Russo, *Time to Wake Up!*, 1994
    This reluctant riser resists his Mom's morning pleas, but ultimately surprises her.
Dr. Seuss, *I Am NOT Going to Get Up Today!*, 1987
    Despite some far-fetched parental efforts to encourage him to get up, a young boy insists that he will stay in bed all day.
Carol Diggory Shields, *I Am Really a Princess*, 1993
    The narrator of this tale appears to be just an ordinary child in an ordinary family, but one who fantasizes the wonderful changes in her life when everyone learns she is really a princess.

1236

JOAN ROTHENBERG, Author/Illustrator

Inside-Out Grandma

(New York: Hyperion Books for Children, 1995)

Subject(s): Grandparents; Holidays, Jewish; Jews
Age range(s): Grades K-2
Major character(s): Rosie, Child; Grandma, Grandmother
Time period(s): 1990s (1995)
Locale(s): United States

Summary: While helping Grandma prepare for Hanukkah, Rosie questions why Grandma wears her clothes inside-out. Grandma's explanation for the inside-out clothes triggers her memory to buy oil for cooking potato latkes and takes Rosie on a memory walk of the family and traditions surrounding the celebration of Hanukkah. The recipe for potato latkes is included. (32 pages)

Where it's reviewed:
Booklist, September 15, 1995, page 172
Five Owls, November 1995, page 44
Horn Book Guide, Spring 1996, page 43
Quill & Quire, October 1995, page 47
School Library Journal, October 1995, page 41

Other books by the same author:
Yettele's Feathers, 1995

Other books you might like:
Malka Drucker, *Grandma's Latkes*, 1992
    While Molly and Grandma make latkes, Molly listens to her grandmother explain the history behind the custom.
Barbara Diamond Goldin, *Just Enough Is Plenty: A Hanukkah Tale*, 1988
    A poor family includes a stranger at their holiday table because Mama can cook enough to be plenty for all.

Eric A. Kimmel, *The Chanukkah Guest*, 1990
Bubba Brayna prepares latkes for the rabbi's visit, but serves them to a bear whom she mistakes for the bearded rabbi.

Malka Penn, *The Miracle of the Potato Latkes: A Hanukkah Story*, 1994
During a drought-caused potato shortage, Tante Golda's faith is rewarded with more than enough potatoes to make the latkes for Hanukkah.

1237

JOAN ROTHENBERG, Author/Illustrator

Yettele's Feathers

(New York: Hyperion Books for Children, 1995)

Subject(s): Jews; Folk Tales
Age range(s): Grades K-3
Major character(s): Yettele Babbelonski, Widow(er); Rabbi, Religious
Time period(s): Indeterminate Past
Locale(s): Ostrow, Ukraine

Summary: From the window of her tiny room over the baker's shop, Yettele has a perfect view of her small town and all the activity in it. Living alone, Yettele has no one to share her favorite pastime—talking—so when she tires of talking to herself she goes outside and talks to anyone she finds. Unfortunately, her conversations about everyone in town are gossip which starts inaccurate and hurtful rumors and soon no one will talk to her. Seeking Rabbi's counsel, Yettele is told to cut the top out of her best pillow and bring it to him. When Yettele attempts to do so, the wind takes the feathers and spreads them all over town. After a day of attempting to gather the wind-blown feathers, Rabbi points out that the feathers are as hard to retrieve as her words, once spoken. As the author's first book concludes, Yettele shares stories with the town's children and their favorite is about Yettele and her feathers. (40 pages)

Where it's reviewed:
Booklist, May 1, 1995, page 1578
Children's Book Review Service, June 1995, page 126
Horn Book Guide, Fall 1995, page 333
Quill & Quire, April 1995, page 43
School Library Journal, April 1995, page 128

Other books by the same author:
Inside-Out Grandma, 1995

Other books you might like:
Adele Geras, *My Grandmother's Stories: A Collection of Jewish Folk Tales*, 1990
An award-winning collection of stories told by a grandmother to her granddaughter includes customs and recipes.

Steve Sanfield, *The Feather Merchants and Other Tales of the Fools of Chelm*, 1991
Thirteen tales drawn from Jewish folklore offer humor and heritage.

Isaac Bashevis Singer, *Stories for Children*, 1984
The collection of tales is inspired by Yiddish tradition.

1238

KRISTA RUEPP
ULRIKE HEYNE, Illustrator

Midnight Rider

(New York: North-South Books, 1995)

Subject(s): Animals/Horses; Beaches; Accidents
Age range(s): Grades 2-4
Major character(s): Charlie, Child, Animal Lover; Mr. Matthew Grimm, Recluse, Neighbor; Starbright, Horse (Mr. Grimm's)
Time period(s): Indeterminate Past
Locale(s): Germany (coast)

Summary: Following the death of her horse, Charlie begins to secretly visit Starbright, hoping to ride him one day. When Charlie bravely approaches grumpy Mr. Grimm with her request to ride Starbright, he coldly dismisses her. That night, as a storm approaches, Charlie sneaks into Starbright's pasture and races him along the beach. Fortunately, the storm awakens Mr. Grimm who finds Starbright missing and rescues Charlie after she is thrown from the horse. Their mutual admiration for the stallion forms a basis for friendship. Translated from the German by J. Alison James (59 pages)

Where it's reviewed:
Booklist, December 1, 1995, page 636
Bulletin of the Center for Children's Books, October 1995, page 67
Horn Book Guide, Spring 1996, page 57
School Library Journal, December 1995, page 90

Other books you might like:
Walter Farley, *The Black Stallion*, 1941
The champion black stallion is featured in 19 books in a series for horse lovers.

Jessie Haas, *Beware the Mare*, 1993
Gram and Gramps don't share Lily's excitement about the new mare that Lily hopes will be hers.

Magdalen Nabb, *The Enchanted Horse*, 1993
Irina's toy horse comes to life at night, carrying her across the moor on secret moonlit rides.

Anna Sewell, *Black Beauty*, 1877
The classic story of a beautiful black horse has been reissued and reillustrated many times.

1239

RONA RUPERT
MICHAEL DOOLING, Illustrator

Straw Sense

(New York: Simon and Schuster Books for Young Readers, 1993)

Subject(s): Mutism; Dolls and Dollhouses; Friendship
Age range(s): Grades 2-4
Major character(s): Shamiema, Aunt; Goolam-Habib Tofie, 5-Year-Old (mute); Saul, Aged Person (kind)
Time period(s): 1990s (1993)
Locale(s): South Africa

Summary: When a lonely, mute boy moves with his aunt Shamiema and her husband to the strawberry fields, he happens upon an old man in a shed making a scarecrow to protect his fields. Fascinated, Goolam-Habib returns and assists Saul in the creation of a straw family. When the family is complete, Goolam-Habib is able to speak again, by first introducing himself to the straw dolls and then to Saul. (32 pages)

Where it's reviewed:
Booklist, November 15, 1993, page 633
Children's Bookwatch, January 1994, page 4
Library Talk, March 1994, page 33
Reading Teacher, April 1994, page 564
School Library Journal, February 1994, page 91

Other books you might like:
Richard E. Albert, *Alejandro's Gift*, 1994
   An old man digs a water hole for the desert creatures who have befriended him.
Ann Grifalconi, *Kinda Blue*, 1993
   Missing her deceased father, Sissy is comforted by her uncle.
Dayal Kaur Khalsa, *The Snow Cat*, 1992
   A lonely girl receives a Snow Cat in answer to her prayers.

1240

BARBARA T. RUSSELL

Last Left Standing

(Boston: Houghton Mifflin, 1996)

Subject(s): Death; Brothers; Friendship
Age range(s): Grades 4-7
Major character(s): Josh, Brother, Child (preteen); Mattie, Grandmother, Artist; Bess Ann, Artist, Learning Disabled Child
Time period(s): 1950s
Locale(s): Florida (small town close to orange groves)

Summary: Unable to face or talk about the death of his brother, Josh spends as much time away from home as he can. One day on his wanders he discovers a cabin in which an older woman and her young granddaughter live. He learns that his brother had been building them a chicken coop. Rather than tell them that Toby is dead, Josh continues what his brother started and falls further into denying his death. It is only when Bess Ann has her own disaster that he is able to face the truth and talk about his brother. (132 pages)

Where it's reviewed:
School Library Journal, October 1996, page 126

Other books you might like:
Marion Dane Bauer, *On My Honor*, 1986
   Joel does not know how to face the death of his best friend Tony and his involvement in it.
Ralph Fletcher, *Fig Pudding*, 1995
   Members of a large family face the death of their brother in different ways.
Barbara Park, *Mick Harte Was Here*, 1995
   A girl describes her feelings as she remembers her brother and his fatal bicycle accident.
Katherine Paterson, *Bridge to Terabithia*, 1977
   Jess makes good friends with Leslie and then must face the sorrow of her death.

Doris Buchanan Smith, *A Taste of Blackberries*, 1973
   A young boy must face the death of his friend from bee stings.

1241

CHING YEUNG RUSSELL
CHRISTOPHER ZHONG-YUAN ZHANG, Illustrator

First Apple

(Honesdale, PA: Boyds Mills Press, 1994)

Subject(s): Gifts; Poverty; Grandparents
Age range(s): Grades 3-5
Major character(s): Yeung Ying, 9-Year-Old; Ah Pau, Grandmother
Time period(s): 1940s
Locale(s): Tai Kong, China (Chan Village)

Summary: Ying's class learns about apples, a fruit she's never tasted. When Ying learns Ah Pau has been dreaming of the taste of an apple since childhood, Ying decides to earn money to buy one for her grandmother's birthday. Despite many frustrations and after she finally has money to buy one, an apple comes to Ying as a gift and she shares it with a very grateful Ah Pau. A brief glossary defines the Chinese words used in the story. (127 pages)

Where it's reviewed:
Booklist, November 1, 1994, page 501
Bulletin of the Center for Children's Books, January 1995, page 177
Horn Book Guide, Spring 1995, page 83
Reading Teacher, September 1995, page 55
School Library Journal, September 1994, page 222

Awards the book has won:
Charlotte Award (New York) Grades 3-5, 1996
Parent's Choice Award, 1996

Other books by the same author:
Water Ghost, 1995

Other books you might like:
Eleanor Frances Lattimore, *Little Pear and His Friends*, 1991
   Six-year-old Little Pear and his friend Big Head find their fun sometimes leads to trouble in their Chinese village.
Elizabeth Foreman Lewis, *Young Fu of the Upper Yangtze*, 1932
   In this Newbery Medal winner a young boy and his mother move from a rural Chinese village to Chungking where the boy's apprenticeship to a coppersmith brings good luck.
Amy Tan, *The Moon Lady*, 1992
   On a rainy day Nai-nai entertains her three granddaughters with stories of her childhood in China.

1242

CHING YEUNG RUSSELL
CHRISTOPHER ZHONG-YUAN ZHANG, Illustrator

Water Ghost

(Honesdale, PA: Boyds Mills Press, 1995)

Subject(s): Grandparents; Cousins; Death
Age range(s): Grades 4-6

Major character(s): Yeung Ying, 10-Year-Old; Ah Pau, Grandmother; Kee, Cousin, 12-Year-Old
Time period(s): 1940s
Locale(s): Tai Kong, China (Chan Village)

Summary: Ying, old enough to attend the annual school campout, must find the money to attend. Ah Pau, who is not in favor of sleeping outside on a hillside at night, reluctantly agrees to allow Ying to go if she raises the money. With Kee also trying to earn his fees, the two squabbling cousins try to cooperate. Ying's guilt following the death of a crippled classmate leads the kind girl to impulsively use her camp money to buy a dead chicken from the girl's grandmother. She endures the ridicule of everyone, until an essay written for a class assignment brings understanding of her actions. Ah Pau depends on Chinese tradition and superstition to make important decisions. A concluding glossary defines the Chinese terms used. (192 pages)

Where it's reviewed:
Booklist, October 15, 1995, page 405
Children's Bookwatch, September 1995, page 1
Horn Book Guide, Spring 1996, page 68
School Library Journal, December 1995, page 108

Other books by the same author:
First Apple, 1994

Other books you might like:
Deborah Nourse Lattimore, *The Dragon's Robe*, 1990
An orphaned weaver girl attempts to appease the rain dragon who creates a drought after noblemen offend the spirit.
Eleanor Frances Lattimore, *More about Little Pear*, 1971
During a school vacation 7-year-old Little Pear helps a neighbor, visits with his grandmother, and learns all about dragons.
Emily Cheney Neville, *The China Year*, 1991
Intrigued by China, but homesick for New York, Henrietta explores a new culture during a year in Beijing where her father is assigned to the university.

1243

MARISABINA RUSSO, Author/Illustrator

Time to Wake Up!
(New York: Greenwillow Books, 1994)

Subject(s): Mothers and Sons; Sleep
Age range(s): Grades K-1
Major character(s): Sam, Child; Mama, Mother
Time period(s): 1990s (1994)
Locale(s): United States

Summary: Mama tickles the toes of reluctant riser Sam to encourage him to get up and get ready for school. While Mama dresses for work, Sam plans a surprise for her. Then they have breakfast and hurry on their way. (24 pages)

Where it's reviewed:
Booklist, June 1, 1994, page 1844
Childhood Education, Fall 1994, page 46
Horn Book, July 1994, page 444
Kirkus Reviews, March 15, 1994, page 403
School Library Journal, May 1994, page 104

Other books by the same author:
Alex Is My Friend, 1992
Where Is Ben?, 1990
The Line-Up Book, 1986

Other books you might like:
Arlene Alda, *Pig, Horse, or Cow, Don't Wake Me Now*, 1994
A peacock's call begins the wake-up process that concludes with a little boy resisting his mother's efforts to get him out of bed.
Sally Grindley, *Wake Up, Dad!*, 1988
Unable to rouse her parents early one morning, a little girl decides to climb in their warm bed and keep them company.
Susan L. Roth, *Princess*, 1993
Despite her mother's repeated attempts to wake her for school, a little girl lingers in bed imagining the freedom she would have if she were a princess.

1244

MARISABINA RUSSO, Author/Illustrator

Trade-In Mother
(New York: Greenwillow Books, 1993)

Subject(s): Mothers and Sons; Family Life; Anger
Age range(s): Grades K-1
Major character(s): Max, Child; Mama, Mother
Time period(s): 1990s (1993)
Locale(s): United States

Summary: Max is having one of those days when nothing seems to go his way and, of course, Mama is seen as the culprit when things go wrong. The proverbial straw to the day comes when Mama will not read his bedtime story one more time. Max announces his intention to trade her in for a mother who would allow him all the things he's missed today. Mama, of course, replies that she will never trade in Max and he reconsiders his plans. (32 pages)

Where it's reviewed:
Booklist, March 1, 1993, page 1237
Horn Book, May 1993, page 325
Publishers Weekly, January 25, 1993, page 85
Reading Teacher, October 1993, page 148
School Library Journal, July 1993, page 70

Other books by the same author:
I Don't Want to Go Back to School, 1994
A Visit to Oma, 1991
The Line-Up Book, 1986 (International Reading Association Children's Book, 1987)

Other books you might like:
Marge Blaine, *The Terrible Thing That Happened at Our House*, 1984
Oh no! Mother has gone to work outside the home and everyone must learn to cope with the resulting chaos.
Dorothea Lachner, *Andrew's Angry Words*, 1995
When Andrew shouts angry words at his older sister he learns how far-ranging the impact of such an outburst can be.
Judith Viorst, *Alexander and the Terrible, Horrible, No Good Very Bad Day*, 1972

Alexander is having one of those days when nothing goes right and his mounting frustration is evident.

1245

KATY RYDELL
DAVID JORGENSEN, Illustrator

Wind Says Good Night
(Boston: Houghton Mifflin Company, 1994)

Subject(s): Bedtime; Nature; Sleep
Age range(s): Grades K-1
Major character(s): Unnamed Character, Child
Time period(s): 1990s (1994)
Locale(s): United States

Summary: In a storyteller's first book for children, a singing mockingbird keeps a young child awake. The night wind implores the bird as well as other insects and animals to stop their activity, but none respond until wind blows a cloud across the moon, providing the catalyst to quiet the noises of the night so that the child sleeps. (32 pages)

Where it's reviewed:
Booklist, April 1, 1994, page 1463
Bulletin of the Center for Children's Books, May 1994, page 301
Children's Book Review Service, May 1994, page 113
Kirkus Reviews, March 1, 1994, page 309
School Library Journal, April 1994, page 112

Other books you might like:
Vivian French, *A Song for Little Toad*, 1995
    Though other animals try to comfort Little Toad with their songs, he finds the croak of his mother's lullaby to be the most soothing.
Reeve Lindbergh, *What Is the Sun?*, 1994
    In a rhyming story a grandmother answers her grandson's bedtime questions about nature.
Fran Manushkin, *Peeping and Sleeping*, 1994
    Barry and his dad seek the source of the peeping sounds that fill the night and keep Barry from sleeping.
Lynn Reiser, *Night Thunder and the Queen of the Wild Horses*, 1995
    Horses from a painting come alive to help a little girl find and quiet the source of loud nighttime noises so she can get back to sleep.
Charlotte Zolotow, *When the Wind Stops*, 1995
    A mother's responses to her son's questions provide reassurance as he settles down to sleep.

1246

JOANNE RYDER
JO ELLEN MCALLISTER-STAMMEN, Illustrator

Bears out There
(New York: Atheneum Books for Young Readers, 1995)

Subject(s): Animals/Bears; Imagination; Nature
Age range(s): Grades K-3
Major character(s): Unnamed Character, Child; Papa, Father
Time period(s): 1990s (1995)

Locale(s): Alaska

Summary: From his morning stretches in a warm bed through his daytime activities, a young boy thinks about the bears who live in the woods surrounding his home and imagines their behavior in relation to his own. As he stands on the porch in the evening, Papa joins him and they both watch, listen, and sense the bears they know are roaming out there. A concluding author's note gives factual information about the black bear. (32 pages)

Where it's reviewed:
Booklist, April 15, 1995, page 1508
Children's Book Review Service, July 1995, page 150
Horn Book Guide, Fall 1995, page 280
School Library Journal, May 1995, page 94

Other books by the same author:
Bambi's Forest: A Year in the Life of the Forest, 1994
A House by the Sea, 1993
The Bear on the Moon, 1991

Other books you might like:
Jim Arnosky, *Every Autumn Comes the Bear*, 1993
    Annually, a bear appears in the woods near a farm seeking a den in which to hibernate.
Dieter Betz, *The Bear Family*, 1992
    A nonfiction title set in the Alaskan wilderness uses photographs to support the story of a grizzly bear and her two cubs.
Jonathan London, *Honey Paw and Lightfoot*, 1995
    A fictionalized account of a year in the life of a bear includes the birth of Lightfoot and the daily life of mother and cub.

1247

JOANNE RYDER
MARK GRAHAM, Illustrator

My Father's Hands
(New York: Morrow Junior Books, 1994)

Subject(s): Fathers and Daughters; Gardens and Gardening; Nature
Age range(s): Grades K-1
Major character(s): Unnamed Character, Child; Unnamed Character, Father, Gardener
Time period(s): 1990s (1994)
Locale(s): United States

Summary: As her father works in the garden, a little girl waits, watching and knowing that soon he will have one of the wonders of nature to show her. The treasures that her father lovingly presents for observation include a pink worm, a gold-colored beetle and a praying mantis. (32 pages)

Where it's reviewed:
Booklinks, November 1994, page 30
Horn Book Guide, Spring 1995, page 53
Kirkus Reviews, July 15, 1994, page 994
Publishers Weekly, July 4, 1994, page 62
School Library Journal, September 1994, page 192

Other books by the same author:
The Good-Bye Walk, 1993

Dancers in the Garden, 1992 (Notable Children's Books in the Language Arts)
Where Butterflies Grow, 1989

Other books you might like:
Nancy White Carlstrom, *Wild, Wild Sunflower Child Anna*, 1987
    Anna enjoys her day outside under the sun and sky, surrounded by grass, flowers, frogs and beetles.
Douglas Florian, *Nature Walk*, 1989
    Two children enjoy a trail hike through the woods learning more about nature.
Anna Grossnickle Hines, *What Joe Saw*, 1994
    Slowpoke Joe is always last in line because he takes the time to enjoy the wonders of nature as he walks.
Elaine Moore, *Grandma's Garden*, 1993
    Together, Grandma and Kim plant their garden, make a scarecrow and repair the damage of an early thunderstorm.

1248

CYNTHIA RYLANT, Author/Illustrator

Dog Heaven

(New York: The Blue Sky Press, 1995)

Subject(s): Animals/Dogs; Death (of a Pet); Angels
Age range(s): Grades K-2
Major character(s): God, Deity
Time period(s): Indeterminate
Locale(s): Dog Heaven, Fictional Country

Summary: Dog Heaven is a special place for deceased dogs watched over by a benevolent God. He gives the animals dog biscuits in the shape of cats, provides lakes of honking ducks, and turns the clouds inside out to make soft beds. (32 pages)

Where it's reviewed:
Booklist, August 1995, page 1956
Bulletin of the Center for Children's Books, October 1995, page 67
Kirkus Reviews, July 1, 1995, page 951
Publishers Weekly, July 17, 1995, page 228
School Library Journal, October 1995, page 115

Other books by the same author:
All I See, 1988
Birthday Presents, 1987
Miss Maggie, 1983

Other books you might like:
Nicholas Allan, *Heaven*, 1996
    While waiting for the angels to come get Dill, Lily and her dog reminisce about their life together, argue about the nature of heaven and say good-bye.
George Ella Lyon, *Ada's Pal*, 1996
    Lonely, dog Ada's grief for the loss of her dog companion is relieved when the family acquires a puppy for her.
Margot Zemach, *Jake and Honeybunch Go to Heaven*, 1982
    Jake and his mule arrive in heaven with such enthusiasm that they are threatened with expulsion if they don't quiet down a little.

1249

CYNTHIA RYLANT
ARTHUR HOWARD, Illustrator

Gooseberry Park

(San Diego: Harcourt Brace & Company, 1995)

Subject(s): Animals; Animals/Squirrels; Fantasy
Age range(s): Grades 3-5
Major character(s): Stumpy, Squirrel, Mother; Kona, Dog; Professor Albert, Aged Person
Time period(s): 1990s (1995)
Locale(s): Gooseberry Park

Summary: An ice storm destroys the tree where Stumpy nests with her three newborn babies. Her devoted friend, Kona, bravely sneaks out of Professor Albert's house during the storm and manuevers himself across the ice to Stumpy's tree. Kona rescues the babies and a bat left as a babysitter, but Stumpy vanishes. After days of tiresome babysitting, Kona, the bat, and Professor Albert's pet hermit crab come up with a plan to help Stumpy find them. (133 pages)

Where it's reviewed:
Booklist, October 1, 1995, page 320
Horn Book Guide, Spring 1996, page 68
Kirkus Reviews, October 15, 1995, page 1500
Publishers Weekly, October 2, 1995, page 74
School Library Journal, December 1995, page 108

Awards the book has won:
Book Links Good Book, 1995

Other books by the same author:
The Van Gogh Cafe, 1995
Missing May, 1992 (Newbery Medal, 1993)
A Blue-Eyed Daisy, 1985

Other books you might like:
Avi, *Poppy*, 1995
    With help from other animals, a young mouse undertakes a journey into the unknown and courageously defeats an owl to improve life for her community.
Dick King-Smith, *Pretty Polly*, 1992
    When Abigail's parents refuse to buy her an expensive parrot, she spends her summer teaching one of the hens to talk with humorous results.
Robert Lawson, *Rabbit Hill*, 1944
    The Newbery Medal winner describes the animal residents of Rabbit Hill pondering their fate as new occupants move into Big House.
Robert C. O'Brien, *Mrs. Frisby and the Rats of NIMH*, 1971
    Needing help, a widowed mouse bravely visits rats, retired from laboratory experiments which have made them wise and long-lived. Newbery Medal.

1250

CYNTHIA RYLANT
SUCIE STEVENSON, Illustrator

Henry and Mudge and the Best Day of All

(New York: Macmillan Books for Young Readers, 1995)

Series: Henry and Mudge

Subject(s): Birthdays; Animals/Dogs; Pets
Age range(s): Grades 1-2
Major character(s): Henry, 8-Year-Old; Mudge, Dog
Time period(s): 1990s (1995)
Locale(s): United States

Summary: When Henry wakes up on the first day of May he immediately realizes it is his birthday. It takes a little effort to convince Mudge today will be wonderful, but as Mudge listens to the plans he begins to suspect Henry may be right. After a day of party games, cake, ice cream, and a pinata, everyone stretches out under a shady tree to rest. (40 pages)

Where it's reviewed:
Booklist, April 15, 1995, page 1509
Bulletin of the Center for Children's Books, May 1995, page 320
Horn Book, May 1995, page 350
Horn Book Guide, Fall 1995, page 289
School Library Journal, May 1995, page 94

Other books by the same author:
Henry and Mudge and the Happy Cat, 1990
Henry and Mudge in the Sparkle Days, 1988
Henry and Mudge under the Yellow Moon, 1987

Other books you might like:
Syd Hoff, *Happy Birthday, Danny and the Dinosaur!*, 1995
    The friendly dinosaur from the museum joins Danny and his friends for a lively birthday celebration.
Elisa Kleven, *Hooray, a Pinata!*, 1996
    Clara becomes so attached to the dog pinata she selects for her birthday party that she doesn't want it broken.
Sue Truesdell, *Addie's Bad Day*, 1993
    To keep Addie, who's having a bad hair day, from missing his party, Max comes up with a plan to make it fun for both of them.

`1251`

CYNTHIA RYLANT
SUCIE STEVENSON, Illustrator

Henry and Mudge and the Careful Cousin
(New York: Bradbury Press, 1994)

Series: Henry and Mudge
Subject(s): Animals/Dogs; Cousins
Age range(s): Grades K-3
Major character(s): Henry, Child, Cousin; Annie, Cousin (fastidious), Child; Mudge, Dog (pet)
Time period(s): 1990s (1994)
Locale(s): United States

Summary: The adventures of Henry and Mudge continue with the arrival of Henry's cousin, Annie. Meeting Annie for the first time and seeing her neat frilly dress, Henry wonders what they will ever find in common. Annie's not interested in his fish because they smell. Offers of cookies fail, too, when Annie sees that Henry stores his cookies in a dusty bag under his bed. Finally, Henry teaches his careful cousin to play Frisbee. Annie surprises Henry, Mudge and herself with her skill at Frisbee and her willingness to enjoy herself, even though it means accepting a little dirt, some dog drool and cookies from a dusty bag. (48 pages)

Where it's reviewed:
Booklist, February 1, 1994, page 1012
Horn Book, March 1994, page 195
School Library Journal, April 1994, page 112

Awards the book has won:
School Library Journal Best Books, 1994

Other books by the same author:
Mr. Putter and Tabby Pour the Tea, 1994
Mr. Putter and Tabby Walk the Dog, 1994
The Dreamer, 1993
Henry and Mudge and the Wild Wind, 1993 (12th book in the series)
When I Was Young in the Mountains, 1982

Other books you might like:
Joyce Champion, *Emily and Alice Again*, 1995
    Best friends, Emily and Alice, share adventures and adversity in the second book about their friendship.
James Howe, *Pinky and Rex*, 1990
    Pinky and Rex, inseparable friends, embark on the first of many shared adventures in this initial book in their series.
Steven Kellogg, *Pinkerton, Behave!*, 1979
    Lovable Pinkerton means well, but this enormous puppy has a way of creating havoc wherever he goes.

`1252`

CYNTHIA RYLANT
SUCIE STEVENSON, Illustrator

Henry and Mudge and the Wild Wind
(New York: Bradbury Press, 1993)

Series: Henry and Mudge
Subject(s): Animals/Dogs; Weather; Fear
Age range(s): Grades 1-3
Major character(s): Henry, Child; Mudge, Dog
Time period(s): 1990s (1993)
Locale(s): United States

Summary: Henry and Mudge share many things including a fear of thunderstorms. When a storm arrives to splatter the house with wind-driven rain, Henry whistles and Mudge hides in the bathroom. Then the lights go out and Henry whistles louder while Mudge buries his big head in the couch. Henry's dad suggests a game which makes the waiting-for-the-storm-to-end time fun and bearable for everyone. (40 pages)

Where it's reviewed:
Booklist, July 1993, page 1980
Horn Book, July 1993, page 485
Horn Book Guide, Fall 1993, page 282
School Library Journal, June 1993, page 88

Other books by the same author:
Henry and Mudge and the Best Day of All, 1995
Henry and Mudge Get the Cold Shivers, 1989
Henry and Mudge in the Green Time, 1987

Other books you might like:
Lena Anderson, *Stina*, 1989
    Visiting her grandfather's home by the sea, Stina is fright-

ened by a storm until grandfather joins her and shares the experience.

Patricia Polacco, *Thunder Cake*, 1990

An understanding grandmother helps her granddaughter overcome a fear of thunder storms by involving her in the baking of a cake.

Anne F. Rockwell, *The Storm*, 1994

A young girl describes a fierce autumn storm from the security of her family home near the sea.

1253

CYNTHIA RYLANT
ARTHUR HOWARD, Illustrator

Mr. Putter and Tabby Bake the Cake

(San Diego: Harcourt Brace & Company, 1994)

Series: Mr. Putter and Tabby
Subject(s): Christmas; Gifts; Cooks and Cookery
Age range(s): Grades 1-3
Major character(s): Mr. Putter, Aged Person; Tabby, Cat; Mrs. Teaberry, Aged Person, Neighbor
Time period(s): 1990s (1994)
Locale(s): United States

Summary: Mr. Putter enjoys making Christmas gifts early, but always has difficulty deciding what to make for Mrs. Teaberry. This year, Mr. Putter plans to bake a light, airy cake for her. The fact that he's never done such a thing and has no cake pans does not deter him at all. He and Tabby stay awake all night Christmas Eve and by the fourth try they achieve a presentable cake. Unfortunately, Mr. Putter is so exhausted that when he brings the cake to Mrs. Teaberry, he falls asleep before eating any with her. (44 pages)

Where it's reviewed:
Booklist, October 15, 1994, page 428
Horn Book, September 1994, page 613
Horn Book Guide, Spring 1995, page 63
Kirkus Reviews, November 15, 1994, page 1548
School Library Journal, December 1994, page 80

Other books by the same author:
Poppleton, 1997
The Bookshop Dog, 1996
The Old Woman Who Named Things, 1996

Other books you might like:
Eileen Christelow, *Don't Wake Up Mama!*, 1992
Five little monkeys are trying to quietly bake a surprise birthday cake for Mama before she awakens.

Maryann Macdonald, *Hedgehog Bakes a Cake*, 1990
In an easy reader, Hedgehog's cake preparations are interrupted repeatedly as friends stop and offer advice.

Toby Speed, *Hattie Baked a Wedding Cake*, 1994
Hattie's preparation of the cake batter is so frenetic that several things which are essential to the wedding fall into the batter and become part of the cake.

Nancy Willard, *The High Rise Glorious Skittle Skat Roarious Sky Pie Angel Food Cake*, 1990
The cake a young girl bakes for her mother's birthday is so fantastic that it attracts three angels hoping for a taste.

1254

CYNTHIA RYLANT
ARTHUR HOWARD, Illustrator

Mr. Putter and Tabby Pick the Pears

(San Diego: Harcourt Brace & Company, 1995)

Series: Mr. Putter and Tabby
Subject(s): Food; Old Age; Animals/Cats
Age range(s): Grades 1-3
Major character(s): Mr. Putter, Aged Person, Gardener; Tabby, Cat; Mrs. Teaberry, Aged Person, Neighbor
Time period(s): 1990s (1995)
Locale(s): United States

Summary: Harvest time is here and Mr. Putter can almost taste pear jelly. First he must pick the pears and that is where the problem arises. With Tabby watching, Mr. Putter braces the ladder against the tree and discovers his "cranky" old legs will not climb. To get the pears down, Mr. Putter tries a slingshot, using fallen apples for ammunition. While he's not successful in knocking down any pears, he enjoys watching the apples sail over his rooftop and away. The next morning, as Mr. Putter and Tabby forlornly ponder the pear problem, Mrs Teaberry arrives with pies, jellies, turnovers, and cider made from all the apples she found in her yard. (44 pages)

Where it's reviewed:
Booklist, January 1996, page 350
Horn Book, January 1996, page 99
Kirkus Reviews, August 15, 1995, page 1194
New York Times Book Review, October 22, 1995, page 41
School Library Journal, October 1995, page 116

Awards the book has won:
ALA Notable Book, 1996

Other books by the same author:
Mr. Putter and Tabby Bake the Cake, 1994
Mr. Putter and Tabby Pour the Tea, 1994
Mr. Putter and Tabby Walk the Dog, 1994

Other books you might like:
Larry Dane Brimner, *Max and Felix*, 1993
Four brief, silly stories describe the friendship of two middle-aged frogs.

Lynne Rae Perkins, *Home Lovely*, 1995
Although Tiffany's first attempt to grow flowers yields vegetables, the kindness of the mailman helps her enjoy her tomato crop and the flowering plants he gives her.

Barney Saltzberg, *Mrs. Morgan's Lawn*, 1993
Fortunately, Mr. Putter does not live next door to Mrs. Morgan who keeps all the balls and toys that accidently land in her yard.

1255

CYNTHIA RYLANT
ARTHUR HOWARD, Illustrator

Mr. Putter and Tabby Walk the Dog

(San Diego: Harcourt Brace & Company, 1994)

Subject(s): Animals/Dogs; Animals/Cats; Old Age
Age range(s): Grades 1-2

Major character(s): Mr. Putter, Aged Person; Tabby, Cat; Zeke, Dog
Time period(s): 1990s (1994)
Locale(s): United States

Summary: When Mr. Putter's neighbor hurts her foot and is unable to walk her bulldog, Mr. Putter offers to do so for her. Mr. Putter and Tabby soon learn that Zeke is not the dream dog he has appeared to be—Zeke is a nightmare. After three days of being pulled, tugged and run to exhaustion by Zeke, Mr. Putter discovers the key to survival is to bribe the dog for good behavior during the walks. (40 pages)

Where it's reviewed:
Booklist, February 1, 1994, page 1013
Book World, May 8, 1994, page 18
Horn Book, May 1994, page 323
Publishers Weekly, January 24, 1994, page 56
School Library Journal, April 1994, page 112

Other books by the same author:
Mr. Putter and Tabby Pick the Pears, 1995
Mr. Putter and Tabby Bake the Cake, 1994
Mr. Putter and Tabby Pour the Tea, 1994

Other books you might like:
Minna Jung, *William's Ninth Life*, 1993
    William is so attached to his owner that when he's given a choice as to where he'd like to spend his ninth feline life, he chooses to return to her cottage by the sea.
Cynthia Rylant, *The Old Woman Who Named Things*, 1996
    Having outlived all her friends, an elderly woman finds companionship by naming the objects that will remain after she is gone; a stray pup complicates her system.
Gene Zion, *Harry and the Lady Next Door*, 1960
    A spotted dog uses some ingenious strategies to try to keep the lady next door from singing.

1256

CYNTHIA RYLANT

The Van Gogh Cafe

(San Diego: Harcourt Brace & Company, 1995)

Subject(s): Restaurants; Magic; Fathers and Daughters

Age range(s): Grades 3-6
Major character(s): Marc, Father, Restauranteur; Clara, 10-Year-Old
Time period(s): 1990s (1995)
Locale(s): Flowers, Kansas

Summary: Marc and Clara believe the magic in their restaurant springs from the walls of the building, originally used as a theater. To non-believers the everyday events at the Van Gogh Cafe might not be magical, but the townspeople know. Each time, the magic begins in a small, inconsequential way and builds to a meaningful event before subsiding, as if resting for the next episode. (53 pages)

Where it's reviewed:
Booklist, June 1995, page 1772
Bulletin of the Center for Children's Books, September 1995, page 28
Horn Book Guide, Fall 1995, page 303
Kirkus Reviews, June 15, 1995, page 861
School Library Journal, July 1995, page 80

Other books by the same author:
Gooseberry Park, 1995
Soda Jerk, 1993
Missing May, 1992 (Newbery Medal, 1993)

Other books you might like:
Molly Bang, *The Paper Crane*, 1985
    After a mysterious customer pays for his dinner with a paper crane, the bird magically comes to life.
Roald Dahl, *The Wonderful Story of Henry Sugar and Six More*, 1977
    Seven fantastic short stories include Henry Sugar's story as well as one about a hitchhiker and another about a boy who talks to animals.
Margaret Mahy, *The Girl with the Green Ear: Stories about Magic in Nature*, 1992
    Trickle is a magical town; nine stories tell of the wondrous events that happen there.

S

1257

CRISTINA SALAT

Living in Secret
(New York: Bantam Skylark, 1993)

Subject(s): Homosexuality/Lesbianism; Kidnapping; Secrets
Age range(s): Grades 5-7
Major character(s): Amelia/Julie Monet/Dreisden, 11-Year-Old; Janey/Megan Dreisden, Worker (house painter); Claire/Kathy Dreisden, Worker (bank employee)
Time period(s): 1990s
Locale(s): Greenport, New York (Long Island); San Francisco, California

Summary: After Amelia's parents divorce and her father is awarded child custody, Amelia wishes she could live with her mother. Her wish comes true when she's kidnapped by her mother, Claire, and her mother's girlfriend Janey, but it's a wish that's hard to live with. Amelia's name and age are changed, she's tutored at home and she feels uncomfortable with all the secrets she has to keep. Though her father finally locates her, Amelia decides to help her mother in the custody battle. (183 pages)

Where it's reviewed:
Voice of Youth Advocates, June 1993, page 94
School Library Journal, February 1993, page 84
Booklist, February 15, 1993, page 1061
English Journal, April 1993, page 91
Los Angeles Times Book Review, June 20, 1993, page 8

Other books by the same author:
Alias Diamond Jones, 1993

Other books you might like:
Lois Duncan, *Don't Look Behind You*, 1989
    April's father testifies against a drug dealer and the family must assume a new identity and life in Florida as part of the Witness Security Program.
Amy Ehrlich, *Where It Stops, Nobody Knows*, 1988
    Nina is startled when her mother is arrested for kidnapping her; she considers Joyce her mother and is upset about joining her birth family.
Norma Klein, *Now That I Know*, 1988
    Nina divides her time between her parents after they divorce, but is unsure what to do when her father announces his homosexuality.

1258

BARNEY SALTZBERG, Author/Illustrator

Show and Tell
(New York: Hyperion Books for Children, 1994)

Subject(s): Schools; Parent and Child; Independence
Age range(s): Grades K-2
Major character(s): Phoebe, Child, Student
Time period(s): 1990s (1994)
Locale(s): United States

Summary: All Phoebe wants to do is take a star-shaped leaf she finds to show-and-tell, but her parents buy a palm tree complete with monkeys for her to share with the class. When other kids laugh, Phoebe decides not to participate in show-and-tell, but her parents have bigger and better plans. Finally, she asserts herself and shares her popsicle collection rather than the herd of cows arranged for by her parents and they begin to understand that Phoebe has good ideas too. (32 pages)

Where it's reviewed:
Booklist, October 15, 1994, page 439
New York Times Book Review, November 13, 1994, page 439
Publishers Weekly, July 18, 1994, page 246
School Library Journal, October 1994, page 97

Other books by the same author:
This Is a Great Place for a Hot Dog Stand, 1995
Where, Oh, Where's My Underwear?, 1994
Mrs. Morgan's Lawn, 1993

Other books you might like:
Joanne Oppenheim, *The Show-and-Tell Frog*, 1992
A beginning reader tells of some unusual adventures for a small, green frog.
Hiawyn Oram, *Reckless Ruby*, 1992
Attempting to reshape her image, Ruby becomes wildly reckless so her overprotective parents will change their ways.
Elvira Woodruff, *Show and Tell*, 1991
The day Andy finds a magic bottle of bubbles to share for show-and-tell, his kindergarten class experiences some unexpected events.

1259

BARNEY SALTZBERG, Author/Illustrator

This Is a Great Place for a Hot Dog Stand

(New York: Hyperion Books for Children, 1995)

Subject(s): Business Enterprises; Food; Individuality
Age range(s): Grades K-3
Major character(s): Izzy, Monster, Businessman; Madame Moola Moo, Monster, Businesswoman
Time period(s): Indeterminate
Locale(s): Fictional Country

Summary: Unhappy painting Baby Beastie horns at a toy factory, Izzy quits his job, builds a cart, and begins life as hot-dog vendor. Once he finds the right location, business is so good he builds a permanent stand on a vacant lot. Soon he's handed an eviction notice because Madame Moola Moo, owner of the land, plans to demolish the block and build a shopping mall. With support from his customers, his own determination, and the lure of a tofu dog, Izzy convinces Madame Moola Moo to spare his hot dog stand from the wrecking ball. (32 pages)

Where it's reviewed:
Booklist, April 15, 1995, page 1508
Horn Book Guide, Fall 1995, page 280
Kirkus Reviews, April 15, 1995, page 562
Publishers Weekly, April 24, 1995, page 72
School Library Journal, September 15, 1995, page 94

Other books by the same author:
Show and Tell, 1994
Where, Oh, Where's My Underwear?, 1993
Mrs. Morgan's Lawn, 1993

Other books you might like:
Molly Bang, *The Paper Crane*, 1985
A paper crane left as payment by a customer comes to life and changes the fortune of a restaurant owner.
Melanie Greenberg, *My Father's Luncheonette*, 1991
A little girl visits her father's diner.
Ethel Kessler, *Stan the Hot Dog Man*, 1990
After retiring from his bakery job, Stan opens a mobile hot dog business which keeps a busload of stranded students well-fed during a blizzard. Co-author Leonard Kessler.
Maryann Kovalski, *Pizza for Breakfast*, 1991
Frank and Zelda soon regret their expressed wish for more customers at their pizza restaurant.

1260

SHEILA WHITE SAMTON, Author/Illustrator

Tilly and the Rhinoceros

(New York: Philomel Books, 1993)

Subject(s): Animals/Geese; Animals/Rhinoceroses; Bullies
Age range(s): Grades K-3
Major character(s): Tilly Gobble, Goose, Friend; Gregor, Rhinoceros, Bully
Time period(s): Indeterminate
Locale(s): Fictional Country

Summary: One morning Tilly and other merchants from her village find the road to the market blocked by a large, cantankerous rhinoceros who refuses to move until someone solves the riddle he proposes. While others try to solve the riddle, kind Tilly brings the disagreeable beast a feather pillow for his head, a quilt to keep him warm, and as the snow falls, a hat. Without realizing it, Tilly solves the riddle, receives the prince's reward, and reaps the benefits of the lesson in kindness which she has taught to a reformed Gregor. (32 pages)

Where it's reviewed:
Booklist, March 15, 1993, page 1361
Horn Book, March 1993, page 201
Publishers Weekly, March 22, 1993, page 78
Quill and Quire, March 1993, page 60
School Library Journal, May 1993, page 91

Other books by the same author:
Oh No! A Naptime Adventure, 1993
Jenny's Journey, 1991
The World from My Window, 1991

Other books you might like:
Diane Marcial Fuchs, *A Bear for All Seasons*, 1995
Bear and Fox disagree about many things but not about the value of their friendship.
Petra Mathers, *Victor and Christabel*, 1993
The kindness of lonely Victor releases Christabel from the spell of her evil cousin.
Todd Starr Palmer, *Rhino and Mouse*, 1994
Despite their differences, Rhino and Mouse enjoy a close friendship.

1261

ROBERT D. SAN SOUCI
BRIAN PINKNEY, Illustrator

The Faithful Friend

(New York: Simon & Schuster Books for Young Readers, 1995)

Subject(s): Friendship; Folk Tales; Wizards
Age range(s): Grades 2-4
Major character(s): Clement Duforce, Young Man, Friend; Hippolyte, Young Man, Friend; Pauline, Young Woman
Time period(s): Indeterminate Past
Locale(s): Martinique

Summary: Two friends, as close as brothers, travel to a nearby town so Clement can ask for Pauline's hand in marriage. Blinded by love, Clement is not deterred by rumors that

Pauline's uncle is a wizard. When the uncle refuses Clement's proposal, the smitten and distraught Pauline leaves home with Clement and Hippolyte. As they walk across the island to Clement's home, Hippolyte overhears three zombies plotting their deaths. Each time, Hippolyte intercedes and prevents the evil plot from succeeding. The final time, in order to preserve his friendship, Hippolyte sacrifices himself. Seeing his friend turn to stone, Clement offers to take on the curse himself if only someone can break it. When the curse is broken, it must be returned to the source and so it is Pauline's uncle and not Clement who turns to stone and everyone else lives happily ever after. (40 pages)

Where it's reviewed:
Booklist, April 15, 1995, page 1499
Children's Book Review Service, March 1995, page 92
Horn Book, September 1995, page 614
Publishers Weekly, March 6, 1995, page 70
School Library Journal, June 1995, page 104

Awards the book has won:
Caldecott Honor Book, 1996
Coretta Scott King Honor Award for Illustration, 1996

Other books by the same author:
The Red Heels, 1996
Sukey and the Mermaid, 1992 (Coretta Scott King Honor Book)
The Talking Eggs: A Folktale from the American South, 1989

Other books you might like:
Virginia Hamilton, *The Dark Way: Stories from the Spirit World*, 1990
    One original story by the author compliments the international collection of myths, legends and folktales about the unexplainable world of the supernatural.
Susan Milford, *Tales Alive! Ten Multicultural Folktales with Activities*, 1995
    The retellings of folktales from around the world include suggestions for activities to make the stories come alive for listeners.
Laurence Yep, *Tree of Dreams: Ten Tales from the Garden of Night*, 1995
    Dreams are central to the folktales from different countries presented in this collection.

1262

CARL SANDBURG
PAUL O. ZELINSKY, Illustrator

More Rootabagas
(New York: Alfred A. Knopf, 1993)

Subject(s): Short Stories; Fantasy; Humor
Age range(s): Grades 3-6
Time period(s): Indeterminate Past
Locale(s): United States

Summary: George Hendrick selects ten previously unpublished stories for inclusion in Sandburg's series of whimsical Rootabaga Stories. Stories of Green Hat-Eating Horses and secret-telling caterpillars inhabit locales such as the Village of Liver and Onions and the Village of Cream Puffs. (94 pages)

Where it's reviewed:
Booklist, December 1, 1993, page 691
Horn Book Guide, Spring 1994, page 82
Kirkus Reviews, October 15, 1993, page 1336
Publishers Weekly, October 11, 1993, page 88
School Library Journal, December 1993, page 116

Awards the book has won:
School Library Journal Best Books, 1993
ALA Notable Book, 1994

Other books by the same author:
Potato Face, 1930
Rootabaga Pigeons, 1923
Rootabaga Stories, 1922

Other books you might like:
Laura Cecil, *Listen to This*, 1988
    The editor has gathered folk tales and short stories from a variety of well-known authors.
Neil Philip, *American Fairy Tales: From Rip Van Winkle to the Rootabaga Stories*, 1996
    The collection includes the works of American authors such as Washington Irving, Louisa May Alcott and Carl Sandburg.
Martin H. Greenberg, *The Newbery Award Reader*, 1984
    With co-editor Martin H. Greenberg, Waugh has assembled excerpts from eighteen Newbery Award winners.

1263

SCOTT RUSSELL SANDERS
HELEN COGANCHERRY, Illustrator

The Floating House
(New York: Macmillan Books for Young Readers, 1995)

Subject(s): Rivers; Frontier and Pioneer Life; Voyages and Travels
Age range(s): Grades K-3
Major character(s): Mary McClure, Settler, Sister (older); Jonathan McClure, Settler, Brother (younger); Wayne Mc-Clure, Settler, Father
Time period(s): 1810s (1815)
Locale(s): Pittsburgh, Pennsylvania (Ohio River); Jeffersonville, Indiana

Summary: With the spring thaw Mary and Jonathan, along with their parents, launch of their flatboat onto the Ohio River for the journey to new territory in Indiana. Wayne McClure steers the flatboat with a long oar while Mary and Jonathan watch for rocks and sand bars in the river. Slowly, they travel with the current until they reach the falls on the Ohio, site of the new settlement of Jeffersonville. Using the wood from the flatboat and the help of other settlers, they build a home on their newly purchased land. (32 pages)

Where it's reviewed:
Booklist, June 1995, page 1789
Children's Book Review Service, May 1995, page 114
Horn Book Guide, Fall 1995, page 280
School Library Journal, June 1995, page 95

Other books by the same author:
Here Comes the Mystery Man, 1993
Warm as Wool, 1992

Aurora Means Dawn, 1989

Other books you might like:
Thomas Locker, *Where the River Begins*, 1984
To help them understand the mystique of the river flowing past their home, two boys and their grandfather plan a camping trip to locate its source.
Joan Sandin, *The Long Way Westward*, 1989
In the sequel to *The Long Way to a New Land*, a family of Swedish immigrants continues their journey to the farmlands of Minnesota.
Jean Van Leeuwen, *Going West*, 1992
A family travels by prairie schooner from their home in the East to a new life on the frontier in Kansas.

1264

SCOTT RUSSELL SANDERS
HELEN COGANCHERRY, Illustrator

Here Comes the Mystery Man
(New York: Bradbury Press, 1993)

Subject(s): Frontier and Pioneer Life; Historical; Storytelling
Age range(s): Grades 1-4
Major character(s): Merchant Meeks, Peddler
Time period(s): 1810s (1811)
Locale(s): Brookville, Indiana

Summary: Twice a year Merchant Meeks visits the Goodwin family, peddling his wares and sharing stories of the world's mysteries. Everyone in the family is eager for these visits and the news the peddler brings, along with the items for sale. The children would love to travel with him, but the chores of the farm beckon, so they content themselves with the dreams and maple sugar candy shared by the peddler. (32 pages)

Where it's reviewed:
Booklist, November 15, 1993, page 634
Horn Book Guide, Spring 1994, page 69
New Advocate, Spring 1994, page 144
Publishers Weekly, July 26, 1993, page 72
School Library Journal, October 1993, page 111

Other books by the same author:
The Floating House, 1995
Warm as Wool, 1992
Aurora Means Dawn, 1989

Other books you might like:
Raymond Bial, *Frontier Home*, 1993
A nonfiction look at the life of pioneer families uses excerpts from diaries to enliven descriptions of the homes and tools of the time.
Brinton Turkle, *Obadiah the Bold*, 1977
The life of the Starbuck family in 19th century Nantucket is presented from a child's point of view.
Ann Turner, *Katie's Trunk*, 1992
During the early days of the Revolutionary War, Katie is trapped inside a trunk while colonist's search her Tory home.

1265

RUTH SANDERSON, Author/Illustrator

Papa Gatto: An Italian Fairy Tale
(Boston: Little, Brown and Company, 1995)

Subject(s): Folk Tales; Animals/Cats; Greed
Age range(s): Grades 2-4
Major character(s): Papa Gatto, Cat, Widow(er); Beatrice, Stepsister; Sophia, Stepsister
Time period(s): Indeterminate Past
Locale(s): Italy

Summary: As adviser to the prince, Papa Gatto frequently travels in his service. Thus, when his wife dies, he hires someone to care for his eight kittens. Sophia, with no interest or talent for work, responds to Papa Gatto's advertisement motivated only by his promise of generous payment. However, when Papa Gatto returns home and finds the house, garden and kittens untended, the only payment Sophia receives is four scratches on her wrist as Papa Gatto snatches off his deceased wife's diamond bracelet. Beatrice then offers her services and Papa Gatto is so charmed by her kindness he recommends her to the prince. Greedy Sophia tries to trick the prince into believing she is Beatrice, but her wrist scars give her away. (32 pages)

Where it's reviewed:
Booklist, December 1, 1995, page 624
Horn Book Guide, Spring 1996, page 94
Kirkus Reviews, October 1, 1995, page 1436
Quill & Quire, September 1995, page 76
School Library Journal, October 1995, page 129

Other books by the same author:
The Nativity, 1993
The Enchanted Wood, 1991 (Irma and James H. Black Award, 1992)
The Twelve Dancing Princesses, 1990

Other books you might like:
Amy Ehrlich, *The Random House Book of Fairy Tales*, 1985
Nineteen familiar fairy tales are included in the illustrated volume.
Margaret Greaves, *Tattercoats*, 1990
The unhappy environment in which Tattercoats lives does not change her good and cheerful nature; a prince who meets her instantly falls in love.
Charles Perrault, *Cinderella*, 1988
In Diane Goode's illustrated translation of a classic tale, kindness once again triumphs over the cruelty of a wicked stepmother and stepsisters.
John Steptoe, *Mufaro's Beautiful Daughters: An African Tale*, 1987
The Caldecott Honor is one of the many awards won by this tale of two sisters, one with physical beauty and a bad attitude; the other whose gentle spirit gives her an unseen beauty.

1266

JOAN SANDIN, Author/Illustrator

Pioneer Bear

(New York: Random House, 1995)

Series: Step into Reading
Subject(s): Photography; Animals/Bears; Frontier and Pioneer Life
Age range(s): Grades 1-3
Major character(s): Andrew Irwin, Child; Bearly, Bear; John Lacy, Photographer
Time period(s): Indeterminate Past
Locale(s): Minnesota

Summary: When Andrew teaches an orphaned cub he is raising as a pet dance, word of the Bearly's talent reaches John Lacy who travels to the Irwin farm to photograph this unusual bear. Andrew, assisted by his siblings, searches all Bearly's favorite places, but cannot find his pet. John Lacy makes a portrait of the family instead and when he returns with the finished picture everyone discovers that Bearly was close by all along. (43 pages)

Where it's reviewed:
Booklist, July 1995, page 1885
Bulletin of the Center for Children's Books, July 1995, page 397
School Library Journal, October 1995, page 117

Other books by the same author:
The Long Way Westward, 1989
The Long Way to a New Land, 1981

Other books you might like:
Jo Carson, *The Great Shaking*, 1994
 Three earthquakes that struck Missouri in the early 1800s are described from the perspective of a surviving bear.
Mary Blount Christian, *Penrod's Picture*, 1991
 In a beginning reader, friends Penrod Porcupine and Griswold Bear share several activities with humorous results.
Natalie Kinsey-Warnock, *The Bear That Heard Crying*, 1993
 A toddler wanders into the woods near the family's colonial home and is cared for by a bear until found by rescuers.
Ida Luttrell, *The Bear Next Door*, 1991
 An entry in the I Can Read series tells about good friends and neighbors Arlo Gopher and Vic Bear.
Jim Murphy, *Backyard Bear*, 1992
 As development reaches the edge of the forest, a young black bear wanders into a neighborhood scaring himself and the residents.

1267

STEVE SANFIELD
SUSAN GABER, Illustrator

Bit by Bit

(New York: Philomel Books, 1995)

Subject(s): Clothes; Storytelling; Family Life
Age range(s): Grades K-3

Major character(s): Zundel, Tailor
Time period(s): Indeterminate Past
Locale(s): Fictional Country (small village)

Summary: Zundel the tailor saves his pennies to buy some beautiful cloth for a new coat which he dearly loves! Over time, as the coat wears out, he converts it into a jacket and then a vest, cap and finally a button, until nothing remains but the threads of a story. The illustrations expand the text and show us the changes in Zundel's personal life as the text describes the adaptations he makes in order to continue using the cloth as it wears out bit by bit. (32 pages)

Where it's reviewed:
Booklist, March 15, 1995, page 1336
Bulletin of the Center for Children's Books, May 1995, page 321
Horn Book Guide, Fall 1995, page 281
Publishers Weekly, March 20, 1995, page 59
School Library Journal, August 1995, page 128

Other books by the same author:
Snow, 1995
Strudel, Strudel, Strudel, 1995

Other books you might like:
May Garelick, *Just My Size*, 1990
 As a young girl grows, her beautiful coat is made into a jacket, vest, cap, knapsack and finally a new coat for her doll.
Phoebe Gilman, *Something from Nothing*, 1993
 A tailor presents his grandson with a beautiful blanket which he remakes into smaller and smaller items as use and age leave less and less usable fabric.
Kevin Henkes, *Owen*, 1993
 Owen's mother cuts his special blanket into small handkerchiefs so he can carry a bit of it with him when he enters school.
Ferida Wolff, *The Woodcutter's Coat*, 1992
 A woodcutter's stolen coat passes through many hands before returning to the woodcutter.

1268

VIVIAN SATHRE
CATHARINE O'NEILL, Illustrator

J.B. Wigglebottom and the Parade of Pets

(New York: Atheneum, 1993)

Subject(s): Schools; Bullies; Brothers and Sisters
Age range(s): Grades 3-5
Major character(s): Jonathan Bradford ''J.B.'' Higgenbottom ''Wigglebottom'', 5th Grader, Bullied Child; Emory Harrison, 5th Grader, Friend (J.B.'s); Buddy Zimmers, 5th Grader, Bully
Time period(s): 1990s (1993)
Locale(s): United States (Lincoln Elementary School)

Summary: In the author's first novel, J. B. is daily subject to Buddy's pranks and insults. Buddy, whose father owns a pet store, thinks he's sure to win first prize in the school's annual Parade of Pets. With a little assistance from Emory and some clever thinking, J. B. prepares to match ingenuity with Buddy's exotic pet and let the best idea win. (89 pages)

Where it's reviewed:
Booklist, March 1, 1993, page 1230
Children's Book Review Service, July 1993, page 152
Horn Book Guide, Fall 1993, page 304
Kirkus Reviews, May 1, 1993, page 603
School Library Journal, July 1993, page 71

Other books you might like:
Jane Cutler, *No Dogs Allowed*, 1993
   Allergies prevent 2 brothers from having pets so 5-year-old Edward decides to become a dog.
N.B. Dorman, *Petey and Miss Magic*, 1993
   Petey comes up with a clever idea for a pet which is within his family's budget, will not bother his sister and, best of all, wins the contest prize.
Bill Wallace, *A Dog Called Kitty*, 1980
   Ricky overcomes his fear of dogs and the taunts of a bully to save a starving stray pup found in his barn.

1269

CAROL P. SAUL
BARRY ROOT, Illustrator

Someplace Else

(New York: Simon & Schuster Books for Young Readers, 1995)

Subject(s): Dwellings; Voyages and Travels; Determination
Age range(s): Grades 1-4
Major character(s): Mrs. Tillby, Mother, Traveller
Time period(s): Indeterminate Past
Locale(s): United States

Summary: After a lifetime in the white house next to the apple orchard, Mrs. Tillby decides it's time for a change. She begins seeking "someplace else" to call home by visiting her son in the city, her daughter at the seashore and another son in the mountains. Initially happy with each change of place, within a few weeks she's on her way to "someplace else." When she has visited all her children, she begins travelling on her own, still not completely satisfied. However, when she spots a travel trailer for sale, she knows she's found the answer to all her problems. Now she can always be "someplace else" while never leaving home. (32 pages)

Where it's reviewed:
Booklist, November 15, 1995, page 565
Bulletin of the Center for Children's Books, October 1995, page 68
Horn Book, November 1995, page 737
Kirkus Reviews, July 1, 1995, page 952
School Library Journal, January 1996, page 95

Other books by the same author:
Peter's Song, 1992

Other books you might like:
Penny Carter, *A New House for the Morrisons*, 1993
   After a day of fruitless searching for a new house, the Morrisons return to the one they like best—their own home.
Emma Chichester Clark, *Across the Blue Mountains*, 1992
   Curiosity leads Miss Bilberry to pack her belongings and travel to the other side of the blue mountains where she finds a home just to her liking.

Mary Lyn Ray, *Alvah and Arvilla*, 1994
   Determined to overcome the demands of farm life that have prevented a vacation for 31 years, Alvah and Arvilla devise a way to bring the animals along for a cross-country trip.

1270

ALLEN SAY, Author/Illustrator

Emma's Rug

(Boston: Houghton Mifflin, 1996)

Subject(s): Crafts; Artists and Art
Age range(s): Grades K-2
Major character(s): Emma, 1st Grader, Artist
Time period(s): 1990s
Locale(s): Japan

Summary: Emma loves to draw and has always gotten inspiration from the colors and patterns on her rug. When she goes to school her pictures win awards and get hung on the wall for all to see. When her mother finds and washes the rug one day, it shrinks and changes and Emma is afraid she will have no more creative ideas without it. Then she steps out into the garden where she senses the things around her and is convinced that she will still make good pictures. (unpaged)

Where it's reviewed:
School Library Journal, September 1996, page 1990
Booklist, October 1, 1996, page 359
Horn Book, September/October 1996, page 587

Other books by the same author:
Stranger in the Mirror, 1995
Grandfather's Journey, 1993
Tree of Cranes, 1991

Other books you might like:
Amy Hest, *Jamaica Louise James*, 1996
   Jamie says that she wants to draw everything she sees and so makes pictures for a birthday party.
Diane Stanley, *The Gentleman and the Kitchen Maid*, 1994
   A little girl is able to paint a picture so that a gentleman in one painting and a girl in the other, can get together.
Max Velthuijs, *Crocodile's Masterpiece*, 1992
   Elephant is given only a blank canvas but is able to imagine all kinds of paintings.
Ewa Zadrzynska, *The Girl with the Watering Can*, 1990
   Characters from paintings in the National Gallery come to life and interact.
Patricia Zelver, *The Wonderful Towers of Watts*, 1994
   Simon collects all kinds of things and makes them into some interesting art forms.

1271

ALLEN SAY, Author/Illustrator

Grandfather's Journey

(Boston: Houghton Mifflin Company)

Subject(s): Grandparents; Voyages and Travels; Japanese Americans
Age range(s): Grades K-3

Major character(s): Unnamed Character, Grandfather, Traveller; Unnamed Character, Immigrant (assumed to be Allen Say)
Time period(s): Indeterminate Past; 1990s (1993)
Locale(s): Japan; San Francisco, California

Summary: A young man's journey to America portrays his awe at all he sees, his return to Japan to marry and bring his wife to this new country, and their subsequent return to Japan unaware that war will intervene to prevent a return to America. The constant pull of native land and adopted home is echoed in the life of the grandson who completes the grandfather's journey. (32 pages)

Where it's reviewed:
Booklist, July 1993, page 1974
Five Owls, November 1993, page 36
Horn Book, September 1993, page 590
Publishers Weekly, August 23, 1993
School Library Journal, September 1993, page 245

Awards the book has won:
Caldecott Medal, 1994
Boston Globe/Horn Book Award, 1994

Other books by the same author:
El Chino, 1990
A River Dream, 1988
The Bicycle Man, 1982

Other books you might like:
Elisa Bartone, *Peppe the Lamplighter*, 1993
    The experience of a young immigrant in turn-of-the-century New York is portrayed in this award-winning book.
Sherry Garland, *The Lotus Seed*, 1993
    An award-winning story of an immigrant's connection to her birthplace through a lotus seed and the sharing of her heritage with children and grandchildren.
Riki Levinson, *Watch the Stars Come Out*, 1985
    A young girl sails with her brother across the ocean to a joyful reunion with other family members in America.
Jirina Marton, *You Can Go Home Again*, 1994
    Hearing stories of now-deceased relatives in the old country, Annie is eager to accompany her mother on a visit to her homeland.

1272

RAGNHILD SCAMELL
JUDITH RICHES, Illustrator

Rooster Crows

(New York: Tambourine Books, 1994)

Subject(s): Animals/Roosters; Animals/Birds; Contests
Age range(s): Grades K-2
Major character(s): Rooster, Rooster; Bluebird, Bird
Time period(s): 1990s (1994)
Locale(s): England (barnyard)

Summary: Pompous Rooster is so confident that his crowing causes the sun to rise that he challenges Bluebird to a contest. Rooster will make the sun rise at midnight. Amidst an audience of supporters, witnesses, challengers and the curious, Rooster produces the loudest and most glorious crowing of his life and . . . a star shoots across the sky. All the animals are

certain that the balance of nature has been disturbed and immediately make private wishes which they hope will restore order. (32 pages)

Where it's reviewed:
Children's Book Review Service, Winter 1995, page 65
Horn Book Guide, Spring 1995, page 54
Kirkus Reviews, September 15, 1994, page 1280
Publishers Weekly, September 19, 1994, page 69
School Library Journal, September 1994, page 192

Other books by the same author:
Buster's Echo, 1993
Three Bags Full, 1993
Solo Plus One, 1992

Other books you might like:
Sheila Cole, *The Hen That Crowed*, 1993
    The town of Bean Blossom learns that there are some advantages to having a rooster who crows at first light.
Bill Peet, *Cock-a-Doodle Dudley*, 1990
    Cocky Dudley thinks that he controls the daily rising of the sun.
Colin Threadgall, *Proud Rooster and the Fox*, 1991
    In his attempt to protect the hen house, rooster enters into a game of hide-and-seek with fox.

1273

RAGNHILD SCAMELL
SALLY HOBSON, Illustrator

Three Bags Full

(New York: Orchard Books, 1993)

Subject(s): Animals; Animals/Sheep; Problem Solving
Age range(s): Grades K-1
Major character(s): Millie, Sheep (generous); Mrs. Farmer, Farmer
Time period(s): 1990s (1993)
Locale(s): England

Summary: Kindly Millie responds so generously to each animal's request for a bit of wool, that she finds herself as bare as a goat. Delighted to be so cool during the hot summer months, she finds herself rather chilly when the seasons change. Mrs. Farmer is disappointed not to have Millie's wool, but kind enough to knit a sweater for Millie. (28 pages)

Where it's reviewed:
Booklist, July 1993, page 1977
Horn Book, September 1993, page 590
Library Talk, January 1994, page 49
Publishers Weekly, April 12, 1993, page 60
School Library Journal, October 1993, page 112

Other books by the same author:
Rooster Crows, 1994
Buster's Echo, 1993
Solo Plus One, 1992

Other books you might like:
Tomie De Paola, *Haircuts for the Woolseys*, 1989
    Spring means haircuts for the sheep on Fiddle-Dee-Dee Farm, but when a cold wind returns, Granny helps the chilly sheep stay warm.

Nancy Shaw, *Sheep in a Jeep*, 1986
Silly sheep fall out of the jeep and land in a heap.
Monica Wellington, *The Sheep Follow*, 1992
When the shepherd falls asleep, the sheep follow so many other animals that they're too tired to follow the shepherd when he wakens.

1274

ELIZABETH SCARBORO

Phoenix Upside Down

(New York: Viking, 1996)

Subject(s): Moving, Household; Sisters; Schools
Age range(s): Grades 4-6
Major character(s): Jamie, 4th Grader; Rachel, 2nd Grader; Celia Opel, Gardener, Aged Person
Time period(s): 1990s
Locale(s): Phoenix, Arizona

Summary: Jamie doesn't want to be in Phoenix; she misses Colorado and her friends there. Rachel seems to be making friends quickly, but the girls find time to explore their new neighborhood and meet a friendly woman who loves to garden. They help her in their spare time and become quite concerned when Miss Opel becomes ill and can't garden. Meanwhile, Jamie and Rachel meet new girls, participate in a three-legged race that does not turn out as expected, and discover other activities and fun to look forward to, especially when the family decides not to return to Colorado. (156 pages)

Where it's reviewed:
Booklist, June 1, page 1724
School Library Journal, June 1996, page 124
Bulletin of the Center For Children's Books, June 1996, page 352

Other books by the same author:
The Secret Language of the SB, 1990

Other books you might like:
Marion Doren, *Nell of Blue Harbor*, 1990
Nell finds it hard to adjust to a new life in Maine after her move from Vermont.
Jan Greenberg, *Just the Two of Us*, 1988
Holly does not want to leave New York city and move to Iowa.
Katharine W. Precek, *The Keepsake Chest*, 1992
Meg does not want to move to Ohio from Colorado until she finds an old chest which reveals old secrets.
Bonnie Pryor, *Rats, Spiders and Love*, 1986
Samantha does not want to move to Ohio from the ocean, where she has always lived.

1275

JUDITH BYRON SCHACHNER, Author/Illustrator

Willy and May

(New York: Dutton Children's Books, 1995)

Subject(s): Aunts and Uncles; Animals/Birds; Christmas
Age range(s): Grades K-3

Major character(s): May, Aunt (great-aunt), Aged Person; Willy, Bird (canary); Unnamed Character, Child, Niece
Time period(s): Indeterminate Past
Locale(s): United States; Whitinsville, Massachusetts

Summary: Twice a year a young girl visits Willy and Great-aunt May. Summer visits are berry picking, swimming in the pond, baking pies, and watching Willy's antics while winter visits are scheduled at Christmas. Great-aunt May's niece is heart-broken the year her mother becomes ill and unable, to drive her to May's home for the summer visit. Great-aunt May then makes plans to visit her niece for Christmas, but even that visit may be cancelled by snowy weather. Fortunately, May and Willy hitch a ride with a jolly man in a sleigh and all ends well. First book both written and illustrated by this children's book illustrator. (32 pages)

Where it's reviewed:
Booklist, November 1, 1995, page 472
Children's Book Review Service, January 1996, page 52
Horn Book Guide, Spring 1996, page 44
Kirkus Reviews, October 1, 1995, page 1436
School Library Journal, October 1995, page 41

Other books you might like:
Nancy White Carlstrom, *Blow Me a Kiss, Miss Lilly*, 1990
Young Sara enjoys the special times she has with an elderly friend.
Steven Kellogg, *Best Friends*, 1986
Kathy and Louise experience the ups and downs of friendship.
Patricia Polacco, *Mrs. Katz and Tush*, 1992
A lonely widow finds a friend in a young boy who brings her a kitten.

1276

URSEL SCHEFFLER
ISKENDER GIDER, Illustrator

The Return of Rinaldo, the Sly Fox

(New York: North South Books, 1993)

Subject(s): Animals/Foxes; Animals; Humor
Age range(s): Grades 2-3
Major character(s): Rinaldo, Fox (trickster); Bruno, Duck, Detective—Police
Time period(s): 1990s (1993)
Locale(s): Fictional Country

Summary: In a beginning chapter book translated from the German by J. Alison James, Rinaldo the Great returns to match wits with Bruno the Detective and any other unsuspecting animal who crosses his path. Rinaldo seems to outfox Bruno, but can he outfox his beautiful dinner companion? (60 pages)

Where it's reviewed:
Booklist, February 15, 1993, page 1061
Horn Book Guide, Spring 1993, page 62
Kirkus Review, October 15, 1993, page 1336
Library Talk, May 1994, page 43
School Library Journal, December 1993, page 93

Other books by the same author:
Rinaldo on the Run, 1995

Rinaldo, the Sly Fox, 1992
The Giant Apple, 1990

Other books you might like:
Eth Clifford, *Flatfoot Fox and the Case of the Bashful Beaver*, 1995
Flatfoot Fox is an overly confident detective, assisted by Secretary Bird, who solves the mystery of Beaver's stolen button bag.
Gerald Hausman, *Coyote Walks on Two Legs: A Book of Navajo Myths and Legends*, 1995
Five stories about trickster coyote include an explanation of his name and two tales in which he is tricked.
Eric A. Kimmel, *Anansi and the Moss-Covered Rock*, 1988
Trickster Anansi discovers a magic rock and uses its power to steal the other animals' food until he is outsmarted and falls victim to the magic rock.
James Marshall, *Fox on Stage*, 1993
A beginning reader which humorously showcases Fox as his attempts at drama sometimes go awry.

1277

URSEL SCHEFFLER
ISKENDER GIDER, Illustrator

Rinaldo on the Run

(New York: North-South Books, 1995)

Series: Rinaldo
Subject(s): Animals; Crime and Criminals; Mystery and Detective Stories
Age range(s): Grades 2-4
Major character(s): Rinaldo, Fox, Thief; Bruno, Duck, Detective; Dustin Polecat, Businessman
Time period(s): 1990s (1995)
Locale(s): Rome, Italy; Chicago, Illinois

Summary: With Bruno the Duck Detective hot on his trail, Rinaldo steals a bag of money from a truck driver offering him a ride to Rome. He buys a disguise and flies to Chicago to pass himself off as the nephew of the wealthy Pizza King. Assuming the role of "Uncle" Dusty's accountant, he soon flim-flams Dustin Polecat out of most of his money and plans his departure. His big mouth, however, lands him back in Bruno's custody until his quick wits can find a way out. Translated from the German by J. Alison James. (60 pages)

Where it's reviewed:
Booklist, May 1, 1995, page 1575
Horn Book Guide, Fall 1995, page 292
School Library Journal, June 1995, page 95

Other books by the same author:
The Return of Rinaldo, the Sly Fox, 1993
Rinaldo, the Sly Fox, 1992
The Giant Apple, 1990

Other books you might like:
Crosby Bonsall, *The Case of the Cat's Meow*, 1965
The four members of the Private Eyes Club solve the mystery of a missing cat.
Doug Cushman, *Aunt Eater's Mystery Vacation*, 1992
Aunt Eater's plans for a relaxing vacation change when

she notices a diamond ring thief, a missing ferry boat captain and a suspicious-looking woman.
James Skofield, *Detective Dinosaur*, 1996
Clutzy Detective Dinosaur seems to cause more mysteries than he solves, but, with Officer Pterodactyl's help, he keeps fumbling along.

1278

GERDA MARIE SCHEIDL
CHRISTA UNZNER-FISCHER, Illustrator

Loretta and the Little Fairy

(New York: North-South Books, 1993)

Subject(s): Fairies; Conduct of Life; Fantasy
Age range(s): Grades 2-4
Major character(s): Loretta, Child; Xydaaqe "Fairy" Bowzd, Mythical Creature; Karen, Child (lonely), Neighbor (Loretta's)
Time period(s): 1990s (1993)
Locale(s): Germany

Summary: Playing alone in her yard, Loretta is surprised to sit upon an invisible fairy. When Fairy materializes, she admits that she's been sent to the human world in order to "grow up" so that she can be granted full fairy powers. Eager to be helpful, Loretta fills her with cherry soup, takes her to school, and teaches her to bake a cake. None of Loretta's ideas about growing up seem to work and a saddened Fairy joins lonely Karen next door, attracting stubborn Loretta's attention. Wanting to be included, Loretta apologizes to Karen for her previous behavior and joins in the play as Fairy vanishes, "grown up" at last. Translated from the German by J. Alison James. (64 pages)

Where it's reviewed:
Horn Book Guide, Fall 1993, page 290
Junior Bookshelf, August 1993, page 142
Kirkus Reviews, April 1, 1993, page 464
School Librarian, August 1993, page 112
School Library Journal, June 1993, page 88

Other books by the same author:
The Crystal Ball, 1993
Can We Help You, Saint Nicholas?, 1992
The Little Donkey, 1988

Other books you might like:
Joanna Cole, *Mixed-Up Magic*, 1987
A girl's friendship with an elf leads to some humorous adventures.
Amy Ehrlich, *Leo, Zack and Emmie*, 1981
When a new girl arrives in class, Leo and Zack wonder if their friendship is strong enough to include her.
Else Holmelund Minarik, *Little Bear's Friend*, 1960
Little Bear and his friend Emily enjoy a fun summer playing with all the animals of the forest.

1279

GERDA MARIE SCHEIDL
JOZEF WILKON, Illustrator

The Moon Man: A Story

(New York: North-South Books, 1994)

Subject(s): Artists and Art; Fantasy; Adventure and Adventurers
Age range(s): Grades K-2
Major character(s): Marion, Child, Artist; Moon Man, Celestial Body (artistic representation); Star Shiner, Worker
Time period(s): Indeterminate
Locale(s): Fictional Country

Summary: Not content to accept the changing phases of the moon, Marion draws Moon Man and hangs the picture above her bed so she can have a full moon all the time. While she sleeps Moon Man goes out in search of some shine so he will really look like the moon. On the way he encounters one predicament after another until the real moon agrees to let Star Shiner share a little star dust with him. Translated from the German by J. Alison James. (24 pages)

Where it's reviewed:
Booklist, August 1994, page 2056
Children's Bookwatch, August 1994, page 2
Junior Bookshelf, June 1994, page 97
Kirkus Reviews, May 15, 1994, page 706
School Library Journal, September 1994, page 193

Other books by the same author:
Pickle & Patch: A Story, 1994
The Crystal Ball, 1993
Flowers for the Snowman, 1988

Other books you might like:
Philip Heckman, *The Moon Is Following Me*, 1991
    On a nighttime family ride, a child observes the full moon ''following'' the car.
Arcadio Lobato, *Paper Bird*, 1994
    A drawing of a bird sets out on a quest to learn to fly.
Amy Tan, *The Moon Lady*, 1992
    Grandmother Nai-nai remembers her childhood journey to see the Moon Lady and ask for a wish to be granted.
Tomi Ungerer, *Moon Man*, 1991
    The man in the moon visits earth with help from a 300-year-old scientist.

1280

DONA SCHENKER

Fearsome's Hero

(New York: Alfred A. Knopf, 1994)

Subject(s): Schools/Middle Schools; Ranch Life; Bullies
Age range(s): Grades 4-6
Major character(s): Tully Webster, 6th Grader; Honey Kotcher, 6th Grader, Bully (reformed)
Time period(s): 1990s (1994)
Locale(s): Matagorda Island, Texas (Diamond Tail Ranch)

Summary: Tully couldn't imagine anything worse than his year in fifth grade with Honey bullying and teasing him all the time. Now, in 6th grade he discovers that life can get worse—now Honey likes him! Her classmates still detest her and do all they can to torment her in retaliation for the years she has made their lives miserable. While Tully would prefer to be ignored by Honey, as he grows to understand some of her behavior as well as his own fear in response to it, he is able to change the peer dynamics in the classroom. (141 pages)

Where it's reviewed:
Booklist, May 15, 1994, page 1680
Bulletin of the Center for Children's Books, February 1994, page 201
Horn Book, July 1994, page 455
Publishers Weekly, May 16, 1994, page 65
School Library Journal, June 1994, page 134

Other books by the same author:
Throw a Hungry Loop, 1991 (Spur Award)

Other books you might like:
Jack Gantos, *Heads or Tails: Stories from the Sixth Grade*, 1994
    Jack keeps a diary to help him cope with the many problems he faces in sixth grade.
D. Anne Love, *My Lone Star Summer*, 1996
    Jill spends the summer filled with the ups and downs of a growing friendship with B.J. on her grandmother's Texas ranch.
Phyllis Reynolds Naylor, *Beetles, Lightly Toasted*, 1987
    Competing against his cousin in a fifth grade essay contest, Andy is inspired to create unique recipes which he tries out on his unsuspecting family and friends.

1281

ALICE SCHERTLE
E.B. LEWIS, Illustrator

Down the Road

(San Diego: Harcourt Brace & Company, 1995)

Subject(s): Country Life; Parent and Child; Independence
Age range(s): Grades K-3
Major character(s): Hetty, Child; Mama, Mother; Papa, Father, Mechanic
Time period(s): 1990s (1995)
Locale(s): United States (rural area)

Summary: Hetty had never walked alone down the dusty road to Mr. Birdie's Emporium and Dry Goods Store. On the day Papa hankers for scrambled eggs for breakfast, he and Mama have no time to walk to the store so Hetty does, carefully carrying her basket of eggs home. Hetty does well with her chore until she attempts to pick three apples from a tree beside the road. When the market basket tips and all the eggs fall out and break, Hetty climbs, dejected, into the tree where her concerned parents find her. They join her high in the branches until their love and support give Hetty the confidence to resume her homeward journey. Breakfast is a delicious apple pie. (40 pages)

Where it's reviewed:
Booklist, September 15, 1995, page 161
Bulletin of the Center for Children's Books, December 1995, page 139

Children's Book Review Service, January 1996, page 53
Horn Book, March 1996, page 191
School Library Journal, April, 1996, page 117

Awards the book has won:
ALA Notable Book, 1996
Booklist Editors' Choice, 1995

Other books by the same author:
How Now, Brown Cow?, 1994
William and Grandpa, 1988
In My Treehouse, 1983

Other books you might like:
Barbara E. Barber, *Saturday at the New You*, 1994
    Saturday is the day that Shauna helps her mother work at
    The New You Beauty Parlor.
Tom Birdseye, *A Regular Flood of Mishap*, 1994
    Six-year-old Ima Bean worries that her family will never
    forgive her for the "flood of mishaps" that her helpful
    efforts create.
Valerie Flournoy, *Tanya's Reunion*, 1995
    Tanya and her grandmother travel to the family farm in
    Virginia to prepare for the upcoming reunion.

`1282`

ALICE SCHERTLE
LYDIA DABCOVICH, Illustrator

Maisie

(New York: Lothrop, Lee & Shepard Books, 1995)

Subject(s): Family Life; Grandparents; Conduct of Life
Age range(s): Grades K-3
Major character(s): Maisie, Mother, Grandmother
Time period(s): 20th century (1905-1995)
Locale(s): United States

Summary: From her birth on a farm to her 90th birthday
celebration, Maisie enjoys a life of simplicity, family and
love. As Maisie grows, attends school, marries, begins her
family, and becomes a grandmother, the text joyfully tells of
the life events while the illustrations expand the story and
keep the reader current with the passage of time through
changing styles. (32 pages)

Where it's reviewed:
Booklist, April 15, 1995, page 1508
Horn Book Guide, Fall 1995, page 281
Kirkus Reviews, March 15, 1995, page 394
Publishers Weekly, January 30, 1995, page 101
School Library Journal, April 1995, page 116

Other books by the same author:
Down the Road, 1995 (Booklist Editors' Choice; ALA Nota-
    ble Book)
How Now, Brown Cow?, 1994 (ALA Notable Book)
William and Grandpa, 1988 (Christopher Award)

Other books you might like:
Virginia Lee Burton, *The Little House*, 1942
    The passage of time and connectedness of family over the
    generations is chronicled in the experiences of a house.
    Caldecott Medal Winner.

Barbara Cooney, *Miss Rumphius*, 1982
    Great-aunt Alice's life is a fulfillment of her childhood
    resolve to travel, live by the sea and leave the world a more
    beautiful place.
Mem Fox, *Sophie*, 1994
    Sophie grows up with Grandpa's comforting presence,
    their roles shift as he ages; after his death, Sophie becomes
    a parent as the cycle of life continues.
Anne Shelby, *Homeplace*, 1995
    While rocking a grandchild, a grandmother traces the
    history of the family from the building of the family
    homestead by the great-great-great-great grandpa to the
    present.

`1283`

JOHN SCHINDEL
JAMES WATTS, Illustrator

I'll Meet You Halfway

(New York: Margaret K. McElderry Books, 1993)

Subject(s): Animals/Turtles; Animals/Frogs and Toads;
Friendship
Age range(s): Grades K-2
Major character(s): Titus Turtle, Turtle, Friend; Fuller Frog,
Frog, Friend
Time period(s): Indeterminate
Locale(s): Fictional Country

Summary: Good friends Titus and Fuller make plans to meet
one another for their first visit in a very long time. Each packs
a home-made gift to give the other and begins the journey to
the halfway point. In his excitement to see Fuller again, Titus
does not notice that the handmade sweater he carries on his
back is unraveling and leaving a trail of red yarn. Nor is Fuller
aware of the birds devouring the cake he has baked for Titus.
When the two friends finally meet it is obvious that nothing is
as important as their friendship. (32 pages)

Where it's reviewed:
Booklist, February 15, 1993, page 1068
Children's Bookwatch, April 1993, page 4
Horn Book Guide, Fall 1993, page 274
Publishers Weekly, March 1, 1993, page 55
School Library Journal, May 1993, page 91

Other books by the same author:
Something's Fishy, 1993
What's for Lunch?, 1993
Who Are You?, 1991

Other books you might like:
Anthony Browne, *Willy and Hugh*, 1991
    The chimp and the gorilla find that their differences con-
    tribute to the success of their friendship.
Robin Michal Koontz, *Chicago and the Cat: The Camping
    Trip*, 1994
    Despite a yucky dinner, a difficult hike and a soaking raft
    ride, Chicago's friendship with Cat makes the trip worth-
    while.
Arnold Lobel, *Frog and Toad Are Friends*, 1970
    In several brief stories, Frog and Toad share some of the
    difficulties as well as the pleasures of friendship.

1284

JOHN SCHINDEL
KEVIN O'MALLEY, Illustrator

What's for Lunch?

(New York: Lothrop, Lee & Shepard Books, 1994)

Subject(s): Food; Animals; Animals/Mice
Age range(s): Grades K-2
Major character(s): Sidney, Mouse, Friend; Shirley, Mouse, Friend
Time period(s): Indeterminate
Locale(s): Fictional Country

Summary: As Sidney stands atop a wall waiting for his lunch date to appear, a cat approaches threatening to devour him. "I don't think so," says Sidney as a dog appears. Each animal is followed by another and Sidney continues his refrain until Shirley appears and yells, "Boo!" scaring all the critters away. Finally, Sidney and Shirley can enjoy their lunch. (24 pages)

Where it's reviewed:
Horn Book Guide, Spring 1995, page 54
Kirkus Reviews, July 15, 1994, page 994
Learning, April 1995, page 71
Publishers Weekly, July 11, 1994, page 77
School Library Journal, September 1994, page 193

Other books by the same author:
I'll Meet You Halfway, 1993
Something Is Fishy, 1993
Who Are You?, 1991

Other books you might like:
Peter Armour, *Stop That Pickle!*, 1993
    Various food items take up the chase after a pickle who runs away to avoid being eaten.
Robert Bender, *A Most Unusual Lunch*, 1994
    As various animals eat their way up the food chain, each takes on characteristics of the animal just eaten, until the lion, offended by his new appearance, belches.
David McPhail, *The Glerp*, 1972
    As the glerp walks, he eats everything in his path until the elephant's tusks become stuck and cause the glerp to cough.

1285

STEPHEN SCHLOSSBERG, Author/Illustrator

Big Red Truck

(Charlottesville, VA: Thomasson-Grant, 1994)

Subject(s): Transportation; Imagination; Family Life
Age range(s): Grades K-2
Major character(s): Ray, Child; Mama, Mother; Papa, Father
Time period(s): 1990s (1994)
Locale(s): Spotsylvania, Virginia

Summary: It's Saturday morning and Ray is too busy pretending his tricycle is a big red truck to help his parent's with the day's chores. However, as he "drives" about the countryside, he encounters a waitress who resembles Mama and a mechanic who resembles Papa. For the services they render to

Ray and his "truck" each demands payment in the form of one of his chores. Author/illustrator's first book. (32 pages)

Where it's reviewed:
Booklist, November 1, 1994, page 509
Bulletin of the Center for Children's Books, November 1994, page 103
Horn Book Guide, Spring 1995, page 54
Publishers Weekly, November 14, 1994, page 66
School Library Journal, February 1995, page 81

Other books you might like:
Harriett Diller, *Grandaddy's Highway*, 1993
    Maggie imagines herself travelling with her truck-driving grandfather all the way to the Pacific coast.
Kirsten Hall, *My Trucks*, 1995
    While playing with his toy trucks, a little boy imagines that he is driving real ones.
Jill Paton Walsh, *Connie Came to Play*, 1995
    After Robert refuses to share his toys, Connie simply imagines some—all bigger and better than Robert's, of course.

1286

ANNIE M.G. SCHMIDT
KAY SATHER, Illustrator

Minnie

(Minneapolis, MN: Milkweed Editions, 1994)

Subject(s): Animals/Cats; Newspapers; Fantasy
Age range(s): Grades 4-6
Major character(s): Miss Minnie, Cat, Human; Mr. Tibbs, Journalist
Time period(s): 1970s (1970)
Locale(s): Europe

Summary: When shy Mr. Tibbs befriends a young woman who has been transformed from a cat to a human, he unwittingly saves his job with the newspaper. The fact that Minnie likes to sleep curled in a cardboard box, purrs while sleeping and is able to communicate with cats does not bother cat-loving Mr. Tibbs. As Minnie grows more accustomed to the idiosyncracies of humans, she must decide whether to remain in this new state or return to her feline life. Originally published in the Netherlands in 1970, the book is translated from the Dutch by Lance Salway. (164 pages)

Where it's reviewed:
Cat Fancy, June 1995, page 50
Children's Book Review Service, November 1994, page 35
Horn Book, March 1995, page 195
Library Talk, January 1995, page 44
School Library Journal, September 1994, page 222

Other books by the same author:
Pink Lemonade, 1992

Other books you might like:
Lloyd Alexander, *The Cat Who Wished to Be a Man*, 1977
    As feline Lionel becomes more familiar with humans, he realizes why the wizard was hesitant to change him into a man.

S.E. Hinton, *The Puppy Sister*, 1995
  A young boy is surprised when his new puppy changes into the shape of a girl and claims to be his loving sister.
Ursula K. Le Guin, *Catwings*, 1988
  Seeking a safe home away from the city, four winged cats are fortunate to find two kind children to shelter them.

1287

ANTONIE SCHNEIDER
CHRISTA UNZNER-FISCHER, Illustrator

You Shall Be King!

(New York: North-South Books, 1995)

Subject(s): Imagination; Play; Friendship
Age range(s): Grades K-2
Major character(s): Unnamed Character, Child, Neighbor; Unnamed Character, Child, Friend; Grandfather, Grandfather
Time period(s): 1990s (1995)
Locale(s): Europe

Summary: When the little girl next door suggests an imaginative game and offers to allow a little boy to be king, he agrees to play. The girl brings all the necessary props, but the boy tires of the activity. Cleverly, the girl shifts the pace of her story to involve the boy in a more interesting way and the imaginary kingdom continues until Grandfather comes home, announcing he'll cook and serve lunch. Translated from the German by J. Alison James. (26 pages)

Where it's reviewed:
Children's Book Review Service, April 1995, page 101
Horn Book Guide, Fall 1995, page 281
School Library Journal, July 1995, page 68

Other books you might like:
Heidi Goennel, *I Pretend*, 1995
  Using her imagination, a little girl has a teaparty with a mouse, becomes a mermaid, and rides on a flying carpet.
Jill Paton Walsh, *Connie Came to Play*, 1995
  When Robert refuses to share his toys, Connie simply pretends to be playing with even better ones.
Tanja Szekessy, *A Princess in Boxland*, 1996
  Imagining herself a princess, Marie uses a magical umbrella to transport her to an enchanted world.

1288

HOWIE SCHNEIDER, Author/Illustrator

No Dogs Allowed

(New York: G. P. Putnam's Sons, 1995)

Subject(s): Animals/Dogs; Hotels, Motels; Vacations
Age range(s): Grades K-2
Major character(s): Mercer, Dog; Mr. Arbuckle, Father
Time period(s): 1990s (1995)
Locale(s): United States

Summary: The Arbuckle family is travelling with their pet Mercer and unable to find overnight accomodations which will accept dogs. In desperation, Mr. Arbuckle stops at a used clothing store and creates a new identity for Mercer which gets the family a room, but soon arouses the suspicions of the hotel guests as well as the management. Fortunately, the vacation is brief because Mercer is eager to be a dog again. (32 pages)

Where it's reviewed:
Booklist, July 1995, page 1884
Horn Book Guide, Fall 1995, page 281
Kirkus Reviews, June 15,1995, page 862
Publishers Weekly, June 19, 1995, page 59
School Library Journal, August 1995, page 128

Other books by the same author:
Uncle Lester's Hat, 1993
Amos Camps Out: A Couch Adventure in the Woods, 1992

Other books you might like:
Debra Barracca, *Maxi, the Star*, 1993
  The third adventure of Maxi and his taxi-driver owner sends them to Hollywood where Maxi makes a commercial. Co-author Sal Barracca.
Susan Meddaugh, *Martha Calling*, 1994
  When Martha wins a weekend for four at a resort with a No Dogs Allowed policy, she accompanys her family anyway—in disguise.
Danny Shanahan, *Buckledown the Workhound*, 1993
  As president of a large corporation, Buckledown is "dog tired" so he plans a vacation at Shirttail Wagon Farm where he learns to lead a dog's life.

1289

STEVEN SCHNUR
STEPHEN T. JOHNSON, Illustrator

The Tie Man's Miracle: A Chanukah Tale

(New York: Morrow Junior Books, 1995)

Subject(s): Holidays, Jewish; Jews; Family Life
Age range(s): Grades 1-4
Major character(s): Mr. Hoffman, Aged Person; Seth, 7-Year-Old, Brother (older); Hannah, Sister (younger)
Time period(s): 1990s (1995)
Locale(s): United States

Summary: As Seth watches for his father to come home on the last night of Chanukah, he sees instead elderly Mr. Hoffman coming up the walk with his box of ties for sale. Initially, Seth resents his intrusion, but as Mr. Hoffman responds to the curious boy's questions he becomes interested in the man who has no family with whom to celebrate a holiday. On this night of remembering, Mr. Hoffman tells Seth, Hannah and their parents about the family whom he "lost" in the war. By sharing with Seth his childhood belief that if all 9 candles in a menorah go out at once the wafting smoke will carry wishes directly to God's ear, Mr. Hoffman may have worked his own miracle. (32 pages)

Where it's reviewed:
Booklist, September 1, 1995, page 59
Five Owls, November 1995, page 44
Horn Book, November 1995, page 730
Kirkus Reviews, October 15, 1995, page 1501
School Library Journal, October 1995, page 41

Awards the book has won:
Booklist Editors' Choice, 1995

Other books by the same author:
The Shadow Children, 1994
The Return of Morris Schumsky, 1987
The Narrowest Bar Mitzvah, 1986

Other books you might like:
David A. Adler, *One Yellow Daffodil: A Hanukkah Story*, 1995
   Invited to celebrate Hanukkah with a neighborhood family, Morris Kaplan finally faces the memories of the family he lost during the Holocaust.
Paula Kurzband Feder, *The Feather-Bed Journey*, 1995
   After tearing their grandmother's beloved feather pillow, Rachel and Lewis learn the special story of the pillow's past in grandmother's childhood Polish home.
Jacqueline Jules, *The Grey Striped Shirt: How Grandma and Grandpa Survived the Holocaust*, 1995
   Frannie learns of her grandparents' experiences during the Holocaust through their responses to her searching questions.
Marissa Moss, *The Ugly Menorah*, 1996
   After Grandpa dies, Rachel is sad to face the first Hanukkah without him, but visiting with Grandma and learning how he made their menorah helps her face his absence.

1290

JOHN SCHOENHERR, Author/Illustrator

Rebel

(New York: Philomel Books, 1995)

Subject(s): Animals/Geese; Nature; Individuality
Age range(s): Grades K-2
Major character(s): Unnamed Character, Goose, Mother; Unnamed Character, Goose, Father; Unnamed Character, Goose (gosling)
Time period(s): 1990s (1995)
Locale(s): United States (pond)

Summary: Annually, a pair of geese return to the same pond, building their nest on a small island and preparing for the birth of their offspring. While the text provides a straightforward narrative of the closely knit family's activities, the pictures reveal one gosling with an independent spirit who not only creates a little extra work for mom and dad, but also is almost left behind when the family prepares to follow nature's call. (32 pages)

Where it's reviewed:
Booklist, December 15, 1995, page 703
Horn Book Guide, Spring 1996, page 44
Kirkus Reviews, September 1, 1995, page 1287
Publishers Weekly, October 2, 1995, page 73
School Library Journal, October 1995, page118

Awards the book has won:
Booklist Editors' Choice, 1995
School Library Journal Best Books, 1995

Other books by the same author:
Bear, 1991

Other books you might like:
Leo Lionni, *Frederick*, 1967
   The other mice do not understand daydreamer and poet Frederick's talents until a winter day when he warms them with memories of summer.
Janet Morgan Stoeke, *A Hat for Minerva Louise*, 1994
   Independent hen Minerva Louise is determined not to let the cold weather curtail her early morning strolls so she finds a hat to keep her warm.
Ellen Stoll Walsh, *Hop Jump*, 1993
   Betsy, a frog who is not content with the monotony of hopping, is inspired by falling leaves to leap, twist and turn.
Piotr Wilkon, *Rosie the Cool Cat*, 1991
   Unlike the others in her family, Rosie expresses her individuality by becoming a rock star.

1291

RONI SCHOTTER
MARYLIN HAFNER, Illustrator

Passover Magic

(Boston: Little, Brown and Company, 1995)

Subject(s): Holidays, Jewish; Relatives; Spring
Age range(s): Grades K-2
Major character(s): Molly, Child, Sister (older); Ben, Child, Brother (younger); Harry, Uncle, Magician
Time period(s): 1990s (1995)
Locale(s): United States

Summary: After weeks of cleaning and preparation, Molly and Ben eagerly greet relatives arriving for celebration of Passover. Uncle Harry, the last to appear, wastes no time demonstrating his famous magic skills. After sunset, the family gathers for the Seder and the traditional celebration of the holiday. A concluding author's note gives information about the story of Passover. (32 pages)

Where it's reviewed:
Booklist, March 1, 1995, page 1249
Horn Book Guide, Fall 1995, page 281
New York Times Book Review, April 9, 1995, page 25
Publishers Weekly, March 20, 1995, page 60
School Library Journal, April 1995, page 116

Awards the book has won:
Notable Children's Trade Books in the Field of Social Studies, 1996

Other books by the same author:
That Extraordinary Pig of Paris, 1994
A Fruit and Vegetable Man, 1993
Hanukkah!, 1990 (National Jewish Book Award)

Other books you might like:
Fran Manushkin, *The Matzah That Papa Brought Home*, 1995
   The award-winning cumulative tale begins with the matzah Papa brings home and continues through the family Seder.
Miriam Nerlove, *Passover*, 1989
   A rhyming text describes the Jewish holy day.
I.L. Peretz, *The Magician*, 1985
   Although they are too poor to have a proper Seder, an

elderly couple befriend a stranger during Passover and are rewarded with a feast. Co-author Uri Shulevitz.

Lauren Wohl, *Matzoh Mouse*, 1991
While preparing for Passover, Sarah, unable toresist temptation, samples the chocolate matzos.

Jane Breskin Zalben, *Happy Passover, Rosie*, 1990
A young bear celebrates her first passover with her family.

Harriet Ziefert, *What Is Passover?*, 1994
Jake and his family prepare a special family seder.

1292

RONI SCHOTTER
DARA GOLDMAN, Illustrator

Warm at Home

(New York: Macmillan Publishing Company, 1993)

Subject(s): Animals/Rabbits; Illness; Play
Age range(s): Grades K-3
Major character(s): Bunny, Rabbit (sick); Mama, Rabbit
Time period(s): 1990s (1993)
Locale(s): United States

Summary: Stuck inside on a rainy day with a cold, Bunny complains of boredom. However, by the time Mama serves a warm bowl of stew for lunch, Bunny has put his imagination to good use and found plenty to do with enough ideas left over for tomorrow when he hopes to feel better and expects the rain to stop. (32 pages)

Where it's reviewed:
Horn Book Guide, Fall 1993, page 274
Publishers Weekly, March 8, 1993, page 77
School Library Journal, June 1993, page 88

Other books by the same author:
That Extraordinary Pig of Paris, 1994
When Crocodiles Clean Up, 1993
Bunny's Night Out, 1989

Other books you might like:
Nancy Carlson, *Take Time to Relax*, 1991
A snowfall forces a very busy beaver family to cancel their plans for the day and stay home.

Sue Porter, *My Little Rabbit Tale*, 1994
Little Rabbit enjoys an active, fun-filled day with his supportive parents.

Rosemary Wells, *Voyage to the Bunny Planet Series*, 1992
In each of the 3 titles in this series a bunny has a bad day which is relived as it should have been during a trip to the Bunny Planet.

1293

ALAN SCHROEDER
BERNIE FUCHS, Illustrator

Carolina Shout!

(New York: Dial Books for Young Readers, 1995)

Subject(s): Street Music and Musicians; African Americans; Individuality
Age range(s): Grades K-3

Major character(s): Delia, Child, Sister (younger); Bettina, Child, Sister (older)
Time period(s): Indeterminate Past
Locale(s): Charleston, South Carolina

Summary: Bettina says she can't hear any music in Charleston, but Delia hears it everywhere. She hears the songs of Charleston in the croaking of bull frogs, the rain drops on the tin roof, and the varied cries and songs of street vendors and workers. Maybe one day Bettina will hear it too. A concluding author's note explains the folklore of street vendors' cries. (32 pages)

Where it's reviewed:
Booklist, October 1, 1995, page 309
Horn Book Guide, Spring 1996, page 45
Kirkus Reviews, August 1, 1995, page 1116
Publishers Weekly, August 28, 1995, page 113
School Library Journal, October 1995, page 118

Other books by the same author:
Satchmo's Blues, 1996
Lily and the Wooden Bowl, 1994
Ragtime Tumpie, 1989

Other books you might like:
Alice Faye Duncan, *Willie Jerome*, 1995
Until Mama takes the time to listen carefully, she thinks Willie Jerome can only make "noise" on his trumpet.

Lynn Joseph, *Jasmine's Parlour Day*, 1994
Jasmine loves parlour day in Trinidad and the cacophony of cries of the various vendors hawking their wares.

George Ella Lyon, *Five Live Bongos*, 1994
Five lively children create the "Found Sound Band" with everyday household items and discards.

Brian Pinkney, *Max Found Two Sticks*, 1994
Max uses two sticks he finds near his urban home to imitate and answer the sounds of the city.

1294

ALAN SCHROEDER
YORIKO ITO, Illustrator

Lily and the Wooden Bowl

(New York: A Doubleday Book for Young Readers, 1994)

Subject(s): Fairy Tale; Folk Tales; Magic
Age range(s): Grades 1-4
Major character(s): Lily, Young Woman; Kumaso, Young Man; Yamoto, Farmer (wealthy), Father (Kumaso's)
Time period(s): Indeterminate Past
Locale(s): Japan

Summary: On her deathbed, Lily's grandmother gives her a wooden rice paddle and a folded paper crane. At the same time she places a large wooden bowl on Lily's head to hide her beauty from unscrupulous people. The grandmother instructs Lily not to remove the bowl and, in return, the bowl, the paddle and the crane will protect Lily. First, the crane magically comes to life to protect her from tormentors. Then, after she is hired by Yamoto to care for his ailing wife, the paddle helps her battle the wicked woman's sorcery as she tries to prevent the marriage of Kumaso and Lily. Finally, Lily's faithfulness to her grandmother is rewarded when, at the moment the marriage ceremony is completed, the bowl shatters, showering the couple with priceless jewels and revealing Lily's beauty. (32 pages)

Where it's reviewed:
Horn Book Guide, Spring 1995, page 109
Kirkus Reviews, October 15, 1994, page 1415
Publishers Weekly, October 31, 1994, page 62
Quill & Quire, January 1995, page 43
School Library Journal, December 1994, page 102

Awards the book has won:
Marion Vannett Ridgway Honor Award, 1995

Other books by the same author:
Carolina Shout!, 1995 (ALA Notable Book, 1996)
Satchmo's Blues, 1995
The Stone Lion, 1994

Other books you might like:
Lensey Namioka, *The Loyal Cat*, 1995
   A cat rescued by a poor priest uses magical powers to gain recognition for the priest and his temple.
Eric Quayle, *The Shining Princess and Other Japanese Legends*, 1989
   A collection of Japanese folktales includes a retelling of the story upon which *Lily and the Wooden Bowl* is based.
Carol Ann Williams, *Tsubu the Little Snail*, 1995
   The love of a poor couple who faithfully care for the snail child sent by the water god in answer to their prayers is rewarde d when the spell is broken and Tsubu becomes a young man.

1295

ALAN SCHROEDER
JERRY PINKNEY, Illustrator

Minty: A Story of Young Harriet Tubman

(New York: Dial, 1996)

Subject(s): Underground Railroad; Slavery; African Americans
Age range(s): Grades 2-4
Major character(s): Araminta ''Minty'', Slave, 8-Year-Old; Mrs. Brodas, Southern Belle; Old Ben, Slave
Time period(s): 1820s
Locale(s): Eastern Shore, Maryland

Summary: Minty's childhood is hard. She is a house slave until the day she spills some cider. Mrs. Brodas takes away her doll and makes her work in the fields. She is beaten for some things she does but the older slaves look after her and Old Ben shows her the way to escape. The first night she has a chance to ride away on a horse she loses her courage and runs back to the cabin, but other chances will come. (unpaged)

Where it's reviewed:
School Library Journal, May 1996, page 108
Horn Book, September/October 1996, page 589

Awards the book has won:
Coretta Scott King Award for Illustration, 1997

Other books by the same author:
Satchmo's Blues, 1996
Carolina Shout!, 1995

Lily and the Wooden Bowl, 1994
Ragtime Tumpie, 1989

Other books you might like:
David A. Adler, *A Picture Book of Harriet Tubman*, 1992
   The life of Harriet Tubman is described in simple terms with illustrations for younger readers.
Joan Anderson, *A Williamsburg Household*, 1988
   The life of slaves and servants in Williamsburg is traced in a photographic story.
William H. Hooks, *The Ballad of Belle Dorcas*, 1990
   A slave woman calls upon a conjure lady to help her save her child from being sold.
Dolores Johnson, *Now Let Me Fly: The Story of a Slave Family*, 1993
   Minnie tries to keep her slave family from being sold and to find freedom.
Connie Porter, *Meet Addy: An American Girl*, 1993
   Addie begins her story as a 9-year-old escapee.

1296

MAXINE ROSE SCHUR
BRIAN PINKNEY, Illustrator

When I Left My Village

(New York: Dial, 1996)

Subject(s): Refugees
Age range(s): Grades 2-5
Major character(s): Menelik, Child, Refugee; Father, Blacksmith, Refugee; Simcha, Brother, Refugee
Time period(s): 1990s (1991)
Locale(s): Gondar, Ethiopia

Summary: Menelik and his family look forward to escaping Ethiopia and moving to Israel where they will join other escaped Ethiopian Jews who have been persecuted. They sneak out of town one night and travel to the Sudan where they join many of their countrymen in a camp. They are forbidden to travel farther, but Father decides they must go on and cuts a hole in the fence. The family escapes by night, eventually reaching a secret airstrip where an airplane takes them to freedom and new friends. (62 pages)

Where it's reviewed:
School Library Journal, March 1996, page 198
Bulletin of the Center for Children's Books, February 1996, page 202

Other books by the same author:
Circlemaker, 1994
Day of Delight, 1994 (prequel to *When I Left My Village*)
Samantha's Surprise, 1986

Other books you might like:
David A. Adler, *One Yellow Daffodil: A Hanukkah Story*, 1995
   A survivor of the holocaust embraces the customs of Hanukkah for one last time.
Karen Ackerman, *The Night Crossing*, 1994
   A Jewish family escapes to Switzerland in 1938.
Patricia Lakin, *Don't Forget*, 1994
   A little girl makes friends with the store owners who wear numbers on their arms from the Holocaust.

Arthur A. Levine, *All the Lights in the Night*, 1991
    Moses and Benjamin have the lights of Hannukah even
    though they traded their menorah for their freedom.
Shulamith Levey Oppenheim, *The Lily Cupboard*, 1994
    A little girl finds protection behind the wall in a house in
    the Netherlands during World War II.

1297

AMY SCHWARTZ, Author/Illustrator

A Teeny Tiny Baby

(New York: Orchard Books, 1994)

Subject(s): Babies; City Life; Parenthood
Age range(s): Grades K-2
Major character(s): Unnamed Character, Child (baby); Mom,
    Mother; Dad, Father
Time period(s): 1990s (1994)
Locale(s): New York, New York (Brooklyn)

Summary: This baby's eye view of the world is one of simple
needs that receive immediate, loving attention from a doting
family. Through the humorous illustrations, this first-born
child shows the adult's perspective of life with an infant in the
house. (32 pages)

Where it's reviewed:
Booklist, July 1994, page 1945
Horn Book Magazine, January 1995, page 53
Kirkus Reviews, September 15, 1994, page 1280
Publishers Weekly, August 29, 1994, page 78
School Library Journal, September 1994, page 193

Awards the book has won:
Booklist Editors' Choice, 1994

Other books by the same author:
Camper of the Week, 1991
Annabelle Swift, Kindergartner, 1988
Oma and Bobo, 1987
Begin at the Beginning, 1983
Bea and Mr. Jones, 1982

Other books you might like:
Catherine Anholt, *When I Was a Baby*, 1989
    A mother and her daughter talk about the girl's life as an
    infant.
Tony Bradman, *This Little Baby*, 1990
    The routine activities of an infant's life are portrayed.
Ann Jonas, *When You Were a Baby*, 1982
    A reassuring look, from the perspective of a capable tod-
    dler, of all the things a baby can and cannot do.
Fiona Pragoff, *Growing: From First Cry to First Step*, 1987
    A colorful overview of the equipment and supplies needed
    by a baby's family.
Vera B. Williams, *More More More Said the Baby: 3 Love
    Stories*, 1990
    This Caldecott Honor Book beautifully portrays the play-
    ful expressions of love between parent and child.

1298

JON SCIESZKA
LANE SMITH, Illustrator

2095

(New York: Viking, 1995)

Series: Time Warp Trio
Subject(s): Time Travel; Museums; Adventure and Adventur-
    ers
Age range(s): Grades 3-5
Major character(s): Joe, Child (member of Time Warp Trio);
    Fred, Child (member of TimeWarp Trio); Sam, Child
    (member of Time Warp Trio)
Time period(s): 1990s (1995); 2090s (2095)
Locale(s): New York, New York

Summary: On a class field trip to the American Museum of
Natural History, Joe, Fred and Sam decide that, rather than
finish an assigned worksheet, they will take a trip using Joe's
magic book. Previous travels have sent them back in time so
this time they decide to explore the future. As usual, they have
problems finding their way back to the present because they
can't locate the magic book. (72 pages)

Where it's reviewed:
Booklist, June 1995, page 1772
Horn Book Guide, Fall 1995, page 304
School Library Journal, Jul 1995, page 81
Tribune Books, March 12, 1995, page 7

Other books by the same author:
Math Curse, 1995
The Good, the Bad, and the Goofy, 1992
Knights of the Kitchen Table, 1991
The Not-So-Jolly Roger, 1991

Other books you might like:
Pam Conrad, *Zoe Rising*, 1996
    In a sequel to *Stonewords*, Zoe travels back to the time of
    her mother's childhood in order to intervene in events and
    save the future.
E.W. Hildick, *The Case of the Weeping Witch*, 1992
    As the kids of the McGurk Organization work on a school
    project, they are somehow transported back in time to the
    1600s where they are charged with witchcraft.
Jenny Pausacker, *Fast Forward*, 1989
    Grandma's new invention enables Kieran to travel either
    back in time or into the future, but he soon learns that using
    the Anti-Boredom Machine creates rather than solves
    problems.
Richard Peck, *Lost in Cyberspace*, 1995
    Josh and Aaron use their school's computer to travel
    through time and impact life situations in the present.

1299

JON SCIESZKA
LANE SMITH, Illustrator

Tut Tut

(New York: Viking, 1996)

Series: Time Warp Trio

Subject(s): Time Travel; Adventure and Adventurers
Age range(s): Grades 3-6
Major character(s): Joe, Time Traveller, 6th Grader; Anna, Time Traveller, Sister; Sam, Time Traveller, 6th Grader
Time period(s): 1990s; Indeterminate Past (from the present to ancient Egypt)
Locale(s): Egypt

Summary: Joe and his friends are finishing their projects on ancient Egypt when Anna comes in and picks up the magic book that sends them all to a pyramid in ancient Egypt. There they meet Hashnet, who is attempting to rob the graves, as well as Thutmose III who befriends them. Their magic tricks don't completely save them as they end up sealed in a tomb. Fortunately Isis and Cleo, Anna's cat, locate the book and bring them back through 3500 years to land in their room. (74 pages)

Where it's reviewed:
School Library Journal, October 1, 1996, page 352
Booklist, October 1, 1996, page 352

Other books by the same author:
Your Mother Was a Neanderthal, 1993
The Stinky Cheese Man: And Other Fairly Stupid Tales, 1992
The Good, the Bad, and the Goofy, 1992

Other books you might like:
Andrew Clements, *The Temple Cat*, 1996
  A cat grows tired of being worshiped and travels to the sea.
Catherine Dexter, *The Gilded Cat*, 1992
  Maggie's purchase of a mummified cat leads to a classic battle of good and evil.
Deborah Nourse Lattimore, *The Winged Cat: A Tale of Ancient Egypt*, 1992
  A servant girl sees the slaying of a sacred cat in ancient Egypt.
Robert Sabuda, *Tutankhamen's Gift*, 1994
  The young pharaoh may have been killed by one of his group.
Kelly Trumble, *Cat Mummies*, 1996
  Tombs of cats have been found that are separate from other tombs. (non-fiction)

1300

JON SCIESZKA
LANE SMITH, Illustrator

Your Mother Was a Neanderthal
(New York: Viking, 1993)

Series: Time Warp Trio
Subject(s): Time Travel; Man, Prehistoric; Humor
Age range(s): Grades 3-5
Major character(s): Joe, Child (member of Time Warp Trio); Sam, Child (member of Time Warp Trio); Fred, Child (member of Time Warp Trio)
Time period(s): 1990s (1992); 400th century B.C. (40,000)
Locale(s): United States; Underground Environment

Summary: Planning their next time travel adventure, the Time Warp Trio decides that the farther back in time they travel the more impressive they and their 20th century things will be to other people. The plan seems a good one until Joe, Sam and Fred find themselves in a Stone Age setting naked, bewildered and without "The Book" which enables them to time travel home. With assistance from cavemen, women and children, including one who looks very much like Joe's mother, the trio manages to return to the present with time to spare. (78 pages)

Where it's reviewed:
Booklist, October 1, 1993, page 346
Childhood Education, Fall 1993, page 48
Horn Book Guide, Spring 1994, page 82
Library Talk, January 1994, page 54
School Library Journal, October 1993, page 130

Awards the book has won:
School Library Journal Best Books, 1993

Other books by the same author:
The Good, the Bad, and the Goofy, 1992
Knights of the Kitchen Table, 1991
The Not-So-Jolly Roger, 1991

Other books you might like:
Edward Eager, *Half-Magic*, 1954
  The children must learn to wish for twice what they want because the coin they've found is only half magic.
Madeline L'Engle, *A Wrinkle in Time*, 1962
  Meg and Charles go on a dangerous mission to find their father in this first book of a fantasy quartet.
H.G. Wells, *The Time Machine*, 1964
  One of many printings telling the story of a young scientist who develops a machine in which he travels through time to another civilization.

1301

ANN HERBERT SCOTT
TED LEWIN, Illustrator

Cowboy Country
(New York: Clarion Books, 1993)

Subject(s): American West; Ranch Life
Age range(s): Grades K-3
Major character(s): Unnamed Character, Cowboy
Time period(s): 1990s (1993)
Locale(s): Nevada

Summary: A young boy receives in introduction to the life of a cowboy from an old buckaroo. While on an overnight trip, via horseback and pack mule to Devil's Canyon, the old, experienced cowboy shares a lifetime of experience with a young boy who aspires to being a cowboy some day. (42 pages)

Where it's reviewed:
Booklist, September 1, 1993, page 66
Horn Book, November 1993, page 760
New Advocate, Spring 1994, page 140
Publishers Weekly, July 26, 1993, page 72
School Library Journal, September 1993, page 218

Awards the book has won:
Book Links Good Book, 1993
School Library Journal Best Books, 1993

Other books by the same author:
A Brand Is Forever, 1993
Grandmother's Chair, 1990

Someday Rider, 1989

Other books you might like:

Russell Freedman, *Cowboys of the Wild West*, 1985
Photographs illustrate the life of a trail-driving cowboy in the late 19th century. (nonfiction)

Dayal Kaur Khalsa, *Cowboy Dreams*, 1990
A city girl wants to become a cowgirl and ride the range out West.

Glen Rounds, *Cowboys*, 1991
A cowboy's work day is long, difficult and sometimes dangerous.

1302

ANN HERBERT SCOTT
GLO COALSON, Illustrator

Hi

(New York: Philomel Books, 1994)

Subject(s): Communication; Mothers and Daughters; Self-Confidence

Age range(s): Grades K-1

Major character(s): Margarita, Child; Unnamed Character, Mother; Unnamed Character, Postal Worker

Time period(s): 1990s (1994)

Locale(s): United States

Summary: When Margarita and her mother enter the post office to mail a package, Margarita cheerfully waves "Hi!" to the people in line, but no one notices or responds to her greeting. As additional people enter the lobby and join the line, Margarita greets each one, but grows progressively more quiet as she continues to receive no response. Finally, the postal clerk answers Margarita's greeting and Margarita leaves happily while telling everyone good-bye. (32 pages)

Where it's reviewed:

Booklist, May 15, 1994, page 1684
Horn Book, July 1994, page 445
Kirkus Reviews, May 15, 1994, page 706
Publishers Weekly, May 30, 1994, page 56
School Library Journal, July 1994, page 89

Awards the book has won:

ALA Notable Book, 1995
Boston Globe/Horn Book Fanfare, 1995

Other books by the same author:

A Brand Is Forever, 1993
On Mother's Lap, 1992
Grandmother's Chair, 1990

Other books you might like:

Kevin Henkes, *Once around the Block*, 1987
A walk around the block gives bored Annie the opportunity to visit with her neighbors.

Fran Manushkin, *Let's Go Riding in Our Strollers*, 1993
Toddlers enjoy a stroller ride through the city to the park.

Elaine Moore, *Good Morning, City*, 1995
As the city comes to life, some go to work and others to school.

1303

VIRGINIA SCRIBNER
JANET WILSON, Illustrator

Gopher Takes Heart

(New York: Viking, 1993)

Subject(s): Bullies; Schools; Self-Respect

Age range(s): Grades 3-6

Major character(s): Matthew "Gopher" Goff, 10-Year-Old, Bullied Child; Fletcher Simpson, 5th Grader, Bully

Time period(s): 1990s (1993)

Locale(s): Rhode Island (Lincoln Elementary School)

Summary: Fletcher shares artistic ability with his imprisoned brother but his antisocial behavior doesn't win him any friends. Because Gopher wins an art contest in which both boys competed, Fletcher bullies him, daily stealing his milk money and eventually the class Valentine Party money which is entrusted to Gopher. In time, Gopher learns to stand up for himself and Fletcher learns an important lesson in friendship. (136 pages)

Where it's reviewed:

Booklist, December 15, 1992, page 739
Children's Book Review Service, March 1993, page 96
Horn Book Guide, Fall 1993, page 304
Kirkus Reviews, December 15, 1992, page 1577
School Library Journal, January 1993, page 103

Other books by the same author:

Gopher Draws Conclusions, 1994

Other books you might like:

Betsy Byars, *The 18th Emergency*, 1973
Mouse tries to avoid bully Marv, but finally decides he must find a way to deal with the problem.

Susan Rowan Masters, *The Secret Life of Hubie Hartzell*, 1990
Already coping with a sick cat and losing his best friend, Hubie now is being threatened by the class bully.

Susan Richards Shreve, *Joshua T. Bates Takes Charge*, 1993
Fifth grader Joshua finally finds the courage to stand up to the school bully and stop his abuse of others.

1304

BRENDA SEABROOKE

The Haunting of Holroyd Hill

(New York: Cobblehill/Dutton, 1995)

Subject(s): Mystery and Detective Stories; Ghosts; Brothers and Sisters

Age range(s): Grades 6-8

Major character(s): Melinda Ryan, 11-Year-Old; Kevin Ryan, 14-Year-Old; Dan Czernikow, Worker (newspaper delivery)

Time period(s): 1990s

Locale(s): Broadfalls, Virginia

Summary: Melinda's displeasure at moving to the country changes when she meets their next-door neighbor Dan and sees her first ghost. Melinda and Kevin make friends with Dan, grandson of a mean old man who chases them out of his orchard. Complexity strikes when Melinda sees not one but two different ghosts and realizes they are somehow tied into a mystery involving Dan's grandfather and the Civil War. (137 pages)

Where it's reviewed:
School Library Journal, April 1995, page 136
Booklist, September 1, 1995, page 66
Children's Book Review Service, Spring 1995, page 143
Children's Bookwatch, July 1995, page 5
Horn Book Guide, Fall 1995, page 304

Other books by the same author:
Looking for Diamonds, 1995
The Dragon That Ate Summer, 1993
The Bridges of Summer, 1992
Judy Scuppernong, 1990

Other books you might like:
Elaine Marie Alphin, *The Ghost Cadet*, 1991
    Benjy helps a ghost find a pocket watch he lost during the Battle of New Market during the Civil War.
George Ella Lyon, *Here and Then*, 1994
    A reenactment becomes real when Abby collects bandages and blankets in response to the voice of a nurse who uses them to help wounded Civil War soldiers.
Karen Weinberg, *Window of Time*, 1991
    Climbing through a window in a basement he's cleaning, Ben Leeds discovers he's landed in the middle of preparations for the Battle of Gettysburg.

1305

BRENDA SEABROOKE
NANCY MANTHA, Illustrator

Looking for Diamonds
(New York: Cobblehill Books/Dutton, 1995)

Subject(s): Grandparents; Country Life; Nature
Age range(s): Grades K-3
Major character(s): Amy, Child; Grandmother, Grandmother; Grandaddy, Grandfather
Time period(s): 1940s
Locale(s): South

Summary: While visiting her grandparents, Amy enjoys the soft comfort of Grandmother's feather bed and a delicious breakfast when she wakens. The activity Amy looks forward to the most is her after-breakfast walk with Grandaddy when they look for diamonds in drops of dew. Today, they spot many signs of animals and a variety of flowers, but no diamonds until they return to the house where Grandmother throws the dirty dishwater onto a backyard cedar, now glistening in the sunlight. (32 pages)

Where it's reviewed:
Booklist, Ocotber 15, 1995, page 413
Children's Bookwatch, November 1995, page 7
Horn Book Guide, Spring 1996, page 45
School Library Journal, October 1995, page 119

Other books by the same author:
The Swan's Gift, 1995
The Chester Town Tea Party, 1991
The Boy Who Saved the Town, 1990

Other books you might like:
Marsha Wilson Chall, *Up North at the Cabin*, 1992
    Memories of earlier vacations mingle with present-day experiences during a family's summer trip.
Helen V. Griffith, *Grandaddy's Place*, 1987
    Janetta visits Grandaddy on his farm, getting to know the mule, the cat, and a simple way of life.
Shulamith Levey Oppenheim, *Fireflies for Nathan*, 1994
    During a visit with his grandparents, Nathan catches fireflies just like his daddy did as a boy.

1306

BRENDA SEABROOKE
WENHAI MA, Illustrator

The Swan's Gift
(Cambridge, MA: Candlewick Press, 1995)

Subject(s): Animals/Swans; Food; Fairy Tale
Age range(s): Grades K-3
Major character(s): Anton, Farmer, Hunter; Rubina, Spouse, Mother
Time period(s): Indeterminate Past
Locale(s): Fictional Country

Summary: The year that the wheat crop fails, Anton and Rubina find themselves unable to feed their seven children. Each winter day, Anton walks the countryside vainly searching for a bird or rabbit to shoot for his family's table. One evening, Anton spots a swan so beautiful that he is unable to kill it despite his family's desparate plight. The magical swan rewards his kindness by dropping water from its wings which hardens into diamonds on the frozen snow. (32 pages)

Where it's reviewed:
Booklist, December 15, 1995, page 710
Horn Book Guide, Spring 1996, page 45
Kirkus Reviews, October 15, 1995, page 1501
Publishers Weekly, October 30, 1995, page 61
School Library Journal, December 1995, page 91

Other books by the same author:
Looking for Diamonds, 1995
The Chester Town Tea Party, 1991

Other books you might like:
Hans Christian Andersen, *Twelve Tales*, 1994
    The collection of Andersen's classic fairy tales is selected, translated and illustrated by Erik Blegvad.
Laura Krauss Melmed, *Prince Nautilus*, 1994
    Kindly Fiona is rewarded when her unselfish actions free a Prince from an evil spell.
Fiona Moodie, *The Boy and the Giants*, 1993
    A kind-hearted fisherboy rescues his beloved Kate from giants.

1307

JOHN SEBASTIAN
GARTH WILLIAMS, Illustrator

J.B.'s Harmonica

(San Diego: Harcourt Brace Jovanovich, Publishers, 1993)

Subject(s): Musicians; Fathers and Sons; Identity
Age range(s): Grades K-3
Major character(s): James "J. B." Bear, Bear, Child; Dad, Bear, Musician; Mom, Bear, Writer
Time period(s): 1990s (1993)
Locale(s): Bearsville

Summary: In the author's first book, J. B. is thrilled to be given his own harmonica until, after hours of practice, someone compliments his playing by comparing J. B. to his father, a concert harmonicist. Then J. B. worries that perhaps he may not want to follow in his father's footsteps. With guidance from Mom and Dad, J. B. learns that he can be himself and still enjoy his harmonica. (32 pages)

Where it's reviewed:
Booklist, March 15, 1993, page 1362
Children's Book Review Service, Spring 1993, page 137
Horn Book Guide, Fall 1993, page 274
Publishers Weekly, April 5, 1993, page 76
School Library Journal, April 1993, page 102

Other books you might like:
Miko Imai, *Sebastian's Trumpet*, 1995
    Initially frustrated, Sebastian finds that, with practice, he can make music with his trumpet.
Robert McCloskey, *Lentil*, 1940
    Others may not see Lentil as a child with musical talent, but he learns to play the harmonica — just in the nick of time too.
William Steig, *Zeke Pippin*, 1994
    Zeke soon learns to play the harmonica which he finds, but discovers that his playing has an unusual effect on others.

1308

J. OTTO SEIBOLD
VIVIAN WALSH, Illustrator
J. OTTO SEIBOLD, Illustrator

Mr. Lunch Takes a Plane Ride

(New York: Viking Press, 1993)

Subject(s): Animals/Dogs; Air Travel; Animals/Birds
Age range(s): Grades K-3
Major character(s): Mr. Lunch, Dog, Traveller; Ambrose, Bird, Companion (to Mr. Lunch)
Time period(s): 1990s (1993)
Locale(s): United States

Summary: Mr. Lunch, professional bird chaser, is excited to be invited to demonstrate his art on a television show. Selecting Ambrose as the token bird to be chased, Mr. Lunch carefully researches plane travel to prepare for his first trip. He anticipates having a bird's eye view of the world, but upon checking in at the airport discovers that dogs must travel in the luggage section. To entertain himself in the windowless space he investigates the contents of some of the luggage, leading to some unexpected events on the TV show. Mr. Lunch's return home to mounds of fan mail concludes the authors' first book. (40 pages)

Where it's reviewed:
Booklist, September 1, 1993, page 71
Children's Book Review Service, Winter 1994, page 65
Horn Book Guide, Spring 1994, page 54
Publishers Weekly, June 28, 1993, page 75
School Library Journal, September 1993, page 218

Other books by the same author:
Mr. Lunch Borrows a Canoe, 1994

Other books you might like:
Debra Barracca, *Maxi, the Star*, 1993
    Maxi is selected to star in a television commercial. Co-author Sal Barracca.
Robert Kraus, *Phil the Ventriloquist*, 1989
    Being a ventriloquist has never brought Phil much acclaim in his family until the day a burglar breaks into the house.
Susan Meddaugh, *Martha Calling*, 1993
    Martha wins a radio contest and a weekend at a resort which does not allow dogs, until they meet Martha.

1309

TOR SEIDLER
FRED MARCELLINO, Illustrator

The Wainscott Weasel

(New York: HarperCollins, 1993)

Subject(s): Animals; Fantasy; Romance
Age range(s): Grades 3-5
Major character(s): Bagley Brown Jr., Weasel, Hero (son of the legendary Wainscott); Zeke Whitebelly, Weasel; Bridget, Fish
Time period(s): 1990s (1993)
Locale(s): Wainscott, Fictional Country (South Fork of Long Island)

Summary: It's Spring and love is in the air. Brash Zeke has fallen in love with a weasel visiting from North Fork while lonely Bagley is smitten with a beautiful striped fish in the pond. Seeing no future in a relationship with a weasel, Bridget does not return Bagley's affection. To save Bridget from certain death at the talons of the pond's osprey, Bagley risks life and limb to remove the osprey's nest from atop a telephone pole, making him the hero of Wainscott. (194 pages)

Where it's reviewed:
Booklist, November 1, 1993, page 519
Children's Book Review Service, October 1993, page 23
Five Owls, January 1994, page 62
Publishers Weekly, September 20, 1993, page 73
School Library Journal, December 1993, page 116

Other books by the same author:
The Tar Pit, 1987
A Rat's Tale, 1986

Other books you might like:

Benedict Blathwayt, *Stories from Firefly Island*, 1993
Tortoise is the resident storyteller for the animals living on Firefly Island.

Kenneth Grahame, *The Wind in the Willows*, 1908
Mole, Ratty, Badger and Mr. Toad are involved in many adventures in this classic story set in the English countryside.

Paul Peabody, *Blackberry Hollow*, 1993
Kindly Parnassus thinks his latest invention will put an end to Tom McPaddy's homesickness.

E.B. White, *Stuart Little*, 1945
In this classic fantasy, Stuart, a mouse, leaves the family home to follow Margolo, a wren he admires.

1310

MARY SERFOZO
JOS. A. SMITH, Illustrator

Benjamin Bigfoot

(New York: Margaret K. McElderry Books, 1993)

Subject(s): Schools; Growing Up; Clothes
Age range(s): Grades K-1
Major character(s): Benjamin, 5-Year-Old; Unnamed Character, Mother; Miss Castle, Teacher (kindergarten)
Time period(s): 1990s (1993)
Locale(s): United States

Summary: When Benjamin wears his dad's old shoes over his sneakers he feels big and grown up. His mother does not agree that he will need to wear the big shoes when he begins kindergarten so Benjamin thinks maybe he will not go to school. A visit to the classroom lets Benjamin meet Miss Castle and discover for himself that his big shoes are a hinderance on the playground. School starts soon and Benjamin is ready to go, wearing his own sneakers. (32 pages)

Where it's reviewed:
Booklist, April 15, 1993, page 1524
Children's Book Review Service, Spring 1993, page 137
Horn Book Guide, Fall 1993, page 275
Kirkus Reviews, March 1, 1993, page 305
School Library Journal, August 1993, page 151

Other books by the same author:
Joe Joe, 1993
Dirty Kurt, 1992
Rain Talk, 1990

Other books you might like:

Dorothy Butler, *My Brown Bear Barney*, 1988
Life is not complete for one young girl unless Barney is her companion.

Miriam Cohen, *Will I Have a Friend?*, 1967
One of the fears of beginning school is happily resolved when Paul finds a friend on the first day.

Kevin Henkes, *Owen*, 1993
Mom helps Owen find a way to carry his special blanket Fuzzy, now disguised as a handkerchief, to school.

Amy Schwartz, *Annabelle Swift, Kindergartner*, 1988
The shared experiences of Annabelle's big sister help Annabelle have a successful first day in kindergarten.

1311

PAMELA F. SERVICE

Stinker's Return

(New York: Charles Scribner's Sons, 1993)

Subject(s): Aliens; Animals/Skunks; Science Fiction
Age range(s): Grades 3-6
Major character(s): Tsynq "Stinker" Yr, Alien; Karen, Child (interested in science fiction), Friend; Jonathan, Child (interested in science fiction), Friend
Time period(s): 1990s (1993)
Locale(s): Planet Twak, Outer Space; Washington, District of Columbia

Summary: In the sequel to *Stinker from Space*, Stinker travels to Earth to return the space shuttle which he used to escape on his previous trip. Jonathan and Karen are still being questioned by government officials regarding their possible involvement in the shuttle's disappearance when Stinker invites them to Washington, D. C. to locate an appropriate souvenir for the High Gryn of Twak. Stinker and friends try to stay one step ahead of NASA officials and the media as everyone tries to learn more about this unique skunk. (96 pages)

Where it's reviewed:
Booklist, April 1, 1993, page 1434
Bulletin of the Center for Children's Books, June 1993, page 329
Horn Book Guide, Fall 1993, page 304
Kirkus Reviews, March 1, 1993, page 306
School Library Journal, May 1993, page 108

Other books by the same author:
Phantom Victory, 1994
Under Alien Stars, 1990
Stinker from Space, 1988

Other books you might like:

Janet Asimov, *Norby Finds a Villian*, 1987
The 6th entry in the series finds Norby the robot and his human friend Jeff trying to free robot-napped Pera.

Gery Greer, *Jason and the Escape from Bat Planet*, 1993
With alien neighbor Coop and a talking cat creature, Jason saves an absent-minded professor from the clutches of the Bat Planet leader. Co-author Bob Ruddick.

Debra Hess, *Alien Alert!*, 1993
Cassie's interest in "sleuthing" leads her to a spaceship in need of repair and a friendship with Zeke, an alien spy-in-training.

1312

TRES SEYMOUR
WENDY ANDERSON HALPERIN, Illustrator

Hunting the White Cow

(New York: Orchard, 1993)

Subject(s): Animals/Cows; Farm Life
Age range(s): Grades K-2
Major character(s): Unnamed Character, Child (daughter); Daddy, Father; White Cow, Cow (stray)
Time period(s): 1900s

Locale(s): Kentucky (rural area, north of Priceville)

Summary: Each attempt to capture a wayward white cow involves more family members and more time; each failure brings more tales of the uniqueness of this tough, smart cow. Not allowed to participate in the searches with the menfolks, the young girl of the family goes off to play and one day near dusk happens upon the cow. Unable to convince the cow to come with her, the girl ties the cow's rope to her wrist before falling asleep. When the girl's father finds the child sleeping on the ground, the cow has escaped again and the tales about her exploits just keep growing. (32 pages)

Where it's reviewed:
Booklist, September 1, 1993, page 71
Horn Book, November 1993, page 738
Kirkus Reviews, August 15, 1993, page 1080
Publishers Weekly, August 19, 1993, page 251
School Library Journal, December 1993, page 93

Awards the book has won:
ALA Notable Book, 1994
School Library Journal Best Books, 1993

Other books by the same author:
Pole Dog, 1993

Other books you might like:
SuAnn Kiser, *The Hog Call to End All!*, 1994
    Minerva is sure that she and her hog, Tilly, will win a blue ribbon in the hog calling contest.
Ogden Nash, *The Tale of Custard the Dragon*, 1936
    Belinda lives with a dragon who, fortunately, comes to her rescue when a pirate comes in the window.
James Stevenson, *Brrr!*, 1991
    The winter of 1908 seems colder each time that Grandpa tells his tale about it.

`1313`

TRES SEYMOUR
DAVID SOMAN, Illustrator

Pole Dog

(New York: Orchard Books, 1993)

Subject(s): Animals/Dogs; Animals, Treatment of; Stories in Rhyme
Age range(s): Grades K-1
Major character(s): Pole Dog, Dog (old and abandoned)
Time period(s): 1990s (1993)
Locale(s): United States (beside a country road)

Summary: A faithful dog abandoned next to a telephone pole waits for his owners' return. Days and nights of cold, hunger and fear pass before the old dog realizes that the yellow truck carrying his owners is simply gone. However, a red car which has driven by daily does stop and a family rescues him. An ending author's note to this first picture book presents factual information on the plight of abandoned animals. (32 pages)

Where it's reviewed:
Booklist, March 15, 1993, page 1362
Children's Book Review Service, March 1993, page 89
Horn Book, July 1993, page 449
Publishers Weekly, February 1, 1993, page 93

School Library Journal, July 1993, page 71

Other books by the same author:
The Smash-up Crash-up Derby, 1995
I Love My Buzzard, 1994
Hunting the White Cow, 1993

Other books you might like:
Robert J. Blake, *Dog*, 1994
    A dog's attempts to make a home with an elderly man are initially rebuffed until the old man sees the similarities between his own lonely existence and that of the dog.
Karen Hesse, *Lester's Dog*, 1993
    Lester's dog has a home and a reputation for meanness that suggests he is mistreated or neglected.
Charlotte Pomerantz, *The Outside Dog*, 1993
    Marisol's wish for a dog comes true when a neighborhood stray ''adopts'' her and wins her reluctant grandfather's heart too.

`1314`

DANNY SHANAHAN, Author/Illustrator

Buckledown the Workhound

(Boston: Little, Brown and Company, 1993)

Subject(s): Animals/Dogs; Work; Vacations
Age range(s): Grades K-2
Major character(s): Buckledown, Dog (overworked); Ms. Bowsa, Secretary; Lenore, Child
Time period(s): 1990s (1993)
Locale(s): United States (Shirttail Wagon Farm)

Summary: Buckledown has worked himself to the bone and now he is dog-tired. At the suggestion of his secretary he vacations at her niece's farm where he learns how to behave like a typical dog. When Lenore announces that her family has an opening for a full-time family dog, Buckledown realizes that he's ready for a career change and turns his company over to Ms. Bowsa so he can begin leading a dog's life. First picture book by the author. (unpaged)

Where it's reviewed:
Booklist, May 1, 1993, page 1606
Children's Book Review Service, July 1993, page 149
Five Owls, May 1993, page 113
Publishers Weekly, May 24, 1993, page 86
School Library Journal, September 1993, page 218

Other books you might like:
Debra Barracca, *Maxi, the Star*, 1993
    The third of adventure of Maxi and his taxi-driver owner sends them to Hollywood where Maxi makes a commercial. Co-author Sal Barracca.
Susan Meddaugh, *Martha Calling*, 1994
    Martha makes the most of the vacation she wins in a radio call-in contest despite the resort's ''No Dogs Allowed'' policy.
Dav Pilkey, *Dog Breath: The Horrible Trouble with Hally Tosis*, 1994
    The Tosis family changes their plans to give away Hally, their dog with bad breath, when her one flaw proves to be the undoing of burglars.

1315

DAVID SHANNON, Author/Illustrator

The Amazing Christmas Extravaganza

(New York: The Blue Sky Press, 1995)

Subject(s): Christmas; Neighbors and Neighborhoods; Change
Age range(s): Grades 1-3
Major character(s): Mr. Merriweather, Father, Neighbor; Mr. Clack, Neighbor
Time period(s): Indeterminate Past
Locale(s): United States

Summary: Until the year a neighborly competition begins, Mr. Merriweather has always been content with simple Christmas decorations. However, this year Mr. Merriweather becomes so focussed on his decorations he loses sight of the meaning of the holiday until the neighbors, led by Mr. Clack, destroy the bothersome displays. Hearing Mr. Merriweather's humble response to their action, the neighbors realize the error of their ways and help clean up the mess they've made before everyone returns to celebrating the holiday in a simpler fashion. (32 pages)

Where it's reviewed:
Booklist, September 15, 1995, page 172
Children's Book Review Service, October 1995, page 16
Five Owls, November 1995, page 44
Kirkus Reviews, October 15, 1995, page 1502
School Library Journal, October 1995, page 41

Other books by the same author:
How Georgie Radbourn Saved Baseball, 1994

Other books you might like:
Mariana, *Miss Flora McFlimsey's Christmas Eve*, 1949
    With help from Timothy Mouse, an angel, and her own belief, Miss Flora has a joyful Christmas that proves wishes do come true.
Dav Pilkey, *Dragon's Merry Christmas*, 1991
    In four episodes of a beginning reader, lovable Dragon demonstrates the true Christmas spirit.
James Stevenson, *The Worst Person's Christmas*, 1991
    The Worst tries to avoid Christmas, but the spirit of the holiday expressed in the children's gift and a neighborhood party finds him.

1316

GEORGE SHANNON
THOMAS B. ALLEN, Illustrator

Climbing Kansas Mountains

(New York: Bradbury Press, 1993)

Subject(s): Fathers and Sons; Summer; Love
Age range(s): Grades K-3
Major character(s): Sam, Child; Unnamed Character, Father
Time period(s): 1990s (1993)
Locale(s): Kansas

Summary: On a hot, lazy summer day, when it looks to Sam as if there's nothing to do, his father suggests that it's time to climb a Kansas mountain. Sam is old enough to know that Kansas is flat, but he willingly accompanies his father. Sure enough, Dad drives him to the only thing to climb in Kansas—the tall grain elevators where he works, giving Sam another view of the world in which he lives and a special shared moment with his dad. (32 pages)

Where it's reviewed:
Booklist, September 1, 1993, page 71
Bulletin of the Center for Children's Books, January 1994, page 168
Publishers Weekly, August 9, 1993, page 477
School Library Journal, December 1993, page 94

Awards the book has won:
School Library Journal Best Books, 1993

Other books by the same author:
April Showers, 1995
Lizard's Song, 1981
The Piney Woods Peddler, 1981

Other books you might like:
Donald Hall, *The Farm Summer 1942*, 1994
    During a summer visit to his grandparents, Peter is introduced to the way of life of a New Hampshire farm.
Patricia MacLachlan, *All the Places to Love*, 1994
    From a young age, Eli is aware that all the places he could ever love are on the family farm.
Alexandra Wallner, *Since 1920*, 1992
    Over the generations, a family home experiences change, decline and renewal of the neighborhhood.
Jane Yolen, *Owl Moon*, 1987
    A father shares a memorable time with his young daughter when they set off into the snowy woods in hopes of seeing an owl on a moonlit night.

1317

GEORGE SHANNON
STEVE BJORKMAN, Illustrator

Heart to Heart

(Boston: Houghton Mifflin Company, 1995)

Subject(s): Animals/Squirrels; Animals/Moles; Friendship
Age range(s): Grades K-2
Major character(s): Squirrel, Squirrel, Friend; Mole, Mole, Friend
Time period(s): 1990s (1995)
Locale(s): Fictional Country

Summary: When Squirrel finds a Happy Valentine's Day card in his mailbox from his good friend Mole, he realizes that he has completely forgotten about Valentine's Day. Hurriedly, he gathers the materials to make a magnificent card, but he can't locate his scissors. However, in his search he discovers one of Mole's lost mittens which gives him an idea for a gift that can only be shared by true friends. (32 pages)

Where it's reviewed:
Booklist, November 15, 1995, page 565
Horn Book Guide, Spring 1996, page 45
School Library Journal, November 1995, page 81

Other books by the same author:
Seeds, 1994
Lizard's Song, 1992

The Surprise, 1983

Other books you might like:

Arnold Lobel, *Frog and Toad Are Friends*, 1970
   In several brief stories, Frog and Toad share some of the
   difficulties as well as the pleasures of friendship.
Thacher Hurd, *Little Mouse's Big Valentine*, 1990
   Little Mouse has made a special valentine, now he's trying
   to find a recipient.
Mariana, *Miss Flora McFlimsey's Valentine*, 1962
   Miss Flora McFlimsey creates original cards to send her
   friends for Valentine's Day.
John Schindel, *I'll Meet You Halfway*, 1993
   Titus and Fuller plan special gifts for each other, but learn
   that the best gift of all is their friendship.

`1318`

GEORGE SHANNON
STEVE BJORKMAN, Illustrator

Seeds

(Boston: Houghton Mifflin Company, 1994)

Subject(s): Friendship; Gardens and Gardening; Moving,
   Household
Age range(s): Grades K-2
Major character(s): Warren, Child, Neighbor; Bill, Gardener,
   Artist
Time period(s): 1990s (1994)
Locale(s): United States

Summary: The intergenerational friendship between Warren
and Bill is interupted when Warren's family moves to another
town. Warren and Bill miss their times together, working in
the garden, sharing stories and playing riddle games. When
Warren writes Bill of his idea to create a garden at his new
home, Bill responds with a package of seeds and a new
storybook idea inspired by Warren. (32 pages)

Where it's reviewed:
Booklist, June 1, 1994, page 1844
Children's Book Review Service, May 1994, page 113
Five Owls, September 1994, page 11
Kirkus Reviews, February 15, 1994, page 233
School Library Journal, April 1994, page 114

Other books by the same author:
Laughing All the Way, 1992
Dance Away!, 1982
Lizard's Song, 1981

Other books you might like:
Monica Hughes, *A Handful of Seeds*, 1993
   Heeding her deceased grandmother's advice, Concepcion
   plants a garden, saving enough seeds from her crop to
   begin again the next year.
Elaine Moore, *Grandma's Garden*, 1994
   Annually, Kim and Grandma plant a garden when the
   spring weather warms the soil.
Joanne Ryder, *My Father's Hands*, 1994
   While digging in the garden, Father shows his patiently
   waiting daughter the treasures of nature that he finds.

`1319`

MARGARET SHANNON, Author/Illustrator

Elvira

(New York: Ticknor & Fields, 1993)

Subject(s): Dragons; Identity; Outcasts
Age range(s): Grades K-2
Major character(s): Elvira, Mythical Creature (dragon), Out-
   cast
Time period(s): Indeterminate Past
Locale(s): Fictional Country

Summary: Gentle Elvira is mocked by the other dragons because of her distaste for fighting or eating princesses and her
preference for making flower chains or adorning herself with
forest finery. When she tires of the teasing, Elvira goes to live
with the princesses who are, initially, not pleased to welcome
a dragon. Elvira enjoys the life of a princess until her father
mistakes her for a very large one and almost eats her, prompting her to return home. The first book for the author was
originally published in Australia in 1991. (32 pages)

Where it's reviewed:
Booklist, August 1993, page 2071
Childrens Book Review Service, September 1993, page 4
Horn Book, September 1993, page 591
Publishers Weekly, June 28, 1993, page 76
School Library Journal, September 1993, page 219

Other books you might like:
Mary Blackwood, *Derek the Knitting Dinosaur*, 1990
   Unlike his ferocious brothers, Derek prefers to knit, a trait
   appreciated by all when the weather becomes cold and
   Derek passes out hand-knit hats and sweaters.
Margaret Hillert, *A Friend for Dear Dragon*, 1985
   A new neighbor with a pet unicorn provides friendship for
   a boy's pet dragon.
Katharine Holabird, *Alexander and the Dragon*, 1988
   The shadow under a fearful boy's bed becomes a dragon
   who, fortunately, has a gentle nature.
Munro Leaf, *Ferdinand*, 1936
   Ferdinand is a bull with a mind of his own and an interest
   in flowers.
Mercer Mayer, *Whinnie the Lovesick Dragon*, 1986
   When a dragon falls in love with a knight, she cannot
   understand his reluctance to develop a relationship.
Dav Pilkey, *A Friend for Dragon*, 1991
   In the first of the tales about lonely Dragon, he makes
   friends with an apple, mourns its inevitable demise and
   rejoices when a new crop of "friends" grows.

`1320`

MARJORIE WEINMAN SHARMAT
MITCHELL RIGIE, Illustrator

Genghis Khan: A Dog Star Is Born

(New York: Random House, 1994)

Series: First Stepping Stone Book
Subject(s): Animals/Dogs; Movie Industry; Kidnapping
Age range(s): Grades 2-4

Major character(s): Duz, Dog; Fred Shedd, Child; Pamela Brinkman, Child, Friend (Fred's)
Time period(s): 1990s (1994)
Locale(s): Hollywood, California

Summary: In a sequel to *The Great Genghis Khan Look-Alike Contest* Duz heads to Hollywood for a year of movie-making in the company of Fred and his parents. Someone, determined to stop Duz's climb to stardom, kidnaps him and Fred calls Pamela for help. (71 pages)

Where it's reviewed:
Booklist, January 1, 1995, page 822
Horn Book Guide, Spring 1995, page 70
School Library Journal, September 1994, page 199

Other books by the same author:
The Great Gengis Khan Look-Alike Contest, 1993
Nate the Great, 1986
Mitchell Is Moving, 1978

Other books you might like:
David A. Adler, *My Dog and the Birthday Mystery*, 1987
    Jenny thinks she is solving the mystery of a stolen bicycle, but she's actually on a trail leading to her surprise birthday party.
Mary Blount Christian, *The Sebastian (Super Sleuth) Series*, 1982-
    Sebastian, an English sheepdog, is the case-solving side-kick of his master John Jones.
Dick King-Smith, *Harry's Mad*, 1988
    When Mad, a talking parrot is stolen, he's smart enough to find his way home again.

1321

MARJORIE WEINMAN SHARMAT
ROSALIND WEINMAN, Illustrator
MARC SIMONT, Illustrator

Nate the Great and the Pillowcase

(New York: Delacorte Press, 1993)

Series: Nate the Great Detective
Subject(s): Mystery and Detective Stories; Humor; Pets
Age range(s): Grades 1-3
Major character(s): Nate "the Great", Detective—Amateur; Sludge, Dog (Nate's pet); Rosamund, Child
Time period(s): 1990s (1993)
Locale(s): United States

Summary: Awakened late one night by his friend Rosamund, Nate begrudgingly agrees to locate her cat's missing pillowcase so they can all get a good night's sleep. With Sludge's help, Nate follows the clues until his slippers are worn out, and once again he succeeds in solving the case. (48 pages)

Where it's reviewed:
Booklist, November 15, 1993, page 626
Horn Book Guide, Spring 1994, page 62
Library Talk, May 1994, page 42
Reading Teacher, September 1994, page 71
School Library Journal, February 1994, page 92

Other books by the same author:
Nate the Great and the Stolen Base, 1992
Nate the Great Stalks Stupidweed, 1989
Nate the Great Goes Undercover, 1978

Other books you might like:
David A. Adler, *Cam Jansen and the Mystery at the Monkey House*, 1985
    In her 10th adventure, Cam Jansen uses her photographic memory and the help of her friends to solve the mystery of disappearing monkeys.
Eve Bunting, *The Skate Patrol*, 1980
    Milton and James meet with success as they track down a thief.
Elizabeth Levy, *The Something Queer Series*, 1971-
    Gwen, Jill and basset hound Fletcher have one adventure after another while they solve mysterious occurrences.

1322

MARJORIE WEINMAN SHARMAT
CRAIG SHARMAT, Illustrator
MARC SIMONT, Illustrator

Nate the Great and the Tardy Tortoise

(New York: Delacorte Press, 1995)

Series: Nate the Great Detective
Subject(s): Animals/Turtles; Mystery and Detective Stories; Animals/Dogs
Age range(s): Grades 1-3
Major character(s): Nate "the Great", Child, Detective—Amateur; Sludge, Dog; Speedy, Tortoise
Time period(s): 1990s (1995)
Locale(s): United States

Summary: To protect the flowers in his yard from an invading tortoise, Nate the Great takes on the mission of locating the animal's home. With Sludge's assistance, Nate first checks with several friends and a veterinary office before he comes up with an idea that leads the pair down the trail to Speedy's owner. (48 pages)

Where it's reviewed:
Booklist, October 1, 1995, page 329
Horn Book Guide, Spring 1996, page 52
School Library Journal, October 1995, page 119

Other books by the same author:
Nate the Great and the Musical Note, 1991
Nate the Great and the Snowy Trail, 1984
Nate the Great, 1977

Other books you might like:
David A. Adler, *Cam Jansen and the Mystery at the Monkey House*, 1985
    In her 10th adventure, Cam Jansen uses her photographic memory and the help of her friends to solve the mystery of disappearing monkeys.
Elizabeth Levy, *The Something Queer Series*, 1971 -
    Gwen, Jill and basset hound Fletcher have one adventure after another while they solve mysterious occurrences.
Lucinda Landon, *The Meg Mackintosh Series*, 1986-
    In a series of solve-it-yourself mysteries, Meg Mackintosh is a winner any way you read the story.

1323

NANCY SHAW
MARGOT APPLE, Illustrator

Sheep Take a Hike

(Boston: Houghton Mifflin Company, 1994)

Subject(s): Animals/Sheep; Hiking; Stories in Rhyme
Age range(s): Grades K-1
Major character(s): Unnamed Character, Sheep
Time period(s): Indeterminate
Locale(s): Fictional Country

Summary: Six sheep set off on a hike which leads them up hills, through underbrush and into a bog where they stay mired until rescued by a moose. Sure that they are hopelessly lost, the sheep are happy to discover tufts of snagged wool on bushes and follow the trail they have unwittingly left home to the comfort of a cup of tea and a warm afghan. (32 pages)

Where it's reviewed:
Booklist, September 15, 1994, page 144
Horn Book, November 1994, page 726
Publishers Weekly, July 4, 1994, page 60
Reading Teacher, October 1995, page 139
School Library Journal, September 1994, page 199

Awards the book has won:
International Reading Association Children's Choice, 1995

Other books by the same author:
Sheep out to Eat, 1992
Sheep in a Shop, 1991
Sheep in a Jeep, 1986

Other books you might like:
Kevin Kiser, *Sherman the Sheep*, 1994
    Sherman is chosen to lead the flock to a new home.
Judith Ross Enderle, *Six Snowy Sheep*, 1994
    Six sheep receive gifts to use in the snow.
Monica Wellington, *The Sheep Follow*, 1992
    All day a flock of sheep follow any animal that passes by and now they are too tired to follow the shepherd.

1324

PEGI DEITZ SHEA
ANITA RIGGIO, Illustrator

The Whispering Cloth: A Refugee's Story

(Honesdale, PA: Boyds Mills Press, Inc., 1995)

Subject(s): Refugees; Grandparents; Artists and Art
Age range(s): Grades 2-4
Major character(s): Mai, Orphan, Refugee (Hmong); Grandma, Grandmother, Refugee (Hmong)
Time period(s): 1990s (1994)
Locale(s): Ban Vinai, Thailand

Summary: Mai's cousins move to America, leaving Mai to sit at the Widow's Store watching the old women stitch *pa'ndau* story cloths. Grandma teaches Mai how to make the uniform stitches of the border, but cautions her that, until she has a story of her own to tell, she is not ready to make the interior story panel. In time, Mai stitches her own story cloth, repre-senting her tragic past and the hope she has for the future. An introductory glossary and author's note give background information and credit to co-illustrator You Yang for stitching Mai's panel. (32 pages)

Where it's reviewed:
Booklist, January 1, 1995, page 827
Children's Book Review Index, March 1995, page 93
Five Owls, May 1995, page 106
Publishers Weekly, December 19, 1994, page 61
School Library Journal, March 1995, page 187

Other books by the same author:
Bungalow Fungalow, 1991

Other books you might like:
Sherry Garland, *The Lotus Seed*, 1993
    When a young girl escapes from Vietnam she carries a lotus seed as a remembrance of her country and its last emperor.
Allen Say, *Grandfather's Journey*, 1993
    A grandson completes his grandfather's journey between homeland and adopted land, memory and desire.
Amy Tan, *The Moon Lady*, 1992
    Now living in the United States, a grandmother reminisces about her childhood in China.

1325

ANNE SHELBY
WENDY ANDERSON HALPERIN, Illustrator

Homeplace

(New York: Orchard Books, 1995)

Subject(s): Family Life; Grandparents; Farm Life
Age range(s): Grades K-2
Major character(s): Unnamed Character, Grandmother; Unnamed Character, Child
Time period(s): 19th century; 20th century (1810-1995)
Locale(s): United States

Summary: While rocking her grandchild, a grandmother tells the origins of the homeplace originally built by the child's great-great-great-great grandpa. Through the generations, additions are made to the home and the family right up to the present day. The text details the continuity of family ties while the illustrations reveal the changes over time. (32 pages)

Where it's reviewed:
Booklist, February 15, 1995, page 1095
Children's Book Review Service, April 1995, page 101
Library Talk, September 1995, page 31
Publishers Weekly, March 6, 1995, page 69
School Library Journal, April 1995, page 118

Awards the book has won:
School Library Journal Best Books, 1995

Other books by the same author:
What to Do about Pollution, 1993
Potluck, 1991
We Keep a Store, 1990

Other books you might like:

Virginia Lee Burton, *The Little House*, 1942

The passage of time and connectedness of family over the generations is chronicled in the experiences of a house. Caldecott Medal Winner.

Donald Hall, *Old Home Day*, 1996

The cycle of growth, decline and renewal of a New England town is described through the history of its settlers.

Patricia MacLachlan, *All the Places to Love*, 1994

A young boy thinks of all the places to love on the family farm that he will share with his baby sister as she grows.

Alice Schertle, *Maisie*, 1994

The story of 90-year-old Maisie's life is also a record of the changes in America during her lifetime and the celebration of family ties.

1326

DYAN SHELDON
SUE HEAP, Illustrator

Harry on Vacation
(Cambridge, MA: Candlewick Press, 1993)

Subject(s): Animals/Cats; Time Travel; Vacations
Age range(s): Grades 3-5
Major character(s): Harry "Destructor Cat", Cat, Alien (from the planet Arcana); Sara Jane "Chicken" Thomas, 10-Year-Old (youngest of 3 siblings)
Time period(s): 1990s (1992)
Locale(s): England

Summary: While their parents may consider a family camping trip the perfect way to spend a summer vacation, Sara Jane and her older siblings are unhappy at the prospect of being stuck together in a car and a tent for 4 weeks. Harry, who is thrilled with the plans, is forbidden to come, but some last-minute trickery enables him to join the tour. The educational, family vacation becomes more than anyone expects thanks to Harry's ability to travel back in time and his penchant for getting even with the teasing siblings. First published in Great Britain in 1992. (138 pages)

Where it's reviewed:
Booklist, June 1, 1993, page 1836
Horn Book Guide, Fall 1993, page 304
School Library Journal, June 1993, page 110

Other books by the same author:
My Brother Is a Visitor from Another Planet, 1993
Harry and Chicken, 1992
Harry the Explorer, 1992

Other books you might like:

Susan Cooper, *The Boggart*, 1993

A family inherits a shape-changing trickster along with a Scottish castle.

Gery Greer, *Jason and the Escape from Bat Planet*, 1993

With alien neighbor Coop and a talking cat creature, Jason saves an absent-minded professor from the clutches of the Bat Planet leader. Co-author Bob Ruddick.

Elisabet McHugh, *Wiggie Wins the West*, 1989

A family car trip through the West gives cat Wiggie ample

opportunity to display his skill and bravery by rescuing family members.

1327

DYAN SHELDON
DEREK BRAZELL, Illustrator

My Brother Is a Visitor from Another Planet
(Cambridge, MA: Candlewick Press, 1993)

Subject(s): Brothers; Aliens; Humor
Age range(s): Grades 4-6
Major character(s): Adam Wiggins, 9-Year-Old, Brother; Keith Wiggins, 13-Year-Old (practical joker), Brother; Midge, 9-Year-Old, Friend (Adam's)
Time period(s): 1990s (1992)
Locale(s): England

Summary: A lifetime of insults and practical jokes from Keith have made Adam wary, but still he falls for the latest one when Keith "confesses" that he's really from another planet and he needs Adam's help to contact his spaceship. The elaborate plot which Keith concocts with help from a friend ensnares Adam and Midge until they discover the truth. Originally published in Great Britain in 1992. (104 pages)

Where it's reviewed:
Booklist, August 1993, page 2063
Children's Book Review Service, August 1993, page 168
Horn Book Guide, Fall 1993, page 304
Instructor, October 1993, page 68
School Library Journal, May 1993, page 108

Other books by the same author:
Harry on Vacation, 1993
Harry and Chicken, 1992
Harry the Explorer, 1992

Other books you might like:

Dennis Haseley, *Getting Him*, 1994

Feigning friendship, Donald instead plans an elaborate hoax to make Harold believe that a spaceship of aliens is coming to earth.

Stephen Manes, *It's New! It's Improved! It's Terrible!*, 1989

He looks like a boy, talks like a television commercial, but is really an alien who's driving Arnold and his friends crazy.

Daniel Manus Pinkwater, *Fat Men from Space*, 1977

While earthlings may count their calories, these aliens are here in search of junk food.

1328

DYAN SHELDON
GARY BLYTHE, Illustrator

Under the Moon
(New York: Dial Books for Young Readers, 1994)

Subject(s): Indians of North America; Dreams and Nightmares; Imagination
Age range(s): Grades 1-4
Major character(s): Jenny, Child

Time period(s): 1990s (1994)
Locale(s): United States

Summary: Finding an arrowhead in her yard prompts Jenny to question life in her commuity long ago. With her mother's guidance she tries to imagine her neighborhood without homes, roads, and cars. That night, as she sleeps in her tent in the yard, she dreams of Indians, tepees and campfires. The experience allows her imagination to recapture that past time when she awakens. (32 pages)

Where it's reviewed:
Booklist, June 1, 1994, page 1845
Bulletin of the Center for Children's Books, May 1994, page 302
Kirkus Reviews, June 1, 1994, page 782
Publishers Weekly, March 21, 1994, page 71
School Library Journal, June 1994, page 113

Other books by the same author:
The Whales' Song, 1991

Other books you might like:
Leigh Casler, *The Boy Who Dreamed of an Acorn*, 1994
    A young Indian boy learns to appreciate the symbolism of his dream about an acorn knowing that it is the source of a mighty tree.
George Ella Lyon, *Dreamplace*, 1993
    While visiting the ruins of ancient cliff dwellings a young girl imagines the life of the people who originally occupied the area.
George Ella Lyon, *Who Came Down That Road?*, 1992
    In response to her daughter's question, a mother lists the people and animals who travelled a road before the two of them.
Audrey Osofsky, *Dreamcatcher*, 1992
    An Ojibway baby sleeps, protected from bad dreams by the traditional dream catcher.

1329

CAROL DIGGORY SHIELDS
PAUL MEISEL, Illustrator

I Am Really a Princess

(New York: Dutton Children's Books, 1993)

Subject(s): Imagination; Parent and Child; Princes and Princesses
Age range(s): Grades K-2
Major character(s): Unnamed Character, Child, Royalty (princess)
Time period(s): 1990s (1993)
Locale(s): United States

Summary: A disgruntled big sister is sure that, when her real parents the king and queen show up, her life will improve. Imagining life as a princess when she can have a pony for a pet and never eat mushy foods like lima beans seems idyllic until the king and queen report that no one tickles, cuddles or snuggles a princess at bedtime. Hmm, is she really a princess? (32 pages)

Where it's reviewed:
Children's Book Review Service, Winter 1994, page 66
Horn Book Guide, Spring 1994, page 54

Language Arts, April 1994, page 298
Publishers Weekly, August 9, 1993, page 477
School Library Journal, November 1993, page 90

Other books by the same author:
Loving a Happy Dog, 1992
Can Dogs Talk, 1991

Other books you might like:
Elisa Kleven, *The Paper Princess*, 1994
    A girl's drawing of a princess blows away on a series of adventures before returning to the artist.
Tony Ross, *I Want to Be*, 1993
    Trying to understand how to grow up while maintaining her individuality, a young princess receives advice from everyone.
Susan L. Roth, *Princess*, 1993
    A reluctant riser imagines life as a princess when she will not go to school.
Ann Turnbull, *The Tapestry Cats*, 1992
    The lonely princess in this story is genuine, but she imagines the cats on her tapestry to be her playmates.

1330

SUSAN RICHARDS SHREVE
DIANE DE GROAT, Illustrator

Amy Dunn Quits School

(New York: Tambourine Books, 1993)

Subject(s): Mothers and Daughters; Single Parent Families; Independence
Age range(s): Grades 4-6
Major character(s): Amy Dunn, 6th Grader, Child of Divorced Parents (perfect); Nicole Dunn, Single Mother, Lawyer
Time period(s): 1990s (1993)
Locale(s): New York, New York

Summary: Supermom's efforts to create a perfect life for Amy lead to pressure and guilt instead as Amy decides to take the day off from all commitments. She skips school, ballet, soccer, piano and the school's Halloween Parade. When Nicole attends the parade to see her daughter in the costume she has made for her, she is surprised to learn that Amy is absent. She hurries home, relieved to find Amy safe and finally able to admit to her mother that she'd like a little unscheduled time in her life. (96 pages)

Where it's reviewed:
Booklist, September 1, 1993, page 62
Horn Book Guide, Spring 1994, page 82
Publishers Weekly, October 25, 1993, page 63
Quill & Quire, March 1994, page 83
School Library Journal, September 1993, page 235

Other books by the same author:
The Formerly Great Alexander Family, 1995
Joshua T. Bates Takes Charge, 1993
The Gift of the Girl Who Couldn't Hear, 1991 (Booklist Editors' Choice)

Other books you might like:
Sandy Asher, *Teddy Teabury's Peanutty Problems*, 1989
    Sixth grader Teddy is overwhelmed by everyone's expectations of him.

Mary Jane Miller, *Fast Forward*, 1993
> Feeling pressured to meet her parent's expectations, Kayla makes a bad decision regarding a school project, but learns from the experience.

Gayle Pearson, *One Potato, Tu: Seven Stories*, 1992
> Seven short stories look at life from the perspective of 12-year-old Lindsey.

1331

SUSAN RICHARDS SHREVE
CHRIS CART, Illustrator

The Formerly Great Alexander Family
(New York: Tambourine Books, 1995)

Subject(s): Divorce; Fathers and Sons; Brothers and Sisters
Age range(s): Grades 3-5
Major character(s): Liam Alexander, 10-Year-Old, Brother; Henry Alexander, Father
Time period(s): 1990s (1995)
Locale(s): Seattle, Washington (Randlewood)

Summary: Liam, the only boy in the absolutely perfect Alexander family, is crushed to learn that his parents are divorcing. After Henry Alexander moves out of the home, Liam is too embarassed to face his friends and drops off the baseball team. During summer vacation, his sisters each suffer in their own way and his mother is always sad. Everyone hopes that, by August, life will be "normal" again. While the summer does not bring his family back to its prior perfect state, it does give Liam some hope that his redefined family will survive. (91 pages)

Where it's reviewed:
Horn Book, November 1995, page 744
Horn Book Guide, Spring 1996, page 69
Kirkus Reviews, June 15, 1995, page 862
Publishers Weekly, June 12, 1995, page 61
School Library Journal, September 1995, page 203

Other books by the same author:
The Gift of the Girl Who Couldn't Hear, 1991
Lucy Forever and Miss Rosetree, Shrinks, 1988
The Flunking of Joshua T. Bates, 1984

Other books you might like:
Eve Bunting, *The In-Between Days*, 1994
> When his widowed father meets a woman he hopes to marry, Georgie wonders how he will fit into his father's new life.

Beverly Cleary, *Strider*, 1991
> As Leigh Botts learns to accept his parents' divorce he find the confidence to join the track team.

Paula Danziger, *Amber Brown Goes Fourth*, 1995
> Amber Brown begins fourth grade coping not only with her best friend's recent move, but also her parents' divorce.

Marilyn Levinson, *No Boys Allowed*, 1994
> Cassie's uncle helps her adjust to the many changes in her life after her father leaves the family.

1332

SUSAN RICHARDS SHREVE
DAN ANDREASEN, Illustrator

Joshua T. Bates Takes Charge
(New York: Alfred A. Knopf, 1993)

Subject(s): Schools; Popularity; Bullies
Age range(s): Grades 3-5
Major character(s): Joshua T. Bates, 5th Grader, Bullied Child; Tommy Wilhelm, 5th Grader (Joshua's enemy), Bully (feared); Sean O'Malley, 5th Grader (new student), Bullied Child
Time period(s): 1990s (1993)
Locale(s): Washington, District of Columbia (Mirch Elementary School)

Summary: In a sequel to *The Flunking of Joshua T. Bates* Joshua is just beginning to recover from the humiliation of being held back in third grade when a new student arrives at his school and his teachers expect him to be Sean's escort and introduction to the school. Because Sean is small and carries a Mickey Mouse lunch box, Tommy and his gang of bullies have fun teasing both Sean and Joshua. Desperate to finally be accepted by his peers and fearing Tommy, Joshua is torn between sympathizing with Sean or distancing himself from him in order to avoid Tommy's humiliating comments. (102 pages)

Where it's reviewed:
Booklist, July 1993, page 1967
Horn Book Guide, Fall 1993, page 305
Instructor, September 1994, page 103
Reading Teacher, September 1994, page 65
School Library Journal, August 1993, page 166

Other books by the same author:
Amy Dunn Quits School, 1993
The Gift of the Girl Who Couldn't Hear, 1991
Lucy Forever and Miss Rosetree, Shrinks, 1988 (Edgar Allan Poe Award)

Other books you might like:
Jeanne Betancourt, *My Name Is Brain/Brian*, 1993
> With support from an understanding teacher and help for his reading problem, Brian comes to a new understanding of friendship and school.

Virginia Scribner, *Gopher Takes Heart*, 1993
> Gopher finds a way to work with Fletcher to end the bully's harrassment of him.

Meredith Sue Willis, *The Secret Super Powers of Marco*, 1994
> To cope in his new home and school, Marco convinces himself that he has super powers which help him befriend bully Tyrone.

1333

SUSAN RICHARDS SHREVE
GREGG THORKELSON, Illustrator

Zoe and Columbo

(New York: Tambourine Books, 1995)

Subject(s): Brothers and Sisters; Adoption; Moving, Household
Age range(s): Grades 3-4
Major character(s): Zoe DeRosa, 9-Year-Old, Sister; Columbo DeRosa, 4th Grader, Adoptee
Time period(s): 1990s (1995)
Locale(s): Lyme, Connecticut; Providence, Rhode Island

Summary: When Zoe and Columbo move from Lyme to Providence, Columbo decides to tell everyone that he and Zoe are twins. In Lyme, Columbo had been proud to be adopted, but now he has no friends while Zoe does; he hates the new school while Zoe likes it; and on Zoe's birthday everyone will realize he's been lying. Feeling heartsick, Columbo stays home from school on Zoe's birthday, but comes to the realization that it's time for him to tell the truth. (71 pages)

Where it's reviewed:
Booklist, December 15, 1995, page 705
Bulletin of the Center for Children's Books, February 1996, page 203
Horn Book Guide, Spring 1996, page 69
School Library Journal, January 1996, page 110

Other books by the same author:
The Formerly Great Alexander Family, 1995
The Gift of the Girl Who Couldn't Hear, 1991 (Booklist Editor's Choice)
Lucy Forever and Miss Rosetree, Shrinks, 1988

Other books you might like:
C.S. Adler, *Youn Hee and Me*, 1995
    When Youn Hee joins the American family that has adopted her brother, she has a difficult time adjusting to the culture of her new country and home.
Matt Christopher, *Double Play at Short*, 1995
    A girl on the opposing team seems somehow familiar to Danny. His curious inquiries lead to new information about his adoption.
Walter Dean Myers, *Mop, Moondance and the Nagasaki Knights*, 1992
    Adopted brothers reach out to help a homeless player on their baseball team.

1334

URI SHULEVITZ, Author/Illustrator

The Golden Goose

(New York: Farrar Straus Giroux, 1995)

Subject(s): Folk Tales; Magic; Humor
Age range(s): Grades K-2
Major character(s): Unnamed Character, Woodsman; Unnamed Character, Aged Person, Wizard
Time period(s): Indeterminate Past
Locale(s): Europe

Summary: In a brightly illustrated retelling of the Brothers Grimm tale, the third son in a family sets off into the forest to cut wood after his two older brothers are injured while trying. The youngest son is considered to be a simpleton, but he is kind to an old man in the woods and that kindness is rewarded with a golden goose. The young man proceeds to an inn with the golden goose and through a chain of events begun by the innkeeper's greedy daughters, he leaves with a parade of townspeople all stuck in a long line behind the goose. The procession causes an unhappy princess to laugh and the simple, kindly young man wins her hand in marriage. (32 pages)

Where it's reviewed:
Booklist, November 15, 1995, page 562
Bulletin of the Center for Children's Books, January 1996, page 171
Kirkus Reviews, October 1, 1995, page 1428
Publishers Weekly, November 6, 1995, page 94
School Library Journal, December 1995, page 97

Awards the book has won:
Book Links Good Book, 1995

Other books by the same author:
The Treasure, 1979
New Monday Morning, 1974
Rain Rain Rivers, 1969

Other books you might like:
L. Leslie Brooke, *The Golden Goose Book: A Fairy Tale Picture Book*, 1992
    The illustrated reissue of a book originally published in 1904 includes four classic fairy tales.
Jacob Grimm, *The Golden Goose*, 1988
    A variation of the Grimm Brothers' humorous fairy tale is retold by Susan Saunders.
Steven Kellogg, *Jack and the Beanstalk*, 1991
    With characteristically zany illustrations, Kellogg portrays lazy Jack, his unusual beans, and the giant's castle with the magical goose.

1335

JUDY SIERRA
WILL HILLENBRAND, Illustrator

The House That Drac Built

(San Diego: Harcourt Brace & Company, 1995)

Subject(s): Haunted Houses; Halloween; Stories in Rhyme
Age range(s): Grades K-3
Major character(s): Drac, Vampire
Time period(s): 1990s (1995)
Locale(s): United States

Summary: In the house that Drac built a cat bites a bat and is chased by a werewolf who is then wrestled by a manticore. By the time the rhyme gets to the trick-or-treaters at the door, a monster, a mummy, a zombie and the fiend of Bloodygore have also appeared. The trick-or-treaters bandage the bat, rewrap the mummy, cage the werewolf, sooth the manticore, and continue on their Halloween way. (32 pages)

Where it's reviewed:
Booklist, September 15, 1995, page 173
Children's Book Review Service, September 1995, page 4

Horn Book, November 1995, page 730
Publishers Weekly, September 18, 1995, page 89
School Library Journal, September 1995, page 186

Other books by the same author:
The Elephant's Wrestling Match, 1992

Other books you might like:
Allan Ahlberg, *Funnybones*, 1981
   In the deep, dark cellar of an old, gloomy house lurk a host of happy skeletons.
Bill Martin Jr., *Old Devil Wind*, 1993
   A small wailing ghost begins a cumulative tale that concludes when the wind blows everything away until Halloween night.
Alvin Schwartz, *In a Dark, Dark Room and Other Scary Stories*, 1984
   An award-winning beginning reader includes seven spooky stories.
Caroline Stutson, *By the Light of the Halloween Moon*, 1993
   One by one scary Halloween creatures are attracted to the bare toe of a young girl playing her violin by the light of the moon.

1336

ERICA SILVERMAN
S.D. SCHINDLER, Illustrator

Don't Fidget a Feather
(New York: Macmillan Books for Young Readers, 1994)

Subject(s): Contests; Animals/Ducks; Animals/Geese
Age range(s): Grades K-1
Major character(s): Duck, Duck; Gander, Goose; Fox, Fox
Time period(s): 1990s (1994)
Locale(s): United States

Summary: Competitive Duck and Gander are determined to outdo one another. Duck can swim faster and Gander can fly higher so they have decided that a freeze-in-place contest will resolve the question as to which one is the "champion of champions." Despite buzzing bees, hopping bunnies, and cawing crows neither bird moves. When a wind blows them into the path of hungry Fox and they are hauled off to be cooked in a stew pot, neither bird "fidgets a feather." At the last moment Duck relinquishes her contest win in order to save her friend. Gander accepts the contest victory but declares that Duck, through her heroism, is truly the "champion of champions." (32 pages)

Where it's reviewed:
Booklist, November 15, 1994, page 615
Children's Book Review Service, Winter 1995, page 66
Instructor, April 1995, page 62
Publishers Weekly, August 22, 1994, page 55
School Library Journal, January 1995, page 93

Other books by the same author:
Fixing the Crack of Dawn, 1994
Big Pumpkin, 1992
Warm in Winter, 1989

Other books you might like:
Jeni Bassett, *The Chick's Trick*, 1995
   Two young chick's find a way to trick their competitive mothers to stop comparing the two offspring.
Arnold Lobel, *Days with Frog and Toad*, 1979
   While good friends Frog and Toad enjoy spending time together, they realize that even friends need some time alone.
James Stevenson, *The Mud Flat Olympics*, 1994
   Annually a group of animal friends hold their own wacky version of the Olympics.

1337

NORMA SIMON
BARBARA SAMUELS, Illustrator

The Baby House
(New York: Simon & Schuster Books for Young Readers, 1995)

Subject(s): Babies; Birth; Pets
Age range(s): Grades K-1
Major character(s): Unnamed Character, Child; Daddy, Father
Time period(s): 1990s (1995)
Locale(s): United States

Summary: In the newly illustrated edition of a story first published in 1955, a young girl describes the anticipated arrival of babies in her family. While waiting, she contents herself with dolls, watching first the cat, then the dog and last her mother grow "rounder and rounder." Just before each birth, she helps Daddy prepare the bed for the new arrivals and, by the conclusion of the story, her wish to have all the babies is realized as she plays with kittens, puppies and a new baby brother. (32 pages)

Where it's reviewed:
Booklist, April 15, 1995, page 1508
Horn Book Guide, Fall 1995, page 282
Kirkus Reviews, March 15, 1995, page 395
School Library Journal, May 1995, page 95

Other books by the same author:
Wet World, 1995
Cats Do, Dogs Don't, 1986
All Kinds of Families, 1976

Other books you might like:
Tom Birdseye, *Waiting for Baby*, 1991
   A young boy eagerly awaits the birth of his brother.
Marisabina Russo, *Waiting for Hannah*, 1989
   Mama tells her daughter of the preparations made in anticipation of her birth.
Mildred Pitts Walter, *My Mama Needs Me*, 1983
   When his baby sister is born, Jason wants to help Mama care for her.

1338

MARILYN SINGER
TED RAND, Illustrator

In the Palace of the Ocean King

(New York: Atheneum Books for Young Readers, 1995)

Subject(s): Fairy Tale; Love; Fear
Age range(s): Grades 1-3
Major character(s): Mariana, Maiden, Heroine; Sylvain, Accident Victim; Ocean King, Royalty
Time period(s): Indeterminate Past
Locale(s): Undersea Environment/Habitat

Summary: While visiting a family friend, Mariana hears a story told by Sylvain which sparks a prophetic dream. During the visit, Mariana falls in love for the first time and is saddened when Sylvain must depart on a long voyage. The prophesy of the merman in the dream comes true when Sylvain's ship sinks and Mariana dives into the ocean that she fears in order to save her beloved from the Ocean King. (32 pages)

Where it's reviewed:
Booklist, July 1995, page 1884
Horn Book Guide, Fall 1995, page 282
Publishers Weekly, April 17, 1995, page 59
School Library Journal, August 1995, page 128

Other books by the same author:
The Painted Fan, 1994
In My Tent, 1992
The Golden Heart of Winter, 1991

Other books you might like:
Hans Christian Andersen, *The Little Mermaid*, 1994
    A retelling illustrated by Michael Hague is one of many variations of the classic tale of a mermaid who loves a human prince.
Emma Bull, *The Princess and the Lord of Night*, 1994
    Through her own initiative a princess frees herself from a lifelong curse by defeating the Lord of the Night.
Leon Garfield, *The Saracen Maid*, 1994
    Forgetful Gilbert is rescued by the Saracen maid who escapes with him to England.
Fiona Moodie, *The Boy and the Giants*, 1993
    Kind Thomas is assisted by animals he has helped in the past when he attempts to rescue his beloved Kate from a kidnapping giant.
Audrey Wood, *Rude Giants*, 1993
    Persuasive Beatrix convinces two rude giants to clean up their act and become good neighbors.

1339

MARILYN SINGER
WENHAI MA, Illustrator

The Painted Fan

(New York: Morrow Junior Books, 1994)

Subject(s): Fairy Tale; Greed; Pearls
Age range(s): Grades 1-3

Major character(s): Lord Shang, Ruler (tyrant); Bright Willow, Maiden, Heroine; Seahorse, Servant
Time period(s): Indeterminate Past
Locale(s): Land of the Seven Caves, China

Summary: When an aged soothsayer warns Lord Shang that a painted fan will be responsible for the end of his rule, he orders all fans destroyed. Bright Willow has one that has been handed down from mother to daughter which she keeps hidden even after Lord Shang she is brought to the palace as his reluctant bride-to-be. Seahorse finds the dropped fan when Bright Willow first arrives, but keeps her secret and the two begin meeting secretly. In order to save her beloved Seahorse from Lord Shang's wrath, Bright Willow agrees to retrieve the legendary Great Pearl. The secret painted fan enables Bright Willow to fulfill her quest and the soothsayer's prophesy. (40 pages)

Where it's reviewed:
Booklist, May 1, 1994, page 1609
Children's Book Review Service, June 1994, page 127
Kirkus Reviews, April 15, 1994, page 564
Publishers Weekly, April 18, 1994, page 62
School Library Journal, May 1994, page 104

Other books by the same author:
In the Palace of the Ocean King, 1995
It's Hard to Read a Map with a Beagle on Your Lap, 1993
Turtle in July, 1989

Other books you might like:
Doreen Rappaport, *The Long-Haired Girl: A Chinese Legend*, 1995
    When Ah-mei discovers a source of water controlled by the God of Thunder, she risks her life to save the villagers of her drought-stricken homeland.
Robert D. San Souci, *The Enchanted Tapestry: A Chinese Folktale*, 1987
    A sorceress assists Li Ju in his quest to recover his mother's tapestry.
Laurence Yep, *Tiger Woman*, 1994
    An old woman who refuses to share food with a beggar learns a lesson about greed.

1340

PETER SIS, Author/Illustrator

Komodo!

(New York: Greenwillow Books, 1993)

Subject(s): Animals/Komodo Dragons; Vacations
Age range(s): Grades K-1
Major character(s): Unnamed Character, Child (boy)
Time period(s): 1990s (1993)
Locale(s): Komodo Island, Indonesia

Summary: A family trip to Indonesia allows a dragon-loving boy to seek a real Komodo dragon. Leaving the crowded, orchestrated tour group, the boy wanders into the jungle and sees for himself what his parents and the other tourists are missing.(32 pages)

Where it's reviewed:
Booklist, April 15, 1993, page 1513
Horn Book Magazine, May 1993, page 325

Kirkus Reviews, May 15, 1993, page 668
Publishers Weekly, May 24, 1993, page 87
School Library Journal, July 1993, page 72

Awards the book has won:
Booklist Editors' Choice, 1993
Boston Globe/Horn Book Honor Book, 1993

Other books by the same author:
The Three Golden Keys, 1994
A Small, Tall Tale from the Far, Far North, 1993
An Ocean World, 1992
Follow the Dream, 1991
Waving, 1988

Other books you might like:
Virginia Harrison, *The World of Lizards*, 1988
 A factual look at lizards and their life. (nonfiction)
Alice Lightner Hopf, *Biography of a Komodo Dragon*, 1981
 Written as a biography of one Komodo dragon, representative of the species, this book is a factual introduction to the life cycle of the Komodo dragon in Indonesia. (nonfiction)
Louise Martin, *Komodo Dragons*, 1989
 Learn more about the life of the world's largest monitor lizard in this nonfiction work. (nonfiction)
Joanne Ryder, *Lizard in the Sun*, 1990
 A little boy really gets into lizards; he spends one day as a green anole. (Just for a Day Series)

1341

PETER SIS, Author/Illustrator

A Small, Tall Tale from the Far, Far North

(New York: Alfred A. Knopf, 1993)

Subject(s): Adventure and Adventurers; Eskimos; Survival
Age range(s): Grades 1-4
Major character(s): Jan Welzl, Adventurer
Time period(s): Indeterminate Past
Locale(s): Arctic

Summary: Seeking a better life, Jan Welzl packs his locksmith tools, loads provisions, and heads for the Far North. Weeks of travel bring him to a vast, empty frozen land where he finds shelter in a cave. Attracted to a glowing mountain in the distance he hikes toward what he thinks is gold and finds himself stuck upside down on a magnetic meteorite. Saved from certain starvation by passing Eskimo hunters, Jan also learns from them survival skills for this harsh land. Author's notes begin and conclude the story, offering factual information about the Czechoslovakian folk hero. (32 pages)

Where it's reviewed:
Booklist, November 15, 1994, page 634
Bulletin of the Center for Children's Books, September 1993, page 24
Horn Book, January 1994, page 66
Publishers Weekly, September 20, 1993, page 72
School Library Journal, September 1993, page 226

Awards the book has won:
ALA Notable Book, 1994
Boston Globe/Horn Book Honor Book, 1994

Other books by the same author:
The Three Golden Keys, 1994
An Ocean World, 1992
Follow the Dream, 1991

Other books you might like:
Pam Conrad, *Call Me Ahnighito*, 1995
 A meteorite discovered by explorer Peary in 1894 is eventually moved to a museum in New York City.
James Houston, *Tikta'liktak: An Inuit Eskimo Legend*, 1990
 A young Eskimo hunter survives the danger of polar bear attack and a long journey home.
Palle Petersen, *Inunguak: The Little Greenlander*, 1993
 Using the knowledge he's learned from his grandfather's stories, Inunguak saves his people from starvation.

1342

MICHELE BENOIT SLAWSON
DEBORAH KOGAN RAY, Illustrator

Apple Picking Time

(New York: Crown Publishers, Inc., 1994)

Subject(s): Country Life; Fall; Work
Age range(s): Grades K-3
Major character(s): Anna, Child; Papa, Father; Mama, Mother
Time period(s): Indeterminate Past
Locale(s): Apple Valley, Washington

Summary: Annually, residents of all ages of an apple-growing area take time from their usual activities to help bring in the apple harvest. Anna has always helped her parents, but never picked a full bin herself. This year she is determined to do so and earn the half-moon punch on her ticket which she can exchange at the orchard office for cash. Papa and Mama each earn several punches by lunchtime. Anna is the last to stop work for the day—when her bin is full and her ticket punched! (32 pages)

Where it's reviewed:
Booklist, September 15, 1994, page 144
Children's Book Review Service, September 1994, page 5
Horn Book, November 1994, page 726
Reading Teacher, May 1995, page 713
School Library Journal, October 1994, page 103

Other books you might like:
Arthur Dorros, *Radio Man = Don Radio: A Story in English and Spanish*, 1993
 Diego uses his everpresent radio to keep up with friends as he and his family follow the crops, bringing in the harvest.
Jane Resh Thomas, *Lights on the River*, 1994
 As her family picks the crops, Teresa's job is to babysit the younger children in a shady spot near the fields.
Sherley Anne Williams, *Working Cotton*, 1992
 Bringing in the cotton is a cooperative effort for Shelan and her family. Caldecott Honor Book; Coretta Scott King Honor Book.

1343

JAN SLEPIAN

Back to Before

(New York: Philomel, 1993)

Subject(s): Space and Time; Death; Cousins
Age range(s): Grades 4-6
Major character(s): Lionel "Linny" Erda, 11-Year-Old, Cousin; Hilary Brier, Cousin
Time period(s): 1990s
Locale(s): Brooklyn, New York; Colchester, Vermont

Summary: Linny spends the summer with his cousin, Hilary, at her new home in Vermont where each is coping with grief. Linny's mother has died in the past year, while Hilary's father has abandoned his family. One day after a bad storm they bicycle on a foggy stretch of road to survey the storm damage. Suddenly it's as though they've fallen through a hole and they're back in Brooklyn exactly one year ago. Linny's mother is still alive and Hilary's father is home; all they have to do is take steps to prevent their world from changing. Before that can happen, they are returned to the present, but not before each has seen the truthfulness of each of their situations and has come to terms with reality. (170 pages)

Where it's reviewed:
School Library Journal, October 1993, page 130
Publishers Weekly, May 24, 1993, page 89
Booklist, September 1, 1993, page 58
Locus, July 1993, page 46
Quill & Quire, August 1993, page 40

Other books by the same author:
Pinocchio's Sister, 1995
Broccoli Tapes, 1989
Night of the Bozos, 1983
The Alfred Summer, 1980

Other books you might like:
Peni R. Griffin, *A Dig in Time*, 1991
    Discovering their grandfather's pipe enables Nan and Tim to time travel in past events in the lives of family members.
Kit Pearson, *A Handful of Time*, 1988
    After observing her mother as a young girl, Patricia is able to accept her parents' divorce.
Cynthia Voigt, *Building Blocks*, 1984
    Brann travels back in time to witness his father's childhood, which helps them build a better relationship.

1344

JAN SLEPIAN
TED LEWIN, Illustrator

Lost Moose

(New York: Philomel, 1995)

Subject(s): Animals/Moose; Mothers and Sons; Nature
Age range(s): Grades K-2
Major character(s): James, Child
Time period(s): 1990s (1995)
Locale(s): United States

Summary: On a wooded, vacation island, young James is making his daily, early morning trek to the duck pond, when he spots an unusual animal that he is convinced is one of Santa's reindeer, sans antlers due to his youth. Following the animal in hopes he will also find Santa, James attempts to dissuade the lost, young moose from going near the busy dining hall just as the mother moose finds her offspring and James' mom finds him. Eyeball-to-eyeball, the two mothers shelter their sons as the moose walks away leaving James with memories of a magical early morning encounter. (32 pages)

Where it's reviewed:
Booklist, March 1, 1995, page 1250
Children's Book Review Service, April 1995, page 101
Publishers Weekly, February 27, 1995, page 103
Quill and Quire, February 1995, page 39
School Library Journal, August 1995, page 129

Other books by the same author:
The Hungry Thing Returns, 1990

Other books you might like:
Jez Alborough, *Where's My Teddy?*, 1992
    As Eddie searches the dark woods for his lost teddy bear he encounters a large bear with a similar problem.
Jeremy Grimsdell, *Kalinzu: A Story from Africa*, 1993
    Separated from her mother, buffalo calf Kalinzu learns to appreciate the bothersome oxpecker birds when they help her find the herd.
Robert McCloskey, *Blueberries for Sal*, 1948
    While blueberry picking with her mother, Sal absentmindedly wanders off as does a young bear eating berries with the mother bear.

1345

TERI SLOAT
NADINE BERNARD WESTCOTT, Illustrator

The Thing That Bothered Farmer Brown

(New York: Orchard Books, 1995)

Subject(s): Animals; Humor; Stories in Rhyme
Age range(s): Grades K-2
Major character(s): Farmer Brown, Farmer
Time period(s): 1990s (1995)
Locale(s): United States

Summary: Farmer Brown's attempt to sleep is disturbed by a troublesome mosquito. As the mosquito buzzes, Farmer Brown swats and whacks, awakening the animals in the barn, but not putting an end to the mosquito. (32 pages)

Where it's reviewed:
Booklist, February 1, 1995, page 1014
Horn Book Guide, Fall 1995, page 282
Publishers Weekly, March 27, 1995, page 85
School Library Journal, March 1995, page 187

Other books by the same author:
From One to One Hundred, 1991
The Eye of the Needle, 1990
From Letter to Letter, 1989

Other books you might like:

Verna Aardema, *Why Mosquitoes Buzz in People's Ears: A West African Tale*, 1975

The folktale which explains, from a mosquito's perspective, why the pesky insects buzz in people's ears won the Caldecott Medal.

Byron Barton, *Buzz Buzz Buzz*, 1973

When a bee stings a bull, a chain of events begins that affects everyone on the farm

Ann McGovern, *Too Much Noise*, 1967

Unable to sleep because his house is too noisy, an old man follows the advice of the village wise man and finally finds the quiet he is seeking.

1346

DAVID SMALL, Author/Illustrator

George Washington's Cows

(New York: Farrar Straus Giroux, 1994)

Subject(s): Animals; Humor; Stories in Rhyme
Age range(s): Grades K-3
Major character(s): George Washington, Gentleman, Farmer
Time period(s): Indeterminate Past
Locale(s): Mount Vernon, Virginia

Summary: With cows dressed in silk, swine for servants, and sheep more learned than he, George Washington decides that farming has turned into a chore that no longer suits him. Historians may quibble, but according to Small, Washington's outlandish animals are the reason he gave politics a try. (32 pages)

Where it's reviewed:
Booklist, November 1, 1994, page 510
Children's Book Review Service, September 1994, page 5
Kirkus Reviews, September 15, 1994, page 1281
Publishers Weekly, August 29, 1994, page 78
School Library Journal, January 1995, page 94

Other books by the same author:
Fenwick's Suit, 1996
Ruby Mae Has Something to Say, 1992
Imogene's Antlers, 1988
Paper John, 1987

Other books you might like:

Amy Ehrlich, *Parents in the Pigpen, Pigs in the Tub*, 1993

Bossy the cow leads the way as the farm animals move into the house forcing the farmer's family to seek space in the barn.

Paul Brett Johnson, *The Cow Who Wouldn't Come Down*, 1993

Miss Rosemary resorts to an ingenious scheme to convince her flying cow Gertrude to land and resume more typical cow behavior.

Toby Speed, *Two Cool Cows*, 1995

Maude and Millie, two cool cows in borrowed boots and sunglasses jump to the moon to frolic with their bovine buddies.

1347

IRENE SMALLS
TYRONE GETER, Illustrator

Dawn and the Round To-It

(New York: Simon & Schuster Books for Young Readers, 1994)

Subject(s): Family Life; African Americans; Problem Solving
Age range(s): Grades K-2
Major character(s): Dawn, 5-Year-Old
Time period(s): 1990s (1994)
Locale(s): United States

Summary: As the youngest in her family, Dawn is the earliest riser and the one most eager to find a parent or sibling to play with her. Daily, each plea for attention is met with the response that the busy family member will play, sing, or read when they "get around to it." While moping at the babysitter's one day Dawn comes up with a creative solution to her problem. (33 pages)

Where it's reviewed:
Booklist, July 1994, page 1956
Horn Book Guide, Fall 1994, page 291
Kirkus Reviews, May 15, 1994, page 707
Publishers Weekly, May 30, 1994, page 54
School Library Journal, September 1994, page 199

Other books by the same author:
Father's Day Blues: What Do You Do about Father's Day When All You Have Are Mothers?, 1995
Jonathan and His Mommy, 1992
Irene and the Big Fine Nickel, 1991

Other books you might like:

Nancy Carlson, *Take Time to Relax*, 1991

The beaver family learns that even busy beavers need to relax sometimes.

John Himmelman, *The Day Off Machine*, 1990

A big snowfall helps Graham use his new invention to convince his busy beaver family to take a day off and relax.

SuAnn Kiser, *The Catspring Somersault Flying One-Handed Flip-Flop*, 1993

Willy perfects an amazing gymnastics move but can find no one in her busy farm family with the time to watch her perform.

1348

NICOLA SMEE, Author/Illustrator

The Tusk Fairy

(Mahwah, NJ: BridgeWater Books, 1994)

Subject(s): Toys; Animals/Elephants; Grandparents
Age range(s): Grades K-1
Major character(s): Lizzie, Child; Elephant, Toy; Grandma, Grandmother
Time period(s): 1990s (1994)
Locale(s): England

Summary: Lizzie and Elephant are exactly the same age. Lizzie has grown bigger while sharing many experiences with Elephant, but her special toy has only grown more worn out. One day his yarn snags on a thorn and he unravels completely leaving only his tusks and trails of yarn which Lizzie sadly gathers. Grandma offers a suggestion which results in a new, almost identical Elephant by morning. First published in England. (32 pages)

Where it's reviewed:
Children's Book Review Service, June 1994, page 125
Horn Book Guide, Fall 1994, page 291
Kirkus Reviews, April 15, 1994, page 564
Publishers Weekly, April 11, 1994, page 63
School Library Journal, August 1994, page 146

Other books by the same author:
The Christmas Story, 1994
A B C, 1993
Finish the Story, Dad, 1991

Other books you might like:
Kim Lewis, *My Friend Harry*, 1995
James and Harry, a toy elephant, go everywhere together until James begins school.
Jean Van Leeuwen, *Emma Bean*, 1993
Molly and her beloved Emma Bean, a stuffed rabbit, begin kindergarten where they meet a little girl with a special teddy bear.
Clara Vulliamy, *Ellen and Penguin*, 1993
Until they meet a little girl with a toy monkey, Ellen and her penguin are too shy to join the children playing at the park.
Selina Young, *Ned*, 1993
Emily agrees with all of Ned's great ideas, but when her special donkey becomes lost on the first day of school, they both agree Ned should stay home on school days.

1349

DORIS BUCHANAN SMITH

Best Girl

(New York: Viking, 1993)

Subject(s): Mothers and Daughters; Family Problems; Self-Acceptance
Age range(s): Grades 5-7
Major character(s): Mary Neal "Nealy" Compton, 11-Year-Old; Mrs. Dees, Neighbor
Time period(s): 1990s
Locale(s): Hanover

Summary: Nealy has a secret refuge spot to which she escapes every time her mother is especially angry and abusive to her; it's under Mrs. Dees' front porch and it's there she keeps her books, pencils and drawing pad. The night Mrs. Dees house burns, Nealy lets the firefighters know that no one's home, but it's another day before she can try to retrieve her treasures. Worst of all, Nealy no longer has a place of refuge. When Nealy's older sister leaves home, her mother becomes more brutal and Nealy is left feeling more unloved then ever before especially without a place to hide. Nealy concentrates her energy on convincing her sister to return home since she is her mother's "best girl" and helping Mrs. Dees repair her home in this touching tale. (144 pages)

Where it's reviewed:
School Library Journal, January 1993, page 103

Publishers Weekly, January 11, 1993, page 64
Booklist, January 15, 1993, page 910
Center for Children's Books. Bulletin, March 1993, page 225
Kirkus Reviews, February 1, 1993, page 154

Other books by the same author:
Remember the Red-Shouldered Hawk, 1994
Karate Dancer, 1987
Return to Bitter Creek, 1986
Kick a Stone Home, 1974

Other books you might like:
Marguerite Murray, *Like Seabirds Flying Home*, 1988
Shelley's father dies after moving his family to an isolated fishing village and, not long afterward, her mother abandons her.
Susan Beth Pfeffer, *Family of Strangers*, 1992
Abby's parents pay no attention to her as they still grieve for a son who died years ago.
Marilyn Sachs, *What My Sister Remembered*, 1992
Separated by an accident that killed their parents, Molly is distressed to hear the secret hurt that her sister, Beth has carried for many years.

1350

DORIS BUCHANAN SMITH

Karate Dancer

(New York: Putnam, 1987)

Subject(s): Martial Arts; Parent and Child
Age range(s): Grades 5-7
Major character(s): Troy Matthews, Artist (cartoonist), Martial Arts Expert; Liesl Trunzo, Dancer (ballerina)
Time period(s): 1980s
Locale(s): Hanover, Georgia

Summary: Troy has two loves, cartooning and karate. Though just a teenager, he draws cartons for his local paper; in karate, he's trying to earn his black belt. Unfortunately, his parents don't show much interest in his martial arts and this hurts Troy. Troy can usually maintain control in karate, but the time he loses his temper his instructor cancels his black belt test and makes him provide a demo of karate to children with muscular dystrophy. Thanks to his girlfriend Liesl, he enrolls in ballet classes and combines all these diffeent experiences to become a "karate dancer." (175 pages)

Other books by the same author:
Remember the Red-Shouldered Hawk, 1994
The Pennywhistle Tree, 1991
Return to Bitter Creek, 1986
Kick a Stone Home, 1974

Other books you might like:
C.J. Cherryh, *The Paladin*, 1988
A science fiction romance set in an alternate Japan where a Samurai swordsman helps a young country girl avenge her family.
Rumer Godden, *Thursday's Children*, 1984
The youngest of six children, Doone is overshadowed by his sister Crystal, until it comes to ballet where he quickly outperforms her.

Gary Soto, *Pacific Crossing*, 1992
Selected as an exchange student to Japan because of his interest in martial arts, Lincoln finds there's much more to Japan than he realized.

1351

JANICE LEE SMITH
DICK GACKENBACH, Illustrator

The Baby Blues: An Adam Joshua Story

(New York: HarperCollins Publishers, 1994)

Series: Adam Joshua Story
Subject(s): Babies; Schools; Pets
Age range(s): Grades 1-3
Major character(s): Adam Joshua, Child; George, Dog; Ms. D, Teacher
Time period(s): 1990s (1994)
Locale(s): United States

Summary: With a two-year-old sister, Adam Joshua doesn't know if he can take having any more babies in his life. His favorite teacher is pregnant which means a substitute and too many changes for Adam Joshua's liking. To make matters worse, Adam Joshua learns that his only confidant, George, has been a little too friendly with the neighbor's dog and will soon become a father. When Ms. D misses the special shower planned by her class due to the early arrival of twins, the class plans a field trip to bring the party to her. (82 pages)

Where it's reviewed:
Booklist, June 1, 1994, page 1823
Horn Book, September 1994, page 584
Horn Book Guide, Fall 1994, page 303
School Library Journal, July 1994, page 90

Other books by the same author:
Nelson in Love, 1992
It's Not Easy Being George, 1989
The Kid Next Door and Other Headaches: Stories about Adam Joshua, 1984

Other books you might like:
Beverly Cleary, *Muggie Maggie*, 1990
Third grade presents many challenges to Maggie, including cursive writing.
Patricia Reilly Giff, *The Secret at the Polk Street School*, 1987
One title in a series about the many adventures of students at Polk Street School.
Suzy Kline, *Herbie Jones and the Class Gift*, 1987
Herbie and Raymond face an unexpected complication when they are sent to pick up the class's gift for the teacher.

1352

JANICE LEE SMITH
DICK GACKENBACH, Illustrator

Serious Science

(New York: HarperCollins, 1993)

Series: Adam Joshua Story
Subject(s): Schools; Brothers and Sisters; Humor

Age range(s): Grades 2-4
Major character(s): Adam Joshua, Child, Brother (older); Amanda Jane, 2-Year-Old, Sister; Nelson, Child, Classmate
Time period(s): 1990s (1993)
Locale(s): United States (elementary school)

Summary: When the fifth and sixth graders have a Science Fair, the primary students lobby successfully for equal time. Adam Joshua is proud of the solar system he constructs and devastated when he finds that Amanda Jane and the family dog have eaten it. With only two days before the Fair, Adam Joshua must come up with a new idea. Inspired by the trouble he and Nelson have with their two-year-old siblings, Adam Joshua creates the "Pest Alert" which is such a hit at the Fair that the older students place orders. (73 pages)

Where it's reviewed:
Booklist, June 1, 1993, page 1836
Horn Book Guide, Fall 1993, 290
New Advocate, Fall 1993, page 294
Reading Teacher, September 1994, page 71
School Library Journal, June 1993, page 89

Other books by the same author:
The Baby Blues: An Adam Joshua Story, 1994
The Turkeys' Side of It: Adam Joshua's Thanksgiving, 1990
The Kid Next Door and Other Headaches: Stories about Adam Joshua, 1984

Other books you might like:
Patricia Reilly Giff, *The Secret at the Polk Street School*, 1987
One title in a series about the many adventures of students at Polk Street School.
Johanna Hurwitz, *Russell and Elisa*, 1989
Elisa is four now, but no less a challenge to big brother Russell.
Suzy Kline, *Herbie Jones and the Class Gift*, 1987
Herbie's adventures continue as he and Raymond are chosen to select the class gift to the teacher.

1353

JANICE LEE SMITH
PAUL MEISEL, Illustrator

Wizard and Wart at Sea

(New York: HarperCollins Publishers, 1995)

Series: I Can Read
Subject(s): Wizards; Magic; Vacations
Age range(s): Grades 1-2
Major character(s): Wizard, Wizard; Wart, Dog, Sidekick
Time period(s): 1990s (1995)
Locale(s): Fictional Country

Summary: Tired of the hardwork of casting spells and mixing potions, Wizard conjures up a vacation trip. While Wizard relaxes on the beach reading, Wart, as always, eats. Wart's activity attracts the usual hungry sea gulls which so frustrate Wizard that he hurriedly spouts a spell and turns the gulls into. . .goats. Wizard continues with some misspells until all the gulls are song birds, the other vacationers are happy and the hotel management is relieved when a tired Wizard and Wart go home to rest. (48 pages)

Where it's reviewed:
Booklist, July 1995, page 1885
Bulletin of the Center for Children's Books, September 1995, page 30
Horn Book Guide, Fall 1995, page 289
School Library Journal, December 1995, page 92

Other books by the same author:
Wizard and Wart, 1994

Other books you might like:
Ida DeLage, *The Old Witch Gets a Surprise*, 1981
  In an Easy Reader, Witch and Wizard's flight on a dragon balloon comes to an unexpected ending.
Mercer Mayer, *Purple Pickle Juice*, 1996
  After trying purple pickle juice and her aunt's magic, Thistle Howl reconsiders her desire to grow in this Step-into-Reading series entry.
Jane O'Connor, *The Bad-Luck Penny*, 1996
  A shiny penny found by a young boy grants wishes, but does not bring the good luck he expects.

1354

LANE SMITH, Author/Illustrator

The Happy Hocky Family

(New York: Viking, 1993)

Subject(s): Family Life; Humor
Age range(s): Grades K-3
Major character(s): Henry Hocky, Child, Brother; Holly Hocky, Child, Sister; Baby Hocky, Child (infant)
Time period(s): 1990s (1993)
Locale(s): United States

Summary: Vignettes of family life star Henry, Holly and Baby in 18 brief "chapters" some of which include a family visit to the zoo, a celebration of a birthday, a cousin's visit, and a balloon. As a parody of "Dick and Jane" style basal readers the Hocky family converses in deceptively simple, repetitive dialogue which is subtly humorous. Keep your eye on the illustrations or you may miss the punch lines! (60 pages)

Where it's reviewed:
Children's Book Review Service, October 1993, page 18
Horn Book Guide, Spring 1994, page 55
Library Talk, May 1994, page 36
Publishers Weekly, July 19, 1993, page 250
School Library Journal, September 1993, page 220

Other books by the same author:
The Big Pets, 1991
Glasses: Who Needs 'Em?, 1991

Other books you might like:
Marjorie Dennis Murray, *Saturday with Little Rabbit*, 1993
  The characters in the beginning chapter book are animals experiencing the ups and downs of childhood.
Jerry Newman, *Green Earrings and a Felt Hat*, 1993
  In a book for beginning readers best friends Susan and Carolyn fall in and out of friendship.
J. Otto Seibold, *Mr. Lunch Takes a Plane Ride*, 1993
  In typical Mr. Lunch fashion, the dog's plane ride in the luggage compartment leads to unexpected events. Co-author Vivian Walsh.

1355

MAGGIE SMITH, Author/Illustrator

Argo, You Lucky Dog

(New York: Lothrop, Lee & Shepard Books, 1994)

Subject(s): Animals/Dogs; Wealth; Lottery
Age range(s): Grades K-3
Major character(s): Argo, Dog
Time period(s): 1990s (1994)
Locale(s): United States

Summary: While his owners are on a business trip, Argo finds a lottery ticket which wins him 17 sacks of money. Promptly burying the sacks in the yard, Argo realizes he's made an unsightly mess and spends some of his winnings having the yard landscaped. Each idea for spending his wealth generates another so that, by the time his owners return, Argo has spent all his winnings and the house and yard have been totally redone. (32 pages)

Where it's reviewed:
Booklist, July 1994, page 1956
Horn Book Guide, Fall 1994, page 291
Kirkus Reviews, May 15, 1994, page 707
Publishers Weekly, May 2, 1994, page 307
School Library Journal, August 1994, page 146

Awards the book has won:
International Reading Association Children's Choices, 1995

Other books by the same author:
Counting Our Way to Maine, 1995
My Grandma's Chair, 1992
There's a Witch under the Stairs, 1991

Other books you might like:
Debra Barracca, *Maxi, the Star*, 1993
  Max's selection to star in a dog-food commercial requires a cross-country trip in his owner's cab. Co-author Sal Barracca.
Nina Laden, *The Night I Followed the Dog*, 1994
  While a family sleeps, their pet dog secretly leads an exciting night life.
Susan Meddaugh, *Martha Calling*, 1994
  Talking dog Martha wins a radio call-in contest and then must come up with a plan for using the prize—a weekend for four at an Inn which does not allow dogs.

1356

SUSAN MATHIAS SMITH
ANDREW GLASS, Illustrator

The Booford Summer

(New York: Clarion Books, 1994)

Subject(s): Animals/Dogs; Animals, Treatment of; Neighbors and Neighborhoods
Age range(s): Grades 3-6
Major character(s): Hayley Larkin, 10-Year-Old; Booford, Dog; Mr. Ben Wood, Neighbor
Time period(s): 1990s (1994)
Locale(s): Virginia

Summary: When taciturn Mr. Wood moves in across the back road from Hayley's home, the animal-loving youngster frets about his neglect of Booford. Already the owner of five stray cats, Hayley is not allowed to acquire any more animals, so she befriends Booford when Mr.Wood is not home. Her inquisitive nature also leads her into a friendship with Mr. Wood as they both learn a lesson in neighborliness. (130 pages)

Where it's reviewed:
Booklist, September 15, 1994, page 137
Horn Book, March 1995, page 221
Kirkus Reviews, September 15, 1994, page 1282
Library Talk, January 1995, page 44
School Library Journal, November 1994, page 108

Other books you might like:
Karen Hesse, *Sable*, 1994
    Tate cares for a stray dog, hoping her parents will allow her to keep the mutt.
Lois Lowry, *Anastasia, Absolutely*, 1995
    Adventurous Anastasia is coping with a new dog, school and an exciting personal life.
Hilary McKay, *Dog Friday*, 1995
    Nursing an injured, lost dog back to health helps Robin overcome the fear of dogs he has felt since being bitten by one.
Phyllis Reynolds Naylor, *Shiloh*, 1991
    In a Newbery Medal winner, Marty finds a lost beagle and tries to hide it from the dog's abusive owner.

1357

ETHEL FOOTMAN SMOTHERS

Moriah's Pond
(New York: Knopf, 1995)

Subject(s): Sisters; African Americans; Grandparents
Age range(s): Grades 4-6
Major character(s): Annie ''Annie Rye'' Moriah, Child; Moriah, Grandmother (Annie Rye's great-grandmother)
Time period(s): 1950s
Locale(s): Mitchell County, Georgia

Summary: Spending the summer with Moriah offers Annie Rye and her two older sisters an opportunity for great adventures before they become old enough to work in the fields with their mother. Swimming and fishing in Moriah's pond, helping Moriah with chores and toting the laundry back and forth to customers' houses keep Annie Rye busy in this sequel to *Down in the Piney Woods*. (111 pages)

Where it's reviewed:
Publishers Weekly, January 23, 1995, page 70
Booklist, January 15, 1995, page 930
School Library Journal, February 1995, page 100
Kirkus Reviews, February 15, 1995, page 232
Library Talk, May 1995, page 44

Other books by the same author:
Down in the Piney Woods, 1992

Other books you might like:
Brenda Seabrooke, *The Bridges of Summer*, 1992
    Sarah Jane summers on an island with her grandmother, a

descendant of slaves, and learns about a heritage that includes a hu hu and a conjure bag.
Eleanora E. Tate, *The Secret of Gumbo Grove*, 1987
    Raisin spends time helping Miss Effie clean out the church cemetery and learns a lot about her black community's history.
Joyce Carol Thomas, *Golden Pasture*, 1986
    Staying on his grandfather's farm, Carl Lee learns patience through caring for a horse.

1358

CAROL SNYDER
MAXIE CHAMBLISS, Illustrator

One Up, One Down
(New York: Atheneum Books for Young Readers, 1995)

Subject(s): Twins; Babies; Brothers and Sisters
Age range(s): Grades K-1
Major character(s): Katie, Sister (older); Ben, Brother, Twin; Adam, Brother, Twin
Time period(s): 1990s (1995)
Locale(s): United States

Summary: When her dad comes home from the hospital with the news that Katie now has two little brothers, life begins to change for everyone. Ben and Adam are opposites in appearance and behavior—when one is dry the other is wet; when one is quiet the other is crying; when one is up the other is down. Katie is a busy and helpful big sister. (32 pages)

Where it's reviewed:
Booklist, June 1, 1995, page 1789
Horn Book Guide, Fall 1995, page 283
New York Times Book Review, October 8, 1995, page 31
School Library Journal, May 1995, page 95

Other books by the same author:
God Must Like Cookies, Too, 1993

Other books you might like:
Catherine Anholt, *The Twins Two by Two*, 1992
    Imitating the bedtime story of Noah's ark, twins Minnie and Max prepare for bed by becoming different pairs of animals.
Beverly Cleary, *Janet's Thingamajigs*, 1987
    When new beds arrive to replace their cribs, twins Janet and Jimmy realize how much they have grown.
Jeffie Ross Gordon, *Two Badd Babies*, 1992
    Mr. and Mrs. Badd have two babies who design their own adventure to the bakery, the movies, the bookstore and home again.
John Himmelman, *J.J. Versus the Babysitter*, 1996
    At first it seems to Stephanie that J.J. is everywhere at once, but the babysitter turns out to be too clever for the twins' tricks.

1359

ZILPHA KEATLEY SNYDER

Cat Running
(New York: Delacorte, 1994)

Subject(s): Family Life; Depression (Economic)
Age range(s): Grades 4-6
Major character(s): Catherine "Cat" Kinsey, 6th Grader; Zane Perkins, 6th Grader
Time period(s): 1930s
Locale(s): Brownwood, California

Summary: Cat's the fastest runner in her class, but she can't compete in the races at her school's annual Play Days, for her father considers it improper for her to wear slacks. Her classmates taunt her and say she's afraid that Zane Perkins, an "Okie," will beat her. Because Cat's so concerned about the dictates from her old-fashioned father, she hasn't paid attention to the poverty in which the Perkins family lives. Though it's the Depression, she doesn't understand the Dust Bowl and what it's like for a family to lose their farm land and begin their life again thousands of miles from their home. Cat's eyes are opened when the youngest Perkins girl catches pneumonia and she and Zane combine their running ability to get help from a doctor. (168 pages)

Where it's reviewed:
Publishers Weekly, November 21, 1994, page 77
School Library Journal, November 1994, page 108
Horn Book, March 1995, page 196
Voice of Youth Advocates, October 1994, page 218
Center for Children's Books. Bulletin, January 1995, page 178

Awards the book has won:
School Library Journal Best Books, 1994

Other books by the same author:
The Trespassers, 1995
Fool's Gold, 1993
Janie's Private Eyes, 1989
The Egypt Game, 1967

Other books you might like:
Emily Crofford, *A Place to Belong*, 1994
    Talmadge's clubfoot often makes him the butt of jokes in a new school and he hates having to move so often during the Depression as his father seeks work.
Kathleen Karr, *The Cave*, 1994
    With their South Dakota farm part of the Dust Bowl, Christine's brother's asthma worsens; finding a cave with running water helps them survive.
George Ella Lyon, *Borrowed Children*, 1988
    Amanda is worn out from taking care of her sick mother; a trip to Memphis helps her recover during the Depression.
Jerry Spinelli, *Maniac Magee*, 1990
    Already a legend for how far and fast he runs, Maniac's greatest triumph is uniting the kids from the black East End and the white West End of town.

1360

ZILPHA KEATLEY SNYDER

The Trespassers
(New York: Delacorte, 1995)

Subject(s): Ghosts; Emotional Problems
Age range(s): Grades 4-6
Major character(s): Cornelia "Neely" Bradford, 6th Grader; Gregory "Grub" Bradford, Child, Brother (Neely's younger); Curtis Hutchinson, Child (emotionally impaired)
Time period(s): 1990s
Locale(s): California (Monterey coast)

Summary: Halcyon House, the old, deserted Hutchinson mansion, holds a fascination for Neely and her younger brother Grub. One day they see an open window in the house's playroom and climb in to see if there's any truth to the rumors about the young girl who died in the house. Their days of exploration appear cut short when a branch of the Hutchinson family moves back into the house, but Neely and Grub are befriended by young Curtis and continue to visit, visits that almost result in tragedy from a very troubled Curtis. (200 pages)

Where it's reviewed:
Voice of Youth Advocates, August 1995, page 166
Booklist, June 1995, page 1773
School Library Journal, August 1995, page 144
Library Talk, September 1995, page 40
New York Times Book Review, October 22, 1995, page 41

Other books by the same author:
Cat Running, 1994
Fool's Gold, 1993
And Condors Danced, 1987
The Velvet Room, 1965

Other books you might like:
Betsy Byars, *The Summer of the Swans*, 1970
    When Sarah's handicapped brother runs away, she finds him visiting the swans in a touching family story.
Paula Fox, *Lily and the Lost Boy*, 1987
    Lily and her brother have always gotten along until they go to Thanos where meeting a young boy disrupts their relationship.
Elizabeth Ladd, *Mystery for Meg*, 1962
    Meg visits her brother on Heron's Neck Island where they explore a locked room found in an old barn.
Cynthia Voigt, *Tree by Leaf*, 1988
    Clothilde's father returns from the war and isolates himself in a cottage, too emotionally upset to be part of his family.

1361

GARY SOTO
ROBERT CASILLA, Illustrator

Boys at Work
(New York: Delacorte Press, 1995)

Subject(s): Mexican Americans; Friendship; Problem Solving
Age range(s): Grades 4-6

Major character(s): Rudy Herrera, 10-Year-Old, Friend (Alex's); Alex, 10-Year-Old, Friend (Rudy's); Slinky, Bully
Time period(s): 1990s (1995)
Locale(s): California

Summary: The hot summer grows even hotter for Rudy when he accidently breaks a Discman borrowed from Slinky. Alex and Rudy desperately think of many plans to earn money and repay Slinky for the Discman. Not all their efforts are as successful as they hope and when Slinky tells them that he borrowed the Discman from the biggest bully in town, all three boys begin to work to pay back the debt. The text includes Spanish words and phrases. (134 pages)

Where it's reviewed:
Booklist, June 1, 1995, page 1773
Bulletin of the Center for Children's Books, September 1995, page 30
Horn Book, September 1995, page 604
Library Talk, May 1995, page 45
School Library Journal, June 1995, page 113

Other books by the same author:
The Pool Party, 1993
The Skirt, 1992
Taking Sides, 1991

Other books you might like:
Betsy Byars, *McMummy*, 1993
  While caring for plants in Professor Orloff's greenhouse, Mozie finds a mummy-shaped pod that seems to have strange powers.
Paula Danziger, *Not for a Billion Gazillion Dollars*, 1992
  Trying to save for a new computer program, Matthew develops an appreciation for the value of money and begins his own business.
Peg Kehret, *The Richest Kids in Town*, 1994
  In his new hometown, Peter meets Wishbone Wyoming who joins him in a series of humorous, but not entirely successful, money-making adventures.

1362

GARY SOTO
SUSAN GUEVARA, Illustrator

Chato's Kitchen
(New York: G. P. Putnam's Sons, 1995)

Subject(s): Animals/Cats; Animals/Mice; Neighbors and Neighborhoods
Age range(s): Grades K-3
Major character(s): Chato, Cat; Novio Boy, Cat, Friend (Chato's)
Time period(s): 1990s (1995)
Locale(s): East Los Angeles, California

Summary: Two cool cats spend an afternoon in the kitchen preparing an appropriate meal as a welcome for the new mouse family that has moved in next door. Being a gracious host, Chato allows the neighbors to bring their friend because he assumes that will simply mean more mice in the tortillas which he and Novio Boy are preparing. Imagine the cats' surprise when the mice arrive riding on the back of their

friend—a dog! A glossary of Spanish terms is listed on the title page although the Spanish words in the text can be understood from context. (32 pages)

Where it's reviewed:
Booklist, March 1, 1995, page 1250
Children's Book Review Service, May 1995, page 112
Horn Book, September 1995, page 591
Publishers Weekly, February 6, 1995, page 84
School Library Journal, July 1995, page 69

Awards the book has won:
ALA Notable Book, 1996
Book Links Good Book, 1995

Other books by the same author:
Too Many Tamales, 1993

Other books you might like:
Arnold Lobel, *Mouse Soup*, 1977
  Mouse has a plan that he hopes will keep him out of Weasel's soup pot.
Jonathan London, *Hip Cat*, 1993
  Oobie-do, a sax-playing cat, hops a train for San Francisco to make his name as a jazz musician.
Susan Meddaugh, *Hog-Eye*, 1995
  A little pig with a mind of her own must put it to good use if she's to escape from the wolf who plans to have her for dinner.
Tony Ross, *Stone Soup*, 1987
  A hen cleverly avoids becoming a wolf's dinner by offering him a taste of her stone soup.

1363

GARY SOTO
ERIC VELASQUEZ, Illustrator

Off and Running
(New York: Delacorte, 1996)

Subject(s): Schools; Mexican Americans; School Spirit
Age range(s): Grades 3-6
Major character(s): Miata Ramirez, 5th Grader, Candidate; Rudy Herera, 5th Grader, Candidate; Alex Garcia, 5th Grader
Time period(s): 1990s
Locale(s): California

Summary: Miata and Rudy are candidates for school president. Miata's platform calls for beautification of the school while Rudy would like more recess. As the campaign heats up, Miata wants to call attention to herself and so tries to give herself a permanent, with disastrous results. Soon all the girls have perms and even some of the boys. The girls are getting crank calls which they first blame on the boys, but then find that it was a younger sister of one of the candidates. The election is close but the girls win as the boys decide to vote for the girls because they want to go out for soccer. (136 pages)

Where it's reviewed:
School Library Journal, September 1996, page 206
Bulletin of the Center for Childrens Books, October 1996, page 77
Booklist, October 1, 1996, page 352

Other books by the same author:
Boys at War, 1995
Taking Sides, 1991
The Skirt, 1990

Other books you might like:
Dean Hughes, *Nutty for President*, 1986
    Another student tries to fix the 5th grade election when Nutty is running.
Johanna Hurwitz, *Class President*, 1990
    Julio discovers that he is the one with leadership skills and is elected even though he was helping his friend run.
Barbara Park, *Rosie Swanson, 4th Grade Geek for President*, 1991
    Rosie is running for president but will truth get in the way?
Erika Tamar, *Alphabet City Ballet*, 1996
    Marisol wins a scholarship to the local ballet school but faces problems in her Hispanic neighborhood.

1364

GARY SOTO
ROBERT CASTILLA, Illustrator

The Pool Party
(New York: Delacorte Press, 1993)

Subject(s): Mexican Americans; Family Life; Peer Pressure
Age range(s): Grades 3-5
Major character(s): Rudy Herrera, 4th Grader; Alex, 4th Grader; Tiffany Perez, 4th Grader, Wealthy
Time period(s): 1990s (1993)
Locale(s): Fresno, California

Summary: Rudy's father is a gardener who depends on the help of the entire family to cut the lawns of the wealthy during the busy summer season. When Rudy receives an invitation to a pool party at a wealthy classmate's home, his friend Alex and everyone in the family offer advice as to how he should behave in such a setting. Rudy, however, is a natural and unselfconsciously enjoys himself at the party oblivious to any class distinction. Tiffany is a gracious hostess and Rudy leaves hoping for another invitation. The dialogue includes Spanish words and phrases with no glossary. (104 pages)

Where it's reviewed:
Horn Book Guide, Fall 1993, page 291
Library Talk, January 1994, page 44
Publishers Weekly, June 7, 1993, page 70
Reading Teacher, September 1994, page 70
School Library Journal, June 1993, page 112

Other books by the same author:
Boys at Work, 1995
Crazy Weekend, 1994
Pacific Crossing, 1992

Other books you might like:
Terry Dunnahoo, *Who Needs Espie Sanchez*, 1977
    After a traffic accident, Espie is befriended by a wealthy young girl who has also been affected by the accident.
Colleen O'Shaughnessy McKenna, *Fifth Grade: Here Comes Trouble*, 1991
    Seeking to change her classmates' image of her, Collette

bravely accepts an invitation to attend a boy-girl birthday party at a wealthy friend's home.
Louis Sachar, *Dogs Don't Tell Jokes*, 1991
    Seeking popularity, Gary learns that his peers don't consider his clowning around to be very funny.

1365

GARY SOTO
ED MARTINEZ, Illustrator

Too Many Tamales
(New York: G.P. Putnam's Sons, 1993)

Subject(s): Christmas; Mexican Americans; Mothers and Daughters
Age range(s): Grades 1-3
Major character(s): Maria, Child (daughter); Dolores, Child, Cousin; Danny, Child, Cousin
Time period(s): 1990s (1993)
Locale(s): United States

Summary: Soon the family celebration of Christmas will begin with grandparents, aunts, uncles, cousins and lots of tamales. While kneading the masa, Maria wears her mother's diamond ring, enjoying the sparkle on her finger. In the excitement of dinner preparation and the arrival of family members, the ring is forgotten . Only later, as Maria visits with her cousins, does she remember the ring. Sure that it can be in only one place, Maria makes her cousins help her eat the tamales in order to find it. Alas, no ring is found, the children are full, the adults have no tamales, and Maria learns that the ring is safe on her mother's finger. (32 pages)

Where it's reviewed:
Booklist, September 15, 1993, page 151
Horn Book, November 1993, page 727
Kirkus Reviews, September 1, 1993, page 1152
Publishers Weekly, August 16, 1993, page 103
School Library Journal, October 1993, page 48

Awards the book has won:
Booklist Editors' Choice, 1993
Book Links Good Book, 1993

Other books by the same author:
Chato's Kitchen, 1995
The Mustache, 1995
Neighborhood Odes, 1992
The Skirt, 1992

Other books you might like:
Marie Hall Ets, *Nine Days to Christmas*, 1959
    Five-year-old Ceci excitedly awaits a traditional pre-Christmas party in Mexico where she will have her own pinata. Co-author Aurora Labastida. Caldecott Medal, 1960.
Pat Mora, *A Birthday Basket for Tia*, 1992
    Cecilia makes a special present for her family's celebration of Great Aunt Tia's 90th birthday.
Leyla Torres, *Saturday Sancocho*, 1995
    Anticipating making chicken sancocho with her grandparents, Maria Lili faces disappointment when she finds her grandparents' kitchen holds only eggs. But Mama Ana's idea makes everyone happy.

1366

PETER SPIER, Author/Illustrator

Father, May I Come?

(New York: Doubleday Book for Young Readers, 1993)

Subject(s): Rescue Work; Shipwrecks; Historical
Age range(s): Grades 1-3
Major character(s): Sietze Hemmes, Child, Historical Figure; Seitze Hemmes, Child
Time period(s): 17th century (1687); 1990s (1993)
Locale(s): Netherlands (small coastal village)

Summary: Presumably based on actual incidents, two boys, separated by centuries yet linked by name and location, spot ships floundering off the coast and alert the rescue crews in time to avoid any loss of life in either incident. The parallel stories contrast the technological changes in rescue work over time, but note the unchanging bravery of the crews. Factual information about the Dutch coast and the modern rescue lifeboat concludes the story. (24 pages)

Where it's reviewed:
Booklist, September 15, 1993, page 161
Horn Book, July 1993, page 450
Kirkus Reviews, July 15, 1993, page 942
Publishers Weekly, July 26 1993, page 71
School Library Journal, September 1993, page 220

Other books by the same author:
And So My Garden Grows, 1992
Tin Lizzie, 1990
Noah's Ark, 1977 (Caldecott Medal, 1978)

Other books you might like:
Barbara Cooney, *Island Boy*, 1988
    Matthais Tibbitts sails the world, choosing to return to his tiny island home in Maine.
Donald Crews, *Harbor*, 1982
    Clear illustrations support an introductory story about the activities of a busy harbor.
Hardie Gramatky, *Little Toot*, 1939
    Content to puff lazily about the river, Little Toot proves his true courage when he assists with a rescue during a storm.

1367

EILEEN SPINELLI
PAUL YALOWITZ, Illustrator

Boy, Can He Dance!

(New York: Four Winds Press, 1993)

Subject(s): Dancing; Fathers and Sons; Cooks and Cookery
Age range(s): Grades K-3
Major character(s): Tony, Child, Dancer; Unnamed Character, Father, Cook (chef at the City Hotel)
Time period(s): 1990s (1993)
Locale(s): United States

Summary: Tony's father expects him to follow in the family business as a chef. However, Tony is only interested in food as a means of acquiring the energy needed to follow his true love of dancing. Dutifully, Tony accompanies his father to the City Hotel to help him prepare for a banquet, but everything Tony does sets his toes to tapping and things in the kitchen to flying. When the hotel manager comes in, frantic because a dancer for the evening show is sick, Tony is given an opportunity to substitute and receive the appropriate recognition for his true talents. (32 pages)

Where it's reviewed:
Booklist, May 15, 1993, page 1696
Horn Book Guide, Fall 1993, page 291
Language Arts, January 1994, page 55
Publishers Weekly, April 19, 1993, page 59
School Library Journal, August 1993, page 152

Other books by the same author:
If You Want to Find Golden, 1993
Somebody Loves You, Mr. Hatch, 1991
Thanksgiving at the Tappleton's, 1984

Other books you might like:
Karen Ackerman, *Song and Dance Man*, 1988
    In a Caldecott Medal winner, Grandpa relives his days on a vaudeville stage for his grandchildren.
Emily Arnold McCully, *The Amazing Felix*, 1993
    Felix's father, a concert pianist expects his son to show the same interest, but Felix seems to have a talent for magic tricks.
Justine Rendal, *The Dancing Cat*, 1991
    A toy cat's ambition to be a dancer is not appreciated by her first owner who gives her away to a boy who recognizes her destiny.

1368

EILEEN SPINELLI
STACEY SCHUETT, Illustrator

If You Want to Find Golden

(Morton Grove, IL: Albert Whitman & Company, 1993)

Subject(s): City Life; Neighbors and Neighborhoods; Mothers and Sons
Age range(s): Grades K-1
Major character(s): Unnamed Character, Child
Time period(s): 1990s (1993)
Locale(s): United States

Summary: If you want to find all the colors of the rainbow and more then follow a young boy and his mother around the city as he describes the best places to find colors from the golden of morning light to the copper of a sunset. (32 pages)

Where it's reviewed:
Booklist, December 1, 1993, page 701
Children's Bookwatch, November 1993, page 4
Horn Book Guide, Spring 1994, page 55
Publishers Weekly, August 9, 1993, page 478
School Library Journal, January 1994, page 99

Other books by the same author:
Boy, Can He Dance!, 1993
Somebody Loves You, Mr. Hatch, 1991
Thanksgiving at the Tappleton's, 1984

Other books you might like:

Angela Johnson, *One of Three*, 1991
    Three sisters are always together in the city unless the little
    one is left behind with Mama and Daddy.

Elaine Moore, *Good Morning, City*, 1995
    The people of a city awaken and begin the varied activities
    that contribute to the bustle of an urban community.

Chris K. Soentpiet, *Around Town*, 1994
    On a summer day, a girl and her mother share a day in New
    York City, enjoying all that a vibrant city has to offer.

1369

EILEEN SPINELLI
MELANIE HOPE GREENBERG, Illustrator

Lizzie Logan Wears Purple Sunglasses
(New York: Simon & Schuster Books for Young Readers, 1995)

Subject(s): Friendship; Moving, Household; Behavior
Age range(s): Grades 2-4
Major character(s): Heather Wade, 8-Year-Old; Lizzie Logan,
    10-Year-Old, Neighbor
Time period(s): 1990s (1995)
Locale(s): United States (Mole Street)

Summary: In a picture-book author's first novel, Heather's
family is greeted on moving day by out-spoken Lizzie who
presents them with a store-bought pie as a welcoming gift
while cautioning them to check it for mold. Lizzie is not like
any other girl Heather has ever known, but the two become
friends in typical friend fashion—fighting and making up—
all summer. (122 pages)

Where it's reviewed:
Booklist, May 15, 1995, page 1648
Horn Book, September 1995, page 605
Instructor, September 1995, page 106
Publishers Weekly, July 3, 1995, page 61
School Library Journal, June 1995, page 113

Other books you might like:

Johanna Hurwitz, *New Neighbors for Nora*, 1979
    Seven-year-old Nora enjoys the excitement of new neigh-
    bors moving into her New York City apartment building.

Maud Hart Lovelace, *Betsy-Tacy and Tib*, 1941
    The warmth of small town neighbors and the activities of
    close friends make this work a timeless classic.

Ann Turner, *One Brave Summer*, 1995
    When her mom rents a mountain cabin for the summer,
    cautious Katy meets out-going Lena May and forms a
    summer friendship of self-discovery and adventure.

Vera B. Williams, *Scooter*, 1993
    Personable and unpredicatable Elana Rose ''Lanny''
    Rosen adjusts easily to a move into a New York apartment,
    meeting neighbors and making new friends.

1370

JERRY SPINELLI

Crash
(New York: Knopf, 1996)

Subject(s): Family Life; Friendship; Conduct of Life
Age range(s): Grades 5-8
Major character(s): John ''Crash'' Coogan, Teenager, Foot-
    ball Player (football player); Penn Webb, Teenager, Run-
    ner (runner); Scooter, Grandfather
Time period(s): 1990s
Locale(s): Springfield, Pennsylvania

Summary: Crash, earning his nickname when he knocks his
cousin over one day, is a typical football jock. His parents are
so busy that they have no time to come watch him play,
though his neighbors go to see their son, Penn, a cheerleader.
Crash's grandfather, Scooter, comes to live with the family
and becomes a big booster of Crash until he has a stroke and is
bedridden. It is then that Crash and his family stand back and
take another look at the way they are living. Crash rethinks the
way he's been acting in school and how he has been treating
Penn. With a chance to prove himself as a runner, he reflects
on the importance of family and what running in the Penn
Relays would mean to Penn and reconsiders his race. (162
pages)

Where it's reviewed:
Horn Book, September/October 1996, page 600
School Library Journal, July 1996, page 124
Booklist, June 1, 1996, page 1724

Awards the book has won:
School Library Journal Best Books, 1996

Other books by the same author:
There's a Girl in My Hammerlock, 1991
Maniac Magee, 1990
Who Put That Hair in My Toothbrush?, 1984

Other books you might like:

Matt Christopher, *Olympic Dream*, 1996
    Doug looks back at his summer and how he changed from
    a video junkie to a self-assured athlete.

Paula Fox, *One-Eyed Cat*, 1984
    A young boy matures when he faces the mistakes he made
    with an air rifle.

David Halecroft, *Benched!*, 1992
    Woody is benched on the basketball team when his grades
    are bad and he is forced to take another look at himself.

Peter Hartling, *Old John*, 1990
    A family faces troubles when the grandfather comes to
    stay with them.

Cynthia Voigt, *The Runner*, 1985
    A teenage boy uses running as a way of avoiding people
    until he sees the value of friends.

1371

JERRY SPINELLI
DONNA NELSON, Illustrator

Tooter Pepperday

(New York: Random House, 1995)

Series: First Stepping Stone Book
Subject(s): Moving, Household; Behavior; Farm Life
Age range(s): Grades 2-4
Major character(s): Tooter Pepperday, Child; Aunt Sally, Aunt, Farmer
Time period(s): 1990s (1995)
Locale(s): Morgantown; Aunt Sally's farm

Summary: Feisty, resourceful Tooter handcuffs herself to the bathroom sink in protest over the family's move, but is overpowered by her mother's tickling approach to problem solving. Finally, two states and three hundred miles from Morgantown, the family arrives at Aunt Sally's farm and Tooter discovers that she is now out of reach of McDonald's, pizza deliveries and cable TV. Understandably, Tooter is miserable, but gradually her attitude changes and she reluctantly accepts her family's new life. (85 pages)

Where it's reviewed:
Booklist, May 18, 1995, page 1575
Bulletin of the Center for Children's Books, June 1995, page 359
Horn Book, September 1995, page 595
Horn Book Guide, Fall 1995, page 292
School Library Journal, July 1995, page 82

Other books by the same author:
Fourth Grade Rats, 1991
The Bathwater Gang, 1990
Maniac Magee, 1990 (Newbery Medal Winner)

Other books you might like:
Beverly Cleary, *Ramona and Her Father*, 1977
   The year that Ramona's father loses his job, Ramona is upset by all the changes in the family routine.
Betsy Duffey, *Hey, New Kid!*, 1996
   Cody is so unhappy to be entering a new school that he makes up a new identity rather than tell people the truthful, boring story of his life.
Susan Patron, *Maybe Yes, Maybe No, Maybe Maybe*, 1993
   Eight-year-old PK is overwhelmed by the rapid changes in her life and unhappy about her family's move to a new apartment.

1372

MICHELLE SOBEL SPIRN
R. W. ALLEY, Illustrator

The Know-Nothings

(New York: HarperCollins Publishers, 1995)

Series: I Can Read Books
Subject(s): Cooks and Cookery; Humor; Behavior
Age range(s): Grades 1-2
Major character(s): Doris, Cook, Friend; Norris, Friend
Time period(s): 1990s (1995)
Locale(s): Fictional Country

Summary: Doris decides to cook for her goofy friends, but no one can decide on just the right thing to eat. Norris suggests that breakfast is a simple meal, so they sit down to wait for that, but become hungry before it arrives and march off to France where they expect to purchase french fries. (64 pages)

Where it's reviewed:
Booklist, July 1995, page 1885
Bulletin of the Center for Children's Books, July 1995, page 398
Horn Book Guide, Fall 1995, page 289
Kirkus Reviews, May 15, 1995, page 716
School Library Journal, November 1995, page 82

Other books you might like:
Harry Allard, *The Stupids Step Out*, 1974
   With their dog Kitty, the Stupid family enjoys a silly, fun-filled day.
Sue Denim, *Make Way for Dumb Bunnies*, 1996
   On a stormy day, a family of three really dumb bunnies go to the beach.
Peggy Parish, *Come Back, Amelia Bedelia*, 1971
   As usual, Amelia Bedelia interprets instructions literally causing her to lose a series of jobs.
Francesca Simon, *The Topsy-Turvies*, 1995
   The unconventional Topsy-Turvy family babysits for a neighbor and unexpectedly scares away a burglar with some unusual hospitality.

1373

KATE SPOHN, Author/Illustrator

Broken Umbrellas

(New York: Viking, 1994)

Subject(s): Homeless; Collectors and Collecting; City Life
Age range(s): Grades 1-3
Major character(s): Unnamed Character, Aged Person, Streetperson
Time period(s): 1990s (1994)
Locale(s): United States

Summary: An elderly woman roams the streets collecting discards, especially her favorite item—broken umbrellas. Contented, perhaps even happy, the woman recycles some items such as the sweaters that she puts into boxes for stray cats and old bread that she feeds to the pigeons. (32 pages)

Where it's reviewed:
Booklist, September 15, 1994, page 145
Children's Book Review Service, Winter 1995, page 66
Horn Book, January 1995, page 54
Kirkus Reviews, September 15, 1994, page 1282
Publishers Weekly, September 19, 1994, page 69

Other books by the same author:
Night Goes By, 1995
Christmas at Anna's, 1993
Fanny and Margarita: Five Stories about Two Best Friends, 1993

Other books you might like:

Dale Gottlieb, *Seeing Eye Willie*, 1992
Spotting a homeless man, a young child imagines what his life may have been like previously.

Donna Guthrie, *A Rose for Abby*, 1988
The sight of an old woman searching through trash cans near her father's church inspires Abby to assist the neighborhood's homeless.

Margaret Wild, *Space Travellers*, 1992
Temporarily without a home, Zac and his mother live in a rocket play structure in a city park.

1374

NANCY SPRINGER
DANIEL MARK DUFFY, Illustrator

The Great Pony Hassle

(New York: Dial Books for Young Readers, 1993)

Subject(s): Stepfamilies; Twins; Animals/Horses
Age range(s): Grades 4-5
Major character(s): Staci Fontecchio, 10-Year-Old, Twin (identical); Toni Fontecchio, 10-Year-Old, Twin (identical); Paisley McPherson, 10-Year-Old, Twin (fraternal)
Time period(s): 1990s (1993)
Locale(s): United States

Summary: A formula for a less-than-successful beginning to a stepfamily: one wedding, joining two parents each with twins, creating four stepsisters one of whom has received a promise of a pony. Bossy Paisley is as much an annoyance to Toni and Staci as her very quiet sister is a puzzle. While the parents are honeymooning, the four girls are arguing, sulking, and gloating over each others' misfortunes. When Paisley's father returns, he realizes that his offer of a pony will work only if he offers one to each of the girls. (75 pages)

Where it's reviewed:
Booklist, June 1, 1993, page 1836
Horn Book Guide, Spring 1994, page 82
Kirkus Reviews, July 1, 1993, page 866
Library Talk, May 1994, page 42
School Library Journal, August 1993, page 166

Other books by the same author:
Music of Their Hooves: Poems about Horses, 1994
Colt, 1991 (Joan Fassler Memorial Book Award)
They're All Named Wildfire, 1989

Other books you might like:

Valerie Beales, *Emma and Freckles*, 1992
Emma's hopes for a pony are realized when she receives Freckles.

Jeanne Betancourt, *A Pony for Keeps*, 1995
The second entry in the Pony Pals series finds Anna trying to improve her grades before her parents take away her pony.

Bonnie Bryant, *Pony Crazy*, 1995
May and Jasmine, best friends and junior members of the Pony Club, are suspicious of the activities of their new neighbors.

1375

SARA ST. ANTOINE

The Green Musketeers and the Fabulous Frogs

(New York: Bantam Books, 1994)

Series: Green Musketeers
Subject(s): Animals/Frogs and Toads; Ecology; Environmental Problems
Age range(s): Grades 3-5
Major character(s): Samantha Ripley, 5th Grader, Activist; Emily Haas, 5th Grader
Time period(s): 1990s (1994)
Locale(s): Berryville

Summary: On a class field trip to Emerson's Bog, Emily spots an unusual, bright green frog which the class learns is an endangered Big Bog Tree Frog, threatened by encroaching development. Determined to preserve the frog's habitat, Samantha and Emily organize their classmates into the Green Musketeers and make plans to publicize the frog's plight by making it the town mascot. Their efforts require teamwork, organizing and energy as they raise money and signatures to solve an important environmental dilemma. (131 pages)

Where it's reviewed:
Publishers Weekly, April 18, 1994, page 63
School Library Journal, April 1994, page 128

Other books by the same author:
The Green Musketeers and the Incredible Energy Escapade, 1994
Ghostwriter: Dress Code Mess, 1992

Other books you might like:

Jean Craighead George, *The Fire Bug Connection: An Ecological Mystery*, 1993
When Maggie's unusual birthday gift fails to develop, she uses her ability to reason scientifically to determine the cause of the fire bugs' death.

Linda Glaser, *Tanya's Big Green Dream*, 1994
Tanya plans an Earth Day project that requires the cooperative efforts of her classmates to be successful.

Bonnie Pryor, *Marvelous Marvin and the Pioneer Ghost*, 1995
Marvin joins forces with his twin Sarah and two other kids to find out who is dumping toxic waste into a local creek.

1376

DIANE STANLEY
DENNIS NOLAN, Illustrator

The Gentleman and the Kitchen Maid

(New York: Dial Books for Young Readers, 1994)

Subject(s): Artists and Art; Love; Museums
Age range(s): Grades 2-4
Major character(s): Rusty, Artist, Student
Time period(s): 1990s (1994)
Locale(s): United States

Summary: For many years two paintings hung facing one another in an art museum. Despite snide comments from subjects in the other paintings, the gentleman loves the kitchen maid. When Rusty selects the portrait of the gentleman to copy, she notices his gaze falls on the painting of a kitchen maid. Perceptively, she solves the couple's dilemma by painting the kitchen maid onto the same canvas as her portrait of the gentleman. (32 pages)

Where it's reviewed:
Booklist, January 15, 1994, page 939
Library Talk, May 1994, page 18
New Advocate, Fall 1994, page 284
Publishers Weekly, November 22, 1993, page 63
School Library Journal, August 1994, page 146

Other books by the same author:
Moe the Dog in Tropical Paradise, 1992
The Conversation Club, 1990
Peter the Great, 1986

Other books you might like:
Johnny Alcorn, *Rembrandt's Beret*, 1991
    While visiting the Uffizi Gallery, a painter observes the paintings come to life.
Barbara Helen Berger, *The Jewel Heart*, 1994
    In this fantasy, the transforming power of Pavelle's love heals injured Gemino.
Petra Mathers, *Victor and Christabel*, 1993
    The loving attention of Victor, a museum guard, frees Christabel from the painting in which she has been imprisoned by her evil cousin.

1377

DIANE STANLEY
G. BRIAN KARAS, Illustrator

Saving Sweetness
(New York: Putnam, 1996)

Subject(s): Orphans; Deserts; Crime and Criminals
Age range(s): Grades K-3
Major character(s): Sweetness, Orphan, Heroine; Sheriff, Guardian, Cowboy; Mrs. Sump, Child-Care Giver
Time period(s): Indeterminate Past
Locale(s): United States

Summary: Sweetness has had enough of the orphanage, where Mrs. Sump makes the girls clean the floor with toothbrushes, and runs away into the desert. When the sheriff comes to rescue her, Sweetness ends up rescuing him instead from thirst, hunger, and a gunslinger. In the end, the sheriff adopts Sweetness, and all the other girls in the orphanage, leaving Mrs. Sump to marry the gunslinger. (unpaged)

Where it's reviewed:
School Library Journal, November 1996, page 93
Bulletin of the Center for Children's Books, November 1996, page 116
Booklist, January 1, 1997, page 857

Awards the book has won:
Booklist Editors' Choice, 1996

Other books by the same author:
Charles Dickens: The Man Who Had Great Expectations, 1993
Moe the Dog in Tropical Paradise, 1992
Bard of Avalon, 1992

Other books you might like:
Caron Lee Cohen, *Bronco Dogs*, 1991
    Bank robbers get into trouble and become ghosts, but they are still best friends.
Roy Gerrard, *Rosie and the Rustlers*, 1989
    Rosie is able to overcome the rustlers, even though she is little.
Tony Johnston, *The Cowboy and the Black-Eyed Pea*, 1992
    A retelling of "The Princess and the Pea" in which the heroine tries to find a real cowboy among her many suitors.
Joan Lowery Nixon, *Beats Me, Claude*, 1986
    Shirley attempts to make an apple pie for Claude but is not successful until the day an orphan comes to try his hand.
Jon Scieszka, *The Good, the Bad, and the Goofy*, 1992
    The Time Warp Trio are in the Wild West meeting cowboys and Indians.

1378

WILLIAM STEIG, Author/Illustrator

Zeke Pippin
(New York: HarperCollins, 1994)

Subject(s): Animals/Pigs; Music; Magic
Age range(s): Grades 1-4
Major character(s): Zeke Pippin, Pig, Runaway
Time period(s): Indeterminate
Locale(s): Fictional Country

Summary: When Zeke finds a harmonica, he cleans it and teaches himself to play. Unfortunately, each time he performs for his family, they fall asleep. Offended by his family's rude behavior, Zeke runs away aboard a raft to float down the river. As he wiles away the time by playing the harmonica, he notices that birds and people on other boats also fall asleep. Recognizing that his harmonica has magic powers, he tries to return to his family. Before he can do so, Zeke must use his new-found knowledge to overpower robbers and a hungry coyote. (32 pages)

Where it's reviewed:
Booklist, November 1, 1994, page 510
Horn Book, January 1995, page 55
Kirkus Reviews, November 15, 1994, page 1544
Publishers Weekly, November 21, 1994, page 76
School Library Journal, December 1994, page 87

Awards the book has won:
School Library Journal Best Books, 1994

Other books by the same author:
The Amazing Bone, 1977 (Caldecott Honor Book)
Abel's Island, 1976 (Newbery Honor Book)
Sylvester and the Magic Pebble, 1969 (Caldecott Medal Winner)

Other books you might like:
Eric A. Kimmel, *Anansi and the Moss-Covered Rock*, 1988
    The sleep-inducing powers of a magic rock are used to

Anansi's advantage until another animal manages to out-wit the trickster.

Robert McCloskey, *Lentil*, 1940

Although he can't carry a tune, Lentil is able to master the harmonica and play in a town celebration.

John Sebastian, *J.B.'s Harmonica*, 1993

Tired of people comparing his playing to his famous father's, J. B. puts his harmonica away temporarily.

1379

JAN ROMERO STEVENS
JEANNE ARNOLD, Illustrator

Carlos and the Cornfield/Carlos y la Milpa de Maiz

(Flagstaff, AZ: Northland Publishing Company, 1995)

Subject(s): Farm Life; Mexican Americans; Fathers and Sons
Age range(s): Grades K-3
Major character(s): Carlos, Child; Papa, Father, Farmer
Time period(s): 1990s (1995)
Locale(s): Espanola Valley, New Mexico

Summary: With the money Carlos earns planting the corn crop in the family garden, he will buy a red pocket knife. For the first few rows, Carlos follows his father's planting instructions carefully, but as the day grows hot and Carlos grows tired, he increases the number of seeds which he puts into each hole so that, when he is "finished," two rows remain unplanted. In time, the corn sprouts and Carlos sees the error of his ways. At first, he tries to transplant the new shoots into the empty row, but he soon realizes he can do only one thing to make it right. He pawns his beloved knife and uses the money to buy more seed to plant into the two empty rows. When the corn is harvested and those two rows yield blue corn, Carlos' secret is obvious to all. The story is written with parallel texts of English and Spanish. (32 pages)

Where it's reviewed:
Booklist, September 1, 1995, page 80
School Library Journal, September 1995, page 186

Other books by the same author:
Carlos and the Squash Plant, 1993

Other books you might like:
Bernice Chardiet, *Juan Bobo and the Pig: A Puerto Rican Folktale Retold*, 1973

Playing a trick on the family pig turns out in a way that Juan does not expect.

Lulu Delacre, *Vejigante/Masquerader*, 1993

Ramon's preparations for and experiences at Carnival are described in a bilingual text.

Douglas Keister, *Fernando's Gift/El Regalo de Fernando*, 1995

Parallel texts in English and Spanish tell the story of a young boy and his family who live in the Costa Rican rain forest.

1380

JANET STEVENS, Author/Illustrator

Coyote Steals the Blanket: A Ute Tale

(New York: Holiday House, 1993)

Subject(s): Animals/Coyotes; Legends; American West
Age range(s): Grades K-3
Major character(s): Coyote, Coyote; Hummingbird, Bird
Time period(s): Indeterminate Past
Locale(s): Southwest

Summary: Ignoring the warnings of Hummingbird, overly confident Coyote continues on the path he has chosen. When he spies the blankets mentioned by Hummingbird, he fails to heed the bird's warnings and grabs a blanket from the rock. Although the consequences are exhausting, they fail to teach the trickster a lasting lesson. (32 pages)

Where it's reviewed:
Booklist, April 1, 1993, page 1428
Horn Book Guide, Fall 1993, page 329
Publishers Weekly, April 19, 1993, page 59
Reading Teacher, October 1994, page 156
School Library Journal, June 1993, page 96

Awards the book has won:
School Library Journal Best Books, 1993

Other books by the same author:
Tops and Bottoms, 1994 (Caldecott Honor Book)
The Town Mouse and the Country Mouse: An Aesop Fable, 1987
The Tortoise and the Hare: An Aesop Fable, 1984

Other books you might like:
Barbara Diamond Goldin, *Coyote and the Firestick*, 1996

Coyote plays the role of the hero rather than the trickster in a retelling of a tale from the Pacific Northwest.

Gerald Hausman, *Coyote Walks on Two Legs: A Book of Navajo Myths and Legends*, 1995

Five traditional tales show Coyote to sometimes be a hero and a fool as well as a trickster.

Gerald McDermott, *Coyote: A Trickster Tale from the American Southwest*, 1994

The retelling of a traditional Zuni tale explains how trickster coyote's fur became the color of dust with a black tip on his tail.

1381

JANET STEVENS, Author/Illustrator

Tops and Bottoms

(San Diego: Harcourt Brace & Company, 1995)

Subject(s): Folk Tales; Animals/Bears; Animals/Rabbits
Age range(s): Grades K-2
Major character(s): Bear, Bear (lazy), Landowner; Hare, Rabbit, Father, Worker
Time period(s): Indeterminate Past
Locale(s): United States

Summary: In an attempt to feed his hungry family, clever Hare enters into a business arrangement with lazy Bear. Bear sleeps and Hare's family plants crops with half the harvest going to Bear in exchange for use of his land. When Bear chooses the top half of the crop, Hare plants root vegetables. When Bear chooses the bottom half, Hare plants celery and broccoli. Angrily, Bear demands a third crop to give him both tops and bottoms so Hare plants corn, takes the middle and leaves Bear the tassels and stalks. Bear now tends his own garden and the Hare family grows rich selling vegetables. (32 pages)

Where it's reviewed:
Booklist, March 15, 1995, page 1329
Bulletin of the Center for Children's Books, April 1995, page 287
Children's Book Review Service, May 1995, page 112
Horn Book, May 1995, page 337
School Library Journal, May 1995, page 103

Awards the book has won:
Caldecott Honor Book, 1996
Booklist Editors' Choice, 1995

Other books by the same author:
How the Manx Cat Lost Its Tail, 1990
The Three Billy Goats Gruff, 1987
The Tortoise and the Hare: An Aesop Fable, 1984

Other books you might like:
Joel Chandler Harris, *Jump! The Adventures of Brer Rabbit*, 1986
Malcolm Jones and Van Dyke Parks have adapted the classic Uncle Remus stories in an illustrated collection.
Linda Hayward, *Hello, House!*, 1988
With customary cleverness, Brer Rabbit outwits Brer Wolf.
Julius Lester, *More Tales of Uncle Remus: Further Adventures of Brer Rabbit, His Friends, Enemies, and Others*, 1988
The famous trickster Brer Rabbit is featured in thirty-seven stories about his activities.

1382

KATHLEEN STEVENS
ROBERT ANDREW PARKER, Illustrator

Aunt Skilly and the Stranger

(New York: Ticknor & Fields Books for Young Readers, 1994)

Subject(s): Animals/Geese; Robbers and Outlaws; Mountain Life
Age range(s): Grades K-3
Major character(s): Aunt Skilly, Aged Person; Buckle, Goose; Unnamed Character, Thief
Time period(s): Indeterminate Past
Locale(s): Which-Way Mountain

Summary: When a stranger from the ''wrong'' side of Which-Way Mountain comes to call, Buckle is immediately suspicious, but Aunt Skilly is as hospitable as always. The thief discovers that her kindliness is not a sign of gullibility when his late-night attempt to steal the home-made quilts which are her year's income is thwarted by Buckle's vigilance and Aunt Skilly's forethought. (32 pages)

Where it's reviewed:
Five Owls, September 1994, page 12

Horn Book, November 1994, page 727
Kirkus Reviews, July 15, 1994, page 996
Publishers Weekly, July 11, 1994, page 78
School Library Journal, October 1994, page 103

Other books by the same author:
Bully for the Beast!, 1990
The Beast and the Babysitter, 1989
The Beast in the Bathtub, 1985

Other books you might like:
Molly Bang, *Wiley and the Hairy Man*, 1976
With help from his mother, Wiley outwits a dreadful creature from the swamp.
Phyllis Root, *Aunt Nancy and Old Man Trouble*, 1996
When Old Man Trouble knocks, Aunt Nancy invites him in and proceeds to outsmart the trickster with her cheerful response to each misfortune he causes.
Cynthia Rylant, *When I Was Young in the Mountains*, 1982
The author shares memories of a childhood spent with grandparents in the Appalachian mountains.

1383

DREW STEVENSON
MARCY DUNN RAMSEY, Illustrator

Toying with Danger

(New York: Cobblehill Books/Dutton, 1993)

Series: Sarah Capshaw Mystery
Subject(s): Mystery and Detective Stories; Inventions; Toys
Age range(s): Grades 3-5
Major character(s): Sarah Capshaw, Detective—Amateur; Clark Lannigan, Child, Friend (Sarah's); Frog Fenniman, Child, Friend (Sarah's)
Time period(s): 1990s (1993)
Locale(s): Wilsonburg, Pennsylvania

Summary: Sarah Capshaw's summer visits with her grandparents provide an exciting change of pace for residents Clark and Frog. Always on the lookout for a mystery to solve, Sarah is not deterred by the boys' fear of Misty Woods and leads them down the lane through the woods at night to investigate a report of a monster at the old Harley farm. They find not only a mystery, but also danger. (128 pages)

Where it's reviewed:
Booklist, February 15, 1993, page 1061
Childhood Education, Fall 1993, page 48
Horn Book Guide, Fall 1993, page 305
Kirkus Reviews, January 1, 1993, page 68
School Library Journal, February 1993, page 95

Other books by the same author:
One Ghost Too Many, 1991 (Sarah Capshaw Mystery)
The Case of the Wandering Werewolf, 1987
The Case of the Visiting Vampire, 1986

Other books you might like:
Avi, *Windcatcher*, 1991
Not eager for a summer visit with his grandmother on the Connecticut shore, Tony finds that learning to sail and searching for lost treasure help him change his mind.
Sharon Cadwallader, *Cookie McCorkle and the Case of the Mystery Map*, 1993

Another entry in the Cookie McCorkle series finds Cookie and friend Walter busy with their detective business as yet another case comes their way.

Eth Clifford, *Never Hit a Ghost with a Baseball Bat*, 1993
When Mary Rose and Jo-Beth accompany their reporter father on assignment to a trolly car museum, they notice the lifeless mannequins seem to be eerily lively.

1384

JAMES STEVENSON, Author/Illustrator

All Aboard!
(New York: Greenwillow Books, 1995)

Subject(s): Animals/Mice; Trains; Adventure and Adventurers
Age range(s): Grades 1-3
Major character(s): Hubie, Mouse
Time period(s): 1930s (1939)
Locale(s): Broadway Blazer; New York, New York

Summary: Hubie and his family board the Broadway Blazer for a trip to the New York World's Fair. At a temporary stop, Hubie curiously gets off and accidently reboards the wrong train. Now aboard the California Comet, Hubie is rapidly heading away from his family and his destination. Through a series of misadventures and a variety of modes of transportation, Hubie finally rejoins his family when he parachutes into the fairgrounds. (32 pages)

Where it's reviewed:
Booklist, April 1, 1995, page 1394
Horn Book, September 1995, page 627
Kirkus Reviews, March 15, 1995, page 396
Library Talk, September 1995, page 29
School Library Journal, June 1995, page 96

Other books by the same author:
The Flying Acorns, 1993
The Stowaway, 1990
The Sea View Hotel, 1974

Other books you might like:
John Burningham, *John Patrick Norman McHennessy: The Boy Who Was Always Late*, 1988
John's teacher does not believe the excuse he gives for his tardiness until an equally unbelievable occurrence happens to him.
Carol Carrick, *Left Behind*, 1988
Returning from a field trip, Christopher becomes separated from his class and finds himself lost in the subway.
Mark Taylor, *Henry Explores the Mountains*, 1975
What was planned to be a simple trip to the woods involves Henry and his dog in a forest fire and a helicopter ride.
David Macaulay, *Shortcut*, 1995
As Albert and his horse travel to market their simple actions effect other travelers in unforeseen ways.

1385

JAMES STEVENSON

The Bones in the Cliff
(New York: Greenwillow, 1995)

Subject(s): Crime and Criminals; Islands; Fathers and Sons
Age range(s): Grades 4-6
Major character(s): Pete, 11-Year-Old; Rosalie Ann "Rootie" Bowditch, 11-Year-Old
Time period(s): 1990s
Locale(s): United States (Cutlass Island)

Summary: Pete knows his father has done something wrong, but he doesn't know what; all he knows is that three times a day he has to meet the ferry that comes to the island to see if there's a cigar-smoking man aboard. His mother is hospitalized with depression and his father is an abusive alcoholic, which combine to create a dismal homelife for Pete. One day he meets Rootie, a native of the island, who shows him island life as newcomers never get to see it. Because Pete and Rootie have so many adventures, Pete misses the ferry the day it carries the hit man to the island in this first novel by a picture book author. (119 pages)

Where it's reviewed:
Publishers Weekly, May 15, 1995, page 74
Booklist, May 1, 1995, page 1567
Five Owls, May 1995, page 103
Horn Book, July 1995, page 461
Library Talk, May 1995, page 44

Other books you might like:
Jay Bennett, *Say Hello to the Hit Man*, 1977
When Fred receives a strange phone call warning him of his upcoming death, he's convinced it's because his father's a gangster.
Barthe DeClements, *Monkey See, Monkey Do*, 1990
Jerry's father violates parole by letting a friend use his car to commit a robbery.
Alice Mead, *Walking the Edge*, 1995
Scott's alcoholic, abusive father makes his life miserable; luckily the Coast Guard apprehends his father during one of his drug-selling activities.

1386

JAMES STEVENSON, Author/Illustrator

The Mud Flat Olympics
(New York: Greenwillow Books, 1994)

Subject(s): Animals; Games; Humor
Age range(s): Grades 1-3
Major character(s): Harold, Owl; Burbank, Opossum; Hugh, Turtle
Time period(s): Indeterminate
Locale(s): Mud Flat, Fictional Country

Summary: The animals of Mud Flat gather annually to conduct their own Olympic games. Harold judges the moles in the digging contest where not only speed, but also glibness of tongue decides the winner. Burbank becomes so bored waiting for the snails to complete the hurdles that he goes out to lunch only to find them all sitting on the finish line when he returns. In the swimming race, Hugh comes out ahead after a mean crocodile tries to knock out the competition and is blown out of the water by two elephants. (56 pages)

Where it's reviewed:
Booklist, September 1, 1994, page 43
Horn Book, November 1994, page 728
Kirkus Reviews, October 15, 1994, page 1416
Publishers Weekly, October 17, 1994, page 81
School Library Journal, October 1994, page 103

Awards the book has won:
Booklist Editors' Choice, 1994

Other books by the same author:
Fun—No Fun, 1994
Oh No, It's Waylon's Birthday!, 1989
The Supreme Souvenir Factory, 1988

Other books you might like:
Arnold Lobel, *Days with Frog and Toad*, 1979
  Good friends Frog and Toad enjoy spending time together.
Margaret Mahy, *The Queen's Goat*, 1991
  At a pet fair, a young queen and her borrowed, runaway goat win an unexpected prize.
Patricia Polacco, *Picnic at Mudsock Meadow*, 1992
  Trying to impress Heather, William enters the many contests at the picnic including seed-spitting and pie-eating.
Erica Silverman, *Don't Fidget a Feather*, 1994
  Two competitive friends learn that some things are more important than winning.

1387

JAMES STEVENSON, Author/Illustrator

A Village Full of Valentines
(New York: Greenwillow Books, 1995)

Subject(s): Animals; Holidays; Humor
Age range(s): Grades 1-3
Time period(s): Indeterminate
Locale(s): Fictional Country

Summary: Brief stories of varying lengths describe the activities in a village as the residents prepare for Valentine's Day. While each has a unique approach to the holiday, all the villagers gather together in the last episode to share their contributions to the day's festivities. (40 pages)

Where it's reviewed:
Booklist, December 15, 1994, page 754
Horn Book, March 1995, page 191
Kirkus Reviews, February 15, 1995, page 233
Publishers Weekly, December 5, 1994, page 77
School Library Journal, February 1995, page 82

Other books by the same author:
The Worst Goes South, 1995
Fun—No Fun, 1994
The Pattaconk Brook, 1993

Other books you might like:
Thacher Hurd, *Little Mouse's Big Valentine*, 1990
  Little Mouse has made a special valentine, now he's trying to find a recipient.

Mariana, *Miss Flora McFlimsey's Valentine*, 1962
  Miss Flora McFlimsey creates original cards to send her friends for Valentine's Day.
George Shannon, *Heart to Heart*, 1995
  When he realizes that he has forgotten Valentine's Day, Squirrel scurries to complete a card for friend Mole.

1388

JAMES STEVENSON, Author/Illustrator

Worse than the Worst
(New York: Greenwillow Books, 1994)

Subject(s): Behavior; Aunts and Uncles; Conduct of Life
Age range(s): Grades K-2
Major character(s): Warren, Child, Nephew; Mr. Worst, Uncle (great-uncle), Aged Person; Daisy, Dog
Time period(s): 1990s (1994)
Locale(s): United States

Summary: When Warren is delivered, uninvited, to Uncle Worst's doorstep, the worst appears to have met his match. Warren orders pizza without asking, takes over his uncle's bedroom and invites all the neighborhood children in to play. Mr. Worst hides in the attic and his dog vanishes. Searching for Daisy helps Warren and Uncle Worst find some common ground, but neither of them want to repeat the experience. (32 pages)

Where it's reviewed:
Booklist, March 1, 1994, page 1271
Bulletin of the Center for Children's Books, July 1994, page 374
Horn Book, May 1994, page 341
Kirkus Reviews, February 15, 1994, page 234
School Library Journal, July 1994, page 90

Other books by the same author:
The Worst Person's Christmas, 1991
The Worst Person in the World at Crab Beach, 1988
The Worst Person in the World, 1978

Other books you might like:
Barbara Bottner, *Bootsie Barker Bites*, 1992
  A little girl dreads being forced to entertain the obnoxious daughter of her mother's friend so she comes up with an idea to beat Bootsie at her own game.
James Marshall, *The Cut-Ups Crack Up*, 1992
  When Spud and Joe get behind the wheel of the Principal's sports car, disaster looms.
Mike Thaler, *The Bully Brothers Trick the Tooth Fairy*, 1993
  Twins Bubba and Bumpo go to extreme measures to make money from the Tooth Fairy until she does some extracting of her own.

1389

JAMES STEVENSON, Author/Illustrator

The Worst Goes South
(New York: Greenwillow Books, 1995)

Subject(s): Neighbors and Neighborhoods; Behavior; Brothers
Age range(s): Grades K-3

Major character(s): Arvin Worst, Brother; Ervin Worst, Brother

Time period(s): 1990s (1995)

Summary: Two grumpy old men with attitude meet when Arvin Worst attempts to escape the noise of a community Harvest Festival near his home by driving to Florida. There he stays in a ramshackle motel operated by a brother he hasn't seen in forty years. It's hard to tell which Worst is worst, but the experience seems to have softened Arvin who returns home on the concluding day of the Harvest Festival and then sends his brother an invitation to drive north for it next year. (32 pages)

Where it's reviewed:
Booklist, September 1, 1995, page 89
Horn Book, September 1995, page 592
Horn Book Guide, Spring 1996, page 46
Parents' Choice, September 1995, page 13
School Library Journal, October 1995, page 120

Other books by the same author:
Worse than the Worst, 1994
The Worst Person's Christmas, 1991
The Worst Person in the World, 1978

Other books you might like:
Eileen Christelow, *The Five-Dog Night*, 1993
    Crabby Ezra wants no advice from helpful, but nosy neighbor Old Betty.
James Howe, *Pinky and Rex and the Mean Old Witch*, 1991
    Pinky and Rex change their plans to seek revenge on a cantankerous old neighbor when they realize she may just be lonely.
Eileen Spinelli, *Somebody Loves You, Mr. Hatch*, 1991
    Unsociable Mr. Hatch receives an anonymous valentine which changes his outlook on life.

1390

JAMES STEVENSON, Author/Illustrator

Yard Sale
(New York: Greenwillow, 1996)

Subject(s): Friendship; Humor
Age range(s): Grades K-3
Major character(s): Crocker, Crocodile; Henry, Raccoon; Matthew, Ox
Time period(s): 1990s
Locale(s): United States (woods near mud flats)

Summary: The woodland animals decide to hold a yard sale. They all have something to buy or sell, from an alarm clock with no alarm to an accordion which ends up being shared. At the end of the day all the animals enjoy a party where they share their new purchases with the former owners. (32 pages)

Where it's reviewed:
School Library Journal, July 1996, page 74
Booklist, March 15, 1996, page 1264

Awards the book has won:
School Library Journal Best Books, 1996

Other books by the same author:
Monty, 1994

The Mud Flat Olympics, 1994
National Worm Day, 1990

Other books you might like:
Artie Ann Bates, *Ragsale*, 1995
    A girl and her mother love to spend time visiting different places to see what they can buy.
Mary Blount Christian, *Penrod's Picture*, 1991
    Penrod Porcupine and Griswold Bear share some amusing adventures.
John Himmelman, *Simpson Snail Sings*, 1992
    Simpson engages in all kinds of activites from a sleep-over to composing a song.
Susan Russo, *Joe's Junk*, 1982
    A young boy builds up collections and then decides to sell them.

1391

DIANNE STEWART
JUDE DALY, Illustrator

The Dove
(New York: Greenwillow Books, 1993)

Subject(s): Floods; Grandparents; Animals/Birds
Age range(s): Grades 1-3
Major character(s): Lindi, Child; Grandmother Maloko, Grandmother
Time period(s): 1990s (1993)
Locale(s): Natal, South Africa (Valley of a Thousand Hills)

Summary: After a flood, Lindi and Grandmother Maloko are grateful for their undamaged home, but concerned about their survival because the ground is too wet for spring planting. Inspired by a dove which landed in the yard on the first sunny day, Lindi uses her grandmother's scraps to make a beaded one which she sells in Durban. Together the two create more doves and other animals, assuring themselves of income while they await the crops. (32 pages)

Where it's reviewed:
Booklist, May 15, 1993, page 1697
Five Owls, September 1993, page 12
Library Talk, March 1993, page 22
Publishers Weekly, May 17, 1993, page 79
School Library Journal, September 1993, page 220

Other books by the same author:
Paper Chase, 1992

Other books you might like:
Rachel Isadora, *Over the Green Hills*, 1992
    Zolani and his mother travel from their rural home on a visit to Grandma Zindzi.
Kioi Mbuga, *Mcheshi Goes to the Market/Mcheshi Aenda Sokoni*, 1991
    A story of a young girl's trip to market with her mother has both English and Swahili text.
Sanna Stanley, *The Rains Are Coming*, 1993
    The daughter of missionaries celebrates the end of a drought in Zaire when the rain begins on her birthday.

1392

SARAH STEWART
DAVID SMALL, Illustrator

The Library

(New York: Farrar Straus Giroux, 1995)

Subject(s): Libraries; Conduct of Life; Stories in Rhyme
Age range(s): Grades K-3
Major character(s): Elizabeth Brown, Collector, Spinster
Time period(s): Indeterminate Past
Locale(s): United States

Summary: Elizabeth Brown loves books. A nonstop reader, Elizabeth prefers buying books to food and reading to eating. One day she recognizes that her book collection has overtaken her home so she generously donates the home and all its contents to the town for a public library while she retires to the home of a friend where she spends her days reading and sipping tea. (32 pages).

Where it's reviewed:
Booklist, March 15, 1995, page 1338
Horn Book, July 1995, page 454
Library Talk, September 1995, page 29
Publishers Weekly, April 10, 1995, page 61
School Library Journal, September 1995, page 187

Other books by the same author:
The Money Tree, 1991

Other books you might like:
Caroline Feller Bauer, *Too Many Books!*, 1984
  Maralou finds a satisying solution to the problem of having an overly large book collection.
Marie Bradby, *More than Anything Else*, 1995
  Based on the childhood of Booker T. Washington, a nine-year-old longs for the day when he is able to read.
Nancy Smiler Levinson, *Clara and the Bookwagon*, 1988
  The arrival at Clara's farm of a horse-drawn book wagon driven by persuasive Miss Mary convinces Papa of the value of allowing Clara to learn to read.
Patricia Polacco, *Aunt Chip and the Great Triple Creek Dam Affair*, 1996
  Elizabeth Brown would never succumb to the temptation of TV, but the residents of Triple Creek do and soon forget how to read.

1393

CATHERINE STOCK, Author/Illustrator

Where Are You Going, Manyoni?

(New York: Morrow Junior Books, 1993)

Subject(s): Animals; Africa; Schools
Age range(s): Grades K-3
Major character(s): Manyoni, Child
Time period(s): 1990s (1993)
Locale(s): Zimbabwe (rural area near the Limpopo River)

Summary: Manyoni is walking from her family's home, past the giant baobab tree, past the dry river bed, through the grove of wild fig trees and past many animals which she seems not to notice. After she crosses the hot dry plains, another child

calls out in greeting and the two continue on to their destination—the village school. A concluding author's note gives factual information and a glossary defines unfamiliar words. (48 pages)

Where it's reviewed:
Booklist, August 1993, page 2071
Five Owls, November 1993, page 35
Horn Book, November 1993, page 739
Library Talk, November 1993, page 32
School Library Journal, December 1993, page 94

Other books by the same author:
Sophie's Bucket, 1994
Armien's Fishing Trip, 1990
Thanksgiving Treat, 1990

Other books you might like:
Jane Cowen-Fletcher, *It Takes a Village*, 1994
  Kokou wanders in the marketplace while his mother peddles mangoes.
Nigel Gray, *A Country Far Away*, 1989
  The lives of two boys are presented for comparison of life in a African village with life in a western country.
Dianne Stewart, *The Dove*, 1993
  Following a crop-destroying flood in Natal, South Africa, Lindi and her grandmother take inspiration from a dove which lands in their yard.

1394

JANET MORGAN STOEKE, Author/Illustrator

A Hat for Minerva Louise

(New York: Dutton Children's Books, 1994)

Subject(s): Animals/Chickens; Clothes; Weather
Age range(s): Grades K-1
Major character(s): Minerva Louise, Chicken
Time period(s): 1990s (1994)
Locale(s): United States

Summary: Other chickens may huddle in the hen house on snowy mornings, but not Minerva Louise. She loves to explore! The only problem is she becomes cold too quickly. Minerva Louise, in her unique way, solves that problem. (24 pages)

Where it's reviewed:
Horn Book, January 1995, page 55
Kirkus Reviews, September 15, 1994, page 1283
Publishers Weekly, August 1, 1994, page 77
School Library Journal, October 1994, page 103

Awards the book has won:
School Library Journal Best Books, 1994

Other books by the same author:
Minerva Louise, 1988

Other books you might like:
Roger Duvoisin, *Petunia*, 1950
  In this first of the Petunia stories, the silly goose thinks that she can gain wisdom by carrying a book with her.
Pat Hutchins, *Rosie's Walk*, 1968
  Unaware that a fox is following her, Rosie enjoys a walk around the barnyard.

Ezra Jack Keats, *The Snowy Day*, 1962
   Peter explores his city neighborhood and the snow brings added pleasures.
Dorothy Stott, *Too Much*, 1990
   A little duck tries and tries to find a suitable place to swim before locating his mother in the pond.

1395

CYNTHIA STOWE
CAT BOWMAN SMITH, Illustrator

Not-So-Normal Norman

(Morton Grove, IL: Albert Whitman & Company, 1995)

Subject(s): Money; Family Life; Problem Solving
Age range(s): Grades 3-5
Major character(s): Anthony, 4th Grader; Norman, Tarantula; Miss Hilda E. Everring, Scientist
Time period(s): 1990s (1995)
Locale(s): United States

Summary: With his father out of work due to a back injury, Anthony decides to establish a pet-sitting service to raise money for his family. The first client, eccentric Miss Everring, delivers Norman prior to her departure for a two-week trip. Concerned when Norman stops eating and responsible for the health of his charge, Anthony takes him to a vet and learns that the spider is simply molting. Another customer with elderly cats adds to Anthony's responsibilities and his sense of accomplishment when he earns $38 to give his parents. (125 pages)

Where it's reviewed:
Booklist, January 15, 1995, page 930
Horn Book Guide, Fall 1995, page 305
Publishers Weekly, December 12, 1994, page 62
School Library Journal, March 1995, page 206

Other books by the same author:
Home Sweet Home, Good-Bye, 1993
Dear Mom, in Ohio for a Year, 1992

Other books you might like:
Tom Birdseye, *Tarantula Shoes*, 1995
   A pet tarantula named Fang helps Ryan earn the money he needs to buy new basketball shoes.
Beverly Cleary, *Ramona and Her Father*, 1977
   Ramona is surprised by the changes in her routine when her father loses his job.
Peg Kehret, *The Richest Kids in Town*, 1994
   Peter's money-making schemes provide a framework for a friendship with Wishbone Wyoming, but don't earn much cash.

1396

SUSAN STRAIGHT
MARISABINA RUSSO, Illustrator

Bear E. Bear

(New York: Hyperion Books for Children, 1995)

Subject(s): Toys; Sisters; Family Life
Age range(s): Grades K-1

Major character(s): Gaila, Child, Sister (older); Delphine, Child, Sister; Bear E. Bear, Bear, Toy
Time period(s): 1990s (1995)
Locale(s): United States

Summary: Poor Gaila! Her special friend, Bear E. Bear, has been dropped in the mud by Delphine. Gaila sits on the dryer and watches Bear E. Bear go around and up and down with the clothes. When he's clean, she waits patiently for the dryer to complete its cycle. While the laundry process is underway, Gaila thinks of how important Bear E. Bear is to her and, when finally he is clean and dry, she hugs him as she settles down to sleep. First children's book for the novelist. (32 pages)

Where it's reviewed:
Booklist, March 15, 1995, page 1338
Horn Book Guide, Fall 1995, page 284
New York Times Book Review, June 4, 1995, page 25
Publishers Weekly, April 3, 1995, page 61
School Library Journal, June 1995, page 96

Other books you might like:
Catherine Anholt, *Bear and Baby*, 1993
   In any kind of weather, a girl and her special teddy bear will be found going places together.
Sarah Hayes, *This Is the Bear and the Bad Little Girl*, 1995
   A boy's beloved teddy bear is stolen by an envious little girl, but his dog chases her and helps to retrieve Fred.
Kim Lewis, *First Snow*, 1993
   While helping Mom feed the animals as snow begins to fall, Sara drops her Teddy. She heads home sad and empty-handed until onof the family dogs appears with Teddy.
Martin Waddell, *Small Bear Lost*, 1996
   When Small Bear is left on a train, he manages to find his way home to the little girl who lost him.

1397

TODD STRASSER

Hey, Dad, Get a Life

(New York: Holiday House, 1996)

Subject(s): Ghosts; Fathers and Daughters; Sisters
Age range(s): Grades 4-7
Major character(s): Kelly Halkit, 12-Year-Old, Child (of single parent); Sasha Halkit, 8-Year-Old, Child (of single parent); Mr. Halkit, Father, Spirit
Time period(s): 1990s
Locale(s): United States

Summary: Sasha and Kelly really miss their father. He was the one who always helped with homework, went to their games, and was a great companion. Now Sasha thinks he may still be alive and after the girls hold a seance in the tree house strange things do begin to happen. Soccer balls react in funny ways during Kelly's games, homework is completed by an unknown being, and Sasha's room is cleaned when she's not there. Mother's nights out with another man are completely ruined and, finally, the spirit of Mr. Halkit appears as a light in the kitchen. When the girls and their mother start doing things together and for themselves, they find that their father is no longer necessary as an active force but the memory of him will always be with the family. (164 pages)

Where it's reviewed:
Booklist, February 15, 1997, page 1024

Other books by the same author:
Friends Til the End, 1991
The Mall from Outer Space, 1987

Other books you might like:
Barthe DeClements, *The Fourth Grade Wizards*, 1990
   A girl and her father must adjust to the death of her mother.
Janice Marriott, *Letters to Lesley*, 1991
   Henry's mother embarrasses him so he writes to Lesley to try to arrange a marriage between their parents.
Mary Jane Miller, *Upside Down*, 1992
   Sara is dismayed when her mother starts to date another man.
Barbara Garland Polikoff, *Life's a Funny Proposition, Horatio*, 1992
   Horatio and his mother move to Wisconsin after his father dies.

1398

EILEEN WALSH STRAUCH

Hey You, Sister Rose

(New York: Tambourine Books, 1993)

Subject(s): Schools/Catholic Schools; Teachers; Teacher-Student Relationships
Age range(s): Grades 4-6
Major character(s): Sister Mary Rose, Religious (nun), Teacher; Arlene Warren, 6th Grader; Eunice Montgomery, 6th Grader (new to the school)
Time period(s): 1950s (1951)
Locale(s): Baltimore, Maryland (St. Anthony's School)

Summary: In the author's first novel, Arlene's worst fears are realized on the first day of school when she discovers that Sister Rose is her teacher. Unfortunately, Sister Rose has not forgotten Arlene's giggling during the Good Friday services last spring and she considers it her duty to assure that Arlene learn proper behavior. Also, Sister Rose encourages Arlene to befriend Eunice who is responsible for her younger siblings since her mother's death. By the end of the year Arlene and Sister Rose have grown sufficiently in understanding of one another to have mixed feelings about parting. (159 pages)

Where it's reviewed:
Booklist, March 1, 1993, page 1231
Children's Book Review Service, April 1993, page 108
Horn Book Guide, Fall 1993, page 305
Publishers Weekly, February 22, 1993, page 96
School Library Journal, June 1993, page 112

Other books you might like:
Barbara Shook Hazen, *Good-Bye, Hello*, 1994
   Sixth grade should be fun, but for Bobbie Jean, stuck in tough Sister Alice's class—what could be worse!
Lois Lowry, *Anastasia, Again!*, 1981
   In the sequel to *Anastasia Krupnik*, Anastasia faces a family move from the city to the suburbs with her characteristic wit and inventiveness.

Colleen O'Shaughnessy Murphy, *The Truth about Sixth Grade*, 1991
   Instant popularity comes to Collette simply because her family knows a teacher considered by the other students to be extremely attractive.
Phyllis Reynolds Naylor, *The Agony of Alice*, 1985
   Motherless Alice is seeking a female role model and the only one available is her despised 6th grade teacher.

1399

CRAIG KEE STRETE

The World in Grandfather's Hands

(New York: Clarion Books, 1995)

Subject(s): Indians of North America; Grandparents; Death
Age range(s): Grades 4-6
Major character(s): Jimmy, 11-Year-Old; Grandfather Whitefeather, Grandfather (Jimmy's grandfather)
Time period(s): 1990s
Locale(s): Southwest

Summary: After Jimmy's father dies, he and his mother leave their pueblo to live in the city with his grandfather. Jimmy misses his desert life and feels hemmed in by the tall buildings and the noise of living in a city. Grandfather Whitefeather tries to explain city life to Jimmy but also reminds him to "carry the pueblo with you wherever you go." Jimmy gradually understands the wisdom of his grandfather's advice. (135 pages)

Where it's reviewed:
School Library Journal, September 1995, page 204
Children's Book Review Service, October 1995, page 20
Center for Children's Books. Bulletin, October 1995, page 71
Kirkus Reviews, June 15, 1995, page 864
Horn Book Guide, Spring 1996, page 69

Other books by the same author:
Big Thunder Magic, 1990 (picture book)
To Make Death Love Us, 1987 (science fiction)

Other books you might like:
Will Hobbs, *Bearstone*, 1989
   Cloyd discovers love, along with his Indian heritage, when he rescues his foster parent Walter from a mining accident in Colorado.
Paul Pitts, *Racing the Sun*, 1988
   When Brandon's grandfather shares a room with him, he teaches Brandon much about his Indian heritage.
Luke Wallin, *Ceremony of the Panther*, 1987
   John is a 16-year-old Indian who's caught in the universal dilemma of blending his family traditions with the expectations and prejudices of the outside world.

1400

JUDITH BERNIE STROMMEN

Champ Hobarth

(New York: Holt, 1993)

Subject(s): Animals/Dogs; Animals, Treatment of; Self-Perception

Age range(s): Grades 5-6
Major character(s): Lawrence Martin "Marty" Hobarth, Volunteer; Leanne Patrice Igler, Volunteer; Champ Hobarth, Dog (Saint bernard)
Time period(s): 1990s
Locale(s): Johnson Falls, Minnesota

Summary: How come everything Marty does is wrong? There's no way he can compete with his family—his father runs marathons, his mother's just completed college and his sister is the town spelling champ. Marty can't even make the local diving team, though he doesn't tell his father this news. What Marty does do is save a stray Saint Bernard from being sent to the pound, though his father won't let him keep it. When the dog eventually ends up at the shelter, Marty and his friend Leanne become volunteers there so he can be near Champ Hobarth. In his own way, Marty proves he's a winner. (179 pages)

Where it's reviewed:
School Library Journal, August 1993, page 166
Horn Book, July 1993, page 461
Library Talk, January 1994, page 42
Booklist, July 1993, page 1968
Kirkus Reviews, June 15, 1993, page 792

Other books by the same author:
Johnson Falls Story, 1995
Grady the Great, 1990

Other books you might like:
Marty Crisp, *Buzzard Breath*, 1995
    Though Will thinks the German shepherd nicknamed Buzzard Breath is not the dog he always dreamed of owning, he can't let him stay in the pound.
Lynn Hall, *Windsong*, 1992
    Marty's saves a greyhound who's the runt of the litter, but then has to find a home for Windsong when her brother's allergies prevent her from keeping him.
Jean Little, *Lost and Found*, 1986
    Happy to find a stray dog when she moves to a new town, Lucy doesn't know what to do when the owner shows up to claim the dog.

1401

VIRGINIA A. STROUD, Author/Illustrator

Doesn't Fall Off His Horse

(New York: Dial Books for Young Readers, 1994)

Subject(s): Indians of North America; Grandparents; Storytelling
Age range(s): Grades 1-3
Major character(s): Saygee, Child, Indian; Grandpa, Grandfather (great grandfather), Indian (Kiowa)
Time period(s): 1990s (1994); Indeterminate Past
Locale(s): Oklahoma

Summary: Saygee listens as her elderly great grandfather recalls the events of his youth which earned him the name Doesn't Fall Off His Horse. With a group of friends, but without the permission of the tribal elders or the knowledge of their parents, several young braves rode to a nearby Comanche village and stole the other tribe's ponies. Grandpa tells

how he rode back to his village despite being wounded by the Comanche thus receiving his warrior name. The author's first picture book includes a glossary of terms. (32 pages)

Where it's reviewed:
Booklist, September 15, 1994, page 145
Children's Book Review Service, December 1994, page 41
Kirkus Reviews, September 15, 1994, page 1283
Publishers Weekly, September 19, 1994, page 71
School Library Journal, November 1994, page 101

Awards the book has won:
International Reading Association Children's Choice, 1995

Other books by the same author:
A Walk to the Great Mystery, 1995

Other books you might like:
Joseph Bruchac, *The Boy Who Lived with the Bears: And Other Iroquois Stories*, 1995
    The award-winning collection of six stories includes tales of humor and drama written for the primary grades.
Paul Goble, *Lone Bull's Horse Raid*, 1973
    With a raiding party, two young Sioux capture horses from a Crow encampment. Co-author Dorothy Goble.
Silky Sullivan, *Grandpa Was a Cowboy*, 1996
    A young, orphaned boy visits his grandfather, hearing stories of his family's history and his grandfather's experiences as a cowboy.
Martin Waddell, *My Great Grandpa*, 1990
    Although her great grandfather is slow and weak, his memory of his travels enables him to take his great-granddaughter to places no one else can.

1402

VIRGINIA A. STROUD, Author/Illustrator

A Walk to the Great Mystery

(New York: Dial Books for Young Readers, 1995)

Subject(s): Indians of North America; Grandparents; Nature
Age range(s): Grades K-3
Major character(s): Ann Beaver, Grandmother, Indian; Dustin, Child, Indian; Rosie, Child, Indian
Time period(s): 1990s (1995)
Locale(s): Fairy Ranch

Summary: Dustin and Rosie's visit with Grandma Ann begins with a walk in the woods behind her home. As the children search for the "Great Mystery" Grandma Ann says little, but offers them each a rock and a flour sack to carry the earth treasures they find. Grandma Ann's lesson, to be attentive to, and appreciative of, the natural world around them, helps them understand that the Great Mystery is both around and within each of them. (32 pages)

Where it's reviewed:
Booklist, July 1995, page 1884
Children's Book Review Service, June 1995, page 127
Horn Book Guide, Fall 1995, page 284
Publishers Weekly, May 29, 1995, page 85
School Library Journal, June 1995, page 96

Other books by the same author:
Doesn't Fall Off His Horse, 1994

Other books you might like:

Joseph Bruchac, *Fox Song*, 1993
As Jamie recalls the nature lessons she learned from her recently deceased grandmother, she knows she will find consolation in the world around her.

Jean Craighead George, *Dear Rebecca, Winter Is Here*, 1993
On the day of the winter solstice, a grandmother writes a letter to her granddaughter describing the changes she sees outside her window.

William T. George, *Fishing at Long Pond*, 1991
While fishing with her grandfather, Katie marvels at the bird, plant and animal life she observes.

Eve Merriam, *Quiet, Please*, 1993
In the stillness of a moment it is possible to observe many things.

1403

CAROLINE STUTSON
KEVIN HAWKES, Illustrator

By the Light of the Halloween Moon

(New York: Lothrop, Lee & Shepard Books, 1993)

Subject(s): Halloween; Ghosts; Animals/Cats
Age range(s): Grades K-3
Major character(s): Unnamed Character, Child
Time period(s): 1990s (1993)
Locale(s): United States

Summary: On a dark night two feet dangle over the edge of a dock attracting the attention of a cat who attracts the attention of a witch and then a bat and so on through ghosts and ghouls. Each looks longingly at the toe, but is prevented from a taste by the next character to appear until finally the girl swats the sprite with her violin. The author's first book concludes with the girl playing a tune for all to dance to under the silvery light of a Halloween moon. (32 pages)

Where it's reviewed:
Booklist, July 1993, page 1977
Children's Book Review Service, September 1993, page 5
Horn Book, November 1993, page 728
Library Talk, May 1994, page 34
School Library Journal, December 1993, page 94

Awards the book has won:
Golden Kite Award, 1993

Other books by the same author:
On the River ABC, 1993

Other books you might like:

Sylvia Andrews, *Rattlebone Rock*, 1995
In the graveyard, tombstones, skeletons and ghosts begin a rhythmic Halloween beat which attracts the attention of the townspeople.

Kenn Compton, *Granny Greenteeth and the Noise in the Night*, 1993
Granny asks her unusual and somewhat spooky housemates to investigate a noise under her bed. Co-author Joanne Compton.

Bill Martin Jr., *Old Devil Wind*, 1993
A ghost begins the Halloween night's noise-making and

the wind concludes it when it whooshes through the old haunted house.

Linda Williams, *The Little Old Lady Who Was Not Afraid of Anything*, 1986
On a night-time walk through the woods an old woman is followed by many scary objects which attempt to frighten her.

1404

VIVECA LARN SUNDVALL
OLOF LANDSTROM, Illustrator

Santa's Winter Vacation

(New York: R & S Books, 1995)

Subject(s): Vacations; Christmas; Behavior
Age range(s): Grades K-3
Major character(s): Reuben Stormfoot, Aged Person, Spouse; Hosannah Stormfoot, Aged Person, Spouse; Johannes Sandworm, 4-Year-Old
Time period(s): 1990s (1994)
Locale(s): Spain; Stockholm, Sweden

Summary: While vacationing, Reuben and Hosannah patiently endure the presence of the Sandworm family who, with the exception of sensitive and quiet Johannes, are totally obnoxious. After returning home, the Sandworm family eagerly awaits the arrival of Santa on Christmas Eve. When he comes, Johannes recognizes Reuben instantly and graciously receives the last three gifts in his pack while his brothers gape in astonishment, still not quite recognizing that they are paying the price for their rude behavior. Translated from the Swedish by Kjersti Board. First published in Sweden in 1994. (32 pages)

Where it's reviewed:
Booklist, September 15, 1995, page 173
Horn Book, January 1996, page 69
Publishers Weekly, September 18, 1995, page 98
School Library Journal, October 1995, page 42

Other books by the same author:
Mimi Gets a Grandpa, 1991
Mimi and the Biscuit Factory, 1989

Other books you might like:

Penny Ives, *Mrs. Santa Claus*, 1990
Not wanting to disappoint the children, Mrs. Santa Claus takes over the Christmas Eve deliveries when Santa and the reindeer become ill.

David McPhail, *Santa's Book of Names*, 1993
Poor reader Edward helps Santa with his list of names and receives a fitting gift in return.

James Stevenson, *The Oldest Elf*, 1996
Elwyn, the oldest elf and retired reindeer Blitzen help Santa for the last time.

1405

ROSEMARY SUTCLIFF
EMMA CHICHESTER-CLARK, Illustrator

The Minstrel and the Dragon Pup

(Cambridge, MA: Candlewick Press, 1993)

Subject(s): Dragons; Fairy Tale; Musicians
Age range(s): Grades 1-4
Major character(s): Unnamed Character, Minstrel; Lucky,
    Mythical Creature (dragon pup)
Time period(s): Indeterminate Past
Locale(s): Fictional Country

Summary: A dragon whose egg has rolled away from its
mother is fortunate enough to hatch at the feet of a minstrel or
perhaps it is the minstrel who is fortunate to have a dragon
hatch at his feet. The two become travelling companions,
singing for their supper throughout the country until an evil,
greedy showman steals the dragon. The minstrel searches
forlornly for Lucky and quite unexpectedly finds him in the
king's zoo. In order to retrieve him, the minstrel plays a tune
which heals the king's son and is granted both the dragon pup
and protection during his travels. This is the first picture book
by the now-deceased author. (42 pages)

Where it's reviewed:
Booklist, March 1, 1993, page 1238
Children's Book Review Service, Spring 1993, page 140
Horn Book, July 1993, page 455
Publishers Weekly, April 12, 1993, page 63
School Library Journal, April, 1993, page 103

Other books you might like:
Wayne Anderson, *Dragon*, 1992
    A dropped dragon egg falls into the sea where it hatches
    into a very confused newborn who searches for his mother
    and his identity.
Kenneth Grahame, *The Reluctant Dragon*, 1938
    A peaceful dragon is befriended by a young boy who must
    convince the villagers and the dragon slayer that the crea-
    ture means no harm.
Michael Hague, *The Book of Dragons*, 1995
    Seventeen short selections for dragon lovers include fan-
    tasy and folktales from different countries.
Margaret Hodges, *St. George and the Dragon: A Golden
    Legend*, 1984
    The 1985 Caldecott Medal winner retells the legendary
    tale of St. George, patron saint of England.

T

1406

MARC TALBERT

A Sunburned Prayer

(New York: Simon & Schuster, 1995)

Subject(s): Grandparents; Animals/Dogs; Hispanic Americans
Age range(s): Grades 4-6
Major character(s): Eloy, 11-Year-Old; Benito, Brother (Eloy's older); Magdalena, Dog (stray)
Time period(s): 1990s
Locale(s): Pedernal, New Mexico

Summary: Eloy defies his parents and makes a seventeen-mile pilgrimage to the Santuario de Chimay to collect some of its sacred dirt. The legend says that if the dirt is tasted, a miracle will occur and Eloy knows his grandmother needs a miracle to overcome the cancer that is wracking her body. As Eloy sets out, he is followed by a stray dog which accompanies him on his trek. When Eloy gets to Chimay, he finds Benito has driven his grandmother to the church in his low-rider car. There she tells Eloy to accept her death and the peace she feels from being in the sanctuary. Though returning home is hard, Grandmother dispels his family's anger and convinces them to let him make a pet of the stray dog, which she refers to as a "gift of God." (108 pages)

Where it's reviewed:
School Library Journal, July 1995, page 82
Publishers Weekly, April 17, 1995, page 61
Booklist, August 1995, page 1950
Horn Book Guide, Fall 1995, page 305
Hungry Mind Review, Winter 1995, page 54

Awards the book has won:
School Library Journal Best Books, 1995

Other books by the same author:
Heart of a Jaguar, 1995
The Purple Heart, 1992
Pillow of Clouds, 1991

Other books you might like:
Patricia Calvert, *Bigger*, 1994
    Tyler sets out on an 800-mile journey to find his dad who didn't return after the Civil War. A "devil dog" he meets trudges with him for the trek.
Jessie Close, *The Warping of Al*, 1990
    The only person in Al's family who talks and listens to him is his beloved grandmother Goopie. When she dies, he wants to leave home.
Libby Hathorn, *Thunderwith*, 1991
    After her mother dies, Lara is convinced she sends her a companion in the form of the magnificent dog she meets in the outback.

1407

ERIKA TAMAR

The Junkyard Dog

(New York: Knopf, 1995)

Subject(s): Animals/Dogs; Stepfathers
Age range(s): Grades 4-6
Major character(s): Katie Lawrence, 11-Year-Old; Jim Grady, Stepfather, Carpenter; Lucky, Dog
Time period(s): 1990s
Locale(s): United States

Summary: Katie's heart breaks when she sees the teenagers throwing stones at the pitiful-looking dog guarding the junkyard. Though the boys are bigger than Katie, she yells at them until they disappear. Determined to help the dog, she gets permission from her mother and stepfather Jim to feed the dog, though she must ask the dog's owner for permission and buy the food with her own allowance. Once the food is settled, Katie finds another obstacle as winter approaches and she sees that the dog, which she names Lucky, needs a doghouse. With determination on Katie's part and help from her stepfather, a new doghouse is built. (185 pages)

Where it's reviewed:
Publishers Weekly, June 19, 1995, page 59
Booklist, May 1, 1995, page 1575

Library Talk, September 1995, page 35
School Library Journal, June 1995, page 114
Horn Book Guide, Fall 1995, page 305

Other books by the same author:
Soccer Mania, 1993
Blues for Silk Garcia, 1982
Good-Bye, Glamour Girl, 1984

Other books you might like:
William Corbin, *A Dog Worth Stealing*, 1987
While Jud is camping, he sees a dog being badly abused by its owner. He feels he has no recourse but to steal the dog.
Lynn Hall, *The Tormentors*, 1990
Sox manages to rescue his stolen dog from a gang that trains dogs for vicious guard work.
Phyllis Reynolds Naylor, *Shiloh*, 1991
Marty decides it's better to lie if it means saving the life of an abused beagle named Shiloh.

1408

HARRIET PECK TAYLOR, Author/Illustrator

Coyote and the Laughing Butterflies

(New York: Macmillan Books for Young Readers, 1995)

Subject(s): Indians of North America; Folk Tales; Animals/ Coyotes
Age range(s): Grades 1-3
Major character(s): Coyote, Coyote
Time period(s): Indeterminate Past
Locale(s): Southwest

Summary: On an errand for his wife, Coyote journeys to the big salty lake to gather salt for her cooking. After a long, hot walk Coyote treats himself to a nap. The butterflies nearby seize the opportunity to play a trick on coyote and carry him home, with his sack still empty. When a very puzzled coyote awakens and finds he has not completed the errand, he promises to go again the next day. Again, Coyote naps and again the butterflies play their tricks. On the third trip, Coyote fills his sack before he naps and the butterflies fly both Coyote and the sack of salt home. To this day, butterflies laugh so hard when they remember these tricks that they cannot fly in a straight line. (32 pages)

Where it's reviewed:
Booklist, July 1995, page 1881
Horn Book Guide, Fall 1995, page 334
School Library Journal, August 1995, page 138

Other books by the same author:
Coyote Places the Stars, 1993

Other books you might like:
Gerald McDermott, *Coyote: A Trickster Tale from the American Southwest*, 1994
Coyote's desire to fly with the crows is fulfilled for only a short time due to his boastful behavior.
Tom Pohrt, *Coyote Goes Walking*, 1995
Four legends present coyote as a mythical creator, a trickster and a victim of his own cockiness.
Janet Stevens, *Coyote Steals the Blanket: A Ute Tale*, 1993
Coyote refuses to accept advice from anyone and suffers the consequences.

Wayne Ude, *Maybe I Will Do Something*, 1993
Seven traditional coyote stories tell of the exploits of a Native American trickster.

1409

MILDRED D. TAYLOR

The Well: David's Story

(New York: Dial, 1995)

Subject(s): Race Relations; Drought; African Americans
Age range(s): Grades 5-7
Major character(s): David Logan, 10-Year-Old; Hammer Logan, 13-Year-Old; Charlie Simms, 14-Year-Old
Time period(s): 1900s
Locale(s): Mississippi

Summary: David, the father of Cassie in *Roll of Thunder, Hear My Cry*, narrates this tale of his early years in Mississippi when all the wells go dry except that of his family. The Logans share their water with everyone else, both black and white, but one white family hates being beholden to blacks. When Charlie Simms takes out his humiliation on David one day, Hammer retaliates and decks Charlie, breaking one of the state's laws that a Negro never hit a white. Though the Logan brothers have to work for the Simms that summer, the attempt by the Simms' to retaliate backfires. (92 pages)

Where it's reviewed:
Booklist, December 15, 1994, page 754
Publishers Weekly, January 2, 1995, page 77
Voice of Youth Advocates, August 1995, page 166
School Library Journal, February 1995, page 100
English Journal, September 1995, page 118

Awards the book has won:
ALA Notable Children's Book, 1996
Jane Addams Children's Book Award, 1996

Other books by the same author:
Let the Circle Be Unbroken, 1981
Roll of Thunder, Hear My Cry, 1976
Song of the Trees, 1975

Other books you might like:
Christopher Paul Curtis, *The Watsons Go to Birmingham— 1963*, 1995
The innocence of the Watson children is lost when a church in Birmingham is blown up, four children killed and they fear they've lost Joetta.
Ossie Davis, *Just Like Martin*, 1992
Ike and his father reconcile their opposite views of civil rights after a church bombing.
Lois T. Henderson, *The Blessing Deer*, 1980
Clarisse helps her white friend understand about prejudice.
Walter Dean Myers, *The Glory Field*, 1994
The Lewis family is sustained and strengthened by a plot of land they call the glory field.

| 1410 |

WILLIAM TAYLOR

Numbskulls

(New York: Scholastic Inc., 1995)

Subject(s): Schools; Family Life; Babies
Age range(s): Grades 4-6
Major character(s): Charlie Kenney, 10-Year-Old, Brother; Jo-Munro Kenney, Child, Sister (younger); Alice Pepper, 10-Year-Old, Neighbor
Time period(s): 1990s (1995)
Locale(s): New Zealand

Summary: In the sequel to *Knitwits* Charlie Kenney is concerned his parents are too laid back in parenting Jo-Munro. His baby sister may turn out to be a poor student just as he is. Certain babies need more focussed instruction, Charlie consults a book *Before Babe's First Steps* and submits himself to Alice Pepper's learning machine. Although he regrets agreeing to pay Alice his allowance for 10 weeks, he does become a capable speller in spite of her intimidating teaching methods. (120 pages)

Where it's reviewed:
Booklist, October 15, 1995, page 405
Bulletin of the Center for Children's Books, December 1995, page 141
Horn Book Guide, Spring 1996, page 69
School Library Journal, October 1995, page 140

Other books by the same author:
Knitwits, 1992
Agnes the Sheep, 1991
Paradise Lane, 1989

Other books you might like:
Betsy Duffey, *How to Be Cool in the Third Grade*, 1993
  Robbie views third grade as an opportunity to mature and change.
Patricia Reilly Giff, *The Beast in Ms. Rooney's Room*, 1984
  One of twelve titles in "The Kids in the Polk Street School" series, this one features Richard "Beast" Best.
Becky Thoman Lindberg, *Thomas Tuttle, Just in Time*, 1994
  Thomas, a procrastinator at heart, tries to improve his school performance by completing his work by the due date.

| 1411 |

MARK TEAGUE, Author/Illustrator

How I Spent My Summer Vacation

(New York: Crown Publishers, Inc., 1995)

Subject(s): American West; Vacations; Stories in Rhyme
Age range(s): Grades K-2
Major character(s): Wallace Bleff, Child, Nephew; Fern, Aunt
Time period(s): 1990s (1995)
Locale(s): West

Summary: As the new school year begins, Wallace tells of being sent by train to vacation at Aunt Fern's home on the plains in order to give his overactive imagination a rest. His parents' plans are waylaid when cowboys kidnap Wallace and

he spends the summer as "Kid Bleff," learning cowboy tricks and living the cowboy life. When the round-up is completed, Aunt Fern invites Wallace and the other cowboys to her home for a barbeque. As Wallace concludes his imaginative oral report, he eagerly anticipates show-and-tell. (32 pages)

Where it's reviewed:
Booklist, September 1, 1995, page 89
Kirkus Reviews, August 1, 1995, page 1117
Los Angeles Times Book Review, August 20, 1995, page 8
Publishers Weekly, July 10, 1995, page 56
School Library Journal, September 1, 1995, page 89

Awards the book has won:
Parent's Choice Award, 1995

Other books by the same author:
Pigsty, 1994
The Field Beyond the Outfield, 1992
Frog Medicine, 1991

Other books you might like:
Sharon Phillips Denslow, *On the Trail with Miss Pace*, 1995
  School teacher Miss Pace begins her long-anticipated summer vacation on a dude ranch and she's surprised to discover two of her students following her everywhere.
Percival Everett, *The One That Got Away*, 1992
  In a silly tale, three cowboys chase errant "ones" and try to herd them into a corral.
Ruth Hooker, *Matthew the Cowboy*, 1990
  Clad in the cowboy suit he received for his birthday, Matthew uses his imagination to travel out West, tame a wild horse, and capture cattle rustlers.

| 1412 |

MARK TEAGUE, Author/Illustrator

Pigsty

(New York: Scholastic Inc., 1994)

Subject(s): Animals/Pigs; Cleanliness; Fantasy
Age range(s): Grades K-2
Major character(s): Wendell Fultz, Child
Time period(s): 1990s (1994)
Locale(s): United States

Summary: When Wendell Fultz's mother likens his room to a pigsty and orders him to clean it, he finds his efforts thwarted by the pig sitting on his bed. During the week, more pigs arrive until finally their antics become too much for Wendell to bear so he organizes the pigs into a cleaning crew. Reluctantly, they work until the room is so clean that the disappointed pigs return to the farm—except for visits on Monopoly night. (32 pages)

Where it's reviewed:
Booklist, September 15, 1994, page 145
Kirkus Reviews, September 15, 1994, page 1284
Parents Magazine, December 1994, page 22
Publishers Weekly, July 11, 1994, page 78
School Library Journal, Ocotber 1994, page 104

Awards the book has won:
International Reading Association Children's Choices, 1995

Other books by the same author:
The Secret Shortcut, 1996
The Field Beyond the Outfield, 1992
Frog Medicine, 1991

Other books you might like:
Suzanne Bloom, *We Keep a Pig in the Parlor*, 1988
    In a rhyming text, a pig explains why he's unsuited for life in the barn and is granted permission to move to the parlor.
Anthony Browne, *Piggybook*, 1986
    Tired of cleaning up after her husband and sons, Mrs. Piggott writes a prophetic note to the "pigs" and leaves them to fend for themselves.
Amy Ehrlich, *Parents in the Pigpen, Pigs in the Tub*, 1993
    The farm animals move into the house and the family heads for the barn in a humorous reversal of roles.
David McPhail, *Pigs Aplenty, Pigs Galore*, 1993
    With his quiet home invaded by messy, noisy pigs ordering pizza for their party, the homeowner loses his patience and demands the pigs clean up before they depart.

1413

SUSAN TEWS
ELIZABETH SAYLES, Illustrator

Nettie's Gift

(New York: Clarion Books, 1993)

Subject(s): Grandparents; Imagination; Fall
Age range(s): Grades K-3
Major character(s): Sarah, 8-Year-Old; Grandma Nettie, Grandmother
Time period(s): 1990s (1993)
Locale(s): Wisconsin

Summary: In her first book, the author draws on childhood memories to present Sarah, a farm girl longing for a playmate other than grandparents. Walking in the woods, Grandma Nettie reminds Sarah that, as a child, she played alone just as Sarah does now. When Sarah visits the remains of her grandmother's childhood home to pick hickory nuts, she imagines herself playing with Nettie, a friend just her age. (32 pages)

Where it's reviewed:
Booklist, March 1, 1993, page 1239
Children's Book Review Service, June 1993, page 124
Horn Book, July 1993, page 451
Publishers Weekly, March 15, 1993, page 87
School Library Journal, June 1993, page 90

Other books by the same author:
Gingerbread Doll, 1993

Other books you might like:
Natalie Honeycutt, *Whistle Home*, 1993
    With her aunt, a young girl enjoys a walk in the woods on a crisp autumn day.
James Howe, *There's a Dragon in My Sleeping Bag*, 1994
    Brothers Alex and Simon have imaginary friends who play with each other, excluding the siblings.
Julie Lacome, *I'm a Jolly Farmer*, 1994
    A little girl uses her dog to assume many roles as they spend a happy day in make-believe play.

Ruth Tiller, *Cinnamon, Mint & Mothballs: A Visit to Grandmother's House*, 1993
    Through a series of haiku poems, the autumn visit of 2 sisters to grandmother's house is vividly described.

1414

ABIGAIL THOMAS
WILLIAM LOW, Illustrator

Lily

(New York: Henry Holt and Company, Inc., 1994)

Subject(s): Animals/Dogs; Pets; Moving, Household
Age range(s): Grades K-2
Major character(s): Lily, Dog; Eliza, Young Woman
Time period(s): 1990s (1994)
Locale(s): Boston, Massachusetts; Vermont

Summary: Lily's complacent, predictable life as the apartment-dwelling pet of a single working woman comes to an abrupt halt one day when everything familiar is stuffed into boxes and two big men load the apartment contents onto a truck. Despite Eliza's words of reassurance, Lily is terrified and drifts off to sleep in the car until it stops at her new home. As soon as the truck arrives to unload, however, Lily realizes that home is right here. (32 pages)

Where it's reviewed:
Booklist, April 15, 1994, page 1542
Children's Book Review Service, June 1994, page 125
New Advocate, Fall 1994, page 286
Publishers Weekly, February 28, 1994, page 86
School Library Journal, August 1994, page 147

Other books by the same author:
Pearl Paints, 1994
Wake Up, Wilson Street, 1993

Other books you might like:
Constance McGeorge, *Boomer's Big Day*, 1994
    Moving day is confusing for Boomer until he is able to explore his new home and find familiar things.
Inga Moore, *Little Dog Lost*, 1991
    After moving to the country, Liz and Tom find new friends while searching for their lost dog Pip.
Rosemary Wells, *Lucy Comes to Stay*, 1994
    Mary Elizabeth delights in her new puppy even when Lucy is mischievous.

1415

ABIGAIL THOMAS
MARGARET HEWITT, Illustrator

Pearl Paints

(New York: Henry Holt and Company, 1994)

Subject(s): Artists and Art; Gifts; Parent and Child
Age range(s): Grades K-2
Major character(s): Pearl, Child, Artist; Peg, Aunt
Time period(s): 1990s (1994)
Locale(s): United States

Summary: A birthday gift of a set of paints, brushes and paper is the catalyst for Pearl's discovery of artistic talent. Her parents worry because she would rather paint than eat or go to school and her brother critiques her work. Only Aunt Peg recognizes that Pearl is an artist who must be allowed to work. When, finally, Pearl's creative energies produce a beautiful mural, she receives recognition, appreciation and more paints. (32 pages)

Where it's reviewed:
Booklist, December 1, 1994, page 688
Children's Book Review Service, February 1995, page 81
Five Owls, November 1994, page 38
Publishers Weekly, October 24, 1994, page 60
School Library Journal, December 1994, page 87

Other books by the same author:
Lily, 1994
Wake Up, Wilson Street, 1993

Other books you might like:
Amy Hest, *Nana's Birthday Party*, 1993
    Maggie, the writer, collaborates with cousin Brette, the painter, to make the best birthday present ever for Nana.
Amy Littlesugar, *Josiah True and the Art Maker*, 1995
    After Patience Cage, the art maker, completes a portrait of his family, she gives Josiah a small brush, trusting that he will learn to use it—and he does.
Patricia Maloney Markun, *The Little Painter of Sabana Grande*, 1993
    A shortage of paper does not deter a young Panamanian artist—he uses the exterior of his adobe house for a canvas.
Sara Yamaka, *The Gift of Driscoll Lipscomb*, 1995
    Annually, Molly receives a brush and a different color of paint from an artist friend until eventually she has all the colors of the rainbow.

1416

FRANCES THOMAS
RUTH BROWN, Illustrator

The Bear & Mr. Bear

(New York: Dutton Children's Books, 1995)

Subject(s): Animals/Bears; Animals, Treatment of; Freedom
Age range(s): Grades K-2
Major character(s): Mr. Bear, Aged Person; Unnamed Character, Bear, Captive
Time period(s): Indeterminate Past
Locale(s): Europe

Summary: Long ago, villagers scorned an unhappy, lonely man by calling him Mr. Bear because of his grumpiness. When he happens into market one day during a carnival, Mr. Bear, touched by the plight of a captive, dancing bear, buys the bear from his cruel owner in order to set it free. Watching the bear awaken to embrace its newly gained freedom gives Mr. Bear a measure of the same release from whatever unseen chains bind his spirit. Originally published in Great Britain in 1994. (32 pages)

Where it's reviewed:
Booklist, January 15, 1995, page 938
Children's Book Review Service, April 1995, page 102
Junior Bookshelf, February 1995, page 12

Publishers Weekly, December 12, 1994, page 62
School Library Journal, March 1995, page 187

Other books by the same author:
The Prince and the Cave, 1992

Other books you might like:
Glenn Halak, *A Grandmother's Story*, 1992
    With no explanation to the neighbors, who suspect she's a bit daft, an old woman rows out to sea until she saves her grandson from drowning.
Patricia Polacco, *Babushka Baba Yaga*, 1993
    In disguise, the feared, mocked, and lonely Baba Yaga enters the village and proves herself to be as loving a care giver as any babushka.
Susan Wojciechowski, *The Christmas Miracle of Jonathan Toomey*, 1995
    Through the kindness of a widow and her young son, Jonathan Toomey begins to free himself from painful memories.

1417

JANE RESH THOMAS
MICHAEL DOOLING, Illustrator

Lights on the River

(New York: Hyperion Books for Children, 1994)

Subject(s): Migrant Labor; Mexican Americans; Family Life
Age range(s): Grades K-3
Major character(s): Teresa, Child, Babysitter; Papi, Father, Worker; Mami, Mother, Worker
Time period(s): 1990s (1994)
Locale(s): United States

Summary: While Mami, Papi, and other relatives labor to pick cucumbers, peaches, or whatever crop is in season, Teresa babysits her younger brother and cousin. Sitting in the cool shade, she thinks about the contrast between her stationary home in Mexico and the one in the United States which changes as the family travels from farm to farm. At the end of a long, tiring day, Mami lights the candle from abuela to remind them of their link to their homeland. (32 pages)

Where it's reviewed:
Booklist, August 1994, page 2053
Five Owls, November 1994, page 37
Kirkus Reviews, September 15, 1994, page 1284
Publishers Weekly, September 19, 1994, page 30
Quill & Quire, November 1994, page 39

Other books by the same author:
Saying Good-bye to Grandma, 1988
Wheels, 1986

Other books you might like:
Linda Jacobs Altman, *Amelia's Road*, 1993
    The frequent moves of her migrant labor family make Amelia long for stability.
Eve Bunting, *Going Home*, 1996
    A Mexican family living and working in America returns home to the parent's village for Christmas.
Michele Benoit Slawson, *Apple Picking Time*, 1994
    For the first time Anna fills one bin with apples she picks

herself, proudly earning a half-moon punched into her very own ticket.

TYNIA THOMASSIE
CAT BOWMAN SMITH, Illustrator

Feliciana Feydra LeRoux: A Cajun Tall Tale

(Boston: Little, Brown and Company, 1995)

Subject(s): Animals/Alligators; Humor; Hunting
Age range(s): Grades 1-3
Major character(s): Feliciana Feydra LeRoux, Child; Grampa Baby, Grandfather, Hunter
Time period(s): Indeterminate Past
Locale(s): Louisiana

Summary: Try as she might, Feliciana can't get an invitation to the one thing she really wants to do—go alligator hunting. When she is tricked out of another hunting trip, Feliciana commandeers one of her brother's pirouges and sets off with only her doll for company. Her confidence wanes when she finds herself face-to-face with an alligator. Fortunately, Grampa Baby and the boys happen along. Unfortunately, when Grampa tries to lasso the alligator's snout, the alligator catches the rope and pulls Grampa into the water. Feliciana loses her fear then and, with her doll in hand, jumps into the swamp, stuffing the doll in the alligator's mouth. Grampa Baby saves himself, rescues Feliciana, and bags the alligator too. (32 pages)

Where it's reviewed:
Booklist, April 1, 1995, page 1429
Children's Book Review Service, May 1995, page 112
Horn Book, September 1995, page 592
Publishers Weekly, May 1, 1995, page 58
School Library Journal, April 1995, page 118

Other books by the same author:
Mimi's Tutu, 1996

Other books you might like:
Anne Isaacs, *Swamp Angel*, 1994
An original tall tale introduces Angelica Longrider who rescues wagon trains mired in Dejection Swamp and skins a huge bear, using his pelt to create a prairie.
Steven Kellogg, *Sally Ann Thunder Ann Whirlwind Crockett: A Tall Tale*, 1995
In a retelling of a tall tale, Sally Ann departs for the frontier on her eighth birthday where she continues her larger than life exploits and marries Davy Crockett.
Mercer Mayer, *Liza Lou and the Yeller Belly Swamp*, 1976
Liza Lou outwits all the witches, haunts and spooks in the Yeller Belly Swamp.
Marcia Vaughan, *Whistling Dixie*, 1995
Dixie Lee rebuts each of her mother's arguments to swamp creatures she's brought home as pets—and she's right.

JAMES THURBER
STEVEN KELLOGG, Illustrator

The Great Quillow

(San Diego: Harcourt Brace & Company, 1994)

Series: Harcourt Brace Contemporary Classic
Subject(s): Fairy Tale; Giants; Problem Solving
Age range(s): Grades 1-4
Major character(s): Hunder, Monster (giant); Quillow, Storyteller, Hero
Time period(s): Indeterminate Past
Locale(s): Fictional Country

Summary: In a newly illustrated version of Thurber's 1944 classic tale, the giant Hunder arrives at a small village with a list of demands. While the frightened villagers worry about how to meet those demands, Quillow, the toymaker, thoughtfully agrees to be the giant's storyteller. Through the story he tells, Quillow plants the seed of doubt in Hunder's mind which will rid the village of the ogre. (56 pages)

Where it's reviewed:
Booklist, December 1, 1994, page 667
Children's Book Review Service, November 1994, page 28
Horn Book, November 1994, page 727
Publishers Weekly, October 31, 1994, page 62
School Library Journal, November 1994, page 91

Other books by the same author:
The Wonderful O, 1990
The 13 Clocks, 1957
Many Moons, 1943 (Caldecott Medal Winner)

Other books you might like:
Roald Dahl, *The BFG*, 1982
The BFG (Big Friendly Giant) kidnaps Sophie because he needs her help to save the Queen and others from the wicked giants.
Walter De la Mare, *Molly Whuppie*, 1983
The newly illustrated presentation of the Celtic story tells of a brave young girl who uses her wits to overcome a giant.
Mary Norton, *Are All the Giants Dead?*, 1997
When young James travels to the land of Happily Ever After he learns a princess must be rescued from the last giant.
Paul Robert Walker, *Giants! Stories from around the World*, 1995
A collection of stories from various folk traditions tell of heroes who use wits and courage to overcome larger foes.

FAYTHE DYRUD THUREEN
ELAINE SANDEEN, Illustrator

Jenna's Big Jump

(New York: Atheneum, 1993)

Subject(s): Courage; Schools; Mothers and Daughters
Age range(s): Grades 3-5

Major character(s): Jenna Wexler, 4th Grader (new student); Kate Bradner, 4th Grader (new student); Buzz, 4th Grader, Bully
Time period(s): 1990s (1993)
Locale(s): Marshall, Minnesota

Summary: Timid Jenna has only one week to be miserable as the new student in class when self-assured Kate arrives. Seeing Kate stand up to Buzz gives Jenna courage and, as their friendship grows, Jenna finds that she can be more like the little girl her mom tells about in her childhood stories. This is the author's first novel for children. (104 pages)

Where it's reviewed:
Children's Book Review Service, May 1993, page 115
Horn Book Guide, Fall 1993, page 305
Kirkus Reviews, March 15, 1993, page 380
Publishers Weekly, May 3, 1993, page 309
School Library Journal, May 1993, page 109

Other books you might like:
Judith Caseley, *Starring Dorothy Kane*, 1992
  With a family move necessitating a change of school and friends, unhappy Dorothy has more to concern her than simply being the middle child.
Patricia Reilly Giff, *Shark in School*, 1994
  Matthew approaches a new school with memories of his friends at the Polk Street School and concerns about making new ones.
Suzy Kline, *Horrible Harry in Room 2B*, 1988
  One of several books about the students in Room 2B, this title focuses on obnoxious Harry.

1421

JEANNE TITHERINGTON, Author/Illustrator

Sophy and Auntie Pearl
(New York: Greenwillow Books, 1995)

Subject(s): Aunts and Uncles; Imagination; Fantasy
Age range(s): Grades K-2
Major character(s): Sophie, Child, Niece; Auntie Pearl, Aunt (great-aunt)
Time period(s): 1990s (1995)
Locale(s): United States

Summary: Sophy is excited to awaken one morning and discover that she has the ability to fly. Her parents are not interested, but next-door Auntie Pearl is willing to join her on an airborne tour of the town. The illustrations reveal children watching the pair float above while adults simply continue with their activities oblivious to the wonder of flight. (24 pages)

Where it's reviewed:
Booklist, August 1995, page 1957
Children's Book Review Service, August 1995, page 159
Horn Book Guide, Spring 1996, page 47
Kirkus Reviews, July 1, 1995, page 953
School Library Journal, September 1995, page 187

Other books by the same author:
Baby's Boat, 1992
A Place for Ben, 1987
Big World, Small World, 1985

Other books you might like:
Arthur Dorros, *Abuela*, 1991
  Riding a city bus with her grandmother, a young girl imagines instead flying with her over New York City.
Jeanne Modesitt, *Lunch with Milly*, 1995
  To provide the forgotten dessert, Milly takes her young luncheon guest on a fanciful journey to collect the ingredients.
Faith Ringgold, *Tar Beach*, 1991
  In an award-winning book, Cassie Lightfoot soars over the rooftops of Harlem, viewing familiar sites from a new perspective.

1422

STEPHANIE TOLAN, Author/Illustrator

Save Halloween!
(New York: Morrow Junior Books, 1993)

Subject(s): Halloween; Christian Life; School Life
Age range(s): Grades 4-7
Major character(s): Johnna Josephine Filkins, 11-Year-Old, Student; T.T. Filkins, Uncle, Religious (evangelist); James J. Filkins, Father, Religious (preacher)
Time period(s): 1990s (1994)
Locale(s): Bradyville, Ohio

Summary: Caught between the crusade of visiting Uncle T. T. and her love for the forbidden holiday of Halloween, Johnna learns to follow her inner guidance. As co-author of the play celebrating the 25th anniversary of Mrs. Teator's 6th grade class' Halloween project for UNICEF, Johnna stands in defiance of her fundamentalist family's beliefs. Having Uncle T. T. arrive to begin a crusade against Halloween only a few weeks before the play creates additional complications for Johnna as she struggles to balance these two worlds. (176 pages)

Where it's reviewed:
Booklist, September, 1, 1993, page 58
Five Owls, September 1993, page 18
Kirkus Reviews, August 1, 1993, page 1008
Publishers Weekly, September 20, 1993, page 31
School Library Journal, October 1993, page 133

Awards the book has won:
Book Links Good Book, 1993
Booklist Editors' Choice, 1993

Other books by the same author:
The Witch of Maple Park, 1992
A Time to Fly Free, 1990
The Great Skinner Enterprise, 1988
The Great Skinner Strike, 1983

Other books you might like:
Patricia Beatty, *Behave Yourself, Bethany Brant*, 1986
  Bethany, a circuit preacher's daughter, has difficulty adjusting to the changes in her life after her mother's death.
Judy Blume, *Are You There God? It's Me, Margaret*, 1970
  Sixth-grader Margaret Simon is coping with her family's unexpected move, changing schools, making new friends, and trying to determine on a religion, her father's Judaism or her mother's Catholicism.

Norma Howe, *God, the Universe, and Hot Fudge Sundaes*, 1984

Alfie's friendship with Kurt helps her at a difficult time and enables her to make some important decisions.

1423

THERESA TOMLINSON

Riding the Waves

(New York: Macmillan, 1993)

Subject(s): Old Age; Sports/Surfing; Friendship
Age range(s): Grades 6-7
Major character(s): Matthew "Matt", Adoptee; Auntie Florrie, Aged Person
Time period(s): 1990s
Locale(s): Seaburn, England

Summary: One of Matt's first assignments from Seaburn Bay Comprehensive School is to deliver a basket of fruit to an elderly person. Somehow he draws the name of Florrie, the best friend of his deceased grandmother. Though years apart in age, the two find great bonds; Florrie reminds Matt of his grandmother and Matt provides Florrie with all the town gossip. Florrie even helps Matt achieve his biggest dream which is to be part of the surfing group of Seaburn Bay. Florrie not only knows all the surfers from the time she ran a chips shop, but she gives Matt the courage to "ride the waves" in this delightful story of friendship. (144 pages)

Where it's reviewed:
Publishers Weekly, May 10, 1993, page 72
Booklist, May 1, 1993, page 1593
School Library Journal, May 1993, page 110
Children's Book Review Service, August 1993, page 168
Kirkus Reviews, May 1, 1993, page 605

Other books by the same author:
The Forestwife, 1995

Other books you might like:
Pat Derby, *Visiting Miss Pierce*, 1986
   As part of a school project, Barry visits nursing home resident, Miss Pierce and finds his life changed by her stories.
Kenneth E. Ethridge, *Viola, Furgy, Bobbi, and Me*, 1989
   Old Mrs. Viola Spencer hires Stephen to do her yard work, but their mutual interest in baseball quickly leads to friendship.
Kristi D. Holl, *No Strings Attached*, 1988
   June and her mother, Anne, live with old, cranky Mr. Cooper in a housing arrangement beneficial for all of them.
Mary C. Ryan, *The Voice from the Mendelsohn's Maple*, 1990
   Thanks to Penny, who hears Miss Cooper calling from the branches of her neighbor's maple tree, Beacon Manor retirement home improves.

1424

ANN TOMPERT
LYNN MUNSINGER, Illustrator

Just a Little Bit

(Boston: Houghton Mifflin Company, 1993)

Subject(s): Animals; Friendship; Play
Age range(s): Grades K-2
Major character(s): Elephant, Elephant, Friend; Mouse, Mouse, Friend
Time period(s): 1990s (1993)
Locale(s): United States (playground)

Summary: When Elephant and Mouse decide to use the seesaw together, Mouse, understandably, is unable to make Elephant's end rise. An assortment of animals come to lend a hand and some needed weight but, even with a menagerie joining Mouse, Elephant does not budge until a small brown beetle lands on Mouse's nose, proving that every little bit helps. (32 pages)

Where it's reviewed:
Booklist, November 1, 1993, page 532
Children's Bookwatch, November 1993, page 5
Horn Book Guide, Spring 1994, page 57
Publishers Weekly, August 9, 1993, page 477
School Library Journal, December 1993, page 95

Other books by the same author:
A Carol for Christmas, 1994
Grandfather Tang's Story, 1990
Nothing Sticks Like a Shadow, 1984

Other books you might like:
Jan Brett, *The Mitten*, 1990
   In one of many adaptations of this folktale, animals crowd into a mitten seeking warmth until the smallest of all tickles the bear's nose. Oops!
Mirra Ginsburg, *Mushroom in the Rain*, 1974
   In an adaptation of a Russian tale, an ant seeks refuge from the rain under a mushroom which somehow expands to keep a number of animals dry.
Jane Yolen, *Mouse's Birthday*, 1993
   When friends arrive at Mouse's tiny house for his birthday, the house becomes fuller, and fuller and. . .

1425

LEYLA TORRES, Author/Illustrator

Saturday Sancocho

(New York: Farrar Straus Giroux, 1995)

Subject(s): Cooks and Cookery; Grandparents; Food
Age range(s): Grades K-3
Major character(s): Maria Lili, Child; Mama Ana, Grandmother, Cook; Papa Angelino, Grandfather
Time period(s): Indeterminate Past
Locale(s): Colombia

Summary: This Saturday begins differently from others when Papa Angelino says there is no money to buy a chicken for the sancocho that Maria Lili looks forward to all week. Resourceful Mama Ana calmly gathers the family's dozen eggs, two baskets, and Maria Lili for a walk to market where her astute bartering skills soon acquire all the ingredients they need to cook the stew. A recipe concludes the book. (32 pages)

Where it's reviewed:
Booklist, April 15, 1995, page 1508
Children's Bookwatch, July 1995, page 7
Horn Book Guide, Fall 1995, page 284
Publishers Weekly, April 24, 1995, page 71
School Library Journal, May 1995, page 97

Awards the book has won:
Book Links Good Book, 1995

Other books by the same author:
Subway Sparrow, 1993

Other books you might like:
Patricia Grossman, *Saturday Market*, 1994
     Vendors in a Mexican village display their homemade and homegrown wares at the weekly market.
Lynn Joseph, *Jasmine's Parlour Day*, 1994
     Jasmine loves parlour day in Trinidad and the cacophony of cries of the various vendors hawking their wares.
Karen Lynn Williams, *Tap-Tap*, 1994
     Sasifi helps her mother sell fruit in the local marketplace.

1426

WILLIAM TREVOR

Juliet's Story

(New York: Simon & Schuster Books for Young Readers, 1994)

Subject(s): Storytelling; Vacations; Growing Up
Age range(s): Grades 4-6
Major character(s): Juliet, Child; Grandmamma, Grandmother
Time period(s): 1990s (1991)
Locale(s): County Tipperary, Ireland

Summary: One of the things that Juliet likes best in her little village is sitting outside the storyteller's cottage, listening to his tales. After the elderly storyteller dies, Juliet is sulky and irritable. As a birthday surprise, Juliet's parents arrange for Grandmamma to take her on a trip by train and boat to Dublin, London and eventually France. As they travel Grandmamma tells her own stories to entertain Juliet, making Juliet long all the more for a story of her own. Originally published in Great Britain in 1991. (105 pages)

Where it's reviewed:
Booklist, July 1994, page 1949
Books for Keeps, January 1994, page 9
Horn Book, September 1994, page 591
Publishers Weekly, May 16, 1994, page 65
School Library Journal, June 1994, page 135

Other books you might like:
William J. Brooke, *A Telling of the Tales: Five Stories*, 1990
     Five classic stories are retold from a contemporary perspective.
Helen Cresswell, *Bagthorpes Abroad*, 1984
     Vacationing in Wales, the Bagthorpe family finds their accomodations are haunted.
Joan Lowery Nixon, *The Gift*, 1983
     While visiting his Irish relatives, Brian tries to prove to a

skeptical great aunt that his great grandfather's tales of Irish folklore are true.

1427

EUGENE TRIVIZAS
HELEN OXENBURY, Illustrator

The Three Little Wolves and the Big Bad Pig

(New York: Margaret K. McElderry Books, 1993)

Subject(s): Folk Tales; Animals/Wolves; Animals/Pigs
Age range(s): Grades K-3
Major character(s): Mother, Wolf, Mother; Unnamed Character, Pig
Time period(s): Indeterminate Past
Locale(s): Fictional Country

Summary: When Mother wolf sends her three children out into the world to make their way she warns them to beware of the big, bad pig. Being cautious little wolves, they build their first house of bricks, but the big, bad pig, in his determination to enter, smashes it with a sledgehammer. Each house the young wolves build is more fortified than the one before, yet each time it is demolished by the big, bad pig and the wolves barely escape with their lives. When they try a totally different approach to house construction they find that their flower home has a soothing effect on the pig who, after several sniffs, decides to become a big, good pig. (32 pages)

Where it's reviewed:
Booklist, September 1, 1993, page 59
Bulletin of the Center for Children's Books, September 1993, page 3
Horn Book Guide, Spring 1994, page 58
Publishers Weekly, June 28, 1993, page 77
School Library Journal, December 1993, page 95

Awards the book has won:
Booklist Editors' Choice, 1993
School Library Journal Best Books, 1993

Other books you might like:
Gavin Bishop, *The Three Little Pigs*, 1989
     The story of three little pigs leaving home to seek their fortunes is illustrated with a hip wolf who sports sunglasses and a walkman, but still ends up in the stew pot.
Jon Scieszka, *The Stinky Cheese Man: And Other Fairly Stupid Tales*, 1992
     The Caldecott Honor book features nontraditional (truly bizarre) retellings of well-known fairy tales.
Vivian Vande Velde, *Tales from the Brothers Grimm and the Sisters Weird*, 1995
     Thirteen classic stories are rewritten with a new twist in a collection of ''fractured'' fairy tales.

1428

ANN TURNBULL

No Friend of Mine

(Cambridge, MA: Candlewick Press, 1995)

Subject(s): Friendship; Social Classes; Identity

Age range(s): Grades 4-6
Major character(s): Lennie Dyer, 11-Year-Old; Ralph Wilding, 11-Year-Old; Bert Haines, Bully
Time period(s): 1930s
Locale(s): Culverton, England

Summary: Every day after school Lennie fears he'll be discovered by Bert the bully; even when he gets home safely, there's no space for privacy within his family's poor home. Then one day he meets Ralph who lives in a big house, has a fine accent, new clothes and a father who's the boss of the mine where Lennie's dad, sick with black lung, used to work. Though from opposite backgrounds, the two become friends which pleases Lennie very much. One day Lennie is accused of stealing something from Ralph's home and the friendship ends when Ralph betrays him. (128 pages)

Where it's reviewed:
Booklist, August 1995, page 1950
Books for Keeps, May 1995, page 10
Junior Bookshelf, April 1995, page 81

Other books by the same author:
Too Tired, 1994
Speedwell, 1992
Frightened Forest, 1975

Other books you might like:
Carol Carrick, *Some Friend*, 1979
    Mike and Rob are friends, but Rob's trait of manipulating people is one that Mike doesn't like.
Alfred Slote, *Tony and Me*, 1974
    When Bill realizes his friend Tony is a thief, besides being a great baseball player, he needs to make some decisions about friendship.
John Tunis, *His Enemy, His Friend*, 1967
    A German boy and a French boy are friends, but the animosity between their two countries affects their friendship.

1429

ANN TURNBULL

Room for a Stranger

(Cambridge, MA: Candlewick Press, 1996)

Subject(s): World War II; Jealousy; Evacuees
Age range(s): Grades 4-6
Major character(s): Doreen Dyer, 12-Year-Old; Lennie Dyer, 15-Year-Old; Rhoda Kelly, 13-Year-Old, Child (evacuee)
Time period(s): 1940s (1941)
Locale(s): Calverton, England (outside London)

Summary: Doreen is looking forward to having an evacuee about her own age come to stay with them, but she is quickly disappointed and jealous of Rhoda when she comes. Rhoda tells them she is the daughter of an actress and constantly talks about her life before she came to the country. When Doreen's brother becomes interested in the new girl and others seem to feel sorry for her, Doreen finally strikes out, accusing Rhoda of not telling the truth and declaring that no one really cares about Rhoda anyway, including her own mother. Rhoda runs off to the deserted mine where an accident almost causes

serious injury. When Rhoda's mother comes, Doreen sees how close to the truth her comments were. (121 pages)

Where it's reviewed:
School Library Journal, March 1996, page 198
Booklist, May 1, 1996, page 1508

Other books by the same author:
Speedwell, 1992
Maroo of the Winter Caves, 1984

Other books you might like:
Nina Bawden, *Carrie's War*, 1973
    Carrie and her younger brother are evacuated to Wales during the war and become involved in unusual local events.
Eve Bunting, *Spying on Miss Mueller*, 1995
    The girls in the boarding school believe their teacher is a German spy and enlist the help of a Jewish student to check on her.
Patricia Reilly Giff, *Lily's Crossing*, 1997
    Two girls are drawn together during World War II because of a mutual feeling of loneliness and loss.
Mary Downing Hahn, *Stepping on the Cracks*, 1991
    Two girls must make a decision whether to turn in a dissenter or not.

1430

ANN TURNBULL
EMMA CHICHESTER-CLARK, Illustrator

Too Tired

(San Diego: Gulliver Books/Harcourt Brace & Company, 1994)

Subject(s): Animals; Floods; Sleep
Age range(s): Grades K-2
Major character(s): Noah, Leader
Time period(s): Indeterminate Past
Locale(s): Earth

Summary: Noah calls the roll as the animals clamber aboard the ark. The sloths have not arrived because they are tired and plan to come tomorrow. Noah will not accept no for an answer and, as the water rises, the other animals (except the cats) try to convince the sloths to climb abroad. First published in Great Britain in 1992. (32 pages)

Where it's reviewed:
Booklist, March 15, 1994, page 1375
Junior Bookshelf, April 1994, page 52
Kirkus Reviews, May 1, 1994, page 638
Publishers Weekly, April 11, 1994, page 64
School Library Journal, April 1994, page 114

Awards the book has won:
ALA Notable Book, 1995

Other books by the same author:
The Sandhorse, 1989

Other books you might like:
Linda Hayward, *Noah's Ark*, 1987
    A retelling of the familiar story of the floating zoo is rewritten for the first level of beginning readers.

Angela McAllister, *When the Ark Was Full*, 1990
  With the ark filled to capacity two land-dwelling whales adapt to a new habitat.
Glen Rounds, *Washday on Noah's Ark: A Story of Noah's Ark According to Glen Rounds*, 1985
  After 40 days of rain, Mrs. Noah takes advantage of the sun to improvise a clothesline and hang out the laundry.
Peter Spier, *Noah's Ark*, 1977
  The 1978 Caldecott Medal winner pictorially reenacts the story of the flood.

1431

ANN TURNER
SANDI WICKERSHAM RESNICK, Illustrator

Apple Valley Year

(New York: Macmillan Publishing Company, 1993)

Subject(s): Seasons; Farm Life; Animals/Foxes
Age range(s): Grades K-3
Major character(s): Ralph Clark, Father, Farmer (apple grower); Tim Clark, Child, Brother; Martha Clark, Child, Sister
Time period(s): Indeterminate Past
Locale(s): United States

Summary: In an apple orchard the seasons of the year determine the work responsibilities for Ralph Clark, his Belgian horses, the bees and the other family members. Each is dependent on the other for a successful crop. Tim and Martha help when they are not in school and look forward to new shoes when the crop is sold. Even the fox living in the orchard plays a part by keeping the mouse population under control. (32 pages)

Where it's reviewed:
Booklist, September 1, 1993, page 72
Horn Book Guide, Spring 1994, page 58
Publishers Weekly, September 6, 1993, page 97
School Library Journal, November 1993, page 95

Other books by the same author:
The Christmas House, 1994
Katie's Trunk, 1992
Dakota Dugout, 1985

Other books you might like:
Thomas Locker, *Family Farm*, 1988
  A family must work together and change with the times to maintain a successful farm.
Karen E. Lotz, *Snowsong Whistling*, 1993
  Autumn brings pumpkins, apples and the first snowsong, foretelling the approach of winter.
Alice Provenson, *The Year at Maple Hill Farm*, 1981
  As the seasons change, the work of a farm continues as the needs of crops and animals change. Co-author Martin Provenson.

1432

ANN TURNER
ROBERT BARRETT, Illustrator

Dust for Dinner

(New York: HarperCollins Publishers, 1995)

Series: I Can Read
Subject(s): Depression (Economic); Drought; Family Life
Age range(s): Grades 1-2
Major character(s): Jake, Child, Brother; Maggy, Child, Sister; Papa, Father, Farmer
Time period(s): 1930s
Locale(s): Oklahoma

Summary: As the drought persists, crops fail, livestock die and Jake and Maggy's family has no income. Sadly, they watch their home and all their possessions auctioned. The next day they pack their pick-up truck with what little they have left and begin the trek to California in hope of finding work. Life is difficult, but finally Papa finds a job and the family once again has a house rather than a tent for a home. (64 pages)

Where it's reviewed:
Booklist, July 1995, page 1885
Bulletin of the Center for Children's Books, September 1995, page 31
Horn Book Guide, Fall 1995, page 289
School Library Journal, October 1995, page 121

Other books by the same author:
One Brave Summer, 1995
Stars for Sarah, 1991
Dakota Dugout, 1985

Other books you might like:
Sid Fleischman, *McBroom the Rainmaker*, 1982
  In a tall tale, MrBroom devises an unusual scheme for bringing rain to the drought-stricken prairie.
Virginia Hamilton, *Drylongso*, 1992
  Out of a dust storm comes Drylongso, a boy who helps a farm family find a source of water on their land so they will survive a drought.
Patricia MacLachlan, *Skylark*, 1994
  In a sequel to *Sarah, Plain and Tall*, drought comes to the prairie farm, testing the family's commitment to the land.

1433

ANN TURNER

Elfsong

(San Diego: Harcourt Brace & Company, 1995)

Series: Elfsong Trilogy
Subject(s): Elves; Music; Animals/Cats
Age range(s): Grades 4-6
Major character(s): Maddy Trevor, 10-Year-Old; Grandpa, Grandfather; Sabrina, Cat
Time period(s): 1990s (1995)
Locale(s): United States

Summary: Maddy looks forward to a relaxing summer vacation at Grandpa's house. This year, from the moment of arrival, she senses magic in the air and experiences the unusual. Sometimes Maddy hears music or bits of a song, or she sees a cat wearing a saddle. Sabrina vanishes and, while searching for her, Maddy meets an elf who trains Sabrina to replace the mount he lost. Maddy learns the elves are being attacked by a great horned owl and enlists Grandpa's help to save them. A glossary defines the elfin terms used in the text. (168 pages)

Where it's reviewed:
Booklist, October 1, 1995, page 321
Bulletin of the Center for Children's Books, December 1995, page 141
Children's Book Review Service, October 1995, page 24
Kirkus Reviews, August 15, 1995, page 1194
School Library Journal, October 1995, page 140

Other books by the same author:
One Brave Summer, 1995
Rosemary's Witch, 1991
Grasshopper Summer, 1989

Other books you might like:
Avi, *Poppy*, 1995
  With help from other animals, a young mouse undertakes a journey into the unknown and courageously defeats an owl to improve life for her community.
Lynne Reid Banks, *The Fairy Rebel*, 1985
  Tiki, a rebellious fairy, risks the wrath of the Fairy Queen to fulfill a human's request.
Janet Taylor Lisle, *Forest*, 1993
  When Amber runs away from home, she stumbles into a world of squirrels in the Upper Forest, initiating a chain of events which will turn violent if she does not act quickly.

1434

ANN TURNER

One Brave Summer

(New York: HarperCollins Publishers, 1995)

Subject(s): Friendship; Fear; Authorship
Age range(s): Grades 3-5
Major character(s): Katy Williams, 10-Year-Old; Lena May Martin, Child, Neighbor; Rachel Williams, Mother, Writer
Time period(s): 1990s (1995)
Locale(s): Sugar Cove (mountains)

Summary: The summer after Katy's fourth grade year in a new school her mother rents a mountain cabin for the summer. Rachel Williams plans to work on a novel, but Katy expects nothing but boredom. Her expectations change when they are greeted upon arrival by Lena May who is eager to have someone her age on the hill. Lena May's exuberance for life and experiences are very different from Katy's cautious, urban approach to adventures. The summer proves to be rewarding for both girls and their families. (163 pages)

Where it's reviewed:
Booklist, October 1, 1995, page 321
Horn Book, September 1995, page 605
Kirkus Reviews, June 1, 1995, page 788
Publishers Weekly, July 3, 1995, page 61
School Library Journal, July 1995, page 82

Other books by the same author:
Street Talk, 1992
Rosemary's Witch, 1991
Grasshopper Summer, 1989

Other books you might like:
Susan Richards Shreve, *Amy Dunn Quits School*, 1993
  Needing some time for herself, Amy Dunn skips school and the many other activities planned for the day by her overly controlling Supermom.
Eileen Spinelli, *Lizzie Logan Wears Purple Sunglasses*, 1995
  On moving-in day, Lizzie Logan greets Heather and her family with a store-bought pie and an offer of friendship.
Elvira Woodruff, *Ghosts Don't Get Goosebumps*, 1993
  While vacationing at her aunt and uncle's farm, Jenna is befriended by Angel, a fast-talking local girl with plans that lead to adventure and mystery.

1435

ANNE TYLER
MITRA MODARRESSI, Illustrator

Tumble Tower

(New York: Orchard Books, 1993)

Subject(s): Princes and Princesses; Cleanliness; Floods
Age range(s): Grades K-2
Major character(s): Princess Molly the Messy the Me, Royalty, Sister; Prince Thomas the Tidy the Ti, Royalty, Brother (younger)
Time period(s): Indeterminate Past
Locale(s): Fictional Country

Summary: Born into a family of neatniks, Princess Molly the Messy is assigned to the tower where her messy living quarters will be less of an embarrassment to her family. Thomas is tidy and perfect, but Molly is content maintaining her private space to suit herself. When the lower level of the castle floods, her family seeks refuge in Molly's "Tumble Tower" and discovers that her lifestyle is perfect for meeting their needs—the outgrown pajamas on the floor fit Thomas, the leftover food from an afternoon snack satisfies hunger and the books left in her bed provide a bedtime story. This is the first picture book by this author of adult novels. (32 pages)

Where it's reviewed:
Children's Book Review Service, Winter 1994, page 66
Horn Book Guide, Spring 1994, page 58
Kirkus Reviews, July 15, 1993, page 943
Publishers Weekly, June 28, 1993, page 76
School Library Journal, September 1993, page 220

Other books you might like:
Pat McKissack, *Messy Bessey's Closet*, 1989
  In a beginning reader coauthored by Frederick McKissack, Bessey learns about sharing while cleaning her messy closet.
Elise Petersen, *Tracy's Mess*, 1995
  Curly-haired Tracy appears to be fastidious, but wait until you see what's behind her bedroom door!
Marjorie Weinman Sharmat, *Mooch the Messy*, 1976
  Mooch's rat hole is such a mess his father tries to implement a clean-up plan which is only temporarily successful.

Harriet Ziefert, *A Clean House for Mole and Mouse*, 1988
   After working to clean their house, mole and mouse stay
   outside all day so the house will remain neat.

U

1436

YOSHIKO UCHIDA
JOANNA YARDLEY, Illustrator

The Bracelet

(New York: Philomel Books, 1993)

Subject(s): Japanese Americans; World War II; Friendship
Age range(s): Grades 2-5
Major character(s): Laurie Madison, 2nd Grader, Friend; Emi, 2nd Grader (Japanese American), Friend
Time period(s): 1940s (1942)
Locale(s): Berkeley, California

Summary: In a newly illustrated reissue of the 1976 title, a saddened and confused Emi faces her family's forced removal from their home and transfer to an internment camp. Emi is consoled to have the bracelet received from her best friend Laurie as a parting gift. Although the bracelet is lost on their first day in a camp, Emi realizes that she will carry the memories of her friendship with Laurie forever in her heart. (32 pages)

Where it's reviewed:
Booklist, September 15, 1993, page 162
Bulletin of the Center for Children's Books, September 1993, page 25
Horn Book, November 1993, page 771
Publishers Weekly, September 13, 1993, page 128
School Library Journal, December 1993, page 95

Other books by the same author:
The Wise Old Woman, 1994
The Magic Purse, 1993
Journey to Topaz: A Story of the Japanese-American Evacuation, 1971

Other books you might like:
Daniel S. Davis, *Behind Barbed Wire: The Imprisonment of Japanese-Americans During World War II*, 1982
A non-fiction account of the Japanese Americans forced into internment camps in 1942.

Kathleen V. Kudlinski, *Pearl Harbor Is Burning! A Story of World War II*, 1991
New to the island of Hawaii, Frank meets Kenji and learns about friendship and patriotism.
Jean Thesman, *Molly Donnelly*, 1993
When World War II begins, Molly faces many changes including the disappearance of her neighbor Emily Tamanaka and her family.

1437

JANICE MAY UDRY
KAREN GUNDERSHEIMER, Illustrator

Is Susan Here?

(New York: Harper Collins, Publishers, 1993)

Subject(s): Parent and Child; Imagination; Family Life
Age range(s): Grades K-1
Major character(s): Susan, Child (imaginative); Unnamed Character, Mother (patient); Unnamed Character, Father (patient)
Time period(s): 1990s (1993)
Locale(s): United States

Summary: Originally published in 1962, this story tells of the day that Susan disappears. All day her parents are assisted with their chores by a series of animals, each one looking suspiciously like a disguised child. At bedtime, as Susan's mother and father sit in her room wishing for her return, they hear a little voice saying "I'm back." (24 pages)

Where it's reviewed:
Booklist, September 15, 1993, page 162
Childhood Education, Winter 1993, page 106
Horn Book Guide, Fall 1993, page 278
Publishers Weekly, June 14, 1993, page 70
School Library Journal, August 1993, page 154

Other books by the same author:
What Mary Jo Shared, 1966
Let's Be Enemies, 1961
A Tree Is Nice, 1957 (Caldecott Medal)

Other books you might like:

Kady MacDonald Denton, *Would They Love a Lion?*, 1995
Using a reversible bathrobe for a costume, Anna ''becomes'' many different animals, each of them loved by her family.

Russell Hoban, *A Baby Sister for Frances*, 1964
Imaginative Frances ''runs away'' as far as the dining room until she overhears her parents plans for celebrating her return with her favorite cake.

Ann Tompert, *Little Fox Goes to the End of the World*, 1984
While her mother sits patiently sewing, Little Fox describes how she will travel to the end of the world, avert danger and return to the safety of her home.

1438

DAVID UPDIKE
ROBERT ANDREW PARKER, Illustrator

The Sounds of Summer

(New York: Pippin Press, 1993)

Subject(s): Animals/Dogs; Death (of a Pet); Summer
Age range(s): Grades 3-5
Major character(s): Homer, Child; Sophocles, Dog (aging)
Time period(s): 1990s (1993)
Locale(s): United States

Summary: In the final book of the quartet about a boy and his dog, Homer's enjoyment of summer is tempered by his realization that his pet is growing old. When Sophocles becomes lost during a storm, Homer and a friend search for him through the night. Although Sophocles is found and receives medical attention, he dies. As the summer progresses, the sounds of wind, birds, and water in the creek help Homer to remember his dog. (39 pages)

Where it's reviewed:
Booklist, September 1, 1993, page 62
Bulletin of the Center for Children's Books, October 1993, page 61
Horn Book Guide, Spring 1994, page 70
School Library Journal, October 1993, page 133

Other books by the same author:
Seven Times Eight, 1990
A Spring Story, 1989
An Autumn Tale, 1988

Other books you might like:

Eleanor Estes, *Ginger Pye*, 1951
A Newbery Award-winning title tells of the Pye family's search for Ginger, their puppy who has disappeared.

Louis Sachar, *Marvin Redpost: Alone in His Teacher's House*, 1994
Marvin's friends think he is lucky to have the opportunity to care for his teacher's old dog while she is away, but when Waldo dies Marvin doesn't feel very lucky.

Mary Stolz, *King Emmett the Second*, 1991
Emmett Murphy faces two difficult problems—his family's move to another state and the death of his pet pig.

1439

JEAN URE

The Children Next Door

(New York: Scholastic, 1996, c1994)

Subject(s): Ghosts; Shyness
Age range(s): Grades 4-7
Major character(s): Laura, 11-Year-Old; Zilla Hobbs, 11-Year-Old; Em, Spirit (appears as a child), Grandmother
Time period(s): 1990s; Indeterminate Past (when Em was young)
Locale(s): London, England

Summary: Laura is very shy and not happy about her new home until she hears some children playing next door. She enjoys watching them play ball and other games. She sees nothing strange about the children until she realizes that these children are from the past. She cannot tell anyone, even the day there is an accident and one of the children is killed. (135 pages)

Where it's reviewed:
School Library Journal, March 1996, page 198
Bulletin of the Center for Children's Books, May 1996, page 317

Other books by the same author:
Supermouse, 1994
Wizard in Wonderland, 1993
The Wizard in the Woods, 1992

Other books you might like:

Vivien Alcock, *The Haunting of Cassie Palmer*, 1980
Cassie has the gift of second sight which enables her to communicate with the other world.

Sarah Ellis, *Next-Door Neighbors*, 1990
Shy Peggy feels lonely after her move to Canada until she meets her strange neighbors.

Mary Downing Hahn, *The Doll in the Garden*, 1989
Ashley and Kriti find an antique doll and discover that it will take them through the hedge and into a different time.

Betty Ren Wright, *The Ghost of Ernie P.*, 1990
Jeff is pushed by his ghostly friend to complete the plan he had started before he was killed in an accident.

1440

EDUARD USPENSKII
VLADIMIR SHPITALNIK, Illustrator

Uncle Fedya, His Dog, and His Cat

(New York: Alfred A. Knopf, 1993)

Subject(s): Animals/Dogs; Animals/Cats; Runaways
Age range(s): Grades 2-4
Major character(s): Uncle Fedya, Child (serious), Runaway; Mr. Matroskin, Cat (talking); Sharik, Dog (talking)
Time period(s): 1970s
Locale(s): Moscow, Russia; Russia (small village in the country)

Summary: Originally published more than 20 years ago, the book is translated from the Russian by Michael Henry Heim and tells the story of Uncle Fedya (so named because of his serious nature) who runs away to the country so that he can have pets. On the way he and Mr. Matroskin meet Sharik and the dog joins them in their new home. To survive they dig up a treasure box, using the treasure to purchase a troublesome cow and a tractor which depends on food for fuel. In time Uncle Fedya's parents find him and the entire menagerie is allowed to accompany Uncle Fedya home. (136 pages)

Where it's reviewed:
Children's Book Review Service, January 1994, page 57
Horn Book Guide, Spring 1994, page 83
Kirkus Reviews, December 1, 1993, page 1530
Publishers Weekly, November 8, 1993, page 77
School Library Journal, November 1993, page 95

Other books by the same author:
Crocodile Gene and His Friends, 1994
The Little Warranty People, 1994

Other books you might like:
Tove Jansson, *Comet in Moominland*, 1959
 In one of several Swedish stories about the Moomintrolls, a journey to the professor provides unexpected adventures for Moomintroll.
Astrid Lindgren, *Pippi Longstocking*, 1950
 Independent Pippi sets up housekeeping with a monkey and a horse for companions and a unique approach to life.
Magdalen Nabb, *Josie Smith*, 1990
 Strong-willed and independent, Josie's great ideas do not always turn out as she expects.

V

1441

VLADIMIR VAGIN, Author/Illustrator

The Nutcracker Ballet

(New York: Scholastic Inc., 1995)

Subject(s): Ballet; Christmas; Fantasy
Age range(s): Grades K-3
Major character(s): Clara, Child; Herr Drosselmeier, Godfather
Time period(s): Indeterminate Past
Locale(s): Germany

Summary: On Christmas Eve, Herr Drosselmeier distributes gifts to all the children. Clara receives a nutcracker which her brother promptly breaks. After the household has quieted for the night, Clara tiptoes into the living room to check on her nutcracker and is surprised to see the Christmas tree grow and the toys come to life as uniformed mice appear. Clara observes a battle and watches her nutcracker change into a prince who takes her to the marzipan castle. In the morning, Clara awakens, remembering the magical evening. (32 pages)

Where it's reviewed:
Booklist, September 15, 1995, page 173
Horn Book Guide, Spring 1996, page 47
Publishers Weekly, September 18, 1995, page 102
School Library Journal, October 1995, page 42

Other books you might like:
Eve Bunting, *The Day Before Christmas*, 1992
    Allie attends a Christmas Eve performance of *The Nutcracker* with her grandfather.
Deborah Hautzig, *The Nutcracker Ballet*, 1992
    The retelling of the classic story in a beginning reader enables children to read the story of Clara's exciting evening for themselves.
Rachel Isadora, *Lili on Stage*, 1995
    Lili is thrilled to have her first role in her ballet company's performance of *The Nutcracker*.

1442

RACHEL VAIL

Daring to be Abigail

(New York: Orchard Books, 1996)

Subject(s): Camps and Camping; Self-Perception; Parent and Child
Age range(s): Grades 4-6
Major character(s): Abigail Silverman, Camper, 11-Year-Old; Dana, Camper; Tiff, Camper
Time period(s): 1990s
Locale(s): United States (Camp Nashaquitsa)

Summary: Abigail arrives at camp determined to be brave and to make new friends. She quickly finds herself part of the in-group and joins in teasing Dana, the last to arrive at camp. Dana turns out to be the only camper who understands the way Abby feels about the death of her father but Abby still teases her and participates in all the tricks played on her. She accepts all dares, including, worst of all, doing something to Dana which is unforgivable and which leads to her being sent home from camp. (128 pages)

Where it's reviewed:
School Library Journal, March 1996, page 198
Booklist, March 1, 1996, page 1184
Hornbook, May/June 1996, page 337

Awards the book has won:
School Library Journal Best Books, 1996

Other books by the same author:
Ever After: A Novel, 1994 (young adult novel)
Do-Over, 1991 (young adult novel)

Other books you might like:
Constance C. Greene, *Double-Dare O'Toole*, 1983
    Fix is game for anything, especially if he is double-dared.
Vicki Grove, *The Crystal Garden*, 1995
    Eliza is determined to be popular at her new school but then she becomes friends with Dierdre, an outsider.

Aileen Jackson, *Crane's Rebound*, 1991
> A boy at camp must cope with homesickness, loneliness and peer pressure.

Mavis Jukes, *Getting Even*, 1988
> Maggie is unable to stop the nasty pranks of her classmate and receives differing advice on how to handle it.

Barbara Park, *Buddies*, 1985
> A thirteen-year old goes to camp wanting to be popular but is hampered by an unattractive cabin mate who wants to be her friend.

Susan Beth Pfeffer, *Truth or Dare*, 1986
> A 6th grader explores the nature of friendship when she tries to make new friends.

1443

AMY VALENS, Author/Illustrator

Danilo the Fruit Man

(New York: Dial Books for Young Readers, 1993)

Subject(s): Magic; Fantasy
Age range(s): Grades K-3
Major character(s): Danilo, Peddler; Ninicchio, Horse; Unnamed Character, Aged Person
Time period(s): Indeterminate Past
Locale(s): Sicily, Italy

Summary: With Ninicchio to pull his cart of oranges, Danilo lives a contented life peddling his fruit to the village residents. One day, travelling down an unfamiliar street, he finds a park with trees of red, pink, and blue fruit. The old man in the garden generously shares the fruit and a riddle. Hurrying to peddle the fruit, Danilo does not heed the message of the riddle and finds that the magical fruit is transformed into rocks. Spring brings another chance for Danilo to learn the old man's lesson. (32 pages)

Where it's reviewed:
Booklist, June 1, 1993, page 1861
Horn Book Guide, Fall 1993, page 278
Publishers Weekly, May 24, 1993, page 86
School Library Journal, July 1993, page 73

Other books by the same author:
Jesse's Day Care, 1990

Other books you might like:
Tomie De Paola, *Strega Nona*, 1979
> The Italian folktale of a witch, Strega Nona, is retold in the first of several tales about her and her bumbling assistant, Big Anthony.

Esphyr Slobodkina, *Caps for Sale*, 1947
> A peddler of caps must use his ingenuity to reclaim his misappropriated wares from a group of monkeys.

Elizabeth Spurr, *The Gumdrop Tree*, 1994
> A little girl is unwilling to eat a bag of gumdrops she receives so she plants them instead and grows a gumdrop tree which bears sweet candies galore.

1444

CHRIS VAN ALLSBURG, Author/Illustrator

The Sweetest Fig

(Boston: Houghton Mifflin Company, 1993)

Subject(s): Dreams and Nightmares; Magic; Animals/Dogs
Age range(s): Grades 3 and Up
Major character(s): Monsieur Bibot, Dentist (uncaring dog owner); Marcel, Dog (Monsieur Bibot's pet)
Time period(s): 1990s (1993)
Locale(s): Paris, France

Summary: Offended that an elderly woman would give him two figs as payment for extracting a tooth, Bibot dismisses her comment that the figs can make his dreams come true and proceeds to eat one fig for his bedtime snack. The following morning, the truth of her statement becomes apparent as he walks Marcel and experiences surreal events that he recalls having dreamed the previous night. Carefully, Bibot plans and prepares himself before eating the second fig. As usual, he has ignored Marcel, the long-suffering dog, who has a plan of his own. (28 pages)

Where it's reviewed:
Booklist, October 1, 1993, page 343
Children's Book Review Service, October 1993, page 18
Horn Book Guide, Spring 1994, page 58
Publishers Weekly, August 30, 1993, page 93
School Library Journal, November 1993, page 110

Awards the book has won:
ALA Notable Book, 1994
Booklist Editors' Choice, 1993

Other books by the same author:
The Widow's Broom, 1992
The Wretched Stone, 1991
Just a Dream, 1990

Other books you might like:
Anthony Browne, *The Big Baby*, 1994
> One day John Young's mother refers to his father as "a Big Baby" and the next morning that's just what they find in the bed.

Anthony Browne, *The Tunnel*, 1990
> A brother and sister stop their bickering long enough to explore a tunnel together and find something totally unexpected at the end.

Demi, *Liang and the Magic Paintbrush*, 1980
> A Chinese boy's dreams come to life with the help of his paintbrush.

Diana Hendry, *A Camel Called April*, 1991
> One morning in the park, Harry is surprised to meet the animals from his dreams.

David Wiesner, *June 29, 1999*, 1992
> Holly's science experiment has some unexpected results when enormous vegetables begin falling from the sky.

1445

NANCY VAN LAAN
MARJORIE PRICEMAN, Illustrator

The Tiny, Tiny Boy and the Big, Big Cow

(New York: Alfred A. Knopf, 1993)

Subject(s): Folk Tales; Animals/Cows; Humor
Age range(s): Grades K-2
Major character(s): Unnamed Character, Child (tiny, tiny boy); Unnamed Character, Cow (big, big); Ma, Mother
Time period(s): Indeterminate Past
Locale(s): Scotland

Summary: A tiny, tiny boy seeks his mother's advice when he is unable to milk the big, big cow who will not stand still. Ma suggests one ploy after another, but the cow is not swayed by offers of tea or gowns of silk. Finally, when the boy and his mother are exhausted, the cow is told to do anything but stand still and, of course, she stands still and is milked. Perhaps she was exhausted too. (32 pages)

Where it's reviewed:
Horn Book, May 1993, page 325
Horn Book Guide, Fall 1993, page 247
Kirkus Reviews, March 15, 1993, page 381
Publishers Weekly, April 19, 1993, page 58
School Library Journal, September 1993, page 221

Other books by the same author:
Mama Rocks, Papa Sings, 1995
Round and Round Again, 1994
Possum Come A-Knocking, 1990

Other books you might like:
Byron Barton, *The Wee Little Woman*, 1995
    A wee little cumulative tale about a wee little woman whose wee little cat has hurt feelings when chastised for drinking all the wee little milk.
Jennifer A. Ericsson, *No Milk*, 1993
    A city boy learns through trial and error how to get milk from a cow.
Rosanne Litzinger, *The Old Woman and Her Pig*, 1993
    When the old woman's newly purchased pig refuses to go over the stile, the old woman calls for help in a lively retelling of a traditional cumulative tale.

1446

JEAN VAN LEEUWEN
THOMAS B. ALLEN, Illustrator

Across the Wide Dark Sea: The Mayflower Journey

(New York: Dial Books for Young Readers, 1995)

Subject(s): Historical; Voyages and Travels; Emigration and Immigration
Age range(s): Grades 1-3
Major character(s): Love Brewster, 9-Year-Old, Traveller; William Brewster, Father, Traveller
Time period(s): 17th century (1620)
Locale(s): At Sea (aboard *Mayflower*); Plymouth, Massachusetts

Summary: With his family and many others, Love Brewster bravely embarks on a journey to a new land in search of religious freedom. Week after week of storms at sea bring despair that land will never be reached, but after nine weeks, the voyage comes to an end. The pilgrims locate a spot for the settlement and hurry to build homes before winter arrives. Many travellers die during that first winter, but Love and his family survive to welcome spring, befriend Indians, and watch the ship sail away, leaving them in the new land. A concluding author's note provides factual information on which the story is based. (32 pages)

Where it's reviewed:
Booklist, September 15, 1995, page 161
Bulletin of the Center for Children's Books, October 1995, page 73
Horn Book Guide, Spring 1996, page 48
Kirkus Reviews, October 1, 1995, page 1437
School Library Journal, September 1995, page 187

Other books by the same author:
Two Girls in Sister Dresses, 1994
Going West, 1992
More Tales of Oliver Pig, 1981

Other books you might like:
Eve Bunting, *How Many Days to America? A Thanksgiving Story*, 1988
    On a small, crowded boat two children and their parents flee their Caribbean island home for freedom in America.
Barbara Cohen, *Molly's Pilgrim*, 1983
    Molly's classmates learn to appreciate the pilgrims' hopes when she depicts a pilgrim's attire in the manner of her family leaving Russia for religious freedom in America.
Linda Hayward, *The First Thanksgiving*, 1990
    The story of the Plymouth Pilgrims is retold in an easy-to-read chapter book.
Kate Waters, *On the Mayflower: Voyage of the Ship's Apprentice and a Passenger Girl*, 1996
    The first voyage of the Mayflower to America is seen through the shipboard experiences of a 12-year-old and a 7-year-old.
Mary Watson, *The Butterfly Seeds*, 1995
    Jake misses his grandfather who did not emigrate with the family, but treasures Grandpa's parting gift.

1447

JEAN VAN LEEUWEN

Blue Sky, Butterfly

(New York: Dial, 1996)

Subject(s): Divorce; Family Life; Gardens and Gardening
Age range(s): Grades 4-7
Major character(s): Christina "Twig", 11-Year-Old, Child of Divorced Parents; Nathan, Brother, Teenager
Time period(s): 1990s
Locale(s): United States

Summary: Twig awakens one day to learn that her parents are separating. Her whole life changes when her mother's depression prevents her from cooking or cleaning and her brother is always away playing sports. When her grandmother comes for a brief visit, things begin to change for the better. Her mother begins to garden and, as the plants begin to grow, so does the family togetherness and understanding. (125 pages)

Where it's reviewed:
Bulletin of the Center for Children's Books, February 1996, page 207
Booklist, June 1, 1996, page 1724
School Library Journal, July 1996, page 126

Other books by the same author:
Bound for Oregon, 1994
Two Girls in Sister Dresses, 1994
Dear Mom, You're Ruining My Life, 1989

Other books you might like:
C.S. Adler, *The Silver Coach*, 1988
   Two sisters face their parent's impending divorce while on a visit to their grandmother.
Marion Dane Bauer, *A Question of Trust*, 1994
   Brad is angry because his mother has left, but becomes reconciled with the help of a mother cat and kittens.
Anne Fine, *Step by Wicked Step*, 1996
   Five children tell the stories of their broken families when they spend the night together on a camping trip.
Alice Mead, *Crossing the Starlight Bridge*, 1994
   Rayanne does not understand why her life must change when her father moves out.
Camille Yarbrough, *The Shimmershine Queens*, 1989
   Angie's cousin helps her face life when her father leaves and her mother becomes depressed.

1448

JEAN VAN LEEUWEN
JAMES WATLING, Illustrator

Bound for Oregon
(New York: Dial Books for Young Readers, 1994)

Subject(s): Frontier and Pioneer Life; Adventure and Adventurers; Historical
Age range(s): Grades 4-6
Major character(s): Mary Ellen Todd, 9-Year-Old, Sister; Louvina Todd, 6-Year-Old, Sister; Abbott L. Todd, Father, Artisan (potter)
Time period(s): 1850s (1852)
Locale(s): Arkansas; Oregon

Summary: When Father decides to take advantage of the opportunities available to those willing to settle in Oregon territory, the family prepares for the long journey and sets off in an ox-drawn covered wagon. Louvina is excited to be travelling, but Mary Ellen is bored by the long days of sitting and worried at the prospect of Indian attacks. During the 6-month journey, the Todds experience danger, hunger, and illness, but they reach Oregon in time to celebrate Christmas in a new home. (176 pages)

Where it's reviewed:
Booklist, October 1, 1994, page 329
Bulletin of the Center for Children's Books, November 1994, page 107
Horn Book, March 1995, page 197
Publishers Weekly, September 5, 1994, page 112

School Library Journal, October 1994, page 128

Other books by the same author:
The Great Summer Camp Catastrophe, 1992
Dear Mom, You're Ruining My Life, 1989
The Great Rescue Operation, 1982

Other books you might like:
Brett Harvey, *Cassie's Journey: Going West in the 1860s*, 1988
   Cassie tells of the hardship and danger to her family during their trip by covered wagon from Illinois to California.
Kathleen V. Kudlinski, *Facing West: A Story of the Oregon Trail*, 1994
   Ben wonders about the dangers ahead as his family departs Missouri for Oregon.
Laura Ingalls Wilder, *Little House on the Prairie*, 1935
   Seeking a better life, the Wilder family travels by covered wagon from the Wisconsin woods to the prairie.
Elvira Woodruff, *Dear Levi: Letters from the Overland Trail*, 1994
   In letters to his younger brother, 12-year-old Austin Ives describes his journey from Pennsylvania to Oregon.

1449

JEAN VAN LEEUWEN
JUAN WIJNGAARD, Illustrator

Emma Bean
(New York: Dial, 1993)

Subject(s): Toys; Animals/Rabbits; Growing Up
Age range(s): Grades K-1
Major character(s): Molly, Child; Emma Bean, Toy (stuffed rabbit)
Time period(s): 1990s (1993)
Locale(s): United States

Summary: When Molly is born, Emma Bean, a stuffed rabbit lovingly made by Molly's mother, is waiting for her. Thus begins the companionship of a girl and her special toy. When Molly is old enough to go to school, Emma Bean's presence helps her through her first days of kindergarten where she meets a little girl with a special teddy bear. (40 pages)

Where it's reviewed:
Booklist, July 1993, page 1977
Horn Book Guide, Spring 1994, page 71
Kirkus Reviews, August 1993, page 1008
Publishers Weekly, August 1993, page 79
School Library Journal, December 1993, page 96

Other books by the same author:
Oliver and Amanda, and the Big Snow, 1995
Going West, 1992
Amanda Pig on Her Own, 1991
Oliver, Amanda, and Grandmother Pig, 1987
Tales of Oliver Pig, 1979

Other books you might like:
Jez Alborough, *Where's My Teddy?*, 1992
   A teddy bear mix-up between a little boy and a bear ends happily when each recovers his own bear.

Miriam Cohen, *Will I Have a Friend?*, 1967
 First-day school fears are put to rest when Paul makes
 friends with Jim.
Don Freeman, *A Pocket for Corduroy*, 1978
 Lisa lovingly sews a pocket on her special teddy bear,
 Corduroy.
Margery Williams, *The Velveteen Rabbit*, 1926
 The love between a toy rabbit and a young boy is so strong
 that eventually the toy becomes a real rabbit.
Selina Young, *Ned*, 1993
 Emily and Ned, her green cloth donkey, are inseparable
 until Ned is lost, and then found again, on the first day of
 school.

1450

JEAN VAN LEEUWEN
ANN SCHWENINGER, Illustrator

Oliver & Amanda and the Big Snow

(New York: Dial Books for Young Readers, 1995)

Series: Easy-to-Read Books
Subject(s): Brothers and Sisters; Family Life; Winter
Age range(s): Grades 1-2
Major character(s): Oliver, Pig, Brother (older); Amanda, Pig,
 Sister
Time period(s): 1990s (1995)
Locale(s): Fictional Country

Summary: Four stories describe the activities of Oliver, Amanda and their parents following a heavy snowfall. Amanda enjoys the snow, but is forever getting lost in snow drifts and needing to be rescued by her patient father. Oliver needs no encouragement to sled on the big hill, but Amanda needs her mother's support to move from the little hill to the big hill. The family plays together and enjoys the snow. (48 pages)

Where it's reviewed:
Booklist, January 1996, page 850
Bulletin of the Center for Children's Books, December 1995,
 page 143
Horn Book, September 1995, page 628
Horn Book Guide, Spring 1996, page 52
School Library Journal, December 1995, page 92

Other books by the same author:
Amanda Pig on Her Own, 1994
Oliver & Amanda's Halloween, 1992
Oliver, Amanda, and Grandmother Pig, 1987

Other books you might like:
Laurie Krasny Brown, *Rex and Lilly Playtime*, 1995
 In an easy reader, brother and sister dinosaurs enjoy three
 fun-filled play activities together.
Maryann Cocca-Leffler, *Ice-Cold Birthday*, 1992
 Although snow interfers with a young girl's birthday party,
 it also provides the venue for some special fun.
Barbara M. Joosse, *Snow Day!*, 1995
 When snow forces the cancellation of school, Robby and
 his family have a day to play outside.
Stephen Krensky, *Lionel in the Winter*, 1994
 In four brief easy-to-read stories Lionel makes the most of
 the winter weather which others in his family dislike.

1451

JEAN VAN LEEUWEN
LINDA BENSON, Illustrator

Two Girls in Sister Dresses

(New York: Dial Books for Young Readers, 1994)

Subject(s): Sisters; Family Life; Clothes
Age range(s): Grades 1-3
Major character(s): Jennifer, 7-Year-Old, Sister; Molly, 5-
 Year-Old, Sister
Time period(s): Indeterminate Past
Locale(s): United States

Summary: As the older sister, Jennifer is alternately jealous of the attention others give to her cute younger sister and protective of Molly when the neighborhood bully picks on her. Wearing their matching hand-made dresses, Jennifer and Molly await the homecoming of their baby brother and ride bikes too quickly down the hill, resulting in skinned knees and torn dresses. The sisters have supportive, understanding parents who offer healing kisses and alternate activities as needed. (49 pages)

Where it's reviewed:
Booklist, April 1, 1994, page 1453
Horn Book, July 1994, page 447
Kirkus Reviews, May 15, 1994, page 709
Publishers Weekly, April 25, 1994, page 78
School Library Journal, June 1994, page 114

Other books by the same author:
Benjy the Football Hero, 1985
Benjy in Business, 1983
The Great Rescue Operation, 1982

Other books you might like:
Beverly Cleary, *Beezus and Ramona*, 1980
 As the big sister, Beezus knows she should be loving
 toward her little sister, however, with a sister like Ramona,
 it's not easy.
Gail Herman, *Flower Girl*, 1996
 With help from a lucky ring, a young girl is able to be the
 perfect flower girl in her sister's wedding.
Ann M. Martin, *Karen's Big Sister*, 1996
 Karen's love for stepsister Kristy is mixed with jealousy
 when Daddy gives Kristy a new pin.
Lisa Westberg Peters, *The Hayloft*, 1995
 Two sisters living on a farm share a memorable summer.
Susan Beth Pfeffer, *Twin Surprises*, 1991
 Betsy tries to keep a surprise birthday party for her twin
 sister a secret with humorous results.

1452

MARCIA VAUGHAN
BARRY MOSER, Illustrator

Whistling Dixie

(New York: HarperCollins Publishers, 1995)

Subject(s): Swamps; Pets; Animals
Age range(s): Grades K-3

Major character(s): Dixie Lee, Child, Animal Lover; Mama, Single Mother; Grandpappy, Grandfather
Time period(s): 1990s (1995)
Locale(s): Hokey Pokey Swamp, South

Summary: Dixie Lee not only whistles as she does her chores, she turns each outing into an animal-finding expedition. First she comes home from the swamp with a young alligator and convinces Mama that this pet should live in the well to fend off churn turners trying to drink Mama's buttermilk. Then she finds a little snake which goes into Grandpappy's gompers jar to keep a bogeyman from stealing Grandpappy's teeth. Over Mama's protests, Dixie Lee comes home with a hoot owl to live in the chimney and protect the house from the mist sisters who bring bad luck. That night, all Dixie Lee's prognostications come to pass and, just as she foresaw, her critters do their job, protecting butter milk, gompers and the luck of the household. (32 pages)

Where it's reviewed:
Bulletin of the Center for Children's Books, May 1995, page 324
Horn Book, September 1995, page 593
Horn Book Guide, Fall 1995, page 285
Kirkus Reviews, April 1, 1995, page 476
New Advocate, Winter 1996, page 64

Other books by the same author:
Dorobo the Dangerous, 1994
The Sea-Breeze Hotel, 1992
Wombat Stew, 1985

Other books you might like:
Mercer Mayer, *Liza Lou and the Yeller Belly Swamp*, 1976
    Liza Lou outwits all the witches, haunts, and spooks in the Yeller Belly Swamp.
Melissa Milich, *Can't Scare Me!*, 1995
    Eugenia loves the stories Papa tells, but they frighten Mr. Munroe so Eugenia has to walk the neighbor home every night.
Tynia Thomassie, *Feliciana Feydra LeRoux: A Cajun Tall Tale*, 1995
    When the menfolks refuse to take her alligator hunting, Feliciana sneaks out to join them in the swamp where she rescues Grampa Baby and brings home an alligator.

1453

MAX VELTHUIJS, Author/Illustrator

Frog Is Frightened

(New York: Tambourine Books, 1995)

Subject(s): Fear; Animals; Friendship
Age range(s): Grades K-1
Major character(s): Frog, Frog, Friend; Duck, Duck, Friend; Pig, Pig, Friend
Time period(s): 1990s (1994)
Locale(s): Fictional Country

Summary: Hearing nighttime noises as he settles into bed, Frog fears a ghost and races to Duck's house to seek refuge. Frog's fright scares Duck and soon both are running through the dark woods to Pig's house. There, despite the sounds of the forest at night, they finally sleep in the comfort of each

other's company. First published in Great Britain in 1994. (32 pages)

Where it's reviewed:
Booklist, March 1, 1995, page 1250
Junior Bookshelf, April 1995, page 68
Kirkus Reviews, March 15, 1995, page 397
School Librarian, May 1995, page 60
School Library Journal, October 1995, page 122

Other books by the same author:
Frog and the Stranger, 1994
Frog in Winter, 1993
Frog and the Birdsong, 1991

Other books you might like:
Russell Hoban, *Bedtime for Frances*, 1960
    Fear of one imagined thing after another keeps Frances from settling down to sleep.
Arnold Lobel, *Frog and Toad Together*, 1972
    Continuing the tale of friendship begun in *Frog and Toad Are Friends*, are five more adventures of the duo.
Beatrix Potter, *The Tale of Mr. Jeremy Fisher*, 1906
    A frog fishing contentedly from his lily pad boat "catches" a frightening and exciting tale, but no fish.

1454

MARTHA M. VERTREACE
SANDRA SPEIDEL, Illustrator

Kelly in the Mirror

(Morton Grove, IL: Albert Whitman & Company, 1993)

Subject(s): Family Relations; Mothers and Daughters; African Americans
Age range(s): Grades 1-3
Major character(s): Kelly, Child; Mamma, Mother
Time period(s): 1990s (1993)
Locale(s): United States

Summary: The author's first children's book features Kelly exploring the attic of her home. When she tries on a cap and sweater that had been her mother's, she notices a resemblance to the picture of Mamma on her first day of school. The discovery reinforces Kelly's sense of belonging to her family and encourages her to suggest a family picture with everyone wearing an item from the attic box. (32 pages)

Where it's reviewed:
Booklist, April 1, 1993, page 1442
Children's Book Review Service, Spring 1993, page 140
Horn Book Guide, Fall 1993, page 278
Publishers Weekly, March 1993, page 56
School Library Journal, August 1993, page 14

Other books you might like:
Melrose Cooper, *I Got a Family*, 1993
    A young girl describes the unique affection she receives from each individual in her caring extended family.
Wade Hudson, *I Love My Family*, 1993
    Special memories of food and fun with the many generations gathered at the annual family reunion are shared by a young boy.
Patricia Polacco, *The Keeping Quilt*, 1988
    A special quilt connects the generations of a family.

1455

JUDITH VIORST
ROBIN PREISS GLASSER, Illustrator

Alexander, Who's Not (Do You Hear Me? I Mean It!) Going to Move

(New York: Atheneum Books for Young Readers, 1995)

Subject(s): Moving, Household; Obstinacy; Parent and Child
Age range(s): Grades K-3
Major character(s): Alexander, Child
Time period(s): 1990s (1995)
Locale(s): United States

Summary: Although his brothers say he's stupid and immature and his parents assure him that all will be well, Alexander is determined NOT to move 1000 miles away from his best friend, his familiar school, his soccer team and his friendly neighbors. Alexander plans to move in with another family or live in a tree, but most assuredly, Alexander is NOT going to move. By the time moving day arrives, Alexander has reluctantly packed for the last time, because after this move he is definitely NOT ever moving again. (42 pages)

Where it's reviewed:
Booklist, August 1995, page 1949
Children's Book Review Service, October 1995, page 17
Horn Book, January 1996, page 66
Publishers Weekly, September 11, 1995, page 85
School Library Journal, October 1995, page 122

Other books by the same author:
The Good-Bye Book, 1988
Alexander, Who Used to Be Rich Last Sunday, 1978
Alexander and the Terrible, Horrible, No Good Very Bad Day, 1972

Other books you might like:
Nancy White Carlstrom, *I'm Not Moving, Mama!*, 1990
  When Little Mouse refuses to move, Mama gently persuades him to come along with the family.
Pamela D. Greenwood, *What about My Goldfish?*, 1993
  Jamie is anxious about the family's move, especially its effect on his pets
Angela Johnson, *The Leaving Morning*, 1992
  A family prepares for their "leaving morning" by saying good-bye to friends, relatives and neighbors before the movers come to load their belongings on a truck.
Patricia MacLachlan, *What You Know First*, 1995
  Slowly, painfully a young girl accepts the need to leave her prairie home, gathering mementos to help her remember what she's known first.

1456

CYNTHIA VOIGT

Bad Girls

(New York, Scholastic, 1996)

Subject(s): Schools; Friendship; Behavior
Age range(s): Grades 5-8
Major character(s): Mikey Alsinger, 5th Grader; Margalo Epps, 5th Grader; Louis Caselli, 5th Grader

Time period(s): 1990s
Locale(s): United States

Summary: Mikey and Margalo are new students who find they have a number of things in common, like their initials and the type of books they read. Teased by Louis, the class trouble-maker, they seek ways to get back at him. Constantly in trouble, the two girls, one overt and the other sneaky, do some really nasty things. As the year progresses, they do not always get along and have no contact outside of school, but in the end, know they will be friends, in spite of the differences in their backgrounds. (277 pages)

Where it's reviewed:
Horn Book, July/August 1996, page 96
Booklist, April 1, 1996, page 1366
School Library Journal, May 1996, page 116

Awards the book has won:
Boston Globe/Horn Book Honor Book, 1996
Bulletin Blue Ribbon, 1996

Other books by the same author:
A Solitary Blue, 1983
Dicey's Song, 1982
Homecoming, 1980

Other books you might like:
Eve Bunting, *Spying on Miss Mueller*, 1995
  The girls in the boarding school fear that their teacher is a German spy and so they spy on her and do nasty things as well.
Ilene Cooper, *My Co-Star, My Enemy*, 1993
  Alison finds out that her co-star on a TV show is out to get rid of her.
Jill Pinkwater, *Mister Fred*, 1995
  A sixth grade class determines to be as bad as they can when they get a new teacher.
Zilpha Keatley Snyder, *Libby on Wednesday*, 1990
  Libby has trouble adjusting to regular school after being home-schooled.
Gina Willner-Pardo, *Jason and the Losers*, 1995
  Jason moves in with his cousin when his parents divorce and begins school by being mean to his cousin's friends because he wants to be popular.

1457

DAVID VOZAR
BETSY LEWIN, Illustrator

M.C. Turtle and the Hip Hop Hare: A Nursery Rap

(New York: Doubleday Book for Young Readers, 1995)

Subject(s): Folk Tales; Animals; Stories in Rhyme
Age range(s): Grades K-3
Major character(s): Hip Hop Hare, Rabbit; M.C. Turtle, Turtle
Time period(s): 1990s (1995)
Locale(s): United States

Summary: A retelling of the traditional *The Tortoise and the Hare* tale takes on a rap beat when Hip Hop Hare challenges a reluctant M. C. Turtle to a race. The distractions for Hip Hop are a little flashier than in the original story, but the outcome is unchanged. Yo, Turtle! (32 pages)

Where it's reviewed:
Booklist, January 1996, page 849
Children's Book Review Service, November 1995, page 28
Horn Book Guide, Spring 1996, page 48
Kirkus Reviews, July 15, 1995, page 103
School Library Journal, October 1995, page 122

Other books by the same author:
Yo, Hungry Wolf! A Nursery Rap, 1993

Other books you might like:
Susan Lowell, *The Tortoise and the Jackrabbit*, 1994
   In this version of the fable, the familiar race is held in a desert of the Southwest.
Frank Remkiewicz, *Fiona Raps It Up*, 1995
   While lost from her flock, a flamingo learns rap from Cap'n Otter.
Janet Stevens, *The Tortoise and the Hare: An Aesop Fable*, 1984
   An illustrated retelling of the classic story of the race between a persevering tortoise and an overly confident hare.

1458

SUE VYNER
TIM VYNER, Illustrator

Swim for Cover!: Adventure on the Coral Reef

(New York: Crown Publishers, Inc., 1995)

Subject(s): Animals/Squid, Octopus; Nature

Age range(s): Grades K-3
Major character(s): Unnamed Character, Octopus
Time period(s): 1990s (1995)
Locale(s): Australia (Great Barrier Reef)

Summary: As an octopus returns to her den, she senses danger behind her and warns each animal that she passes to beware. Each marine animal responds to the warning by telling her of its means of protection. The illustrations show the different defenses used by each and a concluding author's note gives factual information about seven species which live in the coral reef. (32 pages)

Where it's reviewed:
Booklist, August 1995, page 1957
Horn Book Guide, Fall 1995, page 285
New Advocate, Winter 1996, page 71
School Library Journal, July 1995, page 70
Science Books and Film, October 1995, page 212

Other books by the same author:
Arctic Spring, 1993
The Stolen Egg, 1992

Other books you might like:
Joanna Cole, *The Magic School Bus on the Ocean Floor*, 1992
   Mrs. Frizzle drives the magic school bus into the sea for a close-up learning experience about the facts of ocean life.
Dana Meachen Rau, *Undersea City: A Story of a Caribbean Coral Reef*, 1997
   A hermit crab searching for a new shell home is swept out to sea and onto a coral reef.
Bob Weir, *Baru Bay: Australia*, 1995
   Tamara learns about the fragile ecosystem of a coral reef. Co-author Wendy Weir.

W

1459

BERNARD WABER, Author/Illustrator

Do You See a Mouse?

(Boston: Houghton Mifflin Company, 1995)

Subject(s): Animals/Mice; Hotels, Motels; Humor
Age range(s): Grades K-1
Major character(s): Unnamed Character, Mouse; Hyde, Businessman (mouse catcher); Snide, Businessman (mouse catcher)
Time period(s): 1990s (1995)
Locale(s): New York, New York (Park Snoot Hotel)

Summary: From the doorman to the owner, no one believes the complaint about a mouse being spotted in the elegant hotel. To relieve everyone's mind, the owner hires Hyde and Snide, the best mouse catchers in the world, to rid the hotel of any beasts. Despite the fact that alert readers can spot the mouse in every picture, Hyde and Snide deliver a report declaring the hotel free of mice and drive off as the mouse waves good-bye. (32 pages)

Where it's reviewed:
Booklist, April 1, 1995, page 1429
Children's Book Review Service, April 1995, page 102
Horn Book, July 1995, page 454
Library Talk, September 1995, page 29
School Library Journal, September 1995, page 188

Other books by the same author:
Rich Cat, Poor Cat, 1990
Lovable Lyle, 1977
Ira Sleeps Over, 1973

Other books you might like:
Patricia Goehner Baehr, *Mouse in the House*, 1994
    When a mouse is spotted in Mrs. Teapot's house, her new pets try to help locate the culprit.
Henrietta, *A Mouse in the House*, 1991
    A photographic tour of a house shows a mouse eating her way through the birthday party preparations in each room.

Heather Maisner, *Find Mouse in the Yard*, 1994
    By lifting the flaps and following the clues, readers can locate a missing mouse.

1460

BERNARD WABER, Author/Illustrator

Gina

(Boston: Houghton Mifflin Company, 1995)

Subject(s): Friendship; Moving, Household; Stories in Rhyme
Age range(s): Grades K-3
Major character(s): Gina, Child
Time period(s): 1990s (1995)
Locale(s): United States

Summary: Gina is sad to discover that her new apartment building is full of boys her age who won't give her a second look and girls who are either much older or much younger. After days of boredom and loneliness, Gina decides to go out and be herself. The neighborhood boys then discover that Gina is a capable athlete and soon she is a sought-after friend. (32 pages)

Where it's reviewed:
Booklist, September 15, 1995, page 176
Children's Book Review Service, September 1995, page 5
Horn Book Guide, Spring 1996, page 48
Publishers Weekly, August 14, 1995, page 83
School Library Journal, October 1995, page 122

Other books by the same author:
Lyle at the Office, 1994
Ira Says Goodbye, 1988
The House on East 88th Street, 1973

Other books you might like:
Karen Barbour, *Nancy*, 1989
    Inviting children to her birthday party helps Nancy make friends when she moves into a new neighborhood.
Barbara Shook Hazen, *Good-Bye, Hello*, 1995
    Apprehensive about moving from the city, a child finds

that for every good-bye in the city, there is a greeting in the suburbs.

Charlotte Zolotow, *A Tiger Called Thomas*, 1988
Newly moved into his neighborhood, shy Thomas, dressed in a tiger costume for Halloween, learns that his neighbors are interested in meeting him.

1461

BERNARD WABER, Author/Illustrator

Lyle at the Office

(Boston: Houghton Mifflin Company, 1994)

Subject(s): Animals/Crocodiles; Work; Family Life
Age range(s): Grades K-3
Major character(s): Lyle, Crocodile; Mr. Primm, Advertising
Time period(s): 1990s (1994)
Locale(s): New York, New York

Summary: Although Lyle is a very private crocodile, he enjoys being out and about with his family and so he happily accompanies Mr. Primm to work at the advertising agency. When Mr. Primm's boss tries to exploit Lyle in a promotion for a cereal, Mr. Primm refuses to permit Lyle's participation and loses his job. The family pulls together and finds other work until the boss agrees not to use Lyle and rehires Mr. Primm. (48 pages)

Where it's reviewed:
Booklist, June 1, 1994, page 1846
Horn Book, January 1995, page 56
Kirkus Reviews, July 15, 1994, page 997
Publishers Weekly, July 4, 1994, page 61
School Library Journal, September 1994, page 200

Other books by the same author:
Funny, Funny Lyle, 1987
Lovable Lyle, 1969
The House on East 88th Street, 1962

Other books you might like:
John Burningham, *Courtney*, 1994
Courtney, a mongrel with many talents, cooks, juggles and rescues the baby from a fire before he mysteriously vanishes.
Thomas P. Lewis, *Frida's Office Day*, 1989
In a beginning reader, Frida Cat spends a day at her dad's office in the big city.
Susan Meddaugh, *Martha Speaks*, 1992
After dining on alphabet soup Martha develops a gift for gab which fascinates and frustrates her family.

1462

MARTIN WADDELL
PAUL HOWARD, Illustrator

John Joe and the Big Hen

(Cambridge, MA: Candlewick Press, 1995)

Subject(s): Farm Life; Animals/Chickens; Brothers and Sisters
Age range(s): Grades K-2

Major character(s): John Joe, Child, Brother (youngest); Mary, Child, Sister; Sammy, Child, Brother
Time period(s): Indeterminate Past
Locale(s): Ireland

Summary: Although it's Sammy's turn to care for John Joe, he goes to visit a friend on a neighboring farm. Angrily, Mary takes John Joe by the hand and goes to find the irresponsible Sammy. When she leaves John Joe alone in the neighbor's barnyard while she searches, a very large hen walks up close to John Joe. John Joe knows his own hens, but not this strange one so he quickly moves away from her. When Mary returns with Sammy, John Joe is nowhere in sight. With the dog's help they find him sleeping in a field, proud that he has taken care of himself. (26 pages)

Where it's reviewed:
Books for Keeps, January 1996, page 28
Children's Book Review Service, September 1995, page 5
Children's Bookwatch, October 1995, page 5
Horn Book Guide, Spring 1996, page 48
School Librarian, February 1996, page 17

Other books by the same author:
Once There Were Giants, 1995
The Big, Big Sea, 1994
Can't You Sleep, Little Bear?, 1992
Farmer Duck, 1992

Other books you might like:
Margaret Wise Brown, *Big Red Barn*, 1989
The newly illustrated version of the story maintains the rhyming text which introduces the animals living in a barn.
Colby Hol, *A Visit to the Farm*, 1989
When Julie and Martin go to a farm for eggs, cheese and milk, they see many animals.
David McPhail, *Farm Boy's Year*, 1992
Set in the 1800s, the illustraions and story describe a boy's life on a New England farm.
Sandra Jordan, *Down on Casey's Farm*, 1996
Casey's farm is kept in an old drawer, but with Casey's imagination it becomes real.

1463

MARTIN WADDELL
BARBARA FIRTH, Illustrator

Let's Go Home, Little Bear

(Cambridge, MA: Candlewick Press, 1993)

Subject(s): Animals/Bears; Fear; Imagination
Age range(s): Grades K-1
Major character(s): Little Bear, Bear (fearful), Child (imaginative); Big Bear, Bear (comforting), Father
Time period(s): 1990s (1991)
Locale(s): England (snowy woods)

Summary: As Big Bear and Little Bear walk through the snowy woods, Little Bear stops fearfully because of the "Plodder" he hears behind them. Big Bear reassures him the plodding is the sound of his feet and they continue with Little Bear hearing the sounds of "Drippers" and "Ploppers" until he is so overcome with fear that he must continue the walk on Big Bear's shoulders. When they reach their cozy cave, Big

Bear tells him a story and they both enjoy a nap after their tiring walk. Originally published in Great Britain in 1991. (32 pages)

Where it's reviewed:
Booklist, May 1, 1993, page 1597
Children's Bookwatch, May 1993, page 3
Horn Book, March 1993, page 202
Publishers Weekly, March 22, 1993, page 78
School Library Journal, March 1993, page 187

Awards the book has won:
Book Links Good Book, 1993

Other books by the same author:
John Joe and the Big Hen, 1995
Can't You Sleep, Little Bear?, 1992
Once There Were Giants, 1989

Other books you might like:
Jez Alborough, *It's the Bear!*, 1994
 Remembering the bear he met on his last walk in the woods, Eddie is afraid to return there for a picnic with his mom.
Robert McCloskey, *Blueberries for Sal*, 1948
 Sal's blueberry expedition with her mom parallels a bear cub's search for blueberries with his mother as the two youngsters lose their mothers, but find each other.
Else Holmelund Minarik, *Little Bear*, 1957
 Little Bear's understanding mother handles his adventures with humor and grace.

1464

MARTIN WADDELL
ELSIE LENNOX, Illustrator

Little Obie and the Kidnap

(Cambridge, MA: Candlewick Press, 1994)

Subject(s): Frontier and Pioneer Life; Family Life; Behavior
Age range(s): Grades 2-4
Major character(s): Little Obie, Child, Settler; Mrs. Jumping Joseph, Widow(er), Mountain Woman; Effie, Grandmother (Obie's), Settler
Time period(s): Indeterminate Past
Locale(s): Cold Creek, Midwest

Summary: When two sickly orphans in the community need a home, crazy Mrs. Jumping Joseph snatches them and attempts to raise them as best she can. Her child-rearing techniques include lessons in spitting and mud balls so everyone in the community tries to talk to her and find a way to make her give up the children. When reason doesn't work, Effie plots to kidnap the children with the help of Little Obie and his grandfather. Though the plan is successful, eventually Mrs. Jumping Joseph finds the children and a compromise must be reached which considers everyone's needs. First published in Great Britain in 1991. (79 pages)

Where it's reviewed:
Horn Book Guide, Spring 1995, page 85
Junior Bookshelf, August 1992, page 148
School Library Journal, October 1994, page 128
Times Educational Supplement, March 5, 1993, page 12

Other books by the same author:
Little Obie and the Flood, 1992
Harriet and the Robot, 1987
Harriet and the Crocodiles, 1984

Other books you might like:
Brett Harvey, *Cassie's Journey: Going West in the 1860s*, 1988
 Cassie tells of her family's difficult journey by covered wagon from Illinois to California.
Hilda Stahl, *Kayla O'Brian and the Runaway Orphans*, 1991
 With two children from the orphan train, the Larsens expect to celebrate Christmas for the first time on their Nebraska mule farm.
Jean Van Leeuwen, *Going West*, 1992
 In a prairie schooner, a family emigrates from their home in the East across the plains to Kansas.

1465

KAREN WAGGONER
CAT BOWMAN SMITH, Illustrator

Partners

(New York: Simon & Schuster Books for Young Readers, 1995)

Subject(s): Animals/Mice; Brothers and Sisters; Money
Age range(s): Grades 3-4
Major character(s): Jamie Webster, 3rd Grader, Brother; Gordon Webster, Student—Junior High, Brother; Claudia Webster, Sister, Student—High School
Time period(s): 1990s (1995)
Locale(s): United States

Summary: When Claudia's pet cat vanishes for a month, Jamie and Gordon can finally have the mice they've been wanting. Unfortunately, Jamie soon learns that the animals he sees as pets, Gordon sees as profit in a business supplying mice as snake food. Then, to make matters worse, Claudia's cat returns, injured and weak, but still capable of eating a mouse. Sensitive Jamie worries about his pets and his relationship with his siblings until a class math assignment helps him find a solution to his problems. (95 pages)

Where it's reviewed:
Booklist, May 15, 1995, page 1648
Bulletin of the Center for Children's Books, September 1995, page 32
Horn Book, November 1995, page 744
Kirkus Reviews, June 15, 1995, page 865
School Library Journal, June 1995, page 115

Other books by the same author:
The Lemonade Babysitter, 1992

Other books you might like:
Eth Clifford, *Harvey's Horrible Snake Disaster*, 1984
 A visit from cousin Nora always means trouble for Harvey and this year is no exception.
Betsy Duffey, *Throw-Away Pets*, 1993
 Megan and Evie try to find homes for an animal shelter's unclaimed pets before they are euthanized.
Juanita Havill, *Saving Owen's Toad*, 1994
 Owen sees the toads he and his brother find as pets, but

Richard plans to get rich by selling them to eat insects in people's gardens.

1466

JAN WAHL
FRANE LESSAC, Illustrator

Little Gray One

(New York: Tambourine Books, 1993)

Subject(s): Animals/Elephants; Africa; Mothers and Sons
Age range(s): Grades K-1
Major character(s): Mother Elephant, Elephant, Mother; Little Gray One, Elephant, Child
Time period(s): 1990s (1993)
Locale(s): Africa

Summary: Little Gray One and his mother have a quiet day on the African plain. Mother Elephant uses each of Little Gray One's complaints as a basis for instruction so that during the course of the day Little Gray One learns how to find water, pick the sweetest plums and only eat pumpkins when the berries are not yet ripe. The loving relationship of mother and child within the security of the larger community is gently portrayed. (32 pages)

Where it's reviewed:
Booklist, September 15, 1993, page 162
Horn Book Guide, Spring 1994, page 112
Publishers Weekly, August 9, 1993, page 476
School Library Journal, March 1994, page 210
Smithsonian, November 1993, page 188

Other books by the same author:
Little Eight John, 1992
My Cat Ginger, 1992
Dracula's Cat, 1981

Other books you might like:
Jeremy Grimsdell, *Kalinzu: A Story from Africa*, 1993
    When Kalinzu, a buffalo calf, is separated from her mother, ox-peckers help her return to the security of the herd.
Bijou Le Tord, *Elephant Moon*, 1993
    The way of life of elephants and other animals on the African plains is depicted.
Richard Sobol, *One More Elephant: The Fight to Save Wildlife in Uganda*, 1995
    A factual account of the efforts to protect elephant herds in Uganda's Queen Elizabeth National Park.

1467

PAUL ROBERT WALKER

The Sluggers Club: A Sports Mystery

(San Diego: Harcourt Brace Jovanovich, 1993)

Subject(s): Sports/Baseball; Mystery and Detective Stories
Age range(s): Grades 5-6
Major character(s): B.J. Grady, Baseball Player, 12-Year-Old; Medgar "Wash" Washington, Baseball Player, 12-Year-Old; Tony Caldero, Baseball Player, 12-Year-Old
Time period(s): 1990s

Locale(s): Granada

Summary: The Halbertson's Flowers team leads the Little League this season and B.J. is elated that his good friend, Wash, is part of their reason for winning. Wash uses a special bat made of aircraft aluminum but when it's stolen, the team's losses skyrocket and their wins become nonexistent. When other equipment disappears, B.J., Medgar and Tony form the Sluggers Club to investigate various suspects and retrieve Wash's lucky bat. (153 pages)

Where it's reviewed:
Publishers Weekly, February 8, 1993, page 87
Booklist, March 1, 1993, page 1231
Kirkus Reviews, February 1, 1993, page 155
School Library Journal, May 1993, page 110

Other books by the same author:
Big Men, Big Country: A Collection of American Tall Tales, 1993
Method, 1990

Other books you might like:
Matt Christopher, *Hit-Away Kid*, 1988
    Though Barry sometimes bends the rules a little to win, when he sees the dirty tricks of a rival pitcher, he rethinks his own ethics.
Fanny Howe, *Race of the Radical*, 1985
    Alex is devastated when the special BMX racing bike his father designed for him is stolen.
Alfred Slote, *Tony and Me*, 1974
    Bill needs to make a decision about his friend Tony who is a great baseball player, but is also a thief.

1468

BARBARA BROOKS WALLACE

Cousins in the Castle

(New York: Atheneum, 1996)

Subject(s): Adventure and Adventurers; Friendship
Age range(s): Grades 5-7
Major character(s): Amelia Fairwick, Orphan, Kidnap Victim; Primrose "Rosie" Lagoon, Singer; Cousin Charlotte, Kidnapper
Time period(s): 1800s
Locale(s): London, England; New York, New York (aboard ship)

Summary: When her father is killed in an accident in India, Amelia must go to New York to live with her cousins. Aboard ship she meets Rosie, a singer, and the two become friends. On arrival in New York, Cousin Charlotte disappears and Amelia is kidnapped and later escapes to the theater where she thinks Rosie is performing. There she discovers that Rosie is really a boy who helps clean the theater. Together they face the evil people who plan to capture and hold Amelia for ransom until they are rescued by servants in Cousin Basil's house. An incredible surprise awaits them when they find that Basil and Charlotte are the same person and Amelia's father is not dead but has married and come to collect his daughter. (152 pages)

Where it's reviewed:
Booklist, April 1, 1996, page 1363

School Library Journal, May 1996, page 116

Other books by the same author:
The Twin in the Tavern, 1995
The Barrel in the Basement, 1985
Peppermints in the Parlor, 1980

Other books you might like:
Joan Aiken, *Is Underground*, 1993
    Is travels to London to find her lost cousin and finds that children have been fooled and put to work in the mines.
Lloyd Alexander, *The Jedera Adventure*, 1989
    Vesper is involved in returning a library book and finds herself in a mythical kingdom.
Avi, *The History of Hapless Harry*, 1980
    Horatio faces a series of shady characters while his parents are away.
Helen Cresswell, *The Watchers: A Mystery at Alton Towers*, 1994
    Two children run away from an institution and find themselves involved with a bag lady in saving an area for homeless children.
Jan Slepian, *Pinocchio's Sister*, 1995
    Martha travels with her ventriloquist father but is always upstaged by his dummy.

1469

BARBARA BROOKS WALLACE

The Twin in the Tavern
(New York: Atheneum Books for Young Readers, 1993)

Subject(s): Orphans; Twins; Mystery and Detective Stories
Age range(s): Grades 3-6
Major character(s): Taddy Buntz, 10-Year-Old, Orphan; Ebenezer ''Neezer'' Scrat, Thief (cruel), Innkeeper (owner of the Dog's Tail); Beetle, Servant (in service to Neezer)
Time period(s): Indeterminate Past
Locale(s): Alexandria, Virginia

Summary: Alas! Woe is Taddy. His only relations, an aunt and uncle who have cared for him since he was a baby, have died and the crooks who are stealing the belongings from their home find him hiding and haul him off too. The Dog's Tail tavern and the work expected of him under these cruel masters is no better than the feared workhouse which Taddy hoped to avoid. Renamed Toady by Neezer, Taddy develops a friendship with Beetle who has also been trapped into working at the Dog's Tail. Remembering his uncle's dying words to find his twin, Taddy hopes for escape, struggles to know who can be trusted, and ultimately achieves what is rightfully his. (192 pages)

Where it's reviewed:
Booklist, November 1, 1993, page 524
Five Owls, March 1994, page 77
Horn Book Guide, Spring 1994, page 83
Kirkus Reviews, November 1, 1993, page 1399
School Library Journal, October 1993, page 134

Awards the book has won:
Booklist Editors' Choice, 1993
Mystery Writers of America Edgar Allan Poe Award, 1994

Other books by the same author:
Peppermints in the Parlor, 1985

Other books you might like:
Natalie Babbitt, *Goody Hall*, 1986
    The Goody family mansion is the scene of mystery and intrigue.
Sid Fleischman, *The Whipping Boy*, 1986
    A Newbery Medal winner relates the tale of an orphan selected as the whipping boy for Prince Brat and the unexpected reversal of their roles.
Leon Garfield, *Young Nick and Jubilee*, 1989
    Orphaned siblings seeking survival in 18th century London are in the clutches of a pickpocket who pretends to be their father.

1470

BILL WALLACE

Never Say Quit
(New York: Holiday Books, 1993)

Subject(s): Sports/Soccer; Alcoholism
Age range(s): Grades 5-7
Major character(s): Justine Smith, Soccer Player; Randy Black, Soccer Player; Mr. Paul Reiner, Alcoholic
Time period(s): 1990s
Locale(s): Oklahoma

Summary: Rejected by the local soccer team because they just don't belong, Francine, Randy and other kids form their own soccer team and ask Mr. Reiner, a former principal whose alcoholism interfered with his work, to be their coach. He agrees but only if they pay him in beer which they scrounge out of garbage cans. Over several years his rules and coaching methods force them to work together, both on and off the field, as he encourages them to study together and be friends. Kids with learning disabilities becomes friends with ones who can't speak English who becomes friends with those who have no athletic ability in a heart-warming story of a team of ''Misfits'' and one man who can ''never say quit.'' (184 pages)

Where it's reviewed:
School Library Journal, April 1993, page 93
Booklist, April 15, 1993, page 1516
Publishers Weekly, May 3, 1993, page 309
Voice of Youth Advocates, October 1993, page 220
Journal of Reading, October 1993, page 150

Other books by the same author:
Blackwater Swamp, 1994
True Friends, 1994
Danger in Quicksand Swamp, 1989
Trapped in Death Cave, 1984

Other books you might like:
Avi, *S.O.R. Losers*, 1984
    Ten 7th graders spoil the winning record of South Orange River school.
S.S. Gorman, *Soccer Is a Kick*, 1990
    With nicknames that unite them, five athletic boys play on the Tornadoes soccer team in *The High Fives* series.

David Klass, *Breakaway Run*, 1987
American Tony plays soccer in Japan where he's been sent to live while he adjusts to his parents' divorce.
Gordon Korman, *Toilet Paper Tigers*, 1993
Corey's stuck on a Little League baseball team populated by incompetent, klutzy kids and managed by a girl—could his favorite sport become any worse?

1471

BILL WALLACE

True Friends
(New York: Holiday, 1994)

Subject(s): Family Life; Physically Handicapped; Friendship
Age range(s): Grades 4-6
Major character(s): Courtney Ann Brown, 6th Grader; Bill Brown, Brother; Judy Baird, 6th Grader, Handicapped
Time period(s): 1990s
Locale(s): Texas

Summary: Courtney's one of two new students in the sixth grade and is immediately courted by the popular crowd, especially when she makes the cheerleading squad. But just as quickly, her life spins awry. Her brother Bill is accused of dealing drugs, the principal suspects Courtney of stealing money from his office and her stepmother runs off with another man. Judy, the other new student, steps forward to support Courtney, even though she's been shunned because of her reliance on a cane to walk. With Judy's help, Courtney realizes she needs to stand on her own two feet without worrying what everyone else thinks. (169 pages)

Where it's reviewed:
Booklist, October 15, 1994, page 428
School Library Journal, October 1994, page 128
Voice of Youth Advocates, April 1995, page 28
Kirkus Reviews, November 15, 1994, page 1545
Center for Children's Books. Bulletin, November 1994, page 108

Other books by the same author:
Never Say Quit, 1993
Buffalo Gal, 1992
Totally Disgusting, 1991

Other books you might like:
Vicki Grove, *The Fastest Friend in the West*, 1990
Lori's best friend abandons her for the popular crowd; only weird Vern, a new girl at school, wants anything to do with her.
Richard Peck, *Princess Ashley*, 1987
New student Chelsea is thrilled to be part of Ashley's ''in'' group, not realizing she's just being used.
Rachel Vail, *Wonder*, 1991
Jessica's tumultuous seventh grade year finds her seesawing between being a social pariah and having her own clique.

1472

BILL WALLACE
DAVID SLONIM, Illustrator

Watchdog and the Coyotes
(New York: Pocket Books, 1995)

Subject(s): Animals/Dogs; Animals/Coyotes; Self-Confidence
Age range(s): Grades 3-5
Major character(s): Sweetie, Dog (Great Dane); Red, Dog (Irish Setter); Poky, Dog (Beagle)
Time period(s): 1990s (1995)
Locale(s): Scottsdale, Arizona

Summary: For fear of being thrown out of his third home, Sweetie curbs his instinctual behaviors and refuses to bark or to bite anyone or anything rather than receive a one-way ticket to the pound. Thus, Sweetie watches a burglar steal from his owner's home and, with arthritic Red and neighbor Poky, tolerates local coyotes who steal the dogs' food. Red and Poky teach Sweetie that some dog behaviors are acceptable and together they overthrow the bothersome coyotes. When the burglar returns, Sweetie earns the coveted title of Watchdog. (105 pages)

Where it's reviewed:
Booklist, December 15, 1995, page 706
Horn Book Guide, Spring 1996, page 70
School Library Journal, November 1995, page 107

Other books by the same author:
True Friends, 1994
Red Dog, 1987
A Dog Called Kitty, 1980

Other books you might like:
B.B. Calhoun, *Bite Makes Right*, 1994
With help from a stray dog, Fenton assists his paleontologist father with the identification of some dinosaur bones.
John R. Erickson, *The Case of the Kidnapped Collie*, 1996
Hank the Cowdog solves the mystery at the ranch that includes a theft and a kidnapping.
Todd Strasser, *Help! I'm Trapped in Obedience School*, 1995
When Jake's best friend is trapped in his dog's body and vice versa, some humorous situations occur.

1473

NANCY ELIZABETH WALLACE, Author/Illustrator

Snow
(New York: Artists & Writers Guild Books, 1995)

Subject(s): Animals/Rabbits; Winter; Brothers
Age range(s): Grades K-1
Major character(s): Unnamed Character, Rabbit, Brother; Max, Rabbit, Brother
Time period(s): Indeterminate Past
Locale(s): Fictional Country

Summary: In the author's first book, a rabbit reminisces about winter days when he and Max would eagerly await the arrival of snow. When the flakes begin to fall, the brothers bundle up and hurry out to play. Whether sledding, making snow rabbits or throwing snow balls, the brothers conclude each winter day's play by drinking hot chocolate. (32 pages)

Where it's reviewed:
Booklist, November 15, 1995, page 565
Horn Book Guide, Spring 1996, page 48
Kirkus Reviews, September 15, 1995, page 1360
Publishers Weekly, November 6, 1995, page 93
School Library Journal, December 1995, page 93

Other books you might like:
Lois Ehlert, *Snowballs*, 1995
    Simple text and clear collages tell of the creation of a snow family and the inevitable result as the weather warms.
Ezra Jack Keats, *The Snowy Day*, 1962
    Peter explores his city neighborhood and the snow brings added pleasures.
Beverly Komoda, *The Winter Day*, 1991
    On a snowy day, a group of rabbit children find their fun spoiled by a bully.
Steve Sanfield, *Snow*, 1995
    A young boy marvels at the beauty of the newly fallen snow dotted with the tracks of passing animals.
Nancy Willard, *A Starlit Somersault Downhill*, 1993
    A rabbit discovers that hibernating with a bear is not suitable for a creature who wants to be free to somersault down a snowy bank.

`1474`

RUTH WALLACE-BRODEUR
KATHRYN MITTER, Illustrator

Goodbye, Mitch
(Morton Grove, IL: Albert Whitman & Company, 1995)

Subject(s): Animals/Cats; Pets; Death (of a Pet)
Age range(s): Grades K-3
Major character(s): Michael, Child; Mitch, Cat (15-year-old)
Time period(s): 1990s (1995)
Locale(s): United States

Summary: Michael remembers clearly the day that Mitch first refused food despite Michael's coaxing and offering of various tasty treats. After several days and a trip to the vet, Michael's mother gently informs him that Mitch may have an untreatable tumor and all the family can do is make their pet comfortable. As Mitch's health wanes until he dies in Michael's arms, he is loved and supported by Michael just as Michael is loved and supported by his parents. (32 pages)

Where it's reviewed:
Booklist, June 1995, page 1789
Bulletin of the Center for Children's Books, May 1995, page 325
Horn Book Guide, Fall 1995, page 286
School Library Journal, August 1995, page 130

Other books by the same author:
Home by Five, 1992

Other books you might like:
Miriam Cohen, *Jim's Dog Muffins*, 1984
    Jim's first grade classmates share his grief when his dog Muffins is killed.

Amy Ehrlich, *Maggie and Silky and Joe*, 1994
    Joe has grown up with Maggie as his companion but now must accept the changes resulting from the dog's advancing age and eventual death.
Judith Greenberg, *Sunny*, 1986
    With co-author Helen Carey, the nonfiction work describes Bill's reactions as his sick dog dies.
Judith Viorst, *The Tenth Good Thing about Barney*, 1971
    When his cat dies, a young boy consoles himself by thinking of the ten best things he remembers about his pet.

`1475`

ELLEN STOLL WALSH, Author/Illustrator

Hop Jump
(San Diego: Harcourt Brace & Company, 1993)

Subject(s): Animals/Frogs and Toads; Dancing; Individuality
Age range(s): Grades K-1
Major character(s): Betsy, Frog (creative)
Time period(s): 1990s (1993)
Locale(s): United States

Summary: Not content with the monotony of hopping and jumping, Betsy is inspired by the falling leaves to begin leaping, twisting and turning. At first the other frogs reject this new idea which Betsy calls dancing, but soon all but one join in to dance across the pages. Magnanimous as well as creative, Betsy makes room for 1 hopping frog in her chorus line of leapers, twisters, and dancers. (32 pages)

Where it's reviewed:
Booklist, November 1, 1993, page 532
Horn Book, November 1993, page 739
Kirkus Reviews, October 15, 1993, page 1339
Publishers Weekly, September 20, 1993, page 70
School Library Journal, October 1993, page 113

Awards the book has won:
ALA Notable Book, 1994

Other books by the same author:
Pip's Magic, 1994
You Silly Goose, 1992
Mouse Paint, 1989

Other books you might like:
Mary Blackwood, *Derek the Knitting Dinosaur*, 1990
    Green, gentle Derek prefers knitting to ferocious dinosaur activities, a trait appreciated by the others when the world becomes cold and he supplies warm clothes.
Leo Lionni, *Frederick*, 1967
    The other mice are not understanding of daydreamer and poet Frederick's talents until a winter day when he warms them with memories of summer.
Piotr Wilkon, *Rosie the Cool Cat*, 1991
    Unlike the others in her family, Rosie expresses her individuality by becoming a rock star.

1476

ELLEN STOLL WALSH, Author/Illustrator

Pip's Magic

(San Diego: Harcourt Brace & Company, 1994)

Subject(s): Fear; Animals/Reptiles; Self-Confidence
Age range(s): Grades K-2
Major character(s): Pip, Salamander; Old Abra, Turtle, Wizard
Time period(s): Indeterminate
Locale(s): Fictional Country

Summary: To overcome his fear of the dark, Pip searches for Old Abra to ask for some magic. Each place he travels in order to find Old Abra requires him to traverse a dark environment and each time when he arrives, he finds that Old Abra has moved on to another spot on the other side of more darkness. Finally, Pip finds Old Abra just as the sun is rising. In response to Pip's request, Old Abra calmly points out that, through the process of his search, Pip has shown that he already possesses the magic he needs to overcome his fear. (32 pages)

Where it's reviewed:
Booklist, October 15, 1994, page 440
Horn Book, January 1995, page 56
Kirkus Reviews, September 15, 1994, page 1285
Publishers Weekly, August 22, 1994, page 54
School Library Journal, November 1994, page 92

Other books by the same author:
Theodore All Grown Up, 1995
You Silly Goose, 1992
Mouse Paint, 1989

Other books you might like:
Hans Alfredson, *The Night the Moon Came By*, 1993
  Nighttime fears of monsters in the dark are humorously banished.
Natalie Babbitt, *The Something*, 1987
  Using a clay model, Mylo shows his mother the Something scary that comes in his window at night.
Ray Bradbury, *Switch on the Night*, 1993
  With some unexpected help, a little boy conquers his fear of the dark.
Nancy Raines Day, *The Lion's Whiskers: An Ethiopian Folktale*, 1995
  The retelling of an African folk tale describes a stepmother who solves a problem while complying with the wise man's instructions.

1477

WALTER WANGERIN JR.
DEBORAH HEALY, Illustrator

Branta and the Golden Stone

(New York: Simon & Schuster, 1993)

Subject(s): Magic; Animals/Geese; Fairy Tale
Age range(s): Grades 3-5
Major character(s): Papa, Father; Branta, Child (lonely)
Time period(s): Indeterminate Past

Locale(s): Earth (Northernmost island in all the world)

Summary: On his deathbed, Branta's father shares with her the secret of the golden stone, touched by a Baby King many years ago and imbued with great power. In the spring following her father's death, lonely Branta hears the sound of geese and is delighted that they settle on her lake to nest. An early winter storm threatens to kill the geese before they are able to migrate south and Branta does what she must to save them, knowing she will be transformed forever. (34 pages)

Where it's reviewed:
Booklist, November 1, 1993, page 524
Children's Bookwatch, November 1993, page 5
Library Talk, November 1993, page 34
Publishers Weekly, September 6, 1993, page 96
School Library Journal, October 1993, page 134

Other books by the same author:
Elisabeth and the Water-Troll, 1991
The Book of the Dun Cow, 1978 (American Book Award; School Library Journal Best Book)
A Penny Is Everything, 1974

Other books you might like:
Hans Christian Andersen, *The Fairy Tales of Hans Christian Andersen*, 1995
  Collected and retold by Neil Philip, the title includes 12 classic tales by Andersen.
Julie Lawson, *The Dragon's Pearl*, 1993
  In order to prevent the theft of the magical pearl he has found, Xiao Sheng swallows it and is transformed by the pearl's power.
P.K. Page, *A Flask of Sea Water*, 1989
  When a princess falls in love with a goatherd, a fairy godmother uses her magic to assure the satisfying outcome for all.

1478

LEE WARDLAW

101 Ways to Bug Your Parents

(New York: Dial, 1996)

Subject(s): Parent and Child; Money; Family Life
Age range(s): Grades 3-6
Major character(s): Steve "Sneeze" Wyatt, 12-Year-Old, Writer; Hiccup Denardo, 12-Year-Old; Goldie Laux, 12-Year-Old
Time period(s): 1990s
Locale(s): Pittsburgh, Pennsylvania

Summary: Steve is all excited about going to an invention convention and sharing his latest invention, but his parents enroll him, along with his friends, in a creative writing class at summer school. He decides to get back at them by writing a book about different ways to annoy your parents and plans to earn money selling the book. This works well until his teacher is reprimanded for allowing this kind of writing to go on. It is then up to Steve to defend the teacher. (204 pages)

Where it's reviewed:
Booklist, October 1, 1997, page 353
School Library Journal, October 1996, page 128

Other books by the same author:
Seventh Grade Weirdo, 1992

Other books you might like:
Paula Danziger, *Not for a Billion Gazillion Dollars*, 1992
 Matthew tries to earn enough money to buy the computer he really wants.
Peg Kehret, *The Richest Kids in Town*, 1994
 Peter teams up with a new friend to earn enough money to return to his former hometown, but all his plans don't work out.
Hilary McKay, *The Exiles at Home*, 1993
 The Conroy sisters try to raise money to sponsor a boy in Africa but find themselves in all kinds of trouble.
Janet Nichols, *Casey Wooster's Pet Care Service*, 1993
 Casey wants to earn money to travel to visit her mother, but in doing so, she gets to know her stepmother better.
Gary Soto, *Boys at Work*, 1995
 Rudy breaks a discman at a ball game and he and his friends must come up with a way of raising money to pay for a new one.

1479

LEE WARDLAW
RONALD SEARLE, Illustrator

The Tales of Grandpa Cat
(New York: Dial Books, 1994)

Subject(s): Animals/Cats; Grandparents; Storytelling
Age range(s): Grades 1-3
Major character(s): Grandpa Cat, Grandfather, Storyteller
Time period(s): Indeterminate
Locale(s): Catnip Acres, Fictional Country

Summary: Three kittens expect a boring Sunday visit with their grandparents at Catnip Acres. However, Grandpa Cat awakens from his nap when the kittens arrive and takes them for a walk, entertaining them with tales of yesteryear about the escapades of the other senior cats in the retirement community. (32 pages)

Where it's reviewed:
Booklist, October 15, 1994, page 440
Kirkus Reviews, September 15, 1994, page 1285
Publishers Weekly, September 12, 1994, page 89
School Library Journal, February 1995, page 83
Wilson Library Bulletin, February 1995, page 94

Other books you might like:
James Marshall, *Rats on the Range and Other Stories*, 1993
 Eight stories feature animals in humorous and unusual situations.
Barbara Ann Porte, *When Aunt Lucy Rode a Mule and Other Stories*, 1994
 Two children enjoy the stories Aunt Lucy shares about visiting the grandparents' farm as a child.
Ann Tompert, *Grandfather Tang's Story*, 1990
 Grandfather tells of shape-changing fox fairies whose competitive behavior endangers them.

1480

SALLY WARNER

Dog Years
(New York: Knopf, 1995)

Subject(s): Friendship; School Life; Prisoners and Prisons
Age range(s): Grades 4-6
Major character(s): Casey "Case" Hill, 6th Grader; Lily Hill, Child
Time period(s): 1990s
Locale(s): Philadelphia, Pennsylvania

Summary: Knowing his father is serving three years in prison is hard enough, but then Case and his family move away from their home. Now he's adjusting to life in an apartment, attending a new school and being the lonely new kid in class. Trying to complete an English assignment one night, and listening to his little sister Lily explain that she is older than him in dog years, leads him to create a cartoon column for his school newspaper called "Dog Years." As Case realizes, some years are more like dog years than others and this year is one of the dog years of his life. The column brings him instant popularity, but also instant problems when the most popular kid in sixth grade decides to sell his cartoon column. And the "dog years" go on forever in this author's first novel for young readers. (153 pages)

Where it's reviewed:
Publishers Weekly, March 6, 1995, page 70
Booklist, April 15, 1995, page 1501
Library Talk, September 1995, page 36
School Library Journal, April 1995, page 138
Horn Book Guide, Fall 1995, page 305

Other books you might like:
Jay Bennett, *Say Hello to the Hit Man*, 1979
 Fred Morgan disowns his crime boss father, but isn't able to escape his grip, especially when a voice on the phone tells him "You're going to die."
Paul Kropp, *Moonkid and Liberty*, 1988
 Brother and sister support one another as they enter a new school and have to explain their hippie father and unusual family lifestyle.
Gary Paulsen, *The Boy Who Owned the School*, 1990
 Jacob's quest to pass through high school undeteted fails when he falls for Maria who plays the Wicked Witch of the West.

1481

KATE WATERS
MARJORY DRESSLER, Illustrator

The Mysterious Horseman: An Adventure in Prairietown, 1836
(New York: Scholastic Inc., 1994)

Subject(s): Frontier and Pioneer Life; Historical; City Life
Age range(s): Grades 2-4
Major character(s): Andrew McClure, Child, Friend; Thomas Curtis, Child, Friend
Time period(s): 1830s (1836)

Locale(s): Prairietown, Indiana

Summary: When Andrew overhears talk of a headless horseman and a schoolmaster, he is convinced that the story must be about the new schoolmaster in town and hurries to tell Thomas. Later, the boys hear the thud of horse's approaching and, frightened, run to hide. As they peer from the bushes into the afternoon sun, the boys are sure they have seen the headless horseman and hurry to warn the town. When they tell Thomas's father what they've seen, he responds by reading the story of the *The Legend of Sleepy Hollow* to them. Sheepishly, Andrew realizes he has overheard the travellers talking about a new book and not a real event. (40 pages)

Where it's reviewed:
Booklist, September 15, 1994, page 137
Bulletin of the Center for Children's Books, November 1994, page 108
Horn Book Guide, Spring 1995, page 60
Library Talk, September 1994, page 17
School Library Journal, September 1994, page 201

Other books by the same author:
Samuel Eaton's Day: A Day in the Life of a Pilgrim Boy, 1993
The Story of the White House, 1991
Sarah Morton's Day: A Day in the Life of a Pilgrim Girl, 1989

Other books you might like:
Thomas B. Allen, *On Grandaddy's Farm*, 1989
    Summers for a young boy visiting Grandpa's farm include chores, as well as time to play with his cousins.
Washington Irving, *The Headless Horseman*, 1992
    The classic tale of the schoolmaster and the headless horseman is retold as a beginning chapter book by Natalie Standiford.
Megan McDonald, *The Potato Man*, 1991
    Mr. Angelo is a food peddler whose war injuries distort his appearance and make him the brunt of young boys' misperceptions.

1482

MARY WATSON, Author/Illustrator

The Butterfly Seeds
(New York: Tambourine Books, 1995)

Subject(s): Emigration and Immigration; Grandparents
Age range(s): Grades K-3
Major character(s): Jake, Child, Immigrant; Grandpa, Grandfather
Time period(s): Indeterminate Past
Locale(s): S. S. Celtic, At Sea; New York, New York

Summary: Each child on the ship has one special belonging that they are bringing to America. For Jake it is the butterfly seeds from Grandpa. When Jake's family moves into their new home he is discouraged to find that they live three flights up from the street with no land for a garden. Ingenuity and helpful neighborhood vendors enable Jake to create a window box in which he plants Grandpa's seeds. The author's first book conludes as the seeds produce flowering plants which attract butterflies just as Grandpa promised. (32 pages)

Where it's reviewed:
Booklist, September 1, 1995, page 90
Children's Book Review Service, August 1995, page 160
Kirkus Reviews, July 1, 1995, page 954
School Library Journal, November 1995, page 83
Smithsonian, November 1995, page 172

Other books you might like:
Elisa Bartone, *Peppe the Lamplighter*, 1993
    Peppe works hard to support his immigrant family and win his father's respect.
Sherry Garland, *The Lotus Seed*, 1993
    Fleeing her defeated country, Ba carries a lotus seed from the emperor's garden. Years later it is planted and yields seeds to share with her grandchildren.
Riki Levinson, *Watch the Stars Come Out*, 1985
    Grandma relates the story of her voyage to America as a child.
Marissa Moss, *In America*, 1994
    Grandpa explains to his grandson Walter why he chose to leave his homeland and family as a child and come to America.

1483

PETE WATSON
MARY WATSON, Illustrator

The Market Lady and the Mango Tree
(New York: Tambourine Books, 1994)

Subject(s): Food; Greed; Conduct of Life
Age range(s): Grades K-3
Major character(s): Market Lady, Businesswoman (greedy)
Time period(s): 1990s (1994)
Locale(s): Africa (village in West Africa)

Summary: The author's first picture book introduces a merchant who claims as her own every mango that falls from the shady mango tree under which she displays her wares. Hungry, poor children look longingly at the candy Market Lady sells, but settle for the occasional mango that falls to the ground until Market Lady wraps the tree in a net to catch all the mangos to sell. Then she builds traps around all the mango trees in the village so that she becomes rich selling what people once could have for free. Nightmares convince her to change her ways. (32 pages)

Where it's reviewed:
Booklist, February 15, 1994, page 1094
Children's Book Review Service, March 1994, page 90
Library Talk, March 1994, page 33
Publishers Weekly, February 21, 1994, page 253
School Library Journal, June 1994, page 115

Other books you might like:
Lynne Cherry, *The Great Kapok Tree: A Tale of the Amazon Rain Forest*, 1990
    When a kapok tree is threatened by an ax-wielding man, the animals who call the tree home try to convince the tree-cutter to spare the tree.
Walter Dean Myers, *How Mr. Monkey Saw the Whole World*, 1996

During a famine, Mr. Monkey defeats Mr. Buzzard's plan to acquire the food of the other animals.

Robert D. San Souci, *The House in the Sky: A Bahamian Folktale*, 1996

A greedy man who tries to steal food from the spirit folk rather than work for a living almost pays the ultimate price.

1484

SYLVIA WAUGH

The Mennyms

(New York: Greenwillow, 1994)

Subject(s): Dolls and Dollhouses; Family Life; Fantasy
Age range(s): Grades 4-6
Major character(s): Kate Penshaw, Seamstress (deceased); Albert Pond, Professor; Appleby, Teenager (rag doll), 15-Year-Old
Time period(s): 1990s
Locale(s): England (Brocklehurst Grove)

Summary: Forty years ago, Kate Penshaw was a lonely woman who created a life-size family of rag dolls for companionship. After her death, the rag dolls became alive and have occupied her house ever since. They have paid the rent to the sales agent and have lived "normal" lives, though seldom seen by their neighbors. Their lifestyle ends after they receive a letter from Albert Pond who has inherited their property and is coming for a visit. Each family member is frozen at the age they were when created, which means Appleby celebrates her fifteenth birthday every Fourth of July and even her mother is tired of Appleby as a perpetual teenager. As it turns out, the letter is a hoax, a prank by a rebellious teen who's been too long a teen in this first novel! (256 pages)

Where it's reviewed:
School Library Journal, April 1994, page 132
Publishers Weekly, April 4, 1994, page 81
Horn Book, July 1994, page 456
New York Times Book Review, October 9, 1994, page 26
Children's Book Review Service, July 1994, page 156

Other books by the same author:
Mennyms in the Wilderness, 1995

Other books you might like:
Natalie Babbitt, *Tuck Everlasting*, 1975
    The Tuck family is over one hundred years old thanks to a "fountain of youth."
Eve Bunting, *The Ghost Children*, 1989
    After their parents die, Matt and his sister Abby move in with Great-Aunt Gerda who introduces them to "her children," life-sized dolls carved by her husband.
Mary Norton, *The Borrowers*, 1952
    People who are no taller than a pencil live in this special world where they exist on items "borrowed" from regular adult-sized people.
Terry Pratchett, *Truckers*, 1990
    Masklin and his group of gnomes, who feel they're running out of corners in which to live, move to a store where they join forces with more gnomes.

1485

SYLVIA WAUGH

Mennyms Alone

(New York, Greenwillow, 1996)

Subject(s): Dolls and Dollhouses; Family Life
Age range(s): Grades 4-6
Major character(s): Sir Magnus Mennym, Toy (doll), Grandfather; Tulip Mennym, Toy (doll), Grandmother; Lorna Pond, Librarian
Time period(s): Indeterminate Past
Locale(s): England

Summary: The family of life-size rag dolls is concerned that something will happen and they will be returned to the state of dolls everywhere. A new family has come and begins by taking inventory and deciding what to do with the dolls. For a time they are separated and placed in an attic, but then things begin to happen to bring them back to life and back to each other again. (192 pages)

Where it's reviewed:
School Library Journal, September 1996, page 208
Booklist, September 15, 1996, page 242

Other books by the same author:
Mennyms Under Siege, 1996 (sequel to *Mennyms in the Wilderness*)
Mennyms in the Wilderness, 1995 (sequel to *The Mennyms*)
The Mennyms, 1994

Other books you might like:
Anne G. Estern, *The Picolinis and the Haunted House*, 1990
    A group of dolls fashioned after some circus performers have a great time.
Maria Gripe, *Agnes Cecilia*, 1990
    Nora receives a lifelike doll which leads her to discover secrets about her own family.
Helen V. Griffith, *Doll Trouble*, 1993
    Caitlin's doll, Holiday, comes alive and can walk and talk but becomes jealous when Jodi also seems to be alive.
Mary Norton, *The Borrowers*, 1981
    The first in a series about a family of little people who survive by using items the humans throw away.
Justine Rendal, *A Child of Their Own*, 1992
    The Darlings, a doll family, are purchased together and begin a new life wondering if they will be loved or put on a shelf.

1486

SYLVIA WAUGH

Mennyms in the Wilderness

(New York: Greenwillow, 1995)

Subject(s): Fantasy; Dolls and Dollhouses; Family Life
Age range(s): Grades 4-6
Major character(s): Albert Pond, Professor; Soobie Mennym, Teenager (rag doll)
Time period(s): 1990s
Locale(s): England (Brocklehurst Grove); England (Comus House)

Summary: After forty years of living peacefully in Brocklehurst Grove, the Mennyms, a family of rag dolls, find their home threatened by a motorway. The ghost of their creator speaks to her great-nephew, Albert Pond, about the dilemma and he immediately comes to help. Albert moves the rag doll family to another family home well-isolated in the country. Just when the family thinks its troubles are over, a gang of boys captures Soobie to use for its Guy Fawkes bonfire. (255 pages)

Where it's reviewed:

Publishers Weekly, May 8, 1995, page 296
School Library Journal, May 1995, page 110
Booklist, May 1, 1995, page 1576
Horn Book, July 1995, page 462
Library Talk, September 1995, page 38

Other books by the same author:

The Mennyms, 1994

Other books you might like:

Jane Leslie Conly, *R-T, Margaret and the Rats of NIMH*, 1986
    Rat Rasco and his friends must save Thorn Valley from discovery after two children accidentally stumble across it.
Terry Pratchett, *Diggers*, 1991
    The gnomes live in a quarry but when they hear the quarry will reopen, they contact their 15,000 year-old computer to find out what to do.
Rosemary Wells, *Through the Hidden Door*, 1987
    Two boys explore a cave where they dig up an ancient town inhabited by people only two-inches tall.

1487

CAROLE BOSTON WEATHERFORD
YVONNE BUCHANAN, Illustrator

Juneteenth Jamboree

(New York: Lee & Low Books Inc., 1995)

Subject(s): Family Life; African Americans; Holidays
Age range(s): Grades 1-3
Major character(s): Cassandra, Child
Time period(s): 1990s (1995)
Locale(s): Texas

Summary: Beginning her first picture book with an author's note explaining the history of the "Juneteenth" holiday, Weatherford introduces the celebration to Cassandra, a child who has moved with her family to the parent's hometown. Cassandra is aware that something exciting is happening because relatives are cooking, dancing and getting dressed in preparation for a Texas tradition. As Cassandra learns the origins of the holiday, she also begins to feel a part of her new community and extended family. (32 pages)

Where it's reviewed:

Horn Book Guide, Spring 1996, page 49
Publishers Weekly, October 30, 1995, page 61
School Library Journal, January 1996, page 97

Other books you might like:

Sandra Belton, *May'naise Sandwiches & Sunshine Tea*, 1994
    Looking through a photo album with her granddaughter

prompts Big Mama to share memories of a special childhood picnic.
Melrose Cooper, *I Got Community*, 1995
    A rhythmic tale describes the individuals who comprise a young girl's loving and supportive community.
Valerie Flournoy, *Tanya's Reunion*, 1995
    While helping Grandma prepare for a family reunion, Tanya visits and learns about the Virginia farm where Grandma lived as a child.
Wade Hudson, *I Love My Family*, 1993
    Joyfully, a family celebrates the reunion of its members, eating, singing and making a family portrait.

1488

MARYANN N. WEIDT
HENRI SORENSEN, Illustrator

Daddy Played Music for the Cows

(New York: Lothrop, Lee & Shepard Books, 1995)

Subject(s): Farm Life; Family Life; Music
Age range(s): Grades 1-3
Major character(s): Unnamed Character, Child; Daddy, Father
Time period(s): Indeterminate Past
Locale(s): United States (dairy farm)

Summary: A young girl reminisces about her childhood on a dairy farm. The family's life revolves around the cows, the barn and the music Daddy plays for the animals as he milks them. (32 pages)

Where it's reviewed:

Booklist, October 1, 1995, page 327
Children's Book Review Service, November 1995, page 28
Children's Book Watch, November 1995, page 8
Kirkus Reviews, August 1, 1995, page 1118
School Library Journal, October 1995, page 123

Other books by the same author:

Oh, the Places He Went, 1994

Other books you might like:

David McPhail, *Farm Morning*, 1985
    A father and daughter enjoy their mornings on the farm as they feed the animals.
Patricia MacLachlan, *All the Places to Love*, 1994
    Eli has grown up to appreciate that "all the places to love" are on the family farm.
Linda Morris, *Morning Milking*, 1991
    A young girl wishes she could stop time and capture the moments when she helps her father milk the cows each morning.

1489

CATHERINE A. WELCH
LAURIE K. JOHNSON, Illustrator

Clouds of Terror

(Minneapolis: Carolrhoda Books, 1994)

Series: On My Own
Subject(s): Frontier and Pioneer Life; Animals/Insects; Food
Age range(s): Grades 2-4

Major character(s): Erik Lundstrom, 7-Year-Old, Brother; Helga Lundstrom, 9-Year-Old, Sister; Mr. Lundstrom, Settler, Farmer
Time period(s): 1870s
Locale(s): Minnesota

Summary: Helga and Erik expect the cloud on the horizon to bring a sudden prairie storm and so they hurry home. The cloud is not a storm, however, and before they reach shelter, a cloud of grasshoppers descends upon them and their crops. Frantically, the family works to salvage as many crops as they can. Although they are able to save some food to eat, they have lost all their cash crops. Reluctantly, Mr. Lundstrom leaves his family for the winter to find work at a lumber camp to earn the money they need to survive on the harsh prairie. (48 pages)

Where it's reviewed:
Booklist, September 15, 1994, page 147
Horn Book Guide, Fall 1994, page 297
Kirkus Reviews, May 15, 1994, page 709
School Library Journal, August 1994, page 148
Social Education, April 1995, page 221

Other books by the same author:
Danger at the Breaker, 1991

Other books you might like:
Patricia MacLachlan, *Skylark*, 1994
    A drought causes crop failure and forces many families to leave their prairie homes.
Ann Turner, *Grasshopper Summer*, 1989
    A family homesteading in South Dakota faces many hardships including the destruction of their crops by swarms of grasshoppers.
Laura Ingalls Wilder, *On the Banks of Plum Creek*, 1961
    When locusts destroy the harvest, Pa must leave his family temporarily to find work elsewhere.

1490

SHEILA KELLY WELCH
SANDY RABINOWITZ, Illustrator

A Horse for All Seasons
(Honesdale, PA: Boyds Mill Press, 1995)

Subject(s): Animals/Horses; Short Stories
Age range(s): Grades 6-9
Time period(s): 1990s
Locale(s): United States

Summary: Divided into the seasons of the year, this collection of twelve contemporary stories features horses and their young owners. The winning of a ribbon at a summer horse show is the main event in "Costume Class," the fall series of stories includes "Haunted Hayride" in which a young boy scares his sisters during their moonlight hayride and "Hearts and Hoofbeats" describes how a young woman becomes friends with the stable owner's son as they ride together during the cold winter months. (159 pages)

Where it's reviewed:
Voice of Youth Advocates, August 1995, page 166
School Library Journal, January 1995, page 110
Library Talk, March 1995, page 53

Booklist, April 1, 1995, page 1393
Center for Children's Books. Bulletin, January 1995, page 180

Other books by the same author:
Don't Call Me Marda, 1990

Other books you might like:
Betty Cavanna, *Wanted: A Girl for the Horses*, 1984
    Charlotte's life becomes much more interesting when she begins to work as a horse groomer.
Bruce Coville, *Herds of Thunder, Manes of Gold: A Collection of Horse Stories and Poems*, 1989
    This noted author has compiled stories, book excerpts and poems by other authors who write about horses.
Walt Morey, *The Year of the Black Pony*, 1976
    In the early 1900s in Oregon, young Christopher owns and loves his black stallion.

1491

WILLY WELCH
MARC SIMONT, Illustrator

Playing Right Field
(New York: Scholastic Inc., 1995)

Subject(s): Sports/Baseball; Self-Esteem; Stories in Rhyme
Age range(s): Grades K-3
Major character(s): Unnamed Character, Child, Baseball Player
Time period(s): 1990s (1995)
Locale(s): United States

Summary: Always the last one chosen for the team, a little boy dejectedly walks to right field and takes up his customary position watching the dandelions grow. As he daydreams about famous ball players making game-saving plays, he notices his teammates yelling at him and pointing to the sky. He becomes alert just in time to watch a fly ball drop into his glove. Having a new understanding of the importance of his position, he plays it more attentively. The author's first book. (32 pages)

Where it's reviewed:
Booklist, January 15, 1995, page 925
Horn Book, September 1995, page 593
Kirkus Reviews, February 15, 1995, page 234
Library Talk, May 1995, page 15
School Library Journal, March 1995, page 188

Other books you might like:
Brian McConnachie, *Elmer and the Chickens vs. the Big League*, 1992
    Elmer imagines his own field of dreams when he is left on the farm while his big brother goes to a baseball game.
David Spohn, *Home Field*, 1993
    Early one morning, a dad and his son enjoy each other's company while playing baseball.
Richard Wilbur, *A Game of Catch*, 1994
    When gloveless Scho is unable to join his friends in a game of catch, he climbs a nearby tree and directs the action.

1492

ROSEMARY WELLS, Author/Illustrator

Edward's Overwhelming Overnight

(New York: Dial Books for Young Readers, 1995)

Series: Edward the Unready
Subject(s): Animals/Bears; Parent and Child; Growing Up
Age range(s): Grades K-1
Major character(s): Edward, Bear, Friend (Anthony's); Anthony, Bear, Friend (Edward's)
Time period(s): 1990s (1995)
Locale(s): United States

Summary: Initially apprehensive, Edward settles happily into playing in the falling snow at Anthony's house until he receives a phone call from his parents explaining that the roads are no longer safe for travel and Edward must spend the night with Anthony. Decked out in Anthony's new duck pajamas, Edward is still, obviously, miserable and Anthony's parents choose not to prolong the agony, but to simply shovel the driveway, put the chains on the car and follow the snow plow to Edward's house. (22 pages)

Where it's reviewed:
Booklist, September 1, 1995, page 75
Bulletin of the Center for Children's Books, November 1995, page 108
Horn Book, November 1995, page 739
Publishers Weekly, September 18, 1995, page 131
School Library Journal., November 1995, page 84

Awards the book has won:
Booklist Editors' Choice, 1995

Other books by the same author:
Shy Charles, 1988
Timothy Goes to School, 1981
Benjamin and Tulip, 1977

Other books you might like:
Louise Borden, *Albie the Lifeguard*, 1993
    Not ready to join his friends on the swim team, Albie builds his confidence by "guarding" the backyard wading pool.
Robert Kraus, *Leo the Late Bloomer*, 1971
    While father frets, mother patiently waits until the day when son Leo is finally ready to "bloom".
Bernard Waber, *Ira Sleeps Over*, 1973
    An invitation to spend the night at Reggie's house creates a dilemma for Ira—should he bring his teddy?

1493

ROSEMARY WELLS, Author/Illustrator

The Language of Doves

(New York: Dial, 1996)

Subject(s): Death; World War I
Age range(s): Grades K-2
Major character(s): Julietta, 6-Year-Old; Isabella, Bird (dove)
Time period(s): 1990s; 1910s (World War I)
Locale(s): Cape May, New Jersey; Europe

Summary: Julietta's grandfather has talked about raising racing pigeons and on her sixth birthday he gives her one of her own. He then tells her about his youth in Europe and his work with racing pigeons during World War I, especially Isabella who was one of the best at carrying messages but was killed during the war. Julietta takes her pigeon home and lets her go but the pigeon keeps going to her grandfather's house until the day he dies and Isabella returns home to Julietta. (unpaged)

Where it's reviewed:
School Library Journal, September 1996, page 193

Other books by the same author:
Lassie Come-Home, 1995 (retelling)
Lucy Comes to Stay, 1994
The Island Light, 1992

Other books you might like:
Michael Foreman, *War Game*, 1994
    Michael writes from his own life and memories of the time of World War I, including games and holidays.
Natalie Kinsey-Warnock, *The Night the Bells Rang*, 1991
    Mason helps with the chores but he remembers the war as a town bully goes off to fight.
Kathleen V. Kudlinski, *Hero over Here*, 1990
    A young boy has to care for his mother and sister who have influenza while his father and brother fight during World War I.
Staton Rabin, *Casey over There*, 1994
    Aubrey is unhappy that his older brother has gone to Europe to fight in the war and so he writes a letter asking that he be sent home.

1494

ROSEMARY WELLS
SUSAN JEFFERS, Illustrator

Lassie Come-Home

(New York: Henry Holt and Company, 1995)

Subject(s): Animals/Dogs; Poverty; Determination
Age range(s): Grades 3-4
Major character(s): Lassie, Dog (collie); Joe, Child; Duke of Rudling, Nobleman, Wealthy
Time period(s): Indeterminate Past
Locale(s): Greenall Bridge, England (Yorkshire); Scotland

Summary: The adaptation of Eric Knight's original classic about a loyal collie who, after being sold by her impoverished family, struggles against distance, hunger and injury to return home is presented in a beautifully illustrated picture book for older readers. True to the original story, Lassie is Joe's one true friend in the harsh, poor life of a miner's family. When Joe's father loses his job, Lassie is sold to the Duke of Rudling. Three times while still in Greenall Bridge, Lassie frees herself and returns home. After the Duke takes her by train to his castle in northern Scotland, Lassie escapes again. With a thousand miles separating her from Joe, it takes Lassie a year of hardship to find the schoolyard corner where she is accustomed to waiting for him daily, but she overcomes all obstacles and one day Joe finds her, on the brink of death, waiting. (48 pages)

Where it's reviewed:
Booklist, December 1, 1995, page 637
Horn Book, March 1996, page 192
Library Talk, September 1995, page 23
Publishers Weekly, September 18, 1995, page 130
School Library Journal, November 1995, page 84

Other books by the same author:
Lucy Comes to Stay, 1994
Waiting for the Evening Star, 1993
Forest of Dreams, 1988

Other books you might like:
Ruth Brown, *The Ghost of Greyfriar's Bobby*, 1995
    For fourteen years after his master's death, loyal Bobby
    stands vigil at his grave site.
Linda Jennings, *The Best Christmas Present of All*, 1996
    When Mr. Merriweather is taken to the hospital, his grand-
    children try to care for his dog, but Buster runs away in
    search of his owner.
Eric Knight, *Lassie Come-Home*, 1938
    The original novel details Lassie's journey from Scotland
    to Yorkshire and her reunion with her family.
Paul Brett Johnson, *Lost*, 1996
    A young girl never gives up hope that her pet beagle, lost
    in the desert, will survive and come home again. Co-author
    Celeste Lewis.

▮1495▮
ROSEMARY WELLS
MARK GRAHAM, Illustrator

Lucy Comes to Stay
(New York: Dial Books for Young Readers, 1994)

Subject(s): Animals/Dogs; Animals; Family Relations
Age range(s): Grades K-2
Major character(s): Mary Elizabeth, Child; Lucy, Dog
   (puppy)
Time period(s): 1940s (Post World War II)
Locale(s): United States

Summary: Mary Elizabeth loves her puppy, Lucy, so much
that she is never able to scold her for puppy infractions such as
chewed laces on new shoes or blue fur from gnawing a
ballpoint pen. However, to earn the privilege of having Lucy
sleep in her bed, Mary Elizabeth must demonstrate her ability
to care for Lucy and to help her family with other household
chores. (32 pages)

Where it's reviewed:
Booklist, June 1, 1994, page 1846
Children's Book Review Service, September 1994, page 6
Five Owls, September 1994, page 12
Publishers Weekly, May 2, 1994, page 308
School Library Journal, July 1994, page 91

Other books by the same author:
Night Sounds, Morning Colors, 1994
Waiting for the Evening Star, 1993
Forest of Dreams, 1992
Moss Pillows, 1992
Shy Charles, 1988

Other books you might like:
Norman Bridwell, *Clifford, the Small Red Puppy*, 1972
    Emily Elizabeth chooses the smallest puppy in the litter to
    be her pet and, with her loving attention, Clifford grows
    and grows and grows.
Pija Lindenbaum, *Boodil My Dog*, 1992
    Boodil's owner thinks her dog is the perfect pet despite
    what others might consider shortcomings.
Cynthia Rylant, *Henry and Mudge*, 1987
    In this first book of a now classic series, only-child Henry,
    lonely for companionship, begs his parents to allow him to
    have a dog.

▮1496▮
ROSEMARY WELLS, Author/Illustrator

Max and Ruby's First Greek Myth:
Pandora's Box
(New York: Dial Books for Young Readers, 1993)

Subject(s): Animals/Rabbits; Brothers and Sisters; Storytell-
ing
Age range(s): Grades K-3
Major character(s): Ruby, Rabbit, Sister (older); Max, Rabbit,
   Brother (younger)
Time period(s): 1990s (1993)
Locale(s): United States

Summary: In an attempt to keep Max out of her room and her
jewelry box, Ruby tells him her version of the story of
Pandora and her mother's forbidden jewelry box. Max listens
attentively, but it seems unlikely that the tale will curb his
irrepressible curiosity. (28 pages)

Where it's reviewed:
Booklist, July 1993, page 1977
Horn Book, November 1993, page 740
New Advocate, Winter 1994, page 63
Publishers Weekly, June 28, 1993, page 76
School Library Journal, June 1994, page 52

Awards the book has won:
School Library Journal Best Books, 1993

Other books by the same author:
Max and Ruby's Midas: Another Greek Myth, 1995
Max's Dragon Shirt, 1991
Noisy Nora, 1973

Other books you might like:
Ingri D'Aulaire, *D'Aulaire's Book of Greek Myths*, 1962
    A collection of Greek myths has been adapted and illus-
    trated for children. Co-author Edgar Parin D'Aulaire.
James Marshall, *Three Up a Tree*, 1986
    Lolly agrees to tell stories if Sam and Spider will let her
    into the newly built tree house.
Jon Scieszka, *The True Story of the Three Little Pigs*, 1989
    A humorous retelling of a classic tale with a different look
    at just what happened with those three pigs.

1497

ROSEMARY WELLS, Author/Illustrator

Max and Ruby's Midas: Another Greek Myth

(New York: Dial Books for Young Readers, 1995)

Subject(s): Food; Brothers and Sisters; Animals/Rabbits
Age range(s): Grades K-1
Major character(s): Ruby, Rabbit, Sister (older); Max, Rabbit, Brother (younger)
Time period(s): 1990s (1995); Indeterminate Past
Locale(s): United States; Greece

Summary: Attempting to curb Max's insatiable appetite for sweets, Ruby tells him a bedtime story about a young Grecian Prince who preferred sweets to the vegetarian cuisine on which his family dined. Using his laser-beam eyes to transform his meals, the unfortunate prince actually changed his parents and sister into a cherry float, jello and cake. The moral of the tale is lost on Max who feigns sleep and, as Ruby tiptoes out of the room, pulls a cupcake from under his pajama top for a bedtime snack. (32 pages)

Where it's reviewed:
Booklist, May 1, 1995, page 1581
Horn Book, July 1995, page 455
Kirkus Reviews, May 1, 1995, page 641
Publishers Weekly, May 15, 1995, page 71
School Library Journal, May 1995, page 97

Other books by the same author:
Max and Ruby's First Greek Myth: Pandora's Box, 1993
Max's Chocolate Chicken, 1989
Max's New Suit, 1979

Other books you might like:
Stan Berenstain, *The Berenstain Bears and Too Much Junk Food*, 1985
    When Mama Bear decides to change her family's eating habits, Papa has as much difficulty giving up junk food as Brother and Sister do. Co-author Jan Berenstain.
Sarah Hayes, *Eat Up, Gemma*, 1988
    Gemma's brother has an idea that he hopes will encourage the baby to eat her food rather than throw it on the floor.
Robert Kraus, *Near Myths: Dug Up and Dusted Off*, 1996
    The inimitable Kraus has created humorous variations of the stories of mythical and biblical characters such as King Midas and Samson and Delilah.
Jane Read Martin, *Now I Will Never Leave the Dinner Table*, 1996
    Forced by her perfect older sister to remain at the table until she eats her spinach, a young girl imagines that it's easier to get rid of her sister than the spinach.

1498

ROSEMARY WELLS
SUSAN JEFFERS, Illustrator

Waiting for the Evening Star

(New York: Dial Books for Young Readers, 1993)

Subject(s): Farm Life; Brothers; World War I

Age range(s): Grades 1-3
Major character(s): Berty, Child, Brother (younger); Luke, Brother, Farmer
Time period(s): 1910s (1910-1917)
Locale(s): Barstow, Vermont

Summary: Berty is content with the simple life of a farm family, but his older brother Luke longs to see what is beyond the mountains. Berty's recollections draw the reader into the hard-working, supportive community of farmers who labor together, selling or trading any excess they produce. From Berty's earliest memories, Luke has been watching the trains that pass the farm, wondering where they go and waiting for the day he can board one and see for himself. (40 pages)

Where it's reviewed:
Booklist, September 1, 1993, page 72
Five Owls, Summer 1994, page 5
Horn Book, November 1993, page 740
Publishers Weekly, July 19, 1993, page 254
School Library Journal, October 1993, page 114

Other books by the same author:
Forest of Dreams, 1992 (Golden Kite Award)
The Island Light, 1992
Peabody, 1983

Other books you might like:
Candice Christiansen, *The Ice Horse*, 1993
    Jack is proud that he is able to save his uncle's horse when Max plunges into the Hudson River during the annual ice harvest.
Thomas Locker, *Family Farm*, 1988
    Fearing the loss of their farm a family works together to plant additional crops to supplement their income.
Patricia MacLachlan, *All the Places to Love*, 1994
    Eli believes that everything worth loving is right here on the farm and he aims to share his knowledge with his baby sister.
Staton Rabin, *Casey over There*, 1994
    Seven-year-old Aubrey misses his brother Casey when he goes ''over there'' to fight in the Great War.
Cynthia Rylant, *When I Was Young in the Mountains*, 1982
    Set in Appalachia, the book celebrates the needed support of family to endure the hardship of life in the simple beauty of the mountain world.

1499

BRIGITTE WENINGER
ALAN MARKS, Illustrator

Good-Bye, Daddy!

(New York: North-South Books, 1995)

Subject(s): Fathers and Sons; Divorce; Animals/Bears
Age range(s): Grades K-2
Major character(s): Tom, Child of Divorced Parents; Daddy, Father; Unnamed Character, Bear, Toy
Time period(s): 1990s (1995)
Locale(s): Europe

Summary: After an all-day visit with his father, Tom is angry to say good-bye so he hides and ignores Daddy's parting calls and races to his room in tears. Clutching his special bear, Tom hears the teddy bear whispers a story about a similar situation in the bear's life and begins to accept his parent's divorce. The author's first book is translated from the German. (32 pages)

Where it's reviewed:
Children's Book Review Service, August 1995, page 160
Horn Book Guide, Fall 1995, page 286
School Library Journal, June 1995, page 97

Other books you might like:
Crescent Dragonwagon, *Always, Always*, 1984
    Summers with her father, winters with her mother—a child of divorced parents feels confused but begins to see the consistancy in life is her parents' love for her.
Linda Walvoord Girard, *At Daddy's on Saturday*, 1987
    Katie's Daddy moves out of the house and she now sees him only on Saturday visits.
John Schindel, *Dear Daddy*, 1995
    Sad to live far away from his father, Jesse is pleased when a letter finally arrives and the two make plans for a summer visit.

`1500`

MARY WESLEY

Haphazard House
(Woodstock, NY: Overlook House, 1993)

Subject(s): Time Travel; Family Life
Age range(s): Grades 5-6
Major character(s): Lisa Fuller, 11-Year-Old
Time period(s): 1990s
Locale(s): Coldharbor, England (Haphazard House on the Devon/Cornwall border)

Summary: Lisa's father places a bet on a horse on Derby Day, wins a fortune and buys Haphazard House, a dilapidated mansion in an isolated part of England. From the first day the family arrives at the house, it's obvious that everything is very haphazard. Time runs forwards and backwards, grandfather gets younger while their kitten becomes a cat overnight and one time they receive a letter before it's even mailed. Controlling everything seems to be a Panama hat, worn by her father on the day he wins his fortune, worn by the never-seen but always-heard gardner and faced by Lisa when she meets her future in a spookily eerie story. (144 pages)

Where it's reviewed:
Booklist, January 1, 1994, page 828
School Library Journal, August 1993, page 190
Publishers Weekly, June 7, 1993, page 71
Center for Children's Books. Bulletin, October 1993, page 61
Locus, July 1993, page 31

Other books by the same author:
Speaking Terms, 1994
The Sixth Seal, 1993

Other books you might like:
Eileen Dunlop, *Green Willow*, 1993
    Kit's family rents a house and discovers that a ghostly figure keeps appearing in the garden.
William Sleator, *Blackbriar*, 1972
    A mysterious house awaits Danny and his stepmother.

Robert Westall, *Ghost Abbey*, 1988
    Living in an abbey with her mischievous brothers, Maggi's workload increases when a ghost appears from the building's monastery days.

`1501`

ROBERT WESTALL
JOHN LAWRENCE, Illustrator

Christmas Spirit: Two Stories
(New York: Farrar Straus Giroux, 1994)

Subject(s): Christmas; Short Stories
Age range(s): Grades 3-6
Time period(s): Indeterminate Past
Locale(s): England

Summary: In the first story, a young boy delivering Christmas Eve tea to his father at the factory is met by a man that he assumes at first is Santa Claus, but learns is a ghost with a warning. The boy's faith and willingness to communicate first with the ghost and second with the factory workers averts a tragedy. The second tale tells of a young girl's Christmas spent with an unmarried uncle, her friendship with a boy in town and the shelter she secretly offers a pregnant cat. First published in Great Britain in 1991 and 1992. (150 pages)

Where it's reviewed:
Booklist, October 1, 1994, page 329
Horn Book, November 1994, page 715
Kirkus Reviews, October 15, 1994, page 1422
Library Talk, January 1995, page 29
Publishers Weekly, September 19, 1994, page 32

Other books by the same author:
Shades of Darkness, 1994
Demons and Shadows, 1993
The Stones of Muncaster Cathedral, 1993

Other books you might like:
Leo F. Buscaglia, *Seven Stories of Christmas Love*, 1987
    Memories of childhood traditions fill seven short stories about a close, loving family.
Katherine Paterson, *Angels and Other Strangers*, 1979
    A collection of original short stories reflects on some of the mysteries of the Christmas season.
Cynthia Rylant, *Children of Christmas: Stories for the Season*, 1987
    Six short stories present a deeper meaning of the holiday season for those who may be lonely or in need.

`1502`

MARTHA WESTON

Tuck in the Pool
(New York: Clarion Books, 1995)

Subject(s): Animals/Pigs; Fear; Summer
Age range(s): Grades K-1
Major character(s): Tuck, Pig, Brother; Bunny, Pig, Sister; Snyder, Toy, Spider
Time period(s): 1990s (1995)
Locale(s): Fictional Country

Summary: Tuck does not share Bunny's enthusiasm for swimming lessons, especially going underwater and getting water in his eyes and ears. For luck, Tuck brings Snyder along and puts him beside the pool to pat at critical moments. When Tuck discovers that Snyder has fallen in, he overcomes the fear of opening his eyes in the water in order to rescue his good luck toy. (32 pages)

Where it's reviewed:
Booklist, November 15, 1995, page 566
Bulletin of the Center for Children's Books, November 1995, page 109
Horn Book Guide, Spring 1996, page 49
School Library Journal, February 1996, page 91

Other books by the same author:
Apple Juice Tea, 1994
Bea's Four Bears, 1992

Other books you might like:
Louise Borden, *Albie the Lifeguard*, 1993
　　Albie gains confidence ''guarding'' the backyard wading pool and, by summer's end, is able to join his friends at the town pool.
Marc Brown, *D.W. All Wet*, 1988
　　When her family goes to the beach, D.W. is determined to stay out of the water, but her brother, Arthur, helps her enjoy the fun of the water too.
Jonathan London, *Froggy Learns to Swim*, 1995
　　Although Froggy's mother assures him that frogs are born to swim, he does not overcome his fear of the water until he has a mask, snorkel and flippers, as well as his mother's help.

1503

SUZANNE WEYN

My Brother, the Ghost

(New York: HarperCollins, 1994)

Series: House of Horrors
Subject(s): Ghosts; Horror; Brothers and Sisters
Age range(s): Grades 4-6
Major character(s): Sara Buckner, 7th Grader, Sister; Michael Buckner, 6th Grader, Brother
Time period(s): 1990s (1994)
Locale(s): Lakeview (Moonlight Mansion)

Summary: With their parents, Sara and Michael move into the large, old and reputed-to-be-haunted family mansion vacated by their grandmother. Unintentionally, on moving day, the children release a ghost from a long-locked wardrobe thus triggering a frightening series of events which convince Sara and Michael that somehow they must get this evil spirit locked up again or they are doomed. (125 pages)

Where it's reviewed:
Booklist, January 1, 1995, page 822
Publishers Weekly, September 19, 1994, page 26
School Library Journal, December 1994, page 114

Other books by the same author:
Rest in Pieces, 1994
Nicole's Chance, 1993
True Blue, 1991

Other books you might like:
Eve Bunting, *The Haunting of Safekeep*, 1985
　　While working at a Victorian restoration site, Sara encounters two ghosts.
Richard Peck, *The Ghost Belonged to Me*, 1975
　　Spirit Blossom Culp creates some excitement for Alexander before he and Uncle Miles manage to put the ghost to rest.
R.L. Stine, *Let's Get Invisible!*, 1993
　　On his birthday, Max finds a mirror that makes him invisible.
Betty Ren Wright, *A Ghost in the Window*, 1987
　　By revealing the future, Meg's dreams help her learn that some changes in life must be accepted, but also involve her in a mysterious death.

1504

GLORIA WHELAN

The Indian School

(New York: HarperCollins, 1996)

Subject(s): Indians of North America; Orphans; Self-Perception
Age range(s): Grades 2-5
Major character(s): Lucy, Orphan, Student; Raven, Indian, Student; Aunt Emma, Teacher, Religious (missionary)
Time period(s): 1830s (1839)
Locale(s): Michigan

Summary: Lucy comes to live with her aunt and uncle in the missionary school they run for Indians. She finds that students in the school are made to dress in Western clothes and every attempt is made to change their Indian ways. Raven, an Indian girl, is left at the school by her father while he goes off to hunt, but she refuses to follow the strict rules and runs away into the woods where Lucy helps her survive. When Raven's brother becomes ill she is forced to return to the school and is reconciled to Aunt Emma. (89 pages)

Other books by the same author:
Once on This Island, 1995
Night of the Full Moon, 1993
Hannah, 1991

Other books you might like:
Sara H. Banks, *Remember My Name*, 1993
　　A half-Indian girl goes to live with her uncle in Georgia in the 1830's.
Deanna Kidd, *Onion Tears*, 1991
　　A Vietnamese girl tries to adjust to a different lifestyle from what she has known before.
Alice Mead, *Crossing the Starlight Bridge*, 1994
　　Rayanna is not pleased about having to move off the reservation she has known and move in with her grandmother.
Phyllis Root, *The Listening Silence*, 1993
　　A young Indian girl triumphs over her fears and proves herself worthy to be a healer of her tribe.

1505

GLORIA WHELAN
LESLIE W. BOWMAN, Illustrator

Night of the Full Moon

(New York: Alfred A. Knopf, 1993)

Subject(s): Indians of North America; Frontier and Pioneer Life; Indian Captives
Age range(s): Grades 2-4
Major character(s): Libby Mitchell, Settler; Fawn, Indian
Time period(s): 1840s (1841)
Locale(s): Michigan (in the vicinity of Saginaw)

Summary: Libby's mother is in labor, forcing her family to miss the naming ceremony for Fawn's baby brother. Telling her father she is going to gather blackberries, Libby instead runs off to the Indian camp to join her friend. Unfortunately, this is the night that the soldiers come to force the Indians to move farther west and Libby, dressed in Fawn's clothes, is mistaken for an Indian. After 3 days, Fawn's father seizes an opportunity to escape with his family and Libby. With help from Fawn's family, Libby reaches her cabin safely, meets her baby brother and bids a sad good-bye to Fawn. (64 pages)

Where it's reviewed:
Booklist, December 1, 1993, page 691
Five Owls, September 1994, page 5
Horn Book Guide, Spring 1994, page 83
Publishers Weekly, November 8, 1993, page 77
School Library Journal, November 1993, page 110

Other books by the same author:
Hannah, 1993
Goodbye, Vietnam, 1992
Next Spring an Oriole, 1987

Other books you might like:
Sara H. Banks, *Remember My Name*, 1993
    To avoid the Cherokee ''Trail of Tears'' Annie Rising Fawn Stuart and Righteous Cry secretly leave their Georgia home to seek refuge in the Cherokee mountain homelands.
Elizabeth Speare, *The Sign of the Beaver*, 1983
    Left to maintain the frontier homestead while his father brings the other family members, Matt is befriended by an Indian chief and his grandson.
Elisabeth Jane Stewart, *On the Long Trail Home*, 1994
    Separated from her family, 9-year-old Meli finds her brother and the two escape the Trail of Tears to their home in North Carolina.

1506

GLORIA WHELAN

That Wild Berries Should Grow: The Diary of a Summer

(Grand Rapids, MI: Eerdmans, 1994)

Subject(s): Summer; Nature; Grandparents
Age range(s): Grades 4-6
Major character(s): Elsa, 5th Grader; Grandmama, Grandmother (Elsa's German); Grandpapa, Grandfather (Elsa's German)
Time period(s): 1930s (1933)
Locale(s): Detroit, Michigan; Greenbush, Michigan (beside Lake Huron)

Summary: After a year of illness where she misses half of fifth grade, and with her father out of work, Elsa is sent to spend the summer with her grandparents at their lakeside cottage. City-bred Elsa fears the summer will be an empty, boring one but she finds more than enough activities to record in her journal. Getting to know her violin-playing grandfather and stern grandmother, hearing of their victimization during World War I while living in Germany, eating wild berries and learning to fish more than occupy her days in this gentle novel. (125 pages)

Where it's reviewed:
School Library Journal, July 1994, page 104
Publishers Weekly, March 21, 1994, page 73
Booklist, May 1, 1994, page 1602
Horn Book Guide, Fall 1994, page 317
Library Talk, November 1994, page 43

Other books by the same author:
Once on This Island, 1995
A Time to Keep Silent, 1993
Goodbye, Vietnam, 1992

Other books you might like:
Gary Paulsen, *The Cookcamp*, 1991
    For a young boy, World War II means disruption of his family when he is sent to live with his grandmother who's a cook for a logging company.
Ethel Footman Smothers, *Moriah's Pond*, 1995
    Annie Rye and her sisters have a wonderful time spending the summer with Moriah as they swim, fish and help with chores.
Joyce Carol Thomas, *Golden Pasture*, 1986
    Staying on his grandfather's farm, Carl Lee learns patience through caring for a horse.

1507

SUSAN WHITCHER
BARBARA LEHMAN, Illustrator

Moonfall

(New York: Farrar, Straus and Giroux, 1993)

Subject(s): Parent and Child; Fantasy; Imagination
Age range(s): Grades K-3
Major character(s): Sylvie, Child
Time period(s): 1990s (1993)
Locale(s): United States

Summary: In the author's first picture book, Sylvie discovers the moon, battered and dirty under her neighbor's lilac bush. Although she is encouraged to throw it away, Sylvie instead concocts a bath mixture which she hopes will restore the moon to its proper place in the night sky. (28 pages)

Where it's reviewed:
Booklist, August 1993, page 1978
Children's Book Review Service, August 1993, page 162

Horn Book Guide, Fall 1993, page 279
Publishers Weekly, June 14, 1993, page 69
School Library Journal, October 1993, page 114

Other books you might like:

Tim Chadwick, *Cabbage Moon*, 1994
  Albert, a young rabbit, discovers that the moon is a huge cabbage which must be nibbled by hungry bunnies in order to achieve its crescent shape.

Matthew Gollub, *The Moon Was at a Fiesta*, 1994
  An original folktale explaining why the moon is sometimes visible in the morning sky.

Rodney Rigby, *The Night the Moon Fell Asleep*, 1993
  Overtired from too many late nights, the moon falls asleep and crashes to the ground requiring a community effort to restore her to the night sky.

John Rowe, *Rabbit Moon*, 1992
  With the moon hidden by a cloud, Albert puts a fallen party decoration in the sky, satisfied with his success as the moon appears again.

James Thurber, *Many Moons*, 1943
  A Caldecott Medal winner about a Princess whose wish for the moon is finally fulfilled by the Court Jester.

1508

SUSAN WHITCHER
BARBARA LEHMAN, Illustrator

Something for Everyone

(New York: Farrar, Straus and Giroux, 1995)

Subject(s): Friendship; Moving, Household; Imagination
Age range(s): Grades K-2
Major character(s): Elsie Applebaum, Aged Person, Aunt; Tilda, Child, Niece
Time period(s): 1990s (1995)
Locale(s): United States

Summary: When Great-aunt Elsie Applebaum prepares to move to a warmer climate she sets aside the belongings she will leave behind for her relatives, being sure that there is something for each one. When the ungrateful relatives arrive they are disgusted with the items selected for them and each departs, leaving the gift. To Tilda, each object has a special memory of Great-aunt Elsie so she quickly gathers them together and constructs a flying machine. Despite several hazards which almost bring her journey to a halt, Tilda reaches Great-aunt Elsie who has saved the last three cookies for her. (28 pages)

Where it's reviewed:
Horn Book Guide, Spring 1996, page 49
Kirkus Reviews, October 1, 1995, page 1438

Other books by the same author:
Moonfall, 1993

Other books you might like:

Eileen Browne, *No Problem*, 1993
  Mouse receives an unusual construction gift in the mail. When he and his friends finally assemble it correctly, they have transportation to a party.

Marianna Mercer, *Me and My Flying Machine*, 1971
  A young boy finds a barn full of neat things and imagines

the amazing flying machine he will be able to build. Coauthor Mercer Mayer.

Ann Tompert, *Little Fox Goes to the End of the World*, 1984
  Imaginatively, a fox child explains to her mother how she would travel to the end of the world, coping with the dangers she would face and return to her loving mother.

1509

RUTH WHITE

Belle Prater's Boy

(New York: Farrar, Straus, Giroux, 1996)

Subject(s): Cousins; Parent and Child; Identity
Age range(s): Grades 5-8
Major character(s): Woodrow Prater, Cousin, Child; Gypsy, Child, Stepdaughter; Aunt Belle Prater, Mother, Runaway
Time period(s): 1950s
Locale(s): Coal Station, Virginia

Summary: Woodrow has come to live with his grandparents since his mother's disappearance. He makes up stories about all kinds of things that happened on the hillside where he once lived, including what might have happened to his mother. At the same time, Gypsy is having nightmares about her father's death and is unable to talk about it to anyone, until the day the school bully blurts out the truth in class. Gypsy runs home to cut off the long hair which her father dearly loved. The cousins must then face the facts about their families and realize that although the truth is sometimes painful we all have ways of coping with it. (196 pages)

Where it's reviewed:
Horn Book, September/October 1996, page 652
School Library Journal, August 1996, page 158
Booklist, April 15, 1996, page 1434

Awards the book has won:
Newbery Honor Book, 1997
School Library Journal Best Books, 1996

Other books by the same author:
Weeping Willow, 1992 (young adult novel)
Sweet Creek Holler, 1988

Other books you might like:

C.S. Adler, *Daddy's Climbing Tree*, 1995
  Jessica refuses to believe the realities of her father's death.

Sharon Creech, *Walk Two Moons*, 1994
  A girl retraces the steps her mother took when she left home in this Newbery winning title.

Penelope Farmer, *Penelope*, 1996
  Flora is living with her cousin since her father left, but finds herself involved with a former self called Penelope.

Kevin Henkes, *Words of Stone*, 1992
  Blaze deals with feelings for his dead mother as he builds a friendship with the girl next door.

Jan Slepian, *Back to Before*, 1993
  Cousins are transported back in time to when Linny's mother was alive and Hilary's father was still at home.

1510

MARGARET WILD
PAT REYNOLDS, Illustrator

All the Better to See You With!

(Morton Grove, IL: Albert Whitman & Company, 1993)

Subject(s): Family Life; Shyness; Parent and Child
Age range(s): Grades K-2
Major character(s): Kate, Child (nearsighted)
Time period(s): 1990s (1992)
Locale(s): Australia

Summary: With four energetic siblings, quiet Kate's poor vision is not noticed by her parents until the day she "loses" her family on a crowded beach. When the parents question Kate about her vision, they realize she needs to be examined for glasses. Kate's siblings are envious of the new glasses and she is happy to see her family clearly. First published in Australia in 1992. (33 pages)

Where it's reviewed:
Booklist, July 1993, page 1978
Children's Book Review Service, August 1993, page 164
Horn Book Guide, Fall 1993, page 279
Kirkus Reviews, April 1, 1993, page 465
School Library Journal, August 1993, page 154

Other books by the same author:
Going Home, 1994
Our Granny, 1994
The Slumber Party, 1993

Other books you might like:
Libba Moore Gray, *Fenton's Leap*, 1994
   Fenton, the near-sighted frog, sees more clearly after a catfish gives him a pair of glasses found on the bottom of the pond.
Phyllis Reynolds Naylor, *Jennifer Jean, the Cross-Eyed Queen*, 1994
   When Jennifer Jean's beautiful green eyes begin to cross, the doctor prescribes an eye patch and glasses to corect the problem before she enters kindergarten.
Rosemary Wells, *Noisy Nora*, 1973
   Despite Nora's attention-seeking noise, no one in the family really notices her until the day she is so quiet they all fear that she's run away.

1511

MARGARET WILD

Beast

(New York: Scholastic, 1995)

Subject(s): Fear; Bullies
Age range(s): Grades 5-6
Major character(s): Jamie, 11-Year-Old; Brendan, 12-Year-Old, Bully
Time period(s): 1990s
Locale(s): Australia

Summary: Jamie is afraid. He's afraid at night when the beast comes and he's afraid during the day when the school bully Brendan comes after him. Jamie tries to tell his parents about the beast, but no one believes him. It turns out the bully Brendan is an abused child who is jealous of Jamie and his loving family, and Jamie finally realizes that his fear of the beast and his fear of Brendan are one and the same. Getting to know Brendan better helps curtail his fears. (102 pages)

Where it's reviewed:
Voice of Youth Advocates, April 1995, page 29
Book Report, September 1995, page 42
Children's Book Review Service, May 1995, page 120
Library Talk, September 1995, page 36
School Library Journal, February 1995, page 100

Other books by the same author:
But Granny Did!, 1993
Thank You, Santa, 1991

Other books you might like:
Susan Coryell, *Eaglebait*, 1989
   Wardy Spinks is labeled "nerd" when he starts high school, but a year of academic success thwarts his school's bullies.
David Gifaldi, *Toby Scudder, Ultimate Warrior*, 1993
   Trying for the attention he doesn't get at home, Toby acts like a bully in school until he meets his new teacher who has strict rules for class.
Lee Wardlaw, *Seventh Grade Weirdo*, 1992
   With a mother who drives a pink van advertising her mail-order children's book business, Rob is immediately pegged as a weirdo by the school bully.
Gina Willner-Pardo, *Jason and the Losers*, 1995
   As the new kid in school who has to live with his nerdy cousin, Jason retaliates by joining the "cool" kids, picks on his cousin's friends and learns a big lesson.

1512

MARGARET WILD
WAYNE HARRIS, Illustrator

Going Home

(New York: Scholastic, Inc., 1994)

Subject(s): Hospitals; Voyages and Travels; Fantasy
Age range(s): Grades K-1
Major character(s): Hugo, Child, Patient
Time period(s): 1990s (1993)
Locale(s): Australia

Summary: Impatiently awaiting his discharge from the hospital, Hugo discovers that his daydreams about the zoo animals he sees from the window carry him to the distant lands that are home to the animals. Each time, of course, he wears his slippers before getting out of bed to travel to Africa with the elephant, the Amazon jungle with the howler monkey or the Himilayas with the snow leopard. When Hugo is finally able to go home with his family, he whispers the secret of his travels to two other children remaining in the ward. First published in Australia in 1993. (32 pages)

Where it's reviewed:
Booklist, April 1, 1994, page 1463
Horn Book Guide, Fall 1994, page 293
Kirkus Reviews, May 1, 1994, page 638
Publishers Weekly, February 14, 1994, page 88

School Library Journal, April 1994, page 114

Awards the book has won:
ALA Notable Book, 1995

Other books by the same author:
Toby, 1994
The Queen's Holiday, 1992
The Very Best of Friends, 1990

Other books you might like:
Anthony Browne, *Zoo*, 1992
  Surrealistic illustrations suggest an unusual trip to the zoo for Harry and his family.
Liz Rosenberg, *The Carousel*, 1995
  Magically, the animals on a broken carousel come to life and give two sisters an unexpected twilight ride.
Chris Van Allsburg, *Ben's Dream*, 1982
  Dreaming, Ben sees himself passing the great landmarks of the world.

1513
MARGARET WILD
JULIE VIVAS, Illustrator

Our Granny
(New York: Ticknor & Fields Books for Young Readers, 1994)

Subject(s): Grandparents; Individuality; Love
Age range(s): Grades K-1
Major character(s): Granny, Grandmother
Time period(s): 1990s (1993)
Locale(s): Australia

Summary: Grandmothers come in all shapes, sizes and descriptions, but the Granny who lives with the two young children in this story is one-of-a-kind. She has a wobbly bottom, a funny bathing suit, and two grandchildren who adore her. First published in Australia in 1993. (32 pages)

Where it's reviewed:
Booklist, January 15, 1995, page 863
Horn Book, May 1994, page 322
New Advocate, Winter 1995, page 50
Publishers Weekly, January 3, 1994, page 80
School Library Journal, April 1994, page 114

Awards the book has won:
Booklist Editors' Choice, 1994
ALA Notable Book, 1995

Other books by the same author:
But Granny Did!, 1993
My Dearest Dinosaur, 1992
Mr. Nick's Knitting, 1989

Other books you might like:
Nancy Carlson, *A Visit to Grandma's*, 1991
  Tina and her parents are surprised to learn how Grandma has changed since she moved into a Florida condominium!
Kathryn Lasky, *The Gates of the Wind*, 1995
  Desiring to experience a more adventurous life, Gamma Lee moves out of her snug valley home to a windy mountaintop.

Margaret Mahy, *A Busy Day for a Good Grandmother*, 1993
Mrs. Oberon, grandmother extraordinaire, overcomes unusual obstacles to reach and soothe her teething grandson.

1514
MARGARET WILD
DAVID COX, Illustrator

The Slumber Party
(New York: Ticknor & Fields, 1993)

Subject(s): Birthdays; Behavior; Friendship
Age range(s): Grades K-3
Major character(s): Jane, Child
Time period(s): 1990s (1993)
Locale(s): Australia

Summary: To celebrate her birthday, Jane invites 7 friends, her older brother and a cousin to a slumber party. Each guest packs what he or she considers to be the most important items for a sleepover party which leads to diverse, unplanned activities as well as hurt feelings among friends. Eventually, everyone gets some sleep, breakfast is eaten, friendships are mended and all guests go home with plans for their own birthday slumber party. Originally published in Australia in 1992. (32 pages)

Where it's reviewed:
Booklist, October 1, 1993, page 355
Horn Book, September 1993, page 593
Language Arts, September 1994, page 370
Reading Teacher, May 1994, page 648
School Library Journal, October 1993, page 114

Other books by the same author:
Going Home, 1994
My Dearest Dinosaur, 1992
The Very Best of Friends, 1990

Other books you might like:
Stan Berenstain, *The Berenstain Bears and the Slumber Party*, 1990
  Sister and friends have a slumber party that is fun but does not promote sleep.
Amy Hest, *The Pajama Party*, 1992
  Friends Casey, Jenny and Kate enjoy a sleepover complete with cookies and scary stories.
James Howe, *Pinky and Rex Go to Camp*, 1992
  Preparations for their first overnight camping experience test the friendship of two pals.

1515
OSCAR WILDE
JANE RAY, Illustrator

The Happy Prince
(New York: Dutton Children's Books, 1995)

Subject(s): Fairy Tale; Animals/Birds; Death
Age range(s): Grades 2-4
Major character(s): Happy Prince, Royalty; Sparrow, Bird
Time period(s): Indeterminate Past
Locale(s): Fictional Country

Summary: As Sparrow seeks shelter on a beautiful statue, he becomes soaked by tears falling from the statue. The Happy Prince explains that in his lifetime he did not know tears, but since he has been placed on the pedestal to see the misery of others in the city, he weeps. Sparrow resp onds to the Happy Prince's pleas to help others by staying with him even into the winter when the bird freezes to death. By that time, all the statue's gems and gold leaf have been given away to help others so the statue with the broken lead heart is removed and melted. The broken heart and the dead sparrow are thrown on the dust heap. Ray's illustrated adaptation of Wilde's 1888 tale was first published in Great Britain in 1994. (32 pages)

Where it's reviewed:
Booklist, December 15, 1994, page 760
Five Owls, March 1995, page 87
Kirkus Reviews, February 15, 1995, page 235
School Librarian, February 1995, page 23
School Library Journal, March 1995, page 189

Other books by the same author:
The Selfish Giant, 1994
The Devoted Friend, 1986
The Nightingale and the Rose, 1981

Other books you might like:
Leo Lionni, *Frederick*, 1966
    Frederick's winter preparations are not obvious to the other mice until his stories warm their dreary winter days. Caldecott Honor book.
Leo Lionni, *Tico and the Golden Wings*, 1975
    When Tico is born without wings, the bird is given a pair of golden wings which enable him to spread happiness to others.
Jane Yolen, *The Girl Who Loved the Wind*, 1972
    Despite her father's effort to shelter her from all unpleasantness, a Princess hears the voice of the wind tell her about the world beyond the palace walls.

`1516`

NANCY WILLARD
LEO DILLON, Illustrator
DIANE DILLON, Illustrator

The Sorcerer's Apprentice
(New York: The Blue Sky Press, 1993)

Subject(s): Magicians; Magic; Stories in Rhyme
Age range(s): Grades 4-7
Major character(s): Sylvia, Apprentice; Tottibo, Magician
Time period(s): Indeterminate Past
Locale(s): Mount Dragon Eyes, Fictional Country

Summary: Apprenticing herself to Tottibo with the expectation she will learn magic, Sylvia is discouraged to be set the task of sewing clothes for many dragons, gryphons, and other fantastic creatures that inhabit Tottibo's home. As forewarning, Tottibo demonstrates the power of a few drops of magic potion and emphasizes the need for practice lest an incorrectly stated spell produce disastrous results. Feeling overwhelmed by the amount of work and the uncooperative sewing machine, Sylvia sprinkles some magic sand onto the machine which comes to life, sewing everything in sight.

Fortunately, Tottibo awakens and sets things in order again. A concluding note gives factual information about the origins of this cautionary tale. (32 pages)

Where it's reviewed:
Booklist, November 1, 1993, page 529
Five Owls, January 1994, page 60
Horn Book, March 1994, page 193
Publishers Weekly, October 25, 1993, page 59
School Library Journal, January 1994, page 116

Other books by the same author:
Beauty and the Beast, 1992
Pish, Posh, Said Hieronymus Bosch, 1991
The Marzipan Moon, 1981

Other books you might like:
Eric Carle, *Eric Carle's Treasury of Classic Stories for Children*, 1988
    The collection of tales from Aesop, Hans Christian Andersen and the Brothers Grimm is retold and illustrated in Carle's inimitable style.
Marianna Mayer, *The Sorcerer's Apprentice: A Greek Fable*, 1989
    An unskilled apprentice attempts to practice magic in the master's absence with calamitous results.
Neil Philip, *Fairy Tales of Eastern Europe*, 1991
    The collection of 22 traditional tales offers a taste of humor, suspense, adventure and drama.

`1517`

NANCY WILLARD
JERRY PINKNEY, Illustrator

A Starlit Somersault Downhill
(Boston: Little, Brown and Company, 1993)

Subject(s): Animals/Bears; Animals/Rabbits; Stories in Rhyme
Age range(s): Grades K-3
Major character(s): Unnamed Character, Bear; Unnamed Character, Rabbit
Time period(s): 1990s (1993)
Locale(s): United States

Summary: Preparing for winter's hibernation, a brown bear invites a rabbit to share the shelter of his cave. Once inside, rabbit regrets his decision and tries unsuccessfully to awaken his friend. Finally, the lure of the wide-awake world overcomes fears of wolves and owls and the rabbit bounds out of the cave to enjoy the first snow ''in starlit somersaults downhill.'' (34 pages)

Where it's reviewed:
Booklist, October 1, 1993, page 355
Children's Book Review Service, September 1993, page 5
Horn Book Guide, Spring 1994, page 60
Publishers Weekly, July 5, 1993, page 71
School Library Journal, September 1993, page 221

Other books by the same author:
The Alphabet of Angels, 1994
Night Story, 1986
A Visit to William Blake's Inn, 1981

Other books you might like:

Margaret Wise Brown, *Animals in the Snow*, 1995
On a snowy day, five animals are joined by a young boy and girl at play.

Claire Ewart, *One Cold Night*, 1992
The interpretation of hibernation introduces Snow Woman who ensures that the animals are tucked in comfortably for the winter.

Beverly Komoda, *The Winter Day*, 1991
On a snowy day, a group of rabbit children find their fun spoiled by a bully.

Stephen Krensky, *Lionel in the Winter*, 1994
Winter has arrived and Lionel seems to be the only family member to excitedly welcome the cold and snow.

Nancy Elizabeth Wallace, *Snow*, 1995
Memories of a snowy day's activities are shared by an older rabbit as he rocks a younger one.

1518

CAROL ANN WILLIAMS
TATSURO KIUCHI, Illustrator

Tsubu the Little Snail

(New York: Simon & Schuster Books for Young Readers, 1995)

Subject(s): Folk Tales; Poverty; Love
Age range(s): Grades 1-3
Major character(s): Tsubu, Snail; Unnamed Character, Spouse; Water God, Deity
Time period(s): Indeterminate Past
Locale(s): Japan

Summary: When poor, elderly rice farmers pray to the Water God for a child, their answer comes in the form of a little snail or tsubu. The couple are grateful and faithfully care for Tsubu for 20 years. Then, to repay them for his kindness, Tsubu takes the yearly rice tax to the landowner of the rice fields which they work. The landowner offers his daughter in marriage and her unconditional love releases the child of the Water God from his disguise and allows him to be a real person. A concluding author's note cites sources for the folk tale. (24 pages)

Where it's reviewed:
Booklist, June 1995, page 1781
Horn Book Guide, Fall 1995, page 334
Kirkus Reviews, May 1, 1995, page 641

Awards the book has won:
Marion Vannett Ridgway Honor Book, 1996

Other books you might like:

William H. Hooks, *Peach Boy*, 1992
In an easy-to-read adaptation of a Japanese folktale, a childless couple is blessed with a boy born from a peach.

Eric Quayle, *The Shining Princess and Other Japanese Legends*, 1989
Ten Japanese folktales are compiled in an illustrated collection.

Linda Shute, *Momotaro the Peach Boy: A Traditional Japanese Tale*, 1986
A childless couple receives a son who comes from a large peach.

1519

CAROL LYNCH WILLIAMS

Adeline Street

(New York: Delacorte, 1995)

Subject(s): Death; Family Life; Grandparents
Age range(s): Grades 4-6
Major character(s): Leah Orton, 11-Year-Old; Kelly Orton, Sister
Time period(s): 1990s
Locale(s): New Smyrna Beach, Florida

Summary: Continuing the story begun in *Kelly and Me*, Leah struggles to cope with her younger sister's unexpected death from an aneurysm. She and her family find it hard to keep going and even debate whether or not they should celebrate Christmas. Her grandfather finally convinces her that the rest of the world will continue to move on, whether Kelly is with them or not. Gradually a time of acceptance occurs and Leah begins to enjoy her friends and her own life once again in this warm tale of family life. (185 pages)

Where it's reviewed:
Publishers Weekly, January 23, 1995, page 70
Booklist, April 1, 1995, page 1393
Kirkus Reviews, February 15, 1995, page 235
School Library Journal, July 1995, page 82
Library Talk, March 1995, page 53

Other books by the same author:
Kelly and Me, 1993

Other books you might like:

Eve Bunting, *A Sudden Silence*, 1988
Jesse turns his grief into action as he searches for the hit-and-run driver who killed his deaf brother.

Ralph Fletcher, *Fig Pudding*, 1995
Older brother Cliff recounts the year when his gentle brother Brad is killed while riding his bicycle.

Barbara Park, *Mick Harte Was Here*, 1995
Phoebe tells wonderful stories about her brother Mick who would have been alive if he'd worn a bicycle helmet.

Susan Beth Pfeffer, *The Year without Michael*, 1987
Michael leaves home to play softball and never returns. Was he kidnapped? Did he run away?

1520

CAROL LYNCH WILLIAMS

Kelly and Me

(New York: Delacorte Press, 1993)

Subject(s): Sisters; Family Life; Death
Age range(s): Grades 4-6
Major character(s): Leah Orton, 11-Year-Old, Sister; Kelly Orton, 10-Year-Old, Sister; Papa, Grandfather, Widow(er)
Time period(s): 1990s (1993)
Locale(s): New Smyrna Beach, Florida

Summary: After his wife's death, Papa comes to live with Leah and Kelly's family. Sometimes his drinking gets a little out of control, but usually he's a fun, though unconventional, addition to the family. Frequently left in charge of his grandaughters, he teaches them to drive and he allows them to go skinny-dipping at midnight. The shared enjoyment of an exciting summer becomes a cherished memory for Leah when Kelly dies suddenly to conclude the author's first novel. (123 pages)

Where it's reviewed:
Children's Book Review Service, January 1994, page 57
Horn Book Guide, Spring 1994, page 83
Library Talk, May 1994, page 45
Publishers Weekly, September 6, 1993, page 98
School Library Journal, September 1993, page 236

Other books by the same author:
Adeline Street, 1995 (sequel to *Kelly and Me*)

Other books you might like:
Constance C. Greene, *Beat the Turtle Drum*, 1976
    A young girl struggles to adjust to her younger sister's accidental death.
Katherine Paterson, *Bridge to Terabithia*, 1977
    Jess befriends a new girl in his school and then must cope with her accidental death as she tries to reach their favorite meeting spot.
Cynthia Rylant, *Missing May*, 1992
    An award-winning look at the impact of May's death on her husband of many years and their orphaned niece.
Gary Paulsen, *Harris and Me: A Summer Remembered*, 1994
    An unnamed narrator and his cousin Harris wrestle pigs, dodge a feisty barn cat and pee on an electric fence in a memorable summer on a farm.
Richard Peck, *Those Summer Girls I Never Met*, 1988
    Drew and his sister spend the summer aboard a cruise ship with their grandmother, a famous singer from years ago.
Ethel Footman Smothers, *Moriah's Pond*, 1995
    Annie Rye and her sisters have a wonderful time spending the summer with Moriah as they swim and fish and help with chores.

`1521`

KAREN LYNN WILLIAMS
CATHERINE STOCK, Illustrator

Tap-Tap

(New York: Clarion Books, 1994)

Subject(s): Transportation; Mothers and Daughters; Business Enterprises
Age range(s): Grades K-3
Major character(s): Sasifi, 8-Year-Old; Mama, Mother
Time period(s): 1990s (1994)
Locale(s): Haiti

Summary: For the first time Sasifi is allowed to accompany her mother to market to sell their oranges. The walk is long and tiring, but Mama says they do not have the money to ride in a "tap-tap." Impressed with Sasifi's hard work as an orange vendor, Mama rewards her with a new straw hat and some money to make a purchase for herself. After Sasifi views all the treasures of the market, her money is spent riding a "tap-tap" home in style. (34 pages)

Where it's reviewed:
Booklist, April 15, 1994, page 1541

Children's Book Review Service, March 1994, page 91
Five Owls, May 1994, page 106
Horn Book, July 1994, page 445
School Library Journal, June 1994, page 115

Other books by the same author:
Applebaum's Garage, 1993
When Africa Was Home, 1991
Galimoto, 1990

Other books you might like:
Patricia Grossman, *Saturday Market*, 1994
    A Mexican marketplace is busy on Saturday with vendors selling everything from hand-woven rugs to parrots to sandals.
Charles E. Martin, *Summer Business*, 1984
    Heather and her friends earn enough money catering to the needs of the summer visitors to their island to finance a trip to the mainland for the Harvest Fair.
Leyla Torres, *Saturday Sancocho*, 1995
    Maria Lili and Mama Ana visit the market to barter their eggs for the ingredients to make the Saturday Sancocho.

`1522`

SHERLEY ANNE WILLIAMS
CAROLE BYARD, Illustrator

Working Cotton

(San Diego: Harcourt Brace Jovanovich, 1992)

Subject(s): Migrant Labor; Family Life
Age range(s): Grades K-2
Major character(s): Shelan, Child (African American); Daddy, Father, Worker (migrant); Mamma, Mother, Worker (migrant)
Time period(s): 1950s
Locale(s): California

Summary: It's a long day in the cotton fields for Shelan and her family, beginning before dawn and picking until dark. Too young to have her own sack, Shelan piles cotton in the row for her mother, admires the speed with which her father fills his sack and imagines the number of pounds of cotton she will pick when she is older. (32 pages)

Where it's reviewed:
Booklist, September 1, 1992, page 55
Hornbook, January 1993, page 81
Kirkus Reviews, August 15, 1992, page 1068
Publishers Weekly, July 6, 1992, page 55
School Library Journal, November 1992, page 81

Awards the book has won:
Caldecott Honor Book, 1993
Coretta Scott King Honor Book, 1993

Other books you might like:
Linda Jacobs Altman, *Amelia's Road*, 1993
    Amelia wants to change her migratory life and settle in one place long enough for teachers and fellow students to learn her name.
Arthur Dorros, *Radio Man = Don Radio: A Story in English and Spanish*, 1993
    As Diego and his family follow the crops, he searches for his friend, David, succeeding with the help of the ever-

present radio which he carries from cabbage fields to apple orchards.

Michele Benoit Slawson, *Apple Picking Time*, 1994
Too young to pick as rapidly as her parents and grandparents, Anna sets her own goals in the apple orchard and meets them by filling one bin, proudly earning a half-moon punched into her own ticket.

Jane Resh Thomas, *Lights on the River*, 1994
While the adult migrant laborers pick the crops, Teresa serves as babysitter, watching over the picking and the younger children from her shady spot and thinking of her grandmother in Mexico.

1523

VERA B. WILLIAMS, Author/Illustrator

Scooter

(New York: Greenwillow, 1993)

Subject(s): Neighbors and Neighborhoods; Moving, Household; Divorce
Age range(s): Grades 3 and Up
Major character(s): Elana Rose "Lanny" Rosen, Child of Divorced Parents (latch-key child); Petey Timpkin, Child, Neighbor; Mrs. Rachel Greiner, Neighbor, Child-Care Giver
Time period(s): 1990s (1993)
Locale(s): New York, New York

Summary: Not long after Elana Rose Rosen, her Mom, and her scooter move into the Melon Hill Houses, Lanny's scooter hits a bump in the sidewalk and Lanny and Mom have an unexpected cab ride to the Emergency Room. The attraction of stitches, bandages, a scooter, and Lanny's winning personality help Lanny make friends in her new neighborhood. Lanny helps Mrs. Greiner (the Whiner, as Lanny affectionately calls her), to care for Petey, a younger child who does not speak until he is befriended by Lanny. (147 pages)

Where it's reviewed:
Booklist, November 15, 1993, page 626
Five Owls, September 1993, page 14
Horn Book, March 1994, page 202
Publishers' Weekly, October 10, 1993, page 63
School Library Journal, October 1993, page 134

Awards the book has won:
ALA Notable Book, 1994
Booklist Editors' Choice, 1993

Other books by the same author:
More More More Said the Baby: 3 Love Stories, 1990
Cherries and Cherry Pits, 1986
Something Special for Me, 1983
A Chair for My Mother, 1982
Three Days on a River in a Red Canoe, 1981

Other books you might like:
Beverly Cleary, *Ramona Forever*, 1984
Irrepressible Ramona is in third grade now and continuing to approach life in her own way.

Johanna Hurwitz, *Roz and Ozzie*, 1992
Adjusting to a new school is hard enough, but Roz has

Ozzie, her younger neighbor and blabber-mouth uncle, who follows her around making life even tougher.

Johanna Hurwitz, *New Neighbors for Nora*, 1979
Seven-year-old Nora enjoys the excitement of new neighbors moving into her New York City apartment building.

Maud Hart Lovelace, *Betsy-Tacy and Tib*, 1941
The warmth of small town neighbors and the activities of close friends make this work a timeless classic.

Lois Lowry, *Anastasia, Again!*, 1981
Leaving behind friends and a familiar city apartment, Anastasia and her family move to a house in the suburbs.

1524

JEANNE WILLIS
RUTH BROWN, Illustrator

In Search of the Giant

(New York: Dutton Children's Books, 1993)

Subject(s): Giants; Fantasy; Imagination
Age range(s): Grades K-3
Major character(s): Unnamed Character, Child, Sister (older); Unnamed Character, Child, Brother (younger)
Time period(s): 1990s (1993)
Locale(s): England (rural area)

Summary: Along with his older sister, a young boy embarks on a walk in the woods in search of a giant. Is it the power of suggestion or do they really see giants hiding in the gnarled tree trunks and lurking in the twisted vines? When the children hear a loud sound, they imagine it is the roar of a sleeping giant awakening and the walk in the woods comes to an abrupt end. Originally published in Great Britain (28 pages)

Where it's reviewed:
Booklist, July 1994, page 1956
Horn Book, September 1994, page 582
Kirkus Reviews, May 15, 1994, page 709
Publishers Weekly, May 30, 1994, page 56
School Library Journal, August 1994, page 148

Other books by the same author:
Earth Weather, as Explained by Professor Xargle, 1993
Earthlets, as Explained by Professor Xargle, 1989

Other books you might like:
Anthony Browne, *The Tunnel*, 1990
Siblings explore a large tunnel only to find themselves in a very unusual spot at the other end.

Demi, *Liang and the Magic Paintbrush*, 1980
A young Chinese boy's dreams come to life.

John Richardson, *The Hiding Beast*, 1988
Oh no! The beast in Rodney's library book has come to life, or is it only his imagination?

1525

MEREDITH SUE WILLIS

The Secret Super Powers of Marco

(New York: HarperCollins Publishers, 1994)

Subject(s): City Life; Friendship; Self-Confidence
Age range(s): Grades 3-5

Major character(s): Marco, Student, Friend (Tyrone's); Tyrone, Student, Bully; Albert, Uncle (Marco's)
Time period(s): 1990s (1994)
Locale(s): United States (inner city neighborhood)

Summary: When Marco's mother moves the family to a new neighborhood near Uncle Albert's store, Marco must begin a new school with no friends. Lonely, he finds himself getting into trouble and befriending Tyrone, his only classmate without a friend. The relationship proves to be a positive one for both as Marco uses his "power" to see the future for positive change in his behavior. As he accepts Tyrone as his friend while disapproving of some of Tyrone's behavior, the bully begins to be transformed also. (104 pages)

Where it's reviewed:
Booklist, June 1, 1994, page 1823
Horn Book, September 1994, page 592
Kirkus Reviews, June 15, 1994, page 853
Publishers Weekly, June 27, 1994, page 78
School Library Journal, December 1994, page 115

Other books you might like:
Malorie Blackman, *Girl Wonder and the Terrific Twins*, 1993
    With her twin brothers, Maxine tries to be helpful around the house, but usually creates more work not less for poor Mom.
Alice Mead, *Junebug*, 1995
    Rather than celebrate his 10th birthday and face recruitment by a gang or drug dealer, Junebug decides to remain nine and hope that one of his wishes comes true.
Susan Beth Pfeffer, *Sara Kate Saves the World*, 1995
    Sara Kate tries to use her varying superpowers to the best advantage despite the fact that they only work on Tuesdays, Thursdays, and sometimes Saturdays.

1526

PATRICIA WILLIS

Out of the Storm

(New York: Clarion Books, 1995)

Subject(s): Farm Life; Animals/Sheep; Aunts and Uncles
Age range(s): Grades 6-7
Major character(s): Amanda "Mandy" Gates, 12-Year-Old, 7th Grader; Bess Laney, Aunt (Mandy's great-aunt)
Time period(s): 1940s (1946)
Locale(s): Parrish Grove, Ohio

Summary: Mandy's father dies during World War II, her mother loses her job to a returning soldier and her family moves in with her Aunt Bess who lives on a farm. Not only is Mandy unhappy about living with her stern aunt, but she's also displeased that she's responsible for a flock of sheep. During a flood Mandy's faced with a dilemma. If she saves the sheep from drowning, her mother will have the money needed to buy a general store in town, which means Mandy's stuck there forever. On the other hand, how can she possibly let the ewes and lambs drown? (188 pages)

Where it's reviewed:
School Library Journal, April 1995, page 138
Booklist, April 15, 1995, page 1501
Library Talk, September 1995, page 36

Kirkus Reviews, March 15, 1995, page 398
Horn Book Guide, Fall 1995, page 306

Other books you might like:
Joseph Krumgold, *And Now, Miguel*, 1953
    Twelve-year-old Miguel can hardly wait to help the men who pasture their sheep during the summer, as it symbolizes adulthood to him.
Gary Paulsen, *The Haymeadow*, 1992
    This is the summer John grows up as he protects his flock of six thousand sheep against coyotes and bears up in the haymeadow.
Dona Schenker, *Throw a Hungry Loop*, 1990
    Tres Bomer lives up to his grandfather's expectations, as he performs all of his ranch chores on muleback so he can buy a good horse.
Esther Weir, *The Loner*, 1992
    A homeless boy realizes that people do care about him.

1527

GINA WILLNER-PARDO

Jason and the Losers

(New York: Clarion Books, 1995)

Subject(s): Divorce; Cousins; Friendship
Age range(s): Grades 4-6
Major character(s): Jason Gallagher, 5th Grader, Cousin; Everett Taylor, Cousin, 5th Grader
Time period(s): 1990s
Locale(s): United States

Summary: It's not fair! Or so Jason thinks after his parents divorce and he's sent to live with his nerdy cousin Everett. It's not fair that he has to go to a new school where he doesn't know anyone except Everett. To distance himself from his cousin, Jason turns to sports; playing kickball helps him forget everything else for as an athlete he excels. To gain friends, he even joins a group of "cool" kids who heckle and taunt Everett and his friends, who would rather collect stamps and study insects than play ball. Inevitably, Jason learns an important lesson about friendship and bullies, though he still yearns for his former home. (120 pages)

Where it's reviewed:
Booklist, April 15, 1995, page 1501
Publishers Weekly, April 17, 1995, page 60
Children's Book Review Service, Spring 1995, page 144
Library Talk, Spring 1995, page 35
School Library Journal, April 1995, page 138

Other books by the same author:
Hunting Grandma's Treasures, 1994
What I'll Remember When I Am a Grownup, 1994

Other books you might like:
Susan Coryell, *Eaglebait*, 1989
    Wardy Spinks is labeled "nerd" when he starts high school, but a year of academic success thwarts his school's bullies.
David Gifaldi, *Toby Scudder, Ultimate Warrior*, 1993
    Trying for the attention he doesn't get at home, Toby acts like a bully in school until he meets his new teacher who has strict rules for class.

Lee Wardlaw, *Seventh Grade Weirdo*, 1992
With a mother who drives a pink van advertising her mail-order children's book business, Rob is immediately pegged as a weirdo by the school bully.

1528

GINA WILLNER-PARDO
NANCY POYDAR, Illustrator

When Jane-Marie Told My Secret
(1995)

Subject(s): Secrets; Friendship; Jealousy
Age range(s): Grades 2-3
Major character(s): Carolyn Bennett, 3rd Grader, Friend; Jane-Marie, 3rd Grader, Friend
Time period(s): 1990s (1995)
Locale(s): United States

Summary: Carolyn is hurt that her best friend since preschool does not keep the secret entrusted to her. In her anger she refuses to speak to Jane-Marie and makes friends with other girls in the class. Finally, Carolyn is able to accept Jane-Marie's apology and the two seem to be ready to reestablish a friendship that has room for others. (39 pages)

Where it's reviewed:
Booklist, August 1995, page 1950
Bulletin of the Center for Children's Books, October 1995, page 75
Horn Book Guide, Spring 1996, page 58
Kirkus Reviews, July 1, 1995, page 954
School Library Journal, September 1995, page 188

Other books by the same author:
What I'll Remember When I Am a Grownup, 1994

Other books you might like:
Deborah Hautzig, *It's a Secret*, 1988
Although Bert is hurt when Ernie tells his secret to the other Muppets, once their friends know the "secret", they rally to help Bert.
Ann M. Martin, *Karen's Secret*, 1992
When Karen fails to keep Natalie's secret, she must regain her classmates' confidence.
Janice Lee Smith, *The Kid Next Door and Other Headaches: Stories about Adam Joshua*, 1984
Two young boys remain friends despite sharing differing opinions about a variety of topics.

1529

ANNE WILSDORF, Author/Illustrator

Princess
(New York: Greenwillow Books, 1993)

Subject(s): Princes and Princesses; Marriage; Fairy Tale
Age range(s): Grades K-3
Major character(s): Princess, Shepherd; Prince Leopold, Royalty
Time period(s): Indeterminate Past
Locale(s): Fictional Country

Summary: In a translation of a French tale originally published in 1991, Prince Leopold, armed with his mother's list of genuine princesses, sets off to find the girl of his dreams. While none of the princesses on the list suit him, he does meet a young woman named Princess who is just right and so Prince Leopold brings her home to meet the family. When Princess passes the pea under the mattress test, everyone is happy and mother is none the wiser as to just why Princess had such a poor night's sleep. (33 pages)

Where it's reviewed:
Booklist, August 1993, page 2067
Horn Book Guide, Fall 1993, page 279
Kirkus Reviews, June 1, 1993, page 730
Publishers Weekly, May 17, 1993, page 80
School Library Journal, June 1993, page 92

Other books by the same author:
Philomene, 1992

Other books you might like:
Stephanie Calmenson, *The Principal's New Clothes*, 1989
In a twist on the classic Hans Christian Andersen tale of the emperor who likes new clothes, a vain school principal is duped by two tailors.
Ann Campbell, *Once Upon a Princess and a Pea*, 1993
Another version of the classic fairy tale in which the princess must prove her credibility.
Babette Cole, *Princess Smartypants*, 1986
To avoid the unappealing royal suitors, Princess Smartypants concocts a series of tests which all but a multi-talented prince fail.
Sucie Stevenson, *The Princess and the Pea*, 1992
A retelling of the classic Hans Christian Andersen tale which is faithful to the original classic of a princess who is so sensitive she can feel a pea through many mattresses.

1530

GINA WILSON
DAVID PARKINS, Illustrator

Prowlpuss
(Cambridge, MA: Candlewick Press, 1995)

Subject(s): Animals/Cats; Stories in Rhyme
Age range(s): Grades K-3
Major character(s): Prowlpuss, Cat; Nellie Smith, Animal Lover
Time period(s): Indeterminate
Locale(s): England

Summary: Nightly, a rough, tough tomcat with one eye and one ear prowls the alleys until he spots the white cat of his desires and then he serenades her until driven off by the annoyed residents nearby. Unsuccessful, Prowlpuss turns for home, clambering in the window to be warmly greeted by Nellie Smith who sees him as a sweet and cozy pet. (24 pages)

Where it's reviewed:
Children's Book Review Service, July 1995, page 151
Five Owls, May 1995, page 101
Library Talk, September 1995, page 31
School Librarian, May 1995, page 60
School Library Journal, March 1995, page 195

Other books you might like:

Mirabel Cecil, *Lottie's Cats*, 1990

When the favorite of Lottie's seven cats vanishes, she is distraught, but hopeful and Halloween night Friday returns.

Garrison Keillor, *Cat, You Better Come Home*, 1995

Disgruntled Puff leaves home seeking a more gourmet diet; disillusioned, fat and helpless she finally returns to be welcomed by a young boy who's missed her.

Gary Soto, *Chato's Kitchen*, 1995

The coolest cat in East L.A., Chato invites his new neighbors to a welcoming dinner party.

1531

NANCY HOPE WILSON

Becoming Felix

(New York: Farrar Straus Giroux, 1996)

Subject(s): Farm Life; Music; Friendship
Age range(s): Grades 4-8
Major character(s): Felix "JJ" Jacquith II, 12-Year-Old, Musician; Steven Lerner, 12-Year-Old, Musician; Ms. Byron, Teacher
Time period(s): 1990s
Locale(s): West Farley, Massachusetts

Summary: The friendship of JJ and Steven centers on their mutual interest in music. This year, however, it is strained because both have family problems to deal with—JJ is worried about having to sell-off parts of the family farm and Steven is involved in the synagogue. Neither can communicate his concerns even though they see each other at rehearsals for the jazz band. Finally everything reaches a climax when the cows are sold, including JJ's favorite. The boys are successful with their jazz trio and finally take the time to be honest with each other. (184 pages)

Where it's reviewed:
School Library Journal, October 1996, page 128
Booklist, October 15, 1996, page 425

Other books by the same author:
The Reason for Janey, 1994
Bringing Nettie Back, 1992

Other books you might like:

Patricia MacLachlan, *What You Know First*, 1995

When the family farm is sold the daughter wonders what she should tell her little brother so that he can remember the farm.

Susan Sharpe, *Chicken Bucks*, 1992

Mark dreams of raising a prize-winning steer on his family's Minnesota farm.

June Rae Wood, *When Pigs Fly*, 1995

Buddy's parents are having trouble keeping the farm going and have to move, making it harder for Buddy to see her friends.

Jane Breskin Zalben, *Unfinished Dreams*, 1996

Jason risks being called a nerd in order to concentrate on his music.

1532

NANCY HOPE WILSON

The Reason for Janey

(New York: Macmillan, 1994)

Subject(s): Mentally Handicapped; Divorce; Family Life
Age range(s): Grades 5-6
Major character(s): Philura Higley "Philly" Mason, 6th Grader; Danny Stapleton, 6th Grader; Theresa Jane "Janey" Nicoletto, Handicapped
Time period(s): 1990s
Locale(s): Hampton, Massachusetts (Philly's home); Cambridge, Massachusetts (Philly's father's apartment)

Summary: Philly's parents have been divorced for about three years and just recently her mother arranges for Janey, a once-institutionalized mentally handicapped adult, to live with them. Though her father doesn't approve of this stranger living with them, Philly marvels at how much better Janey fits into her family than her father ever did. As Philly gets to know Janey better and sees how kind and loving she is, she tries to reunite Janey with her father, which turns into a major disaster; even Philly's own father is angry with her. Through Janey, Philly discovers the "reason for Janey," which helps her appreciate class brain, Danny Stapleton. (160 pages)

Where it's reviewed:
School Library Journal, May 1994, page 118
Booklist, April 15, 1994, page 1536
Horn Book, July 1994, page 456
Center for Children's Books. Bulletin, June 1994, page 339
Publishers Weekly, March 28, 1994, page 97

Other books by the same author:
Bringing Nettie Back, 1992

Other books you might like:

Rachel Anderson, *The War Orphan*, 1986

Simon's family adopts a Vietnamese orphan, not realizing that he's mentally handicapped.

Vera Cleaver, *Me Too*, 1973

Though Linda's sister is handicapped, Linda is convinced she can make her normal.

Marlene Fanta Shyer, *Welcome Home, Jellybean*, 1978

The return home of an older sister who is mentally handicapped is described by her younger brother.

June Rae Wood, *The Man Who Loved Clowns*, 1992

After her parents die, Delrita learns not to feel ashamed about her kind, loving Uncle Punky who has Down Syndrome.

1533

BARBARA WINSLOW
TERI SLOAT, Illustrator

Dance on a Sealskin

(Seattle: Alaska Northwest Books, 1995)

Subject(s): Eskimos; Coming of Age; Dancing
Age range(s): Grades 2-4
Major character(s): Annie, Child (Yupik Eskimo), Dancer
Time period(s): 1970s

Locale(s): Alaska (Yupik village along the Yukon River)

Summary: With her family, Annie hurries to attend the potlatch in the village kashim where she is to perform a ceremonial dance to signify her coming of age. Although her grandmother who helped her prepare the dance has died, Annie's memory of her is a constant presence during the evening. At the conclusion of Annie's dance (and the author's first book for children), her family gives gifts to all the village in memory of the deceased grandmother and as an expression of pride in Annie's dance. (32 pages)

Where it's reviewed:
Bloomsbury Review, November 1995, page 35
Booklist, August 1995, page 1958
Horn Book Guide, Fall 1995, page 287
Kirkus Reviews, June 15, 1995, page 866
School Library Journal, December 1995, page 110

Other books you might like:
Jeanne Bushey, *A Sled Dog for Moshi*, 1994
   After saving herself and an inexperienced friend from an unexpected storm, Moshi proves that she is ready to care for one of the newborn sled-dogs.
Deborah Davis, *The Secret of the Seal*, 1989
   Kyo faces a difficult decision which requires chosing between loyalty to his family and friendship with a seal.
Margaret Shaw-MacKinnon, *Tiktala*, 1996
   After Tiktala is changed into a seal by the spirit guide she learns to understand seals and the threat of humans to them.

1534

SUSAN WINTER, Author/Illustrator

A Baby Just Like Me

(London: Dorling Kindersley, 1994)

Subject(s): Babies; Sisters; Friendship
Age range(s): Grades K-2
Major character(s): Martha, Child, Sister (older); Sam, Friend (Martha's); Unnamed Character, Child (infant)
Time period(s): 1990s (1994)
Locale(s): England

Summary: Expecting her baby sister to be just like her—able to play with her and laugh at the puppet shows she and Sam perform—leaves Martha very disappointed. However, as Martha's mother promises, the baby grows and is gradually able to interact more with Martha and Sam so that, in time, both feel fortunate to have her around. (32 pages)

Where it's reviewed:
Children's Book Review Service, November 1994, page 28
Horn Book Guide, Spring 1995, page 61
Publishers Weekly, September 12, 1994, page 90
School Librarian, February 1995, page 20
School Library Journal, January 1995, page 95

Other books by the same author:
My Shadow, 1994
I Can, 1993
Me Too, 1993

Other books you might like:
Jennifer Armstrong, *That Terrible Baby*, 1994
   Mark and Eleanor have plans for the terrible baby at their house, but change them when they decide that perhaps the baby is not as bad as they first thought.
Jane Cutler, *Darcy and Gran Don't Like Babies*, 1993
   While Gran and Darcy agree that they don't really like Darcy's smelly, demanding baby brother, both enjoy him more as he grows.
John Hassett, *We Got My Brother at the Zoo*, 1993
   Mary Margaret has some unusual stories to tell about the origins of the new baby at her house. Co-author Ann Hassett.
Russell Hoban, *A Baby Sister for Frances*, 1964
   Frances is not sure about the new addition to the family, but her patient, understanding parents help her adjust to the arrival of a baby sister.
Holly Keller, *Geraldine's Baby Brother*, 1994
   It takes some time for Geraldine to adjust to her noisy baby brother and all the attention he receives.

1535

SUSAN WINTER, Author/Illustrator

My Shadow

(New York: A Doubleday Book for Young Readers, 1994)

Subject(s): Play; Imagination; Animals
Age range(s): Grades K-1
Major character(s): Rosie, Child
Time period(s): 1990s (1994)
Locale(s): England

Summary: Rosie enjoys playing with her shadow whether it's big or small. She likes the way her shadow follows and imitates movements, but she does not like her shadow to hide from her. One day when Rosie wakes up her shadow is nowhere to be found. She asks all the farm animals, but no one can help her. Finally, the rooster crows, the sun pops out and Rosie's shadow returns. (32 pages)

Where it's reviewed:
Booklist, October 15, 1994, page 440
Horn Book Guide, Spring 1995, page 61
School Library Journal, January 1995, page 95

Other books by the same author:
A Baby Just Like Me, 1994
I Can, 1993
Me Too, 1993

Other books you might like:
Michael Bartalos, *Shadowville*, 1995
   Shadowville is the place where all the shadows go after the sun sets to enjoy some degree of independence before the sunrise sends them back to work.
Ann Whitford Paul, *Shadows Are About*, 1992
   On sunny days shadows can be found everywhere until they disappear with the sun at nightfall.
Ann Tompert, *Nothing Sticks Like a Shadow*, 1984
   To win a bet, Rabbit enlists the help of his animal friends in getting rid of his shadow.

1536

ELIZABETH WINTHROP
MARY MORGAN, Illustrator

Asleep in a Heap
(New York: Holiday House, 1993)

Subject(s): Bedtime; Family Life; Play
Age range(s): Grades K-2
Major character(s): Julia, Child (youngest in the family)
Time period(s): 1990s (1993)
Locale(s): United States

Summary: Everyone in the family encourages a very busy little girl to get ready for bed. When Julia finally gets into a bubble bath, she sings a song to her father as he reclines on the floor, lulling him to sleep. Then her mother, sister, the family dog and all the cats come in to check on the progress of the bath and Julia sings each of them to sleep too. With her bath complete, Julia climbs out, dries herself, puts on her nightgown and lies down on the top of the heap and, finally, falls asleep. (32 pages)

Where it's reviewed:
Booklist, November 15, 1993, page 634
Children's Book Review Service, November 1993, page 29
Horn Book Guide, Spring 1994, page 60
Kirkus Reviews, November 1, 1993, page 1400
School Library Journal, January 1994, page 101

Other books by the same author:
I'm the Boss, 1994
Bear and Mrs. Duck, 1989
Maggie and the Monster, 1987

Other books you might like:
Russell Hoban, *Bedtime for Frances*, 1960
Frances is a master at avoiding sleep, but her patient parents have a response for every problem.
Jill Murphy, *A Quiet Night In*, 1994
A bedtime story has the desired soporific effect—unfortunately on the parents and not the kids—leaving the children to put themselves to bed.
Laurence Pringle, *Octopus Hug*, 1993
Active pre-bedtime play with Dad encourages the children to settle into bed before Mom comes home.

1537

ELIZABETH WINTHROP

The Battle for the Castle
(New York: Holiday House, 1993)

Subject(s): Castles; Space and Time; Knights and Knighthood
Age range(s): Grades 4-6
Major character(s): William Edward Lawrence, 12-Year-Old, Gymnast; Jason Stubbs Hardy, Sports Figure (bicyclist); Sir Simon of Hargrave, Royalty
Time period(s): 1990s; 14th century
Locale(s): United States; Mythical Place (a miniature castle)

Summary: William's friend Jason seems, all of a sudden, much older; he's a foot taller, interested in girls and proves his daring by jumping trains. William doesn't feel brave enough to try that stunt, but suddenly has an opportunity to prove his bravery in another way. His former housekeeper mails him a magic token for his birthday, just like the one in *The Castle in the Attic*, which miniaturizes him until he can fit into the model of a castle and sends him back to medieval times. He and Jason transport themselves to the Middle Ages as a scourge of rats menaces the castle. They team up with Sir Simon to rebuff the attack and William discovers he has lots of courage. (211 pages)

Where it's reviewed:
School Library Journal, May 1993, page 111
Booklist, September 1, 1993, page 63
Voice of Youth Advocates, June 1993, page 106
Horn Book, July 1993, page 461
New Advocate, Summer 1993, page 229

Other books by the same author:
The Castle in the Attic, 1985

Other books you might like:
Lynne Reid Banks, *The Indian in the Cupboard*, 1981
Ormi's magic cupboard contains a plastic Indian that has the ability to come to life.
John Bellairs, *The Trolley to Yesterday*, 1989
Johnny Dixon and Professor Childermass board the time travel trolley and wind up in Constantinople in 1453 just before it is invaded by the Turks.
Brian Jacques, *Redwall*, 1986
The evil rat Cluny destroys the peace of ancient Redwall Abbey as he and his hordes of villians attempt to seize control.

1538

WILLIAM WISE
VICTORIA CHESS, Illustrator

Ten Sly Piranhas: A Counting Story in Reverse (A Tale of Wickedness and Worse!)
(New York: Dial Books for Young Readers, 1993)

Subject(s): Animals/Piranhas; Mathematics; Stories in Rhyme
Age range(s): Grades K-3
Major character(s): Unnamed Character, Piranha; Unnamed Character, Crocodile
Time period(s): 1990s (1993)
Locale(s): South America

Summary: One by one, each of ten piranhas, who are not as sly as the title suggests, quietly vanish until there are none. The rhyming text and clever illustrations convey a fun-filled look at the concept of survival of the fittest. (32 pages)

Where it's reviewed:
Booklist, May 1, 1993, page 1597
Hornbook, July 1993, page 452
Kirkus Reviews, May 15, 1993, page 669
Publishers Weekly, May 31, 1993, page 54
School Library Journal, October 1993, page 114

Awards the book has won:
Booklist Editors' Choice, 1993

Other books you might like:

Nan Bodsworth, *A Nice Walk in the Jungle*, 1990
Mrs. Jellaby's class has a most unusual field trip; one by one they are consumed by a boa constrictor.

Roger Chouinard, *One Magic Box*, 1989
Not your typical counting book, this rhyming tale has a surprise ending.

Lois Ehlert, *Fish Eyes: A Book You Can Count On*, 1990
Fish in vibrant colors and imaginative shapes swim through their numbered paces in this rhyming story.

Stan Mack, *Ten Bears in My Bed: A Goodnight Countdown*, 1974
This familiar countdown story starts with ten bears in the bed who, one by one, roll over.

Ellen Stoll Walsh, *Mouse Count*, 1991
Ten sleepy mice do not realize that a hungry snake is nearby.

1539

G. CLIFTON WISLER

Caleb's Choice

(New York: Lodestar, 1996)

Subject(s): Underground Railroad; Slavery
Age range(s): Grades 4-6
Major character(s): Caleb Dulaney, 14-Year-Old; Micah Holland, 15-Year-Old; Lavinia Dulaney, Innkeeper, Grandmother
Time period(s): 1850s
Locale(s): Texas (north of Dallas)

Summary: Caleb's family has lost all its money and he is not welcome at his aunt's house in Houston, so he goes to live with his grandmother. There he meets Micah, who teaches him the work of the hotel as well as plenty of local superstitions. While the boys are cutting wood one day, a storm hits and Caleb is washed away in the river. He is saved by a fugitive slave and finds himself involved with the local Underground Railroad and must decide whether to help save two slaves. (154 pages)

Where it's reviewed:
Bulletin of the Center for Children's Books, November 1996, page 37
School Library Journal, August 1996, page 148
Booklist, August 1996, page 1896

Other books by the same author:
Mr. Lincoln's Drummer, 1995
Jericho's Journey, 1993
Red Cap, 1991

Other books you might like:
Patricia Beatty, *Jayhawker*, 1991
A young, teenage boy becomes involved in freeing slaves in Missouri.

Patricia Beatty, *Who Comes with Cannons?*, 1992
Truth Hopkins and her Quaker family face problems during the Civil War but are able to help slaves escape.

LouAnn Gaeddert, *Breaking Free*, 1994
Richard, an orphan, lives with his uncle but leaves when he is unable to accept his pro-slavery views.

Patricia Hermes, *On Winter's Wind*, 1995
Eleven-year-old Genevieve must decide whether to turn in a slave for the bounty.

Katherine Paterson, *Jip: His Story*, 1996
A young boy discovers that he is an escaped slave and must run away to safety in Canada with the help of his friends.

1540

G. CLIFTON WISLER

Mr. Lincoln's Drummer

(New York: Dutton/Lodestar, 1994)

Subject(s): Civil War; Historical
Age range(s): Grades 4-6
Major character(s): Willie Johnston, Military Personnel (drummer boy)
Time period(s): 1860s
Locale(s): Saint Johnsbury, Vermont; Virginia

Summary: Though Willie is too young to enlist, he follows his dad into the Union Army as a drummer boy. Though in different companies, father and son are both part of the Third Vermont Regiment which eventually marches south through Virginia. Filled with descriptions of the discomforts of camp life and battles, the Civil War becomes real to the reader as Willie stirs the camp in the morning and sounds the retreat in battle. Based on historical records, Willie eventually meets President Lincoln who awards him the Congressional Medal of Honor. (131 pages)

Where it's reviewed:
Booklist, January 15, 1995, page 931
Center for Children's Books. Bulletin, January 1995, page 180
Horn Book Guide, Spring 1995, page 86
Library Talk, May 1995, page 45
New Advocate, Summer 1995, page 207

Other books by the same author:
Jericho's Journey, 1993
Red Cap, 1991
Piper's Ferry, 1990
The Raid, 1985

Other books you might like:
Patricia Beatty, *Charley Skedaddle*, 1987
Charley joins the Union Army, but "skedaddles" during his first battle.

Harold Keith, *Rifles for Watie*, 1957
A young Union soldier offers his view of the fighting in the West during the Civil War. Newbery winner.

Stephen Meader, *Muddy Road to Glory*, 1963
Ben is a member of the Twentieth Maine regiment during the Civil War.

1541

G. CLIFTON WISLER

This New Land

(New York: Walker and Co., 1987)

Series: Walker's American History
Subject(s): Pilgrims and Pilgrimages
Age range(s): Grades 5-7
Major character(s): Richard Woodley, 12-Year-Old
Time period(s): 17th century
Locale(s): Leyden, Netherlands; At Sea (aboard the *Mayflower*); Plymouth, Massachusetts

Summary: Fleeing England to escape religious persecution, the Woodley family first settles in the Netherlands where they live in poverty compared to their life in England. When they have a chance to sail to the New World, they board the *Mayflower* for that historic crossing. Young Richard is a Pilgrim and must obey all the rules of his religion. This is difficult because some of the *Mayflower* passengers are not traveling for the same religious freedom, but rather to find new adventure or because they were asked to accompany the Pilgrims. Through Richard's journal, the reader begins to understand what it was like to make the voyage and live in barren Plymouth where half the colonists die the first winter. (124 pages)

Other books by the same author:
Mr. Lincoln's Drummer, 1994
Jericho's Journey, 1993
Red Cap, 1991

Other books you might like:
Patricia Clapp, *Constance: A Story of Early Plymouth*, 1968
    Constance is a young Pilgrim who sails to America on board the *Mayflower* and records her adventures in a diary.
Evelyn Hammett, *I, Priscilla*, 1960
    Just fifteen years after the first settlers arrive in Massachusetts, young Priscilla travels from there to Connecticut amidst winter snows and Indians.
Scott O'Dell, *The Serpent Never Sleeps: A Novel of Jamestown and Pocahontas*, 1987
    Living in Jamestown, a young girl from England has the chance to meet Pocahontas.

1542

DAVID WISNIEWSKI, Author/Illustrator

The Wave of the Sea-Wolf

(New York: Clarion Books, 1994)

Subject(s): Fairy Tale; Folk Tales; Indians of North America
Age range(s): Grades 3-6
Major character(s): Kchokeen, Indian (Tlingit), Royalty; Gonakadet, the Sea Wolf, Deity
Time period(s): Indeterminate Past
Locale(s): Pacific Northwest

Summary: Blessed with the ability to predict the passing of Gonakadet, creator of huge, destructive waves, Kchokeen protects her people from a foreign ship greedy for fur. Angry when the tribe will not supply more furs, the trader's ship cannons destroy her people's village. Kchokeen senses that a great wave is coming and so with a war party in a canoe she tricks the foreign ship into the path of the wave and the ship is destroyed. Kchokeen's canoe is carried on the crest of the wave until it pierces the trunk of a cedar and so it remains to this day high above the forest floor. A concluding author's note gives background information about the native peoples of the Pacific Northwest. (32 pages)

Where it's reviewed:
Five Owls, January 1995, page 59
Library Talk, January 1995, page 38
New Advocate, Spring 1995, page 125
Publishers Weekly, September 19, 1994, page 71
School Library Journal, October 1994, page 129

Awards the book has won:
New York Times Best Illustrated Book, 1995

Other books by the same author:
Golem, 1996 (Caldecott Medal, 1997)
Sundiata: Lion King of Mali, 1992 (ALA Notable Book)
The Warrior and the Wise Man, 1989

Other books you might like:
Rafe Martin, *The Boy Who Lived with the Seals*, 1993
    A legend of the Chinook people tells of a boy who lives with the seals, but each year presents his tribe with a beautifully carved canoe and paddle.
Gerald McDermott, *Raven: A Trickster Tale from the Pacific Northwest*, 1993
    A Caldecott Medal Honor book explains how shape-changing Raven steals the sun from the Sky Chief in order to bring light to all people.
Michelle Renner, *The Girl Who Swam with the Fish: An Athabascan Legend*, 1995
    Intrigued by the salmon her family catch to preserve for the winter, a young girl slips into the river and lives with the salmon for several years.

1543

SUSAN WOJCIECHOWSKI
P.J. LYNCH, Illustrator

The Christmas Miracle of Jonathan Toomey

(Cambridge, MA: Candlewick Press, 1995)

Subject(s): Artists and Art; Christmas; Friendship
Age range(s): Grades 1-4
Major character(s): Jonathan Toomey, Artisan (wood carver), Widow(er); Mrs. McDowell, Widow(er); Thomas McDowell, 7-Year-Old
Time period(s): Indeterminate Past
Locale(s): New England

Summary: A grumpy woodcarver is mocked by the village children who are ignorant of the reason for Jonathan Toomey's gloomy disposition. When the widow McDowell and her son move to the village, they find that their hand-carved nativity scene has been lost and they seek the services of the best woodcarver in the valley to replace it. Jonathan Toomey agrees to take the job and even tolerates visits from Thomas who aspires to be a woodcarver. Gently Thomas corrects the appearance of the carvings so they will be exactly as he remembers and Jonathan Toomey, with each visit, grows more receptive to Thomas' presence and comments. By the time the nativity set is complete on Christmas morning, a miracle has been worked in the wounded heart of the carver. (40 pages)

Where it's reviewed:
Booklist, September 15, 1995, page 173
Five Owls, November 1995, page 44
Publishers Weekly, September 18, 1995, page 98
Quill & Quire, September 1995, page 76
School Library Journal, October 1995, page 43

Awards the book has won:
ALA Notable Book, 1996
Christopher Award, 1996

Other books by the same author:
The Best Halloween of All, 1992

Other books you might like:
Sharon Chmielarz, *Down at Angel's*, 1994
    Two sisters befriend an elderly, reclusive carpenter, give him a special homemade Christmas gift and receive one of his beautiful tables.
Wendy Matthews, *The Gift of a Traveler*, 1995
    Christine's great-grandmother tells a childhood story of being lost in the snowy woods on Christmas Eve and rescued by a gypsy traveler with a wolf.
Gillian McClure, *The Christmas Donkey*, 1993
    Joseph and Mary begin their trip to Bethlem with an ornery donkey, but as they travel the difficult beast undergoes a transformation.

1544

SUSAN WOJCIECHOWSKI
SUSANNA NATTI, Illustrator

Don't Call Me Beanhead!

(Cambridge, MA: Candlewick Press, 1994)

Subject(s): Family Life; Conduct of Life; Humor
Age range(s): Grades 2-4
Major character(s): Beatrice Lorraine "Beany" Sherwin-Hendricks, Sister (younger), Student; Carol Ann, Friend, Classmate
Time period(s): 1990s (1994)
Locale(s): United States

Summary: Worrywart Beany frets her way through five events wondering how to explain the F she receives on a test while watching an ant or how to get the money to buy artificial fingernails just like Carol Ann's. Even losing a tooth creates a worrisome problem for Beany when she drops her tooth down the bathroom drain. For each calamity, bossy friend Carol Ann has lots of advice, none of it helpful, until finally Beany learns to stand up for herself. (75 pages)

Where it's reviewed:
Booklist, October 15, 1994, page 429
Horn Book Guide, Spring 1995, page 71
Kirkus Reviews, October 15, 1994, page 1418
School Library Journal, October 1994, page 106

Other books by the same author:
Beany (Not Beanhead) and the Magic Crystal, 1997

Other books you might like:
Judy Blume, *Freckle Juice*, 1971
    Gullible Andrew's desire for freckles causes him to be duped by Sharon and her secret formula, but he finds a way to make his own freckles.
Beverly Cleary, *The Ramona Series*, 1952-1984
    Irrepressible Ramona and her family endure school problems, unemployment, and sibling squabbles with love and a sense of humor.
Barbara Park, *Junie B. Jones and a Little Monkey Business*, 1993
    With typical kindergartener logic, Junie B. hears grandma's exclamation that her new baby brother is a cute little monkey and reports that as fact during show-and-tell.

1545

ASHLEY WOLFF, Author/Illustrator

Stella and Roy

(New York: Dutton Children's Books, 1993)

Subject(s): Brothers and Sisters; Bicycles and Bicycling
Age range(s): Grades K-1
Major character(s): Stella, Child (competitive); Roy, Child
Time period(s): 1990s (1993)
Locale(s): San Francisco, California (Golden Gate Park)

Summary: Confident in the speed of her 3-wheeled big wheel, Stella challenges her younger brother Roy, astride a 4-wheeled coaster, to a race around the park lake. Sure enough, Stella is soon far ahead, but while she climbs a tree, Roy rolls by. The race proceeds with Stella enjoying one distraction after another along the way, while Roy patiently rolls and rolls to the finish line. (32 pages)

Where it's reviewed:
Booklist, June 1, 1993, page 1862
Emergency Librarian, March 1994, page 45
Horn Book, September 1993, page 594
Publishers Weekly, June 14, 1993, page 68
School Library Journal, September 1993, page 221

Awards the book has won:
School Library Journal Best Books, 1993

Other books by the same author:
Come with Me, 1990
A Year of Birds, 1988
A Year of Beasts, 1986
Only the Cat Saw, 1985

Other books you might like:
Kristine Church, *My Brother John*, 1991
    Though it seems as if big brothers can do everything, a little girl finds something she can do better.
Janet Stevens, *The Tortoise and the Hare: An Aesop Fable*, 1984
    In this well-known fable, perseverance pays off for the determined tortoise in his race with the over-confident hare.
Linda W. Tyler, *My Brother Oscar Thinks He Knows It All*, 1991

Oscar thinks he's better than his little sister at everything, but little sister has her own ideas.

1546

FERIDA WOLFF
KATIE KELLER, Illustrator

Seven Loaves of Bread

(New York: Tambourine Books, 1993)

Subject(s): Farm Life; Bread; Cooks and Cookery
Age range(s): Grades K-3
Major character(s): Milly, Cook, Sister (ill); Rose, Sister (lazy), Farmer
Time period(s): Indeterminate Past
Locale(s): United States

Summary: When Milly takes to bed sick and is unable to bake the seven loaves of bread she makes daily to distribute to the animals and neighbors, Rose "who only works as hard as she has to" takes over and creates additional work for herself by her shortsightedness when she decides that 7 loaves a day is too much work. By the time Milly is well, Rose has learned her lesson and seven loaves of bread are ready for distribution to animals and neighbors. (32 pages)

Where it's reviewed:
Booklist, September 15, 1993, page 162
Five Owls, January 1994, page 58
Horn Book Guide, Spring 1994, page 61
Publishers Weekly, July 12, 1993, page 78
School Library Journal, November 1993, page 96

Other books by the same author:
The Emperor's Garden, 1994
On Halloween Night, 1994 (Co-author Dolores Kozielski)
The Woodcutter's Coat, 1992

Other books you might like:
Carol Ryrie Brink, *Goody O'Grumpity*, 1937
    A newly illustrated version published in 1994 of the familiar poem presents a baker so renowned for her spice cake that the fragrance attracts the village children.
Heather Forest, *The Baker's Dozen: A Colonial American Tale*, 1988
    When a baker refuses to give the traditional 13 cookies in a baker's dozen, his baking suffers under the curse of a disgruntled customer.
Janet Stevens, *Tops and Bottoms*, 1995
    Industrious Hare is a gardening partner to slumbering Bear in a contemporary interpretation of a trickster tale.

1547

PATRICIA RAE WOLFF
KIMBERLY BULCKEN ROOT, Illustrator

The Toll-Bridge Troll

(San Diego: Harcourt Brace & Company, 1995)

Subject(s): Schools; Problem Solving; Resourcefulness
Age range(s): Grades K-2
Major character(s): Trigg, Student; Unnamed Character, Mythical Creature (troll)

Time period(s): 1990s (1995)
Locale(s): United States

Summary: The author's first book begins as Trigg leaves the house the morning of the first day of school. To reach his school, Trigg must cross a small footbridge where a troll awaits demanding a penny toll. Not wanting to pay a daily fee in order to go to school, Trigg suggests a riddle contest. The troll likes the idea, but can't answer the riddle so Trigg crosses for free. Trigg outsmarts the troll for three days until the troll's disgusted mother sends her son to school with Trigg so he can "get smart" too. (24 pages)

Where it's reviewed:
Booklist, June 1995, page 1789
Five Owls, March 1995, page 86
Horn Book, September 1995, page 594
Publishers Weekly, April 17, 1995, page 57
School Library Journal, June 1995, page 98

Awards the book has won:
ALA Notable Book, 1996

Other books you might like:
Rebecca Emberley, *Three Cool Kids*, 1995
    Three urban goats outwit a hungry, sewer-dwelling rat who tries to keep them from crossing the street to reach a grass-filled, empty lot.
Janet Stevens, *The Three Billy Goats Gruff*, 1987
    An illustrated retelling marches the billy goat brothers across the troll's bridge.
Vivian Vande Velde, *Tales from the Brothers Grimm and the Sisters Weird*, 1995
    Thirteen classic stories are rewritten with a new twist in a collection of "fractured" fairy tales.

1548

AUDREY WOOD, Author/Illustrator

Rude Giants

(San Diego: Harcourt Brace Jovanovich, Publishers, 1993)

Subject(s): Behavior; Neighbors and Neighborhoods; Giants
Age range(s): Grades K-2
Major character(s): Beatrix, Maiden; Gerda, Cow
Time period(s): Indeterminate Past
Locale(s): Fictional Country

Summary: Life is peaceful for Beatrix the butter maid and her best friend Gerda until 2 rude giants enter the happy village and move into the castle on the hill. When a hungry giant takes Gerda home for supper, Beatrix intervenes to save her friend. Her efforts lead to a clean castle and mannerly giants who, while no longer slovenly, are still hungry. To satisfy that problem, Beatrix invites all the villagers to the castle for a giant pot-luck dinner. When the giants' baby turns out to be rude, the parents know just the person to call for help. (32 pages)

Where it's reviewed:
Booklist, March 1, 1993, page 1227
Horn Book Guide, Fall 1993, page 280
Kirkus Reviews, February 1, 1993, page 156
Publishers Weekly, March 1, 1993, page 55
School Library Journal, May 1993, page 92

Other books by the same author:
The Napping House Wakes Up, 1994
Silly Sally, 1992
Weird Parents, 1990

Other books you might like:
John F. Green, *Alice and the Birthday Giant*, 1989
Alice's birthday wish for something big is asleep in her bed and she must figure out where to hide a giant before her party.
Alison Lurie, *Clever Gretchen and Other Forgotten Folktales*, 1980
A collection of 14 stories features clever heroines who take an active role in settling the problems which confront them.
Fiona Moodie, *The Boy and the Giants*, 1993
With assistance from birds and animals, kind Thomas rescues his beloved Kate from the giant's castle.

1549

JUNE RAE WOOD

A Share of Freedom

(New York: G. P. Putnam's Sons, 1994)

Subject(s): Family Problems; Alcoholism; Brothers and Sisters
Age range(s): Grades 5-8
Major character(s): Freedom Jo Avery, 13-Year-Old, Child of an Alcoholic; Jackie Ramsdale, 8-Year-Old, Stepbrother; Mary Margaret Ramsdale, Single Mother, Alcoholic
Time period(s): 1990s (1994)
Locale(s): Gabriel, Missouri

Summary: Freedom thinks her name results from her birth on the Fourth of July. Her persistence to learn more about the identity of her father as well as the secrets of her alcoholic mother's past, and her determination to keep her family intact during her mother's hospitalization lead to some surprising revelations. (255 pages)

Where it's reviewed:
Booklist, September 1, 1994, page 36
Publishers Weekly, September 26, 1994, page 71
School Library Journal, October 1994, page 129

Awards the book has won:
School Library Journal Best Books, 1994

Other books by the same author:
The Man Who Loved Clowns, 1992

Other books you might like:
Paula Fox, *Monkey Island*, 1991
Coping with the difficulties of homelessness in New York City presents challenges to daily life for eleven-year-old Clay.
Patricia MacLachlan, *Journey*, 1991
When Journey and his sister, Cat, are left by their mother at the Grandparents' farm, Journey tries to reconstruct his past with old family photos in hopes of building a future.
Anna Myers, *Rosie's Tiger*, 1994
Sixth-grader Rosie, still grieving her mother's death four years earlier, now must confront the jealousy she feels

when her beloved older brother returns from service in Korea with a wife and child.
Stephanie Tolan, *Who's There?*, 1994
Grieving over the accidental death of their parents, Drew and Evan move in with a long lost aunt at the family home, Rose Hill, only to find themselves in the midst of family ghosts.

1550

ELVIRA WOODRUFF
BETH PECK, Illustrator

Dear Levi: Letters from the Overland Trail

(New York: Alfred A. Knopf, 1994)

Subject(s): Frontier and Pioneer Life; Voyages and Travels; Letters
Age range(s): Grades 4-6
Major character(s): Austin Ives, 12-Year-Old, Orphan; Levi Ives, 9-Year-Old, Orphan
Time period(s): 1850s (1851)
Locale(s): United States (Overland Trail)

Summary: After his father dies on the family's claim in Oregon Territory, Austin is determined to see the only legacy his father left his two boys. Leaving Levi with friends, he joins a family needing assistance on the trail and begins a 6-month journey from Pennsylvania to Oregon. Along the way, he writes to his younger brother telling him of the hardships of the journey, the friends he makes along the way, and the land through which they travel. (119 pages)

Where it's reviewed:
Booklist, July 1994, page 1949
Bulletin of the Center for Children's Books, September 1994, page 28
Horn Book, September 1994, page 592
Library Talk, September 1994, page 45
School Library Journal, August 1994, page 158

Awards the book has won:
International Reading Association Teachers' Choice, 1995

Other books by the same author:
The Magnificent Mummy Maker, 1994
Dear Napoleon, I Know You're Dead, But..., 1992
Awfully Short for the Fourth Grade, 1989

Other books you might like:
Kathryn Lasky, *Beyond the Divide*, 1983
In 1849, Meribah Simon travels with her father by wagon train from Missouri to California.
Eloise Jarvis McGraw, *Moccasin Trail*, 1952
Six years after Indians rescue him from a bear attack, Jim receives a letter from his brother asking him to travel to Oregon to claim the family's homestead.
George Rippey Stewart, *To California by Covered Wagon*, 1954
A non-fiction account story of the first wagono cross America to California in 1844 is based on the diary of 17-year-old Moses Schallenberger who made the trip.

1551

ELVIRA WOODRUFF

JOEL ISKOWITZ, Illustrator

Ghosts Don't Get Goosebumps

(New York: Holiday House, 1993)

Subject(s): Mystery and Detective Stories; Mutism; Friendship

Age range(s): Grades 3-6

Major character(s): Angela "Angel Always" Swope, 11-Year-Old, Friend (Jenna's); Jenna "Jenna Pearl" Connerton, 11-Year-Old, Sister (Nelson's); Nelson Connerton, 5-Year-Old (mute), Brother (Jenna's)

Time period(s): 1990s (1993)

Locale(s): Three Springs, West Virginia (Freedonia Farm)

Summary: Reluctantly vacationing at her aunt and uncle's farm in West Virginia for a month, Jenna meets Angel Always, a fast-talking local girl who considers herself destined to be a TV "soaps" star. Angel decides that, if the girls give Nelson a shock , he will speak again, but before the girls can follow through with the plan, Nelson disappears. Jenna finds him just as they are separated by a fire which endangers Jenna's life. Nelson speaks for the first time in order to lead the rescuers to her. (167 pages)

Where it's reviewed:

Booklist, November 15, 1993, page 626
Horn Book Guide, Spring 1994, page 84
Library Talk, March 1994, page 50
School Library Journal, October 1993, page 136

Other books by the same author:

The Secret Funeral of Slim Jim the Snake, 1993
Dear Napoleon, I Know You're Dead, But. . ., 1992
The Summer I Shrank My Grandmother, 1990

Other books you might like:

C.S. Adler, *One Sister Too Many*, 1989
    Twelve-year-old Case is the only family member suspicious of her baby sister's new sitter. Her suspicions solve the mystery of Meredith's disappearance.

Ann M. Martin, *Eleven Kids, One Summer*, 1991
    The large Rosso family enjoys a summer of mystery and adventure in a rented beach house.

Katherine Paterson, *Flip-Flop Girl*, 1994
    After her father's death Vinnie's family moves, her little brother stops talking and she struggles to deal with her emotions and make friends in her new home.

1552

ELVIRA WOODRUFF

The Magnificent Mummy Maker

(New York: Scholastic, Inc., 1994)

Subject(s): Stepfamilies; Brothers and Sisters; Mummies

Age range(s): Grades 4-6

Major character(s): Andy Manetti, 5th Grader, Stepbrother (Jason's); Jason, 10-Year-Old, Stepbrother (Andy's)

Time period(s): 1990s (1994)

Locale(s): United States

Summary: Overshadowed by his gifted, boastful stepbrother, Andy is an underachiever until the study of Egypt takes his class on a field trip to a museum. There, while viewing a mummy, Andy feels himself filled with mysterious power which gives him artistic talent and seems to grant wishes. Jealous of Andy's class project, Jason dubs him the "Magificent Mummy Maker" and Andy begins to understand how Jason feels when he hears Andy call him "Mr. Gifted." (132 pages)

Where it's reviewed:

Booklist, January 15, 1994, page 931
Children's Book Review Service, June 1994, page 132
Horn Book, September 1994, page 593
Library Talk, March 1994, page 50
School Library Journal, April 1994, page 132

Other books by the same author:

Dear Levi: Letters from the Overland Trail, 1994
George Washington's Socks, 1993
Dear Napoleon, I Know You're Dead, But. . ., 1992
The Summer I Shrank My Grandmother, 1990

Other books you might like:

Susan Beth Pfeffer, *Sara Kate Saves the World*, 1995
    Sara Kate tries to use her varying superpowers to the best advantage despite the fact that they only work on Tuesdays, Thursdays, and sometimes Saturdays.

Zilpha Keatley Snyder, *The Egypt Game*, 1967
    While playing at their recreation of an Egyptian ritual, two children's safety is threatened when a murderer is reported in the neighborhood.

Meredith Sue Willis, *The Secret Super Powers of Marco*, 1994
    Marco's belief that he has super powers helps him to survive a friendship with a hyperactive bully and life in the inner city.

1553

CONNIE NORDHIELM WOOLDRIDGE

WILL HILLENBRAND, Illustrator

Wicked Jack

(New York: Holiday House, 1995)

Subject(s): Folk Tales; Behavior; Conduct of Life

Age range(s): Grades K-3

Major character(s): Jack, Blacksmith; Saint Peter, Angel; Devil, Demon

Time period(s): Indeterminate Past

Locale(s): Virginia (Great Dismal Swamp); North Carolina (Great Dismal Swamp)

Summary: In her first picture book, Wooldridge adapts a tale of a man so ornery and mean that, when he dies, Saint Peter refuses him admittance at the Pearly Gates. Jack then makes the trek down, down, down to the alternative resting spot, but the Devil, remembering the way he was treated by Jack during his lifetime, also refuses to admit the wicked man, leaving Jack to eternally wander the Great Dismal Swamp carrying the Devil's piece of coal. (32 pages)

Where it's reviewed:

Booklist, November 1, 1995, page 475

Horn Book Guide, Spring 1996, page 97
Kirkus Reviews, September 1, 1995, page 1290
Publishers Weekly, October 2, 1995, page 73
School Library Journal, December 1995, page 101

Awards the book has won:
School Library Journal Best Books, 1995

Other books you might like:
Richard Chase, *The Jack Tales*, 1943
    A collection of folk tales from the American South features a variety of Jack stories.
Phyllis Root, *Aunt Nancy and Old Man Trouble*, 1996
    Aunt Nancy turns her troubles into triumphs, confounding Old Man Trouble and sending him on his way to bother someone less clever.
Jan Wahl, *Little Eight John*, 1992
    A mean little boy who defies his mother finds himself confronting Old Raw Head Bloody Bones.

1554

MARY WORMELL, Author/Illustrator

Hilda Hen's Happy Birthday
(San Diego: Harcourt Brace & Company, 1995)

Subject(s): Animals/Chickens; Birthdays; Farm Life
Age range(s): Grades K-1
Major character(s): Hilda Hen, Chicken
Time period(s): 1990s (1995)
Locale(s): Scotland

Summary: Hilda Hen awakens on the morning of her birthday, so assured that others are as absorbed with the day as she is that, everywhere she goes, she sees gifts. Contentedly, Hilda helps herself to the horse's oats, the gardener's apples, the farmer's wife's newly planted flower bed, and the farmer's tea and cookies. Hilda politely thanks each unwitting provider and merrily clucks her way to the next item until she reaches the one, true birthday celebration—a tray of crumbs to share with the rooster and the other chickens.

Where it's reviewed:
Booklist, April 1, 1995, page 1429
Books for Keeps, May 1995, page 29
Horn Book, May 1995, page 331
Publishers Weekly, February 6, 1995, page 84
School Library Journal, April 1995, page 120

Other books by the same author:
Hilda Hen's Scary Night, 1996
Hilda Hen's Search, 1994

Other books you might like:
Roger Duvoisin, *Petunia the Silly Goose Stories*, 1985
    The five stories of a confident, but rather silly goose are gathered in one volume.
Syd Hoff, *Happy Birthday, Henrietta!*, 1983
    Henrietta's friends plan a wonderful surprise party in the barn in honor of her birthday.
Janet Morgan Stoeke, *A Hat for Minerva Louise*, 1994
    When Minerva Louise decides she needs a hat for her walk in the snow, she simply tries items she finds lying around until she locates something suitable.

1555

MARY WORMELL, Author/Illustrator

Hilda Hen's Search
(San Diego: Harcourt Brace & Company, 1994)

Subject(s): Animals/Chickens; Farm Life; Mothers
Age range(s): Grades K-1
Major character(s): Hilda Hen, Chicken
Time period(s): 1990s (1994)
Locale(s): Scotland

Summary: When Hilda Hen is ready to find a spot to lay her eggs, she heads first to the hen house but finds it full. Undaunted, Hilda continues to search, trying and rejecting a cozy basket attached to the handlebars of a bike, a laundry basket filled with comfortable clothes, and the horses' feeding trough. Finally she finds the perfect quiet, comfy, peaceful spot—a dollhouse—and makes her nest. (32 pages)

Where it's reviewed:
Booklist, December 1, 1994, page 688
Kirkus Reviews, October 15, 1994, page 1418
Library Talk, January 1995, page 34
Publishers Weekly, October 31, 1994, page 60
School Library Journal, November 1994, page 93

Other books by the same author:
Hilda Hen's Scary Night, 1996
Hilda Hen's Happy Birthday, 1995

Other books you might like:
Pat Hutchins, *Rosie's Walk*, 1968
    Unaware that she is being followed, Rosie enjoys her walk around the farmyard, unintentionally leading a fox from one accident to another.
Graham Oakley, *Hetty and Harriet*, 1981
    Two chickens with different viewpoints search for the perfect home.
Janet Morgan Stoeke, *Minerva Louise*, 1988
    A confident and very independent hen explores the house with the red curtains.

1556

BETTY REN WRIGHT

The Ghost Comes Calling
(New York: Scholastic, Inc., 1994)

Subject(s): Ghosts; Haunted Houses; Fathers and Sons
Age range(s): Grades 3-4
Major character(s): Chad Weldon, 9-Year-Old; Jeannie Nichols, 11-Year-Old, Neighbor; Tim Tapper, Spirit
Time period(s): 1990s (1994)
Locale(s): Bristol; Perch Lake

Summary: When Chad's father spends the family savings to buy an old, rundown log cabin at Perch Lake, he acquires more than the cabin and surrounding land. Jeannie tries to warn Chad, he's also bought a ghost. The stories Jeannie tells Chad about Tim Tapper prove to be true when his spirit haunts the cabin. In order to enjoy the new vacation home, Chad needs Jeannie's help to solve the mystery of Tim Tapper and put his ghost to rest. (83 pages)

Where it's reviewed:
Booklist, February 15, 1994, page 1083
Bulletin of the Center for Children's Books, March 1994, page 239
Horn Book, September 1994, page 594
Locus, June 1994, page 60
School Library Journal, April 1994, page 132

Other books by the same author:
A Ghost in the House, 1991
Christina's Ghost, 1985
Ghost Beneath Our Feet, 1984

Other books you might like:
Mary Hoffman, *The Four-Legged Ghosts*, 1993
    The excitement of a first pet soon wanes for Carrie and Alex when they discover theirs has the magical power to call up the ghosts of previous animal residents of their old home.
Ellen Leroe, *Ghost Dog*, 1993
    The ghost of a dog in his grandpa's new home creates problems for Artie until he decides to use the dog to help solve a mystery.
Suzanne Weyn, *My Brother, the Ghost*, 1994
    Too late, Sara and Michael discover by opening a long-locked wardrobe they unleash an evil spirit who assumes Michael's appearance.

1557

BETTY REN WRIGHT
KAREN RITZ, Illustrator

The Ghost of Popcorn Hill
(New York: Holiday House, 1993)

Subject(s): Animals/Dogs; Ghosts; Brothers
Age range(s): Grades 3-5
Major character(s): Martin Tracy, Child, Brother (3 years older than Peter); Peter Tracy, Child, Brother; Tom Buffle, Spirit (ghost)
Time period(s): 1990s (1993)
Locale(s): Popcorn Hill

Summary: Martin and Peter are happy when their family moves to an old cabin on the top of Popcorn Hill, until the nightly laughter reveals a lonely ghost and former resident of the cabin looking for companionship. Although their parents allow them to have a small dog, they really want a big one like the sheepdog they see near their home. When the sheepdog turns out to be another lonely ghost, they pair him with Tom Buffle so that both will go away. (81 pages)

Where it's reviewed:
Booklist, February 15, 1993, page 1061
Horn Book, July 1993, page 463
Kirkus Reviews, May 1, 1993, page 606
Publishers Weekly, May 3, 1993, page 309
School Library Journal, May 1993, page 111

Other books by the same author:
Out of the Dark, 1995
The Ghost Comes Calling, 1994
The Secret Window, 1982

Other books you might like:
Susan Cooper, *The Boggart*, 1993
    A family inherits a shape-changing trickster along with a Scottish castle and the children must find a way to send him home.
Mary Hoffman, *The Four-Legged Ghosts*, 1993
    Alex and Carrie find their new pet mouse has unexpected talents as he fills their home with animals that only they can see.
Ellen Leroe, *Ghost Dog*, 1993
    The ghost of a dog in his grandpa's new home creates problems for Artie until he decides to use the dog to help solve a mystery.

1558

BETTY REN WRIGHT
ELLEN EAGLE, Illustrator

The Ghost Witch
(New York: Holiday House, 1993)

Subject(s): Ghosts; Moving, Household; Halloween
Age range(s): Grades 3-5
Major character(s): Jenny Warren, Child; Unnamed Character, Witch, Spirit (ghost); Mrs. Warren, Mother, Widow(er)
Time period(s): 1990s (1993)
Locale(s): United States (Willoughby Lane)

Summary: Jenny does not share her mother's enthusiasm for the old house they've inherited from an elderly friend. Each time Jenny goes to feed the cat, she sees horrible monsters which scare her and the cat. Mrs. Warren thinks her daughter is being imaginative so Jenny takes it upon herself to confront the witch of Willowby Lane and convince her to move into an empty home being used as a haunted house to benefit a local charity. By conquering her own fears, Jenny helps the ghost witch feel useful, aids a charity and rids her new home of the mischievous grandmother of the previous owner. (103 pages)

Where it's reviewed:
Booklist, January 15, 1994, page 931
Horn Book Guide, Spring 1994, page 84
Library Talk, March 1994, page 49
Reading Teacher, September 1994, page 71
School Library Journal, December 1993, page 118

Other books by the same author:
The Ghost Comes Calling, 1994
The Scariest Night, 1991
Christina's Ghost, 1985

Other books you might like:
Avi, *Something Upstairs: A Tale of Ghosts*, 1988
    When Kenny moves into an old home in Rhode Island, he finds it haunted by the ghost of a murdered slave.
Alvin Schwartz, *Scary Stories 3: More Tales to Chill Your Bones*, 1991
    Ghosts and monsters populate the collection of folklore tales retold by the author and illustrated by Gammell.
Ann Turner, *Rosemary's Witch*, 1991
    Finding a 150-year-old witch in the old farmhouse they

hope to make their home creates a dilemma for Rosemary and her family.

1559

BETTY REN WRIGHT

The Ghosts of Mercy Manor

(New York: Scholastic, 1993)

Subject(s): Ghosts; Orphans; Mystery and Detective Stories
Age range(s): Grades 6-7
Major character(s): Gwen Maxwell, Orphan; Tessie Mercy, Child; Jason Mercy, 16-Year-Old
Time period(s): 1990s
Locale(s): Winfield, Wisconsin

Summary: When her elderly great-aunt dies, Gwen is left an orphan and sent to live with a foster family whose home is called Mercy Manor. Though Gwen is happy with young Tessie and teen Jason, she doesn't understand why their parents are so upset when she first tells them of seeing a ghost. Each night the ghost of a young girl beckons Gwen down the back stairs to the cellar. After Mr. Mercy tells Gwen she'll have to leave if she continues to talk about ghosts, she manages to convince Jason to help her. When he also sees the ghost, he helps her solve the mystery which has so unnerved Mrs. Mercy that she's never finished unpacking the family belongings in the basement. (172 pages)

Where it's reviewed:
Booklist, September 15, 1993, page 152
Publishers Weekly, August 2, 1993, page 82
School Library Journal, September 1993, page 236
Voice of Youth Advocates, December 1993, page 304
Horn Book Guide, Spring 1994, page 84

Awards the book has won:
Utah Children's Book Award Winner, 1995
Oklahoma, Sequoyah Children's Book Award, 1996

Other books by the same author:
Out of the Dark, 1995
The Ghost of Popcorn Hill, 1993
The Ghost of Ernie P., 1990
Christina's Ghost, 1985
The Dollhouse Murders, 1983

Other books you might like:
Lynn Cullen, *The Backyard Ghost*, 1993
    As Charlie and Eleanor try to find relics to preserve the past represented by Joseph, their Civil War era ghost, the finding of his bugle allows them to actually meet the ghost.
Lois Duncan, *Stranger with My Face*, 1981
    Laurie's astral twin, Lia, attempts to enter her body so that she can become Laurie and assume her place in the family.
Elizabeth Levy, *The Drowned*, 1995
    Lily sets up a ghost tour of Atlantic City, including the site of a teenage boy's drowning, but doesn't realize she's to be the next drowning victim.

1560

BETTY REN WRIGHT

Haunted Summer

(New York: Scholastic, 1996)

Subject(s): Ghosts; Babysitters; Music
Age range(s): Grades 3-5
Major character(s): Abby Tolson, 9-Year-Old; David Tolson, 11-Year-Old; Hannah Gray, 18-Year-Old, Babysitter
Time period(s): 1990s
Locale(s): United States

Summary: Abby and David do not want a baby-sitter, but the family insists, so Hannah comes out from town to spend the week with the Tolsons. Abby receives a music box from her aunt and notices that it can play by itself, whether it is wound or not. Both Hannah and Abby feel that a ghost is involved in some strange events, but David feels that the girls are being silly. Then one night he follows them when they go to bury the box in the grave of the girl to whom it originally belonged and sees the spirit for himself. (99 pages)

Where it's reviewed:
Booklist, April 1, 1996, page 1367
School Library Journal, May 1996, page 118
Horn Book, July/August 1996, page 466

Other books by the same author:
The Ghosts of Popcorn Hill, 1993
A Ghost in the House, 1991
Christina's Ghost, 1985

Other books you might like:
Elaine Marie Alphin, *The Ghost Cadet*, 1991
    Benjy is surprised to meet a ghost from the Civil War when he goes to visit his grandmother.
Antonia Barber, *The Ghosts*, 1989
    Two girls meet ghosts from another country in their garden.
John Bellairs, *The Ghost in the Mirror*, 1993
    Rose and a white witch are transported back in time to face an adventure in 1828.
Ruth Calif, *The Over-the-Hill Ghost*, 1988
    Elmer, the ghost, brings interest to Jamie's life in the country.
Pam Conrad, *Stonewords: A Ghost Story*, 1990
    Zoe moves in with her grandparents and finds that there is already a ghost living there.
Mary Hoffman, *The Four-Legged Ghosts*, 1993
    Alex and his sister have a pet mouse which can call back all kinds of animals in ghostly form.

1561

BETTY REN WRIGHT
JACQUELINE ROGERS, Illustrator

Nothing but Trouble

(New York: Holiday House, 1995)

Subject(s): Aunts and Uncles; Animals/Dogs; Country Life
Age range(s): Grades 3-5

Major character(s): Vannie Kirkland, Child; Bert Kirkland, Aged Person, Aunt (Vannie's great aunt); Muffy, Dog (Vannie's pet)
Time period(s): 1990s (1995)
Locale(s): Ohio (farm)

Summary: On the way to California to find work, Vannie's parents leave her at Aunt Bert's farm for the summer, promising to send for her when they have jobs and a place to live. Elderly Aunt Bert seems a cantankerous soul who doesn't have much use for a small, yappy dog like Muffy. In a short time, they learn to live together and Vannie helps solve the mystery of vandalism to Aunt Bert's farm house, car and barn. (119 pages)

Where it's reviewed:
Booklist, February 15, 1995, page 1085
Bulletin of the Center for Children's Books, June 1995, page 364
Horn Book Guide, Fall 1995, page 306
School Library Journal, May 1995, page 110

Other books by the same author:
The Midnight Mystery, 1991
Rosie and the Dance of the Dinosaurs, 1989
The Summer of Mrs. MacGregor, 1986

Other books you might like:
John R. Erickson, *The Case of the Kidnapped Collie*, 1996
  Hank the Cowdog solves the mystery at the ranch that includes a theft and a kidnapping.
Margaret Mahy, *Clancy's Cabin*, 1995
  The Harriman children's reluctance to join a camping trip to their father's favorite childhood spot changes to enthusiasm when unusual events enliven the outing.
Gertrude Chandler Warner, *The Guide Dog Mystery*, 1996
  An entry in the Boxcar Children series finds the Alden children helping at a guide dog training school and curious about unusual interest in one particular dog.

1562

COURTNI C. WRIGHT
GERSHOM GRIFFITH, Illustrator

Journey to Freedom: A Story of the Underground Railroad
(New York: Holiday House, 1994)

Subject(s): Underground Railroad; Slavery; African Americans
Age range(s): Grades 1-3
Major character(s): Joshua, 8-Year-Old, Slave; Nathan, 10-Year-Old, Slave; Harriet Tubman, Conductor
Time period(s): 1850s
Locale(s): United States; Canada

Summary: Joshua and Nathan realize how fortunate they are to be travelling to freedom with their parents and others under the guidance of Harriet Tubman. Sleeping by day in safe houses and walking each night, it takes more than three weeks for them to travel from the slavery of a plantation in Kentucky to the safety of Canada. (32 pages)

Where it's reviewed:
Booklist, November 15, 1994, page 605
Horn Book Guide, Spring 1995, page 61
Kirkus Reviews, October 15, 1994, page 1419
Library Talk, September 1995, page 43
School Library Journal, January 1995, page 95

Other books by the same author:
Wagon Train: A Family Goes West in 1865, 1995
Jumping the Broom, 1994

Other books you might like:
Deborah Hopkinson, *Sweet Clara and the Freedom Quilt*, 1993
  Clara designs a quilt which is actually a road map to freedom from slavery for her and other slaves who use it after her escape.
Alan Schroeder, *Minty: A Story of Young Harriet Tubman*, 1996
  An award-winning biographical picture-book introduces eight-year-old Minty, a rebellious slave who dreams of freedom and plots her escape.
Jeanette Winter, *Follow the Drinking Gourd*, 1988
  A song about the Big Dipper is taught to slaves as a way of giving them the information necessary to escape and find a safe route to the North.

1563

COURTNI C. WRIGHT
GERSHOM GRIFFITH, Illustrator

Jumping the Broom
(New York: Holiday House, 1994)

Subject(s): Weddings; Slavery; African Americans
Age range(s): Grades K-3
Major character(s): Lettie, 8-Year-Old, Slave; Tillie, Slave, Bride; Will, Slave, Bridegroom
Time period(s): Indeterminate Past
Locale(s): South

Summary: A slave's life is one of work and hardship, but Sunday is reserved for rest and merriment. For weeks, Lettie and others in the slave quarters have been preparing for the marriage of Lettie's sister Tillie to her beloved Will. Now, the Sunday of the wedding is here, the preparations are complete and all join together for the ceremony of "jumping the broom" and the daylong celebration. (30 pages)

Where it's reviewed:
Bulletin of the Center for Children's Books, July 1994, page 378
Children's Book Review Service, March 1994, page 94
Kirkus Reviews, February 1, 1994, page 152
Publishers Weekly, January 3, 1994, page 81
School Library Journal, April 1994, page 115

Other books by the same author:
Wagon Train: A Family Goes West in 1865, 1995
Journey to Freedom: A Story of the Underground Railroad, 1994

Other books you might like:
William H. Hooks, *The Ballad of Belle Dorcas*, 1990
  When free-born Belle Dorcas falls in love with enslaved

Joshua, she calls on a conjure woman to work the magic that will allow Joshua to stay with her.

Deborah Hopkinson, *Sweet Clara and the Freedom Quilt*, 1993

As a seamstress in the Big House, Clara has access to scraps of cloth and the information needed to turn the scraps into a road map to freedom for escaping slaves.

Hugh Lewin, *Jafta and the Wedding*, 1981

Jafta tells of the week-long festival in his South African village to celebrate his sister's marriage.

1564

KIT WRIGHT
PETER BAILEY, Illustrator

Tigerella

(New York: Scholastic Inc., 1993)

Subject(s): Behavior; Animals/Tigers; Stories in Rhyme
Age range(s): Grades K-3
Major character(s): Ella, Child; Tigerella, Tiger
Time period(s): 1990s (1994)
Locale(s): England

Summary: Polite, cooperative Ella changes into prowling Tigerella at the stroke of midnight. Leaping into the night sky, she bites a piece from the moon, batters the stars and wrestles the Milky Way bear. When she awakens the next morning, quiet Ella blames the family cat for the scratch on her cheek and no one guesses what she's really been doing all night. (32 pages)

Where it's reviewed:
Booklist, September 15, 1994, page 146
Junior Bookshelf, December 1993, page 228
Kirkus Reviews, August 15, 1994, page 1141
Publishers Weekly, July 25, 1994, page 54
School Library Journal, December 1994, page 90

Other books you might like:
Tim Chadwick, *Cabbage Moon*, 1994

Curious Albert discovers that the moon is a giant cabbage that must be nibbled by rabbits such as himself in order to attain the correct size and shape.

Rex Harley, *Mary's Tiger*, 1990

While Mary sleeps, the picture which she has drawn becomes a stuffed tiger.

Katherine Potter, *Spike*, 1994

Quiet Jackson's extroverted, but obnoxious alter ego "Spike" springs forth from a drawing, challenging Jackson to take the initiative in order to control its behavior.

Phyllis Root, *Moon Tiger*, 1985

Jessica Ellen imagines a visit from a tiger who can take her away from her troublesome little brother.

1565

SHARON DENNIS WYETH
RAUL COLON, Illustrator

Always My Dad

(New York: Alfred A. Knopf, 1995)

Subject(s): Fathers; Grandparents; Summer
Age range(s): Grades K-3
Major character(s): Unnamed Character, Child of Divorced Parents; Daddy, Father
Time period(s): Indeterminate Past
Locale(s): United States (rural area)

Summary: A girl and her three younger brothers are spending their summer vacation on their paternal grandparents' farm. Unexpectedly, their father arrives one evening to spend several days with his children, teaching them games from his childhood and drinking sodas at the general store. The children treasure this time and are saddened when Daddy announces he will be leaving the next day to begin a new job. His restless, transient life style prevents him from being a parental caretaker, but he assures his children of his love and reminds them that he will always be their dad. (32 pages)

Where it's reviewed:
Booklist, February 15, 1995, page 1095
Children's Book Review Service, February 1995, page 79
Five Owls, May 1995, page 111
Kirkus Reviews, February 15, 1995, page 236
School Library Journal, December 1995, page 93

Other books you might like:
Mary Hoffman, *Boundless Grace*, 1995

In a sequel to *Amazing Grace* Nana accompanys Grace as she travels to Africa to visit the father she has not seen since she was very young.

Rachel Isadora, *At the Crossroads*, 1991

South African children gather at the crossroads to greet their fathers whose work in the mines keeps them away from home for months at a time.

Dolores Johnson, *Your Dad Was Just Like You*, 1993

When Grandfather shares a boyhood story about Peter's father, Peter begins to have a better understanding of his father.

1566

SHARON DENNIS WYETH
CURTIS E. JAMES, Illustrator

Vampire Bugs: Stories Conjured from the Past

(New York: Delacorte Press, 1995)

Subject(s): Supernatural; African Americans; Short Stories
Age range(s): Grades 4-6
Time period(s): Indeterminate Past
Locale(s): United States

Summary: Whether adaptations of folk tales or fiction inspired by folklore, the six short stories appeal to the desire to be scared. Voodoo queens, ghosts and life during slavery are among the topics covered in a collection of stories. (80 pages)

Where it's reviewed:
Booklist, January 1, 1995, page 823
Bulletin of the Center for Children's Books, April 1995, page 289
Horn Book Guide, Fall 1995, page 375
School Library Journal, March 1995, page 207

Other books by the same author:
The World of Daughter McGuire, 1994
Palmer at Your Service, 1990
Boys Wanted, 1989

Other books you might like:
Virginia Hamilton, *The People Could Fly: American Black Folk Tales*, 1985
   The collection includes traditional trickster tales, tales of the supernatural and stories of slaves' hopes for freedom.
Mary E. Lyons, *Raw Head, Bloody Bones: African-American Tales of the Supernatural*, 1991
   Lyons selects fifteen stories representing folklore from the United States and the Caribbean.
Jane Yolen, *Vampires: A Collection of Original Stories*, 1991
   With co-editor Martin H. Greenberg, Yolen gathers thirteen original stories related to vampires.

1567

SHARON DENNIS WYETH

The World of Daughter McGuire

(New York: Delacorte, 1994)

Subject(s): Interracial Marriage; Prejudice; Identity
Age range(s): Grades 4-6
Major character(s): Daughter McGuire, 11-Year-Old; Connie Boggs, 11-Year-Old; Anna Otake, 11-Year-Old
Time period(s): 1990s
Locale(s): Washington, District of Columbia

Summary: A new neighborhood and a new school are enough for any one person to handle, but all of a sudden Daughter has even more to handle. Daughter, her mother and her two younger brothers move near her grandparents after her father takes an extended leave to write a book. Daughter makes friends with classmates Connie and Anna but then is given a family heritage project. For someone like Daughter who has grandparents who are African American, Italian, Irish-Catholic and Russian-Jewish, that's quite an assignment. When a member of the Avengers gang calls her a ''zebra,'' Daughter sets out to track down her heritage, especially the woman for whom she's named. (167 pages)

Where it's reviewed:
Publishers Weekly, January 24, 1994, page 56
Voice of Youth Advocates, April 1994, page 32
Booklist, May 1, 1994, page 1602
School Library Journal, April 1994, page 132
New York Times Book Review, October 9, 1994, page 26

Other books by the same author:
Boy Crazy, 1991
Heartbreak Guy, 1991
Rocky Romance, 1988

Other books you might like:
Virginia Hamilton, *Arilla Sundown*, 1976
   Part Indian and part black creates an unusual family situation for 12-year-old Arilla.
Joan Kane Nichols, *All but the Right Folks*, 1985
   A young black boy has a chance to experience more of his heritage when he spends the summer with his white grandmother.
Gary Paulsen, *Dogsong*, 1985
   Russell Susskit, a young Eskimo boy, comes of age as he undertakes a perilous dogsled journey seeking the heritage of his ancestors.

Y

1568

SARA YAMAKA
JOUNG UN KIM, Illustrator

The Gift of Driscoll Lipscomb
(New York: Simon & Schuster Books for Young Readers, 1995)

Subject(s): Artists and Art; Birthdays; Friendship
Age range(s): Grades 1-3
Major character(s): Driscoll Lipscomb, Artist, Aged Person; Molly, Child, Friend
Time period(s): Indeterminate Past
Locale(s): United States

Summary: The author's first book tells of the friendship between a painter, Driscoll Lipscomb, and young Molly. Annually, beginning with her fourth birthday, Molly receives from Driscoll Lipscomb a gift of one pot of paint and a brush. For a year, Molly paints with that color. Over time, by saving some of each year's present, Molly collects all the colors of the rainbow and then is finally able to see Driscoll Lipscomb's real gift to her—the ability to see a rainbow of colors anywhere. (32 pages)

Where it's reviewed:
Booklist, June 1995, page 1789
Children's Book Review Service, July 1995, page 151
Horn Book Guide, Fall 1995, page 287
Publishers Weekly, May 15, 1995, page 72
School Library Journal, August 1995, page 131

Other books you might like:
Amy Littlesugar, *Josiah True and the Art Maker*, 1995
Josiah is so entranced by the painting technique of the Art Maker that he treasures the paint brush she gives him and one day becomes an artist himself.
Patricia Maloney Markun, *The Little Painter of Sabana Grande*, 1993
A shortage of paper does not deter a young Panamanian artist who uses his adobe home as his canvas.
Abigail Thomas, *Pearl Paints*, 1994
After receiving a set of paints for her birthday, Pearl puts all her creative energy into a mural on her bedroom wall.

1569

CAMILLE YARBROUGH
TYRONE GETER, Illustrator

The Little Tree Growin' in the Shade
(New York: Putnam, 1996)

Subject(s): African Americans; Slavery; Music
Age range(s): Grades 3-5
Major character(s): Sister, Child; Mr. Witherspoon, Aged Person (96-year-old), Neighbor; Daddy, Storyteller
Time period(s): 1990s
Locale(s): United States

Summary: Sister and her family go to a concert with their neighbor. As they listen to a variety of music, Daddy tells Sister and Brother the history of their people and the kinds of music slaves developed and what the songs mean. Mr. Witherspoon helps by adding details to the songs which the family sings as they listen to the performers. (64 pages)

Where it's reviewed:
Horn Book, September/October 1996, page 590
Booklist, April 1, 1996, page 1367
School Library Journal, August 1996, page 148

Other books by the same author:
The Shimmershine Queens, 1989
Cornrows, 1979

Other books you might like:
Angela Shelf Medearis, *Our People*, 1994
A father and daughter share a trip through African-American history.
Michele Stepto, *Our Song Our Tale*, 1994
Slave stories, facts and music are combined with paintings and sketches from the time period.
Alan Schroeder, *Carolina Shout!*, 1994
The sounds of vendors shouting to sell things in Charleston are explained.
Jeanette Winter, *Follow the Drinking Gourd*, 1988
The words of the song are used to lead the slaves to freedom.

1570

LAURENCE YEP
JEAN TSENG, Illustrator
MOU-SIEN TSENG, Illustrator

The Boy Who Swallowed Snakes

(New York: Scholastic Inc., 1994)

Subject(s): Folk Tales; Poverty; Magic
Age range(s): Grades K-3
Major character(s): Little Chou, Child; Mr. Owyang, Landowner
Time period(s): Indeterminate Past
Locale(s): China

Summary: Little Chou, unaware the basket of silver coins he finds contains a magic snake, takes it home and discovers the small snake coiled around his leg. When the snake returns each time he removes it, his mother takes him to the village wise woman who tells Little Chou he's cursed with the snake. To rid himself of the problem, Little Chou eats the snake despite the wise woman's prediction of certain death. Little Chou lives, but the snake multiplies each time Little Chou devours the ever increasing numbers. Soon Mr. Owyang learns of the good fortune brought by the snake which he tried to lose and demands its return. Little Chou kindly gives him the snake with cooking directions, but Mr. Owyang, motivated by greed, finds eating the snake has fatal results. (32 pages)

Where it's reviewed:
Booklist, December 15, 1993, page 760
Horn Book Guide, Fall 1994, page 295
Library Talk, September 1994, page 50
Publishers Weekly, December 13, 1993, page 70
School Library Journal, April 1994, page 123

Other books by the same author:
The Khan's Daughter: A Mongolian Folktale, 1997
The Junior Thunder Lord, 1994
Butterfly Boy, 1993

Other books you might like:
Demi, *The Magic Boat*, 1990
  For saving a drowning old man, Chang is rewarded with a magical boat he uses to rescue others during a flood until it is stolen by the evil Ying.
Julie Lawson, *The Dragon's Pearl*, 1993
  A young boy swallows a magical pearl in order to protect it from robbers and turns himself into a river dragon.
Ed Young, *Lon Po Po*, 1989
  Young's illustrated translation of the Chinese tale similar to "Red Riding Hood" won many awards including the Caldecott Medal.

1571

LAURENCE YEP
JEAN TSENG, Illustrator

City of Dragons

(New York: Scholastic Inc., 1995)

Subject(s): Prejudice; Giants; Dragons
Age range(s): Grades K-3
Major character(s): Unnamed Character, Child
Time period(s): Indeterminate Past
Locale(s): China

Summary: A boy with a face so sad that it saddens anyone seeing him runs away from home in order to spare his parents the burden of having an unwanted outcast in the family. However, the boy's appearance interfere s with his ability to find work and shelter until he meets a caravan of kindly giants who are moved to tears when they see him. The giants seat the boy atop one of their elephants and proceed into the sea to the City of Dragons. There, the boy's face proves to be an asset when the dragons who see him are moved to cry tears of pearl—the very trade item the giants have come to collect. The boy returns to his village laden with goods and the villagers decide to accept him for what he is inside and not for the way he appears on the surface. (32 pages)

Where it's reviewed:
Booklist, Novmeber 15, 1995, page 566
Horn Book Guide, Spring 1996, page 51
Publishers Weekly, October 2, 1995, page 74
School Library Journal, November 1995, page 86

Other books by the same author:
The Boy Who Swallowed Snakes, 1994
Butterfly Boy, 1993
The Man Who Tricked a Ghost, 1993

Other books you might like:
Michael Hague, *The Book of Dragons*, 1995
  Seventeen short selections for dragon lovers include fantasy and folktales from different countries.
Julie Lawson, *The Dragon's Pearl*, 1993
  In a retelling of a Chinese folktale, a poor boy swallows the magic pearl he has found rather than let it fall into the wrong hands.
Ed Young, *Little Plum*, 1994
  Despite his small size, courageous Little Plum is able to retrieve the villagers' stolen animals.

1572

LAURENCE YEP

Hiroshima

(New York: Scholastic, 1995)

Subject(s): Nuclear Weapons; World War II
Age range(s): Grades 4-6
Major character(s): Riko, 16-Year-Old; Sachi, 12-Year-Old; Colonel Tibbets, Military Personnel, Pilot
Time period(s): 1940s (August 6, 1945)
Locale(s): Hiroshima, Japan

Summary: Perhaps a novella is all anyone should have to read about the horror of Hiroshima. In this slim, quiet book, the terror felt by the Japanese when the atomic bomb is dropped on their country is fully expressed. Sachi and her older sister Riko report to wartime jobs on August 6, 1945 as the *Enola Gay*, piloted by Colonel Tibbets, lumbers its way to its drop site on Hiroshima. Told in alternating chapters, the dropping of the bomb is observed through the eyes of the sisters as well as those of the crew members of the *Enola Gay*. (56 pages)

Where it's reviewed:
School Library Journal, May 1995, page 110
Voice of Youth Advocates, October 1995, page 227
Booklist, March 15, 1995, page 1329
Horn Book, September 1995, page 635
Instructor, November 1995, page 53

Awards the book has won:
Booklist Editors' Choice/Books for Youth, 1995

Other books by the same author:
Thief of Hearts, 1995
American Dragons, 1993
Dragons at the Gate, 1993

Other books you might like:
Karl Bruckner, *Day of the Bomb*, 1963
   Two Japanese children survive the dropping of the atomic bomb and then are able to find their parents.
Toshi Maruki, *Hiroshima No Pika*, 1982
   Though Mii survives the atomic bomb blast, she is left damaged in spirit and in body.
David Rees, *Exeter Blitz*, 1978
   Each member of a family describes what it was like when the Germans bombed their city.

1573

LAURENCE YEP

Later, Gator

(New York: Hyperion Books for Children, 1995)

Subject(s): Chinese Americans; Brothers; Animals/Alligators
Age range(s): Grades 4-6
Major character(s): Bobby, 8-Year-Old, Brother; Teddy, Brother (older); Oscar, Alligator
Time period(s): 1990s (1995)
Locale(s): San Francisco, California (Chinatown)

Summary: When Teddy's mother insists that he buy his brother a ''nice'' gift such as a pet turtle, Teddy chooses an alligator instead, hoping to terrorize perfect Bobby. Much to Teddy's dismay, Bobby loves the alligator and treats it so kindly that all the family and other relatives take an interest in it also. Before Oscar can grow large enough to eat his care-takers, he escapes and dies, but caring for him has given Teddy and Bobby a shared experience that improves their relationship. (122 pages)

Where it's reviewed:
Booklist, May 1, 1995, page 1576
Horn Book, July 1995, page 463
Library Talk, September 1995, page 36
Publishers Weekly, May 8, 1995, page 296
School Library Journal, July 1995, page 82

Other books by the same author:
The Ghost Fox, 1994
The Lost Garden, 1991
The Rainbow People, 1989

Other books you might like:
Jane Cutler, *Rats!*, 1996
   Fourth grader Jason and his younger brother Edward ac-quire pet rats.

Juanita Havill, *Saving Owen's Toad*, 1994
   The squabbling between 9-year-old Owen and his older brother almost lead to disaster as Owen's efforts to save his toad put him in the emergency room.
Phyllis Reynolds Naylor, *Being Danny's Dog*, 1995
   The relationship between T. R. and his older brother is so strong that T. R. thinks of himself as being Danny's loyal, protective dog.

1574

LAURENCE YEP

Ribbons

(New York: Putnam, 1996)

Subject(s): Ballet; Dreams and Nightmares; Grandparents
Age range(s): Grades 4-7
Major character(s): Robin Fox, 11-Year-Old, Dancer; Paw Paw, Grandmother, Aged Person; Madame, Teacher, Dancer
Time period(s): 1990s
Locale(s): San Francisco, California

Summary: Robin loves dancing and is terribly disappointed when her parents tell her they cannot pay for any more dance lessons because her grandmother will be coming to live with them. Paw-Paw moves in and takes over, with her tiny feet, her noisy cane, and her getting in the way. Gradually she and Robin become friends, for they both see beauty in different things. It is with the help of Madame that Paw-Paw insists Robin see the doctor about her own feet and also that she keep dancing with new shoes. (179 pages)

Where it's reviewed:
Bulletin of the Center for Children's Books, February 1996, page 210
Booklist, January 1, 1996, page 836
School Library Journal, February 1996, page 104

Other books by the same author:
City of Dragons, 1995
Hiroshima, 1995
Dragon War, 1992

Other books you might like:
Mary Jane Auch, *Glass Slippers Give You Blisters*, 1989
   Kelly is involved in helping to design a junior high produc-tion.
Sonia Levitin, *The Golem and the Dragon Girl*, 1993
   When Laurel moves to a new house she wants the spirit of her grandfather to move with her.
Lensey Namioka, *Yang the Youngest and His Terrible Ear*, 1992
   A family cannot agree on the relative importance of music and baseball.
JoNelle Toriseva, *Becoming Ballet*, 1995
   Alex is disappointed when she gets new calves for her birthday. She wanted time to go to ballet camp, not raise cows.
Paul Yee, *Tales from Gold Mountain*, 1990
   Chinese immigrants relate their experiences when they moved to America.

1575

JANE YOLEN
JEAN GRALLEY, Illustrator

And Twelve Chinese Acrobats

(New York: Philomel Books, 1995)

Subject(s): Jews; Family Life; Behavior
Age range(s): Grades 2-5
Major character(s): Lyovka ''Lou'' Yolen, Teenager, Brother (older); Velvul ''Wolf'' Yolen, Child, Brother (younger)
Time period(s): 1910s (1910)
Locale(s): Ykaterinislav, Ukraine

Summary: When Lou plays one prank too many on the townspeople, his father sends him to a military school near Kiev. Then word comes that Lou has run away from the school and the family goes into mourning during a long dreary winter. In the spring, lonely Wolf spots Lou leading a troop of Chinese acrobats along the road to the village. Lou's playful nature is unchanged and his father decides that, rather than make Lou fit a mold that doesn't suit his spirit, the parents should take advantage of his strengths by sending him to America to find work and lodging for his family. (54 pages)

Where it's reviewed:
Booklist, March 15, 1995, page 1331
Children's Book Review Service, May 1995, page 116
Horn Book Guide, Fall 1995, page 307
Library Talk, May 1995, page 42
School Library Journal, June 1995, page 115

Other books by the same author:
The Gift of Sarah Barker, 1992
The Dragon's Boy, 1990
The Girl Who Cried Flowers and Other Tales, 1974

Other books you might like:
Miriam Chaikin, *Feathers in the Wind*, 1989
  Yossi understands the rabbi's teachings about curbing an evil tongue when a thoughtless joke backfires.
Riki Levinson, *Boys Here—Girls There*, 1993
  Within the security of her loving Jewish family, six-year-old Jennie faces many changes during the Depression.
Lillian Hammer Ross, *Sarah, Also Known as Hannah*, 1994
  After her father's death, Sarah is sent to live with her aunt and uncle in America.
Sadie Rose Weilerstein, *K'tonton in the Circus: A Hanukkah Adventure*, 1981
  K'tonton accidently joins the circus and celebrates Hanukkah with his new friends.

1576

JANE YOLEN
DAVID SHANNON, Illustrator

The Ballad of the Pirate Queens

(San Diego: Harcourt Brace & Company, 1995)

Subject(s): Pirates; Legends; Adventure and Adventurers
Age range(s): Grades 3-6
Major character(s): Anne Bonney, Pirate; Mary Reade, Pirate
Time period(s): 1720s (1720)

Locale(s): Jamaica (Port Maria Bay)
Summary: With the ship at anchor, the pirate captain and crew spend their time below decks drinking and gaming, leaving the two women to stand guard. Spotting a man-o'-war approaching, Anne and Mary try valiantly to defend their ship against capture. Their efforts are futile, the pirates are imprisoned and all but the two women are hanged. (32 pages)

Where it's reviewed:
Booklist, April 15, 1995, page 1501
Children's Book Review Service, June 1995, page 127
Library Talk, September 1995, page 31
Publishers Weekly, April 17, 1995, page 59
School Library Journal, June 1995, page 126

Awards the book has won:
ALA Notable Book, 1996
School Library Journal Best Books, 1995

Other books by the same author:
Merlin and the Dragons, 1995
The Girl in the Golden Bower, 1994
Good Griselle, 1994

Other books you might like:
Ariane Dewey, *Laffite the Pirate*, 1985
  Based on factual information, the story tells of a pirate who temporarily halts his piracy in order to help the United States during the War of 1812.
Emily Arnold McCully, *The Pirate Queen*, 1995
  Following in her father's footsteps, Irishwoman Grania O'Malley becomes a successful pirate until her capture by the British.
Michael Morpurgo, *The Ghost of Grania O'Malley*, 1996
  Jessie depends on her American cousin and a pirate's ghost to protect her Irish island home from developers.

1577

JANE YOLEN
LAUREL MOLK, Illustrator

Beneath the Ghost Moon

(Boston: Little, Brown and Company, 1994)

Subject(s): Halloween; Animals/Mice; Stories in Rhyme
Age range(s): Grades K-3
Major character(s): Unnamed Character, Mouse, Heroine
Time period(s): Indeterminate
Locale(s): Fictional Country

Summary: With preparations complete for Ghost Eve, the mice sleep soundly, unaware that creepy crawlies have invaded their home to destroy their costumes. Upon awakening, the mice want to abandon their home, but one determined young mouse rallies the others to fight and drive the invaders away. The mice are successful and all but one creepy crawlie, who stays to beg forgiveness and sanctuary, rapidly depart. (32 pages)

Where it's reviewed:
Booklist, September 15, 1994, page 146
Kirkus Reviews, August 15, 1994, page 1142
Library Talk, September 1994, page 16
Publishers Weekly, September 19, 1994, page 25

School Library Journal, September 1994, page 202

Other books by the same author:
Old Dame Counterpane, 1994
Mouse's Birthday, 1993
Owl Moon, 1987 (Caldecott Medal, 1988)

Other books you might like:
Sylvia Andrews, *Rattlebone Rock*, 1995
    In the graveyard, tombstones, skeletons and ghosts begin a rhythmic Halloween beat which attracts the attention of the townspeople.
Kenn Compton, *Granny Greenteeth and the Noise in the Night*, 1993
    Granny asks her unusual and somewhat spooky housemates to investigate a noise under her bed. Co-author Joanne Compton.
Dav Pilkey, *Dragon's Halloween*, 1993
    Dragon creatively solves a scary Halloween problem and unintentionally creates one for others.
Caroline Stutson, *By the Light of the Halloween Moon*, 1993
    One by one, scary Halloween creatures are attracted to the bare toe of a young girl playing her violin by the light of the moon.

`1578`

JANE YOLEN
JANE DYER, Illustrator

The Girl in the Golden Bower

(Boston: Little, Brown and Company, 1994)

Subject(s): Fairy Tale; Magic; Fantasy
Age range(s): Grades 2-4
Major character(s): Aurea ''Curry'', Child; Unnamed Character, Sorceress
Time period(s): Indeterminate Past
Locale(s): Fictional Country

Summary: Mystery surrounds the cottage of a woodsman, his wife and young daughter—a mystery which attracts a sorceress searching for a magic charm. Sensing that the charm is in the cottage, the sorceress stays on to search by posing as a cook. When her mushroom stew poisons Aurea's mother, the dying woman passes on to her daughter a comb, promising that the comb will always protect her. Because young Aurea uses the comb to curry the fur of many woodland animals she befriends, the sorceress mockingly calls her Curry. Eventually, the sorceress realizes that Curry must possess the charm and she lays her plans to own it herself. Although the sorceress puts a spell on Curry, the animal friends and the magic comb protect the child and bring the tale to its happy conclusion. (32 pages)

Where it's reviewed:
Booklist, October 15, 1994, page 440
Bulletin of the Center for Children's Books, October 1994, page 71
Children's Book Review Service, January 1995, page 53
Publishers Weekly, August 15, 1994, page 95
School Library Journal, October 1994, page 106

Other books by the same author:
Tam Lin, 1990

Sleeping Ugly, 1981
The Girl Who Cried Flowers and Other Tales, 1974

Other books you might like:
Hans Christian Andersen, *Twelve Tales*, 1994
    Translated and illustrated by Erik Blegvad, the collection of twelve fairy tales includes both the familiar and the less well-known.
Lauren Mills, *Tatterhood and the Hobgoblins*, 1993
    When her twin Isabella is enchanted, Tatterhood vows to find a way to break the hobgoblins' evil spell.
Ruth Sanderson, *The Enchanted Wood*, 1991
    The youngest of the king's three sons fulfills a quest to free the land from a terrible drought by entering the Enchanted Wood and finding the Heart of the World.

`1579`

JANE YOLEN
DAVID CHRISTIANA, Illustrator

Good Griselle

(San Diego: Harcourt Brace & Company, 1994)

Subject(s): Angels; Babies; Love
Age range(s): Grades 2-4
Major character(s): Griselle, Artisan; Beau, Child
Time period(s): Indeterminate Past
Locale(s): Paris, France

Summary: A kind, but poor lace maker, Griselle's very goodness infuriates the gargoyles of the cathedral who watch her daily movements. On Christmas Eve the gargoyles place a wager with the stone angels on the cathedral that Griselle's goodness will be undone by an ugly child they produce. When Griselle finds the ugly, ill-behaved child on her doorstep, she takes him into her home and her heart, loving him despite what he appears to be. (40 pages)

Where it's reviewed:
Booklist, October 1, 1994, page 335
Horn Book, November 1994, page 761
Kirkus Reviews, October 15, 1994, page 1419
Library Talk, November 1994, page 29
Publishers Weekly, October 17, 1994, page 81

Other books by the same author:
O Jerusalem, 1996
The Girl in the Golden Bower, 1994
Dove Isabeau, 1989

Other books you might like:
Hans Christian Andersen, *Thumbelina*, 1990
    In the retelling by Deborah Hautzig the kindly Thumbelina is transported by a swallow, she saves from freezing, to a warm garden where she reigns as queen.
Emma Bull, *The Princess and the Lord of Night*, 1994
    On her thirteenth birthday a kindly princess born under a curse takes the initiative to free herself forever.
Selma Lagerlof, *The Changeling*, 1992
    Despite the grief a farmer and his wife feel for their lost son, the wife cares for an ugly troll child left in his place and through her kindness secures the return of her son.

1580

JANE YOLEN
MELISSA BAY MATHIS, Illustrator

Grandad Bill's Song

(New York: Philomel, 1994)

Subject(s): Death; Grief; Grandparents
Age range(s): Grades K-3
Major character(s): Jon, 8-Year-Old (grandson); Bill, Grandfather (recently deceased)
Time period(s): 1990s (1994)
Locale(s): United States

Summary: Struggling to understand his feelings following the death of his grandfather, Jon asks family members and friends, "What did you do on the day Grandad died?" As each responds to the question, the young boy not only learns more about his grandfather and his life, but begins to come to grips with his own reaction.

Where it's reviewed:
Booklist, July 1994, page 1957
Children's Book Review Service, June 1994, page 125
Kirkus Reviews, May 15, 1994, page 710
Publishers Weekly, May 23, 1994, page 87
School Library Journal, July 1994, page 92

Other books by the same author:
Before the Storm, 1995
Beneath the Ghost Moon, 1994
Honkers, 1993
Mouse's Birthday, 1993
Owl Moon, 1987 (Caldecott Medal Winner, 1988)

Other books you might like:
Aliki, *The Two of Them*, 1979
Grandfather loved his grandaughter from the moment of her birth; at his death his grandaughter is left with a wealth of memories.
Judith Viorst, *The Tenth Good Thing about Barney*, 1971
Ten wonderful memories of Barney, a young boy's cat who has died, are shared at the funeral.
Charlotte Zolotow, *My Grandson Lew*, 1974
Six-year-old Lew shares his memories of his now-deceased grandfather.

1581

JANE YOLEN, Editor
MARTIN H. GREENBERG, Illustrator
DORON BEN-AMI, Illustrator

The Haunted House: A Collection of Original Stories

(New York: HarperCollins Publishers, 1995)

Subject(s): Ghosts; Haunted Houses; Short Stories
Age range(s): Grades 3-6
Time period(s): 1990s (1995)
Locale(s): United States

Summary: A succession of families occupy "The Close" at 66 Brown's End, a ramshackle house with a past that wants to be told. While adults see nothing unusual in the old house, the children in each family hear, see and experience unusual events. Seven authors describe the lives of seven different families while living at 66 Brown's End, each with a unique and spooky story to tell. (85 pages)

Where it's reviewed:
Booklist, September 1,1995, page 77
Horn Book Guide, Spring 1996, page 135
School Library Journal, November 1995, page 108

Other books by the same author:
Vampires: A Collection of Original Stories, 1991
Things That Go Bump in the Night: A Collection of Original Stories, 1989
Werewolves: A Collection of Stories, 1988

Other books you might like:
Daniel Cohen, *Great Ghosts*, 1990
A haunted house is the setting for each of nine ghost stories flavored with British humor and suspense.
Bruce Coville, *Bruce Coville's Book of Ghosts: Tales to Haunt You*, 1994
The collection of works by different authors features all types of ghosts—some scary, some lonely, some funny.
David Gale, *Don't Give Up the Ghost: The Delacorte Book of Original Ghost Stories*, 1993
A collection of stories by well-known authors focuses on contacts of humans with the supernatural.
Chris Powling, *Faces in the Dark: A Book of Scary Stories*, 1994
Ten stories, most original, vary in setting and time period while sharing elements of spooky humor.
Michael Stearns, *A Wizard's Dozen: Stories of the Fantastic*, 1993
Tales of dragons, giants, and wizards are among the thirteen fantasies presented in this collection.

1582

JANE YOLEN
LESLIE BAKER, Illustrator

Honkers

(Boston: Little, Brown and Company, 1993)

Subject(s): Animals/Geese; Birth; Farm Life
Age range(s): Grades K-3
Major character(s): Betsy, 5-Year-Old (homesick); Grandy, Grandfather, Farmer; Nana, Grandmother
Time period(s): Indeterminate Past
Locale(s): United States

Summary: Saddened, but determined not to cry, Betsy arrives alone by train at her grandparents' farm where she has been sent during her bedridden mother's difficult pregnancy. Nana and Grandy have found an abandoned clutch of goose eggs which Betsy carefully tends until they hatch. Betsy and the honkers spend the summer together under the loving care of Grandy and Nana. (32 pages)

Where it's reviewed:
Booklist, November 1, 1993, page 533
Horn Book Guide, Spring 1994, page 61
Kirkus Reviews, August 1, 1993, page 1010

Publishers Weekly, July 19, 1993, page 252
School Library Journal, January 1994, page 102

Other books by the same author:
The Girl in the Golden Bower, 1994
Letting Swift River Go, 1992 (ALA Notable Books)
Piggins, 1987

Other books you might like:
Donald Hall, *The Farm Summer 1942*, 1994
    During World War II, Peter's parents send him to his
    grandparents' farm where he enjoys a secure, satisfying
    summer of new experiences.
Petra Mathers, *Kisses from Rosa*, 1995
    Rosa lives with relatives far from home while her mother
    recuperates from an illness and finds that leaving them is as
    difficult as coming to them.
John Schoenherr, *Rebel*, 1995
    One of a clutch of five Canadian geese eggs hatches into a
    gosling with a mind of his own.
Pirkko Vainio, *The Snow Goose*, 1993
    A little girl raises a gosling hatched from the egg of a dying
    goose only to watch it join a flock and fly away as the
    summer ends.

`1583`

JANE YOLEN
BARBARA COONEY, Illustrator

Letting Swift River Go
(Boston: Little, Brown and Company, 1992)

Subject(s): Rivers; Country Life; Change
Age range(s): Grades K-3
Major character(s): Sally Jane, Child (daughter); Nancy
    Vaughan, Child, Friend; Papa, Father
Time period(s): 20th century (1927-1946)
Locale(s): Swift River Valley, Massachusetts (from Boston)

Summary: To 6-year old Sally Jane, life is secure and happy
with friends and the routine of a simple, country life. Her
world changes when, in order to provide water for the people
of Boston, the government buys all the towns along the Swift
River, builds a dam and drowns everything that Sally Jane has
ever known. Floating over her former home in a boat with her
father, an older Sally Jane learns to let go of the past in the
same way that the child, Sally Jane, once let go of the fireflies
captured on a summer night. (unpaged)

Where it's reviewed:
Booklist, August 1992, page 2020
Horn Book Magazine, September 1992, page 581
Kirkus Reviews, July 15, 1992, page 929
Publishers Weekly, July 20, 1992, page 248
School Library Journal, September 1992, page 214

Awards the book has won:
ALA Notable Book, 1993

Other books by the same author:
Grandad Bill's Song, 1994
Honkers, 1993
Welcome to the Green House, 1993
Piggins, 1987
Sleeping Ugly, 1984

Other books you might like:
David Bellamy, *How Green Are You?*, 1991
    Through the eyes of a whale, the reader learns of damage
    to the earth and what actions can be taken to counteract it.
Dr. Seuss, *The Lorax*, 1971
    In the name of progress, change and destruction come to
    the homeland of the Lorax, despite his efforts to resist.
Ann Turner, *Heron Street*, 1989
    The herons' marsh habitat changes due to the encroach-
    ment of civilization.
Rosemary Wells, *Waiting for the Evening Star*, 1993
    Two brothers contentment with life in rural Vermont
    changes as the older one's desire to see beyond the moun-
    tains and his subsequent enlistment during the First World
    War separate the two.
Marsha Wilson Chall, *Up North at the Cabin*, 1992
    A young girl shares memories of happy, contented days at
    the family cabin near a lake.

`1584`

JANE YOLEN
BRUCE DEGEN, Illustrator

Mouse's Birthday
(New York: G. P. Putnam's Sons, 1993)

Subject(s): Animals; Birthdays; Stories in Rhyme
Age range(s): Grades K-2
Major character(s): Mouse, Mouse
Time period(s): 1990s (1993)
Locale(s): United States

Summary: Mouse's house, nestled in a corner of a barn is
barely big enough for Mouse. On his birthday his friends
arrive, one by one, bearing gifts and each squeezes into
Mouse's house. When all have arrived, the candle on the cake
is lit, Mouse blows it out and the house is no longer very, very
small. (32 pages)

Where it's reviewed:
Booklist, January 15, 1993, page 925
Horn Book Guide, Fall 1993, page 280
Publishers Weekly, March 8, 1993, page 76
Reading Teacher, May 1994, page 648
School Library Journal, March 1993, page 188

Other books by the same author:
Beneath the Ghost Moon, 1994
Honkers, 1993
Eeny, Meeny, Miney Mole, 1992

Other books you might like:
Jan Brett, *The Mitten*, 1989
    In one of many adaptations of this folktale, animals crowd
    into a mitten seeking warmth until the smallest of all
    tickles the bear's nose. Oops!
Mirra Ginsburg, *Mushroom in the Rain*, 1974
    In an adaptation of a Russian tale, an ant seeks refuge from
    the rain under a mushroom which somehow expands to
    keep a number of animals dry.
Ann Tompert, *Just a Little Bit*, 1993
    Mouse receives help from many animals in order to suc-
    cessfully seesaw with friend Elephant.

1585

JANE YOLEN

Passenger

(New York: Harcourt Brace, 1996)

Series: Young Merlin Trilogy
Subject(s): Legends; Animals/Birds; Feral Children
Age range(s): Grades 4-6
Major character(s): Merlin, Child (feral), 8-Year-Old; Master Robin, Animal Trainer (falconer)
Time period(s): 5th century
Locale(s): England

Summary: Left alone in the woods for a year, a young boy becomes a feral child, caring for himself and unable to remember the words he once knew or where he came from. When a man comes hawking in the woods, the child follows him home, only to be captured and kept to be tamed. It is when the boy helps to save the falconer's birds and hears the word for a young falcon, merlin, that he recognizes his own name. (76 pages)

Where it's reviewed:
Hornbook, July/August 1996, page 466
Booklist, May 1, 1996, page 1508
School Library Journal, May 1996, page 118

Other books by the same author:
Hobby, 1996 (sequel to *Passenger*)
Wizard's Hall, 1991
The Dragon's Boy, 1990
The Devil's Arithmetic, 1988

Other books you might like:
Lloyd Alexander, *The Book of Three*, 1969
    The first book in the fantasy series which introduces the characters, including the assistant pig keeper who becomes a king.
T.A. Barron, *The Merlin Effect*, 1994
    A strange whirlpool attracts Kate and she is drawn into a conflict between Merlin and Vagar.
Peter Dickinson, *Merlin Dreams*, 1988
    This is a collection of tales that come from the dreams of Merlin.
Michael Morpurgo, *Arthur, High King of Britain*, 1995
    A young boy finds Arthur awakening from a nap and hears his story.
Rosemary Sutcliff, *The Light Beyond the Forest*, 1980
    This is a rewriting of stories about the search for the holy grail.

1586

CAROL BEACH YORK
JOHN SPEIRS, Illustrator

The Key to the Playhouse

(New York: Scholastic Inc., 1994)

Subject(s): Cousins; Interpersonal Relations; Behavior
Age range(s): Grades 2-4

Major character(s): Alice Ann, Child, Cousin (Megan's); Megan, Child, Cousin (Alice Ann's); Cissie Wilson, Child, Neighbor
Time period(s): 1990s (1994)
Locale(s): United States

Summary: Annually, Alice Ann and Megan enjoy a two-week vacation with their grandmother, playing in the same playhouse that their mothers had played in as children. This summer they decide the playhouse needs a lock and key to deter robbers when they are not visiting. What begins as a simple safety precaution becomes a means of excluding a new neighbor. When Alice Ann and Megan refuse to share their special playhouse with Cissie, she stays home and creates her own playhouse, giving the cousins a dose of their own medicine. (70 pages)

Where it's reviewed:
Bulletin of the Center for Children's Books, April 1994, page 273
Horn Book, September 1994, page 594
Kirkus Reviews, June 15, 1994, page 854
Library Talk, September 1994, page 44
School Library Journal, June 1994, page 116

Other books by the same author:
Christmas Dolls, 1993
Miss Know-It-All and the Magic House, 1989
Miss Know-It-All Returns, 1985

Other books you might like:
Rumer Godden, *Great Grandfather's House*, 1993
    After three months visiting with her great grandfather, spoiled Keiko learns to behave in a more kind and gentle way.
Elspeth Campbell Murphy, *The Mystery of the Dancing Angels*, 1995
    Annoyed that they must care for spoiled young Patience, three cousins are horrified when they lose her while touring a historical mansion.
Bonnie Pryor, *The Plum Tree War*, 1989
    Robert discovers a different side to bothersome cousin Harriet when the two stop quarrelling long enough to learn that they have a lot in common.

1587

CAROL BEACH YORK
LISA THIESING, Illustrator

Pudmuddles

(New York: HarperCollins Publishers, 1993)

Subject(s): Dwellings; Humor; Behavior
Age range(s): Grades 2-4
Major character(s): Mr. Pudmuddle, Bridegroom, Eccentric; Mrs. Pudmuddle, Bride, Collector
Time period(s): Indeterminate
Locale(s): Fictional Country

Summary: Mr. Pudmuddle's preference for doing things backwards is unusual, but in time his bride becomes accustomed to eating dinner for breakfast and "soodle noup" for lunch. However, she does not tolerate some of the unique features of the house. Eventually, Mr. and Mrs. Pudmuddle work out a happy relationship in their repaired home. (44 pages)

Where it's reviewed:
Booklist, April 1, 1993, page 1435
Horn Book Guide, Fall 1993, page 292
Kirkus Reviews, May 1, 1993, page 606
Library Talk, May 1994, page 43
School Library Journal, May 1993, page 92

Other books by the same author:
The Key to the Playhouse, 1994
Miss Know-It-All and the Three Ring Circus, 1988
Febold Feboldson, the Fix It Farmer, 1980

Other books you might like:
Harry Allard, *The Stupids Have a Ball*, 1978
    The Stupid family celebrates report card day when Buster and Petunia fail every subject.
Peggy Parish, *Amelia Bedelia*, 1963
    In the first of eleven books about beloved Amelia Bedelia, her literal interpretation of instructions leads to humorous events.
Brian Schatell, *The McGoonys Have a Party*, 1985
    With one of them absent-minded and the other one hard of hearing, the McGoonys plans do not always turn out as expected.

1588

RONDER THOMAS YOUNG

Learning by Heart

(Boston: Houghton Mifflin Company, 1993)

Subject(s): Race Relations; African Americans; Family Life
Age range(s): Grades 4-7
Major character(s): Miss Isabella Harris, Housekeeper (Mennonite); Rachel, 10-Year-Old; Callie Thompson, 5th Grader
Time period(s): 1960s
Locale(s): United States (small Southern town)

Summary: In the author's first novel, Rachel reluctantly faces inevitable changes in her life. With the birth of another child expected soon, the family must move from the small apartment behind her parent's grocery store into a house. A "colored" woman is hired to help with the move and child care. Rachel's friendship with Miss Isabella and with Callie Thompson exposes her to prejudicial attitudes of others in her town, but also helps her learn about friendship. (172 pages)

Where it's reviewed:
Booklist, December 15, 1993, page 755
Children's Book Review Service, February 1994, page 84
Horn Book, March 1994, page 203
Publishers Weekly, September 13, 1993, page 137
School Library Journal, October 1993, page 136

Other books you might like:
Deborah M. Newton Chocolate, *NEATE to the Rescue!*, 1992
    When her mother's position on a local council is threatened by a racist, a teenager and her friends take action.
Vaunda Micheaux Nelson, *Mayfield Crossing*, 1993
    When the children of Mayfield Crossing are sent to larger

Parkview Elementary, they are treated as outsiders and judged by the color of their skin.
Mildred D. Taylor, *The Gold Cadillac*, 1987
    When an African-American family from Ohio visits relatives in the South they face the racism that is a part of life in the South in the 1950s.

1589

SELINA YOUNG, Author/Illustrator

Ned

(Charlottesville, VA: Thomasson-Grant, 1993)

Subject(s): Toys; Schools; Imagination
Age range(s): Grades K-1
Major character(s): Emily, Child, Student; Ned, Donkey (toy)
Time period(s): 1990s (1993)
Locale(s): England

Summary: Inseparable companions, Emily agrees to all of Ned's good ideas so it seems only natural for Ned to accompany Emily on her first day of school. Until he "loses" himself, Ned has a wonderful day. Although Ned is found before the school day ends, the next morning he "agrees" with Emily that he should stay home to keep her bedroom free of dragons while she is at school. (26 pages)

Where it's reviewed:
Horn Book Guide, Spring 1994, page 61
Publishers Weekly, September 27, 1993, page 62
School Library Journal, March 1994, page 213

Other books by the same author:
Whistling in the Woods, 1994

Other books you might like:
Jez Alborough, *Where's My Teddy?*, 1992
    A teddy bear mix-up between a little boy and a bear ends happily when each recovers his own bear.
Miriam Cohen, *Will I Have a Friend?*, 1967
    First-day school fears are put to rest when Paul makes friends with Jim.
Kevin Henkes, *Owen*, 1993
    With help from his supportive parents, Owen finds a way to begin school without giving up his beloved yellow blanket.
Jean Van Leeuwen, *Emma Bean*, 1993
    Molly and her beloved Emma Bean, a stuffed rabbit, begin kindergarten where they meet a little girl with a special teddy bear.

1590

KAZUMI YUMOTO

Friends

(New York: Farrar Straus Giroux, 1996)

Subject(s): Old Age; Friendship; Death
Age range(s): Grades 5-8
Major character(s): Yamashita, 6th Grader; Kawabe, 6th Grader; Kiyama, 6th Grader
Time period(s): 1990s
Locale(s): Japan

Summary: When the boys hear about the death of a grand-mother, they're filled with questions about death. They follow an old man from the neighborhood, hoping to catch him when he dies, but become attached to him instead and help him clean and re-plant his yard. Returning from soccer camp, the boys discover that their new friend has died while they were away. But they are satisfied anyway that they've made the end of his life happy. (170 pages)

Where it's reviewed:

Bulletin of the Center for Children's Books, February 1997, page 229

School Library Journal, December 1996, page 124

Awards the book has won:

Mildred L. Batchelder Award, 1997

Japan School Library Book Club Recommended Book, 1993

Other books you might like:

Bruce Brooks, *Everywhere*, 1990
  Two boys wait to see if a grandfather will recover from a heart attack.

Joseph Krumgold, *Onion John*, 1959
  A boy makes friends with an old man.

Jerry Spinelli, *Crash*, 1991
  Crash becomes close to his grandfather and then must deal with his stroke.

Yoko Kaawashima Watkins, *My Brother, My Sister*, 1992
  Two children try to survive in postwar Japan.

Z

1591

JANE BRESKIN ZALBEN, Author/Illustrator

Happy New Year, Beni
(New York: Henry Holt and Company, 1993)

Series: Jewish Holiday
Subject(s): Holidays, Jewish; Jews; Cousins
Age range(s): Grades K-3
Major character(s): Beni, Bear (child); Max, Bear (misbehaving cousin)
Time period(s): 1990s (1993)
Locale(s): United States

Summary: The extended family, including troublesome cousin Max, is gathering at Grandma and Grandpa's to celebrate Rosh Hashanah. Beni and his sister are not eager to spend time with Max and his practical jokes which have spoiled past family gatherings. With Grandpa's help and the sharing of a Jewish tradition Beni and Max both realize that they can begin the New Year with a changed appreciation for one another. (28 pages)

Where it's reviewed:
Booklist, July 1993, page 699
Horn Book Guide, Spring 1994, page 61
Publishers Weekly, September 20, 1993, page 71
School Library Journal, December 1993, page 97

Other books by the same author:
Buster Gets Braces, 1992
Goldie's Purim, 1991
Happy Passover, Rosie, 1990
Beni's First Chanukah, 1988

Other books you might like:
David A. Adler, *A Picture Book of Jewish Holidays*, 1981
Information about a variety of Jewish holidays is presented. (nonfiction)
Malka Drucker, *The Family Treasury of Jewish Holidays*, 1994
With stories, games, songs and recipes, ten Jewish holidays and their traditions are explained. (nonfiction)

Barbara Diamond Goldin, *The World's Birthday: A Rosh Hashanah Story*, 1990
Daniel thinks that the way to celebrate this holiday is to invite the world over for a birthday party.

1592

JANE BRESKIN ZALBEN, Author/Illustrator

Miss Violet's Shining Day
(Honesdale, PA: Boyds Mills Press, 1995)

Subject(s): Animals/Rabbits; Music; Shyness
Age range(s): Grades K-2
Major character(s): Miss Violet, Rabbit, Worker; Sir Reginald Dewlap, Rabbit
Time period(s): Indeterminate Past
Locale(s): Fictional Country

Summary: Timid Miss Violet is so intrigued by the sounds she hears coming from Sir Dewlap's home that she boldly knocks on the door. Sir Dewlap has been playing his cousin's trombone and offers to give Miss Violet lessons. Thus begins such a love for the instrument that Miss Violet is transformed from a simple factory worker into a successful musician. (26 pages)

Where it's reviewed:
Booklist, August 1995, page 1958
Horn Book Guide, Fall 1995, page 288
Publishers Weekly, February 27, 1995, page 102
School Library Journal, April 1995, page 120

Other books by the same author:
Buster Gets Braces, 1992
Happy Passover, Rosie, 1990
Beni's First Chanukah, 1988

Other books you might like:
Barbara Bottner, *Hurricane Music*, 1995
With a clarinet she finds in the basement Aunt Margaret studies the "sounds of life" until, while playing with a hurricane, her instrument blows away.

Dominic Catalano, *Wolf Plays Alone*, 1992

Interested in playing his horn alone in the woods, a wolf finds that his music attracts a succession of noisy animals.

Robert Kraus, *Musical Max*, 1990

When Max stops his annoying practice sessions, the neighbors are just as bothered by the unfamiliar quiet as they were by the noise.

Carol Purdy, *Mrs. Merriwether's Musical Cat*, 1994

A stray cat inspires changes in Mrs. Merriwether's outlook on life and improves her piano students playing.

1593

JANE BRESKIN ZALBEN, Author/Illustrator

Pearl Plants a Tree

(New York: Simon & Schuster Books for Young Readers, 1995)

Subject(s): Trees; Grandparents; Holidays, Jewish
Age range(s): Grades K-2
Major character(s): Pearl, Sheep; Grandpa, Grandfather, Sheep
Time period(s): Indeterminate Past
Locale(s): United States

Summary: After Grandpa shows Pearl the apple tree he planted when he first came to America, she decides to grow one also by putting an apple seed in a little pot. When spring comes Pearl and Grandpa plant the sapling outside and celebrate with a picnic. An author's note gives information about tree-planting holidays around the world and the Tu b'Shvat. (32 pages)

Where it's reviewed:
Booklist, November 15, 1995, page 566
Horn Book Guide, Spring 1996, page 51
School Library Journal, January 1996, page 99

Other books by the same author:
Happy New Year, Beni, 1993
Goldie's Purim, 1991
Happy Passover, Rosie, 1990
Leo and Blossom's Sukkah, 1990
Beni's First Chanukah, 1988

Other books you might like:
Sherry Garland, *The Lotus Seed*, 1993

Fleeing her defeated country, Ba carries a lotus seed from the emperor's garden. Years later it is planted and yields seeds to share with her grandchildren.

Geraldine McCaughrean, *The Cherry Tree*, 1991

After their village is destroyed by war, Taichi and Yumiko find hope in a cherry tree.

Mary Watson, *The Butterfly Seeds*, 1995

Jake plants the seeds given him as a parting gift by Grandpa and is rewarded by plants which attract butterflies and remind him of his homeland.

1594

HARRIET ZIEFERT
LAURA RADER, Illustrator

Pete's Chicken

(New York: Tambourine Books, 1994)

Subject(s): Individuality; Animals/Rabbits; Self-Confidence
Age range(s): Grades K-3
Major character(s): Pete, Student
Time period(s): 1990s (1994)
Locale(s): Fictional Country (Wildwood School)

Summary: Young Pete is proud of his appearance and his uniqueness. Yet, when he draws a multi-colored chicken in art class, the other kids laugh and the teacher does not select Pete's work for display. Dejected he takes the picture home and, after some reflection, decides to ask his mom to display it in the kitchen because, after all, there is no other chicken exactly like his. (40 pages)

Where it's reviewed:
Booklist, September 15, 1994, page 146
Horn Book Guide, Spring 1995, page 62
Publishers Weekly, June 27, 1994, page 78
Reading Teacher, October 1995, page 139
School Library Journal, September 1994, page 203

Awards the book has won:
International Reading Association Children's Choice, 1995

Other books by the same author:
Harry Gets Ready for School, 1991
Little Bunny's Noisy Friends, 1990
Nicky's Picnic, 1986

Other books you might like:
Mary Jane Auch, *The Easter Egg Farm*, 1992

Pauline lays eggs that are not like any other hens, but her supportive owner is able to find a creative use for them.

Miriam Cohen, *No Good in Art*, 1980

With encouragement, a first grader who doubts his artistic ability shows that he is capable of drawing.

Marissa Moss, *Regina's Big Mistake*, 1990

Instructed to draw a jungle, Regina feels unsure of her ability to do so but produces a unique picture which meets her satisfaction.

1595

HARRIET ZIEFERT
LAURA RADER, Illustrator

The Three Little Pigs

(New York: Viking, 1995)

Series: Easy-to-Read Classic
Subject(s): Animals/Pigs; Animals/Wolves; Folk Tales
Age range(s): Grades K-2
Major character(s): Unnamed Character, Wolf; Unnamed Character, Pig
Time period(s): Indeterminate Past
Locale(s): Fictional Country

Summary: The classic story of three little pigs setting out to make their way in the world is retold as a beginning reader. As each pig builds his home, the huffing and puffing wolf arrives to demolish the residences and devour pigs one and two. The third pig proves, once again, to be the wolf's nemesis. (32 pages)

Where it's reviewed:
Booklist, October 1, 1995, page 329
Horn Book Guide, Spring 1996, page 98
School Library Journal, September 1995, page 189

Other books by the same author:
The Little Red Hen, 1995
Three Wishes, 1993
Andy Toots His Horn, 1988

Other books you might like:
Margaret Hillert, *The Three Little Pigs*, 1963
   A simply told version of the folk tale is appealing to younger readers.
James Marshall, *The Three Little Pigs*, 1989
   The inimitable illustrator retells the classic story with humor and originality.
Tony Ross, *The Three Pigs*, 1983
   Fed up with living in a high-rise apartment in the city, three pigs set off to build homes in the countryside with predictable results.
Eugene Trivizas, *The Three Little Wolves and the Big Bad Pig*, 1993
   A familiar tale takes a new turn when the big bad pig tries to outmanuever the three little wolves and ends up surprising himself.

1596

PAUL ZINDEL
JEFF MANGIAT, Illustrator

Attack of the Killer Fishsticks

(New York: Bantam Books, 1993)

Series: Wacky Facts Lunch Bunch
Subject(s): School Life; Friendship; Humor
Age range(s): Grades 3-5
Major character(s): Dave Martin, 5th Grader, Friend; Liz McGinn, 5th Grader, Friend; Max Millner, 5th Grader (new to school), Bullied Child
Time period(s): 1990s (1993)
Locale(s): New Springville

Summary: To survive fifth grade lunch time and have fun too, four friends form the Wacky Facts Lunch Bunch and share trivia and knock-knock jokes daily in the cafeteria. When they notice two bullies picking on a new kid, they go to Max's defense. Dave, Liz and the others are saddened to learn that Max's mother has recently died. Their plan to protect Max and help him be accepted in school leads to his election as the Student Council Representative and a pizza celebration for the Wacky Facts Lunch Bunch. (117 pages)

Where it's reviewed:
Booklist, October 1, 1993, page 347
Publishers Weekly, October 25, 1993, page 64
School Library Journal, October 1993, page 136

Other books by the same author:
One Hundred Percent Laugh Riot, 1994
The Fifth-Grade Safari, 1993
Fright Party, 1993

Other books you might like:
Barthe DeClements, *Nothing's Fair in Fifth Grade*, 1981
   In time, the other fifth graders learn to be supportive of overweight, unhappy Elsie.
Judy Delton, *Only Jody*, 1982
   Jody's mother transfers him to a Catholic school for fifth grade.
Dean Hughes, *Nutty for President*, 1982
   A fifth grade class is determined to elect their classmate to the presidency of the Student Government.

1597

CHARLOTTE ZOLOTOW
JAMES E. RANSOME, Illustrator

The Old Dog

(New York: HarperCollins, 1995)

Subject(s): Animals/Dogs; Pets; Death
Age range(s): Grades K-2
Major character(s): Ben, Child
Time period(s): 1990s (1995)
Locale(s): United States

Summary: A newly illustrated reissue of a 1972 title describes Ben's reaction to the death of his old dog. Nothing is the same on the day Ben's pet dies—no dog greets him when he returns from school and he has no one to throw sticks to when he goes out to play. Finally, Ben simply sits and cries. When his father comes home with a puppy, Ben's tears turn to smiles of joy. (32 pages)

Where it's reviewed:
Booklist, September 1, 1995, page 90
Children's Book Review Service, September 1995, page 6
Horn Book, November 1995, page 762
Publishers Weekly, August 21, 1995, page 65
School Library Journal, December 1995, page 93

Other books by the same author:
Peter & the Pigeons, 1993
Some Things Go Together, 1987
Mr. Rabbit and the Lovely Present, 1962

Other books you might like:
Miriam Cohen, *Jim's Dog Muffins*, 1984
   Jim's first grade classmates share his grief when his dog Muffins is killed.
Amy Ehrlich, *Maggie and Silky and Joe*, 1994
   Joe has grown up with Maggie as his companion but now must accept the changes resulting from the dog's advancing age and eventual death.
Judith Greenberg, *Sunny*, 1986
   With co-author Helen Carey, the nonfiction work describes Bill's reactions as his sick dog dies.

1598

CHARLOTTE ZOLOTOW
STEFANO VITALE, Illustrator

When the Wind Stops

(New York: HarperCollins Publishers, 1995)

Subject(s): Parent and Child; Bedtime; Nature
Age range(s): Grades K-1
Major character(s): Unnamed Character, Child; Unnamed Character, Mother
Time period(s): Indeterminate
Locale(s): Earth

Summary: At bedtime a young boy questions why the day must end and his mother responds that the day does not really end because it begins again somewhere else. Throughout the bedtime ritual, each of the boy's questions is answered by his mother in a reassuring way that shows the continuity of life. Originally published in 1962, the book is revised and reillustrated. (32 pages)

Where it's reviewed:
Booklist, July 1995, page 1879
Five Owls, May 1995, page 108
Horn Book, July 1995, page 455

Publishers Weekly, May 8, 1995, page 298
School Library Journal, August 1995, page 131

Awards the book has won:
ALA Notable Book, 1996
School Library Journal Best Books, 1995

Other books by the same author:
The Summer Night, 1991
William's Doll, 1972
The Sky Was Blue, 1963

Other books you might like:
Margaret Wise Brown, *Little Donkey Close Your Eyes*, 1995
    Animals throughout the world are bid good night in this gentle poem.
Reeve Lindbergh, *What Is the Sun?*, 1994
    In a rhyming story a grandmother answers her grandson's bedtime questions about nature.
Laura Krauss Melmed, *The First Song Ever Sung*, 1993
    Before going to bed a young boy asks family members, his dog and the birds flying by to tell him what was the first song.
Elizabeth Lee O'Donnell, *Sing Me a Window*, 1993
    A young girl requests a bedtime song that details the day's activities with her father.

Award Index

This index lists major awards given to books featured in the entries. Books are listed alphabetically beneath the name of the award, with author name and entry number also indicated.

Time Period Index

This index chronologically lists the time settings in which the featured books take place. Main headings refer to a century; where no specific time is given, the headings INDETERMINATE PAST, INDETERMINATE FUTURE, and INDETERMINATE are used. The 18th through 21st centuries are broken down into decades when possible. (Note: 1800s, for example, refers to the first decade of the 19th century.) Featured titles are listed alphabetically beneath time headings, with author names and entry numbers also provided.

Good Luck, Ronald Morgan! - Patricia Reilly Giff 464

Good Morning, Pond - Alyssa Satin Capucilli 205

Good Night, Gorilla - Peggy Rathmann 1195

Good Night, Sleep Tight - Penelope Lively 884

Good Night, Stella - Kate McMullan 988

Goodbye, Mitch - Ruth Wallace-Brodeur 1474

Gooseberry Park - Cynthia Rylant 1249

Gopher Takes Heart - Virginia Scribner 1303

Gorgonzola Zombies in the Park - Elizabeth Levy 858

Grace and Joe - Maribeth Boelts 120

Gracias, Rosa - Michelle Markel 933

Grandad Bill's Song - Jane Yolen 1580

Grandaddy and Janetta - Helen V. Griffith 519

Grandaddy's Stars - Helen V. Griffith 520

Grandfather's Christmas Camp - Marc McCutcheon 969

Grandfather's Dream - Holly Keller 731

Grandfather's Journey - Allen Say 1271

Grandmas at Bat - Emily Arnold McCully 966

Grandma's Garden - Elaine Moore 1033

Grandma's Shoes - Libby Hathorn 569

Grandma's Smile - Elaine Moore 1034

Grandpa Is a Flyer - Sanna Anderson Baker 62

Granny the Pag - Nina Bawden 90

Grass and Sky - Lisa Rowe Fraustino 426

Great Aunt Martha - Rebecca C. Jones 710

Great Grandfather's House - Rumer Godden 483

The Great Pig Escape - Eileen Christelow 242

The Great Pony Hassle - Nancy Springer 1374

The Great Pumpkin Switch - Megan McDonald 973

The Great Smith House Hustle - Jane Louise Curry 309

Great-Uncle Dracula and the Dirty Rat - Jayne Harvey 568

The Green Bottle and the Silver Kite - Fredericka Berger 101

The Green Musketeers and the Fabulous Frogs - Sara St. Antoine 1375

Green Willow - Eileen Dunlop 373

Gregory Cool - Caroline Binch 107

The Gullywasher - Joyce Rossi 1234

The Hallo-Wiener - Dav Pilkey 1151

Halloween Mice! - Bethany Roberts 1216

The Hanukkah Ghosts - Malka Penn 1128

Haphazard House - Mary Wesley 1500

Happy Birthday, Jesse Bear! - Nancy White Carlstrom 214

The Happy Hocky Family - Lane Smith 1354

Happy New Year, Beni - Jane Breskin Zalben 1591

Harry and Arney - Judith Caseley 218

Harry and Tuck - Holly Keller 732

Harry on Vacation - Dyan Sheldon 1326

Harry's Birthday - Barbara Ann Porte 1166

Harry's Stormy Night - Una Leavy 829

Harvey Slumfenburger's Christmas Present - John Burningham 183

Harvey's Mystifying Raccoon Mix-Up - Eth Clifford 259

A Hat for Minerva Louise - Janet Morgan Stoeke 1394

The Haunted House: A Collection of Original Stories - Jane Yolen 1581

Haunted Summer - Betty Ren Wright 1560

The Haunting of Holroyd Hill - Brenda Seabrooke 1304

The Hayloft - Lisa Westberg Peters 1135

Hazel Saves the Day - SuAnn Kiser 764

Heart to Heart - George Shannon 1317

The Hen That Crowed - Sheila Cole 273

Henry and Mudge and the Best Day of All - Cynthia Rylant 1250

Henry and Mudge and the Careful Cousin - Cynthia Rylant 1251

Henry and Mudge and the Wild Wind - Cynthia Rylant 1252

Henry the Sailor Cat - Mary Calhoun 199

Henry's Baby - Mary Hoffman 636

Herbie Jones and the Birthday Showdown - Suzy Kline 768

Here Comes Henny - Charlotte Pomerantz 1164

Here Comes Tod! - Philippa Pearce 1124

Hey, Dad, Get a Life - Todd Strasser 1397

Hey, New Kid! - Betsy Duffey 368

Hi - Ann Herbert Scott 1302

Hilda Hen's Happy Birthday - Mary Wormell 1554

Hilda Hen's Search - Mary Wormell 1555

Hip Cat - Jonathan London 889

Hob and the Goblins - William Mayne 954

Hog-Eye - Susan Meddaugh 1000

Holding onto Sunday - Kathryn O. Galbraith 436

Home Lovely - Lynne Rae Perkins 1131

Honey Paw and Lightfoot - Jonathan London 890

Hooray for Grandma Jo! - Thomas McKean 982

Hop Jump - Ellen Stoll Walsh 1475

Horrible Harry and the Dungeon - Suzy Kline 769

A Horse for All Seasons - Sheila Kelly Welch 1490

A Horse Like Barney - Jessie Haas 532

Hotter than a Hot Dog! - Stephanie Calmenson 201

Hound Heaven - Linda Oatman High 612

The House That Drac Built - Judy Sierra 1335

How Do You Spell Geek? - Julie Anne Peters 1134

How Emily Blair Got Her Fabulous Hair - Susan Garrison 445

How I Spent My Summer Vacation - Mark Teague 1411

How I Was Adopted: Samantha's Story - Joanna Cole 271

How to Be Cool in the Third Grade - Betsy Duffey 369

How to Get Famous in Brooklyn - Amy Hest 603

How to Grow a Picket Fence - Mary Louise Cuneo 308

Hue Boy - Rita Phillips Mitchell 1023

Humphrey Thud - Camilla Ashforth 48

I Am Really a Princess - Carol Diggory Shields 1329

I Am the Dog, I Am the Cat - Donald Hall 542

I Found Mouse - Pamela D. Greenwood 505

I Got a Family - Melrose Cooper 289

I Hate Company - P.J. Petersen 1137

I Love You, Bunny Rabbit - Shulamith Levey Oppenheim 1097

I Want Answers and a Parachute - P.J. Petersen 1138

I Want to Be - Thylias Moss 1046

I Was a Fifth-Grade Zebra - Nancy J. Hopper 645

I Went to the Zoo - Rita Golden Gelman 447

If Anything Ever Goes Wrong at the Zoo - Mary Jean Hendrick 582

If You Want to Find Golden - Eileen Spinelli 1368

The Iguana Brothers: A Tale of Two Lizards - Tony Johnston 704

I'll See You When the Moon Is Full - Susi Gregg Fowler 421

I'm a Jolly Farmer - Julie Lacome 804

I'm George Washington and You're Not! - Steven Kroll 789

In America - Marissa Moss 1045

The In-Between Days - Eve Bunting 174

In My Mother's Garden - Melissa Madenski 919

In Search of the Giant - Jeanne Willis 1524

In the Rain with Baby Duck - Amy Hest 604

In the Snow - Huy Voun Lee 830

In Trouble with Teacher - Patricia Demuth 339

Indigo and Moonlight Gold - Jan Spivey Gilchrist 469

Insects Are My Life - Megan McDonald 974

Inside a Barn in the Country: A Rebus Read-Along Story - Alyssa Satin Capucilli 206

Inside-Out Grandma - Joan Rothenberg 1236

The Invisible Dog - Dick King-Smith 748

Is Susan Here? - Janice May Udry 1437

Is That Josie? - Keiko Narahashi 1062

Isla - Arthur Dorros 362

It's My Birthday - Helen Oxenbury 1103

It's Pumpkin Time! - Zoe Hall 546

It's the Bear! - Jez Alborough 20

I've Got Chicken Pox - True Kelley 733

J.B.'s Harmonica - John Sebastian 1307

J.B. Wigglebottom and the Parade of Pets - Vivian Sathre 1268

Jack's Garden - Henry Cole 269

Jafta: The Homecoming - Hugh Lewin 864

Jamaica and Brianna - Juanita Havill 570

Jamaica's Blue Marker - Juanita Havill 571

James in the House of Aunt Prudence - Timothy Bush 184

Jason and the Losers - Gina Willner-Pardo 1527

Jazz, Pizzaz, and the Silver Threads - Mary Quattlebaum 1182

Jenius, the Amazing Guinea Pig - Dick King-Smith 749

Jenna's Big Jump - Faythe Dyrud Thureen 1420

Jennifer-the-Jerk Is Missing - Carol Gorman 488

Jennifer, Too - Juanita Havill 572

Jeremy's Muffler - Laura F. Nielsen 1074

Jericho - Janet Hickman 611

A Job for Wittilda - Caralyn Buehner 167

Johnny Rides Again - Jo Ann Muchmore 1048

JoJo's Flying Side Kick - Brian Pinkney 1152

Joshua T. Bates Takes Charge - Susan Richards Shreve 1332

Joshua's Masai Mask - Dakari Hru 658

The Joy Boys - Betsy Byars 194

Julie - Jean Craighead George 451

Juliet's Story - William Trevor 1426

Julius - Angela Johnson 696

Junebug - Alice Mead 998

Juneteenth Jamboree - Carole Boston Weatherford 1487

Junie B. Jones and Some Sneaky Peeky Spying - Barbara Park 1109

The Junkyard Dog - Erika Tamar 1407

Just a Little Bit - Ann Tompert 1424

Just Call Me Stupid - Tom Birdseye 108

Just in Time for Christmas - Louise Borden 125

Just Like My Dad - Tricia Gardella 440

Kalinzu: A Story from Africa - Jeremy Grimsdell 521

Kate's Giants - Valiska Gregory 512

Kelly and Me - Carol Lynch Williams 1520

Kelly in the Mirror - Martha M. Vertreace 1454

The Key to the Playhouse - Carol Beach York 1586

Kid Kibble - Diana Hendry 584

Kinda Blue - Ann Grifalconi 516

Kit and Kat - Tomie De Paola 328

The Know-Nothings - Michelle Sobel Spirn 1372

A Koala for Katie: An Adoption Story - Jonathan London 891

Komodo! - Peter Sis 1340

The Language of Doves - Rosemary Wells 1493

The Last Dragon - Susan Miho Nunes 1085

The Last Noo-Noo - Jill Murphy 1051

The Latchkey Dog - Mary Jane Auch 50

Later, Gator - Laurence Yep 1573

Lavender - Karen Hesse 599

Let's Go Camping with Mr. Sillypants - M.K. Brown 144

Let's Go Home, Little Bear - Martin Waddell 1463

Libbie Sims, Worry Wart - Gayle Rogers Lockwood 887

Libby Bloom - Susan Rowan Masters 948

The Library Dragon - Carmen Agra Deedy 333

The Light on Hogback Hill - Cynthia DeFelice 335

Lights for Gita - Rachna Gilmore 471

Lights on the River - Jane Resh Thomas 1417

Lights Out! - John Himmelman 620

Like Butter on Pancakes - Jonathan London 893

Lila's Little Dinosaur - Wolfram Hanel 553

Lili at Ballet - Rachel Isadora 679

Lili on Stage - Rachel Isadora 680

Lilly's Purple Plastic Purse - Kevin Henkes 587

Lilly's Secret - Miko Imai 676

Lily - Abigail Thomas 1414

Lionel in the Winter - Stephen Krensky 788

Liplap's Wish - Jonathan London 894

21st CENTURY

2000s

2090s

INDETERMINATE FUTURE

INDETERMINATE

Geographic Index

This index provides access to all featured books by geographic settings—such as countries, continents, oceans, and planets. States and provinces are indicated for the United States and Canada. Also interfiled are headings for fictional place names (Spaceships, Imaginary Planets, etc.). Sections are further broken down by city or the specific name of the imaginary locale. Book titles are listed alphabetically under headings, and author names and entry numbers are also provided.

Pudmuddles - Carol Beach York   1587
Quickly, Quigley - Jeanne M. Gravois   494
A Quiet Night In - Jill Murphy   1052
The Rat and the Tiger - Keiko Kasza   722
The Rattlebang Picnic - Margaret Mahy   925
Ready...Set...Read—and Laugh! A Funny Treasury for Beginning Readers - Joanna Cole   272
The Return of Rinaldo, the Sly Fox - Ursel Scheffler   1276
Rex and Lilly Family Time - Laurie Krasny Brown   143
Rhino and Mouse - Todd Starr Palmer   1106
The Royal Nap - Charles C. Black   112
Rude Giants - Audrey Wood   1548
Sheep Take a Hike - Nancy Shaw   1323
Shortcut - David Macaulay   911
Six Snowy Sheep - Judith Ross Enderle   391
Snow - Nancy Elizabeth Wallace   1473
The Snow Queen - Hans Christian Andersen   32
So Much in Common - Laurie A. Jacobs   682
A Song for Little Toad - Vivian French   430
Spider Kane and the Mystery at Jumbo Nightcrawler's - Mary Pope Osborne   1102
The Story of the Three Kingdoms - Walter Dean Myers   1057
Suddenly! - Colin McNaughton   991
Surprise! Surprise! - Michael Foreman   417
The Swan's Gift - Brenda Seabrooke   1306
Tales of the Wicked Witch - Hanna Kraan   782
That's Philomena! - Catherine Bancroft   67
This Is a Great Place for a Hot Dog Stand - Barney Saltzberg   1259
The Three Little Pigs - Harriet Ziefert   1595
The Three Little Wolves and the Big Bad Pig - Eugene Trivizas   1427
Tick-Tock - Eileen Browne   157
Tilly and the Rhinoceros - Sheila White Samton   1260
The Timekeeper - Emily Rodda   1224
Tom, Babette, & Simon: Three Tales of Transformation - Avi   58
A Tooth Fairy's Tale - David Christiana   246
Tuck in the Pool - Martha Weston   1502
Tumble Tower - Anne Tyler   1435
Two Bushy Badgers - Patience Brewster   136
Two's Company - Amanda Benjamin   98
Under the Moon - Vivian French   431
A Village Full of Valentines - James Stevenson   1387
What Would Mama Do? - Judith Ross Enderle   392
What's for Lunch? - John Schindel   1284
The Wizard - Bill Martin Jr.   940
Wizard and Wart at Sea - Janice Lee Smith   1353
Zeke Pippin - William Steig   1378

Ardet Forest
The Dragon and the Unicorn - Lynne Cherry   237

Bear Country
The Berenstain Bears and the New Girl in Town - Stan Berenstain   99

Blackberry Hollow
Blackberry Hollow - Paul Peabody   1123

Blefuscu
Gulliver in Lilliput - Margaret Hodges   628

Catnip Acres
The Tales of Grandpa Cat - Lee Wardlaw   1479

Chestnut Cove
Chestnut Cove - Tim Egan   381

Crag Castle
Day of the Unicorn - Mollie Hunter   664

Dimwood Forest
Poppy - Avi   57

Dog Heaven
Dog Heaven - Cynthia Rylant   1248

Edgerton
That Kookoory! - Margaret Walden Froehlich   432

Firefly Island
Stories from Firefly Island - Benedict Blathwayt   116

Gates of the Wind
The Gates of the Wind - Kathryn Lasky   814

Hambone Hills
A Busy Day for a Good Grandmother - Margaret Mahy   921

Lilliput
Gulliver in Lilliput - Margaret Hodges   628

Mount Dragon Eyes
The Sorcerer's Apprentice - Nancy Willard   1516

Mousopolis
Dogzilla - Dav Pilkey   1149

Mud Flat
The Mud Flat Olympics - James Stevenson   1386

Old Forest
The Story of Santa Claus - Tom Paxton   1122

Pebble Island
An Extraordinary Egg - Leo Lionni   875

Seven Kingdoms
Florizella and the Wolves - Philippa Gregory   510

Sheep Dip Road
Strudwick: A Sheep in Wolf's Clothing - Robert Kraus   786

Slavda
Jacob and the Stranger - Sally Derby   344

Wainscott
The Wainscott Weasel - Tor Seidler   1309

FRANCE

A Boy and His Bear - Harriet Graham   491
Casey over There - Staton Rabin   1184
Dinner at Magritte's - Michael Garland   442
Star of Fear, Star of Hope - Jo Hoestlandt   629
Three Sacks of Truth: A Story from France - Eric A. Kimmel   744
War Game - Michael Foreman   418
What's French for HELP, George? - Helen McCann   961

Paris
A Different Kind of Courage - Ellen Howard   651
Good Griselle - Jane Yolen   1579
The Sweetest Fig - Chris Van Allsburg   1444
The Trouble with Henriette! - Wende Devlin   347

GAMBIA

Boundless Grace - Mary Hoffman   634

GERMANY

Around the Oak - Gerda Muller   1049
Loretta and the Little Fairy - Gerda Marie Scheidl   1278
Midnight Rider - Krista Ruepp   1238
The Nutcracker Ballet - Vladimir Vagin   1441
Sleep Well, Little Bear - Quint Buchholz   165

Black Forest
Kisses from Rosa - Petra Mathers   949

GREECE

Max and Ruby's Midas: Another Greek Myth - Rosemary Wells   1497

GREENLAND

Call Me Ahnighito - Pam Conrad   280
Inunguak: The Little Greenlander - Palle Petersen   1140

GUATEMALA

The People of Corn: A Mayan Story - Mary-Joan Gerson   459

HAITI

Running the Road to ABC - Denize Lauture   823
Tap-Tap - Karen Lynn Williams   1521

INDIA

Heart of a Tiger - Marsha Arnold   42

Tibri
Binya's Blue Umbrella - Ruskin Bond   123

INDONESIA

Komodo Island
Komodo! - Peter Sis   1340

IRELAND

Dog - Robert J. Blake   115
John Joe and the Big Hen - Martin Waddell   1462
Mia the Beach Cat: A Story - Wolfram Hanel   554
Patrick's Day - Elizabeth Lee O'Donnell   1091

Clare Island
The Ghost of Grania O'Malley - Michael Morpurgo   1039

County Tipperary
Juliet's Story - William Trevor   1426

Glenoran
The Secret of the Ruby Ring - Yvonne MacGrory   915

Langley Castle
The Secret of the Ruby Ring - Yvonne MacGrory   915

ISRAEL

West Bank
Sitti's Secrets - Naomi Shihab Nye   1087

ITALY

It Was a Dark and Stormy Night - Allan Ahlberg   16
Papa Gatto: An Italian Fairy Tale - Ruth Sanderson   1265
Silver at Night - Susan Campbell Bartoletti   82

Calabria
Strega Nona Meets Her Match - Tomie De Paola   329

Rome
Rinaldo on the Run - Ursel Scheffler   1277

Sicily
Danilo the Fruit Man - Amy Valens   1443

JAMAICA

The Ballad of the Pirate Queens - Jane Yolen   1576
The Tangerine Tree - Regina Hanson   556

Which-Way Mountain
Aunt Skilly and the Stranger - Kathleen
    Stevens 1382

ALABAMA

Julius - Angela Johnson 696
A Place to Belong - Emily Crofford 305

Birmingham
The Watsons Go to Birmingham—1963 - Christopher
    Paul Curtis 311

ALASKA

Anna's Athabaskan Summer - Arnold Griese 514
Bears out There - Joanne Ryder 1246
Brian's Winter - Gary Paulsen 1119
Child of the Wolves - Elizabeth Hall 545
Dance on a Sealskin - Barbara Winslow 1533
Dogteam - Gary Paulsen 1120
Honey Paw and Lightfoot - Jonathan London 890
The Seasons and Someone - Virginia L. Kroll 794

Kangik
Julie - Jean Craighead George 451

ARIZONA

Phoenix
Phoenix Upside Down - Elizabeth Scarboro 1274

Scottsdale
Watchdog and the Coyotes - Bill Wallace 1472

Tucson
I Want Answers and a Parachute - P.J.
    Petersen 1138
Just Call Me Stupid - Tom Birdseye 108

ARKANSAS

Bound for Oregon - Jean Van Leeuwen 1448

Pickle Springs
Utterly Yours, Booker Jones - Betsy Duffey 371

CALIFORNIA

Amelia Writes Again - Marissa Moss 1043
Amelia's Notebook - Marissa Moss 1044
Boys at Work - Gary Soto 1361
A Day's Work - Eve Bunting 172
Flower Garden - Eve Bunting 173
Frida Maria: A Story of the Old Southwest - Deborah
    Nourse Lattimore 822
In America - Marissa Moss 1045
Just Like My Dad - Tricia Gardella 440
Nine for California - Sonia Levitin 854
Off and Running - Gary Soto 1363
Solay - Mark J. Harris 562
The Trespassers - Zilpha Keatley Snyder 1360
Working Cotton - Sherley Anne Williams 1522

Berkeley
The Bracelet - Yoshiko Uchida 1436
Chevrolet Saturdays - Candy Dawson Boyd 128

Brownwood
Cat Running - Zilpha Keatley Snyder 1359

Cisco
The Iron Dragon Never Sleeps - Stephen
    Krensky 787

East Los Angeles
Chato's Kitchen - Gary Soto 1362

Fresno
The Pool Party - Gary Soto 1364

Fresta
There's an Owl in the Shower - Jean Craighead
    George 452

Hollywood
Genghis Khan: A Dog Star Is Born - Marjorie
    Weinman Sharmat 1320
Maxi, the Star - Debra Barracca 79
Stardust - Alane Ferguson 405

Los Angeles
Gracias, Rosa - Michelle Markel 933
Maybe Yes, Maybe No, Maybe Maybe - Susan
    Patron 1118
Smoky Night - Eve Bunting 177

Lucky Diggins
The Ballad of Lucy Whipple - Karen Cushman 314

Magpie Campground
Earthquake Terror - Peg Kehret 725

Monterey
The Stowaway: A Tale of California Pirates - Kristiana
    Gregory 508

Mountain Terrace
The Girl Who Changed the World - Delia
    Ephron 393

Oakland
Fall Secrets - Candy Dawson Boyd 129
Tikvah Means Hope - Patricia Polacco 1163

San Diego
The 13th Floor: A Ghost Story - Sid Fleischman 409

San Francisco
Earthquake! A Story of Old San Francisco - Kathleen
    V. Kudlinski 798
The Farm Summer 1942 - Donald Hall 541
The Fog Doggies and Me - Gayle Pearson 1125
Grandfather's Journey - Allen Say 1271
Hip Cat - Jonathan London 889
I Want Answers and a Parachute - P.J.
    Petersen 1138
Later, Gator - Laurence Yep 1573
Living in Secret - Cristina Salat 1257
A Place for Grace - Jean Davies Okimoto 1092
Ribbons - Laurence Yep 1574
Stella and Roy - Ashley Wolff 1545
The Warm Place - Nancy Farmer 401

Westmont
Lydia Jane and the Baby-Sitter Exchange - Natalie
    Honeycutt 638

COLORADO

The Banshee Train - Odds Bodkin 119
The Fear Place - Phyllis Reynolds Naylor 1066
Gold in the Hills - Laurie Lawlor 824
Goose and the Mountain Lion - Marian Harris 561

Carter
Someone to Count On - Patricia Hermes 594

Denver
How Do You Spell Geek? - Julie Anne Peters 1134
The Wind Wagon - Celia Barker Lottridge 896

Mesa Verde
Dreamplace - George Ella Lyon 908

Pinevale
The Secret Life of Bethany Barrett - Claudia
    Mills 1017

Tinville
The Gentleman Outlaw and Me—Eli - Mary Downing
    Hahn 539

CONNECTICUT

Herbie Jones and the Birthday Showdown - Suzy
    Kline 768
Josiah True and the Art Maker - Amy
    Littlesugar 883
Song Lee and the Leech Man - Suzy Kline 772
Song Lee in Room 2B - Suzy Kline 773
Tomorrow on Rocky Pond - Lynn Reiser 1206
Who's Orp's Girlfriend? - Suzy Kline 774

Hartford
Orp and the FBI - Suzy Kline 771

Lyme
Zoe and Columbo - Susan Richards Shreve 1333

New Haven
Junebug - Alice Mead 998

Sharon
My Name Is Brain/Brian - Jeanne Betancourt 106

Southwick
The Apprenticeship of Lucas Whitaker - Cynthia
    DeFelice 334

DELAWARE

Come Morning - Leslie Davis Guccione 524

DISTRICT OF COLUMBIA

Washington
The Big Bike Race - Lucy Jane Bledsoe 117
Jimmy Crack Corn - Candice F. Ransom 1188
Joshua T. Bates Takes Charge - Susan Richards
    Shreve 1332
Look Out, Washington, D.C.! - Patricia Reilly
    Giff 465
Nightwalkers - Judy K. Morris 1041
Stinker's Return - Pamela F. Service 1311
A Voice in the Wind - Kathryn Lasky 819
Washington City Is Burning - Harriette Gillem
    Robinet 1218
The World of Daughter McGuire - Sharon Dennis
    Wyeth 1567

FLORIDA

Last Left Standing - Barbara T. Russell 1240
The View from Saturday - E.L. Konigsburg 777

Comfort Creek
Comford Creek - Joyce McDonald 972

East Coconut
The Worst Goes South - James Stevenson 1389

Los Olas
Going the Distance - Mary Jane Miller 1014

New Smyrna Beach
Adeline Street - Carol Lynch Williams 1519
Kelly and Me - Carol Lynch Williams 1520

GEORGIA

Grandaddy and Janetta - Helen V. Griffith 519
Kinda Blue - Ann Grifalconi 516
Pink and Say - Patricia Polacco 1162

Hanover
Karate Dancer - Doris Buchanan Smith 1350

Mitchell County
Moriah's Pond - Ethel Footman Smothers 1357

New Echota
Remember My Name - Sara H. Banks 74

Savannah
Imani and the Flying Africans - Janice Liddell 871

Grand River
Yolanda's Genius - Carol Fenner 404

Greenbush
That Wild Berries Should Grow: The Diary of a Summer - Gloria Whelan 1506

Union City
My Rotten Redheaded Older Brother - Patricia Polacco 1161

MIDWEST
Grandpa Is a Flyer - Sanna Anderson Baker 62
What You Know First - Patricia MacLachlan 918

Cold Creek
Little Obie and the Kidnap - Martin Waddell 1464

Medicine Fire
Black-Eyed Susan - Jennifer Armstrong 38

MINNESOTA
Clouds of Terror - Catherine A. Welch 1489
Good-Bye, Hello - Barbara Shook Hazen 577
Harris and Me: A Summer Remembered - Gary Paulsen 1121
Pioneer Bear - Joan Sandin 1266

Carroll County
Papa Alonzo Leatherby: A Collection of Tall Tales from the Best Storyteller in Carroll County - Marguerite W. Davol 323

Johnson Falls
Champ Hobarth - Judith Bernie Strommen 1400

Marshall
Jenna's Big Jump - Faythe Dyrud Thureen 1420

MISSISSIPPI
The Well: David's Story - Mildred D. Taylor 1409

Cole County
White Socks Only - Evelyn Coleman 275

Lucy
The Shuteyes - Mary James 689

MISSISSIPPI RIVER
Escape into the Night - Lois Walfrid Johnson 700

MISSOURI
The Happy Yellow Car - Polly Horvath 647
Nine for California - Sonia Levitin 854

Clary
Odd Man Out - Gail Radley 1185

Gabriel
A Share of Freedom - June Rae Wood 1549

Mansfield
In the Land of the Big Red Apple - Roger Lea MacBride 912
Little House on Rocky Ridge - Roger Lea MacBride 913

St. Joseph
Keeping Secrets - Joan Lowery Nixon 1075

Warrensburg
Re-Elect Nutty! - Dean Hughes 660

MONTANA
Lucky Morning - Sally Noll 1079
Stolen Bones - Joan Carris 216

The Wimp of the World - Alison Cragin Herzig 596

NEBRASKA
Dandelions - Eve Bunting 171

Cherrygrove
Burton and Stanley - Frank O'Rourke 1101

NEVADA
Cowboy Country - Ann Herbert Scott 1301

NEW ENGLAND
Alvah and Arvilla - Mary Lyn Ray 1199
The Christmas Miracle of Jonathan Toomey - Susan Wojciechowski 1543
Full Worm Moon - Margo Lemieux 835
George Washington's Ghost - Jane Clark Brown 142
Grandfather's Trolley - Bruce McMillan 987
Mary Had a Little Lamb - Sarah Josepha Hale 540
The Storm - Anne F. Rockwell 1222

NEW HAMPSHIRE
Grandmother Bryant's Pocket - Jacqueline Briggs Martin 941
Moon Window - Jane Louise Curry 310
When Willard Met Babe Ruth - Donald Hall 544

Canterbury
Shaker Boy - Mary Lyn Ray 1201

Gale
The Farm Summer 1942 - Donald Hall 541

South Danbury
Lucy's Christmas - Donald Hall 543
Pianna - Mary Lyn Ray 1200

Stark
What Jamie Saw - Carolyn Coman 276

Warren
The Bear That Heard Crying - Natalie Kinsey-Warnock 758

Westfield
Frindle - Andrew Clements 257

NEW JERSEY

Cape May
The Language of Doves - Rosemary Wells 1493

Squan Beach
The Green Bottle and the Silver Kite - Fredericka Berger 101

Tenafly
The Ballot Box Battle - Emily Arnold McCully 963

Trenton
The Fighting Ground - Avi 56

Upper Montclair
The Man in the Ceiling - Jules Feiffer 403

Winter Hill
Make a Wish, Molly - Barbara Cohen 266

Woodside
Down and Up Fall - Johanna Hurwitz 666

NEW MEXICO
A Voice in the Wind - Kathryn Lasky 819

Espanola Valley
Carlos and the Cornfield/Carlos y la Milpa de Maiz - Jan Romero Stevens 1379

Pedernal
A Sunburned Prayer - Marc Talbert 1406

San Juan
The Farolitos of Christmas - Rudolfo Anaya 31

NEW YORK
Amber Brown Is Not a Crayon - Paula Danziger 320
Beyond the Magic Sphere - Gail Jarrow 691
The Case of the Desperate Drummer - E.W. Hildick 615
The Case of the Fantastic Footprints - E.W. Hildick 616
Children of the Longhouse - Joseph Bruchac 159
Make Room for Elisa - Johanna Hurwitz 668
No Boys Allowed - Marilyn Levinson 850
Sunshine Home - Eve Bunting 180
The View from Saturday - E.L. Konigsburg 777
You Can't Eat Your Chicken Pox, Amber Brown - Paula Danziger 322
Youn Hee and Me - C.S. Adler 12

Brooklyn
Back to Before - Jan Slepian 1343
Casey over There - Staton Rabin 1184

Elmont
Pearl Moscowitz's Last Stand - Arthur A. Levine 846

Greenport
Living in Secret - Cristina Salat 1257

Harlem
Willie Jerome - Alice Faye Duncan 372

Hudson River Valley
Drums at Saratoga - Lisa Banim 68

Ithaca
The Up & Down Spring - Johanna Hurwitz 672

Levittown
Our House: The Stories of Levittown - Pam Conrad 282

Long Island
Blue Claws - Walter Lyon Krudop 795

New York
2095 - Jon Scieszka 1298
Alan and Naomi - Myron Levoy 856
All Aboard! - James Stevenson 1384
Amy Dunn Quits School - Susan Richards Shreve 1330
Back to Bataan - Jerome Charyn 234
Bebop-a-Do-Walk! - Sheila Hamanaka 547
The Boardwalk Princess - Arthur A. Levine 845
The Butterfly Seeds - Mary Watson 1482
Call Me Ahnighito - Pam Conrad 280
City of Light, City of Dark: A Comic-Book Novel - Avi 55
Cousins in the Castle - Barbara Brooks Wallace 1468
Dear Fred - Susanna Rodell 1225
Do You See a Mouse? - Bernard Waber 1459
The Dream Jar - Bonnie Pryor 1178
Falcon's Egg - Luli Gray 497
Going to See Grassy Ella - Kathryn Lance 810
Gorgonzola Zombies in the Park - Elizabeth Levy 858
How to Get Famous in Brooklyn - Amy Hest 603
Isla - Arthur Dorros 362
Lili at Ballet - Rachel Isadora 679
Lost in Cyberspace - Richard Peck 1126
Lyle at the Office - Bernard Waber 1461
The Magic Shell - Nicholasa Mohr 1027
Maxi, the Star - Debra Barracca 79
Mendel's Ladder - Mark Karlins 719
The Morning Chair - Barbara M. Joosse 712
My Crazy Cousin Courtney - Judi Miller 1011

Abilene
Santa Calls - William Joyce 715

Amarillo
The Armadillo from Amarillo - Lynne Cherry 236

Curly H Ranch
Armadillo Rodeo - Jan Brett 135

Hermosa
Search for the Shadowman - Joan Lowery
Nixon 1076

Houston
Something Queer in Outer Space - Elizabeth
Levy 861

Langley
The Private Notebook of Katie Roberts, Age 11 - Amy
Hest 607

Matagorda Island
Fearsome's Hero - Dona Schenker 1280

San Antonio
The Armadillo from Amarillo - Lynne Cherry 236
The Brick House Burglars - Peni R. Griffin 517

Temple
Johnny Rides Again - Jo Ann Muchmore 1048

UTAH

The Mud Family - Betsy James 687

Adenville
The Great Brain Is Back - John D. Fitzgerald 408

Ogden
The Trophy - Dean Hughes 662

VERMONT

Beware the Mare - Jessie Haas 529
A Blue for Beware - Jessie Haas 530
Fox Song - Joseph Bruchac 161
Jip: His Story - Katherine Paterson 1113
Lily - Abigail Thomas 1414
A Llama in the Family - Johanna Hurwitz 667
On a Starry Night - Natalie Kinsey-Warnock 759
Sable - Karen Hesse 602

Barstow
Waiting for the Evening Star - Rosemary Wells 1498

Colchester
Back to Before - Jan Slepian 1343

Hamlet
Seven Spiders Spinning - Gregory Maguire 920

Lake Champlain
Little Champ - Jim Arnosky 44

Learning
Soup Ahoy - Robert Newton Peck 1127

Saint Johnsbury
Mr. Lincoln's Drummer - G. Clifton Wisler 1540

VIRGINIA

The Booford Summer - Susan Mathias Smith 1356
The Freedom Riddle - Angela Shelf Medearis 1004
Jimmy Crack Corn - Candice F. Ransom 1188
Mr. Lincoln's Drummer - G. Clifton Wisler 1540
Sees Behind Trees - Michael Dorris 361
Tanya's Reunion - Valerie Flournoy 413
True North - Kathryn Lasky 818
*When Will This Cruel War Be Over? The Civil War
Diary of Emma Simpson* - Barry Denenberg 340

Wicked Jack - Connie Nordhielm Wooldridge 1553

Alexandria
The Twin in the Tavern - Barbara Brooks
Wallace 1469

Blue Ridge Mountains
When the Whippoorwill Calls - Candice F.
Ransom 1190

Broadfalls
The Haunting of Holroyd Hill - Brenda
Seabrooke 1304

Brownsville
Flip-Flop Girl - Katherine Paterson 1112

Coal Station
Belle Prater's Boy - Ruth White 1509

Mount Vernon
George Washington's Cows - David Small 1346

Spotsylvania
Big Red Truck - Stephen Schlossberg 1285

Willow Creek
Pony Crazy - Bonnie Bryant 164

WASHINGTON

The Cabin Key - Gloria Rand 1187
The Pickle Song - Barthe DeClements 331
Second-Grade Pig Pals - Kirby Larson 812
Tough Loser - Barthe DeClements 332

Apple Valley
Apple Picking Time - Michele Benoit Slawson 1342

Marysville
*The Absolutely True Story. . .How I Visited Yellowstone
Park with the Terrible Rupes* - Willo Davis
Roberts 1217

Seattle
The Formerly Great Alexander Family - Susan
Richards Shreve 1331
Yang the Third and Her Impossible Family - Lensey
Namioka 1060

WEST

How I Spent My Summer Vacation - Mark
Teague 1411

Miss Penelope Bartlett's Ranch
On the Trail with Miss Pace - Sharon Phillips
Denslow 342

Red Buttes
Buffalo Bill and the Pony Express - Eleanor
Coerr 262

Three Crossings
Buffalo Bill and the Pony Express - Eleanor
Coerr 262

WEST VIRGINIA

John Henry - Julius Lester 839
More than Anything Else - Marie Bradby 130
Shiloh Season - Phyllis Reynolds Naylor 1068

Buckman
The Boys Start the War - Phyllis Reynolds
Naylor 1064
The Girls Get Even - Phyllis Reynolds Naylor 1067

Muckwater Mountain
Hound Heaven - Linda Oatman High 612

Three Springs
Ghosts Don't Get Goosebumps - Elvira
Woodruff 1551

WISCONSIN

Ellen Anders on Her Own - Karen Hirsch 625
The Kid Who Ran for President - Dan Gutman 527
Mole's Hill - Lois Ehlert 384
Nettie's Gift - Susan Tews 1413
River Day - Jane B. Mason 947
Trick or Trouble? - Ilene Cooper 287

Milwaukee
Nuts to You! - Lois Ehlert 385

Winfield
The Ghosts of Mercy Manor - Betty Ren
Wright 1559

WYOMING

Snowed In - Barbara M. Lucas 903

Big Bend
*The Sweetwater Run: The Story of Buffalo Bill Cody
and the Pony Express* - Andrew Glass 476

Fort Laramie
*The Sweetwater Run: The Story of Buffalo Bill Cody
and the Pony Express* - Andrew Glass 476

Jackson Hole
*The Case of the Missing Cutthroats, an Ecological
Mystery* - Jean Craighead George 448

Morgan
On the Right Track - B.B. Calhoun 198

Yellowstone National Park
*The Absolutely True Story. . .How I Visited Yellowstone
Park with the Terrible Rupes* - Willo Davis
Roberts 1217

VIETNAM

The Lotus Seed - Sherry Garland 443

Tam Nong
Grandfather's Dream - Holly Keller 731

VIETNAM, SOUTH

*Sweet Dried Apples: A Vietnamese Wartime Chldhood
* - Rosemary Breckler 133

VIRGIN ISLANDS OF THE UNITED
STATES

St. Thomas
Rata-Pata-Scata-Fata: A Caribbean Story - Phillis
Gershator 457

WEST INDIES

Captain Abdul's Pirate School - Colin
McNaughton 990

ZIMBABWE

Where Are You Going, Manyoni? - Catherine
Stock 1393

Harare
Do You Know Me? - Nancy Farmer 400

Subject Index

This index lists subjects which are covered in the featured titles. These can include such things as family life, animals, personal and social problems, historical events, ethnic groups, and story types, e.g. Mystery and Detective Stories. Beneath each subject heading, titles are arranged alphabetically with author names and entry numbers also indicated.

AIDS (Disease)

Tiger Flowers - Patricia Quinlan   1183
Too Far Away to Touch - Leslea Newman   1071

Air Travel

Mr. Lunch Takes a Plane Ride - J. Otto
   Seibold   1308

Airplanes

Grandpa Is a Flyer - Sanna Anderson Baker   62

Alcoholism

My Dad - Niki Daly   319
Never Say Quit - Bill Wallace   1470
A Share of Freedom - June Rae Wood   1549
The Trophy - Dean Hughes   662

Aliens

Alien Alert! - Debra Hess   597
Angela's Aliens - Janet Taylor Lisle   876
Insects from Outer Space - Frank Asch   47
Jason and the Escape from Bat Planet - Gery
   Greer   507
My Brother Is a Visitor from Another Planet - Dyan
   Sheldon   1327
The Mystery Machine - Herbie Brennan   134
Ned Feldman, Space Pirate - Daniel Manus
   Pinkwater   1156
Solay - Mark J. Harris   562
Stinker's Return - Pamela F. Service   1311

American Colonies

Drums at Saratoga - Lisa Banim   68
A Spy in the King's Colony - Lisa Banim   69

American West

Armadillo Rodeo - Jan Brett   135
The Bone Stranger - Frank Remkiewicz   1208
Buffalo Bill and the Pony Express - Eleanor
   Coerr   262
Cowboy Country - Ann Herbert Scott   1301
Coyote Steals the Blanket: A Ute Tale - Janet
   Stevens   1380
The Golly Sisters Ride Again - Betsy Byars   193
How I Spent My Summer Vacation - Mark
   Teague   1411
Nine for California - Sonia Levitin   854
Sam's Wild West Show - Nancy Antle   36
A Shooting Star: A Novel about Annie Oakley - Sheila
   Solomon Klass   766
*The Sweetwater Run: The Story of Buffalo Bill Cody
   and the Pony Express* - Andrew Glass   476
Tyrannosaurus Tex - Betty G. Birney   111

Amish

Down Buttermilk Lane - Barbara Mitchell   1021

Amusement Parks

Coaster - Betsy Duffey   367
The Watchers: A Mystery at Alton Towers - Helen
   Cresswell   300

Ancestry

Search for the Shadowman - Joan Lowery
   Nixon   1076

Angels

Dog Heaven - Cynthia Rylant   1248
Good Griselle - Jane Yolen   1579
Snow Angel - Jean Marzollo   945

Anger

Andrew's Angry Words - Dorothea Lachner   802
Carousel - Pat Cummings   307
The Rat and the Tiger - Keiko Kasza   722
Tales of the Wicked Witch - Hanna Kraan   782
Tough Loser - Barthe DeClements   332
Trade-In Mother - Marisabina Russo   1244

Animals

Alejandro's Gift - Richard E. Albert   19
Alvah and Arvilla - Mary Lyn Ray   1199
Arthur's Family Vacation - Marc Brown   147
Aunt Eater's Mystery Christmas - Doug
   Cushman   312
Badger's Bring Something Party - Hiawyn
   Oram   1098
A Bear for All Seasons - Diane Marcial Fuchs   433
Booby Hatch - Betsy Lewin   863
*The Boy Who Lived with the Bears: And Other
   Iroquois Stories* - Joseph Bruchac   158
The Cherry Tree Buck and Other Stories - Robin
   Moore   1035
Dad! I Can't Sleep - Michael Foreman   416
Daisy's Garden - Mordicai Gerstein   460
Fish and Flamingo - Nancy White Carlstrom   213
Flatfoot Fox and the Case of the Missing Whoooo -
   Eth Clifford   258
Frank and Ernest on the Road - Alexandra Day   324
Frog Is Frightened - Max Velthuijs   1453
Geoffrey Groundhog Predicts the Weather - Bruce
   Koscielniak   780
George Washington's Cows - David Small   1346
Good Morning, Pond - Alyssa Satin Capucilli   205
Good Night, Gorilla - Peggy Rathmann   1195
Gooseberry Park - Cynthia Rylant   1249
Hamlet and the Enormous Chinese Dragon Kite -
   Brian Lies   872
Hazel Saves the Day - SuAnn Kiser   764
How the Ostrich Got Its Long Neck - Verna
   Aardema   1
Hungry Hyena - Mwenye Hadithi   536
I Went to the Zoo - Rita Golden Gelman   447
If Anything Ever Goes Wrong at the Zoo - Mary Jean
   Hendrick   582
*Inside a Barn in the Country: A Rebus Read-Along
   Story* - Alyssa Satin Capucilli   206
It's My Birthday - Helen Oxenbury   1103
Jaguarundi - Virginia Hamilton   551
James and the Rain - Karla Kuskin   800
Jazz, Pizzaz, and the Silver Threads - Mary
   Quattlebaum   1182
Just a Little Bit - Ann Tompert   1424
Little Pink Pig - Pat Hutchins   673
Lucy Comes to Stay - Rosemary Wells   1495
Lunch with Milly - Jeanne Modesitt   1025
M.C. Turtle and the Hip Hop Hare: A Nursery Rap -
   David Vozar   1457
Mattie's Little Possum Pet - Ida Luttrell   907
Merry Christmas, Old Armadillo - Larry Dane
   Brimner   138
Moles Can Dance - Richard Edwards   380
A Most Unusual Lunch - Robert Bender   97
Mouse Party - Alan Durant   376
Mouse's Birthday - Jane Yolen   1584
The Mud Flat Olympics - James Stevenson   1386
Mule Eggs - Cynthia DeFelice   336
My Shadow - Susan Winter   1535
*A Newbery Zoo: A Dozen Animal Stories by Newbery
   Award-Winning Authors* - Martin H.
   Greenberg   499

Night Thunder and the Queen of the Wild Horses -
   Lynn Reiser   1204
No More Animals! - Lucia Monfried   1029
Nothing at All - Denys Cazet   227
Parents in the Pigpen, Pigs in the Tub - Amy
   Ehrlich   387
Pepi and the Secret Names - Jill Paton Walsh   1115
The Picnic - Ruth Brown   155
Pig, Horse, or Cow, Don't Wake Me Now - Arlene
   Alda   21
Piggie Pie! - Margie Palatini   1105
Rabbit-Cadabra! - James Howe   657
Rats on the Range and Other Stories - James
   Marshall   937
The Return of Rinaldo, the Sly Fox - Ursel
   Scheffler   1276
Rinaldo on the Run - Ursel Scheffler   1277
The Secret Path - Nick Butterworth   189
A Song for Little Toad - Vivian French   430
Sophie in the Saddle - Dick King-Smith   752
Stories from Firefly Island - Benedict Blathwayt   116
The Story of the Three Kingdoms - Walter Dean
   Myers   1057
The Swoose - Dick King-Smith   756
The Tale of Rabbit and Coyote - Tony Johnston   706
Tales of the Wicked Witch - Hanna Kraan   782
The Thing That Bothered Farmer Brown - Teri
   Sloat   1345
Three at Sea - Timothy Bush   185
Three Bags Full - Ragnhild Scamell   1273
Time for Bed - Mem Fox   422
Too Tired - Ann Turnbull   1430
Tortoise's Flying Lesson - Margaret Mayo   955
Two by Two by Two - Jonathan Allen   26
Two Mice in Three Fables - Lynn Reiser   1207
A Village Full of Valentines - James Stevenson   1387
The Wainscott Weasel - Tor Seidler   1309
What Would Mama Do? - Judith Ross Enderle   392
What's for Lunch? - John Schindel   1284
Where Are You Going, Manyoni? - Catherine
   Stock   1393
Whistling Dixie - Marcia Vaughan   1452
Wipe Your Feet! - Daniel Lehan   832
Zoo - Anthony Browne   156

Animals, Treatment of

The Bear & Mr. Bear - Frances Thomas   1416
The Booford Summer - Susan Mathias Smith   1356
Champ Hobarth - Judith Bernie Strommen   1400
Little Kit or, the Industrious Flea Circus Girl - Emily
   Arnold McCully   967
Pole Dog - Tres Seymour   1313
Throw-Away Pets - Betsy Duffey   370
Time and the Clockmice, Etcetera - Peter
   Dickinson   349
Willa and Old Miss Annie - Berlie Doherty   357

Animals/Alligators

An Extraordinary Egg - Leo Lionni   875
Feliciana Feydra LeRoux: A Cajun Tall Tale - Tynia
   Thomassie   1418
The Gator Girls - Joanna Cole   270
Gertie and Gumbo - Matt Novak   1082
Later, Gator - Laurence Yep   1573

Animals/Armadillos

The Armadillo from Amarillo - Lynne Cherry   236
Armadillo Rodeo - Jan Brett   135

Animals/Badgers

Two Bushy Badgers - Patience Brewster   136

Dog Breath: The Horrible Trouble with Hally Tosis - Dav Pilkey 1148

Dog Days for Dudley - Barbara Moe 1026

Dog Donovan - Diana Hendry 583

Dog Friday - Hilary McKay 980

Dog Heaven - Cynthia Rylant 1248

The Dog Who Cried Woof - Nancy Coffelt 264

Dogteam - Gary Paulsen 1120

Dogzilla - Dav Pilkey 1149

Dream Meadow - Helen V. Griffith 518

Faith and the Electric Dogs - Patrick Jennings 693

Genghis Khan: A Dog Star Is Born - Marjorie Weinman Sharmat 1320

Ghost Dog - Ellen Leroe 836

The Ghost of Popcorn Hill - Betty Ren Wright 1557

Good Luck, Ronald Morgan! - Patricia Reilly Giff 464

Grandfather's Christmas Camp - Marc McCutcheon 969

The Hallo-Wiener - Dav Pilkey 1151

Henry and Mudge and the Best Day of All - Cynthia Rylant 1250

Henry and Mudge and the Careful Cousin - Cynthia Rylant 1251

Henry and Mudge and the Wild Wind - Cynthia Rylant 1252

Hound Heaven - Linda Oatman High 612

I Am the Dog, I Am the Cat - Donald Hall 542

The Invisible Dog - Dick King-Smith 748

Johnny Rides Again - Jo Ann Muchmore 1048

The Joy Boys - Betsy Byars 194

The Junkyard Dog - Erika Tamar 1407

Just in Time for Christmas - Louise Borden 125

Kashtanka - Anton Chekhov 235

Lassie Come-Home - Rosemary Wells 1494

The Latchkey Dog - Mary Jane Auch 50

Lester's Dog - Karen Hesse 600

Lily - Abigail Thomas 1414

Lucy Comes to Stay - Rosemary Wells 1495

Maggie and Silky and Joe - Amy Ehrlich 386

Martha Calling - Susan Meddaugh 1001

Martha Speaks - Susan Meddaugh 1002

Maxi, the Star - Debra Barracca 79

Milton, My Father's Dog - Eric Copeland 291

Mr. Lunch Takes a Plane Ride - J. Otto Seibold 1308

Mr. Putter and Tabby Walk the Dog - Cynthia Rylant 1255

Mrs. Donald's Dog Bun and His Home Away From Home - William Maxwell 953

Murphy and Kate - Ellen Howard 653

Mush, a Dog from Space - Daniel Manus Pinkwater 1155

My Dog Rosie - Isabelle Harper 559

My Dog Talks - Gail Herman 591

Nate the Great and the Tardy Tortoise - Marjorie Weinman Sharmat 1322

The New Puppy - Laurence Anholt 35

The Night I Followed the Dog - Nina Laden 805

No Dogs Allowed - Jane Cutler 317

No Dogs Allowed - Howie Schneider 1288

Nothing but Trouble - Betty Ren Wright 1561

Officer Buckle and Gloria - Peggy Rathmann 1196

The Old Dog - Charlotte Zolotow 1597

One Dog Day - J. Patrick Lewis 866

Out to Lunch - Priscilla Lamont 809

The Outside Dog - Charlotte Pomerantz 1165

A Place for Grace - Jean Davies Okimoto 1092

Pole Dog - Tres Seymour 1313

Posy Bates, Again! - Helen Cresswell 299

The Puppy Sister - S.E. Hinton 623

Sable - Karen Hesse 602

Sebastian (Super Sleuth) and the Copycat Crime - Mary Blount Christian 243

Sebastian (Super Sleuth) and the Flying Elephant - Mary Blount Christian 244

Shiloh Season - Phyllis Reynolds Naylor 1068

A Sled Dog for Moshi - Jeanne Bushey 186

Something Queer in Outer Space - Elizabeth Levy 861

The Sounds of Summer - David Updike 1438

A Sunburned Prayer - Marc Talbert 1406

The Sweetest Fig - Chris Van Allsburg 1444

This Is the Bear and the Bad Little Girl - Sarah Hayes 575

Three Stories You Can Read to Your Dog - Sara Swan Miller 1015

Tornado - Betsy Byars 197

Trouble Will Find You - Joan M. Lexau 870

The Trouble with Henriette! - Wende Devlin 347

The Trouble with Mister - Debra Keller 729

Uncle Fedya, His Dog, and His Cat - Eduard Uspenskii 1440

Watchdog and the Coyotes - Bill Wallace 1472

Animals/Dolphins

A Dolphin Named Bob - Twig C. George 453

Animals/Ducks

Danny's Duck - June Crebbin 297

Don't Fidget a Feather - Erica Silverman 1336

Duncan the Dancing Duck - Syd Hoff 632

Friday Night at Hodge's Cafe - Tim Egan 382

In the Rain with Baby Duck - Amy Hest 604

The Surprise Family - Lynn Reiser 1205

Animals/Elephants

Elephant Moon - Bijou Le Tord 827

Humphrey Thud - Camilla Ashforth 48

Little Gray One - Jan Wahl 1466

My Friend Harry - Kim Lewis 868

Never Ride Your Elephant to School - Doug Johnson 699

Nightwalkers - Judy K. Morris 1041

A Quiet Night In - Jill Murphy 1052

Som See and the Magic Elephant - Jamie Oliviero 1094

The Tusk Fairy - Nicola Smee 1348

Animals/Foxes

Apple Valley Year - Ann Turner 1431

Four Famished Foxes and Fosdyke - Pamela Duncan Edwards 379

Fox on Stage - James Marshall 936

Mole's Hill - Lois Ehlert 384

Peeping Beauty - Mary Jane Auch 52

Rabbit Surprise - Eric L. Houck Jr. 648

Red Fox Running - Eve Bunting 176

The Return of Rinaldo, the Sly Fox - Ursel Scheffler 1276

Animals/Frogs and Toads

Blackberry Hollow - Paul Peabody 1123

An Extraordinary Egg - Leo Lionni 875

Felix's Hat - Catherine Bancroft 66

Froggy Learns to Swim - Jonathan London 888

Good Morning, Pond - Alyssa Satin Capucilli 205

Grandpa Toad's Last Secret - Keiko Kasza 721

The Green Musketeers and the Fabulous Frogs - Sara St. Antoine 1375

Hop Jump - Ellen Stoll Walsh 1475

I'll Meet You Halfway - John Schindel 1283

Jimmy, the Pickpocket of the Palace - Donna Jo Napoli 1061

Let's Go, Froggy! - Jonathan London 892

Peeping and Sleeping - Fran Manushkin 930

Saving Owen's Toad - Juanita Havill 573

That's Philomena! - Catherine Bancroft 67

Animals/Geese

Aunt Skilly and the Stranger - Kathleen Stevens 1382

Branta and the Golden Stone - Walter Wangerin Jr. 1477

The Cuckoo Child - Dick King-Smith 747

Don't Fidget a Feather - Erica Silverman 1336

Goose and the Mountain Lion - Marian Harris 561

Honkers - Jane Yolen 1582

James Bear and the Goose Gathering - Jim Latimer 821

Rebel - John Schoenherr 1290

Tilly and the Rhinoceros - Sheila White Samton 1260

Animals/Giraffes

Emily the Giraffe - Pascal Lemaitre 833

The Warm Place - Nancy Farmer 401

Animals/Goats

One Night: A Story from the Desert - Cristina Kessler 738

So Much in Common - Laurie A. Jacobs 682

Three Cool Kids - Rebecca Emberley 390

Animals/Hippos

Chestnut Cove - Tim Egan 381

So Much in Common - Laurie A. Jacobs 682

Animals/Horses

Be Well, Beware - Jessie Haas 528

Beware the Mare - Jessie Haas 529

A Blue for Beware - Jessie Haas 530

The Carousel - Liz Rosenberg 1231

Dance of the Sacred Circle: A Native American Tale - Kristina Rodanas 1223

Earthquake! A Story of Old San Francisco - Kathleen V. Kudlinski 798

The Enchanted Horse - Magdalen Nabb 1058

The Great Pony Hassle - Nancy Springer 1374

A Horse for All Seasons - Sheila Kelly Welch 1490

A Horse Like Barney - Jessie Haas 532

The Ice Horse - Candice Christiansen 248

Jim-Dandy - Hadley Irwin 677

Midnight Rider - Krista Ruepp 1238

No Foal Yet - Jessie Haas 534

Pony Crazy - Bonnie Bryant 164

Returning Nicholas - Deborah Durland DeSaix 346

Snowy - Berlie Doherty 356

Sophie's Lucky - Dick King-Smith 754

Uncle Daney's Way - Jessie Haas 535

Winni Allfours - Babette Cole 268

Animals/Insects

Bernal & Florinda: A Spanish Tale - Eric A. Kimmel 743

Buz - Richard Egielski 383

Clouds of Terror - Catherine A. Welch 1489

The Fire Bug Connection: An Ecological Mystery - Jean Craighead George 450

Horrible Harry and the Dungeon - Suzy Kline 769

Insects Are My Life - Megan McDonald 974

Insects from Outer Space - Frank Asch 47

Mary Ann - Betsy James 686

Miss Spider's Tea Party - David Kirk 760

Spider Kane and the Mystery at Jumbo Nightcrawler's - Mary Pope Osborne 1102

The Very Lonely Firefly - Eric Carle 210

When the Fly Flew In. . . - Lisa Westberg Peters 1136

Woollybear Good-bye - Sharon Phillips Denslow 343

Bullies

Burglary

Business Enterprises

Camps and Camping

Cancer

Canoeing

Carnivals

Castles

Cartoons and Comics

Caves

Change

Charity

Cheating

Child Abuse

Chinese Americans

Christian Life

Christmas

Grandmother Bryant's Pocket - Jacqueline Briggs
   Martin   941
Harry's Stormy Night - Una Leavy   829
Henry and Mudge and the Wild Wind - Cynthia
   Rylant   1252
I'm George Washington and You're Not! - Steven
   Kroll   789
In the Palace of the Ocean King - Marilyn
   Singer   1338
Kate's Giants - Valiska Gregory   512
King Kenrick's Splinter - Sally Derby   345
The Knight Who Was Afraid to Fight - Barbara Shook
   Hazen   578
Lester's Dog - Karen Hesse   600
Let's Go Home, Little Bear - Martin Waddell   1463
Lights Out! - John Himmelman   620
Little Rabbit Goes to Sleep - Tony Johnston   705
Man Out at First - Matt Christopher   251
Night in the Barn - Faye Gibbons   462
Night Lights: A Sukkot Story - Barbara Diamond
   Goldin   484
On a Starry Night - Natalie Kinsey-Warnock   759
One Brave Summer - Ann Turner   1434
Pip's Magic - Ellen Stoll Walsh   1476
Rabbit Mooncakes - Hoong Yee Lee Krakauer   783
Sarah, Also Known as Hannah - Lillian Hammer
   Ross   1233
Stella's Bull - Frances Arrington   45
Surprise! Surprise! - Michael Foreman   417
Too Much Talk - Angela Shelf Medearis   1006
Tuck in the Pool - Martha Weston   1502
The Up & Down Spring - Johanna Hurwitz   672
Whistle Home - Natalie Honeycutt   639
Wonderful Alexander and the Catwings - Ursula K. Le
   Guin   826

Feral Children

Passenger - Jane Yolen   1585

Fires

Earthquake! A Story of Old San Francisco - Kathleen
   V. Kudlinski   798
Fire in the Wind - Betty Levin   843
The Hen That Crowed - Sheila Cole   273
Smoky Night - Eve Bunting   177
Tikvah Means Hope - Patricia Polacco   1163
The Year of Fire - Teddy Jam   684

Fishing

Blue Claws - Walter Lyon Krudop   795
Deep River - Elaine Moore   1032
Lobster Boat - Brenda Z. Guiberson   525
Lucky Morning - Sally Noll   1079
A Million Fish. . .More or Less - Pat McKissack   986
Moonlight on the River - Deborah Kovacs   781
Rosie's Fishing Trip - Amy Hest   608
Tomorrow on Rocky Pond - Lynn Reiser   1206

Floods

The Dove - Dianne Stewart   1391
No More Water in the Tub! - Tedd Arnold   43
Too Tired - Ann Turnbull   1430
Tumble Tower - Anne Tyler   1435
Two by Two by Two - Jonathan Allen   26

Folk Tales

The Adventures of Hershel of Ostropol - Eric A.
   Kimmel   742
Beware the Brindlebeast - Anita Riggio   1213
The Boardwalk Princess - Arthur A. Levine   845
The Boy and the Giants - Fiona Moodie   1030
*The Boy Who Lived with the Bears: And Other
   Iroquois Stories* - Joseph Bruchac   158

The Boy Who Swallowed Snakes - Laurence
   Yep   1570
The Christmas Blizzard - Helen Ketteman   739
Coyote and the Laughing Butterflies - Harriet Peck
   Taylor   1408
Coyote and the Magic Words - Phyllis Root   1227
The Day Sun Was Stolen - Jamie Oliviero   1093
Diane Goode's Book of Scary Stories and Songs -
   Diane Goode   487
The Faithful Friend - Robert D. San Souci   1261
The Fog's Net - Pat Pflieger   1146
Folks Call Me Appleseed John - Andrew Glass   475
The Freedom Riddle - Angela Shelf Medearis   1004
The Golden Goose - Uri Shulevitz   1334
*Her Stories: African American Folktales, Fairy Tales,
   and True Tales* - Virginia Hamilton   550
How Night Came from the Sea: A Story from Brazil -
   Mary-Joan Gerson   458
How the Ostrich Got Its Long Neck - Verna
   Aardema   1
*How Thunder and Lightning Came to Be: A Choctaw
   Legend* - Beatrice Orcutt Harrell   560
Hungry Hyena - Mwenye Hadithi   536
Jig, Fig, and Mrs. Pig - Peter Hansard   555
John Henry - Julius Lester   839
The Korean Cinderella - Shirley Climo   261
Lazy Jack - Vivian French   428
Lily and the Wooden Bowl - Alan Schroeder   1294
The Lion's Whiskers: An Ethiopian Folktale - Nancy
   Raines Day   325
Little Red Riding Hood: A Newfangled Prairie Tale -
   Lisa Campbell Ernst   394
M.C. Turtle and the Hip Hop Hare: A Nursery Rap -
   David Vozar   1457
Matthew and the Sea Singer - Jill Paton Walsh   1114
The Moon Was at a Fiesta - Matthew Gollub   485
On Cat Mountain - Francoise Richard   1209
Pace and the Witch: A Puerto Rican Folktale - Felix
   Pitre   1157
Papa Gatto: An Italian Fairy Tale - Ruth
   Sanderson   1265
The People of Corn: A Mayan Story - Mary-Joan
   Gerson   459
The Rabbit's Escape - Suzanne Crowder Han   552
*Sally Ann Thunder Ann Whirlwind Crockett: A Tall
   Tale* - Steven Kellogg   734
The Seal Prince - Sheila MacGill Callahan   200
Spooky Stories for a Dark and Stormy Night - Alice
   Low   900
The Story of the Milky Way: A Cherokee Tale - Joseph
   Bruchac   162
Swamp Angel - Anne Isaacs   678
The Tale of Rabbit and Coyote - Tony Johnston   706
Three Cool Kids - Rebecca Emberley   390
The Three Little Pigs - Harriet Ziefert   1595
The Three Little Wolves and the Big Bad Pig - Eugene
   Trivizas   1427
The Tiny, Tiny Boy and the Big, Big Cow - Nancy Van
   Laan   1445
Too Much Talk - Angela Shelf Medearis   1006
Tops and Bottoms - Janet Stevens   1381
Tortoise's Flying Lesson - Margaret Mayo   955
Tsubu the Little Snail - Carol Ann Williams   1518
Two of Everything - Lily Toy Hong   641
Tyrannosaurus Tex - Betty G. Birney   111
The Wave of the Sea-Wolf - David Wisniewski   1542
Wicked Jack - Connie Nordhielm Wooldridge   1553
The Year of No More Corn - Helen Ketteman   741
Yettele's Feathers - Joan Rothenberg   1237

Food

Bertha's Garden - Elisabeth Dyjak   377
The Boy Who Ate Around - Henrik Drescher   365
Cabbage Moon - Tim Chadwick   230
Clouds of Terror - Catherine A. Welch   1489
D.W. the Picky Eater - Marc Brown   151

Four Famished Foxes and Fosdyke - Pamela Duncan
   Edwards   379
Here Comes Henny - Charlotte Pomerantz   1164
How to Make an Apple Pie and See the World -
   Marjorie Priceman   1175
Hungry Hyena - Mwenye Hadithi   536
It's My Birthday - Helen Oxenbury   1103
The Market Lady and the Mango Tree - Pete
   Watson   1483
Max and Ruby's Midas: Another Greek Myth -
   Rosemary Wells   1497
The Miracle of the Potato Latkes: A Hanukkah Story -
   Malka Penn   1129
Molly and the Strawberry Day - Pam Conrad   281
A Most Unusual Lunch - Robert Bender   97
Mr. Putter and Tabby Pick the Pears - Cynthia
   Rylant   1254
Oliver's Vegetables - Vivian French   429
Saturday Sancocho - Leyla Torres   1425
The Sugaring-Off Party - Jonathan London   895
The Swan's Gift - Brenda Seabrooke   1306
This Is a Great Place for a Hot Dog Stand - Barney
   Saltzberg   1259
TV Dinner - Betsy Everitt   398
What's for Lunch? - John Schindel   1284
*Yesterday I Lost a Sneaker (and Found the Great
   Goob Sick)* - David McPhail   996

Animals/Aardvarks

Arthur's First Sleepover - Marc Brown   148
Arthur's New Puppy - Marc Brown   149
D.W. the Picky Eater - Marc Brown   151

Foster Homes

Nightwalkers - Judy K. Morris   1041
Team Picture - Dean Hughes   661

Freedom

The Bear & Mr. Bear - Frances Thomas   1416
The Foot Warmer and the Crow - Evelyn
   Coleman   274
Meet Addy: An American Girl - Connie Porter   1169
Sweet Clara and the Freedom Quilt - Deborah
   Hopkinson   644

Friendship

The Adventures of Sugar and Junior - Angela Shelf
   Medearis   1003
Alan and Naomi - Myron Levoy   856
Albie the Lifeguard - Louise Borden   124
Amber Brown Is Not a Crayon - Paula Danziger   320
Amber on the Mountain - Tony Johnston   702
Amelia's Notebook - Marissa Moss   1044
Andrew Jessup - Nette Hilton   619
Angela's Aliens - Janet Taylor Lisle   876
Annie Bananie Moves to Barry Avenue - Leah
   Komaiko   775
Attack of the Killer Fishsticks - Paul Zindel   1596
B.J.'s Billion-Dollar Bet - Julie Anne Peters   1133
A Baby Just Like Me - Susan Winter   1534
Bad Girls - Cynthia Voigt   1456
Badger's Bring Something Party - Hiawyn
   Oram   1098
A Bear for All Seasons - Diane Marcial Fuchs   433
The Beast and the Boy - Massimo Mostacchi   1047
Becoming Felix - Nancy Hope Wilson   1531
The Berenstain Bears and the New Girl in Town - Stan
   Berenstain   99
Best Friends Together Again - Aliki   25
Beyond the Magic Sphere - Gail Jarrow   691
A Blue for Beware - Jessie Haas   530
A Boy and His Bear - Harriet Graham   491
Boys at Work - Gary Soto   1361
The Bracelet - Yoshiko Uchida   1436

Frontier and Pioneer Life

Gambling

Games

Gangs

Gardens and Gardening

Ghosts

Time Travel

The 13th Floor: A Ghost Story - Sid Fleischman 409
2095 - Jon Scieszka 1298
The Hanukkah Ghosts - Malka Penn 1128
Haphazard House - Mary Wesley 1500
Harry on Vacation - Dyan Sheldon 1326
Lost in Cyberspace - Richard Peck 1126
The Secret of the Ruby Ring - Yvonne
  MacGrory 915
The Timekeeper - Emily Rodda 1224
Tut Tut - Jon Scieszka 1299
Your Mother Was a Neanderthal - Jon
  Scieszka 1300

Toys

The Bag I'm Taking to Grandma's - Shirley
  Neitzel 1069
Barney Is Best - Nancy White Carlstrom 212
Bear E. Bear - Susan Straight 1396
A Bear for Miguel - Elaine Marie Alphin 28
Emma Bean - Jean Van Leeuwen 1449
Good Night, Sleep Tight - Penelope Lively 884
Humphrey Thud - Camilla Ashforth 48
I Love You, Bunny Rabbit - Shulamith Levey
  Oppenheim 1097
The Little Boat - Kathy Henderson 581
My Friend Harry - Kim Lewis 868
The Mystery of the Cupboard - Lynne Reid
  Banks 73
Ned - Selina Young 1589
Nurse Sally Ann - Terrance Dicks 350
Sleep Well, Little Bear - Quint Buchholz 165
The Story of Santa Claus - Tom Paxton 1122
Tom and Pippo and the Bicycle - Helen
  Oxenbury 1104
Toying with Danger - Drew Stevenson 1383
The Tusk Fairy - Nicola Smee 1348

Trains

All Aboard! - James Stevenson 1384
The Banshee Train - Odds Bodkin 119
Mac and Marie and the Train Toss Surprise -
  Elizabeth Fitzgerald Howard 649
The Mighty Santa Fe - William H. Hooks 642
Moony B. Finch, the Fastest Draw in the West - David
  McPhail 993
Pianna - Mary Lyn Ray 1200
The Sunday Outing - Gloria Jean Pinkney 1154

Transportation

The Armadillo from Amarillo - Lynne Cherry 236
Big Red Truck - Stephen Schlossberg 1285
A Busy Day for a Good Grandmother - Margaret
  Mahy 921
Call Me Ahnighito - Pam Conrad 280
Frank and Ernest on the Road - Alexandra Day 324
Grandfather's Trolley - Bruce McMillan 987
Harvey Slumfenburger's Christmas Present - John
  Burningham 183
The Little Black Truck - Libba Moore Gray 495
Tap-Tap - Karen Lynn Williams 1521
The Waiting Day - Harriett Diller 351

Travel

What's French for HELP, George? - Helen
  McCann 961

Trees

Around the Oak - Gerda Muller 1049
Pearl Moscowitz's Last Stand - Arthur A.
  Levine 846
Pearl Plants a Tree - Jane Breskin Zalben 1593

Someday a Tree - Eve Bunting 178
Tanya's Big Green Dream - Linda Glaser 474
When the Monkeys Came Back - Kristine L.
  Franklin 425

Twins

Children of the Longhouse - Joseph Bruchac 159
Double Play at Short - Matt Christopher 249
Egg-Drop Blues - Jacqueline Turner Banks 70
Girl Wonder and the Terrific Twins - Malorie
  Blackman 113
The Great Pony Hassle - Nancy Springer 1374
Harry and Tuck - Holly Keller 732
The New One - Jacqueline Turner Banks 71
Odd Man Out - Gail Radley 1185
On the Trail with Miss Pace - Sharon Phillips
  Denslow 342
One Up, One Down - Carol Snyder 1358
The St. Patrick's Day Shamrock Mystery - Marion M.
  Markham 934
Tarantula Shoes - Tom Birdseye 110
The Twin in the Tavern - Barbara Brooks
  Wallace 1469

Underground Railroad

Caleb's Choice - G. Clifton Wisler 1539
Come Morning - Leslie Davis Guccione 524
Escape into the Night - Lois Walfrid Johnson 700
*Journey to Freedom: A Story of the Underground
  Railroad* - Courtni C. Wright 1562
Minty: A Story of Young Harriet Tubman - Alan
  Schroeder 1295
A School for Pompey Walker - Michael J.
  Rosen 1230
True North - Kathryn Lasky 818

Underground Resistance Movements

Into the Flames - Robert Elmer 388

Unicorns

Day of the Unicorn - Mollie Hunter 664
The Dragon and the Unicorn - Lynne Cherry 237

Vacations

*The Absolutely True Story. . .How I Visited Yellowstone
  Park with the Terrible Rupes* - Willo Davis
  Roberts 1217
Arthur's Family Vacation - Marc Brown 147
Buckledown the Workhound - Danny Shanahan 1314
Grandaddy and Janetta - Helen V. Griffith 519
Harry on Vacation - Dyan Sheldon 1326
How I Spent My Summer Vacation - Mark
  Teague 1411
Juliet's Story - William Trevor 1426
Komodo! - Peter Sis 1340
Lucky Morning - Sally Noll 1079
Martha Calling - Susan Meddaugh 1001
No Dogs Allowed - Howie Schneider 1288
On the Trail with Miss Pace - Sharon Phillips
  Denslow 342
Santa's Winter Vacation - Viveca Larn
  Sundvall 1404
See the Ocean - Estelle Condra 277
Sophie in the Saddle - Dick King-Smith 752
Tomorrow on Rocky Pond - Lynn Reiser 1206
The Up & Down Spring - Johanna Hurwitz 672
Wizard and Wart at Sea - Janice Lee Smith 1353

Vampires

Great-Uncle Dracula and the Dirty Rat - Jayne
  Harvey 568

Little Vampire and the Midnight Bear - Mary DeBall
  Kwitz 801
Rabbit-Cadabra! - James Howe 657

Vietnam War

Sweet Dried Apples: A Vietnamese Wartime Chldhood
  - Rosemary Breckler 133

Violence

Adam's War - Sonia Levitin 853

Voyages and Travels

Across the Wide Dark Sea: The Mayflower Journey -
  Jean Van Leeuwen 1446
Alvah and Arvilla - Mary Lyn Ray 1199
Bluewater Journal: The Voyage of the Sea Tiger -
  Loretta Krupinski 797
Dear Levi: Letters from the Overland Trail - Elvira
  Woodruff 1550
The Floating House - Scott Russell Sanders 1263
Going Home - Margaret Wild 1512
Grandfather's Journey - Allen Say 1271
How to Make an Apple Pie and See the World -
  Marjorie Priceman 1175
*A Journey to the New World: The Diary of Remember
  Patience Whipple* - Kathryn Lasky 815
Mary Patten's Voyage - Richard Berleth 103
Oregon's Journey - Rascal 1191
She Flew No Flags - Joan B. Manley 928
The Snow Queen - Hans Christian Andersen 32
Someplace Else - Carol P. Saul 1269
Wagon Train 911 - Jamie Gilson 473
Wagons West - Roy Gerrard 455

War

War Game - Michael Foreman 418

War of 1812

Abigail's Drum - John A. Minahan 1020
Washington City Is Burning - Harriette Gillem
  Robinet 1218

Wealth

Argo, You Lucky Dog - Maggie Smith 1355

Weather

The Christmas Blizzard - Helen Ketteman 739
First Snow - Kim Lewis 867
The Fog's Net - Pat Pflieger 1146
Geoffrey Groundhog Predicts the Weather - Bruce
  Koscielniak 780
The Gift from Saint Nicholas - Dorothea
  Lachner 803
The Gullywasher - Joyce Rossi 1234
Harry's Stormy Night - Una Leavy 829
A Hat for Minerva Louise - Janet Morgan
  Stoeke 1394
Henry and Mudge and the Wild Wind - Cynthia
  Rylant 1252
How the Sky's Housekeeper Wore Her Scarves -
  Patricia Hooper 643
In the Rain with Baby Duck - Amy Hest 604
James and the Rain - Karla Kuskin 800
Lionel in the Winter - Stephen Krensky 788
Mendel's Ladder - Mark Karlins 719
Outside, Inside - Carolyn Crimi 303
Ruby's Storm - Amy Hest 609
Sail Away - Donald Crews 302
Snow Day! - Barbara M. Joosse 713
The Storm - Anne F. Rockwell 1222

Character Name Index

This index alphabetically lists the major characters in each featured title. Each character name is followed by a description of the character. Citations also provide titles of the books featuring the character—listed alphabetically if there is more than one title—author names, and entry numbers.

A

Aaron (Child)
Matzah Ball: A Passover Story - Mindy Avra Portnoy 1170

Abbajon (Fisherman; Storyteller)
A Million Fish. . .More or Less - Pat McKissack 986

Abbey (Child)
My Island Grandma - Kathryn Lasky 816

Abby (Child)
Mommies Don't Get Sick - Marylin Hafner 537

Abdul (Pirate)
Captain Abdul's Pirate School - Colin McNaughton 990

Abe (Child)
I'll See You When the Moon Is Full - Susi Gregg Fowler 421

Abebe (Child; Stepson)
The Lion's Whiskers: An Ethiopian Folktale - Nancy Raines Day 325

Abercrombie, Horace (Goat)
So Much in Common - Laurie A. Jacobs 682

Abernathy, Clifford Allyn "Cliff" III (12-Year-Old)
Fig Pudding - Ralph Fletcher 411

Abernathy, Joshua (Child)
Fig Pudding - Ralph Fletcher 411

Abigail (Child; Sister)
A Turkey Drive and Other Tales - Barbara Ann Porte 1167

Abuela (Grandmother; Storyteller)
Isla - Arthur Dorros 362

Abuelito (Grandfather; Cowboy)
The Gullywasher - Joyce Rossi 1234

Abuelo (Grandfather; Immigrant)
A Day's Work - Eve Bunting 172

Abuelo (Grandfather)
The Farolitos of Christmas - Rudolfo Anaya 31

Ace (Student—High School; Basketball Player)
Slam Dunk Saturday - Jean Marzollo 944

Adam (Child; Leader)
Adam's War - Sonia Levitin 853

Adam (Immigrant)
The Always Prayer Shawl - Sheldon Oberman 1089

Adam (Grandfather)
The Always Prayer Shawl - Sheldon Oberman 1089

Adam (Uncle; Worker)
My Apron - Eric Carle 209

Adam (Brother; Twin)
One Up, One Down - Carol Snyder 1358

Adam Joshua (Child)
The Baby Blues: An Adam Joshua Story - Janice Lee Smith 1351

Adam Joshua (Child; Brother)
Serious Science - Janice Lee Smith 1352

Adams, Callie (6th Grader)
Nerd No More - Kristine L. Franklin 424

Adams, Nora Jean (11-Year-Old; Cousin)
Harvey's Mystifying Raccoon Mix-Up - Eth Clifford 259

Addario, Ben (Child; Friend)
Starshine and Sunglow - Betty Levin 844

Africa (Slave)
True North - Kathryn Lasky 818

Agnes, Fanny (Farmer)
Fanny's Dream - Caralyn Buehner 166

Ah Pau (Grandmother)
First Apple - Ching Yeung Russell 1241
Water Ghost - Ching Yeung Russell 1242

Ahnighito (Celestial Body)
Call Me Ahnighito - Pam Conrad 280

Aiken, Tammy (Adoptee; Sports Figure)
Double Play at Short - Matt Christopher 249

Aimesworth, Art Atchinson (Brother; Inventor)
Santa Calls - William Joyce 715

Aimesworth, Esther (Sister)
Santa Calls - William Joyce 715

Aisha (Sister)
Magid Fasts for Ramadan - Mary Matthews 951

Aitken, George (13-Year-Old)
What's French for HELP, George? - Helen McCann 961

Al (Aged Person)
Sophie's Lucky - Dick King-Smith 754

Albert (Rabbit)
Cabbage Moon - Tim Chadwick 230

Albert (Uncle)
The Secret Super Powers of Marco - Meredith Sue Willis 1525

Albert (Farmer)
Shortcut - David Macaulay 911

Albert (Aged Person)
Gooseberry Park - Cynthia Rylant 1249

Albert "Meat" (Detective—Amateur; Neighbor)
The Dark Stairs - Betsy Byars 191

Albert "Meat" (Sidekick; Detective—Amateur)
Dead Letter - Betsy Byars 192

Albie (Child)
Albie the Lifeguard - Louise Borden 124

Aleasha (Dog; Sister)
The Puppy Sister - S.E. Hinton 623

Alejandro (Aged Person; Gardener)
Alejandro's Gift - Richard E. Albert 19

Alex (10-Year-Old; Friend)
Boys at Work - Gary Soto 1361

Alex (5-Year-Old)
Carousel - Pat Cummings 307

Alex (Child)
Dancing - Denys Cazet 226

Alex (Child; Classmate)
Father's Rubber Shoes - Yumi Heo 589

Alex (4th Grader)
The Pool Party - Gary Soto 1364

Alex (Child)
River Day - Jane B. Mason 947

Alex (Child; Friend)
Three at Sea - Timothy Bush 185

Alex (Child; Animal Lover)
The Trouble with Mister - Debra Keller 729

Alexander (Child)
Alexander, Who's Not (Do You Hear Me? I Mean It!) Going to Move - Judith Viorst 1455

Alexander, Henry (Father)
The Formerly Great Alexander Family - Susan Richards Shreve 1331

Alexander, Liam (10-Year-Old; Brother)
The Formerly Great Alexander Family - Susan Richards Shreve 1331

Alexander the Grate (Thief)
The Ghastly Gerty Swindle: With the Ghosts of Hungryhouse Lane - Sam McBratney 959

Alice (Child; Dancer)
Dancing Daisy - Kay Gallwey 439

Alice (Child; Neighbor)
Emily and Alice - Joyce Champion   231

Alice (Child; Friend)
Emily and Alice Again - Joyce Champion   232

Alice (Cousin; Librarian)
Meg Mackintosh and the Mystery in the Locked Library - Lucinda Landon   811

Alice (Child)
Someday a Tree - Eve Bunting   178

Alice (Teacher; Religious)
Good-Bye, Hello - Barbara Shook Hazen   577

Alice Ann (Child; Cousin)
The Key to the Playhouse - Carol Beach York   1586

Allegra (Unicorn)
The Dragon and the Unicorn - Lynne Cherry   237

Allen, Donavan (3rd Grader; Collector)
Donavan's Word Jar - Monalisa DeGross   337

Allen, Kitty (3rd Grader)
Mary Marony Hides Out - Suzy Kline   770

Allen, Nicholas "Nick" (5th Grader)
Frindle - Andrew Clements   257

Allfours, Winni (Child; Pony)
Winni Allfours - Babette Cole   268

Alsinger, Mikey (5th Grader)
Bad Girls - Cynthia Voigt   1456

Alvah (Spouse; Farmer)
Alvah and Arvilla - Mary Lyn Ray   1199

Amanda (Child)
Amanda's Perfect Hair - Linda Breiner Milstein   1019

Amanda (Child; Traveller)
Nine for California - Sonia Levitin   854

Amanda (Pig; Sister)
Oliver & Amanda and the Big Snow - Jean Van Leeuwen   1450

Amanda (Child; Niece)
The Palace of Stars - Patricia Lakin   808

Amanda Jane (2-Year-Old; Sister)
Serious Science - Janice Lee Smith   1352

Amani (Buffalo; Mother)
Kalinzu: A Story from Africa - Jeremy Grimsdell   521

Amazing Karlovsky (Magician)
Rabbit-Cadabra! - James Howe   657

Amber (Child)
Amber on the Mountain - Tony Johnston   702

Amber (Dog)
The Latchkey Dog - Mary Jane Auch   50

Ambrose (Bird; Companion)
Mr. Lunch Takes a Plane Ride - J. Otto Seibold   1308

Amelia (10-Year-Old; Writer)
Amelia Writes Again - Marissa Moss   1043

Amelia (9-Year-Old; Writer)
Amelia's Notebook - Marissa Moss   1044

Amelia (Child; Friend)
The Giant - Mordicai Gerstein   461

Amelia (Witch)
Strega Nona Meets Her Match - Tomie De Paola   329

Amos (Dog)
Night in the Barn - Faye Gibbons   462

Amy (Child; Friend)
Lights for Gita - Rachna Gilmore   471

Amy (Child)
Looking for Diamonds - Brenda Seabrooke   1305

Amy (Child; Friend)
Mary Ann - Betsy James   686
The Pink Party - Maryann Macdonald   914

Ana (Cook)
Saturday Market - Patricia Grossman   522

Anders, Ellen (6th Grader)
Ellen Anders on Her Own - Karen Hirsch   625

Andersen, Elise (Twin; Resistance Fighter)
Into the Flames - Robert Elmer   388

Andersen, Peter (Twin; Resistance Fighter)
Into the Flames - Robert Elmer   388

Anderson, Morten (Prisoner)
Into the Flames - Robert Elmer   388

Andrew (Child; Artist)
Andrew's Amazing Monsters - Kathryn Hook Berlan   102

Andrew (Child; Brother)
Andrew's Angry Words - Dorothea Lachner   802

Andrew (Student; Friend)
Sophie Is Seven - Dick King-Smith   753

Andy (Father)
Tom Foolery - Curtis Parkinson   1111

Angel (Railroad Worker; Artisan)
Down at Angel's - Sharon Chmielarz   239

Angel (Child; Friend)
Sycamore Street - C.B. Christiansen   247

Angela (Child)
Angela's Wings - Eric Jon Nones   1080

Angela (7th Grader)
Jericho - Janet Hickman   611

Anica (Grandmother)
The Gift of a Traveler - Wendy Matthews   952

Anna (Child)
Amber on the Mountain - Tony Johnston   702

Anna (Child; Indian)
Anna's Athabaskan Summer - Arnold Griese   514

Anna (Child)
Apple Picking Time - Michele Benoit Slawson   1342
The Gift from Saint Nicholas - Dorothea Lachner   803
The Ice Palace - Angela McAllister   957

Anna (Friend)
I've Got Chicken Pox - True Kelley   733

Anna (Child)
The New Puppy - Laurence Anholt   35

Anna (Aged Person; Musician)
Pianna - Mary Lyn Ray   1200

Anna (Time Traveller; Sister)
Tut Tut - Jon Scieszka   1299

Anna Sarah "Annala" (Child; Immigrant)
Soon, Annala - Riki Levinson   852

Annabel (Pig)
Annabel Again - Janice Boland   122

Anne (Child)
Grandpa Is a Flyer - Sanna Anderson Baker   62

Annie (Dog; Cousin)
Annie and Cousin Precious - Kay Chorao   241

Annie (Child)
Annie Bananie Moves to Barry Avenue - Leah Komaiko   775
Annie Flies the Birthday Bike - Crescent Dragonwagon   364

Annie (Child; Dancer)
Dance on a Sealskin - Barbara Winslow   1533

Annie (Cousin; Child)
Henry and Mudge and the Careful Cousin - Cynthia Rylant   1251

Annie (13-Year-Old; Mentally Challenged Person)
My Sister Annie - Bill Dodds   354

Annie (Stepmother)
My Wicked Stepmother - Norman Leach   828

Annie (Aged Person; Neighbor)
Willa and Old Miss Annie - Berlie Doherty   357

Anthony (Bear; Friend)
Edward's Overwhelming Overnight - Rosemary Wells   1492

Anthony (Brother; Twin)
Girl Wonder and the Terrific Twins - Malorie Blackman   113

Anthony (4th Grader)
Not-So-Normal Norman - Cynthia Stowe   1395

Anthony (Child)
You're a Genius, Blackboard Bear - Martha Alexander   24

Anthony "Ant" (Child)
My Brother, Ant - Betsy Byars   196

Anton (Farmer; Hunter)
The Swan's Gift - Brenda Seabrooke   1306

Antonia (Child)
Returning Nicholas - Deborah Durland DeSaix   346

Applebaum, Elsie (Aged Person; Aunt)
Something for Everyone - Susan Whitcher   1508

Appleby (Teenager; 15-Year-Old)
The Mennyms - Sylvia Waugh   1484

Appleflinger, Alice (Aunt)
Jeremy's Muffler - Laura F. Nielsen   1074

Araminta "Minty" (Slave; 8-Year-Old)
Minty: A Story of Young Harriet Tubman - Alan Schroeder   1295

Arbuckle (Father)
No Dogs Allowed - Howie Schneider   1288

Archer, Jenny (Child)
Get the Picture, Jenny Archer? - Ellen Conford   278

Archibald (Uncle)
King Kenrick's Splinter - Sally Derby   345

Argo (Dog)
Argo, You Lucky Dog - Maggie Smith   1355

Arianna (Child; Royalty)
The Dragon and the Unicorn - Lynne Cherry   237

Arias (Teacher)
The Little Painter of Sabana Grande - Patricia Maloney Markun   935

Armstrong, Annie (10-Year-Old; Sister)
The Baby Grand, the Moon in July, & Me - Joyce Annette Barnes   78

Armstrong, Matthew "Matty" (Musician; Brother)
The Baby Grand, the Moon in July, & Me - Joyce Annette Barnes   78

Arnie (Cat)
Arnie and the Skateboard Gang - Nancy Carlson   211

Arnold (Pig; Bullied Child)
The Wimp - Kathy Caple   204

Arqueta, Rosa (Child-Care Giver)
Gracias, Rosa - Michelle Markel   933

Arrow, Emily (Student)
Look Out, Washington, D.C.! - Patricia Reilly Giff   465

Arthur (Aardvark; Student)
Arthur Writes a Story - Marc Brown   145

Arthur (Chimpanzee; Brother)
Arthur's Camp-Out - Lillian Hoban   627

Arthur (Aardvark; Brother)
Arthur's Chicken Pox - Marc Brown   146
Arthur's Family Vacation - Marc Brown   147

Bear, Jesse (Bear)
Happy Birthday, Jesse Bear! - Nancy White
Carlstrom 214

Bear, Sister (Bear; Student)
The Berenstain Bears and the New Girl in Town - Stan
Berenstain 99

Bearly (Bear)
Pioneer Bear - Joan Sandin 1266

Beatrice (Cat)
The Mushroom Man - Ethel Pochocki 1158

Beatrice (Stepsister)
Papa Gatto: An Italian Fairy Tale - Ruth
Sanderson 1265

Beatrix (Maiden)
Rude Giants - Audrey Wood 1548

Beau (Child)
Good Griselle - Jane Yolen 1579

Beautiful Bengal (Tiger)
Heart of a Tiger - Marsha Arnold 42

Beauville, Jamie (Child)
What Jamie Saw - Carolyn Coman 276

Beauville, Nin (Child)
What Jamie Saw - Carolyn Coman 276

Beauville, Patty (Mother)
What Jamie Saw - Carolyn Coman 276

Beaver, Ann (Grandmother; Indian)
A Walk to the Great Mystery - Virginia A.
Stroud 1402

Becker, Ilana (Child; Sister)
One Yellow Daffodil: A Hanukkah Story - David A.
Adler 14

Becker, Jonathan (Child; Brother)
One Yellow Daffodil: A Hanukkah Story - David A.
Adler 14

Becket, Gilbert (Traveller)
The Saracen Maid - Leon Garfield 441

Beckwith, Mallory (7th Grader)
Really No Big Deal - Margaret Bechard 92

Becky (Child)
Octopus Hug - Laurence Pringle 1177

Bedelia, Amelia (Housekeeper)
Good Driving, Amelia Bedelia - Peggy Parish 1108

Beecher, Uriah (Doctor)
The Apprenticeship of Lucas Whitaker - Cynthia
DeFelice 334

Beeman, Jesse (Child; Friend)
Superbird to the Rescue - Nancy Hayashi 574

Beemer, Charley (Sports Figure)
The Man in the Ceiling - Jules Feiffer 403

Beethoven (Cat)
Mrs. Merriwether's Musical Cat - Carol Purdy 1181

Beetle (Servant)
The Twin in the Tavern - Barbara Brooks
Wallace 1469

Bella (Horse; Toy)
The Enchanted Horse - Magdalen Nabb 1058

Beloved Woman (Aged Person; Indian)
The Story of the Milky Way: A Cherokee Tale - Joseph
Bruchac 162

Ben (Brother; Cousin)
Around the Oak - Gerda Muller 1049

Ben (Gardener; Employer)
A Day's Work - Eve Bunting 172

Ben (6th Grader)
Fruit Flies, Fish & Fortune Cookies - Anne
LeMieux 834

Ben (Child; Brother)
Moonlight on the River - Deborah Kovacs 781

Ben (Child)
The Old Dog - Charlotte Zolotow 1597

Ben (Brother; Twin)
One Up, One Down - Carol Snyder 1358

Ben (Child; Brother)
Passover Magic - Roni Schotter 1291

Beni (Bear)
Happy New Year, Beni - Jane Breskin Zalben 1591

Benito (Child)
Benito's Dream Bottle - Naomi Shihab Nye 1086

Benito (Brother)
A Sunburned Prayer - Marc Talbert 1406

Benjamin (Rabbit)
Babysitting for Benjamin - Valiska Gregory 511

Benjamin (9-Year-Old)
The Barn - Avi 54

Benjamin (5-Year-Old)
Benjamin Bigfoot - Mary Serfozo 1310

Benjamin (Uncle)
Sarah, Also Known as Hannah - Lillian Hammer
Ross 1233

Benjy (Sheep)
Nora's Surprise - Satomi Ichikawa 675

Bennett (Royalty; Friend)
Florizella and the Wolves - Philippa Gregory 510

Bennett, Carolyn (3rd Grader; Friend)
When Jane-Marie Told My Secret - Gina Willner-
Pardo 1528

Benton, Kayo (12-Year-Old)
Don't Go Near Mrs. Tallie - Peg Kehret 724

Bernal (Gentleman)
Bernal & Florinda: A Spanish Tale - Eric A.
Kimmel 743

Bernard (Bear)
Bernard on His Own - Syd Hoff 631

Berra, Yogi (Baseball Player)
My Dad's Baseball - Ron Cohen 267

Berry, Jan (Writer)
Mary Marony Hides Out - Suzy Kline 770

Bert (Farmer; Spouse)
The Great Pig Escape - Eileen Christelow 242

Bertha (Wolf; Gardener)
Bertha's Garden - Elisabeth Dyjak 377

Bertie (Collector)
Plantpet - Elise Primavera 1176

Berty (Child; Brother)
Waiting for the Evening Star - Rosemary Wells 1498

Bess (Grandmother; Healer)
The Moorchild - Eloise Jarvis McGraw 978

Bess Ann (Artist; Learning Disabled Child)
Last Left Standing - Barbara T. Russell 1240

Best, Caroline (Tourist; Divorced Person)
The In-Between Days - Eve Bunting 174

Beth (Child; Sister)
Roommates Again - Kathryn O. Galbraith 437

Betsy (5-Year-Old)
Honkers - Jane Yolen 1582

Betsy (Frog)
Hop Jump - Ellen Stoll Walsh 1475

Bettina (Child; Sister)
Carolina Shout! - Alan Schroeder 1293

Beware (Horse)
Be Well, Beware - Jessie Haas 528
Beware the Mare - Jessie Haas 529

A Blue for Beware - Jessie Haas 530

Bibot (Dentist)
The Sweetest Fig - Chris Van Allsburg 1444

Big Anthony (Assistant)
Strega Nona Meets Her Match - Tomie De
Paola 329

Big Bear (Bear; Father)
Let's Go Home, Little Bear - Martin Waddell 1463

Big Cheese (Mouse; Leader)
Dogzilla - Dav Pilkey 1149

Big Jim (Foster Parent)
Nightwalkers - Judy K. Morris 1041

Big Mama (Grandmother; Storyteller)
May'naise Sandwiches & Sunshine Tea - Sandra
Belton 96

Big Nutbrown Hare (Rabbit; Father)
Guess How Much I Love You - Sam McBratney 960

Big Sister (Teenager)
Red Dancing Shoes - Denise Lewis Patrick 1116

Bijju (12-Year-Old; Brother)
Binya's Blue Umbrella - Ruskin Bond 123

Bilberry (Wanderer; Eccentric)
Across the Blue Mountains - Emma Chichester
Clark 238

Bill (Grandfather)
Grandad Bill's Song - Jane Yolen 1580

Bill (Gardener; Artist)
Seeds - George Shannon 1318

Bills, Walter "Papaw" (Grandfather)
Hound Heaven - Linda Oatman High 612

Billy (Friend)
No More Animals! - Lucia Monfried 1029

Billy Que (Aged Person)
Bobbin Dustdobbin - Susan Patron 1117

Binya (10-Year-Old; Sister)
Binya's Blue Umbrella - Ruskin Bond 123

Bird, Secretary (Bird; Assistant)
Flatfoot Fox and the Case of the Missing Whoooo -
Eth Clifford 258

Birdie (Aged Person)
Beware the Brindlebeast - Anita Riggio 1213

Birdy (Child)
Matthew and the Sea Singer - Jill Paton Walsh 1114

Birgit (Child; Cousin)
Kisses from Rosa - Petra Mathers 949

Bishop, Cordelia (Teacher; Spinster)
Up a Road Slowly - Irene Hunt 663

Bixby, William (9-Year-Old; Cousin)
More than a Name - Candice F. Ransom 1189

Black, Randy (Soccer Player)
Never Say Quit - Bill Wallace 1470

Blackboard Bear (Bear)
You're a Genius, Blackboard Bear - Martha
Alexander 24

Blackfeather, William (Uncle; Indian)
Remember My Name - Sara H. Banks 74

Blair, Emily (1st Grader; Friend)
How Emily Blair Got Her Fabulous Hair - Susan
Garrison 445

Blake, Fanny (Child)
Traveling Backward - Toby Forward 420

Blanche (Sheep; Adoptee)
My Real Family - Emily Arnold McCully 968

Blanco, Cedric Whitgift 57th (Mouse)
The Four-Legged Ghosts - Mary Hoffman 635

Bruno (Duck; Detective—Police)
The Return of Rinaldo, the Sly Fox - Ursel
Scheffler 1276

Bruno (Duck; Detective)
Rinaldo on the Run - Ursel Scheffler 1277

Bryan, Will (Child)
Just in Time for Christmas - Louise Borden 125

Bryant (Healer)
Grandmother Bryant's Pocket - Jacqueline Briggs
Martin 941

Bryant, Sarah (8-Year-Old)
Grandmother Bryant's Pocket - Jacqueline Briggs
Martin 941

Bubbie (Grandmother)
My Rotten Redheaded Older Brother - Patricia
Polacco 1161

Buckle (Goose)
Aunt Skilly and the Stranger - Kathleen
Stevens 1382

Buckle (Police Officer)
Officer Buckle and Gloria - Peggy Rathmann 1196

Buckledown (Dog)
Buckledown the Workhound - Danny Shanahan 1314

Buckner, Michael (6th Grader; Brother)
My Brother, the Ghost - Suzanne Weyn 1503

Buckner, Sara (7th Grader; Sister)
My Brother, the Ghost - Suzanne Weyn 1503

Buckskin Dan (Guide)
Wagons West - Roy Gerrard 455

Buddy (Cat)
Copycat - Ruth Brown 154

Buddy (Rabbit; Daydreamer)
Listen, Buddy - Helen Lester 837

Buffle, Tom (Spirit)
The Ghost of Popcorn Hill - Betty Ren Wright 1557

Buffy (Toad)
Saving Owen's Toad - Juanita Havill 573

Buggins (Dog)
Posy Bates, Again! - Helen Cresswell 299

Bujold, Graciella "Grassy Ella" (Healer; Psychic)
Going to See Grassy Ella - Kathryn Lance 810

Bumblebee (Pony)
Sophie in the Saddle - Dick King-Smith 752

Bun (Dog)
*Mrs. Donald's Dog Bun and His Home Away From
Home* - William Maxwell 953

Bungaroo, Ralph T. (Kidnapper)
Charlie Malarkey and the Singing Moose - William
Kennedy 736

Bunnicula (Rabbit; Magician)
Rabbit-Cadabra! - James Howe 657

Bunny (Pig; Sister)
Tuck in the Pool - Martha Weston 1502

Bunny (Rabbit)
Warm at Home - Roni Schotter 1292

Bunny Rabbit (Toy)
I Love You, Bunny Rabbit - Shulamith Levey
Oppenheim 1097

Buntz, Taddy (10-Year-Old; Orphan)
The Twin in the Tavern - Barbara Brooks
Wallace 1469

Burbank (Opossum)
The Mud Flat Olympics - James Stevenson 1386

Burdle (Dog; Friend)
Out to Lunch - Priscilla Lamont 809

Burton (Stork)
Burton and Stanley - Frank O'Rourke 1101

Bushwick, Cathy (7th Grader)
My Crazy Cousin Courtney - Judi Miller 1011

Buster (Rabbit; Friend)
Arthur's First Sleepover - Marc Brown 148

Butterbarrel, Maxwell (Mythical Creature)
Mendel's Ladder - Mark Karlins 719

Buttons (Raccoon)
Harvey's Mystifying Raccoon Mix-Up - Eth
Clifford 259

Buz (Insect)
Buz - Richard Egielski 383

Buzby (Cat; Hotel Worker)
Buzby to the Rescue - Julia Hoban 626

Buzz (4th Grader; Bully)
Jenna's Big Jump - Faythe Dyrud Thureen 1420

Byner, B.J. (4th Grader; Gambler)
B.J.'s Billion-Dollar Bet - Julie Anne Peters 1133

Byron (Teacher)
Becoming Felix - Nancy Hope Wilson 1531

C

Cabbage Rose (Artist)
Cabbage Rose - Mary-Claire Helldorfer 580

Cage, Patience (Artist)
Josiah True and the Art Maker - Amy
Littlesugar 883

Caldero, Tony (Baseball Player; 12-Year-Old)
The Sluggers Club: A Sports Mystery - Paul Robert
Walker 1467

Caldwell, Terry (7th Grader)
Chive - Shelley A. Barre 80

Caleb (Orphan; Fisherman)
Caleb's Friend - Eric Jon Nones 1081

Caleb (13-Year-Old)
Jim-Dandy - Hadley Irwin 677

Call, Alan (Basketball Player; Friend)
The Trophy - Dean Hughes 662

Callahan, Roberta Jean "Bobbie Jean" (6th Grader)
Good-Bye, Hello - Barbara Shook Hazen 577

Callahan, Sarah "Gramma" (Grandmother; Aged
Person)
Good-Bye, Hello - Barbara Shook Hazen 577

Cally (Teenager)
Beyond the Magic Sphere - Gail Jarrow 691

Calvin "Pa" (Father; Farmer)
Parents in the Pigpen, Pigs in the Tub - Amy
Ehrlich 387

Cambardella, Frankie (12-Year-Old)
Coaster - Betsy Duffey 367

Camilla (Teacher; Traveller)
Nine for California - Sonia Levitin 854

Cannon, Doug (12-Year-Old; Bicyclist)
Olympic Dream - Matt Christopher 252

Capshaw, Sarah (Detective—Amateur)
Toying with Danger - Drew Stevenson 1383

Carlito (11-Year-Old)
The Stowaway: A Tale of California Pirates - Kristiana
Gregory 508

Carlos (Child)
Carlos and the Cornfield/Carlos y la Milpa de Maiz -
Jan Romero Stevens 1379

Carmina (8-Year-Old)
Fernando's Gift/El Regalo de Fernando - Douglas
Keister 728

Carol Ann (Friend; Classmate)
Don't Call Me Beanhead! - Susan
Wojciechowski 1544

Carole (6-Year-Old; Friend)
Pond Year - Kathryn Lasky 817

Caroline (Sister; Cousin)
Around the Oak - Gerda Muller 1049

Caroline (13-Year-Old; Sister)
Dakota Spring - D. Anne Love 899

Caroline (Companion; Southern Belle)
*When Will This Cruel War Be Over? The Civil War
Diary of Emma Simpson* - Barry Denenberg 340

Caroline Rose (Child; Sister)
The Hayloft - Lisa Westberg Peters 1135

Carper, Wilma Letitia "Willy" (Child)
*The Catspring Somersault Flying One-Handed Flip-
Flop* - SuAnn Kiser 763

Carrie (Child)
Catkin - Antonia Barber 75

Carter, Cassandra (6th Grader)
Rosie's Tiger - Anna Myers 1055

Carter, Dawn (Classmate)
Bye, Bye, Bai Kai - Harriett Luger 904

Carter, Josh (6th Grader)
The Light on Hogback Hill - Cynthia DeFelice 335

Carter, Ludwig von Beethoven "Wiggie" (6th
Grader)
Nerd No More - Kristine L. Franklin 424

Carter, Marilyn M. (Mother; Television Personality)
Nerd No More - Kristine L. Franklin 424

Carter, Sam (Grandfather; Rancher)
Someone to Count On - Patricia Hermes 594

Casanova, Brian (Brother)
A Mammoth Mix-Up - Elizabeth Levy 859

Casanova, Brian (2nd Grader; Brother)
School Spirit Sabotage - Elizabeth Levy 860

Casanova, Penny "Pea Brain" (Child; Sister)
A Mammoth Mix-Up - Elizabeth Levy 859
School Spirit Sabotage - Elizabeth Levy 860

Caselli, Louis (5th Grader)
Bad Girls - Cynthia Voigt 1456

Casey (Child; Friend)
Nannies for Hire - Amy Hest 606

Casi Lampu'a Lentemue (Witch)
Pace and the Witch: A Puerto Rican Folktale - Felix
Pitre 1157

Cassandra (Child)
Juneteenth Jamboree - Carole Boston
Weatherford 1487

Castello, Billy (9-Year-Old; Child of Divorced
Parents)
Slam Dunk Saturday - Jean Marzollo 944

Castle (Teacher)
Benjamin Bigfoot - Mary Serfozo 1310

Castleberry, Joe Dean (8-Year-Old)
Woollybear Good-bye - Sharon Phillips Denslow 343

Cat (Cat; Hunter)
Cat, Mouse, and Moon - Roxanne Dyer Powell 1171

Cat (Cat)
The Fat Cat Sat on the Mat - Nurit Karlan 718
I Am the Dog, I Am the Cat - Donald Hall 542
A Question of Trust - Marion Dane Bauer 88

Catherwood, Rob (Animal Trainer)
Away to Me, Moss - Betty Levin 842

Catkin (Cat)
Catkin - Antonia Barber 75

Catwing, Jane (Cat)
Wonderful Alexander and the Catwings - Ursula K. Le Guin 826

Cecilia (Child; Niece)
A Birthday Basket for Tia - Pat Mora 1036

Celeste (Child)
Celeste and Crabapple Sam - Jennifer Brutschy 163

Celie (Child; Sister)
Celie and the Harvest Fiddler - Vanessa Flournoy 414

Cervantes (Mouse)
The Bookstore Mouse - Peggy Christian 245

Cessano, Marsha (3rd Grader)
Good Grief...Third Grade - Colleen O'Shaughnessy McKenna 983

Cessano, Marsha (5th Grader)
Live from the Fifth Grade - Colleen O'Shaughnessy McKenna 984

Chadwick, Beck (Neighbor; Thief)
Grandmother Bryant's Pocket - Jacqueline Briggs Martin 941

Champ Hobarth (Dog)
Champ Hobarth - Judith Bernie Strommen 1400

Chancy (Cat; Blind)
Fat Chance! - Lady Borton 127

Chandler (Friend)
Just in Time for Christmas - Louise Borden 125

Chang (Elephant)
Som See and the Magic Elephant - Jamie Oliviero 1094

Chang, Peter (Child)
The Last Dragon - Susan Miho Nunes 1085

Chapman, John "Appleseed John" (Frontiersman; Backwoodsman)
Folks Call Me Appleseed John - Andrew Glass 475

Chapman, Nathaniel (Brother)
Folks Call Me Appleseed John - Andrew Glass 475

Charlene (Rooster)
The Hen That Crowed - Sheila Cole 273

Charles, Vincent "Vinnie" (8th Grader)
What Happened in Mr. Fisher's Room - Nancy J. Hopper 646

Charlie (Mouse; Cousin)
Charlie and Tyler at the Seashore - Helen Craig 296

Charlie (Cougar)
The Fear Place - Phyllis Reynolds Naylor 1066

Charlie (Child; Animal Lover)
Midnight Rider - Krista Ruepp 1238

Charlie (6th Grader)
My Sister Annie - Bill Dodds 354

Charlie (Animal Lover)
No More Animals! - Lucia Monfried 1029

Charlie (Deaf)
A Place for Grace - Jean Davies Okimoto 1092

Charlie (Child; Brother)
A Question of Trust - Marion Dane Bauer 88

Charlotte (Kidnapper)
Cousins in the Castle - Barbara Brooks Wallace 1468

Chato (Cat)
Chato's Kitchen - Gary Soto 1362

Checha (Indian; Child)
Sees Behind Trees - Michael Dorris 361

Cheko (Sister; Alien)
Star Hatchling - Margaret Bechard 93

Cheng, Lee (Child; Construction Worker)
The Iron Dragon Never Sleeps - Stephen Krensky 787

Chester, Dan (6th Grader; Friend)
My Name Is Brain/Brian - Jeanne Betancourt 106

Chica (Cat)
A Birthday Basket for Tia - Pat Mora 1036

Chicago (Rabbit)
Chicago and the Cat - Robin Michal Koontz 778
Chicago and the Cat: The Halloween Party - Robin Michal Koontz 779

Chicken Man (Aged Person)
White Socks Only - Evelyn Coleman 275

Chief (Outlaw; Leader)
It Was a Dark and Stormy Night - Allan Ahlberg 16

Chin Yu Min (Widow(er))
Chin Yu Min and the Ginger Cat - Jennifer Armstrong 39

Chloe (Child; Friend)
Sycamore Street - C.B. Christiansen 247

Christabel (Crocodile)
Victor and Christabel - Petra Mathers 950

Christina "Twig" (11-Year-Old; Child of Divorced Parents)
Blue Sky, Butterfly - Jean Van Leeuwen 1447

Christine (12-Year-Old)
The Cave - Kathleen Karr 720

Christine (7-Year-Old)
The Gift of a Traveler - Wendy Matthews 952

Christoph (10-Year-Old)
Beethoven Lives Upstairs - Barbara Nichol 1073

Christy (Child; Neighbor)
Be Good to Eddie Lee - Virginia Fleming 410

Chrysanthemum (Mouse; Student)
Chrysanthemum - Kevin Henkes 585

Chuck (Dog)
Chuck and Danielle - Peter Dickinson 348

Chuck (Squirrel; Friend)
Squirrel Park - Lisa Campbell Ernst 396

Cinder Edna (Stepdaughter)
Cinder Edna - Ellen Jackson 681

Cinderella (Stepdaughter)
Cinder Edna - Ellen Jackson 681

Clack (Neighbor)
The Amazing Christmas Extravaganza - David Shannon 1315

Clara (Child; Friend)
The Giant - Mordicai Gerstein 461

Clara (Child; Sister)
The Night Crossing - Karen Ackerman 4

Clara (Child)
The Nutcracker Ballet - Vladimir Vagin 1441

Clara (10-Year-Old)
The Van Gogh Cafe - Cynthia Rylant 1256

Clare (10-Year-Old; Neighbor)
A Sound of Leaves - Lenore Blegvad 118

Clark, Martha (Child; Sister)
Apple Valley Year - Ann Turner 1431

Clark, Ralph (Father; Farmer)
Apple Valley Year - Ann Turner 1431

Clark, Tim (Child; Brother)
Apple Valley Year - Ann Turner 1431

Clarry, Mavis Mae (5th Grader)
B.J.'s Billion-Dollar Bet - Julie Anne Peters 1133

Claudia (Child of Divorced Parents)
Step by Wicked Step - Anne Fine 407

Claudine (Orphan)
A Place for Angels - Clyde Robert Bulla 169

Claus (Artisan)
The Story of Santa Claus - Tom Paxton 1122

Claus, Santa (Philanthropist; Mythical Creature)
Harvey Slumfenburger's Christmas Present - John Burningham 183

Clem (Uncle; Railroad Worker)
Mac and Marie and the Train Toss Surprise - Elizabeth Fitzgerald Howard 649

Cleo (Sister)
Amelia's Notebook - Marissa Moss 1044

Cloud Eyes (Indian; Daydreamer)
Cloud Eyes - Kathryn Lasky 813

Clyde (Bully; Student)
The Wimp - Kathy Caple 204

Coati (Coatimundi)
Jaguarundi - Virginia Hamilton 551

Cochran (Aged Person; Neighbor)
Tangles - Errol Broome 141

Coco (Cat; Neighbor)
Lilly's Secret - Miko Imai 676

Codie (Child; Niece)
Lavender - Karen Hesse 599

Cody, Bill (15-Year-Old; Cowboy)
Buffalo Bill and the Pony Express - Eleanor Coerr 262

Cody, William F. "Buffalo Bill" (13-Year-Old; Frontiersman)
The Sweetwater Run: The Story of Buffalo Bill Cody and the Pony Express - Andrew Glass 476

Coffrey, Slider (Friend)
The Mystery Machine - Herbie Brennan 134

Cohen, Max (7-Year-Old)
My Dad's Baseball - Ron Cohen 267

Cohen, Ron (Father)
My Dad's Baseball - Ron Cohen 267

Cole, Amanda (Crime Victim; Equestrian)
Dead Letter - Betsy Byars 192

Cole, Bertrand "Berti" (Refugee)
A Different Kind of Courage - Ellen Howard 651

Cole, Rosy (Student; Model)
Rosy Cole: She Walks in Beauty - Sheila Greenwald 504

Colin (Child of Divorced Parents)
Step by Wicked Step - Anne Fine 407

Columbine (Sister)
Prince Nautilus - Laura Krauss Melmed 1008

Compton, Mary Neal "Nealy" (11-Year-Old)
Best Girl - Doris Buchanan Smith 1349

Connerton, Jenna "Jenna Pearl" (11-Year-Old; Sister)
Ghosts Don't Get Goosebumps - Elvira Woodruff 1551

Connerton, Nelson (5-Year-Old; Brother)
Ghosts Don't Get Goosebumps - Elvira Woodruff 1551

Conroy, Ruth (13-Year-Old)
The Exiles at Home - Hilary McKay 981

Coogan, John "Crash" (Teenager; Football Player)
Crash - Jerry Spinelli 1370

Cooke, Lila (13-Year-Old)
Bye, Bye, Bai Kai - Harriett Luger 904

Cooke, Suzie (11-Year-Old)
Bye, Bye, Bai Kai - Harriett Luger 904

Cookie (Cook)
Tyrannosaurus Tex - Betty G. Birney 111

Cool, Big (Goat; Brother)
Three Cool Kids - Rebecca Emberley   390

Cool, Little (Goat; Brother)
Three Cool Kids - Rebecca Emberley   390

Cool, Middle (Goat; Sister)
Three Cool Kids - Rebecca Emberley   390

Cooper, Millie (4th Grader; Friend)
Millie Cooper and Friends - Charlotte Herman   590

Cooper, Miranda (12-Year-Old; Deaf)
Cheshire Moon - Nancy Butts   190

Cooper, Sarah-Jane (10-Year-Old; Cousin)
The Mystery of the Dancing Angels - Elspeth Campbell Murphy   1050

Cooper, Tanya (4th Grader)
Tanya's Big Green Dream - Linda Glaser   474

Cordelia (Child)
The Ballot Box Battle - Emily Arnold McCully   963

Corey (Deaf)
Lester's Dog - Karen Hesse   600

Cosgrove, Amanda (Student)
Blabber Mouth - Morris Gleitzman   479

Count, Carlton (Chess Player)
Countess Veronica - Nancy K. Robinson   1219

Courtney (Dog)
Courtney - John Burningham   182

Cousin Jed (Teacher)
Wagons West - Roy Gerrard   455

Coyote (Coyote)
Coyote: A Trickster Tale from the American Southwest - Gerald McDermott   970
Coyote and the Laughing Butterflies - Harriet Peck Taylor   1408
Coyote and the Magic Words - Phyllis Root   1227
Coyote Steals the Blanket: A Ute Tale - Janet Stevens   1380
The Tale of Rabbit and Coyote - Tony Johnston   706

Crabapple Sam (Recluse)
Celeste and Crabapple Sam - Jennifer Brutschy   163

Crawford, Catherine "Kit" (11-Year-Old)
Green Willow - Eileen Dunlop   373

Crocker (Crocodile)
Yard Sale - James Stevenson   1390

Crockett, Davy (Frontiersman)
Sally Ann Thunder Ann Whirlwind Crockett: A Tall Tale - Steven Kellogg   734

Crockett, Sally Ann Thunder (Frontierswoman)
Sally Ann Thunder Ann Whirlwind Crockett: A Tall Tale - Steven Kellogg   734

Crocodile (Crocodile)
How the Ostrich Got Its Long Neck - Verna Aardema   1

Crump (Neighbor)
Mrs. Merriwether's Musical Cat - Carol Purdy   1181

Curry, Derek (6th Grader)
Down and Up Fall - Johanna Hurwitz   666

Curry, Derek (10-Year-Old; Friend)
The Up & Down Spring - Johanna Hurwitz   672

Curtis (Postal Worker)
Good-Bye, Curtis - Kevin Henkes   586

Curtis, Sheldon "Say" (15-Year-Old; Military Personnel)
Pink and Say - Patricia Polacco   1162

Curtis, Thomas (Child; Friend)
The Mysterious Horseman: An Adventure in Prairietown, 1836 - Kate Waters   1481

Custer, George Armstrong (Historical Figure; Military Personnel)
Jim-Dandy - Hadley Irwin   677

Czernikow, Dan (Worker)
The Haunting of Holroyd Hill - Brenda Seabrooke   1304

D

D (Teacher)
The Baby Blues: An Adam Joshua Story - Janice Lee Smith   1351

D.W. (Aardvark; Sister)
Arthur Writes a Story - Marc Brown   145
Arthur's Chicken Pox - Marc Brown   146
Arthur's Family Vacation - Marc Brown   147
Arthur's First Sleepover - Marc Brown   148
Arthur's New Puppy - Marc Brown   149
D.W. Rides Again! - Marc Brown   150
D.W. the Picky Eater - Marc Brown   151

Dad (Father)
The Cabin Key - Gloria Rand   1187
Dad and Me in the Morning - Patricia Lakin   806

Dad (Bear; Father)
Dad! I Can't Sleep - Michael Foreman   416

Dad (Father)
Good Night, Stella - Kate McMullan   988

Dad (Father; Veteran)
Heroes - Ken Mochizuki   1024

Dad (Father)
I Found Mouse - Pamela D. Greenwood   505
I Want Answers and a Parachute - P.J. Petersen   1138

Dad (Father; Handyman)
If I'd Known Then What I Know Now - Reeve Lindbergh   874

Dad (Bear; Musician)
J.B.'s Harmonica - John Sebastian   1307

Dad (Father)
Just My Dad & Me - Leah Komaiko   776

Dad (Father; Alcoholic)
My Dad - Niki Daly   319

Dad (Father)
My Wicked Stepmother - Norman Leach   828

Dad (Father; Babysitter)
Octopus Hug - Laurence Pringle   1177

Dad (Father; Farmer)
The Storm - Marc Harshman   566

Dad (Father)
A Teeny Tiny Baby - Amy Schwartz   1297
When I Grow Bigger - Trish Cooke   285
Your Dad Was Just Like You - Dolores Johnson   698
Zoo - Anthony Browne   156

Daddy (Father)
Always My Dad - Sharon Dennis Wyeth   1565
The Baby House - Norma Simon   1337
Bebop-a-Do-Walk! - Sheila Hamanaka   547
Big Help! - Anna Grossnickle Hines   621
Daddy Played Music for the Cows - Maryann N. Weidt   1488

Daddy (Father; Artist)
Five Live Bongos - George Ella Lyon   909

Daddy (Father)
Good-Bye, Daddy! - Brigitte Weninger   1499
Hunting the White Cow - Tres Seymour   1312
I'll See You When the Moon Is Full - Susi Gregg Fowler   421

Daddy (Father; Frog)
Let's Go, Froggy! - Jonathan London   892

Daddy (Storyteller)
The Little Tree Growin' in the Shade - Camille Yarbrough   1569

Daddy (Father; Artist)
Miranda's Smile - Thomas Locker   886

Daddy (Father)
Mommies Don't Get Sick - Marylin Hafner   537

Daddy (Father; Artist)
The Painter - Peter Catalanotto   224

Daddy (Father)
Peeping and Sleeping - Fran Manushkin   930
Petey's Bedtime Story - Beverly Cleary   256
So Much - Trish Cooke   284

Daddy (Father; Construction Worker)
Tar Beach - Faith Ringgold   1215

Daddy (Father; Worker)
Working Cotton - Sherley Anne Williams   1522

Daisy (Child; Gardener)
Daisy's Garden - Mordicai Gerstein   460

Daisy (Child; Dancer)
Dancing Daisy - Kay Gallwey   439
Moles Can Dance - Richard Edwards   380

Daisy (Elephant)
Nightwalkers - Judy K. Morris   1041

Daisy (Dog)
Worse than the Worst - James Stevenson   1388

Daisy Dare (Mouse)
Daisy Dare - Anita Jeram   695

Daisy Lee (Child)
TV Dinner - Betsy Everitt   398

Dali, Salvador (Artist; Friend)
Dinner at Magritte's - Michael Garland   442

Dalton, Jack (11-Year-Old; Runaway)
Back to Bataan - Jerome Charyn   234

Dan (Pig; Pirate)
The Pigrates Clean Up - Steven Kroll   791

Dan (Farmer)
Kinda Blue - Ann Grifalconi   516

Dana (Camper)
Daring to be Abigail - Rachel Vail   1442

Dancy (Horse)
Jim-Dandy - Hadley Irwin   677

Daney (Uncle)
Uncle Daney's Way - Jessie Haas   535

Daniel (Child; Brother)
Night Lights: A Sukkot Story - Barbara Diamond Goldin   484

Daniel (Child)
Smoky Night - Eve Bunting   177

Danielle (Child)
Chuck and Danielle - Peter Dickinson   348

Daniels, Doug (3rd Grader; Friend)
How to Be Cool in the Third Grade - Betsy Duffey   369

Daniels, Justin (3rd Grader; Friend)
Amber Brown Is Not a Crayon - Paula Danziger   320

Danilo (Peddler)
Danilo the Fruit Man - Amy Valens   1443

Danny (Child; Student)
Danny's Duck - June Crebbin   297

Danny (6-Year-Old)
Happy Birthday, Danny and the Dinosaur! - Syd Hoff   633

Danny (Child)
The Magic Skateboard - Enid Richemont   1211

Danny (Child; Cousin)
Too Many Tamales - Gary Soto   1365

Dunn, Rory (11-Year-Old; Friend)
The Up & Down Spring - Johanna Hurwitz 672

Dunning (Teacher; Stepmother)
Sticky Beak - Morris Gleitzman 480

Dustbobbin, Bobbin (Child; Mythical Creature)
Bobbin Dustdobbin - Susan Patron 1117

Dustbobbin, PapaHob (Father; Friend)
Bobbin Dustdobbin - Susan Patron 1117

Duster, Oakley (Mentally Challenged Person)
Odd Man Out - Gail Radley 1185

Dustin (Child; Indian)
A Walk to the Great Mystery - Virginia A. Stroud 1402

Dutton, Arminda "GrandMin" (Grandmother)
Jericho - Janet Hickman 611

Duz (Dog)
Genghis Khan: A Dog Star Is Born - Marjorie Weinman Sharmat 1320

Dyer, Doreen (12-Year-Old)
Room for a Stranger - Ann Turnbull 1429

Dyer, Lennie (11-Year-Old)
No Friend of Mine - Ann Turnbull 1428

Dyer, Lennie (15-Year-Old)
Room for a Stranger - Ann Turnbull 1429

Dyesal (Child; Student)
Running the Road to ABC - Denize Lauture 823

E

Earth, Germaine (Teacher)
Seven Spiders Spinning - Gregory Maguire 920

Earth, Rilla Harmony (Child)
Monster of the Month Club - Dian Curtis Regan 1203

Earth, Sparrow Harmony (Mother)
Monster of the Month Club - Dian Curtis Regan 1203

Easton, Scott (13-Year-Old)
Walking the Edge - Alice Mead 999

Ebony (Wolf)
Child of the Wolves - Elizabeth Hall 545

Echo Elmo (Radio Personality)
Wolfman Sam - Elizabeth Levy 862

Eddie (Child)
It's the Bear! - Jez Alborough 20

Eddie Lee (Mentally Challenged Person; Child)
Be Good to Eddie Lee - Virginia Fleming 410

Eddington, Sarah (Teacher; Seamstress)
A Shooting Star: A Novel about Annie Oakley - Sheila Solomon Klass 766

Edison (Dog)
Faith and the Electric Dogs - Patrick Jennings 693

Edna (Dog)
Odds on Oliver - Constance C. Greene 500

Edward (Bear; Friend)
Edward's Overwhelming Overnight - Rosemary Wells 1492

Edward (Brother; Twin)
Girl Wonder and the Terrific Twins - Malorie Blackman 113

Edwards, Valvoline (Beauty Pageant Contestant)
McMummy - Betsy Byars 195

Effie (Grandmother; Settler)
Little Obie and the Kidnap - Martin Waddell 1464

Eleanor (Child; Sister)
That Terrible Baby - Jennifer Armstrong 41

Elephant (Elephant; Friend)
Just a Little Bit - Ann Tompert 1424

Elephant (Elephant)
Mouse Party - Alan Durant 376

Elephant (Elephant; Ruler)
The Story of the Three Kingdoms - Walter Dean Myers 1057

Elephant (Toy)
The Tusk Fairy - Nicola Smee 1348

Eli (Child; Brother)
All the Places to Love - Patricia MacLachlan 916

Elijah (Religious)
Dear Elijah - Miriam Bat-Ami 85

Eliza (Young Woman)
Lily - Abigail Thomas 1414

Elizabeth (Aunt)
The Hanukkah Ghosts - Malka Penn 1128

Elizabeth (Aunt; Seamstress)
My Apron - Eric Carle 209

Elizabeth (Aged Person)
William's Ninth Life - Minna Jung 716

Ella (Child)
Tigerella - Kit Wright 1564

Ellen (Child)
My Wartime Summers - Jane Cutler 316

Ellerbee, Pa-Daddy (Unemployed)
Comford Creek - Joyce McDonald 972

Ellerbee, Quinnella "Quinn" (11-Year-Old)
Comford Creek - Joyce McDonald 972

Ellie (Child)
The Wind Garden - Angela McAllister 958

Eloise (Pig)
Chestnut Cove - Tim Egan 381

Eloy (11-Year-Old)
A Sunburned Prayer - Marc Talbert 1406

Elsa (5th Grader)
That Wild Berries Should Grow: The Diary of a Summer - Gloria Whelan 1506

Elvira (Mythical Creature; Outcast)
Elvira - Margaret Shannon 1319

Elvirey (Child; Settler)
The Log Cabin Quilt - Ellen Howard 652

Em (Spirit; Grandmother)
The Children Next Door - Jean Ure 1439

Emi (Child; Friend)
Bebop-a-Do-Walk! - Sheila Hamanaka 547

Emi (2nd Grader; Friend)
The Bracelet - Yoshiko Uchida 1436

Emily (Child; Friend)
Emily and Alice - Joyce Champion 231
Emily and Alice Again - Joyce Champion 232

Emily (Giraffe)
Emily the Giraffe - Pascal Lemaitre 833

Emily (Child; Student)
Ned - Selina Young 1589

Emily (Child; Dancer)
Tanya and Emily in a Dance for Two - Patricia Lee Gauch 446

Emma (1st Grader; Artist)
Emma's Rug - Allen Say 1270

Emma (Teacher; Religious)
The Indian School - Gloria Whelan 1504

Emma Bean (Toy)
Emma Bean - Jean Van Leeuwen 1449

Ennis, Sandra (12-Year-Old; Crime Victim)
The Case of the Fantastic Footprints - E.W. Hildick 616

Ephram (Child; Musician)
Sing to the Stars - Mary Brigid Barrett 81

Epps, Margalo (5th Grader)
Bad Girls - Cynthia Voigt 1456

Erda, Lionel "Linny" (11-Year-Old; Cousin)
Back to Before - Jan Slepian 1343

Eric the Red (Streetperson)
The Bamboo Flute - Garry Disher 353

Ernest (Child; Detective—Amateur)
The Detective Stars and the Case of the Super Soccer Team - Caroline Levine 848

Ernest (Elephant)
Frank and Ernest on the Road - Alexandra Day 324

Ernestine (8-Year-Old)
The Sunday Outing - Gloria Jean Pinkney 1154

Ernesto (Uncle)
The Magic Shell - Nicholasa Mohr 1027

Ernie (Dog)
The Dog Who Cried Woof - Nancy Coffelt 264

Espino, Fernando (Child; Artist)
The Little Painter of Sabana Grande - Patricia Maloney Markun 935

Ethan Allen (Llama)
A Llama in the Family - Johanna Hurwitz 667

Ethel (Farmer; Spouse)
The Great Pig Escape - Eileen Christelow 242

Eunice (Child; Sister)
Ragsale - Artie Ann Bates 86

Eva (Spouse)
The Story of Santa Claus - Tom Paxton 1122

Everest (Bird; Matchmaker)
Mr. Potter's Pet - Dick King-Smith 750

Everring, Hilda E. (Scientist)
Not-So-Normal Norman - Cynthia Stowe 1395

Evie (Student)
Throw-Away Pets - Betsy Duffey 370

Eyefinger, Emily (Child; Detective—Amateur)
Emily Eyefinger and the Lost Treasure - Duncan Ball 64

Eyris, Moel (Artist)
The Painter Who Loved Chickens - Olivier Dunrea 375

F

Fairchild, Ellen (7th Grader)
Who's Orp's Girlfriend? - Suzy Kline 774

Fairwick, Amelia (Orphan; Kidnap Victim)
Cousins in the Castle - Barbara Brooks Wallace 1468

Faith (10-Year-Old)
Faith and the Electric Dogs - Patrick Jennings 693

Fanaye (Stepmother)
The Lion's Whiskers: An Ethiopian Folktale - Nancy Raines Day 325

Fang (Tarantula)
Tarantula Shoes - Tom Birdseye 110

Fanny (Child; Sister)
The Amazing Felix - Emily Arnold McCully 962

Farmer (Farmer)
Three Bags Full - Ragnhild Scamell 1273

Fraser, Edward (5-Year-Old)
No Dogs Allowed - Jane Cutler 317

Fraser, Edward (1st Grader; Brother)
Rats! - Jane Cutler 318

Fraser, Jason (8-Year-Old)
No Dogs Allowed - Jane Cutler 317

Fraser, Jason (4th Grader; Brother)
Rats! - Jane Cutler 318

Freckles (Dog)
What about My Goldfish? - Pamela D.
 Greenwood 506

Fred (Child)
2095 - Jon Scieszka 1298

Fred (Child of Divorced Parents; Brother)
Dear Fred - Susanna Rodell 1225

Fred (Dog)
I'm a Jolly Farmer - Julie Lacome 804

Fred (Bear; Businessman)
The Mighty Movers - Sidney Levitt 855

Fred (Pig)
Pigs Ahoy! - David McPhail 994

Fred (Bear; Toy)
This Is the Bear and the Bad Little Girl - Sarah
 Hayes 575

Fred (Child)
Your Mother Was a Neanderthal - Jon
 Scieszka 1300

Fred (Knight)
The Knight Who Was Afraid to Fight - Barbara Shook
 Hazen 578

Freda (Child)
From Miss Ida's Front Porch - Sandra Belton 95

Freda (Frog; Sister)
That's Philomena! - Catherine Bancroft 67

Freddie (Bear; Toy)
It's the Bear! - Jez Alborough 20

Freeman, Ben (Servant)
Drums at Saratoga - Lisa Banim 68

Fremont, Marvin (4th Grader; Twin)
Marvelous Marvin and the Pioneer Ghost - Bonnie
 Pryor 1179

Fremont, Sarah (4th Grader; Twin)
Marvelous Marvin and the Pioneer Ghost - Bonnie
 Pryor 1179

Frida Maria (Child)
Frida Maria: A Story of the Old Southwest - Deborah
 Nourse Lattimore 822

Friday (Dog)
Dog Friday - Hilary McKay 980

Friday, Roger (3rd Grader)
Good Grief...Third Grade - Colleen O'Shaughnessy
 McKenna 983

Friday, Roger (5th Grader)
Live from the Fifth Grade - Colleen O'Shaughnessy
 McKenna 984

Frisky (Dog)
Dream Meadow - Helen V. Griffith 518

Frog (Frog; Friend)
Frog Is Frightened - Max Velthuijs 1453

Frog, Felix (Frog)
Felix's Hat - Catherine Bancroft 66

Frog, Fuller (Frog; Friend)
I'll Meet You Halfway - John Schindel 1283

Froggy (Frog)
Froggy Learns to Swim - Jonathan London 888
Let's Go, Froggy! - Jonathan London 892

Fronto (Writer)
The Arkadians - Lloyd Alexander 22

Fujikawa, Walter (Child; Friend)
Superbird to the Rescue - Nancy Hayashi 574

Fuller, Lisa (11-Year-Old)
Haphazard House - Mary Wesley 1500

Fultz, Wendell (Child)
Pigsty - Mark Teague 1412

Furby, Alexander (Kitten; Adventurer)
Wonderful Alexander and the Catwings - Ursula K. Le
 Guin 826

Fuzzy (Toy)
Owen - Kevin Henkes 588

G

Gage, Florence (11-Year-Old; Cousin)
A Haunted Year - Ann Phillips 1147

Gaila (Child; Sister)
Bear E. Bear - Susan Straight 1396

Gales, Cory (11-Year-Old)
Zoe's Gift - Sheila Hayes 576

Gallagher, Jason (5th Grader; Cousin)
Jason and the Losers - Gina Willner-Pardo 1527

Gallows, Grudge (Pirate; Thief)
Tingleberries, Tuckertubs and Telephones - Margaret
 Mahy 927

Gamma Lee (Aged Person)
The Gates of the Wind - Kathryn Lasky 814

Gander (Goose)
Don't Fidget a Feather - Erica Silverman 1336

Garcia, Alex (5th Grader)
Off and Running - Gary Soto 1363

Garcilaso (Father; Government Official)
Bernal & Florinda: A Spanish Tale - Eric A.
 Kimmel 743

Garcilaso, Florinda (Gentlewoman)
Bernal & Florinda: A Spanish Tale - Eric A.
 Kimmel 743

Garland, Fairborn Farley "Twef" (Child)
One Dog Day - J. Patrick Lewis 866

Garrow (Widow(er))
The Invisible Dog - Dick King-Smith 748

Garth (3-Year-Old; Brother)
Courtyard Cat - C.S. Adler 10

Garth, Daniel (16-Year-Old)
Green Willow - Eileen Dunlop 373

Gasper, J.J. (Friend; Student)
Search for the Shadowman - Joan Lowery
 Nixon 1076

Gates, Amanda "Mandy" (12-Year-Old; 7th Grader)
Out of the Storm - Patricia Willis 1526

Gator, Allie (Child; Alligator)
The Gator Girls - Joanna Cole 270

Gator, Amy (Child; Alligator)
The Gator Girls - Joanna Cole 270

Gemini, Samona (5th Grader; Friend)
Seth and Samona - Joanne Hyppolite 674

Gemino (Musician)
The Jewel Heart - Barbara Berger 100

Gemma (Child)
Gemma and the Baby Chick - Antonia Barber 76

Gena (Single Mother)
Smoky Night - Eve Bunting 177

General/Buzzard Breath (Dog)
Buzzard Breath - Marty Crisp 304

Genevieve "Gen" (11-Year-Old)
On Winter's Wind - Patricia Hermes 593

Gennard, Charlie "Grandpa" (Grandfather; Store
 Owner)
Little Champ - Jim Arnosky 44

George (Dog)
The Baby Blues: An Adam Joshua Story - Janice Lee
 Smith 1351

George (Child)
Poppa's New Pants - Angela Shelf Medearis 1005

George, Bertie (Student)
Pie Magic - Toby Forward 419

Gerald (Servant; Father)
The Royal Nap - Charles C. Black 112

Gerald (Brother)
See the Ocean - Estelle Condra 277

Geraldine (Pig; Sister)
Geraldine's Baby Brother - Holly Keller 730

Gerda (Cow)
Rude Giants - Audrey Wood 1548

Gerda (Heroine; Friend)
The Snow Queen - Hans Christian Andersen 32

Gershom, Noah (6th Grader; Child of Divorced
 Parents)
The View from Saturday - E.L. Konigsburg 777

Gert (Grandmother)
Annie Bananie Moves to Barry Avenue - Leah
 Komaiko 775

Gertrude (Cow)
The Cow Who Wouldn't Come Down - Paul Brett
 Johnson 701

Ghost (Spirit)
Old Devil Wind - Bill Martin Jr. 939

Ghost Dog (Dog; Spirit)
Ghost Dog - Ellen Leroe 836

The Giant (Child; Human)
A Tooth Fairy's Tale - David Christiana 246

Giddu (Grandmother)
Magid Fasts for Ramadan - Mary Matthews 951

Gifford, Lilian "Lily" (Child; Equestrian)
A Blue for Beware - Jessie Haas 530

Giles (Single Mother; Mother)
Lizzie's List - Maggie Harrison 564

Giles, Lizzie (9-Year-Old; Child of Divorced
 Parents)
Lizzie's List - Maggie Harrison 564

Gina (Child)
Gina - Bernard Waber 1460

Gina (Child; Sister)
Little Champ - Jim Arnosky 44

Ginger Cat (Cat; Fisherman)
Chin Yu Min and the Ginger Cat - Jennifer
 Armstrong 39

Gita (Child; Immigrant)
Lights for Gita - Rachna Gilmore 471

Gladsake (Cat)
The House Gobbaleen - Lloyd Alexander 23

Gloria (Cook; Niece)
King Kenrick's Splinter - Sally Derby 345

Gloria (Dog)
Officer Buckle and Gloria - Peggy Rathmann 1196

Glum, Beverly Sinclair (Castaway)
Faith and the Electric Dogs - Patrick Jennings 693

Little Rabbit Goes to Sleep - Tony Johnston 705

Grandpa (Grandfather; Blind)
Lucy's Picture - Nicola Moon 1031

Grandpa (Grandfather; Artist)
My Dog Rosie - Isabelle Harper 559

Grandpa (Grandfather)
Oliver's Vegetables - Vivian French 429

Grandpa (Grandfather; Sheep)
Pearl Plants a Tree - Jane Breskin Zalben 1593

Grandpa (Grandfather)
Strudwick: A Sheep in Wolf's Clothing - Robert Kraus 786

Grandpa (Aged Person; Grandfather)
Traveling Backward - Toby Forward 420

Grandpa (Grandfather)
The Wind Garden - Angela McAllister 958
Your Dad Was Just Like You - Dolores Johnson 698

Grandpa Cat (Grandfather; Storyteller)
The Tales of Grandpa Cat - Lee Wardlaw 1479

Grandpa Noonie (Grandfather)
Ghost Dog - Ellen Leroe 836

Grandpa Toad (Toad; Grandfather)
Grandpa Toad's Last Secret - Keiko Kasza 721

Grandpapa (Grandfather)
That Wild Berries Should Grow: The Diary of a Summer - Gloria Whelan 1506

Grandpappy (Grandfather)
Whistling Dixie - Marcia Vaughan 1452

Grandy (Grandfather; Farmer)
Honkers - Jane Yolen 1582

Granger, Lorelei (Teacher)
Frindle - Andrew Clements 257

Granite (Dog)
Child of the Wolves - Elizabeth Hall 545

Granny (Grandmother)
Gregory Cool - Caroline Binch 107
Hotter than a Hot Dog! - Stephanie Calmenson 201

Granny (Grandmother; Seamstress)
The Log Cabin Quilt - Ellen Howard 652

Granny (Grandmother)
Our Granny - Margaret Wild 1513

Granny (Detective—Private)
Tingleberries, Tuckertubs and Telephones - Margaret Mahy 927

Granny Blue (Grandmother)
The Mighty Santa Fe - William H. Hooks 642

Grant, Bryan (6th Grader)
Riot - Mary Casanova 217

Grant, Maggie (7-Year-Old)
The Green Bottle and the Silver Kite - Fredericka Berger 101

Grant, Phillip (10-Year-Old)
The Green Bottle and the Silver Kite - Fredericka Berger 101

Grant, Stan (Unemployed)
Riot - Mary Casanova 217

Gray, Hannah (18-Year-Old; Babysitter)
Haunted Summer - Betty Ren Wright 1560

Gray, Henry (Mouse; Brother)
Three Terrible Trins - Dick King-Smith 757

Gray, Orin (13-Year-Old; Mentally Challenged Person)
Fire in the Wind - Betty Levin 843

Gray, Richard (Mouse; Brother)
Three Terrible Trins - Dick King-Smith 757

Gray, Thomas (Mouse; Brother)
Three Terrible Trins - Dick King-Smith 757

Gray Fire (Indian; Handicapped)
Sees Behind Trees - Michael Dorris 361

Grayson, Jerry (Baseball Player; Swimmer)
The Winning Stroke - Matt Christopher 254

Great Aunt (Aunt)
The Last Dragon - Susan Miho Nunes 1085

Great Chief (Deity)
Dance of the Sacred Circle: A Native American Tale - Kristina Rodanas 1223

Great Goob (Monster)
Yesterday I Lost a Sneaker (and Found the Great Goob Sick) - David McPhail 996

Great Grandfather (Grandfather)
Great Grandfather's House - Rumer Godden 483

The Great Sun Father (Deity)
How Thunder and Lightning Came to Be: A Choctaw Legend - Beatrice Orcutt Harrell 560

Greebe, Nicholas (Spirit)
The Ghost of Nicholas Greebe - Tony Johnston 703

Greeley, Elliot (Student—Junior High; Baseball Player)
Bat Boy - Mel Cebulash 228

Green, Archibald "Willy" (11-Year-Old; Bully)
Granny the Pag - Nina Bawden 90

Green, Courtney Alicia (7th Grader; Cousin)
My Crazy Cousin Courtney - Judi Miller 1011

Greene, Lia (7th Grader)
Trick or Trouble? - Ilene Cooper 287

Greenwood, John (3rd Grader)
Herbie Jones and the Birthday Showdown - Suzy Kline 768

Gregor (Rhinoceros; Bully)
Tilly and the Rhinoceros - Sheila White Samton 1260

Gregory (Child; Cousin)
Gregory Cool - Caroline Binch 107

Greiner, Rachel (Neighbor; Child-Care Giver)
Scooter - Vera B. Williams 1523

Griffin, Lily (Animal Lover)
Be Well, Beware - Jessie Haas 528

Griffin, Linwood (Grandfather)
Beware the Mare - Jessie Haas 529

Grillo, Doug (12-Year-Old)
The Fear Place - Phyllis Reynolds Naylor 1066

Grillo, Gordon (14-Year-Old)
The Fear Place - Phyllis Reynolds Naylor 1066

Grimes, Meg (Child)
Hob and the Goblins - William Mayne 954

Grimes, Tom (Child)
Hob and the Goblins - William Mayne 954

Grimm, Matthew (Recluse; Neighbor)
Midnight Rider - Krista Ruepp 1238

Griselle (Artisan)
Good Griselle - Jane Yolen 1579

Gritch (Witch)
Piggie Pie! - Margie Palatini 1105

Groundhog, Geoffrey (Groundhog)
Geoffrey Groundhog Predicts the Weather - Bruce Koscielniak 780

Grover, May (8-Year-Old; Friend)
Pony Crazy - Bonnie Bryant 164

Grunder, Rina (11-Year-Old)
Stolen Bones - Joan Carris 216

Grunt, Althea Finnerty (Mother)
The Happy Yellow Car - Polly Horvath 647

Grunt, Betty (12-Year-Old)
The Happy Yellow Car - Polly Horvath 647

Guardino, Nina (5th Grader; Friend)
Fifth Grade Fever - Michele Granger 493

Gulliver, Lemuel (Captive)
Gulliver in Lilliput - Margaret Hodges 628

Gumbo (Alligator)
Gertie and Gumbo - Matt Novak 1082

Gupta (Businessman; Magician)
Pie Magic - Toby Forward 419

Gutgeld, David (Child)
Jacob's Rescue: A Holocaust Story - Malka Drucker 366

Gutgeld, Jacob "Genyek" (Child)
Jacob's Rescue: A Holocaust Story - Malka Drucker 366

Gwen (Child; Detective—Amateur; Friend)
Something Queer in Outer Space - Elizabeth Levy 861

Gypsy (Child; Stepdaughter)
Belle Prater's Boy - Ruth White 1509

H

Haas, Emily (5th Grader)
The Green Musketeers and the Fabulous Frogs - Sara St. Antoine 1375

Haines, Bert (Bully)
No Friend of Mine - Ann Turnbull 1428

Haktak (Spouse; Aged Person)
Two of Everything - Lily Toy Hong 641
Two of Everything - Lily Toy Hong 641

Halkit (Father; Spirit)
Hey, Dad, Get a Life - Todd Strasser 1397

Halkit, Kelly (12-Year-Old; Child)
Hey, Dad, Get a Life - Todd Strasser 1397

Halkit, Sasha (8-Year-Old; Child)
Hey, Dad, Get a Life - Todd Strasser 1397

Hamilton (Spirit)
The Mighty Movers - Sidney Levitt 855

Hamlet (Pig)
Hamlet and the Enormous Chinese Dragon Kite - Brian Lies 872

Hammond, Arthur (Grandfather)
Celeste and Crabapple Sam - Jennifer Brutschy 163

Hamut (Child; Brother)
Croco'nile - Roy Gerrard 454

Haney, Clyde Elmer "Bo" (3rd Grader; Bully; Student)
How to Be Cool in the Third Grade - Betsy Duffey 369

Hanna (Space Explorer; Teenager)
Star Hatchling - Margaret Bechard 93

Hannah (Child)
I Remember - Fara Lynn Krasnopolsky 784

Hannah (Sister)
The Tie Man's Miracle: A Chanukah Tale - Steven Schnur 1289

Hanni (Spirit; Refugee)
The Hanukkah Ghosts - Malka Penn 1128

Hanson, Hobie (5th Grader; Soccer Player)
Soccer Circus - Jamie Gilson 472

Happy Prince (Royalty)
The Happy Prince - Oscar Wilde 1515

Harabujy (Grandfather)
Peacebound Trains - Haemi Balgassi 63

Hob (Spirit)
Hob and the Goblins - William Mayne 954

Hobarth, Lawrence Martin "Marty" (Volunteer)
Champ Hobarth - Judith Bernie Strommen 1400

Hobbes, Joseph (2nd Grader)
Owen Foote, Second Grade Strongman - Stephanie Greene 501

Hobbs, Zilla (11-Year-Old)
The Children Next Door - Jean Ure 1439

Hobday, Saracen (Orphan; Gardener)
Tingleberries, Tuckertubs and Telephones - Margaret Mahy 927

Hocky, Baby (Child)
The Happy Hocky Family - Lane Smith 1354

Hocky, Henry (Child; Brother)
The Happy Hocky Family - Lane Smith 1354

Hocky, Holly (Child; Sister)
The Happy Hocky Family - Lane Smith 1354

Hodges (Elephant; Cook)
Friday Night at Hodge's Cafe - Tim Egan 382

Hoffman (Aged Person)
The Tie Man's Miracle: A Chanukah Tale - Steven Schnur 1289

Hoffman, Lydia (10-Year-Old; Child of Divorced Parents)
Lydia, Queen of Palestine - Uri Orlev 1100

Holland, Micah (15-Year-Old)
Caleb's Choice - G. Clifton Wisler 1539

Holly (3rd Grader)
Hey, New Kid! - Betsy Duffey 368

Homer (Child)
The Sounds of Summer - David Updike 1438

Honeypaw (Bear; Mother)
Honey Paw and Lightfoot - Jonathan London 890

Hood, Robin (Outlaw; Hero)
Robin's Country - Monica Furlong 434

Hooks (Imposter; Bully)
The House Gobbaleen - Lloyd Alexander 23

Hoong Wei (Child; Sister)
Rabbit Mooncakes - Hoong Yee Lee Krakauer 783

Hoong Yee (Child; Sister)
Rabbit Mooncakes - Hoong Yee Lee Krakauer 783

Hooper, Peter (Baseball Player)
Pressure Play - Matt Christopher 253

Hopbong, Skippy III (Stowaway; Leader)
Space Brat 4: Planet of the Dips - Bruce Coville 293

Horace (Cousin)
The Giant Baby - Allan Ahlberg 15

Horatio (Rabbit; Toy)
Humphrey Thud - Camilla Ashforth 48

Horton, Charles "Chive" (Streetperson; 7th Grader)
Chive - Shelley A. Barre 80

Hotchkiss, Pearl (Student)
Seven Spiders Spinning - Gregory Maguire 920

Houser, Brenda (3rd Grader)
Woollybear Good-bye - Sharon Phillips Denslow 343

Howard (Child)
The Ballot Box Battle - Emily Arnold McCully 963

Howard (Grandfather; Storyteller)
The Year of Fire - Teddy Jam 684

Howgego (Dog; Friend)
Out to Lunch - Priscilla Lamont 809

Hubble, Mildred (Student; Witch)
The Worst Witch at Sea - Jill Murphy 1053

Hubie (Mouse)
All Aboard! - James Stevenson 1384

Hue Boy (Child)
Hue Boy - Rita Phillips Mitchell 1023

Hugh (Turtle)
The Mud Flat Olympics - James Stevenson 1386

Hugh Thomas (Child; Fisherman)
A Million Fish. . .More or Less - Pat McKissack 986

Hugo (Child; Patient)
Going Home - Margaret Wild 1512

Huku (Cat)
The Loyal Cat - Lensey Namioka 1059

Hummer, Freddie (3-Year-Old; Twin)
Nekomah Creek Christmas - Linda Crew 301

Hummer, Lucy (3-Year-Old; Twin)
Nekomah Creek Christmas - Linda Crew 301

Hummer, Robby (10-Year-Old)
Nekomah Creek Christmas - Linda Crew 301

Hummingbird (Bird)
Coyote Steals the Blanket: A Ute Tale - Janet Stevens 1380

Humphrey (Child-Care Giver)
Lydia Jane and the Baby-Sitter Exchange - Natalie Honeycutt 638

Hunder (Monster)
The Great Quillow - James Thurber 1419

Hungry Hyena (Hyena)
Hungry Hyena - Mwenye Hadithi 536

Hutchinson, Curtis (Child)
The Trespassers - Zilpha Keatley Snyder 1360

Hyacinth (Mouse; Mother)
The School Mouse - Dick King-Smith 751

Hyde (Businessman)
Do You See a Mouse? - Bernard Waber 1459

Hyman, Molly (3rd Grader; Immigrant)
Make a Wish, Molly - Barbara Cohen 266

I

Ida (Child)
The Tangerine Tree - Regina Hanson 556

Ida (Neighbor)
From Miss Ida's Front Porch - Sandra Belton 95

Iemanja (Deity; Mother)
How Night Came from the Sea: A Story from Brazil - Mary-Joan Gerson 458

Igler, Leanne Patrice (Volunteer)
Champ Hobarth - Judith Bernie Strommen 1400

Imani (Child)
Imani and the Flying Africans - Janice Liddell 871

Inunguak (Child)
Inunguak: The Little Greenlander - Palle Petersen 1140

Irina (Child)
The Enchanted Horse - Magdalen Nabb 1058

Irwin, Andrew (Child)
Pioneer Bear - Joan Sandin 1266

Isabel (Adoptee)
Bonesy and Isabel - Michael J. Rosen 1229

Isabella (Bird)
The Language of Doves - Rosemary Wells 1493

Isabelle (3-Year-Old)
My Dog Rosie - Isabelle Harper 559

Israel (Fugitive)
On Winter's Wind - Patricia Hermes 593

Ives, Austin (12-Year-Old; Orphan)
Dear Levi: Letters from the Overland Trail - Elvira Woodruff 1550

Ives, Levi (9-Year-Old; Orphan)
Dear Levi: Letters from the Overland Trail - Elvira Woodruff 1550

Ivey (Father; Architect)
Squirrel Park - Lisa Campbell Ernst 396

Ivey, Stuart (Child)
Squirrel Park - Lisa Campbell Ernst 396

Ivy (7th Grader)
The Fog Doggies and Me - Gayle Pearson 1125

Ivy (Child; Sister)
The Hayloft - Lisa Westberg Peters 1135

Iwa (Deity)
Okino and the Whales - Arnica Esterl 397

Izzy (Monster; Businessman)
This Is a Great Place for a Hot Dog Stand - Barney Saltzberg 1259

J

Jabila (Runaway)
The Warm Place - Nancy Farmer 401

Jack (Child)
Cat, You Better Come Home - Garrison Keillor 727

Jack (Cousin)
The Ghost of Grania O'Malley - Michael Morpurgo 1039

Jack (12-Year-Old)
The Ice Horse - Candice Christiansen 248

Jack (Child; Gardener)
Jack's Garden - Henry Cole 269

Jack (Worker)
Lazy Jack - Vivian French 428

Jack (Cat)
My Cat Jack - Patricia Casey 222

Jack (Brother)
Nothing Happened - Bill Harley 557

Jack (Blacksmith)
Wicked Jack - Connie Nordhielm Wooldridge 1553

Jackrabbit (Hare)
The Tortoise and the Jackrabbit - Susan Lowell 901

Jackson (Teacher)
Owen Foote, Second Grade Strongman - Stephanie Greene 501

Jackson, Janetta (8-Year-Old)
Pink Paper Swans - Virginia L. Kroll 793

Jackson, Jason (2nd Grader; Friend)
Dog Days for Dudley - Barbara Moe 1026

Jackson, Matthew (4th Grader; Learning Disabled Child)
Shark in School - Patricia Reilly Giff 468

Jacob (Child; Deaf)
Dad and Me in the Morning - Patricia Lakin 806

Jacob (Young Man; Unemployed)
Jacob and the Stranger - Sally Derby 344

Jacobson, Jake (Child; Brother)
Starlight and Candles: The Joys of the Sabbath - Fran Manushkin 931

Jacobson, Rosy (Child; Sister)
Starlight and Candles: The Joys of the Sabbath - Fran Manushkin 931

Jacquith, Felix "JJ" II (12-Year-Old; Musician)
Becoming Felix - Nancy Hope Wilson 1531

Johnson, Ginger (12-Year-Old; Sister)
Never Trust a Sister over Twelve - Stephen
Roos 1226

Johnson, Jedediah "Jed" (Uncle; Worker)
Uncle Jed's Barbershop - Margaree King
Mitchell 1022

Johnson, Libby (Child)
Annie Bananie Moves to Barry Avenue - Leah
Komaiko 775

Johnson, Lyman (5-Year-Old; Brother)
Never Trust a Sister over Twelve - Stephen
Roos 1226

Johnson, Sugar (Child; Friend)
The Adventures of Sugar and Junior - Angela Shelf
Medearis 1003

Johnson, Suki (9-Year-Old; Sister)
Never Trust a Sister over Twelve - Stephen
Roos 1226

Johnston, Willie (Military Personnel)
Mr. Lincoln's Drummer - G. Clifton Wisler 1540

JoJo (Child; Student)
JoJo's Flying Side Kick - Brian Pinkney 1152

Jolie (Child)
The Trouble with Henriette! - Wende Devlin 347

Jon (8-Year-Old)
Grandad Bill's Song - Jane Yolen 1580

Jonathan (13-Year-Old)
The Fighting Ground - Avi 56

Jonathan (Child)
The Sleeping Porch - Karen Ackerman 5

Jonathan (Child; Friend)
Stinker's Return - Pamela F. Service 1311

Jonathan (Child; Accident Victim)
The Storm - Marc Harshman 566

Jones, Booker (Writer; 12-Year-Old)
Utterly Yours, Booker Jones - Betsy Duffey 371

Jones, Derrick (Friend; Detective—Amateur)
Orp and the FBI - Suzy Kline 771

Jones, Herbie (3rd Grader)
Herbie Jones and the Birthday Showdown - Suzy
Kline 768

Jones, Herculeah (Detective—Amateur; 13-Year-
Old)
The Dark Stairs - Betsy Byars 191

Jones, Herculeah (Detective—Amateur; Child of
Divorced Parents)
Dead Letter - Betsy Byars 192

Jones, Jason (Child)
The Greatest Show off Earth - Margaret Mahy 923

Jones, John Quincy (Detective—Police)
Sebastian (Super Sleuth) and the Copycat Crime -
Mary Blount Christian 243
Sebastian (Super Sleuth) and the Flying Elephant -
Mary Blount Christian 244

Jones, Junie B. (6-Year-Old; Child)
Junie B. Jones and Some Sneaky Peeky Spying -
Barbara Park 1109

Jones, Olivia Elizabeth (8-Year-Old)
Olivia and the Real Live Pet - Charlotte Towner
Graeber 490

Jones, Theodore "Turtleneck" (8-Year-Old;
Baseball Player)
Man Out at First - Matt Christopher 251

Joseck (Student)
The Exiles at Home - Hilary McKay 981

Joseph (Collector)
All the Magic in the World - Wendy Hartmann 567

Joseph, Jumping (Widow(er); Mountain Woman)
Little Obie and the Kidnap - Martin Waddell 1464

Josepha (Teenager; Immigrant)
Josepha: A Prairie Boy's Story - Jim McGugan 979

Josh (Brother; Child)
Last Left Standing - Barbara T. Russell 1240

Josh (Runaway)
The Watchers: A Mystery at Alton Towers - Helen
Cresswell 300

Joshua (Child; Brother)
Celie and the Harvest Fiddler - Vanessa
Flournoy 414

Joshua (Child)
Joshua's Masai Mask - Dakari Hru 658

Joshua (8-Year-Old; Slave)
*Journey to Freedom: A Story of the Underground
Railroad* - Courtni C. Wright 1562

Josie (Child)
Is That Josie? - Keiko Narahashi 1062

Joy, Harry (Child; Brother)
The Joy Boys - Betsy Byars 194

Joy, J.J. (Child; Brother)
The Joy Boys - Betsy Byars 194

Joy-in-the-Dance (Healer)
The Arkadians - Lloyd Alexander 22

Juana (6-Year-Old)
Gracias, Rosa - Michelle Markel 933

Juarez, Carlos (Student)
City of Light, City of Dark: A Comic-Book Novel -
Avi 55

Judith (Worker)
The Bobbin Girl - Emily Arnold McCully 964

Judy (8-Year-Old; Animal Lover)
Jenius, the Amazing Guinea Pig - Dick King-
Smith 749

Judy (Child; Sister)
Willie Jerome - Alice Faye Duncan 372

Julia (Child)
Asleep in a Heap - Elizabeth Winthrop 1536

Juliet (Child)
Juliet's Story - William Trevor 1426

Julietta (6-Year-Old)
The Language of Doves - Rosemary Wells 1493

Juliette (Cat)
Looking for Juliette - Janet Taylor Lisle 879

Julius (Pig)
Julius - Angela Johnson 696

Jump, Maribel (Mythical Creature)
Brigid the Bad - Kathleen Leverich 841

June (Horse)
Shortcut - David Macaulay 911

Junjun (Child)
Rata-Pata-Scata-Fata: A Caribbean Story - Phillis
Gershator 457

Justine (Child; Friend)
Tikvah Means Hope - Patricia Polacco 1163

K

Kael (Wolf; Captive)
Circus of the Wolves - Jack Bushnell 187

Kaeldra (Healer)
Sign of the Dove - Susan Fletcher 412

Kalinzu (Buffalo; Child)
Kalinzu: A Story from Africa - Jeremy Grimsdell 521

Kamornick, Hannah (16-Year-Old; Sister)
Sarah, Also Known as Hannah - Lillian Hammer
Ross 1233

Kamornick, Sarah (12-Year-Old; Sister)
Sarah, Also Known as Hannah - Lillian Hammer
Ross 1233

Kane, Arney (Brother)
Harry and Arney - Judith Caseley 218

Kane, Harry (6-Year-Old; Brother)
Harry and Arney - Judith Caseley 218

Kane, Lillian (Mother)
Harry and Arney - Judith Caseley 218

Kane, Spider (Detective—Amateur; Musician)
Spider Kane and the Mystery at Jumbo Nightcrawler's
- Mary Pope Osborne 1102

Kaplan, Morris (Businessman; Survivor)
One Yellow Daffodil: A Hanukkah Story - David A.
Adler 14

Kapu (Wolf)
Julie - Jean Craighead George 451

Kapugen (Indian; Father)
Julie - Jean Craighead George 451

Kapugen, Julie Edwards Miyax (Indian)
Julie - Jean Craighead George 451

Karen (Child; Neighbor)
Loretta and the Little Fairy - Gerda Marie
Scheidl 1278

Karen (Child; Friend)
Stinker's Return - Pamela F. Service 1311

Kari (Child)
Papa's Stories - Dolores Johnson 697

Karl (Uncle; Student)
Beethoven Lives Upstairs - Barbara Nichol 1073

Kashtanka (Dog)
Kashtanka - Anton Chekhov 235

Kat (Cat; Sister)
Kit and Kat - Tomie De Paola 328

Kate (Child)
All the Better to See You With! - Margaret
Wild 1510

Kate (Kidnap Victim; Artisan)
The Boy and the Giants - Fiona Moodie 1030

Kate (Child; Cousin)
Clean House - Jessie Haas 531

Kate (Child)
Gracias, Rosa - Michelle Markel 933
Kate's Giants - Valiska Gregory 512

Kate (14-Year-Old)
Murphy and Kate - Ellen Howard 653

Kate (Child; Friend)
Nannies for Hire - Amy Hest 606

Kate (Pig; Bride)
The Pigrates Clean Up - Steven Kroll 791

Kate (Child; Friend)
Starshine and Sunglow - Betty Levin 844

Katie (Child)
Dear Bear - Joanna Harrison 563

Katie (Child; Adoptee)
A Koala for Katie: An Adoption Story - Jonathan
London 891

Katie (Sister)
One Up, One Down - Carol Snyder 1358

Katie (Child)
The Snowchild - Debi Gliori 482

Katsumi (Brother)
The Crane Girl - Veronika Martenova Charles 233

Legrand, Bill (Writer)
The Case of the Absent Author - E.W. Hildick   614

Leila (Sister)
On Winter's Wind - Patricia Hermes   593

Lena (Child)
All the Magic in the World - Wendy Hartmann   567

Lennox (Cousin)
Gregory Cool - Caroline Binch   107

Lenore (Child)
Buckledown the Workhound - Danny Shanahan   1314

Leonard (Uncle)
Too Far Away to Touch - Leslea Newman   1071

Leonard, Elizabeth (Mother; Widow(er))
Someone to Count On - Patricia Hermes   594

Leonard, Samantha Marie "Sam" (11-Year-Old)
Someone to Count On - Patricia Hermes   594

Leopold (Royalty)
Princess - Anne Wilsdorf   1529

Lerner, Steven (12-Year-Old; Musician)
Becoming Felix - Nancy Hope Wilson   1531

LeRoux, Feliciana Feydra (Child)
Feliciana Feydra LeRoux: A Cajun Tall Tale - Tynia Thomassie   1418

Leslie (Child; Animal Lover)
If Anything Ever Goes Wrong at the Zoo - Mary Jean Hendrick   582

Lester (Writer; Uncle)
The Man in the Ceiling - Jules Feiffer   403

Lester's Dog (Dog)
Lester's Dog - Karen Hesse   600

Leticia (Child)
The Gullywasher - Joyce Rossi   1234

Lettie (8-Year-Old; Slave)
Jumping the Broom - Courtni C. Wright   1563

Letty (Child)
The Enormous Snore - M.L. Miller   1012

Leudloff (Farmer)
Keep Smiling Through - Ann Rinaldi   1214

Lewis (7-Year-Old; Brother)
The Feather-Bed Journey - Paula Kurzband Feder   402

Lewis, Heather (12-Year-Old)
Lost in Cyberspace - Richard Peck   1126

Lewis, Josh (6th Grader; Time Traveller)
Lost in Cyberspace - Richard Peck   1126

Lightfoot (Bear)
Honey Paw and Lightfoot - Jonathan London   890

Lightfoot, Be Be (Brother)
Tar Beach - Faith Ringgold   1215

Lightfoot, Cassie Louise (8-Year-Old; Daydreamer)
Tar Beach - Faith Ringgold   1215

Ligonier, Boone (13-Year-Old; Artist)
Cheshire Moon - Nancy Butts   190

Lila (7-Year-Old)
Lila's Little Dinosaur - Wolfram Hanel   553

Lili (Child; Dancer)
Lili at Ballet - Rachel Isadora   679
Lili on Stage - Rachel Isadora   680

Lilly (Mouse; 1st Grader)
Lilly's Purple Plastic Purse - Kevin Henkes   587

Lilly (Cat; Friend)
Lilly's Secret - Miko Imai   676

Lilly (Dinosaur; Sister)
Rex and Lilly Family Time - Laurie Krasny Brown   143

Lily (Child; Animal Lover)
Beware the Mare - Jessie Haas   529

Lily (Dog)
Lily - Abigail Thomas   1414

Lily (Young Woman)
Lily and the Wooden Bowl - Alan Schroeder   1294

Lily (Child; Sister)
The Rose Horse - Deborah Lee Rose   1228

Lily (Child)
What's Black and White and Came to Visit? - Evan Levine   849

Lincoln, Abraham (Historical Figure)
The Wagon - Tony Johnston   708

Lindi (Child)
The Dove - Dianne Stewart   1391

Lindsay (11-Year-Old; Sister)
Courtyard Cat - C.S. Adler   10

Lindy (Child)
Drylongso - Virginia Hamilton   549

Lionel (Brother)
Lionel in the Winter - Stephen Krensky   788

Liplap (Rabbit)
Liplap's Wish - Jonathan London   894

Lipscomb, Driscoll (Artist; Aged Person)
The Gift of Driscoll Lipscomb - Sara Yamaka   1568

Lisa (Child; Friend)
The Pink Party - Maryann Macdonald   914

Lito (Grandfather)
Pablo's Tree - Pat Mora   1037

Little Bear (Bear; Child)
Let's Go Home, Little Bear - Martin Waddell   1463

Little Chou (Child)
The Boy Who Swallowed Snakes - Laurence Yep   1570

Little Donkey (Donkey)
Little Donkey Close Your Eyes - Margaret Wise Brown   152

Little Gray One (Elephant; Child)
Little Gray One - Jan Wahl   1466

Little Kit (Orphan; Abuse Victim)
Little Kit or, the Industrious Flea Circus Girl - Emily Arnold McCully   967

Little Lily Goose (Goose)
What Would Mama Do? - Judith Ross Enderle   392

Little Miss (Child)
May'naise Sandwiches & Sunshine Tea - Sandra Belton   96

Little Nutbrown Hare (Rabbit)
Guess How Much I Love You - Sam McBratney   960

Little Obie (Child; Settler)
Little Obie and the Kidnap - Martin Waddell   1464

Little Panda (Bear; Child)
Dad! I Can't Sleep - Michael Foreman   416

Little Panda (Panda)
Surprise! Surprise! - Michael Foreman   417

Little Pink Pig (Pig)
Little Pink Pig - Pat Hutchins   673

Little Rabbit (Rabbit)
Little Rabbit Goes to Sleep - Tony Johnston   705

Little Red Riding Hood (Child)
Little Red Riding Hood: A Newfangled Prairie Tale - Lisa Campbell Ernst   394

Little Thunder (Indian)
Wagons West - Roy Gerrard   455

Little Toad (Toad)
Grandpa Toad's Last Secret - Keiko Kasza   721

Little Toad (Child; Toad)
A Song for Little Toad - Vivian French   430

Little Vampire (Vampire; Brother)
Little Vampire and the Midnight Bear - Mary DeBall Kwitz   801

Littlefeets, Spaulding (Indian; Friend)
Santa Calls - William Joyce   715

Liyan (Mother)
The Burnt Stick - Anthony Hill   618

Liza (Child)
There's a Bear in the Bath! - Nanette Newman   1072

Lizzie (Child)
Grandfather's Christmas Camp - Marc McCutcheon   969
Red Light, Green Light, Mama and Me - Cari Best   104
The Tusk Fairy - Nicola Smee   1348

Logan, David (10-Year-Old)
The Well: David's Story - Mildred D. Taylor   1409

Logan, Dicky (3rd Grader; Bully)
Sara Kate Saves the World - Susan Beth Pfeffer   1143

Logan, Hammer (13-Year-Old)
The Well: David's Story - Mildred D. Taylor   1409

Logan, Lizzie (10-Year-Old; Neighbor)
Lizzie Logan Wears Purple Sunglasses - Eileen Spinelli   1369

Lombardi (Teacher)
A Place for Grace - Jean Davies Okimoto   1092

Lona (Aunt)
A Place for Angels - Clyde Robert Bulla   169

Longrider, Angelica "Swamp Angel" (Frontierswoman)
Swamp Angel - Anne Isaacs   678

Lootna (Alien)
Jason and the Escape from Bat Planet - Gery Greer   507

Lopez, Maria Isabel Salazar (3rd Grader; Immigrant)
My Name Is Maria Isabel - Alma Flor Ada   7

Lord of Night (Sorcerer)
The Princess and the Lord of Night - Emma Bull   168

Loretta (Child)
Loretta and the Little Fairy - Gerda Marie Scheidl   1278

Loring, Haley "Samantha Love" (6th Grader)
Stardust - Alane Ferguson   405

Loring, Joshua (12-Year-Old)
An Island Far from Home - John Donahue   358

Lornge (Bird)
The Shuteyes - Mary James   689

Loud (Child; Student)
Running the Road to ABC - Denize Lauture   823

Louise (Mule)
The Gates of the Wind - Kathryn Lasky   814

Louise (Sister)
Lionel in the Winter - Stephen Krensky   788

Lovejoy, Serena (Chicken; Actress)
Buzby to the Rescue - Julia Hoban   626

Lovello, Lucy (7th Grader)
Cheater, Cheater - Elizabeth Levy   857

Lowe, Patrick (5th Grader; Child of an Alcoholic)
Just Call Me Stupid - Tom Birdseye   108

Lowe, Paulette (Single Mother; Divorced Person)
Just Call Me Stupid - Tom Birdseye   108

Lucian (Accountant)
The Arkadians - Lloyd Alexander   22

Mama (Mother; Traveller)
Nine for California - Sonia Levitin 854

Mama (Mother)
On a Starry Night - Natalie Kinsey-Warnock 759

Mama (Bear; Mother)
One Saturday Morning - Barbara Baker 61

Mama (Mother)
Pablo's Tree - Pat Mora 1037
Priscilla Twice - Judith Caseley 220

Mama (Mother; Librarian)
Red Light, Green Light, Mama and Me - Cari Best 104

Mama (Mother)
Rosie's Fishing Trip - Amy Hest 608
Snow Angel - Jean Marzollo 945

Mama (Mother; Immigrant)
Soon, Annala - Riki Levinson 852

Mama (Mother)
The Tangerine Tree - Regina Hanson 556
Tap-Tap - Karen Lynn Williams 1521
Time to Wake Up! - Marisabina Russo 1243
Trade-In Mother - Marisabina Russo 1244

Mama (Mother; Office Worker)
Valentine - Carol Carrick 215

Mama (Rabbit)
Warm at Home - Roni Schotter 1292

Mama (Mother)
What You Know First - Patricia MacLachlan 918
When the Whippoorwill Calls - Candice F. Ransom 1190

Mama (Single Mother)
Whistling Dixie - Marcia Vaughan 1452
Willie Jerome - Alice Faye Duncan 372

Mama Ana (Grandmother; Cook)
Saturday Sancocho - Leyla Torres 1425

Mama Goose (Goose; Mother)
What Would Mama Do? - Judith Ross Enderle 392

Mamalou (Mother)
Drylongso - Virginia Hamilton 549

Mami (Mother; Worker)
Lights on the River - Jane Resh Thomas 1417

Mamita (Mother)
Bread Is for Eating - David Gershator 456

Mamma (Mother)
Kelly in the Mirror - Martha M. Vertreace 1454

Mamma (Mother; Worker)
Working Cotton - Sherley Anne Williams 1522

The Man (Father; Sailor)
Henry the Sailor Cat - Mary Calhoun 199

Mandell, Roger (Truck Driver; Father)
Flipper's Boy - Mel Cebulash 229

Mandell, Tommy (Basketball Player; Student—High School)
Flipper's Boy - Mel Cebulash 229

Mandy (Child; Equestrian)
A Blue for Beware - Jessie Haas 530

Manetti, Andy (5th Grader; Stepbrother)
The Magnificent Mummy Maker - Elvira Woodruff 1552

Mangiaro, Kelly (Child)
Mush, a Dog from Space - Daniel Manus Pinkwater 1155

Mangold (Pilot)
The Greatest Show off Earth - Margaret Mahy 923

Manuela (2nd Grader)
Second-Grade Pig Pals - Kirby Larson 812

Manyoni (Child)
Where Are You Going, Manyoni? - Catherine Stock 1393

Marc (Father; Restauranteur)
The Van Gogh Cafe - Cynthia Rylant 1256

Marcel (Dog)
The Sweetest Fig - Chris Van Allsburg 1444

Marco (Child; Friend)
The Beast and the Boy - Massimo Mostacchi 1047

Marco (Student; Friend)
The Secret Super Powers of Marco - Meredith Sue Willis 1525

Marconi (Teacher)
Wagon Train 911 - Jamie Gilson 473

Marcy (Child; Activist)
City Green - DyAnne DiSalvo-Ryan 352

Margarita (5-Year-Old; Child)
Born in the Gravy - Denys Cazet 225

Margarita (Child)
Hi - Ann Herbert Scott 1302

Maria (Child)
A Bear for Miguel - Elaine Marie Alphin 28
Too Many Tamales - Gary Soto 1365

Maria Lili (Child)
Saturday Sancocho - Leyla Torres 1425

Marian (Nurse)
Robin's Country - Monica Furlong 434

Mariana (Maiden; Heroine)
In the Palace of the Ocean King - Marilyn Singer 1338

Marianne (Orphan)
Train to Somewhere - Eve Bunting 181

Marie (Sister)
Mac and Marie and the Train Toss Surprise - Elizabeth Fitzgerald Howard 649

Marigold (Rabbit)
Marigold and Grandma on the Town - Stephanie Calmenson 202

Marilyn (Frog; Friend)
An Extraordinary Egg - Leo Lionni 875

Marilyn (1st Grader)
Next Year I'll Be Special - Patricia Reilly Giff 466

Marion (Sister)
Andrew's Angry Words - Dorothea Lachner 802

Marion (Child; Artist)
The Moon Man: A Story - Gerda Marie Scheidl 1279

Marisa (7-Year-Old)
Dumpling Soup - Jama Kim Rattigan 1197

Marisol (Child)
The Outside Dog - Charlotte Pomerantz 1165

Mark (Brother)
I've Got Chicken Pox - True Kelley 733

Mark (Child; Brother)
That Terrible Baby - Jennifer Armstrong 41

Market Lady (Businesswoman)
The Market Lady and the Mango Tree - Pete Watson 1483

Markov (Teacher)
Sweet Notes, Sour Notes - Nancy Smiler Levinson 851

Marks, Jenny (Child; Friend)
Nannies for Hire - Amy Hest 606

Marlin, Luke (14-Year-Old; Brother)
Johnny Rides Again - Jo Ann Muchmore 1048

Marlin, Rose (10-Year-Old; Sister)
Johnny Rides Again - Jo Ann Muchmore 1048

Marlon (Monster)
The Last Noo-Noo - Jill Murphy 1051

Marony, Mary (2nd Grader)
Mary Marony Hides Out - Suzy Kline 770

Marshall, Tate (10-Year-Old)
Sable - Karen Hesse 602

Marshall, Travis (6th Grader)
Frankie Murphy's Kiss List - Donna Guthrie 526

Marta (Teenager; Sister)
The Night Crossing - Karen Ackerman 4

Marta (Mother)
When the Monkeys Came Back - Kristine L. Franklin 425

Martha (Child; Sister)
A Baby Just Like Me - Susan Winter 1534

Martha (Child; Friend)
Bebop-a-Do-Walk! - Sheila Hamanaka 547

Martha (Aunt; Aged Person)
Great Aunt Martha - Rebecca C. Jones 710

Martha (Dog)
Martha Calling - Susan Meddaugh 1001
Martha Speaks - Susan Meddaugh 1002

Martin, Dave (5th Grader; Friend)
Attack of the Killer Fishsticks - Paul Zindel 1596

Martin, Emmie (Cousin)
My Cats Nick and Nora - Isabelle Harper 558

Martin, Lena May (Child; Neighbor)
One Brave Summer - Ann Turner 1434

Martin, Ray (3rd Grader)
Herbie Jones and the Birthday Showdown - Suzy Kline 768

Martinez, Amelia Luisa (Child; Migrant Worker)
Amelia's Road - Linda Jacobs Altman 29

Mary (Child; Sister)
John Joe and the Big Hen - Martin Waddell 1462

Mary (Child; Student)
Mary Had a Little Lamb - Sarah Josepha Hale 540

Mary Ann (Toy)
Good Night, Sleep Tight - Penelope Lively 884

Mary Ann (Child; Neighbor)
Mary Ann - Betsy James 686

Mary Elizabeth (Child)
Lucy Comes to Stay - Rosemary Wells 1495

Mary Ellen (Child)
The Bee Tree - Patricia Polacco 1160

Mary "Ma" (Mother; Farmer)
Parents in the Pigpen, Pigs in the Tub - Amy Ehrlich 387

Mary Rose (Religious; Teacher)
Hey You, Sister Rose - Eileen Walsh Strauch 1398

Mason, Jenna (9-Year-Old; Sister)
Tough Loser - Barthe DeClements 332

Mason, Mike (13-Year-Old; Hockey Player)
Tough Loser - Barthe DeClements 332

Mason, Philura Higley "Philly" (6th Grader)
The Reason for Janey - Nancy Hope Wilson 1532

Massimino (Immigrant; Miner)
Silver at Night - Susan Campbell Bartoletti 82

Matovic, Lisa (Single Mother)
Change the Locks - Simon French 427

Matovic, Steven (11-Year-Old; Brother)
Change the Locks - Simon French 427

Matt (Brother; Child of Divorced Parents)
I Want Answers and a Parachute - P.J. Petersen 1138

Mercy, Tessie (Child)
The Ghosts of Mercy Manor - Betty Ren Wright 1559

Merlin (Child; 8-Year-Old)
Passenger - Jane Yolen 1585

Merlin (Teacher; Wizard)
The Mystery of the Several Sevens - Bill Brittain 140

Merriweather (Father; Neighbor)
The Amazing Christmas Extravaganza - David Shannon 1315

Merriwether (Teacher)
Mrs. Merriwether's Musical Cat - Carol Purdy 1181

Mia (Cat)
Mia the Beach Cat: A Story - Wolfram Hanel 554

Mia (Child; Dancer)
Nutcracker Noel - Kate McMullan 989

Micah (Child)
I Love You, Bunny Rabbit - Shulamith Levey Oppenheim 1097

Michael (Child; Asthmatic)
The Cave - Kathleen Karr 720

Michael (Immigrant)
The Dream Jar - Bonnie Pryor 1178

Michael (Child)
Goodbye, Mitch - Ruth Wallace-Brodeur 1474

Michael (Uncle)
Tiger Flowers - Patricia Quinlan 1183

Michaels, Cody (3rd Grader)
Hey, New Kid! - Betsy Duffey 368

Michaels, Elisa (5-Year-Old; Sister)
Make Room for Elisa - Johanna Hurwitz 668

Michaels, Russell (9-Year-Old; Brother)
Make Room for Elisa - Johanna Hurwitz 668

Michelin, Seth (5th Grader; Friend)
Seth and Samona - Joanne Hyppolite 674

Mickey (Child; Brother)
Mama, Coming and Going - Judith Caseley 219

Midge (9-Year-Old; Friend)
My Brother Is a Visitor from Another Planet - Dyan Sheldon 1327

Midge, Philomena (Hippo; Collector)
So Much in Common - Laurie A. Jacobs 682

Midnight Bear (Bear)
Little Vampire and the Midnight Bear - Mary DeBall Kwitz 801

Mieko (Child; Artist)
Mieko and the Fifth Treasure - Eleanor Coerr 263

Miguel (Child; Student)
Eagle - Judy Allen 27

Mike (Animal Trainer)
A Dolphin Named Bob - Twig C. George 453

Mike (Child; Brother)
Night in the Barn - Faye Gibbons 462

Milford (Royalty; Hippo)
Chestnut Cove - Tim Egan 381

Milkshake (Cat)
Clean House - Jessie Haas 531

Millie (Latch-Key Child)
Palm Trees - Nancy Cote 292

Millie (Sheep)
Three Bags Full - Ragnhild Scamell 1273

Millner, Max (5th Grader; Bullied Child)
Attack of the Killer Fishsticks - Paul Zindel 1596

Mills, Eric (Student; Friend)
I'm George Washington and You're Not! - Steven Kroll 789

Mills, Talliaferro "Tally" (Military Personnel; Boyfriend)
When Will This Cruel War Be Over? The Civil War Diary of Emma Simpson - Barry Denenberg 340

Mills, Violetta (6th Grader)
Wait and See - Virginia Bradley 131

Milly (Friend)
Lunch with Milly - Jeanne Modesitt 1025

Milly (Cook; Sister)
Seven Loaves of Bread - Ferida Wolff 1546

Milo (Cat)
The Bookstore Mouse - Peggy Christian 245

Milsen (Child; Student)
Running the Road to ABC - Denize Lauture 823

Milton (Dog)
Milton, My Father's Dog - Eric Copeland 291

Mimi (Child; Sister)
Roommates Again - Kathryn O. Galbraith 437

Minerva (Child)
The Hog Call to End All! - SuAnn Kiser 765

Minerva Louise (Chicken)
A Hat for Minerva Louise - Janet Morgan Stoeke 1394

Minnie (Cat; Human)
Minnie - Annie M.G. Schmidt 1286

Minter, Claire (Sister)
The Timekeeper - Emily Rodda 1224

Minter, Danny (4-Year-Old; Brother)
The Timekeeper - Emily Rodda 1224

Minter, Patrick (Child)
The Timekeeper - Emily Rodda 1224

Miranda (Child)
Miranda's Smile - Thomas Locker 886

Miranda (11-Year-Old)
Wrapped in a Riddle - Sharon E. Heisel 579

Misha (Child)
The Gift from Saint Nicholas - Dorothea Lachner 803

Miss Kitty (Cat)
The Puppy Sister - S.E. Hinton 623

Missy (Student—College)
A Horse Like Barney - Jessie Haas 532

Mister (Dog)
The Trouble with Mister - Debra Keller 729

Mitch (Cat)
Goodbye, Mitch - Ruth Wallace-Brodeur 1474

Mitchell, Libby (Settler)
Night of the Full Moon - Gloria Whelan 1505

Mitchell, Zoe (11-Year-Old; Psychic)
Zoe's Gift - Sheila Hayes 576

Mo (Child)
The Boy Who Ate Around - Henrik Drescher 365

Mo (4th Grader)
Mayfield Crossing - Vaunda Micheaux Nelson 1070

Moag, Gertrude Elizabeth "Gerty" (Thief; Mother)
The Ghastly Gerty Swindle: With the Ghosts of Hungryhouse Lane - Sam McBratney 959

Mole (Mole)
Badger's Bring Something Party - Hiawyn Oram 1098

Mole (Mole; Friend)
Heart to Heart - George Shannon 1317

Mole (Mole)
Mole's Hill - Lois Ehlert 384

Molly (Child)
Emma Bean - Jean Van Leeuwen 1449

Molly (Child; Friend)
The Gift of Driscoll Lipscomb - Sara Yamaka 1568

Molly (Guinea Pig; Mother)
Jenius, the Amazing Guinea Pig - Dick King-Smith 749

Molly (Child)
Molly and the Strawberry Day - Pam Conrad 281
Outside, Inside - Carolyn Crimi 303

Molly (Child; Sister)
Passover Magic - Roni Schotter 1291

Molly (5-Year-Old; Sister)
Two Girls in Sister Dresses - Jean Van Leeuwen 1451

Molly the Messy, the Me (Royalty; Sister)
Tumble Tower - Anne Tyler 1435

Mom (Mother)
The Bear under the Stairs - Helen Cooper 286

Mom (Single Mother; Worker)
By the Dawn's Early Light - Karen Ackerman 3

Mom (Mother)
The Cabin Key - Gloria Rand 1187

Mom (Single Mother)
Crossing the Starlight Bridge - Alice Mead 997

Mom (Mother)
Flower Garden - Eve Bunting 173
If Anything Ever Goes Wrong at the Zoo - Mary Jean Hendrick 582

Mom (Single Mother; Gardener)
In My Mother's Garden - Melissa Madenski 919

Mom (Mother)
It's the Bear! - Jez Alborough 20

Mom (Bear; Writer)
J.B.'s Harmonica - John Sebastian 1307

Mom (Mother)
No More Animals! - Lucia Monfried 1029
So Much - Trish Cooke 284

Mom (Mother; Farmer)
The Storm - Marc Harshman 566

Mom (Mother; Panda)
Surprise! Surprise! - Michael Foreman 417

Mom (Mother)
A Teeny Tiny Baby - Amy Schwartz 1297

Momma (Mother)
Can't Sit Still - Karen E. Lotz 897

Momma (Mother; Businesswoman)
Saturday at the New You - Barbara E. Barber 77

Momma Bunny (Rabbit; Mother)
The Dumb Bunnies' Easter - Sue Denim 341

Momme (Mother)
The Rose Horse - Deborah Lee Rose 1228

Mommy (Mother)
First Snow - Kim Lewis 867

Mommy (Frog; Mother)
Froggy Learns to Swim - Jonathan London 888

Mommy (Mother)
The Long Weekend - Troon Harrison 565
Mommies Don't Get Sick - Marylin Hafner 537
The Painter - Peter Catalanotto 224
Petey's Bedtime Story - Beverly Cleary 256

Mommy (Single Mother)
Rata-Pata-Scata-Fata: A Caribbean Story - Phillis Gershator 457

Mona (Child)
Sitti's Secrets - Naomi Shihab Nye 1087

Monamie (Mother; Indian)
Full Worm Moon - Margo Lemieux 835

Nathan (6-Year-Old)
Fireflies for Nathan - Shulamith Levey Oppenheim 1095

Nathan (10-Year-Old; Slave)
Journey to Freedom: A Story of the Underground Railroad - Courtni C. Wright 1562

Nautilus (Royalty; Prisoner)
Prince Nautilus - Laura Krauss Melmed 1008

Ned (Child; Brother)
Kid Kibble - Diana Hendry 584

Ned (Donkey)
Ned - Selina Young 1589

Nekatu (Child; Sister)
Croco'nile - Roy Gerrard 454

Nell (Child)
The Crimson Ribbon - Hilary Horder Hippely 624

Nellie (Child; Blind)
See the Ocean - Estelle Condra 277

Nelson (Child; Classmate)
Serious Science - Janice Lee Smith 1352

Nelson (Chameleon)
The Warm Place - Nancy Farmer 401

Nelson, Ray (Child; Friend)
The Sub - P.J. Petersen 1139

Nettie (15-Year-Old)
The Barn - Avi 54

Newcastle, Freedom (12-Year-Old)
Come Morning - Leslie Davis Guccione 524

Newcastle, Nehemiah (Farmer)
Come Morning - Leslie Davis Guccione 524

Newt (Salamander)
Newt - Matt Novak 1084

Newton (Child; Artist)
Not in the House, Newton! - Judith Heide Gilliland 470

Nicholas (Horse)
Returning Nicholas - Deborah Durland DeSaix 346

Nicholas (Aged Person)
The Gift from Saint Nicholas - Dorothea Lachner 803

Nichols, Jeannie (11-Year-Old; Neighbor)
The Ghost Comes Calling - Betty Ren Wright 1556

Nick (Child; Cousin)
Around the Oak - Gerda Muller 1049

Nick (Cat)
My Cats Nick and Nora - Isabelle Harper 558

Nickles, Silver Iris (12-Year-Old; Animal Lover; Orphan)
Hound Heaven - Linda Oatman High 612

Nicoletto, Theresa Jane "Janey" (Handicapped)
The Reason for Janey - Nancy Hope Wilson 1532

Nina (Child; Dancer)
Nina, Nina Ballerina - Jane O'Connor 1090

Ninicchio (Horse)
Danilo the Fruit Man - Amy Valens 1443

Nip (Horse)
Uncle Daney's Way - Jessie Haas 535

Noah (Leader)
Too Tired - Ann Turnbull 1430

Noah (Historical Figure)
Two by Two by Two - Jonathan Allen 26

Noel (Child; Dancer)
Nutcracker Noel - Kate McMullan 989

Noi, Duc (Brother)
Sweet Dried Apples: A Vietnamese Wartime Chldhood - Rosemary Breckler 133

Noi, Lieu (Refugee)
Sweet Dried Apples: A Vietnamese Wartime Chldhood - Rosemary Breckler 133

Noi, Ong (Grandfather; Herbalist)
Sweet Dried Apples: A Vietnamese Wartime Chldhood - Rosemary Breckler 133

Nona (Witch)
Strega Nona Meets Her Match - Tomie De Paola 329

Noodle (Mother; Widow(er))
George Washington's Ghost - Jane Clark Brown 142

Noodle, Celinda (Child; Sister)
George Washington's Ghost - Jane Clark Brown 142

Noodle, Pliny (Child; Brother)
George Washington's Ghost - Jane Clark Brown 142

Nora (Child; Sister)
Emily and Alice Again - Joyce Champion 232

Nora (Child)
Lucky Morning - Sally Noll 1079
Mowing - Jessie Haas 533

Nora (Cat)
My Cats Nick and Nora - Isabelle Harper 558

Nora (Child)
No Foal Yet - Jessie Haas 534
Nora's Surprise - Satomi Ichikawa 675

Nora (5-Year-Old; Orphan)
Train to Somewhere - Eve Bunting 181

Normal, Elliot (Child; Nephew)
Great-Uncle Dracula and the Dirty Rat - Jayne Harvey 568

Normal, Emily (Child; Niece)
Great-Uncle Dracula and the Dirty Rat - Jayne Harvey 568

Norman (Tarantula)
Not-So-Normal Norman - Cynthia Stowe 1395

Norman (Bully)
Pie Magic - Toby Forward 419

Norris (Friend)
The Know-Nothings - Michelle Sobel Spirn 1372

Norstad (Shipowner)
Escape into the Night - Lois Walfrid Johnson 700

Norstad, Libby (12-Year-Old)
Escape into the Night - Lois Walfrid Johnson 700

Nounou (Bear)
A Boy and His Bear - Harriet Graham 491

Novio Boy (Cat; Friend)
Chato's Kitchen - Gary Soto 1362

Number Four (Cat)
Heart of a Tiger - Marsha Arnold 42

Nuna (Dog)
A Sled Dog for Moshi - Jeanne Bushey 186

Nutsell, Frederick "Nutty" (6th Grader)
Re-Elect Nutty! - Dean Hughes 660

O

Oberon (Grandmother)
A Busy Day for a Good Grandmother - Margaret Mahy 921

Oberon, Scrimshaw (Father)
A Busy Day for a Good Grandmother - Margaret Mahy 921

Oberon, Sweeney (Child)
A Busy Day for a Good Grandmother - Margaret Mahy 921

Ocax (Owl; Ruler)
Poppy - Avi 57

Ocean King (Royalty)
In the Palace of the Ocean King - Marilyn Singer 1338

O'Hairy, Scarlett (Mouse; Professor)
Dogzilla - Dav Pilkey 1149

Ohkwa'ri (Indian; Twin)
Children of the Longhouse - Joseph Bruchac 159

Okada, Donnie (Bullied Child)
Heroes - Ken Mochizuki 1024

O'Keefe, Ryan (11-Year-Old)
Tarantula Shoes - Tom Birdseye 110

Okino (Mother)
Okino and the Whales - Arnica Esterl 397

Old Abra (Turtle; Wizard)
Pip's Magic - Ellen Stoll Walsh 1476

Old Armadillo (Armadillo)
Merry Christmas, Old Armadillo - Larry Dane Brimner 138

Old Ben (Slave)
Minty: A Story of Young Harriet Tubman - Alan Schroeder 1295

Old Grampa (Grandfather; Storyteller)
The Year of No More Corn - Helen Ketteman 741

Old Judge (Recluse)
Gold in the Hills - Laurie Lawlor 824

Old Man Hammer (Aged Person; Neighbor)
City Green - DyAnne DiSalvo-Ryan 352

Old Mother Toad (Mother; Toad)
A Song for Little Toad - Vivian French 430

Olga (Teacher)
Nutcracker Noel - Kate McMullan 989

Oli (Child; Brother)
Big Boy - Tololwa M. Mollel 1028

Olinski, Eva Marie (Teacher; Handicapped)
The View from Saturday - E.L. Konigsburg 777

Oliver (Ostrich)
The Cuckoo Child - Dick King-Smith 747

Oliver (Child)
Odds on Oliver - Constance C. Greene 500

Oliver (Pig; Brother)
Oliver & Amanda and the Big Snow - Jean Van Leeuwen 1450

Oliver (Child)
Oliver's Vegetables - Vivian French 429

Ollie (Badger; Friend)
Two Bushy Badgers - Patience Brewster 136

O'Malley, Grania (Pirate; Spirit)
The Ghost of Grania O'Malley - Michael Morpurgo 1039

O'Malley, Oliver (5th Grader; Collector)
Baseball Card Crazy - Trish Kennedy 735

O'Malley, Samantha (7-Year-Old; Sister)
Baseball Card Crazy - Trish Kennedy 735

O'Malley, Sean (5th Grader; Bullied Child)
Joshua T. Bates Takes Charge - Susan Richards Shreve 1332

Omoni (Stepmother)
The Korean Cinderella - Shirley Climo 261

Omri (Child)
The Mystery of the Cupboard - Lynne Reid Banks 73

Onetree, Jo-Beth (8-Year-Old)
Never Hit a Ghost with a Baseball Bat - Eth Clifford 260

Patrick (9-Year-Old)
Patrick's Tree House - Steven Kroll   790

Patrick Edward (Child)
Monster Mama - Liz Rosenberg   1232

Patten, Joshua (Sailor; Spouse)
Mary Patten's Voyage - Richard Berleth   103

Patten, Mary (18-Year-Old; Spouse)
Mary Patten's Voyage - Richard Berleth   103

Patterson, Hadley (11-Year-Old; Child of Divorced
   Parents)
The Light on Hogback Hill - Cynthia DeFelice   335

Patterson, Hartwell "Hart" (12-Year-Old)
Coaster - Betsy Duffey   367

Paul (12-Year-Old; 7th Grader)
The Bamboo Flute - Garry Disher   353

Paul (Child)
The Sugaring-Off Party - Jonathan London   895

Paul (Foster Parent)
Team Picture - Dean Hughes   661

Pauline (Young Woman)
The Faithful Friend - Robert D. San Souci   1261

Paulo (Child)
Amazon Boy - Ted Lewin   865

Pavelle (Dancer)
The Jewel Heart - Barbara Berger   100

Paw Paw (Grandmother; Aged Person)
Ribbons - Laurence Yep   1574

Peabody, Mildred (Grandmother)
Lizzie's List - Maggie Harrison   564

Pear Blossom (Child; Stepdaughter)
The Korean Cinderella - Shirley Climo   261

Pearl (Child; Artist)
Pearl Paints - Abigail Thomas   1415

Pearl (Sheep)
Pearl Plants a Tree - Jane Breskin Zalben   1593

Peck, Darryn (Bully)
Blabber Mouth - Morris Gleitzman   479

Peck, Robert Newton "Rob" (Child; Friend)
Soup Ahoy - Robert Newton Peck   1127

Peckle (Chicken; Mother)
The Chick's Trick - Jeni Bassett   84

Pedro (Artisan)
Saturday Market - Patricia Grossman   522

Peevik, Moomie (Space Explorer)
Space Brat 4: Planet of the Dips - Bruce
   Coville   293

Peg (Aunt)
Pearl Paints - Abigail Thomas   1415

Pendersnarf (Aged Person)
The Christmas Blizzard - Helen Ketteman   739

Pendragon, Arthur (Royalty; Aged Person)
Arthur, High King of Britain - Michael
   Morpurgo   1038

Penguin (Penguin; Royalty)
The Emperor Penguin's New Clothes - Janet
   Perlman   1132

Pennington, Robert (Military Personnel)
An Island Far from Home - John Donahue   358

Penshaw, Kate (Seamstress)
The Mennyms - Sylvia Waugh   1484

Peony (Stepsister)
The Korean Cinderella - Shirley Climo   261

Pepe (Bird)
Booby Hatch - Betsy Lewin   863

Pepi (Child)
Pepi and the Secret Names - Jill Paton Walsh   1115

Peppard, Sam (Blacksmith; Inventor)
The Wind Wagon - Celia Barker Lottridge   896

Peppe (Child; Immigrant)
Peppe the Lamplighter - Elisa Bartone   83

Pepper, Alice (10-Year-Old; Neighbor)
Numbskulls - William Taylor   1410

Pepper, Arlen (10-Year-Old)
Sticks - Joan Bauer   87

Pepperday, Tooter (Child)
Tooter Pepperday - Jerry Spinelli   1371

Percival (Peacock)
Hen Lake - Mary Jane Auch   49

Percy (Gardener; Animal Lover)
The Secret Path - Nick Butterworth   189

Perez, Tiffany (4th Grader; Wealthy)
The Pool Party - Gary Soto   1364

Perina (Girlfriend)
Silver at Night - Susan Campbell Bartoletti   82

Perkins, Zane (6th Grader)
Cat Running - Zilpha Keatley Snyder   1359

Perryman, Laura (14-Year-Old)
The Wreck of the Zanzibar - Michael
   Morpurgo   1040

Pete (11-Year-Old)
The Bones in the Cliff - James Stevenson   1385

Pete (Student)
Pete's Chicken - Harriet Ziefert   1594

Pete (Animal Lover; Worker)
Tornado - Betsy Byars   197

Pete (Cowboy; Assistant)
Tyrannosaurus Tex - Betty G. Birney   111

Pete (Uncle; Unemployed)
Zero's Slider - Matt Christopher   255

Peter (Child; Friend)
Best Friends Together Again - Aliki   25

Peter (Aged Person)
Dog - Robert J. Blake   115

Peter (9-Year-Old)
The Farm Summer 1942 - Donald Hall   541

Peter (Child; Gardener)
Something Is Growing - Walter Lyon Krudop   796

Peter (Child)
Your Dad Was Just Like You - Dolores Johnson   698

Peter (Angel)
Wicked Jack - Connie Nordhielm Wooldridge   1553

Peterson, Ernest "Ernie" (10-Year-Old)
The Big Bike Race - Lucy Jane Bledsoe   117

Peterson, J.P. (4th Grader; Outcast)
Shark in School - Patricia Reilly Giff   468

Petey (Child)
Petey and Miss Magic - N.B. Dorman   359

Petey (Child; Storyteller)
Petey's Bedtime Story - Beverly Cleary   256

Petit Jean (Peddler)
Three Sacks of Truth: A Story from France - Eric A.
   Kimmel   744

Petroff, Eugenia "Jenny" (11-Year-Old)
Tchaikovsky Discovers America - Esther Kalman   717

Phil (Child; Neighbor)
Who Is My Neighbor? - Michael Grejniec   513

Phillips, Nathaniel (Orphan; Runaway)
Drums at Saratoga - Lisa Banim   68

Philomena (Frog; Sister)
That's Philomena! - Catherine Bancroft   67

Philpot, Orin (5th Grader)
Wagon Train 911 - Jamie Gilson   473

Phoebe (5th Grader)
The Accidental Witch - Anne Mazer   956

Phoebe (Servant; Musician)
The Royal Nap - Charles C. Black   112

Phoebe (Child; Student)
Show and Tell - Barney Saltzberg   1258

Piano, Mike (Student—Junior High; Baseball Player)
Bat Boy - Mel Cebulash   228

Pickles, Maisie (Child; Student)
Captain Abdul's Pirate School - Colin
   McNaughton   990

Pierre (Child; Neighbor)
Dinner at Magritte's - Michael Garland   442

Pig (Pig; Friend)
Frog Is Frightened - Max Velthuijs   1453

Pig (Pig; Mother)
Jig, Fig, and Mrs. Pig - Peter Hansard   555

Pig, Garth (Pig; Musician)
Garth Pig Steals the Show - Mary Rayner   1202

Pig, William (Pig; Musician)
Garth Pig Steals the Show - Mary Rayner   1202

Pin (Frog; Royalty)
Jimmy, the Pickpocket of the Palace - Donna Jo
   Napoli   1061

"Pine" (Child)
On the Day I Was Born - Deborah M. Newton
   Chocolate   240

Pinky (2nd Grader; Child)
Pinky and Rex and the Bully - James Howe   654

Pinky (Child; Friend)
Pinky and Rex and the Double-Dad Weekend - James
   Howe   655
Pinky and Rex and the New Baby - James Howe   656

Pip (Child; Baseball Player)
Grandmas at Bat - Emily Arnold McCully   966

Pip (Salamander)
Pip's Magic - Ellen Stoll Walsh   1476

Pippin, Zeke (Pig; Runaway)
Zeke Pippin - William Steig   1378

Pippo (Toy; Monkey)
Tom and Pippo and the Bicycle - Helen
   Oxenbury   1104

Piro (Mythical Creature)
Sign of the Dove - Susan Fletcher   412

Pitts, Annie (3rd Grader; Actress)
Annie Pitts, Swamp Monster - Diane De Groat   327

Pitz, Thomas Osborn "Tom" (12-Year-Old)
*Tom, Babette, & Simon: Three Tales of
   Transformation* - Avi   58

Pixie (Child of Divorced Parents)
Step by Wicked Step - Anne Fine   407

Pizzazz (Hamster)
Jazz, Pizzaz, and the Silver Threads - Mary
   Quattlebaum   1182

PK (8-Year-Old; Sister)
Maybe Yes, Maybe No, Maybe Maybe - Susan
   Patron   1118

Plantpet (Plant)
Plantpet - Elise Primavera   1176

Plowie (Toy)
Plowie: A Story from the Prairie - Patricia
   Kirkpatrick   761

Plumed Serpent (Deity)
The People of Corn: A Mayan Story - Mary-Joan
   Gerson   459

Poetry (Dog)
One Dog Day - J. Patrick Lewis   866

Ratburn (Rat; Teacher)
Arthur Writes a Story - Marc Brown 145

Raven (Bird)
The Day Sun Was Stolen - Jamie Oliviero 1093

Raven (Indian; Student)
The Indian School - Gloria Whelan 1504

Raven (Bird)
Raven: A Trickster Tale from the Pacific Northwest - Gerald McDermott 971

Ravenell, Abigail (Grandmother)
Dakota Spring - D. Anne Love 899

Ray (Child)
Big Red Truck - Stephen Schlossberg 1285

Reade, Mary (Pirate)
The Ballad of the Pirate Queens - Jane Yolen 1576

Rebecca "Rabbit" (Child; Sister)
Maybe Yes, Maybe No, Maybe Maybe - Susan Patron 1118

Red (Dog)
Watchdog and the Coyotes - Bill Wallace 1472

Redmond, Kayla Ann (11-Year-Old; Friend)
Fast Forward - Mary Jane Miller 1013

Reeves, Aaron (Basketball Player; 8th Grader)
One-Man Team - Dean Hughes 659

Reina (Child; Indian)
The Farolitos of Christmas - Rudolfo Anaya 31

Reina (Child; Friend)
The Giant - Mordicai Gerstein 461

Reiner, Paul (Alcoholic)
Never Say Quit - Bill Wallace 1470

Renee (Child; Friend)
Palm Trees - Nancy Cote 292

Retting, Chelsie (6th Grader)
Riot - Mary Casanova 217

Rex (2nd Grader; Child)
Pinky and Rex and the Bully - James Howe 654

Rex (Child; Friend)
Pinky and Rex and the Double-Dad Weekend - James Howe 655

Rex (Child; Sister)
Pinky and Rex and the New Baby - James Howe 656

Rex (Dinosaur; Brother)
Rex and Lilly Family Time - Laurie Krasny Brown 143

Rhino (Rhinoceros; Friend)
Rhino and Mouse - Todd Starr Palmer 1106

Rich, Joey (7th Grader)
Cheater, Cheater - Elizabeth Levy 857

Richard (13-Year-Old; Brother)
Saving Owen's Toad - Juanita Havill 573

Richards, Ryan (2nd Grader)
Ozzie on His Own - Johanna Hurwitz 670

Rightous Cry (Slave)
Remember My Name - Sara H. Banks 74

Riko (16-Year-Old)
Hiroshima - Laurence Yep 1572

Riley, Georgene (Child)
The Face in the Bessledorf Funeral Parlor - Phyllis Reynolds Naylor 1065

Rinaldo (Fox)
The Return of Rinaldo, the Sly Fox - Ursel Scheffler 1276

Rinaldo (Fox; Thief)
Rinaldo on the Run - Ursel Scheffler 1277

Ripley, Samantha (5th Grader; Activist)
The Green Musketeers and the Fabulous Frogs - Sara St. Antoine 1375

Robby (Child)
Snow Day! - Barbara M. Joosse 713

Robert (Child; Friend)
Best Friends Together Again - Aliki 25

Roberts, Katie (11-Year-Old)
The Private Notebook of Katie Roberts, Age 11 - Amy Hest 607

Roberts, Red (Student—College; Bicyclist)
Olympic Dream - Matt Christopher 252

Robeson, Brian (13-Year-Old; Survivor)
Brian's Winter - Gary Paulsen 1119

Robin (Child; Animal Lover)
Eagle Dreams - Sheryl McFarlane 976

Robin (Animal Trainer)
Passenger - Jane Yolen 1585

Robin, Eve (Sister; Student—High School)
Best Enemies Forever - Kathleen Leverich 840

Robin, Priscilla (4th Grader; Sister)
Best Enemies Forever - Kathleen Leverich 840

Rockaway, Joey (Detective—Amateur)
The Case of the Wiggling Wig - E.W. Hildick 617

Rodney (Child; Brother)
Monster Brother - Mary Jane Auch 51

Rogers (Employer)
Good Driving, Amelia Bedelia - Peggy Parish 1108

Rooney (Teacher)
Look Out, Washington, D.C.! - Patricia Reilly Giff 465

Rooney, Pepper (Child)
Trouble Will Find You - Joan M. Lexau 870

Rooster (Rooster)
Rooster Crows - Ragnhild Scamell 1272

Rosa (Child; Cousin)
Kisses from Rosa - Petra Mathers 949

Rosa (Aged Person; Neighbor)
City Green - DyAnne DiSalvo-Ryan 352

Rosalba (Child)
Isla - Arthur Dorros 362

Rosamund (Child)
Nate the Great and the Pillowcase - Marjorie Weinman Sharmat 1321

Roscoe (Outlaw)
The Gentleman Outlaw and Me—Eli - Mary Downing Hahn 539

Rose (Sister; Farmer)
Seven Loaves of Bread - Ferida Wolff 1546

Rose (Pig; Sister)
The Wimp - Kathy Caple 204

Rosemary (Aged Person)
The Cow Who Wouldn't Come Down - Paul Brett Johnson 701

Rosemary (Teacher)
Woollybear Good-bye - Sharon Phillips Denslow 343

Rosen, Elana Rose "Lanny" (Child of Divorced Parents)
Scooter - Vera B. Williams 1523

Rosie (Child; Sister)
The Great Pumpkin Switch - Megan McDonald 973

Rosie (Child)
In My Mother's Garden - Melissa Madenski 919
Inside-Out Grandma - Joan Rothenberg 1236

Rosie (Dog)
My Dog Rosie - Isabelle Harper 559

Rosie (Child)
My Shadow - Susan Winter 1535
Rosie's Fishing Trip - Amy Hest 608

Rosie (Toy)
Stardust - Alane Ferguson 405

Rosie (Child; Indian)
A Walk to the Great Mystery - Virginia A. Stroud 1402

Roslan, Alex (Hero)
Jacob's Rescue: A Holocaust Story - Malka Drucker 366

Roy (Child)
Stella and Roy - Ashley Wolff 1545

Rubina (Spouse; Mother)
The Swan's Gift - Brenda Seabrooke 1306

Ruby (Rabbit; Sister)
Max and Ruby's First Greek Myth: Pandora's Box - Rosemary Wells 1496
Max and Ruby's Midas: Another Greek Myth - Rosemary Wells 1497

Ruby (Child)
Ruby's Storm - Amy Hest 609

Rumplemayer, Fenton (11-Year-Old; Detective—Amateur)
On the Right Track - B.B. Calhoun 198

Rumplemeyer, Bill (Father; Scientist)
On the Right Track - B.B. Calhoun 198

Rundi (Jaguarundi)
Jaguarundi - Virginia Hamilton 551

Rupert (Royalty)
Cinder Edna - Ellen Jackson 681

Rush, Becky (5th Grader)
The Mystery of the Several Sevens - Bill Brittain 140

Rusk, Georgina (Detective; Companion)
Angela's Aliens - Janet Taylor Lisle 876

Rusk, Georgina (Friend)
The Gold Dust Letters - Janet Taylor Lisle 878

Rusk, Georgina (Child; Friend)
Looking for Juliette - Janet Taylor Lisle 879

Rusk, Georgina (Friend)
A Message from the Match Girl - Janet Taylor Lisle 880

Russ (Uncle)
Lobster Boat - Brenda Z. Guiberson 525

Russell (Student)
Jamaica's Blue Marker - Juanita Havill 571

Russell, Priscilla (Foster Parent)
The Promised Land - Isabelle Holland 637

Rusty (Artist; Student)
The Gentleman and the Kitchen Maid - Diane Stanley 1376

Ruth (Worker)
The Bobbin Girl - Emily Arnold McCully 964

Ruth, George Herman "Babe" (Historical Figure; Baseball Player)
When Willard Met Babe Ruth - Donald Hall 544

Ruva (Giraffe)
The Warm Place - Nancy Farmer 401

Ryan, Kevin (14-Year-Old)
The Haunting of Holroyd Hill - Brenda Seabrooke 1304

Ryan, Melinda (11-Year-Old)
The Haunting of Holroyd Hill - Brenda Seabrooke 1304

Ryder (Child)
Bats about Baseball - Jean Little 881

Ryker (Judge; Grandfather)
Wait and See - Virginia Bradley 131

Ryker, Amy (11-Year-Old; 6th Grader)
Wait and See - Virginia Bradley 131

S

Saaski (Child)
The Moorchild - Eloise Jarvis McGraw   978

Sable (Dog)
Sable - Karen Hesse   602

Sabrina (Cat)
Elfsong - Ann Turner   1433

Sachi (12-Year-Old)
Hiroshima - Laurence Yep   1572

Sadie (Orphan; Seamstress)
The Boardwalk Princess - Arthur A. Levine   845

Sailor, Sinker O. (Radio Personality)
Soup Ahoy - Robert Newton Peck   1127

Salah (7-Year-Old; Animal Lover)
The Hundredth Name - Shulamith Levey Oppenheim   1096

Salazar, Stephen (9th Grader)
The Fog Doggies and Me - Gayle Pearson   1125

Sally (Royalty)
Jimmy, the Pickpocket of the Palace - Donna Jo Napoli   1061

Sally Ann (Toy)
Nurse Sally Ann - Terrance Dicks   350

Sally Jane (Child)
Letting Swift River Go - Jane Yolen   1583

Sam (Child)
2095 - Jon Scieszka   1298

Sam (Friend)
A Baby Just Like Me - Susan Winter   1534

Sam (Child; Brother)
Big Help! - Anna Grossnickle Hines   621

Sam (Child)
Climbing Kansas Mountains - George Shannon   1316

Sam (8-Year-Old; Latch-Key Child)
The Latchkey Dog - Mary Jane Auch   50

Sam (Dog)
My Dog Talks - Gail Herman   591

Sam (Cowboy; Entertainer)
Sam's Wild West Show - Nancy Antle   36

Sam (Child)
Time to Wake Up! - Marisabina Russo   1243

Sam (Child; Brother)
A Turkey Drive and Other Tales - Barbara Ann Porte   1167

Sam (Time Traveller; 6th Grader)
Tut Tut - Jon Scieszka   1299

Sam (Child)
Your Mother Was a Neanderthal - Jon Scieszka   1300

Samantha "Sam" (Adoptee)
How I Was Adopted: Samantha's Story - Joanna Cole   271

Sammy (Child; Brother)
John Joe and the Big Hen - Martin Waddell   1462
Sophie and Sammy's Library Sleepover - Judith Caseley   221

Samson (Wolf)
Florizella and the Wolves - Philippa Gregory   510

Samuelson, Rebecca (12-Year-Old)
Dear Elijah - Miriam Bat-Ami   85

Sanchez, Julio (5th Grader; Activist)
School Spirit - Johanna Hurwitz   671

Sandman (Father)
A Tooth Fairy's Tale - David Christiana   246

Sandworm, Johannes (4-Year-Old)
Santa's Winter Vacation - Viveca Larn Sundvall   1404

Sanford, Sally (Child)
Sally's Submarine - Joan Anderson   34

Sapphire (Cat)
Courtyard Cat - C.S. Adler   10

Sara (Child)
First Snow - Kim Lewis   867

Sara (Student)
Wilson Sat Alone - Debra Hess   598

Sara Kate (3rd Grader)
Sara Kate Saves the World - Susan Beth Pfeffer   1143

Sarach, Zina (Refugee)
A Different Kind of Courage - Ellen Howard   651

Sarah (8-Year-Old)
Don't Forget - Patricia Lakin   807

Sarah (Horse Trainer)
A Horse Like Barney - Jessie Haas   532

Sarah (Bear; Runaway)
My Real Family - Emily Arnold McCully   968

Sarah (8-Year-Old)
Nettie's Gift - Susan Tews   1413

Sarah (Friend)
Patrick's Tree House - Steven Kroll   790

Sarah Jean (Niece)
Uncle Jed's Barbershop - Margaree King Mitchell   1022

Sasifi (8-Year-Old)
Tap-Tap - Karen Lynn Williams   1521

Sasparillo (Armadillo)
The Armadillo from Amarillo - Lynne Cherry   236

Saul (Aged Person)
Straw Sense - Rona Rupert   1239

Saunders, Rosie (12-Year-Old)
Don't Go Near Mrs. Tallie - Peg Kehret   724

Sawyer, Humility "Hummy" (Settler; 12-Year-Old)
A Journey to the New World: The Diary of Remember Patience Whipple - Kathryn Lasky   815

Saygee (Child; Indian)
Doesn't Fall Off His Horse - Virginia A. Stroud   1401

Scales, Lotta (Mythical Creature; Librarian)
The Library Dragon - Carmen Agra Deedy   333

Scarecrow (Worker)
Nothing at All - Denys Cazet   227

Schmidt, Veronica (5th Grader)
Countess Veronica - Nancy K. Robinson   1219

Schur, Gordon (6th Grader; Friend)
Tarantula Shoes - Tom Birdseye   110

Scooter (Grandfather)
Crash - Jerry Spinelli   1370

Scott (Child)
Pig, Horse, or Cow, Don't Wake Me Now - Arlene Alda   21

Scraggly Sam (Weasel)
The Sleepy Dormouse - Mark Ezra   399

Scrat, Ebenezer "Neezer" (Thief; Innkeeper)
The Twin in the Tavern - Barbara Brooks Wallace   1469

Scudder, Tobias Michael "Toby" (6th Grader)
Toby Scudder, Ultimate Warrior - David Gifaldi   463

Seabrooke, Dinah (12-Year-Old)
Dinah in Love - Claudia Mills   1016

Seahorse (Servant)
The Painted Fan - Marilyn Singer   1339

Sebastian (Dog; Detective)
Sebastian (Super Sleuth) and the Copycat Crime - Mary Blount Christian   243

Sebastian (Dog)
Sebastian (Super Sleuth) and the Flying Elephant - Mary Blount Christian   244

Second Princess (Royalty)
The Second Princess - Hiawyn Oram   1099

Secret (Cat)
On Cat Mountain - Francoise Richard   1209

Seth (7-Year-Old; Brother)
The Tie Man's Miracle: A Chanukah Tale - Steven Schnur   1289

Shadow (Dog)
My Island Grandma - Kathryn Lasky   816

Shafter, Allen "Alligator" (Fisherman; Teenager)
The Case of the Missing Cutthroats, an Ecological Mystery - Jean Craighead George   448

Shafter, Becky (Housewife)
The Case of the Missing Cutthroats, an Ecological Mystery - Jean Craighead George   448

Shafter, Spinner (Fisherman; 13-Year-Old)
The Case of the Missing Cutthroats, an Ecological Mystery - Jean Craighead George   448

Shamiema (Aunt)
Straw Sense - Rona Rupert   1239

Shang (Ruler)
The Painted Fan - Marilyn Singer   1339

Sharik (Dog)
Uncle Fedya, His Dog, and His Cat - Eduard Uspenskii   1440

Shark (Shark; Ruler)
The Story of the Three Kingdoms - Walter Dean Myers   1057

Sharp, Martha (Hero)
A Different Kind of Courage - Ellen Howard   651

Shauna (2nd Grader)
Saturday at the New You - Barbara E. Barber   77

Shaw, Ebenezer (Aged Person; Blind)
Man Out at First - Matt Christopher   251

Shedd, Fred (Child)
Genghis Khan: A Dog Star Is Born - Marjorie Weinman Sharmat   1320

Shelan (Child)
Working Cotton - Sherley Anne Williams   1522

Shelton, Eric (Child)
Cam Jansen and the Chocolate Fudge Mystery - David A. Adler   13

Shem (Brother; Alien)
Star Hatchling - Margaret Bechard   93

Sheriff (Guardian; Cowboy)
Saving Sweetness - Diane Stanley   1377

Sherman (Sheep; Leader)
Sherman the Sheep - Kevin Kiser   762

Sherwin-Hendicks, Beatrice Lorraine "Beany" (Sister; Student)
Don't Call Me Beanhead! - Susan Wojciechowski   1544

Shetland, Liza (Sheep; Actress)
Sheep Dreams - Arthur A. Levine   847

Shiloh (Dog)
Shiloh Season - Phyllis Reynolds Naylor   1068

Shirley (Mouse; Friend)
What's for Lunch? - John Schindel   1284

Sho (Servant; Animal Lover)
On Cat Mountain - Francoise Richard   1209

Si Ling-Chi (Royalty)
The Empress and the Silkworm - Lily Toy Hong   640

Sidney (Child; Brother)
Monster Brother - Mary Jane Auch   51

Sidney (2nd Grader)
Song Lee and the Leech Man - Suzy Kline   772

Sidney (Mouse; Friend)
What's for Lunch? - John Schindel   1284

Sigfried (Religious)
The Bookstore Mouse - Peggy Christian   245

Silky (Dog)
Maggie and Silky and Joe - Amy Ehrlich   386

Sillypants (Camper)
Let's Go Camping with Mr. Sillypants - M.K. Brown   144

Silverman, Abigail (Camper; 11-Year-Old)
Daring to be Abigail - Rachel Vail   1442

Silverman, Alan (7th Grader)
Alan and Naomi - Myron Levoy   856

Silvia (Child)
New Shoes for Silvia - Johanna Hurwitz   669

Simcha (Brother; Refugee)
When I Left My Village - Maxine Rose Schur   1296

Simms, Charlie (14-Year-Old)
The Well: David's Story - Mildred D. Taylor   1409

Simon (Young Man)
Tom, Babette, & Simon: Three Tales of Transformation - Avi   58

Simon (Fiance(e))
Two's Company - Amanda Benjamin   98

Simon of Hargrave (Royalty)
The Battle for the Castle - Elizabeth Winthrop   1537

Simpkin (Child)
Simpkin - Quentin Blake   114

Simpson, Emma (Writer; Southern Belle)
When Will This Cruel War Be Over? The Civil War Diary of Emma Simpson - Barry Denenberg   340

Simpson, Fletcher (5th Grader; Bully)
Gopher Takes Heart - Virginia Scribner   1303

Sims, Libbie (11-Year-Old; Child of Divorced Parents)
Libbie Sims, Worry Wart - Gayle Rogers Lockwood   887

Sims, Maggie (16-Year-Old; Sister)
Libbie Sims, Worry Wart - Gayle Rogers Lockwood   887

Sims, Ozzie (8-Year-Old)
Ozzie on His Own - Johanna Hurwitz   670

Singer (Store Owner)
Don't Forget - Patricia Lakin   807

Singh, Julian (6th Grader; Immigrant)
The View from Saturday - E.L. Konigsburg   777

Sissy (6-Year-Old)
Kinda Blue - Ann Grifalconi   516

Sister (Child)
The Little Tree Growin' in the Shade - Camille Yarbrough   1569

Sitti (Grandmother)
Sitti's Secrets - Naomi Shihab Nye   1087

Sixteen, John Three (Indian)
Dixie in the Big Pasture - Belinda Hurmence   665

Skilly (Aged Person)
Aunt Skilly and the Stranger - Kathleen Stevens   1382

Skipper (Dog)
Great Aunt Martha - Rebecca C. Jones   710

Skooghammer (Teacher)
Horrible Harry and the Dungeon - Suzy Kline   769

Skunk (Skunk; Friend)
James Bear and the Goose Gathering - Jim Latimer   821

Slade (Businessman; Frontiersman)
The Sweetwater Run: The Story of Buffalo Bill Cody and the Pony Express - Andrew Glass   476

Slagbottom (Anthropologist; Pig)
The Mystery of King Karfu - Doug Cushman   313

Sleuth, Seymour (Detective; Wombat)
The Mystery of King Karfu - Doug Cushman   313

Slinger (Mouse; Teacher)
Lilly's Purple Plastic Purse - Kevin Henkes   587

Slinky (Bully)
Boys at Work - Gary Soto   1361

Slocum, Benjamin (12-Year-Old; Brother)
Bluewater Journal: The Voyage of the Sea Tiger - Loretta Krupinski   797

Slocum, Isabel (Sister)
Bluewater Journal: The Voyage of the Sea Tiger - Loretta Krupinski   797

Slocum, Joshua (Spirit; Sailor)
Moonlight on the River - Deborah Kovacs   781

Sludge (Dog)
Nate the Great and the Pillowcase - Marjorie Weinman Sharmat   1321
Nate the Great and the Tardy Tortoise - Marjorie Weinman Sharmat   1322

Small, Patsy (Child)
Revenge of the Small Small - Jean Little   882

Smallest Hen (Chicken)
The Rooster's Gift - Pam Conrad   283

Smallhorn, David (Indian; Trapper)
Brian's Winter - Gary Paulsen   1119

Smathers, Emmeline Sue (Orphan)
A Shooting Star: A Novel about Annie Oakley - Sheila Solomon Klass   766

Smith (Teacher)
Snowy - Berlie Doherty   356

Smith, Belinda Rainbow "Boo" (Student—Junior High)
The Great Smith House Hustle - Jane Louise Curry   309

Smith, Chad (Bully)
Slam Dunk Saturday - Jean Marzollo   944

Smith, Donald "Donny" (Military Personnel; Veteran)
Following My Own Footsteps - Mary Downing Hahn   538

Smith, Francisco Moonlight "Cisco" (10-Year-Old; Brother)
The Great Smith House Hustle - Jane Louise Curry   309

Smith, Gordon "Gordy" (6th Grader)
Following My Own Footsteps - Mary Downing Hahn   538

Smith, Jennifer "Jennifer-the-Jerk" (Kidnap Victim; Classmate)
Jennifer-the-Jerk Is Missing - Carol Gorman   488

Smith, Justine (Soccer Player)
Never Say Quit - Bill Wallace   1470

Smith, Nellie (Animal Lover)
Prowlpuss - Gina Wilson   1530

Smith, Willie (4th Grader)
Poison Ivy and Eyebrow Wigs - Bonnie Pryor   1180

Snide (Businessman)
Do You See a Mouse? - Bernard Waber   1459

Snodgrass, Martin Elwood (4th Grader)
Poison Ivy and Eyebrow Wigs - Bonnie Pryor   1180

Snow Queen (Sorceress)
The Snow Queen - Hans Christian Andersen   32

Snowdrift (Wolf)
Child of the Wolves - Elizabeth Hall   545

Snowy (Horse)
Snowy - Berlie Doherty   356

Snyder (Toy; Spider)
Tuck in the Pool - Martha Weston   1502

Solay (Alien)
Solay - Mark J. Harris   562

Som See (Child; Niece)
Som See and the Magic Elephant - Jamie Oliviero   1094

Someone (Child; Indian)
The Seasons and Someone - Virginia L. Kroll   794

Song Lee (2nd Grader)
Song Lee and the Leech Man - Suzy Kline   772

Song Lee (2nd Grader; Immigrant)
Song Lee in Room 2B - Suzy Kline   773

Sophia (Stepsister)
Papa Gatto: An Italian Fairy Tale - Ruth Sanderson   1265

Sophie (Child)
Blow Away Soon - Betsy James   685
Sophie and Sammy's Library Sleepover - Judith Caseley   221

Sophie (6-Year-Old)
Sophie in the Saddle - Dick King-Smith   752

Sophie (7-Year-Old; Student)
Sophie Is Seven - Dick King-Smith   753

Sophie (7-Year-Old)
Sophie's Lucky - Dick King-Smith   754

Sophie (Child; Niece)
Sophy and Auntie Pearl - Jeanne Titherington   1421

Sophie (Child; Thief)
Tangles - Errol Broome   141

Sophie (Child)
Weekend Girl - Amy Hest   610

Sophocles (Dog)
The Sounds of Summer - David Updike   1438

Sosi (Child; Indian)
The Mud Family - Betsy James   687

Sparks, Simon (Brother)
The Girl Who Changed the World - Delia Ephron   393

Sparks, Violet Dixie (10-Year-Old)
The Girl Who Changed the World - Delia Ephron   393

Sparrow (Bird)
The Happy Prince - Oscar Wilde   1515

Speedy (Tortoise)
Nate the Great and the Tardy Tortoise - Marjorie Weinman Sharmat   1322

Spencer, Kevin (2nd Grader)
Olivia and the Real Live Pet - Charlotte Towner Graeber   490

Spider (Spider)
Miss Spider's Tea Party - David Kirk   760

Spiny (Dinosaur)
Spiny - Jurgen Lassig   820

Squirrel (Squirrel; Friend)
Heart to Heart - George Shannon   1317

Squirrel, Skip (Squirrel)
Tick-Tock - Eileen Browne   157

Stanley (Stork)
Burton and Stanley - Frank O'Rourke   1101

Stanton, Elizabeth Cady (Suffragette; Historical Figure)
The Ballot Box Battle - Emily Arnold McCully 963

Stapleton, Danny (6th Grader)
The Reason for Janey - Nancy Hope Wilson 1532

Star Shiner (Worker)
The Moon Man: A Story - Gerda Marie Scheidl 1279

Starbright (Horse)
Midnight Rider - Krista Ruepp 1238

Starbuck, Charlotte "Charly" (5-Year-Old; Twin)
A Voice in the Wind - Kathryn Lasky 819

Starbuck, Liberty (12-Year-Old; Twin)
A Voice in the Wind - Kathryn Lasky 819

Starr (7th Grader)
The Fog Doggies and Me - Gayle Pearson 1125

Steadings, Amy (Aged Person)
The Ghastly Gerty Swindle: With the Ghosts of Hungryhouse Lane - Sam McBratney 959

Stebbins, Buddy (12-Year-Old; Orphan)
The 13th Floor: A Ghost Story - Sid Fleischman 409

Stebbins, Liz (Sister; Lawyer)
The 13th Floor: A Ghost Story - Sid Fleischman 409

Stein, Gertrude (Neighbor)
See You Around, Sam! - Lois Lowry 902

Stella (Child)
Good Night, Stella - Kate McMullan 988
Stella and Roy - Ashley Wolff 1545

Stella (Niece; Sister)
When Aunt Lucy Rode a Mule and Other Stories - Barbara Ann Porte 1168

Stellaluna (Bat)
Stellaluna - Janell Cannon 203

Stella's Bull (Bull)
Stella's Bull - Frances Arrington 45

Stephanie (Child; Neighbor)
Tom and Pippo and the Bicycle - Helen Oxenbury 1104

Stewart, Abigail Jane "Abby" (11-Year-Old)
The Winter of Red Snow: The Revolutionary War Diary of Abigail Jane Stewart - Kristiana Gregory 509

Stewart, John Edward (Child)
The Winter of Red Snow: The Revolutionary War Diary of Abigail Jane Stewart - Kristiana Gregory 509

Stillwater, Anne (Student)
First Came the Owl - Judith Benet Richardson 1210

Stormfoot, Hosannah (Aged Person; Spouse)
Santa's Winter Vacation - Viveca Larn Sundvall 1404

Stormfoot, Reuben (Aged Person; Spouse)
Santa's Winter Vacation - Viveca Larn Sundvall 1404

Strata, Melanie "Lanie" (8th Grader)
What Happened in Mr. Fisher's Room - Nancy J. Hopper 646

Straus, Brian (7th Grader)
The Worst Speller in Jr. High - Caroline Janover 690

Strudwick (Sheep)
Strudwick: A Sheep in Wolf's Clothing - Robert Kraus 786

Stuart, Annie Rising Fawn (11-Year-Old; Orphan)
Remember My Name - Sara H. Banks 74

Stubbs, Sarah (Student)
City of Light, City of Dark: A Comic-Book Novel - Avi 55

Stukeley, Sarah (Teenager; Patient)
The Apprenticeship of Lucas Whitaker - Cynthia DeFelice 334

Stumpy (Squirrel; Mother)
Gooseberry Park - Cynthia Rylant 1249

Sullivan, Mary Margaret "Maggie" (11-Year-Old; Friend)
A Spy in the King's Colony - Lisa Banim 69

Sullivan, William (Handicapped; Crime Victim)
Following My Own Footsteps - Mary Downing Hahn 538

Sumi (Child)
Peacebound Trains - Haemi Balgassi 63

Sump (Child-Care Giver)
Saving Sweetness - Diane Stanley 1377

Sun (Celestial Body)
Sun Song - Jean Marzollo 946

Sunipass, Rayanne (9-Year-Old; Indian)
Crossing the Starlight Bridge - Alice Mead 997

Susan (Child; Niece)
The Hanukkah Ghosts - Malka Penn 1128

Susan (Child)
Is Susan Here? - Janice May Udry 1437

Susie (10-Year-Old; Settler)
Black-Eyed Susan - Jennifer Armstrong 38

Sweet Clara (Child; Slave)
Sweet Clara and the Freedom Quilt - Deborah Hopkinson 644

Sweetie (Dog)
Watchdog and the Coyotes - Bill Wallace 1472

Sweetness (Orphan; Heroine)
Saving Sweetness - Diane Stanley 1377

Sweetsong, Stanley (10-Year-Old; Student)
Shoebag Returns - Mary James 688

Swope, Angela "Angel Always" (11-Year-Old; Friend)
Ghosts Don't Get Goosebumps - Elvira Woodruff 1551

Syers, June (Babysitter; Political Figure)
The Kid Who Ran for President - Dan Gutman 527

Sylvain (Accident Victim)
In the Palace of the Ocean King - Marilyn Singer 1338

Sylvia (Apprentice)
The Sorcerer's Apprentice - Nancy Willard 1516

Sylvie (Child; Sister)
All the Places to Love - Patricia MacLachlan 916

Sylvie (Child)
Moonfall - Susan Whitcher 1507

Sylvie (9-Year-Old)
A Sound of Leaves - Lenore Blegvad 118

T

Tabby (Cat)
Mr. Putter and Tabby Bake the Cake - Cynthia Rylant 1253
Mr. Putter and Tabby Pick the Pears - Cynthia Rylant 1254
Mr. Putter and Tabby Walk the Dog - Cynthia Rylant 1255
The Worst Witch at Sea - Jill Murphy 1053

Tacky (Penguin)
Three Cheers for Tacky - Helen Lester 838

Tahsha (Elephant)
Sebastian (Super Sleuth) and the Flying Elephant - Mary Blount Christian 244

Takamura, Corey (8-Year-Old)
Pony Crazy - Bonnie Bryant 164

Takumi (5-Year-Old)
Okino and the Whales - Arnica Esterl 397

Tallie, Hilda (Aged Person)
Don't Go Near Mrs. Tallie - Peg Kehret 724

Tam (Orphan; Farmer)
The Moorchild - Eloise Jarvis McGraw 978

Tangles (Cat)
Tangles - Errol Broome 141

Tante Golda (Cook)
The Miracle of the Potato Latkes: A Hanukkah Story - Malka Penn 1129

Tante Loulou (Aunt)
The Sugaring-Off Party - Jonathan London 895

Tanya (Child; Dancer)
Tanya and Emily in a Dance for Two - Patricia Lee Gauch 446

Tanya (Child)
Tanya's Reunion - Valerie Flournoy 413

Tapiwa (9-Year-Old)
Do You Know Me? - Nancy Farmer 400

Tapper, Tim (Spirit)
The Ghost Comes Calling - Betty Ren Wright 1556

Tara (3-Year-Old; Sister)
Tiger Flowers - Patricia Quinlan 1183

Tatro, Cole (12-Year-Old)
Uncle Daney's Way - Jessie Haas 535

Tavish, Marion McGillicuddy (Spouse; Mother)
The Rattlebang Picnic - Margaret Mahy 925

Taylor, Ardene (Neighbor; Friend)
Falcon's Egg - Luli Gray 497

Taylor, Everett (Cousin; 5th Grader)
Jason and the Losers - Gina Willner-Pardo 1527

Taylor, Ronny (Military Personnel)
Rosie's Tiger - Anna Myers 1055

Taylor, Rosie (6th Grader)
Rosie's Tiger - Anna Myers 1055

Tchaikovsky, Peter Ilich (Composer; Conductor)
Tchaikovsky Discovers America - Esther Kalman 717

Teaberry (Aged Person; Neighbor)
Mr. Putter and Tabby Bake the Cake - Cynthia Rylant 1253
Mr. Putter and Tabby Pick the Pears - Cynthia Rylant 1254

Ted (Bear; Businessman)
The Mighty Movers - Sidney Levitt 855

Teddy (Toy)
First Snow - Kim Lewis 867

Teddy (Brother)
Later, Gator - Laurence Yep 1573

Teitletot, Jenny (9-Year-Old; Magician)
Jazz, Pizzaz, and the Silver Threads - Mary Quattlebaum 1182

Teresa (Child; Babysitter)
Lights on the River - Jane Resh Thomas 1417

Tesfa (Father; Trader)
The Lion's Whiskers: An Ethiopian Folktale - Nancy Raines Day 325

Tess (Child)
Clean House - Jessie Haas 531

Tess (Dog)
The New Puppy - Laurence Anholt 35

Tessie (Child)
I Found Mouse - Pamela D. Greenwood 505

Tetsuzan (Religious)
The Loyal Cat - Lensey Namioka 1059

Thomas (Hero; Fisherman)
The Boy and the Giants - Fiona Moodie 1030

Thomas (Child)
When I Grow Bigger - Trish Cooke 285

Thomas, Andy (12-Year-Old; Researcher)
Search for the Shadowman - Joan Lowery
Nixon 1076

Thomas, Sara Jane "Chicken" (10-Year-Old)
Harry on Vacation - Dyan Sheldon 1326

Thomas the Tidy, the Ti (Royalty; Brother)
Tumble Tower - Anne Tyler 1435

Thompson (Plantation Owner; Bully)
The Foot Warmer and the Crow - Evelyn
Coleman 274

Thompson, Callie (5th Grader)
Learning by Heart - Ronder Thomas Young 1588

Thornbine (Explorer)
Something Is Growing - Walter Lyon Krudop 796

Thornton, Montgomery (3rd Grader)
In Trouble with Teacher - Patricia Demuth 339

Thrush, Brigid (Child)
Brigid the Bad - Kathleen Leverich 841

Thud, Humphrey (Elephant; Toy)
Humphrey Thud - Camilla Ashforth 48

Tia (Aunt)
A Birthday Basket for Tia - Pat Mora 1036

Tibbets (Military Personnel; Pilot)
Hiroshima - Laurence Yep 1572

Tibbs (Journalist)
Minnie - Annie M.G. Schmidt 1286

Tierney, Scott (7th Grader)
Trick or Trouble? - Ilene Cooper 287

Tiff (Camper)
Daring to be Abigail - Rachel Vail 1442

Tiffany (Latch-Key Child; Gardener)
Home Lovely - Lynne Rae Perkins 1131

Tiger (Tiger; Bully)
The Rat and the Tiger - Keiko Kasza 722

Tigerella (Tiger)
Tigerella - Kit Wright 1564

Tikvah (Cat)
Tikvah Means Hope - Patricia Polacco 1163

Tilda (Child; Niece)
Something for Everyone - Susan Whitcher 1508

Tillby (Mother; Traveller)
Someplace Else - Carol P. Saul 1269

Tillie (Hog)
The Hog Call to End All! - SuAnn Kiser 765

Tillie (Slave; Bride)
Jumping the Broom - Courtni C. Wright 1563

Tilly (Child)
The Bear - Raymond Briggs 137

Tim (Child)
What about My Goldfish? - Pamela D.
Greenwood 506

Timmie (Child)
Sunshine Home - Eve Bunting 180

Timpkin, Petey (Child; Neighbor)
Scooter - Vera B. Williams 1523

Tina (Squirrel)
Arnie and the Skateboard Gang - Nancy Carlson 211

Tina (Child of Divorced Parents)
Taxi! Taxi! - Cari Best 105

Tobias (Slave)
Washington City Is Burning - Harriette Gillem
Robinet 1218

Tod (Child)
Here Comes Tod! - Philippa Pearce 1124

Todd, Abbott L. (Father; Artisan)
Bound for Oregon - Jean Van Leeuwen 1448

Todd, Louvina (6-Year-Old; Sister)
Bound for Oregon - Jean Van Leeuwen 1448

Todd, Mary Ellen (9-Year-Old; Sister)
Bound for Oregon - Jean Van Leeuwen 1448

Tofie, Goolam-Habib (5-Year-Old)
Straw Sense - Rona Rupert 1239

Toller, Simon (5th Grader)
The Mystery of the Several Sevens - Bill Brittain 140

Tolson, Abby (9-Year-Old)
Haunted Summer - Betty Ren Wright 1560

Tolson, David (11-Year-Old)
Haunted Summer - Betty Ren Wright 1560

Tom (Child of Divorced Parents)
Good-Bye, Daddy! - Brigitte Weninger 1499

Tom (Iguana; Brother)
The Iguana Brothers: A Tale of Two Lizards - Tony
Johnston 704

Tom (7-Year-Old; Stepson)
My Wicked Stepmother - Norman Leach 828

Tom (Child)
Tom and Pippo and the Bicycle - Helen
Oxenbury 1104

Tom (8-Year-Old)
Tom's Fish - Nancy Coffelt 265

Tom (Pig)
Tom's Tail - Linda Jennings 692

Tomlin, Paula (6th Grader; Child of Divorced
Parents)
The Pickle Song - Barthe DeClements 331

Tommy (Child; Nephew)
Lobster Boat - Brenda Z. Guiberson 525

Tony (Child; Brother)
Baby Jesus, Like My Brother - Margery Wheeler
Brown 153

Tony (Child; Dancer)
Boy, Can He Dance! - Eileen Spinelli 1367

Tooley (Householder; Young Man)
The House Gobbaleen - Lloyd Alexander 23

Toomey, Brian (6th Grader; Dyslexic)
My Name Is Brain/Brian - Jeanne Betancourt 106

Toomey, Jonathan (Artisan; Widow(er))
The Christmas Miracle of Jonathan Toomey - Susan
Wojciechowski 1543

Tooth Fairy (Mythical Creature)
A Tooth Fairy's Tale - David Christiana 246

Toothpick (Bird)
The Pirates' Mixed-Up Voyage - Margaret Mahy 924

Tornado (Dog)
Tornado - Betsy Byars 197

Torrant, Billy (Sports Figure)
Olympic Dream - Matt Christopher 252

Tortoise (Turtle; Storyteller)
Stories from Firefly Island - Benedict Blathwayt 116

Tortoise (Turtle)
The Tortoise and the Jackrabbit - Susan Lowell 901

Tosis, Hally (Dog)
Dog Breath: The Horrible Trouble with Hally Tosis -
Dav Pilkey 1148

Totte (Father; Artisan)
The Rose Horse - Deborah Lee Rose 1228

Tottibo (Magician)
The Sorcerer's Apprentice - Nancy Willard 1516

Trab (Cat)
Augusta & Trab - Christopher De Vinck 330

Tracy, Martin (Child; Brother)
The Ghost of Popcorn Hill - Betty Ren Wright 1557

Tracy, Peter (Child; Brother)
The Ghost of Popcorn Hill - Betty Ren Wright 1557

Trask, Nathan (Collector)
Bess's Log Cabin Quilt - D. Anne Love 898

Travers, Judd (Young Man)
Shiloh Season - Phyllis Reynolds Naylor 1068

Trelling, Christopher "Chris" (Brother)
Up a Road Slowly - Irene Hunt 663

Trelling, Julie (Sister)
Up a Road Slowly - Irene Hunt 663

Trevor, Maddy (10-Year-Old)
Elfsong - Ann Turner 1433

Tribble, Nick (12-Year-Old)
Dinah in Love - Claudia Mills 1016

Trigg (Student)
The Toll-Bridge Troll - Patricia Rae Wolff 1547

Trimble, Bill (Twin; Student)
On the Trail with Miss Pace - Sharon Phillips
Denslow 342

Trimble, Phil (Twin; Student)
On the Trail with Miss Pace - Sharon Phillips
Denslow 342

Troll (Mythical Creature)
Fairy Wings - Lauren Mills 1018

Trouble (Indian)
Guests - Michael Dorris 360

True, Josiah (Child)
Josiah True and the Art Maker - Amy
Littlesugar 883

True, Thomas (Father)
Josiah True and the Art Maker - Amy
Littlesugar 883

Truesdale (Teacher)
Fifth Grade Fever - Michele Granger 493

Truman (Nephew)
Truman's Aunt Farm - Jama Kim Rattigan 1198

Truman, Jonah (7th Grader)
Really No Big Deal - Margaret Bechard 92

Trunzo, Liesl (Dancer)
Karate Dancer - Doris Buchanan Smith 1350

Ts'ina dabju (Child; Indian)
The Day Sun Was Stolen - Jamie Oliviero 1093

Tsubu (Snail)
Tsubu the Little Snail - Carol Ann Williams 1518

Tsugele (Young Woman; Housekeeper)
Tsugele's Broom - Valerie Scho Carey 208

Tsujimoto (Aged Person; Artist)
Pink Paper Swans - Virginia L. Kroll 793

Tubman, Harriet (Conductor)
*Journey to Freedom: A Story of the Underground
Railroad* - Courtni C. Wright 1562

Tuck (Pig; Brother)
Tuck in the Pool - Martha Weston 1502

Tucker, Winnie (10-Year-Old)
The Iron Dragon Never Sleeps - Stephen
Krensky 787

Tucker "Tuck" (5-Year-Old; Twin)
Harry and Tuck - Holly Keller 732

Tunukia-zawadi (Bird)
Big Boy - Tololwa M. Mollel 1028

Turner, Billie (6th Grader; Brother)
Mayfield Crossing - Vaunda Micheaux Nelson 1070

Turner, Jessica (11-Year-Old; Sister)
Daddy's Climbing Tree - C.S. Adler 11

Turner, Judith (Mother; Widow(er))
Daddy's Climbing Tree - C.S. Adler 11

Turner, Max (Boyfriend)
Amber Brown Wants Extra Credit - Paula Danziger 321

Turner, Meg (4th Grader)
Mayfield Crossing - Vaunda Micheaux Nelson 1070

Turner, Tycho (6-Year-Old; Brother)
Daddy's Climbing Tree - C.S. Adler 11

Turtle (Turtle)
The Rabbit's Escape - Suzanne Crowder Han 552

Turtle, M.C. (Turtle)
M.C. Turtle and the Hip Hop Hare: A Nursery Rap - David Vozar 1457

Turtle, Titus (Turtle; Friend)
I'll Meet You Halfway - John Schindel 1283

Tuttle, Thomas (3rd Grader; Friend)
Thomas Tuttle, Just in Time - Becky Thoman Lindberg 873

Tuttlebee, Matilda (Aged Person; Neighbor)
The Great Smith House Hustle - Jane Louise Curry 309

Tutu (Grandmother)
Luka's Quilt - Georgia Guback 523

Tweezers (Neighbor)
Owen - Kevin Henkes 588

Twinkle, Delphinium (Teacher)
Chrysanthemum - Kevin Henkes 585

Twite, Arun (Cousin)
Cold Shoulder Road - Joan Aiken 17

Twite, Is (Cousin)
Cold Shoulder Road - Joan Aiken 17

Tyler (Mouse; Cousin)
Charlie and Tyler at the Seashore - Helen Craig 296

Tyne, Kimberly (8th Grader)
How Do You Spell Geek? - Julie Anne Peters 1134

Tyrannosaurus Tex (Dinosaur)
Tyrannosaurus Tex - Betty G. Birney 111

Tyrconnell, Robert (Child)
The Secret of the Ruby Ring - Yvonne MacGrory 915

Tyrone (Student; Bully)
The Secret Super Powers of Marco - Meredith Sue Willis 1525

U

Uncle Fedya (Child; Runaway)
Uncle Fedya, His Dog, and His Cat - Eduard Uspenskii 1440

Uncle Zeka (Uncle)
Do You Know Me? - Nancy Farmer 400

Unnamed Character (Child of Divorced Parents)
Always My Dad - Sharon Dennis Wyeth 1565

Unnamed Character (Father)
Amazon Boy - Ted Lewin 865

Unnamed Character (Child; Friend)
Andrew Jessup - Nette Hilton 619

Unnamed Character (12-Year-Old)
Arthur, High King of Britain - Michael Morpurgo 1038

Unnamed Character (Thief)
Aunt Skilly and the Stranger - Kathleen Stevens 1382

Unnamed Character (Child)
The Baby House - Norma Simon 1337
A Baby Just Like Me - Susan Winter 1534

Unnamed Character (Bear)
Backyard Bear - Jim Murphy 1054

Unnamed Character (Child)
The Bag I'm Taking to Grandma's - Shirley Neitzel 1069
Bamboozled - David Legge 831

Unnamed Character (Child; Patient)
Barney Is Best - Nancy White Carlstrom 212

Unnamed Character (Child)
Bayou Lullaby - Kathi Appelt 37

Unnamed Character (Bear; Captive)
The Bear & Mr. Bear - Frances Thomas 1416

Unnamed Character (Bear; Toy)
The Bear Santa Claus Forgot - Diana Kimpton 745

Unnamed Character (Bear)
The Bear That Heard Crying - Natalie Kinsey-Warnock 758

Unnamed Character (Child)
Bears out There - Joanne Ryder 1246

Unnamed Character (Monster; Friend)
The Beast and the Boy - Massimo Mostacchi 1047

Unnamed Character (Mouse)
A Beautiful Feast for a Big King Cat - Bill Martin Jr. 938

Unnamed Character (Cat)
A Beautiful Feast for a Big King Cat - Bill Martin Jr. 938

Unnamed Character (Mouse; Heroine)
Beneath the Ghost Moon - Jane Yolen 1577

Unnamed Character (Mother)
Benjamin Bigfoot - Mary Serfozo 1310

Unnamed Character (Child)
Blue Claws - Walter Lyon Krudop 795

Unnamed Character (Witch)
The Boardwalk Princess - Arthur A. Levine 845

Unnamed Character (Kidnapper)
The Boy and the Giants - Fiona Moodie 1030

Unnamed Character (Father; Cook)
Boy, Can He Dance! - Eileen Spinelli 1367

Unnamed Character (Indian)
The Boy Who Dreamed of an Acorn - Leigh Casler 223

Unnamed Character (Father; Indian)
The Boy Who Lived with the Seals - Rafe Martin 943

Unnamed Character (Mother; Indian)
The Boy Who Lived with the Seals - Rafe Martin 943

Unnamed Character (Child; Indian)
The Boy Who Lived with the Seals - Rafe Martin 943

Unnamed Character (Child; Musician)
The Bravest Flute: A Story of Courage in the Mayan Tradition - Ann Grifalconi 515

Unnamed Character (Child)
Bread Is for Eating - David Gershator 456

Unnamed Character (Aged Person; Streetperson)
Broken Umbrellas - Kate Spohn 1373

Unnamed Character (Child)
By the Light of the Halloween Moon - Caroline Stutson 1403
The Cabin Key - Gloria Rand 1187

Unnamed Character (Mythical Creature; Friend)
Caleb's Friend - Eric Jon Nones 1081

Unnamed Character (Child)
Can I Have a Stegosaurus Mom? Can I? Please? - Lois G. Grambling 492
Can't Sit Still - Karen E. Lotz 897

Unnamed Character (Dog)
Can't Sleep - Chris Raschka 1193

Unnamed Character (Sister)
The Carousel - Liz Rosenberg 1231
The Carousel - Liz Rosenberg 1231

Unnamed Character (Cat)
Chicago and the Cat - Robin Michal Koontz 778
Chicago and the Cat: The Halloween Party - Robin Michal Koontz 779

Unnamed Character (Animal Trainer)
Circus of the Wolves - Jack Bushnell 187

Unnamed Character (Dog)
City Dog - Karla Kuskin 799

Unnamed Character (Child)
City of Dragons - Laurence Yep 1571

Unnamed Character (Father)
Climbing Kansas Mountains - George Shannon 1316

Unnamed Character (Child)
Cotton Mill Town - Kathleen Hershey 595

Unnamed Character (Cowboy)
Cowboy Country - Ann Herbert Scott 1301

Unnamed Character (Dentist)
The Crocodile and the Dentist - Taro Gomi 486

Unnamed Character (Crocodile)
The Crocodile and the Dentist - Taro Gomi 486

Unnamed Character (Aged Person)
Crossing the New Bridge - Emily Arnold McCully 965

Unnamed Character (Child)
Daddy Played Music for the Cows - Maryann N. Weidt 1488

Unnamed Character (Orphan; Indian)
Dance of the Sacred Circle: A Native American Tale - Kristina Rodanas 1223

Unnamed Character (Aged Person)
Danilo the Fruit Man - Amy Valens 1443

Unnamed Character (Grandmother)
Dear Rebecca, Winter Is Here - Jean Craighead George 449

Unnamed Character (Mouse)
Do You See a Mouse? - Bernard Waber 1459

Unnamed Character (Dog)
Dog - Robert J. Blake 115

Unnamed Character (Cat)
The Dog Who Cried Woof - Nancy Coffelt 264

Unnamed Character (Animal Lover)
Dogteam - Gary Paulsen 1120

Unnamed Character (Child; Sister)
Down at Angel's - Sharon Chmielarz 239
Down at Angel's - Sharon Chmielarz 239

Unnamed Character (Child; Tourist)
Dreamplace - George Ella Lyon 908

Unnamed Character (Father; Farmer)
Eagle Dreams - Sheryl McFarlane 976

Unnamed Character (Child)
The Earth and I - Frank Asch 46

Unnamed Character (Elephant)
Elephant Moon - Bijou Le Tord 827

Unnamed Character (Aged Person; Blind)
The Enchanted Horse - Magdalen Nabb 1058

Unnamed Character (Child)
The First Song Ever Sung - Laura Krauss
Melmed 1007

Unnamed Character (Indian; Spouse)
The First Strawberries: A Cherokee Story - Joseph
Bruchac 160
The First Strawberries: A Cherokee Story - Joseph
Bruchac 160

Unnamed Character (Child)
Flower Garden - Eve Bunting 173

Unnamed Character (Father)
Flower Garden - Eve Bunting 173

Unnamed Character (Crow)
The Foot Warmer and the Crow - Evelyn
Coleman 274

Unnamed Character (Tiger; Bully)
Friday Night at Hodge's Cafe - Tim Egan 382

Unnamed Character (Duck)
Friday Night at Hodge's Cafe - Tim Egan 382

Unnamed Character (Musician; Wolf)
Garth Pig Steals the Show - Mary Rayner 1202

Unnamed Character (Mother)
Gemma and the Baby Chick - Antonia Barber 76

Unnamed Character (Witch; Spirit)
The Ghost Witch - Betty Ren Wright 1558

Unnamed Character (Child; Orphan)
The Giant Baby - Allan Ahlberg 15

Unnamed Character (Traveller; Gypsy)
The Gift of a Traveler - Wendy Matthews 952

Unnamed Character (Sorceress)
The Girl in the Golden Bower - Jane Yolen 1578

Unnamed Character (Woodsman)
The Golden Goose - Uri Shulevitz 1334

Unnamed Character (Aged Person; Wizard)
The Golden Goose - Uri Shulevitz 1334

Unnamed Character (Bear; Toy)
Good-Bye, Daddy! - Brigitte Weninger 1499

Unnamed Character (Child)
Good-Bye House - Robin Ballard 65

Unnamed Character (Frog)
Good Morning, Pond - Alyssa Satin Capucilli 205

Unnamed Character (Zoo Keeper)
Good Night, Gorilla - Peggy Rathmann 1195

Unnamed Character (Child)
Good Night, Sleep Tight - Penelope Lively 884
Goose and the Mountain Lion - Marian Harris 561

Unnamed Character (Mountain Lion)
Goose and the Mountain Lion - Marian Harris 561

Unnamed Character (Grandfather; Traveller)
Grandfather's Journey - Allen Say 1271

Unnamed Character (Immigrant)
Grandfather's Journey - Allen Say 1271

Unnamed Character (Child)
Grandfather's Trolley - Bruce McMillan 987
Grandma's Shoes - Libby Hathorn 569

Unnamed Character (Child; Niece)
Great Aunt Martha - Rebecca C. Jones 710

Unnamed Character (Cat)
Halloween Mice! - Bethany Roberts 1216

Unnamed Character (Mouse)
Halloween Mice! - Bethany Roberts 1216

Unnamed Character (Dinosaur)
Happy Birthday, Danny and the Dinosaur! - Syd
Hoff 633

Unnamed Character (Cousin)
Harris and Me: A Summer Remembered - Gary
Paulsen 1121

Unnamed Character (Child)
Harvey Potter's Balloon Farm - Jerdine Nolen 1078

Unnamed Character (Mother)
Hi - Ann Herbert Scott 1302

Unnamed Character (Postal Worker)
Hi - Ann Herbert Scott 1302

Unnamed Character (Wolf)
Hog-Eye - Susan Meddaugh 1000

Unnamed Character (Pig; Storyteller)
Hog-Eye - Susan Meddaugh 1000

Unnamed Character (Child)
Homeplace - Anne Shelby 1325

Unnamed Character (Grandmother)
Homeplace - Anne Shelby 1325

Unnamed Character (Child)
Hotter than a Hot Dog! - Stephanie Calmenson 201

Unnamed Character (Spouse)
How Night Came from the Sea: A Story from Brazil -
Mary-Joan Gerson 458

Unnamed Character (Aged Person; Housekeeper)
How the Sky's Housekeeper Wore Her Scarves -
Patricia Hooper 643

Unnamed Character (Child)
How to Grow a Picket Fence - Mary Louise
Cuneo 308

Unnamed Character (Child; Baker)
How to Make an Apple Pie and See the World -
Marjorie Priceman 1175

Unnamed Character (Child)
Hunting the White Cow - Tres Seymour 1312

Unnamed Character (Child; Royalty)
I Am Really a Princess - Carol Diggory
Shields 1329

Unnamed Character (Child)
I Got a Family - Melrose Cooper 289
I Want to Be - Thylias Moss 1046

Unnamed Character (Child; Animal Lover)
I Went to the Zoo - Rita Golden Gelman 447

Unnamed Character (Father)
The Ice Palace - Angela McAllister 957

Unnamed Character (Child)
If You Want to Find Golden - Eileen Spinelli 1368
I'm a Jolly Farmer - Julie Lacome 804

Unnamed Character (Child; Brother)
In Search of the Giant - Jeanne Willis 1524

Unnamed Character (Child; Sister)
In Search of the Giant - Jeanne Willis 1524

Unnamed Character (Mother)
In the Snow - Huy Voun Lee 830

Unnamed Character (Insect)
Insects from Outer Space - Frank Asch 47

Unnamed Character (Farmer)
*Inside a Barn in the Country: A Rebus Read-Along
Story* - Alyssa Satin Capucilli 206

Unnamed Character (Mouse)
*Inside a Barn in the Country: A Rebus Read-Along
Story* - Alyssa Satin Capucilli 206

Unnamed Character (Father)
Is Susan Here? - Janice May Udry 1437

Unnamed Character (Mother)
Is Susan Here? - Janice May Udry 1437

Unnamed Character (Child)
It's My Birthday - Helen Oxenbury 1103

Unnamed Character (Child; Sister)
It's Pumpkin Time! - Zoe Hall 546

Unnamed Character (Child; Brother)
It's Pumpkin Time! - Zoe Hall 546

Unnamed Character (Wizard)
Jacob and the Stranger - Sally Derby 344

Unnamed Character (Child; Classmate)
Josepha: A Prairie Boy's Story - Jim McGugan 979

Unnamed Character (Father; Cowboy)
Just Like My Dad - Tricia Gardella 440

Unnamed Character (Child)
Just Like My Dad - Tricia Gardella 440
Just My Dad & Me - Leah Komaiko 776
Komodo! - Peter Sis 1340

Unnamed Character (Mother)
Lazy Jack - Vivian French 428

Unnamed Character (Child)
Lester's Dog - Karen Hesse 600
Like Butter on Pancakes - Jonathan London 893

Unnamed Character (Father)
Lila's Little Dinosaur - Wolfram Hanel 553

Unnamed Character (Young Man)
The Little Black Truck - Libba Moore Gray 495

Unnamed Character (Child)
The Little Boat - Kathy Henderson 581
Little Donkey Close Your Eyes - Margaret Wise
Brown 152

Unnamed Character (Wolf)
Little Red Riding Hood: A Newfangled Prairie Tale -
Lisa Campbell Ernst 394

Unnamed Character (Child; Brother)
The Lotus Seed - Sherry Garland 443

Unnamed Character (Child)
The Lotus Seed - Sherry Garland 443
Lunch with Milly - Jeanne Modesitt 1025
The Magic Bicycle - Berlie Doherty 355

Unnamed Character (Hare)
The Magic Hare - Lynne Reid Banks 72

Unnamed Character (Aged Person; Spirit)
The Magic Skateboard - Enid Richemont 1211

Unnamed Character (Child)
Mama Is a Miner - George Ella Lyon 910
Mama Zooms - Jane Cowen-Fletcher 294

Unnamed Character (Possum)
Mattie's Little Possum Pet - Ida Luttrell 907

Unnamed Character (Minstrel)
The Minstrel and the Dragon Pup - Rosemary
Sutcliff 1405

Unnamed Character (1st Grader)
Miss Malarkey Doesn't Live in Room 10 - Judy
Finchler 406

Unnamed Character (Mole)
Moles Can Dance - Richard Edwards 380

Unnamed Character (Child; Vacationer)
Monster Beach - Betty Paraskevas 1107

Unnamed Character (Celestial Body)
The Moon Was at a Fiesta - Matthew Gollub 485
The Moon Was at a Fiesta - Matthew Gollub 485

Unnamed Character (Frog)
A Most Unusual Lunch - Robert Bender 97

Unnamed Character (Lion)
A Most Unusual Lunch - Robert Bender 97

Unnamed Character (Mouse)
The Mouse Bride - Joy Cowley 295

Unnamed Character (Farmer)
Mule Eggs - Cynthia DeFelice 336

Unnamed Character (Mole)
The Mushroom Man - Ethel Pochocki 1158

Unnamed Character (Worker)
The Mushroom Man - Ethel Pochocki 1158

Unnamed Character (8-Year-Old)
My Apron - Eric Carle 209

Character Name Index

Unnamed Character (Worker)
The Waiting Day - Harriett Diller 351

Unnamed Character (Child)
Waiting for the Whales - Sheryl McFarlane 977

Unnamed Character (Mother)
Waiting for the Whales - Sheryl McFarlane 977

Unnamed Character (Aged Person; Grandfather)
Waiting for the Whales - Sheryl McFarlane 977

Unnamed Character (Bird)
Washing the Willow Tree Loon - Jacqueline Briggs
Martin 942

Unnamed Character (Child)
Welcome Back, Sun - Michael Emberley 389
What You Know First - Patricia MacLachlan 918

Unnamed Character (8-Year-Old; Brother)
When I Am Eight - Joan Lowery Nixon 1077

Unnamed Character (Child; Camper)
When I Go Camping with Grandma - Marion Dane
Bauer 89

Unnamed Character (Insect)
When the Fly Flew In . . . - Lisa Westberg
Peters 1136

Unnamed Character (Mother)
When the Wind Stops - Charlotte Zolotow 1598

Unnamed Character (Child)
When the Wind Stops - Charlotte Zolotow 1598
Whistle Home - Natalie Honeycutt 639

Unnamed Character (Cat; Spirit)
William's Ninth Life - Minna Jung 716

Unnamed Character (Child; Niece)
Willy and May - Judith Byron Schachner 1275

Unnamed Character (Child)
Wind Says Good Night - Katy Rydell 1245

Unnamed Character (Wizard)
The Wizard - Bill Martin Jr. 940

Unnamed Character (Child)
The Wizard Next Door - Peter Glassman 478
The Year of Fire - Teddy Jam 684
*Yesterday I Lost a Sneaker (and Found the Great
Goob Sick)* - David McPhail 996
Yo! Yes? - Chris Raschka 1194
Yo! Yes? - Chris Raschka 1194

Unnamed Character (Child; Neighbor)
You Shall Be King! - Antonie Schneider 1287

Unnamed Character (Child; Friend)
You Shall Be King! - Antonie Schneider 1287

Unnamed Character (Musician)
Zin! Zin! Zin! a Violin - Lloyd Moss 1042

Unnamed Character (Child; Brother)
Zoo - Anthony Browne 156

V

Valdez, Andy (6th Grader)
Stardust - Alane Ferguson 405

Valentina (Immigrant)
The Dream Jar - Bonnie Pryor 1178

Valerio (Mythical Creature)
The Dragon and the Unicorn - Lynne Cherry 237

Valery, Georges (Cousin)
A Haunted Year - Ann Phillips 1147

van Beethoven, Ludwig (Composer; Deaf)
Beethoven Lives Upstairs - Barbara Nichol 1073

Van Dyke, Gretchen (6th Grader; Friend)
Libbie Sims, Worry Wart - Gayle Rogers
Lockwood 887

Vanegas, Fernando (Child)
Fernando's Gift/El Regalo de Fernando - Douglas
Keister 728

Varmint, Scruffy (Monster)
Listen, Buddy - Helen Lester 837

Vaughan, Nancy (Child; Friend)
Letting Swift River Go - Jane Yolen 1583

Vernon, Mike "Mikey" (10-Year-Old; Child)
Sticks - Joan Bauer 87

Vernon, Poppy (Grandmother)
Sticks - Joan Bauer 87

Veronica (Child; Detective—Amateur)
*The Detective Stars and the Case of the Super Soccer
Team* - Caroline Levine 848

Victor (Child)
Babushka Baba Yaga - Patricia Polacco 1159

Victor (Classmate; Bully)
Insects Are My Life - Megan McDonald 974

Victor (Crocodile; Guard)
Victor and Christabel - Petra Mathers 950

Victoria (Mouse; Student)
Chrysanthemum - Kevin Henkes 585

Victoria (Royalty)
The Swoose - Dick King-Smith 756

Vinson, Luther Wesley "Soup" (Child; Friend)
Soup Ahoy - Robert Newton Peck 1127

Violet (Chimpanzee; Sister)
Arthur's Camp-Out - Lillian Hoban 627

Violet (Mouse)
Shy Vi - Wendy Cheyette Lewison 869

Violet (Rabbit; Worker)
Miss Violet's Shining Day - Jane Breskin
Zalben 1592

Virginia (Slave; Teenager)
Washington City Is Burning - Harriette Gillem
Robinet 1218

Volnik, Emily (12-Year-Old)
The Boggart - Susan Cooper 290

Volnik, Jessup (10-Year-Old; Computer Expert)
The Boggart - Susan Cooper 290

von der Borch, Boris (Pirate)
Tough Boris - Mem Fox 423

Vor, Cooper "Coop" (Alien; Leader)
Jason and the Escape from Bat Planet - Gery
Greer 507

W

Wade, Heather (8-Year-Old)
Lizzie Logan Wears Purple Sunglasses - Eileen
Spinelli 1369

Wafer, Lionel (Pirate; Adventurer)
The Pirates' Mixed-Up Voyage - Margaret Mahy 924

Wald, Zanna (10-Year-Old)
Away to Me, Moss - Betty Levin 842

Walker, Addy (9-Year-Old; Slave)
Meet Addy: An American Girl - Connie Porter 1169

Walker, Danny (Adoptee; Sports Figure)
Double Play at Short - Matt Christopher 249

Walker, Jeremiah (Friend)
A School for Pompey Walker - Michael J.
Rosen 1230

Walker, Pompey Bibb (Slave; Friend)
A School for Pompey Walker - Michael J.
Rosen 1230

Walker, Ruth (Mother; Slave)
Meet Addy: An American Girl - Connie Porter 1169

Wallace, Kathy (12-Year-Old)
The Worst Noel - Ilene Cooper 288

Walnut "Sees Behind Trees" (Indian; Blind)
Sees Behind Trees - Michael Dorris 361

Walter (Child)
In America - Marissa Moss 1045

Walter (Child; Brother)
No More Water in the Tub! - Tedd Arnold 43

Walter, Richard "Dummy" (Orphan)
Robin's Country - Monica Furlong 434

Walters (Teacher)
The Sub - P.J. Petersen 1139

Wanda (Child; Gardener)
Wanda's Roses - Pat Brisson 139

Warner, Alex (5th Grader)
Nothing but Trouble, Trouble, Trouble - Patricia
Hermes 592

Warner, Meg (Child)
Nothing but Trouble, Trouble, Trouble - Patricia
Hermes 592

Warren (Child; Neighbor)
Seeds - George Shannon 1318

Warren (Child; Nephew)
Worse than the Worst - James Stevenson 1388

Warren (Mother; Widow(er))
The Ghost Witch - Betty Ren Wright 1558

Warren, Arlene (6th Grader)
Hey You, Sister Rose - Eileen Walsh Strauch 1398

Warren, Jenny (Child)
The Ghost Witch - Betty Ren Wright 1558

Wart (Dog; Sidekick)
Wizard and Wart at Sea - Janice Lee Smith 1353

Washburn, Jennifer "Jenny Lee" (Basketball Player)
Who's Orp's Girlfriend? - Suzy Kline 774

Washington (Musician; Blind)
Sing to the Stars - Mary Brigid Barrett 81

Washington, Booker T. (9-Year-Old)
More than Anything Else - Marie Bradby 130

Washington, George (Gentleman; Farmer)
George Washington's Cows - David Small 1346

Washington, George (Historical Figure; Military
Personnel)
*The Winter of Red Snow: The Revolutionary War
Diary of Abigail Jane Stewart* - Kristiana
Gregory 509

Washington, Medgar "Wash" (Baseball Player; 12-
Year-Old)
The Sluggers Club: A Sports Mystery - Paul Robert
Walker 1467

Water God (Deity)
Tsubu the Little Snail - Carol Ann Williams 1518

Waterford, Mitch (Computer Expert)
The Fire Bug Connection: An Ecological Mystery -
Jean Craighead George 450

Watkins (Father; Unemployed)
Jimmy Crack Corn - Candice F. Ransom 1188

Watkins, Jimmy (9-Year-Old)
Jimmy Crack Corn - Candice F. Ransom 1188

Watson, Borden (Child)
There's an Owl in the Shower - Jean Craighead
George 452

Watson, Byron "By" (13-Year-Old)
The Watsons Go to Birmingham—1963 - Christopher
Paul Curtis 311

Watson, Dixie (12-Year-Old; 7th Grader)
Dixie in the Big Pasture - Belinda Hurmence 665

Watson, Joetta (Child)
The Watsons Go to Birmingham—1963 - Christopher Paul Curtis 311

Watson, Kenny (10-Year-Old)
The Watsons Go to Birmingham—1963 - Christopher Paul Curtis 311

Watson, Leon (Father; Lumberjack)
There's an Owl in the Shower - Jean Craighead George 452

Wayne (Sheep; Cousin)
Sherman the Sheep - Kevin Kiser 762

Weasel (Child)
The Face in the Bessledorf Funeral Parlor - Phyllis Reynolds Naylor 1065

Weasel (Weasel)
That Kookoory! - Margaret Walden Froehlich 432

Weaver, Jill (11-Year-Old)
Websters' Leap - Eileen Dunlop 374

Weaver, Tad (Teenager)
Websters' Leap - Eileen Dunlop 374

Webb, Penn (Teenager; Runner)
Crash - Jerry Spinelli 1370

Webber, Alice (Librarian)
Nobody's Daughter - Susan Beth Pfeffer 1142

Webster, Claudia (Sister; Student—High School)
Partners - Karen Waggoner 1465

Webster, Gordon (Student—Junior High; Brother)
Partners - Karen Waggoner 1465

Webster, Jamie (3rd Grader; Brother)
Partners - Karen Waggoner 1465

Webster, Tully (6th Grader)
Fearsome's Hero - Dona Schenker 1280

Weinerstein (Scientist)
Hilda and the Mad Scientist - Addie Adam 8

Weldon, Chad (9-Year-Old)
The Ghost Comes Calling - Betty Ren Wright 1556

Wellington (Dog)
The Greatest Show on Earth - John Prater 1174

Wells, Caroline (5-Year-Old; Sister)
Lucy's Christmas - Donald Hall 543

Wells, Lucy (Child; Sister)
Lucy's Christmas - Donald Hall 543

Welzl, Jan (Adventurer)
A Small, Tall Tale from the Far, Far North - Peter Sis 1341

Wendylyn (Noblewoman)
The Knight Who Was Afraid to Fight - Barbara Shook Hazen 578

West, Annie (Teenager; Sister)
Going to See Grassy Ella - Kathryn Lance 810

West, Peggy Jean "Peej" (12-Year-Old; Cancer Patient)
Going to See Grassy Ella - Kathryn Lance 810

Wexler, Jenna (4th Grader)
Jenna's Big Jump - Faythe Dyrud Thureen 1420

Wheeler, Aubrey (7-Year-Old; Brother)
Casey over There - Staton Rabin 1184

Wheeler, Casey (Military Personnel; Brother)
Casey over There - Staton Rabin 1184

Whipple, Amy (Babysitter; 13-Year-Old)
Jennifer-the-Jerk Is Missing - Carol Gorman 488

Whipple, Arvella (Mother; Innkeeper)
The Ballad of Lucy Whipple - Karen Cushman 314

Whipple, California Morning "Lucy" (Settler; Librarian)
The Ballad of Lucy Whipple - Karen Cushman 314

Whipple, Remember Patience "Mem" (Settler; 12-Year-Old)
A Journey to the New World: The Diary of Remember Patience Whipple - Kathryn Lasky 815

Whiskers, Jimmy (Miner)
The Ballad of Lucy Whipple - Karen Cushman 314

Whistle (Babysitter)
Whistle Home - Natalie Honeycutt 639

Whitaker, Lucas (Orphan; Apprentice)
The Apprenticeship of Lucas Whitaker - Cynthia DeFelice 334

Whitcher, Caleb (6-Year-Old)
Shaker Boy - Mary Lyn Ray 1201

Whitcher, Sarah (3-Year-Old; Settler)
The Bear That Heard Crying - Natalie Kinsey-Warnock 758

White Cow (Cow)
Hunting the White Cow - Tres Seymour 1312

Whitebelly, Zeke (Weasel)
The Wainscott Weasel - Tor Seidler 1309

Whitefeather (Grandfather)
The World in Grandfather's Hands - Craig Kee Strete 1399

Whitefox, Willy (Child; Indian)
On the Right Track - B.B. Calhoun 198

Whitney, Caleb (Worker)
Escape into the Night - Lois Walfrid Johnson 700

Whittsen, Marty Louise (1st Grader)
Fat Chance! - Lady Borton 127

Whopper, Frannie (Child)
On the Road with Poppa Whopper - Marianne Busser 188

Whopper, Poppa (Father)
On the Road with Poppa Whopper - Marianne Busser 188

Whyner, Wanda (Mother)
Willy Whyner, Cloud Designer - Michael Lustig 906

Whyner, Wilber (Father)
Willy Whyner, Cloud Designer - Michael Lustig 906

Whyner, Willy (3rd Grader; Inventor)
Willy Whyner, Cloud Designer - Michael Lustig 906

Wickers, Abby (6th Grader)
Ellen Anders on Her Own - Karen Hirsch 625

Wiggins, Adam (9-Year-Old; Brother)
My Brother Is a Visitor from Another Planet - Dyan Sheldon 1327

Wiggins, Keith (13-Year-Old; Brother)
My Brother Is a Visitor from Another Planet - Dyan Sheldon 1327

Wild Willie (Outlaw)
Moony B. Finch, the Fastest Draw in the West - David McPhail 993

Wilder, Almanzo "Manly" (Father)
Little House on Rocky Ridge - Roger Lea MacBride 913

Wilder, Laura Ingalls "Bess" (Mother)
Little House on Rocky Ridge - Roger Lea MacBride 913

Wilder, Rose (9-Year-Old)
In the Land of the Big Red Apple - Roger Lea MacBride 912

Wilder, Rose (7-Year-Old)
Little House on Rocky Ridge - Roger Lea MacBride 913

Wilding, Ralph (11-Year-Old)
No Friend of Mine - Ann Turnbull 1428

Wilhelm, Tommy (5th Grader; Bully)
Joshua T. Bates Takes Charge - Susan Richards Shreve 1332

Will (Slave; Bridegroom)
Jumping the Broom - Courtni C. Wright 1563

Will (Child; Brother)
Moonlight on the River - Deborah Kovacs 781

Will (Brother)
Nothing Happened - Bill Harley 557

Will (Soccer Player; Military Personnel)
War Game - Michael Foreman 418

Willa (Child)
Willa and Old Miss Annie - Berlie Doherty 357

Willard, Joe (Friend)
The Wind Wagon - Celia Barker Lottridge 896

William (Child)
The Bear under the Stairs - Helen Cooper 286
The Mighty Santa Fe - William H. Hooks 642

William (Child; Brother)
No More Water in the Tub! - Tedd Arnold 43

William (Child)
William and the Good Old Days - Eloise Greenfield 502

William (Cat)
William's Ninth Life - Minna Jung 716

Williams, Cassandra "Cass" (Cheerleader; Student—High School)
Fall Secrets - Candy Dawson Boyd 129

Williams, Cassie (5th Grader; Spy)
Alien Alert! - Debra Hess 597

Williams, Danny (10-Year-Old; Child of an Alcoholic)
The Trophy - Dean Hughes 662

Williams, Evan (Father; Alcoholic)
The Trophy - Dean Hughes 662

Williams, Jessie (Actress; Student—Junior High)
Fall Secrets - Candy Dawson Boyd 129

Williams, Katy (10-Year-Old)
One Brave Summer - Ann Turner 1434

Williams, Rachel (Mother; Writer)
One Brave Summer - Ann Turner 1434

Willie (Pig; Brother)
Geraldine's Baby Brother - Holly Keller 730

Willie (Soccer Player)
The Losers Fight Back - Barbara M. Joosse 711

Willie (Child; Brother)
Night in the Barn - Faye Gibbons 462

Willie Jerome (Child; Musician)
Willie Jerome - Alice Faye Duncan 372

Willis, Richard "Ritchie" (5th Grader)
Under the Bridge - Ellen Kindt McKenzie 985

Willis, Rosemary "Rosie" (Child)
Under the Bridge - Ellen Kindt McKenzie 985

Willson, Harvey (12-Year-Old; Cousin)
Harvey's Mystifying Raccoon Mix-Up - Eth Clifford 259

Willy (Bird)
Willy and May - Judith Byron Schachner 1275

Wilma (Witch)
The Fat Cat Sat on the Mat - Nurit Karlan 718

Wilmot, Arthur (3rd Grader; Friend)
Thomas Tuttle, Just in Time - Becky Thoman Lindberg 873

Wilson (Student)
Wilson Sat Alone - Debra Hess 598

Wilson, Cissie (Child; Neighbor)
The Key to the Playhouse - Carol Beach York   1586

Wilson, Mary Jane (Student—Junior High)
The Brick House Burglars - Peni R. Griffin   517

Winkle, Will (Animal Lover; 6th Grader)
Buzzard Breath - Marty Crisp   304

Wise Woman (Aged Person)
Catkin - Antonia Barber   75

Witch (Witch)
Old Devil Wind - Bill Martin Jr.   939

Witch Ellen (Aged Person; Spirit)
Moon Window - Jane Louise Curry   310

Witherspoon (Aged Person; Neighbor)
The Little Tree Growin' in the Shade - Camille
   Yarbrough   1569

Wittilda (Witch; Animal Lover)
A Job for Wittilda - Caralyn Buehner   167

Witting, Anna (Stepdaughter; Sister)
Skylark - Patricia MacLachlan   917

Witting, Caleb (Stepson; Brother)
Skylark - Patricia MacLachlan   917

Witting, Sarah (Stepmother)
Skylark - Patricia MacLachlan   917

Wix (Teacher)
In Trouble with Teacher - Patricia Demuth   339

Wizard (Wizard)
Wizard and Wart at Sea - Janice Lee Smith   1353

Wolf (Wolf)
Strudwick: A Sheep in Wolf's Clothing - Robert
   Kraus   786

Wolf, Dudley (7-Year-Old)
Dog Days for Dudley - Barbara Moe   1026

Wolfgang (Wolf; Companion)
The Bone Stranger - Frank Remkiewicz   1208

Wood, Ben (Neighbor)
The Booford Summer - Susan Mathias Smith   1356

Woodbine (Squirrel)
Forest - Janet Taylor Lisle   877

Woodley, Richard (12-Year-Old)
This New Land - G. Clifton Wisler   1541

Worst (Uncle; Aged Person)
Worse than the Worst - James Stevenson   1388

Worst, Arvin (Brother)
The Worst Goes South - James Stevenson   1389

Worst, Ervin (Brother)
The Worst Goes South - James Stevenson   1389

Worthen, Lyddie (Teacher)
Jip: His Story - Katherine Paterson   1113

Wright, Alec (11-Year-Old)
Stolen Bones - Joan Carris   216

Wyatt, Steve "Sneeze" (12-Year-Old; Writer)
101 Ways to Bug Your Parents - Lee Wardlaw   1478

Wylie, Malcolm (Child)
Jennifer-the-Jerk Is Missing - Carol Gorman   488

Wyoming, Winston "Wishbone" III (4th Grader)
The Richest Kids in Town - Peg Kehret   726

X

Xiao Ming (Child)
In the Snow - Huy Voun Lee   830

Xiao Sheng (Child; Worker)
The Dragon's Pearl - Julie Lawson   825

Y

Yamashita (6th Grader)
Friends - Kazumi Yumoto   1590

Yamoto (Farmer; Father)
Lily and the Wooden Bowl - Alan Schroeder   1294

Yang, Mary Yingmei (Musician)
Yang the Third and Her Impossible Family - Lensey
   Namioka   1060

Yates, Eliza "Elijah Bates" (12-Year-Old; Runaway)
The Gentleman Outlaw and Me—Eli - Mary Downing
   Hahn   539

Yeadon, Meg (12-Year-Old; Cousin)
Fire in the Wind - Betty Levin   843

Yeung Ying (9-Year-Old)
First Apple - Ching Yeung Russell   1241

Yeung Ying (10-Year-Old)
Water Ghost - Ching Yeung Russell   1242

Yoji (6-Year-Old; Cousin)
Great Grandfather's House - Rumer Godden   483

Yolen, Lyovka "Lou" (Teenager; Brother)
And Twelve Chinese Acrobats - Jane Yolen   1575

Yolen, Velvul "Wolf" (Child; Brother)
And Twelve Chinese Acrobats - Jane Yolen   1575

York, Robert Hayes "Robbie" (3rd Grader)
How to Be Cool in the Third Grade - Betsy
   Duffey   369

Yosh (Uncle; Veteran)
Heroes - Ken Mochizuki   1024

Yoshi (Child; Friend)
Mieko and the Fifth Treasure - Eleanor Coerr   263

Yoshiko (Child; Sister)
The Crane Girl - Veronika Martenova Charles   233

Yoshimina, Mari (Detective—Amateur)
The Case of the Wiggling Wig - E.W. Hildick   617

Yoshimura, Mari (Detective—Amateur)
The Case of the Desperate Drummer - E.W.
   Hildick   615

Young Bull (10-Year-Old; Indian)
Cheyenne Again - Eve Bunting   170

Young Jack (Child; Slave)
Sweet Clara and the Freedom Quilt - Deborah
   Hopkinson   644

Young Rooster (Chicken)
The Rooster's Gift - Pam Conrad   283

Yr, Tsynq "Stinker" (Alien)
Stinker's Return - Pamela F. Service   1311

Yungsu (Child; Immigrant)
Father's Rubber Shoes - Yumi Heo   589

Z

Zachariah, Jr. (Child; Friend)
Three at Sea - Timothy Bush   185

Zambezi (Art Dealer; Uncle)
Joshua's Masai Mask - Dakari Hru   658

Zayde (Grandfather)
Sweet Notes, Sour Notes - Nancy Smiler
   Levinson   851

Zeesie (7-Year-Old)
What Zeesie Saw on Delancey Street - Elsa Okon
   Rael   1186

Zeke (Dog)
Mr. Putter and Tabby Walk the Dog - Cynthia
   Rylant   1255

Zekephlon "Zeke" (10-Year-Old; Alien)
Alien Alert! - Debra Hess   597

Zelda (Niece; Sister)
When Aunt Lucy Rode a Mule and Other Stories -
   Barbara Ann Porte   1168

Zeller, Chelsea (5th Grader; Child of Divorced
   Parents)
I Was a Fifth-Grade Zebra - Nancy J. Hopper   645

Zenith (Bird)
Superbird to the Rescue - Nancy Hayashi   574

Zimmer, Aaron (6th Grader; Time Traveller)
Lost in Cyberspace - Richard Peck   1126

Zimmers, Buddy (5th Grader; Bully)
J.B. Wigglebottom and the Parade of Pets - Vivian
   Sathre   1268

Zippy (Dog)
Snow Day! - Barbara M. Joosse   713

Zoe (Child; Niece)
Too Far Away to Touch - Leslea Newman   1071

Zundel (Tailor)
Bit by Bit - Steve Sanfield   1267

Character Description Index

This index alphabetically lists descriptions of the major characters in featured titles. The descriptions may be occupations (astronaut, lawyer, etc.) or may describe persona (amnesiac, runaway, teenager, etc.). For each description, character names are listed alphabetically. Also provided are book titles, author names, and entry numbers.

2-YEAR-OLD

Amanda Jane
Serious Science - Janice Lee Smith 1352

3-YEAR-OLD

Barrett, Brandon
The Secret Life of Bethany Barrett - Claudia Mills 1017

Fine, April
A Llama in the Family - Johanna Hurwitz 667

Garth
Courtyard Cat - C.S. Adler 10

Hummer, Freddie
Nekomah Creek Christmas - Linda Crew 301

Hummer, Lucy
Nekomah Creek Christmas - Linda Crew 301

Isabelle
My Dog Rosie - Isabelle Harper 559

Jimmy
I Hate Company - P.J. Petersen 1137

Tara
Tiger Flowers - Patricia Quinlan 1183

Whitcher, Sarah
The Bear That Heard Crying - Natalie Kinsey-Warnock 758

4-YEAR-OLD

Bly, Gabrielle
Lydia Jane and the Baby-Sitter Exchange - Natalie Honeycutt 638

MacMillan, Chester
Earthquake! A Story of Old San Francisco - Kathleen V. Kudlinski 798

Minter, Danny
The Timekeeper - Emily Rodda 1224

Sandworm, Johannes
Santa's Winter Vacation - Viveca Larn Sundvall 1404

5-YEAR-OLD

Alex
Carousel - Pat Cummings 307

Benjamin
Benjamin Bigfoot - Mary Serfozo 1310

Betsy
Honkers - Jane Yolen 1582

Connerton, Nelson
Ghosts Don't Get Goosebumps - Elvira Woodruff 1551

Dawn
Dawn and the Round To-It - Irene Smalls 1347

Fraser, Edward
No Dogs Allowed - Jane Cutler 317

Harrison "Harry"
Harry and Tuck - Holly Keller 732

Jagamarra, John
The Burnt Stick - Anthony Hill 618

James
The Long Weekend - Troon Harrison 565

Johnson, Lyman
Never Trust a Sister over Twelve - Stephen Roos 1226

Margarita
Born in the Gravy - Denys Cazet 225

Matthews, Mason
Flip-Flop Girl - Katherine Paterson 1112

McClain, Tasha
Junebug - Alice Mead 998

Michaels, Elisa
Make Room for Elisa - Johanna Hurwitz 668

Molly
Two Girls in Sister Dresses - Jean Van Leeuwen 1451

Nora
Train to Somewhere - Eve Bunting 181

Pablo
Pablo's Tree - Pat Mora 1037

Starbuck, Charlotte "Charly"
A Voice in the Wind - Kathryn Lasky 819

Takumi
Okino and the Whales - Arnica Esterl 397

Tofie, Goolam-Habib
Straw Sense - Rona Rupert 1239

Tucker "Tuck"
Harry and Tuck - Holly Keller 732

Wells, Caroline
Lucy's Christmas - Donald Hall 543

6-YEAR-OLD

Bean, Ima
A Regular Flood of Mishap - Tom Birdseye 109

Blue, Andrew
Yolanda's Genius - Carol Fenner 404

Carole
Pond Year - Kathryn Lasky 817

Danny
Happy Birthday, Danny and the Dinosaur! - Syd Hoff 633

Dell
A Sound of Leaves - Lenore Blegvad 118

Jones, Junie B.
Junie B. Jones and Some Sneaky Peeky Spying - Barbara Park 1109

Juana
Gracias, Rosa - Michelle Markel 933

Julietta
The Language of Doves - Rosemary Wells 1493

Kane, Harry
Harry and Arney - Judith Caseley 218

Nathan
Fireflies for Nathan - Shulamith Levey Oppenheim 1095

Palmer, Abby
Earthquake Terror - Peg Kehret 725

Sissy
Kinda Blue - Ann Grifalconi 516

Sophie
Sophie in the Saddle - Dick King-Smith 752

Todd, Louvina
Bound for Oregon - Jean Van Leeuwen 1448

Turner, Tycho
Daddy's Climbing Tree - C.S. Adler 11

Unnamed Character
Pond Year - Kathryn Lasky 817

Whitcher, Caleb
Shaker Boy - Mary Lyn Ray 1201

Yoji
Great Grandfather's House - Rumer Godden 483

7-YEAR-OLD

Bamford, Robert
Gorgonzola Zombies in the Park - Elizabeth Levy   858

Christine
The Gift of a Traveler - Wendy Matthews   952

Cohen, Max
My Dad's Baseball - Ron Cohen   267

Fortune, Kate
The Daydreamer - Ian McEwan   975

Fox, Julie
My Fabulous New Life - Sheila Greenwald   503

Good, Rosie
The Stray - Dick King-Smith   755

Grant, Maggie
The Green Bottle and the Silver Kite - Fredericka Berger   101

Janie
The Invisible Dog - Dick King-Smith   748

Jennifer
Two Girls in Sister Dresses - Jean Van Leeuwen   1451

Keiko
Great Grandfather's House - Rumer Godden   483

Lewis
The Feather-Bed Journey - Paula Kurzband Feder   402

Lila
Lila's Little Dinosaur - Wolfram Hanel   553

Lundstrom, Erik
Clouds of Terror - Catherine A. Welch   1489

Marisa
Dumpling Soup - Jama Kim Rattigan   1197

McDowell, Thomas
The Christmas Miracle of Jonathan Toomey - Susan Wojciechowski   1543

Moscowitz, Mendel
Mendel's Ladder - Mark Karlins   719

O'Malley, Samantha
Baseball Card Crazy - Trish Kennedy   735

Polly
When the Whippoorwill Calls - Candice F. Ransom   1190

Salah
The Hundredth Name - Shulamith Levey Oppenheim   1096

Seth
The Tie Man's Miracle: A Chanukah Tale - Steven Schnur   1289

Sophie
Sophie Is Seven - Dick King-Smith   753
Sophie's Lucky - Dick King-Smith   754

Tom
My Wicked Stepmother - Norman Leach   828

Wheeler, Aubrey
Casey over There - Staton Rabin   1184

Wilder, Rose
Little House on Rocky Ridge - Roger Lea MacBride   913

Wolf, Dudley
Dog Days for Dudley - Barbara Moe   1026

Zeesie
What Zeesie Saw on Delancey Street - Elsa Okon Rael   1186

8-YEAR-OLD

Araminta "Minty"
Minty: A Story of Young Harriet Tubman - Alan Schroeder   1295

Baird, Swiney
In the Land of the Big Red Apple - Roger Lea MacBride   912

Bates, Abigail
Abigail's Drum - John A. Minahan   1020

Bly, Lydia Jane
Lydia Jane and the Baby-Sitter Exchange - Natalie Honeycutt   638

Bobby
Later, Gator - Laurence Yep   1573

Bradley, Cammie
More than a Name - Candice F. Ransom   1189

Bryant, Sarah
Grandmother Bryant's Pocket - Jacqueline Briggs Martin   941

Carmina
Fernando's Gift/El Regalo de Fernando - Douglas Keister   728

Castleberry, Joe Dean
Woollybear Good-bye - Sharon Phillips Denslow   343

Daw, Jack
The Cuckoo Child - Dick King-Smith   747

Diggs, Jamie
The Latchkey Dog - Mary Jane Auch   50

Ernestine
The Sunday Outing - Gloria Jean Pinkney   1154

Fraser, Jason
No Dogs Allowed - Jane Cutler   317

Grover, May
Pony Crazy - Bonnie Bryant   164

Jaikit, Sasha
Hey, Dad, Get a Life - Todd Strasser   1397

Harry
Harry's Birthday - Barbara Ann Porte   1166

Henry
Henry and Mudge and the Best Day of All - Cynthia Rylant   1250

Jackson, Janetta
Pink Paper Swans - Virginia L. Kroll   793

James, Jasmine
Pony Crazy - Bonnie Bryant   164

Jon
Grandad Bill's Song - Jane Yolen   1580

Jones, Olivia Elizabeth
Olivia and the Real Live Pet - Charlotte Towner Graeber   490

Jones, Theodore "Turtleneck"
Man Out at First - Matt Christopher   251

Joshua
Journey to Freedom: A Story of the Underground Railroad - Courtni C. Wright   1562

Judy
Jenius, the Amazing Guinea Pig - Dick King-Smith   749

Lettie
Jumping the Broom - Courtni C. Wright   1563

Lightfoot, Cassie Louise
Tar Beach - Faith Ringgold   1215

Mabel
Gorgonzola Zombies in the Park - Elizabeth Levy   858

Magid
Magid Fasts for Ramadan - Mary Matthews   951

Malloy, Caroline
The Boys Start the War - Phyllis Reynolds Naylor   1064

Merlin
Passenger - Jane Yolen   1585

Muhamad
One Night: A Story from the Desert - Cristina Kessler   738

Onetree, Jo-Beth
Never Hit a Ghost with a Baseball Bat - Eth Clifford   260

Panetta, Antonio
It Was a Dark and Stormy Night - Allan Ahlberg   16

PK
Maybe Yes, Maybe No, Maybe Maybe - Susan Patron   1118

Ramsdale, Jackie
A Share of Freedom - June Rae Wood   1549

Sam
The Latchkey Dog - Mary Jane Auch   50

Sarah
Don't Forget - Patricia Lakin   807
Nettie's Gift - Susan Tews   1413

Sasifi
Tap-Tap - Karen Lynn Williams   1521

Sims, Ozzie
Ozzie on His Own - Johanna Hurwitz   670

Takamura, Corey
Pony Crazy - Bonnie Bryant   164

Tom
Tom's Fish - Nancy Coffelt   265

Unnamed Character
My Apron - Eric Carle   209
When I Am Eight - Joan Lowery Nixon   1077

Wade, Heather
Lizzie Logan Wears Purple Sunglasses - Eileen Spinelli   1369

9-YEAR-OLD

Amelia
Amelia's Notebook - Marissa Moss   1044

Benjamin
The Barn - Avi   54

Bixby, William
More than a Name - Candice F. Ransom   1189

Brewster, Love
Across the Wide Dark Sea: The Mayflower Journey - Jean Van Leeuwen   1446

Brown, Amber
Amber Brown Wants Extra Credit - Paula Danziger   321

Castello, Billy
Slam Dunk Saturday - Jean Marzollo   944

DeRosa, Zoe
Zoe and Columbo - Susan Richards Shreve   1333

Doyle, Patrick "Slugger"
Patrick Doyle Is Full of Blarney - Jennifer Armstrong   40

Feldman, Ned
Ned Feldman, Space Pirate - Daniel Manus Pinkwater   1156

Giles, Lizzie
Lizzie's List - Maggie Harrison   564

Harrall, Angela
The Gold Dust Letters - Janet Taylor Lisle   878

Hastings, Calvin
Jazz, Pizzaz, and the Silver Threads - Mary Quattlebaum 1182

Helen
Star of Fear, Star of Hope - Jo Hoestlandt 629

Henderson, Candy
Ozzie on His Own - Johanna Hurwitz 670

Ives, Levi
Dear Levi: Letters from the Overland Trail - Elvira Woodruff 1550

Jensen, Aristotle "Artie"
Ghost Dog - Ellen Leroe 836

Jess
Dakota Spring - D. Anne Love 899

Johnson, Suki
Never Trust a Sister over Twelve - Stephen Roos 1226

Kellow, Sam
The Big Bazoohley - Peter Carey 207

Kew, Walter
A Message from the Match Girl - Janet Taylor Lisle 880

Larson, Harris
Harris and Me: A Summer Remembered - Gary Paulsen 1121

Lundstrom, Helga
Clouds of Terror - Catherine A. Welch 1489

Mac
Mac and Marie and the Train Toss Surprise - Elizabeth Fitzgerald Howard 649

Mason, Jenna
Tough Loser - Barthe DeClements 332

Michaels, Russell
Make Room for Elisa - Johanna Hurwitz 668

Midge
My Brother Is a Visitor from Another Planet - Dyan Sheldon 1327

Owen
Saving Owen's Toad - Juanita Havill 573

Patrick
Patrick's Tree House - Steven Kroll 790

Peter
The Farm Summer 1942 - Donald Hall 541

Sunipass, Rayanne
Crossing the Starlight Bridge - Alice Mead 997

Sylvie
A Sound of Leaves - Lenore Blegvad 118

Tapiwa
Do You Know Me? - Nancy Farmer 400

Teitletot, Jenny
Jazz, Pizzaz, and the Silver Threads - Mary Quattlebaum 1182

Todd, Mary Ellen
Bound for Oregon - Jean Van Leeuwen 1448

Tolson, Abby
Haunted Summer - Betty Ren Wright 1560

Walker, Addy
Meet Addy: An American Girl - Connie Porter 1169

Washington, Booker T.
More than Anything Else - Marie Bradby 130

Watkins, Jimmy
Jimmy Crack Corn - Candice F. Ransom 1188

Weldon, Chad
The Ghost Comes Calling - Betty Ren Wright 1556

Wiggins, Adam
My Brother Is a Visitor from Another Planet - Dyan Sheldon 1327

Wilder, Rose
In the Land of the Big Red Apple - Roger Lea MacBride 912

Yeung Ying
First Apple - Ching Yeung Russell 1241

10-YEAR-OLD

Alex
Boys at Work - Gary Soto 1361

Alexander, Liam
The Formerly Great Alexander Family - Susan Richards Shreve 1331

Amelia
Amelia Writes Again - Marissa Moss 1043

Armstrong, Annie
The Baby Grand, the Moon in July, & Me - Joyce Annette Barnes 78

Augusta
Augusta & Trab - Christopher De Vinck 330

Babson, Ruth
When Willard Met Babe Ruth - Donald Hall 544

Baylor, Janet
She Flew No Flags - Joan B. Manley 928

Binya
Binya's Blue Umbrella - Ruskin Bond 123

Brogan, Robin
Dog Friday - Hilary McKay 980

Buntz, Taddy
The Twin in the Tavern - Barbara Brooks Wallace 1469

Christoph
Beethoven Lives Upstairs - Barbara Nichol 1073

Clara
The Van Gogh Cafe - Cynthia Rylant 1256

Clare
A Sound of Leaves - Lenore Blegvad 118

Cooper, Sarah-Jane
The Mystery of the Dancing Angels - Elspeth Campbell Murphy 1050

Curry, Derek
The Up & Down Spring - Johanna Hurwitz 672

Delphinium
The Greatest Show off Earth - Margaret Mahy 923

Faith
Faith and the Electric Dogs - Patrick Jennings 693

Fine, Adam
A Llama in the Family - Johanna Hurwitz 667

Fontecchio, Staci
The Great Pony Hassle - Nancy Springer 1374

Fontecchio, Toni
The Great Pony Hassle - Nancy Springer 1374

Fortune, Pete
The Good Fortunes Gang - Margaret Mahy 922

Fortune, Peter
The Daydreamer - Ian McEwan 975

Goff, Matthew "Gopher"
Gopher Takes Heart - Virginia Scribner 1303

Grant, Phillip
The Green Bottle and the Silver Kite - Fredericka Berger 101

Hennings, Kay
Keep Smiling Through - Ann Rinaldi 1214

Herrera, Rudy
Boys at Work - Gary Soto 1361

Hoffman, Lydia
Lydia, Queen of Palestine - Uri Orlev 1100

Hummer, Robby
Nekomah Creek Christmas - Linda Crew 301

Jason
The Magnificent Mummy Maker - Elvira Woodruff 1552

Jessie
The Ghost of Grania O'Malley - Michael Morpurgo 1039

Jibbett, Jimmy
The Man in the Ceiling - Jules Feiffer 403

Kenney, Charlie
Numbskulls - William Taylor 1410

Larkin, Hayley
The Booford Summer - Susan Mathias Smith 1356

Lavine, Annie
The Promised Land - Isabelle Holland 637

Logan, David
The Well: David's Story - Mildred D. Taylor 1409

Logan, Lizzie
Lizzie Logan Wears Purple Sunglasses - Eileen Spinelli 1369

Malloy, Beth
The Boys Start the War - Phyllis Reynolds Naylor 1064

Marlin, Rose
Johnny Rides Again - Jo Ann Muchmore 1048

Marshall, Tate
Sable - Karen Hesse 602

McLaughlin, Lucy
The Secret of the Ruby Ring - Yvonne MacGrory 915

McPherson, Paisley
The Great Pony Hassle - Nancy Springer 1374

Morgan, Bess
Bess's Log Cabin Quilt - D. Anne Love 898

Nathan
Journey to Freedom: A Story of the Underground Railroad - Courtni C. Wright 1562

Orson, Nita
First Came the Owl - Judith Benet Richardson 1210

Orton, Kelly
Kelly and Me - Carol Lynch Williams 1520

Overs, George
A Likely Lad - Gillian Avery 53

Parsons, Abigail
The 13th Floor: A Ghost Story - Sid Fleischman 409

Pepper, Alice
Numbskulls - William Taylor 1410

Pepper, Arlen
Sticks - Joan Bauer 87

Peterson, Ernest "Ernie"
The Big Bike Race - Lucy Jane Bledsoe 117

Potter, Bridget
The Wimp of the World - Alison Cragin Herzig 596

Proctor, Harriet Elizabeth "Hattie"
Gold in the Hills - Laurie Lawlor 824

Putney, Rebecca
The Bobbin Girl - Emily Arnold McCully 964

Rachel
Learning by Heart - Ronder Thomas Young 1588

Rahotep
The Egyptian Polar Bear - JoAnn Adinolfi 9

Smith, Francisco Moonlight "Cisco"
The Great Smith House Hustle - Jane Louise Curry 309

Sparks, Violet Dixie
The Girl Who Changed the World - Delia Ephron 393

Susie
Black-Eyed Susan - Jennifer Armstrong 38

Sweetsong, Stanley
Shoebag Returns - Mary James 688

Thomas, Sara Jane "Chicken"
Harry on Vacation - Dyan Sheldon 1326

Trevor, Maddy
Elfsong - Ann Turner 1433

Tucker, Winnie
The Iron Dragon Never Sleeps - Stephen Krensky 787

Vernon, Mike "Mikey"
Sticks - Joan Bauer 87

Volnik, Jessup
The Boggart - Susan Cooper 290

Wald, Zanna
Away to Me, Moss - Betty Levin 842

Watson, Kenny
The Watsons Go to Birmingham—1963 - Christopher Paul Curtis 311

Williams, Danny
The Trophy - Dean Hughes 662

Williams, Katy
One Brave Summer - Ann Turner 1434

Yeung Ying
Water Ghost - Ching Yeung Russell 1242

Young Bull
Cheyenne Again - Eve Bunting 170

Zekephlon "Zeke"
Alien Alert! - Debra Hess 597

11-YEAR-OLD

Adams, Nora Jean
Harvey's Mystifying Raccoon Mix-Up - Eth Clifford 259

Bates, Rebecca
Abigail's Drum - John A. Minahan 1020

Boggs, Connie
The World of Daughter McGuire - Sharon Dennis Wyeth 1567

Bowditch, Rosalie Ann "Rootie"
The Bones in the Cliff - James Stevenson 1385

Bowser, George "Georgie"
The In-Between Days - Eve Bunting 174

Brodie, Alex
The Four-Legged Ghosts - Mary Hoffman 635

Brooke, Catriona "Cat"
Granny the Pag - Nina Bawden 90

Carlito
The Stowaway: A Tale of California Pirates - Kristiana Gregory 508

Christina "Twig"
Blue Sky, Butterfly - Jean Van Leeuwen 1447

Compton, Mary Neal "Nealy"
Best Girl - Doris Buchanan Smith 1349

Connerton, Jenna "Jenna Pearl"
Ghosts Don't Get Goosebumps - Elvira Woodruff 1551

Cooke, Suzie
Bye, Bye, Bai Kai - Harriett Luger 904

Crawford, Catherine "Kit"
Green Willow - Eileen Dunlop 373

Dalton, Jack
Back to Bataan - Jerome Charyn 234

Davies, Emily Falcon
Falcon's Egg - Luli Gray 497

Dumbello, Chester
The Shuteyes - Mary James 689

Dunn, Rory
The Up & Down Spring - Johanna Hurwitz 672

Dyer, Lennie
No Friend of Mine - Ann Turnbull 1428

Ellerbee, Quinnella "Quinn"
Comford Creek - Joyce McDonald 972

Eloy
A Sunburned Prayer - Marc Talbert 1406

Erda, Lionel "Linny"
Back to Before - Jan Slepian 1343

Field, Strawberry "S.B."
Beyond the Magic Sphere - Gail Jarrow 691

Filkins, Johnna Josephine
Save Halloween! - Stephanie Tolan 1422

Fitzgerald, J.D.
The Great Brain Is Back - John D. Fitzgerald 408

Fortune, Tracey
The Good Fortunes Gang - Margaret Mahy 922

Fox, Alison
My Fabulous New Life - Sheila Greenwald 503

Fox, Robin
Ribbons - Laurence Yep 1574

Fuller, Lisa
Haphazard House - Mary Wesley 1500

Gage, Florence
A Haunted Year - Ann Phillips 1147

Gales, Cory
Zoe's Gift - Sheila Hayes 576

Genevieve "Gen"
On Winter's Wind - Patricia Hermes 593

Green, Archibald "Willy"
Granny the Pag - Nina Bawden 90

Grunder, Rina
Stolen Bones - Joan Carris 216

Hasbrouck, Emily Lathrop
Nobody's Daughter - Susan Beth Pfeffer 1142

Hetherington, Patrick
Change the Locks - Simon French 427

Hobbs, Zilla
The Children Next Door - Jean Ure 1439

Jamie
Beast - Margaret Wild 1511

Jimmy
The World in Grandfather's Hands - Craig Kee Strete 1399

Kelly, Justine
Fruit Flies, Fish & Fortune Cookies - Anne LeMieux 834

Kelly, Peggy
Keeping Secrets - Joan Lowery Nixon 1075

Lacey, Caitlin
Youn Hee and Me - C.S. Adler 12

Lacey, Youn Hee
Youn Hee and Me - C.S. Adler 12

Lafler, Timothea "Timmi"
Grass and Sky - Lisa Rowe Fraustino 426

Landauer, Cassie
No Boys Allowed - Marilyn Levinson 850

Laura
The Children Next Door - Jean Ure 1439

Lawrence, Katie
The Junkyard Dog - Erika Tamar 1407

Leonard, Samantha Marie "Sam"
Someone to Count On - Patricia Hermes 594

Lindsay
Courtyard Cat - C.S. Adler 10

Magruder, Bernie
The Bomb in the Bessledorf Bus Depot - Phyllis Reynolds Naylor 1063
The Face in the Bessledorf Funeral Parlor - Phyllis Reynolds Naylor 1065

Malloy, Edith Ann "Eddie"
The Boys Start the War - Phyllis Reynolds Naylor 1064

Matovic, Steven
Change the Locks - Simon French 427

Mauricette "Coco"
Back to Bataan - Jerome Charyn 234

McGuire, Daughter
The World of Daughter McGuire - Sharon Dennis Wyeth 1567

McKenna, Margy
Fast Forward - Mary Jane Miller 1013

Miranda
Wrapped in a Riddle - Sharon E. Heisel 579

Mitchell, Zoe
Zoe's Gift - Sheila Hayes 576

Monet/Dreisden, Amelia/Julie
Living in Secret - Cristina Salat 1257

Murdoch, Ed Earl
Comford Creek - Joyce McDonald 972

Nichols, Jeannie
The Ghost Comes Calling - Betty Ren Wright 1556

O'Keefe, Ryan
Tarantula Shoes - Tom Birdseye 110

Onetree, Mary Rose
Never Hit a Ghost with a Baseball Bat - Eth Clifford 260

Orton, Leah
Adeline Street - Carol Lynch Williams 1519
Kelly and Me - Carol Lynch Williams 1520

Otake, Anna
The World of Daughter McGuire - Sharon Dennis Wyeth 1567

Overs, William Cobbett "Willy"
A Likely Lad - Gillian Avery 53

Parker, Emily
A Spy in the King's Colony - Lisa Banim 69

Patterson, Hadley
The Light on Hogback Hill - Cynthia DeFelice 335

Pete
The Bones in the Cliff - James Stevenson 1385

Petroff, Eugenia "Jenny"
Tchaikovsky Discovers America - Esther Kalman 717

Raab, Bolivia
The Up & Down Spring - Johanna Hurwitz 672

Redmond, Kayla Ann
Fast Forward - Mary Jane Miller 1013

Roberts, Katie
The Private Notebook of Katie Roberts, Age 11 - Amy Hest 607

Rumplemayer, Fenton
On the Right Track - B.B. Calhoun 198

Ryan, Melinda
The Haunting of Holroyd Hill - Brenda Seabrooke 1304

Ryker, Amy
Wait and See - Virginia Bradley   131

Silverman, Abigail
Daring to be Abigail - Rachel Vail   1442

Sims, Libbie
Libbie Sims, Worry Wart - Gayle Rogers
   Lockwood   887

Stewart, Abigail Jane "Abby"
*The Winter of Red Snow: The Revolutionary War
   Diary of Abigail Jane Stewart* - Kristiana
   Gregory   509

Stuart, Annie Rising Fawn
Remember My Name - Sara H. Banks   74

Sullivan, Mary Margaret "Maggie"
A Spy in the King's Colony - Lisa Banim   69

Swope, Angela "Angel Always"
Ghosts Don't Get Goosebumps - Elvira
   Woodruff   1551

Tolson, David
Haunted Summer - Betty Ren Wright   1560

Turner, Jessica
Daddy's Climbing Tree - C.S. Adler   11

Weaver, Jill
Websters' Leap - Eileen Dunlop   374

Wilding, Ralph
No Friend of Mine - Ann Turnbull   1428

Wright, Alec
Stolen Bones - Joan Carris   216

12-YEAR-OLD

Abernathy, Clifford Allyn "Cliff" III
Fig Pudding - Ralph Fletcher   411

Babson, Willard
When Willard Met Babe Ruth - Donald Hall   544

Benton, Kayo
Don't Go Near Mrs. Tallie - Peg Kehret   724

Bijju
Binya's Blue Umbrella - Ruskin Bond   123

Bradley "Brad"
A Question of Trust - Marion Dane Bauer   88

Brainard, Lane
The Kid Who Ran for President - Dan Gutman   527

Brendan
Beast - Margaret Wild   1511

Caldero, Tony
The Sluggers Club: A Sports Mystery - Paul Robert
   Walker   1467

Cambardella, Frankie
Coaster - Betsy Duffey   367

Cannon, Doug
Olympic Dream - Matt Christopher   252

Christine
The Cave - Kathleen Karr   720

Cooper, Miranda
Cheshire Moon - Nancy Butts   190

DeAngelus, Nettie
The Mona Lisa of Salem Street - Jan Marino   932

Denardo, Hiccup
101 Ways to Bug Your Parents - Lee Wardlaw   1478

Dyer, Doreen
Room for a Stranger - Ann Turnbull   1429

Ennis, Sandra
The Case of the Fantastic Footprints - E.W.
   Hildick   616

Gates, Amanda "Mandy"
Out of the Storm - Patricia Willis   1526

Grady, B.J.
The Sluggers Club: A Sports Mystery - Paul Robert
   Walker   1467

Grillo, Doug
The Fear Place - Phyllis Reynolds Naylor   1066

Grunt, Betty
The Happy Yellow Car - Polly Horvath   647

Halkit, Kelly
Hey, Dad, Get a Life - Todd Strasser   1397

Harte, Mick
Mick Harte Was Here - Barbara Park   1110

Hawkes, Jilly
One Dog Day - J. Patrick Lewis   866

Ives, Austin
Dear Levi: Letters from the Overland Trail - Elvira
   Woodruff   1550

Jack
The Ice Horse - Candice Christiansen   248

Jacquith, Felix "JJ" II
Becoming Felix - Nancy Hope Wilson   1531

Johnson, Ginger
Never Trust a Sister over Twelve - Stephen
   Roos   1226

Jones, Booker
Utterly Yours, Booker Jones - Betsy Duffey   371

Kamornick, Sarah
Sarah, Also Known as Hannah - Lillian Hammer
   Ross   1233

Kee
Water Ghost - Ching Yeung Russell   1242

Laux, Goldie
101 Ways to Bug Your Parents - Lee Wardlaw   1478

Lawrence, William Edward
The Battle for the Castle - Elizabeth Winthrop   1537

Lerner, Steven
Becoming Felix - Nancy Hope Wilson   1531

Lewis, Heather
Lost in Cyberspace - Richard Peck   1126

Loring, Joshua
An Island Far from Home - John Donahue   358

MacMillan, Phillip
Earthquake! A Story of Old San Francisco - Kathleen
   V. Kudlinski   798

McGurk, Jack P.
The Case of the Absent Author - E.W. Hildick   614
The Case of the Fantastic Footprints - E.W.
   Hildick   616

Mercer, Maggie
The Fire Bug Connection: An Ecological Mystery -
   Jean Craighead George   450

Moore, Judson
The Kid Who Ran for President - Dan Gutman   527

Moriarty, Erin
The Worst Noel - Ilene Cooper   288

Musser, Maizie
Maizie - Linda Oatman High   613

Newcastle, Freedom
Come Morning - Leslie Davis Guccione   524

Nickles, Silver Iris
Hound Heaven - Linda Oatman High   612

Norstad, Libby
Escape into the Night - Lois Walfrid Johnson   700

Padgett, Amber
Forest - Janet Taylor Lisle   877

Palmer, Jonathan
Earthquake Terror - Peg Kehret   725

Patterson, Hartwell "Hart"
Coaster - Betsy Duffey   367

Paul
The Bamboo Flute - Garry Disher   353

Pitz, Thomas Osborn "Tom"
*Tom, Babette, & Simon: Three Tales of
   Transformation* - Avi   58

Proctor, Alexander Phimester "Pheme"
Gold in the Hills - Laurie Lawlor   824

Pygenski, Orville Rudemeyer "Orp"
Orp and the FBI - Suzy Kline   771

Sachi
Hiroshima - Laurence Yep   1572

Samuelson, Rebecca
Dear Elijah - Miriam Bat-Ami   85

Saunders, Rosie
Don't Go Near Mrs. Tallie - Peg Kehret   724

Sawyer, Humility "Hummy"
*A Journey to the New World: The Diary of Remember
   Patience Whipple* - Kathryn Lasky   815

Seabrooke, Dinah
Dinah in Love - Claudia Mills   1016

Slocum, Benjamin
Bluewater Journal: The Voyage of the Sea Tiger -
   Loretta Krupinski   797

Starbuck, Liberty
A Voice in the Wind - Kathryn Lasky   819

Stebbins, Buddy
The 13th Floor: A Ghost Story - Sid Fleischman   409

Tatro, Cole
Uncle Daney's Way - Jessie Haas   535

Thomas, Andy
Search for the Shadowman - Joan Lowery
   Nixon   1076

Tribble, Nick
Dinah in Love - Claudia Mills   1016

Unnamed Character
Arthur, High King of Britain - Michael
   Morpurgo   1038

Volnik, Emily
The Boggart - Susan Cooper   290

Wallace, Kathy
The Worst Noel - Ilene Cooper   288

Washington, Medgar "Wash"
The Sluggers Club: A Sports Mystery - Paul Robert
   Walker   1467

Watson, Dixie
Dixie in the Big Pasture - Belinda Hurmence   665

West, Peggy Jean "Peej"
Going to See Grassy Ella - Kathryn Lance   810

Whipple, Remember Patience "Mem"
*A Journey to the New World: The Diary of Remember
   Patience Whipple* - Kathryn Lasky   815

Willson, Harvey
Harvey's Mystifying Raccoon Mix-Up - Eth
   Clifford   259

Woodley, Richard
This New Land - G. Clifton Wisler   1541

Wyatt, Steve "Sneeze"
101 Ways to Bug Your Parents - Lee Wardlaw   1478

Yates, Eliza "Elijah Bates"
The Gentleman Outlaw and Me—Eli - Mary Downing
   Hahn   539

Yeadon, Meg
Fire in the Wind - Betty Levin   843

13-YEAR-OLD

Aitken, George
What's French for HELP, George? - Helen McCann 961

Annie
My Sister Annie - Bill Dodds 354

Avery, Freedom Jo
A Share of Freedom - June Rae Wood 1549

Barnavelt, Lewis
The Vengeance of the Witch-Finder - John Bellairs 94

Caleb
Jim-Dandy - Hadley Irwin 677

Caroline
Dakota Spring - D. Anne Love 899

Cody, William F. "Buffalo Bill"
The Sweetwater Run: The Story of Buffalo Bill Cody and the Pony Express - Andrew Glass 476

Conroy, Ruth
The Exiles at Home - Hilary McKay 981

Cooke, Lila
Bye, Bye, Bai Kai - Harriett Luger 904

David
Team Picture - Dean Hughes 661

Douglas, Hope
Hope - LouAnn Gaeddert 435

Drumm, Jessie
Spying on Miss Mueller - Eve Bunting 179

Easton, Scott
Walking the Edge - Alice Mead 999

Fitzgerald, Tom D. "The Great Brain"
The Great Brain Is Back - John D. Fitzgerald 408

Good, Angela
The Stray - Dick King-Smith 755

Gray, Orin
Fire in the Wind - Betty Levin 843

Harrison
The Barn - Avi 54

Harte, Phoebe
Mick Harte Was Here - Barbara Park 1110

Hatcher, Finis
Beyond the Magic Sphere - Gail Jarrow 691

Jonathan
The Fighting Ground - Avi 56

Jones, Herculeah
The Dark Stairs - Betsy Byars 191

Kelly, Rhoda
Room for a Stranger - Ann Turnbull 1429

Ligonier, Boone
Cheshire Moon - Nancy Butts 190

Logan, Hammer
The Well: David's Story - Mildred D. Taylor 1409

Mason, Mike
Tough Loser - Barthe DeClements 332

Richard
Saving Owen's Toad - Juanita Havill 573

Robeson, Brian
Brian's Winter - Gary Paulsen 1119

Shafter, Spinner
The Case of the Missing Cutthroats, an Ecological Mystery - Jean Craighead George 448

Unnamed Character
The Princess and the Lord of Night - Emma Bull 168

Watson, Byron "By"
The Watsons Go to Birmingham—1963 - Christopher Paul Curtis 311

Whipple, Amy
Jennifer-the-Jerk Is Missing - Carol Gorman 488

Wiggins, Keith
My Brother Is a Visitor from Another Planet - Dyan Sheldon 1327

14-YEAR-OLD

Bradford, Lucy
True North - Kathryn Lasky 818

Dulaney, Caleb
Caleb's Choice - G. Clifton Wisler 1539

Grillo, Gordon
The Fear Place - Phyllis Reynolds Naylor 1066

Kate
Murphy and Kate - Ellen Howard 653

Larson, Glennis
Harris and Me: A Summer Remembered - Gary Paulsen 1121

Marlin, Luke
Johnny Rides Again - Jo Ann Muchmore 1048

Meadows, John
An Island Far from Home - John Donahue 358

Perryman, Laura
The Wreck of the Zanzibar - Michael Morpurgo 1040

Ryan, Kevin
The Haunting of Holroyd Hill - Brenda Seabrooke 1304

Simms, Charlie
The Well: David's Story - Mildred D. Taylor 1409

15-YEAR-OLD

Appleby
The Mennyms - Sylvia Waugh 1484

Cody, Bill
Buffalo Bill and the Pony Express - Eleanor Coerr 262

Curtis, Sheldon "Say"
Pink and Say - Patricia Polacco 1162

Dyer, Lennie
Room for a Stranger - Ann Turnbull 1429

Holland, Micah
Caleb's Choice - G. Clifton Wisler 1539

Landauer, Corinne
No Boys Allowed - Marilyn Levinson 850

Lavin, Maggie
The Promised Land - Isabelle Holland 637

Nettie
The Barn - Avi 54

16-YEAR-OLD

Garth, Daniel
Green Willow - Eileen Dunlop 373

Kamornick, Hannah
Sarah, Also Known as Hannah - Lillian Hammer Ross 1233

Mercy, Jason
The Ghosts of Mercy Manor - Betty Ren Wright 1559

Riko
Hiroshima - Laurence Yep 1572

Sims, Maggie
Libbie Sims, Worry Wart - Gayle Rogers Lockwood 887

18-YEAR-OLD

Babcock, Robert
A Spy in the King's Colony - Lisa Banim 69

Featherbone, Calvin Thaddeus
The Gentleman Outlaw and Me—Eli - Mary Downing Hahn 539

Gray, Hannah
Haunted Summer - Betty Ren Wright 1560

Patten, Mary
Mary Patten's Voyage - Richard Berleth 103

1ST GRADER

Blair, Emily
How Emily Blair Got Her Fabulous Hair - Susan Garrison 445

Emma
Emma's Rug - Allen Say 1270

Fraser, Edward
Rats! - Jane Cutler 318

Jason
I Want Answers and a Parachute - P.J. Petersen 1138

Lilly
Lilly's Purple Plastic Purse - Kevin Henkes 587

Marilyn
Next Year I'll Be Special - Patricia Reilly Giff 466

Paine, Pamela
How Emily Blair Got Her Fabulous Hair - Susan Garrison 445

Unnamed Character
Miss Malarkey Doesn't Live in Room 10 - Judy Finchler 406
Summer's End - Maribeth Boelts 121

Whittsen, Marty Louise
Fat Chance! - Lady Borton 127

2ND GRADER

Casanova, Brian
School Spirit Sabotage - Elizabeth Levy 860

Doug
Song Lee in Room 2B - Suzy Kline 773

Emi
The Bracelet - Yoshiko Uchida 1436

Foote, Owen
Owen Foote, Second Grade Strongman - Stephanie Greene 501

Harry
Horrible Harry and the Dungeon - Suzy Kline 769
Song Lee and the Leech Man - Suzy Kline 772

Hobbes, Joseph
Owen Foote, Second Grade Strongman - Stephanie Greene 501

Jackson, Jason
Dog Days for Dudley - Barbara Moe 1026

Jill
Summer's End - Maribeth Boelts 121

Kelley, Quinn
Second-Grade Pig Pals - Kirby Larson 812

Lee, Song
Horrible Harry and the Dungeon - Suzy Kline 769

Madison, Laurie
The Bracelet - Yoshiko Uchida 1436

Barnes, Dinah
Wagon Train 911 - Jamie Gilson   473

Bates, Joshua T.
Joshua T. Bates Takes Charge - Susan Richards
Shreve   1332

Blue, Yolanda
Yolanda's Genius - Carol Fenner   404

Caselli, Louis
Bad Girls - Cynthia Voigt   1456

Cessano, Marsha
Live from the Fifth Grade - Colleen O'Shaughnessy
McKenna   984

Clarry, Mavis Mae
B.J.'s Billion-Dollar Bet - Julie Anne Peters   1133

Davis, Joey
Chevrolet Saturdays - Candy Dawson Boyd   128

Elsa
*That Wild Berries Should Grow: The Diary of a
Summer* - Gloria Whelan   1506

Epps, Margalo
Bad Girls - Cynthia Voigt   1456

Frank, Patrick
Live from the Fifth Grade - Colleen O'Shaughnessy
McKenna   984

Friday, Roger
Live from the Fifth Grade - Colleen O'Shaughnessy
McKenna   984

Gallagher, Jason
Jason and the Losers - Gina Willner-Pardo   1527

Garcia, Alex
Off and Running - Gary Soto   1363

Gemini, Samona
Seth and Samona - Joanne Hyppolite   674

Gordon, Marty
Fifth Grade Fever - Michele Granger   493

Guardino, Nina
Fifth Grade Fever - Michele Granger   493

Haas, Emily
The Green Musketeers and the Fabulous Frogs - Sara
St. Antoine   1375

Hanson, Hobie
Soccer Circus - Jamie Gilson   472

Harrison, Emory
J.B. Wigglebottom and the Parade of Pets - Vivian
Sathre   1268

Herera, Rudy
Off and Running - Gary Soto   1363

**Higgenbottom "Wigglebottom", Jonathan Bradford
"J.B."**
J.B. Wigglebottom and the Parade of Pets - Vivian
Sathre   1268

Kaufman, Cricket
School Spirit - Johanna Hurwitz   671

Lowe, Patrick
Just Call Me Stupid - Tom Birdseye   108

Manetti, Andy
The Magnificent Mummy Maker - Elvira
Woodruff   1552

Martin, Dave
Attack of the Killer Fishsticks - Paul Zindel   1596

McGinn, Liz
Attack of the Killer Fishsticks - Paul Zindel   1596

Michelin, Seth
Seth and Samona - Joanne Hyppolite   674

Millner, Max
Attack of the Killer Fishsticks - Paul Zindel   1596

O'Malley, Oliver
Baseball Card Crazy - Trish Kennedy   735

O'Malley, Sean
Joshua T. Bates Takes Charge - Susan Richards
Shreve   1332

Ortiz, Celina
Just Call Me Stupid - Tom Birdseye   108

Philpot, Orin
Wagon Train 911 - Jamie Gilson   473

Phoebe
The Accidental Witch - Anne Mazer   956

Pygenski, Chloe
Orp and the FBI - Suzy Kline   771

Rachel
I Was a Fifth-Grade Zebra - Nancy J. Hopper   645

Ramirez, Miata
Off and Running - Gary Soto   1363

Ripley, Samantha
The Green Musketeers and the Fabulous Frogs - Sara
St. Antoine   1375

Rush, Becky
The Mystery of the Several Sevens - Bill Brittain   140

Sanchez, Julio
School Spirit - Johanna Hurwitz   671

Schmidt, Veronica
Countess Veronica - Nancy K. Robinson   1219

Simpson, Fletcher
Gopher Takes Heart - Virginia Scribner   1303

Taylor, Everett
Jason and the Losers - Gina Willner-Pardo   1527

Thompson, Callie
Learning by Heart - Ronder Thomas Young   1588

Toller, Simon
The Mystery of the Several Sevens - Bill Brittain   140

Warner, Alex
Nothing but Trouble, Trouble, Trouble - Patricia
Hermes   592

Wilhelm, Tommy
Joshua T. Bates Takes Charge - Susan Richards
Shreve   1332

Williams, Cassie
Alien Alert! - Debra Hess   597

Willis, Richard "Ritchie"
Under the Bridge - Ellen Kindt McKenzie   985

Zeller, Chelsea
I Was a Fifth-Grade Zebra - Nancy J. Hopper   645

Zimmers, Buddy
J.B. Wigglebottom and the Parade of Pets - Vivian
Sathre   1268

6TH GRADER

Adams, Callie
Nerd No More - Kristine L. Franklin   424

Anders, Ellen
Ellen Anders on Her Own - Karen Hirsch   625

Ayreal
The New One - Jacqueline Turner Banks   71

Baird, Judy
True Friends - Bill Wallace   1471

Barrett, Bethany
The Secret Life of Bethany Barrett - Claudia
Mills   1017

Ben
Fruit Flies, Fish & Fortune Cookies - Anne
LeMieux   834

Bobowick, Mary Ellen
Fruit Flies, Fish & Fortune Cookies - Anne
LeMieux   834

Bradford, Cornelia "Neely"
The Trespassers - Zilpha Keatley Snyder   1360

Brown, Courtney Ann
True Friends - Bill Wallace   1471

Buckner, Michael
My Brother, the Ghost - Suzanne Weyn   1503

Callahan, Roberta Jean "Bobbie Jean"
Good-Bye, Hello - Barbara Shook Hazen   577

Carter, Cassandra
Rosie's Tiger - Anna Myers   1055

Carter, Josh
The Light on Hogback Hill - Cynthia DeFelice   335

Carter, Ludwig von Beethoven "Wiggie"
Nerd No More - Kristine L. Franklin   424

Charlie
My Sister Annie - Bill Dodds   354

Chester, Dan
My Name Is Brain/Brian - Jeanne Betancourt   106

Curry, Derek
Down and Up Fall - Johanna Hurwitz   666

Davis, Annie
Frankie Murphy's Kiss List - Donna Guthrie   526

Dunn, Amy
Amy Dunn Quits School - Susan Richards
Shreve   1330

Dunn, Rory
Down and Up Fall - Johanna Hurwitz   666

Flanagan, Elizabeth "Lizard"
The Miraculous Makeover of Lizard Flanagan - Carol
Gorman   489

Flanagan, Sam
The Miraculous Makeover of Lizard Flanagan - Carol
Gorman   489

Gershom, Noah
The View from Saturday - E.L. Konigsburg   777

Grant, Bryan
Riot - Mary Casanova   217

Hill, Casey "Case"
Dog Years - Sally Warner   1480

Jenkins, Judge
The New One - Jacqueline Turner Banks   71

Jenkins, Jury
Egg-Drop Blues - Jacqueline Turner Banks   70
The New One - Jacqueline Turner Banks   71

Joe
Tut Tut - Jon Scieszka   1299

Kawabe
Friends - Kazumi Yumoto   1590

Kendall, K.J.
My Fabulous New Life - Sheila Greenwald   503

Kinsey, Catherine "Cat"
Cat Running - Zilpha Keatley Snyder   1359

Kiyama
Friends - Kazumi Yumoto   1590

Kotcher, Honey
Fearsome's Hero - Dona Schenker   1280

Landauer, Cassie
No Boys Allowed - Marilyn Levinson   850

Lewis, Josh
Lost in Cyberspace - Richard Peck   1126

Loring, Haley "Samantha Love"
Stardust - Alane Ferguson   405

Marshall, Travis
Frankie Murphy's Kiss List - Donna Guthrie 526

Mason, Philura Higley "Philly"
The Reason for Janey - Nancy Hope Wilson 1532

McLinn, Talmadge
A Place to Belong - Emily Crofford 305

Mills, Violetta
Wait and See - Virginia Bradley 131

Monroe, Loren
Going the Distance - Mary Jane Miller 1014

Montgomery, Eunice
Hey You, Sister Rose - Eileen Walsh Strauch 1398

Morris, Isabel
My Name Is Brain/Brian - Jeanne Betancourt 106

Murphy, Frankie
Frankie Murphy's Kiss List - Donna Guthrie 526

Nutsell, Frederick "Nutty"
Re-Elect Nutty! - Dean Hughes 660

Owen, Jane
The Secret Life of Bethany Barrett - Claudia Mills 1017

Parsons, Sukey
The Pickle Song - Barthe DeClements 331

Perkins, Zane
Cat Running - Zilpha Keatley Snyder 1359

Raab, Bolivia
Down and Up Fall - Johanna Hurwitz 666

Retting, Chelsie
Riot - Mary Casanova 217

Ryker, Amy
Wait and See - Virginia Bradley 131

Sam
Tut Tut - Jon Scieszka 1299

Schur, Gordon
Tarantula Shoes - Tom Birdseye 110

Scudder, Tobias Michael "Toby"
Toby Scudder, Ultimate Warrior - David Gifaldi 463

Singh, Julian
The View from Saturday - E.L. Konigsburg 777

Smith, Gordon "Gordy"
Following My Own Footsteps - Mary Downing Hahn 538

Stapleton, Danny
The Reason for Janey - Nancy Hope Wilson 1532

Taylor, Rosie
Rosie's Tiger - Anna Myers 1055

Tomlin, Paula
The Pickle Song - Barthe DeClements 331

Toomey, Brian
My Name Is Brain/Brian - Jeanne Betancourt 106

Turner, Billie
Mayfield Crossing - Vaunda Micheaux Nelson 1070

Valdez, Andy
Stardust - Alane Ferguson 405

Van Dyke, Gretchen
Libbie Sims, Worry Wart - Gayle Rogers Lockwood 887

Warren, Arlene
Hey You, Sister Rose - Eileen Walsh Strauch 1398

Webster, Tully
Fearsome's Hero - Dona Schenker 1280

Wickers, Abby
Ellen Anders on Her Own - Karen Hirsch 625

Winkle, Will
Buzzard Breath - Marty Crisp 304

Yamashita
Friends - Kazumi Yumoto 1590

Zimmer, Aaron
Lost in Cyberspace - Richard Peck 1126

7TH GRADER

Angela
Jericho - Janet Hickman 611

Beckwith, Mallory
Really No Big Deal - Margaret Bechard 92

Buckner, Sara
My Brother, the Ghost - Suzanne Weyn 1503

Bushwick, Cathy
My Crazy Cousin Courtney - Judi Miller 1011

Caldwell, Terry
Chive - Shelley A. Barre 80

Dawn
Meeting the Make-Out King - Lynn Cullen 306

DeAngelo, Mark
Meeting the Make-Out King - Lynn Cullen 306

Fairchild, Ellen
Who's Orp's Girlfriend? - Suzy Kline 774

Gates, Amanda "Mandy"
Out of the Storm - Patricia Willis 1526

Green, Courtney Alicia
My Crazy Cousin Courtney - Judi Miller 1011

Greene, Lia
Trick or Trouble? - Ilene Cooper 287

Horton, Charles "Chive"
Chive - Shelley A. Barre 80

Ivy
The Fog Doggies and Me - Gayle Pearson 1125

Kelso, Katie
The Worst Speller in Jr. High - Caroline Janover 690

Kirshenbaum, Naomi
Alan and Naomi - Myron Levoy 856

Krupnik, Anastasia
See You Around, Sam! - Lois Lowry 902

Larson, Spud
The Worst Speller in Jr. High - Caroline Janover 690

Lovello, Lucy
Cheater, Cheater - Elizabeth Levy 857

Matzinger, Amanda "Moose"
Really No Big Deal - Margaret Bechard 92

McKibben, Nora
Meeting the Make-Out King - Lynn Cullen 306

Paul
The Bamboo Flute - Garry Disher 353

Pygenski, Orville Rudemeyer "Orp"
Who's Orp's Girlfriend? - Suzy Kline 774

Rich, Joey
Cheater, Cheater - Elizabeth Levy 857

Silverman, Alan
Alan and Naomi - Myron Levoy 856

Starr
The Fog Doggies and Me - Gayle Pearson 1125

Straus, Brian
The Worst Speller in Jr. High - Caroline Janover 690

Tierney, Scott
Trick or Trouble? - Ilene Cooper 287

Truman, Jonah
Really No Big Deal - Margaret Bechard 92

Watson, Dixie
Dixie in the Big Pasture - Belinda Hurmence 665

8TH GRADER

Brueggenmeyer, Lurlene
How Do You Spell Geek? - Julie Anne Peters 1134

Charles, Vincent "Vinnie"
What Happened in Mr. Fisher's Room - Nancy J. Hopper 646

Keller, Ann
How Do You Spell Geek? - Julie Anne Peters 1134

McCurry, Donald
Rosy Cole: She Walks in Beauty - Sheila Greenwald 504

Reeves, Aaron
One-Man Team - Dean Hughes 659

Strata, Melanie "Lanie"
What Happened in Mr. Fisher's Room - Nancy J. Hopper 646

Tyne, Kimberly
How Do You Spell Geek? - Julie Anne Peters 1134

9TH GRADER

Salazar, Stephen
The Fog Doggies and Me - Gayle Pearson 1125

AARDVARK

Arthur
Arthur Writes a Story - Marc Brown 145
Arthur's Chicken Pox - Marc Brown 146
Arthur's Family Vacation - Marc Brown 147
Arthur's First Sleepover - Marc Brown 148
Arthur's New Puppy - Marc Brown 149
D.W. Rides Again! - Marc Brown 150
D.W. the Picky Eater - Marc Brown 151

Aunt Eater
Aunt Eater's Mystery Christmas - Doug Cushman 312

D.W.
Arthur Writes a Story - Marc Brown 145
Arthur's Chicken Pox - Marc Brown 146
Arthur's Family Vacation - Marc Brown 147
Arthur's First Sleepover - Marc Brown 148
Arthur's New Puppy - Marc Brown 149
D.W. Rides Again! - Marc Brown 150
D.W. the Picky Eater - Marc Brown 151

Father
D.W. Rides Again! - Marc Brown 150

Grandma Thora
D.W. the Picky Eater - Marc Brown 151

ABUSE VICTIM

Little Kit
Little Kit or, the Industrious Flea Circus Girl - Emily Arnold McCully 967

ACCIDENT VICTIM

Jonathan
The Storm - Marc Harshman 566

Sylvain
In the Palace of the Ocean King - Marilyn Singer 1338

ACCOUNTANT

Lucian
The Arkadians - Lloyd Alexander 22

ACTIVIST

Kendall, K.J.
My Fabulous New Life - Sheila Greenwald 503

Marcy
City Green - DyAnne DiSalvo-Ryan 352

Moscowitz, Pearl
Pearl Moscowitz's Last Stand - Arthur A. Levine 846

Ripley, Samantha
The Green Musketeers and the Fabulous Frogs - Sara St. Antoine 1375

Sanchez, Julio
School Spirit - Johanna Hurwitz 671

ACTOR

McGill, Matthew
Annie Pitts, Swamp Monster - Diane De Groat 327

ACTRESS

Driscoll, Jessica Charlotte
The Mystery of the Cupboard - Lynne Reid Banks 73

LaFondue, Cashmere
Sheep Dreams - Arthur A. Levine 847

Lovejoy, Serena
Buzby to the Rescue - Julia Hoban 626

Pitts, Annie
Annie Pitts, Swamp Monster - Diane De Groat 327

Shetland, Liza
Sheep Dreams - Arthur A. Levine 847

Williams, Jessie
Fall Secrets - Candy Dawson Boyd 129

ADOPTEE

Aiken, Tammy
Double Play at Short - Matt Christopher 249

Blanche
My Real Family - Emily Arnold McCully 968

DeRosa, Columbo
Zoe and Columbo - Susan Richards Shreve 1333

Isabel
Bonesy and Isabel - Michael J. Rosen 1229

Katie
A Koala for Katie: An Adoption Story - Jonathan London 891

Matthew
Pinky and Rex and the New Baby - James Howe 656

Matthew "Matt"
Riding the Waves - Theresa Tomlinson 1423

Pablo
Pablo's Tree - Pat Mora 1037

Samantha "Sam"
How I Was Adopted: Samantha's Story - Joanna Cole 271

Walker, Danny
Double Play at Short - Matt Christopher 249

ADVENTURER

Furby, Alexander
Wonderful Alexander and the Catwings - Ursula K. Le Guin 826

Wafer, Lionel
The Pirates' Mixed-Up Voyage - Margaret Mahy 924

Welzl, Jan
A Small, Tall Tale from the Far, Far North - Peter Sis 1341

ADVERTISING

Primm
Lyle at the Office - Bernard Waber 1461

AGED PERSON

Al
Sophie's Lucky - Dick King-Smith 754

Albert
Gooseberry Park - Cynthia Rylant 1249

Alejandro
Alejandro's Gift - Richard E. Albert 19

Anna
Pianna - Mary Lyn Ray 1200

Annie
Willa and Old Miss Annie - Berlie Doherty 357

Applebaum, Elsie
Something for Everyone - Susan Whitcher 1508

Bear
The Bear & Mr. Bear - Frances Thomas 1416

Beloved Woman
The Story of the Milky Way: A Cherokee Tale - Joseph Bruchac 162

Billy Que
Bobbin Dustdobbin - Susan Patron 1117

Birdie
Beware the Brindlebeast - Anita Riggio 1213

Callahan, Sarah "Gramma"
Good-Bye, Hello - Barbara Shook Hazen 577

Chicken Man
White Socks Only - Evelyn Coleman 275

Cochran
Tangles - Errol Broome 141

Elizabeth
William's Ninth Life - Minna Jung 716

Florrie
Riding the Waves - Theresa Tomlinson 1423

Flower, Margaret "Peggy"
Mr. Potter's Pet - Dick King-Smith 750

Gamma Lee
The Gates of the Wind - Kathryn Lasky 814

Grandfather
Inunguak: The Little Greenlander - Palle Petersen 1140

Grandpa
Traveling Backward - Toby Forward 420

Haktak
Two of Everything - Lily Toy Hong 641
Two of Everything - Lily Toy Hong 641

Hickathrift, Henrietta "Henny"
The Stray - Dick King-Smith 755

Hoffman
The Tie Man's Miracle: A Chanukah Tale - Steven Schnur 1289

Jane
Dream Meadow - Helen V. Griffith 518

Jenkins, Maynard
The Christmas Blizzard - Helen Ketteman 739

Joe
In My Mother's Garden - Melissa Madenski 919

Kingston, Lydia
Buzzard Breath - Marty Crisp 304

Kirkland, Bert
Nothing but Trouble - Betty Ren Wright 1561

Lipscomb, Driscoll
The Gift of Driscoll Lipscomb - Sara Yamaka 1568

Martha
Great Aunt Martha - Rebecca C. Jones 710

Max
The Palace of Stars - Patricia Lakin 808

May
Traveling Backward - Toby Forward 420
Willy and May - Judith Byron Schachner 1275

Meade, Emily
Falcon's Egg - Luli Gray 497

Moscowitz, Pearl
Pearl Moscowitz's Last Stand - Arthur A. Levine 846

Nicholas
The Gift from Saint Nicholas - Dorothea Lachner 803

Old Man Hammer
City Green - DyAnne DiSalvo-Ryan 352

Opel, Celia
Phoenix Upside Down - Elizabeth Scarboro 1274

Paw Paw
Ribbons - Laurence Yep 1574

Pendersnarf
The Christmas Blizzard - Helen Ketteman 739

Pendragon, Arthur
Arthur, High King of Britain - Michael Morpurgo 1038

Peter
Dog - Robert J. Blake 115

Potter, Peter
Mr. Potter's Pet - Dick King-Smith 750

Putter
Mr. Putter and Tabby Bake the Cake - Cynthia Rylant 1253
Mr. Putter and Tabby Pick the Pears - Cynthia Rylant 1254
Mr. Putter and Tabby Walk the Dog - Cynthia Rylant 1255

Ram Bharosa
Binya's Blue Umbrella - Ruskin Bond 123

Rosa
City Green - DyAnne DiSalvo-Ryan 352

Rosemary
The Cow Who Wouldn't Come Down - Paul Brett Johnson 701

Saul
Straw Sense - Rona Rupert 1239

Shaw, Ebenezer
Man Out at First - Matt Christopher 251

Skilly
Aunt Skilly and the Stranger - Kathleen Stevens 1382

Steadings, Amy
The Ghastly Gerty Swindle: With the Ghosts of Hungryhouse Lane - Sam McBratney 959

Stormfoot, Hosannah
Santa's Winter Vacation - Viveca Larn Sundvall 1404

ARTISAN

Angel
Down at Angel's - Sharon Chmielarz 239

Claus
The Story of Santa Claus - Tom Paxton 1122

Devora
The Fog's Net - Pat Pflieger 1146

Griselle
Good Griselle - Jane Yolen 1579

Kate
The Boy and the Giants - Fiona Moodie 1030

Luka Alexandrych
Kashtanka - Anton Chekhov 235

Morgan, Bess
Bess's Log Cabin Quilt - D. Anne Love 898

Murdoch, Ed Earl
Comford Creek - Joyce McDonald 972

Nasche
A Boy and His Bear - Harriet Graham 491

Pap
Sable - Karen Hesse 602

Pedro
Saturday Market - Patricia Grossman 522

Pudge
First Came the Owl - Judith Benet Richardson 1210

Todd, Abbott L.
Bound for Oregon - Jean Van Leeuwen 1448

Toomey, Jonathan
The Christmas Miracle of Jonathan Toomey - Susan Wojciechowski 1543

Totte
The Rose Horse - Deborah Lee Rose 1228

ARTIST

Andrew
Andrew's Amazing Monsters - Kathryn Hook Berlan 102

Bess Ann
Last Left Standing - Barbara T. Russell 1240

Bill
Seeds - George Shannon 1318

Cabbage Rose
Cabbage Rose - Mary-Claire Helldorfer 580

Cage, Patience
Josiah True and the Art Maker - Amy Littlesugar 883

Daddy
Five Live Bongos - George Ella Lyon 909
Miranda's Smile - Thomas Locker 886
The Painter - Peter Catalanotto 224

Dali, Salvador
Dinner at Magritte's - Michael Garland 442

Emma
Emma's Rug - Allen Say 1270

Espino, Fernando
The Little Painter of Sabana Grande - Patricia Maloney Markun 935

Eyris, Moel
The Painter Who Loved Chickens - Olivier Dunrea 375

Father
Pepi and the Secret Names - Jill Paton Walsh 1115
A Place for Angels - Clyde Robert Bulla 169

Finch, Moony B.
Moony B. Finch, the Fastest Draw in the West - David McPhail 993

Grandpa
My Dog Rosie - Isabelle Harper 559

Jibbett, Jimmy
The Man in the Ceiling - Jules Feiffer 403

Kellow, Vanessa
The Big Bazoohley - Peter Carey 207

Ligonier, Boone
Cheshire Moon - Nancy Butts 190

Lipscomb, Driscoll
The Gift of Driscoll Lipscomb - Sara Yamaka 1568

Magritte, Rene
Dinner at Magritte's - Michael Garland 442

Marion
The Moon Man: A Story - Gerda Marie Scheidl 1279

Matthews, Troy
Karate Dancer - Doris Buchanan Smith 1350

Mattie
Last Left Standing - Barbara T. Russell 1240

Mieko
Mieko and the Fifth Treasure - Eleanor Coerr 263

Newton
Not in the House, Newton! - Judith Heide Gilliland 470

Pearl
Pearl Paints - Abigail Thomas 1415

Rusty
The Gentleman and the Kitchen Maid - Diane Stanley 1376

Tsujimoto
Pink Paper Swans - Virginia L. Kroll 793

Unnamed Character
The Paper Princess - Elisa Kleven 767

ASSISTANT

Big Anthony
Strega Nona Meets Her Match - Tomie De Paola 329

Bird, Secretary
Flatfoot Fox and the Case of the Missing Whoooo - Eth Clifford 258

Pete
Tyrannosaurus Tex - Betty G. Birney 111

ASTHMATIC

Brodie, Carrie
The Four-Legged Ghosts - Mary Hoffman 635

Jane
Nurse Sally Ann - Terrance Dicks 350

Michael
The Cave - Kathleen Karr 720

AUNT

Applebaum, Elsie
Something for Everyone - Susan Whitcher 1508

Appleflinger, Alice
Jeremy's Muffler - Laura F. Nielsen 1074

Aunt Sally
Tooter Pepperday - Jerry Spinelli 1371

Auntie Pearl
Sophy and Auntie Pearl - Jeanne Titherington 1421

Dawsie
The Wimp of the World - Alison Cragin Herzig 596

Driscoll, Jessica Charlotte
The Mystery of the Cupboard - Lynne Reid Banks 73

Elizabeth
The Hanukkah Ghosts - Malka Penn 1128
My Apron - Eric Carle 209

Fern
How I Spent My Summer Vacation - Mark Teague 1411

Fran
Truman's Aunt Farm - Jama Kim Rattigan 1198

Great Aunt
The Last Dragon - Susan Miho Nunes 1085

Henry, Nan
The Root Cellar - Janet Lunn 905

Jess
Olivia and the Real Live Pet - Charlotte Towner Graeber 490

Kirkland, Bert
Nothing but Trouble - Betty Ren Wright 1561

Laney, Bess
Out of the Storm - Patricia Willis 1526

Lona
A Place for Angels - Clyde Robert Bulla 169

Lucy
When Aunt Lucy Rode a Mule and Other Stories - Barbara Ann Porte 1168

Martha
Great Aunt Martha - Rebecca C. Jones 710

May
Willy and May - Judith Byron Schachner 1275

Meade, Emily
Falcon's Egg - Luli Gray 497

Mookie
Kisses from Rosa - Petra Mathers 949

Moore, Alixandra
Lavender - Karen Hesse 599

Pa Nang
Som See and the Magic Elephant - Jamie Oliviero 1094

Pam
You Can't Eat Your Chicken Pox, Amber Brown - Paula Danziger 322

Peg
Pearl Paints - Abigail Thomas 1415

Powell, Odessa
The Sunday Outing - Gloria Jean Pinkney 1154

Prudence
James in the House of Aunt Prudence - Timothy Bush 184

Shamiema
Straw Sense - Rona Rupert 1239

Tante Loulou
The Sugaring-Off Party - Jonathan London 895

Tia
A Birthday Basket for Tia - Pat Mora 1036

BABYSITTER

Batson, Howard "Batty"
McMummy - Betsy Byars 195

Dad
Octopus Hug - Laurence Pringle 1177

Frances
Babysitting for Benjamin - Valiska Gregory 511

Gray, Hannah
Haunted Summer - Betty Ren Wright 1560

Mozer, Robert "Mozie"
McMummy - Betsy Byars 195

Rex
Rex and Lilly Family Time - Laurie Krasny Brown 143

Richard
Saving Owen's Toad - Juanita Havill 573

Rodney
Monster Brother - Mary Jane Auch 51

Sam
Big Help! - Anna Grossnickle Hines 621
A Turkey Drive and Other Tales - Barbara Ann Porte 1167

Sammy
John Joe and the Big Hen - Martin Waddell 1462
Sophie and Sammy's Library Sleepover - Judith Caseley 221

Seth
The Tie Man's Miracle: A Chanukah Tale - Steven Schnur 1289

Shem
Star Hatchling - Margaret Bechard 93

Sidney
Monster Brother - Mary Jane Auch 51

Simcha
When I Left My Village - Maxine Rose Schur 1296

Slocum, Benjamin
Bluewater Journal: The Voyage of the Sea Tiger - Loretta Krupinski 797

Smith, Francisco Moonlight "Cisco"
The Great Smith House Hustle - Jane Louise Curry 309

Sparks, Simon
The Girl Who Changed the World - Delia Ephron 393

Teddy
Later, Gator - Laurence Yep 1573

Thomas the Tidy, the Ti
Tumble Tower - Anne Tyler 1435

Tom
The Iguana Brothers: A Tale of Two Lizards - Tony Johnston 704

Tony
Baby Jesus, Like My Brother - Margery Wheeler Brown 153

Tracy, Martin
The Ghost of Popcorn Hill - Betty Ren Wright 1557

Tracy, Peter
The Ghost of Popcorn Hill - Betty Ren Wright 1557

Trelling, Christopher "Chris"
Up a Road Slowly - Irene Hunt 663

Tuck
Tuck in the Pool - Martha Weston 1502

Turner, Billie
Mayfield Crossing - Vaunda Micheaux Nelson 1070

Turner, Tycho
Daddy's Climbing Tree - C.S. Adler 11

Unnamed Character
In Search of the Giant - Jeanne Willis 1524
It's Pumpkin Time! - Zoe Hall 546
The Lotus Seed - Sherry Garland 443
Snow - Nancy Elizabeth Wallace 1473
Summer Sands - Sherry Garland 444
Tomorrow on Rocky Pond - Lynn Reiser 1206
When I Am Eight - Joan Lowery Nixon 1077
Zoo - Anthony Browne 156

Walter
No More Water in the Tub! - Tedd Arnold 43

Webster, Gordon
Partners - Karen Waggoner 1465

Webster, Jamie
Partners - Karen Waggoner 1465

Wheeler, Aubrey
Casey over There - Staton Rabin 1184

Wheeler, Casey
Casey over There - Staton Rabin 1184

Wiggins, Adam
My Brother Is a Visitor from Another Planet - Dyan Sheldon 1327

Wiggins, Keith
My Brother Is a Visitor from Another Planet - Dyan Sheldon 1327

Will
Moonlight on the River - Deborah Kovacs 781
Nothing Happened - Bill Harley 557

William
No More Water in the Tub! - Tedd Arnold 43

Willie
Geraldine's Baby Brother - Holly Keller 730
Night in the Barn - Faye Gibbons 462

Witting, Caleb
Skylark - Patricia MacLachlan 917

Worst, Arvin
The Worst Goes South - James Stevenson 1389

Worst, Ervin
The Worst Goes South - James Stevenson 1389

Yolen, Lyovka "Lou"
And Twelve Chinese Acrobats - Jane Yolen 1575

Yolen, Velvul "Wolf"
And Twelve Chinese Acrobats - Jane Yolen 1575

BUFFALO

Amani
Kalinzu: A Story from Africa - Jeremy Grimsdell 521

Kalinzu
Kalinzu: A Story from Africa - Jeremy Grimsdell 521

BULL

Stella's Bull
Stella's Bull - Frances Arrington 45

BULLIED CHILD

Arnold
The Wimp - Kathy Caple 204

Bates, Joshua T.
Joshua T. Bates Takes Charge - Susan Richards Shreve 1332

Goff, Matthew "Gopher"
Gopher Takes Heart - Virginia Scribner 1303

Higgenbottom "Wigglebottom", Jonathan Bradford "J.B."
J.B. Wigglebottom and the Parade of Pets - Vivian Sathre 1268

Millner, Max
Attack of the Killer Fishsticks - Paul Zindel 1596

Okada, Donnie
Heroes - Ken Mochizuki 1024

O'Malley, Sean
Joshua T. Bates Takes Charge - Susan Richards Shreve 1332

BULLY

Boomer, Marty
I'm George Washington and You're Not! - Steven Kroll 789

Brendan
Beast - Margaret Wild 1511

Buzz
Jenna's Big Jump - Faythe Dyrud Thureen 1420

Clyde
The Wimp - Kathy Caple 204

Farrow, Ernie
Marvelous Marvin and the Pioneer Ghost - Bonnie Pryor 1179

Fig
Jig, Fig, and Mrs. Pig - Peter Hansard 555

Green, Archibald "Willy"
Granny the Pag - Nina Bawden 90

Gregor
Tilly and the Rhinoceros - Sheila White Samton 1260

Haines, Bert
No Friend of Mine - Ann Turnbull 1428

Haney, Clyde Elmer "Bo"
How to Be Cool in the Third Grade - Betsy Duffey 369

Herman, Chuckie
The Losers Fight Back - Barbara M. Joosse 711

Hooks
The House Gobbaleen - Lloyd Alexander 23

Kevin
Pinky and Rex and the Bully - James Howe 654

Kotcher, Honey
Fearsome's Hero - Dona Schenker 1280

Logan, Dicky
Sara Kate Saves the World - Susan Beth Pfeffer 1143

Melvin the Miffed
The Knight Who Was Afraid to Fight - Barbara Shook Hazen 578

Norman
Pie Magic - Toby Forward 419

Peck, Darryn
Blabber Mouth - Morris Gleitzman 479

Simpson, Fletcher
Gopher Takes Heart - Virginia Scribner 1303

Slinky
Boys at Work - Gary Soto 1361

Smith, Chad
Slam Dunk Saturday - Jean Marzollo 944

Thompson
The Foot Warmer and the Crow - Evelyn Coleman 274

Tiger
The Rat and the Tiger - Keiko Kasza 722

Tyrone
The Secret Super Powers of Marco - Meredith Sue Willis 1525

Unnamed Character
Friday Night at Hodge's Cafe - Tim Egan 382

Victor
Insects Are My Life - Megan McDonald 974

Wilhelm, Tommy
Joshua T. Bates Takes Charge - Susan Richards Shreve 1332

Zimmers, Buddy
J.B. Wigglebottom and the Parade of Pets - Vivian Sathre 1268

BUSINESSMAN

Bowser, David
The In-Between Days - Eve Bunting 174

Sabrina
Elfsong - Ann Turner 1433

Sapphire
Courtyard Cat - C.S. Adler 10

Secret
On Cat Mountain - Francoise Richard 1209

Tabby
Mr. Putter and Tabby Bake the Cake - Cynthia Rylant 1253
Mr. Putter and Tabby Pick the Pears - Cynthia Rylant 1254
Mr. Putter and Tabby Walk the Dog - Cynthia Rylant 1255
The Worst Witch at Sea - Jill Murphy 1053

Tangles
Tangles - Errol Broome 141

Tikvah
Tikvah Means Hope - Patricia Polacco 1163

Trab
Augusta & Trab - Christopher De Vinck 330

Unnamed Character
A Beautiful Feast for a Big King Cat - Bill Martin Jr. 938
Chicago and the Cat - Robin Michal Koontz 778
Chicago and the Cat: The Halloween Party - Robin Michal Koontz 779
The Dog Who Cried Woof - Nancy Coffelt 264
Halloween Mice! - Bethany Roberts 1216
Paper Bird - Arcadio Lobato 885
William's Ninth Life - Minna Jung 716

William
William's Ninth Life - Minna Jung 716

CELESTIAL BODY

Ahnighito
Call Me Ahnighito - Pam Conrad 280

Moon
Cat, Mouse, and Moon - Roxanne Dyer Powell 1171
The Night the Moon Fell Asleep - Rodney Rigby 1212

Moon Man
The Moon Man: A Story - Gerda Marie Scheidl 1279

Sun
Sun Song - Jean Marzollo 946

Unnamed Character
The Moon Was at a Fiesta - Matthew Gollub 485
The Moon Was at a Fiesta - Matthew Gollub 485

CHAMELEON

Nelson
The Warm Place - Nancy Farmer 401

CHEERLEADER

Williams, Cassandra "Cass"
Fall Secrets - Candy Dawson Boyd 129

CHESS PLAYER

Count, Carlton
Countess Veronica - Nancy K. Robinson 1219

CHICKEN

Heckle
The Chick's Trick - Jeni Bassett 84

Hen
The Surprise Family - Lynn Reiser 1205

Hen, Hazel
Hazel Saves the Day - SuAnn Kiser 764

Hen, Hilda
Hilda Hen's Happy Birthday - Mary Wormell 1554
Hilda Hen's Search - Mary Wormell 1555

Henny
Here Comes Henny - Charlotte Pomerantz 1164

Lovejoy, Serena
Buzby to the Rescue - Julia Hoban 626

Minerva Louise
A Hat for Minerva Louise - Janet Morgan Stoeke 1394

Peckle
The Chick's Trick - Jeni Bassett 84

Poulette
Peeping Beauty - Mary Jane Auch 52

Smallest Hen
The Rooster's Gift - Pam Conrad 283

Young Rooster
The Rooster's Gift - Pam Conrad 283

CHIEFTAIN

Unnamed Character
Too Much Talk - Angela Shelf Medearis 1006

CHILD

Aaron
Matzah Ball: A Passover Story - Mindy Avra Portnoy 1170

Abbey
My Island Grandma - Kathryn Lasky 816

Abby
Mommies Don't Get Sick - Marylin Hafner 537

Abe
I'll See You When the Moon Is Full - Susi Gregg Fowler 421

Abebe
The Lion's Whiskers: An Ethiopian Folktale - Nancy Raines Day 325

Abernathy, Joshua
Fig Pudding - Ralph Fletcher 411

Abigail
A Turkey Drive and Other Tales - Barbara Ann Porte 1167

Adam
Adam's War - Sonia Levitin 853

Adam Joshua
The Baby Blues: An Adam Joshua Story - Janice Lee Smith 1351
Serious Science - Janice Lee Smith 1352

Addario, Ben
Starshine and Sunglow - Betty Levin 844

Albie
Albie the Lifeguard - Louise Borden 124

Alex
Dancing - Denys Cazet 226
Father's Rubber Shoes - Yumi Heo 589
River Day - Jane B. Mason 947
Three at Sea - Timothy Bush 185
The Trouble with Mister - Debra Keller 729

Alexander
Alexander, Who's Not (Do You Hear Me? I Mean It!) Going to Move - Judith Viorst 1455

Alice
Dancing Daisy - Kay Gallwey 439
Emily and Alice - Joyce Champion 231
Emily and Alice Again - Joyce Champion 232

Someday a Tree - Eve Bunting 178

Alice Ann
The Key to the Playhouse - Carol Beach York 1586

Allfours, Winni
Winni Allfours - Babette Cole 268

Amanda
Amanda's Perfect Hair - Linda Breiner Milstein 1019
Nine for California - Sonia Levitin 854
The Palace of Stars - Patricia Lakin 808

Amber
Amber on the Mountain - Tony Johnston 702

Amelia
The Giant - Mordicai Gerstein 461

Amy
Lights for Gita - Rachna Gilmore 471
Looking for Diamonds - Brenda Seabrooke 1305
Mary Ann - Betsy James 686
The Pink Party - Maryann Macdonald 914

Andrew
Andrew's Amazing Monsters - Kathryn Hook Berlan 102
Andrew's Angry Words - Dorothea Lachner 802

Angel
Sycamore Street - C.B. Christiansen 247

Angela
Angela's Wings - Eric Jon Nones 1080

Anna
Amber on the Mountain - Tony Johnston 702
Anna's Athabaskan Summer - Arnold Griese 514
Apple Picking Time - Michele Benoit Slawson 1342
The Gift from Saint Nicholas - Dorothea Lachner 803
The Ice Palace - Angela McAllister 957
The New Puppy - Laurence Anholt 35

Anna Sarah "Annala"
Soon, Annala - Riki Levinson 852

Anne
Grandpa Is a Flyer - Sanna Anderson Baker 62

Annie
Annie Bananie Moves to Barry Avenue - Leah Komaiko 775
Annie Flies the Birthday Bike - Crescent Dragonwagon 364
Dance on a Sealskin - Barbara Winslow 1533
Henry and Mudge and the Careful Cousin - Cynthia Rylant 1251

Anthony
You're a Genius, Blackboard Bear - Martha Alexander 24

Anthony "Ant"
My Brother, Ant - Betsy Byars 196

Antonia
Returning Nicholas - Deborah Durland DeSaix 346

Archer, Jenny
Get the Picture, Jenny Archer? - Ellen Conford 278

Arianna
The Dragon and the Unicorn - Lynne Cherry 237

Arthur
Odds on Oliver - Constance C. Greene 500

Aster, Desmond "Diz"
Trouble Will Find You - Joan M. Lexau 870

Aurea "Curry"
The Girl in the Golden Bower - Jane Yolen 1578

Autrie
Indigo and Moonlight Gold - Jan Spivey Gilchrist 469

Babson, Willard
When Willard Met Babe Ruth - Donald Hall 544

Whistle Home - Natalie Honeycutt 639
Willy and May - Judith Byron Schachner 1275
Wind Says Good Night - Katy Rydell 1245
The Wizard Next Door - Peter Glassman 478
The Year of Fire - Teddy Jam 684
Yesterday I Lost a Sneaker (and Found the Great Goob Sick) - David McPhail 996
Yo! Yes? - Chris Raschka 1194
Yo! Yes? - Chris Raschka 1194
You Shall Be King! - Antonie Schneider 1287
You Shall Be King! - Antonie Schneider 1287
Zoo - Anthony Browne 156

Vanegas, Fernando
Fernando's Gift/El Regalo de Fernando - Douglas Keister 728

Vaughan, Nancy
Letting Swift River Go - Jane Yolen 1583

Vernon, Mike "Mikey"
Sticks - Joan Bauer 87

Veronica
The Detective Stars and the Case of the Super Soccer Team - Caroline Levine 848

Victor
Babushka Baba Yaga - Patricia Polacco 1159

Vinson, Luther Wesley "Soup"
Soup Ahoy - Robert Newton Peck 1127

Walter
In America - Marissa Moss 1045
No More Water in the Tub! - Tedd Arnold 43

Wanda
Wanda's Roses - Pat Brisson 139

Warner, Meg
Nothing but Trouble, Trouble, Trouble - Patricia Hermes 592

Warren
Seeds - George Shannon 1318
Worse than the Worst - James Stevenson 1388

Warren, Jenny
The Ghost Witch - Betty Ren Wright 1558

Watson, Borden
There's an Owl in the Shower - Jean Craighead George 452

Watson, Joetta
The Watsons Go to Birmingham—1963 - Christopher Paul Curtis 311

Weasel
The Face in the Bessledorf Funeral Parlor - Phyllis Reynolds Naylor 1065

Wells, Lucy
Lucy's Christmas - Donald Hall 543

Whitefox, Willy
On the Right Track - B.B. Calhoun 198

Whopper, Frannie
On the Road with Poppa Whopper - Marianne Busser 188

Will
Moonlight on the River - Deborah Kovacs 781

Willa
Willa and Old Miss Annie - Berlie Doherty 357

William
The Bear under the Stairs - Helen Cooper 286
The Mighty Santa Fe - William H. Hooks 642
No More Water in the Tub! - Tedd Arnold 43
William and the Good Old Days - Eloise Greenfield 502

Willie
Night in the Barn - Faye Gibbons 462

Willie Jerome
Willie Jerome - Alice Faye Duncan 372

Willis, Rosemary "Rosie"
Under the Bridge - Ellen Kindt McKenzie 985

Wilson, Cissie
The Key to the Playhouse - Carol Beach York 1586

Wylie, Malcolm
Jennifer-the-Jerk Is Missing - Carol Gorman 488

Xiao Ming
In the Snow - Huy Voun Lee 830

Xiao Sheng
The Dragon's Pearl - Julie Lawson 825

Yolen, Velvul "Wolf"
And Twelve Chinese Acrobats - Jane Yolen 1575

Yoshi
Mieko and the Fifth Treasure - Eleanor Coerr 263

Yoshiko
The Crane Girl - Veronika Martenova Charles 233

Young Jack
Sweet Clara and the Freedom Quilt - Deborah Hopkinson 644

Yungsu
Father's Rubber Shoes - Yumi Heo 589

Zachariah, Jr.
Three at Sea - Timothy Bush 185

Zoe
Too Far Away to Touch - Leslea Newman 1071

CHILD-CARE GIVER

Arqueta, Rosa
Gracias, Rosa - Michelle Markel 933

Baba Yaga
Babushka Baba Yaga - Patricia Polacco 1159

Duggan, Zanny
A Voice in the Wind - Kathryn Lasky 819

Greiner, Rachel
Scooter - Vera B. Williams 1523

Humphrey
Lydia Jane and the Baby-Sitter Exchange - Natalie Honeycutt 638

Randolph
Train to Somewhere - Eve Bunting 181

Sump
Saving Sweetness - Diane Stanley 1377

CHILD OF AN ALCOHOLIC

Avery, Freedom Jo
A Share of Freedom - June Rae Wood 1549

Lowe, Patrick
Just Call Me Stupid - Tom Birdseye 108

Williams, Danny
The Trophy - Dean Hughes 662

CHILD OF DIVORCED PARENTS

Barton, Dan
I Hate Company - P.J. Petersen 1137

Brown, Amber
Amber Brown Wants Extra Credit - Paula Danziger 321
You Can't Eat Your Chicken Pox, Amber Brown - Paula Danziger 322

Castello, Billy
Slam Dunk Saturday - Jean Marzollo 944

Christina "Twig"
Blue Sky, Butterfly - Jean Van Leeuwen 1447

Claudia
Step by Wicked Step - Anne Fine 407

Colin
Step by Wicked Step - Anne Fine 407

Davies, Emily Falcon
Falcon's Egg - Luli Gray 497

Dunn, Amy
Amy Dunn Quits School - Susan Richards Shreve 1330

Fred
Dear Fred - Susanna Rodell 1225

Gershom, Noah
The View from Saturday - E.L. Konigsburg 777

Giles, Lizzie
Lizzie's List - Maggie Harrison 564

Grace
Boundless Grace - Mary Hoffman 634
Dear Fred - Susanna Rodell 1225

Harrall, Angela
Angela's Aliens - Janet Taylor Lisle 876

Hoffman, Lydia
Lydia, Queen of Palestine - Uri Orlev 1100

Jones, Herculeah
Dead Letter - Betsy Byars 192

Matt
I Want Answers and a Parachute - P.J. Petersen 1138

Patterson, Hadley
The Light on Hogback Hill - Cynthia DeFelice 335

Pixie
Step by Wicked Step - Anne Fine 407

Priscilla
Priscilla Twice - Judith Caseley 220

Rosen, Elana Rose "Lanny"
Scooter - Vera B. Williams 1523

Sims, Libbie
Libbie Sims, Worry Wart - Gayle Rogers Lockwood 887

Tina
Taxi! Taxi! - Cari Best 105

Tom
Good-Bye, Daddy! - Brigitte Weninger 1499

Tomlin, Paula
The Pickle Song - Barthe DeClements 331

Unnamed Character
Always My Dad - Sharon Dennis Wyeth 1565

Zeller, Chelsea
I Was a Fifth-Grade Zebra - Nancy J. Hopper 645

CHIMPANZEE

Arthur
Arthur's Camp-Out - Lillian Hoban 627

Violet
Arthur's Camp-Out - Lillian Hoban 627

CLASSMATE

Alex
Father's Rubber Shoes - Yumi Heo 589

Boomer, Marty
I'm George Washington and You're Not! - Steven Kroll 789

Carol Ann
Don't Call Me Beanhead! - Susan Wojciechowski 1544

Carter, Dawn
Bye, Bye, Bai Kai - Harriett Luger 904

Kelley, Andrew
Rats! - Jane Cutler 318

Maggie
Insects Are My Life - Megan McDonald 974

Mahoney, Lupe
Flip-Flop Girl - Katherine Paterson 1112

Nelson
Serious Science - Janice Lee Smith 1352

Smith, Jennifer "Jennifer-the-Jerk"
Jennifer-the-Jerk Is Missing - Carol Gorman 488

Unnamed Character
Josepha: A Prairie Boy's Story - Jim McGugan 979

Victor
Insects Are My Life - Megan McDonald 974

COACH

Grandma Nan
Grandmas at Bat - Emily Arnold McCully 966

Grandma Sal
Grandmas at Bat - Emily Arnold McCully 966

Parker
Man Out at First - Matt Christopher 251

COATIMUNDI

Coati
Jaguarundi - Virginia Hamilton 551

COCKROACH

Bagg, Stuart "Shoebag"
Shoebag Returns - Mary James 688

COLLECTOR

Allen, Donavan
Donavan's Word Jar - Monalisa DeGross 337

Bertie
Plantpet - Elise Primavera 1176

Brown, Elizabeth
The Library - Sarah Stewart 1392

Joseph
All the Magic in the World - Wendy Hartmann 567

Midge, Philomena
So Much in Common - Laurie A. Jacobs 682

O'Malley, Oliver
Baseball Card Crazy - Trish Kennedy 735

Pudmuddle
Pudmuddles - Carol Beach York 1587

Trask, Nathan
Bess's Log Cabin Quilt - D. Anne Love 898

COMPANION

Ambrose
Mr. Lunch Takes a Plane Ride - J. Otto
Seibold 1308

Caroline
*When Will This Cruel War Be Over? The Civil War
Diary of Emma Simpson* - Barry Denenberg 340

Lambert, Poco
Angela's Aliens - Janet Taylor Lisle 876

Rusk, Georgina
Angela's Aliens - Janet Taylor Lisle 876

Wolfgang
The Bone Stranger - Frank Remkiewicz 1208

COMPOSER

Tchaikovsky, Peter Ilich
Tchaikovsky Discovers America - Esther Kalman 717

van Beethoven, Ludwig
Beethoven Lives Upstairs - Barbara Nichol 1073

COMPUTER EXPERT

Volnik, Jessup
The Boggart - Susan Cooper 290

Waterford, Mitch
The Fire Bug Connection: An Ecological Mystery -
Jean Craighead George 450

CON ARTIST

Malefetta
Little Kit or, the Industrious Flea Circus Girl - Emily
Arnold McCully 967

CONDUCTOR

Arturo
Arturo's Baton - Syd Hoff 630

Tchaikovsky, Peter Ilich
Tchaikovsky Discovers America - Esther Kalman 717

Tubman, Harriet
*Journey to Freedom: A Story of the Underground
Railroad* - Courtni C. Wright 1562

CONSTRUCTION WORKER

Cheng, Lee
The Iron Dragon Never Sleeps - Stephen
Krensky 787

Daddy
Tar Beach - Faith Ringgold 1215

COOK

Ana
Saturday Market - Patricia Grossman 522

Cookie
Tyrannosaurus Tex - Betty G. Birney 111

Doris
The Know-Nothings - Michelle Sobel Spirn 1372

Fosdyke
Four Famished Foxes and Fosdyke - Pamela Duncan
Edwards 379

Gloria
King Kenrick's Splinter - Sally Derby 345

Hodges
Friday Night at Hodge's Cafe - Tim Egan 382

Mama Ana
Saturday Sancocho - Leyla Torres 1425

Milly
Seven Loaves of Bread - Ferida Wolff 1546

Tante Golda
The Miracle of the Potato Latkes: A Hanukkah Story -
Malka Penn 1129

Unnamed Character
Boy, Can He Dance! - Eileen Spinelli 1367

COUGAR

Charlie
The Fear Place - Phyllis Reynolds Naylor 1066

COUNSELOR

Jim
Lights Out! - John Himmelman 620

COUSIN

Adams, Nora Jean
Harvey's Mystifying Raccoon Mix-Up - Eth
Clifford 259

Alice
*Meg Mackintosh and the Mystery in the Locked
Library* - Lucinda Landon 811

Alice Ann
The Key to the Playhouse - Carol Beach York 1586

Annie
Annie and Cousin Precious - Kay Chorao 241
Henry and Mudge and the Careful Cousin - Cynthia
Rylant 1251

Ben
Around the Oak - Gerda Muller 1049

Birgit
Kisses from Rosa - Petra Mathers 949

Bixby, William
More than a Name - Candice F. Ransom 1189

Brette
Nana's Birthday Party - Amy Hest 605

Brier, Hilary
Back to Before - Jan Slepian 1343

Caroline
Around the Oak - Gerda Muller 1049

Charlie
Charlie and Tyler at the Seashore - Helen Craig 296

Cooper, Sarah-Jane
The Mystery of the Dancing Angels - Elspeth Campbell
Murphy 1050

Danny
Too Many Tamales - Gary Soto 1365

Dawson, Timothy
The Mystery of the Dancing Angels - Elspeth Campbell
Murphy 1050

Dolores
Too Many Tamales - Gary Soto 1365

Erda, Lionel "Linny"
Back to Before - Jan Slepian 1343

Fortune, Pete
The Good Fortunes Gang - Margaret Mahy 922

Fortune, Tessa
Tangled Fortunes - Margaret Mahy 926

Fortune, Tracey
The Good Fortunes Gang - Margaret Mahy 922

Gage, Florence
A Haunted Year - Ann Phillips 1147

Gallagher, Jason
Jason and the Losers - Gina Willner-Pardo 1527

Green, Courtney Alicia
My Crazy Cousin Courtney - Judi Miller 1011

Gregory
Gregory Cool - Caroline Binch 107

Henry
Henry and Mudge and the Careful Cousin - Cynthia
Rylant 1251

Horace
The Giant Baby - Allan Ahlberg 15

Jack
The Ghost of Grania O'Malley - Michael
Morpurgo 1039

Kate
Clean House - Jessie Haas   531

Kee
Water Ghost - Ching Yeung Russell   1242

Larson, Glennis
Harris and Me: A Summer Remembered - Gary
Paulsen   1121

Larson, Harris
Harris and Me: A Summer Remembered - Gary
Paulsen   1121

Lennox
Gregory Cool - Caroline Binch   107

Mabel
Gorgonzola Zombies in the Park - Elizabeth
Levy   858

Macallan, Ellen
Moon Window - Jane Louise Curry   310

Maggie
Nana's Birthday Party - Amy Hest   605

Martin, Emmie
My Cats Nick and Nora - Isabelle Harper   558

McKay, Titus
The Mystery of the Dancing Angels - Elspeth Campbell
Murphy   1050

Megan
The Key to the Playhouse - Carol Beach York   1586

Nakanishi, Yoshito
The Case of the Desperate Drummer - E.W.
Hildick   615

Nick
Around the Oak - Gerda Muller   1049

Prater, Woodrow
Belle Prater's Boy - Ruth White   1509

Precious
Annie and Cousin Precious - Kay Chorao   241

Rosa
Kisses from Rosa - Petra Mathers   949

Taylor, Everett
Jason and the Losers - Gina Willner-Pardo   1527

Twite, Arun
Cold Shoulder Road - Joan Aiken   17

Twite, Is
Cold Shoulder Road - Joan Aiken   17

Tyler
Charlie and Tyler at the Seashore - Helen Craig   296

Unnamed Character
Harris and Me: A Summer Remembered - Gary
Paulsen   1121

Valery, Georges
A Haunted Year - Ann Phillips   1147

Wayne
Sherman the Sheep - Kevin Kiser   762

Willson, Harvey
Harvey's Mystifying Raccoon Mix-Up - Eth
Clifford   259

Yeadon, Meg
Fire in the Wind - Betty Levin   843

Yoji
Great Grandfather's House - Rumer Godden   483

COW

Bossy
Parents in the Pigpen, Pigs in the Tub - Amy
Ehrlich   387

Gerda
Rude Giants - Audrey Wood   1548

Gertrude
The Cow Who Wouldn't Come Down - Paul Brett
Johnson   701

Unnamed Character
The Tiny, Tiny Boy and the Big, Big Cow - Nancy Van
Laan   1445

White Cow
Hunting the White Cow - Tres Seymour   1312

COWBOY

Abuelito
The Gullywasher - Joyce Rossi   1234

Cody, Bill
Buffalo Bill and the Pony Express - Eleanor
Coerr   262

Pete
Tyrannosaurus Tex - Betty G. Birney   111

Sam
Sam's Wild West Show - Nancy Antle   36

Sheriff
Saving Sweetness - Diane Stanley   1377

Unnamed Character
Cowboy Country - Ann Herbert Scott   1301
Just Like My Dad - Tricia Gardella   440

COYOTE

Coyote
Coyote: A Trickster Tale from the American Southwest
- Gerald McDermott   970
Coyote and the Laughing Butterflies - Harriet Peck
Taylor   1408
Coyote and the Magic Words - Phyllis Root   1227
Coyote Steals the Blanket: A Ute Tale - Janet
Stevens   1380
The Tale of Rabbit and Coyote - Tony Johnston   706

CRIME SUSPECT

Magruder, Dolores
The Bomb in the Bessledorf Bus Depot - Phyllis
Reynolds Naylor   1063

CRIME VICTIM

Cole, Amanda
Dead Letter - Betsy Byars   192

Ennis, Sandra
The Case of the Fantastic Footprints - E.W.
Hildick   616

Sullivan, William
Following My Own Footsteps - Mary Downing
Hahn   538

CRIMINAL

Foreman Burglar
The Foxbury Force - Graham Oakley   1088

CROCODILE

Christabel
Victor and Christabel - Petra Mathers   950

Crocker
Yard Sale - James Stevenson   1390

Crocodile
How the Ostrich Got Its Long Neck - Verna
Aardema   1

Fidibus, Anatole
Victor and Christabel - Petra Mathers   950

Lyle
Lyle at the Office - Bernard Waber   1461

Unnamed Character
The Crocodile and the Dentist - Taro Gomi   486
*Ten Sly Piranhas: A Counting Story in Reverse (A
Tale of Wickedness and Worse!)* - William
Wise   1538

Victor
Victor and Christabel - Petra Mathers   950

CROW

Unnamed Character
The Foot Warmer and the Crow - Evelyn
Coleman   274

DANCER

Alice
Dancing Daisy - Kay Gallwey   439

Annie
Dance on a Sealskin - Barbara Winslow   1533

Daisy
Dancing Daisy - Kay Gallwey   439
Moles Can Dance - Richard Edwards   380

Doll, Felicity
Best Enemies Forever - Kathleen Leverich   840

Duncan
Duncan the Dancing Duck - Syd Hoff   632

Emily
Tanya and Emily in a Dance for Two - Patricia Lee
Gauch   446

Fox, Robin
Ribbons - Laurence Yep   1574

Lili
Lili at Ballet - Rachel Isadora   679
Lili on Stage - Rachel Isadora   680

Madame
Ribbons - Laurence Yep   1574

Mia
Nutcracker Noel - Kate McMullan   989

Nina
Nina, Nina Ballerina - Jane O'Connor   1090

Noel
Nutcracker Noel - Kate McMullan   989

Pavelle
The Jewel Heart - Barbara Berger   100

Poulette
Hen Lake - Mary Jane Auch   49
Peeping Beauty - Mary Jane Auch   52

Tanya
Tanya and Emily in a Dance for Two - Patricia Lee
Gauch   446

Tony
Boy, Can He Dance! - Eileen Spinelli   1367

Trunzo, Liesl
Karate Dancer - Doris Buchanan Smith   1350

Unnamed Character
My Mama Had a Dancing Heart - Libba Moore
Gray   496

DAYDREAMER

Buddy
Listen, Buddy - Helen Lester   837

Cloud Eyes
Cloud Eyes - Kathryn Lasky   813

Fortune, Peter
The Daydreamer - Ian McEwan   975

Argo
Argo, You Lucky Dog - Maggie Smith 1355

Bonesy
Bonesy and Isabel - Michael J. Rosen 1229

Boney
The Bone Stranger - Frank Remkiewicz 1208

Bono
The Joy Boys - Betsy Byars 194

Booford
The Booford Summer - Susan Mathias Smith 1356

Buckledown
Buckledown the Workhound - Danny Shanahan 1314

Buggins
Posy Bates, Again! - Helen Cresswell 299

Bun
Mrs. Donald's Dog Bun and His Home Away From Home - William Maxwell 953

Burdle
Out to Lunch - Priscilla Lamont 809

Champ Hobarth
Champ Hobarth - Judith Bernie Strommen 1400

Chuck
Chuck and Danielle - Peter Dickinson 348

Courtney
Courtney - John Burningham 182

Daisy
Worse than the Worst - James Stevenson 1388

Dog
I Am the Dog, I Am the Cat - Donald Hall 542

Dogzilla
Dogzilla - Dav Pilkey 1149

Dooley
Whistle Home - Natalie Honeycutt 639

Duz
Genghis Khan: A Dog Star Is Born - Marjorie Weinman Sharmat 1320

Edison
Faith and the Electric Dogs - Patrick Jennings 693

Edna
Odds on Oliver - Constance C. Greene 500

Ernie
The Dog Who Cried Woof - Nancy Coffelt 264

Fletcher
Something Queer in Outer Space - Elizabeth Levy 861

Fly
Arnie and the Skateboard Gang - Nancy Carlson 211

Freckles
What about My Goldfish? - Pamela D. Greenwood 506

Fred
I'm a Jolly Farmer - Julie Lacome 804

Friday
Dog Friday - Hilary McKay 980

Frisky
Dream Meadow - Helen V. Griffith 518

General/Buzzard Breath
Buzzard Breath - Marty Crisp 304

George
The Baby Blues: An Adam Joshua Story - Janice Lee Smith 1351

Ghost Dog
Ghost Dog - Ellen Leroe 836

Gloria
Officer Buckle and Gloria - Peggy Rathmann 1196

Grace
A Place for Grace - Jean Davies Okimoto 1092

Granite
Child of the Wolves - Elizabeth Hall 545

Harold
Rabbit-Cadabra! - James Howe 657

Henriette
The Trouble with Henriette! - Wende Devlin 347

Henry
The Invisible Dog - Dick King-Smith 748

Hero
Dog Donovan - Diana Hendry 583

Howgego
Out to Lunch - Priscilla Lamont 809

Johnny
Johnny Rides Again - Jo Ann Muchmore 1048

Kashtanka
Kashtanka - Anton Chekhov 235

Kona
Gooseberry Park - Cynthia Rylant 1249

Lassie
Lassie Come-Home - Rosemary Wells 1494

Lester's Dog
Lester's Dog - Karen Hesse 600

Lily
Lily - Abigail Thomas 1414

Lucky
Good Luck, Ronald Morgan! - Patricia Reilly Giff 464
The Junkyard Dog - Erika Tamar 1407

Lucy
Lucy Comes to Stay - Rosemary Wells 1495

Luke
Just in Time for Christmas - Louise Borden 125

Lunch
Mr. Lunch Takes a Plane Ride - J. Otto Seibold 1308

Magdalena
A Sunburned Prayer - Marc Talbert 1406

Maggie
Maggie and Silky and Joe - Amy Ehrlich 386

Marcel
The Sweetest Fig - Chris Van Allsburg 1444

Martha
Martha Calling - Susan Meddaugh 1001
Martha Speaks - Susan Meddaugh 1002

Maxi
Maxi, the Star - Debra Barracca 79

Mercer
No Dogs Allowed - Howie Schneider 1288

Milton
Milton, My Father's Dog - Eric Copeland 291

Mister
The Trouble with Mister - Debra Keller 729

Moose
Earthquake Terror - Peg Kehret 725

Moss
Away to Me, Moss - Betty Levin 842

Mr. Biggins
Grandfather's Christmas Camp - Marc McCutcheon 969

Mudge
Henry and Mudge and the Best Day of All - Cynthia Rylant 1250
Henry and Mudge and the Careful Cousin - Cynthia Rylant 1251

Henry and Mudge and the Wild Wind - Cynthia Rylant 1252

Muffy
Nothing but Trouble - Betty Ren Wright 1561

Murphy
Murphy and Kate - Ellen Howard 653

Mush
Mush, a Dog from Space - Daniel Manus Pinkwater 1155

Mutt
Dog Days for Dudley - Barbara Moe 1026

Nuna
A Sled Dog for Moshi - Jeanne Bushey 186

Oscar
The Hallo-Wiener - Dav Pilkey 1151

Pal
Arthur's New Puppy - Marc Brown 149

Poetry
One Dog Day - J. Patrick Lewis 866

Poky
Watchdog and the Coyotes - Bill Wallace 1472

Pole Dog
Pole Dog - Tres Seymour 1313

Precious
Annie and Cousin Precious - Kay Chorao 241

Puddles
Sophie in the Saddle - Dick King-Smith 752

Red
Watchdog and the Coyotes - Bill Wallace 1472

Rosie
My Dog Rosie - Isabelle Harper 559

Sable
Sable - Karen Hesse 602

Sam
My Dog Talks - Gail Herman 591

Sebastian
Sebastian (Super Sleuth) and the Copycat Crime - Mary Blount Christian 243
Sebastian (Super Sleuth) and the Flying Elephant - Mary Blount Christian 244

Shadow
My Island Grandma - Kathryn Lasky 816

Sharik
Uncle Fedya, His Dog, and His Cat - Eduard Uspenskii 1440

Shiloh
Shiloh Season - Phyllis Reynolds Naylor 1068

Silky
Maggie and Silky and Joe - Amy Ehrlich 386

Skipper
Great Aunt Martha - Rebecca C. Jones 710

Sludge
Nate the Great and the Pillowcase - Marjorie Weinman Sharmat 1321
Nate the Great and the Tardy Tortoise - Marjorie Weinman Sharmat 1322

Sophocles
The Sounds of Summer - David Updike 1438

Sweetie
Watchdog and the Coyotes - Bill Wallace 1472

Tess
The New Puppy - Laurence Anholt 35

Tornado
Tornado - Betsy Byars 197

Tosis, Hally
Dog Breath: The Horrible Trouble with Hally Tosis - Dav Pilkey 1148

Unnamed Character
Can't Sleep - Chris Raschka 1193
City Dog - Karla Kuskin 799
Dog - Robert J. Blake 115
The Night I Followed the Dog - Nina Laden 805
The Story of the Milky Way: A Cherokee Tale - Joseph Bruchac 162
Three Stories You Can Read to Your Dog - Sara Swan Miller 1015

Wart
Wizard and Wart at Sea - Janice Lee Smith 1353

Wellington
The Greatest Show on Earth - John Prater 1174

Zeke
Mr. Putter and Tabby Walk the Dog - Cynthia Rylant 1255

Zippy
Snow Day! - Barbara M. Joosse 713

DOLPHIN

Aster
A Dolphin Named Bob - Twig C. George 453

Bob
A Dolphin Named Bob - Twig C. George 453

DONKEY

Little Donkey
Little Donkey Close Your Eyes - Margaret Wise Brown 152

Ned
Ned - Selina Young 1589

DRIVER

Grandfather
Grandfather's Trolley - Bruce McMillan 987

DUCK

Baby Duck
In the Rain with Baby Duck - Amy Hest 604

Bruno
The Return of Rinaldo, the Sly Fox - Ursel Scheffler 1276
Rinaldo on the Run - Ursel Scheffler 1277

Duck
Don't Fidget a Feather - Erica Silverman 1336
Frog Is Frightened - Max Velthuijs 1453

Duncan
Duncan the Dancing Duck - Syd Hoff 632

Grampa
In the Rain with Baby Duck - Amy Hest 604

Unnamed Character
Friday Night at Hodge's Cafe - Tim Egan 382

DYSLEXIC

Jenkins, Judge
Egg-Drop Blues - Jacqueline Turner Banks 70

Kelso, Katie
The Worst Speller in Jr. High - Caroline Janover 690

Toomey, Brian
My Name Is Brain/Brian - Jeanne Betancourt 106

EAGLE

Fish Eagle
Hungry Hyena - Mwenye Hadithi 536

ECCENTRIC

Bilberry
Across the Blue Mountains - Emma Chichester Clark 238

Fran
Truman's Aunt Farm - Jama Kim Rattigan 1198

Pudmuddle
Pudmuddles - Carol Beach York 1587

ELEPHANT

Chang
Som See and the Magic Elephant - Jamie Oliviero 1094

Daisy
Nightwalkers - Judy K. Morris 1041

Elephant
Just a Little Bit - Ann Tompert 1424
Mouse Party - Alan Durant 376
The Story of the Three Kingdoms - Walter Dean Myers 1057

Ernest
Frank and Ernest on the Road - Alexandra Day 324

Harry
My Friend Harry - Kim Lewis 868

Hodges
Friday Night at Hodge's Cafe - Tim Egan 382

Large
A Quiet Night In - Jill Murphy 1052
A Quiet Night In - Jill Murphy 1052

Little Gray One
Little Gray One - Jan Wahl 1466

Mother Elephant
Little Gray One - Jan Wahl 1466

Tahsha
Sebastian (Super Sleuth) and the Flying Elephant - Mary Blount Christian 244

Thud, Humphrey
Humphrey Thud - Camilla Ashforth 48

Unnamed Character
Elephant Moon - Bijou Le Tord 827

EMPLOYER

Ben
A Day's Work - Eve Bunting 172

Rogers
Good Driving, Amelia Bedelia - Peggy Parish 1108

ENGINEER

Mercer, John
The Banshee Train - Odds Bodkin 119

Ramos, Pedro
The Magic Shell - Nicholasa Mohr 1027

ENTERTAINER

Golly, May-May
The Golly Sisters Ride Again - Betsy Byars 193

Golly, Rose
The Golly Sisters Ride Again - Betsy Byars 193

Maxi
Maxi, the Star - Debra Barracca 79

Nakanishi, Yoshito
The Case of the Desperate Drummer - E.W. Hildick 615

Sam
Sam's Wild West Show - Nancy Antle 36

EQUESTRIAN

Cole, Amanda
Dead Letter - Betsy Byars 192

Gifford, Lilian "Lily"
A Blue for Beware - Jessie Haas 530

Mandy
A Blue for Beware - Jessie Haas 530

EXPLORER

Thornbine
Something Is Growing - Walter Lyon Krudop 796

FANATIC

Nana
Bats about Baseball - Jean Little 881

FARMER

Agnes, Fanny
Fanny's Dream - Caralyn Buehner 166

Albert
Shortcut - David Macaulay 911

Alvah
Alvah and Arvilla - Mary Lyn Ray 1199

Anton
The Swan's Gift - Brenda Seabrooke 1306

Aunt Sally
Tooter Pepperday - Jerry Spinelli 1371

Bert
The Great Pig Escape - Eileen Christelow 242

Brown
The Thing That Bothered Farmer Brown - Teri Sloat 1345

Calvin "Pa"
Parents in the Pigpen, Pigs in the Tub - Amy Ehrlich 387

Clark, Ralph
Apple Valley Year - Ann Turner 1431

Dad
The Storm - Marc Harshman 566

Dan
Kinda Blue - Ann Grifalconi 516

Dat
Down Buttermilk Lane - Barbara Mitchell 1021

Ethel
The Great Pig Escape - Eileen Christelow 242

Farmer
Three Bags Full - Ragnhild Scamell 1273

Father
Snowed In - Barbara M. Lucas 903

Foster, Farmer
Milk Rock - Jeff Kaufmann 723

Goodhart
The Hen That Crowed - Sheila Cole 273

Gramp
Mowing - Jessie Haas 533
No Foal Yet - Jessie Haas 534

Grandad
Baseball Card Crazy - Trish Kennedy 735

Grandfather
The Trouble with Henriette! - Wende Devlin 347

Boundless Grace - Mary Hoffman 634
Branta and the Golden Stone - Walter Wangerin Jr. 1477
Carlos and the Cornfield/Carlos y la Milpa de Maiz - Jan Romero Stevens 1379
Down the Road - Alice Schertle 1281
Dust for Dinner - Ann Turner 1432
Good-Bye House - Robin Ballard 65
Grandfather's Dream - Holly Keller 731
Letting Swift River Go - Jane Yolen 1583
Like Butter on Pancakes - Jonathan London 893
The Matzah That Papa Brought Home - Fran Manushkin 929
The Morning Chair - Barbara M. Joosse 712
On a Starry Night - Natalie Kinsey-Warnock 759
One Round Moon and a Star for Me - Ingrid Mennen 1009
One Saturday Morning - Barbara Baker 61
Papa Tells Chita a Story - Elizabeth Fitzgerald Howard 650
Papa's Stories - Dolores Johnson 697
Priscilla Twice - Judith Caseley 220
Soon, Annala - Riki Levinson 852
The Tangerine Tree - Regina Hanson 556
What You Know First - Patricia MacLachlan 918

Papi
Lights on the River - Jane Resh Thomas 1417

Poppa Bunny
The Dumb Bunnies' Easter - Sue Denim 341

Ragged Robin
The School Mouse - Dick King-Smith 751

Ramos, Pedro
The Magic Shell - Nicholasa Mohr 1027

Rumplemeyer, Bill
On the Right Track - B.B. Calhoun 198

Sandman
A Tooth Fairy's Tale - David Christiana 246

Tesfa
The Lion's Whiskers: An Ethiopian Folktale - Nancy Raines Day 325

Todd, Abbott L.
Bound for Oregon - Jean Van Leeuwen 1448

Totte
The Rose Horse - Deborah Lee Rose 1228

True, Thomas
Josiah True and the Art Maker - Amy Littlesugar 883

Unnamed Character
Amazon Boy - Ted Lewin 865
Boy, Can He Dance! - Eileen Spinelli 1367
The Boy Who Lived with the Seals - Rafe Martin 943
Climbing Kansas Mountains - George Shannon 1316
Eagle Dreams - Sheryl McFarlane 976
Flower Garden - Eve Bunting 173
The Ice Palace - Angela McAllister 957
Is Susan Here? - Janice May Udry 1437
Just Like My Dad - Tricia Gardella 440
Lila's Little Dinosaur - Wolfram Hanel 553
My Father's Hands - Joanne Ryder 1247
Rebel - John Schoenherr 1290
The Shoemaker's Boy - Joan Aiken 18

Watkins
Jimmy Crack Corn - Candice F. Ransom 1188

Watson, Leon
There's an Owl in the Shower - Jean Craighead George 452

Whopper, Poppa
On the Road with Poppa Whopper - Marianne Busser 188

Whyner, Wilber
Willy Whyner, Cloud Designer - Michael Lustig 906

Wilder, Almanzo "Manly"
Little House on Rocky Ridge - Roger Lea MacBride 913

Williams, Evan
The Trophy - Dean Hughes 662

Yamoto
Lily and the Wooden Bowl - Alan Schroeder 1294

FIANCE(E)

Simon
Two's Company - Amanda Benjamin 98

FIREFLY

Unnamed Character
The Very Lonely Firefly - Eric Carle 210

FISH

Bridget
The Wainscott Weasel - Tor Seidler 1309

Fish
Fish and Flamingo - Nancy White Carlstrom 213

Flo
Tom's Fish - Nancy Coffelt 265

Jesse
Tom's Fish - Nancy Coffelt 265

Rainbow Fish
Rainbow Fish to the Rescue! - Marcus Pfister 1145

FISHERMAN

Abbajon
A Million Fish...More or Less - Pat McKissack 986

Caleb
Caleb's Friend - Eric Jon Nones 1081

Ginger Cat
Chin Yu Min and the Ginger Cat - Jennifer Armstrong 39

Granddaddy
Lucky Morning - Sally Noll 1079

Hugh Thomas
A Million Fish...More or Less - Pat McKissack 986

Papa-Daddy
A Million Fish...More or Less - Pat McKissack 986

Shafter, Allen "Alligator"
The Case of the Missing Cutthroats, an Ecological Mystery - Jean Craighead George 448

Shafter, Spinner
The Case of the Missing Cutthroats, an Ecological Mystery - Jean Craighead George 448

Thomas
The Boy and the Giants - Fiona Moodie 1030

FOOTBALL PLAYER

Coogan, John "Crash"
Crash - Jerry Spinelli 1370

FOREMAN

Jim
The Freedom Riddle - Angela Shelf Medearis 1004

FOSTER CHILD

David
Team Picture - Dean Hughes 661

James
Nightwalkers - Judy K. Morris 1041

FOSTER PARENT

Big Jim
Nightwalkers - Judy K. Morris 1041

Paul
Team Picture - Dean Hughes 661

Russell, Priscilla
The Promised Land - Isabelle Holland 637

FOUNDLING

Jip
Jip: His Story - Katherine Paterson 1113

FOX

Flannel
The Foxbury Force - Graham Oakley 1088

Foreman Burglar
The Foxbury Force - Graham Oakley 1088

Fosdyke
Four Famished Foxes and Fosdyke - Pamela Duncan Edwards 379

Fox
A Bear for All Seasons - Diane Marcial Fuchs 433
Don't Fidget a Feather - Erica Silverman 1336
Fox on Stage - James Marshall 936
Mole's Hill - Lois Ehlert 384

Fox, Faraday
What Would Mama Do? - Judith Ross Enderle 392

Fox, Flatfoot
Flatfoot Fox and the Case of the Missing Whoooo - Eth Clifford 258

Fox, Johnny
Rabbit Surprise - Eric L. Houck Jr. 648

Fox, Richard
Rabbit Surprise - Eric L. Houck Jr. 648

Rinaldo
The Return of Rinaldo, the Sly Fox - Ursel Scheffler 1276
Rinaldo on the Run - Ursel Scheffler 1277

Unnamed Character
Peeping Beauty - Mary Jane Auch 52
Red Fox Running - Eve Bunting 176

FRIEND

Addario, Ben
Starshine and Sunglow - Betty Levin 844

Alex
Boys at Work - Gary Soto 1361
Three at Sea - Timothy Bush 185

Alice
Emily and Alice Again - Joyce Champion 232

Amelia
The Giant - Mordicai Gerstein 461

Amy
Lights for Gita - Rachna Gilmore 471
Mary Ann - Betsy James 686
The Pink Party - Maryann Macdonald 914

Andrew
Sophie Is Seven - Dick King-Smith 753

Angel
Sycamore Street - C.B. Christiansen 247

Anna
I've Got Chicken Pox - True Kelley 733

Weekend Girl - Amy Hest   610

Grampa Baby
Feliciana Feydra LeRoux: A Cajun Tall Tale - Tynia
   Thomassie   1418

Grandad
Baseball Card Crazy - Trish Kennedy   735
Patrick's Tree House - Steven Kroll   790

Grandaddy
Grandaddy and Janetta - Helen V. Griffith   519
Grandaddy's Stars - Helen V. Griffith   520
JoJo's Flying Side Kick - Brian Pinkney   1152
Looking for Diamonds - Brenda Seabrooke   1305

Granddaddy
Lucky Morning - Sally Noll   1079

Grandfather
Grandfather's Christmas Camp - Marc
   McCutcheon   969
Grandfather's Dream - Holly Keller   731
Grandfather's Trolley - Bruce McMillan   987
The Luckiest Kid on the Planet - Lisa Campbell
   Ernst   395
Monster Beach - Betty Paraskevas   1107
The Outside Dog - Charlotte Pomefantz   1165
The Trouble with Henriette! - Wende Devlin   347
You Shall Be King! - Antonie Schneider   1287

Grandpa
Bamboozled - David Legge   831
Blue Claws - Walter Lyon Krudop   795
The Butterfly Seeds - Mary Watson   1482
The Cherry Tree Buck and Other Stories - Robin
   Moore   1035
Deep River - Elaine Moore   1032
Doesn't Fall Off His Horse - Virginia A.
   Stroud   1401
Elfsong - Ann Turner   1433
Grandpa Is a Flyer - Sanna Anderson Baker   62
In America - Marissa Moss   1045
Little Rabbit Goes to Sleep - Tony Johnston   705
Lucy's Picture - Nicola Moon   1031
My Dog Rosie - Isabelle Harper   559
Oliver's Vegetables - Vivian French   429
Pearl Plants a Tree - Jane Breskin Zalben   1593
Strudwick: A Sheep in Wolf's Clothing - Robert
   Kraus   786
Traveling Backward - Toby Forward   420
The Wind Garden - Angela McAllister   958
Your Dad Was Just Like You - Dolores Johnson   698

Grandpa Cat
The Tales of Grandpa Cat - Lee Wardlaw   1479

Grandpa Noonie
Ghost Dog - Ellen Leroe   836

Grandpa Toad
Grandpa Toad's Last Secret - Keiko Kasza   721

Grandpapa
*That Wild Berries Should Grow: The Diary of a
   Summer* - Gloria Whelan   1506

Grandpappy
Whistling Dixie - Marcia Vaughan   1452

Grandy
Honkers - Jane Yolen   1582

Great Grandfather
Great Grandfather's House - Rumer Godden   483

Griffin, Linwood
Beware the Mare - Jessie Haas   529

Hammond, Arthur
Celeste and Crabapple Sam - Jennifer Brutschy   163

Harabujy
Peacebound Trains - Haemi Balgassi   63

Howard
The Year of Fire - Teddy Jam   684

John Henry
When Jo Louis Won the Title - Belinda
   Rochelle   1220

Lafler, Grampy Jim
Grass and Sky - Lisa Rowe Fraustino   426

Lito
Pablo's Tree - Pat Mora   1037

Mennym, Magnus
Mennyms Alone - Sylvia Waugh   1485

Noi, Ong
Sweet Dried Apples: A Vietnamese Wartime Chldhood
   - Rosemary Breckler   133

Old Grampa
The Year of No More Corn - Helen Ketteman   741

Papa
Kelly and Me - Carol Lynch Williams   1520

Papa Angelino
Saturday Sancocho - Leyla Torres   1425

Pop
Utterly Yours, Booker Jones - Betsy Duffey   371

Poppa
Poppa's New Pants - Angela Shelf Medearis   1005

Poppy
Fireflies for Nathan - Shulamith Levey
   Oppenheim   1095
Poppy's Chair - Karen Hesse   601

Ryker
Wait and See - Virginia Bradley   131

Scooter
Crash - Jerry Spinelli   1370

Unnamed Character
Grandfather's Journey - Allen Say   1271
Waiting for the Whales - Sheryl McFarlane   977

Whitefeather
The World in Grandfather's Hands - Craig Kee
   Strete   1399

Zayde
Sweet Notes, Sour Notes - Nancy Smiler
   Levinson   851

GRANDMOTHER

Abuela
Isla - Arthur Dorros   362

Ah Pau
First Apple - Ching Yeung Russell   1241
Water Ghost - Ching Yeung Russell   1242

Anica
The Gift of a Traveler - Wendy Matthews   952

Ba
The Lotus Seed - Sherry Garland   443

Beaver, Ann
A Walk to the Great Mystery - Virginia A.
   Stroud   1402

Bess
The Moorchild - Eloise Jarvis McGraw   978

Big Mama
May'naise Sandwiches & Sunshine Tea - Sandra
   Belton   96

Bowman, Grama
Fox Song - Joseph Bruchac   161

Bubbie
My Rotten Redheaded Older Brother - Patricia
   Polacco   1161

Callahan, Sarah "Gramma"
Good-Bye, Hello - Barbara Shook Hazen   577

Dulaney, Lavinia
Caleb's Choice - G. Clifton Wisler   1539

Dutton, Arminda "GrandMin"
Jericho - Janet Hickman   611

Effie
Little Obie and the Kidnap - Martin Waddell   1464

Em
The Children Next Door - Jean Ure   1439

Gert
Annie Bananie Moves to Barry Avenue - Leah
   Komaiko   775

Giddu
Magid Fasts for Ramadan - Mary Matthews   951

Gram
Crossing the Starlight Bridge - Alice Mead   997
Sunshine Home - Eve Bunting   180
Weekend Girl - Amy Hest   610

Gramm
Poppy's Chair - Karen Hesse   601

Gran
Darcy and Gran Don't Like Babies - Jane
   Cutler   315

Grand-mere
The Sugaring-Off Party - Jonathan London   895

GrandAnn
Wrapped in a Riddle - Sharon E. Heisel   579

Grandma
The Big Bike Race - Lucy Jane Bledsoe   117
Busy Bea - Nancy Poydar   1173
Dumpling Soup - Jama Kim Rattigan   1197
The Feather-Bed Journey - Paula Kurzband
   Feder   402
Goodnight Opus - Berkeley Breathed   132
Grandma's Shoes - Libby Hathorn   569
Grandma's Smile - Elaine Moore   1034
Holding onto Sunday - Kathryn O. Galbraith   436
Inside-Out Grandma - Joan Rothenberg   1236
Little Red Riding Hood: A Newfangled Prairie Tale -
   Lisa Campbell Ernst   394
Marigold and Grandma on the Town - Stephanie
   Calmenson   202
My Island Grandma - Kathryn Lasky   816
Sing to the Stars - Mary Brigid Barrett   81
Tanya's Reunion - Valerie Flournoy   413
The Tusk Fairy - Nicola Smee   1348
Valentine - Carol Carrick   215
When I Go Camping with Grandma - Marion Dane
   Bauer   89
The Whispering Cloth: A Refugee's Story - Pegi Deitz
   Shea   1324
White Socks Only - Evelyn Coleman   275
William and the Good Old Days - Eloise
   Greenfield   502

Grandma Jo
Hooray for Grandma Jo! - Thomas McKean   982

Grandma Nan
Grandmas at Bat - Emily Arnold McCully   966

Grandma Nettie
Nettie's Gift - Susan Tews   1413

Grandma Sal
Grandmas at Bat - Emily Arnold McCully   966

Grandma Thora
D.W. the Picky Eater - Marc Brown   151

Grandma Tiny
Poppa's New Pants - Angela Shelf Medearis   1005

Grandmama
Cotton Mill Town - Kathleen Hershey   595
Red Dancing Shoes - Denise Lewis Patrick   1116
*That Wild Berries Should Grow: The Diary of a
   Summer* - Gloria Whelan   1506

Grandmamma
Juliet's Story - William Trevor   1426

Devora
The Fog's Net - Pat Pflieger　1146

Dorabella
Day of the Unicorn - Mollie Hunter　664

Fia
Fairy Wings - Lauren Mills　1018

Gerda
The Snow Queen - Hans Christian Andersen　32

Mariana
In the Palace of the Ocean King - Marilyn
　Singer　1338

Poppy
Poppy - Avi　57

Sweetness
Saving Sweetness - Diane Stanley　1377

Unnamed Character
Beneath the Ghost Moon - Jane Yolen　1577

HIPPO

Midge, Philomena
So Much in Common - Laurie A. Jacobs　682

Milford
Chestnut Cove - Tim Egan　381

HISTORICAL FIGURE

Brewster, William
*A Journey to the New World: The Diary of Remember
　Patience Whipple* - Kathryn Lasky　815

Custer, George Armstrong
Jim-Dandy - Hadley Irwin　677

de Bouchard, Hippolyte
The Stowaway: A Tale of California Pirates - Kristiana
　Gregory　508

Hemmes, Sietze
Father, May I Come? - Peter Spier　1366

Lincoln, Abraham
The Wagon - Tony Johnston　708

Madison, Dolley
Washington City Is Burning - Harriette Gillem
　Robinet　1218

Moses, Phoebe Anne "Annie Oakley"
A Shooting Star: A Novel about Annie Oakley - Sheila
　Solomon Klass　766

Noah
Two by Two by Two - Jonathan Allen　26

Ruth, George Herman "Babe"
When Willard Met Babe Ruth - Donald Hall　544

Stanton, Elizabeth Cady
The Ballot Box Battle - Emily Arnold McCully　963

Washington, George
*The Winter of Red Snow: The Revolutionary War
　Diary of Abigail Jane Stewart* - Kristiana
　Gregory　509

HOCKEY PLAYER

Mason, Mike
Tough Loser - Barthe DeClements　332

HOG

Tillie
The Hog Call to End All! - SuAnn Kiser　765

HORSE

Barney
A Horse Like Barney - Jessie Haas　532

Bella
The Enchanted Horse - Magdalen Nabb　1058

Beware
Be Well, Beware - Jessie Haas　528
Beware the Mare - Jessie Haas　529
A Blue for Beware - Jessie Haas　530

Bonnie
No Foal Yet - Jessie Haas　534

Dancy
Jim-Dandy - Hadley Irwin　677

June
Shortcut - David Macaulay　911

Lucky
Sophie's Lucky - Dick King-Smith　754

Max
The Ice Horse - Candice Christiansen　248

Nicholas
Returning Nicholas - Deborah Durland DeSaix　346

Ninicchio
Danilo the Fruit Man - Amy Valens　1443

Nip
Uncle Daney's Way - Jessie Haas　535

Snowy
Snowy - Berlie Doherty　356

Starbright
Midnight Rider - Krista Ruepp　1238

HORSE TRAINER

Sarah
A Horse Like Barney - Jessie Haas　532

HOTEL WORKER

Buzby
Buzby to the Rescue - Julia Hoban　626

HOUSEHOLDER

Nancy
Wipe Your Feet! - Daniel Lehan　832

Tooley
The House Gobbaleen - Lloyd Alexander　23

HOUSEKEEPER

Bedelia, Amelia
Good Driving, Amelia Bedelia - Peggy Parish　1108

Flower, Margaret "Peggy"
Mr. Potter's Pet - Dick King-Smith　750

Harris, Isabella
Learning by Heart - Ronder Thomas Young　1588

Tsugele
Tsugele's Broom - Valerie Scho Carey　208

Unnamed Character
How the Sky's Housekeeper Wore Her Scarves -
　Patricia Hooper　643

HOUSEWIFE

Arvilla
Alvah and Arvilla - Mary Lyn Ray　1199

Shafter, Becky
*The Case of the Missing Cutthroats, an Ecological
　Mystery* - Jean Craighead George　448

HUMAN

The Giant
A Tooth Fairy's Tale - David Christiana　246

Minnie
Minnie - Annie M.G. Schmidt　1286

Unnamed Character
Pigs Ahoy! - David McPhail　994
Pigs Aplenty, Pigs Galore - David McPhail　995

HUNTER

Anton
The Swan's Gift - Brenda Seabrooke　1306

Cat
Cat, Mouse, and Moon - Roxanne Dyer Powell　1171

Grampa Baby
Feliciana Feydra LeRoux: A Cajun Tall Tale - Tynia
　Thomassie　1418

Unnamed Character
Prize in the Snow - Bill Easterling　378
Red Fox Running - Eve Bunting　176

HYENA

Hungry Hyena
Hungry Hyena - Mwenye Hadithi　536

IGUANA

Dom
The Iguana Brothers: A Tale of Two Lizards - Tony
　Johnston　704

Tom
The Iguana Brothers: A Tale of Two Lizards - Tony
　Johnston　704

IMMIGRANT

Abuelo
A Day's Work - Eve Bunting　172

Adam
The Always Prayer Shawl - Sheldon Oberman　1089

Anna Sarah "Annala"
Soon, Annala - Riki Levinson　852

Ba
The Lotus Seed - Sherry Garland　443

Bram
The Morning Chair - Barbara M. Joosse　712

Gita
Lights for Gita - Rachna Gilmore　471

Hyman, Molly
Make a Wish, Molly - Barbara Cohen　266

Jake
The Butterfly Seeds - Mary Watson　1482

Josepha
Josepha: A Prairie Boy's Story - Jim McGugan　979

Lopez, Maria Isabel Salazar
My Name Is Maria Isabel - Alma Flor Ada　7

Mama
Make a Wish, Molly - Barbara Cohen　266
The Morning Chair - Barbara M. Joosse　712
Soon, Annala - Riki Levinson　852

Massimino
Silver at Night - Susan Campbell Bartoletti　82

Michael
The Dream Jar - Bonnie Pryor　1178

Papa
The Dream Jar - Bonnie Pryor　1178

The Morning Chair - Barbara M. Joosse 712
Soon, Annala - Riki Levinson 852

Peppe
Peppe the Lamplighter - Elisa Bartone 83

Ramos, Jaime
The Magic Shell - Nicholasa Mohr 1027

Singh, Julian
The View from Saturday - E.L. Konigsburg 777

Song Lee
Song Lee in Room 2B - Suzy Kline 773

Unnamed Character
Grandfather's Journey - Allen Say 1271

Valentina
The Dream Jar - Bonnie Pryor 1178

Yungsu
Father's Rubber Shoes - Yumi Heo 589

IMPOSTER

D'Bee, Saratoga
Spider Kane and the Mystery at Jumbo Nightcrawler's - Mary Pope Osborne 1102

Hooks
The House Gobbaleen - Lloyd Alexander 23

INDIAN

Anna
Anna's Athabaskan Summer - Arnold Griese 514

Atuk
Full Worm Moon - Margo Lemieux 835

Beaver, Ann
A Walk to the Great Mystery - Virginia A. Stroud 1402

Beloved Woman
The Story of the Milky Way: A Cherokee Tale - Joseph Bruchac 162

Blackfeather, William
Remember My Name - Sara H. Banks 74

Bowman, Grama
Fox Song - Joseph Bruchac 161

Checha
Sees Behind Trees - Michael Dorris 361

Cloud Eyes
Cloud Eyes - Kathryn Lasky 813

Dustin
A Walk to the Great Mystery - Virginia A. Stroud 1402

Fawn
Night of the Full Moon - Gloria Whelan 1505

Grabber
Children of the Longhouse - Joseph Bruchac 159

Grandmother
Anna's Athabaskan Summer - Arnold Griese 514

Grandpa
Doesn't Fall Off His Horse - Virginia A. Stroud 1401

Gray Fire
Sees Behind Trees - Michael Dorris 361

Jamie
Fox Song - Joseph Bruchac 161

Kapugen
Julie - Jean Craighead George 451

Kapugen, Julie Edwards Miyax
Julie - Jean Craighead George 451

Kchokeen
The Wave of the Sea-Wolf - David Wisniewski 1542

Little Thunder
Wagons West - Roy Gerrard 455

Littlefeets, Spaulding
Santa Calls - William Joyce 715

Mequin
Full Worm Moon - Margo Lemieux 835

Monamie
Full Worm Moon - Margo Lemieux 835

Moshi
A Sled Dog for Moshi - Jeanne Bushey 186

Moss
Guests - Michael Dorris 360

Mother
Anna's Athabaskan Summer - Arnold Griese 514

Ohkwa'ri
Children of the Longhouse - Joseph Bruchac 159

Otsi-stia
Children of the Longhouse - Joseph Bruchac 159

Raven
The Indian School - Gloria Whelan 1504

Reina
The Farolitos of Christmas - Rudolfo Anaya 31

Rosie
A Walk to the Great Mystery - Virginia A. Stroud 1402

Saygee
Doesn't Fall Off His Horse - Virginia A. Stroud 1401

Sixteen, John Three
Dixie in the Big Pasture - Belinda Hurmence 665

Smallhorn, David
Brian's Winter - Gary Paulsen 1119

Someone
The Seasons and Someone - Virginia L. Kroll 794

Sosi
The Mud Family - Betsy James 687

Sunipass, Rayanne
Crossing the Starlight Bridge - Alice Mead 997

Trouble
Guests - Michael Dorris 360

Ts'ina dabju
The Day Sun Was Stolen - Jamie Oliviero 1093

Unnamed Character
The Boy Who Dreamed of an Acorn - Leigh Casler 223
The Boy Who Lived with the Seals - Rafe Martin 943
The Boy Who Lived with the Seals - Rafe Martin 943
The Boy Who Lived with the Seals - Rafe Martin 943
Dance of the Sacred Circle: A Native American Tale - Kristina Rodanas 1223
The First Strawberries: A Cherokee Story - Joseph Bruchac 160
The First Strawberries: A Cherokee Story - Joseph Bruchac 160
The Story of the Milky Way: A Cherokee Tale - Joseph Bruchac 162

Walnut "Sees Behind Trees"
Sees Behind Trees - Michael Dorris 361

Whitefox, Willy
On the Right Track - B.B. Calhoun 198

Young Bull
Cheyenne Again - Eve Bunting 170

INNKEEPER

Dulaney, Lavinia
Caleb's Choice - G. Clifton Wisler 1539

Scrat, Ebenezer "Neezer"
The Twin in the Tavern - Barbara Brooks Wallace 1469

Whipple, Arvella
The Ballad of Lucy Whipple - Karen Cushman 314

INSECT

Buz
Buz - Richard Egielski 383

Hercules
Insects from Outer Space - Frank Asch 47

Unnamed Character
Insects from Outer Space - Frank Asch 47
When the Fly Flew In... - Lisa Westberg Peters 1136

INVENTOR

Aimesworth, Art Atchinson
Santa Calls - William Joyce 715

Parnassus
Blackberry Hollow - Paul Peabody 1123

Peppard, Sam
The Wind Wagon - Celia Barker Lottridge 896

Whyner, Willy
Willy Whyner, Cloud Designer - Michael Lustig 906

JAGUARUNDI

Rundi
Jaguarundi - Virginia Hamilton 551

JOURNALIST

Morgan, Judy
Frindle - Andrew Clements 257

Tibbs
Minnie - Annie M.G. Schmidt 1286

JUDGE

Ryker
Wait and See - Virginia Bradley 131

KIDNAP VICTIM

Fairwick, Amelia
Cousins in the Castle - Barbara Brooks Wallace 1468

Jagamarra, John
The Burnt Stick - Anthony Hill 618

Kate
The Boy and the Giants - Fiona Moodie 1030

Kay
The Snow Queen - Hans Christian Andersen 32

Panetta, Antonio
It Was a Dark and Stormy Night - Allan Ahlberg 16

Smith, Jennifer "Jennifer-the-Jerk"
Jennifer-the-Jerk Is Missing - Carol Gorman 488

KIDNAPPER

Bungaroo, Ralph T.
Charlie Malarkey and the Singing Moose - William Kennedy 736

Charlotte
Cousins in the Castle - Barbara Brooks Wallace 1468

Unnamed Character
The Boy and the Giants - Fiona Moodie   1030

KITTEN

Furby, Alexander
Wonderful Alexander and the Catwings - Ursula K. Le Guin   826

KNIGHT

Dauntless
Day of the Unicorn - Mollie Hunter   664

Fred
The Knight Who Was Afraid to Fight - Barbara Shook Hazen   578

Maladroit
Day of the Unicorn - Mollie Hunter   664

LANDOWNER

Bear
Tops and Bottoms - Janet Stevens   1381

Owyang
The Boy Who Swallowed Snakes - Laurence Yep   1570

LATCH-KEY CHILD

Millie
Palm Trees - Nancy Cote   292

Sam
The Latchkey Dog - Mary Jane Auch   50

Tiffany
Home Lovely - Lynne Rae Perkins   1131

LAWYER

Dunn, Nicole
Amy Dunn Quits School - Susan Richards Shreve   1330

Stebbins, Liz
The 13th Floor: A Ghost Story - Sid Fleischman   409

LEADER

Adam
Adam's War - Sonia Levitin   853

Big Cheese
Dogzilla - Dav Pilkey   1149

Chief
It Was a Dark and Stormy Night - Allan Ahlberg   16

Hopbong, Skippy III
Space Brat 4: Planet of the Dips - Bruce Coville   293

McGurk, Jack P.
The Case of the Desperate Drummer - E.W. Hildick   615

Noah
Too Tired - Ann Turnbull   1430

Sherman
Sherman the Sheep - Kevin Kiser   762

Vor, Cooper "Coop"
Jason and the Escape from Bat Planet - Gery Greer   507

LEARNING DISABLED CHILD

Bess Ann
Last Left Standing - Barbara T. Russell   1240

Jackson, Matthew
Shark in School - Patricia Reilly Giff   468

LEOPARD

Lucky
Spotting the Leopard - Anna Myers   1056

LIBRARIAN

Alice
Meg Mackintosh and the Mystery in the Locked Library - Lucinda Landon   811

Mama
Red Light, Green Light, Mama and Me - Cari Best   104

Pond, Lorna
Mennyms Alone - Sylvia Waugh   1485

Scales, Lotta
The Library Dragon - Carmen Agra Deedy   333

Webber, Alice
Nobody's Daughter - Susan Beth Pfeffer   1142

Whipple, California Morning "Lucy"
The Ballad of Lucy Whipple - Karen Cushman   314

LIGHTHOUSE KEEPER

Bates, Simeon
Abigail's Drum - John A. Minahan   1020

LION

Unnamed Character
A Most Unusual Lunch - Robert Bender   97

LLAMA

Ethan Allen
A Llama in the Family - Johanna Hurwitz   667

LUMBERJACK

Watson, Leon
There's an Owl in the Shower - Jean Craighead George   452

MAGICIAN

Amazing Karlovsky
Rabbit-Cadabra! - James Howe   657

Barnavelt, Jonathan
The Vengeance of the Witch-Finder - John Bellairs   94

Bunnicula
Rabbit-Cadabra! - James Howe   657

Fiddler
Celie and the Harvest Fiddler - Vanessa Flournoy   414

Fidibus, Anatole
Victor and Christabel - Petra Mathers   950

Gupta
Pie Magic - Toby Forward   419

Harry
Passover Magic - Roni Schotter   1291

Hart
Who Is My Neighbor? - Michael Grejniec   513

Teitletot, Jenny
Jazz, Pizzaz, and the Silver Threads - Mary Quattlebaum   1182

Tottibo
The Sorcerer's Apprentice - Nancy Willard   1516

MAIDEN

Beatrix
Rude Giants - Audrey Wood   1548

Bright Willow
The Painted Fan - Marilyn Singer   1339

Mariana
In the Palace of the Ocean King - Marilyn Singer   1338

Unnamed Character
The Saracen Maid - Leon Garfield   441

MARTIAL ARTS EXPERT

Matthews, Troy
Karate Dancer - Doris Buchanan Smith   1350

MATCHMAKER

Everest
Mr. Potter's Pet - Dick King-Smith   750

MECHANIC

Papa
Down the Road - Alice Schertle   1281

MENTALLY CHALLENGED PERSON

Annie
My Sister Annie - Bill Dodds   354

Duster, Oakley
Odd Man Out - Gail Radley   1185

Eddie Lee
Be Good to Eddie Lee - Virginia Fleming   410

Gray, Orin
Fire in the Wind - Betty Levin   843

MENTALLY ILL PERSON

Put
Jip: His Story - Katherine Paterson   1113

MIGRANT WORKER

Martinez, Amelia Luisa
Amelia's Road - Linda Jacobs Altman   29

MILITARY PERSONNEL

Aylee, Pinkus "Pink"
Pink and Say - Patricia Polacco   1162

Bob
My Wartime Summers - Jane Cutler   316

Curtis, Sheldon "Say"
Pink and Say - Patricia Polacco   1162

Custer, George Armstrong
Jim-Dandy - Hadley Irwin   677

Johnston, Willie
Mr. Lincoln's Drummer - G. Clifton Wisler   1540

Meadows, John
An Island Far from Home - John Donahue   358

Mills, Talliaferro "Tally"
When Will This Cruel War Be Over? The Civil War Diary of Emma Simpson - Barry Denenberg   340

Pennington, Robert
An Island Far from Home - John Donahue   358

Moag, Gertrude Elizabeth "Gerty"
The Ghastly Gerty Swindle: With the Ghosts of Hungryhouse Lane - Sam McBratney 959

Molly
Jenius, the Amazing Guinea Pig - Dick King-Smith 749

Mom
The Bear under the Stairs - Helen Cooper 286
The Cabin Key - Gloria Rand 1187
Flower Garden - Eve Bunting 173
If Anything Ever Goes Wrong at the Zoo - Mary Jean Hendrick 582
It's the Bear! - Jez Alborough 20
No More Animals! - Lucia Monfried 1029
So Much - Trish Cooke 284
The Storm - Marc Harshman 566
Surprise! Surprise! - Michael Foreman 417
A Teeny Tiny Baby - Amy Schwartz 1297

Momma
Can't Sit Still - Karen E. Lotz 897
Saturday at the New You - Barbara E. Barber 77

Momma Bunny
The Dumb Bunnies' Easter - Sue Denim 341

Momme
The Rose Horse - Deborah Lee Rose 1228

Mommy
First Snow - Kim Lewis 867
Froggy Learns to Swim - Jonathan London 888
The Long Weekend - Troon Harrison 565
Mommies Don't Get Sick - Marylin Hafner 537
The Painter - Peter Catalanotto 224
Petey's Bedtime Story - Beverly Cleary 256

Monamie
Full Worm Moon - Margo Lemieux 835

Monster Mama
Monster Mama - Liz Rosenberg 1232

Mother
Anna's Athabaskan Summer - Arnold Griese 514
Fly by Night - June Crebbin 298
Princess - Susan L. Roth 1235
The Three Little Wolves and the Big Bad Pig - Eugene Trivizas 1427

Mother Elephant
Little Gray One - Jan Wahl 1466

Mouse, Mama
Mouse TV - Matt Novak 1083

Noodle
George Washington's Ghost - Jane Clark Brown 142

Okino
Okino and the Whales - Arnica Esterl 397

Old Mother Toad
A Song for Little Toad - Vivian French 430

Peckle
The Chick's Trick - Jeni Bassett 84

Pig
Jig, Fig, and Mrs. Pig - Peter Hansard 555

Prater, Belle
Belle Prater's Boy - Ruth White 1509

Queen
Bub: Or the Very Best Thing - Natalie Babbitt 60
The Second Princess - Hiawyn Oram 1099

Rubina
The Swan's Gift - Brenda Seabrooke 1306

Stumpy
Gooseberry Park - Cynthia Rylant 1249

Tavish, Marion McGillicuddy
The Rattlebang Picnic - Margaret Mahy 925

Tillby
Someplace Else - Carol P. Saul 1269

Turner, Judith
Daddy's Climbing Tree - C.S. Adler 11

Unnamed Character
Benjamin Bigfoot - Mary Serfozo 1310
The Boy Who Lived with the Seals - Rafe Martin 943
Gemma and the Baby Chick - Antonia Barber 76
Hi - Ann Herbert Scott 1302
In the Snow - Huy Voun Lee 830
Is Susan Here? - Janice May Udry 1437
Lazy Jack - Vivian French 428
My Working Mom - Peter Glassman 477
Not in the House, Newton! - Judith Heide Gilliland 470
Rebel - John Schoenherr 1290
The Shoemaker's Boy - Joan Aiken 18
Time for Bed - Mem Fox 422
Waiting for the Whales - Sheryl McFarlane 977
When the Wind Stops - Charlotte Zolotow 1598

Walker, Ruth
Meet Addy: An American Girl - Connie Porter 1169

Warren
The Ghost Witch - Betty Ren Wright 1558

Whipple, Arvella
The Ballad of Lucy Whipple - Karen Cushman 314

Whyner, Wanda
Willy Whyner, Cloud Designer - Michael Lustig 906

Wilder, Laura Ingalls "Bess"
Little House on Rocky Ridge - Roger Lea MacBride 913

Williams, Rachel
One Brave Summer - Ann Turner 1434

MOUNTAIN LION

Unnamed Character
Goose and the Mountain Lion - Marian Harris 561

MOUNTAIN MAN

Grandfather
Grandfather's Christmas Camp - Marc McCutcheon 969

MOUNTAIN WOMAN

Joseph, Jumping
Little Obie and the Kidnap - Martin Waddell 1464

MOUSE

Big Cheese
Dogzilla - Dav Pilkey 1149

Blanco, Cedric Whitgift 57th
The Four-Legged Ghosts - Mary Hoffman 635

Cervantes
The Bookstore Mouse - Peggy Christian 245

Charlie
Charlie and Tyler at the Seashore - Helen Craig 296

Chrysanthemum
Chrysanthemum - Kevin Henkes 585

Daisy Dare
Daisy Dare - Anita Jeram 695

Dickory, Tracy
Time and the Clockmice, Etcetera - Peter Dickinson 349

Dormouse
The Sleepy Dormouse - Mark Ezra 399

Field Mouse, Jeremy
Blackberry Hollow - Paul Peabody 1123

Flora
The School Mouse - Dick King-Smith 751

Frances
Babysitting for Benjamin - Valiska Gregory 511

Gray, Henry
Three Terrible Trins - Dick King-Smith 757

Gray, Richard
Three Terrible Trins - Dick King-Smith 757

Gray, Thomas
Three Terrible Trins - Dick King-Smith 757

Hubie
All Aboard! - James Stevenson 1384

Hyacinth
The School Mouse - Dick King-Smith 751

Lilly
Lilly's Purple Plastic Purse - Kevin Henkes 587

Mouse
Cat, Mouse, and Moon - Roxanne Dyer Powell 1171
Just a Little Bit - Ann Tompert 1424
Mouse Party - Alan Durant 376
Mouse's Birthday - Jane Yolen 1584
Newt - Matt Novak 1084
Rhino and Mouse - Todd Starr Palmer 1106

Mouse, Mama
Mouse TV - Matt Novak 1083

Mouse, Papa
Mouse TV - Matt Novak 1083

Muggs, Abbott
The Mystery of King Karfu - Doug Cushman 313

O'Hairy, Scarlett
Dogzilla - Dav Pilkey 1149

Owen
Owen - Kevin Henkes 588

Poppy
Poppy - Avi 57

Ragged Robin
The School Mouse - Dick King-Smith 751

Ragweed
Poppy - Avi 57

Ralph
Babysitting for Benjamin - Valiska Gregory 511

Shirley
What's for Lunch? - John Schindel 1284

Sidney
What's for Lunch? - John Schindel 1284

Slinger
Lilly's Purple Plastic Purse - Kevin Henkes 587

Tyler
Charlie and Tyler at the Seashore - Helen Craig 296

Unnamed Character
A Beautiful Feast for a Big King Cat - Bill Martin Jr. 938
Beneath the Ghost Moon - Jane Yolen 1577
Do You See a Mouse? - Bernard Waber 1459
Halloween Mice! - Bethany Roberts 1216
Inside a Barn in the Country: A Rebus Read-Along Story - Alyssa Satin Capucilli 206
The Mouse Bride - Joy Cowley 295
Two Mice in Three Fables - Lynn Reiser 1207
Two Mice in Three Fables - Lynn Reiser 1207

Victoria
Chrysanthemum - Kevin Henkes 585

Violet
Shy Vi - Wendy Cheyette Lewison 869

Tuttlebee, Matilda
The Great Smith House Hustle - Jane Louise
   Curry   309

Tweezers
Owen - Kevin Henkes   588

Unnamed Character
You Shall Be King! - Antonie Schneider   1287

Warren
Seeds - George Shannon   1318

Wilson, Cissie
The Key to the Playhouse - Carol Beach York   1586

Witherspoon
The Little Tree Growin' in the Shade - Camille
   Yarbrough   1569

Wood, Ben
The Booford Summer - Susan Mathias Smith   1356

NEPHEW

Bleff, Wallace
How I Spent My Summer Vacation - Mark
   Teague   1411

Joel
Tiger Flowers - Patricia Quinlan   1183

Normal, Elliot
Great-Uncle Dracula and the Dirty Rat - Jayne
   Harvey   568

Tommy
Lobster Boat - Brenda Z. Guiberson   525

Truman
Truman's Aunt Farm - Jama Kim Rattigan   1198

Warren
Worse than the Worst - James Stevenson   1388

NIECE

Amanda
The Palace of Stars - Patricia Lakin   808

Cecilia
A Birthday Basket for Tia - Pat Mora   1036

Codie
Lavender - Karen Hesse   599

Gloria
King Kenrick's Splinter - Sally Derby   345

Normal, Emily
Great-Uncle Dracula and the Dirty Rat - Jayne
   Harvey   568

Sarah Jean
Uncle Jed's Barbershop - Margaree King
   Mitchell   1022

Som See
Som See and the Magic Elephant - Jamie
   Oliviero   1094

Sophie
Sophy and Auntie Pearl - Jeanne Titherington   1421

Stella
When Aunt Lucy Rode a Mule and Other Stories -
   Barbara Ann Porte   1168

Susan
The Hanukkah Ghosts - Malka Penn   1128

Tilda
Something for Everyone - Susan Whitcher   1508

Unnamed Character
Great Aunt Martha - Rebecca C. Jones   710
Willy and May - Judith Byron Schachner   1275

Zelda
When Aunt Lucy Rode a Mule and Other Stories -
   Barbara Ann Porte   1168

Zoe
Too Far Away to Touch - Leslea Newman   1071

NOBLEMAN

Duke of Rudling
Lassie Come-Home - Rosemary Wells   1494

NOBLEWOMAN

Dorabella
Day of the Unicorn - Mollie Hunter   664

Wendylyn
The Knight Who Was Afraid to Fight - Barbara Shook
   Hazen   578

NURSE

Marian
Robin's Country - Monica Furlong   434

OCTOPUS

Unnamed Character
Swim for Cover!: Adventure on the Coral Reef - Sue
   Vyner   1458

OFFICE WORKER

Mama
Valentine - Carol Carrick   215

OPOSSUM

Burbank
The Mud Flat Olympics - James Stevenson   1386

ORPHAN

Baird, Swiney
In the Land of the Big Red Apple - Roger Lea
   MacBride   912

Buntz, Taddy
The Twin in the Tavern - Barbara Brooks
   Wallace   1469

Caleb
Caleb's Friend - Eric Jon Nones   1081

Claudine
A Place for Angels - Clyde Robert Bulla   169

Dodge, Gracie
Nobody's Daughter - Susan Beth Pfeffer   1142

Fairwick, Amelia
Cousins in the Castle - Barbara Brooks
   Wallace   1468

Hasbrouck, Emily Lathrop
Nobody's Daughter - Susan Beth Pfeffer   1142

Hobday, Saracen
Tingleberries, Tuckertubs and Telephones - Margaret
   Mahy   927

Ives, Austin
Dear Levi: Letters from the Overland Trail - Elvira
   Woodruff   1550

Ives, Levi
Dear Levi: Letters from the Overland Trail - Elvira
   Woodruff   1550

Kew, Walter
A Message from the Match Girl - Janet Taylor
   Lisle   880

Larkin, Rose
The Root Cellar - Janet Lunn   905

Lavin, Maggie
The Promised Land - Isabelle Holland   637

Lavine, Annie
The Promised Land - Isabelle Holland   637

Little Kit
Little Kit or, the Industrious Flea Circus Girl - Emily
   Arnold McCully   967

Lucy
The Indian School - Gloria Whelan   1504

Mai
The Whispering Cloth: A Refugee's Story - Pegi Deitz
   Shea   1324

Marianne
Train to Somewhere - Eve Bunting   181

Matthew
Matthew and the Sea Singer - Jill Paton Walsh   1114

Maxwell, Gwen
The Ghosts of Mercy Manor - Betty Ren
   Wright   1559

Myron
The Boardwalk Princess - Arthur A. Levine   845

Nickles, Silver Iris
Hound Heaven - Linda Oatman High   612

Nora
Train to Somewhere - Eve Bunting   181

Phillips, Nathaniel
Drums at Saratoga - Lisa Banim   68

Sadie
The Boardwalk Princess - Arthur A. Levine   845

Smathers, Emmeline Sue
A Shooting Star: A Novel about Annie Oakley - Sheila
   Solomon Klass   766

Stebbins, Buddy
The 13th Floor: A Ghost Story - Sid Fleischman   409

Stuart, Annie Rising Fawn
Remember My Name - Sara H. Banks   74

Sweetness
Saving Sweetness - Diane Stanley   1377

Tam
The Moorchild - Eloise Jarvis McGraw   978

Unnamed Character
Dance of the Sacred Circle: A Native American Tale -
   Kristina Rodanas   1223
The Giant Baby - Allan Ahlberg   15

Walter, Richard "Dummy"
Robin's Country - Monica Furlong   434

Whitaker, Lucas
The Apprenticeship of Lucas Whitaker - Cynthia
   DeFelice   334

OSTRICH

Oliver
The Cuckoo Child - Dick King-Smith   747

Ostrich
How the Ostrich Got Its Long Neck - Verna
   Aardema   1

OUTCAST

Elvira
Elvira - Margaret Shannon   1319

Peterson, J.P.
Shark in School - Patricia Reilly Giff   468

OUTLAW

Chief
It Was a Dark and Stormy Night - Allan Ahlberg   16

Featherbone, Calvin Thaddeus
The Gentleman Outlaw and Me—Eli - Mary Downing Hahn   539

Hood, Robin
Robin's Country - Monica Furlong   434

Roscoe
The Gentleman Outlaw and Me—Eli - Mary Downing Hahn   539

Wild Willie
Moony B. Finch, the Fastest Draw in the West - David McPhail   993

OWL

Bardy
There's an Owl in the Shower - Jean Craighead George   452

Blink
Fly by Night - June Crebbin   298

Harold
The Mud Flat Olympics - James Stevenson   1386

Mother
Fly by Night - June Crebbin   298

Ocax
Poppy - Avi   57

Owl, Mournful
Flatfoot Fox and the Case of the Missing Whoooo - Eth Clifford   258

OX

Matthew
Yard Sale - James Stevenson   1390

PANDA

Little Panda
Surprise! Surprise! - Michael Foreman   417

Mom
Surprise! Surprise! - Michael Foreman   417

PARAPLEGIC

Mama
Mama Zooms - Jane Cowen-Fletcher   294

PATIENT

Hugo
Going Home - Margaret Wild   1512

Stukeley, Sarah
The Apprenticeship of Lucas Whitaker - Cynthia DeFelice   334

Unnamed Character
Barney Is Best - Nancy White Carlstrom   212

PATRIOT

Parker, Emily
A Spy in the King's Colony - Lisa Banim   69

PEACOCK

Percival
Hen Lake - Mary Jane Auch   49

PEDDLER

Danilo
Danilo the Fruit Man - Amy Valens   1443

Meeks
Here Comes the Mystery Man - Scott Russell Sanders   1264

Petit Jean
Three Sacks of Truth: A Story from France - Eric A. Kimmel   744

Pumpkin Man
The Pumpkin Man from Piney Creek - Darleen Bailey Beard   91

PENGUIN

Opus
Goodnight Opus - Berkeley Breathed   132

Penguin
The Emperor Penguin's New Clothes - Janet Perlman   1132

Quigley
Quickly, Quigley - Jeanne M. Gravois   494

Tacky
Three Cheers for Tacky - Helen Lester   838

PHILANTHROPIST

Claus, Santa
Harvey Slumfenburger's Christmas Present - John Burningham   183

PHOTOGRAPHER

Grampa
Weekend Girl - Amy Hest   610

Lacy, John
Pioneer Bear - Joan Sandin   1266

Muggs, Abbott
The Mystery of King Karfu - Doug Cushman   313

PIG

Amanda
Oliver & Amanda and the Big Snow - Jean Van Leeuwen   1450

Annabel
Annabel Again - Janice Boland   122

Arnold
The Wimp - Kathy Caple   204

Bunny
Tuck in the Pool - Martha Weston   1502

Dan
The Pigrates Clean Up - Steven Kroll   791

Eloise
Chestnut Cove - Tim Egan   381

Fig
Jig, Fig, and Mrs. Pig - Peter Hansard   555

Fred
Pigs Ahoy! - David McPhail   994

Geraldine
Geraldine's Baby Brother - Holly Keller   730

Hamlet
Hamlet and the Enormous Chinese Dragon Kite - Brian Lies   872

Jig
Jig, Fig, and Mrs. Pig - Peter Hansard   555

Julius
Julius - Angela Johnson   696

Kate
The Pigrates Clean Up - Steven Kroll   791

Little Pink Pig
Little Pink Pig - Pat Hutchins   673

Oliver
Oliver & Amanda and the Big Snow - Jean Van Leeuwen   1450

Pig
Frog Is Frightened - Max Velthuijs   1453
Jig, Fig, and Mrs. Pig - Peter Hansard   555

Pig, Garth
Garth Pig Steals the Show - Mary Rayner   1202

Pig, William
Garth Pig Steals the Show - Mary Rayner   1202

Pippin, Zeke
Zeke Pippin - William Steig   1378

Preston
Suddenly! - Colin McNaughton   991

Rose
The Wimp - Kathy Caple   204

Slagbottom
The Mystery of King Karfu - Doug Cushman   313

Tom
Tom's Tail - Linda Jennings   692

Tuck
Tuck in the Pool - Martha Weston   1502

Unnamed Character
Hog-Eye - Susan Meddaugh   1000
The Three Little Pigs - Harriet Ziefert   1595
The Three Little Wolves and the Big Bad Pig - Eugene Trivizas   1427

Willie
Geraldine's Baby Brother - Holly Keller   730

PILOT

Mangold
The Greatest Show off Earth - Margaret Mahy   923

Tibbets
Hiroshima - Laurence Yep   1572

PIRANHA

Unnamed Character
Ten Sly Piranhas: A Counting Story in Reverse (A Tale of Wickedness and Worse!) - William Wise   1538

PIRATE

Abdul
Captain Abdul's Pirate School - Colin McNaughton   990

Bonney, Anne
The Ballad of the Pirate Queens - Jane Yolen   1576

Dan
The Pigrates Clean Up - Steven Kroll   791

de Bouchard, Hippolyte
The Stowaway: A Tale of California Pirates - Kristiana Gregory   508

Gallows, Grudge
Tingleberries, Tuckertubs and Telephones - Margaret Mahy   927

Lugo, Lumpy "Bugbeard"
Ned Feldman, Space Pirate - Daniel Manus Pinkwater   1156

O'Malley, Grania
The Ghost of Grania O'Malley - Michael Morpurgo   1039

RAT

Finster
Great-Uncle Dracula and the Dirty Rat - Jayne
   Harvey   568

Rat
The Fat Cat Sat on the Mat - Nurit Karlan   718
The Rat and the Tiger - Keiko Kasza   722

Ratburn
Arthur Writes a Story - Marc Brown   145

RECLUSE

Crabapple Sam
Celeste and Crabapple Sam - Jennifer Brutschy   163

Grimm, Matthew
Midnight Rider - Krista Ruepp   1238

Old Judge
Gold in the Hills - Laurie Lawlor   824

REFUGEE

Cole, Bertrand "Berti"
A Different Kind of Courage - Ellen Howard   651

Father
When I Left My Village - Maxine Rose Schur   1296

Grandma
The Whispering Cloth: A Refugee's Story - Pegi Deitz
   Shea   1324

Hanni
The Hanukkah Ghosts - Malka Penn   1128

Mai
The Whispering Cloth: A Refugee's Story - Pegi Deitz
   Shea   1324

Menelik
When I Left My Village - Maxine Rose Schur   1296

Noi, Lieu
Sweet Dried Apples: A Vietnamese Wartime Chldhood
   - Rosemary Breckler   133

Sarach, Zina
A Different Kind of Courage - Ellen Howard   651

Simcha
When I Left My Village - Maxine Rose Schur   1296

RELIGIOUS

Alice
Good-Bye, Hello - Barbara Shook Hazen   577

Elijah
Dear Elijah - Miriam Bat-Ami   85

Emma
The Indian School - Gloria Whelan   1504

Filkins, James J.
Save Halloween! - Stephanie Tolan   1422

Filkins, T.T.
Save Halloween! - Stephanie Tolan   1422

Mary Rose
Hey You, Sister Rose - Eileen Walsh Strauch   1398

Rabbi
Yettele's Feathers - Joan Rothenberg   1237

Sigfried
The Bookstore Mouse - Peggy Christian   245

Tetsuzan
The Loyal Cat - Lensey Namioka   1059

REPAIRMAN

Unnamed Character
Time and the Clockmice, Etcetera - Peter
   Dickinson   349

RESEARCHER

Thomas, Andy
Search for the Shadowman - Joan Lowery
   Nixon   1076

RESISTANCE FIGHTER

Andersen, Elise
Into the Flames - Robert Elmer   388

Andersen, Peter
Into the Flames - Robert Elmer   388

RESTAURATEUR

Marc
The Van Gogh Cafe - Cynthia Rylant   1256

RHINOCEROS

Gregor
Tilly and the Rhinoceros - Sheila White
   Samton   1260

Rhino
Rhino and Mouse - Todd Starr Palmer   1106

RODEO RIDER

Harmony Jean
Armadillo Rodeo - Jan Brett   135

ROOSTER

Charlene
The Hen That Crowed - Sheila Cole   273

Kookoory
That Kookoory! - Margaret Walden Froehlich   432

Rooster
Rooster Crows - Ragnhild Scamell   1272

ROYALTY

Arianna
The Dragon and the Unicorn - Lynne Cherry   237

Babette
*Tom, Babette, & Simon: Three Tales of
   Transformation* - Avi   58

Bennett
Florizella and the Wolves - Philippa Gregory   510

Deodatus
The Seal Prince - Sheila MacGill Callahan   200

Dhutmose
Pepi and the Secret Names - Jill Paton Walsh   1115

Dragon King
The Rabbit's Escape - Suzanne Crowder Han   552

Florizella
Florizella and the Wolves - Philippa Gregory   510

Gordo
The Royal Nap - Charles C. Black   112

Grainne
The Seal Prince - Sheila MacGill Callahan   200

Happy Prince
The Happy Prince - Oscar Wilde   1515

Kchokeen
The Wave of the Sea-Wolf - David Wisniewski   1542

Kenrick
King Kenrick's Splinter - Sally Derby   345

King
Bub: Or the Very Best Thing - Natalie Babbitt   60
The Second Princess - Hiawyn Oram   1099

Kip
Fairy Wings - Lauren Mills   1018

Leopold
Princess - Anne Wilsdorf   1529

Milford
Chestnut Cove - Tim Egan   381

Molly the Messy, the Me
Tumble Tower - Anne Tyler   1435

Nautilus
Prince Nautilus - Laura Krauss Melmed   1008

Ocean King
In the Palace of the Ocean King - Marilyn
   Singer   1338

Pendragon, Arthur
Arthur, High King of Britain - Michael
   Morpurgo   1038

Penguin
The Emperor Penguin's New Clothes - Janet
   Perlman   1132

Pin
Jimmy, the Pickpocket of the Palace - Donna Jo
   Napoli   1061

Prince
Bub: Or the Very Best Thing - Natalie Babbitt   60
Cabbage Rose - Mary-Claire Helldorfer   580

Queen
Bub: Or the Very Best Thing - Natalie Babbitt   60
The Second Princess - Hiawyn Oram   1099

Rahotep
The Egyptian Polar Bear - JoAnn Adinolfi   9

Rupert
Cinder Edna - Ellen Jackson   681

Sally
Jimmy, the Pickpocket of the Palace - Donna Jo
   Napoli   1061

Second Princess
The Second Princess - Hiawyn Oram   1099

Si Ling-Chi
The Empress and the Silkworm - Lily Toy Hong   640

Simon of Hargrave
The Battle for the Castle - Elizabeth Winthrop   1537

Thomas the Tidy, the Ti
Tumble Tower - Anne Tyler   1435

Unnamed Character
I Am Really a Princess - Carol Diggory
   Shields   1329
The Princess and the Lord of Night - Emma
   Bull   168
Three Sacks of Truth: A Story from France - Eric A.
   Kimmel   744
Three Sacks of Truth: A Story from France - Eric A.
   Kimmel   744

Victoria
The Swoose - Dick King-Smith   756

RULER

Elephant
The Story of the Three Kingdoms - Walter Dean
   Myers   1057

Hawk
The Story of the Three Kingdoms - Walter Dean
    Myers 1057

Ocax
Poppy - Avi 57

Shang
The Painted Fan - Marilyn Singer 1339

Shark
The Story of the Three Kingdoms - Walter Dean
    Myers 1057

RUNAWAY

Dalton, Jack
Back to Bataan - Jerome Charyn 234

Hickathrift, Henrietta "Henny"
The Stray - Dick King-Smith 755

Jabila
The Warm Place - Nancy Farmer 401

Josh
The Watchers: A Mystery at Alton Towers - Helen
    Cresswell 300

Katy
The Watchers: A Mystery at Alton Towers - Helen
    Cresswell 300

Krupnik, Sam
See You Around, Sam! - Lois Lowry 902

Phillips, Nathaniel
Drums at Saratoga - Lisa Banim 68

Pippin, Zeke
Zeke Pippin - William Steig 1378

Prater, Belle
Belle Prater's Boy - Ruth White 1509

Sarah
My Real Family - Emily Arnold McCully 968

Uncle Fedya
Uncle Fedya, His Dog, and His Cat - Eduard
    Uspenskii 1440

Yates, Eliza "Elijah Bates"
The Gentleman Outlaw and Me—Eli - Mary Downing
    Hahn 539

RUNNER

Webb, Penn
Crash - Jerry Spinelli 1370

SAILOR

Hare, Timothy
Mary Patten's Voyage - Richard Berleth 103

The Man
Henry the Sailor Cat - Mary Calhoun 199

Patten, Joshua
Mary Patten's Voyage - Richard Berleth 103

Pudge
First Came the Owl - Judith Benet Richardson 1210

Slocum, Joshua
Moonlight on the River - Deborah Kovacs 781

SALAMANDER

Newt
Newt - Matt Novak 1084

Pip
Pip's Magic - Ellen Stoll Walsh 1476

SCIENTIST

Dillon, David A. "Dr. D"
Stolen Bones - Joan Carris 216

Everring, Hilda E.
Not-So-Normal Norman - Cynthia Stowe 1395

Mercer, Maggie
The Fire Bug Connection: An Ecological Mystery -
    Jean Craighead George 450

Rumplemeyer, Bill
On the Right Track - B.B. Calhoun 198

Weinerstein
Hilda and the Mad Scientist - Addie Adam 8

SEA CAPTAIN

Brewster, William
*A Journey to the New World: The Diary of Remember
    Patience Whipple* - Kathryn Lasky 815

Krutch
Pigs Ahoy! - David McPhail 994

Papa
Bluewater Journal: The Voyage of the Sea Tiger -
    Loretta Krupinski 797

SEAL

Deodatus
The Seal Prince - Sheila MacGill Callahan 200

SEAMSTRESS

Eddington, Sarah
A Shooting Star: A Novel about Annie Oakley - Sheila
    Solomon Klass 766

Elizabeth
My Apron - Eric Carle 209

Granny
The Log Cabin Quilt - Ellen Howard 652

Penshaw, Kate
The Mennyms - Sylvia Waugh 1484

Rachel
Sweet Clara and the Freedom Quilt - Deborah
    Hopkinson 644

Sadie
The Boardwalk Princess - Arthur A. Levine 845

SECRETARY

Bowsa
Buckledown the Workhound - Danny Shanahan 1314

SECURITY OFFICER

Unnamed Character
Night of the Gargoyles - Eve Bunting 175

SERVANT

Beetle
The Twin in the Tavern - Barbara Brooks
    Wallace 1469

Freeman, Ben
Drums at Saratoga - Lisa Banim 68

Gerald
The Royal Nap - Charles C. Black 112

Jig
Jig, Fig, and Mrs. Pig - Peter Hansard 555

Phoebe
The Royal Nap - Charles C. Black 112

Seahorse
The Painted Fan - Marilyn Singer 1339

Sho
On Cat Mountain - Francoise Richard 1209

SETTLER

Bonner, Cole Joseph "Coley Joe"
Search for the Shadowman - Joan Lowery
    Nixon 1076

Effie
Little Obie and the Kidnap - Martin Waddell 1464

Elvirey
The Log Cabin Quilt - Ellen Howard 652

Father
Snowed In - Barbara M. Lucas 903

Little Obie
Little Obie and the Kidnap - Martin Waddell 1464

Lundstrom
Clouds of Terror - Catherine A. Welch 1489

Ma
Black-Eyed Susan - Jennifer Armstrong 38

McClure, Jonathan
The Floating House - Scott Russell Sanders 1263

McClure, Mary
The Floating House - Scott Russell Sanders 1263

McClure, Wayne
The Floating House - Scott Russell Sanders 1263

Mitchell, Libby
Night of the Full Moon - Gloria Whelan 1505

Pap
The Log Cabin Quilt - Ellen Howard 652

Sawyer, Humility "Hummy"
*A Journey to the New World: The Diary of Remember
    Patience Whipple* - Kathryn Lasky 815

Susie
Black-Eyed Susan - Jennifer Armstrong 38

Whipple, California Morning "Lucy"
The Ballad of Lucy Whipple - Karen Cushman 314

Whipple, Remember Patience "Mem"
*A Journey to the New World: The Diary of Remember
    Patience Whipple* - Kathryn Lasky 815

Whitcher, Sarah
The Bear That Heard Crying - Natalie Kinsey-
    Warnock 758

SHARK

Shark
The Story of the Three Kingdoms - Walter Dean
    Myers 1057

SHEEP

Benjy
Nora's Surprise - Satomi Ichikawa 675

Blanche
My Real Family - Emily Arnold McCully 968

Grandpa
Pearl Plants a Tree - Jane Breskin Zalben 1593

LaFondue, Cashmere
Sheep Dreams - Arthur A. Levine 847

Millie
Three Bags Full - Ragnhild Scamell 1273

Pearl
Pearl Plants a Tree - Jane Breskin Zalben 1593

Sherman
Sherman the Sheep - Kevin Kiser 762

Gaila
Bear E. Bear - Susan Straight   1396

Geraldine
Geraldine's Baby Brother - Holly Keller   730

Gina
Little Champ - Jim Arnosky   44

Golly, May-May
The Golly Sisters Ride Again - Betsy Byars   193

Golly, Rose
The Golly Sisters Ride Again - Betsy Byars   193

Grace
Dear Fred - Susanna Rodell   1225
Snowed In - Barbara M. Lucas   903

Gracie
My Dad - Niki Daly   319

Hannah
The Tie Man's Miracle: A Chanukah Tale - Steven
   Schnur   1289

Hocky, Holly
The Happy Hocky Family - Lane Smith   1354

Hoong Wei
Rabbit Mooncakes - Hoong Yee Lee Krakauer   783

Hoong Yee
Rabbit Mooncakes - Hoong Yee Lee Krakauer   783

Ivy
The Hayloft - Lisa Westberg Peters   1135

Jacobson, Rosy
Starlight and Candles: The Joys of the Sabbath - Fran
   Manushkin   931

Jenna
Mama, Coming and Going - Judith Caseley   219

Jennifer
Jennifer, Too - Juanita Havill   572
Two Girls in Sister Dresses - Jean Van
   Leeuwen   1451

Jess
Kid Kibble - Diana Hendry   584

Jessann
Ragsale - Artie Ann Bates   86

Jill
Summer's End - Maribeth Boelts   121

Johnson, Ginger
Never Trust a Sister over Twelve - Stephen
   Roos   1226

Johnson, Suki
Never Trust a Sister over Twelve - Stephen
   Roos   1226

Judy
Willie Jerome - Alice Faye Duncan   372

Kamornick, Hannah
Sarah, Also Known as Hannah - Lillian Hammer
   Ross   1233

Kamornick, Sarah
Sarah, Also Known as Hannah - Lillian Hammer
   Ross   1233

Kat
Kit and Kat - Tomie De Paola   328

Katie
One Up, One Down - Carol Snyder   1358

Keisha
Baby Jesus, Like My Brother - Margery Wheeler
   Brown   153

Kenney, Jo-Munro
Numbskulls - William Taylor   1410

Krupnik, Anastasia
See You Around, Sam! - Lois Lowry   902

Leanne
When I Grow Bigger - Trish Cooke   285

Leila
On Winter's Wind - Patricia Hermes   593

Lilly
Rex and Lilly Family Time - Laurie Krasny
   Brown   143

Lily
The Rose Horse - Deborah Lee Rose   1228

Lindsay
Courtyard Cat - C.S. Adler   10

Louise
Lionel in the Winter - Stephen Krensky   788

Lucy
Big Help! - Anna Grossnickle Hines   621

Lundstrom, Helga
Clouds of Terror - Catherine A. Welch   1489

Mackintosh, Meg
*Meg Mackintosh and the Mystery in the Locked
   Library* - Lucinda Landon   811

Maggy
Dust for Dinner - Ann Turner   1432

Magruder, Dolores
The Bomb in the Bessledorf Bus Depot - Phyllis
   Reynolds Naylor   1063

Marie
Mac and Marie and the Train Toss Surprise -
   Elizabeth Fitzgerald Howard   649

Marion
Andrew's Angry Words - Dorothea Lachner   802

Marlin, Rose
Johnny Rides Again - Jo Ann Muchmore   1048

Marta
The Night Crossing - Karen Ackerman   4

Martha
A Baby Just Like Me - Susan Winter   1534

Mary
John Joe and the Big Hen - Martin Waddell   1462

Mason, Jenna
Tough Loser - Barthe DeClements   332

Matthews, Vinnie
Flip-Flop Girl - Katherine Paterson   1112

Maxine "Girl Wonder"
Girl Wonder and the Terrific Twins - Malorie
   Blackman   113

McClain, Tasha
Junebug - Alice Mead   998

McClure, Mary
The Floating House - Scott Russell Sanders   1263

McLinn, Missy
A Place to Belong - Emily Crofford   305

Megan
Maybe Yes, Maybe No, Maybe Maybe - Susan
   Patron   1118

Mequin
Full Worm Moon - Margo Lemieux   835

Michaels, Elisa
Make Room for Elisa - Johanna Hurwitz   668

Milly
Seven Loaves of Bread - Ferida Wolff   1546

Mimi
Roommates Again - Kathryn O. Galbraith   437

Minter, Claire
The Timekeeper - Emily Rodda   1224

Molly
Passover Magic - Roni Schotter   1291

Two Girls in Sister Dresses - Jean Van
   Leeuwen   1451

Molly the Messy, the Me
Tumble Tower - Anne Tyler   1435

Naomi
Night Lights: A Sukkot Story - Barbara Diamond
   Goldin   484

Nekatu
Croco'nile - Roy Gerrard   454

Noodle, Celinda
George Washington's Ghost - Jane Clark Brown   142

Nora
Emily and Alice Again - Joyce Champion   232

O'Malley, Samantha
Baseball Card Crazy - Trish Kennedy   735

Orton, Kelly
Adeline Street - Carol Lynch Williams   1519
Kelly and Me - Carol Lynch Williams   1520

Orton, Leah
Kelly and Me - Carol Lynch Williams   1520

Philomena
That's Philomena! - Catherine Bancroft   67

PK
Maybe Yes, Maybe No, Maybe Maybe - Susan
   Patron   1118

Potter, Bridget
The Wimp of the World - Alison Cragin Herzig   596

Rachel
The Feather-Bed Journey - Paula Kurzband
   Feder   402

Rebecca "Rabbit"
Maybe Yes, Maybe No, Maybe Maybe - Susan
   Patron   1118

Rex
Pinky and Rex and the New Baby - James Howe   656

Robin, Eve
Best Enemies Forever - Kathleen Leverich   840

Robin, Priscilla
Best Enemies Forever - Kathleen Leverich   840

Rose
Seven Loaves of Bread - Ferida Wolff   1546
The Wimp - Kathy Caple   204

Rosie
The Great Pumpkin Switch - Megan McDonald   973

Ruby
Max and Ruby's First Greek Myth: Pandora's Box -
   Rosemary Wells   1496
Max and Ruby's Midas: Another Greek Myth -
   Rosemary Wells   1497

Sherwin-Hendicks, Beatrice Lorraine "Beany"
Don't Call Me Beanhead! - Susan
   Wojciechowski   1544

Sims, Maggie
Libbie Sims, Worry Wart - Gayle Rogers
   Lockwood   887

Slocum, Isabel
Bluewater Journal: The Voyage of the Sea Tiger -
   Loretta Krupinski   797

Stebbins, Liz
The 13th Floor: A Ghost Story - Sid Fleischman   409

Stella
When Aunt Lucy Rode a Mule and Other Stories -
   Barbara Ann Porte   1168

Sylvie
All the Places to Love - Patricia MacLachlan   916

Tara
Tiger Flowers - Patricia Quinlan   1183

Todd, Louvina
Bound for Oregon - Jean Van Leeuwen   1448

Todd, Mary Ellen
Bound for Oregon - Jean Van Leeuwen   1448

Trelling, Julie
Up a Road Slowly - Irene Hunt   663

Turner, Jessica
Daddy's Climbing Tree - C.S. Adler   11

Unnamed Character
The Carousel - Liz Rosenberg   1231
The Carousel - Liz Rosenberg   1231
Down at Angel's - Sharon Chmielarz   239
Down at Angel's - Sharon Chmielarz   239
In Search of the Giant - Jeanne Willis   1524
It's Pumpkin Time! - Zoe Hall   546
Summer Sands - Sherry Garland   444
Summer's End - Maribeth Boelts   121
Tomorrow on Rocky Pond - Lynn Reiser   1206

Violet
Arthur's Camp-Out - Lillian Hoban   627

Webster, Claudia
Partners - Karen Waggoner   1465

Wells, Caroline
Lucy's Christmas - Donald Hall   543

Wells, Lucy
Lucy's Christmas - Donald Hall   543

West, Annie
Going to See Grassy Ella - Kathryn Lance   810

Witting, Anna
Skylark - Patricia MacLachlan   917

Yoshiko
The Crane Girl - Veronika Martenova Charles   233

Zelda
When Aunt Lucy Rode a Mule and Other Stories - Barbara Ann Porte   1168

SKUNK

Skunk
James Bear and the Goose Gathering - Jim Latimer   821

SLAVE

Africa
True North - Kathryn Lasky   818

Araminta "Minty"
Minty: A Story of Young Harriet Tubman - Alan Schroeder   1295

Aylee, Moe Moe Bay
Pink and Say - Patricia Polacco   1162

Aylee, Pinkus "Pink"
Pink and Say - Patricia Polacco   1162

Hezekiah
The Foot Warmer and the Crow - Evelyn Coleman   274

Jim
The Freedom Riddle - Angela Shelf Medearis   1004

Joshua
Journey to Freedom: A Story of the Underground Railroad - Courtni C. Wright   1562

Lettie
Jumping the Broom - Courtni C. Wright   1563

Nathan
Journey to Freedom: A Story of the Underground Railroad - Courtni C. Wright   1562

Old Ben
Minty: A Story of Young Harriet Tubman - Alan Schroeder   1295

Papa
The Wagon - Tony Johnston   708

Rachel
Sweet Clara and the Freedom Quilt - Deborah Hopkinson   644

Rightous Cry
Remember My Name - Sara H. Banks   74

Sweet Clara
Sweet Clara and the Freedom Quilt - Deborah Hopkinson   644

Tillie
Jumping the Broom - Courtni C. Wright   1563

Tobias
Washington City Is Burning - Harriette Gillem Robinet   1218

Virginia
Washington City Is Burning - Harriette Gillem Robinet   1218

Walker, Addy
Meet Addy: An American Girl - Connie Porter   1169

Walker, Pompey Bibb
A School for Pompey Walker - Michael J. Rosen   1230

Walker, Ruth
Meet Addy: An American Girl - Connie Porter   1169

Will
Jumping the Broom - Courtni C. Wright   1563

Young Jack
Sweet Clara and the Freedom Quilt - Deborah Hopkinson   644

SNAIL

Tsubu
Tsubu the Little Snail - Carol Ann Williams   1518

SNAKE

Unnamed Character
A Snake in the House - Faith McNulty   992

SOCCER PLAYER

Black, Randy
Never Say Quit - Bill Wallace   1470

Hanson, Hobie
Soccer Circus - Jamie Gilson   472

Lucy
The Losers Fight Back - Barbara M. Joosse   711

Smith, Justine
Never Say Quit - Bill Wallace   1470

Will
War Game - Michael Foreman   418

Willie
The Losers Fight Back - Barbara M. Joosse   711

SORCERER

Lord of Night
The Princess and the Lord of Night - Emma Bull   168

SORCERESS

Snow Queen
The Snow Queen - Hans Christian Andersen   32

Unnamed Character
The Girl in the Golden Bower - Jane Yolen   1578

SOUTHERN BELLE

Brodas
Minty: A Story of Young Harriet Tubman - Alan Schroeder   1295

Caroline
When Will This Cruel War Be Over? The Civil War Diary of Emma Simpson - Barry Denenberg   340

Simpson, Emma
When Will This Cruel War Be Over? The Civil War Diary of Emma Simpson - Barry Denenberg   340

SPACE EXPLORER

Hanna
Star Hatchling - Margaret Bechard   93

Peevik, Moomie
Space Brat 4: Planet of the Dips - Bruce Coville   293

SPACESHIP CAPTAIN

Blork
Space Brat 4: Planet of the Dips - Bruce Coville   293

SPIDER

Snyder
Tuck in the Pool - Martha Weston   1502

Spider
Miss Spider's Tea Party - David Kirk   760

SPINSTER

Bishop, Cordelia
Up a Road Slowly - Irene Hunt   663

Brown, Elizabeth
The Library - Sarah Stewart   1392

SPIRIT

Boggart
The Boggart - Susan Cooper   290

Buffle, Tom
The Ghost of Popcorn Hill - Betty Ren Wright   1557

Em
The Children Next Door - Jean Ure   1439

Ghost
Old Devil Wind - Bill Martin Jr.   939

Ghost Dog
Ghost Dog - Ellen Leroe   836

Greebe, Nicholas
The Ghost of Nicholas Greebe - Tony Johnston   703

Halkit
Hey, Dad, Get a Life - Todd Strasser   1397

Hamilton
The Mighty Movers - Sidney Levitt   855

Hanni
The Hanukkah Ghosts - Malka Penn   1128

Hob
Hob and the Goblins - William Mayne   954

Kojima
Green Willow - Eileen Dunlop   373

O'Malley, Grania
The Ghost of Grania O'Malley - Michael Morpurgo   1039

Slocum, Joshua
Moonlight on the River - Deborah Kovacs   781

Tapper, Tim
The Ghost Comes Calling - Betty Ren Wright 1556

Unnamed Character
The Ghost Witch - Betty Ren Wright 1558
The Magic Skateboard - Enid Richemont 1211
The Story of the Milky Way: A Cherokee Tale - Joseph Bruchac 162
William's Ninth Life - Minna Jung 716

Witch Ellen
Moon Window - Jane Louise Curry 310

SPORTS FIGURE

Aiken, Tammy
Double Play at Short - Matt Christopher 249

Beemer, Charley
The Man in the Ceiling - Jules Feiffer 403

Doyle, Larry
Patrick Doyle Is Full of Blarney - Jennifer Armstrong 40

Hardy, Jason Stubbs
The Battle for the Castle - Elizabeth Winthrop 1537

McFee, Nicky
Fighting Tackle - Matt Christopher 250

McFee, Terry
Fighting Tackle - Matt Christopher 250

Pug
Patrick Doyle Is Full of Blarney - Jennifer Armstrong 40

Torrant, Billy
Olympic Dream - Matt Christopher 252

Walker, Danny
Double Play at Short - Matt Christopher 249

SPOUSE

Alvah
Alvah and Arvilla - Mary Lyn Ray 1199

Arvilla
Alvah and Arvilla - Mary Lyn Ray 1199

Bert
The Great Pig Escape - Eileen Christelow 242

Ethel
The Great Pig Escape - Eileen Christelow 242

Eva
The Story of Santa Claus - Tom Paxton 1122

Haktak
Two of Everything - Lily Toy Hong 641
Two of Everything - Lily Toy Hong 641

Leatherby, Lulie
Papa Alonzo Leatherby: A Collection of Tall Tales from the Best Storyteller in Carroll County - Marguerite W. Davol 323

McTavish, Jack
The Rattlebang Picnic - Margaret Mahy 925

Patten, Joshua
Mary Patten's Voyage - Richard Berleth 103

Patten, Mary
Mary Patten's Voyage - Richard Berleth 103

Rubina
The Swan's Gift - Brenda Seabrooke 1306

Stormfoot, Hosannah
Santa's Winter Vacation - Viveca Larn Sundvall 1404

Stormfoot, Reuben
Santa's Winter Vacation - Viveca Larn Sundvall 1404

Tavish, Marion McGillicuddy
The Rattlebang Picnic - Margaret Mahy 925

Unnamed Character
The First Strawberries: A Cherokee Story - Joseph Bruchac 160
The First Strawberries: A Cherokee Story - Joseph Bruchac 160
How Night Came from the Sea: A Story from Brazil - Mary-Joan Gerson 458
Tsubu the Little Snail - Carol Ann Williams 1518

SPY

Babcock, Robert
A Spy in the King's Colony - Lisa Banim 69

Hennessey, Violet
Keeping Secrets - Joan Lowery Nixon 1075

Williams, Cassie
Alien Alert! - Debra Hess 597

SQUIRREL

Barker
Forest - Janet Taylor Lisle 877

Brainy
Tick-Tock - Eileen Browne 157

Chuck
Squirrel Park - Lisa Campbell Ernst 396

Squirrel
Heart to Heart - George Shannon 1317

Squirrel, Skip
Tick-Tock - Eileen Browne 157

Stumpy
Gooseberry Park - Cynthia Rylant 1249

Tina
Arnie and the Skateboard Gang - Nancy Carlson 211

Unnamed Character
Nuts to You! - Lois Ehlert 385

Woodbine
Forest - Janet Taylor Lisle 877

STEPBROTHER

Jason
The Magnificent Mummy Maker - Elvira Woodruff 1552

Manetti, Andy
The Magnificent Mummy Maker - Elvira Woodruff 1552

Ramsdale, Jackie
A Share of Freedom - June Rae Wood 1549

STEPDAUGHTER

Briggs, JoEllen
Moon Window - Jane Louise Curry 310

Cinder Edna
Cinder Edna - Ellen Jackson 681

Cinderella
Cinder Edna - Ellen Jackson 681

Gypsy
Belle Prater's Boy - Ruth White 1509

Hennings, Kay
Keep Smiling Through - Ann Rinaldi 1214

Pear Blossom
The Korean Cinderella - Shirley Climo 261

Witting, Anna
Skylark - Patricia MacLachlan 917

STEPFATHER

Grady, Jim
The Junkyard Dog - Erika Tamar 1407

Johnson
Chevrolet Saturdays - Candy Dawson Boyd 128

STEPMOTHER

Annie
My Wicked Stepmother - Norman Leach 828

Dunning
Sticky Beak - Morris Gleitzman 480

Fanaye
The Lion's Whiskers: An Ethiopian Folktale - Nancy Raines Day 325

Hennings, Amazing Grace
Keep Smiling Through - Ann Rinaldi 1214

Omoni
The Korean Cinderella - Shirley Climo 261

Witting, Sarah
Skylark - Patricia MacLachlan 917

STEPSISTER

Beatrice
Papa Gatto: An Italian Fairy Tale - Ruth Sanderson 1265

Peony
The Korean Cinderella - Shirley Climo 261

Sophia
Papa Gatto: An Italian Fairy Tale - Ruth Sanderson 1265

STEPSON

Abebe
The Lion's Whiskers: An Ethiopian Folktale - Nancy Raines Day 325

Tom
My Wicked Stepmother - Norman Leach 828

Witting, Caleb
Skylark - Patricia MacLachlan 917

STORE OWNER

Boney
The Bone Stranger - Frank Remkiewicz 1208

Gennard, Charlie "Grandpa"
Little Champ - Jim Arnosky 44

Leach
Cheshire Moon - Nancy Butts 190

Papa
The Dream Jar - Bonnie Pryor 1178

Ram Bharosa
Binya's Blue Umbrella - Ruskin Bond 123

Singer
Don't Forget - Patricia Lakin 807

STORK

Burton
Burton and Stanley - Frank O'Rourke 1101

Stanley
Burton and Stanley - Frank O'Rourke 1101

STORYTELLER

Abbajon
A Million Fish...More or Less - Pat McKissack 986

Abuela
Isla - Arthur Dorros 362

Bear, James
James Bear and the Goose Gathering - Jim Latimer 821

Big Mama
May'naise Sandwiches & Sunshine Tea - Sandra Belton 96

Daddy
The Little Tree Growin' in the Shade - Camille Yarbrough 1569

Fisher "Pouissant"
From Miss Ida's Front Porch - Sandra Belton 95

Gram
Crossing the Starlight Bridge - Alice Mead 997

Grand-mere
The Sugaring-Off Party - Jonathan London 895

Grandfather
Inunguak: The Little Greenlander - Palle Petersen 1140

Grandpa Cat
The Tales of Grandpa Cat - Lee Wardlaw 1479

Hayman
Can't Scare Me! - Melissa Milich 1010

Howard
The Year of Fire - Teddy Jam 684

Jenkins, Maynard
The Christmas Blizzard - Helen Ketteman 739

Leach
Cheshire Moon - Nancy Butts 190

Leatherby, Papa Alonzo
Papa Alonzo Leatherby: A Collection of Tall Tales from the Best Storyteller in Carroll County - Marguerite W. Davol 323

Old Grampa
The Year of No More Corn - Helen Ketteman 741

Papa
Papa Tells Chita a Story - Elizabeth Fitzgerald Howard 650

Papa-Daddy
A Million Fish...More or Less - Pat McKissack 986

Petey
Petey's Bedtime Story - Beverly Cleary 256

Quillow
The Great Quillow - James Thurber 1419

Tortoise
Stories from Firefly Island - Benedict Blathwayt 116

Unnamed Character
Hog-Eye - Susan Meddaugh 1000

STOWAWAY

Hopbong, Skippy III
Space Brat 4: Planet of the Dips - Bruce Coville 293

STREETPERSON

Eric the Red
The Bamboo Flute - Garry Disher 353

Horton, Charles "Chive"
Chive - Shelley A. Barre 80

Parsons, Sukey
The Pickle Song - Barthe DeClements 331

Unnamed Character
Broken Umbrellas - Kate Spohn 1373

STUDENT

Andrew
Sophie Is Seven - Dick King-Smith 753

Arrow, Emily
Look Out, Washington, D.C.! - Patricia Reilly Giff 465

Arthur
Arthur Writes a Story - Marc Brown 145

Bagg, Stuart "Shoebag"
Shoebag Returns - Mary James 688

Batts, Rowena "Ro"
Blabber Mouth - Morris Gleitzman 479
Sticky Beak - Morris Gleitzman 480

Bea
Busy Bea - Nancy Poydar 1173

Bear, Brother
The Berenstain Bears and the New Girl in Town - Stan Berenstain 99

Bear, Sister
The Berenstain Bears and the New Girl in Town - Stan Berenstain 99

Brickmeyer, Molly
The Library Dragon - Carmen Agra Deedy 333

Chrysanthemum
Chrysanthemum - Kevin Henkes 585

Clyde
The Wimp - Kathy Caple 204

Cole, Rosy
Rosy Cole: She Walks in Beauty - Sheila Greenwald 504

Cosgrove, Amanda
Blabber Mouth - Morris Gleitzman 479

Danny
Danny's Duck - June Crebbin 297

Drumm, Jessie
Spying on Miss Mueller - Eve Bunting 179

Dyesal
Running the Road to ABC - Denize Lauture 823

Emily
Ned - Selina Young 1589

Evie
Throw-Away Pets - Betsy Duffey 370

Filkins, Johnna Josephine
Save Halloween! - Stephanie Tolan 1422

Flora
The School Mouse - Dick King-Smith 751

Fontina, Danny
I'm George Washington and You're Not! - Steven Kroll 789

Gasper, J.J.
Search for the Shadowman - Joan Lowery Nixon 1076

George, Bertie
Pie Magic - Toby Forward 419

Grace, Derrick
Look Out, Washington, D.C.! - Patricia Reilly Giff 465

Haney, Clyde Elmer "Bo"
How to Be Cool in the Third Grade - Betsy Duffey 369

Hotchkiss, Pearl
Seven Spiders Spinning - Gregory Maguire 920

Hubble, Mildred
The Worst Witch at Sea - Jill Murphy 1053

Jamaica
Jamaica's Blue Marker - Juanita Havill 571

Jamie
Snow Angel - Jean Marzollo 945

Jeremy
Jeremy's Muffler - Laura F. Nielsen 1074

Jiminez, Josephine
Shoebag Returns - Mary James 688

Jo Louis
When Jo Louis Won the Title - Belinda Rochelle 1220

Joe
What Joe Saw - Anna Grossnickle Hines 622

JoJo
JoJo's Flying Side Kick - Brian Pinkney 1152

Joseck
The Exiles at Home - Hilary McKay 981

Juarez, Carlos
City of Light, City of Dark: A Comic-Book Novel - Avi 55

Karl
Beethoven Lives Upstairs - Barbara Nichol 1073

Loud
Running the Road to ABC - Denize Lauture 823

Lucy
The Indian School - Gloria Whelan 1504
Lucy's Picture - Nicola Moon 1031

Marco
The Secret Super Powers of Marco - Meredith Sue Willis 1525

Mary
Mary Had a Little Lamb - Sarah Josepha Hale 540

McCurry, Christi
Rosy Cole: She Walks in Beauty - Sheila Greenwald 504

Megan
Throw-Away Pets - Betsy Duffey 370

Miguel
Eagle - Judy Allen 27

Mills, Eric
I'm George Washington and You're Not! - Steven Kroll 789

Milsen
Running the Road to ABC - Denize Lauture 823

Murphy, Maureen "Mo"
My Worst Days Diary - Suzanne Altman 30

Orson, Nita
First Came the Owl - Judith Benet Richardson 1210

Pete
Pete's Chicken - Harriet Ziefert 1594

Phoebe
Show and Tell - Barney Saltzberg 1258

Pickles, Maisie
Captain Abdul's Pirate School - Colin McNaughton 990

Rachel
By the Dawn's Early Light - Karen Ackerman 3

Raven
The Indian School - Gloria Whelan 1504

Russell
Jamaica's Blue Marker - Juanita Havill 571

Rusty
The Gentleman and the Kitchen Maid - Diane Stanley 1376

Sara
Wilson Sat Alone - Debra Hess 598

Sherwin-Hendricks, Beatrice Lorraine "Beany"
Don't Call Me Beanhead! - Susan
Wojciechowski 1544

Sophie
Sophie Is Seven - Dick King-Smith 753

Stillwater, Anne
First Came the Owl - Judith Benet Richardson 1210

Stubbs, Sarah
City of Light, City of Dark: A Comic-Book Novel -
Avi 55

Sweetsong, Stanley
Shoebag Returns - Mary James 688

Trigg
The Toll-Bridge Troll - Patricia Rae Wolff 1547

Trimble, Bill
On the Trail with Miss Pace - Sharon Phillips
Denslow 342

Trimble, Phil
On the Trail with Miss Pace - Sharon Phillips
Denslow 342

Tyrone
The Secret Super Powers of Marco - Meredith Sue
Willis 1525

Unnamed Character
Never Ride Your Elephant to School - Doug
Johnson 699

Victoria
Chrysanthemum - Kevin Henkes 585

Wilson
Wilson Sat Alone - Debra Hess 598

STUDENT—COLLEGE

Has, Capek
The Fire Bug Connection: An Ecological Mystery -
Jean Craighead George 450

Melissa
Team Picture - Dean Hughes 661

Missy
A Horse Like Barney - Jessie Haas 532

Roberts, Red
Olympic Dream - Matt Christopher 252

STUDENT—HIGH SCHOOL

Ace
Slam Dunk Saturday - Jean Marzollo 944

Mandell, Tommy
Flipper's Boy - Mel Cebulash 229

McGill, Mark
Annie Pitts, Swamp Monster - Diane De Groat 327

Robin, Eve
Best Enemies Forever - Kathleen Leverich 840

Webster, Claudia
Partners - Karen Waggoner 1465

Williams, Cassandra "Cass"
Fall Secrets - Candy Dawson Boyd 129

STUDENT—JUNIOR HIGH

Bloom, Noel
Libby Bloom - Susan Rowan Masters 948

Greeley, Elliot
Bat Boy - Mel Cebulash 228

Piano, Mike
Bat Boy - Mel Cebulash 228

Smith, Belinda Rainbow "Boo"
The Great Smith House Hustle - Jane Louise
Curry 309

Webster, Gordon
Partners - Karen Waggoner 1465

Williams, Jessie
Fall Secrets - Candy Dawson Boyd 129

Wilson, Mary Jane
The Brick House Burglars - Peni R. Griffin 517

SUFFRAGETTE

Stanton, Elizabeth Cady
The Ballot Box Battle - Emily Arnold McCully 963

SURVIVOR

Grandma
The Feather-Bed Journey - Paula Kurzband
Feder 402

Kaplan, Morris
One Yellow Daffodil: A Hanukkah Story - David A.
Adler 14

Robeson, Brian
Brian's Winter - Gary Paulsen 1119

SWAN

Fitzherbert
The Swoose - Dick King-Smith 756

SWIMMER

Grayson, Jerry
The Winning Stroke - Matt Christopher 254

TAILOR

Myron
The Boardwalk Princess - Arthur A. Levine 845

Zundel
Bit by Bit - Steve Sanfield 1267

TARANTULA

Fang
Tarantula Shoes - Tom Birdseye 110

Norman
Not-So-Normal Norman - Cynthia Stowe 1395

TAXI DRIVER

Jim
Maxi, the Star - Debra Barracca 79

Papi
Taxi! Taxi! - Cari Best 105

TEACHER

Alice
Good-Bye, Hello - Barbara Shook Hazen 577

Arias
The Little Painter of Sabana Grande - Patricia
Maloney Markun 935

Bishop, Cordelia
Up a Road Slowly - Irene Hunt 663

Byron
Becoming Felix - Nancy Hope Wilson 1531

Camilla
Nine for California - Sonia Levitin 854

Castle
Benjamin Bigfoot - Mary Serfozo 1310

Cousin Jed
Wagons West - Roy Gerrard 455

D
The Baby Blues: An Adam Joshua Story - Janice Lee
Smith 1351

Dickie
My Dad - Niki Daly 319

Dunning
Sticky Beak - Morris Gleitzman 480

Earth, Germaine
Seven Spiders Spinning - Gregory Maguire 920

Eddington, Sarah
A Shooting Star: A Novel about Annie Oakley - Sheila
Solomon Klass 766

Emma
The Indian School - Gloria Whelan 1504

Fenning
Toby Scudder, Ultimate Warrior - David Gifaldi 463

Fisher
What Happened in Mr. Fisher's Room - Nancy J.
Hopper 646

Flores
School Spirit - Johanna Hurwitz 671

Gram
Weekend Girl - Amy Hest 610

Granger, Lorelei
Frindle - Andrew Clements 257

Harvey
Hey, New Kid! - Betsy Duffey 368

Hatchett
The Pirates' Mixed-Up Voyage - Margaret Mahy 924

Jackson
Owen Foote, Second Grade Strongman - Stephanie
Greene 501

Kibble, Kid
Kid Kibble - Diana Hendry 584

Lombardi
A Place for Grace - Jean Davies Okimoto 1092

Mackle
Song Lee in Room 2B - Suzy Kline 773

Madame
Ribbons - Laurence Yep 1574

Malarkey
Miss Malarkey Doesn't Live in Room 10 - Judy
Finchler 406

Marconi
Wagon Train 911 - Jamie Gilson 473

Markov
Sweet Notes, Sour Notes - Nancy Smiler
Levinson 851

Mary Rose
Hey You, Sister Rose - Eileen Walsh Strauch 1398

Merlin
The Mystery of the Several Sevens - Bill Brittain 140

Merriwether
Mrs. Merriwether's Musical Cat - Carol Purdy 1181

Mrs.
Junie B. Jones and Some Sneaky Peeky Spying -
Barbara Park 1109

Muller, Daphne
Spying on Miss Mueller - Eve Bunting 179

Olga
Nutcracker Noel - Kate McMullan 989

Olinski, Eva Marie
The View from Saturday - E.L. Konigsburg 777

Pace
On the Trail with Miss Pace - Sharon Phillips Denslow   342

Ratburn
Arthur Writes a Story - Marc Brown   145

Rooney
Look Out, Washington, D.C.! - Patricia Reilly Giff   465

Rosemary
Woollybear Good-bye - Sharon Phillips Denslow   343

Skooghammer
Horrible Harry and the Dungeon - Suzy Kline   769

Slinger
Lilly's Purple Plastic Purse - Kevin Henkes   587

Smith
Snowy - Berlie Doherty   356

Truesdale
Fifth Grade Fever - Michele Granger   493

Twinkle, Delphinium
Chrysanthemum - Kevin Henkes   585

Unnamed Character
My Name Is Maria Isabel - Alma Flor Ada   7

Walters
The Sub - P.J. Petersen   1139

Wix
In Trouble with Teacher - Patricia Demuth   339

Worthen, Lyddie
Jip: His Story - Katherine Paterson   1113

TEENAGER

Appleby
The Mennyms - Sylvia Waugh   1484

Big Sister
Red Dancing Shoes - Denise Lewis Patrick   1116

Cally
Beyond the Magic Sphere - Gail Jarrow   691

Coogan, John "Crash"
Crash - Jerry Spinelli   1370

Hanna
Star Hatchling - Margaret Bechard   93

Harper, Jessie
Spotting the Leopard - Anna Myers   1056

Josepha
Josepha: A Prairie Boy's Story - Jim McGugan   979

Marta
The Night Crossing - Karen Ackerman   4

Mennym, Soobie
Mennyms in the Wilderness - Sylvia Waugh   1486

Nathan
Blue Sky, Butterfly - Jean Van Leeuwen   1447

Preston, Marty
Shiloh Season - Phyllis Reynolds Naylor   1068

Shafter, Allen "Alligator"
The Case of the Missing Cutthroats, an Ecological Mystery - Jean Craighead George   448

Stukeley, Sarah
The Apprenticeship of Lucas Whitaker - Cynthia DeFelice   334

Virginia
Washington City Is Burning - Harriette Gillem Robinet   1218

Weaver, Tad
Websters' Leap - Eileen Dunlop   374

Webb, Penn
Crash - Jerry Spinelli   1370

West, Annie
Going to See Grassy Ella - Kathryn Lance   810

Yolen, Lyovka "Lou"
And Twelve Chinese Acrobats - Jane Yolen   1575

TELEVISION PERSONALITY

Carter, Marilyn M.
Nerd No More - Kristine L. Franklin   424

THIEF

Alexander the Grate
The Ghastly Gerty Swindle: With the Ghosts of Hungryhouse Lane - Sam McBratney   959

Chadwick, Beck
Grandmother Bryant's Pocket - Jacqueline Briggs Martin   941

Gallows, Grudge
Tingleberries, Tuckertubs and Telephones - Margaret Mahy   927

Moag, Gertrude Elizabeth "Gerty"
The Ghastly Gerty Swindle: With the Ghosts of Hungryhouse Lane - Sam McBratney   959

Rinaldo
Rinaldo on the Run - Ursel Scheffler   1277

Scrat, Ebenezer "Neezer"
The Twin in the Tavern - Barbara Brooks Wallace   1469

Sophie
Tangles - Errol Broome   141

Unnamed Character
Aunt Skilly and the Stranger - Kathleen Stevens   1382
This Is the Bear and the Bad Little Girl - Sarah Hayes   575

TIGER

Beautiful Bengal
Heart of a Tiger - Marsha Arnold   42

Tiger
The Rat and the Tiger - Keiko Kasza   722

Tigerella
Tigerella - Kit Wright   1564

Unnamed Character
Friday Night at Hodge's Cafe - Tim Egan   382

TIME TRAVELLER

Anna
Tut Tut - Jon Scieszka   1299

Joe
Tut Tut - Jon Scieszka   1299

Larkin, Rose
The Root Cellar - Janet Lunn   905

Lewis, Josh
Lost in Cyberspace - Richard Peck   1126

Sam
Tut Tut - Jon Scieszka   1299

Zimmer, Aaron
Lost in Cyberspace - Richard Peck   1126

TOAD

Buffy
Saving Owen's Toad - Juanita Havill   573

Grandpa Toad
Grandpa Toad's Last Secret - Keiko Kasza   721

Little Toad
Grandpa Toad's Last Secret - Keiko Kasza   721
A Song for Little Toad - Vivian French   430

Old Mother Toad
A Song for Little Toad - Vivian French   430

TORTOISE

Speedy
Nate the Great and the Tardy Tortoise - Marjorie Weinman Sharmat   1322

TOURIST

Best, Caroline
The In-Between Days - Eve Bunting   174

Unnamed Character
Dreamplace - George Ella Lyon   908

TOY

Barney
Barney Is Best - Nancy White Carlstrom   212

Bear
Dear Bear - Joanna Harrison   563

Bear, Bear E.
Bear E. Bear - Susan Straight   1396

Bella
The Enchanted Horse - Magdalen Nabb   1058

Bunny Rabbit
I Love You, Bunny Rabbit - Shulamith Levey Oppenheim   1097

Elephant
The Tusk Fairy - Nicola Smee   1348

Emma Bean
Emma Bean - Jean Van Leeuwen   1449

Felix
Mia the Beach Cat: A Story - Wolfram Hanel   554

Fred
This Is the Bear and the Bad Little Girl - Sarah Hayes   575

Freddie
It's the Bear! - Jez Alborough   20

Fuzzy
Owen - Kevin Henkes   588

Harry
My Friend Harry - Kim Lewis   868

Horatio
Humphrey Thud - Camilla Ashforth   48

James
Humphrey Thud - Camilla Ashforth   48

Mary Ann
Good Night, Sleep Tight - Penelope Lively   884

Mennym, Magnus
Mennyms Alone - Sylvia Waugh   1485

Mennym, Tulip
Mennyms Alone - Sylvia Waugh   1485

Paco
A Bear for Miguel - Elaine Marie Alphin   28

Pippo
Tom and Pippo and the Bicycle - Helen Oxenbury   1104

Plowie
Plowie: A Story from the Prairie - Patricia Kirkpatrick   761

Rosie
Stardust - Alane Ferguson   405

Sally Ann
Nurse Sally Ann - Terrance Dicks 350

Snyder
Tuck in the Pool - Martha Weston 1502

Teddy
First Snow - Kim Lewis 867

Thud, Humphrey
Humphrey Thud - Camilla Ashforth 48

Unnamed Character
The Bear Santa Claus Forgot - Diana Kimpton 745
Good-Bye, Daddy! - Brigitte Weninger 1499
Sleep Well, Little Bear - Quint Buchholz 165

TRADER

Tesfa
The Lion's Whiskers: An Ethiopian Folktale - Nancy Raines Day 325

TRAPPER

Smallhorn, David
Brian's Winter - Gary Paulsen 1119

TRAVELLER

Amanda
Nine for California - Sonia Levitin 854

Becket, Gilbert
The Saracen Maid - Leon Garfield 441

Brewster, Love
Across the Wide Dark Sea: The Mayflower Journey - Jean Van Leeuwen 1446

Brewster, William
Across the Wide Dark Sea: The Mayflower Journey - Jean Van Leeuwen 1446

Camilla
Nine for California - Sonia Levitin 854

Harrall, Angela
Angela's Aliens - Janet Taylor Lisle 876

Lunch
Mr. Lunch Takes a Plane Ride - J. Otto Seibold 1308

Mama
Nine for California - Sonia Levitin 854

Tillby
Someplace Else - Carol P. Saul 1269

Unnamed Character
The Gift of a Traveler - Wendy Matthews 952
Grandfather's Journey - Allen Say 1271

TRUCK DRIVER

Mandell, Roger
Flipper's Boy - Mel Cebulash 229

TURTLE

Hugh
The Mud Flat Olympics - James Stevenson 1386

Old Abra
Pip's Magic - Ellen Stoll Walsh 1476

Tortoise
Stories from Firefly Island - Benedict Blathwayt 116
The Tortoise and the Jackrabbit - Susan Lowell 901

Turtle
The Rabbit's Escape - Suzanne Crowder Han 552

Turtle, M.C.
M.C. Turtle and the Hip Hop Hare: A Nursery Rap - David Vozar 1457

Turtle, Titus
I'll Meet You Halfway - John Schindel 1283

TWIN

Adam
One Up, One Down - Carol Snyder 1358

Andersen, Elise
Into the Flames - Robert Elmer 388

Andersen, Peter
Into the Flames - Robert Elmer 388

Anthony
Girl Wonder and the Terrific Twins - Malorie Blackman 113

Ben
One Up, One Down - Carol Snyder 1358

Brown, Caleb
You're an Orphan, Mollie Brown - Mary E. Penson 1130

Brown, Mollie
You're an Orphan, Mollie Brown - Mary E. Penson 1130

Dixon, Kate
The St. Patrick's Day Shamrock Mystery - Marion M. Markham 934

Dixon, Mickey
The St. Patrick's Day Shamrock Mystery - Marion M. Markham 934

Dodge, Alison
The Absolutely True Story. . .How I Visited Yellowstone Park with the Terrible Rupes - Willo Davis Roberts 1217

Dodge, Lewis Q.
The Absolutely True Story. . .How I Visited Yellowstone Park with the Terrible Rupes - Willo Davis Roberts 1217

Edward
Girl Wonder and the Terrific Twins - Malorie Blackman 113

Flanagan, Elizabeth "Lizard"
The Miraculous Makeover of Lizard Flanagan - Carol Gorman 489

Flanagan, Sam
The Miraculous Makeover of Lizard Flanagan - Carol Gorman 489

Fontecchio, Staci
The Great Pony Hassle - Nancy Springer 1374

Fontecchio, Toni
The Great Pony Hassle - Nancy Springer 1374

Fremont, Marvin
Marvelous Marvin and the Pioneer Ghost - Bonnie Pryor 1179

Fremont, Sarah
Marvelous Marvin and the Pioneer Ghost - Bonnie Pryor 1179

Harper, Jordy
Odd Man Out - Gail Radley 1185

Harper, Kit
Odd Man Out - Gail Radley 1185

Harrison "Harry"
Harry and Tuck - Holly Keller 732

Hummer, Freddie
Nekomah Creek Christmas - Linda Crew 301

Hummer, Lucy
Nekomah Creek Christmas - Linda Crew 301

Jenkins, Judge
Egg-Drop Blues - Jacqueline Turner Banks 70
The New One - Jacqueline Turner Banks 71

Jenkins, Jury
Egg-Drop Blues - Jacqueline Turner Banks 70
The New One - Jacqueline Turner Banks 71

McPherson, Paisley
The Great Pony Hassle - Nancy Springer 1374

Ohkwa'ri
Children of the Longhouse - Joseph Bruchac 159

Otsi-stia
Children of the Longhouse - Joseph Bruchac 159

Starbuck, Charlotte "Charly"
A Voice in the Wind - Kathryn Lasky 819

Starbuck, Liberty
A Voice in the Wind - Kathryn Lasky 819

Trimble, Bill
On the Trail with Miss Pace - Sharon Phillips Denslow 342

Trimble, Phil
On the Trail with Miss Pace - Sharon Phillips Denslow 342

Tucker "Tuck"
Harry and Tuck - Holly Keller 732

UNCLE

Adam
My Apron - Eric Carle 209

Albert
The Secret Super Powers of Marco - Meredith Sue Willis 1525

Archibald
King Kenrick's Splinter - Sally Derby 345

Barnavelt, Jonathan
The Vengeance of the Witch-Finder - John Bellairs 94

Benjamin
Sarah, Also Known as Hannah - Lillian Hammer Ross 1233

Blackfeather, William
Remember My Name - Sara H. Banks 74

Bob
My Wartime Summers - Jane Cutler 316

Clem
Mac and Marie and the Train Toss Surprise - Elizabeth Fitzgerald Howard 649

Daney
Uncle Daney's Way - Jessie Haas 535

Ernesto
The Magic Shell - Nicholasa Mohr 1027

Filkins, T.T.
Save Halloween! - Stephanie Tolan 1422

Harry
Passover Magic - Roni Schotter 1291

Joe
The Ice Horse - Candice Christiansen 248

John
The Year of Fire - Teddy Jam 684

Johnson, Jedediah "Jed"
Uncle Jed's Barbershop - Margaree King Mitchell 1022

Karl
Beethoven Lives Upstairs - Barbara Nichol 1073

Landauer, Harry
No Boys Allowed - Marilyn Levinson 850

Leonard
Too Far Away to Touch - Leslea Newman 1071

Lester
The Man in the Ceiling - Jules Feiffer   403

Maladroit
Day of the Unicorn - Mollie Hunter   664

Max
The Palace of Stars - Patricia Lakin   808

Michael
Tiger Flowers - Patricia Quinlan   1183

Narizo
Frida Maria: A Story of the Old Southwest - Deborah Nourse Lattimore   822

Pete
Zero's Slider - Matt Christopher   255

Russ
Lobster Boat - Brenda Z. Guiberson   525

Uncle Zeka
Do You Know Me? - Nancy Farmer   400

Worst
Worse than the Worst - James Stevenson   1388

Yosh
Heroes - Ken Mochizuki   1024

Zambezi
Joshua's Masai Mask - Dakari Hru   658

UNEMPLOYED

Ellerbee, Pa-Daddy
Comford Creek - Joyce McDonald   972

Grant, Stan
Riot - Mary Casanova   217

Jacob
Jacob and the Stranger - Sally Derby   344

Papa
A Bear for Miguel - Elaine Marie Alphin   28

Pete
Zero's Slider - Matt Christopher   255

Watkins
Jimmy Crack Corn - Candice F. Ransom   1188

UNICORN

Allegra
The Dragon and the Unicorn - Lynne Cherry   237

VACATIONER

Dodge, Alison
The Absolutely True Story. . .How I Visited Yellowstone Park with the Terrible Rupes - Willo Davis Roberts   1217

Dodge, Lewis Q.
The Absolutely True Story. . .How I Visited Yellowstone Park with the Terrible Rupes - Willo Davis Roberts   1217

Grandfather
Monster Beach - Betty Paraskevas   1107

Unnamed Character
Monster Beach - Betty Paraskevas   1107
Pigs Ahoy! - David McPhail   994

VAMPIRE

Baby Vampira
Little Vampire and the Midnight Bear - Mary DeBall Kwitz   801

Drac
The House That Drac Built - Judy Sierra   1335

Little Vampire
Little Vampire and the Midnight Bear - Mary DeBall Kwitz   801

VETERAN

Dad
Heroes - Ken Mochizuki   1024

Smith, Donald "Donny"
Following My Own Footsteps - Mary Downing Hahn   538

Yosh
Heroes - Ken Mochizuki   1024

VETERINARIAN

Brand
Be Well, Beware - Jessie Haas   528

VILLAIN

Fishskin
Cold Shoulder Road - Joan Aiken   17

VOLUNTEER

Hilda
Hilda and the Mad Scientist - Addie Adam   8

Hobarth, Lawrence Martin "Marty"
Champ Hobarth - Judith Bernie Strommen   1400

Igler, Leanne Patrice
Champ Hobarth - Judith Bernie Strommen   1400

WANDERER

Bilberry
Across the Blue Mountains - Emma Chichester Clark   238

Hershel
The Adventures of Hershel of Ostropol - Eric A. Kimmel   742

Jessica
An Extraordinary Egg - Leo Lionni   875

WEALTHY

Duke of Rudling
Lassie Come-Home - Rosemary Wells   1494

Perez, Tiffany
The Pool Party - Gary Soto   1364

WEASEL

Brown, Bagley Jr.
The Wainscott Weasel - Tor Seidler   1309

Scraggly Sam
The Sleepy Dormouse - Mark Ezra   399

Weasel
That Kookoory! - Margaret Walden Froehlich   432

Whitebelly, Zeke
The Wainscott Weasel - Tor Seidler   1309

WIDOW(ER)

Babbelonski, Yettele
Yettele's Feathers - Joan Rothenberg   1237

Brogan
Dog Friday - Hilary McKay   980

Chin Yu Min
Chin Yu Min and the Ginger Cat - Jennifer Armstrong   39

Garrow
The Invisible Dog - Dick King-Smith   748

Gramm
Poppy's Chair - Karen Hesse   601

Joseph, Jumping
Little Obie and the Kidnap - Martin Waddell   1464

Leonard, Elizabeth
Someone to Count On - Patricia Hermes   594

McDowell
The Christmas Miracle of Jonathan Toomey - Susan Wojciechowski   1543

Noodle
George Washington's Ghost - Jane Clark Brown   142

Pap
The Log Cabin Quilt - Ellen Howard   652

Papa
Kelly and Me - Carol Lynch Williams   1520

Papa Gatto
Papa Gatto: An Italian Fairy Tale - Ruth Sanderson   1265

Toomey, Jonathan
The Christmas Miracle of Jonathan Toomey - Susan Wojciechowski   1543

Turner, Judith
Daddy's Climbing Tree - C.S. Adler   11

Warren
The Ghost Witch - Betty Ren Wright   1558

WITCH

Amelia
Strega Nona Meets Her Match - Tomie De Paola   329

Baba Yaga
Babushka Baba Yaga - Patricia Polacco   1159

Casi Lampu'a Lentemue
Pace and the Witch: A Puerto Rican Folktale - Felix Pitre   1157

Gritch
Piggie Pie! - Margie Palatini   1105

Hubble, Mildred
The Worst Witch at Sea - Jill Murphy   1053

Nona
Strega Nona Meets Her Match - Tomie De Paola   329

Unnamed Character
The Boardwalk Princess - Arthur A. Levine   845
The Ghost Witch - Betty Ren Wright   1558
My Working Mom - Peter Glassman   477
Tales of the Wicked Witch - Hanna Kraan   782

Wilma
The Fat Cat Sat on the Mat - Nurit Karlan   718

Witch
Old Devil Wind - Bill Martin Jr.   939

Wittilda
A Job for Wittilda - Caralyn Buehner   167

WIZARD

Merlin
The Mystery of the Several Sevens - Bill Brittain   140

Myers
The Wizard Next Door - Peter Glassman   478

Old Abra
Pip's Magic - Ellen Stoll Walsh   1476

Unnamed Character
The Golden Goose - Uri Shulevitz 1334
Jacob and the Stranger - Sally Derby 344
The Wizard - Bill Martin Jr. 940

Wizard
Wizard and Wart at Sea - Janice Lee Smith 1353

WOLF

Bertha
Bertha's Garden - Elisabeth Dyjak 377

Ebony
Child of the Wolves - Elizabeth Hall 545

Kael
Circus of the Wolves - Jack Bushnell 187

Kapu
Julie - Jean Craighead George 451

Mother
The Three Little Wolves and the Big Bad Pig - Eugene Trivizas 1427

Samson
Florizella and the Wolves - Philippa Gregory 510

Snowdrift
Child of the Wolves - Elizabeth Hall 545

Unnamed Character
Garth Pig Steals the Show - Mary Rayner 1202
Hog-Eye - Susan Meddaugh 1000
Little Red Riding Hood: A Newfangled Prairie Tale - Lisa Campbell Ernst 394
Suddenly! - Colin McNaughton 991
The Three Little Pigs - Harriet Ziefert 1595

Wolf
Strudwick: A Sheep in Wolf's Clothing - Robert Kraus 786

Wolfgang
The Bone Stranger - Frank Remkiewicz 1208

WOMBAT

Sleuth, Seymour
The Mystery of King Karfu - Doug Cushman 313

WOODSMAN

Unnamed Character
The Golden Goose - Uri Shulevitz 1334

WORKER

Adam
My Apron - Eric Carle 209

Bradford, Levi "Pap"
True North - Kathryn Lasky 818

Czernikow, Dan
The Haunting of Holroyd Hill - Brenda Seabrooke 1304

Daddy
Working Cotton - Sherley Anne Williams 1522

Dreisden, Claire/Kathy
Living in Secret - Cristina Salat 1257

Dreisden, Janey/Megan
Living in Secret - Cristina Salat 1257

Jack
Lazy Jack - Vivian French 428

Johnson, Jedediah "Jed"
Uncle Jed's Barbershop - Margaree King Mitchell 1022

Judith
The Bobbin Girl - Emily Arnold McCully 964

Mami
Lights on the River - Jane Resh Thomas 1417

Mamma
Working Cotton - Sherley Anne Williams 1522

Mom
By the Dawn's Early Light - Karen Ackerman 3

Papi
Lights on the River - Jane Resh Thomas 1417

Pete
Tornado - Betsy Byars 197

Putney, Rebecca
The Bobbin Girl - Emily Arnold McCully 964

Ruth
The Bobbin Girl - Emily Arnold McCully 964

Scarecrow
Nothing at All - Denys Cazet 227

Star Shiner
The Moon Man: A Story - Gerda Marie Scheidl 1279

Unnamed Character
The Mushroom Man - Ethel Pochocki 1158
The Waiting Day - Harriett Diller 351

Violet
Miss Violet's Shining Day - Jane Breskin Zalben 1592

Whitney, Caleb
Escape into the Night - Lois Walfrid Johnson 700

Xiao Sheng
The Dragon's Pearl - Julie Lawson 825

WORM

Magic
Petey and Miss Magic - N.B. Dorman 359

WRITER

Amelia
Amelia Writes Again - Marissa Moss 1043
Amelia's Notebook - Marissa Moss 1044

Berry, Jan
Mary Marony Hides Out - Suzy Kline 770

Fronto
The Arkadians - Lloyd Alexander 22

Jones, Booker
Utterly Yours, Booker Jones - Betsy Duffey 371

Legrand, Bill
The Case of the Absent Author - E.W. Hildick 614

Lester
The Man in the Ceiling - Jules Feiffer 403

Mom
J.B.'s Harmonica - John Sebastian 1307

Monroe, Cornelia "Nelia"
Going the Distance - Mary Jane Miller 1014

Simpson, Emma
When Will This Cruel War Be Over? The Civil War Diary of Emma Simpson - Barry Denenberg 340

Williams, Rachel
One Brave Summer - Ann Turner 1434

Wyatt, Steve "Sneeze"
101 Ways to Bug Your Parents - Lee Wardlaw 1478

YOUNG MAN

Duforce, Clement
The Faithful Friend - Robert D. San Souci 1261

Hippolyte
The Faithful Friend - Robert D. San Souci 1261

Jacob
Jacob and the Stranger - Sally Derby 344

Kumaso
Lily and the Wooden Bowl - Alan Schroeder 1294

Potter, Peter
Mr. Potter's Pet - Dick King-Smith 750

Simon
Tom, Babette, & Simon: Three Tales of Transformation - Avi 58

Tooley
The House Gobbaleen - Lloyd Alexander 23

Travers, Judd
Shiloh Season - Phyllis Reynolds Naylor 1068

Unnamed Character
The Little Black Truck - Libba Moore Gray 495

YOUNG WOMAN

Eliza
Lily - Abigail Thomas 1414

Lily
Lily and the Wooden Bowl - Alan Schroeder 1294

Pauline
The Faithful Friend - Robert D. San Souci 1261

Tsugele
Tsugele's Broom - Valerie Scho Carey 208

ZOO KEEPER

Unnamed Character
Good Night, Gorilla - Peggy Rathmann 1195

Age Index

This index groups books according to the grade levels for which they are most appropriate. Beneath each grade range book titles are listed alphabetically, followed by the author's name and the entry number.

GRADES K-1

Annabel Again - Janice Boland 122
Annie and Cousin Precious - Kay Chorao 241
The Baby House - Norma Simon 1337
The Bag I'm Taking to Grandma's - Shirley Neitzel 1069
Barney Is Best - Nancy White Carlstrom 212
Bayou Lullaby - Kathi Appelt 37
Bear E. Bear - Susan Straight 1396
Benjamin Bigfoot - Mary Serfozo 1310
Bertha's Garden - Elisabeth Dyjak 377
Big Help! - Anna Grossnickle Hines 621
Born in the Gravy - Denys Cazet 225
Cabbage Moon - Tim Chadwick 230
Can't Sleep - Chris Raschka 1193
The Crocodile and the Dentist - Taro Gomi 486
Daisy Dare - Anita Jeram 695
Do You See a Mouse? - Bernard Waber 1459
Don't Fidget a Feather - Erica Silverman 1336
The Earth and I - Frank Asch 46
Edward's Overwhelming Overnight - Rosemary Wells 1492
Emily and Alice - Joyce Champion 231
Emily the Giraffe - Pascal Lemaitre 833
Emma Bean - Jean Van Leeuwen 1449
Fireflies for Nathan - Shulamith Levey Oppenheim 1095
First Snow - Kim Lewis 867
The First Song Ever Sung - Laura Krauss Melmed 1007
Flower Garden - Eve Bunting 173
Frog Is Frightened - Max Velthuijs 1453
Froggy Learns to Swim - Jonathan London 888
Going Home - Margaret Wild 1512
Good-Bye, Curtis - Kevin Henkes 586
Good-Bye House - Robin Ballard 65
Good Morning, Pond - Alyssa Satin Capucilli 205
Good Night, Gorilla - Peggy Rathmann 1195
Good Night, Sleep Tight - Penelope Lively 884
Good Night, Stella - Kate McMullan 988
Grandpa Toad's Last Secret - Keiko Kasza 721
Guess How Much I Love You - Sam McBratney 960
Halloween Mice! - Bethany Roberts 1216
Harry and Tuck - Holly Keller 732
A Hat for Minerva Louise - Janet Morgan Stoeke 1394
Here Comes Henny - Charlotte Pomerantz 1164
Hi - Ann Herbert Scott 1302
Hilda Hen's Happy Birthday - Mary Wormell 1554
Hilda Hen's Search - Mary Wormell 1555
Hop Jump - Ellen Stoll Walsh 1475
Humphrey Thud - Camilla Ashforth 48

I Love You, Bunny Rabbit - Shulamith Levey Oppenheim 1097
If You Want to Find Golden - Eileen Spinelli 1368
I'll See You When the Moon Is Full - Susi Gregg Fowler 421
I'm a Jolly Farmer - Julie Lacome 804
In the Rain with Baby Duck - Amy Hest 604
Inside a Barn in the Country: A Rebus Read-Along Story - Alyssa Satin Capucilli 206
Is Susan Here? - Janice May Udry 1437
Is That Josie? - Keiko Narahashi 1062
It's My Birthday - Helen Oxenbury 1103
James in the House of Aunt Prudence - Timothy Bush 184
Kate's Giants - Valiska Gregory 512
Kit and Kat - Tomie De Paola 328
A Koala for Katie: An Adoption Story - Jonathan London 891
Komodo! - Peter Sis 1340
The Last Noo-Noo - Jill Murphy 1051
Let's Go Home, Little Bear - Martin Waddell 1463
Like Butter on Pancakes - Jonathan London 893
Lilly's Secret - Miko Imai 676
The Little Black Truck - Libba Moore Gray 495
Little Donkey Close Your Eyes - Margaret Wise Brown 152
Little Gray One - Jan Wahl 1466
Little Pink Pig - Pat Hutchins 673
Lucky Morning - Sally Noll 1079
Mac and Marie and the Train Toss Surprise - Elizabeth Fitzgerald Howard 649
Mama Zooms - Jane Cowen-Fletcher 294
Mary Had a Little Lamb - Sarah Josepha Hale 540
Max and Ruby's Midas: Another Greek Myth - Rosemary Wells 1497
Monster Mama - Liz Rosenberg 1232
Mouse Party - Alan Durant 376
Mr. Bear's Picnic - Debi Gliori 481
My Apron - Eric Carle 209
My Bike - Donna Jakob 683
My Cat Jack - Patricia Casey 222
My Cats Nick and Nora - Isabelle Harper 558
My Dog Rosie - Isabelle Harper 559
My Dog Talks - Gail Herman 591
My Father's Hands - Joanne Ryder 1247
My Friend Harry - Kim Lewis 868
My Shadow - Susan Winter 1535
Naomi Knows It's Springtime - Virginia L. Kroll 792
Ned - Selina Young 1589
The New Puppy - Laurence Anholt 35
No! No! No! - Anne F. Rockwell 1221
Nora's Surprise - Satomi Ichikawa 675

Not in the House, Newton! - Judith Heide Gilliland 470
Nothing at All - Denys Cazet 227
Oliver's Vegetables - Vivian French 429
On the Day I Was Born - Deborah M. Newton Chocolate 240
One Up, One Down - Carol Snyder 1358
Our Granny - Margaret Wild 1513
Outside, Inside - Carolyn Crimi 303
Pig, Horse, or Cow, Don't Wake Me Now - Arlene Alda 21
Pigs Aplenty, Pigs Galore - David McPhail 995
Pole Dog - Tres Seymour 1313
Princess - Susan L. Roth 1235
Quickly, Quigley - Jeanne M. Gravois 494
Rabbit Surprise - Eric L. Houck Jr. 648
Rabbit's Good News - Ruth Lercher Bornstein 126
Sheep Dreams - Arthur A. Levine 847
Sheep Take a Hike - Nancy Shaw 1323
Sherman the Sheep - Kevin Kiser 762
Simpkin - Quentin Blake 114
Snow - Nancy Elizabeth Wallace 1473
So Much - Trish Cooke 284
A Song for Little Toad - Vivian French 430
Stella and Roy - Ashley Wolff 1545
Suddenly! - Colin McNaughton 991
Sunflower - Miela Ford 415
Surprise! Surprise! - Michael Foreman 417
This Is the Bear and the Bad Little Girl - Sarah Hayes 575
Three Bags Full - Ragnhild Scamell 1273
Tick-Tock - Eileen Browne 157
Time for Bed - Mem Fox 422
Time to Wake Up! - Marisabina Russo 1243
Tom and Pippo and the Bicycle - Helen Oxenbury 1104
Tom's Fish - Nancy Coffelt 265
Trade-In Mother - Marisabina Russo 1244
Tuck in the Pool - Martha Weston 1502
The Tusk Fairy - Nicola Smee 1348
The Very Lonely Firefly - Eric Carle 210
When the Wind Stops - Charlotte Zolotow 1598
Who Is My Neighbor? - Michael Grejniec 513
Wind Says Good Night - Katy Rydell 1245
Wipe Your Feet! - Daniel Lehan 832
You're a Genius, Blackboard Bear - Martha Alexander 24

GRADES K-2

Across the Blue Mountains - Emma Chichester Clark 238

GRADES K-3

Charlie Malarkey and the Singing Moose - William Kennedy 736

The Christmas Miracle of Jonathan Toomey - Susan Wojciechowski 1543

Cloud Eyes - Kathryn Lasky 813

Diane Goode's Book of Scary Stories and Songs - Diane Goode 487

The Dragon's Pearl - Julie Lawson 825

Eagle - Judy Allen 27

Fairy Wings - Lauren Mills 1018

The Farolitos of Christmas - Rudolfo Anaya 31

The Feather-Bed Journey - Paula Kurzband Feder 402

The Great Quillow - James Thurber 1419

Here Comes the Mystery Man - Scott Russell Sanders 1264

The House Gobbaleen - Lloyd Alexander 23

Jacob and the Stranger - Sally Derby 344

The Last Dragon - Susan Miho Nunes 1085

Lily and the Wooden Bowl - Alan Schroeder 1294

The Loyal Cat - Lensey Namioka 1059

Luck with Potatoes - Helen Ketteman 740

Matthew and the Sea Singer - Jill Paton Walsh 1114

The Minstrel and the Dragon Pup - Rosemary Sutcliff 1405

The Moon Was at a Fiesta - Matthew Gollub 485

Murphy and Kate - Ellen Howard 653

The Mushroom Man - Ethel Pochocki 1158

My Dad - Niki Daly 319

The Night I Followed the Dog - Nina Laden 805

Night in the Barn - Faye Gibbons 462

One Yellow Daffodil: A Hanukkah Story - David A. Adler 14

Prince Nautilus - Laura Krauss Melmed 1008

The Princess and the Lord of Night - Emma Bull 168

Radio Man = Don Radio: A Story in English and Spanish - Arthur Dorros 363

The Seal Prince - Sheila MacGill Callahan 200

A Small, Tall Tale from the Far, Far North - Peter Sis 1341

Someplace Else - Carol P. Saul 1269

Sophie in the Saddle - Dick King-Smith 752

Sunshine Home - Eve Bunting 180

The Tie Man's Miracle: A Chanukah Tale - Steven Schnur 1289

Tornado - Betsy Byars 197

Under the Moon - Dyan Sheldon 1328

Zeke Pippin - William Steig 1378

Zin! Zin! Zin! a Violin - Lloyd Moss 1042

GRADES 1-5

The Ice Horse - Candice Christiansen 248

See You Around, Sam! - Lois Lowry 902

GRADES 2-3

The Adventures of Sugar and Junior - Angela Shelf Medearis 1003

B.J.'s Billion-Dollar Bet - Julie Anne Peters 1133

The Bone Stranger - Frank Remkiewicz 1208

The Detective Stars and the Case of the Super Soccer Team - Caroline Levine 848

Dog Days for Dudley - Barbara Moe 1026

Frank and Ernest on the Road - Alexandra Day 324

The Gator Girls - Joanna Cole 270

Great-Uncle Dracula and the Dirty Rat - Jayne Harvey 568

Harry's Birthday - Barbara Ann Porte 1166

Holding onto Sunday - Kathryn O. Galbraith 436

Horrible Harry and the Dungeon - Suzy Kline 769

Jennifer, Too - Juanita Havill 577

Lila's Little Dinosaur - Wolfram Hanel 553

Make a Wish, Molly - Barbara Cohen 266

Mary Marony Hides Out - Suzy Kline 770

My Worst Days Diary - Suzanne Altman 30

Nurse Sally Ann - Terrance Dicks 350

Olivia and the Real Live Pet - Charlotte Towner Graeber 490

Peace Crane - Sheila Hamanaka 548

Pinky and Rex and the Double-Dad Weekend - James Howe 655

The Return of Rinaldo, the Sly Fox - Ursel Scheffler 1276

Roommates Again - Kathryn O. Galbraith 437

Second-Grade Pig Pals - Kirby Larson 812

When Jane-Marie Told My Secret - Gina Willner-Pardo 1528

GRADES 2-4

The Always Prayer Shawl - Sheldon Oberman 1089

Amber Brown Is Not a Crayon - Paula Danziger 320

Annie Bananie Moves to Barry Avenue - Leah Komaiko 775

The Ballot Box Battle - Emily Arnold McCully 963

The Berenstain Bears and the New Girl in Town - Stan Berenstain 99

Best Enemies Forever - Kathleen Leverich 840

Brigid the Bad - Kathleen Leverich 841

Buffalo Bill and the Pony Express - Eleanor Coerr 262

Caleb's Friend - Eric Jon Nones 1081

Cat, You Better Come Home - Garrison Keillor 727

Cheyenne Again - Eve Bunting 170

Chin Yu Min and the Ginger Cat - Jennifer Armstrong 39

Clean House - Jessie Haas 531

Clouds of Terror - Catherine A. Welch 1489

Coyote and the Magic Words - Phyllis Root 1227

Dance of the Sacred Circle: A Native American Tale - Kristina Rodanas 1223

Dance on a Sealskin - Barbara Winslow 1533

Dandelions - Eve Bunting 171

Day of the Unicorn - Mollie Hunter 664

Donavan's Word Jar - Monalisa DeGross 337

Don't Call Me Beanhead! - Susan Wojciechowski 1544

The Dragon and the Unicorn - Lynne Cherry 237

Eagle Dreams - Sheryl McFarlane 976

Emily Eyefinger and the Lost Treasure - Duncan Ball 64

The Faithful Friend - Robert D. San Souci 1261

Fox Song - Joseph Bruchac 161

Genghis Khan: A Dog Star Is Born - Marjorie Weinman Sharmat 1320

The Gentleman and the Kitchen Maid - Diane Stanley 1376

Get the Picture, Jenny Archer? - Ellen Conford 278

Ghost Dog - Ellen Leroe 836

The Giant - Mordicai Gerstein 461

The Girl in the Golden Bower - Jane Yolen 1578

Good Griselle - Jane Yolen 1579

Gorgonzola Zombies in the Park - Elizabeth Levy 858

Grandaddy and Janetta - Helen V. Griffith 519

Grandaddy's Stars - Helen V. Griffith 520

The Happy Prince - Oscar Wilde 1515

Harry and Arney - Judith Caseley 218

Herbie Jones and the Birthday Showdown - Suzy Kline 768

Heroes - Ken Mochizuki 1024

Hey, New Kid! - Betsy Duffey 368

How to Be Cool in the Third Grade - Betsy Duffey 369

I'm George Washington and You're Not! - Steven Kroll 789

Imani and the Flying Africans - Janice Liddell 871

In Trouble with Teacher - Patricia Demuth 339

It Was a Dark and Stormy Night - Allan Ahlberg 16

Jenius, the Amazing Guinea Pig - Dick King-Smith 749

The Key to the Playhouse - Carol Beach York 1586

Lavender - Karen Hesse 599

Little Obie and the Kidnap - Martin Waddell 1464

Lizzie Logan Wears Purple Sunglasses - Eileen Spinelli 1369

Look Out, Washington, D.C.! - Patricia Reilly Giff 465

Loretta and the Little Fairy - Gerda Marie Scheidl 1278

Man Out at First - Matt Christopher 251

Maybe Yes, Maybe No, Maybe Maybe - Susan Patron 1118

Meg Mackintosh and the Mystery in the Locked Library - Lucinda Landon 811

Midnight Rider - Krista Ruepp 1238

Minty: A Story of Young Harriet Tubman - Alan Schroeder 1295

Mr. Potter's Pet - Dick King-Smith 750

Mush, a Dog from Space - Daniel Manus Pinkwater 1155

The Mysterious Horseman: An Adventure in Prairietown, 1836 - Kate Waters 1481

The Mystery of the Dancing Angels - Elspeth Campbell Murphy 1050

Nannies for Hire - Amy Hest 606

Night of the Full Moon - Gloria Whelan 1505

No Dogs Allowed - Jane Cutler 317

No More Animals! - Lucia Monfried 1029

Odds on Oliver - Constance C. Greene 500

Olympic Dream - Matt Christopher 252

On Cat Mountain - Francoise Richard 1209

On the Road with Poppa Whopper - Marianne Busser 188

Owen Foote, Second Grade Strongman - Stephanie Greene 501

Papa Gatto: An Italian Fairy Tale - Ruth Sanderson 1265

Patrick Doyle Is Full of Blarney - Jennifer Armstrong 40

Patrick's Tree House - Steven Kroll 790

Pinky and Rex and the New Baby - James Howe 656

Posy Bates, Again! - Helen Cresswell 299

Pudmuddles - Carol Beach York 1587

The Puppy Sister - S.E. Hinton 623

Rats on the Range and Other Stories - James Marshall 937

Rinaldo on the Run - Ursel Scheffler 1277

The St. Patrick's Day Shamrock Mystery - Marion M. Markham 934

Sara Kate Saves the World - Susan Beth Pfeffer 1143

The Saracen Maid - Leon Garfield 441

The School Mouse - Dick King-Smith 751

School Spirit Sabotage - Elizabeth Levy 860

Serious Science - Janice Lee Smith 1352

The Shoemaker's Boy - Joan Aiken 18

Shortcut - David Macaulay 911

Slam Dunk Saturday - Jean Marzollo 944

Sophie Is Seven - Dick King-Smith 753

Sophie's Lucky - Dick King-Smith 754

Spider Kane and the Mystery at Jumbo Nightcrawler's - Mary Pope Osborne 1102

Star of Fear, Star of Hope - Jo Hoestlandt 629

Stories from Firefly Island - Benedict Blathwayt 116

The Storm - Marc Harshman 566

Straw Sense - Rona Rupert 1239

The Stray - Dick King-Smith 755

The Swoose - Dick King-Smith 756

Throw-Away Pets - Betsy Duffey 370

Tooter Pepperday - Jerry Spinelli 1371

Tortoise's Flying Lesson - Margaret Mayo 955

A Turkey Drive and Other Tales - Barbara Ann Porte 1167

Uncle Fedya, His Dog, and His Cat - Eduard Uspenskii 1440

The Up & Down Spring - Johanna Hurwitz 672

Washing the Willow Tree Loon - Jacqueline Briggs Martin 942

When the Whippoorwill Calls - Candice F. Ransom 1190

The Whispering Cloth: A Refugee's Story - Pegi Deitz Shea 1324

Your Mother Was a Neanderthal - Jon
    Scieszka 1300

GRADES 3-6

101 Ways to Bug Your Parents - Lee Wardlaw 1478
Arthur, High King of Britain - Michael
    Morpurgo 1038
The Ballad of the Pirate Queens - Jane Yolen 1576
The Barn - Avi 54
The Booford Summer - Susan Mathias Smith 1356
The Case of the Fantastic Footprints - E.W.
    Hildick 616
Children of the Longhouse - Joseph Bruchac 159
Christmas Spirit: Two Stories - Robert Westall 1501
Daddy's Climbing Tree - C.S. Adler 11
The Daydreamer - Ian McEwan 975
Down and Up Fall - Johanna Hurwitz 666
Drylongso - Virginia Hamilton 549
The Enchanted Horse - Magdalen Nabb 1058
Faces in the Dark: A Book of Scary Stories - Chris
    Powling 1172
Faith and the Electric Dogs - Patrick Jennings 693
Ghosts Don't Get Goosebumps - Elvira
    Woodruff 1551
Gopher Takes Heart - Virginia Scribner 1303
Gulliver in Lilliput - Margaret Hodges 628
The Haunted House: A Collection of Original Stories -
    Jane Yolen 1581
The Light on Hogback Hill - Cynthia DeFelice 335
The Magic Hare - Lynne Reid Banks 72
More Rootabagas - Carl Sandburg 1262
Nightwalkers - Judy K. Morris 1041
Off and Running - Gary Soto 1363
Orp and the FBI - Suzy Kline 771
*Papa Alonzo Leatherby: A Collection of Tall Tales
    from the Best Storyteller in Carroll County* -
    Marguerite W. Davol 323
Pie Magic - Toby Forward 419
Pink and Say - Patricia Polacco 1162
Remember My Name - Sara H. Banks 74
Saving Owen's Toad - Juanita Havill 573
Seven Spiders Spinning - Gregory Maguire 920
Shiloh Season - Phyllis Reynolds Naylor 1068
The Snow Queen - Hans Christian Andersen 32
Soup Ahoy - Robert Newton Peck 1127
Spooky Stories for a Dark and Stormy Night - Alice
    Low 900
Stinker's Return - Pamela F. Service 1311
Tut Tut - Jon Scieszka 1299
Twelve Tales - Hans Christian Andersen 33
The Twin in the Tavern - Barbara Brooks
    Wallace 1469
The Van Gogh Cafe - Cynthia Rylant 1256
The Wave of the Sea-Wolf - David Wisniewski 1542

GRADES 3-7

*The Case of the Missing Cutthroats, an Ecological
    Mystery* - Jean Craighead George 448
Flip-Flop Girl - Katherine Paterson 1112

GRADES 3 AND UP

*A Newbery Halloween: A Dozen Scary Stories by
    Newbery Award-Winning Authors* - Martin H.
    Greenberg 498
Scooter - Vera B. Williams 1523
The Sweetest Fig - Chris Van Allsburg 1444

GRADES 4-5

Fifth Grade Fever - Michele Granger 493
The Great Pony Hassle - Nancy Springer 1374
The Hanukkah Ghosts - Malka Penn 1128
I Was a Fifth-Grade Zebra - Nancy J. Hopper 645
Seth and Samona - Joanne Hyppolite 674

Traveling Backward - Toby Forward 420

GRADES 4-6

The 13th Floor: A Ghost Story - Sid Fleischman 409
*The Absolutely True Story...How I Visited Yellowstone
    Park with the Terrible Rupes* - Willo Davis
    Roberts 1217
Adeline Street - Carol Lynch Williams 1519
Amy Dunn Quits School - Susan Richards
    Shreve 1330
Augusta & Trab - Christopher De Vinck 330
The Baby Grand, the Moon in July, & Me - Joyce
    Annette Barnes 78
Back to Before - Jan Slepian 1343
The Bamboo Flute - Garry Disher 353
The Battle for the Castle - Elizabeth Winthrop 1537
Bess's Log Cabin Quilt - D. Anne Love 898
Blabber Mouth - Morris Gleitzman 479
The Bomb in the Bessledorf Bus Depot - Phyllis
    Reynolds Naylor 1063
The Bones in the Cliff - James Stevenson 1385
The Bookstore Mouse - Peggy Christian 245
Bound for Oregon - Jean Van Leeuwen 1448
Boys at Work - Gary Soto 1361
The Boys Start the War - Phyllis Reynolds
    Naylor 1064
The Burnt Stick - Anthony Hill 618
Burton and Stanley - Frank O'Rourke 1101
Buzzard Breath - Marty Crisp 304
Bye, Bye, Bai Kai - Harriett Luger 904
Caleb's Choice - G. Clifton Wisler 1539
The Case of the Absent Author - E.W. Hildick 614
The Case of the Wiggling Wig - E.W. Hildick 617
Cat Running - Zilpha Keatley Snyder 1359
Child of the Wolves - Elizabeth Hall 545
Come Morning - Leslie Davis Guccione 524
Countess Veronica - Nancy K. Robinson 1219
Courtyard Cat - C.S. Adler 10
Daring to be Abigail - Rachel Vail 1442
Dear Elijah - Miriam Bat-Ami 85
Dear Levi: Letters from the Overland Trail - Elvira
    Woodruff 1550
Dog Friday - Hilary McKay 980
Dog Years - Sally Warner 1480
Double Play at Short - Matt Christopher 249
Drums at Saratoga - Lisa Banim 68
Earthquake Terror - Peg Kehret 725
Egg-Drop Blues - Jacqueline Turner Banks 70
Elfsong - Ann Turner 1433
Ellen Anders on Her Own - Karen Hirsch 625
The Exiles at Home - Hilary McKay 981
Falcon's Egg - Luli Gray 497
Fearsome's Hero - Dona Schenker 1280
Fighting Tackle - Matt Christopher 250
Fire in the Wind - Betty Levin 843
Frankie Murphy's Kiss List - Donna Guthrie 526
Fruit Flies, Fish & Fortune Cookies - Anne
    LeMieux 834
The Girls Get Even - Phyllis Reynolds Naylor 1067
Going to See Grassy Ella - Kathryn Lance 810
Good-Bye, Hello - Barbara Shook Hazen 577
The Great Brain Is Back - John D. Fitzgerald 408
The Greatest Show off Earth - Margaret Mahy 923
The Green Bottle and the Silver Kite - Fredericka
    Berger 101
A Haunted Year - Ann Phillips 1147
Hey You, Sister Rose - Eileen Walsh Strauch 1398
Hiroshima - Laurence Yep 1572
Hob and the Goblins - William Mayne 954
I Remember - Fara Lynn Krasnopolsky 784
The In-Between Days - Eve Bunting 174
In the Land of the Big Red Apple - Roger Lea
    MacBride 912
Jason and the Losers - Gina Willner-Pardo 1527
Jimmy, the Pickpocket of the Palace - Donna Jo
    Napoli 1061
Johnny Rides Again - Jo Ann Muchmore 1048

Juliet's Story - William Trevor 1426
Junebug - Alice Mead 998
The Junkyard Dog - Erika Tamar 1407
Just Call Me Stupid - Tom Birdseye 108
Kelly and Me - Carol Lynch Williams 1520
The Kid Who Ran for President - Dan Gutman 527
Later, Gator - Laurence Yep 1573
Libbie Sims, Worry Wart - Gayle Rogers
    Lockwood 887
A Likely Lad - Gillian Avery 53
The Magnificent Mummy Maker - Elvira
    Woodruff 1552
The Man in the Ceiling - Jules Feiffer 403
Mayfield Crossing - Vaunda Micheaux Nelson 1070
The Mennyms - Sylvia Waugh 1484
Mennyms Alone - Sylvia Waugh 1485
Mennyms in the Wilderness - Sylvia Waugh 1486
A Message from the Match Girl - Janet Taylor
    Lisle 880
Minnie - Annie M.G. Schmidt 1286
The Miraculous Makeover of Lizard Flanagan - Carol
    Gorman 489
Monster of the Month Club - Dian Curtis
    Regan 1203
Moon Window - Jane Louise Curry 310
Moriah's Pond - Ethel Footman Smothers 1357
Mr. Lincoln's Drummer - G. Clifton Wisler 1540
My Brother Is a Visitor from Another Planet - Dyan
    Sheldon 1327
My Brother, the Ghost - Suzanne Weyn 1503
My Fabulous New Life - Sheila Greenwald 503
My Name Is Brain/Brian - Jeanne Betancourt 106
My Wartime Summers - Jane Cutler 316
The Mystery Machine - Herbie Brennan 134
The Mystery of the Cupboard - Lynne Reid
    Banks 73
Nekomah Creek Christmas - Linda Crew 301
Nerd No More - Kristine L. Franklin 424
Never Trust a Sister over Twelve - Stephen
    Roos 1226
*A Newbery Zoo: A Dozen Animal Stories by Newbery
    Award-Winning Authors* - Martin H.
    Greenberg 499
No Friend of Mine - Ann Turnbull 1428
Nobody's Daughter - Susan Beth Pfeffer 1142
Nothing but Trouble, Trouble, Trouble - Patricia
    Hermes 592
Numbskulls - William Taylor 1410
Odd Man Out - Gail Radley 1185
On Winter's Wind - Patricia Hermes 593
Our House: The Stories of Levittown - Pam
    Conrad 282
Passenger - Jane Yolen 1585
Phoenix Upside Down - Elizabeth Scarboro 1274
The Pickle Song - Barthe DeClements 331
The Pirates' Mixed-Up Voyage - Margaret Mahy 924
Poppy - Avi 57
Pressure Play - Matt Christopher 253
The Promised Land - Isabelle Holland 637
Re-Elect Nutty! - Dean Hughes 660
Robin's Country - Monica Furlong 434
Room for a Stranger - Ann Turnbull 1429
The Secret Life of Bethany Barrett - Claudia
    Mills 1017
The Secret of the Ruby Ring - Yvonne
    MacGrory 915
Shoebag Returns - Mary James 688
The Shuteyes - Mary James 689
Soccer Circus - Jamie Gilson 472
Someone to Count On - Patricia Hermes 594
Star Hatchling - Margaret Bechard 93
Stardust - Alane Ferguson 405
Step by Wicked Step - Anne Fine 407
Sticky Beak - Morris Gleitzman 480
Stolen Bones - Joan Carris 216
A Sunburned Prayer - Marc Talbert 1406
Tangled Fortunes - Margaret Mahy 926
Tarantula Shoes - Tom Birdseye 110

Age Index

GRADES 6-9

GRADES 6-12

Illustrator Index

This index lists the illustrators of the featured titles. Illustrators are listed alphabetically, followed by the title, author, and entry number of the book or books in which the artist's work appears.

A

Abolafia, Yossi
Clean House - Jessie Haas 531
Harry's Birthday - Barbara Ann Porte 1166
A Turkey Drive and Other Tales - Barbara Ann Porte 1167

Adinolfi, JoAnn
The Egyptian Polar Bear - JoAnn Adinolfi 9

Aggs, Patrice
Florizella and the Wolves - Philippa Gregory 510

Ahlberg, Janet
It Was a Dark and Stormy Night - Allan Ahlberg 16

Alborough, Jez
It's the Bear! - Jez Alborough 20

Alda, Arlene
Pig, Horse, or Cow, Don't Wake Me Now - Arlene Alda 21

Aldous, Kate
Posy Bates, Again! - Helen Cresswell 299

Alexander, Martha
You're a Genius, Blackboard Bear - Martha Alexander 24

Ali, Abira
The Big Bazoohley - Peter Carey 207

Aliki
Best Friends Together Again - Aliki 25

Allen, Jonathan
Burton and Stanley - Frank O'Rourke 1101
Two by Two by Two - Jonathan Allen 26

Allen, Thomas B.
Across the Wide Dark Sea: The Mayflower Journey - Jean Van Leeuwen 1446
Climbing Kansas Mountains - George Shannon 1316

Alley, R. W.
The Know-Nothings - Michelle Sobel Spirn 1372

Allison, Diane
My Worst Days Diary - Suzanne Altman 30

Ambrus, Victor G.
The Shoemaker's Boy - Joan Aiken 18

Ancona, George
Sally's Submarine - Joan Anderson 34

Andreasen, Dan
Brigid the Bad - Kathleen Leverich 841
Grandma's Garden - Elaine Moore 1033

Grandma's Smile - Elaine Moore 1034
Joshua T. Bates Takes Charge - Susan Richards Shreve 1332

Anholt, Catherine
The New Puppy - Laurence Anholt 35

Anstey, Caroline
Moles Can Dance - Richard Edwards 380

Apple, Margot
Just Like My Dad - Tricia Gardella 440
Sheep Take a Hike - Nancy Shaw 1323

Arnaktauyok, Germaine
A Sled Dog for Moshi - Jeanne Bushey 186

Arnold, Jeanne
Carlos and the Cornfield/Carlos y la Milpa de Maiz - Jan Romero Stevens 1379

Arnold, Tedd
Inside a Barn in the Country: A Rebus Read-Along Story - Alyssa Satin Capucilli 206
My Working Mom - Peter Glassman 477
No More Water in the Tub! - Tedd Arnold 43

Arnosky, Jim
Little Champ - Jim Arnosky 44

Arrington, Aileen
Stella's Bull - Frances Arrington 45

Asch, Frank
The Earth and I - Frank Asch 46

Ashforth, Camilla
Humphrey Thud - Camilla Ashforth 48

Auch, Mary Jane
Hen Lake - Mary Jane Auch 49
Monster Brother - Mary Jane Auch 51
Peeping Beauty - Mary Jane Auch 52

August, Louise
Night Lights: A Sukkot Story - Barbara Diamond Goldin 484

Austin, Virginia
Kate's Giants - Valiska Gregory 512

Ayers, Alan
Maxi, the Star - Debra Barracca 79

Ayliffe, Alex
Lucy's Picture - Nicola Moon 1031

Ayto, Russell
Lazy Jack - Vivian French 428

B

Babbitt, Natalie
Bub: Or the Very Best Thing - Natalie Babbitt 60

Bailey, Peter
Faces in the Dark: A Book of Scary Stories - Chris Powling 1172
Tigerella - Kit Wright 1564

Baker, Leslie
Honkers - Jane Yolen 1582

Ballard, Robin
Good-Bye House - Robin Ballard 65

Barnes-Murphy, Rowan
Sherman the Sheep - Kevin Kiser 762

Barnet, Nancy
Dream Meadow - Helen V. Griffith 518

Barrett, Angela
The Ice Palace - Angela McAllister 957

Barrett, Robert
Dust for Dinner - Ann Turner 1432

Bartlett, Alison
Oliver's Vegetables - Vivian French 429

Barton, Jill
In the Rain with Baby Duck - Amy Hest 604

Bassett, Jeni
The Chick's Trick - Jeni Bassett 84
The Pigrates Clean Up - Steven Kroll 791

Basso, Bill
Ghost Dog - Ellen Leroe 836
Wolfman Sam - Elizabeth Levy 862

Beddows, Eric
The Rooster's Gift - Pam Conrad 283

Begay, Shonto
The Boy Who Dreamed of an Acorn - Leigh Casler 223

Beier, Ellen
Man Out at First - Matt Christopher 251

Ben-Ami, Doron
The Haunted House: A Collection of Original Stories - Jane Yolen 1581
Tornado - Betsy Byars 197

Bendall-Brunello, John
When I Grow Bigger - Trish Cooke 285

Bender, Robert
A Most Unusual Lunch - Robert Bender 97

Benjamin, Amanda
Two's Company - Amanda Benjamin 98

Benson, Linda
Two Girls in Sister Dresses - Jean Van
Leeuwen 1451

Benson, Patrick
The Little Boat - Kathy Henderson 581

Berenstain, Stan
The Berenstain Bears and the New Girl in Town - Stan
Berenstain 99

Berger, Barbara
The Jewel Heart - Barbara Berger 100

Binch, Caroline
Boundless Grace - Mary Hoffman 634
Gregory Cool - Caroline Binch 107
Hue Boy - Rita Phillips Mitchell 1023

Birmingham, Christian
The Magic Bicycle - Berlie Doherty 355

Bittinger, Ned
The Matzah That Papa Brought Home - Fran
Manushkin 929

Bjorkman, Steve
Heart to Heart - George Shannon 1317
Seeds - George Shannon 1318

Blake, Quentin
Simpkin - Quentin Blake 114

Blake, Robert J.
Dog - Robert J. Blake 115
Maggie and Silky and Joe - Amy Ehrlich 386

Blathwayt, Benedict
Stories from Firefly Island - Benedict Blathwayt 116

Blegvad, Erik
A Sound of Leaves - Lenore Blegvad 118
Twelve Tales - Hans Christian Andersen 33

Bloom, Lloyd
One Yellow Daffodil: A Hanukkah Story - David A.
Adler 14

Blythe, Gary
Under the Moon - Dyan Sheldon 1328

Bobak, Cathy
Tom Foolery - Curtis Parkinson 1111

Bolam, Emily
Tortoise's Flying Lesson - Margaret Mayo 955

Bolognese, Don
Buffalo Bill and the Pony Express - Eleanor
Coerr 262

Bootman, Colin
Seth and Samona - Joanne Hyppolite 674

Bornstein, Ruth Lercher
Rabbit's Good News - Ruth Lercher Bornstein 126

Bostock, Mike
Pond Year - Kathryn Lasky 817

Bouma, Paddy
Valentine - Carol Carrick 215

Bowen, Keith
Snowy - Berlie Doherty 356

Bowman, Leslie W.
The Cuckoo Child - Dick King-Smith 747
Night of the Full Moon - Gloria Whelan 1505

Brazell, Derek
My Brother Is a Visitor from Another Planet - Dyan
Sheldon 1327

Breathed, Berkeley
Goodnight Opus - Berkeley Breathed 132

Brett, Jan
Armadillo Rodeo - Jan Brett 135

Brewster, Patience
Two Bushy Badgers - Patience Brewster 136

Briggs, Raymond
The Bear - Raymond Briggs 137

Brown, Jane Clark
George Washington's Ghost - Jane Clark Brown 142

Brown, Kathryn
A Bear for All Seasons - Diane Marcial Fuchs 433
Tough Boris - Mem Fox 423

Brown, M.K.
Let's Go Camping with Mr. Sillypants - M.K.
Brown 144

Brown, Marc
Arthur Writes a Story - Marc Brown 145
Arthur's Chicken Pox - Marc Brown 146
Arthur's Family Vacation - Marc Brown 147
Arthur's First Sleepover - Marc Brown 148
Arthur's New Puppy - Marc Brown 149
D.W. Rides Again! - Marc Brown 150
D.W. the Picky Eater - Marc Brown 151
Rex and Lilly Family Time - Laurie Krasny
Brown 143

Brown, Marcia
How the Ostrich Got Its Long Neck - Verna
Aardema 1

Brown, Ruth
The Bear & Mr. Bear - Frances Thomas 1416
Copycat - Ruth Brown 154
In Search of the Giant - Jeanne Willis 1524
The Picnic - Ruth Brown 155

Brown, Sterling
The Big Bike Race - Lucy Jane Bledsoe 117

Browne, Anthony
The Daydreamer - Ian McEwan 975
Zoo - Anthony Browne 156

Browne, Jane
My Wicked Stepmother - Norman Leach 828

Browning, Colleen
Can't Sit Still - Karen E. Lotz 897

Brunkus, Denise
Junie B. Jones and Some Sneaky Peeky Spying -
Barbara Park 1109

Bryan, Ashley
The Story of the Three Kingdoms - Walter Dean
Myers 1057

Buchanan, Yvonne
Juneteenth Jamboree - Carole Boston
Weatherford 1487

Buchholz, Quint
Sleep Well, Little Bear - Quint Buchholz 165

Buehner, Mark
Fanny's Dream - Caralyn Buehner 166
Harvey Potter's Balloon Farm - Jerdine Nolen 1078
A Job for Wittilda - Caralyn Buehner 167

Buguet, Anne
On Cat Mountain - Francoise Richard 1209

Burningham, John
Courtney - John Burningham 182
Harvey Slumfenburger's Christmas Present - John
Burningham 183

Bush, Timothy
James in the House of Aunt Prudence - Timothy
Bush 184
Three at Sea - Timothy Bush 185

Butterworth, Nick
The Secret Path - Nick Butterworth 189

Byard, Carole
Working Cotton - Sherley Anne Williams 1522

C

Cameron, Scott
Beethoven Lives Upstairs - Barbara Nichol 1073

Cannon, Annie
Whistle Home - Natalie Honeycutt 639

Cannon, Janell
Stellaluna - Janell Cannon 203

Caple, Kathy
The Wimp - Kathy Caple 204

Carle, Eric
My Apron - Eric Carle 209
The Very Lonely Firefly - Eric Carle 210

Carlson, Nancy
Arnie and the Skateboard Gang - Nancy Carlson 211

Carmi, Giora
The Miracle of the Potato Latkes: A Hanukkah Story -
Malka Penn 1129

Carpenter, Nancy
Lester's Dog - Karen Hesse 600
Sitti's Secrets - Naomi Shihab Nye 1087
Washing the Willow Tree Loon - Jacqueline Briggs
Martin 942

Cart, Chris
The Formerly Great Alexander Family - Susan
Richards Shreve 1331

Carter, Abby
Annie Bananie Moves to Barry Avenue - Leah
Komaiko 775
Great-Uncle Dracula and the Dirty Rat - Jayne
Harvey 568
Never Ride Your Elephant to School - Doug
Johnson 699
The Pink Party - Maryann Macdonald 914

Carter, Gail Gordon
Mac and Marie and the Train Toss Surprise -
Elizabeth Fitzgerald Howard 649
May'naise Sandwiches & Sunshine Tea - Sandra
Belton 96

Cartwright, Reg
James and the Rain - Karla Kuskin 800

Caseley, Judith
Mama, Coming and Going - Judith Caseley 219
Priscilla Twice - Judith Caseley 220
Sophie and Sammy's Library Sleepover - Judith
Caseley 221

Casey, Patricia
My Cat Jack - Patricia Casey 222

Casilla, Robert
Boys at Work - Gary Soto 1361
The Little Painter of Sabana Grande - Patricia
Maloney Markun 935

Cassler, Carl
Herbie Jones and the Birthday Showdown - Suzy
Kline 768

Castilla, Robert
The Pool Party - Gary Soto 1364

Catalano, Dominic
Merry Christmas, Old Armadillo - Larry Dane
Brimner 138
Rabbit Surprise - Eric L. Houck Jr. 648

Catalanotto, Peter
*The Catspring Somersault Flying One-Handed Flip-
Flop* - SuAnn Kiser 763
Dreamplace - George Ella Lyon 908
Mama Is a Miner - George Ella Lyon 910
The Painter - Peter Catalanotto 224

Cazet, Denys
Born in the Gravy - Denys Cazet 225
Dancing - Denys Cazet 226

Illustrator Index

Diamond, Donna
Day of the Unicorn - Mollie Hunter　664

Diaz, David
Smoky Night - Eve Bunting　177

Dillon, Leo
Her Stories: African American Folktales, Fairy Tales, and True Tales - Virginia Hamilton　550
The Sorcerer's Apprentice - Nancy Willard　1516

DiSalvo-Ryan, DyAnne
City Green - DyAnne DiSalvo-Ryan　352
Nina, Nina Ballerina - Jane O'Connor　1090
Olivia and the Real Live Pet - Charlotte Towner Graeber　490

DiVito, Anna
I Want Answers and a Parachute - P.J. Petersen　1138

Donahue, Dorothy
Maybe Yes, Maybe No, Maybe Maybe - Susan Patron　1118

Dooling, Michael
Lights on the River - Jane Resh Thomas　1417
The Story of Santa Claus - Tom Paxton　1122
Straw Sense - Rona Rupert　1239

Dorros, Arthur
Radio Man = Don Radio: A Story in English and Spanish - Arthur Dorros　363

Downing, Julie
Cabbage Rose - Mary-Claire Helldorfer　580
A Likely Lad - Gillian Avery　53
Soon, Annala - Riki Levinson　852

Drescher, Henrik
The Boy Who Ate Around - Henrik Drescher　365

Dressler, Marjory
The Mysterious Horseman: An Adventure in Prairietown, 1836 - Kate Waters　1481

Duffy, Daniel Mark
The Great Pony Hassle - Nancy Springer　1374
On the Right Track - B.B. Calhoun　198

Dugan, Karen
School Spirit - Johanna Hurwitz　671

Duke, Kate
One Saturday Morning - Barbara Baker　61

Duncan, Robert
Amber on the Mountain - Tony Johnston　702

Dunrea, Olivier
The Painter Who Loved Chickens - Olivier Dunrea　375

Dusikova, Maja
The Gift from Saint Nicholas - Dorothea Lachner　803

Dyer, Jane
The Girl in the Golden Bower - Jane Yolen　1578
If Anything Ever Goes Wrong at the Zoo - Mary Jean Hendrick　582
Time for Bed - Mem Fox　422

E

Eagle, Ellen
The Ghost Witch - Betty Ren Wright　1558
What's French for HELP, George? - Helen McCann　961

Egan, Tim
Chestnut Cove - Tim Egan　381
Friday Night at Hodge's Cafe - Tim Egan　382

Egielski, Richard
Buz - Richard Egielski　383
Call Me Ahnighito - Pam Conrad　280

Ehlert, Lois
Mole's Hill - Lois Ehlert　384
Nuts to You! - Lois Ehlert　385

Elivia
Grandma's Shoes - Libby Hathorn　569
Hotter than a Hot Dog! - Stephanie Calmenson　201

Emberley, Michael
Welcome Back, Sun - Michael Emberley　389

Emberley, Rebecca
Three Cool Kids - Rebecca Emberley　390

Ernst, Lisa Campbell
Little Red Riding Hood: A Newfangled Prairie Tale - Lisa Campbell Ernst　394
The Luckiest Kid on the Planet - Lisa Campbell Ernst　395
Squirrel Park - Lisa Campbell Ernst　396

Everitt, Betsy
TV Dinner - Betsy Everitt　398

F

Farnsworth, Bill
Grandpa Is a Flyer - Sanna Anderson Baker　62

Fernandez, Laura
Tchaikovsky Discovers America - Esther Kalman　717

Fine, Howard
Piggie Pie! - Margie Palatini　1105

Firth, Barbara
Let's Go Home, Little Bear - Martin Waddell　1463
A Song for Little Toad - Vivian French　430

Fisher, Chris
Under the Moon - Vivian French　431

Fisher, Cynthia
B.J.'s Billion-Dollar Bet - Julie Anne Peters　1133
The School Mouse - Dick King-Smith　751

Fletcher, Claire
The Wind Garden - Angela McAllister　958

Floca, Brian
City of Light, City of Dark: A Comic-Book Novel - Avi　55
Jenius, the Amazing Guinea Pig - Dick King-Smith　749
Luck with Potatoes - Helen Ketteman　740
Poppy - Avi　57

Florian, Douglas
Very Scary - Tony Johnston　707

Ford, George
Baby Jesus, Like My Brother - Margery Wheeler Brown　153

Foreman, Michael
Arthur, High King of Britain - Michael Morpurgo　1038
Dad! I Can't Sleep - Michael Foreman　416
The Long Weekend - Troon Harrison　565
Surprise! Surprise! - Michael Foreman　417
There's a Bear in the Bath! - Nanette Newman　1072
War Game - Michael Foreman　418

Fowler, Jim
I'll See You When the Moon Is Full - Susi Gregg Fowler　421

Frampton, David
My Son John - Jim Aylesworth　59

Franco-Feeney, Betsy
James Bear and the Goose Gathering - Jim Latimer　821

Frazee, Marla
That Kookoory! - Margaret Walden Froehlich　432

French, Fiona
Pepi and the Secret Names - Jill Paton Walsh　1115

Fritz, Ron
My Dog Talks - Gail Herman　591

Fuchs, Bernie
Carolina Shout! - Alan Schroeder　1293

Fulweiler, John
The Iron Dragon Never Sleeps - Stephen Krensky　787

G

Gaber, Susan
Bit by Bit - Steve Sanfield　1267
The Princess and the Lord of Night - Emma Bull　168

Gackenbach, Dick
The Baby Blues: An Adam Joshua Story - Janice Lee Smith　1351
Serious Science - Janice Lee Smith　1352
When I Am Eight - Joan Lowery Nixon　1077

Gallwey, Kay
Dancing Daisy - Kay Gallwey　439

Gamble, Kim
Dear Fred - Susanna Rodell　1225

Gammell, Stephen
Monster Mama - Liz Rosenberg　1232

Gamper, Ruth
The Fog's Net - Pat Pflieger　1146

Garland, Michael
Dinner at Magritte's - Michael Garland　442

Garns, Allen
When I Go Camping with Grandma - Marion Dane Bauer　89

Garrison, Barbara
Josiah True and the Art Maker - Amy Littlesugar　883

Gerrard, Roy
Croco'nile - Roy Gerrard　454
Wagons West - Roy Gerrard　455

Gerstein, Mordicai
The Giant - Mordicai Gerstein　461
Something Queer in Outer Space - Elizabeth Levy　861

Geter, Tyrone
Can't Scare Me! - Melissa Milich　1010
Dawn and the Round To-It - Irene Smalls　1347
The Little Tree Growin' in the Shade - Camille Yarbrough　1569
White Socks Only - Evelyn Coleman　275
Willie Jerome - Alice Faye Duncan　372

Gider, Iskender
The Return of Rinaldo, the Sly Fox - Ursel Scheffler　1276
Rinaldo on the Run - Ursel Scheffler　1277

Gilchrist, Jan Spivey
Indigo and Moonlight Gold - Jan Spivey Gilchrist　469
William and the Good Old Days - Eloise Greenfield　502

Gilleece, David
In the Land of the Big Red Apple - Roger Lea MacBride　912
Little House on Rocky Ridge - Roger Lea MacBride　913

Glass, Andrew
The Booford Summer - Susan Mathias Smith　1356
Folks Call Me Appleseed John - Andrew Glass　475

Two of Everything - Lily Toy Hong   641

Howard, Arthur
Gooseberry Park - Cynthia Rylant   1249
Mr. Putter and Tabby Bake the Cake - Cynthia Rylant   1253
Mr. Putter and Tabby Pick the Pears - Cynthia Rylant   1254
Mr. Putter and Tabby Walk the Dog - Cynthia Rylant   1255

Howard, Paul
John Joe and the Big Hen - Martin Waddell   1462
Rosie's Fishing Trip - Amy Hest   608

Hsu-Flanders, Lillian
Dumpling Soup - Jama Kim Rattigan   1197

Hubbard, Woodleigh
Hip Cat - Jonathan London   889

Hughes, George
Never Hit a Ghost with a Baseball Bat - Eth Clifford   260

Humphries, Tudor
Eagle - Judy Allen   27

Hutchins, Pat
Little Pink Pig - Pat Hutchins   673

Hyman, Trina Schart
The Adventures of Hershel of Ostropol - Eric A. Kimmel   742

I

Ichikawa, Satomi
Nora's Surprise - Satomi Ichikawa   675
Tanya and Emily in a Dance for Two - Patricia Lee Gauch   446

Imai, Miko
Lilly's Secret - Miko Imai   676

Ingraham, Erick
Henry the Sailor Cat - Mary Calhoun   199
Night in the Barn - Faye Gibbons   462

Isadora, Rachel
Lili at Ballet - Rachel Isadora   679
Lili on Stage - Rachel Isadora   680

Iskowitz, Joel
Ghosts Don't Get Goosebumps - Elvira Woodruff   1551

Ito, Yoriko
Lily and the Wooden Bowl - Alan Schroeder   1294

J

Jabar, Cynthia
Good Morning, Pond - Alyssa Satin Capucilli   205
A Koala for Katie: An Adoption Story - Jonathan London   891

Jackson, Shelley
Do You Know Me? - Nancy Farmer   400
Great Aunt Martha - Rebecca C. Jones   710

Jacob, Murv
The Boy Who Lived with the Bears: And Other Iroquois Stories - Joseph Bruchac   158

James, Ann
Tangles - Errol Broome   141

James, Betsy
I Hate Company - P.J. Petersen   1137
Mary Ann - Betsy James   686
No More Animals! - Lucia Monfried   1029

James, Curtis E.
Vampire Bugs: Stories Conjured from the Past - Sharon Dennis Wyeth   1566

Jeffers, Susan
Lassie Come-Home - Rosemary Wells   1494
Waiting for the Evening Star - Rosemary Wells   1498

Jenkins, Leonard
Mayfield Crossing - Vaunda Micheaux Nelson   1070

Jeram, Anita
Daisy Dare - Anita Jeram   695
Guess How Much I Love You - Sam McBratney   960

Jerome, Karen A.
The St. Patrick's Day Shamrock Mystery - Marion M. Markham   934

Johnson, Dolores
Papa's Stories - Dolores Johnson   697
Your Dad Was Just Like You - Dolores Johnson   698

Johnson, Larry
When Jo Louis Won the Title - Belinda Rochelle   1220

Johnson, Laurie K.
Clouds of Terror - Catherine A. Welch   1489

Johnson, Meredith
The Sub - P.J. Petersen   1139

Johnson, Paul Brett
The Cow Who Wouldn't Come Down - Paul Brett Johnson   701
Insects Are My Life - Megan McDonald   974

Johnson, Stephen T.
The Tie Man's Miracle: A Chanukah Tale - Steven Schnur   1289

Johnson, Steve
Cat, You Better Come Home - Garrison Keillor   727

Jones, Jan Naimo
Make a Wish, Molly - Barbara Cohen   266

Joos, Louis
Oregon's Journey - Rascal   1191

Jorgensen, David
Wind Says Good Night - Katy Rydell   1245

Joyce, William
Santa Calls - William Joyce   715

K

Kahn, Katherine Janus
Matzah Ball: A Passover Story - Mindy Avra Portnoy   1170

Kandoian, Ellen
Summer's End - Maribeth Boelts   121

Kang, Johanna
Star of Fear, Star of Hope - Jo Hoestlandt   629

Karas, G. Brian
Like Butter on Pancakes - Jonathan London   893
On the Trail with Miss Pace - Sharon Phillips Denslow   342
Saving Sweetness - Diane Stanley   1377
Truman's Aunt Farm - Jama Kim Rattigan   1198

Karlan, Nurit
The Fat Cat Sat on the Mat - Nurit Karlan   718

Kastner, Jill
Down at Angel's - Sharon Chmielarz   239
Naomi Knows It's Springtime - Virginia L. Kroll   792

Kasza, Keiko
Grandpa Toad's Last Secret - Keiko Kasza   721
The Rat and the Tiger - Keiko Kasza   722

Kaufmann, Jeff
Milk Rock - Jeff Kaufmann   723

Keister, Douglas
Fernando's Gift/El Regalo de Fernando - Douglas Keister   728

Keith, Doug
A Place for Grace - Jean Davies Okimoto   1092

Keller, Holly
Geraldine's Baby Brother - Holly Keller   730
Harry and Tuck - Holly Keller   732

Keller, Katie
Seven Loaves of Bread - Ferida Wolff   1546

Kelley, True
In Trouble with Teacher - Patricia Demuth   339
I've Got Chicken Pox - True Kelley   733
Three Stories You Can Read to Your Dog - Sara Swan Miller   1015

Kellogg, Steven
The Great Quillow - James Thurber   1419
Parents in the Pigpen, Pigs in the Tub - Amy Ehrlich   387
The Rattlebang Picnic - Margaret Mahy   925
Sally Ann Thunder Ann Whirlwind Crockett: A Tall Tale - Steven Kellogg   734
The Wizard Next Door - Peter Glassman   478

Kelly, Jo' Anne
Som See and the Magic Elephant - Jamie Oliviero   1094

Kelly, Laura
The Pumpkin Man from Piney Creek - Darleen Bailey Beard   91

Kennaway, Adrienne
Hungry Hyena - Mwenye Hadithi   536

Kiefte, Kees De
The Cherry Tree Buck and Other Stories - Robin Moore   1035
Chuck and Danielle - Peter Dickinson   348

Kiernan, Anna
The Bear Santa Claus Forgot - Diana Kimpton   745

Kiesler, Kate
Grandfather's Christmas Camp - Marc McCutcheon   969

Kim, Joung Un
The Gift of Driscoll Lipscomb - Sara Yamaka   1568

Kimber, Murray
Josepha: A Prairie Boy's Story - Jim McGugan   979

Kirk, David
Miss Spider's Tea Party - David Kirk   760

Kirkpatrick, Joey
Plowie: A Story from the Prairie - Patricia Kirkpatrick   761

Kiuchi, Tatsuro
The Lotus Seed - Sherry Garland   443
The Seasons and Someone - Virginia L. Kroll   794
Tsubu the Little Snail - Carol Ann Williams   1518

Kleven, Elisa
Isla - Arthur Dorros   362
The Paper Princess - Elisa Kleven   767

Koontz, Robin Michal
Chicago and the Cat - Robin Michal Koontz   778
Chicago and the Cat: The Halloween Party - Robin Michal Koontz   779

Kopper, Lisa
Jafta: The Homecoming - Hugh Lewin   864

Koscielniak, Bruce
Geoffrey Groundhog Predicts the Weather - Bruce Koscielniak   780

Kovalski, Maryann
I Went to the Zoo - Rita Golden Gelman   447

Krakauer, Hoong Yee Lee
Rabbit Mooncakes - Hoong Yee Lee Krakauer   783

McCurdy, Michael
Lucy's Christmas - Donald Hall   543

McDermott, Gerald
Coyote: A Trickster Tale from the American Southwest - Gerald McDermott   970
Raven: A Trickster Tale from the Pacific Northwest - Gerald McDermott   971

McGinnis, Susan
Tanya's Big Green Dream - Linda Glaser   474

McKeating, Eileen
Ozzie on His Own - Johanna Hurwitz   670

McMillan, Bruce
Grandfather's Trolley - Bruce McMillan   987

McMullan, Jim
Nutcracker Noel - Kate McMullan   989

McNaughton, Colin
Captain Abdul's Pirate School - Colin McNaughton   990
Suddenly! - Colin McNaughton   991

McNeill, Shannon
The Trouble with Mister - Debra Keller   729

McPhail, David
Moony B. Finch, the Fastest Draw in the West - David McPhail   993
On a Starry Night - Natalie Kinsey-Warnock   759
Pigs Ahoy! - David McPhail   994
Pigs Aplenty, Pigs Galore - David McPhail   995
Yesterday I Lost a Sneaker (and Found the Great Goob Sick) - David McPhail   996

Meade, Holly
Rata-Pata-Scata-Fata: A Caribbean Story - Phillis Gershator   457

Meddaugh, Susan
Amanda's Perfect Hair - Linda Breiner Milstein   1019
Hog-Eye - Susan Meddaugh   1000
Martha Calling - Susan Meddaugh   1001
Martha Speaks - Susan Meddaugh   1002
That Terrible Baby - Jennifer Armstrong   41

Meisel, Paul
I Am Really a Princess - Carol Diggory Shields   1329
Wizard and Wart at Sea - Janice Lee Smith   1353

Merrill, Christine Herman
A Dolphin Named Bob - Twig C. George   453
There's an Owl in the Shower - Jean Craighead George   452

Messenger, Norman
Hob and the Goblins - William Mayne   954

Meyer, Karen
Double Play at Short - Matt Christopher   249

Miceli, Monica
The Beast and the Boy - Massimo Mostacchi   1047

Minor, Wendell
Red Fox Running - Eve Bunting   176

Minter, Daniel
The Foot Warmer and the Crow - Evelyn Coleman   274

Mitter, Kathryn
Goodbye, Mitch - Ruth Wallace-Brodeur   1474

Miya, Ann
Nothing Happened - Bill Harley   557

Modarressi, Mitra
Tumble Tower - Anne Tyler   1435

Mohr, Mark
The Storm - Marc Harshman   566

Molk, Laurel
Beneath the Ghost Moon - Jane Yolen   1577

Moodie, Fiona
The Boy and the Giants - Fiona Moodie   1030

Moore, Cyd
I Love You, Bunny Rabbit - Shulamith Levey Oppenheim   1097

Morgan, Mary
Asleep in a Heap - Elizabeth Winthrop   1536

Morin, Paul
The Dragon's Pearl - Julie Lawson   825
Fox Song - Joseph Bruchac   161
The Mud Family - Betsy James   687

Moser, Barry
Bingleman's Midway - Karen Ackerman   2
Cloud Eyes - Kathryn Lasky   813
The Farm Summer 1942 - Donald Hall   541
I Am the Dog, I Am the Cat - Donald Hall   542
The Magic Hare - Lynne Reid Banks   72
The Mushroom Man - Ethel Pochocki   1158
My Cats Nick and Nora - Isabelle Harper   558
My Dog Rosie - Isabelle Harper   559
What You Know First - Patricia MacLachlan   918
When Willard Met Babe Ruth - Donald Hall   544
Whistling Dixie - Marcia Vaughan   1452

Moss, Marissa
Amelia Writes Again - Marissa Moss   1043
Amelia's Notebook - Marissa Moss   1044
In America - Marissa Moss   1045

Muller, Gerda
Around the Oak - Gerda Muller   1049

Munsinger, Lynn
Babysitting for Benjamin - Valiska Gregory   511
The Gator Girls - Joanna Cole   270
Just a Little Bit - Ann Tompert   1424
Listen, Buddy - Helen Lester   837
Three Cheers for Tacky - Helen Lester   838

Murphy, Jill
The Last Noo-Noo - Jill Murphy   1051
A Quiet Night In - Jill Murphy   1052
The Worst Witch at Sea - Jill Murphy   1053

Myler, Terry
The Secret of the Ruby Ring - Yvonne MacGrory   915

N

Narahashi, Keiko
Is That Josie? - Keiko Narahashi   1062

Naste, Vincent
Adam's War - Sonia Levitin   853

Natchev, Alexi
Tom, Babette, & Simon: Three Tales of Transformation - Avi   58

Natti, Susanna
Cam Jansen and the Chocolate Fudge Mystery - David A. Adler   13
Don't Call Me Beanhead! - Susan Wojciechowski   1544
Good Luck, Ronald Morgan! - Patricia Reilly Giff   464
Lionel in the Winter - Stephen Krensky   788
Ronald Morgan Goes to Camp - Patricia Reilly Giff   467
Throw-Away Pets - Betsy Duffey   370

Nelson, Donna
Tooter Pepperday - Jerry Spinelli   1371

Newsom, Carol
Alien Alert! - Debra Hess   597

Newsome, Tom
The Mystery of the Cupboard - Lynne Reid Banks   73

Nickens, Linda
Imani and the Flying Africans - Janice Liddell   871

Nolan, Dennis
Fairy Wings - Lauren Mills   1018
The Gentleman and the Kitchen Maid - Diane Stanley   1376

Noll, Sally
Lucky Morning - Sally Noll   1079
Sunflower - Miela Ford   415

Nones, Eric Jon
Angela's Wings - Eric Jon Nones   1080
Caleb's Friend - Eric Jon Nones   1081

Noonan, Julia
A Place for Angels - Clyde Robert Bulla   169

Nordstrom, Joe
The Mystery of the Dancing Angels - Elspeth Campbell Murphy   1050

Novak, Matt
Gertie and Gumbo - Matt Novak   1082
Mouse TV - Matt Novak   1083
Newt - Matt Novak   1084

O

Oakley, Graham
The Foxbury Force - Graham Oakley   1088

O'Brien, Anne Sibley
Jamaica and Brianna - Juanita Havill   570
Jamaica's Blue Marker - Juanita Havill   571

O'Brien, John
The Saracen Maid - Leon Garfield   441
Six Snowy Sheep - Judith Ross Enderle   391
Tyrannosaurus Tex - Betty G. Birney   111

O'Malley, Kevin
Cinder Edna - Ellen Jackson   681
Miss Malarkey Doesn't Live in Room 10 - Judy Finchler   406
What's for Lunch? - John Schindel   1284

O'Neill, Catharine
J.B. Wigglebottom and the Parade of Pets - Vivian Sathre   1268

Ormerod, Jan
The Magic Skateboard - Enid Richemont   1211

Otero, Ben
Mary Patten's Voyage - Richard Berleth   103

Owens, Gail
Down and Up Fall - Johanna Hurwitz   666
Poison Ivy and Eyebrow Wigs - Bonnie Pryor   1180
The Up & Down Spring - Johanna Hurwitz   672

Owens, Mary Beth
Prize in the Snow - Bill Easterling   378

Oxenbury, Helen
It's My Birthday - Helen Oxenbury   1103
So Much - Trish Cooke   284
The Three Little Wolves and the Big Bad Pig - Eugene Trivizas   1427
Tom and Pippo and the Bicycle - Helen Oxenbury   1104

Oz, Robin
Jazz, Pizzaz, and the Silver Threads - Mary Quattlebaum   1182

P

Pak, Yu Cha
Benito's Dream Bottle - Naomi Shihab Nye   1086

Palmer, Kate Salley
Octopus Hug - Laurence Pringle 1177

Palmisciano, Diane
Get the Picture, Jenny Archer? - Ellen Conford 278

Paraskevas, Michael
Monster Beach - Betty Paraskevas 1107

Parker, Nancy Winslow
The Bag I'm Taking to Grandma's - Shirley Neitzel 1069
Here Comes Henny - Charlotte Pomerantz 1164

Parker, Robert Andrew
Aunt Skilly and the Stranger - Kathleen Stevens 1382
Circus of the Wolves - Jack Bushnell 187
Full Worm Moon - Margo Lemieux 835
The Sounds of Summer - David Updike 1438
The Year of No More Corn - Helen Ketteman 741

Parkins, David
Prowlpuss - Gina Wilson 1530
Sophie in the Saddle - Dick King-Smith 752
Sophie Is Seven - Dick King-Smith 753
Sophie's Lucky - Dick King-Smith 754
Tick-Tock - Eileen Browne 157

Parmenter, Wayne
The Stray - Dick King-Smith 755

Paterson, Diane
Gracias, Rosa - Michelle Markel 933

Paulsen, Ruth Wright
Dogteam - Gary Paulsen 1120

Peabody, Paul
Blackberry Hollow - Paul Peabody 1123

Pearson, Tracey Campbell
No Dogs Allowed - Jane Cutler 317
Rats! - Jane Cutler 318

Peck, Beth
Dear Levi: Letters from the Overland Trail - Elvira Woodruff 1550
Sweet Notes, Sour Notes - Nancy Smiler Levinson 851

Pelletier, Gilles
The Sugaring-Off Party - Jonathan London 895

Perkins, Lynne Rae
Home Lovely - Lynne Rae Perkins 1131

Perlman, Janet
The Emperor Penguin's New Clothes - Janet Perlman 1132

Pertzoff, Alexander
The In-Between Days - Eve Bunting 174

Pfister, Marcus
Dazzle the Dinosaur - Marcus Pfister 1144
Rainbow Fish to the Rescue! - Marcus Pfister 1145

Pilkey, Dav
Dog Breath: The Horrible Trouble with Hally Tosis - Dav Pilkey 1148
Dogzilla - Dav Pilkey 1149
Dragon's Halloween - Dav Pilkey 1150
The Dumb Bunnies' Easter - Sue Denim 341
The Hallo-Wiener - Dav Pilkey 1151
Julius - Angela Johnson 696

Pinkney, Brian
The Faithful Friend - Robert D. San Souci 1261
JoJo's Flying Side Kick - Brian Pinkney 1152
Max Found Two Sticks - Brian Pinkney 1153
When I Left My Village - Maxine Rose Schur 1296

Pinkney, Jerry
Drylongso - Virginia Hamilton 549
I Want to Be - Thylias Moss 1046
John Henry - Julius Lester 839
Minty: A Story of Young Harriet Tubman - Alan Schroeder 1295
New Shoes for Silvia - Johanna Hurwitz 669

A Starlit Somersault Downhill - Nancy Willard 1517
The Sunday Outing - Gloria Jean Pinkney 1154
Tanya's Reunion - Valerie Flournoy 413

Pinkwater, Daniel Manus
Mush, a Dog from Space - Daniel Manus Pinkwater 1155
Ned Feldman, Space Pirate - Daniel Manus Pinkwater 1156

Place, Francois
The Wreck of the Zanzibar - Michael Morpurgo 1040

Plecas, Jennifer
I Found Mouse - Pamela D. Greenwood 505
The Outside Dog - Charlotte Pomerantz 1165
Peeping and Sleeping - Fran Manushkin 930
Snow Day! - Barbara M. Joosse 713
What about My Goldfish? - Pamela D. Greenwood 506

Plum, K.D.
The Hayloft - Lisa Westberg Peters 1135

Polacco, Patricia
Babushka Baba Yaga - Patricia Polacco 1159
The Bee Tree - Patricia Polacco 1160
My Rotten Redheaded Older Brother - Patricia Polacco 1161
Pink and Say - Patricia Polacco 1162
Tikvah Means Hope - Patricia Polacco 1163

Poydar, Nancy
The Adventures of Sugar and Junior - Angela Shelf Medearis 1003
Busy Bea - Nancy Poydar 1173
Second-Grade Pig Pals - Kirby Larson 812
Thomas Tuttle, Just in Time - Becky Thoman Lindberg 873
When Jane-Marie Told My Secret - Gina Willner-Pardo 1528

Prater, John
The Greatest Show on Earth - John Prater 1174

Priceman, Marjorie
How Emily Blair Got Her Fabulous Hair - Susan Garrison 445
The Tiny, Tiny Boy and the Big, Big Cow - Nancy Van Laan 1445
What Zeesie Saw on Delancey Street - Elsa Okon Rael 1186
Zin! Zin! Zin! a Violin - Lloyd Moss 1042

Priestly, Alice
Lights for Gita - Rachna Gilmore 471

Primavera, Elise
Plantpet - Elise Primavera 1176

Q

Quackenbush, Robert
Abigail's Drum - John A. Minahan 1020

R

Rabinowitz, Sandy
A Horse for All Seasons - Sheila Kelly Welch 1490

Rader, Laura
Pete's Chicken - Harriet Ziefert 1594
The Three Little Pigs - Harriet Ziefert 1595

Ragins, Charles
Anna's Athabaskan Summer - Arnold Griese 514

Ramos, Mario
Orson - Rascal 1192

Ramsey, Marcy Dunn
One Dog Day - J. Patrick Lewis 866
Pony Crazy - Bonnie Bryant 164
Toying with Danger - Drew Stevenson 1383

Rand, Ted
The Bear That Heard Crying - Natalie Kinsey-Warnock 758
The Cabin Key - Gloria Rand 1187
Don't Forget - Patricia Lakin 807
In the Palace of the Ocean King - Marilyn Singer 1338
A Snake in the House - Faith McNulty 992

Ransome, James E.
Bonesy and Isabel - Michael J. Rosen 1229
Celie and the Harvest Fiddler - Vanessa Flournoy 414
The Old Dog - Charlotte Zolotow 1597
Red Dancing Shoes - Denise Lewis Patrick 1116
Sweet Clara and the Freedom Quilt - Deborah Hopkinson 644
Uncle Jed's Barbershop - Margaree King Mitchell 1022
The Wagon - Tony Johnston 708

Raschka, Chris
Can't Sleep - Chris Raschka 1193
Yo! Yes? - Chris Raschka 1194

Rathmann, Peggy
Good Night, Gorilla - Peggy Rathmann 1195
Officer Buckle and Gloria - Peggy Rathmann 1196

Ray, David
Silver at Night - Susan Campbell Bartoletti 82

Ray, Deborah Kogan
Apple Picking Time - Michele Benoit Slawson 1342
Fat Chance! - Lady Borten 127
Sweet Dried Apples: A Vietnamese Wartime Chldhood - Rosemary Breckler 133

Ray, Jane
The Happy Prince - Oscar Wilde 1515

Rayevsky, Robert
Bernal & Florinda: A Spanish Tale - Eric A. Kimmel 743
Three Sacks of Truth: A Story from France - Eric A. Kimmel 744

Rayner, Mary
Garth Pig Steals the Show - Mary Rayner 1202

Regan, Laura
Sun Song - Jean Marzollo 946

Reiser, Lynn
Night Thunder and the Queen of the Wild Horses - Lynn Reiser 1204
The Surprise Family - Lynn Reiser 1205
Tomorrow on Rocky Pond - Lynn Reiser 1206
Two Mice in Three Fables - Lynn Reiser 1207

Remkiewicz, Frank
The Bone Stranger - Frank Remkiewicz 1208
Froggy Learns to Swim - Jonathan London 888
Horrible Harry and the Dungeon - Suzy Kline 769
The Joy Boys - Betsy Byars 194
Let's Go, Froggy! - Jonathan London 892
Song Lee and the Leech Man - Suzy Kline 772
Song Lee in Room 2B - Suzy Kline 773

Resnick, Sandi Wickersham
Apple Valley Year - Ann Turner 1431

Reynolds, Pat
All the Better to See You With! - Margaret Wild 1510

Rich, Anna
Joshua's Masai Mask - Dakari Hru 658
Saturday at the New You - Barbara E. Barber 77

Riches, Judith
Rooster Crows - Ragnhild Scamell 1272

Rigby, Rodney
The Night the Moon Fell Asleep - Rodney
   Rigby   1212

Riggio, Anita
Beware the Brindlebeast - Anita Riggio   1213
The Whispering Cloth: A Refugee's Story - Pegi Deitz
   Shea   1324

Rigie, Mitchell
Genghis Khan: A Dog Star Is Born - Marjorie
   Weinman Sharmat   1320

Riley, Linnea Asplind
Outside, Inside - Carolyn Crimi   303

Ringgold, Faith
Tar Beach - Faith Ringgold   1215

Ritz, Karen
The Ghost of Popcorn Hill - Betty Ren Wright   1557

Robinson, Aminah Brenda Lynn
A School for Pompey Walker - Michael J.
   Rosen   1230

Robinson, Charles
Nekomah Creek Christmas - Linda Crew   301
Soup Ahoy - Robert Newton Peck   1127

Rockwell, Anne F.
No! No! No! - Anne F. Rockwell   1221

Rodanas, Kristina
Dance of the Sacred Circle: A Native American Tale -
   Kristina Rodanas   1223

Rogers, Jacqueline
Five Live Bongos - George Ella Lyon   909
Nothing but Trouble - Betty Ren Wright   1561
Patrick's Day - Elizabeth Lee O'Donnell   1091
The Puppy Sister - S.E. Hinton   623
Snow Angel - Jean Marzollo   945

Rogoff, Barbara
The Hen That Crowed - Sheila Cole   273

Root, Barry
Alvah and Arvilla - Mary Lyn Ray   1199
Old Devil Wind - Bill Martin Jr.   939
Someplace Else - Carol P. Saul   1269

Root, Kimberly Bulcken
Gulliver in Lilliput - Margaret Hodges   628
If I'd Known Then What I Know Now - Reeve
   Lindbergh   874
The Palace of Stars - Patricia Lakin   808
The Toll-Bridge Troll - Patricia Rae Wolff   1547
When the Whippoorwill Calls - Candice F.
   Ransom   1190

Rosales, Melodye
Meet Addy: An American Girl - Connie Porter   1169
On the Day I Was Born - Deborah M. Newton
   Chocolate   240

Rose, Ted
The Banshee Train - Odds Bodkin   119

Rosenberry, Vera
Binya's Blue Umbrella - Ruskin Bond   123
William's Ninth Life - Minna Jung   716

Rosing, Jens
Inunguak: The Little Greenlander - Palle
   Petersen   1140

Ross, Tony
Amber Brown Is Not a Crayon - Paula Danziger   320
Amber Brown Wants Extra Credit - Paula
   Danziger   321
The Second Princess - Hiawyn Oram   1099
You Can't Eat Your Chicken Pox, Amber Brown -
   Paula Danziger   322

Rossi, Joyce
The Gullywasher - Joyce Rossi   1234

Roth, Robert
Pearl Moscowitz's Last Stand - Arthur A.
   Levine   846
When the Monkeys Came Back - Kristine L.
   Franklin   425

Roth, Roger
The Invisible Dog - Dick King-Smith   748

Roth, Susan L.
How the Sky's Housekeeper Wore Her Scarves -
   Patricia Hooper   643
*How Thunder and Lightning Came to Be: A Choctaw
   Legend* - Beatrice Orcutt Harrell   560
Princess - Susan L. Roth   1235

Rothenberg, Joan
Inside-Out Grandma - Joan Rothenberg   1236
Yettele's Feathers - Joan Rothenberg   1237

Rowe, Gavin
The Sleepy Dormouse - Mark Ezra   399

Ruffins, Reynold
Running the Road to ABC - Denize Lauture   823

Russo, Marisabina
Bear E. Bear - Susan Straight   1396
Good-Bye, Curtis - Kevin Henkes   586
Time to Wake Up! - Marisabina Russo   1243
Trade-In Mother - Marisabina Russo   1244

Ryan, Susannah
Darcy and Gran Don't Like Babies - Jane
   Cutler   315

Rylant, Cynthia
Dog Heaven - Cynthia Rylant   1248

S

Saflund, Birgitta
Remember My Name - Sara H. Banks   74

Saltzberg, Barney
Show and Tell - Barney Saltzberg   1258
This Is a Great Place for a Hot Dog Stand - Barney
   Saltzberg   1259

Samton, Sheila White
Tilly and the Rhinoceros - Sheila White
   Samton   1260

Samuels, Barbara
The Baby House - Norma Simon   1337

Sanchez, Enrique O.
Amelia's Road - Linda Jacobs Altman   29
Saturday Market - Patricia Grossman   522

Sandeen, Elaine
Jenna's Big Jump - Faythe Dyrud Thureen   1420

Sanderson, Ruth
Papa Gatto: An Italian Fairy Tale - Ruth
   Sanderson   1265

Sandford, John
Down Buttermilk Lane - Barbara Mitchell   1021

Sandin, Joan
A Bear for Miguel - Elaine Marie Alphin   28
Pioneer Bear - Joan Sandin   1266

Sather, Kay
Minnie - Annie M.G. Schmidt   1286

Sauber, Robert
The Storm - Anne F. Rockwell   1222

Sawaya, Linda Dalal
How to Get Famous in Brooklyn - Amy Hest   603

Say, Allen
Emma's Rug - Allen Say   1270
Grandfather's Journey - Allen Say   1271

Sayles, Elizabeth
Albie the Lifeguard - Louise Borden   124
The Little Black Truck - Libba Moore Gray   495
Nettie's Gift - Susan Tews   1413
The Night Crossing - Karen Ackerman   4
Not in the House, Newton! - Judith Heide
   Gilliland   470
The Sleeping Porch - Karen Ackerman   5

Schachner, Judith Byron
Jimmy, the Pickpocket of the Palace - Donna Jo
   Napoli   1061
Willy and May - Judith Byron Schachner   1275

Schaefer, Alex
The Wizard - Bill Martin Jr.   940

Schikarioff, Gennady
I Remember - Fara Lynn Krasnopolsky   784

Schindler, S.D.
Charlie Malarkey and the Singing Moose - William
   Kennedy   736
Don't Fidget a Feather - Erica Silverman   1336
The Ghost of Nicholas Greebe - Tony Johnston   703
Little Vampire and the Midnight Bear - Mary DeBall
   Kwitz   801
Odds on Oliver - Constance C. Greene   500
Wonderful Alexander and the Catwings - Ursula K. Le
   Guin   826

Schlossberg, Stephen
Big Red Truck - Stephen Schlossberg   1285

Schneider, Christine M.
Jeremy's Muffler - Laura F. Nielsen   1074

Schneider, Howie
No Dogs Allowed - Howie Schneider   1288

Schoenherr, Ian
One Night: A Story from the Desert - Cristina
   Kessler   738

Schoenherr, John
Rebel - John Schoenherr   1290

Schuett, Stacey
If You Want to Find Golden - Eileen Spinelli   1368

Schutzer, Dena
A Million Fish. . .More or Less - Pat McKissack   986

Schwartz, Amy
My Island Grandma - Kathryn Lasky   816
Nana's Birthday Party - Amy Hest   605
A Teeny Tiny Baby - Amy Schwartz   1297

Schweninger, Ann
Oliver & Amanda and the Big Snow - Jean Van
   Leeuwen   1450

Searle, Ronald
The Tales of Grandpa Cat - Lee Wardlaw   1479

Seeley, Laura L.
The Four-Legged Ghosts - Mary Hoffman   635

Seibold, J. Otto
Mr. Lunch Takes a Plane Ride - J. Otto
   Seibold   1308

Selznick, Brian
Frindle - Andrew Clements   257
Our House: The Stories of Levittown - Pam
   Conrad   282

Sewall, Marcia
The Morning Chair - Barbara M. Joosse   712
Sable - Karen Hesse   602

Shanahan, Danny
Buckledown the Workhound - Danny Shanahan   1314

Shannon, David
The Amazing Christmas Extravaganza - David
   Shannon   1315
The Ballad of the Pirate Queens - Jane Yolen   1576
The Boy Who Lived with the Seals - Rafe Martin   943

Thomas, Angela Trotta
The Mighty Santa Fe - William H. Hooks 642

Thompson, Ellen
Hey, New Kid! - Betsy Duffey 368

Thompson, K. Dyble
My Name Is Maria Isabel - Alma Flor Ada 7

Thorkelson, Gregg
Zoe and Columbo - Susan Richards Shreve 1333

Titherington, Jeanne
Sophy and Auntie Pearl - Jeanne Titherington 1421

Toddy, Irving
Cheyenne Again - Eve Bunting 170

Toft, Lis
Girl Wonder and the Terrific Twins - Malorie Blackman 113

Tolan, Stephanie
Save Halloween! - Stephanie Tolan 1422

Torres, Leyla
Saturday Sancocho - Leyla Torres 1425

Trivas, Irene
Nannies for Hire - Amy Hest 606

Truesdell, Sue
The Golly Sisters Ride Again - Betsy Byars 193
The Losers Fight Back - Barbara M. Joosse 711

Tryon, Leslie
Dear Peter Rabbit - Alma Flor Ada 6

Tseng, Jean
The Boy Who Swallowed Snakes - Laurence Yep 1570
City of Dragons - Laurence Yep 1571

U

Ulrich, George
Emily Eyefinger and the Lost Treasure - Duncan Ball 64
Gorgonzola Zombies in the Park - Elizabeth Levy 858
A Mammoth Mix-Up - Elizabeth Levy 859
School Spirit Sabotage - Elizabeth Levy 860

Unzner-Fischer, Christa
Loretta and the Little Fairy - Gerda Marie Scheidl 1278
You Shall Be King! - Antonie Schneider 1287

Urberuaga, Emilio
Paper Bird - Arcadio Lobato 885

Utton, Peter
Harry's Stormy Night - Una Leavy 829

V

Vagin, Vladimir
Insects from Outer Space - Frank Asch 47
The Nutcracker Ballet - Vladimir Vagin 1441

Valens, Amy
Danilo the Fruit Man - Amy Valens 1443

Van Allsburg, Chris
The Sweetest Fig - Chris Van Allsburg 1444

van Haeringen, Annemarie
Tales of the Wicked Witch - Hanna Kraan 782

Van Nutt, Robert
The Gift of a Traveler - Wendy Matthews 952

Van Zyle, Jon
Honey Paw and Lightfoot - Jonathan London 890

Varley, Susan
Badger's Bring Something Party - Hiawyn Oram 1098

Velasquez, Eric
Off and Running - Gary Soto 1363

Velthuijs, Max
Frog Is Frightened - Max Velthuijs 1453

Vitale, Stefano
Too Much Talk - Angela Shelf Medearis 1006
When the Wind Stops - Charlotte Zolotow 1598

Vivas, Julie
Our Granny - Margaret Wild 1513

Vojtech, Anna
Blow Away Soon - Betsy James 685
The First Strawberries: A Cherokee Story - Joseph Bruchac 160

Vulliamy, Clara
Danny's Duck - June Crebbin 297

Vyner, Tim
Swim for Cover!: Adventure on the Coral Reef - Sue Vyner 1458

W

Waas, Uli
Spiny - Jurgen Lassig 820

Waber, Bernard
Do You See a Mouse? - Bernard Waber 1459
Gina - Bernard Waber 1460
Lyle at the Office - Bernard Waber 1461

Waldherr, Kris
The Seal Prince - Sheila MacGill Callahan 200

Waldman, Neil
Bayou Lullaby - Kathi Appelt 37

Wallace, Ian
The Year of Fire - Teddy Jam 684

Wallace, Nancy Elizabeth
Snow - Nancy Elizabeth Wallace 1473

Walsh, Ellen Stoll
Hop Jump - Ellen Stoll Walsh 1475
Pip's Magic - Ellen Stoll Walsh 1476

Ward, John
Fireflies for Nathan - Shulamith Levey Oppenheim 1095
The Freedom Riddle - Angela Shelf Medearis 1004
Poppa's New Pants - Angela Shelf Medearis 1005

Warhola, James
The Christmas Blizzard - Helen Ketteman 739
The Mystery of the Several Sevens - Bill Brittain 140

Warnes, Tim
Tom's Tail - Linda Jennings 692

Watling, James
Bound for Oregon - Jean Van Leeuwen 1448

Watson, Mary
The Butterfly Seeds - Mary Watson 1482
The Market Lady and the Mango Tree - Pete Watson 1483

Watts, James
I'll Meet You Halfway - John Schindel 1283

Wegner, Fritz
The Giant Baby - Allan Ahlberg 15

Wells, Rosemary
Edward's Overwhelming Overnight - Rosemary Wells 1492
The Language of Doves - Rosemary Wells 1493
Max and Ruby's First Greek Myth: Pandora's Box - Rosemary Wells 1496

Max and Ruby's Midas: Another Greek Myth - Rosemary Wells 1497

Westcott, Nadine Bernard
How to Grow a Picket Fence - Mary Louise Cuneo 308
The Thing That Bothered Farmer Brown - Teri Sloat 1345

White, Michael P.
The Library Dragon - Carmen Agra Deedy 333

Wickstrom, Sylvie
Dog Days for Dudley - Barbara Moe 1026

Wiesner, David
Night of the Gargoyles - Eve Bunting 175

Wijngaard, Juan
Emma Bean - Jean Van Leeuwen 1449

Wilcox, Cathy
Andrew Jessup - Nette Hilton 619

Wilkins, Janet
Bertha's Garden - Elisabeth Dyjak 377

Wilkon, Jozef
The Moon Man: A Story - Gerda Marie Scheidl 1279

Williams, Garth
J.B.'s Harmonica - John Sebastian 1307

Williams, Vera B.
Scooter - Vera B. Williams 1523

Wilsdorf, Anne
Princess - Anne Wilsdorf 1529

Wilson, Gahan
Spooky Stories for a Dark and Stormy Night - Alice Low 900

Wilson, Janet
Gopher Takes Heart - Virginia Scribner 1303
How to Be Cool in the Third Grade - Betsy Duffey 369
Revenge of the Small Small - Jean Little 882
Tiger Flowers - Patricia Quinlan 1183

Wilson, Roberta
Patrick's Tree House - Steven Kroll 790

Wimmer, Mike
All the Places to Love - Patricia MacLachlan 916

Winter, Jeanette
Cotton Mill Town - Kathleen Hershey 595
Shaker Boy - Mary Lyn Ray 1201

Winter, Susan
A Baby Just Like Me - Susan Winter 1534
Henry's Baby - Mary Hoffman 636
My Shadow - Susan Winter 1535

Wisniewski, David
The Wave of the Sea-Wolf - David Wisniewski 1542

Wolff, Ashley
Little Donkey Close Your Eyes - Margaret Wise Brown 152
Stella and Roy - Ashley Wolff 1545

Wood, Audrey
Rude Giants - Audrey Wood 1548

Wormell, Mary
Hilda Hen's Happy Birthday - Mary Wormell 1554
Hilda Hen's Search - Mary Wormell 1555

Y

Yalowitz, Paul
Boy, Can He Dance! - Eileen Spinelli 1367

Yardley, Joanna
The Bracelet - Yoshiko Uchida 1436

Author Index

This index is an alphabetical listing of the authors of books featured in entries and those listed under "Other books by the author" and "Other books you might like." For each author, the titles of books written and entry numbers are also provided. Editors and co-authors are interfiled with Author names. Bold numbers indicate a featured main entry; other numbers refer to books recommended for further reading.

The Pony Pals Series 164, 530
Puppy Love 106
The Rainbow Kid 106

Betz, Dieter
The Bear Family 890, 1246

Bial, Raymond
Frontier Home 1264
Shaker Home 1201

Binch, Caroline
Gregory Cool **107**, 714

Birchman, David F.
The Raggly, Scraggly, No-Soap, No-Scrub Girl 109, 678, 734

Birdseye, Tom
Airmail to the Moon 109
I'm Going to Be Famous 108, 408, 1127
Just Call Me Stupid 106, **108**
A Regular Flood of Mishap **109**, 765, 1281
Soap! Soap! Don't Forget the Soap! An Appalachian Folktale 109, 428, 837
A Song of Stars 108
Tarantula Shoes **110**, 468, 1395
Tucker 108, 276
Waiting for Baby 109, 1337

Birney, Betty G.
Oh Brother! Someone's Afraid of the Dark! 111
Piglet Bakes Half a Haycorn Pie 111
Tyrannosaurus Tex **111**
Walt Disney's Winnie the Pooh and the Missing Pots 111

Bishop, Claire
Twenty and Ten 4

Bishop, Gavin
The Three Little Pigs 1427

Black, Charles C.
The Royal Nap **112**, 345, 1012

Black, Sheila
Santa's Christmas Storybook 1122

Blackman, Malorie
Girl Wonder and the Terrific Twins **113**, 299, 1143, 1525
A New Dress for Maya 113

Blackstone, Stella
Grandma Went to Market: A Round-the-World Counting Rhyme 1175

Blackwood, Mary
Derek the Knitting Dinosaur 1319, 1475

Blaine, Marge
The Terrible Thing That Happened at Our House 1244

Blair, Cynthia
The Double Dip Disguise 70

Blake, Quentin
All Join In 114
Cockatoos 114
Simpkin **114**
Snuff 114

Blake, Robert J.
Dog 115, 1313
The Perfect Spot 115, 759

Blatchford, Claire H.
Nick's Mission 190

Blathwayt, Benedict
Little House by the Sea 116
Stories from Firefly Island 116, 1035, 1057, 1123, 1309

Bledsoe, Lucy Jane
The Big Bike Race **117**

Blegvad, Lenore
Anna Banana and Me 118
Once Upon a Time and Grandma 118, 1033
Rainy Day Kate 118
A Sound of Leaves **118**

Bloch, Marie
Displaced Person 784

Blockman, Mary
Yoo Hoo, Moon! 1084

Bloom, Suzanne
A Family for Jamie: An Adoption Story 891
We Keep a Pig in the Parlor 1412

Blos, Joan W.
A Gathering of Days 1113
The Heroine of the Titanic 963
Nellie Bly's Monkey: His Remarkable Story in His Own Words 1191

Blue, Rose
Me and Einstein: Breaking through the Reading Barrier 106, 108

Blumberg, Rhoda
Bloomers! 963

Blume, Judy
Are You There God? It's Me, Margaret 1422
Freckle Juice 1544
Fudge-a-Mania 318
It's Not the End of the World 850
Otherwise Known as Sheila the Great 645
The Pain and the Great One 1099, 1161
Superfudge 218, 317, 1137, 1138
Tales of a Fourth Grade Nothing 1180

Blundell, Tony
Beware of Boys 1175, 1202

Blyler, Allison L.
Finding Foxes 176

Bodkin, Odds
The Banshee Train **119**

Bodsworth, Nan
A Nice Walk in the Jungle 1538

Boelts, Maribeth
Dry Days, Wet Nights 120, 121
Grace and Joe **120**, 121, 586
Summer's End 120, **121**, 587
Tornado 120, 121

Boggart, Jo Ellen
Gifts 1175

Bojunga-Nunes, Lygia
The Companions 748

Boland, Janice
Annabel 122
Annabel Again **122**

Bond, Michael
A Bear Called Paddington 350
Paddington at the Circus 1174, 1191
The Tales of Olga da Polga 749

Bond, Nancy
The Voyage Begun 448

Bond, Ruskin
Binya's Blue Umbrella **123**
Cherry Tree 123
The Hidden Pool 123
Tales Told at Twilight 123

Bonham, Barbara
Challenge of the Prairie 54

Bonsall, Crosby
The Case of the Cat's Meow 1277
The Case of the Hungry Stranger 1133
Tell Me Some More 333

Booth, Jerry
Big Bugs 686

Borden, Louise
Albie the Lifeguard **124**, 125, 888, 1492, 1502
Caps, Hats, Socks, and Mittens: A Book about the Four Seasons 124, 125
Just in Time for Christmas 124, **125**
The Neighborhood Trucker 124, 125

Bornstein, Ruth Lercher
A Beautiful Seashell 126
Little Gorilla 126
Rabbit's Good News **126**
The Seedling Child 126

Borton, Lady
Fat Chance! **127**, 505
Junk Pile 127

Bos, Burny
More from the Molesons 188

Bottner, Barbara
Bootsie Barker Bites 204, 241, 1388
Hurricane Music 1592

Boughton, Richard
Rent-a-Puppy, Inc. 870, 1026

Boulton, Jane
Only Opal: The Diary of a Young Girl 1201

Bourgeois, Paulette
Too Many Chickens! 375

Bowen, Fred
T.J.'s Secret Pitch 255

Boyd, Candy Dawson
Breadsticks and Blessing Places 128
Charles Pippin 128
Chevrolet Saturdays **128**
Circle of Gold 129
Daddy, Daddy, Be There 129
Fall Secrets 128, **129**, 504
Forever Friends 129
Seasons 128, 129

Bradbury, Ray
Something Wicked This Way Comes 300
Switch on the Night 462, 1476

Bradby, Marie
More than Anything Else **130**, 1230, 1392

Bradley, Virginia
Wait and See **131**, 287, 1142

Bradman, Tony
This Little Baby 1297

Brandenberg, Franz
A Fun Weekend 147, 655

Branscum, Robbie
Cameo Rose 724

Breathed, Berkeley
Goodnight Opus **132**
The Last Basselope: One Ferocious Story 132
Red Ranger Came Calling 132, 715
A Wish for Wings That Work: An Opus Christmas Story 132

Breckler, Rosemary
Hoang Breaks the Lucky Teapot 133
Sweet Dried Apples: A Vietnamese Wartime Chldhood **133**

Brennan, Herbie
Emily and the Werewolf 134
The Mystery Machine **134**, 1156

Brenner, Barbara
Mr. Tall and Mr. Small 722
Wagon Wheels 36, 896

Bresnick-Perry, Roslyn
Leaving for America 1186

Brett, Jan
Annie and the Wild Animals 135
Armadillo Rodeo **135**, 138
Beauty and the Beast 1047
Fritz and the Beautiful Horses 135
The Mitten 1424, 1584
The Trouble with Trolls 135

Brewster, Patience
Rabbit Inn 136
Two Bushy Badgers **136**

Bridgers, Sue Ellen
Home before Dark 353

Bridwell, Norman
Clifford, the Small Red Puppy 35, 291, 583, 1495
Clifford's Good Deeds 182
The Witch Next Door 167

Briggs, Raymond
The Bear 24, **137**, 1072
Father Christmas 137, 183
Jim and the Beanstalk 137
The Snowman 137, 482

Brillhart, Julie
Story Hour—Starring Megan! 221

Brimner, Larry Dane
Cory Coleman, Grade 2 789
Country Bear's Surprise 138
Eliot Fry's Goodbye 138
Max and Felix 25, 138, 619, 1254
Merry Christmas, Old Armadillo 135, **138**

Brinckloe, Julie
Fireflies! Story and Pictures 210, 1095

Brink, Carol Ryrie
Caddie Woodlawn 142, 844, 917
Goody O'Grumpity 1546

Brisson, Pat
Kate Heads West 139, 1043
Kate on the Coast 139, 1225
Magic Carpet 139
Wanda's Roses **139**, 352
Your Best Friend, Kate 672

Brittain, Bill
All the Money in the World 207
My Buddy, the King 927
The Mystery of the Several Sevens **140**
Shape-Changer 140, 507
Who Knew There'd Be Ghosts? 335, 880
The Wish Giver 140, 419
The Wizards and the Monster 140

Brooke, L. Leslie
The Golden Goose Book: A Fairy Tale Picture Book 1334

Brooke, William J.
A Telling of the Tales: Five Stories 1426

Anastasia's Chosen Career 902
Attaboy Sam! 902, 1124
Number the Stars 4, 179, 366, 388,
  651, 856, 902, 1100
The One Hundredth Thing about
  Caroline 174
Rabble Starkey 131
See You Around, Sam! **902**
Taking Care of Terrific 1217

Lucas, Barbara M.
Snowed In **903**

Ludlow, Keren
Benny the Breakdown Truck 324

Luenn, Nancy
Nessa's Fish 186, 514

Luger, Harriett
Bye, Bye, Bai Kai **904**

Lunn, Janet
Double Spell 905
The Root Cellar **905**
Shadow in Hawthorn Bay 905
Twin Spell 905

Lurie, Alison
Clever Gretchen and Other Forgotten
  Folktales 1548

Lustig, Esther
Willy Whyner, Cloud Designer **906**

Lustig, Michael
Willy Whyner, Cloud Designer 719,
  906

Luttrell, Ida
The Bear Next Door 821, 907, 1084,
  1266
Mattie's Little Possum Pet **907**
Milo's Toothache 907
The Star Counters 907
Tillie and Mert 778, 849

Lyon, George Ella
Ada's Pal 1248
Borrowed Children 305, 1359
Cecil's Story 418, 909, 1162
Come a Tide 908, 909, 910
Dreamplace **908**, 910, 1328
Five Live Bongos **909**, 1153, 1293
Here and Then 905, 1304
Here and There 473
Mama Is a Miner 3, **910**
Together 908, 909
Who Came Down That Road? 908,
  910, 1328

Lyon, Nancy
Totem Poles and Tribes 943

Lyons, Mary E.
Raw Head, Bloody Bones: African-
  American Tales of the
  Supernatural 1566

M

Macaulay, David
Black and White 911
Cathedral 911
Shortcut 809, **911**, 1384
Why the Chicken Crossed the
  Road 911

MacBride, Roger Lea
In the Land of the Big Red
  Apple **912**, 913
Little Farm in the Ozarks 912, 913

Little House on Rocky Ridge 912,
  913

Maccarone, Grace
Itchy, Itchy Chickenpox 146, 733

MacDonald, Amy
Rachel Fister's Blister 345
The Spider Who Created the
  World 760

MacDonald, Betty
Hello, Mrs. Piggle Wiggle 924
Mrs. Piggle-Wiggle 420

MacDonald, Elizabeth
John's Picture 729, 832, 993

MacDonald, George
The Light Princess and Other
  Tales 18
The Lost Princess: A Double Story 32

Macdonald, Maryann
Ben at the Beach 914
Hedgehog Bakes a Cake 1253
The Pink Party **914**
Rosie and the Poor Rabbits 914
Secondhand Star 914

MacGrory, Yvonne
The Secret of the Ruby Ring **915**

Mack, Stan
Ten Bears in My Bed: A Goodnight
  Countdown 1538

MacLachlan, Patricia
All the Places to Love 533, **916**, 918,
  1187, 1316, 1325, 1488, 1498
Cassie Binegar 917
Journey 90, 282, 427, 594, 1549
Mama One, Mama Two 916
Sarah, Plain and Tall 54, 174, 899,
  917, 1130
Seven Kisses in a Row 917
Skylark 38, **917**, 1432, 1489
Three Names 916, 918, 1168
Through Grandpa's Eyes 277, 792,
  916, 918, 1031
Tomorrow's Wizard 344
What You Know First **918**, 1455,
  1531

MacMillan, Dianne
Ramadan and Id al-Fitr 951

Madenski, Melissa
In My Mother's Garden 807, **919**
Some of the Pieces 919

Madsen, Ross Martin
Perrywinkle and the Book of Magic
  Spells 568, 801

Maestro, Betsy
Coming to America: The Story of
  Immigration 82

Magnus, Erica
My Secret Place 808

Maguire, Gregory
Missing Sisters 920
Seven Spiders Spinning **920**

Mahy, Margaret
Aliens in the Family 923
The Blood-and-Thunder Adventure on
  Hurricane Peak 923, 924
The Boy Who Was Followed
  Home 242, 387, 921, 925
A Busy Day for a Good
  Grandmother **921**, 925, 1513
The Chewing-Gum Rescue 18, **924**,
  927
The Christmas Tree Tangle 927
Clancy's Cabin 927, 1561

The Dragon of an Ordinary
  Family 921
A Fortunate Name 504, **926**
A Fortune Branches Out 771, **922**,
  926, 927
The Girl with the Green Ear: Stories
  about Magic in Nature 166, 1256
The Good Fortunes Gang 259, 596,
  790, **922**, 926, 1167
The Greatest Show off Earth 922,
  923, 924
The Haunting 923
The Horrendous Hullabaloo 423
The Pirates' Mixed-Up Voyage 441,
  922, **924**
The Pumpkin Man and the Crafty
  Creeper 796, 1176
The Queen's Goat 1386
The Rattlebang Picnic 921, **925**
Seven Chinese Brothers 925
Tangled Fortunes 309, **926**
The Three-Legged Cat 39
Tingleberries, Tuckertubs and
  Telephones **927**

Maisner, Heather
Find Mouse in the Yard 376, 1459

Makris, Kathryn
The Eco-Kids Series 452, 474

Mali, Jane Lawrence
The Wimp of the World **596**

Malotki, Ekkehart
The Mouse Couple: A Hopi
  Folktale 295

Malterre, Elona
The Last Wolf of Ireland 545

Manes, Stephen
It's New! It's Improved! It's
  Terrible! 1327
Make Four Million Dollars by Next
  Thursday! 207, 1127

Manitonquat
The Children of the Morning Light:
  Wampanoag Tales 158, 813

Manley, Joan B.
She Flew No Flags 651, **928**

Manushkin, Fran
Baby, Come Out! 929, 930
Buster Loves Buttons! 930, 931
Latkes and Applesauce: A Hanukkah
  Story 929, 931
Let's Go Riding in Our Strollers 930,
  1302
The Matzah That Papa Brought
  Home **929**, 931, 1291
Peeping and Sleeping 929, **930**, 1245
Starlight and Candles: The Joys of the
  Sabbath **931**

Mariana
Miss Flora McFlimsey's Christmas
  Eve 1315
Miss Flora McFlimsey's
  Valentine 1317, 1387

Marino, Jan
The Day That Elvis Came to
  Town 932
Eighty-Eight Steps to September 932
Like Some Kind of Hero 932
The Mona Lisa of Salem Street **932**

Markel, Michelle
Gracias, Rosa **933**

Markham, Marion M.
The April Fool's Day Mystery 934
The Birthday Party Mystery 934

The St. Patrick's Day Shamrock
  Mystery **934**
The Valentine's Day Mystery 934

Markle, Sandra
The Fledglings 426

Marko, Katherine
Hang out the Flag 1214

Markun, Patricia Maloney
The Little Painter of Sabana
  Grande **935**, 1415, 1568

Marney, Dean
Dirty Socks Don't Win Games 944

Marriott, Janice
Letters to Lesley 1397

Marshall, Edward
Space Case 341

Marshall, James
The Cut-Ups at Camp Custer 620
The Cut-Ups Crack Up 1388
The Cut-Ups Cut Loose 204
Fox Be Nimble 79, 936
Fox on Stage **936**, 1276
Fox Outfoxed 936, 1088
George and Martha 296, 682, 950,
  1106
George and Martha Back in
  Town 381
George and Martha Encore 937
George and Martha Round and
  Round 936
Rats on the Range and Other
  Stories 272, **937**, 1479
Rats on the Roof: And Other
  Stories 937
Red Riding Hood 394
The Three Little Pigs 1595
Three Up a Tree 1496
Wings: A Tale of Two Chickens 49,
  52, 937

Martin, Ann M.
Eleven Kids, One Summer 393, 1551
Karen's Big Sister 1451
Karen's School Surprise 465
Karen's Secret 1528
Karen's Tuba 948
Mallory's Christmas Wish 301
Mary Anne and Camp BSC 437
Mary Anne and the Library
  Mystery 860

Martin, Bill Jr.
Barn Dance! 938
A Beautiful Feast for a Big King
  Cat 695, **938**
Brown Bear, Brown Bear, What Do You
  See? 59
Chicka Chicka Boom Boom 59
Fire! Fire! Said Mrs. McGuire 939,
  940
The Ghost-Eye Tree 45, 600
Listen to the Rain 938
The Maestro Plays 1042
Old Devil Wind **939**, 940, 1335,
  1403
Polar Bear, Polar Bear, What Do You
  Hear? 939, 940
Up and Down on the Merry-Go-
  Round 307, 1231
The Wizard 478, 513, 939, **940**

Martin, Charles E.
Summer Business 1521

Martin, David
Little Chicken Chicken 189

Author Index

Wiggins, Kate Douglas
Rebecca of Sunnybrook Farm 912

Wilbur, Richard
A Game of Catch 118, 1491

Wild, Margaret
All the Better to See You With! **1510**
Beast **1511**
But Granny Did! 1511, 1513
Going Home 1510, **1512**, 1514
Mr. Nick's Knitting 1513
My Dearest Dinosaur 1513, 1514
Our Granny 921, 982, 1510, **1513**
The Queen's Holiday 1512
The Slumber Party 1510, **1514**
Space Travellers 1373
Thank You, Santa 1511
Toby 1512
The Very Best of Friends 1512, 1514

Wilde, Oscar
The Devoted Friend 1515
The Happy Prince 33, **1515**
The Nightingale and the Rose 1515
The Selfish Giant 1515

Wilder, Laura Ingalls
Christmas in the Big Woods 125, 952, 969
Dance at Grandpa's 895
Farmer Boy 142, 248, 543, 667, 912, 973
Little House in the Big Woods 752, 913
Little House on the Prairie 74, 1448
On the Banks of Plum Creek 38, 917, 1135, 1489

Wildsmith, Brian
Carousel 346
Hunter and His Dog 378

Wilhelm, Hans
The Royal Raven 49, 1132

Wilkins, Verna
Dave & Tooth Fairy 246

Wilkon, Piotr
Rosie the Cool Cat 1290, 1475

Willard, Nancy
The Alphabet of Angels 1517
Beauty and the Beast 32, 166, 1516
The High Rise Glorious Skittle Skat Roarious Sky Pie Angel Food Cake 1253
The Marzipan Moon 1516
Night Story 1517
Pish, Posh, Said Hieronymus Bosch 1516
The Sorcerer's Apprentice **1516**
A Starlit Somersault Downhill 1473, **1517**
A Visit to William Blake's Inn 1517

Williams, Carol Ann
Tsubu the Little Snail 1059, 1209, 1294, **1518**

Williams, Carol Lynch
Adeline Street **1519**, 1520
Kelly and Me 1519, **1520**

Williams, David
Grandma Essie's Covered Wagon 854, 979
Walking to the Creek 297, 622, 817

Williams, Karen Lynn
Applebaum's Garage 1521
Baseball and Butterflies 769
First Grade King 196, 654
Galimoto 567, 1521

Williams, Laura E.
The Long Silk Strand 1094

Williams, Linda
The Little Old Lady Who Was Not Afraid of Anything 939, 1403

Williams, Marcia
King Arthur and the Knights of the Round Table 1038

Williams, Margery
The Velveteen Rabbit 350, 1097, 1192, 1449

Williams, Sherley Anne
Working Cotton 29, 363, 1342, **1522**

Williams, Sue
I Went Walking 206

Williams, Suzanne
Edwin and Emily 572

Williams, Vera B.
A Chair for My Mother 77, 910, 1523
Cherries and Cherry Pits 375, 1523
More More More Said the Baby: 3 Love Stories 41, 1297, 1523
Scooter 320, 1044, 1118, 1369, **1523**
Something Special for Me 1523
Stringbean's Trip to the Shining Sea 30
Three Days on a River in a Red Canoe 1523

Williams-Garcia, Rita
Blue Tights 129

Willis, Jeanne
Earth Weather, as Explained by Professor Xargle 1524
Earthlets, as Explained by Professor Xargle 1524
In Search of the Giant **1524**
The Long Blue Blazer 562

Willis, Meredith Sue
The Secret Super Powers of Marco 404, 998, 1143, 1332, **1525**, 1552

Willis, Patricia
Out of the Storm **1526**

Willner-Pardo, Gina
Hunting Grandma's Treasures 1527
Jason and the Losers 407, 1456, 1511, **1527**
What I'll Remember When I Am a Grownup 828, 1527, 1528
When Jane-Marie Told My Secret **1528**

Wilsdorf, Anne
Philomene 8, 1529
Princess **1529**

Wilson, A.N.
Hazel the Guinea Pig 749

Wilson, Gina
Prowlpuss 727, **1530**

Wilson, Nancy Hope
Becoming Felix **1531**
Bringing Nettie Back 1531, 1532
The Reason for Janey 1531, **1532**

Winslow, Barbara
Dance on a Sealskin **1533**

Winter, Jeanette
Follow the Drinking Gourd 1162, 1562, 1569
Klara's New World 913, 1186, 1233

Winter, Susan
A Baby Just Like Me 51, **1534**, 1535
I Can 1534, 1535
Me Too 1534, 1535
My Shadow 1534, **1535**

Winthrop, Elizabeth
Asleep in a Heap 1052, **1536**
The Battle for the Castle **1537**
Bear and Mrs. Duck 1536
Being Brave Is Best 212
The Castle in the Attic 1537
I'm the Boss 1536
Luke's Bully 501
Maggie and the Monster 1232, 1536
Vasilissa the Beautiful: A Russian Folktale 782

Wise, William
Ten Sly Piranhas: A Counting Story in Reverse (A Tale of Wickedness and Worse!) **1538**

Wiseman, Bernard
Halloween with Morris and Boris 779, 1150
Morris and Boris at the Circus 736

Wisler, G. Clifton
Caleb's Choice **1539**
Jericho's Journey 1539, 1540, 1541
Mr. Lincoln's Drummer 1539, **1540**, 1541
Piper's Ferry 1540
The Raid 1540
Red Cap 358, 1539, 1540, 1541
This New Land 815, **1541**

Wisniewski, David
Golem 1542
Rain Player 459, 515
Sundiata: Lion King of Mali 1542
The Warrior and the Wise Man 1542
The Wave of the Sea-Wolf 943, **1542**

Wittbold, Maureen
Mending Peter's Heart 1229

Wittman, Sally
Stepbrother Sabotage 670

Wohl, Lauren
Matzoh Mouse 929, 1170, 1291

Wojciechowski, Susan
Beany (Not Beanhead) and the Magic Crystal 1544
The Best Halloween of All 1543
The Christmas Miracle of Jonathan Toomey 125, 239, 952, 969, 1416, **1543**
Don't Call Me Beanhead! 299, 638, **1544**
Promises to Keep 306

Wolde, Gunilla
Betsy and the Chicken Pox 146, 733

Wolff, Ashley
Come with Me 1545
Only the Cat Saw 1545
Stella and Roy 150, 622, 1104, **1545**
A Year of Beasts 1545
A Year of Birds 1545

Wolff, Ferida
The Emperor's Garden 1546
On Halloween Night 1546
Pink Slippers, Bat Mitzvah Blues 85
Seven Loaves of Bread 193, **1546**
The Woodcutter's Coat 1267, 1546

Wolff, Patricia Rae
The Toll-Bridge Troll **1547**

Wolff, Virginia Euwer
The Mozart Season 426, 489
Probably Still Nick Swansen 690

Wood, Audrey
The Napping House 1052
The Napping House Wakes Up 1548
Oh My Baby Bear! 494
The Rainbow Bridge 458
Rude Giants 1030, 1338, **1548**
Silly Sally 1548
Weird Parents 1232, 1548

Wood, June Rae
The Man Who Loved Clowns 250, 354, 1185, 1532, 1549
A Share of Freedom 427, 594, 662, 810, **1549**
When Pigs Fly 1531

Wood, Marcia
The Search for Jim McGwynn 614

Wood, Phyllis Anderson
Then I'll Be Home Free 131

Woodruff, Elvira
Awfully Short for the Fourth Grade 1550
Dear Levi: Letters from the Overland Trail 473, 1448, **1550**, 1552
Dear Napoleon, I Know You're Dead, But... 1073, 1550, 1551, 1552
George Washington's Socks 509, 1552
Ghosts Don't Get Goosebumps 1434, **1551**
The Magnificent Mummy Maker 1550, **1552**
The Secret Funeral of Slim Jim the Snake 1551
Show and Tell 648, 1258
The Summer I Shrank My Grandmother 419, 1551, 1552
Tubtime 43

Woodson, Jacqueline
Maizon at Blue Hill 234

Wooldridge, Connie Nordhielm
Wicked Jack **1553**

Wormell, Mary
Hilda Hen's Happy Birthday 52, 432, 673, 1164, **1554**, 1555
Hilda Hen's Scary Night 1554, 1555
Hilda Hen's Search 1554, **1555**

Wortis, Avi
The Barn 54
The Fighting Ground 56

Wrede, Patricia
Dealing with Dragons 412

Wright, Betty Ren
Christina's Ghost 1556, 1558, 1559, 1560
The Dollhouse Murders 1559
Ghost Beneath Our Feet 1556
The Ghost Comes Calling 1179, **1556**, 1557, 1558
A Ghost in the House 576, 959, 1556, 1560
A Ghost in the Window 17, 1503
The Ghost of Ernie P. 1439, 1559
The Ghost of Popcorn Hill 584, 635, 836, **1557**, 1559
The Ghost Witch 498, **1558**
The Ghosts of Mercy Manor **1559**
The Ghosts of Popcorn Hill 1560
Haunted Summer **1560**
The Midnight Mystery 1561

Williams, Kate Douglas

Tap-Tap 77, 104, 522, 714, 823, 1425, **1521**
When Africa Was Home 1521

Title Index

This index alphabetically lists all titles featured in entries and those listed under "Other books by the author" and "Other books you might like." Each title is followed by the author's name and the number of the entry of that title. Bold numbers indicate featured main entries; other numbers refer to books recommended for further reading.

A

3 Billy Goats Gruff
Dewan, Ted 390

6th Grade Can Really Kill You
DeClements, Barthe 106

The 13 Clocks
Thurber, James 1419

13 Ways to Sink a Sub
Gilson, Jamie 1139

The 13th Floor: A Ghost Story
Fleischman, Sid **409**

The 18th Emergency
Byars, Betsy 1303

101 Ways to Bug Your Parents
Wardlaw, Lee **1478**

2095
Scieszka, Jon 1224, **1298**

A B C
Smee, Nicola 1348

A Is for Aloha
Feeney, Stephanie 523

A Is for Apple, W Is for Witch
Dexter, Catherine 956, 1053

ABC Mystery
Cushman, Doug 312, 313

Abel's Island
Steig, William 116, 628, 1378

Abigail's Drum
Minahan, John A. **1020**

The Absolutely True Story. . .How I Visited Yellowstone Park with the Terrible Rupes
Roberts, Willo Davis 1063, **1217**

Abuela
Dorros, Arthur 362, 548, 958, 1025, 1215, 1421

The Accidental Witch
Mazer, Anne **956**, 1053

Ace: The Very Important Pig
King-Smith, Dick 751

Across Five Aprils
Hunt, Irene 340, 663

Across the Blue Mountains
Chichester Clark, Emma **238**, 762, 814, 1199, 1269

Across the Creek
Smith, Marya 691

Across the Wide and Lonesome Prairie
Gregory, Kristiana 509

Across the Wide Dark Sea: The Mayflower Journey
Van Leeuwen, Jean 815, **1446**

Adam's War
Levitin, Sonia **853**

Ada's Pal
Lyon, George Ella 1248

Addie Across the Prairie
Lawlor, Laurie 824, 899

Addie Runs Away
Robins, Joan 968

Addie's Bad Day
Truesdell, Sue 1250

Addie's Dakota Winter
Lawlor, Laurie 38, 824

Addie's Long Summer
Lawlor, Laurie 473, 665, 766, 824

Addy Learns a Lesson: A School Story
Porter, Connie 1169, 1230

Addy Saves the Day
Porter, Connie 1169

Adelaide and the Night Train
Rosenberg, Liz 649, 1215, 1232

Adeline Street
Williams, Carol Lynch **1519**, 1520

The Adventures of Ali Baba Bernstein
Hurwitz, Johanna 770

The Adventures of Boone Barnaby
Cottonwood, Joe 472

The Adventures of Hershel of Ostropol
Kimmel, Eric A. **742**

The Adventures of King Midas
Banks, Lynne Reid 72

The Adventures of Opal and Cupid
Tryon, Thomas 1041

The Adventures of Sugar and Junior
Medearis, Angela Shelf 674, 812, **1003**

The Adventures of Taxi Dog
Barracca, Debra 79

The Adventures of Wise Old Owl
Kraus, Robert 785, 786

Aekyung's Dream
Paek, Min 589

Africa Brothers and Sisters
Kroll, Virginia L. 698

African Migration
Adi, Hakim 400

Afro-Bets: Book of Colors
Brown, Margery Wheeler 153

Afro-Bets: Book of Shapes
Brown, Margery Wheeler 153

After Fifth Grade
Mills, Claudia 1017

After-School Monster
Moss, Marissa 1043, 1045

After the Rain
Mazer, Norma Fox 426

Afternoon of the Elves
Lisle, Janet Taylor 876, 877, 878, 879, 880

Agatha's Feather Bed: Not Just Another Wild Goose Story
Deedy, Carmen Agra 333

Agnes Cecilia
Gripe, Maria 1485

Agnes the Sheep
Taylor, William 1410

The Agony of Alice
Naylor, Phyllis Reynolds 577, 887, 1017, 1398

Agua, Agua, Agua
Mora, Pat 1037

Ahoy There, Little Polar Bear
De Beer, Hans 326

Ahyoka and the Talking Leaves
Roop, Peter 361

Airmail to the Moon
Birdseye, Tom 109

Airplane Ride
Florian, Douglas 62

Alan and Naomi
Levoy, Myron **856**

Alaska's Three Bears
Gill, Shelly 1054

Albert the Albatross
Hoff, Syd 632

Albert's Nap
Grejniec, Michael 112

Albie the Lifeguard
Borden, Louise **124**, 125, 888, 1492, 1502

Aldo
Burningham, John 182

Aldo Applesauce
Hurwitz, Johanna 667

Aldo Ice Cream
Hurwitz, Johanna 670, 1180

Aldo Peanut Butter
Hurwitz, Johanna 317, 500, 666

Alejandro's Gift
Albert, Richard E. **19**, 1239

Alex Is My Friend
Russo, Marisabina 1243

Alexander and the Dragon
Holabird, Katharine 1319

Alexander and the Terrible, Horrible, No Good Very Bad Day
Viorst, Judith 1221, 1244, 1455

Alexander & the Wind-Up Mouse
Lionni, Leo 875

Alexander, Who Used to Be Rich Last Sunday
Viorst, Judith 1455

Alexander, Who's Not (Do You Hear Me? I Mean It!) Going to Move
Viorst, Judith 918, **1455**

The Alfred Summer
Slepian, Jan 1343

Alfsong
Turner, Ann 978

Ali Baba Bernstein, Lost and Found
Hurwitz, Johanna 368, 666

Alias Diamond Jones
Salat, Cristina 1257

Alias Madame Doubtfires
Fine, Anne 407

Alice and the Birthday Giant
Green, John F. 333, 1548

Alice in Rapture, Sort Of
Naylor, Phyllis Reynolds 279

Alice Nizzy Nazzy, the Witch of Santa Fe
Johnston, Tony 702

Alice's Adventures in Wonderland
Carroll, Lewis 330

Alien Alert!
Hess, Debra **597**, 1311

Alien Secrets
Klause, Annette Curtis 93, 134, 597, 819

Aliens Ate My Homework
Coville, Bruce 293, 507

Aliens in the Family
Mahy, Margaret 923

All Aboard!
Stevenson, James **1384**

All about Sam
Lowry, Lois 902

All about Stacy
Giff, Patricia Reilly 465

All about Whales
Kovacs, Deborah 781

All but Alice
Naylor, Phyllis Reynolds 287, 306, 489, 1016

All but the Right Folks
Nichols, Joan Kane 1567

All Eyes on the Pond
Rosen, Michael J. 1229

All for the Better: A Story of El Barrio
Mohr, Nicholasa 1027

All I See
Rylant, Cynthia 1248

All in One Piece
Murphy, Jill 1052

All Join In
Blake, Quentin 114

All Kinds of Families
Simon, Norma 1337

The All New Jonah Twist
Honeycutt, Natalie 638, 983

All-of-a-Kind Family
Taylor, Sydney 851

All Sail Set: A Romance of the "Flying Cloud"
Sperry, Armstrong 103, 797

All-Star Fever
Christopher, Matt 251

All the Better to See You With!
Wild, Margaret **1510**

All the Colors of the Earth
Hamanaka, Sheila 547, 548

All the King's Men
Mayne, William 954

All the Lights in the Night
Levine, Arthur A. 845, 846, 847, 1296

All the Magic in the World
Hartmann, Wendy **567**

All the Money in the World
Brittain, Bill 207

All the Places to Love
MacLachlan, Patricia 533, **916**, 918, 1187, 1316, 1325, 1488, 1498

All This Wild Land
Clark, Ann Nolan 38

All Together Now
Hughes, Dean 253

All's Faire
Service, Pamela F. 491

The Almost Awful Play
Giff, Patricia Reilly 466

Along Came a Dog
De Jong, Meindert 348

Alphabet City Ballet
Tamar, Erika 1363

The Alphabet of Angels
Willard, Nancy 1517

Alvah and Arvilla
Ray, Mary Lyn 188, 236, **1199**, 1200, 1201, 1269

Always, Always
Dragonwagon, Crescent 364, 1499

Always and Forever Friends
Adler, C.S. 11, 834, 1013, 1017

Always Gramma
Nelson, Vaunda Micheaux 1070

Always My Dad
Wyeth, Sharon Dennis 698, **1565**

The Always Prayer Shawl
Oberman, Sheldon **1089**

Am I Blue? Coming Out from the Silence
Bauer, Marion Dane 88

Amanda and the Magic Garden
Himmelman, John 958

Amanda and the Witch Switch
Himmelman, John 620

Amanda Pig on Her Own
Van Leeuwen, Jean 631, 1449, 1450

Amanda's Perfect Hair
Milstein, Linda Breiner 292, 445, **1019**

The Amazing Bone
Steig, William 1378

The Amazing Christmas Extravaganza
Shannon, David **1315**

The Amazing Felix
McCully, Emily Arnold **962**, 1367

Amazing Grace
Hoffman, Mary 77, 124, 469, 634, 636, 1022, 1046, 1152

Amazing Gracie
Cannon, A.E. 613

The Amazing Magic Show
Petersen, P.J. 318, 573, 1137, 1138, 1139

The Amazon
Cheney, Glenn Alan 865

Amazon Boy
Lewin, Ted **865**

Amber Brown Goes Fourth
Danziger, Paula 320, 321, 322, 1331

Amber Brown Is Not a Crayon
Danziger, Paula **320**, 322, 465, 772, 775, 1044

Amber Brown Sees Read
Danziger, Paula 321

Amber Brown Wants Extra Credit
Danziger, Paula **321**

Amber on the Mountain
Johnston, Tony 130, 697, **702**, 703, 705, 708

Amelia Bedelia
Parish, Peggy 1587

Amelia Bedelia and the Surprise Shower
Parish, Peggy 1108

Amelia Bedelia Goes Camping
Parish, Peggy 144, 627

Amelia Bedelia Helps Out
Parish, Peggy 1198

Amelia Writes Again
Moss, Marissa **1043**

Amelia's Notebook
Moss, Marissa 30, 145, 320, 1043, **1044**

Amelia's Road
Altman, Linda Jacobs **29**, 363, 1417, 1522

American Dragons
Yep, Laurence 1572

American Dreams
Banim, Lisa 68, 69

American Fairy Tales: From Rip Van Winkle to the Rootabaga Stories
Philip, Neil 33, 431, 1262

American Hero: The True Story of Charles A. Lindbergh
Denenberg, Barry 340

American Tall Tales
Osborne, Mary Pope 323, 739

American Too
Bartone, Elisa 1178

Amos and Boris
Steig, William 1194

Amos Camps Out: A Couch Adventure in the Woods
Schneider, Howie 627, 1288

Amy Dunn Quits School
Shreve, Susan Richards **1330**, 1332, 1434

Amy Loves the Rain
Hoban, Julia 604, 626

Amy Loves the Sun
Hoban, Julia 173

Amy's Goose
Holmes, Efner Tudor 756

Anansi and the Moss-Covered Rock
Kimmel, Eric A. 743, 1276, 1378

Anansi Goes Fishing
Kimmel, Eric A. 986

Anansi the Spider: A Tale from the Ashanti
McDermott, Gerald 971

Anastasia, Absolutely
Lowry, Lois 1356

Anastasia, Again!
Lowry, Lois 577, 1067, 1398, 1523

Anastasia Krupnik
Lowry, Lois 1118, 1226

Anastasia Morningstar
Hutchins, Hazel 1211

Anastasia's Chosen Career
Lowry, Lois 902

And Condors Danced
Snyder, Zilpha Keatley 1360

And It Is Still That Way: Legends Told by Arizona Indian Children
Baylor, Byrd 687

And My Mean Old Mother Will Be Sorry, Blackboard Bear
Alexander, Martha 24

And Now, Miguel
Krumgold, Joseph 1526

And One for All
Nelson, Theresa 1055

And So My Garden Grows
Spier, Peter 1366

And Still the Turtle Watched
Callahan, Sheila MacGill 178, 200

And the Winner Is. . .
Roos, Stephen 1226

And Twelve Chinese Acrobats
Yolen, Jane **1575**

Andrew Jessup
Hilton, Nette 25, 506, **619**, 1225

Andrew Wants a Dog
Kroll, Steven 464, 789, 790, 1165

Andrew's Amazing Monsters
Berlan, Kathryn Hook **102**, 1204

Doesn't Fall Off His Horse
Stroud, Virginia A.   **1401**, 1402

Dog
Blake, Robert J.   **115**, 1313

Dog and Cat
Fehlner, Paul   542, 718

Dog and Cat
Reiser, Lynn   1205

**Dog Breath: The Horrible Trouble
with Hally Tosis**
Pilkey, Dav   264, 347, 953, 1002,
1148, 1149, 1314

A Dog Called Kitty
Wallace, Bill   1268, 1472

Dog Crazy
Feldman, Eve   1026, 1182

Dog Days
Rodowsky, Colby   672

Dog Days for Dudley
Moe, Barbara   602, **1026**

Dog Donovan
Hendry, Diana   347, **583**, 953

The Dog Food Caper
Lexau, Joan M.   870

Dog Friday
McKay, Hilary   602, **980**, 1356

Dog Heaven
Rylant, Cynthia   **1248**

Dog In, Cat Out
Rubenstein, Gillian   542

Dog Magic
Coates, Anna   688

Dog on Third Base
Hiser, Constance   251

Dog Tales
McLean, Janet   799

The Dog That Stole Home
Christopher, Matt   464

The Dog Who Cried Woof
Coffelt, Nancy   **264**, 265

The Dog Who Found Christmas
Jennings, Linda   692

A Dog Worth Stealing
Corbin, William   1407

Dog Years
Warner, Sally   403, **1480**

Dogs Don't Tell Jokes
Sachar, Louis   961, 1364

Dogs in Space
Coffelt, Nancy   264, 265

Dogsong
Paulsen, Gary   1567

Dogteam
Paulsen, Gary   1119, **1120**

Dogzilla
Pilkey, Dav   1148, **1149**, 1151

Doll Face Has a Party!
Conrad, Pam   280, 281

The Doll in the Garden
Hahn, Mary Downing   374, 539,
1147, 1439

Doll Party
Albert, Shirley   764

Doll Trouble
Griffith, Helen V.   1485

The Dollhouse Murders
Wright, Betty Ren   1559

A Dolphin Named Bob
George, Twig C.   452, **453**

Donavan's Word Jar
DeGross, Monalisa   257, **337**

The Donkey's Dream
Berger, Barbara   100

Don't Call Me Beanhead!
Wojciechowski, Susan   299, 638,
1544

Don't Call Me Marda
Welch, Sheila Kelly   1490

Don't Fidget a Feather
Silverman, Erica   632, **1336**, 1386

Don't Forget
Lakin, Patricia   14, 806, **807**, 808,
1296

**Don't Give Up the Ghost: The
Delacorte Book of Original Ghost
Stories**
Gale, David   **438**, 709, 1581

Don't Go Near Mrs. Tallie
Kehret, Peg   **724**

Don't Look Behind You
Duncan, Lois   1257

Don't Make Me Smile
Park, Barbara   1110

Don't Touch My Room
Lakin, Patricia   656

Don't Wake Up Mama!
Christelow, Eileen   605, 1036, 1253

Don't You Know There's a War On?
Stevenson, James   1184

The Doom of the Haunted Opera
Bellairs, John   94

The Doorbell Rang
Hutchins, Pat   284

Dorobo the Dangerous
Vaughan, Marcia   1452

Dorrie and the Museum Case
Coombs, Patricia   329

Double-Dare O'Toole
Greene, Constance C.   1442

The Double Dip Disguise
Blair, Cynthia   70

Double Play at Short
Christopher, Matt   **249**, 250, 253,
254, 1333

Double Spell
Lunn, Janet   905

Double Trouble Squared
Lasky, Kathryn   17, 815, 818, 819

The Dove
Stewart, Dianne   **1391**, 1393

Dove Isabeau
Yolen, Jane   1579

Down and Up Fall
Hurwitz, Johanna   **666**

Down at Angel's
Chmielarz, Sharon   163, **239**, 793,
1543

**Down at the Bottom of the Deep
Dark Sea**
Jones, Rebecca C.   710

Down Buttermilk Lane
Mitchell, Barbara   **1021**

Down by the Pond
Cruickshank, Margrit   379, 938

Down in the Piney Woods
Smothers, Ethel Footman   1357

Down on Casey's Farm
Jordan, Sandra   1462

Down the Road
Schertle, Alice   **1281**, 1282

The Drackenberg Adventure
Alexander, Lloyd   22

Dracula Is a Pain in the Neck
Levy, Elizabeth   858, 859

Dracula's Cat
Wahl, Jan   1466

Dracula's Daughter
Hoffman, Mary   635

Dragon
Anderson, Wayne   1405

The Dragon and the Unicorn
Cherry, Lynne   236, **237**

Dragon Feathers
Dugin, Andrej   743, 744

Dragon Gets By
Pilkey, Dav   1149, 1150

A Dragon in the Family
Koller, Jackie French   497

Dragon-Kite of the Autumn Moon
Reddix, Valerie   872

The Dragon of an Ordinary Family
Mahy, Margaret   921

The Dragon Takes a Wife
Myers, Walter Dean   825, 1057

The Dragon That Ate Summer
Seabrooke, Brenda   1304

Dragon War
Yep, Laurence   412, 1574

Dragonfly's Tale
Rodanas, Kristina   1223

Dragons at the Gate
Yep, Laurence   1572

The Dragon's Boy
Yolen, Jane   1575, 1585

Dragon's Fat Cat
Pilkey, Dav   1150

Dragon's Halloween
Pilkey, Dav   779, **1150**, 1151, 1577

Dragon's Merry Christmas
Pilkey, Dav   1150, 1315

Dragon's Milk
Fletcher, Susan   412

The Dragon's Pearl
Lawson, Julie   **825**, 1477, 1570,
1571

The Dragon's Robe
Lattimore, Deborah Nourse   822, 1242

Drawer in a Drawer
Christiana, David   246

The Dream Factory
Karlan, Nurit   718

The Dream Jar
Pryor, Bonnie   **1178**, 1228

Dream Meadow
Griffith, Helen V.   **518**, 716, 1094

The Dream Quilt
Zerner, Amy   957

The Dream Stair
James, Betsy   685, 686, 687

Dreamcatcher
Osofsky, Audrey   1328

The Dreamer
Rylant, Cynthia   1251

Dreamplace
Lyon, George Ella   **908**, 910, 1328

Dreams
Spier, Peter   906

Dreams of Victory
Conford, Ellen   645

The Dress I'll Wear to the Party
Neitzel, Shirley   1069

Dribbles
Heckert, Connie   716

The Drowned
Levy, Elizabeth   857, 1559

The Drum, the Doll and the Zombie
Bellairs, John   94

Drums at Saratoga
Banim, Lisa   **68**, 69

Dry Days, Wet Nights
Boelts, Maribeth   120, 121

Drylongso
Hamilton, Virginia   **549**, 551, 1432

The Duck in the Gun
Cowley, Joy   295

Ducks!
Pinkwater, Daniel Manus   382

Dulcie Dando, Soccer Star
Stops, Sue   466

The Dumb Bunnies
Denim, Sue   341

The Dumb Bunnies' Easter
Denim, Sue   341

The Dumb Bunnies Go to the Zoo
Denim, Sue   341

Dumpling Soup
Rattigan, Jama Kim   471, 523, 783,
1197, 1198

Dunc and the Scam Artists
Paulsen, Gary   834

Duncan the Dancing Duck
Hoff, Syd   **632**

G

Title Index